March 2–5, 2016
Memphis, TN, USA

Association for
Computing Machinery

Advancing Computing as a Science & Profession

SIGCSE'16

Proceedings of the 47th ACM Technical Symposium on
Computing Science Education

Sponsored by:

ACM SIGCSE

Supported by:

IBM, Google, Oracle, Vocareum, GitHub, Gradescope, Microsoft, Piazza Technologies, Teradata, Turing's Craft, ZyBooks, and ABET

Association for
Computing Machinery

Advancing Computing as a Science & Profession

The Association for Computing Machinery
2 Penn Plaza, Suite 701
New York, New York 10121-0701

ISBN: 978-1-4503-3856-1 (Digital)

ISBN: 978-1-4503-4468-5 (Print)

Additional copies may be ordered prepaid from:

ACM Order Department
PO Box 30777
New York, NY 10087-0777, USA

Phone: 1-800-342-6626 (USA and Canada)
+1-212-626-0500 (Global)
Fax: +1-212-944-1318
E-mail: acmhelp@acm.org
Hours of Operation: 8:30 am – 4:30 pm ET

Printed in the USA

Welcome from the SIGCSE Chair

Welcome to the *47th SIGCSE Technical Symposium on Computer Science Education* (*SIGCSE 2016*) - the premiere technical conference for computer science educators. *SIGCSE 2016* is sponsored by the ACM Special Interest Group on Computer Science Education (the SIGCSE organization).

SIGCSE is an organization of about 2600 members interested in computer science education. Many of these members volunteer for SIGCSE's numerous activities and events held throughout the year. I want to give a large thanks to two very special volunteers for organizing the SIGCSE 2016 symposium, Co-Chairs Jodi Tims and Carl Alphonce. Jodi and Carl have spent countless hours in planning SIGCSE's largest event for about 1300 attendees, and in leading a large committee of over fifty volunteers to help make this SIGCSE Symposium a special. They have created an exciting and engaging program. On behalf of the SIGCSE Organization, I thank Jodi and Carl for their contributions towards the organization and management of this conference.

This conference is a great chance for you to make new connections and to learn about exciting innovations and new pedagogies related to computer science education. This conference is also a chance for us to honor two special people who have made significant contributions to our community. The annual SIGCSE award for Outstanding Contribution to Computer Science Education will be awarded to Jan Cuny. Over many years, Jan has built a community focused on broadening participation in computing that has dramatically increased the access of computing education to many. The annual SIGCSE award for Lifetime Service will be awarded to Barbara Boucher Owens. Barbara has made substantial contributions to the SIGCSE community, including 16 years on the SIGCSE Board and leadership efforts on outreach to computing professionals in several countries. Join me in congratulating both of them with these honors.

This conference is a chance for you to talk to current SIGCSE Board members about issues in computer science education. It is also an election year for the SIGCSE Board. Look for ribbons that identify people as candidates for the SIGCSE Board or current SIGCSE Board members.

Finally, I encourage you to attend the SIGCSE Business meeting on Friday, from 5:10pm to 6:00pm in the Cotton Row room to meet the SIGCSE Board. The other SIGCSE Board members are Vice Chair Paul Tymann, Secretary Judy Sheard, Treasurer Amber Settle, At-Large Board Members Tiffany Barnes, Sue Fitzgerald, and Alison Clear, and Past Chair Renée McCauley. At this annual meeting we will discuss the overall structure of the SIGCSE organization and describe projects SIGCSE members are currently working on. We hope this will be a first step in getting you more involved with SIGCSE that may lead to many rewarding years working with colleagues on computer science education topics. If you are interested in volunteering for SIGCSE, we encourage you to attend this meeting and also to sign up to volunteer using our online form on the sigcse.org site.

Enjoy the conference, meet new colleagues and find something interesting to take back with you!

Susan H. Rodger
SIGCSE Chair, 2013-2016

Message from the Symposium and Program Chairs 2016

Welcome to Memphis and SIGCSE 2016! As you settle in to the relaxed atmosphere of a city famous for good music, civil rights history, and, of course, delicious barbeque, we encourage you to take full advantage of all that this year's symposium has to offer. The many sessions being offered (papers, panels, special sessions, BoFs, posters, workshops, demos and lightning talks) will *Engage, Energize,* and *Empower* you on your journey as a computer science educator.

Our opening plenary address will be delivered by John Sweller, Professor Emeritus (University of Adelaide, Australia) and expert in cognitive load theory. John will challenge us to consider how our understanding of human cognition should impact our instructional procedures to provide the best learning environments for our students. Karen Ashcraft, Professor of Communication (University of Colorado, Boulder, CO) will present at the Saturday luncheon. Her work in the area of social identity will provide valuable insight to issues of gender and diversity in the computing industry. This year's recipient of the SIGCSE Award for Lifetime Service to the Computer Science Education Community, Barbara Boucher Owens (Emeritus Faculty, Southwestern University, Georgetown, TX) will speak at the First Timers' Lunch on Friday and Jan Cuny, recipient of the SIGCSE Award for Outstanding Contributions to Computer Science Education will give the Friday morning plenary address. We look forward to hearing from both of these valued members of the SIGCSE community.

Symposium statistics are presented in the following table. In addition to these refereed session, this year's program includes the usual wide selection of events, including the Thursday evening reception (with a special Memphis treat!), the ACM SIGCSE Student Research Competition, and another challenging SIGCSE puzzle. Our exhibit hall features a number of exhibitors showcasing the latest in hardware, software tools, textbooks and educational programs and research.

Proposal type	*Accepted*	*Received*	*Acceptance Rate*
Paper	105	297	35%
Panel	12	22	55%
Special Session	10	17	58%
Workshop	35	72	49%
Poster	51	89	57%
Birds of a Feather	32	65	49%
Demos	10	29	34%
Lightning Talks	12	23	52%

As of our publication deadline in mid-January, his year's Pre-symposium Event roster includes the following: Universal Design of Teaching in K-12 Computing (Access10K), Computational Thinking: A Chinese Perspective (Ming Zhang), Workshop on Computing for the Social Good: Educational Practices (SIGCAS), Integrating Computing Ethics and Professionalism into the Technical Curriculum (ACM Committee on Professional Ethics), Facilitating POGIL Activities to Support All Students (Helen Hu, et al), Creating Engaging and Relevant Classroom Activities and Assignments (Helen Hu and Beth Quinn), Fulbright for Computer Science Education (CIES), New Educators Workshop (SIGCSE), POSSE Roundup (Gregory Hislop), and Web Development with the MEAN Stack (Adrian German). We encourage you to participate in one of these exciting events.

A symposium as large as SIGCSE 2016 involves the efforts of many people and we wish to thank all of them for their help in making the event a success. Our program committee members (Laine Agee, Ruth Anderson, Bo Brinkman, Tom Cortina, Lynn Degler, Don Goelman, Charles Hardnett, Rachelle Kristof Hippler, Sarah Heckman, Daryl Hepting, Matt Jadud, Martha Kosa, Cary Laxer, Scott McElfresh, Sara Melnick, Larry Merkle, Brad Miller, Christine Moore, David Musicant, Alvaro Monge, Christopher Painter-Wakefield, Jill Pieritz, S. Monisha Pulimood, Samuel Rebelsky, Ann Sobel, Leenkiat Soh, Valerie Henderson Summet, and Jian Zhang) work tirelessly on many details. Associate Program Chairs (Eric Aaron, Don Blaheta, Alistair Campbell, Steve Cooper, Adrienne Decker, Dave Levine, Robert McCartney, Sam Rebelsky, Brad Richards, Jaime Spacco, Tammy Vandegrift, and Ellen Walker) provide meta-reviews for all submitted papers. The International Liaison Committee (Craig Anslow, Paul Denny, Daryl Hepting, Jeisson Hidalgo-Céspedes, Ville Isomottonen, Sridhar Iyer, Mahdi Jazayeri, Carsten Kleiner, Kazushi Ohya, Ian Sanders, Ben Stephenson, Jan Vahrenhold, Gary Wong, and Ming Zhang) works to ensure that attendees from all over the world find SIGCSE 2016 a welcoming and rewarding experience. And finally, we would like to thank the large contingent of student volunteers who pitch in to assist with numerous details such as stuffing conference bags, checking registration badges, distributing t-shirts, and counting attendance at session. Without their assistance, the symposium experience would be greatly diminished.

There are several others who have contributed to the planning of this year's symposium that we would like to thank. Zach Butler (Rochester Institute of Technology) has once again created a Puzzle Challenge that will be sure to be a bit hit. Tracy Camp (Colorado School of Mines) and her CONNECT Team are providing the opportunity for electronic networking during and after the conference. Spryo Spondyl (Digital Media and Design alum of Baldwin Wallace University) designed this year's logo. Each of these volunteers used their talents to enhance your SIGCSE experience.

We'd like to thank all of our supporters, vendors, exhibitors and in-kind donors for the funding and services they provided to make this year's symposium possible. We especially wish to thank Google (platinum), Oracle (gold) , Vocareum (gold), GitHub (silver), Gradescope (silver), Piazza (silver), Teradata (silver), Turing's Craft (silver), ZyBooks (silver), and ABET (bronze).

Your experience at SIGCSE 2016 is influenced in countless ways by the efforts of the planners at Executivevents: Cara Candler, Miki Hodge, and Shannon Cunningham. Your support and guidance in the months leading up to the conference is much appreciated.

A debt of gratitude is owed to Susan Rodger (President) and the entire SIGCSE Board. Additional thanks go to Bob Beck and Scott Grissom (SIGCSE Symposium Site Coordinators), April Mosqus, Ann Lane, Irene Frawley, Donna Cappo, Adrienne Griscti, Stephanie Sabal, and Diana Brantus (ACM staff), Lisa Tolles (Sheridan Publishing), Bill Guckert (WRG Design), Cassandra Taylor, Patrick Aversa, Jessica Harmon, and Alan Waxman (Memphis Cook Convention Center & Visitors Bureau), and David Stewart (Sheraton Memphis Downtown). The assistance of all of these individuals has addressed a myriad of details that go into the planning of a successful conference and we are grateful to each and every one of them. We'd also like to extend a special thank you to Laine Agee, our local events committee member. Laine not only enthusiastically introduced us to all that Memphis has to offer during our site visits, but also stumped local organizations to consider supporting SIGCSE 2016. We are most appreciative of Laine's energy and love of Memphis that was evident throughout our planning.

A special thanks goes to our home institutions (Aarhus University, Baldwin Wallace University, the University at Buffalo, and Virginia Tech) for allowing us the serve the SIGCSE community as organizers of the symposium. It has been a rewarding experience and one that we hope will Engage, Energize, and Empower you on your journey of Computer Science Education.

Jodi Tims
Symposium Co-Chair
Baldwin Wallace University

Carl Alphonce
Symposium Co-Chair
University at Buffalo

Steve Edwards
Program Co-Chair
Virginia Tech

Michael Caspersen
Program Co-Chair
Aarhus University

Table of Contents

Paper Session: Research on Learning

Paper Session: Professional Development

Panel Session

Panel Session

Special Session

Paper Session: Pair Programming

Demonstration Session

Session Chair: Martha Kosa *(Tennessee Tech)*

Paper Session: Big Data

Session Chair: Deepak Kumar *(Bryn Mawr College)*

Paper Session: Teaching with Teams

Session Chair: Leen-Kiat Soh *(University of Nebraska-Lincoln)*

Paper Session: Program Design

Session Chair: Imad Rahal *(Saint John's University)*

Paper Session: Scratch

Session Chair: Mark S. Hall *(University of Wisconsin, Marathon County)*

Special Session

Panel Session

Panel Session

Special Session

Demonstration Session

Session Chair: Tiffany Barnes *(North Carolina State University)*

Paper Session: Peer Techniques

Session Chair: Kim Bruce *(Pomona College)*

Paper Session: Artistic Approaches

Session Chair: Ravi Gandha *(South Seattle College)*

Paper Session: Tests and Outcomes

Session Chair: Don Blaheta *(Longwood University)*

Paper Session: High School Diversity

Session Chair: Howard Francis *(University of Pikeville)*

Panel Session

Panel Session

Panel Session

Panel Session

Paper Session: Problem Solving

Session Chair: Ellen L. Walker *(Hiram College)*

Paper Session: Novel Learning Approaches

Session Chair: Ruth Anderson *(University of Washington)*

Paper Session: CS Ed Research 2

Session Chair: Kathi Fisler *(Worcester Polytechnic Institute)*

Paper Session: K-8 Diversity

Session Chair: Brian Krupp *(Baldwin Wallace University)*

Special Session

Special Session

Panel Session

Panel Session

Demonstration Session

Session Chair: Tiffany Barnes *(North Carolina State University)*

Paper Session: Databases

Session Chair: Cliff Shaffer *(Virginia Tech)*

Paper Session: International Perspectives

Session Chair: Dennis Bouvier *(Southern Illinois University)*

Paper Session: Computer Engineering

Session Chair: Helen Hu *(Westminster College)*

Paper Session: Out-of-school Activities

Session Chair: David J. Stucki *(Otterbein University)*

Paper Session: Classroom Techniques

Session Chair: Sue Fitzgerald *(Metropolitan State University)*

Paper Session: Computing in Middle School

Session Chair: Robert McCartney *(University of Connecticut)*

Paper Session: Games

Session Chair: Joe Hummel *(Loyola University Chicago)*

Special Session

Demonstration Session

Session Chair: Martha Kosa *(Tennessee Tech)*

Paper Session: Security

Session Chair: Judy Sheard *(Monash University)*

Paper Session: Alternative Learning Experiences

Session Chair: Lillian N. Cassel *(Villanova University)*

Paper Session: CS Ed Research 3

Session Chair: Neil Brown *(University of Kent)*

Paper Session: K-12 Teaching

Session Chair: Jan Vahrenhold *(Universität Münster)*

Paper Session: Tools

Session Chair: Bina Ramamurthy *(SUNY Buffalo)*

Special Session

Special Session

Poster Session I

Poster Session II

Birds of a Feather Flock I

Birds of a Feather Flock II

Wednesday Workshops

Friday Workshops

Saturday Workshops

Student Research Competion

SIGCSE 2016 Symposium Committee

Symposium Chairs
Carl Alphonce, *University at Buffalo*
Jodi Tims, *Baldwin Wallace University*

Program Chairs
Michael Caspersen, *Aarhus University*
Stephen Edwards, *Virginia Tech University*

Panels and Special Sessions
Ruth Anderson, *University of Washington*

Workshops
Alvaro Monge, *California State University, Long Beach*
Bo Brinkman, *Miami University*

Publications
Jian Zhang, *Texas Woman's University*

Database Administrators
Brad Miller, *Luther College*
Leenkiat Soh, *University of Nebraska - Lincoln*

Registration
Lynn Degler, *Rose-Hulman Institute of Technology*
Cary Laxer, *Rose-Hulman Institute of Technology*
Larry Merkle, *Air Force Institute of Technology*

Posters
Don Goelman, *Villanova University*

Birds of a Feather
Samuel Rebelsky, *Grinnell College*

Lightning Talks and Demos
Martha Kosa, *Tennessee Technological University*

Student Volunteers and Activities
Sarah Heckman, *North Carolina State University*
S. Monisha Pulimood, *The College of New Jersey*
Sara Melnick, *Bronx Academy for Software Engineering*

Treasurer
Scott McElfresh, *Longwood University*

Evaluations
Christopher Painter-Wakefield, *Colorado School of Mines*

Kids Camp
Valerie Henderson Summet, *Emory University*
Charles Hardnett, *Gwinnett Technical College*

Publicity / Social Media
Christine Moore, *College of Charleston*

Webmaster
Matt Jadud, *Berea College*

Support / Exhibitor Liaison
Tom Cortina, *Carnegie Mellon University*
Dave Musicant, *Carleton College*

Pre-Conference Events & Affiliated Events Liaison
Rachelle Kristof Hippler, *Bowling Green University - Firelands*

K-12 Liaison
Jill Pieritz, *Girls Preparatory School, Chattanooga*

Local Arrangements
Lane Agee, *White Station High School, Memphis*

Student Research Competition
Ann Sobel, *Miami University (Ohio)*

Accessibility Chair
Madeleine Schep, *Columbia College*

International Liaison
Daryl Hepting, *University of Regina, Saskatchewan, CA*

International Committee
Daryl Hepting (Chair), *University of Regina, Saskatchewan, CA*
Craig Anslow, *Middlesex University, United Kingdom*
Paul Denny, *The University of Auckland, New Zealand*
Jeisson Hidalgo-Céspedes, *University of Costa Rica*
Ville Isomottonen, *University of Jyvaskyla, Finland*
Sridhar Iyer, *Indian Inst. of Technology Bombay, India*
Mehdi Jazayeri, *University of Italian Switzerland, Switzerland*
Carsten Kleiner, *Hochschule Hannover, Germany*
Kazushi Ohya, *Tsurumi University, Japan*
Ian Sanders, *University of South Africa*
Ben Stephenson, *Univerisity of Calgary, Canada*
Jan Vahrenhold, *University of Münster, Germany*
Gary K. W. Wong, *The Hong Kong Institute of Education*
Ming Zhang, *Peking University, China*

Associate Program Chairs
Eric Aaron, *Vassar College*
Don Blaheta, *Longwood University*
Alistair Campbell, *Hamilton College*
Steve Cooper, *Stanford University*
Adrienne Decker, *Rochester Institute of Technology*
Dave Levine, *St. Bonaventure University*
Robert McCartney, *University of Connecticut*
Sam Rebelsky, *Grinnell College*
Brad Richards, *University of Puget Sound*
Jaime Spacco, *Knox College*
Tammy Vandegrift, *University of Portland*
Ellen Walker, *Hiram College*

SIGCSE 2016 Reviewers

Donald Acton, *University of British Columbia*
Raman Adaikkalavan, *Indiana University South Bend*Robert Adams, *Grand Valley State University*
Paul Addison, *Ivy Tech Community College*
Rajeev Agrawal, *North Carolina A & T State University*
Shakil Akhtar, *Clayton State University*
Jennifer Albert, *The Citadel*
Farha Ali, *Lander University*
Reem Ali, *University of Minnesota (PhD Student)*
Meghan Allen, *University of British Columbia*
Richard Allen, *St. Olaf College*
Amjad Altadmri, *University of Kent*
Christine Alvarado, *University of California, San Diego*
Ashish Amresh, *Arizona State University*
Peter Anderson, *Rochester Institute of Technology*
Steven K. Andrianoff, *St. Bonaventure University*
Marvin Andujar, *University of Florida*
Karen Anewalt, *University of Mary Washington*
Gabriella Anton, *Northwestern University*
Florence Appel, *Saint Xavier University*
Antonio Araujo, *Faculdade de Engenharia da Universidade do Porto*
Michal Armoni, *Weizmann Institute of Science*
David Arnow, *Brooklyn College*
Charles Ashbacher, *Charles Ashbacher Technologies*
Thushari Atapattu, *University of Adelaide*
John Aycock, *University of Calgary*
Isabel Azevedo, *ISEP*
Dinabandhu Bag, *National Institute of Technology*
Donald Bagert, *Benedictine College*
Doug Baldwin, *SUNY Geneseo*
Catherine Bareiss, *Olivet Nazarene University*
Ian Barland, *Radford University*
David Barnes, *University of Kent*
Tiffany Barnes, *University of North Carolina at Charlotte*
Lewis Barnett, *University of Richmond*
N. Dwight Barnette, *Virginia Tech*
John Barr, *Ithaca College*
Valerie Barr, *Union College*
Martin Barrett, *East Tennessee State University*
Joao Barros, *Instituto Politecnico de Beja - ESTIG*
Phillip Barry, *University of Minnesota*
Austin Cory Bart, *Virginia Tech*
Lina Battestilli, *North Carolina State Universit*
Michael Bauer, *University of Hawaii - Leeward Community College*
Lewis Baumstark, *University of West Georgia*
Robert Beck, *Villanova University*
Brett Becker, *University College Dublin*
Andrew Begel, *Microsoft Research*
Scott Bell, *Northwest Missouri State University*
Tim Bell, *University of Canterbury*
Jens Bennedsen, *Aarhus School of Engineering*
Mikael Berndtsson, *School of Humanities and Informatics, University of Skovde*
Andrew Berns, *University of Wisconsin-La Crosse*
Gian Mario Besana, *DePaul University*
Bradley Beth, *The University of Texas at Austin*
Ivona Bezakova, *Rochester Institute of Technology*
Marie Bienkowski, *SRI International*
William Birmingham, *Grove City College*
Adam Blank, *University of Washington*
Stephen Bloch, *Google*
Cory Boatright, *Grove City College*
Steven Bogaerts, *DePauw University*
Deborah Boisvert, *University of Massachusetts Boston*
Esmail Bonakdarian, *Dominican University*
William Booth, *Baylor University*
Mark Boshart, *Tennessee Technological University*
Durell Bouchard, *Roanoke College*
Dennis Bouvier, *Southern Illinois University Edwardsville*
Kristy Boyer, *North Carolina State University*
James Braman, *The Community College of Baltimore County*
Evelyn Brannock, *Georgia Gwinnett College*
Anna Bretscher, *University of Toronto at Scarborough*
Bo Brinkman, *Miami University*
Ivan Brodenec, *Matej Bel University*
Andrej Brodnik, *University of Ljubljana / University of Primorska*
Neil Brown, *University of Kent*
Gregory Bucks, *University of Cincinnati*
Kevin Buell, *Garmin*
Kevin Buffardi, *California State University, Chico*
David Bunde, *Knox College*
Barry Burd, *Drew University*
Kevin Burger, *Arizona State University*
Debra Burhans, *Canisius College*
Richard Burns, *West Chester University*
Vicky Bush, *University of Gloucestershire*
Candido Cabo, *New York City College of Technology/CUNY*
Mary Elaine Califf, *Illinois State University*
Andre Paul Calitz, *Nelson Mandela Metropolitan University*
Johan Calu, *KULAB*
James Caristi, *Valparaiso University*
Janet Carter, *University of Kent at Canterbury*
Lori Carter, *Point Loma Nazarene University*
Lillian N. Cassel, *Villanova University*
Sheila Castaneda, *Clarke University*
Andrew Cencini, *Bennington College*
Tim Chamillard, *University of Colorado at Colorado Springs*
Maiga Chang, *Athabasca University*
Bruce Char, *Drexel University*

Mahesh Chaudhari, *Arizona State University*
Ranjan Chaudhuri, *Eastern Michigan University*
Peng-Wen Chen, *Oriental Institute of Technology*
Robert Chen, *Framingham State University*
Wei Kian Chen, *Champlain College*
Chia-Chu Chiang, *University of Arkansas at Little Rock*
Donald Chinn, *University of Washington, Tacoma*
Kyoshin Choo, *University of Mississippi*
Radhouane Chouchane, *Columbus State University*
James Church, *University of Mississippi*
Vincent Cicirello, *Stockton University*
John Cigas, *Park University*
Liezel Cilliers, *University of Fort Hare*
Dawn Cizmar, *St. Edward's University*
Michael Clancy, *University of California, Berkeley*
Peter Clarke, *Florida International University*
Alison Clear, *Eastern Institute of Technology, Auckland*
Joe Clifton, *University of Wisconsin, Platteville*
Osvaldo Clua, *Universidad de Buenos Aires*
Porter Coggins, *bemidji state university*
Ben Coleman, *Moravian College*
John Colville, *University of Technology, Sydney*
Tim Comber, *Southern Cross University*
Randy Connolly, *Mount Royal University*
Kevin Coogan, *Blackburn College*
Robert Cook, *Georgia Southern University, retired*
David Cordes, *University of Alabama*
Jose L. Cordova, *University of Louisiana at Monroe*
Thomas Cortina, *Carnegie Mellon University*
Monica Costa, *IPCB*
Mary Courtney, *Pace University*
Michelle Craig, *University of Toronto*
Keeley Crockett, *Manchester Metropolitan University*
James Cross, *Auburn University*
Joyce Blair Crowell, *Belmont University*
Ernesto Cuadros-Vargas, *San Pablo Catholic University*
Diana Cukierman, *Simon Fraser University*
Edwin P. Curran, *University of Ulster*
Pamela Cutter, *Kalamazoo College*
Lawrence D'Antonio, *Ramapo College of New Jersey*
Lucia K Dale, *Sewanee*
Andrew Danner, *Swarthmore College*
Sayamindu Dasgupta, *MIT Media Lab*
Brahma Dathan, *Metropolitan State University*
Don Davis, *UTSA*
Janet Davis, *Whitman College*
Susan Dean, *retired from UMUC - Europe*
Hannah Mary Dee, *Aberystwyth University*
Josh Dehlinger, *Towson University*
Katherine Deibel, *University of Washington Libraries*
Brian Dellinger, *Grove City College*
Robert Deloatch, *University of Illinois Urbana Champaign*
Leigh Ann DeLyser, *CSNYC*
Stavros Demetriadis, *Aristotle University of Thessaloniki*
Marie-Anne Demuynck, *Texas Woman's University*
Yogesh Deshpande, *University of Western Sydney*
Lucia Dettori, *DePaul University - College of Computing & Digital Media*
Scott Dexter, *Brooklyn College*
Kamyar Dezhgosha, *University of Illinois at Springfield*
Darina Dicheva, *Winston Salem State University*
Suzanne W. Dietrich, *Arizona State University*
Adair Dingle, *Seattle University*
Nomusa Dlodlo, *CSIR - Meraka Institute*
William Doane, *Science & Technology Policy Institute*
Zachary Dodds, *Harvey Mudd College*
Michael Doherty, *University of the Pacific*
Marguerite Doman, *Winthrop University*
Toby Donaldson, *Simon Fraser University*
Aijuan Dong, *Hood College*
John Dooley, *Knox College*
Brian Dorn, *University of Nebraska at Omaha*
Mohsen Dorodchi, *University of North Carolina, Charlotte*
Maureen Doyle, *Northern Kentucky University*
Peter Drexel, *Plymouth State University*
John Duncan, *Indiana University*
J. Philip East, *University of Northern Iowa*
Joshua Eckroth, *Stetson University*
Jeffrey Edgington, *University of Denver*
Mary Anne Egan, *Siena College*
Christopher Egert, *Rochester Institute of Technology*
Roger Eggen, *University of North Florida*
Joseph Ekstrom, *Brigham Young University*
Ahmed El-Deeb, *Upland Software*
Richard Enbody, *Michigan State University*
Barbara Ericson, *Georgia Institute of Technology*
Kathleen Ericson, *University of Tennessee at Martin*
Ali Erkan, *Ithaca College*
Yadran Eterovic, *Pontificia Universidad Catolica de Chile*
Henry Etlinger, *Rochester Institute of Technology/Department of Computer Sci*
Cameron Fadjo,
Barry Fagin, *US Air Force Academy*
Daisy Fan, *Cornell University*
Mohammed Farghally, *Virginia Tech*
David L. Feinstein, *University of South Alabama*
Alan Fekete, *University of Sydney*
Maria Feldgen, *Universidad de Buenos Aires*
Ernest Ferguson, *Northwest Missouri State University*
Georgios Fesakis, *University of the Aegean*
Ronald Finkbine, *Indiana University Southeast*
Paul Fodor, *Stony Brook University*
Samantha Foley, *University of Wisconsin-La Crosse*

Timothy Fossum, *SUNY College at Potsdam*
Eric Fouh, *Lehigh university*
Edward Fox, *Virginia Tech*
Susan Fox, *Macalester College*
Diana Franklin, *University of Chicago*
Jason Freeman, *Georgia Tech*
Frank Friedman, *Temple University*
S. Jane Fritz, *St. Joseph's College*
Daniel Frost, *University of California, Irvine*
Mohammad Fuad, *Winston-Salem State University*
Ria Galanos, *Thomas Jefferson High School for Science and Technology*
Jeffrey Galloway, *Western Kentucky University*
Dan Garcia, *UC Berkeley*
Christina Gardner-McCune, *University of Florida*
Charlie Garrod, *Carnegie Mellon University*
Alessio Gaspar, *University of South Florida*
Joe Geigel, *Rochester Institute of Technology*
Judith Gersting, *Indiana University Purdue University at Indianapolis*
Paul Gestwicki, *Ball State University*
Lila Ghemri, *Texas Southern University*
J Paul Gibson, *Telecom Sud Paris*
Mark Goadrich, *Hendrix College*
Don Goelman, *Villanova University*
Michael Goldweber, *Xavier University*
Evan Golub, *University of Maryland*
Mercedes Gomez-Albarran, *Dep. Ingenieria del Software e Inteligencia Artificial*
Pedro Pablo Gomez-Martin, *Universidad Complutense*
Jean Goulet, *Universite de Sherbrooke*
Marco Aurélio Graciotto Silva, *Federal University of Technology - Paraná*
Virginia Grande, *Uppsala University*
Becky Grasser, *Lakeland Community College*
Jonathan Gratch, *State University New York at Oneonta*
Joshua Gross, *Blackburn College*
Andrew Grover, *Thiel College*
Joshua Guerin, *University of Tennessee at Martin*
Carlos Guerrero, *University of the Balearic Islands*
Cengiz Gunay, *Georgia Gwinnett College*
Mark Guzdial, *Georgia Institute of Technology*
Mandlenkosi Victor Gwetu, *UKZN*
Steven Hadfield, *United States Air Force Academy*
Ranette Halverson, *Midwestern State University*
Nadeem Hamid, *Berry College*
Mohammad Hammoudeh, *Manchester Metropolitan University*
Sally Hamouda, *Virginia Tech*
Brian Hanks, *Redfin*
Arthur Hanna, *St. Mary's University*
Stuart Hansen, *University of Wisconsin - Parkside*
Scott Hawker, *Rochester Institute of Technology*
Sarah Heckman, *North Carolina State University*
Phillip Heeler, *Northwest Missouri State University*
Cecily Heiner, *Southern Utah University*
Fredrik Heintz, *Linköpings universitet*
James Heliotis, *Rochester Institute of Technology*
Keith Hellman, *Colorado School of Mines*
Michael Helmick, *Google*
Michael Hewner, *Duke University*
Jose R. Hilera, *University of Alcala*
Curt Hill, *Valley City State University*
Rachelle Kristof Hippler, *Bowling Green State University*
Jalaa Hoblos, *Penn State-Erie*
William Hochstettler, *Antioch University Midwest*
Mark A. Holliday, *Western Carolina University*
William Hooper, *Belmont University*
Charles Hoot, *Northwest Missouri State University*
Cay Horstmann, *San Jose State University*
Hoda Hosny, *The American University in Cairo*
David Hovemeyer, *York College of Pennsylvania*
Brian Howard, *DePauw University*
Wen-Jung Hsin, *Park University*
Chenglie Hu, *Carroll University*
Helen Hu, *Westminster College*
Josh Hug, *UC Berkeley*
James Huggins, *Kettering University*
Deborah Hughes, *Lyndon State College*
Janet Hughes, *University of Dundee*
Chris Hundhausen, *Washington State University*
Dalton Hunkins, *St. Bonaventure University*
Frances Hunt, *Educational Testing Service*
Joshua Hursey, *University of Wisconsin-La Crosse*
Deborah Hwang, *University of Evansville*
Jorge Eduardo Ibarra-Esquer, *Universidad Autonoma de Baja California*
Lubomir Ivanov, *Iona College, Computer Science Department*
Clemente Izurieta, *Montana State University*
Jana Jackova, *Matej Bel University in Banska Bystrica*
Matthew Jadud, *Berea College*
Mark Jaeger, *Baker College*
Osvaldo Jimenez, *University of the Pacific*
Yerika Jimenez, *University of Florida*
Wei Jin, *Georgia Gwinnett College*
Mike Jipping, *Hope College*
David John, *Wake Forest University*
Chris Johnson, *University of Wisconsin, Eau Claire*
Colin Johnson, *University of Kent at Canterbury*
Julie Johnson, *Vanderbilt University*
Michael Jonas, *University of New Hampshire at Manchester*
Edward Jones, *Florida A&M University*
Anthony Joseph, *Pace University*
Alark Joshi, *University of San Francisco*
Mike Joy, *University of Warwick*
Daniel Joyce, *Villanova University*
Maria Jump, *King's College*
Edward Jung, *Kennesaw State University*
Amir Kamil, *University of Michigan*
Alan Kaminsky, *Rochester Institute of Technology*
Pankaj Kamthan, *Concordia University*
Elizabeth Katz, *Millersville University*
David Kauchak, *Pomona College*
David G. Kay, *University of California, Irvine*

Efsun Kayi, *Portland State University*
Siddharth Kaza,
Fereydoun Kazemian, *Rochester Institute of Technology*
Petros Kefalas, *University of Sheffield*
Charles Kelemen, *Swarthmore College*
Tom Kelliher, *Goucher College*
David Kerven, *Georgia Gwinnett College*
Arshia Khan, *University of Minnesota Duluth*
Hassan Khosravi, *Computer Science Department at UBC*
Sami Khuri, *San Jose State University*
Edward Kim, *Villanova University*
Jeff Kinne, *Indiana State University*
Nancy Kinnersley, *University of Kansas*
Jim Kiper, *Miami University*
Michael Kirkpatrick, *James Madison University*
David Klappholz, *Stevens Institute of Technology*
Frank Klassner, *Villanova University*
Carsten Kleiner, *University of Applied Sciences & Arts Hannover*
Joanna Klukowska, *Computer Science*
Joseph Kmoch, *Milwaukee Public Schools*
Jane Kochanov, *Pennsylvania State University - Capital College*
Kyu Han Koh, *Virginia Tech*
Michael Kolling, *University of Kent*
April Kontostathis, *Ursinus College*
Yana Kortsarts, *Widener University, Chester*
David Kosbie, *Carnegie Mellon University*
Janet Kourik, *Webster University*
Alena Kovarova, *Slovak University of Technology*
Douglas Kranch, *North Central State College*
Joan Krone, *Denison University*
Jan Kruger, *Unisa School for Business Leadership*
Beata Kubiak, *Tennessee Tech University*
Amruth Kumar, *Ramapo College of New Jersey*
Deepak Kumar, *Bryn Mawr College*
Benjamin Kuperman, *Oberlin College*
Zachary Kurmas, *Grand Valley State University*
Clif Kussmaul, *Muhlenberg College*
Lynn Lambert, *Christopher Newport University*
Matthew Lang, *Google, Inc.*
Joan Langdon, *Bowie State University*
Yedidyah Langsam, *CIS Department Brooklyn College of CUNY*
David Largent, *Ball State University*
Brian Larkins, *Rhodes College*
Edurne Larraza-Mendiluze, *University of the Basque Country*
Eric Larson, *Seattle University*
Mary Last, *self-employed*
Robert Law, *Glasgow Caledonian University*
Deirdre Lawless, *Dublin Institute of Technology*
Barry Lawson, *University of Richmond*
Alina Lazar, *Youngstown State University*
Christopher League, *Long Island University*
Arthur Lee, *Claremont McKenna College*
Byong Lee, *Bennett College*
Choong-Soo Lee, *St. Lawrence University*
Cornell Lee, *Minnesota State University*
Cynthia Lee, *Stanford*
En-Shiun Lee, *University of Waterloo*
Gilliean Lee, *Lander University*
Chi Un Lei, *The University of Hong Kong*
Terry Letsche, *Wartburg College*
Anany Levitin, *Villanova University*
Dalit Levy, *Zefat Academic College*
Gary Lewandowski, *Xavier University*
Colleen Lewis, *Harvey Mudd College*
John Lewis, *Virginia Tech*
Weidong Liao, *Shepherd University*
Panos Linos, *Butler University*
Jiangjiang (Jane) Liu, *Lamar University*
Jigang Liu, *Metropolitan State University*
Peter Liu, *Seneca College*
Yue Liu, *National University of Defense Technology*
Doug Lloyd, *CS50, Harvard University*
William S. Lloyd, *University of West Georgia*
Kate Lockwood, *The University of St. Thomas*
Sergio F. Lopes, *University of Minho*
Salvador Lopez, *Universidad Nacional Autonoma de Mexico*
Joan Lucas, *The College at Brockport, State University of New York*
Stephanie Ludi, *Rochester Institute of Techology*
Robert Lutz,
Andrew Luxton-Reilly, *The University of Auckland*
Bonnie MacKellar, *St John's University*
Peter Macpherson, *Rogers State University*
Joaquim Madeira, *University of Aveiro*
Manoj Maharaj, *University of KwaZulu-Natal*
Francesco Maiorana, *University of Catania*
Davad Malan, *Harvard University*
Bill Manaris, *College of Charleston*
Daniela Marghitu, *Auburn University*
Mercedes Marques, *University Jaume I*
Fred Martin, *University of Massachusetts Lowell*
Manuel Martins Barata, *ISEL - Instituto Superior de Engenharia de Lisboa*
Dave Mason, *Ryerson University*
Julian Mason, *Google Research*
Suzanne Matthews, *United States Military Academy*
Bruce R. Maxim, *University of Michigan-Dearborn*
Bruce Maxwell, *Colby College*
Chris Mayfield, *James Madison University*
Lester McCann, *The University of Arizona*
Renee McCauley, *College of Charleston*
Robert McCloskey, *University of Scranton*
O. William McClung, *Nebraska Wesleyan University*
Jeffrey McConnell, *Canisius College*
Frank McCown, *Harding University*
Sean McCulloch, *Ohio Wesleyan University*
Chris McDonald, *The University of Western Australia*
Scott McElfresh, *Longwood University*
Monica McGill, *Bradley University*
James McGuffee, *Northern Kentucky University*
Hugh McGuire, *Grand Valley State University*
Bonita McVey, *St. Norbert College*

Pedro Medeiros, *Universidade Nova de Lisboa*
Julie Medero, *Harvey Mudd College*
Lisa Meeden, *Swarthmore College*
António Mendes, *Universidade de Coimbra*
Susan Mengel, *Texas Tech University*
Suzanne Menzel, *Indiana University*
Rachel Menzies, *University of Dundee*
Timothy Meyer, *Edinboro University of Pennsylvania*
Mark Meysenburg, *Doane College*
Razvan Mezei, *Lenoir-Rhyne University*
Lisa Michaud, *Aspect Software*
Gail Miles, *Lenoir-Rhyne University*
Afsaneh Minaie, *Utah Valley University*
Joe Miro, *Universitat de les Illes Balears*
Amitabh Mishra, *University of West Florida*
Sriram Mohan, *Rose-Hulman Institute of Technology*
Selvarajah Mohanarajah, *Claflin University*
Dagmar Monett Diaz, *CS Department, Berlin School of Economics and Law*
Michael Moorman, *Saint Leo University*
Nelma Moreira, *University of Porto*
Patricia Morreale, *Kean University*
Briana Morrison, *Kennesaw State University*
Srikanth Mudigonda, *Saint Louis University*
Christian Murphy, *University of Pennsylvania*
Michael Murphy, *Concordia University Texas*
David Musicant, *Carleton College*
Adity Mutsuddi,
Kristine Nagel, *Georgia Gwinnett College*
Mario Nakazawa, *Berea College*
Tom Naps, *University of Wisconsin - Oshkosh*
Krish Narayanan, *Eastern Michigan University*
Pavol Navrat, *Slovak University of Technology*
Lijun Ni, *UMass Lowell*
Robert Noonan, *College of William and Mary*
Emma Norling, *Manchester Metropolitan University*
Victor Norman, *Calvin College*
Cindy Norris, *Appalachian State University*
Theodore Norvell, *Memorial University of Newfoundland*
Linda Null, *Penn State University*
Keith O'Hara, *Bard College*
William Oblitey, *Indiana University of Pennsylvania*
Rainer Oechsle, *University of Applied Sciences, Trier*
Chris Okasaki, *USMA*
Amos Olagunju, *St. Cloud State University*
Nina Onesti, *Indiana University*
Lawrence Osborne, *Lamar University*
Peter-Michael Osera, *Grinnell College*
Youwen Ouyang, *California State University at San Marcos*
Majdi Owda, *Manchester Metropolitan University*
Barbara Owens, *Southwestern University*
Greta Pangborn, *Saint Michael's College*
Dimitris Papamichail, *The College of New Jersey*
Iraklis Paraskakis, *City College, Intern. Faculty of the University of Sheffield*
Young Park, *Bradley University*
David Parker, *Salisbury University*
Jeff Parker, *Harvard Extension*
James Paterson, *Glasgow Caledonian University*
Laurie Patterson, *University of North Carolina Wilmington*
Richard E. Pattis, *University of California, Irvine*
Arnold Pears, *Uppsala University*
Charles Peck, *Earlham College*
Eileen Peluso, *Lycoming College*
Joslenne Pena, *The Pennsylvania State University*
Bin Peng, *Park University*
Alston Peter, *University of Liverpool*
Teresa Peterman, *Grand Valley State University*
Andrew Petersen, *University of Toronto Mississauga*
John Peterson, *Western State College*
Chrisila C. Pettey, *Middle Tennessee State University*
Jill Pieritz, *Girls Preparatory School*
Vreda Pieterse, *University of Pretoria*
Johanna Pirker, *Graz University of Technology*
Irene Polycarpou, *UCLan Cyprus*
Jeffrey Popyack, *Drexel University*
Leo Porter, *UC San Diego*
Lori Postner, *Nassau Community College*
Jon Preston, *Southern Polytechnic State University*
Barbara Price, *Georgia Southern University*
Roger Priebe, *Texas State University - San Marcos*
David Pritchard, *University of Southern California*
Viera Proulx, *Northeastern University*
William Pugh, *University of Maryland*
Sarah Monisha Pulimood, *The College of New Jersey*
Imad Rahal, *College of Saint Benedict & Saint John's University*
Brian Railing, *Georgia Institute of Technology*
Rajendra Raj, *Rochester Institute of Technology*
Lakshmi Ramachandran, *Pearson*
Muthu Ramachandran, *Leeds Beckett University*
Bina Ramamurthy, *University at Buffalo, SUNY*
Raghuram Ramanujan, *Davidson College*
Saquib Razak, *Carnegie Mellon University*
Michael Redmond, *La Salle University*
David Reed, *Creighton University*
Donna Reese, *Mississippi State University*
Susan Reiser, *UNC Asheville*
Loren Rhodes, *Juniata College*
Catherine Ricardo, *Iona College*
Detlef Rick, *University of Hamburg*
Michael Rieck, *Drake University*
Charles Riedesel, *University of Nebraska - Lincoln*
Kelly Rivers, *Carnegie Mellon University*
Suzanne Rivoire, *Sonoma State University*
Steven Robbins, *University of Texas at San Antonio*
Christian Roberson, *Plymouth State University*

Stefan Robila, *Montclair State University*
Susan H. Rodger, *Duke University*
Guido Roessling, *Technische Universitaet Darmstadt*
Joel Ross, *University of Washington Information School*
Rockford Ross, *Montana State University*
Jerry Roth, *Vanderbilt University*
Krishnendu Roy, *Valdosta State University*
Martin Ruckert, *Munich University of Applied Sciences*
Anthony Ruocco, *Roger Williams University*
Paulo Rupino da Cunha, *University of Coimbra*
Ingrid Russell, *University of Hartford*
Adrian Rusu, *Rowan University*
Amalia Rusu, *Fairfield University*
Rebecca Rutherfoord, *Southern Polytechnic State University*
Mehran Sahami, *Stanford University*
Samuel Sambasivam, *Azusa Pacific University*
Ian Sanders, *University of South Africa*
William Sanders, *University of Hartford*
Vijayalakshmi Saravanan, *Ryerson University , Canada & VIT University*
Allison Sauppé, *University of Wisconsin-La Crosse*
Christelle Scharff, *Pace University*
Walter Schilling, *Milwaukee School of Engineering*
Karl Schmitt, *Valparaiso University*
Jason Schultz, *Ball State university*
Diane Schwartz, *California State University Northridge*
Stephanie Schwartz, *Millersville University*
Michael Scott, *Falmouth University*
Shilad Sen, *Macalester College*
Otto Seppälä, *Aalto University*
Christian Servin, *El Paso Community College*
Amber Settle, *DePaul University*
Behrooz Seyed-Abbassi, *University of North Florida*
Cliff Shaffer, *Virginia Tech*
Bonita Sharif, *Youngstown State University*
Ching-Kuang Shene, *Michigan Technological University*
Mark Sherriff, *University of Virginia*
Swapneel Sheth, *University of Pennsylvania*
Yasuto Shirai, *Shizuoka University*
Keith Shomper, *Cedarville University*
William Siever, *Western Illinois University*
Scott Sigman, *Drury University*
Gavin Sim, *University of Central Lancashire*
Maria Simi, *Universita di Pisa*
Beth Simon, *University of California, San Diego*
Joslyn Smith, *Florida International University*
Peter Smith, *California State University - Channel Islands*
Robert Snapp, *University of Vermont*
Leen-Kiat Soh, *University of Nebraska*
Takako Soma, *Illinois College*
Joel Sommers, *Colgate University*
Raja Sooriamurthi, *Carnegie Mellon University*
Jonathan Sorenson, *Butler University*
Greg Speegle, *Baylor University*
Nathan Sprague, *James Madison University*
Bernhard Standl, *University of Vienna*
Alistair Stead, *University of Cambridge*
Mark Stehlik, *Carnegie Mellon University*
Michael Stein, *Metropolitan State University*
Theresa Steinbach, *DePaul University*
Ben Stephenson, *University of Calgary*
Khadija Stewart, *DePauw University*
Evelyn Stiller, *Plymouth State University*
Jeffrey Stone, *Pennsylvania State University*
Forrest Stonedahl, *Augustana College*
Fred Strickland, *South University*
Kristina Striegnitz, *Union College*
Svetlana Strunjas,
David Stucki, *Otterbein University*
Deborah Sturm, *College of Staten Island CUNY*
Kalpathi Subramanian, *The Univ. of North Carolina at Charlotte*
Ken Surendran, *Southeast Missouri State University*
Rajendran Swamidurai, *Alabama State University*
Robert Tairas, *Vanderbilt University*
Joo Tan, *Kutztown University*
Cara Tang, *Portland Community College*
Michael Tashbook, *Stony Brook University*
Blair Taylor, *Towson University*
Cynthia Taylor, *Oberlin College*
William Thacker, *Winthrop University*
Megan Thomas, *California State University Stanislaus*
Rebecca Thomas, *Bard College*
Stan Thomas, *Wake Forest University*
Alfred Thompson, *Bishop Guertin HS*
Gloria Childress Townsend, *DePauw University*
Christian Trefftz, *Grand Valley State University*
Deborah Trytten, *University of Oklahoma*
Shengru Tu, *University of New Orleans*
Nicoleta Liviana Tudor, *Petroleum-Gas University of Ploiesti*
William Turkett, *Wake Forest University*
William Turner, *Wabash College*
Hakan Tuzun, *Hacettepe University*
Jozef Tvarozek, *Slovak University of Technology in Bratislava*
Luther Tychonievich, *University of Virginia*
Paul Tymann, *Rochester Institute of Technology*
Suleyman Uludag, *The University of Michigan - Flint*
Timothy Urness, *Drake University*
Jaime Urquiza-Fuentes, *Rey Juan Carlos University/Lecturer*
Ian Utting, *University of Kent at Canterbury*
Jan Vahrenhold, *WWU Münster*
David Valentine, *Slippery Rock University*
James Vallino, *Rochester Institute of Technology*
Robert Van Camp, *Marietta College*
James Vanderhyde, *Saint Xavier University*
Jorge Vasconcelos, *National Autonomous University of Mexico*
Troy Vasiga, *University of Waterloo*
Kam Vat, *University of Macau*
Steven Vegdahl, *University of Portland*
Nanette Veilleux, *Simmons College*
J. Angel Velazquez-Iturbide, *Universidad Rey Juan Carlos*

CALL FOR PARTICIPATION

SIGCSE 2017

Inspire, Innovate, Improve!

The 48th ACM Technical Symposium on Computer Science Education

March 8 – 11, 2017, Seattle, Washington, USA

http://www.sigcse2017.sigcse.org

SIGCSE 2017 welcomes colleagues from around the world to present demos, lightning talks, papers, panels, posters, special sessions, and workshops, and to discuss computer science education in birds-of-a-feather sessions and informal settings. The SIGCSE Technical Symposium addresses problems common among educators working to develop, implement and/or evaluate computing programs, curricula, and courses. The symposium provides a forum for sharing new ideas for syllabi, laboratories, and other elements of teaching and pedagogy, at all levels of instruction.

Submissions are welcomed that are in line with the conference theme, **Inspire, Innovate, Improve!** The theme highlights the aim of SIGCSE to inspire all computing educators to innovate new teaching strategies, and to improve those strategies by engaging in the self-reflection and evaluation necessary to deliver the best possible learning outcomes for all.

We are particularly interested in keeping our community connected with interesting educational efforts in upper level courses, open-source software, outreach, and education research. We are continuing to keep our commitment to the inclusion of a wide-variety of submissions in the program that span the spectrum of experience reports to scientifically rigorous educational studies. We are excited for you to be a part of showing our community why we all need to keep computing.

PAPERS

Papers describe an educational research project, classroom experience, teaching technique, curricular initiative, or pedagogical tool. Submitted papers for review will be anonymous. Papers will undergo a blind reviewing process and must not exceed six pages. Accepted papers will need to submit a non-anonymous version for publication in the proceedings after acceptance. Authors will have 25 minutes for their presentations, including questions and answers.

PANELS

Panels present multiple perspectives on a specific topic. To allow each panelist sufficient time to present his or her perspective and still enable audience participation, a panel will normally have at most four panelists, including one moderator. Panel submissions should include a list of the panelists, their affiliations, and a description of the topic, with brief position statements from panelists. Proposals with more than four panelists must provide a statement connecting the extra panelist to the effectiveness of the panel and must convincingly show that each panelist will be able to speak, and the audience able to respond, within the session time. Panel abstracts must not exceed two pages. A panel session is 75 minutes.

SPECIAL SESSIONS

Special sessions are your opportunity to customize and experiment with the SIGCSE conference format. Possible special sessions include a seminar on a new topic, a committee report, or a forum on curriculum issues. More generally, they must be 75 minutes in length, held in standard conference spaces, and justifiably be distinct from the panel, paper, and poster tracks. Within those constraints, the form is yours to design. Special session abstracts must not exceed two pages.

WORKSHOPS

Workshops offer participants opportunities to learn new techniques and technologies designed to foster education, scholarship, and collaborations. A workshop proposal (including abstract) must not exceed two pages. Proposals must specify equipment needs (e.g., participant-supplied laptops, room configurations, and A/V equipment) and any limitation on the number of participants. Workshops are scheduled for a three-hour session and do not conflict with the technical sessions.

BIRDS OF A FEATHER SESSIONS

Birds of a Feather (BoF) sessions provide an environment for colleagues with similar interests to meet for informal discussions. A maximum one-page description (including abstract) is requested to describe the informal discussion topic. A/V equipment will not be provided for these sessions. Each BoF topic is allocated 45 minutes.

POSTERS
Posters describe computer science education materials or research, particularly works in progress. Proposals (including abstract) are limited to two pages. Poster demonstrations are scheduled to permit one-on-one discussion with conference attendees, typically during session breaks. Prepared handouts are encouraged in order to share your work.

LIGHTNING TALKS
Lightning talks describe works in progress, new and untested ideas, or opportunities for collaborative work. The purpose of a lightning talk can be to start a discussion, find collaborators, or receive input and critique about an idea. Proposals are limited to 500 words and will be anonymously reviewed for acceptance. Lightning talk presentations will be 5 minutes each and given without media/slide support.

DEMOS
Demos provide a way to showcase an educational tool or project in a live setting. Not designed to be sales pitches, demonstrations are a way for the community to see the relevance, potential and innovation of the tool and allow time for discussion with its creator. Proposals (including abstract) are limited to two pages and will be anonymously reviewed for acceptance. Proposals must specify any equipment needs (e.g., power, A/V equipment, space needs). Demos will be 30 minutes in length and will occur during break periods at a designated space in the exhibition hall.

STUDENT RESEARCH COMPETITION
Research from all areas of computer science is considered for awards in two categories of competition: graduate and undergraduate. All submissions must represent a student's individual research contribution and a student must be an ACM student member to qualify for awards and travel grants. Entry due date is Monday, September 26, 2016.

PROCEEDINGS AVAILABILITY
The proceedings will be publicly available from the ACM Digital Library 14 days before the start of the conference. Therefore, the official publication date for the proceedings will be February 22, 2017.

IMPORTANT DUE DATES

Friday, August 26, 2016: *Paper, Panel, Special Session, and Workshop submissions*
Monday, September 26, 2016: *Student Research Competition submissions*
Friday, October 21, 2016: *Birds of a Feather, Demos, Lightning Talks, and Poster submissions*

PROGRAM COMMITTEE

Symposium Chairs

Michael E. Caspersen
Aarhus University
mec@cs.au.dk

Stephen Edwards
Virginia Tech
edwards@cs.vt.edu

Program Chairs

Tiffany Barnes
North Carolina State University
tmbarnes@ncsu.edu

Daniel Garcia
University of California, Berkeley
ddgarcia@berkeley.edu

Panels and Special Sessions

Jian Zhang
Texas Woman's University
jzhang@twu.edu

Workshops

Bo Brinkman
Miami University
Bo.Brinkman@MiamiOH.edu

Michelle Craig
University of Toronto
mcraig@cs.toronto.edu

Publications

Ruth Anderson
University of Washington
rea@cs.washington.edu

Registration

Lynn Degler
Rose-Hulman Institute of Technology
degler@rose-hulman.edu

Cary Laxer
Rose-Hulman Institute of Technology
laxer@rose-hulman.edu

Larry Merkle
Computational Optimization Services
l.merkle@ieee.org

Posters

Phil East
University of Northern Iowa
east@cs.uni.edu

Birds Of A Feather

Brian Dorn
University of Nebraska at Omaha
bdorn@unomaha.edu

Lightning Talks

Steven Wolfman
University of British Columbia
wolf@cs.ubc.ca

Demos

Sarah Heckman
North Carolina State University
sarah_heckman@ncsu.edu

Association for Computing Machinery
Advancing Computing as a Science & Profession

SIGCSE
ACM Special Interest Group on Computer Science Education

Student Volunteers and Student Activities

Sarah Heckman
North Carolina State University
sarah_heckman@ncsu.edu

S. Monisha Pulimood
The College of New Jersey
pulimood@tcnj.edu

Sara Melnick
Columbia University
sararielle@gmail.com

Webmaster

Matt Jadud
Berea College
matt_jadud@berea.edu

Treasurer

Paul Tymann
Rochester Institute of Technology
ptt@cs.rit.edu

Evaluations

Alison Clear
Christchurch Polytechnic Institute of Technology
alison.clear@cpit.ac.nz

Support/Exhibitor Liaisons

Tom Cortina
Carnegie Mellon University
tcortina@cs.cmu.edu

Dave Musicant
Carleton College
dmusican@carleton.edu

Pre-Symposium Events & Affiliated Events Liaison

Rachelle Kristof Hippler
Bowling Green State University
rkristo@bgsu.edu

Publicity and Social Media

Christine L. Moore
College of Charleston
moorec@cofc.edu

Kids' Camp

Valerie Henderson Summet
Emory University
valerie@mathcs.emory.edui

Charles R. Hardnett
Gwinnett Technical College
chardnett@gwinnetttech.edu

K-12 Liaison

Leigh Ann Sudol-DeLyser
CSNYC
leighann@csnyc.org

International Liaison

Paul Denny
The University of Auckland
paul@cs.auckland.ac.nz

Local Arrangements

Ruth Anderson
University of Washington
rea@cs.washington.edu

Student Research Competition

Ann Sobel
Miami University (Ohio)
sobelae@miamioh.edu

Database Administrators

Brad Miller
Luther College
bmiller@luther.edu

Leen-Kiat Soh
University of Nebraska, Lincoln
lksoh@cs.unl.edu

Association for Computing Machinery
Advancing Computing as a Science & Profession

SIGCSE
ACM Special Interest Group on Computer Science Education

Recipients of the SIGCSE Award for Outstanding Contributions to Computer Science Education

1981 **William F. Atchison**, *University of Maryland*

1982 **Alan Perlis**, *Yale University*

1983 **Karl V. Karlstrom**, *Prentice-Hall*

1985 **Elliot I. Organick**, *University of Utah*

1986 **Donald Knuth**, *Stanford University*

1987 **Niklaus Wirth**, *ETH, Zurich*

1988 **Grace Murray Hopper**, *Rear Admiral, USN, Digital Equipment Corp.*

1989 **Edsger W. Dijkstra**, *The University of Texas at Austin*

1990 **Curriculum '68 Committee**:
William F. Atchison, Samuel D. Conte, John Hamblen, Thomas E. Hull, Thomas A. Keenan, William B. Kehl, Edward J. McClusey, Silvio O. Navarro, Werner Rheinboldt, Earl J. Schweppe, William Viavant, David M. Young, Jr.

1991 **David Gries**, *Cornell University*

1992 **Daniel D. McCracken**, *City College, City University of New York*

1993 **Alan C. Kay**, *Apple Computer*

1994 **Norman E. Gibbs**, *Software Engineering Institute*

1995 **Robert M. Aiken**, *Temple University*

1996 **Nell B. Dale**, *The University of Texas at Austin*

1997 **Andrew Tannenbaum**, *Vrije University*

1998 **William A. Wulf**, *University of Virginia and National Academy of Engineering*

1999 **Peter J. Denning**, *George Mason University*

2000 **Andries Van Dam**, *Brown University*

2001 **Allen B. Tucker**, *Bowdoin College*

2002 **Elliot Soloway**, *University of Michigan*

2003 **Eric Roberts**, *Stanford University*

2004 **Mordechai Ben-Ari**, *Weizmann Institute of Science*

2005 **Kim Bruce**, *Williams College*

2006 **Richard Pattis**, *Carnegie Mellon University*

2007 **Judith Gal-Ezer**, *Open University of Israel* and **John Hughes**, *University of Technology, Sydney*

2008 **Randy Pausch**, *Carnegie Mellon University*

2009 **Elliot B. Koffman**, *Temple University*

2010 **Sally Fincher**, *University of Kent, Canterbury*

2011 **Matthias Felleisen**, *Northeastern University*

2012 **Harold (Hal) Abelson**, *Massachusetts Institute of Technology*

2013 **Michael Kölling**, *University of Kent, Canterbury*

2014 **Robert M. Panoff**, *The Shodor Education Foundation, Inc.*

2015 **Mark Allen Weiss**, *Florida International University*

2016 **Jan Cuny**, *National Science Foundation*

Recipients of the SIGCSE Lifetime Service Award

1997 **Richard Austing**, *University of Maryland*
1998 **Della Bonnette**, *University of Southwestern Louisiana*
1999 **Robert Aiken**, *Temple University*
2000 **James E. Miller**, *University of Southern Mississippi*
2001 **Lillian N. (Boots) Cassel**, *Villanova University*
2002 **Joe Turner**, *Clemson University and Zayed University*
2003 **Harriet Taylor**, *National Science Foundation and Louisiana State University*
2004 **Bruce Klein**, *Grand Valley State University*
2005 **Andrew McGettrick**, *University of Strathclyde*
2006 **Joyce Currie Little**, *Towson State University*
2007 **John Impagliazzo**, *Hofstra University*
2008 **Dennis Frailey**, *Raytheon Corporation*
2009 **Michael J. Clancy**, *University of California, Berkeley*
2010 **Peter Denning**, *Naval Postgraduate School*
2011 **Gordon Davies**, *Open University*
2012 **Jane Prey**, *Microsoft Research*
2013 **Henry Walker**, *Grinnell College*
2014 **Andrea Lawrence**, *Spelman College*
2015 **Frank H. Young**, *Rose-Hulman Institute of Technology*
2016 **Barbara Boucher Owens**, *Southwestern University*

Cognitive Load Theory and Computer Science Education

John Sweller
Emeritus Professor of Educational Psychology
School of Education
University of New South Wales
Sydney, NSW 2052, Australia
+61 2 9385 1984
j.sweller@unsw.edu.au

ABSTRACT

Cognitive load theory uses our knowledge of human cognitive architecture to devise instructional procedures, most of which are directly relevant to computer science education. There are several basic aspects of human cognition that are critical to instructional design. First, based on evolutionary educational psychology, cognitive load theory assumes that most topics taught in educational and training institutions are ones that we have not specifically evolved to learn. Such topics require biologically secondary knowledge rather than the biologically primary knowledge that we have evolved to acquire. Second, these instructionally relevant topics require learners to acquire domain-specific rather than generic cognitive skills. Third, while generic cognitive knowledge does not require explicit instruction because we have evolved to acquire it, domain-specific concepts and skills that provide the content of educational syllabi, do require explicit instruction. These three factors interact with the well-known capacity and duration constraints of working memory and the unlimited capacity and duration characteristics of long-term memory to delineate a cognitive architecture relevant to instructional design. The working memory limits do not apply to biologically primary, generic knowledge acquired without explicit instruction but do apply to the biologically secondary, domain-specific knowledge that requires explicit instruction and that is relevant to computer science education. Human cognition when dealing with such knowledge constitutes a natural information processing system that has evolved to mimic the architecture of biological evolution. Cognitive load theory uses this architecture to generate a large range of instructional effects concerned with procedures for reducing extraneous working memory load in order to facilitate the acquisition of knowledge in long-term memory. This talk reviews the theory and indicates the instructional implications relevant to computer education.

CCS Concepts

• *Human-centered computing ~ HCI design and evaluation methods*

Keywords

Cognitive load theory; Human cognition; Instructional design

BIO

Dr. Sweller's research reputation is associated with cognitive load theory, an instructional theory based on our knowledge of human cognitive architecture. He initiated work on the theory in the early 1980's. Subsequently, "ownership" of the theory shifted to his research group at UNSW and then to a large group of international researchers. The theory is now a contributor to both research and debate on issues associated with human cognitive architecture, its links to evolution by natural selection, and the instructional design consequences that follow. It is one of the few theories to have generated a large range of novel instructional designs from our knowledge of human cognitive architecture. The following instructional design effects have flowed from cognitive load theory: goal-free, worked example, split-attention, redundancy, modality, element interactivity, isolated-interacting elements, imagination, expertise reversal, completion, variable examples, guidance fading, transient information and collective working memory effects. These effects have been studied by many groups of researchers from around the globe. Based on any commonly used citation index, the work has been cited on between 10,000 and 20,000 occasions.

SIGCSE'16, March 2–5, 2016, Memphis, TN, USA
ACM 978-1-4503-3685-7/16/03.
DOI: http://dx.doi.org/10.1145/2839509.2844549

Service as Rent

Barbara Boucher Owens
Emeritus Faculty
Computer Science Department
Southwestern University
1001 East University Ave.
Georgetown, TX 78628
+1 (512)869-0031
owensb@southwestern.edu

ABSTRACT

"Service is the rent we pay for the space we take up on earth ", my dad's mantra, and one used by many. Participating in professional organizations such as SIGCSE and its parent organization, ACM, has been for me an incredibly rewarding obligation. Many have given of their time and talents to help me on my way. Some of those who have followed in my footsteps have also forged paths of service making mine pale in comparison. This computer science education community affords incredibly rich opportunities for service in venues ranging from local to international. Service in SIGCSE and similar communities can reap untold benefits for both the volunteer and the community served.

CCS Concepts

• Social and professional topics~Computer science education

Keywords

Volunteering; mentoring

BIO

Barbara Boucher Owens retired in 2012 from the Computer Science Department at Southwestern University in Georgetown, Texas. She has been in the computing field since 1967 when she worked at IBM Research in Yorktown Heights, NY and later in San Jose, California, in the area of Computer Assisted Instruction. She began her teaching career in 1970 at Brooklyn College and was a founding member of its Computer Science Department in 1971. Barbara also has held tenured positions at Mercy College in Dobbs Ferry, New York, and St. Edward's University in Austin, Texas. She spent a sabbatical teaching at Uppsala University in Uppsala, Sweden. She is an ACM Distinguished Educator, a past chair of the ACM Special Interest Group on Computer Science Education serving on its board for 16 years, a member of the ACM Council, the ACM Education Council, and until recently, the ACM Council on Women. She is a past-president of the Consortium for Computing Sciences in Colleges, and co-founder of its South Central Conference. She is co-leader of the Computing Educators Oral History Project (CEOHP) and an ABET evaluator. Locally, she serves on the board and is a founding member of the Friends of Georgetown Parks and Recreation, sings in her church choir, and teaches water aerobics for the City of Georgetown. She holds a PhD from NYU, MA from the University of Texas at Austin and BA from Ohio Wesleyan University and was the co-valedictorian of her high school class in Wauseon, Ohio. She and her husband Philip have two daughters, both of whom are in technology fields, and two granddaughters.

SIGCSE '16, March 2–5, 2016, Memphis, TN, USA
ACM 978-1-4503-3685-7/16/03.
http://dx.doi.org/10.1145/2839509.2844550

CS Education: Catching the Wave

Jan Cuny
National Science Foundation
Washington, DC
jcuny@nsf.gov

ABSTRACT

Computer Science (CS) education has caught a wave – of media attention, public support, public/private commitments, broad-based participation by educators, and a surge in student enrollments at the undergraduate level. It is a startling change over just the last 5 years.

Over that 5 years, much has been accomplished at the high school level. The Exploring Computer Science and Advanced Placement® CS Principles courses were created to engage and inspire a diverse mix of students. Hundreds of teachers and university faculty have collaborated to develop course materials, assessments, MOOCS, and models of teacher professional development. Over 2,000 high schools now offer new CS courses, but that leaves out more than 34,000.

Even then, students will need more than a single course, they will need a K-16 CS pathway.

At the K-8 level, CS does not have the decades of research on the teaching and learning that is available to many other, more established disciplines. A stronger evidence base is needed as the basis for pedagogy, curricula, standards, and teacher preparation. The CS community must put greater emphasis on research in CS education and broadening participation, and it must build stronger collaborations with researchers in related disciplines.

Over the last 5 years, college-level CS departments have been inundated with students. This growth is fueled by a strong job market for CS majors and an increasing awareness that computation is fundamental to many other industry sectors and academic disciplines. How will departments cope with increasing numbers without sacrificing access or quality? How will they respond to increasing diversity—of ethnicity and gender, but also of interests, and career goals—of their students?

For those interested in CS education, it's an exciting time, but it comes with some urgency. This talk will discuss how to catch the current wave, using it to full advantage.

Keywords

Computing education; Broadening Participation; K-16; Education Research

SIGCSE '16, March 2–5, 2016, Memphis, TN, USA.
ACM 978-1-4503-3685-7/16/03.
http://dx.doi.org/10.1145/2839509.2844551

BIO

Jan Cuny received her Ph.D. in Computer and Communication Sciences from the University of Michigan. She spent the next 20 years as a faculty member, at Purdue University, the University of Massachusetts, and the University of Oregon. Her research focused on massively concurrent computation, particularly on debugging tools and programming environment support for computational science.

Jan was a long time member, co-chair, and steering committee member of the Computing Research Association's Committee on the Status of Women in Computing Research (CRA-W). That work led to her current position at the National Science Foundation (NSF), where she work to address the longstanding underrepresentation of women, African Americans, Hispanics, Native Americans, and persons with disabilities in computing. CS education is integral to broadening participation.

Focusing first K-12, Jan spearheaded NSF's efforts to build foundational support for CS10K, a national initiative to get engaging, inclusive and rigorous computing courses into America's public schools. Within this effort—named because its initial target was 10,000 teachers in10,000 schools—NSF funded the development of two new courses (Exploring Computer Science and Advanced placement® CS Principles), course materials, assessments, models of scalable professional development, and an online community of practice for teachers. NSF is now partnering with private organizations to pilot and scale these courses with the goal of giving all U.S. students the opportunity to take great computer science courses in high school. Additional efforts will be needed in diversifying and expanding K-8 and undergraduate education, and in building the CS education research enterprise.

Jan is a recipient of a 2006 ACM President's Award, the 2007 CRA A. Nico Habermann Award, the 2009 Anita Borg Institute's Woman of Vision Award, the 2014 Richard A. Tapia Achievement Award, and the University of Massachusetts School of Computing Alumni Award for Outstanding Contributions to Society.

Lean In to the Evidence: Breaking the "Glass Slipper" of Technical Professions

Karen Lee Ashcraft
University of Colorado Boulder
karen.ashcraft@colorado.edu

ABSTRACT

Occupations, like individuals, take on social identities such as gender and race. The social identity of an occupation has profound effects, for example, on wages and prestige, degree of professionalization, and ability to recruit and retain diverse populations. Sifting the historical evidence on technical work, Dr. Ashcraft develops a new concept—the "glass slipper"—which explains how durable associations between occupations and people arise and how they circulate among us like powerful brands. Despite appearances, this process is neither natural nor determined. It is political, however, revealing a reality more daunting than recent advice to "lean in" suggests. But if the social identities of occupations are strategically constructed, they also can be challenged through creative re-branding.

CCS Concepts

• *Social and professional topics~Computing occupations*

Keywords

Occupational identity, (de)segregation, and integration; professionalization and technical professions; brands and branding; gender and race relations; glass slipper

SIGCSE '16, March 2–5, 2016, Memphis, TN, USA
ACM 978-1-4503-3685-7/16/03.
http://dx.doi.org/10.1145/2839509.28460113

BIO

Karen Lee Ashcraft is a Professor of Communication at the University of Colorado Boulder. Her research examines organizations and occupations, with a focus on relations of power and difference such as gender, race, sexuality, and class. Her past research explored the character and sustainability of counter-bureaucratic organization, resulting in several award-winning articles on the potential of hybrid organizational forms. Ashcraft's recent research documents the evolution of professional identity in commercial aviation and other technical contexts. Her resulting development of the "glass slipper" received the 2013 Best Article of the Year Award from the Academy of Management Review. She has published some 50 articles and chapters on these and related themes in the journals of communication and management as well as work and organization studies. Her book with Dennis Mumby, Reworking Gender: A Feminist Communicology of Organization (2004, Sage), received the Book of the Year Award from the National Communication Association. Ashcraft regularly delivers talks and seminars to diverse audiences, including international academic and practitioner communities. She teaches undergraduate and graduate courses on gender and communication; gender, race, and work; organizational communication theory and practice; and qualitative research methods.

Demonstrations

OSBLE+: A Next-Generation Learning Management and Analytics Environment for Computing Education

Daniel M. Olivares, *Washington State University*
Christopher D. Hundhausen, Washington State University
Contact: daniel.olivares@wsu.edu

In order best to support learning analytics in computing education, learning management systems (LMS) should be interfaced with computer programming environments, in which computing students spend much of their time. To this end, we have developed OSBLE+, an outgrowth of the OSBLE (Online Studio-Based Learning Environment) LMS we have been developing over the past eight years. OSBLE+ supports two innovations that make it particularly well-suited to supporting learning analytics in computing education. First, it connects to the Microsoft Visual Studio computer programming environment via a plugin that gives it access to all programming process data within Visual Studio, including edits, compilation attempts, compilation errors, debugging attempts, and run-time exceptions. This enables OSBLE+ to provide students and instructors with a visual analytics environment in which they can explore, compare, and contrast the programming activities of students in the class. Second, the plugin turns Visual Studio into a social programming environment by injecting into it a social media-style activity stream, which enables students (a) to pose and answer programming questions, and (b) to see and explore the programming activities of their peers. Students' social activities within the activity stream are sent to OSBLE+, and are subsequently included as data in the visual analytics environment. OSBLE+ is open source and freely hosted at http://plus.osble.org. While OSBLE+ presently interfaces only with Visual Studio, a plug-in for the Eclipse programming environment is under active development.

Keywords: CS ed; learning analytics; social programming; programming; social process data; learning management systems;

DOI: http://dx.doi.org/10.1145/2839509.2850509

SIGCSE'16, March 2–5, 2016, Memphis, TN, USA.
ACM ISBN: 978-1-4503-3685-7/16/03.

Paper vs. Computer-based Exams: A Study of Errors in Recursive Binary Tree Algorithms

Scott Grissom
Grand Valley State University
Allendale, MI USA
grissom@gvsu.edu

Laurie Murphy
Pacific Lutheran University
Tacoma, WA USA
lmurphy@plu.edu

Renée McCauley
College of Charleston
Charleston, SC USA
mccauleyr@cofc.edu

Sue Fitzgerald
Metropolitan State University
St. Paul, MN
sue.fitzgerald@metrostate.edu

ABSTRACT

This paper reports on a study of goal-plans and errors produced by students who wrote recursive solutions for a binary tree operation. This work extends a previous study of difficulties CS2 students experienced while writing solutions on paper-based exams. In this study, participants solved the same recursive binary tree problem as part of a hands-on computer-based exam where students had access to an IDE and Java API documentation. Not surprisingly, students who took the computer-based exams were more successful than those who took the paper-based exams (58% vs. 17% correct solutions). However, even with the advantage of access to an IDE, documentation, and test cases, 42% of students taking the computer-based exam still made errors, indicating that students exhibit persistent errors even with support. The most common errors observed included incorrect calculations, missing method calls and missing and incorrect base cases.

Keywords

Computer science education research; recursion; data structures; BST; binary search trees; CS2; goal-plan analysis; paper-based exams; computer-based exams.

1. INTRODUCTION

The challenges students face when learning recursion have been widely reported [11]. Unlike many problems often used to introduce recursion (e.g., Fibonacci, factorial, string operations, list traversals), binary search trees (BSTs) are intrinsically linked with recursion: they exhibit structural recursion and the most efficient and natural algorithms associated with BSTs are recursive. At the same time, student misconceptions about BSTs are common [5][6] and previous research studies report student difficulty with tracing and analyzing recursive BST methods [13]. However, little has been written about the challenges students face when writing recursive BST code.

This paper extends a previous study [10] of difficulties CS2 students experience while writing recursive algorithms that operate on BSTs. Data was collected from answers to a paper-based exam. The earlier work reported on the plans students used when writing recursive methods implementing BST operations and the types of errors they made, as well as reporting on linkages between plans and errors.

In this study students solved the same recursive BST problem as part of a hands-on computer-based exam. This paper explores student plans and errors when a compiler and access to Java API documentation are permitted. Our research questions are:

- *What traversal and counting plans do students use when solving recursive problems on computer-based exams?*
- *What errors do students make when solving recursive problems on computer-based exams?*
- *Do students use different plans and/or make different errors on computer-based exams compared to paper-based exams?*

This paper continues as follows: related work is discussed in section 2, the research methodology is covered in section 3, research findings are presented in section 4, and discussed along with their implications for teaching in section 5. Section 6 suggests directions for future work.

2. RELATED WORK

Spohrer, Soloway and Pope [12] analyzed novice Pascal programs using a goal-plan analysis approach. Based on how the solutions deviated from correct plans, errors in code were categorized as malformed, misplaced, missing or spurious. Kopec, Yarmish and Cheung [7] and Yarmish and Kopec [14] adopted the goal-plan analysis technique to evaluate recursive and non-recursive written exam problems. Their advanced novice C-programming students struggled with problems requiring recursion. The students exhibited the most difficulty with base and boundary cases.

Few research studies have focused on the teaching and learning of recursion with data structures. Benander, Benander and Pu [1] investigated students' understanding of recursive algorithms using linked-lists. They compared comprehension of recursive vs.

SIGCSE '16, March 02-05, 2016, Memphis, TN, USA © 2016 ACM.
ISBN 978-1-4503-3685-7/16/03…$15.00
DOI: http://dx.doi.org/10.1145/2839509.2844587

iterative code by examining written explanations of what the code was intended to do. Students were more likely (with statistical significance) to correctly identify a linked-list search operation when it was implemented recursively. However, students were more likely (but not statistically significantly better) to identify a linked-list copy operation if it was implemented iteratively.

In a replication of the Benander et al. [1] study, McCauley, Hanks, Fitzgerald and Murphy [9] found subjects were equally likely to correctly describe the purpose of the search algorithms, regardless of iterative or recursive implementation. Consistent with the findings in the earlier study, subjects were more likely to correctly describe the copy task when it was implemented iteratively rather than recursively. Further, McCauley et al. examined the students' written descriptions of the copy algorithms. Subjects who correctly described the purpose of the copy method wrote abstract summaries. Many of the subjects who did not recognize the purpose of the code, and who answered incorrectly, provided a line-by-line (partial) trace of the code. While revealing some understanding of the execution of the code, these subjects were generally not able to see the forest for the trees. This analysis is analogous to the relational and multi-structural categories of the SOLO taxonomy [3].

Corney et al. [4] also studied recursive program comprehension. They found a strong correlation between ability to explain recursive linked-list code at an abstract level with students' performance on code writing and code reading test problems.

In a debugging study, Benander, Benander and Sang [2] found students were more successful at finding and fixing bugs in recursive linked-list programs than in iterative implementations. Students took about the same amount of time to find and fix bugs regardless of the algorithm's implementation approach.

Although binary trees are often more naturally processed recursively than linked-lists, overall there has been little research on recursion in the context of binary trees. In our prior 2015 study [10], we employed goal-plan analysis to examine plans students used when writing code for a binary tree operation. Students wrote a recursive method to count all the nodes in a binary tree with exactly one child. The problem incorporated two goals: traversing the tree and counting nodes with one child. Three traversal plan variations and four counting plans were observed in student solutions. Over half the students used an arm's-length recursion plan, which tests for the base case before it is actually reached in order to avoid making recursive calls. This strategy resulted in complex and error prone code. Errors were also analyzed, using the Spohrer et al. [12] categorization. Students had particular difficulty with base cases, misplaced calculations, and missing method calls.

3. METHODS

3.1 Participants and Study Context

Study participants were enrolled in a second programming course at a private liberal arts university in the United States. All 42 participants had successfully completed an introductory (CS1) course in Java. Students were asked to write a recursive method to count the number of nodes in a BST with only one child. Eighteen of the students were enrolled in the class in fall of 2013 and submitted their solutions on paper-based final exams (PBE). The other 24 took the course in fall of 2014 and composed their solutions during a computer-based final exam (CBE).

The 15-week course included object oriented design basics; introduction to algorithm analysis; lists, stacks, queues, binary search trees and hash tables; and common sorting algorithms. Recursion and binary search trees were introduced in the middle of the term and about 2½ weeks were devoted to these topics. Students submitted two programming assignments and two written homework problem sets which focused on recursion and trees. One programming assignment required students to write a recursive, text-based Boggle™ game. The second programming assignment required the implementation of numerous BST methods (e.g., size, height, counts of leaves and interior nodes, and pre, post and inorder traversals). An optional 10-question worksheet assignment required students to analyze "perfect" binary trees and to generate and plot height and runtime statistics for randomly generated BSTs. The course included additional exposure to recursion through the study of recursive sorting algorithms and heaps. While the course materials and assignments in both semesters were very similar, the classes were each taught by different instructors using different textbooks.

3.2 Exam Question

The final exams taken by all students comprised 25% of their course grade. However, for the 18 students who took the paper-based exam, the study question was worth 10% of the final exam, while for the 24 students who took both a paper-based and a computer-based exam, the study question was given on the computer-based part and made up 5% of their total exam grade.

The paper-based exam question stated:

> Write a recursive member method for a BST to determine the number of nodes that have one child. (Hint: countParentsOfOne() will call a private recursive method, that you write, that does all the work). Class BinarySearchTree<E> has a field `root` of type Node<E>, and Node<E> has fields `left`, `right`, and `data`.

```
public int countParentsOfOne()
```

The same question was asked on the computer-based exam, although the purpose of the method was stated as a comment in code provided to the students. The code also included a BinaryTreeNode class and other BST methods. Students were also given the hint below regarding nodes with two children.

```
/**
    Counts the number of nodes in the tree
    with exactly one child
    HINT: recall that nodes with two
    children may have descendants with
    only one child
**/
```

PBE students were not permitted to use books or lecture notes, but were allowed to use personal notes written on both sides of an 8.5x11 inch reference sheet. Students who took the computer-based exam were allowed to use their textbooks and worked within the Eclipse IDE, which provided syntax correction and access to the Java API documentation. They were also given a set of JUnit tests with which to test their code that included tests with a variety of trees (empty, one node, skewed, balanced, random). They were not allowed to use any other notes or solutions to their laboratory assignments. All students had nearly two hours to complete the exams, and only a very few students who simply did not know how to answer one or more questions were unable to finish in the allotted time.

3.3 Goal-Plan Analysis

Using goal-plan analysis [12], the researchers identified two goals for this problem: 1) traverse the binary search tree and 2) count nodes with only one child. Each *goal* can be achieved in a variety of ways. Each unique strategy is called a *plan*. Students attempted to achieve the tree traversal and counting goals using several plans. Four researchers classified the unique plans, with all four discussing to consensus on 94% of the categorizations (see Table 1).

Table 1. Goal-Plan Categories

Goal: Traverse tree	
Concise recursion plan	Avoids unnecessary statements and recursive calls (Figure 1-a).
Verbose recursion plan	Includes unnecessary conditionals to prevent passing leaves to the recursive method. This plan is complete and traverses the entire tree. (Figure 1-b).
Incomplete recursion plan	Is missing some conditions or recursive calls such that it does not traverse the entire tree. (Figure 1-c)
Loop plan (not viable)	Attempts to traverse the tree using loop(s), perhaps in combination with recursive method calls (Figure 2).
Other (not viable)	Exhibits no clear plan or is seemingly unrelated to the problem.
Goal: Count nodes with only one child	
Passive counting plan	Uses return statements to passively count nodes with one child without using a local variable (Figure 1-a & 1-b).
Local variable plan	Uses local variable(s) to count nodes with one child (Figure 3-a).
Non-local variable plan	Uses a non-local variable to count nodes with one child (Figure 3-b).
Parameter plan	Uses an extra formal parameter in the recursive method to count nodes with one child (Figure 3-c).
Other: (not viable)	Exhibits no clear plan or is seemingly unrelated to the problem.

Figure 1 illustrates traversal plans adapted from student solutions. Solution 1-a shows a *concise* traversal plan. This approach minimizes the number of statements and is typical of expert implementations. The traversal goal is accomplished with one base case, one conditional and a pair of recursive calls for nodes with one child (left and right children) and another pair of recursive calls for all remaining conditions. Several students used additional conditional statements to avoid recursive calls, in effect short-circuiting the recursion, as seen in Figure 1-b. We call this approach *verbose*. The example shown in 1-c is *incomplete* since it does not traverse the entire tree. Figure 2 shows an example of a *loop* plan that is not viable.

a. concise recursion for traversal

```
public int parentsOfOne(){
  // call to recursive method
  return count(root);
}
private int count(Node t){
  // empty tree
  if (t == null)
    return 0;
  // only one child
  if((t.left != null && t.right == null) ||
       (t.left == null && t.right != null))
     return 1 + count(t.left) + count(t.right);
  // otherwise, keep looking
  return count(t.left) + count(t.right);
}
```

b. verbose recursion for traversal

```
public int parentsOfOne(){
  // check for non-empty tree
  if (root != null)
    return count(root);
  else // empty tree
    return 0;
}
private int count(Node t){
  // empty tree
  if (t == null)
    return 0;
  // leaf node
  else if(t.left == null && t.right == null)
    return 0;
  // only one child (left)
  else if (t.left != null && t.right == null)
     return 1 + count(t.left);
  // only one child (right)
  else if (t.left == null && t.right != null)
     return 1 + count(t.right);
  else // two children
    return count(t.left) + count(t.right);
}
```

c. incomplete recursion for traversal

```
public int parentsOfOne(){
  // call to recursive method
  return count(root);
}
public int count(Node t){
  // empty tree
  if (t == null)
    return 0;
  // does not continue traversing right branch
  else if(t.left == null && t.right != null)
    return 1;
  // does not continue traversing left branch
  else if(t.left != null && t.right == null)
    return 1;
  // does not traverse with two children
  else
    return 0;
}
```

Figure 1. Example plans for achieving the traverse tree goal

attempts to use a loop to traverse tree

```
public int parentsOfOne() {
  while (root != null)
       return count(root);
  return 0;
}
private int count(Node t) {
  int total = 0;
  while(t.left != null) {
    if (t.right == null)
       total++;
    else {
       count(t.left);
       count(t.right);
    }
  }
  return total;
}
```

Figure 2. Example loop traversal plan (not viable)

All examples in Figure 1 achieve the counting goal by adding 1 to the result of a recursive call (except 1-c which does not traverse the tree correctly.) This plan is called passive counting and refers to the absence of any variables to maintain the count. Figure 3 shows segments of several counting plans using local variables, non-local variables and parameters.

a. using a local variable to count

```
  int total = 0;
  if(t.left == null && t.right != null)
    total++;
  if(t.left != null && t.right == null)
    total++;
  total += count(t.right)+count(t.left);
  return total;
```

b. using a non-local variable to count

```
  if(t.left == null && t.right != null)
      global_total++;
  if(t.left != null && t.right == null)
      global_total++;
  count(t.right);
  count(t.left);
  return;
```

c. using a parameter to count

```
private int count(Node t, int total){
  if(t.left == null && t.right != null)
      return count(t.left, total + 1);
  return total;
}
```

Figure 3. Code segment examples of poor counting plans

3.4 Error Categorization

Researchers also identified and categorized coding errors. To establish initial error categories, coding errors were first classified according to programming construct or statement type involved. These included: base case, calculation, conditional, loop, method call, parameter, return value/call/type, and variable. They were then also assigned to one of the error types: *missing*, *malformed*, *misplaced* and *spurious* [12]. This yielded a set of 16 distinct error categories (e.g., missing base case, misplaced return statement, malformed method call, etc.). Three researchers then independently identified the errors in students' code and assigned them to one of the 16 categories. The researchers then worked together to come to agreement on categorizations. At least two researchers agreed on 93% of the 63 total errors identified and all agreed on 85% of the errors. Simple syntax errors and unnecessary code that was not erroneous was noted but not considered an error. The error categories are discussed in detail in Section 4.2.

3.5 Threats to Validity

While all students in the study solved the same problem, those who answered using paper and pencil had far fewer resources (only a single sheet of personal notes) than those who answered on the computer. Students who took the computer-based exam had access to their textbooks, Javadocs and JUnit test cases, and were provided an additional hint (assuming they read it). The test cases in particular, which were reasonably thorough, likely encouraged students to write more complete and correct code than they would have if the tests not been provided, or if they had been directed to write their own tests. These additional resources appeared to improve students' ability to write code, yielding fewer incorrect plans and errors. Yet many of the same erroneous plans and errors appeared in both groups and suggest persistent challenges by novices exist regardless of additional support.

Because this was a small group of students, and they all attended a single institution, results are suggestive rather than significant. Student in the two groups having different instructors and textbooks is also a likely confounding factor.

4. RESULTS

4.1 Goal-Plan Analysis

Forty-two students participated in the study. Eighteen took the paper-based exam (PBE) and twenty-four completed the computer-based exam (CBE) during a different term and with a different instructor.

4.1.1 Traversal Plans

A majority of solutions showed signs of being on the right track with reasonable tree traversal plans (see Table 2). Approximately one-third of the CBE students provided concise solutions for tree traversal compared with one-quarter of the PBE students. Concise and verbose traversal plans are both viable solutions. Considering the combined concise and verbose traversal plans, almost twice as many CBE students provided viable tree traversal plans as compared to PBE students (75% vs. 44%).

The largest distinction between the two groups was the category of incomplete traversal plans. Over one-third of the PBE students (38%) neglected to include all the conditionals or method calls necessary to traverse the entire tree. For example, these solutions might have neglected to include a recursive call when two children were detected. Or the solutions might correctly traverse the left side of the tree but overlook the right side. Less than 10% of CBE participants had similar traversal flaws.

4.1.2 Counting Plans

PBE counting plans were varied. Over one-third of these students used the passive counting plan but some used local variables, non-local variables or parameters to accumulate the number of nodes with only one child. In contrast, a solid majority (71%) of the CBE students used passive counting. No CBE solutions used non-local variables or parameters.

Table 2. Number / Percentage of Students Using Each Plan on Paper-based (PBE) and Computer-based Exams (CBE)

Goal	Plan	PBE	CBE
Traverse tree	Concise recursion	4 (22%)	8 (33%)
	Verbose recursion	4 (22%)	10 (42%)
	Loop (not viable)	2 (12%)	2 (8%)
	Incomplete traversal	7 (38%)	2 (8%)
	Other (not viable)	1 (6%)	2 (8%)
Count parent nodes with one child	Passive counting	8 (44%)	17 (71%)
	Using local variables	3 (17%)	5 (21%)
	Using non-local variables	1 (6%)	0 (0%)
	Using parameters	3 (17%)	0 (0%)
	Other (not viable)	3 (17%)	2 (8%)

4.2 Error Analysis

Table 3 compares the errors made by PBE and CBE students. The data shown are the percentage of students, for each test type, who made at least one error indicted by column and row labels. Some solutions included multiple errors. PBE students made several errors beyond the simple syntax errors common on written exams. Fourteen of the twenty-four CBE students solved the problem with no errors (58%), in comparison to only three of eighteen PBE students who had no errors (17%).

Table 3. Percentage of Student Errors on Paper-based Exams (PBE) and Computer-based Exams (CBE)

Construct / Statement Type	Category PBE / CBE			
	Missing	Malformed	Misplaced	Spurious
Conditional	28% / 12%	22% / 4%		0% / 4%
Method call	56% / 17%			
Base case	39% / 12%	6% / 17%		
Calculation		61% / 29%		
Return stmts	11% / 4%	6% / 0%	0% / 4%	
Variable				
Loop				11% / 8%
Parameter				
At least one error	78% / 25%	67% / 33%	0% / 4%	11% / 12%

4.2.1 *Missing Statements*

Errors identified as *missing statements* resulted in failure to consider certain cases such as an empty tree, failure to search an entire tree (some algorithms only searched down one side of a tree), and failure to make some necessary recursive calls. Missing statements were much more common in PBE solutions (78%) compared to CBE solutions (25%).

4.2.2 *Malformed Solutions*

Malformed solutions included conditionals that attempted to dereference null pointers, conditionals to check if root's data field was null rather than checking for root being null, and incorrect calculation of nodes with only one. Incorrect calculations sometimes counted nodes with no children or two children instead of only one child. Other common errors were to not return the accumulated values or to double count nodes. These errors were more common in PBE solutions (61%) than CBE solutions (29%).

4.2.3 *Misplaced and Spurious Errors*

There was only one *misplaced* return statement. The few *spurious* errors involved use of a loop to traverse the tree. This was observed in two PBE (11%) and two CBE (8%) cases.

4.3 Plans vs. Errors

Table 4 shows the average number of errors for each plan. For example, PBE students who used concise traversal plans had an average of 1.75 errors. This compares to CBE students who had an average of 0.5 errors when using concise traversal. CBE solutions had fewer errors for every plan except for non-viable counting plans.

4.3.1 *Traversal Plans vs. Errors*

For CBE tree traversals, the average number of errors increased as the plan became more complex. The concise plan uses the fewest number of conditional statements and recursive calls and solutions with this strategy had the fewest average number of errors (0.5). On the other end of the spectrum, CBE students without a viable traversal plan had an average of 5.0 errors. (For non-viable plans, many errors can be identified and it is difficult to determine a specific number.) The trend was similar for PBE traversal plans. Students who used concise recursion had fewer errors than those who used non-viable plans (1.75 vs. 6.0).

4.3.2 *Counting Plans vs. Errors*

One could argue that passive counting is the simplest solution with complexity growing as local variables, non-local variables and parameters are used for counting. Again, CBE students using the simplest plan exhibited the fewest errors (0.4) and students with no viable plan had far more errors (5.5). This trend is also observed for PBE students.

Table 4. Average Errors per Plan for Paper-based Exams (PBE) and Computer-based Exams (CBE)

Goal	Plan	PBE Avg (n)	CBE Avg (n)
Traverse tree	Concise recursion	1.75 (4)	0.5 (8)
	Verbose recursion	0.75 (4)	0.5 (10)
	Incomplete	2.6 (7)	1.5 (2)
	Loop (not viable)	4.5 (2)	2.0 (2)
	Other (not viable)	6.0 (1)	5.0 (2)
Count parent nodes with one child	Passive counting	1.1 (7)	0.4 (17)
	Counting with local vars	2.3 (3)	1.8 (5)
	Counting with non-local vars	4.0 (1)	0
	Counting with parameters	2.3 (3)	0
	Other (not viable)	4.3 (4)	5.5 (2)

5. DISCUSSION

Students who took the computer-based exams performed better than those who took the paper-based exams. They had more viable traversal plans and fewer errors.

The groups approached the problem using different plans. In terms of traversal strategies, 75% of CBE students submitted correct solutions employing either concise or verbose recursion, while only 44% of PBE students did the same. With respect to counting strategies, a majority of the CBE students (71%) employed passive counting, while fewer than half of the PBE students (44%) did so. The more concise plans for traversal and counting resulted in fewer errors. This phenomenon was also observed in [10].

Three errors were particularly distinct between the two groups: 1) failure to consider an empty tree, 2) not traversing the entire tree and 3) not accurately counting nodes with only one child.

First, 28% of PBE students failed to account for an empty tree. In contrast, every CBE student at least attempted to address an empty tree even if not done correctly. This superior performance may be due to the unit tests provided by the instructor. CBE students were able to discover through trial and error that the special case of an empty tree was not handled.

A second noticeable difference between the groups was the inability to traverse the entire tree (38% by PBE students as compared to only 8% by CBE students). Several PBE students stopped traversing the tree when the first node with one child was found or otherwise failed to correctly traverse the entire tree (see Figure 1-c). This may suggest that it is difficult for students to visualize traversal of a tree without running their solutions against test cases.

And third, PBE students (61%) were more likely than CBE students (29%) to make errors counting nodes with only one child. Poor strategies included using non-local variables or parameters as accumulators or neglecting to increment the accumulator when a node was detected.

Anecdotally, some students claim computer-based testing is more natural for solving programming problems and that paper exams are too artificial. Results from this study support this perception. Computer-based exams may give students a better opportunity to demonstrate their abilities. These apparent advantages are discussed further in Section 6. However, it is interesting to note that even with the advantage of access to an IDE and test cases, 42% of CBE students still made errors. Students exhibit persistent misconceptions even with support.

This study provides useful insights into the kinds of errors students make when writing recursive code to perform operations on binary trees. Faculty would be well served to focus time and attention on the most common errors – understanding the exact nature of the problem, missing base cases and traversals which do not cover the entire tree.

6. FUTURE WORK

Insights gained through analyzing this small dataset illustrate the potential of using naturally occurring exam data in CS education research [8]. Replicating this study at multiple institutions could confirm persistent misconceptions that should be addressed when introducing BSTs for a variety of students. Using alternative BST problems such as breadth first search or identifying the length of the longest branch may reveal new traversal plans or error types.

As indicated in the Discussion, CBE students had fewer errors which may be due to the support from an IDE, Java documentation and instructor-provided unit tests. Additional data collected at a second institution may provide further insight. Fourteen data structures students were given a programming test that included the countParentsOfOne problem. However, they were not provided hints or test cases as with the current study. A preliminary analysis of goal-plans revealed similar results to those reported in Table 2: 78% of students submitted correct solutions that involved concise or verbose traversal plans, and 93% used passive counting. However, 21% of these CBE students failed to account for an empty tree compared to none in the original data.

It is difficult to identify student conceptions by analyzing exam artifacts only. One-on-one student interviews and using a think-aloud protocol while students solve problems may reveal *why* misconceptions persist. For example, do students truly fail to consider an empty tree or do they think their solutions handle an empty tree? Is writing a concise solution with fewer conditionals and method calls important?

7. ACKNOWLEDGMENTS

We thank Kenneth Blaha for his assistance in collecting data.

8. REFERENCES

[1] Benander, A. C., Benander, B. A., and Pu, H. 1996. Recursion vs. iteration: An empirical study of comprehension. *J. of Systems and Software* 32, 1, 73-82.

[2] Benander, A. C., Benander, B. A., and Sang, J. 2000. An empirical analysis of debugging performance – differences between iterative and recursive constructs. *J. of Systems and Software* 54, 1, 17-28.

[3] Biggs, J. and Collis, K. 1982. Evaluating the Quality of Learning: The SOLO Taxonomy (Structure of the Observed Learning Outcome). Academic Press, New York, NY.

[4] Corney, M., Fitzgerald, S., Hanks, B., Lister, R., McCauley, R., and Murphy, L. 2014. 'Explain in plain English' questions revisited: Data structures problems. In *Proceedings of the 45th ACM Technical Symposium on Computer Science Education* (Atlanta, GA, USA, March 5-8, 2014). SIGCSE '14. ACM, New York, NY, USA, 591-596.

[5] Danielsiek, H., Paul, W., and Vahrenhold, J. 2012. Detecting and understanding students' misconceptions related to algorithms and data structures. In *Proceedings of the 43rd ACM Technical Symposium on Computer Science Education* (Raleigh, NC, USA, Feb. 29-March 3, 2102). SIGCSE '12. ACM, New York, NY, USA, 21-26.

[6] Karpierz, K. and Wolfman, S. A. 2014. Misconceptions and concept inventory questions for binary search trees and hash tables. In *Proceedings of the 45th ACM Technical Symposium on Computer Science Education* (Atlanta, GA, USA, March 5-8, 2014). SIGCSE '14. ACM, New York, NY, USA, 109–114.

[7] Kopec, D., Yarmish, G., and Cheung, P. 2007. A description and study of intermediate student programmer errors. *SIGCSE Bull.* 39, 2, 146–156.

[8] Lister, R., Clear, T., Simon, Bouvier, J., Carter, P., Eckerdal, A., Jacková, J., Lopez, M., McCartney, R., Robbins, P., Seppälä, O. and Thompson, E. 2010. Naturally occurring data as research instrument: analyzing examination responses to study the novice programmer. *SIGCSE Bull.* 41, 4 (January 2010), 156-173.

[9] McCauley, R., Hanks, B., Fitzgerald, S., and Murphy,L. Recursion vs. Iteration: An Empirical Study of Comprehension Revisited, in *Proceedings of the 49th Technical Symposium on Computer Science Education,* (Kansas City, MO, USA, March 4-7, 2015). SIGCSE '15. ACM, New York, NY, USA 350-355.

[10] Murphy, L., Fitzgerald, S., Grissom, S. and McCauley, R. 2015. Recursion vs. iteration: An empirical study of comprehension. In *Proceedings of the 46th ACM Technical Symposium on Computer Science Education* (Kansas City, MO, USA, March 4-7, 2015). SIGCSE '15. ACM, New York, NY, USA, 482-487.

[11] Rinderknecht, C. 2014. A survey on teaching and learning recursive programming. *Informatics in Educ* 13, 1, 87-119.

[12] Spohrer, J. C., Soloway, E., and Pope, E. 1985. A goal/plan analysis of buggy Pascal programs. *Human-Computer Interaction* 1, 2, 163–207.

[13] Tenenberg, J. and Murphy, L. 2005. Knowing what I know: An investigation of undergraduate knowledge and self-knowledge of data structures. *Computer Science Education* 15, 4, 297–315.

[14] Yarmish, G. and Kopec, D. 2007. Revisiting novice programmer errors. *SIGCSE Bull.* 39, 2, 131–137.

Stay on These Roads: Potential Factors Indicating Students' Performance in a CS2 Course

Holger Danielsiek
Department of Computer Science
Westfälische Wilhelms-Universität Münster
48149 Münster, Germany
holger.danielsiek@uni-muenster.de

Jan Vahrenhold
Department of Computer Science
Westfälische Wilhelms-Universität Münster
48149 Münster, Germany
jan.vahrenhold@uni-muenster.de

ABSTRACT

This paper reports on first steps towards identifying factors indicating students' performance in a CS2 course. We discuss a study undertaken to investigate the predictive and explanation power as well as the limits of weekly test items based on concept inventory questions, homework grades, and performance in a preceding CS1 course. We relate our findings for two subgroups to results on academic success in general and performance in a CS1 course in particular.

CCS Concepts

•Social and professional topics → Computer science education; Student assessment;

Keywords

CS1/2; concept inventory; success factors

1. INTRODUCTION

Being able to identify and, ultimately, understand factors influencing students' performance in introductory computer science courses is of central importance for improving the design of such courses. While this holds true for other academic subjects as well, the seemingly unending struggle with recruitment and retention makes this a fundamental issue for many computer science departments.

A large number of studies have been undertaken to investigate factors determining academic success; see the meta-review by Kuh et al. [6]. A major finding is that the "trajectory for academic success in college is established long before matriculation" [6, p. 89]; Kuh et al. also point out, though, that "most students [...] benefit from early interventions and sustained attention at key transition points" [6, p. 94].

A recent meta-analysis by Schulmeister [14] covers almost 300 studies, including 28 large-scale studies based on workload measurements on various levels of granularity and 57 studies addressing other factors determining academic success. The reported results most relevant to our study are that (1) performance is only weakly related to effort [15, p. 949], that (2) class attendance corresponds to performance, but that the effect is greatest at the lowest level [15, p. 951], and that (3) among the *Big Five* personality factors, "*conscientiousness* is strongly and consistently associated with academic success" [9, p. 971]; see also the meta-analysis by Poropat [10]. Regarding effort, Schulmeister [14] reports on a recent large-scale study involving 620 students in, e.g., economics, accounting, mathematics, law, business information management, and IT security. The study could not find a significant relation between (raw) workload and academic success. Also, no significant difference could be observed regarding gender or pre-college subject knowledge [14, Sec. V].

Most research on factors influencing students' success in computer science has focused CS1 courses, see, e.g., [3, 13, 19] and the references therein. Bennedsen and Caspersen [3] found high-school mathematics grades and course work to significantly influence performance in a CS1 course (contradicting earlier results by Ventura and Ramamurthy [18]); these results are in line with the findings by Wilson and Shrock [20] who identified the comfort level, mathematics background, and attribution to luck for success or failure as the three most relevant factors. For the case of a discrete mathematics course, Jamba-Joyner and Klostermeyer found a strong influence of mathematics SAT grades [5]. Because the research reported upon in this paper took place at a German university, it is worthwhile noticing that, according to Schulmeister [14, p. 191], Trapmann [16] concludes from a review of the literature that the factors influencing German high-school graduation grades also influence German college grades. Achievement motivation/expectation of success was found to also influence performance in a CS1 course [13].

Since CS1 exams, at least in the North-American context, frequently exhibit a bimodal grade distribution, researchers have begun to investigate possible explanations for such a distribution [12, 1]. We note in passing, though, that such a distribution cannot be observed in our courses.

Porter et al. [11, 21] established a link between fine-grained peer instruction "clicker questions" and the final exam and can correlate students' performance on such questions with their performance on isomorphic questions in the final exam.

Given the recent efforts to (re-)introduce computer science as part of secondary education, e.g., through the "Hour of Code" initiative, and the fact that computer science already is part of secondary education in several countries, it is not unreasonable to assume that several of the topics currently covered in CS1/2 courses eventually will be integrated into

SIGCSE '16 Memphis, Tennessee USA

ISBN 978-1-4503-3685-7/16/03...$15.00

DOI: http://dx.doi.org/10.1145/2839509.2844591

high-school curricula. Hence, the burden of recruitment and retention might be shifted to current CS2 courses.

2. A CS2 COURSE

This section describes the construction, the learning objectives, and the contents of the CS2 course. The course was taught by the second author. The first author was one of the two graduate assistants assigned to this course.

Class and Recitation Sessions.

The CS2 course is a mandatory course in the second semester of all computer science related programs at the Westfälische Wilhelms-Universität Münster, Germany (WWU). This includes computer science majors and minors (both will be referred to as CS students) as well as business information management (BIM) students. The course is taught during the summer term (14 weeks). In each week, there are two classroom lectures of 90 minutes each plus 90-minutes recitation sessions run in groups of 20 to 30 students. In these recitation sessions, undergraduate teaching assistants review the (graded) weekly homework assignments. Attendance is not mandatory, though.

For CS students, the final grade is determined by the final exam. To be admitted to the exam, however, students have to achieve at least 40% of the points awarded for the homework assignments in either half of the semester. For BIM students, in contrast, there is no such admission barrier. Instead, 20% of the final grade are determined by the homework assignments (provided that the final exam has been passed).

A policy of WWU aimed at supporting teamwork encourages students to work in teams of up to three students when solving homework assignments and to submit only one solution per team. Academic ethics are enforced by routinely checking for duplicate submission across teams and by randomly selecting a team member to present the team's solution during the recitation session.

Learning Objectives and Topics.

After a successful completion of the CS2 course, students should be able to perform the following activities:

- Design solutions for computer science problems.
- Develop and implement algorithms/data structures.
- (Mathematically) Analyze the cost of computations.
- Prove the correctness of algorithms/data structures.
- Select a programming language/paradigm to implement a particular algorithm or data structure.

The CS2 course covers the following topics: Linear data structures, abstract data types (including inductive proofs), analysis of algorithms (including evaluating series), searching/hashing (including loop invariants), sorting (including correctness proofs), divide-and-conquer (including solving recurrences), tree data structures, priority queues, graphs, and graph algorithms. Since the CS2 course at WWU is math-oriented and covers these topics in-depth, there is a second-year *Efficient Algorithms* class that covers advanced algorithmic concepts, such as dynamic programming, not included in the above list.

3. SUBJECTS

The number of subjects participating in the final exam of the CS2 course (summer term 2015) was $n = 201$. Of these, $n_{\text{CS}} = 139$ were CS students, while the remaining $n_{\text{BIM}} = 62$ were BIM students. It should be noted that admission to the computer science courses at WWU is selective: all students in the course reported upon had finished high school with an average grade of at least 2.5/6.0 (in the national system reported upon, the best grade in high school is 1.0, the worst passing grade is 4.0). The distribution of the average final high school grades ($n \approx 79.000$, $\mu = 2.48$, $\sigma = 0.66$) in the state from which WWU draws the majority of incoming students shows a bias in the sense of Trapmann's [16] conjectured common set of factors influencing high-school and academic performance (see Section 1). While the average mathematics grade is lower across all students ($\mu = 2.9$, $\sigma = 1.0$), it is reasonable to expect a certain self-selection bias resulting in a higher average mathematics grade for those taking a CS2 course[1].

As described in Section 2, the grading scheme for BIM students is different from the one used for all other students. As a consequence, we break down our findings with respect to these two groups. This is in line with Schulmeister' recommendation to consider subgroups wherever possible. He even suggests abandoning the quest for global determinants or predictors in favor of trying to understand how variables are distributed across subgroups and to respond to these distributions in class [14, p. 173].

4. TEST ITEMS

In principle, the CS2 course was taught using a traditional model of instruction. In particular, no inverted-classroom techniques, reading assignments, or quizzes were used. The course followed, however, a rapid-feedback concept based on concept-inventory test items [17]. For the sake of self-containedness, we briefly summarize the key features here.

The CS2 classes took place every Monday and Thursday, the recitation sessions are scheduled in parallel Thursday and Friday. During the break of every Monday session, students were asked to complete a paper-and-pencil test. These tests consisted of one to five multiple-choice test items pertaining to the topics covered during the previous week. The development and validation of the distractors for these test items was done using a student-centered feedback loop [17]. The assignment from the answers to students is anonymized through a one-way function, i.e., students can be "tracked" anonymously throughout the semester. As the anonymized ID also encodes the recitation group the student is assigned to, responses can be grouped by recitation group. During the weekly teaching assistants' meeting (held every Tuesday), each teaching assistant learns about the potential deficits of his or her mentees and can respond to their needs in the same week. Serious and/or global misunderstandings can also be addressed during the next lecture (Thursday).

The benefits of this diagnostic and intervention strategy (which are not the focus of this paper) have been confirmed on two occasions (hashing and "big-oh"-notation) where a re-test showed a substantial increase in understanding.

An Attempt to Extrapolate Performance.

The responses from the test items have also been used to compare performance throughout the semester and in the final exam. In a similar study conducted in the context of a

[1]Due to privacy reasons, the high-school grades of the subjects participating in our study could not be accessed.

	n	A	–	+	B	–	+	C	–	+	D	Fail	Difference Items/Exam	
CS Exam	139	0 (0%)	5 (4%)	5 (4%)	7 (5%)	6 (4%)	15 (11%)	17 (12%)	14 (10%)	13 (9%)	20 (14%)	37 (27%)		
Items 1–26 (75%)	101	4 (4%)	2 (2%)	3 (3%)	7 (7%)	2 (2%)	4 (4%)	18 (18%)	10 (10%)	13 (13%)	9 (9%)	29 (29%)	-	no systematic difference
Items 1–26 (50%)	137	4 (3%)	2 (1%)	3 (2%)	8 (6%)	3 (2%)	5 (4%)	21 (15%)	12 (9%)	17 (12%)	13 (9%)	49 (36%)	-	no systematic difference
Items 1–19 (50%)	142	6 (4%)	4 (3%)	5 (4%)	3 (2%)	7 (5%)	14 (10%)	19 (13%)	8 (6%)	20 (14%)	17 (12%)	39 (27%)	-	no systematic difference
BIM Exam	62	0 (0%)	1 (2%)	2 (3%)	1 (2%)	2 (3%)	5 (8%)	10 (16%)	7 (11%)	10 (16%)	12 (19%)	12 (19%)		
Items 1–26 (75%)	40	0 (0%)	0 (0%)	1 (3%)	1 (3%)	3 (8%)	1 (3%)	5 (13%)	1 (3%)	6 (15%)	4 (10%)	18 (45%)	$p \leq .1$	worse than exam
Items 1–26 (50%)	73	0 (0%)	0 (0%)	2 (3%)	1 (1%)	3 (4%)	3 (4%)	8 (11%)	2 (3%)	11 (15%)	5 (7%)	38 (52%)	$p \leq .005$	worse than exam
Items 1–19 (50%)	81	0 (0%)	1 (1%)	2 (2%)	3 (4%)	1 (1%)	4 (5%)	7 (9%)	3 (4%)	11 (14%)	11 (14%)	38 (47%)	$p \leq .005$	worse than exam

Figure 1: Grade distributions for the final exam and their relation to the test item grade distributions after two thirds of the course (for IDs used in at least 50% of the 19 test items) and at the end of the course (for IDs used in at least 50% resp. 75% of all 26 test items). Comparison was done using a Mann-Whitney-U test.

peer-instruction CS1 course, Porter et al. [11] could leverage the clicker technology used and the fact that peer-instruction participation counted towards the grade to establish a link between each individual student's responses and final grades. In our setting, privacy concerns did not allow to establish these individual links. However, as discussed below, the resulting anonymity induced a very low level of stress associated with the test items and allowed for a much lower level of bias regarding presumed desirability of self-assessment questions. It should be noted that the anonymity did not lead to a low response rate. Comparing the number of responses with a quick head-count suggested a response rate of consistently well over 90%. Due to fluctuations in attendance, the number of responses varied between 251 and 136 with a median of 187 and an average of 192.

The "grades" for the test items were extrapolated from the number of correct answers relative to the number of submitted answers (the same scheme was used by Porter et al. [11]). Because no individual links could be established between test items and the final exam, we scaled the extrapolated number of correct answers to the same scale used for grading the final exam and converted this number to a grade.

Results.

In our first study [17], we observed no statistically significant difference between the performance of all students as indicated by the correctness of the test items and the outcome of the final exam. While the same result could be obtained also for this course as long as all students are considered as one group, the results for the CS students and BIM students differ. The results summarized in Figure 1 seem to imply that CS students perform approximately the same on the test items and on the exam while BIM students perform worse on the test items. However, this difference is only weakly significant for BIM students that responded to at least 75% of the test items. As participation in a paper-and-pencil test obviously indicates attendance, these results are consistent with the influence of class attendance on the performance [15]. The change in performance across the three data points for BIM students can also be explained by observing that most students performing less successful on the first 19 test items chose not to take the first final exam (data omitted from this extended abstract).

After two thirds of the course, we administered a questionnaire geared towards the acceptance of the test items as a diagnostic and instructional technique. For this questionnaire, we extrapolated grades for those anonymized IDs used for at least 50% of the test items responded to so far. Among other things, the questionnaire asked students to disclose their extrapolated grade (due to privacy concerns, this required the questionnaire to be completely anonymous) and to report whether they considered this extrapolated grade to properly reflect their knowledge; see Figure 2.

much better	better	similar	worse	much worse
10 (6%)	52 (33%)	57 (36%)	33 (21%)	6 (4%)

Figure 2: "My knowledge is ... compared to the extrapolated grade." Data follows a normal distribution (Shapiro-Wilks test, sig.= .344, $n = 158$).

Figure 3 summarizes the student's assessment of the test-item concept. The first observation is that taking the test items does not (significantly) motivates students to spend extra time on preparation. Moreover (results are omitted due to lack of space), we were unable to find a correlation between extra preparation and extrapolated grades. While this seems less desirable from an instructor's perspective, it is actually quite in line with the fact that study time and performance do not correlate; see Section 1. Also, since the *conscientiousness* personality trait has been shown to strongly influence performance [9, 10], we conjecture that conscientious students tend to prepare anyway and thus do not feel that the test items warrant *extra* preparation time.

The remaining answers indicate that students are comfortable answering the test items and consider them a helpful use of classroom time. These results are consistent with

I spend extra time to prepare for the test items.

n	++	+	○	−	−−
172	5 (3%)	29 (17%)	33 (19%)	43 (25%)	62 (36%)

I feel stressed when answering test items.

n	++	+	○	−	−−
171	4 (2%)	18 (11%)	25 (15%)	57 (33%)	67 (39%)

I consider test items to be useful.

n	++	+	○	−	−−
172	85 (49%)	62 (36%)	17 (10%)	6 (3%)	2 (1%)

The class time spent on test items should have been used to cover more material.

n	++	+	○	−	−−
170	4 (2%)	7 (4%)	23 (14%)	61 (36%)	75 (44%)

Figure 3: Students' assessment of the test-item concept as implemented (++: strongly agree; +: agree; ○: neutral; −: disagree; −−: strongly disagree).

the assessment of short formative web quizzes given during the first weeks of a CS1 course [2]. Moreover, the low level of stress reported implies that this additional testing is not detrimental for the level-of-comfort factor identified by Wilson and Shrock [20].

5. FINAL EXAM

A major question that arises when trying to link test items to final exam is to which extent the competencies needed for mastering the final exam resemble the competencies tested for in the test items. Porter et al. have "anecdotally observed teachers wondering whether [peer-instruction multiple-choice questions] performance will lead to code-writing performance, or whether these skills are just "too different"." [11, p. 54]. In their study, as well as in a recent follow-up study [21], the authors thus were careful to only make causal claims for the predictive power of "clicker questions" regarding isomorphic exam questions. They could show, however, a relation between the performance on "clicker questions" and the overall performance on the CS1 exam.

In addition to understanding and applying algorithms, students in a CS2 course are expected to also learn how to design and formally analyze algorithms for various problems. In the light of the anecdotally observed discrepancy between "clicker questions" and certain competencies needed for CS1 exams, it is thus necessary to investigate these issues for a CS2 course as well. Hence, we will discuss the design of the CS2 final exam and the competencies tested for and relate these to the test items.

Exam Design.

The CS2 course reported upon was designed as an aligned course [4]. In particular, the homework assignments were aligned with the final exam tasks in the sense that they asked students to perform the same activities as they would be asked to perform in the final exam. On top of these, some homework assignments included programming exercises; the final exam, however, required only pseudocode algorithms.

The set of tasks used in the final exam is detailed in Figure 4 and classified according to the following scheme:

Type-I: A Type-I task asks for the reproduction of facts or the execution of a known and practiced procedure. Examples include executing a sorting algorithm or the description of how to delete from a search tree.

Type-II: A Type-II task asks for the explanation of known facts, the reorganization of knowledge, or the guided application of known procedures to new domains. Examples include reconstructing a strict binary tree from a given inorder- and postorder-traversal or solving a recurrence using the master theorem.

Type-III: A Type-III task asks for independent problem-solving, proving, or the reflective discussion of strategies. Examples include solving a problem without a prescribed approach or to devise an algorithm with certain properties and to prove its correctness.

This classification is used predominantly in the design of high-school final exams; such an exam is considered to be of an appropriate complexity if the majority of credits can be earned for Type-II tasks and if less credits can be earned for Type-I tasks than for Type-III tasks [8]. Put differently, no student is supposed to pass by answering only Type-I tasks, but Type-III tasks should only be used to differentiate between "A"-students and "Non-A"-Students. For the sake of well-definedness, the ministry of education has published a set of permissible operators [7] mapped to the different types of tasks. Note, however, that Type-III tasks do not necessarily need be more demanding than Type-II tasks; this classification merely denotes a different set of competencies required to solve a problem. For instance, devising an $\Theta(n \log n)$-algorithm to find an element occurring in each of three unsorted arrays storing n elements in total seems to be less demanding from an experts' point of view than solving the "Dutch flag"-problem. If, however, students have not seen duplicate detection but, as in our course, have solved a 0-1-sorting homework exercise, the tasks' relative complexity is reversed.

In the design of the final exam, we followed this philosophy, keeping in mind that the increased complexity of the subject matter and the relative nature of the above classification scheme still resulted in an adequate increase in complexity of our final exam compared to high-school exams. It should go without saying that the classification shown in Figure 4 has to be seen in the context of the course and, more importantly, the homework assignments.

Results.

The data summarized in Figure 4 shows that the test items administered did not cover the full range of the final exam. Due to the nature of activities required for Type-III tasks, there were no test items corresponding to any of the Type-III tasks. For those of the Type-I and Type-II tasks that had corresponding test items, a significant rank-order correlation regarding students' performance could be established ($n = 5$, $p = .05$, $r_s = 0.90$). This implies that our test items can be used to predict the relative performance in aligned exam tasks. Even if individual correlations could not be obtained due to privacy reasons, this seems to extend the observations of Porter et al. [11] to our aligned CS2 course.

As the final exam was also aligned with the homework assignments and individual grades were available for all students, we performed a regression analysis between these data

Topic	Type	Credits	avg. % (EX)	ρ_{EX}	avg. % (TI)	ρ_{TI}
Lists and arrays; worst-case and amortized analysis	II	12	22	–	–	–
Ordering functions using the "big-Oh"-notation	II	6	71	2	57	2
Solving a recurrence using the master theorem	II	4	61	4	20	5
Proving correctness using a loop invariant	II	10	56	5	33	4
Searching a Young tableau	III	6	16	–	–	–
Finding a common element in three arrays	III	6	41	–	–	–
Solving the "Dutch flag"-problem	II	6	49	–	–	–
Reconstructing a strict binary tree from traversals	II	4	42	–	–	–
Executing AVL-tree operations	I	11	73	1	68	1
Inferring edge weights from Dijkstra traces	II	6	64	3	48	3
Executing heapsort	I	9	58	–	–	–

Figure 4: Tasks in the final exam classified according to the type of activity asked for. For each task, the maximum number of credits, the average percentage of credits given, and the resulting rank ρ_{EX} is reported. If the task was aligned with a test item, the average percentage of points awarded for this item and the resulting rank ρ_{TI} is given. The rank-order correlation is statistically significant ($n = 5$, $p = .05$, $r_s = 0.90$).

sets. The results, obtained with SPSS v22 for a 95% confidence interval, show that these grades significantly correlate; see Figure 5. Because students were asked to work in small teams and to submit only one solution per team, it is not surprising that the explanation power of the regression is rather weak: no more than 25.2% of the variance in the final grades of CS students could be explained by their homework grades. The explanation power greatly diminishes for BIM students (16.7%). Again, this is not surprising given that the homework grade determines 20% of the final grade; anecdotal experiences lead us to assume that some teams consented to have the strongest team member submit the majority of solutions. This is supported by a higher variation in the final grades of the BIM students with "A" homework grades compared to the CS students with "A" homework grades.

	n	B	std. err.	β	sign.	R	R^2_{adj}
CS	139	.571	.083	.507	.000	.507	.252
BIM	62	.302	.083	.425	.001	.425	.167

Figure 5: Regression analysis of the CS2 final exam grade depending on the CS2 homework grade.

Even if only one variable (homework performance) was considered, the above regression analysis matches the explanation power of the model obtained by Bennedsen and Caspersen [3] for the case of a model-driven CS1 course. The major influencing factor in their study, however, was the mathematics grade from high school. Unfortunately, the data available for our study did not include these grades.

Following Trapmann's [16] conjecture that there is a common set of factors influencing high-school and academic performance, we decided to add the performance in the preceding CS1 course to the set of factors for the regression analysis. This data was available because, according to the departmental policy, the CS1 and CS2 courses are taught back-to-back by the same instructor, in this case the second author. Because there were several students who had either recently moved to WWU or had re-taken the CS2 course, i.e., had taken the CS1 course with a different instructor during the previous academic year, the number of data points for CS and BIM students included in this analysis was $n'_{\text{CS}} = 102$ resp. $n'_{\text{BIM}} = 47$.

The results of these regression analyses, given in Figures 6 and 7, show the CS1 performance to be a significant indicator for performance in our CS2 course. This indicator alone explains 60% (CS) resp. 40.9% (BIM) of the variation in the CS2 final grade. Adding the homework grade as a variable actually reduces the explanation power; this can be explained by the fact that this grade is a team grade and thus not awarded on the basis of an individual's performance.

Variables	B	std. err.	β	sign.	R	R^2_{adj}
EX1	.714	.073	-	.000	.779	.399
HW2	.097	.108	-	.372		
EX1	.750	.061	.777	.000	.777	.600
HW2	.681	.126	.476	.000	.476	.219

Figure 6: Regression analysis of the CS2 final exam grades for $n'_{\text{CS}} = 102$ CS students. EX1: CS1 final exam grade; HW2: CS2 homework grade.

Variables	B	std. err.	β	sign.	R	R^2_{adj}
EX1	.469	.115	.533	.000	.677	.433
HW2	.172	.100	.233	.094		
EX1	.572	.100	.649	.000	.649	.409
HW2	.387	.099	.501	.000	.501	.235

Figure 7: Regression analysis of the CS2 final exam grades for $n'_{\text{BIM}} = 47$ BIM students. EX1: CS1 final exam grade; HW2: CS2 homework grade.

6. DISCUSSION

The results reported seem to confirm that concept inventory test items can be used as indicators at least for Type-I and Type-II tasks in the final exam of a CS2 course. Also, grades for homework assignments weakly indicate exam performance. A much stronger indicator identified in our study, however, is the performance in a preceding CS1 course. The significance and explanation power of these indicators varies between the subgroups investigated depending on whether or not homework assignments count towards the final grade.

A potential threat to validity, revalidation of the findings at other institutions aside, is that both courses were taught by the same instructor. Hence, despite the obvious differences in course content, "compatibility" with the style of instruction and testing might the overarching factor.

A more promising explanation comes from the literature: results in educational psychology suggest the *conscientiousness* trait to strongly influence academic success. This explanation would not contradict previous findings regarding the influence of high-school mathematics grades because it is conjectured that there is a common set of factors influencing success in secondary and post-secondary education, i.e., that indeed the "trajectory for academic success in college is established long before matriculation" [6, p. 89]. It could also serve to explain part of the predictive power of test items and "clicker questions" regarding Type-III tasks: conscientious students are known to be well organized, in particular when it comes to preparation and note-taking. We conjecture that such students benefit from mandatory reading assignments or homework assignments that do not count towards the final grade to a larger extent than other students. How to quickly recognize students without such a dominant trait and to empower them to also capitalize on these learning opportunities is subject of future research.

Acknowledgements.

We thank D. Berh for his help with transcribing the weekly responses to the test items. This work was partially supported by the German Federal Ministry for Education and Research (grant 01PB14007A).

7. REFERENCES

[1] A. Ahadi and R. Lister. Geek genes, prior knowledge, stumbling points and learning edge momentum: Parts of the one elephant? In *Proc. Intl. Conf. International Computing Education Research*, pp. 123–128, 2013.

[2] O. Bälter, E. Enström, and B. Klingenberg. The effect of short formative diagnostic web quizzes with minimal feedback. *Computers & Education*, 60(1):234–242, 2013.

[3] J. Bennedsen and M. E. Caspersen. An investigation of potential success factors for an introductory model-driven programming course. In *Proc. Intl. Workshop Computing Education Research*, pp. 155–163, 2005.

[4] J. Biggs and C. Tang. *Teaching for Quality Learning at University*. Open University Press/McGraw Hill, Buckingham, 4th ed., 2011.

[5] L. Jamba-Joyner and W. F. Klostermeyer. Predictors for success in a discrete math course. *SIGCSE Bull.*, 35(2):66–69, June 2003.

[6] G. D. Kuh, J. Kinzie, J. A. Buckley, B. K. Bridges, and J. C. Hayek. What matters to student success: A review of the literature commissioned report for the national symposium on postsecondary student success: Spearheading a dialog on student success. *National Postsecondary Education Cooperative*, 2006.

[7] Ministerium für Schule, Weiterbildung, Wissenschaft und Forschung des Landes Nordrhein-Westfalen. Informatik – Übersicht über die Operatoren, 2005. `http://www.standardsicherung.schulministerium.nrw.de/abitur-gost/getfile.php?file=172` [last accessed: 2015-11-23]. In German.

[8] Ministerium für Schule, Weiterbildung, Wissenschaft und Forschung des Landes Nordrhein-Westfalen. Vorgaben für die Konstruktion von Aufgaben für die schriftliche Abiturprüfung im Fach Informatik, 2010. `http://www.standardsicherung.schulministerium.nrw.de/abitur-gost/getfile.php?file=3383` [last accessed: 2015-11-23]. In German.

[9] M. C. O'Connor and S. V. Paunonen. Big five personality predictors of post-secondary academic performance. *Personality and Individual Differences*, 43(5):971–990, 2007.

[10] A. E. Poropat. A meta-analysis of the five-factor model of personality and academic performance. *Psychological Bulletin*, 135(2):322–338, 2009.

[11] L. Porter, D. Zingaro, and R. Lister. Predicting student success using fine grain clicker data. In *Proc. Intl. Conf. International Computing Education Research*, pp. 51–58, 2014.

[12] A. Robins. Learning edge momentum: a new account of outcomes in CS1. *Computer Science Education*, 20(1):37–71, 2010.

[13] N. Rountree, J. Rountree, A. Robins, and R. Hannah. Interacting factors that predict success and failure in a CS1 course. In *ITiCSE Working Group Reports*, pp. 101–104, 2004.

[14] R. Schulmeister. Auf der Suche nach Determinanten des Studienerfolgs. (Looking for Determinants of Study Success) In J. Brockmann and A. Pilniok, editors, *Studieneingangsphase in der Rechtswissenschaft*, pp. 72–204. Nomos, Baden-Baden, 2014. In German.

[15] H. Schuman, E. Walsh, C. Olson, and B. Etheridge. Effort and reward: The assumption that college grades are affected by quantity of study. *Social Forces*, 63(4):945–966, 1985.

[16] S. Trapmann. *Mehrdimensionale Studienerfolgsprognose: Die Bedeutung kognitiver, temperamentsbedingter und motivationaler Prädiktoren für verschiedene Kriterien des Studienerfolgs.* (Multidimensional prediction of study success: the importance of cognitive, temperamental and motivational predictors of different criteria of academic success) PhD thesis, University of Hohenheim, 2007. In German.

[17] J. Vahrenhold and W. Paul. Developing and validating test items for first-year computer science courses. *Computer Science Education*, 24(4):304–333, 2014.

[18] P. Ventura and B. Ramamurthy. Wanted: CS1 Students. No Experience Required. In *Proc. SIGCSE Techn. Symp. Computer Science Education*, pp. 240–244. 2004.

[19] C. Watson, F. W. Li, and J. L. Godwin. No tests required: Comparing traditional and dynamic predictors of programming success. In *Proc. SIGCSE Techn. Symp. Computer Science Education*, pp. 469–474, 2014.

[20] B. C. Wilson and S. Shrock. Contributing to success in an introductory computer science course: A study of twelve factors. In *Proc. SIGCSE Techn. Symp. Computer Science Education*, pp. 184–188, 2001.

[21] D. Zingaro and L. Porter. Tracking student learning from class to exam using isomorphic questions. In *Proc. SIGCSE Techn. Symp. Computer Science Education*, pp. 356–361, 2015.

BRIDGES: A System to Enable Creation of Engaging Data Structures Assignments with Real-World Data and Visualizations

David Burlinson, Mihai Mehedint, Chris Grafer, Kalpathi Subramanian, Jamie Payton, Paula Goolkasian
University of North Carolina at Charlotte
{dburlins, mmehedin, cgrafer1, krs, payton, pagoolka}@uncc.edu

Michael Youngblood
PARC, A Xerox Company
Michael.Youngblood@parc.com

Robert Kosara
Tableau Research
rkosara@tableau.com

ABSTRACT

Although undergraduate enrollment in Computer Science has remained strong and seen substantial increases in the past decade, retention of majors remains a significant concern, particularly for students at the freshman and sophomore level that are tackling foundational courses on algorithms and data structures. In this work, we present BRIDGES, a software infrastructure designed to enable the creation of more engaging assignments in introductory data structures courses by providing students with a simplified API that allows them to populate their own data structure implementations with live, real-world, and interesting data sets, such as those from popular social networks (e.g., Twitter, Facebook). BRIDGES also provides the ability for students to create and explore *visualizations* of the execution of the data structures that they construct in their course assignments, which can promote better understanding of the data structure and its underlying algorithms; these visualizations can be easily shared via a weblink with peers, family, and instructional staff. In this paper, we present the BRIDGES system, its design, architecture and its use in our data structures course over two semesters.

Keywords

algorithm, data structure, visualization, engagement

1. INTRODUCTION

Over the past several years, enrollment in computer science undergraduate degree programs has been increasing at rates ranging from 6-11% [9]. Despite this increase, retention of CS majors remains a critical concern, especially at the freshmen/sophomore levels, with attrition rates of up to 66% [8]. While the factors that motivate changing majors are many and varied [8], strategies to increase retention are crucial to meet the national needs for graduates that can contribute to a robust and innovative twenty-first century workforce.

Demonstrating a connection between computing and the real world has the potential to increase students' motivation and interest in computing; grounding teaching in familiar, concrete, and relevant examples has been shown to improve learning [4] and has a positive effect on the retention of computing majors, particularly for women students [7]. In practice, however, there is little support for educators who want to incorporate this kind of approach into introductory computer science courses; for most students in introductory computer science courses, there remains a disconnect between the students' own everyday experiences with existing information systems that address real-world problems and the toy examples with small, uninteresting, synthetic data sets they encounter in course assignments that are used to teach students how data structures and algorithms work.

In this paper, we introduce the **BRIDGES** (**B**ridging **R**eal-world **I**nfrastructure **D**esigned to **G**oal-align, **E**ngage, and **S**timulate) system, which (1) facilitates student access to live, real-world data sets for use in traditional data structures programming assignments and (2) makes it possible for students to view and verify (debug) *their own implementations* of data structures, by providing *visualization* capabilities. The goal is to increase the engagement of students enrolled in data structures courses in an effort to improve retention of students in the computer science major. We present the architecture of BRIDGES and sample projects that can be enabled through the use of BRIDGES in a data structures and algorithms course. We describe a study of the application of BRIDGES in two semesters of a sophomore-level course; results show that the majority of students indicate that the BRIDGES-enabled assignments are relevant to career goals and increased their interest in computing.

SIGCSE '16, March 02-05, 2016, Memphis, TN, USA

 ISBN 978-1-4503-3685-7/16/03...$15.00
DOI: http://dx.doi.org/10.1145/2839509.2844635

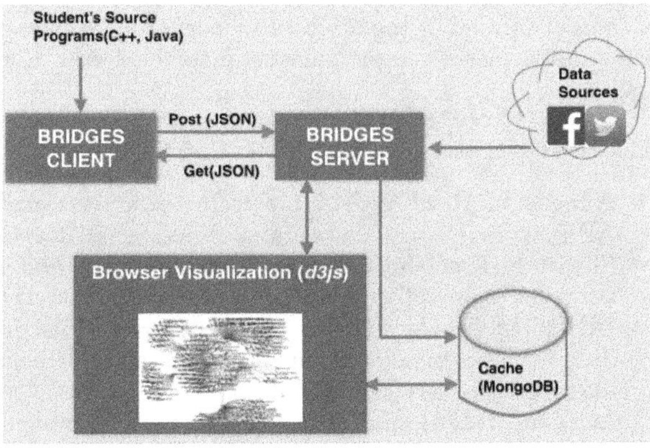

Figure 1: BRIDGES System. Based on a client-server architecture; a user constructs data structure programs using the BRIDGES client classes (Fig. 3) in Java or C++. The data structure representation is sent to the server by the client as a JSON string. After parsing and user authentication, the server stores the assignment on the MongoDB and displays the data structure on a specific web link using D3. The server also has interfaces to retrieve data from external sources upon user requests for use in their programs.

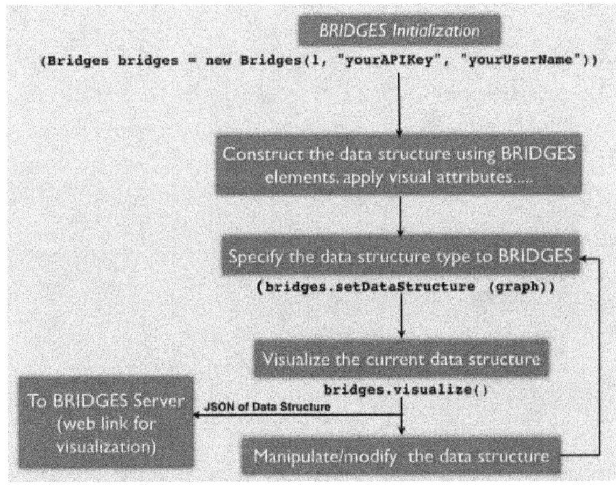

Figure 2: An Example BRIDGES program. Consists of an initialization step to specify user name and id (for authentication), assignment number. This is followed by user's construction of the data structure using BRIDGES client classes. The final 2 steps involve specifying a handle to the data structure (tree root, graph, head of a linked list, etc) and initiating the visualization modules.

2. THE BRIDGES SYSTEM

As illustrated in Fig. 1 the BRIDGES system is based on a client-server model; the client consists of the needed infrastructure for students to implement all of the basic data structures (currently Java and C++ APIs are supported). At any point, a representation of the constructed data structure can be generated and transmitted to the BRIDGES server to generate a visualization. The visualization will be displayed on a specific web link provided to the user. The BRIDGES server provides needed interfaces to data sources that make it easy for the user to make data requests. The acquired data (to be used by the user as part of course projects) is also cached on a Mongo database. Finally the server maintains a gallery of projects created by the user that can be shared. The visualization will appear on the specified web page with some capabilities for interactive manipulation. All projects are held in a database and the client will have access to an interactive gallery under their BRIDGES account.

2.1 An Example BRIDGES Program

We begin with an example template of what a BRIDGES program would look like. Fig. 2 shows the main calls made from an example program and consists of the following steps. The **Bridges** class encapsulates the details of the communication between the client and the server and uses additional helper classes in its implementation.

- **Initialization.** This step creates a BRIDGES class and takes several parameters, including an assignment number, a user id (generated by the user when he/she creates a BRIDGES account) and the corresponding user name. These parameters are used in forming a custom web link for the user's data structure.
- **Data Structure Construction.** In this step, the user constructs and manipulates any of the BRIDGES supported data structures using the BRIDGES client classes (see Section 2.2.1).
- **Specification of Data Structure Type.** This step specifies the handle to the data structure that will be transmitted to the BRIDGES server for visualization. This can be the head of a linked list, root of a tree, graph adjacency list, or array name.
- **Visualization.** This step results in the creation of a JSON string representation of previously specified data structure and its transmission to the BRIDGES server using an HTTP post request. If this is successful, a web link is returned to the user for viewing the visualization. The assignment is also stored in the MongoDB that the user can subsequently access through his BRIDGES account. This step can be repeated any number of times: the data structure can be modified, the handle respecified followed by visualization.

2.2 BRIDGES Design

2.2.1 BRIDGES Client

The BRIDGES client consists of a minimal set of building blocks that are needed by students in a typical sophomore level course on data structures: array, list, tree structures, graph. The class structure is illustrated in Fig. 3, roughly follows the description and implementation of Shaffer[16, 15] contains the following components:

Element. This is the foundational class in BRIDGES. Arrays, lists, tree and graph nodes are constructed using this element. Elements have a unique id, a label (used in the visualization), and visual properties (size, shape, opacity, color). Elements can also be related to another element via a *link*, as would be needed for trees, linked lists and graphs. Links have attributes: color, thickness, and opacity. Elements are declared with a generic parameter, that can be used to hold application specific data (Tweet, actor, movie, etc)

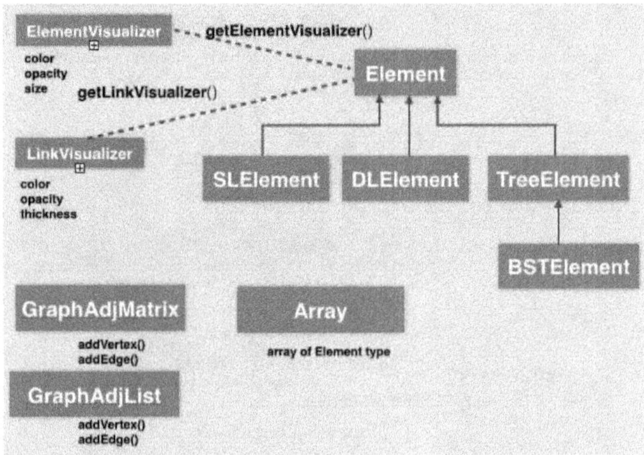

Figure 3: BRIDGES Client. Consists of the basic building blocks to construct data structures, such as arrays, linked lists, binary trees and graphs. The visualizer classes affect the visual attributes (color, opacity, size, thickness) of the elements (nodes) and links, depending on the data structure.

SLElement. Derived from Element, SLelement represents a singly linked element and has a link to the succeeding element, via a *next* pointer.

DLElement. Derived from Element, DLelement represents a doubly linked element and has links to previous and succeeding elements, via *prev* and *next* pointers.

TreeElement. Derived from Element, TreeElement is a binary tree node, with links to its two children, via *left* and *right* pointers.

BSTElement. Derived from TreeElement, augments the TreeNode with *key* value; must be an orderable type.

GraphAdjMatrix. Implemented as a two dimensional hash table, the graph supports vertices indexed by any orderable type (int, float, string, etc).

GraphAdjList. Implemented as a hash table of vertices, with each table entry pointing a singly linked list (of type SLelement);

Array. Arrays represent a list of type Element and support the normal indexing operations of arrays as defined in programming languages; however, each element of a BRIDGES array supports visual attributes.

Implementation. Implementations using the above class structures closely follow the implementation examples in [16, 15]. However, by using the object definitions above, the basic data structure elements can now be augmented with visual attributes that can be exploited by the visualization modules. BRIDGES currently supports both Java and C++ implementations. The Java implementation uses *Java Generics*; while the C++ implementation uses *C++ templates*. Generic implementations make it possible to handle real-world datasets where indexing by string (Twitter or Facebook user name, for example) is needed for graph implementations, bypassing a remapping to integer vertex indices. A second advantage is the ability to incorporate application specific dataset as a generic parameter to the base classes.

2.2.2 *BRIDGES Server*

The BRIDGES server has the following functions:

- **Access to Real-World Data.** As described earlier, APIs to real-world datasets such as social networks (Twitter, Facebook) can be quite complex and beyond the scope of sophomore level CS students. Thus BRIDGES provides an easy to use interface to acquire data from external data sources. To date, implemented interfaces to services include Twitter, RottenTomatoes, and IMDB, and data from Twitter follower lists and timelines from a few public accounts (ieeevis, twitterapi, wired, US geological survey, and earthquake) have been incorporated directly into course projects. Queried data from the various sources is cached in a Mongo database for the sake of efficiency and data reuse.
- **Visualization.** The BRIDGES server is responsible for receiving data structure representations (in JSON string format) from the client and generating a visual representation (students will be provided a web link). All such requests are authenticated, parsed and stored in a database (MongoDB). Uploaded assignments can be accessed with a direct url or via the user gallery and can be made public or private, allowing users to share some visualizations and hide others for later review or modification. Visualizations of arrays, linked lists, binary trees and graphs (node-link diagrams) are supported by BRIDGES.

Implementation. The server-side implementation is a Node.js application, utilizing Jade templating, a MongoDB database, Javascript, and a variety of popular Javascript libraries, such as D3[3], jQuery, and Underscore.js. The database is used to keep a record of all users, projects, and cached datasets.

2.3 BRIDGES Intervention in Data Structures Courses

In our CS program, students take the data structures course at the beginning of their sophomore year, followed by an algorithm analysis course. All BRIDGES projects were assigned to students in the data structures course. Typical enrollment in this course is around 50. The BRIDGES intervention was performed in 1 section of the data structures course in fall 2014 and Spring 2015.

2.3.1 *Fall 2014*

Three BRIDGES projects were assigned in the Fall 2014 semester:

- **Queue:** In this project students to implement and test the Queue ADT, followed by using a live stream of Earthquake Tweet data (US GIS earthquake Tweets). Helper classes were provided to parse the quake data to simplify the data processing tasks. Students had to complete two tasks (a) Given a fixed size queue, incoming tweet data were enqued; if the queue became full, then the oldest tweets were dequed and snapshots of the queue visualizations were to be demonstrated, (b) Given a fixed size queue, incoming data items were to be filtered by quake magnitude prior to entering

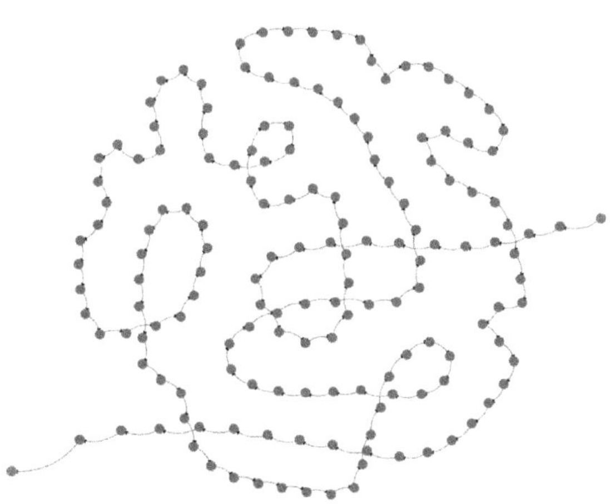

(a) Singly Linked List of IMDB dataset containing 1815 actor-movie pairs. Each node is a unique actor; mousing over a node (not shown) displays a list of that actor's movies.

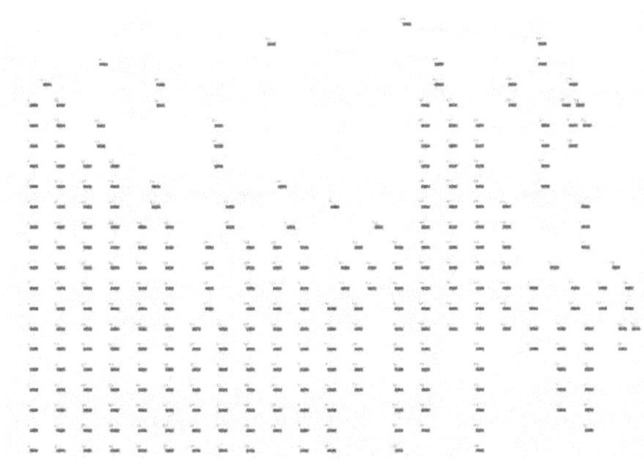

(b) Binary Search Tree of Earthquake Tweet Dataset (US GIS), ordered by quake magnitude.

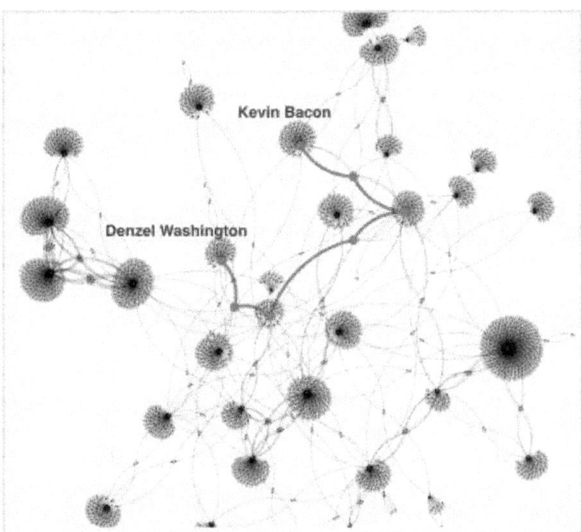

(c) Bacon Number Computation. Actor-Movie Graph of an IMDB dataset containing 1815 actor-movie pairs. Results of the Bacon number computation between Denzel Washington and Kevin Bacon. The red nodes and links display the path from Denzel Washington to Kevin Bacon.

Figure 4: BRIDGES Project Examples

the queue. Various thresholds should be experimented with queue snapshots visualized.

- **Binary Search Tree.** This project continued to use the earthquake Tweet data, but inserted the records (quake magnitude as the search key) into a binary search tree, followed by visualization of the tree structure. Tasks on the search tree included (a) modifying the insertion algorithm to display insertion path, (b) implement the find algorithm and demonstrate (visually) searching for a quake of a particular magnitude. Fig. 4b illustrates the binary search tree sorted by earthquake magnitudes.

- **Graph (Bacon Number Computation).** This project involved building a graph using a reduced version of the IMDB dataset and implementing the Breadth First Search algorithm on a graph to compute the Bacon Number of an actor in an actor-movie graph[14]. The project used a curated IMDB dataset containing 1815 actor-movie pairs. Tasks involved building the actor-movie graph, determining the Bacon Number of any actor in the graph, and highlighting the path from the queried actor to the Kevin Bacon node. Fig. 4c illustrates the actor-movie graph and the path from the actor Denzel Washington to Kevin Bacon.

2.3.2 Spring 2015

Four BRIDGES projects were assigned in the course:

- **Singly Linked List.** The IMDB actor-movie dataset was used in this project. Students had to read in the dataset and build a sorted linked list of the unique set of actors; the data field of each node would contain the list of movies corresponding to the actor. Tasks included finding a specific actor, followed by highlighting the node (if found), adding in new actor-movie pairs and removing an actor. Fig. 4a illustrates the singly linked list sorted by actor names.

- **Stacks: Expression Evaluation.** This project required students to build a linked list-based stack using BRIDGES elements. The stack was then used to evaluate expressions. Bridges visualizations were used to display the contents of the stack after each operation.

- **Binary Search Tree.** This project was similar to the project from the fall 2014 with slight changes in the required tasks.

- **Graph (Bacon Number Computation).** Identical to the Fall 2014 graph project.

3. EVALUATION

We have used BRIDGES in one section of our Data Structures course (ITCS 2214) for the past 2 semesters; the projects that used BRIDGES are described in Sections 2.3.1,2.3.2. The enrollment in each of these 2 sections was capped at 55; the enrollment stabilized at 36 in the Fall 2014 semester and 32 in the Spring 2015 semester. Each BRIDGES project was followed by a project survey with 15 questions relating to the concepts learned in the assignment, the required programming knowledge relative to their own experience, time required for completion of assignment, sources of support

Table 1: Responses to "The assignment was relevant to my career goals" for assignments 1-4.

	#	#Resp	SA%	A%	N%	D%	SD%
Fall 2014	1	29	0.0	48.2	20.7	31.0	0.0
	2	28	17.9	28.6	28.6	17.9	7.1
	3	19	15.8	52.6	15.8	10.5	5.3
Spring 2015	1	27	14.8	14.8	55.6	7.4	7.4
	2	24	29.1	37.5	29.1	4.1	0.0
	3	27	25.9	37.0	29.6	3.7	3.7
	4	28	35.7	25.0	25.0	7.1	7.1

Table 2: Responses to "The assignment was trivial and not essential to learning about computing." for assignments 1-4.

	#	#Resp	SA%	A%	N%	D%	SD%
Fall 2014	1	29	3.5	17.2	24.1	44.8	10.3
	2	28	3.6	10.7	17.9	60.7	7.1
	3	19	5.3	10.5	15.7	42.1	26.3
Spring 2015	1	27	7.4	11.1	25.9	40.7	14.8
	2	24	0	0	25.0	41.6	33.3
	3	27	7.4	0.0	14.8	44.4	33.3
	4	28	10.7	3.6	25.0	21.4	39.2

(mentors, TAs, external sources), relevance of the assignment to career goals, difficulty of the assignment, and degree to which the assignment increased their interest in computing. Responses used a 5 point Likert scale, ranging from strongly agree to strongly disagree. Tables 1,2, and 3 detail the responses to the survey questions, (1) *"The assignment was relevant to my career goals"*, (2) *"The assignment was trivial and not essential to learning about computing."*, and (3) *"The assignment increased my interest in computing"*.

- *"The assignment was relevant to my career goals"*. In the fall 2014 surveys (Table 1), a majority of students agreed on this question, on all 3 projects (48% vs. 31%, 46% vs. 25%, 68% vs. 16%) with the remainder being neutral. In the spring semester, the results were even stronger (29% vs. 14%, 66% vs. 4%, 63% vs. 7%, 61% vs. 14%), except for the first project where there were a large number of neutral responses (55%). This was a more difficult project that should have been assigned in multiple parts; the subsequent projects were corrected, so that students found the tasks more manageable.

- *"The assignment was trivial and not essential to learning about computing"*. In the fall 2014 surveys (Table 2), a majority of students disagreed (55% vs. 38%, 68% vs. 14%, 68% vs. 26%) for all projects and in the spring surveys the results were even stronger (55% vs. 18%, 75% vs. 0%, 77% vs. 7%, 61% vs. 14%).

Table 3: Responses to "The assignment increased my interest in computing" for assignments 1-4.

	#	#Resp	SA%	A%	N%	D%	SD%
Fall 2014	1	29	0.0	20.7	44.8	24.1	10.3
	2	28	10.7	25	32.1	21.4	10.7
	3	19	5.3	42.1	31.6	15.8	5.3
Spring 2015	1	27	3.7	22.2	40.7	14.8	18.5
	2	24	20.8	45.8	25.0	8.3	0.0
	3	27	14.8	48.2	25.9	7.4	3.7
	4	28	21.4	32.1	21.4	17.9	7.1

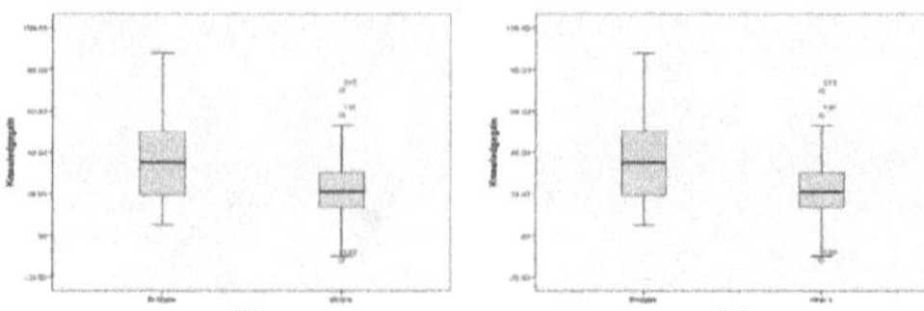

(a) Fall 2014 (b) Spring 2015

Figure 5: Knowledge Gains using BRIDGES

- *"The assignment increased my interest in computing"*. In the fall 2014 surveys (Table 3), the results were mixed, with a minority agreeing on project 1 (21% vs. 34%), slight majority on project 2 (35% vs. 32%), and a majority on project 3 (47% vs. 24%). In the spring 2015 surveys, a minority agreed on project 1 (26% vs. 33%), a majority agreed on the remaining 3 projects (66% vs. 8%, 63% vs. 11%, 53% vs. 25%). As mentioned earlier, project 1 was not modularly designed to help students to complete subtasks as part of the larger assignment, resulting in frustration for many students.

Finally, there was a major version change in BRIDGES between the two semesters. Version 2 of BRIDGES was much more robust, with an improved API (Fig. 3) that was easier to use; additionally, the documentation and tutorials were also vastly improved. Thus, the improvements in student responses across the two semesters were within our expectations.

Knowledge Gains. We also evaluated the knowledge gains of students using BRIDGES compared to students in the remaining sections of data structures. For this we created a knowledge test in data structures with contributions from all instructors teaching the course. A question bank of about 105 multiple choice questions and 38 short answer questions was created. An external project evaluator chose a subset of these questions (35 multiple choice and 6 short answers) to be used for pre/post tests, administered at the beginning and end of the semester. Students from four sections of the fall 2014 data structures course and 4 sections of the Spring 2015 underwent the the knowledge test; 1 section used BRIDGES and the other 3 did not.

Fig. 5 illustrates the knowledge gains using the pre-post scores from the knowledge test. The box plot in Fig. 5 shows knowledge gains from pre-test to post-test, with significant gains for both the BRIDGES section and the control group. It is apparent that the BRIDGES group showed larger gains ($M = 39.12$, $SD = 14.6$) than the control group ($M = 22.\ 00$, $SD = 13.28$), $t\ (93) = 5.33$, $p < .001$. However, each section was taught by a different instructor. As such, the differences in knowledge gains for the groups could be explained at least partially by the differences in instructor emphasis on the knowledge tests; the BRIDGES instructor used part of the knowledge test for the final exam while the other instructors used it as a classroom exercise that did not count toward the final grade. Therefore, it is not possible to definitively pinpoint BRIDGES as a reason for increased knowledge gains.

4. RELATED WORK

Closely related to our work are the approaches in Buckley et al.'s *Socially Relevant Computing* [6] and Bart et al.'s *RealTime Web*[2]; Buckley's work incorporates real world scientific applications into both their introductory and senior capstone courses to make them more interesting and relevant. Bart's *RealTime Web* provides a set of flexible client libraries to request, parse and return real-time data from a number of web sources (Yelp, weather reports, Yahoo Finance, etc.) Our approach goes even further to make the course material relevant; in addiiton to providing easy access to real-world datasets, we provide instantaneous visualizations of the data structures that are built by the students themselves that can help to improve the understanding of the data structure and the algorithms that operate on them.

Visualizations have long been promoted as a way to improve student understanding of data structures and algorithms [1, 12, 5], and the research literature highlighting the ability of interactive visualizations to enhance discovery is vast. Previous efforts to increase engagement have shown promise for the use of visual programming (e.g., Scratch and Alice) [13, 10] for making the first programming steps easier and more engaging. In addition to providing a graphical interface for piecing together programs, these systems let students build graphically interesting programs and encourage them to explore, experiment, and play. Formal evaluations of Alice[11] have shown increased performance and retention in the programing courses and improved attitudes toward computing, especially for at-risk students.

5. CONCLUSIONS

We have presented BRIDGES, a system that provides students with an easy-to-use API for accessing real-world datasets for use in data structures course projects and the ability to explore interactive visualizations of the data structures that are created as part of a BRIDGES-enabled assignment. Rather than look at (uninteresting) textual output of data structures assignments for verification/debugging, students can use BRIDGES to interact with visualizations of the execution of their assignments on real-world data, with the added ability to share their visualizations with peers, friends, and family. Early results of using BRIDGES over 2 semesters in 1 section of our data structures course are promising, with students reporting increased interest in computing after completing assignments.

Currently, we are extending BRIDGES on 3 fronts:

- **External Data Sources.** Ultimately, we expect that BRIDGES will provide access to large variety of interesting external data sources. We also hope to integrate the rich work of *RealTime Web*[2] to complement BRIDGES.

- **Peer Mentoring.** An important component of this project is to build strong connections within the major through peer mentoring, using BRIDGES as a shared interest; specifically, we plan to pair students in data structures courses with the students in the senior-level software development capstone course who are tackling software development projects to extend BRIDGES.

- **Extended Evaluation.** BRIDGES is open source and is available at **http://bridgesuncc.github.io/**. Java and C++ versions are available for deployment by instructors. As more instructors adopt BRIDGES, we plan to perform a larger scale evaluation that measures computing attitudes and engagement in data structures and algorithms courses across institutions.

6. ACKNOWLEDGMENTS

This work was supported by a grant from the National Science Foundation, DUE-1245841.

7. REFERENCES

[1] R. Baecker. Sorting out sorting: A case study of software visualization for teaching computer science. *Software visualization: Programming as a multimedia experience*, 1:369–381, 1998.

[2] A. C. Bart, E. Tilevich, S. Hall, T. Allevato, and C. A. Shaffer. Transforming introductory computer science projects via real-time web data. In *Proc. of the 45th ACM Technical Symposium on Computer Science Education*, pages 289–294, 2014.

[3] M. Bostock, V. Ogievetsky, and J. Heer. D3: Data-driven documents. *IEEE Trans. Visualization & Comp. Graphics*, 2011.

[4] J. D. Bransford, A. L. Brown, and R. R. Cocking. *How people learn: Brain, mind, experience and school.* National Academy Press, 1999.

[5] M. H. Brown and R. Sedgewick. *A system for algorithm animation*, volume 18. ACM, 1984.

[6] M. Buckley, J. Nordlinger, and D. Subramanian. Socially relevant computing. In *Proc. of the 39th SIGCSE Technical Symposium on Computer Science Education*, pages 347–351, 2008.

[7] J. Cohoon. Just get over it or just get on with it. In *Women and Information Technology: Research on Under-Representation.* MIT Press, 2005.

[8] J. Cohoon and L.-Y. Chen. Migrating out of computer science. *Computing Research News*, 15(2), 2003. http://archive.cra.org/CRN/articles/march03/cohoon.chen.html.

[9] Computing Research Association. CRA Taulbee Survey 2010-2011, 2010-2011.

[10] W. P. Dann, S. Cooper, and R. Pausch. *Learning to Program with Alice.* Prentice Hall, 2005.

[11] B. Moskal, D. Lurie, and S. Cooper. Evaluating the effectiveness of a new instructional approach. In *Proc. of the 35th SIGCSE Technical Symposium on Computer Science Education*, pages 75–79, 2004.

[12] W. C. Pierson and S. H. Rodger. Web-based animation of data structures using jawaa. In *ACM SIGCSE Bulletin*, volume 30, pages 267–271. ACM, 1998.

[13] M. Resnick, J. Maloney, A. Monroy-Hernández, N. Rusk, E. Eastmond, K. Brennan, A. Millner, E. Rosenbaum, J. Silver, B. Silverman, and Y. Kafai. Scratch: programming for all. *Communications of the ACM*, 52(11):60–67, 2009.

[14] R. Sedgewick and K. Wayne. *Introduction to Programming in Java.* A Case Study: Small World Phenomenon (http://introcs.cs.princeton.edu/java/home/).

[15] C. Shaffer. *Data Structures and Algorithm Analysis in C++.* Dover Publications, 2011.

[16] C. Shaffer. *Data Structures and Algorithm Analysis in Java.* Dover Publications, 2011.

Computational Thinking as a Liberal Study

Dave Mason
Ryerson University
350 Victoria Street
Toronto, ON,
Canada M5B 2K7
dmason@ryerson.ca

Irfan Khan
Ryerson University
350 Victoria Street
Toronto, ON,
Canada M5B 2K7
irfan1.khan@ryerson.ca

Vadim Farafontov
Ryerson University
350 Victoria Street
Toronto, ON,
Canada M5B 2K7
vadim.farafontov@ryerson.ca

ABSTRACT

Computers and computational thinking are becoming ubiquitous in our world. They are part of the transportation systems we use, the security systems we confront, our entertainment systems, our communication systems, our financial systems, and even our social and political instruments. Computational thinking is a fundamental part of decision-making on a large and increasing number of fronts. It is sometimes hard for a computer scientist to imagine how people without access to those tools can navigate the world in an informed way.

We have designed a course to bring the social, historical, cultural and technical context of these systems to the attention of students and citizens who would not otherwise have access to them, so they can better understand the world in which they will live and work. The course is a Computer Science course because it is talking about the science of computers, albeit in an approachable form for an audience without any assumed previous programming experience.

The course ran in Winter 2014 and Winter 2015 meeting most of its goals, including engaging the non-traditional student who took it.

Categories and Subject Descriptors

D.1.7 [**Programming Techniques**]: Visual Programming; D.2.5 [**Software Engineering**]: Programming Environments; K.4.2 [**Computers and Society**]: Social Issues—*citizenry*; K.8.m [**Personal Computing**]: Miscellaneous—*for non-programmers*

1. INTRODUCTION

Computational thinking as introduced by Jeanette Wing[13] is an approach to take the principles found within Computer Science and bring them to the average person. The primary justification comes from the absolute ubiquity of computing devices, and despite their overwhelming presence the average person remains oblivious of their internal function.

The last time a similar jump in technology resulted in an explosion of knowledge was after the invention of the printing press, which allowed an unparalleled spread of knowledge and ideas through books. This catapulted Western civilization into the Renaissance – a period of great scientific discovery, artistic achievements and unparalleled economic growth. In order to interact with the new social and economic systems, the average person was required to be literate. Without the ability to read and write even the most basic economic functions became problematic.

Today we find ourselves in a similar position, where computational devices are arising in every aspect of our society. However, the understanding and maintenance of these devices is relegated to a special caste of scientists and enthusiasts. Despite the now absolute dependence on these devices, the general population remains oblivious of their inner workings. In order to fully exploit the potential that computational devices have, the principles governing them must become common knowledge.

The course, "Computational Thinking in Our World" is designed as a liberal studies course available for any student at the university. Because of this breadth of audience, there are several interesting challenges: no previous programming experience is assumed, only minimal mathematics is required, and no understanding of technology beyond that of a user is needed. But despite those restrictions, the needs of our students cannot be met with a superficial overview – we aim for deeper knowledge about a broad swath of applications. These challenges have affected the implementation of the environment (described in §3) as well as the way topics are treated (described in §4).

In this paper, we will describe some of the key facets of the course and the decisions we made to keep the course accessible. §4 will lay out the topics that we are covering and some of the rationales behind the choices. §5 will explain the philosophy of the evaluations for the course. §3 will describe the environment we've constructed to facilitate student success in the course. §2 will describe some of the related work in the field that has influenced us. Finally, we'll provide some concluding remarks and project future work.

2. RELATED WORK

Computer science departments have offered introductory courses over the past few years in an effort to attract students from other disciplines. While no other work we could find was directly similar to our research, the rest of the section details some of the work closest to our research.

Mark Guzdial introduced a Media Computation course

SIGCSE '16, March 02-05, 2016, Memphis, TN, USA

DOI: http://dx.doi.org/10.1145/2839509.2844655

for non-majors[4] at Georgia Institute of Technology. The course used a version of the Python programming language called Jython[1]. The language made students' task simpler in learning how to program, and help manipulate sound, images and movies by writing small snippets of code. Guzdial's work makes it clear that most non-major students like to learn programming if it is made simple by eliminating complex syntax and incorporating examples in the course that more directly relate to the real world.

Susan Rodgers'[8, 2] work is another example of introducing computer science to non-majors. Rodgers' goal was to teach students computer science concepts and programming by creating simple animations and building 2D and 3D virtual worlds. Students worked with scripting languages and interactive programming environment like Alice[2], Star Logo[3], Karel++ [1] and JAWAA[4]. Rodgers reports that 75% of the students liked the course. We speculate that some of the students may have been intimidated by the variety of environments they needed to learn, this could be the reason for the course not being liked by all the students.

Stephen Cooper[3] taught a course using animated 3D graphics to prepare novices for CS1. He reports that the students were frustrated by runtime errors they experienced while working in the Alice programming environment, particularly that these cryptic runtime errors left the students with no clue to what the source of such errors were.

Another application of Scratch by Alex Ruthman, Jesse Heines et al[9] was a course teaching computational thinking through musical live coding. This course was jointly offered by the computer science and music departments. This course was intended to attract students with arts and music backgrounds to computer science. Students created small programs applying programming concepts which resulted in music as an output, this was done with the help of Scratch sound blocks.

Shapiro and Hughes[11] made an excellent case for including a level of computer fluency to "be a full-fledged, competent and literate member of the information society". Twenty years later, little progress has been made.

3. PROGRAMMING ENVIRONMENT

The specific programming environment for the course is Phratch, augmented by blocks to directly support the course labs. Phratch[5] is a visual programming environment, based on the Scratch project from MIT,[5] ported to the Pharo programming environment.[6]

The first version of Scratch was publicly launched in May 2007. Since then Scratch has become very popular among young users, with Scratchers from around the world uploading more than 1,500 new projects to the site every day[7]! The goal of Scratch stated by Resnick and Maloney of the Lifelong Kindergarden Group[7] is to help young people (ages 8 and up) develop 21st century learning skills with important mathematical and computational ideas, while also gaining a deeper understanding of the process of design.With Scratch, kids can create their own interactive stories, games, music, and animation and share their creations with one another on the Web.[6]

We have retained the basic programming model of Scratch, but added a significant number of new blocks that facilitate the transformations, sensing and visualizations required for the course labs, as opposed to the multimedia programming that was its original intent The extended blocks implement some of the trickier parts to make student tasks easier since some of the labs contain fairly complex algorithms, and we want students to be able to complete them in a 1-hour lab period. Our goal is to give the students better understanding of the topics and computer science concepts by working through the topics in as simple a manner as possible. Teaching them programming is secondary.

Programming is done by dragging pieces from the left panel into the centre panel, i.e. script area. Most programs start running by clicking the green flag in the top right of the rightmost panel – the stage. For a program to recognize that click, it must contain a "when flag checked" block, which you will find in the Control blocks in the left panel. Besides Control blocks, there are also Operator, Look, Sound, Pen, Sensing, Motion, and Variable blocks.

We chose to use Phratch for all of the current labs. While there may be better languages/environments for some of the labs, with our non-programmer audience we felt it was important to not overwhelm them with new technology to learn on a week-to-week basis.

4. TOPICS, LABS, AND RATIONALE

Each of the topics below is designed to be a one-week, self-contained module. Each consists of 3 hours of lecture and a 1-hour "directed lab."

The lecture portion of each module includes history of the technology, explanation of the underlying computer science involved, and reflection on the social implications - examined through the lens of McLuhan's Tetrad[10].

A conventional Computer Science lab usually simply provides the problem statement and expects the student to imagine and code a working solution to the problem. Remembering our student audience, we can see that this approach would not work well in this course for two reasons:

1. it would lead to a great deal of stress and few students would succeed;

2. few (if any) students could complete a meaningful lab in the 1-hour lab period available.

As our goal is to communicate the computer science behind the week's topic via programming a simplified version of a real system, we have chosen to have the labs guide the students through the problem solving and programming to a successful outcome. Some might consider this too facile, but we believe the result will be maximal understanding with minimal frustration and our experience from the first two runnings of the course supports this. The goal is to connect citizens to computer science principles, not create programmers.

The topic areas were chosen from the world around us, while trying to cover significant fundamental areas of Computer Science. Some may see this as a very ambitious set of topic areas, and so it is. However it actually works well in practice, as attested to by our students and their success.

[1]http://www.jython.org
[2]http://www.alice.org
[3]http://www.media.mit.edu/starlogo
[4]http://www.cs.duke.edu/csed/jawaa2
[5]http://scratch.mit.edu/
[6]http://www.pharo-project.org/
[7]http://llk.media.mit.edu

4.1 Gaming

Gaming is used to introduce computer science concepts to students in a familiar environment. Students are exposed to potential applications of game-mechanics outside of gaming. We also consider how video games have influenced the development of hardware, computer graphics, and how these innovations found application outside of the industry.

Time is taken to explore the structure and culture of the video game industry. Recent issues include the tension between the corporate and independent publishers, and the rise of alternate economic models such as crowd-funding, micro-transactions and free-to-play.

Lab: Students create a version of "Breakout," a game consisting of a paddle, a ball and bricks. The player controls the paddle moving it left and right, attempting to bounce the ball off the surface of the paddle, with the objective of breaking all of the bricks stationed above the paddle. The lab is designed to introduce students to the scratch environment, build confidence and lay down the foundations for the discussion of future topics and labs.

4.2 Communications

Students learn the principles of modern communication; the challenges faced and the implications of the hardware context. This module is intended to act as a precursor to the exploration of the Web and the broader Internet, with the goal of establishing a good understanding of some of the underlying Internet technologies.

We also explore the TCP-IP protocol and students form an understanding of how time-stamps and IP-addresses can be used to gather data.

Lab: Students programmatically send an e-mail using the learned protocols. Byte level knowledge is not expected as they are assisted by a modified Scratch environment. The lab has guided steps that students follow, in order to successfully build the script for sending an email message from the Phratch environment. Blocks designed to support this lab are "**add rfc822 header _ with _ to _**", "**ssl send _**", "**smtp send _ server _**". When the script is started by clicking the green flag in the top right of the stage of the Phratch environment, an information window pops up, which displays the email message built by the user, seen in figure. 1. If the user chooses to send an email using the "**ssl send _**" block, an authentication window pop's up, asking the user to enter a password for the sender's email account as shown in figure 1. They can use the "**ssl send _**" block to send a secure email message or "**smtp send _ server _**" to send insecure mail without requiring any authentication – but this only works with email servers which accept unauthenticated email messages.

A possible solution is shown in figure 1. Note that while the details of the solution may not be readable, it is easy to see that the solution is only a handful of code blocks – which is typical of the labs in the course.

4.3 The Web

This module deals with the exploration of Web technologies and culture. Students are introduced to the protocols used by the Internet and how data moves around the network, time is spent understanding Web-Search functions and the role Spiders and Bots play.

We examine how identity is achieved and maintained on the Web, and what measures have been taken to ensure its

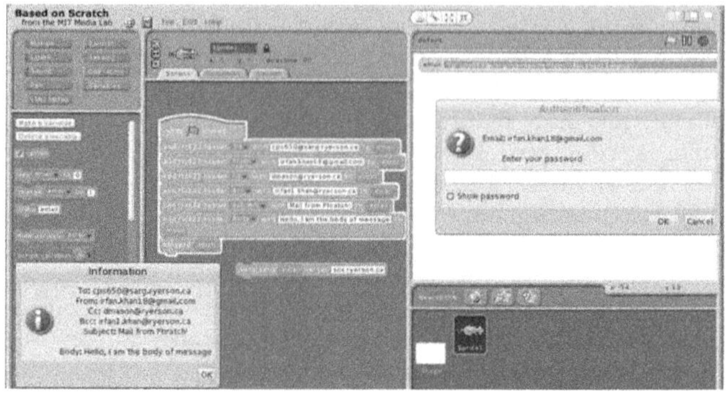

Figure 1: Sending email programmatically

security – actual cryptography is a focus in another section. We finish with the exploration of social networks and their impact as well as the emergence of memes and their role in a cultural context.

Lab: The aim of this lab is to give student's some understanding about web Application Programming Interfaces(API), and how APIs can be used to share, or pull information from Social Networking websites. The studentâĂŹs had guided steps, to help them achieve three taskâĂŹs for this lab:

- Use Twitter REST "Get followers/IDs" API v1.1, to get the followers IDs of their Twitter account, add them to a list, and then iterate over the list, to get the number of followers (i.e. count the number of IDs).
- Get followers of followers IDs into a new list.
- Use the Twitter REST "user lookup" API v1.1, to convert IDs into `screen_names`.

To achieve the above taskâĂŹs from Phratch environment, we designed "**Json extract _ IDs into _**", "**Json extract screen n** ", "**iterate _**", "**replace old item of _ with new _**" and "**current item _**" blocks. A possible solution of one of the task is shown in figure 2.

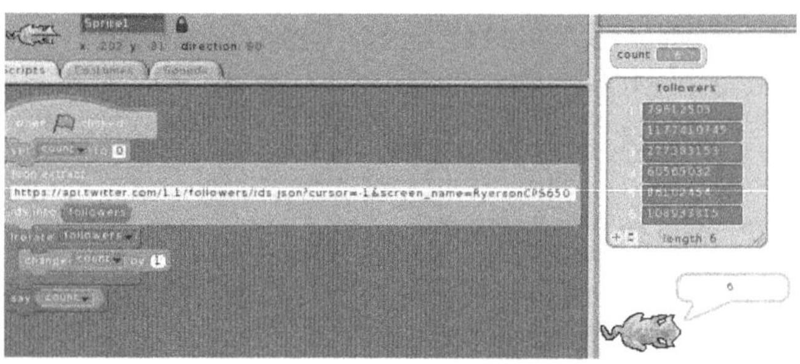

Figure 2: Finding followersID's of UniversityCourse twitter user

4.4 Locations and GPS

Students explore the importance of location-based technologies such as GPS and near-field communication. We look at the dependency of mobile computing to location data and how it extends to fixed computers.

Lab: For the purpose of this lab, we created a 2D virtual GPS system scene which was part of the setup. We designed an animation with three satellite images and three signal images (i.e. sprites), that drift across the stage of the Phratch environment. The three signal images follow the satellite images and leave a circle - like visualization.

Students are supposed to create a script in order to locate the mouse pointer on the stage of the Phratch environment with the help of guided steps. The idea was to create a block that would get the location (i.e. center) and distance of three satellites from the mouse pointer. Once we have a location and distance of three satellites, students draw three circles using the location and distance as the radius to find the intersecting points. The common point among the intersecting points would be the resulting location of the mouseâĂŞpointer. One of the challenges of this lab is to simplify the Math, in order to create an understanding of the GPS technology without excessive expectations of the students. A possible solution for the lab is shown in figure 3.

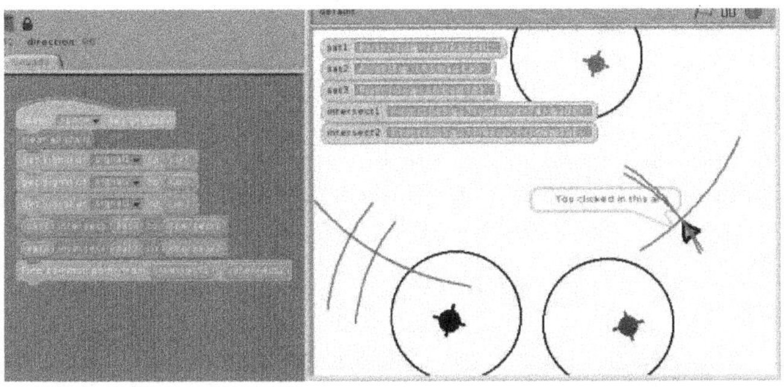

Figure 3: Locating mouse pointer on the stage

4.5 Big Data and Cheap Computation

Students in this section use their previous knowledge and understanding of technology to analyze big-data. By the end of the section, students should have a clear understanding of the problem posed by too much data.

This module also examines data re-sellers and collectors. Students form an understanding of how big-data can be used to guide decisions and delving into the analysis of how information became a commodity.

We explain cloud computing and how map-reduce is used to share processing of large amounts of data over a server farm.

Lab: The lab uses a sprite to plot a graph as an example of a very simple visualisation.

4.6 Robotics

Students explore the challenges of robotics, and it's social impact. We also examine why certain problems are easy for robots, and others exceptionally difficult. Applications of robotics technologies in manufacturing and domestic sectors are analyzed, as well as the changing face of robotics in popular culture.

Lab: For the purpose of this lab, students are supposed to script the robot (i.e. sprite) to solve a Maze, using the Wall follower or Left-hand rule algorithm and TremauxâĂŹs Algorithm. Involves in guiding a simulated robot through a maze. The lab is designed to demonstrate how difficult it is to solve a seemingly trivial problem. The script that students were supposed to achieve with the help of guided steps is shown in figure 4. In order to give more clarity to the students on the path taken by the robot in figure 4 the red circles on the maze indicate the cells visited once by the robot, and the green circles indicate the cells visited twice by the robot.

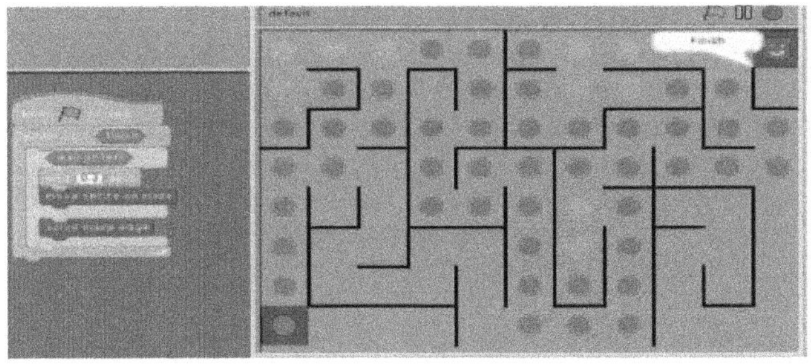

Figure 4: Left-hand-rule maze-solving algorithm

4.7 Secrets and intellectual property

This module introduces the topic of cryptography, its application to secure communication and the technologies it allows. Students learn about public/private key encryption and how it enables HTTPS.

We examine the use of cryptography in CD and DVD players, and discuss RIAA, and the MPAA. Students look at the impact of Copyright, Intellectual Property and Patents in a digital world.

Lab: For the purpose of this lab, we have students focus on the one-time pad encryption algorithm. Students encrypt a message using a one-time-pad algorithm, in order to give hands-on experience with basic cryptography. This section involves heavy use of mathematical concepts and algorithms. Time is taken to ensure the content is presentable to students with a limited math background.

4.8 Politics and Finance

This module centers on analyzing the impact technology has had on politics, contrasted by how politics influenced the development of technology. We examine the role of electronic voting and its security.

Discussion includes the application of computers to the finance sector and their impact on the stock-market. Students also consider the problems created by high-frequency trading.

Lab: Students are tasked with using the Yahoo API to retrieve stock information off the web. The second part of the lab consists of students implementing the Condorcet voting algorithm.

4.9 Security and military uses of computers

A part of this module centers on the concerns and problems of identity in a digital world. We examine the traditional methods of securing an identity, and introduce the concept of biometrics.

We explore the cultural shift created by computerized warfare and technologies such as drones and smart-bombs. We also contrast reality and fiction with "killing by video-game".

Lab: Students are tasked with taking a sterile data-set of access card time stamps, and attempt to match specific individuals to the data. The purpose of the lab is to demonstrate the difficulty of sterilizing data and the implications of pervasive surveillance. Students write a script to access fabricated secure data, which contains information about fabricated persons. The information includes the name of the person, rooms that a person has been to and the time spent in each room.

4.10 Transportation & Medical

Students explore the challenges faced by traffic switching and aircraft traffic control. We also explore the creation of autonomous vehicles and their impact on traditional traffic patterns.

We analyze the application of cheap computation to the medical field. We explore technologies such as medical diagnostic tools, as well as data driven medicine.

Lab: In the first part, we had students focus on how autonomous vehicles work and the importance of sensors in helping autonomous vehicles detect their environment. Students write code for a very simple vehicle which tracks an arbitrary non-crossing line.

The second part is to simulate the function of a CAT-Scan. Students create a script to generate the density values of the scanned object. Perform the scans, using the density values generated, to get some vague image of an object (e.g. diamond, circle, triangle or rectangle) on the stage. A possible solution for the first part of this lab is shown in figure 5

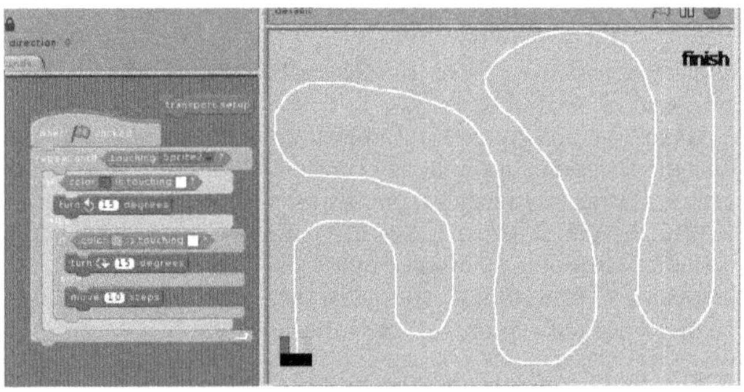

Figure 5: Line Follower Autonomous Vehicle

4.11 Fashion and Design

Students explore the impact of disruptive technologies such as 3D printing and custom fabrication in the manufacturing process. We also discuss the rise of hacker space movements on and maker culture. We also explore computer-aided-design, and the impact of robotic and bespoke manufacturing.

Lab: In the previous iterations of the course there has been no lab for this module. However, 3D printers have become available on campus, so we are exploring the possibility of designing and printing a small object. The challenge is that this would be different software that would be challenging for these students to pick up at the end of a course.

5. EVALUATION

Evaluation for the course is multi-facetted.

1. There is a small mark assigned for each completed lab and for in-class participation for a total of 35%.

2. There are 3 short essays (250-1500 words each) worth a total of 30% on topics of interest from the course, with emphasis on exploring the social/cultural impacts of the chosen technology. This has value in and of itself, but is also a university requirement for courses designated as "Liberal Studies".

3. There is a final exam worth 35%.

The goal of the evaluation is to foment ideas, questioning, and analysis from the students, while ensuring that they have done the work and have an appreciation of how the various technologies work. In the first running of the course the level and frequency of discussion was less than hoped for, so in the subsequent edition we are planning to use TopHat[12] - similar to clickers using the students' own devices.

Student Response

Of the 38 students registered in Winter 2014, 33 earned a grade of B+ or better. Of the 59 students registered in Winter 2015, 40 earned a grade of B+ or better. This is not a case of grade inflation; the students were simply strongly engaged in the course, with several producing very insightful essays.

In the initial delivery of the course, a voluntary survey was taken at the end of each lab. Some of the early ones had very limited participation so we won't provide a table of the questionnaires, but to give a sense of the students' experience, here is the result of 26 participants for the Transportation and Medical lab:

- 58% of the respondents disagreed while 23% of the respondents "slightly agreed" and 19% of the respondents "strongly agreed" on having prior knowledge or understanding about the topic presented.

- 58% of the respondents "strongly agreed" while 42% of the respondents "slightly agreed" on understanding how autonomous vehicles work and how CAT-scan works.

- 69% of the respondents "strongly agreed," 31% of the respondents "slightly agreed" on visualization being helpful in giving them understanding.

- 77% of the respondents "strongly agreed" and 23% of the respondents "slightly agreed" on guided steps helping them successfully complete the lab within 1-hour.

- 57% of the respondents "strongly agreed," 35% of the respondents "slightly agreed" and 8% of the respondents "slightly disagreed" on the topic being presented is important in learning the material of the course Computational Thinking In Our World.

- 23% of the respondents reported the duration of the lab was "short," 77% reported it was "right."

Anecdotal Comments

We have received many positive comments from students of the course, and no complaints. Here we provide some anecdotal comments, grouped by category.

Overall experience of working on the labs. - "overall experience was good, learned about different variety of technologies. The labs gave me better understanding of each topic."

- "At the beginning it was difficult,but it got easier as I got used to the Phratch programming environment."

Favorite lab. - "GPS lab was interesting, because it has good visualization depicting the real-time scenario."

- "Robotics lab was my favorite, because I liked the visualization and the way the robot solved the maze."

Difficulty of lab work. - "Didn't find any lab to be difficult to work on, guided steps made it easy."

- "Voting and finance lab was difficult, due to lack of time."

6. CONCLUSIONS

Computers and computational thinking are becoming a ubiquitous part of modern life and technology. It is important that citizens have sufficient knowledge of the technology they use and depend on to be able to recognize and reason about important policy decisions. It is also important that future leaders understand the technology well enough to understand and question the advice they are given on technology matters.

This course undertakes to give citizens and leaders the understanding that they need in the technological world that is upon us, without overwhelming people who aren't (and have no interest in becoming) programmers.

The use of a block-based programming environment and guided labs has enabled our students – with no prgramming background – to understand the use of computer science and computer technology at a deeper level than if we were simply providing lectures on the topics.

Since the purpose of the course is not to teach programming, we did not analyze to see if guided labs can help non-majors understand programming languages.

The course has been a significant success, doubling in enrollment in the second iteration. The numbers were artificially restricted by a scheduling glitch in W2015, and we anticipate significant growth this coming year.

The electronic resources for the course are accessible at http://cps650.sarg.ryerson.ca.

References

[1] Joseph Bergin et al. *Karel++: A Gentle Introduction to the Art of Object-Oriented Programming.* Wiley, 1996. ISBN: 978-0-471-13809-9.

[2] Stephen Cooper, Wanda Dann, and Randy Pausch. "Alice: a 3-D tool for introductory programming concepts". In: *J. Comput. Sci. Coll.* 15.5 (Apr. 2000), pp. 107–116. ISSN: 1937-4771. URL: http://dl.acm.org/citation.cfm?id=364133.364161.

[3] Stephen Cooper, Wanda Dann, and Randy Pausch. "Using Animated 3D Graphics To Prepare Novices for CS1". In: *Computer Science Education Journal* 13 (2003), pp. 28–29.

[4] Mark Guzdial. "A media computation course for non-majors". In: *SIGCSE Bull.* 35.3 (June 2003), pp. 104–108. ISSN: 0097-8418. DOI: 10.1145/961290.961542. URL: http://doi.acm.org/10.1145/961290.961542.

[5] Jannik Laval. *Phratch.* URL: http://www.phratch.com/ (visited on 09/03/2014).

[6] John Maloney et al. "The Scratch Programming Language and Environment". In: *Trans. Comput. Educ.* 10.4 (Nov. 2010), 16:1–16:15. ISSN: 1946-6226. DOI: 10.1145/1868358.1868363. URL: http://doi.acm.org/10.1145/1868358.1868363.

[7] Mitchel Resnick et al. "Scratch: programming for all". In: *Commun. ACM* 52.11 (Nov. 2009), pp. 60–67. ISSN: 0001-0782. DOI: 10.1145/1592761.1592779. URL: http://doi.acm.org/10.1145/1592761.1592779.

[8] Susan H. Rodger. "Introducing computer science through animation and virtual worlds". In: *SIGCSE Bull.* 34.1 (Feb. 2002), pp. 186–190. ISSN: 0097-8418. DOI: 10.1145/563517.563411. URL: http://doi.acm.org/10.1145/563517.563411.

[9] Alex Ruthmann et al. "Teaching computational thinking through musical live coding in scratch". In: *Proceedings of the 41st ACM technical symposium on Computer science education.* SIGCSE '10. Milwaukee, Wisconsin, USA: ACM, 2010, pp. 351–355. ISBN: 978-1-4503-0006-3. DOI: 10.1145/1734263.1734384. URL: http://doi.acm.org/10.1145/1734263.1734384.

[10] Gregory Sandstrom. "Laws of media – The four effects: A McLuhan contribution to social epistemology". In: *Social Epistemology Review and Reply Collective* 1.12 (2012), pp. 1–6. URL: http://wp.me/p1Bfg0-uc.

[11] J J Shapiro and S K Hughes. "Information Literacy as a Liberal Art: Enlightenment Proposals For a New Curriculum". In: *Educom Review, March/April* 12 (1996), pp. 31–35.

[12] *Tophat – Interactive classroom environment.* http://tophat.com/.

[13] Jeannette M. Wing. "Computational thinking". In: *Commun. ACM* 49.3 (Mar. 2006), pp. 33–35. ISSN: 0001-0782. DOI: 10.1145/1118178.1118215. URL: http://doi.acm.org/10.1145/1118178.1118215.

A Study on the Impact of Multidisciplinary Collaboration on Computational Thinking

Sarah Monisha Pulimood
Department of Computer Science
The College of New Jersey
Ewing, NJ 08628
1-609-771-2788
pulimood@tcnj.edu

Kim Pearson
Department of English
The College of New Jersey
Ewing, NJ 08628
1-609-771-2692
kpearson@tcnj.edu

Diane C. Bates
Dept. of Sociology & Anthropology
The College of New Jersey
Ewing, NJ 08628
1-609-771-3176
bates@tcnj.edu

ABSTRACT

This paper reports on a multi-semester study of the impact on student perceptions of their computational thinking abilities as a result of collaboration between students in computer science (CS) and journalism courses to solve a problem for a community partner, Habitat for Humanity. Interdisciplinary computing collaborations have become a popular mode of instruction in upper-level CS courses. In many cases, these collaborations have been with other STEM disciplines. However, there are non-STEM fields that have been transformed by computer science and can also serve as fruitful test beds for curricular innovation; journalism is one such field. In this study, undergraduate students in CS and journalism courses focused on creating a computational solution to address a real community need. The study investigates whether immersion in multidisciplinary collaborative experiences increases the computational thinking abilities of both CS and non-CS students. 41 CS students participated in the study alongside 96 students in a range of other STEM and non-STEM majors. Quantitative data were collected to gauge students' attainment of concepts and skills constitutive to computational thinking. Pre-test data indicate that CS students were no different from other STEM students in their own assessment of computational thinking and skills. Post-test data indicate that while all students made significant gains in self-assessment of skills and knowledge, CS majors fared significantly better than their peers. It is particularly noteworthy that CS majors' gains outpaced those of computer engineering majors. Further research is planned to gain additional insight into the possible reasons behind these results.

CCS Concepts

• Social and professional topics~Computational thinking • Applied computing~Collaborative learning *• Social and professional topics~Software engineering education • Social and professional topics~Student assessment*

Keywords

Computational thinking; collaboration; community engaged learning.

SIGCSE '16, March 02-05, 2016, Memphis, TN, USA
© 2016 ACM. ISBN 978-1-4503-3685-7/16/03···$15.00
DOI: http://dx.doi.org/10.1145/2839509.2844636

1. INTRODUCTION

To remain competitive in a fast changing global economy, the Unites States must develop a workforce that focuses on the creation, not merely the consumption, of computing technology. This requires a pedagogy that emphasizes problem solving in a gender neutral, culturally and ethnically diverse community, and an authentic learning environment in which students solve real problems as a collaborative community with their peers from other disciplines [17, 24, 25, 28].

Computational thinking [28] can be broadly defined as a way of solving problems that draws on concepts fundamental to computer science, i.e. it requires creating and making use of different levels of abstraction, to understand and solve problems more effectively; thinking algorithmically and applying mathematical concepts such as induction to develop more efficient, fair, and secure solutions; and understanding the consequences of scale, not only for reasons of efficiency but also for economic and social reasons. The Committee for the Workshops on Computational Thinking describes computational thinking as a group phenomenon that can assist specialists in other disciplines to more effectively adopt, use, and develop computational tools [9]. It is therefore reasonable to infer that collaborative learning environments are conducive to fostering this vital set of competencies. Classes focused on computational problem solving in a group context also afford students the opportunity to hone communication and collaboration skills beyond the classroom, and to understand how computer science is applied to particular knowledge domains.

This paper reports on a multi-semester study of the impact on student perceptions of their computational thinking abilities as a result of collaboration between students in CS and journalism courses to solve a problem posed by a community partner.

2. BACKGROUND AND RELATED WORK

2.1 Goals of the Project

The curricular model described here was designed based on the hypothesis that to increase motivation toward, and interest in, computing careers, undergraduate students must be immersed in multidisciplinary collaborative experiences where they are creators of technology-based solutions, and where they internalize the relevance of and interconnectedness between classroom learning and the communities in which they live.

The overarching goal for the project was to formalize a model for courses that collaborate across disciplinary boundaries and with a community partner. The pedagogical goal was to create a model experiential and engaging learning environment through which to immerse both CS and non-CS majors in computational thinking. The research goal was to study the collaborative learning environment, and to articulate the processes, products, challenges and effective strategies that manifest collaborative problem solving. Quantitative and qualitative instruments were developed to measure outcomes in this study, and will ultimately contribute to the knowledge base of STEM workforce preparedness in computing as they are applied beyond our institution.

2.2 Research Base

Computing technologies such as mobile devices, geographic information systems, online social networks, and cloud computing have revolutionized how professionals, including those in non-computing fields, conduct their work. For example, using a hate crimes database obtained from the NYPD Hate Crimes Task Force, and well-designed queries, New York Times reporter Jo Craven McGinty mapped numerous hate crimes[1] in New York based on type, location, frequency, and targeted ethnicity to conclude that Jews are the targets of most NYC hate crimes and that most of the city's hate crimes occur in Brooklyn [23]. Significant effort has been devoted in recent years to designing teaching and research collaborations between computer scientists and those in computing-dependent disciplines as a balanced collaboration between two well-established fields, rather than presenting what is essentially a traditional perspective on computer science through its application [7, 14, 26]. Linked courses have been developed to address the curricular needs in emerging computing-dependent fields such as computational biology and bioinformatics. Computational journalism is an emerging computing-dependent specialty, and the view that all journalists should have at least rudimentary programming and scripting skills is gaining ground among journalism educators [5]. However, an examination of the undergraduate curricula of several leading journalism programs known for their focus on digital innovation reveals limited exposure to computing, and formal collaborations between journalism and CS classes are rare, particularly at the undergraduate level.

Research provides evidence [13, 20] that the level of students' motivation affects their levels of engagement with a task, their enjoyment of activities, how and what they learn, and ultimately, their performance. Students are more motivated by activities they perceive to be useful and socially relevant, and there is evidence that college students care about environmental issues [20]. The benefits of service learning (also referred to as community engaged learning) in CS classes has been discussed at length in the literature [6, 21, 27].

Undergraduates across the country are choosing to leave STEM programs before they graduate with those degrees [16]. While recent nationwide efforts have helped improve the numbers of students enrolling in computing programs, there is still much work to be done to improve recruitment and retention rates, especially among historically under-represented groups. Statistics published by the National Center for Women and Information Technology (NCWIT) [24] include data such as:

- Girls represented 20% of Advanced Placement (AP) CS exam-takers in 2014 (up from 18% in 2009); that is the lowest female representation of any AP exam;
- In 2013 women earned 18% of all Computer and Information Sciences degrees; in contrast, 37% of CS degree recipients in 1985 were women;
- Women hold more than half of all professional occupations in the U.S. but only 26% of all computing-related occupations.

[1] https://www.ire.org/resource-center/stories/22081/

To achieve equity in the computing fields, preconceptions and biases about these fields must change, the culture of the classroom must become more welcoming, and stereotype threats and unconscious biases must be removed. (A stereotype threat is the experience of anxiety in a situation where a person has the potential to confirm a negative stereotype about their social group. This has been shown to reduce the performance of individuals who belong to negatively stereotyped groups [2, 3].) Research in gender and diversity disparity in STEM education [4, 8, 10, 12, 13, 22] asserts that empowerment and mutual respect are key for students. Removing unconscious bias requires a significant change in the culture of the CS classroom so that it supports a diverse, highly interactive community. Inquiry-based pedagogy suggests models of classroom dynamics that focus on teaching both collaborative and individual problem solving strategies that leverage computer science concepts [15, 19, 25].

Three essential themes emerge: (1) creative problem solving requires an authentic inquiry-based pedagogy; (2) computational thinking occurs in a collaborative community; and (3) computational thinking requires diversity of perspectives and background. Expanding participation in the computing pipeline requires inquiry-based student engagement where students are innovators rather than merely users of computing technology. The computing experience must create a supportive and cooperative culture that extends beyond the classroom, in which all members develop confidence and competency [8].

3. PROJECT DESIGN

The principal investigators on this project are a computer science professor and a journalism professor, at a primarily undergraduate institution, who each have industry and academic experience that informed their philosophical inclinations towards project-focused, inquiry-based collaborative learning. The evaluator is a colleague from the sociology department.

The Computer Science (CS) Department has about 130 majors and minors, and is housed in the School of Science, with Biology, Chemistry, Mathematics & Statistics, and Physics. Journalism is offered as a major track within the English Department and has about 100 majors and minors. The department is housed within the School of Humanities and Social Sciences (HSS).

The collaboration occurred over five semesters, but only data for the first four semesters are presented here since data from the most recent semester are still being analyzed. Table 1 shows the classes involved in the collaboration each semester.

Table 1. Collaborating Classes, by Semester

Semester	CS Course	Journalism Course
Spring 2013	Software Engineering	Blogging and Social Media
Fall 2013	Database Systems	Health and Environmental Journalism
	Software Engineering	News Games
Spring 2014	Software Engineering	Future of the News
Fall 2014	Software Engineering	Health and Environmental Journalism
Spring 2015	Software Engineering	Blogging and Social Media

The software engineering course is a requirement for CS and computer engineering majors, as well as for the CS minor. The database systems course is an elective for the CS major and minor. The computer engineering (CE) major is offered by the Electrical and Computer Engineering department that is housed within the School of Engineering. The journalism courses participating in this study are also taken by digital arts, communications, and interactive multimedia majors (IMM), from the School of Arts and Communications (A&C).

3.1 The Problem

The Habitat for Humanity (Habitat) of a neighboring city is part of a global, nonprofit organization that acquires properties and builds, rehabilitates or preserve homes to provide affordable housing for the community it serves. Due to industrialization, the city has many properties that have high levels of particulate matter pollution, toxic discharges, or hazardous waste as determined by the Environmental Protection Agency (EPA)[2]. Habitat frequently has opportunities to purchase properties in the city, only to discover that they are polluted. The costs for construction of new housing in previously industrial urban cores must now include costs associated with environmental testing and mitigation. The cost of mitigating environmental hazards has made it increasingly difficult for Habitat to build homes that are affordable to its target clients. The Executive Director of the local Habitat would like a system that could estimate the level of contamination on any given plot of land prior to expensive environmental testing.

Students in the collaborating classes (see Table 1) are addressing the large and complex problem of developing a web-based system that manages and provides information about potentially polluted properties for Habitat and citizens of the area. The aim is for the system to provide answers to questions such as: Can the cost of clean up for a property be predicted based on data available for neighboring properties? What are the cumulative impacts of different pollutants on the public health of residents? Which organizations (government, private, non-profit, for-profit) are working towards / against pollution control measures?

3.2 The Collaboration

The model described here embraces Kolb's [18] position that experiential learning should be structured as a cyclical process consisting of concrete experience, opportunities for reflection, abstract conceptualization and active experimentation. The authors' experience is consistent with the advice of other researchers about the importance of clearly defining projects, tasks and roles so that expectations are clear to all participants, and project deliverables and milestones are realistic and achievable within the timeframes allotted.

Each class is run separately with its own learning goals, content and deliverables, but major assignments are structured around the goal of the collaboration, i.e. to create a web-based system that provides accurate, accessible and comprehensive information on sites that are likely to contain contaminants. Since this is a complex problem, each semester students identify components of the system that they will develop or enhance. For example, one team worked on making the map module of the system more robust (the map module displays locations of sites in the databases using color-coding and tool tips to indicate the severity of pollution). While students in the CS class focus on technical research, design and implementation, the students in the journalism class identify credible data sources and write content for the website to help users interpret pollution information.

The students met jointly four times in the first semester. At the initial meeting, the executive director and a construction manager from the local Habitat explained how the lack of accurate pollution information complicates their efforts to provide affordable housing. The students brainstormed ideas for software modules that would help address the problem. At a subsequent meeting, an environmental policy expert answered questions about scientific and regulatory issues. The classes also took a field trip to the neighborhood that Habitat is working to redevelop. The teams were required to meet outside of class to continue working on the project. At the end of the semester, the students presented their software modules to Habitat and other stakeholders. Each class also had deliverables that were not directly related to the project. For example, the blogging and social media students created blogs tied to aspects of environmental sustainability, while the software engineering students developed individual projects. Subsequent semesters followed a similar template, but some refinements were made based on observations of the instructors and evaluator, and student feedback. One modification was to have an initial class meeting between students in the two classes, with the guest speakers coming to the second meeting. At the initial meeting, the students explored the existing software system, tested its functionality, and began brainstorming ideas for improvements and questions for the subject matter experts.

Teams are comprised of students from each of the collaborating classes. Project management and source code control occurs through GitHub repositories. Each team works on a branch of the main project. At the end of the semester after the individual modules have been tested, they are merged into the master. Development of the project follows the principles of Humanitarian Free and Open Source Software (HFOSS) [11]. One of the challenges of doing this work with undergraduates is that each semester students are tasked with learning about the issues facing Habitat at the same time that they are learning the journalism or CS content and skills. Despite this, we are moving closer to having a functioning system. The teams' repositories are currently private due to legal issues regarding educational records. Eventually, once the web-based system is stable and the code is anonymized, it will be made public as an HFOSS project.

In addition to a working system that Habitat could use to identify potential sites for constructing new affordable housing, our research documents how students believe they have developed computational and collaborative skills over the course of the semester. Self-assessment reflects whether students perceive themselves as having internalized the knowledge that the professors endeavor to impart.

3.3 Assessing Outcomes

3.3.1 Methods

Student outcomes were measured through self-assessments in pre-tests and post-tests over four semesters. Surveys were administered to all students in the five CS courses and the five journalism courses (some of which were cross-listed as IMM courses, see Table 1 above). In Fall 2013, two courses from each discipline were included in the study; in all other semesters, only one course from each discipline was included. CS and journalism groups are non-equivalent groups, and not genuine controls for one another. Since the software engineering course is required of *all* majors, comparisons to traditional CS instruction was not possible. Similarly, although all journalism classes were electives, there was no attempt to manage enrollment in these classes for experimental design purposes. Pre-tests were administered in person as paper surveys on the first day of class, following an explanation of the project and a review of human subjects protection. Post-tests were administered electronically using Qualtrics software. Students were invited to complete the post-

[2] http://www.epa.gov/.

test during the last week of class, but were able to complete these into the "reading period" before final exams. Pre-test data was collected from 153 individuals. Post-test data was collected from 113 individuals, indicating a response rate of 73.86 percent. Attrition results from students dropping the classes after the first day, or because individual students declined to participate in the post-test. All analysis was completed using SPSS software. The total number of participants for which we have the student major recorded is 138; these were grouped according to the academic unit to which their major pertains: 49 from the School of Science (35.51%; CS = 41, Biology = 2, Mathematics = 1, Physics = 5), 27 from the School of Engineering (19.57%; all CE), 26 from the School of Humanities and Social Sciences (18.84%; Journalism & Professional Writing = 22, English = 3, Psychology = 1) and 36 from the School of Arts and Communication (26.09%; Communication Studies = 2, Digital Arts = 18, IMM = 16).

3.3.2 Operationalization

During the period of study, in traditional assessment less than 4% of the students in the software engineering classes failed to demonstrate achievement of the computational learning goals, by earning a D or F for the course. In this project, our main concern with student learning involved the acquisition or improvement of skills related to collaboration and computational thinking. In addition to traditional assessment, all students were asked a series of questions, derived from ABET's General and Program-Specific (CS) Student Outcomes Criteria for Accrediting Computing Programs [1] and Wing's definition of computational thinking [28]. On both the pre-test and post-test, students were asked, "to what extent do you agree or disagree with each of the following:" with response categories of: Strongly Agree (coded 4), Agree (3), Disagree (2), or Strongly Disagree (1) with the items in Table 2.

Table 2. Items Asked of Students in All Classes

Code	Description
A1	I can apply knowledge of computing appropriate to my major
A2	I can analyze a problem, and then identify and define the computing requirements appropriate to its solution
A3	I understand the impact of computing on society
A4	I can use current computing techniques, skills, and tools necessary in careers for which my major prepares me
A5	I can collaborate with others to design and develop computer based tools and technologies appropriate to careers for which my major prepares me
A6	I can use abstractions
A7	I can use logical thinking
A8	I can use algorithms

There were between 107 and 113 valid cases for each of these items. Reliability analysis of these items as a measure of computational thinking is indicated by a Cronbach's alpha of .806 for pre-test items and .911 for post-test items. These items taken together are a reliable measure of the underlying concept of computational thinking.

Students in the journalism classes rated agreement with two additional items, derived from standards set by the Accrediting Council on Education in Journalism and Mass Communications.

Table 3. Additional Items for Students in Journalism Classes

Code	Description
J1	I can conduct research and evaluate information by methods appropriate to journalism
J2	I can edit

There were 31 cases for item J1. Item J2 could not be evaluated due to an error in the electronic post-test. Reliability analysis of J1 added to items A1-A8 as a measure of computational thinking among these students is indicated by a Cronbach's alpha of .824 for pre-test items and .894 for post-test items.

Students in CS classes were additionally asked to rate agreement with the items in Table 4, derived from ABET learning outcomes.

Table 4. Additional Items for Students in CS Classes

Code	Description
C1	I can design and implement a computer-based system to meet desired needs
C2	I can evaluate a computer-based system to meet desired needs
C3	I can apply algorithmic principles and computer science theory in the modeling and design of computer-based systems
C4	I understand the tradeoffs involved in design choices for computer-based systems
C5	I can apply design and implement principles in the development of computer-based systems of varying complexity

There were 76-77 cases for each of these items. Reliability analysis of the five valid items above added to items A1-A8 as a measure of computational thinking among students in the CS courses is indicated by a Cronbach's alpha of .873 for pre-test items and .947 for post-test items.

4. ANALYSIS

Students from all majors other than those in HSS rated their computational thinking skills comparably in the pre-tests. There were few statistically significant differences between CS, CE, and digital media students in pre-test measures, but journalism majors consistently and significantly rated their own computational thinking skills lower than their peers. The only item for which journalism students were statistically indistinguishable from their peers was "I can use logical thinking". There were no statistical differences between CS and CE students on any pre-test items. There was a single statistical difference between digital media majors taking CS courses and CS students on the item "I can design and implement a computer-based system to meet desired needs" ($p = .017$) on the pre-test, with the digital media students more likely to agree with this statement than CS students. With this minor exception, our data indicates that there were few initial differences among non-journalism students: CS, CE, and digital media students rated themselves similarly.

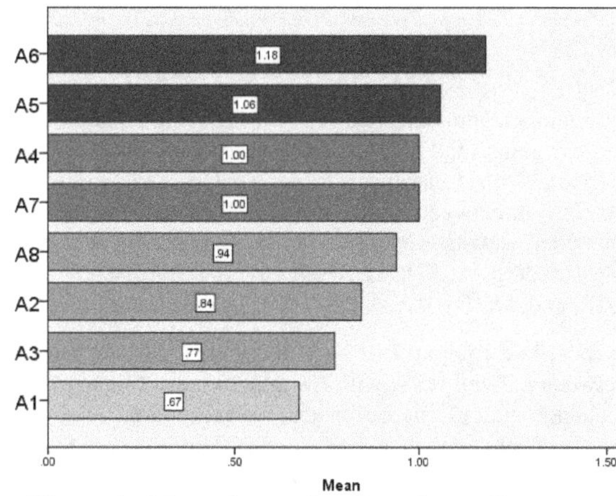

Figure 1: Mean change for all students all semesters

Students from all majors rated their computational thinking and collaboration skills higher on the post-test for all items when compared to their self-ratings in the pre-test, with a full increase of one unit or more in four of eight items. Paired-sample t-tests found statistically significant improvement in all measures from pre-test to post-test (see Figure 1). Given the centrality of computational thinking in all course elements, students in CS classes improved more, as expected; students rated their own knowledge at the end of the semester higher in all items when compared to their self-ratings in the pre-test, with a full increase of one unit in ten of thirteen items (see Figure 2).

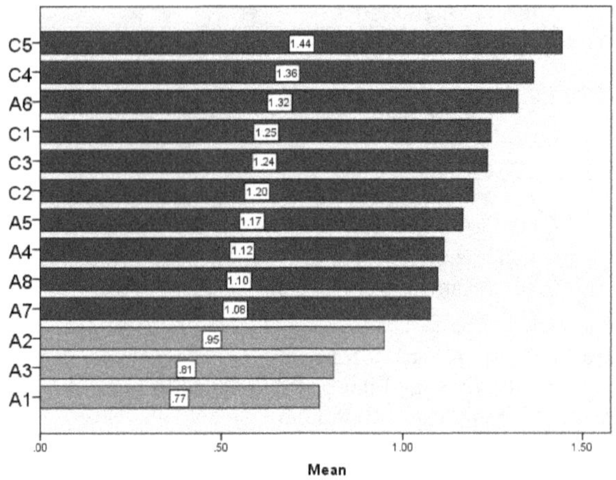

Figure 2: Mean change for students in CS classes

The journalism students rated their own knowledge higher in all items on the post-test when compared to their self-ratings in the pre-test, with an increase of nearly a full unit in four of nine items and at least a half unit increase in all but one item (see Figure 3).

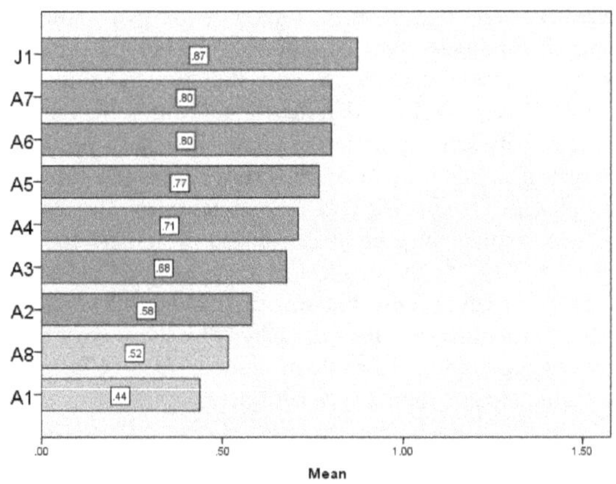

Figure 3: Mean change for students in Journalism classes

Not all majors responded equally to the model. CS majors indicate the largest gains, and these gains are consistently significant in comparison with journalism students; CE and digital media students fall in between these extremes. That said, only four items demonstrated statistically significant differences by major group: A5 (F = 3.029, p = .033), A2 (F = 3.107, p = .030), A4 (F = 3.498, p = .018) and A8 (F = 4.324, p = .007), as shown in Figure 4.

Tukey post-hoc comparisons show that the significant differences are between CS and HSS, with CS majors indicating significantly more change than journalism majors on every item. A&C and CE majors were not statistically different from either CS or HSS majors, but consistently record intermediate levels of change.

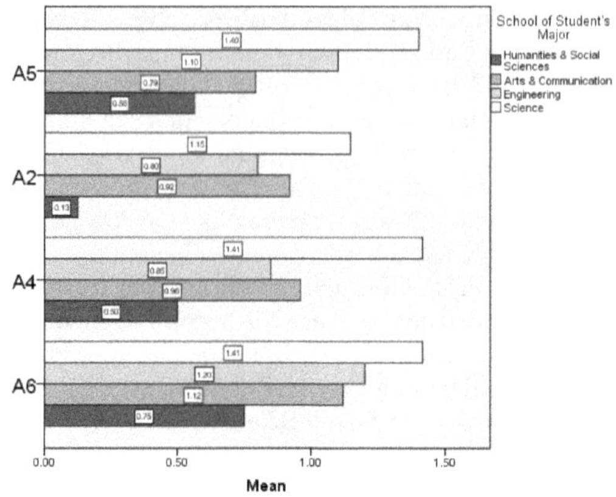

Figure 4: Comparison of Statistically Different Mean Changes by School

Moreover, for all items, computer engineering majors indicated less change than their CS counterparts on every item, as shown in Figure 5. One way analysis of variance (ANOVA) indicates that two items have statistically significant differences between CS and engineering students: C3 (F = 4.996, p =.029) and C4 (F = 4.877, p = .031). Two other items were nearly significant: A4 (F = 3.802, p =.056) and A8 (F = 3.627, p = .061). When the 18 digital media students who had taken CS courses were added to this comparison, they were not significantly different from either CS or engineering students on any item.

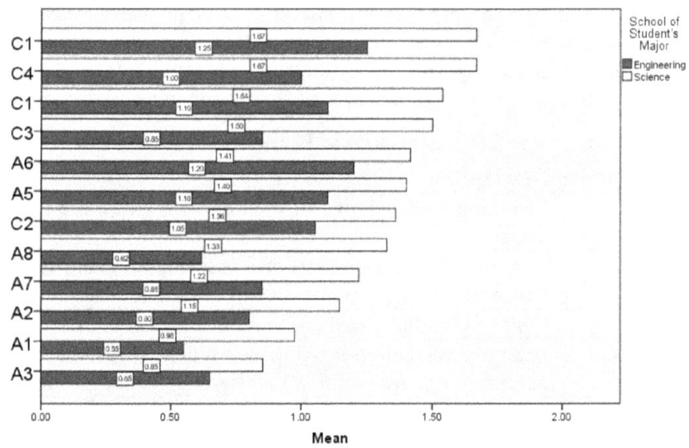

Figure 5: Comparison of Science and Engineering Students

5. CONCLUSIONS

Computational thinking appears to have increased most among students in science majors. Since computer engineering and digital arts majors were not initially different and were exposed to exactly the same class experiences, this raises questions about why computer scientists are different than their peers in computer engineering and digital arts. This is an area for further research. Our project also demonstrates that complex "real-world" problems can be incorporated into the CS curriculum without sacrificing the learning goals of rigorous CS courses.

While the model was designed to make computational thinking be more attractive and relevant to people from underrepresented groups, there was not enough diversity by gender or race/ethnicity in these courses to determine whether the incorporation of a service-learning project had an impact. Since all students experienced gains in computational thinking and because research indicates that service learning increases motivation among historically underrepresented groups, we believe our model holds promise for diversifying the computer science workforce, and increasing computational skills among students from more diverse majors, such as journalism.

6. ACKNOWLEDGMENTS

This material is based on work supported by the National Science Foundation under Grant No. DUE-1141170. Any opinions, findings and conclusions or recommendations expressed in this material are those of the author(s) and do not necessarily reflect the views of the National Science Foundation (NSF).

7. REFERENCES

[1] ABET Computing Accreditation Commission. 2011. Criteria for Accrediting Computing Programs: Effective for Reviews During the 2012-2013 Accreditation Cycle. Retrd April 19, 2015 from http://www.abet.org/uploadedFiles/Accreditation/Accreditation_Process/Accreditation_Documents/Current/cac-criteria-2012-2013.pdf.

[2] Aronson, J., M.J. Lustina, C. Good, and K. Keough. When White Men Can't Do Math: Necessary and Sufficient Factors in Stereotype Threat. Jour. of Experimental Social Psych., Vol. 35, 1999, pp. 29–46.

[3] Bell, A.E., Spencer,S.J., Iserman, E., Logel, C.E.R. Stereotype Threat and Women's Performance in Engineering. Journal of Engg Ed, Oct. 2003 pgs 307-12.

[4] Beyer, S. Rynes, K., Perrault,J., Hay, K., Haller, S. 2003. Gender differences in computer science students. SIGCSE Bull. 35, 1 (January 2003), 49-53.

[5] Bradshaw, Paul. 2012. Two Reasons Every Journalist Should Know About Scraping. Journalist.co.uk August 2, 2012.

[6] Christopher H. Brooks. 2008. Community connections: lessons learned developing and maintaining a computer science service-learning program. SIGCSE Bull. 40, 1 (March 2008), 352-356.

[7] Cassel, L., Holliday, M., Kumar, D., Impagliazzo, J., Bolding, K., Pearson, M., Davies, J., Wolffe, G. S., and Yurcik, W. 2001. Distributed expertise for teaching computer organization & architecture. In Working Group Reports From ITiCSE on innovation and Technology in Computer Science Education ITiCSE-WGR '00. ACM, NY, 111-126.

[8] Chinn, D. and K. Martin, Work in Progress: Adapting the Treisman Model to Computer Science, 36th ASEE/IEEE Frontiers in Education Conference, October 28 – 31, 2006, San Diego, CA, pp 23 – 24.

[9] Committee for the Workshops on Computational Thinking, National Research Council. 2010. Report of Workshop on The Scope and Nature of Computational Thinking. The National Academies Press.

[10] Cohoon, J. M. and W. Aspray, (eds). 2006. Women and Information Technology: Research on Underrepresentation, The MIT Press, Cambridge MA.

[11] Ellis, H.J.C., Jackson, S., Burdge, D., Postner, L., Hislop, G.W., and Joanie Diggs. 2014. Learning within a professional environment: shared ownership of an HFOSS project. In Proc. of the 15th Annual Conf. on Information technology education (SIGITE '14). ACM, NY, 95-100.

[12] Fisher, A. and Margolis, J. 2003. Unlocking the clubhouse: women in computing. In Proc. of the 34th SIGCSE Tech. Symposium on Computer Science Education (Reno, Navada, USA, February 19 - 23, 2003). SIGCSE '03. ACM, NY.

[13] Goode, J., R. Estrella, and J. Margolis, Lost in Translation: Gender and High School Computer Science, in Women and Information Technology: Research on Underrepresentation, The MIT Press, Cambridge MA, 2006. pp 89-113.

[14] Mark Guzdial. 2013. Exploring hypotheses about media computation. In Proceedings of the ninth annual international ACM conference on International computing education research (ICER '13). ACM, New York, NY, USA, 19-26.

[15] Helen H. Hu and Tricia D. Shepherd. 2013. Using POGIL to help students learn to program. Trans. Comp. Ed. 13, 3.

[16] Hurtado, S., Eagan, K. and Chang, M. 2010. Degrees of Success: Bachelor's Degree Completion Rates among Initial STEM Majors. Report from Higher Ed Rsrch. Inst., UCLA.

[17] The Joint Task Force on Computing Curricula, ACM and IEEE Computer Society 2013. Comp. Sc. Curricula 2013. https://www.acm.org/education/CS2013-final-report.pdf.

[18] Kolb, D.A. 1984. Experiential learning: experience as the source of learning and development. Prentice Hall.

[19] Clif Kussmaul and Erica Wenzel. 2012. Analysis of Active Learning Activities Transitions and Patterns in Process Oriented Guided Inquiry Learning (POGIL). In Proc. of the 2012 IEEE 4th Intl Conf. on Tech for Ed. (T4E '12). IEEE Computer Society, Washington, DC, USA, 7-12.

[20] Light, R.J. 2001. Making the most of college: students speak their minds. Harvard University Press. Cambridge, MA.

[21] Chang Liu. 2005. Enriching software engineering courses with service-learning projects and the open-source approach. In Proc. of the 27th intl conference on Software engineering. ACM, New York, NY, USA, 613-614.

[22] Margolis, J., Estrella, R., Goode, J., Holme, J.H., and Nao, K. 2008. Stuck in the Shallow End: Education, Race, and Computing. MIT Press.

[23] Mcginty, Jo Craven. 2005. Breaking Down Hate Crime. New York Times. http://www.nytimes.com/2005/07/23/nyregion/24hate-web.html. Retrieved April 18, 2015.

[24] NCWIT. By the Numbers. https://www.ncwit.org/sites/default/files/resources/btn_04032015_web.pdf. rel. 4/3/15.

[25] Pulimood, S. M. and Wolz, U. Problem Solving in Community: A Necessary Shift in CS Pedagogy. In Proc. of the 39th Tech. Symposium on Computer Science Education (ACM SIGCSE), Portland, Oregon, March 12 – 15, 2008.

[26] Way, T. Cassel, L., Pearson, K. Wolz, U. Tatar, D., Harrison, S. 2010. A Distributed Expertise Model for Teaching Computing Across Disciplines and Institutions, in The 2010 Intl Conf. on Frontiers in Education: Computer Science and Computer Engineering 2010: Las Vegas, NV.

[27] Linda D. Webster and Edward J. Mirielli. 2007. Student reflections on an academic service learning experience in a computer science classroom. In Proc. of the 8th ACM SIGITE conf. on Information tech. ed. (SIGITE '07). ACM, NY, 207-212.

[28] Wing, J. M. 2006. Computational thinking. Commun. ACM 49, 3 (Mar. 2006), 33-35.

Investigating Differences in Wiki-based Collaborative Activities between Student Engagement Profiles in CS1

Adam Eck and Leen-Kiat Soh
Department of Computer Science and Engineering
University of Nebraska-Lincoln
{aeck, lksoh}@cse.unl.edu

Duane F. Shell
Department of Educational Psychology
University of Nebraska-Lincoln
dshell2@unl.edu

ABSTRACT

Introductory computer science courses are being increasingly taught using technology-mediated instruction and e-learning environments. The software and technology in such courses could benefit from the use of student models to inform and guide customized support tailored to the needs of individual students. In this paper, we investigate how student motivated engagement profiles developed in educational research can be used as such models to predict student behaviors. These models are advantageous over those learned directly from observing individual students, as they rely on different data that can be available *a priori* before students use the technology. Using tracked behaviors of 249 students from 7 CS1 courses over the span of 3 semesters, we discover that students with different engagement profiles indeed behave differently in an online, wiki-based CSCL system while performing collaborative creative thinking exercises, and the differences between students are primarily as expected based on the differences in the profiles. Thus, such profiles could be useful as student models for providing customized support in e-learning environments in CS1 courses.

Keywords

Computer Supported, Collaborative Learning; Creative Thinking; Student Modeling; Wiki; CS1

1. INTRODUCTION

Computer science 1 (CS1) courses are being increasingly taught using technology-mediated instruction and/or e-learning environments. For example, CS1 courses have used intelligent tutoring systems [1, 19], computer-supported, collaborative learning (CSCL) systems [4], interactive program visualizations [17] and interactions in e-books [5]. Reported benefits of these technology-mediated instruction and e-learning environments for CS1 courses include more flexibility and broader reach to offer education to a wider range of students, the ability to scale to larger classrooms such as Massively Open Online Courses (MOOCs) [2], and increased student engagement.

Furthermore, increased use of technology to deliver CS1 courses offers the capability to observe and record information about student behaviors during the learning process through passively monitoring how students interact with the technology used for class instruction and assignments. This information can then be used to help educators better understand how students are learning within a course and aid in student evaluation. Combined with models of student behavior, the technology can also be automatically guided to adapt to observed student behaviors and provide customized instruction to individuals and groups in order to more efficiently and effectively improve student knowledge. That is, understanding and modeling student learning behaviors could help support and improve technology-mediated instruction or e-learning environments such as CSCL and MOOCs [2].

Indeed, machine learning and data mining and analysis have been applied to cluster student behaviors and model cognitive styles in e-learning environments in order to adapt learning behaviors, e.g., [3, 7, 8, 9]. In particular, Desmarais & Baker [3] advocated the importance of constructing models of learner behavior, such as through Bayesian Networks, based on observed activities and other key constructs such as learner motivation, emotional and attentional state, metacognition and self-regulated learning. However, these studies constructed their models based on observing student behavior in the e-learning environment, instead of considering student models based solely on learner motivation, metacognition, and self-regulation that might be knowable through surveys or self-reports *a priori* to or separately from the students' use of technology within the learning environment. These studies also have not necessarily focused on CS education or introductory programming courses.

In this paper, we begin to bridge this gap in the literature by investigating how student motivated engagement profiles that have been identified in educational research [11, 15, 16] relate in practice to student learning behaviors in technology-mediated instruction and e-learning environments within CS1 courses. That is, instead of developing empirical models based on observed behavior, we are instead interested in *comparing how students with different motivated engagement profiles identified from student survey questionnaires actually behaved*, as recorded by their interactions with technology during course work. This comparison is important because provided that students indeed behave as predicted, then we have evidence that engagement profiles, which are potentially identifiable prior to learning activities, can be used as models and predictors of student learning behaviors in ways that may guide the customization of e-learning to individual student's motivation and engagement needs in CS courses.

In particular, this paper addresses the following research questions:

RQ1: Do CS1 students with different engagement profiles behave differently in an online CSCL system?

SIGCSE '16, March 02-05, 2016, Memphis, TN, USA © 2016 ACM. ISBN 978-1-4503-3685-7/16/03...$15.00
DOI: http://dx.doi.org/10.1145/2839509.2844615

RQ2: Do different behaviors exhibited by CS1 students in an online CSCL system match the behaviors that would be expected based on their engagement profile?

To answer these questions, we considered data from 249 students within 7 CS1 courses spanning 3 semesters (Fall 2012, Spring 2013, Fall 2013). Each of these students completed a survey identifying their goal orientation, perceived benefits of the course, and emotional/affective states in order to match students to different learning profiles. During their course, students performed group-based creative thinking exercises using CSCL wiki software as part of their CS1 education, where exercises were created on wiki pages. Through their use of the CSCL wiki software, we tracked when students performed different actions needed to complete their assignments. Based on this tracked data, our investigation compared how often each type of action was performed by each student, and we compared the trends in these measures to what should be expected based on their profiles.

Through our investigation, we discovered that: (1) observed student behaviors differed for different engagement profiles, indicating that engagement profiles indeed affect student behavior, and (2) the differences between behaviors for the different profiles largely matched what was predicted by the educational theory behind the engagement profiles, indicating that such profiles are indeed predictors of student behavior in technology-mediated instruction and e-learning environments. This implies that a CSCL tool such as the wiki platform considered in our study can effectively model student learning profiles and have the potential to inform instruction and support student learning at real-time, with important possible benefits for CS1 (and other) courses.

2. BACKGROUND

2.1 Motivated Engagement Profiles

Prior research has identified five distinct motivated engagement profiles among college students [11, 15, 16]. These are:

1. A ***strategic*** learner who demonstrates a high level of motivation, metacognition, and engagement and aspires to master course content and achieve highly in the classroom;
2. A ***knowledge builder*** who is motivated to learn course content for their personal growth, but does not necessarily exhibit high levels of active engagement or metacognitive strategies;
3. A ***surface*** learner who is motivated only by the utility value of the course and engages at superficial rather than deep learning;
4. An ***apathetic*** learner who demonstrates low levels of motivation and engagement; and
5. A ***learned helpless*** student who is motivated to engage but ineffective in their learning and strategies, eventually causing them to lose motivation and begin to disengage.

Recent studies have found these five profiles among undergraduate CS, engineering, and other STEM students taking CS1 courses [6, 11, 16]. In these CS courses, students adopting the strategic and knowledge builder profiles have higher course achievement and learning [11, 16].

2.2 Creative Thinking Exercises

The CS1 courses considered in this study incorporated both computational thinking and creative thinking into CS1 courses to better prepare students to be flexible and resourceful problem solvers, interdisciplinary collaborators, and skilled practitioners of both logic and creativity [18]. This was accomplished through creative thinking exercises designed to challenge established thinking and behavior patterns. These creative thinking exercises consist of a set of activities, some "light bulbs" to help students connect these activities to a given topic, as well as a set of analysis and reflection questions for students to discuss and respond to.

For example, one collaborative creative thinking exercise asked students to *tell a story* collaboratively. Each team of students was assigned a story, with each team member being responsible for a chapter. We provided each chapter with its first and last sentences and required the student responsible for that chapter to fill in 100-200 words between those two sentences. Additionally, the last sentence of the first chapter is the same as the first sentence of the second chapter, the last sentence of the second chapter was the same as the first sentence of the third chapter, and so on. After one week of working on each chapter individually, team members were then required to combine all chapters into a story and address all inconsistencies in the chapter in the second week. Through this process, students learned about logical reasoning, "debugging", and creative problem solving as well.

The other creative thinking exercises included *Everyday Object* where students were asked to describe an everyday object such as a ball-point pen as if the object had never been invented, *Cipher* where students were asked to devise encoding rules to map alphabet letters to numbers and to decipher other teams' code, *Exploring* where students were asked to visit a location on campus and record what they observed through different senses (in addition to sight), and so on.

2.3 Online Wiki-based CSCL System

To collaborate and complete their creative thinking projects, students used an online, wiki-based CSCL platform [4]. This platform was selected because it supports flexible group assignments to setup collaborative work; asynchronous communications between students working together on collaborative writing assignments to promote coordination and cooperation between group members; revision tracking on wiki pages so that students can better understand how content changes over time based on the contributions of different group members; and fine grained tracking of student activities, including who performed an action, what page the action was performed on, when the action occurred, and what type of action was performed.

Using the wiki, each student could perform three key actions toward completing their collaborative creative thinking exercises:

1. **Viewing wiki pages**, including the assignment instructions for each exercise, exemplar examples of solutions to the exercises from past semesters, and the student's group's solutions to the exercises.
2. **Editing wiki pages**, especially by making changes to the student's group's solution to each exercise, building upon and revising the past contributions of team members, and
3. **Commenting on wiki pages** within threaded discussions, leaving messages for group members to read and respond to, in order to discuss and coordinate the students' activities towards completing the creative thinking exercises.

Other actions were also possible within the wiki (e.g., searching for pages, viewing pages intelligently recommended by the system related to the student's current page, rating pages, etc.). However, within the context of the creative thinking exercises, the three key actions (view, edit, comment) outlined above constitute the main behaviors required of students to complete the exercises. Thus, they were the focus of student behavior in this study.

3. DATA

To better understand the relationship between (1) student motivated engagement profiles and (2) student behaviors during technol-

Table 1: Summary of Students
Note: Other indicates class standing not fitting into the standard categories (e.g., non-traditional or graduate students)

Total	249 (100%)
Males	213 (85.5%)
Female	36 (14.5%)
Freshman	117 (47.0%)
Sophomore	79 (31.7%)
Juniors	34 (13.7%)
Seniors	16 (6.4%)
Other	3 (1.2%)
CS Majors	61 (24.5%)
CS Non-majors	188 (75.5%)

Table 2: Motivated Engagement Profile Statistics

Engagement Profiles	Number of Students
Strategic	61 (24.5%)
Knowledge Builders	64 (25.7%)
Surface	51 (20.5%)
Apathetic	39 (15.7%)
Learned Helpless	34 (13.7%)

ogy-mediated instruction and e-learning environments in our CS1 courses, we investigated the behaviors of students completing the creative thinking exercises within the aforementioned CSCL system. In this section, we describe the data collected and analyzed within our investigation.

The creative thinking exercises described in Section 2.2 were deployed to several CS1 courses including a course designed for engineering students and another for CS majors. For this study, we considered data collected from 7 classes at the University of Nebraska-Lincoln across 3 semesters (Fall 2012, Spring 2013, Fall 2013), with a total of 249 students consenting to the use of their engagement profile survey results (described below) and tracked behaviors. Summary statistics for these students are provided in Table 1. In spite of the fact that we considered students from introductory (CS1) courses, the students had a wide variety of experience in school and a range of majors. Thus, our results should generalize to a wide range of potential CS1 students.

Profiles for this study population were derived from a survey battery administered at the end[1] of the course consisting of (1) students goal orientation for the class; (2) students' future time perspective consisting of their ratings of the connectedness between their academic coursework and a STEM career and the perceived instrumentality of their specific course work for attaining STEM academic and career goals; and (3) students' emotional/affective reactions to the course. Students' metacognitive strategies and engagement were assessed with four scales from the Student Perceptions of Classroom Knowledge Building instrument (SPOCK) that assessed metacognitive self-regulation, knowledge building, question asking, and lack of engagement. Students' study time and study effort also were assessed. Profiles were derived using cluster analysis with SPSS. All instruments and procedures are fully described in Shell and Soh [16], Nelson et al. [11], and Flanigan et al. [6].

The students considered in our study provided many students in each engagement profile. The summary statistics for these profiles is provided in Table 2.

[1] The surveys could have also been conducted earlier in the course, providing the system with *a priori* student models.

Student behavior measures from their wiki data were based on the learning processes described in the Unified Learning Model (ULM) [14]. In the ULM, attention, repetition, and connection are the basic processes that underlie all learning. Attention is reflected in a simple page visit. Repetition and connection were operationalized as follows:

Connection: number of unique pages viewed/edited/commented

Repetition: average number of views/edits/comments per page (only considering pages the student interacts with).

4. ANALYSIS

Using the data described in the previous section, we now report the results of our investigation. For each research question, we first introduce our proposed hypothesis, followed by a description of the method employed to evaluate our hypothesis, and finally the results of our analysis.

4.1 RQ1: Differences between Profiles

Recall that our first research question (RQ1) asks whether CS1 students with different engagement profiles indeed behave differently in an online, wiki-based CSCL system. Based on the educational research surrounding student motivated engagement profiles, we hypothesize that:

H1: CS1 students with different engagement profiles will indeed behave differently in an online, wiki-based CSCL system.

That is, we hypothesize that student behaviors measured by connection and repetition (for the different action types: view, edit, and comment) will indeed differ between the engagement profiles. Summary statistics for these measures are provided in Table 3. We provide both the means, as well as the medians, due to (1) the non-normality of the data (determined using the Shapiro-Wilk test, which resulted in p-values all less than 0.001), and (2) the means are skewed due to the presence of outliers, especially at the larger end of the measures.

From Table 3, we observe that there do indeed appear to be differences between student behavior measures across the five engagement profiles in both the mean and median of the behaviors. To formally test for differences across the five engagement profiles, we employed the Kruskal-Wallis non-parametric one-way analysis of variance, rather than parametric ANOVA because of the non-normal empirical distributions of the measures. The null hypothesis of the Kruskal-Wallis tests is that each measure *does not differ* between the five engagement profiles. Rejecting this null hypothesis, instead, would confirm our research hypothesis H1.

We present the results of the Kruskal-Wallis tests in Table 4. From these results, we note that there were statistically significant differences between the five engagement profiles for several of the student behavior measures at 0.05 significance levels. In particular, students differed in: (1) how many times they viewed each wiki page that they visited (Repetition-View), (2) how many pages they edited (Connection-Edit), (3) how many pages they commented on (Connection-Comment), and (4) how many times they commented on each page (Repetition-Comment).

Thus, we reject the null hypothesis for the repetition measure for viewing behavior, connection measure for editing behavior, and both measures for commenting behavior. Instead, we confirm our hypothesis (H1) that *CS1 student behaviors indeed do differ depending on student motivated engagement profiles in an online, wiki-based CSCL system*. Therefore, considering *student motivated engagement profiles can provide clues predicting different behaviors by CS1 students* in a technology-mediated instruction or

Table 3: Average Student Behavior Measures Across Engagement Profiles
Note: Medians are provided in parenthesis due to non-normality and the skew of the measures caused by outliers

Measure	Action	*Engagement Profile* Strategic	Knowledge Builder	Surface	Apathetic	Learned Helpless
Connection	View	11.852 (11)	11.078 (10)	11.647 (13)	10.744 (11)	9.294 (8.5)
	Edit	3.295 (4)	3.125 (3)	3.725 (4)	3.128 (3)	2.441 (2)
	Comment	2.852 (3)	2.797 (3)	3.059 (3)	2.641 (2)	1.824 (1)
Repetition	View	6.475 (5.8)	7.146 (7.798)	7.506 (6.729)	6.084 (5.273)	5.256 (4.059)
	Edit	2.545 (2)	3.122 (2.633)	2.765 (2.4)	2.44 (2.333)	2.118 (1.75)
	Comment	2.46 (2)	3.077 (2.5)	2.645 (2.5)	2.326 (2)	1.709 (1)

Table 4: Results of the Kruskal-Wallis Tests
Note: * indicates statistical significance at the 0.05 level

Measure	Action	X^2	p-value	Significance
Connection	View	4.08	0.3952	
	Edit	11.714	0.0196	*
	Comment	11.257	0.0238	*
Repetition	View	11.484	0.0216	*
	Edit	6.292	0.1784	
	Comment	11.303	0.0234	*

e-learning environment, such as our creative thinking exercises performed within the online, wiki-based CSCL system.

4.2 RQ2: Difference between Profile Predictions and Actual Behavior

Now that we have observed that students with different engagement profiles do indeed differ in observed behaviors, we next turn to our related research question (RQ2) asking whether the differences match what is expected based on the differences between the profiles. That is, we want to know whether the educational research behind the engagement profiles indeed predicts how CS1 students will behave. We hypothesize that:

H2: The different behaviors exhibited by CS1 students in an online CSCL system will indeed match the behaviors that would be expected based on their motivated engagement profile.

In particular, based on the characteristics evidenced by CS1 students in each of the five profiles, we would expect that students in the *strategic* and *knowledge builder* profiles would have high levels of active learning processes that would be reflected in high connection and high repetition. Because of their focus on deep learning and interconnection of knowledge but less active engagement, *knowledge builders* would be expected to be somewhat higher in connection behaviors. *Surface* learners would be expected to be somewhat high in repetition as they are motivated to get good grades and achieve, but they would be expected to be lower in connection as they are not interested in deep learning. *Apathetic* students would be expected to be low in connection and repetition, if they did the exercise at all. *Learned helpless* students are harder to predict. They are motivated and report relatively high engagement and deep learning, but their distinguishing characteristic is that their learning efforts are not being successful. This dysfunction may not be identifiable from their overt behaviors so they may have reasonable levels of connection and repetition, but these may not be paying off in good learning. Conversely, as they lose motivation, they may begin to disengage and have lower levels of these.

To evaluate our hypothesis (H2) and answer our second research question, we compare the differences between the student behaviors across all six measure/action pairs, presented in Table 3. From the results, we make several important observations.

First, we consider the connection behaviors, which measure how many distinct pages students acted upon, and thus how broad their interactions were with the knowledge and exercise content stored in the wiki pages. We observe that students with *strategic* profiles had relatively high (mean and median) connection measures for all three actions (view, edit, comment), whereas students with *apathetic* and *learned helpless* profiles had some of the lowest connection measures. These behaviors match our expectations based on the educational research behind the profiles, described earlier in this subsection.

However, we also observe that contrary to our expectations, students with the *surface* profile had the highest connection measures across all three action types. Thus, it appears that surface learners attempted to maximize their utility (measured by course grades) by interacting with as many pages as possible.

Also contrary to our expectations, students with the *knowledge builder* profile had connection measures somewhere between the more connected (strategic and surface) and less connected (apathetic and learned helpless) profiles. Instead of our expectation that these knowledge builders would connect to a high number of pages, they appear to have instead behaved such that they connected only to the pages needed to build their desired knowledge and complete the exercises.

Second, we consider the repetition behaviors, which measure the average number of times students acted upon each page (considering only the pages they interacted with), and thus how actively engaged students were with the creative thinking exercises. This measures the depth of the students' interactions with the system. We observe again, for all three actions, that students with the *strategic* and *surface* profiles had some of the higher repetitions, whereas students with the *apathetic* and *learned helpless* profiles had some of the lowest repetitions. Again, this matches our expectations based on the definitions of the profiles, described above.

On the other hand, considering the repetition measures, we observe very different behavior for students with the *knowledge building* profile than we observed for the connection measures, in comparison to the other engagement profiles. In particular, knowledge builders had the highest (mean or median) repetition measures for all three actions. Consistent with their focus on deep learning, knowledge builders have *higher engagement* with the pages that they do interact with, possibly in an effort to *maximize the learning from their interactions*. Consistent with their emphasis on constructing knowledge rather than passively receiving it, we observe that the knowledge builders' higher repetition is *greatest for the most intensive actions*: editing and commenting on pages. Whereas viewing is a relatively passive action, editing and commenting on pages requires more thoughtfulness and active participation and contribute more to the advancement of group learning. Thus, knowledge builders contributed more to their collaborative creative thinking exercises than their peers.

Combining these observations, we conclude that CS1 students indeed behaved similarly to what was predicted by their engagement profiles. Upon further reflection, differences in the observed behaviors of knowledge builder and surface learner profiles seem sensible given their differences in passive (viewing) and active (editing, commenting) behaviors. Thus, we have gained new insights into the engagement profiles themselves.

5. DISCUSSION

5.1 Implications

Summarizing the behaviors observed within each engagement profile, we draw the following key implications for each:

1. *Strategic* learners performed high levels of connection and repetition. Thus, strategic learners appear to attempt to perform a large number of interactions in order to achieve their learning goals, according to their motivation.
2. *Knowledge builders* performed moderate levels of connection, but high levels of repetition. Thus, knowledge builders appear to behave such that they *learn efficiently*, only connecting to as many pages as needed to learn and complete assignments, but maximizing their interactions with those pages to deeply learn them.
3. *Surface* learners perform opposite knowledge builders: they performed the highest levels of connection, but lower (comparatively) levels of repetition (especially for the more active actions: editing and commenting). Thus, surface learners appear to behave by performing more passive and less intensive actions than the students from other engagement profiles.
4. *Apathetic* learners performed low levels of connection and repetition, as expected. Thus, these students are unlikely to be actively engaged in technology-mediated instruction and e-learning without prompting, scaffolding, or other engagement from the system itself.
5. *Learned helpless* learners performed the lowest levels of connection and repetition, indicating that in spite of their motivation, their struggles with learning caused them to give up, as predicted. Thus, like apathetic learners, they are unlikely to be actively engaged in technology-mediated instruction and e-learning without prompting, scaffolding, or other engagement from the system itself. However, given their higher motivations, they might be more likely to respond to customization and other help from technology.

Based on our results and the above characterization of the differences in behaviors of CS1 students with different student motivated engagement profiles, we conclude that:

- CS1 students with different engagement profiles *indeed do behave differently* in (at least some) technology-mediated instruction and e-learning environments (e.g., an online, wiki-based CSCL system)
- The engagement profiles themselves describe CS1 students *such that their behavior within technology-mediated instruction and e-learning can be predicted.*

Thus, we now have empirical evidence that student models constructed from educational research, such as the student motivated engagement profiles considered in this paper, can indeed be used to predict student behavior. Interestingly, although we only considered CS1 courses, our students were not just CS majors, and thus *the results should generalize to a wide range of students taking CS1 courses.*

Our results demonstrate that student models such as our engagement profiles could be used by technology (e.g., a wiki-based CSCL system) in order to anticipate student behavior before it occurs, then take intelligent actions to promote good behaviors and discourage, mitigate, or avoid unfruitful behaviors. For example, a system might encourage surface learners to spend more effort in their interactions, instead of performing a large number of less active interactions. Moreover, the system could encourage knowledge builders to teach their peers how to learn more efficiently and more in-depth. Finally, the system could provide customized, tailored support to help learned helpless students overcome their learning difficulties to make their high motivation more fruitful.

Furthermore, in cases where a system does not have an adaptive design, the predictable behaviors from engagement profiles (or other student models based on educational research) could still readily inform instructors during the semester to identify and seek out students with different profiles and perform remediation accordingly, which would be important in engaging and retaining increasingly diverse student populations in CS1 courses. Such information could also be used to form more effective teams for peer instruction and pair programming as well for CS1, for both majors and non-majors [13]. And in general, such information and knowledge helps us understand how students might respond to different assignments, helping plan activities that will benefit all students in the course, as well as prepare steps to help students become engaged with the course material and assignments to maximize learning.

Both of these benefits from student models are especially beneficial in a CS1 setting because (1) CS1 students are often new to college (i.e., freshman) and require guidance on how to learn, and not just in need of new course material, (2) introductory courses are often some of largest courses in terms of the number of students, making individualized support for students more difficult, especially if an instructor or software system must learn the student's characteristics, behaviors, and needs from scratch, and (3) CS1 courses are being increasingly taught with technology-mediated instruction and e-learning environments, where instructor interactions with students are less active, and thus the technology used to support instruction plays an increasingly large role in the student's learning.

Finally, our results here have important implications on to other types of computer-mediated learner support. For example, Piech et al. [12] reported on how they modeled students arriving at their final solution in homework assignments, using machine learning techniques to autonomously create a graphical models progress through a homework assignment in an introductory programming course. Our work could inform their research with additional instructional design—i.e., incorporating threaded discussions and collaborative wikis—as well as enrich their modeling with our engagement profiles. Naps et al. [10] reported the use of visualization to illustrate various concepts in CS; Ericson et al. [5] reported the use of interactive features to engage students in an E-book; Sirkiä & Sorva [17] reported the use of program visualizations of walking through lines of code and displaying results. Because of the primary media of these visualization is computer-based, our study has the potential of enriching these visualization approaches and helping researchers capture vital learner characteristics, thus enabling them to better understand and improve student learning in CS.

5.2 Limitations

Although our study has many promising implications for technology-mediated instruction and e-learning in CS1 (and possibly other) settings, we also note several limitations.

First, our data only includes students who agreed to both take the student engagement profile survey, as well as allow us to track their activities as they used the wiki-based CSCL system. Although we had a large amount of participation, the students who agreed to participate might not have been representative of all students in the courses. We especially expect that lower motivation students (those likely to be in the apathetic or learned helpless profiles) would have been unlikely to participate. Indeed, within the lower performing profiles, our participants might have been skewed towards the more active students of these profile types, implying that these profiles might be expected to perform even fewer connection and repetition behaviors than we observed. Thus, our findings represent only a first look at how profiles might be used to help CS educators understand and intervene with these unmotivated students in technology-mediated and e-learning environments.

Furthermore, we have only considered one type of technology-mediated instruction and e-learning environment: an online, wiki-based CSCL system where students perform collaborative creative thinking exercises. It remains an open question how our results might relate to those in other educational settings (e.g., intelligent tutoring systems, distributed pair programming), which are interesting avenues for future work.

6. CONCLUSIONS

In conclusion, we have studied how student models determined by education research in the form of student motivated engagement profiles [6, 11, 14, 16] can be used to predict student behaviors in technology-mediated instruction and e-learning environments. Considering 7 CS1 courses with 249 students spanning 3 semesters, we investigated how students with different engagement profiles behaved in an online, wiki-based CSCL system while performing collaborative creative thinking exercises. We discovered that not only do students of different profiles behave differently (with respect to how students interact with the exercises and technology), but their behaviors were generally as expected based on the descriptions of the profiles used as student models. As a result, we now have evidence that student models (that could be matched *a priori* before students interact with the technology or assignment based on separate data from system usage) can be used to predict student behavior, and thus could be useful inputs to inform and guide customized educational support tailored to individual student's needs within the e-learning technology.

In the future, we intend to (1) further explore what other types of student behaviors might also be predictable using educational research-informed student models, including in other types of e-learning environments, (2) develop tools for customizing student support exploiting such models, and (3) evaluate the effectiveness of such tools.

7. ACKNOWLEDGMENTS

This material is based upon work supported by the National Science Foundation under grants no. 1122956 and 1431874. Additional support was provided by a UNL Phase II Pathways to Interdisciplinary Research Centers grant.

8. REFERENCES

[1] Cooper, S., Nam, Y.J., & Si, L. 2012. Initial Results of Using an Intelligent Tutoring System with Alice. In *Proc. of ITiCSE'12*, 138-143.

[2] Cooper, S. & Sahami, M. 2013. Reflections on Stanford's MOOCs, *Communications of the ACM*, 56(2):28-30.

[3] Desmarais, M. C. & Baker, R. S. 2012. A Review of Recent Advances in Learner and Skill Modeling in Intelligent Learning Environments. *Journal of User Modeling and User-Adapted Interaction*, 22(1-2):9-38.

[4] Eck, A., Soh, L.-K., & Brassil, C. 2013. Supporting Active Wiki-based Collaboration. In. *Proc. of CSCL'13*, 176-183.

[5] Ericson, B. J., Guzdial, M. J., & Morrison, B. B. 2015. Analysis of Interactive Features Designed to Enhance Learning in an Ebook. In *Proc. of ICER'2015*, 169-178.

[6] Flanigan, A. E., Peteranetz, M. S., Shell, D. F., & Soh, L.K. 2015. Exploring Changes in Computer Science Students' Implicit Theories of Intelligence Across the Semester. In *Proc. of ICER'15*, 161-168.

[7] Jovanovic, M., Vukicevic, M., & Milovanovic, M. 2012. Using Data Mining on Student Behavior and Cognitive Style Data for Improving E-Learning Systems: A Case Study, *Int. Jour. of Computational Intelligence Systems*, 5(3):597-610.

[8] Khandaker, N. & Soh, L.-K. 2010. ClassroomWiki: A Collaborative Wiki for Instructional Use with Multiagent Group Formation, *IEEE Trans. Learn. Technologies*, 3(3):190-202.

[9] Miller, L.D. & Soh, L.-K. 2013. Meta-Reasoning Algorithms for Improving Analysis of Student Interactions with Learning Objects using Supervised Learning. In *Proc. of EDM'2013*, 129-136.

[10] Naps, T. L, et al. 2003. Exploring the Role of Visualization and Engagement in Computer Science Education. *ACM SIGCSE Bulletin*, 35(2):131-152.

[11] Nelson, K.G., et al. 2015. Motivational and Self-Regulated Learning Profiles of Students Taking a Foundational Engineering Course. *J. Eng. Educ.* 104(1):74-100.

[12] Piech, C., et al. 2012. Modeling How Students Learn to Program. In *Proc. of SIGCSE'2012*, 153-160.

[13] Porter, L., Guzdial, M., Mcdowell, C., & Simon, B. 2013. Success in Introductory Programming: What Works? *CACM*, 56(8):34-36.

[14] Shell, D.F., et al. 2010. *The Unified Learning Model: How Motivational, Cognitive, and Neurobiological Sciences Inform Best Teaching Practices*. Springer, New York.

[15] Shell, D.F. & Husman, J. 2008. Control, Motivation, Affect, and Strategic Self-regulation in the College Classroom: A Multidimensional Phenomenon. *J. Educ. Psychol.* 100(2): 443-459.

[16] Shell, D.F. & Soh, L.K. 2013. Profiles of Motivated Self-Regulation in College Computer Science Courses: Differences in Major Versus Required Non-major Courses. *J. Sci. Educ. Technol.*, 22:899-913.

[17] Sirkiä, T., & Sorva, J. 2015. How Do Students Use Program Visualizations within an Interactive Ebook? In *Proc. of ICER'2015*, 179-188.

[18] Soh, L.-K., Shell, D. F., Ingraham, E., Ramsay, S., & Moore, B. 2015. Viewpoint: Improving Learning and Achievement in Introductory Computer Science through Computational Creativity. *CACM*, 58(8):33-35.

[19] Wiggins, J. B., et al. 2015. JavaTutor: An Intelligent Tutoring System that Adapts to Cognitive and Affective States during Computer Programming. In *Proc. of SIGCSE'2015*, 599.

Subgoals Help Students Solve Parsons Problems

Briana B. Morrison
School of Interactive Computing
Georgia Institute of Technology
85 5th Street NW
Atlanta, GA, 30332-0760
bmorrison@gatech.edu

Lauren E. Margulieux
School of Psychology
Georgia Institute of Technology
654 Cherry Street
Atlanta, GA, 30332-0170
l.marg@gatech.edu

Barbara Ericson, Mark Guzdial
School of Interactive Computing
Georgia Institute of Technology
85 5th Street NW
Atlanta, GA, 30332-0760
ericson, guzdial@cc.gatech.edu

ABSTRACT
We report on a study that used subgoal labels to teach students how to write `while` loops with a Parsons problem learning assessment. Subgoal labels were used to aid learning of programming while not overloading students' cognitive abilities. We wanted to compare giving learners subgoal labels versus asking learners to generate subgoal labels. As an assessment for learning we asked students to solve a Parsons problem – to place code segments in the correct order. We found that students who were given subgoal labels performed statistically better than the groups that did not receive subgoal labels or were asked to generate subgoal labels. We conclude that a low cognitive load assessment, Parsons problems, can be more sensitive to student learning gains than traditional code generation problems.

Categories and Subject Descriptors
Social and professional topics~Computer science education

General Terms
Measurement, Design, Experimentation.

Keywords
Subgoal labels, Cognitive Load, Contextual Transfer, Parsons problem.

1. INTRODUCTION
As educators we want to simplify the learning process to present only what is germane to make student learning efficient. As researchers we want to find empirical evidence for effectiveness. One proven method for enhancing learning is to reduce unnecessary cognitive load on the student while they are trying to learn to solve problems [26]. There are several ways to reduce cognitive load, including using worked examples [16].

Worked examples typically include a problem statement along with a step-by-step procedure for solving the problem. Worked examples are most effective when used in worked example-practice pairs [2]. In these pairs, students study a worked example solution and immediately practice by solving a similar problem.

Segmenting worked examples and including subgoal labels have also been shown to be effective in improving learning [2]. Segmenting includes separating portions of the worked example to isolate each step in the process [27]. Subgoal labels are names given to a set of steps in the solution process allowing the user to "chunk" the information to ease learning [10].

While these cognitive load reducing techniques have been empirically tested in math and science disciplines, we have been the first to test these with computer science learning [17]. Margulieux et al. [17] demonstrated learning benefits for subgoal labels with a drag-and-drop programming language. We continued this work to show the effectiveness with textual programming languages [21]. This paper reports on use of a new assessment to measure students' learning.

In our previous experiment [21], we created instructional material to teach introductory programming students about the process of using and writing a `while` loop to solve programming problems. There were three treatment conditions: (1) *no* subgoal labels provided, (2) subgoal labels *given* for each segment of instructions, and (3) subgoal labels *generated*, in which students were asked to generate their own labels for groups of solution statements. Within each treatment group, participants were randomly assigned to either an *isomorphic* or *contextual transfer* group. In the isomorphic transfer group, the problem to be solved in the worked example-practice problem pair was identical to the worked example in both procedural steps and cover story. The differences were the values of the numbers to be calculated. In the contextual transfer group, the problem to be solved in the worked example-practice problem pair involved the same procedural steps but the cover story and numeric values changed. Participants' learning was measured several different ways. In [21] we reported on assessment using novel problem solving tasks by writing code and a post-test. In this paper, we present the results from the Parsons problem assessment and discussion the implications.

Our research questions associated with the experiment were based on previous research on subgoal labels:

- Would students who generated subgoal labels learn better than those who were given the subgoal labels, and would both groups would do better than those who had no subgoals at all?
- What effect would contextual transfer have on student performance? Would those who generated subgoal labels take the least amount of time on the assessment?

2. BACKGROUND
In this section we review the current literature for cognitive load, worked examples, subgoal labeling, and our assessment technique, Parsons problems.

2.1 Cognitive Load
Cognitive load can be defined as the load imposed on an individual's working memory by a particular learning task [32]. The cognitive load required to comprehend materials directly affects how much students learn and affects their performance

SIGCSE '16, March 2–5, 2016, Memphis, TN, USA.

ACM 978-1-4503-3685-7/16/03…$15.00
DOI: http://dx.doi.org/10.1145/2839509.2844617

scores on assessments related to that task [16]. If students have to keep too many things in working memory in order to understand a concept, learning suffers. As designers of instructional material, it is our responsibility to ensure that we do not overload the learner's working memory where possible when presenting new material. We should ensure that students' attention is directed at what is germane learning material rather than extraneous aspects.

The central problem identified by Cognitive Load Theory (*CLT*) is that learning is impaired when the limited capacity of working memory is exceeded [24]. Currently CLT [19, 28, 30] defines two different types of cognitive load on a student's working memory: intrinsic load and extraneous load.

Intrinsic load is a combination of the innate difficulty of the material being learned as well as the learner's characteristics [15]. Extraneous load is the load placed on working memory that does not contribute directly toward the learning of the material---for example, the resources consumed while understanding poorly written text or diagrams without sufficient clarity [15]. Working memory resources that are devoted to information that is relevant or germane to learning are referred to as 'germane resources' [29].

The intrinsic and extraneous loads can be controlled through instructional design. When designing instructional material care should be given to eliminate any possible extraneous load while attempting to minimize the intrinsic load. It is believed that worked examples, when carefully designed, can accomplish both of these goals [24].

2.2 Worked Examples

Worked examples are one type of instruction used to teach students a procedural process for problem solving. Worked examples give learners concrete examples of the procedure being used to solve a problem.

Eiriksdottir and Catrambone argue that learning primarily from worked examples does not inherently promote deep processing of concepts [13]. While it may result in better initial performance because examples are more easily mapped to similar problems, it is less likely result in retention and transfer [13]. When studying examples, learners tend to focus on incidental features rather than the fundamental features because incidental features are easier to grasp and novices do not have the necessary domain knowledge to recognize fundamental features of examples [11]. For example, when studying physics worked examples, learners are more likely to remember that the example has a ramp than that the example uses Newton's second law [11]. A focus on incidental features leads to ineffective organization and storage of information that, in turn, leads to ineffective recall and transfer [6].

2.3 Subgoal Labels

To promote deeper processing of worked examples and, thus, improve retention and transfer, worked examples have been manipulated to promote subgoal learning. Subgoal learning refers to a strategy used predominantly in STEM fields that helps students deconstruct problem solving procedures into subgoals, functional parts of the overall procedure, to better recognize the fundamental components of the problem solving process [1]. Subgoals are the building blocks of procedural problem solving and they are inherent in all procedures except the most basic.

Subgoal labeling is a technique used to promote subgoal learning that has been used to help learners recognize the fundamental structure of the procedure being exemplified in worked examples [8–10]. Subgoal labels are function-based instructional explanations that describe the purpose of a subgoal to the learner. For example, in the problem in Figure 1 for the first two lines of code the subgoal label might read "Initialize Variables." This label provides information about the purpose of that subgoal and the function behind the steps within it. Studies [3, 4, 8–10, 17, 18] have consistently found that subgoal-oriented instructions improved problem solving performance across a variety of STEM domains, such as block-based programming (e.g., [17]) and statistics (e.g., [10]).

Studies have found that giving subgoal labels in worked examples improves student performance when they are solving novel problems without increasing the amount of time they spend studying instructions or working on problems (e.g., [17]). Subgoal labels are believed to be effective because they visually group the steps of worked examples into subgoals and meaningfully label those groups [1]. This format highlights the structure of examples, helping students focus on structural features and more effectively organize information [2].

By helping learners organize information and focus on structural features of worked examples, subgoal labels are believed to reduce the extraneous cognitive load that can hinder learning but is inherent in worked examples [25]. Worked examples introduce extraneous cognitive load because they are necessarily specific to a context, and students must process the incidental information about the context even though it is not relevant to the underlying procedure [30]. Subgoal labels can reduce focus on these incidental features by highlighting the fundamental features of the procedure [25]. Subgoal labels further improve learning by reducing the intrinsic load by providing a mental organization for storing information.

Subgoal labels that are independent from a specific context have been the most effective type of subgoal labels in the past [7, 10]. Catrambone found that learners who were given labels that were abstract (e.g., Ω) and had sufficient prior knowledge performed better than those who were given labels that were context-specific (e.g., isolate x) on problem solving tasks done after a week long delay or in problems that required using the procedure differently than demonstrated in the examples [10]. Catrambone explained this exception by arguing that learners with sufficient prior knowledge were able to correctly explain to themselves the purpose of the subgoal and that by self-explaining the function of the subgoal--the self-explaining presumably due to the abstract label--was more effective than providing labels.

In summary, previous research has found that learners who generate subgoal labels (or self-explain) learn more than those who are given subgoal labels [8, 10]. Additionally those who are given subgoal labels learn more than those who have no subgoal labels. Learners who are given more abstract subgoal labels for problems perform better than those who are given context specific labels. Learners who generate subgoal labels take more time during the learning phase and less time during the assessment phase than those who are given subgoal labels or those with no subgoal labels. Given subgoal labels are considered a lower cognitive load than generating subgoal labels, though both are a higher cognitive load than no subgoal labels; however, no subgoal labels represent no additional learning instructions or cognitive aids for the student. These findings provide the basis for our hypotheses.

2.4 Parsons Problems

One way to make the learning of programming more efficient and effective is to reduce the amount of time that learners struggle with syntax errors. One approach is to use Parsons problems [23] in which correct code is broken into code fragments that have to be put in the correct order with the correct indention. There are several variants of Parsons problems such as including unnecessary code as distractors [12].

Work in this area [12] has found that Parsons problems scores significantly correlate with code writing scores. Parsons problems are simpler than writing code, e.g., students cannot get syntax errors. It has a lower cognitive load because students do not have to focus on issues like syntax while practicing meaning and sequencing within problem solving. This means that Parsons problems might be a more efficient way to practice than the traditional approach, hours of writing code.

2.5 Hypotheses

In this study we sought to combine subgoal labels with a Parsons problem assessment to determine if the performance gains found with subgoal labels still apply with a different type of assessment and if the relative performance speed replicated previous studies.

The contextual transfer was intended to promote deep learning instead of superficial learning as the contextual transfer groups had to do non-superficial transfer during learning [5, 13, 22]. However transfer would not necessarily improve performance on Parsons problems because learners do not have to determine how to apply a conceptual understanding of the procedure to a specific problem since the lines of code in the Parsons problem are provided for them. We entered into the study with the following hypotheses:

H1. Participants who learn with subgoal labels (given or generated) will perform better on low cognitive load assessments.

H2. Changing the context or "cover story" between the worked example and practice problem should have limited effect on student performance on Parsons problem assessments.

H3. Those who generate their own subgoal labels will take less time on assessments than those who are given subgoals or receive no subgoals.

3. METHOD OF STUDY

3.1 Purpose

Participants in introductory programming classes were given instructional material designed to teach them to solve programming problems using `while` loops. This common introductory programming task requires only minimal prior programming knowledge (arithmetic operations and Boolean expressions) to complete at a basic level. This paper reports on data gathered during [21], with additional data collected during the summer of 2015. In this paper we provide only the differences from the study method presented in the original paper.

Participants were recruited from 7 different introductory programming courses at two technical universities in the Southeast United States. At one institution the study was conducted over a two week period; at the other institution the study was done over a month period. Because the courses teach different programming languages (see Table 1), pseudo-code was used in the task to make it independent from any one programming language.

Pseudo-code is relatively easy for programmers to understand regardless of the programming languages that they know [31]. The study was conducted in either a closed lab setting with up to 30 computers in a single room (one institution) or completely through email and over the internet (second institution). Students were given an explanation of the study. They worked independently. The sessions typically lasted between 1 and 2 hours, depending on the rate at which participants completed the tasks.

Table 1. Classes Participating in Study

Programming Language	Majors
C++ or MATLAB	Engineering
C#	Game Development
Java or Python	Computer Science, Information Technology, Software Engineering, Non-Majors

3.2 Instructional Materials

The instructional materials were the same as those used in [21]. Participants were given three interleaved worked examples and practice problems. The worked examples came in three formats, which varied between participants. The first format contained no subgoal labels. The second format grouped steps of the example by subgoal and provided meaningful subgoal labels for each group as is typical in subgoal label research (e.g.,[17]). The third format grouped steps of the example by subgoal and provided a spot for participants to write generated subgoal labels for each group. Exampes of all three formats can be seen in Figure 1. Participant groups were also divided into a *contextual transfer* group or an *isomorphic* problem group. In the *isomorphic* group the "cover story" stayed the same for the worked example and practice problem, only the data values changed. In the *contextual transfer* group the "cover story" between the worked example and practice problem changed. In other words, if the worked example was for averaging tip amounts, the practice problem would involve averaging grades.

No labels	Given Labels	Generate Labels

sum = 0
lcv = 1
 	
WHILE lcv <= 100 DO
  sum = sum + lcv
  lcv = lcv + 1
ENDWHILE
	<u>Initialize Variables</u>
	sum = 0
	lcv = 1
	<u>Determine Loop Condition</u>
	WHILE lcv <= 100 DO
	<u>Update Loop Var</u>
	lcv = lcv + 1
	ENDWHILE
		<u>Label 1:</u> ________
		sum = 0
		lcv = 1
		<u>Label 2:</u> ________
		WHILE lcv <= 100 DO
		<u>Label 3:</u> ________
		lcv = lcv + 1
		ENDWHILE

Figure 1. Partial worked example formatted with no labels, given labels, or placeholders for generated labels.

After completing the instructions, participants completed a Parsons problem to measure their problem solving performance.

3.3 Design

The experiment was a 3-by-2, between-subjects, factorial design: the format of worked examples (unlabeled, subgoal labels given, or subgoal labels generated) was crossed with the transfer distance between worked examples and practice problems (isomorphic or contextual transfer). The dependent variables were performance on the pre- and post-test, problem solving task, and time on task.

3.4 Participants

Participants were 119 students from two technical universities in the Southeast United States (Table 2). Students were offered credit for completing a lab activity or extra credit as compensation for participation. All students from these courses were allowed to participate, regardless of prior experience with programming or using `while` loops. To account for prior experience, participants were asked about their prior programming experience in high school (either regular or advanced placement courses) and college and whether they had experience using `while` loops. Other demographic information collected included gender, age, academic major, high school grade point average (GPA), college GPA, number of years in college, reported comfort with use of a computer, expected difficulty of the programming task, and primary spoken language. There were no statistical differences between the groups for demographic data, which is expected because participants were randomly assigned to treatment groups. Participants also took a multiple-choice pre-test to measure problem solving performance for using `while` loops. Average scores on the pre-test were low, 1.6 out of 5 points, with 23% (28 out of 119) of participants earning no points.

Table 2. Participant Demographics

Age	Gender	GPA	Major
M = 21.6	71% male	*M* = 3.2/4	52% CS major

Many participants did not complete all tasks of the experiment. Participants received compensation regardless of the amount of time or effort that they devoted to the experiment, which might have caused low motivation in some participants. Participants who did not attempt all tasks were excluded from analysis. Participants who answered more than two questions correctly out of the five on the pre-test were excluded from analysis because the instructions were designed for novices.

3.5 Procedure

An outline of the entire study is given in [21]. Briefly, particiants completed a demographic questionnaire and pre-test. This was followed by the instructional period and a 10 item survey designed to measure cognitive load [20].

Once participants completed the cognitive load survey, they started the assessment period which included three types of tasks. Only the Parsons problem assessment task will be discussed here. (See [21] for a complete description and analysis of the initial assessment task, the cognitive load measurement and post test.) The Parsons problem used for assessment was a version of the "rainfall problem" [14]. The problem had 13 different code pieces with between 1 and 3 lines of code in each code piece. The participants were asked to put the code pieces in order with no consideration of indentation. In other words, they indicated the order of the code segments by numbering them. After the assessment period, participants completed a post-test.

Throughout the procedure we recorded the time taken to complete each task. We collected process data throughout the instructional period and performance on the training activities and practice problems to ensure that participants were completing tasks.

4. ANALYSIS AND RESULTS

We scored participants' Parsons problem answers for correct order to create their score. Participants ranked the 13 code pieces from the Parsons problem and we gave them one point for each code piece that was in the correct order relative to the pieces around it. For example, if participants ranked the 4th, 5th, and 6th pieces of the problem as the 5th, 6th, and 7th pieces of their solution, they would receive two out of three possible points for those three pieces. The first piece would be counted as wrong because it is not following the 3rd piece, but the other two pieces would be counted as correct, as they are following the correct piece. This scoring scheme captures participants' understanding than scoring for absolute correct order as it does not penalize correct sequences of code that follow incorrect sequences.

4.1 Accuracy

The effect of the interventions on Parsons problem performance depended on the worked example manipulation. Participants who were given subgoal labels in the worked example performed better than those who generated their own labels or were not given labels, F (2, 113) = 3.8, MSE = 10.6, p = .026, est. ω^2 = .07, f = .18 (see Figure 2). We found no main effect of transfer distance, F (2, 113) = 1.1, MSE = 10.6, p = .303, est. ω^2 = .009. We also found no interaction between worked example format and transfer distance, F (2, 113) = 0.07, MSE = 10.6, p = .937, est. ω^2 = .001.

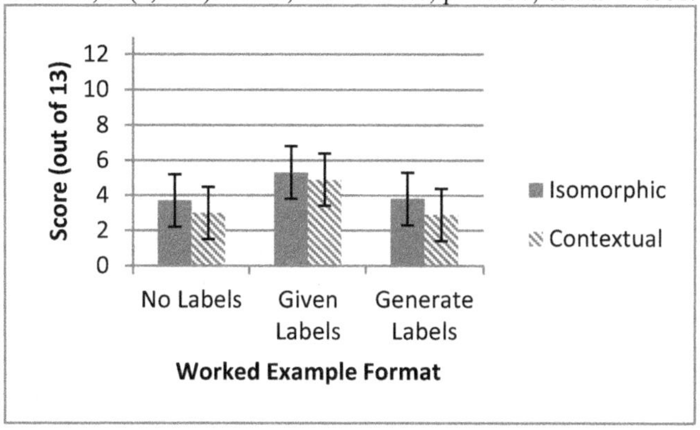

Figure 2. Parsons Problem performance graphed with worked example format on the x-axis, transfer distance as separate colors, and score on the y-axis.

4.2 Time Efficiency

Time spent on the Parsons problem task differed among levels of the worked example manipulation. Participants who generated their own subgoal labels in the worked example (*M* = 2.7 minutes) completed the task faster than those who were not given labels (*M* = 4.2 minutes), F (2, 113) = 4.8, MSE = 5.2, p = .010, est. ω^2 = .07, f = .20 (see Figure 3). We found no main effect of transfer distance, F (2, 113) = 2.2, MSE = 5.2, p = .142, est. ω^2 = .02. We found no interaction between worked example format and transfer distance, F (2, 113) = 2.1, MSE = 5.2, p = .126, est. ω^2 = .03.

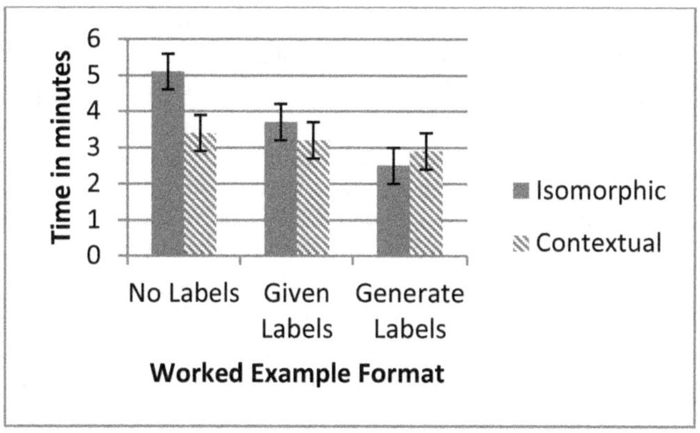

Figure 3. Parsons Problem time graphed with worked example format on the x-axis, transfer distance as separate colors, and minutes on the y-axis.

5. DISCUSSION

In this section we summarize our findings related to our original hypotheses and discuss the implications for teaching.

5.1 Findings

In this study, the results reinforce some of the previous subgoal research. We found that students who were given subgoals performed statistically significantly better than those who had no subgoals or who generated their own subgoals, regardless of transfer condition. In other words, both the Given-Isomorphic and

Given-Contextual Transfer groups performed statistically better than the other groups. In all cases the isomorphic groups did better than their contextual transfer counterpart, however these differences were not significant. We thus have partial support for our first hypothesis: Participants who learn with subgoal labels (given *only*) will perform better on low cognitive load assessments. Because there were no statistical differences between the isomorphic problem groups and the contextual transfer groups, we have support for our second hypothesis, transfer appears to have limited effect on student performance on this task.

The groups that generated their own subgoal labels completed the Parsons problem assessment in statistically less time than those who received no subgoal labels. This is consistent with previous research that indicates those who generate their own subgoal labels can recall the learned information more quickly. However this group did not perform the best, as would have been predicted by previous research. We are not sure why this is the case. One hypothesis is that this group "knew what they knew" and what they did not. They did not want to waste time puzzling out a solution if they predicted they would be unsuccessful. It may also be due to survey fatigue. The Generate groups took the most time during the instructional period (as expected) and the Parson problem assessment was near the end of the study. They may have reached their tolerance level and just wanted to finish.

We would expect the None-Isomorphic group to take the most time on the assessment as they most likely had the most shallow learning. This hypothesis agrees with our findings. There were no statistically significant differences based on the programming language used in the class.

5.2 Implications

Participants that were given subgoal labels performed overall better than those that did not have subgoal labels and those that generated their own subgoal labels. Though participants in the generate labels and no labels conditions performed equally, participants who generated their own labels completed the task faster than those who did not receive labels.

What can we learn from this study? It appears that learning which occurs with a low cognitive load can be assessed with low cognitive load assessments. In our previous work we found that low cognitive load learning did not always lead to better learning performance on high cognitive load assessments like writing code [21]. We can take two implications from these findings.

First, subgoal labels can reduce cognitive load which allows student to focus and learn more efficiently. Students who are given subgoal labels while learning problem solving can most likely recall those labels when needed to arrange code segments into order – the order of the learned subgoal labels. In previous work we have shown that learning subgoal labels also helps with transfer [17]. The subgoal labels provide structure for organization of student learning.

Giving subgoal labels to students may be more beneficial than having them generate their own subgoal labels for two reasons. First, giving the students the subgoal labels requires less time on their part for the learning acquisition phase. It is much quicker to read labels and learn their pattern than generating their own labels. Second, unless the instructor is reviewing and correcting the generated labels, student misconceptions may persist. Students may generate labels that are too context specific and do not transfer to other problems. We saw some evidence of this within the generated labels of the students. This may also explain why the Given Labels groups outperformed the Generate Label groups.

As instructors we should consider providing students with subgoal labels which are consistent across problems – initialization of variables, determining the loop termination / continuation condition, updating the loop control variable, etc. Students who learn the "pattern" of the problem solution can then recall the pattern when asked to order code segments.

Second, we should use more Parsons problems as low cognitive load assessments, either formative or summative, for students. Students who have learned may fail at high cognitive load assessments simply because the cognitive load is too great for them to succeed. Low cognitive load assessments have greater sensitivity. Parsons problems allow students to demonstrate that they understand the meaning and sequence of programs without having to also generate syntax. In summary, if cognitive load is increased in either the learning activity or the assessment activity student performance can suffer.

Previous research found that the transfer condition had a statistically significant effect on the performance of a code writing assessment [21]. Yet it had limited effect on the results of this study. This may be explained by cognitive load. We know that adding transfer between the worked example and practice problem introduces additional cognitive load--students must do non-superficial transfer during learning. This additional cognitive load could alter the learning just enough so that it shows up in a high cognitive load task (writing code from scratch) but not in a low cognitive load task (Parsons problems). Students who can learn the appropriate order of the subgoals may be able to demonstrate that knowledge on Parsons problems, where they may not be able to do so when writing code from scratch [21].

6. CONCLUSION

Research in educational psychology using subgoals in other disciplines indicate that generating subgoals results in deeper learning than given subgoals which results in more learning than receiving no subgoals. In [21] we found partial support replicating these findings. This study found that computer science students who are given subgoal labels (a low cognitive load activity) can perform better on a low cognitive load assessment. They statistically outperform the group who were required to generate subgoal labels and the group that received no subgoal labels. This study provides more evidence that learning programming is inherently different than learning physics or statistics – the educational psychology principles somewhat apply, but are not completely replicable. We believe the answer lies in the cognitive load required to learn programming. Adding even one additional piece to the learning puzzle (contextual transfer, generating subgoals) can have significant effects on learning performance.

Another aspect to consider is student time in both learning and completing the assessments. We found that those who were asked to generate subgoal labels took statistically more time to complete the instructional tasks [21] but completed the assessment task significantly quicker than the other groups. The happy medium may lie with the group that was given subgoal labels. They did not take significantly longer to complete the instructional material or the assessment tasks.

The interventions for this study are strongly grounded in instructional design theory and they were also applied in an authentic educational setting with an authentic educational task. Therefore, we expect that the internal and external validity of this work is high. However, because this study is the first experiment to use this type of task and because the results were different than previous work with subgoal labels, research to replicate these results is needed to ensure the validity of this work.

7. ACKNOWLEDGMENTS

We would like to thank the students who participated in the study and their instructors who graciously gave us the time. This work is funded in part by the National Science Foundation under grant 1138378. Any opinions, findings, and conclusions or recommendations expressed in this material are those of the authors and do not necessarily reflect the views of the NSF.

8. REFERENCES

[1] Atkinson, R.K. et al. 2003. Aiding Transfer in Statistics: Examining the Use of Conceptually Oriented Equations and Elaborations During Subgoal Learning. *Journal of Educational Psychology*. 95, 4 (2003), 762.

[2] Atkinson, R.K. et al. 2000. Learning from examples: Instructional principles from the worked examples research. *Review of educational research*. 70, 2 (2000), 181–214.

[3] Atkinson, R.K. 2002. Optimizing learning from examples using animated pedagogical agents. *Journal of Educational Psychology*. 94, 2 (2002), 416.

[4] Atkinson, R.K. and Derry, S.J. 2000. Computer-based examples designed to encourage optimal example processing: A study examining the impact of sequentially presented, subgoal-oriented worked examples. (2000).

[5] Bjork, R.A. 1994. Memory and metamemory considerations in the training of human beings. *Metacognition: Knowing about Knowing*. MIT Press.

[6] Bransford, J.D. et al. 2000. *How People Learn: Brain, Mind, Experience, and School*. National Academy Press.

[7] Catrambone, R. 1995. Aiding subgoal learning: Effects on transfer. *Journal of educational psychology*. 87, 1 (1995), 5.

[8] Catrambone, R. 1996. Generalizing solution procedures learned from examples. *Journal of Experimental Psychology: Learning, Memory, and Cognition; Journal of Experimental Psychology: Learning, Memory, and Cognition*. 22, 4 (1996), 1020.

[9] Catrambone, R. 1994. Improving examples to improve transfer to novel problems. *Memory & Cognition*. 22, 5 (1994), 606–615.

[10] Catrambone, R. 1998. The subgoal learning model: Creating better examples so that students can solve novel problems. *Journal of Experimental Psychology: General*. 127, 4 (1998), 355.

[11] Chi, M.T. et al. 1989. Self-explanations: How students study and use examples in learning to solve problems. *Cognitive science*. 13, 2 (1989), 145–182.

[12] Denny, P. et al. 2008. Evaluating a new exam question: Parsons problems. *Proceeding of the Fourth international Workshop on Computing Education Research* (Sydney, Australia, 2008), 113–124.

[13] Eiriksdottir, E. and Catrambone, R. 2011. Procedural instructions, principles, and examples how to structure instructions for procedural tasks to enhance performance, learning, and transfer. *Human Factors: The Journal of the Human Factors and Ergonomics Society*. 53, 6 (2011), 749–770.

[14] Johnson, W.L. and Soloway, E. 1985. PROUST: Knowledge-based program understanding. *Software Engineering, IEEE Transactions on*. 3 (1985), 267–275.

[15] Leppink, J. et al. 2013. Development of an instrument for measuring different types of cognitive load. *Behavior research methods*. 45, 4 (2013), 1058–1072.

[16] Leppink, J. et al. 2014. Effects of pairs of problems and examples on task performance and different types of cognitive load. *Learning and Instruction*. 30, (2014), 32–42.

[17] Margulieux, L.E. et al. 2012. Subgoal-labeled instructional material improves performance and transfer in learning to develop mobile applications. *Proceedings of the ninth annual international conference on International computing education research* (2012), 71–78.

[18] Margulieux, L.E. and Catrambone, R. 2014. Improving problem solving performance in computer-based learning environments through subgoal labels. *Proceedings of the first ACM conference on Learning@ scale conference* (2014), 149–150.

[19] van Merriënboer, J.J. and Sweller, J. 2005. Cognitive load theory and complex learning: Recent developments and future directions. *Educational psychology review*. 17, 2 (2005), 147–177.

[20] Morrison, B.B. et al. 2014. Measuring cognitive load in introductory CS: adaptation of an instrument. *Proceedings of the tenth annual conference on International computing education research* (2014), 131–138.

[21] Morrison, Briana B. et al. 2015. Subgoals, Context, and Worked Examples in Learning Computing Problem Solving. *ICER 2015* (Aug. 2015).

[22] Palmiter, S. and Elkerton, J. 1993. Animated demonstrations for learning procedural computer-based tasks. *Human-Computer Interaction*. 8, 3 (1993), 193–216.

[23] Parsons, D. and Haden, P. 2006. Parson's Programming Puzzles: A Fun and Effective Learning Tool for First Programming Courses. *Proceedings of the 8th Australasian Conference on Computing Education - Volume 52* (Darlinghurst, Australia, Australia, 2006), 157–163.

[24] Plass, J.L. et al. 2010. *Cognitive load theory*. Cambridge University Press.

[25] Renkl, A. and Atkinson, R.K. 2002. Learning from examples: Fostering self-explanations in computer-based learning environments. *Interactive learning environments*. 10, 2 (2002), 105–119.

[26] Renkl, A. and Atkinson, R.K. 2003. Structuring the transition from example study to problem solving in cognitive skill acquisition: A cognitive load perspective. *Educational psychologist*. 38, 1 (2003), 15–22.

[27] Spanjers, I.A. et al. 2012. Segmentation of worked examples: Effects on cognitive load and learning. *Applied Cognitive Psychology*. 26, 3 (2012), 352–358.

[28] Sweller, J. et al. 1998. Cognitive architecture and instructional design. *Educational psychology review*. 10, 3 (1998), 251–296.

[29] Sweller, J. et al. 2011. *Cognitive load theory*. Springer.

[30] Sweller, J. 2010. Element interactivity and intrinsic, extraneous, and germane cognitive load. *Educational psychology review*. 22, 2 (2010), 123–138.

[31] Tew, A.E. and Guzdial, M. 2011. The FCS1: a language independent assessment of CS1 knowledge. *Proceedings of the 42nd ACM technical symposium on Computer science education* (2011), 111–116.

[32] van Gog, Tamara and Paas, Fred 2012. Cognitive Load Measurement. *Encyclopedia of the Sciences of Learning*. Springer.

An Examination of Layers of Quizzing in Two Computer Systems Courses

Cindy Norris
Appalachian State University
Department of Computer Science
Boone, NC
norrisca@appstate.edu

ABSTRACT

This paper investigates the impact of layers of quizzing on student performance on subsequent tests and the final exam. The first layer of quizzes are on-line "pre-quizzes" designed to prepare students for follow-on classroom discussions. The second layer quizzes are short "post-quizzes" that are given during class time after discussing questions about the material covered by pre-quizzes. A study involving fifteen semesters of data and 348 students indicated that students performed better on tests and the final exam with this quizzing strategy compared to a more traditional homework based approach. These results agree with the body of research that indicates that testing enhances learning. Significantly, we found an 8 point pass rate increase on the Computer Systems I final exam and a 10 point pass rate increase on the Systems II final.

1. INTRODUCTION

Technological advances have led to an explosion of electronic resources available for educational use including massive open online courses (MOOCs), electronic materials made available by book publishers such as the Mastering system offered by Pearson, numerous online tutorials, videos, and wikis, and course management systems such as Moodle and Blackboard. Many instructors have adopted these technologies to enhance their teaching. One benefit enabled by the technology is the ability to easily create and use on-line quizzes, which provide instant feedback to the student.

In the minds of many educators, as well as parents, too much testing is being performed. There have been frequent complaints about testing, for example, that teachers "teach to the test", that testing takes away from valuable instruction time, and that testing adds to student anxiety. Research indicates that for some students, test anxiety can cause lower performance and students that exhibit test anxiety are likely to be women [8]. This is a particular concern in STEM fields where the attrition rate of women is already high [6]. In addition, there is concern that testing places an emphasis on memorization, sacrificing critical thinking skills. For these reasons and others, many university classes include very few tests, perhaps only a midterm and final while typically the largest portion of a university student's grade is based upon test performance.

SIGCSE '16, March 02 - 05, 2016, Memphis, TN, USA

ISBN 978-1-4503-3685-7/16/03...$15.00
DOI: http://dx.doi.org/10.1145/2839509.2844608

In spite of its questionable reputation, testing can have a very positive impact on learning. Cognitive psychologists have long recognized the "testing effect" in which students remember the material that they have been tested on better than material that they have simply restudied. Roediger and Karpicke equate testing with the Heisenberg uncertainty principle in psychology [10]: "Just as measuring the position of an electron changes that position, so the act of retrieving information from memory changes the mnemonic representation underlying retrieval – and enhances later retention of the tested information." A number of studies have been performed that verify this "testing effect." Some of those studies are described here. A more comprehensive overview can be found at [10].

In a study similar to earlier work by Tulving [17], Karpicke and Roediger compared the results of three different approaches for learning lists of words [11]. In one approach, named SSST, students studied a list of words for three study trials and then were given a recall test. In a second approach, named STTT, students studied a list of words and then were tested on those words during three test trials. In the third approach, STST, students alternated between study trials and test trials. This studying/testing approach was repeated for 5 cycles and one week later students returned to perform a final recall test lasting 10 minutes in length. Students demonstrated incremental learning in all approaches, as seen in the test trial results. However, students participating in the STST approach demonstrated greater learning. In the final learning phase test, students in the SSST group recalled 78% of the words, students in the STTT group recalled 81% of the words, and students in the STST group recalled 88% of the words. In addition, in the final recall test that was performed a week later, students in the STST group demonstrated the greatest amount of recall (57% for the SSST group, 64% for the STTT group, and 68% in the STST group).

The Karpicke and Roediger study [11], as well as others described in [10], demonstrated the "testing effect" in a laboratory setting on recall tests. Other researchers have investigated the "testing effect" using more standard test question formats. For example, a study by Agarwal et. al. [1] found that students demonstrated higher retention of a textbook passage one week later when studying the passage was followed by a short-answer test. In a study described in [10], students studied passages covering scientific topics and were asked to either restudy the passage or take a recall test. All students were then given recall tests 5 minutes, 2 days and 1 week later. The students that restudied rather than taking the test performed better on the recall test taken after 5 minutes. However, in the recall test given 2 days later, the group that took the test produced better retention over those that simply restudied (68% versus 54% recall). In addition, the recall test after 1 week showed a similar gap in performance (56% recall for those that took the test versus 42% for those that simply restudied).

Other researchers have found that the "testing effect" holds true in actual classroom situations (as we have also found). Bangert-Drowns et al. [2] analyzed 35 studies of college (28) and high school (7) classes. Most of the classes in the study were either science or math. 83% of the classroom studies demonstrated a positive effect from frequent testing as measured by the performance on the final exam. In addition, Bangert-Drowns et. al. found that performance on the final exam increases as a function of the number of tests given in the class. Four of those classroom studies also evaluated student attitudes toward testing; in all four studies students gave higher ratings to classes in which they were tested frequently.

In another classroom study, Leeming [13] gave a test at the beginning of each class in an introductory psychology course. He found that the final grades in his "exam-a-day" class were better than the final grades of previous versions of the same class. Pennebaker et. al. [16] employed an approach similar to Leeming. Students in that study were given an on-line quiz at the beginning of each class session. Average performance on the final exam was a half of a letter grade higher than in previous semesters of the course.

There have been few studies of the impact of testing on student learning in Computer Science courses. A study performed by [7] found that students in a CS 1 course performed higher on the final exam when the course included regular "pop" quizzes. In another study involving CS 1 courses, Woit and Mason [18] found that students given weekly quizzes and no midterm performed better on the final exam than students given a midterm and no weekly quizzes. Lacher and Lewis [12] investigated the use of quizzing in conjunction with a flipped classroom. In addition to watching a video prior to coming to class, students completed an on-line, multiple choice quiz based upon the video material. They found that students did *not* earn higher grades when the quizzes were incorporated. In contrast, Zingaro et. al. [19] found that completing reading quizzes positively correlated with other areas of course performance.

This paper demonstrates the positive impact gained in terms of student performance by changing a course from a traditional homework assignments, tests, and final exam assessment format to one that incorporates numerous quizzes, both online and in class, and includes the same type of tests and final exam as the original course. Fifteen semesters worth of data is examined from two courses, Computer Systems I and Computer Systems II. Both courses were taught by the same instructor, using the same textbook for all fifteen semesters, except for a change of edition. For six semesters, these courses were taught using the traditional method; for nine semesters, the course was taught using quizzes rather than homework. The average score on tests and final was consistently higher in the quizzing approach. In addition, a larger percentage of students passed the final exam.

2. LAYERED QUIZZING

Computer Systems I and Computer Systems II are required CS courses at the author's institution and generally recognized as two of the most difficult required courses in the program. Computer Science students typically take these two courses back to back in their junior or senior year of study. The textbook "Computer Systems: A Programmer's Perspective" [4] has been used consistently in both of these courses since 2005, changing only the edition when a new edition was introduced.

In Fall 2010, the author decided to eliminate homework assignments and instead incorporate on-line pre-quizzes. The chief reason to include pre-quizzes was to motivate students to complete reading assignments before class. Like others [5], the author noted an increasing decline in student willingness to complete reading assignments. The author's sense in the decline was intuitive; however, [5] noted a 16-year decline on pop-quiz scores on assigned readings.

Pre-quiz questions include both basic vocabulary and more challenging questions that students were not necessarily expected to complete correctly. All questions on the pre-quizzes are automatically graded; thus the types of questions are restricted to multiple choice, matching, and fill-in-the-blank. Pre-quizzes are very low-stakes; only 5% of the total course grade was based upon performance on approximately 20 pre-quizzes given throughout the semester. In spite of the low-stakes, almost all students attempt the pre-quizzes.

Unlike the homework assignments that were assigned when the course was taught in a more traditional style, the pre-quizzes include some simple, vocabulary questions. These types of questions can be answered without performing a careful reading of the textbook. However, the pre-quizzes also include the same kinds of more challenging problems that were on the homework assignments. For example, one of the questions on a Systems II pre-quiz that quizzes a student's understanding of vocabulary is shown in Figure 1. A more complex question that evaluates a student's understanding of how a cache works included on the same quiz can be seen in Figure 2. Typically, a student will have no difficulty with the first problem, but may not be able to complete the second. However, research indicates that simply attempting to solve a problem will lead to better learning [3].

In addition to motivating students to engage with the reading material, there are several more benefits to the use of on-line pre-quizzes. First, since the quizzes are automatically graded, students receive immediate feedback. We allow our students a second attempt on the pre-quiz, which encourages further engagement with the material. Second, a large number of pre-quizzes can be assigned because the instructor is not burdened with having to grade them by hand. Since we use them to motivate students to be prepared for class, we assign about one per class session. Third, the questions on on-line quizzes can be used to create on-line practice quizzes that students can repeatedly take to prepare for post-quizzes and tests.

Like Just In Time teaching strategies [15], we use pre-quizzes to determine difficulties that students may have with the material and then discuss that material in class. The final question in every pre-quiz is "What problems did you have with this quiz and what would you like your instructor to discuss in class?" This allows us to avoid spending class time discussing material that students are able to pick up on their own without difficulty or were already introduced to in an earlier class. Classroom discussions tend to center around those problems on pre-quizzes that students were unable to complete. This strategy helps to keep students engaged because through the pre-quiz they were able to determine what they didn't understand. In class, they are invested in trying to fill in the gaps in their understanding.

Many instructors have eliminated a reading requirement by providing students with videos that they can watch outside of class, i.e. the flipped classroom. Thus far, we have not taken this approach. We feel that it is important for Computer Science students, particularly upper level students, to develop the skills necessary for reading difficult, technical material.

Class time is spent addressing the difficult material covered by the pre-quizzes and having students complete a written 15-20 minute post-quiz. Post-quizzes are not as comprehensive as pre-quizzes and are not given as frequently. Typically, we give one post-quiz every week or week and a half. Students are encouraged to use the on-line practice quizzes (created out of pre-quizzes) to prepare for post-quizzes. The questions that appear on post-quizzes are *not* identical to questions on pre-quizzes, but they are similar. For example, a post-quiz will contain a question similar to the earlier cache problem, but the cache parameters will be different.

Like pre-quizzes, post-quizzes are also given to contribute to learning. Post-quizzes are not "high stakes" but slightly more weighty than pre-quizzes. In our classes, 15% of the course grade is based upon post-quizzes and about 10 post-quizzes are given. They are not merely in-class group exercises since the quizzes are graded in order to motivate students to prepare for them. They are often given to teams of students (discussed further in section 4), which allows students to learn from each other. Like pre-quizzes, the post-quizzes are given to motivate learning and encourage incremental learning.

At two points during the term, non-cumulative tests are given. Students are encouraged to use post-quizzes and on-line practice quizzes to prepare for those tests. Blank copies of the post-quizzes can be found on-line, as well as the answers, so students can prepare by retaking post-quizzes and checking their answers. The final exam is cumulative. Copies of the tests (both blank and with answers) are provided to help students prepare for the final.

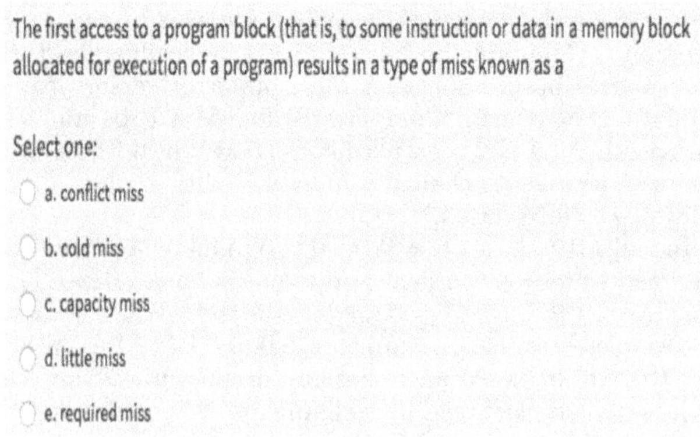

Figure 1: Simple question on pre-quiz

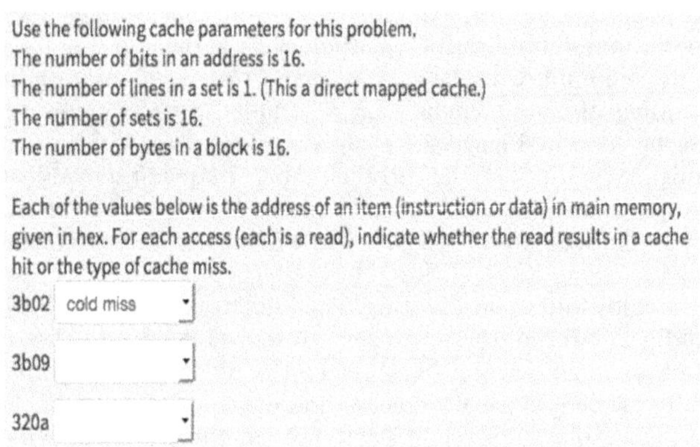

Figure 2: Somewhat challenging question on pre-quiz

3. RESULTS

Six semesters worth of test and exam grades in Systems I and Systems II using a traditional homework strategy was compared to nine semesters worth of test and exam grades in those two courses to measure the impact of the layered quizzing strategy. Overall, the test and final exam results of 348 students are included in the study. The same instructor taught all semesters of these classes and the same textbook was used (with differences in edition). The tests varied from semester to semester (to deal with the possibility of cheating), but the types of questions were the same. For example, a Systems I test will have a problem that requires the students to write assembly code equivalent to provided C code. Each Systems I test has a similar problem but with different C code. Thus, the differences in the results are not due to the instructor being different, differences in the textbook and content, or differences in the tests.

The "No Quizzes" bars in the six figures provided are the results on Systems I and Systems II tests and final from the six semesters those courses were taught in a traditional style. Students were given reading assignments, classroom time was spent on lectures and group exercises, and multiple homework problems were assigned throughout the semester (about 10). No quizzes were given, but the students were provided with the answers to homework problems and tests that they could use for studying.

The "Quizzes" bars in the six figures show the results on Systems I and Systems II tests and final from the nine semesters those courses were taught using the layered quizzing approach. In those classes, homework assignments were replaced by on-line pre-quizzes and in-class written post-quizzes. The same types of in class group exercises, tests, and final were given.

We show the results of the tests and final instead of the course grades because these courses also include a lab component. Although a small portion of a test may be based upon the lab material, the vast majority of each test is based upon the material covered in the textbook. However, 30% of the course grade is devoted to the grades on the labs. For this reason, performance on the tests and final (and not the course grade) is a better measure of the impact of the layered quizzing approach.

Figures 3 and 4 show the average and median score on the final, first test, and second test for the Systems I course. The average score on the second test is about 5 points higher and the average score on the final is about 4 points higher. There is little difference between the average scores on the first test, which is likely because much of the material on the first test is a review of material covered in the required *Discrete Mathematics* and *Introduction to Computer Systems* pre-requisite courses. Thus, this is the third course in which students have been exposed to the material on the first test. There is also a significant difference in the median scores; the median score using the layered quizzing approach is about 6 points higher for the second test and 5 points higher for the final.

Figure 5 compares the pass rates on the final, first test, and second test for the Systems I course. A passing score is 60 points or above. The quizzing classroom technique made a significant difference in the percentage of students that passed the final exam, 93% versus 85% for the traditional technique.

The results for the Systems II class are presented in figures 6, 7, and 8. Again, the results consistently indicate that incorporating quizzes results in better student performance.

4. TEAM QUIZZES

In recent semesters, many of the post-quizzes (about half) offered in the Systems I and Systems II classes were in-class team quizzes, where teams of 2 or 3 students worked together on a quiz and turned in one completed quiz for grading. There are several of benefits of team quizzes. First, as expected, grades on team quizzes are higher than grades on individual quizzes; thus, team quizzes can be less stressful for students than individual quizzes. Second, the quizzes give students a chance to learn from each other. Third, team quizzes reduce the amount of grading required. This

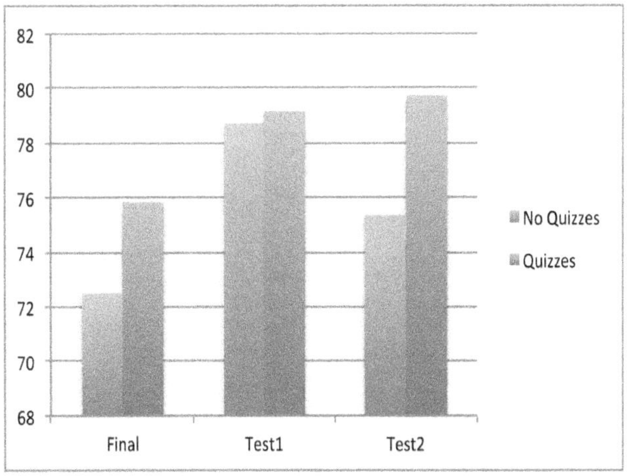

Figure 3: Average score on Final Exam, Test 1, and Test 2 for the Systems I course.

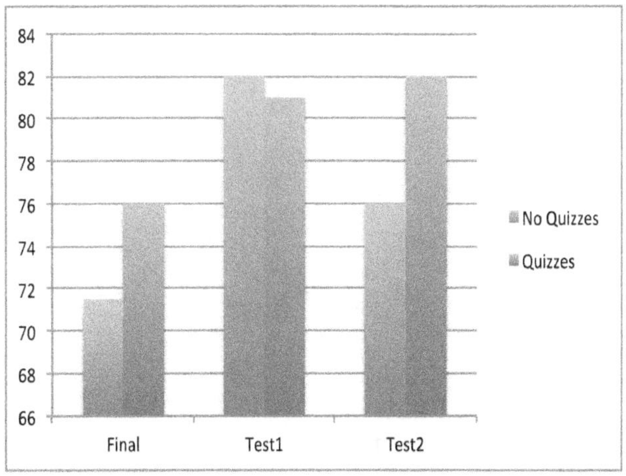

Figure 4: Median score on Final Exam, Test 1, and Test 2 for the Systems I course.

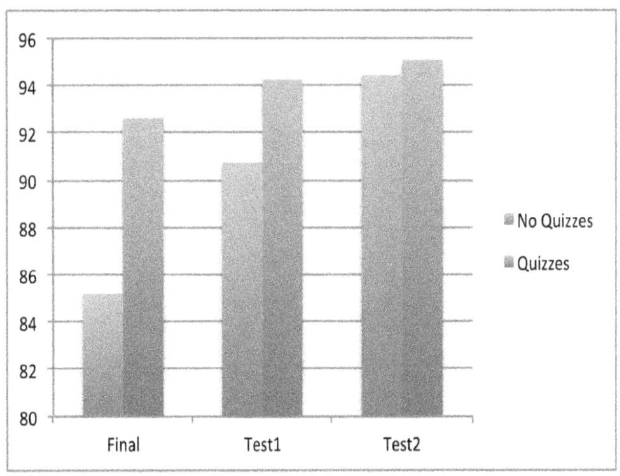

Figure 5: Pass rate on Final Exam, Test 1, and Test 2 for the Systems I course.

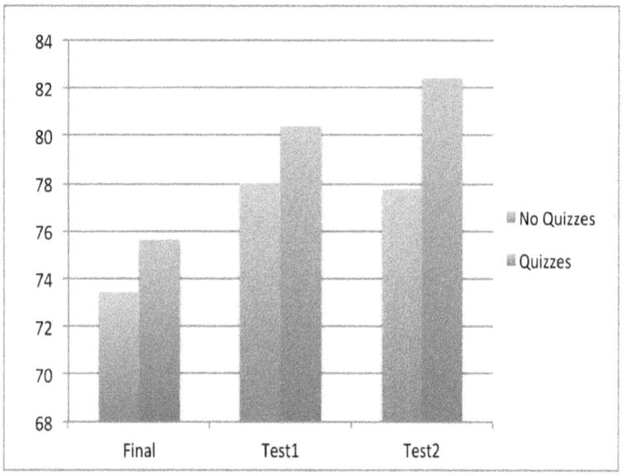

Figure 6: Average score on Final Exam, Test 1, and Test 2 for the Systems II course.

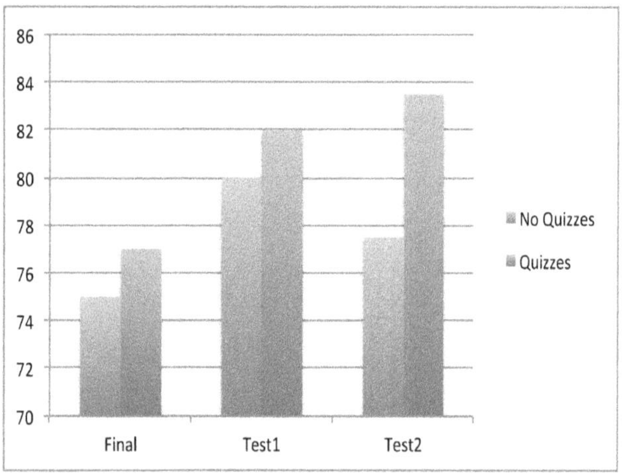

Figure 7: Median score on Final Exam, Test 1, and Test 2 for the Systems II course.

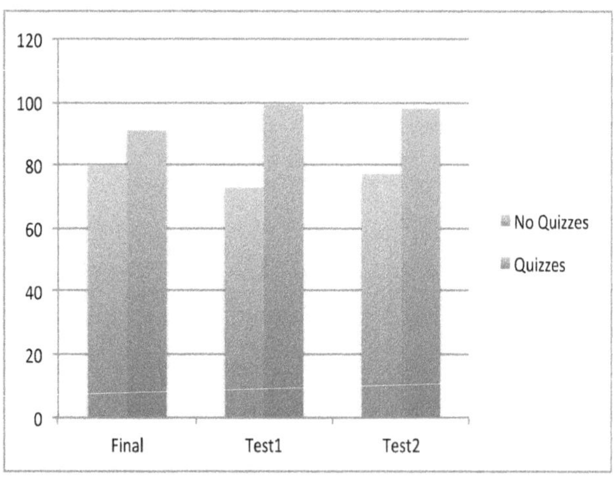

Figure 8: Pass rate on Final Exam, Test 1, and Test 2 for the Systems II course.

1. Compare your enjoyment level of individual to team post-quizzes. I enjoyed the team post-quizzes ...	
Much more	81.8%
Slightly more	18.2%
About the same	0.0%
Slightly less	0.0%
Much less	0.0%

Figure 9: How did students enjoy team quizzes?

2. How much would you prepare for a team post-quiz compared to an individual post-quiz assuming that you know in advance the quiz is to be a team post-quiz? I would	
prepare much more than I would prepare for an individual	4.5%
prepare somewhat more than I would prepare for an	0.0%
prepare about the same as I would prepare for an individual	77.3%
prepare somewhat less than I would prepare for an individual	13.6%
prepare much less than I would prepare for an individual post-	4.5%

Figure 10: How did students prepare for team quizzes?

has become increasingly important to us given dramatically increasing enrollments.

However, team quizzes can be a cause for concern also. For example, will students study for a quiz if they believe the quiz is going to be a team quiz? Our strategy is to inform students when a quiz is going to be given but to not inform the students in advance whether the quiz will be an individual or team quiz. So students don't know whether the quiz is to be a team quiz, but may be willing to take a chance that it will be. We give quizzes to support student learning. Will students learn more or less if the quiz is a team quiz?

In Spring 2015, two classes of students were surveyed to evaluate their opinions about the effectiveness of team quizzes. One class was a Systems II course taught using a layered quizzing strategy. The second class was an Operating Systems course in which a number of in-class quizzes were given. For both classes, some of the in-class quizzes were individual quizzes and some were team quizzes. 41 students were invited to complete the survey; 22 students completed it.

Figure 9 displays the answers to a survey question about enjoyment level. All students indicated that they enjoy team quizzes more than individual quizzes. Figure 10 displays the answer to a survey question about preparation. The majority of the students indicated that they would prepare for a team quiz the same way that they would prepare for an individual quiz, although some students indicated that they would prepare somewhat or much less. Figure 11 indicates that almost all students felt that the team quizzes contributed to their understanding of the material.

5. DISCUSSION AND CONCLUSIONS

3. How much did taking a team post-quiz contribute to your understanding of the material?	
learned a great deal when I took a team post-quiz	68.2%
learned a little from taking a team post-quiz	27.3%
didn't learn anything from taking a team post-quiz	0.0%
would have learned more if it was an individual quiz	4.5%

Figure 11: How did students learn from team quizzes?

Here we address some of the comments and concerns expressed by reviewers. One reviewer commented that students taking many quizzes with similar questions could cause them to become conditioned to a certain type of question. Another concern expressed was that CS students must be able to solve problems that cannot be assigned in a quiz-like format. Admittedly, some skills are best developed and assessed by programming assignments and a lab component of the course serves that purpose. However, quiz questions can certainly require more from students than simply memorizing terms. For example, a pre-quiz question related to programming can require a student to trace through code and determine the output. A post-quiz question can require the student to provide a small amount of code. Similarly, a pre-quiz question can require a student develop but not submit a model in order to solve a problem. We argue that the abundance of quizzes and a variety of quiz questions allow students to develop the skills that we expect them to obtain to perform well on the tests and the final. These expectations should not be a mystery to the student. We believe that it is important that students are made aware of expectations, whether it is the ability to convert a number from one base to another base or the ability to create a model of a cache and analyze the cache performance.

One reviewer expressed an interest in knowing performance results in the semester immediately before the change and the semester immediately after. In fall 2009, 21 students were enrolled in the Systems I course taught using the "traditional" approach. The average grades on the first test, second test, and the final were 75.8, 75.7 and 78.8 respectively. The percentages of students that passed the first test, second test, and the final were 90.5, 90.5, and 95, respectively. One year later, the course with sixteen students was taught by the same instructor using the same textbook and a layered quizzing approach. In that course, the average grades on the first test, second test, and the final were 84.1, 80.3, and 78.3 respectively. Thus, the average was significantly higher on the first and second test, but about the same on the final. More significantly, there was a 100% pass rate on both tests and the final.

This paper investigated the impact of a layered quizzing approach on student learning. The results of 15 semesters of data indicate that quizzes contribute positively to student learning and performance on subsequent assessment artifacts. The results back up the "testing effect", i.e. that students better learn material that they have been tested on.

The pre-quiz questions used in Systems I and Systems II are in Moodle format and are available by contacting the author.

6. REFERENCES

[1] P. K. Agarwal, J. D. Karpicke, S. H. K. Kang, R. L. R. III, and K. B. McDermott. Examining the testing effect with open and closed-book tests. Washington University in St. Louis.

[2] R. L. Banger-Drowns, J. A. Kulik, and C. L. C. Kulik. Effects of frequent classroom testing. *Journal of Educational Research*, 85, 1991.

[3] P. C. Brown, H. L. R. III, and M. A. McDaniel. *make it stick: The Science of Successful Learning.* The Belknap Press of Harvard University Press, Cambridge, Massachusetts, 2014.

[4] R. E. Bryant and D. R. O'Hallaron. *Computer Systems: A Programmer's Perspective, 3rd edition.* Pearson Education, Inc., Upper Saddle River, New Jersey, 2016.

[5] C. M. Burchfield and J. Sappington. Compliance with required reading assignments. *Teaching of Psychology*, (27):56–60, 2000.

[6] X. Chen and M. Soldner. STEM attrition: College students' paths into and out of STEM fields. National Center for Education Statistics, November 2013.

[7] V. A. Cicirello. On the role of effectiveness of pop quizzes in cs1. In *SIGCSE '09: Proceedings of the 40th ACM Technical Symposium on Computer Science Education*, February 2009.

[8] K. Eum and K. G. Rice. Test anxiety, perfectionism, goal orientation, and academic performance. *Anxiety, Stress, & Coping*, 24(2):167–178, March 2011.

[9] H. L. R. III. How tests make us smarter. *New York Times*, July 2015.

[10] H. L. R. III and J. D. Karpicke. The power of testing memory: Basic research and implications for educational practice. *Perspectives on Psychological Science*, 1(3):181–210, 2006.

[11] J. D. Karpicke and H. L. R. III. Repeated retrieval during learning is the key to long-term retention. *Journal of Memory and Language*, 57:151–162, November 2006.

[12] L. L. Lacher and M. C. Lewis. The effectiveness of video quizzes in a flipped class. In *SIGCSE '15: Proceedings of the 46th ACM Technical Symposium on Computer Science Education*, February 2015.

[13] F. C. Leeming. The exam-a-day procedure improves performance in psychology classes. *Teaching of Psychology*, 29:210–212, 2002.

[14] K. B. McDermott, P. K. Argarwal, L. D'Antonio, I. Henry L. Roediger, and M. A. McDaniel. Both multiple-choice and short-answer quizzes enhance later exam performance in middle and high school classes. *Journal of Experimental Psychology: Applied*, 20(1):3–21, 2014.

[15] G. M. Novak, E. T. Patterson, A. D. Gavrin, and W. Christian. *Just-in-time teaching: Blending active learning with web technology.* Prentice Hall, Upper Saddle River, New Jersey, 1999.

[16] J. W. Pennebaker, S. D. Gosling, and J. D. Ferrell. Daily online testing in large classes: Boosting college performance while reducing achievement gaps. *PLoS One*, 8(11):1–6, November 2013.

[17] E. Tulvey. The effects of presentation and recall of material in free recall learning. *Journal of Verbal Learning and Verbal Behavior*, 6:175–184, 1967.

[18] D. Woit and D. Mason. Effectiveness of online assessment. In *SIGCSE '03: Proceedings of the 34th SIGCSE technical symposium on Computer science education*, February 2003.

[19] D. Zingaro, C. B. Lee, and L. Porter. Peer instruction in computing: The role of reading quizzes. In *SIGCSE '13: Proceedings of the 44th ACM Technical Symposium on Computer Science Education*, March 2013.

As CS Enrollments Grow, Are We Attracting Weaker Students? A Statistical Analysis of Student Performance in Introductory Programming Courses Over Time

Mehran Sahami
Computer Science Department
Stanford University
Stanford, CA 94305, USA
sahami@cs.stanford.edu

Chris Piech
Computer Science Department
Stanford University
Stanford, CA 94305, USA
piech@cs.stanford.edu

ABSTRACT

In recent years, enrollments in undergraduate computer science programs have seen tremendous growth nationally. Often accompanying such growth is a concern from faculty that the additional students choosing to pursue computing may not have the same aptitude for the subject as was seen in prior student populations. Thus such students may exhibit weaker performance in computing courses. To help address this question, we present a statistical analysis using mixture modeling of students' performance in an introductory programming class at Stanford University over an eight year period, during which enrollments in the course more than doubled. Importantly, in this setting many variables that would normally confound such a study are directly controlled for. We find that the distribution of student performance during this period, as reflected in their programming assignment scores, remains remarkably stable despite the large growth in enrollment. We then explain how the notion of having "more weak students" and the fact that the distribution of student ability is unchanged can readily co-exist and lead to misperceptions about the quality of incoming students during an enrollment boom.

Keywords

Enrollment growth; mixture modeling; student performance; introductory programming.

1. INTRODUCTION

The past decade has seen tremendous growth in enrollments in computer science programs. Indeed, the Computing Research Association 2014 Taulbee Survey [12] shows a near doubling of the number of newly declared CS/CE undergraduate majors from 2007 to 2014. The increase in majors is correlated with a sharp increase in the number of students taking introductory computer science courses, which has received much attention of late in the popular press [9, 11].

SIGCSE '16, March 02 - 05, 2016, Memphis, TN, USA

ACM 978-1-4503-3685-7/16/03…$15.00
DOI: http://dx.doi.org/10.1145/2839509.2844621

The increasing numbers of students taking CS courses has led some faculty to lament the quality of students entering such programs. Indeed, commentary along these lines is readily found in public online forums frequented by computing faculty. For example, consider the following quote from a former EECS professor at a well-known university [8]:

> *Based on my recent teaching experience, there are definitely many students signing up for CS majors who aren't prepared enough and have difficulty getting through foundational material. Some of them manage to learn through perseverance (retaking courses several times), some don't. They won't be nearly as efficient as median students…*

More anecdotally, we have often heard colleagues questioning whether the students in CS courses today are as strong as those in the past. The thinking along these lines being that when enrollments were lower only the students who had both the aptitude and interest in computing were enrolling. Now, with CS becoming a "hot" major, we are potentially attracting students who have interest, but perhaps less aptitude than before.

Rather than allowing such anecdotal statements to continue unchecked, in this work we seek to provide a statistical analysis of student performance in introductory programming courses during the recent period of large enrollment growth (2007-2014) to quantify the extent to which we may be attracting weaker students into such courses. It is especially important to counter anecdotes with rigorous analysis in such a context. Unsubstantiated statements about "weaker" students can potentially be even more damaging and off-putting to students from under-represented populations who may be particularly susceptible to stereotype threat [3, 7, 10].

Based on building robust statistical models, we find that, contrary to the perception of attracting weaker students, the quality of student work in the introductory programming course we analyze has remained remarkably consistent during the entire eight year period we consider. Indeed, through a mixture modeling approach to fitting the distribution of grades on students' assignments, we find clear evidence that the distribution of student quality (as reflected in assignment scores) is virtually unchanged even in the face of an over 100% increase in enrollment. By examining the implications of the model in more detail we are able to reconcile the quantitative results regarding consistent student populations over time with the reasons that potentially give rise to anecdotes about "more weak students" taking CS courses. In this way, we seek to not only provide a quantitative basis for understanding the implications of enrollment growth, but also help to provide educators with insight about potential misperceptions that can arise in such situations.

The remainder of the paper is organized as follows. In Section 2 we describe the introductory programming course and data we analyze in our study. Section 3 provides details of the statistical methods we use to model the data and gives the results obtained from our statistical analysis. In Section 4 we discuss the results in this study further, highlight our main contributions, and present directions for future work.

2. THE DATA

Analyzing the performance of student populations over time can potentially suffer from many confounding factors, such as the efficacy of different instructors in a course, the impact of different pedagogies on learning, and the use of different assessment instruments. Luckily, in our setting, all these factors are directly controlled for. Specifically, we consider CS106A, an introductory programming course using Java (equivalent to CS1) taught at Stanford University. This course was taught by the same instructor (the first author) every Autumn term for the past eight years (2007-2014). During this time the contents of the course (e.g., textbook, handouts, lectures, section materials) remained largely unchanged (by design) and the same instructional pedagogy was employed. Moreover, the course used the same seven programming projects in every Autumn term offering and employed the same grading rubrics for their evaluation.

The main variable that changed during the period from 2007 to 2014 is the size of the course, which grew from less than 300 students to more than double that size. As a result, the data on student performance in this course (as measured by programming assignment grades) over time provides a highly controlled setting to test hypotheses related to the performance of students enrolling in the course as enrollments have increased.

It is important to be precise about the data that we consider in our study. In order to use a performance measure that is directly comparable across years, we focus on students' aggregate (weighted sum numeric) grade on the seven programming assignments/projects in the course, as these are consistently evaluated across years. In aggregate, the seven programming assignments make up 50% of the overall course grade. We do not include exam data (the course has a midterm and final exam) as the exams are different each term. Thus, exam scores are not directly comparable across terms as difficulty across exams is not directly calibrated. Trying to equate means/variances of exam scores across classes would create statistical distortions in our otherwise controlled data. We recognize that the exclusion of exam scores may present a potential threat to the validity of our results as assignment grades are only one measure of students' ability in a programming course. However, we believe that the distortive effects of exam data normalization across courses would present an even greater threat to the validity of cross-term comparisons. Thus, exam data is not included in our analysis.

We start by considering the full set of students officially enrolled in the course – that is students who have included the course on their study list by the "add" deadline, which is the end of the third week of our 10 week term. Students who then "withdrew" from the course (i.e., dropped the course before the end of the eighth week of the term) are excluded from our dataset of assignment scores (as their set of assignment submissions are intentionally incomplete), but such students are then examined separately so we can determine if there is a significant increase in the percentage of such students over time. This allows us to separately analyze the performance of those students who completed the course from those who withdrew, to have a finer level of resolution in examining student performance.

Next, any students with documented academic integrity issues are excluded from the dataset. The reason for this is that we want the data to be representative of students' *actual* performance, and thus we try to minimize the influence of plagiarism/cheating to the extent that it can be identified. It is important to note that Stanford is an Honor Code school and students were given the opportunity to retract assignments before the end of the course if they felt that the work they submitted was not entirely their own. Any student with one or more such assignment retractions or who was otherwise found to have an academic integrity issue (through the use of plagiarism detection software) was removed from the dataset as their assignment scores no longer entirely reflected their own work. We note that information regarding academic integrity issues at Stanford must be treated with great delicacy as these cases are considered highly confidential. For these reasons, we cannot provide more details with respect to that aspect of the data (e.g., the actual number of data points removed as a result of this filtering, separate analysis of students involved in such issues, etc.), other than to say that the number of data points filtered as a result was generally small and that the filtering process does not qualitatively impact the results we report here.

Finally, to further improve data integrity, we did a manual inspection of all the remaining data to remove any obviously "dirty" data (e.g., students with 0 scores on all assignments/exams who had mistakenly enrolled in the course or forgot to drop, but clearly had no intention of actually trying to complete the class). This final stage resulted in the filtering of very few data points. The remaining data was used in the analysis we discuss presently.

Figure 1 shows the number of students completing the course (i.e., data points after the filtering process above was applied) in the Autumn term of each year as well as the number of students who withdrew from the course in the respective term. The actual numbers are included in the graph above each data point.

We note that the number of students withdrawing from the course in any given offering is very small on a relative basis – never greater than 3.5% of the starting population of the class. In fact, the percentage of students withdrawing from the class in 2007 is essentially the same as that in 2014 (2.8% in both cases) when enrollments were more than double. Since the percentage of withdrawals remains very low and stable during the period in which enrollments grew, it provides no indication—as far as withdrawals are concerned—that the student population enrolling in the course as time goes on is less capable on a relative basis, as we would have expected to see an increase in the *percentage* of withdrawals if that were the case.

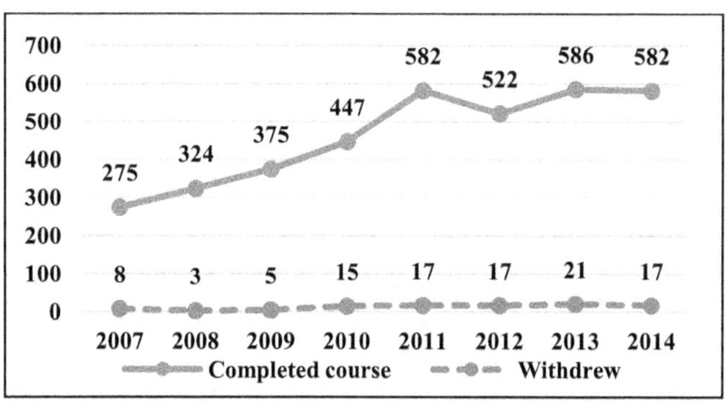

Figure 1. Students completing and withdrawing from course

More importantly, the number of withdrawals is quite small on an absolute basis, and thus would not provide a robust indicator of potential changes in the aptitude of students taking the class even if we saw slightly more fluctuation in this measure. Thus, to see whether the student population has become "weaker" as enrollments have grown we need to consider a detailed analysis of the assignment scores of students who completed the class.

3. RESULTS

3.1 Initial Comparison of Classes

Perhaps the most obvious initial test to consider in determining whether the performance of students in our introductory programming course has changed as enrollments have grown is to consider a T-test of mean assignment scores in the course over time. Setting the 2007 class as the baseline (as it has the smallest enrollment in our controlled data), we perform T-tests between this class and the class in every subsequent year. Essentially, we are looking to see if there is any evidence to reject the null hypothesis, which is that the mean assignment score in the 2007 class is the same as any other class we compare against. We report the p-values from these T-tests (two-tailed, heteroscedastic tests) between the 2007 class and all other years in Table 1. As a side comment, we note that performing ANOVA across all the classes simultaneously would not accurately reflect differences in class means *as enrollments grow* since the test statistic would also be influenced by differences among classes with comparable enrollment levels (e.g., the 2011 and 2014 classes).

Table 1. p-values of T-tests comparing to 2007 class

Class	2008	2009	2010	2011	2012	2013	2014
p-value	0.69	0.69	0.82	0.10	0.11	0.46	0.82

The T-test results in Table 1 do not lead us to reject the null hypothesis at the $\alpha = 0.05$ level for *any* class we compare against, indicating that there does not appear to be a statistically significant difference in the mean scores between the 2007 class and any other class compared against (i.e., classes with much higher enrollments). We do note that the comparison with the 2011 class reaches the $\alpha = 0.10$ significance level, but this is tempered by the fact that *seven* T-tests are being performed, so we would expect some T-tests to result in lower (and potentially close to statistically significant) values even when there is no real difference in the means of the data sets. Interestingly, in comparing the 2007 class with the 2014 class, we find a p-value of 0.82, indicating that it is in fact extremely likely that the means of the two classes are the same, despite the fact that enrollment in the former class is less than half that of the latter class.

To see the stability of class means over time, Figure 2 provides a graph of the assignment means (actual mean values are also given in the graph), with error bars showing one standard deviation around the mean, respectively for each class. Aggregate assignment scores are on a 50 point scale, although a few points of extra credit are possible.

We caution, however, that a lack of statistical significance in the difference of the *means* does not necessarily imply that the *distributions* of the assignment scores are also similar. Indeed, in some cases it is possible for two *distributions* to be quite different, but still yield similar *means* using a T-test (for example, if the distributions have different higher order central moments, such as variance or skewness). To address this point, we next consider analyzing the *distribution* of scores in each class via mixture modeling.

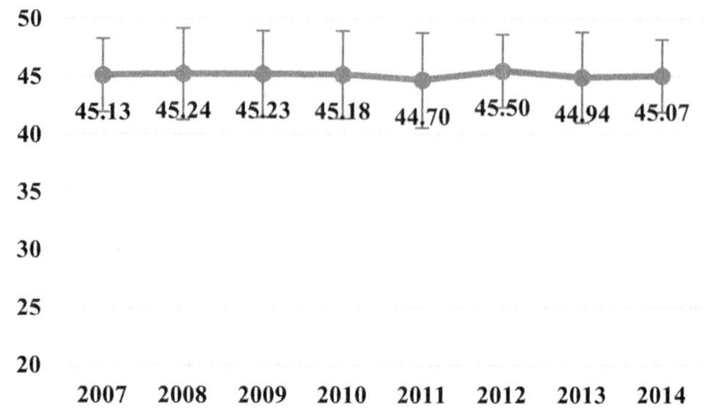

Figure 2. Means of student assignment scores (values labeled), with error bars indicating standard deviation in each class

3.2 Mixture Modeling

At a high level, *mixture modeling* is the task of modeling a probability distribution as a weighted sum of two of more component distributions [5]. Such modeling is often used when a probability distribution may not be fit well by a single parametric distribution (e.g., a single Gaussian), but is more accurately captured by combining two or more such models – for example, a multi-modal distribution.

More formally, a mixture distribution $f(x)$ with K components is a weighted sum of component distributions f_1, f_2, ..., f_K, with respective component weights w_1, w_2, ... w_K, defined by the equation (eq. 1):

$$f(x) = \sum_{i=1}^{K} w_i f_i(x)$$

In our analysis, we consider parametric mixture models, where the component distributions f_i are all Gaussians with different respective means μ_i and variances σ^2_i. The mixture models are fit to the data using the EM (Expectation Maximization) algorithm [1, 2, 4], which is guaranteed to converge to a local optimum of the likelihood function of the data (i.e., it finds parameters μ_i and σ^2_i for all the component Gaussian distributions as well as component weights w_i that jointly maximize the likelihood of the data being fit). While EM is an iterative algorithm that can be sensitive to the starting point chosen (as it is only guaranteed to converge to a local optimum of the likelihood function), we note that given how few parameters are being fit in our models, our results were extremely stable with EM producing exactly the same set of parameters for a given data set when initialized at a variety of different starting points.

To illustrate why mixture models are needed (rather than just fitting a single Gaussian to the data) let us consider the case where we try to model the distribution of student assignment scores with a single Gaussian (which would be equivalent to a mixture model with only one component (i.e., K=1)). Figure 3 shows a histogram of the actual data (student assignment scores) for the 2014 class compared with the values that would be expected using a single Gaussian model with mean and variance fit to the data.

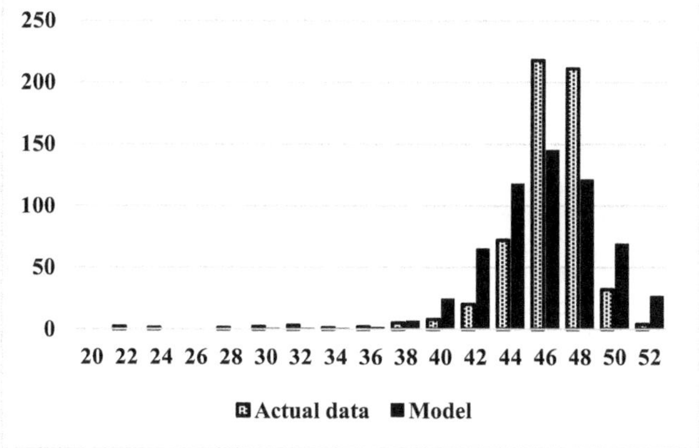

Figure 3. Actual scores compared to a single Gaussian model

As is clear in Figure 3, the single Gaussian provides a poor fit to the actual data as it underestimates the most common score ranges (i.e., 46-48, 48-50) and overestimates other ranges.

Alternatively, we can consider a mixture of two Gaussians (i.e., K=2) fit to the same data (2014 class). We call this the 2-Gaussian mixture model. Figure 4 illustrates the two Gaussian components that are found in the data via the EM algorithm, showing one component that captures much of the lower tail of the distribution (Component 1) and another much more peaked component that reflects the most common score ranges (Component 2).

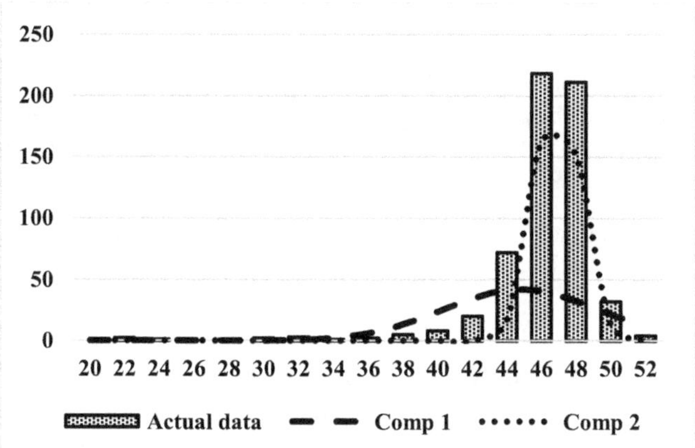

Figure 4. Components in Gaussian mixture model with K=2

We can combine these two components into a single distribution using the mixture model equation (eq. 1) along with the respective component weights also fit using EM. The resulting 2-Gaussian mixture model is graphed alongside the actual data in Figure 5. As can be seen in the figure, the 2-Gaussian model provides a much better fit to the data.

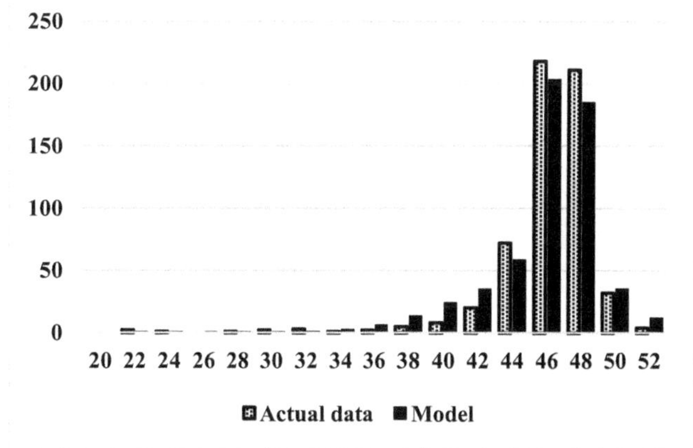

Figure 5. Actual scores compared to a 2-Gaussian model

More importantly than just the accuracy of the model, the 2-Gaussian model gives us greater insight about the distribution of students in the class. Namely, there is one group of students (reflected in Component 2) that is generally doing well and shows a solid understanding of the course assignments as reflected in their scores. There is another group of students (the bottom half of Component 1) which appears to be comprised of "weaker" students with regard to the assignments. This group makes up the tail of the class distribution. We turn our attention to analyzing these two groups over time momentarily.

Here, we pause to observe that it is also possible to fit mixture models with more than two components to the data. Indeed, we considered three-component (i.e., K=3) mixture models and found that they led to qualitatively similar results as the two-component models, but were harder to directly interpret as they had greater model complexity and more parameters. Others [6] have also found that two-component mixture models provide a compelling fit to educational data related to student activity, albeit in a different context than ours. While we could have engaged in Bayesian model selection to determine the number of mixture components more automatically, this would have required the use of a *subjective* prior distribution over the number of model components, which would be open to argument, and would further complicate potential interpretation of the model. Thus, we simply note that it is possible to construct more complex models using the methodology presented here, but for the remainder of our discussion we focus on two-component models for clarity as they provide an excellent fit to the data without overly complicating the interpretation of the model.

3.3 Mixture Components Over Time

After discovering that a two-component model provides both a good fit to the data as well as giving us insight about the subpopulations of students in the course (as reflected in assignment scores), we can look at the evolution of these two components over time by fitting a two-component model to the data set of assignment scores for each respective year.

Figures 6 and 7, graph the respective assignment means for Component 1 and Component 2 in the 2-Gaussian model for each class over time (the actual mean values are also given in the graphs). Error bars in both figures show one standard deviation associated with each respective mean.

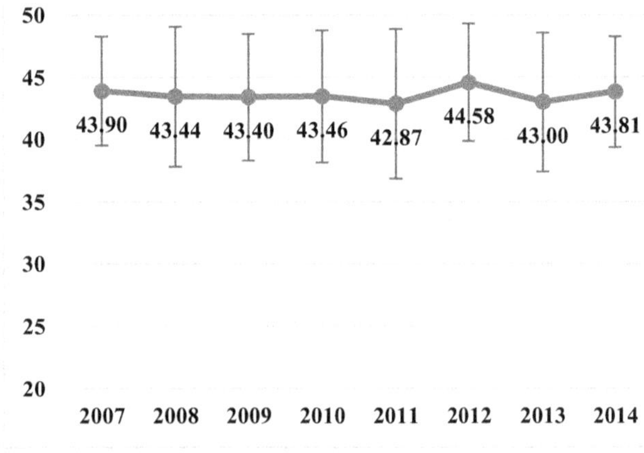

Figure 6. Component 1 means of student assignment scores (values labeled), with error bars indicating Component 1 standard deviation for each class

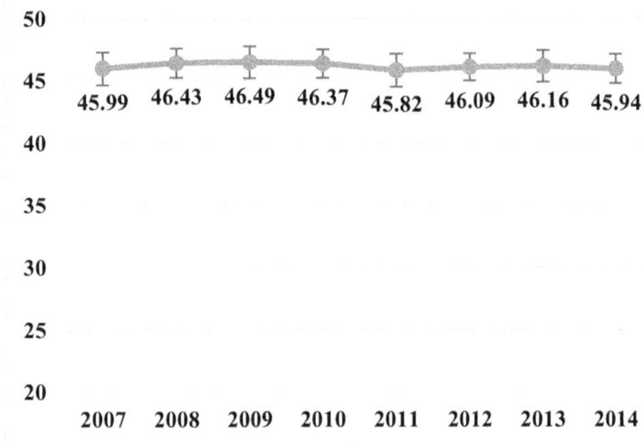

Figure 7. Component 2 means of student assignment scores (values labeled), with error bars indicating Component 2 standard deviation for each class

We see that the Gaussian components, fit *independently* for each data set (year) are remarkably stable over time. Indeed, comparing the 2007 class to that in 2014 shows that the means for both respective components differ by less than one-tenth of one point on an absolute 50-point scale or less than 0.2% on a relative basis. This gives us compelling evidence that the subpopulations of students in the course (at least with respect to assignment scores) have not changed substantially as enrollments have grown over time.

Nevertheless, there is yet one more critical factor we need to examine in such a model. Knowing that the component means (and standard deviations) of the distribution of students in the class has not changed over time reflects that there are two clear and stable subpopulations in the course. However, we must also recall that a mixture model weights the component distributions (with weights w_i) in the sum that forms the mixture distribution. Thus, we must examine if there is a trend in the mixture *weights* over time, which could reflect, for example, that a larger proportion of students might be coming from Component 1 as enrollments increase.

We must pay careful attention to the nuances of such an analysis, as Component 1 overlaps with Component 2 in the mixture model for every class year we fit (see Figure 4 for a graphical example of this phenomenon). Notably, the larger variance of Component 1 allows it to capture two ends of the distribution—both the left-hand tail of "weak" students as well as the right-hand tail of "very strong" students. To address this issue, we consider the proportion of students in each class whose probability of being assigned to Component 1 in that class is greater than that of being assigned to Component 2 (i.e., they are captured by Component 1) and have scores *below the mean* of Component 1. This essentially captures just the left-hand tail of students in each class (i.e., the lower half of Component 1). The graph of the percentage of such students in each class is given in Figure 8 (actual percentages are also given in the graph).

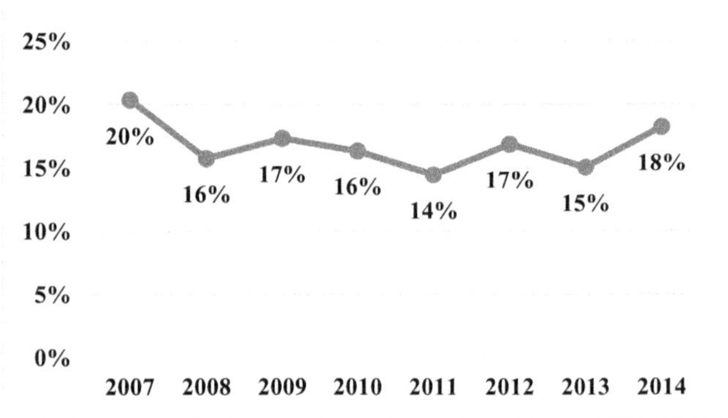

Figure 8. Percentage of students assigned to Component 1 in each class with an assignment score below component mean

Here we find that while the percentage of students in Component 1 who are below the component mean shows some fluctuation over time, there is no positive correlation with the growth in class size. Indeed, a correlation analysis of this percentage with class size reveals a *negative* correlation, but there are so few data points (eight) in measuring this correlation that we cannot conclude that an increase in class size leads to a greater proportion of "strong" students in the course, only that there is no evidence that the proportion of "weak" students grows as enrollments increase.

4. DISCUSSION AND CONCLUSIONS

The series of increasingly refined statistical analyses we conducted on student assignment data showed no evidence for an increase in the proportion of "weaker" students taking the course in the face of significant enrollment increases. Indeed, the statistics bore out a remarkable stability in the student population (and subpopulations) over time. This may lead one to wonder where a perception of an increase in "weak" students came from to begin with. The answer here is somewhat obvious in retrospect, but can now be understood from a rigorous prospective. While the *proportion* (and distribution) of "weak" students remains relatively stable as enrollments grow, that in turn implies that the number of "weak" students grows *on an absolute basis* with enrollments in a linear fashion.

Such students, who tend to struggle more with assignments, are more likely to seek out course staff for assistance, such as attending office hours, sending questions via email, posting to discussion groups, etc. Since such activity is often the most direct communication instructors receive from students, they perceive greater numbers of students struggling as enrollments grow. Naturally, this can lead to the conclusion that more "weak" students are being drawn into the course. In fact, on an absolute scale, more such students are enrolling in the course, but that is simply to be expected from having greater numbers of students in the class overall. As shown in the analysis above, such anecdotal interactions with students should not be construed as indicating that the *population* of students taking the course has somehow shifted in distribution and a greater percentage of "weak" students are enrolling in the course. Thus, our analysis helps to resolve a perceptual paradox that we have seen arise among several faculty in the face of growing enrollments: it is simultaneously possible to see more students struggle in a class and also have there be no change with regard to the *proportion* of "weak" students taking the course. We would encourage instructors to be more cognizant of this fact when making public statements about students choosing to pursue computing courses in the face of growing enrollments so as not to alienate students who may not be as confident in their abilities, especially if they have no prior experience in computing or are part of a population susceptible to stereotype threat.

The main contributions of this work are three-fold. First, we highlight a growing concern among faculty regarding potential changes in the student body taking computing courses in the context of quickly-growing enrollments. Second, we provide a statistical analysis and general methodology, employing the use of mixture models, in a controlled setting to show that no evidence exists in our data to imply that increased enrollments have led to an increase in the proportion of "weak" students. Lastly, we provide an explanation for why faculty may perceive changes in the student population as enrollments grow, when in fact there is little change in the *distribution* of students' facility with the subject.

Importantly, our analysis, while showing results in the limited context our own CS1 course, provides a general methodology that we believe others can use to analyze data at their respective institutions to more rigorously understand the evolution of student performance in their courses. Indeed, our analysis is not meant to be the final word on student performance in computing courses in the face of enrollment increases. Far from it, our goal is to provide a methodology that others use as a starting point in analyzing their own student populations.

In future work, we seek to apply this sort of analysis to other courses at our own institution and elsewhere, as more data with controlled factors becomes available. For example, is the stability we see in student performance in the face of large enrollment growth a more universal phenomenon (at least in introductory CS courses)? We are also interested in seeing how other factors, such as more informed teaching or greater resources for help (e.g., discussion forums, course helpers, etc.) may impact the stability of student performance in computing courses over time.

We are particularly interested in performing such analyses on courses further downstream in our program to better understand the evolution of student populations not only over time, but also through course content. For example, we can try to identify what factors (e.g., prior experience, help-seeking behavior, intended major, etc.) might impact the subpopulation component that a student is associated with. By examining students longitudinally, we can seek to find factors that might be indicative of students moving between subpopulation components as they progress through a series of courses.

On a more theoretical note, this work has pushed us to consider extensions to the EM algorithm applied to multiple disjoint data sets in order to induce mixture models where some of the mixture components share parameters across all the data sets. For example, we could build a 2-Gaussian model where the mean and variance for one of the Gaussians is required to be same across all data sets examined whereas the second Gaussian component is allowed to vary for each data set separately. In the educational setting, this would allow us to see how the "lower" component varies given an "upper" component that is the same across classes.

5. ACKNOWLEDGMENTS

We thank the faculty in our department and at other institutions for discussing issues related to student performance in their computing courses in light of growing enrollments. Such discussions and the attendant views regarding potential changes in the population of students provided the motivation for this work. We also thank Michelle Friend for early discussions of this topic.

6. REFERENCES

[1] Cheeseman, P., *et al*, 1988. AutoClass: A Bayesian Classification System, *Proceedings of the Fifth International Conference on Machine Learning*, 54-64.

[2] Cheeseman, P. and Stutz, J. 1996. Bayesian Classification (AutoClass): Theory and Results. In *Advances in Knowledge Discovery and Data Mining*, AAAI Press, 153-180.

[3] Cheryan, S., Plaut, V. C., Davies, P., and Steele, C. M. 2009. Ambient belonging: How stereotypical environments impact gender participation in computer science. *Journal of Personality and Social Psychology*, 97(6), 1045-1060.

[4] Dempster, A. P., Laird, N. M., Rubin, D. B. 1977. Maximum Likelihood from Incomplete Data via the EM Algorithm. *Journal of the Royal Statistical Society, Series B*, 39(1), 1-38.

[5] Everitt, B.S. and Hand, D.J. 1981. *Finite Mixture Distributions*. Chapman & Hall.

[6] Koller, D., Ng, A., Do, C., and Chen, Z. 2013. Retention and Intention in Massive Open Online Courses: In Depth. *EDUCAUSE Review Online*, June 3, 2013. URL=http://er.educause.edu/articles/2013/6/retention-and-intention-in-massive-open-online-courses-in-depth.

[7] Kumar, A.N. 2012. A Study of Stereotype Threat in Computer Science. In *Proceedings of ITiCSE '12*, 273-278.

[8] Quora.com. *Higher Education: Are there too many students going into Computer Science?* URL=http://www.quora.com/Higher-Education/Are-there-too-many-students-going-into-Computer-Science. Retrieved on August 18, 2015.

[9] Soper, T. 2014. *Analysis: The exploding demand for computer science education, and why America needs to keep up*. GeekWire.com, June 6, 2014. URL=http://www.geekwire.com/2014/analysis-examining-computer-science-education-explosion/.

[10] Spencer, S.J., Steele, C.M., and Quinn, D.M. 1999. Stereotype threat and women's math performance, *Journal of Experimental Social Psychology*, 35(1), 4-28.

[11] Taylor, C. 2014. *From The Ivy League To State Schools, Demand For Computer Science Is Booming*. TechCrunch.com, May 25, 2014.

[12] Zweben, S. and Bizot, B. 2015. 2014 Taulbee Survey. *Computing Research News*. Vol. 27, No. 5 (May 2015), 25.

TEALS: Teacher Professional Development Using Industry Volunteers

Nathaniel Granor
Microsoft/TEALS
New York, NY
nathaniel@tealsk12.org

Leigh Ann DeLyser
NYC Foundation for CS Education
New York, NY
leighann@csnyc.org

Kevin Wang
Microsoft/TEALS
Redmond, WA
kevin@tealsk12.org

ABSTRACT

Rising demand for high school computer science courses in the United States has created pressure to increase the number of computer science(CS) teachers in a short amount of time[2]. In this experience report, we present the TEALS program as a unique, high-touch, professional development model, pairing computing industry professionals with classroom teachers. By combining the relative strengths of the team (content and pedagogy) TEALS has been able to successfully train new CS teachers. We present the history of the TEALS program, the volunteer and teacher recruitment process, the volunteer training program, data from a study of the pedagogical content knowledge of the TEALS volunteers, and program growth and efficacy data. Additionally, we offer achievement of students on the AP CS A exam as an externally valid measurement of learning outcomes in TEALS classrooms.

Keywords

TEALS, Professional Development, Teachers, K12

1. INTRODUCTION

There is an increasing demand for computer science (CS) courses in high schools. In 2012, approximately 2,000 of the 30,000 high schools in the US had AP CS courses. The increase in programs must, by necessity, be accompanied by an increase in teachers who have appropriate pedagogical and content knowledge to effectively teach CS courses at the high school level.

Programs focused on expanding access to CS recognize the need to rapidly increase the number of CS teachers in the country[2]. Ideally, CS teachers would be prepared through a rigorous teacher preparation program that included instruction in both CS content and pedagogical knowledge required to be a teacher[3]. Unfortunately, few pre-service programs for CS Education exist. Many programs attempt to broaden participation in computing by offering summer workshops for teachers[5, 7]. In these workshops, teachers with little or no CS experience learn both CS content and how to teach CS.

In this experience report, we discuss TEALS' (Technology Education And Literacy in Schools) model of teacher professional development(PD). The TEALS program, described in Section 3, places CS experts in the classroom alongside teachers. We will discuss current PD models, the TEALS model specifically, and share data about the growth of TEALS in the United States. We will present data showing the outcomes of TEALS partnerships in transitioning classrooms from volunteer-supported to independent teaching, and share observations from an educational research firm's external evaluation of the TEALS program.

SIGCSE '16, March 02 - 05, 2016, Memphis, TN, USA

ISBN 978-1-4503-3685-7/16/03...$15.00

DOI: http://dx.doi.org/10.1145/2839509.2844589

2. TRADITIONAL MODELS OF TEACHER PROFESSIONAL DEVELOPMENT

Teacher preparation has two phases. Before teachers enter the classroom they are considered pre-service, and the ongoing professional development a teacher completes while employed in a school is considered in-service. This section discusses current models of teacher preparation in CS.

2.1 Pre-service Teacher Education Programs

Pre-service teacher education programs in the United States are often undergraduate or graduate programs that work with students who are not yet teachers. The pre-service programs include coursework in content and pedagogy. For graduate programs, mostly used by professionals seeking a teaching certificate as a secondary career option, there may be fewer content specific requirements as the student would already have significant coursework from a related undergraduate degree if applicable.

Pre-service teacher preparation is rigorous, and despite the debates around its efficacy[1], often requires multiple years to complete. Enacting pre-service teacher preparation for relatively rapid CS teacher training has many barriers. First, pre-service preparation programs require at least one year to complete all of their components. Secondly, pre-service educators are not guaranteed positions at schools, and therefore may not be hired to teach computer science, even after they complete the program. Finally, there are few existing pre-service computer science teacher programs and programs have had difficulty recruiting potential teachers[6].

2.2 In-service Professional Development

In-service teacher education builds the capacity of current teachers in a new subject area or methodology through learning experiences called professional development(PD).

There are many models of in-service education, and a wide variety of providers of such training[8]. TEALS considers itself to be an in-service model of teacher development.

In-service teacher development or professional development can have positive impact on teacher practice[9]. Traditional models of PD have a much shorter time frame between PD implementation and classroom implementation than pre-service options. Because, by definition, in-service teachers are already employed by schools, there is a direct connection between the teacher and a classroom, or school schedule. Many existing models of PD used by the computer science education community rely on spring and summer PD for implementation of new material or new courses the following fall[5, 7]. The length of the PD interventions varies widely by program, some as short as a few days and others requiring many hours of independent study coupled with in person instruction by a provider. Unlike pre-service programs, where prospective teachers study content and pedagogy separately, in-service programs require teachers to develop both at the same time.

3. THE TEALS MODEL OF TEACHER PROFESSIONAL DEVELOPMENT

3.1 History of TEALS

The TEALS program grew from the efforts of its founder, Kevin Wang. After completing a B.S. in CS from UC Berkeley, Kevin worked as a CS teacher for 3 years and earned a Masters degree in Education from Harvard. In 2006, Kevin transitioned to a position at Microsoft to work on a project in distance learning. Kevin began volunteering at an independent school in Seattle, teaching CS 1st period. Other Seattle-area high schools heard about the arrangement, and asked Kevin to teach CS at their schools as well. Not wanting to give up his full-time engineering position, he found other volunteers at Microsoft to serve the additional schools. In the 2010-2011 school year, he formalized this arrangement as TEALS.

In 2011, TEALS formed a partnership with Prof. Stuart Reges at the University of Washington to use Reges' AP CS curriculum. TEALS also partnered with Prof. Dan Garcia at UC Berkeley, and together they created a high school adaptation of Garcia's Beauty and Joy of Computing class using the SNAP! programming language. With a growing cohort of new volunteers, TEALS began a formalized summer training program, aimed at familiarizing volunteers with the curricula, and introducing them to the basics of classroom management and student-centered learning.

The supply of software engineers willing to take on an early-morning part-time job could never scale to provide instructors to each US high school. To address the sustainability of the co-teaching model, TEALS adjusted the program to focus on building teacher capacity in CS. The adjusted model aims to hand off instruction of each CS class to a classroom teacher after 2-3 years of partnership, and holds schools accountable to that goal.

With financial support from Microsoft, TEALS has continued to grow rapidly. In 2014-2015, TEALS served 131 schools in 18 states and Washington DC. Those included 8 private schools, 13 public charter schools, and 110 non-charter public schools. Forty-eight (48) of the schools qualified for Title 1 school-wide programs, indicating that over 40% of their students are eligible for federal free or reduced-price lunch programs.

3.2 The TEALS Model of In-service PD

The TEALS program aims to expand access to computer science in high school by building CS teacher capacity. Partner schools identify a teacher from any discipline who is willing to become a CS teacher, but does not have a CS background. TEALS helps to find and train computer science experts as volunteer instructors, and creates teaching teams of four volunteers plus the partner teacher. The school offers a single section of computer science during first period, early enough for the volunteers to visit before their workday begins. Each volunteer attends class 2-3 times per week. Schools choose to offer either Introduction to Computer Science Principles (a 1-semester subset of the Beauty and Joy of Computing AP CS Principles course) or AP Computer Science A. The TEALS program provides curriculum materials, volunteer training, a community of support, special events and opportunities for students and teachers, and ongoing feedback and observation of partner classrooms.

During two years of partnership, the classroom teacher gradually increases their role in the classroom from learner, to supporter, to primary instructor. At the same time, the volunteers reduce their role from primary instructor to supporter. The TEALS partnership is much longer than most traditional in-service PD models. Over the course of a standard 2-year partnership, a teacher participates in approximately 300 hours of co-teaching with students and subject-matter experts in the classroom. Other styles of PD often rely on teachers attending sessions outside the workday. TEALS partner teachers gain experience in programming and computer science during their normal teaching hours and in their classroom.

3.3 TEALS Volunteers

Volunteers power the TEALS model. TEALS attempts to place 4 volunteers into each CS classroom with a teacher, though this is sometimes limited by availability. A multi-volunteer team reduces the time-commitment, allows flexibility for volunteer travel, and provides redundancy in case of a volunteer withdrawal from the program.

The selection and training process helps to ensure the selection of reliable volunteers with deep content knowledge, and an appropriate classroom demeanor. TEALS regional managers review volunteer applications and conduct interviews with each applicant. Representatives from partner schools attend the interviews to meet the candidates and give input regarding selection. The interview focuses on several areas: the applicant's technical credentials; the program model and commitment; past teaching experience; and presentational style. After the interviews, TEALS regional managers, with input from school representatives, choose which applicants to accept into the program and where to place them.

Volunteers commit to TEALS for one year. TEALS estimates that the total volunteer commitment for a year includes 260 hours of participation. The commitment begins with a summer training program (discussed in the following section), and includes classroom time, commuting to and from the school, preparation for class, regular team meetings, and monthly TEALS events.

In the 2014-2015 school year, TEALS worked with approximately 475 volunteers. The 334 volunteers who specified a current employer represent 144 distinct organizations. 135 (28.4%) of the volunteers work at Microsoft. 107 (22.5%) volunteers are female. TEALS does not collect data on the race or ethnicity of its volunteers.

During their application interviews, volunteers explain their reasons for participating in the program. Many volunteers feel fortunate to have landed in a career they enjoy that supports them well, and they seek an opportunity to give back. Some express interest in helping students from underrepresented groups such as young women and people of color to gain exposure to Computer Science. Other volunteers cite a specific teacher or mentor who inspired them in computer science whom they want to emulate. A few share that they "stumbled onto" CS late in college or after another career and wish they found it sooner. They want to provide today's students with the chance to get in the door earlier.

TEALS volunteers tend to loosely fit into one of three profiles: recent college graduates who don't have many family commitments; mid-career veterans, often with children in high school; and retired former-engineers with lots of time on their hands looking for something worthwhile to do.

3.4 TEALS Volunteer Summer Training

An effective classroom requires an instructor with skill in classroom management and pedagogy, with knowledge of the relevant subject area, and with specific knowledge of how to teach that subject (pedagogical content knowledge or PCK) [4]. The TEALS classroom relies on collaboration between the classroom teacher, who brings skill and experience in managing a classroom and general pedagogy, and the volunteers, who bring a wealth of knowledge of the subject area.

TEALS' summer training program aims to introduce volunteers to the ideas of classroom management and pedagogy, and to walk through parts of the curriculum, emphasizing key pieces of pedagogical content knowledge. Classroom teachers are encouraged, but not required, to attend. TEALS estimates approximately 30% of classroom teachers attended one or more summer training sessions in 2014-2015, but these data were not formally collected.

The format of the summer training program has evolved and changed each year. In 2014-2015, the program consisted of 5 in-person 2.5 hour sessions held every 2 weeks, interspersed with 7 hours of online interactive video modules. In addition to the formal content, volunteers completed the major programming projects for the course, and met with their teaching teams to devise a syllabus and classroom plan.

One set of online training modules focused on the theory behind pedagogy techniques. Other online modules introduced the major curriculum projects and highlighted areas likely to cause students trouble. In-person training sessions provided an opportunity to model good teaching practices like questioning techniques, pacing, and group activities. In a typical interaction, instructors would model an activity, have groups of attendees practice implementing that activity, and then reflect on it.

Table 1 illustrates the breakdown of topics presented in the 2014-2015 TEALS summer training and an approximation of how much time was spent in each major area.

Major Topic (% Time)	Details
Classroom Management (18%)	Creating and implementing classroom procedures; Student notetaking; Setting clear expectations; Use of bonus incentives; Distribution of labor between team members
Pedagogy (35%)	Bloom's Taxonomy; Creating learning objectives (SWBAT); Formative Assessment; Lesson Pacing; Writing lessons; Grading; Homework; Questioning
CS PCK (20%)	Pair programming; Socratic questioning; Design/Problem solving; Group activities; Peer assistance; Encouraging persistence; Debugging; Moving from concrete to abstract; Procedural decomposition; Demo and tutorials; CS Unplugged activities;
Working with Schools (7%)	School roles and personnel; Expectations of staff; Teacher-student relationship; Setting up the classroom; Getting help
Curriculum (12%)	Set of topics; Major projects; Lab ideas; AP Test Prep;
Program Info. (8%)	Administrative topics; Deadlines; Program model

Table 1: TEALS Summer Training Topics

3.5 TEALS Teacher Selection

TEALS considers the selection of a teacher as the most critical component to a successful partnership. Most importantly, that teacher must have several years of classroom experience, and demonstrate personal investment in the successful outcome of the TEALS partnership. TEALS does not specify a required subject area for partner teachers.

TEALS requires schools to nominate a teacher for the partnership when they apply to the program. That teacher must attend the partnership interview and meet the TEALS regional manager. During the interview, TEALS staff inquire about the teacher's educational background, experience, and reasons for participation. The TEALS Regional Manager reviews the model of the program and goal of teacher hand off, and confirms that the teacher wants to participate.

TEALS partner teachers have variable levels of background knowledge in CS. Many partner teachers have no prior CS experience. A few teachers studied CS in college (but have not taught it). Some fall in between these extremes. While the teachers come from many disciplines, Math and CTE (Career & Technical Education) are most common.

3.5.1 Teacher Profile 1: Ada

Ada has completed her 2nd year as a TEALS teacher for the Intro CS course. In 2015-16, she will continue teaching without TEALS support. Ada has 11 years of classroom experience, and taught social studies prior to TEALS. She says, "I feel pretty prepared to teach the course independently. I just need to ensure that I have all the resources we created this year in one place." She likes that TEALS has an online community for volunteers and teachers. "The online forums are helpful for communicating ideas. It all helps me feel that I am not alone in my course issues." Next year, Ada will continue teaching Intro CS independently, and begin a new AP CS class with a team of TEALS volunteers.

3.5.2 *Teacher Profile 2: Jason*

Jason has 7 years of experience teaching English and History. He worked with a team of 4 TEALS volunteers on an Intro CS class, and will continue teaching it on his own in 2015-16. "This year we created two sections of the intro class, which forced me to plan for teaching the later period independently. As a result, I have been able to take the lessons that the volunteers help me to teach, and execute them on my own each day." Jason appreciates the completeness of the TEALS model. He says, "TEALS has helped me to develop and understand a full curriculum, which most other PD does not. Additionally, TEALS has given me multiple thought-partners in terms of implementing ideas in the classroom, whereas most other PD gives you a toolkit and leaves you to try it on your own."

3.5.3 *Teacher Profile 3: Doug*

Doug is a veteran teacher with 35 years of experience in math. After 2 years working with TEALS, Doug will teach AP CS independently in the fall of 2015. "The TEALS [PD] experience ranks among the top 3 or 4 in my career. First, it provides in-the-classroom support. This also encourages conversations and collaboration around planning the instruction and making sense of what the students are producing. My experience was that the volunteers came into the first year with a respect for what I knew about teaching, organizing a classroom, and meeting the needs of students, while they brought content expertise that I lacked. This mutual respect was key to making my initial experience a positive one. I was actually quite skeptical going into the first version of the partnership. Another aspect of the TEALS experience is the long time frame that supported my own learning as a teacher, and the gradual handing over of instructional responsibility to me... It's also been great to have the experience of professional practitioners, who not only bring content expertise to the classroom discussion but also offer insights into how things actually work, patterns of practice in the real world. "

4. INITIAL EVALUATION OF OUTCOMES

TEALS' primary success metric is course "hand offs," where the partner teacher takes over primary instruction of the course. TEALS aims to hand-off courses within 2 years of partnership.

In spring, TEALS regional managers hold a partnership review meeting with each school. The meeting must include the school principal, the partner teacher, and any other administrators involved in the program. During these meetings the group discusses the state of the course, and how students are doing. The teacher outlines their level of participation in the course, and how they feel they are progressing towards hand off, answering the key question: "Would you be comfortable doing this by yourself?" Regional managers report that teachers respond candidly, since overstating their comfort level might result in having to teach without assistance when they aren't ready.

In 2014-2015, TEALS classified each of the 154 partner classrooms with one of these outcomes:

- *Continue as Alumni/TA-Only*: The classroom teacher was already teaching with TA-only support and will continue doing so.
- *Continue Towards Hand Off*: The TEALS partnership will continue with the goal of handing off the course after the following year.
- *Hand Off: Start Additional Course*: The teacher will take over the course, and the school will start a new TEALS partnership with an additional curriculum.
- *Hand Off Course, Alumni Mode*: The partner teacher will take over primary instruction of the course, but continue to seek TEALS volunteers as TA's only.
- *Hand Off Course, No Further Support*: The partner teacher will take over primary instruction of the course, with no additional volunteer support.
- *Withdraw*: The classroom teacher will not teach the CS course in the following year, and TEALS will not return to the school.
- *Replace Teacher*: The classroom teacher leaves the program, but TEALS will continue to engage with the school.

Table 2 shows a summary of the outcomes of TEALS classrooms from the 2014-15 school year. The AP CS column shows the outcomes from classrooms where the AP CS A course was taught. Overall, 80% of the classrooms are progressing through the expected TEALS model, moving either towards hand off, or engaging in a hand off that leaves the course being offered in the school. TEALS successfully executed hand offs in 58 classrooms (37.9%).

Outcome	1st Yr	2nd Yr	>2 Yrs	AP CS	All
Continue To Hand Off	32	3	2	16	37
Continue as Alumni/TA	7	9	12	9	28
Hand Off: Alumni	8	9	12	22	29
Hand Off: Start Additional	7	3	1	2	11
Hand Off: No Further	14	2	2	6	18
Withdraw	7	2	0	5	11
Replace Teacher	12	2	5	11	19
Totals	87	30	34	71	153

Table 2: TEALS Class Outcomes from 2014-15

4.1 TEALS Student AP CS A Performance

In 2014-2015, 72 TEALS classrooms (47%) taught the AP CS A course. TEALS collects the aggregated exam scores of students who take the AP Computer Science exam in each of its partner schools. These scores provide a benchmark to compare student outcomes in TEALS classrooms with those in other computer science classrooms. The aggregated AP test data is a limited proxy for assessing the quality of instruction in TEALS classrooms.

At the time of writing, TEALS was still collecting 2014-2015 AP exam data from its partners. In the 2013-2014 school year, TEALS had 1,281 students enrolled in AP classes at the beginning of the school year. With 2 out of 40 schools not reporting their data, 671 TEALS students took the AP CS exam (See Table 3). The exam is scored out of 5 points, with a 5 being the best possible score. TEALS students averaged 3.28 points, compared to the national AP average of 2.96. Only 19.37% of TEALS students received the lowest score of 1, compared to 31.1% of all AP CS test takers.

Student Scores	TEALS	TEALS %	National	National %
1	130	19.37	12216	31.1
2	65	9.69	3016	7.68
3	130	19.37	6588	16.77
4	179	26.68	9091	23.15
5	167	24.89	8367	21.3
# students	671		39278	
Mean Score	3.28		2.96	
% of scores 3 or higher		70.94		61.22

Table 3: TEALS & National 2013-14 AP Scores

4.2 Evaluation of TEALS Instruction

During the 2013-14 school year, TEALS engaged WestEd, an educational research organization, to perform a qualitative study of TEALS instructional classroom practices. For the study, 8 experienced CS teachers were recruited to serve as observers of 14 TEALS teams in 4 locations. The observers worked with teams in Massachusetts (3), Southern California (3), New York (3), and Northern California (5). Over the course of 6 months observers visited each class 4 times and were asked to complete a post-observation evaluation provided by WestEd. The 8 mentors each completed at least one observation report, yielding a total of 20 reports collected by WestEd.

The post-observation form contained questions from 5 domains (shown in Table 4) and included areas for observers to record challenges, successes and general comments. Table 4 shows the questions provided to observers to report findings. For each question, observers could mark observed, did not observe, or unsure. It is important to note that TEALS does not expect instructors to exhibit all of the described practices in every class session.

The observation form also included open-ended questions for the observers to comment on successes and challenges, and provide any other relevant feedback. Additionally, the WestEd team held a one-hour phone conference to debrief the mentors about logistics, variation in instructional styles and the team dynamic, and challenges. Overall, the observers felt that four observations were not enough to fully represent the classroom dynamic. In the final report submitted by WestEd, the following summary elements were highlighted for observers' comments related to instruction and learning: (1)Most volunteer teams seemed to work well together; (2)There was variation across teams in the roles each volunteer played in the classroom; (3)While instructional style varied, the lesson format was somewhat consistent across sites (i.e., start with lecture then do a problem); (4)Some high school teachers were present and involved in the class, others were not engaged or absent; (5)Observers had difficulty assessing how student learning was measured over time; (6)Information provided to volunteers during summer PD may have been useful, but not easily recalled.

Data from the WestEd observations, as well as from TEALS staff observations, and from volunteer and teacher feedback were used to make significant adjustments to the program for 2014-2015. These changes included: emphasizing teacher participation in materials for schools, creation of teacher self-evaluation tools, expansion of training to multiple geographic regions, a greater emphasis on formative assessment and active learning, and the creation of online training content to present teaching techniques that volunteers can access throughout the year. The program staff intends to continue updating and adjusting the program model each year based on new data.

5. FUTURE GROWTH AND CHALLENGES

The TEALS program began 6 years ago with 4 partner schools in the Seattle area. In the 2015-2016 school year, the program serves 161 partner schools across the US. The growth of the program has been limited by two primary factors: capacity of program staff to manage school partnerships and support volunteers, and number of volunteers available near partner schools. In future years, TEALS plans to continue growing through: hiring more program staff, expanding current geographic regions; forming partnerships in new geographic regions with a known supply of prospective volunteers; and serving schools in other areas through remote instruction with teleconferencing.

For the first time, TEALS has a large cohort of "graduating" partner teachers. During the 2015-2016 school year, TEALS began enlisting former partner teachers to help train volunteers over the summer and mentor new teaching teams. Use of paid master teachers can help facilitate the growth and expansion of the TEALS program by obviating the need for full-time TEALS staff present in every geographic location.

6. CONCLUSIONS

In this experience report we have presented the TEALS model of in-service teacher professional development. TEALS provides deep PD by connecting educators to industry professionals, thereby establishing ongoing connections for teachers and students with the technology industry. The TEALS model works with teachers during their school day, and provides an estimated 300+ hours of professional development through the program (over 2 years). Both teachers and volunteers in the program report successes and overall satisfaction with the process, and data from the AP CS A exam indicates some level of success in student outcomes.

The TEALS program welcomes additional collaborations for recruitment of volunteers from university alumni networks, or research partnerships with faculty to further study the volunteer or teacher participants in the TEALS program.

7. ACKNOWLEDGMENTS

The TEALS program is made possible by the nearly 1,000 volunteers who have given their time, energy and passion to support the growth of high school CS programs, the classroom teachers who have accepted the challenge of a new subject area, and the school and district administrators who have encouraged and enabled these partnerships. The authors would also like to thank WestEd for the contribution of their observational data on the TEALS program.

8. REFERENCES

[1] Ashton, P. Teacher efficacy: A motivational paradigm for effective teacher education. *Journal of teacher education 35*, 5 (1984), 28–32.

Question	Domain	Obs.	Not Obs.	Unsure
Provides clear learning goals	High Expectations	14	3	3
Builds positive rapport with students	High Expectations	14	3	3
Celebrates student successes	High Expectations	9	6	5
Helps students interact with new knowledge	DETP: Content	15	2	3
Organizes for students to practice and deepen knowledge	DETP: Content	14	2	4
Asks questions (and provides support to) struggling students	DETP: Content	16	4	0
Monitors student engagement and reengages when necessary	DETP: Engagement	10	6	4
Provides appropriate scaffolding and pacing	DETP: Engagement	7	4	9
Uses knowledge about student background, skills, & interests	DETP: Engagement	6	11	3
Students have some choice in task completion	DETP: Engagement	8	9	3
Students serve as resources for one another	DETP: Engagement	14	5	1
Establishes, practices, and reinforces standards of conduct	Learning Environment	9	10	1
Responds to student behaviors effectively	Learning Environment	12	7	1
Tracks student progress	Data	9	8	3
Adapts Instruction Based on Student Data	Data	7	10	3
Modifies instruction and planning to meet students' needs	Data	6	8	6
Domains: Centering Instruction on High Expectations, Effective Teaching Practices: Content, Effective Teaching Practices: Engagement, Fostering and Managing a Safe, Positive Learning Environment, and Uses Student Data in Instruction and Planning.				

Table 4: WestEd/TEALS Observation Protocol

[2] Astrachan, O., Cuny, J., Stephenson, C., and Wilson, C. The cs10k project: mobilizing the community to transform high school computing. In *Proceedings of the 42nd ACM technical symposium on Computer science education* (2011), ACM, pp. 85–86.

[3] Berges, M., Hubwieser, P., Magenheim, J., Bender, E., Bröker, K., Margaritis-Kopecki, M., Neugebauer, J., Schaper, N., Schubert, S., and Ohrndorf, L. Developing a competency model for teaching computer science in schools. In *Proceedings of the 18th ACM conference on Innovation and technology in computer science education* (2013), ACM, pp. 327–327.

[4] Cochran, K. F., et al. Pedagogical content knowledge: A tentative model for teacher preparation.

[5] Garcia, D. D., Harvey, B., Barnes, T., Titterton, N., Armendariz, D., Segars, L., Lemon, E., Morris, S., and Paley, J. Ap cs principles and the beauty and joy of computing curriculum. In *Proceeding of the 44th ACM technical symposium on Computer science education* (2013), ACM, pp. 761–761.

[6] Goode, J. If you build teachers, will students come? the role of teachers in broadening computer science learning for urban youth. *Journal of Educational Computing Research 36*, 1 (2007), 65–88.

[7] Goode, J., and Margolis, J. Exploring computer science: A case study of school reform. *ACM Transactions on Computing Education (TOCE) 11*, 2 (2011), 12.

[8] Guskey, T. R., and Huberman, M. *Professional development in education: New paradigms and practices.* ERIC, 1995.

[9] Yoon, K. S., Duncan, T., Lee, S. W.-Y., Scarloss, B., and Shapley, K. L. Reviewing the evidence on how teacher professional development affects student achievement. issues & answers. rel 2007-no. 033. *Regional Educational Laboratory Southwest (NJ1)* (2007).

Implementation and Outcomes of a Three-Pronged Approach to Professional Development for CS Principles

Chrystalla Mouza, Lori Pollock, Kathleen Pusecker, Kevin Guidry, Ching-Yi Yeh, James Atlas, Terry Harvey
University of Delaware
Newark, DE 19716
{cmouza, pollock, klp, krguidry, chingyiy, jatlas, tharvey} @ udel.edu

ABSTRACT

One of the greatest challenges in broadening participation in computer science is teacher preparation, as few middle and high school teachers have a formal background in computing. Further, without a credentialing program, there are limited ways to learn content and pedagogical strategies for effective computer science instruction. As a result, professional development is key to successful reform in the teaching of computer science. In this paper, we describe our three-pronged approach to the design of a professional development model for middle and high school teachers interested in implementing the Computer Science Principles (CSP) curriculum in their classrooms or infusing CSP modules into STEM curricula. We describe our model focusing on content, pedagogical strategies and follow-up classroom support during the academic year. We subsequently report on participating teacher outcomes, in terms of self-rated understandings, attitudes and implementation practices. We share lessons learned and offer recommendations for professional development designers.

Keywords

CS education; computational thinking; K12; CS principles

1. INTRODUCTION

Teachers play a key role in how curricula are presented to students, and effective professional development (PD) is key to helping teachers build capacity to use curricula, such as the Computer Science Principles (CSP) curriculum [1, 8]. Specifically, when teachers receive approximately 49 hours of research-based PD spread over 6-12 months, they can increase student achievement by as much as 21 percentile points [14]. On the other hand, one-shot or short PD experiences lasting less than 14 hours show no statistically significant effect on student learning [7].

While sustained duration is essential, the design features of PD are also critical. Specifically, effective PD is characterized by five elements: (a) helps teachers acquire deeper knowledge of content and how to teach it, (b) is collaborative, (c) provides opportunities for active learning, (d) establishes connections between curriculum and assessment, and (e) includes follow-up support [7, 8]. These elements are particularly important in STEM (Science-Technology-Engineering-Mathematics) fields where teachers need opportunities to deepen their content knowledge as well as pedagogical techniques for their content area. One such field is Computer Science (CS), where the Landscape study found that 75% of the PD providers reported working with participants who were new to CS [5].

The National Science Foundation CS 10K initiative is a systemic effort to transform computing education across the academic pipeline, increase the number of students from under-represented groups studying CS, and prepare 10,000 teachers in 10,000 high schools teaching a new curriculum by 2015 focusing on CSP. The CSP curriculum represents a new approach to CS teaching that breaks down the meaning of computational thinking based on big ideas in computing. Furthermore, the CSP curriculum moves beyond an approach centered on programming and emphasizes applications of computing in real world settings, creativity, and relevance to student needs [6]. Although CS 10K and the CSP curriculum are geared toward high school students, previous work demonstrates the need for changes across the entire computing education pipeline as it is during middle school that students make up their minds about whether CS is boring or worth exploring [3]. As a result, it is important to include middle schools in any pipeline effort since changing only one aspect of the pipeline will not correct the problem [3].

In this paper, we describe a three-pronged approach to the design of a PD model for middle and high school teachers interested in implementing the CSP curriculum in their classrooms or infusing CSP modules into STEM curricula. The PD model was developed by Partner4CS, an NSF CS10K project. We describe the model focusing on content, pedagogical strategies and follow-up classroom support. We subsequently report on participating teacher outcomes, in terms of self-rated understandings, attitudes and implementation practices. We share lessons learned and offer recommendations for PD designers.

2. PD DESIGN

The Partner4CS PD model, launched in the summer of 2012 in Delaware, follows a three-pronged approach that includes: (a) a summer institute, structured around two tracks; (b) follow-up classroom-based support; and (c) online support. The first summer institute track, called *CSP Track,* focuses on high school teachers who are committed to integrating the full CSP curriculum in their classroom (see Fig. 1 for PD schedule). The second track, called *Module Track*, focuses on middle and high school teachers who are interested in infusing CSP modules into existing STEM curricula (see Fig. 2).

SIGCSE '16, March 02-05, 2016, Memphis, TN, USA
 ISBN 978-1-4503-3685-7/16/03…$15.00
DOI: http://dx.doi.org/10.1145/2839509.2844585

2.1. Week-Long Summer Institute

While our PD approach has always recognized that not all participants will implement a full CS curriculum in their classrooms, initially during our week-long summer institute, we separated teachers into a high school and middle school track. The high school track focused specifically on high school teachers with a STEM background who expressed interest in teaching CS. Our expectation was that high school teachers would eventually be implementing the full CSP curriculum in their classrooms once they felt comfortable with CS content and pedagogy. In contrast, we expected middle school teachers to implement CS modules in their respective STEM curricula, but not necessarily implement a full CS curriculum. Therefore, the emphasis was on the integration of CS across STEM curricula. During the first year of our PD design, however, we realized that not all high school teachers had the capacity, flexibility or administrative support within their schools to implement the full CSP curriculum. In fact, some high school teachers were only interested in infusing CSP modules into existing STEM curricula including mathematics, engineering, physics, business etc. As a result, in years 2 and 3, we revised the two tracks to be *CSP Track* and *Module Track*. Thus, rather than separating teachers depending on grade level taught (i.e., high school or middle school), we placed them in tracks based on whether they intended to teach the entire CSP curriculum or integrate CSP modules into existing courses.

In our model, we support the notion that PD which helps infuse CS content into existing STEM curricula has the potential to broaden participation in computing beyond the students who would take a full CS course. Current policy initiatives support this view and emphasize the need to help *all* students acquire a deeper understanding of computing in the world around us, solve real world problems, and understand human behavior by drawing on CS concepts [10, 12].

In terms of design, both tracks include explicit attention to CS content, pedagogical strategies for teaching CS, and strategies for broadening participation in computing. Related to content, the focus is on materials aligned with CSP, specifically the seven key ideas of: (a) creativity, (b) abstraction, (c) data, (d) algorithms, (e) programming, (f) Internet, and (g) impact. Related to pedagogical strategies, teachers learn by participating in pair programming, open-ended projects allowing for creativity, a variety of kinesthetic activities such as CS unplugged, pacing issues, and sustained reflection. The activities are led in a supportive and collaborative environment, which promotes active learning by engaging teachers in experiencing the CSP curriculum as learners. Additionally, *Module Track* participants engage in activities that help them draw connections between the CSP curriculum, the Common Core State Standards for Mathematics, and the Next Generation Science Standards. Both tracks focus on activities that can be directly used or adapted for K-12 classrooms. Specifically for the *Module Track*, discussions about integration and adaptation into a variety of STEM courses occur with each session.

Finally, shared sessions among the two tracks focus on impacts of CS on society, promising practices to recruit and retain diversity in CS, and activities to encourage networking among participants such as *tales from the field* (i.e., implementation stories) presented by teacher leaders.

CSP Track	Monday	Tuesday	Wednesday	Thursday	Friday
9-9:30	Introductions, Purpose, Overview	Pair programming and Scratch projects	Tales from the field - teacher stories	AP Curriculum and performance tasks	CSP: Creativity and projects
9:30-10:15	CSP: Algorithms: Intro/Model lesson	CSP: Programming/impact: Scratch and creating recruiting devices	CSP: Hardware, binary data	CSP: Internet: CS unplugged (Routing)	CSP: Creativity and projects
10:30-12	Hour of code	CSP: Programming/impact: scratch and creating recruiting devices	CSP: Abstraction and data structures	CSP: Advanced programming and web applications	Evaluation surveys, resources, and going forward
12:45-1:15	CSP: Programming: CS Unplugged Harold the robot	CSP: Algorithms: CS unplugged (Battleship)	CSP: Data: CS unplugged (database)	Tales from the field: CSP implementation	
1:15-2:15	CSP: Programming - Directed Scratch lesson with levels	CSP: Algorithms - CS unplugged (Muddy city, ice cream van)	CSP: Generating questions from visualizations	CSP: Impact: Blown to bits discussions and presentations	
2:30-3:30	More directed Scratch lesson	CSP: Impact	CSP: Data: working with large tables	Curriculum, pacing, adaptation, planning	
3:30-4	Reflection	Reflection	Reflection	Reflection	
Homework	*Blown to bits Ch 1*	*outreach activity*			

Figure 1. Schedule for *CSP Track* (2014)

Note: Summer 2014 PD activities utilized Scratch while Summer 2015 activities utilized App Inventor

Module Track	Monday	Tuesday	Wednesday	Thursday	Friday
9-9:30	Introductions, Purpose, Overview	Pair Programming Scratch Project	Tales from the field: teacher stories	Recruiting admin, students, parents	CSP Integration planning
9:30-10:15	CSP: Algorithms: Intro/Model lesson	Scratch Project Deveopment	DSP: Data : Representation, structures, manipulation	CSP: Internet (Routing activity)	CSP Integration sharing and networking
10:30-12	Hour of code	Lesson plan review/mapping to core standards	CSP: Data - lesson activities	Lesson plan review and mapping to core standards	Evaluation surveys, resources, and going forward
12:45-1:15	CSP: Programming: CS Unplugged Harold the robot	CSP: Algorithms: CS unplugged. Battleship	CSP: Data - CS Unplugged (database)	CSP: Impact: Blown to bits jigsaw discussion	
1:15-2:15	CSP: Programming - Directed Scratch lesson with levels	Creating recruiting devices: Interactive Scratch projects	CSP: Data - generating questions from visualizations	CSP: Impact: Blown to bits presentations	
2:30-3:30	More directed Scratch lesson	CSP: Creativity: assessing programs	CSP: Abstraction, data, models	CSP: Internet: CS unplugged (data compression)	
3:30-4	Reflection	Reflection	Reflection	Reflection	
Homework	*Blown to bits Ch 1*	*Outreach activity*			

Figure 2. Module Track (2014)

2.2. Follow-up Classroom Support

While our summer PD institutes provide opportunities for the development of knowledge, skills, and pedagogy in teaching computing, teachers need ongoing support throughout the academic year. To accomplish this goal, we established a *Field Experience* university service-learning course, where Undergraduates directly support teachers in their classrooms. The course, which is open to students who have completed at least one prior CS course, fulfills requirements for a CS major, minor and discovery learning [4]. It has been offered continuously since the spring 2013 and a permanent course number has been established.

The course builds upon earlier efforts to broaden participation in computing such as those of the STARS alliance project [13]. It combines college classroom meetings with visits in middle or high school classrooms where undergraduate participants co-plan and co-teach computing lessons with a practicing teacher. The 75-minute on-campus class time is devoted to identifying and implementing CS teaching resources targeted toward CS principles, modeling classroom lessons with CS unplugged and other resources, discussing teaching pedagogy, preparing and analyzing lesson plans, and reflecting on the field experiences and teacher partnering experiences.

The field experiences take place in local middle and high schools where teachers are working on integrating CS principles into their courses and after-school programs. Undergraduate participants in the course meet with teachers to discuss their role and provide ongoing support directly in teachers' classrooms. Throughout the duration of the project, Undergraduates work collaboratively with teachers to adapt lessons and activities from available resources, lead classroom sessions, and serve as role models for students. They also help plan and lead after-school computing programs where they engage students in programming activities.

2.3. Online Support

We recognize that teachers implementing the full CSP curriculum need additional support. As a result, in Year 3, our team has established a pilot collaboration with the TeachIT-CSP project (https://cs10kcommunity.org/project/1867), which aims to scale the Mobile CSP PD by adapting the curriculum developed by Trinity College and offering it to teachers via a 6-week summer online course [9]. As a result, those teachers who need additional support have the opportunity to enroll in the online course, which also provides ongoing online mentoring during the school year. Research indicates that mentoring is key to improving both teaching practice and student achievement, particularly when the mentors are from the same teaching area [2].

3. METHODS

3.1. Research Question

In this paper, we focus on the following research questions.

1. How does participation in the summer institute influence teachers' knowledge of content and pedagogy towards teaching CS?
2. How do participating teachers implement CS content and pedagogy in their classrooms after their participation in the summer institute?
3. What specific PD activities are valued by participants?

3.2. Data Collection

Data were collected from multiple sources, including teacher surveys, daily reflections during the summer institutes, and weekly reflections by Undergraduates enrolled in the field experience course.

A pre/post survey was administered to all participants during each summer institute. The survey uses a 5-point Likert-scale response format that ranges from *1 (strongly disagree) to 5 (strongly agree)* to examine teachers' knowledge related to: (a) the seven big ideas of computing (creativity, abstraction, data, algorithms, programming, Internet, impacts of computing); (b) career opportunities related to CS in their courses; and (c) generating student enthusiasm about CS related occupations. The survey also assesses teachers' confidence and ability to utilize a range of pedagogical strategies for teaching CS using a 4-point Likert-scale format that ranges from *1 (not well prepared at all) to 4 (well-prepared)*. In addition to Likert-scale items, the survey includes three open-ended questions that ask teachers to explain issues around creativity and computational thinking as well as provide examples of how technology can be used to solve real- world problems. Finally, the survey asks teachers to share their perspective on different PD activities they participated in the summer institute.

Besides the survey, all participants completed daily reflections during the summer institute. All reflections were structured around the same four prompts to facilitate consistent responses:

(a) What (if any) CS skills did you learn from today's session? (b) What (if any) pedagogical strategies for teaching CS did you learn from today's sessions? (c) What questions (if any) do you still have about today's session? and (d) What activities (if any) do you plan to try in your classroom?

Classroom implementation data were collected through weekly reflections completed by CS Undergraduates in the field experience course. Each weekly reflective entry was structured around three prompts: (a) field activities enacted by each participant during the week, (b) identified successes and failures, and (c) recommended steps for future action. Throughout the duration of the project, we have collected approximately 350 undergraduate reflections. The length of each entry varies, with an average of 400 words per entry.

Finally, a follow-up implementation survey was administered to Year 1 and Year 2 summer institute participants that provided information on their CS implementation during the year following their participation in PD. The implementation survey asked teachers to indicate whether they implemented any of the CS principles in the year following their participation in the summer institute, the manner in which they implemented CS, and the number and type of students they reached.

3.3. Participants

Participants for each summer institute are shown on Table 1.

Table 1. PD Participants

	Year 1	**Year 2**	**Year 3**
CSP	14	19	14
Module Track	24	16	8

4. RESULTS

4.1. Teacher Self-Assessed Content Knowledge

Survey responses were analyzed using both quantitative and qualitative methodologies. Quantitative analyses included descriptive statistics and t-tests. Likert-scale items were initially scored and exported into Excel and the Statistical Package for the Social Sciences (SPSS) where means and standard deviations were calculated. To test for the significance of the gain score (post measure-pre measure), a repeated measures t-test was conducted. Results from this analysis are shown on Table 2.

Open-ended responses were analyzed qualitative using inductive approaches. This approach, helped identify common themes that cut across participants' responses. Subsequently, teacher reflections from the summer institute were used to triangulate data. Qualitative analysis on two open-ended questions asking teachers to explain issues around creativity and computational thinking as well as provide examples of how technology can be used to solve real world problems demonstrated increased knowledge of CS principles. In the pre-survey, for instance, explaining what does it mean for students to use creativity to develop computational thinking sample responses included:

I think it means that students need to go beyond playing with technology; and *Students need to think outside the box.*

Similarly, responding to ways in which technology can be used to address real world problems, pre-survey responses included:

The Internet can be used to find new solutions; A GPS can help with navigation; and *Encryption can support secure e-banking.*

For both questions, teachers' responses were more nuanced, detailed and complex in their post-survey responses. A participant from Year 2, for instance, explained in the post-survey:

Computational thinking skills require students to develop and create their own artifacts. Most problems require that you look and analyze the issue from multiple perspectives, creating your own algorithms and original work.

Similarly, a participant from Year 3 responding on how technology can be used to solve real world problems wrote:

One way technology can be used to address real world problems is to collect data on traffic patterns. This data can be analyzed with the help of a computer to look for potential problems in traffic flow, determine where the most congestion occurs and at what times, to work on possible solutions for solving that problem.

4.2. Teacher CS Pedagogical Knowledge

In addition to learning new skills, participants learned a variety of pedagogical strategies for teaching CS modeled during the PD and became more confident in their ability to deliver a CS curriculum. Results from teachers' Likert-scale pre/post responses related to CS pedagogical knowledge are also shown on Table 2. Teacher reflections reinforced those findings. Specifically, when asked to report new CS pedagogical skills acquired during the summer institute, teachers indicated learning about CS unplugged activities, assessment strategies for programming projects, real life examples for introducing algorithms (e.g., following a recipe), designing project-based exercises, pair programming, and code documentation.

4.3. Implementation Outcomes

Data from Undergraduate reflections and data from a follow-up implementation survey indicated that participating teachers implemented a variety of CS modules in their classrooms reaching a broad population of students. Specifically, throughout the duration of the project, Undergraduates worked collaboratively with participating teachers to adapt lessons and activities from available resources (e.g., units on programming, HTML, and Human Computer Interaction), provide hands-on student assistance, and lead classroom sessions. They also helped plan and lead after-school computing programs where they engaged students in programming activities using Scratch, shown to help broaden participation in creating with computing [11]. Throughout the duration of the project, *42 Undergraduates* supported a total of *21 teachers* and approximately *500 students* (not all teachers requested follow-up classroom support).

To date the follow-up implementation survey was administered to teachers who participated in our 2013 and 2014 summer institutes. Of the 38 teachers who participated in the 2013 summer institute, a total of 17 teachers responded. There were 5 respondents who said that they were unable to implement any of the CS principles into their teaching citing lack of flexibility in their curriculum, technology materials, and course time. The remaining 12 teachers implemented CSP modules in high school mathematics, science, engineering as well as CS electives and CS AP courses. Middle school teachers also implemented CSP modules in mathematics, science, business and after-school programs.

Through these efforts, teachers reported teaching CS principles to a total of 217 unique students following their participation in the summer institute. Of these students, the teachers reported that approximately 48% were college bound, 7% vocational, and almost 15% special education. Responses to how did teaching CS principles in a non-CS course affect students' learning included: (a) added relevance to their learning and or their daily lives, (b) created deeper understanding of topics, (c) provided better ways to demonstrate their learning other than tests, and (d) students used and analyzed data and then drew conclusions.

In the spring of 2015, we followed up with teachers who participated in the 2014 summer institute. Of the 15 teachers who responded to the online survey, 14 indicated that they had used CS principles during the school year. Four of those respondents reported teaching a CSP course that lasted throughout the entire school year with nine indicating that they had integrated CSP modules into existing STEM courses. Five respondents also indicated that they were using CSP outside of the classroom such as in Science Olympiad, robotics clubs, and after-school programming clubs.

Table 2. Teacher Self-Assessed Knowledge: Three groups of participants' self-assessed knowledge in CS Principles, Teaching CS, and Career Related CS Opportunities in each year (2013-2015). (* indicates no significance in pre/post score)

	Year 1 (N=37)			Year 2 (N=34)			Year 3 (N=22)		
	Pre (Mean)	Post (Mean)	Sig. (2-tailed)	Pre (Mean)	Post (Mean)	Sig. (2-tailed)	Pre (Mean)	Post (Mean)	Sig. (2-tailed)
	Self-Assessed CS Principles Knowledge *(1 = strongly disagree and 5 = strongly agree)*								
Creativity	2.7	4.1	.001	3.4	4.4	.001	3.1	4.4	.001
Abstraction	2.3	3.8	.001	3.1	4.3	.001	2.6	4.2	.001
Data	2.7	3.9	.001	3.3	4.4	.001	3.0	4.2	.001
Algorithms	2.3	3.6	.001	2.7	4.4	.001	2.7	4.2	.001
Programming	2.3	3.7	.001	3.0	4.4	.001	2.7	4.3	.001
Internet	2.9	3.7	.006	3.7	4.3	.002	3.5	4.5	.001
Impacts	2.5	3.9	.001	3.4	4.5	.001	3.0	4.5	.001
	Self-Assessed Knowledge in Teaching CS *(1 = not well prepared at all and 4 = well prepared)*								
Plan Differentiated Instruction	2.4	2.9	0.013	2.6	3.1	0.007	2.5	3.2	0.004
Teach Computing to Students with Learning Disabilities	1.9	2.3	0.030	2.3	2.9	0.004	2.1	2.9	0.003
Teach Computing to Students with Physical Disabilities	1.7	2.0	*0.088	2.3	2.8	0.016	2.0	3.0	0.001
Teach Computing to ELA Learners	1.7	2.0	*0.067	2.1	2.9	0.001	2.1	3.0	0.003
Provide Enrichment Opportunities for Gifted Students	2.6	3.1	0.013	2.6	3.5	0.001	2.8	3.5	0.003
Encourage Student Internet in Computing	2.6	3.5	0.001	3.0	3.7	0.001	3.0	3.8	0.001
Teach Computing to Girls	2.5	3.1	0.007	3.0	3.6	0.002	3.0	3.8	0.001
Teach Computing to Students Ethnic Minorities	2.4	3.0	0.003	2.9	3.4	0.009	3.0	3.7	0.004
Teach Computing to Low SES Students	2.3	2.9	0.005	2.8	3.3	0.013	2.9	3.5	0.018
Teach Students the Relevance of Computing in Daily Life	2.4	3.4	0.001	2.9	3.5	0.001	2.8	3.6	0.001
	Self-Assessed Knowledge on Career Related CS Opportunities *(1 = strongly disagree and 5 = strongly agree)*								
Knowledge about CS career opportunities	3.1	4.3	0.001	3.6	4.4	0.001	4.0	4.4	*0.062
Confidence in Integrating CS Career Opportunities in Teaching	3.4	4.2	0.001	3.9	4.5	0.001	3.9	4.5	0.008
Confidence in Generating Student Enthusiasm about CS Occupations	4.2	4.3	*0.338	3.9	4.6	0.001	4.0	4.6	0.004

5. DISCUSSION

The three-pronged Partner4CS PD model is informed by evidence-based contributions to research on teacher preparation and PD, teaching and learning of CS, and broadening participation in computing. In turn, our continuous research and evaluation efforts add to the knowledge base by providing insights on PD elements valued by teachers and lessons learned for those involved in the design of PD for CS Principles.

5.1. PD Elements Valued by Teachers

Qualitative analysis of open-ended responses on the best aspects of our PD model, indicated that teachers valued the simultaneous focus on content and pedagogy, engaging with the materials as learners, and working alongside peers, teacher leaders, faculty and Undergraduates. Regarding content, a 2014 participant explained:

I liked how this PD took people on many technology levels (beginner to expert) and was able to teach to each of these different levels adequately.

From a pedagogical standpoint, participants truly enjoyed the CS unplugged activities modeled during the summer institutes and the opportunity to review lessons and activities they could adapt for their own classrooms. Another 2014 participant explained:

I liked how the course was taught through activities that we could immediately use in our classrooms and provided access to a variety of lesson plans we could choose from.

Finally, a number of participants commented on the value of hearing the experiences of teacher leaders and working with their colleagues, which helped them make connections between middle and high school curricula. One 2015 participant explained:

My school is planning on creating a CS pathway for students. We have 4 teachers here, one middle school, and 3 high school teachers. We plan on introducing CS in the middle school and then offering the CS AP courses. Before, I had no idea what my students stepped into after they left my middle school classroom.

5.2. Lessons and Recommendations

Our work and findings to date generated valuable lessons that inform others. Regarding our PD efforts, we have identified the following valuable components of PD for CS teaching:

- Providing simultaneous emphasis on content and pedagogy through a focus on CS curricula and lesson/unit design that helps teachers incorporate new learning into their practice.
- Providing active learning strategies, hands-on learning, and opportunities for teachers to experience CS activities as learners in a supportive and collaborative environment.
- Modeling the lessons that teachers are expected to use in their classroom and providing ample time for reflection on how they would customize those lessons for their own students.
- Grouping teachers from the same disciplines together while working with inquiry activities and discussing the integration of problem-based learning in their curricula.
- Recruiting teacher leaders who generate authentic discussions on their own integration of the PD lessons into their respective classrooms at different levels (i.e., tales from the field).
- Helping teachers draw connections between CS principles and core curricular standards they are expected to cover.
- Providing on-going support as teachers identify areas in their curriculum that work synergistically with CS curricula, look for resources, and implement those modules in their classroom.
- Coordinating our PD efforts with school and district priorities to ensure coherence and improved implementation outcomes.

6. ACKNOWLEDGMENTS

This work is supported by a grant from the National Science foundation (Award # 1240905). All opinions are the authors and do not necessarily represent those of the funding agency.

7. REFERENCES

[1] Barab, S. & Luehmann, A. 2003. Building sustainable science curriculum: Acknowledging and accommodating local adaptation. *Science Education, 87*(4): 454-467.

[2] Beltman, S., Mansfield, C.F., & Price, A. 2011. Thriving not just surviving: A review of research on teacher resilience. *Educational Research Review, 6*(3): 185-207.

[3] Bruckman, A., Biggers, M., Ericson, B., McKlin, T., Dimond, J., DiSalvo, B., Hewner, M, Ni, L., & Yardi, S. 2008. Georgia computes: Improving the entire computing education pipeline. In *Proceedings of the 40th ACM technical symposium on computer science education* (SIGCSE), 2009.

[4] Burns, R., Harvey, T., & Pollock, L. 2012. An experience report on cross-semester student critique and action in an integrated software engineering, service learning course. In *First International Workshop on Software Engineering Education based on Real-World Experiences (EduRex).*

[5] Century, J., Lach, M., King, H., Rand, S., Heppner, C., Franke, B., & Westrick, J. 2013. *Building an operating system for computer science*. Chicago, IL: CEMSE, University of Chicago with UEI, University of Chicago. Retrieved 2015, from http://outlier.uchicago.edu/computerscience/OS4CS/

[6] Cuny, J. 2012. Transforming high school computing: A call to action. *ACM Inroads*, 3(2): 32-36.

[7] Darling-Hammond, L., Wei, R.C., Andree, R., Richardson, N., and Orphanos, S. 2009. *Professional learning in the learning profession: A status report on teacher development in the United States and abroad.* Online: https://edpolicy.stanford.edu/sites/default/files/publications/professional-learning-learning-profession-status-report-teacher-development-us-and-abroad.pdf

[8] Desimone, L. 2009. Improving impact studies of teachers' professional development: Toward better conceptualizations and measures. *Educational Researcher, 38*(3): 181-199.

[9] Morelli, R., Uche, C., Lake, P., & Baldwin, L. 2015. Analyzing year one of a CS Principles PD project. In *Proceedings of the 46th ACM Technical Symposium on Computer Science Education* (SIGCSE '15). ACM, New York, NY, USA: 368-373.

[10] PCAST. 2010. *Prepare and inspire: K-12 education in science, technology, engineering, and mathematics (STEM) for America's future*. Washington, D.C. Retrieved from http://www.whitehouse.gov/sites/default/files/microsites/ostp/pcast-stemedreport.pdf.

[11] Resnick, M., Maloney, J., Monroy-Hernandez, A., Rusk, N., Eastmond, E., Brennan, B., Millner, A., Rosenbaum, R., Silver, J., Silvernman, B., & Kafai, Y. 2009. Scratch: programming for all. *Communications of the ACM, 52*(11).

[12] Royal Society of Engineering. Shut down or restart: *The way forward for computing in UK schools*. 2012. Retrieved from http://royalsociety.org/education/policy/computing-in-schools/report/.

[13] STARS. 201. STARS Alliance. http://www.starsalliance.org

[14] Yoon, K.S., Duncan, T, Lee, L., Scarloss, B., & Shapley, K. 2007. Reviewing the evidence on how teacher professional development affects student achievement. *Issues & Answers Report*, REL 2007–No. 033. Washington, DC.

Deploying Exploring Computer Science Statewide

Helen H. Hu
Westminster College
Salt Lake City, UT 84105
hhu@westminstercollege.edu

Cecily Heiner
Southern Utah University
Cedar City, UT 84720
cecilyheiner@suu.edu

Jay McCarthy
University of Massachusetts Lowell
Lowell, MA 01854
jay.mccarthy@gmail.com

ABSTRACT

Exploring Computer Science (ECS) is a high school introductory computer science class designed to increase student interest in CS. Utah is the first state to offer ECS statewide and use it to meet a high school graduation requirement. Over the past four years, 150 teachers have been trained as Utah ECS teachers and over 10,000 Utah students have taken the class. The Utah initiative is unique because it is the first to deploy ECS in a non-urban environment and with a modified half-year curriculum that includes no additional equipment costs. This paper discusses how the Utah deployment was organized, reports its results and unique difficulties, and offers lessons for deployments with similar characteristics: statewide, rural, and limited resources.

1. INTRODUCTION

Through the Utah Exploring Computer Science (ECS) Initiative, Utah became the first state to offer ECS statewide, adopting a proven curriculum and professional development (PD) model. The original ECS curriculum is based on six units, whereas the Utah initiative pared the curriculum down to three units to create a half-year version of ECS. This modification streamlined adoption because existing Utah graduation requirements include only a half-year of computing.

Over the past four years, 150 Utah teachers have participated in the ECS PD workshops, more than tripling the number of CS teachers in Utah. These teachers prepared to teach ECS, developed their inquiry-based teaching strategies, questioned equity in high school computer science classes, and strengthened the high school CS teacher community. Since 2012, over 10,000 Utah students took ECS in over 100 public and private schools, including urban schools, rural schools, in-custody schools, online schools, non-traditional schools, and schools on Native American reservations. In 2015-16, the Utah ECS Initiative encompasses teachers in 27 of the 41 Utah school districts, including all of the 12 largest Utah school districts. These 27 districts teach 83% of all Utah students enrolled in public schools. Many of the districts that are not teaching ECS are tiny, *e.g.* a single secondary school serving approximately 100 rural students grades 7-12 simply lacks the students and resources for a new course.

SIGCSE '16, March 2-5, 2016, Memphis, TN, USA.

ACM 978-1-4503-3685-7/16/03...$15.00
DOI: http://dx.doi.org/10.1145/2839509.2844622

While ECS has been implemented in urban school districts prior to the Utah ECS Initiative, rolling out ECS statewide in Utah introduced several challenges not experienced elsewhere. Although Utah has some large urban high schools with racially diverse student populations, many Utah schools are predominantly white. The majority of the Utah teachers are white and from rural or suburban areas. The ECS PD curriculum is as much about culture as it is about CS; this created a very different environment for the ECS PD workshops than occurs elsewhere. For instance, when external PD facilitators spoke about a racial equity gap in high school, it was less effective for the local teacher population; but when we focused on a local message about the gender gap in CS, our teachers were more receptive to the equitable teaching practices that will benefit all minority groups in their classrooms. Section 6 develops these lessons for adaptation by others.

2. PRIOR WORK

The origins of ECS are detailed in [4]. In 2008-2009, seven schools in Los Angeles Unified School District (LAUSD) implemented the first ECS curriculum, which was organized around six modular curriculum units and three pillars: core computer science concepts, inquiry, and equity. The original professional development model lasts two years, starting with a five-day summer workshop, followed by four Saturday sessions during the school-year and ending with a five-day summer workshop. The curriculum aims for a "low floor and high ceiling" so any student can succeed and learn something valuable, and students that discover a passion can go much deeper and explore more computer science. ECS integrates a variety of introductory CS approaches, including CS Unplugged and Scratch [1, 6].

The success of ECS in LAUSD spurred its adoption in other areas, beginning with Santa Clara County in 2010 [5] and Chicago Public Schools in 2011[11]. Initially most of these projects were funded by the National Science Foundation, but Code.org has partnered with over 70 school districts, including all seven of the largest school districts in the country to dramatically scale-up ECS adoption [10]. These projects and partnerships have involved largely urban areas with high populations of minorities traditionally underrepresented in computer science. Many have shared their valuable lessons learned in implementing the course, including how equity is central to the ECS program and that ECS professional development is a continual learning process [7, 8]. Project leaders emphasized the importance of partnerships for scalability and sustainability, of engaging and supporting teachers with quality professional development and a learning community, and of aligning ECS into existing district priorities [8]. They also noted the need to look beyond enrollment numbers and to measure whether all students were being engaged and were learning computational thinking [7]. While many of these lessons are applicable to any educational setting, they do not address the specific challenges of deploying ECS statewide for students in all settings, including urban, suburban, and especially rural schools.

3. DEPLOYING ECS STATEWIDE

Utah schools have adopted ECS quickly in part because ECS was modified to solve a widely-recognized Utah problem and to fit within the existing Utah education structure. During Utah Computer Science Teachers Association (CSTA) chapter meetings, high school teachers identified the lack of CS course options for ninth and tenth graders. They also shared general dissatisfaction by parents, students, and guidance counselors with an existing computer literacy course that was required for high school graduation. Adopting a pre-existing curriculum, the Utah ECS Initiative ran its first ECS PD in 2012 on Utah State Office of Education funds, preparing two teachers to pilot ECS in 2012-13, only one year after ECS was first discussed in a Utah CSTA chapter meeting. The National Science Foundation provided the funds to roll-out the program statewide, and state-level champions at the Utah State Office of Education and the State Board of Education created a permanent ECS course and a new ECS endorsement for 2013-14.

Getting ECS approved as a permanent option for high school graduation (as an alternative to the computer literacy course) proved more of a marketing and political project, than a technical or educational one. One author became a regular participant in the local tech industry group's public policy meetings. This industry group's experience with the State School Board and the legislature were invaluable in getting ECS accepted as a high school graduation requirement and including ECS teachers in a salary supplement program. The week before the school board vote, leaders from the tech industry flooded School Board members with messages supporting the importance of computer science education, and a few prominent leaders spoke passionately for the issue at the meeting.

Key to making ECS a successful course was staying vigilant about any state legislation, state and district policy, and implementation changes that would affect ECS. For example, the State Office of Education created a task force in 2013 to consider removing the half-year computer literacy requirement for high school graduation. This task force became an opportunity to have ECS officially added to the graduation requirement. At another point, a large school district was requiring its students to take the original computer literacy course despite having completed ECS, thus disgruntling many parents and students until we reached out to clarify the graduation requirements. Project members presented regularly at state-level and district-level conferences for guidance counselors and high school CS teachers. We also worked with the CSTA state chapter to publicize the ECS course at regional Hour of Code events and with local media including the state newspapers and television news shows. The key lesson is that the success of the Utah ECS Initiative required regular communications with numerous stakeholders.

4. A HALF YEAR ECS CURRICULUM

The full Exploring Computer Science curriculum [3] has six units, which are broken down into 158 days of 55-minute lessons. While the full-year curriculum is preferable because it demonstrates more applications of computational thinking, Utah schools adopted ECS quickly because it could fulfill the existing half-year graduation requirement. Utah's half-year version of ECS includes:

- All 19 days of Unit 1 (Human Computer Interaction)
- All 21 days of Unit 2 (Problem Solving)
- All 30 days of Unit 4 (Programming with Scratch)
- 0-15 days from the 30 days of Unit 5 (Computing and Data Analysis)

Units 3 (Web Design) and 6 (Robotics) were completely cut from the curriculum, to avoid duplicating an existing web design program popular at many Utah schools and to avoid the expense of providing robotics hardware to schools statewide. The main downside of this cut is that the shortened course does not provide application for and emphasis of other ECS principles, and instead can only apply them in one environment (Programming with Scratch.) The Utah State Office of Education has created a second half-year ECS II course that would allow teachers to cover the remaining units, but thus far no public schools in Utah have adopted the full year course.

4.1 A Modified Data Analysis Unit

Initially, we designed a ten-day Unit 5 that was piloted by an experienced ECS teacher. Based on the piloting teacher's challenges and the wide range of classroom pacing across the state, we created three shortened versions of Unit 5: a five-day, ten-day, and 15-day, which are being piloted in multiple classrooms in 2015-2016.

The five-day option contains only the critical foundations of data analysis, such as plots, trends, statistics and data subsetting. Teachers can choose to follow up with either five or ten additional days if time permits. The longer option keeps the inquiry focused group project and much of the most applicable and engaging parts of the original data analysis lessons. The shorter option is based on the longer one, but replaces the group project with a simplified project analysis.

Although the current ECS curriculum allows teachers to select any software platform for Unit 5, the curriculum was originally written for Deducer (a GUI for R) [3], and many teachers found it difficult to teach with other tools. Our version replaces those lessons with lessons designed for online spreadsheet and mapping tools. The result is a shorter lesson module that can work without requiring additional software installation; the new module can be taught by teachers with existing expertise in business technology, a common expertise for our CS teachers.

5. ECS PROFESSIONAL DEVELOPMENT

Many Utah teachers learned about ECS through state-maintained e-mail lists. They registered for our program to meet the five requirements for a Utah ECS teaching endorsement: (1) completion of Code.org's 20-hour Code Studio course; (2) a five-day summer PD workshop; (3) monthly meetings with other first-time ECS teachers in their district; (4) a one-day workshop on Scratch programming; and (5) two additional state-level conferences. They were encouraged but not required to attend another five-day summer workshop in their second year. Stipends were provided to compensate them for their time ($1,500 for the first four requirements of ECS endorsement, and $400 for their second summer PD).

The five-day summer PD also served as a Teaching Methods course for CS endorsement (the state requirement for teaching Computer Programming and CS Principles). Our workshops filled a major gap in the statewide education system, since no Utah universities in the state offered CS teaching methods courses. Teachers seeking a CS endorsement (rather than ECS endorsement) received a $400 stipend for their participation. They immediately recognized that a successful ECS course would increase the enrollments in their other CS courses, and many were able to add ECS to their teaching schedules for the upcoming year.

5.1 Five Day Summer PD

Unlike many traditional textbook curricula, ECS is not a course that can be fully understood without attending a five-day workshop. When teachers read the curriculum alone they do not understand what teaching practices make ECS distinctive. Our project benefitted significantly from an invitation to visit Chicago and participate in one of their professional development workshops. To pay it forward, we hosted a teacher from Maryland and shared materials with Massachusetts.

The five-day summer PD designed by Goode and Chapman inculcates teachers on the three pillars of ECS: (1) computer science concepts; (2) inquiry-based teaching practices; and (3) equity in the classroom.

Nationwide, workshop facilitators first model a few ECS lessons, which all participants experience as if they were high school students. These lessons are followed by a reflective session on how the lesson went and what pedagogical choices were made by the instructors. Many teachers express surprise at how inquiry-based teaching practices can transform a classroom. Eight other ECS lessons are assigned to participants to deliver in groups (preferably groups of four teachers). Equity issues are introduced when participants read and discuss chapters from *Stuck in the Shallow End* [9].

The five-day ECS PD was well-received by Utah CS teachers (4.33 on a 5-point Likert scale by 2014-15 teachers), but could sometimes overwhelm teachers who were completely new to CS. By the last year of the project, we required Utah teachers to complete the 20-hour Code Studio before attending the five-day PD. This exposure to programming helped prepare new-to-CS teachers for the CS concepts covered in the five-day PD.

In response to negative feedback about how equity was discussed in the PD, we shifted the emphasis on equity from race to accessibility, gender, and socio-economic issues in the first half of the week. Recognizing that some Utah teachers had little diversity training or experience teaching racially diverse classrooms, we added short 15-minute sessions to the PD workshop explaining how equity differed from equality, how culture means more than race, how implicit bias is present in everyone, and how to react to micro-aggressions in the classroom. These sessions were designed in response to feedback that teachers wanted more concrete suggestions on equity. In the last iteration, we included too many of these sessions; survey responses suggested the teachers may have been better served by half that many sessions. We discuss this feedback in detail in Section 6.1.

Finally, we partnered with NCWIT's Counselors for Computing (C4C) to share more information about CS pathways and career opportunities. Teachers were especially excited to receive CSTA posters to highlight the multiple facets of computer science.

5.2 District Monthly Meetings

In addition to the five-day summer professional development that was designed primarily as a pre-service activity for new ECS teachers, we ran mandatory monthly meeting groups to provide in-service support for first-time ECS teachers. These groups offered teachers opportunities to discuss local logistics and receive additional training after obtaining some experience in teaching ECS. The monthly meeting groups were generally organized at the end of the workshop. Three to six new ECS teachers were assigned to a group led by either an ECS facilitator or an experienced ECS teacher. Groups met for approximately 90 minutes, followed an established agenda (available at http://www.tinyurl.com/ecs-agenda), and shared their progress by posting their minutes to the CS10K community site.

Our monthly meeting groups were initially organized to limit driving, with groups being assigned geographically based on residence. However, several of our teachers lived in one district and taught in another. As a result, many teachers in our first round of in-service training were attending mentoring groups with teachers who taught in different districts. This made scheduling the meeting times more challenging, and also made discussions regarding district wide issues difficult. In 2014, we changed the model so that teachers were grouped with other teachers who taught in the same district.

Another unique aspect of our monthly meeting groups is that some teachers in rural areas lived too far from other ECS teachers to make face-to-face meetings practical. We resolved this problem by offering online mentoring groups through Google Hangouts. Because district IT was not always friendly for video conferencing, we collected a variety of contact methods including phone numbers. When there were technical connection issues, we were able to fall back on phone conferencing to patch teachers into the meeting. We intentionally kept the maximum size of online groups smaller than in-person groups.

5.3 One Day Scratch PD

In place of the third monthly meeting, we held a full-day combined workshop for new teachers on the Scratch programming unit. Groups of teachers presented on Scratch similar to the practice during the summer. In 2012 and 2013, we did not cover Scratch as part of the summer workshop, and many of the teachers were not prepared to teach effectively during this follow-up. Teachers that were assigned lessons later in the Scratch unit found their assignments especially challenging. In 2014, the teachers received more instruction in Scratch as part of the summer workshop, and they were more prepared to teach Scratch. In 2015, we did even more preparation by having teachers complete 20 hours of coding before attending the summer workshop, and the discussion on programming was much stronger.

5.4 Creating Leaders from ECS Teachers

We identified a pipeline of ECS mentors and facilitators through this process. The second summer of ECS PD was not required, so teachers who attended a second ECS five-day PD were our more committed teachers. Other enthusiastic teachers chose to present at the state-level conferences about ECS. We also observed teachers' ECS classrooms if they were within an hour of Salt Lake City. We invited enthusiastic teachers who demonstrated a good understanding of the inquiry-based teaching practices and equity issues to serve as mentors and to lead the district monthly meetings. Mentors were also invited to observe a third ECS workshop, to prepare them to serve as workshop facilitators in their fourth workshops (following the national ECS model for developing ECS facilitators). Three Utah teachers are trained and experienced ECS workshop facilitators. Two of these teachers were new-to-CS teachers at their first ECS workshop, and two teachers are currently serving as President and Vice-President of our Utah CSTA Chapter.

6. RESULTS

ECS in Utah has experienced astonishing growth (see Table 1), beginning with 53 ECS students in 2012-2013, and reaching over 5000 students in 2015-2016. One downside of this rapid growth is that more than half the ECS schools each year have been new to the program, where the first-time ECS teachers have not yet attended the PD and learned about equity. Thus, the gender breakdown of Utah ECS students has not reached the high percentages achieved in other districts, but is more than double than for other CS courses in Utah (28% female in 2014-15, versus 43.7% female in LAUSD and 13% in other Utah CS courses). On the other hand, because we have targeted large, diverse urban high schools early in the project, the 2014-15 racial diversity of ECS students are higher than those for the state as a whole: 65% white (76% in Utah), 23% Hispanic (16%), 4% Asian (2%), 3% African American (1%), and 1% Native American (1%).

Table 1. ECS Adoption in Utah

	2012-13	2013-14	2014-15	2015-16
Workshops	1 workshop	1	2	3
New Teachers	2 teachers	21	49	78
Total Teachers Trained*	2 teachers in 2 districts	23 in 10	72 in 23	150 in 27
Schools Offering ECS*	2 schools in 2 districts	17 in 9	53 in 22	106 in 26
ECS Students Enrolled	53 students	1205	3461	5375
Total Students	53 students	1258	4719	10,094

* teacher and school counts include public, private and charter schools, but student and district counts only include Utah public school districts

ECS students completed a retrospective pre/post-survey in the last month of the course. On a Likert scale of 1-5 (1=not competent at all to 5=perfectly competent), 2014-15 students had statistically significant gains in their knowledge and problem solving skills in computational thinking (31% increase from 2.86 (σ=0.93) to 3.74 (σ=0.94), p<0.05). Similarly, they showed significant gains in their ability to apply abstractions to problems and to write computer programs (33% increase from 2.86 (σ=1.02) to 3.79 (σ=0.95), p<0.05), and a slight increase in interest in working in pairs or teams (41% to 48% prefer learning best with a peer or group). Students had a significant increase in their likelihood of enrolling in additional CS courses (3.06 (σ=1.25) to 3.71 (σ=1.21), p<0.05) and an increased interest in studying a CS related major in college (17% to 30% of the class population).

6.1 Lesson 1: The Equity Gap is Not Obvious To All Teachers

One of the three pillars of ECS and a motivating factor in the curriculum design is equity. We repeatedly received negative comments about this part of the workshop. We used the book *Stuck in the Shallow End,* which discusses computing, equity, and race in the LAUSD [9] to seed many of our equity discussions. Many of the negative comments were targeted at the book, claiming that it was "outdated" and irrelevant because it was published about LA over a decade ago. One 2015 teacher wrote, "I did not like that book. I understand that my classes need to be equitable without reading about outdated studies done in LA, which is not at all comparable to my school." Another 2015 teacher claimed: "I don't think things [in Utah] are as bad as depicted in this book."

Many teachers expected that they would spend every day learning more computer science lesson plans and practicing concrete technical skills. One teacher wrote, "I do want those students in my class and I will try to engage them, but is it my job to tell them that they should be in those classes when they suggest they are uninterested? Through manipulative tactics? Shouldn't I respect that they have different interests than I do?" Another said, "[Equity] was talked about TOO much. I needed more content information." When they were not asking for more technical content, they simply expressed their emotional exasperation: "I understand the importance of demystifying computer science and reaching more groups [girls/Latinos/etc]; however, I see no reason to beat the subject of Equity 'to death' day after day!" Most concerning, some teachers did not understand what they should do about it. One teacher said, "[I wish we had] more time talking about how we as teachers can address the things that we see in our own schools."

In hindsight, we did not anticipate this resistance (projects in areas with more cultural diversity had not experienced these challenges to this degree), and we did not include enough survey questions to assess change in teachers' viewpoints. We asked teachers to rate their "understanding of equity in the classroom" (2.74 (σ=1.03) to 3.95 (σ=0.77), p<0.05) and their "ability to teach for equity" (2.82 (σ=0.98) to 4.01 (σ=0.78), p<0.05), but these questions are not nuanced enough and assume that teachers believe equity issues exist in classrooms. We should have explicitly asked "Do equity issues exist in your classrooms and schools?" and "What kinds of equity gaps exist?".

Over time, we learned to tailor the presentation of equity to local issues, often starting with the less-threatening socioeconomic status and then branching into accessibility [12], gender and race. Our discussions were more effective when teachers could connect the issues to their own experiences.

Racial equity was especially difficult given Utah's relative racial homogeneity. Our teachers felt it difficult to extrapolate from the book's material to their own experience in their classrooms. One teacher said, "I felt the book and study itself were bias [sic] and not reflective of the nation as a whole, nor do I think it reflects the Utah culture. If you could find a study on gender, that would more appropriately reflect Utah's bias." Our teachers were more willing to confront inequities related to characteristics such as gender, socioeconomic status, religion, and even, in our reservation schools, different tribal affiliations. We were initially not prepared for the strong negative reaction many of our teachers had to the race issues addressed in *Stuck in the Shallow End*, and our surveys did not explore the reasons for these reactions. We hypothesize that some of these reactions may be explained by the dynamics of White Fragility [2].

The cultural challenges of the curriculum were especially clear with ECS lessons like the cornrow curves assignment and the Martin Luther King website analysis. Many of our teachers were extremely uncomfortable with these lessons. Some teachers refused to use the lessons. One teacher was especially candid and explained that they were "afraid to teach a lesson like that" to a classroom of only white students, some of whom may have never seen an African-American in person. They felt they were inadequately prepared to address the cultural issues that were likely to come up in teaching these lessons. In a multicultural setting, these lessons would be connecting CS concepts to pre-existing cultural knowledge for at least some of the students. In our less diverse setting, teachers and students had no relevant pre-existing cultural knowledge, and the curriculum and PD did not adequately scaffold this knowledge for our teachers.

We learned that equity, diversity, and cultural issues have a huge range of meaning across the States. The issues that were relevant and natural during ECS' birth in a racially diverse culture were a challenge to adapt to a middle-America setting with a racially homogeneous population. We needed to think critically about which issues were necessary to discuss (such as giving all students opportunity) and which lessons could be taught using less controversial materials (such as using the Pacific Northwest Tree Octopus website for content analysis). This was an instance where we needed to spend more time making local adaptations. Future deployments of ECS should also consider cultural context.

6.2 Lesson 2: The Professional Development Model of ECS Requires Continual Growth

ECS has its own culture: the foundational pillars are equity, inquiry, and CS concepts, but there is also a strong focus on continual professional development for students and teachers alike. Continual professional development means a continual upward spiral of progression. It also means recognizing that teaching may never be perfect, but it can get better. Even with a fairly specific curriculum, there are many variations on how a lesson can be taught and adaptations that can be made to improve the lesson for a teacher or a student.

Many questions in ECS lessons from the fundamental "What is a computer?" to the more abstract "How do culture and computing relate?" are left deliberately open ended, and often learning is less about arriving at a particular "right" answer than it is about learning how to approach the problem using tools of computation. Many first-time teachers arrived at the workshop wanting "the answer". The lack of direct information dissemination was overwhelming for some teachers as indicated by the comment "The project coordinator was more concerned with our comments rather than giving ideas to us. We had to come up with ideas like our students do, which sometimes is not enough direction to move forward." Another comment indicated "At first it was weird trying to figure out what they meant, but the process of figuring out helped me to really analyze my teaching." Teachers' self reported ratings of their role "to think reflectively about my teaching practices" increased (27% from 3.16 to 4.01, $p<0.01$).

Initially, many returning teachers indicated that they felt that they had learned what they needed to know and did not have anything new to learn. One teacher reported "I took this workshop last year and this [picture activity] was a repeat." Others were overzealous in their desires to tell new teachers how they had taught ECS and how to teach ECS; they wanted to give "the right answer" to the teachers who were asking for it. As we discussed the issue with other facilitators including Gail Chapman, our professional development process for returning teachers evolved. In 2015, we included a letter and additional debriefing sessions at the beginning and end of the workshop day to help them focus more on their own development as well as helping the new teachers develop. We specifically focused on the issue of asking better questions as opposed to providing better answers. In 2015, the 15 returning teachers rated these debriefing sessions 4.2 on a 5-point Likert scale.

6.3 Lesson 3: Local Facilitators Preferred

In our surveys and interactions with our teachers, we repeatedly heard complaints about any facilitator who was perceived as an outsider to Utah culture. Unlike a workshop about a new textbook or a new software tool, the content of an ECS workshop includes more emotional discussions focused on the social and cultural issues that arise in a classroom. Two of the pillars of ECS, equity and inquiry, are about these issues. During PD, facilitators seek to demonstrate inquiry-based learning by having lots of tight interactions with teachers; they seek to expose and confront equity issues directly by talking about them openly. Many of our teachers felt that this created a tense and draining environment where they were being judged by external facilitators for their classroom practices and their cultural background.

Participants would sometimes even question some of our local facilitators on how long they have been in the community and the extent to their involvement. Utah has a strong local custom for modest dress and hairstyles, which immediately brands many visitors and some long-time residents as outsiders. Once we identified this preference for local facilitators, we were able to plan our discussions and approaches differently and create a better connection with the teachers. One teacher commented after their second summer workshop, "I quickly noticed that having a Utah team lead the workshop seemed more inviting and supportive than with the UCLA presenter who facilitated this workshop last summer." One team member experienced this local preference from the opposite direction when she facilitated a workshop in another state and felt the same push-back for being an outsider in that state.

Teachers' ratings of facilitation increased when the facilitation was done by a local team (from 3.91 (σ=0.95) for an external facilitator to 4.37 (σ=0.69) for local facilitators, p=0.01). Our recommendation to future efforts is to pay strict heed to understanding and adapting the curriculum and PD to the dominant culture of teachers and using as many local facilitators as possible, especially for the most pressingly emotional and social issues, so that teachers will buy-in, rather than push-back.

6.4 Lesson 4: Account for Workshop Attrition

Our initial plan was to run a total of eight workshops over four years and train a total of 105 new ECS teachers, with each workshop accommodating approximately 10-20 teachers. Within one year of the project, we realized that we had failed to account for two major factors in our calculations. First, because we were deploying statewide and many teachers did not feel a high degree of accountability to workshop facilitators, many teachers signed up for a workshop but did not attend. Second, ECS workshops are ideally run with 24-32 participants (to allow for 3-4 teachers to present each of the eight lessons). To fix both of these problems, we ran fewer workshops in our second year and began overbooking workshops to account for no-shows. Teachers who provided administration letters committing to two years of ECS courses were offered priority registration, whereas other teachers were admitted on a space-available basis. Our 2014 and 2015 workshops had a 11-23% no-show rate. Asking for letters demonstrating administration support helped reduce the no-show rate, but failed to eliminate it. Even workshops filled exclusively with teachers with letters from their administration still had over 10% of the teachers drop out.

Our smallest workshop had 22 teachers (28 registered) and was offered in a rural area, in part to accommodate teachers from rural areas who might find cities intimidating. Quality discussions can be difficult for the smaller groups, with less opportunity for diversity of thought, controversy, debate, or serious discussion. Our largest workshop had 39 teachers, the result of registering 46 and not having as much attrition as we were expecting. Larger groups made it more difficult to maintain individual accountability in completing homework and participating in workshop discussions. Individual teachers were more likely to show up late, disappear to answer phone calls, and be distracted by their laptops. The quality of the discussion dragged, and teachers and facilitators alike found it much more difficult to emotionally invest in a larger group where sharing deeply personal feelings and potentially controversial ideas is more intimidating.

6.5 Lesson 5: Scaling to Statewide Brings a New Set of Logistical Challenges

Scaling to statewide brought extra logistical challenges. With teachers in rural areas, we had to be more strategic about supplies, help arrange hotels and carpools, and make compromises in the evaluation of their teaching since it was impractical to observe their classrooms.

Recruiting practices differed in effectiveness for different teacher populations. Teachers in Northern Utah and teachers in larger districts were more likely to attend state-level conferences and therefore easier to recruit. Their guidance counselors were similarly easier to reach. To reach out to the smaller districts, we contacted district-level Career and Technical Education (CTE) directors and asked them to help identify appropriate teachers and inform guidance counselors. However teachers sent by school or district administrators were more likely to complain about ECS. Experienced ECS teachers were our best recruiters; many would convince their colleagues from other schools and districts to attend.

School schedules and class schedules often varied tremendously within a single workshop, and we often had teachers on traditional schedules, trimester schedules, A/B day schedules, and project based schedules in the same workshop. When we tried to address scheduling concerns as part of the week long workshop, teachers complained "good but not practical for different schedules." We found that by moving more of the scheduling logistics to the monthly mentoring meetings and by organizing monthly mentoring meetings by district, we were able to provide ECS advice and schedule scaffolding that was relevant and tailored to the teachers' needs.

7. CONCLUSIONS

In conclusion, the Utah Exploring Computer Science Initiative has led the first statewide deployment of ECS. This deployment is unique due to its geographical breadth, diversity of population density, and half-year variation of the ECS curriculum.

This paper has described our experiences during the first four years of this deployment and our contributions of (section 4) a model for adapting the standard ECS curriculum into a half-year variation suitable for credit-hour- and resource-constrained schools; (section 5) a multi-year professional development plan that turns some teachers with no CS experience into instructors, mentors, and workshop facilitators; and (section 6) a set of concrete lessons for adapting ECS to new geographical and cultural settings.

We hope that our results and techniques will be replicated in other states and regions so that the computer science education community can better understand the benefits and challenges of deploying courses like ECS in areas like rural, middle America.

We have created a sustainable program for introductory computer science for all Utah students; our next goal is to use ECS to identify promising teachers who we can train to teach the AP CS Principles course.

8. ACKNOWLEDGEMENTS

We acknowledge the contributions of our evaluation team from SmartStart Evaluation and Research, especially Jessica Martone. We are grateful to Carl Lyman, the State Office of Education, and our Utah and national ECS community. This work is supported by the National Science Foundation Grant No. CNS-1240977.

9. REFERENCES

[1] Tim Bell, Gwenda Bensemann, and Ian H Witten. 1995. Computer science unplugged: Capturing the interest of the uninterested. In Proceedings of the 14th New Zealand Computer Conference.

[2] Robin DiAngelo. 2011. White Fragility. *International Journal of Critical Pedagogy,* 3 (3) (2011), 54-70.

[3] Joanna Goode and Gail Chapman. 2015. Exploring Computer Science. Version 5.0. Downloaded on August 13, 2015 from http://www.exploringcs.org/curriculum

[4] Joanna Goode and Jane Margolis. 2011. Exploring Computer Science: A Case Study of School Reform. Trans. Comput. Educ. 11, 2, Article 12 (July 2011), 16 pages.

[5] Daniel W. Lewis, Lisa Kohne, Timothy Mechlinski, and Mariana Schmalstig. 2015. The Exploring Computer Science Course, Attendance and Math Achievement. In Proceedings of the 2015 ACM Conference on Innovation and Technology in Computer Science Education (ITiCSE '15). ACM, New York, NY, USA, 147-152.

[6] John Maloney, Mitchel Resnick, Natalie Rusk, Brian Silverman, and Evelyn Eastmond. 2010. The Scratch Programming Language and Environment. Trans. Comput. Educ. 10, 4, Article 16 (Nov 2010), 15 pages.

[7] Jane Margolis, Gail Chapman, Joanna Goode, Lucia Dettori, and Dan Lewis. 2013. A Tale of Three ECS Partnerships and Why Scalability ≠ Sustainability. Exploring Computer Science Working Paper #1. Retrieved from http://www.exploringcs.org/research/ecs-working-papers

[8] Jane Margolis, Joanna Goode, and Gail Chapman. 2015. An Equity Lens for Scaling: A Critical Juncture for Exploring Computer Science. In ACM Inroads, 6, 3 (Aug 2015), 58-66.

[9] Jane Margolis, Rachel Estrella, Joanna Goode, Jennifer Jellison Holme and Kim Nao. 2008. Stuck in the Shallow End: Education, Race, and Computing. The MIT Press.

[10] Hadi Partovi. A Comprehensive Effort to Expand Access and Diversity in Computer Science. In ACM Inroads, 6, 3 (Aug 2015), 67-72.

[11] Dale Reed, Brenda Wilkerson, Don Yanek, Lucia Dettori, Jeff Solin. 2015. How Exploring Computer Science (ECS) came to Chicago. In ACM Inroads, 6, 3 (Aug 2015), 75-77.

[12] Andreas Stefik and Richard E. Ladner. 2015. Introduction to AccessCS10K and Accessible Tools for Teaching Programming. In Proceedings of the 46th ACM Technical Symposium on Computer Science Education (SIGCSE '15). ACM, New York, NY, USA, 518-519.

Engaging CS Alumni from Afar

Christine A. Shannon
Centre College
Danville, Kentucky, USA
christine.shannon@centre.edu

James Kiper
Miami University
Oxford, Ohio, USA
kiperjd@miamioh.edu

Samuel A. Rebelsky
Grinnell College
Grinnell, Iowa, USA
rebelsky@grinnell.edu

Janet Davis
Whitman College
Walla Walla, Washington, USA
davisj@whitman.edu

Categories and Subject Descriptors
K.3.2 [**Computers and Education**]: Computer and information science education – *Computer science education.* K.4.0 [**Computers and Society**]: General. K.7.1 [**The Computing Profession**]: Occupations.

General Terms
Human Factors.

Keywords
Alumni engagement; careers; professional development.

1. SUMMARY

Alumni connect an institution to the world beyond its doors. Alumni can help students in many ways, from providing new perspectives on core computer science concepts to providing opportunities for work and experiential learning. Students can envision themselves following in alumni footsteps, and many alumni are eager to help students with whom they share an *alma mater*. Some computer science departments benefit from having their alumni nearby, while others—especially those far away from concentrations of computing and information technology businesses—must find ways to engage alumni from afar.

In the career development community, there has been some discussion of the benefits of student/alumni mentoring programs [3] and a recent analysis of student experiences in these situations [2]. A search of the ACM Digital Library suggests that there has been little discussion about alumni engagement in CS education, until a BoF at SIGCSE 2015 [1].

This panel will illustrate several ways to meaningfully connect CS students with alumni. Some approaches use the Internet to engage alumni at a distance: publishing alumni newsletters, establishing LinkedIn® groups, and teleconferencing alumni into classes. Other approaches bring students and alumni together through events on campus. One new mentoring program combines both approaches in the context of a software development course. We present a Strengths, Weaknesses, Opportunities, Threats (SWOT) analysis [4] of each approach.

2. CHRISTINE SHANNON

Until about three years ago, the Computer Science Program at Centre College could expect the number of sophomores declaring the major to be in the single digits—a few times one could count them on a single hand! As our program has grown, we have continued to nurture close relations with our alumni. For more than ten years, we have published a twice-yearly online alumni newsletter. The newsletter appears shortly after graduation in May or early June and just after the completion of the January term. The newsletter includes stories about current students' work, news of program developments, and brief updates on alumni careers. Every new edition elicits a few more updates to be included in the next edition. Since our email announcement of the newsletter always invites alumni to forward internship and job openings, alumni responses also bring word of opportunities for our students. The archived newsletters are accessible from the program webpage, providing historical snapshots of program activities not just for alumni but also for prospective students.

Homecoming provides an opportunity to bring alumni in contact with current students. In some years, we have run a formal "alumni seminar" where alumni can share their experiences with current students. At other times of the year, nearby alumni are invited to talk in classes or co-curricular sessions; those at a distance can participate online using readily available technologies. Our students have benefitted greatly from alumni, especially recent alumni, who alert us to jobs and internships and who share their experiences with the transition from college to work.

Strengths: Maintains contact with alumni at least twice a year; provides current and prospective students a glimpse of what has been accomplished by alumni as well as "life in the program."

Weakness: Takes time to prepare newsletter and keep track of alumni contact information.

Opportunities: Maintaining contact provides better response to assessment or other surveys and requests for speakers. We often get information about internships and job opportunities.

Threats: As faculty and staff change, it is harder to maintain connections to alumni.

3. JIM KIPER

At Miami University, we have hosted an annual alumni conference for more than ten years. As our department recently celebrated its fiftieth anniversary, we have a large alumni base scattered across the country, and increasingly, around the world. The conference allows alumni to return to campus to mix with students and share their expertise. Alumni are motivated to participate in order to give back to the university, to visit with classmates, and to recruit our students.

The one-day conference includes three or four parallel tracks and a keynote by a distinguished alumna or alumnus. Alumni present technical topics, share their experiences, or give career advice. Some of the most popular sessions are those in which recent graduates report on their transitions from school to work. More experienced alumni help students broaden their views of possible

SIGCSE '16, March 02-05, 2016, Memphis, TN, USA
ACM 978-1-4503-3685-7/16/03.
http://dx.doi.org/10.1145/2839509.2844662

career directions and goals. For example, a student may not envision herself as a CIO until she hears an alumna describe her CIO position. For the past few years, we have hosted a lunch for students and alumni. The lunch and breaks are important for networking—both student to alumni, and alumni to alumni.

Alumni organizers are key to a successful conference. Our department office administrator arranges logistics, but it is beneficial to have alumni plan conference themes and recruit speakers. Lunch, snacks, and advertisements also require financial resources. We have been able to obtain sponsorship from companies at which our alumni work at levels from $1K to $5K.

Strengths: Engagement with alumni; job and internship opportunities for students; funding connections with alumni; industry perspectives for curriculum improvement.

Weaknesses: Planning the conference requires time and effort.

Opportunities: Allows us to connect with companies in ways that may lead to further funding, for instance, as capstone sponsors.

Threats: Without faculty effort, students may not engage with alumni who return to campus.

4. SAM REBELSKY

As Grinnell College students consider and plan for their careers, they face a variety of obstacles beyond our location amongst the cornfields of Iowa and far from the coasts. Most students have little imagination about what you can do with a CS degree. Our career development office, while skilled, does not really understand that applying for computing jobs can be very different from applying for other jobs. And although we tell students about the value of side projects, networking, and other experiences outside the curriculum, students don't necessarily understand how important such work is when they hear it from their faculty.

To address these issues, I offer a 1-credit course, *Learning from CS Alumni*. Each week, an alumni guest speaker visits the class via online conferencing; a few nearby alumni visit in person. And it is no surprise that alumni can help. Alumni have not only chosen a wide variety of careers, they have often switched directions: "When I left college, I never wanted to program again. After a few years, I discovered I really like back-end programming." Alumni can report on things that helped them get desirable positions, even when they didn't know what they were looking for: "Someone noticed my side project on Github and offered me a job because it was close to what they needed." And alumni reinforce the things we tell our current students: "What sets me apart from my colleagues is that I learned to write really well in college."

Strengths: Alumni provide realistic role models and salient career advice. Online conferencing engages many alumni at little cost.

Weaknesses: Typically an overload for the faculty instructor. Organizing the course requires significant effort.

Opportunities: Alumni may inspire students in unexpected ways. Students can get to know some alumni more deeply through host duties or contact after class.

Threats: Not all alumni connect well with students. To succeed, the instructor should know a large number of alumni fairly well. Students get out of it only as much as they put in.

5. JANET DAVIS (MODERATOR)

In a new course at Grinnell College, *Team Software Development for Community Organizations*, teams of 4-6 students design and build software to meet the needs of a community partner. Projects are managed using agile software development methodology, and may continue over several semesters until partners' needs are met. Because it is important for both students and partners to have positive experiences, I want to provide as many resources as possible to help teams succeed—including an involved and experienced mentor. However, I must divide my time amongst several teams, and my experience is limited compared to that of professional software developers. I cannot expect community partners to provide technical mentorship; the nearest software professionals who might volunteer as mentors are an hour away.

Alumni mentors can fill this gap. To identify potential mentors, I used LinkedIn to search for young alumni with appropriate expertise and experiences. After project teams are formed, alumni mentors introduce themselves to the class via teleconference, and teams bid on their preferred mentors. One mentor is assigned to each team. Alumni mentors visit campus for a design workshop early in the semester. Between this workshop and the final presentations, teams and mentors teleconference every other week to conduct iteration retrospectives. Alumni mentors are also available by phone and email to coach students through technical, communication, and project management challenges. In this panel, I will report and reflect on a year of experience with alumni mentors for student software development teams.

Strengths: Deep engagement. Builds relationships between students and alumni. Students learn professional skills and gain confidence in their work. Mentors lessen instructor workload.

Weaknesses: Engages a small number of alumni; not just anyone will do. Costly to fund young alumni travel to campus.

Opportunities: May lead to career opportunities or long-term mentoring relationships.

Threats: Positive experiences depend on responsible students and committed alumni. Students may receive conflicting advice from instructors and mentors.

Acknowledgement: Thanks to Mary Beth Snell for identifying relevant references.

6. REFERENCES

[1] Allen, M., Coleman, B., Horton, D., Lambert, L., and Ng, M. 2015. Sharing best practices for alumni engagement (Abstract Only). In *Proc. 46th ACM Technical Symposium on Computer Science Education* (SIGCSE '15).

[2] Conner, Kristin. 2015. Expectations and experiences of undergraduate students who participated in an alumni mentoring program" *Doctoral Dissertations* Paper 123.

[3] Pfeifer, Sarah E. The Benefits of Establishing a Student/Alumni Mentoring Program, Retrieved August 21, 2015 from Portland State University: https://dus.psu.edu/mentor/old/articles/021007sp.htm.

[4] SWOT analysis. Retrieved August 7, 2015 from Wikipedia: https://en.wikipedia.org/wiki/SWOT_analysis

Rediscovering the Passion, Beauty, Joy, and Awe: Making Computing Fun Again, part 8

Daniel D. Garcia (moderator)
University of California, Berkeley
777 Soda Hall
Berkeley, CA 94720
+1 (510) 517-4041
ddgarcia@cs.berkeley.edu

Josh Caldwell
Code.org
1301 5th Ave, Suite 1225
Seattle, WA 98101
+1 (617) 495-4341
josh@code.org

Pamela Fox
Khan Academy
P.O. Box 1630
Mountain View, CA 94042
510-292-1940
pamela@khanacademy.org

Jeremy Keeshin
CodeHS
1328 Mission St, Suite 8
San Francisco, CA 94103
415-889-3376
jkeesh@codehs.com

Keywords
Computer science education, online learning, self-paced learning

1. SUMMARY

In his keynote at SIGCSE 2007, Grady Booch exhorted us to share the "passion, beauty, joy and awe" (PBJA) of computing [1]. This led to a series of room-packed sessions at the following seven SIGCSE symposia to explore that idea from different angles [2-5]. They have provided a forum for sharing:

- **What we've done / seen**: Highlighting successful PBJA initiatives they have done or seen and wish to trumpet.
- **What we should do (curriculum)**: Pointing out where our curriculum is lacking in PBJA, and how to fix it.
- **How we should do it (pedagogy)**: Sharing how a change in attitude / focus / etc. can make strides to improving PBJA.

While the initial PBJA sessions evolved from a need to understand and combat the enrollment crisis of nine years ago, we are now seeing an explosion of interest in our field. There are colleges where the numbers have vast exceeded historic highs, with computer science enrollments up 22% in 2014 [6]. This PBJA "movement" was born out of this enrollment crisis, but is not tied to it. There is always value in sharing novel best practices and advocating techniques to make computing fun for beginners.

This year we have gathered three educators who represent online, self-paced curriculum, platforms and community that together have reached *millions* of people. How does the online experience support or prevent PBJA in ways traditional classrooms don't? What innovative ideas did they employ to support collaboration, and how do they manage the "bad elements" of their user base? What is the right balance between easy-to-autograde, follow-me curriculum and wide-open, "be creative" experiences for the first-time user? Which works best, blocks-based or text-based programming? How can the "big data" from the mistakes of others be leveraged to give each user a personalized experience? The hope with this panel is to explore best practices of self-paced online offerings in these crucial early years, for participants of any age, in terms of extolling the PBJA of computing.

SIGCSE '16, March 02-05, 2016, Memphis, TN, USA
ACM 978-1-4503-3685-7/16/03.
http://dx.doi.org/10.1145/2839509.2844659

2. JOSH CALDWELL (code.org)

On September 5, 2014, Code.org launched three new computer science courses for K-5 students designed in the style of our popular Hour of Code activities [7]. These activities engage students in fun and challenging puzzle solving tasks that introduce programming and computational thinking skills in an approachable way using characters kids love, like Angry Birds and Plants vs Zombies. Since we launched the Hour of Code, less than a year ago, tens of millions of people discovered the joy of programming through our activities, and those created by the broader community.

While our curriculum is designed to allow students to learn computer science skills completely on their own, we also firmly believe in the importance of skilled teachers in making the learning experience rich, engaging, and accessible to students of all levels. Code.org's K-5 computer science curriculum alternates between our trademark self-paced puzzles and in-person Unplugged activities that engage students in computational thinking through fun games and crafts. Providing these fun Unplugged activities helps students to see the beauty in computational thinking and how it applies to their lives offline as well as online.

To support and strengthen this blended model, we've trained 100 trainers to provide free PD to K-5 teachers across the nation. If we're going to get every student to learn to code, we need to make sure there are great teachers to guide them. Passionate teachers are a huge part of what makes passionate learners - and we've found the teachers working with our K-5 curriculum to have boundless passion!

3. PAMELA FOX (Khan Academy)

Khan Academy provides an environment that teaches JavaScript programming with the ProcessingJS library [8]. The programming environment is entirely online and real-time, so that students see the result of their code changes immediately, enabling them to fail faster and learn more quickly, plus experience the joy of seeing their drawings and animations morph in front of their eyes.

The self-paced curriculum covers all of JavaScript fundamentals, and includes talk-throughs (a more interactive form of videos), challenges, quizzes, and projects. The assessable elements of the curriculum are designed to enable creativity - the challenge graders accept a spectrum of answers and the projects are evaluated by peers with flexible rubrics. Both overall stats and user feedback is collected and used to improve the curriculum, particularly the challenges. For example, we sort challenges by their completion rates, and then improve the graders of the challenges with lowest completion rates by looking at the manually reported feedback of students going through those challenges.

The community is pervasive throughout the Khan Academy programming learning experience. When first learning, a student experiences the community through the questions they ask and the peer evaluations they receive. Many students go on to become "super-members" of the community, spending their time trying out each other's programs (that they find on our "Hot list"), forming programming clubs to create games, participating in self-started contests, and answering thousands of questions from new students. As a teacher, the super-members are what gives me the most joy, because they have such passion for what they're learning that they're so utterly compelled to share it.

4. JEREMY KEESHIN (CodeHS)

CodeHS is a program for helping high schools teach computer science [9]. We provide web-based curriculum, teacher tools, as well as online teacher training. The main courses include Introduction to Computer Science in JavaScript as well as an AP Computer Science in Java course. We start teaching with Karel the Dog and use a thin library in the intro course to allow students to write more interesting programs and focus on concepts.

The curriculum is self-paced and generally used in a blended classroom environment. The curriculum includes short videos, examples, exercises and larger challenge problems. Most problems are autograded for both program functionality and many problems are checked for programming style. Students have access to a Sandbox section to write creative programs outside the curriculum.

We provide lots of resources and tools for both new teachers and experienced teachers alike, including handouts and solution guides, as well as tools to create your own exercises and autograders.

5. REFERENCES

[1] Booch, G. 2007. Readn', writ'n, 'rithmetic... and code'n. *SIGCSE Bull.* 39, 1 (Mar. 2007), 197-197. `doi.acm.org/10.1145/1227504.1227380`

[2] Garcia, D. D., Hutton, M. F., Lemon, E., and Paley, J. 2011. Rediscovering the passion, beauty, joy, and awe: making computing fun again, part 4. In *Proceedings of the 42nd ACM technical symposium on Computer science education* (SIGCSE '11). ACM, New York, NY, USA, 613-614. `doi.acm.org/10.1145/1953163.1953332`

[3] Garcia, D. D., Ericson, B., Goode, J. and Lewis, C. 2012. Rediscovering the passion, beauty, joy, and awe: making computing fun again, part 5. In *Proceedings of the 43rd ACM technical symposium on Computer Science Education* (SIGCSE '12). ACM, New York, NY, USA, 577-578. `doi.acm.org/10.1145/2157136.2157300`

[4] Garcia, D. D., Barr, V., Guzdial, M. and Malan, D.J. 2013. Rediscovering the passion, beauty, joy, and awe: making computing fun again, part 6. In *Proceeding of the 44th ACM technical symposium on Computer science education* (SIGCSE '13). ACM, New York, NY, USA, 379-380. `doi.acm.org/10.1145/2445196.2445308`

[5] Garcia, D. D, Campbell, J; Dovi, R and Horstmann, C. 2014. Rediscovering the passion, beauty, joy, and awe: making computing fun again, part 7. In *Proceedings of the 45th ACM technical symposium on Computer science education* (SIGCSE '14). ACM, New York, NY, USA, 273-274. `doi.acm.org/10.1145/2538862.2538874`

[6] Computer science enrollments rocketed last year, up 22%. `www.networkworld.com/article/2175086/infrastructure-management/computer-science-enrollments-rocketed-last-year--up-22-.html`

[7] Code.org. *Computer science for elementary school.* Accessed 2015-08-28. `code.org/educate/k5`

[8] Khan Academy. *Intro to JS: Drawing & Animation.* Accessed 2015-08-28. `www.khanacademy.org/computing/computer-programming/programming`

[9] CodeHS. *CodeHS - Learn to Code at School or at Home.* Accessed 2015-08-28. `codehs.com`

The Micro-Cluster Showcase: 7 Inexpensive Beowulf Clusters for Teaching PDC

Joel C. Adams
(Organizer) Calvin College
adams@calvin.edu

Jacob Caswell
St. Olaf College
caswell@stolaf.edu

Suzanne J. Matthews
U.S. Military Academy
suzanne.matthews@usma.edu

Charles Peck
Earlham College
charliep@cs.earlham.edu

Elizabeth Shoop
Macalester College
shoop@macalester.edu

David Toth
Centre College
david.toth@centre.edu

James Wolfer
Indiana University, S. Bend
jwolfer@iusb.edu

CCS Concepts

• **Computing methodologies** ~ Parallel computing methodologies • **Computer systems organization** ~ Distributed architectures • **Social and professional topics** ~ Computer science education

Keywords

Architecture; Beowulf; clusters; computer science; computing; distributed; education; GPU; heterogeneous; hardware; inexpensive; multicore; parallel; processes; teaching; threads.

1. SUMMARY

Just as a micro-computer is a personal, portable computer, a *micro-cluster* is a personal, portable, Beowulf cluster. In this special session, six cluster designers will bring and demonstrate micro-clusters they have built using inexpensive single-board computers (SBCs). The educators will describe how they have used their clusters to provide their students with hands-on experience using the shared-memory, distributed-memory, and heterogeneous computing paradigms, and thus achieve the parallel and distributed computing (PDC) objectives of CS 2013 [1].

2. SESSION OBJECTIVE

Most CS educators are aware of the *Raspberry Pi* [8], but many have never heard of more powerful SBCs, such as Adapteva's *Parallella* [3], the Nvidia *Jetson* [6], or the *ODROID C1+* or *XU4* [5]. In this session, our primary objective is to give CS educators the opportunity to:

1. See clusters that their peers have built using SBCs.
2. Hear how their peers are using their clusters to teach PDC.
3. Interact with those peers on a personal basis.

A secondary objective is to inspire other CS educators to create their own clusters. By showcasing these clusters and exploring how they are being using in the classroom, we hope to catalyze a wave of innovation in PDC education.

SIGCSE '16, March 2–5, 2016, Memphis, TN, USA.
ACM 978-1-4503-3685-7/16/03.
http://dx.doi.org/10.1145/2839509.2844670

3. SESSION OUTLINE

Some SBCs are as small as a credit card, allowing our presenters to bring their clusters to the conference. Prior to the session, the presenters will set up their clusters for display and demonstration on tables at the front of the room.

In the first 32 minutes of the session, each presenter will give a 5-minute, 5-slide "lightning talk" on his or her cluster, describing its specifications and how they use it to teach PDC.

The middle 18 minutes will be a "Group Q&A" in which audience members can direct questions to the presenters as a group.

The last 25 minutes will be a "Show&Tell" session in which the presenters will move to their clusters and audience members can approach and interact with the presenters individually.

Table 1 presents a concise overview of the session.

What	Who	Duration
Lightning Talks	Joel Adams	2 min.
- *StudentParallella*	Suzanne Matthews	5 min.
- *PIsToGo*	Jacob Caswell	5 min.
- *HSC-5* and *HSC-6*	David Toth	5 min.
- *Rosie*	Elizabeth Shoop	5 min.
- *LittleFe*	Charlie Peck	5 min.
- *Cu-T-Pi*	James Wolfer	5 min.
Group Q&A	Audience	15 min.
Show&Tell	Everyone	28 min.

Table 1. Session Overview

This 75-minute session thus has three parts: lightning talks, an all-group Q&A, and a Show&Tell.

In the remainder of this section, we provide descriptions of our presenters, the clusters they will present, and how they use those clusters to teach PDC topics. For each of these clusters, the total cost includes everything needed to build the cluster (Gigabit Ethernet interconnect, parts, shipping, etc.), except for a monitor, mouse, and keyboard. The presenters' slides and the disk images for their clusters will be archived at *csinparallel.org* [4].

3.1 Joel Adams (Organizer)

Dr. Adams is a professor of computer science at Calvin College. He has designed and built four Beowulf clusters, including Microwulf [2], a portable sub-\$2500 system that was the first cluster to break the \$100/GFLOP barrier. He will introduce each presenter and moderate the session.

3.2 Suzanne Matthews

Dr. Matthews is an assistant professor of computer science at the United States Military Academy. To incorporate parallel concepts into her department's curriculum, she has created two courses: (i) an elective *Parallel Computing* course that exposes students to a variety of parallel libraries and architectures, including Adapteva's Parallella, an 18-core SBC; and (ii) a required *Computer Organization* course that introduces students to concurrent and shared memory parallel concepts using the POSIX API and x86 architecture. Dr. Matthews also uses two SBC clusters (*StudentPi* and *StudentParallella*) to engage her students in undergraduate research. Both cost about $700 to build.

3.3 Jacob Caswell

Jacob is a junior CS and Physics major at St. Olaf College. He will present *PIsToGo*, a complete, five-node, passively cooled, Raspberry Pi-2 cluster-in-a-briefcase that cost $300. He will also describe *Remora*, a virtual cluster-on-a-flash-drive that can be run on any network of workstations for $3 per node.

3.4 David Toth

Dr. Toth is an assistant professor of computer science at Centre College. He will present his latest "Half-Shoebox Clusters," (*HSC-5* & *HSC-6*) which are portable clusters inexpensive enough for each student to purchase one as lab equipment.

- *HSC-5* has two ODROID C1+ nodes, each with an ARM quad core CPU, at a total cost of $150.
- *HSC-6* has two ODROID XU4 nodes, each with two ARM quad core CPUs and an 8 core MP6 GPU; total cost: $220.

Dr. Toth will discuss his use of HSC clusters to teach OpenMP, MPI, and OpenCL in his *Parallel Computing* course, comparing them to courses in which the students used shared equipment.

3.5 Elizabeth Shoop

Dr. Shoop is a professor of computer science at Macalester College. She will present *Rosie*, a cluster with six Nvidia Jetson-TK1 nodes. Each node has an ARM quad core CPU and a 192 CUDA core Kepler GPU. The nodes share a 500GB hard disk. The total cost was $1350. She will also describe her use of Rosie to teach shared-memory, distributed-memory, and GPU/CUDA computing concepts in two courses: *System Fundamentals* and *Parallel Computing*.

3.6 Charles Peck

Dr. Peck is a professor of computer science at Earlham College. He will present *LittleFe* [7], the original cluster-in-a-suitcase. LittleFe has six custom-built nodes. Each has a dual-core Intel CPU and a 16 CUDA-core Nvidia GPU. The total cost is $2500 (but free for *LittleFe Buildout* participants!), including a shock- and water-proof carrying case. He will discuss his use of LittleFe to teach shared-memory, distributed-memory, and GPU/CUDA concepts in his *Parallel & Distributed Computing* course.

3.7 James Wolfer

Dr. Wolfer is a professor of computer science at Indiana University, South Bend. He will present *CU-T-Pi*, a heterogeneous cluster consisting of one Nvidia Jetson-TK1 and four Raspberry Pi nodes [9]. The total cost of the system was about $500. He has used his cluster to illustrate communication overhead and heterogeneous benchmarking considerations in a *Parallel Programming* course. He has also used it generate random numbers for an *Operating Systems* class by harvesting entropy from a Geiger counter interface, during which it supported remote access by 31 students for sixty 24/7 days.

4. EXPECTATIONS

We believe that hands-on exercises in which students must apply abstract concepts improve their understanding of those concepts. However, the hardware needed for students to experience some PDC topics (e.g., scalability) has traditionally been expensive.

The clusters featured in this session range in price from $150 to $2500, making them much more affordable than traditional Beowulf clusters. People attending this session will thus learn about a range of clusters at a variety of prices, will learn how CS educators are using those clusters, and will have the opportunity to ask detailed questions to those educators.

As a result, this session will be of interest to anyone who is interested in PDC or is teaching a course that covers PDC topics. Such courses include: *Algorithms*, *Computer Architecture*, *Computer Organization*, *Graphics*, *Operating Systems*, *Parallel Computing*, *Software Engineering*, *System Fundamentals*, the *Senior Capstone* course, and others. This special session will thus be of interest to instructors from a wide variety of CS courses.

5. SPECIAL SESSION SUITABILITY

The presenters will bring, display, and demonstrate their clusters, making this 75-minute session a "show and tell" style session. During the first part, the audience will receive an overview of the clusters and how they are being used to teach PDC. The "Group Q&A" part will allow the audience to engage with the presenters in a format that lets everyone hear all questions and answers. In the "Show&Tell" part, presenters will concurrently demonstrate their clusters to interested audience members, who can move from cluster to cluster, view the clusters up close, and ask detailed questions. This session's structure will thus be quite different from that of a typical paper or a panel session.

6. REFERENCES

Parts of this work were supported by NSF DUE #1225739.

7. REFERENCES

[1] ACM/IEEE CS Joint Task Force. "Computer Science Curriculum 2013". Online. Accessed 2015-08-20. https://www.acm.org/education/CS2013-final-report.pdf.

[2] J. Adams and T. Brom. "Microwulf: A Beowulf Cluster for Every Desk", *Proc. of the 39th SIGCSE Technical Symposium*, March, 2008, p. 121-125, DOI= 10.1145/1352135.1352178.

[3] Adapteva. "Parallella". Online, accessed 2015-08-20: http://www.adapteva.com/parallella/.

[4] R. Brown, L. Shoop, J. Adams. "CSinParallel: Parallel Computing in the CS Curriculum". Online, accessed 2015-08-20. http://csinparallel.org.

[5] Hardkernel. "ODROID-XU4 and ODROID-C1+". Online, accessed 2015-08-20: http://hardkernel.com.

[6] Nvidia. "Jetson-Tk1". Online, accessed 2015-08-20: https://developer.nvidia.com/jetson-tk1.

[7] C. Peck, et al. "LittleFe: Parallel and Cluster Computing On The Move". Online, accessed 2015-08-20: http://littlefe.net.

[8] Raspberry Pi Foundation. "Raspberry Pi 2". Online, accessed 2015-08-20: https://www.raspberrypi.org/products/.

[9] J. Wolfer, "A Heterogeneous Supercomputer Model for High-Performance Parallel Computing Pedagogy", *IEEE Global Engineering Education Conference*, March, 2015.

Three Years of Student Pair Programming – Action Research Insights and Outcomes

Ian McChesney
Ulster University
School of Computing and Mathematics
Newtownabbey, Northern Ireland
+44 28 9036 8881
ir.mcchesney@ulster.ac.uk

ABSTRACT

In the software engineering industry the technique of pair programming can be used as a means of enhancing programmer productivity and the quality of the software development process. Pair programming has also been used in computer science education as a mechanism to address some of the educational challenges faced by students learning to program. An action research study is described in which pair programming is used as part of the learning and assessment regime in introductory programming. Module data has been used over a three year cycle to evaluate the impact of pair programming on student performance and confidence in programming, and to gain insights into its practical application. Within-subject analysis confirms previously reported observations of overall improved student performance. Qualitative analysis identifies areas for refinement in the practical application of pair programming for learning and assessment, particularly in relation to pairwise communication, establishing protocols for conflict resolution and development of professional competencies.

Keywords

Pair programming; Introductory Programming; Action Research

1. INTRODUCTION

The challenges of learning and teaching in introductory programming are widely recognized within the computer science education community. Learning to program presents difficulties to students because of the abstractions required and the inherent problem solving necessary for all but the most trivial of programming problems [14]. Learning to program is an incremental and highly integrated endeavor, with each topic in an introductory programming module building upon its predecessors, resulting in students easily falling behind if they have not sufficiently grasped previous concepts. This in turn can lead to diminishing motivation and lack of confidence in completing programming tasks [6], [12].

This paper describes the learning and teaching approach taken in an undergraduate introductory programming module. The module in its current form has been delivered for five years, and has incorporated a range of techniques to enhance student learning and performance. One of these is the use of pair programming for some of the laboratory and assignment work. Initially pair programming was used informally but subsequently a more formal and controlled approach was taken, with the aim of more carefully evaluating the impact of pair programming as introduced in this module – in particular, does it lead to improved student performance and confidence in formal assessment, and how can it be refined to maximize this desired outcome? Adopting an action research approach [8], the aim is to evaluate and revise the implementation of pair programming over a number of cycles of module delivery and to monitor its effect compared to previous published work e.g. [5], [10].

SIGCSE '16, March 02-05, 2016, Memphis, TN, USA
© 2016 ACM. ISBN 978-1-4503-3685-7/16/03…$15.00
DOI: http://dx.doi.org/10.1145/2839509.2844565

2. BACKGROUND

The principles of pair programming have been used in a range of computer science education settings. Recent systematic literature reviews of pair programming in computer science education reveal a consensus that it can improve student understanding, can lead to enhanced confidence in programming, and improved performance in assessment [5], [10]. While not a silver bullet [13], [15] there is evidence of benefit in relation to a student's assessed practical work and, combined with other interventions, is especially helpful for weaker students [3], [7].

As well as its pedagogic benefits, there are professional reasons for introducing students to pair programming. It is a commonly cited technique in agile methods of software development as practiced in industry, methods which place a strong emphasis on the creativity and problem solving capability of the software engineer, with pair programming supporting this approach [1]. Pair programming also provides an opportunity for students to work together, addressing the requirement for team working and collaboration skills in their learning and assessment.

3. APPROACH

In this paper we describe the operation of pair programming in an introductory, undergraduate year 1 programming module, referred to here as Windows Programming 1 (WP1). In the context of on-going improvement in module delivery, action research provides a framework within which to consider the introduction and evaluation of pair programming over a number of cycles [2].

The work described here was approved by the relevant ethics committee within the university. No personal data was gathered from the students. Regarding programming tasks, students were not participating in any activities apart from assessment as part of the normal operation of the module. Student consent was obtained from those students providing additional qualitative feedback.

With the literature suggesting that pair programming is, on balance, a positive intervention in introductory programming [15], the research questions of particular interest in this paper are:

RQ1: Does pair programming improve student performance in programming practical tasks in the module?
and
RQ2: Does pair programming lead to an improved student experience of programming practical tasks in the module?

Consistent with the action research approach, while acknowledging the exercise is specific to one module, it is anticipated that general observations can be made which are relevant to other introductory programming modules.

3.1 Programming Module Description

The WP1 module seeks to introduce students to the foundational concepts of windows-based, event-driven programming, while seeking to develop problem solving skills as an integral part of software development. The module is taught and assessed over two consecutive 12-week semesters. It is assessed through continuous assessment, mainly through practical programming tasks, with two substantive assessments in semester 1, and two in semester 2, in addition to short weekly knowledge and understanding tests.

Table 1. Module WP1 Assessment Breakdown

Assessment	Mode	Weighting%)
a1 (Week 5)	I	15
PP practice	PP	-
a2 (Week 11)	I & PP	20
a3 (Week 17)	I & PP	15
a4 (Week 24)	I	20
Weekly tests	I	30

The assessment breakdown is as shown in Table 1. Assessments 1, 2 and 3 (a1, a2 and a3) are laboratory-based practical assessments of two hours duration each. In semester 1 week 5, students undertake individually (mode I) their first formal practical assessment. In semester 1 week 11 they complete their laboratory-based assessment in part individually and in part as a pair (mode PP). In semester 2 week 5, they do another laboratory-based assignment which is part individual and part pairs, and then a final summative individual practical assessment a4 (outside of laboratory). Laboratory-based assessment typically consists of writing two program in two hours, with both programs equally weighted and of similar difficulty. As such the paired assessment contributes 17.5% of the overall module mark.

In advance of their first pair programming assessment, students are given an introduction to the principles of pair programming plus the opportunity to practice the completion of laboratory exercises in pairs [4]. As such, pair programming is always practiced as a co-located and intensive activity.

3.2 Cohort Profiles

The cohorts studied here consisted of year 1 students on a single honors computing course. On entry, no assumptions are made about students having any previous programming experience.

For practical work in laboratories, students were allocated alphabetically by surname to two groups A and B. In both groups, pairs were allocated randomly and where possible the same pairings were retained from a2 to a3.

3.3 Study Design - Assessments 2 and Assessments 3

Pair programming was used in assessments 2 and 3 (a2, a3). These assessments each involve writing two programs and have been designed to allow for individual work and pair work. At each assessment, the programs to be completed are of similar complexity. Using the above group allocations, the program combinations used were as shown in Table 2, reducing the possibility of performance difference arising from the intrinsic nature of the problems set. In each assessment, individual programming was completed first, followed by the pair programming task.

Table 2. Individual and pair programming in Assessment 2 and Assessment 3

a2		a3	
Group A	Group B	Group A	Group B
a2-P1 (I)	a2-P2 (I)	a3-P1 (I)	a3-P2 (I)
a2-P2 (PP)	a2-P1 (PP)	a3-P2 (PP)	a3-P1 (PP)

Note: (a2 = Assessment 2; a3 = Assessment 3; P1 = Program 1; P2 = Program 2; I = individual; PP = pair programming)

To address the research questions above, we formulate the following hypothesis:

For RQ1: On a within-subject analysis, there is no difference between the student score for individual programming compared with pair programming:

H_0 : Individual mark – pair programming mark = 0

H_1 : Individual mark – pair programming mark < 0

This is tested using the student achieved mark in each assessment a2 and a3.

For RQ2: Considering changes in attitude to the programming experience:

H_0: There is no significant difference in student attitude to pair programming compared with individual programming.

H_1: There is a significant difference in student attitude to pair programming compared with individual programming.

For RQ2, at the end of a2 and a3, attitude was gauged by asking students to reflect on aspects on their pair programming experience, as described in section 4.2 below.

4. RESULTS

In the sections below, data is presented for the three cycles (or three years) of the action research study. Scores presented are percentage scores and are based on the assessment first attempt, including any students who subsequently withdrew from the course.

4.1 Effect of Pair Programming on Student Performance

A within-subject analysis was used to test the hypothesis that students performed better when pair programming compared with individual programming. Two tests were conducted, a one tail, two sample paired t-test and a one tail, Wilcoxon signed ranks test. A significance level of 0.05 was used for analysis.

For a2, the results are shown in Table 3 below.

Table 3. Assessment 2 within-subject analysis comparing individual and pair programming performance.

a2	cohort 1 (n=51)	cohort 2 (n=90)	cohort 3 (n=72)
Mean score (I)	49.84	43.04	58.56
Mean score (PP)	56.51	53.60	58.69
t-test (p)	0.051	<0.001	0.478
Wilcoxon (p)	0.025	<0.001	0.475

Considering the a2 cohort scores for each cycle, the data would suggest there is an improvement arising from pair programming for cohorts 1 and 2 only.

For a3, the results are shown in Table 4. For each cohort, student overall performance was significantly better when pair programming.

Table 4. Assessment 3 within-subject analysis comparing individual and pair programming performance.

a3	cohort 1 (n=52)	cohort 2 (n=84)	cohort 3 (n=68)
Mean score (I)	44.27	46.36	52.59
Mean score (PP)	58.54	53.04	60.65
t-test (p)	<0.001	0.003	0.024
Wilcoxon (p)	<0.001	0.004	0.058

When results were analyzed at the group level within each cohort, some variability was evident as would be expected. For example, for a2 cohort 2, group A exhibited significantly better performance when pair programming (p=<0.001) whereas this was not the case for group B (p=0.328).

There is no surprise that in general pair programming scores are better, since within the pair the weaker student will benefit from the stronger partner's contribution – by definition. To make this explicit in our analysis, we consider the relative performance improvement for weaker students compared with stronger students. For analysis purposes students within a pair were classified as 'high' or 'low' performers depending on their performance in the individual program element of the assessment. Within-subject analysis was repeated for these two groups. For both a2 and a3, results show a significant improvement in the scores for students in the low category ("weaker" students) when programming in pairs but no significant change for the high category ("stronger" students).

By considering within-subject performance from a2 to a3, we gain some insight into individual and pair programming performance over time. To see if there is significance in this data we have:

H_0: a2I - a3I = 0, H_1: a2I - a3I < 0

and

H_0: a2PP - a3PP = 0, H_1: a2PP - a3PP < 0

The data is shown in Table 5. For cohorts 1 and 3, on average individual performance deteriorated whereas pair performance was roughly the same. For cohort 2, there was no significant difference. With individual performance at a3 significantly lower than at a2, a possible explanation is that the students found a3 to be more difficult, but completing the assignment in pairs ameliorated this difficulty. Cohort 3 scores show an overall better performance. A contributing factor to the strong performance of this cohort is possibly the increasing demand for places on the course over the three year cycle, with the result that cohort 3 has a better overall grade profile on their entry qualifications, combined with interventions arising from the action research itself (see section 5.3 below).

Table 5. Analysis of within-subject performance at Assessment 2 and Assessment 3

	cohort 1 (n=50)		cohort 2 (n = 83)		cohort 3 (n = 67)	
mean score	I	PP	I	PP	I	PP
a2	50.04	57.16	44.43	54.02	60.21	59.52
a3	44.28	57.36	45.95	52.10	52.15	59.94
t-test (p)	0.014	0.482	0.268	0.267	0.001	0.447
Wilcoxon (p)	0.006	0.128	0.249	0.307	0.003	0.411

4.2 Student Confidence - Attitudes and Perceptions in Pair Programming

At the end of each of a2 and a3, students were asked to reflect on their experience of pair programming compared with individual programming. The aim was to assess whether they felt more confident when programming in pairs rather than individually. This attitude was explored through seven constructs relating to the pair programming process. There are a range of aspects of pair programming which merit inquiry [5]. The approach here was to consider pair programing with respect to its process (the student experience) and its product (the delivered program). The notion of student confidence is a key question in the action research being undertaken – seeking interventions which help students feel better about programming. Relative to individual programming, students were asked to rate pair programming on perceived difficulty (DIFF), enjoyment of programming (ENJY), stressfulness of the experience (STRS) and productivity or efficiency benefits (PROD). For example, "Compared to individual programming, do you consider pair programming to be less difficult, more difficult, or the same?"

Students were also asked to assess pair programming's effect on program correctness (CRCT), its design quality (DSGN), and overall compliance with the requirements specification (REQS). For example, "Compared to individual programming, is the program delivered via pair programming of poorer quality design, better quality design, or the same?"

To facilitate descriptive analysis, responses were scored -1, 0 and 1 for less, same, and more respectively. Hence an average of 0 would indicate that, overall, there was no change in how individual and pair programming was experienced. Tables 6 and 7 show the results for a2 and a3 respectively. To assess whether a "less" or "more" response was significant, a Chi Square goodness of fit analysis was completed, assuming an even spread of responses within each category as a reference point.

For a2, over the three year cycle, the students felt that compared to individual programming, PP was less difficult and more enjoyable. There was some variation in experience regarding how stressful they found it and whether it was a more productive approach than individual programming. Regarding the finished artefact, they consistently were of the view that it produced better programs. At the group level, there were no significant differences in attitudes between groups A and B in each cohort.

Table 6. Assessment 2 student rating of experience with pair programming compared to individual programming

Rating	DIFF	ENJY	STRS	PROD	CRCT	DSGN	SPEC
cohort 1	-0.34	0.55	-0.22	0.12	0.86	0.50	0.50
cohort 3	-0.40	0.66	-0.29	0.30	0.64	0.53	0.28
cohort 3	-0.21	0.50	-0.31	0.13	0.55	0.57	0.27
χ^2 (p)							
cohort 1	0.007	0.001	0.123	0.107	<0.001	0.001	0.001
cohort 3	<0.001	<0.001	0.002	0.001	<0.001	<0.001	0.003
cohort 3	<0.001	<0.001	0.002	0.275	<0.001	0.001	0.002

For a3 we have similar observations, with student views on pair programming stressfulness and productivity showing some variability across the cohorts. Again, there were no significant differences between the groups in terms of their attitudes.

Table 7. Assessment 3 student rating of experience with pair programming compared to individual programming

Rating	DIFF	ENJY	STRS	PROD	CRCT	DSGN	SPEC
cohort 1	-0.47	0.57	-0.37	0.37	0.72	0.70	0.30
cohort 2	-0.54	0.57	-0.24	0.37	0.65	0.59	0.35
cohort 3	-0.46	0.51	-0.33	0.21	0.68	0.47	0.47
χ^2 (p)							
cohort 1	<0.001	<0.001	0.005	0.005	<0.001	<0.001	0.001
cohort 2	<0.001	<0.001	0.066	0.002	<0.001	<0.001	0.003
cohort 3	<0.001	<0.001	0.002	0.275	<0.001	0.001	0.002

At the cohort level, an analysis of how attitudes changed from a2 to a3 (using a Chi Square test of association) indicates there were no significant changes over time, except in cohort 1 for perceived productivity, where pair programming was considered to be faster (more productive) than individual programming at a3 (0.37, Table 7) compared with a2 (0.12, Table 6).

These results would suggest that students consistently had a positive attitude toward pair programming on the constructs used above, but with an indication of it having some stressful aspects and not always being an efficient process – these points will be discussed further below.

4.3 Student Comments

As well as rating their experience, students were asked to state, in their view, the best and worst aspect of pair programming. A qualitative content analysis using descriptive coding [9] was used to extract key themes from the responses. Over the three cycles of the module, analysis of the "best" aspects of pair programming are shown in Table 8 (n=373 comments). The "worst" aspects are shown in Table 9 (n=257 comments). For the purposes of content analysis a student's response may have consisted of one or more comments.

Regarding the most positive aspect of pair programming, the dominant theme (32% of comments) was that it enabled a better understanding of the problem (e.g. "two minds are better than one"). The necessity of having to discuss towards a solution (29%) was also a strong theme (e.g. "being able to work together. You can talk through problems and issues"). Other comments reflected how partners could often complement each other's strengths and weaknesses or that it helped to develop useful professional skills such as team working.

Table 8. "Best" aspects of pair programming - summary of key themes from student responses

Comment themes:	% comments
Better understanding of problem	32
Discussion required to solve problem	29
Partners had complementary strengths & weaknesses	11
Less stressful than individual programming	9
Resulted in less errors in submitted program	9
Less time to complete program	4
Learning new things from partner	3
Developed soft skills (communication, teamwork)	2
Meeting new person	1

Table 9. "Worst" aspects of pair programming - summary of key themes from student responses

Comment themes:	% comments
Differences of opinion / arguments within pair	25
Requires more time to complete	19
Uneven sharing of workload within pair	14
Both partners can get stuck on the problem	10
Difficulty in sharing keyboard & screen	9
Difficulty in communicating technical concepts	7
A stressful experience	7
Not knowing your partner	4
How to decide on task allocation	3
Personality clash	2

Regarding the worst aspect of pair programming, the dominant theme to emerge was that of differences of opinion or arguments between partners (25%), though only a small number of comments actually referred to this as due to a personality clash. It was also reported by some that pair programming takes longer due to the time required to discuss and explain issues to each other (19%). Other themes to emerge concerned unequal sharing of work, the physical practicalities of keyboard sharing, and difficulties in communicating technical concepts within the pair.

As noted, the above data is summarized over the three year cycle. There was some variation in the relative frequency of these themes from year to year, for example, for cohort 1, 3% of comments were concerned with it being a stressful experience, whereas for cohort 3 this was 14%. Many factors will contribute to an individual's experience and such variation is expected.

5. DISCUSSION

5.1 Research Questions

For RQ1, on balance the results support the hypothesis that pair programming leads to improved student performance. However, as Tables 3 and 4 show, this is not a uniform experience. Cohort 3 a2, for example, did not show any significant improvement in student performance. Note however that the mean individual score for cohort 3 a2 is higher than previous years. As noted earlier, this may be due to improved cohort entry qualifications coupled with the action research intervention in this cycle of enhanced support for weaker students (see section 5.3. below).

When looking at performance over time from a2 to a3, for cohorts 1 and 3 in particular, individual performance deteriorates from a2 to a3, suggesting that a3 is more challenging for the students. (Topics such as lists, arrays and functions are being assessed at this stage.). It could be the case that some of the challenges in the more advanced a3 assessment were ameliorated when working in pairs. This might also suggest that there are benefits in repeated pair programming opportunities within a module.

For RQ2, the results suggest overall a positive experience with pair programming. However, the two aspects where this was not the case related to stress and productivity. Regarding productivity, this is raised by students in their qualitative feedback as one of the worst aspects of pair programming. Of course, the rationale of pair programming is to produce programs of higher quality. In industry, this will take longer during initial development but will lead to overall efficiencies in later testing and maintenance activities. In laboratory-based programming assignments, these quality benefits are limited due to the compressed timescale – the focus is on getting the program to work. And since the two programs in each assessment are swapped between groups for paired completion, the paired programming problem cannot be "made simpler" to address this time constraint arising from pairing.

A possible explanation for the stressfulness experienced is that the time constraint from working in pairs actually contributes to a more stressful experience overall, though stress would also be influenced by factors such as having a difference of opinion with a partner, or working with someone you have not worked with before.

5.2 Insights from Qualitative Data

It is no surprise that many students reported an improved understanding of their programs as a result of working in pairs. However, some individual comments provide helpful insights into student perceptions, even if they were not comments that featured widely throughout the data set.

For example, some saw value in pair programming as a peer learning experience. One student referred to being encouraged to try an aspect of programming they would not have thought useful in the given context – the other student "encouraged me to try code that I previously would have thought is wrong". Other comments in this vein included "Learning about other peoples' methods of coding"; "being able to pick up on anything that you may have forgotten how to do and then be able to remember that for the future" and "Being able to take on my partner's abilities and being able to showcase my own".

There was also insight into the dynamics of the pair programming process. Specific comments included, "there are two people able to try and find notes to help"; "you have additional help and have a different way of thinking. More ideas and conclusions occur" and "When in pairs you are a lot more goal orientated, OK what is the next thing to do? as you constantly communicate and discuss with your partner what is next, is that right or wrong, is it the best way to do it, is it the only way to do it etc.". Not everyone welcomed the experience of pair programming, for example one student reported a "worst" aspect as "Not being able to work with the other person as well as I would have by myself".

The comments suggest two contrasting aspects to the social dynamic of pair programming. On the one hand, students enjoyed the conversational aspect of the experience, e.g. "Getting the chance to meet with others in the class you may not have otherwise got the chance to meet"; "Getting to talk to other people in the class". On the other hand, some students saw this as a pressure situation e.g. "the possibility of embarrassment"; "If one is stressed both become stressed". A more constructive view of this was reported by others in terms of responsibility, e.g. "High level of stress as you are working in a team and want the best score for your team mate"; "Stress in case you bring someone else's marks down"; "The pressure on getting it right. Having shared marks/grade"; "Pressure to do well for both of you".

Some negative comments relate to an observation which had not been anticipated at first, that students found it difficult to explain technical issues or concepts to their partner, sometimes inhibiting their ability to solve a problem. For example, "Two people having a different understanding of what needs to be done. Time then has to be spent explaining and sorting out the issue"; "When trying to explain issues with the code I found it was sometimes difficult to convey what each issue was". This observation is complimentary to [16] where the authors have modelled communication patterns in pair programming; we would add that equipping students with, and reinforcing their understanding of, the necessary technical vocabulary is a valuable part of effective communication in this context. As a student spends more time actually studying programming, their technical vocabulary improves and this might be one reason for repeated pair programming activities being more productive.

5.3 Action Research Outcomes

The work described here has taken place as action research during the teaching of module WP1. The key changes to practice arising from the results and observations are summarized below, and can be viewed as recommended steps for other educators when introducing pair programming. After cohort 1, we sought to *establish and reinforce a clear technical vocabulary for students to use in laboratory work.* As we have noted, students reported a technical communication difficulty when talking about programming. Subsequently, our module delivery has sought to reinforce technical terms during class and to use these consistently in practical sessions and preparation for assessment.

Also after cohort 1, we sought to *establish clear protocols for conflict resolution.* Student comments regarding differences of opinion and arguments led to a greater module emphasis on the mechanisms of the pair programming protocol, with simple strategies for resolving conflict introduced to students.

Cohort 2 results highlighted that for some students, pair programming is seen as a stressful experience. Therefore, in addition to the pair programming practice sessions before a2, we revised our laboratory approach to *encourage students to engage in some pair programming during each weekly laboratory session.* While such collaboration did happen naturally amongst students, this was now more actively promoted. However, the latest results indicate this area needs further work as students continue to report pair programming a stressful experience. Cohort 2 results also highlighted a trend of unexpectedly low individual scores amongst weak students. To address this a more structured regime of formative feedback was introduced.

As an outcome from cohort 3, our next intervention will be to *focus on the transferable skills which can derive from pair programming* and their contribution to professional competencies, ideas which have also been explored by [11]. This positive aspect was something which cohort 1 students had reported but it has not been a feature of student comments since. Generic feedback sessions will be used to identify the particular skills acquired from pair programming which can be transferred to other contexts, focusing on communication skills, shared responsibility and time management.

6. CONCLUSION

While many aspects of module delivery contribute to student outcomes, there is evidence from elsewhere that pair programming contributes positively to student performance and confidence. The results reported here reinforce this view. Students report a positive experience, appreciating the overall benefits of collaborative problem solving while acknowledging there are trade-offs in terms of conflict resolution and time management. The study also suggests that repeated opportunities to practice pair programming enable the dynamics of pair programming to operate more smoothly.

In addition, the approach we have adopted allows students to experience the benefits of collaborative working but in a way which does not detract from the requirement for sufficient individual tasks for assessment validity. Group work is widely recognized as a key component of undergraduate curricula, but does carry disadvantages regarding team overhead, team coordination, and the carrying of "free-riders" within the group. The particular pair programming regime described here can help reduce some of these disadvantages yet give students the benefit of a collaborative programming experience. This lays a foundation for more traditional group work in subsequent modules, equipping students for the challenge of working with diverse groups, conflicting ideas and different levels of commitment.

Finally, the mix of individual and pair programming we have adopted provides the teacher with a mechanism for monitoring paired performance against individual performance as a reference point. The assessment structure outlined above (Tables 1 and 2) provides a framework for innovating without significant perturbation of existing, individual assessment arrangements, and supports the collection and analysis of data for evaluating the benefits or otherwise of the innovation.

7. ACKNOWLEDGEMENTS

The programming laboratory sessions were supported by teaching fellows and other departmental technical staff and their assistance is greatly appreciated.

8. REFERENCES

[1] Beck, K. and Andres, C. 2004. *Extreme Programming explained: embrace change*. Addison-Wesley, Harlow.

[2] Ben-Ari, M., Berglund, A., Booth, S. and Holmboe, C. 2004. What do We Mean by Theoretically Sound Research in Computer Science Education. In *Proc. 9th annual SIGCSE conference on Innovation and technology in computer science education* (ITiCSE '04). ACM, New York, NY, USA, 230-231 DOI = http://doi.acm.org/ 10.1145/1026487.1008059

[3] Braught, G., Eby, L.M. and Wahls, T. (2008) The Effects of Pair-Programming on Individual Programming Skill. In *Proceedings of the 39th SIGCSE technical symposium on Computer science education (SIGCSE '08)*. ACM, New York, NY, USA, 200-204. DOI= http://doi.acm.org/ 10.1145/1352135.1352207

[4] DeClue, T.H. 2003. Pair programming and pair trading: effects on learning and motivation in a CS2 course. *J. Comput. Sci. Coll. 18, 5 (May 2003), 49-56.*

[5] Hanks, B., Fitzgerald, S., McCauley, R., Murphy, L. and Zander, C. 2011. Pair programming in education: a literature review. *Computer Science Education, 21, 2 (June 2011), 135-173.*

[6] Kinnunen, P. and Simon, B. 2012 My program is ok – am I? Computing freshmen's experiences of doing programming assignments, *Computer Science Education, 22, 1 (March 2012) 1-28.*

[7] McDowell, C., Werner, L., Bullock, H. and Fernald, J. 2006. Pair programming improves student retention, confidence, and program quality. *Commun. ACM* 49, 8 (August 2006), 90-95. DOI= http://doi.acm.org/10.1145/1145287.1145293

[8] McNiff, J. and Whitehead, J. 2011. *All you need to know about action research* (2/e). Sage, Los Angeles, USA.

[9] Miles, M.B., Huberman, A.M. and Saldana, J.M. 2013. *Qualitative Data Analysis: A Methods Sourcebook* (3/e). : Sage, Thousand Oaks, USA.

[10] Salleh, N., Mendes, E. and Grundy, J. 2011. Empirical Studies of Pair Programming for CS/SE Teaching in Higher Education: A Systematic Literature Review, *IEEE Trans. Softw. Eng* 37 (4), 509-525.

[11] Schumm, M.; Joseph, S.; Schroll-Decker, I.; Niemetz, M.; Mottok, J., Required competences in software engineering: Pair programming as an instrument for facilitating life-long learning. In *Proc. 15th Intl. Conf. Interactive Collaborative Learning (ICL)*, 2012, pp.1-5, 26-28 Sept. 2012.

[12] Scott, M. and Ghinea, G. 2013. Educating programmers: A reflection on barriers to deliberate practice. In *Proc. 2nd HEA Conference on Learning and Teaching in STEM Disciplines (HEA STEM '13,)*, Paper 028P. DOI: 10.11120/stem.hea.2013.0005

[13] Somervell, J. 2006. Pair programming: Not for everyone? In *Proc. 2006 International Conference on Frontiers in Education: Computer science and computer engineering (FECS'06)*, Las Vegas, NV. 303–307, CSREA Press.

[14] Vickers, P. 2009. *How to think like a programmer*. Cengage Learning, London, UK.

[15] Vihavainen, A., Airaksinen, J. and Watson, C.. 2014. A systematic review of approaches for teaching introductory programming and their influence on success. In Proceedings of the tenth annual conference on International computing education research (ICER '14). ACM, New York, NY, USA, 19-26. DOI= http://doi.acm.org/10.1145/2632320.2632349

[16] Zarb, M. and Hughes, J. 2015. Breaking the communication barrier: guidelines to aid communication within pair programming. *Computer Science Education*, 25, 2 (April 2015) 120-151.

Observations of Pair Programming: Variations in Collaboration Across Demographic Groups

Omar Ruvalcaba
CA State University, Northridge
omar.ruvalcaba@csun.edu

Linda Werner
University of CA, Santa Cruz
linda@soe.ucsc.edu

Jill Denner
Education, Training, Research
jilld@etr.org

ABSTRACT

Sixty-nine pairs of Latino and white middle school students were video recorded as they pair programmed for approximately 20 minutes. We quantitatively analyzed the partners' interactions specifically looking at characteristics of their collaboration. A qualitative analysis of interactions of three girl pairs was conducted to gain insight into how students' experience in diverse cultural communities may relate to their collaboration during pair programming.

Categories and Subject Descriptors

• Human-centered computing ~ Empirical studies in collaborative and social computing

Keywords

Collaboration, Pair Programming, Latinos, Diversity, Middle School

1. INTRODUCTION

Collaboration is an important 21st century skill necessary for students' future success in the work force [13]. The coordination of teamwork toward larger goals is sometimes allowed, but often is not a priority in schools where assignments are often a form of individualized assessment [14]. Pair programming, a collaborative approach to computer programming where two people work sharing the same computer and mouse, may provide a unique context to better understand the process of collaboration. Its use has been shown to increase programming confidence and satisfaction, and has been shown to increase retention in the computer science (CS) major for college students [10]. In the present study, we analyze middle school students' collaboration while pair programming to better understand how they collaborate.

Recent findings shed light on how much remains to be understood about the process of how individuals collaborate. For example, adult groups with women as members outperformed groups without women in a collaborative task [22]. It was found that groups that were sensitive to other's needs, distributed turns in conversation equally, and that had more women performed better than other groups where individuals took traditional individual leadership roles. These findings suggest that skilled collaboration is more important than individual contributions and relates to other aspects of group coordination such as distribution of conversational turn-taking. In addition, collaboration is a complex process that requires frequent assessment by individuals of their joint understanding of the task or problem [15]. Reaching a mutual understanding with partners is important for coordination and moving forward during collaborative work [7]. Understanding the collaborative process during pair programming may further our insight into the process of student collaboration - specifically how students reach mutual understanding and how they coordinate their efforts.

Understanding the process of pair programming is important because of the educational benefits of pair programming for middle school and university students. Previous research using transcripts of middle school girls using pair programming to create computer games has found that different kinds of interactions determined whether the partners got closer to or further from solutions when problem solving [6, 19]. Pair programming has been associated with positive outcomes for university students who were more likely to turn in better quality work and continue with CS coursework than those who worked alone [9, 10]. Additionally, experience with pair programming is related to an increase in university women's interest and retention in the field of CS [21]. Individuals may benefit from zones of proximal development when working with a partner since a partner may support an individual's ability to complete more difficult tasks, such as computer programming [18].

Research suggests that friendship impacts the partner dynamics and learning during pair programming [20]. This finding may be because friends have more experience coordinating with each other than with other children in their school. But two questions remain, what types of interactions are common during pair programming and what do these interactions look like for students of different cultural backgrounds? Research indicates that students from various cultural backgrounds (e.g. Mexican, African American, Indigenous) differ in how and why they collaborate. Students' approaches to collaboration tend to reflect specific experiences with work and activities in their home and community [14]. Children of Mayan-heritage, for example, collaborate with adults as equal contributors in a problem solving discussion. Mothers do not lead the activity; both children and parents equally contribute when they have an idea. This differed from Mayan groups where parents had more experience with European-heritage practices through schooling resulting in scenarios where the parents take control of the activity by dividing the task into smaller jobs and specific roles [3].

In the present study, we build on research on collaboration, pair programming, and culture to understand how middle school students collaborate during pair programming. We hope to gain insight into how collaborative approaches may vary cross-culturally. Our findings should be of interest to CS educators and

SIGCSE '16, March 02-05, 2016, Memphis, TN, USA
© 2016 ACM. ISBN 978-1-4503-3685-7/16/03…$15.00
DOI: http://dx.doi.org/10.1145/2839509.2844558

industry where collaboration between individuals of different cultural backgrounds is becoming the norm. It is our hope that this research spurs CS education researchers to consider the role of cultural practices and experiences in students' approaches to collaborative learning. This research might broaden our understanding of how these cultural experiences relate to learning for each individual in these collaborations.

2. METHOD

2.1 Participants

This study takes data from a larger study looking at the development of computational thinking when creating computer games [19, 20]. Three hundred and twenty-five middle school students worked with partners or individually on computer programming projects. Teachers considered students' preferences when assigning partners. Pairs of students worked together approximately 20 hours throughout the semester. Towards the end of the semesters, during the game creation periods, each pair was video recorded for approximately 20 minutes while pair programming.

Eighty-three middle school student pairs were videotaped while working together. For our purposes, we dropped 14 pairs whose cultural background could not be clearly determined and pairs who were single representatives of their cultural background (e.g. Asian Pacific Islander), leaving 69 pairs for the present analysis. Of those 69 pairs, 14 were Latino student pairs (three girl pairs, nine boy pairs, and two mixed gender pairs), 27 were White student pairs (10 girl pairs, 14 boy pairs, and three mixed gender pairs), and 28 were pairs consisting of one White student and one Latino student that we call Mixed student pairs (seven girl pairs, 19 boy pairs, and two mixed gender pairs).

In addition to the quantitative analysis of these recordings, we present a case study of three pairs to highlight possible cultural variation in students' collaborations. This qualitative analysis includes a pair of Latina students, a pair of White students, and a pair where one student is Latina and another is White.

2.2 Procedure

The classes were held either after-school or an in-school computer programming semester-long class for 20 hours. The students used Alice – a visual computer programming language environment designed for novice use and that allows for the creation of 3D animations. All classes had teachers knowledgeable in Alice. The students programmed using pair programming where each pair shared a computer, mouse, and keyboard and was instructed on the pair programming approach to collaboration, which uses driver and navigator roles. The student as the driver controls the mouse and keyboard. The navigator provides support by checking for input errors and accessing printed resources. Both partners are responsible for design and development of the projects. In each pair, one student first assumed the role of driver and the other student the navigator role. After 10 minutes, they were instructed to switch driver and navigator roles and work for another 10 minutes.

In the first half of the semester-long class or 10 class hours, students played games previously created using Alice, completed self-paced tutorials, and completed guided instructional exercises. In the second half of the class, students were asked to create their own computer games. Towards the end of the semester-long class, the pairs were videotaped for 20 minutes while working on their own game projects. Each pair chose which individual first took the role of driver and navigator. A researcher asked the partners to switch roles after they worked together for 10 minutes.

2.3 Categorization

Using deductive coding [17], we watched a subset of the videos and developed categories to describe non-mutually exclusive observable interactions seen in the recordings. Specifically, we used an approach to deductive video coding that included developing categories of analysis informed by research, theory, and observations [1]. See Table 1.

Table 1. Category definitions and mean G-agreement

Coordination	**Nonverbal Looks** where a student looks over at their partner – 0.86
	Screen Pointing either student points at the screen – 0.89
	Agreement show explicit agreement with a partner's change or a proposed change. Can be verbal or nodding – 0.82
	Disagreement one or both show explicit disagreement with a partner's change or a proposed changed. Includes head shaking – 0.82
Questions	**Question** explicit question but may be indicated by tone inflection or nonverbal gesture (e.g. a student shrugged, pointed at the screen, and looked at partner waiting for a response) – 0.83
	Respond to question student responds to partner's question – 0.87
	Respond to own Question a student asks a question and also answers it moments later – 0.98
	Explanation student spontaneously starts explaining what they are doing or start explaining something difficult – 0.73
Direction	**Controlled Direction** student gives step by step directions to their partner – 0.92
	Suggested Direction student makes a suggestion for next step. Characterized by seeking partner's agreement (e.g. "Do you think we should make a story about a fairy?") – 0.86
Access	**Taking Control with Consent** asks to use mouse/keyboard – 0.98
	Taking Control without Consent takes the mouse/keyboard without explicit consent - 0.94
Antagonis	**Antagonistic Actions** interactions that cause tension including hurtful comments, instigating fights, prodding, putting down partner contributions, and showing annoyance with partner – 0.98

To analyze the recordings for the presence of these types of interactions, we divided each 20-minute recording into 120 ten-second intervals. The researchers chose ten-second intervals based on extensive piloting of the coding system. Ten-second intervals were long enough to capture the interactions of interest. Two research assistants (RAs) were trained in coding the videos using a coding manual. The RAs first watched an entire recording, without categorizing, to gain a sense of a pair's overall collaboration. After the initial viewing, the RAs then determined which, if any, interactions of these types were observed in each ten-second time interval. If an interaction fit a category, the presence of that category would be noted in that ten-second-time interval. Our categorization captured the presence of an interaction in a time interval. We use the term 'observable interaction in an interval' (OII) to refer to the presence of a specific interaction in an interval since we did not measure the frequency of occurrences in each ten-second interval.

Two RAs categorized the data. One RA categorized 100% of the data and the second RA categorized data in 39 (47%) of the 83 videos for inter-rater reliability. For each pair, we calculated Guilford's G, an index of agreement, that adjusts for chance agreement and does not require all marginal frequencies to be nonzero. G-agreement values in most pairs ranged from acceptable agreement, at least 0.60, to perfect agreement with the following exception. The G-agreement was below 0.60 for 'Explanation' for 4 pairs of students. Average G-agreement values were at least 0.82 for all categories except for 'explanation,' which had 0.72 (See Table 1 for all G-agreement values). If there was disagreement, the disagreement was discussed among the researchers until they reached a consensus.

3. RESULTS

3.1 Quantitative Analysis

Table 2. – Mean OIIs for Latino, White, and Mixed student pairs

	Latino Students (n=14)	White Students (n=27)	Mixed Pairs (n=28)	All Students
Nonverbal Looks	25.21	26.56	23.72	25.13
Screen Pointing	13.57	15.89	20.00	17.09
Agreement	10.21	19.11	15.86	15.99
Disagreement	5.57	9.81	9.25	8.72
Question	27.21	32.00	32.36	30.77
Respond to question	16.79	20.70	19.50	19.42
Respond to own question	1.14	2.81	1.57	1.97
Explanation	13.71	29.44	24.46	24.23
Controlled Direction	33.07	39.89	38.46	37.93
Suggested Direction	7.50	14.59	11.79	12.01
Taking control with consent	3.71	3.33	2.11	2.91
Taking control without consent	6.93	4.74	10.57	7.55
Antagonistic Actions	0.93	2.37	1.11	1.57
Average Total	165.57	221.26	209.75	205.29

The means for OIIs for each category are found in Table 2. The means are out of a possible 120 intervals. The most common types of OIIs are 'controlled direction', 'question', 'nonverbal looks', and 'explanation.' The least common types of OIIs are 'antagonistic actions,' 'respond to own question', 'taking with consent', and 'taking without consent.'

The OIIs that included verbal qualities were less commonly observed among Latino student pairs. The means for 'agreement' and 'disagreement' for Latino student pairs were 10.21 and 5.57, respectively, and were approximately half the value of the means for the White student pairs (19.11 and 9.81) and less than the means for the Mixed student pairs (15.86 and 9.25). Means for 'question' and 'respond to partner's question' are lower for Latino student pairs (27.21 and 16.79 respectively) compared to the White student pairs (32.00 and 20.70) and Mixed student pairs (32.36 and 19.50). The means for the 'Direction of Activity' categories are also lower for the Latino student pairs compared to the White and Mixed student pairs; the means for 'controlled direction' are 33.07 vs. 39.89 and 38.46, respectively; and the means for 'suggested direction' are 7.50 vs. 14.59 and 11.79, respectively. 'Explanation' (24.23), 'nonverbal look' (25.13), and 'controlled direction' (37.93) were the most common OIIs across all student pairs.

3.2 Qualitative Analysis – 3 case studies

We draw on qualitative methods [2] to better understand our results. Using a grounded theory approach [17] and informed by previous research and our knowledge of the community, we analyzed the data from three pairs of girl students. Our choice of pairs for the qualitative analysis was motivated by our observations that the Latino student pairs have a substantially lower total average OII. Also, even though a few of the mean OIIs, such as that for 'nonverbal looks,' for Latino student pairs were similar to the mean OIIs for the White student pairs and the Mixed student pairs; some of the Latino pairs were using nonverbal forms of OIIs a larger percentage of the time than most other student pairs (In 36% of Latino pairs, at least a fifth of their interactions were nonverbal looks compared to 11% of White pairs). In addition, nonverbal looks formed a larger percentage of the OIIs for Latino student pairs when compared to White student pairs and Mixed student pairs.

Table 3 – Total OIIs for case study pairs (total possible intervals per video is 120)

	Latina Pair	White Pair	Mixed Pair
Nonverbal Looks	33	24	32
Screen Pointing	6	31	4
Agreement	2	36	24
Disagreement	0	19	2
Question	6	48	33
Respond to question	2	41	23
Respond to own question	1	3	1
Explanation	1	46	18
Control Direction	7	63	26
Suggested Direction	3	26	24
Taking with consent	0	0	0
Taking without consent	6	1	1
Totals	67	338	188

Considering the lack of women and cultural diversity in programming, we decided to focus on girl pairs of diverse backgrounds for the qualitative analyses. We chose three all-female student pairs: one Latina, one White, and one Mixed Latina and White student pair. The pairs where chosen using the criteria that they had at least 18 hours of experience working together before they were recorded and that the partners were engaged with the pair programming activity for most of the recording time. See Table 3 for OII counts for these three student pairs.

Looking at the total OII counts in Table 3, the values are 67, 338, and 188 for the Latina, White, and Mixed student case study pairs respectively. 'Nonverbal looks' accounted for 49% of the total OIIs for the Latina student pair, 7% for the White student pair, and 17% for the Mixed student pair. The nonverbal looks percentage for the three case analysis pairs reflects similar findings in the entire sample with the Latina pair having a higher percentage of 'nonverbal look' OIIs. The percentage average of 'nonverbal looks' for all female pairs is Latina 27%, White 11%, and Mixed 12%; and for all male pairs, Latino 19%, White 15%, and Mixed 13%.

3.3 Details of the Case Studies

Latina student pair. The pair programming session began with the students piecing together where they left off last time. Throughout their pair programming session, they often looked over at each other when discussing next steps. When one partner looked over to check-in with her partner, the other partner often also looked over shortly after and made eye contact. These nonverbal looks often seemed to suggest they were looking for agreement or insight to their partner's understanding of the project. This interpretation is based on the fact that nonverbal looks often followed a question, a suggestion, or a change in the game, and occurred immediately before moving on to a next step (e.g. changes would happen after these looks and often, the other partner would nod). The girls also looked over at each other preceding laughter.

The pair showed signs of openness to their partner taking control when they had suggestions or new ideas. There were brief exchanges of the driver and navigator roles when a partner had a contribution to make. In one instance, the student in the navigator role leaned forward closer to the keyboard and the driver leaned back. The navigator then leaned in closer and typed in a command then leaned back out as the driver leaned back in. This entire interaction occurred without an explicit verbal request or permission. In our scheme this was categorized as 'take control without consent' since there was no explicit verbal agreement of the exchange of roles. Upon closer inspection, this interaction shows evidence that the pair was sensitive to reading cues from body language that our categorization did not capture.

Both partners discussed ideas often while working as either the navigator or driver. Although one partner spoke softer than the other, the other partner appeared to understand the subtle verbal and nonverbal cues. In the driver role, both students often looked over at their navigator partner and waited for a response after stating or suggesting a next step. They verbally discussed ideas and used nonverbal cues to reach some form of agreement before moving forward. Oftentimes, the pair built on each other's ideas by adding suggestions on top of previous contributions made by their partner without eliminating the previous contribution. Sometimes explicit verbal offers to help were also made when the driver hesitated or showed signs that evidenced confusion (e.g. the navigator asked the driver if she needed help typing).

White student pair. Like the Latina student pair, these students also explicitly reminded each other of past progress when they started on their project. Sometimes they looked over at each other ('nonverbal look' OIIs), but the driver often kept her eyes focused on the screen even while she paused – suggesting she was waiting for agreement. Both students often emphasized verbally stating their ideas and worked problems aloud ('suggested direction,' 'controlled direction,' or 'respond to question' OIIs), even when not asked for their feedback. Both students verbally expressed frustration about the problems in the game they were programming.

The partners maintained their roles as driver and navigator with no signs of unexpected role switching. When the navigator made a suggestion, the drive audibly considered the suggestion or simply integrated the navigator's suggestion possibly using some kind of nonverbal response. For example, the first student who took on the navigator role said, "Maybe we should put it in the ocean?" ('suggested direction' OII). The driver responded by shaking her head ('nonverbal look' OII). The navigator then responded, "Right, that wouldn't make sense" ('agreement' OII). Early in the recording they seemed to look for each other's explicit verbal agreement ('nonverbal look' OII). At one point, the navigator leaned forward and moved her hand, possibly in a bid to take control; the driver did not seem to notice since she made no discernable response.

After the pair switched driver and navigator roles when requested by a teaching assistant, discussion of next steps decreased with these new roles. Initially the first driver, now navigator, made statements telling the new driver what to do (e.g. "click there, now there"), ('controlled direction' OIIs). It seemed that the former driver attempted to maintain direct control of the project since her contributions were merely telling the new driver what to do rather than offering suggestions or explanations for what was being typed. The new driver made these changes without looking at her partner. In addition, there was less verbal discussion for the second portion of the collaboration.

Mixed student pair. The student pair with one Latino student and one White student resembled the White student pair in their reliance on mostly verbal communication to reach agreement and coordination; however, there were some interactions that resembled those seen for the Latina student pair. For the Mixed student pair, the White partner took the mouse at the start of their collaboration assuming the driver role and then asked her partner what they should do ('question' OII). This type of check-in characterized the pair throughout their collaboration. Each student often stated her next step in terms of "we" and drew in her partner verbally using 'suggested direction' OIIs.

The Latina partner often looked at her partner ('nonverbal look' OII) after making suggestions ('suggested direction' OII) or asking a question ('question' OII) in both the navigator and driver role. When in the driver role, the White partner mostly maintained her gaze toward the screen, not often looking over to meet her partner's 'nonverbal look' OIIs. When in the navigator role, the White partner looked over at the driver ('nonverbal look' OII) a few times but looked at the screen most of the time. 'Nonverbal look' OIIs were mostly made by the Latina partner. It also seems that these nonverbal looks were less versatile than those we observed in the Latina student pair. For the Mixed student pair, 'nonverbal look' OIIs, were observed for both partners during the same interaction and occurred mostly after 'suggested direction' or 'question' OIIs made by the Latina partner.

Although some of the nonverbal interactions initiated by the Latina partner seemed to have been missed, the White partner interacted by using a more explicit strategy- verbally asking for her partner's feedback and thoughts. Changes in the program were marked by explicit verbal agreements by both students. They often discussed what to do next, how to solve problems, and asked each other for help and feedback. Suggestions by the Latina partner were acknowledged by the White partner when she was driver, but were not always implemented. When not implemented, the White partner often clearly stated why she would not implement the changes. When the Latina partner became driver, she maintained a verbal narrative of the changes she made and incorporated changes that the White partner suggested throughout their collaboration. The Latina partner showed evidence of adapting to her partner's strategy and experience with approaches used by both the Latina and White pairs.

4. DISCUSSION AND LIMITATIONS

Using a system of categories to capture the type of interaction, the quantitative analysis presented in this paper demonstrates that Latina/o student pairs used less verbal OIIs than White or Mixed student pairs when pair programming. Although the Latina student pair case study had fewer total OIIs, the qualitative analysis suggests this may be due to the predominant use of nonverbal communication between these Latino partners. The Latina student pair's use of skilled nonverbal looks and other forms of nonverbal communication, analyzed in the qualitative analysis, may be an important part of how students of these backgrounds approach pair programming. These findings fit with previous research that highlights skilled nonverbal communication by Mexican-heritage and Latino-heritage students [12, 16].

As mentioned, the qualitative analysis provides insight into nonverbal communication patterns. It suggests that Latina students use nonverbal looks for many different purposes that included validation of partner's understanding, asking questions, and seeking agreement. In contrast, the White and Mixed student pairs predominantly used verbal OIIs to check for agreement. The Latina student in the Mixed student pair often looked over at her partner and initiated nonverbal looks that were not always returned by her White partner. The Latina student's point of visual focus shifted from the screen to her partner throughout the collaboration whereas the White student's visual focus mostly remained on the screen. This Mixed pair emphasized verbal communication despite attempts for nonverbal looks by the Latina student, suggesting that the Latina student was experienced in using both modes of communication. Despite these differences and perhaps because of the flexibility shown by the Latina partner, the Mixed pair seemed to collaborate well. Both partners contributed and built on each other's ideas. We don't know whether this is due to cultural differences or to differences in computer confidence, comfort or friendship with the partner, etc. But these examples suggest that given the right support in class, students of diverse backgrounds may be able to learn to cooperate while learning to computer program. Given our small sample, there is a need for future study where types of nonverbal communication are labeled and analyzed to learn more about how nonverbal communication relates to learning computer science for Latina students. If future findings match our analysis of this pair, it may suggest that a purely verbal emphasis in classrooms may put Latina students at a disadvantage.

The pattern of nonverbal interaction fits with previous findings suggesting that Latino-heritage children are skilled in use of nonverbal language when collaborating with peers in various school-like tasks [11]. Although a mix of verbal and nonverbal communication appears to be used in these communities, in certain contexts they are more likely to draw on nonverbal communication to avoid disrupting others around them [11, 16]. It has been suggested that nonverbal communication may support collaboration in ways that are conducive to coordination [16]. In addition to acknowledging the apparent nonverbal skill among Latino students, it is important to acknowledge that Latino-heritage children can be quite verbose in other contexts (e.g. with their families); but in a context that has historically disenfranchised them and focused on controlling their behavior (e.g. emphasizing self control and being quiet), they may rely on their experience with nonverbal communication. It may be that the school context made it easier for them to draw on their skills in reading body language and nonverbal communication.

The present study showcases the strength of using a mixed methods approach to understand computer science learning. Our approach draws from video analysis and case study approaches to gain a better understanding of how children of diverse backgrounds collaborate while programming together on one computer. The quantitative data shows that White student pairs used a higher number of 'explanation' and 'suggested direction' OIIs in their collaboration. We also found that the use of these OIIs was low among the Latino student pairs. The Latino students may instead use skilled nonverbal communication to reach agreement and make suggestions, thus being missed by our system of quantitative analysis. Across all student groups, regardless of cultural background, the two most common OIIs were 'questions' and 'nonverbal looks'. The first most common OII, 'questions,' suggests the importance of teachers encouraging students to ask questions during pair programming. Thus, we suggest it is important that we study what makes students feel comfortable asking questions when learning with technology especially for underrepresented groups such as women and Latinos who may have less experience or confidence with technology [8]. Because prevalence may not directly indicate a connection to positive outcomes, we also suggest future studies look at how different forms of asking questions (including nonverbal forms) may be connected to student learning of computer science concepts. The second most common OII, 'nonverbal looks,' points to the importance of using and reading nonverbal communication and body language for collaborative computer programming -- a form of skilled communication often neglected in computer science education, but often used by women and Latin American- and Indigenous-heritage people. It is important that teachers be aware of subtle nonverbal ways of seeking help.

The largest remaining limitation is the fact that most of our OIIs emphasized verbal communication. Although we were sensitive to nonverbal communication, it seems our categorization system would have benefited from OIIs that could capture differences in the nonverbal communication observed. This would require categories that are able to capture subtle shifts in body language, eye gaze, and context. Using this multifaceted approach to communication may broaden understanding of student approaches to agreement, disagreement, help seeking, or questioning their partners. For example, a partner might signal that they have a suggestion during pair programming by simply hovering their hand over their partner's hand, and then gently taking over when the partner willingly takes their hand off to give their partner a turn. We would like to better understand the use of context and body language in communicating and collaboration during pair programming. We hope to better understand if these patterns hold across Latino, White, and Mixed student groups. To better understand students' views of the collaboration process, we would like to conduct post-participation interviews in future studies.

5. ACKNOWLEDGMENTS

Our thanks go to the teachers and administrators at our seven schools, specifically Anne Guerrero, Shelly Laschkewitsch, Don Jacobs, Sue Seibolt, Karen Snedeker, Susan Rivas, and Katie Ziparo. Thanks also to teaching assistants, Will Park, Chizu Kawamoto, and Joanne Sanchez; and to Pat Rex and Eloy Ortiz, for instructional materials design and technology support. Thanks to UCSC undergraduate research assistants Madelyn Low, Alesandra Roger, Lyanne Rojas, and Inez Amada Solis for their assistance with the development of categories and their video analysis. Thanks to all of the middle school students who participated. This research is partially funded by a grant from NSF 0909733 "The Development of Computational Thinking among Middle School Students Creating Computer Games." Any opinions, findings, conclusions or recommendations expressed in this material are those of the authors and do not necessarily reflect the views of the National Science Foundation.

6. REFERENCES

[1] Angelillo, C., Rogoff, B., & Chavajay, P. (2007). Examining shared endeavors by abstracting video coding schemes with fidelity to cases. *Video research in the learning sciences*, 189-206.

[2] Barron, B. (2000). Achieving coordination in collaborative problem-solving groups. *The Journal of the Learning Sciences*, *9*(4), 403-436.

[3] Chavajay, P. (2006). How Mayan mothers with different amounts of schooling organize a problem-solving discussion with children. *International Journal of Behavioral Development*, *30*, 371-382.

[4] Crabtree, B. F., & Miller, W. L. (Eds.). (1999). *Doing qualitative research*. Sage Publications.

[5] DeLay, D., Hartl, A. C., Laursen, B., Denner, J., Werner, L., Campe, S., & Ortiz, E. (2014). Learning from friends: Measuring influence in a dyadic computer instructional setting. International Journal of Research & Method in Education, 37(2), 190-205.

[6] Denner, J., & Werner, L. (2007). Computer programming in middle school: How pairs respond to challenges. *Journal of Educational Computing Research*,*37*(2), 131-150.

[7] Gibbs, R., & Mueller, R. A. (1990). Conversation as coordinated, cooperative interaction. *Cognition, computing, and cooperation*, 95-114.

[8] Margolis, J. (2008). Stuck in the shallow end. MIT Press.

[9] McDowell, C., Werner, L., Bullock, H., & Fernald, J. (2002). The effects of pair-programming on performance in an introductory programming course. ACM SIGSCE Bulletin, *34*, 38-42.

[10] McDowell, C., Werner, L., Bullock, H. E., & Fernald, J. (2006). Pair programming improves student retention, confidence, and program quality. *Communications of the ACM*, *49*(8), 90-95.

[11] Mejía-Arauz, R., Roberts, A. D., & Rogoff, B. (2012). Cultural variation in balance of nonverbal conversation and talk. *International Perspectives in Psychology: Research, Practice, Consultation*, *1*(4), 207-220.

[12] Mejía-Arauz, R., Rogoff, B., Dexter, A. L., & Najafi, B. (2007). Cultural variation in children's social organization. *Child Development*, *78*, 1001–1014.

[13] Pellegrino, J. W., & Hilton, M. L. (Eds.). (2013). Education for life and work: Developing transferable knowledge and skills in the 21st century. National Academies Press.

[14] Rogoff, B. (2003). *The cultural nature of human development*. Oxford University Press.

[15] Roschelle, J. (1992). The construction of shared knowledge in collaborative problem solving. *The Journal of the Learning Sciences*, 2, 235-276.

[16] Ruvalcaba, O., Rogoff, B., López, A., Correa-Chávez, M., & Gutiérrez, K. (2015, accepted). Children's considerateness of other's activities: *Respeto* in requests for help. *Advances in Child Development and Behavior*, 49.

[17] Straus, A., & Corbin, J. (1990). Basics of qualitative research: Grounded theory procedures and techniques. Sage.

[18] Vygotsky, L. (1978). Interaction between learning and development. In M. Gauvian & M. Cole (Eds.) *Mind and Society* (79-91). Cambridge, MA: Harvard University Press.

[19] Werner, L., & Denner, J. (2009). Pair programming in middle school: What does it look like? *Journal of Research on Technology in Education*, *42*(1), 29-49.

[20] Werner, L., Denner, J., & Campe, S. (2014). Children Programming Games: A Strategy for Measuring Computational Learning. ACM Transactions on Computing Education (TOCE), 14(4), 24.

[21] Werner, L., Hanks, B., & McDowell, C. (2004). Pair-programming helps female computer science students. *Journal on Educational Resources in Computing*, 1-4.

[22] Woolley, A. W., Chabris, C. F., Pentland, A., Hashmi, N., & Malone, T. W. (2010). Evidence for a collective intelligence factor in the performance of human groups. *Science*, *330*(6004), 686-688.

Teaching Mobile Development with Pair Programming

Mohammed Seyam
Department of Computer Science, Virginia Tech
KnowledgeWorks II, Room 1122
2202 Kraft Dr, Blacksburg, VA 24061
+1 540 449 9415
seyam@vt.edu

D. Scott McCrickard
Department of Computer Science, Virginia Tech
KnowledgeWorks II, Room 1118
2202 Kraft Dr, Blacksburg, VA 24061
+1 540 231 6698
mccricks@cs.vt.edu

ABSTRACT
Pair Programming has demonstrated benefits for education, but unique concerns of mobile software design raise questions about the effectiveness of Pair Programming in this evolving field. This paper probes unique challenges for Pair Programming when used in mobile software design classes, focusing on five mobile design topics: dealing with interface and data management, using camera, handling multi-device connectivity, using sensors and collecting GPS data, and using microphones and speakers. The paper highlights successes and challenges for Pair Programming and mobile applications, concluding with recommendations on building assignments, managing student interaction, and implementing Pair Programming for instructors considering using it in their mobile development classes.

Keywords
Computer Science Education; Pair Programming; Mobile development.

1. INTRODUCTION
Agile methods provide techniques, tools, and practices to help software practitioners develop software quickly and efficiently, valuing working software and face-to-face interactions over plans, processes, and documentation [1; 2]. One of the Agile practices that have been used in educational contexts is Pair Programming (PP), which is an approach that features two developers working on the same development task [3; 4]. One developer (usually called the driver) actually writes code, while the other (the navigator) watches the driver, provides advice, and seeks to grasp the overall picture of the task under development [4]. These two roles are exchanged at regular intervals, and the two developers together become the owners of the resulting product—and also become knowledgeable about the development topic.

This paper explores whether PP would help students in a mobile development course to better understand mobile concepts and enhance the quality of their applications. There are fundamental differences in programming topics for mobile, including a very different user interface style centered on a small screen and finger-based interactions, a greater emphasis on parallelism and asynchronous operations, and a large number of sensors. These fundamentally important topics have not been studied with PP previously, but their challenging nature highlight potential benefits for pair-based learning.

SIGCSE'16, March 02 - 05, 2016, Memphis, TN, USA

ACM 978-1-4503-3685-7/16/03…$15.00
DOI: http://dx.doi.org/10.1145/2839509.2844644

The next section provides background on research that has been done on applying PP in classroom settings. We then show how mobile development differs from traditional web/desktop programming. The paper proceeds with showing how we apply PP in our mobile development class. We conclude the paper with a discussion on the findings in five PP sessions we performed, with a set of guidelines that would help instructors facilitate PP sessions in their own mobile development classes.

2. PAIR PROGRAMMING FOR MOBILE DEVELOPMENT CLASS
During the past two decades, PP has been studied in both industrial and classroom settings. For industrial environments, [5] presents studies that have shown that PP enhanced understandability and maintainability of code and design [6], decreased defect rates [7] and supported knowledge transfer [8].

Since we are interested in PP for classroom settings, we focus on studies that have been performed on students, especially in higher education who are enrolled in Computer Science (CS) or Software Engineering (SE) classes. One of the original studies of PP suggested that it is a promising approach to use as a pedagogical tool due to its capability of increasing learning capacity [9], with foundational studies demonstrating how PP as a pedagogical tool that can help students enhance productivity and learn technology design and programming [10-13]. A review of PP studies shows areas of success with evidence suggesting that PP could enhance enjoyment, increase student's confidence level, reduce workload, improve course completion rate, increase homework submission rate, improve exam performance, and facilitate working efficiently on programming assignments [14].

Since it became popular in the 1990s, PP has been used by developers who work on desktop applications. With the rise of web applications, PP became a popular practice for web development. During the past decade, mobile applications became more mainstream, and several approaches and techniques have been developed to serve the goals of mobile application developers. As a result, CS educators started to incorporate mobile development as a core component of their programming classes. Rahimian and Ramsin [15] show that mobile development has certain issues that differentiate it from desktop/web development related to communication, mobility, portability, standards and protocols, power, storage, and user interfaces. Researchers have tried to come up with modern teaching approaches that can accommodate the special nature of mobile application development. Tigrek and Obadat [16] proposed a pedagogy for teaching smartphone programming, which incorporated PP as a practice to encourage guided teamwork. However, PP was just a supporting practice and not at the core of this pedagogy, and the research did not provide details on the results of implementing PP. A recent research paper demonstrated teaching programming for smartwatches as part of an undergraduate mobile development class [17]. This research shows the need to consider several extensions while dealing with mobile development, such as wearable devices, different sensors, and multiple platforms. A focus on design education requires careful consideration of user interface issues. Williams et al. [18] presented a study of using PP for teaching Human Computer Interaction (HCI) class, but they did not show the impact of applying PP on the user interface. Our work explores how PP can be applied while developing mobile applications, and what would be the opportunities and challenges associated with students developing mobile applications in pairs.

Based on these characteristics of mobile development, we believed that students can benefit from PP when working on mobile development in-class activities, with three concerns:

1- Multi-screen mobile development environment. Mobile design relies on multiple screens, indeed multiple platforms, to craft a realistic and meaningful design experience. PP must be adapted to address this issue.
2- Connectivity issues. A definitive feature of mobile devices is that they rely on connectivity both with external devices like smartwatches and health sensors as well as internal hardware like GPS and location data, accelerometers, light sensors, and cameras. PP must account for these features.
3- User interface (UI) and user experience (UX) issues. Mobile devices are very different than more traditional desktop, laptop, and web environments, with challenges and opportunities for PP.

To understand how students would react to these concerns, we examined student course work during pair programming sessions of a mobile development class.

3. PAIR PROGRAMMING SESSIONS

To gain a better understanding for the context of developers in a classroom setting, we conducted expert reviews with two pairs of experienced Android developers. Two active walkthrough PP sessions were conducted to get the participants expert reviews about the process. We observed their interactions throughout the session, and they shared their insights during and after the sessions [19]. The sessions concluded by showing some pitfalls for in-class PP, such as differences in developers' backgrounds and experience levels, poor planning and time management, and not allowing enough time for design prior to coding. The expert reviews also provided some recommendations that the experts think would enhance students' performance, such as considering pairing preferences, handling quality requirements as essential and basic requirements, and explicitly asking for usage scenarios and contextual requirements to be considered.

We applied PP as part of in-class activities for a mobile development course. Our objectives were to:

1- Introduce students to PP as a grounded well-known agile practice that has been used widely in several environments
2- Present different models for software engineering
3- Encourage students to evaluate, compare, and critique different approaches for software development
4- Assess student understanding for mobile topics
5- Study how PP would help students in particular and developers in general to develop better mobile applications
6- Investigate how applying PP can differ between regular web/desktop application development and mobile application development

To achieve these goals, we facilitated five 75-minute PP sessions for the 53-student class, which covered five different aspects related to mobile development:

1- Dealing with interface and data management through fragments
2- Using the camera and processing images
3- Connecting two mobile devices via Bluetooth
4- Using accelerometer and GPS data from mobile device
5- Recording and playing audio via mobile device

The driver and navigator exchanged roles every 15 minutes. The class was managed by a main facilitator for PP and two assistants to answer programming-related questions. Every session started with a 10-minute introduction that worked like a retrospective for previous sessions and preparation for the new one. At the end of every session (except the first introductory one), students were required to fill-in an online questionnaire right after they deliver their application. It was not mandatory for students to answer every question, which means that questions might have different number of responses within the same session. Below is a summary of what was performed in every session, and the outputs from each session.

3.1 Session 1

An introductory session featuring a 10-minute overview of PP and a 5-minute presentation about the activity, which was on creating a simple shopping cart app. PP rounds were 15 minutes each, so each student worked twice as a driver and twice as a navigator. Students could select their partner, select locations, and create their own UI.

3.1.1 Observations

Most students had prior basic knowledge of PP, but with minimum previous practice. They welcomed the idea during the presentation, but seemed uncomfortable during the session. After beginning, they immediately started coding, giving no time to consider the application design. Indeed, they did not design a draft interface until second or third rounds. At this stage, many students struggled to adapt their work to fit the activity's minimal requirements. Therefore, core functionality was present, but with poor attention to UI/UX concerns.

The class instructor noted that the number of questions raised during this session was comparable to other sessions. Students did not pay attention to the time constraints, so the facilitator managed time and ask students to switch roles every 15 minutes.

3.1.2 Questionnaires

There was no questionnaire for this session as it was meant only to get students familiar with PP.

3.1.3 Findings

1- Students got annoyed when asked to work on only one screen (i.e., no second laptop)
2- Students didn't like to switch while in the middle of coding certain code segments, and they ignored the time checks until the driver finishes the part in hand
3- In many cases the navigator put his/her hands on the keyboard to write a piece of code instead of explaining what he wants to do to the driver. Some students said that it happened subconsciously while others argued that it makes them work faster.
4- Upon delivery, when students were asked about UI/UX factors they kept showing how the application is "working as required for the activity", which was the only success factor for them, rather than usable interfaces.

3.2 Session 2

The activity exercised camera and image processing tasks. The session started with instructor comments on student work during the previous PP session, mainly related to the roles of driver and navigator. Students were randomly paired based on a seating location rubric. It was announced that a questionnaire should be filled before leaving the classroom.

3.2.1 Observations

Students were surprised by not being able to self-select pairs. However, they accepted it smoothly and started working with their assigned pairs. The activity involved using the mobile camera, so the navigator has always been responsible for holding the mobile and using the camera. Since the application required students to do image processing on selfies, pairs spent time having fun testing their applications by taking selfies. The fun nature of the application was reflected on the coding and class atmosphere. During this session, the number of questions raised by students was noticeably fewer than in session 1. Similar to the first session, little effort was put towards UI/UX.

Navigators were allowed to hold the mobile devices to test code—augmenting to the traditional PP tasks of watching, testing, and collaborating with the driver on coding. This is a special case for mobile application development as rapid parallel testing is done on another screen, rather than the development screen as in web/desktop apps.

3.2.2 Questionnaires

Out of the 22 responses to the open ended question: "How would you describe your experience of today's Pair Programming session?" 18 students provided positive feedback about the session, while 4 had minor complaints (classroom environment, problems with the code, not being comfortable with the experience). The positive comments were mainly from students who delivered their code on time. It is important to note that students' satisfaction with the activity correlates to their ability to deliver it on time.

3.2.3 Findings

1- Students got more used to switching roles and stick to the assigned turns. However, they needed the facilitator to manage time and remind them when to switch
2- Students managed to give themselves more flexibility in switching time. i.e. to wait until driver finishes what s/he is working on before switching
3- It was still hard to keep pairs working on the same screen, as the navigator sought to use another laptop screen for other supporting functions (online search, displaying class material, looking for previous related assignments)

3.3 Session 3

This session involved using Pebble smartwatches to learn about connectivity issues among wearable devices and mobile phones. Students had freedom to choose their partners for two reasons: to compare their performance against the sessions when they were assigned to random pairs; and to incentivize them to work with the same partners who will work with them on that week's homework assignment. Although students seemed, based on our observations, relieved that they would freely choose their partners, the questionnaire results did not concur with such observations.

3.3.1 Observations

Since it was students' first time to program for Pebble, they were not comfortable dealing with it. Connection issues and multiple coding languages had to be addressed, leading to most of them not to be able to deliver a working piece of code, or even to make much progress either in learning or development. They complained about having short time to work on the activity, affecting the atmosphere of the PP session. There were many questions for instructors during that session, and at times partners were not able to help each other. There was disappointment that pervaded this session: Pebble programming, PP, and programming for wearable devices in general.

3.3.2 Questionnaires

Work distribution among pairs was not as good as the previous session. The 50/50 percentage appeared in free-partner-selection mode less than with random pairs. One major reason for this is that when students work with "strangers", they tend to adhere to rules, be more competitive, and do what's required from them to do. Out of the 34 answers to the open ended question: "How would you describe your experience of today's Pair Programming session?" 14 were negative, mainly discussing the insufficient time to complete the activity. 12 students of those who provided negative feedback delivered less than 50% of the required functionality. More positive feedback came from students who delivered 50%-75% of the required functionality. The scope of the activity was a major drawback for this session, and PP need to adapt to deal with such situation.

3.3.3 Findings

1- In-class activities should balance the difficulty of the task with session time.
2- Topics related to connectivity demand more time even for simple activities. PP sessions need to be tailored to give students time to learn new topics together.
3- For new topics, students may need extra time and preparation in advance prior to working on PP.
4- Student disappointment should identify reasons for the problem, whether from working in pairs, using connectivity protocols like Bluetooth, working with wearables, learning new topics, or working within tight time limitations.

3.4 Session 4

This session featured an activity combining GPS and gyroscope. (Note that students had a previous activity on GPS.) Linking the two topics was new for students. Students were assigned to random pairs. To get students to feel more involved with the sessions, the facilitator displayed anonymous comments from the previous session's questionnaire and discussed them with students during the introduction. That step sought to encourage students to give deeper feedback.

3.4.1 Observations

Since students had a previous lab on GPS, they kept referring to prior material and finding complementary resources online. Discussions among pairs seemed richer and questions to the instructors were much fewer. Differences in knowledge levels between pairs led them to have useful discussions and to get advice on how to proceed with coding. Checking previous materials and online searching was time-consuming but helped pairs complete the activity. A majority of the pairs again objected to the "one screen" rule in PP.

Although the activity introduction asked students to consider how users would use the application, only five groups included guidance for users to be able to use their applications. When students delivered their assignments at the end of the session, the facilitator discussed with them how a user will use their application and why they did not pay attention to that issue. As in previous sessions, students were more worried about providing a functioning project than building a "usable" one.

3.4.2 *Questionnaires*

25 out of the 33 recorded responses indicated they were able to deliver more than 75% of the required functionality. This rate caused the level of satisfaction in students' answers to the open ended questions to be higher than the previous session. 23 of the 29 responses provided positive feedback. Many students indicated that they were able to understand how to use GPS through discussions with their partners.

3.4.3 *Findings*

1- Navigators do not spend the whole time just watching and observing drivers; they want to be more active by looking things up while the driver is coding
2- Students, again, tried to use another laptop screen for tasks other than coding, not stopping until the facilitator asks them to go back to a single screen
3- PP seems to work better when students have prior knowledge about the activity, as this increases their ability to exchange knowledge and learn from each other
4- In situations where a navigator tried to do something other than watching the driver, s/he becomes fully attendant when the driver is facing a problem. This kind of self-organized pairs was common among teams
5- Feedback provided and answers for open-ended questions were lengthier than the previous sessions, perhaps because of the comments discussed in the beginning of the session about the previous questionnaire answers

3.5 Session 5

The objective of the activity was to familiarize students with audio in/out tools. This last PP session of the semester added the statement "You are required to include any components that help users understand and use your app". Based on previous session results, students were assigned to random pairs. One objective was to study how students would consider UI/UX issues when it was explicitly stated as a requirement. Students were also asked to be responsible for time-keeping.

3.5.1 *Observations*

The number of questions directed to instructors was at its minimum during this session. Students were able to explore how to deal with the activities on their own through discussions and web search. As in previous sessions, many tried using other screens to do the online search for some resources despite being directed not to. About half of the groups missed the first switch and needed to be reminded by the facilitator, but only 3 pairs missed it on the second round. On the third and final switch, all pairs managed to switch without reminders.

The final delivered applications had many signs of considering UX requirements, which was not the case with the previous sessions.

3.5.2 *Questionnaires*

23 out of 29 responses provided positive feedback regarding the session. Some students indicated that PP helped them get the required skills needed to work with the activity with no need to ask for instructor's help. Work distribution among pairs is getting much better as the 50/50 workload appeared more than the previous sessions.

3.5.3 *Findings*

1- UX requirements need to be explicitly requested rather than broadly referenced; otherwise students do not realize the need to dedicate time for it.
2- Students are able to practice PP on their own after training
3- Online resources and course material are important during the session. Planning for PP sessions should incorporate such resources within the development process

4. DISCUSSION

Questionnaire results showed how PP affects student performance on in-class activities. For example, the percentage of functionality delivered per session changes with the topic being introduced in such session (see Figure 1). It is clear that the multi-device connectivity activity was the one with the least assignments completed. Therefore, this type of activities should be planned carefully to fit within the allowed time. However, student answers to open-ended questions provided more positive feedback (based on the terms they use to describe the session)—increasingly so as sessions go on (see Figure 2). While this suggests PP was helping students deal with complex problems, it also shows that students work better with PP when they get sufficient practice time.

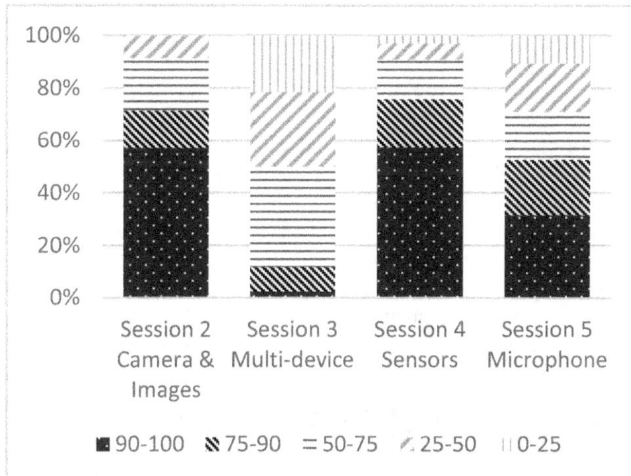

Figure 1. Percentages of delivered functionality

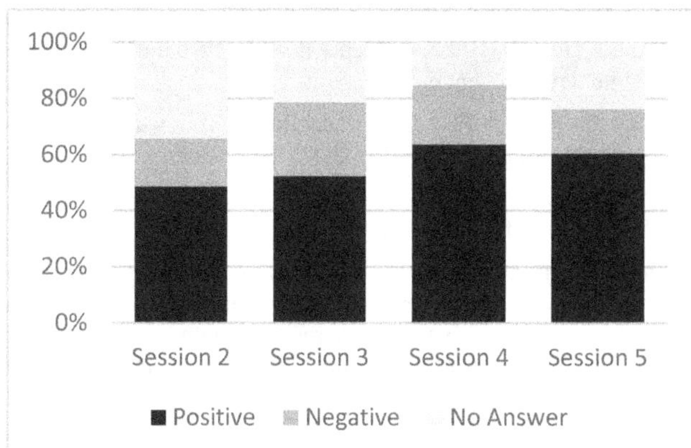

Figure 2. Percentages of positive and negative responses

Along with information from questionnaires, our observations provided different aspects on how students worked with PP. Section 2 postulated three major differences between developing for web/desktop applications and developing for mobile devices. After the five sessions, we discuss in this section what we found relevant and important to consider regarding the differences.

4.1 Unique Nature of Mobile Development

Our PP variant in working on mobile applications allowed a mobile device in the hands of the navigator. We noted that as the driver writes code, the navigator transitions between the driver's laptop screen and the mobile device. The navigator also looks at the mobile screen to the driver occasionally to discuss some issues. Having two screens seems inevitable when students work on mobile applications, but perhaps the small screen size leads to minimal distraction—allowing the navigator to remain connected to the driver's actions.

4.2 Connectivity, Sensors, and Smartwatches

Sessions 3 and 4 required students to program for multiple devices or sensors. Session 3 leveraged Bluetooth to connect mobile device with Pebble watch, while Session 4 leveraged mobile's GPS sensor to control application responses. During these sessions, we observed that interaction between students peaked, although most of them did not deliver the required application on time. Since many mobile applications require multiple-device connectivity (e.g., watches, sensors, wearables), it takes more time and effort of students to be able to learn, understand, and know how to deal with such applications.

Programming for mobile devices cannot be seen as merely writing code—they also searched online resources, checked lecture materials, explored connectivity issues with their mobile devices, and learned core functionality of the new devices. PP discourages parallelism, asking students to work on the tasks as a team. However, it was hard to keep the two students (especially the navigator) working on the same aspect of the task (especially for non-programming tasks). PP does not include explicit guidelines such situations. Further consideration is needed on this issue, perhaps resulting in a PP approach tailored for mobile design.

4.3 Introducing UI/UX Concepts

Students often feel they can start writing code for their assignments without dedicating time for UI/UX issues. However, UI/UX issues are acknowledged as critical for application functionality due to the different factors that affect mobile interfaces (e.g. screen size, orientation, touch and swipe controls). Hence, UI/UX concepts need to be handled carefully in mobile development environments.

During the several PP sessions conducted (both during expert reviews and in-class activities), there have been two approaches to deal with UI/UX concepts:

1- Present only functional requirements of activities

In multiple cases, students start by writing code segments related to the familiar parts, rather than considering the interface. Only after 2-3 rounds do they find themselves with functional code that lacks a usable interface. At this point, they usually delivered products that lack even the basics of UI design concepts.

This approach is more student-based and it helps when the student is a self-learner. The PP approach helps students to elaborate on how users would deal with their applications, shifting from pair "programming" to pair "design". Moreover, this approach is important for mobile development as there are many UI/UX issues that need to be discussed and evolved by the students' own work—not always the case with traditional programming with its less dynamic components.

2- Specify UI/UX issues as essential requirement

As seen in the fifth session, when usage scenarios were a requirement and part of the activity description, students do dedicate time on their first round to discuss interface issues. When they delivered the application, they were keen to explain its usability, and how users can deal with it in different ways.

This second approach can fit with classes that do not have time to do many PP sessions (when lab time is very limited). It directs students from the beginning to consider UI/UX aspects so that they better plan on how to use their time. However, it will lack the ability to show students through practice the importance of these aspects, especially for mobile development.

Both approaches will educate students on UI concepts during PP sessions. However, the first approach encourages experiential learning if student activities are carefully scoped. Whether an instructor decides to go with the first or second approach, it is important not to disregard UI/UX concepts when working on in-class activities, particularly for mobile platforms. PP can help students discuss and focus on those aspects, especially when they work on applications that require extra attention to how users will interact with such applications.

5. RECOMMENDATIONS

Based on our exploratory study for how to introduce mobile development concepts to students using PP, we came to find some practices that can help instructors get the best of PP while achieving their course learning objectives. Below is a list of our recommendations.

1- Allow students to choose partners on the first session, then move to random pairing

The first session lets students unfamiliar with PP focus on learning how PP works instead of figuring out how to deal with an unfamiliar work partner. Based on questionnaire answers and our observations, students tend to be more productive and satisfied when they deal with partner they may not know as well (sessions 2, 4, and 5). Two possible reasons for this are that students are more relaxed when they work with someone they know (no pressure for competency and excellence), and they gain more knowledge from someone whom they did not have interaction with before (as opposed to a friend, whose knowledge about new topics is usually shared among his/her close mates/group).

2- Allow the navigator to look at the mobile device screen while the driver works on coding

Although this contradicts a PP core tenet, this practice seems inevitable for mobile development. Navigators usually need to check the mobile device they are working on, test and debug the application on the mobile device, and work on issues like connectivity and sensors. Asking pairs to keep focused on the coding screen was a constant disappointment for many pairs, with claims that it hindered their progress. It is also important to monitor that navigator gives full attention to coding when the driver faces issues.

3- Decide on the strategy to be used to introduce UI/UX requirements based on the amount of time available for each session

Sessions 4 and 5 show students giving more attention to UI/UX issues much more than the previous sessions. As shown in section 5.3, the instructor should dedicate the first round to only work on UI/UX issues if students will not practice PP themselves. Otherwise, students may be left to learn the importance of including UI/UX thinking the hard way during the multiple sessions. In either case, PP can address UI/UX issues as students exchange views and create scenarios in pairs on how users would deal with their applications. Moreover, since mobile development requires more attention to details when it comes to UI/UX, PP seems that it can be a good fit—but with careful attention from the instructor.

4- Plan for extra time and pre-class preparation for activities that involve using multiple devices and connections

Most mobile development applications require dealing with multiple platforms and connections, new techniques and technologies, different programming interfaces, and multiple sensors. Instructors need to carefully consider whether students can handle all the required tasks within the class time. Moreover, students may be asked to prepare for the task before they come to the class, so that they become ready to work on the assignment within the allowed session time. The value in PP lies in the ability to discuss and exchange ideas, but the reward lies in completing a task. Students' performance and feedback is highly affected by the ability to complete a task. Therefore, it is important to size activities to fit within the allowed time so that students can keep working with good spirit.

6. CONCLUSIONS

Although there has been lots of research on applying PP in CS classrooms, this paper highlights that mobile development requires further investigation on how PP will perform—and how it might change. Our in-class study showed that activities in a mobile development course would differ than regular CS programming course activities in several aspects. Issues related to mobile UI/UX, sensors, and multi-device connectivity introduce unique challenges to students in mobile development classes. PP seems to provide a reasonable approach to handle such challenges, though with changes put in place. For PP to perform better in mobile development classes, instructors should consider how PP has traditionally been applied, as well as why some changes may positively influence student learning and performance. We expect that this work introduces more questions than it answers, and we look forward to learning about the answers through future PP efforts.

7. REFERENCES

[1] 2001. Manifesto for Agile Software Development. http://agilemanifesto.org Accessed: June 15, 2015.

[2] Seyam, M. and Galal-Edeen, G.H., 2011. Traditional versus Agile: The Tragile Framework for Information Systems development. *International Journal of Software Engineering (IJSE) 4*, 1, 63-93.

[3] Williams, L. and Kessler, R., 2002. *Pair Programming Illuminated.* Addison-Wesley Longman Publishing Co., Inc.

[4] Beck, K. and Andres, C., 2004. *Extreme Programming Explained: Embrace Change*. Addison-Wesley Professional.

[5] Plonka, L., Sharp, H., Van Der Linden, J., and Dittrich, Y., 2015. Knowledge transfer in pair programming: An in-depth analysis. *International Journal of Human-Computer Studies 73*(1//), 66-78.

[6] Vanhanen, J. and Lassenius, C., 2007. Perceived effects of pair programming in an industrial context. In *Proceedings of the 33rd EUROMICRO Conference on Software Engineering and Advanced Applications.*

[7] Phaphoom, N., Sillitti, A., and Succi, G., 2011. Pair Programming and Software Defects – An Industrial Case Study. In *Agile Processes in Software Engineering and Extreme Programming*, A. SILLITTI, O. HAZZAN, E. BACHE and X. ALBALADEJO Eds. Springer Berlin Heidelberg, 208-222.

[8] Katriou, S. and Tolias, E., 2009. From twin training to pair programming. In *Proceedings of the 2nd India software engineering conference, ISEC '09* ACM, New York, USA.

[9] Cockburn, A. and Williams, L., 2001. The Costs and Benefits of Pair Programming. In *Proceedings of Second International Conference on Extreme Programming and Flexible Processes in Software Engineering.*

[10] Nagappan, N., Williams, L., Ferzli, M., Wiebe, E., Yang, K., Miller, C., and Balik, S., 2003. Improving the CS1 experience with pair programming. In *Proceedings of the 34th Technical Symposium on Computer Science Education (SIGCSE'03).*

[11] Mcdowell, C., Werner, L., Bullock, H., and Fernald, J., 2006. Pair programming improves student retention, confidence, and program quality. *Communications of ACM 49*, 8, 90-95.

[12] Kuppuswami, S. and Vivekanandan, K., 2004. The effects of pair programming on learning efficiency in short programming assignments. *Journal of Information Education 3*, 2, 251-266.

[13] Simon, B. and Hanks, B., 2007. First Year Students' Impressions of Pair Programming in CS1. In *Proceedings of the Third International Computing Education Research Workshop*, 73-86.

[14] Salleh, N., Mendes, E., and Grundy, J., 2011. Empirical Studies of Pair Programming for CS/SE Teaching in Higher Education: A Systematic Literature Review. *Software Engineering, IEEE Transactions on 37*, 4, 509-525.

[15] Rahimian, V. and Ramsin, R., 2008. Designing an agile methodology for mobile software development: A hybrid method engineering approach. In *Research Challenges in Information Science, 2008. RCIS 2008. Second International Conference on*, 337-342.

[16] Tigrek, S. and Obadat, M., 2012. Teaching smartphones programming using (Android Java): Pedagogy and innovation. In *Information Technology Based Higher Education and Training (ITHET), 2012 International Conference on*, 1-7.

[17] Esakia, A., Niu, S., and McCrickard, D.S., 2015. Augmenting Undergraduate Computer Science Education With Programmable Smartwatches. In *Proceedings of the Proceedings of the 46th ACM Technical Symposium on Computer Science Education* (Kansas City, Missouri, USA2015), ACM, 2677285, 66-71.

[18] Williams, L., McCrickard, S., Layman, L., and Hussein, K., 2008. Eleven Guidelines for Implementing Pair Programming in the Classroom. In *Agile, 2008. AGILE '08. Conference*, 445-452.

[19] Seyam, M. and McCrickard, S., 2015. Collaborating on Mobile App Design through Pair Programming. In *Proceedings of International Conference on Collaboration Technologies and Systems (CTS 2015)*, Atlanta, GA.

Applying the Communal Goal Congruity Perspective to Enhance Diversity and Inclusion in Undergraduate Computing Degrees

Bo Brinkman
Miami University
Department of Comp. Sci. and Software Eng.
Oxford, Ohio 45056
bo.brinkman@miamioh.edu

Amanda Diekman
Miami University
Department of Psychology
Oxford, Ohio 45056
diekmaa@miamioh.edu

ABSTRACT

The lack of diversity in the tech industry is a widely remarked phenomenon. The majority of workers in tech roles are either white or Asian men, with all other groups being under-represented.

Some authors point to cultural factors influencing self-efficacy, leading to a lack of diversity at the start of the "pipeline" of IT talent. Others point to toxic workplace culture that can lead skilled tech workers to drop out of the industry.

While these effects are very real and important, this paper focuses on a third concept contributing to lack of diversity, communal goal congruity. We present a growing body of evidence suggesting that working with others, and in the service of others, are important career goals that many believe tech careers lack. We describe prior work that shows that these beliefs also have a significant impact on the pipeline of tech talent.

We then report on the first pieces of data out of the first long-term intervention designed with this communal goal congruity perspective in mind. We have created a cohort-based service-learning program in computer science, computer engineering, electrical engineering, and software engineering. The result is a program with 26.3% women and 31.6% African American and/or Hispanic students, including 15.8% African American and/or Hispanic women, at an institution that has never previously seen this level of diversity in its computing majors.

Keywords

service learning; diversity;

1. INTRODUCTION

The lack of diversity in the computing professions has been widely remarked. Many people are working on trying to make computing a more diverse and more inclusive field, but not always with great success. U.S. Department of Education data show (see Figure 1) that the share of degrees in computing fields earned by women is less than 20%. Even more puzzling, this is down from a high of 37% in the early 1980s. While other STEM (Science, Technology, Engineering, and Math) fields have shown increasing participation by women over the past 40 years, computing has regressed.

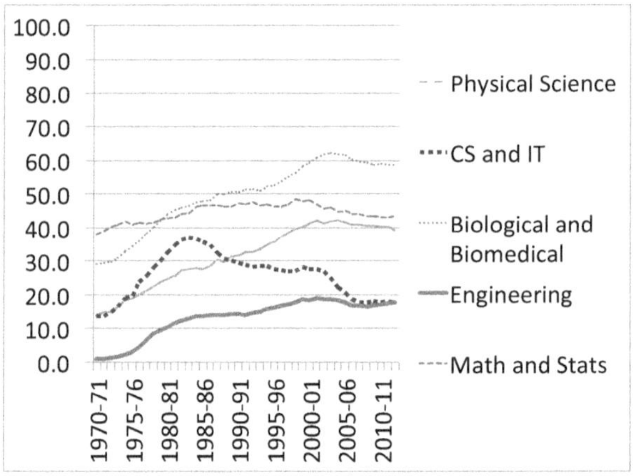

Figure 1: Percentage share of bachelors degrees earned by women, over time, in various STEM fields. Data from: NCES Digest of Education Statistics[23]

Participation rates for most ethnic groups (all groups other than non-Hispanic whites and Asians) are also much lower than those groups' overall share of the U.S. population. These disparities have attracted intense interest from equal rights activists, and caused major tech companies (Yahoo!, Google, LinkedIn, and others) to regularly publish diversity information. Even so, the tech roles at these companies are mostly filled by white and Asian men. Indeed, roughly 80% in tech roles are men, and about 90% are either white or Asian[14, 15, 25]. These figures do not vary much between major tech companies.

In what follows we will first summarize the most well-known explanations for the lack of diversity in tech, which are cultural undermining of self-efficacy and workplace hostility. We will then describe a less well-known, but potentially useful, concept called communal goal congruity. We conclude with a description of how we used communal goal affordance theory to design a new scholarship program at

SIGCSE '16, March 02-05, 2016, Memphis, TN, USA

DOI: http://dx.doi.org/10.1145/2839509.2844562

our institution, and the impressive increase in diversity, at least in initial enrollment, that resulted as a byproduct.

In our review of the literature we found that the computer science education community has not yet started to use and benefit from the communal goal affordance perspective. We consider introducing it to the field one of the main contributions of this paper.

2. LOOKING FOR EXPLANATIONS

Throughout most of what follows we will focus on lack of gender diversity in tech, touching on racial and ethnic diversity wherever we know of research that addresses it.

It is well known that women have now surpassed men in earning college degrees, earning 57.5% of all bachelors degrees in the U.S. [23]. How then do we explain why women earn such a small share of the bachelors degrees in computing and engineering?

2.1 Perceived self-efficacy

In his ground-breaking work on the topic, Albert Bandura argues that the choice of which actions we attempt is influenced by our own expectations of efficacy — whether we have the ability to do what needs to be done in the given situation [1]. He argues that the various types of interventions used in psychological treatments (verbal persuasion, emotional arousal, vicarious experience, and performance accomplishments), though apparently very different, all work by affecting one's perceived self-efficacy.

Much previous work on under-representation of women in computing has focused on computer self-efficacy. We will only mention a few illustrative examples here, as the literature is voluminous. For example, men tend to show higher computer self-efficacy than women [2], and underlying gender differences in computer self-efficacy predict gender differences in signing up for computing courses [17].

More recently, Vekiri and Chronaki found that parental support was the strongest predictor of a child developing computer self-efficacy [24]. What emerges is a theoretical model that argues that low participation by women in computing is due in part to parental and peer discouragement leading to poor self-perceived self-efficacy, resulting in decreased interest in computing.

There have not been many studies on links between race or ethnic identity and computer self-efficacy. Post et al. [20] studied math self-efficacy of black college freshmen. They found that the career considerations of their male subjects were mostly driven by self-efficacy and confidence, while the career considerations of their female subjects were mostly driven by interest. Crisp et al. [7] found no link between racial/ethnic identity, the decision to declare a STEM major, or success in a STEM major. They found that gender, high school preparation, and first-semester success were the main predictors of interest in STEM majors.

Variation in computing self-efficacy thus provides some explanation for gender (but not ethnicity) differences in pursuing computing degrees. Understanding what might motivate female students to engage in computing experiences and thus gain greater self-efficacy remains a key question.

2.2 It's Not (Only) a Pipeline Problem

Another factor discouraging diversity at various points in the tech pipeline is hostility — whether overt or subtle — to individuals who are "outsiders" to tech culture (those who are not white or Asian males).

Our work, as well as the previously mentioned work on self-efficacy, tends to explain the lack of diversity using a pipeline metaphor. As students move through school, at each step along the way, a few more women and students of color leak away, with the result being that very few select tech majors in college. Many commentators believe this ignores a bigger problem, which is a workplace culture that is toxic for women and under-represented minorities. It is perhaps not surprising that academic researchers tend to focus on the pipeline leading to college, since this is what ensures that we have plenty of students to teach.

Jon Evans called this a "trapdoor" problem [12], by which they mean that those that *do* enter the industry tend to find hostile work environments, and drop out again. In an NPR story by Rachel Martin, Laura Gómez (CEO of Atipica, a startup that does job applicant tracking systems) goes as far as to say that "It is not a pipeline issue whatsoever" [16].

Cohoon et al. [5] had slightly more nuanced findings. In a longitudinal study of women in the Computing Research Association's Graduate Cohort program they found that women in CSE doctoral degrees reported less experiences of sexism than "women in other settings report." At the same time, experiences of sexism had a significant impact on thoughts of leaving, and on actual departures, from doctoral degree programs.

Of course it has been well established that implicit bias and stereotyping both play roles in driving women out of computing and engineering. The AAUW book "Solving the Equation" [6] provides quite a bit of evidence, and we refer the interested reader to that work. Chapter 3, for example, summarizes the famous "name" study of Moss-Racusin et al. [18], where science faculty members were given a job application to evaluate. Some managers had an applicant named "John" and some an applicant named "Jennifer," but the applications were otherwise identical. Managers consistently rated the "John" applicant as more competent and more hirable. Another study by Reuben et al. [21] described in the report showed that employers tend to overestimate the mathematical competence of men, while underestimating for women. Implicit biases that associate men with math and science emerge as early as seven [8], and can influence a range of decisions, including college major choice [19].

In addition, "stereotype threat" affects the performance of under-represented groups (including women) in both school and the workplace [22]. Stereotype threat is the fear that one will confirm a negative stereotype of one's group by performing badly. This fear can lead to decreased risk taking and increased anxiety, resulting in worse performance over the long term.

2.3 Is That All?

While we certainly agree that both self-efficacy and workplace climate play key roles in whether a person chooses a computing major, recent research suggests that these differences are not sufficient to completely account for the lack of diversity in some STEM fields.

For example, Eccles surveyed results on gender differences in math self-efficacy. She found that, on the balance, differences in math self-efficacy did *not* predict "gender differences in math course enrollment; the perceived value of the math course did" [11].

Similarly, prejudice may have, at one time, resulted in

girls being discouraged from doing well in math, and have led to women having less math training and ability as a result. Ceci, Williams, and Barnett [3] have studied this question extensively, and argue that this is no longer the case, at least as it applies to selection of college major. They looked at the far right tail of the distribution of standardized math test scores, presumably the group that is prepared for college in a math-related field, and found that women are well represented in that group. They also summarize a body of work that suggests that overt discrimination is unlikely to be the main culprit, though implicit bias and stereotyping are not ruled out.

All of these authors point to women's preferences and choices as having a crucial role in the process. But here we most emphatically *do not* speak of a simple "women do not like computing" explanation for why women are underrepresented in computing! Rather, we need to understand how these preferences are formed, through stereotyping, socialization, and other processes. When Eccles says "the value of the course" determined a woman's interest in taking a math course, this leaves open how that "value" was socially constructed. Similarly, if a woman prefers a particular social role that precludes the possibility of pursuing a STEM career ... how was that social role constructed, and how/when/why was her preference formed?

These issues have been studied by many authors. Ferriman et al. [13], for example, found gender difference in social role preferences and life priorities. These differences intensified over time, and were most pronounced in parents as compared to childless individuals. Cheryan [4] argues that math-related careers are stereotyped as masculine, and that the work involved in math-related careers is stereotyped as incompatible with typical feminine stereotyped life and career goals.

This line of work frames the act of choosing a particular career or college major as opting into a particular social role. What we believe about a particular social role, and whether or not that social role fulfills our personal life goals and preferences, determines whether we pursue it. Our understandings of the available social roles are complicated by stereotyping, leading to systemic perpetuation of the gender divide in these fields.

3. THE COMMUNAL GOAL CONGRUITY PERSPECTIVE

How exactly does this stereotyping of social roles function? What types of career goals are most gender linked? Many of the goals that people have can be classified as either agentic or communal in nature. The communal goal congruity perspective argues that communal goals in particular influence STEM decisions [9]. A communal goal is one that focuses on working with, or in the service of, others, with an altruistic or outward focus. Agentic goals, by contract, focus on the self, self-efficacy, working with things (instead of people), and so on.

Some examples of agentic career goals/experiences:

1. I want to work with the fastest supercomputers in the world
2. I want a job where I'm always learning
3. I love the recognition I get for jumping into a failing project, and rescuing it

Compare these to some communal career goals:

1. I love being part of a team, doing something that we'd never be able to do on our own
2. I want a job where my work has a long-term impact on society
3. I like knowing that, because of my code, people that badly need kidneys are getting them

Using a survey study of 333 undergraduate students from a variety of majors, Diekman et al. [9] showed that there was a strong stereotype that STEM careers do not afford opportunities for pursuit of communal goals, even worse than "male stereotypic" professions as a whole. Students who were particularly interested in communal career goals were particularly disinterested in STEM. Even when controlling for self-efficacy, communal goal affordances still have a significant impact on interest in STEM.

They also found that gender predicted interest in communal goals, and interest in communal goals predicted disinterest in STEM; "the relationship between gender and STEM interest decreased when controlling for communal goal endorsement" [9].

This has motivated a variety of experimental interventions that focus on communal goal affordances in STEM. Diekman (with a different set of co-authors) went on to show that changing beliefs about the communal affordances of a career lead to changes in interest in that career [10]. Subjects (241 undergraduate students) "read about the typical day of an entry-level scientist whose daily activities were framed to be either highly collaborative or highly independent" [10]. While all types of students tended to prefer the "collaborative" version, the effect was much stronger for women than men.

This all points towards a possible path forward: Design programs and messaging that support communal goal affordances in computing professions. One example: Yowell and Sullivan [26], though likely not aware of the communal goal congruity perspective, reported success in increasing diversity in their program using materials from the National Academy of Engineering's (NAE) "Changing the Conversation" campaign — a major component of which emphasizes how engineering "makes a difference."

Another notable success is at Harvey Mudd College. In 2009 their percentage of female computer science majors was 14%, roughly the national average. They then introduced some interventions, and the percentage has risen to about 35-40%, where it has held steady for four years. As reported in "Solving the Equation" [6], Harvey Mudd made three major changes:

- Redesigned their intro course to provide a track for those with no prior experience in programming, and to emphasize real-world uses of programming
- Increased opportunities for participation in research
- Supported female students to attend the Grace Hopper Conference

These last two items, both of which are strongly but not exclusively communal in nature, appear to have had a disproportionately positive impact on women, and their decisions of whether or not to major in computer science.

In this work we report on the first major long-term intervention designed to leverage the communal goal congruity perspective. Ours is a cohort-based service learning program for our computing majors, funded by the NSF S-STEM program. In the next section we describe the design of the program, how the goal congruity perspective influenced the design, and the surprising impact it has had on our student diversity.

4. PREACH SERVICE, REACH DIVERSITY

One of our alumni went to work for a major political campaign. When we asked how he found the job, he said that he had lucked into it. Despite a longstanding interest in politics and political activism it had simply not occurred to him that computer scientists could do that kind of work. He had assumed that his career would consist of working at startups or tech giants, and that he would have to pursue political action in his free time.

This perspective is somewhat depressing, because it illustrates just how bad a job we, as a society, are doing at communicating the impact that computing professionals have on the world. It also illustrates that there are students with communal career goals that are not being satisfied by our current curriculum and messaging. On the other hand, this experience illuminates an avenue for change if these opportunities to integrate service with computing are made visible.

4.1 Service Learning

In what follows it will be useful to the reader to know our definition of service learning. By *service learning* we refer to a very specific type of pedagogy in which neither service nor learning dominates. Students learn through service, and serve through learning. We partner with a local non-profit to fulfill a real community need, and the time spent fulfilling this need allows students to advance towards achieving their course learning outcomes, just as if they had spent that time on reading or homework instead.

We do not, for example, send CS1 students to serve soup at a soup kitchen. Instead, we send them to elementary schools to teach coding clubs, teaching CS1 concepts. Students in a databases course might design and code some new database queries needed by a non-profit that has an existing database.

Our first cohort is currently finishing their first semester, taking our CS1 course. For their service learning, we partnered with Kode2Learn, a student club that delivers hands-on coding experiences before and after school one day a week at three local elementary schools. Our Office of Service Learning handles much of the administrative work: Transportation to and from placements, background checks, liability insurance, etc. We hired an undergraduate to be the Service Learning Coordinator for the class. She worked with the school district to identify the time and place of the clubs, and tracked student attendance. Each student was required to attend five club sessions throughout the 14 week semester.

4.2 Designing a Scholarship Program Around Communal Preferences

We designed a communal goal oriented program within our computer engineering, computer science, electrical engineering, and software engineering majors. What follows is a brief survey of the main elements of the program, some novel, many tried-and-tested by others before us.

- The program is called "Electronics and Computing Service Scholars," and is advertised as a program where students learn "to work together with others to make a difference."
- Students in the first year of the program live together in the dormitory, and have two courses in common during their first semester, to aid in cohort building and cohesion.
- Students apply to the program via essay, and are selected based on merit as demonstrated through the essay. Merit is defined as "evidence of passion for and/or experience with leadership in service."
- Admitted students were awarded scholarships of up to $10,000 per year for 4 years, based solely on financial need.
- Students are required to participate in at least one service activity per year, though this is intended to be satisfied by taking existing service learning designated courses.
- A service learning section of our introductory programming course was created, partnering with a local non-profit that provides coding clubs at local elementary schools.
- A dedicated study space has been allocated where students in the program can meet with each other, peer advisors, and teaching assistants.
- We will supplement our already strong career counseling with additional information about careers in government, non-profits, and B-corporations.
- We will provide guest speakers from government agencies and non-profits to aid in role modeling and career networking.

Our hypothesis is that our program will be more attractive to women than the "normal" computing programs, because the design and messaging of our program clearly communicates a focus on communal career goals.

One important lesson learned from prior S-STEM efforts at our institution is, in advertising, to de-emphasize the scholarship money. Many programs have reported that most students that apply only want the scholarship money, and do not participate in the other support programs. In our advertising and marketing we focus on selling the parts of the program that communicate a communal focus: cohort dorm living, courses in common, peer advisors, service projects, dedicated group study space, and so on. We also required students to describe, in their application form, which of the support services they were most excited about, or would find most helpful. Our hope is that this exercise will help them to initiate the use of the support services.

Though we are just getting started, our results are somewhat startling.

4.3 Results

It is important to note that race, ethnicity and gender were *not* used to select students for the program, or as input in setting scholarship amounts. National Science Foundation guidelines indicate that only merit and need should be used in the selection process.

In Table 1 we report the demographics of our first entering cohort in the Electronics and Computing Service Scholars, and compare it to school and industry norms. Of the 19 scholars in the cohort, all provided self-described gender (free text entry), and 17 of 19 provided self-identified racial and ethnic information using the U.S. federal government categories. Note that "UR/E" denotes under-represented race and/or ethnicity.

The "Baseline" row presents data for students at our institution majoring in computer engineering, computer science, electrical engineering, and software engineering and starting in either August 2014 or August 2015. The "Tech giants" row presents data for employees in tech roles at Yahoo!, Google, and LinkedIn, based on their published 2014 diversity numbers [14, 15, 25]. Because the numbers at the three companies are very similar, we chose to average them together to give a composite for comparison. The other three rows present data for the Electronics and Computing Service Scholars at the three key stages in the admission process. Furthermore, women that self-identify as at least one of black, African American, or Hispanic make up 15.8% of the matriculating EaCSS cohort.

Table 1: Diversity of Service Scholars Compared to Industry Norms

Population	% female	% UR/E
Baseline	12.3%	12.7%
Tech giants	16.7%	6.7%
EaCSS applied	19.2%	21.3%
EaCSS admitted	25.0%	25.0%
EaCSS matriculated	26.3%	31.6%

From the data one can see that the demographics of the group that chose to apply to the program were already significantly more diverse than the baseline population.

In the decision of whether or not to admit, students were ranked based on whether their career goals and/or service experiences were aligned with the program[1], and then we selected the top 32 students to admit. This number was based on available capacity in the program. Many applicants, for example, wrote about their academic achievements, and their desire to start a company or work for a tech giant, but did not address the service aspects of the program at all. It seems likely that some applicants simply re-submitted their standard college essays, without revising them to fit the program criteria. This particular mistake was only made by one female applicant, which at least partly explains the increased percentage of women in the admitted pool compared to the application pool.

The fact that the matriculated pool is even more diverse than the admitted pool is also very interesting. This is the point where we expected the scholarship money to have the biggest impact on whether or not students matriculated at our institution, but the data seem to contradict this. Of the students that received no scholarship money (due to no financial need), 47% still matriculated into the program. Among those that were offered awards, 63% matriculated.

Scholarship sizes were set based on the student's FAFSA data, so that students with higher unmet need received larger awards. There was surprisingly little correlation between the size of the award and whether or not the student matriculated into the program (Pearson's r of 0.206 for the overall sample, 0.202 if restricted to students with financial need).

[1]Students could have been disqualified for having insufficient high school grades and coursework, but no such students applied for the program.

Though far from conclusive, these early results suggest that students are selecting the program in large part for reasons *other* than the scholarship money. In future research we will investigate the matriculated students' reasons for choosing the program, their career goal preferences (whether agentic or communal), and their sense of belonging. But the fact that there is not a clear connection between the scholarships and matriculation is a good sign that students might have chosen the program based on their goals and values, not on purely financial grounds.

4.4 Missteps and Lessons

By far the biggest challenge has been advertising the program. Though the program provides tremendous value to participants, it is surprisingly hard to get students or parents to open an email or read a flier, even when you are offering up to $10k in scholarship money. We tried a variety of ways to reach our target audience. Rather than trying to recruit students that had already expressed an interest in STEM, our goal was to reach students that had expressed an interest in service, and to educate them about the ways that computing can lead to a career of service. A few things we tried:

- Email contact with *all* high school principals in our state. Email open rate was 21.9% and the click rate was 2.3%. We asked that scholarship info be passed on to guidance counselors, students, and/or PTA groups. We see no evidence that this happened.
- Word-of-mouth contact through our alumni, and speaking with students that came for campus visits in the fall. This resulted in 3 applications.
- Email contact in mid-November with *all* high school seniors that submitted a Request For Information to our institution. This resulted in 2 applications.
- Email contact in mid-February with all accepted students to our College of Engineering and Computing. This resulted in 20 applications.
- Email contact in late May with all students that confirmed their admission to our College of Engineering and Computing. This resulted in 28 applications.

This tells a pretty clear story. Students first select which school they will attend, and then look into programs and scholarships after that decision is made.

We argue, therefore, that a broad national campaign is needed to change student attitudes and stereotypes about engineering and computing careers. Intervening during the college selection process is unlikely to work, because the student's focus is on "which college," and little else. We applaud the many organizations are already engaged in this work (e.g. Code for America, Code.org, and the previously mentioned NAE "Changing the Conversation" project).

5. CONCLUSIONS AND FUTURE WORK

The communal goal congruity perspective provides a fresh lens for understanding the lack of diversity in computing, and designing mitigating interventions. We believe that many teachers, scholars, and authors are already making the turn towards increasing service and civic engagement in college curricula, and the communal goal congruity perspective helps provide a theoretical explanation for why this is a good idea.

Our own work, so far, has been much more successful than we expected. Without at any point explicitly focusing on diversity, we have managed to achieve diversity in our S-STEM program simply by designing and marketing the program around communal goal affordances.

Of course the data we have so far is small, and only tells us that our group is diverse. It does not tell us why this is the case, or get at the root causes of the difference between our Service Scholars and the baseline student body in these majors. Over the coming year we will be comparing the students in our service learning CS1 section with students in an honors section of CS1 and a "normal" section of CS1 to investigate how these variations affect belonging, self-efficacy, and other indicators of persistence and retention.

6. ACKNOWLEDGMENTS

Portions of this work were funded by the National Science Foundation, grants #0827606, #1232364, and #1355513.

7. REFERENCES

[1] A. Bandura. Self-efficacy: toward a unifying theory of behavioral change. *Psychological review*, 84(2):191, 1977.

[2] S. Cassidy and P. Eachus. Developing the computer user self-efficacy (CUSE) scale: Investigating the relationship between computer self-efficacy, gender and experience with computers. *Journal of Educational Computing Research*, 26(2):133–153, 2002.

[3] S. J. Ceci, W. M. Williams, and S. M. Barnett. Women's underrepresentation in science: Sociocultural and biological considerations. *Psychological bulletin*, 135(2):218, 2009.

[4] S. Cheryan. Understanding the paradox in math-related fields: Why do some gender gaps remain while others do not? *Sex Roles*, 66(3-4):184–190, 2012.

[5] J. M. Cohoon, Z. Wu, and J. Chao. Sexism: Toxic to women's persistence in CSE doctoral programs. *ACM SIGCSE Bulletin*, 41(1):158–162, 2009.

[6] C. Corbett and C. Hill. *Solving the Equation.* American Association of University Women, 2015.

[7] G. Crisp, A. Nora, and A. Taggart. Student characteristics, pre-college, college, and environmental factors as predictors of majoring in and earning a STEM degree: An analysis of students attending a Hispanic serving institution. *American Educational Research Journal*, 46(4):924–942, 2009.

[8] D. Cvencek, A. N. Meltzoff, and A. G. Greenwald. Math–gender stereotypes in elementary school children. *Child development*, 82(3):766–779, 2011.

[9] A. B. Diekman, E. R. Brown, A. M. Johnston, and E. K. Clark. Seeking congruity between goals and roles: A new look at why women opt out of science, technology, engineering, and mathematics careers. *Psychological Science*, 21(8):1051–1057, 2010.

[10] A. B. Diekman, E. K. Clark, A. M. Johnston, E. R. Brown, and M. Steinberg. Malleability in communal goals and beliefs influences attraction to STEM careers: Evidence for a goal congruity perspective. *Journal of personality and social psychology*, 101(5):902, 2011.

[11] J. S. Eccles. Understanding women's educational and occupational choices. *Psychology of women quarterly*, 18(4):585–609, 1994.

[12] J. Evans. Women In Tech: It's Not Just A Pipeline Problem. http://social.techcrunch.com/2014/08/23/just-another-white-dude-writing-about-diversity/. [Online; accessed 2015-08-03].

[13] K. Ferriman, D. Lubinski, and C. P. Benbow. Work preferences, life values, and personal views of top math/science graduate students and the profoundly gifted: Developmental changes and gender differences during emerging adulthood and parenthood. *Journal of personality and social psychology*, 97(3):517, 2009.

[14] Google, Inc. Diversity - Google. https://www.google.com/diversity. [Online; accessed 2015-07-27].

[15] LinkedIn Corp. LinkedIn's Workforce Diversity. http://blog.linkedin.com/2014/06/12/linkedins-workforce-diversity/. [Online; accessed 2015-07-27].

[16] R. Martin. More Than A Pipeline Problem: In Search Of Diversity In Silicon Valley. http://www.npr.org/sections/alltechconsidered/2015/07/26/426364306. [Online; accessed 2015-08-03].

[17] I. T. Miura. The relationship of computer self-efficacy expectations to computer interest and course enrollment in college. *Sex Roles*, 16(5-6):303–311, 1987.

[18] C. A. Moss-Racusin, J. F. Dovidio, V. L. Brescoll, M. J. Graham, and J. Handelsman. Science faculty's subtle gender biases favor male students. *Proceedings of the National Academy of Sciences*, 109(41):16474–16479, 2012.

[19] B. A. Nosek and F. L. Smyth. Implicit social cognitions predict sex differences in math engagement and achievement. *American Educational Research Journal*, 48(5):1125–1156, 2011.

[20] P. Post, M. A. Stewart, and P. L. Smith. Self-efficacy, interest, and consideration of math/science and non-math/science occupations among black freshmen. *Journal of Vocational Behavior*, 38(2):179–186, 1991.

[21] E. Reuben, P. Sapienza, and L. Zingales. How stereotypes impair women's careers in science. *Proceedings of the National Academy of Sciences*, 111(12):4403–4408, 2014.

[22] C. M. Steele. A threat in the air: How stereotypes shape intellectual identity and performance. *American psychologist*, 52(6):613, 1997.

[23] U.S. Department of Education. Institute of Education Sciences, National Center for Education Statistics. Digest of education statistics. http://nces.ed.gov/programs/digest/current_tables.asp, 2013. [Online; accessed 2015-07-24].

[24] I. Vekiri and A. Chronaki. Gender issues in technology use: Perceived social support, computer self-efficacy and value beliefs, and computer use beyond school. *Computers & education*, 51(3):1392–1404, 2008.

[25] Yahoo!, Inc. Workforce Diversity at Yahoo! http://yahoo.tumblr.com/post/89085398949/workforce-diversity-at-yahoo. [Online; accessed 2015-07-27].

[26] J. L. Yowell and J. F. Sullivan. Who should be an engineer? *Bridge*, 41(2):23–29, 2011.

Enhancing Engagement by Blending Rigor and Relevance

Sarnath Ramnath
CSIT Department; 320-308-4966
St Cloud State Univ., St Cloud MN
sarnath@stcloudstate.edu

John Hoover
School of Education; 320-308-5330
St Cloud State Univ., St Cloud MN
jhhoover@stcloudstate.edu

ABSTRACT
A framework for developing computing courses is presented, that has the potential to increase student engagement by enhancing student perception of relevance. The framework employs established andragogical approaches, course design methodologies, and measurement tools. A preliminary report on the application of this framework is presented. The results are encouraging, and the framework can be easily adapted to a variety of environments

Categories and Subject Descriptors
K.3.2 [**Computers and Education**]: Computer and Information Science Education

Keywords
Rigor, Relevance, Student Perception, Whole-Part-Whole, Integrated Course Design.

1. INTRODUCTION
Experts recognize the need for increasing the level of engagement of students coming into computer science. Several attempts have been made to introduce contexts such as multimedia, game programming [7], music [29] and robot programming [34], to deepen student engagement in introductory programming courses. The need for providing a context for the teaching of programming has received the attention of researchers and practitioners [7, 18]. Several researchers have investigated the effects of context on student motivation [4, 27]. Tew et al [36] extended this research into the teaching of Computer Organization. Other researchers have examined the effects of new curriculums and pedagogies [1]. The effects of tutoring were examined, both in the context of one-on-one human tutoring [9] and through the use of robot-assistants [20]. Barker et al [6] looked at several factors affecting student retention, concluding that student-student interaction proved the most powerful predictor of students' intention to persist. Effectiveness of the methods employed in all these studies has been established by student surveys and retention data.

While these studies have yielded a lot of valuable information, room for improvement in the research exists. Guzdial [18] raised the broader issue of relevance, and the related need to maintain authenticity. In another article [17], he identified problems with use of context, and how these can lead to poor knowledge transfer, and in a recent blog post [16] he has made a case for bringing evidence-based education to Computer Science. In this research we apply established ideas from the field of education to address these concerns. We designed our investigation guided by the following concepts:

1. **The Rigor-Relevance Model**. This is an established theoretical model within which we have attempted to address the issue of student engagement.
2. **Mechanisms that can be used to improve the balance between rigor and relevance.** The Whole Part Whole (WPW) pedagogical approach, and Integrated Course Design (ICD) are well-established methods known to be effective for adult learners.
3. **Measuring student perception of relevance.** This tells if we have been successful in creating in the student, a sense of usefulness and purpose towards constructed knowledge. We use established, statistically rigorous methods for doing this.

We define an evidence-based framework within which practitioners and researchers can design studies to track student engagement. In addition this can be adapted across multiple disciplines, learning styles, and course design techniques. The remainder of this paper is organized as follows: Section 2 explains the components of the Rigor-Relevance model. Section 3 explains the principles of WPW and ICD and their role in the entire process. Section 4 gives examples of applying WPW and ICD to design computing courses. Section 5 describes our instruments for measuring student perception of relevance. Section 6 explains the results of our surveys and Section 7 concludes the paper.

2. THE RIGOR-RELEVANCE MODEL
The Rigor-Relevance model lies at the heart of our research, and the debate between rigor and relevance has been examined in more than one context. In the context of research (e.g., [2]), rigor refers to the manner in which the methods of the discipline are adhered to, and relevance refers to the practical applicability of the results. With all rigor and no relevance we can see studies that are fastidious in their design and analytical sophistication yet fail to address an issue of current relevance (pedantic science). On the other hand, an absence of sufficient rigor can lead to excessively variable results (popularist science). In the context of curriculum development and teaching (e.g., [28]), rigor has been used to denote the formal structures required by the discipline. The presence of rigor is characterized by learning in which students demonstrate a thorough, in-depth mastery of challenging tasks. Rigor develops cognitive skills through reflective thought, analysis, problem-solving, evaluation, or creativity. Relevance is demonstrated by showing value outside the classroom, or phenomenologically, the perceptions of such value.

SIGCSE '16, March 02 - 05, 2016, Memphis, TN, USA

ACM 978-1-4503-3685-7/16/03…$15.00
DOI: http://dx.doi.org/10.1145/2839509.2844554

Why enhance relevance? In their report on a study carried out for the Iowa Department of Education [30], Newmann, King, and Carmichael wrote that:

> *We summarize these distinctive characteristics of authentic intellectual work as construction of knowledge through the use of disciplined inquiry, to produce discourse, products or performances that have* ***value beyond school.***

These and other studies indicate a need for an approach that enhances relevance. Practitioners and investigators have applied ARCS (Attention, Relevance, Confidence, and Satisfaction) in many contexts to measure, sustain and enhance student motivation [20, 22, 23]. Significant association between the students' relevance scores and motivational scores, and between the students' motivational scores and total achievement scores was reported in [16]. Constructivist learning models (e.g., [12]) suggest that learners must build their own knowledge, creating cognitive structures via assimilating new experiences in an idiosyncratic fashion. This construction happens only when the expertise of the course designer (reflected by rigor) adequately affects students' developing cognitive structures. This requires that the student be receptive to the new experiences, and such receptivity is enhanced by the perception of relevance. An optimal learning environment is therefore created with the right balance between rigor and relevance. Several prominent educationists have argued (e.g., [11]), that in order for education to be most effective, content must be presented in a way that allows the student to relate the information to prior experiences, thus deepening the connection with this new knowledge. Relevance helps the learner to see the new information in context, and thus connect it with prior experience. Research has shown that a better rigor-relevance relationship results in better student performance. In a 2004 report, Bottoms, Presson and Han [8] noted that schools enrolling high percentages of minority and/or impoverished students, outperformed schools with comparable demographics when they employed practices that made the curriculum more relevant to students. In another study, Sternberg et al. discovered that students completing more relevant projects (in the sense of being actual industrial applications in an engineering program), performed at higher levels than their peers performing simulated tasks [33].

Measuring Rigor. Rigor can be measured by assessing student learning. The assessment can be standardized by defining outcomes and suitable rubrics to measure the level of attainment. Since these topics are well-studied and their implementation varies considerably across instructors and programs, we do not address this here. In this research, instructors individually ensured that the level of rigor was not compromised.

Measuring Relevance. Our measurement of relevance is done by surveying students. Research has shown that relevance is best determined by student perception [14]. Other studies have affirmed the use of this approach. Himschoot [19] examined students' perception of the relevance of Biology content to everyday life and the methods of instruction that increase it. The work of Malau-Aduli et al [26] suggests that perceived clinical relevance is a contributing factor to the retention of basic science knowledge. Renninger [31] suggests that to understand individuals' motivation to engage, one must focus on individual interest. Perceived utility has been found to correlate well with perceived learning and is a good predictor of satisfaction [32].

3. IMPROVING THE BALANCE

To increase relevance, we should ask ourselves: *What changes should we make to help the learner perceive greater relevance in the course?* In the attempt to address this question, there are two issues here that need to be kept in mind: *(1) Relevance relates to a perception of value,* and *(2) Rigor should not be sacrificed in this quest.* Addressing the first requires that we take into account not only the perspective of the learner, but that of society as a whole. The second issue implies that such a process can only be undertaken by domain experts who recognize the value of enhancing student perception of relevance. The techniques discussed in this section provide a course designer with the ability to intentionally improve student perception of relevance. As with all such methods, it is extremely useful if the instructor can share the reasons for the pedagogical decisions with the learners, and when possible, seek their feedback [32].

3.1 Integrated Course Design

Integrated Course Design (ICD) was proposed by Fink [13], and consists of three main steps:

- *Identifying the Significant Learning Goals.* These goals are identified by incorporating the six dimensions of Significant Learning, which are identified as: Foundational Knowledge, Application, Integration, Human Dimension, Caring, and Learning How to Learn.
- *Constructing the Teaching and Learning Activities.* These are activities designed to foster active learning.
- *Designing Feedback and Assessment.* This is done so that (a) students understand the criteria and standards that will be used to assess their performance and (b) the learning activities prepare students well for eventual assessment activities.

In the process of carrying out these steps, two additional aspects must be taken into account:

- *In-Depth Analysis of Situational Factors.* The design is based on a systematic review of all the major situational factors, in order to define the situational constraints and opportunities of the course.
- *Integration/Alignment.* All components of the course structure reflect and support each other.

The principles and structure of ICD were broadly followed in the design of the courses used for this research.

Other approaches to design courses. There are a few different approaches to that have been used to design courses by looking at all the course objectives (instead of focusing almost entirely on the to-be-covered content). Assignment-based Design [25] and Backward Design [37] start by looking at what students should accomplish (e.g., outcomes) and then focusing on how they will present evidence of their accomplishment (e.g., assignments and tests). The Learning Spiral [3] approach helps instructors construct lessons, activities, or projects targeting the development of students' thinking skills and habits of mind. We found that ICD provides a framework that allows us to incorporate all these approaches and adds dimensions of significance which are not explicitly included in other processes.

3.2 The Whole-Part-Whole Approach

WPW [24] is a pedagogical (to be more precise, andragogical) approach that is used to present learning activities to students, which has been found to be particularly effective in adult learning. The structure of the WPW model is explained in Table 1.

Table 1 Structure of the WPW model

Whole	Parts	Description
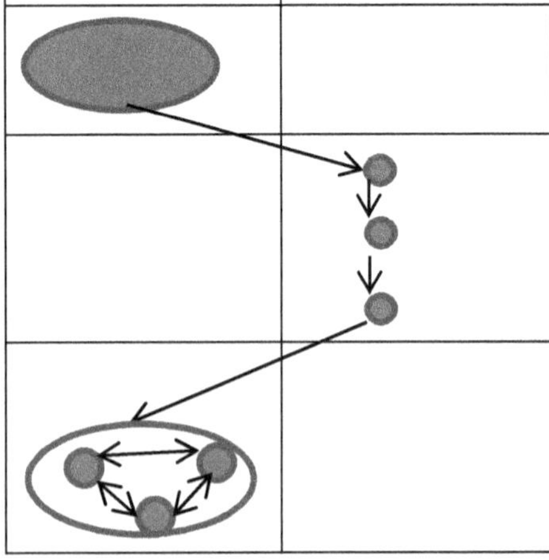		Stage1: Presentation of whole
		Stage2: Focus on individual parts that make up the whole
		Stage3: Return to whole, complete it and connect all the parts.

Each learning experience begins with a presentation of the whole as a black-box view. This allows the instructor to establish relevance without overwhelming the learner with the complexity of the details. In the next stage, the parts are presented so that the learner acquires sufficient mastery. The course designer must ensure that the learners are provided with sufficient background to work on the parts. The parts are assembled to create a white-box view of the whole.

Combing ICD and WPW. There is a certain synergy between ICD and WPW when it comes to designing a program of study. ICD gives us the tools to identify the final set of outcomes in all its complexity, and also define the characteristics of the learning experiences. WPW gives us the means to create concrete learning experiences by assembling the parts that are needed for attaining the expected outcomes.

Other Problem-based approaches. Problem-Based Learning (PBL) methods has been explored by educators. Definitions of PBL vary, as do the implementations. Learning in the PBL environment can be adversely affected by factors like "cognitive load" (e.g., [35]), requiring that the student experiences be well understood and carefully designed. In our courses we have used ICD and WPW to guide us in this process. It remains likely, though not firmly established, that a projects-based approach will be perceived as more relevant on the part of students.

4. APPLYING WPW AND ICD

In this research we report on three computing-related courses: a C++-based "traditional" CS1 course, a senior-level course on Object-oriented Software Design, and a Discrete Math course, required for all Computer Science majors, taught by the Mathematics department. A common thread that unifies all these experiences is that *situational factors* were taken into account. These factors included the nature of the foundational knowledge, and the maturity and diversity of the learners.

4.1 Object-oriented Software Design

The complexity of the topic, makes it an excellent choice for improving student engagement using ICD and WPW. ICD requires a broad view of subject and this was done through two activities:

- looking at a wide variety of textbooks to determine what topics represent essential knowledge
- looking at the tasks assigned to students when they join industry

These activities defined the foundational knowledge, application of this knowledge and its integration. Following this, the final outcome for this course was stated as follows:

> *A student completing the course should have a grasp of the construction process, employ the necessary tools, make good design choices, apply appropriate modeling techniques, work with software architectures, and understand the philosophy and guiding principles of object-orientation.*

Defining the wholes and parts. A single whole that includes all these concepts would overwhelm the learner, and therefore a set of wholes was identified:

1. *Create an object oriented database for a familiar application.* Through this whole the students become familiar with the construction process.
2. *Create a front end for the object oriented database.* Here students learn the fundamentals of finite state modeling and the use of more sophisticated design patterns.
3. *Add features to a simple drawing program.* This requires students to understand software architectures.

The wholes are spread throughout the course, and similar examples are used to guide the students through the construction process. Some periods of traditional lecture-style teaching are interspersed. Students get progressively lesser guidance as the course progresses, thus teaching learners how to learn. One of the challenges in designing such a course is the cognitive load associated with each whole.

4.2 Creating a CS1 Course

Creating a CS1 course poses two other challenges.

- *A diverse student body.* For some STEM majors it serves as a terminal experience; for computing majors, this is a stepping stone. ICD incorporates expectations of all learners when the outcomes are defined.
- *Limited prior experience.* Students have very little exposure to computing. Finding suitable "wholes" which do not overwhelm the student is a challenge.

Diversity is handled by identifying a common expectation, e.g., the need to understand programming as a problem-solving activity. To make the experiences manageable, each whole learning elements is constructed by choosing a small number of parts, and placing these in the context of a larger problem. Two examples of this are described below.

One-dimensional point location. This is a typical learning module that can be used in the early part of CS1. Students explored a divide-and-conquer approach and recognized the need for problem analysis, design and testing.

Creating a simple business application. This is done in two stages; mid-way through the course, a simple version is created using procedural programming, and towards the end, a more complex version (which also serves as a capstone) is created. This requires them to use their understanding of most of the concepts learned in the course, and has apparent value outside the classroom for all students.

Caring and the Human Dimension. In the model of ICD, Caring and the Human Dimension are two important elements of Significant Learning. In both courses, this is done through reflection. Students reflect on the experience by answering questions, relating to both the outcomes that they were expected to attain through the experience, and also how their approach to these problems has changed as a result of going through the experience.

4.3 Creating a Discrete Math Course

A special effort was undertaken to design the Discrete Math course so that the principles of ICD could be applied. Redesigning this posed some unique challenges as well:

- *A diverse student body.* Students from several majors are required to take the Discrete Math course. Integrated Course Design requires that we look at the expectations of all kinds of learners when we define the outcomes for the course.
- *Limited mathematical maturity.* This usually necessitates additional focus on rigor to bring students up to speed.
- *Traditional nature of text books.* Math text books tend to focus on mathematical concepts and rigor and less on application.

To create modules for this course, faculty from other disciplines provided applications. These were presented in the early stages of each module and were used to help students see the relevance of Discrete Math techniques to their chosen disciplines.

5. MEASURING RELEVANCE

At the end of each semester, we administered a course survey whereby students were asked to rate (on a five-point scale) items related to defining relevance for young adult learners, the importance of relevance in learning, the course in general terms, and to evaluate the project-based components of the course. Finally, we also asked students to provide written definitions of relevance as it related to their learning.

We analyzed three aspects of student responses on an exploratory basis. (1) We initiated the analysis via an iterative assessment of relevance that we could apply to the improvement of the whole-part approach and its resulting rigor-relevance balance. (2) We assessed students' perspectives on the whole-part, project orientation as it played out in the course. (3) We examined the effects of the above two metrics on student outcomes with an eye toward validating the approach and determining whether or not, or to what degree, student performance reflected their perceptions of relevance. We intended to develop instrumentation that was reliable, valid, and that could be flexibly applied to a variety of STEM courses.

5.1 Designing a Tool for Measuring Relevance

Scale development and reliability. Initially, we employed principal components analysis [15] to examine the degree to which the relevance items could be organized into defensible components (e.g., the instrument's dimensionality).

We thus subjected 159 cases to principal components analysis (PRINCOMP, factor analysis sans the insertion of prior communality estimates into the main diagonal). Consideration of 1, 2, or 3 factors in the analysis indicated that a 1-factor solution (which we denote F-1) produced the clearest simple structure. An inspection of items suggested that F-1 yielded a scale that can best be entitled "importance and characteristics" [of relevance]. F-1 produced a characteristic root (λ) of 2.21, explaining 24.6% of systematic variance.

As a follow up to PRINCOMP, on an exploratory basis, we evaluated the internal consistency reliability of the resulting instrument utilizing Cronbach's alpha [10], a measure of the degree to which items can be harnessed to measure an entity. The resulting scale yielded a reasonably high α of .62, a level of reliability appropriate for exploratory and research purposes. Since two constructs associated with relevance are combined to form the scale based on F-1 (a) importance, and (b) characteristics) it would prove useful in future to add items to the instrument in each domain with an eye toward generating two more independent, though oblique, constructs each with higher internal consistency values. In short, the scale, while a good start on deciphering relevance of computer science and related courses needs more items—especially more items reliably tapping the characteristics or structure of relevance.

The two items with lower loadings on F-1 appear conceptually related to the interaction between relevance and instructor behavior ("my instructor is probably a better judge of relevance" and "course activities balanced rigor and relevance"). This could reasonably be pursued as a third factor. Finally, we examined students' written responses via a systematic examination of emergent thematic units [21].

6. RESULTS

What does relevance look like? Table 2 shows the seven items along with their loadings on F-1. The items are shown in reverse order by mean value on a scale running from 1-4. By reading down the table, a phenomenological or perceptual picture of relevance emerges.

Qualitative data. Significantly, students' emergent qualitative themes provided insight into their reasoning about relevance (Please write the second author for details on text analysis methodology). The themes (taken from 46 randomly-selected CS1 students) were interconnected and demonstrated considerable overlap, though we did not pursue a statistical analysis of thematic overlap. (1) An overriding theme was that of connections or correlations. That is, students penned responses suggesting that relevance exists when the instructor draws connections between course assignments and a wide variety of life and personal features. The remaining themes are discussed in reverse order by frequency of occurrence (2) Students' discussion of relevance had the course visibly tied to a future orientation—that it clearly connected with some imagined future use of information: (3) The second most common theme to emerge reflected students' definition of relevance in terms of the degree to which activities and assignments "moved" individuals toward degree completion Two sub-themes emerged under the ***future*** orientation, (a.) an undifferentiated future orientation ("the course is relevant when it connects clearly with my future") and (b.) work orientation, that is relevance occurs when an instructor connects course material to an imagined professional future. (4)The fourth-most common leitmotif theme suggested that a course is relevant to the extent that it breaks down barriers between "pure" classroom and real-life skills and applications. This latter construct needs to be examined further; specifically, identifying the elements students classify under "real life." Of particular salience is the degree to which students see theory as "bookish." (5)Many students defined relevance as related to their current situation. The meaning of these statements was often obscure, but suggested that a course

Table 2 Survey items with their loadings

Relevance Variable	N	Loading	Mean	SD	Percent Highest Two Levels	Percent Highest Level (4 of 4)
Relevance, no matter how defined, is important for my learning.	158	0.43	3.6	0.5	98.1	57.0
To the degree that I find course activities as relevant, I learn more from them.	159	0.61	3.4	0.7	92.5	52.2
The relevance of activities in courses deepens my interest in a course (willingness to "dig in,")	158	0.57	3.4	0.7	89.2	53.2
I see assignments as relevant when they seem real—like something a professional in my field might do	158	0.61	3.4	0.8	88.0	54.4
Relevance means that the assignments in a course are related to my major or intended major.	159	0.57	3.3	0.7	88.7	43.4
Relevance is related to a clear link between course assignments and what I see as my future	159	0.52	3.0	0.8	80.5	42.8
The relevance of classroom assignments is related to the links [I see] between course assignments and my interests right now.	158	0.44	3.0	0.7	77.8	20.3
Mean/ Across Items	----		3.3	-----	87.83	46.19

can be made relevant by tapping into students' current interests and concerns, not necessarily related to the future; reading between the lines, students seemed to conflate relevance and engagement. This theme reflected an existing situation or an interpretation: as one student put it, "The course has meaning to me right now."

Validity of the construct. We asked students to rate their level of engagement with computer science related topics on a pre- and post-course basis. The results suggest that perceived relevance of the course (this course balanced rigor and relevance) predicts pre-to-post gains in engagement ($r_{xy} = 0.41$, $p = .031$). We presume that that relational indices will increase as we improve the relevance scale.

7. CONCLUSION AND FUTURE WORK

Results. In this preliminary investigation, student conceptualization of relevance starts to take shape as some combination of future applicability, specifically to further studies (degree attainment) and to an imagined work future. However, students added components via written responses that we had not considered. First, several students seemed to conflate relevance with engagement. A course is relevant to the extent that taps into current goals and interests. Second, and perhaps the element with the most practical implications is students' proclivity to contrast classroom and "real-life" elements. This needs to be explored much more deeply.

Implications for practice. (1) Given the relationship between overall course ratings and relevance indicators, it is safe to say that instructors in CSI courses need to consider relating course materials to students' futures (both occupational and for degree attainment), and to voice the relationship between activities and "real life." (2) In establishing relevance, instructors need to consider two correlated sets of practices. First, efforts should be made to connect with students to identify their present interests and reasons for taking the course; second, our data suggest that instructors would increase students' understanding of relevance via "talk-alouds." That is, openly sharing information with students about why pedagogical decisions were made and eliciting period feedback related to the decisions.

Future research. (1) The elements on engagement and the "real-world-classroom" dichotomy need to be explored further, especially via adding these components to the instrument and conducting interviews with students. (2) We must explore the meaning of rigor as deeply as we have relevance. The balance itself and methods for attaining it remain to be investigated for the case of CS1. (3) Practitioners must explore the relationship between student perceptions of relevance and instructors' willingness to discuss it openly. (4) Finally, more work is needed via development of regression methods to determine to what degree student views of relevance predict student learning.

Acknowledgements. This research was supported in part by a Miller Scholar award, made possible by a generous grant to SCSU by the Miller family. We would also like to thank our colleagues in the Math department, especially Dr.Walk and Dr Zhao, whose support was essential for our success.

8. REFERENCES

[1] Alvarado, C., Lee, C.B., and Gillespie, G., 2014. New CS1 pedagogies and curriculum, the same success factors? Proc. 45th ACM technical symposium on Computer science education, 379-384, 2014.

[2] Anderson, N., Herriot, P., and Hodgkinson, G.P., 2001. The practitioner-researcher divide in Industrial, Work and Organizational psychology: Where are we now, and where do we go from here? Journal of Occupational and Organizational Psychology, v. 74, 391–411, 2001.

[3] Andrade A., 1999. The Thinking Classroom.

[4] Apiola, M., Lattu, M., and Pasanen, T.A., 2010. Creativity and intrinsic motivation in computer science education: experimenting with robots. Proc. 15th conf. on Innovation and technology in computer science education, 26-30, 2010.

[5] Babe, T., 1995. The validation of relevance as an independent dimension of the ARCS motivational model of

instructional design. Unpublished doctoral dissertation, The Pennsylvania State University, University Park.

[6] Barker L.J., McDowell C., and Kalahar K. Exploring factors that influence computer science introductory course students to persist in the major, Proc. ACM SIGCSE, 2009.

[7] Barnes, T., Powell. E., Chaffin, A., and Lipford, H., 2008. Game2Learn: improving the motivation of CS1 students. Proc. 3rd international conference on Game development in computer science education, 1-5.

[8] Bottoms, G., Presson, A., and Han, L., 2004. Rigor, Relevance and Relationships Improve Achievement in Rural High Schools: High School Reform Works When Schools Do the Right Things, SREB, Atlanta, GA, 2004.

[9] Boyer, K. E., Phillips, R., Wallis, M. D., Vouk, M. A., and Lester, J. C., 2009. Investigating the role of student motivation in computer science education through one-on-one tutoring. Comput. Sci. Ed. v. 19, n. 2, 111—135.

[10] Cronbach, L. J. (1951). Coefficient alpha and the internal structure of tests. Psychometrika. 16, 297-334.

[11] Dewey, J., 1938. Experience and Education, 1938. Most recently published by Free Press, ISBN-13: 978-0684838281, 1997.

[12] Duckworth, E.R., 1973. The having of wonderful ideas. In M. Schwebel & J. Raph (eds.), *Piaget in the classroom,* pp. 258–277, New York: Basic Books.

[13] Fink, LD., 2013. Creating Significant Learning Experiences: An Integrated Approach to Designing College Courses, Jossey-Bass, second edition, 2013.

[14] Frymier, A., and Shulman, G., 1995. What's in it for me?: Increasing content relevance to enhance students' motivation. Communication Education. v. 45, 181–199.

[15] Gorsuch, R. L. (1974). *Factor analysis.* Philadelphia, PA: S.

[16] Guzdial M. Computing Education Must Go Beyond Intuition: The Need for Evidence-Based Practice, CACM blog, February 2015.

[17] Guzdial, M., 2010. Does contextualized computing education help? ACM Inroads, v.1 n.4, 4-6, December 2010.

[18] Guzdial, M., 2013. Exploring hypotheses about media computation. Proc. 9th international ACM conf. on International Computing Education Research, 19-26.

[19] Himschoot, A., 2012. Student Perception of Relevance of Biology Content to Everyday Life: A Study in Higher Education Biology Courses. Olivet Nazarene University.

[20] Hung, I., Lee, L., Chao, K., and Chen, N., 2011. Applying ARCS Model for Enhancing and Sustaining Learning Motivation Using Robot as Teaching Assistant. Proc. 6th International Conference on E-learning and Games, Edutainment Technologies, 334-341.

[21] Hunt, K. (1965). Grammatical structures written at three grade levels. NCTE Research report No. 3. Champaign, IL, USA: NCTE

[22] Keller, J. M., 1999. Using the ARCS motivational design process in computer-based instruction and distance education. New Directions for Teaching and Learning, v. 78, 39-47.

[23] Keller, J.M., and Suzuki, K., 2004. Learner motivation and E-learning design: a multinationally validated process. Journal of Educational Media, v. 29, n. 3, October 2004.

[24] Knowles, M.S., Holton, E.F. III, and Swanson, R.A., 2011. The Adult Learner, Sixth Edition: The Definitive Classic in Adult Education and Human Resource Development, Taylor and Francis, seventh edition, 2011.

[25] Kurfiss, J.G., 1988. Critical Thinking: Theory, research, practice and possibilities, ASHE-ERIC Higher Education Report No. 2, 1988. http://eric.ed.gov/?id=ED304041

[26] Malau-Aduli, B.S., Adrian YS Lee, A.Y.S, Cooling, N., Catchpole, M., Jose, M., and Turner, R., 2013. Retention of knowledge and perceived relevance of basic sciences in an integrated CBL curriculum. BMC Medical Education, Approaches to teaching and learning, v. 13.

[27] McGill, M. M., 2012. Learning to Program with Personal Robots: Influences on Student Motivation. ACM Transactions on Computing Education, v. 12 n. 1, 4:1-4:32, March 2012.

[28] McNulty, Raymond J.; Quaglia, Russell J. Rigor, Relevance and Relationships, School Administrator, v64 n8 p18-23 Sep 2007

[29] Misra, A., Blank, D., and Kumar D., 2009. A music context for teaching introductory computing, ACM SIGCSE Bulletin, v.41 n.3.

[30] Newmann, F.M., King, M.B., and Carmichael, D.L., 2007. Authentic instruction and assessment: Common standards for rigor and relevance in teaching academic subjects, 2007.

[31] Renninger, K. A., 2000. Individual interest and its implications for understanding intrinsic motivation. In C. Sansone and J. M. Harakiewicz (Eds.), Intrinsic and extrinsic motivation: The search for optimal motivation and performance. New York: Academic Press.

[32] Roszkowski, M. J. and Soven, M., 2010. Did you learn something useful today? An analysis of how perceived utility relates to perceived learning and their predictiveness of satisfaction with training. Perf. Impr. Qrtly, v. 23, 71–91.

[33] Sternberg S.P.K., Johnson A., Moen D. and Hoover J.H. Delivery and Assessment of Senior Capstone Design via Distance Education, Journal of Engineering Education Volume 89, Issue 2, pages 115–118, April 2000.

[34] Summet, J., Kumar, D., O'Hara, K., Walker, D., Ni, L., Blank, D., and Balch, T., 2009. Personalizing CS1 with robots. Proc.40th ACM technical symposium on Computer Science Education.

[35] Sweller, J., 2006. The worked example effect and human cognition, Learning and Instruction, vol. 16, no. 2, 165–169, 2006.

[36] Tew, A.E., Dorn, B., Leahy, Jr. W.D., and Guzdial, M., 2008. Context as Support for Learning Computer Organization, Journal on Educational Resources in Computing, v.8 n.3, p.1-18, October 2008.

[37] Wiggins, G., and McTighe, J., 2005. Understanding by Design, Expanded 2nd Edition Paperback – July 24, 2005.

[38] Wilhelm, Jeffrey D. (2001). *Strategic Reading.* Portsmouth, NH: Boynton Cook Publishers, Inc

Understanding How Research Experiences for Undergraduate Students May Foster Diversity in the Professorate

Burçin Tamer
Computing Research Association
1828 L Street NW, Ste. 800
Washington, DC 20036
202-266-2935, +1
burcin@cra.org

Jane G. Stout
Computing Research Association
1828 L Street NW, Ste. 800
Washington, DC 20036
202-266-2937, +1
jane@cra.org

ABSTRACT

College and university professors serve as role models and leaders. Unfortunately, in computing fields, only a small fraction of the professorate is women and/or members of minority racial groups. To address this issue, the current research assessed the role of research experiences for undergraduate students (REUs) on underrepresented students' interest in pursuing a career as a computing professor. We found that REUs utilizing a set of specific practices are linked with underrepresented students' interest in becoming a computing professor. On the other hand, no specific REU practice was associated with majority students' (i.e., White and Asian men's) level of interest in becoming a professor. Thus, this research not only identifies aspects of REUs that may be especially important for increasing diversity in the professorate but also highlights that REUs may serve different purposes for underrepresented versus majority students.

Categories and Subject Descriptors

• Social and professional topics ~ Computational science and engineering education • Social and professional topics ~ Race and ethnicity • Social and professional topics ~ Men • Social and professional topics ~ Women

Keywords

undergraduate education; undergraduate research experiences; career; underrepresented students; professor

SIGCSE '16, March 02-05, 2016, Memphis, TN, USA
 ISBN 978-1-4503-3685-7/16/03…$15.00
DOI: http://dx.doi.org/10.1145/2839509.2844573

1. INTRODUCTION

1.1 Background

The computer science academic pipeline lacks diversity among its undergraduate students, graduate students, and faculty [22] [24] [25] [33]. This is a problem for a number of reasons. First, a lack of diversity in computing innovation risks ignoring the needs of significant portions of the population [4] [21]. Furthermore, without contributions from a broad range of perspectives, the field cannot maximize productivity and creativity [16] [32]. In the current paper, we are interested specifically in the lack of diversity in the computing professorate. Research suggests that low diversity in the computing professorate may be inadvertently contributing to low diversity in the computing student body. Extant research indicates that when students experience a dearth of role models who "look like them" in the academy, their performance, motivation, and positive attitudes towards academics suffer (e.g., see [8] [17] [18] [31]). Thus, if the student body within computing is to become more diverse, it is important to showcase a diverse array of role models within the computing professorate.

One way to promote interest in pursuing a professorial job among underrepresented students may be through research experiences for undergraduate students (REUs). REU is an established tool for enhancing the undergraduate experience and increasing students' motivation to pursue graduate study, and academic research careers (e.g., [19] [20] [26] [27]). An ethnographic study of students' perceptions of their REU programs indicated that more than 90% of students' statements about their REU experiences were positive ([28]). Other research indicates that, participation in an REU increases students' persistence in their field ([22]), and undergraduate students to pursue graduate school ([27]).

Importantly, existing research finds that students who are underrepresented men as well as women (URMW) tend to benefit more from REUs than White and Asian male students (i.e., "majority men"; MM). For instance, URMW students show a greater degree of improvement in academic skills, and postsecondary aspirations after participating in undergraduate research than MM students ([5] [6] [10] [27]). Thus a great deal of research suggests that REUs benefit URMW students to a greater degree than MM students, and may serve as a tool to increase the number of URMW individuals interested in pursuing professorial computing professions.

1.2 Understanding the nuances of the benefits of REUs on URMW students

In the current research, we are interested in whether *specific characteristics* of REUs are particularly potent predictors of URMW students' aspirations for the professorate. Although REUs all share a common goal of exposing undergraduate students to scientific research methods, there is considerable variability in REU program components. For instance, while some REUs involve a great deal of collaboration and teamwork, others do not. REUs might also differ in social applicability of their research topic (e.g., Robotics research with medical versus industrial applications). These differences across programs can emerge based on a number of factors, such as the PI's area of expertise and resources available to the program.

Variability in the way REUs are orchestrated may, in turn, have differential impact on students' interest in wishing to pursue computing research in the future. Further, variability in REU infrastructure may have differential effects on different types of students (i.e., URMW versus MM students), such that only a subset of students may leave their REU particularly encouraged to pursue advanced studies in computing. Given that the field of computing research suffers from low diversity at all levels of the academic pipeline, our work sought to pinpoint REU characteristics that are particularly encouraging for URMW students' persistence in academic computing research.

In order to determine the types of REU characteristics that might be relevant for students' future career plans, we turn to the principles of Social Cognitive Career Theory (SCCT) [11] [13] and the extant literature on experiences of underrepresented students in computing.

SCCT indicates that key factors that guide individuals' career choices are outcome expectations (i.e., beliefs about the types of things one can achieve in their career), personal interest, and social support. Previously, scholars found that these factors indeed predicted students' persistence in computing disciplines [14] [15]. In the current study, we are interested in going a step further and teasing out conditions under which URMW students in particular may err towards a career in computing.

For instance, earlier studies have found that some *outcome expectations* for a career in computing carry more importance for URMW students compared to MM students. URMW students tend to be attracted to technical fields that are collaborative and have clear social applications ([9] [30]), suggesting that REUs fostering collaboration and socially relevant research may promote URMW students' *interest* in pursuing research in the future.

Moreover, underrepresented REU students are less likely than their MM peers to have had prior exposure to mentorship (i.e., *social support* from role models and experts; [1] [7] [28]). As such, URMW students may be especially sensitive to the benefits of being mentored during an REU, which involves learning about career options, and gaining exposure to all facets of the research and dissemination process. In this sense, exposure to the research process as well as graduate school preparation during REUs may be more strongly linked with URMW students' intentions to pursue a professorial career compared to the intentions of MM students.

In sum, we have reason to believe that particular REU characteristics might be effective in promoting URMW students' interest in pursuing scholarly computing research as a career path. The current research aims to make a contribution to existing research on the benefits of REUs on URMW students' persistence in computing research by assessing the effect of common REU practices on students' career aspirations.

2. DATA and METHODS

2.1 Participants and procedure

During the fall of 2014, 101 undergraduate students who had completed an REU during the summer of 2014 participated in this study. Students were recruited from computing departments across the United States to complete the Computing Research Association's Center for Evaluating the Research Pipeline (CERP) annual student survey.[1] Students who indicated that they had participated in any of the following during the summer of 2014 were included in our sample: (a) an undergraduate research experience at their home institution, (b) an undergraduate research experience at another institution or (c) a research internship in an industry or government lab.

Within our dataset were two demographic subgroups of interest. The first was underrepresented minority men, including those of Black/African American or Hispanic/Latino descent, and women of all racial and ethnic backgrounds (URMW students, $n = 52$). The second group was White and Asian men. We refer to this group as "majority men" (MM, $n = 49$).

2.2 Measures

The current report focuses on the following subset of measures from CERP's fall 2014 survey that assessed students' career intentions, and experiences during their summer REU:

2.2.1 Outcome variable: Interest in becoming a computing professor.

Students responded to a single item asking "How interested are you in having a computing job like the one below after you finish your highest degree? *College/University professor in computing field*", using a scale ranging from (1) *very disinterested* to (5*) very interested.*

2.2.2 Predictors: REU characteristics.

Students completed a series of survey questions pertaining to their level of exposure to a set of REU characteristics during their REU. While some of the characteristics were measured using a single survey item, other characteristics were aggregate measures that were constructed by averaging across multiple items. Survey items for each REU characteristic variable, and reliability statistics, when appropriate, are listed below.

Collaboration: Collaboration with others was measured via two items (Cronbach's $\alpha = 0.86$): "How much experience did you gain collaborating with colleagues?", (1) *none* - (5) *a lot*; and "How much knowledge have you gained in the following areas as a result of your research experience? *How to work collaboratively with others*", (1) *none* - (5) *a lot.*

Social Impact: Information on how computing can have social impact was measured via a single item: "How much knowledge have you gained in the following areas as a result of your research

[1] CERP administers an annual survey each fall semester to undergraduate student computing majors from a sample of universities and colleges across the county. Survey questions pertain to past research and professional experiences, with a particular focus on factors relevant to career preparation. For more information about CERP's survey research, visit http://www.cra.org/cerp/data-buddies.

Figure 1. Analytical Model

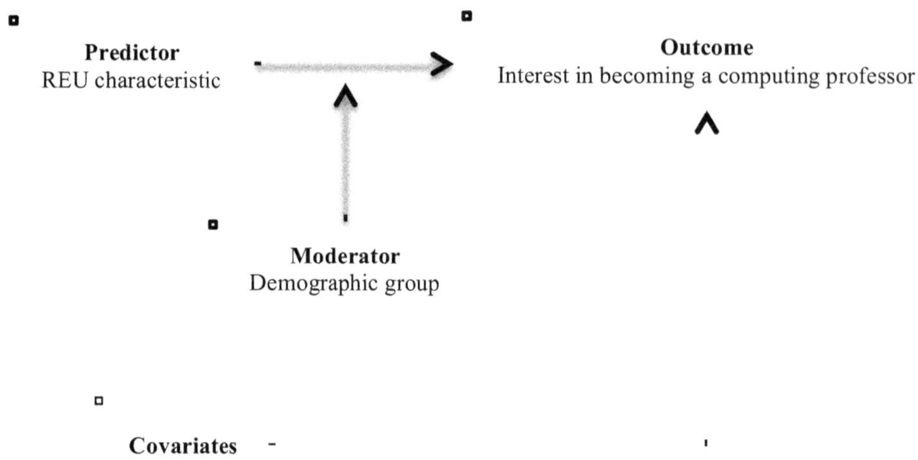

experience? *How computing can make a positive contribution to society*", (1) *none* - (5) *a lot.*

Career Options: Exposure to computing career options was measured via a single item: "How much knowledge have you gained in the following areas as a result of your research experience? *What career options are available within computing*", (1) *none* - (5) *a lot.*

Research Skills: Exposure to research skills was measured via five items (Cronbach's $\alpha = 0.87$): "How much experience did you gain in the following activities? *Using scientific methods to test a hypothesis; Generating hypotheses; Collecting data or conducting experiments; Analyzing data with statistics or other tools; Explaining results*", (1) *none* - (5) *a lot.*

Research Dissemination: Exposure to the research dissemination process was measured via four items (Cronbach's $\alpha = 0.86$): "How much experience did you gain in the following activities? *Summarizing published research results; Writing or co-authoring a research paper or report; Presenting a research paper or report; Publishing a research paper or report*", (1) *none* - (5) *a lot.*

Research Involvement: Involvement in the design of a research project was measured via three items (Cronbach's $\alpha = 0.83$): How much experience did you gain in the following activities? *The design of the research project(s); What research techniques/materials were used; Deciding what to do next (e.g. follow-up studies)*", (1) *none* - (5) *a lot.*

Admissions: Learning about the graduate admission process was assessed via two items (Cronbach's $\alpha = 0.94$): How much knowledge have you gained in the following areas as a result of your research experience? *Criteria for admission to graduate programs, How to select the right graduate program for you*", (1) *none* - (5) *a lot.*

Graduate Student Life: Learning about graduate student life was measured via a single item: "How much knowledge have you gained in the following areas as a result of your research experience? *What it is like to be a graduate student in computer science or computer engineering*", (1) *none* - (5) *a lot.*

2.2.3 Covariates[2]

We measured the following demographic characteristics, which served as covariates during data analyses.

Parental education level: Students indicated parental education level for up to two parents using the following options: Less than high school; High school graduate or GED; Some college or Associate's degree; Bachelor's degree; Master's degree; PhD or Professional degree (MD, JD, Ed.D, etc...). Among students who reported parental education level for two parents, we used the highest parents' education level as our measure of parental education level.

Class standing: Students indicated their class standing using the following categories: first year, second year, third year, fourth year, and fifth year or greater.

Department type: We conducted a content analysis of students' home institutions' computing degree program websites in order to group students' department type by the highest degree granted in their department. Department type was coded into three categories, based on the highest degree awarded in student's home computing department: B.S., M.S., or Ph.D.

Major grade point average: Students reported their grade point average (GPA) in their majors, using a range from 0-4.

3. RESULTS

We ran multiple linear regression analyses to assess whether the relationship between characteristics of an REU program and students' professorial intentions was moderated by (depended on) students' demographic group (URMW vs. MM). Figure 1 illustrates our analytical model showing the moderating role of demographic group in determining the impact of REU

[2] Covariates are known correlates of outcome variables, and are included in statistical models so that any observed effects of predictors and moderators on outcome variables are true *over and above* the effects of our covariates on outcome measures.

Table 1. Simple Effects of Eight REU characteristics for URMW and MM students

REU characteristic	URMW Students			MM Students		
	Average simple effect	95% CI lower bound	95% CI upper bound	Average simple effect	95% CI lower bound	95% CI upper bound
Collaboration	1.61*	0.28	2.84	-0.11	-1.56	1.31
Social Impact	1.46*	0.23	2.68	-0.30	-1.52	0.91
Career Options	0.71	-0.43	1.77	-0.82	-2.02	0.44
Research Skills	0.74	-0.62	2.04	0.80	-0.72	2.42
Research Dissemination	1.08	-0.09	2.27	1.12	-0.23	2.51
Research Involvement	0.80	-0.44	2.10	0.71	-0.93	2.18
Admissions	1.18*	0.21	2.23	0.26	-0.95	1.50
Graduate Student Life	2.01*	0.99	3.01	-0.10	-1.44	1.23

*Note. Simple effects calculated based on an OLS regression model. * $p < .05$.*

characteristics (predictor variable) on undergraduate students' interest in becoming a professor in a computing field (outcome variable). We included a moderating variable in our model to test for the interaction between students' demographic group and REU characteristics. A "moderation" (or interaction) effect occurs when the relationship between a predictor variable (e.g., an REU characteristic) and an outcome variable (e.g., students' level of interest in becoming a college/university professor in a computing field) depends on a moderator variable (e.g., demographic group: MM vs. URMW).

As an example of a moderated relationship, suppose that students who are exposed to a higher degree of collaboration in their REU (predictor variable) are subsequently more interested in becoming a professor of computing (outcome variable). However, the relationship between exposure to collaboration and professorial intentions is stronger for one demographic group of students than another (moderator variable). Specifically, it could be that REUs fostering collaboration are *particularly* likely to promote interest in becoming a professor among URMW students, relative to MM students. Thus, moderation analyses can explain "when" or "for whom" the effects of a predictor variable are related to a particular outcome. In total, we ran eight separate multiple regression models (one for each REU characteristic) using the regression equation seen in Equation 1. We do not present regression output for our full models, given the conditional nature of our analyses (i.e., interpretation of the interaction term in our models is contingent on our dummy coding scheme for Demographic Group, such that output for the Predictor variable is only relevant to students who were coded as 0).[3,4] Instead, we only present output for simple effects of our main predictor and moderator variables in Table 1.

Equation 1. Linear Regression Model

$$\begin{aligned}\text{Interest in Being a Professor}\\ &= \beta_o + \beta_1 \times \text{Parental Education Level}\\ &+ \beta_2 \times \text{Class Standing}\\ &+ \beta_3 \times \text{Department Type} + \beta_4 \times \text{Major GPA}\\ &+ \beta_5 \times \text{ REU Characteristic}\\ &+ \beta_6 \times \text{ Demographic Group}\\ &+ \beta_7 \times \text{ REU Char.} \times \text{Dem. Group}\end{aligned}$$

Simple effects in Table 1 show the effect of a change in the predictor (REU Characteristic) on the outcome for given values of the moderator variable (Demographic Group). Average simple effects shown in Table 1 illustrate the effect of moving from the minimum value of the Likert-type scale (i.e. exposure to REU characteristic = 1) to the maximum value of the scale (i.e. exposure to REU characteristic = 5) for URMW and MM students, respectively. As an example, URMW students who rate their experience of collaboration as "a lot" as opposed to "none" are expected to rate their interest in becoming a college/university professor 1.61 points higher on average.

Our results show that URMW students that experienced greater collaboration (avg. effect = 1.61, 95% CI = [0.28, 2.84]), learned more about the social impacts of a career in computing (avg. effect = 1.46, 95% CI = [0.23, 2.68]), learned more about the graduate school admissions process (avg. effect = 1.18, 95% CI = [0.21, 2.23]), and became more familiar with graduate student life (avg. effect = 2.01, 95% CI = [0.99, 3.01]) during their REU showed greater interest in becoming a computing professor when surveyed the fall after their summer REU. However, MM students' interest in pursuing a career as a computing professor was not influenced by their REU experience.

4. DISCUSSION

The current research was designed to better understand how REUs might be an effective means for promoting diversity in the computing professorate. We found that URMW students who participated in REUs reported greater intentions to pursue a career as a college or university professor when they gained experience collaborating, learned about social impacts of a career in computing research, gained knowledge of the graduate admissions process, and were familiarized with graduate student life. These REU characteristics likely bring URMW students a combination of knowledge and interest necessary to pursue a career as a computing professor. Collaborating within an academic setting on research projects may illustrate to the students that they are capable of taking on tasks that a professor would be performing. In addition to highlighting their capabilities, the experience of collaboration also shows that working in computing research need not be a solitary experience. Furthermore, understanding the social applications of scholarly computing research may reveal to students the potential impact of computing research on their communities. Finally, information on how to get into graduate school as well as exposure to graduate student life may increase students' interest in the professorate by equipping them with the information they need to get started on a professorial career path. These explanations are in line with the theoretical and empirical literature on the experiences of underrepresented students in computing fields as discussed in our introduction section.

[3] For further discussion of conditional interpretation for interaction terms, see [1] [2] [11].

[4] Full regression output is available from the first author.

Interestingly, MM students' level of interest in becoming a professor was not associated with any of the eight REU practices we examined. This suggests that REUs may have a different meaning and purpose for MM students than URMW students. For instance, it could be the case that participating in an REU benefits MM students' resumes, and yields new professional contacts, but does not necessarily influence their personal goals and plans.

An alternative explanation for our observed lack of any association between REU characteristics and intentions to pursue a career as a professor for MM students may be that MM students have systematically higher or lower levels of interest in a professorship than URMW students regardless of how their REU was organized. That is, there may have been less variability in MM students' professorial intentions the URMW students, affording our analytic models less opportunity to predict MM students' intentions. We tested this possibility using a difference of means test URMW students' versus MM students' interest levels in becoming a professor; we found no group difference ($t(98) = 0.72, p = 0.47$).

We acknowledge that the current work cannot make a causal claim about REU dynamics on URMW students' aspirations for the future, because our data were obtained at a single point in time and are therefore correlational. With this caveat in mind, this research suggests that REUs with a certain set of characteristics may be an effective means for diversifying the computing research pipeline in the long term. By promoting interest in the professorate among URMW undergraduate students, REUs have the capacity to diversify the types of role models that future generations of women, and men from racial minority groups interact with and aspire to become.

5. ACKNOWLEDGMENTS

This research is sponsored by two grants from the National Science Foundation awarded to the Computing Research Association: CNS-1246649 and DUE-1431112. We wish to thank Heather Wright for assistance with data collection, and Betsy Bizot, Tracy Camp, and Ama Nyame-Mensah for feedback on an earlier draft of this paper. We also wish to thank participating departments of The Data Buddies Project for contributing to the data source for this paper (participating departments can be found here: http://cra.org/cerp/our-buddies/list-of-data-buddies).

6. REFERENCES

[1] Aiken, L. S., & West, S. G. 1991. *Multiple regression: Testing and interpreting interactions*. Thousand Oaks, CA: Sage.

[2] Bauer, D. J., & Curran, P. J. 2005. Probing interactions in fixed and multilevel regression: Inferential and graphical techniques. *Multivariate Behavioral Research*. 405(3), 373-400.

[3] Bova, B. 2000. Mentoring revisited: The black woman's experience. *Mentoring and Tutoring*. 8, 5-16.

[4] Camp, T. 2012. Computing, we have a problem. *ACM Inroads*. 3, 34 - 40.

[5] Campbell, A., & Skoog, G. 2004. Preparing Undergraduate Women for Science Careers. *Journal of College Science Teaching*. 33, 24-26.

[6] Chang, M., Sharkness, J., Hurtado, S., & Newman, C. 2014. What matters in college for retaining aspiring scientists and engineers from underrepresented racial groups. *Journal of Research in Science Teaching*. 51, 555-580

[7] Committee on Science, Engineering & Public Policy. 2011. *Expanding Underrepresented Minority Participation: America's Science and Technology Talent at the Crossroads*. National Academies Press.

[8] Dasgupta, N. 2011. Ingroup experts and peers as social vaccines who inoculate the self-concept: The stereotype inoculation model. *Psychological Inquiry*. 22, 231-246.

[9] Diekman, A. B., Brown, E. R., Johnston, A. M., & Clark, E. K. 2010. Seeking congruity between goals and roles: A new look at why women opt out of science, technology, engineering, and mathematics careers. *Psychological Science*. 21, 1051-1057.

[10] Jones, M. T., Barlow, A. E. L., & Villarejo, M. 2010. Importance of Undergraduate Research for Minority Persistence and Achievement in Biology. *Journal of Higher Education*. 81, 82-115.

[11] Kam, C. D. & Franzese Jr., R. J. 2007. *Modeling and Interpreting Interactive Hypotheses in Regression Analysis*. Ann Arbor: University of Michigan Press.

[12] Lent, R. W., Brown, S. D., and Hackett G. 1994. Toward a Unifying Social Cognitive Theory of Career and Academic Interst, Choice, and Performance. *Journal of Vocational Behavior*. 45, 79-122.

[13] Lent, R. W., Brown, S. D., and Hackett G. 2002. Social Cognitive Career Theory. In Duane Brown, editor, *Career Choice and Development*, 255-311. John Wiley and Sons, San-Francisco, 4th. Edition.

[14] Lent, R. W., Lopez Jr., A. M., Lopez, F. G., and Sheu, H-B. 2008. Social cognitive career theory and the prediction of interests and choice goals in the computing disciplines. *Journal of Vocational Behavior*, 73, 52-62.

[15] Lent, R. W., Lopez, F. G., and Sheu, H-B., Lopez Jr., A. M. 2011. Social cognitive predictors of the interests and choices of computing majors: Applicability to underrepresented students. *Journal of Vocational Behavior*, 78, 184-192.

[16] Leung, K., Maddux, W., Galinsky, A. D. & Chiu, C-Y. 2008. Multicultural experience enhances creativity: The when and how. *American Psychologist*. 63,169-181.

[17] Lockwood, P., and Kunda, Z. 1997. Superstars and me: Predicting the impact of role models on the self. *Journal of Personality and Social Psychology*. 73, 91-103.

[18] Lockwood, P. 2006. Someone like me is successful: Do college students need same-gender role models? *Psychology of Women Quarterly*. 30,36-46

[19] Lopatto, D. 2004. Survey of undergraduate research experiences (SURE): First findings. *Cell Biology Education*. 3, 270-277.

[20] Lopatto, D. 2007. Undergraduate research experiences support science career decisions and active learning. *Cell Biology Education*. 6, 297-306.

[21] Margolis, J., and Fisher, A. 2001. *Unlocking the clubhouse: Women in computing*. The MIT Press.

[22] Nagda, B. A., Gregerman, S. R., Jonides, J., von Hippel, W., & Lerner, J. S. 1998. Undergraduate student-faculty research partnerships affect student retention. *The Review of Higher Education*, 22(1), 55-72.

[23] National Science Foundation. 2014a. National Center for Science and Engineering Statistics, special tabulations of

U.S. Department of Education, National Center for Education Statistics, Integrated Postsecondary Education Data System, Completions Survey, 2002–12. *TABLE 7-2. Doctoral degrees awarded to women, by field: 2002–12.* Retrieved from: http://www.nsf.gov/statistics/wmpd/2013/tables.cfm

[24] National Science Foundation. 2014b. National Center for Science and Engineering Statistics, special tabulations of U.S. Department of Education, National Center for Education Statistics, Integrated Postsecondary Education Data System, Completions Survey, 2002–12. *TABLE 6-4. Master's degrees awarded to women, by field, citizenship, and race or ethnicity: 2002–12.* Retrieved from: http://www.nsf.gov/statistics/wmpd/2013/tables.cfm

[25] National Science Foundation. 2014c. National Center for Science and Engineering Statistics (NCSES). *Bachelor's degrees awarded, by race or ethnicity, citizenship, sex, and field: 2012. Table 9-7.* Retrieved from http://www.nsf.gov/statistics/wmpd/2013/tables.cfm.

[26] Nyame-Mensah, A. Tamer, N. B. and Stout, J. G. 2015. Understanding How Summer Research Experiences Can Foster Diversity In Computing Research. Computing Research Association: Washington, DC. Available from: http://cra.org/cerp/research-findings.

[27] Russell, S. H., Hancock, M. P., & McCullough, J. 2007. The pipeline: benefits of undergraduate research experiences. *Science.* 316, 548-549.

[28] Seymour, E., Hunter, A.B., Laursen, S. L. and DeAntoni, T. (2004) 'Establishing the benefits of research experiences for undergraduates in the sciences: First findings from a three-year study', *Science Education*, 88(4), 493-534. doi: 10.1002/sce.10131.

[29] Stanley, C. A., & Lincoln, Y. S. 2005. Cross-race faculty mentoring. *Change: The Magazine of Higher Learning.* 37, 44-50.

[30] Stephens, N. M., Fryberg, S. A., Markus, H. R., Johnson, C. S., & Covarrubias, R. 2012. Unseen disadvantage: How American universities' focus on independence undermines the academic performance of first-generation college students. *Journal of Personality and Social Psychology.* 102, 1178-1197.

[31] Stout, J. G., Dasgupta, N., Hunsinger, M., & McManus, M. 2011. STEMing the tide: Using in-group experts to inoculate women's self-concept in science, technology, engineering, and mathematics (STEM). *Journal of Personality and Social Psychology.* 100, 255-270.

[32] Thomas, D. A. 2004. Diversity as strategy. *Harvard Business Review.* 82 (9), 98-108.

[33] Zweben, S., & Bizot, B. 2015. 2014 Taulbee survey: Relentless growth in undergraduate CS enrollment; Doctoral degree production remains strong, but no new record. *Computing Research News*. 27, 5. Available from http://cra.org/resources/crn-online

A (Updated) Review of Empiricism at the SIGCSE Technical Symposium

Ahmed Al-Zubidy, Jeffrey C. Carver
University of Alabama
Tuscaloosa, AL
1-205-348-9829
aalzubidy@crimson.ua.edu
carver@cs.ua.edu

Sarah Heckman
NC State University
Raleigh, NC
1-919-515-2042
sarah_heckman@ncsu.edu

Mark Sherriff
University of Virginia
Charlottesville, VA
1-434-982-2688
sherriff@virginia.edu

ABSTRACT

The computer science education (CSEd) research community consists of a large group of passionate CS educators who often contribute to other disciplines of CS research. There has been a trend in other disciplines toward more rigorous and empirical evaluation of various hypotheses. Prior investigations of the then-current state of CSEd research showed a distinct lack of rigor in the top research publication venues, with most papers falling in the general category of experience reports. In this paper, we present our examination of the two most recent proceedings of the SIGCSE Technical Symposium, providing a snapshot of the current state of empiricism at the largest CSEd venue. Our goal to categorize the current state of empiricism in the SIGCSE Technical Symposium and identify where the community might benefit from increased empiricism when conducting CSEd research. We found an increase in empirical validation of CSEd research to over 70%; however, our findings suggest that current CSEd research minimizes replication precluding meta-analysis and theory building.

Keywords

Systematic literature review, empirical computer science education, scholarship of teaching and learning.

1. INTRODUCTION

The SIGCSE Technical Symposium community is a large, welcoming, and vibrant group of passionate computer science educators. Most of us contribute to other communities of *discipline research* (e.g., software engineering) in computer science and beyond. However, many of the practices that we apply to demonstrate rigor in our discipline research are ignored or actively avoided when performing research in computer science education (CSEd) [2]. As evidence, Valentine [10] classified only 21% of CS1/CS2 papers published in the SIGCSE Technical Symposium between 1984 and 2003 as "experimental". Randolph, et al. [7] used Valentine's categorization and classified 40% of papers sampled from many CSEd venues between 2000 and 2005 as "experimental". However, the definition of "experimental" was broad and many papers reported results that preclude replication, meta-analysis, and theory building [4, 7, 10].

Researchers require evidence to determine the efficacy of teaching and learning interventions. Replications or comparisons of data across studies provide a basis for theory building [1, 4]. Fincher and Petre [4] describe two axes on which CSEd research can be classified: *evidence* – ranging from no evidence to empirical evidence and *argumentation* – ranging from low to high in argumentation or "theory." The authors argue that it would be desirable if the majority of CSEd research could be rated as high in empirical evidence to support theories, as we would expect in any other computer science discipline research [4]. However, they report that most CSEd research has evidence (possibly empirical) but little to no theory exploration [4]. Fincher and Petre [4] suggest that CSEd is "theory scarce" because most publications are not research and do not provide the evidence or replication required for meta-analysis and theory building. An increase in empiricism in CSEd research will move the field from "scholarly teaching" to the "scholarship of teaching and learning" (SoTL) [1] providing the foundation for meta-analysis and the generation of theories about teaching and learning in computer science [4].

Experience reports fall in the category of scholarly teaching rather than CSEd research or SoTL [1, 4]. Scholarly teaching is the application of current ideas or trends about teaching and learning usually due to reflection by an instructor on what did or did not work in the past [1]. SoTL moves scholarly teaching towards rigor, through a formalized plan and empirical evaluation, with the intention of peer review [1]. SoTL is the application of empiricism to CSEd that can build the theory for teaching and learning in computer science. We define empiricism as "validation based on observation of an intervention". An empirical validation reports results from observed evidence rather than argumentation, proof, or some other means [8]. Empirical validation is not solely experimentation or the scientific method, but incorporates the "method of science" [4]. The method of science considers both inductive and deductive paradigms for gathering evidence to answer a research question [4]. An increase in empiricism may help move CSEd research from a "soft" research area into a "hard" computer science sub-discipline [2].

In this paper, we present our examination of the two most recent proceedings of the SIGCSE Technical Symposium, providing a snapshot of the current state of empiricism at the largest CSEd venue. Our goal is to categorize the current state of empiricism in the SIGCSE Technical Symposium [3,11] and identify where the community might benefit from increased awareness of empiricism when conducting CSEd research.

2. PREVIOUS CSED SURVEYS

Several researchers have explored the state of CSEd literature. Valentine [10] reviewed and classified the types of 444 papers about CS1/CS2 accepted to the SIGCSE Technical Symposium between 1984 and 2003. During the years surveyed, Valentine found that 21% of the reviewed papers contained some form of "experimental" evaluation. His experimental category was very

SIGCSE '16, March 02-05, 2016, Memphis, TN, USA
© 2016 ACM. ISBN 978-1-4503-3685-7/16/03…$15.00.
DOI: http://dx.doi.org/10.1145/2839509.2844601

broad and included papers where the "author made any attempt at assessing the 'treatment' with some scientific analysis" [10]. The most common type of paper during the 20-year period was an experience report (what Valentine termed a "Marco Polo" paper). Valentine's data shows that the percentage of experience reports and experimental papers may vary from year to year. The overall trends show that CS1/CS2 experience reports were decreasing while experimental papers had a lull in the late 1980s and early 1990s and were starting to increase at the end of the survey period. However, these data may be skewed due to the selection of only CS1/CS2 papers and the timing of curriculum changes [10].

Valentine's [10] work has several limitations. First, while the period of evaluation was 20 years, he limited his paper selection to CS1/CS2 papers, which was between 25% on average of the proceedings between 1984 and 1993 and 30% on average of the proceedings between 1994 and 2003. A second limitation is that each paper was placed in a single classification when there may be multiple classifications that would work (e.g., there may have been experimental validation on an experience report). Valentine did all categorization himself; but other reviewers may have different interpretations of the categories. In our work, we address these limitations by allowing papers to fall into multiple categories and by allowing papers to be examined by two independent reviewers.

Randolph, et al. [7] reviewed a sample of literature published in multiple venues between 2000 and 2005 to understand the methodological properties of CSEd research during that time. They sampled 352 full papers from the June and December issues of the *SIGCSE Bulletin*, *Computer Science Education*, *Journal of Computer Science Education Online*, SIGCSE Technical Symposium, Innovation and Technology in Computer Science Education Conference, Koli Calling: Finnish/Baltic Sea Conference on Computer Science Education, Australasian Computing Education Conference, and the International Computer Science Education Research Workshop. Their findings suggest that much of the literature, 40% of studies with human subjects, limit their evaluation to anecdotal evidence. Of the 93 papers that reported an experimental or quasi-experimental design (less than one-third of the papers sampled), 54.8% used a post-test only design. The most common measure used to evaluate a paper's research goal was a questionnaire or survey, which consisted of 52.8% of the 123 papers that contained behavioral, quantitative, or empirical research. Randolph, et al.'s [8] work is limited in that several of the inter-rater reliability kappa statistics were low, but the key findings and those listed above were reported to have inter-rater reliabilities of good or fair.

Kinnunen, et al. [6] created a theoretical categorization of CSEd research with a didactic focus. They categorized 67 of the 72 papers published at ICER between 2005 and 2009 to identify commonly researched CSEd subjects. Kinnunen, et al. found that the most common categories of published work were related to students, including student's actions and understanding of learning outcomes, and to pedagogical activities used in the classroom. Of these papers, most were focused at the course level, with a few at the organization or society levels. There were no papers published in several categories suggesting that there are gaps in research coverage especially with teachers and teachers' interaction and engagement with students. The evaluation had at least two reviewers per paper, but no details or inter-rater reliability are reported. Kinnunen, et al. [6] were interested in identifying gaps in the literature for new studies. We are interested in characterizing the current state of the literature.

Prior work like Valentine [10] and Randolph, et al. [7] may have surveyed multiple years and multiple venues, but they did not consider the full proceedings for the SIGCSE Technical Symposium – only a subset. We are evaluating two entire proceedings as a snapshot of the current state of empirical evaluation in the SIGCSE Technical Symposium community. By considering the entire proceedings we can understand the community of the SIGCSE Technical Symposium, the flagship venue for CSEd.

3. METHODOLOGY

Our goal is to categorize the current state of empiricism in the SIGCSE Technical Symposium and identify where the community might benefit from increased awareness of empiricism when conducting CSEd research. We are interested in the following research questions:

RQ1: What percentage of papers in the SIGCSE Technical Symposium have some form of empirical evaluation?

RQ2: Of the papers in the SIGCSE Technical Symposium with empirical evaluation, what are the characteristics of empirical evaluation in the papers?

3.1 Selection Criteria

Prior work [7, 10] has shown a small increase in empirical evaluation of papers in CSEd conferences in general and the SIGCSE Technical Symposium, in particular, between 1984 and 2005. Since we are interested in assessing the current level of empiricism in the SIGCSE Technical Symposium community, we evaluated all accepted full papers in the Proceedings of the 45th and 46th ACM Technical Symposiums on Computer Science Education. We excluded panels, special sessions, posters, workshops, birds-of-a-feather, and keynote papers.

3.2 Data Extraction

For each full paper in the 2014/2015 SIGCSE Technical Symposium proceedings, we determined if the paper contained any empirical evaluation. We defined empirical evaluation as evidence provided from observation, based on the software engineering literature's definition of evaluation (or validation) [8].

Our categorization metrics were chosen to assess the level of empiricism in CSEd research. The classifications of the relationship between the author(s) and evaluation subjects and data origins are a way of measuring the repeatability of the CSEd literature. Replicated evaluations provide a basis for meta-analysis and theory building.

If the paper contained an empirical evaluation, we then identified the following characteristics of the paper:

- Evaluation Type [7]: How were data collected?
  - Experiment: Data were collected through an experiment of some kind
  - Survey: Participants were surveyed about the intervention
  - Retrospective: Analyzing data that was previously collected for another purpose (i.e. not collected for the current study)
- Evaluation Subject [7]: What intervention was evaluated? Intervention types include: tool, pedagogical technique, curriculum, assignment, or other subject.
- Relationship between Author(s) and Evaluation Subject(s): Who developed the evaluation's subject?
  - Paper authors introduce a novel evaluation subject,
  - Paper authors use a novel evaluation subject from their own prior work,

  - Paper authors use a modified version of an existing evaluation subject (modified replication), and
  - Paper authors use an existing evaluation subject with no modifications (replication)
- Number of Students: How many students (if any) participated in the evaluation in the paper?
- Data Collected [7]: What was the actual data collected for the evaluation in the paper?
- Data Origins: Were the data collected for this evaluation or did the data already exist?
  - New: Data used in the evaluation was generated specifically for the evaluation
  - Historical: Data used in the evaluation was originally collected for another purpose
- Comparison [7]: Did the evaluation consider a comparison of the intervention to some other data set?
  - None: Contained no comparison.
  - New: Contained a comparison to something new or within the evaluation design.
  - Historical: Contained a comparison to existing data.
- Threats to Validity: Did the paper contain threats to validity about the evaluation?

Several of our categories are similar to categories used in related work. Table 1 maps the categories in Randolph, et al. [7] to categories that we used for evaluation type and subject. The idea of a control as a comparison is provided in Randolph, et al.'s research design category [7], but we are interested in determining if the control was part of the empirical evaluation or if existing data comprised the control.

3.3 Data Analysis

We reviewed each paper in the proceedings to determine if the paper contained an evaluation, and if so, identify the characteristics of the evaluation. Note that the set of reviewers differed 2014 to 2015 with some overlap. We ensured that some sample of the papers were reviewed by two people (25% in 2014 and 50% in 2015). We used the reviewers' results on these papers to calculate inter-rater reliability. Like Randolph, et al., [7] we measured inter-rater reliability using a free-marginal kappa. For each attribute described in Section 4, we report the kappa value resulting from the inter-rater reliability test to provide some indication of the level of agreement between the two reviewers. The strength of agreement ranges from a kappa value of less than 0.20 as poor agreement to kappa values of greater than 0.81 as very good agreement.

After the initial individual review, the reviewers met to discuss and resolve the discrepancies between their categorizations on some characteristics. A small number of papers required reading by a third reviewer to resolve the categorization. At the end, all reviewers agreed on the final categorization. After resolution, each reviewer revisited the other papers in their set to ensure that they did not need to make any adjustments before merging the results into a final set for counting purposes.

4. RESULTS

The results showed that over 70% of the papers (79/110 in 2014 and 83/104 in 2015) contained some form of empirical evaluation; over three times the percentage reported by Valentine [10] and not quite twice the percentage reported by Randolph, et al. [7]. From the initial evaluation of the papers, the kappa agreement rate was greater than 0.7 in both years, which indicates a "good" level of agreement. The reviewers were able solve all disagreements in a subsequent meeting. The following sections describe the results from characterizing the papers.

Table 1: Mapping of Categories to Randolph, et al. [7]

Source Categories	Our Categories
Evaluation Type	
• Experimental/Quasi-Experimental	• Experimental
• Qualitative	• Experimental
• Causal Comparative	• Experimental
• Correlational	• Experimental
• Survey Research	• Survey
Evaluation Subject	
• Course Org.	• Curriculum / Pedag. Tech.
• Tool	• Tool
• Teaching Programming Languages	• Pedag. Tech. / Assignment / Other
• Parallel Computing	• Other
• Curriculum	• Curriculum
• Visualization	• Other
• Simulation	• Other

4.1 Evaluation Type

To provide some insight into how researchers are evaluating their approaches, the first attribute is the type of evaluation used. Table 2 lists the evaluation types found in the papers along with the number of papers that used each one. Note that since many papers contain more than one type of evaluation, the number of papers is greater than the total in each year. The results show that Survey was the most common evaluation type. In fact, many of the papers that used an experiment or observation also conducted a survey. Most papers that Randolph, et al. [7] sampled with human participants were experimental (64.6%); the least were survey (7.6%). Since the SIGCSE Technical Symposium was the common venue between that paper and ours, this result may suggest that other venues have papers with more experimentation and fewer surveys leading to Randoloph, et al.'s differing results.

Table 2: Evaluation Type

Subject	# of Papers 2014	Percent 2014	# of Papers 2015	Perce nt 2015
Survey	46	58%	42	51%
Experiment	26	33%	35	42%
Others	7	9%	6	7%
Observation	4	5%	2	2%
Retrospective	3	4%	3	3%
Pilot	3	4%	1	1%
Quasi-Experiment	2	3%	0	0%
Exploratory Study	1	1%	0	0%
Not Reported	1	1%	0	0%

The kappa values were .36 (2014) and .32 (2015). These values represent a "moderate' level of agreement. In analyzing the papers, we noticed cases where authors incorrectly named the type of evaluation used (i.e. Pilot study and Quasi-Experiment). Furthermore, in some papers the lack of structure when describing the evaluation made it difficult to identify the evaluation type. This difficulty was likely the cause of the relatively low kappa values.

4.2 Evaluation Subject

The evaluation subject describes what intervention was evaluated: a pedagogical technique, a tool, a course or curriculum, an assignment, or some other subject. Table 3 shows the number of papers that evaluate each type of intervention (again each paper could have more than one). The most common type of evaluation subject was pedagogical techniques; empirical validation methodologies are especially effective for evaluation of a pedagogical technique on students [1, 4]. Our top categories of pedagogical technique, course or curriculum, and tools correspond, roughly, to Randolph, et al.'s [7] top two categories of course organization (50%) and tools (19%).

Table 3: Evaluation Subjects

Subject	# of Papers 2014	Percent 2014	# of Papers 2015	Percent 2015
Pedagogical Technique	38	48%	34	41%
Course or Curriculum	19	24%	18	21%
Tool	17	22%	20	24%
Other	9	11%	14	16%
Assignment	3	4%	1	1%

The kappa values were .23 (2014) and .43 (2015), representing a "slight" and 'moderate" level of agreement respectively. The increase between years likely resulted from the research team obtaining a more consistent understanding of the Evaluation Subjects. We anticipate that the relatively low kappa values were at least partially the result of the fact that many papers had more than one subject, which may have led one reviewer to identify one subject and miss the other. Additionally, the inconsistent paper structure in terms of how the evaluation process was reported made it difficult to correctly identify the Evaluation Subjects.

4.3 Relationship between Author(s) and Evaluation Subjects

If a goal for CSEd research is to build theory, then formalizing repeatable evaluation on common evaluation subjects (e.g., pedagogical techniques, course or curriculum, tool, assignment, etc.) will allow for meta-analysis and generalization. We categorized papers by the creator of the evaluation subject(s):

- Paper authors introduce a novel evaluation subject,
- Paper authors use a novel evaluation subject from their own prior work,
- Paper authors use a modified version of an existing evaluation subject (modified replication), and
- Paper authors use an existing evaluation subject with no modifications (replication)

Each paper reporting an evaluation was only assigned one categorization. The kappa agreement between the two reviewers is 0.41 (2014) and .58 (2015), indicating a "moderate" agreement.

We found that 78% of paper authors in 2014 and 85% of paper authors in 2015 introduced a new evaluation subject. Exceptionally few papers, (six or fewer in both years) replicate prior work implying that there is very little comparison. Further, there is little replication of an author's own evaluation subject(s) in later work (four in 2014 and three in 2015).

The lack of usage of previously established subject(s) and the lack of reuse of an author's own subject(s) makes it challenging to move the discipline of SoTL forward as it becomes increasingly difficult to compare the results of the various studies. A lack of replication precludes meta-analysis and theory building.

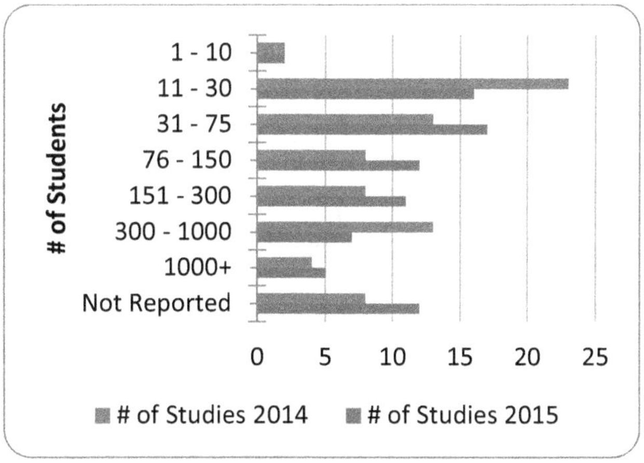

Figure 1: Histogram of Students in Evaluations

The lack of replication could be for a number of reasons:

- Faculty are moved from one course to another and do not have a good way to replicate their previous studies.
- Faculty are not able to recruit others to use their methodologies.
- Faculty tend to move to the "next great idea" when teaching their class and decide not to go back to their old methods.
- Faculty are unaware of other similar studies from which they could build their work upon.
- Papers do not report methodologies clearly enough to allow for replication.

4.4 Number of Students

One of the strengths of the SIGCSE community is the diversity of institutions members call home. Schools of all different sizes and backgrounds are represented by the over 1400 people that attend SIGCSE, which provides a large variety of institutions that can contribute each year. This diversity can be seen in the various papers that were reported in the 2014/ 2015 SIGCSE proceedings.

Figure 1 shows the numbers of students used as subjects in the papers that reported an empirical evaluation. While the most common sample size overall was between 11 - 30 students, there is clearly a split between "small studies" and "large studies." We believe that this split occurs mainly based on the types of data that the researchers were able to use. For smaller studies ($n < 75$), the researchers are mainly looking at pedagogical techniques in smaller classes. The studies that reported more than 1000 students are retrospective studies using data collected for many years. The use of surveys for evaluation fell into both study sizes.

The kappa for this characteristic, 0.60 (2014) and .81 (2015), represent a "good" level of agreement. The disagreement between the reviewers on the number of students ranged from ±1 to ±15 because the number of students was not reported in a structured way. Some of the discrepancies are due to reporting the number of students in the studied population and then reporting a new number of participants due to some non-participation in the study. Multiple evaluations, each with their own set of students confounded agreement.

4.5 Data Collected

Different evaluations and evaluation subjects require different types of data. The papers included data such as: student assignments, quizzes, projects, lab assignments, exams, academic records, surveys, interviews, questionnaires, forums posts, and feedback posts. We grouped those various types of data into two groups: whether data were graded by an instructor (e.g.

assignments, quizzes, etc.), or the data were feedback from the participants (e.g. questionnaires, forum posts, etc.). Table 5 reports the types of data collected and the number of papers that collected those data (again papers could use more than one method). The kappa values of 0.38 (2014) and 0.13 (2015), represent a "fair" and "slight" level of agreement, respectively. Again, we expect that the low kappa value is due to inconsistent reporting of data analyzed. Randolph, et al. [7] collected similar data; the most commonly collected items were questionnaires (53%) and grades (29%). Relying solely on survey data to assess an intervention does not fully measure the impact. However, there is an improvement in the number of studies that considered both a survey and assessment of subject deliverables in the 2015 proceedings.

Table 5: Data Collected

Subject	# of Papers 2014	Percent 2014	# of Papers 2015	Percent 2015
Feedback data from participants	55	69.6%	46	56%
Data graded by an instructor(s)	38	48.1%	19	22%
Both	0	0%	18	21%
Not Reported	1	1.2%	0	0%

4.6 Data Origins

Data origins describes when the data was produced. Papers categorized as "new" report data that was generated specifically for the current evaluation. Papers categorized as "historical" report data that was collected for another purpose. Table 6 shows the data origins and the number of papers for each origin. No papers in 2014 reported only historical data; few papers in 2015 reported historical data. Papers that collected a combination of new and historical data tended to have a comparison of the new data with the historical data (see Section 4.7). The kappa is 0.56 (2014) and .78 (2015), which is a "moderate" and "high" level of agreement, respectively.

Table 6: Data Origin

Subject	# of Papers 2014	Percent 2014	# of Papers 2015	Percent 2015
New	71	90%	70	84%
Combination	8	10%	7	8%
Historical	0	0%	6	7%

4.7 Comparison

A comparison of an intervention with a control group or prior work strengthens the conclusions and provides a basis for theory building [4]. We classified the comparison into three categories:

- None: Evaluation contained no comparison between a treatment group and a control group.
- New: Evaluation contained a comparison between a treatment group and a control group where data for both groups was generated as part of the current study.
- Historical: Evaluation contained a comparison between a treatment group and a control group in which data for the control group was drawn from existing data that were not generated for the current study.

Table 7 reports the number of papers for each of these categories. Only 57% of the papers in 2014 and 48% of papers in 2015 reported any type of comparison between the treatment and a control group. A lack of comparison to a control or prior work weakens the conclusions we can draw from those papers for theory building. Of the papers with comparison, approximately 2/3 compared the treatment to a control within the same study. The kappa is .44 (2014) and .66 (2015), which indicates a "moderate" to "good" agreement.

Table 7: Comparison

Subject	# of Papers 2014	Percent 2014	# of Papers 2015	Percent 2015
None	34	43.0%	41	49%
New	29	36.7%	24	29%
Historical	16	20.2%	18	19%

4.8 Threats to Validity

A threats to validity or limitations section allows for readers to frame the results of the study. Almost 70% of the papers in 2014 and 40% of the papers in 2015 did not report any threats to validity. (This decrease in 2015 is the results of a more liberal interpretation of threats to validity – i.e. not requiring a separate threats to validity section). All studies that involve human subjects have threats to validity due to choices made during the design process. One of the key aspects of study design, which makes it a difficult and time-consuming process when done correctly, is balancing various study designs with their inherent validity threats [4, 8]. It is possible to choose a study design that contains threats that completely invalidate the results of the study. But, more often the threats are less serious.

The biggest concern when papers do not report threats to validity is that readers are not able to properly interpret and apply the results [4, 8]. Without understanding the limitations of the study design, an educator may attempt to apply an intervention in an inappropriate setting, with potentially negative results [4, 8]. Authors should not think that reporting threats to validity weakens their paper, on the contrary it lends more confidence to the reader when he or she can understand the full context. The kappa value is 0.49 (2014) and .61 (2015), which is a "moderate" to "good" level of agreement.

4.9 Emerging Patterns

Overall, we discovered a general increase in the number of empirical studies in the 2014/ 2015 proceedings versus the findings of others from the previous years. The increase may be attributed to our broad definition of empirical evaluation. An alternative explanation is that the review process for SIGCSE is looking more for papers with empirical evaluation, which in turn motivates researchers to include empirical evaluation in their studies.

However, the lack of reuse of evaluation subjects, or even the use of a modified version of a previously published evaluation subject, makes comparing results amongst contrasting pedagogical practices difficult at best. While the motivation appears to be in place to encourage empirical evaluation, researchers are effectively "reinventing the wheel" each time.

As noted in the discussion of many of the specific characteristics, inconsistent paper organization increases the difficulty of finding important information. Details about an empirical evaluation are not always reported in the same way, with the same information, or at the same level of detail. This lack of consistency makes it difficult to compare across papers and to get a full understanding of what really occurred during the study.

5. DISCUSSION AND RECOMMENDATIONS

Our evaluation of empiricism is not an argument to move CSEd literature, specifically at a practitioner conference like SIGCSE, to require an evaluation, but a request for better evaluation when considering interventions. Replication of prior work is a key practice in the advance of any scientific discipline and we see very little of it occurring in our sample precluding meta-analysis and theory building. There are many sources for information about conducting CSEd research that may serve as resources for the community [1, 2, 4, 5, 7, 10]. We advocate for a move from scholarly teaching to SoTL [1]. We propose the following concrete ideas for increasing empirical validation in CSEd research:

- Create an empirical validation or SoTL track at the SIGCSE Technical Symposium with an increase in paper length. Randolph, et al, [7] found that most CSEd research papers lacked a related work section, which may be the first item cut or minimized in a shorter paper. Longer papers would allow for more detail of methodology leading to additional replication. An empirical validation or SoTL track should emphasize replicative and theory-building work.
- Development of workshops co-located with the SIGCSE Technical Symposium and other CSEd venues to train educators in empirical validation techniques and provide feedback and mentorship on experiments.
- Building "laboratory packages" of classical CSEd empirical validation models [9], including qualitative models [5]. Many members of the CSEd community have large teaching loads, which would preclude the creation of a research methodology from scratch. Laboratory packages provide rapid adoption of stronger empirical methodologies and common metrics for replication and meta-analysis [9].
- Creation of datasets of student work for comparison and control.
- Move to consistent use of terminology and reporting of empirical results.

6. STUDY THREATS TO VALIDITY

Our review of the 2014/2015 SIGCSE Technical Symposium full paper proceedings had several threats to validity. We mitigated one threat to internal validity by considering the full proceedings of the two most recent SIGCSE Technical Symposium. However, that contributes to a weakness in our external validity: our conclusions are only about SIGCSE 2014/2015 proceedings. With comparison to prior work, we can make inferences about the general trend of empiricism. Due to variations in the characteristics used to evaluate the literature, we cannot draw stronger conclusions.

A weakness in the construct validity is the inter-rater reliability scores for several of our characteristics. If recommendations for consistent terminology are taken for future work, then future surveys will have an increased construct validity. We considered the inclusion of a characteristic about specifically stating that the authors' Internal Review Board (IRB) approved the study, but decided that many papers may have left out the statement as assumed or due to space limitations. We assume that all evaluative work that used students as human participants received the necessary IRB approval.

7. CONCLUSIONS AND FUTURE WORK.

We have found that the reports of empirical CSEd research have increased when compared with prior surveys of the SIGCSE Technical Symposium. More than 70% of the 2014/2015 SIGCSE Technical Symposium proceedings contained some form of empirical validation. However, many of the evaluations did not consider replication of methodologies or comparisons with other work. As CSEd research matures as a field, we must move toward meta-analysis of the literature for building of theories about CSEd. We plan to organize workshops at future CSEd venues for feedback and mentorship of empirical validation techniques. Additionally, we would like to contribute laboratory packages to help CSEd researchers with the empirical validation of their next teaching innovation.

8. ACKNOWLEDGEMENTS

We thank Kevin Lubick for serving as the second reviewer for the SIGCSE 2014 proceedings and Brantley Collins as a reviewer of the SIGCSE 2015 proceedings. We would also like to thank Lucas Layman of Fraunhofer Center for his input on this work. Jeffrey Carver and Ahmed Al-Zubidy acknowledge partial support from NSF. This material is based upon work supported by the National Science Foundation under Grant Nos. 1305395, 1525028, 1525173, and 1525373.

9. REFERENCES

[1] C. Bishop-Clark and B. Dietz-Uhler, *Engaging in the Scholarship of Teaching and Learning*, Stylus Publishing, Sterling, VA, 2012.

[2] T. Clear, "Valuing Computer Science Education Research?," Proceedings of the 6th Baltic Sea Conference on Computing Education Research, Koli Calling, Uppsala University, Uppsala, Sweden, 2006, pp. 8-18.

[3] J. D. Dougherty and K. Nagel, Conference Chairs, SIGCSE '14 The 45th ACM Technical Symposium on Computer Science Education, Atlanta, GA, USA, March 5-8, 2014.

[4] S. Fincher and M. Petre, eds., *Computer Science Education Research*, Taylor & Francis, The Netherlands, Lisse, 2004.

[5] S. Fincher, J. Tenenberg, A. Robins, "Research Design: Necessary Bricolage," Proceeding of the 7th Int'l Wksp. on Comp. Ed. Res., Providence, RI, August 8-9, 2011, pp. 27-32.

[6] P. Kinnunen, V. Meisalo, L. Malmi, "Have we missed something?: Identifying Missing Types of Research in Computing Education," Proc. of the 6th Int'l Wksp. on Comp. Ed. Res., Aarhus, Denmark, Aug. 8-11, 2010, pp.13-22.

[7] J. Randolph, G. Julnes, E. Sutinen, S. Lehman, "A Methodological Review of Computer Science Education Resarch," *Journal of Information Technology Education*, vol. 7, 2008, pp. 135-162

[8] M. Shaw, "Writing Good Software Engineering Papers," Proceedings of the 25th International Conference on Software Engineering, Portland, OR, USA, 2003, pp. 726-736.

[9] F. Shull, V. Basili, J. Carver, J. C. Maldonado, G. H. Travassos, M. Mendonça, and S. Fabbri, "Replicating Software Engineering Experiments: Addressing the Tacit Knowledge Problem," Proceedings of the 2002 Int'l Symp. on Empirical Soft. Eng., Nara, Japan, October 3-4, 2002, pp.7-16.

[10] D. W. Valentine, "CS Education Research: A Meta-Analysis of SIGCSE Technical Symposium Proceedings," Proc. of the 35th SIGCSE Technical Symposium on Computer Science Education, Norfolk, VA, USA, March 3-7, 2004, pp. 255-259.

[11] A. Decker and K. Eiselt, Conference chairs, SIGCSE '15 The 46th ACM Technical Symposium on Computer Science Education, Kansas City, MO, USA, March 4-7, 2015.

An Effective Approach to Enhancing Compiler Error Messages

Brett A. Becker
School of Computer Science
University College Dublin
Belfield, Dublin 4, Ireland
brett.becker@ucd.ie

ABSTRACT

One of the many challenges novice programmers face from the time they write their first program is inadequate compiler error messages. These messages report details on errors the programmer has made and are the only feedback the programmer gets from the compiler. For students they play a particularly essential role as students often have little experience to draw upon, leaving compiler error messages as their primary guidance on error correction. However these messages are frequently inadequate, presenting a barrier to progress and are often a source of discouragement. We have designed and implemented an editor that provides enhanced compiler error messages and conducted a controlled empirical study with CS1 students learning Java. We find a reduced frequency of overall errors and errors per student. We also identify eight frequent compiler error messages for which enhancement has a statistically significant effect. Finally we find a reduced number of repeated errors. These findings indicate fewer students struggling with compiler error messages.

Keywords

Java; debugging; errors; syntax errors; error messages; compiler errors; feedback; novice; programming; CS1

1. INTRODUCTION

Good compiler error messages provide feedback that is critical for novices [17]. Unfortunately they are frequently inadequate and pose a significant barrier to progress [21], particularly affecting novices more adversely [23]. Error messages and the difficulties they present to students have been pervasive themes in teaching beginners to program for several decades. In 1976, 'cryptic diagnostics' was named by students as one of the primary issues that made programming difficult [25]. Thirty years later Jadud noted that error messages generated by commercial compilers were often uninformative and sometimes misleading [14]. Unfortunately these characteristics are still indicative of the error messages provided by modern languages today, forty years later; cryptic and uninformative, often terse and misleading.

Although this issue spans many (if not all) languages, there is evidence that Java error messages are particularly difficult for novices, and means of learning how to deal with them more effectively are needed. Ben-Ari noted that Java error messages are terse and many novices find it difficult to achieve syntactically correct Java programs [3]. Our experience is that Java compiler error messages, like those in other languages, can be a significant barrier to student success, a view shared by others [7, 8].

It has been shown that the majority of students spend the majority of their time on a minority of errors and that students spend more time solving certain kinds of syntax errors than others [7]. In addition, repeating errors is common, and the number of repeated errors is an indication of struggling students. Jadud found that repeated errors were often the best indicator for how well (or poorly) a student was progressing [14].

In this paper we report on the effects of a Java editor called Decaf which enhances javac compiler error messages. When a student error generates an error message, the offending code and error message are analyzed in an effort to produce an enhanced error message which provides more usable information to the student, in the hope that the error can be rectified more effectively than with the standard error message alone. It is hoped that by presenting both the regular and enhanced errors together, students will learn from the enhanced error messages and avoid making the same mistakes in the future. The main research question is: *Do enhanced compiler error messages have a measurable effect which may help students who are learning to program?* In investigating this we looked at three specific questions: 1. Did enhanced compiler error messages reduce the overall number of student errors? 2. Did enhanced compiler error messages reduce the number of errors per student? 3. What effect to enhanced compiler error messages have on the number of repeated errors?

2. RELATED WORK

Several studies have researched enhanced error messages. A recent paper [8] describes six, and here we present another six. For a more in-depth discussion of these and more, see [2].

Hristova et al. [11] introduced Expresso, a pre-compiler which scans Java programs for 20 common errors. These errors were identified through a survey of their students and faculty at several institutions including their own. Expresso

SIGCSE '16, March 2–5, 2016, Memphis, TN, USA.
© 2016 ACM. ISBN 978-1-4503-3685-7/16/03...$15.00
DOI: http://dx.doi.org/10.1145/2839509.2844584

provides users with explanatory messages provided the error in question is one of those identified. The authors describe their system as an interactive tool that would do a better job generating error messages than existing compilers and also provide suggestions on how to fix the code. However an assessment of Expresso was left to future work.

Thompson and Rigby [19] introduced an Eclipse plug-in called Gild, specifically for novice Java programmers. Gild includes a feature which provides compiler error message explanations and possible causes in plain English. Messages for which the authors felt a longer explanation was required were explained in a wiki. Several online resources were used to generate a list of 51 errors for which Gild could provide enhanced compiler error messages. At the end of the study, 10 of these errors accounted for 68% of all errors. The study had many objectives, with the effects of enhanced compiler error messages making up three of six research questions. In addition, it was an exploratory work with a small number of students – less than 10 for the quantitative results, depending on the sub-study in question. The results were not conclusive as to whether or not students became faster at fixing their errors over the course of the study (one semester), or if their errors changed over the course of the semester. 57% of 28 students found Gild's extra error help feature "useful at least some of the time". It was concluded that Gild needed more specific error messages and better coverage of errors most encountered by students.

Coull [5] introduced a framework for support tools that addresses both program and problem formulation for novices. One of the requirements of such tools is to present both standard compiler error messages and the enhanced messages concurrently. Only one of three systems categorized by Coull met this requirement and focused on syntax errors in high-level languages: CAP [20] which was for Pascal, and often provided exemplar code. Coull also developed SNOOPIE using the framework, for learning Java programming. Although the scope of SNOOPIE was well beyond enhancing compiler error messages, one of the primary objectives of the tool was just that. It was shown that this support was beneficial to a small group of students, particularly for non-trivial syntactic errors.

Hartmann et al. [10] developed HelpMeOut, a 'social recommender system' that aids the debugging of error messages by suggesting solutions that peers have applied in the past. A limited evaluation was carried out and a longer deployment deemed necessary to determine just how successful the system is.

Watson, Li and Godwin [24] developed Bluefix, an online tool integrated into BlueJ [15] which provides varying levels of elaborate feedback, incorporating crowd-sourced error fixes. An evaluation was conducted suggesting a 19% improvement over HelpMeOut and revealing that students viewed the tool positively.

Many of the studies discussed in this section in addition to those discussed in [8] focus on addressing the problem with compiler error messages, but lack empiricism in determining if they make any difference, particularly to novices. Denny, Luxton-Reilly and Carpenter [8] implemented an enhanced feedback system to users of CodeWrite [7], a web-based tool designed to help students complete Java exercises. This 2014 study was the first recent work on the effect of enhancing Java compiler error messages with control and intervention groups. The system was used with students attempting exercises which required them to complete the body of a method for which the header was provided. Students participated for a period of two weeks as part of an accelerated summer course. Students were required to complete 10 lab exercises using the tool with 83 students submitting at least one. The study found no significant effect on the number of consecutive non-compiling submissions, the total number of non-compiling submissions, and the number of attempts needed to resolve the most common kinds of errors.

3. THE TOOL AND METHODS

Decaf analyzes a student's source code and compiler message and presents an enhanced message where possible. A total of 30 error messages result in enhanced messages, which are then customized based on analyzing the offending code. The enhanced message appears alongside the original as recommended by [6]. If no enhanced error message is possible the user is presented with a statement indicating the line number of the first error, and referring the user to the standard javac output which is in the same window (see Figure 1). Decaf only presents an enhanced version of the first error message when more than one are present. This is consistent with other teaching tools such as BlueJ [15] and more recent work [8], but is not always the case, for instance with Expresso [11]. We do not categorize or group compiler error messages unlike previous studies [9, 12, 13] as this can complicate comparison [8].

Figure 1 shows the Decaf error window displaying an enhanced compiler error message resulting from incorrectly calling the length() method of the String class, generating a *cannot find symbol* error message.

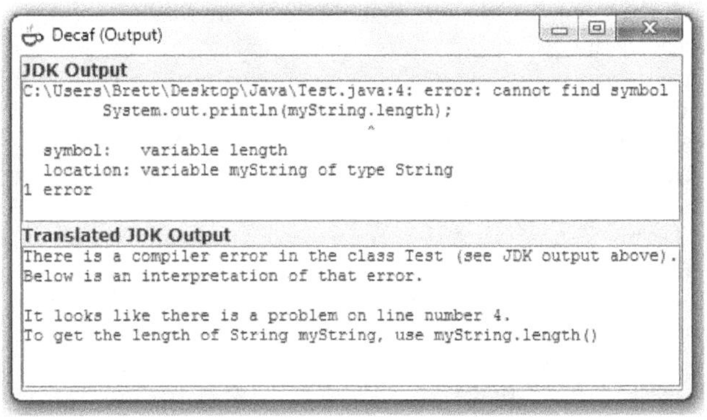

Figure 1: Decaf error window displaying an enhanced compiler error message resulting from incorrectly calling the length() method of the String class which generated a *cannot find symbol* javac error message.

The evaluation study took place at the College of Computing Technology in Dublin, Ireland, in the Semester 1 CS1 module on a BSc in Information Technology program. Anonymous data was logged for a four week period for two groups, each with just over 100 students. The control group received the raw javac compiler error messages and the intervention (enhanced) group received the raw javac messages alongside an enhanced message of the first, should Decaf be able to provide one. The groups took place in consecutive academic years and substantial effort was put into making the learning experience and environment similar for both groups. The same lecturer taught both groups and the

Table 1: Top 10 student errors per compiler error message, control group.

Compiler Error Message	n	%
cannot find symbol	4,614	16.0%
')' expected	3,317	11.5%
';' expected	3,076	10.7%
not a statement	2,142	7.4%
illegal start of expression	1,825	6.3%
reached end of file while parsing	1,406	4.9%
illegal start of type	1,316	4.6%
'else' without 'if'	1,141	4.0%
bad operand types for binary operator	1,138	3.9%
<identifier> expected	1,091	3.8%

course content, lab work, schedule, and other environmental and pedagogical factors were kept as similar as possible.

Unlike some previous studies there were no constructs such as supplied method definitions to be completed by the students. Students were working largely on their own time while studying and working on weekly lab exercises based on: data types, basic mathematics, decision making, logical and relational operators, loops, arrays, user input and type casting.

4. RESULTS

4.1 Comparison of control group with other studies

Before comparing the control and enhanced groups we present the 10 most frequent compiler error messages from the control group (who experienced the standard javac error messages) to facilitate comparison with several other studies. Table 1 shows these error messages and the number of times each was generated. These 10 error messages resulted from 73% of 29,019 student errors.

Figure 2 shows that that the control group aligns well with the previous work of [4, 9, 12, 14, 22]. The fact that some studies group or categorize errors does not seem to complicate this type of comparison much, as we are looking at a frequency-based distribution, not necessarily individual errors. That being said, four of the top five errors are common to all six studies, subject to minor differences due to using different Java versions and study-specific groupings such as some grouping all *cannot find symbol* errors together and others reporting *cannot find symbol (variable/method/etc.)* separately. The top three errors in all six studies are: *cannot find symbol*, *')' expected* or *'bracket expected'*, and *';' expected*. The fourth is mixed: this and two other studies share *not a statement*. The fifth is *illegal start of expression*. Overall the frequency distribution of the top 10 errors (and particularly the top five errors themselves) from this study align well with those from all five previous studies despite some study-specific methodologies and different Java versions.

4.2 Did enhanced compiler error messages reduce the overall number of student errors?

After filtering out data representing students with less than an average of 10 compilation events per week a to-

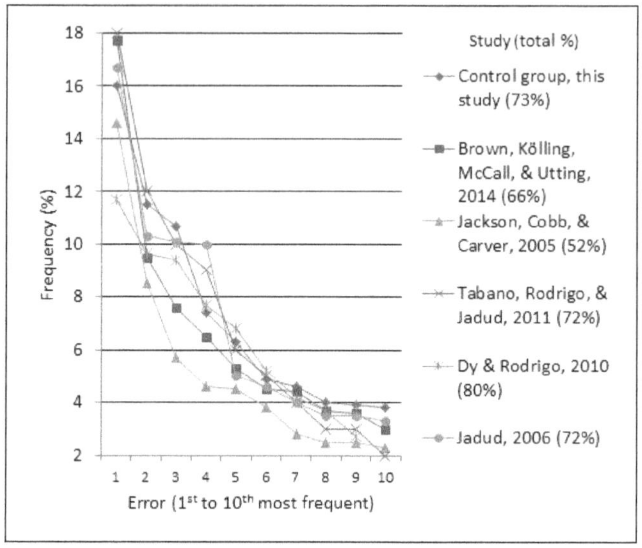

Figure 2: Frequency of the 10 most frequent compiler error messages from six studies.

tal of 48,489 student errors remained, 19,628 for the enhanced group (104 compiler IDs) and 28,261 for control (108). These resulted in 74 unique compiler error messages including all 30 that Decaf enhances. A Wilcoxon signed-rank test (two-tail) showed a significantly lower number of student errors per compiler error message for the enhanced group ($Mdn = 18$) compared to the control group ($Mdn = 34$); $Z = -4.29$, $p < 0.001$.

The top 15 compiler error messages accounted for 86.3% of total errors, 17,144 for the enhanced group and 24,689 for control (102 compiler IDs each). A Wilcoxon signed-rank test (two-tail) showed a significantly lower number of student errors per compiler error message for the enhanced group ($Mdn = 627$) compared to the control group ($Mdn = 1,135$); $Z = -3.17$, $p = 0.002$.

Figure 3 shows a strong linear correlation between groups for all compiler error messages (left) and the 15 most frequent (right). This is somewhat expected; we do not expect enhancing compiler error messages to profoundly alter the errors students make other than possibly reducing their frequencies and the related shifts involved. The slope of both correlations is $> +1$, as the control group (with more error messages overall) is on the y-axes.

Figure 4 shows the number of student errors generating the 15 most frequent compiler error messages for the control and enhanced groups. All but three (*'else' without 'if'*, *illegal start of type*, and *'.class' expected*) are enhanced by Decaf. There are fewer errors for the enhanced group for all errors messages except *'else' without 'if'*, for which the enhanced group is marginally greater. The smallest difference occurs with *'.class' expected.*

4.3 Did enhanced compiler error messages reduce the number of errors per student?

Table 2 shows the average number of errors per student and average number of unique compiler error messages per student for both groups. There was not a significant difference in (student committed) errors per student between groups when taking all errors into account, however for the

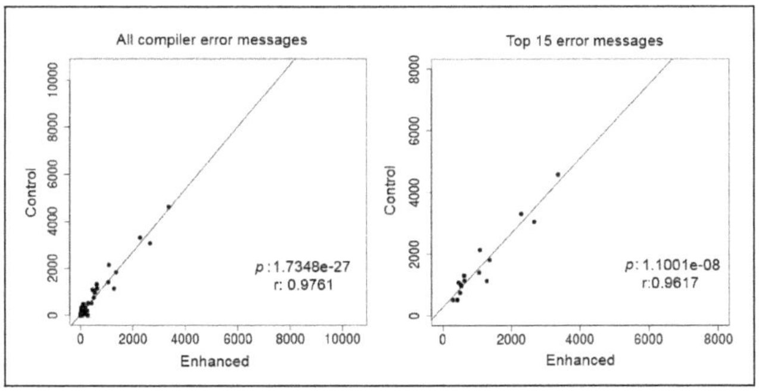

Figure 3: Scatter plots showing linear correlation of number of errors between groups. Each point represents a specific compiler error message.

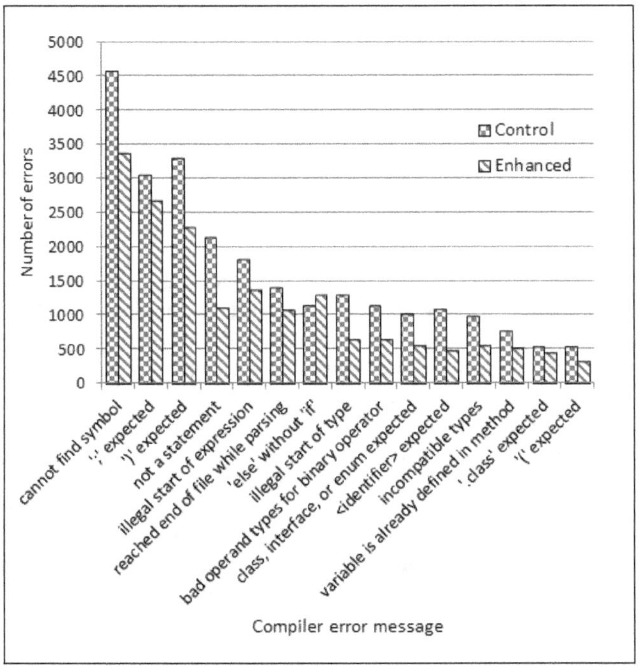

Figure 4: Number of errors for the 15 most frequent compiler error messages.

top 15 compiler error messages (accounting for 86.3% of all errors) a Mann-Whitney U test (two-tail) showed that the number of errors per student was less for the enhanced group ($Mdn = 125$) compared to the control group ($Mdn = 152$); $U = 4,254$, $p = 0.028$.

Investigating individual errors, nine of these 15 had a significant difference between groups, shown in Table 3. Eight of these nine are enhanced by Decaf. The compiler error message that is not (*'.class' expected*) had the smallest difference in number of errors between groups.

4.4 What effect do enhanced compiler error messages have on the number of repeated errors?

To investigate this question we examined the 15 most frequent error messages as they make up 86.3% of all errors. A student is said to have committed a repeated error when two consecutive compilations result in the same error message and originate from a student error on the same line of code. The control group generated 13,849 repeated errors while the enhanced group generated 9,752. Figure 5 shows the number of repeated student errors per compiler error message for the 15 most frequent error messages.

A Wilcoxon signed-rank test (two-tail) showed fewer repeated student errors per compiler error message for the enhanced group ($Mdn = 416$) than for the control group ($Mdn = 742$); $Z = -2.90$, $p = 0.004$. In addition, a Shaprio-Wilk test showed that log transformed data was normal and a paired t-test (two-tail) showed fewer repeated student errors per compiler error message for the enhanced group ($M = 2.68$, $SD = 0.35$) compared to the control group ($M = 2.87$, $SD = 0.30$); $t(14) = 4.73$, $p < 0.001$.

Table 2: Average number of errors per student and average number of unique compiler error messages per student.

Group	Average errors per student	Average unique error messages per student
Control	265	20
Enhanced	188	16

Table 3: The nine of the top 15 compiler error messages with a significant difference between groups (control, c and enhanced, e) sorted by median, *Mdn*.

Compiler Error Message	*Mdn* c, e	p
cannot find symbol	35, 26	0.012
not a statement	10, 6	0.003
illegal start of expression	10, 7	0.042
class, interface, or enum expected	6, 3	0.001
<identifier> expected	4, 2	0.038
incompatible types	5, 3	0.005
variable v already defined in method m	4, 3	0.043
'(' expected	2, 1	0.023
'.class' expected	2, 0	0.006

5. DISCUSSION

We have presented evidence that enhanced compiler error messages reduce the number of errors and number of errors per student, as well as the number of repeated errors per compiler error message. This is presented on the foundation that the control group of this study is comparable to findings from several previous studies, for the same language. However we must identify some threats to validity.

First, the groups were separated by a year. It is possible that the enhanced group simply generated fewer error messages. However as the number of students involved was over 200 and the total number of errors collected was nearly 50,000 we find this unlikely, particularly as attempts were made to make all environmental and pedagogical factors as similar as possible. Students learned the same topics in as similar a way as possible, experiencing the same lecturer, material, labs and other controllable factors. Nonetheless some factors could not be controlled such as scheduling differences, room availability and external pressures on students from other modules.

A more technical threat to validity is the fact that a new

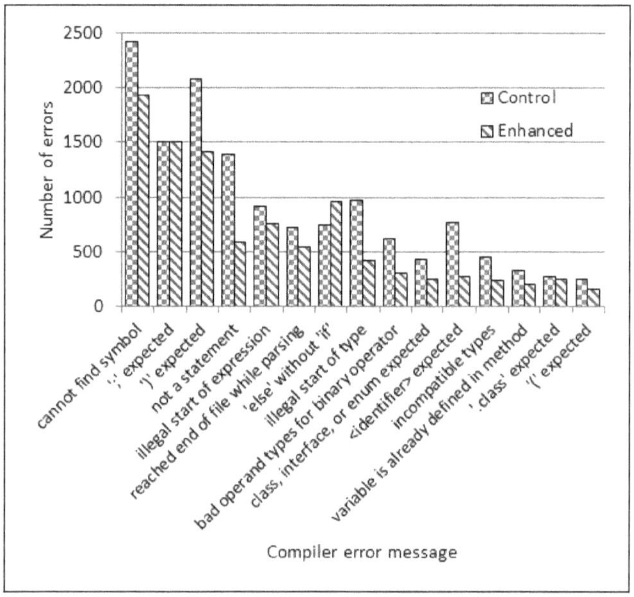

Figure 5: Number of repeated student errors per compiler error message for the 15 most frequent compiler error messages.

anonymous compiler ID is issued when Decaf is reinstalled, perhaps by the same student on the same computer, or by one student on multiple computers. This creates an issue in not having a perfect one to one mapping of compiler IDs to students. It is believed that this did not impact results to a high degree for three reasons. First, the number of compiler IDs was not much above the average attendance and the average number of students submitting lab exercises. Second, filtering data to remove inactive compiler IDs brought the number of compiler IDs even closer to the expected numbers (based on class lists and attendance). Finally and importantly, it was shown that the control group had a similar error profile to other studies. The compiler ID threat will be partially mitigated in future studies with persistent IDs. Related to this, students were encouraged to only use Decaf. A student could choose to use another environment, or use Decaf and another environment, although the lecturer noted very little evidence of this.

The control group was presented with the standard javac error messages (which often involve multiple error messages) making it possible for some students to correct more than one error at a time. Although [8] reported a similar concern, we decided not to interfere with the javac errors at all for the control group. The enhanced group however did only receive one enhanced compiler error message per compilation. It is possible that being presented with only one error reduced confusion for some students, potentially resulting in fewer errors. Future work will investigate this possibility.

We did not anticipate three of the 15 most frequent error messages and therefore Decaf does not enhance them: *'else' without 'if'*, *illegal start of type*, and *'.class' expected*. This however did provide an interesting 'self-contained' control case which spanned both groups. As both groups experienced the same raw Java error messages in these cases, it would be expected that there would be little variation in their frequencies. Indeed for two of these three error messages the frequencies were nearly equivalent. Only *illegal start of type* showed a relatively considerable difference between groups. This could be due to environmental circumstances, or it could be a knock-on effect, where enhancing some compiler error messages helps with other (perhaps related) errors that are not enhanced. See [2] for a discussion on this, which is also a direction for future work.

In [18] McCall and Kölling analyzed actual student errors instead of the diagnostic compiler error messages, noting that analyzing the compiler error messages is imprecise for two reasons. First, a single error (in code) can produce different compiler error messages, depending on context. Second, the same compiler error message can be produced by entirely different errors, again depending on context. In [1] Altadmri and Brown overcame this lack of a one-to-one mapping by parsing the code for offending errors. In the present study the source code is captured at the same time as the error which similarly can overcome this mapping problem in many cases. For instance see Figure 1, where the compiler error message *cannot find symbol* is matched with the source code to produce an accurate error message. Without the source, it would be difficult to provide an accurate message as *cannot find symbol* can occur for a variety of reasons including misspelling an identifier, using an identifier outside its scope, or calling a constructor with an incorrect parameter signature [3]. Nonetheless it should be pointed out that in some cases, matching of the source code and compiler error message does not result in information which can be used to create a usable enhanced error message.

Having presented our results and threats to validity, we do not want to overlook that student surveys revealed a positive experience with the software and enhanced error messages. The enhanced group reported that compiler error messages were less frustrating, and not as much of a barrier to progress compared to the control group. The enhanced group also reported (after spending time with other IDEs) that they found Decaf to make learning to program easier than the control group and that they would recommend Decaf to other learners more than the control group.

6. CONCLUSIONS AND FUTURE WORK

Compiler error messages are frequently inadequate and often a source of discouragement, posing a significant barrier to novices learning to program. Several studies have investigated enhancing compiler error messages but few provide substantial empirical results on their effectiveness. One recent study which did [8] found no effect on the number of non-compiling submissions, the consecutive number of non-compiling submissions, and the number of attempts needed to resolve the three most common kinds of errors.

We designed and implemented an editor providing enhanced compiler error messages and conducted a controlled empirical study with CS1 students learning Java. Comparing the 10 most frequent error messages from the control group representing 79% of 29,019 student errors, we found considerable agreement with other studies. Analyzing nearly 50,000 errors from over 200 students, we found a reduced number of overall errors, errors per student, and repeated errors per compiler error message, for students experiencing enhanced compiler error messages. We also identified eight specific error messages for which enhancement results in a statistically significant reduction in student errors.

Future work involves investigating repeated error messages in greater detail, exploring the possibilities of knock-on effects between enhanced and non-enhanced errors, and applying the rubric of [16] who provide an empirical process for analyzing the effectiveness of error messages and a rubric for understanding the difficulties students have with them.

7. ACKNOWLEDGEMENTS

The author would like to thank Dr. Catherine Mooney of the Royal College of Surgeons in Ireland for her invaluable contributions with data analysis, Dr. Claire McDonnell of the Dublin Institute of Technology for her guidance, and Mr. Graham Glanville and Mr. Ricardo Iwashima of the College of Computing Technology for their insight and support.

8. REFERENCES

[1] Amjad Altadmri and Neil CC Brown. 37 million compilations: Investigating novice programming mistakes in large-scale student data. In *Proceedings of the 46th ACM Technical Symposium on Computer Science Education*, pages 522–527. ACM, 2015.

[2] B. A. Becker. *An Exploration of the Effects of Enhanced Compiler Error Messages for Computer Programming Novices*. Master's thesis, Dublin Institute of Technology, 2015.

[3] M. M. Ben-Ari. Compile and runtime errors in java. www.weizmann.ac.il/sci-tea/benari/software/others/errors.pdf, 2007. Accessed: 2015-08-23.

[4] N. C. C. Brown, M. Kölling, D. McCall, and I. Utting. Blackbox: A large scale repository of novice programmers' activity. In *Proceedings of the 45th ACM technical symposium on Computer science education*, pages 223–228. ACM, 2014.

[5] N. J. Coull. *SNOOPIE: development of a learning support tool for novice programmers within a conceptual framework*. PhD thesis, University of St Andrews, 2008.

[6] N. J. Coull and I. M. M. Duncan. Emergent requirements for supporting introductory programming. *Innovation in Teaching and Learning in Information and Computer Sciences*, 10(1):78–85, 2011.

[7] P. Denny, A. Luxton-Reilly, E. Tempero, and J. Hendrickx. Codewrite: supporting student-driven practice of java. In *Proceedings of the 42nd ACM technical symposium on Computer science education*, pages 471–476. ACM, 2011.

[8] P. Denny, A.a Luxton-Reilly, and D. Carpenter. Enhancing syntax error messages appears ineffectual. In *Proceedings of the 2014 conference on Innovation & technology in computer science education*, pages 273–278. ACM, 2014.

[9] T. Dy and M. M. Rodrigo. A detector for non-literal java errors. In *Proceedings of the 10th Koli Calling International Conference on Computing Education Research*, pages 118–122. ACM, 2010.

[10] B. Hartmann, D. MacDougall, J. Brandt, and S. R. Klemmer. What would other programmers do: suggesting solutions to error messages. In *Proceedings of the SIGCHI Conference on Human Factors in Computing Systems*, pages 1019–1028. ACM, 2010.

[11] M. Hristova, A. Misra, M. Rutter, and R. Mercuri. Identifying and correcting java programming errors for introductory computer science students. *ACM SIGCSE Bulletin*, 35(1):153–156, 2003.

[12] J. Jackson, M. Cobb, and C. Carver. Identifying top java errors for novice programmers. In *Frontiers in Education, 2005. FIE'05. Proceedings 35th Annual Conference*, pages T4C–T4C. IEEE, 2005.

[13] M. C. Jadud. A first look at novice compilation behaviour using bluej. *Computer Science Education*, 15(1):25–40, 2005.

[14] M. C. Jadud. *An exploration of novice compilation behaviour in BlueJ*. PhD thesis, University of Kent, 2006.

[15] M. Kölling, B. Quig, A. Patterson, and J. Rosenberg. The bluej system and its pedagogy. *Computer Science Education*, 13(4):249–268, 2003.

[16] G. Marceau, K. Fisler, and S. Krishnamurthi. Measuring the effectiveness of error messages designed for novice programmers. In *Proceedings of the 42nd ACM technical symposium on Computer science education*, pages 499–504. ACM, 2011.

[17] G. Marceau, K. Fisler, and S. Krishnamurthi. Mind your language: on novices' interactions with error messages. In *Proceedings of the 10th SIGPLAN symposium on New ideas, new paradigms, and reflections on programming and software*, pages 3–18. ACM, 2011.

[18] Davin McCall and Michael Kolling. Meaningful categorisation of novice programmer errors. In *Frontiers in Education Conference (FIE), 2014 IEEE*, pages 1–8. IEEE, 2014.

[19] P. C. Rigby and S. Thompson. Study of novice programmers using eclipse and gild. In *Proceedings of the 2005 OOPSLA workshop on Eclipse technology eXchange*, pages 105–109. ACM, 2005.

[20] T. Schorsch. Cap: an automated self-assessment tool to check pascal programs for syntax, logic and style errors. *ACM SIGCSE Bulletin*, 27(1):168–172, 1995.

[21] A. Stefik and S. Siebert. An empirical investigation into programming language syntax. *ACM Transactions on Computing Education (TOCE)*, 13(4):19, 2013.

[22] E. S. Tabanao, M. M. Rodrigo, and M. C. Jadud. Predicting at-risk novice java programmers through the analysis of online protocols. In *Proceedings of the seventh international workshop on Computing education research*, pages 85–92. ACM, 2011.

[23] V. J. Traver. On compiler error messages: what they say and what they mean. *Advances in Human-Computer Interaction*, 2010, 2010.

[24] Christopher Watson, FrederickW.B. Li, and JamieL. Godwin. Bluefix: Using crowd-sourced feedback to support programming students in error diagnosis and repair. In Elvira Popescu, Qing Li, Ralf Klamma, Howard Leung, and Marcus Specht, editors, *Advances in Web-Based Learning - ICWL 2012*, volume 7558 of *Lecture Notes in Computer Science*, pages 228–239. Springer Berlin Heidelberg, 2012.

[25] R. L. Wexelblat. Maxims for malfeasant designers, or how to design languages to make programming as difficult as possible. In *Proceedings of the 2nd international conference on Software engineering*, pages 331–336. IEEE Computer Society Press, 1976.

Automatic Inference of Programming Performance and Experience from Typing Patterns

Juho Leinonen, Krista Longi, Arto Klami, Arto Vihavainen
Department of Computer Science
University of Helsinki
Finland
{juho.leinonen, krista.longi, aklami, avihavai}@cs.helsinki.fi

ABSTRACT

Studies on retention and success in introductory programming courses have suggested that previous programming experience contributes to students' course outcomes. If such background information could be automatically distilled from students' working process, additional guidance and support mechanisms could be provided even to those who do not wish to disclose such information. In this study, we explore methods for automatically distinguishing novice programmers from more experienced programmers using fine-grained source code snapshot data. We approach the issue by partially replicating a previous study that used students' keystroke latencies as a proxy to introductory programming course outcomes, and follow this with an exploration of machine learning methods to separate students with little to no previous programming experience from those with more experience. Our results confirm that students' keystroke latencies can be used as a metric for measuring course outcomes. At the same time, our results show that students' programming experience can be identified to some extent from keystroke latency data, which means that such data has potential as a source of information for customizing the students' learning experience.

CCS Concepts

•Information systems → Data mining; •Social and professional topics → Computer science education; CS1; •Computing methodologies → Supervised learning by classification; •Security and privacy → *Biometrics;*

Keywords

keystroke latency, biometric feedback, novice programmer identification, programming data, source code snapshots, educational data mining

SIGCSE '16, March 02-05, 2016, Memphis, TN, USA
© 2016 ACM. ISBN 978-1-4503-3685-7/16/03...$15.00
DOI: http://dx.doi.org/10.1145/2839509.2844612

1. INTRODUCTION

Factors that could explain the difficulties in learning to program have been studied since the 1950's [22]. Early research sought to primarily determine whether factors such as the ability to reason correlate with a tendency towards being able to create computer programs. Gender, age, high-school performance, and the performance in various aptitude tests, for example, have been compared with success in programming [10]. More recently, analysis of log data from students' learning activities has gained attention [21]. One stream of research has focused on approaches that extract various metrics from the programming process, and use those as a proxy to course outcomes [2, 7, 14, 29].

One of the common pitfalls is the often-made assumption that students in an introductory programming course have not programmed previously. From the teacher's perspective, this may lead to mistakes with providing constructive feedback, as the feedback should take the student's background and prior performance into account. Misplaced feedback such as praising for success on easy tasks can even be misinterpreted by students [5], potentially leading to undesirable effects on both self-efficacy and motivation, as well as influence the students trust in their teacher. At the same time, information on students' programming background could also be used to adjust the difficulty of provided programming tasks, as well as to help e.g. automatically identify students at risk.

Previously, we have shown that it is possible to identify programmers based on their typing patterns [18]. In this work, we continue on the theme, and study what the students' keystroke latencies tell us about their programming course performance and their previous programming experience. Being able to recognize prior programming experience from keystroke data can be useful for researchers who have already collected such data but without a background survey. Moreover, even if such a survey is given to the students, some may choose not to answer it.

Our analysis is two-fold: as keystroke latencies have previously been used as a proxy to introductory programming course outcomes [24], we perform a partial replication of the study, and explore the applicability of machine learning methods for a similar task. At the same time, we explore the extent to which keystroke latencies can be used to separate novices from non-novices.

This article is organized as follows. First, we visit related work that is relevant for our study, then in Section 3, we discuss our research methodology and data, followed by the description of experiments and results in Section 4. The results are discussed in Section 5, and in Section 6, we conclude the article and outline future work.

2. RELATED WORK

Here, we explore three streams of related work. First, studies on past programming experience and programming course outcomes are discussed, then, we recap studies that have explored the use of keystroke latencies, and finally, we explore the study by Thomas et al. [24] in more detail.

2.1 Past Programming Experience

The connection between past programming experience and programming course outcomes has been studied in a number of contexts. Hagan and Markham found that those who had programmed previously had higher course marks than those with no previous programming [12], while Bergin and Reilly, upon considering their students' past programming experience, found no statistically significant difference between course outcomes [3]. In a more recent study, Watson et al. observed that students with past programming experience had significantly higher overall course points than those with no previous programming experience [28].

The notion of past programming experience has also been extended to ICT experience. For example, Wilson and Shrock combined variables related to programming and computer use, such as formal programming education, the use of internet, and the amount of time spent on gaming, and found that the combination variable had a significant correlation with the midterm score of an introductory programming course [6]. Another study by Wiedenbeck et al. reported that the number of ICT courses taken by students, the number of programming courses taken, the number of programming languages students had used, the number of programs students had written, and the length of those programs, as a single factor, had a weak but significant positive correlation with the introductory programming course outcomes [30]. Overall, the evidence points towards positive correlation despite somewhat mixed results.

2.2 Keystroke Analysis

Keystroke analysis has mainly been used in research on authentication and authorization [15, 19]. Typing pattern properties such as typing speed, keystroke durations and keystroke latencies can be used to identify users [18] . This has been used as an extra level of security in addition to the traditional password and username, as well as for detecting possible moments in which the logged-in user is no longer genuine. As individuals have a specific typing rhythm and latency that can be used to distinguish between them, it is possible, that some parts of the rhythm and latency could be explained by programming experience, and consequently, detected from such data.

Characteristics that can be calculated from keystroke data include duration of keystrokes, pressure of keystrokes, and keystroke latencies, which are commonly used in keystroke analysis [15]. Especially latencies of digraphs – generally considered to be any two adjacent characters – have been widely used [8, 11, 16, 18, 26]. For example, the word `int` includes two digraphs: `in` and `nt`. In addition, features like average keystrokes per minute and amount of errors have been evaluated [23].

Typing patterns can be affected by changes in equipment such as a keyboard. For example, in a study by Villani et al. [26], identification accuracies declined substantially when the keyboards of the studied subjects were changed between recording keystroke latencies and attempting to use new data for identification. On the other hand, the use of both a desktop and a laptop keyboard – when used both during recording keystrokes as well as during identification did not decrease the accuracy noticeably [26].

In addition to equipment, keystroke patterns can be affected by emotional states [9] such as boredom, engagement and stress [4, 27].

2.3 Keystrokes and Programming Performance

Thomas et al. [24] performed two experiments to investigate whether keystroke latencies could be used as an indicator of programming performance. They categorized each digraph – a character pair – into one of 7 categories (explained in more detail in Section 4.1), calculated the mean latency for each category, and analyzed the correlations between these mean latencies and different performance measures.

In the first experiment, 38 participants solved programming exercises using Java in a controlled experiment. The participants had been studying computer science for 2-3 years. The solutions from each student were scored by two experienced programmers. Significant correlations with digraphs for specific categories were observed [24].

In the second experiment, programming sessions of 125 participants were monitored over the course of six weeks. The programming language in these experiments was Ada, and the participants attended an introductory programming class. In the analysis, correlations ranging from -0.3 to -0.4 between the results of the lab exam and digraphs where the characters were of different type, were observed. However, only digraphs where both characters were of a different type but neither is a browsing character, and digraphs composed of numeric characters, had a significant correlation with the results of the written test [24].

Thomas et al. suggested that the results indicate that the mean latencies are related to a learning effect, as the results from the experiments supported each other. However, they also noted that the metrics were not sufficient as they are, and future work was required to enhance the metrics [24].

3. METHODOLOGY

3.1 Context

The data for the study comes from an introductory programming course in Java organized during the Autumn semester in 2014 at the University of Helsinki. The course lasts for a single 7-week period, and during the course the students learn topics such as input and output, variables, loops, lists, and objects. The students' programming process is recorded using a NetBeans-plugin called Test My Code [25].

Unless the students choose to opt-out, the system stores details of every key press within the programming environment that changes the source code. The details include a student identifier, difference created by the change, timestamp, and the identifier of the current assignment.

The students can work on the exercises either in the computer labs, where they may ask for help from teaching assistants, or they can work on the exercises independently at home. That is, the students may change computers – and keyboards – multiple times during a week. A break from programming can also be taken at any time.

3.2 Research Questions

In this work we seek to further study the applicability of keystroke latencies to predicting programming performance and experience. Our research questions are as follows:

RQ 1. To what extent is programming course exam performance explained by keystroke latency data?

RQ 2. Can such keystroke latency data be used to classify programmers into novices and experienced programmers, and if so, with what accuracy?

With the first research question, we wish to both explore the use of keystroke latencies as a factor contributing to introductory programming outcomes, as well as to – depending on the outcomes – consider what a student learns in a programming class. As programming experience is often linked with programming course outcomes, with the second research question, we wish to study the extent to which keystroke latency data could be used to explain experience.

3.3 Data and Preprocessing

Overall, 246 students attended the course. We excluded students who opted out from the data gathering, as well as those who typed less than 2000 characters during the first week of the course. On average, the students type 7500 characters during the first week, which means that only students who worked on more than one quarter of the first week were included. This left us with 226 students in the data for the experiments in sections 4.1 and 4.2. Finally, to investigate whether keystroke latencies can be used to identify students who have previous programming experience, the students who did not volunteer to provide their programming background details were excluded from the study. After this, 223 students were left in the data for the experiment presented in Section 4.3. Out of the 223 students, 125 had no previous programming experience, while 98 had at least some experience of programming.

For the analysis, we excluded all log events that change the code by more than a single character. These events included copy-paste -events, large auto-completion events by the programming environment, refactoring events, as well as long deletions. We also eliminated events for which the duration between the events was too short or too long. This is relevant for latency analysis, as the students did not work in controlled environments, and they were able to take a break or stop working at any time. Therefore, the elapsed time between two characters could even be a couple of days, and including such data could create unnecessary noise in the analysis. Similarly, short events were removed to eliminate short auto-completion events from the programming environment, or other events where two keys are pressed together. At the end, we included all events within the range of of 10ms–750ms, as done also by Dowland and Furnell [8].

4. EXPERIMENTS AND RESULTS

Next, we present the experimental setting we designed to answer each of our research question, as well as the results.

4.1 Exam Performance Correlations

We performed a partial replication of the study by Thomas et al. [24]. In their second experiment, they monitored 125 students in a 6-week introductory programming course in Ada. The participants took two exams, one written test and one laboratory exam, which were graded by professionals. In the analysis, they calculated the Pearson correlation for each digraph type against the exam scores [24].

Several differences exist between our setup and the setup by Thomas et al. In our case, the keystroke data is collected from all programming sessions during the 7-week course, the students program in Java, and the pedagogical approach and context is different (see [17] for additional details). Moreover, only a written exam was offered in our context.

Thomas et al. [24] divided the digraphs collected from the programming process into 7 categories depending on the type of the event, i.e. whether the students were pressing for example alphabetical, numerical, browsing event-related (arrows, home, end) or control-event related (e.g. copy-paste) keys. In the data at our disposal, events that do not change the state of the source code have not been recorded, which means that evaluation of browsing and control events have been excluded. In our case, we divided the digraphs into categories as follows:

- **A** When both characters are alphabetic characters, either lowercase or uppercase
- **N** When both characters are numbers 0-9
- **O** When both characters are other keys
- **E** When the two characters of a digraph are different types

In addition to the previous, Thomas et al. also studied the following categories:

- **B** When both characters are browsing keys, e.g. *left*
- **C** When both characters are control keys
- **H** When one character is a browsing event and the other either alphabetical, number or other key

We evaluated the method using log data ranging from the first week of the course to all the data from the course. The results from correlating the latencies for the above categories with the written test are presented in Table 1.

4.2 Exam Performance Classification

We also explored the applicability of machine learning methods for the task of predicting programming course exam performance. Following the procedure outlined by Ahadi et al. [2], we divided the students into two populations using their median exam score, and sought to identify the students based on their exam score using keystroke latencies as the predictive features. Overall, over 10,000 features (digraph and single character latencies) were initially extracted. After extracting the features, feature selection was performed to reduce overfitting, shorten the training times, and to improve the interpretability of the resulting model. The feature selection was conducted separately for each dataset using the WEKA Data Mining toolkit [13].

After the feature selection, 20-50 features were left in the datasets (discussed in more detail in Section 5.3). This was followed by an exploration of a number of Bayesian, Rule learner, and Decision Tree-based classifiers to classify the students based on their exam performance. The Bayesian Network and Random Forest classifiers had the best average performance in the task, when evaluated with 10-fold cross-validation using classification accuracy and Matthews Correlation Coefficient [20].

Digraph Type	Week 1	Weeks 1-2	Weeks 1-3	Weeks 1-4	Weeks 1-5	Weeks 1-6	Weeks 1-7	Thomas et al. [24]
N (numeric)	-0.049	-0.025	-0.032	-0.047	-0.059	-0.168*	-0.170*	-0.333**
A (alphabetic)	-0.014	-0.023	-0.023	-0.028	-0.034	-0.050	-0.067	-0.183*
O (other)	0.012	0.017	0.007	-0.020	-0.043	-0.060	-0.064	-0.218*
E (edge not B)	-0.112	-0.112	-0.150*	-0.171*	-0.196*	-0.221**	-0.227**	-0.276*
B (browsing)	NA	NA	NA	NA	NA	NA	NA	-0.093
C (control)	NA	NA	NA	NA	NA	NA	NA	-0.083
H (to/from B)	NA	NA	NA	NA	NA	NA	NA	-0.312**

Table 1: Pearson Correlation of exam points with different digraph types in our experiment and in the experiment by Thomas et al. [24] (* indicates $p < 0.05$, ** indicates $p < 0.01$).

The results for the classification accuracy of Bayesian Network and Random Forest classifiers are shown in Tables 2 and 3. Both tables also include the majority class classifier ZeroR, which classifies all instances to the majority class.

Table 2: Exam Performance Classification Accuracy

Dataset	ZeroR	BayesNet	RandomForest
Week 1	52.29	62.46	**65.09**
Week 1-2	52.02	64.59	**65.80**
Week 1-3	52.21	66.89	**67.47**
Week 1-4	52.21	65.66	**66.89**
Week 1-5	52.21	67.95	**68.59**
Week 1-6	52.21	65.53	**68.23**
Week 1-7	52.21	69.71	**71.77**

4.3 Programming Experience

Out of the 226 students, 223 also reported details in their programming background. Out of the 223, 125 had no previous programming experience, while 98 had programmed previously at least to some extent. For the purposes of this study, we sought to automatically classify the students into novices and non-novices.

We followed the same protocol as in Section 4.2, and again, we were left with 20-50 features. We also evaluated the same classifiers using the same 10-fold cross validation approach, which ranked the Bayesian Network and Random Forest classifiers as the top-performers for both classification accuracy and Matthews Correlation Coefficient. Table 4 shows the classification accuracies, and Table 5 outlines the Matthews Correlation Coefficient for the datasets.

5. DISCUSSION

5.1 Latency and Exam Performance

In the first experiment, outlined in Section 4.1, we performed a partial replication of the study by Thomas et al. [24]. Our results are consistent with the original results in that the digraphs consisting of transitions between numeric keys as well as transitions between keys outside the same category had the highest correlations with the exam results (Table 1). The correlations are not evident from the first few weeks of our data, but as the amount of data is increased, the correlations approach the explanatory level achieved by Thomas et al. However, in our data, the correlations remain somewhat lower than those reported in the study by Thomas et al. even when using data from all seven weeks of the course [24].

In the second experiment, outlined in Section 4.2, we extended the previous work by an exploration over all digraphs

Table 3: Exam Performance MCC

Dataset	ZeroR	BayesNet	RandomForest
Week 1	0.00	0.27	**0.31**
Week 1-2	0.00	0.31	**0.32**
Week 1-3	0.00	0.35	**0.36**
Week 1-4	0.00	0.33	**0.34**
Week 1-5	0.00	0.37	**0.38**
Week 1-6	0.00	0.33	**0.37**
Week 1-7	0.00	0.41	**0.44**

Table 4: Programming Experience Classification Accuracy

Dataset	ZeroR	BayesNet	RandomForest
Week 1	60.32	**74.01**	72.61
Week 1-2	59.37	74.63	**75.01**
Week 1-3	58.79	**77.37**	75.11
Week 1-4	58.79	73.91	**74.81**
Week 1-5	58.79	**76.82**	74.76
Week 1-6	58.79	**74.96**	73.69
Week 1-7	58.79	**74.56**	72.54

and single character presses, and explored classifiers with the purpose of distinguishing between students whose performance in the written exam was above or below the class median. The best performing classifier had a correlation of $r = 0.44$ with the binarized exam performance, explaining 19% of the variance.

Whilst the results from Sections 4.1 and 4.2 are not directly comparable, the results indicate that typing velocity may explain a small part of the exam performance. Effectively, this means that the students who type faster, at least at the end of the course, on average, perform marginally better in the exam. This is an interesting phenomenon per se, as it now has been observed in separate contexts.

This observation could partially be explained by previous programming and ICT experience. However, as the observed correlations from the first weeks when such differences should be most evident are poor, further explanations are to be sought after. One possibility is that it takes some time to get used to new tools and environment – details on what tools or environments the students were familiar with were not asked for in the questionnaire. On the other hand, it could be that we are, again, observing a part of "The Elephant" [1].

5.2 Latency and Programming Experience

In Section 4.3, we explored the extent to which keystroke latencies explain previous programming experience. Upon

Table 5: Programming Experience MCC

Dataset	ZeroR	BayesNet	RandomForest
Week 1	0.00	**0.46**	0.43
Week 1-2	0.00	**0.48**	**0.48**
Week 1-3	0.00	**0.54**	0.49
Week 1-4	0.00	0.46	**0.49**
Week 1-5	0.00	**0.53**	0.51
Week 1-6	0.00	**0.49**	0.45
Week 1-7	0.00	**0.48**	0.43

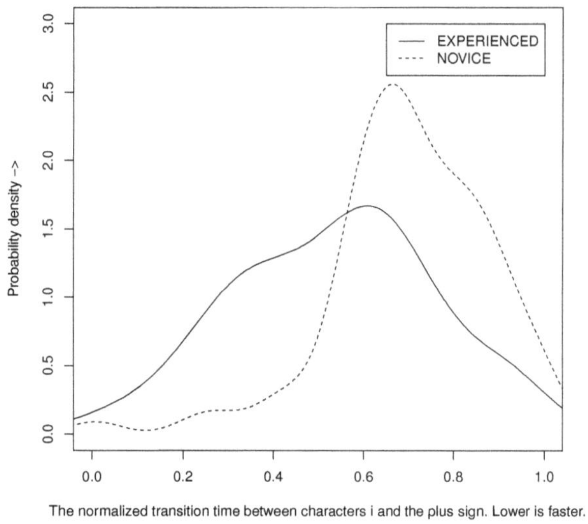

Figure 1: Smoothed probability density function of the times taken between pressing the characters i and + by novice and experienced programmers.

analysis of the results, we observe that the classification accuracy (Table 4) and the Matthews Correlation Coefficient (Table 5) do not increase over time. Throughout the dataset, the Matthews Correlation Coefficient for the included classifiers remains between $r = 0.43$ and $r = 0.54$, explaining 18-29% of the variance.

That is, the keystroke latencies only partially explain previous programming experience. Another observation, which is related to the previous section, is that whilst the classification accuracy of students' exam performance increases over time, the accuracy with which students can be categorized into novices and non-novices remains nearly the same.

This further suggests that the previous observation that the classification accuracy of students' exam performance increases over time, may not, in fact, be related to previous programming experience, but to some additional information that should be explored in the future.

5.3 Analysis of Selected Features

When exploring the applicability of machine learning methods for the tasks in Sections 4.2 and 4.3, feature selection was performed, which helps us now to analyze the individual features. To do this, we performed a qualitative analysis on a combination of the selected features that had the most predictive power over programming experience.

Overall, special keys dominate the list, appearing in nearly 40% of the selected attributes. This is perhaps not surprising, as experienced programmers have probably used them before, and therefore are more familiar with their location on the keyboard. The most relevant digraphs for distinguishing between novices and non-novices are programming-related, and can be categorized into four categories: *common commands*, such as incrementing a variable (`i++`) or using the "OR"-operator (`||`), *common keywords* such as `true`, *transitions between characters that require the use of e.g. shift, ctrl or alt*, such as typing opening and closing brackets (`{}`), and the speed from backspace to various characters, which is likely related to rapid fixing of misspellings.

The difference between the speed with which a novice and non-novice moves typing specific character-combinations, here from typing the character `i` to `+`, is illustrated in Figure 1. In the figure, the typing speeds for the digraph are normalized between 0 and 1 over all the students, and displayed as two probability density functions that depict the novices and non-novices.

6. CONCLUSIONS AND FUTURE WORK

In this work, we explored the applicability of keystroke latency data to analyzing programming performance and past programming experience. To summarize our work, the response to our Research Questions 1, *To what extent is programming course exam performance explained by keystroke latency data?* is as follows: While the most comparable results from Thomas et al. explained up to 11% of variance in the written exam performance, our partial replication of their work reached up to 5%. In another experiment, where the task was made easier by seeking to categorize into two categories based on whether they performed over the class median or not, up to 19% of the variance was explained by the model. We also observed that correlations were rather poor during the early weeks, which may suggest that past programming experience does not explain the differences between the populations. Our results also indicate that the answer to Research Question 2, *Can such keystroke latency data be used to classify programmers into novices and experienced programmers, and if so, with what accuracy?*, is yes, to some extent. The explored models explained 18-29% of the variance in past programming experience.

While our results are far from being able to accurately distinguish those with at least some programming experience from those with none, they show promise in that such identification may be possible. Such knowledge could be used to e.g. improve learning materials and provide targeted guidance, especially in online contexts, where access to teaching resources may be sparse.

As a part of our future work, we will further explore the categories proposed by Thomas et al, by, at least, performing the same study but explicitly looking only at those with no previous programming experience. At the same time, we will be further looking for confounding factors which may explain some of our results.

Acknowledgements

The research was supported in part by the Academy of Finland (project 1266969 and COIN Centre of Excellence) and the Finnish Funding Agency for Innovation (under project Re:Know).

7. REFERENCES

[1] A. Ahadi and R. Lister. Geek genes, prior knowledge, stumbling points and learning edge momentum: Parts of the one elephant? In *Proceedings of the Ninth Annual International ACM Conference on International Computing Education Research*, ICER '13, pages 123–128, New York, NY, USA, 2013. ACM.

[2] A. Ahadi, R. Lister, H. Haapala, and A. Vihavainen. Exploring machine learning methods to automatically identify students in need of assistance. In *Proceedings of the Eleventh Annual International Conference on International Computing Education Research*, ICER '15, pages 121–130, New York, NY, USA, 2015. ACM.

[3] S. Bergin and R. Reilly. Programming: factors that influence success. *ACM SIGCSE Bull.*, 37(1):411–415, 2005.

[4] R. Bixler and S. D'Mello. Detecting boredom and engagement during writing with keystroke analysis, task appraisals, and stable traits. In *Proceedings of the 2013 International Conference on Intelligent User Interfaces*, IUI '13, pages 225–234, New York, NY, USA, 2013. ACM.

[5] G. D. Borich and M. L. Tombari. *Educational Psychology: A Contemporary Approach.* Longman Publishing/Addison Wesley, 2nd edition, 1997.

[6] B. Cantwell Wilson and S. Shrock. Contributing to success in an introductory computer science course: a study of twelve factors. In *ACM SIGCSE Bull.*, volume 33, pages 184–188. ACM, 2001.

[7] A. S. Carter, C. D. Hundhausen, and O. Adesope. The normalized programming state model: Predicting student performance in computing courses based on programming behavior. In *Proceedings of the Eleventh Annual International Conference on International Computing Education Research*, ICER '15, pages 141–150, New York, NY, USA, 2015. ACM.

[8] P. Dowland and S. Furnell. A long-term trial of keystroke profiling using digraph, trigraph and keyword latencies. In Y. Deswarte, F. Cuppens, S. Jajodia, and L. Wang, editors, *Security and Protection in Information Processing Systems*, volume 147 of *IFIP - The International Federation for Information Processing*, pages 275–289. Springer, 2004.

[9] C. Epp, M. Lippold, and R. L. Mandryk. Identifying emotional states using keystroke dynamics. In *Proceedings of the SIGCHI Conference on Human Factors in Computing Systems*, CHI '11, pages 715–724, New York, NY, USA, 2011. ACM.

[10] G. E. Evans and M. G. Simkin. What best predicts computer proficiency? *Comm. of the ACM*, 32(11):1322–1327, 1989.

[11] R. S. Gaines, W. Lisowski, S. J. Press, and N. Shapiro. Authentication by keystroke timing: Some preliminary results. Technical report, 1980.

[12] D. Hagan and S. Markham. Does it help to have some programming experience before beginning a computing degree program? *ACM SIGCSE Bull.*, 32(3):25–28, 2000.

[13] M. Hall, E. Frank, G. Holmes, B. Pfahringer, P. Reutemann, and I. H. Witten. The weka data mining software: an update. *ACM SIGKDD explorations newsletter*, 11(1):10–18, 2009.

[14] M. C. Jadud. Methods and tools for exploring novice compilation behaviour. In *Proceedings of the Second International Workshop on Computing Education Research*, ICER '06, pages 73–84, New York, NY, USA, 2006. ACM.

[15] M. Karnan, M. Akila, and N. Krishnaraj. Biometric personal authentication using keystroke dynamics: A review. *Applied Soft Computing*, 11(2):1565 – 1573, 2011. The Impact of Soft Computing for the Progress of Artificial Intelligence.

[16] K. S. Killourhy and R. A. Maxion. Free vs. transcribed text for keystroke-dynamics evaluations. In *Proceedings of the 2012 Workshop on Learning from Authoritative Security Experiment Results*, LASER '12, pages 1–8, New York, NY, USA, 2012. ACM.

[17] J. Kurhila and A. Vihavainen. Management, structures and tools to scale up personal advising in large programming courses. In *Proceedings of the 2011 Conference on Information Technology Education*, SIGITE '11, pages 3–8, New York, NY, USA, 2011. ACM.

[18] K. Longi, J. Leinonen, H. Nygren, J. Salmi, A. Klami, and A. Vihavainen. Identification of programmers from typing patterns. In *Proceedings of the 15th Koli Calling Conference on Computing Education Research*, Koli Calling '15, pages 60–67, New York, NY, USA, 2015. ACM.

[19] A. Peacock, X. Ke, and M. Wilkerson. Typing patterns: A key to user identification. *IEEE Security & Privacy*, 2(5):40–47, 2004.

[20] D. M. Powers. Evaluation: from precision, recall and F-measure to ROC, informedness, markedness and correlation. 2011.

[21] C. Romero and S. Ventura. Educational data mining: A review of the state of the art. *Systems, Man, and Cybernetics, Part C: Applications and Reviews, IEEE Transactions on*, 40(6):601–618, Nov 2010.

[22] T. C. Rowan. Psychological tests and selection of computer programmers. *J. ACM*, 4(3):348–353, 1957.

[23] M. Rybnik, M. Tabedzki, and K. Saeed. A keystroke dynamics based system for user identification. In *Computer Information Systems and Industrial Management Applications, 2008.*, pages 225–230, June 2008.

[24] R. C. Thomas, A. Karahasanovic, and G. E. Kennedy. An investigation into keystroke latency metrics as an indicator of programming performance. In *Proceedings of the 7th Australasian Conference on Computing Education - Volume 42*, ACE '05, pages 127–134, Darlinghurst, Australia, 2005. Australian Computer Society, Inc.

[25] A. Vihavainen, T. Vikberg, M. Luukkainen, and M. Pärtel. Scaffolding students' learning using test my code. In *Proceedings of the 18th ACM Conference on Innovation and Technology in Computer Science Education*, ITiCSE '13, pages 117–122, New York, NY, USA, 2013. ACM.

[26] M. Villani, C. Tappert, G. Ngo, J. Simone, H. Fort, and S.-H. Cha. Keystroke biometric recognition studies on long-text input under ideal and application-oriented conditions. In *Computer Vision and Pattern Recognition Workshop, 2006. CVPRW '06. Conference on*, pages 39–39, June 2006.

[27] L. M. Vizer, L. Zhou, and A. Sears. Automated stress detection using keystroke and linguistic features: An exploratory study. *Int. J. Hum.-Comput. Stud.*, 67(10):870–886, Oct. 2009.

[28] C. Watson, F. W. Li, and J. L. Godwin. No tests required: comparing traditional and dynamic predictors of programming success. In *Proceedings of the 45th ACM technical symposium on Computer science education*, pages 469–474. ACM, 2014.

[29] C. Watson, F. W. B. Li, and J. L. Godwin. Predicting performance in an introductory programming course by logging and analyzing student programming behavior. In *Proceedings of the 2013 IEEE 13th International Conference on Advanced Learning Technologies*, ICALT '13, pages 319–323, Washington, DC, USA, 2013. IEEE Computer Society.

[30] S. Wiedenbeck, D. Labelle, and V. N. Kain. Factors affecting course outcomes in introductory programming. In *16th Annual Workshop of the Psychology of Programming Interest Group*, pages 97–109, 2004.

CS0 for Computer Science Majors at Ohio University

Cindy Marling
School of Electrical Engineering and Computer Science
Russ College of Engineering and Technology
Ohio University
Athens, Ohio 45701
marling@ohio.edu

David Juedes
School of Electrical Engineering and Computer Science
Russ College of Engineering and Technology
Ohio University
Athens, Ohio 45701
juedes@ohio.edu

ABSTRACT

This paper describes the design and initial implementation of a new CS0 course for CS majors at Ohio University and an associated computer science placement exam. It was our expectation that this course would help improve overall retention and academic performance of CS majors. The new CS0 course was intended for new students with little or no programming experience. Hence, we designed CS0 by selecting some of the best components of other CS0 efforts from the literature, namely, introductory programming in Python, computational thinking, and motivational material aimed at instilling ownership of the major. In order to direct students into CS0 or CS1 appropriately, a placement exam was given to students during orientation. The placement process resulted in a mixed cohort consisting of students with no programming experience as well as other students with programming experience who did not pass the placement exam. Longitudinal analysis of student grades in CS0 and CS1 showed that these were two distinct populations with very different needs. A statistically significant difference was found in the CS1 grades for CS0 students from these populations. Surprisingly, CS0 students without prior programming experience got significantly higher grades in CS1 than CS0 students who had programmed before. We share lessons learned from our experience, including a revised placement process to address these separate populations.

Keywords

Computing Fundamentals; CS0

1. INTRODUCTION

Ohio University is a large, primarily residential, public university with high (but not very high) research activity and selective (but not very selective) admissions. There are over 17,000 undergraduates and over 4,000 graduate students on the main campus, and approximately 33,000 students total, including branch campus and online enrollment. There are more than 250 academic majors for undergraduates to choose from; around 240 undergraduate students major in computer science.

The computer science (CS) program is housed in the Russ College of Engineering and Technology, where it has recently had one of the worst retention rates of any major. To address this issue, we designed and implemented a new CS0 course, which was taught for the first time in Fall, 2014. Due, in part, to the large number of ways in which CS0 is taught at different colleges and universities [3], it was surprisingly difficult to design a CS0 course to meet the needs of Ohio University students. Due, in part, to our large student body, it also proved difficult to place each incoming freshman into the most appropriate introductory computing course. Since nearly every state in the union has at least one large public university like Ohio University, we would like to share our experience in hopes that it may ease CS0 course development and CS placement efforts elsewhere. Contributions include: the design of a new CS0 course for CS majors without prior programming experience; lessons learned about the CS placement process; and an analysis, both quantitative and qualitative, of the intertwined effects on CS1 performance and first-year student retention.

2. GOALS AND MOTIVATION

Our CS0 course was designed for the specific purpose of improving CS major retention. Retention may be affected by many academic and non-academic factors. We began by examining the academic performance of CS majors in CS1. Data was available for the 3.5 year period from Fall, 2010 through Fall, 2013. During that period, 266 majors enrolled in CS1. Of those who enrolled, 27% were unsuccessful, obtaining grades below C (the cutoff for advancing to CS2) or withdrawing. While students can and do retake CS1, we posit that preventing these initial negative experiences will help to boost retention.

We decided that the best way to provide a more positive CS1 experience would be to offer a new CS0 course for freshmen who are not CS1-ready, much as pre-calculus is offered to students who are not calculus-ready. The alternative, revamping CS1 itself, would have had repercussions for the rest of our ABET-accredited curriculum, which we had recently evaluated and revised. Furthermore, many Ohio University students who enter CS1 with prior programming experience enjoy and succeed in CS1. However, we have observed that their enthusiastic in-class participation may adversely affect students without prior programming experience, who may feel intimidated or irremediably behind.

SIGCSE '16, March 02-05, 2016, Memphis, TN, USA

 ISBN 978-1-4503-3685-7/16/03...$15.00
DOI: http://dx.doi.org/10.1145/2839509.2844624

Anecdotal evidence provided by CS1 instructors indicates that the affected non-programmers are disproportionately female or members of other under-represented groups. The detrimental effects of this experience gap have been previously reported by others [9, 14]. CS0 is an opportunity to level the playing field, so that all students get off to a positive start in CS1.

3. THE DESIGN OF CS0 AT OHIO UNIVERSITY

We initially hoped to find an existing CS0 course upon which to pattern our new course offering. However, a literature search revealed a wide variety of CS0 courses, each designed to meet different goals for different student populations, with none quite suited to our goals and our students [4, 5, 8, 12, 13]. Furthermore, we were unable to find a suitable all-inclusive textbook that was neither geared to non-majors nor simply a student-friendly CS1 textbook. However, we found a wealth of good ideas and valuable resources, which, in combination, formed the building blocks of CS0. Particularly helpful were the Harvey Mudd experience [9] and resources for exploring computational thinking [7, 17]. The Harvey Mudd program, designed to attract and retain female CS majors, separates students by experience level, emphasizes computational approaches to problem solving, explores the societal impact of computing, and fosters a sense of self-confidence and belonging among students. Computational thinking encompasses problem-solving skills and processes, which aid in computer programming as well as other intellectual pursuits, and which can be developed in a programming or non-programming environment.

We designed a CS0 course comprising three core components: (1) introductory programming; (2) computational thinking; and (3) CS major ownership. Although these components naturally intertwine, course materials were selected to ensure that each is thoroughly covered.

Introductory programming is included to ensure that no student becomes intimidated by taking CS1 without prior programming experience. However, we do not want to either duplicate or replace CS1, so we selected a different programming language (Python instead of C++), and we spend approximately half as much time on programming as we would in a CS1 course. The textbooks we use for programming are: *Think Python: How to Think Like a Computer Scientist* (chapters 1–6) [6]; and Harvey Mudd's *CS for All* (chapters 1–2) [1]. Both books stress a computational thinking approach to programming, and both are available for free online.

Computational thinking, aside from that incorporated in programming activities, is also taught through a study of the great ideas that empower computation, independent of programming language or even of pseudocode. Our textbook is *Nine Algorithms That Changed the Future: The Ingenious Ideas That Drive Today's Computers* (chapters 1–3 and 6) [11]. It explains step-by-step, at a high level, but without oversimplifying, how the algorithms students actually use everyday, like Google's PageRank, work. This book also enhances the CS major ownership component of our course, in that students clearly see the everyday impact of CS (where would we be without Google?) and develop confidence in their abilities to understand, and ultimately encode, complex computational processes.

The CS major ownership component strives to reinforce, for each student, that CS is an *awesome* major and that CS is *my* major. A variety of motivational materials and activities are incorporated. Profiles of successful computer scientists are included to present diverse role models. TED and TEDx talks provide useful resources for this [15]. Computer science in the news articles, both print and online, help to highlight computing's positive societal impact. Computational fairy tales serve to present complex computing concepts in an entertaining and easy-to-grasp manner [10]. Connections are made between these materials and the skills taught in the other core components.

4. THE FIRST COURSE OFFERING

The first course offering was experimental in nature. A single section was offered and closely monitored in Fall, 2014. The goal was to evaluate and fine tune the course before scaling it up to all CS majors without programming experience.

4.1 Student Placement in CS0

In Summer, 2014, over 4,000 new freshmen attended orientation sessions at which they registered for Fall, 2014 classes. Each orientation session contained 1 or 2 CS majors among 200 other students. Because it was infeasible for the orientation staff to individually assess each student's programming background, a placement test was used to place incoming freshmen into either CS0 or CS1. While math and chemistry placement tests have long been in use at Ohio University, this was the first time a CS placement test had been deployed. A new CS placement test was implemented in Blackboard. Students could take the test in either Java or C++, the two most popular languages among incoming freshmen. Multiple choice questions asked what very short code segments would do, as illustrated in Figure 1. Students who passed the test were directed to CS1, while students who did not were directed to CS0. Once the maximum CS0 enrollment was reached, students who did not pass the placement test were advised to take an introductory programming course for non-majors before taking CS1.

Soon, but not soon enough, the inadequacy of this placement approach became apparent. We had hoped to pilot and analyze a CS0 course for CS majors without programming experience, but instead, we found ourselves piloting and analyzing a CS0 course for a much more diverse student population. Subsequently, we learned some important lessons we had not set out to learn.

4.2 Student Cohort

Twenty CS majors were in the first cohort, including three women and five minorities. The cohort was not the one we had targeted, due to the inadequacy of the placement process. First, an additional four students who were computer engineering (CE) majors, all white males, were inadvertently enrolled, bringing the cohort to 24 students in all. There is overlap between the CS and CE programs, with CE majors taking CS1, typically preceded by an introductory programming course for non-majors. Second, the placement test did not adequately distinguish students without prior programming experience from students who had programmed before but were in need of review or remediation. After the first assignment, an introductory survey, was reviewed, it was discovered that 11 of the CS majors and two of the CE majors had prior programming experience, leaving only nine

Consider the following code segment.

```
public class PlacementTest
{
   public static void main(String[] args)
   {
      int x=3;
      int y=5;
      x += y;
      y += x;
   }
}
```

When the code above executes, what will be the final values of x and y?

```
a.  x:  8, y:  8
b.  x:  5, y:  3
c.  x:  3, y:  5
d.  x:  8, y:  13      // Correct answer
e.  none of the above
```

Figure 1: Sample Java placement test question.

Table 1: Characteristics of the CS0 student cohort.

Major	Computer Science	20
	Computer Engineering	4
Gender	Male	21
	Female	3
Designation	Minority	5
	Non-minority	19
Experience	Novice Programmer	11
	Prior Programmer	13
Demographic	CS Novice Programmer	9
	Other	15

students in the target demographic. Characteristics of the student cohort are summarized in Table 1. Because all 24 students would need to take CS1 and none appeared to be CS1-ready, we believed at the time that the course would be of benefit to all enrolled students. However, course outcomes differed significantly for students with and without prior programming experience, as discussed in the Preliminary Evaluation section.

4.3 Course Procedures

The class met three times a week for 55 minutes per session. Attendance was expected, but not required; it was encouraged by frequent pop quizzes. Most sessions were held in a standard classroom; however, the class moved to a computer lab approximately once a week for programming exercises. Because students are not required to own laptops at Ohio University, the lab was used to provide computer access to all. The lab offers a "virtual desktop," so that students can access lab software away from the lab in order to complete programming assignments. In-lab exercises were instructor guided, intentionally ungraded, practice sessions. Students worked independently, but were encouraged to help each other.

The grading rubric was as follows: homework assignments counted for 25% of the grade; pop quizzes counted for 5%; two midterm exams counted 20% each; and a final exam counted for 30% of the grade. All core components of the course were reinforced and evaluated via assignments, quizzes and exams. Note that computational thinking and CS major ownership were not simply fostered by the overall course environment or subjugated to a primary focus on programming. For example, in an assignment focused on CS major ownership, students found CS in the news articles and presented them as lightning talks to the class. Only half of the homework assignments involved programming.

4.4 Preliminary Evaluation

To fully evaluate the effects of CS0 on CS major retention, students must be monitored until they graduate as CS majors (or not). However, a preliminary evaluation was conducted, using both quantitative and qualitative measures. Data for the four CE majors was not included in the quantitative analysis, as it is not possible to "retain" students in a major they never had. However, because some of the qualitative data was obtained anonymously and majors could not be distinguished, data from all students was included.

4.4.1 Quantitative Evaluation

Three quantitative criteria were used to evaluate CS0 outcomes: first-semester academic probation rate; first-year retention rate; and overall performance in CS1. A statistical analysis was performed using IBM SPSS Statistics, version 22. Statistically significant findings are shown in Figure 2. The full analysis follows.

Mean CS1 grades for CS0 students without prior programming experience were significantly higher than those of CS0 students who had programmed before ($t(15.74)=2.57$, $p=.021$).

CS1 grades and math ACT scores were correlated with $r=.534$, $p=.002$.

Students who were not retained had significantly lower math ACT scores than students who were retained ($t(23.70)=4.03$, $p=.000$).

Students with below average math ACT scores were significantly less likely to be retained than those with above average math ACT scores, with $p=.028$ by Fisher's exact test.

Figure 2: Statistically significant findings.

First semester academic probation is indicative of future retention, because students who are placed on academic probation and do not subsequently improve their grade point averages are involuntarily removed from the major. In 2013, the year before CS0 was introduced, 26% of CS majors were placed on academic probation at the end of their first semester. In 2014, that number dropped to 19% for all CS majors and to 20% for CS majors who had taken CS0. While it is not possible to attribute this improvement solely to CS0, we believe it is an encouraging result.

First-year retention rates were compared for CS majors who had taken CS0 versus those who had not. Ohio University tracks retention for students remaining at the university, regardless of major. In this analysis, we also consider those who switch from CS to other majors. For comparison, the first-year retention rates for the university as a whole and for the Russ College of Engineering and Technology are both 79%. Recently, CS has had one of the lowest retention rates within the Russ College of Engineering and Technology.

This year, 80% of CS majors who took CS0 were retained at the university; however, only 70% were retained as CS majors. The first-year retention rate for main-campus CS majors who did not take CS0 was 79%. Only two students who are still at the university switched majors; both took CS0. Because CS0 appeared to have little effect on first-year retention, we took a closer look at some other factors that could impact first-year retention: gender, minority status, and math ACT scores. Retention rates for different student groups are shown in Figure 3.

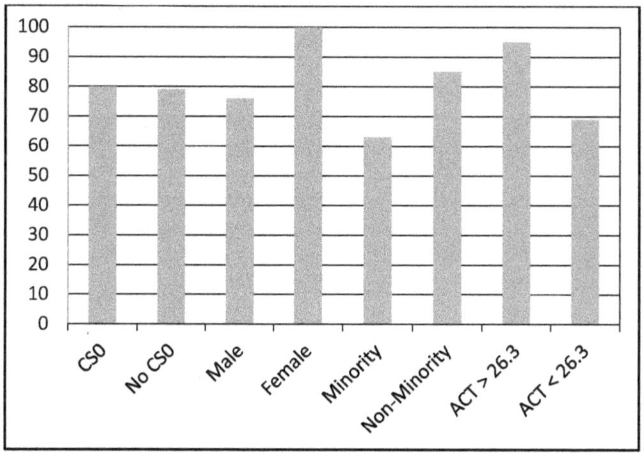

Figure 3: Retention rate for students by CS0 enrollment, gender, minority status, and math ACT score. The mean math ACT score was 26.3.

The only statistically significant factor found to be affecting retention was math ACT scores. The mean math ACT score for freshman CS majors was 26.3. Students scoring above and below this average had significantly different retention rates, as noted in Figure 2. Furthermore, there was a statistically significant difference in the mean math ACT scores of students who were retained (26.8) and those who were not (24.2). Math preparedness (or lack thereof) has long been associated with success (or lack thereof) in computer science [2, 12, 16]. This factor may be overshadowing the potential impact of CS0 on retention; all six CS0 students who either left the university or switched majors had below average math ACT scores.

Next, we compare CS1 grades for freshman CS majors who did and did not take CS0. Eighteen CS0 students enrolled in two sections of CS1 in Spring, 2015. Their grades were compared to those of the other freshman CS majors in the same CS1 sections who had not taken CS0. Note that the other students would have either passed the CS placement test based on past programming experience or taken another introductory programming course. There is no control group of students similar to our CS0 students who went directly into CS1. (While this might have been a better experimental design, it would have been an unacceptable educational experience.) Upon first glance, it appeared that the CS0 students had performed *worse* than the other students in CS1. Although not statistically significant, the mean grade for CS0 students was 1.9, on a 4.0 scale, versus a mean grade of 2.3 for the non-CS0 students.

Upon further analysis, a more interesting and statistically significant finding was discovered. There was a significant difference in CS1 performance for CS0 students with and without prior programming experience. The mean grade for past programmers was 1.4, while the mean grade for those without prior programming experience was 2.6. While this may seem surprising, math preparation may have again come into play. Math ACT scores were correlated with CS1 grades. While mean math ACT scores for CS0 students with and without prior programming experience did not significantly differ, 80% of past programmers had below average math ACT scores versus only 38% of novice programmers. These findings are summarized in Table 2.

4.4.2 *Qualitative Evaluation*

Two instruments were used to gauge student perception of the course: an anonymous Blackboard exit survey and a signed, hand-written exit survey. Students completed these surveys at the end of the semester.

Nineteen students completed the anonymous Blackboard exit survey. Students were asked to rate their level of agreement with each of 16 statements, using a 5-point Likert scale from Strongly Disagree to Strongly Agree. The first nine items stated that a particular course element was valuable. Course elements surveyed were: the *CS for All* textbook; the *9 Algorithms* textbook; the *Think Python* textbook; TED talks; *Computational Fairy Tales*; lightning talks by students; homework assignments; lab exercises; and pop quizzes. More students agreed than disagreed that all nine surveyed course elements were valuable. The elements deemed valuable by the most students were ordered as follows: lab exercises, TED talks, homework assignments, and the *Think Python* textbook.

The remaining items on the anonymous Blackboard survey were general statements about student perception of the course and the field of computer science. Notable responses are shown in Figure 4. Strongly Agree/Agree responses were aggregated, as were Strongly Disagree/Disagree responses. Responses aggregated as Other include Neither Agree nor Disagree, Not Applicable, or item left unanswered. Most disconcerting was that, despite believing they learned a lot they did not already know, 47% of students would have preferred to have skipped CS0 and gone straight into CS1. This perception was backed up by anecdotal reports from faculty members who heard complaints from prior programmers that they should not have been required to take a course for beginning programmers.

Twenty-three students completed the signed, hand-written survey. This survey contained 10 questions with short free form answers. Not all questions yielded clear-cut insights. For example, *Computational Fairy Tales* was listed, by different students, in response to questions about their favorite and least favorite parts of the course. The most informative responses were to the questions: "Are you considering

Table 2: **Comparison of different student groups in CS1.**

Student Group	Number of Students	Mean CS1 Grade	Mean Math ACT	%age Math ACT < 26.3
CS0, new programmer	8	2.6	26.6	38%
CS0, prior programmer	10	1.4	25.6	80%
Did not take CS0	14	2.3	26.7	36%

I understand the field of computer science better than I did before I took CS0.
Agree: 84% **Disagree:** 5% **Other:** 11%

I am a better computer programmer than I was before I took CS0.
Agree: 84% **Disagree:** 11% **Other:** 5%

I already knew a lot of the material covered in CS0 before I took the course.
Agree: 16% **Disagree:** 63% **Other:** 21%

If I could have skipped CS0 and gone straight into CS1 instead, I would have done that.
Agree: 47% **Disagree:** 42% **Other:** 11%

Computer science is an awesome major.
Agree: 89% **Disagree:** 0% **Other:** 11%

Figure 4: Notable responses to the anonymous Blackboard exit survey

switching majors?" and "What grade do you think you will get in CS1 when you take it?" As for switching majors, 18 students answered No, including one who eventually did switch. Three students answered Yes, including one who switched, a CE major considering switching to CS, and a CS major considering switching to CE. Two students answered Maybe. As for CS1 grades, two students left this blank. The average expected CS1 grade for the other 21 students was 3.5 on a 4.0 scale. Although actual CS1 grades were lower (1.9 for the CS majors in CS0), this may be viewed as an indication that CS0 students felt confident that they could succeed in computer science at the end of the course.

5. LESSONS LEARNED

The first CS0 experience was only partially successful, but lessons were learned that may aid in developing CS0 courses and appropriately placing students into them, especially in other large public universities where resources are limited and students are diverse in terms of prior academic preparation. Students in the target demographic, CS majors without prior programming experience, benefitted from the course and did well in CS1, as a whole. Prior programmers, on the other hand, were both *unhappy* that they had been placed into CS0 instead of CS1 and *less successful* in CS1.

To better direct each incoming CS or CE major to the computing course that would best suit their needs, the placement process was overhauled. The new process was carefully documented and communicated to the orientation staff. First, CE majors without prior programming experience were directed to the Introductory Programming in C course. This was the established placement process for CE majors before the advent of CS0, and it has served that major well. Second, the C++ and Java placement tests were replaced by a single, language-independent test, measuring basic computing concepts, as recommended in [5]. Finally, a new process was outlined for administering the test and directing students to one of four existing courses: CS0, CS1, Introductory Programming in C, or Introductory Programming in Java. Note that resource limitations precluded development of additional new courses; our task was to best allocate existing resources to meet student needs.

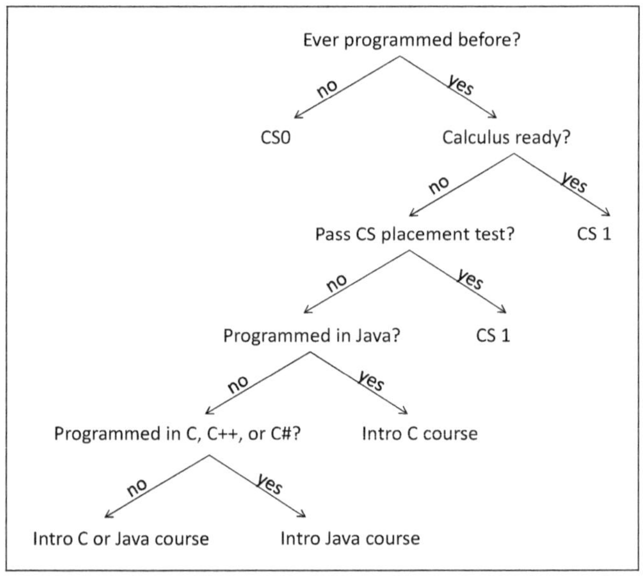

Figure 5: The new placement process for freshman CS majors.

The new placement process for CS majors is shown in Figure 5. The placement test is now only administered to students who say they have programmed before but who are not calculus-ready. Approximately 35% of our incoming CS majors are calculus-ready; many start with pre-calculus. Calculus-ready prior programmers are directed to CS1. Students who say they have no prior programming experience are directed to CS0, regardless of whether or not they are calculus-ready. All other students take the pre-test. Those who pass are directed to CS1. Those who do not pass are directed to an introductory programming course for non-majors in either C or Java, such that, whenever possible, they study a language they have never used before. In this way, weaker programmers will get extra programming experience without feeling like they have been relegated to the novice class. They will also have an extra semester in which to improve their math preparation. Dedicated supplemental math instructors are available to help CS majors struggling with calculus or pre-calculus.

The new placement process was implemented for Fall, 2015. Half of our 60 new freshman CS majors are currently enrolled in two sections of CS0. We will continue tracking progress to measure the impact on retention.

6. SUMMARY AND CONCLUSION

We designed and implemented a new CS0 course for CS majors without prior programming experience and an associated placement exam. We designed CS0 by selecting some of the best components of other CS0 efforts from the literature, namely, introductory programming in Python, computational thinking, and motivational material aimed at instilling ownership of the major. The placement process resulted in a mixed cohort consisting of students with no programming experience as well as other students with programming experience who did not pass the placement exam. Surprisingly, CS0 students without prior programming experience got significantly higher grades in CS1 than CS0 students who had programmed before. Because of this, we have redesigned our placement process to take into account math aptitude as well as prior programming experience. We believe that this new placement procedure will improve overall performance in CS1 and ultimately result in improved CS retention. This new procedure was implemented for the current academic year, and results will be closely monitored.

7. REFERENCES

[1] C. Alvarado, Z. Dodds, G. Kuenning, and R. Libeskind-Hadas. *CS for All.* Harvey Mudd College, Claremont, CA, 2013. http://www.cs.hmc.edu/csforall/, accessed August, 2015.

[2] T. Beaubouef and J. Mason. Why the high attrition rate for computer science students: some thoughts and observations. *ACM SIGCSE Bulletin*, 37(2):103–106, 2005.

[3] S. Davies, J. A. Polack-Wahl, and K. Anewalt. A snapshot of current practices in teaching the introductory programming sequence. In *Proceedings of the 42nd ACM Technical Symposium on Computer Science Education*, pages 625–630. ACM, 2011.

[4] M. desJardins and M. Littman. Broadening student enthusiasm for computer science with a great insights course. In *Proceedings of the 41st ACM Technical Symposium on Computer Science Education*, pages 157–161. ACM, 2010.

[5] C. Dierbach, B. Taylor, H. Zhou, and I. Zimand. Experiences with a CS0 course targeted for CS1 success. *ACM SIGCSE Bulletin*, 37(1):317–320, 2005.

[6] A. Downey. *Think Python: How to Think Like a Computer Scientist.* Green Tea Press, Needham, MA, 2012. http://www.greenteapress.com/thinkpython/thinkpython.pdf, accessed August, 2015.

[7] Google. Exploring computational thinking, 2015. https://www.google.com/edu/resources/programs/exploring-computational-thinking/, accessed August, 2015.

[8] M. Haungs, C. Clark, J. Clements, and D. Janzen. Improving first-year success and retention through interest-based CS0 courses. In *Proceedings of the 43rd ACM Technical Symposium on Computer Science Education*, pages 589–594. ACM, 2012.

[9] M. Klawe. Increasing female participation in computing: The Harvey Mudd College story. *Computer*, 46(3):56–58, 2013.

[10] J. Kubica. *Computational Fairy Tales.* 2012. https://books.google.com/books?id=-L7BlWTtNdAC, accessed August, 2015.

[11] J. MacCormick. *Nine Algorithms that Changed the Future: The Ingenious Ideas that Drive Today's Computers.* Princeton University Press, Princeton, NJ, 2012.

[12] M. Rizvi and T. Humphries. A Scratch-based CS0 course for at-risk computer science majors. In *Frontiers in Education Conference (FIE), 2012*, pages 1–5. IEEE, 2012.

[13] L. Snyder, T. Barnes, D. Garcia, J. Paul, and B. Simon. The first five computer science principles pilots: summary and comparisons. *ACM Inroads*, 3(2):54–57, 2012.

[14] A. Tafliovich, J. Campbell, and A. Petersen. A student perspective on prior experience in CS1. In *Proceedings of the 44th ACM Technical Symposium on Computer Science Education*, pages 239–244. ACM, 2013.

[15] TED. 2000+ talks to stir your curiosity, 2015. https://www.ted.com/talks, accessed August, 2015.

[16] B. C. Wilson and S. Shrock. Contributing to success in an introductory computer science course: a study of twelve factors. In *ACM SIGCSE Bulletin*, volume 33, pages 184–188. ACM, 2001.

[17] J. M. Wing. Computational thinking. *Communications of the ACM*, 49(3):33–35, 2006.

Security Injections 2.0: Increasing Ability to Apply Secure Coding Knowledge using Segmented and Interactive Modules in CS0

Sagar Raina
Towson University
7800 York Rd.
Towson, MD, USA - 21252
443-824-7220
sraina1@students.towson.edu

Siddharth Kaza
Towson University
7800 York Rd.
Towson, MD, USA - 21252
410-704-6310
skaza@towson.edu

Blair Taylor
Towson University
7800 York Rd.
Towson, MD, USA - 21252
410-704-4560
btaylor@towson.edu

ABSTRACT
Student skipping content is common in traditional learning modules that present a large amount of content in a linear format. This can lead to lower student engagement, and may yield poor learning. In this paper, we compare student learning between enhanced learning modules (2.0) and traditional modules (1.0) aimed at providing knowledge on secure coding to students in lower-level programming courses. We discuss the results of a quasi-experiment across two sections of CS0. The study compares students' secure coding awareness, general software security awareness and students' ability to identify security vulnerabilities (integer overflow, input validation and buffer overflow) in three separate code segments. A total of 53 students participated in the study. While results indicate significant improvement in secure coding and general software security awareness in both 1.0 and 2.0 modules, students using 2.0 modules performed significantly better than students using 1.0 modules in applying secure coding knowledge by identifying security vulnerabilities in code segments.

Keywords
Security Injections; integer overflow; buffer overflow; input validation; cs0; cs1; cs2; learning sciences; interactive learning modules; instant-feedback; auto-grading.

1. INTRODUCTION
Cybersecurity education is a crucial component in addressing the cybersecurity crisis [15]. Several cybersecurity learning materials, including module-based, have been developed across United States [2]. Traditional learning modules that present a large amount of content in a linear format may lead to content skipping, lower engagement and poor learning [11, 14]. The original Security Injections @Towson cybersecurity modules, though effective, followed a traditional linear format [15]. One of the issues that was observed by instructors was that students tended to skip content and proceed directly to lab exercises. To address this issue, in our previous study [13], we proposed to incorporate e-learning design principles of segmentation and interactivity and hypothesized – 1) segmentation of content will reduce content skipping, 2) reduced content skipping will increase learning, 3) interactivity will increase engagement and 4) an increase in engagement will increase learning [11, 12, 14]. The results indicated that the enhanced modules significantly increased the student engagement than the traditional modules [13].

SIGCSE '16, March 02–05, 2016, Memphis, TN, USA
© 2016 ACM. ISBN 978-1-4503-3685-7/16/03$15.00
DOI: http://dx.doi.org/10.1145/2839509.2844609

In this paper, we extend our study to examine differences in student learning on concept retention and ability to apply secure coding knowledge between enhanced - (2.0) and traditional (1.0) modules using Security Injections @Towson cybersecurity modules. First, we describe the theoretical framework for segmentation and interactivity; second, we discuss learning differences between interactive and non-interactive systems; third, we describe the enhanced (2.0) modules; and fourth, we discuss the methodology and results of a quasi-experiment across two sections of CS0 that compares students' secure coding awareness, general software security awareness, and students' ability to apply the knowledge they gained by identifying security vulnerabilities (integer overflow, input validation and buffer overflow) in three separate code segments. Previous research has shown that while retention of knowledge is not affected by the interactive nature of the system [5, 6, 9, 17], students perform significantly better on application of knowledge using interactive systems [5, 17]. Based on this we examine the following research questions:

RQ1: Will the enhanced (2.0) and traditional (1.0) modules show the same level of learning for questions related to retention of the material?

RQ2: Will enhanced (2.0) modules show significantly higher learning for identifying security vulnerabilities in code segments (application of knowledge) than traditional (1.0) modules?

2. LITERATURE REVIEW
In this section, we briefly discuss – 1) the theoretical framework for incorporating segmentation and interactivity in traditional linear modules, 2) review previous literature that compares learning in interactive and non-interactive systems.

2.1 Segmentation and Interactivity
Traditional linear web-based modules that present large amount of text on a single page may lead to content skipping and skimming, and lower engagement [11, 14]. Research suggests that skipping in a large web-based hypertext pages could be due to – 1) flexibility to click any of the hyperlinks that links within or

outside the page to gain knowledge and thus loosing context of the original text [3, 11], 2) reading strategy adopted by readers which determines what to read and what to skim [7, 8]. This may lead readers to lose important information, and result in shallow reading, less concentration and attention towards content [4, 8]. Overall, skipping of the content may lead to poor learning [14]. In addition, lower engagement in the traditional linear modules could be due to the less interactive activities, which may also result in less learning [12].

To overcome the issues in traditional linear modules, we proposed to incorporate e-learning design principles of segmentation and interactivity [13]. Segmentation implies breaking large content into smaller chunks and present one chunk at a time on a single screen. Segmentation makes processing, retention and recalling of information easier [1, 10]. In addition, to increase engagement with the module interface, research suggests increasing user-system interactivity [12]. Interactivity in e-learning is the "responsiveness to the learner's actions during learning." We proposed to increase interactivity with dialoguing and controlling. The process of a learner answering a question and receiving feedback on his/her input is referred to as dialoguing. Dialoguing improves learning [16], as learners can relate feedback to the current content. Controlling implies that the learner can determine the pace of the presentation. Controlling helps students learn better by allowing them to process information at their own pace.

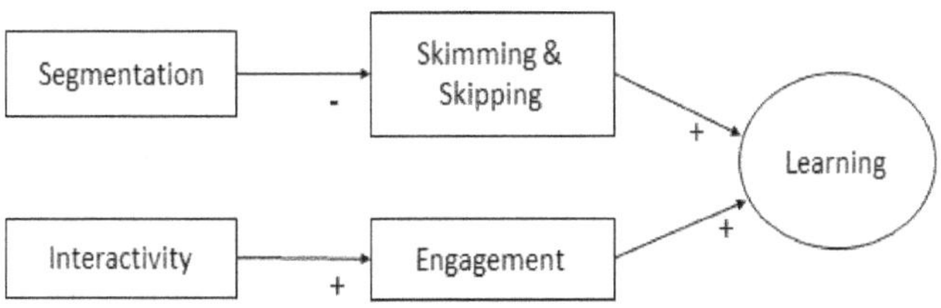

Figure 1. Literature suggests that segmentation and interactivity in modules may increase learning

Overall, segmentation breaks large content into smaller chunks and presents them one at a time, which may result in less reading and less skipping of content. Less skipping of content may lead to increased learning. Interactivity (dialoging and controlling) on segmented chunks leads to engagement and enforces learning (see Figure.1).

2.2 Interactive versus Non-interactive Learning Systems

Hattie [6] state that any kind of educational intervention has a positive effect on student achievement. Then, do interactive and non-interactive systems with similar content will have the same learning effect? A similar study conducted by Evans and Gibbons [5] showed that both interactive and non-interactive systems with same content have same learning when assessment questions examine retention or recall. But, interactive systems performed significantly better than non-interactive system when assessment involved problem-solving.

Another study by Wang et. al. [17] examined impact of animation interactivity on novices' learning of introductory statistics. The study comprised of three groups – 1) static group – provided with static material, 2) simple animation group – animation with input manipulation, and 3) practice group – animation with practice and feedback. The results showed animation interactivity significantly improved students' understanding and lower level applying.

A study by Mayer et. al. [9] found that students performed significantly better on problem solving transfer test due to the interactive feedback provided by the system compared to non-interactive version.

Therefore, based on the literature on interactive and non-interactive systems with same content, we can conclude that interactive systems may not show significant improvement on recall or retention assessments but could show significant improvement on problem-solving assessments where students have to apply their understanding of the knowledge.

3. INCORPORATING SEGMENTATION AND INTERACTIVITY

The original (1.0) modules were developed on the cognitive learning principles of Bloom's taxonomy and adopt a uniform structure. Each module begins with a background section to describe the problem with examples, followed by a "Code Responsibly" section (includes methods to avoid security issues), a laboratory assignment with a security checklist, and discussion questions. The module structure is designed to help students to first *understand* the problem through the background and code responsibly sections, *remember* it through the laboratory assignments, *evaluate* it through checklists, and *apply* the concepts learned through discussion questions. This ensures the implementation of active learning in Security Injection modules.

Using the theoretical framework discussed in section 2.1, we enhanced the 1.0 modules. We implemented segmentation by breaking up the module content per section (background, code responsibly, laboratory assignment, discussion questions) and present each section, one at a time, on the screen. In this fashion, the reader views a small amount of content at a time. We implemented dialoguing using formative assessment with a set of checkpoint questions, both multiple choice and constructed response that include feedback. We selected multiple choice questions, as they can be used to infuse both surface and deep learning, whereas constructed response are known for infusing deep learning among learners. We implement immediate elaborate feedback with the correct answers after students attempt the questions.

Each section in a module is auto-graded using built-in functionality for text and multiple-choice questions. In the background and code responsibly sections, students are required to go through the content and answer a set of checkpoint questions. Each question provides immediate feedback on submit (see Figure 2). The student cannot advance to the next section until all questions are answered correctly. In the Laboratory Assignment and Discussion Question, students answer text-based, multiple-choice questions, and identify vulnerabilities based on a security checklist (see Figure 3). These are also auto-graded.

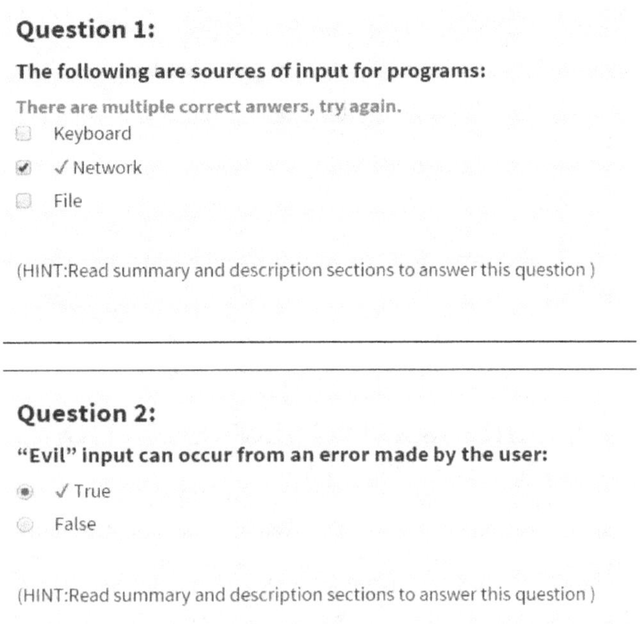

Figure 2. Instant-feedback

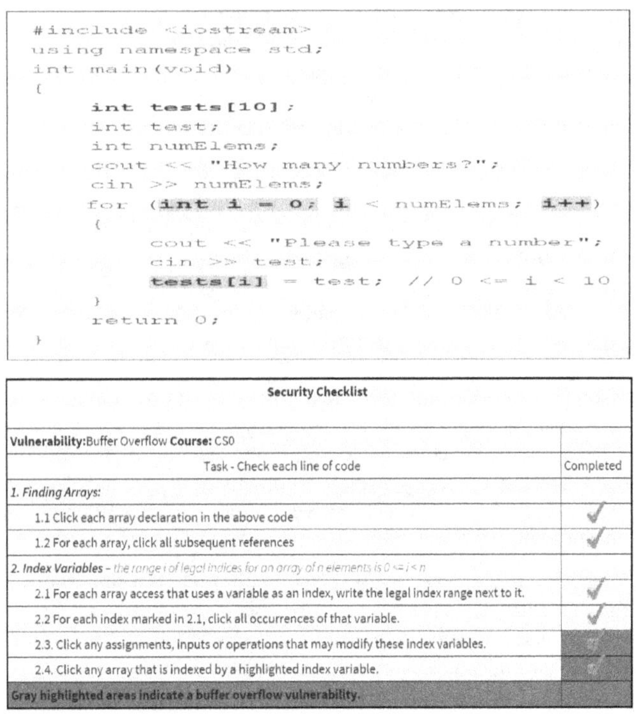

Figure 3. Auto-graded security checklist

4. PILOT STUDY

4.1 Methodology

A quasi-experiment was conducted in two sections of a CS0 course (programming logic using C++) in spring 2015 at a large public university, using a pretest – posttest control group design. Both the sections were taught by the same instructor. One of the sections used the 1.0 version (control group) and the other used 2.0 (treatment group). The study was conducted during the laboratory sessions, which were at different times for each section (11-11:50 AM (control), 12-12:50 PM (treatment)). Three modules - integer error, input validation and buffer overflow - were introduced, in that order, with approximately four weeks between the interventions. Both groups were administered a pre-survey at the beginning and a post-survey at the end of the semester. A total of 53 (26 in the treatment group and 27 in the control group) students participated in the study. See Table 1. for complete student demographics. As can be seen, both groups were comparable.

Table 1. Student Demographics

	Control		Treatment	
	n	%	n	%
Gender				
Male	16	61.5	17	63.0
Female	10	38.5	10	37.0
Age				
20 years or younger	18	69.2	17	63.0
21-25 years	7	26.9	9	33.0
26-30 years	1	3.8	1	3.7
Ethnicity				
White	15	57.7	17	63.0
Black	4	15.4	6	22.2
Hispanic	1	3.8	2	7.4
Asian	5	19.2	2	7.4
Other	1	3.8	0	0.0
Student Standing				
Freshman	7	26.9	10	37.0
Sophomore	10	38.5	7	25.7
Junior	8	30.8	8	29.6
Senior	1	3.8	2	7.4
Major				
Computer Science	14	57.7	11	40.7
Non-Computer Science	12	42.3	16	59.3

4.1.1 Instruments

The survey instruments (both pre-survey and post-survey) used in this study were derived from previous security injections studies [15]. Both the pre-survey and post-survey include multiple choice questions related to student demographics, secure coding awareness and general software security awareness. Secure coding awareness include 5 questions - 2 integer overflow, 2 input validation and 1 buffer overflow; and, 4 questions for general software security awareness. In addition, 3 code segments were added to the post-survey to assess students' ability to apply secure coding knowledge. The code segments were developed by the senior instructors teaching CS0. The students were to identify the potential security vulnerability in the code segments. See Table 3 for security awareness questions and Table 2 for code segments (ability to apply).

Table 2. Code Segments (Ability to apply)

Identify the potential security issues in the following code segment: (Check all that apply)

Code Segment 1
`float price;`
`float totalPrice;`
`cout << "Enter Price" << endl;`
`cin >> price;`
`totalPrice = price + price*.06;`
 	
Code Segment 2
`//assume i < INT_MAX and j < INT_MAX`
`int calc (int i, int j) )`
`{`
`int result = i * j;`
`return result;`
`}`
 	
Code Segment 3
`//assume n < INT_MAX`
`void input(float temperatures[], int n)`
`{`
`for (int i = 0; i < n; i = i + 1)`
`{`
`cout << temperatures[i] << endl;`
`}`
`}`

Table 3. Survey questions (Awareness)

Secure-coding Awareness
Integer Overflow occurs ..
Integer Overflow is caused by ..
Invalid input can come from ..
Which of the following should your well designed program do before processing user input?
Which programming mistake is one of the major vulnerabilities in today applications?
Software-security Awareness
What are the possible consequences of insufficient computer security?
Security Software and Software Security are the same:
When developing secure systems, where does security fit in?
Software security vulnerabilities are the result of software bugs and flaws:
Your code is completely secure if:

Based on the pre-survey and the post-survey scores, we proposed the following set of hypotheses to compare Security Injections 1.0 (control group) and Security Injections 2.0 (treatment group) on the following dependent variables: secure coding awareness, general software security awareness, and ability to apply secure coding knowledge.

H1: The post-survey scores for secure coding awareness (measuring retention) will be significantly higher than the pre-survey scores for secure coding awareness in both control and treatment groups.
Rationale – As discussed in section 2.2, any kind of educational intervention has a positive effect on student achievement. In addition, interactive and non- interactive systems with same content will have the same learning on recall or retention assessments.

H2: The post-survey scores for secure coding awareness (measuring retention) for the treatment and the control group will not be significantly different.
Rationale – As discussed in section 2.2, both interactive and non-interactive systems with same content will have the same learning on recall or retention assessments. Secure coding awareness assesses retention of integer overflow, input validation and buffer overflow knowledge.

H3: The post-survey scores for general software security awareness (measuring retention) will be significantly higher than the pre-survey scores for general software security awareness in both control and treatment group.
Rationale – Same as H1

H4: The post-survey scores for general software security awareness (measuring retention) for the treatment and the control group will not be significantly different.
Rationale – As discussed in section 2.2, both interactive and non-interactive systems with the same content will have same learning for recall or retention assessments. General software security awareness assesses retention of general software security knowledge.

H5: The scores for ability to apply secure coding knowledge in the treatment group will be significantly higher than the control group.

Rationale- As discussed in section 2.2, interactive systems will show significantly higher learning on problem-solving (ability to apply) assessments than the non-interactive systems with same content. The students apply their secure coding knowledge to identify security vulnerability in the code segments.

H1 - **H4** addresses RQ1 and, **H5** addresses RQ2

4.2 Results

A total of 53 (26 in the control and 27 in the treatment) students, including 33 males and 20 females, participated in the study and completed the post-survey. 21 (11 males and 10 females) students in the control group and 24 (14 males and 10 females) in the treatment completed both pre and post survey.

The scores for each category in the survey were calculated based on the correct answers out of - 5 for secure coding awareness (integer overflow (2), input validation (2), buffer overflow (1)), 5 for general software security awareness and 9 for ability to apply secure coding knowledge on code segments (integer overflow (3), input validation (3) and, buffer overflow (3)).

H1 and H3 were tested using Wilcoxson-Signed-Ranks non-parametric test to compare the mean rank of scores between pre-survey and post-survey scores. We picked the non-parametric test because – 1) the Kolmogorov-Smirnov and Shapiro-Wilk test showed that the scores are not normally distributed ($p < 0.05$), and 2) the groups (pre and post) were related samples. H2, H4 and H5 were tested using Mann-Whitney non-parametric test to compare the mean rank of the scores in two groups (control and treatment). We picked non-parametric test because – 1) n for the group were not equal, 2) Kolmogorov-Smirnov and Shapiro-Wilk test showed that the scores are not normally distributed ($p < 0.05$), and 3) the two groups were independent samples.

Comparison for pre-survey and post-survey scores for secure coding awareness in treatment and control group.
In the treatment group, the average score for pre-survey (1.5) and the average score for post-survey (4.0) were found to be statistically significant at the 95% level ($p < 0.05$, $z = -4.02$). In the control group, the average score for pre-survey (1.76) and the average score for post-survey (3.81) were found to be statistically significant at the 95% level ($p < 0.05$, $z = -3.78$). This implies that the use of both Security Injections 1.0 and 2.0 significantly increased the secure coding awareness (measuring retention) among the students in the post-survey compared to the pre-survey. In addition, this verifies that any kind of educational intervention has a positive effect on student achievement, and, interactive and non- interactive systems with same content will have the same learning on recall or retention assessments. This leads us to accept H1 (see Figure 4).

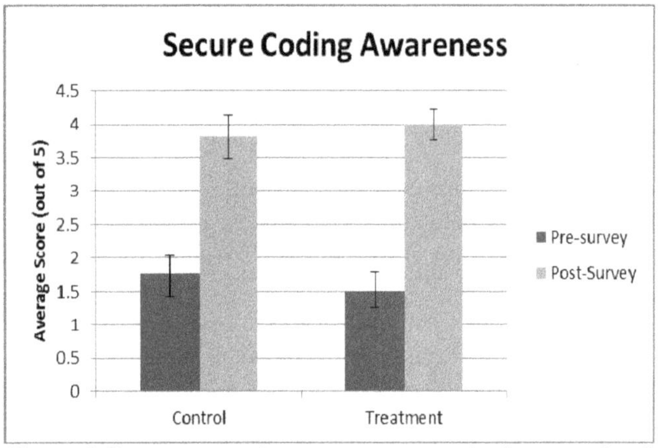

Figure 4. Pre-survey and post-survey scores in the control and treatment groups for security-coding awareness

Comparison of post-survey scores for secure coding awareness in treatment and control groups
In the post-survey, no significant differences were found between the average scores for the treatment group (4.0) and the control group (3.81). This verifies that interactive and non-interactive systems with same content have same learning on recall or retention assessments. This leads us to accept H2 (see Figure 4).

Comparison of pre-survey and post-survey scores for general software security awareness in treatment and control group.
In the treatment group, the average score for the post-survey (4.21) was significantly higher at the 95% level ($p < 0.05$, $z = -3.056$) than the average score for the pre-survey (3.25). In the control group, the average score for the post-survey (4.14) was also significantly higher at the 95% level ($p < 0.05$, $z = -2.20$) than the average score for the pre-survey (3.29). This implies that the use of both Security Injections 1.0 and 2.0 significantly increased the general software security awareness among the students in the post-survey compared to the pre-survey. In addition, this verifies that any kind of educational intervention has a positive effect on student achievement, and, interactive and non-interactive systems with same content will have the same learning on recall or retention assessments. This leads us to accept H3 (see Figure 5).

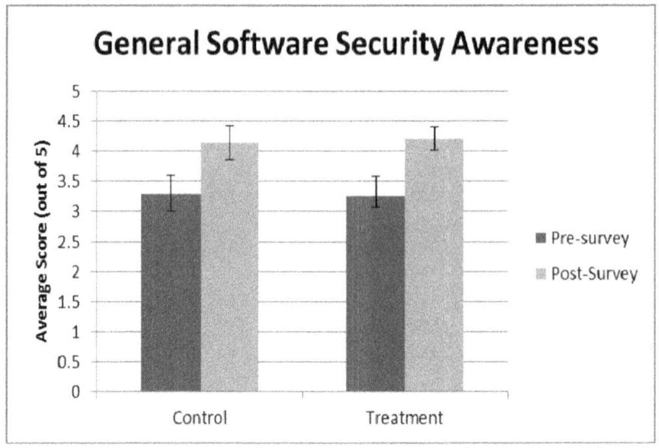

Figure 5. Pre-survey and post-survey scores in the control and treatment groups for general software security awareness

Comparison of post-survey scores for general software security awareness in treatment and control groups
In the post-survey, no statistically significant differences were found between the average scores for the treatment group (4.21) and the control group (4.14). This verifies that interactive and non-interactive systems with same content have same learning on recall or retention assessments. This leads us to accept H4. (see Figure 5)

Comparison of post-survey scores for ability to apply secure coding knowledge in treatment and control groups
In the post-survey, the average score for the treatment group (5.59) was found significantly higher at 90% level ($p = 0.07 < 0.10$, $z = -1.80$) than the average score for the control group (4.27). The students who use enhanced (2.0) modules performed significantly better in identifying security vulnerabilities in three separate code segments than the students who use 1.0. This verifies interactive systems show significantly higher learning on problem-solving (ability to apply) assessments than the non-interactive systems with same content. This leads us to accept H5 (see Figure 6).

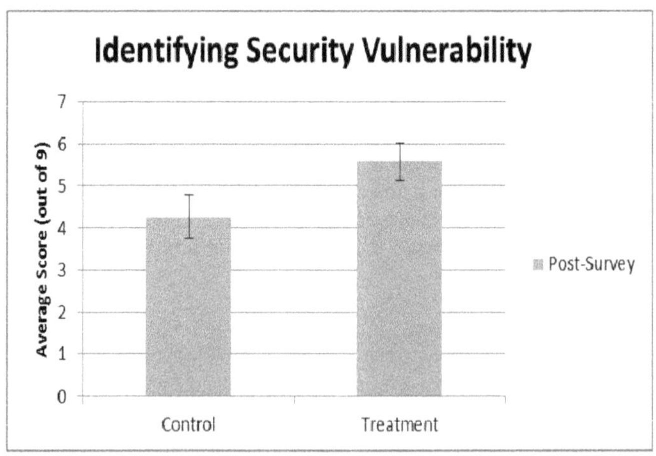

Figure 6. Post-survey scores in the control and treatment groups for ability to identify security vulnerability in three code segments

5. CONCLUSION

In this paper, we extended our previous study to compare student learning between traditional (1.0) and enhanced (2.0) secure coding modules. Traditional modules follow linear format with non-interactive content whereas enhanced module content were segmented and interactive using checkpoint questions, and auto-graded security checklist with instant-feedback. We conducted a quasi-experiment to compare students' secure coding awareness, general software security awareness and students' ability to identify security vulnerabilities (integer overflow, input validation and buffer overflow) in three separate code segments.

Results showed significant improvement in secure coding and general software security awareness (measuring retention) in both 1.0 and 2.0. Additionally, students using segmented and interactive modules performed significantly better in identifying security vulnerabilities in code segments than traditional modules.

In future, we plan to explore the results based on demographics. In addition, we plan to examine another component of our research framework - whether segmentation leads to less skipping and skimming. We plan a usability study in fall 2015 and spring 2016 to record students reading pattern in both 1.0 and 2.0 versions using eye-tracking software.

6. ACKNOWLEDGMENTS

This project is partially supported by NSF DUE-1241738 and 0817267.

7. REFERENCES

[1] Clark, R.C. and Mayer, R.E. 2011. *e-Learning and the Science of Instruction: Proven Guidelines for Consumers and Designers of Multimedia Learning (Google eBook)*. John Wiley & Sons.

[2] Curriculum Resources - Teaching Tools for Educators: *http://niccs.us-cert.gov/education/curriculum-resources*.

[3] DeStefano, D. and LeFevre, J.-A. 2007. Cognitive load in hypertext reading: A review. *Computers in Human Behavior*. 23, 3 (May 2007), 1616–1641.

[4] Duggan, G.B. and Payne, S.J. 2011. Skim Reading by Satisficing: Evidence from Eye Tracking. *CHI 2011* (Vancouver, BC, Cananda, 2011).

[5] Evans, C. and Gibbons, N.J. 2007. The interactivity effect in multimedia learning. *Computers & Education*. 49, 4 (Dec. 2007), 1147–1160.

[6] Hattie, J. 2013. *Visible Learning: A Synthesis of Over 800 Meta-Analyses Relating to Achievement*. Routledge.

[7] Lawless, K.A. et al. 2003. Knowledge, Interest, Recall and Navigation: A Look at Hypertext Processing. *Journal of Literacy Research*. 35, (Jan. 2003), 911–934.

[8] Liu, Z. 2005. Reading behavior in the digital environment: Changes in reading behavior over the past ten years. *Journal of Documentation*. 61, 6 (2005), 700–712.

[9] Mayer, R.E. et al. Multimedia Learning in an Interactive Self-Explaining Environment: What Works in the Design of Agent-Based Microworlds?

[10] Moreno, R. and Mayer, R. 2007. Interactive Multimodal Learning Environments. *Educational Psychology Review*. 19, 3 (Jun. 2007), 309–326.

[11] Protopsaltis, A. and Bouk, V. 2005. Towards a Hypertext Reading/Comprehension Model. *SIGDOC'05* (2005).

[12] Quinn, C.N. 2005. *Engaging Learning: Designing e-Learning Simulation Games*. John Wiley & Sons.

[13] Raina, S. et al. 2015. Security Injections 2.0: Increasing Engagement and Faculty Adoption using Enhanced Secure Coding Modules for Lower-level Programming Courses. *9th World Conference on Information Security Education* (Hamburg, Germany, May 2015).

[14] Rudestam, K.E. and Schoenholtz-Read, J. 2010. *Handbook of Online Learning*. SAGE Publications.

[15] Taylor, B. and Kaza, S. 2011. Security injections: modules to help students remember, understand, and apply secure coding techniques. *Proceedings of the 16th annual joint conference on Innovation and technology in computer science education - ITiCSE '11* (New York, New York, USA, 2011), 3.

[16] Thalheimer, W. 2008. *Providing Learners with Feedback—Part 1: Research-based recommendations for training, education, and e-learning*.

[17] Wang, P.-Y. et al. 2011. The impact of animation interactivity on novices' learning of introductory statistics. *Computers & Education*. 56, 1 (Jan. 2011), 300–311.

Combining Big Data and Thick Data Analyses for Understanding Youth Learning Trajectories in a Summer Coding Camp

Deborah A. Fields
Instructional Technology & Learning Sciences, Utah State University
2830 Old Main Hill
Logan, UT, USA
deborah.fields@usu.edu

Lisa Quirke
Faculty of Information
University of Toronto
140 St. George Street
Toronto, ON, Canada
lisa.quirke@mail.utoronto.ca

Janell Amely, Jason Maughan
Instructional Technology & Learning Sciences, Utah State University
2830 Old Main Hill
Logan, UT, USA
jamely@aggiemail.usu.edu;
jsnmaughan@gmail.com

ABSTRACT
In this paper we explore how to assess novice youths' learning of programming in an open-ended, project-based learning environment. Our goal is to combine analysis of frequent, automated snapshots of programming (e.g., "big" data) within the "thick" social context of kids' learning for deeper insights into their programming trajectories. This paper focuses on the first stage of this endeavor: the development of exploratory quantitative measures of youths' learning of computer science concepts. Analyses focus on kids' learning in a series of three Scratch Camps where 64 campers aged 10-13 used Scratch 2.0 to make a series of creative projects over 30 hours in five days. In the discussion we consider the highlights of the insights—and blind spots—of each data source with regard to youths' learning.

Categories and Subject Descriptors
K.3.2 [Computers and Education]: Computer and Information Science Education – Computer science education

Keywords
computer science education; big data; Scratch; assessment; novice programmers; constructionism

1. INTRODUCTION
One difficulty educators have faced is how to evaluate novice learners' programming or, more broadly, computational thinking [1], especially when projects are open-ended without a single "correct" solution [2]. Since Seymour Papert introduced the idea of constructionism [3], many computer science educators have sought to engage kids in learning through interest-driven, project-based programming. This playful approach to learning-by-designing can be motivating for learners and also useful for developing complex thinking and debugging skills [4]. Learners do not work on identical problems that have a single, favored solution, instead creating original projects, which allow for diverse programming styles such as "structured" or "bricolage" [5]. Being open and free-form, this approach can result in a wide variety of programs that can differ wildly. This creates challenges for educators and researchers who are tasked with measuring and assessing novice learning, especially at larger scales of analysis.

SIGCSE '16, March 02-05, 2016, Memphis, TN, USA
© 2016 ACM. ISBN 978-1-4503-3685-7/16/03…$15.00
DOI: http://dx.doi.org/10.1145/2839509.2844631

Researchers have taken two primary approaches to tackling this problem of assessing novice learning in open-ended programming environments. One approach involves qualitative analysis to gain a rich view of novice learning. Some have approached qualitative analysis by looking at multiple saves of programs at regular intervals in order to see incremental progress [e.g., 6]. Others conduct in-depth think-aloud interviews to capture novices' thinking in the process of solving a targeted problem or bug [e.g., 7]. These provide excellent ways to explore novices' thinking and creating practices, but can only be used across small sets of youth because of the labor involved. An alternative approach includes mining programs with quantitative methods, to capture the learning of large numbers of novice youth. This is particularly useful to study a wide variety of programmers online, for instance on the Scratch website, in order to identify types of programmers [e.g., 8] or types of trajectories [e.g., 9]. However, one of the challenges of this approach is evaluating the quality of programs. Often, the measures of programming are relatively basic, involving simple frequency counts of commands (or blocks) in a program as representative of learners' understanding of a concept.

How then can researchers and educators assess novices' learning of programming in rich ways that also allow for analysis across a wide number of youth? In this paper we explore the potential of an approach that begins with mixed methods, using both qualitative and quantitative means to understand novices' learning. The overarching goal is to develop an approach that applies quantitative measures to the analysis of programming education in a way that moves beyond frequency counts. This approach could be used to assess novices' understanding and use of several programming concepts across a variety of open-ended projects. This paper focuses on the first stage of this endeavor: the development of exploratory quantitative measures of youths' learning of computer science concepts. Our goal is to combine analysis of frequent, automated snapshots of programming (e.g., "big" data) within the "thick" social context of kids' learning, With this information we consider how many times, or over what time period, does it take for kids to pick up a presented concept?

2. BACKGROUND
In recent years researchers have taken several approaches to using "big" data to understanding novice programmers' learning paths (for a review see [10]). A few overarching approaches stand out. First, some use big data to find patterns across hundreds or thousands of participants in free choice environments, participants

who might have vastly different projects. To do this, researchers have sorted individual code blocks into categories of programming concepts. For instance, in Maloney, Peppler, Kafai, Resnick and Rusk's [11] two-year study of a Computer Clubhouse, frequency counts of programming blocks in Scratch stood as measurements for how many youth used various concepts such as loops, variables, conditionals, or Booleans. Building on this general approach, others have used frequency counts of blocks to assess the quality of users' programs on the Scratch site, adding on analytical methods like latent class analyses or K means clustering to document classes of programmers [8] or types of trajectories of programming [9]. The Scrape tool developed by Wolz, Taylor and Hallberg [12], allows any researcher or educator to manipulate this frequency count technique by dragging individual or multiple programs into the tool and categorizing the blocks by type (motion, looks, variables, control, etc.). These studies have carved new territory in making sense of what massive numbers of people are doing on websites such as Scratch, or in large free-choice informal programs. The basic presence of specific blocks in programs, however, does not necessarily denote sophisticated understanding of the related programming concepts. Work by Brennan and Resnick [13] highlights this point, noting the potential for major differences between learners' programs and their actual understanding of how their own code worked.

Alternatively, research may focus on process-based data to gain insights into novices' pathways of learning. In some cases these studies focus on comparing novices' programs to an ideal solution, noting divergences from a "correct" form of solving a problem. For instance, Repenning et al [14] used game code developed by hundreds of kids to assess its similarity to set solutions. Similarly, Blikstein et al [2] captured novices' thinking in the process of solving a targeted checkerboard problem, documenting "sink states" and different pathways to the most efficient solutions. Yet these approaches do not facilitate assessment in open-ended, constructionist-type programming. A few have begun to develop ways to document different pathways to learning in open-ended programming environments. For instance, Werner, McDowell and Denner [15] laid the groundwork to use logfile data from Alice to study "high level actions" as a precursor to analyzing types of problem solving strategies. Similarly, Berland et al [16] used learning analytics to identify students' progress through different programming strategies (tinkering, exploring, and refinement) across two hours of a playful introduction to programming in iPro. While these studies lay the foundation for using big data to study processes of programming over time, we take an approach that uses process-based "big data", or large, automatically-generated quantitative datasets, in conjunction with in-depth qualitative analyses [17] in order to gain insights into the richness of constructionist-based learning that might be hidden by just one method [10, 18].

Our approach is uniquely mixed in methodology: we developed quantitative measures of programming concepts, after deep qualitative analysis of changes in students' projects over time, applying them across more than 600 project saves per student (roughly every 2 minutes). We subsequently evaluated the utility of this approach by comparing these analyses with knowledge from rich case studies of students' changes to projects over time. This allowed us to take an exploratory approach to studying learning in an open-ended programming environment with the long-term goal of using the quantitative measures across a variety of open-ended programming environments. Below we briefly describe the Scratch programming environment, outline our study's methods, and share our findings regarding measures tracking youths' learning of three concepts: initialization, events, and parallelism.

3. CONTEXT: SCRATCH SUMMER CAMP

This study examined ways of developing measures to assess the learning of middle-school youth learning to program using Scratch. Scratch 2.0 (Scratch.mit.edu) is an online, blocks-based visual programming environment, designed to engage children in creating and sharing projects, while learning the foundations of computer programming [19]. Developed by researchers at MIT and launched in 2007, Scratch is one of the most-used programming environments for novices. Scratch and other block-based programming tools (e.g., Alice, Greenfoot, App Inventor) are designed to remove the frustration of syntax errors, while allowing users to develop their knowledge of coding concepts.

The questions examined in this paper emerge from a research study on kids' learning trajectories with Scratch. The project includes data collected at a set of three, week-long "Scratch Camps" held at an intermountain university in partnership with the local 4-H club during the summer of 2014. The camp took place over 30 hours in five days, with approximately 25 hours devoted to programming. Campers aged 10-13 used Scratch 2.0 to make a series of creative projects. They were mentored and taught by one professor and three graduate students, with several high school 4-H club members also offering assistance. We created a series of open-ended, genre-specific project challenges with constraints intended to impel students to learn particular techniques. Campers were given feedback on their projects throughout the camp, and encouraged to use the programming strategies (e.g., initialization, debugging) taught in the daily lessons. We included a variety of projects: Scribble time & Name project (Day 1), Story project (Day 2), Music Video project (Day 3), Video Game project (Day 4), and Free Choice project (Day 5). Scratch Camp concluded with a special gallery walk where interested parents could browse campers' completed work and attend the graduation ceremony.

4. METHODS

4.1 Data Collection

Sixty-four campers (34 girls and 31 boys) consented to participate in the study across three separate Scratch Camps (out of 67 campers total). Campers ranged in age from 10-13. Some had prior experience with Scratch, but most had only played with it for a couple of hours or minutes prior to the camps.

Several types of data were collected. Since the campers were programming on the online version of Scratch 2.0, we were able to use JSON files of student program code collected online with the help of the Scratch Team at MIT, with snapshots of campers' code every time they shifted from editing costumes, backgrounds, or sound, back into coding, and by default every two minutes. This provided 32,465 code snapshots in text-based format, the big data component of our project. Although JSON files contain all of the text of a program, this file cannot be run in Scratch to see if a project works or what it actually looks like while running.

To complement these data, we manually collected projects for 32 campers: five campers from the first camp, five from the second camp, and all campers (22 consenting) from the final camp. These projects were collected roughly once every 75 minutes, at the end of each day's four programming sessions. One researcher also wrote field notes at each camp, focusing on five campers per camp, providing more context on campers' goals, struggles, interactions, and learning moments.

4.2 Analysis

Analysis took shape through three major iterations, and although we include it in the methods section here, the process of analysis is also a significant part of our findings. First, we conducted a qualitative analysis of the 32 campers for whom we had Scratch project saves, creating case studies of these youths' learning. These case studies documented each addition and edit to campers' Scratch projects at the end of each 75 minute session. Every change in projects between sessions was noted and analyzed. Where available, we considered the observational notes to provide context on campers' intentions and any help they received.

Second, with backend data in hand, we began a process of cleaning and reducing it. We created a Scratch JSON parser that captures and quantifies details of each code snapshot (a text-based version of a Scratch project). Then we developed a second layer of analyses that quantified changes in Scratch programs over time. These became a series of quantitative measures in several categories of programming concepts, inspired by Brennan and Resnick's [13] outline, but including other concepts we found pertinent to evaluating youths' learning in the Scratch Camps: Booleans, conditionals, event driven & parallelism, initialization, loops, randomization, and sensing (for more details on all of the measures see: www.workingexamples.org/example/show/727). Each measure was tested and developed iteratively, carefully comparing the quantitative measures with the 32 case studies. Further investigation of campers' Scratch programs was performed as needed to see what each measure revealed about youths' learning and what they missed or glossed over. Finally, we sought to glean which measures were the most useful. Initially we began with a list of 46 measures, and after analyzing them we narrowed the list down to 26 measures to use in further analysis.

Although we included frequency counts of blocks (as done previously in other studies [8, 11, 12]), our quantitative measures of programming concepts include several features that take a next step in terms of evaluating whether youth are using a concept correctly. Each measure we developed only included blocks attached to event hats in Scratch. In Scratch, students can drag blocks into the programming space somewhat randomly—this allows for them to test blocks individually without connecting them to an "event hat" that integrates the test blocks into the program. After some analysis we decided not to include these "floating blocks" in our study of kids' learning in Scratch.

To keep with a constructionist mindset and authentic practices on the Scratch website, we purposefully allowed, and sometimes encouraged, remixing. Remixing is an authentic practice on the Scratch site and can be used effectively to introduce youth to new programming strategies. However, it introduced a large number of blocks that the campers did not program themselves, creating a dilemma in analyzing youths' learning, as we wanted to see only what campers added, not what they had remixed from others' work. After some trial and error, we developed two sets of visualizations. One included all changes, but marked changes that were likely part of a remix (e.g., adding 30 blocks between saves within 2 minutes—see Figure 1). The other included only the changes between saves that involved fewer than 30 blocks, removing any instance where added blocks within 2 minutes numbered over 30. This visualization showed cumulative changes over time (see Figure 2).

5. FINDINGS

In this section we outline three selected measures we developed: initialization, events, and parallelism. These were chosen because they were present in campers' programs early on and throughout the camp allowing us to see how well our methodological approach showed learning over time. We also highlight examples that illustrate how these reveal campers' learning over time.

5.1 Sets of Measures

We begin by briefly describing initialization, events, and parallelism in Scratch, as these concepts may differ in their representation in other languages. Our measures represent the common ways in which our novice campers approached these programming concepts, but do not include every presentation of these concepts in the Scratch environment.

Initialization means setting a starting state or point for all of the actions and actors in a program. In Scratch, *initialization* requires setting the start state of a character (i.e., "sprite"), and needs to be clearly defined by programming. Initialization states in Scratch include: position, direction, costume, graphic effect, layer, showing or hidden, and size. For instance, if a sprite moves, then its starting position needs to be set; if a sprite is hidden, then it needs to be set to *"show"* at a particular time. Although Brennan and Resnick [13] do not include initialization in their outline of programming concepts, we found it to be a challenge for youth to learn and implement in the camps and elsewhere [6].

We initially developed 15 measures for initialization, narrowing them down to 10 that showed the most promise in differentiating campers' learning. The ten measures focus on initialization in position, graphic effects, show/hide, scene (e.g., background), and user-created variables. Five of these measures focus on "missing initialization" where a need for initialization is present. For instance, for the "Missing Position Initialization" measure, if a sprite moves in the program, this measure will increase if there is no programming to set the sprite's starting position. Alternatively, for "Sprites with Position Initialization," we counted the number of sprites that move and whose positions were initialized *before* that movement occurred in the program. By setting the position initialization before the movement of the sprite, the campers' program would return to the correct start position that they had envisioned, instead of restarting in the wrong location.

Event and parallel programming involve coordinating processes and events within a program such that they can be executed sequentially or in parallel without bringing the program to a standstill. In Scratch, coordinating multiple sprites' actions involves learning different forms of synchronization and event driven programming [11]. In particular, events can be triggered with the commands *"broadcast"* and *"when I receive"*. Our measure for events, "Broadcasts Received" includes only broadcasts that have a matching receive (i.e., "broadcast scene 2" and "when I receive scene 2") with some code blocks following the receive. Related to the broadcast event, parallelism in Scratch can be accomplished in two prominent ways (at least for novices): by using multiple event hats such as *"when green flag clicked,* or multiple *"when I receive"* hats to trigger new actions to start at the same time, within or across sprites. We trace these by counting the number of "broadcasts with multiple receives" and "sprites with multiple green flags."

Below we illustrate how these measures, compared with contextual data, provide insight into the learning of one camper, Ginger, a 12 year-old girl with very limited Scratch experience (i.e., "four days") before the camp began.

5.2 Initialization

In our analysis of campers' trajectories, we found that campers learned initialization early but continued to refine their learning throughout the projects they created. As projects became more complex throughout the camp and as new forms of initialization were needed (for instance variables in the Game Project), youth struggled to identify all of the missing initializations in their projects. In other words, although nearly all youth began to introduce initialization into their projects on Day 1, they missed incidences on subsequent days. This became visible in a pattern of spikes and plateaus in the five measures of missing initialization shown in our code snapshots visualization.

Ginger's data on missing initialization (see Figure 1) shows how many initializations are missing at each automated save of her projects. A close look at the spikes and plateaus reveals an interesting insight into her debugging patterns (indicative of

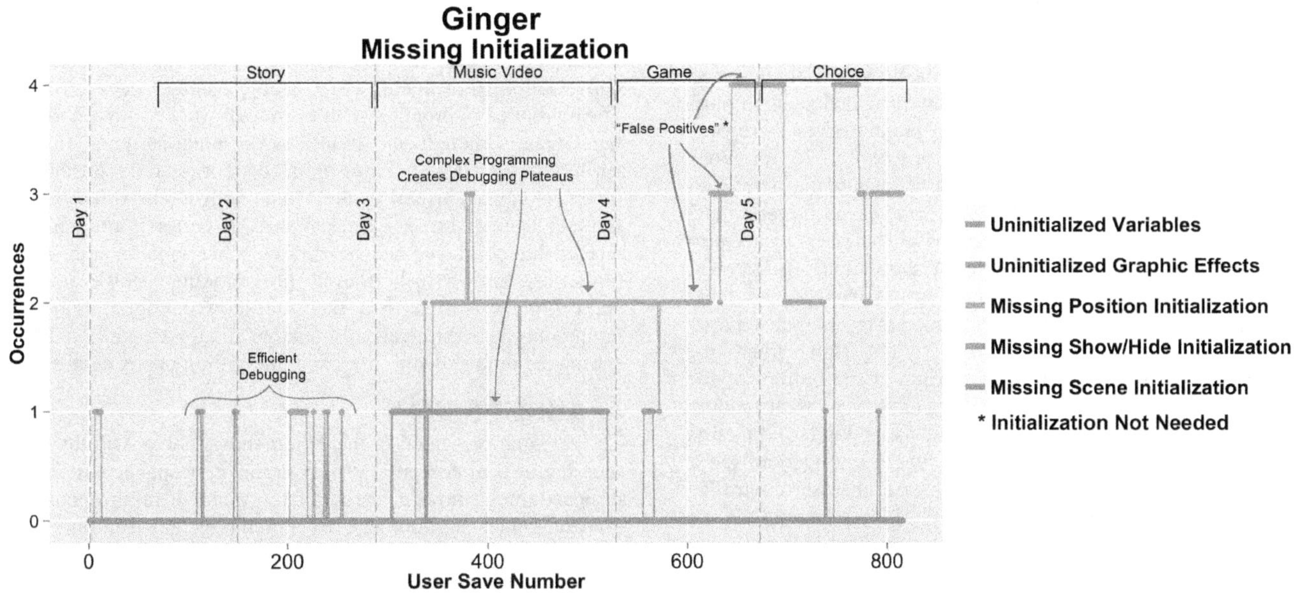

Figure 1. Missing initialization in Ginger's projects across saves. Code snapshot view (includes remixes).

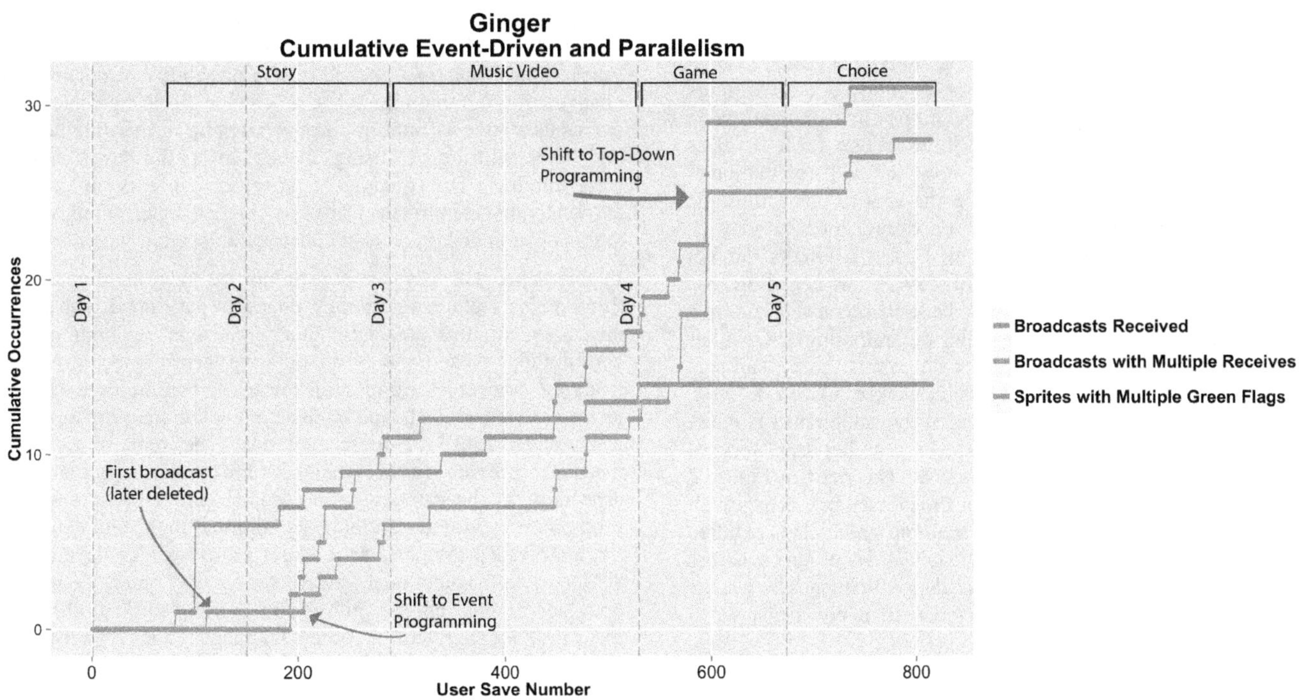

Figure 2. Event-driven and parallel programming in Ginger's projects. Cumulative view (no remixes).

patterns we witnessed in other youth). The spikes represent an introduction of an occurrence of a missing initialization that is almost immediately fixed. For instance, the green spikes on Days 1 and 2 show how Ginger introduced movement into some sprites, and quickly adjusted to set their initial positions. In contrast, the plateaus show where missing initializations remain in her projects across many saves. Plateaus occur for scene initialization (in pink) in Day 3, and both spikes and plateaus for position initialization (in green) begin on Day 3 and continue into Days 4 and 5. These later projects quickly became larger and more complex. For many, it became more difficult to detect and fix missing initializations.

This insight into quick or slow adjustments—the debugging of missing initializations—is a special view provided only through the automated saves. Since our manual project saves were only captured once per session (approximately every 75 minutes), hand-coding could not reveal the quick debugging strategies campers used. Careful study of Ginger's hand-saved projects (.sb2 files), however, reveals some limitations of the current measures for initialization. The chart (Figure 1) shows that Ginger was missing position initialization for four sprites by the end of her game day. However, looking at her game saves, we see a larger perspective. Ginger chose to remix a "catch" game where the player had to move a basket left and right at the bottom of the screen in order to catch an object falling from the sky at random points. The basket did not require the same kind of position initialization needed in other projects, where setting both the x and y coordinates was necessary. In this case, the user-controlled basket only moved left and right. Its initial position had no influence on the game, so it created a false positive in the missing position initialization measure. In a sense, Ginger's project was more sophisticated with its use of user-controlled position than these particular measures could detect.

5.3 Events and Parallelism

While initialization patterns described above were similar among most campers, events and parallel programming revealed several differences. Early on in our analysis we noticed that campers struggled with the concepts of events and parallelism, even when introduced to the concept multiple times in the front of class through targeted instructions and "show and tell" of campers' projects. Some campers picked up on the idea of using multiple green flags in a single sprite early on during the first day as Ginger did, visible in the blue line in Figure 2. Others did not introduce multiple green flags until day 3, or began to use multiple receives with a single broadcast before using multiple green flags (a different use of parallel programming). A similar range of trajectories was apparent with events: some campers began early and used it often, others picked up on it later. Although Ginger was one of the early adopters of event programming in the camps, a closer look at her trajectory of learning shows some interesting moments. The chart in Figure 2 illustrates Ginger's cumulative use of broadcasts, broadcasts with multiple receives, and sprites with multiple green flags. Unlike Figure 1, this chart illustrates only *cumulative* progress across saves with incremental changes (less than 30 changes in blocks between saves), a strategy we adopted with many measures to remove the noise created by remixes.

Shifts in Ginger's programming style become apparent when we compare our qualitative findings with the automated saves. As seen in Figure 2, Ginger first introduced a broadcast late in Day 1, about the time the concept was first presented to the camp. However, she did not add any more broadcasts until part-way through Day 2 (see the flat red line). Qualitative analysis of her projects revealed that she did not use any broadcasts on Day 1: any code that involved broadcasts introduced during instructions was quickly deleted. The stairway-like progression on Day 2 (Figure 2) illustrates Ginger's introduction of new broadcasts and broadcasts with multiple receives. Qualitative analysis revealed a distinct shift in Ginger's programming. Earlier, she programmed very linearly, for instance having Sprite 1 *"say"* something then *"wait 2 seconds"* while Sprite 2 would *"wait 2 seconds"* and then *"say"* something in return. Midway through the second session on Day 2, Ginger began using the broadcast command to coordinate sprites' actions as events, quickly introducing three working broadcasts, most with multiple receives, to orchestrate conversation, movement, and costume changes between sprites. She continued to program with events across the Music Video and the Game, although she found using multiple green flags per sprite (connected with *"wait until"* code triggered with the built-in timer) equally useful in the Music Video. The spike mid-way through Day 4 shows a second shift in Ginger's programming. Before this point, she had steadily built her code on an as-needed basis, also known as bottom-up programming. However, at this spike Ginger shifted to a more top-down programming style, laying out the eight levels of the game all at once with broadcasts, setting the requisite variables, and then filling in any details.

6. DISCUSSION

The research presented in this paper shows one possibility for the measurement of computer programming concepts across time and projects among novice learners using Scratch in an open-ended, constructionist environment. By combining big data and deeply contextual qualitative analyses, our study highlights the insights—and blind spots—of each data source with regard to youths' learning of initialization, events and parallelism. Going beyond frequency counts as representative of learning, allowed us to document the iterative ways that users approached particular concepts (e.g., the way debugging initialization occurred frequently or slowly in simple versus more complex projects). Further, these analyses opened up the possibility of documenting changes in programming styles, as Ginger did in first integrating events as a style of bottom-up programming in multiple projects, and later shifting to using events in a top-down style of programming. The tracing of specific concepts in learners' extremely diverse projects brings us closer to determining ways to assess open-ended projects in constructionist environments.

In this paper due to space constraints we have highlighted only three of the eight programming concepts developed with sets of measures for this analysis. Our goal was to highlight the contributions these types of quantitative measures could make to studying novices' learning trajectories across multiple types of interest-driven projects and to use qualitative analyses to test the interpretive utility of these methods. The remaining sets of measures provide further insights into youths' programming, especially as the campers went deeper into more sophisticated programming with nested loops, conditional logic, and data usage (variables) [20]. As part of the larger project we are developing a "FUN! Tool" (functional understanding navigator), a flexible open source data engine (github.com/ActiveLearningLab) where measures for Scratch or other languages could be input to automatically analyze findings across individual programmers. The tool is meant to help researchers write and share automated data extraction and manipulation techniques with Scratch and other types of programming language.

The multi-method structure of this research strengthened our understanding of learners' developing conceptualizations of programming in ways that a single method could not. Measures of programming concepts applied to frequent saves provided a glimpse at small moves that youth made in their programs not captured in manual saves each session. This provided a clear look into learning that would not normally be captured in qualitative methods. Yet qualitative methods helped not only in creating the original measures, but also in pointing out blind spots in the quantitative measures and in interpreting what they showed. This "thick" approach to data analysis builds robustness into the analysis of "big" data. At the same time, our approach was also limited in certain ways. The lack of pre- and post-tests of youths' performance, for example, and the potential for false positives in some measures, either due to more complex uses of a concept or as a result of remixed content, could be addressed in future research. Our research also took place in a particular time and space with specific pedagogical goals; other approaches could result in different learning and require alternative interpretations of measures or new measures entirely.

Using big data to analyze microgenetic processes of novices' programming [10] has great potential for use across education and research, to assess learners' understanding of key concepts in situ, and potentially reach out to youth to improve learning. This study has particular implications for understanding and mapping the diversity of learning in constructionist environments, formal or informal, which can support novices' interest and creativity while challenging them to deepen their skills and thinking.

7. ACKNOWLEDGMENTS

This material is based upon work supported by a collaborative grant from the National Science Foundation (NSF#1319938) to the first author. The views expressed are those of the authors and do not necessarily represent the views of the National Science Foundation, Utah State University, or the University of Toronto. Special thanks to Sayamindu Dasgupta and Mitchel Resnick of the MIT Media Lab for help collecting data. Nicole Forsgren, Xavier Velasquez, Tori Horton, and Katarina Pantic assisted in analysis. Suzanne Fluty and Whitney King aided in leading the Scratch Camp along with 4-H volunteers.

8. REFERENCES

[1] Wing, J. 2006. Computational Thinking. *Commun. ACM.* 49, 3 (2006), 33-35.

[2] Blikstein, P., Worsley, M., Piech, C., Sahami, M., Cooper, S., and Koller, D. 2014. Programming pluralism: Using learning analytics to detect patterns in the learning of computer programming. *J. Learn. Sci.* 23, 4 (2014), 561-599.

[3] Papert, S. 1980. *Mindstorms: Children, computers, and powerful ideas.* Basic Books, New York.

[4] Kafai, Y. B. 2006. Playing and making games for learning: Instructionist and constructionist perspectives for game studies. *Games and Culture*, 1, 1 (2006), 36-40.

[5] Turkle, S. and Papert, S. 1991. Epistemological pluralism: Styles and voices within the computer culture. *Signs* (1990), 128–57.

[6] Fields, D., Vasudevan, V. and Kafai, Y. B. 2015. The programmers' collective: fostering participatory culture by making music videos in a high school Scratch coding workshop. *Interact. Learn. Envir*, (2015), 1-21.

[7] Murphy, L., Lewandowski, G., McCauley, R., Simon, B., Thomas, L., and Zander, C. 2008. Debugging: The good, the bad, and the quirky – a qualitative analysis of novices' strategies. *ACM SIGCSE Bulletin*, 40: 163–67.

[8] Fields, D. A., Giang, M., and Kafai, Y. 2014. Programming in the wild: Trends in youth computational participation in the online Scratch community. In *Proceedings of the 9th Workshop in Primary and Secondary Computing Education*, (2014). ACM, New York, NY, 2–11.

[9] Yang, S., Domeniconi, C., Revelle, M., Sweeney, M., Gelman, B. U., Beckley, C., and Johri, A. 2015. Uncovering Trajectories of Informal Learning in Large Online Communities of Creators. Paper presented at *L@S 2015 / Learning* (Vancouver, BC, Canada, March 14-18, 2015).

[10] Berland, M., Baker, R. S., and Blikstein, P. 2014. Educational data mining and learning analytics: Applications to constructionist research. *Technology, Knowledge and Learning, 19*, 1-2 (2014), 205-220.

[11] Maloney, J. H., Peppler, K., Kafai, Y., Resnick, M. and Rusk, N. 2008. Programming by choice: Urban youth learning programming with Scratch. *ACM SIGCSE Bulletin*, 40, 1, (2008), 367–371.

[12] Wolz, U., Taylor, B., and Hallberg, C. 2010. Scrape: A Tool for Visualizing the Code of Scratch Programs. Presented at the *ACM SIGCSE* (Dallas, Texas, 2010).

[13] Brennan, K. and Resnick, M. 2012. New frameworks for studying and assessing the development of computational thinking. Paper presented at annual *American Educational Research Association* meeting (Vancouver, BC, Canada, April 2012).

[14] Repenning, A, Webb, D. C., Koh, K. H., Nickerson, H., Miller, S. B., Brand, C., Her Many Horses, I., Basawapatna, A., Gluck, F., Grover, R., Gutierrez, K. and Repenning, N. 2015. Scalable game design: A strategy to bring systemic computer science education to schools through game design and simulation creation. *ACM Trans. Comput. Educ.* 15, 2, Article 11 (April 2015), 31 pages. DOI: http://dx.doi.org/10.1145/2700517

[15] Werner, L., McDowell, C., and Denner, J. 2013. A first step in learning analytics: pre-processing low-level Alice logging data of middle school students. *Journal of Educational Data Mining*, 5, 2, (2013), 11-37.

[16] Berland, M., Martin, T., Benton, T., Petrick Smith, C. and Davis, D. 2013. Using Learning Analytics to Understand the Learning Pathways of Novice Programmers. *J. Learn. Sci.* 22, 4 (2013), 564–99.

[17] Kafai. Y. B. and Fields, D. A. 2013. *Connected Play: Tweens in a Virtual World.* Cambridge, MA: MIT Press.

[18] Grover, S., Pea, R. and Cooper, S. 2015. Designing for deeper learning in a blended computer science course for middle school students. *Comp. Sci. Ed.* 25, 2 (2015), 199-237.

[19] Resnick, M., Maloney, J., Hernández, A. M., Rusk, N., Eastmond, E., Brennan, K., Millner, A. D., Rosenbaum, E., Silver, J., Silverman, B., and Kafai, Y. B. 2009. Scratch: Programming for everyone. *Commun. ACM.* 52, 11 (2009), 60–67.

[20] Velasquez, X. and Fields, D. A. 2015. When good video games promote good programming: Scratch Camp FTW. *Proceedings of the 11th annual Games+Learning+Society Conference.* (Madison, WI, July 2015)

Training Teachers to Integrate Computational Thinking into K-12 Teaching

Rania Hodhod
Columbus State University
4225 University Avenue
Columbus, GA, 31907
706-507-8181
hodhod_rania@columbusstate.edu

Shamim Khan
Columbus State University
4225 University Avenue
Columbus, GA, 31907
706-507-8184
khan_shamim@columbusstate.edu

Yesem Kurt-Peker
Columbus State University
4225 University Avenue
Columbus, GA, 31907
706-507-8187
peker_yesem@columbusstate.edu

Lydia Ray
Columbus State University
4225 University Avenue
Columbus, GA, 31907
706-507-8174
ray_lydia@columbusstate.edu

CSS

• **Social and Professional topics** →Professional Topics

Keywords

Computer Science education; Computational Thinking; K-12 teacher training.

1. SUMMARY

Computational thinking (CT), which encompasses strategies for problem analysis and solution design, is highly applicable in all STEM disciplines, including computer science, for learning concepts as well as solving problems. Yet, the exposure of K-12 students to CT in many schools is practically non-existent. For students to acquire this important skill, teachers require in-depth knowledge of the problem solving strategies that define CT, and strategies for integrating CT into their lesson plans. The proposed special session will be both a tutorial on CT and an interactive session for sharing the experience and results from a CT workshop held at Columbus State University for middle and high school STEM subject teachers. This workshop, offered as a part of the ACT4STEM (Applying Computational Thinking for STEM Disciplines) project, took place in the summer of 2015. It brought together teachers from the metropolitan Columbus area in Georgia with priority given to teachers from high-need schools (as determined by the GA Department of Education [1]). The workshop introduced the participants to CT concepts and demonstrated how CT strategies of pattern recognition, generalization, problem decomposition and algorithmic thinking can be used to improve student learning of STEM concepts. The proposed special session will present sample CT modules developed for the ACT4STEM workshop in the form of a tutorial and projects and lesson plans designed by participants during the workshop. It will include interactive, hands-on activities and discussions in addition to results from the teachers' actual experiences on applying these lesson plans in their classes. This special session will benefit K12 teachers of STEM subjects interested in improving their students' comprehension of discipline related concepts and their application. Moreover, computer science faculty interested in helping K-12 teachers by organizing training sessions will gain valuable insights from the first-hand accounts of the presenters of their own experience with such an effort.

SIGCSE'16, March 2–5, 2016, Memphis, TN, USA.
ACM ISBN: 978-1-4503-3685-7/16/03.
DOI: http://dx.doi.org/10.1145/2839509.2844675

2. OBJECTIVE

Computational Thinking (CT) nowadays is being recognized as the essential 21st century skill that can enable anyone, regardless of their discipline, to take advantage of the enormous power of computing and information technology [2]. The use of computational thinking in K-12 STEM teaching and learning can supplement the current nationwide effort to promote STEM education to produce a smart workforce ready for today's knowledge economy. The proposed special session is motivated by the need to increase awareness of the role CT can play in improving teaching and learning. It attempts to address the current lack of knowledge among K-12 teachers about CT and how they can use it in their classrooms for better learning outcomes.

The specific objectives of the proposed session will be to:

- introduce computational thinking as a skill essential for learning problem analysis and solution design;
- demonstrate how the components of CT can be applied to improve student learning at middle and high school levels; and,
- disseminate the experience gained from a teachers' workshop on CT aimed at achieving the above two objectives.

The session will be organized in the form of a tutorial with hands-on activities for both K-12 teachers and computer science faculty interested in teaching problem solving. School teachers will benefit from learning about CT and how it can be integrated into their lesson plans – not just for teaching computer science, but for all other STEM disciplines as well. The tutorial will offer opportunities for interaction through hands on activities and group discussions. Attendee school teachers will be asked for feedback on the lesson plans shared with them and suggestions will be invited for utilizing CT in lesson plans in their own fields. With the mix of audience consisting of both CS faculty and K-12 teachers from all over the country as well as overseas, this would be an important opportunity for everyone to gauge opinion on the suitability and perceived benefits of infusing CT into the classroom.

3. OUTLINE

- Introduction (5 min.) – Topics of the session: How the idea came about, funding, format of the workshop, recruitment of participating teachers, and results from the workshop. (Presenter: Yesem Kurt-Peker)
- Demo of modules - Part 1 (15 min.) – Demonstration of sample modules on decomposition and algorithmic thinking (Presenter: Lydia Ray)
- Demo of modules - Part 2 (15 min.) – Demonstration of sample modules on pattern recognition and generalization (Presenter: Shamim Khan)
- Small group activity (10 min.) - Audience will work in small groups on one of the hands on activities from the ACT4STEM workshop, namely, Towers of Hanoi. In particular, they will explore how Towers of Hanoi can be used to explain various aspects of CT. Material will be provided by the presenters.
- Sample projects and lesson plans (10 min.) – Presentation of a sample of the final products from the ACT4STEM workshop including projects and lesson plans developed by participants (Presenter: Rania Hodhod)
- Brainstorming by audience (10 min.) – Audience will be invited to comment on presented lesson plans, suggest improvements and come up with additional ideas for integrating CT into various STEM disciplines. The brainstorming of ideas and sharing of experience will be continued after the workshop in an online forum set up especially for this special session.
- Final remarks, sharing of experiences, Q&A (10 min.)

4. EXPECTATIONS

The proposed special session is designed for K-12 teachers of STEM subjects and computer science educators. K-12 teachers should gain an appreciation of the usefulness of computational thinking in student learning and be able to take home ideas on how to integrate CT into their STEM lesson plans. Computer science educators and faculty interested in conducting their own teacher training workshops similar to the one described in this session can benefit from our experience and results, in addition to using the modules we present in the session.

Through audience participation in group discussions and resulting exchange of ideas, we expect to receive valuable feedback on the efficacy of our own efforts and improvements for the future.

5. SUITABILITY FOR A SPECIAL SESSION

The proposed session concerns computational thinking and ideas and activities related to its use in improving teaching and learning. It consists of a tutorial on computational thinking and its possible applications in teaching. The tutorial is formatted as an interactive session including hands-on activity that aims to provide the audience with an experience similar to that of teachers who attended a recent CT workshop organized by the authors. Much of the session will be devoted to Q&A and group discussions to help the audience share experiences and enable direct feedback from K-12 teachers and CS educators. Given its content and format, special session appears to be the most suitable forum for this effort.

6. REFERENCES

[1] Teacher Quality Grant, http://teacherquality.coe.uga.edu/wp-content/uploads/2014/08/High-Need-LEAs-2015-2016.pdf

[2] J. Wing, "Computational thinking and thinking about computing," in *Philosophical Transactions Series A, Mathematical, Physical, and Engineering Sciences*, vol. *366*(1881), 2008, pp. 3717–3725.

Demystifying Computing with Magic, part III

Daniel D. Garcia
University of California, Berkeley
777 Soda Hall
Berkeley, CA 94720-1776
+1 510-517-4041
ddgarcia@cs.berkeley.edu

David Ginat
Tel-Aviv University
Sharet Building; Ramat Aviv
Tel-Aviv, Israel
+972 3-640-8151
ginat@post.tau.ac.il

SUMMARY

One man's "magic" is another man's engineering.
– Robert A. Heinlein

Some beginning students have fuzzy mental models of how the computer works, or worse, sincerely believe that the computer works unpredictably, "by magic" [2]. We seek to demystify computing for these students using analogy, by showing them something that even magic itself isn't really mystical, it is just computation. This is a continuation of our standing-room only SIGCSE 2012 and SIGCSE 2013 special sessions [4, 7].

Magic is one of the most colorful examples of "unplugged" (i.e., without-computer, active learning) activities. It adds a unique facet in that it holds a *hidden secret* that the audience can be challenged to unfold. Once solved, students are often enthusiastic to perform the magic in front of others. In this session, we will share a variety of new magic tricks whose answer is grounded in computer science: modulo arithmetic, human-computer interfaces, algorithms, binary encoding, invariants, etc. For each trick, we will have an interactive discussion of its underlying computing fundamentals, and tips for successful showmanship. Audience participation will be critical, for helping us perform the magic, discussing the solution, and contributing other magic tricks.

Keywords
Computational thinking, magic, card tricks, unplugged activities

1. OBJECTIVE

Magic is a lot of fun. Yet, it can be more than fun – it can be used to illustrate and teach scientific and mathematical notions, including those of computer science [1, 3, 5, 6]. Our objective in this special session is to show how magic can motivate particular computational ideas, by challenging the students to figure out the idea *behind* the trick, then elaborating on these notions and relating them to the material. Students may also be encouraged to practice the magic, and even perform in front of the class. In our primary experience, students (majors and non-majors) are enthusiastic to take part.

SIGCSE '16, March 02-05, 2016, Memphis, TN, USA
ACM 978-1-4503-3685-7/16/03.
http://dx.doi.org/10.1145/2839509.2844679

2. OUTLINE

The session will be an interactive seminar. It will include motivation, illustrations, audience participation, and conclusion. The general structure will be as follows.

- **Rationale.** The relevance of magic, as a special unplugged activity, will be described and presented. An emphasis will be put on magic's baffling impact on one hand, and the enthusiastic characteristic to discover the secret – on the other.
- **Aspects and illustrations.** We will display several magic tricks. The presentations will sometimes involve volunteers from the audience. The secrets behind the presented magic will be related to a variety of CS principles. Suggestions will be offered on how one may elaborate on the underlying CS notions following a magic presentation.
- **Audience participation.** The audience will participate in three ways. Volunteers may take part in some presentations. The audience will be challenged to discover the secrets. Audience participants may offer further, enriching, unplugged ideas for magic, including those presented, and will be invited to perform them, if they wish.
- **Suggestions for educators.** Pedagogical lessons of ways to embed magic will be displayed and discussed. We will share our experience with students, who like to perform (sometimes more than once) in front of their friends. This yields active assimilation of studied principles.

Here are but a few of the magic tricks we will perform. We will have more ready to present, if time permits.

2.1 The Game You Can Always Win (or Lose)

The magician asks a spectator to choose three (any odd number, actually) numbers from the set {4, 5, 6, 7}, duplicate numbers are allowed. The magician and the spectator now play a game in which on each turn, the players can take as much as they'd like from any of the numbers (at least one, but the numbers can't get lower than zero), with the goal to make all numbers 0. The magician moves first, but the spectator even gets to choose which number the magician must change. The flourish is that at almost any stage in the game, the magician can ask the spectator whether the spectator would like to win or lose, and it always happens.

Youngest group: Grade School (~7 years old)
Lesson: Algorithms, invariants, binary representation.

2.2 The One Where The Tone Gives It Away

The blindfolded magician hands a deck of cards to a spectator who deals them into six piles. The spectator chooses a card from the middle of any pile, puts it on top of any pile, and puts the piles back together in whatever order they like. One by one they turn a card over, saying the card's name out load. When they get to the card they picked, claiming the tone of their voice gave it away, the magician stops the proceeding and announces the chosen card [6].

Youngest group: Grade School (~7 years old)
Lesson: Algorithms, pre-computation.

2.3 The Force All To Choose The Same Card

The magician claims to be able to make the entire audience choose the same card. The magician shows five cards (using PowerPoint) and asks the audience to look at one card *only*, and memorize it, raising their hand when they were done. After some time, the screen is blanked for a while and only four cards remain (with no gaps, so the card that was removed isn't obvious). The audience is told to raise their hand if their card is missing, and everyone raises their hands [6].

Youngest group: Grade School (~7 years old)
Lesson: Algorithms, computer vision, design principles.

2.4 The Two Wrongs Make a Right Trick

The magician shows the audience the contents of the shuffled deck and puts the Ace of Spades on top. He then asks the audience for a relatively small number, taps the deck and claims the Ace of Spades just jumped that number deep in the deck. The magician deals out that number of cards and turns the next card over to an "aha", but it isn't the card. The magician places the cards back on top and asks for a slightly larger number, tries again, but again it isn't the card (he puts the cards back on top again to reset). Flustered, the magician says "well, maybe it was the difference between those numbers", taps the deck one final time, deals out the difference number of cards, and the next card is the Ace of Spades! [6]

Youngest group: Grade School (~7 years old)
Lesson: Algorithms, Stack data structure.

2.5 The Unfolded Swap

A participant from the audience comes to the table on the stage, and orders a fork, a knife, and a spoon, in a line. The magician looks at the table, and turns around. The participant swaps pairs of pieces 10 times (any two pieces at any swap), and calls out loud the swapped pieces. Then, the participant performs another swap without telling what she swapped. Then, again, she swaps pairs of pieces for 10 times, and calls out loud every swap. All the swaps are made quickly, so that the magician will not be able to memorize the line of pieces throughout the game. After all the swaps end, the magician turns around, and tells the swap in the middle of the process, which was not called out loud.

Youngest group: Grade School (~7 years old)
Lesson: Sufficient partial information, the notion of complement.

2.6 Zig-Zag Colors

A participant from the audience orders 8 cards - 4 red ones and 4 black ones in a line, in any order she wishes (only the colors matter). The magician looks at the line, and makes zero, one, or two swaps of card locations. (But, no more than two swaps.) Then, the magician collects the cards, in the order they are on the table, into a pack, so that they are all face down. Then, he operates the following process: he turns the top card and puts it on the table face up; picks the next and puts it in the bottom of the pile (face down); then, turns the top card, and puts it to the right of the one put earlier; picks the next and puts it in the bottom of the pile; and so on - until all the cards are put face up on the table in a line. They all form a line of interchanging colors. How did he do that?

Youngest group: High School
Lesson: Pre-processing, ordering, recursion, complement.

3. EXPECTATIONS

The intended audience for the special session is the broad community of computing educators, especially those who enjoy magic but have not used it in their classes or during occasions of computing outreach. They will hear (and hopefully, contribute) magic tricks, the computing fundamentals behind them, showmanship tips, and how to direct a follow-up discussion.

4. SUITABILITY

Our presentation is interactive and engaging, with active audience participation. Anyone in attendance who knows magic tricks based on computing fundamentals is encouraged to contribute. A special session affords and encourages this unique format with the most audience involvement.

5. REFERENCES

[1] CS Unplugged. *Error Detection.* Retrieved January 1, 2012 from `http://csunplugged.org/error-detection`

[2] Clancy, M. Misconceptions and attitudes that interfere with learning to program. In *Computer Science Education Research*, s. Fincher and M. Petre, eds. Taylor and Francis Group, London, 2004, 85–100.

[3] Curzon, P. and McOwan, P. W. 2008. Engaging with computer science through magic shows. In *Proceedings of the 13th Annual Conference on innovation and Technology in Computer Science Education* (Madrid, Spain, June 30 - July 02, 2008). ITiCSE '08. ACM, New York, NY, 179-183. `http://doi.acm.org/10.1145/1384271.1384320`

[4] Garcia, D. and Ginat, D. 2012. DeMystifying computing with magic. In *Proceedings of the 43rd ACM technical symposium on Computer Science Education* (SIGCSE '12). ACM, New York, NY, USA, 83-84. `http://doi.acm.org/10.1145/2157136.2157164`

[5] Ginat, D., Garcia, D., and Gasarch, W. 2002. Aha! an illuminating perspective. In *Proceedings of the 33rd SIGCSE Technical Symposium on Computer Science Education* (Cincinnati, Kentucky, February 27 - March 03, 2002). SIGCSE '02. ACM, New York, NY, 1-2. `http://doi.acm.org/10.1145/563340.563342`

[6] CS4FN. 2012. *The Magic of Computer Science.* Retrieved September 6, 2012 from `http://www.cs4fn.org/magic/`

[7] Daniel D. Garcia and David Ginat. 2013. Demystifying computing with magic, continued. In*Proceeding of the 44th ACM technical symposium on Computer science education* (SIGCSE '13). ACM, New York, NY, USA, 207-208. DOI=10.1145/2445196.2445262 http://doi.acm.org/10.1145/2445196.2445262

Panel: Engage in Reasoning with Tools

Gregory Kulczycki
Virginia Tech
Computer Science Department
Falls Church, VA 22043
1-703-538-8370
gregwk@vt.edu

Murali Sitaraman
Clemson University
School of Computing
Clemson, SC 29634
1-864-656-3444
murali@clemson.edu

Nigamanth Sridhar
Cleveland State University
Electrical Engineering & Computer Science
Cleveland, OH 44115
1-216-687-5341
n.sridhar1@csuohio.edu

Bruce W. Weide (Moderator)
The Ohio State University
Computer Science and Engineering
Columbus, OH 43210
1-614-292-5813
weide.1@osu.edu

SUMMARY

A central goal of computer science education is to teach students how to reason about the correctness of the code they write. Typically, students use a trial and error process and check that their logic "works" by running it on test inputs. Typically, instructors encourage them towards logical reasoning through manual tracing of the code. Rarely reasoning tools are used in the process, at least partly because few instructors are familiar with them and fewer have the time to investigate and experiment. The purpose of this panel is to introduce the attendees to a variety of reasoning tools the presenters have used in their classrooms. In some cases, the tools have been used in only one or two classes of a course to illustrate specific points. In other cases, entire projects have been done using the tools. The courses range from the introductory sequence and discrete structures to software engineering and graduate-level courses. The tools are freely available on the web and attendees will be encouraged to experiment with the reasoning tools on their own laptops to solve simple reasoning problems.

CCS Concepts

Software and its engineering—software creation and management—software verification and validation—formal verification
Software and its engineering—software notations and tools

Keywords

Automated tools, components, correctness proofs, programming by contract, specification, verification, and web tools.

Helping students learn how to reason that the code they write behaves as expected is a central goal of computer science education. This panel will demonstrate the use of tools in achieving this objective. There are several advantages of using reasoning tools, some of which are freely available through online interfaces.

SIGCSE '16, March 02-05, 2016, Memphis, TN, USA
ACM 978-1-4503-3685-7/16/03.
http://dx.doi.org/10.1145/2839509.2844657

Inside the classroom, reasoning tools make it possible to demonstrate quickly certain non-trivial aspects of reasoning, helping students ask and answer a variety of "what if" questions that would be difficult or impossible to do in the absence of tools. Outside the classroom, students can learn to check the logic of their code at their own pace at a place and time of their convenience, and understand the ideas using a number of exercises. The overall goal is to help educators see the potential benefits of using reasoning tools in the context of introductory computer science, discrete structures, programming languages, and software engineering courses. The panelists will use a variety of examples to illustrate the ideas, ranging from simple straight-line code with subtle errors to code involving objects, loops, and recursion.

The panel will be organized as follows. Each panelist will present a reasoning concept or two in about 8 minutes, and then follow it up with 8 minutes of "what if" questions from either from the panelist to the attendees or from the attendees to the panelist (asked in the style of students learning the topic). The goal is to motivate and demonstrate how one might approach teaching rigorous reasoning about software correctness. Some of the exercises might involve the attendees trying the tools on their own laptops. The goal is to introduce a range of concepts that can be effectively taught with tools using various course contexts so that the attendees to incorporate the ideas in their own courses.

1. BRUCE W. WEIDE

Reasoning tools have been used in the second semester of the *introductory sequence* in "software" for CS majors at Ohio State. The software sequence (designed by Weide and others) consists of two semester-long courses, the second of which is taken concurrently with the first of two courses in "foundations." The first software course introduces some logic concepts and notations so that students can read and understand (but not write) formal specifications, and the second one also instructs them in how to write some specifications. In the first foundations course, students become familiar with some proof techniques. This means that by late in the second software course, all these concepts can be tied together nicely via examples using automated verification tools that students should increasingly be expected to encounter in the workplace shortly after graduating.

Bruce W. Weide is Professor Emeritus of Computer Science and Engineering at The Ohio State University. He and his colleagues in the RSRG at Ohio State have studied and taught design, specification, and verification of component-based software for over 30 years. Weide and his colleague, Tim Long, were awarded the IEEE Computer Society Computer Science and Engineering Undergraduate Teaching Award in 2000 for their innovations.

2. MURALI SITARAMAN

In three required courses for CS majors at Clemson, Sitaraman and other instructors have used a web-based reasoning tool supported by the RESOLVE verifying compiler, details of which may be found in [1, 2]. For connecting proofs with establishing software correctness in a *discrete structures* course, he has used a variety of exercises, including ones that involve inductive proofs and recursive code, for example [3]. Clemson has also used the reasoning tool more extensively in a software engineering course for underscoring the role of formal contracts in establishing the correctness of component-based code in a modular fashion. Details of these reasoning projects may be found in [4].

Murali Sitaraman is Professor of Computer Science in the School of Computing at Clemson University. His research spans a spectrum of foundational, practical, and educational topics in software engineering. He has been involved in developing tools and techniques for enhancing mathematical reasoning in undergraduate CS education for nearly 25 years. He has offered tutorials and workshops to educators on teaching mathematical reasoning at SIGCSE several times, including four of the last five years.

3. NIGAMANTH SRIDHAR

At Cleveland State University, Nigamanth Sridhar uses reasoning tools in two different courses. In the senior-level course on *software engineering*, students learn the role of formal assertions in the context of specifying software interfaces. Students work in the Visual Studio environment and use Code Contracts [5] to check correctness of code with respect to specifications. The other is a graduate-level formal methods course that is focused exclusively on tools for model checking and software verification, such as Dafny, NuSMV, RESOLVE, and SPIN.

Nigamanth Sridhar is an Associate Professor in Electrical Engineering and Computer Science at Cleveland State University. He co-directs the graduate program in Software Engineering. For the last several years, Sridhar has worked on the application of formal methods in reasoning about correctness of software for small embedded systems. Sridhar, along with his colleagues, is currently running an NSF-funded project to train high school teachers across Ohio to teach the new CS Principles course.

4. GREG KULCZYCKI

Greg Kulczycki has introduced reasoning tools in *Object-Oriented Software Specification and Construction*, a course in the core curriculum for software engineering graduate students at George Mason University. The course uses [6] to present a specification-centric view of Java development and introduces assertions such as requires clauses, ensures clauses, abstraction functions, and representation invariants. The course uses Dafny [7], an object-oriented language that can be annotated with assertions. Using the Dafny compiler, code exercises can be written, compiled, and verified online, though Dafny is limited in its support of abstraction and modularity.

Gregory Kulczycki served as an assistant professor at Virginia Tech and has worked as a formal methods researcher at Battelle Memorial Institute. He is currently a professor of practice at Virginia Tech and is coordinating the Computer Science Department's involvement in the online Masters of Information Technology program. He has been introducing students to formal reasoning in one form or another for over a decade and has significant experience with instruction via online courses.

5. PANEL AUDIENCE

The panel should be of interest to all educators who might be interested in infusing tools to engage students and help them see the benefits of logical reasoning. Since examples from a variety of courses using different tools will be presented, the audience will be quickly introduced to a number of ideas with which they can experiment in their classrooms. SIGCSE routinely has a sizeable contingent of attendees interested in mathematical thinking [8], code analysis, and tools. The panel will be of interest to a good number of these attendees who are looking for ways to help students learn to reason better about their code. The panel will involve significant tool demonstration and active audience participation to make it engaging.

6. ACKNOWLEDGMENTS

We acknowledge NSF grants CCF-1161916, CCF-1162331, DUE-0942542, and DUE-1022941. Any opinions, findings, conclusions, or recommendations expressed here are those of the authors and do not necessarily reflect the views of the National Science Foundation.

7. REFERENCES

[1] Sitaraman, M., Adcock, B., Avigad, J., Bronish, D., Bucci, P., Frazier, D., Friedman, H.M., Harton, H., Heym, W., Kirschenbaum, J., Krone, J., Smith, H., and Weide, B.W., "Building a Push-Button RESOLVE Verifier: Progress and Challenges," *Formal Aspects of Computing 23*, 2011, 607-626.

[2] Cook, C.T., Harton, H.K., Smith, H., and Sitaraman, M., "Specification Engineering and Modular Verification Using a Web-Integrated Verifying Compiler," *Proc. 34th International Conference on Software Engineering*, IEEE/ACM, 2012, 1379-1382.

[3] Drachova,S. V., Hallstrom, J. O., Hollingsworth,J. E., Krone, J., Pak, R., and Sitaraman, M.. 2015. Teaching Mathematical Reasoning Principles for Software Correctness and Its Assessment. *ACM Trans. Computing Education 15*, 3, Article 15 (August 2015), 22 pages. DOI=10.1145/2716316 http://doi.acm.org/10.1145/2716316

[4] Cook, C.T., Drachova, S. V., Sun, Y-S., Sitaraman, M., Carver, J., and Hollingsworth, K. E., "Specification and Reasoning in SE Projects Using a Web-IDE," *Proc. 26th Conference on Software Engineering Education and Training*, IEEE, 2013.

[5] Fahndrich, M., Barnett, M., Leijen, D., and Logozzo, F,, "Integrating a Set of Contract Checking Tools into Visual Studio," *Procs. Second International Workshop on Developing Tools as Plug-ins (TOPI 2012)*, IEEE, 2012.

[6] Liskov, B. and Guttag, J., *Program Development in Java*, Pearson, 2000.

[7] Dafny Tutorial, http://rise4fun.com/Dafny/tutorial (5 Sept 2014)

[8] Baldwin, D., "Math-thinking-l – Mathematical reasoning in CS curricula", at: http://mail.geneseo.edu/mailman/listinfo/math-thinking

Demonstrations

The Speech Recognition Virtual Kitchen Toolkit

Rebecca Bates, *Minnesota State University, Mankato*
Euisung Kim, *Minnesota State University, Mankato*
Contact: bates@mnsu.edu

Speech recognition and natural language processing are interesting and relevant applications of many CS principles. Unfortunately, the barrier to entry for using existing tools is quite high, often requiring many hours installing, compiling, testing, and debugging tools before students can even begin exploring the technical concepts. The "Speech Recognition Virtual Kitchen" environment is an NSF-sponsored collaborative research infrastructure project that has the goals to promote community sharing of research techniques, foster innovative experimentation, and provide solid reference systems as a tool for education, research, and evaluation. The core of the research infrastructure is the use of virtual machines (VMs) that provide a consistent experimental environment. We liken the virtual machines to a "kitchen" because they provide the infrastructure into which one can install "appliances" (e.g., speech recognition tool-kits), "recipes" (scripts for creating state-of-the art systems), and "ingredients" (language data). A web-based community platform allows physically disconnected users to jointly explore VMs, learn from each other, and collaborate in research. This demo will provide an overview of available VMs, suggestions for use in undergraduate and graduate computer science courses and capstone projects, and a demonstration of our teaching VM, highlighting the ease of working with available tools. We invite participation in our community through downloading and uploading VMs, which can be an entry to open-source software development. More information can be found at speechkitchen.org.

Keywords: Automatic speech recognition, virtual machines, toolkit, research infrastructure

DOI: http://dx.doi.org/10.1145/2839509.2850506

SIGCSE'16, March 2–5, 2016, Memphis, TN, USA.
ACM ISBN: 978-1-4503-3685-7/16/03.

VisMap: Exploratory Visualization Support for Introductory Data Science and Visualization

Dugald Ralph Hutchings
Elon University
Elon, North Carolina, USA
dhutchings@elon.edu

Megan Squire
Elon University
Elon, North Carolina, USA
msquire@elon.edu

ABSTRACT
We present VisMap, a Web-based software tool that supports student exploration of possible data visualizations during a typical process of data science practice. Specifically, we detail visualization approaches within three major kinds of data analysis (part-to-whole and rank, correlation, and geospatial) and discuss how VisMap allows students to visually explore visualization options that correspond to the kind of analysis. The discussion is rooted in our experiences developing an introductory undergraduate course in data science and in our classroom observations of the limitations of existing software tools. These limitations include inefficiency of visualization comparison, difficulty in manipulating data to achieve visualization goals, and current challenges novices face when using professional tools simultaneous with learning about visualization. We finally offer a variety of future paths to further evaluate and refine VisMap.

Categories and Subject Descriptors
- **Human-centered computing~Visualization systems and tools**
- **Social and professional topics~Information science education**
- **Applied computing~Interactive learning environments**

Keywords
Visualization, data science, education, VisMap

1. INTRODUCTION
Everyday readers of news media, whether in print or online, are likely to encounter data visualizations as components of articles and occasionally even as standalone features. Some visualizations are simple, such as a static line chart showing the value of a stock over time, or an annotated map indicating where different events in a news article occurred. Other visualizations can be more complex, such as combination charts (line, bar, map) showing weather patterns over an entire year, or an interactive map of social indicators (crime, race, income) that can be viewed at the national, state, or local levels. The ubiquity of such data visualizations in print and online media provides a valuable classroom opportunity to teach students how to use data to learn something about their word and tell a compelling story, from any number of domains: news, business, science, education, public policy, *etc.*

SIGCSE '16, March 02-05, 2016, Memphis, TN, USA
© 2016 ACM. ISBN 978-1-4503-3685-7/16/03…$15.00
DOI: http://dx.doi.org/10.1145/2839509.2844572

Over the past several years we have developed an undergraduate introductory course examining the typical data science process, with particular emphasis on visualizing data. During this time we have observed a number of drawbacks inherent in existing software tools, particularly in how these tools support visualization *education* and the needs of novices. Consequently, we have developed a Web-based software tool entitled *VisMap* to mitigate the drawbacks and better support our course design (see a demo at http://www.hutchmap.com). In the following sections we discuss development of the course, detail existing visualization tool disadvantages, explain the influence of related work, provide description and illustration of the VisMap tool, and discuss future work in deployment, evaluation, and design iteration.

2. COURSE DEVELOPMENT
Beginning in 2011 our institution transitioned from an undergraduate program in information systems to a program in information science with an emphasis on areas related to data science. The faculty developed an innovative introductory course entitled *Data Science and Visualization* that exposes students to engagement in data acquisition, storage, cleaning, manipulation, visualization, and analysis [12]. In particular, this course strongly emphasizes the critical thinking skills needed to select, develop, and evaluate data visualizations effectively. The course is open to all undergraduate students at the institution but targets three main groups:

- Students with an inherent interest in data science (*i.e.*, future majors or minors);
- Students with a general interest in the computing sciences (*i.e.*, possible majors or minors); *and*
- Students with a specific interest in the concepts and skills taught in the course, such as aspiring communications, business, education, or science majors who are likely to have data analysis or presentation components in their work throughout their careers.

Our institution employs a 4-semester hour system rather than the traditional 3-semester hour system, so the twice-a-week Data Science and Visualization course meets for 100 minutes in each class period. When designing the course, the faculty members sought to exploit the lengthy course periods by offering a lab experience in (nearly) every class period, and by limiting lecture and lecture-style discussion to no more than 10 minutes at the start of each class. During each lab, students create a brief report of their investigations by describing the following aspects [12].

- Nature of investigation: either *directed* (one or more specific questions to be addressed via the data science and visualization process) or *exploratory* (description of an available dataset and possible areas of inquiry to learn what analysis of the data may reveal)
- Data acquisition and storage: where (and possibly how) the data was obtained and where it will be stored

- Data cleaning: how the dataset's elements were altered to facilitate later analysis or visualization (common examples include creating abbreviated data labels, creating labels to group data in ad hoc ways, removing data irrelevant to the investigation, fixing obvious data errors, or applying uniform formatting to textual data)
- Data manipulation: any actions on the data that resulted in the creation of new information (common examples include adjusting monetary values for inflation, extracting month, day, or hour data from a timestamp, calculating summary statistics for groups of data, or calculating incidence rates from raw counts and another data field, such as population)
- Data visualization: (1) presentation of the visualizations themselves and (2) discussion of the key advantages of the specific visualization type and/or crucial decisions made in constructing the visualization
- Investigation analysis: (1) any conclusions that can be drawn from the process above, particularly the visualization step, and (2) aspects of the investigation that may call the conclusions into question, such as validity of the data source, arbitrary decisions made in the cleaning process, or alternative explanations of obvious visualization interpretations

3. SOFTWARE SUPPORT

The lab-based approach and variety in student backgrounds, motivations, and goals lead to selection of support software tools that are readily available outside of the classroom environment and that have relatively low barriers to use. Consequently, the faculty members teaching the course employ two major types of software:

- Spreadsheet tools (like Microsoft Excel and Google Sheets) that support both data analysis and visualization, and may be familiar to undergraduate students; *and*
- Web-based visualization tools (like the very recently retired IBM ManyEyes system [7]) that focus on graphic creation rather than data analysis, but are very easy to use with pre-formatted data.

Following more than a dozen course section offerings, we have observed a number of positive outcomes of using these tools, but we have also consistently observed several shortcomings. We detail limitations of these software tools in subsequent subsections.

3.1 Comparing Graph Types

With both Microsoft Excel and Google Sheets, there is a limited ability to *rapidly explore and compare* visualization types using the target data set. For example, the user can very easily visualize a data set as a bar graph, pie chart, scatter plot, *etc.*, but each graph must be created separately. Neither of these tools allows an *automated, simultaneous visual comparison* of graph types using real data. By forcing the student to create each visualization separately, the student tends to choose a graph and stick with it, rather than opt to create and evaluate multiple graphs and then choose the best one. Textbooks teach critical thinking about visualization by showing the same data in multiple graph types (for example, in Few's work [2], which we use in our class). Ideally then, a system that automatically created sensible representations of the data using all of the possible visual approaches would facilitate rapid comparison and selection by the student. Such a system would allow the student to create a subsequent detailed visualization using a tool of choice (spreadsheet or Web-based), with confidence that the student had chosen the best visualization type for the data set.

3.2 Customizing Graphs

With existing tools, there is also a limited ability to *explore the impact of smaller, but crucial, visual choices* for a graph. For example, what is the visual and storytelling impact of changing the scale of the y-axis on a bar chart? What is the visual impact of removing outliers in a scatterplot? Spreadsheet tools allow a wide variety of visual choices but, as with the issues of selecting type, the novice student must go through a cumbersome process of trial-and-error. Given a discussion of y-axis choices, for example, a student may wish to try different axis scales, but will quickly experience this as time-consuming and frustrating since the graph has to be re-drawn in a separate window after each choice. Each axis choice will involve more clicks and more user interface navigation to view the results. Some students will anticipate needing to make three or four graphs with different axis choices, so they will create multiple charts and change each one in different ways. This is better, but also very time-consuming because each chart still has to be constructed through significant user interface interaction. Students could benefit from a software tool that lets them compare the impact of multiple visual choices at the same time. Then, they can either use that visualization directly or they can mimic it in their spreadsheet or Web-based tool of choice.

3.3 Visualization-related Data Conversion

In addition to manipulating graphical factors (like chart type or axis scales), we occasionally encourage students to perform simple data conversions in order to create more effective images. For example, a common visual tactic is to reduce visual clutter by combining small categories into a larger "*other*" category. We find that existing tools lack *simple* data conversion capabilities like these, especially at the point where the student is actually constructing the graph or chart. In the case of creating a simple "*other*" category, spreadsheet tools will require nontrivial, manual data manipulation to create the category, and even more time to refine the category if the user would like to consider different groupings. Web tools also generally require that data manipulation has already taken place before the graph is created, and to our knowledge, no Web tool automatically creates an "*other*" category. As with the other shortcomings, we notice that students spend a great deal of time on the more mechanical aspects of creating *any* visualization instead of considering and comparing options to create the *best* visualization.

3.4 Professional Visualization Tools

While there are some existing data and/or visualization tools that are candidates for addressing these shortcomings (such as Tableau Public [14] or iVisDesigner [11]), these tools exhibit drawbacks in the lab environment. Key drawbacks are listed below.

- Students find these tools to be difficult to learn since the tools generally assume that the user is already familiar with all basic and some advanced visualization concepts
- Even when guided by an instructor, learning the tool is time-consuming and often replaces time spent on critical thinking or evaluation of visual choices
- After students learn to use the tool, they often neglect to exploit its advanced features. They use it in a way that is not much more advanced than any other spreadsheet or Web-based tool
- Software licensing and other restrictions may mean students cannot use professional desktop software outside of the lab environment unless the students themselves purchase the (typically expensive) software

Summarizing the subsections 3.1-3.4, we thus find four key shortcomings based on our observations of student interactions in the lab: limited ability to compare broad graph types, limited ability to compare the impact of visual customizations of a graph, inability to convert data to support more effective graphical choices, and limited utility of professional tools in a lab environment. In order to improve upon these shortcomings with existing tools, we have developed VisMap. Before we begin discussion of VisMap we further contextualize the development of the tool by describing its role in teaching data science and visualization to novices.

4. OTHER RELATED WORK

We have designed VisMap by incorporating a key piece of recent literature about non-expert design of visualization. Grammel *et al.* executed a lab-based study of undergraduate business students tasked with understanding unfamiliar sales data and presenting their analysis to a (fictitious) supervisor [3]. Of particular note was a finding that "support[s] the need for tools that suggest potential visualizations" which we shortly demonstrate as a key feature of VisMap. Other findings from that work include recommendations for "[tools] that provide explanations and help with learning." We currently implement this recommendation in the classroom environment via instructor interaction, but such enhancements could be implemented more directly in later versions of VisMap itself. Further discussion of design approaches to support novice visualization creation can be seen the visualization democratization work of Huron et al. [5].

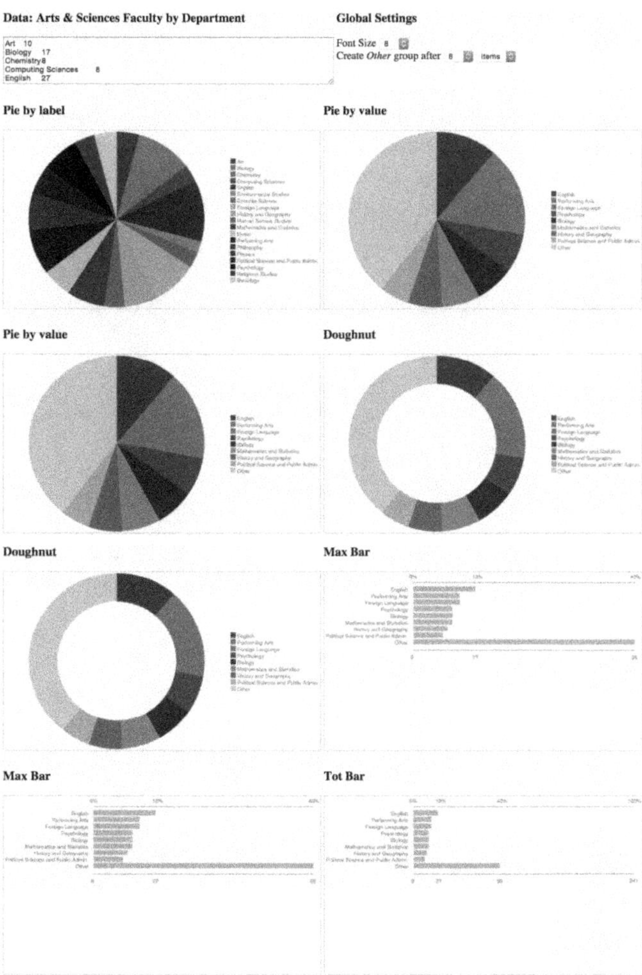

Figure 1. A typical part-to-whole and rank analysis view.

We contribute to a growing body of literature describing courses introducing data-related computing issues to students. A key similarity of our Data Science and Visualization course to other work is the inclusion of visualization as key course material. Within the SIGCSE community, Sullivan presented a data-oriented course introducing students to computer science that has a 1-week section on data visualization in 2013 [13] and Plaue and Cook presented a graduate-level data journalism course with a data presentation section constituting approximately 35% of the course in 2015 [9]. Looking beyond our institution's curriculum [4], our literature review revealed only one comprehensive undergraduate data science model curriculum. Anderson's *et al.* SIGCSE 2014 presentation indicated a topmost learning objective of managing large datasets and includes *Graphics and Visualization* as a main component [1]. We posit that development of tools to aid visualization novices can extend to a variety of courses with data emphases.

5. VISMAP DEVELOPMENT

We designed VisMap to allow students to learn how to make good visualization choices, without all the shortcomings of existing tools used in the lab environment, as outlined in Section 3. VisMap was also designed to be as easy as possible to use outside of the lab environment, including on mobile devices like smartphones and tablets where (perhaps surprisingly) students engage in some out-of-class coursework. VisMap employs common Web technologies and runs in any browser capable of rendering the HTML5 *canvas* tag and executing the JavaScript *Canvas* API [8]. Both the desktop and mobile versions of each of the current five most popular browsers of Chrome, Firefox, Internet Explorer, Opera, and Safari support and run VisMap code.

We further designed VisMap to be based on the kind of analysis rather than visualization type. This approach corresponds to our lab designs and aligns with the textbook commonly used in the course [2]. The three kinds of analysis that we discuss in this paper are part-to-whole and ranking analysis, correlation analysis, and geospatial analysis (which refers to overlaying color, shape, or other visual elements on a map or other visual representation of geography).

Regardless of domain, creating visualizations in VisMap is very straightforward: the user pastes data (such as from a text file or spreadsheet) into a textbox on a Web page, and then the VisMap tool automatically creates a variety of visualizations, which is very similar to the IBM ManyEyes data approach that we have observed to be successful in our classroom [7]. Unlike with ManyEyes, however, users may also edit the data directly in the textbox, for example to perform tests ("What would happen if this data point were set to zero?"). VisMap further provides settings specific to the kind of analysis the student is performing at that moment. As soon as the student edits data or updates settings, VisMap immediately refreshes the visualizations, providing instant feedback. We now describe the VisMap settings in detail in each kind of analysis.

5.1 Part-to-Whole and Rank Analysis

We suggest part-to-whole and rank analysis when the elements of a dataset combine to form a whole, such as departments in an academic institution or states in the USA. For example, if a student wants to address how many faculty are working in each academic department at a university, the student may wish to use part-to-whole or rank analysis to show how the number of faculty compare in each department. To explore visualization types, the student pastes data into VisMap and can immediately see several sample visualizations for this data. The student will also be given the option to consolidate lower-frequency items into an "*other*" category. Figure 1 illustrates sample results of this process.

Right away VisMap helps the student see that some of these visualizations are more effective than others for this data set. We now discuss each of the four rows of visualizations to explain their advantages for visualization *education* and in specific support of a lab exercise.

Row 1. On the left we have a pie chart sorted alphabetically by label and ignoring the *other* category (exactly what Microsoft Excel or Google Sheets would do with the data as entered). On the right we have a pie chart sorted by value and using the "*other*" category. It is far easier to make visual comparisons by using the right-hand chart, especially with respect to rank and combined size of the smaller departments.

Row 2. The same pie chart sorted by value from the previous row is juxtaposed with a doughnut chart also sorted by value. On the left, the user's natural inclination is to compare the area of the pie wedges whereas on the right the inclination is to compare the length of the sections. Length comparisons are far easier to make for users [2] and suggests that the doughnut chart is the superior approach for this dataset. Repeating the display of the pie chart from the previous row uses more space (not a problem for an electronic display) but encourages the kind of direct visual comparison we have designed VisMap to promote to students.

Row 3. A doughnut chart is juxtaposed with a bar chart, two very different types of displays. An advantage of the doughnut chart is that it is easier to see the cumulative percentage among the departments. An advantage of the bar chart is that length comparisons are side-by-side instead of end-to-end (thus easier to make) and easily labeled with both percentages and actual values. Depending on the context of the investigation, the ability to compare the visualizations may prompt the student to favor one type of visualization, elect to use both visualizations, or use the detailed spreadsheet visualization design tools to incorporate the advantages of each visualization into a single display (such as a Pareto chart [2]).

Row 4. The same bar chart from the previous row is compared against a bar chart in which the axis is scaled to 100% rather than to the maximum percentage among the individual values. Seeing how individual values relate to the whole is easier while length comparisons are still easy to make despite some loss of precision. Cumulative percentage estimations are eased slightly but generally remain difficult despite the scale change.

To create the set of visualizations in Figure 1 in a spreadsheet tool would require significant data manipulation time (because creating a flexible "*other*" category is time-consuming and error-prone) and visualization creation time (requiring the creation of at least 5 charts and possibly multiple copies of the data, since most spreadsheet charting tools automatically adjust the visualization in response to re-sorting the data). VisMap creates several detailed visualization types using the actual dataset and can result in both significant time savings and a fuller understanding of the consequences of visualization selection for the given dataset.

5.2 Correlation Analysis

When a dataset contains many variables, it may be of interest to examine whether any of these variables appear to relate to other variables. Correlation analysis can show whether violent crimes and property crimes correspond, or whether higher salaries correspond to better performance for professional athletes and professional teams. In the case of looking at exactly two variables common approaches include the scatterplot, point plot (with 2 differently scaled, overlaid y-axes), and juxtaposed bar charts. In the other case of examining whether any relationships may exist among more than two variables, common approaches include a series of juxtaposed bar charts (first explored by Rao's and Card's Table Lens work [10]), heatmap matrix (similar to the Table Lens but using color scaling instead of bars), and scatterplot matrix (not currently implemented but planned in future development).

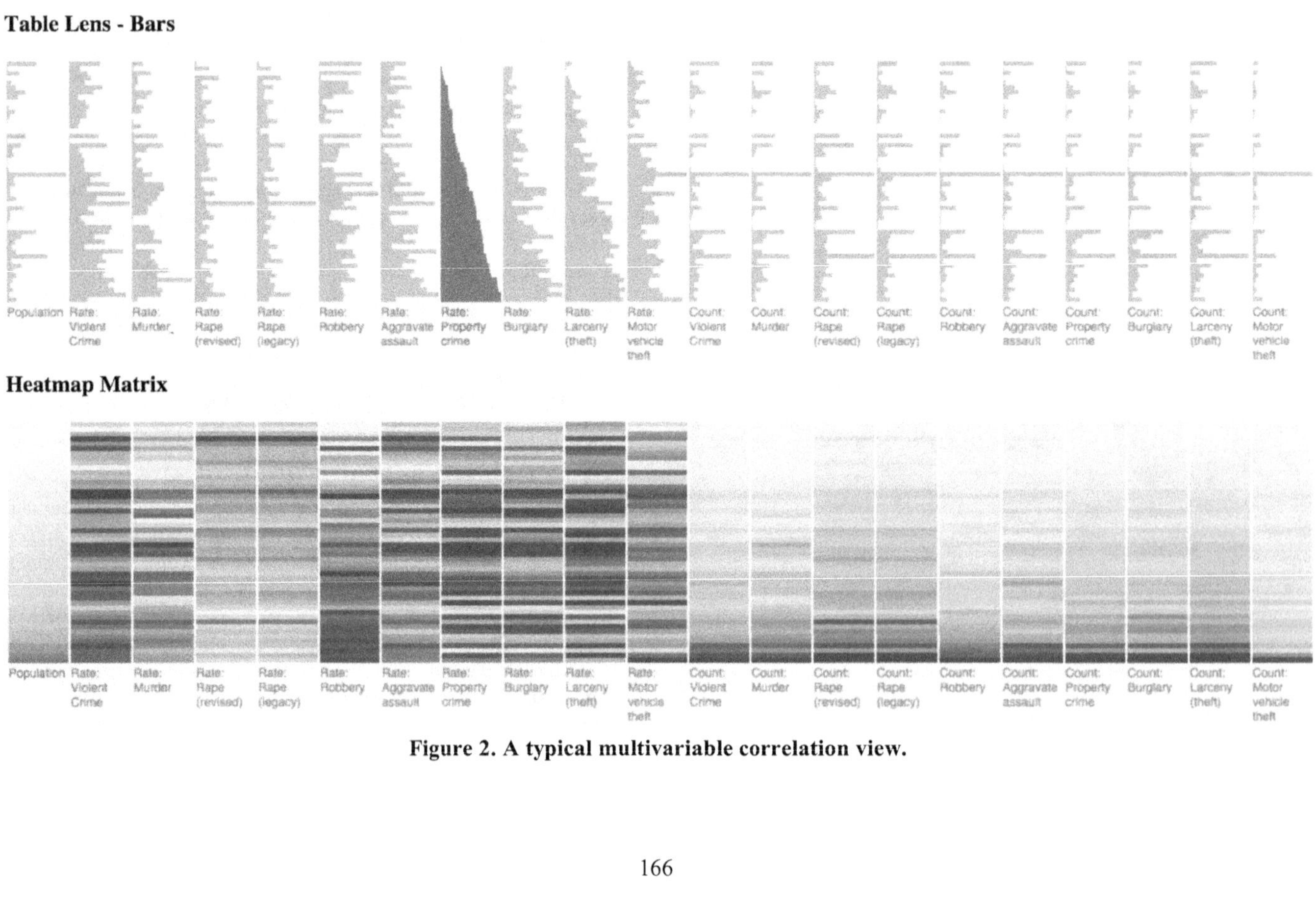

Figure 2. A typical multivariable correlation view.

Figure 2 illustrates what happens when a student pastes some data into the VisMap correlation screen. In this case the data is USA crime counts and per capita incident rates by state, and the student selects property crime rate as the sort variable. A Table Lens (top) and a heatmap matrix (bottom) each appear. Notice that the length of the bars generally follows the same pattern in the two columns to the right of property crime rate, indicating a possible correlation, but other possible relationships are weak or not at all apparent. This can help students (especially in exploratory analysis assignments) quickly identify questions and analysis areas to target rather than explore possibly many hypotheses with few interesting results. Further, while spreadsheet tools allow the creation of similar displays, time costs are significant. For example, Microsoft Excel allows data cells to be conditionally formatted using colors or bars, but require the user to repeat the process for each column of data and then use a variety of formatting and zooming tricks to make sense of the display. Existing Web-based tools allow quick selection of any two variables (*i.e.*, indirect design iteration), but to our knowledge do not provide an overview of all the variables at one time (*i.e.*, direct design comparison).

The dataset used in Figure 2 also facilitates learning about a common general issue with correlation analyses: false correlations. The first column (state population) and the rightmost 10 columns (crime counts) appear to have roughly the same bar shape or color pattern. While it is true that population is highly correlated with the count of any type of crime, few of the crime types themselves are truly correlated. But if a student inspected robbery and burglary using the counts and not the rates without the ability to see all of the data at once, the student might quickly (and falsely) conclude that the crime types correlate. The automatic creation of the overall view allows the student an opportunity to consider the data more carefully and it also allows instructors to select datasets to best illustrate their lessons.

Another benefit of the VisMap approach is that as soon as the student selects one variable for the overview visualizations, a scatterplot and dot plot are also created, with an ability to easily select or change the second variable as well as to remove outliers from either variable at the student's discretion. For example, Figure 3 (top row) illustrates the scatterplot that is created when the student selects motor vehicle theft rate for the *x*-axis and murder rate for the *y*-axis. Noting 3 potential outlying values on the *x*-axis and 1 on the *y*-axis, the user has elected to remove those values to recreate the scatterplot (bottom row). Spreadsheet tools do not easily support this type of flexible adjustment of outlying values because either the values need to be deleted (which quickly destroys the integrity of the data) or the data re-sorted. Web-based tools enforce re-creation of the data set with outliers manually omitted.

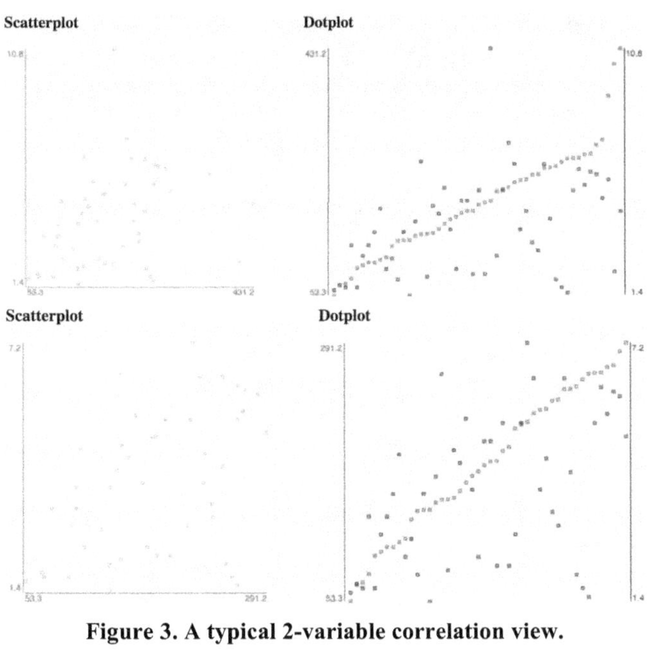

Figure 3. A typical 2-variable correlation view.

5.3 Geospatial Analysis

When data includes a geographical component, such as the crime data from each of the 50 states of the USA used in the previous subsection, one line of analysis involves inspecting the data relative to geographical positioning. Using geography allows a user to literally see *where* the data is and look for regional patterns or exceptions that may otherwise be missed in the analysis. Issues like mismatches in land area and population size and necessity of comparing irregularly-shaped states can give a false impression of these patterns.

We designed VisMap to offer a number of alternative, abstract geographical data views.

- Land-area based: each state is drawn in proportion to its land area, but using a rectangle in a 2:1 aspect ratio in order to simplify shape comparisons
- Population-based: each state is drawn using a size proportional to the population of the state rather than the land area of the state, also using 2-by-1 rectangles
- Uniform: each state is drawn as a square in a grid

Our current design improves upon the options provided in existing tools but does have some limitations, discussion of which appears in the next section. Figure 4 illustrates a sample set of abstract USA maps using property crime rate data. Note that the user can control whether to show state labels, which is especially helpful in seeing the color of small states or looking for a color pattern without being distracted by text. We have provided one view with labels and one without labels in Figure 4 strictly for demo purposes.

6. FUTURE WORK

VisMap was conceived and designed based on our observations of the strengths and limitations of current tools for *students* of introductory data science and visualization but the tool has not yet been evaluated in a classroom setting. We believe that use of

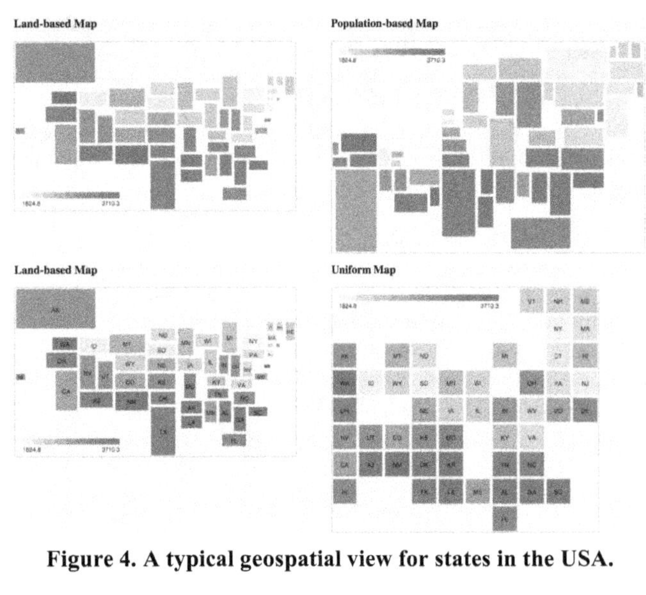

Figure 4. A typical geospatial view for states in the USA.

VisMap in the classroom will significantly aid the quality of student work and students' overall understanding of data visualization principles and approaches. We further believe that close observation of student usage of the tool will aid future development in a number of ways:

- Understanding the specific strengths and weaknesses of juxtaposition and exposure to broad visualization types;
- Validating the current design and suggesting ways to both amend and expand VisMap; *and*
- Suggesting efficient paths to usage of professional tools

We also envision several ways that the current state of VisMap can be improved without classroom deployment.

- Develop treemaps for part-to-whole visualization [6]. We have avoided treemap implementation in the initial design because treemaps are suitable only when data is organized in hierarchy of two or more levels, and because data layout strategies to support treemap visualization vary widely among existing tools
- Allow additional depth of analysis in correlation displays, such as allowing scatterplot data to be grouped and visualizing groups using different shapes or colors
- Allow adjustment of the population-based USA map to use the population of the state at the time of the data (such as when visualizing crime data from a previous era), or based on some other data dimension of the user's choosing (such as population within a certain age range, race, ethnicity, gender identity, etc.)
- Implement deeper interactivity in the visualizations such as allowing the user to tap or click a point in a scatterplot to reveal identity information

A key challenge we face in expanding the capabilities of VisMap is striking a balance between giving the students choices and guiding them to the elements of a visualization that matter most. For example, consider color selection. We have observed students spending inappropriately lengthy amounts of time adjusting the color palette and color selections of a spreadsheet visualization in ways that add no analytical power or storytelling effectiveness to the visualization. But we also observe complaints that Web-based tools may offer only one color palette and if that palette is particularly offensive to the student, then the student may avoid creating what is otherwise a very effective visualization type. Determining the right amount of design choice will be an ongoing challenge for us to consider after completing the initial study of the effect of VisMap's core functionality on learning outcomes.

7. ACKNOWLEDGEMENTS

We wish to thank Shannon Duvall for her contributions to the development of this paper. Our work was supported by a fellowship program at Elon University.

8. REFERENCES

[1] Anderson, P., Bowring, J., McCauley, R., Pothering, G., and Starr, C. 2014. An undergraduate degree in data science: curriculum and a decade of implementation experience. In *Proceedings of the 45th ACM technical symposium on Computer science education* (SIGCSE '14). ACM, New York, NY, USA, 145-150. DOI= http://doi.acm.org/10.1145/2538862.2538936

[2] Few, S. 2009. *Now You See It: Simple Visualization Techniques for Quantitative Analysis*. Analytics Press, Oakland, CA, USA.

[3] Grammel, L., Tory, M., and Storey, M. 2010. How Information Visualization Novices Construct Visualizations. *IEEE Transactions on Visualization and Computer Graphics* 16, 6 (November 2010), 943-952. DOI= http://dx.doi.org/10.1109/TVCG.2010.164

[4] Heinrichs, L. R., Hutchings, D., Kleckner, M., and Squire, M. Charting a new curriculum for a data-driven world. *Issues in Information Systems* 12, 2 (2011), 256-263. http://iacis.org/iis/2011/256-263_AL2011_1731.pdf

[5] Huron, S., Carpendale, S., Thudt, A., Tang, A., and Mauerer, M. 2014. Constructive visualization. In *Proceedings of the 2014 conference on Designing interactive systems* (DIS '14). ACM, New York, NY, USA, 433-442. DOI= http://doi.acm.org/10.1145/2598510.2598566

[6] Johnson, B. and Shneiderman, B. 1991. Tree-Maps: a space-filling approach to the visualization of hierarchical information structures. In *Proceedings of the 2nd conference on Visualization '91* (VIS '91), IEEE Computer Society Press, Los Alamitos, CA, USA, 284-291.

[7] Many Eyes. Accessed August 19, 2015. http://www-01.ibm.com/software/analytics/many-eyes/

[8] Mozilla Developer Network. Canvas API. Accessed August 19, 2015. https://developer.mozilla.org/en-US/docs/Web/API/Canvas_API

[9] Plaue, C. and Cook, L. R. 2015. Data Journalism: Lessons Learned While Designing an Interdisciplinary Service Course. In *Proceedings of the 46th ACM Technical Symposium on Computer Science Education* (SIGCSE '15). ACM, New York, NY, USA, 126-131. DOI= http://doi.acm.org/10.1145/2676723.2677263

[10] Rao, R. and Card, S. K. 1994. The table lens: merging graphical and symbolic representations in an interactive focus + context visualization for tabular information. In *Proceedings of the SIGCHI Conference on Human Factors in Computing Systems* (CHI '94). ACM, New York, NY, USA, 318-322. DOI= http://doi.acm.org/10.1145/191666.191776

[11] Ren, D., Hollerer, T., Yuan, X. 2014. iVisDesigner: Expressive interactive design of information visualizations. *IEEE Transactions on Visualization and Computer Graphics* 20, 12 (December 2014), 2092-2101. DOI= http://dx.doi.org/10.1109/TVCG.2014.2346291

[12] Squire, M. Outline and exercises for a novel course in Data Science and Visualization. *Issues in Information Systems* 13, 1 (2012), 382-390. http://iacis.org/iis/2012/76_iis_2012_382-390.pdf

[13] Sullivan, D. G. 2013. A data-centric introduction to computer science for non-majors. In *Proceedings of the 44th ACM technical symposium on Computer science education* (SIGCSE '13). ACM, New York, NY, USA, 71-76. DOI= http://doi.acm.org/10.1145/2445196.2445222

[14] Tableau Public. Accessed August 19, 2015. https://public.tableau.com/s/

A Practical and Sustainable Model for Learning and Teaching Data Science

Bina Ramamurthy
Computer Science and Engineering Department
University at Buffalo
345 Davis Hall, Buffalo, NY 14260
716-634-3182, bina@buffalo.edu

ABSTRACT

This paper details our experiences with design and implementation of data science curriculum at University at Buffalo (UB). We discuss (i) briefly the history of project, (ii) a certificate program that we created, (iii) a data-intensive computing course that forms the core of the curriculum and (iv) some of the challenges we faced and how we addressed them. Major goal of the project was to improve the preparedness of our workforce for the emerging data-intensive computing area. We measured this through assessment of student learning on various concepts and topics related to data-intensive computing. We also discuss the best practices in building a data science program. We highlight the importance of external funding support and multi-disciplinary collaborations in the success of the project. The pedagogical resources created for the project are freely available to help educators and other learners navigate the path to learning data science. We expect this paper about our experience will provide a road map for educators who desire to introduce data science in their curriculum.

Categories and Subject Descriptors

H.3 [**Information Storage and Retrieval**] H.3.2 [Information storage] File organization H.3.4 [**Systems and Software**]: Distributed systems. K.3.2 [**Compute and information systems education**]: Computer science education, information system education.

General Terms

Algorithms, Design, Experimentation.

Keywords

Data Science; curriculum; cloud computing; data analysis; Hadoop; MapReduce; Spark

SIGCSE '16, March 02-05, 2016, Memphis, TN, USA
© 2016 ACM. ISBN 978-1-4503-3685-7/16/03…$15.00
DOI: http://dx.doi.org/10.1145/2839509.2844603

1. Introduction

We are witnessing explosive growth in applications that deal with data: some consume enormous volumes of variety of data [8,9], several others deal with storage and analytic models for large scale data [3,4], and yet others generate and/or gather data [20] at high velocity. All these have resulted in a rich ecosystem that is collectively referred to as data-intensive computing. People with data analysis skills are in high demand in the workplace. Educators are eager to teach data-intensive computing fundamentals, algorithms, tools and techniques that will enable their students to learn and practice data skills. Research universities and data-driven businesses have established strong data oriented infrastructures and applications. However we are lacking in the methods for adopting these resources into the curriculum at 2-year colleges and undergraduate programs at the 4-year college level. It is this gap between advances in data-intensive computing and their adoptability to college-level instructions that we address in our project and in this paper.

1.1 A Little Bit of History

Around 2007 we observed a new wave of technology solutions built around "data". Google became a popular application and the details of the Google file system, data infrastructures and algorithms were published in a landmark paper [5]. In 2008 National Science Foundation (NSF) with the help of Yahoo! hosted a Big-Data Study Group at Sunnyvale, CA to disseminate the early information about this emerging area and the newer infrastructures and processing models introduced by such companies as Google and Facebook. NSF selectively supported travel funds for a few educators to attend the Yahoo! summit [22] and the author of this paper was one of them. From the various presentations at the Summit we found out that data aggregation and mining formed the core of most data advances. Traditional science and engineering curriculum was lagging behind these newer models of computing used at technology companies. We decided to address this gap by exploring the area, in particular the material presented at the Yahoo! Summit. We built a 4-node Hadoop [3] network and studied the working of the Hadoop-MapReduce [5], the new programming paradigm to process big-data. A team of students worked on independent research under the guidance of the author to adapt the concepts into pedagogical modules and a course curriculum. Armed with this knowledge we wrote a proposal to NSF DUE CCLI program to create a novel course in data-intensive computing and a certificate program centered on this course. The grant was awarded (in 2009) and the project **Timely Introduction of Data-intensive computing (TIDE)** began in 2010 after course approvals.

1.2 Related Work

Importance of data science is apparent in the proliferation of Data Science programs at all levels. Schools with strong Computer Science program such as Berkeley and Stanford have introduced data science concepts (algorithms and data structures) into the CS1 and CS2 level courses. Columbia University and University of Washington have established Data Science institutes and comprehensive certificate programs. MOOCs (massive open online courses) such as Coursera and Udacity have several Data Science courses targeted for general public. An extensive list of the programs, schools and courses can be found in [13]. Our focus is on establishing a comprehensive data science curriculum (courses and/or certificate) for a 4-year undergraduate program. The goal is to support educators navigate through myriad of options, technologies and pedagogies to help students acquire critical data science competencies and integrate these within their ***regular curriculum***.

2.0 The TIDE Project

Two new courses Distributed System (CSE486) and Data-intensive Computing System (CSE487) were designed and offered. **A Data-intensive Computing certificate** program was created that incorporated these courses.

2.1 The Certificate Program

The goals in the design of the certificate program included (i) efficient coverage of the data science concepts and skills (ii) easy to follow requirements for the students as well as educators, and (iii) sustainability (beyond the grant period). The program was designed to be similar to a track of specialization in a certain area with a set of foundational courses, two applied courses related to Data Science and a capstone project course for 1-3 credits. We discuss how we accomplished these goals in the next sections, with quite extensive discussion on the curriculum.

2.1.1 Intended Audience for the certificate program

Any entering CSE undergraduate easily can satisfy the certificate requirements if they plan right. This certificate program is also suitable for non-CSE engineering majors, Math majors, bioinformatics majors and any student wishing to pursue a minor in CSE. This program also serves members of the local industrial workforce who are considering retraining and those who are interested in focused instruction and training in data-intensive computing and technologies. Any matriculated undergraduate student can possibly enroll in this program irrespective of the major, thus emphasizing the importance of ***multidisciplinary*** nature of data-intensive computing. This program facilitates a data-intensive computing track for a CS student, and possibly a minor in CS with emphasis in Data-Intensive Computing for non-majors.

2.1.2 Sustainability

Initially there was reluctance in applying for New York-state-level (SUNY) certificate program since this takes a considerable time for approval. However with encouragement from the external consultant on the project, Dr. Neal, we applied for a SUNY-level certificate program. The SUNY chancellor's education committee at Albany, New York approved (in 2011) the certificate program expeditiously with no change in our application. Perhaps, that committee recognized the urgency in educating our students about big data and data-intensive computing. A major implication of this SUNY-level approval is that the data-intensive certificate program created is offered by the university as an ***institutional offering*** rather than as a local department-level certificate by the CSE department. This certificate program is permanent and thus assured the sustainability of the program by the university beyond the grant period. Currently the certificate program is listed in the official undergraduate catalog [21] and promoted by the university for all incoming students.

2.2 The Curriculum

The program consists of required courses in CSE, one elective course from the major discipline of the student and a capstone project course that applies the concepts in the earlier courses of the certificate. The uniqueness of the certificate program is that the newly designed courses are built on top of the existing foundational courses, thus aligning the program with existing curriculum. The course requirement for the certificate are (i) CS1 (Introduction to Computer Science I), (ii) CS2 (Introduction to Computer Science II), (iii) Distributed Systems, (iv) Data-intensive Computing, (v) a technical elective course of student's choice in her own major and (vi) a capstone project. The Data-intensive Computing course is the main feature of the program and was specifically created for this program. The interest in the program was evaluated through this course. Though this course is offered at the junior/senior level course it is also cross-listed as an entry level graduate course. We consider Data Science as a program level entity consisting of the Data-intensive computing course that we discuss next.

2.3 Data-intensive Computing Course

We provide below the course description of CSE487 Data-intensive Computing and the list of expected outcomes. The other course CSE486 Distributed Systems has become a core course for the undergraduate and graduate program and is offered as a regular course by the CSE department.

2.3.1 Course Description

Data-intensive computing deals with storage models, application architectures, middleware, and programming models and tools for large-scale data analytics. In particular we study approaches that address challenges in managing and utilizing ultra-scale data and the methods for transforming voluminous datasets (big data) into discoveries and intelligence for human understanding and decision making. Topics were chosen to cover all aspects of data-intensive computing: intelligent representation of data, approaches discovering intelligence in data, data-driven computing, storage requirements of big data, organization of big data repositories such as Google File System (GFS), characteristics of Write-Once-Read-Many (WORM) data, data-intensive programming models such as MapReduce, fault-tolerance, privacy, security and performance, services-based cloud computing middleware, and scalable analytics and visualization. This course has four major goals: (i) understand **data-intensive computing**, that has been defined as *the fourth paradigm* for Sciences by the late Jim Gray [10], (ii) study, design and develop solutions using ***data-intensive computing models*** such as MapReduce [5], (iii) perform predictive analytics and visualization using packages such as R [16] and Google analytics [9] and (iv) focus on methods for scalability using *the* ***cloud computing infrastructures*** such as Google App Engine (GAE), and Amazon Elastic Compute Cloud (EC2).

2.2.2 Course outline

On completion of this course students will be able to analyze, design, and implement effective solutions for data-intensive applications with very large scale data sets. The concepts were chosen to provide effective coverage of critical data-related processes. More specifically a student will be able to:

a) Describe data-intensive computing concepts
b) Compute with data-intensive computing concepts
c) Recognize a data-intensive problem.
d) Identify the scale of data.
e) Analyze the data requirements of a problem.
f) Describe the data layout and define the data repository format (Ex: Google File System)
g) Decide the algorithms (Ex: MapReduce) and programming models and algorithms (Ex: Bayesian)
h) Define application-specific algorithms and analytics (Ex: Finite State Element analysis)
i) Design the data-intensive program solution and system configuration; implement and test it for functional correctness and non-functional requirements.
j) Research algorithmic improvements; experiment with them.
k) Write a report summarizing the solution and results.
l) Incorporate services from cloud computing platforms.
m) Study the foundational concepts enabling cloud computing: services-based interfaces, programmatic consumption of services, virtualization, PKI-based security, large-scale storage, load-balancing, machine images and on-demand services.
n) Formulate data-intensive visualization solutions for presenting the results.

2.2.3 Evaluation

We evaluated the outcomes using two different instruments (i) the traditional 40-question survey designed by the evaluator on the project to evaluate the course and (ii) an online instrument on the pre and post survey designed for assessing the student learning. The course evaluation form for the course were designed by the external educational consultant on the project and were IRB (Internal Review Board) approved. The students filled up the paper forms anonymously and the forms were directly collected and delivered to the external consultant. She tabulated and evaluated the outcomes and discussed the responses with the PI at a pre-arranged time and recommended adjustments. Some of the initial concerns were about lack of proper text book and accessibility to data-intensive infrastructure. We eventually found good text books [12, 15] and also improved the infrastructure using offerings from Amazon and Google. It turned out that we did not need any departmental infrastructure after all since students worked on virtual machines on their laptops and on web services offered by educator's grants from cloud providers.

We discuss in detail the assessment of student learning from the spring 2014 offering of the course in Data-Intensive Computing (CSE487/587). This process gave us a real measure of student learning and some interesting observations.

We present below the results of student learning outcomes. We evaluated 8 different aspects: skills such as (i) **coding** as in program design and implementation, and (ii) **communication** as in technical presentations, and their familiarity with study areas of (iii) **data visualization**, (iv) **machine learning**, (v) **probability & statistics**, (vi) **mathematics,** and (vii) **computer science,** and their (viii) **domain expertise** in any application area e.g., biology, automobile engineering. We conducted this anonymous survey through the Blackboard facility meant for the course, once in the first week of classes (PRE-Test) and next during the last week of classes (POST-Test). The results of PRE-Test (top half) and the POST-Test (bottom half) are shown in each of the blocks below. The inspiration for this evaluation comes from the text used in the course, Doing Data Science [15].

2.3.4 Learning Outcome Analysis

The number of students who responded to the PRE-Test is 70 (N=70) and the POST-test is 84 (N=84). The increase in number of responses is a positive outcome. We feel that this is an indicator that students were engaged and interested in the course.

Each skill is evaluated on a 7-level scale: Excellent, Very Good, Good, Somewhat Good, Fair, Poor, and Unanswered. These levels are indicated by the different colors and are represented from left to right. Perusal of all the charts at a high level shows the distributions shown by histograms skewing to the left towards "Excellent" and "Very good" levels showing significant student learning for most of the charts, though at varying measures. We also observe that there is no anomalous response, such as all responses pointing to "Excellent" for any of the skills. We will discuss here the improvement for each of the skills.

Coding: Most of the students have reasonable coding skills when they enter the course (34% of the respondents have "Very Good" or "Excellent" skill level, as expected from Juniors/Seniors in CSE). By the end of the course this percentage improved to nearly 75%, nearly doubling due to the rigors of the projects in the course.

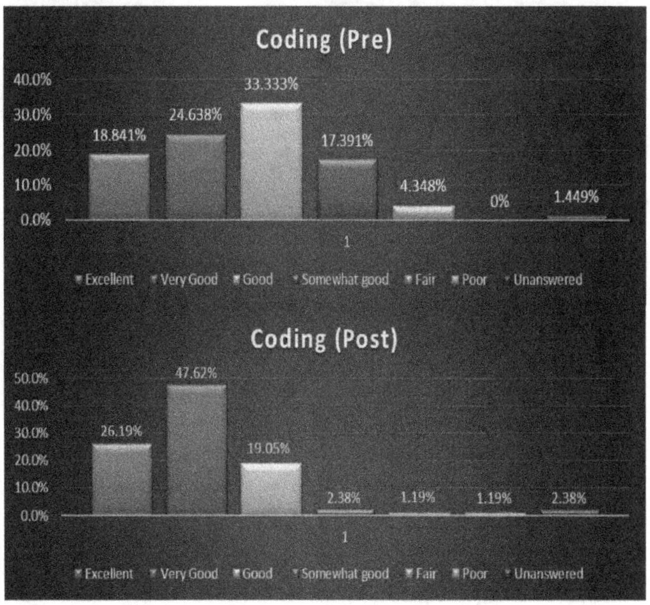

Data Visualization: Unlike coding, only about 23% responded to have good visualization skills in the beginning and this improved to 42% at the end. There was also a significant peak (36%) at the "Good" skill level moving people from the lower poorer levels into this level. We did cover R language [16] based graphical plotting and visualization and also Google visualization.

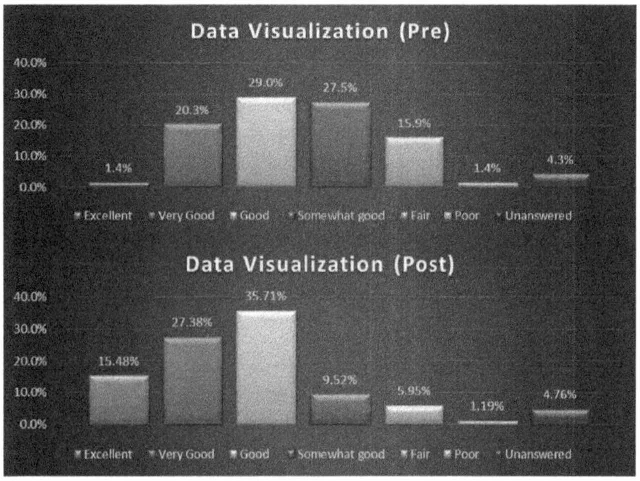

Machine Learning (ML): We introduced the machine learning algorithms at a very high level; but students learned how to apply the algorithms to data analytics using R and also transformed these applications into parallel version using MapReduce and Hadoop Distributed File System - HDFS [3] infrastructure to analyze big-data. So the focus is on big-data processing using the machine learning algorithms for clustering and classification. The skill level on entry is low at about 8% (for the upper levels) and that improves to about 28% and there is also a significant peak of 31% at the "Good" level in the POST-Test. Obviously the course is not ML focused as truly reflected in the evaluation.

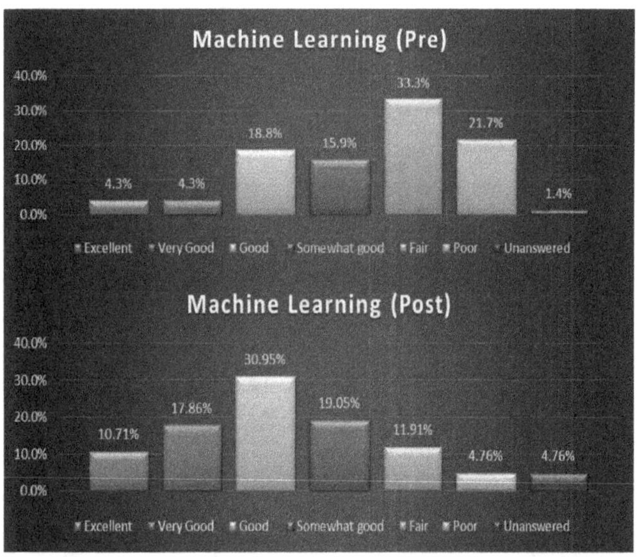

Probability and Statistics: We introduced statistical models (eg. logistic regression), probabilistic algorithms (eg. Naïve Bayes) and R programming language for performing exploratory data analysis. This topic also shows an improvement from 23% to 42% with a peak at the "Good" level. Students learned to apply probabilistic algorithms and statistical methods to big data.

Mathematics: For the mathematics skills distributions change between PRE-Test and Post-Test shows negative trend. Perhaps the course material made them realize that there is lot more to learn in mathematics.

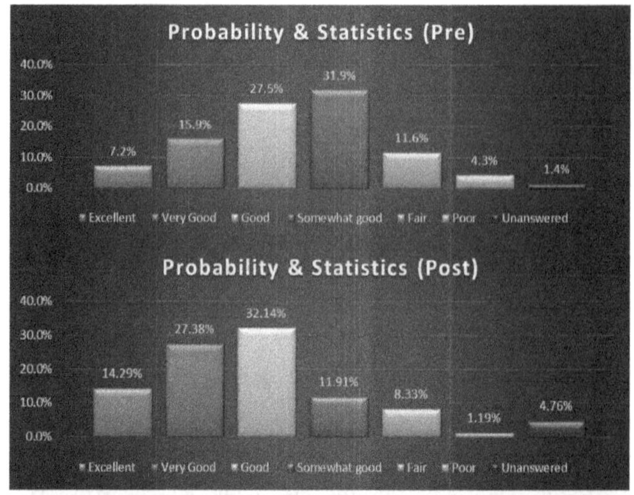

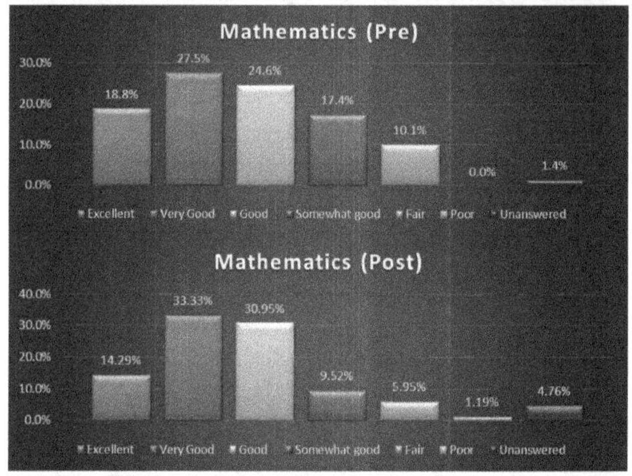

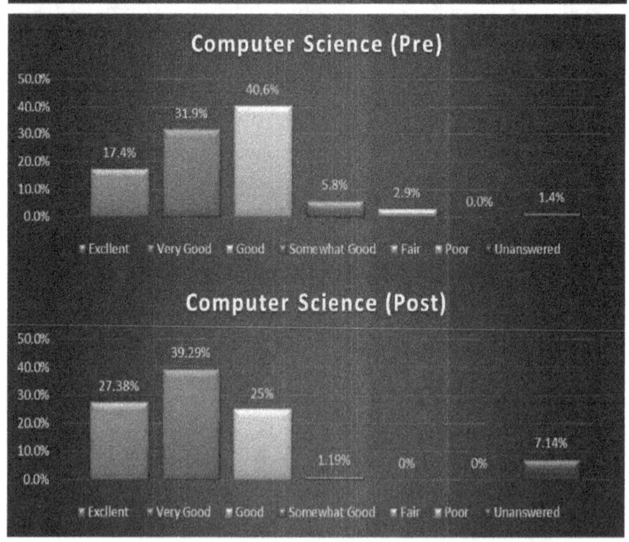

Computer Science: For Computer Science "skill" there is improvement but not that significant as some of the other areas discussed above (40% to 57%), and appropriately so. We did not teach any core concepts in CS like algorithmic complexity and efficiency of data structures. This is reflective in the outcome chart.

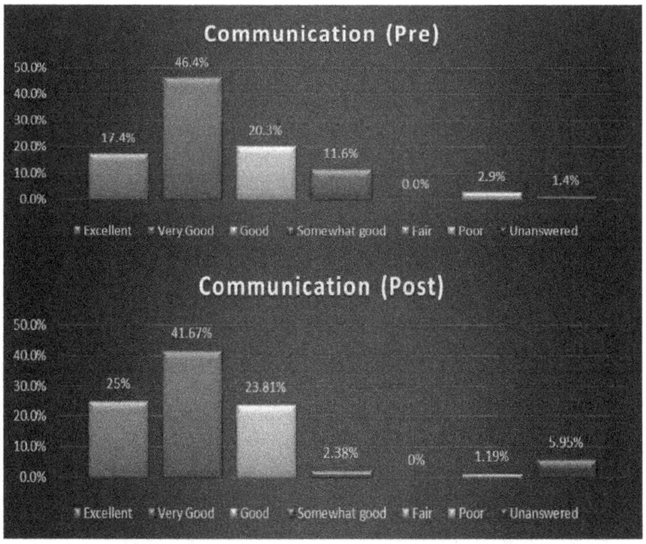

Figure 1: Distribution of PRE-Test and POST-Test Responses

Communication & Domain expertise: These topics are somewhat dependent on the prior experience and preparation of the students. The course did not cover the "communication" skill explicitly except for the project report preparation. The domain expertise was developed based on the application areas students chose to solve the big-data problems in. Though there is improvement in each of these categories, it is modest.

Overall the assessment of student learning outcome showed significant learning improvement in Data Science related areas.

3. Significant Outcomes

Any matriculated undergraduate student can possibly enroll in this program irrespective of the major, thus emphasizing the importance of ***multidisciplinary*** nature of data-intensive computing. This program facilitates a data-intensive computing track for a CS student, and for non-CSE majors a minor in CS with emphasis in Data-Intensive Computing. The certificate program was approved in 2011 for the institution and we could advertise it for enrollment in Fall 2011. Allowing for a two year time for completing the required courses, it is only now that we are filling the pipeline with students who plan to follow the data-intensive computing track. This grant program supported students with stipends, many of whom moved onto higher studies and employment in the same area. A crowning achievement of the project is that a student who was supported by the project went on to win SIGCSE undergraduate research competition and then went on to win the grand finale of all the ACM SIG competition for the undergraduate research category [1]. This student is currently enrolled in a prestigious Ph.D. program in Computer Science.

Even though course enrollment for Data-intensive Computing course (CSE487) was high, many took this course at the Junior/senior level and could not plan the certificate program requirements into their plan of study. Moreover many got their internships and jobs based on the material and skills they learned in the CSE487 course, and did not have time to complete the requirements for the certificate. Now that the program is listed in the undergraduate catalog, there are many inquiries from students entering the university. Many are choosing to plan their study around this program. We expect the data-intensive computing certificate to be become integral part of the undergraduate program ensuring sustainability.

4. Best Practices in Creating a Data Science Program

So far we discussed the curriculum, evaluation of student learning and the sustainability of the project. In this section we discuss practical details for adopting and/or adapting the curriculum developed as discussed above (the TIDE project). First step in realizing the data science curriculum at any level is the preparation of the educators.

1. Educator development: Educators who desire to introduce Data Science need professional development to learn about data-intensive computing. This can be achieved by educators attending workshops at conferences such as SIGCSE and other ACM and IEEE conferences focusing on data. Most of the conferences have educators' track with some travel support.

2. Curriculum development: While this is a daunting task, we suggest a light-weight approach for especially the novices to this area. The light weight approach involves a development of a single new course in Data Science/Data-Intensive computing that eventually will lead to a full track of data concentration or a certificate program. The second approach is the one we followed and is quite aggressive in that a whole new certificate program needed to be developed. The latter requires strong commitment from the faculty and/or some external funding from sources such as NSF. Our recommendation is to combine a set of existing courses in the curriculum with one or more newer courses. The latest curriculum for the data-intensive computing course that we developed can be found here [17].

3. Hands-on laboratory components: The implementation of the data science curriculum requires large volumes of storage and compute clusters for working with newer models of computation. The best approach is to rent compute facilities on the cloud, thus introducing the students to computing on the cloud, a valuable skill to have. The most common compute models such as Amazon AWS, Google compute engine and IBM Bluemix have free or educator's versions available that the students in the course may use. Some of these businesses have a dedicated educators' grant [2, 11] for teaching courses using their cloud resources.

4. Capstone Project: The capstone project is the highlight of the certificate program. Students work on applying the data-intensive concepts studied in the earlier courses to a research problem in their area of interest, typically in their major discipline of study. Some of the projects are pure applications and others are projects resulting in research publication. For example, one such research project by a student won the ultimate undergraduate research award given by ACM student research competition.

5. Continuous improvement: Data science area is in a state of flux. The data ecosystem consisting of the infrastructure, computing models and algorithms and applications are rapidly evolving. Continuous monitoring of the data ecosystem and corresponding updating of the curriculum are imperative. The professional development for the educators and a reliable cloud computing infrastructure are indispensable to address this challenge. Thus the course topics given in Section 2.2.2 need to be improved with every offering of the course.

6. Outreach: The stakeholders for the data-intensive computing come from many disciplines (STEM as well as humanities) and from all levels, high schools and community colleges and also local industrial workforce requiring retraining in this data sciences. Thus the course developed can be publicized to communities of interest to enroll more students as well as to explore realistic use cases for data. We did demonstrate pieces of the course to community colleges and K-12 schools. We also offered custom training to local industries based on the curriculum we developed.

5. Multi-Disciplinary Collaboration

The grant NSF-DUE-CCLI-0920335, Timely Introduction of Emerging Data-intensive Computing to Undergraduates was indeed timely and highly successful in developing students and several interdisciplinary collaborations (ART, BIO, EDU, ENG and MTH). The Biological Sciences and Mathematics collaborations have resulted in inter-disciplinary talks, discussions, joint proposals some of which were funded and have become highly impactful and successful projects in STEM [14, 18, 19]as well as social sciences areas [6, 7]. We have also created a data-driven Emerging Applications and Technology course for an international degree program. We found that many of the interesting use cases for data-driven applications are from outside computer science. Thus the introduction of data-intensive computing in a department's curriculum has opened up tremendous opportunities for collaboration and interactions.

6. Summary

We learned that it takes a lot of effort, time, support and relentless perseverance to (i) design courses in emerging areas (ii) establish a certificate program, and (iii) integrate these into CSE curriculum for sustainability beyond the grant period. The exploratory analysis of the assessment data shows significant improvement and awareness among learners for data-related technologies, applications and practices. The two featured courses CSE486 Distributed Systems and CSE487 Data-intensive Computing have become popular and permanent core courses of the CSE department, and the SUNY-wide certificate program has been institutionalized. 1113 college level students have directly benefitted by these two courses during the grant period 2009-2014. Many more stakeholders from K-12 students, educators and adult learners benefitted from the outreach efforts and lectures. Future plans include targeted dissemination to colleges nationwide using in person and distance learning methods.

7. Acknowledgements

The author would like to thank the reviewers for their thoughtful feedback. Thanks to Xiang Lin and Tarun Gauba for preparing the charts. This work would not have been possible without a grant from NSF CCLI program grant NSF-DUE-CCLI-0920335.

8. References

[1] ACM Student Research Competition 2015, http://src.acm.org/, Last viewed Aug. 2015.

[2] Amazon Web Services: Cloud Computing Services, aws.amazon.com, last viewed August 2015.

[3] Apache Hadoop. https://hadoop.apache.org/, August 2015.

[4] Apache Spark: Lightning Fast Cluster Computing. http://spark.apache.org/, last viewed August 2015.

[5] Dean, J. and Ghemawat, S. 2008. MapReduce: simplified data processing on large clusters. *Communication of ACM* 51, 1 (Jan. 2008), 107-113.

[6] Digital Choreographic Lineage. Techne award from the prestigious Techne Institute, highly synergistic collaboration with Prof. Aceto of Theater and Dance department: 2013-2015.

[7] A Global Access and Preservation Framework. Innovative Micro-Programs Accelerating Collaboration in Themes (IMPACT) grant from VPR for Research and Development at SUNY Buffalo, 2014-2015. With Prof. Aceto of Theater and Dance Department.

[8] Google Cloud Platform. https://cloud.google.com/, Aug. 2015.

[9] Google Analytics Platform. https://developers.google.com/analytics/, August 2015.

[10] Gray, J. Distributed Computing Economies. Computer Systems Theory, Technology and Applications, from Object-Relational Mappers Vol. 6, No. 3 - May/June 2008, http://www.acmqueue.org/modules.php?name=Content&pa=showpage&pid=545, last viewed August 2015.

[11] IBM Bluemix, http://www.ibm.com/cloud-computing/bluemix/, last viewed August 2015.

[12] Lin, J. and Dyer, C. Data-Intensive Text Processing with MapReduce. Morgan Claypool, 2010.

[13] Master's Programs in Data Science. http://www.mastersindatascience.org/schools, last viewed 2015.

[14] NSF OCI CI-TEAM/NSF-ACI-1041280: A *Cloud-enabled* Evolutionary Genetics Learning Tool for Engaging the Net-Savvy Generation. This is in collaboration with Dr. Poulin and Dr. Dittmar De la Cruz of Biological Sciences department.

[15] ONeil, C. and Schutt, R. Doing Data Science, ISBN:978-1-4493-5865-5. Oreilly Media, Doing Data Science, http://shop.oreilly.com/product/0636920028529.do, 2013.

[16] The R Project for Statistical Computing. https://www.r-project.org/, last viewed August 2015.

[17] Ramamurthy, B. Data-intensive Computing Curriculum Page. http://www.cse.buffalo.edu/faculty/bina/DataIntensive, last viewed August 2015.

[18] SUNY Innovation in Instructional Technology Grant (IITG): SUNY Collaboratory on Immersive Virtual Learning Environments for STEM Learning, CO-PI with *Education Department at SUNY Albany*, 2012-2013 (Phase I), SUNY Games (Phase II), 2013-2014.

[19] SUNY Innovation in Instructional Technology Grant (IITG): Development and Assessment of Mobile Device Instruction in STEM Education at K-21 Level, CO-PI with Biology Dept., 2012-2013 (Phase I), Development and assessment of a multiplayer, cloud module for teaching population genetics (Phase II), 2014-2015.

[20] Twitter. https://twitter.com. Last viewed August 2015.

[21] University at Buffalo, Undergraduate Catalog, Data-intensive Computing Certificate program, http://undergrad-catalog.buffalo.edu/academicprograms/dic.shtml, 2014.

[22] Yahoo! Big Data Summit and Big Data Study group, http://www.cra.org/ccc/visioning/visioning-activities/big-data-computing, 2008.

Teaching Big Data with a Virtual Cluster

Joshua Eckroth
Math/CS Department
Stetson University
jeckroth@stetson.edu

ABSTRACT

Both industry and academia are confronting the challenge of *big data*, i.e., data processing that involves data so voluminous or arriving at such high velocity that no single commodity machine is capable of storing or processing them all. A common approach to handling big data is to divide and distribute the processing job to a cluster of machines. Ideally, a course that teaches students how to work with big data would provide students access to a cluster for hands-on practice. However, a cluster of physical, on-premise machines may be prohibitively expensive, particularly at smaller institutions with smaller budgets.

In this report, we summarize our experiences developing and using a *virtual cluster* in a big data mining and analytics course at a small private liberal arts college. A single moderately-sized server hosts a cluster of virtual machines, which run the popular Apache Hadoop system. The virtual cluster gives students hands-on experience and costs less than an equal number of physical machines. It is also easily constructed and reconfigured. We describe our implementation, analyze its performance characteristics, and compare costs with physical clusters and the Amazon Elastic MapReduce cloud service. We summarize our use of the virtual cluster in the classroom and show student feedback.

Keywords

big data; virtual machines; cloud computing; curriculum

1. INTRODUCTION

Today's data scientists work with larger datasets than ever before. Known as "big data," these datasets are so massive that new tools, techniques, and expertise are required. Many of these tools and techniques have emerged only in the last few years and have not yet transitioned into the undergraduate curriculum. We believe computer science and information technology students should learn the theory and practice of big data. Doing so may greatly improve their standing in the job market and their ability to keep up with a rapidly changing technology landscape.

Teaching big data presents a challenge. The challenge is not due to a lack of data. A variety of large datasets are publicly available without cost from myriad sources. The challenge is obtaining sufficient computational and storage resources to work with big data. Because big data is normally too large for processing or storage on a single commodity machine, i.e., anything short of a supercomputer, multiple machines must be used in tandem. Machines are often networked into a cluster and the data are stored and processed in a distributed, parallel fashion. However, the costs of building a cluster may present a serious obstacle for smaller computer science departments hoping to give students hands-on experience with big data.

In order to reduce costs while still offering a hands-on big data infrastructure, we developed a *virtual cluster* using virtual machines rather than physical machines. This system was used in a *Big Data Mining and Analytics* course at Stetson University in Spring 2015. The virtual cluster proved successful for the course and was procured with relatively low cost.

In the following sections, we describe the technical details of the virtual cluster (Section 2). In Section 3, we examine the costs of this system and alternatives. This is followed by an evaluation the virtual cluster's performance under a variety of configurations in Section 4. Our system's performance and costs are compared to the Amazon Elastic MapReduce cloud service in Section 5. Discussion follows in Section 6. We then report on our experiences with the virtual cluster in the classroom (Section 7), summarize related work (Section 8), and offer conclusive remarks and plans for future work in Section 9.

2. IMPLEMENTATION

Rather than purchase a number of physical machines to form a cluster, we upgraded an existing server to host virtual machines. Details about the hardware and associated costs are presented in Section 3. In this section, we discuss the software that configures and runs the virtual cluster. We chose only open source software due to cost and the ubiquity of such software in industry and academia.

We opted to make use of the Apache Hadoop platform. Hadoop is a common open source software system for managing distributed storage and processing. Many software packages enhance the Hadoop system, and are commonly used by data scientists. The variety and popularity of Hadoop-based tools greatly enhances the value of Hadoop in an ed-

SIGCSE '16, March 02-05, 2016, Memphis, TN, USA

DOI: http://dx.doi.org/10.1145/2839509.2844651

ucational setting. Some examples of Hadoop-based tools include the following.

- Apache Hive provides SQL-like language for querying against large datasets.
- Apache Pig provides the PigLatin language to more easily describe complex dataflow processing tasks.
- Apache Mahout provides algorithms for machine learning applications.

Hadoop stores data in the Hadoop Distributed File System (HDFS) [7]. HDFS is designed to manage the storage of very large datasets with high reliability. It does so by splitting the data into chunks and storing each chunk on a different machine in the cluster. Furthermore, each chunk is replicated on other machines to ensure the original data can be pieced back together if a small number of machines go offline or lose their data.

In a typical Hadoop data processing scenario, the job is split into stages, distributed to multiple machines, and executed in parallel. Ideally, each machine holds the subset of data it is required to process, thus limiting communication over the virtual or physical network. Results from each machine are collected and merged in a final processing stage.

A typical Hadoop system consists of three or more machines (virtual or physical): a ResourceManager, a NameNode, and $N \geq 1$ additional nodes that both store and process data. The ResourceManager is responsible for managing the processing jobs. The NameNode is responsible for managing the HDFS index. The ResourceManager and NameNode are not required to be installed on separate machines, but it is common to do so in order to reduce resource contention. The number of nodes N should be decided based on expected workload. Below, we evaluate a range of values for N in our virtual cluster environment.

Hadoop can be set up in one of two ways:

- *Local-Hadoop*, which runs normal Hadoop jobs but does not actually distribute the workload. All processing is performed by a single machine hosting the local-Hadoop system. Data are stored on the local filesystem, not distributed in HDFS. Local-Hadoop is commonly used for testing purposes.
- *Cluster-Hadoop*, which runs jobs in a distributed fashion across N nodes, and stores data in HDFS. Unlike local-Hadoop, this setup takes advantage of distributed data storage and processing.

Our goal was to give students hands-on experience with Hadoop. This could be accomplished in several ways:

1. Ask students to install local-Hadoop on their own machines.
2. Install local-Hadoop on each student-accessible lab computer.
3. Give students access to a physical cluster of machines running cluster-Hadoop.
4. Give students access to a virtual cluster of machines (hosted on one physical machine) running cluster-Hadoop.
5. Give students access to a cloud service capable of running cluster-Hadoop, such as Amazon Elastic MapReduce, Microsoft Azure HDInsight, or Google Cloud.

Option (1) is untenable because not all students have access to sufficiently powerful personal machines. Both options (1) and (2) do not give students experience with distributed parallel computing since local-Hadoop processes jobs only on a single machine. Options (3) and (4) differ in two dimensions: as shown below, a physical cluster (option 3) may be more expensive than a virtual cluster (option 4), but a physical cluster may also be more performant. We investigate these dimensions below in Sections 3 and 4, respectively. Option (5) presents a different cost model in which a student or school pays for each data processing job rather than one up-front cost. We examine this option in Section 5.

We used LibVirt and the KVM/QEMU hypervisor on a CentOS Linux host machine to run the virtual machines. Each virtual machine runs Ubuntu Linux 14.04. Hadoop version 2.6 was installed in each virtual machine. Vagrant and Ansible were used to automatically generate and configure the virtual machines just by executing a single command. Our cluster configuration software[1] consists of Vagrant and Ansible scripts that build or restart the virtual machines, install and configure Hadoop, and configure student access to the web-based Hadoop management system. The configuration software supports several virtualization platforms, including VirtualBox and VMWare, and a configurable number of nodes N. When used without the Vagrant component, our configuration scripts are able to install and configure Hadoop and related tools on each machine in a physical cluster as well. These scripts enable instructors and/or IT personnel to easily build and manage a virtual or physical cluster. Students likewise can begin using the system without any special configuration on their own machines.

The configuration software consists of a couple primary commands. We assume the number of nodes N is predefined in the Vagrant script.

- `vagrant up` — creates N virtual machines and, if necessary, installs Hadoop and related utilities on each.
- `setup-hadoop.sh` — installs Hadoop configuration to ensure each node is aware of the others and to enable the Hadoop web-based management system.

These two commands build and configure the entire virtual cluster. After they complete, Hadoop jobs may be executed from the host machine (the server hosting the virtual machines) with commands like:

- `hadoop jar wc.jar WordCount /input.txt /output`

Students may view the status of their jobs by accessing the web interface. In our case, we showed students how to communicate with the host server via Secure Shell tunnels. After connecting to the host server, they were able to access the web interface in their normal browser.

Students used Eclipse and a local-Hadoop installation to test jobs on small datasets before submitting them to the virtual cluster. We also provided a local-Hadoop installation on a separate virtual machine for those who did not wish to install Hadoop on their own machines.

[1]https://github.com/StetsonMathCS/hadoopvirtualcluster

3. COSTS

One of the two differences between physical clusters and virtual clusters is their costs. The other difference is performance. We evaluate performance of the virtual cluster in Section 4, below. Here, we compare the prices of new hardware for a single server capable of hosting virtual machines and forming a virtual cluster, and the prices of new hardware to form a physical cluster.

While we did not purchase all new hardware for our Spring 2015 course, we have identified a comparable new machine from Dell. We choose Dell in these cost comparisons simply for convenience, as Dell sells a wide variety of hardware. The top section of Table 1 estimates the cost of a server with the same performance characteristics and storage capacity of the server used in our course. This proposed server is capable of hosting a large number of virtual machines, perhaps up to fifty. We did not test with so many virtual machines because we experienced diminishing returns after about twenty.

We estimate that a new server or cluster of servers will require significant upgrades after three years of use. We estimate the power costs assuming three years of continuous usage multiplied by the US national average electricity cost. Other incidental costs, such as personnel required for maintenance, space for housing the computers, air conditioning, etc. are not included in our calculations, as they vary widely and depend on the particulars of the institution.

The cost for an *equivalent* physical cluster is difficult to estimate. Virtualization adds some overhead. Johnson et al. [4] found that KVM-based virtualization adds little overhead for CPU and memory access, but may significantly diminish network performance (communication between virtual machines). It is not clear how a typical Hadoop job is impacted by this observation. Even so, assume that one virtual machine on the proposed server has nearly equal performance characteristics to the low-end servers shown in the table. Suppose the virtual cluster consists of N nodes in addition to the ResourceManager and NameNode. Then the cost of an equivalent physical cluster would be $N \times \$982 + (N+2) \times \$810 + \$2,272$, as shown in the table. Thus, whenever $N \geq 3$, a virtual cluster is cheaper than an equivalent physical cluster.

Assuming three years of use before significant upgrades, the cluster may be used across six academic semesters. Further assume that each class involves 20 students, as is common for smaller colleges and universities, and the curriculum includes five big data projects. Finally, assume each student submits an average of five processing jobs per project. This amounts to 500 jobs submitted per semester, or 3000 jobs over the lifetime of the cluster. Thus, the cost per job for our proposed server is \$2.82. Assuming a 10-node physical cluster, the cost per job is \$7.27. In Section 5, we will compare these numbers with the average cost per job for Amazon Elastic MapReduce under various configurations.

The potential cost benefits of a virtual cluster over a physical cluster should be considered against their relative performance characteristics. We were not able to evaluate the performance of a physical cluster. However, the following section addresses performance evaluation of virtual clusters.

Proposed server:	
Dell R430	\$7,400
Power for three years:	\$1050
Cluster of low-end servers:	
Dell R220 for ResourceManager	\$982
Dell R220 for NameNode	\$1,086
Dell R220 for N nodes	$N \times \$982$
Power for three years for all servers	$(N+2) \times \$810$
Network switch	\$204

Table 1: Costs for proposed virtual cluster server and alternative physical cluster hardware configurations. Configuration specifics follow. Dell PowerEdge R430: Intel Xeon E5-2640, 128 GB memory, hard drives totaling 28 TB; Dell PowerEdge R220: Intel i3-4150, 8 GB memory, 2 TB hard drive; or 16 GB memory for NameNode; Power usage of proposed server estimated at 400 watts, and each low-end server estimated at 300 watts [1]; Power costs estimated assuming US national average electricity rate of \$0.1009/kWh; Network switch: 1 Gbit Cisco 200 series. Prices accurate as of June, 2015.

4. PERFORMANCE EVALUATION

We measured the performance of virtual clusters under various loads and with various node counts N. Such an evaluation can tell us the number of nodes that maximizes job throughput under various loads. With this information, the virtual cluster can be configured with the ideal number of nodes and the Hadoop scheduler configured to support a certain maximum number of simultaneous jobs. We expect that these optimal values depend on the specific hardware and virtualization platform.

Our evaluation consisted of executing a number of equivalent jobs on virtual clusters with various node counts. The job was a typical word count on a 2 GB text file. The text file was uploaded to HDFS as multiple copies to ensure the chunks of each copy were evenly distributed across the nodes. This ensures that the jobs are executed on the widest distribution of nodes, i.e., those that hold chunks of the input text, rather than all executing on the same node.

Figure 1 shows the results of our evaluation. We see that the general trend is low throughput for few simultaneous jobs, then a peak, followed by a modest decline in throughput. This trend indicates that a cluster's resources are not fully utilized until a modest number of simultaneous jobs are submitted. This peak appears to occur around 4-6 jobs in our tests. When more jobs are submitted, and resources are overstressed, one of two contingencies may occur. Jobs may execute in parallel and consume each other's resources, slowing the execution of all jobs. Or, jobs may be postponed by the scheduler until sufficient resources become available. We observed both of these cases occurring, sometimes simultaneously.

A second trend to notice is that $N = 15$ or $N = 20$ is better than $N = 10$ in terms of overall throughput. With fewer nodes, jobs are forced to share a smaller pool of resources. Our host server has 32 CPU cores, so $N = 30$ nodes or so should be feasible before CPU utilization reaches its maximum capacity. As N increases, the number of simultaneous disk input/output operations increases, which reduces overall performance, since there is only one disk (or one array of disks). There is evidence of this phenomenon at 12 simultaneous jobs. A configuration with 10 nodes handles 12

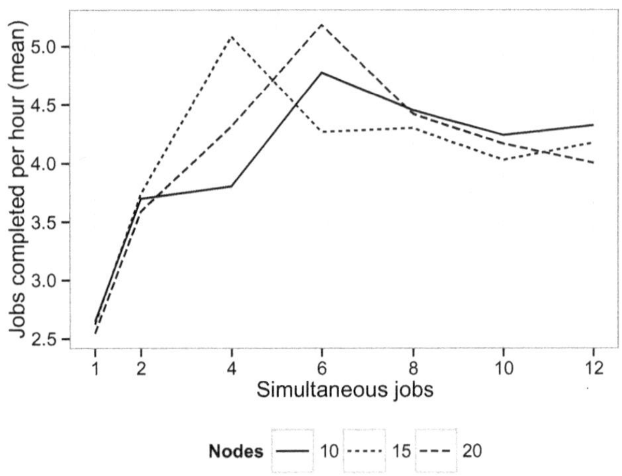

Figure 1: Jobs completed per hour (throughput) for a range of counts of simultaneous jobs and nodes (labeled N in the text). The tests were performed on the virtual cluster described in the text. Throughput was measured as the mean of three tests in each case.

simultaneous jobs better than 15 or 20 nodes because some of the jobs are placed in a queue, waiting for free resources on one of the 10 nodes. Even with this waiting period, jobs complete faster because there is less contention for the disk. Each node was given 8 GB of memory (except the NameNode, which was given 16 GB of memory), but our word count job did not consume enough memory to make memory capacity a limiting factor.

5. COMPARISON WITH AMAZON EMR

Cloud services provide an alternative to housing one or more servers on-premise. In this section, we evaluate Amazon's Elastic MapReduce (EMR) service, though alternatives such as Microsoft's Azure HDInsight and Google's Cloud are available. Elastic MapReduce is capable of executing normal Hadoop jobs on a configurable number of cluster nodes. Furthermore, the nodes may be one of several types with different performance characteristics and costs. We evaluate the m1.medium, m1.large, and m1.xlarge types.

The cost of a processing job is calculated based on the duration of the job multiplied by the number of nodes and the cost of the node type. For example, suppose a job requires 35 minutes of processing time, and 10 nodes of type m1.large are utilized. One extra node (of the same type) is needed to manage the Hadoop job. The cost of an Elastic MapReduce m1.large node is \$0.197 per hour (at the time of writing), which is calculated by adding the cost of an m1.large node (\$0.175/hour) and the cost of Elastic MapReduce (\$0.022/hour). Thus, the cost of the job is $35/60 * 11 * \$0.197 = \$1.26$. In fact, processing times are rounded up to the nearest hour, so the actual cost is $60/60 * 11 * \$0.197 = \$2.17$. Our costs reported below are not calculated by rounding-up to the nearest hour; rather, the exact number of minutes required to complete the job is used in our calculations.

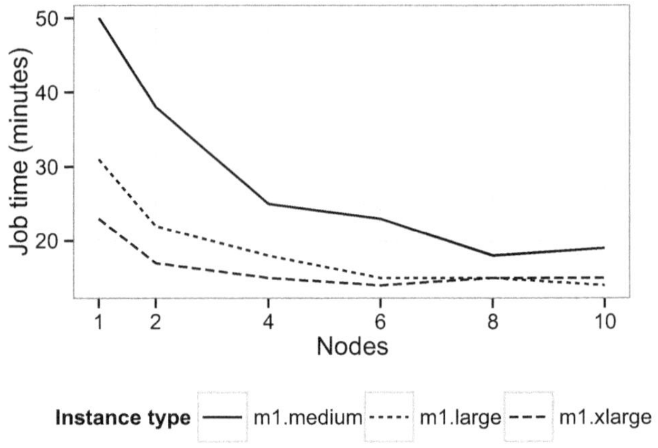

Figure 2: Processing time for a single job under various configurations of Amazon Elastic MapReduce jobs. The job submitted was a word count on a 2 GB text file.

Platform	Job time	Job cost
Virtual cluster	334 min	\$2.82
Physical cluster	–	\$7.27
Amazon EMR, m1.medium	101 min	\$2.02
Amazon EMR, m1.large	56 min	\$2.02
Amazon EMR, m1.xlarge	34 min	\$2.32

Table 2: Processing times and costs (estimated for virtual and physical clusters) for a word count job on a 37 GB text file. In each case, the cluster is configured with 10 nodes. We did not build and test a physical cluster.

We executed the same 2 GB word count job on the three different node types with varying number of nodes. As expected, the more expensive node types (e.g., m1.xlarge) performed better than the cheaper types (e.g., m1.medium). Figure 2 shows the general trend as the number of nodes increases.

Since the job cost is partly calculated according to the processing time, we expect that node configurations that complete a job faster are more expensive. Figure 3 shows exactly that trend. Thus, it is clear that for cloud services, faster and cheaper are competing desiderata.

We can directly compare performance and costs of the virtual cluster solution and Elastic MapReduce by submitting a larger job. In this case, the job is a word count of a 37 GB text file. The processing times and costs are shown in Table 2. Note that we did not build and test a physical cluster, so we do not know the exact processing time for such a configuration. Conclusions that may be drawn from this table are discussed in the following section.

6. DISCUSSION

Our evaluation of a single server hosting several virtual machines, an equivalent physical cluster, and Amazon's cloud service yields several interesting insights. First, a physical

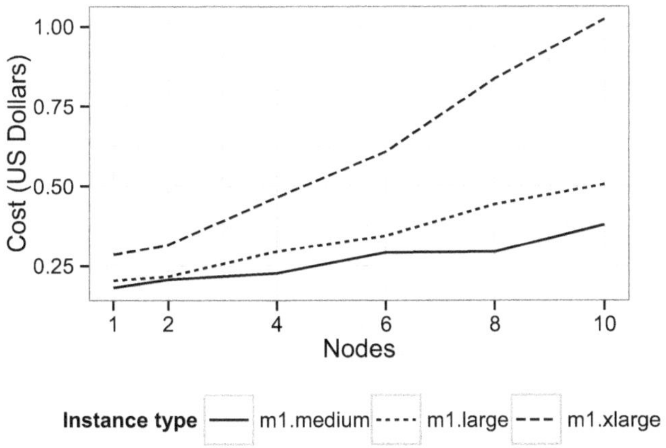

Figure 3: Costs for a single job under various configurations of Amazon Elastic MapReduce jobs. The job submitted was a word count on a 2 GB text file.

cluster is significantly more expensive, per job, than either a single equivalent server or Amazon's offering. Second, Amazon offers a very competitive Hadoop platform both in terms of price and performance.

Before we consider Amazon's service, it is important to point out the Achilles' heel of the virtual cluster solution. The virtual cluster suffers from a performance limitation that is not present in a physical cluster or a cloud platform. Hadoop is designed to make use of the resources of distinct physical machines. In particular, it assumes that when machine A reads or writes data, these operations do not impact machine B's ability to read/write its data. This is because HDFS stores data on each machine and only asks each machine to process the data that it stores. However, in a virtual cluster, there is only one physical hard drive, or array of drives that share a single input/output channel. When virtual machine A accesses data, virtual machine B may need to wait for the input/output channel to become available. Disk input/output becomes a bottleneck in virtual clusters. This bottleneck is especially apparent when processing the 37 GB text file, shown in Table 2, and less apparent when processing the 2 GB text file. When processing the larger text file with more than 10 virtual nodes, I/O contention was so prevalent that some nodes failed to receive any data in a reasonable time and were abandoned by the Hadoop ResourceManager.

Amazon's cloud service is both cheaper and more performant than our virtual cluster solution. We expect similar results from Microsoft's and Google's cloud offerings. This makes cloud services very compelling for computer science education. However, the cost model is fundamentally different. Cloud services are paid for on a per-job basis. If students are required to pay for their own jobs, we expect that they will be reluctant to submit any jobs due to fear of job failure or wrong answers, which require correcting and submitting new jobs. Costs may also accumulate due to accidental failure to terminate the nodes. If a student forgets to turn off 11 m1.large nodes (10 processing nodes plus the Hadoop manager node) over the course of a weekend (48 hours), the student will be presented with a \$104.02 bill. Further work is needed to determine how students approach an assignment when out-of-pocket costs are involved.

7. EXPERIENCES IN THE CLASSROOM

Twenty students made use of the virtual cluster. They authored, submitted, and monitored Hadoop jobs, uploaded and downloaded data from HDFS, executed Hive queries, and trained machine learning models with Mahout.

Five projects involved the virtual cluster.

1. A typical word count introductory exercise.
2. "Analyze BackBlaze's hard drive monitoring data[2] to determine if some group of hard drives failed more often than others." The dataset was 4.2 GB in size.
3. "Analyze StackExchange's entire database of questions and answers[3] to determine if persons with high reputation typically answer questions faster." The dataset was about 116 GB in size.
4. "Use image processing and clustering to determine if a dataset of 10,000 cat images is comprised of cats of distinct breeds, based on the cat's colors." The dataset was 4.2 GB in size.
5. "Build a spam classifier model for 75,419 email messages in the TREC 2007 dataset."[4] The dataset was about 0.7 GB in size.

Depending on the project, students crafted MapReduce jobs, wrote Hive queries, and/or executed Mahout commands. In many cases, they were not required to use these tools, but chose to out of necessity or convenience. We wanted students to gain an understanding of why various tools exist, even Hadoop itself. They came to these realizations by discovering that they could not easily solve a problem, such as processing huge datasets without splitting the task with Hadoop, or merging user data and question/answer data in the StackExchange project without SQL-like table joins with Hive.

The system proved very reliable and was never unavailable due to load or system failure. However, we did observe some drawbacks during the course. The fair scheduler described above was not installed at the time, so jobs often waited in a first-in, first-out (FIFO) queue for quite some time. Students found it hard to predict the amount of time a job would take, partly due to the FIFO queue but also due to their inexperience with large processing tasks. Extensive benchmarks, like those presented above, were not performed until after the course ended. Some *ad hoc* adjustments to the number of nodes N were performed during the course to better balance the computational load. These changes disrupted some jobs and could have been avoided with better planning.

Student comments that relate to the virtual cluster and big data tools are shown below. Responding to the question, "Which aspects of this course helped you learn the most?" some students wrote,

[2] `https://www.backblaze.com/hard-drive-test-data.html`

[3] `https://archive.org/details/stackexchange`

[4] `http://plg.uwaterloo.ca/~gvcormac/treccorpus07/`

- "The practice with the various tools and software used in the class."
- "Hands on experience with current trends in the industry."

Those two comments give us reason to believe that the virtual cluster was a success. However, responding to the question, "Do you have suggestions for improving any aspects of the course?" one student wrote,

- "Add additional servers for student use."

More computational power would certainly reduce processing times and increase student satisfaction with the course and tools. However, more investigation is required to find the right tradeoff between budgetary concerns and additional student resources. We also note that these three comments are not necessarily representative of the entire class. In the future, we plan to explicitly ask students about their experiences with the virtual cluster.

8. RELATED WORK

Virtual clusters designed for student use have been developed by computer science departments in several small institutions. For example, St. Olaf College built both virtual and physical clusters using the KVM and the Beowulf platforms [3, 4], respectively. They describe the clusters' architectures and use cases. They also look at energy usage and the costs of cooling a room full of servers. In a more recent report by Brown and Shoop [2], they report that virtual clusters are less performant than physical clusters. A precise characterization of the performance penalty of virtualization depends on the workload. Brown and Shoop also discuss issues of cluster management. They do not compare physical and virtual cluster costs.

Ngo et al. [5] report on their increasingly more sophisticated clusters for teaching about big data with Hadoop. They do not address the costs of building a cluster nor analyze its performance characteristics. They report significant learning on several dimensions and high student satisfaction with their hands-on big data experiences.

Finally, Rabkin et al. [6] review their experiences teaching with cloud clusters provided by Amazon Web Services. A cloud cluster is an on-going expense, unlike a physical or virtual cluster which is a fixed expense. Their work was supported by a grant, so the costs were not passed on to the students. They find that students utilized an average of $45 worth of cloud resources during the semester. However, the efficiency of a student's solution could impact their costs. Even subtle features of code like object creation, string parsing, etc. could produce a substantial effect when processing big data. Some students also had a habit of leaving cloud services running unnecessarily, incurring costs without actually making use of the resources. Overall, the authors conclude that cloud services are a good platform for very large class sizes but costs are difficult to estimate and control.

9. CONCLUSION AND FUTURE WORK

This report summarized our experiences developing and using a virtual cluster for a big data course at a small private liberal arts college. Because we were able to upgrade existing equipment, we found that the virtual cluster design was cost-effective and sufficiently performant for a class of twenty students. Students expressed mostly positive feedback about the virtual cluster, though at least one student felt that the virtual cluster did not provide enough computational resources. The most significant drawback of the virtual cluster design is I/O contention, which dramatically lowers performance on large processing jobs. Experimentation with Amazon's Elastic MapReduce cloud service showed that cloud services can be cheaper and more performant than a virtual cluster solution. However, costs for cloud computing are charged on a per-job basis, which may fundamentally change how students decide to submit a job if they are responsible for the costs.

In future work, we plan to evaluate a wider variety of workloads, such as Hive queries and Mahout machine learning tasks. We are also considering ways in which to bring cloud services into the classroom in a manner that is least impactful to students in terms of costs.

10. ACKNOWLEDGEMENTS

This project was supported by the Brown Center for Faculty Innovation & Excellence at Stetson University.

11. REFERENCES

[1] S. Barielle. Calculating TCO for energy. *IBM Systems Magazine: Power*, pages 38–40, November 2011.

[2] R. Brown and E. Shoop. Teaching undergraduates using local virtual clusters. In *IEEE International Conference on Cluster Computing (CLUSTER)*, pages 1–8. IEEE, 2013.

[3] R. A. Brown. Hadoop at home: Large-scale computing at a small college. In *ACM SIGCSE Bulletin*, volume 41, pages 106–110. ACM, 2009.

[4] E. Johnson, P. Garrity, T. Yates, R. Brown, et al. Performance of a virtual cluster in a general-purpose teaching laboratory. In *IEEE International Conference on Cluster Computing (CLUSTER)*, pages 600–604. IEEE, 2011.

[5] L. B. Ngo, E. B. Duffy, and A. W. Apon. Teaching HDFS/MapReduce systems concepts to undergraduates. In *Parallel & Distributed Processing Symposium Workshops (IPDPSW), 2014 IEEE International*, pages 1114–1121. IEEE, 2014.

[6] A. S. Rabkin, C. Reiss, R. Katz, and D. Patterson. Experiences teaching mapreduce in the cloud. In *Proceedings of the 43rd ACM Technical Symposium on Computer Science Education*, pages 601–606. ACM, 2012.

[7] K. Shvachko, H. Kuang, S. Radia, and R. Chansler. The Hadoop distributed file system. In *IEEE 26th Symposium on Mass Storage Systems and Technologies (MSST)*, pages 1–10. IEEE, 2010.

Evaluating Student Teams: Do Educators Know What Students Think?

Anya Tafliovich
University of Toronto
Scarborough
anya@cs.toronto.edu

Andrew Petersen
University of Toronto
Mississauga
petersen@cs.toronto.edu

Jennifer Campbell
University of Toronto
campbell@cs.toronto.edu

ABSTRACT

The subject of this work is evaluation methods of student software development team projects. Over a two year period in three courses, we study student preferences for team evaluation methods, the reasons behind their preferences, the changes in preference that occur within a single course and across courses, and misconceptions that educators hold about student preferences.

Data was collected from peer evaluations and surveys. We find evidence that students' preferences for evaluation method are influenced by their year of study, familiarity with teammates, and overall happiness with the team experience. Other factors we explored, including gender and perceived ability, did not appear to influence evaluation preferences in our courses.

Keywords

student teamwork; evaluation; motivating students; undergraduate software development project

1. INTRODUCTION

Employers of Computer Science and Software Engineering graduates greatly value their employees' ability to work effectively in teams. Team projects are central to some CS and SE undergraduate courses, yet there is no agreed-upon approach or best practice for forming, managing, and evaluating student teams [19].

The aim of the current study is to explore students' preferences in teamwork evaluation methods and educators' perceptions of those preferences. We have reported preliminary results of the (now two-year-long) study in [24]. At the time, we were left with more questions than answers. In this work, we report on the analysis of an additional body of data, and the insights it provides into evaluation methods of student team projects, and the students' and educator's perceptions of these evaluation methods.

SIGCSE '16, March 02 - 05, 2016, Memphis, TN, USA

ISBN 978-1-4503-3685-7/16/03...$15.00

DOI: http://dx.doi.org/10.1145/2839509.2844647

2. RELATED WORK

The majority of research into team formation, team management, and team evaluation that we studied, was conducted in the domain of management or health care and policies. We note the evident need for more research into team management and team evaluation in education, and in particular in Computer Science and Software Engineering education, since the domain of our interest and the stakeholders' qualifications, level of maturity, and personal objectives are all very different in our setting.

Many groups have looked at team composition and at attributes of the team members that negatively impact the team's performance [2, 6, 14, 20, 22]. Faraj et al. found that a team's performance is affected by their communication and coordination styles [4], and Karn and Cowling found that personality issues that lead to disruptions were the most significant factor impacting quality of work [15].

Several studies focus on the impact of rewards on teams. Researchers in management cite the need to reward personal achievement to maximize productivity [13]. However, Hoffman et al. argue that a need for cooperation between teammates necessitates more equal sharing of rewards [11]. Similarly, in the classroom, students must balance the need to cooperate with teammates with the urge to demonstrate personal ability (for a better mark). Hazzan's 2003 study asked students to distribute a financial award within a team and observed their behaviour and found that the students tended to divide the majority of the funds equally, reserving a small portion to reward personal achievement [8]. Several groups have worked to teach teamwork skills in the context of software engineering teams and to raise awareness of the tension between collaboration and reward [9, 12, 21].

Self and peer assessments are critical elements in assessment for student team software projects, but some have expressed concerns about the effectiveness of peer assessment [1, 5, 17]. They found evidence of teams colluding to make sure that marks were shared equally — or to punish a single group member [16, 7]. Herbert found that students are both too generous *and* too hard on themselves, suggesting that students' perceptions of effort are not objective [10]. In contrast, Dunsmore et al. notes that peer critiques of contribution were consistent and correlated with perceptions of how much work was completed by team members [3]. Smith and Smarkusky propose a competency based framework for assessment to assist students in making more objective judgments [23].

Tarmazdi et al. [25] developed a software tool to allow instructors to monitor online student teamwork in real-time.

	Team portion (% of the total grade)	Individual portion (% of the total grade)
Option 1	100%	0%
Option 2	80%	20%
Option 3	50%	50%
Option 4	20%	80%
Option 5	0%	100%

Table 1: Survey Question Phase 1

	Team portion (% of the total grade)	Individual portion (% of the total grade)
Option 1	100%	0%
Option 2	90%	10%
Option 3	80%	20%
Option 4	70%	30%
Option 5	50%	50%
Option 6	30%	70%
Option 7	20%	80%
Option 8	10%	90%
Option 9	0%	100%

Table 2: Survey Question Phase 2

One purpose of this tool is for instructors to more effectively observe student interactions in order to provide students with timely feedback, including identify teams work are functioning poorly.

Willcoxson et al. [26] introduces an approach for team assessment that involves a framework for objective assessment, in addition to subjective assessment. Subjective assessment may not yield accurate results due to students factoring self-interest and peer-pressure into their subjective self- and peer-evaluations. Willcoxson's frame is also intended to serve as a resource to instructors who have the challenging task of assigning grades to individual team members.

3. ENVIRONMENT

The study was performed at a large, North American research-intensive university, over a period of two academic years. It included students from six sections of a second-year course and two sections of a forth-year course. Each course included a significant team-based software project within a twelve week term.

3.1 Courses Involved in the Study

The second-year course (we will call it SE2) introduced students to the programming language Java (the first year is taught in Python), basic Android development, object-oriented analysis and design, simple design patterns, basic version control, and introduction to software modelling. This is the first course in the program that involves significant and structured teamwork, though the students may opt to work with a partner in first year courses. The course project spanned seven weeks (roughly the second half of the term) and consisted of three distinct stages. The end product of the project was a simple Android application. The first stage was the design stage, done in groups of two. The second and third stages involved revisiting the design and developing the application; these were done in groups of four. The teams followed a prescribed, simplified, Scrum-like software development process, closely monitored by the course teaching assistants. The study participants were enrolled in four sections of the course offered in the Fall term of 2013 (first phase of the study) and in two sections of the course offered in the Winter term of 2015 (second phase of the study). The course offerings were extremely similar, and the project teamwork component was managed identically between the offerings. In total, the six course sections had over 800 students at peak enrolment.

The fourth-year course (SE4) is an advanced software engineering course. The students worked on a large (200K+ lines of code) open source project, in teams of six or seven in the Winter term of 2014 (first phase of the study) and in teams of five in the Winter term of 2015 (second phase of the study). In the course of the project, the students performed reverse engineering and analysis of the code base, completed at least two bug fixes, and investigated, designed, and implemented at least one new feature. The project spanned 10 weeks of the course in a twelve-week term. The teams chose their own software development process, with the vast majority choosing Agile development (Scrum or modified Scrum). The two offerings of the course involved over 140 students at peak enrolments.

3.2 Team Formation and Peer Evaluation

In all instances of SE2, the students formed teams of two for the first stage of the project. The course instructors then formed teams of four for the second and third stages of the project by merging the pairs from the first stage.

In SE4, we allowed students to request a single partner for the team. The course instructors then formed teams and, when possible, put the requested partners on the same team.

We used CATME team formation and peer evaluation software to form the teams in all three courses [18]. The team formation criteria included personal schedules (to maximize time available for group meetings), gender (females are not outnumbered in a team), GPA (to group students with dissimilar GPAs), and commitment level (to group students with similar self-reported commitment). We shoud note that, as a result of students partner requests, the team composition does not solely depend on these factors.

In all course offerings we also used CATME to perform a peer evaluation after each stage of the project. The students ranked themselves and their teammates, on a scale of 1 to 5, on (1) contributing to the team's work, and (2) interacting with teammates.The students were also invited to provide additional comments to the instructor. Based on these criteria (except for the comments), the CATME software calculates an *adjustment factor* for each student.

In SE2, the individual grade for a project stage was calculated as $0.8 \times \textit{team grade} + 0.2 \times \textit{adjustment factor} \times \textit{team grade}$, with the adjustment factor capped at 1.05. In SE4 the formula was $\textit{adjustment factor} \times \textit{team grade}$, where the adjustment factor was capped between 0.8 and 1.05.

In the second phase of the study, in addition to ranking their teammates, the students were also asked to rank, on a scale of 1 to 5, their agreement with the following statements: (1) I am satisfied with my present teammates, (2) I am pleased with the way my teammates and I work together, (3) I am very satisfied with working in this team.

3.3 Preferences of Team Evaluation

The information was collected at several points during the course of each term involved in the study.

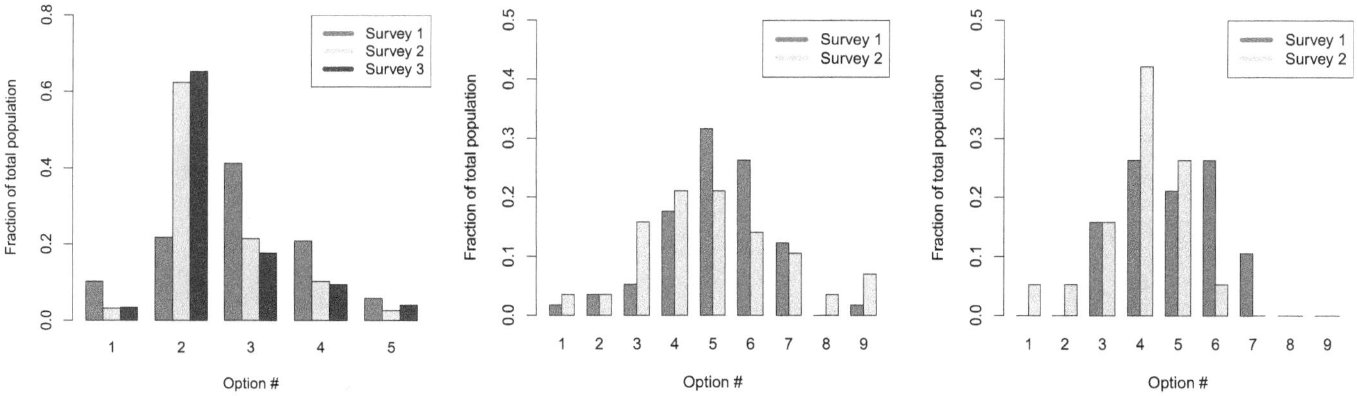

(a) SE2 — Phase 1 of study (b) SE2 – Phase 2 of study (c) SE4 – Phase 2 of study

Figure 1: Changes in evaluation preference

In the first phase of the study (2013 – 2014), at the beginning of the term, during lecture, we administered a survey that asked participants for: (1) whether the student is majoring in CS, (2) gender, (3) GPA, (4) whether English is the student's first language, and (5) expected grade in the course. In the second phase of the study (2014 – 2015), we asked for different information: (1) the number of team projects with 3+ team members, in which the participant was involved prior to the current course, (2) the method of forming the team in the last team project, in which the participant was involved (team formed by the instructor or by the students), (3) the participant's level of satisfaction with the team in this last team project, and (4) the participant's level of confidence in the instructors' and peers' ability to evaluate individual team member's contribution in a team project.

To assess the students' preference of team project evaluation policies, the students were also asked the following question:

> Assume that you are a member of a student team working on a course project that involves developing software. Your project grade will consist of two portions: Team and Individual. In the Team portion of the grade, each team member *receives the same grade.* In the Individual portion of the grade, each team member's grade is allocated *based on his/her individual performance* on the project. The table below outlines [five/nine] grading options:
>
> *[See Table 1 and Table 2 for the tables in the two surveys.]*
>
> Which grading option would you prefer? (Circle one) [1]

At the time of the survey, students were asked to provide informed consent. This information was provided to the investigators at the end of the term. The investigators also received access to all consenting students' term and final grades, as well as all term peer evaluation data, also after the end of each term.

In the first phase of the study, in SE2, the students answered the above question three times: (1) before the project teams were formed, (2) after the teams were formed but before they completed a project stage, and (3) at the end of the term. In the second phase of the study, the questions were answered (1) after the partners were declared, but before the four-member teams were formed, and (2) at the end of the term.

In SE4 in both phases of the study, the students answered the questions twice: (1) at the beginning of the term before teams were formed and (2) at the end of the term.

Each time, the students were informed that their survey responses were made anonymous for the purposes of the study, and that their responses had no impact on the actual method of project evaluation performed in the course.

[1]Notice that the students in the second phase of the study were given more options to select from.

4. RESULTS

A total of 509 participants provided consent for the study described in this paper: 430 from SE2 (342 in the first and 88 in the second phase of the study, or 60% and 55%, respectively) and 79 from SE4 (42 in the first and 37 in the second phase of the study, or 67% and 69%, respectively).

4.1 Team Evaluation Preference Changes

In support and in addition to the results reported in [24], the data analysis shows that:

- students' preferences with regards to evaluation of team projects change, both from year to year and within the course,
- students preferences shift towards putting more weight on the team's work, rather than on individual contribution, and
- the change and the preference for a larger teamwork component occurs as soon as the students know their team.

Figure 1 shows the changes in evaluation preferences. Please, note that because of the differences in the timing of administering the surveys in the two study phases, Survey 1 in Phase 2 of the study was administered at the time of Survey 2 in Phase 1 of the study. We also observe that given more evaluation options, the students clearly *prefer a more balanced split between the team and the individual component, although they still shift towards putting more weight on teamwork as soon as they know their teammates.*

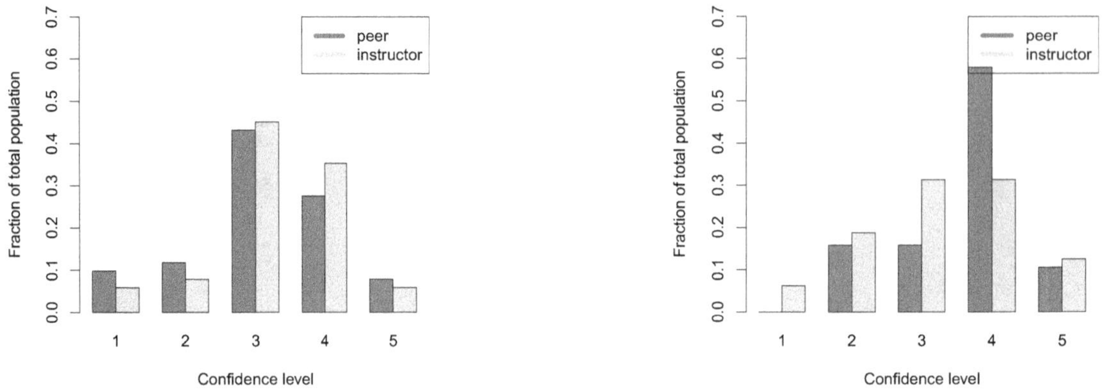

(a) Second year (b) Fourth year

Figure 2: Confidence in instructor and peer evaluation of individual contribution into a team project

4.2 Team Evaluation Preference: Any Predictors?

We used statistical software package R to perform linear regression tests to answer the following question:

Which, if any, of the factors of interest are predictors of the students' initial and/or final preferred option of team project evaluation?

In the first phase of the study, the factors we considered were: (1) gender, (2) being in a CS program, (3) English as first language, (4) GPA prior to this course, (5) expected grade in the course, (6) student's individual performance in the course (as measured by grades on pieces of work submitted individually in the course), (7) the student's peer evaluation scores in a recently completed project phase, (8) the student's evaluation of his or her peers in a recently completed project phase, and (9) the grade in this project phase.

In the second phase of the study, the factors were: (1) the number of team projects with 3+ team members, in which the participant was involved prior to the current course, (2) the method of forming the team in the last team project, in which the participant was involved (team formed by the instructor or by the students), (3) the participant's level of satisfaction with the team in this last team project, and (4) the participant's level of confidence in the instructors' and peers' ability to evaluate individual team member's contribution in a team project, (5) student's individual performance in the course (as measured by grades on pieces of work submitted individually in the course), (6) the student's peer evaluation scores in a recently completed project phase, (7) the student's evaluation of his or her peers in a recently completed project phase, (8) the grade in this project phase, and (9) the student's reported satisfaction with the team, as measured by three questions below:

- I am satisfied with my present teammates,
- I am pleased with the way my teammates and I work together, and
- I am very satisfied with working in this team.

Contrary to what we consider to be a popular belief among Software Engineering educators, and supporting and adding to the preliminary results reported in [24], we found that ***none** of the above are predictors* of either the initial (as reported in the beginning of the term) or the final (as reported at the end of the term) student's preference of team project evaluation option, *in any of the course offerings* involved in the study, except for the following:

In SE2, the level of satisfaction with the previous team project, in which the participant was involved, prior to this course, is a predictor of the initial preferred team project evaluation option, as reported in the beginning of the term — the more satisfied the student is with the previous project, the more she is likely to prefer to be evaluated as a team, rather than individually ($p = 0.0004$, $R^2 = 0.26$).

Interestingly, the same does not hold in SE4. Moreover, the satisfaction with the previous project (outside of this course) no longer matters for the evaluation preference, when the students in SE2 are asked the same question at the end of the term.

Surprisingly, we do not observe a similar correspondence in the results of the end-of term study, namely: Is the satisfaction with the team in this course a predictor of the evaluation preference option in SE2, as reported at the end of the term? The answer to this question is No.

4.3 Change in Preference: Any Predictors?

We performed additional linear regression tests to answer the following question:

Which, if any, of the factors of interest are predictors of the change in students' preferred option of team project evaluation?

Similar to the results in Section 4.2, we find that none of the factors under consideration are predictors of the change in students' preference, except for the rating of the statement: *I am very satisfied with working in this team.*

Here we have a negative correlation between the level of satisfaction with the working in the current team and the change in the preferred option. In other words, students who are happier working in their team are more likely to prefer to be evaluated as a team, rather than individually ($p = 0.0037$, $R^2 = 0.1476$).

We would like to bring the reader's attention to the fact that peer evaluation scores — both the student's peer evaluation scores in a recently completed project phase and the student's evaluation of his or her peers in a recently completed project phase — are **not** predictors of the change. Clearly, the students make a distinction between evaluating performance of their teammates and evaluating their satisfaction with the teamwork experience! We will elaborate on this in Section 4.5.

Anecdotal evidence suggests that educators are frequently surprised that the student's level of satisfaction with his or her teammates' performance is *not* positively correlated with opting for a higher team portion, and neither is it the case that stronger students prefer an evaluation option with a higher individual portion. Two years worth of data clearly shows that this is not the case — it is a misconception on the part of the educators.

4.4 Trust in Evaluation of Individual Contribution?

One hypothesis that came up in discussion of the possible explanations of *why* peer evaluations in the current project do not affect the evaluation preference option, despite the fact that these evaluations had, at least in the courses in this study, a direct affect on the students' grades, is the possibility that students do not trust these evaluations.

To this end, we collected data on the participant's level of confidence in the instructors' and peers' ability to evaluate individual team member's contribution in a team project. Figure 2 shows that the students do, in fact, trust both the instructor's and the peer's ability to evaluate and report individual contribution into the team project. Moreover, the confidence in peer evaluation grows dramatically from second to fourth year course, while confidence in instructor evaluation decreases.

4.5 Analysis of Student Comments

Since the quantitative data did not provide us with an insight into *why* the students differentiate between their evaluation of their team mates and their evaluation of the teamwork experience (with the second one being a predictor of the evaluation preference, while the first one is not), we set out in search for more data.

At the end of the project in the fourth year course and after the second and third phases of the second year course, students were asked to evaluate themselves and their teammates. As part of the evaluation, students were offered the opportunity to write a comment about their experience. A total of 160 comments were received from 111 students.

These comments were coded in two steps. First, 20% of the comments were selected randomly and analyzed without any preexisting codes. This generated four broad categories: the team, issues that had been encountered, workload, and self-evaluations of ability. Within the category of issues, we distinguished between comments that specified a problem and those that offered a cause for the issue. Second, we analyzed the full set of comments (including the 20% from before), using the categories identified as a guide. A fifth category was introduced part of the way through the second pass: a meta-category, for comments about the survey itself or the way that course was being conducted. These comments were fairly rare.

Table 3 provides a summary of the extracted tags, with their counts. There are a number of interesting aspects to note here, such as (1) the overwhelming number of comments on the positive team experience, (2) the majority of perceived problem causes and issues being related to communication, and (3) isolating a problem teammate, each of which warrants additional research.

Analysis of the student comments provided insight into

Issues	Android Tools	2
	Communication	16
	Debugging	1
	Design Conflicts	6
	Problem Teammate	36
	Scheduling Meetings	10
	Understanding Content	7
Perceived Causes		
	Commute	2
	Differences in Motivation	3
	Ego	3
	Inability to meet	5
	Lack of Communication	13
	Misrepresenting Progress	1
	Personal Issues	9
	Quality of Work	7
	Unequal Ability	5
Meta-comments		5
Self-evaluation	Lack of confidence	5
	Confidence	6
Team-evaluation	Negative	16
	Neutral	11
	Positive	73
Workload	Equal Division	4
	Difficulties Dividing Work	5
	Unequal Division	16

Table 3: Tags extracted from student comments

the lack of direct relationship between peer evaluation scores and overall teamwork satisfaction scores. For example:

> It was great working with — and — on this project, they were both respectable and responsible group members and I enjoyed being a part of the team. — was still not present during this third phase, so it was a bit of a struggle on our end to account for one less team member. Although all of our work loads increased, I think we were able to manage through helping each other with what we learned while completing our individual tasks, such as solving common issues regarding saving, layouts and etc.

Here the student isolates a problem team member and yet admits an overall positive teamwork experience.

> I feel like I approached working with a group in computer science with a lot of ... distrust before this course. Over the phases of this project I've realized that if the group interacts regularly and effectively it isn't so bad. If we had a shot at taking on another similar project again I think we'd do a lot better with what we've learned.

This student went into the team project with little trust towards the team members, and, judging by the last comment, there were issues along the way. Yet, the student is able to see this as a valuable learning experience, and foresees that in the future he or she would be a happier team member.

5. CONCLUSIONS

Our data analysis demonstrates that the student's preference for the method of evaluation in a software development team project changes dramatically depending on the year of study, as well as on the point during the term when the preference is expressed. In particular, simply knowing who their teammates are, shifts their evaluation preference towards putting more weight on teamwork and less on the individual contribution.

We also show that students do trust the instructors'

and the peers' ability to assess individual contributions in a team project, and that, over time, the trust in peer evaluation increases significantly while the trust in instructor evaluation decreases somewhat.

With two years worth of data, we dispel a myth that students with higher grades prefer to be evaluated individually, while weaker students prefer to be evaluated as a team. We also examine a large number of factors as potential predictors of the students' evaluation preference. We find that, among all the factors under consideration, such as gender, whether the student is majoring in CS, GPA, whether English is the student's first language, expected grade in the course, individual performance in the course, the student's peer evaluation scores in a recently completed project phase, the student's evaluation of his or her peers in a recently completed project phase, the grade in this project phase, the number of team projects with 3+ team members, in which the student was involved prior to the current course, the method of forming the team in the last team project, in which the student was involved (team formed by the instructor or by the students), the student's level of satisfaction with the team in this last team project, and the student's level of confidence in the instructors' and peers' ability to evaluate individual team member's contribution in a team project, most are *not* predictors.

We find that, in a second year course, the level of satisfaction with the previous team project, in which the participant was involved, prior to this course, is a predictor of the initial preferred team project evaluation option, as reported in the beginning of the term — the more satisfied the student is with the previous project, the more she is likely to prefer to be evaluated as a team, rather than individually. However, this factor no longer has any effect on the preference once the students know their teammates in the current project.

We also show that the level of overall satisfaction with teamwork in the current project is a predictor of the *change* in the students' preference: happier team members shift towards favouring a larger portion of team weight.

Interestingly, the students make a distinction between evaluating their team mates and evaluating their own overall teamwork experience.

We identify the need to conduct student interviews with the aim of better understanding the students' reasoning behind these aspects. Since our current results indicate that educators hold several misconceptions about students' preferences in teamwork evaluation, we still identify a lack of available research data that would help explain these preferences, and the need for such data.

6. REFERENCES

[1] N. Clark, P. Davies, and R. Skeers. Self and peer assessment in software engineering projects. In *Proceedings of the 7th Australasian Conference on Computing Education*, volume 42, pages 91–100, 2005.

[2] Y. Dubinsky and O. Hazzan. Using a role scheme to derive software project metrics. *Journal of Systems Architecture*, 52(11):693–699, 2006.

[3] H. E. Dunsmore, D. P. Moffet, and S. T. Ward. Software engineering team project group member evaluations: Some empirical results. *SIGCSE Bull.*, 21(2):40–45, 1989.

[4] S. Faraj and L. Sproull. Coordinating expertise in software development teams. *Management Science*, 46(12):1554–1568, 2000.

[5] A. Gates, N. Delgado, and O. Mondragon. A structured approach for managing a practical software engineering course. In *30th Annual Frontiers in Education Conference*, 2000.

[6] N. Gorla and Y. W. Lam. Who should work with whom?: Building effective software project teams. *Commun. ACM*, 47(6):79–82, 2004.

[7] J. H. Hayes, T. C. Lethbridge, and D. Port. Evaluating individual contribution toward group software engineering projects. In *Proceedings of the 25th International Conference on Software Engineering*, pages 622–627, 2003.

[8] O. Hazzan. Computer science students' conception of the relationship between reward (grade) and cooperation. *SIGCSE Bull.*, 35(3):178–182, 2003.

[9] O. Hazzan and Y. Dubinsky. Students' cooperation in teamwork: binding the individual and the team interests. In *Proceedings of the ACM International Conference on Object Oriented Programming Systems, Languages, and Applications*, pages 151–152, 2010.

[10] N. Herbert. Quantitative peer assessment: Can students be objective? In *Proceedings of the Ninth Australasian Conference on Computing Education*, volume 66, pages 63–71, 2007.

[11] J. R. Hoffman and S. G. Rogelberg. A guide to team incentive system. *Team Performance Management: An International Journal*, 4(1):23–32, 1998.

[12] J. M. Hogan and R. Thomas. Developing the software engineering team. In *Proceedings of the 7th Australasian Conference on Computing Education*, volume 42, pages 203–210, 2005.

[13] D. Ian Brown. Team-based reward plans. *Team Performance Management: An International Journal*, 1(1):23–31, 1995.

[14] M. Ikonen and J. Kurhila. Discovering high-impact success factors in capstone software projects. In *Proceedings of the 10th ACM Conference on SIG-information Technology Education*, pages 235–244, 2009.

[15] J. Karn and T. Cowling. A follow up study of the effect of personality on the performance of software engineering teams. In *Proceedings of the 2006 ACM/IEEE International Symposium on Empirical Software Engineering*, pages 232–241, 2006.

[16] D. Kaufmann, R. Felder, and H. Fuller. Accounting for individual effort in cooperative learning teams. *Journal of Engineering Education*, 89:133–140, 2000.

[17] R. Layton and M. Ohland. Peer ratings revisited: Focus on teamwork, not ability. In *Proceedings of American Society for Engineering Education Annual Conference*, 2001.

[18] R. A. Layton, M. L. Loughry, M. W. Ohland, and G. D. Ricco. Design and validation of a web-based system for assigning members to teams using instructor-specified criteria. *Advances in Engineering Education*, 2(1):1–28, 2010.

[19] R. Lingard and E. Berd. Teaching teamwork skills in software engineering based on an understanding of factors affecting group performance. *Frontiers in Education*, 3, 2002.

[20] V. Pieterse, D. G. Kourie, and I. P. Sonnekus. Software engineering team diversity and performance. In *Proceedings of the 2006 Annual Research Conference of the South African Institute of Computer Scientists and Information Technologists on IT Research in Developing Countries*, pages 180–186, 2006.

[21] A. Radermacher, G. Walia, and D. Knudson. Investigating the skill gap between graduating students and industry expectations. In *Companion Proceedings of the 36th International Conference on Software Engineering*, pages 291–300, 2014.

[22] S.-T. Shen, S. Prior, A. White, and M. Karamanoglu. Using personality type differences to form engineering design teams. *Engineering Education*, 2:54–66, 2007.

[23] H. H. Smith, III and D. L. Smarkusky. Competency matrices for peer assessment of individuals in team projects. In *Proceedings of the 6th Conference on Information Technology Education*, pages 155–162, 2005.

[24] A. Tafliovich, A. Petersen, and J. Campbell. On the evaluation of student team software development projects. In *Proceedings of the 46th ACM Technical Symposium on Computer Science Education*, pages 494–499, 2015.

[25] H. Tarmazdi, R. Vivian, C. Szabo, K. Falkner, and N. Falkner. Using learning analytics to visualise computer science teamwork. In *Proceedings of the 2015 ACM Conference on Innovation and Technology in Computer Science Education*, pages 165–170, 2015.

[26] L. E. Willcoxson. "it's not fair!": Assessing the dynamics and resourcing of teamwork. *Journal of Management Education*, 30(6):798–808, 2006.

Teaching Global Software Engineering by Simulating a Global Project in the Classroom

Yang Li, Stepan Krusche, Christian Lescher and Bernd Bruegge
Technische Universität München
Chair for Applied Software Engineering
Munich, Germany
{liya, krusche, lescher, bruegge}@in.tum.de

ABSTRACT

Globalization has long since found its way into software engineering. Many companies transfer part of their development activities to distributed countries in order to ensure their global competitiveness, gain access to local markets and react to the prevailing lack of specialized workforce. The global distribution of project teams introduces new challenges: Geographic separation, different time zones, remote communications, and culture and language barriers make the collaboration between team members more difficult.

Instructors in universities are faced with the problem of how to make students with little or no experience aware of the challenges of Global Software Engineering and equip them with skills to deal with them. International practical courses are effective but require high organizational effort. In this paper, we describe an exercise for teaching Global Software Engineering in a single classroom and report on our experiences. The exercise simulates a global software project within three sites. Through the exercise, students experienced some of the aforementioned challenges and tried to deal with them in a simulated environment.

Keywords

Global Software Engineering; Simulation; Classroom; Education; Project Management

1. INTRODUCTION

Software engineering is increasingly a globally-distributed undertaking [14]. Development teams are often distributed over multiple sites and countries. A variety of motivations, including proximity to markets or customers, access to talent regardless of location and cost competitiveness are driving this move. While the advantages are tempting, Global Software Engineering (GSE) also introduces new challenges: Geographic separation, working in different time zones and different cultures make the collaboration between team members more difficult than in co-located projects.

SIGCSE '16, March 02-05, 2016, Memphis, TN, USA

ISBN 978-1-4503-3685-7/16/03...$15.00
DOI: http://dx.doi.org/10.1145/2839509.2844618

Typical collaboration problems in GSE include ineffective communication, unclear responsibilities, and low team cohesion. Geographically distributed teams lack effective communication such as face-to-face conversations to effectively deliver messages in multiple channels (e.g. voice, emotions and body language) and get instant feedback. Miscommunication occurs repeatedly in ineffective communication, which is one major cause for issues such as cost overruns, quality problems and project delays [8]. Additionally, responsibilities between teams are unclear, due to a reduced level of awareness about who is currently working on which topic. This delays task assignment and other types of decision making especially when change occurs. Finally, team cohesion – team members stick together to pursue a common goal – is often used to measure team performance. High team cohesion leads to enhanced motivation, increased morale, greater productivity, harder work, more open communication, and higher job satisfaction compared to non-cohesive groups [5, p.52]. However, team cohesion is more difficult to achieve between globally distributed teams.

Instructors in universities are faced with the problem of how to teach GSE, imparting not only theoretical knowledge, but also practical skills required for globally distributed projects. Previous work [13, 6] presented a systematic review on teaching GSE and the learning environments used. A common approach is to set up an international practical course, involving students from multiple universities who then work jointly over distance on a software project.

We reported on our experience with teaching three distributed software engineering project courses [2], namely JAMES [1, p.725], PAID and STARS. Students from Carnegie Mellon University in Pittsburgh, USA and from Technische Universität München (TUM) in Munich, Germany collaborated to specify, design, and realize software for a real industrial client located at Stuttgart, Germany and Detroit, USA. The three project courses aimed to address team management, client collaboration and rationale capture in a global software project setup. In the Global Studio Project students from Carnegie Mellon University, International Institute of Information Technology Bangalore, Monmouth University, Pontifical Catholic University of Rio Grande de Sul, University of Limerick and TUM jointly worked on a software project [14, p.183]. We also conducted NEREID (Network of Engineering univeRsities Educating in Intercultural Design), involving students from Mexico, Chile, France and Germany [12]. Gloor et al. [7] described a global project course they taught for six years that involves 30–40 students from two to four sites, located in the USA and Europe.

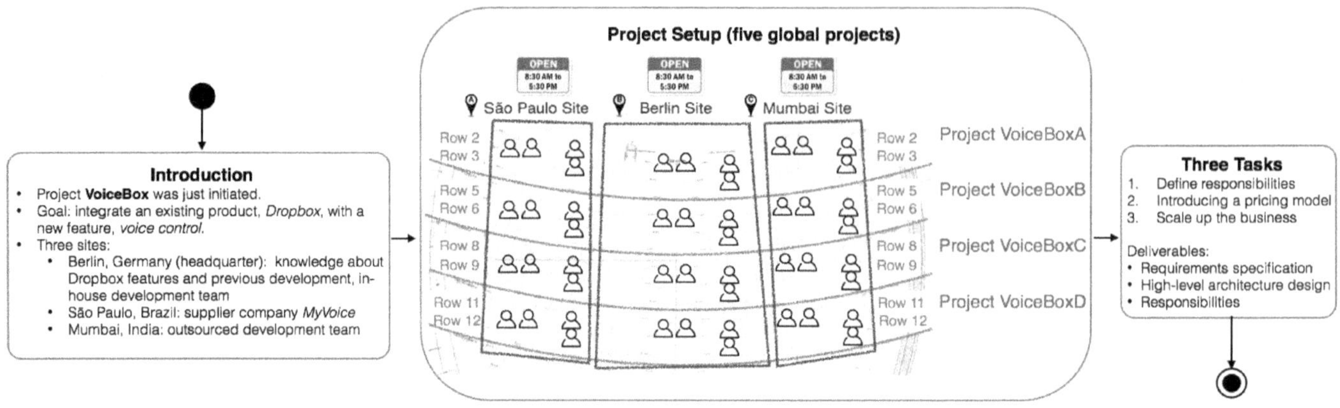

Figure 1: Exercise workflow

Although the approach of an international practical course was found to be effective, it has the disadvantage of requiring high organizational effort. To set up such a course is a globally distributed project in itself, where instructors from multiple universities need to agree on common objectives, a time schedule which fits to the semester timetable of all involved sites, a harmonized evaluation scheme, etc.

In this paper, we present an alternative way of teaching GSE in the classroom, simulating a global project. The simulation exercise can be carried with low overhead and has shown to be effective in addressing typical GSE challenges and in applying first strategies to overcome them. The rest of the paper is organized as follows: Section 2 introduces the workflow and detailed design of the simulated global project. Then we share our findings and lessons learned in Section 3. Finally we conclude the paper in Section 4.

2. COURSE DESIGN

To simulate a global project with competitiveness of different talents and technical skills, our strategy is to simulate GSE projects with three sites: one site is the in-house development team at headquarters; a second site is an outsourced development team; and the third site has a unique set of technologies and domain knowledge. The goal is to integrate a *special technology* provided by the third site with an *existing product* developed by the other two sites.

One of the biggest challenges of the simulated project is how to prepare students to become a domain expert within a short amount of time and only by using the materials provided in the exercise. This is especially hard for the third site. We have brainstormed for ideas and researched for available resources that we can provide to students for fast learning. After study and discussions, we have chosen "voice control" as the *special technology* that the third site provides. For students in computer science, the idea and main functionalities of voice control are not difficult. However, only few of them are aware of the approaches and technologies behind. For example, how speech recognition works and how vocabularies are customized. Nuance is a leading speech-recognition technology company. It provides rich documentation[1] for developers who want to integrate Nuance speech services. We provide students the Nuance developers documentation to obtain domain knowledge. As for the *existing product* that will be integrated with speech recognition, we chose Dropbox[2], due to its popularity. Most students are already familiar with Dropbox, so the overhead of gaining knowledge to understand the product and requirements is low.

The exercise workflow is shown in Figure 1. At the beginning of the 1.5 hours exercise, the instructor gives an overview. Afterwards four global projects (i.e. A, B, C, D) are set up in the classroom. Three different tasks are assigned and conducted by students. In the following, we elaborate the exercise introduction, project setup, and each of the three tasks.

2.1 Exercise Introduction

Before the project starts, the instructor first introduces the context, goal, and organization of the global project. In our course, we defined the exercise context as follows:

"Project *VoiceBox* was just initiated. The goal of the project is to integrate an existing product, *Dropbox*, with a new feature, voice control. To gather domain expertise in the new voice control technology, your company recently acquired the supplier company *MyVoice*[3] in São Paulo, Brazil. The main development sites are in Berlin, Germany (headquarters) and Mumbai, India. While the team in Berlin has rich knowledge about Dropbox features and previous development, the team in Mumbai consists of good coders who are inexperienced with Dropbox however."

In addition, we specified the following constraints within the global projects:

- Project members may not leave their site. Exception: each project has one and only one liaison from the Berlin site, who can travel to the other development sites. He/she can talk to the developers only during local business hours (8:30 am - 5:30 pm).
- Each project may select their own communication mechanism (phones, Skype, and chat), but they can respond only during local business hours.

[1]Documentation is available on Nuance developers homepage: http://dragonmobile.nuancemobiledeveloper.com

[2]Dropbox allows users to securely share and synchroize files. Dropbox official website: www.dropbox.com

[3]MyVoice is an imaginary technology we named. The description and materials about MyVoice were adapted from Nuance documentation.

- Use the project Confluence[4] space to document meetings and deliverables.
- Projects may request extra hours after usual business hours, however this will lead to additional costs.

2.2 Project Setup

After exercise introduction, global projects are organized in the classroom. We have grouped the students into four projects. Each project reflected the introduced three-sites organization, i.e. São Paulo, Berlin and Mumbai sites. We used a chart to illustrate the project setup (see Figure 1), a map of the classroom where the course took place. Depending on the number of students and the classroom layout, this "matrix-organization" may be adjusted. Additionally, the instructor showed a time zone map (see Figure 2) to visualize the time zones at the three sites. After students join the projects, each project has five minutes to decide and setup the project communication mechanisms. Then the first task is introduced by the instructor.

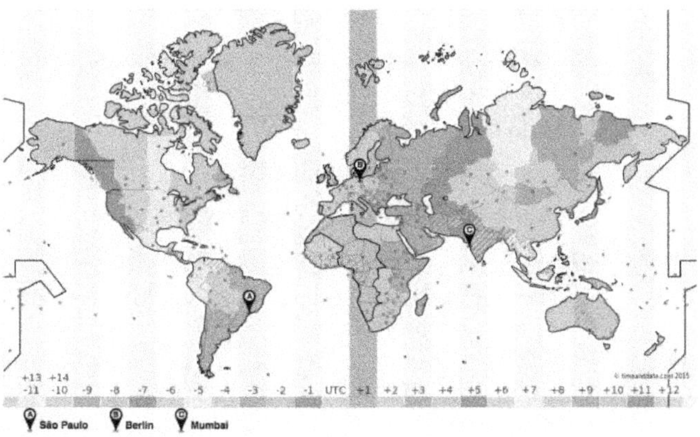

Figure 2: Time zone map of the three sites (created on timeanddate.com)

2.3 Task I

Duration: Students have in total 20 minutes to work on this task which correspond to four real world hours[5]. The simulated time for this task is at Berlin Time 10:00 am. This corresponds to São Paulo time 05:00 am and Mumbai time 1:30 pm. Project members at São Paulo site are still sleeping and do not work at the beginning of the exercise. The instructor shows Figure 3a to students that visualizes current local time in the three different time zones.

Task description: At the headquarters in Berlin, the team first specifies the requirements. Afterwards, the Berlin team arranges a meeting with the Mumbai team to discuss requirements, architecture, and responsibilities of each site. Open questions to the São Paulo site are listed.

Instructions (work breakdown structure): The following instructions were given to the students during the task.

- Berlin Site:
  - Specify early requirements for VoiceBox.
  - Provide information about existing architecture of Dropbox.
  - Organize meetings.
  - Lead other sites to refine requirements, architecture and responsibilities.
- São Paulo Site:
  - Read the provided materials about MyVoice.
  - Prepare yourself to be the MyVoice experts.
- Mumbai Site:
  - Read the provided programmer's guide of MyVoice.
  - Give input about how to integrate MyVoice into the current product.

Process: After clarifying the task and instructions, the instructor distributes initial requirements to the Berlin site and programmer's guide to the Mumbai site. Since it is at 5:00 am in São Paulo, this site is not involved in meetings with the other two sites. Instead, students at this site use the time to become experts in the MyVoice technology. Custom vocabularies guide and programmer's guide of MyVoice and a pricing model (see Table 1) are provided to the São Paulo site. In this task, the goal is that students from each site understands the setup, the roles they are playing and obtain domain knowledge. Especially students will experience for the first time in software projects, that one site (São Paulo) is not reachable due to time difference.

	Silver Platinum (\$999/year)	**Gold Platinum** (\$3999/year)	**Platinum** (\$9999/year)
Cloud-based automatic speech recognition (ASR) for dictation and web-search	yes	yes	yes
Vocabularies for ASR customization	Up to 200 phrases Up to 40 vocabularies	Up to 1000 phrases Up to 80 vocabularies	Up to 300 phrases Up to 160 vocabularies Vocabularies update
Cloud-based Text-to-Speech (TTS)	English	English, Spanish, Arabic, French, German, Chinese and Japanese	40+ languages
Platforms	iOS and Android	iOS, Android, and HTTP REST interface	iOS, Android, and HTTP REST interface
Production Pricing	Free up to 2k transactions/Day/App Above 2k: \$.008/transaction	Free up to 10k transactions/Day/App Above 10k: \$.008/transaction	Free up to 20k transactions/Day/App Above 20k: \$.005/transaction

Table 1: Pricing model of MyVoice (material provided to the São Paulo site)

2.4 Task II

Duration: Students again have in total 20 minutes to work on this task. The simulated time for this task is at Berlin Time 2:00 pm. This corresponds to São Paulo time 09:00 am and Mumbai time 5:30 pm. This means that Mumbai just finished local business hours. The instructor shows Figure 3b to students that visualizes current local time in the three different time zones.

Task description: The São Paulo site receives the listed questions of Task I and answers them right away. The pricing model of MyVoice is also introduced by the São Paulo site. Requirements, architecture and responsibilities need to be refined based on the new information about MyVoice. Be careful, the office hour at the Mumbai site is about to end.

Instructions (work breakdown structure): The following instructions were given to the students during the task.

[4]Confluence is a Wiki provided by Atlassian. We set up the space for the students before the exercise.
[5]Every 5 minutes one real world hour passes.

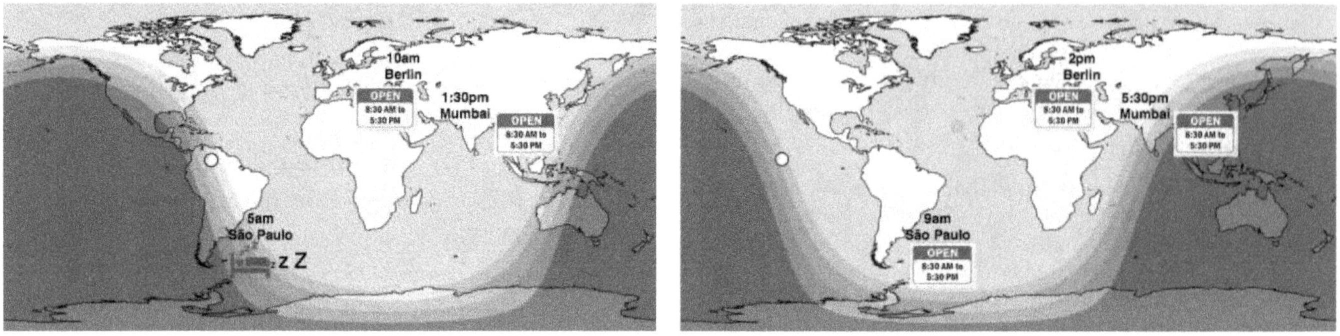

(a) Local times for Task I

(b) Local times for Task II

Figure 3: World map showing daylight and the current time of the three sites

- Berlin Site:
  - Make business decisions of VoiceBox based on new information from other sites.
  - Provide information about existing architecture of Dropbox.
  - Lead other sites to refine requirements, architecture and responsibilities.
- São Paulo Site:
  - Answer the questions about MyVoice.
  - Introduce the MyVoice Pricing Model.
- Mumbai Site:
  - Give input about how to integrate MyVoice into the current product.

Process: After Task I, students are prepared for diving into details about the project. In this task, the instructor expects the students to organize meetings cross sites. The pricing model introduced by the São Paulo site is a surprise to the other two sites as they do not know about it. Due to the pricing model, the project might change the development plan they discussed before. Cross-site negotiation might be involved and delay in communication and decision-making will occur. Students will also need to decide if the Mumbai site needs to take extra working hours for the meeting or not. Until now, students should also use at least one mechanism to communicate and to document the artifacts such as meeting minutes and decisions in a global setup. The goal is, that students will face common GSE challenge such as ineffective communication, miscommunication between sites, unclear requirements and lack of transparent information.

2.5 Task III

Duration: Students have in total 20 minutes to work on this task. However, this time students will define the current time and inform the instructor about the meeting time slots.

Task description: After the previous meeting, the Berlin headquarters identified new requirements for VoiceBox to support the increasing business. Define a time slot for a meeting, where you address these new requirements. Refine requirements, architecture and responsibilities.

Instructions (work breakdown structure): The following instructions were given to the students during the task.

- Berlin Site:
  - Schedule a meeting with other sites.
  - Address new requirements.
  - Lead other sites to refine requirements, architecture and responsibilities.
- São Paulo Site:
  - Answer questions about MyVoice.
  - promote different MyVoice services.
- Mumbai Site:
  - Give input about how to integrate MyVoice into the current product.

Process: The instructor distributes new requirements to the Berlin site. The new requirements include supporting a larger user base and localized languages. It also requires that VoiceBox will work on multiple platforms. The Berlin site is expected to discuss with the Mumbai site about the feasibility and difficulty of realizing the new requirements. They might also want to discuss with the São Paulo site about different services come with different prices.

In order to find a suitable time slot to meet, students will propose different strategies. They might request the Mumbai site to take more extra hours and discuss the issues as soon as possible. To avoid taking extra hours, an alternative is, that the Berlin site can meet with São Paulo site first and wait until the second day to meet with the Mumbai site. This is a typical extra working costs vs. delay costs situation. Via the meeting scheduling, students will take serious account of working hours and time differences in global projects. This is a valuable point that is worth discussing in a retrospective session. In particular, the instructor can interview students about their meeting time and strategy. He can relate the situation to global projects that often have shifted local business hours (different from other local companies) to maximize overlapping hours with other sites.

3. FINDINGS AND LESSONS LEARNED

We conducted the GSE exercise in the course of *Software Engineering II: Project Organization and Management* in summer term 2015. The target audience of this course were students who had basic knowledge about software development and wanted to enhance their knowledge in project management. The course covered concepts such as agile

#	Statement	Strongly Agree	Agree	Neutral	Disagree	Strongly Disagree
S1	... it is difficult to coordinate time	34%	50%	11%	4%	2%
S2	... there is communication overhead	23%	52%	18%	5%	2%
S3	... there is a lack of informal communication	27%	43%	23%	5%	2%
S4	... it is difficult to communicate changing requirements	21%	45%	23%	11%	0%
S5	... expertise is not shared with relevant stakeholders	18%	46%	18%	16%	2%

Table 2: Evaluation results of the GSE exercise with Likert scale responses to statements: The exercise addressed the challenge in global projects that ...

methods, configuration management and continuous delivery [9, 10], as well as team-based software development [3, 4]. 450 computer science students registered for the course, including half bachelor students in their second year and half master students. About 100 students participated in the GSE exercise. In the following we present the findings and lessons learned from conducting the exercise.

3.1 Findings

We were amazed at how diverse the documents and communication logs were. Each project had established its own communication mechanism. Project A and C used Confluence to share important information and questions to other sites. Project B was communicating mainly on an online chatting platform. Project D had a liaison who traveled between sites throughout the whole project, while Project A had a liaison only for Task III. Project D also created a Facebook group so that everyone could communicate online. Among the four projects, we have observed that Project D had the most effective communication, the best team performance, and high quality documentation. The liaison played an important role in face-to-face communication and motivating other sites when visiting them. Project A was frustrated at the beginning, but was able to catch up after all sites had improved the communication. In Project C, the team was underperformed and many of the GSE difficulties were shown. Students had ineffective communication (only using Confluence to share documents but no chatting or visiting). The Mumbai site got unmotivated. Project C didn't have a leader to motivate and organize the team.

We evaluated the exercise in an online questionnaire. 56 students took part in the questionnaire and reported about their experience of GSE challenges in the exercise by assessing between "strongly disagree" to "strongly agree" (five-level Likert scale) to statements shown in Table 2. 84% respondents agreed that the exercise addressed time coordination challenges. This indicates that despite being in the same classroom, the students were able to experience synchronization issues and that the simulation of the time differences worked well. 75% respondents agreed that the exercise addressed communication overhead because of the geographical separation of project teams. The respondents reported communication challenges they experienced between the three different sites. For instance, one project reported that they have agreed on using one communication channel, but some team members were still trying to initialize other communication mechanisms. Another reported communication challenge was caused by the different time zones. When developers at one site wanted to discuss with other sites, but unluckily they were out of business hours or they had to request for extra hours.

About 70% respondents agreed that the exercise had presented the lack of informal communication in global projects. This result corresponds to our observation during the exercise. 66% respondents agreed that in the exercise it was difficult to communicate changing requirements between the different sites. However, in another question, 46% respondents reported that they were able to address changing requirement. They reported that creating a page in the Confluence wiki which includes a notification mechanism for changes, was an effective measurement to deal with the problem. The challenge of sharing expertise with relevant stakeholders was addressed in the exercise for 64% respondents. They reported that it was difficult enough to find the right person and still they have to overcome the communication barriers.

We also asked which communication channels the students used. They could choose multiple answers. 21% used Skype as chatting application. 61% used Facebook, some of them used its chatting feature, others used the group feature that offered commenting and like functionality. 48% used Confluence as Wiki to create pages with important knowledge and communicating with comments. 39% traveled between the different sites, especially for negotiation tasks.

Finally, 53% respondents agreed that they liked the global software engineering exercise, in particular they liked to experience the different challenges in a condensed but yet very practical way and in real time. One student wrote: "The whole execution was interesting, effective and fun! Never thought it would be possible to emulate a global project management inside a class". For the unsatisfied students, they disliked the exercise because of its high complexity and the frustration caused by the GSE challenges. This implies again the exercise was effective to address GSE issues that often reoccur in the real world. Nevertheless, a retrospective discussion with the students about the frustration that reflects GSE challenges and how to address them would be helpful.

On the other hand, the students also suggested possible improvements that we consider for the next GSE exercise. Some indicated that the overall exercise was too complex and should be simpler, especially regarding the technical documentation that was handed out. Others had problems to understand the exercise and were confused about the different tasks. They asked for more time and information and more explicit requirements. One student suggested to also include cultural differences into the exercise.

3.2 Lessons Learned

From our own observation and students' feedback we identified the following lessons learned.

Project Context. The project context was well defined. The idea of integrating voice control in Dropbox was easy to understand, but domain knowledge is required to specify requirements and architecture. Therefore, the three sites were able to play distinct roles in the project. According to students' performance, we consider the defined context is at an appropriate level of difficulty for the exercise.

Time Management. The exercise time was a little too tight. We did not have time to conduct a retrospective discussion to reflect GSE issues students experienced. We recommend to plan two hours for the exercise, which include a 10 minutes retrospective session. We also suggest to allocate 30 minutes for Task I instead of 20 minutes as we did. This allows students to have sufficient time to understand the project and read the provided materials.

Multimedia Support. We used three projectors in the classroom to present world clock, task description and instructions. This helped us greatly in handling the complexity of the exercise. We distributed hardcopies of the pricing model to the São Paulo site. We also created tinyurl links for the downloadable developer's guides, so that students could easily fetch the materials. All of these need to be planed in advance. The practice we suggest is to write a script for screen projection and schedule material distribution.

Curriculum Design. The GSE exercise is suitable for bachelor / master level software engineering courses. In our case, we designed the tasks with a focus on project management. Depending on course goals, the tasks can be adjusted. For example, in a course that focuses on modeling and software design, tasks can be to decompose subsystems and draw UML class diagrams for each subsystem. For courses that have only short time slots for exercises, we recommend other smaller in-class GSE exercises that are described in [11].

Privacy. While privacy is an important concern in industrial projects, we did not focus on it in our exercise. The students were free to choose their own preferred communication mechanism. For example, some students used services such as Facebook or Skype which might not be allowed in enterprises. However, enterprises usually have other mechanisms for secure communication such as private wikis or customized chat services that can only be used internally.

4. CONCLUSIONS

In this paper we described a global software engineering exercise that can be carried out in the classroom. We shared the exercise design and our experience. We consider the first conduction of the exercise successful. The students had experienced work with different timezones, lack of effective communication and other GSE issues that are typical in the real world. In an online questionnaire we found anecdotal evidence that the simulated global project in the classroom was able to address key GSE challenges. We have also identified areas to improve for the next exercise. For instance, we plan to refine the task instructions to make them more precise for students to understand what exactly needs to be done. Additionally, the time management needs to be improved, so a retrospective session can be included. We hope the simulation exercise serves as an example for other university instructors. The exercise can be further adapted and customized to fit into their curricula.

5. ACKNOWLEDGMENTS

We want to thank all students taking part in the exercise.

6. REFERENCES

[1] B. Bruegge and A. Dutoit. *Object-Oriented Software Engineering Using UML, Patterns and Java: International Version.* Prentice Hall, 3rd edition, 2010.

[2] B. Bruegge, A. H. Dutoit, R. Kobylinski, and G. Teubner. Transatlantic project courses in a university environment. In *Proceedings of the Seventh Asia-Pacific Software Engineering Conference, APSEC 2000*, pages 30–37. IEEE, 2000.

[3] B. Bruegge, S. Krusche, and L. Alperowitz. Software engineering project courses with industrial clients. *ACM Transactions on Computing Education.*, 2015.

[4] B. Bruegge, S. Krusche, and M. Wagner. Teaching Tornado: from communication models to releases. In *Proceedings of the 8th Educators' Symposium*, pages 5–12. ACM, 2012.

[5] E. Carmel. *Global Software Teams – Collaborating Across Borders and Time Zones.* Prentice Hall, 1999.

[6] L. Fortaleza, T. Conte, S. Marczak, and R. Prikladnicki. Towards a GSE international teaching network: Mapping Global Software Engineering courses. In *Proceedings of Collaborative Teaching of Globally Distributed Software Development Workshop*, pages 1–5. IEEE, 2012.

[7] P. Gloor, M. Paasivaara, C. Lassenius, D. Schoder, K. Fischbach, and C. Miller. Teaching a global project course: experiences and lessons learned. In *Proceedings of the 2011 Community Building Workshop on Collaborative Teaching of Globally Distributed Software Development*, pages 1–5. ACM, 2011.

[8] D. J. Hoch, S. K. Lindner, C. R. Roeding, and G. Purkert. *Secrets of Software Success: Management Insights from 100 Software Firms around the World.* Harvard Business School Press, 1999.

[9] S. Krusche and L. Alperowitz. Introduction of Continuous Delivery in Multi-Customer Project Courses. In *Companion Proceedings of the 36th ICSE*, pages 335–343. IEEE, 2014.

[10] S. Krusche, L. Alperowitz, B. Bruegge, and M. Wagner. Rugby: An agile process model based on continuous delivery. In *Proceedings of the 1st Workshop on RCoSE*, pages 42–50. ACM, 2014.

[11] C. Lescher, Y. Li, and B. Bruegge. Teaching global software engineering: Interactive exercises for the classroom. In *Proceedings of the IEEE 9th International Conference onGlobal Software Engineering (ICGSE),*, pages 163–172. IEEE, 2014.

[12] F. Matthes, C. Neubert, C. Schulz, C. Lescher, J. Contreras, R. Laurini, B. Rumpler, D. Sol, and K. Warendorf. Teaching Global Software Engineering and International Project Management: Experiences and Lessons Learned from Four Academic Projects. In *Proceedings of the 3rd International Conference on Computer Supported Education (CSEDU)*, 2011.

[13] M. Monasor, A. Vizcaino, M. Piattini, and I. Caballero. Preparing students and engineers for global software development: a systematic review. In *5th IEEE International Conference on Global Software Engineering*, pages 177–186. IEEE, 2010.

[14] R. Sangwan, M. Bass, N. Mullick, D. J. Paulish, and J. Kazmeier. *Global Software Development Handbook.* Auerbach Publications, 2006.

Exploring Lightweight Teams in a Distributed Learning Environment

Stephen MacNeil
UNC Charlotte
smacnei2@uncc.edu

Celine Latulipe
UNC Charlotte
clatulip@uncc.edu

Bruce Long
UNC Charlotte
nblong@uncc.edu

Aman Yadav
Michigan State University
ayadav@msu.edu

ABSTRACT

In both flipped classroom settings and distance learning, educational content is typically delivered via video lectures that students watch alone. While flipped classrooms typically provide students with opportunities for social interaction that feature active learning, online learners are not typically afforded these opportunities. Cooperative learning techniques like Lightweight Teams [15] provide social, collaborative learning opportunities to students in flipped classrooms but extending these techniques to distance learning settings is not straightforward. In this paper, we present our experiences with online, distributed Lightweight Teams. We present an in-the-wild study that compares learning outcomes and student preferences between co-located and distributed Lightweight Teams against the base case of individual learning. Our results show that while there are no significant learning differences between the two team conditions and the individual condition, students significantly prefer the team conditions.

Keywords

Distance learning; Team-based Learning; Lightweight Teams; Distributed Teams; Synchronous Learning

Categories and Subject Descriptors

K.3.2 [**Computer Science Education**]: Computer and Information Science Education

1. INTRODUCTION

Flipped classroom learning environments have been receiving much attention over the past few years; partly because they help to provide more opportunities for active and engaged learning. Flipped classroom setups tend to foster collaborative peer learning, which has been shown to improve learning outcomes [14, 8, 1, 17]. Researchers are investigating how instructional design techniques that leverage collaboration in face-to-face classrooms can be extended or applied in distance learning. This research has become even more relevant with the recent surge of Massively Open Online Courses (MOOCs). Traditional distance learning classes and MOOCs both share similarities with flipped classrooms in that students typically consume educational content by watching lecture videos alone. However, with flipped classrooms, these lecture videos are then supplemented with face-to-face active learning activities in the classroom that are often collaborative in nature. In distance learning, this type of interaction either doesn't happen at all or has to be mediated by technology. Keeping distributed students engaged and encouraging collaborative peer learning in distance environments is challenging. Extending effective face-to-face teaching techniques to an online context requires an understanding of the challenges that distance creates as well as strategies for mitigating those challenges [21].

We build on our previous work with Lightweight Teams [15], which were used in a face-to-face flipped classroom environment, by creating an online version. Lightweight Teams (LWT) are a cooperative learning approach in which teams of students are assigned to work together throughout a course, but where the activities performed by the team are lightweight and have little or no direct impact on each individual student's grade. This approach leverages the benefits of peer learning while removing the stress typically associated with team-based learning.

Our contributions in this paper are: (1) to present an online, distributed version of LWT; (2) to provide a comparative study to investigate learning in co-located LWT, distributed LWT, and students learning individually; (3) to elicit student preferences to determine whether the latent, non-performance-specific benefits of social learning - such as engagement, enjoyment and relationship building - translate to an online environment; (4) and finally, to provide a discussion that highlights the challenges of moving LWT online and describes some unexpected benefits.

2. RELATED WORK

2.1 Lightweight Teams

We previously define Lightweight Teams (LWT) as small teams in which students collaborate throughout the semester on tasks that do not represent a significant portion of their final grade [15]. In our initial implementation, teams en-

SIGCSE '16 March 02-05, 2016, Memphis, TN, USA

ACM ISBN 978-1-4503-3685-7/16/03.
DOI: http://dx.doi.org/10.1145/2839509.2844577

gaged in various activities such as peer-instruction clicker quizzes, structured active-learning challenges, and sharing course notes. Each of these were specifically designed to promote team cohesion and encourage collaborative peer learning. Students sit together in class to develop cohesion and eliminate any potential anxiety experienced by freshmen students entering large classes, who might wonder who they should sit with, whether anyone will want to sit with them or talk to them, etc.

An important activity for LWT was the clicker quizzes, which followed a modified peer instruction method [6]. After each question was projected on screen, students discussed the question with their teammates and then answered individually, without necessarily forming a consensus. In our initial implementation and in this study, clicker quizzes accounted for only 10% of each student's grade, which was enough to ensure participation, but not enough to cause stress associated with having unprepared teammates.

Previously, we observed positive qualitative feedback from the majority of students that used LWT, with students reporting that they liked being on their teams. In addition, 62% of student respondents noted that they had made 5 or more new friends as a result of taking the class. Students also performed better in a follow-on programming course than students who took a traditional lecture-based course instead. These results demonstrate that LWT create a positive and engaging learning environment. Furthermore, this approach mimics real world environments where graduates must be able to work with others.

Approaches like these provide scaffolding for team-work and for self-regulated learning where students can observe from their peers' study habits and correct their own as necessary. These opportunities for observation and imitation lead to improvements in self-regulation [22].

2.2 Online Learning

Increasingly, employers expect employees to adjust their skills to meet changing markets and demands. As a result, employees must be lifelong learners who are capable of self-guided learning. For many working adults, the need for continuing education is met through online learning environments, though this is often a frustrating and lonely experience. In addition, a large population of the developing world, connected via the Internet, are reaching out for online educational opportunities that are not readily available locally [7, 3].

Despite surging popularity and the promise of continuing and global education, online learners face many unique challenges. Many of the original challenges described in the canonical work 'Distance Matters" [21] - such as establishing common ground, coupling in work, collaboration readiness, and technology readiness - are still issues today. Some challenges associated with working remotely are not limited to remote contexts. For example, establishing trust is challenging in both a remote [2] and face-to-face environment [19].

Some challenges, such as cultural differences, are more unique to remote collaboration. These cultural challenges remind us that distance is both physical and cultural [23]. Some of these cultural aspects of distance are both positive and negative - distance provides more perspectives; however, managing conflicts that naturally arise from multiple perspectives can be challenging to resolve [9, 12].

There are also some unique benefits afforded by distance and computer-mediated communication (CMC) in educational settings. For example, students' inhibitions about participating in discussions can be alleviated in online contexts [10]. Similarly, online worlds like Second Life provide contextualization, recreating historically accurate environments that no longer exist in the real world [25].

Finally, distance implies geographic diversity which can naturally deter homophily, the tendency people have to associate with people similar to themselves [18]. And peer learning, which is an effective way of developing positive race relationships [24], is well situated to take advantage of this geographic diversity; especially for MOOCs, where many cultures are potentially interacting [7, 3].

Recent research has aimed to provide a social learning environment online via synchronous and asynchronous discussions. Synchronous techniques include textual chat and video conferencing. Some recent examples are a series of studies that investigate learning in discussion forums [4, 5], how new students benefit from interactions with alumni that continue to participate in an IRC chatroom for a course [20], and the online video-chat discussion system, Talkabout [13].

Previously, we investigated an online, modified version of LWT. This modified version, "Low-Stakes Teams" [16], used the peer-instruction and low-stress aspects of LWT but ignored the aspects of temporality and team cohesion. This one-off controlled experiment provided insights about instantaneous learning gains, but didn't address latent benefits - such as engagement, enjoyment, preference - which require longitudinal studies where teams develop strong cohesion.

Table 1: Experiment Design: conditions were counterbalanced so that each student experienced each of the three conditions over the three week period.

Team	Week1	Week2	Week3
Teams 1-3	Face-to-Face	Distributed	Individual
Teams 4-6	Distributed	Individual	Face-to-Face
Teams 7-9	Individual	Face-to-Face	Distributed

3. COMPARATIVE STUDY

For two years, we have been using LWT in our CS1/2 courses. Students in teams of 5 sit together each week and work on clicker quizzes and other activities together during class time. We were interested in extending this approach to support students socially when learning online.

To investigate the effect of adding distance to LWT, we conducted a three week experiment that allowed students to learn in three environments: individually in a traditional lecture format, as co-located LWT, and finally as distributed LWT collaborating remotely. Each participant rotated conditions each week so that they experienced every condition (see Table 1). This resulted in a partially counter-balanced design which accounted for some of the ordering effects and variations in the difficulty of the topics from week to week. As an in-the-wild study, we designed our experiment with as few changes as possible to the normal course flow.

By using the same teams that had been working together co-located in class through the semester, we were able to mimic a long-term team dynamic in our study, preserving team cohesion. Role negotiation was informal and students were only guided by the clicker questions. Each week of the experiment consisted of a quiz where students had an opportunity to engage with material and a post test to gauge how their interaction with the material transferred to isomorphic questions (questions that have the same structure or form, but differ in actual content). Each week we booked two classrooms: (1) the normal classroom where students engaged in co-located LWT, (2) a classroom for the "lecture" where students worked alone. In addition to these two rooms, some students worked remotely using Google Hangouts. These differences are described in more detail in the next section. Generally, the quizzes took 45 minutes and the distributed team typically took at least 15 minutes more than other conditions. It is also important to note that in our comparative study, discussion with the instructor is replaced by an explanation slide after each question to control for multiple instructors engaging differently with the groups.

We provided a few tutoring sessions on Google Hangouts leading up to the experiment weeks to get students familiar with using the platform. The tutoring sessions were in the form of review sessions before each test and provided opportunities to promote technology readiness [21]. Approximately 10 students attended each session which served as an opportunity for working out the kinks of using this kind of communication. The week before our first experiment all students were asked to join a Google Hangout as a team and invite the TA to their session to collect attendance. This ensured that all students tested Google Hangouts.

3.1 Study Methodology

We used a counter-balanced design with three conditions:

Individual (I): Students were in a lecture hall where they took a clicker quiz individually. Students were not able to discuss the questions. This approach mimics the traditional lecture. After each question, the correct answer was shown on the screen, along with an explanation. The students took the post-test individually, online or on paper.

Group Co-located (GC): Students were in their normal classroom engaging in LWT to answer each clicker question. After discussing each question, they answered individually, without necessarily having reached consensus. Unlike LWT, the instructor didn't discuss the answers with the class. Instead, the answer was shown after each question and students could discuss the answer. Students took the post-test online, individually.

Group Distributed (GD): Students in this condition took the clicker quiz online using Socrative instead of the clicker software used in the other two conditions. Team members discussed clicker questions using audio and video on Google Hangouts. In each Hangout, a TA was present to observe team behavior. The TA was also responsible for pacing the clicker quiz. After all team members answered the question, the TA displayed the explanation followed by the next question. Students in this group left the Google Hangout session and answered the post-test questions online, individually.

Our general research question is whether LWT can provide educational benefit, in terms of learning outcomes and social engagement, to students who are learning at a distance. We had the following hypotheses:

1. Learning gains will be highest for the students in the co-located group.
2. Learning gains will be higher for students in the distributed group than for students working alone.
3. Team conditions will be perceived as being more enjoyable, more rewarding, and requiring less effort than learning alone.
4. Team conditions will be preferred to learning alone.

3.2 Participants

Our experiment consisted of 58 student participants in their normal scheduled class period for three weeks. After removing incomplete cases, we analyzed the results for 52 students. Those 52 students contributed 156 observations for each condition over the course of three weeks, where each observation represents a normalized test score. These observations were counterbalanced so that each participant contributed only one observation each week.

3.3 Statistical Analysis

Our experiment investigates students' performance as measured at three points in time. These points correspond to a different week covering a specific topic and a different condition as each participant rotates through all of the conditions. For example, in the first week students learned about enumerated types and in the second week they learned about threads. It is unclear whether these topics are equivalent in terms of difficulty. As a result, our analysis needed to model participant, team and content-related error terms.

Given these considerations, we analyzed the data using multilevel mixed effects models; fit by restricted maximum likelihood estimation. Condition was a fixed effect and both time and students nested within their groups were modeled as random effects. This and the counterbalanced design mitigate some effects of multiple instruments measuring the same construct. When significant, comparisons between groups were made using Tukey contrasts applied to the model. These results are reported using normally distributed Z values. To control family-wise error rates, p-values were adjusted using the single-step method. We checked assumptions of normality. Homoscedasticity of standardized residuals and model fitness were checked using residual-to-predicted plots and Q-Q plots (quantile-quantile).

Table 2: Clicker quiz score differences between conditions out of 10 questions.

Comparison	Difference	$P(>\|z\|)$
Co-located - Distributed	-0.312	0.722
Co-located - Individual	0.771	0.160
Distributed - Individual	**1.084**	**0.018**

3.4 Quantitative Results

We modeled both the clicker quiz and the post-test scores using a multilevel mixed effects model. Assumptions were upheld, but we did observe a slight bias for both models when plotting fitted against residuals. Only the model for clicker quizzes showed significant differences and those differences were explored using Tukey contrasts, shown in Table 2. Generally, teams did better than individuals on the clicker quizzes; although, this was only significant for distributed LWTs. This difference didn't appear to translate to post-test scores. High performance during collaboration which doesn't translate to post-test scores partially supports our previous work with Low-Stakes teams [16].

There are a number of explanations for this: (1) explanations were provided after each question (2) the post-test was too short to delineate differences in understanding (3) isomorphic questions may not have been challenging enough to distinguish between partial and holistic understanding. It is unclear whether LWT provide benefits that apply immediately to transfer questions. Our results also may not reflect the learning gains that could be achieved through long-term sustained engagement and effort.

In our analysis, Week 1 clicker data was not used. In Week 1, both team conditions outperformed individuals; however, distributed teams were paced by all teams instead of being individually paced. Consequently, they took nearly twice as long to finish. This was fixed in Weeks 2 and 3.

4. SUMMATIVE ATTITUDINAL SURVEY

To elicit student preferences about each condition we created a summative survey with 11 questions. The first 9 questions were Likert scale questions that asked students about the perceived effort, rewards, and enjoyment associated with each condition. Following these 9 questions, we asked them to rank the conditions by overall preference and then finally we provided them with an open-ended text box where they could comment on any aspect of the study. The preference survey was provided after finals to ensure that students didn't feel obligated to complete it and to make sure it didn't interfere with their preparation for their finals. As a result, only 16 students completed this survey.

4.1 Statistical Analysis

We analyze both the rankings of conditions and attitudes about each condition based on a 5-point Likert scale. Ranks and Likert data are ordinal and consequently we used non-parametric tests to analyze them. We used the Friedman test because each participant provided ranks for all conditions. To analyze significant differences, we performed a post-hoc analysis using Fisher's LSD test for multiple comparisons. We adjusted p-values using the Bonferroni method to control family-wise error rates. The Bonferroni method is typically overly conservative in its adjustments but this adjustment is safest given our small sample size.

Table 3: Rankings between conditions. A low rank indicates that it was selected as best condition more.

Comparison	Rank-Sum	P-Value
Co-located - Individual	**-25**	**0.002**
Co-located - Distributed	**-14**	**<0.001**
Distributed - Individual	**-11**	**0.015**

4.2 Quantitative Results

We investigated two aspects of our survey data: (1) overall rankings for each condition (2) Likert data related to perceived effort, enjoyment, and rewards.

Table 4: Preference differences across conditions on a 5-point Likert scale (Strongly Disagree - Strongly Agree). Higher rank-sums indicate agreement.

Preference	Comparison	Rank-Sum Difference	P-Value
Effort	Col - Ind	-9.0	> 0.99
	Col - Distr	-22.0	> 0.99
	Distr - Ind	35.5	> 0.99
Enjoyment	**Col - Ind**	**86.0**	**<0.001**
	Col - Distr	**39.5**	**0.029**
	Distr - Ind	**46.5**	**0.003**
Rewards	**Col - Ind**	**56.5**	**<0.001**
	Col - Distr	27.5	0.655
	Distr - Ind	29.0	0.464

The Friedman test found a significant difference between conditions in their rankings of overall preference between conditions ($\chi^2 = 19.63, p < 0.001$). Post-hoc analyses also revealed significant differences for all pairwise comparisons. Participants ranked co-located teams as their most preferred condition and working individually as their least favorite condition (see Table 3).

To investigate people's Likert responses we conducted a Friedman test and found a significant difference in terms of preference ($\chi^2 = 53.72, p < 0.001$). Post-hoc analyses also revealed significant differences for some pairwise comparisons. All the comparisons of interest are shown in Table 4.

With a limited sample size and a conservative p-value adjustment, we still obtained significant findings. Specifically, people strongly prefer being face-to-face and are ambivalent about working in distributed teams; however, they generally don't like to work alone. This evidence supports our fourth hypothesis and is compelling because it indicates that students may be more willing to engage in these team-based alternatives than traditional lectures which supports previous findings [5, 13].

Revisiting our other hypotheses, team conditions were significantly more enjoyable than working alone, shown in Table 4. Our hypothesis that the team conditions would be more rewarding was only significant for face-to-face teams and not for the distributed version, as shown in Table 4. This may relate to the fact that distributed teams typically took at least 15 minutes longer than either of the other conditions. Finally, we did not observe any significant differences between conditions for perceived effort. This was surprising; however, it may be that the reduced cognitive load due to multiple people collaboratively answering a question is offset by the effort of communicating.

5. QUALITATIVE RESULTS

The TAs used a rubric to code behaviors, team dynamics and technical difficulties. These rubrics guided observations and served as common ground for analysis. Many students mentioned that they liked Google Hangouts because they could work from home. Students found new common ground; for example, students discussed hobbies based on cues they observed in each other's environments, such as a motorcycle poster in one student's room and a guitar in another student's room. Figure 1 shows two examples where

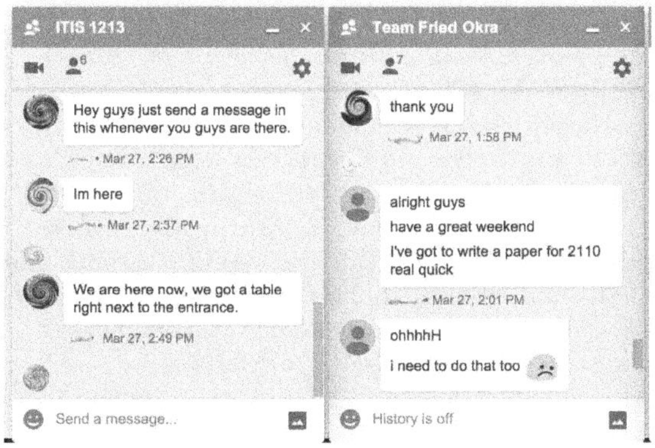

Figure 1: Students used Google Hangouts and Chat to answer questions, and this led into socializing. In these two distributed teams' sessions, members met after class for lunch and to work on a paper deadline.

students met up for food based on a discussion that started in Google Hangouts and continued in Google Chat. Students continued to use Google Chat throughout the semester to remind each other about deadlines and to meet up to study.

In addition to these advantages, there were some challenges. In one distributed team, a student was watching TV and continued to watch TV even after his teammates mentioned it. He only lowered the volume. Online it is more difficult to hold teammates accountable for their actions since many actions are not as overt as this one. A second challenge is related to time. Students experienced technical difficulties or arrived late and the teams were disrupted as a result. In one case, a student's laptop battery died and her team waited for her to charge it. One student even participated in the Hangout while driving to campus.

It is important to consider the implications of these observations for future implementations of distributed LWT. Features like supporting teams on mobile devices may or may not be preferable. Similarly, social accountability, which is a key component to successful collaborative work [11], becomes challenging when students can multitask discreetly.

6. DISCUSSION

Our findings suggest that the successes associated with LWT may be primarily associated with the more frequent social interactions occurring between students and increased engagement over the course of the semester. In our study, specific short-term performance benefits were not seen when students were asked to answer isomorphic transfer questions. The team conditions generally didn't do any better than the students working alone; however, all conditions received the same explanations for each question. This suggests that students working alone with explanations and supplemental material may be able to perform similarly to teams on similar questions. On the other hand, students drastically preferred working in distributed LWT than working alone in a traditional lecture format. As a result, students may be more willing to interact with the material for longer duration. Although distributed teams took the longest of the three conditions and despite technical glitches, students still preferred learning in distributed teams to working alone.

We encountered numerous challenges in moving LWT online. Even though we provided tutoring sessions using CMC to ensure technology readiness, students still experienced moderate technical difficulties, such as battery life, lack of headphones in public places, latency, and microphone problems. Despite an effort to ensure common ground, students weren't always respectful of each other's time: arriving late, and multi-tasking while participating.

We think that these study results make an extremely strong case for the importance of studying face-to-face educational methods in an online context before actually deploying them online at large scale. Even with design considerations that specifically accounted for distance, we still experienced many challenges associated with distance. Furthermore, design decisions like using small groups to increase accountability may be problematic if students don't respect each others' time and skip a scheduled discussion.

Finally, we think there are some specific changes that we could investigate in the future to improve the efficacy of distributed LWT. First, we think that the group size is very important for online discussions. Specifically, it is much easier for students to become distracted online and there are less overt signs that they have become distracted. We think that by limiting the size of the groups students might be accountable to each other and less able to discreetly multitask. We also found that question pacing is a double edged sword. In the first week all distributed teams were paced by one quiz and as a result some teams had significant down-time between questions. Different teams experienced down-time but generally we noticed that this "positive down-time" may have been beneficial. Students discussed weekend plans and asked about each other's interests. That week, distributed teams took nearly twice as long as the other conditions.

7. LIMITATIONS

Our study had some limitations, mainly due to the in-the-wild nature of the setup. We integrated this study into a class where we were teaching real students. We considered their learning goals most important and our study secondary. As a result, we were forced to make some concessions in our study, namely: (1) groups were not modified in any way, (2) explanations were provided after each question to ensure students could learn the material, (3) post-tests were short so students weren't significantly taxed by additional work, (4) post-tests were optional and ungraded, (5) the instructor didn't interact with students during the clicker quiz (as they traditionally would), to eliminate differences in teaching style and teaching ability, and (6) students in this course typically learn in face-to-face LWT so they may have been more comfortable with this modality.

8. CONCLUSIONS

We presented an in-the-wild comparative study of LWT where students learned individually, face-to-face and online. Our distributed version of LWT was similar in terms of performance to the original implementation of LWT; however, in our study students were unable to interact with the instructor. Our results provide insight about the potential for distributed LWT. In terms of performance, we only saw a significant difference on the clicker quizzes, which didn't translate to the post-test. However, we did show strong evidence that students prefer working in LWT and enjoyed working in them. Our main qualitative findings convey the difficulties of learning remotely. As we show in this paper, the challenges that distance creates are difficult to address.

Given that distributed and co-located LWT performed similarly and that students strongly preferred these environments to learning individually, distributed LWT show promise as a social, collaborative learning approach that may alleviate some of the loneliness associated with distributed learning and may help to ameliorate low retention rates in online classes.

9. ACKNOWLEDGEMENTS

This work was partially supported by the U.S. Department of Education under grant P200A130088. Any opinions, findings, conclusions, or recommendations expressed in this material are those of the authors and do not necessarily reflect those of the sponsor.

10. REFERENCES

[1] J. Bergmann and A. Sams. *Flip your classroom: Reach every student in every class every day.* International Society for Technology in Education, 2012.

[2] N. Bos, J. Olson, D. Gergle, G. Olson, and Z. Wright. Effects of four computer-mediated communications channels on trust development. In *Proceedings of the SIGCHI conference on human factors in computing systems*, pages 135–140. ACM, 2002.

[3] L. Breslow, D. E. Pritchard, J. DeBoer, G. S. Stump, A. D. Ho, and D. T. Seaton. Studying learning in the worldwide classroom: Research into edX's first MOOC. *Research & Practice in Assessment*, 8(1):13–25, 2013.

[4] D. Coetzee, A. Fox, M. A. Hearst, and B. Hartmann. Chatrooms in MOOCs: all talk and no action. In *Proceedings of the first ACM conference on Learning@ scale conference*, pages 127–136. ACM, 2014.

[5] D. Coetzee, S. Lim, A. Fox, B. Hartmann, and M. A. Hearst. Structuring interactions for large-scale synchronous peer learning. In *CSCW: ACM Conference on Computer Supported Collaborative Work*, 2015.

[6] C. H. Crouch, J. Watkins, A. P. Fagen, and E. Mazur. Peer instruction: Engaging students one-on-one, all at once. *Research-Based Reform of University Physics*, 1(1):40–95, 2007.

[7] J. DeBoer, G. S. Stump, D. Seaton, and L. Breslow. Diversity in MOOC students' backgrounds and behaviors in relationship to performance in 6.002 x. In *Proceedings of the Sixth Learning International Networks Consortium Conference*, 2013.

[8] J. Foertsch, G. Moses, J. Strikwerda, and M. Litzkow. Reversing the lecture/homework paradigm using eTEACH web-based streaming video software. *Journal of Engineering Education-Washington*, 91(3):267–274, 2002.

[9] P. J. Hinds and D. E. Bailey. Out of sight, out of sync: Understanding conflict in distributed teams. *Organization science*, 14(6):615–632, 2003.

[10] J. M. Hudson and A. Bruckman. Disinhibition in a CSCL environment. In *Proceedings of the Conference on Computer Support for Collaborative Learning: Foundations for a CSCL Community*, pages 629–630. International Society of the Learning Sciences, 2002.

[11] D. W. Johnson and R. T. Johnson. Making cooperative learning work. *Theory into practice*, 38(2):67–73, 1999.

[12] S. Kiesler and J. N. Cummings. What do we know about proximity and distance in work groups? a legacy of research. *Distributed work*, 1:57, 2002.

[13] C. Kulkarni, J. Cambre, Y. Kotturi, M. S. Bernstein, and S. Klemmer. Talkabout: Making distance matter with small groups in massive classes. In *Proceedings of CSCW 2015: ACM Conference on Computer Supported Collaborative Work*, 2015.

[14] M. Lage, G. Platt, and M. Treglia. Inverting the classroom: A gateway to creating an inclusive learning environment. *The Journal of Economic Education*, 31(1):30–43, 2000.

[15] C. Latulipe, N. B. Long, and C. E. Seminario. Structuring flipped classes with lightweight teams and gamification. In *Proceedings of the 46th ACM Technical Symposium on Computer Science Education*, pages 392–397. ACM, 2015.

[16] S. MacNeil, C. Latulipe, and A. Yadav. Learning in distributed low-stakes teams. In *Proceedings of the eleventh annual International Conference on International Computing Education Research*, pages 227–236. ACM, 2015.

[17] M. L. Maher, C. Latulipe, H. Lipford, and A. Rorrer. Flipped classroom strategies for CS education. In *Proceedings of the 46th ACM Technical Symposium on Computer Science Education*, SIGCSE '15, pages 218–223, New York, NY, USA, 2015. ACM.

[18] M. McPherson, L. Smith-Lovin, and J. M. Cook. Birds of a feather: Homophily in social networks. *Annual review of sociology*, pages 415–444, 2001.

[19] L. K. Michaelsen and M. Sweet. Fundamental principles and practices of team-based learning. *Team-based learning for health professions education: A guide to using small groups for improving learning. Sterling (VA): Stylus Publishing*, pages 9–31, 2008.

[20] M. Nelimarkka and A. Vihavainen. Alumni & tenured participants in MOOCs: Analysis of two years of MOOC discussion channel activity. In *Proceedings of the Second (2015) ACM Conference on Learning@ Scale*, pages 85–93. ACM, 2015.

[21] G. M. Olson and J. S. Olson. Distance matters. *Human-computer interaction*, 15(2):139–178, 2000.

[22] D. H. Schunk and B. J. Zimmerman. Social origins of self-regulatory competence. *Educational psychologist*, 32(4):195–208, 1997.

[23] L. D. Setlock, S. R. Fussell, and C. Neuwirth. Taking it out of context: collaborating within and across cultures in face-to-face settings and via instant messaging. In *Proceedings of the 2004 ACM conference on Computer supported cooperative work*, pages 604–613. ACM, 2004.

[24] R. E. Slavin. Cooperative learning. *Review of educational research*, 50(2):315–342, 1980.

[25] S. Warburton. Second Life in higher education: Assessing the potential for and the barriers to deploying virtual worlds in learning and teaching. *British Journal of Educational Technology*, 40(3):414–426, 2009.

Can Students Design Software? The Answer Is More Complex Than You Think

Chenglie Hu
Carroll University
Waukesha, WI 53186
262-524-7170
chu@carrollu.edu

ABSTRACT

In this paper, we first present an assessment on students' software design abilities based on qualitative data from a design class. We will then provide, using the assessment as a backdrop, a discussion on the nature of software design, the challenges of teaching design, and ways to improve design education.

CCS Concepts

CCS → Applied computing → Education, CCS → Software and its engineering → Software creation and management → Designing software

Keywords

Software design, Teaching of Software Design, Design Education

1. INTRODUCTION

It is a widely-held view that the most critical ingredient in ensuring a software system's quality and longtime success is its design [23]. ABET Accreditation Criteria (retrievable at www.abet.org) stipulates that a computer-science graduate should have an ability to apply mathematical foundations, algorithmic principles, computer science theory, and design principles in the modeling and design of computer-based systems of varying complexity in a way that demonstrates comprehension of the tradeoffs involved in design choices. However, studies [7, 8, 13, 20], over a span of six years, seem to have concluded that graduating computer science students were generally unable to design software, and a significant number appeared to lack even minimum knowledge of design. The researchers also found that increased educational attainment has little effect on students' valuation of key design characteristics.

As an ABET program evaluator, the author noticed that computer science programs take different approaches to teaching software design. While some programs have a dedicated course about design, most seem to teach design in a software engineering or software development course. We do offer a dedicated design course in our own computer science program. Given the aforementioned studies, we asked this question to ourselves: In what way can our students design software after they received some significant formal education on design? We will present our findings in the next section.

SIGCSE '16, March 02-05, 2016, Memphis, TN, USA.
 ISBN 978-1-4503-3685-7/16/03…$15.00.
DOI: http://dx.doi.org/10.1145/2839509.2844563

But a viewpoint we try to make in this article is that designing software is an inherently complex, and undefined process. Thus, assessing students' software design competencies requires substantially different measures from design artifacts students produce. We will make our case in Section 3, and discuss the kind of design abilities we want our students to acquire in a design course. Furthermore, we will look at issues surrounding teaching of design in a larger context in Section 4. We will briefly conclude in Section 5.

2. CAN SOPHMORE STUDENTS DESIGN SOFTWARE?

2.1 Background Information and Data Description

To evaluate students' designs, the authors of [8] developed certain categories to "measure" the quality of a student design. These are:

- Nothing – little or no intelligible content,
- Restatement – merely restating requirements in some fashion from the task description,
- Skumtomte – a small amount restatement of the task with a small amount of information in text, or a drawing of a GUI, or some unimportant implementation details with no description of its design,
- First step – some significant work beyond the description: either a partial overview of the system with the parts identified, but generally no identification of how they are related in the system, or the design of one of the system's components, such as the GUI or the interface to the database,
- Partial design – providing an understandable description of each of the parts and an overview of the system that illustrates the relationships between the (maybe incomplete) parts without completely described communications between the parts, and
- Complete – showing a well-developed solution, including an understandable overview, part descriptions that include responsibilities, and explicit communication between the parts.

Using these categories, we "measured" students' performances on the same design task (a super software alarm clock) used in the aforementioned studies after students had been exposed to what we considered a reasonably good amount of design theory and practices in a course termed "Software Design".

To put learning in context, we believe that a design class is not where we make every student a good designer, but where students gain understanding of what it would take to become a good designer (our philosophical viewpoints about teaching of software design were documented in [12]). With that belief, we placed an emphasis on learning to effectively evaluate and hence make design choices in a non-prescriptive, multi-paradigm approach [4].

Table 1. Student Performance Data

Student A: The class diagram has these entities: *Student* (with encapsulated data structures) using *MenuInterface*, *Day*, and *Alarm* with two subtypes *WakeUp* and *SleepReminder*. The assignment of functional behaviors to the entities appeared appropriate. The sequence diagram describes interactions amongst the designed entities with some mislabeled communications. However, there was a lack of overall control modules in the design, thus, the design was categorized as a ***partial design***.

Student B: The class diagram appropriately describes relations among these entities: *GUI* using *Student* and *Clock* controlled by *ClockControl*, which uses *Calendar* and *DBRecord* (for data store and retrieval). The sequence diagram depicts method calls representing sequence of software events. Although there were minor issues regarding the behavior of some entities, we thought the design was essentially ***complete***.

Student C: The class diagram involves these entities: *AlarmInitializer* aggregating *Student* and *Clock* that uses *TimeTrackingSystem*, which in turn aggregates *WakeupAlarm* and *SleepAlarm*, with entity *Clock* using *SleepAwakeDatabase*, which aggregates an interface *Record* with implementing classes *SleepRecord* and *AwakeRecord*. The sequence diagram captures the major software events, yet was unclear about the communication with entity *SleepAwakeDatabase* (the design of which appeared flawed). Nonetheless, we thought that the design was virtually ***complete***.

Student D: The class diagram has these entities: *DAO* (interface) with implementing class *AlarmDataStructure* used by *AlarmEventHandler*, which has *AlarmClock* aggregating *Clock* and *Notification*. The sequence diagram depicts a sequence of software events with some missed communications, and involves entities that are not defined. The entities lack detailed behaviors. Thus it was a ***partial design***.

Student E: The class diagram has entities: *SuperAlarmClock* (containing main method) using *SleepDataHandler*, aggregated in *Student*, which uses *WakeupHandler* and *SleepHandler*. The sequence diagram is vague on object interaction. There is no design on how data is to be handled. There is also lack of overall control mechanism. The design appeared merely a ***first step***.

Student F: The class diagram has these entities: *AlarmApp* (containing main method) using *AlamManager* that has a list of objects typed *Alarm*, which uses an entity of *Student*. The sequence diagram has unlabeled communications. Communication with *AlarmManager* is not specified. Data store and retrieval are also missing. It was a ***partial design***.

Student G: The class diagram has entities: *SupperAlarmApp* aggregating instance of *SuperAlarmClock*, which uses an interface *IUserInterface* with its implementing class *ConsoleBasedUI* using *Student* and *ClockManager* interacting with *DAO* objects for data handling and managing a collection of *Alert* objects and an instance of *AlarmCollection* – a *HashMap* data structure of *Alarm* instances, and a *Factory* entity to create alarms and alerts. The sequence diagram shows all events involved although the timelines of the events were hidden. The design was considered ***complete***.

Student H: The class diagram has entities: *AlarmClock* encapsulating a list of *Alarm* instances, and interacting with *Student*, *Alarm*, *SleepAlert*, *Report*, and *DataAccessLayer*. No sequence diagrams were given. Thus the design was considered a ***partial design***.

Student I: The class diagram has entities: *AlarmHandler* that aggregates *SupperAlarmClock* with a *HashMap* of *String* to *Timer*, which in turn has an instance of *EventStore* (a *DAO* entity) to handle instances of *AlarmEventObject*. The design uses *Observer* design pattern. Although there is a sequence diagram, but the communication between event occurring and notifying listeners is not clear. The design was considered a ***partial design***.

Student J: The class diagram has entities: *AlarmClock* aggregating *CurrentTime*, *WakeUp*, *AboutToSleep*, *SleepReminder* that uses *SleepDeprived*, which encapsulates an instance of *EmergnecyContact*, *SendDataToDB*, and *Student*. These entities together, even with the flow of a sequence diagram, are essentially a restatement of the requirements. However, the student did include code that shows a flow of control. Thus, the design was consider a ***first step***.

Student K: The class diagram has entities: *AlarmManager* with a *HashMap* from *String* to a list of instances of *AlarmClock* – one student corresponding to a list of alarms, which aggregates *DAO*, *ConsoleUI*, *AlarmClock*, and *Student* with *AlarmClock* using entity *Time* with two subtypes *ActualTime* and *AlarmTime*. The sequence diagram depicts event setting, but not event handling. There is a lack of overall control. Thus, the design was considered a ***partial design***.

Student L: The class diagram has entities: *AlarmClockPanel* (which main method invokes) aggregating *TimeManager*, which interacts with *Student*, *Alarm*, and *AlertManager*, and independent entities *DataManager* (interacting with an instance of *Student*), *Alarm*, and *Guardian*. The sequence diagram describes change of panel mode and the associated events. The design was considered ***complete***.

In every design assignment, we required students to implement what they had designed in order for them to develop a good sense of accuracy and implementability of a design.

In our experiment of a spring 2013 class, students were assigned the aforementioned "super alarm clock" design task as the 6th design assignment roughly at ¾ time mark of a 15-week semester. It was a week-long assignment to be completed on an individual basis. Students were expected to produce an architectural diagram about the software elements they designed and their relations, interaction diagrams of their choosing, and skeleton code based on the design. Although a complete implementation of a design wasn't a requirement of the assignment, the fact that the students implemented all five design assignments prior to this assignment did speak for certain degree of validity of their designs sketched in Table 1. Two designs by students who were professional programmers at the time were excluded. All students were fairly motivated and reasonably prepared in their technical skills, although they differ naturally in cognitive strengths. Figure 1 is a chart-view of the data to provide some intuition (note that categories with zero instance were not graphically represented).

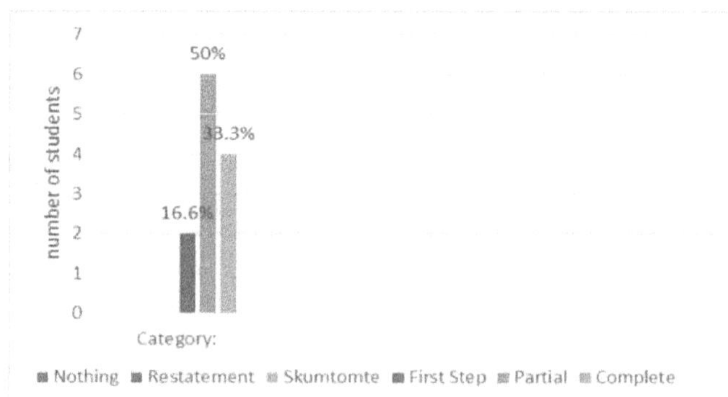

Figure 1. Chart for student design completeness

To evaluate whether the submitted design artifacts represent complete and appropriate designs, we used the following criteria:

- The elements created appear adequate in serving the needs for software operation;
- The behavior of each element appears reasonable;
- Relations (association, aggregation, inheritance) are correctly labeled;

- A data-structure element must indicate its underlying storage structure;
- There must be an interaction diagram or a piece of code that describes the flow of software operation in terms of event monitoring and handling in an appropriate sequence using the elements identified.

The design evaluations, performed by the same instructor, were consistent, although they were only as accurate as the instructor's domain expertise warrants.

We also asked students to complete a survey at the end of a design class with two primary items for them to respond: (1) Describe your typical design process including an evaluation of elements interaction and design iteration; (2) Describe the most difficult part in your learning experience. Our summary of students' responses is organized in Table 2 with our interpretation of the design processes (students described) to match the process patterns we defined. We actually did another round of data collection in the spring of 2014, but the data did not render new insights.

Table 2. Novices' design processes

Noun-extraction approach – They start a design by defining classes, interfaces, and data structures that the problem description seems to support or imply. When they start coding, they fix the problems along the way to make the already-started structure work, even if things become convoluted.
Task-oriented process – Student may start with some tasks he/she may have had experience before, and appears to know what needs to be done. He/she then starts coding with modules or tasks that seem less likely to be abandoned later, and uses objects only when the requirements seem to suggest. He/she changes or modifies code often, but not likely tries to improve the overall design.
Console-dialog-oriented process – Some students developed a habit in elementary programming classes to place a dialog loop in the main method asking for inputs of task selection, and then invoke methods to perform the specified task. So they would start a design by finding such action methods, and their hosting classes. They would then try to make it work even when the approach becomes problematic.
Code-first approach – They do not produce design artifacts other than the code (with the concerns that ideas not implemented would not work for them). They start with some simple tasks to code, and gradually move to more demanding ones; they may change many things back and forth, and test along the way.
Design iteration – Few students experienced design iteration to evolve design architecture. For many, design iteration means: (1) fixing problems that happen across several parts of the program, going back and forth in a random fashion or an ad-hoc order, or (2) adding or removing classes, modifying local code structures on the fly depending upon what's coming into one's mind, or (3) filling in details of a skeleton structure gradually. ***Experienced difficulties*** (in descending order of frequency) – (1) How to effectively start a design, (2) weighing design options mentally, (3) use of object-oriented design principles to refactor a design.

2.2 Data Analysis

In this section, we interpret the data and reflect on the students' attainment of expected learning outcomes. As a qualitative analysis tool, reflection allows practitioners to step outside their pre-conceived beliefs and seek evidence that affirms or refutes the assumptions underpinning their practice. We used a reflection framework suggested by Watson and Wilcox based on a metaphor of reading a book [22]. Like reading stories, there are three modes to reflect on an experience: (1) a "quick scan" to provide an initial impression on the range of issues in the experience, (2) "zooming in" to pursue a fine-grained analysis of a particular aspect of the issue, and (3) synthesizing and evaluating the experience by "zooming out" to enable restructuring our sense of issues and the relative significance of these issues to extend reflection from the local level to a larger context. We do "zooming-in" analysis in this section, and provide some "zooming-out" discussions in the rest of the sections.

Students responded very well to the design class they experienced, which they considered to be very demanding, but rewarding. They valued what they were exposed to. Many said that the class significantly changed the way they approached problem solving. Even though some were not satisfied with the attainment of the learning outcomes they demonstrated, they expressed confidence going forward as they believed they would surely improve their design abilities over time. Compared to where they were at the start of the class, many probably had made conceptual and methodological improvements by leaps and bounds.

Most of our students take a design class in the second semester of sophomore year following a data structures course. Figure 1 shows that about 80 percent of the students were able to either complete a design or do so to a considerable extent (same was true for the classes of spring 2014 and 2015). As we observed, that cohort had improved their design skills with varying degrees at the time they did their capstone projects. In other words, students of that cohort were generally able to design software at the time of graduation if that ability was to merely provide artifacts deemed "complete".

However, we asked a different question: Were students able to apply design principles to modeling software in a way that demonstrates comprehension of design tradeoffs? Our answer to the question was generally negative given the responses to the survey questions summarized in Table 2, and our observation on students' overall performances. There was generally little evidence that students were able to effectively evaluate design tradeoffs and ramifications of different choices of software elements, their communication mechanisms, and data structures.

In our experience, most students were unable to approach a design architecturally, even though they learned the importance of requirement analysis that leads to architectural decisions from "day one" of the class. They generally were unable to identify opportunities to create useful structural design elements. Many created design elements and their behaviors often based on intuition, not analysis. Lack of requirement analysis often led students to a difficult start of a design process as a significant number of students experienced, especially when they had no prior experiences of solving similar problems. When asked how they would typically start a design, three popular answers were: starting with (1) some types you definitely want to keep, (2) some methods, or (3) some domain entities. As self-described, students' thought processes appeared to be task oriented, asking themselves questions such as: Do I need this class? What should I do if multiple objects seem to need this behavior or this data? How do I replace this if-else structure with an object structure? Do I need to group these operations in an interface? What kind of "manager" should I create – data manager, or process manager, or both?

Lack of analysis was also observed when students produced diagrams. A typical first trial of a diagram by a student in the class, regardless of a style, was merely a kind of restatement of the original requirements without rendering much architectural significance. In fact, many students had difficulty understanding the semantic requirements of the diagram constructions. As a result, few actually found diagramming useful.

Students also appeared to perform poorly in design iteration. They tended to make the design they started with work unless something really went wrong. To many, design iteration was meant to do local fixes if things became "not working". They were unlikely to update a design if they deviated from it during implementation. A number of students reflected that they tended to apply design principles along the lines of avoiding the past mistakes, not exploring new design ideas. While they understood the object-oriented design concepts such as "dependency inversion" and their roles in design refactoring, few could actually apply these ideas in seeking improvements of their own designs.

But there were also examples where thinking appeared at a broader level, as this quote shows: "For example with this assignment, first I was thinking about using a factory to create actions to manage all operations, but I slowly realized this would lead to passing too many variables too embedded in the program, so I scrapped the idea entirely and went with state pattern to delegate tasks…". Some students were also able to work on a design subconsciously as shown in this quote: "I usually read over the problem statement right away with the best intentions of working on the design ahead of time, but always end up working on all of my other homework first with design ideas always floating around in the back of my head. This subconscious mulling over my design actually aids me greatly."

In general, even though most of designs students produced could be considered "complete" in varying degrees, the overall quality of design remained largely a "work in progress". This phenomena is probably not unexpected however as cognition is a process by which the sensory input is transformed, reduced, elaborated, stored, recovered, and used [15]. Because of the nature of design (which we will discuss in the next section), there might be a significant (knowledge) elaboration period students would need to gradually overcome their default modes of thinking, and develop perceptions, design-analysis abilities, and a sound judgment on valid uses of the design theory and practices.

3. DISCUSSION

3.1 Complexity of Designing Software

What are key design characteristics? It might be a reasonably understanding of design that a design is an expression of software elements and their interaction schemes, and a "blueprint" of the software that fulfills the requirements. In the business world however, requirements often endure changes, and so might a design. Thus, software design is meant to be more of a dynamic process enduring design refactoring than a product delivered before construction takes place. As a design evolves, the sensibility of software elements and their interaction methods to requirement changes may affect sustainability of the design. Thus, it is widely recognized that a quality design should be structurally extendible to accommodate requirement changes and overlooked environment constraints – a key design characteristic as we understand. A good designer must be able to weather the unpredictable, and make sound decisions based upon effective evaluation of design options and their tradeoffs.

However, "software design, as an engineering process, is not well understood in terms of what effective software designers would do when they design, and in terms of well-founded guidance about how to match method to context" [1]. Design is a modeling and simulation process that proposes solutions yet allows them to fail – a process that happens inside one's brain at a speed faster than lightening [10]. Design is driven by what's termed "design thinking"– a mental ability to tolerate ambiguity, maintain sight of the big picture, handle uncertainty, make decisions, think as part of a team and in several design languages [1; 2; 5]. As believed, "design thinking" involves cycles of convergent thinking – driven by reasoning questions operated in one's knowledge domain leading to facts, and divergent thinking – stimulated by generative questions operated in a concept domain, exploring the possibilities that the known facts can diverge to [5]. Figure 2 places perceived design-thinking elements in a 2D operational environment.

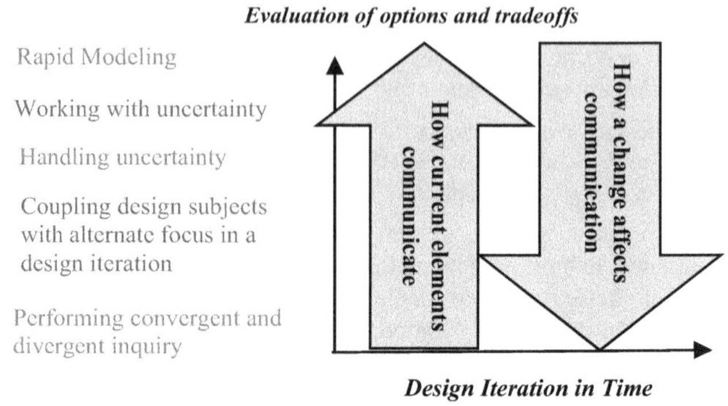

Figure 2: Dynamic view of design thinking

Design as an intelligent process, in fact, has been long perceived. Dasgupta described design to be generally a descriptive, not a prescriptive, human activity that is cognitive, intellectual, and psycho-biological in nature [6]. Winograd et al. argued that an ability to design software goes beyond the ability to be creative in solving problems [24]. Baker et al. portrayed design as being inherently an interdisciplinary subject, influenced by a large number of human factors that confound what's already a muddled picture of how design truly progresses [1].

Meanwhile, software design in the real world is diversely practiced, often driven by a focus or a featuring aspect of the development. In particular, professionals who advocate agile software-development practices may believe that design is not only highly iterative, but emergent, and models often lie. Thus, only coding, running tests, and refactoring the code reveal the truth about a design. Hence, code is an ultimate design, they argue [18]. The "threat" from agile practices to the conventional software-design process was so real that a keynote speech at an OOPSLA conference was dedicated in its entirety to addressing what many might have wondered: Is design dead [9]?

The subtle nature of software design is likely the reason that even a design textbook (for example, [19]) may not bother defining what software design is. Yet educators argued decades ago that there are plausible reasons why students need to know a rational design process even if one has to fake it [16]. We understand that central to learning a rational design process is the learning of "design thinking". Arguably, design thinking shares many elements with, and is a form of, computational thinking [11], which we think that not only our students, but general public should also achieve. At the heart of computational thinking is computational modeling of what is to be computed. Arguably also, learning and doing software design is perhaps one of the most relevant ways for students to acquire and nurture their computational thinking abilities.

Therefore, it is our view that we should assess students' software design abilities not only by the design artifacts they produce, but more importantly, also by the ways they approach design decision making. In fact, the same researchers of [8] noticed that some students indeed knew more about the design than was produced on paper during the interviews. In our practice, we required students to describe the thought process in each of the assignments to go with the submitted artifacts. We also asked impromptu design questions in class, and asked randomly-picked students to provide answers allowing only a small amount of time for them to think about. Moreover, at the end of each design class, we required students to complete a self-evaluation about their experiences of learning to apply design-thinking elements. In other words, we tried, in a way, to understand each student's profile of thinking when approaching a design question or task, even though this understanding can still be coarse. It is thus logical to argue that given designing software being an unspecified, complex mental process, we should assesse one's ability to design software by the way he or she handles uncertainty and complexity.

3.2 What We Expect Students to Achieve

In our case, we expected students to gain in a design class: 1) factual knowledge of design theory, techniques and common practices, 2) an ability to engage in a design process by applying elements of design thinking, and 3) improved understanding of some key computing concepts and methodologies. Even though we placed significant emphasis on object-oriented design, we believe that students have to develop design skills applicable in a multi-paradigm design environment. This is consistent with the nature of design. This also makes learning of design more empirically relevant, as "the real world has experienced a resurgent of multi-paradigm programming as today's technology is often developed under diverse platforms" [21].

Frequent requirement changes can make existing software documentation obsolete quickly. As a result, organizations in the business world have diverse practices towards design documentation. Nonetheless, we think that only when students have known how to meaningfully document a design would they be able to determine whether, when, or how much they should document later in their professional lives.

Learning design must also acknowledge, we think, the fact that many organizations in the real world practice agile development methodologies. There might be diverse views in academia in terms of teaching agile methods in an academic setting. Learning to evaluate design tradeoffs is a process of learning incremental design improvement, ways to make software architecture extendible, and design refactoring to make elements more cohesive and less coupled – the same process where agile methods are supposed to be useful. Thus, we believe that learning design would naturally integrate key agile practices into the learning. However, we do believe that students must learn to produce an upfront architectural design given the current requirements even though some agilists may denounce the "big, upfront design".

The challenge we faced was not how much technical material we expect students to learn, but how we would be able to integrate the materials into one coherent learning experience. The difficulty of learning to design software can be comparable to that of learning to do mathematical proofs [12]. Learning may also be against unhealthy programming habits students may have developed. Thus the learning necessarily carries high intrinsic cognitive loads, and it challenges perhaps even the most carefully-designed pedagogies. Expectedly, each student would achieve learning outcomes at a different level. But minimally yet essentially, we expected all students to attain an ability to proceed a design with appropriate analysis, and produce an implementable design with correct utilization of the design methods and tools.

4. A FEW PEDAGOGICAL HEURISTICS

4.1 The Focus of a Design Course

According to Software Engineering Body of Knowledge (www.swebok.org), the knowledge of software design may include design-enabling techniques and process knowledge. The former involves design principles and methodologies, key concepts in regard to design abstraction, decomposition, and modularization, as well as design tools. Students actually start learning these in various courses once they know how to program. In contrast, students do not seem to understand what sort of information a software system design should include and how that information might be communicated [13]. In other words, students may not understand what to accomplish, much less "how", in a design process. So the focus of a design course, we think, is on exposing students to, in order for them to gain, process knowledge.

What is process knowledge? Design is a modeling process, which traditionally begins with requirement analysis, leading to design formation followed by software construction and testing. This process maps software requirements in the problem domain to software elements in a solution domain. However, this is not a process of 'linear progression"; it is highly iterative to allow for evaluation of "how decisions made in one part of the design may influence those made in other parts" [1]. Besides, process knowledge may also include knowledge of "process paradigms" practiced in the business world driven by a business domain, by the model, by the behaviors of software elements, or simply by a practice (such as test-driven design). But again, learning design thinking would naturally enable learning of process knowledge, as one's thinking dictates the way one applies design paradigms, makes design decisions, and moves a design process forward.

4.2 Nurturing Students' Design Skills

Students in a design class are in fact hardly "design novices". They start learning rudimentary program design in elementary programming courses such as the "top-down" design principle. They continue to learn various aspects of design in more advanced courses. But why increased attainment of computing education may have little effect on improving students' design skills, or simply on their valuation of basic characteristics of design (suggested in the aforementioned studies)?

We think that inconsistency and lack of coordination in teaching the aspects of design may have contributed to this dilemma. Students do not achieve design competency in one course. Thus, there must be a collaborative effort in a computing program to nurture students' design skills over time, over different computing contexts, and over diverse environments and platforms where software operates. This effort of collaboration may require that we teach design principles, methods, techniques, and practices consistently across the curriculum. But at the very least, students should not experience unlearning what they have learned in a prior course. Inconsistent learning experiences in learning problem solving can easily make students retrieve their default thinking, thus being stagnant in developing their problem-solving skills.

Nurturing students' design skills may also mean to enable, not to restrict, learner's thinking. As instructors, we may unintentionally impede effective thinking if we put a restriction on a design method or tool to use, ideas to follow, or the kind of design to be expected. It is part of a learning process that students select, with their own judgement, design methods, techniques, or tools to use when approaching a design task. Our own experience suggests that we may facilitate, and thus enable, this learning by reminding them of the characteristics of different methods, techniques, or tools, by demonstrating later "how I would start", or by critically comparing their design ideas, as well as the completed design artifacts.

4.3 Teaching Design in a Larger Context

Whenever there is computational modeling, there is design. Thus, it might make sense to promote a design culture in our computing programs so that when we teach computing concepts, theory, or practices in different courses, we do so consistently with full awareness about their use in design. For instance, when students learn the concept of "interface" in a programming class, they need to also learn the use of interfaces in writing reusable code.

A design culture would also encourage sharing of responsibilities of teaching design. For instance, many design patterns are data structures of certain kinds. Particularly, Chain of Responsibility pattern is essentially a linked list. Including some design patterns in a data structures class can not only pepper a possibly dull learning environment with some fun, yet useful materials, but also give students some good dose of the idea behind design patterns. By the same token, learning flowcharts, UML activity diagrams (or "glorified flowcharts"), or those with "object swim lanes" could happen in different courses; but if we teach as a "team", we can not only improve student's achievement of learning diagramming with various kinds of "flowcharts", but also raise the bar to encourage students to diagram creatively in design activities.

Can effective inquiry, the systematic interplay between divergent and convergent questions, be taught or promoted [5]? We probably can at least promote such a way of thinking if we work together. Critical thinking is a deliberate meta-cognitive (thinking about thinking) and cognitive (thinking) act whereby a person reflects on the quality of the reasoning process simultaneously while reasoning to a conclusion [14]. Design thinking is a kind of critical thinking built on the basic thinking elements – thinking to motivate a solution intent, ask exploratory questions, make assumptions, retrieve relevant information, form solution viewpoints, conceptualize a solution framework, reach a solution, and weigh the implications. Students can learn this process of thinking in virtually all computing classes. Once students are in a design class, they would be then facing not the learning of design thinking, but applying the thinking skills they already have to new situations.

5. CONCLUSION

It was assessed almost a quarter century ago that software design education students received in a typical computer science program had been inadequate [17]. The studies on students' design performances mentioned earlier may have suggested that this situation likely has continued to this day. Teaching design in many computing programs is still an isolated endeavor that lacks coordinated efforts, consistent pedagogical strategies, and even basic instructional support (frankly, finding an appropriate design textbook can be a challenge these days). The difficulty of teaching design is exacerbated by widely-varied design practices in the real world, and our poor design codification beyond a few design patterns. Nonetheless, we are still obligated to provide students a good design education, and we need a community effort to do so.

As software-based technologies evolve rapidly, they demand our abilities to produce designs that are structurally stable, adaptive, and lasting. Fred Brooks called for great designers suggesting a tenfold difference between great and regular designers [3]. What makes this tenfold difference by a great designer, as we understand, is the ability to effectively evaluate design tradeoffs in such a way that ensures design elegance (the author of [19] has some view about what that means) against software constraints and varying requirements. To ensure that our graduating students meet the challenges, improving design education is thus not an option, but a necessity. We have reasoned in this article that a graduating student of a computer science program should, and generally can design software in an intelligent way if we all work together to support a quality design education.

6. REFERENCES

[1] Baker, A.et al. (2012). Studying Professional Software Design, IEEE SOFTWARE, Jan. /Feb. 2012, 28-33.

[2] Baker, A. and Van der Hoek, A. (2010). Ideas, Subjects, and Cycles as Lenses for Understanding the Software Design Process, Design Studies, 31(6), 590–613.

[3] Brooks F. (1986) "No Silver Bullet — Essence and Accident in Software Engineering". Proceedings of the IFIP Tenth World Computing Conference: 1069–1076.

[4] Coplien, J. (1999). Multi-Paradigm Design for C++, Addison-Wesley, Boston, MA.

[5] Dym, C. et al. (2005) Engineering Design Thinking, Teaching, and Learning, Journal of Engineering Education, January, 2005, 103-120.

[6] Dasgupta, S. (1991) Design Theory and Computer Science, Cambridge University Press, UK.

[7] Eckerdal, A. at al. (2006). Can Graduating Students Design Software Systems? In Proceedings of the 37th SIGCSE Technical Symposium on Computer Science Education, ACM, New York, NY, 403-407.

[8] Eckerdal, A. el al. (2006) Categorizing student software designs: Methods, results, and implications, Computer Science Education Volume 16, Issue 3, 2006, Special Issue: Koli Calling 2005 Conferenc, pages 197-209

[9] Fowler, M. (2000). Is Design Dead? Retrievable at http://martinfowler.com/articles/designDead.html.

[10] Glass, R. (2006). Software Conflict 2.0: The Art and Science of Software Engineering. Developer.*Books.

[11] Hu, C. (2011). Computational Thinking: what it might mean and what we might do about it, in Proceedings of the 16th Annual Conference on Innovation and Technology in Computer Science Education, ITiCSE '11, ACM Press, 223-227.

[12] Hu, C. (2013). The Nature of Software Design and Its Teaching: An Exposition (a comprehensive article). ACM Inroads, ACM Press, Vol. 4, No. 2, 62-71.

[13] Loftus, C et al. (2011). Can Graduating Students Design: elaborated, in Proceedings of the 42nd ACM technical symposium on Computer Science Education, ACM, New York, NY, 105-110.

[14] Moore, D. (2006) Critical Thinking and Intelligence Analysis, Joint Military Intelligence College, Occasional Paper 14, May 2006, pg. 2.

[15] Neisser, U. (1967). Cognitive Psychology. Meredith Publishing Company.

[16] Parnas, D. and Clements, P. (1986). A Rational Design Process: How and why to fake it. IEEE Transactions on Software Engineering, Volume 12, Issue 2, 251-257.

[17] Pierce, K et al. Teaching software design in the freshman year, Software Engineering Education (Lecture Notes in Computer Science Education, Volume 536) Springer Berlin / Heidelberg, 1991, 219-231.

[18] Reeves, J. (2005). Code as Design: Three Essays by J. Reeves at: http://developerdotstar.com/mag/articles/reeves_design_main.html

[19] Skrien, D. (2009). Object-Oriented Design Using Java, McGraw Hill.

[20] Tenenberg J. et al. (2005). Students Designing Software: a Multi-National, Multi-Institutional Study. Informatics in Education, 2005, Vol. 4, No. 1, 143–162.

[21] Wampler, D. and Clark, T. (2010). Multi-paradigm Programming. IEEE Software, Vol.27, No.5, 20-24.

[22] Watson, J., & Wilcox, S. (2000). Reading for understanding: Methods of reflecting on practice. Reflective Practice, 1(1), 57-67.

[23] Welcome Message of ICSE, (2011) The 33rd International Conference on Software Engineering. Honolulu, Hawaii, May 2011, Retrievable at: http://2011.icse-conferences.org/content/welcome.

[24] Winograd, T., Bennett, J., De Young, L., & Hartfield, B. (eds.) (1996). Bringing Design to Software. Stanford University and Interval Research Corporation, Addison-Wesley.

On the Interplay Between Bottom-Up and Datatype-Driven Program Design

Francisco Enrique Vicente Castro
Department of Computer Science
Worcester Polytechnic Institute
100 Institute Road, Worcester, MA, USA
fgcastro@wpi.edu

Kathi Fisler
Department of Computer Science
Worcester Polytechnic Institute
100 Institute Road, Worcester, MA, USA
kfisler@wpi.edu

ABSTRACT

When students are faced with a programming problem unlike any they have solved before, prior research suggests that they develop code backwards from essential computations in the problem. Some curricula, however, teach students to first write scaffolding code based on the type of the input data. How do these two approaches interact? We gave CS1 students who were taught to write scaffolding code a programming problem unlike any they had seen before. We found that while students put essential computations into the scaffolds, they often overuse affordances of the scaffolds in ways that lead to plan-composition errors. We propose that steering students away from on-the-fly decomposition while programming could help avoid some of these errors.

Keywords: Novice programmers; models of code development; plan composition

1. INTRODUCTION

Most models of how novices program suggest that they use previously learned examples or solutions as starting points for new programs [3, 4, 10]. What happens, however, when a new problem is sufficiently different that previously-learned examples don't apply?

In studies with students learning Pascal, Rist [5, 6] determined that novices write down a statement or expression that captures the essence of some program task (the *focus*), then work backwards to integrate this into the overall program. In contrast, pedagogic approaches such as *How to Design Programs* (henceforth HTDP) aim to be more systematic, teaching students to first write scaffolding code that exploits the structure of input data. These two perspectives, one a model developed from observing students programming procedurally and one a process designed to scaffold traversal of recursively-defined datatypes (as taught in some CS1 courses that use functional languages), could either complement or interfere with one another. What role does each play in helping students develop correct solutions to new problems? What hindrances does each introduce?

SIGCSE '16, March 02 - 05, 2016, Memphis, TN, USA

ISBN 978-1-4503-3685-7/16/03. . . $15.00

DOI: http://dx.doi.org/10.1145/2839509.2844574

This paper explores the interplay of bottom-up programming and datatype-driven design, using Rist's model and HTDP as concrete instances of each. We report on a study in which HTDP students were given a problem that required program structures they had not yet learned. We video-recorded their sessions, looked for how students used each of focal-expressions and HTDP scaffolds in attempting to solve the problem, and extract insights on the affordances and limitations of each approach. In part, this work explores how bottom-up programming manifests in functional programming. In part, it tries to identify ways to leverage each perspective towards developing pedagogic techniques that help students tackle new programming problems.

2. BACKGROUND

2.1 Rist's Focal Expansion Model

Several papers from the mid 1980's proposed models of how students create new programs by adapting known solutions to similar problems (we review these in section 2.3). Rist's *focal-expansion model* [5, 6] expanded on these to cover situations in which students lacked similar problems on which to build. His model identifies two states that students can enter when encountering a programming problem:

1. **Plan Retrieval**: If a novice knows a solution to a similar problem, she will retrieve it (from memory) and reproduce the code in a top-down fashion.
2. **Plan Creation**: If a novice does not know a solution to a similar problem, she will start from a small code fragment for an identified computation within the problem. This code fragment is called the *focus* or *focal computation.* She will then expand the code around the focus in bottom-up fashion to integrate the new code into the rest of the program.

When a known solution applies to a more difficult problem, the model predicts that students switch to bottom-up creation mode after retrieval. As a programmer's experience increases, she makes heavier use of retrieval.

Intuitively, the focus is the essential computation for an identifiable *task* within the program. For the task to sum a sequence of numbers, an expression like `sum := sum + n` would be the focus (where `n` would be defined subsequently, perhaps by reading the next input from the sequence). In the problem of averaging a sequence of numbers, there are three focal expressions, one for each of the required tasks of summing the elements, counting the elements, and dividing the sum by the count. Rist's model does not address which focal a student would handle first. Rather, it claims that one of the expressions `sum := sum + n`, `count := count + 1`, or `average = sum / count` would be written and expanded upon first, rather than more generic code such as "iteratively read input" (which would only occur first in retrieval mode).

Rist developed this model from watching students produce code (in Pascal) for problems such as calculating the volume of a box-like house or sorting weights into ascending order. The essence of the model lies in (a) new plan creation starting from a focal computation, and (b) the construction of code being either top-down or bottom-up, depending on whether a plan is being created or retrieved.

2.2 How to Design Programs

How to Design Programs (HTDP) is a CS1 curriculum that teaches a step-by-step "recipe" for designing programs [2]. Its two core ideas are *write test suites first* and *design programs from the shape of the input data*. A student trained in HTDP first writes down the input and output types of a function, followed by several examples (test cases) of the function's behavior (including both inputs and outputs), followed by a *template* for the function. The template captures code that is dictated by the shape of the data, leaving holes to fill with problem-specific computations.

As an example, consider a function to determine whether a list of strings contains "pie". A student would first write the type signature (as a comment) and several examples (a.k.a. `check-expects`). We present code in Racket, as that is the language used in both our study and the HTDP textbook (though the principles apply more generally).

```
; containsPie? : list-of-string -> boolean
(check-expect (containsPie? empty) false)
(check-expect (containsPie? (list "apple" "pie")) true)
(check-expect (containsPie? (list "bread" "tea")) false)
```

Next, the student would write the *template*: code that exhausts what is known about the shape of the input data (in this case a list of strings):

```
; containsPie? : list-of-string -> boolean
(define (containsPie? alst)
  (cond [(empty? alst) ... ]
        [(cons? alst) ... (first alst)
                      ... (containsPie? (rest alst)) ]))
```

The template has a conditional that checks whether the list is empty. If it is, the template simply contains a hole for the function's result in that case. If not, then the list must have both a first element and the subsequent elements (rest). The latter is itself a list of strings, and hence should also be processed by `containsPie?`. The template therefore includes a recursive call on the rest of the list. The template has holes in place of concrete code for combining the first element with the result from the recursive call. Note that nothing in the template is specific to the computation required for `containsPie?`: the template simply traverses the input data.

To finish the function, the student fills in the holes with details specific to `containsPie?`. The student can leverage the test cases to do this (details of how to do this are not relevant to this paper). The next box shows the final code: the student filled in `false`, a comparison to the string `"pie"`, and the `or` operator to complete the function.

```
; containsPie? : list-of-string -> boolean
(define (containsPie? alst)
  (cond [(empty? alst) false]
        [(cons? alst) (or (string=? "pie" (first alst))
                          (containsPie? (rest alst)))]))
```

Templates are at the heart of the difference between HTDP and Rist's model. They scaffold development of code, giving students systematic rules to follow to get beyond a blank page when starting a programming problem (in Rist's creation state). HTDP teaches students concrete rules (not described here) for creating templates from datatypes; these rules scale to rich data structures including binary and n-ary trees, graphs, and other mutually-recursive data. This set of uniform rules across datatypes provides a detailed *process* for designing programs, particularly on new datatypes. As students write multiple functions over the same datatype, templates can also serve as *schemas* for other programs over that datatype. Many students appear to internalize these schemas, without having to use the rules to create templates afresh each time.

2.3 Other Related Work

Early studies by Pirolli *et al.* on novices learning recursive programming observed that people rely heavily on known solutions when developing new programs [3, 4]. Novices modify already-learned solutions to fit the context of the new problem. Spohrer and Soloway's studies of the end-product programs of students and their talk-aloud protocols (verbal reports of planning, implementation, and debugging steps taken in programming a solution) echo this [10]. They suggest that students, when writing code for a problem, either (1) use previously learned programming knowledge (programming plans) to write the code, or (2) translate relevant non-programming knowledge (non-programming plans) into code. Students then proceed to a testing phase where they detect problems (or impasses) within their code, then enter a debugging phase to repair these impasses.

Spohrer and Soloway observed that most novice programming mistakes are due to difficulties with *plan composition*, the putting together of program fragments to form a working program [9]. They analyzed buggy programs in terms of their *goals* relative to their *plans* (groups of code that work together [7, 8]). Goals and plans are cognitively plausible, deep structure knowledge that programmers have, based on knowledge of working programs. For example, programmers do not perceive an expression like `sum += sum` merely as an assignment statement (code-specific: surface structure), but as part of a plan for a running sum (deep structure). Reasoning through a goal/plan perspective, and not merely through surface-structure language constructs, considers chunks of code as single units. Spohrer and Soloway identified several issues that make plan composition difficult for novices, including cognitive load problems, unexpected cases, and optimization problems, among others [9].

3. AN EXPLORATORY STUDY

By design, HTDP templates should defer entry into Rist's "creation" mode, giving students a schema to retrieve based solely on the type of input to a function. If students have not solved a similar problem to the overall function, Rist's model predicts that students would then write focal computations. However, Rist's notion that students write the focal computation then build context around it differs from the HTDP process, in which students would place focal computations either in template holes or in auxiliary (a.k.a. helper) functions. Seeing what HTDP students do after writing templates should give insights into whether and how Rist's model, and the general idea of bottom-up programming, play out in the context of data-traversal schemas for recursive programs.

To better understand the interplay between Rist's model and HTDP, we conducted a study in a single HTDP-based CS1 class at a university in the USA. We gave students a programming problem over an input datatype they knew (a list of numbers), but that required additional programming techniques that they had not yet seen. This combination should have put students into Rist's creation mode (perhaps after retrieving the template). We video-captured the students' programming sessions, then analyzed the videos to see when students wrote each of HTDP templates and Rist's focal computations, and how they edited around these pieces to complete the program.

In particular, we sought insight on the following questions:

1. When do HTDP-trained students use templates?
2. How does Rist's idea of focal computations manifest in HTDP programs?
3. How and when do HTDP students integrate focal computations into existing code?

Our questions attempt to avoid bias in favor of either Rist's model or HTDP's claimed benefits. While we expected students to follow HTDP's process (as this was a key part of the course), we did not assume that students had internalized that process enough to actually do so. This is an exploratory study, asking whether (a) Rist's focal-expansion theory applies to functional programming through HTDP and (b) HTDP provides useful scaffolding to students on problems that require significantly different programming techniques than what they have already seen.

3.1 The Problem: Adding Machine

Our study used a programming problem called *Adding Machine* that consumes and produces a list of numbers:

> Design a program called `adding-machine` that consumes a list of numbers and produces a list of the sums of each non-empty sublist separated by zeros. Ignore input elements that occur after the first occurrence of two consecutive zeros.
>
> Example:
> `(adding-machine (list 1 2 0 7 0 5 4 1 0 0 6))`
> should produce `(list 3 7 10)`

Adding Machine involves four tasks:

a) Ignoring data after the double-zero
b) Identifying sublists separated by single zeros
c) Summing the elements in each sublist
d) Building the output list from the sums of the sublists

Students trained in functional programming would write a recursive solution. Viable recursive approaches include:

- **Reshape the data first**: The sublists in the input are embedded in a flat list of elements delimited by zeros. The input could be reshaped into a list of lists that omits the zeros. For example, the input `(list 1 2 0 7 0 5 4 1 0 0 6)` could be reshaped as `(list (list 1 2) (list 7) (list 5 4 1))`. Separate functions would iterate over this list and sum each individual sublist.
- **Accumulate sums in a parameter**: The recursive function could take an additional parameter for the sum of the current sublist. When a 0 is detected at the front of the input list, this parameter would be concatenated onto the result of processing the rest of the input list with the sum parameter initialized to 0.
- **Recur on a new list containing the sublist sum**: Since the recursive function takes the list to process as an input, the first position of the list can be used to store the running sublist sum. For example, the call `(adding-machine (list 1 2 0 5))` would generate the call `(adding-machine (list 3 0 5))`. This approach is distinctly functional, as imperative solutions rarely modify a list mid-iteration. Special care is required, however, if a sublist can sum to 0.
- **Recur on a new list that skips the first sublist**: A function could recur on the suffix of the list without the first sublist, using a separate function to produce the sum of the prefix corresponding to the first sublist.

Detecting the consecutive-zero termination pattern adds a bit of complexity, as solutions must check both the length of the remaining input (an input that doesn't contain the 00 pattern might have only one element) and the values of the first two elements. Solutions can either truncate the input data at the double-0 in a separate pre-traversal, or integrate checking for the pattern into the core computation.

This problem seems excellent for studying the interactions between Rist's model and HTDP. Lists of numbers are a familiar datatype to HTDP students: many will have already internalized the schema for flat lists. Each of the high-level solutions outlined above, however, uses some more-advanced programming concepts: parameters that accumulate data or recur on something other than the rest of the list are covered after trees in HTDP. While basic mastery of lists would suffice to reshape data, students would not be exposed to the *idea* of doing so until much later. Thus, if HTDP students are given this problem after a couple of weeks of programming with lists, they will have a schema that appears to apply (the basic list template), but no experience with "similar" solutions that draw on these more advanced concepts. Many students should end up in the plan-creation state while working on this problem, even if they initially retrieve the list-of-numbers template.

3.2 Data Collection and Logistics

We collected data in Spring 2015 in a CS1 course taught using HTDP in Racket. Neither author was on the course staff. Students were given roughly 40 minutes to work on *Adding Machine* during a weekly lab session. Each student used the SnagIt video-capture tool to record all activity within the window for the course IDE (DrRacket). Students uploaded both the video and their final source-code file at the end of the lab session. In total, 138 students submitted data; we randomly sampled 25 to analyze in this study. In terms of final course grades, the sampled population earned

```
1 Test AM 3
2 Template-list AM
3 AM buildsumlist (cons (helper1 first-L)
                         (AM rest-L))
4 Template-list helper1
5 helper1 sumelts (+ first-L (helper1 rest-L))
6 helper1 singlezero (= 0 first-L (AM rest-L))
7 AM singlezero (= 0 first-L)
8 Test helper1 3
```

```
;; ListofNumber->ListofNumber
;; adds together elements of a sublist and returns
    them as a list
(check-expect
     (adding-machine (list 1 2 0 7 0 5 4 1 0 0 6))
     (list 3 7 10))
(check-expect (adding-machine empty) empty)
(check-expect
     (adding-machine (list 5 15 22 0 7 0 8 1))
     (list 42 7 9))

(define (adding-machine lon)
  (cond [(empty? lon) empty]
        [else (cons (findzero (first lon))
                    (adding-machine (rest lon)))]))
```

Figure 1: Sample coding sequence (top) and the actual program code (bottom)

5 As, 13 Bs, 3 Cs, 3 fails, and 1 incomplete. We thus had a good mix of students relative to mastery of the material and likelihood of needing help.

We conducted the study five weeks into the academic term, after students had roughly 16 lectures (50-minutes each), 4 labs (50 minutes each), and 4 multi-exercise programming assignments for homework. Before this point, the course had covered defining and calling functions, composing functions, conditionals, recursive functions over lists, and the HTDP design process (including test-first development of functions and templates, as described in section 2.2). The students had written several functions over lists of numbers, strings, and records prior to doing the study. The course had not yet covered trees, accumulating results of computations in additional parameters, or recursive calls on an argument other than the rest of the list.

3.3 Coding Programming Edits

When analyzing the videos, we recorded several events:

1. **Template use**: Students wrote an HTDP-prescribed template for a new function.
2. **Task-specific computation**: Students wrote code related to one of the four problem tasks. We recorded the actual code, the task it belongs to, and the function in which students put the code. The tasks were recorded with the following labels:
   - **singlezero**: handling single-zero delimiters
   - **doublezero**: handling the double-zero sentinel
   - **sumelts**: summing elements (of a sublist)
   - **buildsumlist**: building the list of sublist sums
3. **Test case use**: Students wrote test cases for a specific function. We recorded the function name and number of tests written for it before the next event occurred
4. **Other**: Students made edits that did not fall into one of these categories

Figure 1 shows an example of our analysis summary, along with its corresponding Racket program (the program shows the code as of step 3 in the summary). In the summary, `AM` refers to the *Adding Machine* function. The student wrote another function named **findzero**, replaced with the alias, **helper1**, in the summary. Names for helper functions were replaced with aliases with the format **helper<number>** to facilitate consistency in the coding as the students would sometimes change the names of helpers as they programmed their solutions. We produced a summary such as this for each of the 25 sampled programs.

4. ANALYSIS AND INTERPRETATION

None of the sampled students produced working solutions for *Adding Machine*, despite evidence that they used templates, developed focals, and tried to decompose the problem. Plan composition was the main hurdle, particularly when students tried to reuse template code inappropriately in multiple smaller-scale plans.

All but one student (24 of 25) used the list-of-numbers template (same as the `containsPie?` template in section 2.2). From there, students took many approaches. Table 1 shows two examples of the directions students took: the student on the left created a helper function to handle both single-zero delimiters and computing the sum of sublists, while the student on the right tried to handle both the double-zero and sum tasks within the template for *Adding Machine*. Both show plan-composition errors which we will explain as we describe general patterns in our data.

4.1 Focals After Templates?

We hypothesized that students would enter creation mode after retrieving the template. As such, we looked at what code students wrote immediately after the template and where they put it, checking whether it captured focals. As Table 2 shows, all but 3 students wrote expressions that took on specific tasks. Most (19) students put this new code into the template for the *Adding Machine* function. This matches focal-expansion theory, as well as HTDP pedagogy. Most template holes get filled by focal-like expressions, though some decomposition (through helpers) also goes there.

Whether students had entered creation mode, however, isn't clear. Summing a list is a standard HTDP programming problem; students may have retrieved the `+` code as done in Table 1 (right). The single- and double-zero tasks are about termination of computations. As such, they resemble base cases of recursive functions (even though the usual base case of a recursive function on a list handles the empty list). Students may have retrieved the pattern of terminating a traversal, adapting it to recognize patterns of zeros. The left student in Table 1 wrote base-case-like code to catch the single-zero in the `adder` function.

Overall, 21 students who started with templates immediately filled in holes in that template with focal expressions for a specified program task and 2 began to decompose the problem by creating a helper function (in both cases to handle *Double zero*). Of the remaining 4, one wrote a focal computation (*Single zero*) within a non-template function, and 3 wrote something not clearly linked to a problem task.

4.2 Plan Composition

Whether students retrieved or created plans for the problem tasks, they still had to compose them into an overall

Table 1: Code samples: (Left) A task identified is pulled out into a separate function; (Right) Interleaving function calls within one function without decomposition.

```
(define (adding-machine lon)
  (cond [(empty? lon) empty]
        [else (cons (adder lon)
                    (adding-machine (rest lon)))]))

(define (adder lon)
  (cond [(empty? lon) 0]
        [(= 0 (first lon))
         (adding-machine (rest lon))
        [else (+ (first lon) (adder (rest lon)))]))
```

```
(define (adding-machine lon)
  (cond
    [(empty? lon) 0]
    [else
      (if (and (= (first lon) 0) (= (second lon) 0))
          (list 0)
          (+ (first lon)
             (adding-machine (rest lon))))]))
```

Table 2: First tasks coded, with location (*Note: T = within template, NT = not in template*)

Task	Within AM	New Helper
Sum sublist	6	0
Output list	3	0
Single zero	9 (T) + 1 (NT)	0
Double zero	1	2
None/Other	3	

Table 3: Where code for each task appears

Task	Just in Main	Just in Helper	Both
Single zero	7	3	10
Double zero	4	1	2
Sum sublist	9	5	6
Output list	8	0	0

program. Here, students displayed significant difficulties. Each solution in Table 1 illustrates one of these challenges.

The solution on the right tries to integrate the plans for sum and double-zero by sharing template code: the template base-case (the `empty?` check) returns a 0 as in the sum plan, while the "new" base case for double-zero returns a list (the output type of the overall function). In attempting to share the recursive call (which would be syntactically identical in both the sum and truncate-at-00 plans), the student created an inconsistency in the output type of the program. Only 5 students even wrote both the sum and double-zero tasks; 3 of these put these tasks in the same function. Six students put both the single-zero and double-zero tasks in the same function, missing that each terminates a different other task (processing a sublist and identifying input to process, respectively).

In the solution on the left, the student tried to decompose the problem via a helper function. The output task stayed in the main template, while the sum and single-zero tasks moved into the helper. This approach was on the right track, but had two key errors (aside from the missing plan for double-zero): the single-zero detection needed to be a base case (and return 0) in the helper, and the recursive call in the main function needed to take the suffix without the first sublist as input (rather than the entire rest of the list). Despite these flaws, this student at least had a largely consistent view of the output type of each function (the erroneous single-zero base case answer notwithstanding). This reflects an understanding (missed in the solution on the right) that one use of template code can return only one type of output.

Eleven students moved the sum-sublist task into a helper (as in the solution on the left). None modified the portion of the list passed on the recursive call, instead using the recursive call verbatim from the template. Overall, 16 students created a helper function that took a list of numbers as input and included some program tasks. Table 3 summarizes the number of students who covered each task in each of helper functions, the main *Adding Machine* function, or both.

Even when students realized to create helpers, they often failed to effectively decompose the problem around those helpers: 12 of 25 created helpers that they never called from their main function. These helpers attempted combinations of the single-zero, double-zero, and sum-sublist tasks. This seems a different manifestation of thinking through focals: rather than integrate a focal computation into an existing function (their original templates), students tried to put them in separate functions. This is not unreasonable, as each of these three tasks involves traversing a list, and students had been taught to use recursive functions to traverse lists. Of the students who created helper functions, 8 used templates in writing all helper functions (2 more did so sometimes), again suggesting a strong HTDP influence. These observations suggest that upon entering the creation state (after setting up templates), students resort to building their functions with a characteristic tinkering behavior [1] by patching up the holes in the template with familiar constructs and function calls, even when these result in output inconsistencies and essentially, plan composition problems.

Several students put the same tasks in both the main and helper functions (last column of Table 3). Task-replication seems to depart from Rist's focal model, which suggests that students would write the focal computations once within their existing code, then build around them. This again reflects students' difficulties in decomposing the problem around the tasks.

4.3 Advanced Techniques

Both accumulating intermediate data in parameters and reshaping the data into a list of sublists are advanced patterns that students had not seen in the course (and thus could not have retrieved). Only 1 student attempted to add a parameter for the running sublist sum. Only 3 attempted to reshape the data; none did so successfully. The coding sequences for the latter students suggests that as soon as students pulled out tasks to attempt to reshape the data, they proceeded into tinkering in and around these helpers. Students who tried this step (which would have been valuable had it worked) were clearly not thinking through focals, as data reshaping is not a computational task suggested in the problem statement (even though the problem hints at the flattened state of the data).

5. DISCUSSION AND FUTURE WORK

The study in this paper was motivated by an apparent underlying tension between HTDP templates and Rist's model of bottom-up programming. Rist's work suggests a cognitive process that students follow on new programming problems: write a core computation for a problem task (the focus), then augment the program to produce the data needed for the focal computation. The potential tension with HTDP lies in the sub-expressions that templates introduce: these provide a *context* into which students will place focal computations. That context could either help or interfere with students' thinking as they integrate focals into a larger program.

Our data suggest that students largely work through problem tasks: they write focal computations on the front elements of the input list, or create new functions for problem tasks. They often appear to retrieve plans, in the form of individual recursive functions, for individual tasks (such as summing a list). As such, our students often introduced focals as entire functions, not small expressions (as in Rist). This may have deferred students' entry into creation mode, shifting more burden to plan composition.

Our students struggled to compose plans: some failed to adjust the portion of the list being recurred over, others tried to perform two tasks with different output types (summing and building lists) within the same recursive traversal (rather than accumulating the sum or creating a helper). In both cases, our students used template expressions verbatim, rather than adjust them to the need of the computation at hand. Given that they had not seen programs that adjusted template code, this behavior is not particularly surprising. More generally, they lacked schemas for *composition*, instead retrieving insufficient, lower-level, plans.

Does this mean that templates, and the context they provide, interfere more than help students? Not necessarily. The recursive calls are still needed, even if on slightly different inputs in some (but not all!) cases. Students had simply not learned when to decompose problems into multiple instances of templates, and the templates failed to help them discover or resolve the issue. Given prior work on the importance of retrievable schemas, HTDP's templates fit squarely within known results on how people program.

Arguably, the key issue is that students are decomposing the problem *on the fly around code they have already written.* This arises whether students use HTDP (which prescribes the context) or bottom-up programming (in which students' existing code provides the context). If the prior context isn't well-suited to the problem at hand, students will struggle with composition. Decomposing the *problem* up front, into tasks that can be composed cleanly into a solution, should make the actual coding less error prone.

Can we teach students to effectively decompose problems? Both Rist's work and ours show that students think in terms of core program tasks. Decomposing problems (rather than code) is about grouping the tasks of a problem into chunks that can reasonably be handled together. What if we could teach students to use concrete examples to work out problem decompositions? In the case of *Adding Machine*, for example, a student could start with

```
(adding-machine (list 1 2 0 7 0 5 4 1 0 0 6))
```

then write that this should produce the same answer as

```
(list (+ 1 2) (+ 7) (+ 5 4 1))
```

Realizing this might suggest specific functions that a student could write to transform the first expression into the second. Something systematic such as this seems preferable to expecting students to just keep experimenting until their bottom-up process hits on a workable solution. Just as students currently internalize schemas for writing code, we might expect they can learn to internalize schemas for decomposing problems through concrete examples. The question at least warrants further study.

We suspect that some tension between Rist's model and HTDP arises from differences between functional and imperative programming. Deciding what Rist's model might mean within functional programming took considerable discussion among the authors. Rist's description of "bottom up" references code organization typical of imperative programs: variable declaration and initialization at the top, computation in the middle, and results and output on the bottom. Functional programs are organized differently: variables are initialized when functions are called, and outputs are typically composed from nested expressions within the middle of a function. For this project, we chose to interpret "bottom up" as "write contextual code after the focus". Functional programs also tend to decompose problems into several functions, whereas imperative solutions for CS1-level programs often live within a single procedure. This changes the decomposition patterns that students need for problems such as *Adding Machine*. This raises various questions for how cognitive behavior in creation mode might differ based on the (affordances of the) programming language at hand.

Acknowledgments.

We thank Joe Beck for letting us collect data in his course and Mike Clancy for pointing us to the *Adding Machine* problem. This research is partially funded by the US NSF under grant number CCF1116539.

6. REFERENCES

[1] M. Berland, T. Martin, T. Benton, C. P. Smith, and D. Davis. Using learning analytics to understand the learning pathways of novice programmers. *Journal of the Learning Sciences*, 22(4):564–599, Oct 2013.

[2] M. Felleisen, R. B. Findler, M. Flatt, and S. Krishnamurthi. *How to Design Programs.* MIT Press, 2001.

[3] P. L. Pirolli and J. R. Anderson. The role of learning from examples in the acquisition of recursive programming skills. *Canadian Journal of Psychology/Revue canadienne de psychologie*, 39(2):240–272, 1985.

[4] P. L. Pirolli, J. R. Anderson, and R. G. Farrell. *Learning to program recursion*, pages 277–280. 1984.

[5] R. S. Rist. Schema creation in programming. *Cognitive Science*, pages 389–414, 1989.

[6] R. S. Rist. Knowledge creation and retrieval in program design: A comparison of novice and intermediate student programmers. *Hum.-Comput. Interact.*, 6(1):1–46, Mar 1991.

[7] B. Shneiderman. Exploratory experiments in programmer behavior. *International Journal of Computer and Information Sciences*, 5(2):123–143, June 1976.

[8] E. Soloway and K. Ehrlich. Empirical studies of programming knowledge. *IEEE Transactions on Software Engineering*, SE-10(5):595–609, September 1984.

[9] J. C. Spohrer and E. Soloway. Novice mistakes: Are the folk wisdoms correct? *Commun. ACM*, 29(7):624–632, July 1986.

[10] J. C. Spohrer and E. Soloway. *Simulating Student Programmers*, pages 543–549. IJCAI '89. Morgan Kaufmann Publishers Inc., 1989.

Modernizing Plan-Composition Studies

Kathi Fisler
WPI
kfisler@cs.wpi.edu

Shriram Krishnamurthi
Brown University
sk@cs.brown.edu

Janet Siegmund
University of Passau
siegmunj@fim.uni-passau.de

ABSTRACT

Plan composition is an important but under-studied topic in programming education. Most studies were done three decades ago, under assumptions that miss important issues that today's students must confront. This paper presents rationale and details for a modernized study of plan composition that accommodates a broader range of programming languages and problem features. Our study design has two novelties: the problems require students to deal with data-processing challenges (such as noisy data), and the questions ask students to not only produce but also evaluate programs. We present preliminary results from using our study in multiple courses from different linguistic paradigms. We discuss several future studies that are prompted by these results.

CCS Concepts

•**Social and professional topics** → **Model curricula; CS1;**

Keywords: Plan composition, imperative programming, functional programming

1. INTRODUCTION

Most non-trivial programs encompass multiple tasks that collectively perform a computation. Computing the number of employees with low salaries, for example, involves searching a collection of employee records, determining which have low salaries, and counting the number of identified employees. A program that performs the computation could approach this problem in several ways: it could detect low salaries and count employees while traversing the employee collection, it could extract low-salary employees then count the results, it could first sort all employee salaries, and so on. Organizing the tasks of a problem into a program is called *plan composition* [9]. It is a key skill to develop in learning to program.

Plan composition is relevant whether or not a student plans to major in computer science or become a professional programmer. Many students seek just enough programming education to solve problems in other disciplines: for example, a biology student may wish to write scripts to process data from a research project. Such scripts often involve integrating multiple tasks. Deferring problem decomposition and plan composition to later CS courses is therefore not an option: we need effective pedagogies for this material in CS1 and non-major courses.

Existing plan-composition studies are dated by problem tasks, rubrics that failed to consider high-level variations in code structure, and implicit assumptions about the languages and constructs that students might use. Most studies (1) used imperative programming (2) with few data structures on (3) problems dominated by I/O. Today's students often learn different languages (functional, dynamic/scripting, OO), libraries, and a richer set of constructs for processing data. If teaching plan composition is important, we need to understand the impact of different languages, constructs, and pedagogies on how students structure code. We also need to modernize the study questions to encompass both linguistic differences and current computing contexts.

This paper makes three contributions in this direction. First (§ 2), we propose a concrete set of problems and questions that refine prior plan-composition studies. Second (§ 3), we present data from a preliminary, multi-national, multi-university study with these problems: three courses used functional programming and two used imperative programming. Third (§ 5), we identify additional study questions and design constraints that emerged from analyzing our data. These findings sharpen the goals of future plan-composition studies, while also suggesting an overarching framework for designing such studies.

SIGCSE '16, March 02 - 05, 2016, Memphis, TN, USA

ISBN 978-1-4503-3685-7/16/03...$15.00

DOI: http://dx.doi.org/10.1145/2839509.2844556

2. STUDYING STUDENT PLANS

Prior planning studies focused analysis on the errors students made and the process by which students developed code [3, 12]. Our interests go farther: we want to identify factors that influence students' code structures, and the ways in which curricula, pedagogy, and programming language affect these factors. We therefore ask students to not only *produce* programs but also *assess* solutions (operationally, to provide a partial-order preference ranking of code we give that represents different plans). The latter helps us identify issues that students consider when thinking about program structure, a question with little prior research.

While prior planning studies featured simple console I/O, today's students program in a data-rich world. There are many operations—common at a high-level, different in their details—that students may need for processing data. Planning problems should exercise these operations. Concretely, we focus on three particular data-processing challenges: noisy data that should be *cleansed* prior to computation; flattened structured data that could be *reshaped*; and monolithic data from which relevant parts must be *extracted*. We also include problems over data that are *already structured* yet admit multiple interleavings of tasks.

We considered candidate problems from the computing education literature, technical papers, and course assignments. By design (to reduce bias), some authors are fans of each of functional and imperative programming. We rejected problems that struck any of us as "unnatural" (in our subjective opinions) for CS1 students learning our preferred style of programming; all authors approved of all selected problems. Ultimately, we chose six problems that include at least two samples of many of our data-facing criteria. We limited ourselves to six problems of relatively modest complexity because instructors would balk at adding a lengthy assignment to already-full classes.

We now present our proposed set of problems. In our preliminary study (§ 3), we gave the first three as programming problems. The latter three were given as ranking problems, with students provided correct, working code in the language of the course. Other partitions would also make sense, though we recommend putting one problem from each data-processing criterion into each activity. Students should do the programming problems first, to reduce bias from seeing the solutions in the ranking problems. Due to space limits, we present only summaries of the problem statements and solutions. The full, exact problem statements, as well as our coding rubric, can be found at cs.brown.edu/research/plt/dl/sigcse2016plancomp/

Programming Problems.

Palindrome A palindrome is a string with the same letters in each of forward and reverse order (ignoring capitalization). Design a program called `isPalindrome` that consumes a string and determines whether the string with all spaces and punctuation removed is a palindrome. Treat all non-alphanumeric characters as punctuation.

Sum Over Table Assume that we represent tables of numbers as lists of rows, where each row is itself a list of numbers. The rows may have different lengths. Design a program `sumLargest` that consumes a table of numbers and produces the sum of the largest item from each row. Assume that no row is empty.

Adding Machine Design a program called `addingMachine` that consumes a list of numbers and produces a list of the sums of each non-empty sublist separated by zeros. Ignore input elements that occur after the first occurrence of two consecutive zeros.

Ranking Problems.

For ranking, students were given multiple programs that solved each problem (10–20 lines per solution in functional code, a little longer in Java). Here we describe the code structure in prose. Our solutions are described in terms of helper functions, but the code could also be (and in Java, was) written using loops and variables that accumulate answers. The text marked with black bars (not given to students) summarizes the design decisions within each solution.

Rainfall Design a program called `rainfall` that consumes a list of real numbers representing daily rainfall readings. The list may contain the number -999 indicating the end of the data of interest. Produce the average of the non-negative values in the list up to the first -999 (if it shows up). There may be negative numbers other than -999 in the list (representing faulty readings). Assume that there is at least one non-negative number before -999. The solution options are:

A One function (or helper function) that iteratively accumulates three values: the remaining numbers, the total so far, and the number of days so far. When the numbers are exhausted, it returns the average using the other two parameters.

B One function that iteratively computes the sum of rainfalls. Another function that iteratively computes the number of days. Each one duplicates the cleansing logic. A main computation that uses these two functions, then computes the average.

C One function to cleanse the data. A main function that invokes the cleanser, then uses library or helper functions to compute the sum of rainfalls and number of days, and computes the average.

> Solution **A** uses a *single traversal* of the data, while the others use multiple traversals. We call solution **C** "clean first" and solution **B** "clean multiple".

Length of Triples Design the program `maxTripleLength` that consumes a list of strings and produces the length of the longest concatenation of three consecutive elements. Assume the input contains at least three strings. The solution options are:

A A helper function converts the flat list into a list of triples. The main function first uses this to generate triples of strings, then converts these to triples of numbers, then calls a function to find the maximum one.

B A helper function converts the flat list into a list of triples. The main function first converts the input into a list of numbers, then uses the helper to generate triples of numbers, then calls a function to find the maximum.

C A helper function iteratively accumulates the list of remaining strings, the maximum length so far, and the two previous lengths. It is then invoked on the appropriate arguments.

> Solutions **A** and **B** employ reshaping, and hence have multiple traversals of data. Each solution comes with a data structure (e.g., a class) for a single triple. Solution **C** uses a single traversal.

Shopping Cart An online clothing store applies discounts during checkout. A shopping cart is a list of the items being purchased. Each item has a name (a string like `"shoes"`) and a price (a real number like 12.50). Design a program called `checkout` that consumes a shopping cart and produces the total cost of the cart after applying the following two discounts:

1. if the cart contains at least 100 worth of shoes, take 20% off the cost of all shoes (match only items whose exact name is `"shoes"`)
2. if the cart contains at least two hats, take 10 off the total of the cart (match only items whose exact name is `"hat"`)

	Language	Country	Students	Timing
US1-IM	Java	USA	261 [70]	CS1-end
US1-FP	Racket, OCaml	USA	144 [42]	CS1-end
US2-FP	Racket	USA	106 [0]	CS1-end
FR-FP	OCaml	France	35 [18]	FP-end
GM-IM	Java or Python	Germany	80 [24]	CS2-start

Table 1: Students column reports total students and the number sampled when looking at code solutions.

The problem statement included specific data structures for representing items. The solution options are:

A The set of shoe entries is extracted, and their discount calculated. The set of hat entries is extracted, and their discount calculated. The total cost is calculated, and the two discounts applied.

B A helper function iteratively accumulates the cart contents, the total cost so far, the shoe costs, and the hat costs. When the cart is empty, the discounts are computed and applied to the total cost.

> Solution **A** performs a separate traversal per discount. Solution **B** traverses the data only once.

Problem Characteristics.

Rainfall and *Palindrome* require cleansing. *Adding Machine* and *Length of Triples* could leverage reshaping, while *Sum Over Table* has clean, already-structured data. *Rainfall* and *Adding Machine* examine only a prefix of data. *Shopping Cart* suggests future extensibility (for additional discounts), and also illustrates the potential for *separation of concerns* [6]. Each admits a variety of solution structures.

3. PRELIMINARY STUDY

As a formative exercise, we used the study described in § 2 to explore differences across programming languages. We wanted both to check whether these six problems, and the combination of programming and ranking, were useful for eliciting cross-linguistic planning nuances, and to identify candidate differences for further study.

We asked students to provide code for the first three problems and to preference rank (ties allowed), with justification, solutions for the latter three problems. We gathered data from five courses (three functional and two imperative) across three countries. None was taught by the authors.

Table 1 summarizes the courses: names indicate the country and programming paradigm (functional vs imperative; the latter in either an OO or scripting context). The two US1 courses were from parallel CS1-CS2 sequences in the same department (both lead into the major). GM-IM was a Java-based CS2 course that students came to after CS1 in either Python or Java. FR-FP was a first course in functional programming for third-year engineering students. US2-FP was a functional CS1 course that only did the ranking problems (and hence had no sampled students).

Prior studies on Rainfall [3, 8, 9] suggest that imperative solutions typically traverse the input exactly once while functional ones often perform multiple traversals. These trends are consistent with each paradigm's programming patterns. We thus analyzed traversal preferences in both the programming and ranking problems. When sampling programming solutions for detailed analysis within each course, we selected an even distribution in how often students preferred single-traversal solutions in the ranking problems.

Logistics: US2-FP did the ranking problems only, in a 40 minute lab setting after 6 weeks of CS1. All other courses gave the task as a homework assignment with multiple days to solve it (the exact duration varied by course). In all cases, at least a majority of students wrote predominantly correct solutions, confirming that the problems were within their abilities and that the assessment below is of program structures that were not written in haste or under pressure (e.g., in a timed exam). US1-IM, US1-FP, and FR-FP gave the study as a homework assignment towards the end of the semester. GM-IM used similar conditions, but at the start of CS2. All students worked in a programming environment. We customized the problem wordings for each course to accommodate its default data structures (lists versus arrays), vocabulary ("program" versus "method"), and naming conventions (`isPalindrome` versus `is-palindrome`). Staff from each course reviewed the problems, both to fine-tune the customizations and to confirm that the problems were reasonable for the students. Two of the authors manually read all the responses and coded them according to the rubric linked in § 2.

3.1 Results: Programming Problems

We hypothesized that most imperative students would write single `for`-loops that interleaved all problem tasks, while the functional students would frequently handle some tasks in separate functions. Each of *Palindrome* and *Adding Machine* contradicted part of this hypothesis. *Adding Machine* also highlighted key nuances within single-traversal solutions. We discuss each question in turn.

***Palindrome*:** Our version of palindrome has three tasks: "skipping" punctuation and whitespace, ignoring capitalization (which we'll call "normalizing"), and checking the core palindrome property on the resulting characters. We clustered solutions by how they interleaved the first two tasks with the third: Mequal solutions handled both skipping and normalization before the main reverse-equality check; Mcase handled skipping before a main equality check that also performed normalization; Mskip handled normalization before a main equality check that also performed skipping; Mboth handled both skipping and normalization in the main equality check with a single traversal. (None reflects missing or unintelligible programs.)

	Mequal	Mcase	Mskip	Mboth	None
US1-IM	81%	7%	3%	0%	9%
US1-FP	56%	41%	0%	0%	2%
FR-FP	83%	0%	6%	11%	0%
GM-IM	71%	4%	8%	0%	17%

The table shows that Mequal, which performs the equality check in a *separate* traversal, was the most popular in every course. Across all four courses, only two students (both from FR-FP, a functional course) did single-traversal solutions. What explains the lack of single-traversal solutions, especially amongst the imperative students?

The answer is library functions for manipulating or comparing strings or lists (of characters). Many Java solutions used `replaceAll` or `toLowerCase`; Racket solutions often used a case-insensitive string-comparator. Primitives thus have significant influence on program structure. This may not sound surprising, but it has pedagogic consequences. Classic plan-composition papers [9, 12] focused on the integration of new statements into existing procedures. With primitives, the problem shifts to include *decomposition* of problems around tasks covered by primitives. Problem decomposition is a different skill than code composition.

***Adding Machine*:** Nearly every solution, whether functional or imperative, used a single traversal. Nevertheless, there were significant differences across the paradigms, some with pedagogic implications. Not surprisingly, functional students used recursion, while imperative students used `for`-loops. Within each pattern, solutions differed in which intermediate values they accumulated in parameters or top-level variables: the running sum of the current sublist, the output so far, both, or neither ("neither" can occur in a recursive solution that recurs on a new list with the running sublist sum in the first position). The following table summarizes solution structures based on the accumulated values. AccBoth plans accumulated both the sublist sum and the output so far. AccSum accumulated only the current sublist sum. Reshape created lists of sublists before computing the sums. Other solutions accumulated sublists or used nested loops (rather than top-level variables) for the sublist sums. None had no code relevant to the problem.

	AccBoth	AccSum	Reshape	Other	None
US1-IM	56%	0%	0%	27%	17%
US1-FP	10%	36%	14%	40%	0%
FR-FP	22%	17%	6%	33%	11%
GM-IM	48%	0%	9%	22%	22%

Solutions were more distributed in the functional courses. This likely reflects flexibility from having the input list be a parameter in recursive solutions: a solution could, for example, store the running sum in the first position of the list. `For`-loop solutions lack this flexibility. Only one imperative student (in US1-IM) used recursion: this solution passed a modified input list on the recursive call, but was missing too many tasks to reflect a clear structure.

Functional and imperative solutions seem prone to different errors:

- Several imperative students ran into trouble using the "enhanced" form of `for` (e.g., `for (i : anArray) ...`). In this form, it is impossible to determine the next element, which is essential for this problem (to check for two consecutive zeros). When trapped in this situation, many students inadvertently confused array contents with indices, e.g., comparing `i` with zero (rightly treating `i` as the content) but also comparing `i + 1` with zero (accidentally treating it as an index). (We conjecture that using the variable name `i`, which is usually associated with indices, makes this problem more likely, and suggest that users of enhanced for loops use a variable name more likely to suggest content than an index.)

- Students who used index-based `for` loops avoided this problem, but fell prey to (the usual) out-of-bounds errors when doing arithmetic on indices to detect consecutive zeros.

- Recursive solutions sit squarely between these two forms of loops: the recursive list is an inductive structure, so even though the program lacks index variables, it can still access subsequent elements of the list from the current head. Functional students who kept the running sublist sum in the first position of the list typically produced solutions that would fail on a non-empty sublist whose sum is zero.

- Imperative solutions that used the current sum to detect consecutive zeros fell prey to the same problem, but imperative students used a wider range of patterns for detecting consecutive zeros in the first place.

3.2 Results: Ranking Problems

For the ranking problems, we were primarily interested in whether the language students learned correlated with preferences for single-traversal solutions. § 2 outlines the structure of the solutions. We implemented each solution using typical structures from each language (e.g., we did not write recursive solutions in Java), but without primitives or operators that traversed data (such as built-in iterators or higher-order functions). We did not lead the students with particular issues to consider, but merely asked for free-form comments that justified their rankings.

The following table reports the percentage of *all* students (not sampled) who ranked the single-traversal solution as one of their top choices. (It is worth noting that even though ties were permitted, they never exceeded 15% for first-place choices, and were usually closer to 6–8%, indicating that students really did choose to express a preference.) On all three problems, students in the imperative courses had strong preferences for single-traversal solutions. Curiously, each functional course had a much stronger preference for single traversals on one problem, with a different problem preferred in each course. We do not yet have an explanation for this, but suspect it says something about curricular or pedagogic differences among the courses.

	Rainfall	*Length of Triples*	*Shopping Cart*
US1-IM	90%	93%	94%
US1-FP	71%	34%	48%
US2-FP	33%	33%	65%
FR-FP	60%	86%	43%
GM-IM	88%	81%	78%

Students' written justifications (sampled) cited issues such as runtime efficiency, readability, space consumption, code layout, separation of concerns, use of variables, lines of code, clarity of computations, and support for future code modification. No issue was raised consistently either within a course or within those who preferred a particular structure. Not surprisingly, however, efficiency was one of the top two cited issues (readability, in various forms, was the other). Some students raised it as a deciding factor (in favor of a single-traversal solution), but others cited it as a difference between solutions that was outweighed by another concern.

Three observations around efficiency comments warrant deeper investigation. First, in US1-IM, students often based decisions on efficiency, even though the professor insisted that he not only did not teach it, he expressly told his students to not consider it. Because most students in the class have no prior programming experience, their concern is unlikely to stem from their previous preparation. One possibility is that the large teaching assistant population (all undergraduate students who previously took the same course) is sending a different message that contradicts the professor's.

Another is that this is an inherent concern in how students think about computing—at least those that choose a Java-based course. We believe this warrants further investigation to understand the mindset of students.

Second, concern with efficiency and counting the number of traversals is not consistent with using library functions (such as `replaceAll` in *Palindrome*) that perform additional data traversals. In both imperative courses, roughly half of the students who used `replaceAll` also selected single loop solutions with justifications that cited efficiency. This suggests that students might have a weak cost model of library functions. There seem to be significant open questions here about what cost models students have, how they develop, and what role they should or do play in planning.

Third, several imperative students (16 of 59 in US1-IM, for example) criticized creating intermediate data as inefficient (each multi-traversal solution explicitly created such data). Creating intermediate data structures is common in functional programming, though less typical in imperative introductory courses. Again, however, library functions obscure intermediate data creation. In addition, in some languages it is *syntactically* much more concise to define an intermediate data structure than in others: creating the datatype and constructor for a flat triple of data needs only a single line in Racket, but at least 7 lines in Java. Built-in iterators (such as filters in functional programming) create intermediate data with a single operation; doing the same task manually requires several lines of code, which can make the program look more complicated. It is therefore unclear whether students' concerns about efficiency are truly about the run-time cost or actually statements about the syntactic appearance of code.

4. RELATED WORK

Historically, studies of program planning focused on how students interleaved I/O (including detecting sentinels and re-prompting on bad input) with computation. *Rainfall* is the classic planning problem [9, 10], with other I/O-focused problems proposed in other studies [11, 12]. Given that I/O mechanisms vary widely across models, problems with multiple tasks that arise from the problem data should be better suited to cross-course and cross-language studies.

In many early *Rainfall* studies [9, 11], students had not learned data structures or multiple forms of iterating over data. This vastly constrains the range of viable plans, leaving little to study beyond program errors [3, 8, 9, 13]. Students today learn a richer collection of constructs and libraries, thus letting us study relationships between the plans students choose and instructors' pedagogic decisions (which languages to use, primitives and patterns to teach, etc.) that influence students' choices.

Our project studies the relationship between programming languages (and their corresponding coding styles and pedagogies) and students' code structure. Ebrahimi [3] did the first cross-lingual *Rainfall* study in 1994. He compared rates of certain low-level errors across solutions written in four languages. He did not analyze high-level differences in solution structures (as we do), seemingly because the students had learned similar programming patterns across the languages [personal communication].

Fisler [4] studied *Rainfall* with functional programming students, finding that they produced diverse solutions, often correlated with use of library functions. One goal of our paper was to see whether those results generalized to problems other than *Rainfall*. This paper also adds the ranking questions component, which was not part of Fisler's work.

Theories of how people select plans and program structure [1, 7, 11] likely explain some of students' planning choices (such as which looping structures they use). These theories do not, however, fully account for design decisions such as whether to clean or parse data before processing it. Those decisions reflect general design principles. Ideally, studies should explore when and how students develop an appreciation for such design concerns.

The program structures that we consider here, based on cleaning and reshaping, as well as consideration of different kinds of iteration, represent programming patterns that one can teach explicitly. Ginat and Muller's work on Pattern-Oriented Instruction [5] shows that explicitly teaching patterns can improve student performance in problem decomposition and programming. Several (though not all) of the patterns that they teach correspond to standard primitives and higher-order operators from functional programming. Clancy and Linn [2] summarize approaches to teaching programming patterns, highlighting that such instruction must be multi-faceted, relating to both problem descriptions and a model of program execution. Their work may provide a lens for investigating differences across our study courses.

The ranking-problems portion of our study loosely relates to other work on code comprehension using *Rainfall*. Another part of Ebrahimi's study compared the correctness of students' *Rainfall* solutions with their performance on a code-comprehension task. Venables et al. [13] related student performance on writing programs including *Rainfall* with their ability to trace and explain programs with procedural loops. They found that students who could not trace accurately could not produce correct programs. Our study did not ask students directly to comprehend code; indeed, students could rank the problems based on surface features without deep understanding of how the programs worked. Nevertheless, a handful of students ruled out solutions believing them to be incorrect.

5. TOPICS FOR FUTURE STUDIES

Different programming languages embody different ways of structuring data and computations. We would expect the structure of students' code to vary somewhat across programming languages. This variance has not been studied sufficiently, especially with respect to skills like plan composition. Many early studies of student programming were done within single linguistic styles. Given the variety of languages and styles currently used for beginning students, the community needs a much deeper understanding of the interplay between core skills and linguistic factors.

This paper proposes a set of problems and a general framework for cross-linguistic studies of plan composition. The framework tries to identify parameters that can yield a robust set of problems for studying plan integration. Prior to our preliminary study, these parameters emphasized the nature of the tasks within programming problems. We took a data-processing approach, embracing challenges that many casual programmers are expected to confront: noisy data, flattened data, and selecting subsets of data. Our initial study suggests two additional parameters: (1) the existence (and student knowledge) of common library functions that align with some problem tasks, and (2) dependencies between data elements (such as relationships between consecutive elements) for some problem tasks. We posit that varying these parameters will deepen the value of planning studies.

Deeper analysis of library functions and language constructs should shed light on the aspects of different languages that matter for plan composition. For instance, Python is taught imperatively by some and functionally by others. We see such variation in the solutions students produce. Indeed, this challenges whether the typical paradigm classification of languages is even sensical.

We are also exploring students' views on program structure by having them assess code, not only produce it. Asking students to rank and comment on different solutions provides insight into the criteria that students are internalizing about "good" programs. We suspect these criteria are often not taught explicitly (as we saw with efficiency concerns). This kind of implicit knowledge acquisition is a vital but under-studied aspect of computing education.

Contrasting students' preferences in ranking solutions with the code they produced raised questions about the cost models that students have for library functions. We saw several students embrace primitives that traverse data multiple times when programming, only to castigate these same approaches as inefficient when ranking. Perhaps the conciseness of code written with primitives blinds students to their costs. Perhaps students cite efficiency because no other criterion comes to mind. A followup study should have some ranking problem solutions use primitives while others use equivalent computations written manually. This could help tease apart both students' cost models and whether, as we conjecture, concise code is perceived as more efficient.

Our data also reveal that some students criticize intermediate data for efficiency reasons, while others praise "thinking ahead" to other potential uses of such data (such as potentially reusing clean data from *Rainfall* in another, related, computation). We suspect that these reactions are learned from the problems students have seen in class. It is possible that simply showing imperative-programming students solutions that create intermediate data, even without directly discussing efficiency concerns, would alter perceptions that the inefficiency of such data is inherently bad.

With student populations changing, CS courses are increasingly called on to prepare a broader range of students to write not-too-complicated (but not trivial) scripts for data processing. For these students, teaching them to effectively use primitives and to write separate functions for separate tasks is likely less error prone than teaching them to interleave tasks into single-traversal functions. Put differently, our student population may call for shifting the goal of "plan composition" studies to look at how to teach *problem decomposition* as much as *code composition.* Classic plan-composition studies arguably emphasized the latter, at least as evidenced by evaluation metrics. Instead, we need to refine the rubrics that we use in planning studies to account for each of the decompositions of tasks around functions or traversals, errors within tasks, and errors in composing tasks and traversals. Our work with *Adding Machine* taught us that we also need to track the specific constructs through which students implement individual traversals. We similarly see value in tracking constructs in Python due to the different styles engendered by explicit loops versus constructing loops implicitly through comprehensions.

Should we deem this shift valuable, researchers should also query *instructors* about their ranking preferences and perceived value of efficiency. We have discussed different solutions to our study problems with multiple colleagues, many of whom teach introductory courses. Informally, we see faculty who work in imperative programming question solutions that perform multiple traversals (on the grounds of inefficiency), while faculty who program functionally raise principles (such as "clean data first" and "separate concerns") behind their multi-traversal solutions. Other projects, such as Ginat's pattern-oriented instruction [5] explicitly promote solutions that interleave tasks for sake of efficiency. A broader discussion among faculty as to what we will consider "well composed" programs may be in order to smooth existing differences in solutions across languages.

Finally, this study has refined our sense of what background information might help understand factors that influence planning. Our data suggest that meaningful "prior-knowledge" surveys should explore what datatypes students know, what iteration patterns they have learned over each, and which libraries they have used. This is more nuanced than "how many courses", or "what languages have you used", while targeting specific prior knowledge that might affect students' program structures.

Acknowledgments.

We thank Joe Beck, Amy Greenwald, Alan Schmitt, Peter Thiemann, and Andy van Dam. We appreciate Ardra Hren's feedback. Mike Clancy presented us the adding machine problem. This work is partially funded by the US NSF.

6. REFERENCES

[1] J. R. Anderson, R. Farrell, and R. Sauers. Learning to program in LISP. *Cognitive Science*, 8:87–129, 1984.

[2] M. J. Clancy and M. C. Linn. Patterns and pedagogy. *SIGCSE Bulletin*, 31(1):37–42, Mar. 1999.

[3] A. Ebrahimi. Novice programmer errors: language constructs and plan composition. *International Journal of Human-Computer Studies*, 41:457–480, 1994.

[4] K. Fisler. The recurring rainfall problem. In *Proceedings of ICER*, 2014.

[5] O. Muller, B. Haberman, and D. Ginat. Pattern-oriented instruction and its influence on problem decomposition and solution construction. In *Proceedings of ITiCSE*, 2007.

[6] D. L. Parnas. On the criteria to be used in decomposing systems into modules. *Communications of the ACM*, 15(12):1053–1058, Dec. 1972.

[7] P. L. Pirolli. *Problem Solving by Analogy and Skill Acquisition in the Domain of Programming.* PhD thesis, Carnegie Mellon University, Department of Cognitive Psychology, 1985.

[8] Simon. Soloway's Rainfall problem has become harder. *Learning and Teaching in Computing and Engineering*, pages 130–135, 2013.

[9] E. Soloway. Learning to program = learning to construct mechanisms and explanations. *Communications of the ACM*, 29(9):850–858, Sept. 1986.

[10] E. Soloway, J. Bonar, and K. Ehrlich. Cognitive strategies and looping constructs: An empirical study. *Communications of the ACM*, 26(11):853–860, Nov. 1983.

[11] J. C. Spohrer. *MARCEL: Simulating the Novice Programmer.* Intellect Books, 1992.

[12] J. C. Spohrer and E. Soloway. Simulating student programmers. In *International Joint Conference on Artificial Intelligence*, pages 543–549, 1989.

[13] A. Venables, G. Tan, and R. Lister. A closer look at tracing, explaining and code writing skills in the novice programmer. In *Proceedings of ICER*, pages 117–128, 2009.

Initialization in Scratch: Seeking Knowledge Transfer

Diana Franklin[§], Charlotte Hill[♭], Hilary A. Dwyer[♮], Alexandria K. Hansen[♮], Ashley Iveland[♮], Danielle B. Harlow[♮]

[§]Center for Elementary Math and Science Education
University of Chicago
1100 E. 58th St
Chicago, IL 60637
dmfranklin@uchicago.edu

[♮]Gevirtz School of Education
[♭] Department of Computer Science
UC Santa Barbara
Santa Barbara, CA 93106-9490
{hdwyer, akillian, aockey, dharlow}@education.ucsb.edu
charlottehill@cs.ucsb.edu

ABSTRACT

With the growing movement to use visual block-based languages (VBBLs) in elementary and middle school classrooms, questions arise about the learning outcomes of such activities. While some schools are content to use VBBLs to spark interest and motivation for the future pursuit of computing, others are asking, "Does this early exposure produce knowledge that transfers to traditional text-based languages (TBLs)?" If transfer is a goal, then a corollary is, "How do we design the transition to maximize the transfer?" This paper focuses on initialization of state and variables, exploring the differences between Scratch and two TBLs: C and Java. Based on observations of 9-12 year old students in a VBBL curriculum, we identify four "pieces of knowledge" that are critical for C and Java but are not nearly as obvious in Scratch, including whether, when, and how to perform initialization. We conclude with suggestions for instruction and development environment that may improve transfer.

Keywords

Initialization; Scratch; VBBLs; K-6; knowledge transfer

1. INTRODUCTION

For decades, computer scientists have been developing activities for young students in an effort to engage them in computer science early, leading to many educational programming platforms[7, 14], activities[3, 13] and outreach programs[21, 9]. Two goals of such early exposure to computer science include recruitment[6, 15] and computational thinking skills. It is hoped that early exposure to computer science makes students more likely to either become computer scientists, work with computer scientists, or program as needed. Block-based programming languages were developed to allow students to learn fundamentals of programming without the overhead of typing or memorizing commands. An open question is how much of what they learn is useful only for programming in VBBLs, and how much helps them when moving to a TBL. In this paper, we restrict ourselves to *imperative* and *object-oriented* languages. This question has gained importance as the Hour of Code and other efforts have piqued the interest of elementary schools. Recent research has shown that some knowledge does transfer between VBBLs and TBLs when "bridging" and "hugging" techniques to support transfer are used[1, 8].

SIGCSE '16, March 02-05, 2016, Memphis, TN, USA.
© 2016 ACM ISBN 978-1-4503-3685-7/16/03$15.00
DOI: http://dx.doi.org/10.1145/2839509.2844569

Here, we consider transfer to occur if a student applies principles from one context to another, even when the learning environment and language details differ and consider the conditions of the two types of languages (VBBLs and TBLs) that support and hinder transfer. In this study, we closely examine initialization of variables and objects as accomplished in Scratch, C, and Java, and the relationship between these. The contributions of this paper are:

- Detailed comparison of the data models in Scratch and C/Java.
- Identification of key concepts that are integral to initialization in C/Java but overlooked by students in Scratch.
- Suggestions for the development environment and instruction that may improve transfer.

The rest of the paper is organized as follows. We provide background on visual block-based languages, prior work on transfer, and our theoretical framework in Section 2. Section 3 describes initialization in more detail. Sections 4 and 5 present our curriculum from a high level and the methodologies derived from educational research used in our study. We then present our results in Section 7. Finally, Section 8 contains our conclusions and future work.

2. BACKGROUND

There are several visual block-based development environments, including Alice[7], Scratch[14], and LaPlaya[12] with common attributes like, a drag-and-drop development environment to replace much of the typing, available commands displayed visually, images are favored over numerical and textual output, and "sprites" are created with a friendly interface hiding variables such as position, orientation, and size.

In our work, we use a variant of Scratch, a common programming environment for novices in a variety of contexts[16]. Scratch differs from more traditional, text-based languages in both control and data. First, while it has some similar control structures (loops, conditionals), the program paradigm is entirely event-driven, with no single thread of control in the program. Second, the "data" consists mostly of "sprites" represented by 2D images with attributes such as size, position, orientation, and visibility that can be manipulated.

Block-based languages have been used at the college and pre-college levels to provide an early introduction to computing with a transition to a traditional language either within the same first course (college)[8] or in a second course (pre-college)[1]. Two types of approaches have been used. Some courses present each concept first in a block-based language, and then in the traditional language. Other courses present a set of concepts in a block-based language, and then transition to a traditional language, revisiting each of those concepts in the new language.

The difference between visual block-based languages and "traditional" languages is debatable. In this work, we assume two major differences between the types of languages. First, the programming environment differs, with traditional languages depending on typing on a blank screen, and much less scaffolding of the available instructions and syntax. Second, the type of data operated on differs. VBBL projects are multimedia projects, operating mostly on graphical data (2D or 3D), and the languages provide primitives to manipulate these attributes (changing size, location, orientation, etc.); Traditional languages typically operate on strings and numbers.

Perkins and Salomon[18] define two techniques, "bridging" and "hugging," that help students transfer knowledge from one context to another. Bridging refers to how the concept is taught in the first context. These principles can be applied to computer science when teaching general concepts within a single language. When presenting a new topic in the language, a bridging discussion would describe how the general concept is applied to other contexts (e.g. real-world or other languages) to prepare students for the use in other languages. This gives students a broader understanding of the concept, allowing them to more easily apply it to the new language. Hugging refers to how the concept is taught in the second language. Initial examples are chosen to make the second context as similar to the first as possible in order to encourage students to see the relationship between the two languages. More examples follow that show the different ways this concept can be applied to the second concept.

Dann et al.[8] applied bridging and hugging to a college-level blended Alice/Java course. Student achievement increased across the entire course - improving their final scores from 61% to 85% and 82% (with similarly large gains with every subject in the course) compared to a Java-only course. Another pertinent result was that in order to improve hugging, the block-based language sometimes must fundamentally change in order to allow for simpler correlating examples in the second language. In particular, parallelism and inheritance are not subjects that match well between Alice and Java at this time.

Armoni et al.[1] performed a study in two different classrooms. First, they taught students Scratch in a middle-school course. Then, some students enrolled in a high school CS1 course in which they were mixed with students who had not taken the Scratch course. They found that the students who had taken the Scratch course did significantly better (20 percentage points) than the other students in bounded and conditional loop execution, but there was no difference in variables and conditionals. In addition, teachers covered the material more quickly when students had already taken the courses. They found that students' knowledge was very limited to the contexts in which they had been taught, lending credence to the importance of bridging and hugging.

One line of work seeks to build learning progressions for young VBBL learners. Seiter[19] used existing projects across different grade levels to identify how computational thinking concepts varied by level in their Progression of Early Computational Thinking (PECT) Model. However, existence of a block in a project is not evidence of learning, as Brennan et al.[4] found out when interviewing Scratch contributors.

In order to understand how students learn a topic, learning progressions have been proposed that illustrate a path (or choice of paths) that students go through in understanding a particular topic, with the final goal being some level of understanding appropriate to the student's age. When thinking of computer science from a learning progressions perspective, it is tempting to consider the learning of VBBL programming at the bottom of the progression *leading to* skills and understanding for traditional languages. However, programming in VBBLs may require *different* ideas and skills than TBLs, making the learning process more complex than the linear learning progression model depicts and more akin to transferring knowledge between related fields of knowledge than directly building knowledge. In fact, other scholars have made the argument that learning progression models, in general, are too simple to capture the learning process. Hammer and Sikorski[11] argue that a particular level of understanding requires different pieces of knowledge. These pieces of knowledge may not have a particular order to them and may be activated differently depending on the learning context.

```
int index = 0;
int index = x+5;
```
(a)

```
Sprite(int s, int dir, int x, int y){
    size = s;
    direction = dir;
    xPos = x;
    yPos = y;
}
Sprite mySprite(100, 90, 0, 0);
```
(b)

```
void init_sprite(sprite *sp, int s,
        int dir, int x, int y){
    sp->size = s;
    sp->direction = dir;
    sp->xPos = x;
    sp->yPos = y;
}
sprite s;
init_sprite(&s, 100, 90, 0, 0);
```
(c)

Figure 1: (a) Primitive type declaration / initialization, C/Java
(b) Class constructor definition and use, Java
(c) Struct function definition and use, C

This perspective learning is related to earlier work by Hammer[10] in which he proposed the idea that, rather than large concepts, learners had smaller ideas that are neither correct nor incorrect on their own, but may be activated appropriately or inappropriately by a context. An important perspective in this work is to break concepts down into smaller chunks. It is not sufficient to study whether students "learned loops" or could "transfer their knowledge of loops" or any other single concept. The idea of transfer (or learning) from this perspective becomes activating appropriate combinations of smaller ideas in a new context.

The goal of this study is to better understand initialization of variables and objects in Scratch and TBLs. More specifically, we seek to identify pieces of knowledge (from student work and observation) and hypothesize what aspects make transfer challenging without careful bridging and hugging.

3. VARIABLE INITIALIZATION

In this section, we describe initialization in Scratch compared to C and Java. We focus on two aspects: the variable types and mechanisms for initializing values, and the lifetime of variables. In the interest of space, we simplify the concepts. In addition, we do not evaluate whether it is *easier* or *harder*; we merely discuss the *differences*.

In C and Java, there are two kinds of variables. Primitive types use simple assignment operators to initialize (Figure 1a). Variables may also be grouped. In Java, a class provides the ability to define functions that operate on variables in an object of that class. In addition, a constructor, contains all initialization of variables in the class (Figure 1b). In C, the user may define an initialization function, but the system does not explicitly support it differently than any other function (Figure 1c).

Variables are created and destroyed throughout the program. The longest lived variables are global variables, which are created when a particular execution begins and destroyed when it ends. All variables should be initialized (written to) before they are used

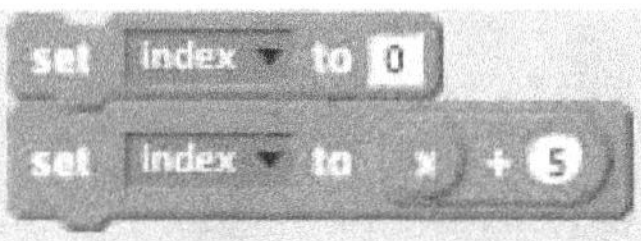

Figure 2: Blocks that modify named variables

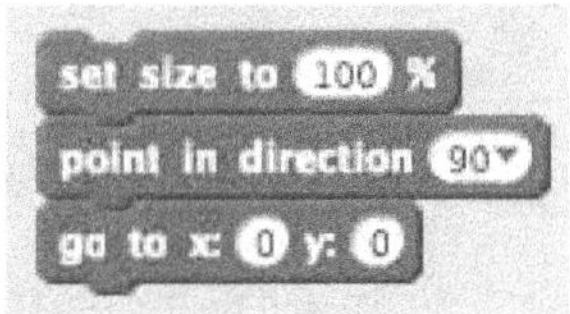

Figure 3: Blocks that initialize sprite attributes

(read from). If the programmer forgets to initialize before use in C, then the variable could have any value in it. For most variables, the value will begin with whatever value was already in that memory location – the ending value of another variable that is no longer present in the program. This leads to unpredictable behavior, and it is difficult to track down such bugs. In Java, however, uninitialized variables are detected by the compiler.

In Scratch, programming occurs in a combined development / runtime environment. There are also two types of variables. Variables can be declared explicitly by the programmer, and standard operators are provided for those (Figure 2). More common, however, are groups of variables in sprites. These are created with a "new sprite" button and given a first costume (image). When a sprite is created, it starts with a default set of values. Although the variable values may not be displayed directly, the visual effect is clear. Figure 3 shows blocks that can be used to initialize such attributes. There are two major differences between these blocks and traditional variable manipulation. First, the blocks are specific to the purpose (size, direction, pen down or up). Second, while some of them do have explicit variable names on which one can operate (e.g., x, y, size), many of them have no way to read the values, only set them (pen up or down, hide/show).

Scratch variables are created during program development rather than program execution. When the program is run twice in a row, the starting values are the same as the ending values from the previous execution. When the program is stored, the current values of all variables are also stored.

Finally, a complicating factor in initialization in Scratch is that there exists no definite "beginning" of a Scratch program. As stated previously, a Scratch program opens in its previously saved state. Scratch is an event-based program, so a program could consist entirely of events such as mouse clicks or key presses. The convention is to begin the program on the green flag, so this is where initialization would occur. However, because this is merely a convention, with no system enforcement, it may not be evident to novice Scratch programmers. In addition, there is no explicit support for initialization like a constructor, and programmers may not create functions.

4. CURRICULUM

Research on how children learn often depends on the curriculum that supports that learning. This is true of our work, as well. Our curriculum is intended to help students develop ideas about computational thinking with two types of activities: activities done off the computer (modeled on CS Unplugged activities[4]) and programming activities done on the computer. The computing concepts covered are the minimum set of concepts necessary to successfully complete a digital storytelling project in Scratch and included two lessons on initialization. The context of the projects were varied and selected to be interesting and accessible to our population of 4th graders (8-9 years old). We also included bonus projects for students who finish early and would like to explore more creatively.

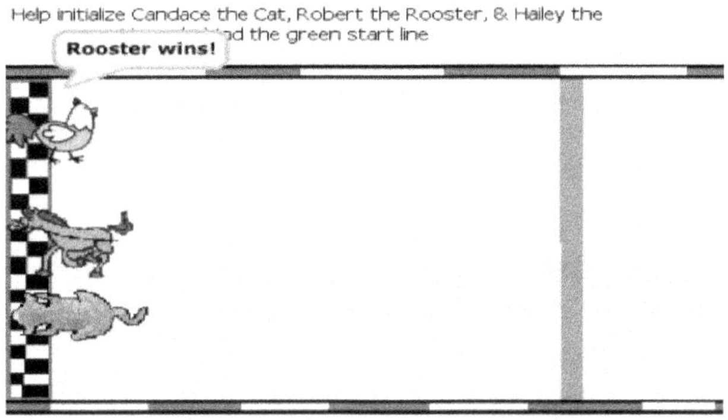

Figure 4: The Animal Sprint stage after the race has occurred.

We included an explicit lesson on initialization (see Figure 4) called Animal Sprint. This lesson animates a race between a horse, rooster, and cat. The animals begin in the correct positions so that students can see where each animal should begin. Then each animal starts running when clicked. When the green flag is clicked to reset the race, only the horse moves to back its initial position at the starting line. The rooster and cat, in contrast, are not properly initialized. For the rooster, both the location and orientation need to be initialized because of its non-linear path to the finish line. For the cat, both the location and size need to be initialized because it stopped and ate several items, growing bigger, on its way to the finish line. In this study, we focus only on the initialization of the cat. Because of the difficulty students had completing this project, we added a second project (Piñata) that required only initializing position.

5. METHODS

We used design-based research, using both qualitative and quantitative data to simultaneously inform curriculum development, research, and practice[2, 4, 23], improving our curriculum as we learned about student learning. Design-based research is "a systematic but flexible methodology aimed to improve educational practices through iterative analysis, design, development, and implementation, based on collaboration among researchers and practitioners in real-world settings, and leading to contextually-sensitive design principles and theories"[23].

This study involved ten 4th-6th grade classrooms (aged 8-12) at five schools across California. In two of these schools (schools B and E), we collected only student project snapshots. In the other three schools (A, C, and D), we observed instruction and interviewed students. Schools varied in numbers of classrooms, grades participating, start dates, and order of projects.

Being present in three classrooms as participant observers[22] allowed us to discover concepts the students were struggling to learn. Researchers wrote field notes following each school visit. In addition, in both distant and local classrooms, for every project, we stored not only the final projects, but also snapshots during the development process. A snapshot was taken and stored into a zip file each time a project was run (*when green flag clicked*) if at least 4 changes had been made.

Computer science researchers read the field notes and inspected a subset of student projects to explore how the code deviated from what was intended. They then identified the specific features of projects that indicated a different view of initialization than we anticipated. After identifying these features, the entire set of student projects was automatically assessed to count how often those features manifested themselves in projects.

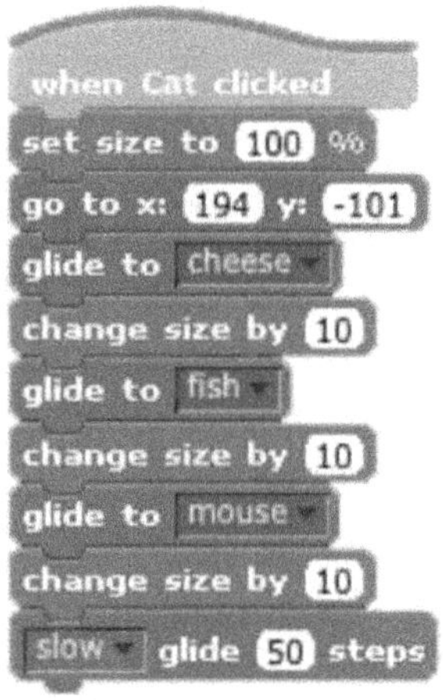

Figure 5: Resetting just before the sprint.

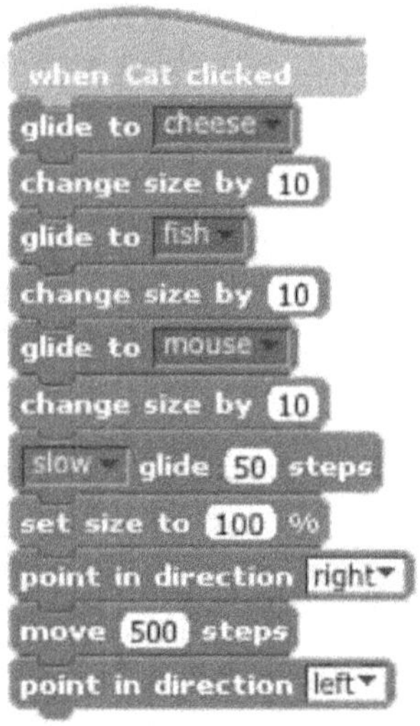

Figure 6: Resetting just after the sprint.

The computer science and education researchers then met together to discuss any conceptual issues, sources of those conceptual issues, and changes to make to the lessons, projects, and/or programming environment. These conversations focused on points where students made what appeared to be "errors" *from the perspective of experts in computer science.*

These conversations made visible understandings about initialization held by the computer scientists that derived from traditional languages and may not have been applicable to Scratch. The disciplinary knowledge of experts differs considerably from that of novices, making it difficult for experts to anticipate where novices will struggle and, in some cases, making them assume an unnecessary ordering of how information is learned, a phenomenon termed "expert blind spot" [17].

While the students programmed in a VBBL, the experts' knowledge was developed and reified largely through TBLs. As such, our analysis of projects, fieldnotes, and challenges, brought to light differences between the VBBL and TBLs. In some cases, these differences made it difficult for the students to develop the knowledge useful for TBLs through the VBBL curriculum.

This process was repeated with each subsequent wave of classrooms. Finally, at the end of the process, the computer scientists and education researchers identified key pieces of knowledge that were necessary for initialization in TBLs, how those were expressed in Scratch, and the challenges in matching the two languages.

6. RESULTS

Our final results are the pieces of knowledge[10] *derived from the lens of traditional languages but expressed in a way that is applicable to Scratch.* We also present the different expressions of that knowledge observed in student projects and discuss the implications on transfer between Scratch and other languages. Finally, for some results (due to space limitations), we also present data as to how often students demonstrated use of concepts in their projects. We present this data to give a sense of the variance and challenge involved in teaching initialization rather than to make precise conclusions.

In this study, we focus on initialization of the cat in the activity called Animal Race. The correct script initializes two attributes: size and location. That is, the cat's size is reset to 100%, and the cat is placed in the proper starting location.

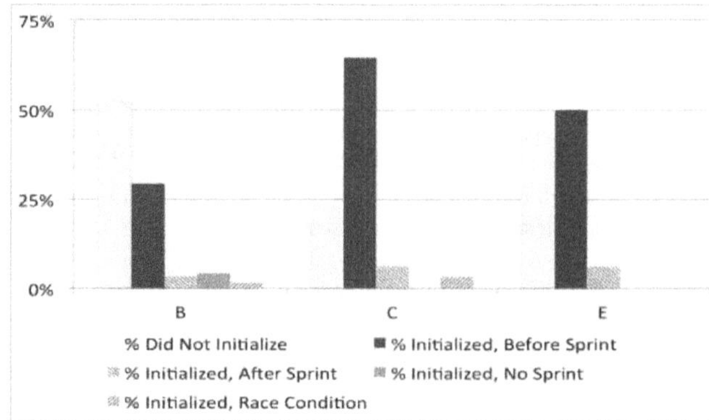

Figure 7: Existence and timing of initialization for cat's position in final snapshot of a given student's project.

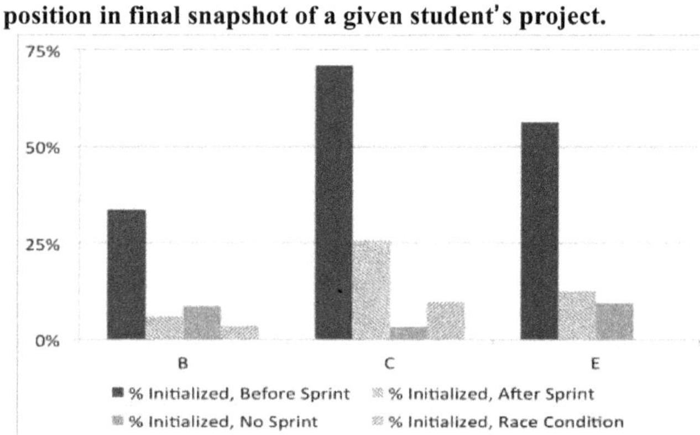

Figure 8: Existence and timing of initialization for cat's position in any snapshot of a given student's project.

For each project, we looked at two types of data - snapshots and final projects. We looked at final projects to gauge how students ended their programs, and we looked at all snapshots to identify what techniques students used along the way. Many students (47% at school B, 77% at school C, and 56% at school E) successfully initialized the cat to the starting line by their final submission, as seen in Figure 7. Variances in completion rates were due to the number of sessions schools spent on initialization, when they encountered the lesson (later schools' curriculum had been improved), and the ages of the students.

6.1.Initialization Before Use

In traditional languages, it is imperative that the variable be initialized before it is used. In Scratch, however, this is not as obvious, since all variable states are stored between executions, and the expression of the variables (sprite attributes) are already visible before program execution. Therefore, we found three additional ideas that students needed to understand in order to initialize in Scratch. Although perhaps not obvious, it is actually critical in Scratch to initialize at the beginning rather than the end – execution can be stopped at any time, so only initialization at the beginning is guaranteed to occur.

1a: Initialization cannot occur at the end of a program.

Many students initialized at the very end of the race. Figure 5 is a script that initializes at the beginning of the script, and Figure 6 is an example of initialization at the end of the script.

Figure 8 shows all the places initialization occurred during students' development. We can see that, at one time or another, 26% of the students from school C placed initialization after the sprint. In addition, almost 10% introduced a race condition

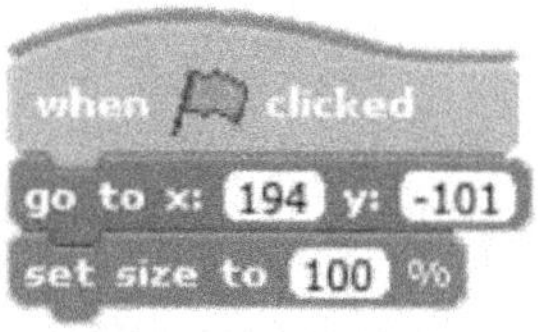

Figure 9: Expected script.

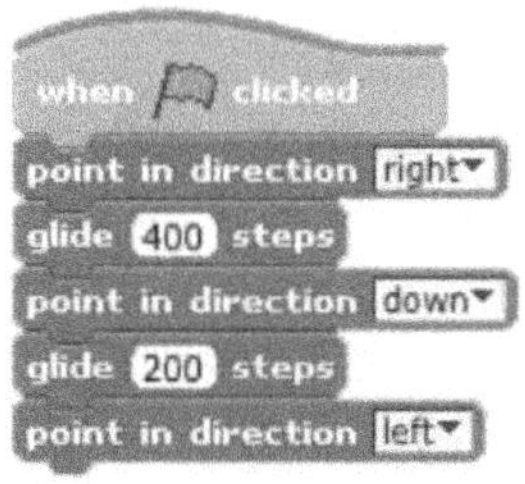

Figure 10: Initializing before race, assuming end position of race.

because they used *when sprite clicked* rather than *when green flag clicked* as the trigger event (creating a second *when sprite clicked* script that ran in parallel with the given sprint script). Finally, several students in classes B and E altered their sprint code enough during their development that the cat no longer reached the finish line (if sprinting from the starting line).

Figure 7 shows that only school C, which spent 3 sessions on Animal Sprint and received very targeted help, had a majority of students complete initialization before the sprint. About half of the projects in the other classrooms had no initialization at all.

The frequency of students initializing after execution shows the effect that carrying the state through alters students' ideas of initialization. It makes sense to students to initialize, or "reset" the state at the end because that will be held. Therefore, unless students are taught explicitly to initialize at the beginning, students may attempt to initialize at the end in traditional languages, as well.

1b: Initialization should occur on the green flag

In TBLs, the only requirement is initialization before use. In Scratch, however, all attributes of sprites are visible, even before the program is running. When, then, should initialization occur? By convention, execution starts when the green flag is pressed, so initialization should occur as the first actions in the green flag script (Figures 9 & 10); all other events are part of the running program. Many students, instead, initialized with the *on cat clicked* script, which made initialization occur immediately before or after the race.

1c: Initialization should be hidden from the user.

In Java and C, not only does initialization occur first, but it is a separate, unique action. Constructors are special pieces of code that are not explicitly called by the user or programmer: the system calls them automatically when a new variable is created. This challenged us to find a way to express the specialness and separateness of initialization in an environment in which the expression of the values are already visible before execution.

We identified this problem through iterative observation and discussion. Initially, several students used blocks that were unexpected to the computer scientists on the team. For students who placed initialization code before the action (e.g., prior to the sprint in Animal Sprint or at the start of the Piñata Project), they chose one of two block types: *go to* (instantaneous) or *glide* (a visible, slow movement).

Figure 11 shows what blocks students used in their final submissions of the Animal Sprint and Piñata projects. In schools C and D, all students used the *go to* block, whereas at schools B and E, many students used the *glide* block. In School D, for the Piñata projects, the presenter explicitly pointed out that it looked "silly" for the candies to slowly glide up to the piñata. Therefore, students had explicit instruction to use the *go to* block. At school E, no directions were given. In discussions about this concept, we discovered that the computer scientists' expectation of

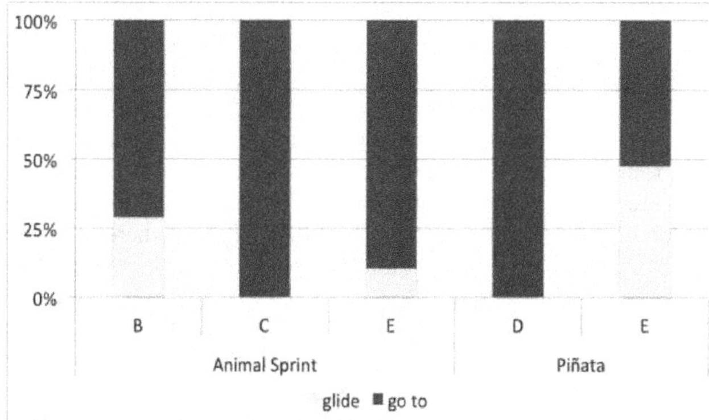

Figure 11: Instantaneous vs gradual initialization in last submission only for projects that included initialization before the action

instantaneous blocks was a manifestation of the belief that initialization is special and should not be confused with normal execution. Those who were encountering initialization only through Scratch (education researchers and students) did not see this distinction.

The important question is whether teaching this distinction would help students transfer their knowledge to TBLs. More specifically, would teaching that initialization is a special, distinct action that occurs at the beginning of the program and should not be viewed as part of the program, help transfer their knowledge? While teaching that seeing the initialization "looks silly" may have resulted in the students using the instantaneous blocks, it is unlikely that students learned any generalizable concept.

6.2.Initialization does not use prior state

In traditional languages, nothing can be assumed about state prior to initialization. In Scratch, the state is dependent entirely on that variable's end state. This influences the instructions / blocks used for initialization.

2a: Absolute blocks need to be used rather than relative blocks.

In traditional languages, absolute instructions (e.g., int x = 5) must be used for initialization (as opposed to int x += 5). Likewise, in Scratch, there are absolute blocks (set size to X%) and relative blocks (change size by X).

In Scratch, because initial state is the same as end state, the case for absolute blocks is not obvious. Figure 8 shows initialization based on an absolute "go to" block, whereas Figure 9 shows a script that moves the cat back to the starting point assuming it had been left at the end point. This works only in the most expected use case: the program is running from beginning to end each time. Unfortunately, this does not work properly if someone accidentally presses the green flag twice without waiting for it to complete, or if someone stops execution in the middle.

Table 1: The four pieces of knowledge identified that results in robust implementations in both Scratch and traditional langs.

Initialization should occur at the beginning of the program
Initialization should occur in the green flag script
Initialization should be hidden from the user
Absolute blocks must be used to initialize

7. DISCUSSION

These findings can be analyzed from several levels. First, we identified several "pieces of knowledge", summarized in Table 1, that signify principles about initialization derived from domain experts' expectations of Scratch projects. We found that because Scratch saves state across executions and the state is visible as sprite attributes, even the most basic pieces of knowledge of initialization in traditional languages, "Initialize before Use" and "Assume no Prior State", are not obvious to a novice Scratch programmer. Other attributes of Scratch, such as the lack of a definite starting point and the variety of blocks used to alter state, makes it much more difficult to identify exactly where to put the code (the event) and which blocks to use (absolute vs relative).

One might be tempted to conclude that these are irrelevant, especially when using Scratch with no desire for the knowledge to transfer to other languages. Three out of the four principles, however, apply to Scratch projects themselves – only the question of instantaneous vs. gradual initialization has no clear answer in Scratch. Because students appear to design for the simple case (executing the project to the end each time) they often initialize in locations that do not work in other conditions. Once those conditions are encountered, it is difficult to fix their program, especially if they are not present to move everything back.

What about if transfer is one of the goals? We found that, despite explicitly teaching initialization, these principles were not obvious to the students. Therefore, the development environment, language, and instruction will need to be revised to better align these concepts. Within Scratch, students could be shown what happens when a project is interrupted part way through in order to develop a practice of initializing first and with absolute blocks. In addition, bridging should occur to present more general, high-level principles including the separate, special nature of initialization. It should occur in the green flag script (or a special script created just for initialization), and perhaps it should be instantaneous. In addition, a Scratch variant could provide a separate event for initialization that must be executed before the green flag. Finally, hugging could occur when students encounter traditional languages to relate what they learned in Scratch to what they see in the new context. Students need to be explicitly taught that variables are destroyed every time the program ends, so they need to be initialized anew each execution.

8. CONCLUSIONS

We have discussed the details of initialization of state as they are expressed in Scratch projects, presented several pieces of knowledge necessary to understand initialization, and suggested instructional strategies and Scratch modifications that could increase the chances of successful knowledge transfer.

Initialization is just one of several important concepts for creating digital storytelling projects. Similar analysis needs to be undertaken for sequential execution, events, message-passing, costumes, and scene changes, identifying how 4th graders learn these concepts in VBBLs, and how that might affect their understanding of traditional languages.

9. ACKNOWLEDGMENTS

This work is supported by the National Science Foundation CE21 Award CNS-1240985. We would also like to thank all of the teachers, students, and schools involved in this project.

10. REFERENCES

1. Armoni, M., Meerbaum-Salant, O., and Ben-Ari, M. 2015. From Scratch to "Real" Programming. *Transactions on Computing Education.* 14, 4, Article 25 (February 2015)
2. Barab, S. and Squire, K. Design-based research: Putting a stake in the ground. *The Journal of the Learning Sciences*, 13(1):1–14, 2004.
3. Bell, T., Witten, I. H. and Fellows, M. *Computer Science Unplugged.* 2006.
4. Brennan, K. and Resnick, M.. New frameworks for studying and assessing the development of computational thinking. In *AERA*, 2012.
5. Brown, A. L. Design experiments: Theoretical and methodological challenges in creating complex interventions in classroom settings. *The Journal of the Learning Sciences*, 2(2):141–178, 1992.
6. Lori Carter. 2006. Why students with an apparent aptitude for computer science don't choose to major in computer science. *SIGCSE Bulletin* 38, 1, 27–31.
7. Dann, W., Cooper, S., and Pausch, R. Making the connection: programming with animated small world. ITiCSE, 2000.
8. Dann, W., Cosgrove, D., Slater, D., Culyba, D., and Cooper, S. Mediated transfer: Alice 3 to Java. In *Proceedings of the 43rd SIGCSE Symposium.* ACM, New York, NY, 141–146, 2012.
9. Franklin, D., et. al. Animal Tlatoque: attracting middle school students to computing through culturally-relevant themes. In *Proceedings of the SIGCSE Symposium*. 2011.
10. Hammer, D., Elby, A., Scherr, R. E., & Redish, E. F.. Resources, framing, and transfer. *Transfer of learning from a modern multidisciplinary perspective*, 89-120, 2005.
11. Hammer, D., and Sikorski, T. Implications of complexity for research on learning progressions. *Science Education, 99*(3) 424-431, 2015.
12. Hill, C., et al. Floors and Flexibility: Designing a programming environment for 4th-6th grade classrooms" In SIGCSE '15. ACM Press, 2015.
13. Hood, C. S., and Hood, D. J. Teaching programming and language concepts using LEGOs. In the *Conference on Innovation and Technology in Computer Science Education* (ITiCSE), June 2005.
14. Maloney, J., et al. The scratch programming language and environment. *Trans. Comput. Educ.*, 10(4):1–15, Nov. 2010.
15. Margolis, J., and Fisher, A. *Unlocking the Clubhouse: Women in Computing*. MIT Press, Cambridge, MA, 2003.
16. Meerbaum-Salant, O., Armoni, M.,and Ben-Ari, M. Learning Computer Science Concepts with Scratch. In the *International Workshop on Computing Education Research (ICER10)*, Aaarhus, Denmark, pp. 69-76, 2010.
17. Nathan, M.J., and Petrosino, A. Expert blind spot among preservice teachers. *American educational research journal*, *40*(4), 905-928, 2003.
18. Salomon, G., and Perkins, D. Teaching for transfer. *Educational Leadership*, 22-32, September, 1988.
19. Seiter, L. and Forman, B. Modeling the learning progressions of computational thinking of primary grade students. In the International Workshop on Computing Education Research (ICER13). ACM, 2013.
20. Spradley. J. P. Participant observation. Holt, Rinehart and Winston, 1980.
21. The stars alliance: A southeastern partnership for diverse participation in computing. NSF STARS Alliance Proposal. http://www.itstars.org/.
22. Vygotsky. L. *Mind in society: The development of higher psychological processes*. Harvard Uniersity Press, 1978.
23. Wang F., and Hannafin, M. Design-based research and technology-enhanced learning environments. Educational Technology Research and Development, 53(4):5–23, 2005.

ITCH: Individual Testing of Computer Homework for Scratch Assignments

David E. Johnson
School of Computing, University of Utah
50 S. Central Campus Drive, #3190
Salt Lake City, UT USA
1-801-585-1726
dejohnso@cs.utah.edu

ABSTRACT
In this paper, we describe ITCH, an automatic testing system for projects in the Scratch programming language. While Scratch lacks traditional input/output mechanisms, ITCH overcomes this by exploiting the persistent saved project state to embed ITCH-specific lists that retain project output. In addition, the ITCH system replaces Scratch user input commands with automatically assigned test values. ITCH can gather variable state from running code, redirect output to a file, and capture drawings done by a Scratch project to save in a report format. The ITCH system has been successfully used in a large computer science explorations class where small practice code questions are assigned before extending work to larger, more creative projects without further burdening course graders. Examples of course projects and the ITCH-tested practice questions are given.

1. INTRODUCTION
Educational programming languages aid novice students in rapidly developing engaging projects. Educational languages such as Alice [3] and MIT's Scratch [9] have seen widespread deployment over a range of age groups and institutions. However, as Scratch increasingly gets used in higher-education courses, some of its shortcomings become more apparent. One shortcoming is the difficulty of evaluation of Scratch homework projects, as Scratch runs in an isolated environment without traditional output mechanisms; instead, evaluation typically requires substantial and time-consuming mouse clicking and key pressing.

Scratch has been used as a gentle introduction to programming in our university's pre-major CS course. As computer science enrollments have increased nationally, this course has grown to over 200 students. Homework assignments based on Scratch have required significant time to grade. One consequence of this time-intensive grading is that instructors may be reluctant to assign the type of short practice questions ("write code to count from 1 to 10") that can aid students in mastery of Scratch constructs.

SIGCSE '16, March 02-05, 2016, Memphis, TN, USA © 2016 ACM.
ISBN 978-1-4503-3685-7/16/03...$15.00 DOI:
http://dx.doi.org/10.1145/2839509.2844600

To aid grading of Scratch projects, we have developed ITCH, Individual Testing of Computer Homework, which is a Python tool to transform and run Scratch 2.0 projects, provide different test inputs, record outputs, and generate a report on the success or failure of the code. Eventually, we would like to develop a web system that would also allow students to test their code while developing it.

The ITCH system is aimed at automated testing of small Scratch programs, although well-defined larger projects can also be tested. It is not aimed at projects such as games, where continuous control is needed to navigate through the project. However, ITCH can be usefully deployed in the grading of small building-block questions that can aid students in the final development of more complex and creative assignments.

2. BACKGROUND
There is substantial prior work in automated grading of programming assignments [6]. In general, automated testing is an important part of the software engineering process [5]. Testing can use static analysis, where the code is examined for common errors [4], or run-time testing with different sets of input designed to evaluate the overall correctness of the running code [8].

2.1 Testing of GUIs
Automated testing of graphical user interface (GUI) applications has increased in importance as interface-heavy phone and tablet "apps" become more prominent. Methods for GUI-testing includes capturing an underlying model of the system so that different aspects can be exercised [10], capture and replay [1] of user interactions (such as is used by Selenium for web testing), and GUI "ripping", which parses user-interface elements and extracts properties and values for testing [7].

2.2 Testing in Scratch
The ITCH testing environment is designed to work with Scratch 2.0. Scratch is an educational programming language from MIT [9] with a rich set of high-level instructions that aid rapid development of creative projects. Scratch uses a block language designed to reduce syntax errors. Because of this, most problems with Scratch projects occur at run-time, and these errors are typically difficult for new programmers to detect and correct. Similarly, evaluation of Scratch projects typically requires careful hands-on running of a project.

Prior work for Scratch project testing and analysis includes Hairball [1], which is focused more on static analysis of Scratch 1.4 projects. Hairball supports checking for initialization of program state, synchronization of sound and text, message broadcast and receive matching, and checking for program complexity, such as used in animating a sprite.

Another Scratch-focused analysis tool is Scrape [11], which analyzes block-usage in Scratch projects or across groups of projects. These systems do not provide run-time analysis of Scratch projects, which is the main goal of the ITCH tool.

3. SYSTEM DESIGN

The goal of the ITCH system is to provide automatic testing of student Scratch projects and to generate a summary report from that testing. The fundamental difficulty of automated testing for Scratch projects is that the projects run within a graphical environment with little connection to the rest of the computer. For example, there is no mechanism to write files from a running project or any way to override standard user input with an external source. However, we can exploit one property of Scratch projects, which is that the values in variables and the state of the Scratch world are all saved as part of a saved Scratch project.

ITCH uses this persistent state to embed the results of testing in a saved Scratch project and then parses the saved file to extract the results. The fundamental process used by most of the ITCH system is parsing and replacing blocks in the saved project file. In the following sections, we describe this process.

3.1 The Structure of Scratch files

A saved Scratch 2.0 project is really a zipped folder containing resources and the program file. The program file is a JSON file with key:data pairs, where the data is often a list with human-readable text naming the blocks used and any arguments used with the block. For example, a small Scratch script to draw a square is shown on the left and the corresponding portion of the saved JSON is on the right in Figure 1.

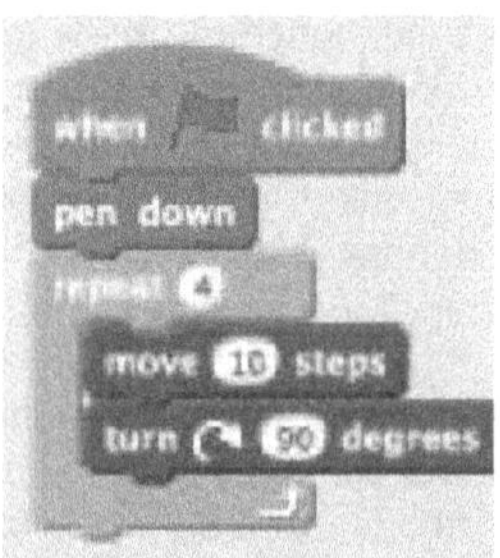


```
[["whenGreenFlag"],
        ["putPenDown"],
        ["doRepeat", 4,
          [["forward:", 10],
           ["turnRight:", 90]]]
```

Figure 1: The Scratch script on the left and corresponding saved JSON file structure on the right.

3.2 Block Replacement

The ITCH system loads the JSON file into a Python dictionary data structure. ITCH functions allow script blocks to be replaced with a different block. For example, a "when space pressed" event block can be turned into a "when green flag" block for easier running by the test program. More commonly in the ITCH system, blocks that provide temporary output to the screen are replaced with blocks that save output, and blocks that require input are replaced with sets of testing values.

3.3 Storing Output

Scratch projects typically use cartoon-like text bubbles to output information to a user. These text bubbles are generated with a say block, which accepts a string or other data as the information to be displayed. In order to record output the ITCH system first makes a Scratch list variable named "output" by inserting the appropriate text into the project JSON file. Then, the system recursively searches the Scratch project scripts for a say block and replaces the say block with the appropriate code to add the displayed data to the "output" list. When the modified program is run and saved, the state of the "output list" is stored in the saved file and the information can be extracted. The ITCH system can also report on the values stored in variables at the beginning or end of a script without requiring a say block to be part of the original program.

Figure 2 shows an example transformation of a script that counts from 1 to 10. The "when 1 key pressed" block has been replaced with a green flag start for ease of automating. An informational comment has been added so the report shows which script is activated. Finally, the say block has been replaced with a block that adds the said value to the ITCH-generated "output" list.

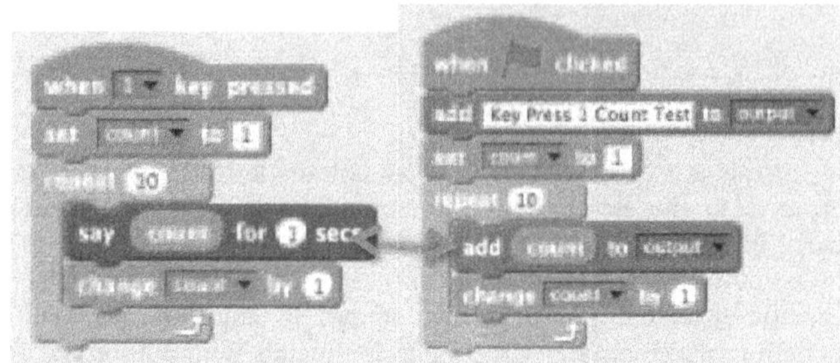

Figure 2: On the left is a small script to count from 1 to 10. On the right is the ITCH-augmented script with a replaced start event block, an added informational comment block, and a transformation from a text-bubble "say" block to storage in the ITCH "output" list.

3.4 Testing Scripts

Scripts that take human input are similarly modified to accept input from a list of test values at run-time. In a Scratch program, an ask block prompts the user for information. The user-supplied answer is stored in a system variable called "answer". The ITCH system creates a new variable called "fakeAsk" and adds it to the project JSON file. Then, the ask blocks are replaced by creating blocks to assign "fakeAsk" to the desired test data and "fakeAsk" replaces appearances of the system "answer" block in the script. This prevents the system from pausing to wait for human input and provides consistent testing with a set of test data for scripts.

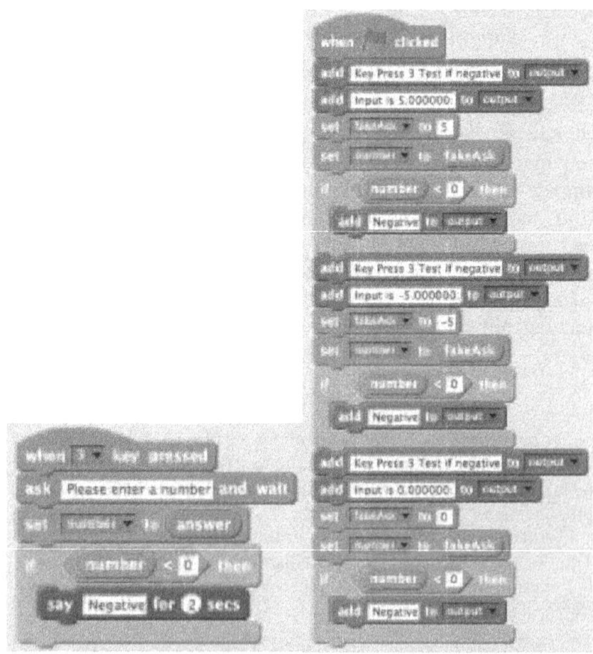

Figure 3: An example transformation from user input to automated testing.

Figure 3 shows an example of this process. The original script asked the user for a number and then tested the answer for negativity. The tester specifies a set of test inputs, in this case [5, -5, 0], and the ITCH system replaces the user-input with setting the ITCH-created "fakeAsk" variable to each element of the test set and replicates the blocks for each test value. ITCH also sends the input values to the "output" list for later viewing in the summary report. Note that the ITCH system provides consistency in testing, such as checking the zero boundary case that a teaching assistant may or may not remember to do.

3.5 Static Analysis

There have been some assignments where static analysis is useful to make sure the student is fulfilling the requirements of the assignment. For example, one assignment problem requires that the student create and use a custom block, Scratch's version of a subroutine. The ITCH system can search for the existence of certain blocks, like the custom block call, and report on its existence. There are also routines for counting loops, nesting of loops, and checking the visibility of sprites.

3.6 Interacting with ITCH

The ITCH tool is a set of Python scripts. A test is setup by calling the scripts and providing specific events and data to test. In a typical test program, different events are specified and turned into green flag events that run in sequence (by means of artificial delays added in between the different actions).

Most tests start by specifying the kind of event to look for.

```
findKeyPressAndMakeGreenFlag(data,"2")
```

The above example shows taking a key press "2" event and turning it into a green flag event for testing consistency. Other green flag events have been stashed out of the way for later retrieval at this point. Along with these specialized routines to look for key press events, other ITCH routines look for any Scratch "hat" block (or event) associated with a particular sprite. In the above code, data is the parsed Scratch JSON file.

Messages can be added at the beginning or end of Scratch scripts. These messages are intended to provide guidance to graders.

```
findGreenFlagsAndStartWithMsg( data, "Key Press 2:
Floor of Number - should answer 1,1,-1")
```

This message is giving the problem being exercised and the results expected from given test values. The message will be stored in the output file after running the tests.

Then, a single user input "ask" block is replaced with a variable that is assigned different numbers in succession. The example below sends 1.3, 1.7, and -0.7 to a student script exercising the floor function.

```
replaceAskWithValue(data,[1.3, 1.7,-0.7])
```

The script is actually repeated 3 times, once for each test case entered in the command.

The scripted testing that ITCH uses works well for student assignments. The physical layout of projects varies widely between students, but things like the names of sprites can be specified, allowing interaction via script.

While much of this Python interaction with ITCH could be replaced with a more user-friendly front-end text language, we are still exploring the uses of ITCH and some advanced possibilities include using the Python language to do things like count block usage and conditionally report on the answer, which is hard to capture in a very simple interface.

3.7 Report Generation

The modified Scratch project is run and saved by Apple's Mac OS X Automator, which can open files and repeat GUI actions such as clicking on the green start flag and saving a file. Then the ITCH system again parses the saved JSON project file and extracts the "output" list information. Additional data can be pulled out of the project. For example, any drawing done on the stage is saved as an image file in the project folder, and these can also be added to the report. The ITCH system makes a large pdf with each student on a page for easy grading evaluation. The ITCH system frees up grader time for the more creative portions of the assignment.

Some example reports are shown in Section 4 along with a description of the problems and larger assignment they support. Note that the report format evolved over the course of the semester as additional tools were found to be desirable. While the formatting of the reports is not too sophisticated, it is still much faster to skim the report than open up the Scratch project, click various keys to trigger scripts, and note the results.

4. ITCH Usage Examples

In our CS0 course there are 5 Scratch assignments. The first few assignments practice basic programming constructs and the rest explore important CS concepts with Scratch implementations. These assignments are described so that the integration of Scratch testing with the main part of the assignment can be seen. Each assignment has a main part and then support questions which are automatically graded by the ITCH system.

Assignment 1 has students convert an algorithm from pseudocode to Scratch and also make a simple game where the player must avoid enemies who bounce around the screen. The support questions ask the student to make different counting loops and also exercise conditionals with a positive-zero-negative number test and a maximum value number test. An exemplar student report is shown in Figure 4.

```
test1.sb2  Results:
[2, 3, 4, 5, 6, 7, 8, 9, 10, 11, 12]
test2.sb2  Results:
[10, 20, 30, 40, 50, 60, 70, 80, 90, 100]
test3.sb2  Results:
['Input is 3:', 'Positive',
'Input is 0:', 'Zero',
'Input is -5:', 'Negative']
test4.sb2  Results:
['Input is 1:', 'Input is 2:', 'Input is
3:', 'The maximum value is', 3,
'Input is 3:', 'Input is 2:', 'Input is
1:', 'The maximum value is', 3,
'Input is 1:', 'Input is 3:', 'Input is
2:', 'The maximum value is', 3]
```

Figure 4: A sample student report for assignment 1.

Assignment 2 uses a more open-ended adventure game assignment with state variables, conditionals, and message passing between sprites. Errors with any of those can be difficult to find when embedded in a complex game. The support questions ask students to test for a number range with if-then-else blocks, alternate hiding and showing a sprite using a state variable, draw a 2D array of triangles, and use message passing to make another sprite say "hello" (see Figure 5).

test1.sb2
Results:
Input is -5.000000: Far from zero.
Input is -4.999000: Near zero.
Input is 0.000000: Near zero.
Input is 4.999000: Near zero.
Input is 5.000000: Far from zero.

Part 2:

Part 3: Starting visibility status is [True, True]
Part 3: Ending visibility status is [False, True]
Part 4:
Results: ['Hi Cat!']

Figure 7: A sample report for assignment 2 showing testing with different inputs and capturing drawings on the stage.

Assignment 3 has students implement a destructive selection sort. This is the first assignment where the underlying algorithm moves beyond trivial complexity and students struggle with seeing how the larger problem can be broken into smaller steps. The support questions have students build a list of random numbers, output each item in a list, increment a counting variable, copy a list, and removing and moving an item in a list (see Figure 6). Many of these questions are difficult for a TA to grade as scripts that say output to the screen are slow to execute.

Assignment 4 practices binary-decimal conversion. The support questions practice some Scratch skills necessary for easier implementation, such as changing sprite costumes (when flipping bits from 0 to 1), using the floor function, concatenating strings (used to build up the binary result), and making a custom block subroutine to double a number. This report shows an example of some static analysis from ITCH: a block that calls a custom block is searched for in the project (see Figure 7). ITCH also performed testing on the main conversion part of the assignment, allowing TAs to concentrate on code analysis.

test5.sb2 Results:
'Key Press One Values'
'12 15 19 13 5 18 18 14 18 11'

'Key Press Two Say All Items in Values'
12 15 19 13 5 18 18 14 18 11

Part 3: Starting count status is 0
'Key Press Three Changed Value'
1
'Key Press Three Changed Value'
2
'Key Press Three Changed Value'
3

'Key Press Four: Make a Copy'
'12 15 19 13 5 18 18 14 18 11'
'Key Press Five: Copy Item by index'
'Input is 10:'
'12 15 19 13 5 18 18 14 18 11 11'

Figure 8: A sample student report for assignment 3.

test1.sb2 Results:
'Key Press 1 Switch Costume': 1
'Key Press 1 Switch Costume': 2
'Key Press 1 Switch Costume': 1

'Key Press 2 Floor of Number'
'Input is 1.300000:' 1
'Key Press 2 Floor of Number'
'Input is 1.700000:' 1

'Key Press 3 Add a': 'a'
'Key Press 3 Add a': 'aa'
'Key Press 3 Add a': 'aaa'

'custom block call used - probably good'
'Key Press 4 Double entered number'
'Input is 1.000000:' 2
'Key Press 4 Double entered number'
'Input is 1.500000:' 3
'Change by 8 Testing': 41 33 41
'Decimal to Binary Testing':
'Input is 3.000000:' : '11'
'Input is 255.000000:': '11111111'

Figure 6: A report showing static analysis in searching for a custom block call.

test1.sb2 Results:
'Key Press 1 Num Values'
'Input is 1: 'The number of Values is 2'
'Input is 2: 'The number of Values is 4'
'Input is 8: ''The number of Values is 256'

'Key Press 2 Max Value'
'Input is 1:' 'The maximum value is 1'
'Input is 2:' 'The maximum value is 3'
'Input is 8:' 'The maximum value is 255'

'Digitize 30 to 4 levels': 33.33333333333
'Digitize 100 to 2 levels': 100
'Digitize 75 to 2 levels': 100

Figure 5: A sample report for a digitizing assignment.

Assignment 5 explores digitizing analog values given a sample rate and sample bit size. The assignment uses audio loudness as the audio signal and draws a digitized signal given slider settings for sample rate and sample size. The support questions force students to program and test key portions of the assignment in isolation from the larger project. The questions ask students to write scripts that compute the number of values a number of bits can represent and the maximum value on a zero to maximum integer range for those number of bits along with test scripts that send user input to those custom blocks. ITCH tested those small problems and also tested the overall digitization process, as shown in Figure 8.

5. DISCUSSION AND CONCLUSION

The approach of working with Scratch through its saved state via an external program was used in contrast to modifying the Scratch executable directly partly to decouple the testing from Scratch and also to avoid having to dig into the large Scratch stand-alone code.

The ITCH system does not provide automated evaluation, just reporting of results. Some of this is because of Scratch's procedural nature – there is no concept of returning a value from a script, so it is harder to isolate a result from testing. We could have added additional analysis of the generated output to provide some validation of results and will be exploring this in the future.

While the ITCH system has not been formally evaluated in terms of student achievement, the tool has been successfully used in a 200 student CS0 course to provide automatic evaluation of small practice code Scratch projects. The ITCH system was able to parse and modify all the student projects and generate an appropriate report. The teaching assistants anecdotally report happiness with using the generated report to assist their grading.

Some students failed to follow basic guidelines on which events to use to trigger actions and others had problems with infinite loops or other time delays, in which case the testing would time out before completion. In that case, the assignments would be graded by hand, but these have been a small percentage of assignments. Even in these cases, the testing script provides guidance to graders about expectations for evaluation.

The ultimate goal for ITCH is to improve the front-end to the ITCH system to allow structuring of testing without direct Python coding and to provide testing access via the internet to support student testing of Scratch projects during development.

6. ACKNOWLEDGMENTS

Thanks to the teaching assistants of the CS0 course who willingly used the ITCH reports for grading.

7. REFERENCES

[1] Andersson, J. and Bache, G. 2004. The Video Store Revisited Yet Again: Adventures in GUI Acceptance Testing. Lecture Notes in Computer Science, Springer-Verlag Heidelberg, vol. 3092, pp. 1-10.

[2] Boe, B., Hill, C., Len, M., Dreschler, G., Conrad, P. and Franklin, D. 2013. Hairball: lint-inspired static analysis of scratch projects. In *Proceeding of the 44th ACM technical symposium on Computer science education* (SIGCSE '13). ACM, New York, NY, USA, 215-220.

[3] Dann, W., Cooper, S., and Pausch, R. 2008. *Learning to Program with Alice* (2 ed.). Prentice Hall Press, Upper Saddle River, NJ, USA.

[4] Darwin, I. 2008. *Checking C Programs with Lint,* O'Reilly.

[5] Edwards, S. 2003. Rethinking computer science education from a test-first perspective. In *Companion of the 18th annual ACM SIGPLAN conference on Object-oriented programming, systems, languages, and applications* (OOPSLA '03). ACM, New York, NY, USA, 148-155. DOI=10.1145/949344.949390 http://doi.acm.org/10.1145/949344.949390

[6] Jackson, D. and Usher, M. 1997. Grading student programs using ASSYST. In *Proceedings of the twenty-eighth SIGCSE technical symposium on Computer science education* (SIGCSE '97), James E. Miller (Ed.). ACM, New York, NY, USA, 335-339. DOI=10.1145/268084.268210 http://doi.acm.org/10.1145/268084.268210.

[7] Memon, A., Banerjee, I., and Nagarajan, A.. 2003. GUI Ripping: Reverse Engineering of Graphical User Interfaces for Testing. In *Proceedings of The 10th Working Conference on Reverse Engineering*, Nov. 2003.

[8] Myers, G. 1979. *The Art of Software Testing*, John Wiley and Sons, New York, New York.

[9] Resnick, M., Maloney, J., Monroy-Hernandez, A., Rusk, N., Eastmond, E., Brennan, K., Millner, A., Rosenbaum, E., Silver, J., Silverman, B., and Kafai, Y. 2009. Scratch: Programming for All. *Communications of the ACM.* 52, 11 (Nov. 2009). 60-67.

[10] Silva, J., Campos, J., and Paiva, A.. 2008. Model-based User Interface Testing With Spec Explorer and ConcurTaskTrees. *Electron. Notes Theor. Comput. Sci.* 208 (April 2008), 77-93.

[11] Wolz, U., Hallberg, C. and Taylor, B. 2011. Scrape: A tool for visualizing the code of scratch programs. Poster presented at the 42nd ACM Technical Symposium on Computer Science Education, Dallas, TX., March 2011.

Multi-Track Programming Competitions with Scratch

Jason Arnold Heather Bort Ryan Naugle Casey O'Hare Dennis Brylow
Department of Mathematics, Statistics and Computer Science
Marquette University
1313 West Wisconsin Avenue
Milwaukee, WI 53201–1881
firstname.lastname@marquette.edu

ABSTRACT

High school programming competitions often follow the traditional model of collegiate competitions, exemplified by the ACM International Collegiate Programming Contest (ICPC). This tradition has been reinforced by the nature of Advanced Placement Computer Science (AP CS A), for which ICPC-style problems are considered an excellent practice regimen. As more and more students in high school computer science courses approach the field from broader starting points, such as Exploring Computer Science (ECS), or the new AP CS Principles course, an analogous structure for high school outreach events becomes of greater importance.

This paper describes our work on developing a Scratch-based alternative competition for high school students, that can be run in parallel with a traditional morning of ICPC-style problems.

Keywords

Scratch; programming competition; K-12 outreach

1. INTRODUCTION

Computer programming competitions for high school students are a time-tested method of outreach and engagement that have been widely used by academia and industry.

Universities organize and execute programming competitions for high school students for several reasons:

1. Competitions raise the visibility of a campus and its academic computing offerings among future students,
2. Competitions offer an opportunity for universities to directly encourage promising future students,
3. Bringing teams to campus offers a rare window of opportunity for networking and professional development for those teams' computer science teachers, and
4. Many college students view helping run such a competition as worthy community service, and/or as preparation for the collegiate-level competition.

Conversely, high school computer science students and their teachers attend programming competitions because:

SIGCSE '16, March 02-05, 2016, Memphis, TN, USA
© 2016 ACM. ISBN 978-1-4503-3685-7/16/03...$15.00
DOI: http://dx.doi.org/10.1145/2839509.2844634

1. Students who take up an interest in computer science often would like a place to hone their skills and be recognized for their accomplishments,
2. Students are eager to see college campuses and meet college students in a likely area of future study, and
3. Students often view such competitions as valuable practice for subsequent, high-stakes testing such as the Advanced Placement exam in Computer Science.

In most states in the U.S., more than 85% of high schools have no computer science teacher, and thus no computer science courses. High school programming contests held at college campuses in our region have been attractive only to a very narrow, elite band of high schools. Those schools are overwhelmingly suburban schools in orbit about metropolitan areas. Participants from those schools tend to be mostly white or Asian males, from middle-class backgrounds. Many are planning to major in computer science already.

Beginning in 2014, a National Science Foundation grant project started to roll out professional development for area teachers in schools with no computer science presence. Due to this project, 18 new school districts in our state began teaching ECS [6], and over 600 new high school students were taking computer science for the first time. We quickly realized that our traditional model of high school programming competitions was a poor match for the wave of new students entering computer science with broader introductory courses.

In response, we have adapted our traditionally-structured high school programming contest to make it more attractive to this new population of students. We added a second, parallel track to the traditional Java-based competition that uses the Scratch programming language to welcome students from courses such as ECS, or the new AP CS Principles [4] (AP CSP) course. Broadening the reach of this outreach beyond those schools with existing, well-established programs that culminate in Advanced Placement CS A is essential to engaging a more diverse set of participants. Our novel structure requires problems that can be quickly judged, but allow open-ended solutions rewarding creativity and artistic merit. Most significantly, two of the 11 schools participating this year were coached by brand-new ECS teachers, from districts that previously had no CS teacher or courses.

Although years of experience with traditional contest models have produced robust contest management software[1], a rich pool of existing and reusable contest tasks[2], and deep institutional knowledge about how to successfully engineer

[1]http://www.ecs.csus.edu/pc2/
[2]http://uva.onlinejudge.org/

and execute an event, there has been little published work on designing a Scratch-based competition with short-term, open-ended challenge tasks that must run in parallel with a traditional ICPC-style Java track.

This paper presents the first two years of our experience with the challenge of designing and fielding just such a competition.

2. BACKGROUND

Programming competitions have been used to foster and encourage student interest in computing since at least the early 1970s [2]. In this section, we briefly summarize the large body of prior and related work.

2.1 Collegiate Programming Competitions

The Association for Computing Machinery (ACM) International Collegiate Programming Competition (ICPC) is among the oldest and most respected institutions for bringing computing students together in competition from around the world. The typical format has teams of three students working on eight or more complex algorithmic thinking tasks with a five-hour time limit and only one computer. [2]

Regional and local competitions at the collegiate level frequently follow the model of the ICPC, using the vast repository of past contest tasks as both practice and competition problems.

The International Olympiad in Informatics [11] is billed as, "the most prestigious international algorithmic programming competition at the high-school level". National bodies, such as the USA Computing Olympiad [18], hold internal competitions to select a team of delegates to participate in the international competition, not unlike the Olympic Games for athletics.

For USACO, the internal rounds consist of online competitions, supplemented by many hours of free, online training.

Separately, the American Computer Science League [1] offers asynchronous, school-based competition with both a written exam component and a solo programming component. The asynchrony allows ACSL to scale to many schools, by allowing individual teachers to offer the competition during the school day at a time that suits the local context in the high school building.

A wide variety of corporate-sponsored coding contests and web portals compete for the attention of high school students with a strong interest in computer science and related fields. A thorough survey of the landscape of programming competitions is provided in [8].

With many decades of experiences running programming competitions for high school students, more recent research has sought to classify and clarify the categories of competitions and tasks commonly found. Pohl [16] provides a taxonomy of computer science competitions, contests and challenges. Ragonis [17] classifies common questions types found in computer science challenge problems. Hakulinen [9] provides a survey of challenge task development. Forišek [8] gamely suggests new possible problem categories, and discusses an Internet Problem Solving Contest (IPSC) designed to escape some of the more common tropes found in ICPC- and IOI-style competitions.

Despite the longevity and popularity of the traditional model for such events, it is clear that there is room for improvement. Critics point out that time-bound contest problems evaluated solely through automated black box testing discourage many of the most important pedagogical goals of modern computer science [3]. The emphasis on speed in the ICPC-style contest crowds out documentation, refinement and design. The emphasis on platform-independent programming languages and development environments, as well as black-box testing, usually discourages the use of graphics and sound, sharply limiting the creative universe of both problem tasks and their solutions.

Finally, researchers have been commenting on the lack of diversity of participants attracted by the traditional contest model since at least the 1990s [7].

2.2 Alternative Competitions

While the ICPC-style competition is likely to persist in some form, many alternative competition styles have been proposed to address its known shortcomings, including its lack of participant diversity [7].

Alternatives such as the Kansas City Computer Science Fair [7] and the College of Charleston's alternative competition [3] emphasize quality-of-process by judging criteria based on both technical and artistic merit, rather than just black box testing [3]. We reused these ideas in order to encourage creativity and reward artistic merit.

Others have combined CS Unplugged [14] activities with competition-style programming problems [19] to produce an effective hybrid. A wide variety of robotics-based competitions [15] allow participants to branch out beyond text-based input and output, as well as simple black-box testing.

Brebas [5] (Lithuanian for, "Beaver"), is an international, online competition series with divisions open to grades 5 through 12, and intended for those interested in computing regardless of skill level. Individual tasks are typically short, taking 3 minutes or so to solve. Typical Brebas tasks are not programming tasks, but use a computer to solve interactive and/or multiple-choice prompts. In contrast, our work retains the focus on algorithmic design and programming, using the Scratch [12] programming language.

2.3 Scratch Competitions

Competitions that use Scratch or SNAP [13] take advantage of these language's attractive, block-based graphical programming environment to make the programming task more welcoming to novices. Scratch prevents standard syntax errors, and offers a simple set of primitives to manipulate *sprites* (graphical elements with attached method behaviors) on a *stage* (background). Emphasis is on animation, sound, and reactive programming features such as mouse clicks and keyboard events.

The annual Harvard SCRatch International Programming Trial (SCRIPT)[3] began in 2012. Students ages 6-15 can participate in groups of 2-4, and submit a Scratch project under one of six categories: greetings, games, music and dance, stories, simulations, and educational software. Both Georgia Tech[4] and University of New Brunswick[5] have also offered a Scratch-based competition in several past years similar to SCRIPT described above.

Like many other alternative competition formats, all three of these alternative Scratch competitions differ from our

[3]http://scratched.gse.harvard.edu/discussions/events/scratch-competition-symposium-script-2014

[4]http://home.cc.gatech.edu/TeaParty/346

[5]http://www.unb.ca/saintjohn/sase/dept/csas/competitions/jr-high/index.html

work by focusing on online, long-term tasks, rather than an on-site track co-located with traditional ICPC-style contestants. However, all three efforts seek to accomplish similar goals to our work:

- Building students' sense of belonging in computing,
- Encouraging students to code, and
- Encouraging local teachers to teach Scratch.

The use of Scratch in the Syrian Olympiad in Informatics [10] is the clearest antecedent to our current work. Like our contest tasks, the SOI participants were given sprites and a stage, and asked to add behavior. The overall structure of the SOI differs markedly from our typical high school outreach event, and was not designed to bring a growing community of Scratch-using high school students into a parallel competition track.

3. YEAR ONE COMPETITION

For the Spring 2014 edition of our high school programming competition, we decided to add a new, parallel, Scratch-based track to our existing ICPC-style competition that allowed Java, Python and C++ solutions. We knew that the Scratch Division needed to remain open-ended to promote creativity while completing in the same timespan as the other competition.

At that time, we could find no readily available resources that suggested previously successful task prompts for such a competition. Existing models (see prior section) generally relied on much longer competition times, and also on longer judging times. There were no examples of on-site, open-ended, Scratch-based tasks suitable for grades 9-12, or corresponding judging rubrics.

3.1 Task Prompt

The final design envisioned a single, three-hour challenge task centered on a particular, classic fairy-tale motif. Students were asked to retell the story of *The Three Little Pigs*.

The task description included a summary of *The Three Little Pigs* and key requirements such as a minimum of three scenes, repetition of appropriate dialogue, and a conclusion that emphasizes the moral of the story – that hard work shall be rewarded when challenging times come.

Participants were admonished that their work should be original. They could use any of the sprites, backgrounds, audio and other narrative elements that are available through the Scratch.mit.edu site, but should not reuse or adapt existing Scratch projects.

3.2 Judging

The existing PC2 contest management software was determined to be unsuitable for running the Scratch Division. Because the entries would only be judged at the end, there was no need for features handling rapid submission, testing and feedback. Moreover, the complex and somewhat intimidating default interface of the software was deemed likely to detract from the overall welcoming message behind the Scratch Division in the first place.

A panel of faculty judges evaluated work submitted using four criteria including originality, creativity, elegance, and sophistication.

The small number of Scratch Division participants in the first year allowed judging to be completed successfully. However, entirely subjective judging went slowly, and three hours per task allowed participants to produce elaborate artifacts

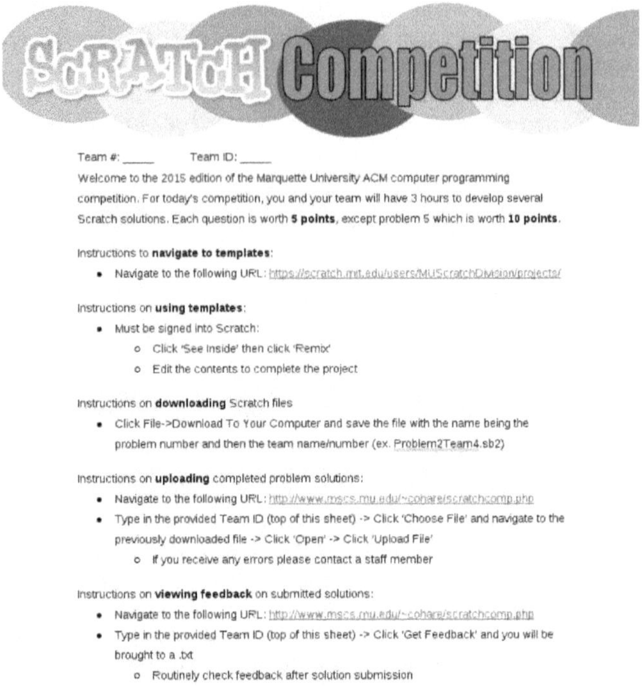

Scratch Competition

Team #: _____ Team ID: _____

Welcome to the 2015 edition of the Marquette University ACM computer programming competition. For today's competition, you and your team will have 3 hours to develop several Scratch solutions. Each question is worth **5 points**, except problem 5 which is worth **10 points**.

Instructions to **navigate to templates**:

- Navigate to the following URL: https://scratch.mit.edu/users/MUScratchDivision/projects/

Instructions on **using templates**:

- Must be signed into Scratch:
  - Click 'See Inside' then click 'Remix'
  - Edit the contents to complete the project

Instructions on **downloading** Scratch files

- Click File->Download To Your Computer and save the file with the name being the problem number and then the team name/number (ex. Problem2Team4.sb2)

Instructions on **uploading** completed problem solutions:

- Navigate to the following URL: http://www.mscs.mu.edu/~cohare/scratchcomp.php
- Type in the provided Team ID (top of this sheet) -> Click 'Choose File' and navigate to the previously downloaded file -> Click 'Open' -> Click 'Upload File'
  - If you receive any errors please contact a staff member

Instructions on **viewing feedback** on submitted solutions:

- Navigate to the following URL: http://www.mscs.mu.edu/~cohare/scratchcomp.php
- Type in the provided Team ID (top of this sheet) -> Click 'Get Feedback' and you will be brought to a .txt
  - Routinely check feedback after solution submission

Figure 1: Scratch Division Instruction Page

that were difficult for judges to fully explore in the time allotted.

4. YEAR TWO COMPETITION

In the second year, we made several important changes to the structure of the Scratch Division in order to more easily scale problem judging, while retaining the distinctive character of the competition.

Competitors were still permitted to compete in pairs, or individually. While high school students were the target audience, one coach requested and received permission to bring an advanced middle school team.

The competitors were given a packet of competition questions, including detailed instructions on how to access templates and submit their work. Additionally, the packets were created to be colorful and playful (compared with the traditional, no-frills ICPC-style specifications) in order to encourage participants to maintain a creative and open mindset. (See Figure 1.)

A mix of both closed- and open-ended questions were used, meaning quicker judging for the technical points during the competition, allowing more time for the judging of creative merit.

Under the question type taxonomy suggested in [17], this task set included:

- Type 1: Developing a Solution (tasks 1, 2, 3, 4)
- Type 2: Developing a Solution that Uses a Given Module (tasks 1, 2), and
- Type 7: Completing a Given Solution (problem 1).

4.1 Task 1 - The Maze

For the first task, the designers sought to present the students with a straightforward, recognizable, and easy to implement question. Given a maze backdrop and a sprite, along with incomplete code blocks, the participants were expected to program the sprite to maneuver through the maze. They were expected to provide the test loop to determine when the sprite should stop moving (e.g. hitting a wall, crossing the finish line).

The designers intended for this problem to be solvable by all teams. Although not all teams received full marks, each team submitted a functioning copy of the sprite and maze. Not all of the teams were able to end the game successfully.

4.2 Task 2 - The Fly Swatter

Figure 2: Flying Hippo Swatter and He-Man Sings

The second question required students to make a fly swatter game. Participants were given a fly sprite, swatter sprite, and a kitchen background. The fly was pre-programmed to randomly move around the kitchen, and the students were to map the swatter sprite to the user's mouse, "squashing" the fly sprite when clicked. The question's main objective was to see if students were able to make the game work well, which required the bug to wait a certain amount of time before moving again. If this was not present in the participant's submission, it would be difficult to win at all.

All eight of the participating groups produced a submission for this problem, with only 6 receiving full points.

Despite the relatively structured nature of this task, participants still incorporated creativity into their solutions. Some teams replaced sprites, while others created elaborate win animations, such as in Figure 2, which incorporated a winged hippopotamus instead of the simple fly, and a popular Internet meme from that month[6].

[6]http://knowyourmeme.com/memes/he-man-sings

4.3 Task 3 - Rock-Paper-Scissors

The third task asked the participants to develop a working *rock-paper-scissors* game using the given sprites and their own animations. They were also required to find their own background to complement their game and animation, as well as promote the creativity of the question.

Creative solutions to the animation subtask included spinning the selection, keyboard movement for selection, and moving towards the opposing sprite.

4.4 Task 4 - Pong

The fourth task in the competition asked the participants to create a working two-dimensional one-player pong game (Figure 3) and for extra credit they could implement a custom artificial intelligence algorithm as a second player. This was intended to be the most challenging task in the Scratch Division.

As expected, this slightly more difficult problem did not elicit as much creative flourish as the earlier, easier problems.

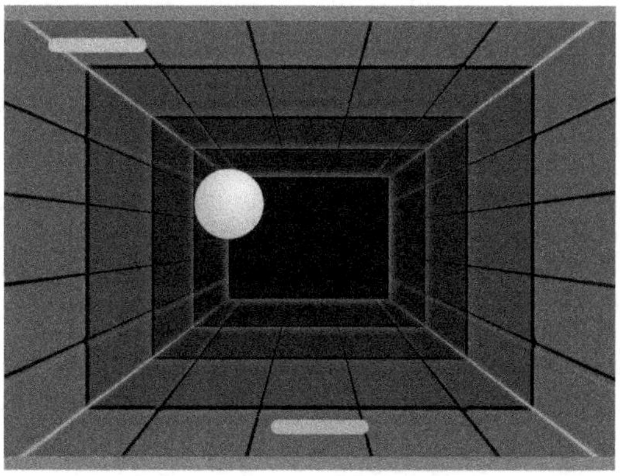

Figure 3: Task 4 - Pong

4.5 Task 5 - Sunken Ship Narrative

The fifth task was designed to be the most open-ended, allowing participants to demonstrate both their Scratch-fluency and creativity (Figure 4). Similar to our first year competition's sole task, the fifth task provided a story prompt and directed participants to finish the story. The plot included a tale of a sunken ship; however, it was up to the participants to provide their own developments to the story, conclude it with a somewhat logical ending, and include the required elements (e.g., underwater animation, loops, at least two sound clips). The participants were also asked to include as many additional objects as they saw fit. We made sure to emphasize that creativity was the ultimate goal for this question, and informed them that it was a very important qualifier for grading.

All eight groups submitted answers to this problem, with greatly varying levels of whimsy. One group made an incredibly creative story, but had difficulty implementing every requirement of the prompt, such as the code requirements.

In an echo of results from the previous year, the most creative code made the requirements difficult for judges to identify. On the far end of the spectrum, some groups made sure to hit every program requirement for the task, but did not invest time into adding creative touches to their sub-

Figure 4: Task 5 given water, rock and ship sprites

mission. In the happy middle, some teams met not only the basic requirements, but retained a logical program structure.

One group developed a game in which user could maneuver a character to collect all the coins within a sunken ship while avoiding the sharks on the screen. This group even included a winning and losing screen. (See Figure 5.)

Although this question was the most difficult to grade, it provided the largest variety of solution types. This not only allowed each individual group to set themselves apart and present their personalities, but allowed us to take a look into how these groups performed "in the wild". We were thus able to observe how the participants built their own blocks of code, while allowing them to personalize it and have fun along the way.

Anecdotal feedback from the teams confirmed that this question was both the judges' and the participants' favorite.

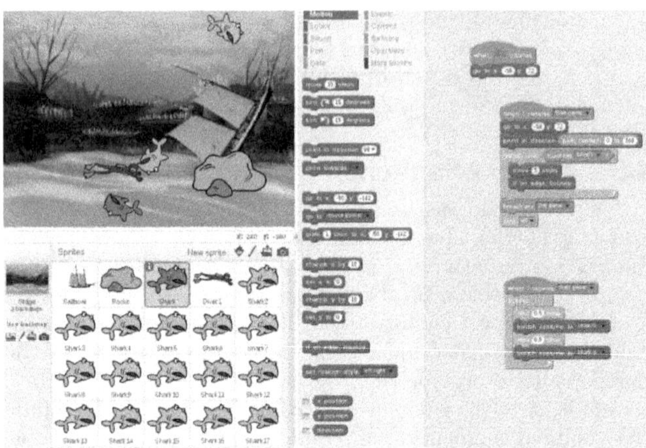

Figure 5: Task 5 Shark Sprite skin choices and Code

4.6 Submission and Judging

We deployed a simple, PHP-driven web submission system for the Scratch Division. This was deemed to be a simpler, lighter-weight and more theme-appropriate solution than the standard PC2 contest management software. (PC2 was still used for the Java Division.)

The judging rubric included a five point system the participants needed to fulfill in order to get full points. While grading submissions, the judges filled out corresponding feedback.txt files that marked whether their submission was correct or incorrect. If incorrect, then feedback was given in order for the team to attempt corrections. The teams could view their feedback using the same aforementioned web system with unique key.

Tasks one to four were worth five points each with an extra three points of extra credit possible for task four. All partial credit was awarded three points as long as the submission had at least three of the problem's criteria working for their submission. Open-ended task five was worth ten points; seven points were awarded if they reached the minimum requirements.

5. RESULTS AND DISCUSSION

In total, 36 teams participated in our year two high school programming competition – 28 teams in the traditional, ICPC-style Java Division, and eight in the Scratch Division. More than 120 students from 11 high schools across our state competed from 9am-Noon, taking up all five of the computer science department's instructional laboratories, as well as many other spaces to host registration, the coaches' meeting, judging, contest headquarters, etc.

Most significantly, two of the 11 participating schools were coached by brand-new ECS teachers. Those schools had previously had no CS teacher or courses, and had sent no previous teams to our events, but this year were able to join in on the Scratch Division.

Thanks to generous support from industrial sponsors and alumni, we were able to award prizes to the top 25% of teams in both the Java and Scratch Divisions, ranging from flatpanels to Arduino starter kits, to wireless peripherals.

Feedback from coaches and participants were overwhelmingly positive. In evaluating the success of the Scratch Division, one of our most experienced ECS teachers noted that most of the tasks resembled the in-class assessments she gives her students at the end of units. We take this as confirmation that we are on the right track. The number of ECS and CSP teachers in our area is growing sharply, due in part to outreach and professional development efforts led by our institution; a fall survey of teachers in our network suggests that we can expect both divisions to grow by another 25-50% in spring of 2016.

In practice, the design of the second year competition scaled well to triple the number of Scratch Division students from the previous year.

What we did not expect was the rather creative turn the participants took with the objective-based questions. For instance, the fly swatter problem (task 2) was rather straightforward; however, a team redesigned it to track how many times the fly was clicked and when it reached one-hundred-and-eleven whacks a spinning animation of a picture from the internet was displayed along with sound. The originality made it more difficult to grade some submissions, but it is the opinion of the authors that this was a worthy trade-off, and one that we look forward to making again next year.

Finally, we were surprised to learn on competition day that the contestants in the Scratch Division varied more widely in age than expected. Despite ECS being intended as a 9th-grade course, our participants from ECS schools ranged from middle school students to high school seniors.

The total number of Scratch Division participants was still less than 20 this year, so it is not yet feasible to make statistically valid claims about the demographic shift we are seeing in the population participating in the Scratch Division. Anecdotally, the Scratch Division has had a better gender balance than the Java Division in both years.

5.1 Future Work

The originality and creativity that some students implemented indicates a need for more open ended questions. For several prompts, we outlined many of the steps and provided a template of sprites and some code fragments that contestants should use. This may have restricted some of the creativity that students could display. In the future, it may serve us better to give a general paragraph of what we require, and expect groups to take different routes to completing the prompt.

Moving forward, we expect to grow the competition next year, as more schools are affected by efforts to increase the number of new CS teachers in the state. We are considering creating a third division, based on previous work on CS Fairs, that would directly model one of the non-programming performance tasks expected for AP CSP.

As the number of participants grows, we hope to complete a statistically valid analysis of the differences between the populations in the two tracks. Our hypothesis is that the Scratch Division attracts a higher percentage of women than the current Java Division, and draws teams from schools with a larger population of underrepresented students.

6. CONCLUSION

We have presented the structure and rationale for an alternative, Scratch-based track that we have added to our existing ICPC-style high school programming competition. The design of this track incorporates both relatively constrained tasks that can be quickly judged, and more open-ended tasks that can be rewarded for creativity and artistic merit. Our overriding goal was to include in our annual outreach event the growing number of Scratch programmers coming out of broader introductory CS courses such as ECS and AP CSP. Students participate in the same, on-campus event, with a different set of tasks, proctors and judges, and participate in the same awards ceremony.

The competition ran well, and attracted markedly more participants than the previous years. The presence of a Scratch Division allowed new schools to participate who had previously never sent a team to such an event. Furthermore, while numbers are still small, it seems likely that the demographic balance of the Scratch Division will at least initially beat the traditional Java Division competition.

Acknowledgments

The authors would like to thank the high school teachers of the CSTA Wisconsin-Dairyland chapter for their guidance and support in creating our event, and for bringing their teams of students. We are grateful to the Marquette University student chapters of ACM and Upsilon Pi Epsilon for the logistical and volunteer support that made our events possible. Aspects of the competition were supported by generous donations from Marquette computer science alumni as well as local employers, such as Rockwell Automation and Direct Supply.

Some of the authors were supported in part by NSF CE21 grant #CNS-1339392, the results of which are driving the need for high school programming contests that appeal to a broader audience in our region.

7. REFERENCES

[1] American Computer Science League. http://www.acsl.org/, Accessed: 2015-05-14.

[2] Association for Computing Machinery (ACM). ICPC factsheet. http://icpc.baylor.edu/worldfinals/pdf/Factsheet.pdf, Accessed: 2015-05-14.

[3] J. F. Bowring. A new paradigm for programming competitions. In *Proceedings of the 39th SIGCSE Technical Symposium on Computer Science Education*, SIGCSE '08, pages 87–91, Portland, OR, 2008. ACM.

[4] College Board. Computer science: Principles. http://www.csprinciples.org/, Accessed: 2015-05-14.

[5] V. Dagiene and G. Futschek. Bebras, a contest to motivate students to study computer science and develop computational thinking. In *WCCE 2013: Tenth World Conference on Computers in Education*, Torun, Poland, July 2013.

[6] Exploring Computer Science. Curriculum v6.0. http://www.exploringcs.org/, Accessed: 2015-05-14.

[7] S. Fitzgerald and M. L. Hines. The computer science fair: An alternative to the computer programming contest. In *Proceedings of the Twenty-seventh SIGCSE Technical Symposium on Computer Science Education*, SIGCSE '96, pages 368–372, Philadelphia, PA, 1996. ACM.

[8] M. Forišek. Pushing the boundary of programming contests. *Olympiads in Informatics*, 7:23–35, 2013. ISSN 1822-7732.

[9] L. Hakulinen. Survey on informatics competitions: Developing tasks. *Olympiads in Informatics*, 5:12–25, 2011. ISSN 1822-7732.

[10] A. Idlbi. Taking kids into programming (contests) with Scratch. *Olympiads in Informatics*, 3:17–25, 2009. ISSN 1822-7732.

[11] International Olympiad in Informatics. http://www.ioinformatics.org/, Accessed: 2015-05-14.

[12] MIT Media Lab. Scratch. https://scratch.mit.edu/, Accessed: 2015-05-14.

[13] U. of California at Berkeley. Snap (build your own blocks). https://snap.berkeley.edu/, Accessed: 2015-05-14.

[14] U. of Canterbury. CS unplugged: Computer science without a computer. http://csunplugged.org/, Accessed: 2015-05-14.

[15] P. Petrovič. Ten years of creative robotics contests. In *Proceedings of Select Papers, ISSEP 2011: 5th International Conference on Informatics in Schools: Situation, Evolution and Perspectives*, pages 201–212, Bratislava, Slovakia, October 2011.

[16] W. Pohl. Computer science contests for secondary school students: Approaches to classification. *Informatics in Education*, 5(1):125–132, 2006.

[17] N. Ragonis. Type of questions – the case of computer science. *Olympiads in Informatics*, 6:115–132, 2012. ISSN 1822-7732.

[18] USA Computing Olympiad. http://www.usaco.org/, Accessed: 2015-05-14.

[19] J. Voigt, T. Bell, and B. Aspvall. *A New Learning Paradigm: Competition Supported by Technology*, pages 207–234. CEDETEL, Boecillo, Spain, 2009.

Special Session: ACM Joint Task Force on Cyber Education

Diana Burley
George Washington University
Graduate School of Education and Human Development
44983 Knoll Square, suite 147
Ashburn, VA 20147
+1 703-553-3761
dburley@gwu.edu

Matt Bishop
University of California, Davis
Department of Computer Science
One Shields Avenue
Davis, CA 95616
+1 530-752-8060
mabishop@ucdavis.edu

Elizabeth Hawthorne
Union County College
STEM Divison-Computer Science
1033 Springfield Avenue
Cranford, NJ 07016
+1 908-497-4232
hawthorne@ucc.edu

Siddharth Kaza
Towson University
Department of Computer and Information Sciences
8000 York Road
Towson, MD 21252
+1 410-704-3868
skaza@towson.edu

Scott Buck
Intel Corporation
2200 Mission College Blvd.
Santa Clara, CA 95054
+1 480-552-2341
scott.buck@intel.com

Lynn Futcher
Nelson Mandela Metropolitan University
School of Information and Communication Technology
Summerstrand Campus (North), R149
+27 41 504 9128
lynn.futcher@nmmu.ac.za

CCS Concepts

• **Social and professional topics** ~ Computing education • **Social and professional topics** ~ Model curricula • **Social and professional topics** ~ Computing education programs • **Social and professional topics** ~ Accreditation

Keywords

Curriculum; Cybersecurity education; security education; cyber sciences

1. SUMMARY

In this special session, members of the ACM Joint Task Force on Cyber Education to Develop Undergraduate Curricular Guidance will provide an overview of the task force mission, objectives, and work plan. After the overview, task force members will engage session participants in the curricular development process.

2. BACKGROUND

In the context of computer security and information assurance, cyberscience is a computing-based discipline involving technology, people, and processes aligned in a way to enable "assured operations" in the presence of risks and adversaries. It involves the creation, operation, analysis, and testing of computer systems (including network and communication systems) designed to be secure, as well as the study of how to employ operations, reasonable risk taking, and risk mitigations to further that design goal. It is an interdisciplinary course of study, and includes aspects of law, policy, human factors, ethics, risk management, and other topics directly related to the success of the activities and operations dependent on such systems, often in the context of an adversary.

SIGCSE'16, March 2–5, 2016, Memphis, TN, USA.
ACM ISBN: 978-1-4503-3685-7/16/03.
DOI: http://dx.doi.org/10.1145/12345.67890

Recent reports [1, 2] have pointed to the need for developing curricular standards for cybersecurity education. Currently the 2013 ACM Curricular Guidelines for Undergraduate Degree Programs in Computer Science (CS2013) [3] treats information assurance and security (IAS) as a specific knowledge area as well as material that spans other knowledge areas. The IAS knowledge area explores aspects of information assurance and security in depth; in other knowledge areas the information assurance and security material is tied to that particular area.

Unfortunately, those curricular guidelines do not treat computer security and information assurance as a cyberscience. The goal of the ACM Joint Task Force on Cyber Education is to develop undergraduate curricular guidance in information assurance and security that teaches computer security and information assurance so students see it as a cyberscience.

3. OBJECTIVE

The objective of this special session is to introduce the work of the ACM Joint Task Force on Cyber Education to Develop Undergraduate Curricular Guidance and to engage the computer science education community in the curricular development process. The session will communicate the objectives and status of the development work, and elicit input from community members. Task force members will engage session participants through general session presentations and small group discussions. In the general session, task force members will highlight the joint task force members and objectives, summarize the work of the Cyber Education Project and how the joint task force will leverage this work, and will provide a roadmap for the development process. This session will provide an opportunity for follow up on the Cyber Education Project's Learning Outcomes Working Group session held at the 2015 SIGCSE Technical Symposium and will support continued community engagement in the curricular development process.

4. OUTLINE

The 75-minute session will be organized to allow ample time for audience participation. The tentative session outline is:

- Session overview, Introduction of the Joint Task Force structure and objectives (10 minutes) – Task Force co-chairs Diana Burley, Matt Bishop
- Background - Cyber Education Project, Cyber Sciences (15 minutes) – Task Force members Beth Hawthorne, Sidd Kaza
- Discussion of stakeholder engagement strategy (10 minutes) – Task Force members Lynn Futcher, Diana Burley
- Audience Engagement (40 minutes) – Task force members will divide the audience into 4 small groups in order to engage in specific discussions on the curricular development process. Small groups will discuss topics for 20 minutes then reconvene as a large group to report out from the small groups (5 minutes per group).

5. EXPECTATIONS

The special session is intended for all participants of the SIGCSE conference who teach or are stakeholders in undergraduate security curricula. Since cybersecurity is interdisciplinary by nature, we expect participants from all areas in the computing sciences including computer science, information systems and information technology. The session will provide participants with the background and current status of the joint task force activities. In addition, through the facilitated small group discussions, participants will be able to provide direct input to the development process. Session participants will also be encouraged to stay engaged with task force members after the SIGCSE special session.

6. SUITABILITY

This session will provide an opportune time for community engagement in this important curricular development process. The 2016 SIGCSE meeting will be held approximately 6 months after the task force has been launched. As such, task force members will have had sufficient opportunity to develop initial work products upon which community members will be able to offer constructive feedback. As an ACM-sponsored task force, the SIGCSE community represents a primary set of potential adopters of the guidance being developed. Participants are encouraged to review the following resources prior to the session:

- *The Future of Cybersecurity Education* in IEEE Computer - www.computer.org/csdl/mags/co/2014/08/mco2014080067-abs.html
- *Usable Cybersecurity: Human Factors in Cybersecurity Education Curricula* in the National Cybersecurity Institute Journal - www.excelsior.edu/static/journals/nci-journal/1-1/offline/download.pdf#page=5
- *Final Report: Workshop on Cybersecurity Education* - NSF, https://research.gwu.edu/sites/research.gwu.edu/files/downloads/CEW_FinalReport_040714.pdf
- *Toward Curricula Guidelines for Cybersecurity: Report of a Workshop on Cybersecurity Education and Training*, ACM - www.acm.org/education/TowardCurricularGuidelinesCybersec.pdf
- *Blueprint for a Science of Cybersecurity* in The Next Wave, Cornell University - www.cs.cornell.edu/fbs/publications/SoS.blueprint.pdf

7. REFERENCES

[1] McGettrick, A. 2013. Toward Curricular Guidelines for Cybersecurity. ACM.

[2] Hogan, M., & Newton, E. 2015. Report on Strategic U.S. Government Engagement in International Standardization to Achieve U.S. Objectives for Cybersecurity (draft). National Institute of Standards and Technology

[3] ACM Computer Science Curriculum 2013: Curriculum Guidelines for Undergraduate Degree Programs in Computer Science (Dec. 2013); doi: 10.1145/2534860

[4] Cyber Education Project. http://cybereducationproject.org/about/

Technology We Can't Live Without!, revisited

Daniel D. Garcia (moderator)
University of California, Berkeley
777 Soda Hall
Berkeley, CA 94720
+1 (510) 517-4041
ddgarcia@cs.berkeley.edu

Leslie Aaronson
Forshay Learning Center
3751 S. Harvard Blvd
Los Angeles, CA 90018
+1 (323) 854-6815
leslieaaronson01@gmail.com

Shawn Kenner
Sharon High School
181 Pond St.
Sharon, MA 02067
+1 (781) 784-1554
shawn5678 at gmail.com

Colleen Lewis
Harvey Mudd College
301 Platt Blvd.
Claremont, CA 91711
+1 (909) 607-0443
lewis@cs.hmc.edu

Susan Rodger
Duke University
Dept. of Computer Science
LSRC D237, Box 90129
Durham, NC 27708
rodger@cs.duke.edu

Keywords
Computer science education; technology and teaching

1. SUMMARY

The pace of technology for use in computing education is staggering. In the last few years, the following technologies have completely transformed our teaching: *Piazza*, *GradeScope*, *Google Docs*, *YouTube*, *Doodle* and *whenisgood.net*, *Skype* and *Google Hangout*, and *Khan Academy* among others. Hardware has also played a part – we love our *Zoom digital voice recorder* (for recording CD-quality lecture audio), *Blue Yeti USB mike* (for audio/videoconferences), and *iClickers* (for engaging students in class).

This panel is an outgrowth of a *Technology that Educators of Computing Hail (TECH)* Birds of a Feather session that we've held at SIGCSE for seven years, and the panel from SIGCSE 2015 [1] that served as a springboard for a regular column in ACM Inroads [2]. It will provide a chance for seasoned high school and university educators to show you the technologies that have "bubbled to the top" for them, and what key problems they solve. Like concert musicians, they will give live demonstrations and reveal the particular configuration options required to make their technology "sing". We hope this forum will allow the presenters to dive deeply into the common use cases of these technologies, highlight why they are invaluable, share any "gotchas" they've uncovered, and explain how others can adopt them at their institutions. The highlight of the panel is when the audience, inspired by the presentations, is invited to share their favorite "can't live without" technologies as well.

2. LESLIE AARONSON

I can't live without the free website authoring tools *Weebly* and *Wix* [3, 4]. I have taught high school students for three years at the Foshay Tech Academy in South Los Angeles. Every student starting in the 10th grade creates projects using Scratch, JavaScript, and HTML, and they need a portfolio to keep their work and make it available when they apply for jobs, programs, and scholarships. The students simply pick their authoring site and choose a template. If needed, the web-savvy kids can go in and fine-tune their sites by hand-coding HTML – it's easier in Weebly. At the end of the day, everyone else gets a free, professional-looking website that organizes their projects and makes them ready for any upcoming opportunity at a moment's notice. If they wish, they can purchase their own URL to transfer their data. It takes them from high school to college to career and keeps everything organized in one place. Students have remarked that they have been hired based on their portfolio alone!

The other tool I can't live without for classroom management is *Edmodo* [5]. It is a great way for me to keep track of student assignments, and for them to submit them to me. We can write comments to each other, and they can use it to track their grade in the class. It also has a library for me to upload resources that I can attach to assignments or add as a note. It connects to their Google Drive accounts and has a "backpack" in the cloud that allows them to safely save their work. Since discovering the tool, the students have stopped relying on Flash drives and have gotten better at file management. I can testify that students have improved their work based on conversations inside Edmodo.

3. SHAWN KENNER

If previous experience is any guide, then the app or website I fall in love with this year I don't even know about yet. Five years ago, moodle [6] and Poll Everywhere [7] were my essential go-to tools. More recently, *Socrative* [8], *EDpuzzle* [9] and *Kahoot!* [10] have been playing a larger role in my instruction and assessment strategies.

Socrative is terrific for quick bell-ringers, mid-unit formative assessments and even student surveys. With this easy-to-use website, I no longer need to drag out the bag of clickers; students can simply use their phones to respond to quizzes I've prepared in advance. At the conclusion of the assessment, I select how I want the results and am emailed a prepared PDF or spreadsheet.

SIGCSE '16, March 02-05, 2016, Memphis, TN, USA
ACM 978-1-4503-3685-7/16/03.
http://dx.doi.org/10.1145/2839509.2844668

While I tend to use Socrative in class, EDpuzzle is a great way to customize and personalize homework. It allows me to search for or upload relevant videos, trim them to any desired length, and add questions. I'm able to inspect students' answers before class, at which point I can comment directly and privately to individual students; for me, this is especially useful on constructed response items. The third tool, Kahoot!, should probably come with a warning sign; use of this whole-class quiz tool – where both accuracy and speed are rewarded – absolutely brings the house down. I use this site primarily for end-of-unit review. Many teachers have contributed quizzes to the site, making it easy to drag an existing Kahoot into my library where I can then make any edits appropriate for my own class.

Finally, are you using Shoutkey [11] or Google tone [12] yet? You must! These are two great tools for sharing websites with a class quickly. Shoutkey is a standard URL shortener, but instead of a gibberish URL, it cleverly produces a URL of the form `shoutkey.com/`***`EnglishWord`***, e.g., `shoutkey.com/eat`. When your students get used to it, you just have to say to them "shoutkey eat" and they know where to go. Google tone [10] is a Google Chrome add-on, has a similar purpose, but magically transfers URLs to the class through computer-generated tones.

4. COLLEEN LEWIS

I try to set boundaries with students. For example, I don't reply to email after 8:30pm. If I am up late working, I used to save emails as drafts and wait until the morning to send them. Now I use *Boomerang for Gmail* [13], which is integrated into *Gmail* [14] and allows me to pick a time that the email will be sent. I can write the email, click "Send Later" and easily *appear* consistent with the boundaries I have set.

I also try to stay organized and maintain my to-do list. However, I am consistently overly optimistic about what I can get done and these aspirational to-do items clutter up my (already packed) to-do list. Now I use *Any.do* [15], a to-do list app that runs on my computer and phone. Any.do has a category "Someday" where I can park my purely aspirational to-do items. It also makes it easy for me to go through all of the things I planned to do that day and set reminders (as well as to be realistic and push items to some future time, or into the "Someday" pit).

Finally, I try to schedule weekly meetings with my student researchers when everyone can attend. However, *Doodle* [16] polls to find a overlapping hour sometime in a 50-hour work week are unmanageable! Now I use *WhenIsGood* [17], a web tool to facilitate scheduling. It allows poll participants to "paint" over the times that they are available rather than clicking a radio button for each option. It is significantly easier to use than Doodle when there are many possible meeting times.

5. SUSAN RODGER

In teaching introductory programming with Python, I can't live without the online interactive python book "How to think like a computer scientist – interactive edition" [18], which is part of the *Runestone Interactive Project*. With this book I can demo code in lecture, and students can experiment with concepts in the book as they learn them. With a free account, it keeps track of what you have read and problems you have already answered. There are many other online interactive textbook platforms for hosting textbooks such as *OpenDSA* [19], which specializes in algorithm animations.

The second tool I can't live without is *Python Tutor* [20], which uses visualizations to help students form a mental model of how Python works (especially with lists, maps, and tracing how parameters work with functions). You can step through code and visualize the values of variables and data structures. A few more "can't live withouts" include reading quizzes on Sakai, Google forms and Piazza. With the reading quizzes I create on Sakai, I can assign reading and a reading quiz and have the reading quiz turn off when class starts. With growing enrollments I cannot live without Google forms and have a separate web page just for forms for students to request regrades, special accommodations, scheduling makeup exams, etc. We also use Google forms in class as a substitute to clickers.

6. REFERENCES

[1] Daniel D. Garcia, Eric Allatta, Manuel Pérez-Quiñones, and Jeff Solin. 2015. Technology We Can't Live Without!. In *Proceedings of the 46th ACM Technical Symposium on Computer Science Education (SIGCSE '15)*. ACM, New York, NY, USA, 597-598. DOI=10.1145/2676723.2677336 **`doi.acm.org/10.1145/2676723.2677336`**

[2] Daniel D. Garcia. 2015. TECH launch with Gradescope: exam grading will never be the same again!. *ACM Inroads 6*, 2 (May 2015), 82-83. **`doi.acm.org/10.1145/2747883`**

[3] weebly. *Create a Free Website or Blog*. **`www.weebly.com`**

[4] WIX.com. *Free Website* Builder. Aug. 2015. **`www.wix.com`**

[5] Moodle. *Open Source Software for Online Learning*. August 2015. **`moodle.com`**

[6] Poll Everywhere. August 2015. **`www.polleverywhere.com`**

[7] Edmodo. *Connect With Students and Parents in Your Paperless Classroom*. 2015. **`www.edmodo.com`**

[8] Socrative. August 2015. **`www.socrative.com`**

[9] EdPuzzle. August 2015. **`edpuzzle.com`**

[10] Kahoot. *Game Based Learning Platform*. **`getkahoot.com`**

[11] ShoutKey. August 2015. **`shoutkey.com`**

[12] Google tone. August 2015. **`g.co/tone`**

[13] Baydin. *Boomerang for Gmail*. August 2015. **`www.boomeranggmail.com`**.

[14] Google Inc. *Gmail*. August 2015. **`www.gmail.com`**

[15] Any Do. August 2015. **`www.any.do`**

[16] Doodle AG. *Doodle*. August 2015. **`doodle.com`**

[17] WhenIsGood. *When Is Good*. July 2015. **`whenisgood.net`**

[18] How to think like a computer scientist - Learning with Python - Interactive Edition 2.0, accessed August 25, 2015. **`interactivepython.org/runestone`**

[19] OpenDSA, May 2015. **`algoviz.org/opendsa`**

[20] Python Tutor. August 2015, **`www.pythontutor.com`**

igniteCS: Addressing Undergraduate CS Retention

Erin Mindell Cannon
(moderator)
Google
3300 N. Interstate 35
Austin, TX 78705
mindell@google.com

Priya Chawla
University of Cincinnati
1522 Ashbury Woods Dr.
Dayton, OH 45458
chawlapa@mail.uc.edu

Katherine Lo
University of California, Irvine
6210 Donald Bren Hall
Irvine, CA 92697-3425
kmlo@uci.edu

Haley Adams
Rhodes College graduate
27186 With Marlin Dr.
Orange Beach, AL 36561
haleytoadams@gmail.com

1. SUMMARY

Retention and attraction of undergraduate women in computer science has remained remarkably low over the past decade despite an increase in demand for computing jobs; fewer than 15% of the Bachelor's degrees in Computer Science and Computer Engineering in 2014 were earned by women [6]. In spring 2015, Google piloted a program, igniteCS, to address the retention problem in diverse student populations at the undergraduate level[1, 2, 4]. Using a near-peer model grounded in current research [3, 5], college students created programs to teach CS to middle and high school children, many of whom were also from underrepresented CS backgrounds. The college students were able to work toward a common goal and become mentors. Through voluntary pre-service, in-service, and post-service surveys, we found that the college mentors—of whom ~75% were from groups underrepresented in CS—were more interested in a CS career, felt more prepared for a CS career, felt more confident in their CS abilities, and were better able to make connections between CS and other interests after completing their mentoring program. Google funded ten Association for Computing Machinery-Women (ACM-W) chapters across the US and one in Puerto Rico, reaching more than 150 university students. This panel consists of students from three of the pilot schools.

2. ERIN MINDELL CANNON (moderator)

Erin is a program manager for Google's EngEDU team, where she helps develop quality education tools and resources to advance new approaches in computer science education. Erin developed the igniteCS project which is aimed at addressing critical retention issues at the undergraduate level. By collecting longitudinal data on igniteCS' current and future iterations, Google hopes to better understand the retention challenges facing underrepresented groups in computer science and find ways to tackle them directly. By understanding and collaborating with other effective interventions, Erin hopes to help build a holistic approach to attracting and retaining underrepresented students in CS at the undergraduate level. Other programs that Erin has led on the Google Education team in the past include Computer Science for High School (CS4HS), which provides professional development training program for k-12 teachers of computer science and Call to Code—a national coding competition for students in Ireland aged 13-18, which just finished its second year.

3. PRIYA CHAWLA

Priya founded and is serving as the President of the ACM-W chapter at UC, despite many roadblocks faced during its inception. Priya has been able to help grow the philanthropic and community initiatives at the university through collaborative partnerships.

In spring 2015, the ACM-W chapter used their igniteCS funding to create their own community service initiative to help a local area high school. Some of the challenges in creating a sustainable program included creating an inclusive volunteering program for all UC students, attracting volunteers, and enhancing the value of mentoring for students in underprivileged school districts. Through planning and coordination, her chapter initiated a program with Hughes STEM High School where they developed the Bearcat Coders program, which allows for UC to tap into their longstanding partnership with Hughes through the support of the UC Center of Community Engagement. Overall, the program was a success; the UC ACM-W chapter was awarded the "*International 2015 ACM Student Chapter Excellence Award for Outstanding Community Service*" and was the only ACM-W chapter and American chapter to receive and excellence award this year.

Currently, volunteers from UC tutor and mentor 9th-11th grade students at Hughes during their IT/CS programming and web development classes. Because of igniteCS mentoring, there has been an increase in retention of high school students in the IT/CS Pathway program. There has also been interest from some volunteer undergraduate students to switch into CS majors and minors.

4. KATHERINE LO

Katherine Lo is a doctoral student in Informatics at the University of California, Irvine. Her research examines the dominant narratives that motivate diversity initiatives in technology and how they are differently enacted in practice (e.g., scholarship programs, coding camps, student affinity groups). She serves as a graduate advisor to UC Irvine's Women in Information and Computer Sciences (WICS) undergraduate organization.

With WICS, Katherine led the development and execution of a three-week program of technology workshops at La Quinta High School in Garden Grove, CA. This program comprised two-hour workshops with primarily high school underclasswomen. WICS collaboratively designed a program that addressed occupational pathways, personal interest and accessibility. Workshops featured activities around exploring interdisciplinary career paths in technology, combined crafting and coding projects using Makey Makeys and Scratch, and an introduction to Python. Undergraduate students of WICS served as mentors and instructors during the workshops, with each undergraduate committing to a team of four to five high school girls.

WICS mentors took notes and collected extensive feedback throughout the workshop series from high school students' mentees. They met for one to two hours after each workshop to reflect on its execution, discuss challenges and failures, consider different forms of evaluation, and adjust curriculum as they

SIGCSE'16, March 2–5, 2016, Memphis, TN, USA.
ACM ISBN: 978-1-4503-3685-7/16/03.
DOI: http://dx.doi.org/10.1145/2839509.2844658

progressed. These sessions for reflection, combined with the extensive time dedicated to developing the workshops, provided ample opportunities for mentorship between graduate and undergraduate students and bolstered the sense of camaraderie and commitment within WICS.

Guidance for details of implementation beyond curriculum would be a valuable resource to assist students in programs like igniteCS. The most daunting obstacles of starting the workshops were balancing the time commitment limitations of undergraduate students with the time commitment required for a program that is impactful for the high school students, developing productive relationships with high school district facilitators and extensive administrative obligations.

In 2016, Katherine is facilitating two workshop series through igniteCS, the first at Kennedy High School in Richmond, CA with college students from UC Berkeley, Mills College, and Contra Costa Community College, the second at La Quinta High School in Garden Grove, CA, again with WICS. She will study how the programs can be situated differently to these communities, both of which are economically underserved and hold a high density of ethnic minorities.

5. HALEY ADAMS

Camp Codette was created to devise a dynamic educational program that would expose young women to the basics of computer science and inspire them to pursue it further. Haley and her team provided an array of activities that included working with Lego Mindstorm, Makey Makey, 3D printing, Scratch and App Builder. The camp was hosted for three one week sessions over summer recess on the campus of Rhodes College in Memphis, TN and was geared towards middle school girls. The program had tremendous success in maintaining engagement by varying instructional sessions and including outdoor activities. Mentors implemented a project-based approach, to encourage creativity and independence among participants.

As with any pilot program, Camp Codette faced unanticipated issues. Some students were not able to work with the prepared materials exactly as they were presented, which meant improvising. Other campers came from households without computers and were not able to continue practicing at home; these students were at a disadvantage due to limited computer access.

Camp Codette faces additional issues as it moves into its next iteration. It is currently only active during the summer. It will be necessary to maintain more continuous contact with the students, otherwise previous campers are liable to lose interest after time has passed. The transitory nature of the program also makes it difficult to track any tangible success.

It should be noted that this group was not economically diverse, perhaps because due to the enrollment fee and the need for private transportation to campus. Scholarships were available and to some extent utilized, but the low turnout of kids from low socio-economic backgrounds is telling. While making the program free might solve some issues, it would make it impossible for the camp to remain self-sustaining.

Opportunities like igniteCS are imperative to areas in the South that have a dearth of computer science education. The majority of students in these areas never realize what programming is or that it is a viable interest to pursue due to a complete lack of exposure. This becomes even more apparent for young women, who face more deterrents than just ignorance.

6. REFERENCES

[1] Alvarado, C., Dodds, Z. 2010. Women in cs: An evaluation of three promising practices. In *Proceedings of the 41st ACM Technical Symposium on Computer Science Education* (Milwaukee, March 10-13, 2010).

[2] Cohoon, J.M. 2001. Toward improving female retention in the computer science major. *Communications of the ACM.* 44, 5 (May 2001, 108-114).

[3] Horwitz, S., Rodger, S.H. 2009. Using peer-led team learning to increase participation and success of under-represented groups in introductory computer science. In *Proceedings of the 40th ACM Technical Symposium on Computer Science Education* (Chattanooga, March 4-7, 2009). DOI=10.1145/1508865.1508925.

[4] Krause, J., Polycarpou, I., Hellman, K. 2012. Exploring formal learning groups and their impact on recruitment of women in undergraduate cs. In *Proceedings of the 43rd ACM Technical Symposium on Computer Science Education* (Raleigh, February 29-March 3, 2012).

[5] Zaidman, M. 2011. Inspiring future female scientists. In *Frontiers in Education Conference* (Rapid City, Oct. 12-15, 2011). DOI=10.1109/FIE.2011.6142706.

[6] Zweben, S., Bizot, B. 2015. 2014 Taulbee survey: Relentless growth in undergraduate cs enrollment; doctoral degree production remains strong, but no new record. *Computing Research News*. 27, 5 (May 2015, 2-51).

Instructional Design is to Teaching as Software Engineering is to Programming

Austin Cory Bart and Clifford A. Shaffer
Virginia Tech
{acbart, shaffer}@vt.edu

Categories and Subject Descriptors

K.3.2 [**Computer and Information Science Education**]: Computer Science Education

Keywords

Instructional Design; Teaching; Software Engineering; Dick & Carey; Formal Methods

1. SUMMARY

This special session will explore practical results from the educational theory of Instructional Design (ID), with particular focus on the widespread similarities between a process for creating successful courses and a process for creating successful software. We present a small set of specific practices that should be easy for CS educators to adopt. In particular, the session will cover the popular Dick & Carey model, meant for beginners to ID. This model helps instructors rigorously define *who* they will teach to, *what* they will teach, *how* they will assess, and (only then) *how* they will teach. The approach is parallel to Software Engineering techniques such as Test-Driven Development, Requirements Engineering, and Iterative Development.

The session will be a blend of presentation, participation, and assessment. Participants will work in small groups both to foster discussion and to provide learning support. The content of the presentation will particularly focus on how the model can be applied practically. It is our hope that attendees, whether new to teaching or experienced, will adopt or be influenced by the model in order to approach their courses with the same rigor they apply to software development.

2. OBJECTIVE

Instructional Design is the iterative, systematic design of effective learning experiences by following a coherent process that gives measurable results. Its history stretches back into the 1930s [2], but there has been surprisingly few published cases of its use in Computer Science Education. Going the other way, there is a body of research on how Software Engineering techniques can be applied to ID [3, 4, 6]. Within CS, what little research that exists focuses on pedagogical tools and tactics [1, 5] rather than holistic, cohesive processes.

Figure 1 gives an overview of the phases of the Dick & Carey Model. Notice that the actual development and testing of instructional materials and strategy is saved for the final phases of the model, rather than the beginning. Instead, instructors begin by analyzing their "users" (the learners) and their instructional goals, then determine concrete objectives and measurements (tests), and finally focus on design and development. Similar to how Software Engineering does not dictate architecture but rather focuses on process, such as how to do documentation and testing, ID promotes process for things like documentation and organization over constricting your pedagogy. ID is compatible with other popular educational theories, including Constructivist Learning, Active Learning, and Collaborative Learning.

We will present a number of beneficial strategies with specific implementation recommendations, including:

Course Alignment (≈ Quality Management) ID leads to explicit definitions for learning objectives, assessments, and course activities, making it clear how components fit together.

Templated Instruction (≈ Design Patterns) Development of instructional strategy and material can be guided by templates.

Assessment Evaluation (≈ Unit Testing) Instructional faults can be pinpointed, and further isolated and resolved by using techniques such as Item Response Theory to increase the coverage and validity of the assessment instruments.

Course Documentation (≈ Design Documentation) Good instructional design practice is self documenting. Collaborators can be given more than the course materials. They can get instructional strategy, assessments, and the rationale behind the instruction.

This session will be organized as a blend of tutorial and hands-on, small-group exercise. We will introduce a new, practical educational theory to attendees, many of who may be unfamiliar with it. ID should resonate with instructors that have an engineering background and yearn for similar structure in their design of learning experiences.

SIGCSE '16, March 2–5, 2016, Memphis, TN, USA.
ACM ISBN 978-1-4503-3685-7/16/03.
DOI: http://dx.doi.org/10.1145/2839509.2844674

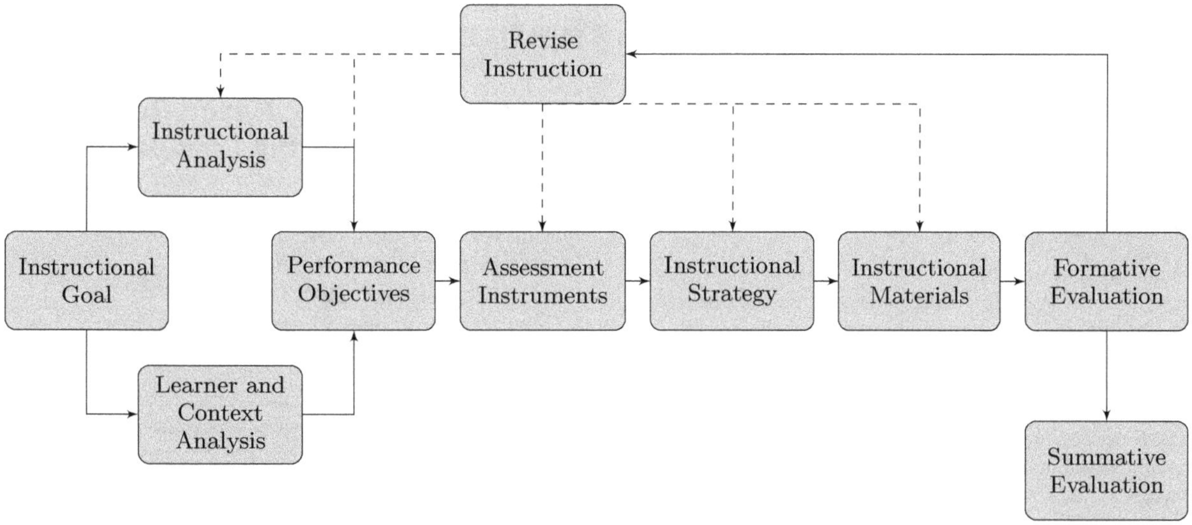

Figure 1: The Dick & Carey Model of Instructional Design

3. OUTLINE

Introduction: (15 minutes) Overview of the ID model, its pros and cons, and practical strategies for using it.

Case Study: (15 minutes) Walk through of the Dick & Carey model and our experiences using it.

Practice Problems: (20 minutes) Small group exercise. Attendees will get to apply the model to solidify their knowledge.

Post-Test: (15 minutes) Attendees will be given a brief, optional "post-test" to help them identify if they learned the material of the session.

Discussion: (10 minutes) Attendees will discuss how the model could be applied to their own classrooms, and their reaction to this special session.

4. EXPECTATIONS

The expected audience is computer science instructors, although anyone interested in educational theory should find the session useful. No prior experience with ID is expected. This session will cover an overview of the Dick & Carey model and demonstrate how it can be used in Computer Science classrooms at any grade level (K-12, undergraduate, etc.), any experience level, and any setting. We expect that instructors with prior knowledge of ID will also benefit from exposure to this concrete method.

The session will cover how instructors can get more information about the model, to promote long-term transfer of the material. Feedback will be solicited from attendees using a survey, and there will also be a pre- and post- assessment (both meant as a formative evaluation of the materials and to guide attendees' learning).

5. SUITABILITY FOR A SPECIAL SESSION

The presenters believe that this session is particularly suitable as a Special Session rather than a paper or panel because it requires hands-on experience and sufficient time to do so. Although a workshop would be a suitable alternative to this format, we suspect that few attendees will be sufficiently knowledgeable of Instructional Design to be willing to invest money in attending it. But we hope that after initial exposure, instructors will be motivated to learn more. The Special Session format allows us to provide the SIGCSE community with a low-stakes introduction to a powerful new technique that could revolutionize the way we design our lessons.

6. ACKNOWLEDGMENT

This material is based upon work supported by The National Science Foundation Graduate Research Fellowship, Grant No. DGE 0822220

7. REFERENCES

[1] D. Damian, A. Hadwin, and B. Al-Ani. Instructional design and assessment strategies for teaching global software development: A framework. In *Proceedings of the 28th International Conference on Software Engineering*, ICSE '06, pages 685–690, New York, NY, USA, 2006. ACM.

[2] W. Dick, L. Carey, and J. O. Carey. The systematic design of instruction. 2005.

[3] I. Douglas. Instructional design based on reusable learning objects: applying lessons of object-oriented software engineering to learning systems design. In *Frontiers in Education Conference, 2001. 31st Annual*, volume 3, pages F4E–1–5 vol.3, 2001.

[4] I. Douglas. Issues in software engineering of relevance to instructional design. *TechTrends*, 50(5):28–35, 2006.

[5] S. Hadjerrouit. Learner-centered web-based instruction in software engineering. *Education, IEEE Transactions on*, 48(1):99–104, Feb 2005.

[6] S. Tripp and B. Bichelmeyer. Rapid prototyping: An alternative instructional design strategy. *Educational Technology Research and Development*, 38(1):31–44, 1990.

Demonstrations

Creating and Grading IPython/Jupyter Notebook Assignments with NbGrader

Jessica B. Hamrick, *University of California, Berkeley*
Contact: jhamrick@berkeley.edu

Many courses in scientific fields require students not just to write code, but to also visualize their data, work through a mathematical derivation, or write a paragraph interpreting their results. The Jupyter notebook (formerly known as the IPython notebook) is an ideal platform for creating assignments that include all of these question types, due to its interactive document format that weaves together code, prose, images, and math. Instructors can provide students with self-contained notebooks that include instructions, coding exercises, and written responses all in the same place. Students can write and execute code in these notebooks, and any text or images produced by the code are displayed immediately beneath the input that produced them. However, while having all exercises in the same place makes for better assignments, it also makes them difficult to grade. This demo presents *nbgrader*, an open-source tool developed by the Jupyter project that solves this problem by providing an interface that blends the autograding of notebook-based assignments with manual human grading. Additionally, *nbgrader* streamlines the process of assignment creation, distribution, collection, grading, and feedback—a process that is often logistically difficult for instructors. To give students access to the notebook, this demo illustrates how it can be deployed in the cloud, and how this complements the grading process. Information about the Jupyter notebook can be found at http://jupyter.org/, and a demo of the notebook at https://try.jupyter.org/. Information about nbgrader can be found at https://github.com/jupyter/nbgrader. ***A laptop is recommended for this demo. Handouts will be provided.***

Keywords: autograding; Jupyter; IPython; notebook assignments

DOI: http://dx.doi.org/10.1145/2839509.2850507

CodeSnaps: Block-Based Robotic Programming for the Low-Budget Classroom

Jennifer Sabourin, *SAS Institute*
Lucy Kosturko, *SAS Institute*
Scott McQuiggan, *SAS Institute*
Contact: Jennifer.Sabourin@sas.com

Robotics and block-based languages have been growing in popularity as a way to introduce computer science topics to young audiences. This approach focuses on capturing interests by reducing the complexity required to learn to program. Unfortunately, many K-12 classrooms do not have the budgets necessary to provide each student with the technologies required by these approaches. As a solution, we developed CodeSnaps, a tool that provides an engaging coding experience for an entire classroom with minimal technology requirements. CodeSnaps brings the interest and simplicity of block-based robotic programming to any student in a classroom with at least one iPad and one Sphero Robot (www.sphero.com). With CodeSnaps, students can program at their desks independently or in groups using printable paper coding blocks similar to Blockly (developers.google.com/blockly). When their program is ready, students can "snap" their code (i.e., take a picture) with the iPad. The CodeSnaps app then translates their work to a digital version that is finally executed by Sphero. The CodeSnaps environment will also be freely available with the goal of reaching as many budding computer scientists as possible.

Keywords: Low-budget; block-based; robotics; K-12 education

DOI: http://dx.doi.org/10.1145/2839509.2850508

SIGCSE'16, March 2–5, 2016, Memphis, TN, USA.
ACM ISBN: 978-1-4503-3685-7/16/03.

The Sweep: Essential Examples for In-Flow Peer Review

Joe Gibbs Politz† Joseph M. Collard° Arjun Guha° Kathi Fisler‡ Shriram Krishnamurthi†
†Brown University °UMass Amherst ‡WPI
sk@cs.brown.edu

ABSTRACT

In in-flow peer review, students provide feedback to one another on intermediate artifacts on their way to a final submission. Prior work has studied examples and tests as a potentially useful initial artifact for review. Unfortunately, large test suites are onerous to produce and especially to review. We instead propose the notion of a *sweep*, an artificially constrained set of tests that illustrates common and interesting behavior. We present experimental data across several courses that show that sweeps have reasonable quality, and are also a good target for peer review; for example, students usually (over half the time) suggest new tests to one another in a review.

1. EXAMPLES, TESTS, AND PEER REVIEW

Testing is an integral skill for students to learn, and writing tests before writing code is a theme in both industrial programming and in educational contexts. Some pedagogies, like *How to Design Programs* [6], make writing a few example invocations of a function a required step in writing programs, with exhaustive tests added as the function is fleshed out. Others teach the more rigid protocol of test-*driven* development [1], where students must write a test for each incremental piece of functionality before implementing it.

Seemingly orthogonal to testing, peer review is another important skill for students to learn. In-flow peer review (IFPR) [3] is a contributing student pedagogy [8] that integrates peer (code) review into assignments with low overhead. In particular, IFPR assignments have students submit parts of their work early on to be used as artifacts for peer review. Students can then use the feedback from review to improve their work before the final submission.

Prior work has combined these software engineering skills, using tests as an initial artifact [10]. Tests are an especially good review artifact: they can be read relatively independent of each other; they describe only expected behavior, before having to identify an implementation strategy; and they force the author and reader to consider all of program's input and output space. Reviewers can point out both *correctness* mistakes that misunderstand problem behavior, and *thoroughness* issues that don't cover important cases. IFPR has been used as early as first-year college courses.

SIGCSE '16, March 02-05, 2016, Memphis, TN, USA
 ISBN 978-1-4503-3685-7/16/03. . . $15.00
DOI: http://dx.doi.org/10.1145/2839509.2844626

2. SUITES AND SWEEPS

Following this other research, we have been experimenting with IFPR in courses that use a test-first (but not test-driven) style of program development. Students are required to submit test suites for review. As test suites, they are expected to comprehensively cover the problem space. Students receive feedback from others well in time to use it for their final submissions.

Unfortunately, from conversations with students (and from numerous complaints filed with TAs), it quickly became apparent that writing and reviewing a complete test suite in isolation was quite a difficult task, for three main reasons.

- We wanted students to submit tests early—usually two days into a week-long assignment. This is very onerous, and many tests only become clear after students have done some implementation, which they usually have not yet begun.
- While in principle unit tests should be written independent of an implementation, in practice it is hard to write them without being able to check for at least basic properties like type-correctness and well-formedness of values.
- Most of all, students were encouraged (by our grading system: section 3) to write comprehensive test suites, resulting in suites with hundreds of tests. These were onerous to review, leading to low-quality reviews and disaffected students.

Consequently, we decided to focus the initial submissions on artifacts that could be both produced and reviewed in a short amount of time, while still containing useful content. Concretely, we instructed students to initially submit 5–10 interesting, representative examples, dubbed the *sweep*,[1] rather than a comprehensive suite. This unburdens students from covering an entire input space, and lets them focus on exploring the interesting parts of the problem. Rather than exhaustively testing the program, they are instead coming up with representative *examples* that illustrate (and check!) important features of the program's behavior.

It is worth noting that the sweep idea has independent value. API documentation needs small sets of carefully-chosen examples. Exploring a new library for the first time involves coming up with interesting examples inputs to try. Separating feature-critical, first-priority tests from more in-depth system tests is a useful software engineering skill. Thus, the idea behind the sweep shows up in many later, professional contexts.[2]

---

[1] "Sweep" is a term from archaeology for an area containing a non-comprehensive, but interesting, survey of artifacts (https://en.wikipedia.org/wiki/Archaeological_field_survey#Fieldwalking_.28transects.29). We have also heard the term used in geology, to refer to a similar overview sample of rocks.

[2] In this paper: *tests* refer to comprehensive suites; *examples* are

Eventually—with the final submission—students must construct a strong test suite, going beyond the sweep. Shifting the focus of peer review from test suites to sweeps raises several questions, which we explore in this paper:

- Are sweeps sophisticated enough to cover an interesting part of the problem space, or does their brevity inhibit their value?
- Do students all test the same cases in their sweeps?
- Are sweeps (nearly) as comprehensive as full test suites, so full test suites were somewhat unnecessary all along?
- Do students give useful review feedback on sweeps?
- Do students share ideas about tests when reviewing sweeps?
- Are sweeps so simple that students don't make any errors for reviewers to point out, removing a useful kind of feedback?

We proceed by first discussing some of the mechanics of sweep-based assignments, including assessing test cases and the workflow of review (section 3), and the data we collected for this study (section 4.1). We then examine the behavior of student sweeps and suites for thoroughness and correctness (section 4.2). Finally, we explore the students' reviewing activity when giving feedback on one another's sweeps (section 4.3).

3. ASSESSING SUITES AND SWEEPS

When testing is an explicit part of an assignment, it ought to be assessed. There are a number of metrics we could use to do this.

One is code coverage – how much of the student's implementation is covered when running the test cases? For example-first approaches, this metric doesn't make much sense because the tests are written independent of the student's implementation! Once the student finishes the problem, including an implementation, coverage could be used to assess their tests, so the sweep could be held in reserve until the end of the assignment and assessed then. Two problems remain: first, it is difficult for a student to predict whether a particular sweep would cover all paths in a final implementation since that is dependent on a yet-unknown structure, and second, the sweep doesn't necessarily cover all cases by design, so grading strictly based on code coverage could be unfair.

Another technique is to run students' tests against one another's implementations, and give points for bugs caught [5]. It becomes necessary to avoid double-counting bugs caught if students, say, copy tests with minor permutations. One solution is to only count the number of other student solutions caught, rather than the number of tests that catch them. Again, this requires waiting until the end of the assignment to assess the sweep.

In section 1, we hinted at two metrics for evaluating tests:

- *Correctness* – do they have the right input/output behavior?
- *Thoroughness* – do the tests cover the input space?

Thoroughness is distinct from code coverage. It measures how thoroughly the *problem input space* is covered, not one particular implementation. For example, a function that uses division could have tests with perfect code coverage that still lack thoroughness, because they don't trigger a possible divide-by-zero exception.

Given these two metrics, how do we apply them to particular student tests? One way to evaluate correctness is to run the tests against a correct reference implementation to check that they pass, which we call a *gold* implementation. The more tests passed, the better the correctness of the suite or sweep. To check thoroughness, we can run the tests against several incorrect implementations or *coals*, and check if the tests fail. If some test fails on a coal that didn't fail on the gold implementation, the we give the student credit for *detecting* that bad implementation. This gold/coal grading technique is useful for evaluating tests in general, and it is related to *mutation testing* [4], an existing technique in software engineering for ensuring the quality of a testing process.

When we introduced the sweep, students rightfully pointed out that it would be unfair to grade sweeps against the same standard as full test suites. To assess sweeps, we set some fraction of (often easier) coals as the number that needed to be caught for full credit on the sweep. The full set was used to assess final submissions.

Finally, human judgment is a useful way to assess tests: an expert can relatively quickly determine what problems could slip through a set of tests unobserved. In some testing cases, it's difficult to automate assessment with coals because the problem has multiple interacting pieces (so it's not clear what part to make the "coal"), or may involve visual components that aren't easy to automatically check. As a result, in some cases test cases were assessed manually by course staff, rather than through an automated process.

4. EFFECTIVENESS OF SWEEPS

The research questions in section 2 target the potential benefits of sweeps in peer review, as well as their potential limitations. Our formal analysis of those questions uses both quantitative and qualitative analyses: we use the gold/coal methodology outlined in section 3 to assess the correctness, thoroughness, and diversity of sweeps, and we manually analyze the content of reviews and review feedback to assess how students perceived the value of sweep-based peer review. Parts of these analyses explore sweeps independent of peer review, while others combine aspects of sweeps and peer review. Usually this will be clear from context, but we will also make this explicit where there might be doubt.

We intentionally do not attempt to compare peer review with sweeps to peer review with "full" test suites. A proper study of this form would require a controlled experiment, ideally with the same students doing sweeps on some assignments and not on others. The sweep arose because students found peer review with full test suites burdensome to the point that it was having adverse impacts on their experience in the course. Rather than (irresponsibly) prolong a bad pedagogic decision for the sake of a study, we instead chose to analyze sweeps on their own, letting our negative experience with the original model speak for itself.

4.1 Study Logistics

Courses and Population.

In this study, we use data collected from assignments in 3 courses across 2 institutions, both in the United States. Figure 1 summarizes the courses. CSPL is a programming languages course taught to sophomores through graduate students. CS1.5 is an accelerated introduction to data structures and algorithms for first-semester college students. CS2 is an introduction to data structures, algorithms, and object-oriented programming. The Assignments column lists the number of assignments per course that reviewed sweeps.

Assignment and Reviewing Workflow.

Assignment length varied from 4-5 days to two weeks, with most lasting one week. For week-long assignments, students submitted

exploratory checks, usually written before and independent of the implementation; and *sweeps* are small example suites meant to capture interesting behavior rather than acheive complete coverage.

Tag	Institution	Enrollment	Assignments
CSPL	I1	62	5
CS1.5	I1	60	7
CS2	I2	144	4

Figure 1: Courses with assignments involved in the study

sweeps by midnight on the second day. For example, an assignment released Friday and due the following Thursday midnight would have sweeps due by Sunday midnight. When assignment duration varied, the sweep deadline was roughly a third of the way through.

Students were explicitly instructed to submit 5-10 examples in the sweep. A single example was usually a single testing assertion (checking for two values being equal, for a predicate being true, etc.), but sometimes one logical example required multiple checks, so students submitted sweeps with more than 10 assertions.

All work was submitted through a Web interface that managed submissions, review assignment and authoring, and feedback. Upon submission, students were assigned other sweeps to review immediately if available, or put in a queue for review assignment if not. Sweeps were assigned to students until they had been reviewed 3 times each, and each student received 3 sweeps to review (TAs could fill in reviews for the last few submissions if needed).

Reviews followed a rubric that varied across courses and the semester, but asked roughly the same 3 questions:

- Are the tests correct?
- Do the tests cover an important and interesting set of cases?
- What did you like about the tests?

Students could browse code and mark incorrect tests with inline comments describing what was wrong, and give freeform feedback on the other questions. There were also Likert scales provided to quantitatively report on correctness and thoroughness.

Students could give two kinds of feedback on the review process. First, they could provide feedback on the helpfulness of individual reviews, including flagging them for inappropriate content (students didn't flag any reviews as hostile, though they did flag some for having negligible content). Then, after each assignment, students could fill out a survey indicating what changes they made both as a result of reviews they received and other sweeps they saw. Both kinds of feedback were visible only to the course staff.

Reviews *did not* count towards students' grades. The software we used wouldn't let students move on to their final submission without completing reviews, so they had to provide some content in the review form. We sent some messages via email (outside the system) to students who submitted reviews late to remind them of the review deadline, but this did not negatively affect their grade. Our experience thus reflects students' review habits unmotivated by any particular grading structure for them.

Altogether, students submitted around 1106 sweeps and 1975 reviews across the 16 sweep-based assignments. The rest of this section examines different parts of that corpus, starting with the sweeps themselves, before exploring the reviews.

4.2 Sweep Characteristics

We begin by analyzing the quality of sweeps themselves. For peer review to be valuable pedagogically, the artifacts to review need to contain issues for students to comment on, be deep enough

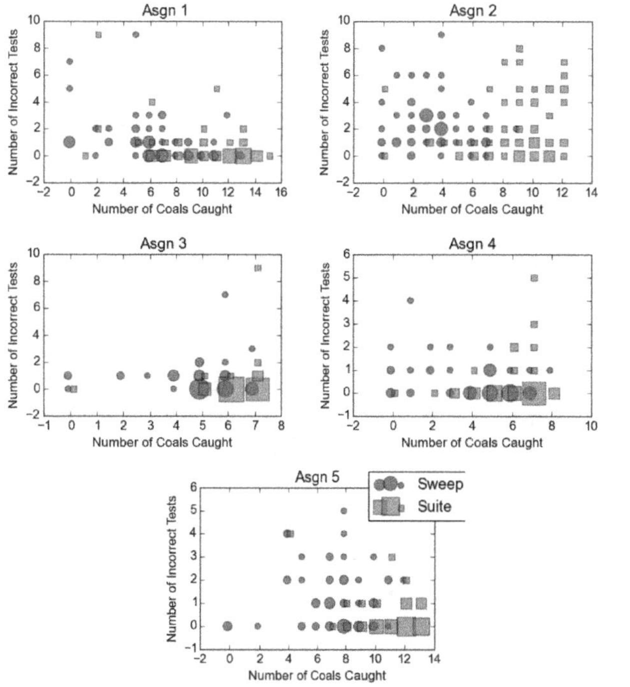

Figure 2: Sweep and suite test assessment

for students to find value in reading them, and be diverse enough that students don't all submit the same thing.

We limit our quantitative analysis (Section 4.2.1 and section 4.2.2) to assignments from CSPL, which had the most readily automatable gold/coal infrastructure. Our qualitative analysis (section 4.3) addresses peer review data from all courses.

4.2.1 Sweep Thoroughness and Correctness

CSPL staff wrote 6-16 coals for each assignment, depending on the complexity of the assignment and its amenability to coal implementation. The coals were intentionally designed to span a range of difficulty, with some containing obvious errors in simple base cases, and the hardest having subtle bugs in specific circumstances. Thus, we expected students to initially catch some easy coals, and eventually build a thorough suite to detect most or all of them.

Figure 2 summarizes both thoroughness and correctness of both sweeps and students' final test suites, with one plot for each assignment. Circles indicate sweep counts, and squares indicate final suite counts. Larger (proportionally) dots indicate more submissions were assessed with the values at that particular point. The x-axis shows the number of coals caught, so dots further to the right indicate more broad sets of tests. The y-axis shows the number of *incorrect* test cases, so dots closer to the bottom indicate more correct sets of tests. Thus, submissions at the bottom right do as well as possible by this metric, and those at the top left are the worst.

In these plots, we are most interested in whether sweeps contain errors (for reviewers to comment on) and cover multiple coals (suggesting depth in the sweeps, even though they should not be comprehensive by design). The plots largely show both in each assignment. We include the data on the final test suites to show that students' work progresses significantly beyond the sweeps, as one would hope. That final suites cover more coals and converge

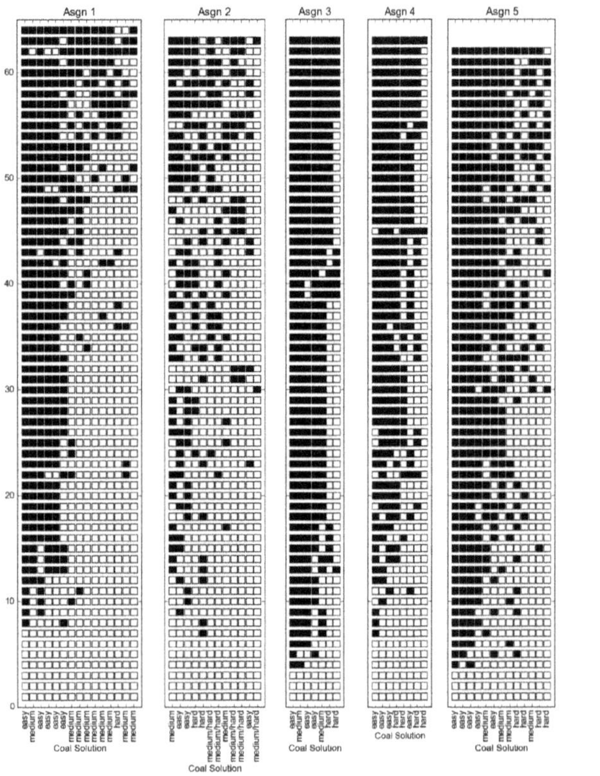

■/□ – Coal caught/not caught by sweep (each row is a sweep submission)

Figure 3: Sweep variety measured by coal detection

on the lower right is neither surprising nor interesting. Comparing numbers of incorrect tests across sweeps and suites is tricky, given that the number of examples is limited in sweeps but not in suites. Overall, these data suggest that sweeps are sufficiently deep and error-prone that they are worthy of peer review.

4.2.2 *Sweep Diversity*

Next we explore whether sweeps are *diverse* enough across students to enable valuable peer review. We measure diversity as the distribution of coals detected by sweeps for the same assignment. The sweeps that caught each coal are shown for the same five assignments in figure 3. In each plot, rows represent submissions and columns represent coals. A square is filled if the sweep caught the coal, and empty if not. The submissions are ordered decreasing from top to bottom by number of coals detected, and coals are ordered decreasing from left to right by total number of students detecting each. The labels on the columns indicate the course staff's intent (before running anything) of how difficult each coal would be to detect. The layout allows us to observe a few things at a glance:

- In all 5 assignments, all coals were caught by some sweep, including the intentionally difficult ones. So students' sweeps cover the breadth of coals designed for assessment.
- In all assignments, there are some coals that are commonly caught by sweeps, and some that aren't. For example, the last "hard" coal on assignment 4 is caught by very few sweeps, while the first "easy" coal is caught by most.

Assignment	In	Out	Assignment	In	Out
CSPL/3	47	15	CS1.5/A	35	25
CSPL/4	41	21	CS1.5/B	39	21
CSPL/5	40	22	CS1.5/C	38	22
			CS1.5/D	37	23
CSPL/All	37	12	CS1.5/All	19	8
CSPL/Once	50	25	CS1.5/Once	52	41

Assignment numbers for CSPL are the same as in figure 2 and 3. Assignments 1 and 2 in CSPL did not allow students to opt out.

Figure 4: Student choice in assignments with opt-out

- All assignments show some variety in the sweeps as measured by coal, with some exhibiting much more than others. Assignments 3 and 4 show particularly little variety, and 1, 2, and 5 show more. We note that assignments 3 and 4 are also the assignments with fewer coals (the instructional staff reported that those problems were trickier to design interesting coals for). In these cases, we may be seeing the lack of diversity in coals more than the lack of variety in sweeps.

This analysis shows one measure of variety between sweeps, which is the different behaviors they exercise across coal solutions. There may be others; for example, the sweeps may use a different test structure or style that affords greater clarity, or they may detect the same coals with a more concise set of tests. However, just by the metric of coal detection, we see interesting variety across students in these assignments, which is a promising indicator of the value, in terms of test diversity, students could get when seeing one another's submissions during review.

4.3 Peer Review of Sweeps

Our quantitative analysis suggests that sweeps are artifacts worthy of peer-review: they have interesting content, they contain mistakes, and they provide a space of differences among students. We now turn to more qualitative analyses to determine whether sweeps are useful review artifacts in practice. We explore both students' impressions of sweep-based peer review and the content of the reviews themselves, checking whether students provide actionable recommendations in their reviews.

4.3.1 *Student Opinion and Engagement*

Since the semester for CSPL started with a non-sweep version of assignments, and we switched styles in part to respond to student feedback, we surveyed the students in that class to find out if they found the sweep helpful. We asked: *Since switching to the sweep (the new style of test submission), review has been helpful when I've participated, whether receiving or writing reviews.* 37 of 62 students responded, with 5 strongly agreeing, 17 agreeing, 10 slightly agreeing, 3 slightly disagreeing, and only 1 each disagreeing and strongly disagreeing. We took this as positive feedback that students were at least *perceiving* value from the process.

In addition, in both CSPL and CS1.5, students were given the option of opting out of sweep-based peer review a few assignments into the semester. This was mainly in response to concerns about the time burden of peer review. As a result, students could choose at sweep submission time on each assignment whether or not to participate in review. Students who opted out of review still had to

	CS1.5		CSPL		CS2		α
LGTM	16.8%	(74)	24.8%	(71)	45.4%	(163)	*
ERR	38.3%	(169)	20.3%	(58)	18.9%	(68)	.81
SPEC	33.6%	(148)	14.0%	(40)	12.5%	(45)	.55
TEST	58.0%	(256)	64.0%	(183)	42.1%	(151)	.88
NEG	1.4%	(6)	0.0%	(0)	2.2%	(8)	.00
TIP	28.6%	(126)	9.8%	(28)	11.1%	(40)	.72
REV	4.5%	(20)	4.5%	(13)	2.2%	(8)	.85
POS0	11.3%	(50)	23.1%	(66)	30.9%	(111)	.37
POS1	63.7%	(281)	62.6%	(179)	54.9%	(197)	
POS2	24.9%	(110)	14.3%	(41)	14.2%	(51)	

Figure 5: Results of coding reviews of sweeps

submit a sweep—because of our use of example-first programming practices—which was graded against the same standards; they only did not receive or provide reviews.

The results for students opting in are shown in figure 4. Between 30 and 40% of students opted out of review, which was roughly constant across both courses. Perhaps more remarkable is that 60–70% of students voluntarily participated in doing the extra work of peer review, which we believe argues for the (perceived) value of this process. The "All" row shows how many students made the choice to opt in or out consistently across all assignments, and "Once" shows how many students made the choice at least once. By this metric, in CSPL students were much more consistent with their choices than in CS1.5. We do not have a clear explanation for the difference between the two; in part it may just be that across four assignments in CS1.5 there was more opportunity for churn.

We do know that some students simply did not want to bother with an extra step in assignments, and were happy with their achievement already. It is tempting to believe that allowing students who aren't engaged to opt out may improve the reviews of all those who were motivated to participate. However, review improvement from opt-out isn't inevitable, as the students who opt out could actually the best reviewers, and removing them from the review pool would reduce the overall quality of review. For example, it's worth noting that CSPL has a more uniform cross-section of that department's population, while CS1.5 consists of students who placed into the accelerated course, and are thus more likely to view themselves as "hot shots". We leave the effects of student attitudes like these on review participation and quality for a future study.

4.3.2 Review Content Analysis

We manually analyzed a random sample of 1088 reviews from all the courses. Reviews can be valuable in many ways: they can point to errors in understanding the problem, suggest additional (concrete) examples, suggest changes to code style, or provide encouragement. Sometimes, reviewers gain insight from the work they are reviewing. In contrast, reviews that offer only cursory comments or are hostile devalue peer review. Our analysis looked for these positive and negative traits in reviews of sweeps.

A Rubric for Evaluating Reviews.

We developed a category-based rubric for coding reviews, iteratively checking inter-coder reliability and refining the categories. We settled on seven categories, which we summarize here:

- **(ERR) Identified (Potential) Mistake** – Did the reviewer claim to identify a programming mistake or incorrect testt?
- **(SPEC) Discussed or Disputed Problem Specification** – Did the reviewer remind the reviewee of correct behavior or point out an incorrect input/output pair? This can, but doesn't necessarily, overlap with ERR.
- **(TEST) Suggested Additional Test(s)/Identified Untested Feature** – Did the reviewer point out a specific gap in the thoroughness of the tests?
- **(POS) Complimentary/Positive (Scale of 0-2)** – Did the reviewer have specific praise for (parts of) the sweep?
- **(NEG) Hostile/Negative** – Was the review unnecessarily sarcastic, or blatantly hostile?
- **(TIP) Coding or Style Tip/Test Structure Comment** – Did the review give advice unrelated to the sweep or problem specification, like a coding trick or advice on test structure?
- **(REV) Reviewer Gained/Confirmed Understanding** – Did the reviewer indicate that they learned from performing the review, or confirm their own understanding?

Data Assessment and Rubric Agreement.

Figure 5 summarizes the results across the sample for these rubric categories, except for the the LGTM row, which we explain shortly. The last column reports Krippendorff's α calculated per category across 3 coders (each involved in at least one of the study courses) on 200 samples. Under this measure, strong agreement occurs at .8 and above, with tentative agreement above .67. As POS is scalar, its α score is aggregated in the row for POS0. When there was disagreement between coders in the 200 samples used for reliability testing, we counted the coding chosen by two of three coders.

The α column shows strong inter-coder agreement on three categories and no agreement on SPEC, POS, and NEG. We suspect that the low agreement on SPEC arose because the coders were not experts on all the assignments being coded; deciding if particular comments were about the assignment itself was very difficult. The POS category was highly subjective: coders had difficulty agreeing on the degree of positive tone in reviews. The NEG category has a 0 alpha score because there was only one case of a negative review labelled in the overlap, and the coders disagreed.

Observations on the Reviews.

The most common feature of reviews was a suggestion of a new test (category TEST): this happens in over half the reviews we sampled. Since sweeps are not comprehensive by design, we should expect that students *could* identify additional tests to suggest. This figure shows that students *do* share testing ideas through reviews. In addition, if we take a somewhat naïve understanding of the percentages in the categories and assume they happen uniformly, we could predict that roughly half of reviews will suggest a test to a student. That means that a student receiving just 2 reviews on a sweep ought to get some benefit (we have not analyzed this hypothesis).

The second most common feature is a reviewer claiming to identify out some kind of error (category ERR), whether a programming mistake or an input/output misunderstanding. This happened more rarely than suggesting an additional test, which could be for a number of reasons: errors are rarer because sweeps are short, or errors are simply harder to find than additional tests are to suggest (especially given the diversity of sweeps across students). Again, if we take a naïve interpretation, a student receiving 3 reviews ought to expect to get an error reported most of the time (this is more clearly naïve than for additional tests, since students with no errors in their sweeps ought to not have errors pointed out to them). Nevertheless, any identification of purported errors is clear evidence of students attempting to perform a conscientious job of reviewing.

We gauged how often students received cursory (largely content-free but non-empty) reviews through an LGTM[3] category which we computed from categories in the rubric. We labelled a review LGTM if it had no other high-reliability category selected (we ignore SPEC, POS, and NEG since they aren't reliable). Since fewer than half the reviews are LGTM by our measure, this suggests that students getting multiple reviews are likely to get *some* non-vacuous feedback from peer review of their sweep.

There are other interesting observations across courses. First, the ordering of percentages are the same in all three courses—TEST, ERR, SPEC, TIP, REV, NEG—suggesting some cross-course consistency. In contrast, the magnitudes of the different categories differ quite a bit between courses. CS2 has the highest LGTM percentage and lowest percentage across the other categories. CS2 had a few major differences from the other two courses in the study that we could conjecture as explanations for the higher rate of LGTM reviews, and use as hypotheses in future studies. It (a) was a mandadory course, (b) had largest enrollment, and (c) didn't provide students with an opt-out for peer review. Finally, if we take these categories as indications of review utility, CS1.5 had the most useful reviews, which would fit an understanding that matches student motivation to review performance–CS1.5 is an advanced introductory course with prerequisite programming exercises required to enter. Further studies are required to probe at these questions of class size, review options, and motivation.

5. RELATED WORK

Testing and peer code review are well-studied topics in computer science education; we focus on work that emphasizes both, or is especially related to the example-driven style of the sweep.

Buffardi and Edwards study automated, rather than peer-written, feedback on test cases [2]. The feedback was different in three main ways: the style was test-driven, with students encouraged to maintain complete code coverage; the feedback took the form of hints on students' *solutions*, rather than tests; and the feedback was *earned* by submitting good tests. On different assignment styles (or at different stages of the same assignment), the two approaches could be complimentary.

Kulkarni, et al. study the impact of early exposure to examples in creative work, specifically drawings [9]. While their work is not programming-related, the sweep has similar goals in exposing students to diverse examples early on in the assignment process. Their work finds that when exposed to a variety of examples early on, subjects produced more varied final results in their own work, which is related to students suggesting new test ideas during review.

Smith, et al. don't do test-first programming, but do have students test one another's implementations [12]. Similarly, Reily, et al. use test cases as part of a code review feedback rubric [11]. These are different in that students are specifically testing an implementation, but similar in that tests and reviews are closely linked. A test in their workflows is a concrete piece of feedback that can be used to reproduce bugs in the other student's submission. Our process emphasizes generating ideas and understanding of a shared problem specification, while theirs is targeted at feedback on robustness and bug-finding in an existing implementation.

Gaspar, et al. report on Peer Testing, where students share test suites but do not review them [7], which was positively received by students. Since students do not produce reviews, the value comes from sharing tests, a value present in sweep-based assignments as well. This corresponds to the REV category in our coding rubric, where reviewers indicated that they learned something.

[3]An abbreviation for "Looks good to me". In some settings, it describes lazy reviews that do not indicate whether or not the reviewer actually analyzed the submission.

Acknowledgments.

This work is partially supported by the US National Science Foundation. We thank courses' staffs, especially Justin Pombrio.

Bibliography

[1] Kevin Buffardi and Stephen H. Edwards. Impacts of Teaching Test-Driven Development to Novice Programmers. *International Journal of Information and Computer Science*, 2012.

[2] Kevin Buffardi and Stephen H. Edwards. Impacts of Adaptive Feedback on Teaching Test-Driven Development. In *Proc. Special Interest Group on Computer Science Education*, 2013.

[3] Dave Clarke, Tony Clear, Kathi Fisler, Matthias Hauswirth, Shriram Krishnamurthi, Joe Gibbs Politz, Ville Tirronen, and Tobias Wrigstad. In-flow Peer Review. In *Proc. Innovation and Technology in Computer Science Education*, 2014.

[4] Richard A. DeMillo, Richard J. Lipton, and Fred G. Sayward. Hints on test data selection: Help for the practicing programmer. *IEE Computer*, 1978.

[5] Stephen H. Edwards, Zalia Shams, Michael Cogswell, and Robert C. Senkbeil. Running students' software tests against each others' code: New life for an old "gimmick". In *Proc. Special Interest Group on Computer Science Education*, 2012.

[6] Matthias Felleisen, Robert Bruce Findler, Matthew Flatt, and Shriram Krishnamurthi. How to Design Programs. MIT Press, 2002.

[7] Alessio Gaspar, Sarah Langevin, Naomi Boyer, and Ralph Tindell. A Preliminary Review of Undergraduate Programming Students' Perspectives on Writing Tests, Working with Others, & Using Peer Testing. In *Proc. Special Interest Group on Information Technology Education*, 2013.

[8] John Hamer, Quintin Cutts, Jana Jackova, Andrew Luxton-Reilly, Robert McCartney, Helen Purchase, Charles Riedesel, Mara Saeli, Kate Sanders, and Judithe Sheard. Contributing Student Pedagogy. *SIGCSE Bulletin* 40(4), pp. 194–212, 2008.

[9] Chinmay Kulkarni, Steven P. Dow, and Scott R Klemmer. Early and Repeated Exposure to Examples Improves Creative Work. In *Proc. Design Thinking Research*, 2014.

[10] Joe Gibbs Politz, Shriram Krishnamurthi, and Kathi Fisler. In-flow Peer Review of Tests in Test-First Programming. In *Proc. International Computing Education Research*, 2014.

[11] Ken Reily, Pam Ludford Finnerty, and Loren Terveen. Two peers are better than one: Aggregating peer reviews for computing assignments is surprisingly accurate. In *Proc. ACM International Conference on Supporting Group Work*, 2009.

[12] Joanna Smith, Joe Tessler, Elliot Kramer, and Calvin Lin. Using Peer Review to Teach Software Testing. In *Proc. International Computing Education Research*, 2012.

The Effects of Peer- and Self-assessment on the Assessors

Joonsuk Park
Cornell University
Ithaca, NY
jpark@cs.cornell.edu

Kimberley Williams
Cornell University
Ithaca, NY
kw299@cornell.edu

ABSTRACT

Recently, there has been a growing interest in peer- and self-assessment (PSA) in the research community, especially with the development of massive open online courses (MOOCs). One prevalent theme in the literature is the consideration of PSA as a partial or full replacement for traditional assessments performed by the instructor. And since the traditional role of the students in assessment processes is the assessee, existing works on PSA typically focus on devising methods to make the grades more reliable and beneficial for the assessees.

What has been missing in the picture is the *assessor*: How are those conducting peer- and self-assessment impacted by the process? This question has become relevant from educational perspective, because in PSA, the students take on the role of the assessor, as well.

We present PSA as an active learning exercise for the assessors and examine its impact. For this, we incorporated PSA into a university-level Introduction to Natural Language Processing (NLP) course consisting of more than 100 students and analyzed student surveys and exam results of peer-, self-, and no-assessment groups. The final exam performance suggests that PSA is helpful for learning, which is consistent with the student survey results. Also, students generally enjoyed conducting PSA.

Keywords

Active Learning; Peer-assessment; Self-assessment

1. INTRODUCTION

Assessing the quality of student work, whether summative or formative, has long been a core element in most classes. It serves as feedback for both students and instructors, with the following potential uses, among others: Students can distinguish concepts they understand well from those with whch they are less familiar and allot their time accordingly. Also, course instructors can gain a better estimate of the level of understanding in their students, which can be valuable when adjusting the content or the structure of the current or future classes to better accommodate the students' needs.

Conducting assessments, however, can be labor intensive. This is especially the case for Massive Open Online Courses (MOOCs), in which a handful of staff[1] has to support tens of thousands of students. The need for a scalable means of performing assessments has led to an active research on peer- and self-assessment (PSA), the act of providing grades and feedback on peers' and his or her own work [16, 17]. Because existing works on PSA typically focuses on how PSA would partially or fully replace traditional assessment methods, they tend to examine the benefits for the assessees, and methods to achieve reliable grades [9, 12].

While an immediate goal of assessments is evaluating the quality of student work, performing assessments has additional benefits of promoting learning in the assessor. Though several researchers have reported the benefits of PSA for the assessor, this is still an understudied aspect of PSA with a limited number of studies based on rigorous experiments [15, 7, 3, 14].

A more systematic study is necessary to better understand the impact of PSA on the assessors. This will allow the instructors to decide the time and resources that should be reserved for PSA in their courses. Also, positive findings will motivate the students to perform assessments more carefully, which can benefit both the assessees and the assessors [18].

In this paper, we detail our effort to analyze the effects of PSA on the assessors. Specifically, we compare the exam performance of more than 100 students after they conduct peer-, self-, and no-assessment in a semester long course on natural language processing (NLP). In addition, we analyze student surveys on PSA. The final exam performance suggests that PSA is helpful for learning, which is consistent with the survey in which students reported that they found PSA beneficial. Also, students generally enjoyed conducting PSA.

2. RELATED WORK

PSA or peer-assessment without self-assessment has been studied in many domains, including more open-ended ones like writing [4] and oral presentation [8], as well as more objective ones like computer programming [14] and algorithms [3]. In this project, PSA was conducted on problem sets consisting of conceptual and computational ques-

[1]"staff" refers to the instructors and teaching assistants.

SIGCSE '16, March 02-05, 2016, Memphis, TN, USA
© 2016 ACM. ISBN 978-1-4503-3685-7/16/03...$15.00
DOI: http://dx.doi.org/10.1145/2839509.2844602

tions requiring knowledge in linguistics and probability theory. The questions are quite objective in that the questions mostly had definite answers, though multiple approaches may be possible depending on the question.

Different researchers are concerned with different aspects of PSA. For instance, Bauer et al. study how students feel about online vs in-person assessment [1]. With the advent of MOOCs, where the size of staff is significantly smaller than that of the students, research efforts have focused on ways to acquire reliable grades from peers [9, 12]. Also, many have concentrated on the impact of PSA on the assessees [10]. Some have reported that the assessors benefit from PSA, as well [18]. However, not many systematic studies have been conducted to analyze how the assessors are affected as this project does.

The work by Chinn is one of the few works that look at PSA from the perspective of the assessors [3]. Chinn reports that the quality of peer-assessment and exam performance are correlated, though the direction of causality cannot be determined. In this project, we do not take the quality of assessments into consideration. This is because we are interested in the impact of PSA regardless of the assessors' levels of understanding, which is one of the factors influencing the quality of assessments.

By viewing PSA from the perspective of the assessors, we are effectively treating PSA as an active learning exercise for the assessors. Novel active learning strategies are often developed for classroom settings, where the goal is to make the traditional lecture style classes more active and engaging for the students [2, 11, 13]. Our implementation of PSA, however, takes place *outside* the classroom and thus is complementary to the active learning activities performed in classrooms.

3. METHODOLOGY

3.1 Overview

This work is based on experiments and observations made in a university-level Introduction to Natural Language Processing course. There were over 100 students enrolled, where the majority of them were junior and senior level undergraduate and master's students, mostly majoring in Computer Science.

The experiment consisted of two cycles of problem set, PSA, and survey, followed by the final exam. The problem sets and the final exam covered topics as shown in Table 1. Note that the final exam also covered topics that were not covered in the problem sets, such as those covered in programming projects. These, however, are not mentioned in the table, as they are not part of the experiment.

Of the 103 students who completed the course, 94 students completed PSA for both problem set 1 and 2, and their final exam performance is used for the quantitative analysis in Section 4. Also, 67 students completed the survey after performing PSA for problem set 1, and 71 after performing PSA for problem set 2.

3.2 Experiment Components

Problem Set. The students individually completed problem sets, each consisting of problems covering three topics that later appeared in the exam. The questions were designed to be as objective and clear as possible, involving concepts mostly from linguistics and probability. However, because the subject involves language and real world applications which are inherently subjective and open-ended, the questions still had room for variations in approach.

Topic	Problem Set 1	Problem Set 2	Final Exam
LM	o		o
POS	o		o
WSD	o		o
CD		o	o
(P)CFG		o	o
Parsing		o	o

Table 1: Topics Covered in Problem Sets and Exams

*LM : Language Models, POS : Part-of-Speech Tagging, WSD : Word Sense Disambiguation, CD : Computational Discourse, (P)CFG : (Probabilistic) Context-Free Grammar, Parsing : Syntactic Parsing.

The grade was broken down with an intention to motivate the students to perform PSA with more care: The peer- and self-assessments students conducted were graded by the staff for an extrinsic motivation to get good grades, and the peer-assessment results were accounted for the peers' grades for an intrinsic motivation to be fair as assessors. Numerically, 10% of the grade is based on the quality of PSA, judged by the staff, and the remaining 90% on the solutions to the problem set—81% is from the staff's grade, and 9% is from the average of peer-assessment grades.

Peer- and Self-assessment. The students performed double-blinded PSA on problem set submissions using a solution manual and a brief grading rubric provided for them soon after the problem set deadline. For each question being assessed, the students were to give a numeric score and written feedback.

In order to compare the effects of peer-, self-, and no-assessment on the exam performances, we needed to have students perform different types of assessment on the problem set submissions. One approach we considered was to split students into three groups, each with a designated type of assessment. This approach, however, couples assessment types and individuals too tightly: Even if a statistically significant difference is observed in the final exam performance among the groups, it would not be distinguishable whether it is caused by the effectiveness of the assessment methods or the abilities of the students who happened to be assigned to the groups. Also, the students in the peer-assessment group would have to do much more work than those in other groups. Similarly, as the difficulty of the topics could vary, we did not want to assign specific assessment type for each topic.

To minimize the impact of the variations in student abilities and topic difficulties on the experiment results, we set up PSA in a way that decouples individuals and topics from the assessment types: Each student was assigned to a group with a designated topic to peer-assess (6 peers' work) and another topic to self-assess, leaving the remaining topic for no-assessment. For instance, students in PSA Group 1 for problem set 1 peer-assessed LM questions for 6 peers, self-graded POS questions and did no-assessment for WSD questions.

While the assignment to the groups was done randomly,

the number of students in each group was kept as uniform as possible. This means that for each topic, there were roughly the same number of students performing each type of assessment. Under this setup, the exam result for each student-topic pair is associated with a single assessment type, and the final exam results can be clustered by the assessment type. This way, each student contributes to all three assessment types evenly, and so does each topic, minimizing the impact of the variations in student abilities and topic difficulties on the experiment results. In analysis, each score is divided by the best student score instead of the maximum possible score to partially control for the variations in topic difficulties.

Survey. After completing PSA, the students filled out a post PSA survey. Participating in a survey was one of many ways, such as contributing to in-class or online forum discussions, to earn 5% participation points for the course. As it was largely voluntary, roughly 30% of students neglected to participate in the survey, as mentioned in the beginning of this section.

Most questions were 5-level Likert items, where a statement is presented and the respondent selects from one of five choices ranging from *Strongly Disagree* to *Strongly Agree.* Here are the question prompts presented :

1. *Grader X's grades are fair.* and *Grader X's feedback is helpful.* for each of the 6 peer assessors that assessed the given respondent's problem set.
2. *My grades are fair.* and *My feedback should be helpful.*
3. *Performing PSA helped me learn the materials better*
4. *Knowing my peers' level of understanding gave me more confidence*
5. *Performing PSA was beneficial overall.*
6. *I self-assessed every question, regardless of the PSA assignment.*

Items 1 and 2 were presented to compare the peer- and self-reported quality of the assessments, items 3 - 5 were presented to measure the benefits of PSA, and item 6 was presented to determine how PSA was executed in real life.[2]

In addition to these Likert items, there were short questions asking for reasons for their choices on Likert items, as well as any comments about their experience and opinions about PSA.

Exam. After completing two cycles of problem set, PSA, and survey, students took the final exam. For each student, the grade with respect to each topic was recorded separately.

As discussed, each student's final exam performance on each topic is associated with an assessment type. We group the scores based on the assessment type to form 3 clusters of scores corresponding to peer-, self- and no-assessment, where each score is uniquely associated with a student and a topic. Then, the average scores of these score clusters are compared to measure the effectiveness of the assessment types.

Standard tests of statistical significance such as (paired) t-test are not applicable in this case, because the dependence among the scores is a bit idiosyncratic: given two assessment types under comparison, you can pair scores by the student, but the scores themselves are on different topics. Thus, we chose to take the generally applicable bootstrapping approach, where 10,000 datasets are created via sampling with replacement and the percentage of the time the same or greater difference is observed is used as the estimate for the p-value [6].

[2]We were concerned that students may self-grade every topic, not just assigned ones, because that would break the experiment setup in which scores are clustered by the assessment method. See **Peer- vs Self-assessment** in Section 4 for more discussion.

4. RESULT 1 : EFFICACY OF PSA

The averages of the scores of each assessment type are presented in Table 2. Also, note that indented quotes that appear throughout the result sections are exemplar quotes from the student surveys. These quotes serve as anecdotal evidence for the qualitative analysis portion of the study.

Assessment Type	Peer	Self	No
Mean Score	74.6%*	74.8%*	72.8%
Standard Deviation	11.4%	10.6%	12.3%

Table 2: Comparison of Final Exam Performance

* The performance gain over no-assessment is statistically significant ($p<0.05$).

Peer- and Self- vs No-assessment. Peer- and self-assessment scores are higher than no-assessment scores. The difference is small, but statistically significant. This is consistent with our hypothesis, and student survey as shown in Figure 1. There are several benefits to PSA:

1. PSA makes students review the topics soon after the problem sets are due:

   > "[...] I enjoyed the peer grading experience because in most classes, after an assignment is due, most people just forget it since "the work is done." [...]"

   As depicted by Ebbinghaus's *forgetting curve*, frequent reviewing is crucial for retaining newly acquired knowledge, though the frequency can be lowered over time [5]. Performing PSA soon after the problem set deadline prevents the students form missing early review opportunities.

2. PSA exposes students to approaches different from the ones they are familiar with, which may or may not be correct:

   > "I actually got more out of grading peers work than my own because it allowed me to see other ways of approaching the same problems."

   > "It was a nice experience getting to know how others think. Also, it was a nice opportunity to see common mistakes."

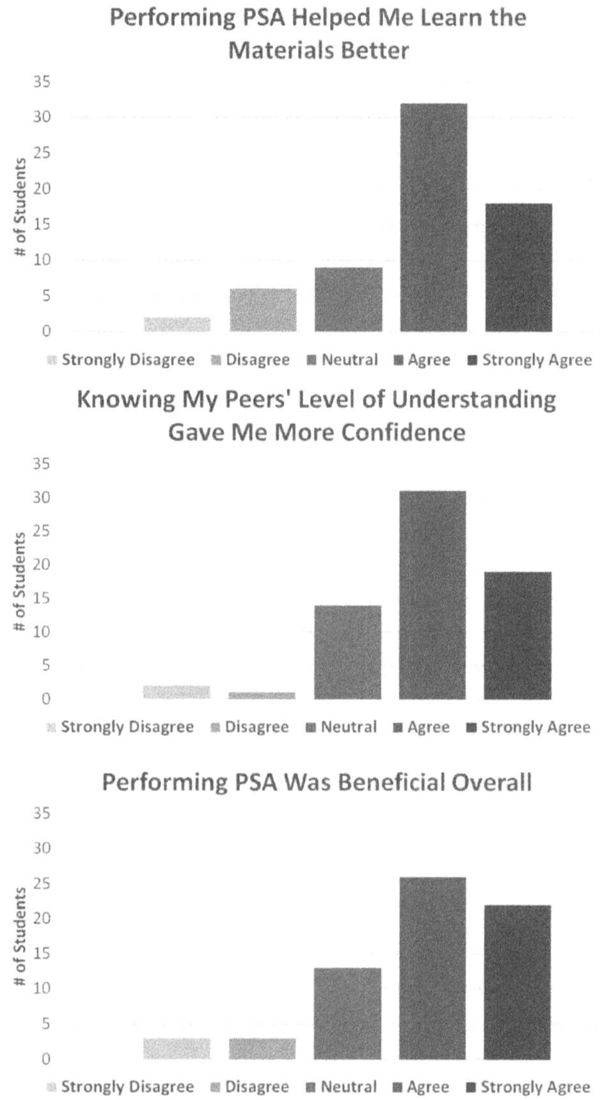

Figure 1: Post-PSA Survey Results

The students have to reason through various approaches to evaluate their correctness. Such critical thinking, as well as gaining multiple perspectives of a given problem, should be helpful for learning.

3. Students have additional intrinsic motivation to carefully study the concepts, because they want to be fair to their peers:

> "Personally, I understood the concepts even better than before because I studied it more in depth just so that I could grade accurately. [...]"

Everyone is driven by unique motivations. Also, existing motivations, such as the grades, are mostly extrinsic in nature. Providing an additional source intrinsic motivation in this way can fulfill the needs of certain students.

4. PSA satisfies students' curiosity:

> "It's always interesting to see others' answers."

Students gain access to other students' work through PSA. Satiating the curiosity, along with other benefits, may keep them interested in the subject.

Peer- vs Self-assessment. What is less intuitive about the average exam scores from the experiment is that peer-assessment is no more beneficial than self-assessment. Note that benefit 2 and 3 above are effects of peer-assessment, specifically. Even then, why is there no significant difference in the exam scores between peer- and self-assessment groups?

One reason is that peer-assessment may not always be more beneficial than self-assessment. This is covered in more detail as we discuss the third case in **When PSA fails to be beneficial**.

Also, students may have done self-assessment for the topic assigned for peer-assessment. The average response to survey item 6, "I self-assessed every question, regardless of the PSA assignment," was 3.03. In this case, 1 means that the given student self-assessed neither of the 2 remaining topics, and 5 means that they self-assessed both of the topics. Since 3.03 sits right in the middle of the scale, we can see that the students self-assessed 1 of the 2 remaining topics on average. Given the statistically significant difference in the average exam scores between no-assessment and the rest, we conjecture that the 1 additional self-assessment was performed on the topic the given student was assigned to peer-assess. This sounds reasonable as well, because this is the topic that requires less additional work: After all, the student has already assessed 6 peers' work on that topic and is familiar with the correct solution. But it is also possible that the additional, voluntary self-assessment was done evenly across different topics, in which case the performance gain over no-assessment would be bigger in real life than what is shown in Table 2.

When PSA fails to be beneficial. Just like any learning exercise, PSA is not too helpful when the assessor understands the concepts well already:

> "I don't think it added much to the process given that I had already spent so long on the problems and for the most part understood the approaches."

The average final exam scores of the students who (strongly) disagreed survey item 5, "Performing PSA Was Beneficial Overall," is significantly higher than that of those who (strongly) agreed with the statement, 81.83% and 70.2%, respectively. This suggests that students who thinks they know the concepts too well to benefit from an additional assignment like PSA indeed know the concepts well, instead of wrongly thinking that they do. However, it is still unclear whether they really did not benefit from PSA.

Also, when the assessee has a strong command over the materials, thus their solutions resemble those in the solution manual closely, there is little for the assessor to gain from PSA:

> "[...] An assignment with many mistakes will force us to think what goes wrong and look for place for partial credit if any. However, with perfect homework, one can learn nothing from peer grading."

In an extreme case, the assessee's solution could be identical to the sample solution. In such cases, though, the assessor has not much to lose either, except for the opportunity cost perhaps, since it will take little to no time to assess the student work.

Before we discuss the third case in which PSA is not helpful for the assessor, consider the following comment:

> "[...] On the last homework I found it useful to repeatedly go through the process of seeing how they arrived at answers. On this homework however, some of the peer solutions (while still with the correct answer) may not have solved it the same way I did. *Thinking about multiple ways to solve a problem can in some ways make it more confusing*, as I have a specific way most comfortable for me to correctly solve such problems."

This brings up an important point: To benefit from PSA, the student assessors need to have a sufficient level of command over the relevant concepts. They need to have the capacity to critically analyze and determine the correctness of a peer's approach that is different from the sample solution. Also, they need to be ready to absorb multiple correct approaches without getting them confused.

The level of sufficiency depends on how open-ended the question is. The more open-ended the question is, the more likely it is for the peers to take approaches that are divergent from the sample solution provided for them. Then, should the instructor prepare questions with little to no room for alternative approaches? In such cases, however, there may be little benefit for the assessors, because it is more likely to be in the aforementioned cases. Thus, the degree of subjectivity has to be carefully determined to balance the amount of benefit that can be gained from PSA and the level of understanding required to reap the benefit.

In our case, most students found PSA helpful, but some were ready for more challenges:

> "It's a lot more useful for assignments where there is more subjective grading criteria, such as essays. I'd rather peer grade the projects than the homeworks, honestly, since there's a lot more room for diverse solutions in the former."

5. RESULT 2 : STUDENT SATISFACTION

> "This is my first time to do things like PeerGrade. This is really helpful!"

> "Surprisingly, I enjoyed peer grading."

> "Hopefully we do this again!"

Students are generally happy about PSA, perhaps because they found PSA to be helpful as discussed in the previous section. But there are other factors that contributed to the generally positive sentiment toward PSA.

Workload. When incorporating PSA into our class, we were very cautious about keeping the workload reasonable, because it requires work additional to all other assignments and responsibilities asked of the students. The students seem to appreciate it:

	PSA for PSet 1		PSA for PSet 2	
Judged by	Grade	Feedback	Grade	Feedback
Assessor	4.65(.57)	4.56(.59)	4.72(.70)	4.71(.69)
Assessee	4.61(.82)	4.48(.85)	4.72(.71)	4.72(.66)

Table 3: Average Survey Response Scores on the Quality of Peer-assessment (SD in parentheses)

The responses were given on a scale from 1 (Strongly Disagree) to 5 (Strongly Agree). Each value on the "Self" row is the average of self-reported quality scores of the assessments provided to the peers. (E.g. *My feedback should be helpful* and *My grades are fair.*) Each value on the "Peers" row is the average of quality scores of the assessments received from the peers. (E.g. *Grader X's feedback is helpful* and *Grader X's grades are fair.*)

> "I'm glad that you guys gave us a reasonable chunk of peer grading since it didn't take too long."

Is it necessarily good that students are happy about the workload? What additional benefits would a more demanding implementation of PSA bring? These are interesting and practical questions that cannot be answered with our results. But what we can claim with our experience is that with manageable workload, PSA can be enjoyable to the students, even though they know that it incurs extra work.

Perceived assessment quality. Table 3 summarizes how the students thought about the quality of the assessments they provided and received. Students are generally satisfied with the numeric grades and written feedback they received from the peers, which may partially explain the positive sentiment toward PSA. While this is not generalizable to all assessors, some assessors are quite meticulous, to a degree in which the staff cannot afford to be due to the limited resources:

> "I liked the way peers have explained the flaws. They have pointed out minute details of my homework. It definitely helps me to do better in my next home work. Overall, they have done a good job!"

Even if a student is assigned less meticulous peer-assessors for a given problem, he or she still receives feedback from multiple people, including a staff member. Thus, the feedback can collectively cover more aspects of the student work than it would in a no PSA setting.

Also, peers tends to be more lenient than the staff. Again, this depends on the assessor, but perhaps some are lazy, do not understand the concept well enough to take off points and argue a case for it, or just want to be lenient to people in the same boat as they are:

> "[...] I did find that overall instructors were a bit harsher than peers in grading"

6. THREATS TO VALIDITY

This work details the experience and results from a study done in an NLP course with primarily senior-level students. Two of the implications are as follows:

First, the good balance between objectivity and open-ended nature in the questions may make NLP a good fit for PSA, which in turn may have led to the promising results observed in this study. For instance, in *language modeling*, a question may ask the students to assign a probability to a sentence. Roughly speaking, students are to estimate the probability of seeing the given sentence in an unseen document, based on the number of occurrences of the substrings of the sentence in a provided corpus. Depending on the choice of preprocessing and *smoothing*, the answer may vary. However, given a complete description of an assessee's approach, there is little ambiguity in the steps and result. How effective would PSA be in other subjects? While this cannot be directly answered, the discussion at the end of Section 4 remains relevant.

Second, the maturity of the students could have had a significant role in making the overall experience beneficial and pleasant. It takes knowledge and character to evaluate others' work and provide constructive feedback. Can we expect to see similar maturity in younger students? To answer this question, additional experiments with students in earlier stages of their education is necessary.

7. CONCLUSIONS

We present PSA as an active learning exercise for the assessors and study its impact. After incorporating PSA into an Introduction to Natural Language Processing course consisting of more than 100 students, we analyze student surveys and exam results of peer-, self-, and no-assessment group. The majority of the students found peer- and self-assessment to be helpful according to the survey, which is confirmed by the exam results. The final exam performance suggests that PSA is helpful for learning, which is consistent with the survey in which students reported that they found PSA beneficial. Also, students generally enjoyed conducting PSA.

This work compliments the vast literature on PSA that focuses on how the assessees are benefited, and methods to obtain reliable grades, by completing of the picture, and providing additional motivations for students to perform more careful assessments for peers and themselves. For future work, we would like to explore different design decisions in implementing PSA in classes to maximize the benefit we see in this work.

8. REFERENCES

[1] C. Bauer, K. Figl, M. Derntl, P. P. Beran, and S. Kabicher. The student view on online peer reviews. In *Proceedings of the 14th Annual ACM SIGCSE Conference on Innovation and Technology in Computer Science Education*, ITiCSE '09, pages 26–30, New York, NY, USA, 2009. ACM.

[2] C. C. Bonwell and J. A. Eison. Active learning : creating excitement in the classroom. *ASHEERIC Higher Education Report No. 1*, 1991.

[3] D. Chinn. Peer assessment in the algorithms course. In *Proceedings of the 10th Annual SIGCSE Conference on Innovation and Technology in Computer Science Education*, ITiCSE '05, pages 69–73, New York, NY, USA, 2005. ACM.

[4] A. DiPardo and S. W. Freedman. Peer response groups in the writing classroom: Theoretic foundations and new directions. *Review of Educational Research*, 58(2):pp. 119–149, 1988.

[5] H. Ebbinghaus. Uber das gedachtnis leipzig, dunker. *Translated by Ruger HA and Bussenius CE (1913) Teachers College, Columbia University.[WWW document] http://psychclassics. yorku. ca/Ebbinghaus/index. htm (last accessed August 16 2004)*, 1885.

[6] B. Efron and R. Tibshirani. An Introduction to the Bootstrap, 1993.

[7] S. Fallows and B. Chandramohan. Multiple approaches to assessment: Reflections on use of tutor, peer and self-assessment. *Teaching in Higher Education*, 6(2):229–246, 2001.

[8] D. Grez, Valcke, and Berings. Peer assessment of oral presentation skills. *Procedia - Social and Behavioral Sciences*, 2(2):1776 – 1780, 2010. Innovation and Creativity in Education.

[9] C. Kulkarni, K. P. Wei, H. Le, D. Chia, K. Papadopoulos, J. Cheng, D. Koller, and S. R. Klemmer. Peer and self assessment in massive online classes. *ACM Trans. Comput.-Hum. Interact.*, 20(6):33:1–33:31, Dec. 2013.

[10] N.-F. Liu and D. Carless. Peer feedback: the learning element of peer assessment. *Teaching in Higher Education*, 11(3):279–290, 2006.

[11] M. Prince. Does active learning work? a review of the research. *J. Engr. Education*, pages 223–231, 2004.

[12] K. Raman and T. Joachims. Bayesian ordinal peer grading. In *NIPS 2014 Workshop on Human-Propelled Machine Learning*, 2014.

[13] B. Simon, R. Anderson, C. Hoyer, and J. Su. Preliminary experiences with a tablet pc based system to support active learning in computer science courses. *SIGCSE Bull.*, 36(3):213–217, June 2004.

[14] J. Sitthiworachart and M. Joy. Effective peer assessment for learning computer programming. In *Proceedings of the 9th Annual SIGCSE Conference on Innovation and Technology in Computer Science Education*, ITiCSE '04, pages 122–126, New York, NY, USA, 2004. ACM.

[15] D. Sluijsmans, F. Dochy, and G. Moerkerke. Creating a learning environment by using self-, peer- and co-assessment. *Learning Environments Research*, 1(3):293–319, 1998.

[16] K. Topping. Peer assessment between students in colleges and universities. *Review of Educational Research*, 68(3):pp. 249–276, 1998.

[17] K. Topping. Self and peer assessment in school and university: Reliability, validity and utility. In M. Segers, F. Dochy, and E. Cascallar, editors, *Optimising New Modes of Assessment: In Search of Qualities and Standards*, volume 1 of *Innovation and Change in Professional Education*, pages 55–87. Springer Netherlands, 2003.

[18] I. van den Berg, W. Admiraal, and A. Pilot. Design principles and outcomes of peer assessment in higher education. *Studies in Higher Education*, 31(3):341–356, 2006.

Differences in the Learning Principles Dominating Student-Student vs. Student-Instructor Interactions while Working on Programming Tasks

Alessio Gaspar
Department of Computer Science & Engineering
University of South Florida
813-974-2932
alessio@usf.edu

Joni Torsella & Nora Honken
Department of Engineering Education
University of Cincinnati
513-556-1224
joni.torsella@uc.edu
honkenna@ucmail.uc.edu

Sohum Sohoni
School of Computing Informatics and Decision Systems Engineering
Arizona State University
480-727-1590
sohum.sohoni@asu.edu

Colin Arnold
Department of Computer Science & Engineering
University of South Florida
813-974-3780
cdarnold@usf.edu

ABSTRACT

Peer learning principles have been successfully applied to novice programmers. Pedagogies such as Pair Programming, Peer Testing, Peer review of code or tests, or, more generally Peer Instruction, have repeatedly demonstrated their effectiveness in improving both individual performance and retention rates.

This paper proposes to supplement the existing literature by investigating how students interact with one another during collaborative programming tasks. More specifically, we are interested in comparing the learning principles used during student-student interactions with those used during student-instructor or student-teaching assistant dialogs.

Students in online and face to face courses, who worked collaboratively on programming assignments, were surveyed to gain an understanding of the frequency with which they engaged in specific activities. These that are representative of the learning principles that have been supported by research to promote learning.

Results suggest that some learning principles, may be absent from student-student interactions. We discuss how the success of collaborative programming pedagogies put into question the role of these principles and whether they may contribute to further improve peer-based approaches.

Keywords

Novice Programmers; Peer Learning; Learning Principles

1. INTRODUCTION

1.1. Motivation

Active learning and constructivist pedagogies have paved the way for computer science educators to transition from being "Sages on the stage" to being "Guides on the side"; e.g. **[1, 2]**. Among them, pedagogies based on peer learning such as peer instruction **[3, 4]**, pair programming **[5, 6]** and peer testing **[7, 8]** have been repeatedly reported as successful at improving student grades, retention, motivation and individual programming skills.

This success invites researchers to further investigate the nature of the didactic dialog which students establish with one another, and whether this dialog is related to learning principles that have been proven to be beneficial. Also of interest is how similar, or different, student-student interactions are from those between students and instructors or teaching assistant. Gaining insights on this has potential to help us better understand why collaborative programming activities are so beneficial to students.

This research is further motivated by the growth of online programs. Within the context of the previous research question, we also want to assess whether our findings are stable when switching from face-to-face to online delivery modality. Means et al. **[9]** state that solid empirical research on implementations of online learning is limited, and is lagging behind technological innovations that act as game-changers. Although a body of knowledge exists on teaching and learning online, researchers are discovering that different aspects of online learning need to be explored in more detail within specific contexts (**[9]**, p. 37).

1.2. Specific Objective of this Study

This paper is a first step towards investigating the specifics of how students help one another while working on programming tasks. Unlike previous studies, it is the didactic nature of the interactions that was examined, rather than measurements of the impact collaborating has on improving grades, individual skills, motivation, or retention rate in the discipline.

While the long term goals of this project are to understand the impact of the didactic exchanges among students, and to drive new pedagogies based on these findings, this paper is an initial necessary step in this direction. Based on Fincher and Petre's method of science approach **[10]** p.16, this paper may be viewed as a step towards developing an explanatory theory preliminary to a predictive one. The data collection and analysis we leveraged in this study is consistent with this phase of a theory's development.

1.3. Conceptual Framework

In 2008 a group of researchers, brought together by the Association of Psychological Sciences and the American Psychological Association, accumulated a list of learning principles that had been proven through research to lead to learning. Their purpose was to disseminate the list to practitioners with the hope of improving learning in schools **[11]**. We reasoned

SIGCSE'16, March 2–5, 2016, Memphis, TN, USA.
© 2016 ACM. ISBN 978-1-4503-3685-7/16/03…$15.00.
DOI: http://dx.doi.org/10.1145/2839509.2844627

that if learning actually takes place during collaborative programming assignments that some of the principles should be present. After reviewing the 25 Learning Principles, we felt that *deep questioning* and *desired difficulty* had a strong potential to support collaborative programming activities. As such, we decided to focus our first study on these.

The first principle, **Deep Questioning**, is related to asking *why*, *how*, *what-if* questions. These types of questions have been shown to promote deeper comprehension and learning at a deeper level **[11, 12]**. Collaborative work creates opportunities for students to ask each other *such* questions. It also enable them to treat different solutions emerging in the group as *what if* scenarios they may justify to one another.

The second principle we investigated is **Desirable Difficulty**. It involves the learner having to exert effort during acquisition and retrieval of information. It has been shown that, when students have to organize their thoughts on a topic, learning is enhanced **[11]**. This learning principle is relevant to collaborative programming scenarios in so far that participants are not necessarily allowed to indulge in a passive pupil role. Instead, they are expected to contribute equally by their peers. The latter implies investing efforts in understanding explanations from other members who are not solely dedicated to help them.

Due to their established relevance to computing education **[1, 2, 13]**, we also considered **constructivism** and **instructivism**. Constructivists theorize that learners construct their knowledge through experiences, while instructivists theorize that an instructor is at the center of learning and are responsible to pass on their knowledge to the student. In collaborative programming tasks, we hypothesize that one participant rarely assumes a dedicated teacher role. While it is easy to assume that this entails a form of constructivism, no study has, to the best of our knowledge, characterized student-student interactions as such. As an extension of the above, we also considered the **pupil's independence** as a way to identify passive learning or instructivist pedagogies.

Last but not least, we then supplemented the above via the concepts of **knowledge transfer sequences** vs. **collaborative sequences**. In **[14]**, Haller et al. use conversation analysis as a method to understand how students learn from each other in cooperative groups. Although the study was conducted in a chemical engineering class, it has implications in the broad context of science and engineering courses using teamwork. The authors classify the conversations into two kinds of teaching-learning interactions, *transfer of knowledge sequences*, and *collaborative sequences*. In the former, the students engage in a teacher-pupil dialog but with a dialogic feedback loop that is usually not present in a classroom. In the collaborative sequences, learning is accomplished through shared thinking, and knowledge-building through discussion.

The above principles and pedagogies served as the framework of our study and dictated the design of a survey instrument.

1.4. Hypothesis

This study aims at gaining insights about how students learn while working on programming tasks together. More specifically, we seek to establish whether, and how, student-student didactic interactions differ from those they have with instructors or teaching assistants. Our hypothesis is that the nature of both didactic dialogs should reflect the focus of instructors and teaching assistant to support their interlocutor's learning, while peer might be more focused on completing assignments successfully. Differences in the interactions themselves would suggest that, while successful, student-student interactions may be further improved by integrating elements from educational practices which have already demonstrated their effectiveness in non-peer learning settings.

1.5. Terminology

In the remainder of this paper, "Programming tasks" will encompass both graded and non-graded programming activities. "Working together" will describe dynamics ranging from informal study groups, to supervised activities; e.g. pair programming or team assignments. "Student-instructor" will refer to interactions between students and either faculty or teaching assistants (TA).

2. METHODS

Given our objectives, our primary source of information is the students themselves. We therefore adopted a cross-sectional study research design using an online anonymous survey administered in Survey Monkey to students at three different universities.

2.1. Overall Survey Design & Organization

The survey was designed to gather the same information in two distinct scenarios; when the respondents are working with other students, and when they are working with instructors or teaching assistants. As a result, the survey was divided in two parts respectively dedicated to each scenario. In order to keep responses comparable, we used the same questions in both, albeit after adapting the phrasing to fit the specifics of the scenario.

We also used three "pivot" questions. These allowed us to determine whether a responded had indeed participated in collaborative programming activities with other students or instructors / teaching assistants. Based on their responses to these questions, we skipped the parts of the survey focused on interactions they didn't experience personally.

The core questions of our survey, which are detailed in the following subsections, allowed respondents to express the frequency with which they engaged in various behaviors. These frequency levels were expressed via 5-point Likert items ranging from *almost never* (1) to *most of the time* (5). During analysis, the two lowest levels were aggregated into a nominal category *seldom*. Similarly, the two highest level 3 was kept as *sometimes*, and level 4 and 5 were aggregated into *often*.

2.2. Types of Assistance Received

Each of the two main parts of the survey started with a question about how often respondents experienced specific scenarios when requesting help in programming tasks.

You have problems implementing a part of the project and you ask ___ for help. Rate the frequency with which each of the following situations occurs.

1. *The __ tells me exactly how to fix it without fixing the problems for me*
2. *The ___ fixes the problems for me without explaining*
3. *The ___ directs me to the part of the lecture I misunderstood without fixing the problems for me*
4. *The ___ and I work together and both contribute equally to fix the problems*
5. *The ___ fixes the problems for me while explaining*
6. *The ___ explains what is wrong but not how to fix it and does not fix the problems for me*

The above template was used as **Q7** in the first part of the survey and **Q12** in the second. The blanks were respectively replaced with "*another student*" and "*the instructor or teaching assistant*". Based on our conceptual framework, the six items were carefully phrased. **Table** 1 shows which items are related to scenarios illustrating either high or low independence on the part of the pupil – i.e. the respondent. It also shows which scenarios reveal teaching-learning interactions based on knowledge transfer sequences, collaborative sequences, and one scenario is used to capture situations where such sequences are absent; item #2.

Table 1 – Learning Principles Captured in Q7 / Q12

Learning Principles		Items
Pupils' Independence	High	3, 4, 6
	Low	1, 2, 5
Teaching-Learning Interactions	KT-Sequence	1, 2, 5, 6
	C-Sequence	4
	None	2

2.3. Types of Explanations Received

Last, we used another frequency level question in each part of the survey to gain more detailed insights regarding the nature of the explanations received by respondents when they asked for help.

You have problems implementing a part of the project and you ask ___for help. Rate the frequency with which each of the following situations occurs.

1. *Their explanations take into consideration my mistakes or misunderstandings*
2. *Their explanations relate other learning situations or concepts I encountered*
3. *Their explanations only describe the steps to solve the problem*
4. *Their explanations take into consideration my current understanding or knowledge*
5. *Their explanations include what-if scenarios*
6. *Their explanations require me to put effort into understanding them*
7. *Their explanations focus on **why** a piece of code works*
8. *Their explanations focus on **how** a piece of code works*

The above template was used as **Q9** in the first part of the survey and **Q14** in the second. The blanks were respectively replaced with "*another student*" and "*the instructor or teaching assistant*".

Table 2 – Learning Principles Captured in Q9 / Q14

Learning Principles	Items
Deep Questioning	5, 7, 8
Desirable Difficulty	6
Constructivism	1, 2, 4
Instructivism	3

Table 2 shows how each item in these questions was phrased to relate to the two previously selected learning principles, i.e. Deep Questioning and Desirable Difficulty. We also phrased items so that some would also relate to Instructivism or Constructivism.

2.4. Population & Sample

The survey was administered using *surveymonkey*. Instructors disseminated the URL to their students at the end of the spring 2015 semester. Participation was entirely optional, with no additional incentive provided. The survey was anonymous, not gathering any identifying or even demographic information about respondents. The sample was therefore self-selected solely on the basis of respondents' inclination to volunteer for this study. No questions were mandatory, allowing respondents to skip questions for which they didn't feel they had a meaningful or relevant response. This resulted in a variable number of responses for different questions, as noted during our data analysis.

The surveyed population consisted of engineering undergraduate students in US institutions, all enrolled in offerings with a strong programming requirement. Four of the offerings in which the study was conducted were taught in an online Information Technology BS degree in a research-intensive university; "Object Oriented Programming", "Programming Concepts", "IT Program Design" and "Data Structures". These span the sophomore to senior years and rely on the C, C++ and Java programming languages. Students are assigned programming assignments and interact with the instructor via emails, forums posts and weekly, optional, "live" online sessions. The latter are organized in a flipped manner since the lecture material is already conveyed via reading assignments or recorded videos. Most enrolled students are adults, work full time, and value the flexibility afforded by online delivery.

"Systems Fundamentals" was also offered online. It covers number systems and arithmetic, Boolean algebra, logic gates, truth tables, finite state machines, and logic circuits. A significant portion of the grade is on individual and team projects where students implement simple circuits in behavioral Verilog; e.g. counters, simple ALU's.

"Microprocessors" was delivered as both a face-to-face and a separate online offering. It covers microcomputer architecture, instruction set, assembly language programming, I/O and memory interfacing, and exception/interrupt handling. A significant portion of the grade is based on individual and team projects which involve programming tasks in MIPS-like assembly.

The online versions of the Systems Fundamentals and the Microprocessor course were offered as part of a fully-online Software Engineering BS degree in a research-intensive university. The Systems Fundamentals course was also taken by students in a fully-online Information Technology BS degree. Both courses saw a distribution of students in all four years, with a majority of sophomores and juniors.

"Models II", a required freshman course, was taught face-to-face in a department of Engineering Education in a research-intensive university. The course focusses on programming with MATLAB®. The overwhelming majority of the students in this course were traditional college students. Multiple sections, taught by different instructors, were surveyed.

2.5. Analysis

Data was analyzed using the Minitab software. Descriptive statistics were calculated and Chi Square Goodness of Fit tests were run to determine if the distribution of responses was different between online and face to face courses.

3. RESULTS

3.1. Response Rates

The survey was disseminated to 479 students in the six online classes and 478 in the four face-to-face ones. Respective response rates were 17% (81 responses) and 11% (51). Overall, we had 132 respondents for a 14% response rate.

3.2. Identifying Dominant Scenarios

Table 5 and **Table** 6 show the raw data that was collected during this study. Each table respectively provides the data about one of two pairs of questions.

Table 5 summarizes the data related to the types of assistance received (questions **Q7** and **Q12**). **Table** 6 does the same for the pair of questions related to the types of explanations (**Q9** and **Q14**). A Chi-Square test was used to examine the significance of relationships between our two nominal level variables: class type and level of frequency. Class type includes two categories: face-to-face courses – **F2F** – and online courses – **ONL**. Level of frequency includes *seldom*, *sometimes* and *often*.

In each table, the first question focuses on student-student interactions, while the second focuses on student-instructor ones. Each table lists the response items used in both questions of the corresponding pair. We are interested in the number of responses in each of our categories.

Our goal is to compare student-student interactions with student-instructors ones. To this end, we need to characterize how the distribution of responses, both ONL and F2F, varies when comparing the first question of the pair to the second. Let us detail the process we used to do so by considering an example.

Questions **Q7** and **Q12** both refer to the types of assistance received respectively in student-student and student-instructor interactions. Item #4 describes a scenario where both the student, and the person they are working with, contribute equally to solving the problems encountered.

Table 5 identifies the nominal category with the most respondents, for this item.

For face-to-face students;

- For **Q7**, the mode is in the *often* category (22 as opposed to 9 for *seldom* and 14 for *sometimes*).
- For **Q12**, the mode is in *sometimes* (15 as opposed to 11 for *often* and 10 for *seldom*).

Thus in a F2F situation, it is more common to have equal contribution to solving a problem when students are collaborating.

For online students;

- In **Q7**, the mode is in *seldom* (15 vs. 10 or 7).
- In **Q12**, *often* is the least popular response while *sometimes* and *seldom* are really close (resp. 6 and 5 respondents).

In an online situation equal contribution is more frequently noted when the interaction is between the student and TA/instructor, although it is not dominantly frequent even there.

This example illustrates that a given scenario might be slightly more frequently reported in one of the two types of interactions, while still being globally infrequent. To identify such a situation, we then look at whether the mode in one of the questions is not in the *often* category. We do so for both ONL and F2F students.

In the above example;

- We first look at face-to-face students (F2F) in student-student interactions (**Q7**). The *often* responses dominate. For online students (ONL), it fails to clearly dominate.
- We then look at student-instructor interactions (**Q12**) and notice that, for both face-to-face and online students, the dominant number of responses is not in *often*.

Therefore, it seems that item #4's scenario is less frequent in student-instructor interactions than student-student ones.

4. DISCUSSION

Table 3 shows the result of applying this process to all items from questions **Q7** and **Q12**. **Table** 4 shows similar data for questions **Q9** and **Q14**. In some instance, the item was not found to dominate in either type of interactions (=). The last column revealed that, most of the time, both student-student and student-instructor interactions did not feature a mode in the *often* category for either online or face-to-face students ("both").

The following subsections respectively review the summary tables related to the types of assistance and the types of explanations.

4.1. Differences in Types of Assistance

We first applied the above-defined process to the data in **Table** 5. Questions **Q7** and **Q12** prompted respondents to estimate the frequency of six scenarios each capturing specific learning principles. **Table** 3 shows the resulting summary information. Reviewing the survey item results in

Table 5 individually, we discover some interesting results. Several practices identified by our question items clearly do not dominate student behavior; e.g. strategies whereby students are provided step-by-step ways to fix their problems, or even worse, have their problems fixed without having to solve issues themselves. These practices are *weak* in both face-to-face vs. online, along with, student-student vs student-instructor scenarios. These observations are actually positive, as such practices do not align with what educators recognize as efficient in teaching.

Table 3 – Q7 / Q12 – Summary Comparison

Item #	Student-student vs. Student-instructor			
	Most frequent F2F	Most frequent ONL	Mode is in "often" Student	Mode is in "often" Instructor
1	Student	=	NO	NO
2	=	=	NO	NO
3	=	Instructor	NO	NO
4	Student	Instructor		NO
5	=	=	NO	NO
6	Instructor	Instructor	NO	

Similarly, the practice of providing help by referring the student to study material, e.g. lectures, without further help is not dominant in any of the scenarios either. This might actually suggest an improvement to both face-to-face and online delivery approaches; as well as, student-student vs. student-instructor didactic dialogs. Assuming that pointing students to revisit relevant study material, given the specific difficulties they are encountering, is an instance of the Desirable Difficulty principle, then this result suggests that we might want to better prepare instructors and students alike.

Reviewing the results as they pertain to our defined learning principle pattern, we find the responses to the three items corresponding to pupil high independence (3, 4 and 6) show a strong dominance for instructors in online settings, and a mixed dominance in face-to-face ones. The responses to the three items corresponding to pupil low independence (1, 2 and 5) do not show any clear dominance in either setting or interaction type with the highest dominant vote being sometimes for item 5; thus neither students nor instructors are providing answers without explanation. Therefore we find that, in online settings, instructors are more likely to use constructivist techniques. Further, due to the mixed results for student-student interaction in both scenarios we see that students would potentially benefit from being taught some learning strategies to reap the benefits seen in student-instructor dialogs.

The responses to the question corresponding to collaborative sequences (item 4) suggest that face-to-face students often work together sharing knowledge and discussing problems to be able to learn, and to a lesser extent, with instructors. However, in online settings we find that students seldom have such conversations with either other students or instructors. Not surprisingly, we find that students seldom engage in a knowledge transfer sequence when working with other students. However, we find mixed results in students-instructors interactions. In face-to-face settings, we find that instructors explain how to fix the problem while explaining why it was wrong. In online settings, instructors more often explain what is wrong but not how to fix it. Lastly, we sometimes find instructors who, regardless of the setting, fix the problem without explanation.

4.2. Differences in Types of Explanations

We then applied the same process to the data provided in **Table** 6 and obtained the summary presented in **Table** 4. The responses to the item representing desirable difficulty suggest that this learning principle is less often leveraged when students work with one another than when they work with an instructor.

The three items representing the deep questioning learning principles revealed that this practice occurs more frequently when students work with the instructor than with peers. Similarly, it occurs more frequently in face-to-face than online settings. However, results also show that the number of responses in the *often* frequency level do not represent a majority of respondents in any scenario; i.e. student-student vs. student-instructor, or face-to-face vs. online. This suggests that this learning principle might be particularly important to introduce to both instructor and students.

Table 4 – Q9 / Q14 – Summary Comparison

Item #	Student-student vs. Student-instructor			
	Most frequent F2F	Most frequent ONL	Mode is in "often" for...	
			Student	Instructor
1	Instructor	Instructor		
2	Instructor	Instructor	NO	
3	Instructor	Instructor	NO	NO
4	Instructor	=	NO	
5	=	Instructor	NO	NO
6	Instructor	Instructor		
7	=	Instructor		
8	Instructor	Instructor	NO	NO

The three items representing constructivist learning principles led to similar results with respect to when they occur most frequently. However, only student-student and online showed a lack of dominance for the *often* level, thus narrowing down the scenarios in which remediation should be applied.

The item capturing an instructivist pedagogy was, interestingly, more frequent in face-to-face settings and when working with the instructor. However, it also revealed that none of the scenarios, i.e. student-student vs student-instructor and face-to-face vs. online, featured a dominant proportion of respondents in the *often* level.

4.3. Threats to validity

The anonymous nature of the survey, its online administration and the lack of any added incentive to participate, provided both potentially positive and negative effects on the results.

This setting helped ensure that respondents shared their genuine opinions by mitigating biases based on perceptions of what would be "ideal responses". The lack of incentive prevented random responses provided just to get to the reward.

However, voluntary participation always invites the so-called self-selection sampling bias. Those who are motivated to respond, often do so under strong opinions, whether positive or negative.

In the same line of thought, we ensured that the survey would randomize items in questions in order to prevent biases induced by arbitrary response patterns.

While our sample size allowed us to draw statistically significant conclusions, the response rates were low. It is reasonable to assume that the lack of incentive is at least partially responsible. However, it is difficult to assess whether the low response rates might have been more detrimental than the various biases enabled by incentives. The anonymity of the survey prevented us from supplementing our analysis with a profiling of the non-respondents, which may have helped characterize respondents' motivations. In subsequent studies, we will seek funding to attempt to incentivize participation. However, we will do so using an option for students to skip responding and just get the incentive when they open the survey. We previously used this technique to mitigate random responses provided by respondents who are solely incentive-driven.

Another potential threat lies in the nature of online asynchronous courses. In such courses, the nature of student interactions is much more diversified and less easy to trace; e.g. emails, web-meetings, face-to-face study groups, in-lab supervised collaborative work... This is not taken into account in this study.

5. Conclusions & Future work

The results from this pilot study merit a more comprehensive investigation of the didactic dialog students establish with each other. This next step of our study will be conducted in partnership with additional faculty who are invited to contact us to express an interest in participating in a broader study on this topic.

We plan on using the results of such a larger-scale validation study to provide foundations for modifying peer learning interventions in order to lead students to further minimize interactions in which they provide each other with "too much" information which results in reducing the pupil's independence.

Once we have gathered sufficient quantitative data, we plan on integrating more qualitative research designs to help us understand *why* students rely on the specific type of didactic interactions the quantitative study identified. This will involve explaining the observed behaviors through focus group, interviews, and other qualitative approaches such as linguistic analysis of student dialog transcribed from video recording of work sessions.

6. ACKNOWLEDGMENTS

This material is based in part upon work supported by the National Science Foundation under award #0836863 Any opinions, findings, and conclusions or recommendations expressed in this publication are those of the author(s) and do not necessarily reflect the views of the National Science Foundation.

The authors are also indebted to Drs. Kastner, and Bucks from the University of Cincinnati for kindly disseminating the link to the online survey to their "Models II" students.

7. REFERENCES

[1] T. Wulf. 2005. Constructivist approaches for teaching computer programming. In Proceedings of the 6th conference on Information technology education (SIGITE '05). ACM, New York, NY, USA, 245-248.

[2] A.K. Lui, R. Kwan, M. Poon, and Y.H.Y. Cheung. 2004. Saving weak programming students: applying constructivism in a first programming course. SIGCSE Bull. 36:2, 72-76.

[3] B. Simon, J. Parris, and J. Spacc. 2013. How we teach impacts student learning: peer instruction vs. lecture in CS0. In *Proceeding of the 44th ACM tech. symp. on Computer science education* (SIGCSE '13). ACM, New York, NY, USA, 41-46.

[4] D. Zingaro and L. Porter. 2014. Peer instruction: a link to the exam. In *Proceedings of the 2014 conference on Innovation & technology in computer science education* (ITiCSE '14). ACM, New York, NY, USA, 255-260.

[5] K. Beck and C. Andres. 2004. Extreme Programming Explained: Embrace Change. Addison-Wesley Professional.

[6] G. Braught, T. Wahls, and L. Marlin Eby. 2011. The Case for Pair Programming in the Computer Science Classroom. Trans. Computing Education 11, 1, Article 2 (February 2011)

[7] M. H. Goldwasser. 2002. A gimmick to integrate software testing throughout the curriculum, presented at the Proceedings of the 33rd SIGCSE Technical Symposium on Computer Science Education, ACM, New York, NY, pp. 271-275

[8] A. Gaspar, S. Langevin, N. Boyer, and R. Tindell. 2013. A preliminary review of undergraduate programming students' perspectives on writing tests, working with others, & using peer testing. In *Proceedings of the 14th annual ACM SIGITE conference*. ACM, New York, NY, USA, 109-114.

[9] B. Means, M. Bakia, and R. Murphy. 2014. Learning online: What research tells us about whether, when and how. Routledge.

[10] S. Fincher, M. Petre. 2004. Computer Science Education Research. Taylor & Francis. ISBN: 9026519699

[11] A.C. Graesser, D.F. Halpern, and M. Hakel. 2008. 25 principles of learning. Washington DC. Task Forces on Lifelong Learning at Work and at Home. Retrieved 10/10/2014 from https://activelearningps.files.wordpress.com/2014/07/25-learning-principles-to-guide-pedagogy.pdf

[12] S. D. Craig, J. Sulling, A.Witherson, and B. Gholson. 2006. The deep-level reasoning effect: The role of dialogue and deep-level-reasoning questions during vicarious learning. Cognition and Instruction 24, 565-591.

[13] A. Gaspar, S. Langevin, N. Boyer. 2007. Constructivist Apprenticeship through Antagonistic Programming Activities, Encyclopedia of Information Science and Technology, Vol. 2.

[14] C. Haller, V. Gallagher, T. Weldon, R. Felder. 2000. Dynamics of Peer Education in Cooperative Learning Workgroups. Journal of engineering education. 39:3, pp. 285 – 293.

Table 5 – Q7 / Q12 – Items Comparisons

#	Q	Seldom		Sometimes		Often		χ^2	p
		F2F	ONL	F2F	ONL	F2F	ONL		
1	7	19	27	16	4	10	1	14.164	.001
	12	17	7	11	5	8	1	1.366	.505
2	7	30	26	9	3	6	2	2.802	.246
	12	28	9	7	3	1	1	0.719	*
3	7	18	21	23	8	4	3	5.596	.061
	12	8	3	17	6	11	4	0.006	.997
4	7	9	15	14	10	22	7	7.957	.019
	12	10	5	15	6	11	2	1.230	.541
5	7	17	25	20	3	8	4	13.616	.001
	12	17	8	16	4	3	1	0.826	.662
6	7	26	21	13	8	5	3	0.336	.845
	12	12	1	11	4	13	8	3.808	.149

* Expected count is one, Chi-Square probably invalid

Table 6 – Q9 / Q14– Items Comparisons

#	Q	Seldom		Sometimes		Often		χ^2	p
		F2F	ONL	F2F	ONL	F2F	ONL		
1	9	10	20	23	7	12	5	12.923	.002
	14	3	5	19	4	14	4	6.467	.039
2	9	8	18	19	9	18	8	12.939	.002
	14	1	4	17	7	17	2	9.780	.008
3	9	20	24	17	6	8	2	7.236	.027
	14	14	6	12	6	10	1	2.267	.322
4	9	22	22	19	7	4	3	3.589	.166
	14	8	4	24	8	4	1	0.433	.805
5	9	12	23	19	6	14	3	15.584	.000
	14	1	4	17	5	18	4	8.283	.016
6	9	7	19	18	11	20	2	20.340	.000
	14	1	5	12	3	23	5	11.341	.003
7	9	5	15	23	12	17	5	13.184	.001
	14	0	5	13	6	23	2	18.499	.000
8	9	9	17	18	7	18	8	9.216	.010
	14	1	2	15	5	20	6	2.662	.264

Computational Art - Introducing High School Students to Computing via Art

Zoë J. Wood
Computer Science
California Polytechnic State University
San Luis Obispo, CA 93407
zwood@calpoly.edu

Paul Muhl
Santa Barbara High School
700 E. Anapamu St.
Santa Barbara, CA
pmuhl@sbunified.org

Katelyn Hicks
Computer Science
California Polytechnic State University
San Luis Obispo, CA 93407
khicks@calpoly.edu

ABSTRACT

Introducing computer science to high school students in a creative context, and fitting such a course into an overly packed high school curriculum, is a challenge. This paper describes a fruitful collaboration to create and teach an alternative introductory computing curriculum for high school students targeted at introducing students to computing via an artistic context. This curriculum allows students to be introduced to computing in a highly interest based context, attracting diverse student body participation (25% female students in the first offering and 38% female students in the present offering). This curriculum also fulfills student's fine art course requirement making it more readily accessible to a wide audience to 'try out' CS while making progress on their academic goals. This curriculum has been used as a successful introduction to computing at the Santa Barbara High School CS Academy in the 2014-2015 school year and is currently being offered again this year. In this paper, we present the curriculum and evaluation of this initial offering.

Keywords

Introductory programming, computer science education, applied computing - fine arts, k-12 education

1. INTRODUCTION

Context based introduction to computer science has been consistently shown to be a positive way to introduce computing concepts [11, 8, 9, 6]. Presenting computer science within a context helps students to recognize the importance of computing to a field or theme they are interested in and creates a greater sense of investment in the course material and projects. Numerous themes have been proposed and various universities have adopted context based introductory courses.

Nationwide, computational art (closely related to media computation and generative art), is a relatively under-utilized introductory computing context, however this context has been shown to be successful at various institutions [7, 4, 10], with recent work by Guzdial [10] presenting long term analysis of the success of the Media Computation course at Georgia Tech.

Meanwhile, high schools have been tackling the problem of introducing computing to a wide audience in an attractive context. In addition, high schools face the challenge of an already impacted school day with numerous required courses, leaving students with little opportunities to explore computing as an elective course. This kind of exploratory enrollment is essential for students to be able to try out computer science to discover the joys of problem solving and programming.

This paper addresses the need for high school curriculum that allows students to fulfill course requirements and build an interest and understanding of computing in a creative and interesting context. Building off of a University level introduction to computing course focused on computational art, this paper describes a collaboration focused on developing a yearlong high school computational art course. This course simultaneously introduces students to computer science and to art and design principles in a hands-on creative manner, allowing students to fulfill their fine arts requirement while also teaching them to program in Java.

In this paper, we present the computational art curriculum and initial evaluation detailing the successes of the year long high school course. This course was attractive to a wide audience and received overwhelming positive responses for both shifting student's identities positively towards computing and encouraging them to enroll in subsequent computer science courses.

1.1 Context

Santa Barbara High School (SBHS) is committed to computer science education for all high school students and started teaching computer science again in 2012 after a break from offering such classes, followed by a School Board approved Computer Science Academy in 2014. The Academy operates as a school within a school serving those students who self identify as interested in the computer science (examples of other academies at the same school include Visual Arts and Design and Media Arts and Design Academies). This high school of about 2200 students and includes a diverse student body with 56% Latino, 49% low socioeconomic status and 55% first generation college bound students. The CS Academy offers four courses in computing, Exploring CS, AP CS, Mobile computing and Computational Art.

SIGCSE '16, March 02 - 05, 2016, Memphis, TN, USA

ISBN 978-1-4503-3685-7/16/03...$15.00

DOI: http://dx.doi.org/10.1145/2839509.2844614

The Computational Art course was designed as a collaborative effort with Professor Wood in order to offer an alternative entry-way into computer science. This course attracts a diverse student body; the initial offering in 2014-2015 included 25% female students (versus the Exploring CS course with 10% female students) and the 2015-2016 course has 38% female students. Taught by the CS Academy Director, Paul Muhl, this course allows students to fulfill their fine arts requirement[1] while learning to program in Java. Of all the courses offered by the CS Academy, this course best reflects the general student population and is an attractive entry to computer science for students of any grade level.

The collaboration on this high school level course comes out of the success of the introductory computational art course, which has been taught at Cal Poly for the last four years as a CS0 course. The course material explores the relationship of aesthetics and computation. Students write text based computer programs that generate two-dimensional digital art using the Processing development environment. The course allows students to explore the joy of using mathematics to define shapes, curves, relationships, color and animations to create artistic expressions. No prior programming experience is assumed. This course is one of five context based courses offered as a CS0 course for majors and has been shown to be successful at preparing students for subsequent computer science courses. Other context options include mobile, security, robotics and video games. The computational art offering has attracted larger than its share of female students then the other CS0 courses offered at Cal Poly (assuming an even distribution of female students across all contexts).

1.2 The Basics of the Curriculum

The purpose of the SBHS Computational Art course is to introduce, broaden and enhance a student's ability to generate both static and dynamic digital art (static art is most equivalent to an image, while dynamic art includes animation or changes based on user interaction). This course fulfills student's fine arts requirement and therefore has a solid grounding in art and design principles. The medium used to introduce these principles is the Processing development environment, which allows them to simultaneously develop their artistic and programming skills. Processing is an open source programming language and IDE, which is built on the Java programming language. It was designed by Casey Raes and Benjamin Fry at the MIT Media Lab and was built to allow for the teaching of fundamental programming concepts in a visual context.

2. RELATED WORKS

There is a large body of work addressing the multitude of challenges (including failure rates [1]) in introductory computer science curricula, including context-based computing, small courses and the use of labs early, making use of pair programming, etc. [9, 6, 12, 5, 3]. In the high school setting, all of these challenges exist in addition to the challenge of fitting computer science into an already packed curriculum.

Previous research has suggested that computational art can serve as a socially relevant, contextualized, real-world context for the introduction of computer science concepts. For example, Greenburg, Kumar & Ku evaluated the success of an art-focused creative-coding environment designed to emphasize excitement, creativity, and innovation within computer science and found that their "approach is successful and appears particularly appealing to women" [7]. Data suggested that major and non-major students taking the computational art course were more "positively inclined to take additional CS courses," and "more likely to spend extra time on a homework assignment for 'fun'." Guzdial [10], in a review of research over 10 years focused on efforts to teach introductory computer science courses with a media-focused context, found that the introduction of this Media Computation course improved retention.

Qualitative analysis suggested that retention was linked to students experiences in the course as "a welcome opportunity to be creative," and as contextualized and relevant [10]. Of special relevance, analysis indicates that not only did more women enroll in these courses than other introduction to CS courses, but more women succeeded - in some cases at a higher rate than men. While more research is necessary to fully account for the factors that lead to these higher interest and higher success rates for women in these classes, these findings make intuitive sense given women's higher participation in AP art courses. In 2013 women made up 75% of AP exam takers in AP Studio Art: Drawing; 74% of AP exam takers in Studio Art: 2D Design; 71% of AP exam takers in Studio Art: 3D Design; and 66% of AP exam takers in Art History [2]. These numbers indicates a fruitful area for creating compelling computer science courses, appealing to female students in particular.

3. OUR SOLUTION

In order to address the need for a creative and engaging high school course of interest to a wide audience of participants, we designed the computational art course to allow students to learn and apply key art and design principles and key technical programming principles to the production of both static and dynamic digital art.

In the computational art course, students gain an understanding of digital media production, including the production of such art via text based programming. Students' understanding comes from viewing, discussing and creating their own digital media projects. Students study fundamentals of digital art (color, shape, composition, relationships, perspective, texture, light, and animation principles and timing). Through the study of these fundamentals, students create multiple artistic pieces demonstrating an understanding of these principles. Students also develop their own personal style for the creation of both static digital art pieces and dynamic, interactive or animation visual art projects.

Students simultaneously develop their technical understanding of key technical concepts relating to computational art production including data representations, control flow, iteration and the application of logic to control the interaction and story of their creations, in addition to mastering the appropriate Java programming syntax. Students then apply this knowledge to implement computer programs that produce artistic artifacts.

The course is broken into six units, each of which includes material focused on art and design concepts. Students engage with the concepts by learning from existing examples

[1]Specifically for the context of this high school, students in California applying to UC schools are required to complete a year of fine arts

and then mastering relevant technical skills and material to produce computational art demonstrating the particular concept.

The six fundamental units include:

- Principles of design, color, shape, and space
- Principles of design, composition, scale and perspective
- Principles of Design: generative & repetition and organic shapes & curves
- Principles of design: texture and light
- Digital Image representation and manipulation
- Principles of animation

The primary learning modality for the course beyond introduction, demonstration, and exploration of each concept included associated assignments to be completed by students in the computer lab with the instructors assistance for each of these units. This hands-on learning allows students to create computational art demonstrating their understanding of the relevant art and design concept as well as their mastery of the technical material.

Each of the unit topics are enumerated in detail below. Each unit contains subtopics related to the global principle and example assignments and the associated key technical concepts (related to programming) that are covered with each topic and assignment. The learning outcomes for each unit are encapsulated in the subtopics and closely related technical skills, with each outcome enumerated and expanded upon for each individual assignment. For each subtopic the curriculum is designed such that students will learn and understand the principles for each subtopic and technical skill and be able to apply that knowledge via the production of an assignment that illustrates their use. Example assignments for each subtopic and the related technical skills are briefly enumerated here to illustrate the copasetic relationship between both the art and design principles and the programming principles being introduced to the students.

The order in which the art and design topics are introduced has some flexibility, however, the units are currently designed in this specific order to allow students to scaffold their technical skills in such a way to build more and more complex computer programs.

3.1 Principles of Design, Color, Shape, and Space

This first unit allows students to begin to develop their art and design vocabulary along with introducing them to the development environment and programming syntax. See Figure 1 for an example of some of the student's art from the 2014-2015 offering of the computational art course at SBHS related to this unit.

- **Subtopic:** Shapes and order

  Assignment 2D pixel space: design a face
  Technical Introduction to the Processing development environment and syntax

- **Subtopic:** Shapes, order, and color

  Assignment Overlapping shape composition: design a creature
  Technical order of commands, color picker and shape syntax

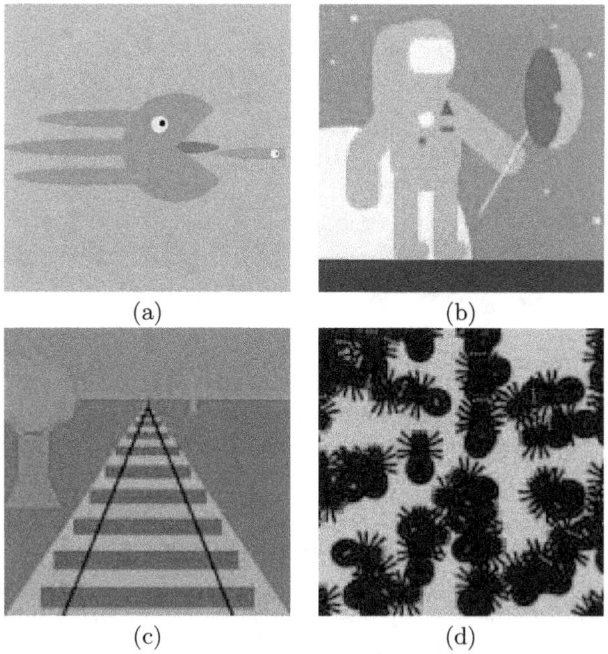

Figure 1: Student work from the 2014-15, assignments focused on: (a) creatively understanding shape and 2D space (pair programmed E. Ornelas and D. Panchi), (b) an assignment exploring composition through the study, reproduction and modification of a Blexbolex design (E. Diaz) (c) exploring perspective and the application of scale (E. Heffernan) (d) exploring repetition and generative art creation (E. Rojas)

- **Subtopic:** Mastering 2D space and ordering

  Assignment Growing and shrinking dots
  Technical the use of variables to control size

- **Subtopic:** Color (warm/cool and representation)

  Assignment Warm/cool lab
  Technical the use of variables to control color

3.2 Principles of Design, Composition, Scale and Perspective

This second unit builds on student's vocabulary and art and design concepts and allows students to practice their basic programming skills. See Figures 1 and 2 for examples of static art produced for this unit.

- **Subtopic:** Introduction to composition

  Assignment Golden ratio lab
  Technical variable practice

- **Subtopic:** Composition, scale and mood

  Assignment Composition exploration - Blexbolex
  Technical introduction to transforms to rescale and reposition a character

- **Subtopic:** Perspective and vanishing points

  Assignment Vanishing point lab
  Technical practice with transforms

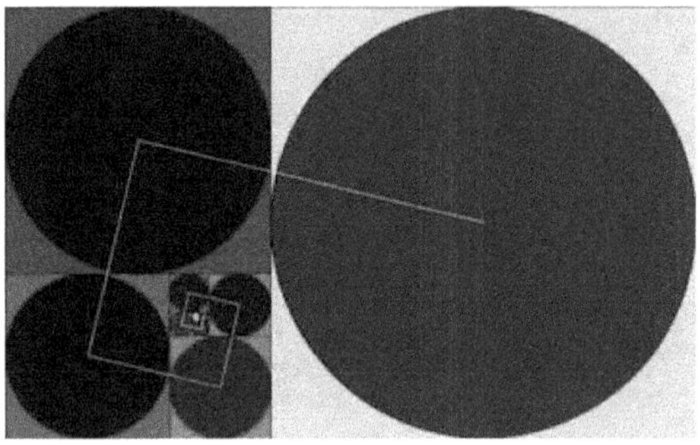

Figure 2: Student result for an assignment practicing using variables to control a sketch that conforms to the golden ratio and practices art and design concepts of composition and scale (A. McKaba)

3.3 Principles of Design: Generative & Repetition and Organic Shapes & Curves

This third unit allows students to explore the differences between generative art using random numbers and repition and careful design. This unit also introduces the use of mathematical functions (parametric curves) in order to allow students to create organic shapes. In this unit students enhance their programming skills to add more control flow tools to apply repetition to the creation of their art pieces. See Figure 1 for some examples of static art produced for this unit.

- **Subtopic** Generative art, iteration and random #s

  Assignment Exploring repetition - random repetition
  Technical loops
- **Subtopic** More generative art

  Assignment Further repetition: face with many teeth
- **Subtopic** Organic shape: Parametric functions for lines, curves and circles

  Assignment Creating flowers
  Technical loops (emphasis on loop control parameters)
- **Subtopic** Organic shape continued

  Assignment Creating spirals and other natural forms
  Technical loops and mathematical background

3.4 Principles of Design: Texture and Light

This fourth unit introduces fundamental art and design concepts relating to mood via light and texture. Students expand and apply their understanding of loops to include nested loops in order to create painterly renderings. See Figure 3 for some examples of students work.

- **Subtopic** Texture

  Assignment Comparative textures lab (lines, points, strokes and hash marks)
  Technical nested loops and variables for strokes
- **Subtopic** Light and form

  Assignment Difference between a circle and sphere
  Technical loops
- **Subtopic** Light, form and texture

  Assignment Parametric curves and stroke textures
  Technical loops and mathematical background
- **Subtopic** Light, form and texture

  Assignment Implicit curves and stroke textures
  Technical loops and mathematical background

3.5 Digital Image Representation & Manipulation

This fifth unit introduces students to the digital representation of images. This unit encourages students to take self portraits with their cell phones and then modify them programmatically in creative ways. It includes an examination of pop-art such as Andy Warhol and combines creativity and technology in a compelling way for students to practice and deepen their understanding of data representations and loops. Examples can be seen in Figure 3.

- **Subtopic** Introduction to images

  Assignment Painterly strokes applied to images
  Technical 2D arrays and indexing (loops)
- **Subtopic** Pop-art and Images

  Assignment Andy Warhol filter
  Technical 2D arrays and conditionals
- **Subtopic** Images changing over time

  Assignment Image processing: morph
  Technical 2D arrays and indexing (loops)
- **Subtopic** Images: 2D arrays, indexing

  Assignment Image processing: edge detection
  Technical 2D arrays and indexing (loops)
- **Subtopic** Images and shapes together

  Assignment Images with windows defined by shape
  Technical 2D arrays and 2D space conditionals

3.6 Principles of Animation

This final unit introduces a few of the principles of animation [13] in order to help students create compelling animations. Some more advanced technical skills, such as objects, are introduced to allow students to see more powerful datastructures in action. This unit includes a capstone experience for the course in the form of team based final animation that tells a story.

- **Subtopic** Introduction to motion and time (history of animation and keyframing)

  Assignment Animation loop
- **Subtopic** Animation timing basics: frame rate and velocity

  Assignment Make a character move/respond
  Technical interaction with the mouse
- **Subtopic** Procedural animation

  Assignment Make many moving creatures
  Technical array practice
- **Subtopic** Principals of animation: squash and stretch, staging and story

  Assignment Curve following with squash and stretch

Figure 3: Further samples of student work created with this curriculum. On the left top row is an example of an Andy Warhol filter (E. Diaz). On the right top is an example of an assignment exploring the use of parametric curves to create organic shapes and designs (A. McKaba), while below this is a 'painterly' sketch with the use of defining various shapes to represent strokes is applied to a scene defined by implicit curves, allowing students to explore texture (B. Saguache). Bottom row, example student's work from an assignment focused on digital image representation including the implementation of simple edge detection and compositing (A. Gaona, D. Ocampo, A. McKaba).

- **Subtopic** Intro. to physically based animation: particles

  Assignment Fireworks
  Technical Introduction to objects
- **Subtopic** Intro. to hierarchical modeling for animation

  Assignment Build a duck
  Technical Use of the matrix stack
- **Subtopic** Hierarchical modeling for animation II

  Assignment Make the duck walk and fly
  Technical Use of the matrix stack
- **Capstone** Final Project: An original animation

4. EVALUATION AND REFLECTION

Overall, this course has been a successfully collaboration to create an engaging context based introduction to computing. We are very satisfied with the curriculum and with student's engagement with the course.

4.1 Survey results

At the conclusion of the yearlong course, twenty-eight students responded to a survey about the course. Of those students responding to the survey, when asked "How interested are you in learning more programming/computer science?", twenty responded that they were either "very interested" (i.e. planning to enroll in a CS related course the following year) or "possibly interested" (considering enrolling in a CS related course). Only two students responded that they were "not interested" in taking future CS courses (with the final 6 responding that they 'might try one more course' at some future time). The fact that 71% of the students who took this course are interested in taking more courses indicates that the course was a success at inspiring student's interest in computer science.

Students were asked at the beginning and end of the course, what they identified as: technologist, artist, both, or neither. When asked what they identified as at the beginning of the year, nine students identified as technologists, twelve as artists, five as both, and two as neither. When asked to reevaluate their identity at the end of the year, eight identified as technologists, five as artists, fourteen as both, and one as neither. Nine students began the year identifying as only a technologist or only an artist, but now identify as both a technologist and an artist. We see this switch in identity as a very positive outcome for the course as one of the targets of the course is to expose a wide variety of students to the joys of computer science, even those who perhaps initially only identified with the context domain of art.

We asked students to list their top three favorite assignments and their final animation assignment (creating a simple story) was an overwhelming favorite. With the next most popular assignments being an animation assignment focused on simulating fireworks using a particle system and an image processing assignment including both edge detection and image composition (see Figure 3).

One-way to measure the students' engagement is to ask them about extra time and which assignments they showed to others. The top assignment in both of these categories was the final animation assignment – again indicating a strong correlation in student satisfaction with this capstone experience of being able to create and code a story programmatically. The other assignments that students told their friends and family about were "Images - morph" and "Images - Andy Warhol", again indicating studentsâĂŹ enthusiasm for being able to work programmatically with the more complex data structure.

4.2 Instructor Reflections

Overall, the course worked extremely well. Though the coding component started slowly in favor of an early emphasis on art principles, by the end of the course more computer science topics were covered in more depth than would be required or expected at this class level. The end result is that the students moving up to the AP course from Computational Art are very well prepared, with an early exposure to concepts such as object oriented programming and some advanced data structures. Furthermore, a wide variety of math concepts were introduced and used above and beyond what some of the students had yet learned in their math courses. These math concepts were made accessible to all students in the class either through explanation and derivation or simply as "black-box" formulas whose effects could be understood through experimenting with input parameters to see immediate, visual results. Again, the end result was a clear demonstration of the close relationship between math and programming, and a confidence to use code in a modular way. The Animation unit was the only one that proved to be a bit too difficult, coming at the end of the year, and representing the full synthesis of all the most complicated concepts. Students were still able to achieve a basic level of success with the first sub-topics of the unit and the final animation project, but in retrospect this unit will need to be presented differently in the future.

4.3 Examples of student work

At the conclusion of the year, the instructor and several students from the course participated in a district wide art show, demonstrating the students work to a public audience and receiving positive feedback from the audience in response to the student's art in addition to an "innovation award" for the student art.

Throughout the year students produced a wide variety of both static and dynamic art pieces shown in Figures 1, 2 and 3. We include static figures of sample student work, which is just a subset of the lab assignments to provide examples of the type of work created by students.

5. CONCLUSIONS

This preliminary offering of computational art at the high school level was a great success. Of the computer science course offerings at SBHS, it had and has the most diverse student population. The collaborators were able to restructure the college level curriculum to an appropriate level for the high school students and expand the curriculum to more clearly address the related art and design principles. This enhanced emphasis on art and design skills also allowed the course to fulfill student's fine art requirement, making it accessible for a wide audience of students to 'try out' CS. Surveys show that the course overwhelming inspired students to pursue learning more about computer science and that taking the course shifted students' identities positively towards computer science. The fact that the second year of the course offering has an even larger female student population, 38% female, is likewise a huge indicator of the course's success. We plan to make the entire curriculum publicly available in the next year and hope that other high schools are inspired to use this highly successful course in their curriculums.

6. ACKNOWLEDGMENTS

We wish to thank all the 2014-2015 SBHS computational art students for their enthusiasm and art.

7. REFERENCES

[1] J. Bennedsen and M. E. Caspersen. Failure rates in introductory programming. *SIGCSE Bull. 39*, pages 32–36, 2007.

[2] C. Board. The 10th annual AP report to the nation - subject supplement. http://apreport.collegeboard.org/, 2014.

[3] K. E. Boyer, R. S. Dwight, C. S. Miller, C. D. Raubenheimer, M. F. Stallmann, and M. A. Vouk. A case for smaller class size with integrated lab for introductory computer science. In *Proceedings of the 38th SIGCSE Technical Symposium on Computer Science Education*, SIGCSE '07, pages 341–345, New York, NY, USA, 2007. ACM.

[4] R. Bryant, R. Weiss, G. Orr, and K. Yerion. Using the context of algorithmic art to change attitudes in introductory programming. *J. Comput. Sci. Coll.*, 27(1):112–119, Oct. 2011.

[5] J. P. Cohoon and L. A. Tychonievich. Analysis of a CS1 approach for attracting diverse and inexperienced students to computing majors. In *Proceedings of the 42Nd ACM Technical Symposium on Computer Science Education*, SIGCSE '11, pages 165–170, New York, NY, USA, 2011. ACM.

[6] Z. Dodds, R. Libeskind-Hadas, C. Alvarado, and G. Kuenning. Evaluating a breadth-first CS1 for scientists. In *ACM SIGCSE Bulletin*, volume 40, pages 266–270. ACM, 2008.

[7] I. Greenberg, D. Kumar, and D. Xu. Creative coding and visual portfolios for CS1. In *Proceedings of the 43rd ACM Technical Symposium on Computer Science Education*, SIGCSE '12, pages 247–252, New York, NY, USA, 2012. ACM.

[8] M. Guzdial. Teaching computing for everyone. *J. Comput. Sci. Coll.*, 21(4):6–6, Apr. 2006.

[9] M. Guzdial. Does contextualized computing education help? *ACM Inroads*, 1(4):4–6, Dec. 2010.

[10] M. Guzdial. Exploring hypotheses about media computation. In *Proceedings of the Ninth Annual International ACM Conference on International Computing Education Research*, ICER '13, pages 19–26, New York, NY, USA, 2013. ACM.

[11] M. Haungs, C. Clark, J. Clements, and D. Janzen. Improving first-year success and retention through interest-based CS0 courses. In *Proceedings of the ACM Technical Symposium on Computer Science Education*, 2012.

[12] N. Nagappan, L. Williams, M. Ferzli, E. Wiebe, K. Yang, C. Miller, and S. Balik. Improving the CS1 experience with pair programming. *SIGCSE Bull.*, 35(1):359–362, Jan. 2003.

[13] F. Thomas and Johnston. *Disney Animation - the illusion of life*. Abbeville Press, New York, NY, USA, 1981.

The MoveLab: Developing Congruence between Students' Self-Concepts and Computing

Kayla DesPortes
Georgia Institute of Technology
85 5th Street NW
Atlanta, GA 30308
ksdesportes@gatech.edu

Monet Spells
Georgia Institute of Technology
85 5th Street NW
Atlanta, GA 30308
monet.spells@gatech.edu

Betsy DiSalvo
Georgia Institute of Technology
85 5th Street NW
Atlanta, GA 30308
bdisalvo@cc.gatech.edu

ABSTRACT

The MoveLab was an educational research intervention centering on a community of African American and Hispanic girls as they began to transform their self-concept in relation to computing and dance while creating technology enhanced dance performances. Students within underrepresented populations in computing often do not perceive the identity of a *computer scientist* as aligning with their interests or value system, leading to rejection of opportunities to participate within the discipline. To engage diverse populations in computing, we need to better understand how to support students in navigating conflicts between identities with computing and their personal interest and values. Using the construct of self-concept, we observed students in the workshop creating both congruence and dissension between their self-concept and computing. We found that creating multiple roles for participation, fostering a socially supportive community, and integrating student values within the curriculum led to students forming congruence between their self-concept and the disciplines of computing and dance.

Keywords

Physical computing; STEAM education; self-concept; underrepresented minorities; women; dance

1. INTRODUCTION

Students within underrepresented populations in computing often perceive the identity of a *computer scientist* as one that does not align with their interests or values [16, 23]. This misalignment of identities and values often leads to rejection of opportunities to participate in computing [13, 15]. Identity is a complex concept with many theories and methods for exploration. Some studies have explored misaligned identity issues by providing face-saving excuses for activities with computing [8], or contextualized computing in relevant cultures [9]. However, the underlying identity misalignment might best be explored through the processes of students forming congruence or dissension between their self-concept and computing. Forming congruence is the process when a student creates alignment between how she views herself and how she views computing. In contrast, dissension refers to when a student breaks or distances her view of herself from how she views computing. Research has yet to address what characteristics within the learning environment promote congruence, and how educators can better support an environment conducive to this. To shed light on these questions, we observed students and leaders collaborating within a *community of learners* [20]. Throughout this process the students and leaders evolved their perspectives and participation with computing and dance, allowing us to investigate how this supported students in aligning their self-concept with these disciplines. We look at self-concept as one's belief of themselves and particularly focus on how that belief can transform to create *self-occupational congruence* [3] with computing and dance. Self-concept was chosen as the construct to explore these issues because of the previous work using it to understand academic performance [25], gender roles [28], and examining occupational choices [17]. Self-concept theory allows us to explore the misalignment of identities and focus on self-beliefs about one's self and the outside world – both critical influencer on persistence in CS and academics more generally [3, 17].

A community of learners [20] brings together learners with different levels of knowledge and expertise. The MoveLab was a STEAM (Science, Technology, Engineering, Art, and Math) educational experience that brought together leaders who were experts in dance or computing, to work with middle school and high school girls from economically distressed urban areas to create technology enhanced dance performances. The variations in background allowed the students and experts to both contribute to the community as teachers and as learners, enabling a greater balance of power, chances for leaders to model learning behavior, and a wider variety of roles for participation among the students. As the participants worked to produce a technology enhanced dance performance we uncovered many themes that suggest a starting point to investigate how to enable students to foster congruence between their self-concept and computing. More specifically we explored:

What characteristics of a learning environment help students develop congruence between their self-concept and the disciplines of computing and dance?

2. RELATED WORK

2.1 STEAM in Computing Education

STEAM has been defined as interdisciplinary education that includes the arts with STEM in ways to promote creativity and reflection [4]. The arts have often been used as a "*hook*" to get students with interests that lie outside the computing domain engaged with computing. Some investigations have looked at E-Textiles as a way to couple fashion and making with computing [5, 19]. Other studies have investigated the use of creativity with Scratch [18], using robots for artistic creativity [29], or coupling

SIGCSE '16, March 02 - 05, 2016, Memphis, TN, USA

ACM 978-1-4503-3685-7/16/03 $15.00
DOI: http://dx.doi.org/10.1145/2839509.2844586

dance with the Alice programming environment [14]. In general, dance has seen little attention in STEM education efforts, however, dance is a promising domain because it has the affordances of improving creativity and problem-solving, engaging the students in abstract thinking, and giving the students an embodied mode of expression [11].

2.2 Community of Learners

While some STEAM interventions create an equitable educational environment for teaching the arts at the same level as the STEM disciplines [10], it is often the case that the arts education takes a back seat to STEM. We sought to create an equitable educational environment, balancing the arts and STEM, by creating a community of learners. A community of learners, as defined by Rogoff, attempts to engage everyone in the community through their participation in different roles. It is centered around "the idea that learning and development occur as people participate in the sociocultural activities of their community" [20]. We created a community within the MoveLab in which the participants from varying disciplines brought in their sociocultural backgrounds and methods of practice. Through design exercises, students identified themes that were unique to their teenage experience and relevant to their lives allowing them to explicitly share their knowledge. The investigation focused on the interaction between the learners as they shared and applied their distinct knowledge. Incorporating dancers and technology leaders gave students exposure to a diversity of perspectives and backgrounds. Although most of the students did not have discipline knowledge in dance or technology, they contributed their own perspectives thereby integrating their values.

2.3 Adolescent Self-Concept

One's self-concept is composed of abstract self-beliefs that become recognized and more organized throughout adolescence [26]. It consists of multiple dimensions of varying hierarchy. Part of the hierarchical structure of one's self-concept places self-beliefs on a spectrum of stability [24]. At the bottom are the least stable beliefs, which are the ones that are most easily influenced. These consist of decisions about the self in relation to specific experiences, "not only does the individual develop a description of himself in a particular situation or class of situations, he also forms evaluations of himself in these situations" [24]. As you go up the hierarchy of stability, the beliefs become more abstract and contain more stable beliefs about the self in a general sense. For example, if someone does well on an algebra test they now have an experience in which they proved their knowledge of algebra, which then might support a self-belief that they are *good at math*. Aggregation of the experiential self-beliefs begin to shape the higher order beliefs about the self [24]. Our intervention is just one experience that has the possibility to affect higher level beliefs within the students' self-concepts. While one's self-concept is internal, it is shaped by the social environment within these experiences [27] necessitating that we understand the effects of the social environment within our educational setting.

In Byrne and Shavelson's investigation they illustrate a multidimensional organization of self-concept with "perceptions of behavior at the base moving to inferences about the self in sub-areas (e.g., academic—English, mathematics), then to inferences about the self in academic and non-academic areas, and finally to inferences about the self in general" [6]. Within these dimensions adolescents begin to develop *self-occupational congruence* which aligns one's self-concept to the roles one associates with certain occupations [3]. Between the ages of 10 to 18, the exploration of self-concept in terms of occupational roles increases significantly [17] signifying middle and high school as an important time if we hope to influence how students view themselves in relation to computing occupations. The findings from the MoveLab are intended to use empirical evidence to begin to understand how we can create congruence between a student's self-concept and computing such that we can engage more students.

3. METHODS

3.1 Location and Logistics

The MoveLab was a five-day workshop investigating a community of learners [20] as they embarked on a STEAM endeavor to create a technology enhanced dance performance. The leaders consisted of two lead researchers (both women, who also served as technology leaders), two additional technology leaders (both men), and four dance leaders (all women). Leaders collaborated with 13 middle school and high school girls (ages 11 to 15). We recruited students from underserved regions of a large metropolitan city through working with Wondrous Threads[1]. This community organization supports girls and young women (ages 11-19) through building self-esteem, creating healthy living habits, and broadening their horizons through new experiences. We used this method for recruitment because we intended the workshop to be an outreach program to engage students who might not typically get an opportunity to participate with CS and engineering.

The workshop was held at PinWheel, a local performing arts center, and took place during the students' Thanksgiving school break. The workshop ran from 10am to 5pm for the first four days and ended with a half day, running from 10am to 2pm, on the fifth day. Student participation fluctuated throughout the workshop due to family commitments and other obligations. Two weeks after the workshop, there was a Saturday rehearsal and a Sunday recital open to the public, allowing the students to present their dances to a broader audience.

3.2 Curriculum and Learning Goals

The MoveLab consisted of curriculum that exposed and taught the students about dance and computing. The computer scientists and engineers created a microcontroller curriculum using Arduinos and Processing. The curriculum consisted of introduction to sensors and other peripheral components, such as accelerometers, capacitive touch sensors, RGB LED strips, and motors. The technology leaders directed students through the coding process, offering hands on instruction and functional examples as the students typed and performed the coding tasks. We strove for a high-level understanding of the material due to the short duration of the workshop and the students' minimal prior exposure to circuitry and programming.

The dancers and choreographers created a curriculum introducing students to choreographic techniques such as *call-and-response*, *ripples*, and *cannons*, while bringing attention to size, speed, and space. The curriculum consisted of group exercises to get the students moving, improve their body awareness, and introduce them to choreography. We strove for broad exposure to the material, to help students connect different techniques to the choreography in their performances.

---

[1] All organizations and names have been given aliases to protect their identity.

As the workshop progressed, the dance and technology curriculums merged through the students' creation of their dance routines. The technology was applied to the costumes, props, and environment, and incorporated into the dances as the students interacted with the components through their dance moves.

3.3 Dance Themes and Technology

The young women's' design of the technology enhanced dance performance was scaffolded in an effort to make their performances expressive of themes relevant to their values and lives. Leaders conducted a participatory design activity with the young women to understand the pertinent issues in their lives. We used this activity to group young women who were passionate about the same or similar topics, resulting in three equally divided groups. The groups chose to focus on bullying, resisting peer pressure, and the harms of deforestation. One example of how the technology was incorporated is the shirt in Figure 1 from the bullying group. This group used LED lights, capacitive touch sensors, and a piezo buzzer to express emotion and conflict between the bully and the bullied.

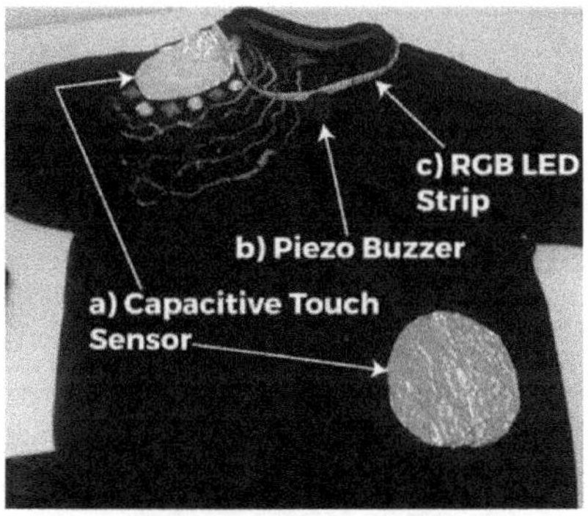

Figure 1. One of the costume tops for the bullying-themed dance, which included a) two capacitive touch sensors, b) a piezo buzzer and c) an RGB LED strip.

3.4 Data Analysis

We administered pre-study surveys to gather background information on the students and capture a baseline understanding of their interests in dance and technology. Post-study surveys gathered information about summative changes in perspectives about dance and technology. Due to the variability in participation, only 6 participants completed both the pre- and post-study surveys. In conjunction with the surveys we conducted observations, and had the leaders capture their real-time observations in a journal. At the end of each day we audio recorded a debrief session with the leaders to gather their observations. At the end of the workshop, semi-structured interviews were conducted with 6 students and 4 leaders. Interviews asked about learning and teaching opportunities during the workshop, the different ways participants contributed to the performance, the participants' use of technology and dance, and their self-concept in relation to technology and dance. The interviews were audio recorded and transcribed.

The interviews, observations, and leader debriefs were reviewed and analyzed for emergent themes by two researchers. They used pattern coding [22] to solidify themes into codes within the codebook (Table 1) to describe the data. After the codes were agreed upon, the two researchers reviewed the data, identified any missed or controversial codes, and discussed and resolved any disagreements. The researchers identified codes within the codebook, which identified characteristics that led to both congruence and dissension between the students' self-concepts and the disciplines of computing and dance.

4. FINDINGS & DISCUSSION

Through our analysis we identified characteristics within the learning environment that influenced the students' transformation of their self-concepts in relation to computing and dance. This was not a straightforward evolution, but more of a negotiation between the students' changing views of dance and technology, in conjunction with their understanding of themselves. As their perspectives evolved over the course of the project, they navigated the incorporation of new aspects of these disciplines into their self-concepts. We found instances in which there was congruence formed between their self-beliefs and the disciplines, as well as instances in which there was dissension formed between their self-beliefs and the disciplines. For space considerations we are focusing on the qualitative data from our study; however, our findings within the survey data are consistent with the findings we will present.

4.1 Developing Congruence

We identified three characteristics within the MoveLab that enabled students to form congruence between their self-concepts and the computing and dance material: (1) creating multiple roles for participation, (2) fostering a socially supportive community, and (3) integrating student values within the themes.

Multiple Roles for Participation. The open-ended project nature of the MoveLab created many roles for the students to get involved with both dance and computing. Many students took on specific roles in their groups such as the role of circuit builder or choreographer. These roles were important for creating agency and facilitating the leaders in guiding the students. Bandura showed that agency could be viewed as an artifact of perceived self-efficacy, which in turn often positively aligned one's perception of themselves within a discipline [2]. The agency the students assumed within the MoveLab enabled them to take on more tasks and engage more deeply with the content in ways that were beneficial to the students and others in the community: *"I was actually kind of surprised because I'm not usually that great...with technology or any of [the] elements surrounding technology. Once I caught onto the computer programming and hooking up different wires...I would help the other people in my group to...catch on with it as well and hook up different sensors." — Janelle (student).*

Like Janelle, we found that by encouraging students to form a narrow expertise, we increased their ability to develop a deeper understanding of a topic rather than a breadth of superficial knowledge. These roles served as a guide for the leaders to understand what piqued the interest of each of the students and to understand where each of them was gaining expertise, so the leaders could then push the students in the directions necessary to engage more deeply with the topics. This deeper engagement created knowledge disparities between the students, allowing them to serve as technical resources for others. This is a key characteristic within communities of learners, which allows for integration and thus appreciation of various types of knowledge in the community [21]. Even the programming aspects had tangible results once uploaded to the microcontrollers. This externalization provided a way for students to gain recognition as others acknowledged and appreciated their contributions. Having a supportive community allowed students to take more risks and not be as afraid of failure.

Table 1. Pattern Codebook used to identify code similarities and extract consistent themes in the data.

Code: Description	Sample Quotes
Developing Congruence	
Agency: Taking initiative to get involved	Some of the students wanted to cut the wires and build the circuits while others jumped to program on the computers.
Pride: Pride over success with material	Once I caught onto the computer programming and…hooking up different wires …I would help the other people in my group.
Narrowing Expertise: Narrowing focus to a particular topic	Students noticed that I'm a little bit more hands-on for the technology side of things and the lead dance instructors are more hands-on for the dancing side of things.
Developing Identity as a Group: Working within the social norms of the group	When it came to coming up with the different sensors and building the sensors, I was more on that end and my other group member was helping more with the dance and costumes.
Expression of Values: Expressing personal values and interests through work	I worked on a project, one that really got me thinking about what I didn't like in the world and what I didn't like within my community.
Developing Dissension	
Preconceived Ideas: Previous ideas influencing participation with material	I would never have thought to put dance and technology together. Until, of course, this workshop.
Avoidance of Failure: Avoiding activities for fear of failing	She was putting on a facade of "I don't care" but in reality she was too nervous to do anything.
Conflicting Values: Previous self-concepts conflicting with work	Because I'm not that big of a dancer…This was definitely a new experience for me, in terms of working with actual dancing. I've never done that because I'm pretty…very STEM focused.
Group Resistance: Resisting participation against the social norms of the group	She was having a lot of trust issues in the teamwork because we were trying to build teams and it was about teamwork and especially in the very beginning, she was really anxious letting the other partner even touch [the sensor].

For example, one of the students reflected on how the environment enabled her to try something new: *"Since I'm so used to doing something strict and technical like ballet, it was a bit out of my comfort zone because I'm not used to just doing freeform whatever...But, um, since it was just the girls I guess it was fine." — Janelle (student).* Creating a place where students could interact in new ways with material they originally felt uncomfortable with, led many of the students to re-evaluate their initial rejection of the material. One student originally only wanted to participate with the technology, but found herself also contributing to the choreography: *"I was actually proud of myself for this. I made up a dance move. I was like 'yay!' because I never make up dance moves." — April (student).* The importance of these experiences ties back to the hierarchical nature of one's self-concept, in which the student's evaluation of herself during specific experiences shapes her higher order beliefs of how she views herself in terms of certain disciplines [24].

Integrating Student Values. We created an initial design activity to enable the students to have control over their performance themes to express values and interests relevant to them. This structured design activity enabled students to talk about issues they were grappling with and helped them represent those issues through dance and technology. Interviews demonstrated that this was an important aspect of the educational experience that differentiated it from other experiences they have had: *"You're still learning but it's more fun and it's not all about learning, it's about helping with life and stuff like that." — Malia (student).* By allowing the students to choose their themes, they began to see how the concepts they learned could be integrated into topics they cared about. When April was asked what her favorite thing about the dance was, she stated: *"My favorite thing is the message behind it...Because we're basically saying that you should not put someone down and that the person that is being put down can, you know, stand up and not take the bullying or the hurt." — April (student).* This expression led students to think of their work as relevant outside of just the workshop, placing it in the context of the *real world.* This change in perspective of the discipline changed what they viewed as authentic to the discipline broadening their initial view of computing and dance. It was clear how important this was to the students and for many this characteristic differentiated the MoveLab from the students' other learning experiences.

4.2 Developing Dissension

Throughout the workshop, students also developed dissension between their perspective of dance and technology and their self-concept. We identified three characteristics that cultivated this dissension: (1) their perspectives of the disciplines (2) fear of failure, and (3) working in a group environment.

Perspectives. The students entered the workshop having already built some ideas around dance and technology. As the leaders worked with the students many of these conceptions were revealed, and they often came out in ways to show how students previously disengaged with the material. Some of their perspectives of the material centered on how they saw the disciplines situated in society. This led to views about who should be participating in certain forms of dance: *"one girl said that...poor kids don't get to go to good schools. And she had drawn a picture of a girl doing ballet that was happy and the rich school...and then a picture of the sad poor girl doing hip-hop" — Whitney (dance leader).*

Many viewed the computing and engineering material from the perspective of their previous experiences in school: *"I learned* [in the MoveLab] *that science doesn't always have to be in the book. It can also be fun. Or you could like use it in life, in real world experiences." – Maila (student).*

Some of the students already had strong identities around dance and/or technology based on their value system: *"I'm not really much of a dancer, but I'm definitely going to be doing more technology." — April (student).* Another student, Harmony, continuously disengaged with the programming aspects of her dance even though she was one of the students with the most experience coding, having attended coding and engineering camps. For example, when one of the leaders asked if she wanted to work on the code for her dance, she quickly ran to the costuming table saying, *"I'm not a technology person."— Harmony (student).*

Our workshop was clearly not the first exposure these students had with either dance or technology. Through the media, school, and informal educational programs, the students had many beliefs and ideas about the topics we presented to them. We observed how these previous experiences seemed to cause them to disengage with the material, making them reluctant to participate. Bringing these beliefs to light enabled our leaders to work with and around perspectives that were creating dissension between the students' self-concepts the material. When a student's value system was conflicted, it was important to be aware and sensitive to them, as it was imperative that activities are done with a respect for students. Research supports the usefulness of revealing students misconceptions about material at the beginning of the learning process [5]. Our study suggests it might also be useful to understand what students' perspectives and values are of a discipline, to reveal how students might view themselves in terms of what participation in these disciplines represents.

Fear of Failure. Many times throughout the workshop, we saw students attempting to do things with either dance or technology and struggling with their self-esteem. If they got to a point in which they were unhappy with themselves, it would often lead to the students disengaging with a particular activity: *"She tried really hard and I think she was doing well, but I think the self-judgment...or whatever her expectation, was not meeting with whatever we were doing. So that put her down and she kept pulling herself down each time" — Aiza (dance leader).* When this happened it would also make it more difficult to get the students to participate with the material in the future because they did not want to be put in that situation again. Students also avoided the material even before they experienced failure. For example, Harmony put forth several inventive ideas, but when asked to think deeper about them and flesh them out more technically, she shut down; we perceived she feared not being able to answer correctly.

The workshop was only five days and the students were novices in both dance and computing, resulting in a performance that could have been improved with more time or previous experience. Some students expressed fear of the final performance being a failure, or had parents who publicly expressed concern that the performance was not of a high enough quality for their child to participate. A few of the students who expressed fear or heard the parent's comments did not show up to the final performance, which we believe was due to avoidance of failure. This type of fear of failure is of particular concern with authentic artistic engagement. Because this was a real performance, at a real art venue, it set an expectation that the quality of the performance needed to be high. However, the limited time working with the students who were not experts created an environment where we sacrificed production quality for student leadership that allowed their ideas to drive the project. By placing the art as central to our STEAM endeavor, rather than just a "*hook*", we unwittingly created a higher bar to reach for authenticity. This raised expectations, and therefore created a greater opportunity for public failure that worked as a barrier to participation.

As we create these experiences for students we need to understand how to help them deal with failure in a way that is healthy and productive, because failure is an important aspect of the creation process for both dance and computing. At the same time we need to understand how to prepare students such that they can feel proud of their final artistic expression. Extending the time to work on the dance and creating a space for them to show their work in ways they are comfortable, are important considerations.

Group Collaboration. While there were many benefits to working in a group, a few of the students had negative reactions to some of the group activities. One of the girls was having difficulties at first working with others: *"So the first day, I thought she is not going to work, like teamwork, so I tried to just talk to her and help her understand that it's a team [activity] and we could make mistakes and we could also correct them." — Aiza (dance leader).* This type of group resistance was much more common at the beginning of the workshop and subsided as the girls became accustomed to the expectations, each other, and the dance and technology material.

We found that the students had trouble working with the group for a number of reasons; for example, failure avoidance, conflicting values, or preconceived ideas. The leaders were often able to understand and work through the student's resistances outside of the group activities. By taking it out of the social context we avoided publicly embarrassing the students or making them feel any additional discomfort. There are a variety of reasons that students might be resistant to participation. It is essential that these moments be handled in ways that do not marginalize the student or their choice to not participate

5. CONCLUSION

Our findings highlight important factors for consideration when attempting to integrate students who might not relate to the computing culture. The interdisciplinary nature of the workshop created opportunities that would not have existed without both dance and technology. Although, the sample size was small, the findings presented provide evidence of important characteristics within the learning environment to understand and explore in order to help students develop congruence between their self-concept and computing. We found that creating multiple roles for participation, fostering a socially supportive community, and integrating student values within the themes, helped develop this congruence. Conversely, student perspectives of the disciplines, their fear of failure, and working in a group setting, caused tensions that created dissension between the student's self-concept and computing. Within these interdisciplinary learning environments it is important to respect the students' values while understanding their perspectives of the disciplines. Educators can then help students learn in ways that fit within their value system. This research offers a first step in understanding students' self-concepts in relation to computing.

6. Acknowledgements

We would like to thank the community organizations and students we worked with on the MoveLab, and Georgia Institute of Technology's GVU Center and IPaT seed funding that enabled this project.

7. REFERENCES

[1] Bandura, A. et al. 2001. Self-Efficacy Beliefs as Shapers of Children's Aspirations and Career Trajectories. *Child Development*. 72, 1 (2001), 187–206.

[2] Bandura, A. 1982. Self-Efficacy Mechanism in Human Agency. *American Psychologist*. 37, 1 (1982), 122–147.

[3] Betz, N.E. 1994. Self-concept theory in career development and counseling. *The Career Development Quarterly*. 43, 1 (1994), 32–42.

[4] Boy, G.A. 2013. From STEM to STEAM: Toward a Human-Centered Education, Creativity & Learning Thinking. (2013), 3.

[5] Buechley, L. et al. 2008. The LilyPad Arduino: using computational textiles to investigate engagement, aesthetics, and diversity in computer science education. *Proceedings of the SIGCHI conference on Human factors in computing systems* (2008), 423–432.

[6] Byrne, B.M. and Shavelson, R.J. 1987. Adolescent Self-Concept: Testing the Assumption of Equivalent Structure Across Gender. *American Educational Research Journal*. 24, 3 (Jan. 1987), 365–385.

[7] Dempsey, J. et al. 2015. The Emerging Role of Self-Perception in Student Intentions. (2015), 108–113.

[8] DiSalvo, B. et al. 2014. Saving Face While Geeking Out: Video Game Testing as a Justification for Learning Computer Science. *Journal of the Learning Sciences*. 23, 3 (Jul. 2014), 272–315.

[9] Eglash, R. et al. 2013. Culturally Responsive Computing in Urban, After-School Contexts Two Approaches. *Urban Education*. 48, 5 (2013), 629–656.

[10] Freeman, J. et al. 2014. Engaging underrepresented groups in high school introductory computing through computational remixing with EarSketch. (2014), 85–90.

[11] Hanna, J.L. 2008. A nonverbal language for imagining and learning: Dance education in K–12 curriculum. *Educational Researcher*. 37, 8 (2008), 491–506.

[12] Hayes, G.R. et al. 2004. Audience in computer learning: a constructionist interpretation. *Proceedings of the 6th international conference on Learning sciences*. (2004).

[13] James DiSalvo, B. et al. 2011. African American men constructing computing identity. *Proceedings of the SIGCHI Conference on Human Factors in Computing Systems* (2011), 2967–2970.

[14] Leonard, A.E. and Daily, S.B. The Dancing Alice Project: Computational and Embodied Arts Research in Middle School Education.

[15] Margolis, J. 2008. *Stuck in the shallow end: Education, race, and computing*. MIT Press.

[16] Martin, C.D. 2004. Draw a computer scientist. *ACM SIGCSE Bulletin* (2004), 11–12.

[17] Montemayor, R. and Eisen, M. 1977. The development of self-conceptions from childhood to adolescence. *Developmental Psychology*. 13, 4 (1977), 314.

[18] Oh, J. et al. 2013. Development and Application of STEAM Based Education Program Using Scratch: Focus on 6th Graders' Science in Elementary School. *Multimedia and Ubiquitous Engineering*. J.J. Park et al., eds. Springer Netherlands. 493–501.

[19] Peppler, K. 2013. STEAM-powered computing education: Using e-textiles to integrate the arts and STEM. *Computer*. 9 (2013), 38–43.

[20] Rogoff, B. 1994. Developing understanding of the idea of communities of learners. *Mind, Culture, and Activity*. 209–229.

[21] Rogoff, B. et al. 1996. Models of teaching and learning: Participation in a community of learners. *The handbook of education and human development*. (1996), 388–414.

[22] Saldaña, J. 2012. *The coding manual for qualitative researchers*.

[23] Shashaani, L. 1993. Gender-Based Differences in Attitudes Toward Computers. *Computers Education*. 20, 2 (1993), 169–181.

[24] Shavelson, R.J. et al. 1976. Self-Concept: Validation of Construct Interpretations. *Review of Educational Research*. 46, 3 (1976), 407.

[25] Skaalvik, E.M. and Skaalvik, S. 2006. Self-concept and self-efficacy in mathematics: Relation with mathematics motivation and achievement. *Proceedings of the 7th international conference on Learning sciences* (2006), 709–715.

[26] Steinberg, L. and Morris, A.S. 2001. Adolescent Development. *Journal of Cognitive Education and Psychology*. 2, 1 (2001), 55–87.

[27] Swann, W.B. 1983. Self-Verification: Bringing Social Reality into Harmony with the Self. *Sociological Perspectives on The Self*. 33–66.

[28] Trauth, E.M. et al. 2012. Embracing intersectionality in gender and IT career choice research. *Proceedings of the 50th annual conference on Computers and People Research* (2012), 199–212.

[29] Turbak, F. and Berg, R. 2002. Robotic design studio: Exploring the big ideas of engineering in a liberal arts environment. *Journal of Science Education and Technology*. 11, 3 (2002),237–253.

Creative Computation in High School

Dianna Xu
Computer Science
Bryn Mawr College
Bryn Mawr, PA (USA)
dxu@brynmawr.edu

Aaron Cadle
Computer Science
Fort Worth Country Day School
Forth Worth, TX (USA)
aaron.cadle@fwcd.com

Darby Thompson
Computer Science
Sidwell Friends School
Washington, DC (USA)
thompsond@sidwell.edu

Ursula Wolz
RiverSound Solutions
Montclair, NJ (USA)
http://riversoundsolutions.com
riversoundsol@gmail.com

Ira Greenberg
Computer Science & Engineering
Southern Methodist University
Dallas, TX (USA)
igreenberg@smu.edu

Deepak Kumar
Computer Science
Bryn Mawr College
Bryn Mawr, PA (USA)
dkumar@brynmawr.edu

ABSTRACT
In this paper we describe the success of bringing Creative Computation via Processing into two very different high schools that span the range of possibilities of grades 9-12 in American education. Creative Computation is an emerging discipline that requires a thorough grounding in both media arts and computing. We report on how contextualized computing that supports integration of media arts, design, and computer science can successfully attract and motivate students to learn foundations of programming and come back for more. The work of two high school teachers with divergent pedagogical styles is presented. They successfully adapted a college-level Creative Computation curriculum to their individual school cultures providing a catalyst for significant increases in total enrollment as well as female participation in high school computer science.

CCS Concepts
• **Social and professional topics~K-12 education**

Keywords
K-12; CS0; CS1; education; creative computation; Processing.

1. INTRODUCTION
Contextualized computing provides a means through which a diverse student population gains insight into the foundations of computer science [Cassel & Wolz 2013]. At the college level this includes media computation [Guzdial 2004], robots [Summet et al 2009, Kumar et al 2008], games/animation [Xu et al 2008, Bayless & Stout 2006], and music [Beck et al 2011]. Extensions into the K-12 curriculum are beginning to occur, but the primary emphasis is on computing principles applied to a sampling of disciplines rather than immersion in an interdisciplinary domain.

SIGCSE'16, March 02–05, 2016, Memphis, TN, USA
 ISBN 978-1-4503-3685-7/16/03…$15.00.
http://dx.doi.org/10.1145/2839509.2844611

Based on successful outcomes at the university level [Greenberg et al 2012, Greenberg et al 2013], the project described here explores high school level immersive experiences in *creative computation* -- a highly interdisciplinary area combining theory and methodology from Computer Science and Engineering with aesthetic principles and creative practices from the fine arts [Maida 2001].

Using a qualitative research approach we studied how creative computation can be applied at the high school level with an eye toward curriculum appropriate for both the existing CS AP A exam and the emerging CS Principles program. Creative computation also has potential for technology, art and media instruction within the common core standards for grades 6-12 (e.g. middle to high school [Wolz et al 2011]).

Two very different high schools (public:James Martin High School, Dallas, TX and private:Sidwell Friends School, Washington, DC) were chosen as the initial participants both because of their school cultures and for the marked difference in teacher pedagogical styles. These differences suggest that creative computation can be adapted across a broad spectrum of school cultures by teachers with a range of organizational and accountability constraints and levels of expertise. More formal analysis of a larger set of schools is underway.

James Martin High School (MHS), located in the Arlington School District in Dallas, TX, is a large (> 3000 student) public high school (grades 9-12) with rigorous standardization at the state level. Sidwell Friends School (SFS), located in Washington, DC is an east-coast elite private PK-12 day school with a total enrollment of approximately 1000 and a deep Quaker tradition.

Both teachers emphasize extensive student-initiated problem solving. Aaron Cadle (MHS) provides a highly structured, more traditional delivery of instruction style using a huge corpus of materials he developed; Darby Thompson (SFS) approaches the material through quick face-to-face delivery followed by extensive one-on-one and small group interaction. Both are experienced computer science teachers and hold undergraduate or higher degrees in computer science.

The two teachers adapted the college-level creative computation, CS1 course to a Level 3B course (proposed CSTA K-12 Curriculum [Seehorn et al 2011]) integrated into their specific curricula. As expected, they took different approaches based on their school culture. Both schools are (1) leaders in their respective geographical areas, (2) have teachers who are proficient in Computer Science, and most importantly (3) have serious commitments from their school heads. We can claim now to have a corpus of exemplars of a Level 3B course that we believe offers an easy on-ramp for high school teachers with experience in computer science, information technology or media studies.

2. CREATIVE COMPUTATION FOR CS1

Creative Computation is an emerging discipline that requires a thorough grounding in both media arts and computing. Put simply, it is the discipline and theory of visual arts rendered through computer code. On top of programming principles students learn essential graphics operations such as transformations, iteration and randomization; algorithmic drawing, animations, basic physics, and interactivity. Areas of focus include creative use of image processing and emergent systems: two and higher-dimensional arrays are natural data structure choices for pixel-based image manipulations as well as implementing Cellular Automata such as Game of Life. Finally, text and data visualization round out the fusion of artistic design and computing.

Students engage in artistic creative acts to practice and master essential concepts. As a vehicle for teaching introductory computer science our design is consistent with a traditional Java-based CS1, however application of these core concepts is taught through highly individualized artistic expression. In other words, we teach the same material as the standard CS1 course, but instead of solving for roots of polynomials, simulating gas station/cash registers, or implementing graphics rendering techniques, we create art, interactive media and visualizations using algorithms and code.

The college level course upon which the high school experience is based comprises the following topics, in typical order of presentation during the semester. Topics 10-12 add advanced material appropriate for visualization and medium-to-large datasets:

1. Introduction to programming and drawing primitives.
2. Variables, data types and expressions
3. Control structures and simple physics simulations
4. Animation, Iterations
5. Using APIs and writing Functions
6. Coordinate systems, trigonometry, geometry and matrix transformations
7. Object-oriented Programming and Design
8. Arrays
9. Inheritance, abstract classes and interfaces
10. Recursion
11. Image processing and emergent systems (2D arrays)
12. Text and Data visualization
13. Transition to CS2 with full Java

Figure 1: Student submissions for assignment 1, after 1 week of lecture

Exercises designed for the course include a sequence of programming projects that utilize the concepts being introduced in the lectures as detailed above. Every exercise has a well-defined basic part and offers students the opportunities to explore open-ended creative projects. This is critical for the retention of student interest and motivation. Students take ownership of their work. Also, as a consequence, each submitted work is a unique program. No two programs are the same.

3. PROCESSING AND FISH TANKS

The curriculum assumes use of the Processing IDE (processing.org). It also assumes an art studio approach of iterative project development based on formal and informal critique. Students develop a visual portfolio of their work as they proceed through the course. Portfolio-based assessments enhance student awareness of the process of gaining and applying programming knowledge and skills especially during the Pilot III efforts being carried out during the development of the CS Principles course [Arpaci-Dusseau et al 2013].

Our perspective follows in the footsteps of John Maeda, who is both a formally trained artist and computer scientist. Inventor of the programming environment Design by Numbers, a precursor to Processing, he pioneered an approach to "Creative coding" that radically *recontextualized* computer code–from an applied math notation to a creative medium, on par with charcoal, paint, clay, etc. Creative coding is an exploratory and aesthetically driven approach, where students build visual designs and artworks iteratively as they expand their programs [Maida 1999].

Processing is built on top of Java with a simplified syntax and an API that focuses on graphics/media programming. It is a robust and full-featured language that has use both in the classroom and beyond; it is used widely in industry and growing quickly in popularity. It supports code writing in Java, Python and JavaScript. A Processing project is developed in a simple IDE that dispenses with the complexity of creating a complex

Figure 2: Class aquarium populated by students, spring 2012

collection of classes, instead using Java inner classes that provide

a gentle introduction [Koffman & Wolz 1999] to object-oriented programming.

For example, a student-favorite among the assignments is a collaborative class aquarium (virtual fish tank) project where students use OOP principles to design an animated (possibly interactive) sea creature of their choosing. Instructors provide an interface - the fish tank and generic fish as a super class or abstract class; and the students contribute customized implementations (sea creature class, physics class, etc). In this exercise they learn OOP principles: classes, objects, inheritance, polymorphism, and also team programming. The aquarium is then populated with student's creatures and displayed in a public space. Figure 2 provides an example, but doesn't do justice to the animated effect of the objects moving in its own way.

4. FROM COLLEGE TO HIGH SCHOOL

The curriculum outlined above has been in place within undergraduate introductory courses at Bryn Mawr College, Bryn Mawr, PA and Southern Methodist University, Dallas, TX for over six years. These institutions saw a significant increase in introductory computing enrollments prior to the more recent national surge. These surges are directly attributable to the creative computation approach (as reported in [Greenberg et al 2012, Greenberg et al 2013]). In addition, we report evidences of this context attracting women and non-STEM or undecided majors to computer science. 20% of Bryn Mawr's all-female freshmen class now takes CS1 (lottery still required), while SMU reports 41% female in Processing-based CS1 classes and 50% women majors in its new Creative Computation program.

Bryn Mawr College is a small, all-women's liberal arts college in the suburbs of Philadelphia that enrolls 1,300 undergraduates. The Computer Science Department offers a B.A. in Computer Science as well as a minor in Computer Science and in Computational Methods.

Southern Methodist University is a private university of 11,000 students near the vibrant heart of Dallas, TX. The university offers nationally competitive undergraduate, graduate and professional programs. The Creative Computation Program is supported through both the School of the Arts and the Department of Computer Science and Engineering housed in the School of Engineering and offers degrees in both Computer Science and Computer Engineering.

In both institutions Creative Computation has been successfully adopted to fit the local intellectual culture. Ten different instructors successfully offered our curriculum more than twenty times. As a curriculum intended to support the bridge from high school to college, a natural consequence was to investigate how it could be adapted to the cultures of high school. The remainder of this paper reports on the experience of bringing Creative Computation into high schools at opposite ends of the of a spectrum. Please visit the project website at www.cs.brynmawr.edu/visual for more information.

5. COACHING FOCUS AT SIDWELL FRIENDS SCHOOL

Sidwell Friends School (SFS) provides the kind of intimate, student-centered setting that is ideal for highly individual, rigorous instruction. The implementation of Creative Computation as elective subject matter at SFS provides a model for schools that can support a highly collaborative environment with close contact between students, faculty and parents in which rigorous engagement by students is expected.

5.1 School Description

Sidwell Friends School is a private coeducational PK-12 Quaker school in Washington, DC. The school offers a rich and rigorous interdisciplinary curriculum designed to stimulate creative inquiry, intellectual achievement and independent thinking. Virtually 100% of students enroll in four-year colleges upon graduation. The students routinely attend a wide variety of colleges and universities including the full range of the most selective institutions in the country. At the start of this project in 2013, The Upper School (grades 9-12) offered computer science as an elective to 480 and had 62 students enrolled (16% female) in academic year 2012-2013.

The computer science curriculum at SFS offers a variety of semester-long courses ranging from introductory programming to data structures and algorithms, artificial intelligence and game development, to dynamic web design. The intention of this curriculum is two-fold: firstly, to provide an accelerated track for students who are already highly motivated to learn computer science and secondly to engage students who might never have considered computer science as a potential major after graduation.

5.2 Pedagogical Style and Curriculum

Darby Thompson has been teaching computer science at SFS for five years and developed the current curriculum from scratch. Previously, she spent five years teaching introductory CS courses at the George Washington University while pursuing her PhD in Computer Science focusing on robotics and user interfaces.

Thompson's teaching style and her school culture de-emphasize worksheet/small task exercises and emphasizes project work. This approach is a direct outcome of her experience with the 'Mindstorms' pedagogy of Seymour Papert. Her resources are organized into 'Labs.' The labs are available on request from the author, and the sequence from the 2014-2015 curriculum implementation is shown in Table 1.

Topics	Lab
1Programming	001_Bouncing_Ball 01_Kindergarten_Picture
2 Functions, variables, basic loops, 2D Arrays	02_Image_Processing
3 Fundamentals, Control structures	03_Andy_Warhol 04_Green_Screen
4 Algorithm development	05_Finding_The_Robots_Ball
5 OOP:Classes, Polymorphism, animation	01_BouncingBall 02_SeaCreature
6 OOP and Design	03_SpaceInvaders
7 Abstraction Strings	04_DataVisualization
8 OOP:Interfaces	05_SwimmableObject 06_Paint
9 OOP:Inheritance	07_SeaCreatureInheritance
10 Recursion	08_HanoiTower
11 Algorithm development, OOP: Encapsulation	09_RobotMaze

Table 1: Articulation of Curricular with High School Labs

Topics 1-4 in Table 1 are covered in an introductory semester-long course, immediately following a 4-week introduction to programming in Python. Topics 5-11 are covered in the follow up intermediate semester-long course with the emphasis on learning OOP. Each course has an open-ended final lab. Her intermediate course final lab is a side scroller/platform game intended to pull together concepts from Object Oriented Programming.

Thompson presents material in a lightening-lecture fashion as the start of a new project. Students are then encouraged to collaborate to develop the basic concepts and skills to complete the project with direct one-on-one support from Thompson. Assessment occurs through rubric-based project evaluation. Student work is displayed throughout the school on large-screen monitors.

5.3 Outcomes Academic Year 2013 – 2014

Sidwell Friends School offers an Introduction to CS course. In the fall semester (2013) this course continued to use Python to explore variables, conditionals, loops and functions. Creative Computation was incorporated into a second semester course: Intermediate Computer Science (Spring 2014). Students engaged in the projects with an emphasis on object-oriented programming and the Java Language. Enrollment in Intermediate CS was 33.

Creative Computation also had a place in Advanced CS. Students used Processing to create data structures (Linked Lists, Trees) and built in data structures to program standard sorting, searching and graphing algorithms. Of the 33 enrolled in Intermediate CS, 8 were graduating seniors, and 22 of the remaining 25 students continued onto Advanced CS giving a retention rate of 88%.

Artificial Intelligence and Game Design is an advanced course, which in this academic year was populated by students who did not have a Creative Computation background. However students intermittently used Processing to develop AI behaviors and program AI players for games such as 4x4 Tic-Tac-Toe.

Ratio of female students doubled to 32% from 16% in 2012-2013.

5.4 Outcomes Academic Year 2014 – 2015

Creative Computation migrated into the Introduction to CS Course and contributed to a dramatic increase in interest in computer science. The curriculum was modified to transition from Python to Processing after the first 4 weeks of the course instead of at the end with positive feedback from the students. In Fall 2014, Thompson taught 4 sections of Introduction to CS with an enrollment of 61 students and 1 section of Advanced CS with a full enrollment of 18 students. The courses were over enrolled. An extra section of Introduction to CS was added. Students faced a lottery to determine if they could take the class. In the spring, 48 students continued on from the introductory class to take Intermediate CS. The 78% does not reflect a significant a downturn in retention, but rather was impacted by the need to limit the number of sections offered.

Ratio of female students again improved to 37% in 2014-2015. Most encouragingly, current female ratio reached 52% in 2015-2016. Fall 2015 will witness our first section with more female students than males and the preliminary signups for Advanced CS for Fall 2015 are 50/50 for the first time since the creation of the program in 2010.

5.5 Curricular Change – Lessons Learned

Creative Computation has been fully embraced at Sidwell Friends School. Initial concern with including Creative Computation in the introductory course was rapidly mitigated as students in the intermediate course produced stunning projects that excited members of the school-wide community. The doubling of interest in computer science between the two years is, of course, significant, as well as the rapidly increasing percentage of female students. It should be noted again that Thompson built the computer science program over a five-year period. Creative Computation sparked the interests of students school-wide.

Students at SFS are noticeably more vocal and confident about their work in the CS courses since the transition to Creative Computation. The approach is more natural to apply to group projects than traditional text-based assignments. In addition, regular reflection is required of the students. Their projects are demonstrated to their classmates and teacher in class, but also to the entire school via a display in the hallway. This has increased the visibility of the CS program at SFS. Although SFS takes a project-based approach, repetition and drills of the basic concepts still play an important role in the course. The open-endedness and creative aspect of the assignments have allowed the courses to be successful for students with a very wide range of abilities.

6. MATERIAL SUPPORT LEARNING AT JAMES MARTIN HIGH SCHOOL

James Martin High School (MHS) has a very different school culture than Sidwell Friends School. It is a large public high school that accommodates a diverse population with a full range of socio-economic needs. As such, expectations for achievement require significant reinforcement via extensive use of highly structured materials. The computer science program at MHS is targeted toward Advanced Placement (a metric used to evaluate the quality of the education unnecessary at schools like SFS). The school culture, in combination with the personal style of CS teacher Aaron Cadle, result in an equally successful experience, but one with significantly more support materials.

6.1 School Description

James Martin High School enrolls over 3300 students in grades 9-12 and is the largest public secondary school in the Arlington independent school district in Dallas, TX. 68% of students who graduate attend a four-year college. In order to serve such a large and diverse population, the school offers over 20 different Advance Placement classes. At the start of this project in 2013, 140 students were enrolled in the Computer Science program (28% female). The CS program consists of three courses at MHS: Pre-AP Computer Science (CS0 at college level), AP Computer Science (CS1 at the college level) and Advanced Computer Science III. Due to early introduction of Processing into the curriculum independent of this project starting in 2010, MHS has enjoyed a higher percentage of female students in the CS program, especially in Pre-AP Computer Science, where much of the Processing instruction concentrated before the start of this project. For the three years 2010-2013, Pre-AP Computer Science consistently enrolled 32%-34% female students, but upper level CS courses rarely saw any female participation.

6.2 Pedagogical Style

Aaron Cadle holds a B.S. in Computer Science from Texas A&M University. He is currently in his 7th year teaching computer science at MHS. Beginning with 45 students and a very traditional CS curriculum in 2008-2009, MFS has grown the program to 140 students as an early adopter of Creative Computation. Beginning in 2010 he redesigned the introductory course (Pre-AP Computer Science) to include elements of Creative Computation using Processing, game development using Scratch, object oriented programming using Jeroo, and hardware design using Logg-O. Currently his Pre-AP Computer Science course covers the first three topics in Table 1. Students typically take this course in 9th grade.

This combination allows students unfamiliar or uncomfortable with computer science to obtain a general understanding while expecting enough rigor to prepare students for a more advanced second year course (AP Computer Science). All second year students are required to take the AP CS exam. AP students boast a 94% passing rate (3 or better) with 80% of those students making a 4 or better on the exam. A third year course (CS III) explores data structures for one semester while focusing on creative computation with Processing and Microsoft Kinect during the second semester.

Cadle employs teaching strategies that support large-class, large-school, diverse-population techniques. He has developed a corpus of approximately 100 individual items in order to keep students engaged and accountable. These include:

- Slide decks: for full class problem solving; both outlines for live writing and completed solutions for review.
- Student worksheets and quizzes, tests.
- Warm ups: quick puzzles assigned to students to solve at the start of class.

Following highly structured presentations and individual assignments via worksheet, he provides 'labs' that are similar in focus and style to Thompson, and indeed provide one-on-one coaching support from the instructor. Assessment occurs through regular quizzes and tests. Materials are available on request from the author.

6.3 Outcomes Academic Year 2013 – 2014

Students used Processing exclusively to implement Creative Computing projects in Pre-AP Computer Science. The syllabus covered basic programming concepts in including variables, conditionals, loops, but also advanced into CS1 territory with introductory object-oriented concepts of methods, and classes. Enrollment for Pre-AP Computer Science reached 125 students (29% female) for the 2013-2014 school year.

In AP Computer Science, Processing was used intermittently to reinforce topics traditionally covered in a CS1 course (Arrays, 2D Arrays, Objected-oriented programming, ArrayLists, Inheritance). 60 students (15% female) took AP Computer Science during the 2013-2014 school year.

Advanced Computer Science III – Students used Processing and a Microsoft Kinect to create motion control games. Students spent the first semester learning the fundamental data structures for Computer Science (LinkedLists, BinaryTrees, Sets, Maps). The second semester students learned how to interact with a Microsoft Kinect through Processing. They spent the entire second semester developing an interactive game using the motion capture features of the Kinect and the graphical abilities of Processing. Enrollment for Advanced Computer Science III was 7 students (14% female) for the 2013-2014 school year.

The number of students taking Computer Science grew from 140 students for the 2012-2013 school year to 193 students for the 2013-2014 school year due to the full-scale introduction of Creative Computation in the classroom. AP CS also more than doubled to 60 from 27 in 2012-2013. A second CS teacher was hired to help with the course load.

6.4 Outcomes Academic Year 2014 – 2015

183 students took computer science in 2014-2015, despite staffing constraints that forced enrollment limits for the first time in Pre-AP Computer Science. 2014-2015 was a building year for MHS's CS program while bringing the second CS teacher to speed. Courses already implemented using Creative Computation and Processing only instituted incremental changes to their curriculum. The second CS teacher taught all four sections of Pre-AP Computer Science and readily adopted Processing as her teaching tool of choice. Enrollment for Pre-AP Computer Science was 107 students (32% female) for 2014-2015, down slightly from 2013-2014 entirely because of the enrollment caps. AP Computer Science enrolled 47 students (13% female), and enrollment for Computer Science III increased from 7 students in 2013-2014 to 29 students (7% female) for 2014-2015.

In addition, currently AP CS in 2015-2016 enrolls 29% female students (45 total). It is the first time in history that AP CS has approached the critical threshold of 30% women.

6.5 Curricular Change – Lessons Learned

Cadle had a head-start on adapting Creative Computation to high school curricula, using Processing in the classroom as early as 2010. However, in the last two years the focused emphasis on the Processing IDE and artistic design significantly influenced the increased interest in and sustainability through computing course offerings. Note that MHS courses are year-long. Sustained enrollment from the Pre-AP to AP course was impacted by limits on section offerings and class size. However the significant outcome is the tripling of the number of students enrolled in Computer Science III. Of the 60 students in AP Computer Science from 2013-2014, 27 chose to continue to CS III in 2014-2015. A 45% retention rate at an academically rigorous public high school is extraordinary, given the competing demands on student attention and time. The increasing participation of female students in upper level CS courses beyond Pre-AP is also very encouraging.

Processing is an event-driven language that requires a "re-thinking" of traditional labs. The first program is no longer "Hello World" but a graphical picture – possibly a smiley face, a robot, or a skyline? Processing allows teachers to contextualize their labs to their environments. Processing allows for more individual exploration as well due to the simplicity of starting a program. Minimal syntax is needed to make a sketch work and the examples on the processing.org website are easy to understand. Some concepts, like recursion, are more readily engaged with students willing to work on a recursive graphical lab much longer than a traditional recursive lab (e.g. code the Fibonacci sequence). Typical worksheets should be redesigned as well. A worksheet on loops now requires students to draw multiple shapes rather than just a sequence of numbers. A combination of both old problems and new Processing problems is a great way to prepare students for a subsequent course that may be more traditional.

7. ANALYSIS

James Martin High School and Sidwell Friends School teachers have successfully adapted the college-level creative computation model to the following course:

- An introduction to computer science course that starts with 4 weeks of Python following by Processing. The course covers materials traditionally associated with CS1 with an introduction to classes but without inheritance.

- An introduction to computer science course that uses Processing exclusively and covers material traditionally associated with CS0.
- An advanced computer science course that parallel expectations for a traditional CS1/CS2 experience exclusively taught in Processing.
- An AP CS course that requires students to sit for the AP exam. Processing and Creative Computation projects are used intermittently because this approach is not well aligned with the test.
- An Artificial Intelligence and Game Design course that has evolved into a significant example of Creative Computation that goes beyond the fine arts.
- An advanced computer science class that covers material traditional found in CS2 as well as providing opportunities for kinesthetic game design.

These courses are taught in two schools at the extreme end of the spectrum of high school cultures, using pedagogy that is similar in the emphasis on project work, but markedly different in use of materials and presentation style.

In both cases enrollment in Computer Science increased significantly, as did female participation. Because the research to date is qualitative on a tiny sample size we cannot draw conclusions about either causality or coincidence. Nation-wide, the CS Principles movement is providing evidence that contextualized computing in safe, uncomplicated IDEs supports increased participation in computer science classes. The conclusion we can draw from this experience is that Creative Computation has a place in the arsenal of appropriate curricula.

8. NEXT STEPS

The authors are concluding a National Science Foundation project in which over a dozen high school teachers have been introduced to our high school Creative Computation curricula. Four 'mini grants' (two public and two private schools) have been awarded to high school teachers to adopt the course and adapted curricula to their own institutions. We anticipate providing more substantive evidence of adaptability to high school within the coming year.

The authors are also developing a publicly available indexed repository that will allow instructors to locate relevant materials by media as well as computing topic, traditional course relevance, and teaching style. Options will be available for curated contributions to the repository.

Finally we address the question of the relevance of this curriculum to (1) current advanced placement preparation, (2) as general preparation for undergraduate level computer science. Creative Computation was used in classes that span 9th – 12th grade, exposing students to material in the CS AP (and in one instance directly preparing them for the exam.) Our experience was not merely 'pushing down' a college level course, but in adapting curricula to the expectations of high school curricula. Our next step is to understand the role these curricula might play in offering the new 'CS Principles AP' as more information emerges.

Regarding the question of transition to an undergraduate experience: the Computer Science Teachers Association (CSTA.org) takes a strong stand on the need to bring computing into the K-12 curriculum. One size does not fit all. The experiences related here suggest a need for rigorous study of impact K-12 curricula for developmentally appropriate experiences. Our report suggests that Creative Computation has a definite place in the high school experience.

9. ACKNOWLEDGMENTS

This project is supported in part by grants from The National Science Foundation (DUE-0942626, DUE-0942628, DUE-1323463, DUE-1323305, CCF-0939370, and CCF-1140489), and from Bryn Mawr College and Southern Methodist University.

10. REFERENCES

[1] [Arpaci-Dusseau *et al* 2013] A. Arpaci-Dusseau, M. Bauer, B. Franke, J. Griffin, R. Morelli, O. Astrachan, M. Carrell, C. Gardner, R. Kick, D. Muralidhar, D. Barnett, R. Dovi, J. Gray, A. Kuemmel, and R. Brook Osborne. Computer Science Principles: Analysis of a Proposed Advanced Placement Course. In *Proceedings of SIGCSE 2013.* ACM Press 2013.

[2] [Bayless & Stout 2006] Jessica D. Bayless and Sean Strout. Games as a "Flavor" of CS1. In *proceedings of SIGCSE 2006.* ACM Press 2006.

[3] [Beck et al 2011] Robert E. Beck, Jennifer Burg, Jesse M. Heines, and Bill Manaris. Computing and Music: A Spectrum of Sound. *Special Session, SIGCSE 2011.* Dallas, TX, March 2011.

[4] [Cassel & Wolz 2013] Cassel, L. and Wolz, U Interdisciplinary Computing, Successes and Challenges. In *Proceedings of SIGCSE 2013.* ACM Press 2013.

[5] [Greenberg et al 2012] Ira Greenberg, Deepak Kumar and Dianna Xu. Creative Coding and Visual Portfolio for CS1. In *Proceedings of SIGCSE 2012.* ACM Press 2012.

[6] [Greenberg et al 2013] Ira Greenberg, Dianna Xu, and Deepak Kumar. *Creative Coding and Generative Art in Processing 2.0.* friends Of ed/Apress 2013.

[7] [Guzdial 2004] Mark Guzdial. *Introduction to computing and programming with Python: A Multimedia Approach.* Prentice-Hall, 2004.

[8] [Koffman & Wolz 1999] Koffman, E. and Wolz, U. CS1 using Java language features gently. In *Proceedings of SIGCSE/ITiCSE 1999.* ACM Press 1999.

[9] [Kumar et al 2008] Deepak Kumar, Doug Blank, Tucker Balch, Keith O'Hara, Mark Guzdial, Stewart Tansley, Engaging Computing Students with AI and Robotics. *Symposium on Using AI to Motivate Greater Participation in Computer Science*, 2008.

[10] [Maida 2001] John Maeda *Design by Numbers*, MIT Press 2001.

[11] [Seehorn et al 2011] K-12 Computer Science Standards, CSTA 2011.

[12] [Summet et al 2009] Jay Summet, Deepak Kumar, Keith O'Hara, Daniel Walker, Lijun Ni, Doug Blank, and Tucker Balch. Personalizing CS1 with Robots. In *Proceedings of ACM SIGCSE 2009.* ACM Press 2009.

[13] [Wolz et al 2011] Wolz, U., K. Pearson, S.M. Pulimood, M. Stone, M. Switzer. Computational Thinking and Expository Writing in the Middle School: A novel approach to broadening participation in computing, *Transactions on Computing Education*, 2011, Volume 2, article 9.

[14] [Xu et al 2008] Dianna Xu, Douglas Blank, and Deepak Kumar. Games, Robots and Robot Games: Complementary Contexts for Introductory Computing Education. In *Proceedings of Third International Conference on Game Development in Computer Science Education* (GDCSE'08), 2008.

Impact of Student Achievement Goals on CS1 Outcomes

Daniel Zingaro
Math and Computational Sciences
University of Toronto Mississauga
daniel.zingaro@utoronto.ca

Leo Porter
Computer Science and Engineering
University of California, San Diego
leporter@ucsd.edu

ABSTRACT

Achievement goals are cognitively-represented end states that individuals strive to reach in competence situations. Well-studied by educational psychologists, achievement goals are robust predictors of grades, interest, and motivation of students. In this paper, we apply achievement goal theory to measure CS1 students' achievement goals and consequent interest in CS and final exam grade. We find that students aiming for topic mastery become interested in CS and, contrary to theoretical expectations, perform well on the exam. A more complex pattern of results surrounds students who orient toward competence demonstration or normative comparison, and the link between such performance goals and outcomes is less clear. We argue for the continued appropriation of educational theory to inform our studies of CS success.

1. INTRODUCTION

Why are some students successful in CS1 and others are not? The answers that we uncover depend on at least three choices: the predictors that we measure, the outcome measures that we collect, and the particulars of the learning process and how the course is taught. Many researchers have investigated this question, but often make these choices in similar ways. Studies often investigate predictors that are thought to be unique to the CS context, collect exam grade or final course grade as the outcome measure of success, and do so in a lecture-based CS1. Authors have since argued that all three decisions should be problematized in the CS research literature: we should consider theory-based predictors from other subject domains, measure outcomes such as interest and self-efficacy in addition to course grades, and do so in courses where new pedagogical tools are in use [21].

Researchers have recently used achievement goal theory to investigate links between students' achievement goals and interest, enjoyment, and grades in CS1 [22]. They found that achievement goals relate to these CS1 outcomes, but in ways discordant with the educational psychology literature in which the framework was developed. In the present paper, we replicate and extend the main findings of that work using a different student pool and different measures of achievement goals that disaggregate larger performance goal constructs. We find that students oriented toward subject mastery become interested in CS and perform well on the CS1 final exam. On the other hand, aiming to outperform peers or publicly demonstrate competence can in some cases be positively related to exam grade, but the link is comparatively less clear.

SIGCSE '16, March 02-05, 2016, Memphis, TN, USA

DOI: http://dx.doi.org/10.1145/2839509.2844553

2. LITERATURE REVIEW

2.1 Predicting CS1 Performance

As carefully outlined by Robins [17], the CS education community has been long intrigued by the possibility of finding factors that separate programmers from non-programmers. Researchers have considered cognitive capacity, learning style, personality, developmental, and other factors that might explain why some students readily succeed at programming compared to others. Research, however, remains inconclusive and contradictory on most if not all of these factors [2]. Mathematical ability is a robust and powerful predictor of programming ability, but it is unclear whether this link measures anything beyond the obvious link between intelligence and programming aptitude [17]. In addition to persevering in the search for discipline-specific predictors, we might make additional progress using predictors known to be important in other domains. While such predictors are unlikely to explain the alleged bimodal distribution in CS1 [17], for two reasons we believe this line of inquiry remains worthwhile. First, there is recent debate around the bimodality of such grades, and whether there really are two separate student populations [13]. Second, it may be that grades are indeed bimodal, but other valued outcomes are not.

2.2 Interest as Valued Outcome

The grade earned by students on exams or in the course itself is one important measure of what has been learned. Indeed, many studies take grades as the sole measure of CS1 success [3, 20].

As noted by educational psychology researchers [10], however, interest in a foundational course can be more important than grades for determining whether students continue to enroll in further courses in that discipline. Early work in CS education suggested that students take CS courses for many reasons, including enjoyment working with computers, desire for a high-paying job, challenging material, and

Goal	Brief Explanation
Mastery	Learn and master the course material
Performance-Appearance	Show others that one is smart and/or good at class-work
Performance-Normative	Perform better than other students

Table 1: Summary of Achievement Goals.

interest in using CS in another field [4, 7, 12]. Recent anecdotal evidence suggests that challenging oneself and learning socially-relevant skills remain compelling reasons for a student to take CS courses [1]. Grades, therefore, do not capture the variety of outcomes that are relevant to students. We suggest that interest in CS is in itself a valued outcome to be cultivated and measured.

2.3 Achievement Goals

The goals adopted by students can have dramatic effects on course performance and intrinsic interest [9]. Achievement goal theory examines those achievement-related goals that reflect the desire to develop, attain, or demonstrate competence [9]. Research suggests two particularly important types of achievement goals: mastery goals and performance goals. A summary of these achievement goals appears in Table 1.
Mastery Goals: Mastery goals are self-referential, focusing on task-based standards or, more commonly, personal improvement. Students with such goals try to learn as much as possible and are thought to seek challenge and persist through difficulty. There is much to suggest the adaptive nature of mastery goals. For example, students that adopt mastery goals are thought to involve themselves deeply in learning processes, use elaborative study strategies, and become interested in academic domains [19]. Indeed, much early literature espoused a mastery goal perspective, arguing that mastery goals should be the sole type of goal adopted by students, and that any positive effects associated with adopting performance goals would be outweighed by their drawbacks [11].
Performance Goals: The effects of performance goals have been much contested, in no small part due to the performance goal label subsuming at least two separable goal types [11]. One type of performance goal is related to **appearance**: demonstrating competence to peers or teachers, possibly also with an evaluative component based on outperforming others. The other type of performance goal is purely **normative**: trying to competitively outperform others with regard to objective standards. This distinction is important, because appearance goals are typically negatively related to course performance, whereas normative goals tend to be positively related to course performance [11].
Multiple Goals: A multiple goals perspective acknowledges the possibility that mastery and performance goals can each contribute to desirable interest and performance outcomes. One statistical pattern supporting this perspective occurs when performance goals predict one valued outcome and mastery goals predict another [19]. For example, one study [10] used a longitudinal design in order to investigate the relationship between achievement goals and interest and performance outcomes. The authors found that students who adopted mastery goals became more interested in psychology and enjoyed lectures more than students who did not adopt mastery goals. On the other hand, students who adopted performance goals earned higher grades in the course and higher semester GPA than did students lacking performance goals. Each type of goal was therefore indicative of a desirable outcome. Outperforming others is not inconsistent with attaining task mastery, and this is borne out by data showing that students can simultaneously adopt both goal strivings [9].
Goals in CS: In a previous study of achievement goals in CS1, the author found support for the mastery goal perspective [22]. Mastery goals were positively related to exam grade, enjoyment of CS1, and interest in CS. Performance goals, on the other hand, were negatively related to exam grade and, in one section of the course but not the other, were related to lower interest and enjoyment in CS. This is at odds with the findings in educational psychology research [19], suggesting that optimal goal strivings in CS may be different than those in other academic areas. However, in that CS1 study, the two facets of performance goals described earlier — appearance and normative — were aggregated into a single performance goal measure. Indeed, not until recently has the importance of separating these strivings been acknowledged [11]. To that end, the goal of the present study is to examine relationships between achievement goals (mastery, appearance, and normative) with valued outcomes (grades and interest in CS).

3. METHOD

3.1 Study Context

We report on a CS1 course taught in Fall 2014 at an undergraduate campus of a large research-intensive university. The course was taught using the Peer Instruction (PI) pedagogy. Briefly, this involves a shift away from lecture and toward classes driven by conceptual questions. Students use clickers to respond to these questions and engage their peers in deliberations over the correct answer. For recent reviews of PI in CS, and expected benefits in terms of learning and instruction, see [16, 23, 24].

The instructor began the course by introducing the rationale for using PI, covering some of the research findings and goals for the peer discussions. Prior to each lecture, students completed a reading quiz; the instructor read the responses to help shape the following lecture. The reading quizzes were graded based on completion (not correctness) and were worth 4% of students' final grade; in-class clicker participation accounted for a further 5% of students' grade. Each lecture was focused on three to four PI questions, with mini-lectures interspersed when planned by the instructor or when performance was poor. The course instructor was a lecturer with significant PI and CS teaching experience, and had taught CS1 using PI several times.

The course took place over 12 weeks, with three 50-minute lectures and one lab session per week. Students were enrolled in one of two sections, both lockstepped in delivery (including the same assignments and exams) and taught by the same instructor. Python was used as the programming language through which traditional imperative CS1 topics were taught. In the final three weeks of class, some CS2 topics were briefly introduced: sorting, complexity, and object-oriented programming.

3.2 Questionnaire Administration

At the start of the semester, students were invited to participate in the research study. Students were introduced to the field of Computer Science Education, and were told that the purpose of the study was to understand whether and why particular types of students succeed in CS courses. This information, along with a link to the first questionnaire, was included in the introductory course slides and sent by email to all students. A small course credit was given to students who completed both waves of the study; students received this credit whether or not they opted to allow us to use their responses in data analysis.

Goals Wave: The first questionnaire was made available for two weeks beginning at the start of the semester. The items (all seven-point, from "not at all" to "very") were intended to measure students' adoption of mastery, appearance, and normative goals. The mastery and normative items were obtained from the Achievement Goal Questionnaire - Revised [6], and the appearance goal items were taken from the Patterns of Adaptive Learning Scales (PALS) instrument [14]. (Some of the PALS items were slightly modified to remove references to importance in favour of explicit goal strivings.) The reliability of each scale was adequate, with Chronbach's alphas of 0.77 (mastery), 0.93 (appearance), and 0.82 (normative). These questionnaire items appear in the appendix.

Interest Wave: In week 10, students were reminded in class that the study contained two questionnaires and that the second questionnaire would now be made available. Again, students were emailed a link to the questionnaire. This questionnaire contained 7-point items assessing students' interest in CS and enjoyment of the specific course and are based on items used by Harackiewicz et al. [10]. Those authors distinguish interest from enjoyment by conceptualizing interest as a substantive interest ("hold" interest) and enjoyment as an affinity for specific course features ("catch" interest). The questionnaire was accessible after students had received most of their graded term work but before the study break leading to the final exams. The interest scale (see appendix) proved highly reliable ($\alpha = 0.91$), but the reliability of the enjoyment scale was low ($\alpha = 0.51$). We therefore do not report further on the enjoyment scale.

Grades: As a measure of course performance, we use students' final exam grade. This is preferred to course grade as a whole because students worked with partners on labs and assignments, and those measures necessarily conflate ability with the ability of their partner and effort in general. Final exams are far from perfect measures of ability [15, 19], but do match the usage in the vast majority of those CS1 studies concerned with student performance.

3.3 Data Analysis

Table 2 details the distributions of the continuous variables; together, the range and standard deviation (SD) suggest considerable spread in response choices. Table 3 contains the zero-order correlations below the diagonal and associated p-values above the diagonal. Across both sections, 298 students wrote the final exam, and 135 (45%) provided all of the required data for the study. The final dataset for this study contained 125 students: 7 students were removed because they spent less than 30 seconds on one or both questionnaires, and a further 3 were removed because their influence statistics were large. (Re-running the models with these students included does not change the overall results.) There was no statistically significant difference between course sections in initial goals, interest in CS, or exam grade, so data were collapsed across sections for analysis. In addition, gender was not a significant predictor in any model (on its own or interacting with other predictors), and so gender was similarly excluded.

Variable	Range	Mean	SD
Mastery	1-7	6.14	0.91
Appearance	1-7	3.31	1.61
Normative	1-7	5.47	1.31
Interest	1-7	5.61	1.14
Exam	0-100	60.69	19.17

Table 2: Range, mean, and standard deviation for continuous variables.

	Mastery	Normative	Appearance	Interest	Exam
Mastery	0.00	0.00	0.88	0.00	0.17
Normative	0.34	0.00	0.00	0.24	0.55
Appearance	0.01	0.44	0.00	0.08	0.52
Interest	0.36	0.10	-0.15	0.00	0.00
Exam	0.12	0.05	-0.06	0.43	0.00

Table 3: Correlations (below diagonal) and p-values (above diagonal) for continuous variables.

Multiple linear regression was used to test the effects of goals on final exam grade and interest in CS. Initial models were constructed to include mastery goals, appearance goals, normative goals, and all two-and three-way interactions. Continuous variables were centred but not standardized. Higher-order interactions were removed from models when nonsignificant. None of the models violated assumptions of constant variance or autocorrelation [8]. The residuals of the interest model were non-normal according to a Shapiro-Wilk normality test. While the non-normality was correctable using a power transformation and did slightly improve the model fit, it did not affect the significance of coefficients. Therefore, to facilitate comparisons with the grade model, we report on the untransformed interest scores and resultant model.

4. RESULTS

Table 4 contains the coefficients, standard errors, and significance symbols for each of the two regression models. As an example of interpreting this table, consider the Mastery row. It shows that a one-point increase in mastery goals is associated both with a 0.40 increase in interest and a 4.75% increase in exam grade. The stars affixed to each number show that these relationships are both statistically significant. The Intercept row gives the mean interest score and exam grade for students at the midpoint of each of the goal predictors.

4.1 Interest

The overall interest model was found to be significant ($f(3, 121) = 7.75, p = 0$). Mastery goals were positively and significantly related to interest in CS ($t = 3.80, p = .0002$), and appearance performance goals were negatively related to interest in CS ($t = -2.03, p = .04$).

	Interest	Exam Grade
(Intercept)	5.67***	63.40***
	(0.09)	(1.81)
Mastery	0.40***	4.75*
	(0.11)	(2.10)
Normative	0.06	−2.96
	(0.08)	(1.84)
Appearance	−0.13*	0.80
	(0.06)	(1.27)
Normative:Appearance		−3.13***
		(0.88)
R^2	0.16	0.11
Adj. R^2	0.14	0.08

***$p < 0.001$, *$p < 0.05$

Table 4: Multiple regressions for interest in CS and exam grade. $a : b$ is used to denote the interaction between a and b.

		Normative		
		low	**medium**	**high**
Appearance	**low**	59	62	65
	medium	67	63	59
	high	75	65	54

Table 5: Interaction of appearance and normative performance goals on final exam grade (%).

4.2 Exam Grade

The overall grade model was found to be significant ($f(4, 120) = 3.85, p = .006$). Mastery goals were positively and significantly related to final exam grade ($t = 2.27$, $p = .025$). The two performance goal main effects (appearance and normative) were not significant, though their interaction was significant ($t = -3.54, p = .0006$). To break down the interaction, we predicted final exam grade for low, medium, and high appearance goals, at each of low, medium, and high normative goals. ("Low" refers to one standard deviation below the mean, and "High" refers to one standard deviation above the mean.) The results appear in Table 5. By examining trends within each column or row of the table, one finds that poor performance is associated with a high level of both goals or a low level of both goals. Students with a low level of one type of goal and a high level of the other perform considerably better. Simple slope analyses confirm that, when one goal is at a high level, the other goal has a significant negative relationship with exam grade.

4.3 Prior Experience

One may wonder whether the reported mastery-goal relationships with interest and grades are spurious, reflecting instead a link between prior experience and these outcomes. Is it that those with prior programming experience are more likely to adopt mastery goals? It appears not.

As a measure of prior experience, we asked students on the first questionnaire to indicate the number of years they had programmed before taking the course. Correlations between prior experience and mastery ($r = .16$), appearance ($r = -.01$) and normative goals ($r = -.07$) are all non-significant ($p > .05$). In addition, adding prior experience to the interest and grades regressions, we find that the patterns of significance and non-significance remain unchanged. Unsurprisingly, prior experience does significantly predict interest ($p = .025$) and grades ($p = .047$) in these augmented models, but there is no evidence that controlling for prior experience explains the relationships between goals and outcomes.

5. DISCUSSION

5.1 Who Becomes Interested in CS?

We find that mastery goals are positively correlated with interest, normative goals are not significantly correlated with interest, and appearance goals are negatively correlated with interest. The mastery link with interest is well-documented in other fields [10]; perhaps more surprising is the negative link between appearance goals and interest. Why might this be so in CS, particularly a PI-based CS1? Indeed, the finding appears counterintuitive. Consider one of the appearance statements: "One of my goals is to show others that I'm good at my class work". PI, with its focus on group discussion and argumentation, gives students many opportunities to show their peers that they are "good" at their class work. One might therefore expect students who score highly on such appearance items to enjoy PI and thereby become interested in CS. However, the opposite was found. This may be a case where student interviews could yield fruitful results.

In the meantime, we offer one hypothesis: perhaps it is difficult in PI discussions for students to prove that they are good at their class work! We strive for one- to two-thirds of students to answer each PI question incorrectly. In such circumstances, it is unlikely that students can answer many questions correctly on their own. This motivates the group discussions as students work collaboratively and pool their knowledge resources to arrive at a correct answer. Appearance-goal students may want to demonstrate their knowledge, but are unable to do so without the group discussion and argumentation. That is, these students might prefer to be able to tell their groupmates the correct answer to each question rather than negotiate the correct answer. There is evidence that performance-oriented students do exhibit unique behaviour patterns in group settings; for example, they are intolerant to ideas that are obviously wrong and dismiss inaccurate information [19]. It is worth pursuing this understanding further, particularly the possible effects of appearance-oriented students on others in their group.

5.2 Who Does Well in CS?

Replicating previous findings [22], we find a positive correlation between mastery goals and exam grade. This result is unexpected if one holds to a multiple goals perspective. In considerable educational psychology research, mastery goals are unrelated to grades [10, 18]. Furthermore, the multiple goals perspective contends that performance goals do positively correlate with grades, but we do not find clean evidence of that here. Appearance goals **can** positively correlate with exam grade, but only when normative goals are low. Similarly, normative goals **can** positively correlate with exam grade, but only when appearance goals are low. Striving for both types of performance goals simultaneously is maladaptive. As mastery goals do not interact with these performance goals and are independently and positively predictive of exam grade, our evidence presented here supports a mastery goal perspective. We hypothesize that our results in CS differ from findings in other fields due to different styles of exams and effective means for studying for those exams.

5.2.1 *Differing Examination Practices*

If we compare our CS exams to typical introductory psychology exams, differences are immediately apparent: psychology exams are often normatively-graded multiple-choice exams, whereas CS1 exams tend toward comprehensive code-writing [10, 15]. The exam for the present course consisted of large code-writing questions, multiple-choice questions, and code-explaining and tracing questions, in approximate thirds. Some contend that performance-goal students, with their superficial study strategies, can perform well on multiple-choice tests but not tests requiring synthesis and integration [18]. Yet, recent research suggests that performance goals are in fact more adaptive than mastery goals on difficult tasks compared to easy tasks [18]. Understanding why and how performance goals operate in the face of difficult material may help us remedy the unclear link between performance goals and CS1 exam grades.

As ancillary analyses, we separately investigated both the multiple-choice and code-writing portions of the exam. The pattern of findings remained intact; in particular, mastery goals positively predicted these subsets of exam grades. Therefore, on both small conceptual questions and integrative code-writing questions, it appears that mastery goals are advantageous. Methodical research on this point is warranted.

5.2.2 *Differing Student Studying Strategies*

We know from the achievement goal literature that mastery and performance goals are each associated with a somewhat distinct set of study practices [5, 19]. The core distinction in study practices is between surface strategies (e.g. memorizing, re-reading) and deep strategies (e.g. elaborating). Though both mastery and performance goals have been associated with both types of studying, mastery goals are more often linked to deep strategies and performance goals are more often linked to surface strategies [5]. One reason that mastery-focused students may perform well on exams is that their mastery goals can lead to deep study strategies which in turn can lead to increased exam grades. We wonder to what extent this may be uniquely true in CS. Others have noted the tightly-interconnected nature of CS concepts [17], so that if a student fails to learn one topic then they are increasingly likely to fail to learn future topics. Given such coupling, it seems plausible that deep study strategies, where students make connections between topics and seek synthesis of ideas, would prove advantageous on exams. This suggests that educators should explicitly model and encourage connection-building between concepts, both to highlight the ways that concepts tend to relate and interact in CS, and to encourage this integrative approach to studying and learning.

6. CONCLUSION

The CS education research community has gamely proposed and studied numerous predictors of CS success, with mixed results. Under-studied, however, is the appropriation of theoretical frameworks from other disciplines that might prove to be useful in CS as well. To this end, we have continued the nascent investigation of achievement goal theory as the guiding framework. We find that goals do predict performance and interest in CS1. Mastery goals positively predict interest and exam grades, whereas some performance goals are negatively related to interest and interact to positively or negatively predict exam grades. It seems worthwhile to continue this investigation: if we can clearly link goal strivings and success, then we might be able to influence students' achievement-related behaviour and thereby their interest and grades in CS1. We encourage the community to take up these concerns as we further discover what achievement goal theory can teach us about student success.

7. REFERENCES

[1] Why so many harvard students take computer science. www.businessinsider.com/why-so-many-harvard-students-take-computer-science-2014-9. Accessed November 10, 2015.

[2] A. Ahadi, R. Lister, H. Haapala, and A. Vihavainen. Exploring machine learning methods to automatically identify students in need of assistance. In *Proceedings of the Eleventh Annual International Conference on Computing Education Research*, pages 121–130, 2015.

[3] J. Bennedsen and M. E. Caspersen. An investigation of potential success factors for an introductory model-driven programming course. In *Proceedings of the first international workshop on Computing education research*, pages 155–163, 2005.

[4] L. Carter. Why students with an apparent aptitude for computer science don't choose to major in computer science. *SIGCSE Bulletin*, 38(1):27–31, 2006.

[5] A. Elliot, H. McGregor, and S. Gable. Achievement goals, study strategies, and exam performance: A mediational analysis. *Journal of Educational Psychology*, 91(3):549–563, 1999.

[6] A. J. Elliot and K. Murayama. On the measurement of achievement goals: critique, illustration, and application. *Journal of Educational Psychology*, 100(3):613–628, 2008.

[7] A. Fisher, J. Margolis, and F. Miller. Undergraduate women in computer science: experience, motivation and culture. *SIGCSE Bulletin*, 29:106–110, 1997.

[8] J. Fox and S. Weisberg. *An R Companion to Applied Regression*. Sage, second edition, 2011.

[9] J. M. Harackiewicz, K. E. Barron, and A. J. Elliot. Rethinking achievement goals: When are they adaptive for college students and why? *Educational Psychologist*, 33(1):1–21, 1998.

[10] J. M. Harackiewicz, K. E. Barron, J. M. Tauer, S. M. Carter, and A. J. Elliot. Short-term and long-term consequences of achievement goals: Predicting interest and performance over time. *Journal of Educational Psychology*, 92(2):316–330, 2000.

[11] C. S. Hulleman, S. M. Schrager, S. M. Bodmann, and J. M. Harackiewicz. A meta-analytic review of achievement goal measures: Different labels for the same constructs or different constructs with similar labels? *Psychological Bulletin*, 136:422–449, 2010.

[12] T. Jenkins. The motivation of students of programming. *SIGCSE Bulletin*, 33(3):53–56, 2001.

[13] R. Lister. Computing education research: geek genes and bimodal grades. *ACM Inroads*, 1(3):16–17, 2010.

[14] C. Midgley, M. L. Maehr, L. Z. Hruda, E. Anderman, L. Anderman, K. E. Freeman, M. Gheen, A. Kaplan,

R. Kumar, M. J. Middleton, J. Nelson, R. Roeser, and T. Urdan. *Manual for the Patterns of Adaptive Learning Scales (PALS)*. University of Michigan, 2000.

[15] A. Petersen, M. Craig, and D. Zingaro. Reviewing CS1 exam question content. In *Proceedings of the 42nd ACM technical symposium on Computer science education*, pages 631–636, 2011.

[16] L. Porter, C. B. Lee, and B. Simon. Halving fail rates using peer instruction: A study of four computer science courses. In *Proceedings of the 44th ACM technical symposium on Computer science education*, pages 177–182, 2013.

[17] A. Robins. Learning edge momentum: A new account of outcomes. *Computer Science Education*, 20(1):37–71, 2010.

[18] C. Senko, A. M. Durik, L. Patel, C. M. Lovejoy, and D. Valentiner. Performance-approach goal effects on achievement under low versus high challenge conditions. *Learning and Instruction*, 23:60–68, 2013.

[19] C. Senko, C. S. Hulleman, and J. M. Harackiewicz. Achievement goal theory at the crossroads: Old controversies, current challenges, and new directions. *Educational Psychologist*, 46:26–47, 2011.

[20] P. Ventura and B. Ramamurthy. Wanted: CS1 students. no experience required. *SIGCSE Bulletin*, 36:240–244, 2004.

[21] D. Zingaro. Peer instruction contributes to self-efficacy in CS1. In *Proceedings of the 45th ACM technical symposium on Computer Science Education*, pages 373–378, 2014.

[22] D. Zingaro. Examining interest and performance in computer science 1: A study of pedagogy and achievement goals. *Transactions on Computing Education*, 15(3), 2015.

[23] D. Zingaro, C. Bailey-Lee, and L. Porter. Peer instruction in computing: the role of reading quizzes. In *Proceedings of the 44th ACM technical symposium on Computer Science Education*, pages 47–52, 2013.

[24] D. Zingaro and L. Porter. Peer instruction in computing: The value of instructor intervention. *Computers & Education*, 71:87–96, 2014.

APPENDIX

A. MASTERY AND PERFORMANCE

These questions make up the mastery- and performance-goal scales, as asked of students on the start-of-course questionnaire. Mastery and performance labels were not included.

Indicate the extent to which each statement is true of you from 1 (not at all) to 7 (very):

Mastery [6]:

- My aim is to completely master the material presented in this class.
- I am striving to understand the content of this course as thoroughly as possible.
- My goal is to learn as much as possible.

Performance, appearance [14]:

- One of my goals is to have other students in my class think I am good at my class work.
- One of my goals is to show others that I'm good at my class work.
- One of my goals is to show others that class work is easy for me.
- One of my goals is to look smart in comparison to other students in my class.
- I aim to look smart compared to others in my class.

Performance, normative [6]:

- My aim is to perform well relative to other students.
- I am striving to do well compared to other students.
- My goal is to perform better than the other students.

B. INTEREST

These questions make up the interest scale, as asked of students on the end-of-course questionnaire.

Indicate the extent to which each statement is true of you from 1 (not at all) to 7 (very) [10]:

- I think what we are learning in this class is interesting.
- I think I will be able to use what I learn in this course in other courses.
- I would recommend this class to others.
- I am enjoying this computer science class very much.
- I think the field of computer science is very interesting.
- This class has been a waste of my time.
- I'm glad I took this class.
- I think the course material in this class is useful for me to learn.
- I would like to take more computer science classes after this one.
- I am more likely to register for another computer science class because of my experience in this course.

Introducing and Evaluating Exam Wrappers in CS2

Michelle Craig
Computer Science
University of Toronto
mcraig@cs.toronto.edu

Diane Horton
Computer Science
University of Toronto
dianeh@cs.toronto.edu

Daniel Zingaro
Math & Computational Sciences
University of Toronto Mississauga
daniel.zingaro@utoronto.ca

Danny Heap
Computer Science
University of Toronto
heap@cs.toronto.edu

ABSTRACT

In addition to their role as a summative measure, midterm tests can provide formative feedback that can be used by students to identify areas of weakness and adjust studying approaches. Unfortunately, low levels of test pickup often preclude this type of learning from tests. Even when students do collect their marked tests, it is unclear how much they reflect on or learn from the feedback.

Exam wrappers have been designed and used in other sciences to promote reflection on tests and improve study practices. In this paper, we introduce exam wrappers into a CS course. We outline our adoption of exam wrappers, and illustrate how we as educators can learn from student responses on exam wrappers. We also describe an experiment comparing three styles of exam wrapper. Although it did not find significant differential impact on exam scores, we find, for all wrapper styles, improved test pickup rates and qualitative evidence that students successfully reflect on past behaviour and recognize improved study strategies.

1. INTRODUCTION

Responding to elevated failure rates [9] and disappointing student understanding [5], CS researchers and educators have implemented a wide range of strategies to promote student success. New pedagogical approaches [11], early-warning feedback mechanisms [10], and connecting to students' contextual interests [3], among others, demonstrate the creativity and efficacy of these strategies. Frequent and timely feedback to students is important in many of these efforts. For example, Peer Instruction, a research-based pedagogical approach, involves offering feedback to students several times per class [11], and some teaching tools are based primarily on short exercises paired with immediate feedback [1, 7]. Under-explored in this literature, however, is the use of this type of feedback to encourage student reflection and self-regulated learning [6]. Yet, if students do not reflect on and learn from the feedback we provide, it is unlikely that the feedback will inform future behaviour and improvement.

SIGCSE'16, March 02–05, 2016, Memphis, TN, USA.

http://dx.doi.org/10.1145/2839509.2844561

In this paper, we explore the use of "exam wrappers" in CS2. As further discussed in the next section, exam wrappers scaffold students' use of the feedback made available when marked exams are returned. To our knowledge, exam wrappers have not been used in CS. This paper introduces our discipline-specific modifications to the concept of exam wrappers, evaluates the results of an experiment comparing three types of exam wrappers, and studies student responses to the wrappers themselves.

2. BACKGROUND

2.1 What are Exam Wrappers?

Exam wrappers were introduced by Marsha Lovett in response to students' poor study strategies and inability to use feedback to learn about their learning difficulties [6]. Exam wrappers are structured reflection activities that students engage in after their instructor has marked and returned an exam. They help students practice metacognitive skills such as planning, evaluating performance, and changing behaviour based on past successes and failures.

Lovett discusses three types of questions that compose her exam wrappers:

Reflecting on Preparation. The goal of these questions is to have students reflect on the choices that they made when studying for the exam. For example, how much time was spent, where was the focus, what study strategies were used?

Kinds of Errors. Having reflected on their studying, students are asked to categorize the types of errors they made. One hope is that students will connect suboptimal study strategies with certain types of mistakes on the exam. For example, reading and rereading the same material is likely to be a poor study strategy, perhaps evidenced by lost marks on application- or synthesis-type questions.

Changes for Next Time. The ultimate goal of the exam wrapper and its focus on metacognition is student improvement. For these questions, students are asked how they intend to improve for next time. Student responses should be guided by their reflection on where they lost marks and how their existing study strategies were inadequate.

Exam wrappers can be completed quickly by students, target important metacognitive skills and, as we discuss below, are readily adapted to new disciplinary contexts.

2.2 Research on Exam Wrappers

There are few evaluations of the benefits of exam wrappers. In the paper introducing them [6], wrappers were evaluated in four courses: biology, chemistry, physics and calculus. The author provides three complementary findings. First, looking at wrapper responses themselves revealed that students intended to use a variety of study strategies in the future. Unfortunately, there is no evidence that students did use these strategies or that these strategies were productive if indeed used. Second, on an end-of-semester survey asking students how their study strategies had changed, more than half of the students mentioned specific strategies that they had adopted. And third, the number of courses taken by a student in which exam wrappers were used positively correlated with increases in metacognitive strategies and productive study strategies.

Other research indirectly supports the potential utility of exam wrappers. Extra help, resources, examples, and review sessions provided by an instructor often have little effect on the targeted students [2]. One reason is that low-performing students for whom the help is offered often do not avail themselves of the support. By making an exam wrapper "mandatory", *i.e.*, allocating marks for completing it, an instructor can increase the number of students that may benefit. Second, if the students don't see concrete connections between an intervention and the ways in which it relates to course success, then students may lack the motivation or support to adopt new strategies. Exam wrapper questions can make explicit the connection between the use of new strategies and the reasons why those strategies are thought to be beneficial.

3. THE STUDY

We implemented exam wrappers in a large CS2 course at a research-intensive Canadian university during the winter term of 2015. The course took place over 12 weeks, with two one-hour lectures and a two-hour lab session each week. The course uses Python and students study object-oriented programming, recursion, linked lists, implementations of trees, abstract data types, and complexity. In addition to labs, students completed three assignments, and wrote two term tests and a final exam. After each term test, students were given a wrapper activity; those who completed the wrapper earned 1% towards their course grade.

We conducted an experiment by randomizing students into three treatment groups, each of which received a different type of wrapper. We then sought to detect differential impact of wrapper types by comparing grades on the final exam for students who submitted wrappers for both tests. We also studied how test pickup behaviour compared to the previous year when we did not use wrappers.

Finally, we used an inductive coding approach to analyze the responses to the test-1 wrappers. The second author coded each textual response with relevant codes and then combined the codes into larger thematic units. These themes were accepted if they subsumed multiple related codes. Note that the codes and themes were not agreed upon a priori but were generated from the data-analytic process itself.

3.1 Wrapper Types

Two factors influenced our choices of wrapper questions on the two term tests. First, our reading of the literature suggested that wrappers are likely to have positive impacts and certainly no negative impacts. Second, our use of wrappers is borne out of a concern that students do not carefully read and reflect on the feedback given on their graded tests. In fact, our experience is that a significant fraction of the class does not even pick up their tests.

We anticipated that explicitly understanding where marks were lost would go a long way toward mobilizing metacognitive processes that might support improvement on future tests. To give all students this possible benefit, all three types of wrappers began with a question asking students to indicate the number of marks that they lost for each reason in a list of possibilities. (See Table 5). Categories were based on our knowledge of relevant skills and test-specific content, the latter of which changed on each term test. The questions on each wrapper given after these "marks-lost" questions are as follows (see appendix for more details):

Placebo. For this wrapper group, students were given a page of placebo questions related to interest in and enjoyment of CS. The purpose of these questions was simply to increase the work required to complete the placebo wrapper to make it comparable to that required by students from the other groups.

Metacognition. This wrapper group was asked questions intended to scaffold reflection and planning. The first questions concerned how the student had prepared for the test. They were asked to report the total amount of time they spent studying and how they distributed this time across various studying activities. Items on the list itself demonstrated good study practises, and we hoped that asking students to examine their investment in each would be beneficial. The remaining questions required students to reflect on what worked well and how they plan to improve their studying.

Content. This wrapper group was asked to answer a programming question on content similar to that given on the test. On its own, yet another practice problem is unlikely to help students improve. In this case, however, the content question was presented after asking students to carefully go through their test and add up lost marks. For this reason, we thought it possible that completing the programming question would further assist students in learning material of obvious importance in the course.

Wrote both tests	516
Completed both wrappers and gave informed consent	259
Placebo	81
Metacognition	86
Content	92

Table 1: Number of participants

Prior to term test 1, students were randomized into one of these three wrapper groups. Students were instructed to pick up their test, to which a wrapper page had been stapled. This page gave a table in which students could work out their marks-lost responses, and a link and login token for a website where their responses, including marks-lost, were to be entered. Once the student logged-in, they were asked the wrapper questions corresponding to their randomly-assigned group. The wrapper group assigned to a student on term test 1 was then used again on term test 2, to increase the "dosage" of wrapper answered by each student, and to cleanly separate effects of different wrapper types. See Table 1 for participation rates.

4. RESULTS

Prior to any other analysis, we verified that the grades on the first term test between the three wrapper groups were statistically indistinguishable. This would validate that our randomization was effective in balancing the initial skill of our three groups. A one-way ANOVA of wrapper group on term test 1 grade shows that there is no evidence of difference ($f(2, 256) = 0.1, p = 0.91$).

4.1 Wrapper Type and Exam Grade

Did the type of wrapper have an effect on students' final exam grade? Table 2 answers this question using a one-way ANOVA on the exam grades of the three student groups. 259 students who submitted both wrappers are included in this analysis. In the row labeled "group", we see a p-value of 0.67 which is above the 0.05 threshold for significance. There is therefore no evidence that the groups differ; the type of wrapper given to students did not influence their exam grades.

	Df	Sum Sq	Mean Sq	F value	Pr(>F)
group	2	89.50	44.75	0.40	0.6727
Residuals	256	28857.50	112.72		

Table 2: Effect of exam wrapper group on final exam grade.

Focusing in particular on the content wrapper, it is unlikely that the programming question answered by this group would have a global effect on exam grades as a whole. After all, the exam covers many topics, most of which would not be covered by a single content-related programming question. Instead, perhaps there are content-specific improvements for the content wrapper group that are visible on the exam. On the wrapper for term test 1, we asked the content group to design a `Fraction` class and associated methods. One of the questions on the final exam similarly asked students to design a class, and we wondered whether the content group would exhibit gains on this question. Table 3 shows this not to be the case, as the p-value of 0.97 is above the 0.05 significance threshold. (We ran a corresponding analysis for the content group on test 2 with similar results.)

	Df	Sum Sq	Mean Sq	F	P
group	2	0.19	0.09	0.02	0.9763
Residuals	256	1000.32	3.91		

Table 3: Effect of exam wrapper group on final exam class design grade.

4.2 Time Taken to Complete Wrappers

As Table 4 shows, the median time taken to complete the wrapper questions for test 1 is substantially different across wrapper types. (Results on term test 2 are similar.) The placebo group took the least time, followed by the metacognitive group, followed by the content group. Medians were used rather than means because of skew in the time taken by the content group. In future, we will work to better balance these time demands. But the imbalance does allow us a claim here: the content group failed to outperform the other groups on the exam in spite of allotting more time to their wrapper questions.

group	time (seconds)
placebo	61.21
metacognitive	255.66
content	716.75

Table 4: Median time taken to answer wrapper questions.

4.3 Influence of Wrappers on Test Pickup

As was done in past offerings of the course, graded tests were returned in lecture, and students who did not pick up their tests at that time were invited to pick them up in office hours. Historically, we observe that a disheartening fraction of the class does not pick up their graded tests, which unfortunately precludes those students learning from the provided feedback. In winter 2014 we observed a correlation between test pickup and exam performance: students who picked up tests had median exam scores significantly higher than those who didn't (Wilcoxon rank-sum tests with $p < 0.0004$ (test 1) and $p < 0.02$ (test 2)). We expected that our introduction of exam wrappers would influence this behaviour, because completion of each wrapper contributed 1% towards a student's grade in the course and test pickup was required to obtain the login token to complete the wrapper questions. Indeed, this effect was seen. In winter 2014, prior to the use of wrappers, we found for both tests that 54% of students picked up their graded test. With our addition of exam wrappers, 2015 pickup rates rose to 87% (test 1) and 74% (test 2).

Figure 1 shows the percentage of students who collected their graded test 1 broken down by quartiles of student performance on that test. The increase attributed to the introduction of wrappers is seen equally in all quartiles of the class.

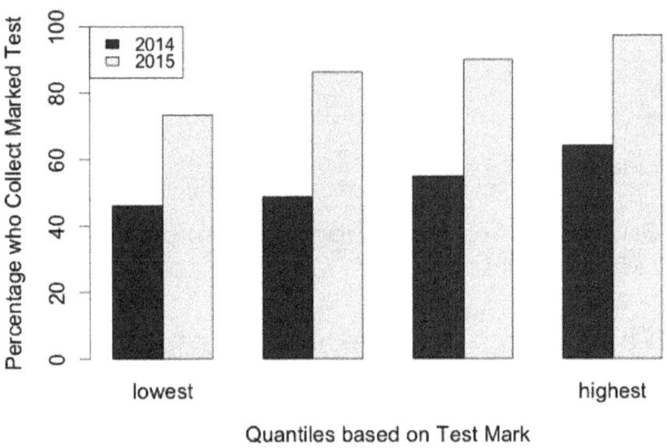

Figure 1: Test One Pickups by Quartile prior to and after the introduction of test wrappers.

Reason	S	M
Not knowing how to translate the question description into code	88	2.0
Not understanding self	62	1.3
Not knowing how to write the special methods `__init__` and/or `__eq__`	147	1.0
Not being able to correctly trace a call to a recursive function	148	2.4
Not knowing what to put in the parent class vs. the child class	89	1.6
Not understanding exceptions	49	1.5
Not being fluent with the prerequisite material that the course presumes you already know	54	1.8
Misunderstanding what the question was asking	119	1.9
Syntax errors or careless mistakes (where you knew the answer conceptually)	209	1.7
Not being able to come up with the algorithm needed to solve the problem	52	1.9

Table 5: Number of students (out of 373) who reported losing marks for each reason on our list (S), and mean number of marks lost among those students (M). The test was out of 25.

4.4 Students' Reflection on Lost Marks

Here we provide a qualitative analysis of the 373 responses to test-wrapper 1.

All wrapper types included the questions about where students lost marks. Table 5 shows the number of students who reported losing marks for each of the reasons we anticipated. Reasons are listed in the order in which we provided them on the wrapper. If a single error fell under multiple categories, students were asked to include that error in each relevant category. The most common reason cited for losing marks was "Syntax errors or careless mistakes (where you knew the answer conceptually)". The marking scheme was not punitive for syntax errors that did not reflect a lack of understanding. Therefore, this large number of responses likely represents students' misattributing their errors and overestimating their understanding of the material. Many students reported losing marks due to issues with specific programming constructs and concepts. Many also lost marks due to lack of higher-level skills or prerequisite knowledge.

Students could also provide up to three other reasons for losing marks. We categorized their free-text responses in Table 6. One might expect students to have been primed by our question and to give similar reasons to those that we listed. Yet, the most common responses concerned students managing the test-writing situation, including time management and being careful; our list did not prime students for this. We see this category of responses as incorporating elements of metacognition and self-reflection, and are encouraged by students' awareness of the importance of these skills.

Category	n
Managing yourself on the test	36
Recursion	21
Object-oriented programming	10
Other general programming issues	9
Reading and interpreting the questions	6
Quality of code (not correctness)	5

Table 6: Categorization of free-form text responses indicating where marks were lost for reasons other than those listed in Table 5.

4.5 Metacognition Wrapper

We asked students in the metacognition group to report on how they prepared for the test. We next analyze the 122 metacognition-group answers submitted for test-wrapper 1. The median self-reported study time was 5.0 hours and the mean was 9.3 hours. The mean was inflated by one outlier who declared having studied for 170 hours.

Table 7 shows how students divided their study time across various activities that we listed. By far, the most time was devoted to reading lecture notes and example programs. On average, 55% of study time was spent on activities that did not involve writing code. Of code-writing activities, the most time was devoted to solving old tests and exams and re-doing lab activities, both of which are productive ways to prepare for a test. Relatively few students (8%) took the initiative to invent their own coding tasks. This is an important skill that we may wish to help students develop, perhaps through a Contributing Student Pedagogy [4].

It is not clear whether students who solved old tests and exams were doing so on paper or were running their code. Practising on paper does simulate the test environment, however students also need to develop their ability to know when their answer is correct. One student's comment about redoing lab activities demonstrates that this skill is sometimes lacking: "I redid all the lab exercises but the extra exercises had no solutions to them so I didn't do them because I wasn't sure if it would have been making the best use of my time".

Activity	Study Time	M.E.	I.T.
Creating a summary of the course course concepts	13%	14	5
Going to office hours/ help centre with questions	2%	1	21
Discussing the course concepts with a friend	8%	7	8
Reading the lecture notes and example programs	27%	26	11
Editing and running the example programs	9%	8	6
Re-doing the lab activities	11%	36	26
Reading the textbook	5%	5	3
Writing other relevant Python code for practise	8%	11	13
Solving old tests and exams	17%	24	8
Other responses	1%		

Table 7: Test preparation activities listed by students on the 122 metacognition wrappers, average percentage of study time devoted to each, number of students who reported that it was the most effective activity (M.E.), and number who reported that they devoted insufficient time to it (I.T.).

We also asked students which activities provided the most effective preparation and to which activities they felt they had devoted insufficient time. Table 7 shows the number of students who chose each of our provided responses.

Re-doing lab activities was most often cited as the most effective activity, and it was also an activity to which many students indicated that they had not dedicated sufficient time. On average, only 2% of study time was spent seeking help at office hours or the help centre; however, again many said that they had devoted insufficient time to it. Using this type of feedback to advise future students is an active area of research [8].

In addition, 20 students identified as most effective some activity not on our list. These responses were either very broad (for instance, "keep practising") or were given by only one or two students. No interesting categories emerged in the analysis of these responses. 41 students identified some activity not listed by us as one they had insufficiently undertaken. Most often they referred to specific concepts, particularly recursion. 11 students reported that they planned to change little or nothing.

The final portion of the meta-cognition wrapper asked students to project forward by listing "at least three things that you plan to do differently as you prepare for the next test." Table 8 shows a categorization of student responses. The most frequent responses focused on strategies for studying. Many of the strategies students gave were ones we had listed as answer options for the question about how students had divided their study time. We expected, and in fact hoped, to see students listing these good practices. Very few students mentioned specific course material. Rather, the focus was on higher-level strategies and self-regulation. What we don't know is the extent to which they acted on these reflections; this is an important open question.

Category	Subcategory	n
Strategies	use resources	125
	use course staff or friends	72
	practise	51
	summarize	14
	study examples	4
	memorize	3
	total	**277**
Self-regulation	keep up	22
	study more	16
	use lecture or lab better	7
	study more thoroughly	5
	be more careful on test	5
	sleep more	4
	miscellaneous	3
	total	**62**
Significant change not needed	planned no change	7
	listed fewer than 3 changes	8
	total	**15**
Content-related	syntax	5
	recursion	2
	total	**7**
Other	total	**8**

Table 8: Categorization of responses from the 122 students in the metacognition group to the question on areas for improvement in their test preparation.

5. CONCLUSIONS AND FUTURE WORK

What is the role of test wrappers in CS courses? Our analysis of student responses suggests engagement with the test wrapper questions and evidence of student awareness of effective and ineffective regulatory and learning processes. Students demonstrated mature reflection on what went wrong on their tests, why things went wrong, and what they can do in the future to improve. That said, we found no difference in exam grades between our three experimental conditions. This leads to three related areas of future work.

First, given existing evidence of test wrapper effectiveness in other sciences [6], we were not comfortable here with a pure placebo group where students answer no questions of relevance. However, we wonder whether our "no experimental effect" was due in part to the marks-lost questions providing baseline gains for all wrapper types. We plan to run a true placebo study to disentangle possible gains hidden by the marks-lost questions. Second, metacognitive advances are less potent when the target of learning, and the skills that are most effective, are unknown [8]. That is, while our test wrappers may have highlighted effective strategies, it may not be clear to students how to implement those strategies and how these strategies should be mobilized to learn particular content. Future work might therefore include using learning analytical data to make students aware of links between study practices and course success. Finally, we suggest that post-course follow-up (interviews or a third survey) would help determine the extent to which students "do what they say" on the test wrappers. Are students mindful of and do they take seriously their intentions as written on their test wrappers? Are there gaps between intention and action where we can intervene?

We see test wrappers as a new and largely-unexplored technique for increasing what our CS students learn from their tests. We have demonstrated that wrappers can be applied to CS and have introduced several types of questions that we see as particularly relevant. We hope the community will help us move this research forward as we seek to understand the optimal use and potential benefits of test wrappers in the CS curriculum.

6. REFERENCES

[1] Problets. www.problets.org. Accessed July 22, 2015.

[2] L. Deslauriers, S. E. Harris, E. Lane, and C. E. Wieman. Transforming the lowest-performing students: an intervention that worked. *Journal of College Science Teaching*, 41:80–88, 2012.

[3] M. Guzdial. Exploring hypotheses about media computation. In *Proceedings of the Ninth Annual International ACM Conference on International Computing Education Research*, pages 19–26, 2013.

[4] J. Hamer, Q. Cutts, J. Jackova, A. Luxton-Reilly, R. McCartney, H. Purchase, C. Riedesel, M. Saeli, K. Sanders, and J. Sheard. Contributing student pedagogy. *SIGCSE Bulletin*, 40(4):194–212, 2008.

[5] R. Lister, E. Adams, S. Fitzgerald, W. Fone, J. Hamer, M. Lindholm, R. McCartney, J. Moström, K. Sanders, O. Seppälä, B. Simon, and L. Thomas. A multi-national study of reading and tracing skills in novice programmers. *SIGCSE Bulletin*, 36(4):119–150, 2004.

[6] M. Lovett. Make exams worth more than the grade. In M. Kaplan, N. Silver, D. LaVague-Manty, and D. Meizlish, editors, *Using reflection and metacognition to improve student learning: Across the disciplines, across the academy.* 2013.

[7] D. Marchena Parreira, A. Petersen, and M. Craig. PCRS-C: Helping students learn C. In *Proceedings of the 2015 ACM Conference on Innovation and Technology in Computer Science Education*, pages 347–347, 2015.

[8] C. Ott, A. Robins, P. Haden, and K. Shephard. Illustrating performance indicators and course characteristics to support students' self-regulated learning in CS1. *Computer Science Education*, 25(2):174–198, 2015.

[9] C. Watson and F. Li. Failure rates in introductory programming revisited. In *proceedings of the 19th conference on innovation and technology in computer science education*, pages 39–44, 2014.

[10] C. Watson, F. W. Li, and J. L. Godwin. No tests required: Comparing traditional and dynamic predictors of programming success. In *Proceedings of the 45th ACM Technical Symposium on Computer Science Education*, pages 469–474, 2014.

[11] D. Zingaro and L. Porter. Peer instruction in computing: The value of instructor intervention. *Computers & Education*, 71(1):87–96, 2014.

APPENDIX: Test 1 Wrapper Questions

All wrapper types

Look back carefully over your test and compare your answers to the sample solutions posted on the course website. In the table below, select the number of marks lost on the test for each of the categories. Lost marks can count in multiple categories, so the total does not need to match the total number of lost marks on your paper, but every mark you lost on the paper should appear in at least one category." Answer options are shown in Table 5 in the order in which they were presented to students.

Metacognition wrapper

-Approximately how many hours, in total, did you spend preparing for this midterm?
-Now consider what you did to prepare for this midterm. Approximately what percentage of your preparation time did you spend on each of the following activities? (Answer options shown in table 7.)
-Of the activities listed above, which do you think was the most effective as preparation for the test?
-What did you NOT do (or didn't spend enough time doing) that you realize would have been effective?
-List at least three things that you plan to do differently as you prepare for the next test.

Placebo wrapper

Indicate the extent to which each statement is true of you from 1 (not at all) to 7 (very):
-I think what we are learning in this class is interesting.
-I think I will be able to use what I learn in this course in other courses.
-I would recommend this class to others.
-I am enjoying this computer science class very much.
-I think the field of computer science is very interesting.
-This class has been a waste of my time.
-I'm glad I took this class.
-I think the course material in this class is useful for me to learn.
-I would like to take more computer science classes after this one.
-I am more likely to register for another computer science class because of my experience in this course.
-The lectures in this class really seem to drag on forever.
-I don't like the lectures very much.
-I like my professor.

Content wrapper

Design and implement a class called Fraction. It needs to record a numerator and a denominator, which do not have to be in their simplest form. For example, we could have 8/2 or 6/8. Write just these two methods: 1. an initializer that is passed the numerator and denominator, and 2. a method to multiply the fraction by another fraction and return a new fraction containing the result. You must include docstrings, but you are not required to write doctest examples.

Measuring Effects of Modality on Perceived Test Anxiety for Computer Programming Exams

Robert Deloatch, Brian P. Bailey, Alex Kirlik
Department of Computer Science
University of Illinois
Urbana, IL 61801
{deloatc2, bpbailey, kirlik}@illinois.edu

ABSTRACT

The modality students use to complete programming-centric exams is shifting from paper to computer. We developed and distributed a survey to investigate how exam modality affects student perceptions of test anxiety and performance during programming-centric exams. We examine the distribution of modality preference among students and understand how students cope with test anxiety. We found a majority of students report at least moderate perceived anxiety (rating $\geq$ 4 on 7-pt scale) on paper- (69%) and computer-based (64%) exams. Though moderate anxiety was experienced by a majority of the students, we found 1 in 5 students had no strategy to cope with anxiety. Additionally, we examine how students perceived anxiety during testing affects their thought process and behavior. We found computer-based exams were perceived as more beneficial to the quality and speed of student's solutions and a majority of students preferred computer-based testing (67%). Lastly, we introduce possible technological solutions to benefit students experiencing test anxiety while not impeding less anxious students.

Keywords

Test anxiety, computer-based testing, programming-centric exam

1. INTRODUCTION

Students experiencing high levels of test anxiety struggle to remain focused while competing with pessimistic expectations, irrational outcomes, and physical feelings of sickness [1]. Test anxiety can lead to lower levels of academic achievement, self-esteem, and motivation [1, 7, 12]. Test anxiety has typically been studied in courses that use paper-based exams [7]. As computer-based exams have become more common, researchers have begun to study how this change in modality affects student's test anxiety. However, these studies have been typically performed in context of exams with forced choice questions (e.g. multiple-choice or true-false), whereas we are interested in programming-centric exams [10, 20].

A programming-centric exam is an exam in which students must write code to solve open-ended problems. These types of exams are also becoming more computer-based. Access to a compiler, debugger, and the ability to execute code provides students with a programming exam experience that is more representative of the conditions programming is normally performed [2, 6, 8, 25]. Students have responded favorably to such exam environments, with up to 75% of students preferring computer-based assessment to traditional paper-based assessment [25]. The favorable responses from students and the potential advantages of reduced grading time, dynamic content, increased possibilities for feedback, improved grading consistency, and alternative testing styles make it likely that computer-based testing will continue to grow in courses that teach programming [14, 18, 25].

In this paper, we report the results of a large-scale survey examining student perceptions of anxiety and performance when taking programming-centric exams on paper and computer. We also survey student preferences for exam modality (paper vs. computer) for programming-centric exams and collect self-reported strategies for coping with test anxiety. Though we focus on anxiety in testing situations, similar phenomena can be seen in programming-centric job interviews and work places with tight programming deadlines.

The survey was first distributed to students enrolled in two programming courses and later to all undergraduate students enrolled in the computer science program at our institution (N=391). Our key findings include: (1) 22% of students reported high test anxiety (rating $\geq$ 6) and this was not affected by exam modality, (2) 67% of students preferred taking programming-centric exams on a computer, (3) students perceived an increase in solution quality and completion time for computer-based exams, (4) women reported higher levels of perceived anxiety for computer-based exams compared to paper-based exams whereas the opposite pattern was detected for men, and (5) though many coping strategies were reported (e.g. taking a mental break or outlining psuedocode), 22% of students reported having no strategy for coping with test anxiety. Lastly, we describe technological solutions that would benefit students experiencing test anxiety without impeding less anxious students.

2. RELATED WORK

In section 2.1, we define test anxiety, describe its effects, and discuss how examining perceived anxiety for programming exams with differing modalities contributes to this lit-

SIGCSE '16, March 02-05, 2016, Memphis, TN, USA
 ISBN 978-1-4503-3685-7/16/03...$15.00
DOI: http://dx.doi.org/10.1145/2839509.2844604

erature. In section 2.2, we describe how we extend previous work on the effects of modality on test anxiety and other measures.

2.1 Studies of Test Anxiety

Test anxiety is defined as a combination of physiological and emotional responses in conjunction with worry and catastrophizing that occur while preparing for and during testing situations [1]. Early studies lend support to a two-factor model of test anxiety. The cognitive factor, "worry," contains mental behaviors, such as pessimistic expectations, absent-mindedness, self-criticism, and irrational outcomes. The second factor, "emotionality," affects heart rate, feeling of sickness, sweating, and tense muscles [16]. More recently, studies using factor analytic methods still include worry, but have decomposed the emotionality factor into three distinct factors – tension, test-irrelevant thinking, and bodily reactions [3, 23].

In a meta-analysis of test anxiety studies, Hembree found test anxiety negatively correlated with IQ, aptitude, and achievement tests, problem-solving and memory tasks, course grades, and cumulative GPA [12]. For example, Blankstein found that students with higher levels of test anxiety scored lower on the Academic Problem-Solving Inventory [4]. In addition, high test anxious students display strong fears of negative evaluation and lower levels of self-esteem [12]. Further troubling is the prevalence of test anxiety. Previous studies have found between 25-48% of students experience test anxiety [1, 13, 17] and that it disproportionately affects women [21]. Reduction of test anxiety has increased scores on IQ, aptitude, and standardized tests as well as increased GPA [12]. Therefore, educators should be aware of the test anxiety that students experience and attempt to reduce it.

Test anxiety is often measured using questionnaires that focus on test-taking independently of modality, such as the Reactions to Tests and the Cognitive Test Anxiety scale [7, 23]. Performance on multiple choice exams or psychological tests are then used as dependent measures to compare students of different test anxiety levels [5, 10, 22]. In our work, we use a custom questionnaire because we are interested in examining student's perceived anxiety for different exam modalities and eliciting their coping strategies. In addition, we focus specifically on exams that require students to write code that solve open-ended problems.

2.2 Effects of Modality on Test Anxiety and Other Measures

Previous work has examined the effect of modality on test anxiety in programming courses. Haghighi conducted a study where students completed a two-section final exam [9]. The first written section contained concept questions, diagrams, and flowcharts. The second computer-based section required programming. The authors found that students with less programming experience reported higher levels of anxiety for the computer than on paper. We extend this work by studying the effects of exam modality on perceived anxiety using a larger population of students from various years of study, courses, and prior exam experiences. In addition, we collect and analyze the coping strategies that students reportedly use in these situations.

Other researchers have studied the effect of modality on logical thinking in programming courses, student and instructor perceptions of programming exams, and reading comprehension. For example, Kim found logical thinking scores were unaffected in separate semester long courses where one required computer programming and the other required written logical thinking exercises [15]. In addition, Barros found that a majority of students perceived computer-based exams as contributing to a better final grade [2]. When learning was assessed using computer-based exams, instructors felt more confident in their evaluation of student learning [8]. Our work is similar to these studies because we also measure the effects of exam modality. However, we differ because we investigate the effects of modality on perceived anxiety, preference, and coping strategies.

3. METHOD

The goal of our study was to answer these questions:

1. How does the modality of a programming-centric exam affect student perceptions of test anxiety and performance?
2. What percent of students prefer paper versus computer-based exams and how does this vary by year of study and experience with each modality?
3. For those students that experience test anxiety, how does it affect them and how do they cope with it? How do students cope differently between modalities?

The first question is important because the transition to more computer-based programming exams could lead to increased anxiety. This is interesting because a change in self-perception has been shown to correlate with changes in motivation and academic achievement [24]. From the second question we hope to replicate findings from prior work about preference and contribute new findings about how year of study and modality experience affect this preference. The third question was intended to learn coping strategies used by students. This will provide insight into how instrumentation of computer-based exams might support students who experience test anxiety. To answer these questions we conducted a large-scale survey.

3.1 Survey

The survey contained nine 7-point Likert questions and three open-ended questions. It was developed as a Google Form. The survey instructed participants that the programming exams referenced in the survey questions pertains to exams where they were specifically asked to write coding solutions. The survey was piloted in Fall 2014 and refined based on the preliminary data. Key questions from the survey are shown in Table 1. This survey was distributed to two large undergraduate courses (see below). The survey was then modified to include additional open-ended questions, while some of the rating questions were removed to maintain reasonable completion time. The survey took about 15 minutes to complete and participants were entered in a drawing to win two $25 gift cards. This variation was then disseminated to the computer science departments undergraduate listserv. Students that participated in any prior surveys were removed. A subset of the open-ended questions can be seen in the last four rows of Table 1. In Table 1, the scale for Quality and Speed ranged from 1 (least favorable) to 7 (most favorable), with 4 indicating no effect. For Anxiety, the scale ranged from 1 (no anxiety) to 7 (high

Question Key	Question
Quality	What effect does taking a programming exam with [paper/computer tools] have on the quality of your solutions?
Speed	What effect does taking a programming exam with [paper/computer tools] have on your ability to finish quickly?
Anxiety	How much anxiety do you typically experience on programming exams given with [paper/computer tools]?
Preference	Please indicate your preference for how programming exams are given.
Cope	What are some of the ways you cope with anxiety during a programming exam?
Process	Think back to some of your previous programming exams. How did your anxiety affect your thought process, behavior, and/or experiences on the exam?
Challenge	What are the largest challenges you've experienced when taking a programming exam with [paper/computer tools]?
Benefit	What are the largest benefits you've experienced when taking a programming exam with [paper/computer tools]?

Table 1: Eight questions asked in the survey. The first four questions asked for ratings on a Likert scale, whereas the last four asked for open-ended responses. Note that [paper/computer tools] indicates the question was repeated for both modalities.

anxiety). For Preference, it ranged from 1 (strongly prefer paper) to 7 (strongly prefer computer) with 4 indicating no preference.

3.2 Courses and Participants

The survey targeted undergraduates at a large midwestern university who have taken courses requiring exams with computer programming. To recruit participants two courses were contacted via email with a link to a survey. The email was sent to a Spring 2015 Computer Architecture course with 329 students and a Computer Systems & Programming course with 326 students. We chose these courses because the instructors were using computer-based exams that required students to write code. The email was also sent to all undergraduate students in the computer science department–1,235 students–to gain broader perspectives.

We received responses from 391 participants meeting the stated qualification of having taken an exam that required them to write programming code on either paper or computer, yielding a response rate of 25%. The participants identified as 79% men and 21% women. (80%) of participants declared a major or minor of computer science and 18% declared a major or minor of electrical engineering or computer engineering. Participants included 25% in their first year, 45% in their second year, 19% in their third year, and 10% in their 4th year or more. In addition, 23% of participants had only taken computer programming exams using paper, 8% of participants had only taken a computer programming exam on the computer, and 69% had taken exams on both paper and computer.

4. SURVEY RESULTS

Figure 1 shows the frequency distribution of the perceived anxiety participants reported for each modality. It shows that 22% (n = 61) of students perceive high anxiety (rating ≥ 6) when writing code on paper-based exams and 23% (n = 64) perceive high anxiety when writing code on computer-based exams. In addition, a majority of students report at least moderate levels of perceived anxiety (rating ≥ 4) for paper-based (69%; n = 189) and computer-based (64%; n = 176) exams. Figure 2 shows the frequency distribution of the modality preference for participants. Strong preference (rating ≥ 6) for computer-based testing (49%; n = 135) was observed. Additionally, a majority of participants had at least a moderate preference (rating ≥ 5) for computer-based testing (67%; n = 185). 12% (n = 33) of participants had a strong preference (rating ≤ 2) for paper based exams and 21% (n = 58) had at least a moderate preference (rating $\leq$ 3) for paper based exams.

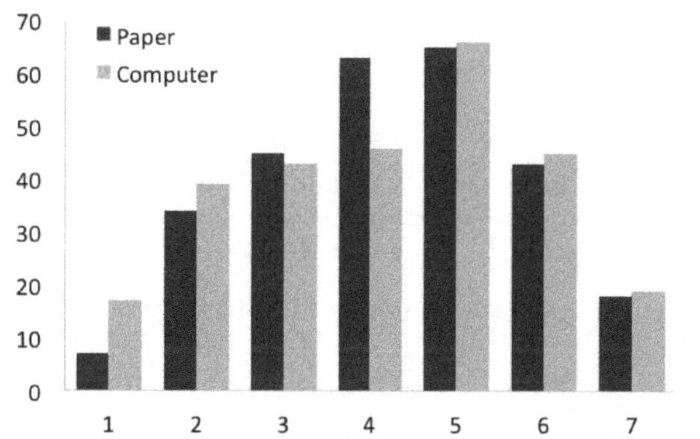

Figure 1: The frequency distribution of perceived anxiety reported by participants per modality. Darker bars represent paper and lighter bars indicate computer (N= 275). The x-axis ranges from 1 (no perceived anxiety) to 7 (high anxiety).

Question Key	Paper	Computer
Quality	3.62 (1.44)	5.09** (1.35)
Speed	3.40 (1.58)	4.94** (1.55)
Anxiety	4.26 (1.51)	4.15 (1.67)
Preference	58	185**

Table 2: The means and standard deviations for survey responses Quality, Speed, and Anxiety. The fourth row shows the counts for the survey responses to the Preference question. ** means p < .001

We conducted four planned comparisons within the data. The means and standard deviations can be seen in Table 2. A Wilcoxon signed rank test showed that when exams were administered on a computer, students perceived their solutions to be of higher quality ($\mu = 5.09$), and perceived faster development of those solutions ($\mu = 4.94$) compared to when performing exams on paper ($\mu = 3.62$, $p < .001$, $\delta = 1.03$; $\mu = 3.40$, $p < .001$, $\delta = .98$; respectively). Another Wilcoxon signed rank test revealed participants reported no

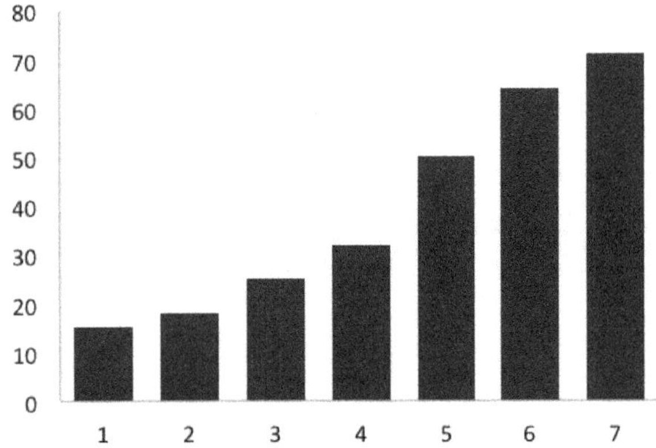

Figure 2: The frequency distribution of reported modality preferences (N=275). The x-axis ranges from 1 (strongly prefer paper) to 7 (strongly prefer computer).

Modality	Women	Men
Paper	4.27 (1.52)	4.25 (1.51)
Computer	4.78* (1.51)	3.99* (1.67)

Table 3: The means and standard deviations for the survey response Anxiety for women (N = 55) and men (N = 220). * means p < .05

difference in perceived anxiety for paper (μ = 4.26) and computer-based exams (μ = 4.15, p = .39). A one-sample Wilcoxon signed rank test was used to compare the student modality preferences against no preference (rating = 4). The test showed a significant preference for computer-based testing ($\mu = 5.04$, $\sigma = 1.8$, $p < .001$, $d = .82$).

We also investigated gender differences, as test anxiety has been found to disproportionately affect women [21]. Table 3 shows the means and standard deviations for perceived anxiety reported by gender for each modality. Two Wilcoxon signed rank tests revealed women reported higher levels of perceived anxiety for computer-based exams (μ = 4.78) than paper-based exams (μ = 4.27; p = .05). Men reported the opposite pattern: they reported lower perceived anxiety for exams taken on a computer (μ = 3.99) than on paper (μ = 4.25; p = .05). No gender differences were detected for perceptions of solution quality, speed, or modality preferences.

We also examined if preferences differed between students whose only exam experiences consisted of paper, computer, or both and if a difference existed as year in school increased. A Kruskal-Wallis test showed that no difference existed between modality experiences ($\chi^2 = 2.09$, $p = .35$). A Jonckheere-Terpstra Test showed that there was a significant trend in preference for paper-based testing as year in school increased (1st year, μ = 5.57; 4th+ year, μ = 5.06; p = .0386). This could indicate that as the complexity of course content increases, students perceive fewer benefits from using tools to write code on exams.

Coping Strategies. The open-ended responses were segmented into idea units. An initial pass of the data assigned thematic codes to each unit. Subsequent passes were then performed to aggregate the existing codes and form more abstract categories. This continued until the themes were perceived to be reasonably exclusive. When reporting each theme, we give the number of participants who shared that response. The responses to the Cope question yielded 3 common themes. The first theme, "Relaxation Techniques," included responses centered around breathing or taking a break (n = 31). For example, P58 stated *"Take some time to calm and simply zone out and take a mental break for a bit."* The second theme was participants that experienced anxiety, but had no strategy for coping (n = 25). For example, P64 stated *"I don't [have a strategy]. Haha. Programming exams are super stressful."* The third theme was "Writing," which includes behavior such as drawing pictures, writing checklist, or writing pseudocode (n = 12). P28, for example, wrote *"[I write] loads of comments to help me flesh out my thoughts."*

The responses to the Process question yielded three themes. The first theme, "Difficulty Focusing," consisted of behaviors, such as blanking out or being easily distracted (n = 27). P80, for example, stated that it is *"really hard to think clearly and logically"*. The second theme, "Increased Mistakes," focuses on small mistakes that participants perceive they make that they wouldn't if not for feeling anxious (n = 17). For example, P96 stated, *"my anxiety made it harder...causing me to make mistakes I normally wouldn't."* The third theme, "Increased Worry," focuses on behavior such as feelings of being unconfident in their solutions to easy questions, continuously checking answers, and worrying about forgetting simple things (n = 10). For example, P85 stated *"I have a tendency to second-guess things I would otherwise be sure of."*

The responses to the Challenge question when asked regarding paper exams, yielded four major themes. The first theme, "Organization," focuses on responses involving making edits, space constraints, and legibility (n = 44). For example, P60 stated, *"Basic formatting, cleanliness, and erasing mistakes."* The second theme, "Remembering syntax," contains challenges such as remembering function names, forgetting semicolons, and other small errors (n = 40). For example, P52 states, *"remembering the syntax or function names."* The third theme is "Confidence," which contains responses about being unable to compile or being confident that portions of their code work as expected (n = 28). For example P3 stated, *"I have a hard time being confident in my programming answers."* The fourth theme is "Pace." This contained responses around running out of time during the exam due to slow writing speed, hand cramps, or spending too long debugging (n =19). For example, P23 stated *"The sheer amount of time it takes to write stuff out."*

When the Challenge question was asked regarding computer-based exams, two themes were discovered. The first theme, "Anxiety," contains responses from students feeling increased stress, panicking, or feeling scared due to the testing environment, debugging, or time pressure (n = 24). For example, P30 states *"When I find a bug in my code and time is running out, I tend to panic."* The second theme, "Partial Credit," focuses on students stating a decrease in their exam score versus when on paper, due to less partial credit (n = 12). For example, P11 states, *"It's usually all or nothing. Not a lot of partial credit if you make a mistake."*

The Benefit question was also asked about both modalities. When discussing paper testing, this question yielded two themes. The first theme focused on cognition. This theme contained responses about the modality helping participants think about the problem better or helped them learn the process better when studying (n = 28). For example, P116 states *"Makes you think critically about the problem without relying on a compiler."* The second theme "Partial Credit," focused on gaining points even if the program doesn't entirely work (n = 27). For example, P58 stated *"Graders tend to be more lax with partial credit."* In addition, 28 participants reported perceiving no benefit to writing code on a paper-based exam. When discussing computer-based testing, this question yielded 3 themes. The first theme, "Feedback," consisted of responses around being able to compile, use IDE tools, and increased confidence (n = 47). For example, P12 stated *"I can be more confident in my answer before moving onto the next problem."* The second theme, "Organization," focused on the ability to edit and organize code clearly (n = 16). The third theme, "Familiarity," focused on the environment being more realistic and familiar (n = 10). For example, P8 stated that *"it more closely resembles an actual programming environment."*

5. DISCUSSION

Our goal was to investigate how exam modality affected student perceptions of test anxiety and performance, learn student preferences for exam modality, and how they are affected by and cope with test anxiety. A majority of students reported at least moderate anxiety (rating ≥ 4) during both paper (69%) and computer (64%) exams. A notable percent of students reported high levels of perceived anxiety (rating ≥ 6) when taking exams on paper (22%) and computer (23%). This finding further supports prior work on test anxiety prevalence [1, 13]. 67% of students at least moderately preferred (rating ≥ 5) computer-based testing. This result was consistent with prior work showing that 75% of students preferred computer-based testing [25]. We found that participants perceived an improvement in their solution quality and speed of solution development during computer-based exams. Modality had differential effects on gender, with women reporting higher perceived anxiety for computer-based exams than paper-based exams and men reporting lower perceived anxiety for computer-based exams than paper-based exams. This finding is consistent with prior work showing that women experience disproportionately higher anxiety relative to men [21]. However, for programming-centric exams, our results show that this difference is present only when the exams are taken on a computer.

Our results, however, slightly contradict Haghighi's work where students preferred computer-based testing as their programming experience increased [9]. This difference might exist because the participants in Haghighi's work were all in the same introductory course where programming experience was measured as a binary variable, having none or having some, whereas we measure programming experience as a year of study in an undergraduate program. From the open-ended survey responses, we found that coping strategies did not differ between modalities. To cope, students used relaxation techniques, drew pictures, and wrote pseudocode, yet 22% of students did not report a coping strategy.

Relevant theory divides coping strategies into problem-focused methods and emotion-focused methods [4, 11]. When people employ problem-focused coping strategies they perform "behaviors designed to reduce or eliminate the problem in question" [4]. An example is writing an action plan for a problem. When people employ emotion-focused strategies they exhibit "behaviors designed to reduce negative emotional reactions" [4]. Some examples are wishful thinking and tension-reduction. Previous work has shown that problem-focused strategies are more effective than emotion-focused strategies [4], yet emotion-focused strategies are employed more often by students in testing situations [19]. In our study, relaxation techniques, one form of an emotion-focused strategy, were found to be the most prevalent with 27% of students adopting this strategy. Encouraging more problem-focused strategies, such as writing pseudocode or developing a solution plan, may be more effective. We found only 10% of students used these approaches. In addition, students that have not developed coping strategies, such as the 22% in this study, could learn effective techniques.

Coping strategies could be embedded in computer-based exams, leveraging the preference for and increased use of this modality. One approach could be giving students the ability to pause the exam and engage in a prompted coping strategy. Students could then write about possible solutions or about the source of experienced emotions. Also, visualizations could be used to encourage more relaxed breathing patterns. To ensure that students unaffected by test anxiety do not perceive their peers as gaining an unfair advantage, all students could be provided with a specified number of "timeouts" during which the coping strategies are performed.

Our study had several limitations. First, we measured perceived anxiety through the use of self-reports on a custom survey. It was not realistic to validate these subjective ratings against objective measures (e.g. physiological measures). The survey also measured anxiety holistically, and did not tease apart its multiple dimensions as found in longer instruments targeting anxiety, such as the Reactions to Tests [23]. Second, our participant selection was limited to a single university. A third limitation is that we sampled mostly computer science and computer engineering students, which may not be representative of the entire population that take programming-centric exams. A final limitation is that we did not investigate if student experiences and preferences correlated with perceived course difficulty and course grade. These factors could influence how student's perceived the modality used in that particular course.

6. CONCLUSION AND FUTURE WORK

Open-ended computer-based programming exams provide a realistic environment to measure student coding proficiency. Our main goal was to investigate how exam modality affects perceived test anxiety during these types of exams. We found that a majority of student participants perceived at least moderate levels of anxiety during exams regardless of modality (69% paper; 64% computer) and a notable portion of students perceived high anxiety (22% paper; 23% computer). We also found that women reported higher levels of perceived anxiety for computer-based testing than paper-based testing, whereas men reported the opposite effect. In addition, participants reported taking mental breaks, writing comments, and outlining pseudocode to cope with anxiety. However, 22% of participants reported no strategy for coping with test anxiety.

We see at least four promising directions for future work. First, we would like to generalize our findings by conducting a similar survey at additional institutions and including populations of students who learn to program in disciplines outside of computer science (and STEM). Second, we would like to deepen and extend our findings by conducting interviews with students and collecting physiological measures of anxiety. Third, it may be fruitful to explore instrumentations of computer-based exams that would enable theoretically-based coping strategies for students experiencing high anxiety. Finally, it would be interesting to compare how our results and implementation of coping strategies would generalize to related situations such as programming under stress in the workplace (e.g. due to tight deadlines).

7. ACKNOWLEDGMENTS

This project was funded in part by a grant from the Strategic Instructional Innovation Program within the College of Engineering at the University of Illinois Urbana-Champaign.

8. REFERENCES

[1] Asghari, A., Kadir, R., Elias, H., and Baba, M. Test anxiety and its related concepts: A brief review. *GESJ: Education Science and Psychology 22* (2012), 3–8.

[2] Barros, J. a. P., Estevens, L., Dias, R., Pais, R., and Soeiro, E. Using lab exams to ensure programming practice in an introductory programming course. *SIGCSE Bull. 35*, 3 (2003), 16–20.

[3] Benson, J., and El-Zahhar, N. Further refinement and validation of the revised test anxiety scale. *Structural Equation Modeling: A Multidisciplinary Journal 1*, 3 (1994), 203–221.

[4] Blankstein, K. R., Flett, G. L., and Watson, M. S. Coping and academic problem-solving ability in test anxiety. *Journal of Clinical Psychology* (1992), 37–46.

[5] Bradley, R. T., McCraty, R., Atkinson, M., Tomasino, D., Daugherty, A., and Arguelles, L. Emotion self-regulation, psychophysiological coherence, and test anxiety: results from an experiment using electrophysiological measures. *Applied psychophysiology and biofeedback 35*, 4 (2010), 261–283.

[6] Califf, M. E., and Goodwin, M. Testing skills and knowledge: Introducing a laboratory exam in cs1. *Proceedings of the 33rd SIGCSE Technical Symposium on Computer Science Education* (2002), 217–221.

[7] Cassady, J. C., and Johnson, R. E. Cognitive test anxiety and academic performance. *Contemporary Educational Psychology 27*, 2 (2002), 270 – 295.

[8] Chamillard, A. T., and et al. Using lab practica to evaluate programming ability. *Proceedings of the Thirty-second SIGCSE Technical Symposium on Computer Science Education* (2001), 159–163.

[9] Delir Haghighi, P., and Sheard, J. Summative computer programming assessment using both paper and computer. In *Proceedings of the 2005 Conference on Towards Sustainable and Scalable Educational Innovations Informed by the Learning Sciences: Sharing Good Practices of Research, Experimentation and Innovation*, IOS Press (2005), 67–75.

[10] Epstein, M. L., Lazarus, A. D., Calvano, T. B., Matthews, K. A., Hendel, R. A., Epstein, B. B., and Brosvic, G. M. Immediate feedback assessment technique promotes learning and corrects inaccurate first responses. *The Psychological Record 52* (2002), 187–201.

[11] Folkman, S., and Lazarus, R. S. If it changes it must be a process: study of emotion and coping during three stages of a college examination. *Journal of personality and social psychology 48*, 1 (1985), 150–170.

[12] Hembree, R. Correlates, causes, effects, and treatment of test anxiety. *Review of Educational Research 58*, 1 (1988), 47–77.

[13] Kavakci, O., Semiz, M., Kartal, A., Dikici, A., and Kugu, N. Test anxiety prevalance and related variables in the students who are going to take the university entrance examination. *The Journal of Psychiatry and Neurological Sciences 27* (2014), 301–307.

[14] Kika, F. M., McLaughlin, T., and Dixon, J. Effects of frequent testing of secondary algebra students. *The Journal of Educational Research 85*, 3 (1992), 159–162.

[15] Kim, B., Kim, T., and Kim, J. Paper-and-pencil programming strategy toward computational thinking for non-majors: Design your solution. *Journal of Educational Computing Research 49*, 4 (2013), 437–459.

[16] Liebert, R. M., and Morris, L. W. Cognitive and emotional components of test anxiety: A distinction and some initial data. *Psychological reports 20*, 3 (1967), 975–978.

[17] McDonald, A. S. The prevalence and effects of test anxiety in school children. *Educational Psychology 21*, 1 (2001), 89–101.

[18] Noyes, J. M., and Garland, K. J. Computer-vs. paper-based tasks: are they equivalent? *Ergonomics 51*, 9 (2008), 1352–1375.

[19] Parker, J. D., and Endler, N. S. An assessment of appraisal, anxiety, coping, and procrastination during an examination period. *European Journal of Personality 3* (1989), 195–208.

[20] Powers, D. E. Test anxiety and test performance: Comparing paper-based and computer-adaptive versions of the gre general test. *ETS Research Report Series 1999*, 2 (1999), 1–32.

[21] Putwain, D., and Daly, A. L. Test anxiety prevalence and gender differences in a sample of english secondary school students. *Educational Studies 40*, 5 (2014), 554–570.

[22] Putwain, D. W., Connors, L., and Symes, W. Do cognitive distortions mediate the test anxiety–examination performance relationship? *Educational Psychology 30*, 1 (2010), 11–26.

[23] Sarason, I. G. Stress, anxiety, and cognitive interference: reactions to tests. *Journal of personality and social psychology 46*, 4 (1984), 929–938.

[24] Skaalvik, E. M., and Valås, H. Relations among achievement, self-concept, and motivation in mathematics and language arts: A longitudinal study. *The Journal of Experimental Education 67*, 2 (1999), 135–149.

[25] Zilles, C., Deloatch, R., Bailey, J., Khattar, B., Fagen, W., Heeren, C., Mussulman, D., and West, M. Computerized testing: A vision and initial experiences. *122nd ASEE* (2015).

Investigating the Role of Being a Mentor as a Way of Increasing Interest in CS

Jody Clarke-Midura
Utah State University
2380 Old Main Hill
Logan, UT
jody.clarke@usu.edu

Vicki Allan
Utah State University
429 Old Main Hill
Logan, UT
vicki.allan@usu.edu

Kevin Close
Utah State University
2380 Old Main Hill
Logan, UT
kevin.close@usu.edu

ABSTRACT
In order to affect career decisions, it is important to reach youth at early ages. While some have focused on using mentors in order to successfully teach mentees, few have focused on the benefits to the mentors themselves. To our knowledge, no other research has been conducted on the effect that serving as a near-peer mentor has on increasing the *mentors'* interest, self-efficacy, value-beliefs, and skills in computer science. Our paid mentorships provided youth two weeks of participation in computer science camps using App Inventor. The mentors in our pilot study increased self-efficacy and interest after the mentoring activity, on average. This all-female mentoring experience provided opportunities to transcend barriers such as negative stereotyping and lack of role models. We feel that being able to reach high school girls at a critical stage makes this pedagogical approach ideal. The positive results, even with the short duration of the intervention, are encouraging.

Keywords
Near Peer Mentoring; App Inventor; Girls; Self-Efficacy

1. INTRODUCTION
Despite effort to broaden participation, the numbers of women and minorities earning bachelor degrees in computer science (CS) is still low [39]. The low numbers of women in CS contradict the trends of higher numbers of women obtaining college degrees and increases in the number of women in other technical fields [10]. Both recruitment and retention of women are of interest, as women tend to leave the major at higher rates than do males. This lack of gender diversity produces unfavorable development solutions for industry and highlights a need for research on how we can increase participation in CS, particularly for women and minorities [27].

Research indicates the importance of reaching youth at early ages, in time to make important decisions about acquiring math and computer skills before college [13][26]. Yet, computer science is not prevalent in K-12 education [5]. To our knowledge, no state requires computer science for graduation, and only half of the states allow computer science to substitute for math requirements [9]. Thus, it is unclear how to reach students when access to computer programming instruction is often non-existent, even in high school [27].

SIGCSE '16, March 02-05, 2016, Memphis, TN, USA
© 2016 ACM. ISBN 978-1-4503-3685-7/16/03…$15.00
DOI: http://dx.doi.org/10.1145/2839509.2844581

In order to engage middle and high school girls in computing, some researchers have focused on mentors as a way to transcend some of these barriers [2][10]. For example, the National Center for Women & Information Technology (NCWIT) AspireIT program focuses on summer camps and after school programs for middle school girls using near-peer (high school aged) mentors. While these camps serve mentees, in this study, we focused on the mentors. Specifically, we explored the effect of acting as a near-peer mentor on high school girls' self-efficacy, interest, and skill in computer science. Though recent literature highlights the importance of social encouragement and identity-forming activities in girls' computer science lessons, to our knowledge, no other research has been conducted on the effect of acting as a near-peer mentor as a pedagogical approach to increase the *mentors'* interest, self-efficacy, and programming skills in computer science [14][34]. Considering the effectiveness of pair programming among girls in middle school and undergraduate courses and the theoretical underpinnings contributing to the success of pair programming (e.g. increased metacognition, reciprocal teaching, etc.), there is reason to believe that playing a role of near-peer mentor could lead to increased learning and interest in computer science [37]. In this paper, we present results of our pilot study where we studied the effect of being a mentor on high school girl's self-efficacy, interest, and skill in computer science. In the following sections, we briefly provide background and context for our study, our camp, the research design followed by findings and conclusions.

2. PREVIOUS RESEARCH
While there is much discussion about the role of mentors in technology fields, the research focuses on the advantage to the protégées, not on the benefits to the mentors themselves. Goals for mentoring include: providing role models, providing advice, giving support, offering validation, alleviating fears, and addressing isolation [19]. Historically, none of the goals consider the advantages to the mentors. Mentoring is key in recruitment and retention of the protégées in computing [2][10]. Role models, relatives, and the peer group may influence choices [11], with peer support as an especially important factor [20][25][30].

There is a need for research on the mentors themselves and how the role of acting as a mentor may affect knowledge of programming and interest in computer science courses or interest in computer science as a career. The idea of near-peer mentoring has proven successful in increasing the mentors' learning and interest in academics and career in the medical field [31], geoscience [12], as well as in undergraduate science education [17]. Feldon et al [17] found that graduate student teaching experiences improve research skills. Furthermore, Karcher [21] found that high school students mentoring near-peers exhibited increased feelings of school connectedness. Yet, there is a lack of research on the mentors in computer science education. In this research, we build on prior work and study the effect of mentoring on the mentor's computer skills, self-efficacy, and interest in computer science.

When providing guidance, mentors must exercise many essential skills across a diverse set of problems, such as decoding error messages, determining what features to include, and organizing the components. In contrast, learning on one's own provides fewer opportunities for social interaction and justification of decisions, because an individual typically only works on one project at a time. As a mentor of multiple campers, participants in our study engaged with multiple, diverse sets of issues specific to each project's demands, providing a form of varied practice [32]. A further anticipated benefit to mentors is that they need to express their reasoning orally when they provide guidance to campers. Research evidence suggests that when students engage in such self-explanation, they develop more effective problem solving techniques [8][32]. As they explain how to think about a problem, they reinforce their own learning [8]. While the mentors were immersed in coding during the week of mentoring, it was different than doing their own coding therefore we were interested to see if their computational skills improved from mentoring. This benefit to learning occurs as a joint benefit of both practice and self-explanation that occurs during mentoring. Increased skills and motivation has been shown to link to social learning, peer tutoring, and group problem solving. Research has shown that one's perception of their skills is more important to their success than the actual skills they possess [3]. Our goal was to evaluate both the acquisition of skills and perception of skill mastery. The research questions that guided our study were:

- *Does acting as a mentor affect participants' self-efficacy and confidence in their ability to program?*
- *Does acting as a mentor affect participants' interest in computer science careers/academics?*
- *Does acting as a mentor affect participants' programming skill?*

3. METHODS

The purpose of our study was to explore the effect of acting as a near peer mentor on high school girls' programming skills, self-efficacy of their skills, and interest in a technical career. In this section we describe the App Camps and research design.

3.1 App Inventor camp

During the summer of 2015, we held four App Camps; one was focused on preparing mentors to use App Inventor. The other three were camps for middle school students. All of the camps lasted five days, four and a half hours per day. The curriculum was the same in all camps and mentors programmed the same apps as the campers. The curriculum focused on ten apps including: Talk to Me, Paint, Women Speak, Personal Message, Timer, Mole Mash, Chore List, and Walking Tour. The apps focused on important concepts in computing such as Boolean logic, lists, variables, procedures, parameters, conditional statements, looping, incrementing, random selection, use of media files, and event-driven programming. Each camper worked at their own computer and had their own device for testing the apps. Campers and mentors were allowed to take the devices home to show their friends and family what they created.

In addition to the ten cell phone apps that each camper created, we played games to learn terminology. Campers had a chance to step away from their computers, get exercise, and socialize while pantomiming and blurting out computer terms. We also offered career coaching, in the form of a visit from the dean of engineering for each camp, where she led a discussion of job prospects for computer scientists. We also showed a video made by Code.org to show how exciting jobs in computer science could be. We emphasized the ability of programmers to develop apps that help people. We also utilized games to create a relaxed attitude among the mentors and campers.

3.2 Mentor training

In addition to the week-long pre camp training, the mentors were involved in an hour and a half of mentor training each day after the camp. This time was used to discuss learning styles, allow mentors to create blog entries discussing specific successes and challenges, and work on programming challenges. The non-technical part of mentor training gave the mentors ownership of the camp as they could suggest improvements to the organization. It was also a time for reflection as we talked about what went well and why.

The duration of the intervention for each mentor was short – one week for training and one week for mentoring. While we expect that the improvements would be more dramatic in a longer intervention, it is noteworthy that others have found significant changes are possible in a short period of time [18]. This is important as, during the summer, it is challenging to find mentors with long periods of availability or the resources to conduct long interventions.

3.3 Sample

Our sample consisted of twenty-six high school female mentors from four different high schools in northern Utah. The racial makeup of our sample was African-American (8%), Asian/Pacific Islander (15%), Latina (4%), and Caucasian (73%). The average age of the mentors was 16.17 years. The mentors were required to be entering ninth through twelfth grades, but because of the large number of applications, we gave first preference to older mentors who would have fewer opportunities to participate in such a program.

Twenty-five of the mentors have computers at home and access to the Internet. Twenty-one of the mentors have taken a Computer Education and Technology (CET) class in their school. The CET course is a required course intended for students to learn concepts associated with key application software, basic computing fundamentals, and appropriate behavior while using technology as a tool in the classroom and in life. One mentor had experience with the Scratch programming language through a local workshop.

3.4 Procedures

Mentors completed an application and indicated which week they could mentor. Based on their availability, we randomly divided the mentors into three groups: A, B, and C. All three combined groups attended the week-long App Training camp on a college campus. Prior to the camp, all participants took pre surveys in which they were asked about their computer self-efficacy and interest (described in the next section). At the end of the camp, all participants took identical post surveys on their self-efficacy and interest and a programming skills test. The following week, Group A mentored an all girl camp. They received mentor training immediately following each day of camp for four days. At the end of the first camp, Group A took identical delayed post surveys with the skills test. Two weeks later, group B took the surveys and then mentored a mixed gender camp. They received mentor training following each camp session for four days. At the end of the camp, group B took the delayed post surveys. The following week group C mentored a group of all girl campers. They received mentor training after each camp session. After the camp, they took the delayed post surveys.

3.5 Measures

3.5.1 Affective measures

In order to assess whether acting as a mentor had an effect on their self-efficacy and interest in computer science, we piloted an affective survey that was developed from three instruments: The Social Cognitive Career survey [7], Motivational Beliefs and Assessment survey [33], and Student Perceptions of ICT survey [24]. Our instrument contained 41 items and asked students to rate the items on a scale of 1-6 from strongly disagree to strongly agree. One item was eliminated because it was worded awkwardly and did not fit in the initial factors. To aid the interpretation, we conducted a commonly used exploratory factor analysis technique [1], orthogonal varimax rotation, in SPSS. Varimax clarifies each factor and set of variables by enhancing the load of variables on a single factor and reducing their load on the remaining set [29]. Three factors explained 53.234% of the variance: self-efficacy, interest, and value-beliefs. Self-efficacy contains items like, “I can succeed in a computer science class” and “I am confident in my ability to program.” Interest contains items like, “I am interested in studying computer science in the future” and “Working in the computer science is an interesting occupation.” Value-belief contains items related to personal and social beliefs: “It is important for me to improve my computer programming skills” and “It is useful to have programming skills” as well as supports: “My parents think that being good at computer programming is useful for my future.”

Composite scores were created for each of the three factors, based on the mean of the items, which had their primary loadings on each factor. Higher scores indicated greater self-efficacy, interest, and value-beliefs. Internal consistency for each of the scales was examined using Cronbach’s alpha, a widely used measure of scale reliability [15]. The alphas were high: interest $\alpha = 0.9566$ (19 items), self-efficacy $\alpha = 0.8769$ (11 items), and value-belief $\alpha = 0.7933$ (10 items). Descriptive statistics are presented in table 1.

Overall, these analyses indicated that three distinct factors were underlying mentors responses and that these factors were internally consistent.

Table 1. Descriptive Statistics of Affective Factors

Graphics	Items	Mean (SD)	Alpha
Interest	19	4.61 (.87)	.96
Self-efficacy	11	5.21 (.56)	.88
Value-belief	10	5.13 (.48)	.80

3.5.2 Programming skills

In order to assess whether acting as a mentor affected mentor’s programming skills, we administered a 25 item, multiple-choice test modified from the Evaluation for App Inventor test developed by Erickson [16], before they mentored (SKILL 1) and then again after they mentored (SKILL 2).

The questions assessed a variety of skills: basic understanding of App Inventor terminology, basic programming skills, and detailed understanding of programming logic. Sample skill questions were “Our variables typically had a name beginning with "global". What does that imply?” “The Loop property of the player tells the player to do what?” and “In the following piece of code, what is the value of global total when global meal is 20 and global tipPicker is 15?”

4. RESULTS

Our first two research questions focused on whether high school students’ self-efficacy and interest changed after mentoring. As mentioned above, we surveyed mentors on 41 items that fit into 3 factors: self-efficacy, interest, and value-belief. We conducted a one way repeated measures ANOVA to compare the effect of time on each of these three factors before App Training (T1), Before Mentoring (T2), and after mentoring (T3). We then conducted post hoc comparisons between the conditions (time1-time2, time2-time3 and time1-time3) to look for significant differences. Descriptive statistics for each of the three factors are presented in Tables 2, 3, and 4.

Table 2. Descriptive Statistics of Interest (N=25)

	Mean	Std Dev	Std Error	Median	Range
Pre-App Camp (T1)	4.59	0.67	0.13	4.47	2.21
Pre-Mentoring (T2)	4.51	1.01	0.20	4.82	3.68
Post-Mentoring (T3)	4.71	0.95	0.19	4.84	2.89

Table 3. Descriptive Statistics of Self-Efficacy (N=25)

	Mean	Std Dev	Std Error	Median	Range
Pre-App Camp (T1)	5.01	1	0.12	5	2.64
Pre-Mentoring (T2)	5.22	0.52	0.10	5.27	1.82
Post Mentoring (T3)	5.38	0.52	0.10	5.55	1.91

Table 4. Descriptive Statistics of Value-beliefs (N=25)

	Mean	Std Dev	Std Error	Median	Range
Pre-App Camp (T1)	5.14	0.47	0.09	5.1	1.70
Pre-Mentoring (T2)	5.07	0.43	0.09	5.1	1.80
Post-Mentoring (T3)	5.15	0.53	0.11	5.2	2.00

As you can see in Table 3, the mentors in our sample reported an increase in self-efficacy at each time interval, on average. As shown in Table 2 and Table 4, there was a slight decrease, on average, for interest and value-beliefs from T1 to T2. However, this decrease was not significant. Given the typical decrease in interest experienced by many new programmers, we appear to be experiencing an initial loss in interest that we hypothesize mentoring is able to overcome.

4.1 Interest

We measured mentors' interest in Computer Science three times. As mentioned above, the mentors in our sample reported a slight decrease in interest from Pre-App Camp (T1) to Pre-Mentoring (T2). Not surprisingly, when we conducted a one-way repeated measures ANOVA, we did not find a significant effect of time on interest, *Wilks' Lambda = .860, F(2, 23) = 1.866, p=.177.* However, we did find a significant difference in interest when we made post hoc comparisons between the conditions.

The data did not meet all assumptions for normality, so we conducted Wilcoxon Signed-ranks tests to make comparisons. The tests indicated that mentors' interest was higher after mentoring (time 3, Median = 4.84) than before mentoring (time 2, Median = 4.82), *Z = 1.941, p< .05, r =.3882.* On average, the girls in our sample, who acted as mentors for their middle school peers at a camp on how to program apps using App inventor, saw a statistically significant increase in their interest in computer science from before they mentored to after they mentored.

Interviews and surveys hinted at reasons for the increase in interest. Mentors remarked, "It was really interesting to see all the things I could do and how all the things fit together." "I was surprised that programmers work with a bunch of people. The idea of getting a team together to work on things, that was new to me." "I enjoyed working with the campers and helping them solve their problems. It made me feel very smart." "I am definitely more likely to follow a career in computing, because now I understand what it would be like more." "Before I thought only super smart people were in computing degrees. I really enjoy working with computers, after actually being able to see myself progress and be able to understand things I never thought I would!"

4.2 Self-Efficacy

We conducted a repeated measures ANOVA to look for an effect of time on self-efficacy. Mauchly's test indicated that the assumption of sphericity had been violated, $\chi^2(2)$ = 14.252, p= .001. Therefore, degrees of freedom were corrected using Greenhouse-Geisser estimates of sphericity (ε = .684). The results show that there was a significant effect of time on mentors self-efficacy, *F(1.368, 32.835) = 7.677, p= .005.* These results suggest that mentors self-efficacy increased over time after mentoring their younger peers.

There was a significant difference in self-efficacy between all occasions. A Wilcoxon Signed-ranks test indicated that mentor self-efficacy was higher after the initial App Inventor training (time 2, Median = 5.27) than before App Training (time 1, Median = 5), *Z = 2.062, p< .0392, r =.4124.* Mentor self-efficacy was higher after mentoring (time 3, Median = 5.54) than before mentoring (time 2, Median = 5.27), *Z = 2.538, p< .0112, r =.5076.* Finally, mentor self-efficacy was higher after mentoring (time 3, Median = 5.54) than prior to their App Camp training (time 1, Median = 5), *Z = 2.951, p< .0032, r =.5902.* The girls in our sample saw an increase in their self-efficacy after being a near-peer mentor. Their self-efficacy increased over time.

4.3 Value-beliefs

We conducted a one-way ANOVA with repeated measures followed by post hoc comparisons of mentors' value beliefs on the three occasions. We did not find a significant effect of time on value beliefs or significant differences between the three occasions. Thus, even though there was a slight decrease in value beliefs from Pre-App Camp (T1) to Pre-Mentoring (T2) and then an increase after mentoring, none of these differences were statistically significant. These results suggest a need for further research into the development and growth of value beliefs.

4.4 Programming Skills

Our third research question explores whether acting as a mentor affects participants' programming skills. The mean, standard deviation, and standard error of SKILL 1 and SKILL 2 are presented in Table 5. Our data met assumptions of normality. In order to see if there was a difference between mentors programming skills before and after mentoring, we conducted a paired t-test between the mean of SKILL 1 and SKILL 2. While participants scored higher on SKILL 2 on average (mean = 17.95833) than SKILL 1 (mean = 17.33333); the difference was not significant, $t(23) = 1.4288, p = > 0.$

Table 5. Descriptive Statistics of Programming Skill (n=24)

	Mean	Std Deviation	Std Error
SKILL 1 (Pre-Mentoring)	17.33	3.73	.75
SKILL 2 (Post-Mentoring)	17.96	4.46	.91

5. DISCUSSION

We set out to explore whether the role of being a near-peer mentor to middle school peers on App Inventor has any positive effect on high school girls' self-efficacy, interest, and skill in computer programming. In our pilot, we found a relationship between the role of being a near-peer mentor and participants' self-efficacy and interest, on average. While we can't make any causal claims, the results of our pilot are exciting and have broader implications for new research in the field.

5.1 Changes in affect

The girls in our sample, on average, saw a significant increase in their self-efficacy over time. There was also a significant increase in their interest in computer science from before they mentored to after they mentored, on average. The significant increase in self-efficacy over all three occasions is promising because it suggests that short interventions of one week have the potential to have positive effects. This also aligns with research that has shown that mentoring improves academic self-esteem [21]. Similarly, Scott et al [28] found that their hands-on, female-centered information technology camp also increased the students' sense of self as a technosocial manipulator. Finally, other social pedagogies for programming have also shown increased self-efficacy and interest among girls, particularly pair programming [23][37].

Retention of women is an important issue in computer science. Despite efforts to broaden participation, retention rates of women remain low [2][4][10]. It was not surprising that, on average, girls' interest went down after the first App training. However, after mentoring, the girls in our sample reported a statistically significant increase in interest. These findings suggest that placing girls in the role of mentor has the potential to increase retention in CS. Further research is needed to understand how mentoring increases interest in CS and how we can use mentoring as a pedagogical approach to broaden participation in CS.

We did not see a similar change in value-belief that we saw in self-efficacy or interest. We believe there is a reason for this. First, we didn't emphasize the career aspects or value of programming for a wide variety of careers. We have already started conversations with some industry partners and plan to develop videos of women talking about their CS careers. Our future camps will not only place more emphasis on the variety of options a CS career offers, but we also hope to develop career pathways for the mentors through partnerships with industry and the potential of internships. We hope that this will lead to increased value-belief.

5.2 Changes in skill

Assessing programming skills remains a challenge [35]. We struggled to find a good measure that we could use to show change in skill after mentoring. The multiple-choice questions we administered, while useful, were insufficient to understand the learning that can happen in such a short intervention. However, for the purpose of our pilot research, our findings confirm what we observed in each of the camps: the mentors were learning programming skills and we need to find a way to measure this. Researchers are currently looking for ways to assess programming and computational thinking [36][38], and we hope to utilize some of these resources in our future studies.

There is a critical need to find innovative pedagogies that broaden participation in computer science. Our findings are promising because they suggest that the role of acting as a mentor has the potential to increase girls' self-efficacy and interest in computer science and programming. The camaraderie that developed with an all-female group of mentors was key in helping them find role models and friends in the group and allowing them to crack the stereotype of computer programmers. The negative stereotype of computer scientists was further weakened by the admiration of the campers. Not only were the mentors esteemed as role models in fashion, humor, and accomplishments, they were appreciated in their role as technology experts.

6. FUTURE WORK

Our pilot results were promising and encourage us to continue pursuing research on how mentoring affects the mentor's self-efficacy, interest, value beliefs and skills in CS. In future camps, we will place more of an emphasis on the social encouragement that occurs [34]. Cell phone apps are compelling as they utilize pictures, music, text, vibration, and motion. In addition to sparking creativity, the use of media allows for a discussion of file types, pixels, screen coordinate, color, and file manipulation. Apps have the added advantage of being shareable as students take the phones home to show family, friends, and neighbors. This utilization of audience is important in changing attitudes of members of the mentor's support groups. [22]. While campers did take the devices home to show off what they created, mentors were less likely to do the same. As part of the mentor training, we will encourage them to share their apps.. We intend to use observation and interviews to further understand the mechanisms that lead to change in mentors' affect and skill development. We also plan to study the effects of mentoring for a longer period (with two separate camps) to see if the repetition further improves skill development.

We saw a change in interest after mentoring, but that is largely unexplored. What about mentoring increases interest? Certainly the skill acquisition and self-efficacy makes increased interest possible. Other reasons could include: knowledge of job opportunities, knowledge of personal skills, understanding what computer science really is, understanding of the work environment, breaking down of stereotypes, and the presence of role models (in other mentors and faculty). We intend to study the factors that influence change in mentors' attitudes and skills.

7. CONCLUSION

Finding ways to increase girls' participation in computer science is a national priority. A recent study on what factors influence women to pursue CS careers found social encouragement, academic exposure, career perceptions, and self-perception to be the most critical [34]. In this paper, we share a promising pedagogical approach: placing high school girls in the role of mentor to their middle school peers, that has the potential to increase participation in CS while encompassing these four factors.

By offering paid mentorships, we were able to attract young women to a computing experience who are too old for the typical camp experience, yet closer to a career decision. Using near-peer mentors was key to making the camp successful for the campers, but it is equally important to note that by providing a mentoring experience, we were able to attract young women to a computing experience who have few opportunities for such experiences. We feel that being able to reach high school girls at a critical stage make this pedagogical approach ideal.

8. REFERENCES

[1] Abdi, H. 2003. Factor Rotations in Factor Analyses. In M. Lewis-Beck, A. Bryman, & T. Futing (Eds.), *Encyclopedia of Social Sciences Research Methods*. Thousand Oaks, CA: Sage.

[2] Ashcraft, C., Eger, E., & Friend, M. 2012. Girls in IT: the facts. *National Center for Women & IT. Boulder, CO.*

[3] Bandura, A. 1997. Self-efficacy: The exercise of self-control. Gordonsville, VA: WH Freeman & Co.

[4] Bunderson, E. D., & Christensen, M. E. 1995. An analysis of retention problems for female students in university computer science programs. Journal of Research on Computing in Education, 28(1), 1-18.

[5] Barr, V., & Stephenson, C. 2011. Bringing computational thinking to K-12: what is Involved and what is the role of the computer science education community?. ACM Inroads, 2(1), 48-54.

[6] Brunner, C., Bennett, D., & Honey, M. 2000. Girl games and technological desire. From Barbie to Mortal Kombat: Gender and Computer Games, ed.

[7] Carrico, C., & Tendhar, C. 2012. The Use of the Social Cognitive Career Theory to Predict Engineering Students' Motivation in the PRODUCED Program. In *American Society for Engineering Education*. American Society for Engineering Education.

[8] Chi, M. T., Leeuw, N., Chiu, M. H., & LaVancher, C. 1994. Eliciting self-explanations improves understanding. Cognitive science, 18(3), 439-477.

[9] Code.org Website

[10] Cohoon, J. M. 2011. Promising Practices: Encouragement Works in Academic Settings (Case Study 1). Boulder, CO: National Center for Women & Information Technology.

[11] Cozza, M. 2011. Bridging Gender Gaps, Networking in Computer Science.Gender, Technology and Development, 15(2), 319-337.

[12] DeFelice, A., Adams, J. D., Branco, B., & Pieroni, P. 2014. Engaging underrepresented high school students in an urban environmental and geoscience place-based curriculum. Journal of Geoscience Education, *62*(1), 49-60.

[13] Denner, J. 2011. What Predicts Middle School Girls' Interest in Computing? International Journal of Gender, Science and Technology, *3*(1).

[14] Denner, J., Werner, L., Bean, S., & Campe, S. 2005. The Girls Creating Games Program. Frontiers: A Journal Of Women Studies, 26(1), 90-98.

[15] DeVellis, R. 2003. Scale Development Theory and Applications. Thousand Oaks, CA: SAGE Publications

[16] Erickson, B. 2015. (retrieved http://home.cc.gatech.edu/ice-gt/311).

[17] Feldon, D. F., Peugh, J., Timmerman, B. E., Maher, M. A., Hurst, M., Strickland, D., & Stiegelmeyer, C. 2011. Graduate students' teaching experiences improve their methodological research skills. Science, 333(6045), 1037-1039.

[18] Hulleman, C. S., & Harackiewicz, J. M. (2009). Promoting interest and performance in high school science classes. *Science*, *326*(5958), 1410-1412.

[19] Hupert, N. 2002. Telementoring: Using Online communication for a student mentoring project, http://cct.edc.org/publications/telementoring-using-online-communication-student-mentoring-project, accessed 1/22/2015.

[20] Jenson, J., De Castell, S., & Bryson, M. 2003. "Girl talk": gender, equity, and identity discourses in a school-based computer culture. In Women's Studies International Forum (Vol. 26, No. 6, pp. 561-573). Pergamon.

[21] Karcher, M. 2009. Increases in academic connectedness and self-esteem among high school students who serve as cross-age peer mentors. Professional School Counseling, 12(4), 292-299.

[22] Marcu, G., Kaufman, S. J., Lee, J. K., Black, R. W., Dourish, P., Hayes, G. R., & Richardson, D. J. 2010, Design and evaluation of a computer science and engineering course for middle school girls. In Proceedings of the 41st ACM technical symposium on Computer science education (pp. 234-238). ACM.

[23] McDowell, C., Werner, L., Bullock, H. E., & Fernald, J. 2003, May. The impact of pair programming on student performance, perception and persistence. In Proceedings of the 25th international conference on Software engineering (pp. 602-607). IEEE Computer Society.

[24] McLachlan, C., Craig, A., & Coldwell, J. 2010, January. Student perceptions of ICT: a gendered analysis. In Proceedings of the Twelfth Australasian Conference on Computing Education-Volume 103 (pp. 127-136). Australian Computer Society, Inc.

[25] Moorman, P., & Johnson, E. 2003, June. Still a stranger here: Attitudes among secondary school students towards computer science. In ACM SIGCSE Bulletin (Vol. 35, No. 3, pp. 193-197). ACM.

[26] Powell, R. M. 2008, March. Improving the persistence of first-year undergraduate women in computer science. In ACM SIGCSE Bulletin (Vol. 40, No. 1, pp. 518-522). ACM.

[27] Scott, K. 2009. The new digital divide: Where are our girls?. LeadCast Blog, http://www.niusileadscape.org/bl/?p=404.

[28] Scott, K., Aist, G. & Zhang, X. 2014. Designing a Culturally Responsive Computing Curriculum For Girls. International Journal of Gender, Science and Technology,6(2), 264-276.

[29] Stevens, J. 2002. *Applied Multivariate Statistics for the Social Sciences* (4th ed.). Mahwah, NJ: Lawrence Erlbaum Associates.

[30] Teague, J. 2002. Women in computing: What brings them to it, what keeps them in it? ACM SIGCSE Bulletin, 34(2), 147-158.

[31] Tenenbaum, L. S., Anderson, M. K., Jett, M., & Yourick, D. L. 2014. An Innovative Near-Peer Mentoring Model for Undergraduate and Secondary Students: STEM Focus. Innovative Higher Education, 39(5), 375-385.

[32] VanLehn, K. 1996. Cognitive skill acquisition. Annual review of psychology, 47(1), 513-539.

[33] Vekiri, I., & Chronaki, A. 2008. Gender issues in technology use: Perceived social support, computer self-efficacy and value-beliefs, and computer use beyond school. Computers & Education, 51(3), 1392-1404.

[34] Wang, J., Hong, H., Ravitz, J., & Ivory, M. 2015. Gender Differences in Factors Influencing Pursuit of Computer Science and Related Fields. In Proceedings of the 2015 ACM Conference on Innovation and Technology in Computer Science Education (pp. 117-122). ACM.

[35] Weintrop, D., & Wilensky, U. 2015. Using Commutative Assessments to Compare Conceptual Understanding in Blocks-based and Text-based Programs. In Proceedings of the eleventh annual International Conference on International Computing Education Research (pp. 101-110). ACM.

[36] Werner, L., Denner, J., Campe, S., & Kawamoto, D. C. 2012. The fairy performance assessment: Measuring computational thinking in middle school. In Proceedings of the 43rd ACM technical symposium on Computer Science Education (pp. 215-220). ACM.

[37] Werner L., Denner J. 2009 Pair programming in middle school: What does it look like? Journal of Research on Technology in Education (ISTE), 42(1), 29-49.

[38] Werner, L., McDowell, C., & Denner, J. 2013. Middle school students using Alice: what can we learn from logging data?. In Proceeding of the 44th ACM technical symposium on Computer science education (pp. 507-512). ACM.

[39] Zweben, S., & Bizot, B. 2014. 2013 Taulbee Survey. COMPUTING, 26(5).

Towards More Gender Diversity in CS through an Artificial Intelligence Summer Program for High School Girls

Marie E. Vachovsky*
Stanford University
Stanford, U.S.A.
mvachovs@stanford.edu

Grace Wu*
Stanford University
Stanford, U.S.A.
gracew2@stanford.edu

Sorathan Chaturapruek*
Stanford University
Stanford, U.S.A.
sorathan@cs.stanford.edu

Olga Russakovsky*
Stanford University
Stanford, U.S.A.
olga@cs.stanford.edu

Richard Sommer
Stanford University
Stanford, U.S.A.
sommer@stanford.edu

Li Fei-Fei
Stanford University
Stanford, U.S.A.
feifeili@cs.stanford.edu

ABSTRACT

The field of computer science suffers from a lack of diversity. The Stanford Artificial Intelligence Laboratory's Outreach Summer (SAILORS), a two-week non-residential free summer program, recruits high school girls to computer science, specifically to Artificial Intelligence (AI). The program was organized by graduate student and professor volunteers. The goals of the pilot program are to increase interest in AI, contextualize technically rigorous AI concepts through societal impact, and address barriers that could discourage 10th grade girls from pursuing computer science. In this paper we describe the curriculum designed to achieve these goals. Survey results show students had a statistically significant increase in technical knowledge, interest in pursuing careers in AI, and confidence in succeeding in AI and computer science. Additionally, survey results show that the majority of the students found new role models, faculty support, and a sense of community in AI and computer science.

Keywords

Artificial Intelligence, K-12 Education, Outreach, Gender and Diversity, Summer Camps, Recruiting Women, Computer Science Education

1. INTRODUCTION

Recent diversity reports demonstrate a large gap between the percentage of women holding computing jobs compared to the percentage of men [1]. This disparity pervades in academia as well: in 2011, only 17.6% of Bachelor's degrees and 20.2% of Doctoral degrees in computer and information sciences from U.S. institutions were awarded to women [2].

*Equal contributions

SIGCSE '16, March 02 - 05, 2016, Memphis, TN, USA

ISBN 978-1-4503-3685-7/16/03. . . $15.00

DOI: http://dx.doi.org/10.1145/2839509.2844620

In this paper, we evaluate the Stanford Artificial Intelligence Laboratory's Outreach Summer (SAILORS) as a way of addressing the lack of diversity in Artificial Intelligence (AI). SAILORS recognizes that the AI field needs greater diversity, and sees AI's potential for technical and social impact education as a way to attract more women to the field of computer science (CS) as a whole. This potential has been untapped in high school CS education. SAILORS is the first AI camp for high school students that gives them a large-scope overview of the humanitarian applications of the field as well as the technical methods behind these applications. We evaluate the pilot program, a two-week nonresidential free[1] program run by 40+ graduate student and professor volunteers. The program focuses on gender diversity by targeting rising 10th grade girls, and has the following goals: 1) increase interest in AI among the students; 2) contextualize AI technical concepts through societal impact; and 3) address barriers that could discourage 10th grade girls from pursuing CS in the future.

Increase interest in AI. SAILORS exposes students to AI topics such as natural language processing (NLP) and computer vision, introduces these topics through technical skills, and gives them the opportunity to have close interactions with faculty and students from the Stanford AI Lab. Through these topics and opportunities, we aim to spark the students' curiosity and motivation.

Contextualize AI through social impact. SAILORS balances the technical skills with their application and frames technical skills as a stepping stone towards a larger goal. Within SAILORS curriculum, these problems have a humanitarian focus, which shows an alternative to the types of problems the stereotypical computer scientist works on. For example, girls chose from research projects that each applied AI technical skills towards a humanitarian purpose: making hospitals safer, assisting disaster relief, identifying cancer cells through the genome, and making driving safer (see section 4.5).

Address barriers for girls in computer science. SAILORS focuses on the gender-gap problem of recruitment within AI.

[1]Funded by sponsors.

The program addresses three of the barriers that women in CS face at the undergraduate level, so that when SAILORS alumni reach university level, they will be equipped to handle these barriers. SAILORS addresses 1) lack of exposure to technical concepts early on [3, 4]; 2) limited perception of CS as a field [3, 5, 6]; and 3) lack of faculty and same-sex peer-to-peer support [3, 6, 7].

2. RELATED WORKS

Based on our literature review, SAILORS is unique in three ways: 1) it is the only summer AI program in the U.S. geared specifically towards high school girls; 2) it is the only high school summer program in the U.S. that teaches multiple subfields of AI (instead of focusing on only one, such as robotics [8] or bioinformatics [9]); and 3) it is the only summer program to teach these subfields through technically rigorous and socially relevant research projects.

CS programs for girls. There exist many out-of-school programs that target the same demographic as SAILORS; some of these work or worked towards similar goals. Girls on the Go was a week-long residential summer program held at Miami University for female high school sophomores and juniors [10]. Related to our goals, the camp introduced students to computing by exposing them to fields computer scientists collaborate with. Specifically, Girls on the Go taught girls to create an app that allows zookeepers to record animal behavior. The University of Delaware held an eight week half-day summer program for high school girls called Girls' POWER [11]. The camp's structure was similar to SAILORS's: the teaching was done by CS professors, the camp introduced girls to role models in CS research and industry, and there was a programming exercise after lectures.

AI programs for minorities. Some camps targeting underrepresented groups focused on one aspect of AI. Young Women in Computing (YWIC) was a five-week long summer program at New Mexico State University that targeted female high-school students [9]. Like SAILORS, YWIC aimed to increase interest, peer mentoring, and role models in CS. The program included a two-week long bioinformatics session, where students completed research projects in the field, e.g. investigated genes associated with particular illnesses. Additionally, the University of Minnesota Center for Distributed Robotics and the Digital Technology Center conducted a week-long day camp geared towards middle-school students underrepresented in CS (girls, African-Americans, Latinos) [8]. The camp, like SAILORS, was run by graduate student volunteers, and also found success in offering students real laboratory experience through robotics lessons. However, robotics and bioinformatics are only two topics in the larger field of AI. SAILORS aims to introduce students to the foundational technical concepts in AI, such as classifiers, and include topics from many concentrations in the field.

3. PROGRAM RECRUITMENT

We recruited students to apply for the program primarily through email. We emailed high school teachers in the bay area as well as students within the Stanford summer camp database (i.e. students that had applied for a Stanford camp before). As a pilot program, we found this method necessary to directly reach interested students. We welcomed students from all income levels and backgrounds to apply. Interested students completed a free online application composed of short response questions about their previous activities and classes, a longer question about their understanding of AI, and a teacher recommendation form. Students submitted a transcript. By the application deadline, we received 213 applications for 24 spots in the program. Overall, the following criteria were used throughout the admissions process: high academic performance in math and science classes, demonstrated leadership ability, enthusiasm for AI as exhibited through responses, strong teacher recommendations, and critical thinking as exhibited through the essay. Although previous CS experience was not a factor in admissions, all admitted students had some previous experience. Experience ranged from self-taught to AP CS; about half of the students taught themselves basic CS and 20% took a CS class in school (less than or equivalent to CS1). Our pool of admitted students consisted of girls passionate about technology who performed strongly in academics, but did not necessarily have much exposure to AI. All admitted students had high GPAs and many participated in science fairs and other extracurricular activities. A majority of them were Asian, reflecting our applicant pool, which was roughly 75% Asian. Additionally, all but two of the students came from California, as SAILORS is a non-residential program.

4. PROGRAM CURRICULUM

The two-week schedule was designed to fulfill the overall goals of SAILORS, and introduced girls to concepts in AI through a variety of engaging avenues. The first half of the daily schedule introduced students to research topics in AI and CS while the second half of the day allowed students to have first hand experience with some of the topics. Each activity targeted a combination of SAILORS's three goals, and balanced technological theory/rigor and social impact through AI. This balance is a part of what strongly differentiates SAILORS's curriculum from other CS camps. Because most students came in with a wide range of programming experience, the curriculum was designed assuming they had little to no programming knowledge.

4.1 Professor Lectures

Each morning began with breakfast with a professor, followed by an hour-long professor lecture. Students enjoyed the chance to speak personally with the professor about their research before the formal lecture. After breakfast, professors presented on the main topics and applications of their research. Topics included computer vision, cognition, biomedical informatics, robotics, information networks, natural language processing, human-robot interactions, computational sustainability, and aeronautics/astronautics. The lectures emphasized real-world applications to excite and inform the students about the types of problems AI and CS can solve. For example, one professor lectured on air controllers, and how he used dynamic programming to reduce air traffic collisions while also decreasing unnecessary flight path changes. Post-lecture breaks gave students an opportunity to interact closely with the professor, so that they may be inspired to learn more about the topic after the lecture.

4.2 Classroom Sessions

Following the professor lecture, graduate students explained in detail one technical component of the lecture. The graduate student instructors began with a lecture-style explanation; the students then worked on relevant problems to practice the concept. For example, one postdoctoral fellow gave a talk on Fisher's exact test. Students then used real data from a computational biology research site to compare genes based on varying parameters. For another session, students learned about inductive reasoning: when given a partial pattern of numbers, they guessed numbers that should belong, and compared the probability of their guesses to probabilistic programs that do the same. Other topics included nearest neighbor algorithm, correlation, graph search algorithms, and PID controllers. The classroom sessions gave students the confidence that they themselves can use the technical methods used in AI, and that they have the ability to delve into the technical aspects of the field.

4.3 Personal Growth Sessions

The personal growth sessions aimed to give girls the skills they need to be successful as women working in STEM. These skills were not AI specific and gave students the ability to thrive in the face of the more general challenges—microaggressions, working in teams, etc.—of both university level classes and of the AI/STEM workplace. The sessions were 1) talk with AI women; 2) team dynamics; 3) scientific communication; 4) industry panel; 5) design thinking; 6) how to recognize and react to microagressions; 7) time management; and 8) staying involved in AI/CS.

Excluding the panels, 1) and 4), the sessions were led in a seminar setting by a professional in the area. For example, a professor from Stanford Design school led the design thinking session. The sessions transitioned between short lectures, facilitated discussions, and interactive activities. The panels were conducted Q&A style, and the students asked relevant questions to the panelists.

4.4 Social Hour

Social hour gave the students a space to build friendships and community outside of their project work. Two social hours were spent exploring technology on campus: self-driving car and haptic surgical simulation; the remainder were unstructured.

4.5 Research Projects

A two hour time block each day was dedicated to research projects. The students were split up into four groups of six, with two graduate students leading each team. Project topics included computer vision, robotics, NLP, and computational biology; the students ranked the topics by preference and worked on the same project for the entire program. The project topics were carefully selected to be engaging, to emphasize the real-world impact of AI, to be technically stimulating, and to showcase the variety and depth of problems AI can solve. Additionally, the research projects were designed to closely mimic current AI research. Students could thus get a first-hand experience of what researchers in the field work on, and gain confidence that they can work on the same. In this way, the projects aimed to increase students' understanding of the technical methods used in AI as well as their excitement towards research in the field.

The coding for all of the projects was done in Python through the programming environment Jupyter. Each project included a short general introduction to coding. During the projects, the students implemented their code individually but worked in pairs to brainstorm ideas.

4.5.1 Making Hospitals Safer with Computer Vision

Students learned how to develop computer vision algorithms that can automatically understand actions in videos in order to monitor hand washing in hospitals. Their objective was to develop an algorithm that can recognize whether or not a doctor uses the hand sanitizing dispenser before he/she enters a room. First, to consturct a dataset, the students recorded a video and labeled each frame as having used the sanitizer or not. Then, instructors presented an overview of machine learning classifiers and introduced the background subtraction algorithm.

The students worked in pairs to code this algorithm. The instructors provided simple skeleton code, guidance when needed, and the evaluation code with the F-score metric; students largely coded the background subtraction algorithm independently. Manually choosing a threshold was the most technically rigorous portion. The students experimented with the size and location of the crop region for the algorithm as well as what to threshold (color channels, image difference, etc). After some manual trial and error, the students learned how to use the machine-learning assessment technique cross validation to automatically choose the thresholds.

In the remaining days, the students learned about and programmed a linear classifier. Because of limited time, the whole group with the instructors collectively coded the classifier on the board. Then, the students implemented it separately and compared the F-score of the background subtraction algorithm and the linear classifier. They discovered that the linear classifier performed much better than background subtraction. The students left with a broad understanding of the full pipeline of how to train and deploy an activity recognition model for a real-world healthcare application.

4.5.2 Assisting Disaster Relief with Natural Language Processing (NLP)

Students learned how to use NLP to determine which area of the world needs disaster relief, and which relief is needed (such as food, water, medical care). Students took a real corpus of tweets made during Hurricane Sandy, and automatically determined which of the tweets were relief requests for food. Each student built their own Naive Bayes classifier to classify the tweets.

Students began by exploring the raw data of tweets. Using the data, they created a simple rule-based classifier by writing the rules function in the classifier starter code. The students saw that this classifier does not generalize well, and, as an alternative, the instructors introduced Naive Bayes as a statistical model. For a hands-on demo, instructors used plastic cups to represent classes, grapes to represent instances, and grape color to represent features.

Students first used the Naive Bayes algorithm hands-on to classify Set cards by color, pattern, and number of icons. Using instructor starter code, they coded their algorithm. They then revisited the tweets, and explored the pros and cons of Naive Bayes as applied to tweets. Students wrote the code to extract features from a tweet, calculate class probabilities, calculate conditional probabilities, and predict the class of an unseen tweet. Students ran their final programs on the data, and compared the results to the rule-based classifier. At the end of the two weeks, the students saw that they have the ability to create something that processes real data to have a social impact.

4.5.3 Decoding DNA: Finding Meaning in the Genome

Students learned some of the technical methods used in computational biology. Students focused on gene expression data from several types of cancer, and used different classifiers to distinguish between normal and tumor samples, as well as between cancer types and stages of progression.

Students first learned the high-level concept of classifiers. As a hands-on example, students were given training grapes and tomatoes and developed features to distinguish them. This example intuitively demonstrated the k-nearest neighbors algorithm. After gaining the conceptual knowledge, students explored the online dataset of genes and the performances of k-nearest neighbor algorithm on various k (with working code written by the instructors). Then, students programmed the k-nearest neighbor algorithm themselves, working from instructor-written starter code. Students tested the performance of their algorithm on various datasets (provided by the instructors) with various parameters.

Student pairs brainstormed their own final experiments. One group tested the effect of random feature selection with k-nearest neighbors classification, while another tested the effects of balanced versus unbalanced datasets. By the end of the two weeks, students understood the basic biology of cancer, as well as several computational techniques used for analyzing cancer datasets to identify and classify tumors.

The Python code of the project, including the student's code, can be viewed online at goo.gl/okTkdj.

4.5.4 Self-Driving Cars and the Future of Personal Transportation

Students implemented a basic control system for a compact robotic car to navigate a system of roads represented by lines. Each day the instructors first presented a concept used by real autonomous cars, and then translated the concept to their robots, Pololu m3pi. The instructors taught three levels of control: 1) low level trajectory tracking, 2) motion planning, 3) routing.

In the first week, students learned control for low level trajectory tracking. The students focused on the algorithms, while communication infrastructure, data structures, etc. were prepared by the instructors. More specifically, the students programmed a proportional-integral-derivative (PID) controller to make a compact robotic car follow lines on a small road network using light sensors. They then iteratively tested the robots and adjusted control parameters and control strategies until the robot correctly and smoothly completed the task.

In the second week, students implemented Dijkstra's algorithm in Python to find the shortest path for the car. The students first independently wrote a function to return the cost of a path given the nodes of the path. The instructors then explained Dijkstra's algorithm, and the students worked in groups of two or three to implement Dijkstra's in code. The instructors provided a package to allow the students to see a visualization of their algorithm on a graph. Near the end of the week, students practiced route planning with other robotic cars on the line roads, simulating real roads. Students were able to receive information about the locations of other robotic cars and use Dijkstra's to choose a path to avoid collisions. In addition to technical knowledge, students gained an understanding of the potential value and societal impact of autonomous vehicles.

The Python code of the project, including the student's code, can be viewed online at goo.gl/kEWm3z.

4.6 Field Trips

The camp featured two field trips, one to the Computer History Museum with a tour led by Turing Award winner Ed Feigenbaum, and the other to Google to listen to a panel of Google female engineers and have lunch with the engineers. The first showed the students the rich history of computer science with an emphasis on AI, as told by the "father of expert systems". The second showed the students what an industry workplace looks like and what computer scientists in industry do on a day to day basis, with an emphasis on women in computer science. The students thoroughly enjoyed speaking with these professionals.

5. EVALUATION

We administered two sets of surveys. The first set included relevant questions from [12], as well as AI-oriented questions, and allowed us to establish a baseline for the attitudes and abilities of our admitted students. Relevant materials include [13, 14]. The second set of surveys focused on the admitted students pre and post participation in the 2 week summer program. Because the survey was AI specific, we did not use a validated instrument.

5.1 Baseline Survey

Students were asked questions about their attitudes towards math and science, their comfort level with peers at school, STEM career knowledge, humanitarian career interest, AI social interest, AI technical interest. For the analysis and for all following analysis, the Likert scale was quantified from 1 to 5, where 1 is the most negative and 5 is the most positive. For robustness of analysis, the questions were grouped based on the topic they measured. For each group, a scaled mean was calculated per participant. The resulting means suggest that the students have strong math and science backgrounds, and are passionate in engineering, humanitarian issues, and AI (mean above 4 in these areas). The survey also suggests students entered the program successful in general areas that SAILORS targets, for example STEM career knowledge and comfort in STEM classes (mean above 4 in these areas). For this reason, the second survey asks more specific questions about SAILORS's goals.

Before and after analysis was done on the baseline survey, with the same grouping as above. 11 paired t-tests were performed on 11 of the groups. Using the Benjamini-Hochberg procedure to control for false positive discovery rate, none of the t-tests were statistically significant. We speculate the high means did not leave much space for significant increase.

5.2 Pre/Post Survey

Students entered the program expressing a strong interest in CS and AI. At the end of the 2 week program, we found a statistically significant increase in their confidence and likelihood to pursue CS and AI. To test for a change in the students between the start and end of the program, paired analysis was done. The Likert scale questions were tested using a paired t-test. There were 11 such questions (Table 1). The two questions measuring interest in AI (Q13

Table 1: **Mean value changes in survey responses of the 24 SAILORS students before and after the program.**

#	Question	Mean Before	Mean After	p-value
12	How likely is it that you will have a career in AI in the future?	3.50	4.08	.0002
3	How likely do you think it is that you attain that position [your dream computer science position]?	3.33	3.83	.001
8	When I am learning CS, I know girls who I am comfortable asking for help.	3.08	3.92	.001
10	How likely is it that you will study AI?	3.79	4.25	.002
15	I can succeed in AI.	4.17	4.50	.002
9	How likely is it that you will major in computer science in the future?	4.29	4.58	.005
14	I can succeed in CS.	4.33	4.58	.011
11	How likely is it that you will have a career in CS in the future?	4.17	4.46	.016
Grouped 13,17	Grouped: 1) I want to learn more about AI. 2) I want to do research in AI.	4.71	4.75	.664
16	I want to do research in CS.	4.50	4.50	1.000

and Q17) were grouped together when tested, giving a total of 10 t-tests. The paired t-test analysis with Benjamini-Hochberg procedure found that questions 3, 8, 9, 10, 11, 12, 14, and 15 show a statistically significant ($\alpha = .05$) positive difference between pre-SAILORS student answers and post-SAILORS. Thus, there exists statistically significant evidence that SAILORS relates to 1) increase in confidence in CS (Q3 and Q14); 2) increase in confidence in AI (Q15); 3) increase in likelihood of pursuing CS (Q9 and Q11); 4) increase in likelihood of pursuing AI (Q10 and Q12); and 5) increase in same-sex peer-to-peer support (Q8).

The survey also asked technical questions to gauge the technical skills they learned at SAILORS (for example: "What is the main focus of controls engineering?"). The technical questions were tested using McNemar test performed as binomial exact test with Yates continuity correction. The test uses categories incorrect and correct, paired before and after. There is a statistically significant ($\alpha = .05$) change between answers for three out of five of the questions. For these three questions, we see an increase in the number of correct answers from before to after. These three questions addressed high-level technical concepts used in AI, as well as general CS, while the other two addressed simple probability and coding. Thus, there exists statistically significant evidence that SAILORS relates to an increase in CS and AI technical knowledge.

Students were asked if they had advisors in CS, role models in CS, and role models in AI (other than their parents). These questions were tested using McNemar test, with categories yes (student has advisor or role model) and no (does not have), paired before and after. There was a statistically significant ($\alpha = .05$) positive change between answers for AI role model ($p = .0002$). Thus, there exists statistically significant evidence that SAILORS relates to increase in AI role models. In the pre-survey, no student cited university level faculty as a CS advisor or role model. In the post-survey, 64% of those who have CS role models cited SAILORS-affiliated faculty, and 79% of those who have CS advisors cited SAILORS-affiliated faculty. Thus, there also exists statistically significant evidence that SAILORS relates to increase in faculty role models and faculty support.

When asked to give a short answer on what kind of problems people in AI work on, students first gave high-level answers along the lines of solving societal problems to make human lives easier. After the program, students gave more specific answers such as: "People in AI work on making models and graphs to predict or classify a range of items from diseases to birds." Additionally, when asked if their perception of who can be successful in CS changed and how, 83% of students responded yes, with the most cited responses being that anyone can be successful in CS, computer scientists can have other interests outside of CS, and other qualities besides academic strength (teamwork, problem solving) are also required to be successful in CS. Finally, we asked the students to elaborate on a problem in the world they are passionate about and what specific technical methods in AI can be used to solve that problem. Before the program, students cited "coding" and "robots". We saw an increase in the students' knowledge of which technical methods could be used to solve the problem. For example, one student stated that we can use the k-nearest neighbors algorithm to classify trash and recycling in order to prevent waste.

In addition to the questions above, we asked students for feedback on specific components of the curriculum. When asked to respond on Likert scale to the statements "The projects I built can help people" and "The projects I built were interesting", 95.8% of the students replied with strongly agree. 83.3% of students strongly agreed with the statement, "I am proud of what I built" and 75% of students strongly agreed with the statement "I am confident that I can work on a similar project in the future". For the personal growth sessions, when asked to respond to "There are people like me in AI", "There are people like me in CS fields", "I can find support in a CS field", and "I am comfortable speaking up for myself in a CS field", the students all responded with an average above 4 on the quantified Likert scale.

5.3 Limitations

Despite positive results, the pilot program had several limitations. First, the survey was unanonymized for internal purposes; future years should anonymize the survey. Second, the staff knew of the goals, and discussed some of the goals with the students, perhaps resulting in confirmation bias. Third, SAILORS did not reach low-income, African American, or Latino students. Since students of these backgrounds were not included in our study, we cannot draw conclusions from our results towards those demographics. Based on their applications, our students had access to other opportunities to learn about CS; while SAILORS may have been the only opportunity for them to learn AI, future years may target girls who do not have many technical opportunities.

6. CONCLUSION

The results show a positive impact of SAILORS upon the pilot-year students. Namely, the results support achieving goals 2 (contextualize technical AI concepts through social impact) and 3 (address barriers for girls in CS), and some support in achieving goal 1.

In support of goal 2, students' perception of AI and CS shifted to include a wider variety of people who can successfully work in the field. They also left knowing concrete, specific technical methods that can solve the problems they are passionate about. Research projects successfully allowed students to technically work on real-world applications.

In support of goal 3, students gained faculty support, same-sex peer-to-peer support, exposure to technical methods, and increased their AI and CS confidence. For faculty support, students gained faculty role models and advisors in CS and AI. For same-sex peer-to-peer support, students' comfort asking girls for help increased, and they cited SAILORS as a community. The personal growth sessions successfully allowed girls to relate to each other and other women in the field. The program has also created a community for SAILORS's volunteer faculty at the AI lab. For technical exposure, students were exposed to many technical methods used in AI; by the end of the program they had built classifiers, and correctly answered questions about technical methods used in AI. For confidence, students left feeling more likely to succeed in both AI and CS, as well as more likely to go into both fields. Students were also proud of their research projects, and their ability to engage real-world applicable technical methods.

The results do not directly show support for increase in interest. We speculate students already came in with a very high level of interest in AI (Likert scale mean 4.7/5) because of our admissions criteria. However, the increase in likelihood to go into AI suggests a potential increase in longer term interest.

All in all, SAILORS was successful this year in achieving its short-term goals. Our hope now is that the excitement and confidence the girls feel about AI and CS, as well as the community they have found, persist. To facilitate, we plan to hold events with both the students and AI faculty. Ultimately, SAILORS's pilot year has proven to be an effective way to educate students in AI and the societal impact of CS. In future years, we hope to reach a more diverse demographic of students as well as see the long term impact of the program.

7. ACKNOWLEDGEMENTS

We are grateful to all of the SAILORS staff, students, generous sponsors, and anonymous reviewers.

8. REFERENCES

[1] National Center for Women and Information Technology. Women and Information Technology By the Numbers, 2015. Retrieved August 21, 2015 from http://www.ncwit.org/sites/default/files/resources/btn_04032015_web.pdf.

[2] Degrees in computer and information sciences conferred by degree-granting institutions, by level of degree and sex of student: 1970-71 through 2010-11, 2012. Retrieved August 21, 2015 from http://nces.ed.gov/programs/digest/d12/tables/dt12_349.asp.

[3] Jane Margolis, Allan Fisher, and Faye Miller. The Anatomy of Interest: Women in Undergraduate Computer Science. *Women's Studies Quarterly*, 28(1/2):pp. 104–127, 2000.

[4] Greg Scragg and Jesse Smith. A Study of Barriers to Women in Undergraduate Computer Science. *SIGCSE Bull.*, 30(1):82–86, March 1998.

[5] Lori Carter. Why students with an Apparent Aptitude for Computer Science Don't Choose to Major in Computer Science. In *Proceedings of the 37th SIGCSE Technical Symposium on Computer Science Education*, SIGCSE '06, pages 27–31, New York, NY, USA, 2006. ACM.

[6] Neil Anderson, Colin Lankshear, Carolyn Timms, and Lyn Courtney. Because it's boring, irrelevant and I don't like computers: Why high school girls avoid professionally-oriented ICT subjects. *Computers & Education*, 50(4):1304 – 1318, 2008.

[7] J.M. Cohoon. Must there be so few? Including women in CS. In *Software Engineering, 2003. Proceedings. 25th International Conference on*, pages 668–674, May 2003.

[8] Kelly R. Cannon, Katherine A. Panciera, and Nikolaos P. Papanikolopoulos. Second annual robotics summer camp for underrepresented students. *SIGCSE Bull.*, 39(3):14–18, June 2007.

[9] Inna Pivkina, Enrico Pontelli, Rachel Jensen, and Jessica Haebe. Young women in computing: Lessons learned from an educational & outreach program. *SIGCSE Bull.*, 41(1):509–513, March 2009.

[10] Janet E. Burge, Gerald C. Gannod, Maureen Doyle, and Karen C. Davis. Girls on the Go: A CS summer camp to attract and inspire female high school students. In *Proceeding of the 44th ACM Technical Symposium on Computer Science Education*, SIGCSE '13, pages 615–620, New York, NY, USA, 2013. ACM.

[11] Lori Pollock, Kathleen McCoy, Sandra Carberry, Namratha Hundigopal, and Xiaoxin You. Increasing high school girls' self confidence and awareness of CS through a positive summer experience. *SIGCSE Bull.*, 36(1):185–189, March 2004.

[12] *Manual for Observing Patterns of Adaptive Learning (OPAL): A Protocol for Classroom Observations.*

[13] B. H. Loyd and C. P. Gressard. Computer attitude scale. *Journal of Computing Research.*, 15(3):241–259, June 1996.

[14] Brian Dorn and Allison Elliott Tew. Empirical validation and application of the computing attitudes survey. *Computer Science Education*, 25(1):1–36, 2015.

Sisters Rise Up 4 CS: Helping Female Students Pass the Advanced Placement Computer Science A Exam

Barbara J. Ericson
Georgia Institute of Technology
801 Atlantic Drive
Atlanta, GA, 30332
+1-404.385.2107
ericson@cc.gatech.edu

Miranda C. Parker
Georgia Institute of Technology
85 Fifth Street NW
Atlanta, GA, 30332
miranda.parker@gatech.edu

Shelly Engelman
SageFox Consulting Group
675 Seminole Ave NE Suite 303
Atlanta, GA 30307
+1-404-633-9005
sengelman@sagefoxgroup.com

ABSTRACT

Female students are underrepresented in computing careers and in computing majors at the college or university level. This underrepresentation starts in high school. Only 20% of Advanced Placement (AP) Computer Science (CS) A exam takers in 2014 nationally were female. In addition to being underrepresented, female students tend to have a lower pass rate on the exam than male students. Failing the exam could reduce interest in computing as a career. Sisters Rise Up 4 CS was created at the Georgia Institute of Technology (Georgia Tech) to help more female high school students pass the AP CS A exam. It offers help sessions, near-peer role models, exposure to a college campus, and a community of learners. Sisters Rise Up 4 CS is based on Project Rise Up 4 CS, which was also created at Georgia Tech to help increase the number of African-American students that pass the AP CS A exam. However, Sisters Rise Up 4 CS does not include the financial incentives offered by Project Rise Up 4 CS. Project Rise Up 4 CS has resulted in statistically significant positive changes in attitudes for participants and a large increase in the participants' perception of their ability to pass the exam. Even students who did not pass the exam have reported positive benefits from being in Project Rise Up 4 CS. This paper summarizes the findings from Project Rise Up 4 CS from 2013-2015 and presents the findings from the pilot of Sisters Rise Up 4 CS from 2014-2015. We used a mixed-methods approach to evaluate the project and to judge the effectiveness of the project elements.→

Keywords

Advanced Placement Computer Science; Near-peer mentors; Gender Issues; Underrepresented Minorities; Financial Incentives

1. WOMEN IN COMPUTING

The percentage of women in earning bachelor's degrees in computer and information science in the United States grew quickly from 16% in 1973-1974 to 37% in 1983-1984. Since then it declined to 18% in 2010-2011 [2]. This underrepresentation in computer science can be seen in high school as well. Women were only 20% of Advanced Placement (AP) Computer Science (CS) A exam takers nationally in 2014 [1].

SIGCSE '16, March 2-5, 2016, Memphis, TN, USA.
© 2016 ACM. ISBN 978-1-4503-3685-7/16/03…$15.00.
DOI: http://dx.doi.org/10.1145/2839509.2844623

Female students pass the Advanced Placement (AP) Computer Science (CS) A exam at a lower rate than male students both nationally and in our state [1]. The AP CS A course is intended to be equivalent to a college level CS1 course for majors. Scores on the exam range from 1 to 5 with a 3 as the threshold for passing. In 2014, the national pass rate for female students on the exam was 57% and the male pass rate was 68%. In 2014, the female pass rate in Georgia on the exam was 42% while the male pass rate was 47%. Failing the exam may not be a problem if you weren't really trying to pass it, but it could discourage those who were trying to pass the exam from considering a career in computing. Research has shown that belief that you can succeed in a field is a critical factor in choosing a career [10]. Additionally, when girls fail they tend to blame themselves and lose confidence in their ability whereas boys tend to blame external factors, so failure can have a more debilitating effect on females [9].

2. PROJECT RISE UP 4 CS

We created Project Rise Up 4 CS at Georgia Tech to help more African-American high school students pass the Advanced Placement (AP) Computer Science (CS) A exam in Georgia [12]. African-Americans have the lowest pass rate on the AP CS A exam of any racial group both in Georgia and nationally [1]. Project Rise Up 4 CS offers twice a week webinars, once a month in-person hands-on sessions, near-peer role models, exposure to a college campus, competitions, and a community of learners. It has also offered a financial incentive for passing the exam (offered the last 3 years) and for attending the required number of help sessions (offered in the 2nd and 3rd year).

We created a free ebook to help prepare high school students for the AP CS A exam and have added content to it each year [11]. Participants in Project Rise Up 4 CS always have access to the most recent version of that ebook and we make the new version publically accessible after the exam. The ebook contains information about what is on the exam, common mistakes, worked examples, and lots of practice problems. Research on worked examples shows that they are an efficient and effective way to learn [17]. Research also highlights the importance of worked examples and practice to build skill [18].

The design of Project Rise UP 4 CS was based on two successful projects: The Advanced Placement Incentive Program and Glitch. The Advanced Placement Incentive Program (APIP) started in Texas and has offered financial incentives for both students and teachers as well as additional help sessions for students in order to increase the number of students who take and pass AP exams [14]. The Glitch Project at Georgia Tech was created to increase Black male high school students' interest in studying computer science by paying them to be game testers and also teaching them computing concepts.[8]. Glitch featured near-peer role models, instruction in computing, and exposure to a college campus. Near-peer role models are "near" to the target population in some way: age, ethnicity, gender, and/or interests. Bandura's social learning theory posits that people learn by observing, imitating, and modeling what they learn from other people and are more likely to imitate those that they feel are "similar" to them [3]. The majority of Glitch participants continued studying computer science after high school graduation even though only 20% were originally interested in a career in computing [8].

2.1 First Year – Jan 2013 to May 2013

Originally Project Rise Up 4 CS offered a $100 financial incentive if the participants attended at least four help sessions and passed the exam with a score of 3 or higher [12]. That year 27 students enrolled in the project at Georgia Tech and 14 (52%) students completed four or more help sessions as shown in Table 1. Thirteen of the 14 students who completed four or more help sessions took the exam. Nine of the 13 passed the exam for a pass rate of 69%. The pass rate for all African-American students in Georgia that year for AP CS A was 22%. A total of 28 African-American students passed the exam in Georgia in 2013, which was a record number. Twenty-two students had passed the exam in Georgia in 2012, which was the prior record. We cannot know how many students would have passed without Project Rise Up 4 CS, but at least some of the students told us that they didn't think that they would have passed otherwise.

Table 1. Summary of Project Rise Up 4 CS: 2013 - 2015

Year	Num	# Sessions Required	Completed	Took Exam	Passed
2013	27	4	14 (52%)	13	9 (69%)
13-14	33	6	15 (45%)	15	6 (40%)
14-15	21	4	16 (76%)	15	5 (33%)

2.2 Second Year – Oct 2013 – May 2014

In response to participants' suggestions, we started the second year of Project Rise UP 4 CS in October of 2013. Since we started earlier, we required that participants attend six help sessions rather than four to be considered as completers. Thanks to a Google RISE grant, we offered participants $100 if they attended six help sessions and an additional $100 if they passed the exam. Our hypothesis was that this additional financial incentive would encourage more students to attend the minimum number of help sessions. That year 33 students enrolled at Georgia Tech and 15 (45%) attended the minimum number of help sessions, as shown in Table 1. Six of those 15 participants passed the exam for a pass rate of 40%. The pass rate for all African-Americans in Georgia that year was 23%. A total of 35 African-American students passed the exam in 2014 in Georgia, which was also a new record. Contrary to our hypothesis, the completion rate actually fell from 52% in year one to 45% in year two. However, this decrease in the completion rate could have been due to our increasing the required number of help sessions from four to six. While one of the participants mentioned the financial incentive as a reason why he joined the project during a focus group, some of the students who earned the $100 didn't even fill out the paperwork to receive the money.

2.3 Third Year – Oct 2014 – May 2015

In 2015, we went back to requiring participants to complete four help sessions rather than six to assess if that would result in a higher completion rate. Due to the need to spend out the Google RISE grant before the end of 2014, we offered prizes worth at least $100 if students attended the required number of help sessions and a prize worth at least $100 if the student passed the exam. Twenty-one students enrolled at Georgia Tech and 16 (76%) of them attended four or more help sessions as shown in Table 1. Fifteen students took the exam and 5 passed (33%). The completion rate did increase when we required four help sessions (76%) versus six (45%) and it was also above the original completion rate without the additional $100 financial incentive (52%). This supported our hypothesis that the additional financial incentive for attending the required number of help sessions would improve the completion rate. However, three of the students didn't pick up their prizes. In addition, the pass rate for completers decreased. While the financial incentives were mentioned by some of the students in a focus group as part of the motivation for joining the project, they didn't seem to be important to others.

3. SISTERS RISE UP 4 CS – 2014 - 2015

Georgia Tech created Sisters Rise Up 4 CS in the fall of 2014 to help more female students pass the AP CS A exam. We retained the same components as Project Rise Up 4 CS *except for the financial incentives*. Participants were entered into a raffle for a prize worth $150-200 if they sent us their scores on the AP CS A exam before the end of July. This was to encourage students to send us their scores in a timely fashion. Our research questions were *1) Would we see similar results in terms of attitude changes in Sisters Rise Up as we had seen in Project Rise Up?* and *2) Would we see similar completion and pass rates without a financial incentive?*

3.1 Recruitment and Application

We sent emails to our mailing list of AP CS A teachers in our state and asked them to notify their students about the project. Students had to fill out an online application that asked for their contact information, grade, gender, ethnicity, the computing courses they had taken, school name, teacher name, computing experience such as summer camps and robotics teams, textbook, development environment, how they got interested in computer science, and why they wanted to be part of the project. Thirty students applied.

3.1.1 Themes from the applications

Eighteen (60%) of the applicants said that they became interested in computer science because of a family member, teacher, or friend. *"I got interested in computer science because my brother would often show me some of the cool things he could do with Python and MATLAB as a student at Georgia Tech." "My computer science teachers at [my school] encouraged me."* Thirteen (43%) talked about how interesting and valuable the field was. *"I first got interested when I realized the career fields out there involving computer science."* Four (13%) became interested because of a summer camp or prior computing course. *"(The) Introduction to programing class, specifically working with Python Program, motivated me to be involved in computing."* Four (13%) of them said that they became interested at a young age.

These themes are not surprising given recent research from Google on the factors that influence women in computing [19].

In particular, researchers *"found that encouragement and exposure are key controllable indicators for whether or not young women decide to pursue a computing-related degree. [19]"* The research also showed that encouragement from both family and non-family (peers, teachers, role models) sources had more of an effect on girls than on boys.

3.2 Enrollment

Of the 30 students who applied, 21 completed the required parent consent and student assent forms to enroll in Sisters Rise Up 4 CS at Georgia Tech. Eight students enrolled in November of 2014. Thirteen students enrolled in February of 2015. At the enrollment session students took a pre attitudinal survey and completed a 20-question multiple-choice content knowledge pretest. We gave parents and students a presentation on the breadth of research being done by women in computing at Georgia Tech. Parents attended a session on computer science at Georgia Tech while the participants were taking the pre attitudinal survey and pretest. Our goal was to encourage the parents to support their daughters' interests in computer science.

Of the twenty-one enrolled students, one (5%) was in 9th grade, eight (38%) were in 10th grade, three (14%) were in 11th grade, and nine (43%) were in 12th grade. Of the twenty-one enrolled students one (5%) was Latina, three (14%) were African-American, four (19%) were Caucasian, and 13 (62%) were Asian.

The enrolled students came from nine different schools as shown in Table 1. Most of the students came from highly ranked schools (with 1 as the highest and 399 as the lowest).

Table 2. School Information for Sisters Rise Up 4 CS

School	% Free/ Reduced Lunch	Rank of 399	Num Students	Num ≥ 4 Help Sessions	Num Passed Exam
1	13%	5th	5	4	2
2	11%	9th	2	1	1
3	8%	13th	7	2	3
4	5%	14th	1	1	1
5	28%	25th	1	0	1
6	41%	53rd	1	0	0
7	55%	201st	1	1	0
8		Private	2	2	1
9		Private	1	1	0
		Total	**21**	**12**	**9**

3.3 Program Details

We hired two Caucasian female undergraduate students and one male Caucasian high school senior student to serve as near-peer role models and to lead the webinars and in-person help sessions. The high school senior had previously passed the AP CS A exam with a 5. One of the undergraduates was a junior and one was a senior. In the spring, one of the female role models acquired another position; to fill her spot, we moved one of the Asian male undergraduate students who had been working with Project Rise Up 4 CS to Sisters Rise Up 4 CS. Prior research has shown that both males and females can serve as role models for female students provided that they do not reinforce or promote stereotypes about computer scientists [6].

We trained the leaders on how to use Blackboard Collaborate, the webinar software that we used. We instructed them to make the webinars interactive by asking the participants to explain concepts, predict results, and explain why the answers to multiple-choice questions were right or wrong. Prior Project Rise Up 4 CS students had commented that they enjoyed the interaction on the webinars [13]. We incorporated findings from education research into the webinars and in-person sessions. In particular, we encouraged our role models to use active learning, worked examples and practice, and to encourage learning from mistakes [4; 5; 7].

We spent less than $3,000 total on Sisters Rise Up 4 CS. We paid the undergraduate students and high school student who led the webinars and in-person sessions, paid for food for the in-person sessions, and bought prizes for the competitions and raffle. We held a practice multiple-choice exam competition, called the AP Bowl, at Georgia Tech in April of 2015 and awarded prizes to the top scorers from Sisters Rise Up 4 CS and Project Rise Up 4 CS. We also entered all of the female students who sent us their scores on the exam into a raffle for a prize worth $150 to $200.

3.4 Results

Participants were required to attend at least four help sessions to be considered to have completed the project. Twelve (57%) of the 21 participants attended at least four help sessions. Some participants attended many more than four help sessions as seen in Figure 1. One person attended 14 help sessions, which suggests that she found the sessions valuable.

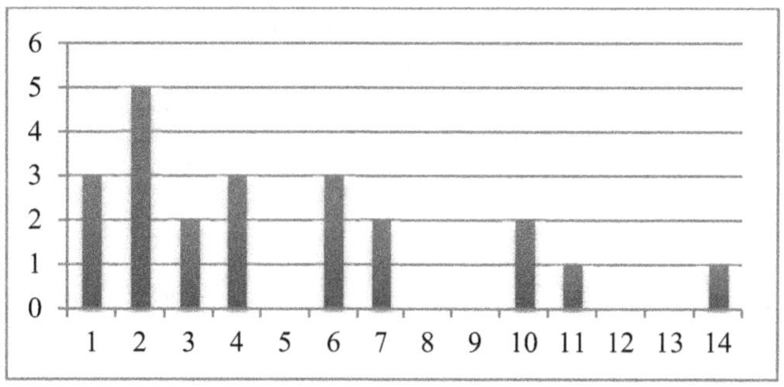

Figure 1. How many attended each number of help sessions

Of the 12 participants who attended four or more help sessions, 11 took the exam, and 6 of the eleven passed (55%) with a score of 3 or higher. Of the 21 original participants, a total of 9 of the 21 (43%) students passed the exam. However, three of the 21 students did not take the exam. For comparison, the pass rate for females in our state in 2015 on the AP CS A exam was 48%.

As displayed in Table 3 six (67%) of the nine students who passed the exam identified as Asian. Two (22%) identified as White, and one (11%) identified as African-American.

Table 3. Information on students who passed the exam

Id	Grade	Race	Num Help	School	Pre test score	Exam Score
1	9th	White	10	3	13	5
2	12th	AA	10	1	9	4
3	12th	White	4	8	3	3
4	12th	Asian	2	2	8	4
5	10th	Asian	6	4	6	3
6	10th	Asian	4	3	8	5
7	11th	Asian	3	5	8	4
8	12th	Asian	4	1	7	4
9	10th	Asian	1	3	18	4

As shown in Table 4, four (57%) of the seven non-completers who took the exam failed the exam. Five (45%) of the 11 completers, who took the exam, failed the exam. A higher percentage of the non-completers failed the exam than the completers. None of the students at the two lowest ranked schools passed the exam, as seen in Table 2.

The student from school 7, a low ranking school, was actually taking the course virtually, since her school didn't offer the course. She attended 11 help sessions, but still failed to pass the exam. In an email she said, *"I'm sending this score with a good bit of shame as it was my 1st one out of all 10 AP tests I've taken. I do want to clarify that though I did terrible on the exam, I think a lot of it had to do with me learning through (the) GA Virtual School (which was a struggle in itself because it's the only class I've taken online ever). The Sisters Rise Up program definitely taught me a lot (helping me end up with an A in the actual class) and I'm still glad I participated in it despite the outcome. As for the ebook, it was extremely helpful in teaching things in an easier/broken-down way rather than how I was learning it online. I'm planning to major in CM (Computational Media) at (Georgia) Tech this coming Fall, so this program definitely still kept me interested in coding despite my miserable experience with the class."* It is encouraging to see that even though she failed the exam she credited Sisters Rise Up 4 CS with helping her earn an A in her course and for maintaining her interest in a career in computing.

Table 4. Score breakdown for completers and non-completers

AP CS A Score	# Completers	# Non-completers
1	3 (27%)	3 (43%)
2	2 (18%)	1 (14%)
3	2 (18%)	
4	2 (18%)	3 (43%)
5	2 (18%)	
Did not take exam	1	2

4. EVALUATION

A mixed methods approach was used to evaluate Sisters Rise Up 4 CS. We administered a pre attitudinal survey and a pre content knowledge assessment when the students enrolled. We asked students to complete a retrospective post attitudinal assessment and a post content knowledge assessment in April of 2015. However, very few students took the post-content knowledge assessment, so we are not reporting on that here. The attitudinal surveys are available on request and the pre and post content knowledge assessments are available in the ebook [11]. A focus group was conducted in the spring of 2015 with three members of Sisters Rise Up 4 CS in order to gain deeper insight into the participants' experience. In addition, we conducted individual interviews with several students in the summer of 2015 in order to gather feedback from more of the participants.

4.1 Attitudinal Survey Results

Twelve of the participants in Sisters Rise Up 4 CS completed the retrospective post attitudinal survey. These students showed gains across all eight attitudinal constructs from "before" the program to "now" as shown in Table 5 (top row in each section). This may indicate that the program was effective in enhancing females' positive attitudes towards computing. In particular, students show statistically significant ($p<.05$) gains in their attitudes towards gender equity in computing. Likewise, growth in their perceptions of the importance and usefulness of computing is trending toward significance at $p=.089$. There was also a significant, positive correlation between the number of sessions that participants attended and growth (from before to now) in "Motivation to Succeed" at $p=.012$ and in "Identity and Belonging" at $p=.008$. This suggests that attending more help sessions increased their motivation to succeed and their feeling of belonging in computing.

Thirteen of the participants in Project Rise Up 4 CS completed the retrospective post attitudinal survey. These students demonstrated statistically significant gains in confidence, enjoyment, and motivation to succeed as shown in Table 5 (second row in each section).

Table 5. Retrospective Attitudinal Survey Results for both Sisters Rise UP 4 CS and Project Rise Up 4 CS participants for 2014-2015

Construct	Sample Item	Before	Now	Paired Samples t-test
Computing Confidence	*I can get good grades in computing.*	3.58	3.83	0.166
		3.62	4.27	0.005*
Computing Enjoyment	*Computers are fun.*	3.00	3.27	0.216
		3.38	3.96	0.001*
Importance & Perceived Usefulness	*I will use computing in many ways throughout my life.*	4.00	4.32	0.089
		4.31	4.38	0.502
Motivation to Succeed	*When a computing problem arises that I can't immediately solve, I stick with it until I have the solution.*	2.92	3.04	0.674
		3.58	4.12	0.024†
Identity and Belonging	*I feel like I "belong" in computing.*	2.40	2.50	0.726
		3.69	4.15	0.082
Gender Equality	*Girls can do just as well as boys in computing.*	4.25	4.63	0.032†
		4.77	4.77	1.000
Creativity in Computing	*I am able to be expressive and creative while doing computing.*	3.00	3.31	0.266
		3.87	4.08	0.193
Intent to Persist	*I see myself working in a computing field.*	3.29	3.75	0.183
		4.15	4.54	0.086

* $p < 0.01$, † $p < 0.05$. Sisters Rise Up 4 CS results are shown in the top row in each section and Project Rise UP 4 CS results are shown in the second row in each section (shaded). For Sisters Rise Up n = 12 and for Project Rise Up n = 13.

It is important to note that the "now" results for the Sisters Rise Up 4 CS participants for only two constructs exceeded 4.0 on a 5-point Likert scale. This is in contrast to the "now" results for Project Rise Up 4 CS in which nearly all averages are above 4.0. Together, these findings indicate that while the attitudinal gains among Sisters Rise Up 4 CS participants are promising, there is still considerable room for further growth.

There was also a positive correlation ($r=0.569$ and $p=0.014$) between performance on the pre content knowledge assessment and performance on the AP CS A exam. One Sisters Rise Up 4 CS participant had a pretest score of three out of 20, yet she still passed the exam with a score of three as shown in Table 3. Given her low score on the pre content knowledge assessment she appeared to be at risk of failing the exam when the project started, which implies that she made strong gains in her content knowledge during Sisters Rise Up 4 CS.

4.2 Sisters Rise Up Focus Group Interviews

Qualitative data gleaned from a focus group with three Sisters Rise Up 4 CS participants revealed many of the same themes that we had seen in prior Project Rise Up 4 CS focus groups [13]. Participants valued the in-person sessions, the webinars, the near-peer leaders, and the focus on the exam. Some students praised their AP CS A course teachers. Others said that their course teachers made them learn mostly on their own. One participant reported that her teacher didn't cover the material on the exam or help them prepare for the exam. Research suggests that minimally guided instruction is inefficient and less effective than direct instruction [15].

The subsections below highlight comments that we have not encountered before in our prior focus groups.

4.2.1 Computer Science is Different

When asked to elaborate on their reasons for enrolling in the project, one student responded, *"I thought it would be very helpful, because computer science is different. You never learn anything about it before. Unlike biology and chemistry, you have some background knowledge on it. But it's a whole new subject. So, any extra help would be helpful."* Other research has found that boys tend to develop interest in computer science at an earlier age than girls, so girls often have less prior experience [16].

4.2.2 Exam Tips and Tricks

Participants appreciated the exam tips and tricks that they learned from Sisters Rise Up 4 CS, *"They help you go into the problems much faster and save time on the test."* There are 40 multiple-choice questions on the exam and the students only had 75 minutes to answer those questions, so it is important to be able to answer the questions quickly.

4.2.3 Reaction to the webinars

Some students found the webinars more engaging than they originally expected, *"This is actually fun. I want this to be longer."* Some students had trouble attending the webinars, *"for the webinars, that's what we have problems with because time-wise 8:00 to 9:00, I'm studying for tests the next day. So, it's a struggle."* Some students liked that you could watch the recordings of the webinars *"you can go back and watch it, which was really helpful."* Some students reported technical problems with the first webinar. The leaders had problems with their Internet connection during that webinar.

4.2.4 Importance of the College's Prestige

Participants felt that it was important that the program was offered through a prestigious college. *"I think the perception of the name adds more to it. So, you know that you actually get something good from it, rather than being a program that you're not really sure about whether it will be worth your time or no., because the drive is far. So, I think if it wasn't Georgia Tech, then maybe a lot of people wouldn't attend."*

4.2.5 Increased Interest in Computer Science

One student credited Sisters Rise UP 4 CS with increasing her interest in computer science. *"I used to not like computer science at all. The only reason I took the course is because my dad told me. Then here, I really like seeing the students and how kind of passionate I guess they are about it and seeing other people that do it, too. So, it made me more interested."*

4.3 Individual Interviews

To gather more information on participants' experiences in the program, we conducted remote individual interviews with two additional participants in late summer of 2015. Both interviewees passed the AP CS A exam; however, one attended 10 help sessions while the other attended only 2 help sessions. We were particularly interested in learning why the second interviewee had only attended two help sessions.

We interviewed a ninth grade participant who attended ten help sessions and achieved the top score, a five, on the AP CS A exam. She described Sisters Rise Up 4 CS as *"the place that I could ask questions and get answers."* She valued the responsiveness of the webinar leaders, *"if I asked a question and they didn't know the answer on the spot, they would always answer it a little bit later maybe, and they would definitely find the answer to my questions."* She also valued the exam taking tips and strategies *"They have some good advice there on how to succeed on the computer science exam, like how to get points even (though) you don't understand the problem."* Participating in the program did not further increase her interest in computer science as her interest was high to begin with, *"I always really liked CS and I was really interested in it, so I don't think it can get more interesting for me."* When asked to offer suggestions for improvement, she recommended including more timed exams and additional practice on the free response aspect of the exam. She appreciated the AP Bowl, which was a timed practice exam of 40 multiple-choice questions held at Georgia Tech, "*It was a great practice, it helped me a lot because I didn't know how...like timing plays a big role on the AP exam*".

We also interviewed a twelfth grade participant who only attended two sessions, but scored a four on the exam. She said that she enjoyed going to the in-person session where she programmed a robot, *"I thought they did a nice job trying to engage the students in learning about computer science in more than like a textbook way."* She wanted to attend more in-person help sessions but she lived too far away, "*It was like 40 minutes to an hour, and I started working, so the hours didn't work out for me."* She tried to attend the webinars, but encountered technical difficulties installing the necessary software, *"I don't know why but my computer wouldn't work with that program."* Even though she only attended two help sessions she credited the sessions with increasing her interest in computer science, *"before I wasn't really thinking about majoring in computer science, but I think because of that those sessions and the class I changed my major to computer science."*

5. DISCUSSION

Our two research questions were 1) *Would we see similar results in terms of attitude changes in Sisters Rise Up as we had seen in Project Rise Up?* and 2) *Would we see similar completion and pass rates without a financial incentive?* Participants in both Project Rise Up 4 CS and Sisters Rise Up 4 CS in 2014-2015 had positive gains in attitudes towards computing. However, the participants in Sisters Rise Up 4 CS started out lower in all categories and ended lower as well (as shown in Table 5), so more can be done to improve the Sisters Rise Up 4 CS participants' attitudes towards computing. The completion rate for Project Rise Up 4 CS (76%) in 2014-2015 was higher than that of Sisters Rise Up 4 CS (57%), but Sisters Rise Up completion rate was higher than the completion rate for Project Rise Up 4 CS in each of the first two years (52% in 2013 and 45% in 2013-2014). Project Rise Up 4 CS offered participants $100 for attending the required number of help sessions for the last two years, while Sisters Rise Up 4 CS did not. The pass rate for completers for Sisters Rise Up 4 CS was 50% compared to a pass rate for Project Rise Up 4 CS in 2014-2015 of 33%. The Sisters Rise Up 4 CS completion rate and pass rate indicate that the financial incentives are not necessary for Sisters Rise Up 4 CS to be at least as effective as Project Rise Up 4 CS. More work will need to be done to determine how much the financial incentives matter to the success of Project Rise Up 4 CS.

Qualitative data gleaned from focus groups and interviews show that participants in Sisters Rise Up 4 CS valued the project. Likewise, there is evidence to suggest that several participants were motivated to pursue additional computing courses and/or a college major in computing as a result of participating in the project. Additional research is needed to track participants long-term to see if the impact of the project is sustained through college.

6. CONCLUSION

Women are underrepresented in computing careers and on the Advanced Placement (AP) Computer Science (CS) A exam. Helping more women pass the exam could improve the representation of women in computing. Sisters Rise Up 4 CS is a low cost intervention that resulted in positive changes in attitudes towards computing. It was based on Project Rise Up 4 CS, except that it did not include the financial incentives in Project Rise Up 4 CS. The financial incentives in Project Rise Up 4 CS for the last two years were $100 for students who attend the required number of help sessions and another $100 for passing the exam. The completion rates and pass rates for Sisters Rise Up 4 CS were not substantially different from Project Rise Up 4 CS. Given the low cost of this intervention and its success; more colleges and universities should consider starting similar projects at their institutions. Project Rise Up 4 CS has already been successfully replicated at other institutions [13]. Sisters Rise Up 4 CS can also be easily replicated. The materials (ebook, handbooks for the project coordinator, and handbooks for webinar and help session leaders) are freely available. It's a low-cost but significant-impact intervention.

7. ACKNOWLEDGMENTS

The funding for Project Rise Up 4 CS and Sisters Rise Up 4 CS came from National Science Foundation grant CNS-1228352 as well as RISE awards TFR14-00363 and TFR14-03256 from Google. We thank the undergraduate and high school students who were involved in both Project Rise Up 4 CS and Sisters Rise Up 4 CS and the high school teachers who encouraged them to apply to these programs.

8. REFERENCES

[1] Advanced Placement Data College Board http://research.collegeboard.org/programs/ap/data.

[2] Degrees conferred by degree-granting institutions from 1970 to 2011. National Center for Education Statistics.

[3] BANDURA, A., 1977. *Social learning theory*. Prentice-Hall, Englewood Cliffs, NJ.

[4] BJORK, E.L. and BJORK, R.A., 2011. Making things hard on yourself, but in a good way: Creating desirable difficulties to enhance learning. *Psychology and the real world: Essays illustrating fundamental contributions to society*, 56-64.

[5] BRANSFORD, J.D., BROWN, A.L., and COCKING, R.R., 2000. How People Learn NATIONAL ACADEMY PRESS, Washington D.C.

[6] CHERYAN, S., DRURY, B.J., and VICHAYAPAI, M., 2013. Enduring Influence of Stereotypical Computer Science Role Models on Women's Academic Aspirations. *Psychology of Women Quarterly 37*, 1 (March 2013), 72-79. DOI= http://dx.doi.org/10.1177/0361684312459328.

[7] CLARK, R.C. and MAYER, R.E., 2011. *E-Learning and the Science of Instruction: Proven Guidelines for Consumers and Designers of Multimedia Learning* Pfeiffer.

[8] DISALVO, B., GUZDIAL, M., MEADOWS, C., PERRY, K., MCKLIN, T., and BRUCKMAN, A., 2013. Workifying games: successfully engaging African American gamers with computer science. In *Proceedings of the 44th ACM technical symposium on Computer science education (SIGCSE)* (Denver, Colorado, USA2013), ACM, 317-322.

[9] DWECK, C., 1986. Motivational Processes Affecting Learning. *American Psychologist 41*, 10, 1040-1048.

[10] ECCLES, J.S., 2009. Who Am I and What Am I Going to Do With My Life? Personal and Collective Identities as Motivators of Action. *Educational Psychologist 44*, 2, 78-89.

[11] ERICSON, B., Java Review for the AP CS A Exam. **http://tinyurl.com/JavaReview**

[12] ERICSON, B., ENGELMAN, S., MCKLIN, T., and TAYLOR, J.Q., 2014. Project rise up 4 CS: increasing the number of Black students who pass advanced placement CS A. In *Proceedings of the Proceedings of the 45th ACM technical symposium on Computer science education* (Atlanta, Georgia, USA2014), ACM, 2538937, 439-444. DOI= http://dx.doi.org/10.1145/2538862.2538937.

[13] ERICSON, B. and MCKLIN, T., 2015. Helping African American Students Pass Advanced Placement Computer Science: A Tale of Two States. In *Proceedings of the RESPECT conference* (Charlotte, NC, USA2015), IEEE.

[14] JACKSON, C.K., 2010. A little now for a lot later: A look at a Texas Advanced Placement incentive program. *Journal of Human Resources 45*, 591-639.

[15] KIRSCHNER, P.A., SWELLER, J., and CLARK, R.E., 2006. Why Minimal Guidance During Instruction Does Not Work: An Analysis of the Failure of Constructivist, Discovery, Problem-Based, Experiential, and Inquiry-Based Teaching. *Educational Psychologist 41*, 2, 75-86.

[16] MARGOLIS, J. and FISHER, A., 2003. *Unlocking the clubhouse: women in computing*. MIT Press.

[17] SWELLER, J. and COOPER, G., 1985. The Use of Worked Examples as a Substitute for Problem Solving in Learning Algebra. *Cognition and Instruction 2*, 1, 59-89.

[18] TRAFTON, J.G. and REISER, B.J., 1993. The contributions of studying examples and solving problems to skill acquisition. In *Proceedings of the Proceedings of the 15th Annual Conference of the Cognitive Science Society* (Hillsdale, NJ1993), Lawrence Erlbaum Associates, Inc., 1017–1022.

[19] WANG, J., HONG, H., RAVITZ, J., and IVORY, M., 2015. Gender Differences in Factors Influencing Pursuit of Computer Science and Related Fields. In *Proceedings of the 20th Annual Conference on Innovation and Technology in Computer Science Education (ITiCSE)* (Vilnius, Lithuania, Jul 04-08, 2015 2015), ACM.

Panel: Future Directions of Block-based Programming

Neil C. C. Brown
School of Computing
University of Kent
Canterbury, CT2 7NF
UK
nccb@kent.ac.uk

Jens Mönig
Communications Design
Group (CDG), SAP Labs
1025 Westwood Blvd.
Los Angeles, CA, USA 90024
jens@moenig.org

Anthony Bau
Phillips Exeter
Academy
NH, USA
dab1998@
gmail.com

David Weintrop
(moderator)
Northwestern University
Evanston, IL, USA 60208
dweintrop@
u.northwestern.edu

1. SUMMARY (DAVID WEINTROP)

Blocks-based programming is becoming the way that learners are being introduced to programming and computer science. Led by the popularity of tools like Scratch, Alice, and Code.org's Hour of Code activities, many new programming environments and initiatives are employing the blocks-based modality. This trend can be seen in the growing number of classroom computer science curricula incorporating blocks-based environments into their materials. Despite this rise in use, many open questions remain surrounding blocks-based programming. In this panel, we discuss the current state of blocks-based programming environments, review what we know about learning with blocks-based tools, and look to the future, discussing what form next-generation blocks-based, or blocks-inspired, programming environments might take.

Research looking at blocks-based programming is revealing that modality matters: that the representations used to present programming concepts affect learners' conceptual understanding [6], programming practices [3], and perceptions of programming and computer science [5]. This panel brings together leading designers and researchers looking to advance graphical, blocks-based programming through new, innovate designs. The panel will open with a review of current research literature on learning with blocks-based programming and then continue with presentations of three recently designed blocks-based programming environments (Greenfoot 3, GP, Pencil Code), each of which look to push the boundaries of the approach in different directions. These short presentations will frame the discussion of pertinent questions facing designers and educators who use blocks-based programming environments. As part of the panel discussion, the following questions with be explored:

Why do blocks-based programming environments work? Blocks-based tools weave together a myriad of features to produce accessible, engaging programming environments. The color and shape of commands, the organization and easily navigable way blocks are displayed, and the drag-and-drop composition mechanism all contribute to supporting novices in writing successful programs. Drawing on research and our own experiences, we discuss why the current generation of blocks-based tools look the way they do, and what are the key features of successful block environments.

What are the challenges associated with designing blocks-based editors? In the creation of a programming environment, countless design decisions are made, including aspects of the interface and layout, questions of language design, and consideration of how the blocks-based programming component will interact with the runtime environment. In answering this question, we discuss the tensions and trade-offs inherent in creating blocks-based programming environments, and discuss elusive features we have yet to figure out how best to incorporate into blocks-based tools.

What are the challenges we face in bringing blocks-based programming into the classroom? With this question we explore technological, pedagogical, and perceptual challenges of teaching with blocks-based programming in formal settings. This includes confronting the perception that blocks are not "real" programming and other hurdles towards adoption of blocks-based tools in formal contexts.

What are the pros and cons of blocks-based programming (especially relative to text-based alternatives)? Research is revealing that the blocks-based modality can support learners' conceptual understanding, help novices advance more quickly, and engage underrepresented populations with computer science. At the same time, text still retains some advantages over blocks. In addressing this question we reflect on the current state of blocks-based environments and discuss how we as designers, researchers, and educators might address the current limitations.

What are the gaps between blocks- and text-based programming? How can they be bridged by design or pedagogy? A major open question is if, and how, concepts and practices learned in introductory blocks-based environments transfer to more conventional text-based languages. Research has reported both successful and unsuccessful transfer. With this question we explore the gaps that exist between the two modalities and discuss potential design solutions to address them.

What is the future of blocks-based programming? This final question looks to the future, thinking about what blocks-based programming might look in the near and not-so-near future. As part of this question we discuss the long-term role of blocks-based programming and whether or not we think blocks-based (or blocks-inspired) environments will supplant text-based programming.

These questions, along with questions from the audience, will be explored as part of this panel session.

SIGCSE '16 March 02-05, 2016, Memphis, TN, USA

ACM ISBN 978-1-4503-3685-7/16/03.
DOI: http://dx.doi.org/10.1145/2839509.2844661

2. NEIL BROWN (GREENFOOT 3)

Neil Brown, Michael Kölling and Amjad Altadmri are designing the new Greenfoot 3 "frame-based" editor [1]. Frame-based editing is intended to combine the best parts of block-based programming and text-based programming. Frames are very similar to blocks, but crucially, keyboard entry is supported by use of a "frame cursor" which occupies the space between frames and allows single keypress insertion of new frames. The cursor also allows for easy selection and manipulation of frames in a similar way to text. For example, holding shift while moving the cursor creates a frame selection, which can be cut/copied/pasted. This keyboard support is accompanied by many further usability improvements to better support intermediate and experienced users.

The frame-based language in Greenfoot 3 is named Stride. Stride is very similar to Java, with a near-identical semantic model, and allows full use of Java libraries. Where most block based systems have a finite set of commands, all of which are shown on a potentially overwhelming palette, Stride has a single, generic "method call" frame which can be used to call any Java method, without complicating the set of available frames. A classic code completion interface helps users select available methods.

Neil and his colleagues believe that blocks-based programming, as enhanced in their frame-based programming, has the potential to surpass text-based programming in terms of usability – that by adding keyboard support and further improvements for program manipulation, readability and navigation, it is possible to bring together the best of blocks- and text-based programming into a single unified system.

3. JENS MÖNIG (GP AND SNAP!)

Jens Mönig, John Maloney, and Yoshiki Ohshima are developing GP, a portable, extensible, general purpose blocks programming language for casual programmers [4]. The GP class library and programming environment are written in GP itself, so all code can viewed, edited, and debugged as blocks. So far, the GP developers have used conventional text editors on the textual representation of GP code as a way to bootstrap the system, but we hope to develop techniques to allow us – and advanced GP users – to evolve and extend the GP system using only blocks-based editing tools.

Blocks languages offer many advantages to the beginner or "casual" programmer. They eliminate syntax issues, allow the user to work with logical program chunks, provide affordances such as drop-down menus, and leverage the fact that recognition is easier than recall. However, as users gain experience and start creating larger programs, they encounter two inconvenient properties of pure blocks languages: blocks take up more screen real-estate than textual languages and dragging blocks from a palette is slower than typing.

We will describe two techniques that address these problems in GP. The first technique, which addresses the screen-real estate and code readability (and "skim-ability") issues, is to switch to an alternate block rendering style that removes block outlines and colors, changes fonts, and shrinks the vertical and horizontal spacing. The result looks and reads like text (in the same amount of screen space), yet retains the underlying structure and affordances of blocks.

The second technique explores ways to input and edit blocks using only the keyboard. This effort was initially inspired by an interest in making GP accessible to users with visual or physical impairments, but we quickly realized that keyboard-based block editing benefits all GP users. Like Greenfoot's frame editor, GP's keyboard block editor introduces a "block input cursor" that can be moved around using navigation keys. To insert a new block at the cursor, the user starts typing any word that appears on the desired block. As they type, the system shows a menu of the top five matching blocks. It usually takes just a few keystrokes to select a given block from GP's current palette of approximately 250 blocks. Keyboard entry avoids the overhead of selecting a category in the blocks palette, finding the block in that category, dragging it out, and dropping it into the correct location – thus saving a great deal of time.

4. ANTHONY BAU (PENCIL CODE)

Anthony Bau is developing Droplet, a new block editor used in David Bau's Pencil Code environment and Code.org's Applab. Droplet is a block-based editor that can load and edit code in text languages. This provides many of the advantages of blocks (a palette, less typing, assistance with syntax, and a visualization of the program) while allowing students to use text language runtimes and participate in text language communities.

Currently, block languages generally fall short of text languages in expressiveness and in the maturity of their developer communities. There is also a disconnect in students' minds between block programming and their perception of "real" programming [2]. These problems could be solved by creating more advanced block languages; however, they could also be solved by bringing the benefits of block languages to existing text languages. Droplet is designed to do the latter, by allowing students to work in blocks with real-world text programs in mainstream languages, and to switch between blocks and text at any time.

Even as visual languages improve, Anthony believes that text languages will always be a staple of computer science education. Block editing for text programs, like Droplet, will be a way for students and professionals to take advantage of the simplicity of blocks while learning to code in text.

5. REFERENCES

[1] M. Kölling, N. C. C. Brown, and A. Altadmri. Frame-based editing: Easing the transition from blocks to text-based programming. In *WiPSCE '15*, pages 29–38, 2015.

[2] C. M. Lewis. How programming environment shapes perception, learning and goals: Logo vs. scratch. In *SIGCSE '10*, pages 346–350, 2010.

[3] O. Meerbaum-Salant, M. Armoni, and M. Ben-Ari. Habits of programming in scratch. In *ITiCSE '11*, pages 168–172, 2011.

[4] J. Mönig, Y. Ohshima, and J. Maloney. Blocks at your fingertips: Blurring the line between blocks and text in GP. In *Blocks and Beyond workshop*, 2015.

[5] D. Weintrop and U. Wilensky. To block or not to block, that is the question: Students' perceptions of blocks-based programming. In *IDC '15*, pages 199–208, 2015.

[6] D. Weintrop and U. Wilensky. Using commutative assessments to compare conceptual understanding in blocks-based and text-based programs. In *ICER '15*, pages 101–110, 2015.

Why Don't Some CS0 Students Succeed? How Important Are Background, Experience, Culture, Aptitude, Habits and Attitude?

Daniel D. Garcia (moderator)
University of California, Berkeley
777 Soda Hall
Berkeley, CA 94720
+1 (510) 517-4041
ddgarcia@cs.berkeley.edu

Colleen Lewis
Harvey Mudd College
Department of Computer Science
Claremont, CA 91711
+1 (909) 607-0443
lewis@cs.hmc.edu

Stuart Reges
University of Washington
Box 352350
Seattle, WA 98195
+1 (206) 685-9138
reges@cs.washington.edu

Nathan Ensmenger
Indiana University
School of Informatics & Computing
Bloomington, IN 47408
+1 (812) 855-0705
nensmeng@indiana.edu

Keywords
Computer science education, hidden prerequisites, litmus test

1. SUMMARY

There are always some students who succeed and some students who don't. Our four panelists are committed to the success of all students, but have different explanations for students' lack of success. This panel discussion will highlight both their shared beliefs and disagreements between veteran CS educators Stuart Reges and Dan Garcia, CS education researcher Colleen Lewis, and Professor of History and Philosophy of Science Nathan Ensmenger. We hope this lively discussion will bring together divergent and complementary positions and expertise, as well as invite significant audience participation.

2. DANIEL D. GARCIA

After ten years of teaching our non-majors introductory computing classes, to hard-working students who have never programmed before, I have noticed several common features of students who succeed: **logical thinking** (e.g., debugging skill, or noticing that `XOR(a,b)` is really just `a!=b`), **problem solving** (e.g., knowing when a solution is a dead-end, how to back up to the last decision branch, where that branch is, and what the other possibilities are from that branch), **lateral "out of the box" thinking** (e.g., able to generate creative, non-linear solutions), **persistence in the face of challenge** (i.e., "grit"), **a love of "tinkering"** (i.e., pleasure in casually playing with an artifact), **comfort in a world of unknowns balanced with a drive to make sense of it** (e.g, getting a new electronic toy with lots of buttons and wanting to try each one out), and the ability to **abstract** (removing irrelevant details, generalizing something by noticing common patterns, etc.).

I believe all students who put in the time and effort can succeed in introductory computing classes (and beyond), and when some don't, it's *our* fault. We should make sure the climate doesn't have bias and is fully conducive to their learning. We may also be operating under a false assumption that all students have all the features listed above. Those who did succeed may have honed these skills in another context and transferred their knowledge over! We should make these prerequisites explicit, and/or provide activities in our classes to help develop them.

SIGCSE '16, March 02-05, 2016, Memphis, TN, USA
ACM 978-1-4503-3685-7/16/03.
http://dx.doi.org/10.1145/2839509.2844667

3. STUART REGES

My 27 years of teaching programming to novices has left me with some deep intuitions about how people learn to program. I share Don Knuth's belief that there is a mode of thinking that is particular to computer science (CS) and that some students have a greater aptitude than others. As Knuth has written, "I conclude that roughly 2% of all people 'think algorithmically,' in the sense that they can reason rapidly about algorithmic processes" [5]. My own intuition about this is that there are students who think this way naturally, but we can build up this ability in a broad range of students with exercises that allow them to practice this thought process. I have presented some questions that I hypothesize measure what Knuth calls "algorithmic reasoning" [9], although another study failed to replicate the result [8], so there is still no conclusive evidence to support this intuition that many of us have.

Whether or not CS aptitude exists, most of us who teach introductory CS classes observe wide variation in how students take to programming. Many students who expect to enjoy it because they enjoyed using video games or other software are surprised to find that they don't enjoy the process of programming. Other students who had no clue that they would enjoy programming are surprised to find that they thoroughly enjoy the mental challenge presented by it. Often it is men who are disappointed and women who are pleasantly surprised, although surprises happen in the other direction as well.

Even though I believe that some students more easily pick up programming than others, I also believe that we can design introductory courses in which every student can succeed. Instructors should:

- present coding topics incrementally with lots of examples
- provide a strong safety net for students who need help
- point out common programming patterns and include exam questions that reward students who learn these patterns
- include non-programming, "mechanical" questions on exams
- emphasize that effort is at least as important as aptitude in predicting success

Of course, you don't want to tailor your course too much for the students who struggle because you want to make sure that there is enough intellectual content to attract the students who end up loving it. This is a delicate balancing act that I feel I have struggled with throughout my career.

4. COLLEEN LEWIS

A common occurrence in the United States is that students arrive at college without programming experience. At many institutions, these students have a rich set of skills and deep knowledge in domains other than CS. Certainly, educating these students should be easier than educating younger, less skillful, and less knowledgeable students. Unfortunately, as a CS education community, we have few techniques for building upon students' out-of-domain knowledge and skills. Even worse, we have no clear understanding of how, when, and why various out-of-domain knowledge and skills are productive in CS.

My hypothesis of what makes students successful is that they, without being instructed, apply the right out-of-domain knowledge and skills. Other students may have the right knowledge and skills, but do not apply them. My research [7] attempts to identify productive out-of-domain knowledge and skills for reasoning about computer programs. If we better understand what is required to master computer programming, we can make these requirements explicit and support them in developing these competencies.

The hypothesis that there exists an innate ability for CS is flawed and deeply problematic. In decades of research, there have been no factors that reliably predict an individual's success learning to program [10]. Why would there exist an innate ability, uncorrelated with other abilities, for a task (CS) that did not exist one hundred years ago? The potential for discouragement and discrimination in assuming there exists an innate ability for CS seems obvious. As evidence of this potential for discouragement, students' belief in an innate ability for CS appears to be consequential for students' decision to major in CS [6]. In addition, it has been shown that students who believe intelligence is innate avoid taking intellectual risks [3], which is the exact opposite of the behavior we want from our students.

We are far too young as a field to assume that students who are not successful cannot be successful. As a community we should start identifying relevant out-of-domain knowledge and skills and developing teaching techniques to build upon them.

5. NATHAN ENSMENGER

From the establishment of the Curriculum '68 [1] guidelines to the present, there has existed a long-running debate within the academic CS community about what skills, abilities, training (and even personality type) are required to be a successful computer scientist. I am especially interested in the relationship between the formal curriculum in CS education and the informal subculture that is often associated with the computing professions. I argue that the distinctive cultural norms and practices of certain computing communities, which draw on or appeals to tacit knowledge, skills, and other cultural affinities independent of the actual intellectual content of the CS curriculum, send subtle message to potential CS students about who does (and, more importantly, does not) belong. Educators who are sensitive to the influence and effects of this subculture can use it to encourage a broader and more diverse range of students. This is particularly true in regard to gender diversity, an issue of concern to many CS departments.

Much of my historical research focuses on the role of women in computing, and I find that including this history in the curriculum both helps with the recruitment and retention of women, but also encourages all students to appreciate the value of a broad and inclusive perspective on their discipline [4]. There is a also growing body of research that suggests that not only can historical case studies be useful in teaching core concepts in CS, but that they can help students better appreciate the value – to themselves, and to society – of a CS education.

6. REFERENCES

[1] ACM Curriculum Committee on Computer Science. 1968. Curriculum 68: Recommendations for Academic Programs in CS. Comm. ACM 11, 3 (Mar. 1968), 151-197.

[2] Briggs, A. and Snyder, L. 2012. Computer science principles and the CS 10K initiative.ACM Inroads 3, 2 (June 2012), 29-31. `doi.acm.org/10.1145/2189835.2189847`

[3] Dweck, C. (2007). Mindset: The new psychology of success. New York, NY: Random House, Inc.

[4] Ensmenger, Nathan. "Making Programming Masculine." In Gender Codes: Why Women Are Leaving Computing, edited by Thomas Misa, Wiley, 2010.

[5] Knuth, D. 2004. Selected Papers on Computer Science. CSLI.

[6] Lewis, C. M., Yasuhara, K., & Anderson, R. E. (2011). Deciding to Major in Computer Science: A Grounded Theory of Students' Self-Assessment of Ability. Proceedings of the International Computer Science Education Research Workshop. Providence, RI. 3-10.

[7] Lewis, C. M. (2012). Applications of Out-of-Domain Knowledge in Students' Reasoning about Computer Program State. (Doctoral dissertation). Retrieved from ProQuest Dissertations and Theses. (Accession Order No. 12710).

[8] Lewis, C. M., Khayrallah, H., & Tsai, A. (2013). Mining data from the AP CS A exam: patterns, non-patterns, and replication failure. Proceedings of the International Computer Science Education Research Workshop. San Diego, CA, USA. 115-122.

[9] Reges, S. The mystery of "b := (b = false)." Proceedings of the 39th SIGCSE technical symposium on Computer Science education.

[10] Robins, A. (2010). Learning edge momentum: a new account of outcomes in CS1. CS Education, 20(1), 37-71.

Scrum and Agile Methods in Software Engineering Courses

Jennifer Campbell
University of Toronto
campbell@cs.toronto.edu

Stan Kurkovsky
(moderator)
Central Connecticut State University
kurkovsky@ccsu.edu

Chun Wai Liew
Lafayette College
liewc@lafayette.edu

Anya Tafliovich
University of Toronto
Scarborough
atafliovich@utsc.utoronto.ca

Categories and Subject Descriptors

• Software and its engineering → Agile software development.
• Social and professional topics → Software engineering education

Keywords

Scrum; Agile software development; Software engineering

1. SUMMARY

Agile software development has been formally introduced in 2001 in the "agile manifesto" [4]. Agile methods are best described as an amalgamation of four core principles describing lightweight iterative software processes:

- Individuals and interactions over processes and tools;
- Working software over comprehensive documentation;
- Customer collaboration over contract negotiation;
- Responding to change over following a plan.

Over the years, a number of agile frameworks, such as Extreme Programming and Scrum, have evolved and matured. The underlying philosophy of Scrum recognizes that the customers often change their mind about the product they want and that the development challenges are unpredictable by their nature. Consequently, Scrum embraces the fact that the problem being solved cannot be fully understood or described from the start. Instead, Scrum focuses on maximizing the ability of the development team to quickly deliver in response to emerging requirements.

The aim of this panel is to present the experiences and challenges of practicing Scrum and agile methods at a variety of computer science programs.

2. OUR EXPERIENCE

This section describes the experience of each panelist (in alphabetical order).

2.1 Jennifer Campbell

At the University of Toronto, we offer a second-year course [1] in which we teach the fundamentals of software design and give students an opportunity to apply what they are learning in designing and developing Java and Android applications. Students are also introduced to the basics of software engineering and follow a prescribed Scrum-like software development process as they complete a team project. Each semester, between 200 and 400 students enroll in this course.

The software development process involves an instructor generated project feature set, multiple software design and development phases, subsets of the feature set for each project phase, planning meetings, status meetings, and post-phase peer- and self-evaluations. These loosely correspond to key Scrum elements including product backlog, sprints, sprint backlog, sprint planning, daily scrums, and sprint retrospective. We introduce students to a variety of software tools to support their project, including version control (Subversion) and a fully featured IDE (Android Studio). We also use the CATME web tool (www.catme.org) for team formation and team member evaluations.

For most students, this project is their first team software development project and by introducing this Scrum-like process we aim to keep the multi-week multi-phase team projects on track. Exposing students to a software development process at this stage of their academic program also allows us to foreshadow the third-year software engineering course that involves an agile software development project.

2.2 Stan Kurkovsky

At Central Connecticut State University students have at least two opportunities to experience Scrum.

Students may choose to get an in-depth experience with Scrum in a game development course, which is based on the book written by one of our graduates [2]. Typically, students take this course immediately after Data Structures and have a limited experience with software development processes or working as a part of the team. This course introduces students to the core principles of Scrum using a broad range of agile games, some of which are based on those from tastycupcakes.org. Students learn about the Scrum roles; sprints and their planning, reviews, and retrospectives; product backlog, user stories and their prioritization.

A few weeks into the course, student teams are ready to begin applying Scrum in a game development project lasting until the end of the semester. The course is structured so that there is enough time for at least three 2-week sprints. The instructor plays

SIGCSE'16, March 2–5, 2016, Memphis, TN, USA.
ACM ISBN: 978-1-4503-3685-7/16/03.
DOI: http://dx.doi.org/10.1145/2839509.2844664

the role of the Scrum Master with all sprint planning and review meetings taking place during the class time in the second half of the semester.

As a part of a required formal senior Software Engineering course, all students in our program are introduced to Scrum in a 3-hour long LEGO-based simulation [5], which prepares them for an agile course project that focuses on short iterations with evolving requirements.

2.3 Chun Wai Liew

At Lafayette College students take a second year course in which we teach the fundamentals of software engineering and students learn about the basic tools and techniques involved in developing group projects [3]. This course serves two purposes in our curriculum. Firstly, it teaches the students about the software development tools that they will need in the upper level courses -- software repositories, time management/planning/scheduling tools, weekly status and bug reporting tools. Secondly, they learn the basics of the agile process - (1) repeated short iterations, (2) unit testing from the beginning, (3) interleaving of specification development, prototyping and design.

For our students, this is (a) their first group development project, and (b) their first "medium-sized" project. They learn how to keep the projects on track (most of the time) and also how to coordinate their activities as a group. This experience allows us to have richer projects in the upper level courses and also to offer a capstone software engineering course with external clients.

We also have a second software engineering course (the capstone) where students apply the scrum/agile methodology that they have learned on a project with external (to the college) clients.

2.4 Anya Tafliovich

At the University of Toronto Scarborough, we have a sequence of three courses that involve aspects of Agile software development, to various degrees. The first in the sequence is a second-year course described above. The students who complete this course have had experience with a 6-7 weeks long team project, in which they follow a fairly rigidly prescribed Scrum-like simplified development process. They are familiar with the ideas of source control (subversion), iterative development (prescribed project phases), backlogs (feature lists for each phase, prescribed by the instructor), and the different kinds of meetings involved.

The second course in the sequence is a third-year Introduction to Software Engineering course. In this course the students are introduced (in lecture) to all aspects of Agile development; we look at Scrum and XP in detail. The course has a 10-week long team project, in which the students have hands-on practice with all aspects of Agile development. We do not follow either Scrum or XP religiously, as we found this to be counter-productive in a course setting. Instead, we have developed an Agile hybrid process suitable for third-year computer science student teams, in a large class (we expect over 20 teams in the coming term). We bring in a real client, with a real need for software. The client is non-technical (a member of a different department), which gives the students practice with the challenges of requirements gathering. The students practice writing user stories, producing release plans and iteration plans, using state-of-the-art tools that support Agile development (GitHub, online project management tools, etc.), and following through with iterative development, re-planning and re-estimation as needed, until the final product is ready for the final presentation to the client at the end of the term. Crucial to the success of the course are weekly deliverables and weekly meetings with the team TA—these keep the projects on track.

The third course in the sequence is a fourth-year course, in which the student teams participate in a large open-source project hosted on GitHub. If there is enough interest, we can elaborate on this course and the use of Agile methods in it during the panel.

3. CHALLENGES

The panelists are also planning to have an open discussion focusing on lessons learned, challenges, and their possible solutions:

- Why should we teach Scrum/Agile?
- What are the biggest obstacles to adopting Scrum/Agile in teaching Software Engineering?
- How to fit Scrum process into a class schedule? (daily meetings are usually impossible)
- Who plays the roles of the Scrum Master and Product Owner?
- Are two courses necessary to introduce Scrum/Agile? Can the approach work if the students only have one experience? What carries over from the first course to the second?
- What aspects of the Scrum/Agile process are most difficult for the students to master?
- Is there a difference in teaching Scrum/Agile to first/second year students as opposed to fourth year students?

4. REFERENCES

[1] Campbell, J. and Tafliovich, A. 2015. An experience report: using mobile development to teach software design. In *Proceedings of the 46th ACM Technical Symposium on Computer Science Education* (SIGCSE '15). 506-511.

[2] Keith, C. 2010. *Agile Game Development with Scrum.* Addison Wesley.

[3] Liew, C. W. 2005. Teaching software development skills early in the curriculum through software engineering. In *Proceedings of the 10th Annual SIGCSE Conference on Innovation and Technology in Computer Science Education* (ITiCSE '05). ACM, New York, NY, USA, 133-137.

[4] Manifesto for Agile Software Development. 2001. http://www.agilemanifesto.org/

[5] Paasivaara, M., Heikkilä, V., Lassenius, C. and Toivola, T. 2014. Teaching students scrum using LEGO blocks. In *Companion Proceedings of the 36th International Conference on Software Engineering* (ICSE '14). ACM, 382-391.

How to Use Open Source Software in Education

Judith Bishop
Microsoft Research
Redmond, WA, USA
jbishop@microsoft.com

Carlos Jensen
Oregon State University
Corvallis, OR, USA
jensenca@eecs.oregonstate.edu

Walt Scacchi
University of California, Irvine
Irvine, CA, USA
wscacchi@ics.uci.edu

Arfon Smith
GitHub Inc
San Francisco, CA, USA
arfon@github.com

Keywords

Open source software; industrial collaboration; games; FOSS; capstone projects

1. SUMMARY

There are many papers about projects that release their software as open source. Our panel looks at why open source is a good idea for education, and how it can best be leveraged. The panel represents industry and academia and its members have years of experience in the field. Specific questions that panelists will address, in addition to their position statements, are:

- What makes open source particularly attractive for educators and students?
- What are barriers to use?
- What areas of computer science and what levels of study are most appropriate for introducing open source?

Finally, this panel takes a step back and looks at the broad issues associated with using that software in education. We will mention the specific details of releasing, curating, licensing and using open source software. But most of all this panel wants to explore how, for educators, open source works. We believe it is because open source fosters an ecosystem of collaborators who can pool resources and expertise to build new collaborative ways of solving hard research projects. We look forward to the contributions from the audience and energetic debate.

NOTE: There are many definitions of Open source software (OSS) and Free/Open Source Software (FOSS). OSS emphasizes community development and sharing, but the software might not be free. FOSS ensures free code, but does not guarantee shared development.

2. JUDITH BISHOP (MODERATOR)

OSS is a powerful way of advancing software development. The free aspect of FSS has always been attractive to academics who wish to put diverse software in the hands of their students. Software companies such as Microsoft are now routinely putting research projects, as well as key software, in open source repositories for both community development and free use. An example can be seen at http://research.microsoft.com/opensource .

SIGCSE'16, March 2–5, 2016, Memphis, TN, USA.
ACM ISBN: 978-1-4503-3685-7/16/03.
DOI: http://dx.doi.org/10.1145/2839509.2844665

Academia has long wanted access to industrial projects, but now that it is a reality, what exactly can be done and by whom? There are several options, notably:

- instructors can use the software as illustration in their classes [10]
- capstone projects can be based on OSS [13];
- software can be extended for research purposes [5]
- in hackathons, often in conjunction with industry [12].

It is expected that students will have difficulties in working with other people's code [13], but the learning benefits of getting acquainted with industrial strength software are deemed to be worth it. What we are now seeing is that the growing diversity of available OSS projects presents an even greater hurdle for educators who are faced with selecting suitable projects for integration into a course [5] [10].

With quality open source software being released by industry daily, educators face a real dichotomy between staying with what they know and moving onto the next new thing. In order to help with the choice, curated hubs have been become popular. Openhub.net has some categorization and reflects which projects are popular. OSSPAL.org and Microsoft Research's portal[Error! Bookmark not defined.] concentrate on classifying software into categories.

Another problem for educators is that raw dumps on repositories such as GitHub can be meaningless to students without some additional guidance and back-up. Even at the research level, software on its own is not enough for a successful transfer of ideas, or the establishment of an engagement. As discussed in [12], even Hackathons need careful planning. I shall pose some solutions to these problems.

3. CARLOS JENSEN

Free/Open Source Software (FOSS) is an increasingly important part of the computing eco-system. Teaching students how to participate in FOSS not only gives students meaningful and highly marketable skills [11], it presents novel opportunities for recruiting and motivating both traditional and non-traditional [3][4], and can have a lasting positive effect beyond the classroom. That said, figuring out how to successfully contribute to FOSS is a daunting challenge for students, and often fraught with dangers [1], especially for women [2]. New tools must often be used, and students and instructors must both learn to navigate new social and technical processes, large code-bases and deal with active and distributed developer communities [4]. How then can instructors help students navigate the joining process and successfully incorporate FOSS in the classroom, where student success and inclusion are top concerns? I will address these issues, as well as ethical and logistic hurdles to using and incorporating FOSS development in the classroom.

4. WALT SCACCHI

FOSS is now a widespread approach to the development of software systems by groups of loosely-coupled developers working in geographically and temporally distributed settings [9]. FOSS development projects are now responsible for major software systems that underlie the ongoing operation of World-Wide Web servers and browsers, modern search engines, social media, e-commerce, global financial services, military defense systems, and more including operating systems, programming language compilers and interpreters, database management systems, networking, computer graphics, interactive development environments, public source code repositories, and other technologies central to the theory and practice of Computer Science [7][9]. Computer games are software applications that now represent among the most complex and most comprehensive embodiment of CS knowledge to date. Computer games have also become a global software industry, with large shares of computer users, especially those in the 8-30+ year old demographic, frequent game players. My interest is in examining how, where, when, and by whom do these two worlds of software come together, and to what ends [6][8]? I will identify what lies at the intersection and union of these two worlds of software, and what such knowledge may offer to CS educators who are looking for new ways and means to engage and challenge the next generation of undergraduate CS students.

5. ARFON SMITH

Whether consuming, contributing or producing, open source software for many industries is the 'new normal'. It's therefore critical that our students are exposed early to the open source ecosystem and learn how to become active members of the community. I'll concentrate on outlining some strategies for open source newcomers wishing to either release their first open source software or contribute to an existing project. In addition, I'll devote some time to talk about a new tool GitHub has developed to reduce the barrier to entry for teachers wishing to use GitHub in a classroom setting including creating assignments, inviting groups of students to a course and keeping on top of their progress.

6. ABOUT THE PANELLISTS

Judith Bishop is Director of Computer Science at Microsoft Research. She is leader of the Open Source Software Initiative which brings together projects from Microsoft and Microsoft Research that are of interest to academics.

Carlos Jensen is associate professor at Oregon State University. He has studied the barriers for entry into Open Source, and finding ways we can get more people, including students, involved in Open Source.

Walt Scacchi is Senior Research Scientist, Research Faculty, Institute for Software Research, and Research Director, Institute for Virtual Environments and Computer Games. His research includes organizational studies of FOSS development and the acquisition of OSS (including governance, procurement, licensing, software engineering, deployment, operations and field support).

Arfon Smith is a Chief Scientist at GitHub Inc, the world's largest host of software on the planet. He supports researchers who are using the GitHub platform for capturing the process of scientific discovery and seeks to elevate the role of research software within academia at large.

7. REFERENCES

[1] King, S., Kuechler, V., Jensen, C.: Joining Free/Open Source Software Communities: An Analysis of Newbies' First Interactions on Project Mailing Lists. 44th Hawaii International Conference on System Sciences (2011).

[2] Kuechler, V., Gilbertson, C., Jensen, C.: Gender Differences in Early Free and Open Source Software Joining Process. Open Source Syst. Long-Term Sustain. 78–93 (2012).

[3] Morelli, R., Tucker, A., Danner, N., De Lanerolle, T.R., Ellis, H.J., Izmirli, O., Krizanc, D., Parker, G.: Revitalizing computing education through free and open source software for humanity. Commun. ACM. 52, 67–75 (2009).

[4] Morgan, B., Jensen, C: Lessons Learned from Teaching Open Source Software Development. OSS, 133-142 (2014)

[5] Nascimento, D.M.; Cox, K.; Almeida, T.; Sampaio, W.; Almeida Bittencourt, R.; Souza, R.; Chavez, C., Using Open Source Projects in software engineering education: A systematic mapping study, in *Frontiers in Education Conference, IEEE* , 1837-1843 (2013)

[6] Scacchi, W., Modding as an Open Source Approach to Extending Computer Game Systems, *Intern. J. Open Source Software and Processes*, 3(3), 36-47, (2011). Reprinted in S. Koch (Ed.), *Open Source Software Dynamics, Processes, and Applications*, 177-188, Information Science Reference, IGI Global.

[7] Scacchi, W. and Alspaugh, T.A. Understanding the Role of Licenses and Evolution in Open Architecture Software Ecosystems, *Journal of Systems and Software*, 85(7), 1479-1494 (2012)

[8] Scacchi, W, and Cooper, K.M. Research Challenges at the Intersection of Computer Games and Software Engineering, *Conf. Foundations of Digital Games* (2015)

[9] Scacchi, W, Crowston, K, Jensen, C, et al. Towards a Science of Free/Open Source Systems, FOSS Workshop Final Report, Prepared for the Computing Community Consortium, Fall. (2010)

[10] Therese Mary Smith, Robert McCartney, Swapna S. Gokhale, and Lisa C. Kaczmarczyk. Selecting open source software projects to teach software engineering. In *Proceedings of the 45th ACM technical symposium on Computer science education*, SIGCSE, 397-402. (2014)

[11] Trapasso, E., Vujanic, A.: Accenture Newsroom: Investment in Open Source Software Set to Rise, Accenture Survey Finds. (2010).

[12] Trainer, E.H., Chaihirunkarn, C., Kalyanasundaram, A., Herbsleb, J.D., Community Code Engagements: Summer of Code & Hackathons for Community Building in Scientific Software. *ACM Conference on Supporting Groupwork (GROUP)*, (2014).

[13] Jari Vanhanen, Timo O. A. Lehtinen, and Casper Lassenius. 2012. Teaching real-world software engineering through a capstone project course with industrial customers. In *Proceedings of the First International Workshop on Software Engineering Education Based on Real-World Experiences* EduRex, 29-32 (2012)

A Course on Programming and Problem Solving

Swapneel Sheth
Christian Murphy
Department of Computer and Information Science
University of Pennsylvania
Philadelphia, PA, USA
swapneel@cis.upenn.edu
cdmurphy@cis.upenn.edu

Kenneth A. Ross
Department of Computer Science
Columbia University
New York, NY, USA
kar@cs.columbia.edu

Dennis Shasha
Department of Computer Science
New York University
New York, NY, USA
shasha@cs.nyu.edu

ABSTRACT

At its core, Computer Science is the study of algorithmic problem solving. Although it is necessary to teach programming, data structures, computer organization, etc., students should ultimately learn to use these things to solve problems, understand what is good and bad about their solutions, and share their solutions with others.

This paper describes a course that focuses on the four steps of the problem solving process: algorithmic thinking, implementation, analysis, and communication. This course, based on Knuth's popular seminar at Stanford, has been extremely successful at the authors' three institutions. In addition to discussing the course's objectives and methodology, we present sample problems, summarize the outcomes and feedback from students, and give advice to other educators looking to create a similar course.

Keywords

problem-based learning; open-ended problems; soft skills

1. INTRODUCTION

Although modern Computer Science curricula focus on programming, data structures, computer organization, software engineering, etc., we must not lose sight of the fact that the goal of CS is to use algorithms to solve problems, and that problem solving in CS is a collaborative activity that involves analyzing and communicating solutions, not just implementing them.

This paper introduces a unique course that focuses on problem solving in CS. This course, based on Knuth's popular seminar in the 1970's and 80's, has been taught at the authors' three institutions for over 15 years, and develops students' problem solving skills using techniques that they have learned during their CS training. In the course, students work together to use programming techniques to solve open-ended problems from the domains of optimization, simulation, etc. There are no "correct" answers to these problems; rather, the focus is on the four steps of the problem solving process: algorithmic thinking, implementation, analysis, and communication.

This paper describes the course's objectives and methodology, presents a sample problem, summarizes the outcomes and feedback from students, and serves as a roadmap to other educators looking to create a similar course.

SIGCSE '16, March 02-05, 2016, Memphis, TN, USA

DOI: http://dx.doi.org/10.1145/2839509.2844594

2. HISTORY

Donald Knuth started teaching CS204, "A Programming and Problem Solving Seminar," at Stanford in 1976. This class was designed to be taken by new CS PhD students during their first quarter. He taught the class roughly every two years, and transcripts of those classes can be found as Stanford Technical Reports (e.g., [4, 21]). Video of the 1985 class can be found at http://scpd.stanford.edu/free-stuff/engineering-archives/donald-e-knuth-lectures under the heading "Aha Sessions."

In the preface for the 1976 class report [4], Knuth states,

> The purpose of CS 204 is to teach skills needed for research in computer science, as well as programming skills. I assigned five programming problems drawn from different areas of computer science; none of these problems was easy, but they were all intended to be sufficiently enjoyable that the students would not mind working overtime.

The main features of the class were to:

- Work on open-ended problems.
- Work on several different types of problems.
- Use programming as a way to gain knowledge about a problem (and potentially solve it).
- Have fun working on challenging problems.
- Work in small groups.
- Openly discuss approaches with students doing most of the talking; the instructor serves primarily as moderator.
- Collaborate (building on one another's ideas as the class progresses through a problem) rather than compete (keeping one's ideas private until the end).

In 1999, the third author, who had the privilege of being Knuth's teaching assistant at Stanford, created a new course at Columbia University based on the Stanford model. The course was aimed at both undergraduate and graduate students and was called "Programming and Problem Solving." A transcript of the first instance of the class is available [17]. As of summer 2015, the class has been offered fifteen times at Columbia University. The first two authors took this course as graduate students at Columbia University in Fall 2006 and Fall 2004, respectively. After joining the faculty at the University of Pennsylvania they introduced this class there in 2013 and as of this writing it has been offered five times.

A similar class, "Heuristic Problem Solving," has been taught at New York University since 2001. While writing a book on great computer scientists [18], the fourth author revisited some of the problems Knuth had used at Stanford. Recognizing that students learn best when they do rather than when they sit and allegedly listen, the Heuristic Problem Solving course (taught for the 16th time in Fall 2015) is structured around simple-to-state but hard-to-solve puzzles, many drawn from the fourth author's columns in Scientific American and Dr. Dobb's Journal.

3. COURSE DETAILS

In this section, we describe in detail the course's goals and educational objectives and the overall course structure.

3.1 Educational Objectives

Computer Science can be thought of as an algorithmic problem-solving activity in which we create, implement, analyze, and communicate solutions. The main objective of this course is to strengthen students' abilities in these four areas, specifically by having them do the following:

- Identify appropriate algorithms, data structures, etc. to use in order to solve a problem.
- Apply programming skills as a means of implementing an algorithmic solution.
- Develop intuition to enable students to come up with creative approaches to problems.
- Reuse and modify code.
- Collaborate with other students on programming projects.
- Develop skills for analyzing solutions.
- Incorporate feedback from others in order to enhance the quality of the solution.
- Improve communication skills (group discussion, written, presentation, teamwork).

More formally, using Bloom's taxonomy of educational objectives [1], most CS courses focus on the lower two levels, i.e., "knowledge" and "comprehension," with partial coverage of the third level, "application." This course, on the other hand, assumes that knowledge and comprehension have already been gained in a variety of CS classes. It thus focuses primarily on the upper levels of the taxonomy, namely "analysis," "synthesis," and "evaluation." Although capstone and project courses often touch on these particular aspects, there are few, if any, classes with these specific objectives in a traditional CS curriculum.

3.2 Intended Audience

This course is appropriate for upper-level undergraduates and graduate students, and serves as a capstone experience for them in that it builds on what they have learned in terms of algorithms, data structures, and programming and requires them to apply those as "tools" in solving problems.

In terms of prerequisites, data structures, algorithms, and at least two years of programming experience are required. Upper-level courses like Artificial Intelligence and Machine Learning are recommended.

3.3 Course Structure

There are no lectures in the course; rather, the course uses the Problem-Based Learning [20] methodology throughout the semester. The course consists of four cycles, each lasting approximately three weeks. In each cycle, the instructor first presents the problem to be solved. All the problems are open-ended and there are no "correct" solutions. We describe an example problem called "Organisms" in Section 4.1.

For each problem, the instructor provides a simulator that implements the rules and logic and that allows students to evaluate their solutions and/or compete against other teams' implementations in a variety of configurations. Students program to a given interface as part of their solution. The students can thus focus on the implementation of their approach/algorithm and not worry about implementing the details related to simulating the problem itself.

After the initial discussion of the problem, teams are formed (details below) and students work with their groups outside of class time. Subsequent class meetings consist of discussions of the students' insights into the problem and the work they have done in their group. There are a series of team "deliverables" due over the course of the problem cycle, and each group demonstrates their progress to the rest of the class in each class meeting.

At the end of the problem cycle, a tournament is held to determine the "best" solution, by an agreed-upon definition of "best," for a variety of configurations according to the problem. Although tournament results are not necessarily related to the students' grade, they are indicative of the quality of the solution and serve as a motivating factor.

3.4 Class Size and Teams

Due to the nature of the course, class size is typically limited to 25–30 students. Teams usually consist of three or four students, thus resulting in six to eight teams overall. For each problem cycle, new teams are created and group membership necessarily changes. The constraint that we add is that two students cannot work together more than once, as long as feasible. This gives everyone an opportunity to work with different people, leading to a greater diversity of ideas and approaches.

3.5 Open Source Nature

What perhaps makes this class even more unique compared to others typically offered in most CS departments is the open source nature of the class. Teams are allowed (and encouraged) to take ideas and even code from other teams, as long as they are appropriately attributed and cited. This allows for a freer exchange of ideas in the class discussions and it is very common to have a team say: "We really liked what team X proposed and since they were pursing another approach, we decided to implement their idea this weekend."

3.6 Communication and Presentation

An important pedagogical goal of this course is to improve students' communication and presentation skills in technical subjects. Towards this end, at the end of each problem cycle, every team submits a final report, which includes details of the team's solution, critical analysis of their approach, an overview of the implementation, and analysis of the tournament results. Every team also does a short presentation in the last class for each cycle.

3.7 Evaluation and Grades

For each problem, the grade is based on the students' implementation and deliverables, including:

- the novelty of the approach
- the thoroughness of the report
- the clarity of the report presentation
- the quality of the code
- the correctness and generality of the proposed solution
- the efficiency of the proposed solution

A large part of the course grade is also based on class and group participation. As such, class attendance is mandatory and missing several classes will result in a significant drop in the grade. Likewise, (for some of us), students evaluate each other at the end of each cycle, and these evaluations are used in calculating the final course grade.

4. SAMPLE PROBLEMS

One of the main contributions of this paper is to provide a large repository of existing problems that can be used by instructors at different institutions. There are three different sets of problems maintained by authors at the three institutions. There are over 85 problems available in total; for all the problems, software support (code, simulators, and GUI) is available either on request or directly through our website at http://programming-and-problem-solving.github.io/.

4.1 Organisms

We now describe an example problem called "Organisms." This problem has been used several times and is one of the most popular as voted by the students. The description below is the handout given to the class at the start of the problem cycle.

Consider an electronic world consisting of an m by n grid. Virtual "organisms" can exist on this grid, with an organism able to occupy a cell on the grid. Organisms have energy that can be gained or lost in a variety of ways. When an organism runs out of energy it dies, and vacates the cell it formerly occupied. An organism can have at most M units of energy. An organism may do one of several things during a virtual time cycle:

- Move one cell horizontally or vertically in any direction. The world wraps, so that an organism traveling off the right edge of the grid appears on the left edge, and similarly for the top and bottom edges. A move uses some energy.
- Stay put and do nothing. This move uses a small amount of energy.
- Reproduce. An organism can split in two, placing a replica of itself on an adjacent square. Each resultant organism has slightly less than half of the initial energy of the original organism since reproduction costs some energy.

An illegal move (such as trying to move or reproduce onto an occupied square) results in a "stay put" outcome.

There will be food scattered over the grid. One unit of food corresponds to u units of energy. Food reproduces according to the following rules:

- An empty square has a small probability p of having a single unit of food "blow in."
- For cells already containing food, but no organisms, every food unit on a nonempty square has a small probability q of doubling. This doubling is independent of other food units on the cell. So, a cell with three units of food may have anywhere between three and six units of food on the next cycle. Nevertheless, no cell may have more than K units of food at any one time, due to space constraints.
- Cells with organisms never obtain additional food. (The organisms block the light.) In fact, an organism that is on a cell with food, and which has energy no larger than $M - u$, will consume a unit of food and add u units of energy to its store. If an organism is hungry, it can eat one unit of food per cycle until either the food runs out, or it achieves energy greater than $M - u$.

An organism has an *external* state that is an integer between 0 and 255. This state may be changed by the organism during the course of the simulation. The external state is visible to other organisms, as described below.

An organism can "see" in the four orthogonal directions. An organism gets information about:

- Whether there is food or not on a neighboring square (but not how much food).
- Whether there is another organism on a neighboring square. If there is, then the external state of the neighboring organism is also available.
- The amount of remaining food on the organism's current cell.
- The amount of energy currently possessed by the organism.
- Values of the simulator parameters s (energy consumed in staying put), v (energy consumed in moving or reproducing), u, M, and K, but not p, q, m, or n.

An organism's "brain" is a program that you will write. Since there will be many organisms on the grid simultaneously, each will run a separate instance of the brain code. Each instance will have access only to the local environment of the organism. Organisms are placed randomly on the grid, and don't know their coordinates. The brain can keep a history of local events for the organism if it's useful.

Organisms cannot identify their neighbors. Neighbors may be of the same species (i.e., have the same programmed brain), or of a different species (i.e., have a different brain). This will be important for simulations in which multiple organisms from different groups are placed on the same grid. (How might you use the external state to help in identification? What about impostors?)

Organisms act one-at-a-time from top-left to bottom-right, row by row. We number the top-left cell as (1,1) and the bottom-right cell as (m, n). That means that the state of the virtual world seen by an organism at (x, y) reflects the situation in which all organisms in positions (x', y') lexicographically less than (x, y) have already made their moves, while organisms in positions lexicographically after (x, y) have not yet moved. This convention allows all operations to happen without any need for resolving conflicts between organisms (for example trying to move to the same cell). However, it leads to some slightly unintuitive effects:

- An organism that is sensed to the west is usually in its final position for the cycle (can you think of an exception?), while an organism sensed to the east may or may not be in its final position.
- An organism moving east can be sensed from the west, while an organism moving west cannot be sensed from the east. (There's an exception to this observation: what is it?)

We'll provide an organism "simulator" that reads in one or more organism brains, places one organism for each such brain randomly on the grid, and lets the organisms behave according to their brains' instructions.

There are several goals for this problem:

1. Your organism should be able to survive and replicate in an environment where it is the only kind of organism present. This may not be as easy as it sounds. Overpopulation may lead to consumption of all the food. If p is sufficiently small, extinction may ensue. The goal is to achieve the highest long-term stable population.
2. Your organism will be tested in environments containing other organisms. The goal here is primarily to survive, and secondarily to survive in higher numbers than competing organisms. Can your organisms populate the grid faster than their competitors? (Is that even the right strategy given the possibility of everybody going extinct?) How might you program your organisms to "recognize" different organisms based on their state and/or behavior? If you can distinguish members of your species, how might you behave differently to members of another species? Your goal here is not necessarily to obliterate other species, but to maximize your fraction of the population.
3. In the discussion so far, we haven't limited the size of organisms' brains. How might your programs change if (to simulate an organism's limited brain size) we limited the complexity of the brain code? For example, what if we eliminated all looping constructs (while, for, etc.) from brains?

5. OUTCOMES

This course has been taught several times at the three institutions: the first two authors have taught this course five times over three years at University of Pennsylvania; the third author has taught this course almost every year since 1999 at Columbia University; the fourth author has taught this course thirteen times at New York University.

The student experience at all three institutions has been overwhelmingly positive. Overall course quality scores range between "Very Good" and "Excellent." We now describe the qualitative feedback from the various offerings of this course. The feedback comes from a variety of sources including end of semester wrap-up sessions, official university evaluations, and email sent to the authors. The feedback is grouped into the following categories:

Overall Course: This course has consistently been very highly rated and has been very popular with students. Selected comments include: "One of the best courses I've taken."; "I would not only recommend this to any CS student, but would demand that they take it, even make it a core course of the program."; "It is the most unique course in the department."; "This is the best thing that happened to me here. The course structure is great, the problems were well chosen."

Course Structure: The open-ended nature of the problems was very appealing to students. Selected comments include: "These open ended problems excited an interest and an enthusiasm that I've never seen in almost any other class."; "The open-ended nature of the problems really helped to develop my skills of independent problem solving."; "This also changed my idea of how a course SHOULD be taught—namely using competitions and open-ended projects as motivating devices."

Course Workload: Students felt that the course entailed a lot of work but that it was worth the effort. Selected comments include: "This is the hardest, best class I have ever taken. It made me weep it was so hard, but I never have learned more or had so much fun as in this class."; "The work was VERY heavy, but was reasonable considering the nature of the class."

Teamwork, Discussion, and Communication: Students mentioned that a strong positive aspect of the course was the emphasis on teamwork and presentation and communication skills. Selected comments include: "The class discussions really helped open me to new perspectives on the problems, and the regular presentations helped develop my skill in communicating technical matters."; "The open discussions in the bi-weekly classes definitely facilitates the evolution of new ideas as students need not worry about their own plans being copied by other teams – in fact one wishes that his or her ideas are borrowed by the participants as credit will be given to them."; "It's also a class where teamwork is key and good communication is vital."

Class Size: As class sizes are growing at most universities, students found the small class size in this course to be a very unique and beneficial aspect. Selected comments include: "Having a small class is a wonderful thing."; "The small class size and that too of hand-picked students really made the discussions to be of very high quality."; "Having fewer people in the class makes me more comfortable and gives me the chance to speak my mind. Something I have not had in ANY class up to this point."

While there has been occasional negative feedback from students, it almost always concerns being in a group with a team member who was not willing to pull their weight. Because groups switch after every problem cycle, nobody is paired with the same partner more than once.

6. RELATED WORK

This course builds on and complements existing work on flipped classrooms and active learning, project-based courses, simulation-oriented games, and integrating soft skills in Computer Science classes. We summarize the important related work in this section.

Problem-Based Learning (PBL) and the inverted/flipped classroom [14] have become popular pedagogical tools. In PBL, appropriate problems are used to increase knowledge and mastery of the material. Group learning is a key part of PBL and the goal is not "only the acquisition of knowledge but also several other desirable attributes, such as communication skills, teamwork, problem solving, independent responsibility for learning, sharing information, and respect for others" [20]. Using aspects of PBL, in the inverted/flipped classroom, activities that traditionally happen in the classroom (such as lectures) happen outside the classroom and vice-versa. Students review slides before coming to class and class time is used to review the material and practice problems. This approach has been been used successfully in a variety of CS classes. Lockwood and Essenstein [15] describe using an inverted classroom to teach introductory programming. Gehringer and Peddycord [7] use an inverted classroom to teach computer architecture. Kurtz et al. [13] describe using tablets for active learning in lectures. Our course leverages and complements all of this prior work in that learning occurs outside the classroom while students are working on their solutions and class meeting time is focused on discussion.

Projects have been and are being used as a significant component in many different courses. We describe only the recent related work for sake of brevity. Krutz et al. [12] use real-world open source projects for teaching software testing. Szabo [19] describes using existing projects with real bugs for teaching software maintenance. Bloomfield et al. [2] describe a two-semester capstone project where students develop software for local non-profit organizations. Whereas the projects described in these related works are generally based on implementing a particular specification, our course and project structure (as described in Section 3) is different in that the problems are open-ended and the emphasis is on devising, analyzing, and communicating solutions, in addition to implementing them.

There has been a lot of work in using simulation-oriented games for teaching various aspects of CS. SimSE [16] uses a game-based simulation environment for teaching software process and software engineering. Wu's Castle [5] is a game to teach students basic programming constructs such as loops and arrays. Gibson and Bell [8] have conducted a large survey that evaluates games for teaching CS. Their survey (and the references therein) lists games on a variety of topics such as binary numbers, basic programming concepts, graph algorithms, and network protocols. All these papers focus on teaching a very specific CS aspect and are, by definition, narrow in scope. Our course is designed to do the opposite—it is intended as a broad upper level course that builds on courses such programming, data structures, algorithms, and software engineering and uses them as tools in solving problems.

Finally, soft skills such as communication and teamwork are becoming an increasingly important aspect for a Computer Scientist [6] and are found to be "unfortunately lacking in many new graduates" [11]. There has been some recent work that aims to integrate soft skills in various CS classes. Hoffman et al. [10] describe using "workplace scenarios" to teach communication skills in various classes. Hazzan and Har-Shai [9] draw the analogy between soft skills and soft computer science concepts such as abstraction and propose that both these can be learnt gradually by students over a period of time. Burns et al. [3] describe their efforts on teaching soft skills by having student teams partner with middle school teacher teams to help the latter integrate computing into their teaching and curriculum. Our course also aims to improve students' soft skills and is complementary to all of these efforts.

7. RECOMMENDATIONS

We conclude this paper with recommendations for others who might want to adopt this course.

7.1 Teaching the Class

The role of the instructor in this class is, paradoxically, to avoid instructing. As discussion of a problem progresses, the ideas should be coming from the students during (and between) class discussions. The role of the instructor is to structure the discussion so that progress can be made. Our advice on the instructor's role during class time is summarized below.

- Have a structure for class discussions. There should be an expectation that every student will be called on at some point, even when their hand is not raised. Discussions can be based upon results obtained since the previous class, with the focus moving from group to group. Or discussions can be open and broad, particularly in the first class for a problem cycle.
- Listen to a student present an idea, then highlight any insights and restate them in a parsimonious way. Sometimes ideas come up that could take the discussion in a whole new direction. If the previous direction of the discussion still has room for elaboration, put the new idea aside and come back to it later. It's easier to have discussions in a depth first rather than breadth first manner.
- If a student asks a question, pose the question to the class rather than trying to answer it.
- Avoid trying to solve the problems ahead of time. That way, the instructor won't inadvertently push the discussion in a particular direction. The most inspiring moments for an instructor happen when students come up with good ideas that the instructor would never have thought of.
- Be strict about participation. This means (a) eliminating side conversations and prohibiting the use of cell-phones and laptops during class discussions, and (b) limiting the number of allowed absences to a very small number.

Instructor preparation for a particular class hour is small, and the instructor will improvise as the discussion follows an unpredictable course. By improvising in this way, students get to see a more natural "way of thinking" about CS. The primary preparation effort for the class occurs before the class starts, when selecting a set of problems for the term.

7.2 What makes a good problem?

We recommend trying to choose different types of problems over the course of the semester if possible. Games are a good because they seem to get students motivated by friendly competition. If one chooses more than one game-type problem, try to make them different (e.g., one two-player game and another many-player game). We suggest choosing problems that could have come from the real world, and are phrased within the context of simulating a (somewhat abstracted) real-world scenario. It's important to choose problems that have good visualizations, preferably interactive ones. A high quality interface can give the students direct feedback about the mechanics (and bugs) of their solutions, both in class and outside of class. Other important considerations include choosing/controlling the appropriate level of difficulty (using several parameters such as board size or number of players), whether the problem (or a close variant of it) has been solved before or extensively studied in the literature, and reusing problems used in the past (or from our repository) so that students can potentially have access to previous work done and build on it. Finally like Knuth, we aim to choose problems that are open-ended, and likely to be fun.

8. ACKNOWLEDGMENTS

The authors would like to thank their hard-working teaching assistants, without whom the courses would not have been nearly as successful.

9. REFERENCES

[1] B. S. Bloom. *Taxonomy of Educational Objectives: The Classification of Education Goals. Cognitive Domain. Handbook 1.* Longman, 1956.

[2] A. Bloomfield, M. Sherriff, and K. Williams. A service learning practicum capstone. In *Proceedings of the 45th ACM Technical Symposium on Computer Science Education*, SIGCSE '14, pages 265–270, New York, NY, USA, 2014. ACM.

[3] R. Burns, L. Pollock, and T. Harvey. Integrating hard and soft skills: Software engineers serving middle school teachers. In *Proceedings of the 43rd ACM Technical Symposium on Computer Science Education*, SIGCSE '12, pages 209–214, New York, NY, USA, 2012. ACM.

[4] M. J. Clancy and D. E. Knuth. A Programming and Problem-Solving Seminar. Technical Report stan-cs-77-606, Computer Science Department, Stanford University, 1977. http://infolab.stanford.edu/pub/cstr/reports/cs/tr/77/606/CS-TR-77-606.pdf.

[5] M. Eagle and T. Barnes. Experimental evaluation of an educational game for improved learning in introductory computing. *SIGCSE Bull.*, 41:321–325, March 2009.

[6] H. A. Etlinger. A framework in which to teach (technical) communication to computer science majors. In *Proceedings of the 37th SIGCSE Technical Symposium on Computer Science Education*, SIGCSE '06, pages 122–126, New York, NY, USA, 2006. ACM.

[7] E. F. Gehringer and B. W. Peddycord, III. The inverted-lecture model: A case study in computer architecture. In *Proceeding of the 44th ACM Technical Symposium on Computer Science Education*, SIGCSE '13, pages 489–494, New York, NY, USA, 2013. ACM.

[8] B. Gibson and T. Bell. Evaluation of games for teaching computer science. In *Proceedings of the 8th Workshop in Primary and Secondary Computing Education*, WiPSE '13, pages 51–60, New York, NY, USA, 2013. ACM.

[9] O. Hazzan and G. Har-Shai. Teaching computer science soft skills as soft concepts. In *Proceeding of the 44th ACM Technical Symposium on Computer Science Education*, SIGCSE '13, pages 59–64, New York, NY, USA, 2013. ACM.

[10] M. E. Hoffman, P. V. Anderson, and M. Gustafsson. Workplace scenarios to integrate communication skills and content: A case study. In *Proceedings of the 45th ACM Technical Symposium on Computer Science Education*, SIGCSE '14, pages 349–354, New York, NY, USA, 2014. ACM.

[11] J. L. Kayfetz and K. C. Almeroth. Creating innovative writing instruction for computer science graduate students. In *Frontiers in Education Conference, 2008. FIE 2008. 38th Annual*, pages T4F–1. IEEE, 2008.

[12] D. E. Krutz, S. A. Malachowsky, and T. Reichlmayr. Using a real world project in a software testing course. In *Proceedings of the 45th ACM Technical Symposium on Computer Science Education*, SIGCSE '14, pages 49–54, New York, NY, USA, 2014. ACM.

[13] B. L. Kurtz, J. B. Fenwick, R. Tashakkori, A. Esmail, and S. R. Tate. Active learning during lecture using tablets. In *Proceedings of the 45th ACM Technical Symposium on Computer Science Education*, SIGCSE '14, pages 121–126, New York, NY, USA, 2014. ACM.

[14] M. J. Lage, G. J. Platt, and M. Treglia. Inverting the classroom: A gateway to creating an inclusive learning environment. *The Journal of Economic Education*, 31(1):30–43, 2000.

[15] K. Lockwood and R. Esselstein. The inverted classroom and the cs curriculum. In *Proceeding of the 44th ACM Technical Symposium on Computer Science Education*, SIGCSE '13, pages 113–118, New York, NY, USA, 2013. ACM.

[16] E. O. Navarro and A. van der Hoek. SimSE: an educational simulation game for teaching the software engineering process. In *Proc. of the 9th annual SIGCSE conf. on Innovation and technology in CS education*, ITiCSE '04, pages 233–233, 2004.

[17] K. A. Ross and S. R. Shamoun. Programming and Problem Solving: A Transcript of the Spring 1999 Class. Technical Report cucs-018-99, Department of Computer Science, Columbia University, 1999. http://www.cs.columbia.edu/~library/TR-repository/reports/reports-1999/cucs-018-99.pdf.

[18] D. Shasha and C. Lazere. *Out of Their Minds: The Lives and Discoveries of 15 Great Computer Scientists.* Springer-Verlag, New York, August 1995.

[19] C. Szabo. Student projects are not throwaways: Teaching practical software maintenance in a software engineering course. In *Proceedings of the 45th ACM Technical Symposium on Computer Science Education*, SIGCSE '14, pages 55–60, New York, NY, USA, 2014. ACM.

[20] D. F. Wood. Problem based learning. *Bmj*, 326(7384):328–330, 2003.

[21] C. V. Wyk and D. E. Knuth. A Programming and Problem-Solving Seminar. Technical Report stan-cs-79-707, Computer Science Department, Stanford University, 1979. http://infolab.stanford.edu/pub/cstr/reports/cs/tr/79/707/CS-TR-79-707.pdf.

The Influence of Problem Solving Abilities on Students' Performance on Different Assessment Tasks in CS1

Alex Lishinski
Michigan State University
College of Education
East Lansing, MI
lishinsk@msu.edu

Aman Yadav
Michigan State University
College of Education
East Lansing, MI
ayadav@msu.edu

Richard Enbody
Michigan State University
Department of Computer Science and Engineering
East Lansing, MI
enbody@cse.msu.edu

Jon Good
Michigan State University
College of Education
East Lansing, MI
goodjona@msu.edu

ABSTRACT

Previous research has suggested that cognitive tests, including instruments seeking to measure problem solving, are significant predictors of students' programming performance. This paper seeks to expand upon this previous research by using a more theoretically grounded approach to measuring problem solving as a means of predicting performance in an introductory undergraduate programming course. Programming course performance has typically been measured by overall course grades; however, in this paper we used a more fine-grained approach to measuring student programming performance. Specifically, we utilized different types of course assignments (projects and tests) to measure programming outcomes. Results from this study indicate that problem solving ability significantly correlates with performance on programming assignments, but does not correlate with performance on multiple-choice exams.

Keywords

CS1, Assessment, Problem Solving

1. INTRODUCTION

Problem solving is an important set of cognitive skills that are highly valued in education as a set of skills that are applicable to many different academic disciplines [8]. Researchers in computer science education have long been interested in the relationship between problem solving skills and programming abilities [16, 15]. Previous research has suggested that there exists some connection between the generic set of skills that constitute problem solving, and the specific set of skills that is involved in solving programming problems; however, previous research is ambiguous about this relationship.

Previous research on the cognitive processes involved in learning to program has considered generic problem solving skills to be a sort of *telos* of programming instruction [12]. Generic problem solving skills are seen as emerging from the specific declarative and procedural knowledge that is acquired through learning to program, as one moves from novice to expert [16]. However, the existing research has generally not presented a theoretically well-grounded picture of problem solving. Without such a framework, it is difficult to justify a choice of instrument, much less any causal inferences [16].

The other side of the relationship between programming and problem solving is the notion that problem solving ability is predictive of success in programming [15]. However, there is limited research on using problem solving as a predictor of programming performance, compared to the research that has examined improved problem solving abilities as an outcome [19]. Nevertheless, the studies that have looked at problem solving as a predictor are located within a much more extensive body of literature on predictors of programming performance [5]. This body of research presents a relatively uniform picture of the positive predictive value of different sorts of cognitive measures (for example: the embedded figural relations test, the iconic pattern recognition test, and various other reasoning tests) that could reasonably be classified alongside problem solving as measures of "thinking skills" [9, 11, 4]. These results suggest that a measure of generic problem solving would likely have a similar relationship with programming performance.

Type of outcome measure is one element of the relationship between problem solving and programming that has not been substantially explored. Previous studies on predictors of programming ability have generally not discussed the implications of the choice of outcome measure. The outcome typically used is the grade obtained in a programming course or the score on a programming exam. The choice of course grades and exam scores as outcome measures has generally not been described in detail nor justified [15, 4, 22]. This lack of attention to choice of outcome measure persists de-

SIGCSE '16, March 02 - 05, 2016, Memphis, TN, USA

ISBN 978-1-4503-3685-7/16/03...$15.00

DOI: http://dx.doi.org/10.1145/2839509.2844596

spite evidence that different types of assessment can reflect student understanding and ability to substantially different degrees [20]. In particular, research has suggested that the use of multiple choice as opposed to constructed response assessments can greatly affect the validity of assessment in computer science courses [3]. The choice of outcome measure in studies of predictors of programming performance, therefore, becomes critically important.

The focus on the type of assessment draws its significance from the notion of a hierarchy of programming skills, which ranks programming related competencies from easy to difficult. Research into such a hierarchy is relatively new [14] and the results have suggested that a hierarchical model of programming skills is a viable one [17, 21, 13, 18]. Drawing from this research, this study attempted to account for the connection between problem solving ability and programming outcomes in such a way that is consistent with the hierarchical model.

In this study, we examined the relationship between CS1 students' problem solving skills and their programming outcomes as measured by programming projects and multiple choice exams. In order to assess problem solving skills, we used items from the problem solving section of the Programme for International Student Assessment (PISA). These items were chosen because the PISA test focuses on generic, content-agnostic problem solving and because they have not been previously used to examine the relationship between problem solving and programming performance. Furthermore, the PISA test is a well tested and validated instrument based on a theoretical foundation of problem solving, making it ideal for this study.

The contributions of this work include:

- We found that there was a significant connection between problem solving ability and programming performance as measured by grades on programming assignments.
- We found no significant connection between problem solving ability and programming performance as measured by grades on multiple choice exams.
- We found a significant, but moderate, statistical connection between student performance on multiple choice exams and programming project performance, consistent with hierarchical accounts of programming knowledge.
- We found that the variance in programming project performance is uniquely explained by problem solving performance, which suggested that problem solving ability contributes to programming skill at the highest level of the hierarchy of programming skills.
- We piloted the use of an assessment of problem solving that had not previously been used in CS education, which addresses the need for a generic measure that is theoretically well-grounded.

2. THEORETICAL BACKGROUND

Fredericksen (1984) presented a review of the cognitive theoretical framework for problem solving[8]. Drawing largely from Newell and Simon's (1972) account of problem solving, Fredericksen laid out the prevailing key theoretical elements. The first key element Fredericksen discussed was *Problem representation*, which includes the notion of a *task environment* and a *problem space*. Problem representation includes the structure of the problem and the information and concepts that make up the problem definition. Another key element discussed by Fredericksen was problem solving procedures, which included *means-end analysis*, *hypothesize and test*, and *pattern recognition*. Means-end analysis is the process of comparing the present state to the goal state, and devising a series of subgoals to transform the current state into the goal state. Hypothesize and test, drawn from Simon (1980), is the process of looking for confirmatory (and disconfirmatory) evidence for suppositions about the task environment. Lastly, pattern recognition, drawn in this context from studies by Simon and Chase (1973) and Reitman (1976) on chess and go players, refers to the ability to combine disparate elements of the problem space into discrete units for more efficient mental processing.

2.1 Programming and Problem Solving

Previous research on the relationship between problem solving and programming has largely focused on the potential causal relationship between instruction in programming and generic problem solving ability, and less on the predictive power of generic problem solving ability on programming course outcomes. Palumbo (1990) reviewed the literature on the potential causal relationship extensively, and found that overall, the causal connection between problem solving and programming was not well supported empirically[16]. However, certain instructional factors, such as greater programming exposure and deliberate instruction in metacognitive strategies, have been found to influence problem solving.

Research on problem solving as a predictor of programming performance has been less common. Many studies have examined predictors of programming performance based on cognitive abilities of various sorts (see for example [9, 11, 4]) and results have been generally been significant. Fewer studies have examined problem solving *per se* as a predictor. Mayer (1986) examined problem solving as a predictor of programming performance, and vice versa[15]. The results of that study highlighted the significance of problem solving as a predictor. However, the problems chosen to indicate problem solving ability in his study were math word problem translation tasks, which is not aligned with the framework adopted in this study of problem solving as a generic, content-agnostic skill set.

2.2 Hierarchy of Programming Skills

The BRACElet project was a series of workshops and associated studies conducted between 2004 and 2010 with the goal of understanding how students learn various programming skills. The studies established a number of results related to the establishment of a hierarchy of programming skills. Lopez et al. (2008) formally established the hierarchy of skills, developing a model of programming skills that included basics like syntax at the low end, code tracing in the moderate level, explaining at an upper moderate level, and code writing as the highest level [14]. Other results have corroborated the existence and ordering of the hierarchy; Philpott et al. (2007) found that code tracing failures predicted code explaining failures [17].

Additional previous research has empirically examined the relationships between these higher and lower level programming skills. Venables et al. (2009) found relationships between code-writing tasks and lower level tracing and explaining tasks that were consistent with the hierarchical model [21]. Lister et al. (2009) similarly looked at the relationship between these dimensions, finding significant relationships between tracing, explaining and writing [13]. Porter et al. (2014) examined clicker data as a predictor of student performance, and found that the clicker data was equally predictive for multiple choice and code-writing questions, which is consistent with the hierarchical model [18].

2.3 Outcome Measures: Types of Assessment

Previous research on types of assessment has distinguished between multiple choice (MC) assessments and constructed response (CR) assessments. This prior research has shown a significant difference between student results on these two types of assessment, with MC assessments being more suited for assessing students' understanding of factual content with unambiguous correct answers, and CR assessments being better suited for measurement of students' thinking and problem solving processes. Azalov et al. (2004) examined the differences between student results on MC and CR assessments in an undergraduate introductory CS course and found that students' scores on a CR assessment predicted final course grades to a much greater extent than an analogous MC assessment [3]. Kuechler and Simkin (2003) also examined the relationship between multiple choice questions and code-writing questions in an introductory programming course and found significant, but moderate, connections between MC questions and code-writing questions, which is consistent with the hierarchical model [10].

Therefore, the purpose of this study was to examine the relationship between problem solving and different types of assessments (multiple choice exams vs. programming projects) in order to establish whether there is a relationship with one or both. The next section discusses the methodology and data collection to address the research questions.

3. METHODS

Participants: 41 undergraduate students enrolled in a CS1 class at a large midwestern university participated in the study. The sample included 29 males and 9 females (3 non-responses) with an average GPA of 3.19.

Setting: Participants were recruited from an online section of a CS1 course at a large Midwestern University in the Spring Semester 2015. The online course followed a standardized format consisting of the use of pre-recorded video lectures, in lieu of in-person class meetings, to cover the course content. The course exams were conducted in-person and the course used Python as the programming language.

3.1 PISA Problem Solving Framework

The PISA problem solving items used in this study were based on an account of problem solving as generic and content-agnostic. The authors of the PISA problem solving framework contended that a problem is essentially a situation where a novel strategy is required to arrive at a solution [2]. The content-agnostic nature of problem solving thus emerges from the notion that previous knowledge must not be directly applicable in problem solving. The authors contrasted a problem with an exercise, which is a situation that allows for the application of prior knowledge and previously used strategies to generate a solution.

To develop the problem solving items, the authors first developed a problem solving theoretical framework drawn in large part from Mayer (1992). The PISA framework centers around the following definition of problem solving ability: *An individual's capacity to engage in cognitive processing to understand and resolve problem situations where a method of solution is not immediately obvious.* The framework lists deductive, inductive, analogical, and combinatorial as the primary types of reasoning that are used to solve the PISA problem solving tasks. Furthermore, the framework contains a list of cognitive processes involved in problem solving, which include:

- *Exploring and understanding* the information associated with the problem.
- *Representing and formulating* the problem with various representations and formulating hypotheses about the relevant factors and relationships.
- *Planning and executing*: devising a plan, setting goals and subgoals and executing the steps of the plan.
- *Monitoring and reflecting*: monitoring progress, reacting to feedback, reflecting on the solution, the strategy used, or information associated with the problem.

This framework of the processes involved in problem solving maps neatly onto the account given by Fredericksen (1984). Exploring and understanding the problem corresponds to Newell and Simon's notion of problem representation. Representing and formulating the problem corresponds to pattern recognition and hypothesize and test strategies. Planning and executing corresponds to means-end analysis and hypothesize and test strategies.

The NCES (National Center for Education Statistics) technical report (2007) [6] on the assessment of problem solving in two major international assessments (TIMSS and PISA) assessed the validity of the approaches to problem solving used in these two assessments. Drawing from problem solving theory, the authors of the report identified a set of factors that define problem solving, which largely align with the framework used to develop the PISA problem solving assessment. In particular, whether or not a strategy is easily found is key, according to the authors. If a strategy that the individual has previously used in similar situations works in this situation, then it cannot be said to be an instance of problem solving. The NCES report therefore corroborated the theoretical approach to problem solving used by the authors of the PISA problem solving items.

The PISA problem solving items are divided into 3 subtypes. Four items are termed *Decision Making*; given the constraints of a problem situation, the student must select which of a number of outcomes are acceptable or optimal given those constraints. Four items are termed *System Analysis and Design*; given some examples or information about the way that a system is structured, the student must predict how a system will behave in a given situation, or determine what will satisfy the relations and constraints of the system. The remaining two items address *Troubleshooting*; given a situation in which certain characteristics of how a system should behave are described, the student must identify what is causing a given problem.

To measure participants' problem solving skills, we selected items from the released problem solving items from the 2003 PISA test (see Appendix A for example item) [1]. The released items consisted of 10 distinct problem situations, each of which was accompanied by 1-3 questions. Of the 10 released items, 4 items were chosen for this study. Of the 4 items, two were systems analysis and design, one was decision making, and one was troubleshooting. The items were chosen on the basis of difficulty level and skill relevance. Specifically, item difficulty was identified using the percentage of students who answered the items correctly on the 2003 PISA test. Skill relevance was selected based on the framework of computational thinking. Specifically, items were chosen that were judged to best link generic problem solving with the more generically applicable elements of computational thinking, such as algorithms, pattern recognition, and debugging.

3.2 Study Design and Data Collection

The course grade consisted of multiple choice midterm exams that included mostly code tracing and syntax questions, a cumulative final exam with the same format, programming projects, and weekly lab assignments (see Appendix B for archive of exams and programming projects). The programming projects allowed students to write a substantive piece of code to meet a set of specified assignment requirements in service of a coherent larger goal. For example, one project required students to write a program to open and process text files to extract particular information. These programs were scored by a teaching assistant using a multidimensional rubric based upon the requirements for each assignment.

Of the assignment types used in the course, we chose to focus on the multiple choice exams and programming projects for two main reasons. These two assignment types were the most significant components of students' overall grade, and the programming projects were judged to be the best exemplar of a code-writing assignment in the course.

3.3 Data Analysis

To analyze the data, each of the PISA items were weighted and scored individually in order to create a composite problem solving score for each participant. Specifically, individual question results from actual PISA administrations were used to identify difficulty level of each item and more difficult items were weighted more heavily than the easier items in participants' composite problem solving score. For example, the library system question awarded 1 point to students who correctly answered the initial 1 blank question and a total of 4 points to students who correctly answered the flowchart design question, which had 8 blanks.

To analyze the connection between the problem solving assessment and course outcomes, scores on the programming projects were combined and used as one measure of course performance, and scores on the 2 midterm exams were combined and used as a second measure of course performance. Correlation and regression analysis were used to examine these connections. To avoid bias in the coefficient estimates, students who recorded a zero, indicating that no assignment was submitted, for any of the programming projects or either of the exams were excluded from the data analysis.

4. RESULTS

After removal of those students with missing data, the final analysis included 28 students who completed all of programming projects and exams. The distribution of student scores on programming projects was significantly negatively skewed, and the distribution of students' scores on the problem solving assessment deviated significantly from normality. In order to meet the assumptions of the Pearson product-moment correlation coefficient and linear regression, both variables were transformed using the standard square root transformation. The square root transformation resulted in an approximately normal distribution of values for both variables. The distribution of total exam scores satisfied the normality assumption without transformation. Cumulative GPA was also included in the analysis, and the distribution was negatively skewed, so it was transformed to approximate normality with a natural log transformation.

4.1 Correlation Analysis

The Pearson product-moment correlation coefficient was calculated for the relationships between problem solving score, total exam score, and total project score (see table 1). The results of these correlations shed light on the connection between problem solving and the 2 course outcomes. The relationship between problem solving and programming project scores was moderately strong and significant (r = .4099, p = .0152), but the relationship between problem solving score and exam grade was insignificant (r = -.0088, p = .5176). However, exam and project scores correlated substantially with one another (r = .427, p = .0117), which suggested that, while the two course assessments were related, problem solving ability accounts for performance on programming projects above and beyond exam scores.

4.2 Regression Analysis

To further explore these results, linear models were created, regressing total project scores on problem solving scores and total exam scores, both individually and in combination. An R^2 value of .1824 (Adj: .1509) was observed for the regression of project score on exam score, and an R^2 value of .168 (Adj: .136) was observed for the regression of project score on problem solving score. The combined model had an R^2 value of .3534 (adj: .3017). The ΔR^2 for both variables was calculated for the combined model (see table 2), with a ΔR^2 of .1711 being observed for problem solving scores, and a ΔR^2 of .1855 being observed for combined exam scores. The η_p^2 value of 0.21 for problem solving indicates a medium effect size for problem solving as a predictor. This pattern of results supports the notion that MC and CR assessments in this course are hierarchical, because problem solving only explains performance on higher level skills, but it makes a unique contribution to this explanation. The knowledge assessed by the multiple choice test (tracing, comprehension, etc.) is, therefore, foundational for the skills assessed by the programming projects (writing code). To put it another way, the lower level skills are necessary but not sufficient for the upper level skills.

Previous data from this CS1 class showed that the best predictor of student success in this course is cumulative GPA [7]. For this reason, the connections between cumulative GPA, the two course outcome scores, and problem solving scores were examined. Of particular interest is the relationship between problem solving scores and GPA, because we wanted to know whether the correlation between problem solving and programming project scores was independent or subsumed by another known covariate. The connection between GPA and course outcomes was verified by the fact that

	Cum. GPA (log)	Problem Solving (sqrt)	Prog. Project (sqrt)	Exam Score
Cum. GPA (log)	1.00	0.18	0.36	0.36
Problem Solving (sqrt)	0.18	1.00	0.41	-0.01
Prog. Projects (sqrt)	0.36	0.41	1.00	0.43
Exam Score	0.36	-0.01	0.43	1.00

Table 1: Correlation Matrix

	SSR	df	η_p^2	ΔR^2	SSE	SST
(Intercept)	0.30	1.00	0.00		81.72	126.39
Problem Solving	21.62	1.00	0.21	0.17	81.72	126.39
Exam Score	23.44	1.00	0.22	0.19	81.72	126.39

Table 2: Model change with Exam Score and Problem Solving

	SSR	df	η_p^2	ΔR^2	SSE	SST
(Intercept)	2.17	1.00	0.03		79.06	126.39
Problem Solving	18.03	1.00	0.19	0.14	79.06	126.39
Exam Score	15.30	1.00	0.16	0.12	79.06	126.39
Cum. GPA	2.66	1.00	0.03	0.02	79.06	126.39

Table 3: Model change with GPA, Exam Score and Problem Solving Score

cumulative GPA correlated significantly with both course outcome variables (r = .360, r = .358, see table 1). The regression model was recalculated, adding GPA as a predictor. The delta R-squared statistic for this additional predictor was small ($\Delta R^2 = .0210$), and the values for the other 2 predictors were reduced somewhat (exam score: $\Delta R^2 = .1211$, problem solving score: $\Delta R^2 = .1427$, see table 3). The η_p^2 value of 0.19 for problem solving indicates that the effect size is still medium for problem solving as a predictor, even accounting for the effect of GPA in the model. In the resulting model, problem solving score surpassed exam score as the predictor that explained the largest proportion of variance in programming project outcomes. Therefore, the predictive value of problem solving scores was largely independent of previous GPA, although previous GPA substantially contributes to explaining variation on both assessments. The results of this analysis, therefore, further support the conclusion that problem solving uniquely explains differences in higher level programming skills.

5. DISCUSSION

In this study, we examined the use of problem solving as a predictor of beginners' programming outcomes. In particular, we were interested in the extent to which problem solving might be related to the different types of assessment used in a CS1 course. We found that the problem solving scores measured at the beginning of the term are predictive of student outcomes, but only the outcomes on the constructed-response programming assignments, and not the outcomes on multiple choice exams. Similar to Porter et al. (2014), this study corroborated the association between code-writing and multiple choice grades. However, unlike Porter et al. (2014), the results of this study identified a predictor of programming success that is able to differentiate between the two types of assignment. Furthermore, this predictor is especially valuable because it is a preexisting characteristic measured at the beginning of the semester.

While Porter et al.'s observation that you must be able to trace code in order to write code appears true, it does not follow of course that the ability to trace entails the ability to code. There is an association between the lower and higher level programming skills, as this study confirmed, the question remains however, what can explain the differences in outcomes for higher level skills beyond the foundational effect of the lower level skills? This study found that problem solving ability is uniquely predictive of higher level skills above and beyond the effect of lower level skills. These results not only provide evidence for the notion that programming knowledge/ability is hierarchical, but they also suggest what abilities underlie the upper level skills and distinguish them from the lower level skills. Problem solving is a means by which we can explain this distinction between higher and lower level skills. Furthermore, the finding that controlling for previous GPA did not significantly detract from the predictive value of problem solving further supports the conclusion that problem solving ability has a unique predictive value for success on higher level programming tasks. These findings offer a basis for early identification of students who may encounter difficulties at higher level programming tasks.

6. CONCLUSION

In this paper, we have found evidence that programming ability is hierarchical, and goes beyond what can be assessed by a multiple choice test. We have observed that the variability of outcomes at the higher levels of the programming skills hierarchy is associated with generic problem solving skills. These results support the hierarchy of programming skills developed by Lopez et al. (2008) and the other BRACElet studies, and also provide a more substantive picture of what differentiates higher level skills like code writing from lower level skills like code tracing, using the theoretical framework of problem solving[14, 17, 21, 13, 18]. Problem solving ability helps explain success on the most difficult programming tasks.

7. REFERENCES

[1] PISA Problem Solving Items and Scoring Guides, 2003.

[2] The PISA 2003 Assessment Framework. Technical report, Organisation for Economic Co-operation and Development, 2003.

[3] P. Azalov, S. Azaloff, and F. Zlatarova. Work in Progress - Comparing Assessment Tools in Computer Science Education: Empirical Analysis. *Proceedings of 34th ASEE/IEEE Frontiers in Education Conference, 20-23 October 2004*, 2:18–19, 2004.

[4] R. J. Barker and E. a. Unger. A predictor for success in an introductory programming class based upon abstract reasoning development. *ACM SIGCSE Bulletin*, 15(1):154–158, 1983.

[5] S. Bergin and R. Reilly. Predicting introductory programming performance: A multi-institutional multivariate study. *Computer Science Education*, 16(February 2015):303–323, 2006.

[6] J. A. Dossey, S. S. Mccrone, C. O. Sullivan, P. Gonzales, and M. Schneider. Problem Solving in the PISA and TIMSS 2003 Assessments. Technical report, 2007.

[7] R. J. Enbody, W. F. Punch, and M. McCullen. Python CS1 as preparation for C++ CS2. *Proceedings of the 40th ACM technical symposium on Computer science education - SIGCSE '09*, page 116, 2009.

[8] N. Frederiksen. Implications of Cognitive Theory for Instruction in Problem Solving. *Review of Educational Research*, 54(3):363–407, 1984.

[9] D. C. Gibbs. The effect of a constructivist learning environment for field-dependent/independent students on achievement in introductory computer programming. *ACM SIGCSE Bulletin*, 32(1):207–211, 2000.

[10] W. Kuechler and M. Simkin. How well do multiple choice tests evaluate student understanding in computer programming classes? *Journal of Information Systems Education*, 14(4):389–399, 2003.

[11] B. L. Kurtz. Investigating the relationship between the development of abstract reasoning and performance in an introductory programming class. *ACM SIGCSE Bulletin*, 12(1):110–117, 1980.

[12] M. C. Linn. Cognitive Consequences Instruction in Classrooms Programming The. *Educational Researcher*, 14(5):14–16,25–29, 1985.

[13] R. Lister, C. Fidge, and D. Teague. Further evidence of a relationship between explaining, tracing and writing skills in introductory programming. *ACM SIGCSE Bulletin*, 41(3):161, 2009.

[14] M. Lopez, J. Whalley, P. Robbins, and R. Lister. Relationships between reading, tracing and writing skills in introductory programming. *Proceeding of the fourth international workshop on Computing education research - ICER '08*, pages 101–112, 2008.

[15] R. E. Mayer, J. L. Dyck, and W. Vilberg. Learning to program and learning to think: what's the connection? *Communications of the ACM*, 29(7):605–610, 1986.

[16] D. Palumbo. Programming Language / Problem-Solving Research : A Review of Relevant Issues. *Review of Educational Research*, 60(1):65, 1990.

[17] A. Philpott, P. Robbins, and J. L. Whalley. Assessing the Steps on the Road to Relational Thinking. In *20th Annual Conference of the National Advisory Committee on Computing Qualifications, Nelson, New Zealand.*, page 286, 2007.

[18] L. Porter, D. Zingaro, and R. Lister. Predicting student success using fine grain clicker data. In *Proceedings of the tenth annual conference on International computing education research - ICER '14*, pages 51–58, 2014.

[19] W. M. Reed, D. B. Palumbo, A. L. Stolar, W. M. Reed, and D. B. Palumbo. The Comparative Effects of BASIC and Logo Instruction on Problem-Solving Skills. *Computers in the Schools*, 4(3-4):105–118, 1988.

[20] M. G. Simkin and W. L. Kuechler. Multiple-Choice Tests and Student Understanding: What Is the Connection? *Decision Sciences Journal of Innovative Education*, 3(1):73–98, 2005.

[21] A. Venables, G. Tan, and R. Lister. A Closer Look at Tracing, Explaining and Code Writing Skills in the Novice Programmer. In *Proceedings of the Fifth International Workshop on Computing Education Research Workshop - ICER '09*, pages 117–128, 2009.

[22] B. C. Wilson and S. Shrock. Contributing to success in an introductory computer science course: a study of twelve factors. *ACM SIGCSE Bulletin*, 33(1):184–188, 2001.

APPENDIX

A. PISA TEST ITEM EXAMPLE

Adapted from PISA Problem Solving Items and Scoring Guides available at http://nces.ed.gov/surveys/pisa/pdf/items2_solving.pdf [1]

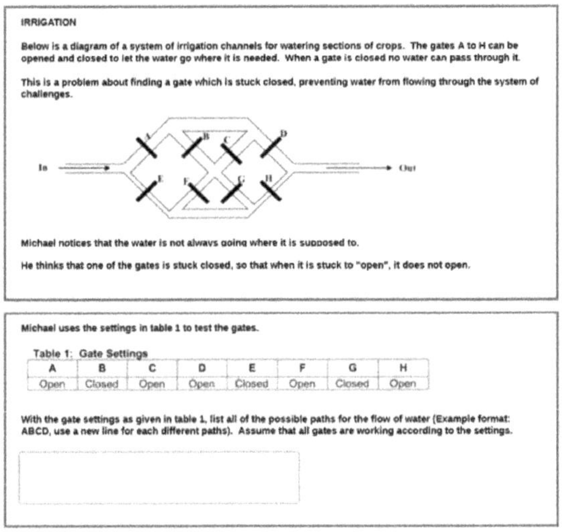

IRRIGATION

Below is a diagram of a system of irrigation channels for watering sections of crops. The gates A to H can be opened and closed to let the water go where it is needed. When a gate is closed no water can pass through it.

This is a problem about finding a gate which is stuck closed, preventing water from flowing through the system of challenges.

Michael notices that the water is not always going where it is supposed to.

He thinks that one of the gates is stuck closed, so that when it is stuck to "open", it does not open.

Michael uses the settings in table 1 to test the gates.

Table 1: Gate Settings

A	B	C	D	E	F	G	H
Open	Closed	Open	Open	Closed	Open	Closed	Open

With the gate settings as given in table 1, list all of the possible paths for the flow of water (Example format: ABCD, use a new line for each different paths). Assume that all gates are working according to the settings.

Figure 1: Troubleshooting Item: Irrigation (Question 1)

B. COURSE MATERIALS

Archive of programming assignment examples: http://www.cse.msu.edu/∼cse231/PracticeOfComputingUsingPython/

Archive of exam assignment examples: http://www.cse.msu.edu/ cse231/Exams/

Online CS1: Who Enrols, Why, and How Do They Do?

Diane Horton
Dept of Computer Science
University of Toronto
dianeh@cs.toronto.edu

Jennifer Campbell
Dept of Computer Science
University of Toronto
campbell@cs.toronto.edu

Michelle Craig
Dept of Computer Science
University of Toronto
mcraig@cs.toronto.edu

ABSTRACT

When students can choose to take a course online or face-to-face, who chooses each format? Why do students select one format instead of the other? We compare an online section of CS1 to a concurrent face-to-face section and find that the populations in the two sections are very different. In particular, students in the online section have less prior programming experience and are less likely to intend to major in computer science. We also examine the reasons why students choose their section, many of which relate to convenience, desire for interaction with others, and degree of familiarity with the course material. Finally, we compare course outcomes for the two sections. We find significant differences in drop rates, but not in final exam scores. We investigate whether the differences we find can be explained by differences in the populations who choose to take the course online vs face-to-face.

1. INTRODUCTION

Online learning has been around as long as the internet, but the term has been understood to mean different things at different times. Older studies often consider an online course to consist of the distribution of static slides or readings, perhaps accompanied by access to a community discussion board and email contact with course staff. Some online courses consist of synchronous activities such as video-conferenced lectures and live chat-room help sessions with course staff and perhaps other students. Currently, a wide variety of formats are being used to teach CS1 topics, including interactive coding platforms, online games, and puzzle design websites [7]. Some online materials are also being used in on-campus courses [2, 1].

Studies of online offerings of introductory computer science (CS1) are few. Preston and Wilson [10] replaced face-to-face lectures with pre-recorded video in one section of a large CS1 course, keeping all other activities (office hours, assignments, tests) the same. Students self-selected into what was dubbed the "lecture anytime" section. Face-to-face students perform marginally better, but no statistical tests of significance are reported.

In contrast, McDonald et al. [8] provide statistical analyses in a 3rd-year database course and find that face-to-face students perform better than online students in terms of course grade. Again, the online students are self-selected, but the researchers argue that the two populations in this study are not statistically significantly different in terms of incoming GPA, enrolled major, or number of credit hours completed.

Olson [9] attempts to control for the variations due to self-selection by inviting students to enlist in the study and indicate their desire to have an online experience, and then randomly assigning the applicants to the online section or a traditional (face-to-face) section. This provides three comparison groups: traditional (those not wanting online), experimental (those wanting online who got it), and control (those wanting online who got traditional). He finds no difference in completion rates among the three groups, but the control and experimental groups both scored lower on the weekly quizzes. Olson attributes this to the population difference between those who volunteered for the online section and those who did not, arguing that the students may have been selecting the online course because they were looking for an easy option. It is of note that Olson's course, while called CS1, does not include any programming.

In another controlled study, Korhonen et al. [6] randomly assigned students in a first-year data structures course either to complete algorithm simulation exercises online or in a classroom, or to complete more challenging design exercises in a classroom. Among the first two groups, who were given identical exercises, there was no difference in course completion rate or exam marks, but the students doing the online exercises were likely to drop the course earlier than those in the control group.

In this paper, we compare online and face-to-face offerings of CS1 in a context where students had a choice between the two formats. This differs from some of the related work in which students were randomly assigned to a format; those studies may not generalize to this context. Given that our institution, and possibly others, plans to continue to offer courses in both online and face-to-face formats, an investigation of the efficacy of this approach is warranted. We examine who it is that chooses online as opposed to face-to-face, why they make that choice, and what the outcomes are for students taking the course in each format.

SIGCSE '16, March 02-05, 2016, Memphis, TN, USA
 ISBN 978-1-4503-3685-7/16/03...$15.00
DOI: http://dx.doi.org/10.1145/2839509.2844578

2. METHODOLOGY

2.1 The Course

This study took place at the University of Toronto, a research-intensive North American public university. Our face-to-face CS1 course has been delivered in a flipped fashion since 2013, and has been discussed previously [1, 5, 4]. In fall 2014, the course was offered for the first time in an online format. At registration time, students chose either the online section or one of the four flipped sections, which were available at four time slots, each with its own instructor.

Students in the online and flipped sections experienced much of the course in the same way. Course content was delivered through videos for all students. They all completed the same out-of-class programming tasks — weekly exercises and three assignments — and wrote the same in-person final exam. (The final exam was the only element of the course that required online students to be present on campus.) All students had access to help through an online discussion board, online office hours, and traditional in-person office hours. The primary difference was that flipped students met face-to-face and completed exercises during lecture periods as described in [1], while the online students instead did analogous exercises asynchronously and online.

The online exercises were delivered through the PCRS system [11], which provided immediate feedback on the correctness of students' solutions. To parallel the just-in-time teaching that occurred in the flipped section, the online students had access to explanatory videos in which an instructor solved the exercises and addressed anticipated misconceptions. Neither the in-class exercises of the flipped students nor the online exercises of the online students counted as credit towards the course.

One additional difference between sections concerned the midterm. The flipped students wrote a traditional midterm on paper, while the online students completed their midterm online. Because of the limited question types supported by our Learning Management System (Blackboard), and the fact that the online students could not be monitored during the test, their midterm was worth only 5% of the course grade, as opposed to 14% for the flipped students. The remaining weight was added to the final exam, which was worth 59% rather than 50%.

2.2 The Study

We had a number of hypotheses and research questions about the population, participation, performance, and perception of students in the flipped and online sections. To address these, we conducted surveys in the first and final week of term (see Appendix A). Regardless of whether they gave informed consent to participate in our study, students who completed both the initial and final survey earned 1% towards their course grade. We also had access to students' GPA prior to taking the course (unless the students were in their first year and hence had no GPA), their GPA for the term, all course grades for the CS1 course, and the results of the university's standard course evaluations.

We set a p-value of 0.05 for statistical significance. We report exact values for p, to three decimal places, unless it is $< .0001$.

2.3 Populations

In total, 929 students consented to participate in our study: 170 in the online section and 759 in the flipped section. Of those, 105 (62%) and 553 (73%) completed both the initial and final surveys.

Although students chose their section, and hence chose an online or flipped format, some could not get the section they wanted due to enrolment pressures. With this in mind, on the initial survey question that asked why they chose online or flipped, we included an answer option for students who preferred the other section but were unable to enrol in it. 31.6% of online students wanted to enrol in flipped and 1.5% of flipped students wanted online. In Section 3.1, where we examine who chooses each format, our analyses omit students who were unable to enrol in the format of their choice. Elsewhere, these students are included.

3. RESULTS AND DISCUSSION

3.1 Who Chooses Online vs Flipped?

Here, we examine the populations who chose to enrol in the online and flipped sections. Knowing who the online section is serving helps in planning how often to offer the online section and whether to tailor it to a certain type of student. It is also important to know how similar the populations are when we compare course outcomes for the two sections (see Section 3.4).

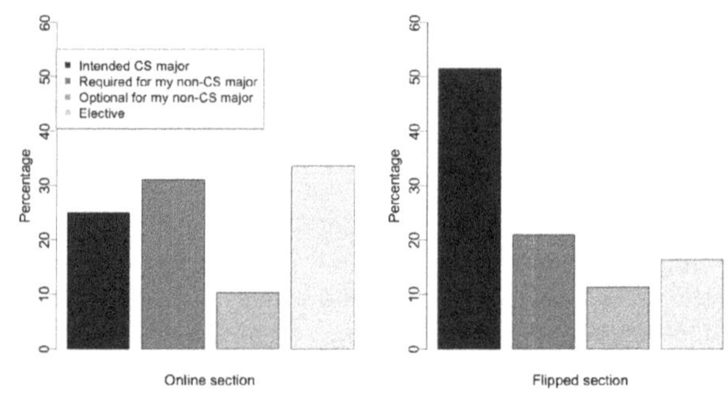

Figure 1: Percentage of students who cited each reason for taking CS1.

Reason for taking CS1

Figure 1 shows, for each section, the reasons why students took CS1 in terms of the role that it played in their university studies. A Pearson's Chi-squared test confirms that these proportions are significantly different ($\chi^2 = 35.3872$, df= 3, $p < 0.0001$). Intended CS majors constituted a much lower proportion of the online section than the flipped section. The online section had a higher constituency of students required to take the course for another major, or taking the course purely as an elective.

The vast majority of students intending to major in CS preferred to enrol in the flipped section. Of those who were able to enrol in their preferred section, only 7% of intended CS majors chose online.

Prior programming experience

Students self-reported their prior programming experience on a scale of 1 (no experience) to 5 (a lot of experience).

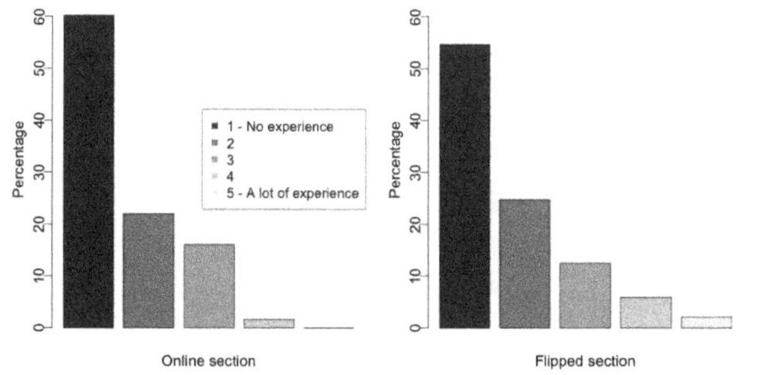

Figure 2: Degree of prior programming experience.

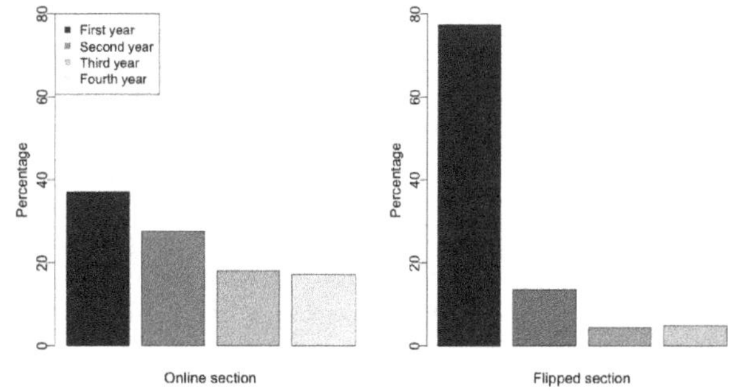

Figure 3: Year of study.

Although the majority of students in both the online and flipped sections had never programmed before (Figure 2), students in the flipped section had more experience (online μ =1.59, flipped μ = 1.76). A Welch Two-sample T-test comparing the means of the two distributions finds the difference to be significant ($p = 0.049$).

Prior GPA

McDonald et al. [8] use incoming GPA to compare their study populations. Because many of the students in our course were in their first term of university, only some in each section had a GPA prior to taking CS1. The average incoming GPA among the 86 online students who had one was 2.43; the average among the 266 flipped students with an incoming GPA was 2.36. A Welch Two-sample T-test finds no statistical difference in these values ($p = 0.508$).

Retakers

Some of the students in the course were previously enrolled in CS1 (retakers). They may have dropped the course before or are repeating it to raise their grade. We hypothesized that retakers would be more likely to enrol in the online section than students who are taking the course for the first time. They may feel they don't need to attend every lecture again, or may be embarrassed about having to retake the course. Our hypothesis was supported by the data. We found that 13.5% of the students enrolling in online were retaking the course while only 6.5% of those who enrolled in flipped were retakers. The difference is significant ($\chi^2 = 6.3864$, df= 1, $p = 0.012$).

Course load

The online section had more part-time students (22%) than the flipped section (13%). A Pearson's Chi-squared test shows that this difference is significant ($\chi^2 = 6.3873$, df= 1, $p = 0.011$).

Year of study

Although it is a first-year course, our CS1 is taken by many students in their second, third, or fourth year of university (see Figure 3). We hypothesized that students who are not in first year would be more likely to enrol in the online section than first-year students, resulting in a lower fraction of first-year students in the online section than the flipped section. The data support this hypothesis: The online section had 37% first-year students while the flipped section had 77%, and a Pearson's Chi-squared test shows that the difference is significant ($\chi^2 = 77.8344$, df= 1, $p < 0.0001$).

Gender

The online section had a slightly higher percentage of female students (47.5%) than the flipped section (42%).

3.2 Why Choose Online vs Flipped?

Table 1 shows the reasons students gave for choosing the online or the flipped section. Unsurprisingly, the most common reason was that the student either preferred to attend or not to attend lectures. Very few said they chose online because they preferred not to interact with their instructor or their classmates face-to-face. In contrast, the majority of flipped students cited a preference for face-to-face interaction with their instructor and with their classmates. We wondered whether some would choose online because they had a very strong background and thought they could perhaps save some time in the online section. However, nearly as many online students said that having very *little* background was a reason for choosing online. In the flipped section, approximately a third of the class chose flipped because they had little background, but very few chose it because they had strong background.

Among the other reasons given for enrolling in the online section, the vast majority concerned conflicts in their timetable or outside commitments, and flexibility in scheduling course activities. A few appreciated the ability to work at home and avoid commuting. For the flipped students, some were simply unaware of the online section, while others expressed uncertainty about what the online section would be like or their ability to self-regulate their learning behaviour in an online course.

3.3 How Satisfied Are Students?

We compare the results of the university-run course evaluations for the online and flipped sections. Our university administration values two measures in particular: the "institutional composite mean", a mean of five questions (each with scales from 1 to 5), and the question *Overall, the quality of my learning experience in this course was...* on a scale of 1 (Poor) to 5 (Excellent). Table 2 shows these scores. The course overall was well-received; evaluation scores on these two key measures were above the departmental average in every section. More importantly, scores for the online section were on par with the flipped sections. One notable

Reasons for enrolling in the online or flipped section	Online n	Online %	Flipped n	Flipped %
No space in other section.	52	30.6%	11	1.5%
Prefer not to attend lectures.	59	34.7%	-	-
Prefer to attend lectures.	-	-	582	76.6%
Prefer not to interact with my instructor face-to-face.	4	2.4%	-	-
Prefer to interact with my instructor face-to-face.	-	-	473	62.2%
Prefer not to interact with my classmates face-to-face.	8	4.7%	-	-
Prefer to interact with my classmates face-to-face.	-	-	393	51.7%
I think the online section will be less work.	7	4.1%	-	-
I think the on-campus section will be less work.	-	-	21	2.8%
I think the online section will be more work.	2	1.2%	-	-
I think the on-campus section will be more work.	-	-	31	4.1%
I already know quite a bit of the course material.	14	8.2%	29	3.8%
I know very little of the course material.	11	6.5%	257	33.8%
None of these apply.	16	9.4%	10	1.3%
Other (summarized in Section 3.2)				

Table 1: Reasons for enrolling in the online or the flipped section. Students could choose all responses that applied.

Section	Institutional Composite Mean	Quality of Learning Experience	Response Rate
Online	4.2	3.9	30% (n=49)
Flipped A	4.2	3.9	44% (n=88)
Flipped B	4.2	3.8	47% (n=81)
Flipped C	4.2	3.9	41% (n=79)
Flipped D	4.0	3.7	41% (n=83)
Dept. Avg.	3.9	3.5	N/A

Table 2: Course evaluation results.

		Section: Online	Section: Flipped
Everyone	n	170	756
	Drop	55 (32%)	132 (18%)
	Fail	18 (11%)	59 (8%)
	Pass	97 (57%)	565 (75%)
Completers	n	115	624
	Pass	97 (84%)	565 (91%)

Table 3: Outcomes (drop, fail, or pass) for online and flipped sections, and pass rate among students who did not drop the course ("completers").

difference between online and flipped is that the response rate for the online section is lower.

Our final survey for the study included a question about how well students had enjoyed the course relative to their other courses. Students in both sections gave very similar responses. With the categories "much less" to "much more" mapped to values 1 to 5, the means were 3.7 for online and 3.8 for flipped. We also asked students which course section they would enrol in if they could start over. Though students' enjoyment of the course was comparable across sections, a smaller proportion (65%) of online students than flipped students (78%) said that they would choose the same section again.

3.4 Course Outcomes

Successful completion

Each student who registers for the course either drops the course, or completes the course with either a failing or passing grade. Table 3 shows, for each section, the number and percentage of students with each of these outcomes.

The drop rate is nearly twice as high in the online section as in the flipped section, and the difference is highly significant ($\chi^2 = 18.1873$, df$= 1$, $p < 0.0001$). This is consistent with the results from [6]. However, Korhonen et al. ran a true experiment, where students were randomly assigned to treatment groups. In our case, students self-selected online or flipped sections, so any differences in course outcomes could be due to differences in the populations. Prior programming experience is a predictor of course outcomes [3], and as noted above, students in the online section had less prior experience than flipped students. In addition, compared to the online section, the flipped section had more students who intended to major in CS or required CS1 for another major. Because they need the course, they may be less inclined to drop it. To investigate how much of the difference in drop rates is due to the different populations, we ran a nested regression with whether or not a student dropped the course as the outcome, and using why they took CS1, their prior programming experience, and their section as the predictor variables. The ANOVA table is in Table 4 and the regression model is shown in Table 5. We see that the format of the section (online or flipped) was still a significant predictor ($p = 0.026$) even once the dropping behaviour had been modelled by the other predictors. In other words, students are more likely to drop out of the online section, even once we control for these other factors.

The pass rate was also lower in the online section (Table 3) than in the flipped section. However, much of the difference in pass rates is accounted for by the fact that many fewer students completed the course in the online section. When

	Resid. Df	Resid. Dev	Df	Deviance	Pr(>Chi)
1	914	856.48			
2	913	833.92	1	22.56	0.0000
3	912	828.97	1	4.95	0.0261

Table 4: Effect of role, prior experience and format on dropping

Dropping modeled by role and section	
(Intercept)	$-1.23\ (0.26)^*$
role.elective	$1.23\ (0.23)^*$
role.option	$0.65\ (0.30)^*$
role.required	$0.69\ (0.23)^*$
prior.exp	$-0.54\ (0.12)^*$
format.online	$0.46\ (0.21)^*$
Num. obs.	918
R^2	0.088

$^*p < 0.05$

Table 5: Statistical model: Dropping behaviour

we consider the pass rate among completers of the course, the difference is much smaller: 84% in the online section compared to 91% in the flipped section. This does not meet our bar for statistical significance (Pearson's Chi-squared test, $p = 0.067$).

We have seen that the drop rate is much higher in the online section than in the flipped section. Students in the online section also drop the course earlier than flipped students (see Figure 4[1]).

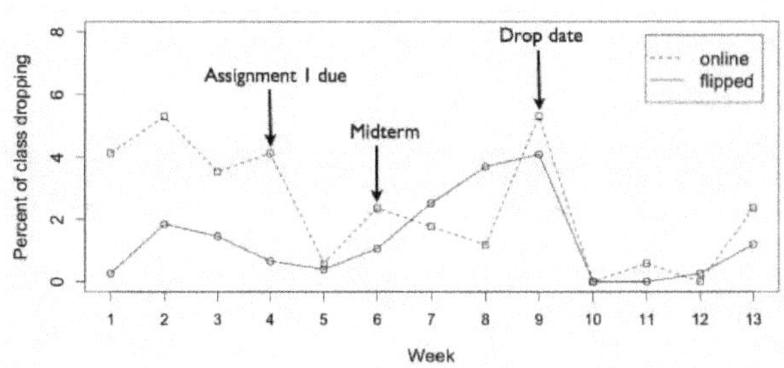

Figure 4: Percentage of the class that drops the course each week of term. Percentages are based on enrolment at the start of term.

Learning

We hypothesized that learning, as measured by final exam grades, would not be significantly different in online than in flipped. The data supports our hypothesis. Students in the online section did not perform as well (exam averages were 65.8% for online section and 69.1% for flipped), however, a Welch Two-sample T-test does not meet our bar for statistical significance ($p = 0.088$).

Although the difference in exam scores was not significant, we are still interested in knowing to what degree course format, as opposed to other factors, influences these scores. Other researchers in related but not identical contexts [8] found the most significant predictor of exam grades in the course under study to be the incoming GPA of the students. Since most of our students are in their first semester, they do not have a GPA prior to the study. As an alternative to incoming GPA, we use the GPA for courses other than CS1 that the student completed in the semester of the study. This "semester GPA" (or SGPA) is an operational definition for the strength of a student in this particular semester. It could be a better predictor of exam grades than incoming GPA because it is likely influenced not only by scholarly ability but also by any global factors that were influencing the student's academic performance at the time of the study, such as work commitments or personal issues. One threat to validity of using SGPA as a measure of a student's strength in that semester is that the student's positive (or negative) experience in CS1 may have had a spill-over effect onto performance in other courses taken concurrently.

We find that SGPA is lower for online students (online: 2.57, flipped: 2.91) and that the difference is significant (Welch Two-sample T-test, $p = 0.008$). Unsurprisingly, we also find SGPA to be highly correlated to final exam grade (Pearson's product-moment correlation $p < 0.0001$, $r = 0.62$). We perform a linear regression of exam grades modelled by section (and hence format) and SGPA for the 649 students for whom we have complete data (an exam mark and an SGPA). Table 6 contains the resulting model; the corresponding ANOVA table is in Table 7. We see the expected significant relationship between SGPA and grades, and no interaction between SGPA and format. When we add format to the model containing only SGPA, the p-value is 0.86, suggesting that there is no significant relationship between format and grades. However, it is important to remember that this categorical variable (format) is observed and not assigned; instead of a true experiment where participants were assigned to either the online or flipped section, participants in this study self-selected their section. As a result, it is not possible to truly disentangle the effects of the online delivery itself from the types of students who select online.

Grades modeled by section and SGPA	
(Intercept)	$24.99\ (1.32)^*$
format.online	3.34 (2.96)
SGPA	$8.00\ (0.42)^*$
format.online:SGPA	-1.32 (1.02)
Num. obs.	649
R^2 .088	0.39

$^*p < 0.05$

Table 6: Statistical model: Grades

	Res.Df	RSS	Df	Sum of Sq	F	Pr(>F)
1	647	66614.85				
2	646	66611.57	1	3.28	0.03	0.8584

Table 7: Effect of SGPA and Format on Grades.

In summary, we have seen that the difference in exam grades between the online and flipped sections is not signifi-

[1]The drop figures shown for week 13 include students who dropped during the final exam period.

cant. Furthermore, with the caveat noted above, it appears that what difference does exist is explained by differences in SGPA between the two sections, rather than by course format.

4. SUMMARY AND FUTURE WORK

We observed large differences in the population of students who chose to take CS1 online rather than in our face-to-face flipped format. Students who completed the online CS1 liked the course, giving it course evaluation scores comparable to the flipped section and above departmental averages. Students who completed the course also earned final exam grades that were not significantly different between the online and flipped sections. However, many online students did not make it to the course evaluation and final exam stage: the drop rate was significantly higher in the online section, even when we controlled for important differences between the online and flipped populations. We are doing two things to address this issue. First, we are looking more closely at who drops the course, with particular attention to the role of skills for self-regulated learning. We are investigating whether strong self-regulated learning skills predict good outcomes, and whether this is true to a greater degree in the online section. We saw earlier that students themselves expressed concern about lacking these skills sufficiently to succeed online. Second, we are implementing measures for the coming year intended to reduce the drop rate in the online format. These measures aim to foster a greater sense of community, and to give students a better awareness of their standing in the course so that they know when they have fallen behind and have an opportunity to recover.

5. ACKNOWLEDGMENTS

The development of the online course was funded by the Ontario Ministry of Training, Colleges and Universities. We thank Daniel Zingaro for assistance with the statistical analyses.

6. REFERENCES

[1] J. Campbell, D. Horton, M. Craig, and P. Gries. Evaluating an inverted CS1. In *Proceeding of the 45th ACM Technical Symposium on Computer Science Education*, SIGCSE '14, pages 307–312, 2014.

[2] P. Carter. An experience report: On the use of multimedia pre-instruction and just-in-time teaching in a cs1 course. In *Proceedings of the 43rd ACM Technical Symposium on Computer Science Education*, SIGCSE '12, pages 361–366, 2012.

[3] D. Hagan and S. Markham. Does it help to have some programming experience before beginning a computing degree program? *SIGCSE Bulletin*, 32:25–28, 2000.

[4] D. Horton and M. Craig. Drop, fail, pass, continue: Persistence in cs1 and beyond in traditional and inverted delivery. In *Proceedings of the 46th ACM Technical Symposium on Computer Science Education*, SIGCSE '15, pages 235–240, 2015.

[5] D. Horton, M. Craig, J. Campbell, P. Gries, and D. Zingaro. Comparing outcomes in inverted and traditional cs1. In *Proceedings of the 2014 Conference on Innovation & Technology in Computer Science Education*, ITiCSE '14, pages 261–266, 2014.

[6] A. Korhonen, L. Malmi, P. Myllyselkä, and P. Scheinin. Does it make a difference if students exercise on the web or in the classroom? In *Proceedings of the 7th Annual Conference on Innovation and Technology in Computer Science Education*, ITiCSE '02, pages 121–124, 2002.

[7] M. J. Lee and A. J. Ko. Comparing the effectiveness of online learning approaches on cs1 learning outcomes. In *Proceedings of the Eleventh Annual International Conference on International Computing Education Research*, ICER '15, pages 237–246, 2015.

[8] M. McDonald, B. Dorn, and G. McDonald. A statistical analysis of student performance in online computer science courses. In *Proceedings of the 35th SIGCSE Technical Symposium on Computer Science Education*, SIGCSE '04, pages 71–74, 2004.

[9] D. Olson. A comparison of online and lecture methods for delivering the cs 1 course. *J. Comput. Sci. Coll.*, 18(2):57–63, Dec. 2002.

[10] J. A. Preston and L. Wilson. Offering cs1 on-line reducing campus resource demand while improving the learning environment. In *Proceedings of the Thirty-second SIGCSE Technical Symposium on Computer Science Education*, SIGCSE '01, pages 342–346, 2001.

[11] D. Zingaro, Y. Cherenkova, O. Karpova, and A. Petersen. Facilitating code-writing in PI classes. In *Proceeding of the 44th ACM Technical Symposium on Computer Science Education*, SIGCSE '13, pages 585–590, 2013.

Appendix A: Surveys

The survey questions that we discuss in this paper are included below. All questions also had the option "Prefer not to answer."

Initial Survey

- *Why are you taking csc108? Note: By "program" we mean specialist, major, or minor.* (a) I am pursuing or considering a program in computer science. (b) I am pursuing or considering a program in a subject other than computer science for which CSC108 is required. (c) I am pursuing or considering a program that includes CSC108 in a list of options that count towards my degree requirements. (d) I am not pursing or considering any program that requires CSC108, but I am taking it as an elective.
- *Many CSC108 students have no prior programming experience, while others have some. Rate the amount of prior programming experience that you have.* Scale: no experience (1) to a lot of experience (5).
- *How many full credits do you have at UofT already (including any transfer credits from another school)?* (a) fewer than 5.5 (first year) (b) 5.5 to 10.0 (second year) (c) 10.5 to 15.0 (third year) (d) more than 15.0 (fourth year)
- *What is your gender?* (a) Female (b) Male (c) Other
- *In a past semester, have you ever enrolled in CSC108?* (a) Yes, I took CSC108 before and dropped it. (b) Yes, I took CSC108 before and failed it. (c) Yes, I took CSC108 before and passed it. (d) No, I have not taken CSC108 before.
- *Why did you enrol in the on-campus/online section? Check all that apply.* See Table 1 for the options.

Final survey

- *How much did you enjoy this course compared to other university courses you have taken?* Scale from 1 (much less) to 5 (much more)
- *If you could start over, which section would you choose to enrol in?* (a) on-campus (b) online

Just-In-Time Learning for the Just Google It Era

Elizabeth Boese
University of Colorado - Boulder

Elizabeth.Boese@colorado.edu

ABSTRACT
Computer Science education has to change - the students are demanding a new paradigm in this Just Google It era [3][8]. This paper discusses what Just in Time Learning is, how it is more effective than the traditional educational process, and how to change education to embrace the Internet through incorporating the Just-In-Time Learning model. There are five parts to incorporating the Just-In-Time Learning model: one – recognizing that the textbook is dead, as students Just Google It, two – help students learn how to vet the information they find online, three – incorporate real-world problems and support creative student ideas, four – modify the classroom to include an active-learning environment to fully support Just-In-Time Learning, and five – the role of the teacher is now as a tutor, helping students learn and learn how to learn. By incorporating these five parts of the Just-In-Time Learning model, there is no longer the concept of cheating, and students are learning the core necessary skills: problem-solving, critical thinking, good decision making, self-learning, and effective communication.

Categories and Subject Descriptors
K.3.2 [**Computers and Education**]: Computer and Information Science Education – *computer science education, information systems education, curriculum.*

Keywords
Computer Science Education, Just-In-Time Learning Model, Just-In-Case Learning Model, Just Google It, Active-Learning, Flipped Classroom.

1. INTRODUCTION
Traditionally students learn through the Just-In-Case Learning model, learning everything up front in the hopes that they will need it and actually remember it later. However, this is not very effective for retention [7] and lacks the critical motivation for students – the answer to the question, "Why learn this?" [21]

With the Internet has come rampant cheating. Current and old assignments and their solutions are posted online. Sometimes these are for sharing in what would be considered 'cheating', but many times students are making use of online discussion boards to get help with their programs from experts in the community (the median response time on StackOverflow is only 21 minutes). Either way, the solutions are available on the Internet and students find and submit them as their assignments. There are also many websites that offer to do a student's assignment for a mere ten dollars! Essentially we have lost the war on cheating.

Why shouldn't the students copy off the Internet? These students grew up on the Internet, where search has always been a part of their daily lives. It is also how we do it at work every day, because it is an efficient way to find ideas and solutions as well as get help on problems. We can change the educational model to encourage students to search the Internet, by having problems for them to work on that are not already available online and make use of the Internet in effective ways to help students learn.

The goal of a computer science education is to help students learn how to: think critically and creatively, solve problems, make good decisions, apply concepts in new contexts, learn how to be a self-learner, and communicate effectively. None of these are focused on memorization and regurgitation. By focusing on the goal of a computer science education, the vision of what we want students to walk away with when they graduate, we can make better decisions about computer science curricula. The remainder of this paper discusses the Just-in-Time Learning model and five ways to incorporate Just-in-Time Learning to improve student retention and understanding.

2. JUST-IN-TIME LEARNING MODEL
Just-in-Time Learning Model is when students move away from reading the full background on a topic, and instead focus on just the research they need to answer a question or solve a problem. This technique is more motivational as students have a focal point for their research. A Just-in-time model answers the critical motivation question – the "Why?" question. Why learn this? Now students would have a reason for learning – because it is to answer this question or solve this problem.

There are five parts to incorporating the Just-in-Time Learning Model: one – recognizing that the textbook is dead, as students follow the Just Google It methodology, two – help students learn how to vet the information they find online, three – incorporate real-world problems and support creative student ideas, four – modify the classroom to include an active-learning environment to fully support Just-In-Time Learning, and five – the role of the teacher is now as a tutor, helping students learn and learn how to learn.

2.1 Part 1: The Textbook is Dead
"Reading programming textbooks is an incredibly boring and soul-crushing experience."
-Student in Object-Oriented Analysis & Design course

The textbook is dead. And I'm saying that as a textbook author! Students no longer read sequentially through a four hundred-page textbook. Most students don't even buy the books anymore! Even when the book costs as little as $35, and a version of it is available

SIGCSE'16, March 2–5, 2016, Memphis, TN, USA.

ACM 978-1-4503-3685-7/16/03…$15.00.
DOI: http://dx.doi.org/10.1145/2839509.2844583

Table 1. Do students read the readings?

Course	YES	NO	I don't use or have the book	Yes, it helps a lot	Yes, it helps a little	No, it doesn't match the lecture	No, the topics are too hard	No, it's too confusing	No, other reasons	No. Responses	% Responding
CS1	36%	24%	40%	28%	8%	8%	1%	6%	9%	311	82%
Methods & Tools	16%	23%	65%	1%	15%	8%	3%	1%	11%	105	89%
OO Analysis & Design	12%	64%	24%	-	-	-	-	-	-	79	75%

online for free, students still do not want to read it (4% read all of it, 18% read some of it). This is the Just Google It era, and that is what students are doing.

A Senior in Object-Oriented Design & Analysis course gave this feedback concerning textbooks, *"Reading programming textbooks is an incredibly boring and soul-crushing experience. I find it far more pleasant AND easy to learn in a format where I can learn the basics of the topic via lecture slides or something similar, then deepen my knowledge and understanding of the material by doing exercises on it."* Another student in the course said, *"Never have I had to read for a CS class. And I am learning how to program well here at the University of Colorado. There is not a dependency between reading a book and OOD knowledge. Let us learn the way we want without reading and just keep teaching. We learn well from time in class."*

Most flipped or inverted classrooms will still require students to read the book and enforce this by having them take a quiz on the material either before class or in the beginning of class [1]. These have been used successfully in a variety of computer science courses ranging from CS1 [4] to a systems course [5] and more. However, most of these implementations are still set up to support the Just-in-Case Learning model, forcing students to read the material in the hopes that they will then need what they read on the quiz.

The quiz concept could work as a Just-in-Time Learning method if the quiz questions are available to students *as they read the material*, not *after* they read the material. If students have access to the questions before reading, most will probably Just Google It to find the answers (or use search within the online reading material) and still may not read the full text *unless you design your quiz questions in such a way to force full coverage of the material.*

Instead of fighting to make students read the book, we should embrace the Internet into education and support the Just Google It methodology that students are doing. If we design our courses to optimize learning knowing that students Just Google It, then we can maintain control over ensuring students still gain the full understanding and context of the content we expect them to learn.

One of the problems with the Just Google It method is that students may be only gaining a superficial understanding of the material. This became really apparent when I opened up the exams in a Software Engineering Methods & Tools course to be done online, with 40 minutes to answer 20 questions (2 minutes per question) during class time. Students admitted after the exam that 65% of them had not studied at all since the exam was open-Google, open-note. But that is a problem, because it takes time to *learn* it. The idea of an open-Google exam is to help you recall the fine details or exact wording/structure/etc., but it does not work to try to learn the material during the exam! Students also tried to argue for partial credit, but when they simply copy-pasted from the Internet and did not even try to apply it to what the question was asking then I refused. This is another important aspect of grading when students have access to Google and their notes. It is no longer enough to be able to regurgitate the formula or some information; the questions need to pose critical thinking and application to a particular context and be graded as such.

2.2 Part 2: Loss of Context

When we Just Google It for our information, we lose context. The concern of many instructors is the superficial level of understanding that students get when they Just Google It for their information, and grab the sentence they find but do not read the greater context in which it belongs. An example of this problem is a study in communications that has been misquoted extensively for years in online sites and published books. In Mehrabian's work in communication, he found that 7% is communicated through the words that are said, 38% through the tone of your voice, and 55% through general body language [15]. However, if you read the paper more closely, this only applies when talking about attitudes or feelings – it does not transfer to other types of communication such as business meetings or scientific discussions. Yet tons of business websites and published books site these results for *all* communication.

Context of information is becoming just as important as the information itself. We need to help students learn how to vet the material they find online. We can do this by having them go to multiple websites to find the most reputable ones, and read the comments on articles and blogs to learn about errors in the post and different opinions on the solution. A nice side effect of vetting the information is that they really learn the material by seeing it presented in multiple ways.

This effects our assignments and assessments when we allow students to access the Internet for answers. In the Software Engineering Methods & Tools course, we allowed open-Internet on three mid-term exams set up to last only forty minutes. Students found random websites with odd wordings and mis-interpretations that they used to argue for credit for their wrong answer. This is related to two problems – finding the answer without looking at the context as well as some of the references were either out-right wrong or simply someone's opinion. To fix this, our policy for all open-Google assignments and assessments is that only readings and material from the course (vetted by the course staff) can be referenced when defending their answers in the case they get marked wrong. But this still highlights the huge problem of the need to vet information found on the Internet as correct and separate fact from opinion, especially when students rely on Just Google It for their information.

2.3 Part 3: Real Problems to Work On

One of the problems of cheating is that everyone is working on the same 'toy' problems and the answers are on the Internet. This is not as motivational for students, when they could be working on real-world problems from industry or their own creative ideas.

A better way to engage students is to have them work on real problems that will be used by others, or students' own creative ideas. This has been proven to get students more engaged [6][14]. There are three ways to bring in real-world problems: the first is to have students work on actual problems that industry is working on, the second is to support students' creative ideas, and the third is to design context-rich problems for students. All of these problem types are motivational for students and help engage the students.

2.3.1 *Industry Problems*

We are fortunate in computer science to have multiple options to enable students to work on real-world industry problems. Students can get involved with real-world problems in a variety of ways:

- Contribute to open-source software, including ones such as the Humanitarian Free and Open Source Software project, known as HFOSS (http://hfoss.org) which have projects such as helping Rwanda monitor the spread of disease and programs to assist victims of an earthquake,
- Refactor or extend freely available software code bases,
- Recruit local companies to provide a semester long or year long project (e.g., Senior capstone course),
- Download a data set and create an application that uses or displays the information (e.g., Go Code Colorado http://gocode.colorado.gov/),
- Participate in a coding contest (e.g., Google's Code Jam https://code.google.com/codejam, HP's High School contest http://www.hpcodewars.org/)
- Start their own business.

Students also gain valuable experience working with experts in the field. They have access to ask questions and learn much more beyond the scope of the course. These experts can be much more helpful than the instructor in a classroom who may or may not have experience in a student's chosen project. This also gives students practice asking questions and communicating with the community, a valuable skill for the workplace.

2.3.2 *Creative Student Ideas*

Students become very invested and engaged when working on their own creative ideas [18]. Industry also has been embracing this idea, with many companies and education research referencing Google's 20% time as a successful example [20].

In our introduction to programming course for non-majors, students had projects at the end of the semester that included requirements such as using a loop, at least three conditional statements, a graphical interface, etc. Example projects include a full 2-player board game, an outfit mixer that rotates through pictures of her with various tops and bottoms, a super hero creator, and a Jeopardy game. These students typically reported working well over one hundred hours on their projects – well beyond anything we would ever ask or expect from them! They became so engaged in making their ideas work that they invested the time into learning how to make it happen. Seniors who were computer science majors were jealous of what these freshmen non-majors produced!

2.3.3 *Context-Rich Problems*

We can write problems for students in such a way as to aid in knowledge transfer through designing the problem with context [10][11][18][19]. Traditionally many computer science courses may have an assignment such as, "Write a program that takes in a data file of numbers and store the values into an array and calculate the average by using a loop through the array." By transforming these problems into context it gives students motivation and an example of its application. This approach was successfully used across four universities [2] and examples of creative assignments available at Nifty Assignments hosted at Stanford (http://nifty.standford.edu).

For example, we have incorporated a breadth of fields into the assignments in CS1. Assignments include implementing football statistics for simple calculations, a dungeon maze game for conditionals, political science voting program for manipulating files, DNA analysis using actual DNA data files to predict susceptibility for Type-2 Diabetes, encryption and decryption of messages for functions, an artificial intelligence ELIZA program using arrays, and a mini-Netflix challenge using classes. For each assignment we get students asking how to learn more about that application of computer science, and we direct students to the appropriate professor or university department where they could look into options for a major or minor relating programming to another field. This works extremely well in CS1 as we have students across all the majors and undecided majors taking our introductory course on programming, and this gives them ideas of how it applies across various disciplines.

2.3.4 *Personalized Learning*

Through the use of students working on unique problems we can direct learning on a personalized level. Hulleman adds to the idea of connecting what they are learning to their own personal lives, "A more effective approach is to 'encourage students to generate their own connections and discover for themselves the relevance of course material to their lives.' " [13] Personalized attention is becoming an important part of the brick-and-mortar school as a distinction from the anonymity of MOOCs [14]. The personalized attention is also helpful for recruitment and retention [9].

The biggest concern for personalized attention is usually on how to handle grading, especially as course enrollments scale up. Work done at the University of Colorado – Boulder was able to perform fifteen-minute one-on-one grading interviews for assignments in CS1 with loads of over seven hundred students in a semester [9]. This enables students to be working on their own projects and still be feasible to grade.

2.4 Part 4: Classroom Time is Not a Lecture

"Lecturing is that mysterious process by means of which the contents of the note-book of the professor are transferred through the instrument of the fountain pen to the note-book of the student without passing through the mind of either." -Edwin Slosson

The traditional 'lecture' is dying too, because any one-way conversation about a topic, which is essentially what the word 'lecture' means, can be recorded as a video and put online. Classroom time needs to hold more value for students these days. Just as students do not want to sit around and read through a four hundred-page textbook, they also do not want to sit through a one-way lecture about a topic either. Both of these modes of learning follow the traditional Just-In-Case Learning model, which lacks motivation to go through and is proven to provide minimal retention [16].

While lecture can still be a portion of class time in a hybrid model, the focus of class time should be on the value provided in this communal face-to-face environment. The physical act of being in the classroom together provides an opportunity for authentic connections and a raw, collective experience. Highly successful class time could have students saying, "*I could not have had that experience if I did not go to class.*"

Class time can still be designed in a variety of different formats. Active Learning is proven to be successful [1] [17]. Example options for active-learning include: clicker questions, in-class quizzes (group or individual), cooperative problem-based and Process Oriented Guided Inquiry Learning [17] [12], student-built wiki, and discussions. Many flipped classrooms require videos or readings before class with an auto-graded quiz to be done before class or clicker questions in the first few minutes of class; this gives the instructor a quick analysis of any confusion points for students and can address them during lecture, and follow-up with group exercises in class for an active-learning environment.

"It is not realistic to expect us to read ahead of time, when there is a chance you will cover the material, we read afterwards if it was confusing since that is more efficient."
– Student in Object-Oriented Analysis & Design

Many have found students prefer a hybrid class with a mini-lecture and active-learning exercises. The mini-lecture goes over the material *quickly* to point out confusing or important parts, provides a chance to review the material, and an opportunity for students to ask questions about the material. Table 2 shows the student responses to how they like the active-learning exercises in addition to a shortened lecture (over 90% of students across all courses wanted at least some lecture during class time, so the table is based on having at least some lecture as part of class). CS1 has 3 classes and one recitation per week, Methods & Tools has 2 classes and one 2-hour lab, and Object-Oriented Analysis & Design has only 3 classes per week. The Methods & Tools course is a bit different than other courses because we cover over 20 distinct topics ranging from regex to git to REST APIs to SQL to Intellectual Property. Due to the non-building-upon format of the course content and therefore the constant introduction of distinct methods and tools, the use of a more traditional lecture is desired by a lot of students over additional exercises in class since they already have a lab each week for such exercises.

Some courses implement the Just-in-Time Learning model by cancelling one or two lectures per week to allow time for students to learn through the readings. But this defeats the purpose of the brick-and-mortar schools that students chose over online courses, which is supposed to provide a rich community environment of face-time with the instructor and their peers. It is essential to maintain the face-time with the students, and find ways to provide value during this class time.

Table 2. How students like active-learning exercises [in addition to a mini-lecture] during class time
[CS1 and Methods & Tools have a lab in addition to lecture, OOAD has only a lecture]

Course	Helpful	Not Helpful	Don't Attend Class	# Responses
CS1	95%	5%	-	311
Methods & Tools	59%*	37%	4%	200
OO Analysis & Design	87%	8%	5%	121

The Methods & Tools course question was worded as: Easier to just have a lecture on it and practice in the labs vs. Practice in lecture is also helpful when the topic works for it [or I don't go to lecture].

2.5 Part 5: Teachers are Tutors

"You can't teach people everything they need to know. The best you can do is to position them where they can find what they need to know when they need to know it."
– Professor Seymour Papert, MIT

With lectures, textbooks, and many websites available online, students are able to learn through a variety of methods outside of class time. Class time spent as a lecture is no longer considered valuable use of this quality time together. Teachers are no longer lecturers imparting their wise knowledge about a topic. That's the Internet's job, to be the disseminator of information. The role of the teacher is now that of a tutor, guide, or facilitator helping students learn, and learn how to learn. It is our job as tutors to help inspire students to be tomorrow's leaders.

3. NO MORE CHEATING!

By incorporating these five parts of the Just-in-Time Learning model into computer science education, there is no longer the concept of cheating. If students are working on unique problems from industry or their own creative ideas, allowed to Just Google It, and encouraged to collaborate with their peers and online communities – then how can they "cheat"?

4. INTRODUCING STUDENTS TO JUST-IN-TIME LEARNING MODEL

The best practice to introduce a new way of learning into courses is to do so from the beginning of the course. There is less disruption of changing how things work mid-semester, which can cause confusion for students. It has also been found that being up-front on the first day about how the course is organized can help students decide whether they wish to take your course or perhaps find an alternative course or instructor if the option is available. Students may also need some additional guidance early on to adjust to this new way of structuring a course until this becomes more mainstream.

5. SUMMARY

The Internet is an enabler, and we should embrace it into the educational process. It enables fast research across the vast amount of data available through the Internet.

Relying on the Internet as the main source for information introduces new problems with context and correctness. We need to teach students how to vet the information they find including recognizing when they need more context of information, identify errors as well as separate facts from opinions.

Enabling students to work on real-world problems either from industry or students' own creative ideas helps engage them in the course. There are many options for computer science courses to make use of real-world problems especially through contests and open-source software projects.

Adjusting the classroom time to support a "Just-in-Time Learning" model can include a hybrid of lecture and group exercises for an active-learning environment. This enables students to practice communication and teaching each other, pair programming, problem-solving, critical-thinking, and vetting the material they find through a guided communal experience.

These changes also modify the role of the teacher to recognize our role is that of a tutor instead of a lecturer. If we can rely on the Internet to disseminate the information, then our expertise is to help guide students in their learning as a "guide on the side" instead of the "sage on the stage".

By incorporating these five "Just-in-Time Learning" techniques we have effectively removed the concept of cheating. We have simulated more closely to the workplace environment where students can use the Internet to help them solve problems where the problems don't already have answers available on the Internet. This also leads towards personalized and individualized teaching and learning that is more effective in helping students learn the fundamental skills necessary for the workforce.

Through adopting the Just-in-Time Learning Model we have embraced the Internet and incorporated into the curriculum what students are doing anyway. We can then focus on what humans do well, by helping students learn how to solve problems, think critically, make good decisions, and communicate effectively.

6. REFERENCES

[1] Adam, M. et. al. Flipped Classroom Field Guide. Retrieved April 18, 2015. https://docs.google.com/document/d/s36ihFbG5jzh5-WFu2rIZ9Q/headless/print

[2] Anderson, R., Ordonez, R., Pham, P., Tribelhorn, B. A Data Programming CS1 Course. 2015. In *Proceedings of the 46th ACM Technical Symposium on Computer Science Education,* SIGCSE '15, March 4–7, 2015, Kansas City, MO, USA.

[3] Boese, E. The Internet Has Killed Education As We Know It | TEDxCU. Retrieved Aug. 11, 2015 from YouTube: https://youtu.be/B1AiU7yAyOg

[4] Carter, P. 2012. An experience report: on the use of multimedia pre-instruction and just-in-time teaching in a CS1 course. *In Proceedings of the 43rd ACM technical symposium on Computer Science Education (SIGCSE '12).* ACM, New York, NY, USA, 361-366. DOI=10.1145/2157136.2157244 http://doi.acm.org/10.1145/2157136.2157244

[5] Davis, J. 2009. Experiences with just-in-time teaching in systems and design courses. In *Proceedings of the 40th ACM technical symposium on Computer science education* (SIGCSE '09). ACM, New York, NY, USA, 71-75. DOI=10.1145/1508865.1508895 http://doi.acm.org/10.1145/1508865.1508895

[6] Detmer, R., Li, C., Dong, Z., and Hankins, J.. 2010. Incorporating real-world projects in teaching computer science courses. In *Proceedings of the 48th Annual Southeast Regional Conference* (ACM SE '10). ACM, New York, NY, USA, , Article 24 , 6 pages. DOI=10.1145/1900008.1900042 http://doi.acm.org/10.1145/1900008.1900042

[7] Gallagher, S. 2013. The Science Of Learning, Retention, & Sustainment Training. *The Cambridge Handbook of the Learning Sciences Science.* Cambridge University Press.

[8] Ganapathy, S. Karl Kapp On How to Train Millennials. Retrieved April 18, 2015. http://www.mindtickle.com/blog/karl-kapp-train-millennials/

[9] Grunwald, D., Boese, E., Hoenigman, R., Sayler, A., Stafford, J. 2015. In *Proceedings of the 46th ACM Technical Symposium on Computer Science Education,* SIGCSE '15, March 4–7, 2015, Kansas City, MO, USA.

[10] Heller, P. and Hollabaugh, M. 1992. Teaching Problem Solving through Cooperative Grouping. Part 2: Designing Problems and Structuring Groups. *American Journal of Physics*, 60(7), pp. 637-44.

[11] Heller, P., Keith, R. and Anderson, S. 1992. Teaching Problem Solving through Cooperative Grouping. Part 1: Group Versus Individual Problem Solving. *American Journal of Physics*, 60(7), pp. 627-36.

[12] Hu, H., Kussmaul, C. 2012. Promoting student-centered learning with POGIL. In *Proceedings of the 43rd ACM technical symposium on Computer Science Education* (SIGCSE '12). ACM, New York, NY, USA, 579-580. DOI=10.1145/2157136.2157302 http://doi.acm.org/10.1145/2157136.2157302

[13] Hulleman, C. S., Godes, O., Hendricks, B. L., & Harackiewicz, J. M. 2010. Enhancing Interest and Performance With a Utility Value Intervention. *Journal of Educational Psychology*. Advance online publication. DOI=10.1037/a0019506

[14] Lovell, E. 2014. Promoting constructive mindsets for overcoming failure in computer science education. In *Proceedings of the tenth annual conference on International computing education research* (ICER '14). ACM, New York, NY, USA, 159-160. DOI=10.1145/2632320.2632331 http://doi.acm.org/10.1145/2632320.2632331

[15] Mehrabian, A., Ferris, S. 1967. Inference of attitudes from nonverbal communication in two channels. *Journal of Consulting Psychology, 31,* 248-252.

[16] Newmann, F. M., Marks, H. M., & Gamoran, A. 1995. Authentic pedagogy: Standards that boost student performance. *Issues in Restructuring Schools*, 8, 1–4.

[17] Nilson, L. 2010. *Teaching at It's Best: A Research Based Resource for College Instructors*, 3rd Edition. John Wiley & Sons, Inc., CA.

[18] Ogilvie, C. 2009. Changes in students' problem-solving strategies in a course that includes context-rich, multifaceted problems. *Physics Review Special Topics - Physics Education Res*earch, 5, 020102.

[19] VanDeGrift, T. 2015. Supporting Creativity and User Interaction in CS 1 Homework Assignments. In *Proceedings of the 46th ACM Technical Symposium on Computer Science Education,* SIGCSE '15, March 4–7, 2015, Kansas City, MO, USA.

[20] Von Jan, K. 2011. Pursue Passion: Demand Google 20% Time at School. *Huffington Post Education,* http://www.huffingtonpost.com/katherine-von-jan/unstructured-classroom_b_1024404.html

[21] Yeager, D., Henderson, M.; Paunesku, D., Walton, G., D'Mello, S.; Spitzer, B.; Duckworth, A. 2014. Boring but important: A self-transcendent purpose for learning fosters academic self-regulation.

Hackathons as an Informal Learning Platform

Arnab Nandi
Computer Science & Engineering
The Ohio State University
arnab@cse.osu.edu

Meris Mandernach
University Libraries
The Ohio State University
mandernach.1@osu.edu

ABSTRACT

Hackathons are fast-paced events where competitors work in teams to go from an idea to working software or hardware within a single day or a weekend and demonstrate their creation to a live audience of peers. Due to the "fun" and informal nature of such events, they make for excellent informal learning platforms that attract a diverse spectrum of students, especially those typically uninterested in traditional classroom settings. In this paper, we investigate the informal learning aspects of Ohio State's annual hackathon events over the past two years, with over 100 student participants in 2013 and over 200 student participants in 2014. Despite the competitive nature of such events, we observed a significant amount of peer-learning – students teaching each other how to solve specific challenges and learn new skills. The events featured mentors from both the university and industry, who provided round-the-clock hands-on support, troubleshooting and advice. Due to the gamified format of the events, students were heavily motivated to learn new skills due to practical applicability and peer effects, rather than merely academic metrics. Some teams continued their hacks as long-term projects, while others formed new student groups to host lectures and practice building prototypes on a regular basis. Using a combined analysis of post-event surveys, student academic records and source-code commit log data from the event, we share insights, demographics, statistics and anecdotes from hosting these hackathons.

1. INTRODUCTION

Hackathons are events where computer programmers and others involved in software development, including graphic designers, interface designers and project managers, collaborate intensively on software projects in a short period of time, typically 24-36 hours. Traditionally software companies have held or sponsored these events to induce problem solving through creativity. Though hackathons have existed since the late 1990s, few have focused on emphasizing the key aspects of learning as a focal point of the event. A university-sponsored hackathon gives developers an opportunity to compete, develop products, and potentially make important academic connections with faculty and labs. At Ohio State, the first university-wide, full-scale hackathon was held in November 2013 over a 24 hour period. There were 103 participants, constituting 34 teams of which 26 gave demonstrations of their work. Building on the success of the first year, in October 2014, a 36 hour hackathon featured over 200 participants comprising 59 teams.

SIGCSE '16, March 02 - 05, 2016, Memphis, TN, USA

ISBN 978-1-4503-3685-7/16/03...$15.00
DOI: http://dx.doi.org/10.1145/2839509.2844590

Figure 1: 2 hours remaining: The 2013 Hackathon

In 2013, projects built during the Hackathon ranged from an app to aid suicide prevention (a collaborative project built by a Psychology graduate student and 3 CSE students), to an alarm that read the weather, to a class selector for CSE that bundled class dependencies using clustering. In 2014, projects ranged from an app for checking into events from doctor appointments to class attendance; to a motorcycle-mounted sensor data collection device.

2. RELATED EFFORTS

There is a tremendous amount of interest in making education more engaging and interesting to students. Beyond traditional curriculum, several programs have adopted project-based approaches [15] that allow students use a critical problem-solving approach while simultaneously integrating information from a variety of topical lectures and multiple disciplines. Though informal education [6, 9, 17] has been considered an exciting and compelling way to get students introduced to Computer Science in higher education, the barrier to entry has always been relatively high because of the steep learning curve and specificity of concepts used in the discipline. This paper examines informal learning through a hackathon by analyzing team activity (e.g., commit histories), participant academic performance vs. non-participant performance (e.g., GPAs), and individual feedback from hackathon participants.

Competitive Settings: One way to reduce barriers in the learning process is to shape education around competitive platforms. Johnson and Johnson [14] discussed several strategies of adapting pedagogy to include cooperative, competitive, and individualistic learning in the classroom. Competitive events [11] provide an excellent venue to facilitate learning since they simultaneously enforce a structure (i.e., rules of the competition) and allow for out-of-the-box and imaginative thinking. The introduction of gaming as a learning vehicle has also been studied heavily [26]. While coding competitions and hackathons [10, 23] have been considered before, the focus is typically entrepreneurial or industry driven [13], rather than learning outcomes. The hackathon model provides a fun and engaging format for students [1] akin to flipped classroom settings [22] and has been adapted to other disciplines [7] as well.

Industry-focused learning: Hackathons have been popular in industry settings [5, 23] and open source communities [8] – they are often seen as an efficient way to rapidly prototype [21] on ideas outside of the project schedule, or as a community exercise [4]. By designing aspects of the hackathon to focus on informal learning by and mentorship of students new opportunities emerge. Programs such as Yahoo! Inc.'s "Hack U" have brought industry partners into the university setting, allowing them an opportunity to both educate students about industry-relevant technologies and recruit students for internships or full-time positions [5]. For several industry partners, this is a rare opportunity to mentor and interview prospective employee candidates for an extended and intensive period of time.

Group and Peer Learning: Programming is often a solitary exercise and therefore it does not easily lend well to a cooperative, peer-based setting. However, for both graduate work and in industry, the ability to work in teams and leverage peer-assisted and self-directed learning are essential [3]. While the impacts of group learning, especially in computer-based education, have been well studied [12], specifically designing competitive events to exploit peer-learning techniques is challenging [24].

Addressing Diversity: As a discipline, Computer Science has faced a history of gender and diversity challenges [16]. Scragg and Smith [20] suggest that very few women even consider Computer Science as a possible major, and that efforts need to be made not just to retain, but to recruit students in to the field. Blum, et. al. [2] posit that the reasons for gender challenges include the *environment* and *perception* of the field. Thus, creating an appealing, collegial setting for women to learn new concepts without the formal and onerous requirements of coursework was a critical consideration when developing our hackathon events.

Libraries as Informal Learning Environments: Libraries have long served as a discipline neutral space where ideas can be presented and debated. In academic settings, libraries are spaces where learning can be both formal and informal. Students are able to meet and study and learn from each other or work independently and use it primarily as a study space. Walton and Matthews [25] point out that libraries are poised to contribute to the evaluation of informal learning spaces because librarians have the expertise and experience of developing spaces. More recently, libraries have evolved to support more non-traditional learning experiences by providing services related to makerspaces [19], 3D printing [18], hack spaces, and generally supporting the *DIY* (do-it-yourself) movement. As spaces evolve, so must library services. Libraries are thus primed to support the informal learning inherent in hackathons, and also have the required event infrastructure (e.g., wireless internet).

3. THE ANATOMY OF A HACKATHON

3.1 Objectives and Event Format

The primary goals of the hackathon were to raise awareness of technical talent at Ohio State and foster a competitive, yet cooperative, culture for talented individuals to showcase their knowledge. It also allowed participants to connect with faculty, labs, centers on campus, and most importantly, with each other. *"We didn't know each other before we did this"*, said one team, who went from being strangers to working together over 20+ hours and producing a demonstrable project.

The event format both years included a tech talk that kicked off the hackathon, a set period of hacking which included technical help from individuals from industry, followed by judging. The top teams were announced immediately following judging and public voting was conducted for crowd favorites. This was followed by an awards ceremony and networking event, allowing participants to showcase their projects in a science-fair format.

3.2 Demographics

For the 2013 event, there were 103 participants, constituting 34 teams, all from Ohio State. In 2014, this number roughly doubled to 202 participants in 59 teams. The opening up of the event to non-Ohio State students brought in 18 participants from other nearby universities: Bowling Green State University, Kent State University, University of Akron, University of Cincinnati, Wright State University and Youngstown State University. Based on a combination of registration data and student records, we present demographic information for the Ohio State participants below.

Gender: In terms of gender, there were 11 women participants in 2013. In 2014, this number increased to 30, i.e., 16%. While this is roughly comparable to the representation of women in Computer Science, we plan to continue to address diversity and inclusion issues, as described in the previous sections.

Figure 2: Diversity of disciplines: Hardware projects at the 2014 Hackathon

Majors of Study: As shown in Table 1, while the event was predominantly Computer Science-focused, there were a considerable number of non-Computer Science majors who participated. Given that a workable output was expected from this hackathon, it was not surprising that Computer Science Engineering majors comprised the majority of the participants. However, as the popularity of the event grows, the number of non-Computer Science students is expected to rise, both through raising awareness of hackathons amongst the non-Computer Science communities, and also through affiliated domain-focused events, such as the 50+ participant *Makeathon* conducted in April 2015 which focused on building hardware projects over a 24-hour period.

Major	'13 (%)	'14 (%)
Computer Science & Engineering	79	71
Electrical Engineering	8	12
Physics & Engineering Physics	6	3.5
Mechanical Engineering	1	3
Misc / Exploration	1	3
Business	0	2
Chemistry & Chemical Engineering	0	1
Biomedical	0	1
Architecture & Planning	0	1
Geography	2	0.5
Aero, Astronomy, & Astrophysics	2	0.5
Mathematics	0	0.5
Civil Engineering	0	0.5
Industrial Systems Engineering	0	0.5
Psychology	1	0

Table 1: Demographics: Major

Event	1st yr	2nd yr	3rd yr	4th yr	Grad
2013 (# students)	6	19	22	33	23
2014 (# students)	12	33	37	78	24

Table 2: Demographics: Year in School

Year of Study: The hackathon was a predominantly undergraduate focused, as shown in Table 2. However, there was a strong and significant representation of graduate students. Based on post-interviews and contributed resumes, the graduate students who participated had a history of involvement in competitive events during their undergraduate education. Some graduate students used the event to collaborate with individuals from other disciplines in order to bring their ideas to fruition, such as a psychology graduate student who partnered with CSE students to build a suicide prevention Android application. Other Computer Science graduate students used the hours as a focused way of building upon their existing research projects.

3.3 How Teams Work

In 2014, we introduced compulsory use of source control, sponsored by Github. Each team was required to save their code to a private repository on a regular basis, thereby promoting collaboration and responsible coding practices. Access to these repositories allowed for a unique opportunity: **we could, on a fine-grained per-commit basis, discover insights on how 200 students collaboratively built software over a 36-hour time period.** We present our findings from analyzing the source code commit logs next, as shown in Figures 3–5. It should be noted that due to the scale and diversity of student teams, and since performance evaluations and surveys were anonymous, we use this analysis to gain insights and adapt our event to aid learning, and not as an absolute metric of student performance.

Self-pacing and Productivity: The extended nature of this event made pacing an important factor for productivity and learning. As described in the previous sections, we took care to provide resources and an initial orientation about taking care of themselves during such an event. However, in terms of the project, it was up to the participants to pace themselves and plan out how they would achieve their desired goals. In addition to qualitative and anecdotal data, the source code commit logs depicted noticeable patterns. As shown in Figures 4 and 5, productive teams kept a steady pace of progress throughout the event, saving code on a regular basis. In the 2013 event, we had noticed that several inexperienced teams gave up due to burnout. Feedback also indicated that an additional 12 hours would allow participants to sleep without worrying about completing their projects. The 36-hour format allowed students to take breaks and compete in a more relaxed environment. This is evidenced by the lull in activity of commits during the early hours of Saturday, when most students took a break after an initial flurry of coding activity, and returned the next day to continue their project.

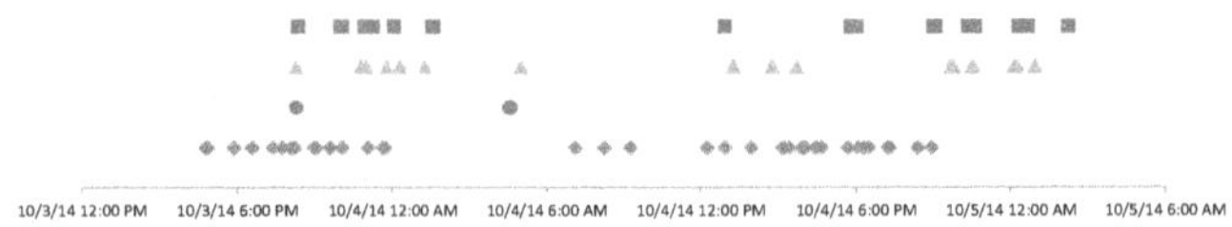

(a) Team taking turns to work, complementary commit patterns (relay model)

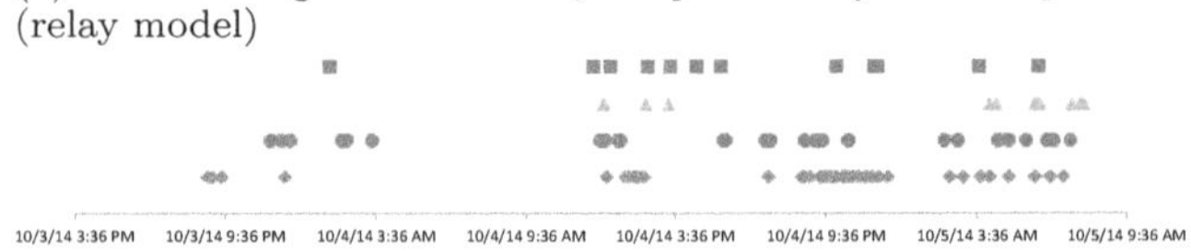

(b) Team working in coordinated schedules, taking breaks at the same time (waves model)

Figure 3: Models of collaboration over time (x-axis): each dot is a `git` commit from a team member (each student is represented by a different color / shape).

Different Models of Collaboration: Another interesting insight from the commit log data was that it evidenced the students teamwork. Two noticeable patterns of collaboration emerged. The first model (the *relay* approach, as seen in Figure 3a) involved teams taking turns working on the project. After an initial period of coordinated and simultaneous work, the team divided tasks, and one or two students took breaks while the other students in the team worked. One consideration to keep in mind is that not all productivity is immediately visible in the source code: e.g., if a student was acting as a project manager, or if two students were working in pairs / as a group, but using one computer. However, the log data shows this approach whereby the commits alternate between members of the group.

A contrasting approach used by other teams was the *waves* model (Figure 3b), where teams would meet on a frequent basis to work together and coordinate for brief periods, and then take breaks at the same time, or go off to work individually. Based on observations during the event, the particular team in Figure 3b was highly collaborative with all team members actively writing code, and used the source control system as a way to share code.

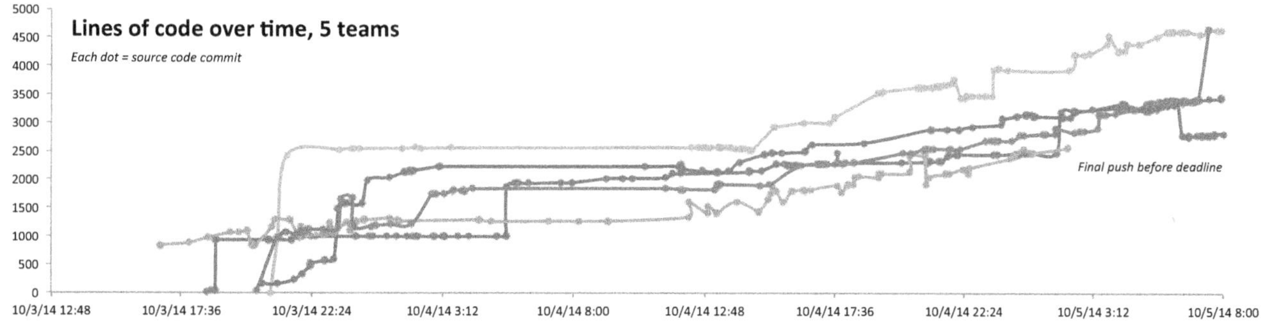

Figure 4: Projects being built over a 36 hour period: The x-axis represents time, and the y-axis represents number of lines of code. Each dot is a team member pushing their code to the repository.

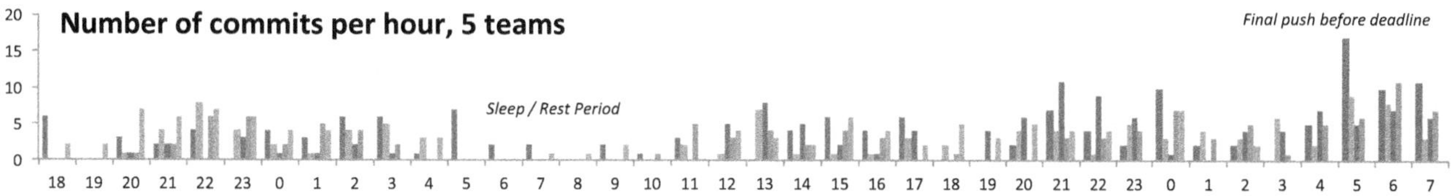

Figure 5: Number of commits over 36-hour Hackathon period.

In addition to individual team peer-to-peer learning, students regularly sought help from technical mentors, members of the Open Source Club, and other peers from other participating teams to figure out how to work past stumbling blocks during the events. Several individuals mentioned these approaches in their post-event surveys.

4. POST-EVENT SURVEYS

In addition to gathering feedback throughout the planning process, we conducted an anonymous post-event survey each year. Students rated the 2013 event at a **4.5** on **5** (20% response rate), and the 2014 event at **4.6** on **5** (36% response rate). Drilling down to actual ratings, the 2014 event had a overwhelmingly positive rating: 50 students rated it a **5/5**, and **91%** rated it at 4 or above. In addition to objective ratings, the surveys provided a lot of qualitative insight, which we have factored into our long-term planning.

On in-class vs practical learning: Due to the scale and diverse nature of the event, it is hard to objectively measure or correlate learning outcomes. However, as an initial insight, quotes from the students are highly encouraging:

- *"Enjoyed the opportunity to build an application from start to finish. I learned a lot and truly understood how to apply my classroom/personal learnings."*
- *"Had a challenging but great weekend coding, really made my brain burn, which feels great."*
- *"It allowed me to participate and gain experience in a group programming setting, something that is not too stressed in my current/past classes."*
- *"Ability to create something useful and learn from others. Meeting more CSE students to collaborate with is always a positive."*
- *[What I liked:] "The ability to sit down for an extended period of time and just work on a project* ***allowed me to accomplish more in 24 hours than I have since the start of the school year*** *and it made me feel like I actually did something useful for once."*
- *"I loved the fact that this event gave me time to learn how to implement real world applications of [computer science]."*

On team skills: As organizers, we were ourselves very surprised at the level of teamwork. Some teams were formed at the event itself, while some other teams were formed during a "team match making" event organized by the ACM-W student group a week before the 2014 event.

- *"I enjoyed working with a team to create the application. It was a good learning experience, because* ***I had only just met my teammates.****"*
- *"I felt like I got a lot done and really accomplished something cool. I enjoyed working with my team.* ***We will continue working on our project****, so it helped us get off the ground."*
- *"[What I liked was] The teamwork and collaboration between teams."*
- *"I loved being able to work in an environment with my peers."*
- *"I liked being around a lot of bright people. I was able to learn a lot, and I look forward to more hackathons."*

On the availability of mentors: Having alumni come back to the University as technical mentors created the opportunity for them to be role models for students participating in the hackathon. They were able to help with experience and insights, e.g., providing advice into scoping projects conservatively due to the time limitations. We were pleasantly surprised by the participation levels of some mentors. Several used these opportunities to wander around and visit with hackathon participants, discuss jobs or internships at their companies, and provide hints to help solve pesky problems that arose in students' code. Many of the mentors were Ohio State alumni who work in the tech industry in the city and beyond. While mentors had initially committed to spending 4 hours with the students, some ended up spending 24+ hours since they enjoyed the process.

- *"It was a great opportunity to learn, meet peers, and network with professionals."*
- *"The motivation from the mentors was extremely helpful. The mentors themselves were awesome."*
- *"The availability of mentors was very nice, and they were for the most part approachable and helpful."*
- *"I enjoyed working with mentors as well as meeting people from other schools who had come to compete."*
- *"I really liked the energy of the people in the event as well as the organization of the mentors within a structured setup. The best part was the free food that was given all weekend, which tied with the excellent help and support given by the mentors."*

- A first time participant noted: *"While working on a project with friends was fun, and I learned a lot from it, the chance to talk to other like-minded people and meeting mentors was definitely one of the most invaluable experiences from the event."*
- *"Awesome mentors - they really made it for me."*

5. ACADEMIC PERFORMANCE

In Table 3, we present a term-by-term analysis of Cumulative and Term GPAs for Undergraduate students during the existence of our program. (Some numbers / measures are withheld for institutional privacy and administrative reasons.) While we do not expect a single weekend event each year to have a measurable impact on a student's performance, does the long-term impact on student morale, community, self-confidence and peer-learning have a bearing on academic performance? One concern is that the sustained time involvement of such extracurricular events compete with homework and class projects, and are a timesink in a student's already busy academic schedule: they may have a *negative* impact on in-class performance. In our analysis of student grades, we found this concern to be unwarranted: our analysis revealed that the hackathon-participating students have small (2–5%) but consistently higher GPAs than non-participating students. When comparing performance in individual to see if students who participated in the Hackathons got better, worse, or stayed roughly the same from one term to the next ("better" / "worse" defined as a GPA increase / decrease of 0.1 or more), we were unable to find any significant patterns. Thus, while we cannot claim that the Hackathon causes or impacts better GPAs, our conjecture is that such activities seem to consistently self-select a higher achieving group of students.

There are two ideal followups to this analysis: a cohort study isolating student "profiles" by analyzing not just averages, but the distribution of GPAs in each of these groups. Second, a large-scale, longitudinal study tracking the entirety of a student's progress through each term in college would allow us to control for a variety of possible impactors – these are ideal future work.

Category / Measure	Au 13	Sp 14	Au 14	Sp 15
Hackathon Undergrads				
Count	129	132	160	148
Term GPA	3.136	3.073	3.155	3.131
Cumulative GPA	3.243	3.218	3.177	3.193
Degree-Seeking Undergrads				
Term GPA	3.031	3.066	3.073	3.121
Cumulative GPA	3.071	3.088	3.088	3.112
Hackathon CSE-BS				
Count	70	71	71	64
Term GPA	3.192	3.124	3.204	3.141
Cumulative GPA	3.254	3.242	3.224	3.231
Non-Hackathon CSE-BS				
Count			621	
Term GPA			3.025	
Cumulative GPA			3.123	

Table 3: Average Cumulative and Term GPAs for Undergraduate students. Hackathon-participating students have small (2–5%) but consistently higher GPAs than non-participating students.

6. LEARNING OUTCOMES

Industry Relevance: Both judges and mentors from local and national industry participated in the events. They were able to use these events to network and recruit students from Ohio State. They also were able to make valuable connections with each other as they waited for students to approach them and ask questions. This way, sponsors have two potential outcomes of the event: recruitment of current students and engaging with colleagues from other companies.

The planners of the hackathon included several student organizations. Through these student organizations several events happened prior to the hackathon and served to market the event to potential attendees as well as facilitate the organization of teams, teach students the basics of GitHub commits, as well as coordinate tech talks from industry sponsors. These individuals learned valuable lessons related to project management, key details of navigating the infrastructure of higher education, reaching out to local news agencies, and soliciting sponsorships from vendors.

Long-term projects: There were several excellent examples of long-term projects that germinated at these events. Our source code repository showed signs of activity days, and even weeks after the Hackathon – a sign that students were working on their projects well after they were due. One group that did not make it to the top ten projects at the awards ceremony continued working on their project and received undergraduate research scholarships that let them complete their project in the following semester. In the longer term, we additionally expect to see entrepreneurial activity based on both the projects prototyped and social connections developed during the event.

Long-term team skills: One particularly interesting observation was a team comprising 4 students, each from a different university. Through in-person conversations and further followups, we learned that the team went to the same high school, and they used university hackathon events such as ours to reconnect and collaborate using skills learned at different institutions.

7. ANCILLARY OUTCOMES

Industry-facing Skills: Yen et al. [27] suggest that skills most needed by information systems professionals in industry include interpersonal behavior and communication skills, personal motivation and working independently, and critical and creative thinking. These are exactly the skills developed through events such as hackathons. This informal learning and skill development better equips students to market themselves for internships and jobs after college.

All of the mentors and judges who participated in the hackathons mentioned that they enjoyed the large amount of face-to-face time they had with students. They were able to use the mentoring opportunities as an extended interview and really understood the capabilities of the students after working with them through the course of the hackathon. Additionally, university-industry collaboration is always time-intensive because project-development and relationship-building are iterative and complex. Using the hackathon format to develop work strategies allows industry sponsors to jumpstart productivity on specific projects and by providing mentors they're able to iterate quickly with the hackathon participants.

In-University Benefits: In addition to the specific benefits of creating a tech culture at Ohio State University, there were some unforeseen benefits that have arisen from the hackathon events. Several students enrolled into courses such as "Mobile app development" or specific capstones after attending the event, demonstrating the promise of the Hackathon serving as both an on-ramp into a university's course offerings, and also a venue to demonstrate skills learned from these courses. From the 2013 event, one team developed an app to train for a large charity bike ride and they were contacted by that organization and hired to continue their hackathon project. One key benefit for the university and for students is that students are able to be recruited from this event for specific research assistantships. Most notably, students were contacted by Computer Science faculty and recruited to be part of labs. Though few of the teams chose to work on staff-suggested projects, one plan for the future is to advertise projects earlier and market them to students as potential job leads should they choose to work on the projects. This allows university units to leverage the hackathon as source of creativity for those who need help specific developing apps or web interfaces to augment their domain-specific research.

Future Events: The interest from the events has led to the formation of the "Buckeye Hackers Club", with an active membership of over 40 individuals. Funds, insights, and infrastructure from the hackathon events were used to enable other related events, such as *TownHack*, a city and community-focused hackathon (Nov 2014), and the Electronics Club-hosted *Makeathon* hardware hackathon (April 2015). Planning for the 2015 hackathon is underway.

8. CONCLUSION

The hackathons held at Ohio State have provided a structure for increased informal learning. They have spawned creativity and have resulted in continued enthusiasm amongst students, and established valuable mentorship connections with alumni. Given the time constraints of the competition, students are able to quickly teach and learn from their peers (not just teammates) in order to produce a workable product in time for the showcase. Students learn to compress their development process into a short time frame, allowing them to hone their problem solving, project management, and prioritization skills – all while still maintaining a fun, enthusiastic, and engaging experience. In addition to surveys and activity information from the event itself, additional data indicates that students participating in a Hackathon tend to have stronger GPA than their peers.

What started as an idea to host a single hackathon has blossomed into a complete program dedicated towards creating informal settings for learning in a variety of different areas. The program is now sponsoring students to attend other hackathons, funding related events, and soliciting greater partnerships with industry. These initiatives focus on fostering an inclusive tech culture focused on informal learning (both individual and peer-based) and higher levels of engagement with the technology industry.

Acknowledgements: The first author was supported in part through U.S. National Science Foundation CAREER award #1453582. We would like to thank Christopher Wallace, Matt Faluotico, Elizabeth Burl, George Kvaratskhelia, Barry Brinkley, Eric Schnell, Daniel Dotson, Charlene Brenner, Krysta Kirsch, Robert VanDyne, Linda Katunich, Swaroop Joshi, Neelam Soundarajan, Paulo Sivilotti, Rajiv Ramnath for providing support, data, and valuable feedback towards both the paper and the events.

9. REFERENCES

[1] J. A. Artiles and D. R. Wallace. Borrowing from Hackathons: Overnight Designathons as a Template for Creative Idea Hubs. *WEEF*, 2013.

[2] L. Blum, C. Frieze, et al. A Cultural Perspective on Gender Diversity in Computing. *SIGCSE*, 2006.

[3] D. Boud, R. Cohen, and J. Sampson. *Peer Learning in Higher Education: Learning from and With Each Other.* Routledge, 2014.

[4] D. Boud and H. Middleton. Learning from Others at Work: Communities of Practice and Informal Learning. *Journal of Workplace Learning*, 2003.

[5] G. Briscoe and C. Mulligan. Digital Innovation: the Hackathon Phenomenon. *Creative Works*, 2014.

[6] R. R. Burton and J. S. Brown. An Investigation of Computer Coaching for Informal Learning Activities. *International Journal of Man-Machine Studies*, 1979.

[7] M. Calco and A. Veeck. The Markathon: Adapting the Hackathon Model for an Introductory Marketing Class Project. *Marketing Education Review*, 2015.

[8] L. Christopherson et al. Developing Scientific Software Through the Open Community Engagement Process. *Technical Report*, 2013.

[9] F. Coffield. *The Necessity of Informal Learning.* Policy Press, 2000.

[10] K. Goetz. Hackathon: 2 Days, 1,000 Developers, Lots of Caffeine. *All Things Considered*, 2010.

[11] J. Grimes et al. Robotics Competition: Providing Structure, Flexibility, and an Extensive Learning Experience. *FIE*, 2008.

[12] S. Hooper. Effects of Group Composition on Achievement, Interaction & Learning Efficiency. *ETRD*, 1991.

[13] L. Irani. Hackathons and the Making of Entrepreneurial Citizenship. *Science, Technology & Human Values*, 2015.

[14] D. W. Johnson et al. *Learning Together & Alone: Cooperative, Competitive, & Individualistic Learning.* Prentice-Hall, 1987.

[15] J. J. Kellar, W. Hovey, et al. A Problem Based Learning Approach for Freshman Engineering. *FIE*, 2000.

[16] J. Margolis, A. Fisher, and F. Miller. The Anatomy of Interest: Women in Undergraduate Computer Science. *Women's Studies Quarterly*, 2000.

[17] V. J. Marsick and K. E. Watkins. Informal and Incidental Learning. *New Directions for Adult and Continuing Education*, 2001.

[18] H. Michele Moorefield-Lang. Makers in the Library: Case Studies of 3D Printers and Maker Spaces in Library Settings. *Library Hi Tech*, 2014.

[19] A. Pashia. Empty Bowls in the Library Makerspaces Meet Service. *College & Research Libraries*, 2015.

[20] G. Scragg and J. Smith. A Study of Barriers to Women in Undergraduate Computer Science. *SIGCSE Bulletin*, 1998.

[21] A. Sigfridsson, G. Avram, A. Sheehan, and D. K. Sullivan. Sprint-driven Development: Working, Learning and the Process of Enculturation in the PyPy Community. *Open Source Development, Adoption and Innovation*, 2007.

[22] M. Skirpan and T. Yeh. Beyond the Flipped Classroom: Learning by Doing Through Challenges and Hack-a-thons. *SIGCSE*, 2015.

[23] S. Sousa. Lessons learnt from a public–private big data hackathon. *Big Innovation Centre Report*, 2013.

[24] K. J. Topping. Trends in Peer Learning. *Educational Psychology*, 2005.

[25] G. Walton and G. Matthews. Evaluating University's Informal Learning Spaces: Role of the University Library? *New Review of Academic Librarianship*, 2013.

[26] U. Wolz, T. Barnes, I. Parberry, and M. Wick. Digital Gaming as a Vehicle for Learning. *SIGCSE Bulletin*, 2006.

[27] D. C. Yen, S. Lee, and S. Koh. Critical Knowledge/Skill Sets Required by Industries: an Empirical Analysis. *Industrial Management & Data Systems*, 2001.

The Video Collaboratory as a Learning Environment

Vikash Singh, Sarah Abdellahi, Mary Lou Maher and Celine Latulipe
Department of Software and Information System
University of North Carolina at Charlotte
Charlotte, NC, USA

{vsingh7, sabdella, m.maher, clatulip}@uncc.edu

ABSTRACT
Video usage in educational environments has increased significantly with the expansion of online learning opportunities. However, current video-based applications used for learning are designed for passive consumption of video content and do not support small-group collaboration. Specifically, they lack interaction affordances for active and collaborative learning through video materials. In this paper, we present the affordances and user experience of a web-based video application called Video Collaboratory that is designed with multiple affordances for group-based learning around video content. We surveyed students and analyzed the use of the Video Collaboratory in an HCI course. Students found the Video Collaboratory helpful because they could learn from their peers. Students also used the application beyond the activities required for credit.

Keywords
Computer-supported collaborative learning, flipped courses, video annotation, collaborative computing

1. INTRODUCTION
The growth of Massive Open Online Courses (MOOCs) in recent years shows the huge potential of video as a medium for education. Video lectures and tutorials are the primary method of instruction in MOOCs, delivered either through YouTube as in the case of Udacity, or native video applications as in Coursera and edX. Besides MOOCs, other approaches for online learning include blended or hybrid methods that involve face-to-face interactions among students in addition to online video-based instruction. The flipped classroom approach requires students to come to class after viewing the required materials so that they are ready to engage in learning activities [1,10,12]. Learning materials such as lectures and presentations are delivered to students through an alternate medium such as podcasts or video-on-demand services [5,10,15,17]. Students can view these materials on their own time prior to coming to the class, allowing the use of class time for active learning. In-class activities include quizzes, collaborative learning exercises, and working in a group towards a project goal. Various strategies for flipped classroom learning in CS education are described in Maher et al [13].

SIGCSE '16, March 02-05, 2016, Memphis, TN, USA
ACM 978-1-4503-3685-7/16/03.
DOI: http://dx.doi.org/10.1145/2839509.2844588

A challenge in using video in online education environments is the inability to tailor video environments for collaborative learning. In the case of MOOCs, the video lectures are not directly connected to the discussion about the video. For example, the students on MOOCs generally post their comments about video lectures in a separate forum or send an email to their instructors with their question. Such disjointed interaction may create confusion, waste time and increase miscommunication. In some MOOC platforms such as Udacity, the users are presented with formative quizzes to test users' learning but these assessments are targeted to individuals and lack a collaborative approach to learning. The lack of collaborative engagement leads to the individual user passively consuming the videos [11] rather than actively interacting with the video as a group.

In this paper, we discuss some of the video-based educational platforms and demonstrate a lack of affordances for collaborative learning through video. Then we present the Video Collaboratory application, a tool for video-centered collaborative learning. We used the Video Collaboratory for collaborative learning around video lectures in our HCI course in the Spring 2015 semester and we present our analysis of student perceptions and usage of the tool in this course.

2. RELATED WORK
Collaboration and peer learning are important components of the learning process. Through collaboration and peer learning, students develop critical thinking skills and discover important issues found by other students [18]. Collaborative learning allows students to interact with their peers to achieve a common learning goal [14]. A three years study of students' performance on final exam scores between control and experimental student groups showed higher scores for students who completed collaborative exercises than those who were in a traditional lecture-based course that focused on individual learning [4].

A review of active learning methods clearly suggests that, like other instructional practices, collaborative learning has strong advantages [14]. Many groups have explored the idea of using video annotation interfaces as a support tool for educators to enhance active learning. However, most of the education-specific video software systems lack support for collaboration among students and between students and instructor.

In the education domain, there are many popular web-based or standalone video interfaces used for content delivery. Some popular examples are Coursera[1], edX[2], Udacity[3], GoReact[4], and

[1] http://coursera.com
[2] http://edx.org
[3] http://udacity.com
[4] http://goreact.com

edPuzzle[5]. Other examples include MRAS [3], videoANT [8], and TrACE [7]. Most of these applications focus on content delivery and have their own novel design features to support communication between instructors and students. These features not only enhance the video watching experience by supporting different ways of video navigation (edX, videoANT) but also increase interactivity with the lecture videos by allowing instructors to embed quizzes in the lectures (Udacity, edPuzzle). Other features such as the ability to evaluate a video with rating scales (GoReact) and add text annotations to different parts of the video (videoANT, GoReact, TrACE) contribute to interactions between the instructors and the students.

However, none of these tools are designed for collaborative sense-making, an important component of the learning process. Many applications support embedding quizzes inside a video lecture but the process of embedding quizzes is done before student consumption of video content and although it adds some interactivity to the video, it doesn't support student-student or student-instructor collaboration (Udacity, edPuzzle). Similarly, video annotations are supported for videos more for self-reference (edX) and are not synchronously or asynchronously available to other users for collaboration. Some systems support sharing of annotations through email (videoANT, MRAS) but using a separate channel for sharing annotations makes the discussion disjointed from the video.

The lack of affordances for collaboration in these systems inhibits collaborative discussion and does not offer an engaging video experience. To address this need for a collaborative platform for video-centered discussion, we have designed and developed the Video Collaboratory system.

In the classic CSCW time-space matrix for groupware [9], collaboration among group members can happen synchronously or asynchronously depending on whether the group members are present at the same time or not. Similarly, whether the participants are co-located or collaborating remotely also affects the choice of groupware. Sense-making of an online lecture video is an asynchronous process where different students watch a video at their own time. Using the Video Collaboratory for sense-making of video lectures falls into the asynchronous-remote quadrant. In the next section, we discuss the various affordances in the Video Collaboratory system that allow collaboration among students.

3. VIDEO COLLABORATORY

The Video Collaboratory (VC) is a web-based platform that provides unique interaction techniques and a user experience that is customized towards enabling group collaboration around video (Figure 1). VC allows small groups to create text and sketch annotations on existing videos: enabling effective and creative collaboration centered around video artifacts. The Video Collaboratory has been developed through an iterative process following a research through design approach [19] where the design of the collaborative environment led to insights on affordances for collaboration around video content. A major contribution is an environment for collaboration that connects annotations and comments directly to video content and eliminates the need for a separate channel for discussion around a video.

[5] http://edpuzzle.com

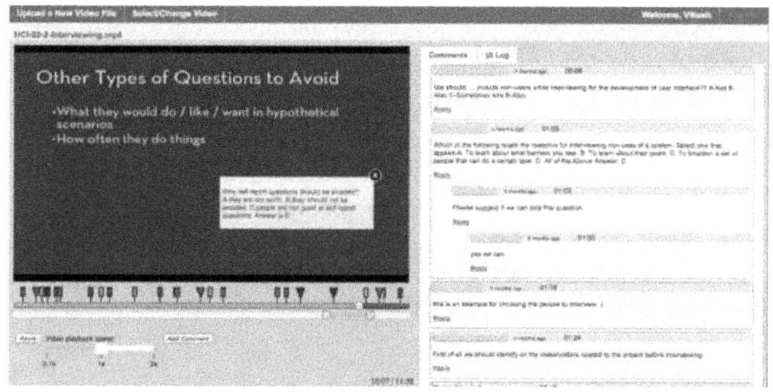

Figure 1. Video Collaboratory main screen.

3.1 Affordances for Video-centered Collaboration

The affordances for video-centered collaboration include:

3.1.1 Context awareness

Awareness and notifications are two important aspects of both synchronous and asynchronous collaboration [2]. While working with collaborators, it becomes important to know the context of the communication content to facilitate discussion [6]. In the case of video-centered collaboration, a video's timeline represented by a scrubber is an important signifier as it represents the full length of a video. In the Video Collaboratory, the markers on the scrubber provide affordances for recognizing the context of a comment or annotation, and are signifiers for the specific location on the video timeline for specific comments. When moving a mouse or other pointing device over a marker, the user has a preview of the comment at that point in time at a glance or can navigate to that point on the video by clicking. This feature is important for collaboration because while engaging with a video lecture it becomes easier to note interesting or important sections by noticing the density and distribution of comment markers on the video timeline.

3.1.2 Contextual navigation

In the Video Collaboratory, the video could be navigated through comments in the right panel or the markers on the timeline. When a user clicks on a comment on the panel to the right of the video window, the video relocates on the timeline and automatically loops to display annotations in context. Two different kinds of markers are used to signify whether the marker represents a comment on a frame (rectangular) or on a segment of video (inverted triangle). This contextual navigation is important for collaboration because it helps collaborators quickly interpret the meaning of comments from other group members by seeing the video segment that is the context for each comment.

3.1.3 Color-coding

A different color codes each member's comments, allowing collaborators to visually identify different members' comments from a list of comments. This facilitates collaboration as it allows users to quickly follow the activities of another group member.

3.1.4 Threaded discussion

Threaded commenting is an important design affordance for collaborative interaction. It facilitates discussion among collaborators by allowing replies to a posted comment. In the Video Collaboratory, the 'Reply' button at the bottom of each comment signifies that a threaded discussion is supported in the system. The threaded conversation retains the color-coding of different collaborators, clearly representing the participants in a discussion.

3.1.5 *Multi-modal annotations*

Multiple modalities allow users to collaborate around videos in different ways. Sketching on the video frame allows users to specify spatial context that is not possible with text comments. The sketching modality is important to collaboration because it allows users to communicate spatial information and to sketch ideas onto the content in the video.

3.2 User Interface

After launching the VC application, the user enters login details for authentication and identification so the source of comments can be associated with a specific individual. Each registered user has access to a set of assigned videos and can select one for viewing and interaction. The collection of videos is presented in a tree like structure where each root node represents a collection of videos assigned to a group of users for a course or project. When a root node is clicked, all the videos inside that folder are displayed in a tile format (Figure 2). The user can hover their cursor over any of the videos to get a preview of the video. The user can then click on any of the tiled videos to open the main screen of the Video Collaboratory for that video. The main screen of the application has a two-column layout. The left column contains the video panel and the right column contains the comments panel with all the comments posted on that video (Figure 1). The video controls are located in the first column below the video. The annotation tools and palette are on top of the video panel.

3.3 User Interaction

The Video Collaboratory supports a wide array of interactions with video. In addition to supporting the default controls for video such as a play/pause, toggle, and video scrubbing, it supports some novel interaction techniques that are specially designed for video-based collaboration. Some of the user interactions supported by the application are described next.

3.3.1 *Inserting Comments*

On the main screen, comments can be inserted on the video timeline in two different modalities by clicking the 'Add Comment' button. Once a user chooses to insert a comment, he can choose between text or sketch or a combination of both modalities. The comments can be added to a point (frame) or to a selected segment of any length of the video. Once a comment is submitted, it is added to the list of comments in the comments panel on the right and a color-coded marker appears over the video timeline showing the position of the inserted comment on the video timeline. A user can reply to a comment by clicking on the reply button at the bottom of each comment on the right panel.

3.3.2 *Exploring and Editing Comments*

Posted comments can be explored in two different ways. A user can click on any comment in the comments panel or on a colored marker on the video timeline. Either action moves the video play-head to the appropriate part of the video and loops the playback between 2 seconds prior and 2 seconds after the comment point. For segment comments, the video loops over the specified segment of the video. Comments related to that marker are then overlaid on the main video. Users can view, edit or delete their own comments, but can only view the comments of others.

3.3.3 *Annotations Preview*

When many collaborators use a video, the timeline could potentially become crowded with comments. If a user is looking to revisit a comment, or wants to get a quick sense of the types of comments found in one part of the video, she can hover her cursor over the comment markers. This helps the user browse and navigate without having to click on each individual annotation marker. Additionally, as a user hovers over a segment marker, the length of the segment is highlighted on the Segment Selector as a preview.

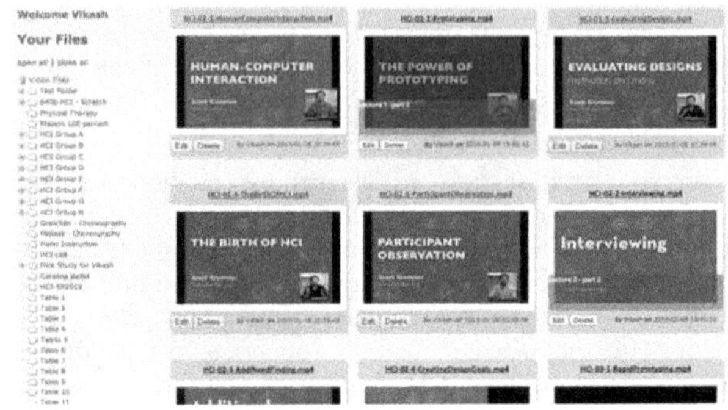

Figure 2. Tiled videos on video selection screen.

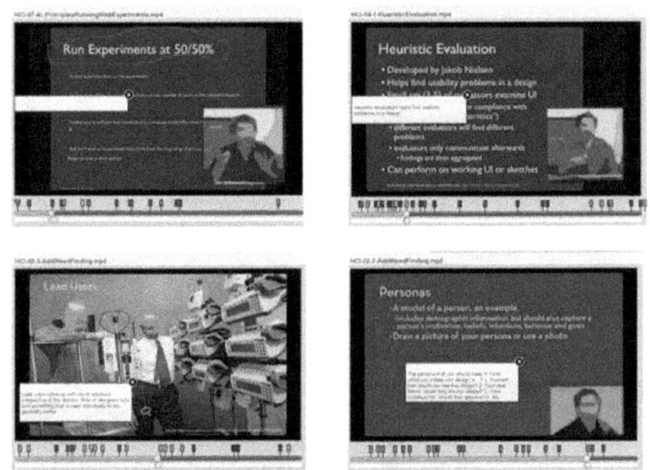

Figure 3. Examples of sketching on lecture videos by students.

4. VIDEO COLLABORATORY USE IN A FLIPPED CLASS

In the Spring 2015 semester, we used the Video Collaboratory system for the Human Computer Interaction course at our institution. The course was taught as a flipped class, with video lectures watched outside of class, and hands-on group activities during scheduled class time. There were 121 students enrolled in the class: 62 graduate students and 59 undergraduate students.

The students were placed in groups where each group was all undergraduate or graduate students. The students were divided into 14 groups with a minimum of 6 and a maximum of 9 students per group. We kept the undergraduates and graduate students separate for pedagogical reasons that were independent of the evaluation of the use of the VC. As we reported the usage of the VC separately for graduates and undergraduates, we noticed different levels of engagement with the lecture material, possibly due to different levels of maturity and attention to the course. In future use of the VC, we plan to develop different strategies in creating assignments and activities around lecture videos for different levels of students.

4.1 Active Learning around Video Lectures

The students in each group shared access to the same weekly lecture and therefore shared their comments and annotations through the Video Collaboratory. That is, each group had their own folder on the Video Collaboratory with their own private copy of the lecture videos. This design was purposeful: first, small group collaboration can help students feel more comfortable and less intimidated than they might if they had to post comments seen by 120 other students. Second, by limiting interaction around each video instance to a smaller group of people, the timeline would not become too cluttered with annotation markers. This makes it possible for students to see each other's markers and get to know each other's marker colors, helping to create a visual image of who is commenting and where. This would not be feasible with 120 different colors and hundreds of markers on a single video.

Each student was required to enter 3 comments on the assigned lecture each week to identify 3 multiple-choice questions as the significant content of the video lecture. Each group was then asked to reach a consensus on two questions to be sent to course TAs prior to the start of the class each week. These two questions from each of the 14 groups formed the question pool for that week's clicker quiz class activity. The TAs then selected 4-6 questions from the question pool and other resources to create that week's clicker quiz.

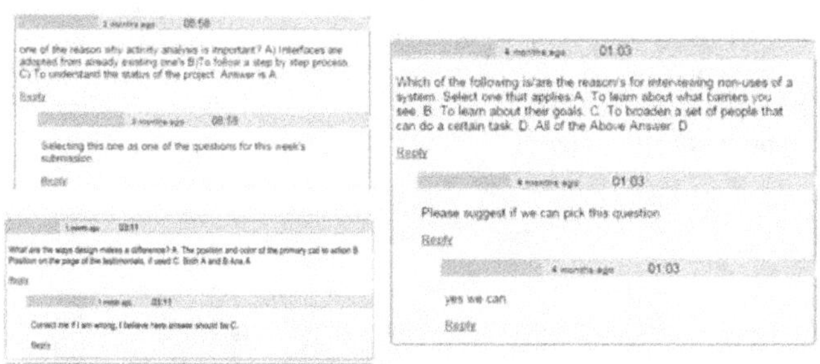

Figure 4. Examples of discussions among students about weekly quiz questions.

Students were motivated to produce the multiple-choice questions in 3 ways. First, groups with the best choice of questions during the semester were given extra credit. Second, each individual student had to participate in a clicker quiz with questions partly chosen among the aggregated questions submitted by the groups each week. These quizzes were graded as a part of the students' final grade and groups with the best choice of questions had the chance to answer questions designed by their own group in the clicker quiz. Third, the annotations, multiple choice questions, and comments from the entire class were collected and made available to the students as a study guide for the mid-term and final exams.

4.2 Data Collection and Analysis

We gathered two sets of data during the semester: survey data and VC usage data. The survey included questions about the students' perception of the flipped classroom learning experience. Some of the questions students answered in the survey are relevant to the VC and are shown in Table 1.

We conducted the same survey before the mid-term and then again before the final exam to see if student perceptions of the flipped classroom had changed. 110 students participated in the mid-term survey and 98 students completed the survey before the final exam.

Table 1. Survey results - Mean and median of responses on a 7 point Likert scale

	How helpful were the online videos for learning HCI methods?	**Other students helped me to understand the right answers while we were discussing quiz questions.**	**I helped other students to understand the right answers while we were discussing quiz questions.**
Mid-term Average *(Median)*	4.35 *(4)*	4.73 *(5)*	5.01 *(5)*
Final Average *(Median)*	4.03 *(4)*	4.44 *(4)*	4.68 *(4)*

The survey tool was developed to examine student perceptions of flipped classrooms and had a total of 24 questions. Here we only report on the 3 questions relevant to the use of the Video Collaboratory. The results for questions about the online lecture videos and the collaborative approach to quizzes are shown in Table 1. While there was a drop in the average value on the Likert scale for these questions, this difference is not significant. Students generally liked using the videos on the Video Collaboratory. They also liked the collaborative nature of the application that allowed them to prepare for the quizzes together. In the Video Collaboratory the students posted questions for each other and let other members of the group answer the questions. Many students used the Video Collaboratory application as a tool for creating references on the video for self-study. Some students used sketching to write answers of self-created quiz questions on the video as shown in Figure 3.

We gathered data on the use of comments, annotations, and replies in the VC. We aggregated the data into student groups. We looked specifically for evidence of collaboration on the VC for coming to consensus on choosing group questions. The reason for gathering this data is to compare the actual number of comments to the required number of comments as an indicator of the usability of the VC and as an indicator of the students' perceived value of video engagement. Since the VC supports more than just watching video lectures, the VC usage data also allows an analysis of how engaged the students are with the video lectures beyond a record of how much time they spent watching the video.

We found that the students added more comments on the videos than the amount required for the assignment. Since each group had up to 9 members, and each person was required to provide 3 comments per week, the maximum required number of comments per week is 27. As shown in Figure 5 and 6, most of the time groups added more comments than required for grades. In several cases, up to four times the expected number of comments was observed. The recorded data shows as many as 111 comments from a single group in one week. The analysis of the data on the number of comments on video lectures shows interesting patterns in students' use of the VC, and is an indicator of student engagement in the lecture material. A visual representation of the

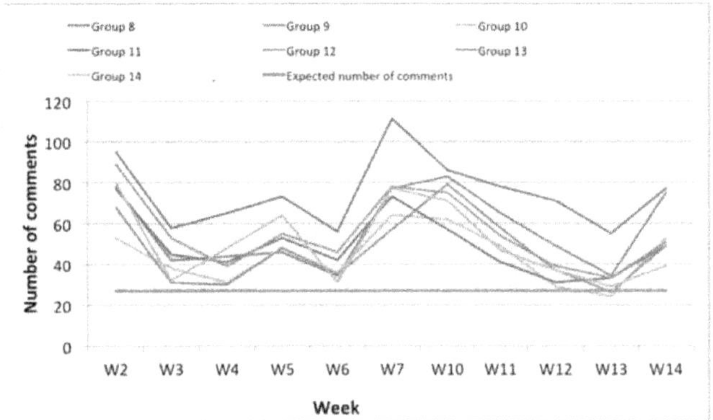

Figure 5. Number of comments posted by graduate groups on VC each week compared to the expected number in each assignment.

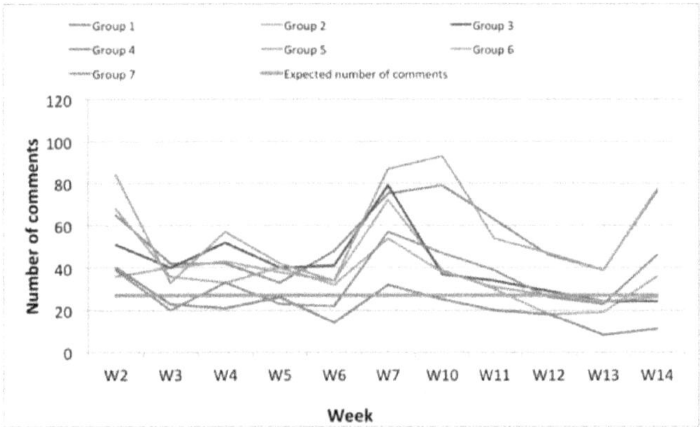

Figure 6. Number of comments posted by undergraduate groups on VC each week compared to the expected number by the assignment number in each assignment.

data on students' use of VC is available in Figure 5 for graduate students and Figure 6 for undergraduate.

The flat green line in Figures 5 and 6 represents the required number of comments for each week. While some groups did significantly more than required (groups 8, 9, 10, 12, 13, 14) and others did less (groups 4 and 7), all groups had a strong start at the beginning of the semester and a decrease in the amount of work after the second week. All groups had a significant increase in the amount of comments placed on the videos the week before and after the midterm exam, and the week before the final exam. The groups had fewer comments in the VC during weeks with project submission deadlines (weeks 6 and 13).

The significance of visualizing this usage data is the additional information it provides to the instructor about student preparation, engagement, and collaboration. Where most video platforms for online education provide the instructor with information about how many students viewed the video and for how long, the VC provides information about how much the students engaged with the video content by showing their comments and annotations.

We observed a significant difference in the amount of work done by graduate students in the class (groups 8 to 14) compared with the undergraduates (groups 1 to 7). While the graduate groups placed up to 4 times the expected number of comments on the videos, undergraduate groups moved closer to the required amount of work, and 2 groups (groups 4 and 7) didn't complete the required work in some weeks. Again, the significance of visualizing the difference between the graduate student groups and the undergraduate student groups is the feedback this provides to the instructor. The graduate students were more engaged with the lecture material than the undergraduates. This is important information when interacting with the students during in-class activities and when evaluating their projects. This analysis of the use of the VC could lead the instructor to be more strategic about assignments that would encourage a more uniform engagement with video content.

The extra comments posted by the groups on the videos were not limited to the quiz design assignments. The content of comments placed by the students also included:

- Finalizing the quiz questions and decision-making about the group submission.
- Highlighting, and summarizing important points mentioned in the videos.
- Discussing confusion about course material in the video and helping each other to understand the material.

While students had been required to post quiz questions on the VC, using it as a medium for the three other purposes mentioned above was their own choice. Choosing the VC for communication about course material confusion and to ask peers for help supports the importance of context awareness in collaboration. Also, using the VC to highlight the important points supports both the importance of context awareness and contextual navigation as it allows them to review the course material by navigation through the comments and review the related video, in addition to providing the possibility of reviewing the points considered important by their peers.

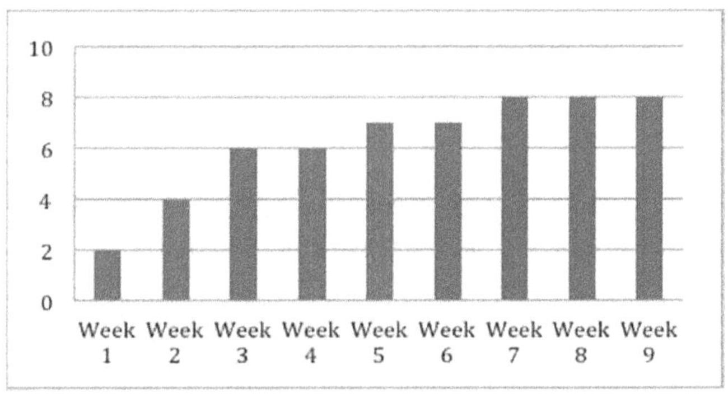

Figure 7. Number of groups using VC reply option for discussion around the assignment each week number by the assignment number in each assignment.

An indication of collaborative communication is the number of times the groups used the reply option. Figure 7 shows how many groups used the reply option each week. More groups used the VC as a collaborative communication media at the end of the semester compared with the start of the semester. While in the first week two groups were using the reply feature on the VC for discussion around the activity, after week 7, 8 groups had used that feature for discussion around the assignment. These groups did more than just enter their quiz questions on the videos, and used the VC communication features (commenting and replying) for choosing the group's best questions for submission each week. In the beginning of the semester the groups were using other communication channels such as email for exchanging thoughts about the group weekly assignment, but by the end of the semester more groups were relying on the commenting and reply features of the VC for conversation around the quiz questions, consensus and decision making, and clarifying misunderstandings. Figure 4 shows a few examples of these uses by some of the groups. This type of analysis of the annotations on educational video content could lead to more strategic use of video and activities around video.

5. SUMMARY AND CONCLUSION

Collaborative learning is a complex social process and any software environment intended to support collaborative learning should afford and encourage ideas from multiple viewpoints that can be further developed as students approach consensus [16]. The Video Collaboratory provides affordances to support this social process around video material. Students can watch a video, mark up and annotate different points and segments of the assigned videos. The Video Collaboratory not only allows students to reach a consensus on weekly tasks but also helps them create collective self-study material. The design of the VC has focused on asynchronous collaboration, and future developments include a signifier for presence of others viewing and annotating the same video as an affordance for synchronous collaboration.

Our analysis of the use of the VC in a flipped classroom learning environment shows that students engaged with the video content more than was required, implying that the students found value beyond that needed to get the credit for commenting on video content. The students' video comments and annotations also provided the instructor with a better understanding of student engagement with video lecture content since this data shows more than just the amount of time they watch the video: including data about their active note taking and communication with others around the video content.

The design of the features and affordances in the VC has focused on the collaborative user experience, assuming that the user is collaborating around video content. In the context of education, the VC user experience has focused on the student as user and instructional material as content. As we gain more experience with the use of VC in a learning environment, we are planning the development of the user experience for the instructor. The analysis of student engagement can lead to different educational strategies around online lectures, beyond embedding quizzes as is typical in current online learning environments. Our analysis of the student engagement with video content required extracting the logged data and performing an analysis outside the VC. Future versions of VC should provide this analysis as a built-in aid to the instructor.

6. REFERENCES

[1] Ellen R. Auster and Krista K. Wylie. 2006. Creating Active Learning in the Classroom: A Systematic Approach. Journal of Management Education 30, 2: 333–353.

[2] Ronald Baecker, Dimitrios Nastos, Ilona Posner, and Kelly Mawby. 1993. The user-centered iterative design of collaborative writing software. ACM Press, 399–405.

[3] D. Bargeron, A. Gupta, J. Grudin, and E. Sanocki. 1999. Annotations for streaming video on the web. CHI '99 Extended Abstracts, 278–279.

[4] Leland Beck and Alexander Chizhik. 2013. Cooperative learning instructional methods for CS1: Design, implementation, and evaluation. ACM Transactions on Computing Education (TOCE) 13, 3.

[5] Jacob Lowell Bishop and Matthew Verleger. 2013. The Flipped Classroom: A Survey of the Research. 120th ASEE Annual Conference.

[6] J. J. Cadiz, Anop Gupta, and Jonathan Grudin. 2000. Using Web Annotations for Asynchronous Collaboration Around Documents. Proceedings of the 2000 ACM Conference on Computer Supported Cooperative Work, ACM, 309–318.

[7] Brian Dorn, Larissa B. Schroeder, and Adam Stankiewicz. 2015. Piloting TrACE: Exploring Spatiotemporal Anchored Collaboration in Asynchronous Learning. Proceedings of the 18th ACM Conference on Computer Supported Cooperative Work, ACM, 393–403.

[8] Brad Hosack, Charles Miller, and David Ernst. 2009. VideoANT: Extending Video beyond Content Delivery through Annotation. Proceedings of World Conference on E-Learning in Corporate, Government, Healthcare, and Higher Education 2009, AACE, 1654–1658.

[9] Robert Johansen. 1988. GroupWare: Computer Support for Business Teams. The Free Press, New York, NY, USA.

[10] Maureen J. Lage, Glenn J. Platt, and Michael Treglia. 2000. Inverting the Classroom: A Gateway to Creating an Inclusive Learning Environment. The Journal of Economic Education 31, 1: 30–43.

[11] Fei Xue Larissa Schroeder. 2013. Flipping three different mathematics courses: Common conclusions and plans for the future. MathAMATYC Educator 4, 2: 63–68.

[12] Kate Lockwood and Rachel Esselstein. 2013. The inverted classroom and the CS curriculum. Proceeding of the 44th ACM technical symposium on Computer science education, ACM, 113–118.

[13] Mary Lou Maher, Celine Latulipe, Heather Lipford, and Audrey Rorrer. 2015. Flipped Classroom Strategies for CS Education. Proceedings of the 46th ACM Technical Symposium on Computer Science Education, ACM, 218–223.

[14] Michael Prince. 2004. Does Active Learning Work? A Review of the Research. Journal of Engineering Education 93, 3: 223–231.

[15] Nancy M. Schullery, Robert F. Reck, and S. Schullery. 2011. Toward solving the high enrollment, low engagement dilemma: A case study in introductory business. International Journal of Business, Humanities and Technology 1, 2: 1–9.

[16] Gerry Stahl. 2000. A model of Collaborative Knowledge-Building. Fourth International Conference of the Learning Sciences, 70–77.

[17] Roxanne Toto and Hien Nguyen. 2009. Flipping the work design in an industrial engineering course. Proceedings of the 39th IEEE international conference on Frontiers in education conference, IEEE Press, 1066–1069.

[18] William M. Waite, Michele H. Jackson, Amer Diwan, and Paul M. Leonardi. 2004. Student Culture vs Group Work in Computer Science. Proceedings of the 35th SIGCSE Technical Symposium on Computer Science Education, ACM, 12–16.

[19] John Zimmerman, Jodi Forlizzi, and Shelley Evenson. 2007. Research Through Design As a Method for Interaction Design Research in HCI. Proceedings of the SIGCHI Conference on Human Factors in Computing Systems, ACM, 493–502.

A Multi-institutional Study of Peer Instruction in Introductory Computing

Leo Porter[1], Dennis Bouvier[2], Quintin Cutts[3], Scott Grissom[4], Cynthia Lee[5], Robert McCartney[6], Daniel Zingaro[7], and Beth Simon[1]

[1]University of California, San Diego
[2]Southern Illinois University Edwardsville
[3]University of Glasgow
[4]Grand Valley State University
[5]Stanford University
[6]University of Connecticut
[7]University of Toronto Mississauga

ABSTRACT

Peer Instruction (PI) is a student-centric pedagogy in which students move from the role of passive listeners to active participants in the classroom. Over the past five years, there have been a number of research articles regarding the value of PI in computer science. The present work adds to this body of knowledge by examining outcomes from seven introductory programming instructors: three novices to PI and four with a range of PI experience. Through common measurements of student perceptions, we provide evidence that introductory computing instructors can successfully implement PI in their classrooms. We find encouraging minimum (74%) and average (92%) levels of success as measured through student valuation of PI for their learning. This work also documents and hypothesizes reasons for comparatively poor survey results in one course, highlighting the importance of the choice of grading policy (participation vs. correctness) for new PI adopters.

1. INTRODUCTION

Peer Instruction (PI) has gained considerable traction among computer science educators and there have been a number of studies demonstrating its efficacy in a variety of dimensions. Students value PI [5, 8, 10] and learn more in PI classes compared to traditional lecture classes [11, 13]. PI is also associated with low failure rates [6] and increased retention of majors [9].

The vast majority of PI studies in CS take the form of evaluating a single instructor [5, 8, 10] or implementation at a single institution [5, 6, 9]. As such, one concern is that the reported PI results overrepresent those occasions where PI has proven successful. Given the current trend of increased PI adoption, it is important to establish the kinds of outcomes that can be expected across larger datasets and institution types. In addition, it is important to begin studying the ways in which new adopters adopt PI. To what extent is PI adopted wholesale? How are the steps of PI altered to suit the instructor or student demands?

This paper reports on a set of PI adoptions with a broad range of class parameters and types of institutions. Only one other paper has offered such a multi-institution view, but it examined only small classes at private liberal-arts colleges [8]. In the present study, seven instructors and their students, from multiple institutions of different types, were surveyed. The instructors range from new adopters of PI to experienced PI users. The level of success was not uniform across the instructors.

Our key findings are:

- Consistent with previous studies, a supermajority of students in all studied classes liked and would recommend PI.
- Successful PI implementation requires that the instructor's motivations for using PI are clear to students.
- The grading policy attached to in-class PI question responses appears to have an effect on student engagement and satisfaction.

2. RELATED WORK

PI is characterized by asking challenging, in-class conceptual questions of students. For each question, students individually respond, discuss the question in small groups, and respond again based on their new understanding [1]. These questions should target common misconceptions and/or core course concepts. To be most effective, PI requires other supporting course changes. For example, many instructors require additional preparation from students before class in order to make best use of limited class time. This preparation can consist of pre-lecture reading and associated quizzes [1, 14] or clicker quizzes at the start of class [14].

Interactive classrooms, including PI classrooms, have shown significant increases in student learning in physics [4]. In

SIGCSE '16, March 02-05, 2016, Memphis, TN, USA

DOI: http://dx.doi.org/10.1145/2839509.2844642

Table 1: Institution, course, and instructor characteristics. For major, (decl.) and (ant.) denote declared and anticipated, respectively. N/A denotes data not available.

Identifier	N-A	N-B	N-C	E-D	E-E	E-F	E-G
Institution	R1	PUI	PUI	R1	R1	R1	PUI
Size	Large	Large	Large	Large	Large	Large	Small
Public/Private	Public	Public	Public	Public	Public	Public	Private
Course	CS1.5	CS1	CS1	CS1	CS0	CS1	CS1
Language	Java	Java	Java	Python	Alice	Matlab	Java
Times Taught this Course	6	10+	10+	10+	2	1	0
Courses Taught using PI	0	0	0	0[a]	10	3	1
Students Enrolled at End of Course	64	30	36	151	87	98	19
Survey participants	62	29	13	65	87	92	15
Percentage of CS majors	34% (decl.) 59% (ant.)	50%	29% (decl.)	70% (ant.)	1%	6.4%	44% (ant.)
Freshman	3%	40%	36%	>95%	34%	34%	37%
Sophomore	40%	27%	42%	N/A	45%	16%	26%
Junior	37%	27%	13%	N/A	14%	33%	22%
Senior	21%	6%	9%	N/A	8%	17%	16%
Percentage of Students who Previously used Clickers	77%	28%	22%	3%	N/A	31%	25%
Avg. # of PI Questions per class	7	7	6	5	5	4	5
Length of class (min)	75	50	75	60	80[b]	50	80
(D)eveloped or (A)dopted Questions	D	D	D	D	D	D	A

[a] Instructor of course E-D had not taught a class using PI, but had been part of PI research and course development. As such, that instructor is considered experienced in PI.

[b] 30 minutes each week was spent on a practice code-writing quiz.

CS, a number of studies have reported on the success of PI, including improved student satisfaction [5, 8, 10], student learning [7, 15], final exam grades [11, 13], failure rates [6], and retention of majors [9].

The present work provides additional evidence that, for both new and seasoned adopters of PI, students widely laud the change to the course structure. As noted in earlier research [10], it is not always the case that PI is adopted following all recommended practices. The results of the present work lead us to examine ways in which PI is adopted, and we find suggestive evidence that student satisfaction can be significantly impacted by grading clicker results on correctness rather than participation.

3. METHOD

Each of the seven instructors in this study reported the teaching of one introductory programming course. Four of the instructors had experience with PI, either by having taught a course in PI or by having participated significantly in the development of a PI course. The other three instructors were new to PI. We label our courses with two letters: N (novice) or E (experienced) to indicate the instructor's PI experience, and a letter A-G to differentiate each course (assigned, within N and E categories, by decreasing years of teaching experience for the instructor). Course and instructor characteristics are provided in Table 1.

A brief description of each course is provided below.

Course N-A: CS 1.5 - Object-Oriented Design and Programming: This course concentrates on the object-oriented paradigm, particularly encapsulation, inheritance, and polymorphism. Programming assignments emphasize graphics and event-driven interaction.

Course N-B: CS1 – Computer Science I: This course is an introduction to programming and computer science whose topics include: simple and structured data types, program control structures, problem analysis, algorithm design, and implementation using a high-level language (Java).

Course N-C CS1– Introduction to Computing I: This Java course covers types/variables, assignment, conditions, loops, classes/objects, files, and arrays.

Course E-D: CS1: This course is an introduction to procedural programming in Python for CS majors covering basic types, expressions, state, control structures, function definition and use, and lists.

Course E-E CS0 – Fluency in Information Technology: This non-majors computing course is required for all psychology majors and as a general education requirement for a subset of university students (those within a specific "college"). The goals of this "general education" course in computing include computational thinking and communicating and collaborating about computational artifacts (in this case Alice programs and Excel sheets).

Course E-F: CS1 – Introduction to Programming in Matlab: This course is an introduction to MATLAB programming for the Cognitive Science department and uses the Media Computation approach [3]. Students study foundational programming constructs such as data manipulation, conditional statements, for-loops, while-loops, and various types of vector and matrix indexing.

Course E-G: CS1 – Computer Science I: This course is a required course for CS and Mathematics majors taught using Media Computation [3]. Concepts include variables, objects, methods, loops, conditionals, and class design.

Table 2: Student feedback on the value of PI. Percentages reflect student agreement. Agreement values under 80% are highlighted.

Question/Identifier	N-A	N-B	N-C	E-D	E-E	E-F	E-G
Thinking about clicker questions on my own, before discussing with people around me, helped me learn the course material.	68%	86%	100%	94%	95%	95%	100%
Most of the time my group actually discusses the clicker question.	90%	93%	100%	88%	98%	97%	100%
The immediate feedback from clickers helped me focus on weaknesses in my understanding of the course material.	74%	96%	100%	95%	99%	91%	100%
Knowing the right answer is the only important part of the clicker question.*	37%	14%	15%	12%	23%	17%	20%
Generally, by the time we finished with a question and discussion, I felt pretty clear about it.	69%	90%	100%	94%	97%	84%	93%
Clickers helped me pay attention in this course compared to traditional lectures.	58%	93%	100%	95%	90%	90%	100%
Clickers with discussion is valuable for my learning.	74%	93%	100%	100%	94%	91%	93%
I recommend that other instructors use this approach (reading quizzes, clickers, in-class discussion) in their courses.	71%	90%	100%	98%	93%	87%	100%

One instructor, experienced in teaching PI, is known by all instructors and actively assisted the novice instructors in weekly half-hour Skype meetings during their first PI term. The instructors surveyed their students using a common instrument, which enabled comparison of responses across courses.

4. RESULTS

In student self-report surveys, we asked for views on the value of the PI approach in supporting various aspects of the learning experience and views on the instructor's implementation of PI in the classroom.

4.1 Student Perception of the Value of PI

Students reported on their perception of the value of PI (see Table 2). For all but one question (denoted with a *), higher percentages are better. Responses below 80% positive are highlighted. We note two trends in Table 2.

The first trend is that students overwhelmingly value PI. They report that they pay better attention in class, believe it helps them identify weaknesses earlier, and believe the process helps them learn. As a result, the vast majority of students (91% per class on average) recommend that more instructors use PI in their courses. In two classes, 100% of students would recommend that other instructors use PI. These results demonstrate that across a wide range of institutions and instructors, students both value PI and desire that PI be used by more instructors.

The second trend is that the students in Course N-A perceive PI considerably differently than students in other courses. Compared to students in other courses, the students in Course N-A recommend PI less often, felt discussion was less valuable, and generally reported less value from the PI process. Perhaps most striking is the large percentage (37%) of students who believe the value of a clicker question is only in having the correct answer. We will revisit this anomalous result in the Discussion.

4.2 Student Perception of PI Implementation

Table 3 indicates student satisfaction with how PI was implemented regarding difficulty and timing. To express dissatisfaction, students could respond either "too long"/"too difficult" or "too short"/"too easy."

The majority of classes saw high degrees of satisfaction with the PI implementation. Both Courses N-A and E-F stand out as having lower levels of satisfaction with the implementation, but recall that only Course N-A experienced the overall lower value of PI.

Question Difficulty. In Course N-A, some students (23%) felt that questions were too difficult. Only two other courses had more than 4% of students who reported that questions were too difficult: Course E-F with 14% and Course E-G with 13%.

Question Time Allowed. In general, if students were unsatisfied with the time allowed for the initial vote, then they felt that they had too little time (notably in Courses N-A, N-C, E-D, E-E, and E-G) rather than too much time. Course N-A was again an outlier with 21% of students responding that they had too little time relative to 7% who felt they had too much time. Although instructors set the questions (and drive the pace), it is critical for students to be given time to think through the questions on their own. Question design (e.g. word choice, clarity, answer options) can seriously impact student time needed to read the question.

Discussion Time Allowed. An interesting trend appears regarding time allowed for peer discussion. Of those students who were not satisfied with the time allowed for peer discussion in the courses of all four experienced instructors, more students felt that too much time was allowed. A possible reason for this is that experienced PI instructors are more comfortable spending time on peer discussion, and may have personal evidence suggesting the value of providing students with more time to talk among themselves. For novice instructors, time circulating in the classroom or silently standing up-front can be initially unnerving, and at the very least is a change in their teaching style. However, results in Course N-A more closely match those of courses taught by experienced instructors in that unsatisfied students felt that too much time was allowed. As can be observed from Figure 1, this may be related to the comparatively fewer students in Course N-A who report always discussing with their peers: if some students are not discussing, then they are waiting for class to move forward.

Table 3: Student feedback on the implementation of PI. Percentages reflect students responding "OK" or "About right". Values under 80% are highlighted.

Question/Identifier	N-A	N-B	N-C	E-D	E-E	E-F	E-G
From the point of helping me learn, the content of clicker questions was: (too hard, okay, too easy)	76%	83%	100%	88%	94%	78%	80%
In general, the instructor gave us enough time to read and understand the questions before the first vote: (too short, about right, too long)	72%	89%	92%	81%	87%	78%	87%
The amount of time generally allowed for peer discussion was: (too short, about right, too long)	89%	87%	92%	79%	86%	77%	73%
In general, the time allowed for class-wide discussion (after the group vote) was: (too short, about right, too long)	70%	86%	100%	64%	81%	63%	93%

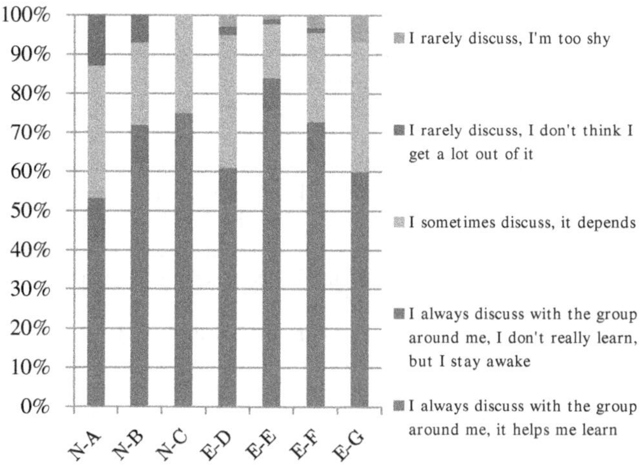

Figure 1: Student responses to the question: Which of the following describes your discussion practices this term?

Figure 2: Student responses to the prompt: The professor explained the value of using clickers in this class.

Class-wide Discussion Time Allowed. Regarding class-wide discussions, unsatisfied students felt that they had too much time in Courses N-A, E-D, E-E, and E-F. Course E-F had the most students reporting that too much time was spent on class-wide discussion (26% too much compared with 11% too little). This instructor had little experience with the programming language used in the course; it is possible that this caused a mismatch between where students struggled and where the instructor anticipated struggles.

Student Behavior during Discussion. Figure 1 provides the breakdown of student responses regarding their discussion habits. For all but one course, the majority of students reported valuing the discussion with their group as it helped them learn. For all courses, only a small minority of students either did not discuss because they did not value discussion or because they were too shy.

Explanation of the Purpose of PI. Figure 2 provides the breakdown of student responses regarding the explanation from the instructor on why clickers were being used. For all but Instructor N-A, more than 90% of students thought that the instructor explained the use of clickers well or did so too much. Instructor N-A had a considerably larger percentage of students reporting that they were unclear why they were using clickers. The other anomalous course result was Course E-G, where 20% of students felt that the instructor explained the use of clickers too much.

5. DISCUSSION

5.1 Value to Students and Instructors

Our results suggest that PI can be successfully adopted at a variety of institutions in introductory computing courses. At least 71% of students (avg. 91%) would recommend that other instructors use this approach in their courses.

The seven instructors in this work all reported a dramatic change in their usual classroom experience upon implementing PI. These instructors varied in terms of reasons for adoption, amount and type of adoption support, and teaching experience. Instructors had varying comfort levels with the courses and varying support for developing and implementing clicker questions. In fact, some had no more to go on than a notion of allowing students to "test" their knowledge. Some read publications on its use, some reviewed clicker slides prepared and used in computing courses, and some had the opportunity to TA for or repeatedly observe an experienced PI instructor. *Independent of these background factors, all instructors report that the next time they teach this class, they will teach it with PI.*

This said, one course (N-A) stands out as yielding poor survey results compared to the other courses. We next reflect on why this may be the case.

5.2 Exploring Course N-A Differences

Differences between N-A and the other courses can be seen fairly uniformly in both the valuation and implementation surveys. Through reflective discussion and our reading of PI reports in other disciplines, we highlight two structural issues for discussion. First, the instructor required correctness for a portion of the PI grade (each question was worth 2 points: 1 for correctness and 1 for participation). Second, a notable 25% of the class felt that the instructor did not sufficiently explain why clickers were being used. Together, we posit that these two issues contributed to a very different classroom culture regarding PI, as evidenced by the markedly different student survey responses. In sum, students in Course N-A (more than those at other institutions):

1. Felt that clicker questions were too hard
2. Felt that too little time was allotted to read and understand questions
3. Did not always discuss with their peers
4. Did not find value in hearing other students provide explanations in class-wide discussion and,
5. Reported lesser perception of the value of PI for their learning.

5.2.1 Grading on Correctness

We suspect that the change from grading on participation to grading on correctness fundamentally changes the atmosphere of the course. Consider the first four points in the above list. This kind of student affect — feelings that questions are too hard and that discussion is not useful — make sense if students perceive PI questions as "standard quiz" questions rather than peer discussion questions. The fact that Instructor N-A gave points for correctness, even though he/she also gave points for participation, may have factored into students perceiving questions as a test of something they should already know, rather than tools designed to build their understanding.

There are two other concerns related to grading on correctness rather than participation. The first is that students become concerned about arguing their interpretation of the question, and this can disrupt the learning process. A focus on learning is hampered when an incorrect answer in the learning process itself has grade-based implications. The second, related issue, is that questions cannot be too difficult or will be viewed as unfair. This is problematic when the recommended correctness range for the individual vote on PI questions is 35-70% [1] and when there is evidence that students benefit considerably more from difficult questions [15]. Instructors who both grade on correctness and recognize the limits that this poses on difficulty may respond in-kind by offering easier questions. This shying away from difficult questions may explain why many students thought that PI was not beneficial for their learning.

We can see evidence of students experiencing Course N-A differently than the other courses through open-ended student responses. For example, a student in Course N-A reports:

In this lecture I am more focused on trying to guess the answers to the questions than on internalizing and understanding the course content. In standard lectures I am focused on taking clear and thorough notes and absorbing the material.
–Student in Course N-A

A quote from a student in Course E-G may provide more insight into the importance of the grading structure, based on their report of clicker use in a different class:

I have another clicker course, this one is far better. In the other course, every clicker question is graded. It feels too much like the professor just wants to play game show host and puts to [sic] much weight on the correct answers and not the process of getting the answer. This is opposite for this course. I feel like participation should just be graded.
–Student in Course E-G

Given this criticism of grading on correctness, it is essential to examine Course E-E. Like Course N-A, Course E-E had a correctness requirement, but it was differently implemented in a manner that reinforced the role of clicker questions in the learning process rather than the assessment process. In Course E-E, students were graded on participation, but they had to get at least 50% of all questions (including individual and group responses) in each lecture period correct to get those participation points. This approach was devised based on experience in an earlier offering of the course, which required only participation and where students were noted answering randomly and engaging in unrelated activities in the classroom. The instructor believed that a change in policy was needed based on the fact that the course was a required, non-majors course. Students generally did not start the course with a great deal of enthusiasm, nor much understanding of what value the course held for them. In explaining the "half correct" policy, the instructor was able to reiterate that clicker questions are for helping students engage in developing expert analysis and argumentation skills. The policy reinforced Instructor E-E's primary course learning goal: getting students to learn how computing people see problems.

A student from Course E-E discusses this policy, noting his/her need to prepare, but expressing satisfaction with the awarding of discussion points:

This class was very different from my other classes as it truly made me be on top of my game. I did like the grading structure and how participation points were fair.
–Student in Course E-E

And some students did appear to get the message that their engagement in reasoning about the question, not simply getting points, was the goal.

[I]n [this course], discussion and proof of understanding is a vital part of lecture. With clicker questions, as a student, I was able to engage in thoughtful reasoning.
–Student in Course E-E

5.2.2 Explaining Pedagogical Change

It is critically important to explain (repeatedly) to students any deviation from expected classroom norms. Students have both experience with and expectations of college classroom learning. They know what happens in a lecture and have techniques that they expect to use in order to learn and measure their progress toward success. From our collective experience, we can report that students claim that they "have to sit at the front of the class" in order to learn/stay awake, want the instructor to "just explain it," or complain that the lack of lecture "forced me to learn it all myself." PI completely pulls the rug out from under the students by challenging them to re-examine their established, comfortable, and often perceived successful learning habits.

In a popular 2-page "Tips for Successful Clicker Use" summary, Douglas Duncan (Univ. of Colorado, Astronomy) lists as his second tip: "You MUST MUST MUST explain to students why you are using clickers. If you don't, they often assume your goal is to track them like Big Brother, and force them to come to class. Students highly resent this." (emphasis original)[12]. Perhaps more tellingly, the first item on his list of Practices that Lead to Failure is "1. Fail to explain why you are using clickers." [2]

In Course N-A, 74% of students report that their instructor explained to the class why he/she was using clickers. However, the remaining 26% of students who felt that clickers were not explained adequately (or at all) was the highest percentage among the courses. This emphasizes the importance of explaining the value of PI not just once and in not just one way. Moreover, for Course N-A, it is likely that students were especially sensitive to this issue as most students had previously taken an introductory course where the instructor used clickers to take attendance. The presence of these kinds of non-pedagogical uses of clickers only heightens the need to explain the pedagogical goals of PI.

5.2.3 Other Factors

Note that, in addition to the two structural issues we have highlighted, Course N-A also differs from other courses in other ways. The course is a CS 1.5 course (not a CS1 course), many of the students used clickers in the past, and the proportion of freshmen is lower. There is little precedence for these differences contributing to the outlying survey results for this course, however. The earliest experience reports of PI in CS report on successful adoption in CS1.5 courses [10], and we know of no evidence suggesting that any novelty of clickers wears off after a single course.

6. CONCLUSION

In this multi-institutional study of student satisfaction in Peer Instruction (PI) courses, we find further evidence of PI being highly valued by students. We also find that one course yielded lower student satisfaction than the other courses. We have argued that this lower satisfaction may have stemmed from two adoption decisions: grading on correctness, and not convincingly arguing to students why clickers and PI are being used. We offer two conclusions here. First, new adopters of PI can expect levels of success similar to those reported by others with considerable PI teaching and development experience. Second, it is important to evaluate adoption decisions. A pedagogy so widely-applicable as PI will inevitably engender debate over the particulars of day-to-day implementation and interaction with students. We encourage all PI instructors to reflect on and make explicit the reasons undergirding their PI-based decisions so as to maximize the value of PI for students.

7. ACKNOWLEDGEMENTS

Thank you to the reviewers for their helpful suggestions. This work was supported in part by NSF grant 1140731.

8. REFERENCES

[1] C. H. Crouch and E. Mazur. Peer instruction: Ten years of experience and results. *American Journal of Physics*, 69, 2001.

[2] D. Duncan. *Tips for Successful "Clicker" Use*, 2008. Accessed 8/24/15.

[3] M. Guzdial. A media computation course for non-majors. *ACM SIGCSE Bulletin*, 35(3):104–108, 2003.

[4] R. R. Hake. Interactive-engagement vs. traditional methods: A six-thousand-student survey of mechanics test data for introductory physics courses. *American Journal of Physics*, 66(1), 1998.

[5] C. B. Lee, S. Garcia, and L. Porter. Can peer instruction be effective in upper-division computer science courses? *Transactions on Computing Education*, 13(3):12:1–12:22, Aug. 2013.

[6] L. Porter, C. Bailey Lee, and B. Simon. Halving fail rates using peer instruction: A study of four computer science courses. In *Proceeding of the 44th ACM Technical Symposium on Computer Science Education*, 2013.

[7] L. Porter, C. Bailey-Lee, B. Simon, and D. Zingaro. Peer instruction: Do students really learn from peer discussion in computing? In *7th Annual International Computing Education Research Workshop*, 2011.

[8] L. Porter, S. Garcia, J. Glick, A. Matusiewicz, and C. Taylor. Peer instruction in computer science at small liberal arts colleges. In *Proceedings of the 18th ACM Conference on Innovation and Technology in Computer Science Education*, 2013.

[9] L. Porter and B. Simon. Retaining nearly one-third more majors with a trio of instructional best practices in cs1. In *Proceeding of the 44th ACM Technical Symposium on Computer Science Education*, 2013.

[10] B. Simon, M. Kohanfars, J. Lee, K. Tamayo, and Q. Cutts. Experience report: Peer instruction in introductory computing. In *Proceedings of the 41st SIGCSE technical symposium on computer science education*, 2010.

[11] B. Simon, J. Parris, and J. Spacco. How we teach impacts student learning: Peer instruction vs. lecture in cs0. In *Proceeding of the 44th ACM Technical Symposium on Computer Science Education*, 2013.

[12] C. Wieman. *Clicker Resource Guide*. CWSEI - Carl Wieman Science Education Initiative at the University of British Columbia, 2015. Accessed 8/24/15.

[13] D. Zingaro. Peer instruction contributes to self-efficacy in cs1. In *Proceedings of the 45th ACM technical symposium on Computer Science Education*, pages 373–378, 2014.

[14] D. Zingaro, C. Bailey Lee, and L. Porter. Peer instruction in computing: The role of reading quizzes. In *Proceeding of the 44th ACM Technical Symposium on Computer Science Education*, 2013.

[15] D. Zingaro and L. Porter. Peer instruction in computing: The value of instructor intervention. *Computers & Education*, 71:87–96, 2014.

Developing a Computer Science Concept Inventory for Introductory Programming

Ricardo Caceffo
Institute of Computing
State University of Campinas
Campinas, SP, Brasil
rec@ic.unicamp.br

Steve Wolfman
Computer Science
University of British Columbia
Vancouver, BC, Canada
wolf@cs.ubc.ca

Kellogg S. Booth
Computer Science
University of British Columbia
Vancouver, BC, Canada
ksbooth@cs.ubc.ca

Rodolfo Azevedo
Institute of Computing
State University of Campinas
Campinas, SP, Brasil
rodolfo@ic.unicamp.br

ABSTRACT

A Concept Inventory (CI) is a set of multiple choice questions used to reveal student's misconceptions related to some topic. Each available choice (besides the correct choice) is a distractor that is carefully developed to address a specific misunderstanding, a student wrong thought. In computer science introductory programming courses, the development of CIs is still beginning, with many topics requiring further study and analysis. We identify, through analysis of open-ended exams and instructor interviews, introductory programming course misconceptions related to function parameter use and scope, variables, recursion, iteration, structures, pointers and boolean expressions. We categorize these misconceptions and define high-quality distractors founded in words used by students in their responses to exam questions. We discuss the difficulty of assessing introductory programming misconceptions independent of the syntax of a language and we present a detailed discussion of two pilot CIs related to parameters: an open-ended question (to help identify new misunderstandings) and a multiple choice question with suggested distractors that we identified.

Keywords

concept inventory, data structures, misconceptions

1. INTRODUCTION

A Concept Inventory (CI) is a multiple choice questionnaire used to reveal students' misconceptions related to a subject or topic. For each question the answer choices, aside from the right one, is a distractor designed to address a specific misunderstanding—a wrong yet common way of thinking among students.

SIGCSE '16, March 02-05, 2016, Memphis, TN, USA
© 2016 ACM. ISBN 978-1-4503-3685-7/16/03...$15.00
DOI: http://dx.doi.org/10.1145/2839509.2844559

In this paper, we discuss our experience developing a CI for introductory programming courses that cover topics related to basic programming skills, such as variables, conditional commands, loops and iterations, procedures and functions, basic sorting algorithms, vectors and matrix representations, and elementary structures. These topics are far from exhaustively studied in the CI literature. Our study is part of a multi-institutional project to develop and validate CIs for introductory programming courses that can be used with a peer instruction approach.

2. RELATED WORK

Herman et al. [7] identify a CI as a standardized test that has been statistically validated. Unlike a typical classroom exam, a CI is not comprehensive. It only covers critical concepts for a topic. Each concept is tested multiple times to ensure the CI's validity and reliability [7]. A CI can be used by an instructor to adjust material to students' needs. The idea of a CI was originally applied to fundamental physics: the Force Concept Inventory (FCI) [8] was created to identify students' common misunderstandings about Newton's Laws of Force.

CIs can also be used to measure the impact of educational methodologies, such as comparing traditional and interactive engagement educational methods [5]. This is achieved using pre- and post-tests at the beginning and end of the term to determine the learning gain of each student through the course, taking into account any initial knowledge students may have had when the course started.

Some studies reported in the literature [3, 10] developed CIs based on the flowchart development process proposed by Almstrum et al. [1]. The first step in developing a CI is identification of fundamental concepts through synthesis of various sources (experts, textbooks, papers, etc.). This often follows a pre-defined path, passing through the development of open-ended questions, pilot multiple-choice questions, a student-based investigation, a trial period, and a statistical analysis, leading to final deployment of the CI. Because CI development is costly, novel approaches are under development, such as the open-source approach of Porter et al. [12] and the CS1 exam developed by Tew & Guzdial that uses pseudo-code questions [14].

A number of initiatives in Computer Science have created, validated, and applied CIs. Although different methodologies were used, Computer Science CIs can be categorized into two groups: (1) misconception identification, related primarily to topics and themes that emerge from students' misconceptions, and (2) where after identifying misconceptions a pilot CI is developed and validated.

Misconceptions in computer science have been identified and CI questions proposed for *binary search trees* (2 questions) [3, 10], *digital logic* (19 questions) [7], *hash tables* (1 question) [10], and *operating systems* (10 questions) [16]. Misconceptions but no questions have been identified for *Boolean logic* [6], *heaps* [3], *loops and iteration* [9], *memory models and allocation* [4, 9], *object concepts* [9], *parameter scope* [4], and *recursion* [4].

Another approach, proposed by Sorva [13], allows learners to interact and cognitively engage with a Visual Program Simulation (VPS). Sorva mapped from the literature 162 misconceptions and categorized them as General, VarAssign (variables, assignment and expression evaluation), Control (flow of control during execution), Calls (subprogram invocations and parameter passing), Recursion, Refs (references and pointers) and OOP (Object-Oriented Programming).

3. METHODOLOGY

We looked at an introductory algorithm and computer programming course at the State University of Campinas (Brasil), a mandatory course for all engineering students. More than 500 students enrol each semester and attend four 50-minute lectures (theoretical classes) and two 50-minute labs (practical classes) every week. Each week students are given a practical problem related to theoretical concepts seen in lecture. They then develop a C programming language program to solve the problem. This usually requires an additional four out-of-class hours each week. We developed a CI for the course following an approach similar to Almstrum et al. [1], which is depicted in Figure 1.

Figure 1: CI development methodology, based on Almstrum et al. [1]

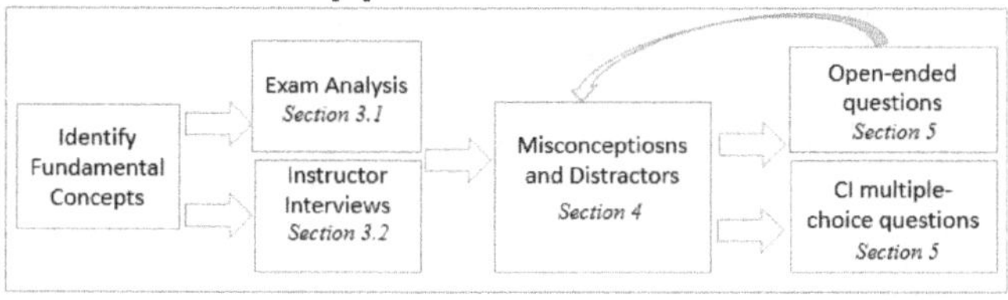

Key steps included identification of student misconceptions through analysis of exam papers and instructor interviews, and development of open-ended and multiple-choice questions for CI items that reflect the misconceptions.

3.1 Exam Analysis

We analysed two course exams, each having four questions. The exams were taken individually by 66 and 60 students in the same term, at the end of the second and fourth months, respectively. We classified student's errors in exams according to misunderstandings that might explain incorrect answers.

The first question in Exam 1 presented a C program with two functions each called from inside a loop within `main()`. Students were to identify the local and global variables and describe the expected outputs from `printf` statements. The second question asked students to write a C program to input an integer and print all of its divisors. The third question asked students to write a C program to input a year and print whether or not it was a leap year. The fourth question asked students to write a C program to verify whether an input n is Pythagorean (n is Pythagorean iff there are integers a and b such that $a^2 + b^2 = n$).

The first question in Exam 2 presented a C function that correctly implemented *Insertion Sort* and received as a parameter an `int` array to be ordered. Students were asked to create a `Date` structure composed of year, month, and day fields, and then change the function to sort an array of `Date` structures. The second question asked students to write a C function to receive an `int` matrix and verify whether it followed some pre-defined rules (e.g., the first and last rows should contain the number 0). The third question asked students to write a C function to receive an array and two `int` pointer parameters and return via the first pointer the average value of the array and via the second pointer an element closest to the average value. The fourth question asked students to write a recursive C function to calculate the floor of the logarithm base 2 of an `int`.

Based on exam papers students submitted, we identified misconceptions and collected them into initial categories that grouped similar items. We eliminated misconceptions that fell outside of the scope of our investigation.

3.2 Instructor Interviews

We conducted semi-structured interviews [11] with 5 course instructors. We asked them about the main misconceptions they believed students in the course had and we asked them to comment on our exam analysis findings. They were also asked to identify and separate higher-level critical thinking misconceptions from lower-level syntax misconceptions and explain how they might apply our CI in their course.

Based on these interviews, we refined misconception categories to reflect the main topics necessary for correct understanding in an introductory programming course. We believe a comprehensive CI for an introductory programming course must have questions from each of these categories.

3.3 Development of Pilot Items

We developed open-ended and multiple-choice questions covering the categories of misconceptions identified in earlier steps, with distractors for each multiple-choice question drawn from examples in students' exam papers. These were used in pilot studies to test the validity of the CI.

4. MISCONCEPTIONS

We identified seven misconception categories. Each category has one or more misconceptions for which we found evidence in the exams or in our interviews with instructors. Categories represent similar types of misconceptions and thus offer opportunities to identify linkages between misconceptions by providing multiple distractors from the category in a single CI item. For each category we describe below the type of misconceptions that characterize it and we give examples drawn from our analysis of exam papers and our interviews with instructors. We provide the percentage and number of instances we found of each misconception.

Categories are described in decreasing order of their prevalence.

We also identified an eighth category, which arose in the interviews, regarding differences between conceptual misunderstandings and misunderstandings about the specific syntax of a construct in a particular programming language. We discuss that after the seven that arose from students' exams.

4.1 Function Parameter Use and Scope

This was by far the largest source of misconceptions, identified in both exams and instructor interviews. Students do not understand function calls and parameters passing. We identified three misconceptions in this category.

Call by reference vs. call by value semantics (44% – 29/66 in Exam 1 and 5% – 3/60 in Exam 2). The association between *actual parameters* (arguments) and *formal parameters* depends on the particular mechanism used by a language. C uses call-by-value exclusively for all parameters, yet on both exams students thought if they changed the content of a formal parameter inside a *called function*, the actual parameter variable located outside in the *caller function* would also change.

Parameters as local variables (17% – 11/66). On Exam 1 we identified cases in which students did not consider function parameters to be local variables. This misconception is a distinct category because it is specific to the scope of function parameters.

Initialization of formal parameters (12% – 7/60). On Exam 2, students didn't appear to understand how parameters work, specifically, how they are initialized. Students apparently did not realize that function calls initialize parameters so they sometimes gave parameters specific values either by explicit assignment or from an external source at the beginning of function execution, rather than using the caller's supplied values.

Candidate Distractors: Possible distractors cover situations where (a) parameters are used as if passed by reference, (b) parameters are accessed outside their scope, and (c) the original parameter value is changed by an external source such as `scanf()`.

The most instances of errors similar to distractor (a) were in the first question of Exam 1, in which students had to `printf` a local variable after calling a function that receives the variable as parameter and changes its value. Another instance of distractor (a) was in the third question of Exam 2, in which students were to implement a function based on the following prototype:

```
void f(double v[], int n, double *a, double* b)
```

Students should calculate the average value of the elements of `v`, putting its value into the memory address pointed by `a`. Some students instead declared a local variable `x`, set it to be the average value, and then set `a = &x`, perhaps expecting that some variable in the caller function corresponding to `a` would change.

Distractor (b) was proposed by instructors in interviews but was never observed in student responses. It may therefore be inappropriate for a CI. We plan to test this in a multiple choice format and will discard the item if it elicits few incorrect responses. If it is popular, we will follow up with think-aloud interviews to assess whether students really choose the distractor for the reasons we heard in instructor interviews.

Distractor (c) was identified in both exams. Some students replaced the caller-provided value for a parameter with a value drawn from some other source. For example, in Exam 2, some students began a function that received a parameter that was a matrix of integers by creating a loop to read all matrix elements with `scanf("%d", &x)`. In interviews, some instructors identified cases in which students started functions by initializing parameter variables with hard-coded numbers, losing the original values that had been passed.

4.2 Variables, Identifiers, and Scope

On Exam 1 students did not understand declarations of variables or rules for assignment and scope in a program. This category excludes parameters, as explained in the previous section.

Out of scope assignment (33% – 22/66). Variables declared inside functions were not considered local to the function. Students classified variables from one function as being part of another function. Local variables were used as if they were global.

Function names (6% – 4/66). Students classified function names in function prototypes as global variables (they are global, but they are not variables).

Candidate Distractors: Distractors include (a) using non-variables as variables, (b) using local variables as global variables, (c) using global variables as local variables, and (d) having multiple variables with the same name but declared in different scopes (e.g., global and local variables with the same name).

In the first question of Exam 1, students were asked to identify the local and global variables inside a program. Some identified non-variables, such as function names in prototype declarations, as variables (distractor (a)), some identified local variables as global (distractor (b)), while others identified global variables as local variables (distractor (c)). In the same question, students analysed a program that had a loop within the main function that used an `int` variable `i` as iterator. The loop had a call to a function that accessed an `int` global variable also named `i`. Some students got confused and thought the value of `i` inside the function was the value of the local variable `i` inside `main`, instead of the value of the global variable `i` (distractor (d)).

4.3 Recursion

On Exam 2 students had three misconceptions about the application of recursion in problem-solving.

Bounded recursion (15% – 9/60). The expression for a return value had an embedded recursive call with a parameter that was larger than the parameter to the current invocation, leading to an inifite loop because the level of recursion increases indefinitely.

Stopping condition (12% – 7/60). Appropriate checks to terminate recursion when a base case is encountered were not provided.

Self-reference (7% – 4/60). Functions required to be recursive did not call themselves.

Candidate Distractors: Possible distractors are: (a) a recursive function without a call to itself, (b) a recursive call that grows its parameter and thus leads to an infinite recursive loop, (c) lack of a stopping condition, and (d) use of an improper stopping condition.

Distractors examples were identified in the fourth question of Exam 2, in which students were asked to implement a recursive function `int logRec (int n)` that calculates the floor of the logarithm base 2 of `n`. Some students wrote most of the function code correctly, but didn't insert a recursive call to the function itself (distractor (a)); other students inserted the correct stopping condition (`n == 1`) but the recursive call was made with an increased `n` (e.g., `logRec (n+1)`) leading to an infinite loop (distractor (b)); other students didn't insert the stopping condition (distractor (c)); and some students inserted an incorrect stopping condition (e.g., `while n == 1`), which represents an instance of distractor (d)).

4.4 Iteration

On Exam 1 students seemed not sure when iteration should be used or how the number of loop iterations is managed.

Basic loop behavior (14% – 9/66). Students used a loop to perform some calculation but had a call to `printf()` for the result value that appeared inside the loop, not outside the loop.

Logic of looping count (14% – 9/66). Students did not pass all required values (from 1 to n) to an auxiliary function. Instead, they only called the function once, without any looping structure.

Candidate Distractors: Possible distractors are (a) premature final result calculation or reporting before the loop is over, (b) solving a problem that requires iteration without having a loop, (c) improper initialization of the loop counter, and (d) improper updating of the loop counter.

An instance for distractor (a) was identified in the fourth question of Exam 1, in which students were supposed to verify if an integer `n` is Pythagorean. The correct answer involves a loop to check all possibile pairs of numbers. Some students inserted inside the loop a `printf` stating whether `n` was or was not Pythagorean before testing all possible number combinations. In the same question, some students implemented an auxiliary boolean function that receives three parameters `a`, `b`, and `n` and verified if the condition for `n` to be Pythagorean was satisfied for the parameters `a` and `b` but some of those students only called the function once, without making a loop to check all possibilities for `a` and `b` (distractor (b)).

An instance for distractor (c) was identified in the first question of Exam 1, in which students were asked to print all numbers that are divisors of some integer `n`. Some students initialized a `for` loop with `i = n` instead of `i = 1`. In the same question, some students correctly coded the iteration as `for (int i = 1; i < n; i++)` but added inside the loop another increment `i++` of the iterator `i` (distractor (c)).

4.5 Structures

On Exam 2 students did not understand how to declare and use C-style structs.

Accessing fields (27% – 16/60). Students tried to use the struct as an atomic unit (e.g., to compare it to a number or to another struct), without accessing any of the struct's inner fields.

Multi-key sorting (17% – 10/60). Given an array of `Date` structs, students created three variants of the insertion sort function that had been provided and sorted the array first by `year`, then by `month`, and finally by `day`. They instead should have made a single multi-key sort function.

Candidate Distractors: A possible distractor relates to the use of the whole struct when only a field is needed. For example, on the second question of Exam 2, students should compare two `Date` structs (`a` and `b`) with day, month, and year fields. Instead of comparing the struct through their fields (e.g., `a.day > b.day`, `a.month > b.month`, and so on) the distractor would compare the entire struct using the statement `a > b`.

4.6 Pointers

On Exam 2 students did not understand the concepts of memory addresses and pointers, nor why and how pointers should be used.

Returning values through pointers (3% – 2/60). Students created a local variable containing the value to be returned by a function and assigned its memory address to the pointer parameter, rather than dereferencing the pointer parameter to assign the value to be returned to a memory location external to the function.

Assign values to pointers (12% – 7/60). Students assigned to a pointer variable a specific value instead of a memory address.

Candidate Distractors: Possible distractors are: (a) assigning a value to an address, (b) assigning an address to a value, and (c) assigning to a pointer an invalid address.

For example, in the third question of Exam 2, students should make a function that receives two `double*` variables `a` and `b` and changes the values pointed to by `a` and `b` to some calculated `double x`. Some students assigned `x` to an address, for example `a = x` (distractor (a)); some assigned the address of `x` to the value pointed to by `a` using the statement `*a = &x` (distractor (b)); and others assigned to the pointer the address of `x` using `a = &x`, which would point to an invalid address after the function returns (distractor (c)). The expected answer was `*a = x`.

4.7 Boolean Expressions

Students did not understand boolean expressions' meanings or their evaluation.

Truth tables (12% – 8/66). Incorrect use of the `||` and `&&` operators.

Candidate Distractors: Possible distractors cover (a) translation from English sentences to incorrect Boolean expressions, which don't have the expected precedence order or semantics; and (b) attempts to create a Boolean expression without boolean operators (e.g., without 'and' (`&&`) and 'or' (`||`)).

An instance for distractor (a) was identified in the third question of Exam 1, in which students were asked to verify if a number `n` represents a leap year. Leap years are multiples of 400 **or** they are multiples of 4 that are **not** multiples of 100. Some students were not able to correctly translate this sentence to a Boolean expression. For example, some used only `&&` or `||` operators without including parenthesis to delimit the precedence order. Other students tried to solve the problem through an `if` sequence, not using any Boolean operators at all. Although not technically wrong, this workaround does not contemplate the purpose of the exercise (distractor (b)).

4.8 Syntax vs. Conceptual Understanding

In our interviews, instructors raised concerns about distinguishing between learning/conceptual misconceptions and highly language-specific syntactic misconceptions. For example, could one or more CI items distinguish between a student who does not grasp the concept of pointer addressing and one who understands the concept but not the C progamming language syntax for pointer addressing? The consensus of the instructors who were interviewed was that the nature of the subject (programming) makes it hard to elaborate conceptual questions entirely independent of the particular programming language being used. This conclusion is similar to findings in the literature [9].

Another concern raised by instructors focused on the typical use of CIs as pre- and post-tests. Unlike the Force Concept Inventory [8], where college students have everyday experience of basic Newtonian force concepts and may even have studied them, many students' first contact with most programming concepts happens in college introductory programming courses. A CI that assumes knowledge of programming language syntax at the start of the term would not be effective; it could even frighten students. To address this issue, we propose an approach similar to that discussed by Porter et al. [12], where the pre-course CI consists of conceptual questions, not related to programming language syntax, and the post-course CI has those same questions, but with additional specific programming language questions added. This approach is related to Commonsense Computing, an attempt to get at deep computing concepts in ways accessible to people with no computing background [15].

This leads to the development, for the same misunderstanding, of two types of CI questions: conceptual or analogy questions, accessible to all students at any point in the course, and technical or language-dependent questions, where knowledge of the chosen programming language syntax is required. This approach supports the measurement of learning gains; it is still possible to compare the initial subset of questions that are in both the pre- and post-course tests. Developing such questions remains a goal.

5. PILOT TEST QUESTIONS

As Almstrum et al. propose [1], the next step in this kind of research is the creation of open-ended or multiple-choice pilot items based on categories of misunderstandings. In open-ended questions students can write the answers in their own words, allowing discovery of new misconceptions. Multiple-choice questions have the advantage of being easier to analyse than are open-ended questions, but they require creation of distractor options to address each identified misconception.

We explored the open-ended questions approach during the exam analysis described in Section 3.1. We opted to create both new open-ended questions (to identify new misconceptions) and multiple-choice pilot items. Due to space limitations we present here only two questions, which relate to the topic **Function Parameter Use and Scope** as examples to illustrate our approach. Question 1 (Q1) is an open-ended question, to help identify new misconceptions related to the topic. Question 2 (Q2) is a multiple-choice question that has distractors for the misunderstandings identified already in our study.

Q1. Function usage. Write a program in C that asks the user to enter two `int` numbers, `a` and `b`. Then, if `a` is equal or greater than `b`, calculate and print `a-b`. Otherwise, calculate and print `b-a`. You must write one (and only one) auxiliary (helper) function that performs the subtraction.

Discussion: This open-ended question was developed to help find new misconceptions related to function parameters' use and scope. The fact that the student must write just one auxiliary function verifies if the student understands how parameter passing works. This question can also help identify misconceptions related to variable assignment and scope and boolean expression evaluation.

Q2: Scope of variables. The following code includes a function that adds five to a number. This is called on `x` in the `main` function.

```
int addFiveToNumber (int n) {
      int c = 0;
      // Insert a Line Here
      return c;
}

int main ( ) {
      int x = 0;
      x = addFiveToNumber(x);
}
```

The correct line to be inserted is:

(a) `scanf ("%d", n);`
(b) `n = n + 5;`
(c) `c = n + 5;`
(d) `c = x + 5;`

Discussion: Aside from the right answer (option (c)), each other option matches a specific distractor presented in Section 4.1: option (a) relates to the change of the original parameter value by an external source; option (b) relates to the misunderstanding that parameters are passed by reference, and option (d) relates to the misunderstandings that a variable can be accessed outside its scope. Our interest in piloting this question is how attractive the distractors are.

For example, the `scanf()` distractor does not include any addition of 5. Will students avoid it for that reason? As we further develop the question, we will tailor it to try to elicit the actual misconceptions that students hold, based on our experience with the pilot exam.

6. CONCLUSIONS AND FUTURE WORK

We have begun to identify misconceptions appropriate to introductory computing courses using the C programming language that cover concepts related to basic programming skills, such as variables, conditional commands, loops, functions, pointers, and structs. Through a careful exam analysis, we first identified the main misunderstandings associated with each topic. Then, aided by instructor interviews, we categorized the misconceptions, extracting the distractors. We are now applying these data to generate a pilot CI, composed of 21 open-ended and multiple-choice questions, classified either as conceptual or analogy questions or as programming language-dependent questions.

The CI is available at the **http://edu.ic.unicamp.br/caceffo** website.

In future work, we plan to test our pilot CI to statistically validate it and use think-aloud interviews to identify new, not-yet-addressed misconceptions. We plan to apply the conceptual/analogy questions as a pre-course test, and to also include them in the post-course test as a means to measure learning.

Another approach that we plan to take is an adaptation of the Peer Instruction methodology [2], called CSPI (Computer Science Peer Instruction). Currently in development, CSPI addresses Computer Science-specific needs, for example, supporting the use of classroom clickers to test specific misunderstandings of programming concepts such as a program's execution flow control. We plan to apply the CI that we develop to measure the CSPI's educational impact in CS1 courses. Future work will continue the multicultural approach in the work to date, with the CI application tested in universities from different countries, with different native languages, and different student backgrounds.

7. ACKNOWLEDGMENTS

This research was supported in part by the São Paulo Research Foundation (FAPESP) under grants #2014/07502-4 and #2015/08668-6 and by the Natural Science and Engineering Research Council of Canada (NSERC) under grant RGPIN 116412-11.

8. REFERENCES

[1] V. L. Almstrum, P. B. Henderson, V. Harvey, C. Heeren, W. Marion, C. Riedesel, L.-K. Soh, and A. E. Tew. Concept inventories in computer science for the topic discrete mathematics. *SIGCSE Bull.*, 38(4):132–145, June 2006.

[2] C. H. Crouch and E. Mazur. Peer instruction: Ten years of experience and results. *American Journal of Physics*, 69:970–977, 2001.

[3] H. Danielsiek, W. Paul, and J. Vahrenhold. Detecting and understanding students' misconceptions related to algorithms and data structures. In *Proceedings of the 43rd ACM Technical Symposium on Computer Science Education*, SIGCSE '12, pages 21–26, New York, NY, USA, 2012. ACM.

[4] K. Goldman, P. Gross, C. Heeren, G. L. Herman, L. Kaczmarczyk, M. C. Loui, and C. Zilles. Setting the scope of concept inventories for introductory computing subjects. *Trans. Comput. Educ.*, 10(2):5:1–5:29, June 2010.

[5] R. Hake. Interactive-engagement versus traditional methods: A six-thousand-student survey of mechanics test data for introductory physics courses. *Am. J. Phys.*, 66(1):64–74, January 1998.

[6] G. L. Herman, M. C. Loui, L. Kaczmarczyk, and C. Zilles. Describing the what and why of students' difficulties in Boolean logic. *Trans. Comput. Educ.*, 12(1):3:1–3:28, Mar. 2012.

[7] G. L. Herman, M. C. Loui, and C. Zilles. Creating the digital logic concept inventory. In *Proceedings of the 41st ACM Technical Symposium on Computer Science Education*, SIGCSE '10, pages 102–106, New York, NY, USA, 2010. ACM.

[8] D. Hestenes, M. Wells, and G. Swackhamer. Force Concept Inventory. *Phys. Teach.*, 30(3):141–158, March 1992.

[9] L. C. Kaczmarczyk, E. R. Petrick, J. P. East, and G. L. Herman. Identifying student misconceptions of programming. In *Proceedings of the 41st ACM Technical Symposium on Computer Science Education*, SIGCSE '10, pages 107–111, New York, NY, USA, 2010. ACM.

[10] K. Karpierz and S. A. Wolfman. Misconceptions and concept inventory questions for binary search trees and hash tables. In *Proceedings of the 45th ACM Technical Symposium on Computer Science Education*, SIGCSE '14, pages 109–114, New York, NY, USA, 2014. ACM.

[11] J. Lazar, J. H. Feng, and H. Hochheiser. *Research Methods in Human-Computer Interaction*. Wiley Publishing, 2010.

[12] L. Porter, C. Taylor, and K. C. Webb. Leveraging open source principles for flexible concept inventory development. In *Proceedings of the 2014 Conference on Innovation #38; Technology in Computer Science Education*, ITiCSE '14, pages 243–248, New York, NY, USA, 2014. ACM.

[13] J. Sorva. *Visual Program Simulation in Introductory Programming Education*. PhD thesis, Aalto University, Finland, 2012.

[14] A. E. Tew and M. Guzdial. The FCS1: A language independent assessment of CS1 knowledge. pages 111–116, 2011.

[15] T. VanDeGrift, D. Bouvier, T.-Y. Chen, G. Lewandowski, R. McCartney, and B. Simon. Commonsense computing (episode 6): Logic is harder than pie. pages 76–85, 2010.

[16] K. C. Webb and C. Taylor. Developing a pre- and post-course concept inventory to gauge operating systems learning. In *Proceedings of the 45th ACM Technical Symposium on Computer Science Education*, SIGCSE '14, pages 103–108, New York, NY, USA, 2014. ACM.

A Data-Driven Analysis of Informatively Hard Concepts in Introductory Programming

R. Paul Wiegand
Institute for Simulation & Training
University of Central Florida
Orlando, FL, USA
wiegand@ist.ucf.edu

Anthony Bucci
119 Amory St.
Cambridge, MA, USA
anthony@bucci.onl

Amruth N. Kumar
Ramapo College of New Jersey
Mahwah, NJ, USA
amruth@ramapo.edu

Jennifer L. Albert
The Citadel
171 Moultrie Street
Charleston, SC, USA
jalbert@citadel.edu

Alessio Gaspar
University of South Florida
4202 E. Fowler Avenue
Tampa, FL, USA
alessio@usf.edu

ABSTRACT

What are the concepts in introductory programming that are easy/hard for students? We propose to use Dimension Extraction algorithm (DECA) inspired by coevolution and co-optimization theory to answer this question. We propose and use the metrics of *informatively easy/hard* concepts to identify programming concepts that are solved correctly by the most "dominated student" versus solved incorrectly by the most "dominant student". As a proof of concept, we applied DECA to analyze the data collected by software tutors called problets used by introductory programming students in Spring 2014. We present the results, i.e., informatively easy/hard concepts on a dozen different topics covered in a typical introductory programming course. It is hoped that these results will inform programming instructors on the concepts they should (de)/emphasize in class. They will also contribute towards creating a concept inventory for introductory programming.

CCS Concepts

•Social and professional topics → Computer science education; •Applied computing → Education;

Keywords

introductory programming education; dimension extraction; multiobjective optimization, performance analysis; problets

1. INTRODUCTION

Attrition in the introductory programming course is legendary. Students find programming to be hard. What are the concepts in introductory programming that are hard/easy for students? Knowing this would help educators better target the hard concepts, provide focused support to students, and possibly improve retention in the course.

Typically, a study of hard programming concepts would be conducted in the context of creating a concept inventory. However, no formal concept inventory exists for programming concepts. Delphi process has been proposed as one mechanism for identifying hard concepts [6]. While this process relies on the expertise and consensus of educators, the results still need to be empirically validated.

In this paper, we propose a data-driven approach for identifying easy and hard programming concepts. In addition to easy and hard concepts as traditionally understood, we propose the notions of *informatively easy* and *informatively hard* concepts. As proof of concept, we apply our approach to data collected by software tutors for programming, called problets (problets.org) in Spring 2014. We present the results and discuss their significance.

The data-driven approach we propose is based on *dimension extraction coevolutionary algorithm* (DECA) and inspired by coevolution and co-optimization theory [2]. The algorithm identifies structural relationships amongst students and problems by constructing a geometry of problems and students that illustrates how student performance can be distinguished in fundamentally different ways. While the algorithm has been used in technical applications such as analyzing game playing strategies, it has seen very little application in educational domains such as identifying difficult programming concepts in computer science education.

SIGCSE '16, March 02 - 05, 2016, Memphis, TN, USA

ISBN 978-1-4503-3685-7/16/03...$15.00

DOI: http://dx.doi.org/10.1145/2839509.2844629

2. BACKGROUND

2.1 Hard Concepts in Programming

Defining and measuring the hardness of concepts is important for scaffolding learning according to Vygotsky's Zone of Proximal Development (ZPD) theory [15]. One of very few attempts to identify hard concepts in programming [6] recently identified a list of topics using Delphi process and ranked them according to importance and difficulty (see Table 1 for the subset used in this study). A second study [7] surveyed instructors of CS1 and CS2 on how much time they spent on various topics and correlated that importance with student performance. However, neither study delved into individual concepts within each topic.

Usually, researchers enumerate concepts and assess their level of hardness when creating a concept inventory on a subject. In Computer Science, concept inventories have been attempted on various subjects (e.g., digital logic, operating systems, algorithms) [13] but none has been completed on introductory programming. Two recent attempts have both been preliminary, one identifying topics [6] and another identifying some high-level concepts [14]. To create a concept inventory for introductory programming, assessment items must be created on a continuum of specific concepts within each topic that students do not understand. We address this issue of granularity [12] by proposing to identify low-level concepts on most of the topics typically covered in introductory programming, particularly those concepts whose hardness can be measured using data-driven analysis.

2.2 Co-optimization and Coevolution

The challenge of defining hard and easy problems arises in the study of *co-optimization* problems and *coevolutionary* algorithms [11]. Co-optimization problems are distinguished from optimization problems by the presence of two or more types of entity (e.g., student or problem) that might vary and can interact with one another with a measurable outcome or score. In the present context we have computer science students and a variety of computer programming problems we might present to those students; any student can attempt–interact with–any of the problems, and they receive a score. Therefore, the real-world domain of students solving problems resembles a co-optimization problem, and we believe the tools and techniques developed in the study of those algorithms can be fruitfully applied to this domain.

One foundational line of work in co-optimization and coevolutionary algorithms concerns *dimension extraction* methods [3, 4, 2, 5]. Abstractly, this work hypothesizes that the information gleaned from interactions, for instance the scores of students solving problems, can be decomposed into a vector-space-like *coordinate system*. Within a coordinate system, there are potentially *multiple axes* or *dimensions*, consisting of a linearly ordered subset of the set of all entities. Entities further along a given axis are "no worse than" those preceding it. Across two different axes, entities are incomparable to one another, in the sense that an entity on one axis will be better in some ways, but worse in other ways, than an entity on another axis. This method has been used for a number of purposes, including automatically identifying key conceptual tactics in the game of Nim [5].

We will apply a minor variant of the dimension-extraction algorithm presented in [4] to analyze data about populations of students. A "student axis" will be a subset of the students, which might be thought of as a "learner type". Students further along the axis they are in tend to be better on the collection of problems they attempted than the students preceding them on the axis. This analysis will help us distinguish student performance, a key insight of this paper.

3. METHODS

3.1 Problets

The software tutors used in this study, problets (problets.org), cover topics typically studied in introductory programming courses. Each problet addresses one topic, but covers several concepts (see Table 1). The concepts address different skills: evaluating expressions, tracing programs (e.g., predicting the output), debugging programs and identifying the state of variables in a program. An advantage of using data collected by problets is that problets have been used by third-party educators in their introductory courses for over a decade and have been continually and extensively evaluated (e.g., [9, 10]).

Problets are adaptive, i.e., they tailor the sequence of problems to the learning needs of the student. Initially, each problet presents the student with one test problem per concept. Thereafter, it only presents practice problems on concepts on which the student incorrectly solved the test problem. Since the purpose of this study was to identify easy/hard concepts, we used only the data from the initial test administered by each problet — this data represented a snapshot of what the students knew/did not know before using the problet but after attending one or more lectures on the topic in class.

Table (1) lists the topics on which problets are available, and the number of concepts covered by each problet. It lists the number of students who solved all the test problems in each problet, and their schools in Spring 2014. Participants were students of introductory programming from high schools, community colleges and four-year colleges, who usually used the problets for after-class assignments after the topic had been covered in class.

Topic	Concepts	Schools	Students
Arithmetic	25	29	982
Relational	24	20	582
Logical	21	16	572
Assignment	19	15	599
Selection	12	21	774
Switch	12	12	221
while	9	18	523
for	10	18	700
do-while	15	13	175
Advanced Loops	13	8	161
Functions/Bugs	9	7	282
Functions/Tracing	10	8	449
Array	14	14	221
Class	18	4	125

Table 1: Concepts per topic and number of schools/students who used each problet in Spring 2014

3.2 Dimension Extraction

Dimension Extraction Coevolutionary Algorithm (DECA) [4] is a coevolutionary algorithm that uses a dimension extraction method, as outlined in Sect. 2.2, at its core. While the coevolutionary algorithm searches through *candidate solutions* and *tests*, for our purposes here we will be using its internal dimension-extraction algorithm to analyze students and problems.

In a *problem analysis*, the students are the candidates and the problems are the tests. The result is a coordinate system of problems, where each dimension orders a subset of the problems. Problems further along a dimension are not passed by at least the same students than those lower on the dimension. Problems on different dimensions are those on which students performed incomparably. Intuitively, each dimension corresponds to a different concept that differentiated student performance and the problems that are highest on each dimension are the problems the most students did not solve.

Dually, in a *student analysis*, the problems are the candidates and the students are the tests. The result is a coordinate system of students this time, where each dimension orders a subset of students in terms of the number of problems they solved correctly. Students on different dimensions perform incomparably on the tests. In this sense, each dimension corresponds to a different pattern in which students performed on problems or intuitively speaking a "type" of learner. The students furthest along an axis solve the most problems, and in that sense are the best-performing representatives of each type.

Application of these analyses to the performance of students on problets potentially provides several sources of insight. First, the number of dimensions extracted from problem analysis gives an implicit measure of the number of distinct *concepts* that appear in the problem set; that is, the number of different ways that problems distinguish student performance. Likewise, the number of dimensions extracted from student analysis gives an implicit measure of the number of distinct *types of learner* that appear in the student set, or in other words the number of different ways students can be grouped in terms of differences in performance.

Additionally, such analyses allow us to highlight the importance of how informative different problems are. It is simplistic to assign a "difficulty" measure to problems based purely on how many students solve or do not solve a problem. For instance, if Garry Kasparov were to play a classroom of intermediate chess students, he would likely beat them all, and it would be impossible to determine which students were among the best in the class. Likewise, if someone who never played chess was used as the opponent, this person would likely lose to everyone, and we would be equally uninformed about the relative performance of students. Similarly, a problem that most students miss (or get right) may not be an informative problem because it might not provide distinctions to help educators know where students are having problems.

Instead, we want challenging problems that distinguish student performance as much as possible. As educators, we should be interested in constructing problems that lie in a *zone of proximal development* [15] — problems of varying levels of difficulty that are on the boundary of where students perform in fundamentally different ways and, consequently, where true performance can best be judged. To begin to address this shortfall, we introduce two new terms grounded in our dimension extraction analysis, *informatively hard* and *informatively easy*.

For each dimension extracted in a student analysis, i.e. type of learner, we identify the *most dominant student* as the one who solved the most problems among students on that dimension. We count each problem not passed by such students, for all of the most dominant students. Likewise, we identify the *most dominated student* as the one who solved the fewest problems among students on their dimension. We count each problem solved correctly by such students, for all of the most dominated students. Then, a problem is **informatively hard** if it is most often solved incorrectly by the most *dominant* students. Similarly, a problem is **informatively easy** if it is most often solved correctly by the most *dominated* students.

These two measures do not coincide with their traditional counterparts. For example, it is possible for a problem to be missed by everyone *but* the strongest students, for an otherwise challenging problem to be solved by the weakest students. When such things happen, it is likely that student behavior is confounding a linear expectation of performance, and is therefore interesting. Measures such as informatively easy and hard highlight and preserve the idea that different students understand different concepts in different ways. An informatively easy concept may be understood in the context of Zone of Proximal Development as the concept nearest to some other concept, whereas an informatively hard concept is farthest from any other concept.

By contrast, we define a problem as (traditionally) **hard** if it is solved incorrectly by most students and as **easy** if it is solved correctly by most students.

As we will see in the next section, rarely is an informatively easy concept also easy, or an informatively hard concept also hard, although our intuitive notions of monotonicity of hardness would dictate this. Recall that informatively hard concepts are determined by the most dominant students vis-a-vis the general population, and informatively easy problems are determined by the most dominated students. The more interesting, although rare, cases are when an informatively easy concept is hard and an informatively hard concept is easy. The former corresponds to when it is easy for the general population to make mistakes while solving a problem. The latter corresponds to when it is easy for the general population to guess the answer.

3.3 Consistency with the Data

We will begin to demonstrate the utility of our approach in the next section; however, an important preliminary question is whether or not our method for identifying informatively hard and informatively easy remains relatively consistent across a given data set. Our discussion below describes our analysis for identifying informatively hard problems; however, the same analysis was also conducted for informatively easy problems.

To address the question of consistency, we performed the following experiment. For each topic, we split the data so that students were assigned to one of two groups independently and uniformly at random. We extracted dimensions on both groups and used the results to identify informatively hard problems. Since there can be multiple problems that are equally informatively hard, when the two extractions produced an overlap in the set of identified problems, we considered that split to have been "*consistent*". This was repeated 50 times, where each splitting was independent.

Traditional proportions or goodness of fit tests are not possible in this case because the algorithm can return multiple results for a given split. Instead, we first computed per-trial probabilities combinatorially, noting that given that one split produces k informatively hard problems while another produces j informatively hard problems over n such problems, the probability of random subsets overlapping is given by: $1 - \frac{(n-k)!\,(n-j)!}{(n-k-j)!\,n!}$.

For each topic, we averaged these probabilities across the 50 trials, which were then used to compute theoretical values for how many trials should have produced matches in the 50 trials, assuming a random process. After that, we used a traditional one-tailed difference of two proportions statistical test. The results were significant ($\alpha = 0.05$) for both informatively hard and informatively easy calculations, for all but two topics. The *Functions/Bugs* topic did not produce significant results, and the *while* topic results were significant for only informatively easy calculations. Overall, this suggests that the method is fairly consistent; however, when many potential informative cases are identified, consistency issues can arise. However, in such scenarios, the algorithm is not necessarily reporting random information. Since many of the problems are equally discriminating, the specific data set being analyzed simply becomes the biggest factor in identifying informative problems.

4. RESULTS: EASY AND HARD CONCEPTS

Students used problets in sufficient numbers on 13 topics in Spring 2014 for our analysis to be meaningful, as listed in table 1 (We combined the results of the two functions tutors). For each of these topics, we list below the informatively easy and informatively hard concepts as determined by the Dimension Extraction algorithm, along with easy and hard concepts as traditionally understood.

Arithmetic Expressions:
Easy: Evaluating expressions such as $8 - -5$, which involve subtracting a negative number; • evaluating fully parenthesized expressions, such as $(14/((6-3)+2))$, where the order of evaluation of operators is fully dictated by parentheses.
Hard: Evaluating expressions such as $12\%5 + 5\%12.0$, containing remainder operator along with real operands.
Fully parenthesized expressions can be evaluated without knowledge of precedence and associativity rules. Remainder operator and data types are both novel concepts first taught in programming classes.
Informatively Easy: Evaluating expressions involving divide-by-zero error: e.g., $9/3/0$.
Informatively Hard: Evaluating expressions featuring integer division: e.g., $5/3 + 3 * 5$
Integer division is also a novel concept, specific to programming. Dividing by zero is informatively easy since it is emphasized as a problem in math.

Relational Expressions:
Easy: Evaluating expressions where the two operands are the same: e.g., $5 >= 5$
Hard: Evaluating expressions featuring chained relational operators: e.g., $3 > 7 >= -1$
Chaining of relational operators results in errors in Java, and yields surprising results in C++. Both are a clear departure from math, and are novel to programming.
Informatively Easy: Evaluating expressions that involve both arithmetic and relational operators, both being at the lower level of precedence in their respective groups (e.g., + in arithmetic, != in relational), such as $3 - -5 \;\; != \;\; 3+5$
Informatively Hard: Evaluating expressions containing both arithmetic and relational operators, the two being at different levels of precedence at their respective groups, e.g., $-3 * -4 \;\; != \;\; 6 * 2$
Expressions involving both arithmetic and relational operators, but no parentheses, seem to be both informatively easy and hard at the same time. The difference could be that students already understand the concept of subtracting a negative number, but not so much multiplying two negative numbers.

Assignment Expressions:
Easy: Evaluating pre-fix assignments: e.g., `5 + ++var1`
Hard: Evaluating pre- and post-fix assignments: e.g., `var2 = ++var1` and `var2 = var1++`
Both pre- and post-fix assignment operators are inherently confusing to students. That prefix increment also features in the easy expression leads us to speculate that students guess the answer to this problem more often than not.
Informatively Easy: Evaluating coercion during assignment: e.g., `double var1 = 3 + 5`
Informatively Hard: Evaluating postfix decrement operator: e.g., `var2 = var1--`)
By the time students learn assignment expressions, it is likely they are already familiar with the concept of coercion.

Logical Expressions:
Easy: Evaluating fully parenthesized expressions, e.g., `(true && (true && (true || false)))` that do not involve short-circuit evaluation or need for precedence rules; and • expressions evaluated left to right with easy evaluation semantics: e.g., `true && false && true`.
Hard: Evaluating C++ expressions wherein numerical values are used as boolean operands: e.g., $3 * 0 \&\& 3 + 0$
Again, these support the hypothesis that difficulty is linked to novel concepts, specific to programming.
Informatively Easy: The same as the fully parenthesized easy expression described before.
Informatively Hard: The same as the non-parenthesized easy expression described before — even though this is easy, the best students still make mistakes when evaluating it.

Selection Statements:
Easy: Identifying the output of nested `if` statements.
Hard: Identifying the output of an `if-else` statement with a condition that evaluates to true.
The hard problem was designed to be the simplest on `if-else` statements. Lack of familiarity with the user interface may explain why students solved it incorrectly in larger numbers — selection being the first tutor and this problem being the first problem in the tutor. It is surprising that students found nested `if` statements to be easy, suggesting that the bifurcation of control flow is what is complicated about selection statements, not conditional execution.
Informatively Easy: Predicting the output of multiple back-to-back `if` statements.
Informatively Hard: Tracing the output of an `if-else` statement whose condition evaluates to false; • an `if` statement whose condition evaluates to true; • nested `if` statements.
Once again, user interface may be to blame for why students found the first two concepts informatively hard.

`switch` Statement:
Easy: Tracing the output of a `switch` statement whose condition matches no case; • a `switch` statement in which the body of a `case` statement is empty.
Hard: Identifying the output of a `switch` statement with a missing `break` statement.
Both easy concepts entail code not generating any output, and may be traced with only a cursory glance.
Informatively Easy: Specifying the output of nested `switch` statements; • identifying as syntax error when the `case` value is not an integer expression.
Informatively Hard: Predicting the output of multiple back-to-back `switch` statements.
Both informatively easy concepts come as a surprise, since

the correct answer to neither is easily guessable, and cursory glance is not sufficient to arrive at the correct answer. This is an example where data-driven analysis contradicts intuition.

`while` **Loop:**

Easy: Predicting the output of a loop that iterates only once; • a loop that never iterates because its condition evaluates to false on the first try.

Hard: Identifying the output of multiple back-to-back loops, wherein the behavior of the second loop depends on the execution of the first loop.

The two easy concepts require students to trace not so much the repeated execution of the loop as the independent one-time evaluation of the condition and the loop body.

Informatively Easy: Identifying the output of nested loops, wherein execution of the inside loop is independent of that of the outside loop.

Informatively Hard: Predicting the output of • nested loops, with the inner loop's behavior dependent on that of the outer loop; • loop that never iterates because its condition fails immediately; • loop whose condition variable is updated before it is printed inside the loop; • loop with sentinel value changing on each iteration; • code that appears and is executed after the loop exits.

Informatively hard concepts involve behavior that deviates from that of a simple loop. The informatively easy concept of independent nested loops might suggest that nesting is not so much a problem as unexpected behavior of code.

`for` **Loop:**

Easy: Predicting the output of a zero-iteration loop, which results in no output for the code.

Hard: Tracing the output of two back-to-back loops, where second loop's counter depends on the first loop.

Informatively Easy: Identifying the output of a loop which iterates exactly once.

Informatively Hard: Identifying the output of nested dependent loops, wherein the inner loop's counter depends on the outer loop's execution.

All the above findings concur with those on `while` loop.

`do-while` **Loop:**

Easy: Specifying the output of a loop that iterates only once.

Hard: Identifying the output of a C++ loop whose condition is an assignment statement.

The empirically hard problem has been a long-known source of error for novice programmers [8].

Informatively Easy: Tracing the output of a loop whose condition is a disjunctive logical expression.

Informatively Hard: Predicting the output of a loop whose condition is a conjunctive logical expression.

Presumably, disjunctive expressions such as `status == 's' || status == 'f')` are easier to evaluate than conjunctive expressions such as `limit >= 0 && limit <= 100`.

Advanced loop concepts:

Easy: Identifying that modifying the value against which the condition variable is compared results in an infinite loop..

Hard: Predicting the output of a loop containing `continue` statement.

Surprisingly, identifying an infinite loop turned out to be easy, possibly because of the emphasis placed on it in class.

Informatively Easy: Predicting the output of a loop containing `continue` statement.

Informatively Hard: Identifying the bug when a `break` statement appears outside any loop or `switch` statement.

The informatively easy concept is also hard. This suggests that it is easy to make mistakes when tracing loops with `continue` statement, even when one understands the underlying concepts. The informatively hard concept corresponds to a pathological use of the language.

Functions:

Easy: Tracing the output when a function is called as part of an expression; • identifying as a bug when the caller tries to use the value returned by a function with `void` return type.

Hard: Predicting the output when a variable is passed by value to a function; Identifying as a bug when • return statement is missing in the definition of a non-`void` function; • data type of the value in the return statement is incompatible with the return type of the function.

In accord with our previous findings, easy concepts correspond to scenarios where functions are treated like math functions, and hard concepts deal with novel programming-specific constructs. Please note that parameter passing by reference was not included in problets.

Informatively Easy: Tracing the behavior of a function that has multiple conditional return statements; • Identifying bugs due to type incompatibility between formal and actual parameters; • Identifying bugs due to type incompatibility between returned value and return type of a function.

Informatively Hard: *Not* identifying as a bug when two variables with the same name appear in two different functions; • Identifying the C++ bug wherein a function is called before it is defined or prototyped.

Informatively hard concepts deal with advanced concepts of scope and extent . Informatively easy concepts should both be familiar to students by the time functions are introduced.

Arrays:

Easy: Specifying the contents of a fully initialized array; • predicting the behavior of referencing a random element.

Hard: Identifying the contents of an array declared with incomplete initialization.

The hard concept is among the pathological cases often skipped in lectures, but must be known to students nevertheless. Problets are designed to cover these concepts.

Informatively Easy: Predicting the behavior when an element of an array is referenced before it is initialized.

Informatively Hard: Identifying type mismatch when an array is passed as parameter to a function.

Although students are familiar with parameter passing and type mismatch by now, applying these concepts to arrays turns out to still challenge them.

Access in classes:

Easy: Identifying the behavior when a `public` object member is accessed by a member function of the class.

Hard: Tracing the behavior of the default constructor when an object is created.

Constructors are hard because they are the first example of call-back functions that students study. (While `main` is also a call-back function, it is usually not introduced as one.)

Informatively Easy: Identifying mismatching numbers of actual / formal parameters when calling member functions.

Informatively Hard: Tracing the behavior of constructors, with or without parameters, when an object is created. While students have had additional opportunities to learn about parameter-passing, call-back constructors are novel.

5. DISCUSSION

Informatively easy or hard concepts overlapped with traditional easy or hard concepts only occasionally. This supports our claim that the use of DECA to identify them have the potential to bring new insights to educators.

Our results show that the novelty of a concept significantly influences whether the concept is easy or hard, e.g., integer division and remainder operator are novel and therefore, hard. This is consistent with previous research [7]. As a corollary, what is informatively easy or hard changes throughout a semester, as exposure to and familiarity with specific concepts increases, e.g., data type compatibility. Another recurring theme is that students found it easier when they could relate programming concepts to math concepts they already knew. So, instructors may want to highlight the relationship between concepts in programming and math.

We found that some concepts that are intuitively thought to be hard turned out to be easy (e.g., independent nested `while` loops) and vice versa (e.g., conjunctive logical condition in a `do-while` loop). Clearly, there is a need for data-driven analysis to confirm or refute intuitive notions in Computer Science education and inform educators.

We expect the easy, hard, informatively easy, and informatively hard concepts enumerated in the previous section to contribute to a concept inventory for introductory programming. Since these concepts are supported by data-driven analysis, their inclusion in the concept inventory will better reflect the needs of students.

Our results apply to C++, Java and C#, although some concepts identified as easy/hard are specific to C++. The concepts we considered relate to code analysis (program tracing, debugging and expression evaluation), but not synthesis (code design, writing) or evaluation (e.g., refactoring) skills in Bloom's taxonomy [1].

A confounding factor of this study is that the set of concepts identified for each topic were meant to be representative but not exhaustive or exclusive. Still, the approach we used for data analysis would be applicable to an exhaustive set of concepts, should one be collected; and the results of this study, while not a concept inventory in its entirety, will contribute to one when it is created.

In future, we will also examine the consistency of the dominance relationships produced by the algorithm. Additionally, we will use DECA to identify concepts and redundancies in the problem data. Further, we will examine how the structure uncovered by these methods might relate to "learning trajectories". Overall, this tool has great potential to help instructors design informative problem sets that will better elucidate student performance differences.

6. ACKNOWLEDGMENTS

This material is based in part upon work supported by the National Science Foundation under awards #1504634, #1502564, and #1504634.

7. REFERENCES

[1] L.W. Anderson, D.R. Krathwohl, P.W. Airasian, K.A. Cruikshank, R.E Mayer, P.R Pintrich, J. Raths, and M.C. Wittrock. *A taxonomy for learning, teaching, and assessing: A revision of BloomâĂŹs Taxonomy of Educational Objectives.* New York: Longman, 2001.

[2] A. Bucci. *Emergent Geometric Organization and Informative Dimensions in Coevolutionary Algorithms.* PhD thesis, Brandeis University, Boston, MA, 2007.

[3] A. Bucci, J.B. Pollack, and E.D. de Jong. Automated extraction of problem structure. In *Proceedings of the 7th Annual Conference on Genetic and Evolutionary Computation*, GECCO '04, pages 501–512, 2004.

[4] E.D. de Jong and A. Bucci. DECA: Dimension extracting coevolutionary algorithm. In *Proceedings of the 8th Annual Conference on Genetic and Evolutionary Computation*, GECCO '06, pages 313–320, New York, NY, USA, 2006. ACM.

[5] E.D. de Jong and A. Bucci. Objective set compression: Test-based problems and multi-objective optimization. In *Multi-Objective Problem Solving from Nature: From Concepts to Applications.* Springer, 2008.

[6] K. Goldman, P. Gross, C. Heeren, G. Herman, L. Kaczmarczyk, M.C. Loui, and C. Zilles. Identifying important and difficult concepts in introductory computing courses using a delphi process. *ACM SIGCSE Bulletin*, 40(1):256–260, 2008.

[7] M. Hertz and S.M. Ford. Investigating factors of student learning in introductory courses. In *Proceeding of the 44th ACM Technical Symposium on Computer Science Education*, SIGCSE '13, pages 195–200, New York, NY, USA, 2013. ACM.

[8] A. Koenig. *C Traps and Pitfalls.* Addison-Wesley Professional, 1989.

[9] A.N. Kumar. The effectiveness of visualization for learning expression evaluation. In *Proceedings of the 46th ACM Technical Symposium on Computer Science Education*, SIGCSE '15, pages 362–367, New York, NY, USA, 2015. ACM.

[10] A.N. Kumar. Solving code-tracing problems and its effect on code-writing skills pertaining to program semantics. In *Proceedings of the 20th Annual Conference on Innovation and Technology in Computer Science Education, ITiCSE 2015, Vilnius, Lithuania, July 6-8, 2015*, pages 314–319, 2015.

[11] E. Popovici, A. Bucci, R.P. Wiegand, and E.D. de Jong. Coevolutionary principles. In *Handbook of Natural Computing*, pages 987–1033. Springer, 2012.

[12] L. Porter, C. Taylor, and K.C. Webb. Leveraging open source principles for flexible concept inventory development. In *Proceedings of the 2014 conference on Innovation & technology in computer science education*, pages 243–248. ACM, 2014.

[13] C. Taylor, D. Zingaro, L. Porter, K.C. Webb, C.B. Lee, and M. Clancy. Computer science concept inventories: past and future. *Computer Science Education*, 24(4):253–276, 2014.

[14] A.E. Tew and M. Guzdial. Developing a validated assessment of fundamental cs1 concepts. In *Proceedings of the 41st ACM technical symposium on Computer science education*, pages 97–101. ACM, 2010.

[15] L.S. Vygotski. *The Collected Works of LS Vygotsky.* Springer, 1987.

Differentiating for Diversity: Using Universal Design for Learning in Computer Science Education

Alexandria K. Hansen[1], Eric R. Hansen[2], Hilary A. Dwyer[1], Danielle B. Harlow[1], Diana Franklin[3]

[1]Department of Education
Gevirtz Graduate School of Education
UC Santa Barbara
Santa Barbara, CA 93106- 9490
{akillian, hdwyer, dharlow}
@education.ucsb.edu

[2]Hope Elementary School
3970 La Colina Road
Santa Barbara, CA 93110
eric.robert.hansen@gmail.com

[3]Center for Elementary Math
and Science Education
University of Chicago
1100 E. 58th Street
Chicago, IL 60637
dmfranklin@uchicago.edu

ABSTRACT

As computer science moves from an outreach activity to a normal classroom activity in the multi-subject, mainstream elementary school classroom, curricula need to be examined to ensure they are meeting the needs of diverse students. In this paper, we present how Universal Design for Learning (UDL) was used to develop and refine a programming environment and curriculum for upper-elementary school classrooms (students aged 9-12). We then present our accommodations and modifications to emphasize the ways our development environment and/or curriculum enabled such uses. Ensuring introductory computer science experiences are equitable and accessible for a wide range of student learners may broaden the diversity of individuals who perceive themselves as capable of pursuing computer science in the future.

Categories and Subject Descriptors

K.3.2 [**Computing Milieu**]: Computer and Information Science Education– *computer science education, curriculum.*

General Terms

Design, Human Factors, Languages, Theory.

Keywords

Computer science education; graphical programming; differentiation; culturally responsive pedagogy; elementary school

1. INTRODUCTION

There has been a recent push to include more computer science (CS) and programming in schools. Over 4.5 million 4th-6th grade students participated in the 2014 Hour of Code, hosted by Code.org [1]. Other programming platforms have recently been developed, increasing the available opportunities that young students have to program (e.g., Scratch, Alice, Blockly, Tinker, etc.). Although this early exposure creates awareness and interest in CS, more attention needs to focus on attending to student learning differences and ensuring that instruction is accessible to a wide range of student learners.

It is widely acknowledged that individuals in the field of computer science are not equally representative of the diverse, larger population. In the United States, for example, women comprise only 18% of CS undergraduates. Additionally, only 7% of CS undergraduates are Hispanic (compared to 17% of the population), and less than 5% are Black or African American (compared to 13% of the population) [2]. Similar trends are observed in U.S. high school enrollment for the Advanced Placement CS Exam [3].

SIGCSE '16, March 02-05, 2016, Memphis, TN, USA
©2016 ACM. ISBN 978-1-4503-3685-7/16/03…$15.00
DOI: http://dx.doi.org/10.1145/2839509.2844570

There have been some focused efforts to attract underrepresented minority students through content in CS, such as the Multimedia approach [5] and by discouraging faculty from using sports-heavy examples. However, most of these approaches occur at the undergraduate level, despite research indicating that students' academic interests before high school are largely predictive of their future career choices [4]. To diversify the workforce and diversify the population of individuals familiar with computer science, efforts are needed to focus on earlier exposure to CS for a wider range of individuals.

CS has typically been offered in schools as an elective and there appears to be limited attention focused on adjusting the curriculum to fit the needs of diverse students of varying skill levels. However, as CS is more frequently integrated into the school day, schools and teachers need resources for meeting the needs of *all* students, providing equitable opportunities to participate and experience success in CS at an earlier age.

We are an interdisciplinary team of educational researchers and computer scientists who developed and tested a CS curriculum and programming environment for upper elementary school students (aged 9-12). From the onset, we selected programming task examples and content to be gender-neutral and appropriate for the ethnic and linguistic populations we worked with, which included a large number of native Spanish speaking children. As we tested and iteratively revised our curriculum, we recognized the need to further adjust our curriculum to meet our students at their current cognitive, language, and mathematical levels. We leveraged the research and recommendations on differentiated instruction and universal design for learning. Here we describe how this helped us move toward a curriculum and interface design that supported the needs of diverse students studying computer science.

2. RELATED WORKS

2.1 Differentiated Instruction

Differentiation is "a process to approach teaching and learning for students of differing abilities in the same class. The intent of differentiating instruction is to maximize each student's growth and individual success by meeting each student where he or she is, and assisting the learning process" [6]. Tomlinson [7] describes differentiation as "the efforts of teachers to respond to variance among learners in the classroom." Differentiation is necessary for students of varied abilities in a classroom. Varied abilities may result from many factors such as students with diagnosed learning disability (e.g. dyslexia), students with conditions such as autism or attention deficit hyperactivity disorder (ADHD), students learning English as a second language, students who are considered gifted, or students who lack sufficient support at home. Differentiation in computer science must also attend to differences in access to technology at home.

The concept of differentiated instruction comes from research traditions in special education and the learning sciences [8]. Recently, there has been a greater push to include more students needing special education services in the general education classroom; this is called inclusion [9]. This also ensures students are in the least restrictive environment (LRE), a legal mandate from the Individuals with Disabilities Education Act [10]. Now, more general education teachers are required to differentiate their instruction in order to meet the needs of a diverse student population.

While research traditions in special education and the learning sciences often focus on cognitive aspects of learning, other research has considered issues of culture and diversity and their effects on learning. Heath's seminal work [11] investigated different home communication patterns among families of varying cultural backgrounds and socioeconomic statuses. She found that schools most often replicate communication patterns found in middle class, European American/White households, while ignoring potentially beneficial aspects of communication in other types of families. Additionally, students from different cultural backgrounds were often unprepared for the types of questions and interactions found in the traditional, U.S. classroom. This work led to investigations around how schools can better serve students of varying cultural backgrounds, with Ladson-Billings popularizing the theory of culturally responsive pedagogy (CRP) as a promising solution [12].

CRP is now a common technique used to meet the needs of students from traditionally underrepresented minorities, and is emphasized in many teacher education programs nationwide. CRP is described as, "an approach to teaching that incorporates attributes, characteristics, or knowledge from students' cultural background into the instructional strategies and course content in an effort to improve educational outcomes" [13]. At the core of CRP is the belief that *all* students are capable of excelling academically, regardless of their culture, language, socioeconomic status, or family background. It is a mindset that considers the culture of students as transformative and empowering in the classroom, not as a deficit to be overcome through schooling.

CRP is also related to Moll's Funds of Knowledge theory [14], the idea that "historically accumulated and culturally developed bodies of knowledge and skills essential for household or individual functioning and well-being" are useful. For example, residents of an agricultural community might have funds of knowledge that include information about ranching, farming, crops or soil irrigation. This information learned informally at home is beneficial to draw upon in the classroom setting. In the field of education, it is widely accepted that students learn best when the content connects to, and builds from, their previous experience [15]. It then follows that culturally responsive pedagogy should make use of students' funds of knowledge. To do so, teachers and curriculum developers need to be cognizant of their students' rich culturally based funds of knowledge.

More recently, Santamaria [8] proposed a new framework for meeting the varied needs of students who have been historically unsuccessful in the general education classroom setting—Culturally Responsive Differentiated Instruction (CRDI). CRDI combines differentiated instruction and culturally responsive pedagogy. The hybrid model speaks to best teaching practices, which "consider all learners in a classroom setting and pay close attention to differences inherent to academic, cultural, linguistic, and socioeconomic diversity" [8]. Ultimately, teachers must get to know their students on a personal level, continually making adjustments to the classroom, curriculum, and instruction to ensure that all students are capable of achieving academically.

2.2 Universal Design for Learning

At the core of differentiated instruction is the concept of universal design for learning (UDL). UDL is a framework that teachers can use to create an inclusive classroom. It highlights the need to design features of instruction that are **essential** for some students, **beneficial** to others, and **not detrimental** to any. UDL emphasizes the importance of flexible instruction (presented in a variety of formats) to meet the needs of diverse learners, reducing possible barriers to learning, and maintaining high achievement expectations for all students [16]. An example of UDL for non-native English speakers is to provide increased visuals for new vocabulary words. Providing additional visuals is necessary for students learning English, is beneficial for other students (such as students with audio-processing disorders, or visual learners), and is not detrimental to any student. All teachers should design instruction to fit within the UDL framework.

2.2.1 Accommodations and Modifications

Even with UDL, some students are outside of the range of variation supported by the curriculum. There are two categories of changes that teachers can make to differentiate instructions for individual students: 1) Accommodations and 2) Modifications.

Accommodations allow students to "complete the same assignment or test as other students, but with a change in the timing, formatting, setting, scheduling, response and/or presentation" [17]. Accommodations do not significantly alter the content that a student learns, or what an assessment measures; rather they allow the student to access the content or assessment in another way. Examples of accommodations include a student who is blind taking an assessment in Braille, or a student who has ADHD working in a quiet space to limit distractions. In both cases, the content or assessment is unchanged, but accommodations are provided, allowing the student to access the general education curriculum.

In contrast, modifications involve an "adjustment to an assignment or a test that changes the standard or what the test or assignment is supposed to measure" [17]. By changing the standard that a student is expected to meet, modifications allow struggling students to experience success in the classroom. Modifications are often used for students with more severe learning disabilities, but they can be helpful for many types of students. Examples of modifications include shortening an assignment, or requiring the student to complete one section of a larger assignment, focusing on mastery of key concepts. Other examples of modifications include using recognition tests (fill-in-the blank, matching, true-false) as opposed to longer, written responses, and letting a student re-submit an assignment or assessment to receive a higher score. Modifications are also used to provide additional challenge on assignments for gifted students.

During the iterative curriculum development process, we identified student struggles in the classroom and how these related to the design of our curriculum and programming environment. These led to changes in the curriculum and classroom instruction. In this paper, we report on changes directly related to differentiation and culturally responsive pedagogy to illustrate how these concepts play an important role in computer science education.

3. METHODS

3.1 The Study

As part of a larger NSF-funded project, we had two primary goals: 1) to design a curriculum to teach basic programming and computational thinking to 4th-6th grade students (aged 9-12), and 2) to develop and test a learning progression for computational thinking at the upper elementary school level. Here, we report on findings related to concepts necessary to program a digital story in our block-based programming environment, a modified version of Scratch [18]. For more information on our changes to Scratch, see [19]. Targeted concepts in the curriculum included sequential execution, event-based programming, initialization, message passing, costume changes, and scene changes.

3.2 Research Design

We used design-based research methodology [20] to iteratively inform the development of our curriculum, programming environment, and research [21]. This systematic and flexible approach involves researchers and practitioners collaborating in real-world settings with the aim of improving educational practices. Changes to the curriculum and programming environment were made over time in response to what was learned about student learning.

In the 2013-2014 school year, we tested our curriculum and programming environment in fifteen classrooms from five different California schools, with approximately 400 participating students (aged 9-12). Schools included local schools (within 50 miles of the university) and distant schools. Participating schools ranged from 2%-82% designated English language learners, and 4%-100% of students qualifying for free or reduced lunch (a proxy for socioeconomic status). Schools generally had equal numbers of female and male students. Some schools had a designated computer teacher lead lessons during computer lab time. Other schools had general education classroom teachers lead lessons, some during computer lab time, and others during normal class time. We tested our curriculum again during the 2014-2015 school year with 1,500 students. We had a similar number of local schools participating, but increased the amount of distant schools.

In local schools, graduate student researchers (GSRs) attended each classroom meeting and recorded detailed field notes about student learning. Depending upon the comfort level of the teacher, GSRs sometimes assisted in teaching lessons or reviewing content. In addition, GSRs collected video recordings of each class meeting, audio recordings of students asking questions, and interviews with teachers and students. We also collected final student projects, and automated snapshots of projects to show the development process over time. After each class period, GSRs wrote analytical memos [22] that were shared with the research group. In distant schools, we only collected student work.

3.3 Data Analysis

Our research team met weekly to discuss observations and reflections from the previous week. These discussions often revolved around analytical memos. Frequently, analytical memos captured incidents that deviated from what was expected to occur in the classroom, and served as a consideration for possible change, in alignment with design-based research methodology.

In cases where students struggled or did not meet the pre-identified learning goals, we realized that we, as developers, or the classroom teacher, had unintentionally hindered student learning, or failed to provide an additional support that would have made the content more accessible. Over time, these cases became "rich points" [23] that prompted serious consideration of how we were (or were not) differentiating instruction. In this paper, we report on rich points that prompted a significant change to the classroom-learning environment. In the following section, we share how we identified each rich point and what changes were made to ensure our curriculum and programming environment fit within the UDL framework. We separate changes into three categories: 1) UDL changes made to the programming environment or curriculum, 2) Accommodations, and 3) Modifications made by the classroom teacher or GSRs.

4. FINDINGS

4.1 Universal Design for Learning Changes

In this section, we report on changes made to the curriculum and/or programming environment. This differentiation fits within the UDL framework—changes that were necessary for some students, beneficial for others, and not detrimental to any.

4.1.1 Designing for English Proficiency

Upon entering schools, we quickly learned that we needed to differentiate further for students with limited English proficiency. Ultimately, we determined that we would make changes to address English proficiency for all students as these changes would benefit some and not be detrimental to any students' learning of computer science. The following excerpt depicts a realization that our student population greatly struggled with reading English.

<u>12/1/2013: Analytical Memo from GSR</u>

> Many students would call me [the researcher] over and ask what to do, as opposed to reading the instructions themselves. I would then direct them to reading the instructions aloud, which often resulted in sighs...My overall impression is that reading is hard for these students, and, as a result, they tend to avoid it if at all possible.

More classroom observations and conversations with teachers confirmed that some students struggled more than others to read and understand English.

<u>2/19/2014: Analytical Memo from GSR</u>

> [The teacher] said that there were some special education students in the class, and I could tell that a couple of students weren't that comfortable with English - I saw at least one student write part of his in Spanish.

Specific instances with students also revealed that the language we selected for instructions and programming commands were not always accessible.

<u>11/17/2014 & 12/1/14: Analytical Memos from GSRs</u>

> The largest confusion that I noticed was around the motion blocks. Many students did not connect the word "glide" to move/walk.
>
> It took most students multiple attempts at reading the blocks to pinpoint the differences. One student kept reading, "grilled" instead of "glide."

Students continued to ignore our written instructions, hints, and feedback, as well as the accompanying worksheets. This caused us to reconsider what text we wanted students to read, and why. The resulting conversations led to several UDL changes that made our curriculum and programming environment more accessible.

First, we eliminated student worksheets, at the request of teachers who felt students largely ignored them. We then embedded more text in the interface, and greatly reduced the difficulty of reading required. Instructions were simplified, and key words were underlined or bolded. This works was done by GSRs with teaching experience, and reviewed by a special education teacher.

Next, we decided to add an audio read back function, allowing students to have instructions read aloud via headphones. We are currently in the process of implementing this change, but feel it will greatly reduce the amount of required reading, allowing students to focus on mastery of CS concepts.

4.1.2 Designing for Math Proficiency

Similar to English, students had varying mathematical skill levels. Additionally, some of the math content embedded in our initial curriculum was above a fourth-grade level (students aged 8-9), particularly the following concepts: 1) x/y coordinate plane system, 2) negative numbers, and 3) decimals and percentages. For a full report on our investigation of these mathematical concepts within our curriculum, see [19]. Here, we focus on the concept of the x/y coordinate plane system, and the UDL changes made to ensure this content was accessible to more students.

We noticed that students were unfamiliar with the x/y coordinate plane system when we asked them to use the "Go to X: Y: " block. To use this block successfully, students had to recognize there was an x/y coordinate plane system embedded in the program's stage, and understand how to plot x/y coordinates. Teachers attempted to accommodate while teaching this lesson- one used the metaphor of an address to represent a coordinate, another projected an image of a coordinate plane system – but the students had not learned this content before. To address this need, a change to the programming environment was required.

We did not want to remove the coordinate plane system because identifying a location is essential for some CS concepts. Removing the x/y coordinate plane system would require removing these key concepts from the curriculum, and may be detrimental to the students' learning of CS in the future. As a result, we modified the programming environment without removing the coordinate plane system entirely, allowing more students to access the content.

First, we removed negative numbers from within the coordinate system. To do this, we placed the origin (0, 0) at the bottom left corner as opposed to in the center. Next, we added a "grid button" that students could use to display grid lines for counting purposes on the coordinate plane system (see Figure 1). This change provided additional help for students who needed it, but also allowed us to keep the coordinate plane system within our programming environment.

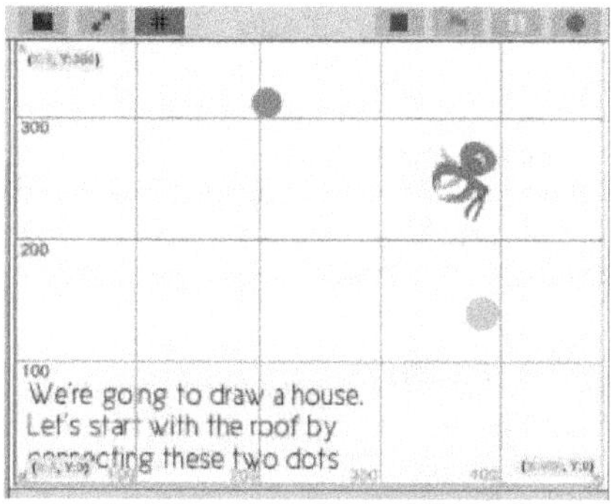

Figure 1. Programming stage with coordinate plane and grid lines.

4.1.3 Designing for Culture

Before designing our curriculum, we conducted interviews with local students to understand how they related computer science concepts to their everyday lives. During these interviews, we were cognizant of students' cultural and ethnic backgrounds, and how they interacted with our activities.

For example, when discussing the concept of sequencing in CS, making a peanut butter and jelly sandwich (and the order of steps therein) is the traditional example used. However, when conducting initial student interviews, we realized that our local students did not eat peanut butter and jelly sandwiches often. This prompted us to ask what types of food they do eat for lunch. A common response that also had a simple set of steps was a quesadilla. This insight caused us to change our initial lesson idea from using a peanut butter and jelly sandwich to a quesadilla. In these interviews we also learned that piñatas were an important part of celebrations, which caused us to include an initialization activity that required students to put the candy into the piñata to correctly initialize the program.

Despite attempting to align our curriculum to our students' culture ahead of time, we still identified instances where we failed to do so. One example is captured in the observation below.

1/9/2015: Analytical Memo from GSR

> Students were confused by the words "tortoise" and "hare". [The teacher] and I told students they could substitute the words turtle and rabbit, if they felt more comfortable. I don't think that many students were familiar with the story "The Tortoise and the Hare."

In a lesson that included the classic story of the tortoise and the hare, we realized we had unintentionally created a barrier to learning by relying on what we assumed was a familiar story. In fact, many students in our classes were not familiar with this story. In other words, we assumed a different fund of knowledge than what the students actually had. This caused them to focus on the words "tortoise" and "hare" as opposed to learning the CS skills in our lesson. As a simple fix, we removed the words "tortoise" and "hare," from our example, and provided an overview of the story beforehand. This fix was necessary for some, beneficial to all, and not detrimental to any student.

Another more extreme example emerged when students were working to complete their final project- programming a digital story. Students were allowed to select any topic for their story, but many decided to program stories about friends, family, and themselves. One girl recognized that few of the character sprites possessed physical attributes like her, and reported to her teacher, "Nobody looks like me." This was also captured in the following observation.

3/3/2015: Analytical Memo from GSR

> I was working with one girl who is usually hesitant to engage in programming. On her storyboard, she had drawn herself having a conversation with [a friend]. But, she couldn't find any sprites that looked like her or [her friend] (i.e. darker skin, darker eyes).

While we had included sprites of varying ethnicities in the programming tasks, we had failed to include these same sprites in the blank templates students used to create their digital stories. What was an unintentional oversight on our part resulted in one student receiving the message that she could not program a story about herself or friends. We added sprites of varying ethnic backgrounds to the available library for blank projects, ensuring that any student who participated in our curriculum could find a sprite that looked like him or herself.

4.1.4 Designing for Pace

Another differentiation opportunity emerged in one classroom where we noticed that students completed their work at varied speeds. What took one student five minutes to complete sometimes took another student an hour. This observation (and suggestion for change) was captured in the following excerpt:

12/20/13: Analytical Memo from GSR

> I saw students who quickly finished the activity and then sat for extended periods of time without another task. [We] advised these students to change colors and sizes of sprites, but I think this time could be more valuably spent. I would consider adding a challenge assignment for students who have mastered [the lesson] early.

This led our research team to add another feature to our programming environment—the Sandbox. This new feature opens a blank project for students, and provides all available blocks. Previously, blocks were slowly introduced in lessons as students learned new skills. The Sandbox provided an area for students who finished their work early to play, practice, and experiment.

4.1.5 Taking a Multimodal Approach

Another opportunity to align our practices with the UDL framework was made at the request of a teacher who noticed that her students were struggling to upload their projects to our server at the end of each lesson.

1/31/2014: Email Communication from General Education Teacher

> One low-tech thing I thought might help would be to make a poster outlining, in detail, each step of the submission process. This would also aid those students who are not able to remember how to do it from one week to the next.

We promptly made the poster, which hung in the computer lab for the rest of the school year. At first, students frequently relied on the poster for instructions. Through time, fewer students needed it for reference because they received more practice in uploading their work. Often, these posters are referred to as anchor charts in a classroom because they help anchor the learning process for students in the form of a visual representation.

4.2 Accommodations

In this section, we discuss accommodations that were made in the classroom by teachers or GSRs. Accommodations do not change the learning goals of a lesson, but provide students another way to access the content.

4.2.1 Re-teaching and Small Group Instruction

Throughout our time in classrooms, the most common strategy used when large amounts of students were confused was re-teaching. An example of re-teaching is shown below.

2/11/2014: Analytical Memo from GSR

> I told the kids I forgot what we did last week and asked if they could help me remember. This was really fun because they did remember a lot—even big words like initialization. As they said each "big word" I would ask what that meant so we spent time reviewing vocabulary—upload, download, initialization, sprite, scripts, blocks. The kids still don't have a strong grasp of the different words so talking about it together seemed to help.

Re-teaching is an effective tool when the majority of students in a class need help reviewing. However, there are often times in a classroom when only a small group of students would benefit from re-teaching a lesson. This accommodation is called small-group instruction. An example of small group instruction is captured below during a lesson when students were learning about broadcasting and receiving messages.

2/24/2014: Analytical Memo from GSR

> While some of the class was [working in the Sandbox], I worked with students who were moving slower...they were understanding the idea of broadcast/receive too, though needed some extra one-on-one-- someone to read through what they were writing, help mirror the logic of what they produced back to them.

Small group instruction is an accommodation that allows a teacher to work with a smaller amount of students, providing targeted support and direct feedback during the learning process. With this support, students are able to accomplish much more than they would alone.

4.2.2 Modeling

Modeling is another instructional strategy (and accommodation) that aided in reinforcing learning objectives. When modeling, an instructor demonstrates the procedure for students to follow.

1/28/2014: Analytical Memo from GSR

> There was still a lot of confusion over how to use the direction and glide blocks...It was almost like they couldn't recall/remember that GLIDE meant move and the [other blocks] all mean direction. I tried to mimic [the activity] to help. They had to "program" me to walk to the nearest bookshelf. Unless they said glide I didn't actually move forward, only turned in circle. This seemed to help a little bit.

In this event, students were confused over motion blocks. The GSR modeled how the blocks functioned by acting out the actions of the blocks. The students provided the "commands" necessary to move her around the room, similar to how a sprite would move around the stage. Modeling helped students to kinesthetically connect their everyday experience to that of abstract programming commands.

4.3 Modifications

Sometimes, even with accommodations, students still struggle to meet a lesson's objective. In these instances, modifications are necessary. Modifications change the standard that individual students are expected to meet to better fit their individual levels. In this section, we report on modifications made by teachers and GSRs in the classroom. We discuss modifications made for: 1) the whole class, 2) struggling students, and 3) advanced students.

4.3.1 Modifications for the Whole Class

An example of a modification for the whole class is captured in the reflection below during a lesson about changing scenes using broadcast and receive.

3/20/2014: Analytical Memo from GSR

> When the majority of the class was still struggling with scene changes, the teacher and I discussed what to do. We decided that instead of requiring the students to program all three, scene changes, we would have them program only one. If a student was able to do that, then s/he could move onto the other scenes.

This specific lesson proved more difficult for students than we anticipated, and required a change during class. Instead of requiring students to program three scene changes, we modified the lesson to only require students to program one scene change. This modification allowed struggling students to experience success (without being overwhelmed with the lesson's requirement), but provided the flexibility for more advanced students to complete all three, scene changes if they were ready to move on.

4.3.2 Modifications for Struggling Students

An unforeseen benefit of the Sandbox (open programming environment) was captured in an interview with a special education teacher.

4/30/2015: Special Education Teacher Interview

> The Sandbox was great because I could direct my struggling students there. If a student had a difficult time completing the lesson, they could take a break in the Sandbox and play. Or, if a student was unable to complete the lesson at all, I was still able to create smaller, personalized assignments in the Sandbox. Instead of making the car go up, down, right, and left with arrow keys, maybe we only try to get the car to move right.

What we assumed would be a feature used primarily by students who finished early turned into a differentiation opportunity for struggling students as well. The Sandbox provided a space for overwhelmed students to take a break from an activity, but still gain experience programming. It also provided a space for teachers to create their own modified assignments in real time, based on their individual students' needs.

4.3.3 Modifications for Advanced Students

Modifications are not only used for students who are struggling, they can also support advanced students who are ready to go beyond the lesson's objectives. In one classroom, a teacher designated a small group of students with more technology experience as "computer helpers." The identified students were comfortable uploading and downloading work, excelled in the programming tasks, finished their work early, and were willing to help their peers. As "computer helpers," these students were expected to assist their confused peers during class. They were given the freedom to walk around the classroom after finishing their own work, answering classmates' questions. This freed up the teacher to assist students who needed more directive support, and provided the advanced students an opportunity to act as experts, sharing their knowledge with peers.

5. DISCUSSION

In this paper, we leveraged the Universal Design for Learning framework to illustrate differentiation opportunities that were necessary for our diverse students studying computer science in elementary school. We discussed accommodations and modifications as tools for differentiating curriculum and classroom instruction to better meet the needs of diverse students. Differentiation was necessary to provide a more equitable and accessible introductory computer science learning experience for our target population. As U.S. schools continue to diversify in culture, language, ethnicity, skills and interests, curriculum developers and teachers need to be cognizant of this diversity, and ways in which to leverage this diversity for the advancement of student learning.

6. ACKNOWLEDGMENTS

This work is supported by the National Science Foundation CE21 Award CNS-1240985. We'd also like to thank all of the teachers, students, and schools involved in this project.

7. REFERENCES

[1] Alvarado, C. (2014). CS Ed Week 2013: The hour of code. *ACM SIGCSE Bull*, *46*,1, 2-4.

[2] U.S. Department of Education. Institute of Education Sciences, National Center for Education Statistics, (2009).

[3] College Board. (2011). *The 10th Annual AP report to the nation.* Retrieved from: http://apreport.collegeboard.org.

[4] Tai, R. H. (2006). Career choice: Enhanced: Planning early for. *Life Science*, *1*, 0-2.

[5] Guzdial, M. J., & Ericson, B. (2009). *Introduction to Computing and Programming in Python, A Multimedia Approach.* Prentice Hall.

[6] Hall, T. (2002). *Differentiated instruction.* Wakefield, MA: National Center on Accessing the General Curriculum.

[7] Tomlinson, C. A., Brighton, C., Hertberg, H., Callahan, C. M., Moon, T. R., Brimijoin, K., ... & Reynolds, T. (2003). Differentiating instruction in response to student readiness, interest, and learning profile in academically diverse classrooms: A review of literature. *Journal for the Education of the Gifted*, *27*(2-3), 119-145.

[8] Santamaria, L.J. (2009). Culturally responsive differentiated instruction: Narrowing gaps between best pedagogical practices benefiting ALL learners. *Teachers College Record*, *111*(1), 214-247.

[9] Idol, L. (2006). Toward inclusion of special education students in general education a program evaluation of eight schools. *Remedial and Special education*, *27*(2), 77-94.

[10] Osborne, A. G., & Dimattia, P. (1994). The IDEA's least restrictive environment mandate: Legal implications. *Exceptional Children*, *61*(1), 6-14.

[11] Heath, S. B. (1982). What no bedtime story means: Narrative skills at home and school. *Language in Society*, *11*(1), 49-76.

[12] Ladson-Billings, G. (1995). Toward a theory of culturally relevant pedagogy. *AM EDUC RES J*, *32*(3), 465-491.

[13] Howard, T. C. (2012). Culturally responsive pedagogy. *Encyclopedia of Diversity in Education*, 1-7.

[14] Moll, L. (1992). Funds of knowledge for teaching: Using a qualitative approach to connect homes and classrooms. *Theory into Practice*, *32*, 2, 132-141.

[15] Fosnot, C. T., & Perry, R. S. (1996). Constructivism: A psychological theory of learning. *Constructivism: Theory, perspectives, and practice*, 8-33.

[16] King-Sears, P. (2014). Introduction to Learning Disability Quarterly Special Series on Universal Design for Learning. *Learning Disability Quarterly*, *37*(2), 68-70.

[17] PACER Center. (2013). School accommodations and modification ideas for students who receive special education services.

[18] Resnick, M., Maloney, J., Monroy-Hernández, A., Rusk, N., Eastmond, E., Brennan, K., ... & Kafai, Y. (2009). Scratch: programming for all. *COMMUN ACM*, *52*(11), 60-67.

[19] Hill, C., Dwyer, H. A., Martinez, T., Harlow, D., & Franklin, D. (2015). Floors and flexibility: Designing a programming environment for 4th – 6th grade classrooms. *SIGCSE '15.* ACM.

[20] Barab, S., & Squire, K. (2004). Design-based research: Putting a stake in the ground. *J LEARN SCI*, *13*(1), 1-14.

[21] Wang, F., & Hannafin, M. J. (2005). Design-based research and technology-enhanced learning environments. *Educational Tech Research and Development*, *53*(4), 5-23.

[22] Saldaña, J. (2009). *The Coding Manual for Qualitative Researchers.* Thousand Oaks, CA: Sage Publications.

[23] Agar, M. (2000). Border lessons: Linguistic "rich points" and evaluative understanding. *New Directions for Evaluation*, *2000*(86), 93-109.

Empowering All Students: Closing the CS Confidence Gap with an In-School Initiative for Middle School Students

Philip Sheridan Buffum
psbuffum@ncsu.edu[1]

Megan Hardy Frankosky
rmhardy@ncsu.edu[2]

Kristy Elizabeth Boyer
keboyer@ufl.edu[3]

Eric N. Wiebe
wiebe@ncsu.edu[4]

Bradford W. Mott
bwmott@ncsu.edu[1]

James C. Lester
lester@ncsu.edu[1]

[1] Computer Science, North Carolina State University, Raleigh, North Carolina, USA
[2] Psychology, North Carolina State University, Raleigh, North Carolina, USA
[3] Computer & Information Sciences & Engineering, University of Florida, Gainesville, Florida, USA
[4] STEM Education, North Carolina State University, Raleigh, North Carolina, USA

ABSTRACT

The important goal of broadening participation in computing has inspired many successful outreach initiatives. Yet many of these initiatives, such as out-of-school activities or innovative new computer science courses for secondary school students, may disproportionately attract students who already have prior interest and experience in computing. How, then, do we engage the silent majority of students who do not self-select computer science? This paper examines this question in the context of ENGAGE, an in-school outreach initiative for middle school students. ENGAGE's learning activities center on a game-based learning environment for computer science. Results reveal that the initiative improved the computer science attitudes of students who were not already predisposed to study computer science, in a way that a corresponding after-school program could not. The results illustrate how an in-school initiative can empower young students who might not otherwise consider studying computer science.

Categories and Subject Descriptors

K.3.2 [**Computers & Education**]: Computer and Information Sciences Education --- *Computer Science Education*

Keywords

In-school outreach, middle school, broadening participation.

1. INTRODUCTION

Computing skills are increasingly integral to many 21st century jobs. Nonetheless, computer science remains a "niche" subject in the United States, studied by a generally small, non-diverse population of students. Consequently, many current initiatives in the United States seek to broaden participation in computing. Many of these initiatives involve out-of-school activities such as summer camps [1]. Other initiatives focus on formal, in-school coursework through the development of innovative pre-college curricula such as Exploring Computer Science [10] and AP Computer Science Principles [2, 11]. Fundamental to all of these initiatives is the mission to engage students who are historically underrepresented in computer science, including female students.

DOI: http://dx.doi.org/10.1145/2839509.2844595

Yet for both of these types of initiatives—out-of-school activities and in-school computer science courses for secondary school students—questions remain as to just how effective they are in broadening participation [17]. Both these types of initiatives are likely to involve self-selection, attracting a certain subset of students rather than a truly representative sample. In other words, even if a given initiative has a large percentage of underrepresented students (e.g., female students) among its participants, these students likely either already have interest in studying computer science or have someone in their lives encouraging them to study computer science. Of course, this does not negate the value of these initiatives: nurturing a student's pre-existing interest in computing and empowering her with new skills may contribute greatly to her persisting in the field.

To fully address the goal of broadening participation, however, we must also reach out to students who do not have predispositions or existing influences to study computer science or to participate in extracurricular computing activities. This paper provides evidence that the key is to develop *in-school* initiatives that enroll a broad population of students (i.e., not students specifically seeking a computer science elective). Furthermore, it is crucial to create such in-school initiatives at the *pre-secondary level*, as students begin their career trajectory as early as middle school [14]. Indeed, researchers have looked specifically at how the underproduction and underrepresentation issues in undergraduate computer science departments may be traced back to lack of exposure as early as middle school [25, 28].

Our team has embarked on one such initiative, in which we hope to leverage the engaging nature of game-based learning environments to spark interest in computing. Over the past three years, we have developed ENGAGE, an immersive game-based learning environment that adapts learning objectives from the AP CS Principles course [2] to be middle-grade appropriate. We then integrated this computing content with an existing middle school science curriculum and trained middle school science teachers to teach this course in four diverse middle schools. The results show that the in-school implementation of ENGAGE improved the computer science attitudes of students with no prior computer science experience, in a way that the corresponding after-school implementation could not.

This paper explores the potential of situating an outreach initiative within an in-school course for middle school students. Section 2 provides a review of related work, highlighting three elements that can make in-school initiatives successful. Section 3 describes the development and in-school implementation of ENGAGE. This includes software development, curriculum development, and teacher development. Finally, Section 4 reports on the initiative's success at improving computer science attitudes of those students who were less predisposed to study computer science. Overall, the paper highlights the potential of a pre-secondary, in-school initiative to reach students who might not otherwise consider computer science as a field of study, and to improve their attitudes toward computer science.

2. RELATED WORK

To attain a full understanding of the recent work on in-school computer science outreach initiatives, we performed a comprehensive literature review of the past five SIGCSE conferences (2011-2015). Of the approximately 500 full papers presented at these conferences, we identified 113 papers focusing on K-12 education. Slightly more than half of these K-12 papers reported on out-of-school initiatives (e.g., summer camps), and another quarter of them focused on in-school computer science electives for secondary school students, such as AP Computer Science Principles. This paper reviews the remaining literature (in-school, pre-secondary) that address the key question: *How can we create in-school outreach initiatives that reach those students who do not necessarily have a predisposition to study computer science?* Performing studies on such a general population of students, rather than on a subset of students who self-select to attend computer science activities, can provide greater insight into how all students learn computer science, regardless of prior knowledge or interest. For example, in-school research studies have examined the programming abilities of primary students as related to their reading abilities [24] and to their general academic performance in other subjects [19], in both cases providing better understanding on how *all* students learn programming, and not just those who self-select computer science. Crucially, research has also looked at how to design in-school initiatives with an emphasis on sustainability [13].

Reaching K-12 students with computer science content during school hours ultimately requires empowering K-12 teachers to teach that computer science content. It is important to note that the instructors for after-school and summer initiatives are often different than those who would teach an in-school course for middle school. Accordingly, a significant amount of research in this area has addressed *teacher professional development*. Perhaps the most popular approach for this has been to introduce K-12 teachers to computer science content through summer workshops [12, 16]. Other research has looked at introducing computer science content to student teachers through pre-service teacher education [3, 30], or to in-service teachers with research experience in computer science labs at local universities [26]. While these workshops have been shown to be effective at having an immediate impact on teachers' knowledge and attitudes, less research has been done to examine how likely teachers are to keep teaching the content year after year [13]. Moreover, little research has been reported on how effectively these teacher benefits translate into measurable impacts on *students*, and particularly on students who are not predisposed to study computer science.

We might reasonably expect greater and more sustainable impacts if teachers have an established *curriculum* to accompany their professional development. One middle school curriculum uses a "braided teaching" approach by interleaving a number of computer science concepts throughout a course for middle school students [20]. Another middle school curriculum focuses on improving computer science attitudes by highlighting the breadth of the field, an approach that should perhaps start at the primary school level [8]. Several recent efforts have created pre-secondary computer science curricula by leveraging existing tools also popular with out-of-school initiatives, such as Scratch [23] and Alice [21]. These pre-existing tools offer great functionality. The sheer breadth of possibilities that an open-ended learning environment like Scratch affords, however, can make it difficult for K-12 teachers unfamiliar with computer science to ensure that student work is adhering to a curriculum's learning objectives, perhaps making it less likely that the teachers will fully adopt it [15, 18]. More work needs to be done to investigate whether relying on these ubiquitous tools privilege students who have already used them in prior computer science activities.

Most initiatives involve some software system, but there has been comparatively little recent work that reports on developing software systems specifically for in-school initiatives. The research that has been reported has led to valuable insights. AgentSheets has been used to assess middle school students' computational thinking [4]. Most importantly for the goal of broadening participation in computing, research on the AgentSheets system has explored ways to use computer science pedagogy to improve computer science attitudes among female students [27]. Another large-scale effort, Bootstrap, uses its custom software tool WeScheme to integrate computing concepts with middle school algebra [31]. This custom software enables Bootstrap to reinforce algebra content in ways that a pre-existing tool like Scratch would not, and this ability makes it particularly appealing to math teachers [22]. With both AgentSheets and Bootstrap, we see the great potential value of developing software systems tailored to the curriculum.

In the related literature on in-school pre-secondary initiatives, we see the importance of three key types of development: professional development for teachers, development of curricula, and development of software that links strongly to the curriculum. This is not to say that all successful in-school initiatives need each of these elements. Rather, we argue that they each have great potential to help produce in-school initiatives that are sustainable and have positive impacts on a broad population of students. Below we describe how we endeavored to incorporate all three of these elements into a middle school initiative. As part of a three-year project, we first developed a game-based learning environment along with a computer science curriculum, and then ran a Teacher Institute so that we could deploy the resulting course in four diverse schools during the 2014-15 school year. As noted above, our overarching goal at each stage of development was to create an initiative that would reach students who might not otherwise consider computer science, and positively impact their computer science attitudes.

3. DESIGN OF IN-SCHOOL INITIATIVE

3.1 Development Process

Our research and development team developed both the ENGAGE game-based learning environment and its accompanying computer science curriculum synchronously over two years. Although the game-based learning environment[1] can be deployed within a

[1] This game-based learning environment is one in which students learn by playing the game, in contrast to learning by building games.

wider curriculum (including non-gameplay lessons with complementary learning activities), we designed the game so that it could feasibly operate in a stand-alone fashion. Students with no prior computer science knowledge can play the game from beginning to end, developing their computational thinking skills with only the in-game activities scaffolding their learning. This provides more flexibility in how ENGAGE can be deployed, allowing for out-of-school and in-school implementations.

Crucially, designing the game-based learning environment in this way also eases the burden on the teacher for in-school implementations. We anticipated that our middle school teachers would have limited prior computer science knowledge, so we sought to create a software environment that would ease the burden of teaching an unfamiliar subject. We hoped this step would positively influence how likely the teachers would be to teach the course again and maintain "curriculum integrity" [13].

In developing the curriculum for in-school implementation, we planned for a 20-session course, with each session lasting an hour. We envisioned a schedule in which gameplay sessions would alternate with non-gameplay sessions. During a given gameplay session, we planned for students to receive an introduction to a certain computational concepts within the game-based learning environment. Then the next day's session would center on a classroom activity that would reinforce the concept. As we progressed with the development of the game, we thus generated ideas for activities that would extend students' understanding of the material, while not being integral to success in the game.

During game development, we delayed drafting lesson plans for the non-gameplay activities because we wanted to include the eventual classroom teachers as co-creators. Ultimately, with the support of district-level stakeholders, we integrated our computer science content with an existing quarterly science elective focused on oceanography. Our partner schools offer this course to students each quarter of the academic year during normal school hours, and it draws a diverse population of students. The entire course consists of 45 hour-long sessions. Our in-school implementation plan thus became to integrate three types of sessions: gameplay sessions, non-gameplay sessions that reinforced computational concepts, and non-gameplay sessions that focus on the pre-existing science content. We approached this task in close collaboration with classroom teachers, as detailed in Section 3.2.

3.2 Overview of System and Curriculum

The ENGAGE game-based learning environment engages the student in a narrative in which she is a computer scientist tasked with solving a socially relevant mystery. As the student advances through the immersive, three-dimensional game world (Figure 1), she must employ computational thinking skills to overcome challenges. With the curriculum's learning objectives derived from the AP CS Principles curriculum framework, some of these challenges require the student to write programs in a block-based programming interface, but the emphasis is on students deepening their conceptual understanding rather than only developing programs. Additionally, the narrative of the game reinforces the idea of the student becoming a computer scientist. By focusing the game's goals on student conceptual understanding and identity formation, the goal is to avoid overly privileging students with prior programming experiences. The project keenly hopes to empower all students to view computer science as a possible future subject of study.

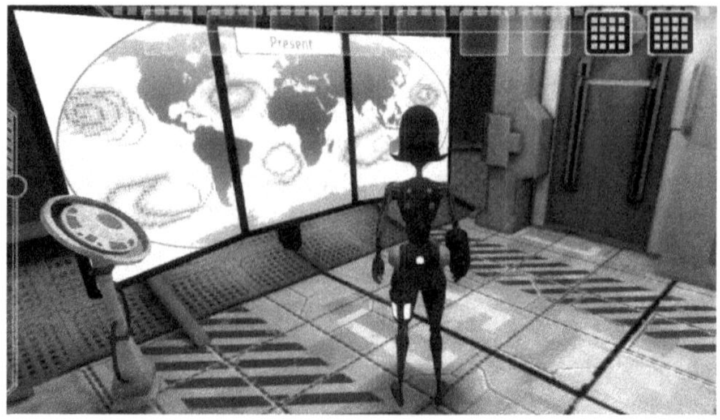

Figure 1. The ENGAGE game-based learning environment.

The game is divided into three levels. The first level introduces students to basic programming concepts such as sequencing and iteration. The students will later apply these concepts in more sophisticated programs in the subsequent levels. The second level focuses on binary numbers. Students learn how a binary system works, how to interpret binary numbers, and how computers use binary numbers to represent other forms of data, such as text and images. The third and final level focuses on exploration of data. Students write programs to make sense of data they receive from other characters in the game. In addition to learning about algorithms such as sorting and filtering data, students solve challenges that require the use of large data sets to solve globally-relevant problems.

3.3 Teacher Institute

In summer 2014, we held a six-day Teacher Institute, which included a total of 40 hours of workshop activities with middle school science teachers. We recruited four teachers from four different middle schools, each serving a diverse student population. In addition to attending the Teacher Institute, these four science teachers all committed to teaching our integrated curriculum during one of their class periods for the 2014-15 school year. As described below, the teachers co-designed this integrated curriculum with the research team, supplementing the research team's *computer science education* and *game-based learning* expertise with the teachers' *science education* and *middle school teaching* expertise.

In preparation for the Teacher Institute, the research team created a teacher kit that included a project overview, a proposed classroom implementation plan, guidelines for survey administration, and a summary of key locations in the game. These key locations consisted of 1) challenges that students might find particularly difficult, and 2) areas in which the teacher might especially impact deeper student learning by asking targeted questions about the given topic. Additionally, the teacher kit contained placeholders for lesson plans that would be created collaboratively during the workshop sessions. We aimed to produce detailed lesson plans specifying the learning objectives, necessary materials, and connection to the content in the game-based learning environment. We also planned for the Teacher Institute to produce an updated in-school classroom implementation plan, clarified by teacher input.

In designing the structure for the Teacher Institute of 2014, we built upon our experience conducting a series of workshops the previous summer [6]. We devoted the first day of this new Teacher Institute to an overview of the project. This included an introduction to the game-based learning environment, a summary of the computer science content, and our vision for how we might integrate the computer science content with the existing science curriculum. On each subsequent day, we used the morning hours to provide the teachers a solid understanding of both the project and the content knowledge. Since these teachers did not enter with backgrounds in computer science, we needed first to teach them the computer science topics that the students would be learning in the curriculum. We then used afternoon sessions to give the teachers time to draft lesson plans that would incorporate this computer science content into the existing science curriculum.

By the end of the Teacher Institute, we had produced a detailed in-school implementation plan, endorsed by all teachers. As noted above, the entire curriculum was designed for an academic quarter lasting approximately two months. We expected that the implementation plan would remain consistent from quarter to quarter, but, anticipating the need to refine the plan iteratively, we only solidified a calendar for the first academic quarter. The goal was to set dates for certain lessons so that members of the research team could coordinate with the teachers in preparing those class sessions. As described below, members of the research team worked closely with the teachers during the first quarter to troubleshoot issues with the game-based learning environment, to provide content knowledge support to the teachers, and to gather observations on how to improve the classroom implementation.

3.4 Study Implementation

Due to school constraints and other factors, not all teachers taught this curriculum each quarter of the 2014-15 academic year. During the first quarter in which each teacher taught the course, members of the research team attended most gameplay sessions and all non-gameplay sessions that involved computer science content. Teachers had the responsibility of delivering all lessons, but could request assistance from the research team member in the case of any uncertainty. For the most part, the teachers did not need to rely on in-class support from the research team. They reported satisfaction with the training that they received during the Teacher Institute, as well as appreciation for how the game-based learning environment supported instruction.

The classroom study saw over 200 students complete the course during the 2014-15 academic year. Students overwhelmingly responded positively to the experience on post-surveys, and classroom observations further established the game's success at engaging students. Furthermore, preliminary studies have revealed significant learning gains, as measured by ENGAGE's purpose-built knowledge assessment instrument [5, 7]. The rest of this paper, however, will focus on another dimension of the initiative's success: reaching a diverse student population, as measured by computer science attitudes.

4. COMPARISON OF STUDENTS WITH AND WITHOUT PRIOR PROGRAMMING EXPERIENCE

As discussed above, the desire to reach a diverse student population motivated our in-school implementation strategy. The fundamental goal of our project is to broaden participation in computing. While there exist many useful approaches to supporting this grand goal, we focus on reaching *students who might not otherwise consider computing fields*, helping them build their computational thinking skills, and positively impacting the attitudes that they hold towards computer science.

This requires us to go beyond merely looking at traditional demographic information to evaluate our success. In previous pilot studies, conducted as out-of-school initiatives, we succeeded in recruiting a large percentage of female students [6]. Yet the self-selection that is inherent to such out-of-school initiatives allows for the possibility that we may only have been reaching the female students who already felt predisposed to study computer science, or who had parents who encouraged them to study computer science. Furthermore, even if we "hid" computer science content within some out-of-school activity advertised as another discipline, which can be successful at reaching students who are not predisposed to computer science [9], we still might face issues of access that in-school activities largely avoid.

Thus, while we want to ensure that our initiative appeals to student groups generally underrepresented in computer science (and we have, in fact, analyzed ways in which it does so [7]), we also want to measure the success of our initiative at specifically impacting students with less of a predisposition toward studying computer science. To begin examining this, we can compare the computer science attitudes of students based on their prior computing experiences. This paper reports on the data of one our partner schools, Ada Middle School,[2] which offered the course each quarter of the 2014-15 academic year. Ada is an urban middle school serving a racially and ethnically diverse community, with over one third of its students receiving free or reduced lunch. It must be noted that Ada does provide its students a relatively high degree of exposure to computing due to its STEM theme and its proximity to a technology hub.

Of the 84 total students who completed all surveys (including pre- and post-surveys on computer science attitudes), 31 were female students and 53 were male students. As for race or ethnicity, the in-school implementation included 12 African-American students, 19 Asian students, 6 Latino/a Students, 1 Middle Eastern student, 6 mixed/multiracial students, 19 South-Asian students, and 21 white students. Meanwhile, on the survey item, "Have you ever participated in any activities that involve computer science or computer programming?", 48 of the participants reported "yes" and 36 reported "no".

To compare the computer science attitudes of those with and without prior programming experience, we utilized an attitude survey that was originally validated for college students [29], and which was modified for middle school students. This computer science attitudes (CSA) survey includes three subscales: *confidence* in computer science skills, *usefulness* of computer science, and *motivation* to study computer science. Perhaps unsurprisingly, the students with prior programming experience scored higher on this CSA survey overall and on all three subscales, as seen in Table 1.

Table 1. Computer science attitudes (CSA) on pre-survey of students with and without prior programming experience

	Prior Programming	No Prior Programming
CSA Overall	3.64 (SD = .62)	3.11 (SD = .65)
Confidence Subscale	3.88 (SD = .74)	3.08 (SD = .85)
Usefulness Subscale	3.59 (SD = .81)	3.23 (SD = .80)
Motivation Subscale	3.44 (SD = .75)	3.01 (SD = .64)

[2] Names of schools are pseudonyms. We report only on the data from this school here so that we can make a clearer comparison to students in an after-school initiative, described below.

One-way ANOVAs found all these differences to be significant with p–values less than .05. The confidence subscale saw an especially stark difference ($p < .001$). We expected to see such differences in computer science attitudes on this pre-survey. Students with prior programming experience may express more positive computer science attitudes because of prior programming experiences they have had. They may also have participated in those prior programming experiences due to their existing predispositions toward studying computer science.

The reinforcing interplay of *participation* and *interest* in computer science activities seems to start early. With this in mind, our in-school implementation aims to have particularly strong positive impacts on middle school students who *do not* have prior exposure to computer programming. To measure the initiative's success in this goal, we can look at the results of the CSA post-survey. As Table 2 shows, the pre-existing differences in computer science attitudes largely disappeared by the time students took this post-survey.

Table 2. Computer science attitudes (CSA) on post-survey of students with and without prior programming experience

	Prior Programming	No Prior Programming
CSA Overall	3.53 (SD = .9)	3.32 (SD = .86)
Confidence Subscale	3.6 (SD = 1.05)	3.41 (SD = .95)
Usefulness Subscale	3.54 (SD = .96)	3.27 (SD = 1.02)
Motivation Subscale	3.46 (SD = .94)	3.29 (SD = .82)

On the post-survey, neither the CSA overall nor any of the subscales revealed any significant differences between students with and without prior programming experience. The most dramatic shift occurred in the confidence subscale, where students with no prior programming experience increased their confidence to near the level of those with prior programming experience. A repeated-measures ANOVA found this increase from pre-survey to post-survey to be statistically significant ($F(1, 35) = 5.039$), $p < .05$). In many ways, this should be expected; following their participation in this initiative, all students on the post-survey now have some prior programming experience, so in some ways they all leave the initiative in the same category. If we had not situated this initiative in-school, however, we may never have reached those students with no prior programming experience. Now, students in this crucial demographic leave the initiative feeling empowered, and perhaps more motivated to study a subject that they had never before considered.

To further illustrate the potential value of in-school initiatives, we compare the in-school implementation to an after-school activity our research team conducted in Spring 2015. For this activity, we advertised for student participants at Hopper Middle School, which is *not* one of the middle schools where our course is offered during the school day, but is in the same district. Compared to Ada, Hopper Middle School has even larger percentages of students from underrepresented groups and a slightly larger percentage with free or reduced lunch (over 40%). Similar to Ada, Hopper provides its students a relatively high degree of exposure to computing due to its STEM focus, enhanced even further by its close proximity to an engineering university.

The participating students stayed after school each day for two weeks, during which they played through the entirety of the ENGAGE game-based learning environment. We accepted anyone who wished to participate, but we placed an emphasis on attracting female students in order to have a relatively even gender split. A total of 18 students ended up participating in this after-school activity: 10 male students and 8 female students. There were 11 white students, 3 African-American students, 2 Asian students, and 2 Latino students. We see here an over-representation of white students from a school population in which about two-thirds of students are non-white, and this is consistent with study results of other out-of-school initiatives [17]. Furthermore, all but one of the after-school participants reported "yes" to the survey item, "Have you ever participated in any activities that involve computer science or computer programming?"

In other words, although we attracted a participant pool that contained a fair representation of female students, this after-school activity failed to provide the diversity of participant pool that could help us understand how the game-based learning environment impacts students who have no pre-existing interest in computer science. Unsurprisingly, these students all reported positive computer science attitudes, with an overall 3.89 (SD = .49). Indeed, these after-school participants reported positive computer science attitudes even in comparison to the in-school students with prior programming experience (reporting an average of 3.64, as seen above in Table 1). These differences in computer science attitudes get at the root of the problem we face with the out-of-school study implementation. Students who participate in these types of activities may already have an above-average interest in computer science. For an initiative such as ours that aims to reach a broad population of students, these out-of-school study implementations may not provide valid and generalizable assessments of how well our initiative affects students' learning and attitudes.

5. CONCLUSION

This paper highlights an area of need in K-12 computer science education research: in-school initiatives. Many current outreach initiatives involve some degree of self-selection. In the case of out-of-school initiatives, such as summer camps or after-school clubs, participants tend to already feel motivated to study computing. Further, these activities often place demands on the participants' families (e.g., transportation to and from the activity) that may disadvantage students from underrepresented backgrounds. Innovative curricula for computer science electives at the secondary school level address this issue of access, but they still likely enroll students who enter with higher computer science attitudes than the overall population. Furthermore, some evidence suggests that secondary school may be too late for significantly impacting computer science attitudes. To fully support the goal of broadening participation in computing, we must create in-school initiatives at the pre-secondary level.

Merely looking at demographic information (e.g., gender) does not provide enough information as to whether an initiative is reaching a truly broad population of students. We must reach out to students who would not otherwise consider computer science as a subject of study, in addition to nurturing the computing careers of underrepresented students who already have pre-existing interest in the field. Through research on initiatives with this goal, we can gain insight into how best to design learning activities that appeal to young students with little incoming computer science experience and low predisposition for computer science interest.

In future work, it is important to investigate how the various areas of development (teacher professional development, curriculum, and purpose-built software) interact with one other to produce the most effective initiatives. A key issue is sustainability. While many projects have reported on the immediate results of an initiative, we need to follow up to see whether, and how, teachers are continuing in successive years. Finally, as the overarching goal is to recruit underrepresented students into computing, it will be critical to conduct longitudinal studies to measure the extent to which these in-school outreach initiatives empower students to study computer science at advanced levels.

6. ACKNOWLEDGEMENTS

This work is supported in part by the National Science Foundation through Grants CNS-1453520 and CNS-113897. Any opinions, findings, conclusions, or recommendations expressed in this report are those of the participants, and do not necessarily represent the official views, opinions, or policy of the National Science Foundation.

7. REFERENCES

[1] Aritajati, C. et al. 2015. A Socio-Cognitive Analysis of Summer Camp Outcomes and Experiences. *Proceedings of SIGCSE '15*, 581–586.

[2] Arpaci-dusseau, A. et al. 2013. Computer Science Principles : Analysis of a Proposed Advanced Placement Course. *Proceedings of SIGCSE '13*, 251–256.

[3] Bell, S. et al. 2014. Spreading the Word: Introducing Pre-Service Teachers to Programming. *Proceedings of SIGCSE '14*, 187–192.

[4] Bennett, V.E. et al. 2013. Computing Creativity: Divergence in Computational Thinking. *Proceeding of SIGCSE '13*, 359–364.

[5] Buffum, P.S. et al. 2015. A Practical Guide to Developing and Validating Computer Science Knowledge Assessments with Application to Middle School. *Proceedings of SIGCSE '15*, 622-627.

[6] Buffum, P.S. et al. 2014. CS Principles Goes to Middle School: Learning How to Teach "Big Data." *Proceedings of SIGCSE '14*, 151–156.

[7] Buffum, P.S. et al. 2015. Leveraging Collaboration to Improve Gender Equity in a Game-based Learning Environment for Middle School Computer Science. *RESPECT - IEEE Special Technical Community on Broadening Participation* (2015), 1-8.

[8] Carter, E. et al. 2012. Bringing the Breadth of Computer Science to Middle Schools. *Proceedings of SIGCSE '12*, 203-208.

[9] Franklin, D. et al. 2011. Animal Tlatoque: Attracting Middle School Students to Computing Through Culturally-Relevant Themes. *Proceedings of SIGCSE '11*, 453–458.

[10] Goode, J. and Margolis, J. 2011. Exploring Computer Science. *ACM Transactions on Computing Education*. 11, 2 (Jul. 2011), 1–16.

[11] Gray, J. et al. 2015. A Mid-Project Report on a Statewide Professional Development Model for CS Principles. *Proceedings of SIGCSE '15*, 380–385.

[12] Kay, J.S. et al. 2014. Sneaking in Through the Back Door: Introducing K-12 Teachers to Robot Programming. *Proceedings of SIGCSE '14*, 499–504.

[13] Koh, K.H. et al. 2013. Will it Stick ? Exploring the Sustainability of Computational Thinking Education Through Game Design. *Proceedings of SIGCSE '13*, 597-602.

[14] Lent, R.W. et al. 1994. Toward a Unifying Social Cognitive Theory of Career and Academic Interest, Choice, and Performance. *Journal of Vocational Behavior*. 45, (1994), 79–122.

[15] Levy, R.B.-B. and Ben-Ari, M. 2007. We Work So Hard and They Don't Use It: Acceptance of Software Tools by Teachers. *Proceedings of the 12th Conference on Innovation and Technology in Computer Science Education - ITiCSE '07*, 246-250.

[16] Liu, J. et al. 2014. Making Games a "Snap" with Stencyl – A Summer Computing Workshop for K-12 Teachers. *Proceedings of SIGCSE '14*, 169–174.

[17] McGill, M.M. et al. 2015. Does Outreach Impact Choices of Major for Underrepresented Undergraduate Students? *Proceedings of ICER '15*, 71–80.

[18] Ni, L. 2009. What Makes CS Teachers Change?: Factors Influencing CS Teachers' Adoption of Curriculum Innovations. *ACM SIGCSE Bulletin*. 41, 1 (Mar. 2009), 544–549.

[19] Oliveira, O.L. et al. 2014. Quantitative Correlation Between Ability to Compute and Student Performance in a Primary School. *Proceedings of SIGCSE '14*, 505–510.

[20] Pasternak, A. and Vahrenhold, J. 2012. Design and Evaluation of a Braided Teaching Course in Sixth Grade Computer Science Education. *Proceedings of SIGCSE '12*, 45–50.

[21] Rodger, S. et al. 2012. Integrating Computing into Middle School Disciplines through Projects. *Proceedings of SIGCSE '12*, 421–426.

[22] Schanzer, E. et al. 2015. Transferring Skills at Solving Word Problems from Computing to Algebra Through Bootstrap. *Proceedings of SIGCSE '15*, 616–621.

[23] Schofield, E. et al. 2014. MyCS: CS for Middle-Years Students and their Teachers. *Proceedings of SIGCSE '14*, 337–342.

[24] Seiter, L. 2015. Using SOLO to Classify the Programming Responses of Primary Grade Students. *Proceedings of SIGCSE '15*, 540–545.

[25] Shashaani, L. 1994. Gender Differences in Computer Experiences and Its Influence on Computer Attitudes. *Journal of Educational Computing Research*. 11, (1994), 347–367.

[26] Tashakkori, R.M. et al. 2014. Research Experience for Teachers: Data Analysis & Mining, Visualization, and Image Processing. *Proceedings of SIGCSE '14*, 193–198.

[27] Webb, D.C. et al. 2012. Toward an Emergent Theory of Broadening Participation in Computer Science Education. *Proceedings of SIGCSE '12*, 173–178.

[28] Webb, H.C. 2011. Injecting Computational Thinking Into Career Explorations for Middle School Girls. *2011 IEEE Symposium on Visual Languages and Human Centric Computing VLHCC*. (2011), 237–238.

[29] Wiebe, E.N. et al. 2003. *Computer Science Attitude Survey*. Dept. of Computer Science, North Carolina State University Technical Report TR-2003-1.

[30] Yadav, A. et al. 2011. Introducing Computational Thinking in Education Courses. *Proceedings of SIGCSE '11*, 465-470.

[31] Yoo, D. et al. 2011. WeScheme: The Browser Is Your Programming Environment Danny. *Proceedings of ITiCSE '11*, 163-167.

How Early Does the CS Gender Gap Emerge? A Study of Collaborative Problem Solving in 5th Grade Computer Science

Jennifer Tsan
Computer Science
North Carolina State Univ.
Raleigh, NC, USA
jtsan@ncsu.edu

Kristy Elizabeth Boyer
Computer Science
University of Florida
Gainesville, FL, USA
keboyer@ufl.edu

Collin F. Lynch
Computer Science
North Carolina State Univ.
Raleigh, NC, USA
cflynch@ncsu.edu

ABSTRACT

Elementary computer science has gained increasing attention within the computer science education research community. We have only recently begun to explore the many unanswered questions about how young students learn computer science, how they interact with each other, and how their skill levels and backgrounds vary. One set of unanswered questions focuses on gender equality for young computer science learners. This paper examines *how the gender composition of collaborative groups in elementary computer science relates to student achievement.* We report on data collected from an in-school 5th grade computer science elective offered over four quarters in 2014-2015. We found a significant difference in the quality of artifacts produced by learner groups depending upon their gender composition, with groups of all female students performing significantly lower than other groups. Our analyses suggest important factors that are influential as these learners begin to solve computer science problems. This new evidence of gender disparities in computer science achievement as young as ten years of age highlights the importance of future study of these factors in order to provide effective, equitable computer science education to learners of all ages.

CCS Concepts

•**Social and professional topics → Computer science education; Student assessment; K-12 education;**

Keywords

K-12, elementary, gender diversity, collaboration

1. INTRODUCTION

The benefits of introducing computer science to students at a young age are starting to be recognized [14]. Students often choose not to take computer science classes or enter a career in the field based upon misconceptions [3]. By reaching students earlier in their school years, we may be able to prevent students from forming these misconceptions and help them to make more informed decisions about a future career in computer science. However, bringing effective computer science learning opportunities to K-5 students is a challenging proposition [11]. There are many unanswered questions about effective teaching practices and how to assess students' skills, practices, and knowledge in age-appropriate ways [13, 20].

A very important category of unanswered questions centers around gender equity. The challenges of fostering and sustaining a diverse group of computer science learners has been long recognized at the postsecondary, high school, and even middle school levels, where evidence of gender disparity is clear [2, 3]. However, there has been very little research on these issues at the elementary school level. Research in math has shown that gender disparities in that area can begin as early as first grade [18]. Math gender stereotypes also emerge in elementary school and may have an effect on how students of each gender relate to math [7]. The community has yet to collect a strong body of evidence on gender disparities in computer science at the elementary school level.

This paper reports on a project to develop and implement an in-school computer science elective course at an urban elementary school in the southeastern US. We co-designed the course with an elementary school technology teacher, piloted it as an after-school course, and then offered the 30-contact-hour elective in school four quarters during the 2014-2015 academic year. We initially hypothesized that if we could recruit girls into this elective, there would be no gender gap in achievement between girls and boys. Our team conducts research on diversity in computer science education; the team itself is diverse; and we designed the curriculum, projects, and activities to have broad appeal to both genders. However, our in-class observations suggested that there were indeed differences in the quality of artifacts produced by students depending on the gender composition of their collaborative groups.

This paper investigates the following research question: *How is gender composition of collaborative groups in elementary computer science related to student achievement?* We examine the context of collaboration based on the long-recognized importance of collaboration for computer science practice [4, 9] and in light of evidence that learning collab-

SIGCSE '16, March 2-5, 2016, *Memphis, Tennessee USA*
© 2016 ACM. ISBN 978-1-4503-3685-7/16/03...$15.00
DOI: http://dx.doi.org/10.1145/2839509.2844605

oratively is beneficial to students in computer science [16].

We collected students' programs from one project in the 5th grade computer science course. These programs were rated for quality, and the results show that all-female groups produced significantly lower-scored artifacts than groups with at least one male. This finding is consistent with field observations made by the team and suggests that there is a gender disparity in computer science performance even at the young age of ten years old. We present the code quality comparison as well as a set of case studies to illustrate factors that are influential in the achievement of collaborative groups of computer science students at the elementary level, and suggest ways in which computer science education research can make advances in addressing this gender gap.

2. RELATED WORK

Recent years have seen an increase in efforts to engage elementary students in computer science, both in formal education and outreach programs. These projects span in-school and after-school interventions.

2.1 Elementary School Interventions

The KELP curriculum is a modular computer science curriculum for upper elementary school students [10]. The curriculum was designed around LaPlaya, a programming language and environment based on Scratch [13]. LaPlaya was built specifically to scaffold 4th-6th grade students in learning programming. The development of this curriculum and the preparation required to make the implementation successful have yielded informative insights. For example, some of the research findings suggest that it is important to reinforce content knowledge from other subject areas, construct an environment that fosters collaborative work, and provide careful feedback that emphasizes that there may be many solutions to a particular problem [11]. In interviews students were asked predictive questions such as what would happen when a user pressed the run button [8]. The results showed that some visual cues can be confusing: for example, some students believed that the location of blocks in the editing area determined the order in which the blocks would run.

Code Club, an after-school programming club in the UK, reached children in 1000 elementary schools in 2014 [22]. The goal of Code Club was to get elementary students excited about programming. Survey data showed that students were comfortable with the programming concepts they learned, and a third of the schools reported that over two thirds of the students in the club continued to use some form of digital creation outside of the club.

In Scotland, an in-depth study of 29 games created by pairs and groups of 60 students between the ages of 8 and 11 revealed the types of games students chose to create, the computer concepts used within the game, and how the code was organized and the game was designed [23]. The games were designed over the course of eight weeks. The authors' discussion suggested that the students were able to learn and apply their programming knowledge. 97% of the games had at least some functionality and 28% of the games had full functionality. The authors also note that, given more lessons and time to work, it was likely that students would have created more complex games with increasing functionality.

One question that arises with the introduction of computer science to young students is how the students' knowledge and skills should be evaluated. The PECT (Progression of Early Computational Thinking) Model was introduced to assess the computational thinking skills of students from the ages of 6-12 through their Scratch programs [20]. The model was applied to 25 projects found online in the Scratch community. The authors found that students in lower grades modified the sprites' looks and had them move and converse, but they often did not have any other features in their projects, such as collision and scoring. Upper elementary students had the same features as the lower elementary students but they also integrated collision, interaction, and scoring into their projects more often.

2.2 Collaboration in Elementary School

Research on how to foster, practice, and evaluate collaboration in computer science classrooms is ongoing for many ages of learners. For elementary computer science learning, some work has investigated collaborative problem solving. Notable work has examined the equity of students' relationships as they solve computer science problems in pairs [21, 15]. That work focused on elementary students who participated in a summer computer science course, and the authors analyzed the paired dialogues in terms of how much the students spoke to each other and the content of their conversations. The authors concluded that equity is contextualized and may be a result of certain students' desire to complete projects quickly.

Outside of computer science, a study of elementary students' collaboration revealed that female-male relationships in subjects such as physical education, reading, language art, social studies, and art are not equal [17]. Boys appear to benefit more from female-male pairings by developing their leadership skills and increasing their self-efficacy in problem solving, whereas these pairings can reinforce gender stereotypes for girls.

Given these findings, the importance of investigating gender and collaboration for elementary computer science education is clear. The remainder of this paper reports on a study to examine one aspect of gender and collaboration, the quality of artifacts produced. We also examine some possible factors influencing artifact quality through case studies.

3. ELEMENTARY CLASS & STUDY

In 2014 a team consisting of two computer science Ph.D. students, one computer science undergraduate, and a local elementary school technology teacher collaboratively designed a 30 hour 5th grade computer science curriculum. In this class students engage in problem solving, writing, and collaborative projects that span a series of topics in algorithmic thinking and programming, robotics, AI, and computers in society. The content of the curriculum was inspired by the intersection of CS Principles [1], Exploring CS [12], and the CSTA K-8 guidelines [5], which were adapted with the help of the teacher for 5th grade. The teacher had no formal background in computer science and the team introduced necessary topics to the teacher as they collaboratively designed and built the curriculum.

The curriculum was first piloted as a 13-day after-school club in Spring 2014, then was expanded and refined during Summer 2014 to fit the in-school 30-day, 45-minute class slot requested by our partner elementary school.[1] The school's

[1]The curriculum is modularly designed, so others who wish to use it may adopt smaller portions if desired.

demographics were 53.1% African American, 32.6% Caucasian, and 14.3% Hispanic, Latino, Native American, Asian, or mixed race. 47.4% of students received free or reduced lunch.

Each quarter during the 2014-2015 school year, teachers enrolled students in electives based on the students' expressed preferences. There was a total of 55 students enrolled in the computer science elective (16 girls, 39 boys).

Table 1: Class gender by quarter.

Quarter	Girls	Boys	Total
1	6	8	14
2	3	12	15
3	5	10	15
4	2	9	11

As part of exploratory work on the effectiveness of the curriculum, we collected the following: pre- and post-interviews, videos of students working in class, screen recordings of student programming, student short essays, and handwritten design artifacts including conditional trees and storyboards. A researcher observed the class an average of three times per week and made field notes.

The students in the class completed three major projects: two Scratch programming projects, and one research project on computer science and society. The analysis reported in this paper investigates the first programming project, in which students selected a fairy tale to implement as an interactive program. The teacher made the decision as to how the students could be paired. For some quarters he allowed the students to choose their partners and intervened only when he felt it was necessary. For other quarters he choose the pairs himself. Although most of the students worked in pairs, there were also cases where students worked in groups of three or four, or, as seen in one case study in Section 5, individually. The students were required to incorporate two instances of cause and effect from the fairy tale, and two instances of user input where the user's input decided the path the story took.

The project spanned approximately six class days and it began after students received between four and six days of instruction on using conditionals and loops, broadcasting and receiving signals, and moving sprites in Scratch. The project days were structured, with design and planning time required before students started programming. The paper-based design packet included a sheet for determining collaborative tasks and tracking their completion. On the first day the students selected and read their fairy tales, identified two instances of cause and effect and user input, and drew conditional trees. The next day the students identified the characters and backgrounds they would use in their program, drew a storyboard, and created a rough code plan. The third day was the only day reserved for the students to choose or make their characters and backgrounds. On the remaining days the students pair programmed, switching the "driver" at 15 minute intervals.

4. ANALYSIS AND RESULTS

The goal of this analysis is to examine the relationship between gender composition of groups and the quality of the final project they submitted. The sample size for this analysis is 18 pairs or groups (and in one case an individual): 4 all-female, 4 female-male, and 10 all-male.

First, quality of the submitted projects was rated. We created and iteratively refined a rating scheme inspired by previous work using the SOLO (Structure of the Observed Learning Outcome) taxonomy to rate 4th grade student programs [19]. Given students' completed work for assigned learning tasks, the SOLO taxonomy measures the complexity of the work. Each student's work is assigned to one of five levels depending on the criteria it meets. We found that for some important factors of the student programs, this taxonomy was not fine-grained enough, while in other cases it was too fine-grained. We ultimately rated the project based on three factors:

- Requirements: How well the project runs and meets the requirements given by the teacher (includes two instances of cause and effect and two instances of user-input).
- Consistency: Whether the project runs consistently (resetting appropriately before or after the code runs).
- Usability: Whether the project is intuitive for users (e.g., uses prompts to clearly guide the user).

Table 2 displays the four-level coding scheme for the Code Requirements factor. Consistency and Usability were rated on a binary scale.

Table 2: Coding scheme for Code Requirements.

Level	Criteria
0	Did not attempt to write the program
1	The program contains blocks but does not function, or it functions but does not show cause and effect or utilize user input
2	The program shows an instance of cause and effect and user input
3	The program shows two instances of cause and effect and user input

After rating the 18 projects, their overall weighted score was computed as $(0.7{*}Requirements)+(0.2{*}Consistency)+(0.1*Usability)$. We determined the weights before starting our analysis. The weights were based on the emphasis the teacher placed on each criterion. The median of all project scores was 0.62, with a minimum of 0.23 and a maximum of 1.0.

We divided the groups as follows: all-female (FF), female-male (FM), and all-male (MM). Figure 1 shows a scatter plot of each pair's code score. The programs of all four all-female groups scored below the median, and their scores were clustered together. The scores of the female-male groups were also relatively close to each other, with their lowest scores being equal to the highest score of the all-female groups and their highest score being slightly lower than most of the all-male groups. The all-male groups displayed the widest range of scores, with both the highest and lowest scoring groups out of all the categories (however, note that the all-male group was also largest, with n=10). Seventy percent of the all-male groups scored 0.77 or higher.

We ran a Fisher's exact test to investigate whether there were differences in average code quality score between the groups. Because of the small sample, we first binned into high and low scores based on median, and considered a

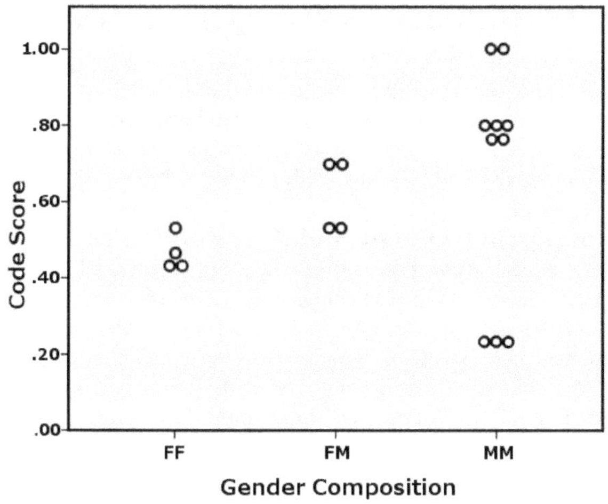

Figure 1: Code score vs. group gender composition.

Table 3: Results of the Fisher's exact test on gender composition and code score.

	Code Score		
	Low	High	Total
All Female	4 (100%)	0 (0%)	4 (100%)
1+ Male	5 (35.7%)	9 (64.3%)	14 (100%)
Total	9 (50%)	9 (50%)	18 (100%)

two-way split of gender composition: all-female (n=4) and at-least-one-male (n=14).[2] The results revealed that *none* of the all-female groups, and 64% of the at-least-one-male groups, achieved a high code score. This difference was statistically significant (p=0.04).

We also examined the all-male (n=10) and at-least-one-female (n=8) groups separately. In this split, 70% of all-male groups and 25% of at-least-one-female groups achieved high code scores, and this difference was not statistically significant (p=0.08).

5. CASE STUDIES

In order to better elucidate group dynamics, we examine selected case studies. These case studies are based on collected videos and the first author's field notes from observing the class. The cases were selected to illustrate the results and are not comprehensive.

5.1 Individual: Xavier

Xavier[3] took the class during the second quarter. The teacher mentioned that Xavier had experience from participating in the after-school pilot in Spring 2014; however, the project analyzed here was not part of that pilot. At first Xavier was paired with another student with less experience. However, the teacher noticed that Xavier's partner quickly became disengaged. The teacher moved Xavier's partner to another team and Xavier completed the project individually.

[2]Although this split resulted in unbalanced group sizes, it was necessary to investigate the hypothesis which arose from our classroom observations, that the presence of a male substantially altered group dynamics.

[3]All student names are pseudonyms.

When completing his design packet, Xavier bypassed the sprites, stages, and outline sections. However, his was one of six groups that completed the code plan, and he produced one of the two highest-rated conditional trees. Most groups drew two separate conditional trees that illustrated two instances of cause and effect. Although those trees met the requirements the teacher gave, they did not show any connection between two major events that occurred in their chosen fairy tale. In contrast, Xavier's conditional tree was unified and resembled a flow chart. Xavier's code plan was also detailed, included drawing chunks of Scratch blocks in the order he would later put them in, and he drew arrows to show how the program should flow. Xavier completed his project implementation work early, and when the teacher suggested he extend his project, Xavier added an alternate stage to the program when the player selected a specific ending. Xavier's program was one of two programs that received a perfect score.

5.2 Female-Male Pair: Mia and John

Mia and John participated in the class the during the final quarter of the 2014-2015 school year. Prior to the project, they were observed working well together (spontaneously) on basic programming exercises. However, sharing a computer proved more difficult for them. Mia often overrode John's ideas, choosing instead to ask the teacher for help. The team rarely solved a problem on their own due to the frequency with which they summoned the teacher. Mia was also reluctant to switch from the driver to the navigator role when the teacher announced that it was time to switch; she sometimes even took the mouse from John when he was the driver. The pair also spent much of their time modifying their sprites in Scratch and less time programming and problem solving.

Mia and John's program met the requirements of conditional branching. However, it did not run consistently and had a low usability score. To run the program from beginning to end, users had to take actions in addition to answering questions, but there were no prompts or user guidance. Still, Mia and John, along with one other pair, achieved the highest project scores out of the four female-male pairs. Even this score was only slightly higher than the overall median.

Figure 2 displays a screen capture of Mia and John's program running and Figure 3 shows the code for one of the characters, a prince. Mia and John did not use some of the concepts they learned in class, such as loops, broadcasting, and receiving messages. They only accounted for one user answer to their first question, and some actions were triggered by clicking on the sprite or pressing a key, but these available actions were not made apparent to the user. Overall, Mia and John failed to form a unified vision of their work and it appears that they did not successfully apply their potential when they were placed into a collaborative pair.

5.3 Female-Female Pair: Willow and Daphne

During the first quarter, Willow and Daphne were two of the six girls in the class. The girls asked to work as a team because they were friends and had worked together during the prior Scratch lessons. Willow and Daphne worked well together and were creative. Like Xavier, they also bypassed the sprites, stages, and outline section, completing

Figure 2: Screen capture of Mia and John's stage.

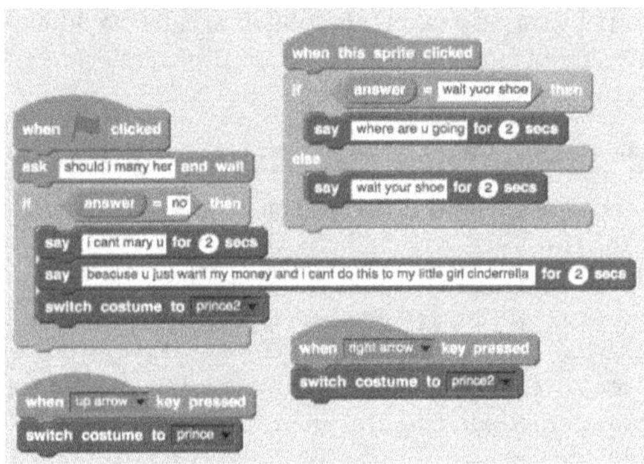

Figure 3: Screen capture of Mia and John's code.

the other components instead. The conditional trees Willow and Daphne drew expressed two conditionals based on user input, but like many of their peers, the two conditions were not linked in an overall flow. Like Xavier's, their code plan included some hand-sketched Scratch blocks, but theirs included only the user input options, not the condition that resulted from each one.

When it came to implementation, Willow and Daphne did not implement the required cause-and-effect. Their code did run consistently and the user prompts were clear, but their characters' conversations were incoherent. The missing requirements were reflected in their score of 0.53, which although it was the highest among all of the all-female groups, was still well below the overall median.

5.4 Male-Male Pair: Greg and Harry

Greg and Harry participated in the last quarter of the school year. Both students had enthusiasm for programming and they often took creative liberties during the Scratch lessons. Although the pair worked well together and seemed to follow a similar line of thinking, Harry would sometimes get distracted by a friend in a different group, even leaving his seat to visit the other group. They were animated while brainstorming ideas for their "Jack and the Beanstalk" game, but spent less time on their design document, only completing about half of it.

This trend continued through their implementation, when they were engaged in off-task behavior with unrelated blocks. They only introduced one instance of cause and effect, and their program scored low for usability and consistency. Their code score was the lowest, shared by two other all-male groups.

6. DISCUSSION AND LIMITATIONS

Our results suggest that there is a relationship between gender and the artifacts produced by collaborative groups in a 5th grade computer science elective. While our analyses do not definitively answer our original research question, they do suggest factors that are influential and are important for future study.

Supporting Design and Planning. One important factor is the extent to which students engaged in design and planning. While these activities were scaffolded with a carefully designed paper-based packet, we observed a phenomenon that is often seen in computer science education. Namely, students often preferred to bypass design and planning, instead preferring to implement immediately or "tinker." While tinkering has been shown to have potential benefits, our results suggest that it is important to investigate how to foster the collaborative design and planning process for young learners.

Fostering Collaborative Skills and Practices. In addition to these concerns regarding design and planning, collaboration skills and practices are a very important area for future study. Young learners have had little opportunity to practice collaboration, and they display tendencies to separate rather than collaborate (as we saw with Xavier and his partner, as well as with Mia and John). This tendency, of course, is often observed with more sophisticated learners, as one of the authors of this paper can attest: even in second and third programming courses, she finds herself needing to remind students constantly not to just attempt to *divide* the implementation tasks in a collaborative project, but to work *together* and share ideas. If we can identify ways to support good collaborative habits as early as elementary school, perhaps those habits can propagate into students' future education and careers.

Investigating Cognitive and Social Constructs. Differences in performance at young ages is almost certainly related in part to influences that occur prior to the class itself. For example, there is a systematic gender difference between toys marketed to young children. Legos and robots are more likely to be marketed for boys, while dolls and kitchen sets are more likely to be marketed for girls. It is possible that the traditionally "boy" toys foster spatial and programmatic reasoning skills more than traditionally "girl" toys, and recent literature suggests a correlation between spatial reasoning and computer science performance [6].

Limitations. As mentioned above, there are important limitations due to the small sample size and exploratory nature of the study described here. The sample size, n=18, was partially due to the fact that not all projects were submitted. This points to a bigger-picture discrepancy between required versus elective in-school classes. Ours was offered as an elective, which was not permitted to include exams, and for which grades were assigned in a much less structured way than required courses such as mathematics and language. It will be important to explore this phenomenon on a larger dataset in the future.

Another limitation to the study stems from the evolution of the course across quarters. As is often the case, the course was refined and improved over time. The course was also confined to a single instructor and thus the teacher effect cannot be eliminated. Finally, it is important to note that the researcher making field notes was not always able to achieve the ideal role as a silent observer in the classroom. Because this classroom teacher was still developing computer science skills and knowledge, the researcher provided input and support when needed.

7. CONCLUSION AND FUTURE WORK

This paper has examined the first of a series of projects created by students in an in-school 5th grade computer science elective. We examined 18 group projects and investigated whether there was a difference between gender composition of groups and the quality of the final artifact they produced. Classroom observation suggested that a difference did exist, and results demonstrated that all-female groups achieved significantly lower program quality than groups with at least one male. The analyses suggest that numerous factors play important roles, including the extent to which students were willing to engage in design, students' collaborative practices, and other cognitive and social factors.

There are several important directions for future work. The finding of a possible gender discrepancy in computer science achievement as early as elementary school highlights the need for research on diversity and equality in K-5. More broadly, there is a need for increased computer science education research, curriculum building, and integration with other subject areas at the elementary level. As a computer science education community of practitioners and researchers, we have the opportunity to expand our focus on computer science learners to include younger children, as they make their way toward becoming the next generation of computer scientists.

ACKNOWLEDGEMENTS This work is supported in part by the Wake County Public School System and the National Science Foundation through Grant CNS-1453520. Any opinions, findings, conclusions, or recommendations expressed in this report are those of the participants, and do not necessarily represent the official views, opinions, or policy of the National Science Foundation.

8. REFERENCES

[1] AP Computer Science Principles Draft Curriculum Framework, 2014.

[2] S. Beyer, K. Rynes, J. Perrault, K. Hay, and S. Haller. Gender differences in computer science students. *SIGCSE Bulletin*, 35(1):49–53, 2003.

[3] L. Carter. Why students with an apparent aptitude for computer science don't choose to major in computer science. In *SIGCSE '06*, pages 27–31, 2006.

[4] B. Coleman and M. Lang. Collaboration Across the Curriculum: A Disciplined Approach to Developing Team Skills. In *SIGCSE '12*, pages 277–282, 2012.

[5] I. Computer Science Teachers Association, Association for Computing Machinery. Computer Science K-8: Building a Strong Foundation, 2012.

[6] S. Cooper, K. Wang, M. Israni, and S. Sorby. Spatial Skills Training in Introductory Computing. In *ICER'15*, pages 13–20, 2015.

[7] D. Cvencek, A. Z. Meltzoff, and A. G. Greenwald. Math-Gender Stereotypes in Elementary School Children. *Child Development*, 82(3):766–779, 2011.

[8] H. Dwyer, C. Hill, A. Hansen, A. Iveland, D. Franklin, and D. Harlow. Fourth Grade Students Reading Block-Based Programs: Predictions, Visual Cues, and Affordances. In *ICER'15*, pages 111–119, 2015.

[9] K. Falkner, N. J. Falkner, and R. Vivian. Collaborative Learning and Anxiety: A phenomenographic study of collaborative learning activities. In *SIGCSE '13*, pages 227–232, 2013.

[10] D. Franklin, D. Harlow, H. Dwyer, J. Henkens, C. Hill, A. Iveland, A. Killian, and Staff. Kids Engaged in Learning Programming (KELP-CS) -Module 1 Digital Storytelling. A computer science curriculum for elementary school students. https://discover.cs.ucsb.edu/kelpcs/educators/KELPCSIntro.pdf, 2014.

[11] D. Franklin, C. Hill, H. Dwyer, A. Iveland, A. Killian, and D. Harlow. Getting Started in Teaching and Researching Computer Science in the Elementary Classroom. In *SIGCSE '15*, pages 552–557, 2015.

[12] J. Goode and G. Chapman. Exploring Computer Science: A High-School Curriculum Exploring what Computer Science is and What it Can Do. https://www.exploringcs.org/curriculum, 2013.

[13] C. Hill, H. A. Dwyer, T. Martinez, D. Harlow, and D. Franklin. Floors and Flexibility: Designing a Programming Environment for 4th-6th Grade Classrooms. In *SIGCSE '15*, pages 546–551, 2015.

[14] E. Kazakoff and M. Bers. Programming in a Robotics Context in the Kindergarten Classroom: The Impact on Sequencing Skills. *Journal of Educational Multimedia and Hypermedia*, 21(4):371–391, 2012.

[15] C. M. Lewis and N. Shah. How Equity and Inequity Can Emerge in Pair Programming. In *Proceedings of ICER'15*, pages 41–50, 2015.

[16] C. M. Lewis, N. Titterton, and M. Clancy. Using collaboration to overcome disparities in Java experience. In *ICER '12*, pages 79–86, 2012.

[17] M. E. Lockheed and A. M. Harris. Cross-Sex Collaborative Learning in Elementary Classrooms. *American Educational Research Journal*, 21(2):275–294, 1984.

[18] J. P. Robinson and S. T. Lubienski. The Development of Gender Achievement Gaps in Mathematics and Reading During Elementary and Middle School: Examining Direct Cognitive Assessments and Teacher Ratings. *American Educational Research Journal*, 48(2):268–302, 2011.

[19] L. Seiter. Using SOLO to Classify the Programming Responses of Primary Grade Students. In *SIGCSE '15*, pages 540–545, 2015.

[20] L. Seiter and B. Foreman. Modeling the Learning Progressions of Computational Thinking of Primary Grade Students. In *ICER '13*, pages 59–66, 2013.

[21] N. Shah, C. Lewis, and R. Caires. Analyzing Equity in Collaborative Learning Situations: A Comparative Case Study in Elementary Computer Science. In *ICLS*, pages 495–502, 2014.

[22] N. Smith, C. Sutcliffe, and L. Sandvik. Code Club: Bringing Programming to UK Primary Schools through Scratch. In *SIGCSE '14*, pages 517–522, 2014.

[23] A. Wilson, T. Hainey, and T. Connolly. Evaluation of computer games developed by primary school children to gauge understanding of programming concepts. In *Proceedings of the European Conference on Games Based Learning*, pages 549–558, 2012.

AP Computer Science and Service Learning with We.org

Sandy Czajka
Riverside Brookfield High School
Riverside, IL 60546
+1 708-442-7500
czajkas@rbhs208.net

Lien Diaz (lead contact)
College Board, AP Program
Duluth, GA 30096
+1 770-225-4012
ldiaz@collegeboard.org

Crystal Furman
College Board, AP Program
Duluth, GA 30096
+1 770-225-4065
cfurman@collegeboard.org

Categories and Subject Descriptors

K.3.2 [**Computer and Information Science Education**]: computer science education, service learning, curriculum

General Terms

Design, Experimentation

Keywords

CS0, CS1, computer science education, service learning, active learning. computing applications

1. SUMMARY

College Board is thrilled to announce the launch of a pilot program, Advanced Placement® (AP) with We.org Service, in a partnership with international charity and educational partner, Free the Children. AP Computer Science is among six AP courses that will participate in this pilot program. The College Board and Free The Children share a passion for enriching students' learning experiences and developing well-rounded citizens. The program combines the academic challenge and rigor of AP Computer Science with Free The Children's WE.org education and citizenship model. AP Computer Science with WE.org Service creates an opportunity for students to consider their classroom work and how it applies to the real world, while working closely with peers to address social issues.

Through its partnership with Free The Children, the College Board hopes to:

- Encourage teachers and students to apply the knowledge they gain in an AP Computer Science class by locally developing and enacting service initiatives that address opportunities and challenges in their own or others' communities.
- Allow for broader discussions of demanding academic material due to the interactive and problem-based nature of service-learning projects.
- Provide the relevant tools and resources for educators and students to design and implement their own service-learning programs.
- Motivate an increase in participation with a diverse group of students, especially with females and underrepresented students in computing.
- Encourage higher education institutions to recognize service-learning within a rigorous academic context.

This session will provide information regarding the AP Computer Science curriculum modules and lessons that have been developed as part of the partnership with We.org. The lessons include opportunity for students to select a service learning project and consider solutions that they will develop as part of their AP Computer Science course work. Participants will engage in a brief activity to become familiar with the goals of this program and to learn how the lessons integrate the We.org service-based learning framework and resources into the AP Computer Science courses. They will understand how the lessons help students to identify local priorities and translate classroom learning into-hands-on innovation and problem solving. A student who completes an AP Computer Science course with a WE.org Service component will earn a recognition that will appear on their AP score reports that he or she sends to colleges and universities. High schools will also have the option to indicate on students' transcripts that they have completed an AP course with a service-learning component.

SIGCSE'16, March 2–5, 2016, Memphis, TN, USA.
ACM ISBN: 978-1-4503-3685-7/16/03.
DOI: http://dx.doi.org/10.1145/2839509.2844676

2. SESSION OBJECTIVES

The current AP Computer Science course and Exam has been the subject of substantial discussion and debate. How should computer science be introduced? What topics should be included? What pedagogy is appropriate? In addition, there will be a new AP Computer Science Principles course in which high schools will begin offering in fall of 2016. This session seeks to introduce a different approach for engaging students in the study of computer science and motivate an increase in participation with diverse students, especially females and other underrepresented students in computing. This impetus leads to the following session objectives:

- Review information regarding the AP with We.org Service Program and learn about how the program is being piloted in schools.
- Examine how effective service learning is shown to increase students' sense of self-esteem, enhance students' ability to relate to culturally diverse groups, help students apply learning in the "real world" and have a positive impact on problem analysis, critical thinking and cognitive development.
- Learn how service learning increases students' skills for career development and awareness.

- Review the AP Computer Science service learning lessons and learn how Service-Learning can be integrated into AP Computer Science classes as well as entry level university computer science courses.

- Examine how service learning has potential to attract and retain women and underrepresented groups in computer science.

3. OUTLINE OF THE SESSION

The following outline envisions questions and discussion during the last 20 minutes of the session. Realistically, some questions may arise during the initial presentations, so the question-answer time may be revised as the session progresses.

- Overview of the AP with We.org Service Program. Diaz – 10 minutes
- Development of the AP Computer Science Service Learning Modules and Lessons. Furman – 15 minutes
    - Overview of content and integration of service learning options
- Implementation of the AP Computer Science Service Learning Modules and Lessons. Czajka – 30 minutes
    - Description of classroom activities
    - Engage participants in a brief activity
- Questions, audience feedback, discussion --- 20 minutes

4. EXPECTATIONS

This proposed session will serve several audiences:

- Teachers of introductory computer science (at high school and college levels) who are interested in nation-wide trends and practices regarding their courses.

- Educators and administrators who want to better understand the role of service learning integrated with computer science education.

- Guidance counselors and student advisors who want to guide students in the transition from high school CS courses to college courses.

- Department chairs and deans who are monitoring placement and credit policies regarding AP courses.

- AP Computer Science teachers who are interested in providing students effective and engaging learning opportunities that incorporates service learning.

With the diversity of practices regarding introductory CS at the college level, the results reported in this session will likely generate considerable discussion and debate. Thus, the session will conclude with a 20-minute question-answer-feedback session involving attendees.

5. SUITABILITY FOR A SPECIAL SESSION

This special session responds to many inquiries over the years regarding the extent to which AP Computer Science relates to introductory CS courses at the college level. Thus, this special session serves as something of a report by the AP Program and subject matter experts in service learning and AP Computer Science.

- *The session does not represent a traditional SIGCSE paper:* The material presented discusses the direction the AP Computer Science program is taking. The session is not a presentation of educational research or pedagogy, following the form for usual SIGSE papers.

- *The session does not bring together multiple viewpoints as would be found in a typical SIGCSE panel:* The session leader represents AP Computer Science, and the session will discuss practices used by the College Board and the AP Computer Science course development over the next few years.

Altogether, the material for this session continues an on-going dialog between the AP Computer Science program and the broad computing community, the nature of the session does not seem to fit well with either a paper or panel format, but the content seems of general interest to the overall community. The special session framework seems best suited for this type of discussion.

6. ACKNOWLEDGMENTS

The Advanced Placement Program thanks We.org and Free the Children for the opportunities provided by this partnership to bring a unique and rigorous implementation to the study of college level computer science course work.

7. REFERENCES

[1] Janet S. Eyler, Dwight E.Giles, Jr., Christine M. Stenson, and Charlene J. Gray. *What We Know about The Effects of Service-Learning on College Students, Faculty, Institutions and Communities*. August, 2001.

[2] College Board, *The Computer Science A Course Description*, 2014. https://secure-media.collegeboard.org/digitalServices/pdf/ap/ap-computer-science-a-course-description.pdf.

[3] College Board, *AP Computer Science Principles Curriculum Framework*, September 2014.

CS10K Teachers by 2017? Try CS1K+ students NOW! Coping with the Largest CS1 Courses in History

Daniel D. Garcia (moderator)
University of California, Berkeley
777 Soda Hall
Berkeley, CA 94720
+1 (510) 517-4041
ddgarcia@cs.berkeley.edu

Jennifer Campbell
University of Toronto
Department of Computer Science
Toronto, ON Canada M5S 2E4
+1 (416) 978-6320
campbell@cs.toronto.edu

John DeNero
University of California, Berkeley
781 Soda Hall
Berkeley, CA 94720
+1 (510) 643-7354
denero@cs.berkeley.edu

Mary Lou Dorf
University of Michigan
4636 Beyster Bldg.
Ann Arbor, MI 48109
+1 (734) 615-9916
mdorf@umich.edu

Stuart Reges
University of Washington
Box 352350
Seattle, WA 98195
+1 (206) 685-9138
reges@cs.washington.edu

Keywords

Computer science education, CS1, Over-enrollment, Diversity

1. SUMMARY

"Be careful what you wish for, you just might get it." – Proverb

In 2005, computing education was experiencing a crisis. Enrollments had "fallen to such an extent that some academic computing programs were facing significant reductions in staffing levels or even elimination" [1]. The community responded, with panels to investigate and highlight ways to infuse "passion, beauty, joy and awe" into the introductory experiences [2], the CS10K project to bring computing to 10,000 teachers and 100,000 students [3], and better messaging of career opportunities [4], to name a few of the initiatives to bring students back into our seats.

Well, by golly, it worked! It certainly didn't hurt our cause that Wall Street almost collapsed [5], young whiz kids were becoming TECH billionaires, an inspiring video and an interactive website led millions of people to code for an hour every December, or smart devices put computing into the hands of young people, and social media became the killer app. Whatever it was, CS became hot again [6]. And we mean HOT. There are now several institutions around the world that have well over a thousand students taking CS1 in the Fall of 2015. There's just so much lemonade one can make [7] before the seams start to burst, and the wheels come off the bus, as many shared at SIGCSE 2015 at the Birds of the Feather session [8].

The goal of this panel is to bring together educators who were charged with delivering face-to-face CS1 on the grandest scale the field has ever seen. How did they cope? Does it become all people management with an army of Teaching Assistants? What were the differences and common themes in their survival plans? What is working? What mistakes were made? How are they supporting differential learning for the students who don't have the same experience as others? How is diversity being affected? Finally, what advice would they have for others interested in venturing into the tsunami, and broaden participation at a massive scale?

SIGCSE '16, March 02-05, 2016, Memphis, TN, USA
ACM 978-1-4503-3685-7/16/03.
http://dx.doi.org/10.1145/2839509.2844660

2. JENNIFER CAMPBELL

At the University of Toronto, nearly 1,200 students enrolled in CS1 in Fall 2015 and a couple hundred more would have taken the course if space permitted. Over the past few years, we've seen a significant increase in demand for CS1, which has led to an increase in both the number and size of sections. This Fall, CS1 will be taught in five sections (one online and four flipped) of 220-250 students. Each section has its own instructor, but exercises, assignments, and the final exam are shared. Office hours for the course are delivered through a CS1 help centre staffed by teaching assistants and course instructors.

In addition to instructors for each section, the course also has a Course Coordinator (CC). The faculty member who takes on the CC role receives teaching credit equivalent to teaching a single section of CS1, in addition to any credit received for teaching the course. The CC role involves working with instructors to ensure consistent delivery of the course material, supervising teaching assistants, managing grades, handling academic offense cases, and other administrative tasks.

3. JOHN DENERO

The main CS1 course at UC Berkeley is now the largest course on campus, with 1,400 students enrolled in a *single lecture section* for the Fall 2015 semester. Rather than splitting students into separate lecture sections that might actually fit in the available rooms on campus, this single section is served primarily through videos that contain both exposition and brief discussion questions. Students engage in the material during 3 hours each week of 30-student discussion and lab sections that typically have high attendance rates throughout the semester. Drop-in office hours are available for at least 32 hour each week, staffed by the teaching assistants.

The course's scale has allowed for substantial software development efforts to reduce redundant work by the course staff and allow students to make progress independently. An updated version of *Online Python Tutor* that fully depicts the behavior of higher-order functions made our students substantially more self-sufficient [9]. Online exam grading through Gradescope has proven indispensable [10]. Interactive feedback to check students' understanding of problem specifications dramatically reduced the number of clarifying questions asked by students about their projects. Feedback about program style and composition given online has replaced the need to print, collect, and distribute paper copies of programs [11]. The course infrastructure allows the teaching assistants to focus on high-value interactions, such as answering conceptual questions and helping students debug and understand challenging examples.

4. MARY LOU DORF

It would have been really nice if there were somewhere I could have found information on how to handle the 50% increase in enrollments each year over the last few years. I have found that every time enrollments double, the administration for the course needs to change. What worked for 100, no longer works for 200. What worked for 200, no longer works for 400, What worked for 400, no longer works for 800. I am currently planning on how to handle the next major increase. We have an enrollment of 1,600 at the University of Michigan, split over 4 different CS1 courses and multiple lectures. However, each of the courses are highly coordinated with the same topics in each lecture on the same day, the same projects, the same assignments, the same book with the same readings, the same exams, etc.

Right now my primary concern is on diversity and how to improve. Current numbers are about 1/3 of the students are females and 10% are minority across all the CS1 courses. However the pipeline leaks and the issues are many: how to make sure all the courses are on the same page with supporting underrepresented students, how to determine why students either don't continue to the next course or withdraw from the course, how to get buyin from all faculty involved in 4 different CS1 courses to change some of their policies, how to assure these students thrive in CS1, how to make sure they are prepared for success in CS2 and CS3, etc. Our statistics show that once they get through that 3rd course, they continue within the major to graduate with a CS degree. We're getting there.

5. STUART REGES

The University of Washington has seen steady increases in enrollment for four years to the point where we now have over 2,800 students taking our CS1 course, which is just shy of 50% of the undergraduates. We have managed to have mostly open enrollment, which has helped us to attract more women to the computer science major. Our undergraduate TA program has allowed us to scale up while also maintaining high quality instruction. The TAs run small group discussion sections of 20 to 25 students. Because we have such a strong sense of community among the TAs, we continue to get 5 to 10 applicants for each TA that we hire. We have also invested in online tutoring tools for students and online grading tools for TAs. We hired a full-time programmer to manage these tools in 2014-2015 and we are adding a half-time administrative staff support person as well.

Our greatest challenges have been logistical as we keep running out of seats in every auditorium that we are able to reserve. We have also found it challenging to preserve community at this scale and have introduced new activities and procedures like a "TA buddy" program to ensure that we continue to have a vibrant community even as we grow.

6. REFERENCES

[1] Lillian (Boots) Cassel, Andrew McGettrick, Mark Guzdial, and Eric Roberts. 2007. The current crisis in computing: what are the real issues?. In *Proceedings of the 38th SIGCSE technical symposium on Computer science education* (SIGCSE '07). ACM, New York, NY, USA, 329-330. doi.acm.org/10.1145/1227310.1227426

[2] McGettrick, A., Roberts, E., Garcia, D. D., and Stevenson, C. 2008. Rediscovering the passion, beauty, joy and awe: making computing fun again. In *Proceedings of the 39th SIGCSE Technical Symposium on Computer Science Education* (Portland, OR, USA, March 12 - 15, 2008). SIGCSE '08. ACM, New York, NY, 217-218. doi.acm.org/10.1145/1352135.1352213

[3] Briggs, A. and Snyder, L. 2012. Computer science principles and the CS 10K initiative. *ACM Inroads* 3, 2 (June 2012), 29-31. doi.acm.org/10.1145/2189835.2189847

[4] ACM. *Computing Degrees and Careers*. August 2015. computingcareers.acm.org

[5] Network World. *Wall Street's collapse was computer science's gain.* Accessed August 2015. www.networkworld.com/article/2176789/data-center/wall-street--39-s-collapse-was-computer-science--39-s-gain.html

[6] NY Times. *CS Programs Make a Comeback in Enrollment.* www.nytimes.com/2009/03/17/science/17comp.html

[7] Steven A. Wolfman. 2002. Making lemonade: exploring the bright side of large lecture classes.*SIGCSE Bull.* 34, 1 (February 2002), 257-261. DOI=10.1145/563517.563441 doi.acm.org/10.1145/563517.563441

[8] Josh Hug and Daniel D. Garcia. 2015. Handling Very Large Lecture Courses: Keeping the Wheels on the Bus (Abstract Only). In *Proceedings of the 46th ACM Technical Symposium on Computer Science Education* (SIGCSE '15). ACM, New York, NY, USA, 697-697. doi.acm.org/10.1145/2676723.2691867

[9] Philip J. Guo. 2013. Online python tutor: embeddable web-based program visualization for cs education. In Proceeding of the 44th ACM technical symposium on Computer science education (SIGCSE '13). ACM, New York, NY, USA, 579-584. doi.acm.org/10.1145/2445196.2445368

[10] Tyler, Christine. 2013. Professor Spearheads New System to Streamline Grading, save Time." *In The Daily Californian.*

[11] John DeNero and Stephen Martinis. 2014. Teaching composition quality at scale: human judgment in the age of autograders. In Proceedings of the 45th ACM technical symposium on Computer science education (SIGCSE '14). ACM, New York, NY, USA, 421-426. doi.acm.org/10.1145/2538862.2538976

Booming Enrollments – Survey Data

Tracy Camp
(Moderator)
Dept. of EECS
Colorado School of Mines
Golden, CO 80401 USA
+1 303-384-2184
tcamp@mines.edu

Stu Zweben
Dept. of CSE
The Ohio State University
2015 Neil Avenue
Columbus, OH 43210 USA
+1 614-354-8871
zweben.1@osu.edu

Duncan Buell
Dept. of CSE
Univ. of South Carolina
315 Main. Street
Columbia, SC 29208
+1 803-777-7848
buell@cse.sc.edu

Jane Stout
Center Eval. Research Pipe
Computing Research Assoc.
1828 L Street, NW.
Washington, DC 20036 USA
+1 202-266-2937
jane@cra.org

ABSTRACT
The main goal of this panel is to share survey data being collected on booming enrollments in computer science. Survey data are being collected from two source types: institutions and students. The institution data are being collected through both the CRA Taulbee Survey, which represents computer science departments in North America with doctoral degrees, and the ACM NDC Survey, which represents computer science departments at U.S. 4-year and master's universities and colleges. The student data are being collected via the Data Buddies Project, run by the CRA's Center for Evaluating the Research Pipeline. The institution data will allow us to answer questions such as "what 'boom' are institutions seeing and how are different types of institutions responding to this boom?" The student data will allow us to answer questions such as "why are students suddenly eager for our classes?". The survey data will help us understand (1) the intensity of the "boom" at different types of institutions, (2) how institutions are responding to the increasing demand for computing education, and (3) whether the current enrollment "boom" represents the "third bubble" or whether it is here to stay. The data will also allow us to ask questions that attempt to understand the impact of the boom on underrepresented students. Data collection is ongoing; we will present results "hot off the presses".

1. INTRODUCTION
Universities and colleges are facing a significant increase in students' enrollment in computing courses and computing degree programs [1]. Many institutions are seeing the following "booms":

(1) The major: the total undergraduate enrollment in computing majors among U.S. computer science departments rose over 44% at a sample of Ph.D. granting institutions from 2011-12 to 2013-14 [2]. A sample of CS programs from non-Ph.D.-granting departments reported over 26% growth in enrollment from 2012-13 to 2014-15 [3].

(2) Interest in low-level non-major courses in computing: for instance, the demand for introductory computer science at Hiram College was the highest it has been between 2010-2015, even though the incoming class size was the smallest it had been between 2010-2015 [4].

SIGCSE '16, March 2–5, 2016, Memphis, TN, USA.
ACM 978-1-4503-3685-7/16/03.
http://dx.doi.org/10.1145/2839509.2844663

(3) Non-majors enrolling in advanced major courses: for example, according to the Registrar, approximately 30% of students taking Algorithms (a senior level course) at the Colorado School of Mines in Fall 2015 are non-CS majors, and include students from petroleum engineering, mechanical engineering, and geophysics.

At some institutions, the current "boom" is exceeding previous "booms", and there is a general sense that this boom is substantially different than the mid-1980's and late 1990's. The questions on many minds are "how is the boom different?" and "will the boom continue?".

2. CRA'S BOOMING ENROLLMENTS COMMITTEE RESEARCH QUESTIONS
The Computing Research Association (CRA) created a committee to investigate several questions related to the booming enrollments, including:

1. How are departments responding to the "boom"?
2. Is the "boom" affecting all levels of the curriculum?
3. What impact are non-majors/minors having on enrollment?
4. Are all departments feeling the enrollment surge equally?
5. Why are students so interested in computing?
6. How will the current "boom" impact diversity in an already demographically homogenous field?

In the formation of this committee, the CRA Booming Enrollment committee learned that several other organizations had initiated booming enrollment efforts as well (e.g., NCWIT, ACM Education Council). In an attempt to avoid duplicate efforts, individuals from these organizations were invited to participate on the CRA Committee on Booming Enrollments.

The CRA Booming Enrollment Committee quickly realized that two sub-groups were needed, in order to address the different questions that the community wants answered. The institution sub-group (members marked with an 'i' in the following list) were tasked with gathering data to answer high-level questions such as "how are departments handling the boom?" The student sub-group (members marked with an 's' in the following list) were tasked with gathering data to answer high-level questions such as "why are students so interested in computing?"

The Committee, which has been meeting regularly since Spring 2015 semester ended, includes:

- Tracy Camp, Chair of the Committee and on both sub-groups (student=s) and (institution=i), Colorado School of Mines

- Rick Adrion (i), University of Massachusetts
- Betsy Bizot (i), Computing Research Association
- Susan Davidson (i), University of Pennsylvania
- Mary Hall (i), University of Utah
- Susanne Hambrusch (i), Purdue University
- Stuart Zweben (i), The Ohio State University
- Duncan Buell (s), University of South Carolina
- Ed Lazowska (s), University of Washington
- Leen-Kiat Soh (s), University of Nebraska
- Jane Stout (s), Computing Research Association
- Jodi Tims (s), Baldwin Wallace College

Jan Cuny and Lida Beninson, from the National Science Foundation, are also actively involved.

3. INSTITUTIONAL SUB-GROUP

Members of the CRA Booming Enrollment Committee institutional sub-group finalized an *institutional survey* that is being sent to (1) all U.S. CRA Member Taulbee institutions with a computer science degree program, and (2) all ACM Non Doctoral Computing (NDC) institutions with a computer science degree program. The institutional survey data is currently being collected, allowing for data analysis and reporting in early 2016.

The institutional survey includes questions to allow us to understand how much control a given institution has on the "boom" they are experiencing. For example, some institutions (e.g., University of Utah and University of Washington) have control over the number of undergraduate majors in a given degree program, while other institutions have little control over the number of undergraduate students in a given degree program (e.g., Purdue University and Rice University). It is imperative to understand the local situation in order to fully understand the "boom" that a given degree program is facing.

The institutional survey also includes questions to understand how pervasive the "boom" is across computing programs in the U.S. For example, the CRA Taulbee Survey and the ACM NDC Survey document significant increases in computing majors. Importantly, majors are not the only source of demand on computing faculty. Thus, we also ask: How pervasive is the "boom", and what problems are institutions encountering due to the "boom"? These questions (and more) are part of the institutional sub-group survey.

4. STUDENT SUB-GROUP

Members of the CRA Booming Enrollment Committee student sub-group is working with the Center for Evaluating the Research Pipeline (CERP) in order to gather data concerning students' interest and experiences in introductory computing courses and the computing major. CERP is a research and evaluation center housed at the Computing Research Association (CRA), and funded by the National Science Foundation (CNS-1246649; DUE-1431112). CERP's flagship program is the Data Buddies Project, which distributes surveys annually to undergraduate and graduate students enrolled in a nationally representative sample of computing programs across the United States. Data Buddies surveys measure students' motivation for engaging in computing courses and/or a computing degree, as well as predictors and evidence of professional development in computing career tracks. CERP is particularly interested in using Data Buddies data to study the experiences of underrepresented student groups in computing, such as women, as well as men of racial minority.

To date, more than 100 departments have participated in the Data Buddies Project, and participation is continually rising. Notably, participating departments show diversity in institution type (e.g., PhD granting; Liberal Arts Colleges) and population demographic (e.g., Historically Black Colleges and Universities; women's colleges). Data Buddies samples are intentionally diverse and large in order to assess the experiences of particularly underrepresented student groups in computing (e.g., African American women; students with disabilities). CERP has successfully been collecting data via the Data Buddies Project since 2011.

CERP's Data Buddies survey, which was launched in late October/early November, includes questions that gauge students' (1) career aspirations (i.e., *How interested are you in having job _____ after you finish your highest degree?*), (2) career goals (i.e., *How important to you is it that your future career allows you to give back to the community?),* and (3) perceived ability to meet personal goals via a computing career. Students enrolled in a first year computing class are also being asked "why did you enroll in an introductory computing class?" as well as how the students rate themselves compared to others of a similar age (e.g., artistic ability, computer skills, and drive to achieve).

5. CONCLUSION

Our response to the current "boom" in computing will likely shape our community for years. Understanding the "boom" is a first step in determining how to meet student demand, and ensuring the boom's impact on diversity is positive. We are confident we will have interesting results that will engage SIGCSE participants in further discussion.

6. REFERENCES

[1] S. Zweben and B. Bizot, 2015. 2014 Taulbee survey: Relentless growth in undergraduate CS enrollment; Doctoral degree production remains strong, but no new record. *Computing Research News*. 27, 5 (2015).

[2] S. Zweben and B. Bizot, 2014. 2013 Taulbee Survey: Second consecutive year of record doctoral degree production; Continued strong undergraduate CS enrollment. *Computing Research News*, 26, 5 (2014).

[3] J. Tims, S. Zweben, Y. Timanovsky and J. Prey, 2015. The 2015 Survey of Non-Doctoral Granting Departments in Computing, *ACM Inroads*, 6, 3 (2015), 16-30.

[4] T. Camp, S. Zweben, E. Walker, and L. Barker, Booming Enrollments – Good Times? Proceedings of SIGCSE 2015, 2 pages, 2015.

Demonstrations

OnRamp to Parallel and Distributed Computing: Web-portal for Teaching Parallel and Distributed Computing

Samantha S. Foley, *Univ. of Wisconsin-La Crosse*
Joshua Hursey, *Univ. of Wisconsin-La Crosse*
Contact: ssfoley@cs.uwlax.edu

The OnRamp project provides a web portal which coaches users, primarily computer science (CS) undergraduate students, through a collection of interactive curriculum modules teaching them about parallel computing and the software ecosystem while allowing them to launch parallel applications on parallel compute environments (PCEs) from day one. There are a number of hurdles for instructors to incorporating a parallel and distributed computing (PDC) curriculum module into an existing course – from setting up the materials to preparing the students to work on a remote PCE. The OnRamp project removes these hurdles allowing instructors to easily connect to PCEs, deploy existing PDC curriculum modules, and setup user accounts for a course in just a few minutes. This demonstration of the OnRamp project will show the process an instructor will go through to set up a "workspace" for a class with a few PCEs and curriculum modules. Additionally, we will show how students will interact with this workspace to explore the curriculum module and launch parallel jobs on actual PCEs. We will have time for questions following the demonstration and provide materials for instructors to get started using OnRamp in their courses.

Keywords: parallel and distributed computing; web portal; learning environment.

DOI: http://dx.doi.org/10.1145/2839509.2850511

Education Modules for Networking, Cloud Computing, and Security in Systems Courses

Jay Aikat, *UNC – Chapel Hill*
Michael Reiter, *UNC – Chapel Hill*
Kevin Jeffay, *UNC – Chapel Hill*
Contact: aikat@cs.unc.edu

We have developed education modules for topics in networking, security, and cloud computing. A networking instructor could use our modules to enhance the teaching of basic concepts by demonstrating these concepts with real experiments on GENI testbeds. Any systems instructor could use our security or cloud computing modules to begin teaching new topics, or enhance existing topics by adding hands-on experiments on GENI and CloudLab testbeds. Our NSF funded projects to develop these curricular modules have been successfully used by several instructors. Attendees at SIGCSE would comprise exactly the kind of audience, from varied institutions and dedicated to enhancing their curriculum, for whom we've built these modules. Our modules are freely available, and we are committed to helping instructors use our modules in their courses. The underlying testbeds, GENI and CloudLab, are also NSF-funded and thus freely available for instructors to use. Attendees will be provided a handout that contains relevant information, including contact for help, as they go back and begin using our education modules in their curriculum.

Keywords: networking; security; cloud computing; education modules

DOI: http://dx.doi.org/10.1145/2839509.2850514

SIGCSE'16, March 2–5, 2016, Memphis, TN, USA.
ACM ISBN: 978-1-4503-3685-7/16/03.

Students' Syntactic Mistakes in Writing Seven Different Types of SQL Queries and its Application to Predicting Students' Success

Alireza Ahadi
University of Technology Sydney
Australia
Alireza.Ahadi@uts.edu.au

Vahid Behbood
University of Technology Sydney
Australia
Vahid.Behbood@uts.edu.au

Arto Vihavainen
University of Helsinki,
Finland
Arto.Vihavainen@cs.helsinki.fi

Julia Prior
University of Technology Sydney
Australia
Julia.Prior@uts.edu.au

Raymond Lister
University of Technology Sydney
Australia
Raymond.Lister@uts.edu.au

ABSTRACT

The computing education community has studied extensively the errors of novice programmers. In contrast, little attention has been given to student's mistake in writing SQL statements. This paper represents the first large scale quantitative analysis of the student's syntactic mistakes in writing different types of SQL queries. Over 160 thousand snapshots of SQL queries were collected from over 2000 students across eight years. We describe the most common types of syntactic errors that students make. We also describe our development of an automatic classifier with an overall accuracy of 0.78 for predicting student performance in writing SQL queries.

Categories and Subject Descriptors

H.2.3 [**Database Management**]: Languages – query languages.

General Terms

Management, Measurement, Human Factors.

Keywords

Online assessment; databases; SQL queries; Machine learning.

1. INTRODUCTION

The Structured Query Language (SQL) is the standard language for relational and object-relational databases. A better understanding of student SQL errors and misconceptions would improve the teaching and learning of SQL. It would also serve the writing of textbooks and other instructional materials. As with any other computer language, SQL queries may contain semantic or syntactic errors. The focus of the previous studies of novices in writing SQL queries has been on the nature of semantic errors. There has been little attention to analyzing the syntactic mistakes made by students when writing SQL queries.

In this paper we use data collected over eight years, from 2300 students, to quantitatively study the syntactic errors committed by students at the authors' institution. We review these mistakes among seven different types of SQL queries and compare syntactic errors of students who were successful versus students who were unsuccessful in writing a correct query. We also show how this information can be used to train a rule-based classifier to predict student success at writing an SQL query.

This paper is structured as follows. In section 2, we review the literature on analysis of semantic errors in SQL. In section 3, we describe how the data was collected and how the classifier was trained. In section 4, we review our findings on syntactic error analysis and demonstrate how the information obtained from student snapshots can be used to predict their performance in writing SQL queries under exam condition. Section 5 expands and discusses our findings. Section 6 presents our conclusions.

2. RELATED WORK

Many reports have been published about online SQL tutoring/assessment tools. However, most of those reports focus on the functionality of the tool itself, or on how the system supports a certain pedagogical model [1-6]. Those reports do not analyze the data collected by those systems to determine the syntactic errors that students face when writing SQL queries.

There are some papers in which authors review different semantic errors encountered in writing SQL queries. Reisner [8] categorized queries generated by subjects into three categories: "correct", "minor error(s) only", and "major error(s). Wetly and

SIGCSE '16, March 02-05, 2016, Memphis, TN, USA
© 2016 ACM. ISBN 978-1-4503-3685-7/16/03…$15.00
DOI: http://dx.doi.org/10.1145/2839509.2844640

Stemple [7] and used a more elaborate categorization scheme: "correct, "minor language error", "minor operand error", "minor substance error", "correctable", "major substance error", "major language error", "incomplete" and "unattempted". Wetly and Stemple studied how subjects faired at writing SQL queries in comparison to a a more procedural query language (TABLET). Later in 1985, Welty [9] ran an experiment on a small number of subjects (N=39) to test how assistance with error correction would affect SQL user performance. In that study, errors are categorized into "minor syntactic", "complex errors", "group by", "semantic error", "incorrect" and "unattempted". Buitendijk [10] categorized SQL errors into the categories of "existence", "comparison", "extension" and "complexity". In that work, a classification of natural language questions was introduced to give insight into possible errors in SQL queries. Smelcer [11] reports seven different type of common mistakes in writing SQL queries, which are "omitting the join clause", "AND/OR difficulties", "omitting quotes", "omitting the FROM clause", "omitting qualifications", "misspellings" and "synonyms". In that work, a model of query writing is developed that integrates a GOMS-type analysis of query writing with the characteristics of human cognition. Brass [12] reports an extensive list of conditions that are strong indications of semantic errors. Although all those works give a fundamental understanding of semantic errors in SQL, none of them reviewed syntactic errors.

3. METHOD

3.1 Data Collection

The data collected in this study forms a total number of ~161000 SQL SELECT statements from ~2300 students. We collected our data in an online assessment system, AsseSQL [5, 6]. The students in this study were all novice undergraduate students enrolled in an introductory database course at the authors' university. Most of the students enrolled in this course were studying for a Bachelor degree in Information Technology or Software Engineering. Each semester there is an online SQL test assessing student's performance in writing SQL SELECT statements. In the online test, students were allowed 50 minutes to attempt seven SQL questions. Each question examines the students' ability to write a SELECT statement which covers a fundamental concept. Table 1 represents these question and the total number of snapshots collected from students' attempts. Each of the seven questions presented to a specific student is chosen at random from a small pool of questions.

Table 1. Number of snapshots generated by students for different SQL SELECT statements.

Type of SELECT statement required in answer	Number of SQL statements collected from students
Group by with having	31484 (20%)
Self-join	27350 (17%)
Group by	24422 (15%)
Natural join	24248 (15%)
Simple subquery	18860 (12%)
Simple, one table	18440 (11%)
Correlated subquery	15856 (10%)

3.2 Error Categorization

In order to collect the execution result of students' attempts, all the students' SQL statements were re-executed in PostgreSQL and the execution results generated by the DBMS were collected. Based on the execution message returned by DBMS, we define a *syntactic error* as an error message which is returned by PostgreSQL engine. In contrast, a *semantic error* is produced by a successfully running query that does not produce the correct answer. For the sake of clarity, we redefine *syntax error* (Error code 42601) as a type of syntactic error which is due to either a typo or the exclusion of a semicolon at the end of the query. Table 2 reviews these error codes and their frequency among students' queries.

Table 2. PostgreSQL error codes and their frequency in student's attempts

PSQL Error code	Description	Frequency
Error 42601	Syntax error	34504 (21%)
Error 42703	Undefined column	20689 (13%)
Error 42803	Grouping error	15442 (10%)
Error 42P01	Undefined table	5548 (3%)
Error 42702	Ambiguous column	4844 (3%)
Error 42883	Undefined function	2534 (2%)
Error 42804	Data type mismatch	1262 (1%)
Error 22008	Date time field overflow	975 (0.61%)
Error 22007	Invalid text representation	849 (0.53%)
Error 22P02	Invalid date time format	536 (0.33%)
Error 3F000	Invalid schema name	457 (0.28%)
Error 42704	Undefined object	134 (0.08%)
Error 42712	Duplicate alias	108 (0.07%)
Error 42P10	Invalid column reference	96 (0.06%)
Error 42P02	Undefined parameter	47 (0.03%)
Error 42725	Ambiguous function	21 (0.01%)

In many cases, an error might arise for multiple reasons. As a result, the error code alone might not be sufficiently self-explanatory to express exactly where the problem lies within the corresponding SQL statement. Therefore, we categorized those error codes which might arise due to different reasons into sub-categories that are summarized in Table 3.

3.3 Classification

In order to investigate the predictive value of the syntactic errors of students' attempts, we trained a classifier to see to what extent this information can be used to distinguish between successful students and unsuccessful students. To that end, information on syntactic errors (i.e. the top eight syntactic errors in Table 2), the number of semantic errors and the total number of attempts of 480 students were used to build the training set. AsseSQL selects questions for each student on a random basis from a question pool. As a result, we decided to train the classifier on the proportion of students who were assigned with the same identical question. This training set included 240 students who were successful in answering a GROUP BY question correctly (Positive set) as well as 240 students who were not able to answer a GROUP BY question (Negative set). We chose to study the GROUP BY question as it had a particularly high ratio of syntactic errors in students' attempts. The classifier trained in this study is PART, a rule based classifier which, in each iteration, builds a partial C4.5 and re-expresses the best leaf as a rule [13]. The PART classifier was selected for two main reasons. First PART handles missing values caused by student queries which no syntactic errors of a given kind. Second, PART provides a clear explanation of the rules generated within the C4.5 iterations. Feature selection and classifier evaluation was performed using the WEKA Data Mining toolkit [14].

Table 3. PostgreSQL error codes and underlying reasons.

PSQL Error code	Reason	Occurrence
42601	Wrong syntax	33482 (97%)
	Chunk of code not closed	681 (2%)
	Invalid subquery syntax	268 (<1%)
	Other rare syntactic errors	73 (<1%)
42803	Aggregate function may not be used in GROUP BY clause	13019 (84%)
	Aggregate function may not be used in WHERE clause	2294 (14%)
	Aggregate function may not be nested	104 (2%)
42883	Operator does not exist	1628 (64%)
	Function does not exist	906 (36%)
42804	Argument of AND must be type Boolean	547 (44%)
	Argument of OR must be type Boolean	437 (35%)
	Argument of HAVING must be type Boolean	271 (21%)

4. RESULTS

4.1 Syntactic Errors Have a High Frequency Ratio Among Students' Attempts

Among ~161000 students' attempts, more than half of those attempts result in a syntactic error (54%). Around 40% of all executions do not include a syntactic error, but include semantic errors. Thus only the remaining 6% of executions result in a successful execution capable of producing the correct result table. A low percentage of successful executions is to be expected, as a student stops attempting a question in the online system as soon as they have generated a correct answer. However, this low percentage of correct answers does reflect: (1) the long sequence of incorrect queries, both syntactic and semantic, typically generated by students before arriving at the correct answer, and (2) the many students who never generate a correct answer to some questions.

Table 4 reviews the frequency of incorrect SQL statements written by students. As can be seen, the number of syntactic errors in most categories is more than the number of semantic errors. Examining the last attempt of unsuccessful students revealed that half (51%) of unsuccessful students abandoned the question when they were not able to fix a syntactic error. As shown in Table 2, error 42601 ("syntax error") is the biggest category of syntactic errors. The main cause of this error is typos. The second largest category of encountered errors is error 42703 which is generated when the referenced column does not exist (which may also be caused by a typo).

Table 4. Incorrect SQL statements and syntactic errors. Second column represents the percentage of incorrect queries among all queries collected for each query type. Third column represents the percentage of incorrect queries among all incorrect queries per query type where the incorrectness is due to syntactic errors.

SELECT statement type	Percentage of unsuccessful statements	Unsuccessful due to syntactic errors
Simple, one table	89%	54%
Group by	93%	68%
Group by with having	96%	61%
Natural join	94%	66.%
Simple subquery	92%	64%
Self-join	98%	38%
Correlated subquery	93%	55%

4.2 Syntactic errors in different types of SQL SELECT statements

To better understand which syntactic errors students encounter in writing different types of SQL statements, we investigated the error codes generated by their attempts in answering seven different types of SQL questions. We chose these seven types of queries because the relative difficulty of these seven types has been studied and established by Ahadi *et. al.* [15]. As can be seen in Table 5, a limited number of error codes form the majority of the total population of most encountered errors in the seven different query types. However, the frequency of these errors varies between the seven query types. For each query type, with the exception of the self-join, more than half of the students who did not get a right answer gave up when they were not able to fix the syntactic error produced by their SELECT statement.

4.3 Successful vs. Unsuccessful: Syntactic Error Comparison

To characterize students as "successful" or "unsuccessful" according to their syntactic errors, for each SQL query type we selected an equal number of students (N >300) and compared the total number of semantic and syntactic errors (Table 6). As an example of how this table was constructed, consider the 81% figure shown in the top left of Table 6. For error code 42601, from the total number of queries generated by successful and unsuccessful students, 81% are from unsuccessful students.

According to the information presented in Table 6, unsuccessful students tend to have more syntactic and semantic errors compared to successful students. Although the number of encountered syntactic errors differs from query type to another, the majority of syntactic and semantic errors in each error category are from unsuccessful students.

Table 5. Most encountered errors in different SQL statements.

SQL type	1st error	2nd error	3rd error	All Other Errors
Simple, one table	42601 (46%)	42703 (19%)	42803 (13%)	22%
Group by	42601 (52%)	42803 (26%)	42703 (11%)	11%
Group by with having	42601 (45%)	42803 (29%)	42703 (15%)	11%
Natural join	42703 (38%)	42601 (27%)	42P01 (12%)	23%
Simple subquery	42703 (33%)	42601 (28%)	42803 (13%)	26%
Self-join	42601 (37%)	42703 (23%)	42P01 (11%)	29%
Correlated subquery	42601 (35%)	42703 (32%)	42P01 (11%)	22%

4.4 Syntax Error Based Prediction of Unsuccessful Students

As we were able to characterize successful and unsuccessful students according to their syntactic errors, we decided to see to what extent a student's degree of struggle would be a good predictor of student's success in eventually writing the correct query. We therefore trained the PART classifier on an equal number (240) of successful and unsuccessful students in answering GROUP BY questions (i.e. N=480). On a 10-fold cross validation training mode, the classifier was able to correctly classify 77% of students correctly. Table 7 provides further details on the performance of the classifier.

To reduce the number of overlapping features, reduce over fitting, and to improve predictive accuracy of the feature set, feature selection was performed. We used correlation-based feature subset selection, where the individual predictive ability of each feature along with the degree of redundancy between the features was evaluated using three methods; (1) genetic search, (2) best first method and (3) greedy stepwise method. After feature selection, four features were used to train this classifier. Those features were: (1) how many times a student's queries contained error 42803, (2) contained error 42601, (3) a semantic error, and (4) total number of attempts student at the question.

Using those four features, five rules were generated by PART. Inspection of the rules identified features distinguishing successful and unsuccessful students. For example, two of the rules generated by our classifier are:

- If the total number of attempts is higher than 30 and there is at least one syntactic error of code 42803, then the student is not successful.
- If the student has not encountered a semantic error in answering the question, then the student is not successful. (A complete absence of semantic errors usually indicates that all the student's attempts contained syntactic errors.)

We discuss these rules, and other findings, in the next section.

5. DISCUSSION

According to our analysis, the majority of students' mistakes in writing SQL SELECT statements are either syntax errors or an incorrect referred column in different clauses of the SELECT statement. While the former seems to be a result of lack of practice, the second category gives us some insights into student's understanding. The most common mistake among students' attempts in writing a simple join query is an incorrect column name in either the SELECT or WHERE clause. In some cases, this is simply due to a typing error. In cases where the incorrect column name is not a typing error, perhaps the complexity of the provided entity relationship diagram leads students to make a mistake in choosing the right field name.

Table 6. Distribution of errors for unsuccessful students compared to successful students in different query types. The values in the table represents the proportion of unsuccessful students from the total mistake for each error and cross different query types.

PSQL Error code	Simple, one table	Group by	Group by with having	Natural join	Simple subquery	Self-join	Correlated subquery
Error 42601	81%	70%	71%	73%	70%	73%	72%
Error 42702	63%	90%	75%	70%	69%	46%	75%
Error 42703	73%	81%	68%	70%	61%	58%	72%
Error 42803	84%	69%	71%	70%	72%	73%	61%
Error 42804	89%	76%	76%	85%	77%	76%	50%
Error 42883	85%	85%	71%	74%	88%	60%	69%
Error 42P01	77%	86%	78%	65%	74%	64%	78%
semantic error	75%	61%	61%	61%	53%	50%	59%

Table 7. PART classifier's performance in classifying successful and unsuccessful students in writing a GROUP BY query.

TP Ratio	FP Ratio	Precision	Recall	F-Measure	ROC Area	Class
0.84	0.30	0.74	0.84	0.79	0.84	Unsuccessful
0.70	0.16	0.81	0.70	0.75	0.84	Successful
0.77	0.23	0.77	0.77	0.77	0.84	Weighted Avg.

We were surprised to find that error 42803 is the third most common mistake in writing a simple SELECT statement on one table, accounting for 13% of all syntax errors. When this error occurred, it almost always occurred in the WHERE clause. A simple SELECT doesn't require a GROUP BY clause, which probably indicates a serious misconception.

Inspecting the top three most encountered syntactic mistakes among seven different categories of SQL queries, error 42P01 (i.e. undefined table) is observed in four different types of queries:

a) When there is a need to perform a natural join between two relations.

b) When writing a simple subquery

c) When there is a need to join a table to itself.

d) When writing a correlated subquery.

What these four categories of queries share is the presence of either more than one table in the SELECT statement or the presence of more than one SELECT clause. This might be an indicator of students' lack of skill in identifying the correct tables from which to extract the desired information. On the other hand, investigating a small number of their queries shows that the main mistake they make is mistyping the correct name of the table, even though the number of tables used in each entity relationship diagram is small.

The results from different machine learning algorithms with the same goal can be extremely context-dependent. Even with the same algorithm, variation can even occur with variations in the exact training data used. We trained a wide range of models to classify student's performance in the online test and for each classifier, we obtained a prediction accuracies ranging from 60% to 79%. Each of these classifiers has a different set of generated rules and selected features

6. CONCLUSION

Our study goes a small way to addressing that imbalance in the computing education literature between the study of novices writing programs and novices writing SQL queries. Our data is from a relatively large data set (over 161000 SQL queries collected from ~2300 students) for a range of different syntactic errors that novices make in writing SQL statements. Our findings show that, in general, students make more syntactic errors than semantic errors. Furthermore, a syntactic error and not a semantic error is what in most cases causes a student to abandon answering a question. Syntax errors in different clauses of the SELECT statement, undefined referred column errors, and grouping errors are the most common mistakes that novices make in writing their SQL statements. The prevalence of syntactic errors, and in particular the fact that syntactic errors is what leads students to abandon attempting a question, indicates that the teaching of SQL queries needs to place greater emphasis on syntax and syntax errors. While we believe that semantic errors are the more intellectually demanding errors, students will not come to grips with semantic errors while their query formulation remains dominated by syntax errors.

7. REFERENCES

[1] Brusilovsky, P., Sosnovsky, S., Lee, D., Yudelson, M., Zadorozhny, V., and Zhou, X. 2008. An open integrated exploratorium for database courses. *ITiCSE* '08. pp. 22-26.

[2] Brusilovsky, P., Sosnovsky, S., Yudelson, M. V., Lee, D. H., Zadorozhny, V., and Zhou, X. 2010. Learning SQL programming with interactive tools: From integration to personalization. Trans. Comput. Educ. 9, 4, Article 19 (January 2010).

[3] Mitrovic, A. 1998. Learning SQL with a computerized tutor. SIGCSE '98, pp. 307-311.

[4] Mitrovic, A. 2003. An intelligent SQL tutor on the web. Int. J. Artif. Intell. Ed. 13, 2-4 (April 2003), pp. 173-197.

[5] Prior, J., and Lister, R. 2004. The backwash effect on SQL skills grading. ITiCSE 2004, Leeds, UK. pp. 32-36.

[6] Prior, J. 2014. AsseSQL: an online, browser-based SQL skills assessment tool. ITiCSE 2014. pp. 327-327.

[7] Wetly, C. and Stemple, D. 1981. Human factors comparison of a procedural and a nonprocedural query language. ACM Transactions on Database Systems (TODS) 6;4:626-629

[8] Reisner, P. 1977. Use of psychological experimentation as an aid to development of a query language. IEEE Trans. Softw. Eng. SE-3, 3 (1977), 218-229.

[9] Wetly, C. 1985. Correcting user errors in SQL. International Journal of Man-Machine Studies 22(4): 463-477.

[10] Buitendijk, R. B., 1988. Logical errors in database SQL retrieval queries. Computer Science in Economics and Management 1 (1988) 79-96

[11] Smelcer, J. B. 1995. User error in database query composition. Int. J. Human-Computer Studies (1995) 42, 353-381

[12] Brass, S. and Goldberg, C. 2006. Semantic error in SQL queries: A quite complete list. The Journal of Systems and Software 79 (2006) 630–644.

[13] Frank, E. and Witten, I. H. 1998. Generating accurate rule sets without global optimization. (Working paper 98/2). Hamilton, New Zealand: University of Waikato, Department of Computer Science.

[14] Hall, M., Frank, E., Holmes, G., Pfahringer, B., Reutemann, P. and Witten. I. H. 2009. The WEKA data mining software:

an update. ACM SIGKDD explorations newsletter, 11(1):10-18, 2009.

[15] Ahadi, A., Prior, J., Behbood, V. and Lister, R. 2015. A quantitative study of the difficulty for novices of writing seven different types of SQL queries. ITiCSE (2015) Proceedings of the 2015 ACM Conference on Innovation and Technology in Computer Science Education 201-206.

chidb: Building a Simple Relational Database System from Scratch

Borja Sotomayor
University of Chicago
borja@cs.uchicago.edu

Adam Shaw
University of Chicago
ams@cs.uchicago.edu

ABSTRACT

We present **chidb**, a medium to large-scale programming project where students implement the main components of a relational database management system, including B-tree data structures for tables and indexes, a database machine with registers and a selection of high-level and low-level instructions, and a SQL compiler targeting that machine. Moreover, **chidb**'s SQL compiler's internal representation is a direct encoding of the relational algebra, whereby the theory that might otherwise be relegated to notes and blackboards is directly connected to practice and experience. The project uses the C programming language and is demonstrably suitable for use in advanced undergraduate courses; we have administered this project through five iterations of our databases course for advanced undergraduates. **chidb** is freely available online and customizable to suit the needs and tastes of any particular instructor.

Keywords

computer science education; databases; relational database management systems; SQL

1. INTRODUCTION

Teaching subjects that have immediate practical applications, like databases, often involves balancing the practical with the theoretical. Both kinds of knowledge are important; they are, ideally, mixed in such a way as to give students solid instruction in both areas, stinting on neither.

At the University of Chicago, this principle is apparent in many of our systems-oriented courses (Operating Systems, Networks, Databases, *etc.*), most of which involve an extensive hands-on programming project with a strong theoretical connection. Furthermore, these projects are designed to be as realistic as practicable during a quarter-long project. For example, instead of having students in our Operating Systems course implement standalone components of the OS, such as writing a memory allocator as an isolated programming assignment, they work in teams to implement an x86 OS kernel nearly from scratch using the Pintos project [3]. Similarly, students in our Networks class must implement a version of TCP that is RFC-compliant to the extent that, at the end of the quarter, they are able to write socket-based applications (capable of communicating over the Internet) that use their TCP implementation instead of the operating system's.

Of course, few students will be asked in their careers (whether in industry or academia) to write an operating system or their own network stack directly, and doing so arguably takes time away from gaining more immediately applicable skills. Even so, we believe that this approach allows students to understand and appreciate the core concepts of a subject, making the connection between theory and practice clearer, and enabling them to better engage with the subject matter after they complete the class.

Our first foray into this style of teaching began in our major-level *Introduction to Databases* course, where we developed **chidb**: a quarter-long C programming project where students have to implement a relational database management system (RDBMS) largely from scratch, from the file-based B-trees all the way up to the SQL compiler. By the end of the quarter, students are able to bootstrap their own database (without using any instructor-provided samples) and run a variety of `SELECT`, `INSERT`, and `CREATE` statements on that database within the system they build themselves. More importantly, when students run a SQL statement, they will have written most of the code that is run from the moment the SQL statement is parsed to when individual blocks of the B-tree file are read from disk.

The **chidb** project makes the following contributions to the teaching of databases:

- Provides a framework for a database course to explore the complete implementation of a realistic RDBMS, including B-trees, its internal architecture, cursors, compilation of SQL queries, and query optimization. Ours is one on the only projects that spans all these layers, providing an integral view of the entire RDBMS.

- Allows students to engage directly with concepts that are typically only covered in the abstract. Notably, our internal representation of SQL queries is based on relational algebra (containing `sigma`, `pi` and `rho` abstract syntax tree nodes, for example), reinforcing in a working system what the students have otherwise seen only on paper. The relational algebra is, furthermore, an especially congenial representation for both reasoning about and implementing query optimizations.

SIGCSE '16, March 02 - 05, 2016, Memphis, TN, USA

ISBN 978-1-4503-3685-7/16/03...$15.00

DOI: http://dx.doi.org/10.1145/2839509.2844638

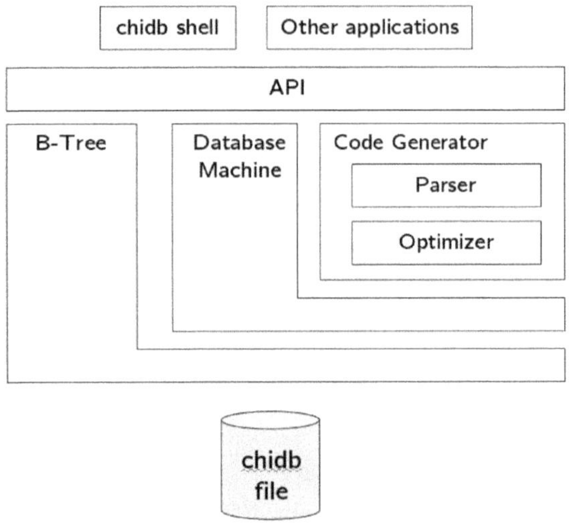

Figure 1: `chidb` architecture

- The project is structured as an open-ended architecture, not as a fixed set of assignments. So while we provide a number of assignments ourselves, it would be relatively easy for other instructors to build additional assignments. All the code is freely available under a BSD license at http://github.com/uchicago-cs/chidb, and we provide documentation on `chidb`'s architecture and assignments at http://chi.cs.uchicago.edu/chidb.

The rest of this paper is structured as follows. We begin by describing the architecture of `chidb` in Section 2, followed by a summary of the assignments we currently use in Section 3, and a discussion of our experience so far with `chidb` in Section 4. Next, we discuss related work in Section 5, and present our conclusions and future work in Section 6.

2. ARCHITECTURE

Consistent with the style of teaching we described in the previous section, `chidb`'s architecture is guided by two main principles:

1. It must replicate, as closely as possible, the architecture of a real RDBMS. We chose to base the architecture of `chidb` on SQLite [2], particularly by using a file format that is a subset of the SQLite file format (all `chidb` files are valid SQLite files, but not the other way around.) This feature provides the benefit that `chidb` databases can be viewed and operated on from within the SQLite shell.

2. It must be structured in such a way that students can focus on database-specific implementation tasks, with an apparent connection to the theory of databases, without getting bogged down in orthogonal and uninteresting implementation details.

In this section, we discuss the `chidb` architecture in its fully implemented state, which is summarized in Figure 1. Section 3 focuses on which implementation tasks could be assigned to students as part of specific assignments.

2.1 File Format

Like SQLite, `chidb` uses a single file to store a relational database. In fact, the `chidb` file format is a subset of the SQLite file format and, thus, a `chidb` file can store any number of tables, physically stored as a B^+-tree (referred to as a *table B-tree*), and each table can have records with any number of fields of different datatypes. Indexes are also supported, and are stored as B-trees (referred to as *index B-trees*).

A detailed file format specification is available in the `chidb` website. In summary, a file is divided into equally-sized *pages* (typically 1–4 kilobytes), each storing one *node* of a B-tree. Each node can contain multiple *cells*, with a different cell structure depending on the type (table or index) and level (internal or leaf) of the node. Of special note are the leaf nodes of table B-trees, where the cells contain a ⟨*key*, *database record*⟩ pair, where each record represents one row of the table. Finally, each B-tree has at least one *root node*, and the location of this root node is stored in a special *schema table* (itself a table B-tree) rooted in page 0 of the file.

Although the file format is remarkably close to the SQLite file format, to the point that valid `chidb` files can be read by SQLite, we do allow students to make the following simplifying assumptions:

- Each table must have an explicit primary key (SQLite allows tables without primary keys to be created), and the primary key must be a single unsigned 4 byte integer field.
- Indexes can only be created for unsigned 4-byte integer unique fields.
- Only a subset of the SQLite datatypes are supported.
- The size of a record cannot exceed the size of a file page (more specifically, SQLite overflow pages are not supported). This effectively also limits the size of certain datatypes (such as strings).
- A user is assumed to have exclusive access to the database file.

These assumptions were made to simplify the implementation of many low-level details, so that students can focus on tasks that directly relate to database concepts (while still requiring a healthy amount of low-level programming). For example, although supporting database records that span multiple pages is a necessary feature in production databases, its implementation requires a fair amount of low-level programming that is algorithmically dull (at least when compared with algorithms for B-tree insertion, query optimization, etc.), and ultimately irrelevant to the main thread of our curriculum.

2.2 B-trees

The B-tree module of `chidb` is the only part of the `chidb` code that reads and manipulates `chidb` files. It has a well-defined API with functions to create new B-trees, insert records, search for records with a given key, *etc.*

2.3 Database Machine

The database machine (or DBM) is a virtual machine specifically designed to operate on `chidb` files, and includes low-level assembly-like instructions such as `Integer`, which loads an integer constant into a register, and `Eq`, which jumps to a specified address if the contents of two registers is the same, as well as high-level database-specific instructions such as `CreateTable`, which creates a new table B-tree and stores its root page number in a register, and `Seek`, which moves a cursor to point to the first entry in a B-tree with a given key k, and jumping to a given address if no such entry exists in the B-tree.

The DBM is inspired by SQLite's VDBE[1] and, in fact, supports many of the same instructions. There are 36 DBM instructions, each with up to four operands: P1, P2, P3, and P4. P1 through P3 are signed 32-bit integers, and P4 is a pointer to a null-terminated string. The implementation of these instructions often requires using functions from the B-tree module.

An instance of the DBM includes the following:

Program A sequence of one or more DBM instructions. The program is typically produced by the code generator, but we also provide the ability to load arbitrary programs easily for the purposes of testing.

Program Counter Keeps track of what instruction is currently being executed. Certain instructions can directly modify the program counter to jump to a specific instruction in the program.

Registers A machine can have an arbitrary number of registers, each of which can contain a 32-bit signed integer, a pointer to a null-terminated string or to raw binary data, or a NULL value.

Cursors A cursor is a pointer to a specific entry in a B-tree.

2.4 SQL Compiler

The SQL compiler consumes plaintext SQL programs and produces DBM programs. We provide a SQL parser that parses a small but significant fraction of the SQL language, including, for example, `WHERE` conditions and natural joins, but excluding certain others like groupings or nested subqueries which are, in our experience, infeasible to implement within our time frame. The internal representation the parser targets is an abstract syntax tree that matches the notation of relational algebra (σ, π, ρ). From a pedagogical standpoint, this has the effect of unifying the theoretical treatment of certain optimizations—pushing sigmas, for example—with their practical implementations.

2.5 API

`chidb` exposes all the above functionality through a simple API that can be accessed from other C programs simply by including a `chidb.h` header file, and linking with a `libchidb` library produced by our Makefile. This means that, given a fully-implemented `chidb` system, `chidb` databases can be used from other C programs in the same way that SQLite databases can be used through the SQLite API[2].

The `chidb` API, shown in Figure 2, provides functions to open and close database files, execute SQL statements, and, in the case of `SELECT` statements, provide access to the results of the query.

[1]https://www.sqlite.org/opcode.html

[2]https://www.sqlite.org/capi3ref.html

```
/* Functions to open and close a database file */
int chidb_open(const char *file, chidb **db);
int chidb_close(chidb *db);

/* Takes a SQL statement and compiles it. The resulting
   database machine (DBM) is stored in the "stmt"
   output parameter */
int chidb_prepare(chidb *db, const char *sql,
                                 chidb_stmt **stmt);

/* Frees all the resources associated with a DBM
   previously created with chidb_prepare */
int chidb_finalize(chidb_stmt *stmt);

/* For SELECT queries, step to the next row
   in the results */
int chidb_step(chidb_stmt *stmt);

/* Column access functions */
int chidb_column_count(chidb_stmt *stmt);
int chidb_column_type(chidb_stmt *stmt, int col);
const char *chidb_column_name(chidb_stmt* stmt, int col);
int chidb_column_int(chidb_stmt *stmt, int col);
const char *chidb_column_text(chidb_stmt *stmt, int col);
```

Figure 2: `chidb` API

2.6 Shell

We provide a command-line shell that can be useful for interactively testing a `chidb` implementation (even an incomplete one). It provides the following functionality:

- Running SQL statements and, in the case of `SELECT` statements, displaying their results.
- Running arbitrary DBM programs.
- Parsing SQL and showing the syntax tree produced by the parser.
- An `EXPLAIN` directive which, given a SQL statement, shows the DBM program produced by the code generator.

3. ASSIGNMENTS

The `chidb` architecture can support countless assignments and, in fact, could be used in more that just a databases course. A data structures class could assign the implementation of the B-tree module; an introductory systems course could focus on implementing the DBM; and, a compilers course could focus on scanning, parsing, optimizing, and generating code for the DBM set of instructions. This is not to mention the many ways in which `chidb` could be modified or extended even in the context of a databases course.[3]

We have chosen to structure the `chidb` project somewhat differently in each of the years of our teaching it; the most recent format we used divided the project into four assignments, the first of which is done in pairs, and the latter three done in teams of four students each.

Assignment 1: B-trees Students implement the B-tree module, starting only from the API specification of that module. At the end of this assignment, fully working

[3]For example, `chidb` has never been used in a semester length course, which would necessitate some adaptation.

student implementations (of which there have always been a few) are chosen as reference B-tree implementations for the rest of the quarter, and shared with the rest of the class.

Assignment 2: Database Machine (DBM) This assignment provides students with the instructors' implementation of the core DBM (registers, program loading, etc.), but leaving the implementation of the DBM instructions up to the students. Students must also implement the cursor data structure, and must do so in a way that allows the cursor to move to the next or previous entry in a B-tree in amortized $O(1)$ time.[4]

In the past, students had to implement the entire DBM from scratch themselves. This had the advantage of giving students the freedom to design their implementation however they wanted, within the context of a tight specification, of course, instead of being given it by their instructors. However, as a practical matter, this made it impossible for our graders to automate testing of all the different DBM implementations, since they did not know quite what they would be getting, and we have since standardized the internal representation of the DBM.

Assignment 3: Code Generation Students must implement a code generator which, given a simple `SELECT`, `INSERT`, `CREATE TABLE` or `CREATE INDEX` statement, will generate the appropriate DBM program. A SQL lexer and parser is already provided for them (implemented in `lex` and `yacc`) which produces an abstract syntax tree representation of the SQL statement. Students needed to be able to compile `SELECT` statements with any number of fields or * (for which consulting the database schema is necessary), conjunctions of comparisons in their `WHERE` clauses, and two-way natural joins (which also entails examining the database schema), among a few others.

Assignment 4: Query Optimization Students must modify the compiler to optimize certain queries where possible. This includes using indexes when indexes are available, or transforming the tree representation of the query in accordance with certain well-known optimizations, such as sigma-pushing and sigma coalescing.

Students had two or three weeks to complete each of these phases of the project. In all but the last assignment, students are provided with an extensive set of unit tests they can use to test their implementation.

Although this is the way we have structured the project, other instructors could take the `chidb` architecture, described in the previous section, and create new assignments or variations on the existing ones. For example, a possible new assignment could involve adding support for concurrent access and transactions. A variation on an existing assignment could involve providing a complete implementation of the DBM (including all the instructions), to spend more time on the code generation and query optimization assignments, covering a larger portion of the SQL language (a greater variety of `SELECT` statements, for example, or `DELETE` and `UPDATE` statements). Modifying the compiler to do join order analysis, for example, or to support n-way joins, would be natural extensions of the optimization exercises.

[4]See Section 4 for colorful feedback on this point.

4. EXPERIENCE

As mentioned above, our department teaches an advanced undergraduate course entitled *Introduction to Databases.* The prerequisites for the course at our department are three quarters of introductory study in computer science, including two quarters doing a substantial amount of C programming and systems programming, with some assembly language. These prerequisites have worked in the context of our curriculum and our student population, and may not directly translate to other programs of study. In general, students working on this project must have acquired enough knowledge of C programming and software development to tackle a relatively large C programming project, as well as enough of a sense of the low level operations of a machine to understand what code generation requires of them. Furthermore, while students in our course work on `chidb` while simultaneously learning about databases for the first time, `chidb` could also be used in an advanced databases course where students are assumed to already be familiar with fundamental database concepts.

We have taught `chidb` in the databases course each of the last five times we have offered it, in five non-consecutive years between 2009 and 2015. The enrollments in these courses have ranged from a minimum of 6 students in 2010 to a maximum of 62 students most recently in 2015. (Our department's enrollments have, of late, surged across the board.)

There are two ways to discuss our experience of having taught `chidb`. One is from our perspective, and the other is from the students' perspective. We will begin with the students.

Our evidence about students' experience with `chidb` is, admittedly, not statistically rigorous. We have anecdotal evidence from working with the students directly, since the authors have been involved in teaching this course five and three times, respectively, and we also have the students' course evaluations, which are available online internally at our institution.

Although we have not quantified our experience of working with students in person, anecdotally and having interacted with the by now more than 100 students who have taken this course in some form over the last five years, the project is generally well liked and valued by those who have undertaken it. This is not to say it has been universally well liked, because some students' work on this project, for the usual variety of reasons, has been less than stellar. Nonetheless, every time we have taught `chidb`, the project has been the source of great interest and spurred countless interesting discussions about the inner workings of this kind of system. It is a project that appeals very strongly to students who like to roll up their sleeves and write a lot of code!

As recorded in the college's post-course surveys, the students' feelings towards the course are positive, on the whole. The surveys the students are given do not (unfortunately) ask the students outright whether they liked and/or valued the course itself; the questions are mostly about the instructor. Nevertheless, in their comments, students commented favorably on `chidb`:

> The chidb project really is a great learning experience and also is very cool.

They shared impartial observations on its difficulty:

> The projects were very intense and required an immense investment of time.

And they vented their frustrations:

> [The project was] at times an absolute nightmare...

as well as

> I cringe when I hear the word Cursor.

Nevertheless, when the survey asked the students directly "Were the demands of the course reasonable?", in the most recent batch, 34 students responded that yes, the demands were reasonable, and only one responded no[5] (and this is roughly in line with previous years).

As instructors, per our internal measures, we feel the project has been a great success! The fact that it has not received unanimous acclaim from students is, we believe, entirely to be expected, given its difficulty. The students emerge with what we hope and expect is a relatively deep understanding of the diverse machinery that needs to come together for data to be stored on disk in a sensible way and efficiently retrieved by queries. Furthermore, having implemented basic SQL queries "only" up to natural join and indexes, students develop a great appreciation for the achievements of a full SQL compiler. In other words, the knowledge and experience the students gain is well beyond what they would get merely by writing and executing SQL queries, however serpentine and clever those queries might be. When we consider the content of this course alongside the database courses we took at similar points in our educations, what our own students learn from having worked on `chidb` is much richer in depth and detail.

Still furthermore, and looking at this work as part of the students' education more broadly, it is important for students to have grappled with a file format and set of data structures that are engineered for actual use, and are not exercises contrived for the students' benefit. Real data structures (such as B-trees whose nodes fit disk blocks) have a shape, texture and scope that reaches beyond what students are able to work with in the usual sandboxes of their introductory coursework.

5. RELATED WORK

The SimpleDB project [5], while different from `chidb` in nearly every particular, is the most current, most similar work to ours in terms of the role it plays in database instruction. `chidb` was developed roughly concurrently and independently of any knowledge of SimpleDB, so `chidb` is in no way a response to or a critique of SimpleDB. The philosophies of the two projects are quite different. Broadly speaking, `chidb` is in our judgment a narrower project, but a deeper one in its area. `chidb` deals with the particular concerns of storing data in B-trees and compiling SQL queries to operate on that data, in a particular virtual machine framework following SQLite's example. SimpleDB, by contrast, is concerned with the larger scope of database systems, including major units on transactions and concurrency. SimpleDB treats topics that are not part of `chidb` at all, including user authentication, buffer management, deadlock detection, recovery, and more. If these latter elements of database systems are of particular importance to a particular curriculum, then SimpleDB is surely the appropriate choice among these two.

[5]Not all students respond to the surveys, or to every question in the surveys.

```
struct RA_s {
   enum RA_Type t;
   union {
      struct { char *name; } table;
      struct { RA_t *ra; Condition_t *cond; } sigma;
      struct { RA_t *ra; Expression_t *expr_list; } pi;
      struct { RA_t *ra1, *ra2; } binary;
      struct { RA_t *ra;
               Expression_t *to_rename;
               char *new_name;} rho;
   };
   Column_t *columns;
};
```

Figure 3: Excerpt of the RA (relational algebra) data structure

Within the area of overlap between the two projects, there are enough technical dissimilarities between them to make them substantially different from one another:

- `chidb` stores table data, indexes, and even database schema information in B-trees. SimpleDB uses a linear data store for tables.
- `chidb` uses an internal representation that hews closely to relational algebra; see Figure 3 for an excerpt.
- The back end of `chidb` compilation is code generation to a target virtual machine.
- SimpleDB follows a client/server architecture, with databases stored in collections of files; `chidb` is a library that other programs can link with, with each database stored in a single file.

As a practical matter, SimpleDB is written in Java, while `chidb` is in straight C. This might make SimpleDB or `chidb` suitable or unsuitable for different academic programs, depending on which programming languages students know and are expected to use. Unlike `chidb`, SimpleDB is supported by a textbook [6].

Going back a bit further, the Minibase framework [4] is also similar in its educational approach. It is an important predecessor to SimpleDB, and named as such in the abstract of the SimpleDB paper. Like SimpleDB, and like `chidb`, Minibase is designed for students to learn databases by implementing an RDBMS. With respect to its technical details, Minibase implements B^+-tree indexes, as `chidb` does, but stores record data in unordered heap files, unlike `chidb`. Furthermore, database queries are implemented in Minibase as different kinds of iterators: iterators for simple queries, for selection, for joins, *etc.* This differs from the compiled-query approach taken by `chidb` and following SQLite.

As far as we can tell, Minibase is not an active project, although we were able to find adaptations of it in recent use (for example, a Java version of Minibase was taught at Purdue as recently as 2012).

MinSQL [7] is a project similar in design and scope to Minibase, although its implementation is in Java. We do not believe this to be an active project. It also worth noting that a course taught at Berkeley and CMU [1] favored modifying the codebase of an actual database system (Postgres, in this case) to working with an educational system (Minibase), on the grounds that the latter was insufficiently representative of real-world software.

6. CONCLUSIONS AND FUTURE WORK

We have described `chidb`, a simple relational database management system that is small enough to comprehend, and even implement, over the course of a quarter or semester, yet complete enough to provide functionality found in many existing database systems, including the ability to run a variety of SQL statements. Furthermore, `chidb`'s architecture lends itself easily to design a variety of programming assignments.

Our experiences using `chidb` have been, overall, positive. However, there are still a number of aspects in which `chidb` can be improved. The biggest gap in `chidb` is its assumption that the database file will be used by a single user; there is no attempt to implement any sort of locking, and concurrent access to the database will likely result in an inconsistent state. This is an arguably fair assumption if we want students to focus on implementing the DBM or the SQL compiler, but it does not meet our standard of producing a system that is as realistic as possible, and it also precludes instructors from designing assignments revolving around transactions.

We have in mind a number of medium-scale improvements to be made in the near future, including the following:

- We have never been fully satisfied with the query optimization assignment, since the SQL queries that are currently supported only lend themselves to some limited optimizations. Also, the result of these optimizations is hard to test automatically. While we consider the first three assignments to be relatively stable, we expect our next efforts will focus on improving the fourth assignment.
- We would like to streamline the data structures that represent relational algebra expressions, and provide better documentation for them.
- Although our suite of tests gives students the ability to load arbitrary DBM programs, we realize that debugging those DBM programs using traditional debuggers can be challenging. We will address this by including a tool that allows students to run a DBM program step by step, providing a dump of the DBM registers and cursors at each step.

Acknowledgments

We owe a large debt of gratitude and inspiration to the creators of SQLite. It is a remarkably robust, elegant, compact system, not to mention an immensely popular one. SQLite has no publications in the academic record, so we are unable to provide a paper citation, but `chidb` is its direct descendant. We acknowledge our colleague Sharon Salveter, who taught the `chidb` course in its first two iterations, and so got the ball rolling with what was at the time untested work. We are also grateful to Allen Nelson, who implemented the current incarnation of the SQL parser that is included with `chidb`. We appreciate the thoughtful comments of our anonymous reviewers; they improved the paper.

7. REFERENCES

[1] A. Ailamaki and J. M. Hellerstein. Exposing undergraduate students to database system internals. *SIGMOD Rec.*, 32(3):18–20, Sept. 2003.

[2] D. R. Hipp. SQLite (http://www.sqlite.org), 2015.

[3] B. Pfaff, A. Romano, and G. Back. The Pintos Instructional Operating System Kernel. *SIGCSE Bull.*, 41(1):453–457, Mar. 2009.

[4] R. Ramakrishnan. The Minibase Home Page (http://research.cs.wisc.edu/coral/mini_doc/minibase.html), 1996.

[5] E. Sciore. SimpleDB: A Simple Java-based Multiuser System for Teaching Database Internals. *SIGCSE Bull.*, 39(1):561–565, Mar. 2007.

[6] E. Sciore. *Database Design and Implementation*. Wiley, 2008.

[7] G. Swart. MinSQL: A simple componentized database for the classroom. In *Proceedings of the 2Nd International Conference on Principles and Practice of Programming in Java*, PPPJ '03, pages 129–132, New York, NY, USA, 2003. Computer Science Press, Inc.

SQL: From Traditional Databases to Big Data

Yasin N. Silva
Arizona State University
ysilva@asu.edu

Isadora Almeida
Arizona State University
isilvaal@asu.edu

Michell Queiroz
Arizona State University
mfelippe@asu.edu

ABSTRACT

The Structured Query Language (SQL) is the main programing language designed to manage data stored in database systems. While SQL was initially used only with relational database management systems (RDBMS), its use has been significantly extended with the advent of new types of database systems. Specifically, SQL has been found to be a powerful query language in highly distributed and scalable systems that process Big Data, i.e., datasets with high volume, velocity and variety. While traditional relational databases represent now only a small fraction of the database systems landscape, most database courses that cover SQL consider only the use of SQL in the context of traditional relational systems. In this paper, we propose teaching SQL as a general language that can be used in a broad range of database systems from traditional RDBMSs to Big Data systems. This paper presents well-structured guidelines to introduce SQL in the context of new types of database systems including MapReduce, NoSQL and NewSQL. A key contribution of this paper is the description of an array of course resources, e.g., virtual machines, sample projects, and in-class exercises, to enable a hands-on experience with SQL across a broad set of modern database systems.

Categories and Subject Descriptors

K.3.2 [**Computers and Education**]: Computer and Information Science Education

General Terms

Design, Experimentation

Keywords

Databases curricula; SQL; structured query language; Big Data

1. INTRODUCTION

The Structured Query Language (SQL) is the most extensively used database language. SQL is composed of a data definition language (DDL), which allows the specification of database schemas; a data manipulation language (DML), which supports operations to retrieve, store, modify and delete data; and a data control language (DCL), which enables database administrators to configure security access to databases. Among the most important reasons for SQL's wide adoption are that: (1) it is primarily a declarative language, that is, it specifies the logic of a program (*what* needs to be done) instead of the control flow (*how* to do it); (2) it is relatively simple to learn and understand because it is declarative and uses English statements; (3) it is a standard of the American National Standards Institute (ANSI) and the International Organization for Standardization (ISO); and (4) it is, to some extent, portable among different database systems. Even though SQL was initially proposed for traditional relational databases, it has also been found to be an effective language in several new types of database systems, particularly Big Data management systems (BDMSs) that process large, fast and diverse data. While BDMSs have significantly changed the database landscape and traditional RDBMs represent now only a small fraction of it, most books and database courses only present SQL in the context of RDBMs.

SIGCSE '16, March 02 - 05, 2016, Memphis, TN, USA

ACM 978-1-4503-3685-7/16/03…$15.00
DOI: http://dx.doi.org/10.1145/2839509.2844560

In this paper we propose learning SQL as a powerful language that can be used to query a wide range of database systems, from traditional relational databases to modern Big Data systems. The main contributions of this paper are:

- The description of the new database landscape and the identification of broad types of Big Data systems where SQL can be effectively used.
- The presentation of well-structured guidelines to prepare course units that focus on the study of SQL on new types of database systems including MapReduce, NoSQL and NewSQL.
- A detailed description of class resources for each unit to enable a hands-on experience with SQL across a broad set of modern database systems. These resources include virtual machines, data generators, sample programs, projects, and in-class exercises.
- Files of all the resources made available to instructors [1]. The goal is to enable instructors to use and extend these resources based on their specific needs.

The rest of the paper is organized as follows. Section 2 describes the new database landscape and the types of BDMSs where SQL can be used. Sections 3, 4, and 5 present the details of how SQL can be introduced in the context of the new types of database systems (MapReduce, NoSQL, and NewSQL). These sections describe many class resources which will be made available in [1]. Section 6 presents a discussion of the integration of the proposed units into database courses. Section 7 concludes the paper.

2. NEW DATABASE LANDSCAPE

The development and widespread use of highly distributed and scalable systems to process Big Data is considered as one of the recent key technological developments in computer science [3, 4, 5, 6]. These systems have significantly extended the database landscape and are currently used in many application scenarios, e.g., social media data mining, scientific data analysis, recommendation systems, and web service analysis. BDMSs are usually composed of clusters of commodity machines and are often dynamically scalable, i.e., nodes can be added or removed as needed. The area of BDMSs has quickly developed and there are now dozens of BDMS-related open-source and commercial products. Some of these systems have proposed their own query languages or application program interfaces but several others have recognized the benefits of using SQL and support it as a query language. The use of SQL in DBMSs is expanding and some top database researchers believe that many more systems will move to support SQL [2]. The authors propose that SQL should be taught in the context of the following types of BDMSs in addition to traditional RDBMSs:

- **MapReduce**. It is considered to be one of the main frameworks for Big Data processing. It enables building highly distributed programs that run on failure-tolerant and scalable clusters. Apache Hadoop [7] is the most widely used MapReduce implementation. Examples of systems that support SQL to query data in Hadoop are: Hive [8] and Spark (Spark SQL) [9].
- **NoSQL**. These data stores have been designed to provide higher scalability and availability than conventional relational databases while supporting a simplified transaction and consistency model. Some examples of NoSQL data stores are: MongoDB [10], Apache HBase [11], Google's BigTable [12], and Apache Cassandra [13]. While many NoSQL systems do not support SQL natively, several systems have been proposed to enable SQL querying on these systems. Examples of such systems are: Impala [14], Presto [15] and SlamData [16].
- **NewSQL**. These systems aim to have the same levels of scalability and availability of NoSQL systems while maintaining the ACID properties (Atomicity, Consistency, Isolation and Durability), relational schema, and SQL query language of traditional relational databases. Examples of NewSQL systems are: VoltDB [17], MemSQL [18], NuoDB [19], and Clustrix [20].

3. SQL IN MAPREDUCE SYSTEMS

MapReduce is an extensively used programming framework for processing very large datasets. Apache Hadoop is its most popular implementation. A MapReduce program divides a large dataset into independent chunks that can be processed in a parallel fashion over dynamic computer clusters. The overall processing is divided into two main phases: *map* and *reduce*, and the framework user needs to provide the code for each phase. The *map* and *reduce* functions have the following form:

map: (k1,v1) → list(k2,v2)
reduce: (k2,list(v2)) → list(k3,v3)

The input dataset is usually stored on an underlying distributed file system and different chunks of this dataset are processed in parallel by different *map* tasks. Each *map* task processes an input chunk one record or line at the time. Each *map* function call receives a key-value pair (k1,v1) and generates a list of (k2,v2) pairs. Each generated key-value pair is sent over the network to a reduce node (*shuffle* phase). The framework guarantees that all the intermediate pairs with the same key (k2) will be sent to the same *reduce* node where they will form a single group. Each *reduce* call processes a group (k2,list(v2)) and outputs a list of (k3,v3) pairs, which represent the overall output of the MapReduce job.

While MapReduce is a powerful framework to build highly distributed and scalable programs, it is also complex and difficult to learn. In fact, even simple data operations, like joining two datasets or identifying the top-K records, require relatively complex MapReduce programs. This is the case because MapReduce requires users to build a program using a procedural language that needs a detailed specification of how a processing task should be carried out. Considering this limitation, several systems have been proposed to: (1) enable the use of SQL-like languages on top of MapReduce-based systems, e.g., Apache Hive [8] and Apache Pig [22], and (2) integrate SQL with MapReduce-based computations, e.g., Spark SQL [9].

3.1 Hive: SQL Queries on Hadoop

Apache Hive [8] is a system that supports the processing and analysis of data stored in Hadoop. Hive allows projecting structure onto this data and querying the data using HiveQL, a SQL-like query language. One of the key features of Hive is that it transparently converts queries specified in HiveQL to MapReduce programs. This enables the user to focus on specifying *what* the query should retrieve instead of specifying a procedural MapReduce program in Java. Hive uses indexing structures to accelerate the execution of queries and was particularly built to support data warehouse applications, which require the analysis of primarily read-only massive datasets (data that does not change over time). While HiveQL is Hive's main query language, Hive also allows the use of custom *map* and *reduce* functions when this is a more convenient or efficient way to express a given query logic.

HiveQL supports many of the features of SQL but it does not strictly follow a full SQL standard. Hive supports multiple DDL and DML commands such as CREATE TABLE, SELECT, INSERT, UPDATE and DELETE. Moreover, starting with Hive 0.13, it is possible to support transactions with full ACID semantics at the row (record) level.

We propose the following in-class activity to introduce HiveQL.

Using Virtual Machines. Since many Big Data systems rely on distributed architectures, a computer cluster is needed to enable a direct interaction with these technologies. Many institutions, however, do not have such clusters available for teaching. A solution that the authors recommend is the use of virtual machines (VM) with all the required packages already installed and configured. In the case of Hive, the authors recommend the use of Cloudera's VM [23] which includes: (1) CentOS Linux as the operating system, (2) Hadoop, (3) Hive, and (5) Hue, a web-based application that can be used to write and run HiveQL queries.

Data Generators and Datasets. The queries presented in this section use *MStation2*, a synthetic dataset of meteorological station data prepared by the authors. The dataset has two tables: *Station* (*stationID*, *zipcode*, *latitude*, *longitude*) and *WeatherReport* (*stationID*, *temperature*, *precipitation*, *humidity*, *year*, *month*). The data generator and a sample dataset are available in [1]. The generator can be modified to produce datasets of different sizes and data distributions for additional exercises or projects.

Loading and Querying the Data. The commands for this activity are listed in Fig. 1. To start interacting with Hive, students can open a terminal window using Cloudera's VM and start the Hive console using command C1. Students can then create the database *MStation* (C2) and use the DDL commands C3 and C4 to create tables *stationData* and *weatherReport*, respectively. Students can then load the data generated by the MStation2 data generator into both tables using commands C5 and C6. Both, the Hive console and the Hue application, can be used next to run SQL queries. Students can use the available tables to write queries such as (Q1-Q4 in Fig. 1):

- Q1: For each zipcode, compute the average precipitation level.
- Q2: Group the data by station and output the average humidity level at each station.
- Q3: Identify the minimum and maximum temperatures reported by each station considering years greater than 2000.
- Q4: Compute the tenth highest temperatures ever reported. List the temperature, zip code, month and year.

Fig. 2 shows the result of queries using the Hive console and Hue.

```
C1: sudo hive

C2: CREATE database MStation;

C3: CREATE TABLE stationData (stationed int, zipcode int,
latitude double, longitude double, stationname string);

C4: CREATE TABLE weatherReport (stationid int, temp double,
humi double, precip double, year int, month string);

C5: LOAD DATA LOCAL INPATH '/home/cloudera/datastation/
stationData.txt' into table stationData;

C6: LOAD DATA LOCAL INPATH '/home/cloudera/datastation/
weatherReport.txt' into table weatherReport;

Q1: SELECT S.zipcode, AVG(W.precip) FROM stationData S JOIN
weatherReport W ON S.stationid = W.stationid GROUP BY
S.zipcode;

Q2: SELECT stationid, AVG(humi) FROM weatherReport GROUP BY
stationid;

Q3: SELECT stationid, MIN(temp), MAX(temp) FROM weatherReport
WHERE year > 2000 GROUP BY stationid;

Q4: SELECT S.zipcode, W.temp, W.month, W.year FROM
stationData S JOIN weatherReport W ON S.stationid =
W.stationid ORDER BY W.temp DESC LIMIT 10;
```

Figure 1. Hive Commands and Queries

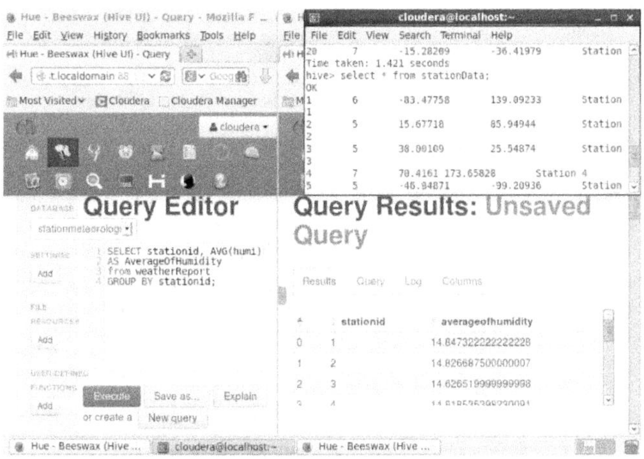

Figure 2. Executing SQL queries in Hive

3.2 Spark: Integrating SQL and MapReduce

Apache Spark [9] is a highly distributed data processing framework. In contrast to Hadoop's two-stage disk-based MapReduce approach, Spark works by loading the data into a cluster's memory and querying it using a wider set of processing primitives (which also include operations similar to *Map* and *Reduce*). Spark's performance has been reported to be up to one hundred times faster than Hadoop's for some applications [9]. For distributed storage, Spark can work with Hadoop Distributed File System (HDFS), OpenStack, Amazon S3, etc. Spark uses the notion of Resilient Distributed Datasets (RDD). An RDD is an immutable collection of objects that are partitioned and distributed across multiple physical nodes of a cluster, which allows the data to be processed in parallel. Once an RDD has been instantiated, the user can apply two types of operations: transformations and actions. Transformations return new RDDs while actions generate outputs. Spark SQL is one of the key tools supported by Spark. Spark SQL is the Spark module for structured data processing, and uses DataFrames (equivalent to relational database tables) as its main programming abstraction. The data in a DataFrame is organized into named columns. DataFrames can be created from already existing RDDs, Hive tables, or JSON files. Spark SQL supports many of the features of SQL and, therefore, it is a powerful tool to learn SQL while working with big datasets.

```
C1: wget http://real-chart.finance.yahoo.com/table.csv?
s=AAPL&d=6&e=4&f=2015&g=d&a=11&b=12&c=1980&ignore=.csv

C2: mv table.csv?s=AAPL table.csv

C3: hadoop fs -put ./table.csv /data/

C4: spark-shell --master yarn-client --driver-memory 512m --
executor-memory 512m

C5: import org.apache.spark.sql._

C6: val base_data = sc.textFile("hdfs://sandbox.hortonworks.
com:8020/data/table.csv")

C7: val attributes = base_data.first

C8: val data = apple_stocks.filter(_(0) != attributes(0))

C9: case class AppleStockRecord(date: String, open: Float,
high: Float, low: Float, close: Float, volume: Integer,
adjClose: Float)

C10: val applestock = data.map(_.split(",")).map(row =>
AppleStockRecord(row(0), row(1).trim.toFloat,
row(2).trim.toFloat, row(3).trim.toFloat, row(4).trim.toFloat,
row(5).trim.toInt, row(6).trim.toFloat,
row(0).trim.substring(0,4).toInt)).toDF()

C11: applestock.registerTempTable("applestock")

C12: applestock.show

C13: applestock.count

C14: output.map(t => "Record: " + t.toString).collect().
foreach(println)

Q1: val output = sql("SELECT * FROM applestock WHERE close >=
open")

Q2: val output = sql("SELECT MAX(close-open) FROM applestock")

Q3: val output = sql("SELECT date, high FROM applestock ORDER
BY high DESC LIMIT 10")

Q4: val output = sql("SELECT year, AVG(Volume) FROM applestock
WHERE year > 1999 GROUP BY year")
```

Figure 3. Spark Commands and SQL Queries

We describe next an in-class activity with Spark SQL. Hortonworks Sandbox [24] is an excellent virtualization environment to provide students with hands-on experience in Spark SQL. This virtual machine comes with Apache Spark fully installed and enables the execution of commands from a terminal. The dataset to be used in this activity contains the historical prices of the Apple stock (AAPL, 1980-2015) and was obtained from the Yahoo! Finance website [25]. The dataset can be downloaded as a comma-separated values (CSV) file. Each record contains the stock values of a single date and includes the following attributes: *date*, *open price*, *high price* (highest stock value), *low price* (lowest stock value), *close price*, *volume*, and *adjClose* (close price adjusted for dividends and splits). An additional attribute *year* (extracted from date) is added to enable de specification of some interesting queries.

Fig. 3 shows the sequence of commands to load and query the data using the Hortonworks VM. The student downloads first the dataset (C1), renames it to *table.csv* (C2), copies the file into Hadoop's HDFS (C3), and starts the Spark shell (C4). Then, C5 is executed to import a library that is needed to use Spark SQL. Command C6 creates the RDD *base_data* using the dataset stored in the HDFS. C7 and C8 create a new RDD (*data*) which contains all the records in *base_data* with the exception of the record with the headers. C9 creates the class *AppleStockRecord* which specifies the attributes and data types of the Apple stock dataset. C10 parses the records of *data*, creates an instance of *AppleStockRecord* for each record, and populates the RDD *applestock* with the created instances. C11 registers *applestock* as a DataFrame. This DataFrame can now be used as a relational table. C12 and C13 show the top 20 records and the number of records of *applestock*, respectively. Students can now be assigned to write SQL queries such as (Q1-Q4 in Fig. 3):

- Q1: Report the records where the close price is greater or equal than the open price.
- Q2: Identify the record with the largest difference between the close and the open prices.
- Q3: Report the ten records with the highest high prices.
- Q4: Report the average stock volume per year, considering only years greater than 1999.

A key feature of Spark is that the output of SQL queries can be used as the input of MapReduce-like computations. This is, in fact, done in C14 to print the results of the SQL queries.

4. SQL IN NOSQL SYSTEMS

NoSQL (Not only SQL) is a broad class of data stores that aims to provide higher scalability and availability than traditional relational databases. NoSQL systems have the following core properties: (1) they usually use a distributed and fault-tolerant architecture where more computers can be easily added, (2) data is partitioned among different computers, (3) data is replicated to provide fault tolerance, and (4) they often support a simplified transaction/consistency model, for instance *eventual consistency* (given a sufficiently long period of time in which no changes are made, all the previous updates are expected to eventually propagate through the system). There are different types of NoSQL such as: (1) Key-Value stores, e.g., Cassandra and Riak, which store data in a schema-less way using key-value pairs; (2) Document stores, e.g., MongoDB and CouchDB, which store documents in a given format (XML, JSON, binary, etc.); and (3) Tabular data stores, e.g., HBase and BigTable, which store tabular data that can have many attributes and records.

While originally most of the NoSQL systems did not adhere to the relational database model and did not support SQL for data manipulation, one of the key recent developments in this area has been the recognition that a declarative, highly expressive and standardized query language like SQL can be an effective way to query NoSQL systems [2]. This is reflected in a number of systems that enable SQL querying on common NoSQL data stores, for instance Impala [14], SlamData [16] and Presto [15] support SQL queries on HBase, MongoDB, and Cassandra, respectively.

4.1 Impala: SQL to Query HBase Tables

Impala [14] is an open-source query engine that allows running SQL queries on top of HBase tables (Impala also supports HDFS as storage sub-system). HBase [11] is an open-source NoSQL database that runs on top of HDFS and provides a fault-tolerant way of storing and processing large amounts of sparse tabular data. HBase provides efficient random reads and writes on top of HDFS (HDFS does not directly support random writes). Impala has been built leveraging and extending key components of Hive, e.g., SQL syntax, metadata and schema. While both system support SQL, Hive is best suited for long-running batch processing and Impala provides a better support for dynamic analytic queries.

We propose the following in class activity to introduce SQL in Impala. For this activity students can use the Cloudera VM [14] which has Impala, HBase and Hive already installed. The list of commands is presented in Fig. 4. The dataset used in this activity contains information about occupations in the U.S. The dataset can be found in the VM under the *dataset* folder (*sample_007.csv*). It has four attributes: *code* (occupation ID), *description*, *total_emp* (number of employees), and *salary* (combined income). We renamed the data file as *occupations.csv*. Students should first open a terminal window in the VM and start the HBase shell (C1). Next, the HBase table *OccupationsData* is created using command C2.

```
C1: hbase shell
C2: create 'OccupationsData', 'code', 'description',
'total_emp', 'salary'
C3: exit
C4: hive
C5: CREATE EXTERNAL TABLE Occupations (key STRING, description
STRING, total_emp int, salary int) ROW FORMAT DELIMITED FIELDS
TERMINATED BY ',' STORED BY 'org.apache.hadoop.hive.hbase.HBa
seStorageHandler' WITH SERDEPROPERTIES ("hbase.columns.mappin
g" = ":key, description:description,total_emp:total_emp,salary
:salary") TBLPROPERTIES("hbase.table.name"="OccupationsData");
C6: hbase.org.apache.hadoop.hbase.mapreduce.ImportTsv '-
Dimporttsv.separator=,' -Dimporttsv.columns=HBASE_ROW_KEY,
details:code,details:description,details:total_emp,details:sal
ary OccupationsData /home/cloudera/occupations.csv;
C7: impala-shell
C8: invalidate metadata [[default.]Occupations]
Q1: SELECT description, salary FROM Occupations ORDER BY
salary DESC LIMIT 10;
Q2: SELECT description, salary/total_emp AS PerPersonSalary
FROM Occupations ORDER BY PerPersonSalary DESC LIMIT 10;
Q3: SELECT SUM(salary)/SUM(total_emp) AS AvgSalary FROM
occupationsIncomeHBase WHERE description LIKE '%computer%';
Q4: SELECT code, description, salary FROM Occupations WHERE
Salary IN (SELECT MAX(salary) FROM Occupations);
```

Figure 4. Impala Commands and SQL Queries

At this point, students should switch into Hive (C3 and C4), create an external table (*Occupations*) that is linked to *OccupationsData* (C5), and load the data (C6). After this, students can start the Impala shell (C7) where they can write and execute SQL queries. Because Impala and Hive share the same metadata database, once the table is created in Hive, it can be queried in Impala. Command C8 is needed to make Impala aware of the recently created table. Students can now write an execute queries such as (Q1-Q4 in Fig. 4):

Q1: Show the occupations with the 10 highest combined salaries

Q2: Show the occupations with the 10 highest per-person salaries.

Q3: Show the average per-person income of the occupations in the Computer field.

Q4: Show the occupation that has the highest combined income.

4.2 SlamData: SQL on MongoDB

SlamData [16] is a system that allows running SQL statements on MongoDB [10], an extensively used document-oriented and open-source NoSQL database. MongoDB does not natively support SQL or multi-object transactions and works with documents as basic units of data. Documents use a JSON-like structure (BSON) and are equivalent to rows in relational databases. A set of documents forms a collection (table). Each document is composed of field and value pairs similar to JSON objects. The values of fields can be other documents, arrays, and arrays of documents. These embedded documents and arrays reduce the need for joins.

We propose the following in-class exercise to introduce the use of SQL in the context of MongoDB and SlamData. The commands for this exercise using MS Windows are listed in Fig. 5. The dataset is the 2012 U.S. Income Tax Statistics per ZIP code reported by the IRS (CSV file) [26]. We use the following attributes: *STATE*, *ZIPCODE* (99999 is the aggregation of all ZIP codes with less than 100 returns, 0 represents the whole state), *N1* (number of returns, which approximates the number of households), *N2* (number of exemptions, which approximates the population), *A00100* (AGI), and *A00200* (salaries and wages, in thousands of dollars).

The first step is to download [10] and install MongoDB (we installed it in *C:\mongodb*). A required data directory is created in C1. MongoDB is started in C2 and a connection through the mongo.exe shell is stablished in C3. C4 can be used to list the available databases (initially, there should be one called *local*). At this point, SlamData should be downloaded [16] and installed. To run queries, students need to mount a MongoDB cluster in SlamData and host it somewhere. We will do this using the free tier of MongoLab [27]. After creating a MongoLab account, students should create a new MongoDB deployment (select *single-node* and *standard line*) and provide the database name (*project*). After the deployment is created, students can set the database user name and password by clicking on the new deployment. Then, students will import the CSV file into the MongoDB deployment. This can be done using one of the pre-filled commands provided by MongoLab under the Tools/Import-Export tab. The CSV section in this tab provides a command formatted as C5. Students need to run this command on a MS Command Prompt window. Next, students will open the GUI-based SlamData application and mount the MongoDB database. To do this, students will click on the Mount icon in SlamData and use a connection URI (formatted as C6) that can be obtained in the recently created MongoDB deployment in MongoLab. Students can now use the SlamData application to write SQL queries such as (Q1-Q4 in Fig. 5):

- Q1: Identify the number of households in your ZIP code.
- Q2: Estimate the population in each ZIP code of New York.
- Q3: Identify the zip codes with the 10 largest total gross income in the state of NY.
- Q4: Compute the average wages and salaries amount per state.

```
C1: md \data\db
C2: C:\mongodb\bin\mongod.exe
C3: C:\mongodb\bin\mongo.exe
C4: show dbs
C5: C:\mongodb\bin\mongoimport.exe -h <host:port> -d <your
database name> -c <collection> -u <dbuser> -p <dbpassword> --
type csv --file <path to .csv file> -headerline
C6: mongodb://<dbuser>:<dbpassword>@<host:port>/<dbname>
Q1: SELECT N1 FROM "/project/taxes" WHERE ZIPCODE=85304
Q2: SELECT N2, ZIPCODE FROM "/project/taxes" WHERE STATE='NY'
Q3: SELECT ZIPCODE, A00100 FROM "/project/taxes" WHERE
STATE='NY' AND ZIPCODE!=0 ORDER BY (A00100) DESC LIMIT 10
Q4: SELECT DISTINCT STATE, AVG(A00200) FROM "/project/taxes"
WHERE ZIPCODE!=0 AND ZIPCODE!=99999 GROUP BY STATE
```

Figure 5. SlamData Commands and SQL Queries

5. SQL IN NEWSQL SYSTEMS

NewSQL is a class of database systems that not only offers the same levels of scalability and availability of NoSQL systems but also preserves the ACID guarantees, relational data model, and SQL query language of traditional relational databases. NewSQL systems are divided into three groups: (1) New architectures, e.g., VoltDB and NuoDB, these are new systems designed to work on a distributed cluster of shared-nothing nodes that can dynamically scale; (2) Optimized SQL Engines, e.g., MySQL Cluster and Infobright, these systems support the same programming interface of traditional systems like MySQL but have better scalability; and (3) Transparent sharding, e.g., dbShards and ScaleBase, these systems provide a middleware layer to automatically fragment and distribute databases over multiple nodes.

Most NewSQL databases can be used to learn SQL considering the application scenarios commonly used to teach traditional RDBMs, e.g., university, employee, or inventory databases. A better approach, however, is to consider application scenarios that require the capabilities of NewSQL systems, e.g., the need of processing large or fast data in the stock market, social media networks and online games. Moreover, educators should consider applications that take advantage of the features of the NewSQL system used in class, e.g., an application that requires processing a high number of short transactions per second would be a good fit for VoltDB.

5.1 Learning SQL with VoltDB

VoltDB [17] is an in-memory and ACID-compliant NewSQL database system that uses a shared-nothing architecture as well as partitioning and replication mechanisms to achieve high transaction throughputs. The system is open-source and was designed by well-known database researchers. VoltDB aims to give solutions to real-time analytic problems, extracting insights from fast flowing data. VoltDB can be installed on Linux and Mac OS X computers and provides client libraries for Java, Python, PHP, C++, C#, etc.

VoltDB can be used to learn many aspects of SQL using hands-on class activities. For instance it can be used to learn the SQL data definition and data manipulation languages. Using a VM is also an effective way to enable a hands-on interaction with NewSQL systems like VoltDB. In this case, instructors can use the VM available at VoltDB's web site [17]. The VM includes the installed VoltDB software and a set of sample applications and tools for application development. The sample applications are useful resources to learn about VoltDB. They include: (1) a system that simulates a telephone-based voting process, (2) a memcache-like cache implementation using VoltDB, (3) a Key-Value store backed by VoltDB, and (4) a system that uses a flexible schema and JSON.

VoltDB also made available an application gallery [21] that contains many applications that can be used to develop learning activities. We propose the use of the Ad Performance application that can be downloaded from [21] and installed in VoltDB's VM. This application simulates a high velocity stream of ad events (impressions, clickthroughs and conversions) that are augmented and stored in real time. Instructors can use the following in-class activity working with this application. Students first analyze and execute the provided scripts that start the database server, create tables and views, and run a client application that creates the stream of ad events. Fig. 6 shows the statement (C1) that creates the table *event_data,* which stores all the received and processed events. During the execution of the client application, students use the provided web-based interface, shown in Fig. 7, to monitor in real-time the stream of events and the costs and rates associated with ad campaigns. Next, students can use VoltDB's Management Center to write and run SQL queries. Fig. 6 shows several queries prepared by the authors to compute various ad real-time statistics.

- Q1: For each website that shows ads, compute the number of received ad events, impressions, clicks and conversions, and the total ad cost.
- Q2: For each advertiser, get the number of processed ad events, impressions, clicks and conversions, and the total ad cost.
- Q3: For each advertiser, compute the daily number of ad events, impressions, clicks and conversions, and the daily ad cost.
- Q4: Identify the 10 ads with the largest associated cost.

This learning activity also provides a good opportunity to highlight some of the key properties of this type of NewSQL system, e.g., high transaction throughput (transactions/second) and low latency (time to process the events).

C1: `CREATE TABLE event_data (utc_time TIMESTAMP NOT NULL, creative_id INTEGER NOT NULL, cost DECIMAL, campaign_id INTEGER NOT NULL, advertiser_id INTEGER NOT NULL, site_id INTEGER NOT NULL, is_impression INTEGER NOT NULL, is_clickthrough INTEGER NOT NULL, is_conversion INTEGER NOT NULL);`

Q1: `SELECT site_id, COUNT(*) AS records, SUM(is_impression) AS impressions, SUM(is_clickthrough) AS clicks, SUM(is_conversion) AS conversions, SUM(cost) AS cost FROM event_data GROUP BY site_id;`

Q2: `SELECT advertiser_id, COUNT(*) AS records, SUM(is_impression) AS impressions, SUM(is_clickthrough) AS clicks, SUM(is_conversion) AS conversions, SUM(cost) AS cost FROM event_data GROUP BY advertiser_id;`

Q3: `SELECT advertiser_id, TRUNCATE(DAY,utc_time) AS utc_day, COUNT(*) AS records, SUM(is_impression) AS impressions, SUM(is_clickthrough) AS clicks, SUM(is_conversion) AS conversions, SUM(cost) AS spent FROM event_data GROUP BY advertiser_id, TRUNCATE(DAY,utc_time);`

Q4: `SELECT creative_id AS ad, SUM(cost) AS cost FROM event_data GROUP BY creative_id ORDER BY cost DESC LIMIT 10;`

Figure 6. VoltDB SQL Queries

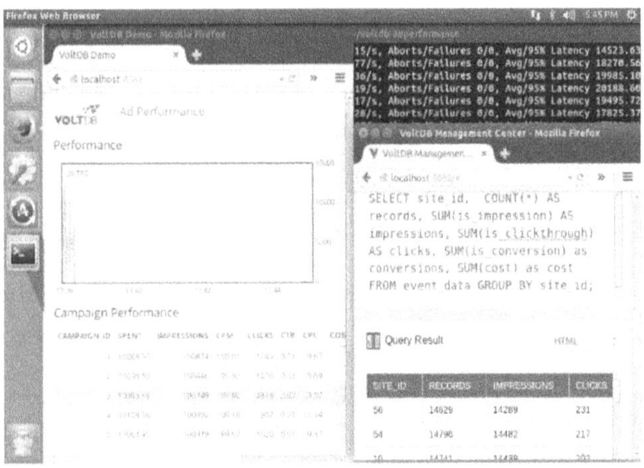

Figure 7. Executing SQL queries in VoltDB

6. DISCUSSION

The proposed modules can be integrated into several introductory and advanced database-related courses. One approach is to adopt Big Data management systems as a replacement of the traditional relational databases currently used in most introductory database courses. We recommend using a NewSQL system, e.g., VoltDB, for this approach since it supports both the relational model and SQL. An alternative approach for introductory database courses is to complement the use of a traditional database with a Big Data system. In this case, instructors can teach database fundamentals using traditional databases and then show how the same or similar concepts can be applied to modern Big Data systems. Another approach it to integrate the study of SQL beyond traditional databases as part of a course in Big Data. This course can study the use of SQL in MapReduce, NoSQL and NewSQL systems, and compare it with other native query languages. The authors have previously integrated the study of NewSQL systems in a Big Data course and are currently integrating the study of SQL in a Big Data system as part of an undergraduate database course. We plan to report the results of these experiences in a future work.

7. CONCLUSIONS

Many application scenarios require processing very large datasets in a highly scalable and distributed fashion and different types of Big Data systems have been designed to address this challenge. Many of these systems have recognized the strengths of SQL as a query language. Most database courses, however, focus solely on traditional relational databases. In this paper we propose that SQL should be taught consider the new and broader database landscape. This exposure will enable students to get better insight from the data on a wider array of systems and applications. This paper presents a set of guidelines and a wide array of class resources to integrate the study of SQL with three core types of Big Data systems: MapReduce, NoSQL, and NewSQL.

8. REFERENCES

[1] ASU. SQL: From Traditional Databases to Big Data - course resources. http://www.public.asu.edu/~ynsilva/iBigData.

[2] Barron's. Michael Stonebraker Explains. http://blogs.barrons.com/techtraderdaily/2015/03/30/michael-stonebraker-describes-oracles-obsolescence-facebooks-enormous-challenge/.

[3] D. Kumar. Data science overtakes computer science? ACM Inroads, 3(3):18–19, Sept. 2012.

[4] A. Cron, H. L. Nguyen, and A. Parameswaran. Big data. XRDS, 19(1):7–8, Sept. 2012.

[5] A. Sattar, T. Lorenzen, and K. Nallamaddi. Incorporating nosql into a database course. ACM Inroads, 4(2):50–53, June 2013.

[6] Y. N. Silva, S. W. Dietrich, J. Reed, L. Tsosie. Integrating Big Data into the Computing Curricula. In ICDE 2015.

[7] Apache. Hadoop. http://hadoop.apache.org/.

[8] Apache. Hive. https://hive.apache.org/.

[9] Apache. Spark SQL. https://spark.apache.org/sql/.

[10] 10gen. Mongodb. http://www.mongodb.org/.

[11] Apache. Hbase. http://hbase.apache.org/.

[12] F. Chang, J. Dean, S. Ghemawat, W. C. Hsieh, D. A. Wallach, M. Burrows, T. Chandra, A. Fikes, and R. E. Gruber. Bigtable: A distributed storage system for structured data. ACM Trans. Comput. Syst., 26(2):1–26, 2008.

[13] Apache. Cassandra. http://cassandra.apache.org/.

[14] Cloudera. Impala. http://impala.io/.

[15] Presto. https://prestodb.io/.

[16] SlamData. SlamData. http://slamdata.com/.

[17] VoltDB. Voltdb VM. https://voltdb.com/run-voltdb-vmware.

[18] MemSQL. MemSQL. http://www.memsql.com/.

[19] NuoDB. Nuodb. http://www.nuodb.com/.

[20] Clustrix. Clustrix. http://www.clustrix.com/.

[21] VoltDB. Application gallery. http://voltdb.com/community/applications.

[22] Apache. Pig. https://pig.apache.org/.

[23] Cloudera. Cloudera VM 4.7.0. http://www.cloudera.com/content/cloudera/en/downloads.html.

[24] Hortonworks. Hortonworks Sandbox on a VM, HDP 2.3. http://hortonworks.com/products/hortonworks-sandbox.

[25] Yahoo Finance. Historical Prices - AAPL. http://finance.yahoo.com/q/hp?s=AAPL+Historical+Prices.

[26] IRS. Tax Stats. http://www.irs.gov/uac/SOI-Tax-Stats-Individual-Income-Tax-Statistics-2012-ZIP-Code-Data-(SOI).

[27] Mongolab. Mongolab. https://mongolab.com/.

The Performance of Female Computer Science Students across Three Caribbean Islands

Daniel T. Fokum and Daniel N. Coore
The University of the West Indies, Mona
Department of Computing
Kingston, Jamaica
{daniel.fokum|daniel.coore}
@uwimona.edu.jm

Yewande E. Lewis-Fokum
The University of the West Indies, Mona
School of Education
Kingston, Jamaica
yewande.lewis@uwimona.edu.jm

ABSTRACT

We examine the gender balance of students in the Computer Science programme at a prominent Caribbean university—with campuses in Jamaica, Barbados, and Trinidad—from three perspectives: enrollment, retention and completion. In the US, in 2011, females accounted for approximately 17.7% of all graduands with a computing degree. These numbers are considered low, especially since when all subjects are taken into account, women account for more than 50% of American college graduates. On one campus of the Caribbean university, for the same year, the proportion of females graduating in Computer Science was 44.2%. These numbers are higher than the US national averages, even after normalizing them for the high female student population on the campus (approximately 70%). We introduce the notion of gender neutrality to represent these normalized ratios. Notably, we did not observe any statistically significant difference in the average performance of males and that of females, which is similar to the result found in the US. We discuss the methods that we used to make these comparisons.

Categories and Subject Descriptors

K.3.2 [**Computer and Information Science Education**]: Computer science education

Keywords

Performance, Female, Graduation odds

1. INTRODUCTION

In the United States in 2012 approximately 18% of the Computer Science graduates were women, whereas they comprised 58% of the baccalaureate graduates in all other disciplines [20]. As a result, there is great interest [10, 13] in boosting diversity in Computer Science, as this would ultimately benefit the technology industry [13]. In this paper we seek to determine if the gender differences in CS and IT observed in the US are accurately reflected in the anglophone Caribbean. We also highlight the reasons why some of the women in developing countries choose CS and IT. This paper considers how female students in Computer Science perform in three Caribbean nations, which are all developing countries, albeit middle income nations. To the best of our knowledge all of the previous work on diversity in Computer Science has only considered developed nations. In North America, there is great interest in increasing female enrollment in Computer Science programs. As a result, a secondary objective of this paper is to determine how the female enrollment in computing courses in these Caribbean nations has evolved over time.

Most of the data in this paper comes from The University of the West Indies (UWI), a regional university serving the anglophone Caribbean with campuses in Mona, Jamaica; St. Augustine, Trinidad; and Cave Hill, Barbados. Bachelor's degrees in Computer Science are awarded across all three campuses. The contribution of this paper is to compare the performance of computing students across genders and the enrollment, retention, and graduation from the computer science major. We introduce a normalizing measurement called gender neutrality to do these comparisons.

The rest of this paper is laid out as follows: Section 2 presents literature on diversity in Computer Science. Section 3 briefly describes our methods. In Section 4 we present our results. Section 5 provides some additional context for our findings, while Section 6 provides concluding remarks.

2. LITERATURE REVIEW

One of the significant challenges facing computing education is the perceived lack of diversity in computer science education in terms of gender, race, and geographic diversity. Gender differences in Computer Science (CS) majors as well as differences between Computer Science majors versus non-majors are examined in [5]. Beyer *et al.* [5] "found no gender differences in quantitative ability, interest in CS, stereotypes and knowledge of CS, or attitudes towards CS courses and instructors." However, [5] found that women's computer confidence was much lower than men's. Furthermore, female CS majors were found to have even less confidence in their computer skills than male non-majors. This lack of confidence was presented as the major barrier to female advancement in Computer Science.

Katz *et al.* [12] examined the role of gender and race in predicting achievement in Computer Science. Katz *et*

SIGCSE '16, March 02-05, 2016, Memphis, TN, USA
© 2016 ACM. ISBN 978-1-4503-3685-7/16/03...$15.00
DOI: http://dx.doi.org/10.1145/2839509.2844566

al. [12] discovered some gender differences in practices such as experimentation that influence performance in Computer Science. However, [12] also observed that women experiment with programming tutorials more than they think they do.

A follow-up study examined the role of gender in achievement and persistence in an undergraduate computer science programme [11]. This study explored why "high-achieving students" leave undergraduate computer science programmes. It was found that factors that predict achievement also predict persistence in Computer Science beyond the first two courses in the major [11]. Katz *et al.* [11] also found that men who received less than a B grade in an introductory CS course were more likely to take the next course in the CS curriculum than were women who earned less than a B.

A 2014 study by Google identified encouragement and exposure as the leading factors that influenced girls to study Computer Science [10]. The Google study stated that anyone can help increase female participation in Computer Science, regardless of their technical abilities or background. Furthermore, they also noted that uncontrollable factors, like ethnicity and household income, were statistically insignificant when compared with controllable factors, like encouragement and exposure [10]. The Google study concluded by stating that encouragement and exposure of girls to Computer Science are steps that could be taken to increase female participation in CS [10].

Google's findings are somewhat aligned with Settle *et al.*'s [18] study. This research study observed that a numerical minority of female students were more likely to feel "isolated" in CS programs, and that tutors should find ways to help their female students connect with student organizations as a means to address social isolation. Ultimately encouragement to connect with others could boost the confidence and participation of female students in CS programs [18].

Sax *et al.* [17] reported that while men are more likely than women to major in Computer Science, the interest in the discipline has varied over time for both genders. Sax *et al.* [17] stated that two traits which tend to discourage women from Computer Science are: 1) weaker math confidence, and 2) stronger artistic orientation relative to men are now less predictive of women's intent to major in Computer Science. On the other hand students who have a father with a STEM career or who place greater emphasis on status or on wealth are more likely to major in CS, regardless of gender [17].

One of the characteristics of education in Jamaica is the wide difference in achievement between male and female students. CAPRI (Caribbean Policy Research Institute) has noted that in Jamaica "girls outperform boys on [sic] all levels of the education system" [6]. CAPRI's report also stated that gender inequity has increased at the tertiary level (between 2000 and 2008) in part due to fewer males meeting the requirements for entry into tertiary education [6]. With respect to computer science education, prior work [9] has shown that the teaching of IT in Jamaican schools is hindered by the ability to attract trained teachers.

Our literature review has shown that a lack of confidence among female students appears to be a great barrier to increasing the level of female enrollment in computer science. Furthermore, there appear to be no gender differences in quantitative ability between male and female Computer Science. In Section 4 we will determine if the claims of [5] also hold true in the Caribbean.

3. METHODOLOGY

The data in this paper was largely drawn from a single query that was run at each campus to select all students who had registered for a first year course in Computer Science or Information Technology at that campus between Semester I 2003/2004 and Semester I 2014/2015. There were 2,064 distinct records selected for Mona, 3,852 records for St. Augustine, and 1,991 records for Cave Hill. Each record had the student's gender as well as a list of all Computing courses attempted along with matching grades and the years and semesters in which the courses were taken. This data was imported into a Microsoft Access database and additional post-processing was done to split the list of Computing courses. The results of this process allowed us to compute each student's GPA in Computing courses.

A second, and smaller dataset, was also drawn from the university's Student Administration System. This dataset contained the aggregate information—such as distribution of male and female students, total enrollment, and grade distribution—for every Computing course offered between Semester I 2004/05 and Semester I 2013/14.

4. RESULTS

The results in this section are mainly drawn from students who have attempted at least 15 credits of computing courses. This condition allowed us to capture students who had attempted at least one academic year's worth of computing courses regardless of whether they had passed all 15 credits. The data was exported from Microsoft Access and statistical analysis was done with R [16].

4.1 Female Performance

4.1.1 Mona

Fig. 1 shows a boxplot with the GPA in Computing courses grouped by gender and campus. The black line in each box represents the median GPA for each gender. The lower and upper vertical boundaries of each box in the boxplot represent the 25th and 75th quartiles, respectively. Fig. 1 shows that at Mona the sample median Computing GPA (2.052) for female students is slightly higher than that for men (1.911).

At Mona there was a significant difference in the mean Computing GPA for male ($n = 798$, $\mu = 2.171$, $\sigma = 1.221$) and female ($n = 535$, $\mu = 2.343$, $\sigma = 1.222$) students; $t(1144.9) = 2.513$, $p = 0.012$. The 95% confidence interval for the difference between the mean Computing GPA for both populations is [0.038 : 0.305]. These results suggest that at Mona there is a significant difference between the performance of males and females in Computing courses. Furthermore, these results are a confirmation of CAPRI's claim that in Jamaica girls outperform boys at all levels of the education system [6].

4.1.2 St. Augustine

Fig. 1 shows that at St. Augustine the sample median Computing GPA (1.512) for female students is about the same as that for men (1.496). At St. Augustine there was no significant difference in the mean Computing GPA for male ($n = 529$, $\mu = 1.634$, $\sigma = 1.067$) and female ($n = 293$, $\mu = 1.710$, $\sigma = 1.136$) students; $t(571.9) = 0.946$, $p = 0.344$. The 95% confidence interval for the difference between the

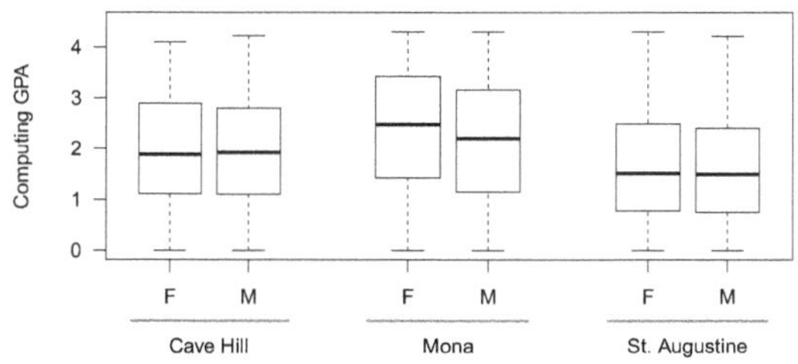

Figure 1: Boxplot showing GPA in computing courses for each UWI campus grouped by gender

mean Computing GPA for both populations is $[-0.082 : 0.236]$. These results suggest that at St. Augustine there is no significant difference between the performance of males and females in Computing courses.

4.1.3 Cave Hill

Fig. 1 shows that at Cave Hill the sample median Computing GPA (1.884) for female students is slightly lower than that for men (1.925). At Cave Hill there was no significant difference in the mean Computing GPA for male ($n = 196$, $\mu = 2.035$, $\sigma = 1.201$) and female ($n = 68$, $\mu = 2.027$, $\sigma = 1.039$) students; $t(133.7) = -0.051$, $p = 0.959$. The 95% confidence interval for the difference between the mean Computing GPA for both populations is $[-0.309 : 0.294]$. These results suggest that at Cave Hill there is no significant difference between males and females in performance in Computing courses.

4.2 Quantifying Gender Bias

In examining the ratio of males to females in any particular group, we might be tempted to make absolute comments about ratios that are far from 1. However, it is important that any gender biases in the population be taken into account, before any such comparisons are made. For the purposes of this paper, we shall define the notion of "gender neutrality" as a measure of the gender balance of a group, after normalising for any population biases. Formally, the *gender neutrality* of a group is the ratio of men to women in the group divided by the ratio of men to women in the population. So, for a group that is drawn from a population of equal numbers of of men and women, if it has a gender neutrality measure of ν, then it contains men and women in a $\nu : 1$ ratio.

We can algebraically define gender neutrality as follows. The table below illustrates the case when the number of males in, and out of, the group are a and b respectively, and those for females are c and d, respectively.

	M	F
In Group	a	c
Out of Group	b	d

The total number of males is $a + b$ and that for females is $c + d$, so by definition,

$$\nu = \frac{a}{c} / \frac{(a+b)}{(c+d)} = \frac{a}{a+b} / \frac{c}{c+d}$$

The second form provides an alternative, but equivalent, way to measure of gender neutrality: it is the ratio of the proportion of males in the group to the proportion of females in the group.

4.2.1 Comparison of gender neutrality to odds ratio

A common statistical measure used for pairs of categories of binary data is the odds ratio. In this particular discussion, the odds ratio, comparing males to females, would be the ratio of the odds for a man being in the group to those for a woman being in the group. In other words, its value would be $\frac{ad}{bc}$. From the algebraic expression, it is clear that the odds ratio is not numerically equal to the gender neutrality measure (ν). In fact, it is straightforward to algebraically show that ν is always closer to 1 than the odds ratio (smaller for odds ratios larger than 1, but larger for odds ratios smaller than 1). We submit that the gender neutrality measure is a more intuitive concept than the odds ratio, and therefore is worthwhile reporting instead of the odds ratio. To illustrate this, if we knew that a programme had a gender neutrality measure of 2.0 in a university where enrollment is typically 60% male, then we would expect that the programme would have about $2.0 \times .6/.4 = 3.0$ times as many males as females enrolled in it. On the other hand, an odds ratio of 2.0 tells us that the odds of a male student getting a CS degree are twice those of a female student, which does not translate in a direct way to the expected ratio of males to females to enrol in the programme. This is because the odds ratio does not take the ratio of the overall population into account, whereas the gender neutrality measure does.

4.3 Female Enrollment

The number of women enrolled in Computer Science programmes is a subject of great interest. In this section we show the changes in the proportion of female students enrolled in Computing courses. We examine trends in enrollment at Cave Hill, Mona, and St. Augustine.

4.3.1 Mona

These statistics ought to be interpreted against the backdrop of female enrollment at The UWI, Mona campus. Statistics from the 2012/13 academic year (the most recent available) show that about 69% of the students at The UWI, Mona were women [4].

Fig. 2 shows the evolution of the average proportion of females in computing courses from 2008/09 Semester I to 2013/14 Semester II. Since the 2008/09 academic year, the average proportion of female students in Year 1 Computing courses has remained below 40% in all semesters. The average enrollment in Year 2 Computing courses has also remained below 40% in all semesters since 2008/09. In fact, the average proportion of female students in Year 2 is generally below the corresponding number for Year 1. Finally, the average proportion of female students in the Year 3 courses is also generally below 40%, with the exception of the 2008/09 academic year. Furthermore, the average proportion of female students in Year 3 courses is mostly greater than the corresponding number for Year 2 courses.

4.3.2 Cave Hill and St. Augustine

Fig. 3 shows the evolution of the average proportion of females in computing courses at Cave Hill and St. Augustine from 2008/09 Semester I to 2013/14 Semester II.

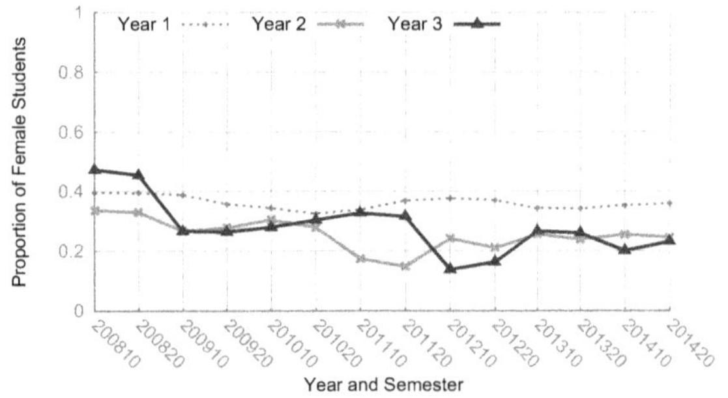

Figure 2: Average proportion of female students in Computing Courses at Mona

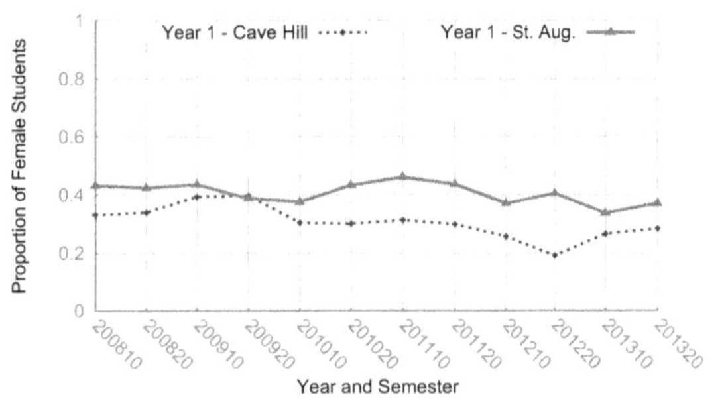

Figure 3: Average proportion of female students in Computing Courses at Cave Hill and St. Augustine

At Cave Hill the average proportion of female students in Year 1 Computing courses has been at or below 40% in all semesters. At St. Augustine, on the other hand, the proportion of female students has risen as high as 48%, but in recent years it has declined. The University's most recent annual report [4] shows that about 69% of the students at Cave Hill are female, while about 64% of the students at St. Augustine are female. It is curious to note that St. Augustine has the highest average proportion of female students in Year 1 courses, even though there are proportionately fewer women on that campus.

4.4 Graduation of Female Students

Tables 1 and 2 summarize data showing the number and sex of students graduating from university in the US and at The UWI, Mona respectively. From Tables 1 and 2 we calculated the gender neutrality of graduating with a computing degree, as well as the corresponding odds ratios, for each academic year from 2008 to 2011. The gender neutrality of a computing-related degree in the US was consistently between 6.027 and 6.248 for the years that we measured it. While at UWI, Mona, the values ranged between 3.894 and 23.072. In 2011/12, the neutrality of a computing-related degree at UWI was less than that of the US, but we cannot make summative statements about the comparison in general, without more data points, because the 95% confidence interval on the UWI data is too wide. Nevertheless, it is quite clear from the data that—apart from 2010/11—computing degrees appear to be somewhere between 4 and 7 times as attractive to males as it is to females. This is true for both UWI, Mona as well as the US, but in the US, that number is more tightly measured to lie between 6.027 and 6.248. The odds ratios paint a similar picture, but interpreting them is less direct.

From Table 1, we can infer that the odds of a male student in the US choosing a Computer Science degree are over 6.0 times the odds of his choosing a degree in a different discipline. Table 2 shows that at Mona the same odds ratio is slightly lower for two of the academic years between 2008/09 and 2011/12, and higher than the US number in the other two years. Table 3 shows that at Cave Hill the odds of a male student in Barbados choosing a Computer Science degree are between 7 to 11 times the odds of his choosing a degree in another discipline. These odds are consistently higher than the corresponding measurement for the USA.

4.5 Retention of Female Students in computing-related courses

Considering Fig. 2 it is hard to make definitive statements about whether the DoC is losing several female students between first and third years because the data includes statistics for both core and elective 3rd year courses. If we examine core courses for Computer Science such as Mathematics for Computing (1st year), Discrete Mathematics (2nd year), and Operating Systems (3rd year) the data does not suggest that the DoC is losing many female students. The strongest conclusion that we can infer from this data is that the 3rd year elective courses for the Computer Science major probably have a stronger gender bias towards males than the core courses do. To properly gauge gender bias in retention in the Computer Science major, we would have needed to analyze longitudinal data.

We did not have sufficient data to perform exact measures of retention rates throughout the programmes, but we had enough to determine good proxies for progression through the Computer Science major. We tallied all the students who had registered for a 1st year course between 2004 and 2011 inclusive. These would be the students who did the first semester of the Computer Science programme; but not all of them have any intention to major in Computer Science. At The UWI it is common for first year students to take at least one science course outside their major. We also counted the number of students who registered for the core algorithms course, as well as those who registered for the final project. Since the project course has the algorithms course as a prerequisite, and is also core to the major, the fraction of students who register for the project course relative to the number that register for the algorithms course is a reasonable approximation of the retention rate to the final year. We shall refer to this ratio as those *Advancing*. If we consider the students who register for the 1st year of the programme as only potential majors, then we can consider the fraction of them who go on to register for the algorithms course as the ones that we have successfully attracted to the programme. Consequently, we shall refer to this ratio as *Attracted* to the programme.

Table 4 shows that the gender neutrality measure of the students attracted to the computer science major was 1.454, and that for the students advancing in the major was 1.292. Both of those numbers are quite a bit smaller than the gender neutrality for the graduation data. The fact that the gender neutrality of the retention rate is only slightly higher than 1 means that the dropout rate of females is probably not a significant contributor to the high bias towards males graduating with a computing-related degree. That high gen-

Table 1: Graduation statistics for the USA by sex. Sources: [19, 20]

Major	2011–12 M	2011–12 F	2010–11 M	2010–11 F	2009–10 M	2009–10 F	2008–09 M	2008–09 F
CS graduates	38,773	8,611	35,478	7,594	32,410	7,179	31,215	6,779
Non-CS graduates	726,544	1,017,118	698,655	974,186	674,223	936,202	654,167	909,207
Odds Ratio (M:F)	6.30		6.51		6.27		6.40	
Gender Neutrality (M:F)	6.035		6.248		6.027		6.154	

Table 2: Graduation statistics for The UWI, Mona by sex. Sources: [7, 8, 14, 15, 1, 2, 3]

Major	2011–12 M	2011–12 F	2010–11 M	2010–11 F	2009–10 M	2009–10 F	2008–09 M	2008–09 F
CS graduates	29	23	36	5	25	12	32	22
Non-CS graduates	571	1,830	543	1,901	536	1,861	447	1,686
Odds Ratio (M:F)	4.041		25.206		7.233		5.486	
Gender Neutrality (M:F)	3.894		23.702		6.956		5.187	

Table 3: Graduation Statistics for The UWI, Cave Hill by sex. Sources: [21, 22, 23, 24]

Major	2011–12 M	2011–12 F	2010–11 M	2010–11 F	2009–10 M	2009–10 F	2008–09 M	2008–09 F
CS graduates	37	11	43	10	33	12	36	18
Non-CS graduates	322	839	288	791	230	789	224	784
Odds Ratio (M:F)	8.764		11.810		9.434		7.000	
Gender Neutrality (M:F)	7.964		10.406		8.375		6.169	

Table 4: Retention Statistics for the UWI, Mona by Sex

	Attracted M	Attracted F	Attracted Tot	Advancing M	Advancing F	Advancing Tot
Yes	308	143	451	167	60	227
No	517	414	931	141	83	224
Total	825	557	1382	308	143	451
Odds Ratio (M:F)	1.724			1.638		
Neutrality (M:F)	1.454			1.292		

der neutrality value for graduation combined with a nearly neutral retention rate implies that the intake of new students in computing related subjects is probably also high gender biased. We did not have an opportunity to verify this though.

4.6 Survey Results

We conducted a survey of female students at Mona who graduated between 2009 and 2015 in order to determine which factors might have attracted them to Computing and why they chose to persist in the discipline. Only 21 students responded to the survey. The survey had 21 questions including who might have encouraged them to study computing at university and which subjects were taken in high school. Eight of the students stated that a teacher was responsible for their choosing to major in Computer Science. Five students stated that their decision to major in CS was influenced by friends. Most of the students (81%) stated that their mathematical skills in high school were above average. This result is not surprising, as our data shows that female students who have attempted over 12 credits of Computing courses generally have better CAPE (Caribbean Advanced Proficiency Examination) Mathematics and Computer Science grades. This finding is statistically significant.

Most of the students felt that they had a positive university experience studying Computing. About 71% of the students stated that their CS lecturers had created an environment in which they felt comfortable asking questions. About 2/3 of the respondents stated that they were likely to recommend that others major in Computer Science.

This survey, while small, gives an indication of which factors might be important to boost female enrollment in Computer Science, at least in the Jamaican context. We learned that high school teachers have a great part to play in influencing students to study Computer Science at university. Thus, institutions need to reach out to teachers telling them about programme prerequisites and helping the teachers better prepare their students for university.

5. DISCUSSION

The gender neutrality measure for the academic year 2010-11 at Mona, Jamaica is probably an outlier. No other year since then, or even before, has seen so few females graduating in Computer Science, but we do not have a good explanation for why that number is so small. If we were to omit the 2010-11 measurement from our computation, then the mean gender neutrality of graduation from the CS major at Mona would become 5.346, which is slightly lower than the US national average, but still quite heavily gender biased. The relatively few years over which the average was computed means that we have to be cautious about reading too much into the comparison of those two numbers, but the difference does bear further investigation to determine whether it can be attributed to a cultural or contextual difference.

The cultural norms for Jamaica, insofar as gender roles are concerned, are not too far from those of the US and Western Europe. This is not too surprising, given Jamaica's history as a former British colony. However the prevalence of women in tertiary educational institutions, and the relatively commonplace examples of women in powerful or prominent positions probably has an empowering influence on young girls who are trying to decide what to study. For example, the head of Government is currently female, there are many female holders of public office, and many school principals are females. So, there are many examples of prominent women as role models for young girls, though none are in computing-related careers. On the other hand, there is an absence of local role models in these careers for boys as well. Yet, a Computer Science degree is still viewed as being highly marketable, and therefore is attractive to both genders.

So, while it is possible that the apparent difference in gender neutrality between the Jamaican and the US contexts for graduating Computer Science majors is only noise, it may also be a real reflection of some of these differences in role models for girls.

In the end though, the real message in the values of the gender neutrality measures for students graduating with a Computer Science major, whether in Jamaica, the USA or Barbados, was that they are more similar to each other than they are different. So, the gender bias to earning Computer Science degrees appears to span cultural and national boundaries.

6. CONCLUSIONS

We have investigated the gender bias of the Computer Science major at The UWI on the three physical campuses in Jamaica, Barbados and Trinidad, with particular attention to the programme at Mona, Jamaica. We introduced a measurement for quantifying gender bias, which we have called *gender neutrality*. We then measured the gender neutrality of four aspects of the major: enrollment at first year, retention from first to second year, retention from second to third year, and graduation.

We found that the gender neutrality of the retention measures, both to the 2nd year, as well as to the 3rd year, were close to 1, signifying that the retention rate was almost the same for both males and females. On the other hand, the gender neutrality of graduation from the Computer Science major was sufficiently far from 1 to signify heavy gender bias in that aspect. In fact, the bias is so significant that in spite of a near 2:1 ratio of women to men on the UWI campuses, there were consistently more men than women in 1st year CS courses, as well as graduating from the major. Interestingly the magnitude of this bias in Jamaica was less than the bias in the US, which in turn was lower than that of Barbados.

This paper also reviewed the performance of female computer science students across three Caribbean islands. We found that, with the exception of Jamaica, there is no statistically significant difference in performance in Computer Science courses between males and females. For Jamaica our findings were consistent with prior work that showed that females do better than males at all levels of the educational system.

7. REFERENCES

[1] *Statistical Review: Academic Year 2008/2009.* The University of the West Indies, 2010.

[2] *Statistical Review: Academic Year 2009/2010.* The University of the West Indies, 2010.

[3] *Annual Report 2011/2012.* The University of the West Indies, Mona, Jamaica, 2013.

[4] *The University of the West Indies Annual Report 2012/2013.* University of the West Indies, 2014.

[5] S. Beyer, K. Rynes, J. Perrault, K. Hay, and S. Haller. Gender Differences in Computer Science Students. In *Proc. 34th SIGCSE Technical Symp. Computer Science Education*, SIGCSE '03, pages 49–53, Reno, NV, USA, Feb. 2003. ACM.

[6] Caribbean Policy Research Institute and PREAL (Programa de Promocion de la Reforma Educativa en America Latina y el Caribe). Prisms of Possibility: A Report Card on Education in Jamaica, 2012.

[7] D. N. Coore. Department of Computing Report. 2008/2009, Aug. 2009.

[8] D. N. Coore. Department of Computing Report. 2009/2010, Aug. 2010.

[9] P. Daley-Morris. *Introduction of Information Technology to Schools in Jamaica.* Education for all in the Caribbean: Assessment 2000 Monograph Series. Office of the UNESCO Representative, 2000.

[10] Google, Inc. Women Who Choose Computer Science—What Really Matters. Report, May 2014.

[11] S. Katz, D. Allbritton, J. Aronis, C. Wilson, and M. L. Soffa. Gender, Achievement, and Persistence in an Undergraduate Computer Science Program. *SIGMIS Database*, 37(4):42–57, Nov. 2006.

[12] S. Katz, J. Aronis, D. Allbritton, C. Wilson, and M. L. Soffa. Gender and Race in Predicting Achievement in Computer Science. *Technology and Society Magazine, IEEE*, 22(3):20–27, Fall 2003.

[13] D. Khanna. We Need More Women in Tech: The Data Prove It, Oct. 26 2013.

[14] E. K. Mugisa. Department of Computing Report. 2010/2011, Aug. 2011.

[15] E. K. Mugisa. Department of Computing Report. 2011/2012, Aug. 2012.

[16] R Core Team. *R: A Language and Environment for Statistical Computing.* R Foundation for Statistical Computing, Vienna, Austria, 2014.

[17] L. J. Sax, K. Lehman, J. A. Jacobs, A. Kanny, G. Lim, L. N. Paulson, and H. Zimmerman. Anatomy of an Enduring Gender Gap: The Evolution of Women's Participation in Computer Science. In *Proc. American Educational Research Association*, Apr. 2015.

[18] A. Settle, J. Lalor, and T. Steinbach. Reconsidering the Impact of CS1 on Novice Attitudes. In *Proc. 46th ACM Technical Symp. Computer Science Education*, SIGCSE '15, pages 229–234, New York, NY, USA, Mar. 2015. ACM.

[19] T. D. Snyder and S. A. Dillow. *Digest of Education Statistics 2011.* National Center for Education Statistics, 2012.

[20] T. D. Snyder and S. A. Dillow. *Digest of Education Statistics 2012.* National Center for Education Statistics, Dec. 2013.

[21] The University of the West Indies Cave Hill Campus Barbados. Statistics 2008/2009, 2010.

[22] The University of the West Indies Cave Hill Campus Barbados. Statistics 2009/2010, 2011.

[23] The University of the West Indies Cave Hill Campus Barbados. Statistics 2010/2011, 2012.

[24] The University of the West Indies Cave Hill Campus Barbados. Statistics 2011/2012, 2013.

Alice in the Middle East: An Experience Report from the Formative Phase

Saquib Razak
Computer Science
Carnegie Mellon University
Doha, Qatar
srazak@qatar.cmu.edu

Huda Gedawy
Computer Science
Carnegie Mellon University
Doha, Qatar
hgedawy@qatar.cmu.edu

Wanda Dann
Alice Project, Emerita
Carnegie Mellon University
Pittsburgh, PA
wpdann@andrew.cmu.edu

Don Slater
Alice Project
Carnegie Mellon University
Pittsburgh, PA
dslater@andrew.cmu.ed

ABSTRACT

In this paper, we describe the initial results of the formative phase of a project that crosses international borders. Alice in the Middle East (Alice ME) is a project designed to adapt the Alice software, develop new curricular materials, and provide professional development for teachers and students in the Middle East. For those who may be considering a collaborative project that would be conducted across international borders, we share lessons learned.

CCS Concepts

• **Social and professional topics~K-12 education**

Keywords

Alice; Computing Curriculum; K-12; Internationalization; Computational Thinking

1. INTRODUCTION

Alice is a program visualization software tool for introducing computational thinking and programming concepts in the context of creating 3D animations [13, 14]. In Alice, 3-D models of objects (e.g., people, animals and vehicles) populate a virtual world and students use a drag and drop editor to manipulate the movement and activities of these objects. Alice has been remarkably successful in North America, where formal studies [9, 10] have shown improved student enthusiasm, achievement, and retention. The use of program visualization with educational software tools such as Alice, Scratch, and Greenfoot is continuing to gain acceptance as an educational approach, particularly in K-12 classrooms. In the Alice Project, this growth is measured by analytics such as software downloads (now more than 1.4 million annually) and membership in the Alice Educator's Listserve (~ 2500).

We are currently working on a project that aims to adapt the Alice software for a conservative Middle Eastern culture, develop curricular materials, and provide professional development workshops for teachers and students in the Middle East. The target population for Alice in the Middle East (Alice ME) is teachers and students at the middle school level. The focus of this effort is to create curriculum that introduces computational thinking and problem solving skills in students. Alice ME is a collaborative project between the Alice Project at Carnegie Mellon University (CMU) in Pittsburgh, PA, and the Alice ME team at Carnegie Mellon University in Qatar (CMU-Q).

The Alice Project currently supports two versions: Alice 2 (version 2.4) and Alice 3 (version 3.1). Alice ME project is based on Alice 2 due to its object-based approach, which is more appropriate for the middle school grades. The Alice ME project is motivated by the efforts of the Alice Project to internationalize the software and support materials. Internationalization will provide access to students and teachers around the world. Internationalization efforts, over the last three years, have focused on translation of both Alice 2 and Alice 3 to Spanish and Portuguese.

Computer science education research projects conducted by investigators across international borders may take advantage of rare opportunities for broader impact. In the Alice ME project, for example, the partnership is between a team in the US and a team in Qatar. Qatar is the size of Connecticut and is a single-state nation having a ministry of education, known as the Supreme Education Council (SEC). The SEC manages the educational system of the entire country. Working with an agency such as the SEC provides an opportunity for influencing education standards at a national level. This, in turn, may influence neighboring countries that share a common culture and language, like United Arab Emirates, Saudi Arabia, Bahrain, Egypt, and Kuwait. Qatar aims to be a leader for educational innovation in the Middle East, spurred by the Qatari government leaders' recognition of the importance of computing "know-how" and a vision for a knowledge-based society [15].

In this paper, we describe our experiences during the formative phase of the Alice ME project. We present our approach with the realization that there is an effort towards globalization of education systems. There is a trend for countries, to evaluate curriculum from other cultures, and then try to bring the successful curriculum to their own school systems. This trend is largely because societies have started realizing the importance of education and knowledge. Qatar's efforts towards building knowledge-based society and upgrading their higher education infrastructure are proofs of this realization. The challenge is to recognize that although a strong curriculum is necessary, simply porting a successful curriculum to a different environment is not sufficient to guarantee success. Here we share our attempt to take a tool with associated curriculum and apply it in an environment with a very different culture and social values. Our findings include that religion and culture are an intricate part of the society in the Middle East and contents of the academic curriculum have to conform to the social norms. As a result of this finding, we removed several existing 3-D models from Alice that were

SIGCSE '16, March 2–5, 2016, Memphis, TN, USA.
 ISBN 978-1-4503-3685-7/16/03…$15.00.
DOI: http://dx.doi.org/10.1145/2839509.2844593

inappropriate for the conservative local culture and added several that are relevant to local culture. We also discovered that there is a dearth of resources in Arabic language and any effort to introduce new curricula will require development of resources, like student textbooks, in Arabic. We also present our experience in addressing the challenge of getting endorsement from different stakeholders to introduce curricular material that requires students to think and be creative. Such material is considered "hard" for the students and in general resisted. After overcoming several challenges, we implemented the curriculum in several local schools. Our initial results from a pilot test of this curriculum indicate that students were able to demonstrate higher level of logical thinking skills. We hope that readers can benefit from this experience.

In the Gulf-region, which consists of countries like United Arab Emirates (UAE), Qatar, Bahrain, Saudi Arabia, Kuwait, and Oman, there has been a positive shift of focus towards education. "The Kingdom of Bahrain is one example of a wider regional trend toward policy borrowing and the importation of foreign systems and practices in education" [19]. Top universities from US and Europe have setup their branches in the region. Carnegie Mellon University and HEC Paris in Qatar, New York University in UAE, and University College London in Bahrain are examples of some of these institutions. In order to provide a steady stream of well-qualified students for these institutes, these countries are working hard to upgrade their K-12 education systems. There is a big opportunity for professionals working in education around the world to contribute towards this progress. We are hoping that our work in this project will motivate some of these efforts.

2. PREVIOUS WORK

In 2004, Alice 2 was officially released as a *program visualization* tool for introductory programming courses. Program visualization, as defined here, refers to the use of computer graphics to directly relate individual lines of program code with visualized actions that are performed by objects at runtime. Early examples of program visualization are Logo [11] and Karel the Robot [12]. In the case of Alice, the visualized objects are instances of 3D model classes. Rather than manipulating strings and numbers in an abstract setting, students learn concepts of logic and computational thinking (e.g., iteration, conditionals, objects and classes, and methods and parameters) by manipulating data common in the contexts of digital storytelling, video game production, and movie-making: actors, scenes, and sound samples.

Because the Alice ME project is using the latest version of Alice 2, we present a summary of previous studies with a restriction to those performed with Alice 2.

Alice 2 has been used successfully as an intervention to draw at-risk students into computing [2, 3, 4]. At-risk students were defined as those students who had demonstrated less success in math or those who had little previous programming experience. A textbook [5] was developed and pilot tested in introductory computer programming courses (pre-CS1) offered at Saint Joseph's University and Ithaca College. Additionally, a detailed set of curricular materials [1], including curricular models, presentations, lab exercises, and many other components, was composed. These studies resulted in the following significant results [9]:

- The average grade for at-risk students exposed to Alice was a 3.0 GPA in CS1, which is comparable to the grades of students who were at no risk or low risk. The average grade for at-risk students not exposed to Alice was a 1.2 GPA in CS1.
- 88% of at-risk students exposed to Alice enrolled in CS2 after CS1. Only 47% who were not exposed to Alice enrolled in CS2 ($p < .05$, chi-squared).

Investigators in this study concluded that the Alice approach doubled retention rates of at-risk students and increased achievement by at least one letter grade.

Other investigators have performed studies in other courses and other settings and have reached supportive conclusions. For example, Mullins, Whitfield, and Conlon [10] concluded: "Retention data shows that the incorporation of Alice into the programming sequence has increased the number of students that pass the courses and decreased the number of withdrawals. Also, the number of students enrolling in Alice has increased by 10% as the number of majors has dropped by 50%."

We ask the reader to note that the studies described above were performed with students primarily at early college levels. For the middle school population, only two studies have been conducted. In 2006, Kelleher and Pausch [7] studied the use of Storytelling Alice (a variant of Alice 2) with middle school girls. This study was conducted in an informal setting with Girl Scouts who participated in one-time Saturday sessions. Kelleher found it was necessary to provide pre-built high-level animations for the 3D models as well as provide a guided template for storyboarding.

A second project involving middle school teachers and students is the Alice ITEST project led by Rodger, Cooper, Stalvey and Schep. The major activity in this project is professional development workshops for middle and high school teachers, where teachers attend a workshop and then develop lesson plans that are contributed to an online repository [16]. One-year follow-ups are conducted to track effectiveness. The ITEST project is still underway.

This is, of course, not the first effort in importing successful curricula to the Middle East. Kingdom of Bahrain partnered with Singapore to develop teacher education programs for the Kingdom. Although this effort was started in 2005 and came into effect in 2008, "the borrowing of the model, to date, has not made any significant impact in student attainment or teacher efficacy, in part due to the slow rate of contextualization of the materials, leading to inappropriate curricula and models that are not fit for purpose" [19]. Kirk further reports that areas of conflict that impede the successful porting of these successful curricula from Singapore are "language issues, cultural appropriateness of materials and resources, and the sense of "loss of ownership" of national education systems" [19].

3. OVERVIEW

The Alice ME project is targeted at middle school (grades 6-8) teachers and students in the Middle East. The overall goal of the project is to adapt the Alice 2 software to the local cultures, develop new instructional materials appropriate for local systems, and test the effectiveness of the Alice approach at the middle school level. The "Alice approach" – using program visualization to teach/learn analytic, logical, and computational thinking, problem solving skills and fundamental programming concepts in the context of animation – remains the same as described in the above studies.

3.1 Major objectives

3.1.1 *Software modification*

The first objective of this project is modification of the Alice software for greater diversity. The modification includes the development of new 3D models that provide animation objects encountered in student's daily lives (animals, buildings, clothing, and vehicles) as well as artifacts that reflect and respect the heritage of Middle Eastern culture. The new models provide characters and images that reflect local culture, thereby supporting the local aspiration for maintaining a balance between embracing modernization and preserving tradition. To make room for the new models and to improve the download time for access in remote regions, the size of the gallery was decreased to a core set of 3D models.

3.1.2 *Curriculum Development*

A second, but equally important, objective is the development of new curriculum and instructional materials for the middle school level. Existing instructional materials, were designed and developed for high school and early college students. New materials are needed with a lower reading level and slower pace. Although the reading level and pace are changing, the focus is still on programming concepts, analytic and logical thinking, and problem solving skills in the context of creating animations. To create the animation, students will need to logically decompose the problem, create an algorithm, and implement the code. These are computational thinking skills, applied in the innovative, modern context of creating animation.

3.1.3 *Teacher Training*

The third objective is to provide workshops for local teachers in learning and using the Alice pedagogy of innovative techniques for teaching logical thinking and problem solving skills with the technology of the 21st century. This objective involves development of new training materials for teachers and workshops for teachers as well as providing ongoing support as the teachers learn how to adapt and integrate new techniques and pedagogy in their own classroom setting with their students.

3.1.4 *Evaluation*

The fourth objective is evaluation of the effectiveness of this project in achieving the above objectives and the effect of this approach with participating teachers and students at the middle school level. The evaluation task is divided into two phases. The first phase is the formative phase where we use an advisory board to help understand local culture, student level, and teachers' expertise. We also create a pilot curriculum and teacher training associated with this curriculum. We use a pilot study in a controlled setting using a few classes within one or two schools. This study will test the quality and appropriateness of this curriculum, both from students and teachers perspectives. The emphasis during this phase is evaluating the curriculum to meet the educational and cultural needs of the school. During this phase, we also determine the correct level, duration, and approach for teacher training workshop. The feedback from this phase will help shape the summative phase of the project where we conduct a formal study to determine the effectiveness of the curriculum to reach the educational goals of computation thinking, logical reasoning, and analytical skills of the students. The summative phase will use pre- and post- tests to evaluate the merit of our curriculum.

4. FORMATIVE PHASE

In the formative phase, our goal was to understand the environment and local culture and evaluate the opportunities and challenges. The lessons learned in this phase are being used to formulate the future direction of our research. This section details the *tasks performed* in this phase and *lessons learned* from this experience.

4.1 Advisory board

To get started on creating an initial set of 3-D models that would be relevant to the Middle Eastern culture, we formed an advisory board. The advisory board was tasked with the following goals:

- Help us understand the Middle East culture and determine which themes and models would be relevant to the society
- Help us understand the educational systems in terms of grade levels and curriculum
- Help us understand student and teacher skill sets
- Preview new models for Alice ME and give us feedback
- Help us pilot test early models and evaluate results of this test

The advisory board consisted of members from the curriculum development department of the SEC, ICT (Information and communications technology) teachers from local secondary schools, and principals of these schools. Schools in Qatar are mainly of two categories: public schools that follow the SEC curriculum guidelines, and international schools that mostly follow British or US curriculum standards. The public schools use Arabic as the language of instruction while private schools use English. The advisory board had representation from both types of schools.

Although the Middle Eastern countries are rapidly modernizing, the desire to maintain traditional norms is strong. For this reason, we compiled two lists of models. One list was of existing models in the Alice gallery that are not appropriate for the Middle Eastern culture. Qatar (and Middle East in general) is a religious society that follows conservative norms in dress for both men and women. We used the following principles learned from the advisory board for making the list of models to remove:

- Models depicting females that are not appropriately covered (long sleeve shirts, and long pants or dresses) were removed.
- Models with men wearing tank-tops (construction workers) or shorts (swimmers, fishermen) were removed
- Models related to magic and sorcery were deleted
- Models associated with mythology were also removed

The second was a list of models that would be interesting and relevant to the Qatari society. These lists helped us determine those models that might be modified, removed, or added to the gallery. We found that Qatar is a cultural society with a lot of emphasis on local customs. Local hospitality, religion, and traditional professions like pearl diving, fishing, and policemen have special place in society. We also discovered that people in general and boys in particular, have a special respect for camels and the desert.

We also learned which grade levels (7th, 8th, and 9th) the advisory board felt was the most appropriate target for our research. Although we determined, based on existing curriculum and assessments, that these levels are more or less comparable to those of the US or UK, there is a marked difference in IT or computing related topics in Qatar schools. Based on conversations with advisory board members, we concluded that the main reasons are

Computer Science as a field is not well understood in the society, there is no local software industry, and a high level of prestige is associated with more traditional engineering and medical fields. The result is that topics related to these traditional engineering and medical fields receive greater emphasis in school curricula.

The existing curriculum in most schools is based on learning to use technology but not creating technology. Students learn the use of productivity tools, multimedia and graphics, and some web development using WYSIWYG development tools. Since most schools in Qatar have strong financial support, there is widespread use of technology within classrooms and computer labs are available for student use.

The advisory board also helped us determine the proficiency level of local ICT teachers. We found that most teachers are professionally trained in IT related fields but lack continuing professional training opportunities. This has resulted either in teachers having to learn new content and techniques on their own or in resisting adoption of newer technology.

4.2 Developing new 3D Models

As part of our work with the Advisory board, we conducted a needs assessment using surveys with teachers, administrators, and students at a well-known private school in Doha to determine a prospective list of models that would be appropriate for local cultures and interests. We also explored art resources online and in local art museums seeking relevant artifacts related to the history of this geographic region. The lists were compiled and prioritized in terms of relevance and estimated time for constructing the models.

Armed with this prioritized list, we first developed three prototype models. The prototypes were imported and previewed with professional character artists (for review of model animation functionality) and local school administrators (for review of faithfulness to cultural and everyday-life artifacts). A lesson learned in this process was that open-ended questions on needs assessment surveys did not provide sufficient detail regarding cultural appropriateness. We had to follow-up the surveys with research into historical and contemporary artifacts.

Thus far, thirty-five new Middle-East-themed 3D models have been designed and developed, based on the results of the needs assessment activities and feedback obtained from the students and teacher during pilot test phase. These new models were incorporated into a new version of the Alice 2 software. Figure 1 shows screenshots of some of these models. The new models have been added to the Alice 2 gallery, in a collection named Middle East. The model at the top left of Figure 1 is a local Fort known as Fort Zubara. This fort has a special significance in Qatari history and students study it in primary school as part of the social studies and history lessons. The second model is that of a tea-pot and tea-cup, a sign of local hospitality. The third model is a pearl shell (historically pearl diving was an important part of the local economy) and the fourth model represents a religious scholar or Imam.

In Alice, the models are used in animations where users animate parts of models or complete models based on some predefined functions. For example, a user may want to show a flying dragon by moving the dragon in the air and at the same time moving dragon's wings up and down to simulate flapping of wings while flying. The left side of figure 2 shows an example of different components of a model of a man.

Using these models during pilot study in our formative phase, we realized that one of the obstacle for students was to determine the name for each part. Local school student take their subjects and instructions in Arabic and although, they are able to use most software applications in English, the level of knowledge required to understand these models caused a cognitive overload for the students. As an improvement to the 3-D models we are translating all models in the Alice gallery to Arabic text in the summative phase of our project. The right side of figure 2 shows the translated model for the religious scholar from Figure 1.

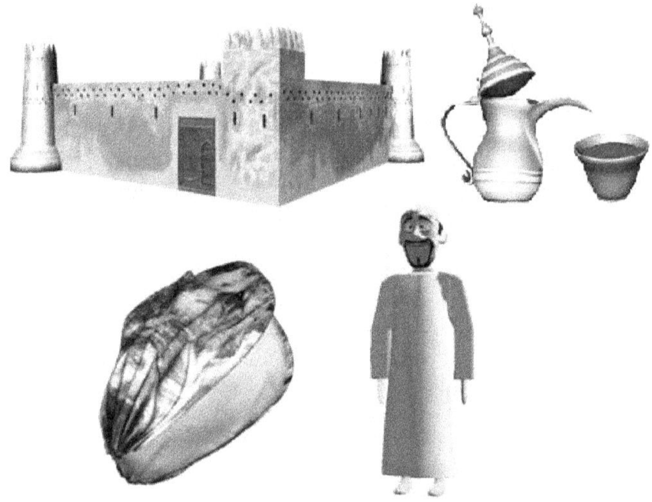

Figure 1. Examples of 3-D models

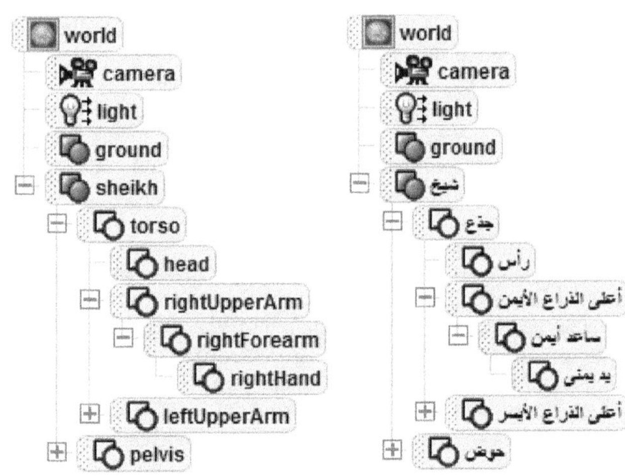

Figure 2. Body parts of the religious scholar from Figure 1 with Arabic translation

4.3 Curriculum and instructional material

Although feedback from the advisory board was vital to the design of curriculum and instructional material, any teaching material developed without collaboration with ICT teachers would be inadequate. We approached different private and public schools to work with us on developing and pilot testing Alice-based computational curriculum in their schools. We learned that schools are very skeptical in adapting new technology for reasons that we had not anticipated. We can imagine that schools and teachers are concerned about the educational well-being of the students, so new and unproven curriculum would be undesirable for them. That was not the biggest concern for the schools as they realize that the existing curriculum being used is obsolete and useless. Our main obstacle was their skepticism of our motives. The region in general and Qatar in specific is financially affluent and different organizations and companies are actively trying to sell their products to the local entities. Microsoft's efforts to introduce their MS products based International Computers Driver's License (ICDL) [21] in local schools systems, is example of one of such efforts. Schools have found that these organizations sell them curricula and products that "promise the world" to them and end up being useless in classrooms. The biggest hurdle we had to cross was to convince the concerned parties that we are educationalists and are working on this project to promote computing education and not for financial gains.

The second lesson we learned was that in public schools, teachers have no power and they are told what to teach and how to teach it from the Ministry of Education (Supreme Education Council or SEC). The curricular material is developed by the SEC and then implemented in each school. We decided to take advantage of this situation by influencing the professionals at the SEC. Convincing the experts at that level about the effectiveness of Alice in teaching computing seemed the most prudent way of gaining access to the public schools. Well-prepared presentations showing the results of previous formal studies were the key to success.

We created the curriculum in collaboration with one private school and the Supreme Education Council. Creating artifacts in isolation and expecting the educational systems to adopt them is recipe for disaster [22]. Working with the two school systems, we learned that current ICT and computing curriculum is based on step-by-step instructions that students are expected to follow and reproduce. There is a lack of stress on student learning, creativity, and application. Even courses in Visual Basic walk the students through step-by-step instructions on how to create a calculator application. At end of the term, students are able to create their own calculator application from scratch using these directions. Curriculum that is based on student creativity and thinking is considered difficult for students and hence undesirable.

A considerable segment of education system is realizing this shortcoming and there seems to be a desire to fix these problems. Any education reformer should be able to make a big difference in the quality of education in the Middle East, as long as they are mindful of the local cultures and customs.

4.3.1 Curriculum development and pilot testing

The first artifact that we created was a weekly breakdown of computing topics. The academic year plan consisted of following topics:

- Introduction to Alice, getting started, and installation
- Storyboarding and procedural decomposition
- Learning to use the Alice IDE
- Creating objects and using object properties and methods
- Creating animations using sequential execution
- Creating animations using concurrent execution
- Using sounds and camera in animations
- Using conditional execution for more complex animations
- Using loops in animations for repetitive tasks
- Functional decomposition and implementation
- Event driven programming for games

As we mentioned earlier, one of the challenges for introducing a new curriculum is the lack of resources in the medium of instructions at the schools – which happened to be Arabic in our case. We had to create Arabic version of all our curricular materials including writing a textbook for the students. In the absence of these resources, any adaptation or change become hard.

During the evaluation of the pilot testing of our curriculum, we visited schools and attended classes to get first-hand impressions of the progress. We realized that it is not enough to use the Arabic curriculum without modifying the language of the tool. The Alice software is still in English and it imposes a cognitive overload on students. For example, if we want the students to move a camel, all body parts of the camel like "frontleftleg", "frontrightleg", "backleftleg", etc. are in English. Its takes a lot of effort for students to determine each item's name. As part of our summative phase of the project, we are working on translating the models to Arabic. An initial sample translation is shown in figure 2.

4.4 Pilot workshops

Most ICT teachers in Qatar, both in public and private schools, are trained ICT professionals. At the same time, most of these teachers are not familiar with program visualization tools such as Alice and have not taught fundamental programming concepts in their classes. As a result, the need for professional development workshops is urgent. We have conducted several workshops for teachers to help them use Alice during the pilot study of the curriculum. Teachers usually attend two workshops, where each workshop lasting three days. In the first workshop we cover topics on how to use Alice. After the workshop, we let teachers use Alice over a couple of months to give them a chance to learn Alice, its features and capabilities. Following this first workshop, we offer a second workshop where we discuss topics and techniques that allow the teachers to understand how to teach computing and problem solving techniques using Alice.

5. RESULTS

We conducted a pilot test of the curriculum, instructional materials, and the new 3-D models in the Alice gallery for middle school students in one private English school and two public Arabic schools. The pilot test involved more than 400 students in the three schools combined. Once the students were familiar with the tool and had used several different 3-D models, we conducted a survey to obtain initial feedback regarding the 3D models from the Middle East gallery (students have access to all models that are part of Alice's core gallery). We asked students to indicate the 3-D models they liked best in the Middle East-themed gallery as well as asking them for ideas of models they would like to see in the gallery. The results of the survey drove our efforts in creating new 3-D models. Through the student surveys, we observed that props and objects that students used in everyday life were very popular when it came to using models in Alice.

In addition to student surveys, we interviewed teachers and school administrators at the participating schools. The teachers requested the curriculum be expanded to provide instructional material for a two-year program. In addition, the school administrators want to use Alice as part of their plan to implement the National Curriculum of England for computing programs of study [12].

One of the most important skills that is essential for building the future generation is critical thinking. Although, we are currently only looking at the acceptability of the newly created 3-D models and usability of our curriculum and instructional material, we are still curious about the effectiveness of this curriculum in teaching computational thinking. Although studying these effects are the focus of the summative phase of our project, the initial results are very encouraging. The teacher in the private school administered a quiz to the students from different levels in her school. The quiz was designed to measure the problem solving skills. The results showed an impressive change in the skill set the students presented. Several questions were designed to measure the critical thinking skill in problem solving without any reference to Alice. Around 76% of the students in grade 7 who studied Alice-based curriculum answered the questions correctly, while only 67.6% of the students from grade 9 answered them correctly. We hope that this result is directly related to the students' experience with Alice, as it works on making the students think about the problem from different perspectives. We acknowledge that still more formal work needs to be done in order to support our hypothesis.

6. NEXT STEPS AND FUTURE WORK

The next steps in the Alice ME project include updates and expansions to the first draft of instructional materials for middle school teachers and students. The updates will include changes to example problems as well as an increased number of examples, tutorials, and videos. In response to teachers and school administrator feedback, we are currently mapping the Alice middle school curriculum to the National Curriculum of England, specifically for Key Stage 3 [17]. The Alice middle school curriculum will be expanded to provide content for a two-year program, where the classes meet twice a week.

With these steps completed, formal testing will ensue and results will be collected and analyzed. As a result of pilot tests during the formative phase, the SEC has agreed to use Alice in six schools for the upcoming academic year. The formal testing at these schools will include conducting pre- and post- tests for students in schools using Alice and then comparing them with schools that are not.

If the summative testing yields successful results, we plan to make Alice ME and the middle school curriculum and instructional materials available to educators in other Middle Eastern countries, such as Jordan, Kuwait, Bahrain, Saudi Arabia, and Egypt.

7. ACKNOWLEDGMENTS

This paper was made possible by NPRP grant # 5-1070-2-451 from the Qatar National Research Fund (a member of Qatar Foundation). The statements made herein are solely the responsibility of the author[s].

8. REFERENCES

[1] Alice 2 instructional materials. Online. Retrieved 9/2/2014 from http://www.aliceprogramming.net

[2] Cooper, S., Dann, W., & Pausch, R. 2003. Teaching objects first in introductory computer science. *Proceedings of the 34th SIGCSE technical symposium on Computer science education* (Reno, Nevada, USA). ACM Press.

[3] Dann, W., Cooper, S., & Pausch, R. 2000. Making the connection: programming with animated small worlds. In *Proceedings of the 5th annual conference on Innovation and Technology in Computer Science Education* (Helsinki, Finland), 41-44.

[4] Dann, W., Dragon, T., Cooper, S., Dietzler, K., Ryan, K., & Pausch, R. 2003. Objects: Visualization of behavior and state. *Proceedings of the 8th annual conference on innovation and technology in computer science education* (Thessaloniki, Greece), 84-88.

[5] Dann, W. P., Cooper, S., & Pausch, R. 2005. Learning to program with Alice. Prentice-Hall: Upper Saddle River, NJ.

[6] Greenwood, C., Horton, B., & Utley, C. 2002. Academic engagement: Current perspectives on research and practice. *School Psychology Review, 31*, 328–349.

[7] Kelleher, C. and Pausch, R. 2006. Lessons Learned from Designing a Programming System to Support Middle School Girls Creating Animated Stories. VL/HCC 2006, 165-172.

[8] Marks, H. 2000. Student engagement in instructional activity: Patterns in elementary, middle and high school years. *American Educational Research Journal, 37*,153–184.

[9] Moskal, B., Lurie, D., & Cooper, S. 2004. Evaluating the effectiveness of a new instructional approach. *Proceedings of the 35th SIGCSE technical symposium on Computer Science Education.* (Norfolk, Virginia).

[10] Mullins, P., Whitfield, D., and Conlon, M. 2008. Using Alice2.0 as a first language. *Journal of Computer Science in Colleges,* 24(3), 136-143.

[11] Papert, Seymour. 1980. Children, Computers, and Powerful Ideas. Basic Books: New York.

[12] Pattis, Richard E. 1981. Karel the Robot: A Gentle Introduction to the Art of Programming, John Wiley & Sons.

[13] Pausch, R. (head), Burnette, T., Capeheart, A.C., Conway, M., Cosgrove, D., DeLine, R., Durbin, J., Gossweiter, R., Koga, S., White, J. 1995. Alice: rapid prototyping system for virtual reality, *IEEE Computer Graphics and Applications*.

[14] Pierce, J. S., Christiansen, K., Cosgrove, D., Conway, M., Moskowitz, D., Stearns, B., et al.1998. Alice: Easy to learn interactive 3d graphics, *CHI 98 conference summary on* Human factors in computing systems. (Los Angeles, CA).

[15] Qatar, G. S. D. P. "Qatar National Vision 2030." *Doha, General Secretariat for Development* (2008).

[16] Rodger, S. Duke Adventures in Alice Programming, Online at: http://www.cs.duke.edu/csed/alice/ Accessed 9/3/2014.

[17] National Curriculum in England for Computing. Online at: https://www.gov.uk/government/publications/national-curriculum-in-england-computing-programmes-of-study. Accessed 9/3/2014.

[18] Slavin, R. 2003. Educational psychology: Theory and practice. Boston: Pearson Education.

[19] Kirk, D. 2014. The "Singapore of the Middle East": The Role and Attractiveness of the Singapore Model and TIMSS on Education Policy and Borrowing in the Kingdom of Bahrain. *Education for a Knowledge Society in Arabian Gulf Countries,* (London: Emerald), 127–150

[20] Kirk, D. 2008. Local voices, global issues: A comparative study of the perceptions student teachers hold in relation to their pre-service training in the United States of America, United Kingdom and United Arab Emirates. Ph.D. dissertation, University of Georgia, Athens, GA.

[21] ICDL - International Computer Driver's License. Online. Retrieved 9/2/2014 from http://www.ecdl.org/programmes/ecdl_icdl

[22] Kirk, D. Innovate or Replicate? Education Reform Initiatives in the Gulf Cooperation Council States. *The Muslim World* 105.1 (2015): 78-92

Piloting Computer Science Education Week in Mexico

Nora A. Escherle
School of Education
University of Applied Sciences
Northwestern Switzerland (FHNW)
Windisch, Switzerland
nora.escherle@fhnw.ch

Silvia I. Ramirez-Ramirez
Department of Computer Sciences
Tecnológico de Monterrey - Campus Monterrey
Monterrey, Mexico
iliana.ramirez@itesm.mx

Ashok R. Basawapatna*
Department of Mathematics, Computer & Information Science
SUNY, Old Westbury
Old Westbury, NY 11568
basawapatnaa@oldwestbury.edu

Dorit Assaf
School of Education
University of Applied Sciences
Northwestern Switzerland (FHNW)
Windisch, Switzerland
dorit.assaf@fhnw.ch

Alexander Repenning[§]
School of Education
University of Applied Sciences,
Northwestern Switzerland (FHNW)
Windisch, Switzerland
alexander.repenning@fhnw.ch

Carmine Maiello
School of Education
University of Applied Sciences
Northwestern Switzerland (FHNW)
Windisch, Switzerland
carmine.maiello@fhnw.ch

Yasko Ch. Endo
Department of Computer Science
University of Colorado – Boulder
Boulder, CO 8030
yasko.endo@colorado.edu

Juan A. Nolazco-Florez
Department of Computer Sciences
Tecnológico de Monterrey
Monterrey, Mexico
jnolazco@itesm.mx

ABSTRACT

programming tools embedded with tutorials, report large participation numbers. However, to truly broaden participation, activities need to be made accessible in international contexts. In 2014, Tecnológico de Monterrey and Instituto de Innovación y Transferencia de Tecnología de Nuevo León, modified the Scalable Game Design CS Ed Week activity to include a Mexican feasibility pilot study. The goal of the pilot was to broaden participation in Computer Science in Mexico by creating interest and demand in further activities, including launching of 2015 Mexico CS Ed Week. This paper reviews the initial results of this 2014 pilot, including the discussion of the unique challenges faced in this context, and examines efforts to make this activity more accessible and successful. In addition to pilot data highlighting future activity improvements, initial retention results show that despite challenges, Mexican students were able to effectively use the modified activity to create games on par with U.S. students.

Keywords

Broadening Participation; Computer Science Education; International Research; Computer Science Education in Mexico; Computer Science Education Week; Experience Report; Globalization of Programming Activities.

1. INTRODUCTION

Thanks to many reforms and initiatives in the sector of education, Mexico achieved a school enrollment of 94% of all children

[1*]Additionally affiliated to the Dept. of CS, Univ. of Colorado - Boulder

[§]Additionally affiliated to the School of Education, FHNW

SIGCSE '16, March 2–5, 2016, Memphis, TN, USA

DOI: http://dx.doi.org/10.1145/2839509.2844598

Computer Science Education Week activities, featuring online

between age 6 and 14 by 2010. However, according to the 2012 OCDE Education Report on Mexico, drop out rates are alarmingly high [14]. The transition to high school and further education shows a dropout rate of 43% for students between 15 and 19 [5]. Among the reasons to drop out school are poverty, ethnic inequality and gender. Dropout rates are far higher than in the United States, where in 2013 an average of 6.8% of all students dropout of high school before graduation [12].

Regarding students' access to ICT (Information and Communication Technologies) and the status of computer science education in Mexico, numbers are even worse. According to Martínez (2012), only 42.3% of the public schools at the elementary level have been equipped with computers, while only 18% have access to the Internet [10]. Again, this is in stark contrast to 97% of USA's public elementary schools having Internet connectivity at some level [11]. Furthermore, in Mexico the educative resources are not evenly distributed among schools, as the OCDE's quality index evidence shows Mexico to have the largest variances [14].

For several years now, many initiatives and reforms have been undertaken to improve the education system in Mexico [20]. An essential part of these envisioned improvements are efforts to effect the massive integration of ICT into basic education [19] because increased digital literacy and guaranteed access to ICT are considered vital to students' education and future careers. In order to effect these improvements in the field of ICT, educational reforms and programs have been launched by the state government and by institutions like universities and non-governmental organizations. A main goal of programs such as Enciclomedia or Digital Abilities for Everyone (known in Spanish as HDT) was to mitigate the gross lack in technology infrastructure and equip schools with computers and software. Enciclomedia began to distribute computers to public schools from 1st to 9th grade in 2004 [20]. The program was interrupted, however, when some studies showed that the technology by itself did not improve education [10, 19]. Governmental programs aiming at the dissemination and integration of ICT while improving the educational and social conditions include-Mexico, ProNap online (a website to keep teachers updated), Red Escolar (a school network of educational computer science), and EduSat (education through television, based on satellite technology) [18, 20].

Importantly, the efforts in Mexico to implement the national ICT education objectives resulted in the creation of a new curriculum [21] that is based on the ISTE NETS standards [5], also used in many schools in the U.S., and includes the transversal teaching of ICT both on elementary and secondary school levels. Those standards strive to develop skills in six fields, including those of "Creativity and Innovation" and "Critical thinking, problem solving and decision taking" [21]. In these two fields, computer science activities are particularly relevant for student skills development. According to the Educational Studies Center, however, the new curriculum does not translate into specific activities enabling transversality and the actual development of abilities [19]. This major shortcoming and the many remaining challenges as yet unsolved by existing programs result in the ongoing demand for computer science education activities that can be integrated into school curricula in order to develop high level abilities in the above mentioned fields. The pedagogical ideas and classroom activities of the U.S. Scalable Game Design project were considered promising candidates for meeting these demands because they are aligned with the ISTE NETS standards and have an established track record regarding their integration in school curricula [16].

Scalable Game Design (SGD) has successfully broadened computer science participation in the United States through engaging teachers and students in game and simulation design [16]. This research builds upon previous SGD work on engaging students in computers science education with reference to cyberlearning [15] and computational thinking [23]. This engagement is based on a theory entitled the Zones of Proximal Flow [2]. This theory combines Vygotsky's Zone of Proximal Development [22] with Csíkszentmihályi's theories on Flow [3] and is aimed at keeping students motivated through simulation and game design. Part of this strategy includes providing tools for cyberlearning, online programming environments, real time classroom management [1], implementation and evaluation of computational thinking [16], teacher professional development [16], and providing resources supporting low threshold/high ceiling curricula [2, 7]. So far, the SGD project has helped over 20,000 students in the U.S. create their first games and simulations [16]. Furthermore, SGD successfully launched the Swiss Computer Science Education Week (CS Ed Week) activity in 2014 [4, 17], extending its scope to Europe.

The acknowledgement of SGD's track record of success in the US and beyond resulted in the SGD Mexico project, which is a partnership between the U.S. based SGD project on the one hand and Tecnológico de Monterrey (ITESM) and Instituto de Innovación y Transferencia de Tecnología de Nuevo León (I2T2). The aim of the 2015 SGD Mexico project is to help reinvent and invigorate computer science education in Nuevo León, Mexico, through innovative, engaging, and motivating game design programming and computational thinking activities proven to be effective through research. In 2015, SGD Mexico was awarded a Google RISE Partnership Award aimed at broadening participation in Computer Science and increasing access to Computer Science Education in Mexico. Due to the interest generated about SGD in Mexico, the team was also awarded research funds from the Mexican National Council on Science and Technology (CONACyT) to add a research data collection component to the activities, to measure student motivation and learning.

One of the goals of the SGD Mexico project was to launch CS Ed Week in Mexico with a small pilot in 2014 using an accessible online activity tailored to the needs of Mexican students. To this end, SGD Mexico, ITESM and I2T2 worked together to develop and test a pilot study, using a modified SGD CS Ed Week activity, in Nuevo León, Mexico, on December 7-13, 2014. This pilot was run in ITESM. The small-scale recruitment, conducted with the help of I2T2 and the Secretaría de Educación de Nuevo León, focused primarily on public schools. In the U.S., SGD has worked with hundreds of teachers and partnered with national organizations to advertise various activities. The infrastructure that exists in the U.S. to help broaden participation in computer science does not exist as deeply in Mexico. Professor Ramírez had to develop partnerships in order to recruit the greatest number of students possible. Many of the participating pilot teachers were computer science teachers that had worked with robotics programs in the past or had formerly collaborated with ITESM in coding activities, and were highly motivated to take part in this activity. Post pilot implementation in 2015 will have a larger scale recruitment strategy that in part will include a marketing, radio and social network campaign as well as recruitment from not just public schools but also direct recruitment from private schools.

The principal aim of the Mexican pilot, conducted in parallel to the full-scale 2014 U.S. and Swiss SGD CS Ed Week activities, was to get a baseline idea of the challenges that need to be overcome for a full-scale 2015 Mexican CS Ed Week rollout. Hopefully, the project challenges identified, and new strategies and resources developed, will help broaden participation in Mexico, and can be applied to broaden participation in similar international contexts and even feedback into the U.S. For example, it has been reported that English Language Learners are one of the most underrepresented groups in the U.S. in CS and STEM fields [13]. It is our hope that the multilingual resources developed for Mexico and Switzerland can transfer back to the U.S. and be integrated into a cohesive strategy helping to motivate second language learners in computer science.

Generally, CS Ed Week activities are highly scaffolded online introductions to programming. They are advertised as self-guided, with embedded tutorials [9]. The model is equivalent to providing a link to a webpage and hoping that the activity scaffolding will be sufficient to keep students engaged. However, in international contexts more thought must go into tailoring the activity for the intended target. Assumptions pertaining to the languages students understand and technology schools have access to might not be valid [8]. The international challenge for CS Ed Week activities is, in addition to motivating student-interest in computer science, that they must first be well matched to students' and teachers' environments and abilities. Although the SGD CS Ed Week activity is self-contained, novice teachers have to be supported in doing it, for example, in case something went wrong with student projects. In 2014, professors from the Mexican project attended the annual SGD Summer Institute professional development in the U.S. These professors, alongside CS student volunteers of ITESM, were present for the hour-long pilots in Monterrey public schools. Furthermore, the organizers launched a SGD Mexico website offering online support including classroom materials.[2]

[2] http://www.csedweek.mx/

Figure 1. Scalable Game Design AgentCubes Online CS Ed Week Activity.

The idea was to provide Mexican participants with online resources such as tutorials and lesson plans, which are well established in the U.S. SGD project. Some of these electronic materials were already available during the pilots.

The aim of this Mexican CS Ed Week pilot was to identify major challenges in Nuevo León and prepare the activity for a full rollout in 2015. The hypothesis, based on discussions with our contacts in Mexico, is that resource constraints at some of the schools, especially regarding technology limitations, could result in issues that negatively affect student activity retention. The research question investigated is what are the specific factors that might affect this retention. Subsequent sections will first describe the SGD CS Ed Week activity, then outline the primary challenges in modifying the activity for Mexico, and then present initial activity retention results along with a brief discussion.

2. The 3D FROGGER ACTIVITY

The Scalable Game Design CS Ed Week activity is an HTML5 browser based exercise wherein users program a 3D-Frogger game inspired by the 80's classic arcade game Frogger in AgentCubes Online.[3] The positive motivational aspects of the Frogger activity have already been established on the basis of experiences reported by thousands of students [16]. AgentCubes Online is a browser based visual programming tool that enables users to build their own games and simulations. The tool implements the pedagogical approach of a strong correlation between student motivation resulting from the experience of ownership and the opportunity of being creative on the one hand and learning progress on the other hand [16]. Students can create their own individual 3D-characters called "Agents" from scratch with the built-in graphics editor and select their self-made characters listed in the "Agent Gallery" (Fig. 1, label 1) to design their own virtual 3D-worlds. Users create in-game interactions between the characters by composing character behavior rules. These rules consist of programming blocks from the "Conditions"-palette (Fig. 1, label 2) and the "Actions"-palette (Fig. 1, label 3), which are assembled in the "Behavior Editor" (Fig. 1, label 4) by drag-and-drop programming. Apart from the syntactic support provided by drag-and-drop programming, the tool also offers semantic support through conversational programming, which uses graphic annotations to visualize what the program will do at any given stage and thereby facilitates the debugging of faulty code. Equipping AgentCubes Online with an embedded video tutorial in English, Spanish, German, Italian, and French (Fig. 1, label 5), the CS Ed Week activity enables students to build a complete 3D-Frogger game guided by the tutorial's step-by-step verbal and visual instructions. The video itself is supplemented by an interactive table of its contents consisting of indexed links allowing students to (re-)access instructions for each single programming step (Fig. 1, label 6). Students who follow the video tutorial will complete similar 3D-Frogger games consisting of identical rules. Figure 1 is a screenshot of this activity when the student has programmed the frog-truck collision and the tutorial shows how to switch to first-person view.

After the activity, students are not only able to play their own games and share them with others but are also given a link to their games, which allows them to return whenever they want to modify their games. (In the context of the Google RISE Partnership Award, the Mexican pilot's participants were granted AgentCubes Online licenses for one year). Hypothetically, students could return to their games at any point in time after the activity introduction to make modifications.

Conducting the CS Ed Week Mexican pilot consisted of adapting the activity to the Mexican context, which primarily involved addressing language and technology challenges. In terms of language, the whole activity had to be translated into Spanish since even Mexican students at the middle school level often have little fluency in English. The translated elements included the audio narration of the embedded video tutorial (Fig. 1, label 2) and the indexed video links allowing users to access specific instructions on how to program a given interaction in Frogger (Fig. 1, label 3). Previous experiments, in German, looked at changing the conditions and actions, in Figure 1 labels 4 and 5, to students' native language. However, it was decided that to keep

---

[3] http://www.csedweek.us.

consistency between the visual language environments, the program would instead provide a tooltip in the native language (in this case Spanish) when the cursor hovers over a given condition or action. The hope was that these changes would allow the Mexican students to understand the embedded video instruction along with the environment, including the mechanics of game creation. In terms of technology, limited Internet access was anticipated to be the main issue. As mentioned before, only 18% of the public schools at primary and secondary level have access to the Internet [9]. These circumstances are quite disadvantageous for conducting a browser based programming activity. For those cases where Internet access was not available or the bandwidth was too limited for conducting the activity online, students had to use the English desktop version of AgentCubes and were provided with the video tutorial on a USB-stick or with printed instructions.

3. METHODOLOGY

To assess the overall efficacy of the activity and its adaptation for use in Mexico, we used participant retention as an evaluation instrument. Retention in this case meant how long a student remained with the activity before stopping. Every time a user modifies their program for a given agent in AgentCubes Online, by adding methods, rules, conditions, and actions, an XML file corresponding to that agent's programmed behaviors is modified on the server. Analyzing all the XML files corresponding to each agent allows for an operationalization of program length akin to a lines of code metric. The complete tutorial-guided 3D-Frogger activity consists of 215 lines of code in AgentCubes Online, which we calculate by analyzing the XML files. We surmise that by looking at retention data, conclusions can be drawn on the effectiveness of the video tutorial to relay the programming activity's instructions, as well as learn about factors that may lead to students discontinuing the activity. As explained above, the CS Ed Week 3D-Frogger video tutorial provides step-by-step instructions that lead to students building identical games with the same rules and lines of code. Each step of the programming taught by the tutorial directly correlates to a known and consistent set of lines of codes in student projects. Because of the direct relationship between the steps of taught by the tutorial and the actual lines of code that students create, a project's number of lines of code correlates directly to how far a student followed the tutorial and at what point in the tutorial he or she left the activity.

In past classroom SGD observations, students usually get to a program length of around 46 or 59 within an hour. In the CS Ed Week activity these two lengths correspond to the Frog moving in all four directions, at a program length of 46, and the win state of the game wherein the player wins if the frog jumps on a target at the end of the level, at a program length of 59.

4. RESULTS

Despite all these difficulties and some as yet unresolved challenges, the pilot was successfully launched. In total, 5 schools, 11 classes, and over 350 mainly middle-school students participated in the event, and every participating pilot teacher has already expressed interest in continuing participation with the 2015 activity. From those participating in the activity, we were able to gather and analyze both qualitative data, in the form of in-class observations and statements of participating students, and quantitative data, in the form of student retention through the activity. The data shows that the adaptation of the activity to the Mexican context had promising results. Qualitative data was gathered from all teachers and their students. However, due to some schools' lack of the required bandwidth of the Internet access, many students had to conduct the activity using the desktop version of AgentCubes. Therefore we only gathered and analyzed quantitative data in the form of XML files from those 109 students who could do the activity using AgentCubes Online. On the basis of these data, we employed retention as an instrument to assess the efficacy of the activity.

4.1 In-Class Observations

In-class observations from the Mexican CS Ed Week activity indicate that, despite of language and technology related challenges, students enjoyed the activity and wanted to continue. Teachers reported that students were very motivated and attentive while performing the activity. Some students commented that they should have more activities like this in their computer lab. At the end of the activity many students asked for the link so they could continue their work at a later time. The students seemed to prefer doing the activity by themselves or in pairs, which was found to be more efficient than following class instructions as a group. Finally, students worked at different rates; most students were able to work effectively for an hour.

Figure 2. A Girl drawing a Car "Agent" during the Mexican Pilot using the Desktop Version of AgentCubes and following Printed Out Instructions.

As anticipated, the main challenges encountered during the activity were related to language and technology. Regarding language students were confused when the narration of the video tutorial occasionally used Spanish words to refer to parts of the programming environment that are in English. Some students had to use English desktop version leading to more time between steps and greater dependence on the in-class support team.

Technology challenges were much more extensive. Bandwidth constraints limited many students from properly loading the embedded video tutorial in their browsers while doing the activity in AgentCubes online. Some schools maintained a single YouTube connection to screen the tutorial for all students. In case of even greater bandwidth limitations, students either received memory sticks containing the video tutorial or had to use written instructions. At two of the five schools bandwidth limitations were so dire that students could not even do the activity in AgentCubes online and had to use the software's desktop version instead. As mentioned before, from these students using the desktop version of AgentCubes, we could not gather quantitative retention data. In terms of hardware, some computers were outdated running Windows XP with 512 of RAM, which adversely affected students using the offline desktop version of AgentCubes. The main software issue was that some computers only had Internet Explorer installed. This caused an AgentCubes online error due to writing invalid XML (recommended browsers include Chrome, Firefox and Safari with WebGL enabled). Once the error was encountered students could not continue their project on AgentCubes online.

These observations and experiences of the pilot study are of great value because they identified the above challenges to the activity, which we can attempt to eliminate with the full-scale 2015 rollout. Examples could include well-prepared contingency plans if bandwidth issues are encountered, making sure computers have the correct software, and updating the activity narration.

4.2 Retention

The first-time data collected in the Mexican pilot resembles data collected in the 2014 CS Ed Week activities in the United States and Switzerland. Figure 4 shows the student retention through every program length in 3D-Frogger (maximum program length of 215) for the SGD CS Ed Week Activity in Mexico, the U.S. and Switzerland. We start at 100% at the program length of 1 and, as we increase, we lose students as their numbers drop off at each program length greater than 1. Estimating these points could show student deviation from student engagement. Figure 3 shows that the data from all three main participating countries in the activity, i.e. U.S., Switzerland (CH), and Mexico (MX), fit a negative exponential trend well.

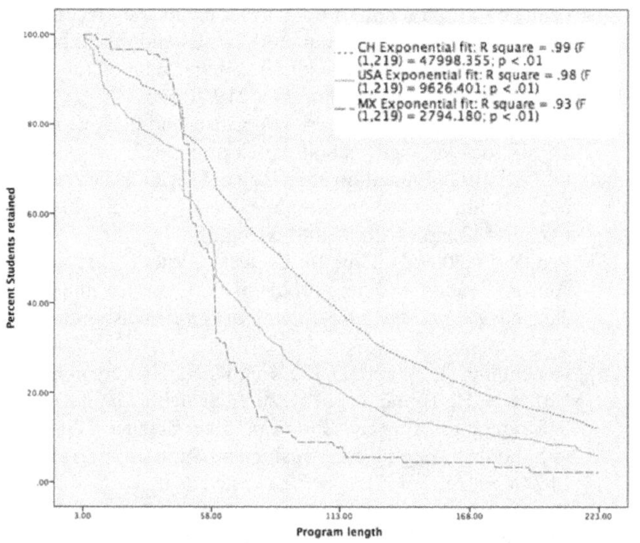

Figure 3. Percentage of Retained CS Ed Week Activity Students by Country.

The nature of student retention in all three countries followed the same general trend, regardless of language or environment. The negative exponential fit also implies that in every country the activity retained a higher percentage of students at each step as the activity went on. These results are promising for the Mexican pilot. Figure 4 depicts the mean program length of each country with associated error bars. According to ANOVA, countries differ with reference to the mean game complexity ($F(2,4768)=65.932$; $p<.01$). Post hoc tests (Scheffé) reveal that the only significant differences are between Switzerland (M=95.149) and the US (M=60.507) as well as between Switzerland and Mexico (M=50.890). No significant differences were found between the more established U.S. activity and the Mexican pilot. In general, the comparison between U.S., Mexico and Switzerland may primarily reflect shortcoming regarding hardware and bandwidth, which assumedly led to generally shorter program lengths. As shown by figure 3, clear points of inflection occur at program lengths of 45 and 59 independent of the country. In prior classroom observations, students creating 3D-Frogger got to a program length of about 46 to 59 in the first hour, the mean program length of around 50 for Mexican students, and 59 in the

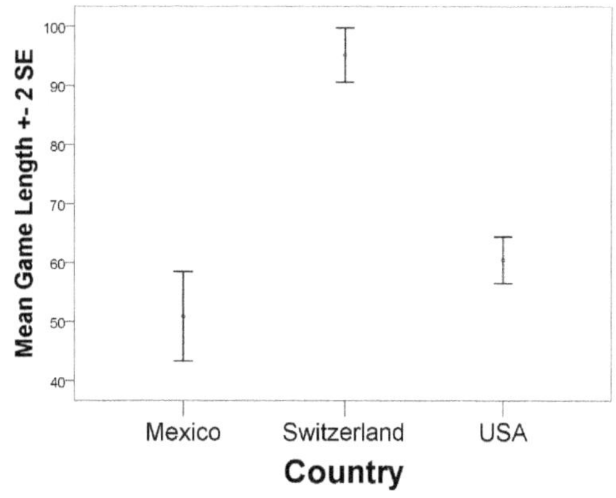

Figure 4. Mean Game Program Length by Country with Error Bars.

U.S students, is right within this expected range.

Despite the challenges encountered, students in the Mexican pilot study using the modified AgentCubes online activity performed on par with U.S. students. The Switzerland games produced were significantly longer than those of both Mexico and the U.S. in terms of lines of code.

5. DISCUSSION

As suggested by the mean game length with error bars, the retention in Mexico was not significantly different statistically from the retention in the U.S. However, the distribution of the Mexican retention is wider and includes more students creating only relatively small programs. In Figure 3, this can be seen in the relative low Mexican retention after the 59 lines of code point. The 59 lines of code point coincides with the "win state is detected" activity checkpoint, which most students reach after about one hour. This pronounced retention drop suggests that most of the participating schools only spent one hour. Similarly, the retention of students in the USA or Switzerland dropped less because they continued beyond one hour of coding in school or even at home. After one hour, students are encouraged to submit their games. When they do, they receive an email including a link to their game allowing them to continue working on the project. Due to their generally more limited computer access at home, however, Mexican students were far less likely to continue with their game projects than Swiss and U.S. students. The really high retention beyond the first hour in Switzerland may be due to the timing of the activity [4]. During CS Ed Week, many Swiss schools have so-called project weeks where teachers are free to dedicate multiple school sessions to special projects. Furthermore, the fact that games of Swiss students were significantly longer than those of U.S. and Mexican students could be due to additional support provided to the Swiss activity including a 10 hour a day phone-in help line and email support consisting of a staff of 3 full-time workers during CS Ed Week [4]. This might be something that could be extended to the Mexican and U.S. activities to better deal with technical issues that may come up during the activity.

In spite of the relatively low retention beyond one hour in Mexico, the number of students retained in the first hour is remarkably high, exceeding the Swiss and U.S. retention. This is difficult to explain because it appears to contradict anticipated impacts of infrastructure and language challenges. The Mexican, U.S., and Swiss retention need to be compared carefully as the number of participants in Mexico during the pilot was almost two orders of magnitudes smaller (n(Mexico) =109). The number of participants alone is not likely to have caused this effect but perhaps the nature of the project in Mexico still being in a pilot stage did. Possibly, pilot schools in Mexico were recruited more strategically, resulting in higher levels of commitment among teachers and students. The fact that ITESM computer science students were present during the activity to support both teachers and students may be another reason for the high number of retained students within the first hour. Additionally, the bandwidth problems discussed earlier resulted in some schools playing the tutorial video theater style in front of students. In contrast to each student playing the video at his or her own speed this lockstep approach may have resulted in high retention by making it difficult for student to drop out.

6. CONCLUSION

Despite Mexico being a developing country, with very little infiltration of Internet connectivity and computer science education into public schools, the pilot was able to broaden participation in computer science in Mexico. Additionally, the students produced games of similar complexity like those of the U.S. students using the AgentCubes Online activity, and teachers and students expressed interest in pursuing further activities in the future. The results of this pilot bode well for the upcoming Google RISE Partnership and full rollout of the 2015 Mexican CS Ed Week. The high level of the students' interest and engagement during the 2014 CS Ed Week pilot was a catalyst for an entire state to get excited about coding and to commit to the goal of giving all students in Mexico more access to CS activities. By including a more comprehensive teacher professional development, and the development of the program Chic@s Code, which is especially aimed at broadening Latina participation in computer science, we can build upon this pilot experience to motivate the greatest number of students possible, engaging Mexico in computer science through CS Ed Week and beyond.

7. ACKNOWLEDGMENTS

This work is supported by the Google K-12 Education Outreach Fund Tides Foundation (grant #TFR14-03105), the National Science Foundation (grants #1138526 and #1312129), and the Hasler Foundation. Any opinions, findings, and conclusions or recommendations expressed in this material are those of the authors and do not necessarily reflect the views of the NSF We thank the ITESM; the I2T2 de Nuevo León; and the Secretaría de Educación de Nuevo León for logisitic help; and the Instituto Tecnológico y de Estudios Superiores de Monterrey, Computer Science's student association, AgentSheets Inc., the Computational Thinking Foundation and CONACyT for funding.

8. REFERENCES

[1] Basawapatna, A. R., Repenning, A., and Koh, K. H. 2015. Closing The Cyberlearning Loop: Enabling Teachers To Formatively Assess Student Programming Projects. In *Proc. SIGCSE '15*, 12-17.

[2] Basawapatna, A. R., Repenning, et al., 2013. The Zones of Proximal Flow: Guiding Students through a Space of Computational Thinking Skills and Challenges. In *Proc. ICER '13*, 67-74.

[3] Csíkszentmihályi, M. 1977. *Beyond Boredom and Anxiety*. San Francisco: Jossey-Bass.

[4] Escherle, N. A., Assaf, D., Basawapatna, A. R., et al. 2015. Launching Swiss Computer Science Education Week. In *Proc. WIPSCE '15*, 11-16.

[5] Instituto Nacional de Estadística y Geografía (INEGI), 2015. Cuéntame: Población de México. http://cuentame.inegi.org.mx/poblacion/asistencia.aspx?tema=P.

[6] ISTE. 2015. ISTE Standards for Students. http://www.iste.org/standards/ISTE-standards/standards-for-students.

[7] Koh, K. H, Nickerson H., Basawapatna, A. R., and Repenning, A., 2014. Early Validation of Computational Thinking Pattern Analysis. *ACM* (June 2014). 213-218.

[8] Kraemer, K. L., Dedrick, J., and Sharma, P. 2009. One Laptop Per Child: Vision vs. Reality. In *Commun. ACM* 52, 6 (June 2009). 66-73.

[9] Kumar, D. 2014. Digital Playgrounds for Early Computing Education. In *ACM Inroads* 5, 1 (Mar. 2014). 20-21.

[10] Martínez, N. 2012. En escuelas de México, amplia brecha digital. *El Universal*, martes 4 de septiembre, 2012.

[11] National Center for Education Statistics (NCES). 2001. Internet Access in U.S. Public Schools and Classrooms: 1994-2000. http://nces.ed.gov/pubs2001/2001071.pdf.

[12] National Center for Education Statistics (NCES). 2014. Percentage of high school dropouts among persons 16 through 24 years old (status dropout rate), by sex and race/ethnicity: Selected years, 1960 through 2013. http://nces.ed.gov/programs/digest/d14/tables/dt14_219.70.asp.

[13] NSF Report. 2013. Women, Minorities, and Persons with Disabilities in Science and Engineering: 2013.

[14] OECD. 2012. Education at a Glance: OECD Indicators. Mexico. http://www.oecd.org/mexico/EAG2012%20-%20Country%20note%20-%20Mexico.pdf.

[15] Pea, R. D. 2007. A Time for Collective Intelligence and Action: Grand Challenge Problems for Cyberlearning. In *NSF Cyberinfrastructure Team Workshop*, Washington, D.C.

[16] Repenning, A., Webb, D. C., Koh, K. H., Nickerson H., Miller, S. B., Brand, C., et al. 2015. Scalable Game Design: A Strategy to Bring Systemic Computer Science Education to Schools through Game Design and Simulation Creation. In *TOCE '15*, 2. 1-31.

[17] Repenning, A., Assaf, D., Basawapatna, A.R., et al. 2016. The Retention of Flow. In *Proc. SIGCSE '16*.

[18] Romero, J. L. R. 2006. Las Tecnologías de la Información y la Comunicación en la Educación en Cuatro Países Latinoamericanos. In *Revista Mexicana De Investigación Educativa*, 11, 28. 61-90.

[19] Santiago, D. 2015. Dejan 28 mil escuela en NL. In *El Norte* Sunday August 23.

[20] Santibanez, L., Vernez, G. and Razquin, P. 2005. *Education in Mexico: Challenges and Opportunities*. Santa Monica, CA: RAND Corporation. http://www.rand.org/pubs/documented_briefings/DB480.html.

[21] Secretaría de Educación Pública (SEP). 2012. Reforma Integral de la Educación Básica. http://basica.sep.gob.mx/tiempocompleto/pdf/memorias2012/articulacion_educ_bas.pdf.

[22] Vygotsky, L.S. 1980. *Mind in Society: The Development of Higher Psychological Processes*. Harvard University Press.

[23] Wing, J. M. 2006. Computational Thinking. In *Commun. ACM* 49, 3. 33-35.

Testing Strategies for the Automated Grading of Student Programs

Chris Wilcox
Computer Science
Colorado State University
1873 Campus Delivery
Fort Collins, Colorado 80523
wilcox@cs.colostate.edu

ABSTRACT

Enrollments in introductory computer science courses are growing rapidly, thereby taxing scarce teaching resources and motivating the increased use of automated tools for program grading. Such tools commonly rely on regression testing methods from industry. However, the goals of automated grading differ from those of testing for software production. In academia, a primary motivation for testing is to provide timely and accurate feedback to students so that they can understand and fix defects in their programs. Testing strategies for program grading are therefore distinct from those of traditional software testing. This paper enumerates and describes a number of testing strategies that improve the quality of feedback for different types of programming assignments.

CCS Concepts

•Social and professional topics → Computing education; Student assessment;

Keywords

automated assessment; automated grading

1. INTRODUCTION

Automated grading addresses some of the logistical challenges posed by increasing enrollments in introductory computer science courses. More importantly, automated grading gives students immediate feedback on their programs, allowing them to make progress without an instructor or teaching assistant by their side. The use of automated grading is widespread and generally thought to be beneficial [1]. We make the further claim that the use of grading systems has become an economic necessity for many institutions.

During our paper presentation at SIGCSE 2015, we were able to survey attendees concerning their use of automated assessment. Because of the venue, our survey risks a bias in favor of committed users of automated grading. Even so, the results provide a first approximation of tool usage. Figure 1 shows a summary of the responses in which it appears that the majority of attendees that use automation often or extensively also use homegrown tools. Such a high usage of homegrown tools motivates the need to study and disseminate effective testing strategies.

Many papers have presented frameworks for automated grading, including Web-CAT [2], Marmoset [6], APOGEE [4], and Infandango [5]. More recently, commercial software has become available for online grading, including Vocareum, Zybooks, Turings Craft, and Pearson Revel. Such software is commonly based on regression testing, a technique widely used for quality control in industry. However, we maintain that the goals of program grading differ significantly from those of software production.

In previous work we find evidence that automated grading contributes to student achievement and frees up teaching resources for better uses [7]. This paper puts aside the question of pedagogical benefit, and focuses instead on the pragmatic concern of how to improve the feedback from automated grading, using a variety of strategies that have not to our knowledge previously appeared in the literature. These strategies allow instructors to tailor tests to a wide range of programming assignments.

The goal of regression testing as practiced in industry is to verify that code changes do not introduce new defects. Developers initially create a test suite, then they write software that can pass some or all of the tests. When the test suite is run, the results can be archived and checked for correctness. Test suites are then run periodically during further development (or maintenance) of the software to identify defects that may have been introduced.

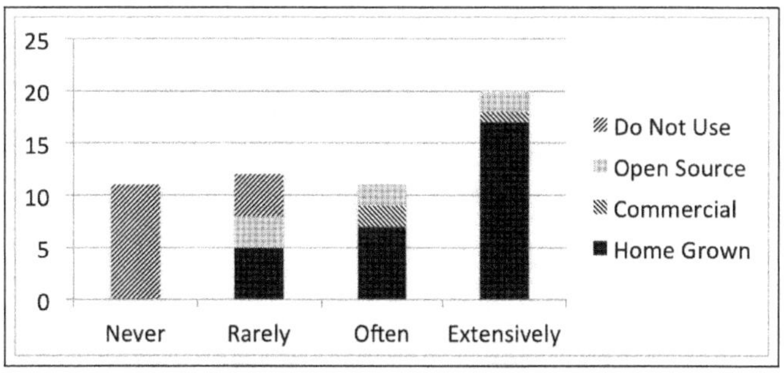

Figure 1: Automated Grading Survey Results.

SIGCSE '16, March 02-05, 2016, Memphis, TN, USA
© 2016 ACM. ISBN 978-1-4503-3685-7/16/03...$15.00
DOI: http://dx.doi.org/10.1145/2839509.2844616

Contrast this with the process for automatic grading of student programs, in which the instructor specifies an assignment, develops a solution, and creates a test suite. As with regression testing, test results from the solution are archived for use as an oracle. Student programs are submitted and tested by executing the test suite on them and comparing the outcome to the archived results. A mismatch with the oracle implies an error in the student program.

One of the key challenges of program grading is designing feedback to the student to help them understand defects in their program. We start this topic with an overview of grading frameworks (Section 2), followed by our central discussion of strategies for writing effective test programs (Section 3). We conclude with a discussion of several issues that arise in the context of grading frameworks (Section 4).

2. GRADING FRAMEWORKS

The key features of grading frameworks are 1) to provide feedback to the student about errors in their programs, 2) to automate the rote task of running student programs and scoring the results, and 3) to help instructors write effective test programs. Of equal importance, in our opinion, is a repository of test programs that can be leveraged for new assignments, thereby avoiding the necessity of developing unique test code for each assignment.

As with many institutions, we fulfill these requirements with a homegrown grading framework that provides a high degree of flexibility when developing test programs. The back-end of our framework is a set of shell scripts that automate the batch grading of student programs. A front-end web interface allows the instructor to offer real-time, interactive testing. The combination of script-based and web-based technologies is a third-generation system, as defined in the review of automated assessment by Douce [1]. Figure 2 shows the user interface and Figure 3 a block diagram of our grading system, which has previously been described [7].

Our automated tools rely on test scripts and program written by the instructor. These scripts specify test names, a scoring rubric, and a command for each test case. To support the range of testing strategies described in this paper, our grading framework allows the instructor to specify the entire Linux command line for each test case. A benefit of command line approach is that any programming language for which the platform has support can be tested. The command lines are executed in a Linux shell, and therefore can combine Linux commands and scripts, test programs, and any other software that runs in the Linux environment.

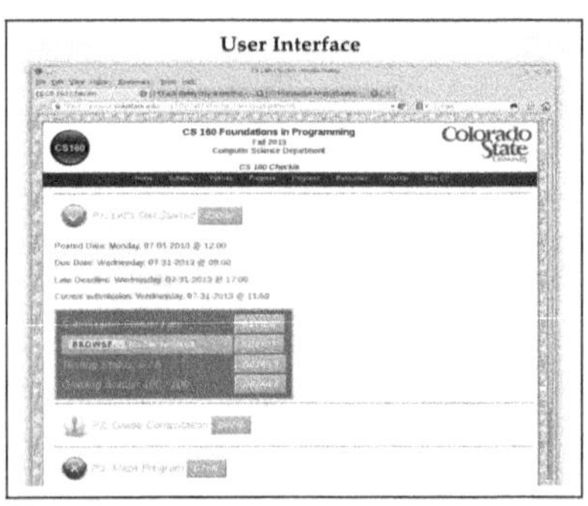

Figure 2: Automated Grading Interface.

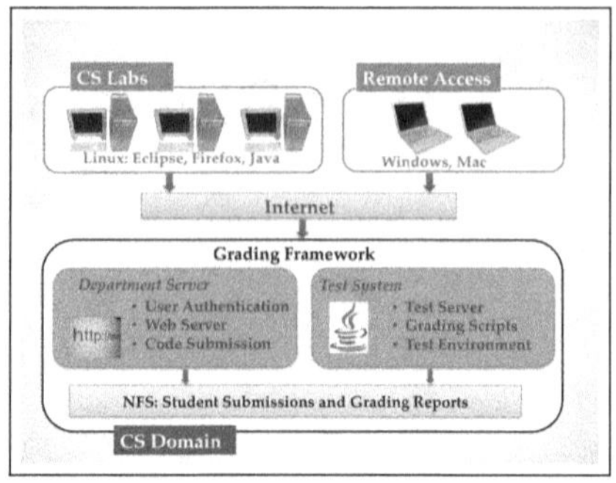

Figure 3: Automated Grading Framework.

3. TESTING STRATEGIES

In this section we focus on a number of strategies for the automated grading of student programs that have not to our knowledge been previously enumerated in the literature. These depend on a robust and flexible automated grading framework. To handle diverse assignments we employ eight strategies, listed below by increasing complexity.

3.1 Output Comparison

Output Comparison is similar to regression testing as practiced in industry. The strategy compares textual output from student programs to an oracle created from a correct solution to the assignment. Output can be captured from the standard output or error streams, and our framework allows the instructor to select a subset of the output lines to be compared. Our tests can restrict the capture to the granularity of a method call, using a Java feature that allows redirection of console streams.

To implement the strategy, our framework compiles and runs the student program, compares the resulting output to the oracle, and produces a grading report. The report contains comparison results, test scores, and compiler errors and warnings from the student code. Figure 4 shows a comparison in which the student submitted a program with a spelling error, a wrong answer, and extra output.

Frameworks assign scores based on the extent to which the student's output matches that of the oracle. A direct comparison is inflexible about capitalization and spelling errors and minor white space differences. For this reason, some frameworks allow customization of the comparison tool, which can be as rudimentary as a call to the Linux *diff* command, or can incorporate more advanced features such as color coding. Output comparison is primarily for console programs, and does not support feedback beyond direct program output. However, no separate test program needs to be written to use this strategy. Figure 5 shows a block diagram of the output comparison strategy.

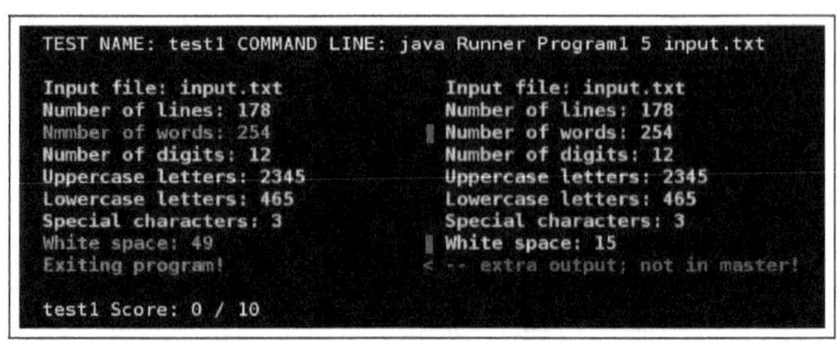

Figure 4: Test Results from Output Comparison.

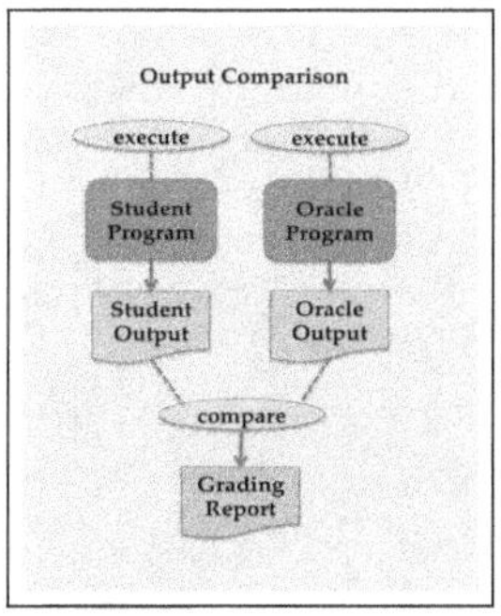

Figure 5: Output Comparison Strategy.

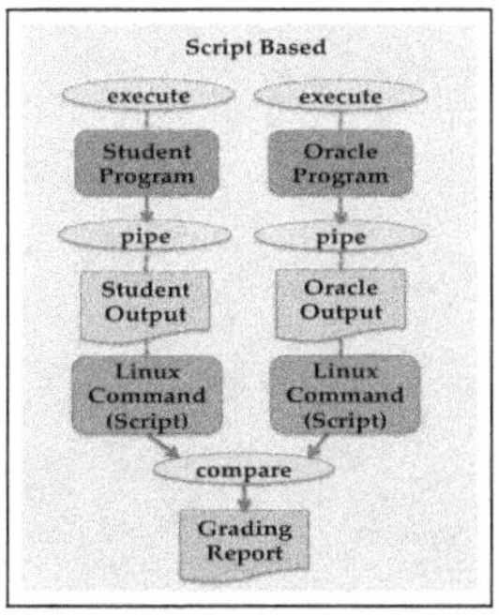

Figure 6: Script Based Strategy.

3.2 Script Based

Script Based testing extends the previous strategy by letting instructors specify a command line for each test, thereby introducing the use of Linux commands, scripts, redirection, pipes, and other shell programming features. We commonly pipe the textual output of student programs to Linux commands such as *grep*, *awk*, and *sed*, and we introduce custom shell scripts into the command line to post-process program output, which allows us to filter, sort, and otherwise interpret student results.

For example, a test case can use the Linux commands *sort* to sort, *grep* to filter, and *head* or *tail* to select output. Figure 6 shows a block diagram of script based testing in which the program output is piped to a single Linux command. However, the command line can invoke an unlimited number of commands and scripts, thus making the technique more powerful. Additional feedback can be incorporated by echoing text into the output stream.

3.3 Output Analysis

Output Analysis allows us to add custom test programs to the Linux command line to further analyze or post-process the output of the student program. We do not include in this strategy test programs that instantiate student classes or execute student programs as child processes. Such programs are described in subsequent sections. To implement output analysis, the test script pipes the student output to the test program, which then produces output for the comparison. As with the previous strategy, the instructor can incorporate Linux commands and scripts or other third-party software to help with the desired analysis.

An advantage of this approach is that instructors can write more sophisticated test programs than can be easily encapsulated into a Linux script. Test programs can be written in any language to verify student programs in any other language. For example, the instructor can write a Perl or Python script to evaluate Java, C, or C++ programs. Specifying test scripts as a set of Linux command lines has the additional benefit of removing any restriction on the programming language used to write test code. Additional feedback can be inserted at any point by the test program to further explain the test results to the student.

Furthermore, the test program can do more than simply manipulate the program output. It can interpret the output and derive its own conclusions about the behavior of the student program. For example, a test program can implement fuzzy comparison of floating-point values when grading programs where the numerical accuracy is not strictly specified, thus allowing a range of student solutions to be accepted as correct. Test programs can also measure and evaluate the performance characteristics of the student program for performance testing. Figure 7 shows a block diagram of the output analysis strategy.

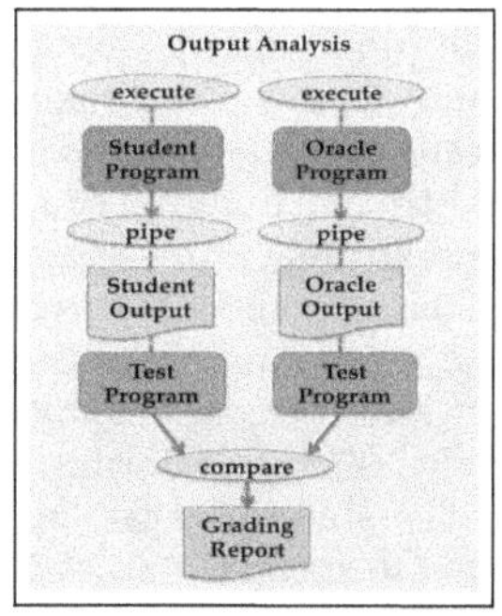

Figure 7: Output Analysis Strategy.

3.4 Stream Control

Stream Control is a strategy for console programs that interleave input and output streams. The test output for such programs combines program output, including prompts, and program input. Ideally, these should appear in the same order that the user would see if they ran the program interactively. This is problematic in the batch environment where input data is redirected from a file to simulate the user typing, since without special handling the input stream will not be echoed to the output stream. Many grading frameworks and online tutorials avoid this problem by displaying separate windows for input and output.

Figure 8 shows test results where the input and output have been ordered correctly using stream control. The assignment from which these results were generated prompts for income data and reads the data with a Java scanner, performs a tax calculation, and outputs results. A capitalization error has caused a failure, which is color coded for easy recognition, and the user input for this example is redirected from a file. By interleaving prompts, input, and output, the feedback to the student is more like what they would see when running the program.

Our solution for stream control is implemented in a test program called Runner that handles a variety console-based programs, regardless of the number of inputs or content of the prompts. Runner executes the student program within a child process, then spins up threads to process the program's input and output. The output handler continually reads and prints output from a buffered reader attached to the output stream of the student program. The input handler intercepts the input stream and detects when the program is waiting for input. It then feeds the inputs to the program and echoes them to the output stream. Figure 9 shows a block diagram of the stream control strategy.

The primary technical challenge for stream control is to reliably detect when a program or process is waiting on input. We have now developed two solutions, both of which are dependent on the Linux platform. The first is a Perl script that queries the state of the Linux process, and the second uses Java code to snoop the stack trace of the student program during execution. The latter is embedded in the source code for Runner. Runner also has a timeout thread to terminate student programs that enter infinite loops or expect the wrong number of inputs, based on an amount of time specified by the instructor. The termination problem is discussed in more detail in Section 4.

3.5 Object Instantiation

Object Instantiation is implemented through test programs that directly instantiate student classes in order to verify their implementation through method calls and member accesses. This approach models unit testing, which we believe is an important concept for students. Instantiation can additionally support module testing by verifying the interactions between methods and state. To implement an instantiation test, the instructor must customize test code for each method call or member access.

The main method in the student code is not usually tested via instantiation, however this is technically possible. Some instructors require the students to write test code for their class in main, and such test code is easily verified within our framework. A limitation of the strategy is that students must specify all of the methods with correct parameters (in order), return types, and attributes, otherwise the compile will fail and the student will receive a zero on the assignment. If the program does compile, then detailed feedback can be provided on the functionality of the student program.

A workaround for the compile problem is to require students to implement an interface in their classes. This forces students to correctly specify methods to allow their programs to compile. Another solution is to use Java reflection, which is discussed as a separate strategy. Figure 10 shows a block diagram of the object instantiation strategy.

3.6 Instrumentation

Instrumentation is a strategy that is useful when classes are supplied to the student as part of the assignment. The basic idea is to ignore the output of the student program, and embed test code into the supplied classes instead. For example, we often introduce graphical user interface (GUI) into assignments in our introductory courses. Students at this level are not usually advanced enough to program GUI applications, but students find assignments that incorporate user interface to be compelling.

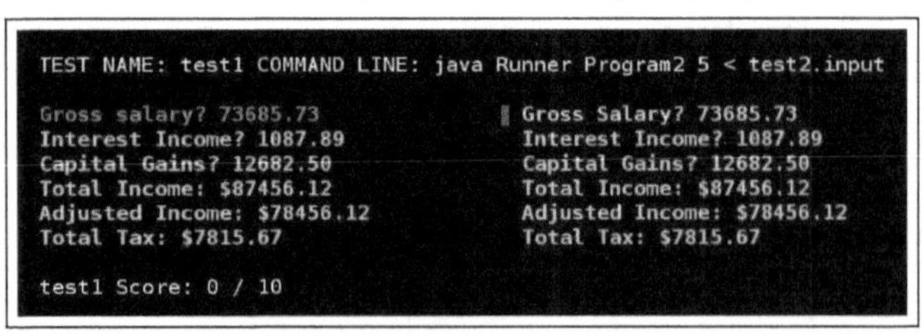

Figure 8: Test Results from Stream Control.

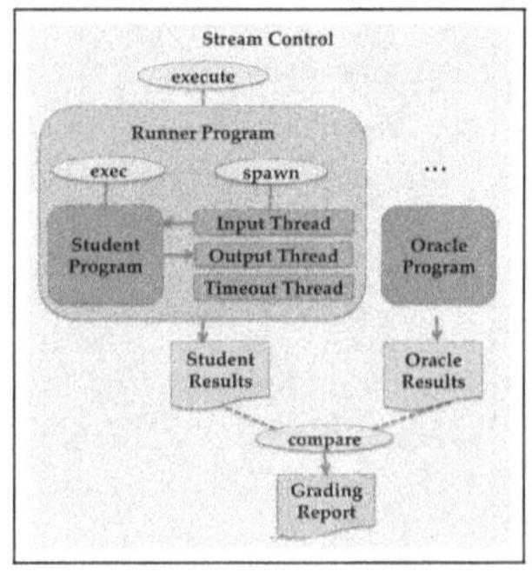

Figure 9: Stream Control Strategy.

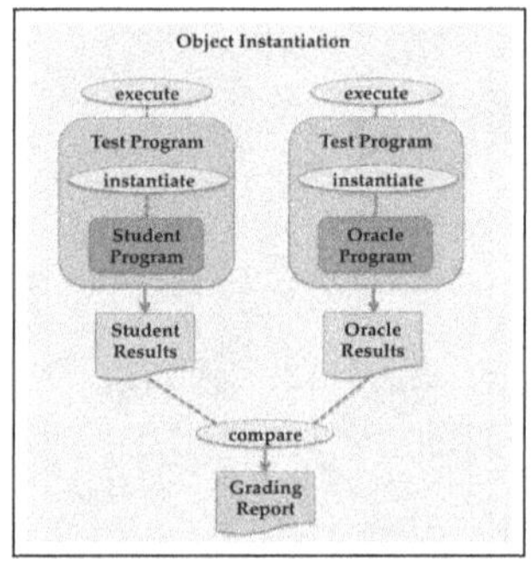

Figure 10: Object Instantiation Strategy.

When using instrumentation, testing proceeds through instrumentation of the supplied classes that captures how and when methods are called. The test script discards standard output, thereby ignoring output from the student code. Test output from the supplied classes is sent to standard error, which is used exclusively for comparison against the oracle. In addition, we can remove GUI calls from the supplied class to make testing faster and more efficient. The benefit of instrumentation is targeted and detailed feedback on the behavior of the student program. Figure 11 shows a block diagram of the instrumentation strategy.

To further understand instrumentation testing we consider two assignments. The first is a maze program in which the student code instantiates a supplied GUI object and writes code to control the behavior of a character in a maze. The second is a plotting program in which the student code reads data from a file and uses a GUI object to display color charts and graphs. For both assignments the student must

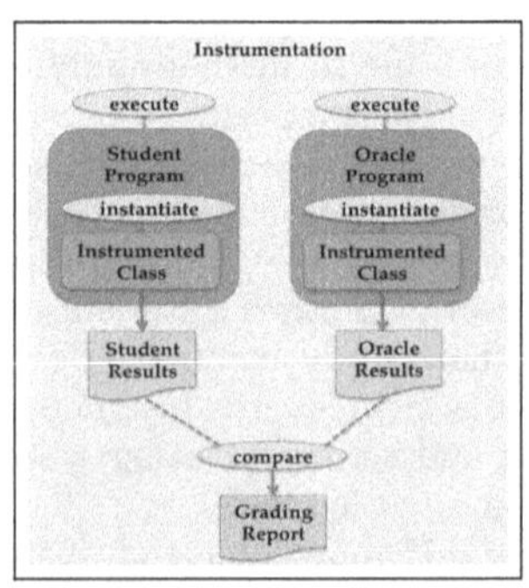

Figure 11: Instrumentation Strategy.

instantiate the supplied GUI class and invoke methods on it. The structure of the student code is not specified for these assignments, so there is no way to directly test student code. Instead we verify the student program indirectly by checking method calls to the supplied object to make sure the student code has implemented the correct behavior.

For the maze program, the supplied code simply prints out the direction each time the student code calls our object to move the character. If the student correctly follows the specified algorithm, then their moves will be identical those of the oracle program. Incorrect, superfluous, or duplicate moves will cause test failures. For the plotting program, we check the size and contents of the data arrays by printing them. If student code fails to read the file correctly, or fails to allocate arrays dynamically, then test failures will occur. Supplied code can check other behaviors such as the order and number of method calls.

3.7 Reflection

Programming languages such as Java and Python provide reflection, which enables introspection of class members and methods. This feature has proven to be highly useful in writing tests. Reflection code can enumerate members and methods in student classes, and invoke methods without instantiation. Enumeration includes data types, access modifiers, static keyword, return values, and generic (nameless) declarations of method parameters. This information provides the student with feedback on how closely their class matches the specification.

The ability to invoke methods without instantiating is a key advantage. Reflection also allows private members and methods to be examined and invoked. Thus partial credit can be awarded for methods that are implemented correctly, without the compile errors that can result from instantiation. This strategy therefore provides more precise feedback than instantiation testing. Figure 12 shows a test result where methods in a student class are enumerated. The student has failed the test because a method was declared as private instead of public. Figure 13 shows the reflection code that enumerates the methods in a class.

Reflection tests are easy to leverage from previous assignments, since the code to enumerate methods and member variables is identical from one assignment to the next. However, method invocations and functional tests have to be tailored to the assignment. This strategy is useful for languages that support reflection, as well as programming languages such as C++ that have third party solutions for reflection. Figure 14 shows a block diagram of the reflection strategy.

```
TEST: test1 CMD LINE: java TestProgram3

Your Output/Master Output:

  Verifying methods in Program3.java:
  public static int Program3.sumArray(int[])
  public static char[] Program3.createChars(java.lang.String)
  private static double Program3.findLargest(double[])
  public static int[] Program3.translateChars(char[])

  Verifying methods in Program3.java:
  public static int Program3.sumArray(int[])
  public static char[] Program3.createChars(java.lang.String)
  public static double Program3.findLargest(double[])
  public static int[] Program3.translateChars(char[])

test1 Score: 0 / 10
```

Figure 12: Test Results from Reflection.

```java
// Java reflection code to enumerate methods in a class
public static boolean queryMethod(String className) {

    // Reflection code to enumerate methods in a class
    try {

        // Search for class
        Class<?> c = Class.forName(className);

        // Enumerate methods
        Method[] allMethods = c.getDeclaredMethods();
        for (Method m : allMethods) {

            // Get method declaration
            String methodDeclaration = m.toGenericString();

            // Print method declaration
            System.err.println(methodDeclaration);
        }

    } catch (ClassNotFoundException x) {
        System.err.println("Could not find: " + cName);
    } catch (InstantiationException x) {
        System.err.println("Could not instantiate: " + cName);
    } catch (IllegalAccessException x) {
        System.err.println("Could not access: " + cName);
    }
}
```

Figure 13: Listing of Reflection Code.

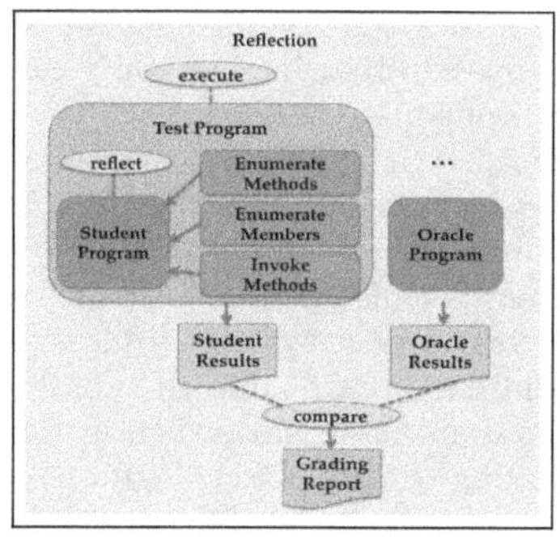

Figure 14: Reflection Strategy.

3.8 Code Analysis

With a flexible framework, the instructor is not limited to functional testing as described above. Test programs can also read and parse student source code, thus opening the door for various kinds of analysis. Code analysis can be implemented as a custom test program, or in some cases by using other tools such as static analysis programs.

To date we have made limited use of code analysis by verifying that the program header is correctly formatted, that sufficient comments are provided, that required methods are called, and that proscribed methods are not. However, we can easily envision grading based on program style, code complexity, code coverage, and so on. Figure 15 shows a block diagram of the code analysis strategy.

4. ISSUES

Regardless of the implementation of an automated framework, several issues consistently emerge. The first is that programs submitted by students often fail to terminate, thus requiring a robust timeout mechanism in the framework. The second is security, which must be addressed to protect against inadvertent and intentional attempts to compromise the testing system. The third is the performance required to make a grading system interactive.

4.1 Non-Terminating Programs

Student programs often exhibit non-terminating behaviors that interfere with automated grading. We commonly encounter programs that have infinite loops (with no input or output), that produce infinite output, or that expect the wrong number or type of inputs. The latter may hang waiting for unspecified input that is never provided. The prevalence of such programs has led us to incorporate timeout code into the grading framework, as have other institutions [3]. One such mechanism is provided by the Runner program, which has previously been presented. In addition to stream control, Runner differentiates between infinite loops and student programs that expect too much or too little input, and can truncate excessive output.

4.2 Security Issues

Testing frameworks must consider the possibility that code submitted by a student could compromise the test system. These threats include (but are not limited to) unauthorized access to class materials, theft of submissions from other students, access to or modification of grades, and damage to the integrity of the test system. Students in our introductory courses have not proven to be sophisticated enough to intentionally attack the grading system, but we have had at least one submission that inadvertently caused a problem by overwriting input files.

We have identified and implemented a number of strategies to maintain security in our framework. The first line of our defense is authentication, in which our framework verifies that a student is registered in the course and holds valid credentials for department systems. Anyone that does not pass the authentication is unable to submit to or interact with the test system. Beyond authentication, we increase security by isolating testing from class directories to prevent access to exam and assignment solutions and other sensitive materials. One way to do this is to have the framework set file protections to prevent student code from reading or writing files that they should not have access to. A variant of this technique is to run student code under a different Linux user or group to prevent access.

We are investigating solutions that provide even more protected environments. One proposal is to perform testing using the Linux *chroot* command. Another proposal is to test student programs in the context of a virtual machine. Either method precludes access to class directories and other materials, and helps protect the integrity of the test system. A more elaborate security system could detect and log student submissions that attempt unauthorized access or other damaging actions. Commercial system for automated grading will undoubtedly have to address these concerns in the future in order to sell into academic markets.

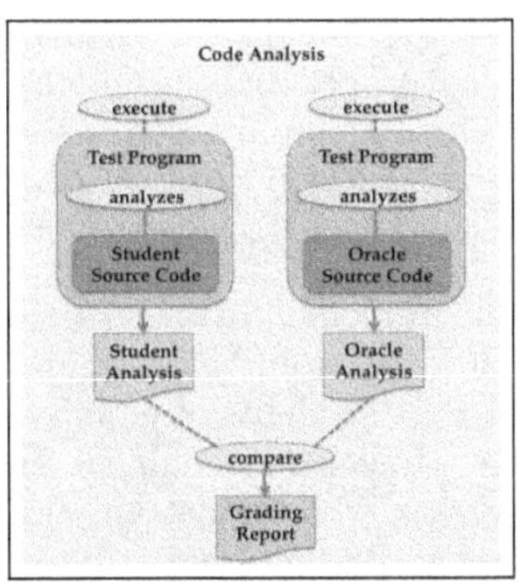

Figure 15: Code Analysis Strategy.

4.3 Grading Performance

To support interactive testing, a grading system should be able to test a student submission in a small number of seconds. The performance of our framework is less than a second per test case per student, not counting the duration of the student program. Since programs in introductory courses usually execute quickly, we can support interactive testing with only a single-threaded server running on a single system. In batch mode, classes with several hundred students can usually be graded in under an hour, without supervision. This represents a large time savings compared to manual grading. Future plans include a test server that is multi-threaded to decrease latency.

5. CONCLUSIONS

This paper has described a set of strategies for testing student programs that are more effective than regression testing at providing detailed and relevant feedback to students. In addition, we have discussed some of the issues that arise in the context of automated grading and their solutions.

6. ACKNOWLEDGMENTS

The author would like to acknowledge Fritz Sieker for writing the automated grading framework, and Jack Applin for writing the initial version of the Runner program.

7. REFERENCES

[1] C. Douce, D. Livingstone, and J. Orwell. Automatic Test-based Assessment of Programming. *Journal Educational Resources Computing*, 5(3), Sept. 2005.

[2] S. Edwards. Using Test-Driven Development in the Classroom: Providing Students with Automatic, Concrete Feedback on Performance. In *Proc. International Conf. on Education and Information Systems: Technologies and Applications (EISTA 03)*, pages 421–426, 2003.

[3] S. H. Edwards, Z. Shams, and C. Estep. Adaptively identifying non-terminating code when testing student programs. In *Proceedings of the 45th ACM Technical Symposium on Computer Science Education*, SIGCSE '14, pages 15–20, New York, NY, USA, 2014. ACM.

[4] X. Fu, B. Peltsverger, K. Qian, L. Tao, and J. Liu. APOGEE: Automated Project Grading and Instant Feedback System for Web Based Computing. In *Proc. of the 39th SIGCSE Technical Symposium on Computer Science Education*, SIGCSE '08, pages 77–81, New York, NY, USA, 2008. ACM.

[5] M. J. Hull, D. Powell, and E. Klein. Infandango: Automated Grading for Student Programming. In *Proc. of the 16th Annual Joint Conf. on Innovation and Technology in Computer Science Education*, ITiCSE '11, pages 330–330, New York, NY, USA, 2011. ACM.

[6] J. Spacco, D. Hovemeyer, W. Pugh, F. Emad, J. K. Hollingsworth, and N. Padua-Perez. Experiences with Marmoset: Designing and Using an Advanced Submission and Testing System for Programming Courses. In *Proc. of the 11th Annual SIGCSE Conf. on Innovation and Technology in Computer Science Education*, ITICSE '06, pages 13–17, New York, NY, USA, 2006. ACM.

[7] C. Wilcox. The role of automation in undergraduate computer science education. In *Proceedings of the 46th ACM Technical Symposium on Computer Science Education*, SIGCSE '15, pages 90–95, New York, NY, USA, 2015. ACM.

A Strategy to Combine Test-Driven Development and Test Criteria to Improve Learning of Programming Skills

Bruno Henrique Pachulski Camara
Federal University of Technology - Paraná
PPGI, Cornélio Procópio, PR, Brasil
Faculdade Integrado, Campo Mourão, PR, Brazil
brunohenrique@grupointegrado.br

Marco Aurélio Graciotto Silva
Departamento Acadêmico de Computação
Federal University of Technology - Paraná
Campo Mourão, PR, Brazil
magsilva@utfpr.edu.br

ABSTRACT

Students usually have difficulties assimilating basic contents of introductory programming disciplines. Test-Driven Development (TDD) is an interesting approach to address this issue, but it does not focus on quality with respect to software testing. This study aims to verify the effectiveness of the use of software testing criteria for producing test cases with higher quality in the context of education with TDD. We used the test-driven development technique with a change in the refactoring step, adding an activity for creating test cases using software testing criteria. We performed two experimental studies to evaluate the effectiveness of the technique. Each study comprised two groups: one using traditional TDD and the other using TDD with test criteria, both having developed the same software. The results showed that groups applying the proposed intervention produced better test cases, with greater coverage, and not disrupting TDD. Moreover, we could observe that, in general, the test set for groups using TDD with criteria was more efficient, getting greater coverage with fewer test cases than groups using plain TDD.

Keywords

test-driven development; TDD; software testing; structural testing; computing education

1. INTRODUCTION

Reflection in action fosters learning with proper comprehension of problems [10], avoiding the usual acting on trial and error [10, 18]. Instead, doubts found on learning activities are addressed with micro-experiments, whose hypotheses are carefully studied before trying to solve them. In the introduction to programming, techniques relying on software testing or test-driven development support reflection in action, yet promoting incremental software development and early detection of defects [8, 10, 17].

On one hand, several studies report that requiring software testing techniques for programming courses allow students to produce better software, evidenced by higher test suite coverage and defects detection [4, 25, 26]. On the other hand, there are plenty of approaches using TDD for education: development of software for different (and more motivating) domains, such as Web [23], games [16]; intelligent tutoring systems [14], automatic assessment mechanisms [3, 9, 10, 27], and others. However, few studies consider integrating both. Software testing is often used to grade assignments, considering test cases coverage [8, 11]. Moreover, the explicit use of software testing techniques is not considered when designing test cases, even when using TDD.

In fact, TDD does not focus on applying software test techniques and creating effective test sets with respect to some test criteria. Recently, some studies focused on integrating TDD and software testing, evaluating improvements on the test set quality (coverage), time required for development and overall source code quality [6, 7]. Nonetheless, this has not been investigated in the educational context, thus devising a strategy that could be successfully used by students.

Considering this scenario, our study establishes an approach for integrating test-driven development with software testing techniques. Our goal is to improve reflection in action by using criteria when developing test cases. Thus, we have changed the TDD workflow, adding an activity to create test cases based upon control-flow test criteria. This action is complementary to test cases created at the beginning of TDD, avoiding major changes to the usual TDD workflow.

The impact of this change and the adoption of basic structural test criteria are intentional, reducing the need for introducing concepts that could be an obstacle for students. At the same time, we expect the approach to guide students in creating better test sets, avoiding *ad hoc* approaches and improving the reflection in action.

The remainder of this paper is organized as follows. We provide the main concepts regarding TDD and test criteria required by our approach on Section 2. We evaluated it by an experimental study with students from a graduation course on Information Systems, as described on Section 3. The students were organized in two groups, allowing the comparison between traditional TDD and TDD with test criteria. We could observe that students who employed TDD with test criteria produced software with better internal quality, *i.e.*, test sets that covered most test requirements, yet with similar test set size, as reported on Section 4. Threats to the validity of our study are analyzed on Section 5. We compared our study with related work on TDD with test criteria on Section 6, followed by conclusions and

SIGCSE '16, March 2–5, 2016, Memphis, TN, USA.

DOI: http://dx.doi.org/10.1145/2839509.2844633

considerations for further evaluation of the current strategy and improvements on Section 7.

2. TEST-DRIVEN DEVELOPMENT WITH TEST CRITERIA

Test-driven development (TDD) is an iterative software design technique organized in three stages [2, p. 9]. The first one requires the definition of test cases regarding the functionality to be implemented in the iteration. In the software testing community, this stage is known as test-first. Meanwhile, this stage is nicknamed as *red* by the TDD community, as every test case created will fail. The implementation of code required to pass the test case is the goal of the second stage (*green*). The last stage comprises refactoring the code, improving the solution design without changing the functionality just implemented. After refactoring, a new iteration can be commenced, selecting new functionalities for implementation [2, p. 9].

However, TDD was created as a design technique, contributing to high cohesion, and low coupling [18]. An important rule in TDD is: "If you can't write a test for what you are about to code, then you shouldn't even be thinking about coding" [13]. Indeed, testability is often asserted as a driver for (requirement) quality. For TDD, such quality attribute is enforced by extensive use of unit testing, driving the creation and modification of code. Nonetheless, despite the importance of test cases, they are not created with respect to some test criteria [1, 2].

Software testing criteria aim the reduction of the input domain while determining most errors [21, p. 43]. Criteria are defined based upon testing techniques which use some information source to derive test requirements. Finally, test cases should be defined to satisfy the requirements, defining a coverage measurement. For instance, source code can be used to derive requirements regarding control-flow using structural software testing techniques. In this study, we considered two criteria:

- All-nodes or statement coverage. Every code block must be covered by at least one test case [21]. For structural testing, the application is represented as a control flow graph, whose nodes represent a sequence of statements and edges represent changes of flow between blocks. In this paper, we use only the term "statement coverage".
- All-edges or branch coverage. Every edge must be covered by at least one test case [21]. This criterion subsumes "All-nodes", as covering edges requires covering their source and destination nodes, but usually provides more test requirements than the former. In this paper, we use only the term "branch coverage".

In fact, test criteria are not considered throughout TDD [2], relying upon developers' experience to derive test cases. Empirically, adding more test cases reveals errors and improves the software quality. However, *ad hoc* test technique increases the costs of development and can negatively impact the adoption of TDD. Recently, some studies have been conducted to address this, with promising results [5, 24]. Nonetheless, the definition and evaluation of test strategies that combine test techniques, employing a test criterion of increasing strength within each stage and iteration, must be further investigated. Moreover, if we are willing to improve education on programming and testing to foster software quality, such strategy must consider the requirements regarding students, especially those who are commencing on Computing.

Our approach considers the adoption of test techniques to derive test cases, guiding students on when and which test criteria should be applied. Considering the usual TDD cycle, depicted on Figure 1, we supplemented the refactoring phase with activities related to the definition of new test cases, improving the coverage with respect to control-flow test criteria, step-wisely increasing, after each iteration, the criterion strength.

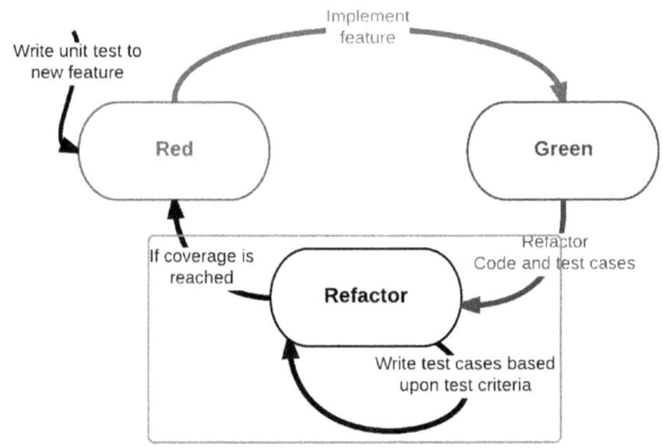

Figure 1: Workflow for TDD augmented with test criteria.

The incremental strength of adopted test criteria not only fosters quality, but also supports scaffolding, as students learn simpler test techniques and improve their design and, after satisfying the test criterion, can use stronger ones. Thus, such strategy allies incremental quality improvement, provided by rigorous software testing, with development of design abilities, which is desirable for students.

3. METHOD

Considering the efficacy of test-driven development in the academic and enterprise settings, and promising results on adopting test techniques into TDD [5, 24], we defined a strategy guided by software test criteria applied to TDD aimed at undergraduate students. Thus, we proposed a change to the usual TDD workflow, adding an activity to create test cases while refactoring. The test set must satisfy a given coverage with respect to a test criterion, otherwise the refactoring activity cannot be finished and a new TDD iteration cannot start.

The research hypothesis is that the quality of the software using TDD can be improved with the adoption of test techniques and test criteria. Moreover, we want to evaluate whether such intervention might impair TDD.

The strategy is targeted toward undergraduate students with basic programming skill, but who do not practice test-driven development and are not familiar with software testing. Our technique, by combining TDD and simple test criteria, provides a scaffolding approach to develop skills that can significantly improve the quality of the software developed by the students, and whose results can endure throughout their academic and professional life.

In this study, we defined a strategy based upon structural testing and unit testing. We have changed the activities developed at the refactoring stage: the student should, besides refactoring, create test cases that cover test requirements with respect to statement criteria, and, yet in the same iteration, reach most requirements for branch coverage. The group could start a new TDD iteration only when both coverage thresholds were reached.

The strategy was evaluated with a controlled experiment [22]. We controlled the problem to be solved by the students (Bowling Game), the programming language (Java), test framework to be used when defining test cases (JUnit), the environment for development (Eclipse) and submission of source code for evaluation. For each subject (student) of this study, we established its profile, identifying previous experience on programming, TDD and software testing. The subjects were organized in two groups:

- "Group A" (control). Subjects that will implement software requirements (functionalities) using plain TDD.
- "Group B" (intervention). Subjects that will implement software requirements using TDD based upon test criteria. Besides implementing at least one test case for each functionality, every subject must develop a test set, in the refactoring stage, that satisfies some test criteria, as defined in our strategy.

At the beginning of the experiment, every student was trained on TDD, basic concepts on software testing, and control-flow test criteria. After training, we evaluated whether the students correctly understood the concepts and developed the required abilities on TDD and software testing.

The subjects that succeeded were randomly assigned to groups A and B. Then, the instructor supplied the description of the software. Resembling a typical TDD workflow, the development was organized in iterations. As suggested by Shelton *et al.* [24], each iteration comprised of a single functionality to be implemented. The description of a new functionality was delivered to the group only after finishing the current iteration. This approach is similar to a typical software development environment and conceals information from future iterations that could be a confounding factor.

Both groups were assigned to the same project and, for each iteration, they were given the same functionality to implement. The groups did not know they were using different TDD strategies, and could not interact with one another, avoiding influences between groups.

For each iteration and software delivered at its end, we collected the source code of the application and test cases, and processed related data, such as date and time of the end of the iteration. Using these data, we could extract information considered relevant to analyze TDD experiments: size of the application and test cases (number of line of codes), internal quality (statement and branch coverages) [20].

4. RESULTS

Considering the method described in the previous section, we conducted two experiments with students from a graduation program on information systems. The first trial took place on April 2014 with a cohort of four students, and the second trial was on November 2014 with a cohort of sixteen students. The organization into groups, training and analysis of the results are discussed in the following subsections.

4.1 Grouping and training

The subjects of the first trial were four students of the second-to-last term of the course. Overall, they have similar grades for Mathematics and Computing courses, easing the provision of balanced groups. Thus, the subjects were randomly assigned to groups A (control) and B (intervention).

In this trial, training was initiated with video-lectures on TDD, demonstrating traditional software development, and development using TDD, highlighting the benefits of the latter technique. Along the lecture, the instructor developed an example, which was also implemented by the students. Afterward, another activity was proposed, exercising the concepts just learned. Finally, the instructor evaluated the results of the exercises, which he considered satisfactory.

The subjects of the second trial were sixteen students of the last term of the course. Differently from the first trial, instead of a video, the professor taught TDD as usual. After lecturing, the students were assigned six activities on TDD, which were evaluated by the instructor. Based on this evaluation, four students were excluded from the trial, as their proficiency on TDD was inadequate.

4.2 Activity and intervention

The software developed in both trials was "Bowling Game" [19], an application commonly used in studies about TDD [5, 6, 12]. This application is expected to provide the score of a player in a bowling game using a set of rules regarding tries and knocked down pins. In our experiment, we considered a subset of its functionality, organizing it in three software development iterations:

- First iteration: The game has ten tries and, for each try, the player can roll the ball twice. Each roll can achieve at most ten points (number of pins knocked down). The score should be provided at any moment of the game (before or after every roll).
- Second iteration: If the player gets ten points in the first roll of a try, he gets a strike. The player cannot play the second roll of the try, but the current try will be awarded the points of the next one.
- Third iteration: The player gets two extra rolls if he gets a strike on the tenth try. If the player gets a spare (knock down all pins with two rolls) in the tenth try, he gets one extra roll.

For each iteration, Group A used traditional TDD and Group B employed TDD with test criteria to develop the software, as defined in Figure 1. For our experiment, Group B created test cases with respect to statements and branches coverage while in the refactoring stage. Only after the students noticed they had covered most statements or branches (in our study, this represents at least a 90% coverage), the intervention group could start a new iteration.

After each iteration, groups submitted the code to the instructor through the institution virtual learning environment. The instructor collected coverage information for each submission employing Eclemma, extracting data as shown in Table 1. The name of each group was suffixed with the trial number to ease the interpretation of the data.

4.3 Analysis

We analyzed the data for internal quality attributes: number of test cases, and coverage of test requirements.

Table 1: Results from experiments.

			Iteration 1			Iteration 2			Iteration 3		
			Statements	Branches	Test cases	Statements	Branches	Test cases	Statements	Branches	Test cases
Trial 1	Student 01	A1	93.3	54.8	5	96.7	93.3	6	95.4	71.4	7
	Student 02	A1	91.2	44.3	2	87.7	43.0	3	88.6	44.4	4
	Average	**A1**	**92.25**	**49.55**	**3.5**	**92.20**	**68.15**	**4.5**	**92.00**	**57.90**	**5.5**
	Student 09	B1	95.4	78.6	2	82.7	75.0	4	95.1	89.6	6
	Student 10	B1	98.7	100.0	2	98.9	100.0	4	98.7	100.0	4
	Average	**B1**	**97.05**	**89.30**	**2.0**	**90.80**	**87.50**	**4.0**	**96.90**	**94.80**	**5.0**
	Diff. B1 A1		**4.85**	**39.75**	**-1.5**	**-1.40**	**19.35**	**-0.5**	**4.90**	**36.90**	**-0.5**
Trial 2	Student 03	A2	77.8	33.3	1	85.2	66.7	2	82.2	68.8	3
	Student 04	A2	93.4	100.0	1	96.4	100.0	2	96.4	100.0	4
	Student 05	A2	89.4	62.5	1	79.2	77.8	1	89.0	61.8	1
	Student 06	A2	91.1	66.7	4	85.1	66.7	2	89.1	71.4	3
	Student 07	A2	80.0	50.0	2	94.9	83.3	7	95.5	83.3	10
	Student 08	A2	91.3	75.0	11	92.8	73.1	11	97.1	73.3	12
	Average	**A2**	**87.17**	**64.58**	**3.3**	**87.17**	**77.93**	**4.1**	**91.55**	**76.43**	**5.5**
	Student 11	B2	89.6	100	1	80.1	100	1	93.6	100	4
	Student 12	B2	88.2	100	2	92.9	100	5	87.1	80.6	9
	Student 13	B2	93.2	100	3	94.2	100	4	96.9	100	8
	Student 14	B2	98.2	90	3	99.4	81.2	3	99.0	88.7	3
	Student 15	B2	100	100	3	100	100	4	99.8	88.8	5
	Average	**B2**	**93.84**	**98.00**	**2.4**	**93.32**	**96.24**	**3.4**	**95.28**	**91.62**	**5.8**
	Diff. B2 A2		**6.67**	**33.42**	**-0.9**	**6.15**	**18.31**	**-0.7**	**3.73**	**15.19**	**0.3**

* Group A is control (traditional TDD) group and Group B is intervention (TDD+Test Criteria) group.

For this study, we considered statement and branch coverage for test requirements evaluation. Overall, groups using TDD with test criteria developed test sets with higher coverage with respect to statements and branches coverage and with less test cases than groups using traditional TDD.

In Table 1, considering the first trial, we can notice that, in the first iteration, Group A1 developed on average 3.5 test cases covering 92.25% statements and 49.55% branches, while Group B1 developed on average 2 test cases, covering 97.05% statements and 89.30% branches. For the next iterations, Group A1 added on average one test case per iteration. Meanwhile, Group B1 doubled their test set size (although yet smaller than the one of Group A) and, in the third iteration, they added just one test case. Concerning coverage of test requirements on the second and third iteration, Groups A1 and B1 kept similar averages for statements coverage, but the same does not apply for branch coverage: Group B1 always kept a higher average than Group A1, on a minimum of 20% difference.

For the second trial, the difference for statements and branches coverage was clearer. Group A2 achieved an average of 64.58% for branch coverage while Group B had 98.00% using fewer test cases for the first iteration. For statements coverage, the difference was smaller, but Group B2 still had a better coverage.

Based on the average checked on Table 2 of the two groups in the first iteration, group A averaged 3.38 test cases with 88.44% statement coverage and 60.83% branch coverage against an average of 2.29 test cases with 94.76% statement coverage and 95.51% branch coverage. For the second and third iterations, the difference is smaller, with both groups developing on average 5 test cases, but yet with significant difference between coverage of test requirements: 89.75% versus 92.60% regarding statement coverage, and 75.49% versus 93.74% for branch coverage. Indeed, the difference of statement coverage between groups A and B is not statistically significant. This result agrees with studies that evaluate coverage for test cases developed by students using TDD [11]. However, for branch coverage, the difference is significant at a level of 0.05 applying Mann-Whitney Test U (merging data from both trials). Merging data from all iterations, statement coverage is also statistically significant.

An expected result is the improvement of software quality due to application of test criteria without impairing TDD, despite the additional effort to create better test cases and impact of this activity in the refactoring state. So far, our results show that test criteria act as a guide to create test cases, allowing the definition of more consistent test sets with respect to number of test cases and quality (coverage). In the short-term, the effort saved by defining fewer test cases is an interesting result of the technique. On the longer term, the higher quality of the test set can contribute to reduce the effort required on specific software testing activities or enable the usage of more sophisticated test techniques, considering test criteria with better strength and comprehensive integration and system testing.

After the experiment, we surveyed the students about the use of traditional TDD and TDD with test criteria. Overall, they perceived test cases as an integral part of the software, which they could not deliver it without implementing the

Table 2: Summary of the results from the experiment.

	Statements				Branches				Test cases			
	TDD	TDD+TC	Diff.	p-value	TDD	TDD+TC	Diff.	p-value	TDD	TDD+TC	Diff.	p-value
Iteration 1	88.44	94.76	6.32	0.094	60.83	95.51	34.69	**0.006**	3.38	2.29	-1.09	1.000
Iteration 2	89.75	92.60	2.85	0.397	75.49	93.74	18.26	**0.031**	4.25	3.57	-0.68	0.860
Iteration 3	91.66	95.74	4.42	0.189	71.80	92.53	20.73	**0.014**	5.50	5.57	0.07	0.682
Iter. 1 + 2 + 3	89.95	94.37	3.85	**0.007**	69.37	93.93	24.56	**0.00009**	4.38	3.81	-0.57	0.818

* TDD is control (traditional TDD) group and TDD+TC is intervention (TDD+Test Criteria) group.

required functionalities and test cases (keeping them all "green"). With respect to TDD with criteria, the groups considered satisfying test requirements as much a goal as satisfying software requirements, *i.e.*, while the requirements for the iteration are not fulfilled, the software is not ready for delivery.

Moreover, when questioned about the efficacy of applying test criteria with TDD, the students asserted the approach had helped them to better define their test cases and check which part of the code required further testing. One student, that had previous experience on TDD, complemented that he was accustomed to *ad hoc* techniques to create test cases, while the current approach provided a better experience, establishing "guidelines" on writing test cases.

5. THREATS TO VALIDITY

An important threat is the evaluation of whether students correctly applied TDD. We tried to address this by training sessions. For instance, on the second trial, we excluded two students that could not perform TDD as expected after those training sessions.

The correct application of control-flow test criteria should be considered when analyzing results. For both trials the students did not use tools to directly evaluate the coverage with respect to the criteria in question. Despite this, we could observe that the coverage data are consistent with the hypothesis that students considered the statements and branches criteria when developing test cases. Analyzing the data, we could notice that coverage did not reach 100% mostly due to "getters" and "setters" methods created by the students with automatic assistance of the development tool, and for which they constantly forgot to design test cases. Nonetheless, future work should provide the students tools to address this threat. We are modifying an Eclipse plugin, based on Eclemma [15], which will compute this information, and automatically collect and send it for analysis by the instructor. Furthermore, we will analyze the impact of code automatically created and verify their impact on test coverage.

The subjects of our study were students from the last year of their graduation courses. This reduces the impact of lack of programming experience, improving the effectiveness of TDD. Therefore, such population do not have the same characteristics of those students from introductory computing classes, who we would also like to evaluate. That is a factor we must consider when applying the strategy for beginners (CS1 and CS2 students). The test strategy we adopted in this study may also require use of different test criteria. Thus, we are considering to evaluate functional test criteria, such as equivalence partitioning and boundary value analysis.

6. RELATED WORK

As we have discussed on Section 2, the usual focus of research related to test-driven development is improvement of software design, helping programmers to define better solutions for the scenario to be addressed [1, 2, 10]. Software testing is not an explicit goal, at least with respect to a test criterion or test phase.

Even with no explicit goal on software testing, test cases must be somehow defined. Considering this fact, Shelton *et al.* [24] evaluated test cases with respect to mutant analysis at the end of each development iteration. Their goal was to increase the quality of the test set after completing refactoring, enabling the developer to assess the mutation score and to define new test cases to improve that score. Another goal was to evaluate the impact of such activity in the TDD workflow. Their study was conducted along with three professional programmers, who were proficient on TDD and use of software testing frameworks. The results showed improvement at the quality of the test, discovering more defects after using mutation analysis. The statement coverage, originally at 91%, reached 100%, and the mutation score ranged from 40% to 96.9% [24]. Overall, the programmers were receptive to the novel TDD approach, stating that the development pace was not affected, and that they found it easier to refactor code and find defects for the application with improved test set [24].

Causevic *et al.* defined a method to improve quality of software within TDD: TDD^{HQ} (Test-Driven Development High Quality). Before starting an iteration, a quality improvement aspect should be chosen. Then the programmer selects a software testing technique that can contribute toward satisfying that aspect. At the end of the iteration, the programmer restarts the workflow, choosing between implementing a new functionality and improving another quality aspect [5]. The efficacy of the approach on defect detection was evaluated with a controlled experiment. Two students' groups were organized: one who used TDD^{HQ} and another that employed traditional TDD. The chosen quality improvement aspects were functionality and robustness, which were evaluated with equivalence partitioning test criterion. The results of the study revealed improvement of the quality of the test set developed by the TDD^{HQ} group, showing test cases that had exercised invalid input data (*bad-path*) were more effective at finding defects than those that had considered only valid input (*happy-path*), as usual in traditional TDD. However, it was not possible to rebut the hypothesis that TDD^{HQ} has better results than traditional TDD to find defects [5].

Differently from those studies, our approach was designed to help students initiating on Computing. For instance, Causevic *et al.* [5] define a flexible model that supports several quality assurance activities, but they evaluated it with graduated students (ongoing master's degree programs). Shelton *et al.* [24] adopts mutation analysis, which is a more sophisticated software testing technique, requiring more effort from the student to grasp the rationale for detection of defects and the development of reflection in action.

7. CONCLUSIONS

The hypothesis we have evaluated was whether the application of test criteria to test-driven development could improve the quality of software developed by students, and foster reflection in action. The development of test cases, by itself, contributes toward this, but, in our study, we could observe that the use of test criteria improved the quality of the test set without significant disturbance to the TDD workflow.

Likewise, in related studies the experiment was rather short, comprising just three iterations. Longer term effect of the approach should be evaluated, employing more iterations and measuring the effort for developing test cases using *ad hoc*, structural or another testing technique. Considering test criteria, can we observe the saturation effect regarding coverage and use such information to employ criterion with greater strength than control-flow ones, and, if so, can students cope with such criteria? Another question is whether there are other improvements besides test set quality with respect to coverage. For instance, can the usage of TDD with criteria contribute to even better design than traditional TDD? Does the effort for improved testing alleviate the effort for testing the software?

Our next step comprises of further evaluation of the current strategy for longer iterations, and applying functional test criteria. We will also focus on students from introductory computing courses, and evaluate more students (cohorts of up to 40 students), reducing bias concerning profiles and enabling the proper statistical evaluation of our hypothesis.

8. REFERENCES

[1] M. F. Aniche and M. A. Gerosa. How the practice of TDD influences class design in object-oriented systems: Patterns of unit tests feedback. In *26th Brazilian Symposium on Software Engineering*, pages 1–10, 2012.

[2] K. Beck. *Test-Driven Development: By Example.* Addison-Wesley Professional, USA, 1 edition, Nov. 2002.

[3] K. Buffardi and S. H. Edwards. Exploring influences on student adherence to test-driven development. In *17th Conference on Innovation and Technology in Computer Science Education*, pages 105–110, 2012.

[4] K. Buffardi and S. H. Edwards. Effective and ineffective software testing behaviors by novice programmers. In *9th Conference on International Computing Education Research*, pages 83–90, New York, NY,USA, 2013.

[5] A. Causevic, S. Punnekkat, and D. Sundmark. TDD^{HQ}: Achieving higher quality testing in test driven development. In *39th Euromicro Conference Series on Software Engineering and Advanced Applications*, pages 33–36, 2013.

[6] A. Causevic, R. Shukla, S. Punnekkat, and D. Sundmark. Effects of negative testing on TDD: An industrial experiment. In *14th Conference on Agile Software Development*, pages 91–105, 2013.

[7] A. Causevic, D. Sundmark, and S. Punnekkat. Impact of test design technique knowledge on test driven development: A controlled experiment. In *13th Conference on Agile Software Development*, pages 138–152, 2012.

[8] D. M. de Souza, S. Isotani, and E. F. Barbosa. Teaching novice programmers using ProgTest. *International Journal of Knowledge and Learning*, 10(1):60–77, 2015.

[9] S. H. Edwards. Rethinking computer science education from a test-first perspective. In *18th Conference on Object-Oriented Programming, Systems, Languages, and Applications*, pages 148–155, New York, NY, USA, 2003. ACM.

[10] S. H. Edwards. Using software testing to move students from trial-and-error to reflection-in-action. In *35th Technical Symposium on Computer Science Education*, pages 26–30, New York, NY,USA, 2004.

[11] S. H. Edwards and Z. Shams. Do student programmers all tend to write the same software tests? In *19th Conference on Innovation and Technology in Computer Science Education*, pages 171–176, New York, NY,USA, 2014.

[12] D. Fucci and B. Turhan. On the role of tests in test-driven development: A differentiated and partial replication. *Empirical Software Engineering*, 19(2):277–302, Apr. 2014.

[13] B. George and L. Williams. A structured experiment of test-driven development. *Information and Software Technology*, 46(5):337–342, Apr. 2004.

[14] M. Hilton and D. S. Janzen. On teaching arrays with test-driven learning in WebIDE. In *17th Conference on Innovation and Technology in Computer Science Education*, pages 93–98, 2012.

[15] M. R. Hoffmann et al. EclEmma - Java code coverage for Eclipse. Software, Aug. 2006.

[16] V. Isomöttönen and V. Lappalainen. CSI with games and an emphasis on TDD and unit testing: piling a trend upon a trend. *Inroads*, 3(3):62–68, Sept. 2012.

[17] D. Janzen and H. Saiedian. Test-driven learning in early programming courses. In *39th Technical Symposium on Computer Science Education*, pages 532–536, 2008.

[18] D. S. Janzen and H. Saiedian. Test-driven learning: intrinsic integration of testing into the CS/SE curriculum. In *37th Technical Symposium on Computer Science Education*, pages 254–258, 2006.

[19] R. C. Martin. The Bowling Game Kata. Site: http://butunclebob.com/ArticleS.UncleBob.TheBowlingGameKata, 2005.

[20] H. Munir, M. Moayyed, and K. Petersen. Considering rigor and relevance when evaluating test driven development: A systematic review. *Information and Software Technology*, 56(4):375–394, Apr. 2014.

[21] G. J. Myers. *The Art of Software Testing.* John Wiley & Sons, New York, NY,USA, 2 edition, 2004.

[22] S. L. Pfleeger. Design and analysis in software engineering: the language of case studies and formal experiments. *Software Engineering Notes*, 19(4):16–20, Oct. 1994.

[23] S. Schaub. Teaching CS1 with web applications and test-driven development. *Inroads*, 41(2):113–117, June 2009.

[24] W. Shelton, N. Li, P. Ammann, and J. Offutt. Adding criteria-based tests to test driven development. In *5th International Conference on Software Testing, Verification and Validation*, pages 878–886, 2012.

[25] D. M. d. Souza, J. C. Maldonado, and E. F. Barbosa. ProgTest: An environment for the submission and evaluation of programming assignments based on testing activities. In *24th Conference on Software Engineering Education and Training*, pages 1–10, 2011.

[26] J. Spacco, D. Hovemeyer, W. Pugh, F. Emad, J. K. Hollingsworth, and N. Padua-Perez. Experiences with Marmoset: designing and using an advanced submission and testing system for programming courses. In *11th Conference on Innovation and Technology in Computer Science Education*, pages 13–17, New York, NY,USA, 2006.

[27] M. Thornton, S. H. Edwards, R. P. Tan, and M. A. Pérez-Quiñones. Supporting student-written tests of GUI programs. In *39th Technical Symposium on Computer Science Education*, pages 537–541, 2008.

Tool Design and Student Testing Behavior in an Introductory Java Course

Grant Braught
Department of Mathematics and Computer Science
Dickinson College
Carlisle, PA 17013
+1 (717) 245-1401
braught@dickinson.edu

James Midkiff
Department of Mathematics and Computer Science
Dickinson College
Carlisle, PA 17013
+1 (717) 245-1401
midkiffj@dickinson.edu

ABSTRACT
This paper examines the effects of tool design on student testing behavior in an introductory course. Two tools are considered: BlueJ and WebCAT. A small modification was made to the BlueJ test recording interface to encourage students to engage more deeply in the testing process. A larger percentage of tests submitted by students using the modified BlueJ interface were correct. Further, the solutions they submitted contained fewer lines of code while being similarly complete and correct. Evidence is given that students using both BlueJ versions often rely on Web-CAT to validate their solution methods before testing the methods themselves. In response a new Web-CAT grading plug-in is proposed that we believe will better promote an incremental code-a-little test-a-little development style.

CCS Concepts
• Social and professional topics~Computer science education • Social and professional topics~CS1 • *Software and its engineering~Integrated and visual development environments*

Keywords
Testing Tools; Java; JUnit; BlueJ; Web-CAT;

1. INTRODUCTION
The need to teach more software testing has received significant attention in the CS education literature [e.g. 1,2]. In response, faculty have integrated testing into courses, including starting from the very first course [e.g. 3,4,5]. While there has been success having introductory students learn both coding and testing simultaneously [6], quite a few authors caution that novice programmers have difficulty doing so and that a good set of tools that simplify, incentivize and reinforce the testing process is essential [7,8,9]. Other research suggests that when such tools are used the benefit to students is more than simply leaning testing techniques. Proulx [9] has argued that student understanding of OO design may be improved by working with quality testing libraries. Edwards [16] advanced the idea that part of the benefit of having students engage in testing is to provide "practice in hypothesizing about the behavior of their programs and then experimentally verifying (or invalidating) their hypotheses." He argues that this practice moves students from a "trial-and-error" approach to a more mature "reflection-in-action" approach where students have a deeper understanding of their programs and their programming process.

This paper reports on the first steps of a new project, in a vein similar to recent work by Buffardi and Edwards [10,11], that aims to improve and empirically assess changes to testing tools that have been designed for use in the computer science classroom. When designing our introductory course to explicitly include testing, we adopted two excellent tools for beginners: BlueJ and Web-CAT. We have been extremely happy with the quality of these tools and we have seen that novices coming to our course are able to learn both programming and testing together. However, we have also observed that some specific features in each of these tools have unintended consequences and have led students to adopt undesirable development and testing behaviors. Thus, our new project sets out to empirically verify our anecdotal observations of student testing behavior with these tools, envision changes to the tools to address these behaviors and then to implement and quantitatively evaluate the effects of these changes.

In what follows, we focus first on a student behavior with BlueJ's test recording interface and assess the effect that a change to the BlueJ Test Recording dialog had on student test and code quality. We then present data that confirms observations that students are relying on features of Web-CAT to verify the correctness of some methods in their programs before testing them themselves. Finally, we propose a design for a new Web-CAT grading plug-in that we hope will change the observed behavior and state our plans to study it.

2. SETTING
Our studies were conducted in the first course in computer science (COMP131) at Dickinson College, which uses both BlueJ and Web-CAT to introduce students to programming and unit testing.

2.1 Dickinson College
Dickinson College is a highly selective liberal arts college in South Central Pennsylvania with approximately 2500 enrolled students. The computer science faculty consists of 3 full-time tenured faculty, 1 full-time lecturer/technician and approximately 1-2 adjunct instructors per term. The program typically graduates 8-15 computer science majors per year.

SIGCSE '16, March 02-05, 2016, Memphis, TN, USA

DOI: http://dx.doi.org/10.1145/2839509.2844641

2.2 COMP 131

COMP131 provides an Objects First introduction to programming and generally follows the BlueJ text [12]. It is our first course in computer science – taken by both majors and non-majors. The course satisfies general education requirements for laboratory science and quantitative reasoning and can also be used as an elective for the mathematics major. The course meets for 50-minutes three times per week and also for a 2-hour lab once per week. Full-time faculty teaches both the class meetings and lab period, and undergraduate TAs help field questions during the lab periods.

Class meetings are typically a mixture of short lectures interspersed with live-coding demonstrations and hands-on activities. Testing using the BlueJ test recording feature is explicitly taught in class. Initially, one full class period is dedicated to introducing unit testing and the BlueJ test recorder. Then, as new language features and data structures are introduced, additional time is spent discussing techniques for testing them. For example, when conditionals are introduced the idea of statement coverage is introduced in conjunction with it. Throughout the semester an incremental "code-a-little test-a-little" development cycle is emphasized and illustrated during live-coding demonstrations.

Student programming assignments in COMP131 include exercises that are a part of approximately weekly homework assignments, a mixture of one and two-week lab assignments and lab exams. After about the fourth week of the course students are required to submit (to Web-CAT) recorded unit tests that achieve statement coverage for all programming exercises. Lab assignments use an Objects In Context approach [13], where students are asked to code and test classes that are used by a larger application that provides a compelling context. This approach, which allows students to focus on programming in the small, is a natural fit for introducing unit testing and simplifies the creation of reference solutions and instructor reference tests. All labs are completed using pair-programming. Students elect to do homework in whatever way they learn best (individually, in pairs, or in larger groups) and lab exams are completed individually under exam conditions.

3. TOOL DESCRIPTIONS

Both BlueJ and Web-CAT have served as excellent tools in COMP131. However, over many years of use we have observed elements of their operation that allow or even reward poor or unproductive testing behaviors.

3.1 BlueJ

BlueJ is a widely used IDE for beginner programmers and includes syntax boxing and highlighting, improved compile time error reporting, a simplified debugger and a test recording facility [14]. Of specific interest to this work is BlueJ's Method Result dialog box shown in Figure 1. This dialog box appears when a method is invoked while recording a unit test in BlueJ. The user is able to select the type of assertion to be made (e.g. "equal to", "not same", "true" etc.) and enter the result that the method must return for the test to pass.

As can be seen in Figure 1 this dialog also displays the value (e.g. 10) that the student's implementation method returned when it was invoked. We have found this to be problematic as we regularly observe students blindly copying the returned value into the assertion box. In doing so they are simply accepting the output of their solution code as the correct result because it is more expedient than thinking carefully about the proper value for the assertion. Thus, students adopting this behavior short-circuit the process of hypothesis formation and testing that Edwards has argued moves them from "trial-and-error" to "reflection-in-action".

To assess the effects of this feature on student behavior we made a small change to the BlueJ interface so that it displays a "?" in the "returned" box of the Method Result dialog in place of the value returned by the student method. We then used this modified BlueJ in our spring 2015 offerings of COMP131. This has allowed us to compare student solution and test code from a past semester of COMP131 (using the original BlueJ) to that from a more recent semester (using our modified BlueJ). The specifics of this comparison are given in Section 4.

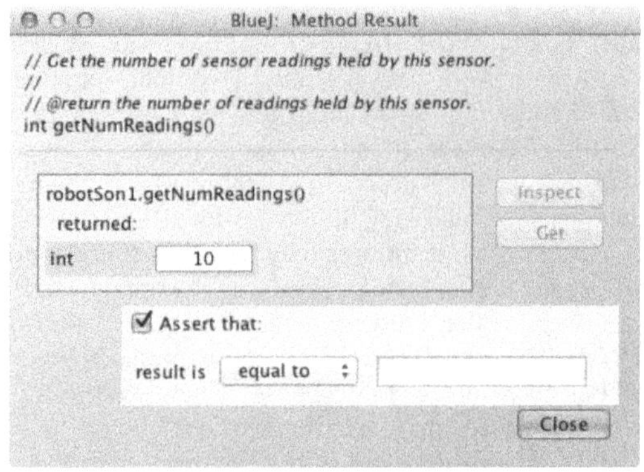

Figure 1: BlueJ Method Result Dialog that is used to specify JUnit assertions when recording unit tests.

3.2 Web-CAT

Web-CAT [16] is an on-line service that provides both automated and instructor generated feedback for student submitted assignments. Web-CAT's grader plug-in architecture supports assignments in a variety of languages, including Java via the Java-TDD plug-in that is of interest here. With the Java-TDD plug-in, students can submit their solution and tests as many times as they like as they work on it. They then receive automated feedback in response to each submission. The feedback provided includes: the percentage of reference tests passed; hints for to help with fixing code that caused failed reference tests; suggestions for improving coding style and format; and information about testing quality in terms of code coverage. When the due-date for the assignment has passed the instructor can also add additional feedback for the student.

When using Web-CAT with the Java-TDD plug-in, we have frequently observed the following undesirable, but time efficient, behavior. Students write a large percentage of their implementation, testing some parts of it but not testing it completely – often leaving the most difficult parts untested. They then submit this work to Web-CAT in order to receive its hints on how to correct any errors that have been detected by the instructor's reference tests. Students then improve their implementation based on these hints, resubmitting as necessary. Finally, only when their implementation passes all of the instructor tests do they set about, pointlessly and begrudgingly, writing unit tests for code that they already know is correct. Our observations are consistent with a number of other studies that argue that without proper incentives students will not adopt good testing behaviors [7,8]. In Section 4, we present empirical evidence from past offerings of COMP131 that support this anecdotal observation and in Section 5 we suggest an design for a new Web-CAT grading plug-in that we plan to study during the current academic year.

4. METHODS AND RESULTS

4.1 The Data Set

The data used in this study was collected from Web-CAT submissions by 92 students in four sections of COMP131 during the 2014-15 academic year. 51 students in two sections used the original BlueJ and 41 students in two sections used the modified BlueJ. These sections were taught by three experienced Ph.D. faculty with one teaching a section in the fall and another in the spring. All faculty taught from a common set of lecture notes, examples and activities and the students in all sections were given the same homework, lab and lab-exam assignments.

Because we are interested in how our modification to BlueJ affects student testing behavior, we want to consider students who make a sincere attempt at testing. Thus, unless otherwise noted, we have included in our analysis only those submissions that achieve least 75% statement coverage. This is similar Buffardi and Edward's technique of discarding their neglectful testers [10] to better focus on students that are making an effort to test. In addition, we limit our analysis to submissions made on lab-exams where we know that the students worked individually, which is essential for the statistical analysis that accounts for individual differences in students. Finally, we note that four students from the modified BlueJ sections who had downloaded and used the original BlueJ from bluej.org were recoded into the original BlueJ group for all analyses.

4.2 Statistical Methods

The results reported in sections 4.3 - 4.5 were produced using linear mixed effects models [17] in R [18] with the lme4 package [19]. Each model analyzed the relationship between a target variable and the BlueJ version (original or modified) as a fixed effect and random effects with varying intercepts for each assignment, instructor and student. All p-values reported for the significance of fixed effects were obtained via likelihood ratio tests of the model including the effect against the model without the effect [17]. The results of these tests will be reported using the format ($\chi^2(1)=5.23$, $p=0.057$) where 1 is the number of degrees of freedom, 5.23 is the χ^2 value of the test and 0.057 is the p-value of the test.

4.3 Individual Test Methods

To examine the effects of our modification to the BlueJ test recording interface, we can classify individual test methods submitted by the students as follows:

	Student Test is Correct	Student Soln. Passes
Class1	Y	Y
Class2	N	Y
Class3	Y	N
Class4	N	N

Table 1: Student test method classification. A student test method is correct if it passes when run against the instructor reference solution. The student solution passes if the student test passes when run with the student solution.

The distinction between Class 2 and Class 3 test methods provides a way to assess our modification to the BlueJ test recording interface. In Class 2 test methods, both the student test and the student solution are incorrect (the solution passes an incorrect test). Such methods would result when the student has copied the return value from incorrect solution code as the assertion value (only possible with the original BlueJ) or has implemented and tested consistently but based on an incorrect understanding of the problem. In Class 3 test methods, the student has created a correct test method despite having incorrect solution code, which suggests that the student has thought carefully through the test and determined the correct assertion to be made. Thus, a reduction in Class 2 test methods and/or an increase in Class 3 test methods would be indicative of a positive change in student testing behavior.

In the following analysis we include the first submission of every test method submitted by every student. Subsequent submissions of test methods with the same name by the same student are not included. This ensures we count each test method only once and isolates the effect of our BlueJ modification from the effects of Web-CAT feedback. Of these (n=1614) test methods, 90%, for each BlueJ version, were Class 1 where both the student test and the student solution are correct. Because the percentage of Class 1 tests is equal between the groups, we examine the Class 2, 3 and 4 tests separately.

Table 2 shows the division of the remaining (n=159) test methods among classes 2, 3 and 4. Notably, almost no submissions (1.1%) using the original BlueJ fall in to Class 3, where a student who had written incorrect solution code thought carefully enough to produce a correct test. The 21.6% greater proportion of Class 3 submissions by modified BlueJ users suggests that these students are thinking more carefully about the test methods they create. This conclusion is further reinforced by the reduction in Class 2 and Class 4 submissions, which reflect the submission of incorrect test methods. Results from running linear mixed effect models with the binary variable of membership in Class 2 or Class 3 as the target variable confirm these observations. The likelihood ratio tests are significant at the $p<0.1$ level for the effect of BlueJ version on both Class 2 ($\chi^2(1)=3.79$, $p=0.052$) and Class 3 ($\chi^2(1)=2.79$, $p=0.095$) as target variables. The model with Class 4 as a target variable did not converge.

	Class 2	Class 3	Class 4
Original BlueJ	82.8%	1.1%	16.1%
Modified BlueJ	71.2%	22.7%	6.1%
Difference	-11.6%	21.6%	-10.0%

Table 2: Percentage of Class 2, 3, and 4 test methods for students using the original and modified BlueJ test recording interface.

4.4 First Submissions

In addition to considering individual test methods, we examined the effect of BlueJ version on students' entire first submission to Web-CAT. Considering full submissions allows us to examine the effect of our BlueJ modification not only on students' test code but also on the quality of their solution code. We ran linear mixed effect models on students' first submission with following target variables:

- Normalized Solution NCLOC: The number of Non-Comment, non-blank Lines Of Code (NCLOC) in the submitted student solution normalized to the mean solution NCLOC of all first submissions to the assignment.
- Normalized Test NCLOC: The NCLOC in the submitted student unit tests normalized to the mean test NCLOC of all first submissions to the assignment.

- % Statement Coverage: The percentage of student solution lines in the submission that were executed at least once by the student's unit tests.
- TSSS (Test Statement Per Solution Statement) [20]: The ratio of Test NCLOC to Solution NCLOC.
- % Reference Tests Passed: The percentage of instructor generated unit tests that were passed by the student's solution.
- % Student Tests Correct: The percentage of the student's submitted unit tests that were correct (i.e. passed when run with an instructor reference solution).

Table 3 gives the mean values of these metrics for the original and modified BlueJ groups and summarizes the results of the likelihood ratio tests on the linear mixed effect models. This table shows statistically significant effects of the BlueJ version, at the $p<0.1$ level, for three metrics. Students in the modified BlueJ group submitted fewer lines of solution code, achieved a higher TSSS and a greater percentage of the tests that they submitted were correct. The first two of these are closely related. The modified BlueJ students submitted fewer lines of solution code than the original BlueJ students, but the amount of test code is similar between these groups. Thus, we would expect the TSSS for the modified BlueJ group to be larger. One explanation for this would be that the modified BlueJ group was completing less of the assignment prior to their first submission. However, both groups pass a similar percentage of the instructor reference tests. Based on this, we conclude that both groups were completing similar amounts of the assignment prior to their first submission to Web-CAT. Thus, the modified BlueJ students appear to be submitting shorter but equally complete and equally correct solutions. The greater percentage of student tests that were correct for the modified BlueJ users corresponds to the changes in Class 2, 3 and 4 test methods, as described above in Section 4.3. It is also worth noting that a somewhat smaller percentage of first submissions by the modified BlueJ group achieved at least 75% statement coverage on their first submission. This suggests that fewer members of the modified BlueJ group are adopting and sticking to a desirable test-a-little, code-a-little development routine.

	Original BlueJ	Modified BlueJ	
Submissions Included	76% 67/88	69% 48/70	Likelihood Ratio Test Results
NorSoln NCLOC	1.06	0.96	$\chi^2(1)=8.25$, **p=0.004**
NorTest NCLOC	1.06	1.04	$\chi^2(1)=0.07$, p=0.793
% Stmt Cover	94.1%	92.8%	$\chi^2(1)=1.10$, p=0.295
TSSS	1.32	1.47	$\chi^2(1)=3.63$, **p=0.057**
% Ref Test Pass	83.7%	82.2%	$\chi^2(1)=0.07$, p=0.795
% Stu Test Corr	90.1%	96.1%	$\chi^2(1)=3.56$, **p=0.059**

Table 3: Comparison of metrics and likelihood ratio test results for students' first submission to Web-CAT. The Submissions Included row indicates the percentage and raw number of all first submissions that were included in the analysis (i.e. those with >75% statement coverage).

4.5 Final Submissions

To investigate the effects of feedback from submission to Web-CAT we followed up on our analysis of the first submissions by looking at the same metrics applied to students' final submissions. These results are shown in Table 4. In final submissions, the BlueJ version has a statically significant effect on solution size and statement coverage. The difference in solution size is discussed further in section 4.6. The difference in statement coverage may be statistically significant but does not seem to be practically important as both groups of students achieve very high statement coverage (averages of 95% & 98% with the majority reaching 100%). They do so as a consequence of Web-CAT's scoring mechanism, which allows unlimited submissions and rewards high statement coverage. This scoring mechanism also explains the increase in the percentage of submissions with greater than 75% statement coverage as compared to the first submissions.

	Original BlueJ	Modified BlueJ	
Submissions Included	90.1% 100/111	89.7% 78/87	Likelihood Ratio Test Results
NorSoln NCLOC	1.1	0.98	$\chi^2(1)=10.3$, **p=0.001**
NorTest NCLOC	1.2	1.1	$\chi^2(1)=0.76$, p=0.384
% Stmt Cover	97.8%	94.9%	$\chi^2(1)=8.62$, **p=0.003**
TSSS	1.48	1.59	$\chi^2(1)=0.94$, p=0.331
% Ref Test Pass	88.2%	85.2%	$\chi^2(1)=0.85$, p=0.357
% Stu Test Corr	92.3%	94.2%	$\chi^2(1)=0.62$, p=0.431

Table 4: Comparison of metrics and likelihood ratio test results for students' last submission to Web-CAT. Normalization for NCLOC was done using final, rather than first, submissions to the assignments.

4.6 Solution Size

In Sections 4.4 and 4.5, results showed that modified BlueJ users, both before and after Web-CAT feedback, were submitting fewer lines of solution code while passing similar percentages of reference tests. Table 5 compares the actual number of non-comment, non-blank lines of code in the student solutions between BlueJ versions for first and final submissions on each of the lab exams. Comparing the size of submissions by the original and modified BlueJ groups shows that both the first and last solutions for both the first and second lab exams were smaller for the modified BlueJ group.

	Lab Exam 1		Lab Exam 2	
	Original BlueJ	Modified BlueJ	Original BlueJ	Modified BlueJ
First Submission	59.8	52.4	77.7	72.0
Last Submission	61.5	52.5	81.1	75.1

Table 5: Comparison of solution NCLOC in first and last submissions with at least 75% statement coverage.

To explore further, we examined the source code submitted for the first lab exam by a randomly selected sample of students from the original and modified BlueJ groups. In examining their solutions to the lab exam, it appears that students in the modified BlueJ group were making more extensive use of logical operators in conditional statements than were students in the original BlueJ group. A number of possible explanations exist for this observation. It could well be that the instructors and/or the TA for the modified BlueJ sections emphasized conditional operators more heavily. The modified BlueJ students' backgrounds may have been different (e.g. more math majors having taken discrete math in the fall before taking COMP131 in the spring). Or possibly, being forced by the BlueJ modification to think more carefully through complex test cases in prior labs and homework involving conditionals and logical operators increased this group's comfort level with these structures. We currently do not have enough information to resolve this question. We plan to return to this potentially interesting question bringing in data from past semesters of COMP131 that used the original BlueJ as well as data from future sections of COMP131 that will use our modified version of BlueJ.

4.7 Testing Behavior with Web-CAT

When introducing Web-CAT in section 3.2 we described an undesirable behavior in which students delay at least some testing until after using Web-CAT to confirm the correctness of their solution. Observations based on the data we have collected support our anecdotal observation that this behavior is occurring. If we compare the solution sizes of the first and last submissions in Table 5 with the similar data about student submitted tests in Table 6. From Table 5 it is clear that student's first submissions contain largely complete solutions. For student submitted tests, however, Table 6 shows that while test sets are substantial at the first submission, they increase in size from first to last submission much more than do the solutions. Thus, it appears that students are waiting to add tests for some solution code that had been submitted earlier.

	Lab Exam 1		Lab Exam 2	
	Original BlueJ	Modified BlueJ	Original BlueJ	Modified BlueJ
First Submission	77.7	78.0	103.2	101.3
Last Submission	91.8	87.0	114.8	109.8

Table 6: Comparison of test NCLOC in first and last submissions with at least 75% statement coverage.

Figure 1 further illustrates this point, showing the normalized size of student solution and test set submissions over time. Unlike earlier tables, this figure includes all submissions (regardless of test coverage) of all types of assignments (homework, labs and lab exams). It shows that solutions tend to be nearly complete even in early submissions, but that test sets grow over time; incrementally adding test code for solution code that was already present but untested in earlier submissions.

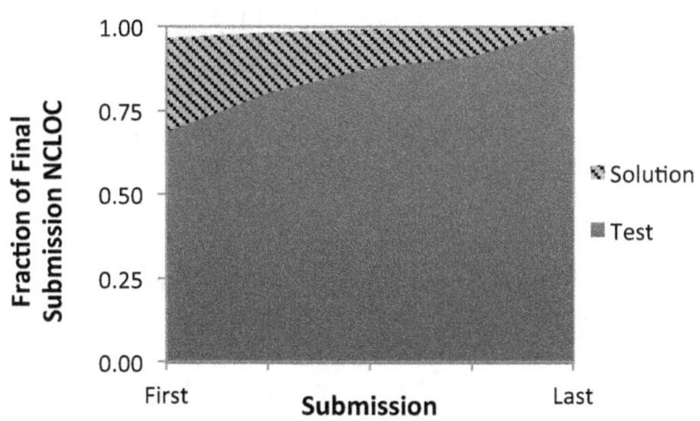

Figure 1: Average size of student solutions and test sets as a fraction of their final size from the first to last Web-CAT submissions.

Changes in the percentage of correct student tests from the initial submissions (Table 3) to the last submissions (Table 4) are also suggestive of the undesirable Web-CAT behavior. In going from the first to last submissions, the percentage of original BlueJ users' tests that were correct increased while that of the modified BlueJ users decreased. The behavior of students submitting untested code to Web-CAT until it is correct and then writing tests is one possible explanation for this observation. A student exhibiting this behavior with the original BlueJ will be given the correct assertion in the Method Result dialog because his/her code is already correct. The modified BlueJ user exhibiting the same behavior, however, will still have to figure out the correct assertion to make and thus, particularly on more complex methods and under lab exam time pressures, would be likely to make more mistakes. Incidentally, this explanation also suggests that the percentage of Class 2 test methods observed for the original BlueJ group in section 4.3 is probably an underestimate as many more Class 2 submissions would likely occur if not for this undesirable Web-CAT behavior.

5. A New Web-CAT Grading Plug-in

We have found Web-CAT to be an excellent tool and very effective at encouraging students to create tests for their solutions. However, as seen in the previous section, students do not necessarily fully test their solutions as they are developed. Instead, some exploit Web-CAT's feedback and miss some of the potential benefits to be gained by fully engaging in the process of testing their own code. The Java-TDD grading plugin for Web-CAT enables this behavior because it will provide feedback on the correctness of submitted solution code that the student has not yet tested.

We propose a new Web-CAT grading plug-in that will more explicitly encourage students to develop their solutions using a code-a-little test-a-little (or vice-versa if you prefer) approach. The key features of the plug-in are that it:

- provides direct feedback about the correctness of the tests submitted by the student.
- returns reference test results and associated hints only for code that the student has tested.

Providing direct feedback on the correctness of student submitted tests encourages students to think about the correctness of their solution in terms of their own tests. Running the submitted student test methods against an instructor provided reference solution can generate this feedback. Student tests that pass when run with the reference solution will be marked as correct and those that fail will be marked as incorrect. When a student's solution passes a correct test, she learns about the correctness of her program in a natural way, from her own tests. When a student's solution fails a correct test, he is better equipped to track down the problem because he wrote the test. And when a student's test is incorrect, the structure of the plug-in feedback will ensure that the best way forward is for her to think more carefully about the test and correct it.

The above is sufficient for students to ensure that everything that they test is correct. However, to encourage students to fully test their solutions (e.g. edge cases, etc.) a set of instructor reference tests will still be used. The feedback that the student receives from each reference test will depend upon whether or not the student's own tests have covered the lines used by the reference test. If the student has tested all of the solution lines used by the reference test then her feedback will indicate if the reference test passed or failed and if it failed a hint can be provided. If any of the lines used by the reference test have not been covered by a student test, then his feedback will not give the results of the reference test, and it will count as a failure in the computed score. In this case, the student will be presented with a list of solution methods that were used by the reference test and any containing uncovered lines will be indicated. Thus, again the plug-in ensures that best way forward is through improved testing.

Providing feedback in the way described will also better support a code-a-little test-a-little development approach than the current Java-TDD plug-in. The current Java-TDD plug-in returns randomly selected hints from the reference tests that fail, possibly providing hints on some parts of the solution the student has not yet begun and omitting hints on parts that he has. The proposed plug-in does better by ensuring that the feedback the student receives is on exactly the parts of her program on which she has worked. We can be sure of this because she has tested them. Thus, a student can write and test a single method and submit it knowing that he will receive feedback relevant to that method. In addition, we believe that this plug-in will make student testing more authentic and intrinsically valuable because students will learn about the correctness of their solution, not through an inscrutable oracle, but by creating correct test methods. An implementation of the proposed Web-CAT grading plug-in has been developed and is currently in beta testing. It is scheduled to be used in COMP131 during the 2015-16 academic year. Data from this use will then be analyzed in summer 2016.

6. Summary

We have reported on an empirical investigation into student testing behavior with BlueJ and Web-CAT, two testing tools that are widely used in introductory computer science courses with novice programmers. We found that a change in the BlueJ test recording interface led to a higher percentage of student recorded test methods being correct. Our finding that modified BlueJ users submitted equally complete and equally correct solutions using fewer lines of code may lend additional support to assertions that having students engage in testing benefits them in learning to code as well. However, our results also suggested that all students, but more so the modified BlueJ users, were not reliably practicing a desirable code-a-little test-a-little development strategy when interacting with Web-CAT. In response, we proposed a new Web-CAT grading plug-in that we believe will help move students toward a more desirable incremental development and testing approach. We anticipate collecting data for its evaluation during the 2015-16 academic year and doing an analysis during summer 2016.

7. ACKNOWLEDGMENTS

Partial funding for the development of the COMP131 materials was provided by the National Science Foundation under a CCLI-A&I grant (DUE-0511264). We would like to thank Dr. Stephen Edwards of Virginia Tech for supporting our use of Web-CAT and Dr. Jeffery Forrester of Dickinson College for his assistance in identifying appropriate statistical techniques and introducing us to R.

8. REFERENCES

[1] Terry Shepard, Margaret Lamb, and Diane Kelly. 2001. More testing should be taught. *Commun. ACM* 44, 6 (June 2001), 103-108.

[2] Edward L. Jones. 2001. Integrating testing into the curriculum — arsenic in small doses. In *Proc. 32nd SIGCSE tech. symp. on Computer Science Education*. ACM, New York, NY, USA, 337-341.

[3] Chetan Desai, David S. Janzen, and John Clements. 2009. Implications of integrating test-driven development into CS1/CS2 curricula. In *Proc. of the 40th SIGCSE tech. symp. on Computer science education*. ACM, New York, NY, USA, 148-152.

[4] David Janzen and Hossein Saiedian. 2008. Test-driven learning in early programming courses. In *Proc. 39th SIGCSE tech. symp. on Computer science education*. ACM, New York, NY, USA, 532-536.

[5] D. Steinberg. 2001. The effect of unit tests on entry points, coupling and cohesion in an introductory Java programming course. XP Universe, Raleigh, NC, 2001.

[6] Chetan Desai, David Janzen, and Kyle Savage. 2008. A survey of evidence for test-driven development in academia. *SIGCSE Bull.* 40, 2 (June 2008), 97-101.

[7] Vesa Lappalainen, Jonne Itkonen, Ville Isomöttönen, and Sami Kollanus. 2010. ComTest: a tool to impart TDD and unit testing to introductory level programming. In *Proc. 15th annual conf. on Innovation and technology in computer science education*. ACM, New York, NY, USA, 63-67.

[8] Jaime Spacco and William Pugh. 2006. Helping students appreciate test-driven development (TDD). In *Companion to the 21st ACM SIGPLAN symp. on Object-oriented programming systems, languages, and applications*. ACM, New York, NY, USA, 907-913.

[9] Viera K. Proulx. 2009. Test-driven design for introductory OO programming. In *Proc. 40th SIGCSE tech. symp. on Computer science education*. ACM, New York, NY, USA, 138-142.

[10] Kevin Buffardi and Stephen H. Edwards. 2013. Impacts of adaptive feedback on teaching test-driven development. In *Proc. 44th SIGCSE tech. symp. on Computer science education*. ACM, New York, NY, USA, 293-298.

[11] Kevin Buffardi and Stephen H. Edwards. 2014. A formative study of influences on student testing behaviors. In *Proc. 45th SIGCSE technical symposium on Computer science education*. ACM, New York, NY, USA, 597-602.

[12] David J. Barnes and Michael Klling. 2011. *Objects First with Java: A Practical Introduction Using BlueJ* (5th ed.). Prentice Hall Press, Upper Saddle River, NJ, USA.

[13] Grant Braught and Tim Wahls. 2008. Teaching objects in context. *J. Comput. Sci. Coll.* 23, 5 (May 2008), 101-109.

[14] Andrew Patterson, Michael Kölling, and John Rosenberg. 2003. Introducing unit testing with BlueJ. In *Proc. 8th annual conf. on Innovation and technology in computer science education*, David Finkel (Ed.). ACM, New York, NY, USA, 11-15.

[15] Stephen H. Edwards. 2004. Using software testing to move students from trial-and-error to reflection-in-action. In *Proc. 35th SIGCSE tech. symp. on Computer science education*. ACM, New York, NY, USA, 26-30.

[16] Stephen H. Edwards. 2003. Improving student performance by evaluating how well students test their own programs. *J. Educ. Resour. Comput.* 3, 3, Article 1 (September 2003).

[17] Winter, B. 2013. Linear models and linear mixed effects models in R with linguistic applications. arXiv:1308.5499.

[18] R Core Team 2015. R: A language and environment for statistical computing. R Foundation for Statistical Computing, Vienna, Austria. URL http://www.R-project.org/.

[19] Bates D, Maechler M, Bolker BM and Walker S. 2015. Fitting Linear Mixed-Effects Models using lme4. ArXive-print; in press, URL: http://arxiv.org/abs/1406.5823.

[20] Buffardi, K. & Edwards, S.H. 2012. Impacts of Teaching Test-Driven Development to Novice Programmers. International Journal of Information and Computer Science, Vol. 6, No 1.

An Experience Report Assessing A Professional Development MOOC For CS Principles

Jeff Gray
University of Alabama
Tuscaloosa, AL, USA
gray@cs.ua.edu

Jonathan Corley
University of Alabama
Tuscaloosa, AL, USA
corle001@crimson.ua.edu

Brian P. Eddy
University of West Florida
Pensacola, FL, USA
beddy@uwf.edu

ABSTRACT

CS Principles is a new AP course being developed by the College Board and introduced into high schools across the nation. To aid and encourage the adoption of the new CSP course, we have developed a Massively-Open Online Course (MOOC) over the past two years that serves as a professional development (PD) offering for CS Principles. Additionally, we have provided a parallel face-to-face workshop for a smaller group of MOOC participants. In this paper, we discuss our experiences conducting PD using a MOOC. We investigated the impact of the face-to-face event and online community on participants' completion and performance in the course. Our analysis suggests that participants who have even just a few days of face-to-face engagement tend to be more successful in completing a multi-week MOOC.

Keywords

MOOC; Professional Development; Hybrid Learning Env.

1. INTRODUCTION

CS Principles (CSP) is a new AP CS course being introduced into high schools across the nation, with the first exam targeted for May 2017 [1]. To aid and encourage the adoption of AP CSP, we offered a Massively-Open Online Course (MOOC) providing a gentle introduction to the CSP Curriculum Framework (CF) and Performance Tasks (PTs) [2]. The MOOC evolved from a non-majors course at the University of Alabama (with special focus on Secondary Math Education majors and 67% enrollment by women) that was a College Board pilot course. The university-focused course served as the basis for an NSF-supported project (NSF CE21: NSF#1240944) that offers year-long CSP training to high school teachers across the state of Alabama. The MOOC curriculum is driven by a combination of the university course and shared resources developed by the teachers in the NSF project [9]. The content delivery needs led to an online version of the course that evolved into a free MOOC coupled with a one week local face-to-face meeting, the CS4Alabama PD workshop, held for the teachers in the NSF project. The MOOC, CSP4HS [2], has been supported by Google for two offerings of the course in 2014 and 2015. The most recent offering enrolled over 1,065 educators from 48 states (sans Wyoming and Vermont) in the USA and 39 other countries. Six other states used our MOOC for their CSP content mixed with their own local 3-5 day face-to-face meetings. This paper reports on the Alabama experiences.

The current version of the MOOC is teacher-facing and designed for professional development (PD) of teachers who have little background in computer science. However, we offer a variety of resources that we strive to update for each new offering. Thus, we also provide some content of value to past participants. The current offering of the course includes six units of instruction spanning topics of the Big Ideas of CSP utilizing the following key components.

1. Course Materials[1] provided to participants include:
    a) training modules for the CSP CF and PTs
    b) over 120 videos[2] for teachers and students
    c) lesson plans developed by teacher leaders
    d) lesson slides
    e) quizzes and exams
    f) a pacing guide and syllabus
2. Piazza-based community of practice for teachers participating in the course
3. Course-wide broadcast through Google Hangouts on Air for synchronous interaction with MOOC instructors as well as invited guests
4. Virtual Face-To-Face through Google Hangouts

A certificate is available for those participants who complete all quizzes and exams, along with a solo version of the Create PT. Although focused on summer participation, the MOOC resources are available year-round.

The driving philosophy behind both the NSF project and MOOC is the idea of "for teachers, by teachers." Many of the MOOC resources have been created and vetted by teachers from our NSF project. The MOOC co-instructors are also high school teachers who have been teaching CSP for several years. This philosophy has contributed to what we feel is the major success of this MOOC, a vibrant and active

[1]http://tinyurl.com/CSP4HS-2015-Resources
[2]http://tinyurl.com/CS4Alabama-YouTube

SIGCSE '16 March 2–5, 2016, Memphis, TN, USA

DOI: http://dx.doi.org/10.1145/2839509.2844654

Figure 1: CSP4HS Participants in Continental USA

community of practice driven by the needs, concerns, and suggestions of classroom teachers.

In this paper, we present an experience report describing our activities, challenges, and lessons learned offering a MOOC for teacher PD. We begin in Section 2 by introducing the key components of the MOOC along with some demographic information describing the participant diversity. Section 3 discusses the primary challenges encountered in development of the MOOC, including the following:

1. coordinating rapid, large scale communication from course participants
2. creating and adapting curriculum content in the presence of evolving changes from the College Board development process
3. managing the grading and communicating the results of assessment instruments
4. significantly underestimating the initial time needed to develop course materials for an online presence
5. intgrating a cocktail of tools that were used to deliver the course
6. understanding how to address differentiated needs among many participants with varied backgrounds and abilities

Additionally, whereas prior work in the area has explored the concerns of face-to-face PD [8], we investigated the impact of face-to-face meetings and an online community on participants' completion and performance in the course.

2. OVERVIEW OF CSP4HS

In this section, we introduce the key components of the MOOC and the face-to-face workshop, and we present demographic data regarding enrollment in the course and the face-to-face event.

2.1 CSP CS4HS 2015: A CSP PD MOOC

The MOOC had four primary components: the course materials, Piazza (an online forum designed for integration into the classroom), Hangouts on Air (Google Hangouts broadcast to YouTube), and virtual face-to-face (small group Google Hangouts facilitated by our instructors).

2.1.1 Course Materials

The primary course materials consisted of a Google Course Builder course [2], a set of quizzes and exams built using Google Forms, and a set of Lesson Videos hosted on YouTube. Google Course Builder [4] was used to craft a set of six units each consisting of several lessons. A complete lesson contained the lesson videos (embedded in the page), links to a variety of relevant sources including the slides from the lesson video, links to freely available resources, relevant videos from our face-to-face event, and a textual guide discussing all the content that ties together the overall lesson with sample activities and discussion questions. Very frequently, we would also direct participants in the course to post on Piazza regarding certain aspects of the lessons. These discussions sparked conversation between participants and enabled us to directly converse with course participants regarding the content of the lessons.

A common component of all course lessons was links to external sources relevant to the lesson topic. This was a key feature of the course designed to expose participants to the vast wealth of other CSP resources available online. Because preparing educators to teach CSP concepts was a primary goal of the course, we included links to videos and activities covering key lesson concepts (*e.g.,* YouTube videos, Code.org activities, or CS Unplugged activities). We also directed participants to lesson plans and teaching resources relevant to course topics from a variety of sources[3].

2.1.2 Asynchronous Community Discussion Forum

The course used Piazza [6] as an open forum for discussion among all participants involved in the course (participants and instructors). The instructors could post announcements, run polls, post questions, answer questions, and endorse answers and posts made by participants. Most threads were public and available to all participants, but we also allowed private threads between a single participant and the instructors, or within a specific subgroup (*e.g.,* the six other states that used our MOOC for content, but provided their own face-to-face meetings each had their own subgroup). We maintained dedicated threads for each les-

[3]These sources include but are not limited to http://apcsprinciples.org/, https://cs10kcommunity.org/, https://apcommunity.collegeboard.org/

son, each HOA (discussed in Section 2.1.3), and other central concepts. These dedicated threads helped maintain discussion of a specific topic within a single location, but many other topics were discussed and numerous private threads were posted. There were over 3,800 posts to the Piazza community, with an average response time of 33 minutes for replies to posted questions.

2.1.3 *Live Guest Talks*

Hangouts on Air (HoA) is a Google Hangout [5] that simulcasts (with slight delay) and archives to a YouTube channel. The HOAs provided an opportunity for the entire class to listen to a broadcast from a guest speaker(s) who is very influential in the CSP community, and to ask questions via a dedicated Piazza thread. Several HOAs have also been incorporated into the lessons as a video resource (*i.e.,* embedded YouTube video of a previously recorded HOA broadcast).

2.1.4 *Synchronized Group Office Hours*

We used traditional Google Hangouts [5] to serve as virtual office hours (*i.e.,* face-to-face meetings) among a small group of participants (10 or less) facilitated by one of our instructors; *i.e.,* High School teachers with several years experience teaching CSP (two are national College Board Pilot instructors) recruited to assist with the course. The Hangouts focused on discussing current topics related to the course, and were offered nearly daily during the initial six weeks of the course. The Hangouts were filled in a first-come, first-served basis and scheduled through a dedicated Piazza thread for each Hangout.

2.2 Face-to-Face Meetings

We held a face-to-face PD workshop designed to prepare 47 teachers from across Alabama to teach CSP, as part of our multi-year PD model. This workshop is part of an NSF grant (NSF CE21) that funds activities to train teachers along with developing curriculum for the AP CSP course.

The workshop reinforced several concepts introduced in the MOOC, including programming using Snap!, recruitment strategies, as well as deep discussions and group activities surrounding the CSP PTs. The workshop lasted one week running from 9am to 4pm most days with 2 evening activities. We had returning participants from previous workshops as well as new participants. We often offered parallel sessions to allow our returning participants to cover more advanced or expanded topics. Our MOOC was also used by six other states who were funded by Google CS4HS. The online content of our MOOC was supplemented by face-to-face meetings within each state.

2.3 Course Demographics

As a freely available online course, we attracted a large and widely diverse group of participants. To capture the widely varying demographics for the course, we took an initial survey of all those interested in the course. With over 1,065 participants completing this survey of interest, we immediately observed several interesting trends.

2.3.1 *Intent to Complete the Course*

Our MOOC attracted a number of participants only interested in browsing the course materials, including some who had taken a previous iteration of the course in 2014. Nearly

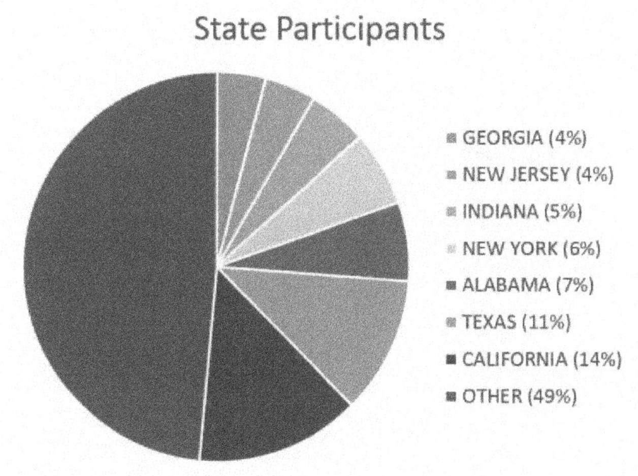

Figure 2: Participants per State

5% of our participants indicated an interest in browsing the materials, but not in completing the course requirements to earn the various PD certificates. Even more notable, over 30% of respondents indicated they intended to partially complete the course, but would not strive to earn any of the PD certificates. Some of these two groups indicated they had previously completed the course and were browsing for new material and updates. Others still indicated they were passively interested in the course materials and intended only to seek a general understanding of the concepts covered by the course. Most interesting to us is that 65% of the participants indicated that they wished to pursue the complete course, including earning the certificate. However, only about 13% completed the majority of certificate requirements. A focus of this paper is to understand why participant follow-through has been so low, as common to other MOOCs.

2.3.2 *Gender Diversity*

We also teach a CSP course for non-majors at the university level, which has been a national College Board Pilot since 2011. The Fall 2015 course enrollment has 67% women. There is a similar gender tilt toward women in our MOOC, with the participants at 57% women.

2.3.3 *Geographically Dispersed*

Our original hope was to draw participants from across our state and even some participants from across the nation into our online community. To our surprise and delight, these expectations have been met and well surpassed. The enrollment for the 2015 offering of this course included 48 states and over 39 countries. Fig. 1 displays the geographic spread across the continental US, and Fig. 2 illustrates the states with the largest enrollment in the course.

2.3.4 *Teaching Focus*

The course was offered primarily as PD in support of the new AP CSP course. As such, our primary audience was high school educators. To gain a better understanding of the diversity of educators, we asked several questions regarding where, how, and what our respondents teach. Fig. 3a illustrates the type of school at which our participants teach. The vast majority teach at public schools

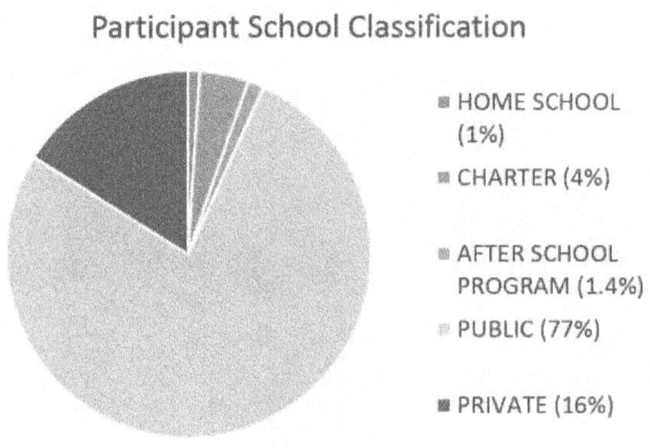

(a) Classification of Schools

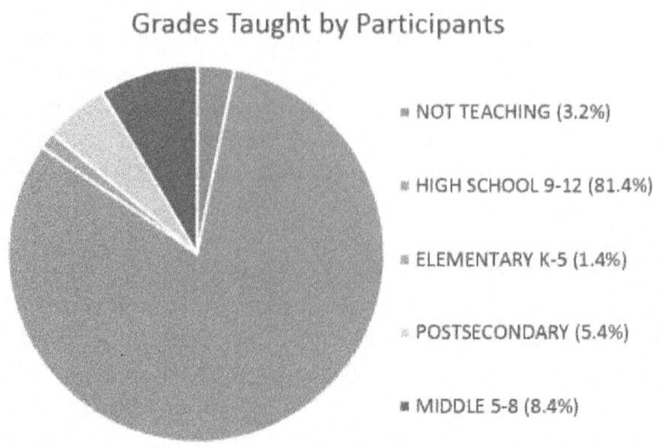

(b) Grades Taught

Figure 3: Teaching Demographics of MOOC Participants

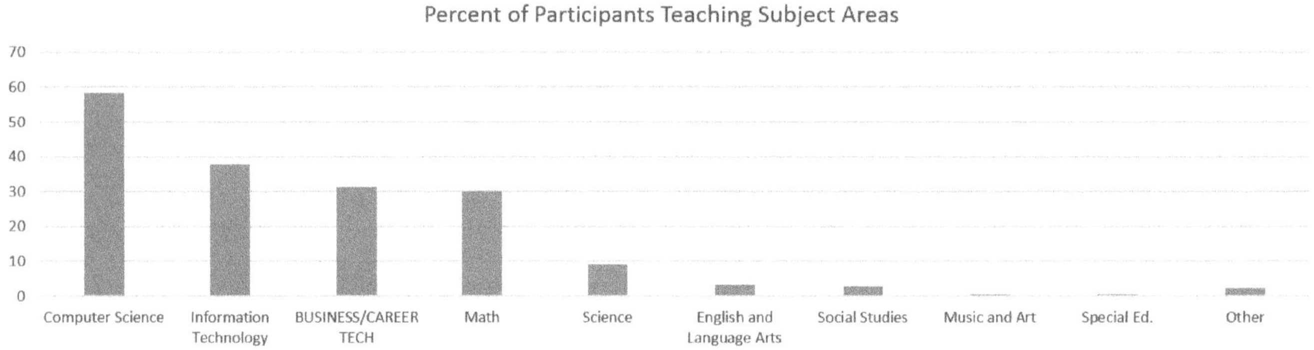

Figure 4: Subject Areas Taught by Participants

(77%) with the next largest group being private schools (16%). However, there were also participants from charter schools (4%), homeschool programs (1%), and even after school programs (1.4%). When queried about which grades they taught (Fig. 3b) , the vast majority taught High School (81.4%) as expected for the AP course material, but we also had participants who teach Elementary (1.4%), Middle (8.4%), and Post-secondary (5.4%). Finally, Fig. 4 displays the percentage of participants who teach at least one course in a specific subject area.

We were also interested in whether the participants currently or planned to teach CSP. We found that 15% currently teach CSP, and 45% plan to teach CSP in the future. Only 3% indicated they would not consider teaching the course, with the remaining 37% open to the possibility of teaching CSP at some point in the future.

2.3.5 *Prior Knowledge*

A key concern of managing the course and materials was understanding the experience of the participants. Therefore, we asked a set of questions to gather information regarding our participants CS education, CS teaching experience, and knowledge of programming languages and environments. We found that approximately 46% of participants had taken one or two courses covering CS topics; 16% had taken 3-4 courses; and a surprisingly sizeable 38% had taken 5 or more courses covering CS.

Regarding CS teaching experience, 43% indicated little or no experience teaching CS courses. Of the remainder, 25% had notable experience teaching CS and 27% indicated they had experience teaching CSP. We believe the expressed interest in the course is driven by recent changes to the Curriculum Framework by the College Board and the addition of new resources (*e.g.,* lesson plans) being advertised as available through the MOOC that are specifically designed to aid teachers who plan to explore CSP.

We also identified the programming languages known or used by the participants, and were surprised at the variety of languages listed. In total, participants listed 121 languages. The top languages and environments included Scratch (used by 51%), Java (51%), C++ (35%), Javascript (32%), Python (31%), Alice (29%), and App Inventor (27%). Nearly 10% of participants had no experience with any programming language or environment.

3. LESSONS LEARNED

This section summarizes some of the challenges that we faced in offering the MOOC, as well as an assessment that we made on the impact of face-to-face and online communities toward course completion and content mastery.

3.1 Challenges Encountered During the MOOC

Our MOOC is in its second version, which has allowed us to reflect back on some of the experiences during its development. The main challenges we faced are summarized in the following subsections.

3.1.1 *Creating and Developing Course Materials and Curriculum*

As with most reports of online course development [7], the amount of time needed to curate and design the set of curricular resources is significantly greater compared to teaching a face-to-face course. A particular challenge has been the changes to the CSP Curriculum Framework during the College Board's pilot development, which forced us to revisit and recreate videos and resources from the previous year's offering.

3.1.2 *Managing Communication at Scale*

Even though our MOOC was a much more modest offering than more large-scale courses (we had barely more than 1,000 participants in 2015), we still experienced the shock of scale during the initial communication with course participants. Before the Piazza community began to settle in its role, we received over 850 emails on the first day of the course opening. Coordinating the community responses and replies from the course instructors required considerable planning.

3.1.3 *Managing Grading at Scale*

Several online courses have used automated tools, as well as peer grading, to handle the challenges of assessing student performance in a course. We had approximately 3,065 quizzes that were graded automatically using Flubaroo [3] (a Google Docs plugin for managing forms-based quizzes), which provided a summary of all quiz responses for analysis and also communicated results to the participants. To achieve consistency in grading the Create PT homework, we developed a rubric and a subset of our course instructors graded the homework submissions, rather than using peer grading.

3.1.4 *Differentiated Learners at Scale*

In the same way that a traditional classroom has students with mixed abilities requiring the practice of differentiated learning strategies, the issue is even more evident in a MOOC. With participants who have a very deep background, to those who have never programmed before, we needed to create special opportunities to challenge those with more experience while offering additional instruction for those who are newly initiated to CS.

3.1.5 *Integrating Disparate Tools to Create a Cohesive Course Environment*

We used a cocktail of tools to support the online experience, including: Google Course Builder for hosting the main course site, Piazza for forming the community of practice discussion area, Google Docs and Flubaroo for surveys and assessments, Google Drive for course resources, YouTube for video resources, and both Hangouts and Hangouts on Air for synchronous communication. These tools often did not integrate with each other natively (*e.g.,* Course Builder and Flubaroo), and the number of different tools needed to participate and follow along in the course was confusing to some participants. A more integrated MOOC experience would likely reduce any stress associated with completing the course.

3.2 Impact of Face-to-Face

The face-to-face portion of the course included the PD workshop for our Alabama teachers. The purpose of the face-to-face portion of the course was to provide teachers who were planning to teach CSP in the future with a more interactive learning environment where they could work more closely with the instructors of the course than was possible through online instruction alone. Our goal was to help teachers develop the confidence they needed to succeed in teaching the course, as well as help them to build and establish a community of practice among peers.

We evaluated whether the teachers who participated in our own statewide face-to-face session went on to complete the course and if they were more successful in completing the material than those who did not participate in the face-to-face workshop. To this aim, we analyzed the results of the course in terms of the percentage of the course and scores on course assessments for teachers who completed the face-to-face versus participants who did not. For our comparisons, we looked at only those teachers who had full interest in completing the course as judged by the pre-course surveys.

3.2.1 *Impact of Face-to-Face on Course Completion*

We first looked at whether there was a difference between the completion rates of the teachers who participated in the face-to-face event and those who did not. We judged this based off of the percentage of lessons completed, the completion of the course midterm, and the completion of the course's Create PT homework. We found that on average, the teachers who completed the face-to-face event completed 88% of the course, while the teachers who did not complete the face-to-face event only completed 21% of the course on average. We performed a Wilcoxon rank-sum test between the two groups, which is the non-parametric analogue of the t-test, and found a significant difference ($p < 0.05$) between the two groups. We consider this observation to be a major finding and contribution of this paper toward better understanding the importance of face-to-face workshops on completion of hybrid PD courses.

3.2.2 *Impact of Face-to-Face on Course Assessments*

Second, we looked at the results of the course midterm and the course's Create PT. On average, the teachers who participated in the face-to-face event scored an 89% on the course midterm on average and 80% on the Create PT on average. Teachers who did not participate in the face-to-face scored a 92% on the course midterm on average and a 78% on the Create PT on average. While the midterm percentage is slightly higher for the group that did not participate in the face-to-face, a statistically significant difference was not found between the groups. Furthermore, the percentage of the teachers who completed the face-to-face who also completed the midterm was 88%, whereas the percentage was only 13% for those teachers who did not. We believe that the face-to-face session gave teachers, who typically would not have completed the midterm or homework, the confidence to do so.

3.2.3 *Impact of Face-to-Face on Participation in Online Discussion*

Finally, we were interested in whether the teachers who completed the face-to-face event were more likely to participate in the online discussion. We looked at both the percentage of the teachers who participated in some form of online discussion and the number of contributions each participant in this group made to the online discussions. We found that on average, the teachers who participated in the face-to-face event made 9 contributions to the online discussion and 88% of the teachers participated in some form of online discussion. For the teachers who did not participate in the face-to-face event, we found that they made on average 6 contributions to the online discussion and only 35% participated in the online discussion. For those teachers who participated in the online community, we did not find a significant difference in the number of contributions between those that participated in the face-to-face event and those who did not.

3.3 Impact of Online Community

The online community allowed teachers to communicate asynchronously with their peers and instructors to ask questions, discuss the course material, and to learn about additional material related to CS and to teaching CS in the classroom. In addition, it was included as a way for teachers to build a network of their peers that they may not have been able to otherwise. Teachers could participate in the online community regardless of whether they participated in the face-to-face or not.

We evaluated whether the teachers who participated in the online community were more successful at completing the material than those who did not. Like the analysis of the face-to-face event, we analyzed the results of the course in terms of the percentage of the course and scores on course assessments for teachers who participated in the online community versus teachers who did not. Again, we looked at only those teachers who had full interest in completing the course as judged by the pre-course surveys.

3.3.1 Impact of Online Community on Course Completion

Similar to the face-to-face workshop, we first looked at whether there was a difference between the completion rates of the teachers who participated in the online community and those who did not. We found that on average, the teachers who participated in the online community completed 35% of the course, while the teachers who did not participate in the online community only completed 15% of the course on average. We found a significant difference ($p < 0.05$) between the two groups.

3.3.2 Impact of Online Community on Course Assessments

We then looked at the results of the course midterm and the course's Create PT. On average, the teachers who participated in the online community scored a 93% on the course midterm on average and 84% on the Create PT on average. Teachers who did not participate in the online community scored 92% on the course midterm on average and a 78% on the Create PT on average. For both the course midterm and for the Create PT, the averages were higher for teachers who participated in the online community. While no significant difference was found between the course midterms, a difference was found between the Create PT averages of the two groups. Furthermore, the percentage who participated in the online community who also completed the midterm was 22% and the Create PT was 17%, whereas the percentage was only 8% for midterms and 6% for the Create PT for those who did not participate in the online community.

4. CONCLUSIONS AND FUTURE WORK

Over the course of two offerings of a MOOC for PD on CSP, we have encountered a number of challenge that range from managing simple concerns (*e.g.,* participant communication) to more complex issues (*e.g.,* addressing differentiated course needs among a large group of participants with varying backgrounds and abilities). In this paper, we discussed our experiences with these challenges and the lessons learned. Furthermore, we investigated the impact of our face-to-face event and online community with respect to participants' completion and performance in the course.

As future work, we hope to investigate further the impact of the various key course components through additional data collection and analysis. Our goal is to understand the benefits of providing online and face-to-face interactions among participants and how these interactions impact success in the course. Additionally, we hope to be able to gather information regarding use of MOOC materials in classrooms and as reference resources for past participants.

5. ACKNOWLEDGMENTS

This work is supported by NSF CE21 (CNS 1240944) and Google CS4HS.

We would like to thank the following who assisted with the instruction and development of the MOOC: Jeff Baker, Roy Black, Lydia Eubanks, Rachael Giles, Gina McCarley, Deepa Muralidhar, Michele Roberts, Lauri Springer, Jake Trower, Jill Westerlund.

6. REFERENCES

[1] AP CS Principles. http://apcsprinciples.org/. Accessed: 08-29-2015.

[2] CSP4HS. https://csp-cs4hs.appspot.com/preview.

[3] Flubaroo. http://www.flubaroo.com/. Accessed: 08-29-2015.

[4] Google Course Builder. https://www.google.com/edu/openonline/index.html. Accessed: 08-29-2015.

[5] Google Hangouts. https://plus.google.com/hangouts. Accessed: 08-29-2015.

[6] Piazza. https://piazza.com/. Accessed: 08-29-2015.

[7] J. Burge. Insights into teaching and learning: Reflections on mooc experiences. In *Proceedings of the 46th ACM Technical Symposium on Computer Science Education*, SIGCSE '15, pages 600–603, Kansas City, MO, 2015.

[8] S. Cooper, S. H. Rodger, M. Schep, R. H. Stalvey, and W. Dann. Growing a k-12 community of practice. In *Proceedings of the 46th ACM Technical Symposium on Computer Science Education*, SIGCSE '15, pages 290–295, Kansas City, MO, 2015.

[9] J. Gray, K. Haynie, S. Packman, M. Boehm, C. Crawford, and D. Muralidhar. A mid-project report on a statewide professional development model for cs principles. In *Proceedings of the 46th ACM Technical Symposium on Computer Science Education*, SIGCSE '15, pages 380–385, Kansas City, MO, 2015.

Two Teachers, Two Perspectives on CS Principles

Jean Griffin
College of Education
Temple University
Philadelphia PA, USA
jean.griffin@temple.edu

Tammy Pirmann
Springfield Township High School
Montgomery County PA, USA
and Gwynedd Mercy University
Gwynedd Valley PA, USA
tammy_pirmann@sdst.org

Brent Gray
George Washington Carver High
School of Engineering and Science
Philadelphia PA, USA
bhgray@philasd.org

ABSTRACT

This paper reports on an investigative, qualitative case study of the teaching practices of two public high school Computer Science teachers as they teach courses that are fully or partially aligned with the CS Principles framework. One teaches at an urban, high minority STEM school, the other at a middle class suburban school. Ethnographic methods were used to collect data via classroom observations and teacher interviews. Within-case and across-case analyses are presented which characterize the teachers' practices regarding pedagogy, curricula, creative activities, problem-solving activities, and management of social interactions. The findings provide detailed insights regarding the challenges these teachers face and the strategies they use, which may be useful to teachers in a variety of settings at both the high school and college/university levels.

Keywords

CS Principles; CS1; K-12; pedagogical content knowledge; PCK-CS, Pair Programming; POGIL.

1. INTRODUCTION

In an effort to increase the number and diversity of American high school students who engage with Computer Science (CS) as an academic discipline, the National Science Foundation has partnered with the College Board during the past decade to develop a framework for a new Advanced Placement Computer Science course called *CS Principles* [4, 16, 18, 46]. The longstanding AP CS-A course and exam, which focus on programming with the Java language, will continue to be offered after the official launch of AP CS Principles, slated for 2016-17. While the CS Principles framework features some aspects found in the traditional AP course such as programming, algorithms, abstraction, and data, it includes other "big ideas" of CS such as creativity and the Internet, as well as the ethical, social, and global impacts of computing. It also emphasizes certain *computational thinking* skills: collaborating, communicating, connecting, and creating along with analyzing and abstracting [2, 27, 48]. This attention to the creative and social dimensions of computing is intended in large part to be attractive to young people from groups that have been underrepresented in computing courses and careers in the United States, such as females and people from racial or ethnic minorities [7, 15, 22, 32, 33, 49].

SIGCSE '16, March 02-05, 2016, Memphis, TN, USA
© 2016 ACM. ISBN 978-1-4503-3685-7/16/03···$15.00
DOI: http://dx.doi.org/10.1145/2839509.2844630

2. BACKGROUND

2.1 The CS Principles Framework

It is noteworthy that CS Principles is a *framework*, not a set curriculum. Teachers are free to use whatever computing technologies they want as long as the learning objectives are met. The framework is an emerging one that has evolved in an iterative process beginning with a few dozen college and high school pilot offerings in 2010-12 [3, 11, 45]. Some of the pilot instructors required their students to learn just one computing technology; others required several and/or made some optional. In total, a wide range of technologies was taught for animation, games, robots, mobile apps, web programs, traditional text-based programs, etc. As the pilot instructors experimented with pedagogies and curricula, the CS Principles project team fine-tuned the framework so teachers could prepare students for the AP CS Principles exam, slated to launch in 2016-17.

As CS Principles evolved, a portfolio requirement was added; it requires students to complete both a research performance task (Explore) and a creative/constructive performance task (Create) [5]. Additional pilot courses that addressed the portfolio requirement were offered [19, 37]. Several teams developed and shared course curricula aligned with CS Principles and initiated teacher professional development programs [6, 17, 19, 35, 37, 47]. Others developed and shared curricular modules and pedagogies aligned with CS Principles [14, 25, 38] .

2.2 Adoption and Enactment of Curricula

The fact that CS Principles is a framework, rather than a set curriculum, presents opportunities as well as challenges. It has fueled the fires of creative innovation as evidenced by the varied and engaging courses and curricula designed by educators and technologists involved with CS Principles. This freedom of choice can also be problematic as teachers and school administrators decide what choices to make for their students. Although some research has been conducted on the issues CS teachers face regarding the adoption of new curricula [39], teachers and administrators could benefit from specific guidance about navigating the dizzying array of choices related to CS Principles.

After the choice of curriculum is made, there are still decisions to make about how it will be realized in the classroom. Research studies indicate that the efficacy of curricula in terms of student achievement depends in part on how it is enacted [24, 41]. Pedagogical approaches for enacting curricula in one school setting may not be effective in another. CS teachers and school administrators can benefit from learning how CS Principles curricula are enacted by experienced CS teachers in a variety of school settings.

2.3 Problem Solving & Creative Construction

High school Computer Science lies at the crux of two contrasting computing education paradigms. Formal CS education developed largely in the mathematical tradition within institutions of higher education. Many college-level introductory CS classes have a primary emphasis on problem solving. For example: "Write a program or algorithm to solve this problem." It's not unusual for undergraduate degree programs to have numerous introductory courses focused on problem solving, with capstone courses towards the end that focus on design tasks.

In contrast, the most famous learning theory related to computing for youth is Seymour Papert's Constructionism, which encourages beginners to construct knowledge by creating personally meaningful computational artifacts and to share them in a public setting [40]. This learning theory emerged alongside the Logo language and *turtle graphics*. It has gained renewed attention recently with the invention of numerous educational technologies for creative computing including Alice, Bootstrap, LightBot, Lilypad Arduino, Processing, Scratch, Snap!, and MIT App Inventor for Android. Some of these technologies that were designed for middle schoolers are increasingly finding a foothold in high school and undergraduate courses.

The CS Principles framework essentially seeks to bridge these two paradigms, an ambitious but worthy goal. For teachers accustomed to the "primarily problem solving" paradigm, it can be difficult to incorporate creative activities due to a lack of experience with assigning creative projects and concerns about evaluating them appropriately. For teachers who have more of a creative background, it can take time to learn the terms, concepts, and problem solving skills important in a foundational CS course. Teachers need strategies for incorporating both paradigms within a single course, and can benefit from learning how experienced teachers in a variety of settings do so.

2.4 Social Interactions within a Course

Social interactions constitute an important dimension of learning. In higher education, CS has traditionally been taught via lecture along with a lab period where students often work alone. Many high school CS classes follow suit. CS Principles disrupts this pattern with rules that require students to complete some tasks with a partner. Even with these constraints, teachers of CS Principles still have many choices to make about establishing norms of social interaction. For example: how are students paired for the Create performance task? how do students work on other activities – alone, with a partner, in a free form group, in a group where members have roles? how much time is spent on lecture? is there an online discussion board? if so, are there rules of etiquette?

3. RESEARCH QUESTIONS

The research questions that frame this study are:

1. What pedagogical practices, curricula, and technologies do teachers in diverse settings employ while teaching courses fully or partially aligned with the CS Principles framework?
2. How do these teachers balance problem-solving activities with creative/constructionist activities?
3. What norms of social interaction do these teachers establish regarding the time students spend working individually, with a partner, with a group, or in whole-class discussions?
4. How are these teachers' practices similar and different?

4. METHODS

4.1 Research Design

This study was an investigative case study that used qualitative ethnographic methods to learn how two experienced high school Computer Science teachers approach the teaching of courses aligned fully or partially with the CS Principles framework.

4.2 Settings and Participants

The participants are a convenience sample of two high school CS teachers. Both work at schools in close proximity to the university with which the first author, an education researcher and the first-person voice of this paper, is associated. Both teachers have a high degree of academic preparation and experience with teaching CS. In the spirit of practitioner inquiry, they also served as co-researchers on this project and co-authors of this paper [13]. All three authors are on the board of Philadelphia's chapter of the Computer Science Teachers Association (CSTA-Philly) and have collaborated to develop curricular modules for CS Principles.

Springfield Township High School in Montgomery County PA is a public, middle class, low-minority school located in the suburbs of Philadelphia. According to the 2015 *U.S. News and World Report*, 14% of Springfield's population of 1,196 students is minority; 13% are economically disadvantaged; 79% are proficient in math; and 82% are proficient in literature. The gender balance is roughly 50-50. The participating teacher from Springfield is Tammy Pirmann. Pirmann has an undergraduate degree in Management and Information Systems and a master's degree in Education. She has taught high school CS for over ten years and is pursuing a doctorate in Educational Leadership at Gwynedd Mercy University in Gwynedd Valley PA.

George Washington Carver High School of Engineering and Science is a public magnet school located in Philadelphia PA. Carver has admission requirements including A's and B's in major subjects, 85+% on standardized test scores, an excellent attendance record, and no disciplinary reports. According to the 2015 *U.S. News and World Report*, 97% of Carver's population of 750 students is minority; 53% are economically disadvantaged; 94% are proficient in math; and 98% are proficient in literature. According to the school's website, the population is 76.6% African American, 9.3% Asian, 6.9% Latino, 3.8% Caucasian, and 3.4% Other. The gender balance is approximately 40% female to 60% male. The participating teaching from Carver is Brent Gray. Gray holds master's degrees in both Engineering (Computer Science) and Education. He has over ten years of experience at the high school level teaching both Mathematics and CS.

4.3 Data Collection and Measures

Classroom observations were conducted in spring 2015; teacher interviews took place in the spring and summer of 2015. Data sources include: field notes from nine 90-minute classroom observations of Pirmann and six 90-minute classroom observations of Gray (consisting of a description of the initial state of the classroom each day, descriptions of activities with begin and end times, and summary); notes from teacher interviews held at the conclusion of each observed class; clarifications to these notes (shared online) made by the teachers in the interest of *member checking*; researcher memos; curricular materials including the CS Principles framework [2]; and audiotaped interviews with each teacher using the interview protocol found below in Table 1.

Table 1. Teacher Interview Protocol *(question 4 abbreviated)*

1. What is your current teaching position?
2. What is your teaching load and what balance do you have between teaching CS and non-CS courses?
3. Describe the school culture with respect to Computer Science. For example, are CS course required? Are there any other CS teachers?
4. Questions about the observed course: course name; student demographics; length (semester/year); grade levels of students in the course; what does the course count for at your school; how does it fit in the school sequence of courses; topics and technologies; how much autonomy do you have in shaping the course; how does the course relate to CS Principles framework if at all; what has your involvement been with the CS Principles project; has your teaching practice changed since your involvement with CSP; how do you manage the social interactions during class and for out-of-class assignments (e.g. students work alone, with a partner, or group); do you have a personal philosophy about teaching the course: guiding principles/ideals; how might your course evolve in the future.
5. What is your academic background?
6. Regarding CS Education, what are your own goals and/or goals you would like to see your students achieve?
7. Is there anything else we should discuss?

4.4 Analysis

Classroom activities were encoded as they took place in field notes using pre-determined codes [34]. Two sets of codes were used simultaneously. One categorized social interactions: lecture, class discussion, individual work, and paired/partner work. During the observation period an additional code was added to this set, for structured small group work (where students assume specific roles). This set of codes proved to be robust; it provided a useful measure for patterns of social interaction in the classroom. A second set of codes categorized conceptual activities in the classroom either as problem solving or creative/constructionist. This set of codes did not prove to be as useful. Many activities are a combination of the two, and some activities such as student research were not easily categorized. Instead, the ways in which the teachers balanced and blended these paradigmatic modes of activity were informed by a constellation of factors including curricular choices, interview responses, assessments, and so forth.

The hour-long audiotaped teacher interviews were transcribed and coded according to themes corresponding to the research questions, for example, how teachers balanced analytical activities with creative activities and how they managed social interactions. Additional themes emerged during the study such as the role of writing, and the constraints and affordances of technologies. At the conclusion of the study, I prepared a draft within-case analysis of each setting and a cross-case analysis. These were shared with the teachers. Their feedback was incorporated in an iterative process until consensus was reached.

5. FINDINGS

5.1 Case 1: Pirmann at Springfield High

Pirmann teaches several CS courses including the traditional CS AP-A course (with Java), a CS Principles course, a game design course, and a web development course. She also teaches a course taken by most ninth graders to fulfill her school's graduation requirement, a course she describes as "CS Principles Light."

Pirmann's CS Principles course, the subject of Case 1 in this study, is a semester-long, 5-days/week class closely aligned with the CS Principles framework. On a typical day, six females and four males attended the class in a room lit by natural sunlight due to an expansive wall of windows. The room had approximately eight 4'x6' tables. As students arrived they sat at tables facing their current group members. They often kept their school-issued laptops in backpacks until they were asked to take them out.

Pirmann's course is a modified version of the Mobile CSP course [35]. Like Mobile CSP, it has a unit on "What is a computer?" (covering the basics of hardware and software, and some history of computing), multiple units on programming mobile apps with MIT App Inventor for Android, and an Internet unit. Pirmann added web programming (with HTML, CSS, and some JavaScript) to her version of the Internet unit because she wants all of her students to develop their own website. Next year she plans to add a text-based language such as Python or Processing.

Homework often involves readings from the book *Blown to Bits: your life, liberty, and happiness after the digital explosion* [1]. This facilitates the learning of technical material within a social context. It also gives students ideas for choosing an aspect of computing to investigate for the Explore performance task. Such activities that highlight the social and ethical aspects of computing have expanded Pirmann's practice beyond the traditional programming-heavy AP curriculum.

> *I have a lot more examples now than I did before... I can talk about transportation, home automation, there's just so many things that... have been added to my repertoire... Teaching CS Principles has given me I guess a renewed appreciation that Computer Science is there in every news story, you just have to ferret it out.*

The Explore and Create performance tasks both require written reports. Pirmann assigns even more writing assignments than demanded by the framework. For homework, she asks students to post reflections about the readings on an online discussion board: three posts, one of which can be a question. Her rules of etiquette for these posts serve as an added layer of civic education. Pirmann also requires her students to keep learning blogs.

> *I believe reflecting on your learning is very valuable... they have an assignment where they have to... read over their progress through the course — their learning blogs, their reflections. And then they give me a summative "this is what I learned in this course." It's a reflection on the entire course.*

Pirmann is a proponent of active learning. Her classes typically involve short periods of lecture less than 15 minutes long. When introducing a new programming concept, she demonstrates (for roughly a half hour) by writing code that is projected on a screen. Students use laptops to replicate the code individually. She then provides a few challenges, typically extensions to the code, e.g. to add a score or level to a game. Students work on them with a partner using Pair Programming, taking turns writing code on one computer [10]. Pirmann signals when it's time for partners to change "drivers" (coders) by snapping her fingers. She generally pairs students who are at similar levels of mastery, and keeps partners together for a few weeks before changing partnerships.

Pirmann employs *Mastery Learning* techniques to accommodate the varying rates at which students master course concepts [8, 9]. Before a unit assessment, she gives students a practice test to complete individually. This formative assessment includes questions similar to ones that she thinks will be on the written portion of the AP CS Principles exam. Over the subsequent week, she addresses each question one by one, calling students who missed each question to meet with her in a small group to review the relevant concepts. This selective review process takes place while students work on their Explore or Create projects. Approximately a week after the practice test, students take the unit assessment individually.

Pirmann grades the Explore and Create tasks using CS Principles guidelines. I observed Pirmann's students as they showcased their Create projects on the last day of class. As the framework dictated, each student had collaborated with a partner to create a program (a mobile app); they worked alone on a related one. The class created an impressive collection of mobile apps. Without exception the students displayed pride in their work.

A distinctive feature of Pirmann's practice is her use of structured small groups, where each member of a small team assumes a specific role. She uses Process Oriented Guided Inquiry Learning (POGIL), which was originally developed for chemistry education and later adapted for other subjects [26, 29, 36]. With POGIL, the teacher acts as a facilitator rather than a lecturer. POGIL activites for CS may or may not involve computers. Pirmann uses them (typically for a class period) to introduce thematic units.

5.2 Case 2: Gray at Carver High

Over the past decade, Gray has primarily been a Math teacher, secondarily an AP CS teacher. Three years ago he changed jobs to work at Carver so he could teach more CS. Although he is happy to teach more CS now, it has been a difficult adjustment because Math (as a testable subject in the current high-stakes testing climate) is treated as more important than CS, which has implications for students' time management. Gray teaches several courses, including a dual-credit CS AP-A and Discrete Math class. All Carver students must take a yearlong 5-days/week CS1 course; virtually all 9th graders take it. Gray teaches two of the six sections; one of them is the subject of Case 2 in this study. Gray describes this course as *trending towards* a CS Principles course. He coordinates with the other two teachers of the course while gradually adopting aspects of CS Principles.

Gray's classroom is a bright but windowless oblong room. Tables spanning the long sides of the room have desktop computers, one for each student. On a typical day a gender-balanced group of twenty-six students attends Gray's class. As students arrive they log on to the course website to complete a 5-minute "Do Now" activity, typically a thought provoking question that Gray posts (using Geddit or Socratic) to get the class rolling and to help students focus. Students can see the results for the whole class update dynamically on the screen at the front of the room. They can also change their answers; this tends to spark lively conversation. Gray then lectures for about 10 minutes, covering the day's learning objectives, goals, and key concepts. He describes the remainder of the class as having two or three different arcs of complexity (where students develop or utilize concepts), each followed by 5 minutes of lecture for clarification and synthesis.

> *On a concept invention day where we're using Scratch as the technology they will either do one Scratch project that they successively add features to... or they'll do 5 or 6 little mini-projects where each one is a separate discrete thing. And usually I plan that out as a longer arc with what I know is going to be the defining project. There's* ***always*** *a project. My goal sometimes with these is... to have the mini-projects basically be a library... to complete the main project.*

Gray thinks it's important to introduce his students to multiple programming languages, not just to allay boredom:

> *I think it's important, because that's the abstraction right? If I had to pick the main thing I'm teaching in this course, it's abstraction... an abstraction of some underlying idea, like iteration.*

As a conceptual tool for making these abstractions explicit, Gray's students keep a "programming diary". Rather than asking students to write long paragraphs, he uses other techniques for reflection and summation. For example, students create a table where each row is a programming construct such as an if-statement or a loop. Each column is for a different programming language. For a given row the first column might contain a screenshot of an if-statement in a block-based language, the second column could have a screenshot of comparable code in JavaScript, and the third column could be for Python.

Gray asks each student to develop a project whenever they learn a new technology. Although students work individually, he encourages discussion and collaboration during the process. It's not unusual for his students to have three full class periods to work on a project. During these periods he typically walks around the classroom every ten minutes or so to check on each student. If he notices several students struggling with the same issue, he'll make an announcement that anyone struggling with the problem should come to see him or one of the students who has had success with it. I observed several classes when students worked on web pages of their own design. My field notes on one of those days reports:

> *Student projects were creative with a range of topics such as dance, fashion, celebrities, games, etc. Today (as with Tuesday), some students didn't want to leave when the bell rang.*

Rather than using the CS Principles framework for assessing projects, Gray uses his own rubrics.

> *I want to get them used to reading specifications. I make my rubrics like specifications... You will get a C if your project does the following things. You will get a B if your project does all the C stuff plus the following. You will get an A if you do all the C and B stuff plus the following. So I make it eminently easy to predict your grade.*

After spending a few weeks on a technology, Gray gives the students a break from coding. He may show a movie such as *Social Network* and facilitate a discussion about it, or ask students to work on a research project such as "great computer scientists" or the history of computing. On occasion he asks students to make presentations using Scratch to act out skits. He credits CS Principles for broadening his concept of a computing course to include topics beyond programming:

> *I've tried to broaden the way in which I assess, and [broaden the scope of] activities that I give them. So from that point of view I think I've evolved incredibly in the last two years.*

Gray also gives tests involving conceptual understanding and problem solving. Like Pirmann, he gives practice tests to help students prepare for the unit assessment. A source of frustration for Gray is the constraints of the desktop computers. He wishes his CS students had laptops so they could easily work in groups as his Math students do. He occasionally uses POGIL activities, designed for groups of 3-4 students with assigned roles. His students typically do POGIL activities with their table neighbors, without assigning roles.

5.3 Cross Case Analysis: Pirmann and Gray

A cross-case analysis in light of the research questions follows.

5.3.1 Pedagogical practices, curricula, technologies

Both teachers structure their courses so that all students who work hard can succeed. Both advocate active learning, typically starting the day with a 10-15 minute lecture and interspersing even shorter lectures between long periods of student engagement. Both employ Mastery Learning techniques: they precede end-unit analytical and problem solving assessments with formative assessments and provide supplemental support as needed. For creative projects, both provide clear rubrics with measurable goals when the projects are assigned, and avoid arbitrary aesthetic evaluation.

Both report that CS Principles has expanded their practice, for example to include more socially relevant material. Pirmann follows the Mobile CSP curriculum closely while making changes as she sees fit. Gray has carefully studied the framework and developed his own sequence of topics and activities that address many of its learning objectives.

Regarding technologies, both teach block-based programming and then web programming. Gray also introduces popular text-based languages, to promote awareness of abstraction and to demystify the languages taught in subsequent CS courses. Pirmann plans to cover at least one such language in future course offerings. Each of Pirmann's students has a laptop; Gray's students use desktop computers but he wishes they had laptops to facilitate group work.

5.3.2 Balancing problem solving and creativity

Both teachers structure their courses around thematic units and interleave strands of problem-solving activities with creative ones for the duration of each unit (~ 4-6 weeks). Example unit themes include the basics of: hardware, logic, programming, computers and society, and the Internet. The teachers often start a unit with a POGIL activity to promote concept invention and collaboration.

Regarding problem solving, both teachers give a test at the end of each unit, based on learning objectives, that focuses on conceptual understanding and analysis. Various activities prepare students to master these summative assessments: teacher demonstrations, short lectures, assignments, hands-on activities, practice tests followed by remediation as needed, and so forth.

Creative activities in Gray's class typically have the lifespan of a unit. As the unit progresses, he provides opportunities for creative expression incrementally. This builds up to a multi-day period at the end to work on a project, for which students are given a rubric and creative freedom. Pirmann also assigns short creative tasks regularly and incrementally, but her alignment with CS Principles means that the time her students spend completing the time-intensive performance tasks spans several units.

It is normative in both teachers' classrooms to have some students working on mastering problem solving skills while others work on creative projects, with flexible amounts of time devoted to each.

5.3.3 Norms of social interaction

Both teachers intentionally structure the social climate of the classroom. While Gray takes a less formal approach to Pair Programming and POGIL than Pirmann regarding assigning and changing roles, he agrees with the underlying philosophy:

> *Kids at that developmental stage need models for interaction... Just the social negotiation of knowledge within a group is really hard for them... It's hard for a quieter kid... to put their opinion in. ... I really do very much believe that you have to give them roles or rules for trying to negotiate that social minefield.*

Pirmann describes her moderation of the online discussion board:

> *If I see some tendencies of somebody saying... "that's a stupid idea" or "I can't believe you thought that" I step in right away. And so within the first two weeks the students learn... the etiquette. I do remind them... it's an academic discussion, and it's graded, and it's recorded.*

5.3.4 Similarities and Differences

The prior sections highlight several similarities and differences in the teachers' practices. Perhaps the greatest difference is in their treatment of narrative writing. Pirmann requires students to fulfill the substantial writing requirements of the Explore and Create tasks plus additional ones such as bulletin board posts and learning/reflection blogs. While Gray also requires his students to conduct research, create reports, and formulate reflections, he requires less narrative writing but more alternative modes of expression such as visual diaries, animations, and concise arguments. He conveys his position and student sentiment about lengthy writing assignments:

> *I'm in an engineering school. A lot of kids selected it because they really want to do [technical work]. "Really dude? I want to do math problems. I want to program! What is this? This is social studies! I don't want to write sentences!"... It's a hard thing to balance.*

While some may argue that a lot of narrative writing is important, Gray takes a pragmatic approach: *I'm trying to get kids who like me, who like my course, who want to go on in Computer Science.*

Other differences are that Pirmann assigns more homework; Gray teaches more languages and moves at a faster clip. The schools differ markedly in socio-economic status (SES) and minority enrollment. Pirmann's suburban school (with the higher SES and lower minority population) has nicer classrooms and better computers. On the other hand, Gray's urban school is a selective STEM school with higher performing students overall. Students at both schools are highly motivated. Differences in teaching practice due to SES or minority enrollment were not apparent.

6. Discussion

This study documents the practices of two high school teachers as they teach courses fully or partially aligned with CS Principles. It describes their choices of pedagogies, curricula, and technologies; their techniques for balancing problem solving with creativity; and their means of establishing social norms. Both are strong proponents of active learning: lectures are short and students spend ample time working hands-on. Both teach a block-based language and web programming; one teaches additional languages. Both use multi-week units with frequent creative explorations and summative assessments for which students are prepared through Mastery Learning techniques. Both are proactive in establishing social norms, e.g. with Pair Programming and POGIL. The teachers differed in several respects, notably in the amount of narrative writing they require. Frequent and/or lengthy writing assignments may discourage some of the very students that the CS Principles project hopes to attract. Alternatives include audio-visual reports, reflections, and summaries.

This study has several limitations. Carver is a STEM magnet school with high admission standards; findings about it cannot be generalized to other urban high-minority or low-SES schools. Both teachers have a high degree of professional preparation; their ability to adapt to the CS Principles framework can't be generalized to other teachers. As the primary researcher, I have known both teachers for several years; this may have facilitated the research process but could account for some degree of bias.

This study contributes to the understanding of the types of knowledge, beyond content knowledge, that contribute to effective teaching of CS. After Shulman introduced the concept of pedagogical content knowledge (PCK) [43, 44], researchers tailored it to subjects such as mathematics [31] and technology [28, 42]. Studies demonstrate positive correlations between student achievement and teacher PCK [23]. The findings reported here contribute to the understanding of PCK for Computer Science (PCK-CS) [12, 20, 21, 30] and are applicable widely to high school and college/university settings. A primary goal of the CS Principles project is to broaden participation in computing. Given the high degree of flexibility of the framework, more studies of practitioners who teach CS Principles courses and modules are warranted in order to inform teachers, instructional designers, school administrators, and professional development programs. The framework and methodology described in this paper can be replicated for such studies.

7. REFERENCES

[1] Abelson, H. et al. 2008. *Blown to Bits: your life, liberty, and happiness after the digital explosion*. Addison-Wesley Professional.

[2] AP Computer Science Principles Curriculum Framework: *https://secure-media.collegeboard.org/digitalServices/pdf/ap/ap-computer-science-principles-curriculum-framework.pdf*. Accessed: 2015-12-02.

[3] Arpaci-Dusseau, et al. 2013. Computer science principles: analysis of a proposed advanced placement course. *Proceedings of the 44th ACM technical symposium on Computer Science Education* (2013), 251–256.

[4] Astrachan, O. and Briggs, A. 2012. The CS Principles Project. *ACM Inroads*. 3, 2 (2012), 38–42.

[5] Astrachan, O. and Osborne, B. 2012. Computer Science Principles: Portfolio-based Assessment. *SIGCSE Bulletin*. 44, 4 (2012), 4.

[6] Beauty and Joy of Computing: *http://bjc.berkeley.edu/*. Accessed: 2015-08-15.

[7] Beyer, S. 2014. Why are women underrepresented in Computer Science? Gender differences in stereotypes, self-efficacy, values, and interests and predictors of future CS course-taking and grades. *Computer Science Education*. 24, April 2015 (2014), 153–192.

[8] Block, J.H. ed. 1974. *Schools, Society, and Mastery Learning*. Holt, Rinehart, and Winston.

[9] Bloom, B.S. 1968. Learning for Mastery. *UCLA Evaluation comment*. 1, 2 (May 1968).

[10] Braught, G. et al. 2011. The Case for Pair Programming in the Computer Science Classroom. *ACM Transactions on Computing Education*.

[11] Briggs, A. and Snyder, L. 2012. Computer science principles and the CS 10K initiative. *ACM Inroads*.

[12] Buchholz, M. et al. 2013. PCK and reflection in computer science teacher education. *Proceedings of the 8th Workshop in Primary and Secondary Computing Education* (2013), 8–16.

[13] Cochran-Smith, M. and Lytle, S.L. eds. 1993. *Inside/Outside: Teacher Research and Knowledge*. Teachers College Press.

[14] Code.org's CS Principles Curriculum: *https://code.org/educate/csp*. Accessed: 2015-12-01.

[15] Cohoon, J.M. and Aspray, W. 2006. *Women and information technology: Research on underrepresentation*. The MIT Press.

[16] csprinciples.org: *http://csprinciples.org/*. Accessed: 2015-12-01.

[17] Cuny, J. et al. 2014. CS Principles Professional Development: Only 9,500 to go! Lessons Learned from our CS10K Summer 2013 PD. *Proceedings of the 45th ACM technical symposium on Computer science education*. (2014), 543–544.

[18] Cuny, J. 2012. Transforming high school computing. *ACM Inroads*. 3, 2 (2012), 32.

[19] Gray, J. et al. 2015. A Mid-Project Report on a Statewide Professional Development Model for CS Principles. *Proceedings of the 46th ACM Technical Symposium on Computer Science Education*. (2015), 380–385.

[20] Hazzan, O. et al. 2008. A model for high school computer science education: the four key elements that make it! *ACM SIGCSE Bulletin* (2008), 281–285.

[21] Hazzan, O. and Gal-Eezer, J. 2010. How to Establish a Computer Science Teacher Preparation Program at Your University? *ACM Inroads*. 1, 1 (2010), 35–39.

[22] Hill, C. et al. 2010. *Why So Few? Women in Science, Technology, Engineering, and Mathematics*. American Association of University Women, 1111 Sixteenth Street NW, Washington, DC 20036.

[23] Hill, H.C. et al. 2005. Effects of Teachers' Mathematical Knowledge for Teaching on Student Achievement. *American Educational Research Journal*.

[24] Hill, H.C. and Charalambous, C.Y. 2012. Teaching (un)Connected Mathematics: Two teachers' enactment of the Pizza problem. *Journal of Curriculum Studies*.

[25] Hu, H. 2015. Using POGIL Activities to Teach CS Principles to Diverse Students. *poster section of Proceedings of the 46th ACM Technical Symposium on Computer Science Education* (2015), 676–676.

[26] Hu, H. and Shepherd, T.D. 2013. Using POGIL to Help Students Learn to Program. *ACM Transactions on Computing Education (TOCE)*. 13, 3 (2013).

[27] Kick, R. and Trees, F.P. 2015. AP CS Principles: Engaging, Challenging, and Rewarding. *ACM Inroads*. 6, 1 (2015), 42–45.

[28] Koehler, M. and Mishra, P. 2009. What is technological pedagogical content knowledge (TPACK)? *Contemporary Issues in Technology and Teacher Education*. 9, 1 (2009), 60–70.

[29] Kussmaul, C. 2012. Process Oriented Guided Inquiry Learning (POGIL) for Computer Science. *Proceedings of the 43rd ACM Technical Symposium on Computer Science Education* (2012), 373–378.

[30] Lapidot, T. and Hazzan, O. 2003. Methods of teaching a computer science course for prospective teachers. *ACM SIGCSE Bulletin*. ACM.

[31] Loewenberg, D. et al. 2008. Content Knowledge for Teaching: What Makes It Special? *Journal of Teacher Education*.

[32] Margolis, J. et al. 2008. *Stuck in the shallow end: Education, race, and computing*. The MIT Press.

[33] Margolis, J. and Fisher, A. 2003. *Unlocking the clubhouse: Women in computing*. The MIT press.

[34] Miles, M.B. and Huberman, M.A. 1994. *Qualitative Data Analysis*. Sage Publications.

[35] Mobile CSP Project: *http://mobile-csp.org*. Accessed: 2015-05-01.

[36] Moog, R.S. and Spencer, J.N. 2008. *Process oriented guided inquiry learning (POGIL)*. Oxford University Press.

[37] Morelli, R. et al. 2015. Analyzing Year One of a CS Principles PD Project. *Proceedings of the 46th ACM Technical Symposium on Computer Science Education*. (2015), 368–373.

[38] Musicant, D.R. et al. 2015. Engaging High School Students in Modeling and Simulation through Educational Media. *Proceedings of the 46th ACM Technical Symposium on Computer Science Education*. (2015), 464–469.

[39] Ni, L. et al. 2010. How do computing faculty adopt curriculum innovations?: The story from instructors. *Proceedings of the 41st ACM technical symposium on Computer science education*. (2010), 544–548.

[40] Papert, S. 1980. *Mindstorms: children, computers, and powerful ideas*. Basic Books, Inc.

[41] Remillard, J.T. 2005. Examining Key Concepts in Research on Teachers' Use of Mathematics Curricula. *Review of Educational Research*.

[42] Schmidt, D.A. et al. 2009. Technological Pedagogical Content Knowledge (TPACK): The Development and Validation of an Assessment Instrument for Preservice Teachers. *Journal of Research on Technology in Education*. 42, 2 (2009), 123–149.

[43] Shulman, L.S. 1987. Knowledge and teaching. *Harvard Educational Review*. 57, 1 (1987), 1–22.

[44] Shulman, L.S. 1986. Those Who Understand: Knowledge Growth in Teaching. *Educational Researcher*.

[45] Snyder, L. et al. 2012. The first five computer science principles pilots. *ACM Inroads*.

[46] The College Board: AP Computer Science Principles: *https://advancesinap.collegeboard.org/stem/computer-science-principles/*. Accessed: 2015-12-01.

[47] Thriving in Our Digital World: *https://institute.uteach.utexas.edu/cs/digitalworld*. Accessed: 2015-12-01.

[48] Wing, J.M. 2006. Computational thinking. *Communications of the ACM*.

[49] Zweben, S. and Bizot, B. 2014. 2013 Taulbee Survey. *Computing*. 26, 5 (2014).

Lessons Learned from "BJC" CS Principles Professional Development

Thomas W. Price
North Carolina State Univ.
Raleigh, NC
twprice@ncsu.edu

Veronica Cateté
North Carolina State Univ.
Raleigh, NC
vmcatete@ncsu.edu

Jennifer Albert
The Citadel
Charleston, SC
jalbert@citadel.edu

Tiffany Barnes
North Carolina State Univ.
Raleigh, NC
tmbarnes@ncsu.edu

Daniel D. Garcia
Univ. of California, Berkeley
Berkeley, CA
ddgarcia@cs.berkeley.edu

ABSTRACT

Computer Science Principles (CSP) will become an Advanced Placement course during the 2016-17 school year, and there is an immediate need to train new teachers to be leaders in computing classrooms. From 2012-2015, the Beauty and Joy of Computing team offered professional development (PD) to 133 teachers, resulting in 89 BJC CSP courses taught in high schools. Our data show that the PD improved teachers' confidence in our four core content categories and met its primary goal of training teachers in equitable, inquiry-based instruction. In this paper, we present the evolution of the BJC PD, its challenges and lessons that we learned while continually adapting to teachers' needs and contexts.

Keywords

Professional Development; Computer Science Principles

1. INTRODUCTION AND BACKGROUND

Computer Science Principles (CSP) is a new course designed to appeal to a broad audience and provide high school students with an introduction to computing [2]. CSP will become an Advanced Placement course in 2016-17 and is a key part of the National Science Foundation's CS10K project which aims to teach 10,000 new, highly qualified high school teachers in computing. Since 2012, we have been offering professional development (PD) to help prepare cohorts of teachers to teach the Beauty and Joy of Computing[1] (BJC) version of CSP. The BJC course and PD support novices in learning computing using the Snap*!* visual programming language and emphasize equitable pedagogies, such as pair programming. In this paper, we report outcomes and lessons learned through 4 years of BJC PD workshops with 133 high school teachers. By conveying the story and outcomes of our program, we hope to contribute to a better understanding of teacher PD for CS.

[1] bjc.berkeley.edu

SIGCSE '16, March 02 - 05, 2016, Memphis, TN, USA

ISBN 978-1-4503-3685-7/16/03...$15.00
DOI: http://dx.doi.org/10.1145/2839509.2844625

In the last few years, a growing body of research has focused on CS PD for K-12 teachers in the US [5, 7, 8, 9]. The Exploring Computer Science (ECS) curriculum built by Joanna Goode, Jane Margolis and colleagues is taught in PD using strategies from educational research [7]. It emphasizes inquiry-based learning, teacher-learner-observer models and cultivating a professional learning community. These central features of the ECS PD provide teachers with pedagogical content knowledge and time to collaborate. The PD emphasizes active, engaged and creative learning and models what should take place in the ECS classroom.

Gray's CSP PD project found that providing time for teachers to collaborate is an important aspect of successful PD [8]. Leaders from the Mobile CSP PD [9] and Chicago's Taste of Computing PD [6] found it important to provide a positive experience for teachers so that teachers will be more likely to use the full curriculum in their courses. The BJC PD project described here supports these findings, and evolved to emphasize teacher collaboration during the PD.

In addition to the challenges of learning CS content and pedagogy, high school CS teachers are uniquely isolated, often with only 1-2 teachers teaching CS courses at a given school, or even in a whole district. The "current isolation of HS CS teachers further indicates the need for supporting [these teachers]" [10]. Communities of practice support learning "in part through social interaction and the circulation of narrative." These "groups of practitioners are particularly important, for it is only within groups that social interaction and conversation can take place" [3]. BJC PD provides a community of practice throughout the school year in a Piazza forum and monthly meetings online.

2. THE BJC CS PRINCIPLES PD

The goal of our PD project was to train 100 teachers and have 50 teachers adopt the BJC CSP course. BJC features weekly pair-programming labs, a final project of the students' choosing, lectures that highlight computing topics from artificial intelligence to the internet, and discussions on current events and the Blown to Bits text [1]. The BJC PD centered on learning the principles of computing through hands-on, collaborative labs, and learning to use equitable pedagogies known to support women, underrepresented minorities, and students with less prior computing experience. From 2012-2015, we exceeded our goals, with 133 teachers participating in PD and 51 going on to teach a BJC course, for a total 89 courses.

The BJC PD lasts 6 weeks, with Weeks 1 and 6 held in person and Weeks 2-5 held online. All teachers in the PD are initially added to Piazza - an online question and answer wiki and forum we used to organize the PD schedule, resources, and teacher work and questions. Week 1 prepares teachers to learn the programming content with hands-on lessons on the first 5 Snap*!* labs, taught just as teachers are expected to teach the labs in class, using pair programming. During Weeks 2-5, participants complete the remaining labs and readings, as well as the CSP "Create" and "Explore" tasks[2]. In the Create task, students work in pairs to create a program, while the Explore task is a writing assignment to report on the potential benefits and harms of a computing innovation. Week 6 emphasizes methods for recruiting and supporting diverse students, mapping the curriculum to each teacher's specific course schedule, as well as pedagogical content knowledge (PCK), or "how to teach CS." These PCK methods include pair programming, ways of connecting computing to students' daily lives, ways to help students reflect on the impacts of technology, and ways to motivate BJC topics, such as CS Unplugged activities.

In the remaining sections, we discuss the evolution of the BJC PD in three main phases: the pilot year (2012), the restructuring year (2013), and the evolved PD (2014-15). The PD is held at two primary sites, in North Carolina (NC) and California (CA). We focus here on experiences from the NC site, which were distinct in Phase I but similar to CA for the remaining years.

2.1 Phase I (2012)

In 2012, the NC Department of Public Instruction recommended 10 Career and Technical Education (CTE) teachers to take the BJC PD. Since these CTE teachers had experience teaching high school programming courses, we assumed that teachers were fluent in both CS and in PCK for CS. In Week 1, teachers worked all the labs, with the PD facilitator discussing how each lab related to a larger CS context. For Weeks 2-5, teachers were asked to adapt an existing BJC unit into a lesson plan for their own classroom, instead of finishing the BJC course as students would. In Week 6, teachers presented their lesson plans to one another. Two of the teachers created quality lesson plans, with the remaining teachers creating powerpoint slides, or web resource links. Few teachers reported making contact with each other over the summer, and those teachers who did attempt the assignment felt the directions were unclear.

By the end of the PD, it became clear most of the participating teachers were not fluent in either CS content or CSP pedagogies. Many teachers only had experience teaching business and software applications courses, and even those who had taught programming courses were underprepared to discuss CSP from an advanced perspective. Because we assumed more expertise than the teachers possessed, the level of PD instruction was too high, and teachers felt unprepared to teach BJC the way it was presented. We learned that teachers want and need to be taught as if they were students in the course, so they can model their teaching after their experiences in the PD. Further complicating matters, many teachers had already been assigned their course schedule for the following year, and knew they would not be teaching a BJC course, leading to a lack of motivation to learn the material. To address these problems, we implemented major PD revisions for 2013.

2.2 Phase II (2013)

In 2013, we required certification that teachers would be teaching CSP within the next 2 school years but assumed no prior CS or pedagogical content knowledge. We also invited PD alumni back for Week 6 to review and prepare for future courses, and to help newer attendees. The PD focused on training teachers from the ground up, to understand both the CS content and the pedagogy for BJC. Week 1 still focused on the use of Snap*!* and the CS concepts in each lab. However, instead of emphasizing computational elegance in each lab, we emphasized basic guidance on using the programming interface and accomplishing the lab goals. Teachers were required to work in pairs, to learn together, answer each other's questions, and help debug programs. In Weeks 2-5, teachers were requested to complete the BJC course online, and to use Piazza to ask questions and collaborate. In Week 6, teachers collaborated to adapt the BJC curriculum to their own high school scheduling constraints. One teacher in particular stood out, developing a pacing guide, curriculum blueprints (mapping the CSP curriculum framework and learning objectives to BJC labs and units), and sample exam material. Because of these efforts, we were able to promote the course, since each of these documents was required for wider adoption in our state high schools. This experienced teacher was an invaluable resource to other teachers both during and after the PD, demonstrating the value of sharing expertise among teachers and creating a community for their ongoing mutual support.

2.3 Phase III (2014/2015)

Based on our observation that teachers were more satisfied with the PD the more they interacted with other teachers, we shifted PD leadership from university faculty to experienced high school teachers and PD alumni. We expanded emphasis on strategies for recruiting and diversity, and collaborative lesson planning, with high school teacher facilitators. To prepare these 'master teacher' facilitators, a new branch of the PD was created specifically to train master teachers to lead BJC PD on their own.

In Week 1, experienced high school teachers were brought to the PD from the Tapestry Workshop [4]. Tapestry is a community of teachers and professors sharing strategies, research-based practices, and field-tested ideas for teaching CS in a way that reaches all students regardless of sex or ethnicity. On the last two days of the Week 1 PD, the Tapestry teachers shared their strategies for pedagogy and recruiting diverse students into their computing courses. The BJC PD teachers valued the time and insights from fellow teachers and suggested that we continue to emphasize peer teaching.

The main BJC PD is now run primarily by high school teachers, who lead 60-80% of the workshop content, with BJC professors leading more advanced topics by request of the attending teachers. Flexibility is scheduled into the PD so that teachers can request further discussion on topics they find relevant. The first week is still primarily geared towards understanding Snap*!* and the BJC mission. During the

[2]www.apcsprinciples.org

Year	CA	NC	Total	Alum	Taught BJC Total	Taught BJC New
2012	12	13	25	–	7	2
2013	9	12	21	3	29	21
2014	38	17	55	8	24	17
2015	18	14	32	21	29	11
Total	**77**	**56**	**133**	**32**	**89**	**51**

Table 1: The number of teachers who attended each PD site and the number of confirmed BJC courses taught. We also include the number of "Alumni" teachers who attended more than 1 PD.

four-week online course, teachers complete the remaining BJC curriculum through an edX MOOC (Massively Open Online Course). This same course can then be used as a resource for participants when they teach the material to their own students. Piazza is used for answering questions and maintaining notes and discussion over the course of the whole PD, and later serves as a way to keep in touch and troubleshoot over the school year.

The PD Week 6 focuses on pedagogy and teaching strategies specific to computing and BJC, i.e. PCK. Teachers work in groups to develop a lesson plan for a BJC unit of their choice, and give short presentations to the rest of the teachers so they can use each other's plans in the coming year. This in-class presentation of ideas allows teachers to take ownership of the course, demonstrating their own ability to teach the material. In addition, these teacher-led lessons provide opportunities for teachers to reflect on the course as students and observers.

2.4 Summary

In the first 3 years of the PD for the BJC curriculum, we actively adapted the PD course to improve our instruction, to better support teacher learners from diverse backgrounds and to individualize their learning experience to meet their needs. We worked to centralize online support and resources, which were originally spread across many platforms. Our teaching practice shifted from having university faculty explaining the intricacies of the BJC curriculum, to having teachers training fellow teachers to understand and teach CS concepts. Our initial, rigid schedule was adjusted to allow extra days to explore the topics participants found most interesting. These changes led to a PD that was more effective and led to higher teacher confidence and adoption, as is explored in the next section.

3. OUTCOMES

To assess the outcomes of the BJC PD, we surveyed participants before and after attending the PD. For participants who went on to teach a computing course, we collected post-course surveys from both the participants and their students. Previous work has investigated student post-course surveys [11], suggesting that the course was generally appealing to students, and the BJC curriculum was equally effective for students from diverse backgrounds. Table 1 shows the number of teachers who attended the PD from 2012-2015 and how many BJC courses were taught each year. These numbers only include courses we could *confirm* through surveys and forum posts and likely underestimate the true numbers. During this time, we were also able to train over 80 teachers across the U.S. in shorter BJC workshops. In the remainder of this section, we will focus on analysis of the pre- and post-PD surveys from the summer 2014 PD at the NC and CA sites, for which we have the most complete data (2015 survey data was not available at the time of this writing).

Gender:	Female	20	54%
	Male	17	46%
Race/ Ethnicity:	American Indian	0	0%
	Asian	3	8%
	Black/African-American	4	11%
	Hawaiian/Pacific Islander	1	3%
	White	28	76%
	Hispanic	6	16%

Table 2: The 2014 PD participant demographics.

3.1 Population and Survey Content

The pre-PD survey included 57 participants: 38 attended in CA; 13 attended in NC; 6 attended at both CA and NC. The post-PD survey included 50 participants: 32 attended in CA; 12 attended in NC; 6 attended at both CA and NC. In total, 37 of the respondents completed both pre- and post-surveys. Any analysis comparing surveys was limited to these respondents. Respondents had an average of 10.7 years of teaching experience (range = 0-40; median = 9.5) but an average of only 3 years of experience teaching CS (range = 0-22; median = 1). Demographic information is presented in Table 2.

The pre-survey included a number of questions on participants' backgrounds, including demographics, the number of years they had taught in K-12 and high school classrooms, the number of college-level CS courses they had taken and any degree or teaching certificates they had been awarded. Participants also reported any computing courses they had taught previously, or anticipated teaching. The post-survey asked participants to rate various aspects of the PD on a 5-point scale, including applicability, efficacy, quality of instruction and use of time. Participants were also asked to give an overall rating to the PD on a 5-point scale.

Both the pre- and post-surveys included a set of identical questions to assess the effects of the PD. Participants were asked what percent of their course they expected to be based on the BJC materials. They also reported their perceived ability to teach a CS Principles course in four categories which correspond to the goals of the BJC curriculum: Content, Inquiry, Equity and Differentiation. Each category consisted of 6 to 13 five-point Likert scale items.

Content questions asked participants to rate their fluency with CS principles concepts and teaching tools. Inquiry questions concerned participants' ability to foster inquiry and engagement within their students in CS courses. Equity questions concerned participants' ability to teach equitably and incorporate elements of social justice into their instruction. Differentiation questions concerned participants' ability to teach to a diverse student body, including students with physical or learning disability, racial/ethnic minorities and females. All responses were self-reported and reflect perceived abilities.

3.2 Teacher Ratings of the PD

The PD was well-rated overall, with 76% of post-survey respondents describing it "Excellent" or "Above Average."

Category	Pre	Post	p<	*d*
Content	2.726 (0.742)	2.962 (0.649)	0.001	0.338
Inquiry	2.431 (0.683)	2.633 (0.559)	0.025	0.341
Equity	2.562 (0.801)	2.862 (0.663)	0.025	0.408
Diff.	2.403 (0.761)	2.742 (0.686)	0.005	0.467

Table 3: Average scores (and standard deviations) in each of the four categories for the pre- and post-survey. Each showed a significant improvement. P-values and Cohen's *d* (effect size) are given.

Content	Pre	CS	HS	R^2	p <
M1	0.699**			0.663	
M2	0.639**	0.342**		0.732	0.005
M3	0.630**	0.276*	0.232+	0.764	0.05
Equity	Pre	K12			
M1	0.424**			0.247	
M2	0.394**	0.418*		0.378	0.05

+ p < 0.1, * p < 0.05, ** p < 0.005

Table 4: The construction of models for post-survey Content and Equity ratings. Each row shows Beta-weights for the model produced by adding an additional variable. R-squared is given for each model, along with p-values from comparing each model to the previous. The final model for each category is last, in bold.

Participants also rated a number specific aspects of the PD:

PD facilitators were highly rated, with 88% of respondents agreeing or strongly agreeing with the statement "The facilitator was knowledgeable and helpful," 84% with the statement "The facilitator was well prepared," and 87% with the statement "The facilitators helped me understand how to implement my learning." In the 2014 PD, instructors included both university faculty and returning teachers, who had previously taken the PD and taught a BJC course. When asked the best aspect of the course, many mentioned the quality of instruction and instructors:

The instructors were great. [The facilitators] were all excellent. I especially loved the different point of views, opinions, and approaches they all took. As someone that is new to teaching (especially regarding CS), it was valuable to provide such a diverse set of instructors and modeling.

The PD content was also well rated, with 89% of respondents agreeing or strongly agreeing with the statement "The content of the professional development is relevant to my professional responsibilities" and 95% with the statement "This professional development will extend my knowledge, skills, and performances."

Participants also noted areas where the PD could be improved, specifically in the area of organization and time management. Only 52% of respondents agreed or strongly agreed with the statement, "Time was used efficiently and effectively," and 62% with the statement "The professional development goals and objectives were clearly specified."

I know that you were trying to be flexible, but at times in Week 6, I didn't feel like the schedule was well planned out and followed. There were times when we get a topic that was really interesting and then it would cut short for one that wasn't so interesting.

3.3 Perceived Ability to Teach a BJC Course

To assess the impact of the PD on teachers' perceived ability to teach CSP, we investigated their pre- and post-survey ratings in each category: Content, Inquiry/Engagement, Equity and Differentiation. For each category, we summed item responses to produce a numeric value, and tested for differences between pre- and post-survey responses using a Wilcoxon signed-rank test, as the data did not appear normal. In each category there was a significant improvement, as shown in Table 3.

3.4 Modeling PD Outcomes

To understand the potentially differential impact of the PD based on the prior experience of participants, we investigated the relationship between participants' teaching experience and various outcome measures of the PD's effectiveness. The pre-survey attributes we investigated were: number of years teaching high school (`HS`), number of years teaching K-12 school (`K12`), and number of college-level CS courses taken (`CS`). Each of the numeric variables was converted to a binary value, where the variable was true if the participant had at least the median years of experience. The PD outcomes we investigated in the post-survey were: perceived ability to teach CSP in each of the 4 categories, and how much of future course curricula the teacher intended to base on BJC.

We used a linear regression to model the relationship between each outcome variable and the binary attribute variables. In each of our models, we included the pre-survey response as a covariate. We built the models in a forward step-wise fashion, using Akaike Information Criterion (AIC) as our selection criterion to balance model complexity with accuracy. After each model was computed, we added the variables in, one at a time, and stopped if any variable failed to produce a statistically significant improvement in the model, as measured by an F-test. After this procedure, two models were non-trivial and are given in Table 4.

The first model suggests that Content understanding improved more after the PD for participants with at least the median 2 college-level CS courses. The model also suggests a similar trend for high school teaching experience, but the teaching experience variable was not significant. Similarly, the second model suggests that Equity understanding improved more after the PD for participants with at least the median 8 years of K-12 teaching experience.

It is important to note that these models are intended to be descriptive rather than predictive. For instance, the first model can be interpreted to say that participants without a CS background are getting less out of our CS content instruction, and additional effort is needed to help them keep up. We offer this as an example of how data can be used to inform future PD instruction, rather than relying solely on anecdotal evidence.

3.5 BJC Adoption

One of the primary goals of the PD was to encourage and enable teachers to teach a BJC-based course. To better understand the impact of the PD on teacher intentions to teach BJC, we compared participant responses to the question "About how much of your course do you expect to be based on BJC materials?" on the pre- and post-surveys. The distribution of pre and post- survey responses is shown in

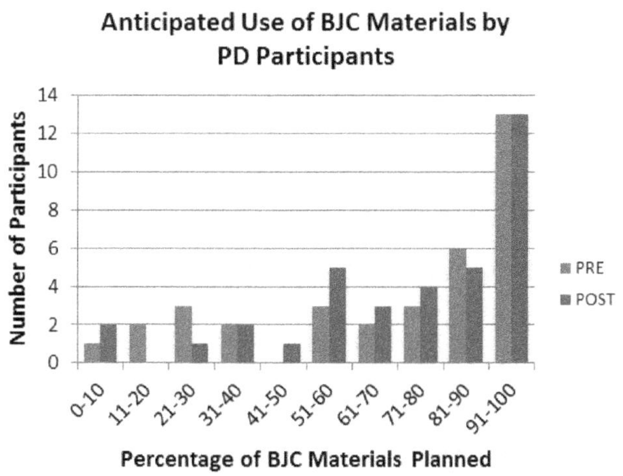

Figure 1: Anticipated BJC use reported in the pre- and post-surveys. Despite similar distributions, pre-survey responses were not predictive of post-survey responses.

Figure 1. On the whole, we see the majority of participants intend to use most or all of the BJC curriculum. Historical data from Table 1 suggests that in reality, adoption rates are not this high. While the distributions look quite similar, it is important to note that many participants' intentions did change from pre to post, but the changes were in different directions for different teachers. In fact, the Spearman rank-order correlation coefficient between participants' pre- and post-survey responses to this question was 0.33. This tells us that participants' understanding of the BJC curriculum, and how the curriculum can meet their needs, evolved over the course of the PD.

4. CHALLENGES AND LESSONS

Throughout the previous sections, we have noted many of the considerations, challenges and lessons learned in designing and iterating on the PD. Here we highlight some of our key findings, which can be used to improve future PD.

4.1 Challenges and Our Responses

Evaluation. It is difficult to measure exactly how successful the PD was in encouraging participants to teach BJC courses. For instance, from 2012-2014 we sent out yearly surveys to our PD participants during the school year to determine if they were teaching BJC that year; however, our response rates were low, ranging from 31-50%. We also offered stipends to teachers with BJC courses who were willing to respond to short surveys once every two weeks, giving a quick update on the material they had taught, the tools they used and how the students perceived the material. However, we struggled to convince busy professionals to take time out of their days to respond during the school year, and response rates remained low. Because the data we do have comes from those participants who chose to respond to surveys, and many of these are the most enthusiastic teachers, this data is likely to be strongly influenced by selection bias.

Response: Instead of impersonal surveys, we found that offering a single in-depth interview in-person at the end of the semester evoked a better response rate and provided us with more detailed data. For the pre- and post-PD surveys, we found that giving participants time to complete the survey during the PD ensured a high response rate and a representative sample. We also found that forum activity offered good, if incomplete, evidence of teachers' adoption of BJC. The adoption numbers reported in Table 1 come largely from confirmations on the Piazza forum. However, because most online forums, including BJC's Piazza, have low average participation, it is likely that we have underestimated the number of teachers who have taught BJC.

Institutional Barriers. One consistent challenge throughout the PD was helping newly-trained participants to implement a computing course at their institutions. Despite training 133 new teachers from 2012-2015, we could only confirm that 51 (38%) went on to teach a BJC course. We found that institutional barriers played a strong role in preventing PD participants from teaching a BJC course. Some teachers came into the PD assuming they would be teaching a computing course the next semester, only to see that course changed, delayed or canceled by administrators. Changing administrative policies can also affect computing courses. One school district, for instance, implemented a policy which limited each school to teaching no more than two different programming languages. Some impacted teachers were forced to alter their curricula to compensate, while others were unable to teach the course. In many districts, high teacher attrition rates exacerbate these problems.

Response: While we cannot directly control institutional policies, we have found that these problems can be mitigated to some extent by providing teachers with adequate support and encouraging community once the PD has concluded. We accomplish this in part through a forum on Piazza where teachers can post challenges they face (both institutional and content-based) and facilitators and other teachers can provide support. We further encourage formation of and participation in local chapters of the Computer Science Teachers Association (CSTA), which provide a similar support function.

Teacher Communities. While strong communities can provide invaluable support to participants as they transition into teaching a computing course, developing those communities is a serious undertaking. Our participants came from across the United States, many from districts where they may be the only computing teacher. Others came from remote or rural areas, making it difficult to be involved in support groups, such as the CSTA, when meetings are far away. For those that do have access to a community of computing teachers, their resources and curricula are often diverse and fragmented, making it difficult for teachers to share them and offer support.

Response: We addressed this in part by creating a virtual community for our participants. They have access to various online resources, such as a Piazza support forum, a resources wiki[3], and the edX course, with activities for their students. The Piazza forum has over 350 members, 31% of whom have actively posted, with almost 200 questions answered by members (30%) and instructors (70%) alike. By giving teachers shared training, shared resources, and a shared space for addressing problems that arise, we hope to give them the support they need, even if it is not

[3]beautyjoycomputing.wikispaces.com

available at their institution. However, this is not a comprehensive solution. We still find that many teachers use these resources when a problem arises (posting on the forum, using a resource in the wiki), but it is much more difficult to get participants to contribute content, for instance, by adding to the wiki. These responsibilities are still largely fulfilled by PD facilitators.

4.2 Lessons Learned

Address Participants' Needs. The BJC curriculum was initially designed for college students. However, AP courses are meant to be taken by high school students for college credit, so it was important that our PD meet the needs of high school teachers. This required a number of adjustments along the way. Because our original facilitators were university faculty, they naturally taught the PD in a way that would meet the needs of professors like themselves, providing resources and a framework for using them, paced for a semester's duration. This did not match the needs of our participants, who were accustomed to year-long courses, or semester-long courses with significantly more contact hours, with detailed lesson plans provided to teachers in advance. An experienced high school teacher helped us to develop a more detailed pacing guide that participants found much more useful. In addition, we encouraged PD alumni to attend PD in subsequent years to provide them with more time and opportunities to learn enough computing and pedagogical practices to prepare them for the classroom.

Model Teaching in the PD. The first year that we taught the PD, we expected participants to come in with a background in CS and experience with pedagogy and lesson planning. As such, the PD focused on the importance of the high-level concepts in the BJC curriculum. In reality, our participants came from diverse backgrounds, with a variety of teaching experiences, and many had no CS experience at all. We learned to recognize that our teachers were students themselves, and they needed to understand the BJC materials before they could learn to teach them. This gave us the opportunity to use the PD to model how to teach the BJC curriculum to a group of diverse learners. Drawing upon lessons learned from other CS PD, e.g. [7], we adapted the course to focus on inquiry-based learning, with teachers exploring the materials as their students would, and later presenting this back to other participants as teachers.

Encourage Community through Collaboration. We have stressed the importance of community in helping participants to overcome the institutional and classroom challenges that come with teaching a new course. We have found that one of the most effective ways to encourage community during the PD is through collaboration on assignments. The BJC curriculum is already designed to foster collaboration among students, with an emphasis on pair programming and team assignments. Getting teachers to model this during the PD not only shows them the importance of collaboration for their students; it helps to form the basis for the community that will help support them throughout the coming semesters.

5. CONCLUSIONS

The BJC PD led to the training of 133 teachers and at least 89 implemented high school courses. Our data show that the PD improved teachers' confidence in each of our four core content categories, and met its primary goal of training teachers in equitable, inquiry-based instruction. To accomplish this, we had to constantly adapt the PD, think creatively, and borrow the best ideas from other PD efforts, in order to provide more opportunities for teachers to experience the content and connect with a supportive community. Our hope is that this account and analysis will help other PD facilitators to learn from our experience and create more effective PD in the future.

6. ACKNOWLEDGEMENTS

The research reported here was supported by National Science Foundation (NSF) grants 1346922, 1138588, and 1138596. The views expressed are those of the authors and do not represent the views of supporting agency.

7. REFERENCES

[1] H. Abelson, K. Ledeen, and H. R. Lewis. *Blown to Bits: Your Life, Liberty, and Happiness After the Digital Explosion*. 2008.

[2] O. Astrachan, T. Barnes, D. D. Garcia, J. Paul, B. Simon, and L. Snyder. CS Principles: Piloting a New Course at National Scale. In *Proc. of the 42nd Annual ACM SIGCSE Conf.*, pages 397–398, 2011.

[3] J. S. Brown, A. Collins, and P. Duguid. Situated Cognition and the Culture of Learning. *Educational Researcher*, 18(1):32–42, 1989.

[4] J. Cohoon, J. Cohoon, and M. Soffa. Focusing high school teachers on attracting diverse students to computer science and engineering. In *Proc. of the ASEE/IEEE Frontiers in Education Conf.*, 2011.

[5] J. Cuny, D. A. Baxter, D. D. Garcia, S. Hall, J. Gray, R. Morelli, and D. Baxter. CS Principles Professional Development: Only 9,500 to go! In *Proc. of the 45th Annual ACM SIGCSE Conf.*, pages 543–544, 2014.

[6] L. Detorri, R. I. Greenberg, S. McGee, and D. Reed. The Impact of Meaningful High School Computer Science Experiences in the Chicago Public Schools. In *Proc. of the 1st Annual RESPECT Conf.*, 2015.

[7] J. Goode, J. Margolis, and G. Chapman. Curriculum is Not Enough: The Educational Theory and Research Foundation of the Exploring Computer Science Professional Development Model. *Proc. of the 45th Annual ACM SIGCSE Conf.*, pages 493–498, 2014.

[8] J. Gray, K. Haynie, S. Packman, M. Boehm, C. Crawford, and D. Muralidhar. A Mid-Project Report on a Statewide Professional Development Model for CS Principles. In *Proc. of the 46th Annual ACM SIGCSE Conf.*, pages 380–385, 2015.

[9] R. Morelli, C. Uche, P. Lake, and L. Baldwin. Analyzing Year One of a CS Principles PD Project. In *Proc. of the 46th Annual ACM SIGCSE Conf.*, 2015.

[10] L. Ni, M. Guzdial, A. E. Tew, B. Morrison, and R. Galanos. Building a Community to Support HS CS Teachers: the Disciplinary Commons for Computing Educators. *Proc. of the 42nd Annual ACM SIGCSE Conf.*, pages 553–558, 2011.

[11] T. W. Price, J. Albert, V. Catété, and T. Barnes. BJC in Action : Comparison of Student Perceptions of a Computer Science Principles Course. In *Proc. of the 1st Annual RESPECT Conf.*, 2015.

Seeing Is Believing: Helping Students Visualize Multithreaded Behavior

Joel C. Adams (adams@calvin.edu)
Patrick A. Crain (pac3@students.calvin.edu)
Christopher P. Dilley (cpd5@students.calvin.edu)
Serita M. Nelesen (snelesen@calvin.edu)
Javin B. Unger (jbu2@students.calvin.edu)
Mark B. Vander Stel (mbv26@students.calvin.edu)

Department of Computer Science
Calvin College
Grand Rapids, MI 49546

ABSTRACT

Multicore processors are now the standard CPU architecture, and parallel and distributed computing (PDC) is in the CS2013 core curriculum [9]. It is now the task of CS educators to begin creating pedagogical materials that will help their students understand PDC concepts. In this paper, we present TSGL (the *thread-safe graphics library*), a C++11 library that safely supports multithreaded graphics. We also present several multithreaded visualizations that illustrate how TSGL can be used to visualize the *Parallel Loop* design pattern, and present evidence that TSGL can improve student mastery of this parallel abstraction.

CCS Concepts

• Human-centered computing~Visualization toolkits • Computing methodologies~Parallel computing methodologies • Computing methodologies~Graphics systems and interfaces • Social and professional topics~Computer science education

Keywords

Graphics; image processing; integration; library; loop; Mandelbrot set; multithreading; parallel; safe; thread; visualization.

1. INTRODUCTION

Today's phones, tablets, laptops, and desktops all contain multicore CPUs, and parallel computing has moved into the core CS curriculum [9]. With this change, CS educators must now begin creating educational materials and tools to help their students understand essential parallel computing concepts.

One of these essential parallel concepts is the *Parallel Loop* (also known as "Loop Parallelism"), which is often used to implement the *Data Decomposition* pattern [5]. Sequential programs that process large data sets typically spend the vast majority of their time in a data processing loop. If such a loop can be replaced by a *Parallel Loop* that scales with the number of available cores, such a program can run faster on a multicore computer. Like other abstractions, many students have difficulty understanding this *Parallel Loop* concept.

SIGCSE '16, March 02-05, 2016, Memphis, TN, USA

DOI: http://dx.doi.org/10.1145/2839509.2844557

The subject of this paper is a tool called TSGL – the *thread safe graphics library*. As its name implies, this tool provides a library by which multiple threads can safely perform graphical operations and simultaneously draw to the screen, in approximate real-time.

Using TSGL, a CS educator can take a multithreaded application and annotate it with graphics calls so that each thread draws to the screen as it computes. By visually displaying its contribution to the overall computation, such an application can help students see exactly how the application is using parallelism to solve the problem. In short, CS educators can use TSGL to build visualizations of multithreaded concepts like the *Parallel Loop*.

1.1 Objectives

If multiple threads can simultaneously call a function/method without producing a race condition, even when the calls will access shared data, then the function/method is called *thread-safe*. In this paper, we use the term *safe* as shorthand for thread-safe.

With this in mind, our list of objectives for TSGL included:

- An easy-to-use *Canvas* class supporting 2D graphics, to which multiple threads can safely draw (or read) pixels.
- A *Shape* class hierarchy for drawing basic shapes such as triangles, rectangles, circles, polygons, and so on.
- A thread-safe *CartesianCanvas* class (a subclass of *Canvas*) for conveniently creating Cartesian coordinate systems.
- A *Function* class hierarchy for easily plotting functions.
- The ability to safely create and display multiple *Canvas* or *CartesianCanvas* objects, simultaneously or sequentially.
- Support for reading, writing, displaying, and processing PNG, JPEG, and BMP image files; plus safely getting and/or setting the individual pixels in such images.
- Support for *Canvas* interaction using a mouse or keyboard.
- Platform independence and high performance.
- Support for each thread to draw using a unique color, so that items drawn by different threads can be easily identified.
- Support for easily delaying a thread's execution, if slowing down a computation is desired.
- Operability with C++11, OpenMP, and POSIX threading.
- HTML-based API documentation similar to the Java API.

In a nutshell, our goal is that when a computation creates a TSGL *Canvas* object, that action will open a new window on the user's screen; any of the computation's threads sharing that *Canvas* may then invoke safe methods to draw shapes on, load images into, read pixels from, or write pixels to the shared *Canvas*; any effects of those methods will be rendered on the *Canvas* "immediately."

1.2 Related Work

Others have built graphics libraries for CS education to help students visualize program behavior. One of the earliest was a mid-1990s C library from Stanford [7]. More recent efforts (e.g., [3], [6], [8]) have focused on Java, which is not commonly used for parallel / high performance computing. More critically, none of these libraries guarantees thread safety.

We also examined existing C++ graphics libraries, including:

- *Qt* (*qt-project.org*). Qt provides a rich C++ graphical class hierarchy. Unfortunately, it is not thread-safe [4].
- The *Fast Light Toolkit* (*www.fltk.org*). FLTK supports many of our objectives, and can be configured to be thread-safe, but it is not thread-safe by default. In the end, we decided against using it because one could not easily take an existing multithreaded application and annotate it with graphics calls to create a visualization of that application's parallel behavior.
- The *MPE* library [10]. MPE permits multiple C or C++ *processes* to safely perform graphical operations in parallel; but its graphics calls are not thread-safe as of this writing.

Being unable to find a library that fully realized our objectives, we were motivated to build TSGL.

In Section 2, we describe our design and implementation of TSGL. In Section 3, we present some examples that demonstrate its capabilities. In Section 4, we present evidence that TSGL can help students understand abstract parallel computing concepts.

2. TSGL

We begin with the design and implementation of our library.

2.1 Design

To help achieve the objectives of Section 1.1, we designed a class hierarchy, some of which is shown in Figure 1:

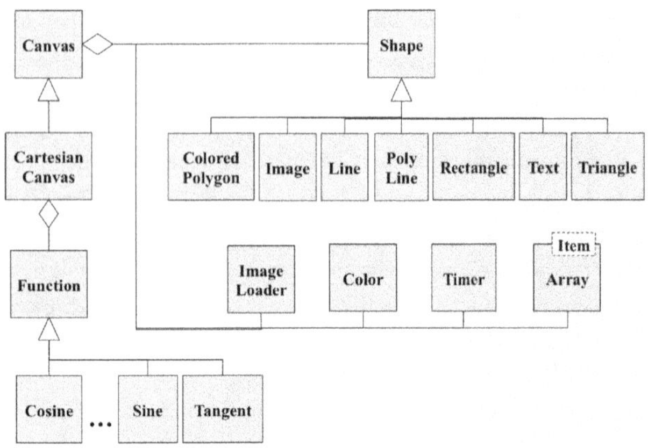

Figure 1. A Partial TSGL Class Structure Diagram

The *Canvas* class in Figure 1 plays a central role in TSGL, as it provides the methods to draw the various shapes in the *Shape* class hierarchy. The color in which a shape is drawn may be controlled using the *Color* class, which provides different methods by which threads may get unique and contrasting colors.

The *Canvas* class also provides methods for loading, storing, displaying, and manipulating images in the bitmap (BMP), joint photographic experts group (JPEG), or portable network graphics (PNG) formats. These methods rely heavily on the *Image* and *ImageLoader* classes of Figure 1, which provide most of the functionality for handling the different image formats.

Canvas also serves as the superclass for our *CartesianCanvas* class, which makes it easy to create a window containing a Cartesian coordinate system. The *CartesianCanvas* class provides methods for conveniently displaying the x-y axes of a Cartesian coordinate system, transparently mapping (x,y) coordinates in that system to the corresponding pixel coordinates, and plotting *Function* objects. The *Function* class hierarchy defines subclasses for a variety of commonly used functions, and makes it easy to plot any other function implemented as a subclass of *Function*.

Given modern processor speeds, many graphical computations occur too quickly for a person to see essential details, especially if we want to visualize individual thread behaviors. To allow an educator to control a computation's speed, our *Canvas* class includes methods to slow a thread's execution, so that individual steps of the thread's behavior can be observed.

2.2 Implementation

To implement our design, we used:

- *C++11* as our programming language to ensure that TSGL works with C++11, OpenMP, and POSIX threads. This made it straightforward to create the classes shown in Figure 1, which we built with both versions 4.9 and 5.1 of GNU g++.
- *OpenGL* as the graphical foundation for our *Canvas* class, to ensure platform independence. For handling OpenGL extensions conveniently, we used the OpenGL Extensions Wrangler (GLEW) library (*glew.sourceforge.net*). For interacting with the *Canvas* using a mouse and/or keyboard, we used the GLFW library (*glfw.org*).
- The C++11 *std::chrono* library to build our *Timer* class. This new-in-C++11 library provides support for durations, clocks, time points, and a variety of utility functions, as well as support for handling C-style dates and times.
- The *libjpeg* (*www.libjpeg.org*) and *libpng* (*www.libpng.org*) libraries, to handle the image data of JPEG and PNG files. We processed BMP files without external libraries.
- The *Doxygen* documentation generator (*www.doxygen.org*) to document our library's API in HTML format.

If the same thread performs graphical rendering and computation, then that thread will be unable to perform any computation while it is rendering the graphical content. To avoid this problem, each *Canvas* has its own "render-thread" that renders the graphical content being drawn, independent of any compute-threads that are invoking its methods.

To allow a compute-thread to safely draw on a *Canvas*, we use the *Shared Queue* parallel design pattern. More precisely, when a compute-thread invokes a *Canvas* method to draw a *Shape*, that method safely adds the *Shape* to be drawn to the *Array* member of the *Canvas*. The *Canvas*' render-thread safely retrieves *Shape*s from the *Array* and converts them to textures in OpenGL's framebuffer, which the GPU then draws on the *Canvas*.

3. EXAMPLES

TSGL includes tutorials and over forty examples to show its use. Here, we present some examples using the *Parallel Loop* pattern.

3.1 Integration (Area Under the Curve)

For CS students who have had integral calculus, integration should be a familiar concept, and they may be interested in learning how integration can be performed computationally.

While there are a variety of methods that can be used, one that is easy for students to understand is to compute the area between the function's graph and the x-axis for the specified range of x values. A pseudo-code algorithm to compute the integral of **f(x)** from **a** to **b** using the "rectangle method" might be given as follows:

```
heights = 0.0;
recWidth = (b-a) / NUM_RECTANGLES;
halfRecWidth = recWidth / 2.0;
for (i = 0; i < NUM_RECTANGLES; i++) {
   xLo = a + i * recWidth;
   xMid = xLo + halfRecWidth;
   y = f(xMid);
   heights += y;
}
return heights * recWidth;
```

For each rectangle, the algorithm's loop accumulates the sum of the rectangles' "heights" (from the rectangle's midpoint on the x-axis up to the curve) in the variable **heights**. When the loop is completed, we multiply those accumulated "heights" by the width of the rectangle to compute the return value.

To convert this algorithm into a parallel multithreaded algorithm, we can use OpenMP's directives for the *Parallel Loop* pattern. To help students see how the algorithm works, we can use TSGL to (i) give each thread a color, and (ii) have the thread draw its rectangles, as shown in the following pseudo-code:

```
heights = 0.0;
recWidth = (b-a) / NUM_RECTANGLES;
halfRecWidth = recWidth / 2.0;
CartesianCanvas canvas(MAX_X, MAX_Y);
canvas.showAxes();
canvas.drawFunction(f);
#pragma omp parallel reduction(+:heights)
{
 threadID = getThreadID();
 Color color = canvas.getMyColor(threadID);
 #pragma omp for
 for (i = 0; i < NUM_RECTANGLES; i++) {
   xLo = a + i * recWidth;
   xMid = xLo + halfRecWidth;
   y = f(xMid);
   canvas.drawRec(xLo, 0, xLo+recWidth, y, color);
   heights += y;
 }
}
return heights * recWidth;
```

That is, we (1) create a *CartesianCanvas* object that all threads will share; (2) tell that canvas to display its axes; and (3) tell that canvas to draw the function we are integrating. We then (4) direct OpenMP to create a parallel block, launching the desired number of threads; (5) have each thread retrieve its id number; (6) use that id number to give each thread a unique color; and (7) direct OpenMP to divide the iterations of the for loop among the threads launched in step 4. Within the loop, (8) each thread draws the current rectangle on the canvas, using its unique color.

Figure 2 shows two screenshots of a running implementation of this algorithm, using a quarter of the unit circle function for **f()** and one thread. In the left shot, **NUM_RECTANGLES** == 10; in the right shot, **NUM_RECTANGLES** == 100.

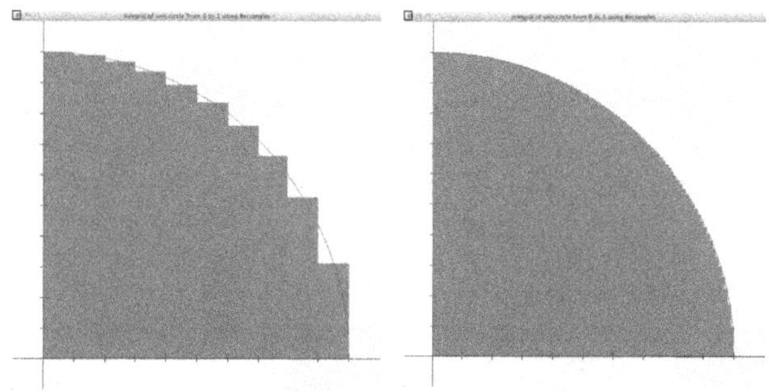

Figure 2. Integration With One Thread: (a) 10 Rectangles; (b) 100 Rectangles

Since a single thread is performing the integration, each rectangle is drawn using the same color (red). This program lets us specify the number of rectangles and threads from the command-line, so Figure 3 shows the same computation using two and four threads:

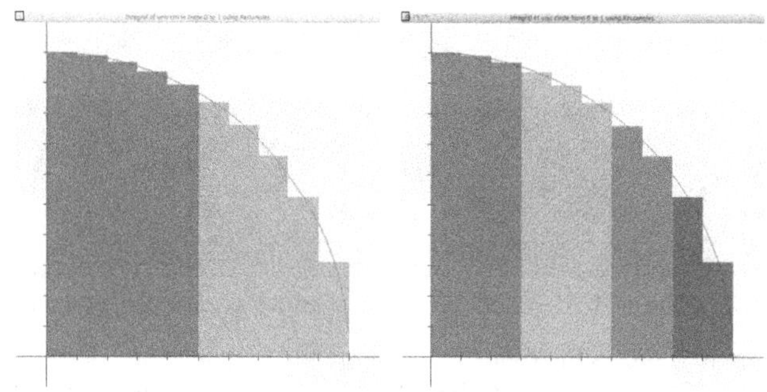

Figure 3. Integration With 10 Rectangles: (a) Two Threads; (b) Four Threads

Using words to explain how the *Parallel Loop* pattern works can be challenging, but TSGL lets us see how the pattern works. Figure 3a shows that for two threads, the pattern divides the iteration range into two contiguous "chunks"; Figure 3b shows that for four threads, it divides the range into four such "chunks". Since each thread is coloring its "chunk" using its unique color, we can infer (and verify) that for N threads, the pattern divides the iteration range into N contiguous "chunks". It is also easy to see how this pattern divides the iterations when they are not evenly divisible by the number of threads, as can be seen in Figure 3b.

By letting us color-code each thread differently, TSGL lets us see how a computation's workload is divided among its threads.

3.2 The Mandelbrot Set

The Mandelbrot set is a well-known fractal figure. A pseudo-code algorithm to draw it might be simplistically given as follows:

```
Canvas canvas(MAX_X, MAX_Y);
for (y = 0; y < MAX_Y; y++) {
   for (x = 0; x < MAX_X; x++) {
      Color color = mandelColor(x, y);
      canvas.drawPoint(x, y, color);
   }
}
```

In this algorithm, we have hidden the computation of whether a given (x,y) point is in the Mandelbrot set within a **mandelColor()** function. This function is sufficiently time-consuming (i.e., it contains another loop) that on many computers, one can see the individual rows of the figure being drawn.

As with the integration example in Section 3.1, the *Parallel Loop* pattern can be used to divide the iterations of this algorithm's outer loop into "chunks" performed by different threads.

However, unlike the integration example, the time to perform a given iteration in the Mandelbrot set can vary widely, depending on the (x,y) point being computed. TSGL lets students see this; if we use the *Parallel Loop* pattern and 8 threads, we observe behavior like that shown in Figures 4 and 5:

Figure 4. Mandelbrot Using Eight Threads; In Progress

Figure 4 shows the figure in an intermediate state in which threads 0 and 1 have completed the top two eighths of the figure, threads 6 and 7 have completed the bottom two eighths, and threads 2, 3, 4, and 5 are still working on their respective eighths, as indicated by the four gray bands in the middle of the figure.

This behavior occurs because points within the Mandelbrot set (the black portion of the figure) take longer to compute than points outside the set. Since the threads drawing the middle rows have more inside-the-set points to compute, it take them longer to complete their "chunks". TSGL's near real-time drawing thus lets students see the effects of non-uniform workloads, which can be used to motivate the introduction of other parallel design patterns that do a better job of load balancing across the threads.

When finished, we have each thread draw a colored rectangle around the portion of the figure it drew, as shown in Figure 5.

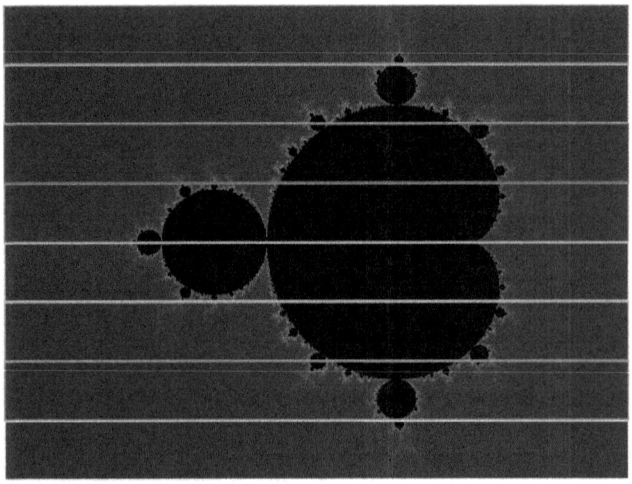

Figure 5. Mandelbrot Using Eight Threads; Finished

This application also lets a user "zoom in" by dragging the left mouse button over a point of interest in the figure. Clicking the right mouse button will "zoom out", and clicking the middle mouse button will reset the view to the original perspective.

3.3 Image Processing

The preceding examples may be interesting to students who have studied integral calculus and/or complex numbers, but they may not be interesting to first-year students. For students who have spent their teen years taking pictures with smart phones, applying a transformation to a large digital image may be more motivating.

For example, Figure 6 presents a large and colorful PNG image being displayed using a TSGL *Canvas*.

Figure 6. A Colorful PNG Image

In the rest of this section, we present the *color inversion* transformation of this image.

There are different algorithms for inverting a color image, depending on how the RGB color information is stored. If a color's RGB components are integers between 0 and 255, a pseudo-code algorithm might be given as follows:

```
Canvas canvas1, canvas2;
canvas1.loadImage(imageFile);

for each y in canvas1.getRows() {
   for each x in canvas1.getColumns() {
      Pixel p = canvas1.getPixel(x,y);
      newR = 255 - p.getR();
      newG = 255 - p.getG();
      newB = 255 - p.getB();
      canvas2.setPixel(x, y, newR, newG, newB);
   }
}
```

If the image being processed is sufficiently large and a single thread performs the algorithm, then that thread's progress may be slow enough that it can be seen in real time. (For smaller images, the TSGL *Canvas* provides methods to slow the processing as needed for the human eye to see the thread's progression.)

In this algorithm, each pixel's value is retrieved and modified independently of all other pixel values. Since each of the loop's iterations is independent of the others, we can once again use the *Parallel Loop* pattern to parallelize this algorithm. Figure 7 shows a TSGL visualization of this, using four threads to invert the image from Figure 6, with the computation about 2/3 finished:

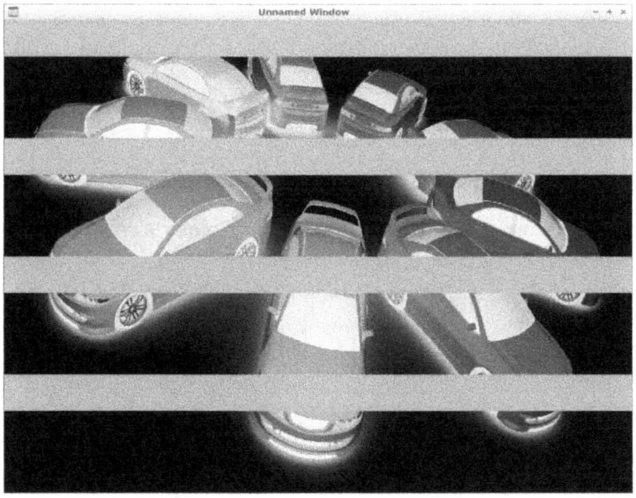

Figure 7. Color Inversion Using Four Threads; In Progress

In Figure 7, the four gray bands indicate the portions of the image that remain unprocessed; the other areas show Figure 6 pixels that have been inverted. Unlike the Mandelbrot computation in Figure 4, the four threads' gray bands are equal-sized, because the time required to invert each pixel is the same. TSGL thus lets a student see: (i) *what* work each thread is doing; (ii) *when* that work is being done, in relation to the other threads' work; and (iii) *how fast* each thread is working, compared to its peers.

At the end of the computation, we again have each thread use a unique color to draw a bounding box around its portion of the image, to indicate its contribution toward the overall computation, as shown in Figure 8.

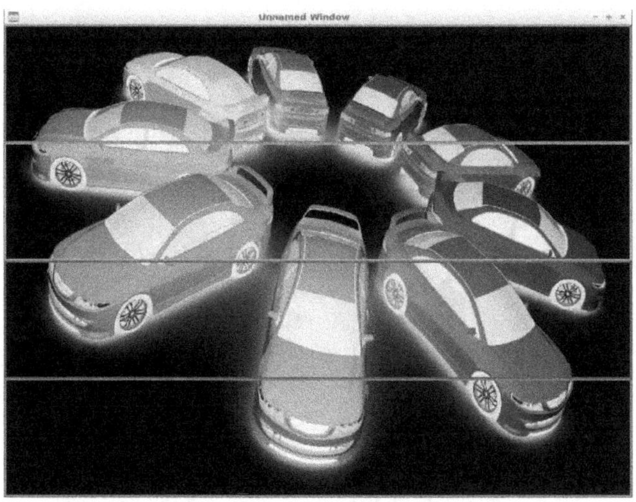

Figure 8. Color Inversion Using Four Threads; Finished

TSGL makes it possible to provide a student with a sequential, graphical version of any of the common image transformations (e.g., color-to-grayscale, sepia tinting, resizing, brightening, sharpening, blurring, etc.) and have the students time the operation. If they then parallelize the operation's processing loop and rerun the program, they will see and experience the difference in speed and behavior between the original sequential version and their parallel version. By interactively varying the number of threads in such a parallel program and seeing the result, first-year students can develop an intuitive understanding of abstract concepts like scalability, load balancing, and so on.

4. ASSESSMENT

Since 2012, we have devoted a week in our CS2 (*Data Structures*) course to OpenMP multithreading [1]. This week includes three classroom sessions, plus a hands-on lab session in which students use the *Parallel Loop* pattern to speed up slow operations, and measure their runtimes using 1, 2, 4, 6, 8, 10, 12, 14, and 16 threads. To assess our students' learning of this material, our final exam includes four questions that explore their understanding of:

1. What OpenMP is.
2. How an OpenMP parallel block behaves.
3. What thread behaviors produce race conditions.
4. How an OpenMP thread can discover its identity number.

The 50 students in our Spring 2015 course were spread across two lab sections of 27 and 23 students. To assess the effect of TSGL-visualization on student learning, we ran an experiment using these two lab sections as the control and experimental groups:

- Group 1 (the control group) completed the same exercise as the students in preceding semesters: speeding up the addition and transpose operations for large matrices.
- Group 2 (the experimental group) sped up the inversion of a large image, using TSGL to visualize the running computation.

Both lab exercises used the *Parallel Loop* pattern in similar ways, repeatedly timing a program with varying numbers of threads, but the output for Group 2 was much more visual (see Section 3.3).

To assess how well students understood this pattern's behavior, we added the following fifth question to the final exam (but we did not count it toward a student's exam score):

5. Suppose that two threads perform the following for loop:

```
vector<int> v(8);
#pragma omp parallel for
for (unsigned i = 0; i < v.size(); i++) {
   cout << v[i] << endl;
}
```

Which of the following is true?
A) Thread 0 will output the items in v[0] through v[3],
thread 1 will output items in v[4] through v[7].
B) Thread 0 will output the items in v[0], v[1], v[6], v[7];
thread 1 will output the items in v[2], v[3], v[4], v[5].
C) Thread 0 will output the items with even index values (0,2,4,6);
thread 1 will output the items with odd index values (1,3,5,7).
D) Thread 0 will output the items with odd index values (1,3,5,7);
thread 1 will output the items with even index values (0,2,4,6).
E) Thread 0 will output four items with random index values;
thread 1 will output the remaining items.
F) None of these are true.

Our null hypothesis was that students in the two groups would do equally well on each of the five exam questions, using a 1-tailed T-test to examine the significance of any differences in their responses. Figure 9 summarizes our two groups' performances on these questions and the statistical significance of their differences:

Question	Group 1	Group 2	p-value
1	77.8%	85.0%	*0.26764*
2	85.2%	80.0%	*0.32762*
3	18.5%	30.0%	*0.19133*
4	88.9%	85.0%	*0.23201*
5	**7.4%**	**40.0%**	***0.00685***

Figure 9. Percentage of Correct Question-Responses by Group

Our null hypothesis held for the original four questions, but our results lead us to reject the null hypothesis for question #5. This suggests that an exercise that lets students see multithreaded behaviors like the *Parallel Loop* pattern can significantly improve their understanding of such abstractions.

We also compared our two groups' aggregate responses to questions 1-4. There were no significant differences in the correctness of their responses to these questions (*p=0.36166*).

(It may be worth mentioning that the correct answer to question 3 was "all of the above"; most students gave a partly correct answer, but only the percentages shown gave the fully correct response.)

We also compared our two groups' responses on questions 1-4 to the responses of the 183 students from our 2012-2014 semesters. There were no significant differences between the correctness of the responses of students from previous semesters and our control group (*p=0.19232*), nor our experimental group (*p=0.42134*).

Our TSGL visualization thus had no effect (positive or negative) on student mastery of the parallel concepts assessed by our four original exam questions, but it did improve student understanding of the *Parallel Loop*'s default behavior. Since it significantly improved student learning, we plan to replace our non-visual matrix lab exercise with our visual image-processing exercise the next time our CS2 course is taught.

Both groups used the same *Parallel Loop* pattern to accelerate an operation on a 2-dimensional data structure, but the fact that Group 1's structure was a matrix while Group 2's structure was an image represents a potential confounding factor. This might be addressed by conducting a follow up experiment in which two groups parallelize an image-processing operation, but only one group uses TSGL to see the parallelization happening as the program is running. We conjecture that such an experiment will produce the same results as those reported here; if we conduct such an experiment, it will be the subject of a future report.

5. CONCLUSIONS

Since parallel computing is now in the core CS curriculum, it is time for CS educators to begin developing the pedagogical materials to help students understand parallel concepts, as well as tools to create those materials.

Taking the adage *"A picture is worth 1000 words"* as our motto, we have developed TSGL, a tool by which a sequential or multithreaded application can be safely annotated with graphical calls to indicate each thread's contribution to the computation in near real-time. This permits us to build multithreaded applications in which a person can see (i) *what* work each thread is doing; (ii) *when* that work is being done, relative to other threads; and (iii) *how fast* that work is being done, relative to other threads.

In Section 3, we presented examples showing how TSGL can be used to teach CS students about the *Parallel Loop* design pattern. These examples differ in the amount of background knowledge they require on the part of the student: the third example has been successfully used with first-year university students, while the first two examples might be best suited to older students.

In Section 4, we have presented experimental evidence that our TSGL visualization improved student understanding of the *Parallel Loop* pattern's precise behavior. We believe that TSGL holds great potential for creating visualizations to help students understand abstract concepts, whether parallel or sequential.

When creating such visualizations, it is important that they be *scalable*: a program should make it easy for the student to change the number of threads being used without recompiling; the visualization's behavior should change accordingly, in both appearance (see Figure 3) and execution-time.

The current release of TSGL is available on GitHub [2] as free, open-source software under the GNU Public License (v. 3). It was developed on Ubuntu Linux 14.0.4 and has been successfully tested on both MacOS X Yosemite and Windows 7.

TSGL is a work in progress. While the examples presented here have all used a *Data Decomposition* pattern (i.e., the *Parallel Loop*), we are currently working on components to help visualize other patterns (e.g., *Task Decomposition*, *Shared Queue*, etc.). We are also working on other interesting visualizations, including *Parallel Mergesort*, the *Dining Philosophers Problem*, and so on.

We invite interested instructors and students to use TSGL and/or contribute to the project. We look forward with anticipation to seeing the visualizations that others create with it.

6. ACKNOWLEDGMENTS

We are grateful to the National Science Foundation, whose grant NSF-DUE #1225739 made it possible to develop TSGL.

7. REFERENCES

[1] J. Adams. Injecting Parallel Computing into CS2. *Proc. 45th SIGCSE Tech. Symposium on Computer Science Education* (Mar. 2014), 277-282. DOI=10.1145/2538862.2538883.

[2] J. Adams, P. Crain, C. Dilley, M. VanderStel. TSGL. Online: https://github.com/Calvin-CS/TSGL Accessed 2015-08-15.

[3] K. Bruce, A. Danyluk, T Murtagh. 2010. Introducing Concurrency in CS1. *Proc. 41st SIGCSE Tech. Symposium on Computer Science Education* (Mar. 2010), 224-228. DOI=10.1145/1734263.1734341.

[4] Digia pic. 2014. Qt reentrancy and thread safety. Online: http://qt-project.org/doc/qt-4.8/threads-reentrancy.html. Accessed 2015-08-15.

[5] T. Mattson, B. Sanders, B. Massingil, *Patterns for Parallel Programming*, Addison Wesley, 2004.

[6] N. Parlante. 2004. Graphics and Java. *ACM SIGCSE Bulletin* (36)2, June 2004. 26-27. DOI= 10.1145/1024338.1024364.

[7] E. Roberts. 1995. A C-based Graphics Library for CS1. *Proc. 26th SIGCSE Tech. Symp. on Computer Science Education* (Mar. 1995), 163-167. DOI=10.1145/199688.199767.

[8] E. Roberts, K. Bruce, J. Cross II, R. Cutler, S. Grissom, K. Klee, S. Rodger, F. Trees, I. Utting, F. Yellin. 2006. The ACM Java Task Force: Final Report. *Proc. 37th SIGCSE Tech. Symposium on Computer Science Education* (Mar. 2006), 131-132. DOI=10.1145/1121341.1121384.

[9] M. Sahami, et al. Computer Science Curricula 2013. Online: http://www.acm.org/education/CS2013-final-report.pdf. Accessed 2015-08-15. DOI=10.1145/2534860.

[10] O. Zaki, E. Lusk, W. Gropp, D. Swider. 1999. Toward Scalable Performance Visualization with Jumpshot. *International Journal of HPC Applications*, (13)3, August 1999, 277-288.

A Survey of Ethical Agreements in Information Security Courses

Benedict Chukuka
University of Calgary
Dept. of Computer Science
602 ICT
2500 University Dr. NW
Calgary, Alberta T2N 1N4
bchukuka@ucalgary.ca

Michael Locasto
University of Calgary
Dept. of Computer Science
602 ICT
2500 University Dr. NW
Calgary, Alberta T2N 1N4
locasto@ucalgary.ca

ABSTRACT

Existing ethical agreements, as applicable in the teaching of information security courses, typically spell out rules on what students should and should not do. The main problem is that the question of what students should or should not do is not a settled issue, because personal stances on questions of morality and ethics fundamentally influence the ethical recommendations that teachers present to their students. In light of the growing level of malice in the computing domain, experts have highlighted the importance of information security ethics by debating the need for a standard code of ethics for information security. Arguably, differences in ethical stance, with the effect of divergent ethical agreements, will not efficiently serve the purpose of effective universal application of ethics in the field of information security education. Examining current ethical policies in information security courses can provide insight about the prevailing ethics within the information security community. Moreover, understanding what the prevailing philosophies on ethics are within the community, in terms of how they actually diverge or converge, will present a good projection of how a standard policy on ethics may be feasibly applicable in a future regulatory environment. This way, we may be able to forecast the nature of ethical norms that future professionals will accept or allow to be imposed on them. Therefore, in our survey, we analyze ethical agreements on information security courses to identify the nature of existing agreements. We determine the commonalities of these agreements and derive an ethical policy prototype that includes the common elements of 329 ethical policies.

1. INTRODUCTION

The subject of Ethics is commonly applied in the education of students in higher institutions of learning, mainly as an instrument for shaping individual students into future responsible professionals. Professional codes of ethics [1, 6], which are usually communicated to students in the learning process, exist to support this fact. In addition to standard professional codes of ethics, institutions essentially maintain codes of ethical conduct [9], which serve to guide students on the importance of upholding principles of integrity and academic honesty in their pursuit of knowledge. More specifically, the field of Computer Science highlights the importance of ethical behaviour through emphasis on the existing ACM and/or IEEE codes of ethics, where students are essentially guided on the need for professionalism and good conduct with regard to engaging in the Computing profession.

SIGCSE '16, March 2–5, 2016, Memphis, TN, USA.

ISBN 978-1-4503-3685-7/16/03...$15.00

DOI: http://dx.doi.org/10.1145/2839509.2844580

The question of ethics in Computer Science education is especially visible in the teaching of information security courses to Computer Science majors. Application of ethics to information security courses is imperative due primarily to the ample potential for unintended consequences, with negative outcomes. The relevance of ethics is particularly underscored by the fact that while information security courses serve to teach students how to defend computer systems, they create the paradox of affording students the opportunity and capability to attack systems, thereby causing harm to others. Evidence that ethics in general and ethical agreements in particular, are necessary for students in information security classes can be seen from ongoing debate by experts, actual student breach cases, and certain rules that standard codes of ethics contain.

In 2012, a university student attacked his institution's network, exposing more than 650,000 personal and sensitive records belonging to students, parents, and employees [10]. On the premise of the growing level of malice in the computing domain, Greenwald et al. [4] argue the need for a code of ethics that caters specially to information security. This magnitude of attention being given by experts to information security ethics serves to highlight the importance of the subject of ethics to the domain. For its part, the ACM code of ethics echoes the acknowledgment of malice in the computing domain and makes a case for the importance of ethics with the moral imperative, "Avoid harm to others". While students might often have acquired knowledge of general computing ethics prior to taking an information security course, this knowledge may not adequately prepare them for the kind of ethical challenges that arise from being exposed to dangerous skills through information security courses [4]. This possible limitation of general computing ethics further underscores the importance of ethical impartation in the special context of information security courses.

Unintended consequences can especially ensue as a side effect of fickleness in individual disposition toward ethical and moral theories [5] in the course of time. Consequently, it can be difficult to determine *ex ante*, how acquired information security knowledge and skills will be eventually put to use, within the context of future ethical demands. Thus, teachers of information security courses often design sets of ethical rules (or agreements) for their students, with the intent that these agreements can serve as important pedagogical tools for guiding them on proper behaviour and dissuading them from nefarious use of acquired information security knowledge and skills. In this regard, ethical agreements as designed to cater to the special nature of information security courses, present a framework that helps prevent students from being entangled in ethical pitfalls and legal hassles as a result of taking these courses.

While the plausibility of applying rules of ethics in the teaching of information security courses is obvious, a fundamental issue lies in the fact that current agreements may not present a universally acceptable structure by reason of being divergent in nature. This is especially against the backdrop of the debate on the need for a standard code of ethics for information security [4]. Therefore, we explore through this survey, the nature of existing ethical agreements as applicable in the teaching of information security courses. In particular, our work serves to address two pertinent and key questions. First, what is the nature of existing ethical agreements in information security courses? Second, what are the common elements of these ethical agreements? By our analysis of many ethical agreements and derivation of a prototype policy from commonalities existing among them, we equally provide an empirical basis for assessing the feasibility of a standard code of ethics that caters to information security.

2. RELATED WORK

Ethics, as an important component of the pedagogical process in any domain of learning and research, receives regular attention in the general discourse of issues bordering on pertinent moral and ethical questions. More often than not, the potential for harm is a primary determinant of the need for ethics, where ethics assumes the crucial role of shaping good conduct and preserving same in persons engaging in learning and research. In relation to information security ethics research, perspectives on topics that range from the use of human subjects in research, to proposition of the teaching of malware, to argument about the need for a "universal" code of ethics, have been presented in recent literature.

The work by Aycock et al.[2], addresses the issue of ethics in research, with focus on the effectiveness of existing policy mechanisms regarding human research ethics, as it affects the field of Computer Security. The importance of teaching students research ethics is advocated, while issues on existing policy mechanisms with regard to lack of adequate understanding of computer security research by Institutional Review Boards (IRBs), are also highlighted. The work essentially projects the need for ethics regulations (e.g. through reviews done by IRBs) and the tools (policies) that drive these regulations to be correctly executed, toward meeting intended goals over the domain of computer security research. Similar to the idea of this work, we consider elements and features of current policy instruments on ethics in relation to information security education. However, our work differs in the sense that we examine a wide range of ethical policies.

Ledin in his article [7], emphasizes the critical need for students of Computer Science to be taught the intricacies of malware as a necessary means of protecting society in general against the growing malware problem. He highlights the ample scale of this contemporary problem by analyzing the increasing motivation and sophistication of tactics employed by malware herders; a development he warns requires that computer science students be taught malware to enable them successfully defend against extant as well as yet-to-be-known malware instances. While opponents to this proposal keep dismissing the idea of arming students with knowledge about malware as a catastrophe waiting to happen, the compelling argument and instances presented in support of the case for malware education in university classrooms, serve to amplify the ethical dilemma that characterizes certain forms of instruction in information security education.

Sullins [8] projects an active standpoint on the subject of ethics in relation to malware research. In this sense, the work advocates early teaching of ethics to malware researchers (or students), with the pedagogical approach entailing that which engages students, not as passive recipients of rules and thoughts on ethics but as active participants whose mindsets are ultimately modelled and sustained in favour of positive ethical choices. In other words, students should not just be handed codes of ethical conduct without real effort in the direction of molding behaviour that helps guarantee that the potential problem of malevolent application of knowledge is satisfactorily kept in check. To this end, classroom discussions and reflections, in addition to high stakes exam processes, are suggested as possible effective pedagogical mechanisms.

In debating the necessity of a code of ethics that specially caters to the peculiar needs and nature of the Information Security field, Greenwald et al. [4] present four different positions of thought. First is that the field of Information Security needs a specialized code of ethics. The premise of this argument lies in the notion that current codes of ethics (e.g. that of the ACM), as generally applicable in the Computer Science domain, are built on an ideology which assumes a world that is void of the propensity for malice. And in this sense, these codes of ethics do little good to the Information Security field; a field that is evidently fraught with malice. Second is the position that while ethics is necessary for the field, it would be difficult to derive a specialized code of ethics because of implementation challenges. Third is that a specialized code of ethics may not be needed because default ethics already exists in computer security. The primary suggestion here is that computer security professionals by virtue of the nature of their work, for example, are able to inherently acquire and internalize positive ethical traits as much as a code of ethics may be able to offer. Finally is the position that a specialized code of ethics is not needed because of the many bottlenecks that attempts at formulating ethical policies and enforcing ethics will bring. While the proponents of these positions disagree on the need for a specialized code of ethics, they compromise on the need for a set of "core values". Interestingly, a set of core values may equally behave like a code of ethics, as the common de-

Table 1: Distribution of Institution Types

Institution Type	Count	Percentage
Public	121	60.2%
Private	40	19.9%
Community College	29	14.4%
Private College	4	2%
Other	7	3.5%

Table 2: Categories of Ethics Documents Collected

Category	Count	Perc.
Category 1: Signable Agreements	72	21.8%
Category 2: Acceptable Use Policies	47	14.3%
Category 3: Warning Notes	122	37.1%
Category 4: Standard Codes of Ethics	59	17.9%
Category 5: Other Security Policies	29	8.8%

nominator remains that of grooming and preserving positive personal and professional norms for the common good.

3. DATA CORPUS

3.1 Data Collection Methodology

We searched the web and collected many ethics documents, which govern student behaviour in information security courses, as taught in higher institutions. The search involved first identifying postsecondary institutions that offer courses in information security. Subsequently, we visited various information security course pages and obtained the documents directly from those pages. The entire dataset was obtained from publicly available course information on the web, and there was no human involvement in the process. During our search, there were a few cases where it was apparent that an information security course did not require an ethical agreement, at least from information available online. It would have been interesting to consider the proportion of these courses, relative to all the courses we came across during our search. However, the focus of our work is more on providing information to the community on the nature of current ethical agreements. Thus, in our search, we concentrated only on courses that incorporate ethical agreements as course requirement, and did not consider courses without ethical agreements. Our dataset consists of 329 agreement documents across 273 courses and 201 higher institutions. The courses were taught between the years 1999 and 2014, inclusive.

3.2 Data Sources

Most of the documents came from North American sources, with a representation of 94% (308 documents) of the dataset, while the remaining 6% percent were from other regions of the world. These other regions of the world, with indication of the number of documents collected from sources there, include: Europe (11 documents), Asia (5), Middle East (3), and Oceania (2), totaling 21. Out of the 201 institutions, 60% are public research schools, 20% private, 14% community colleges, 2% private colleges, and 3.5% classifiable as Other. Institutions that fall under this category of Other are non-traditional institutions that teach cyber security in their curriculum. The Cybersecurity Institute, Oracle Academy, and the Canadian Institute of Professional Studies are prime examples of these institutions. Table 1 shows the distribution of types of institutions, as representative of our dataset.

While collecting data, we paid particular attention to institutions designated as Centers of Academic Excellence in Information Assurance (IA) - CAE/IA. These institutions represent one-third of the total number of institutions (at a total number of 62.) With respect to specific representation of the CAE/IA institution types, 53% are of type CAE/IAE (education focused CAE institution), 18% of type CAE/R (research focused CAE institution), while 29% are CAE institutions that focus on both education and research in Information Assurance. In general, 51 of these CAE institutions are information security education-oriented, while 29 are research-oriented; that is, when one considers the institutions that are of the Research and Education type, altogether.

3.3 Categories of Ethics Documents

With respect to the forms and contents of the ethics documents, our dataset comprises five categories. Table 2 shows the distribution of these categories of documents in terms of number and percentage representation in our dataset.

Category 1 represents agreements as explicitly executed by the instructor in charge of the information security course. These documents contain at a minimum, ethical guidelines and clauses, the student's name, signature, and date. Students are usually instructed to sign and agree to the terms of the document prior to the first day of class.

Category 2 documents are those that exist as Acceptable Use Policies (AUPs), where in general, specific rules are spelt out as to what students should and should not do with computer systems and networks. These AUPs are usually executed at institutional or departmental levels. Students are referred to the AUPs by virtue of their participation in the information security course.

Category 3 represents warning notes to students on the course website, syllabus, or lecture materials. These warnings specifically point out to students, the potential danger of being exposed to the attack techniques that will be taught in the course. Students are then told that the sole purpose of teaching them system vulnerabilities and exposing them to tools and techniques on how to attack systems, is to enable them learn how to better defend the systems. Finally, a firm advise is given against applying the knowledge and skills from the course to unethical and/or irresponsible use.

Category 4 consists of existing standard codes of ethics (e.g. ACM, IEEE, $(ISC)^2$, AITP, CIPS, The Ten Commandments of Computer Ethics.) Here, students are pointed to these codes of ethics with particular focus on the ethical principles and guidelines they contain, the motive being that of encouraging students to uphold principles of good behaviour with regard to the potentially dangerous knowledge and skills they will be acquiring in the course.

Category 5 refers to documents that we obtained for cases where computer security ethics-related policies exist at departmental or institution-wide level, but information security courses do not specifically provide ethical guidelines online. For cases like these, instructors rather than come up with their separate personal policy for a security course, would fall back to the already existing one, and may altogether not be inclined to making this existing policy explicitly available on their course website. We assume that where these security-related policies exist at an institution and contain elements that address the ethics of computer usage, students of information security courses are likely being told about the polices.

4. EVALUATION OF ETHICAL POLICIES

4.1 Methodology

We assessed the entire dataset against seven core criteria. This assessment forms the basis for identifying the common features among the various ethical agreement documents. The criteria we consider include: Main Idea; Specific Rules or Guidelines; Legal, Privacy, and Security underpinnings; Structure; Length; Motive; and Penalties included. We determined these criteria on the basis of the fact that from observing our dataset, these are attributes that ethical policies predominantly incorporate. In looking at the Main Idea criterion, we consider the fundamental message of ethics that a particular policy bears. Rules or Guidelines concern the specific forms of ethical injunctions in relation to expected behaviour, as stipulated in the document. By Legal, Privacy, and Security underpinnings, we consider whether the general theme focuses on legal, privacy, or security issues. In looking at Structure, we focus on the general form and composition of a policy, including how clauses are set. By Length, we consider how long a policy document is in terms of the number of pages. Through the Motive criterion, we examine what the underlying concerns are on the part of an instructor, in presenting a particular ethical policy to students. Finally, through the Penalties criterion, we look at the question of if and what specific punitive measures are being put forward in the event of violation of a policy. These core criteria enabled us to perform a detailed manual analysis of our dataset.

In performing our manual analysis, we examined each ethical policy document to determine whether or not it contained features that align with any of our selected criteria. If any such features were observed with a policy document, we noted it against this document. After examining the entire dataset against these criteria in this manner, we determined the percentage of documents bearing commonality for each feature. This assessment process resulted in the common policy features as shown in Table 3. As we can observe from Table 3, these common features derive directly from the seven criteria upon which we base our analysis.

4.2 Findings

Our analysis shows that ethical policies currently exist in various forms in terms of structure, content, and disposition on the subject of ethics. This is particularly reflected by the information we presented in Section 3.3. While this observation goes to indicate a fractured approach to the form and nature of ethical agreements currently in use within the information security education community, we were able to identify some features that are common to the policies, based on our analysis using the various criteria discussed in section 4.1. We present these commonalities in Table 3, where we show nine main features together with the proportion (in percentage) of the ethical policies in our dataset that incorporate each feature.

As Table 3 shows, thematic focus on ethical or responsible conduct; legal, privacy, and security underpinnings; as well as one-to-two page of document length, are features that

Table 3: Common Features of Ethical Policies

Policy Feature	Perc.
Theme urges ethical and/or responsible conduct	99.6%
Addresses security	98%
Addresses privacy	95%
Addresses legal issues	90%
Length is between 1 and 2 pages	75%
Concerns about unethical use of skills from course	57%
Includes ethical guidelines, sections, and clauses	50%
Addresses consequences for policy violation	49%
Contains some general ethical principles	18%

are overwhelmingly common among these documents. On the other hand, the features of consequences (or penalties) for policy violation; concerns about unethical use of skills learnt in the course; and inclusion of ethical guidelines, sections, and clauses (in relation to document structure), show commonality across the ethics policies only at moderate levels. While these moderate proportions indicate limited occurrence of these features in ethical policies, we posit that the levels are significant enough to indicate that they are currently generally included in ethical policies. The very low proportion (at 18%) of the feature on inclusion of general ethical principles, indicates that principles of ethics as specifically spelt out in the ACM or IEEE codes of ethics, are sparsely included in ethical policies.

4.3 Common Elements

Based on the results of our analysis as discussed in Section 4.2, where we identify the main features that are common to currently applicable policies on ethics, a universally applicable ethical policy may consist of the following elements: fundamental principles on ethics; guidelines that spell out expected behaviour; emphasis on ethical and responsible conduct with knowledge acquired from the course; emphasis on the legal, security, and privacy implications of unethical behaviour; a maximum length of two pages; specific penalties for violation of the policy; and distinct sections. To portray what such an ethical policy document will look like, we manually developed a prototype that incorporates these elements. Listing 1 shows this prototype. Further, we performed automated summarization of all the policy documents in our dataset by running them against the *Free Summarizer* text summarization tool [3]. Listing 2 is the output of this automated summarization. In Listing 2, we redact actual institution name with "Institution X".

Listing 2 shows the actual features (in terms of contents and theme) of the policy documents from our dataset. A close look at this summary clearly reveals features of these policy documents as discussed in preceding sections. For example, features that address security, legal, and privacy issues can be easily seen. Equally obvious are specific guidelines as generally spelt out in these policies. Furthermore, the feature that urges students to uphold responsible behaviour is evident in the third paragraph. Comparing this automated summary of Listing 2 with our manual prototype, we can observe that these features of the actual ethical policies in our dataset adequately reflect the features we include in our prototype. This comparison enables us to gauge the extents to which our manual prototype is accurate, in terms of how well we have incorporated common policy features from various sources.

Listing 1: Prototype of Ethical Agreements

Computer Security Course Ethical Agreement
Course Title: *Course Number:*
Name of Institition: *Name of Instructor:*

1.0 Preamble. *This Agreement outlines important ethical principles and guidelines every student enrolled in this course is expected to abide by. As a student participating in this course, you will be exposed to tools and techniques that can be used to exploit existing vulnerabilities on computer systems and networks. By exposing you to these tools and techniques, this course exclusively aims to educate you with knowledge necessary for defending computer systems. Exploiting vulnerabilities on systems without explicit authorization from system owners and/or appropriate authorities is unethical and can have far-reaching security, privacy, or legal consequences. In this regard, you must continually play the role of a good ambassador of computer systems defense by not engaging in any conduct that amounts to nefarious use of your knowledge from this course. If at any time you are not sure of the consequences of your actions, contact the instructor for proper guidance and advice.*

2.0 Ethical Principles. *While enrolled in this course, you are required to be guided by the following general principles of ethics:*
1. Be a good citizen.
2. By all means, avoid causing harm to others.
3. Always uphold ethical and responsible conduct.
4. Respect the persons and privacy of others.
5. Respect the intellectual property rights of others.
6. Uphold the highest standard of professional behaviour.
7. Maintain the integrity of all systems and networks.
8. Always take full responsibility for all your actions.

3.0 Guidelines for Ethical and Responsible Conduct. *With regard to the knowledge you will gain in this course, and as a responsible citizen of society, you agree that:*
1. All the concepts and skills you will learn in this course are only for purposes of education.
2. You will use the tools taught in the course only for purposes of instruction in the class environment.
3. You will apply all your knowledge from this course responsibly.
4. You will abide by the institution's policy on acceptable use of computing resources.
5. You will not engage in any unethical computer system-related activity.
6. You will not use the skills you acquire in this course for criminal activity.
7. You will not use the tools taught in class to unlawfully break into systems or aid others in doing so.
8. You will not attempt to exploit any vulnerabilities on systems without appropriate authorization.
9. You will not employ computer systems to willfully violate the privacy of others, within and/or outside the school environment.
10. You will not intentionally create malicious programs (viruses, Trojan horses, worms, etc) to compromise systems.

4.0 Penalties. *Applicable penalties for violation of this agreement include:*
1.Dismissal from the class and indicating the violation in your transcript.
2.Failing the course.
3.Expulsion.
4.Suspension of access to campus systems.
5.Civil fines and criminal prosecution.
6.Other sanctions, as permissible by law and the governing rules of this institution.

Student's Acknowledgment/Agreement:
I acknowledge that I have read the ethical principles and guidelines set forth in this Agreement as part of the requirements I am expected to meet in the course. I understand in entirety, the contents herein, including the stated penalties for violation. I undertake that I will abide by all the stipulations and refrain from any behaviour that will bring harm to others or impact on the well-being of society. I hold myself responsible and liable for any unethical behaviour on my part as a direct consequence of my enrollment and involvement in this course. I fully indemnify the institution and the instructor teaching this course. Where I am not sure of the legal, privacy, and/or security implications of any of my actions, I will not hesitate to seek clarification from the instructor.

Student's Name: *Student's ID:*
Student's Email: *Student's Signature:*
Agreed to On:____ *Day of* ____, *20*__.

Listing 2: Automated Summary of Ethical Policies

Respect the rights of others. Inappropriate behaviors include: altering system configuration; accessing/monitoring other people's accounts without their permission; misrepresentation of self or others' identity; misuse of computing resources to diminish efficiency; breaching or attempting to breach computer security systems, whether with or without malicious intent; engaging in any activity that might be harmful to systems or to any stored information such as creating or propagating viruses, worms, Trojan Horses, or other rogue programs; disrupting services; or damaging files; violating copyright and/or software license agreements; using computing resources to threaten or harass others or transmitting obscene or fraudulent messages; Installing or operating computer games on university-owned computers for purposes other than academic instruction; Downloading or posting to university computers, or transporting across university networks, material that is illegal, proprietary, in violation of university contractual agreements; or in violation of university policy; and Violating local, State or Federal laws.

Do not use the department's computing and networking resources to download any unauthorized or illegal software or data in any form including audios, texts, videos, images, and animations. Do not install any unauthorized software or store any unauthorized or illegal files in any form on the department's computers. Do not use the department's computing resources to duplicate electronically any unauthorized or illegal documents. Do not harass or threaten any user by sending messages via email or any other way. Do not engage in any subverting activities such as deleting or modifying system files, installing unauthorized hardware, tampering with existing hardware, infecting computer systems with virus. Do not disrupt and attack services on department's servers. Do not reveal or attempt to reveal private information of other users using any hardware or software tools. Never use the computing resources of the department to attack any computer or network in the university or on the Internet. Users are prohibited from changing or circumventing access controls to allow themselves or others to perform actions outside their authorized privileges. Users must not intentionally introduce or use malicious software such as computer viruses, Trojan horses, or worms. Users must not download/install or run security programs or utilities that reveal or exploit weaknesses in the security of a system.

Members of the University community are expected to follow certain principles of behavior in making use of computers and network systems, in particular, to respect, and to observe policies and procedures governing: the privacy of or other restrictions placed upon data or information stored in or transmitted across c omputers and network systems, even when that data or information is not securely protected; an owner's interest in proprietary software or other assets pertaining to computers or network systems, even when such software or assets are not securely protected; the finite capacity of computers or network systems by limiting use of computers and network systems so as not to interfere unreasonably with the activity of other users.

I agree to: Only examine the special course accounts for privacy vulnerabilities (if applicable). Report any security vulnerabilities discovered to the course instructors immediately, and not disclose them to anyone else. Maintain the confidentiality of any private information I learn through the course exercise. Actively use my course account with the understanding that its contents and actions may be discovered by others. Hold harmless the course instructors and Institution X for any consequences of this course. Abide by the computing policies of Institution X and by all laws governing use of computer resources on campus.

I agree to NOT: Attempt to gain root access or any other increase in privilege on any Institution X workstation. Disclose any private information that I discover as a direct or indirect result of the course exercises. Take actions that will modify or deny access to any data or service not owned by me. Attempt to perform any actions or use utilities presented in the laboratory outside the confines and structure of the labs.

---

5. DISCUSSION

The divergent nature of ethical agreements, as we have demonstrated through our analysis of existing documents, confirms a fractured approach to the application of ethics in information security education. This fractured approach in the impartation of ethical norms over the malice-fraught field of information security, potentially undermines the effective application of ethics in a universal sense. Conveying a universally acceptable message of ethics in the teaching of information security courses is important with regard to effectively addressing ethical pitfalls that may arise from exposing students to potentially dangerous information security concepts and skills. This is especially because the tough ethical questions and potential problems that surround the teaching of these information security concepts, are universal in nature. In being universal, ethical problems are not confined to the boundaries of distinct backgrounds or ideologies. As such, these problems require a platform of mitigation that caters to diverse backgrounds. While disparity in personal stance on questions of morality and ethics remains a key determinant of the sort of ethical agreements or policies that teachers currently present to students, divergence in the nature of these policies may be compensated for by the commonality of features among them. In this regard, an ethical policy resulting from existing commonalities may engender a harmonized approach to the ethical impartation process within the information security education community. A harmonized approach in this manner can result in the pursuit of a common purpose of ethical impartation in the community. Unity of purpose would mean that students are taught information security with ethical policies that are more inclusive with regard to ethical message and general structure, in contrast to the status quo.

6. CONCLUSION

We have looked at ethical agreements on information security courses from multiple and diverse sources and examined their contents and structure. Our analysis has shown that ethical agreements currently in use are divergent in structure and theme and as such would not efficiently serve the purposes of universal acceptance and application. We analyzed these agreements to identify existing commonalities among them. Based on the commonalities identified, we have demonstrated the possibility of a universally applicable and acceptable ethical agreement or policy in the teaching of information security courses.

7. REFERENCES

[1] ACM. Code of Ethics - Association for Computing Machinery. http://www.acm.org/about/code-of-ethics.

[2] J. Aycock, E. Buchanan, S. Dexter, and D. Dittrich. Human subjects, agents, or bots: Current issues in ethics and computer security research. In *Financial Cryptography and Data Security*, pages 138–145. Springer, 2012.

[3] freesummarizer.com. Free Summarizer. http://freesummarizer.com/#summarizecontainer.

[4] S. J. Greenwald, B. D. Snow, R. Ford, and R. Thieme. Towards an ethical code for information security? In *Proceedings of the 2008 workshop on New security paradigms*, pages 75–87. ACM, 2009.

[5] C. E. Harris. *Applying moral theories.* Wadsworth Publishing Company, 1997.

[6] IEEE. IEEE Code of Ethics. http://www.ieee.org/about/corporate/governance/p7-8.html.

[7] G. Ledin Jr. The growing harm of not teaching malware. *Communications of the ACM*, 54(2):32–34, 2011.

[8] J. P. Sullins. A case study in malware research ethics education: When teaching bad is good. In *Security and Privacy Workshops (SPW), 2014 IEEE*, pages 1–4. IEEE, 2014.

[9] UofC. University of Calgary : K.1 Statement of Intellectual Honesty. http://www.ucalgary.ca/honesty/.

[10] J. Vijayan. Undergrad suspected in massive Univ. of Nebraska breach, 2012.

Assessing the Tier-1 Core Learning Outcomes of CS2013

James W. McGuffee
College of Informatics
Northern Kentucky University
Highland Heights, KY 41099 USA
+1.859.572.7931
mcguffeej1@nku.edu

E. Kent Palmer
MacMurray College
447 E College Ave
Jacksonville, IL 62650 USA
+1.217.479.7048
kpalmer@goshen.edu

Indira R. Guzman
Trident University International
5757 Plaza Dr. #100
Cypress, CA 90630 USA
+1.714.816.0366 x2561
Indira.Guzman@trident.edu

ABSTRACT

In December 2013, the ACM and IEEE-Computer Society sponsored joint Task Force on Computing Curricula released the comprehensive Computer Science Curricula 2013 (CS2013). At the same time, a geographically diverse group of volunteers, known as the CS2013 Assessment Council, met to begin the work of creating a valid three option multiple-choice exam to comprehensively assess the tier-1 core learning outcomes of CS2013. This project has been facilitated by the Institute for the Certification of Computing Professionals (ICCP). This paper describes the motivation and desire to create an assessment exam for the CS2013 tier-1 core learning outcomes, a brief review of the relevant research in psychometrics and educational assessment, the process used to create test items for this exam, the alpha testing and analysis of test questions, the beta testing and analysis of the complete exam, and the current state of the completed exam that is now available for use.

Keywords

Assessment; Evaluation; Exam; Accreditation; Certification; Computer Science Curricula 2013; Learning Outcomes

1. BACKGROUND

In this section, we describe the body of knowledge presented in the Computer Science Curricula 2013, the relevance of the tier-1 core topics, and the need for a comprehensive computer science exit exam. We also give an overview of the history, current status, and relevancy of the Institute for the Certification of Computing Professionals.

SIGCSE '16, March 02-05, 2016, Memphis, TN, USA
© 2016 ACM. ISBN 978-1-4503-3685-7/16/03...$15.00
DOI: http://dx.doi.org/10.1145/2839509.2844613

1.1 CS2013 and Assessment

In December of 2013, a joint task force comprised of members from ACM and the IEEE-Computer Society formally presented their recommendations for a major revision to the previous computer science curricula guidelines (CS2001). In the report, the task force identified ten guiding principles that were used in the creation of the new guidelines. These principles included flexibility for educational institutions, defining an expected level of mastery of topics by computer science graduates, and managing the overall size of the essential knowledge for an undergraduate degree in computer science. In order to address these various principles, CS2013 categorized the computer science body of knowledge into three distinct categories: tier-1 core, tier-2 core, and elective topics. Of these three categories, only the topics in the tier-1 core are expected to be covered by all undergraduate computer science degree programs [5].

The tier-1 core learning outcomes span fifteen different defined knowledge areas and represent 166 hours of coverage. CS2013 does not define specific courses nor does it define a certain sequencing of topics. Rather, the CS2013 task force wanted to give individual institutions flexibility in how they cover and teach these essential core learning outcomes [5,6].

This flexibility in defining tiered knowledge areas does leave a potential gap in assessment of computer science degree learning outcomes. In the past, it might have been easy to determine if a degree program did or did not contain the essential number and variety of computer courses. Then, for an overall degree assessment, all that would be required would be a summary of the individual course assessments in the degree program. However, under these new curricula guidelines, there needs to be a way to assess the computer science learning outcomes at a program level without any assumption of what courses may or may not be offered.

Given the structure and purpose of CS2013, the authors of this paper believe that having an independent measurement of assessment for overall learning outcomes for a computer science degree program has many benefits. We specifically advocate for an exit exam that objectively measures the tier-1 core learning outcomes of the various knowledge areas of CS2013. The choice of limiting the exam to the assessment of tier-1 core learning outcomes was made because the tier-1 core sections are the only outcomes that are required of all computer science degree programs that wish to consider themselves in compliance with the recommended CS2013 guidelines. This is not to say that tier-2 core learning outcomes are not important. In fact, all computer science programs are expected to cover most of the tier-2 core learning outcomes. However, all programs are not required to cover all tier-2 core learning areas [5].

A review of the literature also lends support for the benefits of an external exit exam. In 1997, Bishop documented the correlation between achievement and the use of an exit exam [4]. More recently, Ahmad et. al. have written of the benefits of using exit exams in evaluating engineering degree programs [3]. An objective external exam can also be used to effectively document the effectiveness of a program for accreditation.

1.2 Institute for the Certification of Computing Professionals (ICCP)

In 1973, ACM along with seven other professional societies related to computing created the ICCP as a non-profit organization charged with the creation of creating independent certification assessments in the information and computing sciences [7]. Today, ICCP is seen as the non-profit standard bearer for broadly applicable and internationally recognized certification programs for professionals in the information systems, information technology, and computing fields [2]. One measure of ICCP's global impact is the groups that choose to affiliate themselves with ICCP. As of 2015, ICCP is comprised of four constituent societies:

- ACM (Association for Computing Machinery)
- AITP (Association of Information Technology Professionals)
- CIPS (Canadian Information Processing Society)
- CPCI (Consejo Profesional en Ciencas Informaticas),

seven affiliate societies:

- ABRS (Professional Learning Services of Hong Kong)
- BTA (Business Technology Association)
- CMG (Computer Measurement Group)
- HKCS (Hong Kong Computer Society)
- DAMA International
- ISCA (Information Systems Consultants Association)
- Society of Computer Professionals,

and seven business partners:

- ASIT (Advanced Solutions Institute)
- ACBSP (Accreditation Council for Business Schools and Programs)
- BPM (Business Process Management Institute)
- Excelsior College
- IBM
- SOX Institute
- TDWI (The Data Warehouse Institute).

In addition to professional certification in specific areas, ICCP has been involved in the creation of assessments that map to suggested curriculum guidelines. A little over ten years ago, ICCP developed an outcome assessment examination reflecting the objectives and learning units espoused in the IS2002 Model Curriculum. IS2002 was created by a joint task force from ACM, AITP, and AIS (Association for Information Systems). IS2002 defined model curricula for undergraduate information systems degree programs. As part of the development of this examination, ICCP formed the CCER (Center for Computing Education Research) to provide the assessment examination and related institutional feedback on programmatic preparation of graduates consistent with the IS2002 Model Curriculum [8,9].

2. CREATING THE EXAM

2.1 Timeline

On December 6-8, 2013, a group of geographically disparate faculty met in Cleveland, Ohio to begin initial planning for the creation of a comprehensive multiple choice exam to measure the tier-1 core learning objectives of CS2013. This group of faculty is collectively known as ICCP's CS2013 Assessment Council. Note: While ICCP provided logistical support for exam creation and travel to meetings, all faculty members of the CS2013 Assessment Council were unpaid volunteers.

For the first meeting in December of 2013, there were two main tasks. First, the various knowledge areas of CS2013 were divided among the faculty council members who then became responsible for writing questions and recruiting volunteers to help write questions for those knowledge areas. Second, the council met with John Whitehouse (a professional psychometrician employed by ICCP) who covered the essentials of assessment exam creation, testing, and validation. This included explaining the format and mechanics of the testing software and the data that could be attained and used to improve exam questions and whole exams during the alpha and beta testing phases of exam creation.

Over the next several months, the council met monthly via the internet until the next in person meeting on March 28-30, 2014 in Dallas, Texas. At the meeting in Dallas, the CS 2013 Assessment Council evaluated each test question that had been written and tested (i.e. a group of students had taken the exam with the questions being reviewed). There was a significant learning curve in learning how to evaluate the validity of individual questions. For each question, the council members could graphically see how many student had answered each option, how the students relative strength on other questions compared to their answers on this question, and the correlations between these metrics. For a more detailed explanation of how these metrics were used, please see section 3.1 below.

After the meeting in Dallas, the various members of the CS2013 Assessment Council re-wrote questions that needed re-writing and generated new questions. In late spring, another group of students took the exam with all the new and revised questions. This new set of questions was evaluated during an in person meeting on July 31 - August 3, 2014 in Chicago, Illinois. After this summer meeting, a full round of alpha testing took place in the fall of 2014.

The council met again in Chicago on November 15-16, 2014 to review the comprehensive results from alpha testing and to prepare for formal beta testing of the exam which took place during the first six months of 2015. On July 16-19, 2015 the CS 2013 Assessment Council had a joint meeting with ICCP's Certification Council, reviewed the results from beta testing, and finalized plans for the official rollout of the exam in fall 2015.

2.2 Levels of Mastery and Item Generation

According to the Computer Science Curricula 2013 document, each learning outcome listed in the knowledge areas is classified in to one of three different levels of mastery. The three levels are familiarity, usage, and assessment. Familiarity is the first level and is concerned with a basic awareness of the concept. The next level is usage and deals with a student's ability to apply the concept in a concrete way. Assessment is a level of mastery that involves the ability to choose an appropriate approach from alternatives [5].

In trying to write multiple choice questions for each learning outcome, it was easiest to write questions for the familiarity level outcomes. However, to be a robust exam, it was decided that questions must not only be written for all knowledge areas but also for all three types of levels of mastery. This means that hundreds of exam questions were created. Many tier-1 core learning outcomes had three or more unique questions written to assess the mastery of the specific learning outcome.

In the CS2013 guidelines, there is no correlation between the number of learning outcomes listed in a particular knowledge area and the amount of time that CS2013 recommends be spent on each area. Thus, while questions were created for all levels of all tier-1 core learning outcomes, not all questions will be given to each student taking each exam. For each knowledge area, a set of questions are pulled from the databank of questions related to that knowledge area. One advantage of this method is that students seated next to each other will most likely have very different exams. Each exam instance can be dynamically created because all instances of exams are administered via secure software developed by ICCP.

In addition to the different questions on different exams, the ordering of the options that a student will have to choose from will vary from exam to exam. Again, this is made possible because the exam is given on a computer via software that generates a unique exam for each student. The impact on exam question creation is that no option may take on the form of "none of the above" or "all of the above" because each option may appear in any order. Each option must be a stand-alone option that may appear in any order of the options.

When creating test questions, care was taken to move as much information to the stem of the question (the part of the question that is common to all options) and thus minimize the length of options. This was done to try to reduce the amount of time it will take to complete the exam. Also, care was taken to make sure each option (the answer and the distractors) were of the same form and of similar length. During testing of the exam, results indicated that when options were dissimilar it provided a clue to exam takers. A principle of a good multiple-choice exam is that students who have mastered the learning outcome should choose the correct answer and that students who haven't mastered the learning outcome will choose one of the distractors (i.e. incorrect answer).

2.3 Three Option Multiple-Choice Questions

Early in the development of the exam, the CS2013 Assessment Council realized that this was going to be a very lengthy exam. Our group tried to brainstorm many different options. One option considered was to have a stem that would be part of many questions. This ultimately turned out to be a non-implementable solution due to the nature of ICCP's exam administration software. Additionally, because of the decision that each instance of an exam would be a unique generation and ordering of questions, the sharing of information between two or more questions was infeasible. Another option that seemed to hold promise was to change all questions from a four option to a three option multiple-choice question. By simple reasoning, this reduction should cut down the time to read the options for a question by 25%.

Also, when we were analyzing results from initial testing, we noticed that with a four option multiple choice question there would inevitably be an answer that was very rarely chosen (i.e. an underperforming distractor). In plain terms, two of the distractors would be "doing their job" but one of the distractors was doing nothing more than taking up space. We then performed a literature search and found that the psychometric and statistical testing literature supported the notion that an exam with three option multiple choice questions was just as statistically valid in measuring knowledge as an exam with four option multiple choice questions [10].

Given these two factors, the decision was made that all questions in the exam would be three option multiple choice questions. In other words, each question would have one correct answer and two incorrect distractors. Further testing demonstrated that students were indeed able to answer more questions in a shorter period of time and by statistical measurement the exam was just as valid in assessing the tier-1 core learning outcomes of the various knowledge areas of CS2013.

3. TESTING THE EXAM

3.1 Item and Alpha Exam Testing

Each question tested was rigorously examined according to several metrics. The first metric examined was the number of exam takers choosing each of the three options (i.e. the correct answer and the distractors). For acceptable questions, there should be a relatively good distribution among all options chosen. When the Council saw that a distractor was not performing well, a choice was made of whether that question should be re-written and re-tested or whether that question be discarded.

Another metric reviewed was the relative overall exam score of each test taker. Then, for each question, the correlation between good performers and poor performers and the options they chose were graphically displayed. In simple terms, the correct answer should be chosen more often by good performers and poor performers should choose distractors at least as frequently as they choose the correct answer. The graphical display allowed the committee of reviewers to quickly see the relative strong or poor performance of individual questions. Once again, after this analysis a decision was made of whether to keep the question, discard the question, or attempt to re-write the question.

When it was decided to try and re-write a question, several factors were considered. These factors included:

- Examining the question for clarity.
- Emphasizing with capitalization when a 'not' term was used.
- Insuring that graphics were displayed correctly.
- Removing regionally and culturally biased phrases.
- Insuring that the answer and two distractors were similar in structure and length.
- Moving as much information as possible to the stem of the question.
- Removing wordiness that did not contribute to an understanding of what the question was asking.

3.2 Beta Testing

During beta testing, individual questions were examined with the same thoroughness that occurred during previous testing. However, at this stage of exam development, a question was much more likely to be removed from the database rather than try to edit it if the question had performed poorly in testing. Again, poor performance was measured the same way as in earlier stages of testing.

In addition to question by question performance, the exam performance as a whole was considered. Some examples of questions asked include: did a certain set of students perform unexpectedly well or poor in one or more knowledge areas, were students able to complete the exam in a reasonable amount of time, and did the exam seem to unfairly favor any group of students?

While the beta testing is now complete, it is important to realize that testing of the exam is never complete. Every time someone takes an instance of an exam, more information is gathered on the performance of questions. Periodically, these questions will be reviewed and if a question begins to perform poorly, it will be removed. Also, over time new questions will be added. In addition to the questions that will be assessed, it is planned that up to ten trial questions may be asked during any particular exam instance. The results of these questions will not be part of the student's score but will be used to make improvements on the exam over time.

4. CURRENT EXAM

The current CS2013 assessment exam is divided into two parts of 83 questions each. It is estimated that each part will take no more than two hours to complete. Both parts may be taken in one sitting or on different days. The numbers of questions per knowledge area were determined by the number of hours assigned to each tier-1 core learning outcomes. In other words, the question topics are assigned proportional to the number of hours assigned that topic in the CS2013 model curricula. Here is the complete listing of both parts of the exam with associated knowledge areas and number of questions.

CS2013 Exam Part 1

Number of Questions	Knowledge Area Covered
19	AL – Algorithms and Complexity
37	DS – Discrete Structures
11	SP – Social Issues and Professional Practice
4	NC – Networking and Communications
4	OS – Operating Systems
8	PL – Programming Languages

CS2013 Exam Part 2

Number of Questions	Knowledge Area Covered
43	SDF - Software Development Fundamentals
18	SF – Systems Fundamentals
6	SE – Software Engineering
4	HCI – Human-Computer Interaction
3	IAS – Information Assurance and Security
1	IM – Information Management
5	PD – Parallel and Distributed Computing
2	GV – Graphics and Visualization
1	CN – Computational Science

This exam is administered with care for functionality, ease of use, and security to maintain the validity of the exam results. In order to take an exam, an examinee must insert a physical USB drive that is supplied by ICCP. All exam software and the entire database of all questions are securely saved and encoded on this physical device. When the exam is finished, the results are saved on the USB drive and the USB drive is physically returned to ICCP.

At the end of the exam, the person taking the exam will be able to see their results. This gives immediate feedback to the person taking the exam (i.e. the person does not have to wait for the exam to be sent away to be evaluated). At the completion of the exam the person taking the exam is also giving the option of printing the results of his/her detailed exam results. This feedback includes a score by individual CS2013 knowledge area.

ICCP is also able to produce additional reports for institutions by student, groups of students, and by knowledge area. Institutions are able to use these reports to assess how well their computer science program is meeting the tier-1 core learning outcomes of CS2013. It is important to remember that this exam is not intended to assess every learning objective of every computer science program. For example, a reasonable expectation of a computer science graduate might be the ability to work in teams to complete a software project. A multiple choice exam simply can't measure that learning outcome. However, as an exam that assesses all of the tier-1 core learning outcomes of CS2013 and generates reports broken down by the knowledge areas of CS2013, this exam is singularly unique.

5. FUTURE WORK

There are three main areas of future work related to this project that are currently being explored. First, members of ICCP's CS2013 Assessment Council are exploring how the tier-1 core knowledge areas map to the Accreditation Board for Engineering and Technology's (ABET) expected outcomes for a computer science graduate [1]. With this mapping, ICCP's CS2013 exam may prove to be a useful tool in the accreditation process.

Second, ICCP is considering the creation of a computer science certification. ICCP has over 40 years of experience in certification and believes that a computer science certification would be a potentially useful credential. While the exam alone would not be all that is involved in the certification process, the CS2013 exam could be a foundational part of the certification process.

Third, ICCP is in the very initial stages of exploring the possibility of creating an exam for the tier-2 core learning outcomes of CS2013. One challenge for this exam would be that not all tier-2 core learning outcomes are covered by every computer science program and these programs would most likely like to choose which of the tier-2 knowledge area topics would be covered in an exam given to students in their program.

6. ACKNOWLEDGMENTS

The authors would like to specifically acknowledge their colleagues who served with them on ICCPs CS2013 Assessment Council:

- Paulette Alexander (University of North Alabama)
- Kewal Dhariwal (ICCP, executive director)
- Terry Linkletter (Central Washington University)
- Patricia Roden (University of North Alabama)

Beyond the CS2013 Assessment Council, many people helped support this project by submitting questions in various knowledge areas. The authors would like to thank the following for their contributions to the creation of ICCP's CS2013 assessment exam:

- Maureen Doyle
- Eric Emrick
- Richard Fox
- Nick Meyer
- Bruce White
- John Whitehouse

We also acknowledge the support of the ICCP staff with particular thanks to Cindy Blaese and Tracey Byron. If you have any questions about the exam described in this paper, please contact the ICCP office. Complete contact information may be found by going to http://iccp.org/contact.

7. REFERENCES

[1] ABET Computing Accreditation Commission (2014). 2015-2016 Criteria for Accrediting Computing Programs, <www.abet.org/wp-content/uploads/2015/05/C001-15-16-CAC-Criteria-03-10-15.pdf>: accessed 23 Aug 2015.

[2] Adelman, C. (2000). A parallel universe certification in the information technology guild. *Change: The Magazine of Higher Learning*, 32(3):20-29, doi: 10.1080/00091380009601732

[3] Ahmad., M. A., Marzouqi, A. H. A., and Hussien, M. (2014). Exit exam as academic performance indicator. TOJET : *The Turkish Online Journal of Educational Technology*, 13(3), 58-67.

[4] Bishop, J. H. (1997). The effect of national standards and curriculum-based exams on achievement. *The American Economic Review*, 87(2), 260-264.

[5] Joint Task Force on Computing Curricula, Association for Computing Machinery (ACM) and IEEE Computer Society (2013*), Computer Science Curricula 2013: Curriculum Guidelines for Undergraduate Degree Programs in Computer Science*. ACM, New York, NY, USA.

[6] Linkletter T. and Whitehouse J. (2013), How do we know our students have learned the BS outcomes? : an overview of assessment, accreditation, the model curricula, and certification --- in information systems and in computer science. *Journal of Computing Sciences in Colleges*, 29(1):96-97.

[7] McCracken, D.D. (1979). ACM President's Letter: the institute for certification of computer professionals: a call for ACM action. *Communications of the ACM* 22(3):145-146. doi: 10.1145/359080.359081

[8] McKell, L.J., Reynolds, J.H., Longenecker, H.E., Landry, J.P., and Pardue, H. (2004). Integrating program evaluation and a new certification for information technology professionals. *CITC5 '04 Proceedings of the 5th conference on information technology education* :283. doi: 10.1145/1029533.1029616

[9] McKell, L.J., Reynolds, J.H., Longenecker, H.E., and Landry, J.P. (2011). Aligning ICCP certification with the IS2002 model curriculum: a new international standard. *International Business & Economics Research Journal*, 2(9):87-92.

[10] Rodriguez, M. C. (2005), Three options are optimal for multiple-choice items: a meta-analysis of 80 years of research. *Educational Measurement: Issues and Practice*, 24: 3–13. doi: 10.1111/j.1745-3992.2005.00006.x

Updating Curricular Guidelines for Associate-Degree Computer Science Programs

Cara Tang
Portland Community College
12000 SW 49th Avenue
Portland, OR 97219
+1-971-722-4447
cara.tang@pcc.edu

Cindy S. Tucker
Bluegrass Community and Technical College
500 Newtown Pike
Lexington, KY 40508-1207
+1-859-246-4634
cindy.tucker@kctcs.edu

Elizabeth K. Hawthorne
Union County College
1033 Springfield Ave
Cranford, NJ 07016
+1-908-497-4232
hawthorne@ucc.edu

Keywords
Community College; Two-Year College; Computer Science Education; Cybersecurity Education; CS2013; Curriculum Guidelines.

1. SUMMARY
This special session, led by the ACM CCECC (Committee for Computing Education in Community Colleges), will engage participants in the curriculum development process for associate-degree programs in Computer Science, with emphasis on the importance of cybersecurity.

As a standing committee of the ACM Education Board, the CCECC has produced curricular guidelines for community college computing programs in the five areas outlined by ACM and IEEE-CS in CC2005 (The Overview Report) [2]. Most recently the CCECC published guidelines for IT programs in *ACM Competency Model of Core Learning Outcomes and Assessment for Associate-Degree Curriculum in Information Technology* [4] in October 2014.

Guidelines for Computer Science programs at the associate-degree (2-year) level have generally followed the publication of Computer Science guidelines at the bachelor's degree (4-year undergraduate) level. The most recent set of associate-degree Computer Science guidelines were published in 2009 by the CCECC [3] following the 2008 *Computer Science Curriculum 2008: An Interim Revision of CS 2001* [1].

In December of 2013, the ACM and IEEE-Computer Society published *Computer Science Curricula 2013: Curriculum Guidelines for Undergraduate Degree Programs in Computer Science* (CS2013) [5], representing a comprehensive revision over previous guidelines. A growing diversity of topics and rapid evolution of technology necessarily leads to an evolving body of knowledge (BoK). Beyond technology advances however, the CS2013 BoK was redefined as "a result of rethinking the essentials necessary for a Computer Science curriculum" [5]. One of these essentials is the increased importance of cybersecurity, reflected in CS2013 in the integration of security learning outcomes throughout the BoK as well as the new knowledge area Information Assurance and Security (IAS). The importance of Cybersecurity is also demonstrated in the ACM Education Board's formation of a curricular task force to develop undergraduate guidance in Cybersecurity [6].

SIGCSE '16, March 02-05, 2016, Memphis, TN, USA
ACM 978-1-4503-3685-7/16/03.
http://dx.doi.org/10.1145/2839509.2844671

Following changes in the discipline and the publication of CS2013, as well as increased focus on and importance of cybersecurity in computer science, new curricular guidelines for associate-degree Computer Science programs are needed. The ACM CCECC has initiated the creation of such guidelines. The guidelines should be compatible with CS2013, fostering inter-institutional cooperation and student articulation. They should emphasize the critical importance of cybersecurity throughout the BoK. They should reflect the opportunities, constraints, and characteristics of the community college environment, facilitating use and adoption at community colleges and similar post-secondary institutions worldwide.

Prior to the special session at SIGCSE, the CCECC will have conducted a survey of community college educators on knowledge units from CS2013 that may be applicable at the lower division undergraduate level. An initial draft of the associate-degree BoK will be constructed. This prior work will serve as inputs to the work carried out at the special session.

2. OBJECTIVE
This special session will engage those interested in Computer Science at the undergraduate, lower division level in the development of curricular guidelines. Participants will have the opportunity to review the current draft and related materials, to recommend changes, plan further revisions, and otherwise assist in crafting the curricular guidance. The session will serve an important role by engaging the broader community to provide input and dialog on opportunities, challenges, local needs, and successful models of computing curricula to shape the new guidelines.

3. OUTLINE
The 75-minute session will be organized as follows:

3.1 Introduction (15 minutes)
Members of the ACM CCECC will describe the work of the committee, the current curricular project, and the goals for this special session. Presenters include Elizabeth Hawthorne (CCECC Chair, and member of the CS2013 steering committee), Cara Tang (CCECC Vice-Chair), and Cindy Tucker (CCECC member).

3.2 Body of Knowledge Work (45 minutes)

The current draft of the proposed associate-degree body of knowledge will be presented. Participants will break into small groups, with each group to consider a subset of the BoK with respect to CS2013, results from the CCECC's survey, and other materials as appropriate. The small group discussion may include suitability of BoK topics for associate-degree programs, associated student learning outcomes, assessment metrics, and missing topics. After a time, each small group will report out to the whole group and further discussion will take place.

3.3 Summary and Wrap-Up (15 minutes)

Changes to the BoK that were proposed during the session will be summarized. The presenters will describe ways in which participants may continue to be involved in or stay connected to the curricular project.

4. EXPECTATIONS

The intended audience for this session includes community college faculty, division chairs, and program coordinators, as well as educators from 4-year programs interested in 2-year curricula and computer science articulation. The session will provide an overview of existing curricular guidelines for Computer Science, with the majority of time in the session spent working on and contributing to the creation of curricular guidance for associate-degree Computer Science programs.

5. SUITABILITY FOR A SPECIAL SESSION

At SIGCSE 2015 a BOF sponsored by the ACM CCECC with the topic "Perspectives on How Computer Science Curricula 2013 Influences Two-Year College Programs" drew a standing-room-only crowd of community college educators and others. Now embarking on a curricular project on the same topic, the CCECC desires to engage the interested community more deeply than is possible in a BOF. The session is designed to be highly interactive and would not be suitable as a paper or panel.

6. REFERENCES

[1] ACM/IEEE-CS Joint Interim Review Task Force. 2008. *Computer Science Curriculum 2008: An Interim Revision of CS 2001*. ACM, New York, NY, USA.

[2] ACM/IEEE-CS Joint Task Force for Computer Curricula. 2005. Computing Curricula 2005: The Overview Report. DOI= http://doi.acm.org/10.1145/1124706.1121482.

[3] ACM Two-Year College Education Committee. 2009. *Computing Curricula 2009: Guidelines for Associate-Degree Transfer Curriculum in Computer Science*. Available at http://ccecc.acm.org/files/publications/2009ComputerScienceTransferGuidelines.pdf. Accessed 30 November 2015.

[4] Hawthorne, E., et al. 2014. *Information Technology Competency Model of Core Learning Outcomes and Assessment for Associate-Degree Curriculum*. ACM, New York, NY, USA. DOI= http://dx.doi.org/10.1145/2686614.

[5] Joint Task Force on Computing Curricula, Association for Computing Machinery (ACM) and IEEE Computer Society. 2013. *Computer Science Curricula 2013: Curriculum Guidelines for Undergraduate Degree Programs in Computer Science*. ACM, New York, NY, USA. DOI= http://dx.doi.org/10.1145/2534860.

[6] Minutes of the ACM Education Council meeting, August 24, 2015, Denver, CO.

Uncommon Teaching Languages*

Mark C. Lewis
(moderator)
Trinity University
1 Trinity Place
San Antonio, TX
mlewis@trinity.edu

Douglas Blank
Bryn Mawr College
Bryn Mawr, PA 19010
dblank@cs.brynmawr.edu

Kim Bruce
Pomona College
Claremont, CA 9171
kbb04747@gmail.com

Peter-Michael Osera
Grinnell College
Grinnell, IA 50112
osera@cs.grinnell.edu

CCS Concepts

•Applied computing → Education; •Software and its engineering → General programming languages; *Object oriented languages; Functional languages;*

Keywords

CS1; CS2; Programming-Languages

1. SUMMARY

Most courses of study in computer science begin with students learning to think algorithmically, and to express the solutions to problems using a programming language. The choice of *which* programming language is usually considered secondary to the choice of concepts, but the reality is that the vehicle we choose for teaching concepts shapes the way that students understand those concepts, and enables or inhibits the learning of certain concepts.

Most departments use one of a small number of mainstream languages that are well-established in industry and are backed by teaching and learning resources. A minority of departments choose to work with non-mainstream languages, finding that the advantages of those languages outweigh the disadvantages. What issues should we consider when choosing a programming language for our introductory courses?

A. Use in the "real world". A department may be pressured to use a language that is prevalent in local industry, local feeder schools, or standardized tests. For example, local companies might like students to be prepared for internships by being taught in whatever language they use for production. Unfortunately, "real world" languages often come with complex features, that, while useful on large industrial projects, make them unsuitable for students, particularly beginning students, and have a tendency to become less pure, more complex, and harder to teach over time.

B. Available resources. More teaching resources can mean less work for the instructor and can make life easier for students looking to answer questions. Unfortunately, it also means that cheating is easier and that students get lazy. After all, why figure out your own approach when you can find the answer on *StackOverflow*?

C. Pedagogical benefits. Does the language have a clear syntax that teaches the students the vocabulary of the programming paradigm? Does it have a straightforward semantics for expressing algorithms? Does it add to the essential difficulties of learning how to express algorithms its own set of "accidental difficulties" that distract students from learning the essentials?

The idioms natural to a particular language can encourage beginning students to develop specific programming habits. Does the language and its libraries encourage habits, such as clear interfaces, single-responsibility methods or functions, model-view separation, and test-driven development, that will serve students well regardless of language? Or does the language encourage techniques that don't transfer well to other languages?

D. Integration with the curriculum. Students need a path from the introductory language to languages used in later courses; this argues for using the same or similar languages. However, students should also be exposed to a variety of styles of language during their degree program; this argues for using radically different languages at different stages in the program.

SIGCSE '16 March 2–5, 2016, Memphis, TN, USA

ACM ISBN 123-4567-24-567/08/06...$15.00
DOI: 10.475/123_4

2. OCAML (PETER-MICHAEL OSERA)

OCaml is a strongly-typed functional programming language derived from ML. At the University of Pennsylvania, we start our CS2 course in OCaml and then transition into Java in the second half. This approach seems to violate several of the desiderata presented in Section 1: OCaml is neither a common language found in industry nor elsewhere in our curriculum and there are comparatively few resources for teaching OCaml at this level. However, OCaml strongly supports the type-directed, test-driven design process and usage of immutable data structures that we emphasize in the course.

While OCaml possesses object-oriented features, we elect to use a small functional subset of the language which allows the students to immediately jump into the course and solve problems without being bogged down in syntax. Furthermore, the fact that OCaml is not widely used becomes a boon because it "levels the playing field" between our students who have a wide range of programming experience, particularly with Java. Finally, utilizing a functional programming language early in the curriculum allows us to draw meaningful comparisons between the object-oriented paradigm and other, lesser known paradigms.

3. GRACE (KIM BRUCE)

Grace [2] is by design an object-oriented language for novices, in the same way that Pascal was by design a procedural language for novices. It is simpler syntactically and semantically than Java, yet includes more powerful and expressive modern features. It provides better support for object-oriented features than Python. It omits many of the features that make industrial languages so hard for novices.

Grace supports two different graphics libraries and a library for supporting animations. There is also a well-designed data structures library. A draft textbook, *Programming with Grace*, based on the `objectdraw` library and event-driven programming, is freely available. Grace programs can be written and run in a web browser, so Grace can be run on all platforms just by visiting a URL.

Dialects (like those of Racket) can be used to add new constructs to the language or to restrict the language to allow students and instructors to focus on key concepts. Grace has a simple syntax that avoids most of the "noise" that pollutes code in other languages; for example, there is no `public static void main`, and the visibility defaults are exactly what novices require. Programs can be anywhere in the spectrum from completely dynamically typed to fully statically typed.

Grace was designed to make it easy for students to move on to languages like Java, Scala, and Python. In our experience, the only difficulty in shifting from Grace to Java is getting used to the weird special cases in Java that get in the way of the programmer. Picking up Python should be even easier. Many of Grace's features are similar to Scala, so we see a smooth path from Grace to Scala.

4. JIGSAW, SCHEME, AND PROCESSING (DOUGLAS BLANK)

Jigsaw is a drag-and-drop, block-oriented language designed to help transfer knowledge between languages from Scratch to Python. Jigsaw is one of the languages used in the Calico system [3], all of which can share libraries. For example, the same graphics or robot library can be used in Jigsaw and Python. This allows students to use the same library API in the two languages. Holding the library constant and switching languages is thought to enable better migration between programming paradigms [3]. Scheme is a commonly mentioned uncommon language for computing, and there are some very good Schemes designed for use in education (e.g., Racket [4]). Calysto Scheme is a version of Scheme implemented in Python that uses all of Python's libraries [1]. Thus, Calysto Scheme has many of the advantageous that make Python popular, including being cross-platform, and providing an extensive library of functions. Processing is a language and environment that attempts to make Java as easy to use as Python, and is designed to allow the creation of beautiful and compelling art [6]. Processing allows some Java shorthand, so that the full Java language can be avoided, and many libraries are included by default.

Although all three of these uncommon languages are arguably better than Python, I argue that none will become common. In fact, I believe that the set "common languages for CS1" will remain small. This has little to do with the details of any particular language. Rather, "common languages" will comprise those that have the best support communities for teachers.

5. SCALA (MARK LEWIS)

Scala is a functional/OO hybrid language that runs on the JVM and is #14 on the RedMonk language ranking[5].

A. Scala is a rising language in industry, but does not have nearly the market penetration of Java, C++, or Python. Being based on the JVM does make the inevitable task of learning Java later easier.

B. Scala falls in a middle ground for resources. The educational resources are still thin, but there are well over a million questions that have been answered about the language on StackOverflow. Fortunately, it is easy to create problems for which no online solutions currently exist.

C. Scala is a statically-typed language with a uniform syntax, a REPL, and a scripting environment that encourages students to develop a Java-like coding style while also allowing coverage of functional concepts. Being a "real" language evolving to support professional developers does mean that it has complexities not found in teaching languages.

D. Unlike many languages, Scala is very good at both programming-in-the-small and programming-in-the-large. The main professional uses cases are Web Development, Big Data Processing, and any application that needs to scale up, so it can work well with later curricular elements. We adopted it at Trinity because it was good at covering all the concepts we wanted for CS1 and CS2.

6. REFERENCES

[1] Calysto Scheme. github.com/Calysto/calysto_scheme, 2015. [Online; accessed 28-August-2008].

[2] A. P. Black, K. B. Bruce, M. Homer, J. Noble, A. Ruskin, and R. Yannow. Seeking grace: A new object-oriented language for novices. In *Proceeding of the 44th ACM Technical Symposium on Computer Science Education*, SIGCSE '13, pages 129–134, New York, NY, USA, 2013. ACM.

[3] D. Blank, J. S. Kay, J. B. Marshall, K. O'Hara, and M. Russo. Calico: A multi-programming-language, multi-context framework designed for computer science education. In *Proceedings of the 43rd ACM Technical Symposium on Computer Science Education*, SIGCSE '12, pages 63–68, New York, NY, USA, 2012. ACM.

[4] R. B. Findler, J. Clements, C. Flanagan, M. Flatt, S. Krishnamurthi, P. Steckler, and M. Felleisen. Drscheme: A programming environment for scheme. *J. Funct. Program.*, 12(2):159–182, Mar. 2002.

[5] M. Odersky, L. Spoon, and B. Venners. *Programming in Scala, 2nd Edition.* Artima Inc, 2011.

[6] C. Reas and B. Fry. *Getting Started with Processing.* Make Books - Imprint of: O'Reilly Media, Sebastopol, CA, 1st edition, 2010.

Lightning Talks

Computational Making: What Does this Theory Mean for SIGCSE?

Jennifer A. Rode, *Univerisity of Siegen & Drexel*
Andrea Marshall, *Drexel University*
Houda El Mimouni, *Drexel University*
Jennifer Booker, *Drexel University*
Contact: jen@acm.org

While unquestionably research on CSE education is centered in the SIGCSE conference, other venues such as the International Joint Conference on Pervasive and Ubiquitous Computing (Ubicomp), and the Conference on Tangible, Embedded and Embodied Interaction (TEI), and the Conference on Interaction Design and Children (ICD) explore CS education focusing on educational play and novel off the desktop techniques for CS education. Unfortunately, this literature remains isolated from the mainstream CSE literature, and this lightning talk attempts to help contribute to rectifying this by presenting a core recent educational theory "Computational Making" and discuss its contributions to CSE.
Rode et al published a paper "From Computational Thinking to Computational Making" at UbiComp 2015 which argues the skills encompassed by computational thinking are too limited to account for the range of skills required for STEAM. The paper challenged computer science educators to engage with maker culture and the arts to increase diversity in computing, and in doing so laid out new skills beyond those of computational thinking. This paper presented an ethnographic study of children learning to program as part of a Lilypad Arduino e-textile activities. Our data shows that skills to support aesthetics, creativity, construction, visualizing multiple representations, and understanding materials were all vital to STEAM programming activities using ubicomp. This lightning talk presents these findings at their highest level and explains their relevance for helping to promote diversity in computing.

Keywords: Computational Thinking; Computational Making, Ubiquitous Computing

DOI: http://dx.doi.org/10.1145/2839509.2850522

You Wouldn't Know It from SIGCSE Proceedings, but We Don't Only Teach CS1

Colleen Lewis, *Harvey Mudd College*
Contact: lewis@cs.hmc.edu

Let's talk about how we teach upper-division courses! CS pedagogical content knowledge - i.e., knowledge of how to teach computer science - is mostly undocumented. This is particularly true for upper-division courses and in some cases this upper-division content is much more difficult to teach than CS1 or CS2 content! CSTeachingTips.org is an NSF-sponsored project to help curate tips that allow teachers to anticipate students' difficulties and build upon students' strengths. The lightning talk will be a call to action: first to share tips on Twitter @CSTeachingTips and at our CSTeachingTips booth and second to create research directions that will help us develop pedagogical content knowledge that extends beyond CS1.

Keywords: Pedagogical Content Knowledge; teaching tips; upper-division CS

DOI: http://dx.doi.org/10.1145/2839509.2850523

Complexity Tutor: Developing an Interactive Tutoring System for Computational Complexity

Mark McCartin-Lim, *Univ. of Massachusetts Amherst*
Contact: markml@cs.umass.edu

This lightning talk describes the development of Complexity Tutor, an interactive tutoring system to assist students in understanding theoretical models of computation and computational complexity. Many computer science students, especially ones lacking a strong background in mathematics, struggle to learn these subjects with the traditional regimen of lectures and written homework assignments. When they are in the process of developing proofs for these homework assignments, they receive no immediate feedback that would illuminate their errors. We intend to remedy this. The main components of our system will entail a novel framework for constructing proofs, as well as a framework for producing algorithmic reductions. The first framework provides continuous feedback to the student on their approach and progress toward the needed proof. The second framework involves analyzing code the student writes in a pseudocode-like language, such as Python. Currently, we have prototypes, which show how to use our frameworks to construct NP-completeness reduction proofs. We are planning to test the efficacy of this system in theoretical computer science courses at the University of Massachusetts Amherst.

Keywords: teaching theoretical computer science; intelligent tutoring systems; computational complexity; proofs; reductions

DOI: http://dx.doi.org/10.1145/2839509.2850524

A Body of Knowledge for Usable Security and Privacy Education

Yousra Javed, *UNC Charlotte*
Heather Richter Lipford, *UNC Charlotte*
Contact: yjaved@uncc.edu

The importance of usability in security and privacy technologies is now widely accepted. A vibrant and growing research community in usable security and privacy has contributed a wide range of results in the past 15 years. Despite this, the vast majority of computing students are being exposed to very little of this discipline. In this presentation, we describe our ongoing efforts to

SIGCSE'16, March 2–5, 2016, Memphis, TN, USA.
ACM ISBN: 978-1-4503-3685-7/16/03.

enable broader education in this area. We are leading the construction of a body of knowledge for usable security and privacy education, to serve as an organizing framework for the discipline. We are also creating online learning modules for several key topics, as resources for faculty and students. We seek feedback on these resources as well as faculty participants who are interested in utilizing and evaluating the learning modules.

Keywords: Usable security and privacy education; body of knowledge

DOI: http://dx.doi.org/10.1145/2839509.2850517

U.S. Army's Cyber Leader Development Program

James Finocchiaro, *United States Military Academy*
Contact: james.finocchiaro@usma.edu

This lightning talk describes the U.S. Army's Cyber Leader Development Program (CLDP) which is a recently implemented initiative designed to increase and improve undergraduate cyber education for United States Military Academy (USMA) and Reserve Officers' Training Corps (ROTC) cadets.

The CLDP takes a holistic viewpoint towards cyber education. Its methodology provides a model for all educators on how to integrate out-of-class enrichment opportunities with an in-class curriculum. CLDP is a voluntary program that has about 800 hours of required out-of-class activities. These required activities include being assigned a formal mentor, participation in a security or hacking club, attending a security conference, participating in security training, and participating in an internship. This program is in its inaugural year with ROTC and in its second year at the United States Military Academy.

The focus of this lightning talk will be to highlight the central aspects of the program and to describe how such programs would improve the holistic development of any students, security or otherwise. CLDP is not just a working military program – it is an exportable concept that presents an applicable model for the development of cyber security students destined to support corporate America as well as government agencies at federal, state, and local levels.

Keywords: Department of Defense; US Army; Cyber; Leadership; Student Development; CLDP

DOI: http://dx.doi.org/10.1145/2839509.2850518

Using Instant Chat for Fun and for Profit to Run a Large Class

Michael Ball, UC Berkeley EECS
Contact: michael.ball@berkeley.edu

This lightning talk describes the idea of "chat ops" applied to the classroom. Chat Ops is a (growing) industry practice which uses instant messaging (such as IRC, or Slack) to automate common development or monitoring tasks, such as maintaining and deploying a website. Instead of deploying a site, we use the process of ChatOps to help run large classes, and even individual class sections by automating tasks that are tedious or error prone. We've extended a bot framework, Hubot, with the tools that we need. We can automate releasing student scores, updating student's access to assignments, or handling in-class check offs with just a line of plain text. Chat messages also have the benefit that they are loggable and show everyone on the staff what's going on and why. We'd like to show why augmenting traditional email systems with chat messages can help improve communication and save time, but can also be an enjoyable way to build a community.

Keywords: chat; chatops; class management; automation; bot; Hubot;

DOI: http://dx.doi.org/10.1145/2839509.2850526

Crossing the Streams: Exploring the Interplay between Students' Online Social Activity and Programming Behavior

Adam S. Carter, Washington State University
Christopher D. Hundhausen, Washington State University
Contact: cartera@wsu.edu

With the widespread availability of massive amounts of student programming data, we are witnessing a digital gold rush as researchers attempt to make sense of students' programming behaviors. In prior research, we incorporated programming data into a statistical model that accounted for a significant amount of a student's course performance. In a separate line of research, we explored how online social networking tools might be leveraged for pedagogical purposes.

Rather than treating our explorations of students' programming and social behaviors as separate research spaces, we are next considering the interplay between social behavior, programming behavior, and course performance. As a first step, we incorporated online social participation into our statistical model of programming behaviors. The outcome was quite promising: we witnessed a 30% increase in our model's effect size. This result would seem to indicate that neither programming behavior nor social behavior alone can fully account for student performance.

Encouraged by this result, we are now considering how social interaction influences programming decisions and vice versa. In particular:

1) After receiving help on a social network, what changes are made to code? Are these changes more or less likely to move the student closer to a correct solution?

2) How do students address coding problems when their questions are left unanswered?

3) At what points in the programming process are students more likely to pose questions? Similarly, when are students more willing to offer help?

4) How can we use this knowledge to better identify students who are struggling?

Keywords: social networking; programming behavior

DOI: http://dx.doi.org/10.1145/2839509.2850519

SIGCSE'16, March 2–5, 2016, Memphis, TN, USA.
ACM ISBN: 978-1-4503-3685-7/16/03.

Social Network Analysis as a Tool for Understanding Student Interaction in Project-based Courses

Bonnie MacKellar, *St John's University*
Contact: mackellb@stjohns.edu

Many university software engineering/capstone courses attempt to teach students the importance of communication by having them work collaboratively on a large scale project. This can be a sink-or-swim approach. There is a real risk of complete project failure, and while students may learn that coordination is important, it isn't clear they learn how to do it effectively. The CoordinationTracker project uses social network analysis both to study coordination in student project teams, and to develop an automated tool to support students learning this skill. In this talk, I will briefly present some results using social network analysis and socio-technical congruence measures to study communication in a software engineering course, and then will describe the design of the proposed CoordinationTracker tool, which will use socio-technical congruence measures to give feedback to students. For example, as a student works on a file, an automated reminder capability will suggest who the student should be communicating with in order to prevent unwanted effects on components dependent on the file. The system also will have a reporting component which will allow each student, as well as the instructor, to view his or her coordination performance via graphs. Once CoordinationTracker has been implemented, it will be tested on several iterations of the software engineering course in order to determine whether students improve their coordination while using the tool. I am interested in audience feedback on the design of this tool as well as possible involvment with the project.

Keywords: software engineering education; communication analysis; socio-technical congruence; student learning support tools

DOI: http://dx.doi.org/10.1145/2839509.2850520

Enhancing Teaching of Big Data by Using Real World Datasets

Anurag Nagar, *University of Texas at Dallas*
Contact: axn112530@utdallas.edu

This lightning talk will focus on our experience of teaching a graduate level Big Data course. Traditionally, such courses have relied on "WordCount" style problems, which involve computing the simple count of words in a corpus of documents using the distributed MapReduce framework. While this is certainly a good way of introducing the students to the BigData framework, more real world examples are needed to motivate students. Further, since a majority of courses require students to work on a large project as part of this course, it is essential that they have access to a diverse and interesting set of data. In our course, we experimented with various data sources, such as text from real-time, streaming news articles, twitter feeds, and property price data from various zip codes in a county. The students were involved in gathering the data, designing and implementing MapReduce style algorithms for distributed processing, and presenting their findings. The feedback was extremely positive and we would like to develop this approach further. In this talk, we will present some ideas on how to collect and analyze real world datasets that are suitable for Big Data analysis. We would also encourage further inputs from the audience about this topic.

Keywords: Big Data teaching; Distributed Computing teaching; Datasets for teaching Big Data

DOI: http://dx.doi.org/10.1145/2839509.2850516

Collaborative Learning Eliminates the Negative Impact of Gender Stereotypes on Women's Self-Concept

Jane Stout, *Computing Research Association*
Burçin Tamer, *Computing Research Association*
Contact: jane@cra.org

Cultural stereotypes about women's "fit" and ability in technical fields, like computing, are alive and well. These cultural beliefs can make their way into women's personal belief system. When this happens, women's self-conceptions in computing suffer, namely, self-efficacy, sense of belonging, and identification with computing. The current research examines whether collaborative learning methods (pair programing; supplemental instruction) can erase the negative relationship between women's endorsement of negative gender stereotypes and their computing self-concept. Longitudinal survey data from 48 women computing majors indicated that participation in collaborative learning activities nullified the negative impact of gender stereotype endorsement on women's self-efficacy, sense of belonging, and identification with computing. These findings showcase the benefits of existing pedagogical strategies in computing on increasing the likelihood that women will persist in a computing career path.

Acknowledgements: This research is sponsored by two grants from the National Science Foundation awarded to the Computing Research Association: CNS-1246649 and DUE-1431112.

Keywords: women; self-concept; gender stereotypes; collaborative learning

DOI: http://dx.doi.org/10.1145/2839509.2850515

A "Grand Tour" of Computer Science: Re-Designing CS1 for Breadth and Retention

Natalie Linnell, *Santa Clara University*
Nicholas Tran, *Santa Clara University*
Contact: nlinnell@scu.edu

We have transformed our first programming course from an introduction to programming, to an introduction to Computer Science. We have done this in part by broadening the topics discussed. We now incorporate discussion of social topics like privacy and humanitarian technology, and "big ideas in CS" like how the Internet and databases work. We have also embedding many of our programming examples in applications from fields like biology and psychology. The other major feature of this course is that we have separated teaching problem-solving from teaching a programming language. In lecture, we discuss problem-solving

SIGCSE'16, March 2–5, 2016, Memphis, TN, USA.
ACM ISBN: 978-1-4503-3685-7/16/03.

with high-level programming constructs like conditionals and loops, using only pseudocode. In our new lab section, students are taught how to translate those ideas into C++ code. This allows us to free the initial learning of problem-solving from the complications of a language like C++.

A unique feature of these changes is that it is possible to offer multiple different labs, in different languages, in conjunction with the same lecture section. It is our intention to start offering labs in different languages starting in Fall 2016.

Our primary goal in making these changes was to improve recruitment and retention, especially among women. We also hoped to improve the course's utility as an elective for non-majors. Our evaluation of a pilot offering suggests that the re-designed course is likely to improve retention, without negatively impacting programming knowledge. We have now completely adopted the re-designed course, and are continuing to gather data to evaluate the new design.

Keywords: CS1; Retention

DOI: http://dx.doi.org/10.1145/2839509.2850521

Raising the Awareness of Accessibility Needs in Block Languages

Amber Wagner, *Kennesaw State University*
Jeff Gray, *University of Alabama*
Daniela Marghitu, *Auburn University*
Andreas Stefik, *University of Nevada, Las Vegas*
Contact: awagne30@kennesaw.edu

Block languages (e.g., Scratch, Snap!, Alice, App Inventor, Blockly) offer a gentle introduction to programming and have been adopted widely in both K-12 and CS0 courses. However, block languages often are dependent on the mouse/keyboard for input and typically are visual in their output and representation. Because of these dependencies, students with a disability (e.g., mobility limitations or vision impairment) generally are unable to use block languages, thereby reducing the opportunities for broader participation in computational learning activities. Given the increasing need to broaden the participation of computing to those with diverse skills and backgrounds, it is important that the tools used to initiate the earliest entre into computing do not erect immediate roadblocks that impede initial interest and opportunity. There are many variations of user interfaces and assistive technologies that benefit those who may have difficulties utilizing traditional Graphical User Interfaces (GUIs), but these tools often cannot be used universally across block languages. As more block languages are being developed and integrated into K12 and University curriculum, it is imperative that accessible solutions are discussed and implemented. These discussions require participation from the block language developer community, accessible computing community, and those educators who encounter accessibility needs among the students in their classrooms. The goal of this lightning talk is to call attention to the need for more accessible block-based programming environments and to spark conversation surrounding possible standard accessibility APIs that could possibly be supported by block language environment tool developers.

Keywords: Accessibility; Block languages; Broadening participation

DOI: http://dx.doi.org/10.1145/2839509.2850525

SIGCSE'16, March 2–5, 2016, Memphis, TN, USA.
ACM ISBN: 978-1-4503-3685-7/16/03.

Undergraduate Assembly Language Instruction Sweetened with the Raspberry Pi

Jalal Kawash
Department of Computer Science
University of Calgary
Calgary, Alberta, Canada
+1 403 220 6619
jkawash@ucalgary.ca

Andrew Kuipers
Department of Computer Science
University of Calgary
Calgary, Alberta, Canada
+1 403 220 6015
amkuiper@ucalgary.ca

Leonard Manzara
Department of Computer Science
University of Calgary
Calgary, Alberta, Canada
+1 403 220 3518
manzara@cpsc.ucalgary.ca

Robert Collier
School of Computer Science
Carleton University
Ottawa, Ontario, Canada
+1 613 520 4333
robert.collier@scs.carleton.ca

ABSTRACT

It is widely recognized that motivating students in an undergraduate assembly language course is a tremendous challenge, principally because of the perception that the subject matter is both difficult and tedious. The Raspberry Pi is a small and inexpensive single-board computer that was created for educational purposes, and in this paper we describe how we successfully incorporated this device into the curriculum of an undergraduate assembly language course. We describe, in detail, the objectives for this course and the dedicated lab that uses the Raspberry Pi as an embedded device, and then evaluate the effectiveness of our approach. Our findings (obtained by exploring changes in student performance and examining the results of an engagement/enjoyment survey) strongly indicate that the introduction of the Raspberry Pi was well received by the students and contributed positively to their learning outcomes.

Keywords

Computer Science Education, Raspberry Pi, Assembly Language Programming, Hardware/Software Interface

1. INTRODUCTION

In recent educational practice, computer science students are typically introduced to programming by learning a high-level computer language. Although the importance of being able to program in a high-level language is undeniable, it would be difficult to argue that learning assembly language is not crucial for understanding the underlying computer architecture. Unfortunately, although assembly language remains a fundamental topic in computer science, novice assembly language programmers often find the process of programming in it tiresome and frustrating. This is not surprising, since programming in assembly is typically a tedious process, and is often described as "dry" [1], "difficult to learn", and "confusing" [2]. Naturally, this impression can be exaggerated if the course is concerned with difficult advanced assembly language programming techniques, despite the fact that these techniques are considered essential in many computer science, information technology, and engineering programs. As a result, post-secondary educators are strongly motivated to make the process of learning assembly language more engaging and rewarding for students.

SIGCSE '16, March 02-05, 2016, Memphis, TN, USA
© 2016 ACM. ISBN 978-1-4503-3685-7/16/03…$15.00
DOI: http://dx.doi.org/10.1145/2839509.2844552

The Raspberry Pi, released in 2012 as an educational tool for computer science, is an affordable, relatively small device that contains an ARM11 [6] processor and supports a wide range of peripherals. Its inclusion of a General Purpose Input/Output (GPIO) interface [7] makes it especially suitable for teaching a wide variety of I/O protocols. Our decision to use the Raspberry Pi in an assembly language programming course was motivated by the desire to make the process of learning assembly language more enjoyable for the students, while offering them exposure to a contemporary architecture (similar to what they may encounter in today's ubiquitous mobile devices). It is also our belief that both seeing and closely working with an actual physical device (as opposed to an invisible and remote server) will help students break down the conceptual barrier between software and hardware. Hence, the main research question this paper intends to answer is whether the adoption of the Raspberry Pi can improve both the learning experience and outcomes of students.

The Raspberry Pi is usually equipped with a Linux operating system, and educational institutions that employ the Pi typically use it as a stand-alone computer (running Linux). Our approach, in contrast, is to use the Pi as an embedded device. Programming for direct hardware control is not possible when there is an overprotective operating system guarding hardware resources, so we use a minimal OS (employing only a first-stage bootloader) on the Pi, which allows students to program the hardware directly.

Although the Raspberry Pi has been adopted as an educational tool by many colleges (and, in [8], as a motivator for high school students), the novelty of the device entails that there are only a few studies that analyse these experiences in depth. For example, Brock et al. discuss how the Pi is being used across a range of secondary-school computer courses [5], while Foltz discusses how it is used to teach network administration at the undergraduate level [9]. Although Hooper discusses (at an introductory level) how to program the Raspberry Pi at a low level using C++ and ARM assembly in a workshop [10], to the best of our knowledge our use of the Raspberry Pi to teach low-level programming in an undergraduate computer science course is unique.

There are alternatives to the Raspberry Pi for teaching the hardware/software interface (for example, embedded devices such as the Arduino or FPGAs have been used for this purpose), but these devices often do not feature a comparable set of built-in peripheral interfaces. Also, it is possible to use an architecture that supports an operating system with a "real-mode" (allowing direct access to hardware) and the course described in this paper evolved from a course that used Windows 98 running in real-mode on the x86 architecture [3]. Nevertheless, the results of our investigation indicate that the Raspberry Pi is a viable alternative platform that improves both student engagement and performance.

The remainder of this paper is organized into seven sections. Section 2 and Section 3 are used to describe the course and the typical hardware/software setup of a workstation in our lab. The course objectives are discussed in Section 4 and Section 5 gives a brief description of the format and topics of the previous version of the course (for comparison). Section 6 gives a comparative (and quantitative) assessment of student performance in each version of the course, and detailed student feedback on the use of the Raspberry Pi is discussed and analyzed in Section 7, with our final discussions presented in Section 8 to conclude the paper.

2. THE COURSE

The subject of this paper is the *Computing Machinery II* (CPSC 359) course at the University of Calgary. It is a required course for students pursuing an undergraduate degree in computer science at the University of Calgary, and is a prerequisite course for the third-year courses *Computer Structures*, *Computer Networks*, and *Principles of Operating Systems*. As suggested by the course title, this is the second of a pair of early (second-year) undergraduate courses, both of which are mandatory for a Bachelor's degree in Computer Science. In the prerequisite course, students are exposed to assembly language programming and general computer architecture and organization concepts, while in CPSC 359 the emphasis is on the hardware/software interface. Students enrolled in this course are exposed to digital logic design, microarchitecture design, interrupts and interrupt handling, and hardware I/O. It should be noted that, out of all these topics, this paper is concerned primarily with hardware I/O.

The enrollment in the course for the Fall 2013, Winter 2014, and Winter 2015 semesters were 61, 112, and 120 students, respectively, with students divided into groups of at most 22 students per lab tutorial. A typical week consisted of 150 minutes of lecture time complemented by 100 minutes of lab time. The lab sessions, designed to parallel the lectures by providing a hands-on experience with the Raspberry Pi in a specialized lab (Section 3), were conducted by graduate teaching assistants.

The main student deliverable in the Raspberry Pi component of the course is an interactive video game developed entirely in ARM assembly language, using a Super Nintendo™ Entertainment System (SNES) controller [12] as an input device, and an HDMI monitor for output. The game is required to run on "bare metal" (on the ARM processor without an operating system), in a manner that is typical for many embedded systems. Although the game itself would vary between semesters, a representative example would be a game that required the player to traverse a maze. In addition to the actual graphical representation of the maze itself, the students would also need to draw a title screen and menu elements. The player would only be permitted a finite number of actions and would need to collect items in order to proceed, all of which comprises game data that the program must track and report to the user. The game would receive input from the SNES controller (opening doors and moving a character), and present the player with success and failure messages as required. It should also be noted that students were evaluated on the quality of their code, and that the students were given the option to work in groups of up to three members.

3. LAB SETUP

Writing bare-metal assembly code for the Raspberry Pi introduces a set of challenges not encountered when developing programs directly on a Pi equipped with a full-featured operating system such as Linux. The principal difficulty is that the Raspberry Pi will be running a minimal operating system that does not provide a compiler and system-level I/O. Consequently, compilation and debugging cannot take place on the device itself, but instead must be performed on a host computer. Basic user input also poses a problem. While the Raspberry Pi is equipped with a USB interface, it is unreasonable to expect second-year undergraduate students to write a USB keyboard or mouse driver in assembly, and providing a library or pre-made driver to handle user input does not help them understand how input is handled at the lowest software level. To solve these challenges, a dedicated lab was created with 30 student workstations, each of which includes a host computer and a suite of supporting hardware that interfaces with the Raspberry Pi. The details of these workstations, from both the hardware and software perspectives, are described below.

3.1 Hardware Setup

In order to facilitate students writing bare-metal assembly code for the Raspberry Pi, the workstations need to provide support for cross compiling a program targeted to the ARM architecture, transferring compiled programs to the Raspberry Pi, debugging programs running on the Raspberry Pi, and facilitating user I/O. The additional hardware connected to the Raspberry Pi (not including the host computer) is shown in Figure 1, and includes:

a) Raspberry Pi
b) Custom Breakout Board
c) Segger™ JLink EDU Debugger [11]
d) Super Nintendo™ Entertainment System (SNES) Controller
e) HDMI Interface
f) USB to TTL Serial Interface

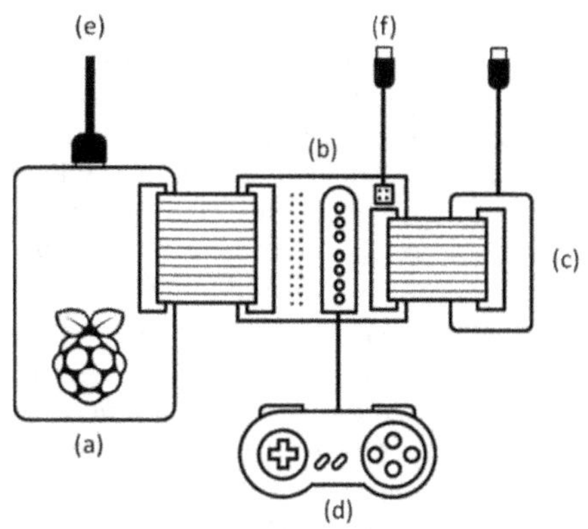

Figure 1. Workstation Hardware Suite.

Much of the hardware used in the workstations needs to communicate over the Raspberry Pi's General Purpose Input / Output (GPIO) interface, and so a custom breakout board (b) was created to connect the Raspberry Pi's 26-pin GPIO header to the various devices used in the workstation. Programs compiled on the host computer are transferred to the Raspberry Pi and remotely debugged using the JLink EDU debugging unit (c), which connects to the host computer's USB interface and to the Raspberry Pi across the GPIO interface. The USB to TTL serial interface (f) also connects the host computer to the Raspberry Pi across the GPIO interface, and provides a means of performing text-based serial input and output. The SNES controller (d) is also connected to the GPIO interface, and provides an additional method of user input. Finally, the Raspberry Pi's native HDMI interface (e) is connected to a monitor, which provides a means of graphical output from the Raspberry Pi.

3.2 Software Setup

Writing bare-metal assembly for the Raspberry Pi involves a different software setup than would be used to write and run programs directly on the device itself. Given that the Raspberry Pi will not be using a full-featured operating system (that is, instead of Linux we use a simple operating system that does not provide facilities such as text editors, compilers, or debuggers), students must edit and compile their programs on a different computer system, herein referred to as the *host*. The compiler on the host must be able to cross-compile source code to produce executable binaries that run on the Raspberry Pi. Debugging provides an additional challenge, since the host debugger is interacting with a program running on a remote system.

The software setup used on the workstations involves a distribution of the Linux operating system. A version of the GNU Compiler Collection (gcc), built to target the Raspberry Pi's ARM11 architecture, was installed on the workstations, providing a cross-platform compiler and debugger. Additionally, the GNU Debugger (gdb) Server provided by Segger™ (JLinkGDBServer) was installed on the host computers to allow communications between the gdb debugging client on the host and the JLink EDU remote debugging unit connected to the Raspberry Pi.

In order to establish a connection between the JLink EDU remote debugging unit and the Raspberry Pi, the GPIO lines used for JTAG communication must be set to the correct mode using a sequence of software commands. To accomplish this, a "minimal" kernel image with just enough code to enable the JTAG GPIO lines is compiled by the students and copied to the SD card from the host computer, and the Raspberry Pi is powered on with this SD card inserted. One difficulty here is that, at the time that this paper was authored, the details of the first-stage bootloading process were not currently publicly available, so students were not able to recreate this stage of the bootloading process themselves. To solve this problem, an SD card is first written with the original Raspbian distribution (available on the Raspberry Pi website, and which includes the first-stage bootloader), and then modified by overwriting the kernel image file used in the second-stage of the bootloading process with the "minimal" kernel image.

Once the Raspberry Pi is powered on with an SD card containing the "minimal" kernel image, the JLinkGDBServer can be started on the host computer. After a successful connection has been made and the debugger server is running, the students can start the ARM-targeted gdb client using a kernel image they have compiled with the ARM-targeted compiler, and establish a remote debugging connection to the JLinkGDBServer instance. At this point, the student executes a command in the gdb client to upload the kernel image to the Raspberry Pi's memory, sets the Raspberry Pi's program counter register to the beginning of the kernel image, and continues execution on the device. If successful, the student's new kernel image will now be running on the device.

3.3 Additional Considerations

While the overall experience of working with the Raspberry Pi was generally advantageous to students, it should be noted that the specialized lab we created came with a price tag of more than $30,000 (CAD) for about 34 workstations (including 4 workstations for instructional staff). Although this cost might be considered prohibitive for some institutions, it is worth noting that the lab was constructed with completely new equipment, including new top-of-the-line host machines and dual monitors (one for the host and a HDMI monitor for the Raspberry Pi). Consequently, it should be noted that this price tag could be reduced substantially by simply equipping an existing lab of host machines; the add-on price for converting an existing lab to make it Raspberry Pi-ready can be very minimal, and would include only the price for HDMI monitors (if necessary), JLink devices, and a few inexpensive accessories. Furthermore, there are cheaper display options than the HDMI monitors used in our lab that can be used with the Raspberry Pi's RCA video output.

The cost of the Raspberry Pi itself and its accessories is very low; the price for an assembled kit (which includes a power supply adapter, SIM card, cables, and protective case) was about $85 (CAD) in Winter 2015. Note that all students were required to purchase the Pi and accessories when registering for the course.

It should also be noted that, with the enrollment in the winter semester exceeding 100 students, the students were struggling to find lab time and space during peak times close to assignment due dates. Not being able to work from home (due to the specialized hardware required) was a clear disadvantage to students, but duplicating a lab workstation at home incurs a relatively low cost, and can be encouraged in future offerings. Students would need only an extra HDMI screen, a JLink EDU device, and our locally-manufactured breakout board.

4. COURSE OBJECTIVES

As this paper describes the use of the Raspberry Pi for assembly language instruction, it is worth noting that several Raspberry Pi topics are considered course objectives, including (but not limited to) the following:

Advanced ARM Assembly Programming: Students are exposed to stacks, the concept of subroutines (as implemented in assembly language), two-dimensional arrays, and interrupt service routines.

General-Purpose Input/Output: GPIO is a well-known mechanism used to provide flexible I/O for microcontrollers. GPIO allows the students to connect a wide range of I/O devices to the Raspberry Pi. However, a substantial amount of programming is required to write device interface functions (i.e., GPIO is not plug-and-play). Students are expected to become proficient in the use of GPIO registers, including those that set the function for a GPIO line (e.g., input, output, or a special function) and those that read or set the values of the GPIO lines [7].

Universal Asynchronous Receiver/Transmitter Protocol: UART is a low speed serial protocol used ubiquitously for simple communication between devices. The Raspberry Pi provides support for UART (and a reduced implementation called mini-UART) through its GPIO interface. The protocol is relatively easy to present to students, and students are required to implement a driver for a generic UART device from scratch.

Video Programming: The Raspberry Pi provides support for video programming via a frame-buffer architecture accessed through memory-mapped I/O (that is, the frame-buffer is accessed through memory load and store instructions). On the Raspberry Pi, the buffer is initialized through a mailbox interface, and is used to establish communication between the ARM core and the video core (or GPU). A suite of registers in addition to RAM is used for this communication, and the use of these registers, along with the protocol for initializing the frame-buffer [7,13], are both areas in which the students must become proficient.

Interrupts and Exceptions: The ARM architecture has a number of different execution modes, and software or hardware exceptions (i.e., interrupts) change the execution mode of the processor. Writing and registering exception handlers requires the students to understand the vector table architecture, and how to use the Current Program Status Register (CPSR) and the Saved Program Status Register (SPSR) on the ARM CPU [6]. Students learn to program an interrupt service routine to handle a hardware event such as a rising or falling edge on a GPIO line.

5. PREVIOUS VERSION

It is worth noting that the previous version of this course covered similar topics using a different platform. The lab for the predecessor course was based on an Intel x86 platform running Windows 98. This setup allowed students to work in real address mode, which enabled direct access to hardware. In order to develop an interactive video game (which, in the current iteration of this course, remains a significant course deliverable), the students had to write specialized device drivers without relying on privileged operating system calls. Unfortunately, the more recent versions of the Windows operating system no longer provide this option, and other operating systems (e.g., Linux) are too overprotective and do not allow developers to write programs that access the hardware directly.

The nature of the video game deliverable did not change significantly when this course was adapted to the Raspberry Pi. In the predecessor course, students needed to use a low-level video library (the VESA BIOS Extension (VBE) [15]), necessitating that they work with both port-mapped and memory-mapped I/O. It was also necessary for students to work with XGA monitors (with a resolution of 1024 × 768 with 256 colors), and develop specialized PS/2 keyboard and/or mouse drivers (requiring that they program and register their own interrupt handlers).

As noted previously, versions of Windows subsequent to Windows 98 do not permit students to work in real address mode and, consequently, the previous version of the course also required a specialized lab (i.e., x86 machines with Windows 98). Although this was suitable to fullfil the objectives of the course, there were two significant issues with this lab setup. First, in spite of a substantial explanation that course concepts were universal and still applicable (regardless of the computing environment), many students reported that they were not convinced that the course was relevant to current computing practices. Feedback received from the students indicated that a significant number of them were discouraged when working with a computing environment that they literally characterized as "ancient".

The second issue that arose was related to the sustainability of a lab that consisted of x86 machines running Windows 98. Unsurprisingly, it was becoming progressively more difficult to repair and find spare parts for any failing machines. To address this, we resorted to DOSBox [17] in subsequent offerings of the course [3], but we were ultimately dissatisfied with the quality of experience the students were receiving while using an emulator rather than working directly with the actual hardware.

6. COMPARATIVE ASSESSMENT

According to the undergraduate grading system at the University of Calgary, letter grades between F and A+ are mapped to grade point values between 0.0 and 4.0, inclusively (with A's and A+'s worth 4.0, A- worth 3.7, B+ worth 3.3, etc.) Consequently, if the letter grades assigned to each student for their respective performance on the exam that followed the x86 / ARM course module are mapped to grade point values according to this scheme, it is possible to calculate mean grade point values for different categories of students. Since the Raspberry Pi was first adopted for this course in the Fall semester of 2013, the body of students that have completed this course in the last three years can be divided into two categories: those that completed the *Computing Machinery II* while the x86 architecture was in use, and those that completed the course since the Raspberry Pi was adopted. We should note that in both course versions, the ARM and x86 material was tested in an exam separate from other course topics. The marks presented here are for this exam. It should be highlighted that current and previous versions were taught by the same instructor. In both formats, no textbooks were required, but we recommended in each case a book that covered the basic parts of speech of each assembly language (x86 and ARM). Hence, the platform and the lab were the only major changes.

In the available data, there were 138 students in the former category (i.e., those that took the course with the x86 between September 2012 and April 2013) and 319 students in the latter category (i.e., those that took the course with the Raspberry Pi, after September 2013). After mapping the letter grades to numeric values, we observe a mean grade point value of 2.542 (0.846 standard deviation) for the students in the former category, and a mean grade point value of 2.986 (0.730 standard deviation) for the students in the latter. These results correspond to a mean letter grade of between C+ and B- for the students that completed the course with the x86, and a mean letter grade of B for those that completed the course with the Raspberry Pi. The distribution of the marks for each population of students is plotted in Figure 2.

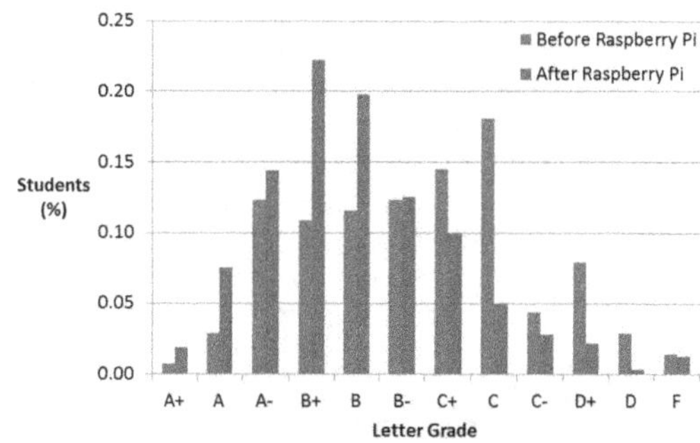

Figure 2. Distribution of the ARM/x86 Exam Grades.

It was necessary to test the normality of these data sets before testing whether the difference between the mean grades was statistically significant. As evidenced by the quantile-quantile plots in Figure 3, the distribution of grades across the cohort of students that completed the course with the x86 was not quite normal (n.b., an R^2 of 0.9085 for the quantile-quantile plot trend line) and, thus, required an unpaired, nonparametric student t-test to demonstrate statistical significance.

This test showed that the difference was extremely statistically significant (p-value < 0.0001), and so it is not unreasonable to interpret it as evidence that the use of the Raspberry Pi has had a very positive impact on student performance. This result is consonant with the feedback provided by the students, as discussed in the following section.

7. SURVEY RESULTS

Students registered under the new format of the course were asked to participate in a voluntary, anonymous survey that assessed their enjoyment, learning experience, motivation, and independent learning. We have received a total of 198 valid instruments from students in two consecutive semesters, from a total enrollment of 337 students (i.e., an overall response rate of 58%).

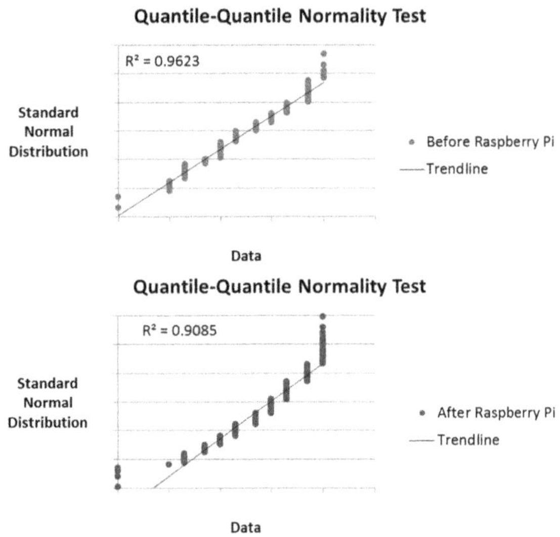

Figure 3. Normality Testing with Quantile-Quantile Plots.

7.1 Quantitative Summary

Tables 1 and 2 show the basic frequency statistics for the survey. To clarify, these tables show the fraction of survey participant responses associated with each of the five different values from the Likert scale used on the instrument (i.e., Strongly Agree, Agree, Neutral, Disagree, and Strongly Disagree).

Table 1 shows the proportion of the survey participants that responded with each of the different responses to items about working with the Raspberry Pi. It is clear from these results that the students felt very positively about the impact of the Raspberry Pi, with a substantial 82.32% majority reporting agreement that their learning was enhanced. The other responses expressed similarly positive reactions concerning enjoyment and motivation.

	Item (a) I enjoyed working on the Raspberry Pi.		Item (b) The use of the RPi enhanced my learning.		Item (c) The use of the RPi motivated me...	
Strongly Agree	22.73%	**66.16%**	29.29%	**82.32%**	23.74%	**67.17%**
Agree	43.43%		53.03%		43.43%	
Neutral		20.71%		15.66%		24.75%
Disagree	7.58%	**13.13%**	1.01%	**2.02%**	5.05%	**8.08%**
Strongly Disagree	5.56%		1.01%		3.03%	

Table 1. Survey Responses Concerning the Raspberry Pi.

Table 2 presents similar data for items about the feeling students reported concerning pursuing future studies. The majority of the participants responded with agreement for each of the items (i.e., low-level programming, game programming, and independent studies). In all cases, the majority of the survey participants have reacted positively to the use of the Raspberry Pi.

To facilitate further analyses, study participants were grouped into two classes: the "Enjoyers", who agreed or strongly agreed to item (a), and the "Non-Enjoyers", who were neutral, disagreed, or strongly disagreed with the same item. By translating the Likert scale responses on the other items into numerical values (between 1 and 5 inclusive, with 1 and 5 assigned to responses of "Strongly Agree" and "Strongly Disagree", respectively), the results could be subjected to additional statistical analyses.

	Item (d) I would like to learn more about low-level programming.		Item (e) I would like to learn more about game programming.		Item (f) I would like to pursue independent learning with similar topics.	
Strongly Agree	16.67%	**52.53%**	38.89%	**71.21%**	24.75%	**60.61%**
Agree	35.86%		32.32%		35.86%	
Neutral		18.69%		14.65%		19.70%
Disagree	18.69%	**28.79%**	7.07%	**14.14%**	10.61%	**19.70%**
Strongly Disagree	10.10%		7.07%		9.09%	

Table 2. Survey Responses Concerning the Future Studies.

When comparing the responses of the Enjoyers with the Non-Enjoyers, item (b) was used to assess whether the participants felt that the use of the Raspberry Pi enhanced their individual learning experiences. The mean translated response from the Enjoyers (4.29) corresponds to a response between agreement and strong agreement, while the value from the Non-Enjoyers (3.69) corresponds to a response between neutrality and agreement. Although the mean responses would characterize both groups as feeling "positively" about their learning with the Raspberry Pi, the difference between the mean translated responses were extremely statistically significant (p-value < 0.0001).

Similarly, in item (c) (assessing whether the students felt that the Raspberry Pi contributed positively towards their individual motivation), the mean translated responses were 4.08 and 3.24, for the Enjoyers and the Non-Enjoyers respectively. This indicates, once again, that the mean response from the Enjoyers corresponds to agreement / strong agreement, in contrast to the mean response from the Non-Enjoyers, corresponding to a response between neutrality and agreement. The difference between the mean translated responses was, once again, extremely statistically significant (p-value < 0.0001) and for both this item and the previously explored item (b), the survey results indicate that those who enjoyed using the Raspberry Pi thought that the experience contributed to both enhanced learning and improved motivation.

7.2 Qualitative Summary

The survey participants were also given the opportunity to explain their choices in a free-form format, and these were subjected to a qualitative analysis. This analysis, restricted to those instruments on which the students reported "Neutral", "Disagree", or "Strongly Disagree" with item (a) (i.e., "I enjoyed working on the Raspberry Pi") indicated the presence of two underlying themes.

The first theme saw the majority of these students express dissatisfaction about the "fragility" and "awkwardness" of the working environment. One student (with a neutral rating) stated this clearly: "*The fact that we're working on relevant hardware is nice; however, the experience was terribly tarnished by system instability, over-complication, and J-Link being absolutely awful.*" This student goes on to say: "*The relevance of the Raspberry Pi to modern day technology is interesting.*" Another student who strongly disagreed with the question under discussion stated: *"ARM is a current technology and the Raspberry Pi is super novel, but painful due to hic-ups in the system.* S/he further explains: *"The method for communication/work with/on the Raspberry Pi was over complicated by J-Link."*

The second theme was centered on the workload of the course itself and the scarcity of lab space and time, or the inability to work from home. A representative student states: *"Although I enjoyed the idea of the RPi, the projects consumed a lot of my time, more than any other course by far. [...] It was interesting to work below the OS [...], but the projects required a lot of troubleshooting and we could only work on the RPi on campus.*"

8. CONCLUSION

Teaching assembly language programming at the undergraduate level is often challenging, and this can often be attributed to the perceptions (of the students) that the topic is dull and tedious. Earlier attempts to offset this bias (in the predecessor *Computing Machinery II* course discussed herein) included the incorporation of video game development to introduce a "fun factor" into the student experience. While we have retained this element in our present course design, we looked at incorporating a contemporary platform that students would find more relevant to the current state of the computer industry. The use of a credit card-sized computer with an ARM processor served this purpose, largely because of prevalence of mobile devices in the students' daily lives. In this paper, we show that a significant majority of the students were more motivated to learn about the hardware/software interface and assembly language due to the use of the Raspberry Pi as a learning platform. Another majority also indicated that the Raspberry Pi improved their learning experience and enjoyment of the topic.

These results, compiled from the "self-assessments" provided by the students on the survey instruments, closely align with our own quantitative analysis of student performance. We found that there was a significant increase in mean grade point value for the exam associated with this module of the Computing Machinery II course when the course switched to the Raspberry Pi from the x86 platform. Furthermore, a reduced standard deviation (in the context of a greater mean grade value and in conjunction with a visual inspection of the distributions from Figure 2) indicates that fewer students are being "left behind" in this challenging subject.

On the task of improving the experience further, it should be noted that the Raspberry Pi seemed to convince only about 30% of the surveyed students to pursue future independent learning about low-level programming. Although this is certainly a respectable result, the task of increasing this value further remains daunting. This result raises the following question: If a student enjoys programming with assembly on the Raspberry Pi and indicates that this was a memorable learning experience, why would they remain unconvinced to learn more about the subject independently, and what can be done to address this?

Finally, while the experience was generally advantageous to a large majority of students, qualitative analysis also indicated two areas for improvement: the "unfriendly" development environment, and the accessibility to the lab. There is not much that can be done to address the perception of the development environment as "unfriendly", since cross-compilation and the use of the JLink debugging device is, at the moment, a necessary complication. Improving lab access is also difficult, since increasing the size of our lab facilities requires finding new space when space is scarce, and expending more money. One possible solution is to provide help and resources for students who wish to duplicate the development environment on a home computer. The additional cost to students is relatively minor (and, of course, entirely optional if they would rather work on campus).

There will always be trade-offs when choosing particular platforms to achieve general pedagogic aims. As we have shown, the use of a specific platform to teach general concepts by exposing them to real-world experiences can be very beneficial to students, but, special care must be taken to ensure that "platform-specific details do not swamp pedagogic objectives." [14]

9. ACKNOWLEDGMENTS

Our thanks go to the students of CPSC 359 who took part in this study. We also thank the anonymous reviewers.

10. REFERENCES

[1] C. Zilles. 2005. SPIMbot: an engaging, problem-based approach to teaching assembly language programming. In *Proc. of the 2005 workshop on Computer architecture education: in conj. with the 32nd Int'l Symp. on Computer Architecture* (WCAE '05). ACM, New York, NY, USA.

[2] D. Crookes. 1983. Teaching Assembly-Language Programming: A High-Level Approach. *Software Microsystems*, vol. 2, no. 2, pp. 40-43.

[3] J. Kawash and R. Collier. 2012. Using Video Game Development to Engage Students of Assembly Language Programming. In *Proc. of the 14th annual ACM SIGITE conf. on Information technology education* (SIGITE '13). ACM, New York, NY, USA, 71-76.

[4] www.raspberrypi.org

[5] J. D. Brock, R. F. Bruce, and M. E. Cameron. 2013. Changing the world with a Raspberry Pi. *J. Comput. Sci. Coll.* 29, 2 (December 2013), 151-153.

[6] ARM. 2010-2011. *ARM Compiler Toolchain, Using the Assembler* (pages 3 to 21). http://infocenter.arm.com/help/topic/com.arm.doc.dui0473c/DUI0473C_using_the_arm_assembler.pdf

[7] Broadcom Corporation.2012. *BCM 2835 ARM Peripherals.*

[8] J. Black, J. Brodie, P. Curzon, C. Myketiak, P. W. McOwan, and L. R. Meagher. 2013. Making computing interesting to school students: teachers' perspectives. In *Proc. of the 18th ACM conf. on Innovation and technology in computer science education* (ITiCSE '13). ACM, New York, NY, USA, 255-260.

[9] C. Bryan Foltz. 2014. Network administration with the Raspberry Pi. *J. Comput. Sci. Coll.* 29, 5 (May 2014), 66-67.

[10] W. H. Hooper. 2013. Easy as Raspberry Pi: an inexpensive platform for machine language instruction. *J. Comput. Sci. Coll.* 29, 1 (October 2013), 102-103.

[11] www.segger.com/jlink-debug-probes.html

[12] www.gamefaqs.com/snes/916396-snes/faqs/5395

[13] Broadcom Corporation. *VideoCore® IV 3D Architecture Reference Guide.*2013.

[14] Joint Task Force on Computing Curricula, ACM and IEEE Computer Society. 2013. *Computer Science Curricula 2013: Curriculum Guidelines for Undergraduate Degree Programs in Computer Science.* ACM, New York, NY, USA.

[15] VESA. Retrieved 2013/05/20 from: www.vesa.org

[16] DOS Protected Mode Interface (DPMI) Specification: Version 0.9 Printed 1990/07/26. Retrieved 2013/05/20 from: http://homer.rice.edu/~sandmann/cwsdpmi/dpmispec.txt

[17] DOSBox, an x86 emulator with DOS. Retrieved 2013/05/20 from www.dosbox.com

Droning On: Reflections on Integrating UAV Technology into a Computer Engineering Design Laboratory

Meriel Huggard
School of Computer Science and Statistics
Trinity College Dublin
Dublin 2, Ireland
Meriel.Huggard@tcd.ie

Ciarán Mc Goldrick
School of Computer Science and Statistics
Trinity College Dublin
Dublin 2, Ireland
Ciaran.McGoldrick@tcd.ie

ABSTRACT

Unmanned aerial vehicles, also known as drones, are often characterized as representing the next big disruptive change in our everyday interaction with technology. Indeed some commentators have suggested that their impact will be as significant as that of the Internet. It is thus incumbent upon modern, foresightful educators to integrate these platforms into the curriculum in order to more fully equip the next generation of professional engineers and computer scientists with the skillsets and competences needed to realize the full potential of these devices.

In this paper we reflect on the challenges encountered when integrating drone technology into an existing project-based freshman design module. The objective was to introduce the drone as a relatively seamless extension of an existing problem set for a design project involving an autonomous vehicle. In doing so, critical factors such as engineering ethics, health and safety, and regulatory constraints; in addition to implementation challenges; are directly addressed and quantified. Lessons learned and reflections on best practice for the use of drone technology in the laboratory are adduced and articulated.

Keywords

Unmanned Aerial Vehicles; Drones; Collaborative Learning; Engineering Design; Practical; Laboratory; Experiential Learning

1. INTRODUCTION

The goals, content and means of delivery of many electronic and computer engineering design modules has evolved radically over the past decade due to the rise in the availability of affordable, open-source programmable, microcontrollers and accessible wireless communication devices [28] [15] [26] [14].

Many engineering modules have evolved or have been extended to more closely integrate the underlying technologies and systems with modern engineering practice. One of the more enticing recent developments is the commoditization of unmanned aerial vehicles (UAVs) or drones. Whilst many commentators have focused on public fears over the intrusiveness of drone technology, they have a wide range of real-world applications, and the full potential of these devices has yet to be explored by either industry or educators [21].

It is clear that drones offer enormous potential for engaging students and developing new classroom learning paradigms [21] [20] [30]. Drones offer a challenging evolution for existing computer engineering design modules where students presently face challenges in electronics, control, programming and project management. Educators seeking to incorporate drones within their modules must be cognisant of both the new technical challenges, and the necessity to create a safe environment in which students can gain hands on experience with the technology.

In this paper we reflect on the challenges encountered when integrating drone technology into an existing project-based freshman design module. In particular, we address the challenges facing those who wish to implement or extend robotic laboratory tasks to incorporate the use of unmanned aerial vehicles, and propound some thoughts on best practice for same. The paper identifies the technical constraints that bound any such endeavor and describes how they may be addressed in the context of experiential learning, ethical awareness and the development and reinforcement of responsible professional practice.

The contributions comprise i) a strategy for the inclusion of drones within the existing wireless control activity and requirement set for a freshman laboratory; ii) a functional description of the implementation of a "hypervisor" to safely enable (wireless) direct student control of operational drones in flight; iii) requirements of an enabling layer that provides technical translation, validation and control capabilities, whilst also policing and enforcing responsible use and engagement. The paper concludes with reflections on lessons learnt and best practice for managing the incorporation of drones within the curriculum.

2. UNMANNED AERIAL VEHICLES

UAVs are generally autonomously functional, remotely controlled and reusable. They entered the populist consciousness approximately a decade ago through their use by the military in battle and conflict scenarios. More recently drones have been attracting attention for the broad range of civilian and industrial uses to which they are being put. Some have referred to the advent of wide scale domestic drone deployments as being akin to a "flying Internet" in

SIGCSE '16, March 02 - 05, 2016, Memphis, TN, USA

ISBN 978-1-4503-3685-7/16/03...$15.00

DOI: http://dx.doi.org/10.1145/2839509.2844650

terms of the green-field opportunities it presents to innovators and entrepreneurs alike. It is clear from the diversity of use-case scenarios currently being pursued, for example in conservation, search and rescue, surveying and commercial delivery, that drones will have a marked impact on many future workplaces and, consequently, on the employability skill sets educators should be targeting for their students.

Figure 1: An Unmanned Aerial Vehicle [5].

There are a wide variety of commercially produced UAVs available for purchase, ranging in cost from c.$40 to tens of thousands of dollars. Regardless of cost, these UAVs share many similar features in terms of the available on-board equipment e.g. cameras, GPS and the wireless communications protocols used e.g. WiFi. Two UAVs that have been successfully used in educational settings [22] [10], [25] are the Parrot AR.Drone 2.0 [1] and DJI Phantom 2 Vision [5]. These relatively low cost UAVs are equipped with cameras and WiFi. The latter not only enables the UAVs to transmit images it also permits the end-user to control them using mobile devices. For both of these drones the SDK provided [2][4] allows the device to be controlled using Simple API commands. The typical battery lifetime is such that the drones can fly continuously for up to 25 minutes.

3. UAVS AND THE LAW

The military applications of UAVs have been discussed in the media for well over a decade [29] [23]. However, interest in the potential civilian and academic uses of these devices has only taken off in recent years [21].

Governments are being proactive in their support of the much anticipated UAV revolution as they are fast-tracking the development of the law and policy needed to enable their deployment. For example, the European Commission has drawn up a policy framework which will enable the progressive development of the commercial drones market while safeguarding the public interest [3].

The response from the existing aviation regulators, such as the U.S. Federal Aviation Administration (FAA) and the European Aviation Safety Agency (EASA) has also been positive: the FAA are developing regulations for the use of UAVs in public airspace [21] while the EASA are developing a new regulatory approach for safely operating UAVs [19]. These new standards will address issues such as safety, security, privacy, data protection, insurance and liability.

The international demand for changes in the law and in policy in relation to the civilian use of UAVs has been driven by multi-nationals such as Google and Amazon and by collective bodies such as the Small UAV Coalition (www.smalluavcoalition.org). There has also been demands for regulatory changes from those in academia as they seek to explore the full potential of these devices for both research and educational purposes.

4. UAVS IN THE CLASSROOM

While many recognize the potential of unmanned aerial vehicles in the classroom, there has been little focus on their integration within the existing curriculum. This may be due to concerns related to safety, security, privacy and liability. However, such arguments are invalidated by the fact that many have successfully incorporated UAVs into their existing outreach activities to encourage students to pursue careers in science and engineering [20], [8], [25]. One possible reason for the slow uptake of this technology may be that they are often viewed as "toys" (as, for example, in [8]), rather than as autonomous aerial vehicles with the potential to revolutionize the computer engineering curriculum [13].

Where UAVs have been successfully integrated into the curriculum, these are often in the form of single classes or one day events. Nitschke et al. have developed a one day contest that is suitable for undergraduate and taught postgraduate students [22]. The interdisciplinary design competition required participants to make use of open-source libraries to develop a program capable of autonomously guiding a UAV from a start point to a destination. The UAV navigated its way along the course using visual markers. The authors found that while there was a steep learning curve, the students developed a deep understanding of the potential and limitations of the technology. Yokokawa et al. used the UAV to develop teaching materials for a single freshman class. Their study found that the teaching materials developed were successful in motivating students to learn more about control engineering and image processing [25].

Eriksen, Ming and Dodds explored the use of a UAV in the implementation of a location based "lab-escape" challenge [12]. The UAV was placed in a previously mapped room and the challenge was to determine its location and then proceed to the exit. Their study detailed the prototype that was developed using a UAV [1] and a Microsoft Kinect sensor, however, it did not extend to the actual deployment of drones in a classroom setting.

Winterfeldt and Hahne [30] developed a master's level module that integrated UAVs into an application design module taken by a group of 17 students. The objectives were to design an application to make use of several input devices, e.g. an android phone or a gamepad, to control the UAV. The course was split into 12 units where each unit lasted for three hours. The authors found that the use of UAVs in the classroom led to an effective, application-based learning approach that engaged students and improved performance on the module. The study did not explore how such a module could be scaled to classroom scenarios beyond the small group setting described.

5. AUTONOMOUS VEHICLES IN COMPUTER ENGINEERING DESIGN

It is widely accepted that engineering design needs to be incorporated across the curriculum [11][9], and that it should not be relegated to a single capstone module that meets the minimum requirements of accrediting bodies [17]. As a consequence many institutions now take an integrated approach to the inclusion of design aspects across the undergraduate computer engineering curriculum. A key feature of many of these design modules is that they foster the lifelong learning skills expected of graduates. In particular, they often incorporate elements of creative thinking, active learning, collaborative learning, teamwork, conflict resolution, decision making and communication. Pedagogically these module are often considered key elements of the curriculum as they contribute significantly to a range of professional accreditation goals, both nationally and in line with Washington Accord [6] outcomes.

Design courses seek to introduce students to all elements of the product development process so they gain experience of what it is like to work as a professional. The technologies, task and professional skills development elements of such design modules are explicitly chosen to be of direct benefit to all students, regardless of their specialism. For example computer engineering design courses may also incorporate elements of mechanical and electrical engineering [14].

Many design modules have focused on the development of small autonomous vehicles that are designed to carry out a specific task e.g. to sumo wrestle with each other [18] [24], or to emulate an urban light rail system [14]. The autonomous vehicles are often equipped with a variety of sensors that enable them to safely navigate their way through their surroundings. They may make use of visual tracking systems to estimate their position and their direction of motion. A wide variety of tracking approaches are possible and these may be categorized as marker and marker-less methods [7]. Marker-based systems follow a known pattern or image e.g. a straight white line on a black background, while marker-less systems may employ Simultaneous Localisation and Mapping (SLAM) techniques to navigate through their environment.

6. EXISTING MODULE OVERVIEW

One of the key objectives of this work is to explore the integration of UAVs within an existing computer engineering design module. The module chosen seeks to introduce students to all elements of the product development process so that they gain experience of what it is like to work as a professional engineer. This module runs over 12 weeks and is taken by approximately 170 second year undergraduate students annually. It is classified as a small group, project-based module. The academic staff who run the module are drawn from the Department of Electronic and Electrical Engineering (EE) and the School of Computer Science and Statistics (SCSS) within the host university.

Each student has four timetabled laboratory hours each week, split evenly between EE and SCSS. In addition there is one lecture hour timetabled each week. This hour is used to provide students with more in-depth information on the technologies they encounter in the course of the module. It is also used to provide broad guidance and advice on the tasks they should be engaging in at each phase of the design project. Students are expected to engage in self-directed learning associated with this module for an additional twelve to fifteen hours each week. Structured programming support services are also available [27] [16]. While the students taking this module are engineering majors, this module is taken before they specialise into specific branches of engineering. The module is carefully structured to ensure that the technologies encountered, the design task and the key professional skills to be developed are all aligned with the over-arching degree program objectives.

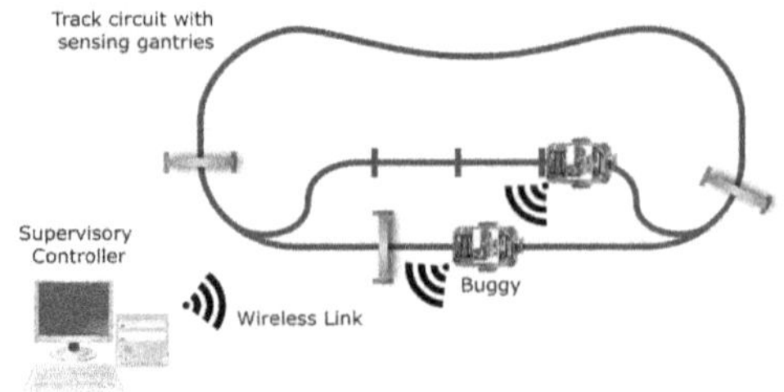

Figure 2: Overview of the Track for the Existing System

7. EXISTING DESIGN TASK

The high level metaphor used in presenting and describing the project task is that of a light-rail or tram system. Such systems travel on tracks laid in the city streets, incorporate points systems for track and junction changes, have remote signaling systems and communications capabilities, and are electrically powered. Students are required to implement a full emulation of such a light-rail system in the laboratory.

A marker based navigation system is deployed using a high contrast black line, known as the track, for the autonomous vehicles to follow. This track has both an outer and an inner "express" loop. Infrared sensing gantries are placed above the track at key locations and are used to help the vehicle determine its location. A PC is used to communicate wirelessly with the vehicles and it acts as a supervisory controller. Fig 2 provides an overview of the high-level system.

Students are tasked with the create of an autonomous vehicle based on a small, two-motor chassis with line following capabilities. Wireless communication functionality between each autonomous vehicle and the supervisory controller is achieved using XBee modules.

Each student group is provided with a rudimentary, motive chassis to use in their autonomous vehicle. The underside of each vehicle is equipped with Infrared emitters (LEDs) and detectors. These are intended for use in the line (track) following part of the task. A simple microcontroller is also provided. The main purpose of this microcontroller is to make Infrared detection decisions and to interact with the motor driver circuit.

The students design, lay out, build, test and debug their own motor control boards which must interface with the vehicle chassis. The chassis also contains a "daughter" board that manages and controls the autonomous vehicle's more complex interactions with its environment.

Evaluation and assessment of student performance and achievement occurs through informal laboratory engagement, formal graded deliverables, an individual quiz and a final practical system demonstration and interview for each group. Feedback from each student on their experience of peer group engagement and learning, and their sense of the strengths and weaknesses of their engagement, is explicitly mandated within each deliverable. A strategy for the extension of this task set to inclusion UAVs within the existing robotic wireless control activity and requirement set is discussed below.

8. INCORPORATING UAVS

The present laboratory task includes a prescribed control vocabulary. Instructions include forward, stop, speed xx, branch, and disco. The branch command causes a vehicle to follow a branch line from the main track for overtaking, parking or obstacle avoidance purposes. Upon receipt of the disco command the vehicle advances to the parking bay, awaits the arrival of all other vehicles on the track and then they all perform a synchronized 180 degree turn so that they all face in the opposite direction. Finally, the vehicles proceed to complete the prescribed tasks in reverse.

Upon successful demonstration of fully supervised control of all vehicles, students were offered the opportunity to extend their activities to include control of an inflight drone. The original task requirements specified that the command set vocabulary be implemented in an extensible fashion within the students control strategy. Open air drone flight necessitates that the current inter command timings for completing the on-track task be linearly scaled in order to achieve similar outcomes in the outdoor arena. This constitutes the first stratum of attainment in open-air drone control for the students.

During these flights the students attention is drawn to the various real world constraints and limitations that accompany drone flights. These include (i) the very limited power source that limits flying time, (ii) environmental factors that affect the predictability, e.g. wind, and viability, e.g. precipitation, of flight, (iii) regulatory issues, e.g. is licensing required to fly and (iv) legal constraints, including privacy, ethical and health and safety concerns. Students then proceed to implement their solutions to these challenges.

The following section provides a functional description of the implementation of a "hypervisor" to safely enable (wireless) direct student control of operational drones in flight.

9. THE "HYPERVISOR"

The hypervisor is the "brain" of the classroom drone management system. In effect it is an electronic "big brother" that assesses, moderates and ultimately penalizes operators, i.e. student groups, based on the likelihood of their instruction resulting in an unacceptable risk or failure event.

In its simplest form, the hypervisor has a geofenced map of the open air arena in which the drones are to fly. It also has mappings for obstacles i.e. physical impediments, that the drone cannot fly into or through. The geofenced area exists as a set of 3D co-ordinate boundary sets. Typically these will be set to ensure that the drone remains above the reach of human hands, below elevations at which it could either require regulatory licensing or interfere with licensed air traffic (e.g. at or below the height of adjacent buildings) and sufficiently distant from neighboring buildings so as to avoid significant airflow disturbance or constitute a significant source of noise pollution. In practice outdoor sports fields make an ideal flight arena for these purposes.

The hypervisor receives incoming commands from the operator, in this case the specific wireless interface to the student group's PC. The commands can be in the form of a complete route with intersectoral timings, or as an ongoing "live" stream of commands. The command is validated by the hypervisor and then translated into an outcome if applied to the current drone position, elevation and speed and direction. The time to intersection with the geofence is approximated and compared with the duration of instruction, if one has been provided. If the requested time is excessive this is recorded and the instruction is amended, if necessary on-the-fly, to cause the drone to continue to the boundary but no further. At all times instructions are subject to processing and validation by the hypervisor prior to being executed. Route following or target hunting activities are deemed complete when the drone positions itself within a defined radius of the goal and hovers there for 10 seconds.

The hypervisor also has a variety of supervisory override functions that can be triggered remotely by the supervising academics or teaching assistants. In particular, there is an emergency "big red button" capability that immediately overides all ongoing flight and returns the drone at full power to a safe hover in the center of the arena geofence. This is a conservative strategy that maximizes the safety margins in the event of an unknown or unexpected occurrence e.g. significant wind gust or direction shift, malicious command attack, etc. In this mode control is only accepted from a separate, secure, encrypted channel available to the instructor, and the only subsequent command accepted is "land" where the UAV returns to its origin and lands autonomously. There is also a pause command available to the instructors that causes the drone to immediately stop and enter hover in its current location and at its current elevation. This locks out commands from the student operators until the "unlock" function is activated. This allows instructors to safely demonstrate, in flight, how and where potential faults may be developing in the groups control strategy.

The requirements from an enabling layer that provide both technical translation, validation and control capabilities, whilst also policing and enforcing responsible use and engagement is considered below.

10. THE ENABLING LAYER DESIGN

The enabling layer for integrating our existing laboratory based activity with the drone has its origins in the organic fashion in which the extant laboratory structure has evolved.

The present laboratory task uses XBee modules for communication between the robot and the controller PC. The students transmit their control instructions to/from the control station and the vehicle. The drones used for prototyping include the DJI Phantom 2 Vision units [5] as these represent an effective trade-off between price, capabilities and performance. Other UAVs, for example the Parrot AR.Drone 2.0 [1] or the open-source ardupilot (ardupilot.com), would also be suitable. The DJI platform was closed source at the time work commenced on the design of this laboratory experience; however, an API has subsequently been released that provides some of the requisite data and functional access to the DJI flight control.

The key facets of working with the DJI drones, as they pertain to the work described herein, were: control between the ground and drone is across a 5.8 GHz connection, and conveys telemetry and live video preview data. The device remote includes a range extender, based on openWRT, which provides a WiFi network that android and iOS clients can connect to in order to control and interact with the UAV via the DJI provided apps. The flight controller communicates with the drone during flight through port 2001 using a ser2net style connection.

It should be noted that the control system detailed above contains additional complexities due to the way in which the existing laboratory task has evolved and some of the challenges addressed above may not arise in other scenarios. For example, if redesigning the cumulative task from scratch, we would converge on using WiFi as the communication medium between the robot and control station, and between the drone and control station. We would also update our command API and vocabulary definitions to be more readily compatible with those used by DJI and in the open source autopilots that are available.

11. BENEFITS ACCRUING FROM INTEGRATING UAVS IN THE CLASSROOM

The experiential and developmental benefits that result from the use of UAVs for education purposes should not be underestimated. A poorly controlled and operated drone constitutes a hazard for persons, animals, infrastructure, and itself. In this sense it provides valuable opportunities for introducing, reinforcing and evaluating a variety of personal and professional developmental skills that we expect our graduate to possess, but which we, as educators, are often poor at elucidating and conveying.

To take some simple examples, accreditation bodies place strong emphasis on the development of good professional practice, ownership of assigned activities and instillation of strong ethical awareness and responsibility. The extant laboratory activity required, and assessed, all three of these elements as fully as was reasonably practicable. Tools used included summative and formative assessments; for example demonstrations, interviews and individual assessments.

UAV flight implicitly necessitates good professional practice: Their operators must be aware of everything from the environmental factors at play; the potential risks associated with device failure, e.g. due to a crash or power loss; the consequences of poor control or loss of control e.g. crash, damage, injury, lawsuits, etc. In addition, those wishing to use UAVs for commercial purposes may have to overcome some of the negative perceptions that surround them. For example, there has been much public debate on their military use for unmanned aerial assaults and on their deployment for more voyeuristic intrusion into the private lives on celebrities. Introducing UAVs into the laboratory provides opportunities to engage students with wider issues surrounding the use of technology in the real world outside of a formal academic setting.

The hypervisor controls and monitors all instructions received from the operator i.e. from each student group. Any "failure" and corrective action are then reported back to the screen, with an associated penalty weighting to be applied to the overall task performance score. This "penalty" can be conceived as comprising elements arising from failings in good professional practice, failings in ownership of and responsibility for the UAV, health and safety failings through causing a hazard, and failings under the broader "Engineering Ethics" heading. The scale of the weighting is graduated in proportion to the potential consequence of the transgression - a drone instructed to exit the arena at 100% power accrues a much higher penalty than a drone that overshoots slightly whilst slowing itself.

As students are learning to control the UAV it is almost inevitable that they will experience a crash or loss of supervisory control event. Thus they will find themselves confronted with the consequential reality of this failure, and see it recorded as a number or a weighting on their overall grade. The evolutionary responses in strategy to this penalty approach are most interesting and subject to ongoing exploration and research.

Achievable solutions, at this academic stage, include use of GPS elevation data from the drone to maintain consistent flight elevation - thereby reducing or obviating hazard to licensed airspace users; use of GPS speed and position data to ensure that drone speeds and locations are safe and appropriate, and that safety margins to pre-mapped obstacles are maintained. Senior undergraduates could be expected to operate the drones safely in 3D, mapping and maintaining "flight corridors" for separation purposes; and utilizing the camera(s) for target identification, tracking and landing.

Secondary and tertiary assessment examples include accurate management of flight elevation so as not to constitute a hazard to other UAVs or aircraft at higher elevations, controlled target identification and simulated medicines delivery to remote dispensaries, etc. If one wished to extend this experience to graduate students, then they could further develop these concepts through the integration of peripherals into the drone e.g. ultrasonics or LIDAR, with the concomitant benefits that these will bring to safety and performance.

12. REFLECTIONS ON LESSONS LEARNT AND BEST PRACTICE

The system and approach described herein arose from seeking to integrate UAVs into an existing practical line following robotics task for freshman students. There are many similar practical classroom tasks documented in the International literature that can be inspired by, and evolve from, this work.

The approach is not tied to any specific platform or UAV technology, and includes strategies for integrating both open and closed source platforms.

The use of a supervisory control and override mechanism is essential on a number of grounds: health and safety (of students, staff, onlookers and infrastructure), legal compliance, overall drone meta control (both single drones and multiple in-flight drones), and to provide positive reassurance and feedback for both staff and students alike.

It is reasonable to assume that attackers (other groups or third parties) may seek to compromise the simple communications exchanges, so securing the two-way communication between the drone and controller is an important facet of any implementation.

Having a separate, prioritized "master" control channel, supporting a very small number of "safe" behaviors, is advisable. In practice one behavior was found to be sufficient - that of returning the drone to the center of the arena upon activation of the signal. Initial implementation saw the UAV task constitute an extension activity for students who demonstrated fully-supervised control of the ground based robots. In this way the risk profile associated with direct student flight of UAVs was mitigated.

The initial "delta" or step in transitioning from 2D ground-based robotics tasks to 3D air-based UAV tasks must appear small in order to avoid discouraging or demotivating students at the outset. This work describes a simple "scaling" factor that is directly applied to the ground based instruction set to appropriately magnify the in-air duration of each action. Speed and elevation are held constant in this initial transition stage for each group.

A quantifiable focus on professionalism, good practice, ethics and sensitivity to environmental concerns are directly evoked through the task requirements and operation of the hypervisor. This accords well with the educational requirements sought from progammes by professional Engineering and Accreditation bodies.

13. CONCLUSION

This paper provides one of the first descriptions of the structured integration of UAV technology into an existing freshman laboratory based Computer Engineering Design course. A protocol for providing seamless transition from ground based robotic vehicle control to in-flight UAV control is set out, and the supporting software and systems implementations are characterized in detail. Elucidation and assessment of key complementary skills is integrated into the technical framework described, as are the more traditional group and peer learning modalities. The paper concludes with a summary of our reflections on best practice in the integration, design and implementation of drone technology in the classroom

14. REFERENCES

[1] *The Navigation and Control Technology Inside the AR.Drone Micro UAV*, Milano, Italy, 2011.

[2] AR.Drone 2.0 Developer Guide. http://ardrone2.parrot.com/developer-zone/, 2012. Accessed: 2015-12-01.

[3] *A new era for aviation - Opening the aviation market to the civil use of RPAS in a safe and sustainable manner.* Communication from the Commission to the European Parliament and the Council, 2014.

[4] DJI Developer API Doc. https://dev.dji.com/api_doc, 2015. Accessed: 2015-12-01.

[5] PHANTOM 2 User Manual. http://dl.djicdn.com/downloads/phantom_2/en/PHANTOM2_User_Manual_v1.4_en.pdf, 2015. Accessed: 2015-12-01.

[6] W. Accord http://www.washingtonaccord.org/, 2012. Accessed: 2015-08-23.

[7] F. Bonin-Font, A. Ortiz, and G. Oliver. Visual navigation for mobile robots: A survey. *J. Intell. Robotics Syst.*, 53(3):263–296, Nov. 2008.

[8] J. Burg, V. P. Pauca, W. Turkett, E. Fulp, S. Cho, P. Santago, D. C. nas, and H. D. Gage. Engaging non-traditional students in computer science through socially-inspired learning and sustained mentoring. In *Proc. 46th ACM SIGCSE*, pages 639–644, 2015.

[9] C. Charyton. Creative engineering design: The meaning of creativity and innovation in engineering. In *Creativity and Innovation Among Science and Art*, pages 135–152. Springer, 2015.

[10] I. Deaconu and A. Voinescu. Mobile gateway for wireless sensor networks utilizing drones. In *13th RoEduNet Conference: 8th RENAM Joint Event*, pages 1–5, Sept 2014.

[11] C. L. Dym, A. M. Agogino, O. Eris, D. D. Frey, and L. J. Leifer. Engineering design thinking, teaching, and learning. *J. Eng. Ed.*, 94(1):103–120, 2005.

[12] C. Eriksen, K. Ming, and Z. Dodds. Accessible aerial robotics. *J. Comput. Sci. Coll.*, 29(4):218–227, 2014.

[13] J. Froyd, P. Wankat, and K. Smith. Five major shifts in 100 years of engineering education. *Proc. IEEE*, 100:1344–1360, May 2012.

[14] M. Huggard, F. Boland, and C. Mc Goldrick. Using cooperative learning to enhance critical reflection. In *44th Annual Frontiers in Education Conference, IEEE*, pages 1–8, Oct 2014.

[15] M. Huggard and C. McGoldrick. Incentivising students to pursue computer science programmes. In *36th Annual Frontiers in Education Conference, IEEE*, pages 3–8, Oct 2006.

[16] M. Huggard and C. McGoldrick. Lessons Learnt from a Decade of Structured Support for Novice Programmers. In *14th Int. Conference on Engineering Education*, pages FR.A.SB 11.230–7, 2011.

[17] N. Kartam. Integrating design into a civil engineering education. *Int. J. Eng. Ed.*, (2):130–135, 1998.

[18] C. McGoldrick and M. Huggard. Peer learning with lego mindstorms. In *34th Annual Frontiers in Education, IEEE* , pages S2F–24–9 Vol. 3, Oct 2004.

[19] G. S. McNeal. Amazon and Google Delivery Drones Will Likely Fly in Europe First. *Forbes*, March 2015.

[20] C. Molina, R. Belfort, R. Pol, O. Chacon, L. Rivera, D. Ramos, and E. Rivera. The use of unmanned aerial vehicles for an interdisciplinary undergraduate education: Solving quadrotors limitations. In *44th Annual Frontiers in Education, IEEE*, pp 1–6, 2014.

[21] L. V. Morris. On or coming to your campus soon: Drones. *Innovative Higher Ed.*, 40(3):187–188, 2015.

[22] C. Nitschke, Y. Minami, M. Hiromoto, H. Ohshima, and T. Sato. A quadrocopter automatic control contest as an example of interdisciplinary design education. In *14th Int. Conf. on Control, Automation and Systems (ICCAS)*, pages 678–685, Oct 2014.

[23] T. Padgett. Drones join the war against drugs. *Time Magazine*, June 2009.

[24] C. F. Panadero, J. Román, and C. D. Kloos. Impact of learning experiences using lego mindstorms® in engineering courses. In *Education Engineering (EDUCON)*, pages 503–512. IEEE, 2010.

[25] S. Rahok Yokokawa, H. Oneda, S. Osawa, and K. Ozaki. Development of a teaching material that can motivate students to learn control engineering and image processing. In *17th Int. Conf. on Comput. Sci. and Eng. (CSE)*, pages 413–419, Dec 2014.

[26] M. Shuman, D. Heer, and T. Fiez. A manipulative rich approach to first year electrical engineering education. In *38th Annual Frontiers in Education, IEEE*, pages F1D–10–F1D–15, Oct 2008.

[27] I. Stamouli, E. Doyle, and M. Huggard. Establishing structured support for programming students. In *34th Annual Frontiers in Education, IEEE*, pages F2G–5–9 Vol. 2, Oct 2004.

[28] R. Traylor, D. Heer, and T. Fiez. Using an integrated platform for learning trade; to reinvent engineering education. *IEEE Trans. Ed.*, 46(4):409–419, 2003.

[29] T. Wall and T. Monahan. Surveillance and violence from afar: The politics of drones and liminal security-scapes. *Theoretical Criminology*, 15(3):239–254, 2011.

[30] G. Winterfeldt and C. Hahne. Controlling quad-copters a project-based approach in the teaching of application design. In *Global Engineering Education Conference (EDUCON), IEEE*, pages 961–968, 2014.

Effects of a Program Integrating Course for Students of Computer Science and Engineering

Viggo Kann
KTH Royal Institute of Technology
Stockholm, Sweden
viggo@csc.kth.se

Anna-Karin Högfeldt
KTH Royal Institute of Technology
Stockholm, Sweden
akhog@ece.kth.se

ABSTRACT

Study programs are a central component of the higher education system, in particular for professional education. However, for many education programs, especially in engineering, a large part of the beginner students fail to reach graduation. A reason for this could be lack of program coherence. In order to strengthen the program coherence of the computer science and engineering program at KTH, a program integrating course was introduced in 2010. The course runs at low speed through the first three years of the program. It consists of reflection seminars in small cross-grade groups of students, led by a professor as a mentor. In the seminars the students exercise self-regulated learning abilities, such as metacognitive skills, when reflecting, discussing and acting upon different topics, such as study techniques, procrastination, studying abroad, plagiarism and responsibility, and the professional life after the studies.

We have studied and found both perceived and measurable positive effects of the program integrating course. In this paper we describe effects on the students' study skills, their ability to reflect and interest in exchange studies.

Keywords

program coherence; reflection; self-regulated learning

1. INTRODUCTION

The use of the terms metacognition, self-regulation (SR) and self-regulated learning (SRL) in research studies has been trustworthily analyzed by Dinsmore et al. [6]. The authors find that SR and SRL have increased in popularity the latest years, and the term metacognition is meeting a "reemerging interest". Metacognition could be defined as a person's capability to be "thinking about thinking". While metacognition has its focus on the individual, SR and SRL look at "the interaction of the person with the environment".

Dinsmore et al. emphasize that "conceptions of these constructs are not stagnant or fixed, rather they continue to move and take shape over time". Still, some general patterns are revealed. All three terms share the conceptual commonality on how well "individuals make efforts to monitor their thoughts and actions and to act accordingly to gain some control over them. It is, in effect, a marriage between self-awareness and intention to act that aligns these bodies of work" [6]. Typically, SRL research aims at combining the two others and "deliberately attempting to address the interaction of cognitive, motivational, and contextual factors" [6], in order to find "how students become masters of their own learning" [17].

Zimmerman describes how academic success is linked to students' use of learning strategies, such as "self-evaluation, organization and transformation, goal setting and planning, information seeking, record keeping, self-monitoring, environmental structuring, giving self-consequences, rehearsing and memorizing, seeking social assistance (peers, teacher, or other adults), and reviewing (notes, books, or tests)" [17]. Research shows that merely telling students about these strategies will not suffice.

Kolb and Kolb argue that "educators can pave the way by placing learning about learning on the agenda of their educational programs" [12]. This can be done using for instance reflection tasks. Zimmerman argues that in order for students to develop long-lasting self-regulated learning skills, they will need to be trained in long-term efforts that "offer direction and insight into the processes of self-regulated learning" [17]. Nilsson reports that engineers in work life have difficulties finding relevance of the actual learning and studies within the engineering educational program. Looking back, the educated engineers "view their education as compartmentalized or fragmented, and they lack a main thread in the educational programme" [14].

Program coherence is a concept that has become common in discussions and research on professional education [2, 3]. How well courses and units are linked together to create a meaningful whole, how well theory and practice are interwoven, and how well 'connections, sequences, timing and logical flow of assessment tasks across the whole program' [10] are created to lead to complex professional degree outcomes, is the main focus for the concept of program coherence. It is argued that professionals in the fields of engineering, law, nursing, social working and education among others, are not well prepared enough when entering real life, and that this is because professional education has not achieved well when it comes to program coherence.

Our Program Integrating Course, studied in this paper, is designed to meet the needs of program coherence and

SIGCSE '16, March 2–5, 2016, Memphis, TN, USA

DOI: http://dx.doi.org/10.1145/2839509.2844610

Table 1: Hierarchy of reflection levels [8]

1. *Technical writing* just describing personal experience, events and action in a specific situation.
2. *Descriptive reflection* analyzing one's performance, giving reasons for actions taken.
3. *Dialogic reflection considering alternatives* exploring alternative viewpoints and alternative ways to solve problems.
4. *Critical reflection from a broader perspective* thinking about the effects upon others of one's actions, taking account of the society.

the development and training of students' long-term skills. Reflection assignments, orally and in writing, are used as a tool to strengthen the program coherence over the years and to promote self-regulated learning among our students. The students are, throughout the three years' course, given reflection assignments on different topics related to Zimmerman's learning strategies mentioned above [17]. Early, we noticed that we would need to encourage the students to write deeper reflections. It is known that students may experience difficulties when being asked to reflect on given topics, which can manifest in more descriptive than reflective texts [4, 8].

In order to help students to improve their ability to reflect more deeply, Hatton and Smith have defined a hierarchy of levels of reflection, summarized in Table 1 [8]. We have found these to be useful in order to support our students to create more sophisticated reflections and to use their reflections to become better self-regulated learners.

Automatic assessment of the reflection level of student texts is not much studied. There is no such system at all for Swedish text. For English text, Ullmann suggested an architecture for such a system and implemented parts of it [15]. The system uses natural language processing techniques for finding indications of the reflection level of the text. Parts of the system are fully automatic and parts of the system are used for computer-supported classification. Ullmann et al. compared the decisions of the system to human judgement, and found the system to perform well [16].

We will first describe the *Program Integrating Course* and motivate why it improves the program coherence and the academic integration of the students. We have investigated the effects of the course with respect to the students' ability to reflect, their interest in exchange studies and their study skills. We will describe the results and how the effects were measured. We conclude with a discussion of the opportunities given by a program integrating course.

2. THE COURSE

The Program Integrating Course (PIC) has been given since 2010 as a mandatory course to the students of the five year Degree Program in Computer Science and Engineering at KTH. It was inspired by a similar course at the Media Technology program at the same university.

PIC runs over the first three years of the program, at low speed. It enables the students to develop their self-regulated learning abilities and shows the main thread of the program, for example how the courses are linked. PIC gives an opportunity to focus on "softer" program learning outcomes, that are hard to cover fully in ordinary technical courses. The number of students starting the course in their first year is between 170 and 180. The number concluding the course in their third year is between 120 and 140, due to drop out.

The course consists of reflection seminars, 4 times a year, in small cross-grade groups with a professor as a facilitator and mentor. The only lectures in the course are a single introduction lecture at the beginning of each year and a few information meetings with the study counselor.

Before each seminar all students write a text reflecting both on the topic of the seminar and their recent studies in the courses taken in parallel. The reflection documents are read by everyone in the group before the seminar. In order to encourage the students to improve their reflections we started using the four levels of reflection in Table 1, both in the given questions and in the mentor's assessment of the reflection documents. For the *procrastination* topic, this would look like the following:

1. *Technical writing:* Do you procrastinate? How? When?
2. *Descriptive reflection:* Why do you procrastinate?
3. *Dialogic reflection considering alternatives:* Choose, from the list of 50 anti procrastination tips, one that you should promise to try for 60 days. Motivate your choice and suggest methods ensuring that you keep your promise.
4. *Critical reflection from a broader perspective:* Reflect about how your and others' procrastination could influence you and/or others, for example while studying in groups or in project work.

3. CHARACTERISTICS AND FUNCTIONS OF THE COURSE

3.1 Characteristics

The five key concepts that characterize successful activities for academic integration and improved student completion, according to Andersson et al. [1], are successfully matched with the program integrating course, as motivated below.

1. An overall perspective

The course runs for the whole first three years of the education and is mandatory for all students. All categories of personnel who are directly involved in the program are involved in the course: the program directors, the study counselor, and 13 professors who are teaching courses in the program. PIC ties together all mandatory courses and guides the students in their choices of elective courses and specializations. It covers the studies, the objectives of the education and the courses, the execution and development of the courses, and the profession and lifelong learning.

2. Student activity

The students meet in small cross-grade groups four times each year, in the same group and with the same mentor each time. Before each seminar each student should write a reflection and read the written reflections of the other members in the group. During the seminar the written reflections are discussed. PIC is permeated by student activity.

3. Personal meetings

The seminar groups consist of about 12–13 students from different grades (1–3). In the yearly evaluation the students often emphasize that the meetings with students in other grades are especially fruitful. Since the students meet the same professor as mentor for three years, a mutual trust is developed, which is utilized at the end of the third year, when the mentor meets each student individually for 15 minutes and discusses the important choice of specialization in the master program. The students also meet the study counselor at least once a year within the course.

4. Forward-pointing

Our intention is that the course members should become professional and conscious self-regulating students, knowing the objectives of their education and why the program is composed in the way it is, and knowing how to choose to get precisely the vocational training and education that they seek. The discussions about current courses, in the second half of each seminar, show younger students what they will meet in one or two years.

5. Discourse awareness

The first lecture in the first year of the program is a PIC lecture, where the students learn how the mandatory courses of the program are linked, how the program is run and developed, which course administrative systems exist, where students can find answers to questions and get help, and similar knowledge that simplifies life as a student. The textbook gives further insight into the academic discourse. Each seminar has a topic that raises the consciousness about some academic discourse, which makes the students aware of many discourses spread out over the three years that the course is given. The most popular topic are shown in Table 2. The topics rotate in a 3 year cycle.

Since PIC meets all five key concepts characterizing successful activities for academic integration and improved student completion, it is likely that PIC is a successful activity.

3.2 Functions

Kann [11] argues that PIC fulfills the following functions:
1. academic introduction
2. increased understanding of the program
3. connections between teachers and students
4. exchange of experiences between students from different years of the program
5. training in written and oral communication and reflection
6. covering subjects that other courses are not covering
7. information about elective courses and studies abroad
8. follow-up of academic results
9. education of the professors involved
10. quality enhancing evaluation of the program

The motivation of the eight first functions should be clear from the above characterization, so only the two last functions need to be motivated here.

The education of the professors acting as mentors, in function 9, is of two kinds: First, PIC gives knowledge about the program, its objectives, contents and courses. Second, the professors will learn how the students feel about their studies, how they study and prioritize. The professors can then use this knowledge to improve their own courses and make these more suited for the program.

There are several common problems with ordinary course evaluations that PIC solves. Many course evaluations have low participation, but in PIC the evaluations are mandatory, because one of the objectives of the course is "critically analyze and reflect on the structure and performance of the programme and their own study achievements". Also, the evaluations in PIC can have program perspective, which is harder in a course evaluation. Furthermore, the course reflections ending each seminar give direct feedback on the current courses, independently of which department they belong to. This feedback is collected by the mentor and presented to the other mentors (including the program directors) at a short meeting over a cup of coffee the day after the seminars. Hence, the last function is motivated.

Table 2: The eight top results of the evaluation question: "Which two [three for the third year] seminar topics do you think, as a whole, were most fruitful?"

65%	Procrastination
45%	Study motivation and study skills
35%	Master programs
31%	Plagiarism and responsibility
29%	Studying and working abroad
23%	The professional life as a CS engineer
21%	Learning outcomes, criteria and assessment
19%	Life-long learning

4. MEASURED EFFECTS

We have tried to measure some effects of the program integrating course and will report the results below.

4.1 The yearly course evaluation

At the end of each academic year a questionnaire is distributed to all PIC students, with some questions evaluating PIC itself. Since the questionnaire is included as a learning activity (see above), we have 100% response rate for this evaluation. In May 2013, the first-year students who started the course back in 2010 graduated from the course (in year 3). Therefore their answers to the evaluation questions were particularly interesting. The third-year students were asked "Have the reflection seminars been fruitful?". 94% of the students answered *yes*, of which 14% answered *yes, to a large extent*, and 80% answered *yes, to some extent.* 4% answered *no*, and 2% answered *don't know.* On the question about whether a similar course should be given to the other programs at the same university, 65% answered *yes*, 10% *no*, and 25% *don't know.*

One question asked which three seminar topics were most fruitful. The first and second year students were asked which two seminar topics were most fruitful. The results of these questions in 2014 can be found in Table 2. Since the students in year 1 and 2 had not yet participated in all seminars, the results are given as proportions of students that had participated in the seminar.

4.2 Measuring the level of reflection

In order to analyze the progression of the reflective ability of the students in an objective way, we developed a Swedish NLP classifier based on the architecture by Ullmann [15]. We have translated the premise and conclusion indicating keywords (such as because, since, whereas, and therefore, hence, consequently) using several English-Swedish dictionaries. Since our system should measure the reflection levels of Hatton and Smith, we identified keywords and phrases that were typical for each level, see some examples in Table 3, translated to English. We identified about 50 key-

Table 3: Examples of keywords indicating reflection

level 2	level 3	level 4
reason	would	organisation
due to	possibility	development of society
since	disadvantage	external
above all	for example	engineer
thanks to	choose	team
despite	change	employed
obviously	alternatively	the education

words for each level. Since words may occur in different inflections (in Swedish nouns have 8 different inflections), we tagged many of the keywords with *lemma*, meaning that any inflection of the keyword should be matched. Some keywords are homonymous in Swedish, for example the word *så* which could be either an adverb (*so*) or a verb (*sow*). These were tagged with the relevant word class, so that our system could match the words only if the occurred in the correct sense in the text, using a disambiguating parts-of-speech tagger [5].

The process of determining the reflection value for a document consists of four steps:

1. Convert the PDF document into a text document.
2. Use a Swedish parts-of-speech tagger to tag each word with its word class and lemma form [5].
3. Check which reflective keywords (including premise and conclusion indicators) that occur in the text and to which level of reflection they are linked.
4. Compute the reflection value of the text by adding the levels of the found keywords and normalize it with respect to the length of the text.

We matched all reflection documents from 2010 to 2015 (over 7.000) to their author and sorted them chronologically – each student writes 11 reflection documents during the course. In order to measure the progression in reflection of the students we then, for each student, computed the mean reflectional value for the texts that were written in the first year and the mean reflectional value for the texts that were written in the third year. The mean reflectional values for each starting year can be found in Figure 1. For 2009 the course started in year 2 and for 2013 the data from the last year are from year 2. Some of the documents were stored in formats that we were not able to automatically extract text from. The data in Figure 1 are from the students exclusively handing in documents that we were able to analyze, which fortunately were the majority. The reflection level model was introduced in the course in 2012. From this year on, we gave a higher grade to reflections reaching level 3 or 4, but only for second and third year students. We can see in Figure 1 that the students reflect on a higher level in the last year than in the first year. The difference was quite small before we introduced the reflection level model and very much larger afterwards. Since the topics are different each year, some variation between different years should be expected. But the mean reflectional value of first year students only varies between 210 and 217, except for year 2011.

In the course evaluation questionnaire given 2015 to the students who started in 2012, we asked about the perceived ability to write reflections. The results in Figure 2 show that

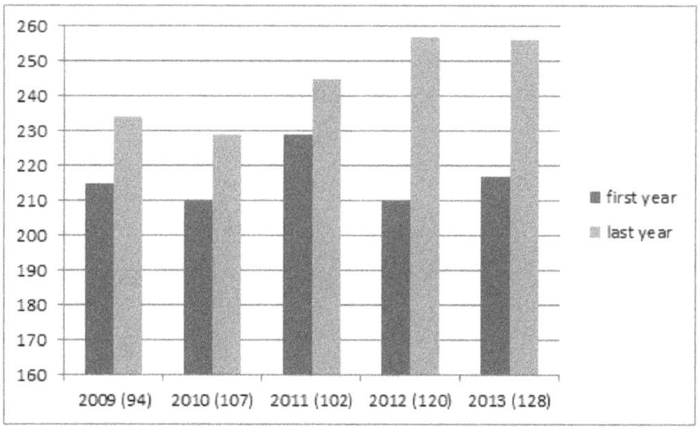

Figure 1: Mean reflectional values for the students starting 2009–2013 in their reflections from the first and last year of the course. The number of investigated students in parentheses.

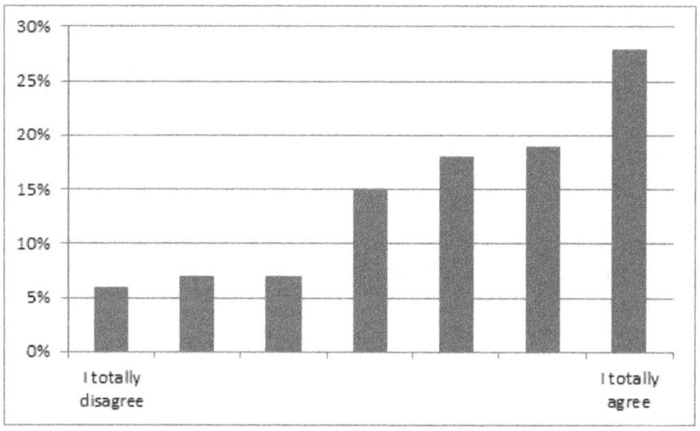

Figure 2: Results from the question "I feel that I'm better at writing reflections now than when I started the course".

most students perceive a progression, and only very few do not perceive any improvement at all.

4.3 Inspiration for exchange studies

Our university has the ambition that half of the students should become international exchange students during their studies. The Computer science and engineering program has always been very far from this goal. Therefore we decided to insert a seminar on the topic *studying and working abroad* into the program integrating course. Before the seminar, the students had to read about how exchange studies work and how and when to apply for exchange studies. Furthermore the students should read three travel reports from students who have studied abroad (each exchange student has to write such a report). The reflection questions that the students should answer before the seminar were:

- The travel reports give many reasons for going on exchange. Which reasons would you rate highest? Could exchange studies be a merit when you apply for a job? Reflect!
- Why do travel reports focus that little on the studies?
- Are you interested in exchange studies? If so, when?

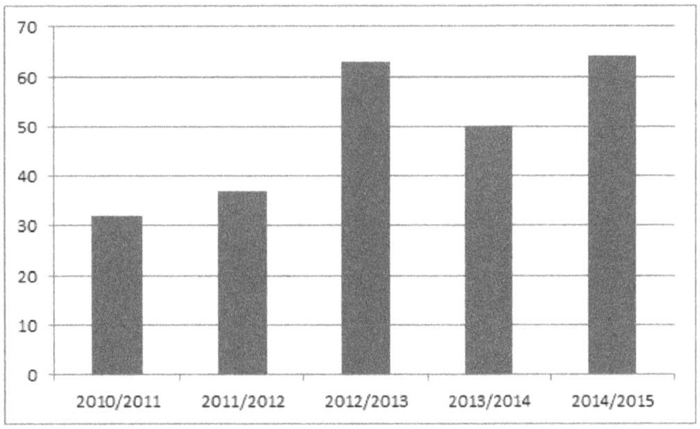

Figure 3: Number of students studying abroad. The new seminar was given in 2011/2012.

Our idea was that, by requiring each student to reflect on exchange studies, the number of students really applying for exchange studies should increase. Before we inserted the seminar, there only was an information session open for the interested students, and there might have been students who knew too little to be interested enough to go to such a session, but if they had known, they would be interested.

The real numbers of students going on exchange studies, presented in Figure 3, confirm this assumption. Before the seminar, about 30–35 students per year were studying abroad. After the seminar, about 25 students more each year were studying abroad.

4.4 Improving study skills

A way to increase the productive time of the students is to make them learn study skills. The first seminar topic for the first-year students in PIC is study motivation and study skills. The study skills module of the course is structured in the following way, which can be seen as an example of how we implement a topic in the course:

First the students look at some short videos where study skills are explained and motivated and read a book on study skills. The students then write a text where they reflect on how they have studied for the last week and how they are planning to study in the future, and also choose at least one new study skill to try for the next months. The students read each others' texts and meet and discuss at seminar 1. After 6 weeks, the students write a new text, reflecting on how the attempt to try a new study skill fell out, and discuss this at seminar 2, where another topic is also introduced. A graphical overview of the structure is found in Figure 4.

In 2014, when the students had tried the new study skill(s) for about 7 weeks, they were given a mandatory questionnaire evaluating the perceived effects of the new skill(s). The main results are given in Table 4. The numbers are percentages of the number of students trying each skill. Each of the 169 students should try at least one new skill. The reason that we asked about the study skills presented in the table was that they were presented in the videos that the students were required to look at, before they chose which study skill(s) to try. 20 students chose to try some skill not on the list. We can see that many student perceived an obvious effect, and only a few did not notice any effect. The skills with highest perceived effect were "planning your studies the upcoming week" and "trying to stop procrastinating". For more detailed results of the study skills intervention, see [9].

Table 4: Perceived effects on the students' learning of trying a new study skill

What is your perception of the effects on your learning of...	Obvious effect	Most likely effect	No noticed effect
...preparing before lectures?	23%	69%	8%
...taking smart notes at lectures?	23%	57%	21%
...going through the previous day's and week's teaching?	23%	63%	15%
...planning your studies the upcoming week?	49%	40%	11%
...maintaining a study diary?	23%	45%	32%
...read the course literature in three steps?	44%	37%	19%
...trying to stop procrastinating?	59%	31%	10%
...doing some other change?	43%	57%	0%
In total	35%	51%	14%

Table 5: Results from the question "Has PIC promoted you to analyze and adapt your study habits?", posed to the students at the end of each year

Year	Number of students	Yes, to a high degree	Yes, to some degree	No	Don't know
2011					
1	141	25%	57%	16%	3%
2	134	10%	70%	20%	0%
3	120	7%	61%	27%	5%
2012					
1	155	18%	68%	12%	2%
2	154	14%	68%	13%	4%
3	151	10%	68%	18%	5%

Study skills is a special topic of the course, since it is brought up and discussed at every seminar (four times each year for three years), always related to the current seminar topic and the courses that the students in the different years currently take. Therefore we expect to see an effect also on the students in the second and third year, and not only on the students in the first year who had taken the study skills module. In the course evaluation questionnaire at the end of each year we have for many years asked the students about the perceived effects of PIC with respect to study skills. The results for two classes, starting PIC year 2011 and 2012, are presented in Table 5. About 20–25 percent of the first year students believe that they have improved their study skills to a high degree because of the course. The effect is largest during the first year, but there is an effect to some degree for most students throughout the three years of the course. Only a small share of the students believe that they did not improve their study skills because of the course. The reason could be either that they already have good enough study skills or that they did not benefit from the course.

5. DISCUSSION AND CONCLUSIONS

In this study we have chosen to present some of the effects of the Program integrating course for computer science and engineering students that has been running for five years. We have found that the course is an excellent solution to the problem with the lack of sufficient program coherence.

Of the ten functions of the program integrating course presented in Section 3.2, the function *training in written*

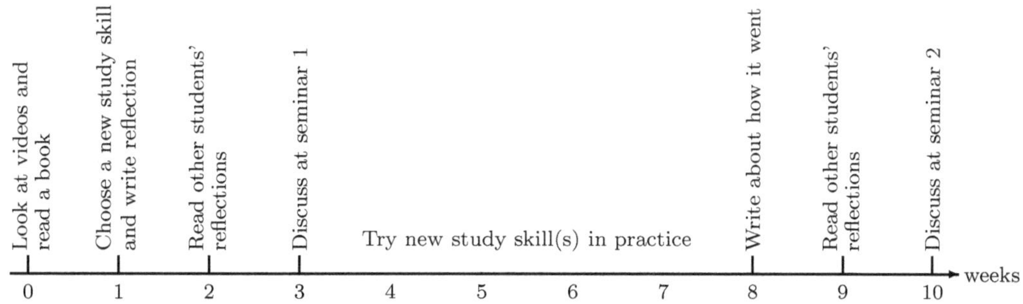

Figure 4: The structure of the study skills module.

and oral communication and reflection is the key for the students to exercise their metacognitive skills. The other functions promote the program coherence in different ways.

We would like the effects of the course to be long-term. Zimmerman concludes: "limited attempts at instruction that focus on only one or two processes are unlikely to promote long-term effects. Instead, attention must be directed toward developing all three dimensions of self-regulated learning in students: metacognitive, motivational, and behavioral." [17]. The PIC course indeed develops metacognition, motivation as well as good habits (for example new study skills and how to handle procrastination), so the effects might well be long-term. Furthermore the course runs for three whole years. which should improve the long-term effect even more. This is in line with Light et al. [13] who argue that students will need to develop learner autonomy, control, adaptability and self-efficacy, which are improved by long-term commitment and extended concentration

Edwards et al. observe that reflective writing assignments alone did not have significant impact on student procrastination [7]. They suggest that extending the intervention such as having students discuss their reflections could improve its effectiveness. This was confirmed by our study.

We have seen that both study skills and the ability to reflect improve from the beginning to the end of the course. Can a topic at a single seminar also have an effect? Yes, this is shown by our exchange studies study.

The course evaluations show that the students enjoy the course, and that half of the students even are more positive to the course at the end than at the beginning.

At our university a dozen educational programs now have started a program integrating course, inspired by PIC. The course has even spread to some other Swedish universities.

6. REFERENCES

[1] S. Andersson, J. Andersson Chronholm, and B. Victor. Working actively with student integration and retention. In *Proc. 3rd Development Conference for Swedish Engineering Educations*, 2011.

[2] M. Atkins. Oven-ready and self-basting: taking stock of employability skills. *Teaching in Higher Education*, 4(2):267–280, 1999.

[3] D. P. Baker. The educational transformation of work: towards a new synthesis. *Journal of Education and Work*, 22(3):163–191, 2009.

[4] Å. Cajander, M. Daniels, R. McDermott, and B. R. von Konsky. Assessing professional skills in engineering education. In *Proc. 13th Australasian Computing Education Conf. Vol. 114*, pages 145–154, 2011.

[5] J. Carlberger and V. Kann. Implementing an efficient part-of-speech tagger. *Software-Practice and Experience*, 29(9):815–32, 1999.

[6] D. L. Dinsmore, P. A. Alexander, and S. M. Loughlin. Focusing the conceptual lens on metacognition, self-regulation, and self-regulated learning. *Educational Psychology Review*, 20(4):391–409, 2008.

[7] S. H. Edwards, J. Martin, and C. A. Shaffer. Examining classroom interventions to reduce procrastination. In *Proc. ACM ITiCSE 2015*, pages 254-259. ACM, 2015.

[8] N. Hatton and D. Smith. Reflection in teacher education: Towards definition and implementation. *Teaching and teacher education*, 11(1):33–49, 1995.

[9] B. Hedin and V. Kann. Improving study skills using program integrating reflection seminars. Submitted, 2015.

[10] T. Jessop, Y. El Hakim, and G. Gibbs. The whole is greater than the sum of its parts: a large-scale study of students' learning in response to different programme assessment patterns. *Assessment & Evaluation in Higher Education*, 39(1):73–88, 2014.

[11] V. Kann. A program integrating course with many functions (in Swedish). *Proc. 3:rd Development Conference for Sweden's Engineering Programs*, pages 153–156, 2011.

[12] A. Y. Kolb and D. A. Kolb. The learning way meta-cognitive aspects of experiential learning. *Simulation & Gaming*, 40(3):297–327, 2009.

[13] G. Light, S. Calkins, and R. Cox. *Learning and teaching in higher education: The reflective professional.* Sage, 2009.

[14] S. Nilsson. On the meaning of higher education in professional practice: the case of physicians and engineers. *Journal of Education and Work*, 23(3):255–274, 2010.

[15] T. D. Ullmann. An architecture for the automated detection of textual indicators of reflection. In *Proc. 1st European Workshop on Awareness and Reflection in Learning Networks*, pages 138–151, 2011.

[16] T. D. Ullmann, F. Wild, and P. Scott. Comparing automatically detected reflective texts with human judgements. In *Proc. 2nd Workshop on Awareness and Reflection in Technology-Enhanced Learning*, pages 101–116, 2013.

[17] B. J. Zimmerman. Self-regulated learning and academic achievement: An overview. *Educational psychologist*, 25(1):3–17, 1990.

Meeting Graduate Employability Needs through Open-source Collaboration with Industry

Matthew Forshaw, Ellis Solaiman, Oonagh McGee, Hugo Firth
School of Computing Science
Newcastle University, United Kingdom
{matthew.forshaw,ellis.solaiman, oonagh.mcgee,h.firth}@ncl.ac.uk

Paul Robinson, Ryan Emerson
Red Hat Inc
Newcastle upon Tyne, United Kingdom
{paul.robinson,remerson}@redhat.com

ABSTRACT

This paper describes the development and delivery of a course, in close collaboration with industry, over a ten-year period. We describe the details of this collaboration, which aims to equip students with collaborative software development experience, incorporating open source, *Enterprise Middleware* technologies and industry best practices. In presenting our case study we share valuable insights, into the challenges and opportunities, for all parties involved. We present the reflections of all stakeholders, including; the course leader, the industrial partner, lab demonstrators, and students. We also present the results of our investigations to track the employment of our graduates over the last five years, identifying that all students who responded are employed within relevant positions or undertaking further study. Based on our successful delivery of the course, in this paper we make all tools and teaching materials available to the open source community, for delivery at other institutions. We emphasise the importance of the continued involvement of industry partners to inform pedagogical practices within Computer Science.

Keywords

industrial collaboration; outreach; employability; middleware; pedagogy; open source

1. INTRODUCTION

The software industry is an ever-changing and competitive environment, and expectations for graduate software engineers entering industry are high. Highly skilled graduates are key resources to drive continuous innovation and development of new computing applications and technologies. This provides a unique opportunity for CS educators to continually reflect and redesign the curriculum in order to deliver learning methods and resources capable of providing students with skills that are relevant to industry.

SIGCSE '16, March 02 - 05, 2016, Memphis, TN, USA

ISBN 978-1-4503-3685-7/16/03... $15.00

DOI: http://dx.doi.org/10.1145/2839509.2844649

Graduates are expected to possess a blend of cognitive, applied and interpersonal skills [14, 17, 8]. This presents a pedagogical challenge; *how do we balance the teaching of theoretical frameworks whilst empowering students with a holistic set of skills to succeed in this environment?*

Academia acknowledges the need to enhance programmes to equip students with skills for employment, yet there exists a disparity between industry expectations and existing curriculum frameworks [15]. This can be addressed by increased involvement of industry partners in the design and development of computing science programmes; important factors determining the success of such initiatives are highlighted in the literature, including the proximity of academic institution to industry partner [6], and the delivery of material in a real-world context [11].

In this paper we present a unique case study of over ten years of collaboration, between the School of Computing Science, Newcastle University and industrial partner, Red Hat [1], the world's largest provider of open source solutions.

We specifically describe the collaboration between Newcastle University and Red Hat on the design and delivery of the *Enterprise Middleware* course within our Advanced MSc programmes. The uniqueness of this study, compared to other capstone courses, stems from a long standing relationship, and from the close proximity of the school to the Red Hat Cloud Research Centre, created in 2010 at Newcastle University[1], co-located on Newcastle University's new Science Central campus. This initiative drives investment in research on enterprise technologies such as cloud, virtualisation, and middleware technologies.

The remainder of this paper is organised as follows. Relevant related work is presented in Section 2, and we describe our teaching initiative in Section 3. In Section 4 we highlight key challenges of running a course in collaboration with industry, identifying potential solutions to these. Section 5 presents student, academic, and industrial perspectives on the benefits of delivering a collaborative course. We explore student satisfaction through University-administered surveys and volunteered testimonials from recent graduates in Section 6. Section 7 presents student outcomes and employability data, and provides a recommendation for further longitudinal study. Section 8 presents our tools and teaching materials, available to the open source community for delivery at other institutions.

[1] http://www.redhat.com/en/about/press-releases/2963

2. RELATED WORK

A number of initiatives which seek to bring industrial relevance to computer science courses, are presented in the literature. The mode and extent of industry involvement in the design and delivery of these courses varies significantly.

A great body of work relates to academic initiatives seeking to emulate industry through cross-site project work. Rusu *et al* [15] provide a survey of previous efforts, and describe their initiative, combining theoretical software engineering content with an industry-informed collaborative working in paired teams across multiple universities.

Collaborations have also been initiated by industry, e.g. Chandran *et al* [3] presents work by Intel, to promote the field of electronics packaging in Malaysian university programmes, leading to the employment of over thirty students.

Further initiatives seek to expose students to industrial practices outside the structure of a degree programme, e.g. Larsen *et al* [7] present a multi-disciplinary summer school delivered in collaboration with Bang and Olufsen, Denmark, and emphasise the importance of students developing soft competencies in multi-disciplinary international teams.

Other studies obtain input to curriculum design through industry advisory boards, and guest speakers [18]. Tenenberg [16] provides an alternative argument and presents the *Industry Fellows* model, emphasising the importance of industry involvement in the classroom, and describes a course featuring an industry partner from Google as a co-lecturer.

Our initiative demonstrates novelty compared to those in the literature in the following aspects; *a)* closeness of collaboration and proximity between academia and the industry partner, *b)* we present insights gained through a decade-long initiative, *c)* we document issues around enhancing future iterations of the course, *d)* we make our tools and teaching materials available open source for use by other educators.

3. COURSE DESCRIPTION

The initiative we describe in this paper forms the practical component of an *'Enterprise Middleware'* course (or *'module'*) delivered to our Advanced MSc students, including UK, EU and International students. The course runs for four weeks, split evenly between two weeks (16 hours) of practical work, and 2 weeks (16 hours) of lectures. Assessment for the course comprises a 90-minute closed-book, summative written examination at the end of Semester 1, and a programming assignment and accompanying report worth 30% of the course mark. While the written examination focuses on theoretical aspects of distributed computing, the coursework assignment is a highly practical application of these concepts and principles, which also seeks to incorporate industry best practices. This close relationship between lecture/examination and practical components embodies the principles of constructive alignment and constructivist learning theory [2], i.e. *active learning* and *collaborative learning.*

This coursework covers the development of an enterprise application using Java Platform Enterprise Edition (Java EE) technologies deployed to a Platform as a Service (PaaS) cloud. Students are introduced to modern production-grade enterprise middleware technologies and their application to build a multi-tier distributed *'holiday booking'* application. Hawthorne *et al* [5] acknowledge the benefits of teaching such integration platforms to reinforce students' knowledge of architectural styles, patterns, techniques and principles.

We aim to reflect industry, where developers commonly work on existing codebases; we provide students with a significant *'base project'* which they should extend to provide additional functionality, described in a detailed specification. This is often a student's first experience working with someone else's code, especially at this scale. We assist the students throughout the challenge of familiarising themselves with the base code, by providing detailed guidance materials and comprehensive source code documentation.

The assignment begins with individualised self-guided work, supported by group discussion, where students develop a cloud-based booking service (e.g. *'Taxi'*, *'Flight'*, *'Hotel'*). In a final exercise, students are required to work collaboratively, to integrate their solutions with those of two colleagues in order to develop an integrated holiday booking system. Informal formative feedback is offered, through demonstrator support, during 16 hours of supervised practical labs. Assessment focuses on the tangible artefacts produced through collaboration, acknowledging complexities in assessing the process [13]. Students are expected to produce a short written report, providing technical documentation of their solution, demonstrate understanding of core concepts, and to reflect on their experiences and personal learning.

In addition to the summative assessment of submitted source code and report, students undertake a 15-minute demonstration/viva held two days before the submission deadline. Vivas are an informal process where students describe their technical solution and experiences on the course, are asked open questions related to core concepts, and receive formative feedback prior to submission.

The purpose of the assignment goes beyond a means of assessment, but seeks to empower students with skills and real-world experience developing a large software artefact, resources not available through other courses. Students' solutions are intentionally *'full stack'*, comprising front- and backend technologies, such that they may form a compelling portfolio piece when seeking employment. This offers a unique opportunity for the students to demonstrate their abilities and use this for their continued career progression.

4. CHALLENGES AND OPPORTUNITIES

A number of challenges exist when delivering courses with industry which exhibit significant technical complexity and collaborative elements. In this section we discuss our course, challenges encountered, and document the interventions we put in place to ameliorate their effects.

4.1 Development of course materials

Generalisability: A common issue, where industry collaboration is concerned, surrounds the generalisability of industry-informed taught content. Care must be taken to ensure that external input is relevant on a wider scale, and not specific to the industrial partner involved. This is particularly important when considering international cohorts, whose employment destinations may span global job markets, each exhibiting cultural variation.

We are confident students' expertise gained on the course may be easily generalised, due to; *a)* we focus on Java EE and cloud technologies which see widespread industrial use, *b)* Red Hat tools are open source and are reference implementations of Java standards, and *c)* ongoing efforts to ensure clear links between the practical elements of the course and theoretical concepts. This objective is shared by our industry partner; *"We have been very careful to ensure that Red Hat technologies are simply used as a vehicle to learning generally applicable skills and technologies."*

Scalability: The issue of scalability is often underestimated when formulating delivery and assessment methods, and selecting the level of difficulty for a course. Techniques appropriate for a particular size of cohort may be intractable if student numbers rise. The need for lightweight assessment mechanisms is felt particularly when collaborating with industry partners, whose availability is often limited.

As the complexity of coursework rises, so too does its assessment. For example; in the context of distributed computing, significant environment setup complicates being able to execute student code in a time efficient manner. This issue is exacerbated as the number of students rises.

In response to a significant rise in student intake in recent years, we have successfully employed the *'viva'* assessment activity, as described in Section 3. The vivas were well received by students, and demonstrators found them extremely effective in assessing understanding, identifying cases of collusion, and ensuring the fairness of marking. Adding the viva assessment means we have been able to retain complexity while simplifying marking.

Accessibility: It is trivial to formulate industry-inspired curricula focused towards more experienced and competent students. A much greater challenge is ensuring that the material remains accessible to less capable students while retaining the intended learning outcomes. This represents a trade-off between realism and difficulty; making the course too difficult would alienate some students, while oversimplifying aspects of the course may overly protect students from real-world issues.

We believe our initiative should represent a positive experience for all students, allowing them to gain confidence in their real-world software development experience. Hence, we place a strong emphasis on providing students with *ipsative feedback*, acknowledging the personal learning experience of each student in the assessment process [9]. We also provide students the opportunity to reflect on their experiences through the viva and written report assessment components.

Providing an environment where the teaching methods and assessment are accessible to all, poses a challenge. We seek to combat this through these blended assessment methods, and collaborative nature of the course.

4.2 Reconciling academic and industry needs

In designing a course with industry involvement, it is essential to reconcile the two, sometimes conflicting, viewpoints of academia and industry. Academics need to demonstrate the application of theoretical concepts using current technologies, and professionals need to ensure they focus less on the minutae of a particular technology, but the broader learning outcomes.

Key issues surround managing the expectations of both parties, with regards to establishing an appropriate level of difficulty of the course, and ensuring the assignment accurately reflects industrial practice, whilst enhancing and adhering to university regulations.

In the context of this course, our industrial partner possesses Masters-level and PhD degrees from our academic institution, so understands the academic context we operate within, and what is required from our students. Therefore, in the design of our *'Enterprise Middleware'* course, we involve industry partners closely in the design of the marking scheme and validation of the assessment. Our industry partner also engages at the marking stage, co-marking a subset of the students' work to ensure fairness of marking and contributing to written summative feedback. This moderation affords a unique opportunity for the integration (in the mark scheme) of industry perspectives with academic learning outcomes. In doing so, we provide students with feedback and feed forward specifically informed by industry input. We advocate academic partners actively engaging with industry prior to, during, and following the course.

4.3 Maintainability

Operating within the ever-changing environment of industry best practice and tooling, necessitates keeping course content up-to-date. This requires significant development work by university staff, in consultation with Red Hat to ensure the *base project* provided to students supports desired learning outcomes. By selecting a *lead demonstrator* to liaise with the industrial partner and perform required changes, three months prior to the beginning of the course, we are able to ensure the smooth delivery of the course.

In addition to the effort required to keep the course in line with current industry best practices, significant up-front development effort has been required each year to ensure the compatibility of the coursework solution, as software versions, cloud platforms and local infrastructure changes.

We have recently ameliorated these issues by contributing the *base project* to the open-source community as a JBoss Developer *"Quickstart"*, a *"use-case code examples tested with the latest stable product releases"* [2]. The maintenance of the project will now be carried out by the industry partner, ensuring compatibility with subsequent software releases. We retain responsibility for updating additional documentation, the coursework specification and model solutions.

Great care is taken to ensure the course could endure a change in personnel. For our demonstrators we encourage an apprenticeship model, whereby the current lead demonstrator trains new demonstrators to take their place in subsequent years. This is important when drawing from a pool of PhD students, who change every three or four years.

The issue of staff turnover is a risk common to all courses which are delivered with industry participation. There has been significant investment by Red Hat in the development of the course over a ten-year period, alongside two changes in academic course leader. In light of this, we are confident of ongoing industry support if staff changeover were to occur.

5. STAKEHOLDER REFLECTION

In order for the continued success and effective delivery of the course it is necessary to actively engage with key stakeholders. These include the demonstrators, course leader, industry partners and students.

5.1 Demonstrators

The delivery of practical labs on the course relies heavily on the support of demonstrators (graduate teaching assistants), comprising PhD students from the School of Computing Science. Whilst demonstrators provide a valuable contribution to courses across the department, their contribution to this course is integral to its operation.

[2]http://www.jboss.org/developer-materials/

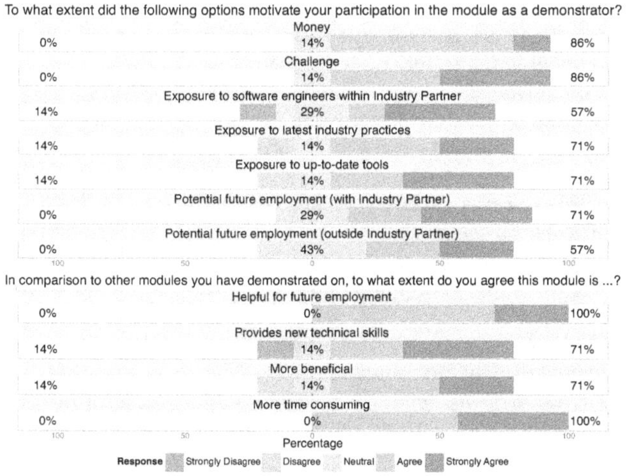

Figure 1: Demonstrator survey results

This course differs in that it requires significant advanced knowledge and substantial preparatory work to deliver the course. Demonstrators commonly acknowledge that demonstrating on this course is more time consuming and challenging than other courses. Despite these potential barriers to demonstrator recruitment, each year we have been successful in recruiting the required demonstrators to assist on the course, with all demonstrators participating in multiple consecutive years throughout their PhDs.

In order to better understand demonstrator's motivations for demonstrating on the course, and in doing so secure sustainable demonstrator provision, we have surveyed every demonstrator on the course between 2010 and 2015, with results presented in Figure 1. The width of the figure represents 200% of the sample size, with percentage values showing the proportion of negative, neutral and positive responses respectively. Each row is horizontally aligned so that neutral responses are centred, in order to more easily observe overall sentiment.

Although "financial incentives" were cited as being a significant motivator for demonstrating on this course, students were not financially remunerated proportionally for the additional workload required in comparison to demonstrating on other courses within the department. Hence we believe further factors motivate students. We see demonstrators value exposure to latest industry practices and tools, and consider their participation to be beneficial to career prospects, with the industry partner and also generally.

We supplement our survey results with volunteered testimonials from demonstrating staff involved in the course between 2010 and 2015; one demonstrator who was previously a student on the course, and now works at Red Hat, comments; *"I felt that the module was the most beneficial to me during my masters. I wanted to contribute to help new students in the hope they would gain as much as me."* The same demonstrator goes on to cite *"contributions to the open-source community"* as an additional factor motivating his participation on the course.

Finally, demonstrators reported that their participation on the course enhanced their own skills, e.g. *"helps PhD students keep up to date with industry trends outside of their research area"*. Further empirical evidence supports that the content is useful to our PhD research students, with a number of doctoral students requesting to attend each year.

Our survey results and empirical evidence suggests our course benefits not only the students enrolled on the course, but also empowers our demonstrators, enhancing them as lifelong learners through continued skill development.

5.2 Lead Demonstrator

One *lead demonstrator* (also a graduate teaching assistant) each year is responsible for *a)* co-ordinating and administering demonstrator provision, *b)* liaising with the industry partner on developing the course materials, *c)* allocation and moderation of marking.

"The experience of acting as lead demonstrator on this module posed significant additional workload, but afforded me the opportunity to enhance my knowledge of industry-specific tools and provided me with improved technical skills.

"The module has exposed me to the tools and techniques required for curriculum development and provided me the opportunity to actively contribute to the development and enhancement of the assessment framework. Within the development of the assessment a further challenge arose, that of the individual student learning journey. As a consequence, additional fluidity was introduced into the marking scheme."

"This combined experience proved invaluable when applying for a lecturing position on completion of my PhD."

5.3 Course Leader

The course leader is responsible for delivering lectures, and for the coordination of course activities (e.g. deciding course content, methods of delivery, and assessment), and of ensuring that the course aim and objectives are met. Here the course leader speaks of the benefits of industry collaboration in relation to the delivery of the course, and the wider impact of this engagement on research supervision.

"Ongoing collaboration with Red Hat industry leaders in open-source middleware technologies, allows for the curriculum to be continually informed by the current needs of industry. This enables us as educators to energise teaching materials to reflect latest middleware technologies and development methodologies."

"This collaboration has further exposed me to current research challenges, enabling me to provide research supervision at Masters and PhD levels which exhibit greater industrial relevance and impact."

5.4 Industry

The involvement of industry is driven by two key objectives; seeding technologies, and talent acquisition. Within this section we consider these and include a reflection from the industry partner.

Seeding technologies: There has been a move in recent years towards the democratisation of decision making software development, driven by the increased popularity of open source and cloud technologies [10]. The increasing adoption of open source software has alleviated commercial software licensing costs, which were traditionally prohibitive to individuals. Similarly, the significant capital expenditure once associated with hardware purchasing has now been ameliorated by cloud computing. Consequently, software developer preference is gaining influence in organisations' technology procurement decisions.

Naturally, vendors now seek to target developers early in their career, exposing them to their technologies in the hope

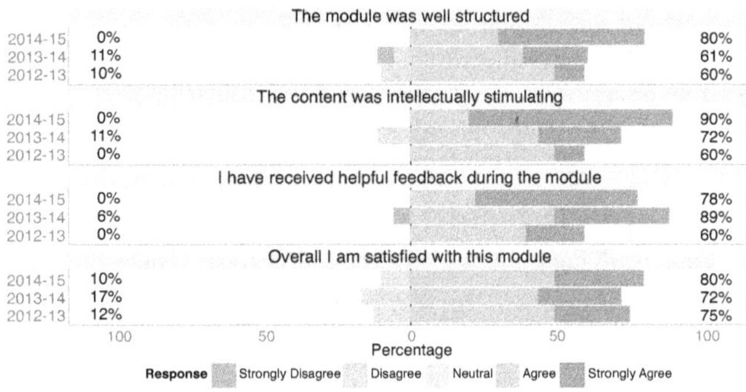

Figure 2: Student survey results

that they will go on to use these in their career. An effective mechanism which is increasingly appearing as part of many vendors' *'Developer Relations'* strategies is to target future developers during their studies through collaboration on curriculum design, incorporating vendor technologies.

The industry partner is highly motivated to provide a positive experience for the students in using their tools and software. This encourages their continued use of the product upon completion of the course.

Talent acquisition: Our industry partner has an established talent acquisition pipeline for our students. Students may apply for internships while carrying out their capstone project, working closely with industry over a period of four months. The course has led to a number of internships being offered to students, some leading to job offers. Internship and employment statistics are presented in Section 7.

Work experience has been shown to be highly beneficial for graduate employment [4], and students' contributions to open source projects throughout their internship further enhances their appeal [10].

Our industry partner expresses positive sentiments around the initiative; *"In my opinion an academic initiative like this has the potential to offer a good return on investment whilst also being very low risk."*

Overall Reflection: *"The opportunity to have an input into the design and delivery of the CS curriculum provides Red Hat with access to graduates with skills valued by industry. Given the increasing skills gap and disparity between the delivery of education and the needs of employers, this relationship is critical for providing a continued pipeline of students into industry, and the development of a suitable curriculum which benefits the students."*

6. STUDENT SATISFACTION

Here we consider student satisfaction evaluation, using formal University surveys and volunteered testimonials.

The results from a University-administered survey, on a five-point Likert scale, are presented in Figure 2. We began a major coursework refresh to include cloud technologies at the beginning of the 2013/14 academic year, so we consider feedback following the update to better ensure our results are comparable.

Our results suggest that our ongoing efforts to enhance the course have lead to students considering the course better structured and more intellectually stimulating than previous years. We also observe a significant increase in the number of students who *'Strongly Agree'* that they have received helpful feedback. Despite increasing complexity of the coursework assignment in recent years, we see increases in overall satisfaction with the course.

Furthermore, we supplement these survey results with volunteered testimonials from our alumni, which suggest that students value the course's real-world and collaborative elements.

"This gave us an idea how challenging it is to tackle actual real world problems."

"covers a lot of aspects that are neglected or not thought about when doing assignments from other programming modules."

"helped students to collaborate and share ideas which each other when stuck at a problem."

"These are the type of situations that industries face and that require soft skills to manage and make decisions appropriately."

A number of students who have since graduated and joined industry discuss the course's benefits when seeking employment; e.g.: *"I believe this experience was highly valuable especially during the job hunting period for a student as I could mention about concepts and technologies learnt doing this assignment which are valuable to the industry."*

This positive feedback reinforces the practices and tools we have put in place on the course, highlighting areas of strength to further enhance in future iterations of the course.

7. STUDENT OUTCOMES

Table 7 shows the results of an investigation into the employment status of graduates, that have undertaken the *Enterprise Middleware* course over the last five years. Results were obtained through; the University alumni association, personal contact, and professional website LinkedIn. We also show the number of Red Hat internship, job and PhD studentship offers made to students from each cohort.

We observe a significant increase in cohort size from 2011-12 onwards. This is a consequence of the course being offered on a new MSc programme. Furthermore, 2013-14 sees a larger intake of international students, a trend which has continued in current academic year 2014-15. All graduates we have made contact with report they are either in relevant employment or undertaking further study.

We see that Red Hat consistently offers between one and two paid internships to students each year, which may lead to future employment. There is further evidence of Red Hat valuing doctoral study, providing a number of partially- and fully-funded PhD studentships.

Overall response rates for cohorts range between 55-87.5%. The Higher Education Statistics Agency (HESA) Destinations of Leavers from Higher Education (DLHE) survey [3] seeks response rates of 75% for home students and 20% for international students, which we achieve for each cohort. Despite maintaining close contact with Home UK/EU students, with 77.8-100% response rate, we experienced lower response rates from our International graduates. Contributing factors to this are considered by [12].

We consider not only this snapshot of graduates' current employment status, but also explore the stability and quality of employment [17]. We further examine graduates' employment history, finding destinations to be stable and at an appropriate level (e.g. 'software developer', 'systems devel-

[3]https://www.hesa.ac.uk/stats-dlhe

Year	Program Enrollment			Survey Responses			Employed			Red Hat Offers		
	Total	Home	Int.	Total	Home	Int.	Industry	PhD	Other	Intern	Job	PhD
2013–14	27	7 (25.9%)	20 (74.1%)	16 (59.3%)	6 (85.7%)	10 (50%)	10	5	1	2	2	0
2012–13	14	7 (50%)	7 (50%)	9 (64.3%)	6 (85.7%)	3 (42.9%)	7	2	–	2	1	1
2011–12	20	9 (45%)	11 (55%)	11 (55%)	7 (77.8%)	4 (36.4%)	8	3	–	1	1	0
2010–11	7	3 (42.9%)	4 (57.1%)	5 (71.4%)	3 (100%)	2 (50%)	5	0	–	1	2	2
2009–10	8	5 (62.5%)	3 (37.5%)	7 (87.5%)	5 (100%)	2 (66.7%)	7	0	–	1	1	0

Table 1: Employment statistics for graduates over the last five years, including Red Hat job offer statistics.

oper'). When considering students from earlier cohorts, we see clear pathways to career progression, with many graduates entering senior and managerial roles.

Further work is required to conduct a longitudinal study to capture graduate career progression, alongside qualitative feedback on the impact of the course. In light of our ongoing interest in ensuring the applicability of our course to global job markets, particular attention will be given to maintaining better contact with international students.

8. OPEN SOURCE COURSEWARE

Based on the successes seen within Newcastle University, we have made the course materials available open source on GitHub[4], for delivery at other institutions. These materials include a detailed tutorial introducing the tools used in the coursework and their configuration, and a detailed coursework specification. Model solutions and sample mark schemes are also available, stored in a private repository limiting access to instructors only.

This delivery of coursework materials also represents industry best practices for software documentation, written in AsciiDoc and made available through version control.

Delivering the content externally is mutually beneficial. From an academic perspective, the delivery of the course in other institutions leads to further scrutiny and accepted enhancements to the coursework materials will benefit the delivery of the course in subsequent years.

Furthermore, close cooperation between academia and industry for the production of courseware naturally requires significant time, effort, and resources. Thus, providing our materials for use externally is of huge benefit to institutions that may not have sufficient access to such resources.

Our industry partner comments; *"I see providing general material to multiple universities as a great way to scale the program, reaching a much greater number of students with only a slight increase in resources."*

Our open source course content was first delivered remotely in a trial at Durham University, UK in the 2014-15 academic year to a cohort of 30 students. We now seek to engage with other institutions and industry to highlight the issues around delivering an open courseware with external institutions, by means of a cross-site study.

9. REFERENCES

[1] *Red Hat Inc. (Homepage).* http://redhat.com/.

[2] M. Ben-Ari. Constructivism in computer science education. *JCMST*, 20(1):45–73, 2001.

[3] D. P. K. Chandran, Y. K. Sow, M. Harizan, C. C. Kooi, T. T. Hoy, and C. K. Foong. Success Story Of Collaboration Between Intel And Malaysian Universities To Establish And Enhance Teaching And Research In Electronic Packaging. In *IEEE IEMT*, 2010.

[4] L. Harvey. Embedding and integrating employability. *New Directions for Institutional Research*, 2005(128):13–28, 2005.

[5] M. J. Hawthorne and D. E. Perry. Software engineering education in the era of outsourcing, distributed development, and open source software: challenges and opportunities. In *Software Engineering Education in the Modern Age*, pages 166–185. 2006.

[6] C. K. Hobbs and H. H. Tsang. Industry in the Classroom: Equipping Students with Real-World Experience A reflection on the effects of industry partnered projects on computing education. In *ACM WCCCE '14*, 2014.

[7] P. G. Larsen, J. M. Fernandes, J. Habel, H. Lehrskov, R. J. Vos, O. Wallington, and J. Zidek. A multidisciplinary engineering summer school in an industrial setting. *EJEE*, 34(6):511–526, 2009.

[8] T. C. Lethbridge. A survey of the relevance of computer science and software engineering education. In *IEEE CSEED '98*, 1998.

[9] D. Nicol. From monologue to dialogue: improving written feedback processes in mass higher education. *Assessment & Evaluation in Higher Education*, 35(5):501–517, 2010.

[10] S. O'Grady. *The New Kingmakers.* O'Reilly Inc., 2013.

[11] S. Palkar. Industry-academia collaboration, expectations, and experiences. *ACM Inroads*, 4(4):56–58, December 2013.

[12] S. R. Porter and P. D. Umbach. Student survey response rates across institutions: Why do they vary? *Research in Higher education*, 47(2):229–247, 2006.

[13] P. Race. *A briefing on self, peer & group assessment*, volume 9. LTSN, 2001.

[14] A. Radermacher and G. Walia. Gaps between industry expectations and the abilities of graduates. In *SIGCSE '13*, pages 525–530. ACM, 2013.

[15] A. Rusu, R. Docimo, C. Santiago, and M. Paglione. Academia-academia-industry collaborations on software engineering projects using local-remote teams. In *SIGCSE '09*, pages 301–305. ACM, 2009.

[16] J. Tenenberg. Industry fellows: bringing professional practice into the classroom. In *ACM SIGCSE*, 2010.

[17] A. Tymon. The student perspective on employability. *Studies in higher education*, 38(6):841–856, 2013.

[18] G. Ushaw, W. Blewitt, and G. Morgan. Adopting commercially inspired practices within an academic teaching course: A case study of a computer games engineering degree. In *CSEDU '14*, 2014.

[4]http://EnterpriseMiddlewareCoursework.github.io/

Agile Software Development Study Away

Maureen Doyle
Department of Computer Science
Northern Kentucky University
Highland Heights, KY 41099
+1 859-572-5468
doylem3@nku.edu

Candace Gibson,
Michelle Melish
Office of Education Abroad
Northern Kentucky University
Highland Heights, KY 41099
+1 859-572-6908
gibsonc3@nku.edu
melishm1@nku.edu

Rees Storm
College of Informatics
Northern Kentucky University
Highland Heights, KY 41099
+1 859-572-7593
storm@nku.edu

ABSTRACT
We describe and report on a study away course held in the spring of 2015 that brought computer science students from a Midwestern university to visit companies in the Bay Area in California as part of their study of agile software development. While it may be a sufficient goal to offer study away as an encouragement for future participation in study abroad programs, study away has benefits in and of itself. In actuality, study away can build students' self-confidence, aid them in being accepting of different ideas, and help them to understand a different area of the world. The class was offered as a 1-credit computer science course and students met weekly leading up to the trip, then once again after. The class included a one-week visit to the San Francisco area, with visits to two universities and five high-tech companies. Eight undergraduates and one post-baccalaureate participated at a cost of $1700 each. Students were required to submit a five-page paper and were separated into two teams to develop and present posters at the university's student research symposium. The course was a success due to the investment of the Chief Information Officer of the university, the Office of Education Abroad, the department of Computer Science, and academic advising. Students reported upon immediate return—then once again three months later—that their interest in computer science had increased, that they had gained an understanding of a different region of the United States and that they were more accepting of different ideas.

General Terms
Management, Documentation.

Keywords
Software Engineering, Experiential Learning, Study Away, Agile Software Development, Scrum.

1. INTRODUCTION
Northern Kentucky University (NKU) is one of six regional universities in Kentucky and enrolls around 12000 undergraduates. The university is in the greater Cincinnati region and is largely a commuter college, with more than 80% of the students coming from a 50-mile radius. In 2014, more than 53% of the first-time full-time students were first-generation college students. Most of the students who graduate from one of the undergraduate programs in computer science and computer information technology go directly to industry. The Computer Information Technology (CIT) degree and Computer Science (CS) degree program are the first and fifth top enrolled degrees at the university for the fall 2015 semester and, while there is a high demand for our graduates in our area, we wanted to expose our students to another region and build their career confidence.

SIGCSE '16, March 02 - 05, 2016, Memphis, TN, USA

ACM 978-1-4503-3685-7/16/03…$15.00
DOI: http://dx.doi.org/10.1145/2839509.2844571

One of the goals for student success in Northern Kentucky University's five-year strategic plan is to expand international educational experiences. The university understands the importance of preparing its students to work in a global environment. At the time this paper was being written, the world was awaiting the results of Greece's referendum regarding the bailout proposal from the International Monetary Fund. Such a decision doesn't affect just Greece or Europe but the entire world. We are now living in a society that is globally interdependent and companies now seek employees who can operate effectively abroad as well as in the U.S. Study abroad programs can help give students the skills needed to function in this global market including intercultural understanding, leadership, confidence, and an understanding of diversity[3].

Study abroad is not new to the university; Northern Kentucky University has had an Office of Education Abroad (OEA) for over 25 years. The office is a member of several nationwide organizations for study abroad including *NAFSA: Association of International Educators (NAFSA)* and the *Forum on Education Abroad.* Not all students are ready to take such a leap into the unknown and out of their comfort zone. Only about 3% of our students participate in our study abroad programs. Many of our students have families, full time jobs, and/or are the first generation in their family to go to a university. Therefore, simply leaving the region can seem daunting. This past year the office, based on successes at other universities, began offering domestic programs within the United States [8], since many of the benefits from study abroad have been realized in these programs. We use the term "Study Away" to refer to the programs which have travel to a United States destination integrated into the course. Study away courses introduce our students to the outside world without leaving behind all the comforts of home. The first domestic program was taught in the spring of 2015 and was titled: Agile in Theory and Practice.

Computer science students were targeted intentionally for this program. From 2009 to 2014 less than 1% of NKU students who studied abroad were majoring in Computer Science, despite it being one of the top five degrees within the university. This issue of few CS students studying abroad exists throughout the United

States. While a 2005 ITiCSE working group argued in favor of an international component for the computer science degree [5]; according to the Institute of International education, of the 10% of students who were Mathematics or Computer Sciences majors in 2011-2012, they were only 2% of all study abroad students. Because of the high number of CS students at NKU and low participation in Study Abroad, NKU's OEA hoped to engage more students in study away programs.

In this paper we present this computer science study away course that integrates travel into the course. We propose that a faculty member, as one course of their normal course load, could easily teach this course. Faculty effort was spent on course development, delivery, grading, advising content to companies, and serving as one of two group leaders on the trip. The faculty hours were not excessive, and although more than this is typical for a one-credit course, it was significantly less than a traditional three-credit course.

2. RELATED WORK

The benefits and need of study abroad programs for students is well documented [3][5], however many students do not take advantage of the offerings. NKU has relationships with foreign universities, including an exchange program with the computer science department at Babeş-Bolyai University in Romania, where our students studying in Romania have the benefit of their classes being taught in English. The university subsidizes students' travel so that they are not charged more for studying abroad than they would for a semester at home. That said, only one computer science student has chosen to do a semester abroad in Romania since 2009. NKU is sending it second CS student to study at Babeş-Bolyai University in spring 2016.

This class, Agile in Theory and Practice, is similar to other study abroad and study away programs in that a trip could not easily be added to pre-existing curriculum. Instead, a course was created for students to study agile development with minimal prerequisites. We did this primarily as a way to expand the number of interested students.

There are publications defining and sharing about study abroad programs for computer science majors [4][5]. Baylor University's program[4] is a Summer study abroad program where students take two Baylor courses in the Netherlands. Similar to our program, the classes were tailored for the study away program and therefore students had classes with students who were only from their home university. The two programs offer students different experiences since Baylor's program follows a traditional study abroad program for its classes taught in the Netherlands. Our program was shorter (one week versus 41 days), cost much less ($1700 versus their $6,400 fee in 2004) and was taught by a professor from the home institution. The ITiCSE working group paper proposes study abroad for all CS students to gain international experience and knowledge, and does not address issues related to different localities in the United States.

3. Agile Study Away

This course was the culmination of work by the NKU OEA, Computer Science Faculty and the College of Informatics (COI) Advising Center. Our university's Chief Information Officer (CIO) also provided critical support by engaging his network in Silicon Valley, who welcomed us with grace and enthusiasm. Students were recruited through faculty referrals, advising and student word-of-mouth. The pre-requisites to enroll in the course were sophomore level standing or permission of the instructor. All technology majors were encouraged to participate; in fact, CS, CIT, and Media Informatics majors and one alumnus with degrees in Physics and Mathematics signed up for the experience. We had 9 participants - all male - and two facilitators – a CS Faculty and a COI Advisor.

3.1 Design

The design of the course and study away experience encompassed a twofold intent and was based on a learner-centered model:

3.1.1 Introduction and exploration of the concept and controversy of Agile Software Development

Agile Software Development (ASD) is trendy and often misunderstood. It is a project management methodology specifically intended for software development and it was designed with best practices and high philosophical ideals in mind. However, *how often is ASD implemented in the tech industry? Is ASD in compliment to or in conflict with business needs? What do working software developers perceive as the cost and benefits of working in an ASD framework? In sum, how is the theory applied in the real world?* The class was designed to explore these questions through readings and discussions, and then through informational interviews on site at several firms in the Silicon Valley.

3.1.2 Immersion in the San Francisco Bay Area and its tech and cultural offerings through the context of exploring the practice of agile development

During the week of the university's spring break, the class stayed the week in San Francisco at a youth hostel in the Tenderloin District – an intensely urban and vibrant location. Central location public transportation cards (provided by the program) allowed the students to explore the city and its offerings during their free time. Meanwhile, the formal itinerary was packed with 6 full days of site visits and cultural visits. One full free day was also provided. Examples of site visits include, Workday, SAP, Adobe and Cisco. Examples of cultural sites we visited as a group include Alcatraz, North Beach, and Pier 39. In addition, we conducted a self-guided walking tour of Stanford University and we attended presentations of graduate-level data science students at University of California, San Francisco (UCSF). With only a couple of exceptions when logistics demanded a rented bus, we used public transportation extensively – cable car, bus, subway, and train – to give students an immersion into urban life. We were often 'commuting' during peak hours with San Franciscans during their flow to and from work. We were treated to an in-depth look at each site we visited and were also able to either participate in an interactive activity or conduct interviews around the topic of ASD. At one site, we were allowed to observe a "daily scrum" in action. A daily scrum is a central component of the ASD methodology and, according to best practice, small development teams should meet daily to go over their progress on a particular task, called a 'story.'

3.2 Activities

3.2.1 Reading and discussion of Agile Software Development Theory and Best Practices

Students had the assigned text *"Agile!: The Good, the Hype and the Ugly"* by Bertrand Meyer, Springer, 2014, ISBN-10 3319051547. Students had six weekly reading assignments of 2-3 chapters from Meyer's text and met weekly to discuss the readings. The readings and discussions gave the students the historical context to think critically about ASD in advance of the study away experience. Students were responsible for reading the last chapter of the text prior to the trip; the final chapter and final interview preparation was discussed while on the trip.

3.2.2 *Interviews and Travel Preparation*

Several weekly meetings were built in to the semester schedule to cover interview preparation and travel preparation. The SOA presented on travel and safety tips and were given an overview of tourist sites in the Bay Areas well before the experience to help the students plan their free time activities. For the interview preparation, a Journalism faculty member volunteered her time to share professional interview techniques and then she returned to critique the proposed interview questions.

3.2.3 *Site Visits*

As mentioned, site visits were an integral part of the experience. We enjoyed unprecedented access due to the connections made for us by our CIO. Four companies - Workday, SAP, Adobe and Cisco – greeted us, fed us, and allowed us unexpected opportunities to understand their companies mission and culture. At Cisco, we were treated to their gallery of emerging technology. At SAP, we participated in a Design Thinking Workshop. At Adobe, we heard from developers who were responsible for introducing ASD to their team about how they had evolved the process to work within their division's needs. And at Workday, we observed a scrum in action and learned how they are used to revolutionize cloud based enterprise software. We had the added treat at Workday of connecting with an NKU alumnus charged with maintaining a public service app that he had developed while a student.

Figure 1. Study Away Group at Adobe

We also spent a few hours visiting a Bay Area high-tech company campus and conducted a self-guided walking tour of Stanford University. Lastly, we sat in on group presentations of graduate level data science students at UCSF and our students got to see recruiting in action as many tech company reps were also in the audience.

3.2.4 *Professional Development*

The course included a focus on how to communicate professionally both visually and verbally. We required casual professional dress and professional conduct. Students were not allowed to use their phones during meetings, however laptop-use was acceptable for taking notes. The faculty and advisor modelled appropriate behavior by fully participating in the meetings, although the students primarily asked the questions and engaged in conversation. When circumstances allowed, we encouraged them to engage one-on-one with the developers we were meeting. For most, this was their first chance to see inside both well-established and up-and-coming global tech companies.

3.2.5 *Cultural Immersion*

While in San Francisco, we stayed in a youth hostel downtown in the Tenderloin district. The location and proximity to public transportation was the perfect launching off point to explore the city and its highlights. The hostel itself was bustling with travelers and college-age students using it as a temporary residence while conducting interviews and participating in internships. Other residents were from all over the world and, with many scheduled social activities, there was ample opportunity for interaction. Two group dinners were included on the itinerary and helped us explore the fishing piers and North Beach neighborhoods. We also had arranged a trip to Alcatraz that afforded us a great view of the Bay and the San Francisco skyline. An international art exhibit at Alcatraz gave us a chance to broaden our horizons while learning some of the controversial history of the area.

3.3 Student Assessment

Student feedback—via surveys and faculty evaluations, along with student learning through final papers and projects—indicates that the class was successful. In total, eight undergraduates and one post-baccalaureate enrolled in the class. Of the eight undergraduates, one student was a freshman, two were sophomores, three were juniors, and two were seniors. The post-baccalaureate did not take the course for credit and therefore did not participate in assessment.

3.3.1 *Evaluation*

Students were asked to complete three assessments of the course and trip.

3.3.1.1 *Trip Surveys*

Two trip surveys were developed to evaluate the success of the study away experience, the students' interest in computer science and their interest in participating in future learning experiences either away or abroad. Students were given a paper survey at the airport on the return trip and an online survey three months after their return. The paper surveys were given out and collected by the COI Advisor. Students were not required to provide their name; however anonymity was not guaranteed. The survey given three months later was anonymous and online in order to determine if students' enthusiasm for the experience persisted, but also to counter any concern of bias on the paper surveys.

All eight undergraduates completed the paper survey. Students were asked to take the three-month survey via email. Six of the eight (75%) students completed the voluntary three-month survey. Students answered from 1 to 5 given a set of statements, with 1 being Strongly Agree and 5 being Strongly Disagree. Table 1 documents the results for both surveys.

Table 1. Survey Responses

Survey Questions	Return n=8		3 months n=6	
	Mean	SD	Mean	SD
My ability to adapt to new and uncertain situations has increased.	2	0.75	1.50	0.54
I have grown self-confident.	1.75	0.88	1.83	0.75

I am more accepting of different ideas.	1.63	0.74	2.0	0.89
I have gained an understanding of a different region of the United States.	1.13	0.35	1.17	0.40
My interest in computer science has increased.	1.38	0.74	1.0	0

A simple t-test on the different questions showed no significant difference between the mean of the answers.

Since one objective is to break down barriers to traveling and considering different employers, this trip empowered students to consider the Bay Area as a possible job location. Student comments about San Francisco ranged from "...it actually helped me realize I probably do not want to live out west," and "There was some culture shock when we passed through the poor part of the city," to "I loved city life. Especially using public transportation. I met and talked to many interesting people in the street."

Student comments about the course were at least fairly positive, an example being "...I learned a good amount." Others showed more enthusiasm, such as "I was really unsure what to expect going in. My advisor suggested it...It was an incredible experience, to be able to see inside these successful companies and understand how they develop software."

3.3.1.2 Course and Faculty Evaluations

The course and faculty evaluation survey was available for the last two weeks of the semester. Six of the eight students logged onto the evaluation system. Students who log onto the evaluation system can opt out of doing the survey or complete the survey. Regardless, they receive their course grades as soon as the grades are available. Students who do not log onto the evaluation system are required to wait an additional two weeks to receive their final grades.

Four of the six students who logged onto the evaluation system completed the survey for a total response rate of 50%. Students reported spending 0-3 hours per week on course readings, but some commented that they still fell behind. Two of the four students commented that this was the most exciting class of their career and that they learned the most in this class.

The faculty evaluations were very positive, and students only expressed enthusiasm for the course and support for the faculty member.

3.3.2 Student Learning Assessment

A month after our return the students participated in the annual research poster symposium, which is held on campus each spring. Each team prepared posters around a specific theme of the experience and were on-hand to discuss their learning at the event. In addition students were required to submit a five-page paper discussing Agile Development.

Students were assessed based on a final report and a team poster presentation. Students were divided into two teams for the poster presentation. The first team is shown in Figure 2 at the spring celebration of student research.

Figure 2. Students presenting Agile Methods Poster

Their poster presented their findings on how agile methods, and scrum in particular, is being used in different businesses in the Bay Area. The other team created and showed a poster detailing the entire trip. The latter poster will be used in future study abroad and study away recruitment activities.

Students were also required to write a five-page paper. The assignment was: "Define agile development and compare agile to scrum, as defined in Meyer's text. In addition, please discuss the similarities and differences between scrum in theory and in practice. Please include specific examples from your visits to support any claims. Conclusion should include your opinion about scrum and its practice."

The submitted papers ranged from fairly well written to excellent in quality, as well as quite wrong about agile to correctly argued analysis in content. In particular, two of the students seemed to believe scrum was a synonym for agile which led them to defend a company that was meeting scrum guidelines but missing key principles from the Agile Manifesto. This confusion seems to be grounded in the lack of assessment for the text readings and hopefully will be corrected in future offerings.

3.4 Project Strengths

The project strengths fell into two main areas, the trip, including its logistics, and the course itself.

3.4.1 Logistics

The OEA managed and coordinated the logistics for transportation, lodging and meals. In addition, they took care of setting and collecting all student fees for the project. The Office also provided additional funds and student and faculty training about group travel.

3.4.1.1 Before the Trip

As stated earlier, the OEA planned the trip. A notable strength was that planning was done with regular input from the faculty member and the advisor. Both the faculty member and advisor had lived in the Bay Area and provided tips and ideas for the lodging, transportation and activities.

Arranging to schedule meetings with the companies seemed impossible when we first considered the trip. We were fortunate to be able to reach out to others in our university who have contacts with high tech businesses. Our university, like most, purchases a lot of software and hardware through the CIO, and our CIO offered and then followed up by reaching out to a number of companies he has relationships with and coordinated our visits to SAP, CISCO and Adobe. We also involved a center on campus that works with various companies as a collaborator. The center director, who also happens to be the CIO, contacted Workday, Inc. and coordinated and scheduled the visit with them.

We cannot overstate how valuable working with the CIO was for arranging visits to the high tech companies. We did visit one other company, who will not be named, that was not coordinated through him. The faculty member and a student coordinated the visit through the company's college recruiters. We were escorted by two non-technical college recruiters and given a typical tourist tour. Our visit was two hours and consisted of some photo opportunities, lunch and a trip to their gift shop. This was a great trip for a high school or for vacation, but it was not an experiential learning opportunity since it did not help our students learn anything about agile software development. We will not include visits like this in future trips.

Another strength was partnering up with an experienced study abroad advisor. The COI advisor on this trip is the head of advising for our college and has led multiple trips to Mexico. She managed all discipline with the students and the logistics while traveling. An ancillary benefit of this experience was our advisor participated in all activities and came away with a deeper understanding of software engineering and agile software development.

3.4.1.2 While traveling

All attendees enjoyed staying at the hostel. It was centrally located in San Francisco. There were four students to a small room, while the advisor and faculty member had a private room with an en suite. The hostel had many activities to encourage mingling and meeting other people.

We also utilized a free smart phone app to keep in touch with all students. We wanted students to have access to us 24x7, but did not want to give out our cell phone numbers. We looked at free burner numbers but they had too short a life. We used Life 360[7] to stay connected. Life 360 has both an Android and iPhone app. It allows a user to sign up and be able to text and contact others in a group without sharing personal information. When the app was on we could see where everyone was and send and receive texts. One student who did not have a smart phone was paired up with one who did and they had to travel together.

3.4.2 Course

The course, Studying Agile in Theory and Practice, is not a standard computer science course but is ideal for a study away class. The selected text, "Agile! The Good, the Hype and the Ugly" by Bertrand Myer text[8] was a strength. The text is short, easily readable yet includes a thorough review of agile principles, groups them so they are more easily understood and then presents different agile models, with enough information on scrum so that students were prepared for company visits. Serendipitously, there were two ACM webinars by Myer during the semester on this topic and are recommended for this course[9].

The ability of studying agile in practice could not have occurred without company visits. This project was successful due to the commitment of the companies we visited to share their experiences and time with us.

Another strength was the inclusion of the journalism professor. The interviewing module took two class sessions, however we recommend including this to anyone wanting to replicate the class. The students and faculty were well prepared for the sessions with the company; The students asked intelligent and meaningful questions and they were also able to ask questions that arose during the discussion, providing them with a deeper learning experience.

3.5 Lessons Learned

3.5.1 Before the Trip

We believe we could have done a better job letting students know about this trip and why it would be useful to them. Advisors advertised the trip, and it was shared in the study abroad fairs as well as on the web and via email. We do not believe that this was enough because students came up afterwards telling us they had not heard about it. Similarly, one of the students who decided to go had mentioned in his survey that "the interviews seemed cut-and-dry. It was the best surprise that it was so much more than that. .. You can ask real people from your favorite companies the questions you've only wished you could and actually learn." In the future we will visit classes directly to encourage students to sign up for the trip.

In addition, we were disappointed that no females registered for the trip. We reached out to any who had expressed interest in the trip, however the cost was prohibitive at $1700. This was not unique to females and was shared by many males who expressed interest but did not participate. We hope to be able to offer financial scholarships to students to help defray the cost in future course offerings.

This was the first study away class, and we hope to study if students decide to participate in additional study away or study abroad experiences, and we will develop reliable and validated instruments for a longitudinal study.

3.5.2 While traveling

Communication with the tech companies could have been managed better. The trip coordination and contacts were with the CIO, and three of the companies expected him to be there. All handled his absence graciously. We will be clearer in future offerings; however, we recognize that their hospitality may diminish without bringing the executive who makes the purchasing decisions with us. We also had issues communicating with the companies during the trip. We had scheduled visits almost daily, but businesses wanted to confirm everything the day before our arrival at their company. We could not talk with them until the evening because we were at a different company causing some stress on both sides. In future trips, OEA has agreed to handle the last minute logistic phone calls for us.

One other lesson learned that we considered important is overbooking. We arrived on Saturday, students had Sunday on their own, and then were scheduled daily for most of the week. In discussions and in survey responses, students asked for at least one afternoon and evening off midweek. They felt that there was just too much going on and we concur.

Finally, we would adjust our schedule to go on an officially guided tour of Stanford. The tour times did not fit easily into our schedule, so we tried to do the tour ourselves since we had alums on the trip. We got lost a few times and only managed to save the tour thanks to the help of online resources and a Stanford undergraduate (an acquaintance of one of the students on the trip) who joined us part way through.

3.5.3 Course

The next offering of this class will be for three credits instead of one credit to include more background material on software development and more assessment. Our institution has a senior-level Software Engineering course and, to avoid duplication of material, we only briefly went over the history of software development methodologies. As evidenced by the students' final papers, this was a mistake. We will keep the necessary background to fewer than three weeks. This course would work well at institutions that teach Software Engineering at the freshmen or sophomore level.

The lack of assessment during the semester was a lesson learned. The class was held like a seminar and we discussed the readings in class. Unfortunately, it was hard to tell who had read the material and who had not, versus who was confused about the readings. In the future, quizzes will be added throughout the course to ensure that students understand the readings, instead of waiting to do so until the final paper when it is too late.

3.6 Conclusions and Future Work

The first study away for computer science students was a success by most measures including faculty and staff satisfaction, student satisfaction and student feedback. Staff from OEA and the COI advisor met with the other computer science faculty to encourage them to consider organizing a similar class, enabling students to visit a different geographic region each year. There were a number of ideas, but no faculty member agreed to offer a class for this academic year. Faculty expressed concerns about how to tie a visit to another location so that it is relevant for the class they are teaching. There have been proposals for security courses tied with international travel, as well as travel to internationally known computer museums. In the future we will set up a repository for study abroad and study away courses in computer science to be shared among the community.

The faculty member who offered the class in 2014-2015 will offer an updated version in 2016-2017 and is considering visiting the East Coast instead of the San Francisco. Students will vote on location in the fall semester. Future offerings will include a software engineering text like Rod Stephens, *Beginning Software Engineering*, published by Wrox in 2015.

Future work will also include keeping track of any additional study away and study abroad travel for students who participated in this trip. We will also use, develop or implement reliable and valid evaluation instruments to measure the effectiveness of the programs as well as improved assessments demonstrating students meeting learning objectives[2].

4. ACKNOWLEDGMENTS

Thanks first to the Office of Education Abroad and Tim Ferguson, CIO of Northern Kentucky University and Director of the Center of Applied Informatics. We thank the Office of Education Abroad for suggesting, encouraging, subsidizing and organizing this trip. The visits to the companies were set up and coordinated by Tim Ferguson and without his huge efforts this trip would not have been such a success.

The department of Computer Science, COI Dean's Office and the COI Advising Center promoted and supported this project.

We thank journalist faculty member, Michele Day, for working with our students to prepare them for interviews at the different companies. We also thank Dr. David Uminsky and University of San Francisco's Data Science program for such a warm welcome and inclusion in the Data Science colloquium.

All that is grammatically correct in this paper is a credit to Liz Gauck, and errors indicate when the authors did not heed her advice. Thank you, Liz, for helping to improve the quality of this work.

The success of this trip rests on the shoulders of the four companies who opened their doors and welcomed us to spend time with them. A special thanks to Michael Joseph Parks and CISCO, Scott Jones and SAP, Charlie Boyle and the staff from Workday and Keith Spencer and Rob Sargent from Adobe.

5. REFERENCES

[1] Belyavina, R., Li, J., and Bhandari R., *New Frontiers: U.S. Students Pursuing Degrees Abroad, a 2-year analysis of key destinations and fields of study*, Institute of International Education, May 2013.

[2] Durrant, M. B. and Dorius, C. R. Study Abroad Survey Instruments: A Comparison of Survey Types and Experiences. *Journal of Studies in International Education*, 11, 1 2007), 33-53.

[3] Engberg, M. E. The Influence of Study Away Experiences on Global Perspective-Taking. *Journal of College Student Development*, 54, 5 2013), 466-480.

[4] Fry, C. C. 2004. The Development of a Summer Study Abroad Program for Engineering and Computer Science Students at Baylor University, In *Proceedings of the 34th Annual Frontiers in Education,* (Savannah, Georgia, Oct 20-23) 2004. DOI= 10.1109/FIE.2004.1408525

[5] Fuller, U., Amillo, J., Laxer, C., McCracken, W. M. and Mertz, J. Facilitating student learning through study abroad and international projects. *SIGCSE Bull.*, 37, 4 2005), 139-151.

[6] Leggett, K. Encouraging STEM Students to Study Abroad. *International Educator (1059-4221)*, 20, 4 2011), 44-47.

[7] Life 360 [mobile computer software], (2015, August 26) Retrieved from http://www.life360.com.

[8] Myers, B., *Agile Methods: The Good, the Hype and the Ugly*, Springer, Switzerland , 2014.

[9] ACM Webinars, Retrieved August 28, 2015, Meyers, B., http://learning.acm.org/webinar/

[10] Sobania, N. and Braskamp, L. A. Study Abroad or Study Away: It's Not Merely Semantics. *Peer Review*, 11, 4 (Fall2009 2009), 23-26.

Computer History on the Move

Graham Farr, Barbara Ainsworth, Chris Avram and Judy Sheard
Monash Museum of Computing History, Faculty of I.T., Monash University,
900 Dandenong Road, Caulfield East, Victoria 3145,
Australia
+61 3 9905 4000
{Graham.Farr, Barbara.Ainsworth, Chris.Avram, Judy.Sheard}@monash.edu

ABSTRACT

Computer history tours are a new way to educate people about our discipline and its history. We describe the introduction of such tours and their use in curriculum enrichment, outreach, and academic community-building. These tours give historical and social context to the development of topics in the curriculum, and demonstrate to students the universality of some of the principles they learn. The city of Melbourne, Australia, serves as an illustration, but computer history tours can be run in many cities of various sizes, and we give advice on how to do this.

Keywords

Computer Science education; outreach; computer history; computer museum; computer tour.

1. INTRODUCTION

As a transformative discipline, information and communications technology (ICT) looks much more to the future than the past. But the field is now old enough that its past has much to teach about the evolution of technology and its relationship with society. ICT history shows the stages that led to its present, and gives clues about how it may yet develop.

Interest in the history of the field has increased markedly in recent years. It wasn't so long ago that most of the pioneers were still alive. As that first generation passes, the next generation becomes more conscious of the value of their heritage and the need to preserve it. Computer history collections have been developed in museums around the world (such as the Science Museum in London and Deutsches Museum in Munich), and whole museums devoted to computer history have been founded in several places. Physical computer history museums include: the Computer History Museum [7,27,40] in California; Heinz Nixdorf MuseumsForum [20,33] in Paderborn, Germany; The National Museum of Computing (TNMoC) [36] in the UK, and its neighbour, Bletchley Park [4]; the Nexon Computer Museum [31] in Jeju, Korea; and the Monash Museum of Computing History [28] in Melbourne, Australia. There are also virtual museums, such as the Virtual Museum of Computing [39] and the Information Processing Society of Japan (IPSJ) Computer Museum [22]. Through these endeavours, many important historical artefacts have been restored and displayed. Anniversaries of pioneers are celebrated, most notably with Alan Turing Year 2012 [8]. Conferences have been devoted to the field [9,35].

SIGCSE '16, March 02-05, 2016, Memphis, TN, USA
ACM 978-1-4503-3685-7/16/03.
http://dx.doi.org/10.1145/2839509.2844575

The study of the history of computing is included in some university IT programs either as a separate course or woven into the curriculum of various courses [30]. For example, Draper et al. [11] describe a curriculum in which the history of computing is presented to students using technology as a framework, whereas Papadimitriou [32] proposes using a historical context to add interest to technical subjects. Impagliazzo & Lee [21] and Zhang & Howland [41] provide many reasons for studying the history of computing but also highlight the lack of resources for teaching this topic.

In this article we introduce a new way of presenting ICT history: *computer history tours*. In such a tour, people visit a series of sites related to the history of computing. The tour provides a framework for education on individual topics, with specific reference to experiences in the tour location (in our case, Melbourne) providing a context for presenting the overall development of the field. The tours serve several purposes: raising the profile of our discipline and awareness of its history; communicating the historical context of changes in technology and the computer industry; supplementing undergraduate education by illustrating and reinforcing concepts; using historical computers to show undergraduate students the universality of some of the principles they learn; providing enrichment opportunities for students; and academic and professional community-building. Other benefits include enhancing the international student experience, by providing a day of sightseeing that ties in with their education, and making contact with industry veterans who are able to provide new historical information.

Our tours attract a variety of participants including students, university staff, alumni, computer industry employees or veterans, computer hobbyists, and ordinary citizens looking for an unusual day out. We use a mix of walking and public transport. Among the places we visit are museums, sites (past and present) of notable companies and projects, and a cathedral. Artefacts studied include early calculators, an early commercial transistor-based computer, and the oldest surviving complete computer in the world. On the way, we see many historic buildings and enjoy breaks at cafés. Participants are encouraged to ask questions throughout the tour and this leads to many varied interesting technical and historical discussions.

Different kinds of computer history tours have been run in other places. Computer history museums typically offer tours of their collections. Some companies offer guided tours by vehicle of sites in Silicon Valley [1,3]. Alan Turing Birthday Walks have been held annually in Manchester since 2009 [17].

We conjecture that our tour is unique in that it is the first computer history tour anywhere that satisfies any one of the following: (a) takes place outside Silicon Valley; (b) is a free organised group tour; or (c) uses walking and public transport only. Our tour is not an event- or person-specific activity but rather makes an attempt to show the evolution of computing in different fields including academic, commercial and technical innovations. The tour covers many locations and differs from tours of one specific site such as a museum. The tour has evolved in response to our experiences and feedback from participants.

We also conjecture that computer history tours of this type could be run in many other places, and give advice on how to do this, with some potential examples.

2. HISTORY OF THE TOUR

The initial inspiration for our tours was a Mathematics Tour of Melbourne devised by Jill Vincent [38], which focuses on geometry in architecture and is aimed at secondary school mathematics students. Our tour differs in its subject matter and historical focus.

Our first Computer History Tour took place on 16 August 2008. It had 21 participants and took 6½ hours. Since then, we have conducted an average of just over two tours each year, making eighteen to date. The tour takes most of a day and covers many sites with connections to the earliest days of computing [12]. Each typically involves a group of 20-30 people travelling through inner Melbourne by a mix of walking and tram travel, stopping at about eight sites, sometimes for five minutes, sometimes for an hour. The tour is bookended by two museums: the Monash Museum of Computing History [28], and Melbourne Museum, the home of CSIRAC [25,29], the oldest surviving complete computer in the world. (Melbourne Museum is part of Museum Victoria.) The tour on 1 December 2012 was part of the Alan Turing Year programme of events and dedicated to Turing's memory.

Within our university, the tour is promoted by our usual electronic channels to students and staff. Externally, in Melbourne, the tour has become known by media coverage, some public presentations, and word-of-mouth. In May 2009, just before our third and fourth tours, we were contacted by *The Age* newspaper in Melbourne. The resulting article [14] generated great public interest and a long waiting list of people for future tours. Other media coverage [6,13,37] has added to the profile of the tours.

3. DESCRIPTION OF TOUR

Our tour begins at the Monash Museum of Computing History and ends at sites related to CSIRAC. Our website contains a guide to the tour schedule and background notes on the sites and points of discussion. The group is led by a team from the Faculty of IT, Monash University. Members of the team have specialist knowledge and they provide short commentaries as well as answer questions.

We follow a fixed route until reaching the south side of central Melbourne. The route through central Melbourne varies, as there is a number of sites scattered around this area and there is insufficient time to visit them all. After leaving the north side of central Melbourne, we finish the tour with sites connected with CSIRAC.

Here we review the "bookends" in more detail and browse some of the sites between them.

Figure 1: MMoCH calculator display

3.1 Beginning of Tour : Monash Museum of Computer History

The Monash Museum of Computing History (MMoCH) (Figure 1, 2) was established in the Faculty of Information Technology at the university's Caulfield campus in 2001. Its aims are "to provide a visual display of computing history as well as establish a reference collection demonstrating the use of computing technology at the university" [28].

Figure 2: MMoCH, central section: 'A Digital Evolution' and (right) Ferranti Sirius display

The Museum is located in a foyer, outside a set of lecture theatres and classrooms, so its displays are frequently viewed by passing students. The display is divided into sections with an introduction to calculators (Figure 1), early computers and personal computers and a biographical component on key figures in Monash University's computing history. The central section of the display (Figure 2) presents the evolution of computer technology against a photographic backdrop illustrating the concurrent evolution of society. The Museum is a teaching resource and a focal point for the history of computing. We run a programme of public outreach including several visits each year by groups of school students. The Museum area is open to the public when the university is open and is free of charge.

The major item in the collection is Monash University's first computer, a Ferranti Sirius (1962), which was an early commercial transistor-based computer (Figure 3). The history of this machine is described by Ainsworth [2]. The display includes a short film which was produced in 1963 to explain the workings of a computer to office staff.

The tour starts in this Museum, though we usually gather at a nearby café first, which gets the day off to a good start socially. We explain the purpose and layout of the museum, and tell people about the Ferranti Sirius.

Figure 3: Ferranti Sirius at Monash University

© Trevor Hicks (Monash University)

3.2 Middle of tour

We then take a half-hour tram journey, which travels along two streets which were home to many computer companies in the early days of the industry. (We call this stretch the 'Silicon Mile', by analogy with the Golden Mile, a term used informally elsewhere in Melbourne.) We stop at an architecturally significant building, called 'Stanhill', which was the home of the Melbourne Computer Centre (Figure 4). This was a commercial computer bureau run by the British firm, Ferranti Ltd. It provides an opportunity to discuss the nature of the computer industry, and the way computers were used in business, during the 1960s .

Figure 4: Stanhill

We then pass Monterey Apartments, where code-breaking was done during the Second World War, and continue up Silicon Mile to Melbourne Observatory (Figure 6). This observatory was established in 1863 (Figure 5) from the relocation and merger of Williamstown Observatory (est. 1853) and Flagstaff Observatory (est. 1858). It has been part of the Royal Botanic Gardens since 1997. There, we have lunch in a café, and take people to a particular window of the original observatory building so that they can see Melbourne's first Computer Room, which dates back to 1863. This was the workplace for the observatory's *human computers*, who were all unmarried women. This leads into a discussion of the evolution of the meaning of "computer", the naming conventions of computers (in particular, names ending in –AC, for Automatic Computer, or Mark I), changes in the opportunities for women in employment, and the importance of computation in astronomy then and now.

After lunch, we pass Victoria Barracks, an Australian military installation, which used to house a Cray supercomputer used in cryptanalysis in the 1980s. We then visit St Paul's Cathedral, where we inspect a list of former Deans that contains the name of a great-great-grandson of Charles Babbage (Figure 7). Here we take the opportunity to talk about Babbage's work and the origin of the concept of a computer.

Figure 5: Melbourne Observatory, 1863

Figure 6: Computer History Tour visits Melbourne Observatory, August 2008

Figure 7: List of Deans of Melbourne, St Paul's Cathedral

Figure 8: State Library of Victoria (then, the Public Library), late 19th century

Our routes through central Melbourne have varied. We may, for example, visit a plaque recording the first telegraph station in the southern hemisphere (1854), and Lonsdale Exchange where we can talk about the history of email and some network concepts such as packet switching and circuit switching. We may visit the State Library of Victoria (Figure 8), which introduced some innovative ways of using computers to improve information access, including one of Australia's first internet service providers, Vicnet [19]. We may visit some former sites of the Bureau of Meteorology, where computers were introduced in the 1960s to handle their own "big data" deluge and from the 1990s contributed to the work of the Intergovernmental Panel on Climate Change [5].

3.3 End of tour: CSIRAC

CSIRAC was Australia's first computer, and is commonly agreed to have been the world's fourth (if we insist that the term "computer" requires stored-program architecture) [25,29]. It is the only complete surviving first-generation computer in the world, although it is no longer in working order. CSIRAC is also significant for the world's first computer music (1951). It is on permanent display at Melbourne Museum (Figure 9).

Figure 9: CSIRAC, in Melbourne Museum

This computer was designed and built by Trevor Pearcey and Maston Beard in the Radiophysics Laboratory of the Council for Scientific and Industrial Research (CSIR) in Sydney from 1947. It was initially called CSIR Mark I and became operational in November 1949. In the same year, CSIR became the Commonwealth Scientific and Industrial Research Organisation (CSIRO).

CSIRO decided to devote more resources to rainmaking (unsuccessful) than computing (revolutionary) in the 1950s. CSIR Mark I was closed down and moved to the University of Melbourne in 1955. It was re-named CSIRAC (thereby switching between the two main computer-naming conventions of the day) and started work again in 1956. Among other achievements, it was used for Australia's first computer-based weather forecast in 1956. It remained at the University of Melbourne, operating very productively (with about 10% downtime), until it was retired in 1964. Fortunately, its custodians had the foresight, unusual at the time, to preserve it and placed the computer into the care of Museum Victoria.

In studying CSIRAC, we point out the various parts of the CPU, including the Arithmetic-Logic Unit, memory (mercury delay lines, and a later magnetic drum), and peripherals including paper tape devices, circular cathode ray displays (to show contents of memory registers), control switches, and a subroutine library (a collection of paper tape rolls in a box of pigeonholes). We outline how it worked, taking the opportunity to mention load-store architecture and the fetch-execute cycle. Students can see how fundamental and universal some of the principles they learn are, since they were present in these earliest computers.

During this last stage of the tour, we also visit the University of Melbourne to see the building that housed CSIRAC, from 1956 to 1964. The substantial gap between ground level, where we stand, and floor level above, indicates the large under-floor space which was an important source of cool air for temperature control.

While at the University of Melbourne, we pause outside the Richard Berry building, which housed Australia's first internet connection. This began operation on 23 June 1989. We discuss the differences between network layers (with the physical link to the US being from Sydney but the TCP/IP link from Melbourne). We note how internet speeds have changed: initially, the entire *country* was connected to the US by a 56kbps link, while today, most *individuals* would find that speed inadequate.

4. HOW TO CREATE A COMPUTER HISTORY TOUR

Melbourne is fortunate to have a number of important links to the early days of ICT. But, in fact, a tour like ours could be run in many other places around the world. To design a tour we recommend the following steps.

a) Investigate local museums. They may have displays of old computer and communications equipment.
b) Look for displays of old equipment at universities. It is not uncommon for Computer Science or Electrical Engineering departments to have such displays.
c) Every city had a first computer, at some stage. In some cases, this may be well known. In other cases, it may be identified with the help of computer industry veterans or the staff of large computer-using organisations such as universities, research laboratories, financial institutions, industrial plants, and of course computer companies.
d) Find out about historic astronomical and meteorological observatories in your area. These often employed human computers [18] and some had a computer room.
e) Find out about the introduction of telecommunications in your area, from local telecommunications companies or historical websites [15] and books [34]. Sites of early telegraph offices give an opportunity to draw historical parallels with the development and impact of the internet. Sites of old semaphore ("optical telegraph") stations [23] can serve a similar purpose, although fewer survive.
f) Kahn's book [24], and the journal *Cryptologia*, can help identify cryptographic sites.
g) Investigate major libraries in the area. Some of these may have been pioneers in new methods of information access for their community. Academic staff in librarianship and information management may have good suggestions.
h) Search the timeline at the Computer History Museum [7]. Another useful website is Digibarn [10].
i) Ask your colleagues for suggestions.

Some examples will indicate what is possible.

Sites in London include: the Science Museum (Babbage artefacts, reconstructed Difference Engine No. 1, and large computer section); several Charles Babbage sites, including his likely birthplace at Walworth, the site of the former Babbage home in Marylebone (with plaque), and his grave in Kensal Green cemetery; a plaque to Ada Lovelace at St James's Square; the house where Alan Turing was born, in Warrington Crescent; the City and Guilds Technical College site, in Leonard St, Finsbury, where the flip-flop was invented; the Royal Greenwich Observatory, which employed computers for just over 100 years from 1836; the Computer Museum at the University of Greenwich [26]; a plaque on the BT Centre in Newgate St to mark Marconi's wireless transmission there; an optical telegraph site in West Square, Kennington; and the grave of Thomas Bayes in Bunhill Fields (talk about Bayesian methods in machine learning).

New York City's Columbia University was the site of Herman Hollerith's work on tabulating machines, and of the first working model of the first personal computer, Simon, whose design had been outlined by Edmund Berkeley. Grace Hopper was born in New York City, studied at Vassar College, and worked there later. The famous chess match in which Deep Blue defeated world champion Garry Kasparov took place at the Equitable Center in 1997. Many human computers were employed in the New York Hydrographic Office at the Hudson Terminal Building [18]. ICT companies based in NYC include AOL, DoubleClick and Tumblr.

Chicago has the Museum of Science and Industry, and was the birthplace of the first online bulletin board system, CBBS, due to Ward Christensen and Randy Suess (1978). The key-driven mechanical calculators known as comptometers were developed there by Felt & Tarrant. Elisha Gray, of the Western Union Telegraph Company in Chicago, was pipped by Bell in patenting the telephone in 1876. Teletype was introduced in Chicago by Charles Krumm and his son in 1907. The University of Chicago has a long history of computational work, going back to 1939 when it hosted the Cowles Commission for Economic Research, with its team of human computers, until 1955.

Paris has, for a start, its Musée de l'Informatique (from 2008), Musée des Arts et Métiers (from 1794) (including a calculator invented by Blaise Pascal), historic Paris Observatory, and the church Saint-Étienne-du-Mont where Pascal is buried.

Tokyo has the National Science Museum which includes Japan's first electronic computer, the FUJIC (designed by Okazaki Bunji, completed in 1956); Waseda University, where FUJIC was located for a time; the NTT History Center of Technologies; the Ridai Museum of Modern Science at the Tokyo University of Science; Nishamura Computers Collection (by appointment) at the Tokyo University of Agriculture Technology, and sites associated with companies including Fujitsu and Hemmi and other early computers such as MUSASINO-1.

In each of these cases, the lists we give are by no means comprehensive, and could doubtless be extended and improved by people with more local knowledge.

Smaller cities can support such tours as well. The city of Geelong is 75km south-west of Melbourne, and has a population of about 180,000. Historically, it has been a centre for the wool industry and manufacturing. At first glance, one might not expect to find much ICT history there. But it has four important sites: an automatic punched-card weaving loom from 1910, still working, at the National Wool Museum; the Geelong Telegraph Station (1857), surmounted by a timeball; the first automatic telephone exchange in the southern hemisphere (1912); and the site of the first telephone call in Australia (1877). We ran group tours of the first three of these sites in May 2014 and April 2015.

Any list of sites needs to be considered for feasibility, to determine if there is a safe route enabling them to be visited in a reasonable time, and in some cases to determine arrangements for group access.

We have found that a tour group size in the low 20s works well. We are able to meet all participants over the course of the day, and make reasonable progress through the day. Our tour takes a full day and requires careful planning, allowing realistic times for transitions and moving around. Well-timed breaks are important. Some participants do not stay for the whole day. Seasonal weather is a factor in scheduling — in Melbourne, we avoid the hotter summer months. Our website [12] is designed to be usable for self-guided tours as well.

5. CONCLUSIONS AND INVITATION

We have described a new approach to interpretative heritage for ICT by combining the built environment with physical exhibits in formal museum displays in a guided tour to present the technological and cultural evolution of the field.

The development of the computer history tours of Melbourne has been a rewarding activity on many different levels, and has had a number of different outcomes. It has illustrated and reinforced technical concepts from the undergraduate curriculum, and demonstrated how fundamental and universal some of them are. It has raised awareness of the historical and social aspects of ICT, and given context for the technical concepts. It has given staff, students and alumni some extra value from their connection with the university. The program has stimulated research into topics for the tour as well as brought to light more sites of interest.

The tour has enabled us to meet many computer industry veterans with valuable recollections. It would be good to collect the memories and stories we come across in a more systematic way. We encourage participants to record their experiences and send the details, however there is scope for using technology to facilitate the systematic collection of this material.

While we have established a structured format for the tour, it is always evolving and more sites are being included as options. Future work on our tour could include a virtual online tour of some kind, or an app for a self-guided tour.

Although Melbourne is fortunate in its rich connections with the early days of computing, many other cities could support computer history tours too. We invite you to organise your own computer history tour and share your experiences.

6. ACKNOWLEDGMENTS

We are very grateful to the many people and organisations who have provided information and assisted with our visits to the various sites. Many of these are listed on our tour web page [12]. Special thanks are due to David Demant and Melbourne Museum for their work as curator and custodians of CSIRAC and their assistance with our visits there. We also acknowledge the invaluable work done by the CSIRAC Team, led by Peter Thorne, in ensuring its preservation, both at the time of its closure in 1964 and now as Research Associates with Melbourne Museum.

7. REFERENCES

[1] A Friend in Town, Silicon Valley -San Jose Sightseeing Tour, http://www.toursanfranciscobay.com/tours/silicon-valley-san-jose.html.

[2] Ainsworth, A.B., The Ferranti Sirius computer at Monash University, August 2008, http://www.infotech.monash.edu.au/about/museum/papers/first-computer-at-monash-university-v7.pdf

[3] Alegro Private Tours, http://alegroprivatetours.com/tours/silicon-valley-tours/

[4] Bletchley Park, http://www.bletchleypark.org.uk/

[5] Bureau of Meteorology, *50 Years of Computing in the Bureau of Meteorology*, 2013.

[6] Cincotta, Katie , Top 11 things to do, *Green Guide* (`livewire' section), pp. 20-21, *The Age* (Melbourne), 1 December 2011, http://www.theage.com.au/digital-life/top-11-things-to-do-20111130-1o5mz.html

[7] Computer History Museum, Mountain View, Ca., http://www.computerhistory.org/

[8] Cooper, S. B. (ed.), Alan Turing Year, http://www.turingcentenary.eu/.

[9] De Mol, L., and Primiero, G. (chairs), *International Conference on the History and Philosophy of Computing (HaPoC)*, Ghent University, Nov. 2011, http://www.computing-conference.ugent.be/

[10] Digibarn Computer Museum, http://www.digibarn.com/

[11] Draper, G., Kessler, R., and Riesenfeld, R. A History of Computing Course with a Technical Focus. *Proceedings of the 40th ACM Technical Symposium on Computer Science Education (SIGCSE 2009),* ACM, 458-462.

[12] Farr, G., Ainsworth, B., Avram, C., and Sheard, J., Computing in Melbourne: A Historical Tour, http://www.csse.monash.edu.au/~gfarr/tour/.

[13] Farr, G., radio interview by Hilary Harper, 774 ABC Melbourne, 22 August 2009, ~ 6:10am for ~ 5 mins, http://blogs.abc.net.au/victoria/2009/08/22/ (scroll down).

[14] Farrer, Gordon, Computer tour spins web of interest, *The Age* (Melbourne),14 May 2009, p24; online (without photo) at http://www.theage.com.au/national/computer-tour-spins-web-of-interest-20090513-b3au.html?page=-1

[15] R. Freshwater, UK Telephone History, http://www.britishtelephones.com/histuk.htm

[16] Giangrandi, P. and Mirolo, C., Enhancing the general background of CS students through a computing history course. In: *Proceedings of the Innovation and Technology in Computer Science Education Conference (ITiCSE)*, Madrid, Spain (2008), 301-305.

[17] Glinert, E. (organiser), private communication, 30 March 2014; URL for walks: http://www.newmanchesterwalks.com/event/alan-turing/

[18] Grier, D.A., *When Computers Were Human*, Princeton University Press, 2005.

[19] Hardy, G., Hall, S., Bates, A., and Kurzeme, I., VICNET and the web in the wider Victorian community, in: R S Debreceny and A E Ellis (eds.), *AusWeb95 – Proceedings of the First Australian World Wide Web Conference*, Norsearch Publishing, Lismore, NSW, 1995. http://ausweb.scu.edu.au/aw95/libraries/hardy/

[20] Heinz Nixdorf MuseumsForum, http://www.hnf.de/

[21] Impagliazzo, J. and Lee, J. A. N., Using computing history to enhance teaching. In J. Impagliazzo & J. A. N. Lee (Eds.), *History of Computing and Education*, Kluwer Academic Publishers, Boston (2004), 165-175.

[22] Information Processing Society of Japan (IPSJ) Computer Museum, http://museum.ipsj.or.jp/

[23] Jones, R.V., Optical Telegraphy, http://people.seas.harvard.edu/~jones/cscie129/images/history/chappe.html

[24] Kahn, D., *The Codebreakers*, MacMillan, 1967, 1996.

[25] McCann, D., and Thorne, P., *The Last of the First: CSIRAC: Australia's First Computer*, Department of Computer Science and Software Engineering, University of Melbourne, 2000. http://www.cis.unimelb.edu.au/about/csirac/the-last-of-the-first-csirac-ebook.pdf

[26] Mann, T., and Fedorec, A., Computer Museum, School of Computing and Mathematical Sciences, University of Greenwich, *IEEE Annals of the History of Computing*, **26** (1) (2004) 69-70.

[27] Marsh, A., Revolution: The first 2,000 years of computing. *Technology and Culture* **54** (3) (2013), 640-649.

[28] Monash Museum of Computing History, http://www.infotech.monash.edu.au/about/museum/

[29] Museum Victoria, CSIRAC: Australia's First Computer, http://museumvictoria.com.au/csirac/

[30] Nakano, H., Styles, M. G. and Draper, G. M., A call for champions: Why some 'History of Computing' courses are more successful than others. *ACM Inroads,* **4**(1)(2013),26-28.

[31] Nexon Computer Museum, http://www.nexoncomputermuseum.org/

[32] Papadimitriou, C. H., *Mythe*mati**CS**: In Praise of Storytelling in the teaching of CS and Math, *Proc. 8th Ann. Conf. on ITiCSE*, *Inroads* (SIGCSE Bulletin) **35** (3) (Sept. 2003), 7-9.

[33] Ryska, N. and Viehoff, J., The Heinz Nixdorf Museums-Forum, central venue for the "History of Computing". In: *Making the History of Computing Relevant: IFIP WG 9.7 Internat. Conf., HC 2013* (2013), 47-52, Springer.

[34] Standage, T., *The Victorian Internet*, Walker & Co., 1998.

[35] Tatnall, A. (ed.), *History of Computing: Learning from the Past, IFIP WG 9.7 Internat. Conf., HC 2010,* Springer, 2010.

[36] The National Museum of Computing, http://www.tnmoc.org/

[37] Tolerton, Jane, Look at how far computing has come, *The Dominion Post* (Wellington, NZ), 27 December 2008, pB3.

[38] Vincent, Jill, *Shrine to University: A Geometry Journey along St. Kilda Road and Swanston Street*, Math. Assoc. of Victoria, Brunswick, Vic., Australia, 1999. Later edition: http://www.mav.vic.edu.au/studact/im/IM_06.pdf.

[39] Virtual Museum of Computing, http://museums.wikia.com/wiki/VMoC

[40] Williams, M. R., The computer history museum. *ACM SIGCSE Bulletin inroads,* **35**(4) (2003), 12-13.

[41] Zhang, C. and Howland, J. E., Brief and yet bountiful: The history of computing, why students need you? *Journal of Computing Sciences in Colleges,* **20**(4) (2005), 308-314.

Picture credits:
Drawing of Melbourne Observatory (1863) and photo of the State Library of Victoria (1870-1889): State Library of Victoria (both out of copyright). Ferranti Sirius: Monash University Archives (IN6378), © Trevor Hicks (photographer). All other photos by Chris Avram (August 2008 or July 2010).

Improving Engagement in Introductory Courses with Homework Resubmission

Amanda M. Holland-Minkley
Washington & Jefferson College
60 South Lincoln Street
Washington, PA, United States
ahollandminkley@washjeff.edu

Thomas Lombardi
Washington & Jefferson College
60 South Lincoln Street
Washington, PA, United States
tlombardi@washjeff.edu

ABSTRACT
This paper describes the introduction of a feedback-revision-resubmission cycle for homework assignments in two introductory courses. The goal was to increase student engagement with homework assignments as an important tool for concept practice and mastery. A review of the effects in both an object-oriented programming course and a relational databases course shows positive outcomes as reflected in both course evaluations and a decision tree analysis of student performance on assignments.

Keywords
Programming; Databases; Problem-based Learning.

1. INTRODUCTION
While courses vary widely in their specific syllabus structure, it is generally the case that introductory computer science courses, particularly those with a coding component, assess students through a mix of homework assignments and exams. From an instructor's perspective, homework carries a central learning purpose; completing homework assignments successfully ensures success in the course because of its role in concept mastery. In contrast, because exams typically carry a higher weight value than homework assignments, by design, many students perceive of homework as less important than exams. This can result in students misallocating their efforts in courses in a manner that detracts from their ultimate learning.

In our case, we had been offering introductory object-oriented programming and relational databases courses that presented students with challenging, problem-based homework assignments. In both courses, we frequently encountered low student engagement with homework, including students "giving up" on homework and expressing the intent to instead really learn the content for the exams. As expected, in practice students who did not engage with homework rarely mastered course content sufficiently to subsequently perform well on exams.

In the face of these challenges and inspired by concurrent revisions to a shared writing-intensive course, we incorporated a cycle of feedback, revision, and resubmission for homework assignments in these two courses. The result was improved student engagement with homework, both by student self-report and as evidenced by a decision tree analysis of student grades.

SIGCSE'16, March 02-05, 2016, Memphis, TN, USA

ACM 978-1-4503-3685-7/16/03…$15.00.
DOI: http://dx.doi.org/10.1145/2839509.2844576

2. BACKGROUND
We have been fortunate in our department to coordinate the faculty in adopting a shared problem-based learning (PBL) approach across our courses. The value of constructivist approaches to education, and computer science education in particular, have been well discussed elsewhere [2, 6]. The merits of the PBL variant of constructivism have also been well explored [12, 16]. PBL specifically calls for student learning to be centered on realistic and ill-structured problems, thus engaging students in problem exploration and definition. Through these self-structured problems, students then self-discover course content. In this context, syllabi place problem solving and student engagement at the center of the coursework.

Our program offers two no-prerequisite introductory coding-focused courses serving both our majors and students from across the institution, particularly the sciences. These are an introductory course in object-oriented programming taught using Java and an introductory course in relational databases taught using SQL. In both courses, regular homework assignments are used to present students with robust problem-solving challenges, consistent with PBL practices. Exams are given for evaluative purposes, but our goal is to have the primary student engagement be with these homework problems. In part, this is reinforced with the course grading scheme, with homework assignments worth between 10% and 25% of the final grade in the course (depending on course and section), which requires most students to complete homework assignments satisfactorily to achieve their desired grade.

Through multiple offerings of both courses, it was evident that syllabi adjustments were called for to increase student engagement with the homework assignments. It is well understood that learners who are new to PBL often struggle with teaching approaches focused on robust problems as they are still developing their skills in self-sufficient problem solving. Supportive scaffolding for these new learners is recommended to both support skill development and motivate students to work through challenging assignments [16]. Students in our object-oriented programming course frequently demonstrated the type of frustration and burn-out that would be predicted with insufficient scaffolding. This manifested itself through students turning in homework assignments late or submitting incomplete assignments rather than engaging in the deep problem-solving intended. This then resulted in very low exam grades, as students had not sufficiently engaged with course content prior to testing.

Similarly, within the relational databases course, many students failed to engage seriously with assigned homework. Here too, these students suffered on exams due to a lack of practice. Several students were caught cheating on assignments. The students recorded their frustrations in no fewer than eight negative comments on evaluations specifically related to homework assignments. The course's final cumulative review homework received particular criticism such as in this comment: "One or two of the assignments, especially assignment 8, seemed like pure busy work because we learned and applied all of the concepts earlier in the course." Within the structure of the course, the intent of this assignment is to have students integrate previously covered content and prepare for the final exam. However, these sorts of criticisms suggest many students did not understand the purpose of the assignment to offer review and exam preparation. At the same time, many students mentioned not feeling prepared for exams, suggesting a need for reviewing how homework assignments were presented to and perceived by students.

At the same time as the instructors of these two courses were identifying this issue, they were also working with the institution's writing instruction coordinator on strategies for improving student writing in a departmental history of computing course taught on rotation by department faculty and satisfying the college's general education writing requirement. We were encouraged to adopt frequent cycles of writing, feedback, and revision to improve student writing, with early versions being minimally graded or not graded at all. Within writing instruction, self-reflection supported by external feedback leading to revision is widely accepted as a best practice [3, 9].

In addition to incorporating this best practice in our history of computing course, we decided to also adapt the practice in our programming course in the format of a feedback, revision, resubmission cycle for homework assignments. After a successful pilot there, we then introduced homework resubmissions effectively into the databases course as well.

3. INTRODUCTION OF REVISION AND RESUBMISSION

The original syllabi structures of the programming and database courses are shown in Tables 1 and 3. In both cases, there are a significant number of short homeworks assigned in the first half of the course, designed to reinforce core course content through problem solving tasks. For example, within the object-oriented programming course, Homework 6 provided students with a potential desired usage for an object class including sample method calls and asked the students to design an object with methods that manage data internal to the object appropriately and consistently. Similarly, Homework 2 in the database course asked students to normalize data appropriately for a data-driven application. Thus, students are given a plausible problem-solving context and a degree of freedom in designing a robust solution. In both cases, grading is based on not just pure correctness of output, but also coding style and the elegance of the solution.

In our adjusted syllabi, we give students the (non-mandatory) option of resubmitting any homework after receiving feedback and an initial grade on their code; if the student does resubmit, the new grade replaces 75% of their original grade on the assignment. Feedback takes the form of narrative reflections on the submission, generally handwritten on a hardcopy of the assignment, covering issues with correctness, adherence to the assignment, and stylistic issues. This individualized feedback may include suggestions for test data or references to particular course content to review. With this structure, students have an incentive to engage early with challenging problems with less pressure to completely master these problems on their first attempt. Revision after feedback encourages students to continue to develop and refine their problem-solving skills by incorporating reflection. To help manage the workload produced by resubmission, students are required to submit a copy of the feedback from their original submission along with their revision in order to receive credit. Late submissions are also no longer accepted to enable prompt review and turn-around of submissions.

The two courses underwent adjustment to accommodate the resubmission deadlines in the timing of the course. In the case of the programming course, the two assignments covering the use of built-in classes were combined into one as shown in Tables 1 and 2. In the original syllabus, the second homework (HW5 in Table 1) was included to give students additional practice with using classes as many were performing poorly on the first homework on the topic (HW 4). Students were also given slightly less time to complete each assignment; with the opportunity to revise and resubmit, this resulted in roughly the same amount of total time available to work on each homework. In the database course, the number of homework assignments was cut from eight to four without removing content as shown in Tables 3 and 4. This was achieved by combining topics into larger, single problems. This also had the side effect of presenting students with more robust problem-solving opportunities within each homework, consistent with the course's PBL pedagogy.

Table 1: Assignments before resubmits (*Programming*)

Assignment	Points	Topic
HW1	25%	Program Structure, Output
HW2		I/O, Arithmetic Statements
HW3		Graphics Applets
HW4		Using classes: Math, String, Random
HW5		Using classes: Math String Random
HW6		OO design: writing simple classes
HW7		OO design: writing interacting classes
Project1	30%	GUIs, events, if statements, OO design
Project2		Loops, Arrays, Threads
Participation	10%	All class sessions
Exam1	10%	I/O, Arithmetic, Using classes, Applets
Exam2	10%	OO Design
FinalExam	15%	Comprehensive Exam

Table 2: Assignments after resubmits (*Programming*)

Assignment	Points	Topic
HW1	20%	Program Structure, Output
HW2		I/O, Arithmetic Statements
HW3		Using classes: Math, String, Random
HW4		Graphics Applets
HW5		OO Design: writing simple classes
HW6		OO Design: writing interacting classes
Project1	30%	GUIs, events, if statements, OO design
Project2		Loops, Arrays, Threads, Inheritance
Participation	5%	All class sessions
Exam1	10%	I/O, Arithmetic, Using classes
Exam2	10%	OO Design: writing simple classes
Exam3	10%	OO Design: writing interacting classes
FinalExam	15%	Comprehensive Exam

Table 3: Assignments before resubmits (*Database Course*)

Assignment	Points	Topic
HW1	5	Collect sample data
HW2	5	Normalization, ER Diagrams
HW3	5	SQL: Data Definition Language
HW4	5	Queries in Graphical Environment
HW5	5	SQL: Data Manipulation Language
HW6	5	Database Forms
HW7	5	Database Reports and Menus
HW8	5	Review: Normalization and SQL
Project1	25	Database Design
Project2	25	Database Implementation
Exam1	40	Normalization, ERD, Queries
Exam2	40	DDL, DML, GUI
FinalExam	70	Comprehensive Exam

Table 4: Assignments after resubmits (*Database Course*)

Assignment	Points	Topic
HW1	20	Data Types, Relations, 1NF
HW1R		
HW2	20	Normalization, 3NF, ERD
HW2R		
HW3	20	SQL: DDL + DML
HW3R		
HW4	20	DB GUIs: Menus, Forms, Reports
HW4R		
Project1	80	Database Design
Project2	80	Database Implementation
Quizzes (8)	80	All topics
Participation	80	
Exam1	80	Normalization, ERD
Exam2	80	SQL: DDL and DML
Exam3	80	Database GUIs
FinalExam	160	Comprehensive Exam

In our first pilot of resubmissions, the new grade replaced 100% of the original grade. This mimicked a frequent practice in writing exercises of having first drafts be ungraded. However, we found that this resulted in some students considering only the resubmission deadline as the "real" deadline and as the course progressed received more initial submissions that reflected minimum effort. By having a portion of the grade based on the original submission, students are encouraged to put concerted effort into their original submissions; we found that this adjustment did have the expected effect, with only a very small number of original submissions reflecting minimum effort.

Another deviation from the common application of revision for writing exercises is that we did not make resubmission mandatory. Both courses hold no pre-requisites and attract students from our major and from across the sciences and social-sciences. As such, there is a wide range of backgrounds for students in the courses, and the initial homework assignments are by necessity fairly straightforward. It is common for attentive students with a strong background to score perfectly on these initial assignments, while less experienced students may only earn half the possible points on their first attempt. Given the performance on the low end, it would be undesirable to make the assignments more challenging. By making resubmissions optional, more experienced students are rewarded for making a strong effort early by being able to skip the revision. At the same time, less experienced students are given the opportunity to "catch up" with their classmates.

The practice of homework resubmissions bears similarities to the practice of integrating code reviews into introductory courses. Peer review has been found to be effective in leading students to engage with feedback and improve mastery of course content [1, 14]. Pedagogical code review [7, 8] where review involves both peer student reviewers and an expert moderator demonstrates similar benefits. Hundhausen et al [7] found that in introductory courses, pedagogical code review can also have positive effects on student awareness of their learning. Within our classes, we have not chosen to adopt code review at the introductory level though we have begun adopting it within some intermediate courses. In the context of relatively small classes with a broad diversity of student background, we find individual instructor feedback on each assignment currently plays a valuable role in identifying needed interventions to assist with retention. Further, by relying on instructor feedback we can ensure that students are provided with primarily high-level conceptual and design input at the feedback stage, encouraging a focus on problem solving concerns over syntactic concerns. However, our current practice could be adapted to be based on peer review rather than instructor review depending on course size and other course goals. This is also consistent with writing instruction best practices, where it has also been found that the act of peer review or writing can effectively be used as an alternative to instructor feedback, with benefits to the reviewing student as well as the reviewed student [4].

4. ASSESSMENT

Following the adoption of a feedback, revision, resubmission cycle in our two introductory courses, we were able to observe the benefits for both student attitude and student engagement through an inspection of course evaluations as well as applying tools from educational data mining.

4.1 Course Evaluation Feedback

Through course evaluations, we have evidence that students found resubmissions helpful. Prior to resubmissions, many evaluations for the programming course mentioned the homework as a negative, particularly those portions that were most reflective of their role as a tool for engagement with new material. For example, students were critical of homework that was more complex than in-class examples; a feature of the assignments intended to guide students to integrate isolated concepts in a single program. With the introduction of resubmissions, student mentions of homework were more positive, with many students explicitly mentioning that resubmitting homework helped them learn. Said one, "The homework resubmissions were very convenient. Since some of the coursework took practice to master, the ability to re-do the assignment after more practice and learning what you did wrong was beneficial."

Similarly, the student feedback in the databases course after the changes took effect reflected many of these notions. In fact, the new course format produced a number of enthusiastic responses including the following representative comment: "I liked how we could resubmit the homework assignments. That really helped me learn the concepts and made the class less stressful. It made sure that you really understood the material before moving onto the next lesson". One student demonstrated a clear understanding of the organizing principle for the course: "Loved the re-submit option for homework. The homework assignments were at first very challenging, but given the opportunity to resubmit, it gave me the chance to evaluate what I did and improve, ultimately helping me do well on the exams."

Though course evaluations showed that students felt resubmissions helped their learning, these self-reports are not sufficient to determine that instructor goals are being met. It remained possible that students spoke favorably of resubmissions because they believe they make the course easier (for example, perhaps they do not try as hard on their first attempts), the opposite of the pedagogical intent of higher engagement.

4.2 Decision Tree Analysis of Course Data

Comparing grades between offerings is not a valid assessment of effectiveness in our case because the content and difficulty of our assignments changed alongside the introduction of resubmissions. However, we were able to draw on the tools of educational data mining (EDM) and decision tree analysis to assess the effect of introducing resubmissions into our courses. Decision trees have been widely recognized in the data mining literature for their interpretability [18], and this has been successfully applied to the domain of educational data. The ease of interpretation in part explains its broad adoption for many research goals in the EDM community. Romero et al. state that decision trees produced by algorithms like C4.5 and CART are straight-forward for educators to interpret [15]. Superby et al. used decision trees to understand the factors contributing to the success or failure of first-year university students [17]. Dekker et al. predicted student drop-out rates with decision trees [5]. Moreover, decision trees have been used for rubric evaluation [13], student success prediction [10] and student remediation [5, 17].

In particular, many researchers have embraced decision trees as descriptive devices for modeling and exploratory analysis. Pechenizkiy et al. put it this way: "Instead of trying to achieve the highest possible accuracy, our goal was finding descriptive or discriminative patterns providing us with an insight and evidence supporting a particular hypothesis" [11]. We utilize this insight and focus on the descriptive aspects of decision trees to discriminate patterns in student assessment data that provide insight into the effects of our syllabus changes.

We used constructed decision trees with the C4.5 and CART algorithms, using each of gain ratio, information gain, and gini index. The minimum node size for splitting was four, and the minimum leaf node size was two; this ensures that we do not generate a class of size one to avoid overfitting and issues related to student privacy. Our data comprise five semesters of course assessment in two courses with student grades organized as seen in Tables 1-4; in all cases n<=20. All data were cleansed to remove identifying information from the data set. Students who withdrew from the course prior to completion were removed. We devised a distance metric to gauge empirically the effectiveness of each tree based on the distance between the decision tree's predicted final grade and the student's actual final grade.

Unlike other data mining techniques, the decision trees we produce can be compared as descriptions across semesters and even classes. For example, the entropy and impurity metrics used to construct these trees are more resilient to changes in measurement scale than other data mining techniques [18]. The trees, therefore, can be compared even if the number of assignments or the weights of assignments change.

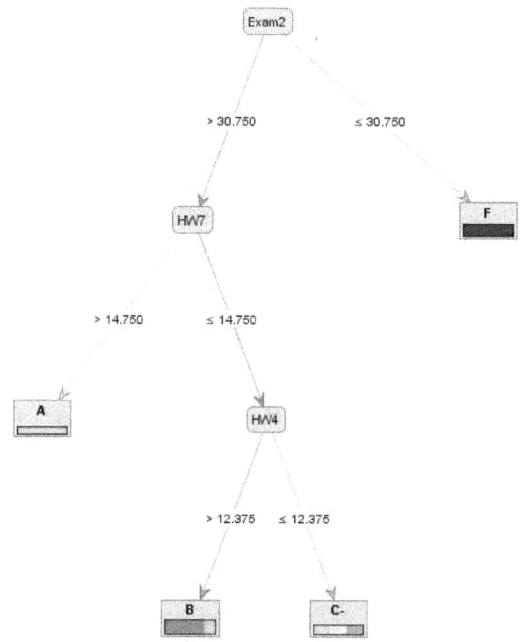

Figure 1: Decision Tree for Student Assessments in *Programming Course* before Resubmissions.

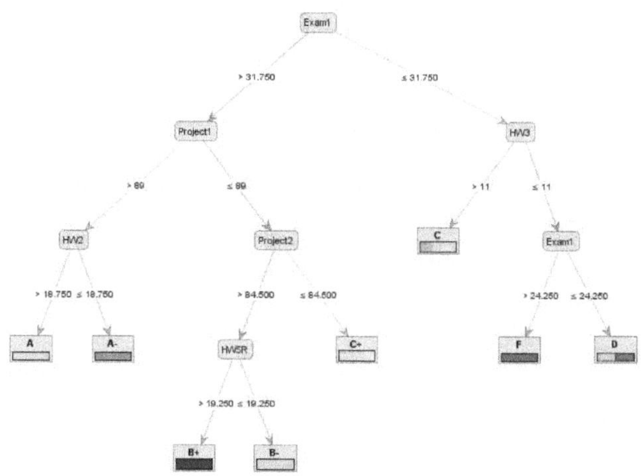

Figure 2: Decision Tree for Student Assessments in *Programming Course* after Resubmissions.

In our case, we hope to see that, with their role as an engagement activity, homework assignments will have the most importance in the learning process, as compared to primarily grade-determining activities such as exams. This should be the case even if the exams have a relatively large point value; from the perspective of where the act of learning takes place, it is the problem solving homework assignments and projects that have highest importance. This would be represented as a decision tree constructed over all course assessments that shows homework, projects and participation providing the most information and thus populating the top of our decision trees, as the root node in a decision tree represents the entity yielding the greatest information gain. In contrast, when our syllabi or instructional techniques conflict with those goals we expect exams and quizzes at the top of the decision trees. In general, our generated trees only include a small subset of the total set of assessments factoring into the final grade, representing those with the greatest discriminative power in classifying students earning different letter grades.

Applying this analysis to student grades for our two introductory courses both before and after introducing resubmissions of homework, we do in fact see a shift from decision trees with exams as root nodes and low effects from homework assignments to decision trees showing greater predictive power of student outcomes from homework performance.

4.3 Object-Oriented Programming Analysis

Before introducing homework resubmissions, given the observed low engagement with homework assignments among many students, we expect to see exams taking a more prominent role in the decision tree generated from student grade data than would be ideal. In Figure 1, we see the most prominent node is Exam 2. Within the course design, some of the most significant learning is intended to come from the two projects which fall in the second half of the course and require students to engage with larger authentic problems. However, neither project appears in the tree, despite their educational primacy and their significant proportional contribution to the final grade.

We contrast this with the tree in Figure 2 representing the most recent offering of the course, after resubmissions were introduced. In this case, both course projects feature prominently in the tree, as well as two homework assignments and one homework resubmission. It is noteworthy that the significant homework resubmission is for the first assignment requiring students to work with object-oriented design – the topic covered by Exam 2.

Exam 1 does still figure strongly in our post-resubmission decision tree. We take a few lessons away from this. First, we see this as a signal that while our adjustments to the course are helping achieve our pedagogical goals, we should continue to look for ways to provide students with effective scaffolding, particularly early in the course. We also observe that this was the first time the course was offered with three in-class exams rather than two, due to the course moving from a Tuesday/Thursday to a Monday/Wednesday/Friday schedule. The difficulty and scope of the first exam was also reduced, in part to allow students to use it to practice taking a coding-based exam in a timed setting. Exam 1 prominence in the tree may be reflective, then, of the importance of students learning to take coding-based exams. It remains for the course instructor to determine whether this is overly detrimental to the intended PBL approach of the course.

4.4 Relational Databases Analysis

Based on student comments and instructor impressions, we expect exams to dominate the structure of decision trees prior to the use of homework resubmission. In Figure 3 the final exam is clearly the most important node in the determination of the grade with Exam 2 also exerting an important influence. This bears out our intuition that many students were not well prepared for the exams. This tree also shows the only homework contributing significant information is Homework 8 which was designed to be a review assignment to help students prepare for the final. Overall, the decision tree generated for these data support our interpretation of the student comments: students misunderstood the purpose of the assignments and failed to focus properly on assignments outside of class. These issues contributed to student grades varying more widely than expected or desired on exams.

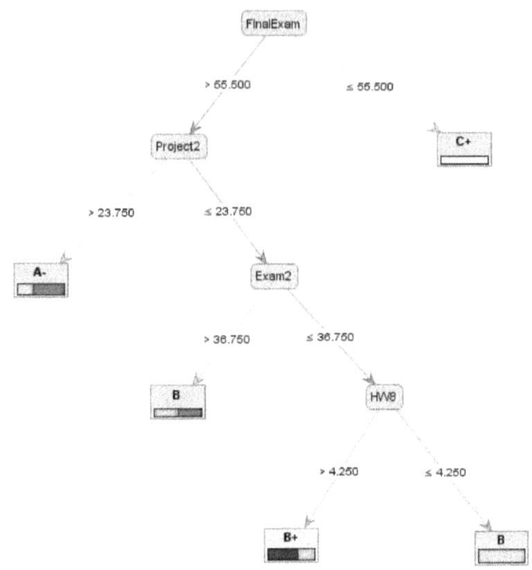

Figure 3: Decision Tree for Student Assessments in *Database Course* before Resubmissions

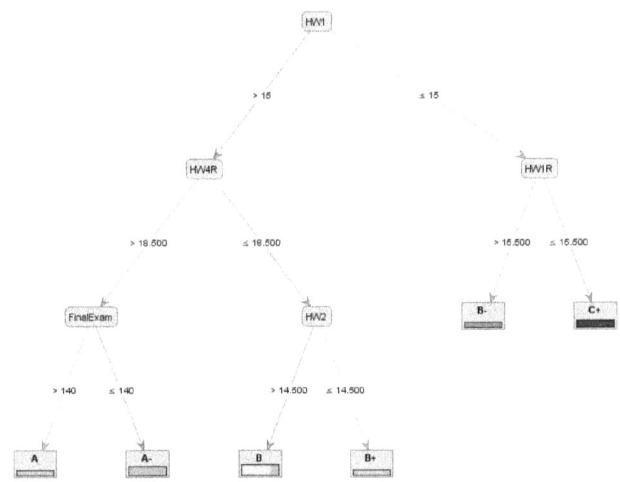

Figure 4: Decision Tree for Student Assessments in Database Concepts after Resubmissions

Figure 4 displays a decision tree derived from student assessment data for the last available semester after the adoption of resubmissions. In a sense, the tree in Figure 4 is an inverted version of Figure 3. In Figure 4, homework assignments and resubmitted homework dominate the tree structure with the final exam serving only to distinguish between A and A- students. This structure emphasizes the assignments on which students spend the most time rather than on those graded events that have the most weight. The instructor was particularly encouraged to see that assignments related to normalization (HW1, HW1R, HW2) provided important information. Exams other than the final exam have fallen out of the tree completely. Although the final exam still does contribute, it is significantly less dominant. Overall, the decision tree validates the student feedback and the instructors' intuition regarding this change to the syllabus.

5. DISCUSSION

In addition to the benefits to student engagement, these changes offered advantages to the course instructors. By implementing resubmission on an optional basis, the effects of different student backgrounds is smoothed out. High-performing students benefit from early effort and engagement, and instructors obtain a positive mechanism for directing struggling students towards additional help early in the course when it is of the most benefit.

While unanticipated, we have also found less student resistance to point deduction due to stylistic or other more subjective assessments of their submissions. Because students have the opportunity to revise and resubmit, feedback on stylistic concerns such as non-standard naming, suboptimal typing choices, or inefficiencies can be offered productively and students are able to act on it. As an instructor, this has in turn made us more prone to note such potential improvements rather than focusing largely on functionality issues. In some cases, the portion of the points on an assignment allocated to style issues has even been increased because of a perception of it being more "fair" to grade based on subjective assessments with the potential for revision.

Taken together, we have found resubmissions to be an invaluable addition to our introductory courses in object-oriented programming and relational databases. We have been able to increase student engagement with challenging problem-based homework assignments, resulting in improved student satisfaction and improved alignment of student learning with course goals.

6. ACKNOWLEDGMENTS

We thank the many students who persevered through our courses in all of their iterations, Dr. Tara Fee who inspired us to think about revision as a learning tool, Dr. Matthew North who crafted the original version of our databases course upon which this one is based, and our institution's IRB for their review of our work.

7. REFERENCES

[1] Anewalt, K. 2005. Using peer review as a vehicle for communication skill development and active learning. J. Comput. Sci. Colleges 21, 2, 148–155.

[2] Ben-Ari, Mordechai. 1998. Constructivism in computer science education. In *Proceedings of the 29th SIGCSE technical symposium on Computer science education (SIGCSE '98)*, ACM, New York, NY, USA, 257-261.

[3] CCCC Committee on Assessment. (November 2006). Writing Assessment: A Position Statement. *National Council of Teachers of English.* Retrieved from http://ncte.org/cccc/resources/positions/writingassessment

[4] Cho, K. and MacArthur, C. 2011. Learning by reviewing. *Journal of Educational Psychology*. 103, 1 73-84.

[5] Dekker, G., Pechenizkiy, M and Vleeshouwers, J. 2009. Predicting Students Drop Out: A Case Study. In *Proceedings of the International Conference on Education Data Mining (EDM)*. International Working Group on Educational Data Mining, Cordoba, Spain, 41-50.

[6] Duffy, T., & Jonassen, D. 1992. *Constructivism and the technology of instruction: A conversation.* Philadelphia: Lawrence Erlbaum.

[7] Hundhausen, C., Agrawal, A., Fairbrother, D., and Trevisan, M. 2009. Integrating pedagogical code reviews into a CS 1 course: an empirical study. In *Proceedings of the 40th ACM technical symposium on Computer science education (SIGCSE '09)*. ACM, New York, NY, USA, 291-295.

[8] Hundhausen, C. Agrawal, A., and Agarwal, P. 2013. Talking about code: Integrating pedagogical code reviews into early computing courses. *Trans. Comput. Educ.* 13, 3, Article 14 (August 2013), 28 pages. DOI=10.1145/2499947.2499951

[9] International Network of WAC Programs. (February 2014). Statement of WAC Principles and Practices. *Writing Across the Curriculum Clearinghouse.* Retrieved from http://wac.colostate.edu/principles/statement.pdf

[10] Kumar, S.A. and Vijayalakshmi, M. N. 2011. Efficiency of Decision Trees in Predicting Student's Academic Performance. In *Proceedings of the 1st International Conference on Computer Science, Engineering and Applications, CS and IT 02*, Dubai, 335-343.

[11] Pechenizkiy, M., Calders, T., Vasilyeva, E. and De Bra, P. 2008. Mining the Student Assessment Data: Lessons Drawn from a Small Scale Case Study. In *Proceedings of the 1st International Conference on Educational Data Mining*, 187-191.

[12] Pedersen, S. and Liu, M. 2002. The transfer of problem-solving skills from a problem-based learning environment: The effect of modeling an expert's cognitive processes. *Journal of Research on Technology in Education*, 35.

[13] Quevedo, J.R. and Motañes, E. 2009. Obtaining rubric weights for assessments by more than one lecturer using a pairwise learning model. In *Proceedings of the International Conference on Educational Data Mining.* International Working Group on Educational Data Mining, Cordoba, Spain. 289-298.

[14] Reily, K., Finnerty, P. L., and Terveen, L. 2009. Two peers are better than one: Aggregating peer reviews for computing assignments is surprisingly accurate. In *Proceedings of the ACM International Conference on Supporting Group Work.* ACM Press, New York, 115–124.

[15] Romero, C., Ventura, S., Espejo, P.G., and Hervas, C. 2008. Data Mining Algorithms to Classify Students. In *Proceedings of the 1st International Conference on Educational Data Mining*, 8-17.

[16] Savery, J. 2006. Overview of problem-based learning: Definitions and distinctions. *The Interdisciplinary Journal of Problem-Based Leraning.* 1(2), 9-20.

[17] Superby, J.F., Vandamme, J.-P., and Meskens, N. 2006. Determination of factors influencing the achievement of first-year university students using data mining methods. In *Proceedings of the Workshop on Educational Data Mining at the 8th International Conference on Intelligent Tutoring Systems (ITS 2006)*, 37-44.

[18] Witten, I., Frank, E., and Hall, M. 2011. *Data Mining: Practical Machine Learning Tools and Techniques.* Elsevier.

Animated Examples as Practice Content in a Java Programming Course

Roya Hosseini
University of Pittsburgh
roh38@pitt.edu

Teemu Sirkiä
Aalto University
teemu.sirkia@aalto.fi

Julio Guerra
University of Pittsburgh
jdg60@pitt.edu

Peter Brusilovsky
University of Pittsburgh
peterb@pitt.edu

Lauri Malmi
Aalto University
lauri.malmi@aalto.fi

ABSTRACT

Code examples are commonly used learning resources that help students grasp various programming structures and concepts. However, example code usually requires explanations about what each line or part of the code does. Otherwise, students may find it difficult to follow an example. In this paper, we compare two types of code examples that use different techniques to describe important concepts in the code: annotated and animated examples. The former displays an explanation for a subset of lines in plain text, whereas the latter visualizes code execution. We studied the use and impact of these enhanced examples, provided as non-mandatory practice content, in three introductory Java courses. Our results suggest that animated examples are more engaging and have a positive impact on students' learning. As compared to annotated examples, students spent more time with animated examples and more likely completed them. Also, a positive relationship was found between the number of explored animated examples and the overall course grade.

Keywords

code examples; learning; Java programming; annotated examples; animated examples; program visualization

1. INTRODUCTION

Understanding program dynamics (i.e., how program execution is carried out in computer memory) is one of the central challenges of learning computer programming. Du Boulay [7] wrote "...there are difficulties associated with understanding the general properties of the machine that one is learning to control, the notional machine, and realizing how the behavior of the physical machine relates to this notional machine." These difficulties are generally related to the abstract nature of program execution.

CS teachers and researchers have developed numerous methods and tools to support students in learning program dynamics. One basic method is annotating program code to explain what happens when each line is executed. A more advanced method is *program visualization*, a whole research direction [15] that focuses on building specialized software tools and interactive techniques to support following and exploring program execution in a graphical form.

Even though sophisticated tools have been developed and evaluated, they frequently fail to meet their goals, because teachers and students simply do not use them [12]. Packaging interactive learning content into online practice systems such as Codingbat[1] has recently emerged as a way to decrease the teacher engagement threshold: teachers can now point students to these systems, rather than master these tools to integrate individual content items into their teaching. However, practice systems still face the problem of student engagement. Since practice content is usually offered for students' own benefit while awarding no additional credit, students tend to skip practice materials to focus on tasks that give them credits. Turning examples from practice to mandatory content is not an optimal solution either, because it can lead to mindless clicking through the content to gain points without any understanding. A relevant overall research question in this area remains: *what kind of non-compulsory learning resources are both beneficial and engaging for students in programming education?*

In this paper, we examine the value of animated program examples as practice content for both educational impact and prospects for engagement. To examine the added value of *animated examples*, we compare them to *annotated examples*, which are a more traditional way to support students in learning to understand programs. Both types of resources in our study were provided as voluntary practice materials.

2. RELATED WORK

A printed textbook, which could be considered as a traditional medium to present program examples to learners, provides little help in delivering the essence of an example or helping students to locate more relevant examples. At most, a textbook author could provide line-by-line example code explanations. This approach has been used in a number of textbooks, and in some cases, has defined the nature of a textbook [9]. To overcome these limitations and to provide better support for learning from examples, instructors and researchers have suggested a range of interactive computer tools. Roughly, the work on these tools could be classified

[1] http://codingbat.com/

SIGCSE '16, March 02-05, 2016, Memphis, TN, USA

DOI: http://dx.doi.org/10.1145/2839509.2844639

in three directions. One direction has focused on providing better access to the right example at the right time - although the examples could still be traditional, plain-code examples [6, 16]. The other two directions have focused on augmenting the examples themselves. One has focused on adding richer expert explanations to the example code by using interactive linking [4]. The other has attempted to promote deeper knowledge of language semantics by offering visual animations of example code [15]. Below, we briefly review some work along the latter two directions that are most relevant to the paper.

The concept behind interactive explained examples is to add expert comments on the role of different constructs in achieving the goal of the provided code, as well as other related comments. These kinds of worked-out examples are known in many other science and engineering domains; however, programming was one of the first areas where interactive systems were developed to support these kinds of examples. Starting from the pioneering work of Linn and Boyle [2, 10], a number of researchers explored systems that offer access to explained examples [4, 6]. In providing access to explanations without breaking the example code, these systems typically used interactive hypermedia features.

Animated examples, which fall in the area of program visualization, are a more advanced and complicated technology. The idea of animated examples is to make the dynamic execution or program examples visible. Without such visualization, novice students are not able to see how the given code is really executed, because the execution process is normally invisible. This may lead to different kinds of misconceptions that prevent learning new concepts, as the code does not behave as expected. Animated examples make the execution process visible so that novice students can easily see and follow all the important steps.

A recent review of the existing program visualization tools [15] indicates that many different tools have been developed for novice programmers to create animated examples. The earliest tools appeared in the 1980s; however, it is only over the past 10 years that this technology has become broadly available for instructors. One well-known program visualization system is Jeliot 3 [1] and its ancestors. They have been used for almost two decades in introductory programming. Jeliot 3 is a Java-based application for Java programs that can even visualize students' own code. Many research papers have presented positive learning results when Jeliot 3 is used in CS1 courses (eg. [5]). One newer tool for creating animated examples is the Online Python Tutor [8], which can create embeddable animated examples that run in a browser.

3. TOOLS USED IN THE STUDY

3.1 Mastery Grids Portal for Practice Content

All practice content in our study was accessed through the Mastery Grids portal [11], which integrates three kinds of content: code execution problems, annotated examples, and animated examples [4, 13]. In integrating external content, Mastery Grids portal follows the suggestions of the recent ITiCSE working group report [3]. Instead of directly embedding each kind of examples into the portal, all interactive examples are technically external resources that are hosted by separate content servers. This design allows for reuse of content in multiple portals or course management systems.

To engage students to work with the content, the Mastery Grids portal provides visual personal progress tracking, as well as social comparison visualizations, which allow a student to compare her progress to the progress of the rest of the class or with the most advanced students. Mastery Grids organizes the content in topics that are represented as a series of colored cells, which get darker as the student completes the content within a topic. A part of the topic cells of the programming course can be seen in Figure 1, where an animated example from the topic "Strings" is shown overlaying Mastery Grids. For a detailed explanation of the Mastery Grids interface, see previous work [11]. In line with its practice nature, the use of the system and any of its content was not mandatory.

3.2 Exploring Examples with Jsvee

Jsvee [13] is a JavaScript library to create animated examples. The library is language-independent, but can be extended to have language-specific features: for example, there is limited support for built-in Java libraries that are needed in the animations. The main idea of the Jsvee library is that the original code is transformed into an intermediate language that the library can visually execute. Jsvee is able to produce smooth expression-level visualizations, which means that all the intermediate steps to evaluate the current line are shown. For example, the order of evaluating arithmetic operations or nested function calls are visible. With textual descriptions or line-based visualization tools, such as Online Python Tutor [8], it is difficult to explain or demonstrate these important evaluation steps.

These interactive visualizations (see Figure 1) can be embedded into online course materials or used as individual small exercises. They are pure HTML, CSS, and JavaScript, which allows them to be also used with mobile devices, because plugins (such as Flash) are not required. Jsvee also automatically generates short explanation texts for the animation of each step.

To get information how the students use animated examples, Jsvee collects log traces. Every time when a student uses the controls, such as "step forward" or "undo," a log entry with the timestamp and current step number is created. Entries are sent to the server every 20 seconds, as well as after the example is completed. With this data it is possible to measure, for example, how much time students have spent on each step.

3.3 Exploring Examples with WebEx

WebEx is a web-based system for the interactive exploration of programming examples. The key idea behind the Webex system is to generate self-sufficient interactive examples by adding explanations to example code. With WebEx, the code of the example is shown as an easy-to-grasp single chunk, while line-by-line explanation are accessible by clicking on lines of interest. As a result, from being a passive reading activity, the work on examples changes to an interactive exploration.

Starting in 2001 with several dozen annotated programming examples in C, this technology has been used to produce a large volume of annotated examples for several programming languages (C, Java, SQL) with explanations that address both the semantics and pragmatics of the examples [4]. Figure 2 shows a typical WebEx example in Java for teaching students the concept of *pre/post-increment*. A green bullet to the left of a code line indicates the availability of

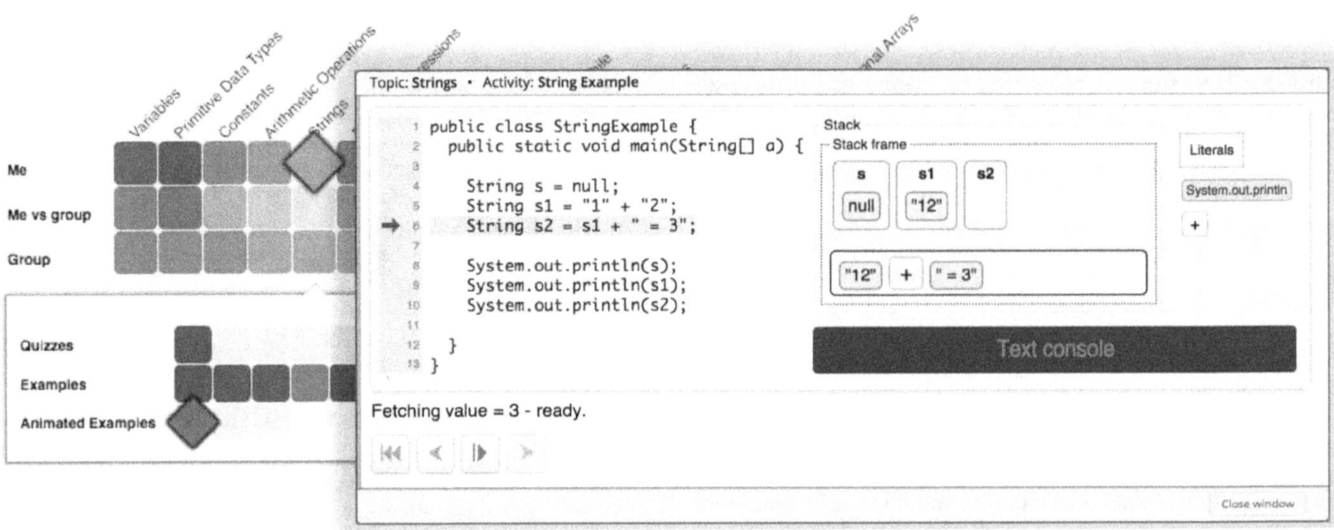

Figure 1: An illustration of an animated example in Mastery Grids. When a student clicks on an animated example, the activity is shown in an iframe that overlays Mastery Grids, and the student can click on the forward button to see the animations. For example, in the current line (line 6), the value of the variable `s1` will be concatenated with the literal value `"= 3"`. Jsvee demonstrates how the local variables are updated by showing all the intermediate steps of fetching values and evaluating the operator - not simply the final result.

explanations for this line. Explanations are shown as the student clicks on each bullet. The WebEx system logs all user interactions with the tool, which enables seeing how students work with examples in the context of real courses.

4. THE STUDY

To investigate the impact of different example types, we analyzed the data of classroom studies that were carried out at the University of Pittsburgh (PITT) and Winston-Salem State University (WSSU) during the fall 2014 and spring 2015 semesters. The subjects were undergraduate students taking an introductory course in Java programming. All students were informed by course instructors to access supplementary materials for the course through the Mastery Grids portal. A pretest and post-test was administered at the beginning and end of the course to measure students' learning at the end of the course. Both tests had the same questions.

The practice content offered by the course through the Mastery Grids portal included three types of interactive content, organized under 19 topics: annotated examples, animated examples, and parameterized code execution problem. A code execution problem provides a fragment of code to a student and asks about the value of a specific variable or the content printed on a console after the code is executed. The system evaluates the student's answer and reports whether the answer was correct or incorrect. Students can try the same problem many times. Each time, the code is generated with randomly selected values for the problem parameters, and as a result, the correct answer will be different each time. Table 1 provides more details for the number of students and practice content items in the studied groups.

Table 1: Classroom studies: participants and course materials

	PITT 2014	PITT 2015	WSSU 2014
Students registered in the course	65	61	28
Students logged into the portal	56	33	20
Problems	101	111	111
Annotated examples	79	104	104
Animated examples	31	52	52

5. THE RESULTS

We evaluated the impact of annotated and animated examples on students' engagement and learning from the following four aspects: engagement level, problem solving performance, amount of learning, and course grade. In the following subsections, we describe the analyses we performed to discover the importance of examples to these aspects of learning.

5.1 Engagement Level

Here, we evaluated the level of user engagement by defining a set of usage measures that summarize students' attempts on example activities. The measures that we used are as follows: (1) the number of distinct examples viewed; (2) the percentage of viewed examples (that is the number of distinct examples viewed divided by the number of available examples); (3) the total time spent on examples (seconds); (4) the average percentage of example completion; and (5) the average time spent per example. The average completion was calculated by dividing the average clicks actually made by the total number of clicks needed to view the whole example. Only started examples were taken into account. For WebEx examples, a click means an action to view an explanation, and for animated examples, a click means a step to move forward. Since the work with the system was non-mandatory, the amount of work with practice content done by the students offers a good approximation of engagement.

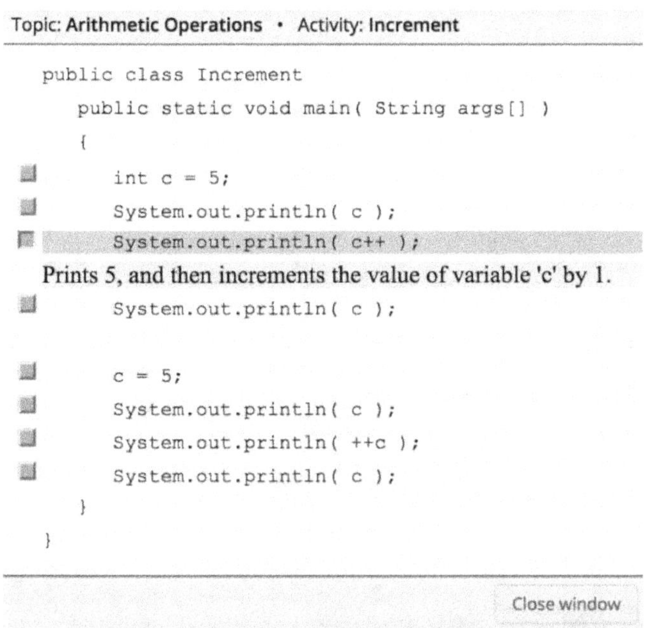

Figure 2: A WebEx example for demonstrating a *pre/post-increment* concept in the *Arithmetic Operations* topic. When a student clicks on the green bullets, an explanation appears below the line.

Table 2 provides summary statistics for the above measures. As the table shows, students viewed significantly more annotated examples than animated examples (Kruskal-Wallis test: $\chi^2(1) = 10.177, p = .001$). Also, the average total time spent on annotated examples was significantly higher than animated examples ($\chi^2(1) = 15.048, p < .001$). However, these numbers should be considered with care, since the number of more easy-to-author annotated examples in the system was considerably larger.

Looking at the percentage of example completion, we found that students completed an average of 95.0% of each animated example that they viewed. This was significantly larger (23.6% more) than the percentage of completed annotated examples ($\chi^2(1) = 29.424, p < .001$). Moreover, students spent twice as much time interacting with an animated example than with an annotated example ($\chi^2(1) = 78.667, p = .001$). It indicates that both kinds of examples were engaging; however, individual animated examples were more engaging, and motivated students to stay longer and follow more lines. Whether this longer work was beneficial for learning will be addressed in the rest of this section.

Note that annotated and animated examples differ considerably in their interactivity and freedom of navigation. Their usage should be compared with understanding this nature. In particular, it is easy to navigate through annotations in any order skipping less important lines, while the sequential nature of animations allows for comparatively little freedom, with no skipping or random access.

5.2 Problem Solving Performance

As mentioned earlier, the practice content offered by the course in the Mastery Grids portal included parameterized code execution problems for self-assessment of students' knowledge. We assumed that problem solving performance

Table 2: Comparison of engagement level between annotated & animated examples

Usage summary	Annotated ex. Mean (SE)	Animated ex. Mean (SE)
Distinct examples	29.7 (2.4)	8.7 (1.0)
Distinct examples (%)	33.0% (3.0%)	24.0% (3.0%)
Total time (sec)	2196.5 (285.6)	1585.7 (426.5)
Avg. completion (%)	71.4% (3.5%)	95.0% (1.5%)
Avg. time per example	61.1 (6.3)	128.2 (22.1)

(correctness of problem answers) could be used to evaluate student knowledge and attempted to explore the impact of annotated and animated examples on student knowledge by looking into the relationship between *success rate* in answering problems and the usage of different example types.

Success rate is defined as the number of correct attempts on problems divided by the total problem attempts. Using data from all students ($n = 109$), a significant negative correlation was found between the number of distinct annotated examples that students viewed and their success rate. A higher number of annotated example views was associated with a lower success rate ($\rho = -0.22$, $p = .029$). This result looks counter-intuitive, but it is important to remember that the content to practice is freely selected by students. As we observed, those failing to answer problems turned to examples in a hope to bridge the knowledge gap. Moreover, annotated examples were much more frequently accessed after a failure. Following 19.71% of failures to solve a problem, students seek help in easy-to-parse annotated examples, while in 3.91% of failures, they turned to animated examples. Considering all attempts to access each type of example, 20.01% of all annotated examples and 13.61% of animated examples were accessed immediately after failure, which largely makes failures a remediation tool, rather than just a learning tool. As a result, two opposite processes connecting the work with examples and performance took place. It is likely that examples do help students to increase knowledge (positive connection between student work with examples and performance), but on the other hand, due to free content choice, lower knowledge and failures led to the increased use of examples (negative connection between examples and performance). As we see, in case of annotated examples, the latter process overcame the effect of learning from examples.

We further investigated the parameters that influence problem solving performance by fitting stepwise regression models to predict the number of correct problem attempts in terms of activities on topics, examples, and problems; time spent on examples; pretest scores; and the group that a student belongs to. Table 3 shows the result of the model with the highest goodness-of-fit (*Adjusted* $R^2 = 0.95$, $F(7, 89) = 253.6$, $p < .001$) that uses the data of all students who used the system ($n = 109$). We found that the number of viewed topics, attempted problems, viewed animated examples, total time spent on annotated examples, and students' groups were reliable predictors for the number of correct attempts on problems, while annotated examples and time spent on animated examples were not.

More specifically, as expected, students with a higher pretest score had more correct attempts on problems; one

Table 3: Summary of the regression model for number of correct problem attempts ($n = 109$)

Predictor	Estimate	Std. error	p-value
Topics covered	3.47	0.24	<.001
Problem att.	0.08	0.02	<.001
Distinct animated ex.	0.48	0.09	<.001
Time on annotated ex.	-7.6e-4	2.7e-4	.006
Pretest	7.28	3.23	.027

unit increase in the normalized pretest score increased the number of correct attempts on problems by 7.28 ($SE = 3.23$). Also, every additional topic that was covered increased the number of correct problem attempts by 3.47 ($SE = 0.24$). Attempting a problem and an animated example increased the number of correct problem attempts by 0.08 ($SE = 0.02$), and 0.48 ($SE = 0.09$), respectively. On the other hand, each second of time that is spent on annotated examples decreased the correct problem attempts by -7.6e-4 (SE =2.7e-4). This data hints that students are likely learning more from animated examples. As a result, the positive impact of examples overcame the negative process of associating examples with poor knowledge, and their joint impact is still positive. In contrast, annotated examples appeared to be less useful for learning, allowing the reverse process to overcome the positive impact on knowledge. These findings reveal a stronger impact of animated examples on problem solving performance; however, more data and more careful analysis should be made to determine a reliable conclusion.

5.3 Amount of Learning

We measured learning by predicting students' post-test scores at the end of the semester. We considered various predictors, including system usage factors (covered topics, total attempts on code execution problems, correct attempts on problems, distinct annotated/animated examples viewed, and time spent on annotated/animated examples), prior knowledge of students as measured by pretests, and the group that indicates the course and semester that study was performed. Pretest and post-test scores were normalized in the 0–1 range. Also, out of 83 students who had taken both the pretest and the post-test, there were 8 students whose post-test score were less than their pretest. We discarded data from those students, as we assumed that no unlearning occurs. Table 4 summarizes the final results of the stepwise regressions for the model, which explains 61% of the variance for the remaining 75 students (*Adjusted* $R^2 = 0.61$, $F(7, 67) = 17.43$, $p < .001$).

As expected, student prior knowledge measured by pretest was among the reliable post-test predictors. One unit increase in the pretest score increased the normalized post-test by 0.615 ($SE = 0.099$) units. Among measures related to student work with practice content, the following four achieved at least a marginal impact on the scores of the post-test: correct attempts on problems, distinct views on annotated examples, and animated examples were all marginally significant (p <.10), and the total time spent on animated examples was significant at the 0.035 level. In particular, similar to the previous analysis, we observed that a switch from annotated to animated examples turns the connection between amount of work and performance from negative to positive: each explored annotated example *decreased* the normalized post-test

Table 4: Summary of the regression model for post-test scores ($n = 75$)

Predictor	Estimate	Std. error	p-value
Correct problem att.	1.4e-3	7.2e-4	.050
Distinct annotated ex.	-0.003	0.002	.077
Distinct animated ex.	0.007	0.004	.088
Time on animated ex.	-8.9e-6	4.1e-6	.035
Pretest	0.615	0.099	<.001

Table 5: Summary of the regression model for course grade ($n = 75$)

Predictor	Estimate	Std. error	p-value
Correct problem att.	8.2e-4	3.1e-4	.010
Distinct annotated ex.	-0.003	0.001	.003
Distinct animated ex.	0.006	0.002	.015
Pretest	0.173	0.050	.001

by 0.003 ($SE = 0.002$) while each explored animated example *increased* the post-test by 0.007 ($SE = 0.004$). While spending too much time with animated examples doesn't add enough extra knowledge to overcome the negative process, the overall connection is still negative: every additional second that students spent on animated examples decreased the normalized post-test by -8.9e-6 (SE=4.1e-6).

5.4 Course Grade

To explore the relationships between the example usage and *course grade*, we used the data of students for whom we had access to their course grades ($n = 82$). Spearman correlation showed marginally significant positive correlation between the number of distinct animated examples that students viewed and their course grade. More views of animated examples was associated with a higher course grade ($\rho = 0.19$, $p = .085$).

Regression analysis was performed to predict the final course grade of students in terms of the same predictors, as mentioned in 5.2. Among 82 students for whom we had access to their grades, 7 had missing pretest and were excluded from the analysis. So, data of 75 students were used in the regression model and Table 5 shows the effect of each predictor on students' grade in the best fitted model (*Adjusted* $R^2 = 0.27$, $F(5, 69) = 6.353$, $p < .001$). As the table shows, the number of correct problem attempts, animated example views, and pretest score positively influenced the course grade. Every additional problem attempt or view of distinct animated examples increased the course grade by 8.2e-4 (SE =3.1e-4) and 0.006 ($SE = 0.002$), respectively. For every unit increase in the normalized pretest score, there was a corresponding predicted increase of 0.173 ($SE = 0.050$) in the course grade. But, the number of views on annotated examples had a negative effect on the course grade: every single view of a distinct annotated example decreased the course grade by 0.003 ($SE = 0.001$). This is another case where a switch to animated examples turns the balance positive.

5.5 Student Feedback

Students from the PITT group were surveyed at the end of the term about the usefulness of the system. One of the questions was about animated examples ("Animated examples helped me to learn Java") and was answered in a

5-point Likert scale, from *Strongly disagree* = 1 to *Strongly agree* = 5. A total of 48 students who used the system and saw animated examples at least once completed the questionnaire. The results show a mildly positive opinion (Mean = 3.44, Median = 4 (Agree), and Mode = 4). Certain differences in the response patterns among low and high pretest groups exist, as well. Students in the low pretest group have a strong tendency to Agree: 58% (14) of them give value 4. By contrast, students in the high pretest group are more heterogeneous: 29% (6) give no opinion (value 3), 29% agreed and 24% (5) strongly agreed (value 5). No significant correlation was found between the answer to this question and the usage of the system (number of animated examples viewed), but a marginal significant negative correlation was found between question responses and the pretest score for high pretest group B= -.345, p=.05, N=21. Very high pretest students found animated examples to be less useful.

6. CONCLUSION AND FUTURE WORK

This paper compared the impact of traditional annotated examples with more advanced animated examples as practice content for learning Java programming. Our results indicated that animated examples better engaged students increasing their interest in completing examples. Animated examples also provided better impact on several performance measures such as problem solving success, post-test scores, and course grade turning the relationship between the amount of work with examples and performance from negative to positive.

The present work confirms previous findings about the usage of animated examples. A recent research by Sirkiä and Sorva [14] studied usage of animated examples as a part of an electronic textbook. Similar to what we observed in this work, students viewed almost all animated examples that they started, and viewing animated examples in the textbook was associated with higher course grades. An interesting difference between these two studies is in the treatment of examples. While in our study examples were offered as additional non-mandatory practice content, in the Sirkiä and Sorva [14] study, animated examples were the core part of the course, and were embedded into the course materials together with text. As expected, core content got more attention than practice content: in that study, students viewed on average 65.3% of embedded animated examples, 63.2% higher than in the case of practice content offered by the Mastery Grids portal.

In the future, we plan to combine the ideas of annotated and animated examples by adding annotation support for animated examples. This means that a teacher can add custom texts to animations in order to emphasize and explain the most important steps in more detail. The current automatically-generated explanations frequently fail to explain what is actually happening. Teachers can create better explanations, just as they can now in WebEx, but instead of explaining the whole line, the explanation can refer to a single animation step, which is only a part of the line. In this way, students are able to follow the animated examples with deeper understanding.

7. ACKNOWLEDGEMENTS

This work is supported by the Advanced Distributed Learning (ADL) Initiative. The views and conclusions contained in this document are those of the authors and should not be interpreted as representing the official policies, either expressed or implied, of the Department of Defense or the Joint Staff. The U.S. Government is authorized to reproduce and distribute reprints for government purposes. Also, the authors want to thank Rebecca Caldwell, Darina Dicheva, and Dmitry Babichenko for their help with data collection.

8. REFERENCES

[1] M. Ben-Ari, R. Bednarik, R. B.-B. Levy, G. Ebel, A. Moreno, N. Myller, and E. Sutinen. A decade of research and development on program animation: The Jeliot experience. *Journal of Visual Languages & Computing*, 22(5):375 – 384, 2011.

[2] T. Boyle, J. Gray, B. Wendl, and M. Davies. Taking the plunge with CLEM: the design and evaluation of a large scale CAL system. *Computers & Education*, 22(1):19–26, 1994.

[3] P. Brusilovsky, S. Edwards, A. Kumar, L. Malmi, L. Benotti, D. Buck, P. Ihantola, R. Prince, T. Sirkiä, S. Sosnovsky, et al. Increasing adoption of smart learning content for computer science education. In *Proceedings of the Working Group Reports of the 2014 on Innovation & Technology in Computer Science Education Conference*, pages 31–57, 2014.

[4] P. Brusilovsky and M. Yudelson. From WebEx to NavEx: Interactive Access to Annotated Program Examples. *Proc. of the IEEE*, 96(6):990–999, 2008.

[5] S. M. Čisar, R. Pinter, D. Radosav, and P. Čisar. Effectiveness of program visualization in learning Java: a case study with Jeliot 3. *International Journal of Computers, Communications & Control*, 6(4), 2011.

[6] A. Davidovic, J. Warren, and E. Trichina. Learning benefits of structural example-based adaptive tutoring systems. *IEEE Transactions on Education*, 46(2):241–251, 2003.

[7] B. du Boulay. Some difficulties of learning to program. *Studying the Novice Programmer*, page 283, 2013.

[8] P. J. Guo. Online python tutor: embeddable web-based program visualization for cs education. In *Proceeding of the 44th ACM technical symposium on Computer science education*, pages 579–584. ACM, 2013.

[9] A. Kelley and I. Pohl. *C by dissection : The essentials of C programming*. Addison-Wesley, New York, 1995.

[10] M. Linn. Can experts' explanations help students develop program design skills. *International Journal on the Man-Machine Studies*, 36:511–551, 1992.

[11] T. Loboda, J. Guerra, R. Hosseini, and P. Brusilovsky. Mastery Grids: An open source social educational progress visualization. In *9th European Conference on Technology Enhanced Learning (EC-TEL 2014)*, pages 235–248.

[12] T. Naps, G. Rossling, J. Anderson, S. Cooper, W. Dann, R. Fleischer, B. Koldehofe, A. Korhonen, M. Kuittinen, C. Leska, M. McNally, L. Malmi, J. Rantakokko, and R. J. Ross. Evaluating the educational impact of visualization. *ACM SIGCSE bulletin*, 35(4):124–136, 2003.

[13] T. Sirkiä. A JavaScript library for visualizing program execution. In *Proceedings of the 13th Koli Calling International Conference on Computing Education Research*, Koli Calling '13, pages 189–190. ACM, 2013.

[14] T. Sirkiä and J. Sorva. How do students use program visualizations within an interactive ebook? In *Proceedings of the eleventh annual International Conference on International Computing Education Research*, pages 179–188. ACM, 2015.

[15] J. Sorva, V. Karavirta, and L. Malmi. A review of generic program visualization systems for introductory programming education. *ACM Transactions on Computing Education*, 13(4):1–64, 2013.

[16] G. Weber. Individual selection of examples in an intelligent learning environment. *Journal of Artificial Intelligence in Education*, 7(1):3–31, 1996.

Memory Diagrams: A Consistant Approach Across Concepts and Languages

Toby Dragon and Paul E. Dickson
Ithaca College
Computer Science Department
953 Danby Rd.
Ithaca, NY 14850, USA
(tdragon, pdickson)@ithaca.edu

ABSTRACT

Hand-drawn memory diagrams are frequently used in computer science to demonstrate new programming concepts and support students' understanding of program functionality. These diagrams often vary among courses, instructors, and languages, which confuse students moving through the curriculum. Consistent memory diagrams throughout a curriculum not only alleviate confusion but offer a scaffold for students to transfer their understanding between courses taught at different levels of complexity and in different languages. We describe our standardized system for memory diagrams as it is used in our curriculum to demonstrate this scaffolding process through multiple concepts and programming languages.

CCS Concepts

•Social and professional topics → Computer science education;

Keywords

Memory Diagram, Tracing, Computer Science Education, Program Memory Traces, Pedagogy

1. INTRODUCTION

Memory diagrams, created by tracing code, are frequently used in computer science courses to teach concepts at various levels of complexity. Tightly integrating memory diagram creation by hand into introductory courses has been shown to be beneficial to students [3]. A useful memory diagram can illustrate basic functionality and expected outcomes for introductory programming. By introducing more complexity, memory diagrams can clarify precisely how memory is organized and managed, which varies among programming languages.

Often, these memory diagrams are drawn by hand. This technique is used for various reasons, including the ease of creation and the lack of any technological requirements. Hand-drawn diagrams can easily be created by both teachers and students. This is helpful in a learning scenario, for rapid work, and also in real-life scenarios when debugging tools may not be present or familiar to programmers. Hand-drawn diagrams often vary greatly among courses and professors. This variation can be purposeful, to demonstrate specific points but can also be arbitrary. In either case the differences can result in confusion for students, particularly when the students are unaware of which differences are purposeful and which are arbitrary. Our own experience at Ithaca College has demonstrated this phenomenon. Six of our seven tenure track faculty members teach students to create memory diagrams by hand as a regular part of class time within our core computer science courses. These courses are taught in three main languages: Python, Java, and C++. Students have noted that the combination of instructors' diagram styles and programming languages was confusing.

To remedy this problem, a subset of our faculty has worked together to develop a standardized approach to memory diagrams, removing arbitrary differences. Furthermore, as we introduce new topics, we increase complexity of diagrams to add additional information rather than make alterations to the previously learned diagramming style. This progression provides students with visual and procedural representation of the concepts. The entire faculty is adopting the memory diagraming methodology presented in this paper, and we believe this consistent approach is reducing both student confusion and faculty effort.

This work seeks to offer the community support for improving memory diagrams within their own curricula in two ways. First, we offer a standardized method for creating memory diagrams. We find this method generically applicable to undergraduate computer science education. Second, we describe the manner in which we use this diagramming method to support the introduction of new concepts in our curriculum with various programming languages. This demonstrates the way we utilize memory diagrams to lead students into a deeper and more refined understanding of memory organization and management.

2. RELATED WORK

Previous research offers a wealth of information about both the motivation and the effectiveness of memory diagrams. Most of that work is focused on computerized visualization of computer memory or program visualization

SIGCSE '16, March 2–5, 2016, Memphis, TN, USA.

DOI: http://dx.doi.org/10.1145/2839509.2844607

in general. This work is intricately related to hand-drawn diagrams and we looked for lessons learned and guiding principles of memory diagrams within these publications. Nap et al. [7] present several best practices around program visualization. The most relevant to our efforts are that visualization should adapt to the knowledge level of the user, include execution history, and support learner-built visualizations. Our diagramming style fulfills these recommendations. Sorva et al. [8] present a thorough review of computerized systems for program visualization. They present dozens of systems and studies that demonstrate various levels of success with improving learning gains and student motivation. The authors note that these systems generally present a single level of complexity rather than provide a scheme capable of demonstrating different levels of complexity. In contrast, we discuss our methods for presenting a consistent diagramming technique that can be used for increasingly complex concepts.

Certain related work in visualization argues that hand-drawn diagrams are tedious and therefore less useful than visualization software [2]. While we understand this perspective, we consider there to be trade-offs between the two techniques. When seeking to explain the lack of adoption of visualization software, Sorva et al note reasons for teachers not adopting software visualization to include "the lack of teacher time for learning about systems or configuring them..." and "poor fit with specific aspects of the course (e.g., programming language, teachers' personal pedagogical styles)" [8]. Hand-drawn diagrams alleviate these concerns by allowing teachers to quickly and easily implement and adopt our technique, an idea also noted by Hertz et. al. [3].

Several related works focus specifically on diagrams related to object oriented programming [4, 2, 6]. We are encouraged by their work that demonstrates the helpfulness of memory diagrams, but we also see that the limited application can be problematic. Vainio et al. [9] state that one main problem with current memory diagraming techniques is caused by using single programming language for all example programs. Hertz et al. [3] present an argument quite similar to our own, namely that tightly integrated hand-drawn memory diagrams can improve learning. Their focus was demonstrating the specific learning gains offered in a single course in order to validate the memory diagramming approach.

This prior research demonstrates the promise of diagramming techniques but is limited in scope and often with access limited by software and hardware requirements. As evaluation is often the focus, this work offers no detailed examples of precisely how traces cover a variety of situations. Some sources offer more detail in their trace technique but lack a thorough description of the educational value [1, 5]. We demonstrate a method of creating memory diagrams that can cover a larger portion of curriculum and describe in detail our tracing methodology that can be applied across various concepts and languages.

3. MEMORY DIAGRAMS

We draw all memory diagrams by hand on paper or whiteboard in our classes. One hand-drawn example is given to show the authentic product (Figure 5), but for legibility other diagrams in this paper will be computer generated in the same form as a hand-drawn diagram would appear. We will present the different aspects of our memory diagramming standard with increasing complexity, as students would have the information presented throughout their education at our institution. In this way, reading through the following sections should provide not only a description of our standard with concrete examples but also an understanding of how these diagrams can be used at different levels of complexity and with different languages.

3.1 Basic Stack Diagrams

The first memory diagrams we teach students to create are basic and initially used only on primitive data types. Strings are treated primitives in introductory level diagrams because giving greater detail will only cause confusion. Strings are readdressed when students have greater knowledge. This type of diagram is used to demonstrate the correspondence between variable names (*identifiers*) and the *value* of that current variable. Students are taught to trace each line of code individually, adding new variables above old variables and replacing values by crossing out and writing new values when an identifier is used multiple times (*overwriting*). An example of a complete memory diagram for a short Python program is shown in Figure 1.

```
s = "hello"
x = 4
y = 6
x = 8
total = x + y + x
print(total)
```

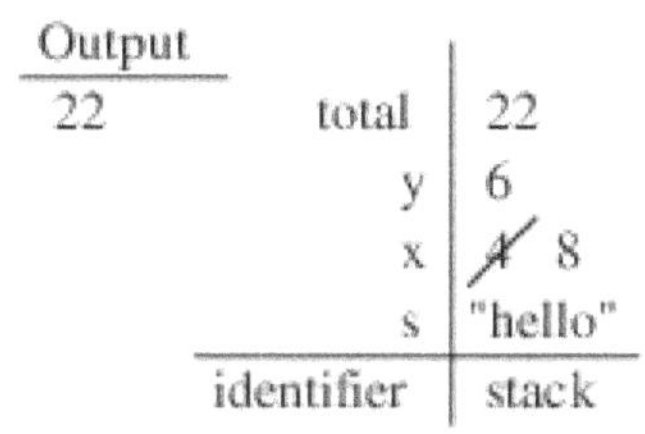

Figure 1: Basic Python example.

This diagram is not perfectly accurate because Python uses references for all variables, and therefore there is not one memory slot for the variable x as indicated. We find this distinction to be overwhelming and counterproductive to our student's learning process at the introductory level. Additionally, acknowledging this aspect creates greater differences in the diagrams of different languages, such as Java and C++. The simplistic view of simple variables at an early stage allows a base for understanding. Tracing behavior as demonstrated in Figure 1 allows for correct prediction of results with a simple, consistent model across several languages.

3.2 Function Calls

The next step to increase complexity in our curriculum and memory diagrams is the introduction of functions (Figure 2). Functions introduce the concepts of *scope*, *return values*, and *parameters*. To represent scope, we place a box on the stack, with the name of the function to the left of the box representing that specific function call. All variables created or accessible within that function call will be represented within this box. Students are instructed to consider only the top box on the stack while still tracing code from that function call. When the function returns, that box is crossed out. This process is presented with brief discussion of the concept of scope and several worked examples and exercises of the practical impact. This creates a procedural understanding of the effects of scope before formally addressing the concept.

```
def here(valHere):
  valHere = valHere + 1
  return valHere

output=3
output=here(output)
output=here(output)
```

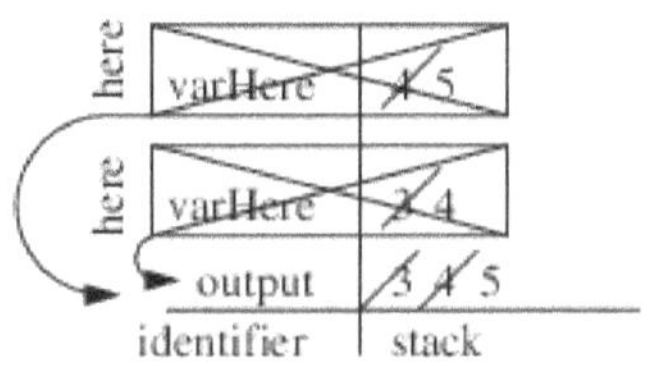

Figure 2: Functions in Python.

Return values are represented with arrows. If the value returned from a function call is caught with a variable (in our case, the variable output), an arrow is drawn from the lower left corner of the box to the specific variable that will receive the return value. Students are taught to draw this arrow when the function is called. The student completes the trace within the function, which ends with the return value replacing the value pointed to by the arrow.

This process supports students in recognizing common errors when handling return values. Students are forced to recognize where the return value of the function will be saved before starting the trace of the function, which can easily be forgotten during the trace of the function. The arrow also helps as a check for missing return statements or missing variables to catch the return value. If students see the arrow when exiting a function but have not encountered a return statement, they are made aware of a flaw in the program. Similarly, if they reach a return statement and there is no arrow from the current function call box, they are made aware that the return value of this function is not caught in the original call. These errors are extremely common with novice programmers and this standardized diagram gives students a visual reminder and procedure to follow in order to support their conceptual understanding.

Function calls also introduce the concept of *parameters* and *arguments*. We teach students to add the parameters and arguments to the function call box when initially creating the box. They view the function definition to find the appropriate identifiers for the parameters and the function call to find the corresponding values for the arguments. The correspondence between parameters in the function declaration and arguments in the function call is a major conceptual hurdle for novice programmers. An example of a complete memory diagram for a short Python program demonstrating all of these concepts is given in Figure 2.

Once again, a true understanding of Python will demonstrate this to be inaccurate in that Python does not pass parameters or return values by value (as we have presented) but rather passes references to the heap in each of these scenarios. However, since these data types are immutable there is no functional difference to this simplified conceptual model. This simplified view offers a usable description of memory that is generally applicable across Python, Java, and C++, even though all three of these languages handle this specific scenario is different ways. The concept of mutable data introduces the need to understand deeper concepts of pass by reference vs. pass by value.

3.3 Collections, Mutability, and the Heap

The next conceptual hurdle is collection data types: arrays, lists, two-dimensional arrays, associative arrays, etc. We use these collections as a basis for introducing the concept of *mutability*. Outside of functional programming, these collection data types are mutable and therefore the concept of references is necessary to accurately trace programs, particularly considering parameters and return values.

All the tracing techniques used thus far remain intact when considering mutability. We extend our diagrams by adding another section representing the *heap*. We inform students that all of these mutable data types (e.g., collections) are created in this heap section rather than in the section where they normally create their values (the stack). An arrow is drawn from the identifier (which remains in the normal location) to the heap where this mutable data can be found (Figure 3). We show that when something from this heap area is passed as either a parameter or return value, it is not copied but rather a new arrow is drawn to the same data in the heap. The most important aspect of this new diagramming technique is the recognition that changing the data within a function can have *side-effects*. This also leads to the concept of *pure functions*. While this is challenging for students, there is a practical hook for them when introducing references and collections together, namely large amounts of data. We reinforce the practical reason programming languages choose to pass single variables by copying but would not want to copy of a collection of one million items.

```
def change(listIn):
  listIn[0]=0
  return listIn

numList=[5,7,17,24]
numList2=change(numList2)

dict = {'Name': 'Seth', 'Age': 2};
```

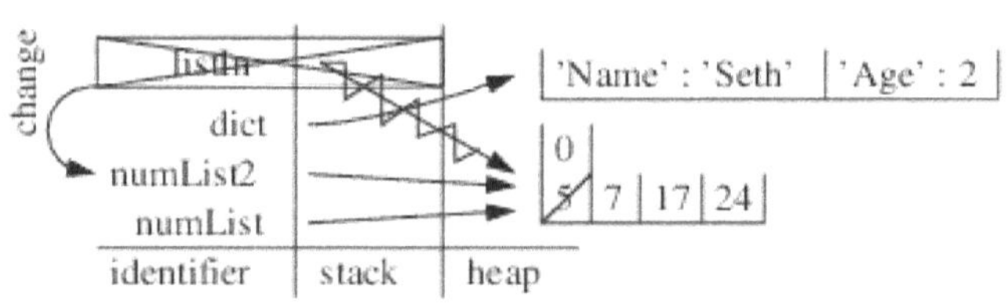

Figure 3: Lists and dictionaries in Python.

This significant new concept builds on previous memory diagram knowledge, expanding rather then relearning the diagram process. This offers a practical and procedural knowledge of mutable data, references, and the heap without overwhelming with technical definitions or ungrounded conceptual knowledge. Figure 3 demonstrates our extended diagram that includes mutable data on the heap.

We use Python when introducing these concepts (both in class and in this paper) partially for the simplicity of the list data type. Students can begin with collections quickly and easily in Python. However, this concept gives a useful mapping of these data types in Python, Java, and C++. It must be noted that this simplified view is not exactly accurate for any of these three languages. An example is that although all collections are in the heap for both Python and Java, C++ allows the programmer to decide where allocation will take place. We simplify in this scenario and introduce the complexity in a later course when C++ is being used.

3.4 Object Oriented Programming

When *Object Oriented Programming* (OOP) is introduced, we treat the diagrams as a continuation of the traces of mutable data discussed in Section 3.3. Students are taught that objects are mutable data and therefore are drawn in the heap with arrows (references) connecting them to their identifiers (Figure 4). Each instance contains a copy of the classes' data members. Each object is drawn as a circle and labeled with the corresponding class name. Inside this circle, students draw the internal state of the object represented by instance-level identifiers and values. When a method is called on an object, the method call is represented by a box in the diagram (as any other function) with the addition of the identifier that allows access to the member variables (*self* in Python, *this* in Java / C++). When a function returns, the references are crossed out. Physically crossing out the arrow intuitively connects students to the concept of references, and that references can be removed without removing/altering the actual location in memory. This becomes crucial to understanding of dynamic memory, dangling pointers, and memory leaks in C++.

```
class Person:
  def __init__(self, name, age):
    self.name = name
    self.age = age

  def getAge(self):
    return self.age

p1=Person("Seth",2)
p2=Person("Elyse",3)
ageOut=p1.getAge()
```

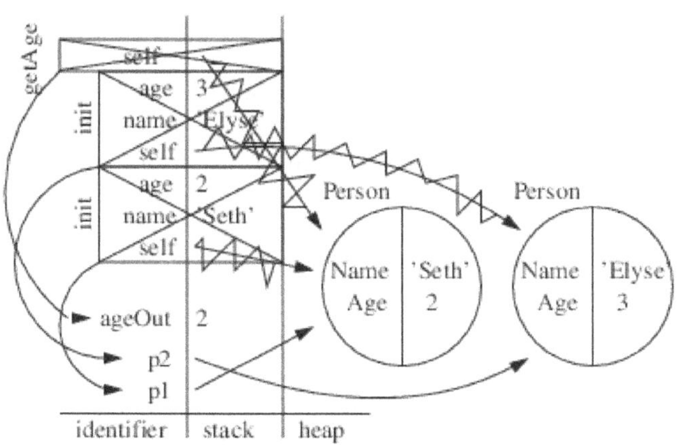

Figure 4: Objects in Python.

This diagram visually represents many of the challenging concepts that accompany a shift from imperative programming to OOP. First and foremost, students can see the concept of a *class* versus an *object* in that they use the class definition (code) to create each individual object (actual circles in the diagram). This clarifies the concept of *instances.* Similarly, this style of diagram reinforces the shift in scope when tracing method calls. Students have the explicit reference (self or this) that clarifies the object being referenced within any given method call. They are prompted to create this reference because they are accustomed to creating all parameters when calling a function (self being an explicit parameter in Python). All of these new concepts are introduced as extensions to the types of diagrams students have already been practicing, allowing students to understand OOP as an extension of their prior experience rather than a totally new concept (Figure 4).

We introduce OOP using Python but only briefly toward the end of our introductory class. Of the main OOP concepts, we focus almost exclusively on *encapsulation.* We then move to Java, where students receive more rigorous training in OOP that covers the concepts of *privacy, inheritance,* and *polymorphism.* We believe that consistent memory diagrams across both languages helps to smooth the language transition for students, helping them recognize the similarity between languages.

Figure 5 illustrates the basics of inheritance and polymorphism in Java. We see the effects of inheritance when representing an object of a child class. We note the parent class name as well as the child class name when creating the circle representing the object, and we ensure that the data members of both classes are then represented within the object. Students see the effects of polymorphism when the getInfo method is called on the SavingsAccount class. This diagram also demonstrates an actual hand-drawn example that we expect from students (during in-class exercises, quizzes, or exams).

Objects are handled almost identically in Python and Java (Figures 4 and 5) and would be handled similarly for OOP code in C++ . The difference in the code for a C++ example would be explicit pointer data types and virtual functions to ensure proper polymorphism. These types of differences can be seen as extensions to the diagram rather than as changes. In the next section we discuss one of these extensions, explicit pointers, and its usefulness.

3.5 Memory Management

Thus far we have not discussed the concept of *memory management*, namely how memory is allocated, organized, and freed. These concepts are mentioned from time to time throughout our early curriculum. We discuss *allocation* when discussing the creation of variables, particularly objects. We discuss *organization* briefly in the separation between the stack and the heap sections of the diagram. Least discussed is *deallocation*, when all references to a memory location are released and that memory can then be freed by the garbage collector and reused. As opposed to formal discussion in the early stages, the memory diagrams offer an intuitive sense about these topics and support students when these topics are brought to the forefront.

```
public class Account {
  private String id;
  private double balance;
  public Account(String id, double deposit){
    this.id = id;
  this.balance = deposit;
  }
  public String getInfo(){
    return "ID: " + this.id + "\tBalance:" +
      this.balance;
  }

  public static void main(String[] args) {
    Account test = new SavingsAccount("Jane Doe",
      100, 0.0025);
    String acctInfo = test.getInfo());
  }
}

class SavingsAccount extends Account {
  private double apr;
  public SavingsAccount (String id,
      double deposit, double apr){
    super(id, deposit);
    this.apr = apr;
  }
  public String getInfo(){
    String acctInfo = super.getInfo();
    return acctInfo + "\tAPR: " + apr;
 }
}
```

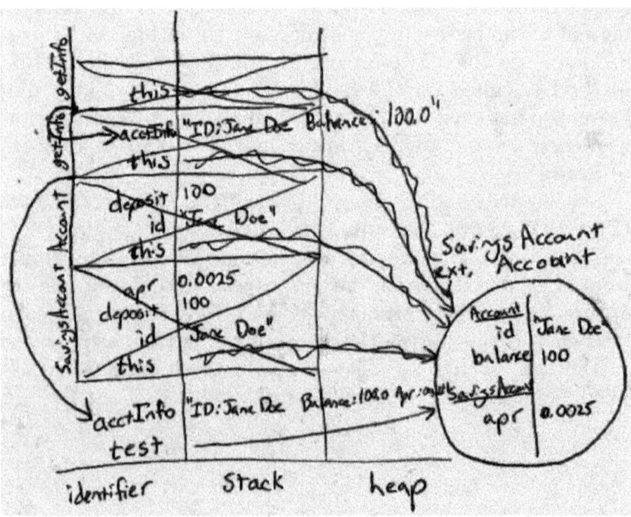

Figure 5: Objects in Java.

We choose to withhold these topics for two reasons. First, we want to keep things as simple as possible in the early stages. Our memory diagrams support this concept by giving students a visual and intuitive understanding of memory management without the necessity of formal discussion. Students see the circles and arrows being created, understand that memory is divided into different sections, and can recognize in a diagram that references to specific memory can be lost (e.g., creating an object within a function and not returning a reference to this object). This allows students the procedural knowledge to accurately model the inner workings of memory without overwhelming with high-level definitions and formalisms. Second, we delay this discussion because of language choice. When working in higher-level garbage-collected languages like Python and Java, these concepts can be treated more intuitively. Our curriculum now turns to C++ for exactly this reason. C++ offers exposure to a lower-level control that creates an opportunity and a need to gain a much deeper understanding of memory management.

We rely on the shift from Java to C++ to expose students to deeper concepts, including *memory addressing*, *pointers*, and *explicit vs. implicit allocation and deallocation*. All of these concepts can be considered incremental extensions of a familiar memory diagramming scheme.

The example given in Figure 6 demonstrates a simple C++ program that helps students understand these different concepts. Moving to C++, we discuss how Java and Python are more limited in the control they offer over memory management. In Java and Python, the language itself decides which types of variables are assigned memory in the stack and which are assigned memory in the heap. All heap memory uses a reference (arrow in our diagram). C++ offers us choices and control over these aspects. To add these possibilities to our diagram, we need only consider each arrow drawn to represent an actual memory address. In C++ these variables are their own data types called pointers. These pointers can hold memory addresses within the stack or the heap, as seen in Figure 6.

```
#include <iostream>
using namespace std;
int main () {
  int stackX = 5;
  int* stackPtr = &stackX;
  int* heapPtr = new int;
  *stackPtr = 10;
  *heapPtr = 20;
  cout << "\n on stack:" << stackX;
  cout << "\n on heap:" << *heapPtr;
  delete heapPtr;
  heapPtr = nullptr;
  return 0;
}
```

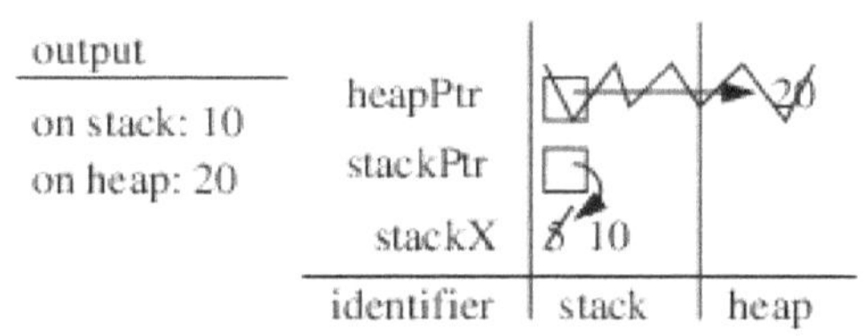

Figure 6: C++ pointer example.

We can also see the difference between explicit and implicit allocation in our code. When stackX is declared, it is also implicitly allocated on the stack. If we want to explicitly allocate memory, we can create a pointer (heapPtr) and then explicitly call for memory allocation in the heap by using the keyword "new". Students are used to the idea that the heap and the stack are different part of memory and that they are used for different types of data. The preparation scaffolds acceptance of the new concepts of explicit pointers and control over the location of the variable (stack versus heap). Finally, students need to recognize that implicitly allocated memory will be deallocated by the system but that memory allocated explicitly (on the heap) needs to be explicitly deallocated. This concept is represented visually by the separation of the stack and the heap in the diagram. A simple procedural rule for students to follow is that everything in the heap must be explicitly deallocated. This supports their practical thinking about the abstract concept of explicit deallocation.

At this point in the curriculum we have arrived at an almost completely accurate representation of computer memory in C++ . The small inconsistencies and assumptions of our previous diagrams have been replaced with the details of the actual inner workings of C++. With our completed diagramming knowledge we now can revisit previous languages with a better understanding. We engage in this process in our Programming Languages course later in the curriculum.

4. CONCLUSIONS

We have presented brief, clear examples of memory diagrams to highlight specific concepts. Obviously, real classwork involves more complex code and hand-drawn diagrams can become arduous and confusing. We manage this difficulty by tracing with a purpose. We choose key points where diagrams can be best utilized in class and on quizzes. The first demonstration of a new concept is often best accompanied by a diagram. Debugging erroneous examples is another key use for diagrams. Students discovering program faults by using hand-drawn diagrams can solidify their understanding of common mistakes.

Our memory diagrams offer teachers and students a standardized way to visualize program traces across different languages and at different levels of complexity. These diagrams strike a balance by offering the consistency necessary to support students along with the generality necessary to move from basic to more advanced concepts in the curriculum. The consistency across languages compliments this process by allowing instructors to use different languages to highlight different concepts. We have invested heavily in the design of our introductory curriculum with particular focus on the order in which concepts and languages are introduced and these memory diagrams are crucial part of the process. The memory diagram technique we have presented can be a valuable tool to achieve consistency across a department, providing students with consistency and scaffolding that can help their learning process.

5. REFERENCES

[1] cs.stolaf.edu. Memory diagram format. http://www.cs.stolaf.edu/wiki/index.php/Memory_diagram_format. Accessed: 2015-08-28.

[2] Andrew R. Dalton and William Kreahling. Automated construction of memory diagrams for program comprehension. In *Proceedings of the 48th Annual Southeast Regional Conference*, ACM SE '10, pages 22:1–22:6, New York, NY, USA, 2010. ACM.

[3] Matthew Hertz and Maria Jump. Trace-based teaching in early programming courses. In *Proceeding of the 44th ACM Technical Symposium on Computer Science Education*, SIGCSE '13, pages 561–566, New York, NY, USA, 2013. ACM.

[4] Mark A. Holliday and David Luginbuhl. Cs1 assessment using memory diagrams. In *Proceedings of the 35th SIGCSE Technical Symposium on Computer Science Education*, SIGCSE '04, pages 200–204, New York, NY, USA, 2004. ACM.

[5] itcsolutions.eu. Tutorial java - #8 understand stack and heap. http://www.itcsolutions.eu/2011/02/06/tutorial-java-8-understand-stack-and-heap/. Accessed: 2015-08-28.

[6] Linxiao Ma, John D. Ferguson, Marc Roper, Isla Ross, and Murray Wood. Using cognitive conflict and visualisation to improve mental models held by novice programmers. In *Proceedings of the 39th SIGCSE Technical Symposium on Computer Science Education*, SIGCSE '08, pages 342–346, New York, NY, USA, 2008. ACM.

[7] Thomas L. Naps, Guido Rossling, Vicki Almstrum, Wanda Dann, Rudolf Fleischer, Chris Hundhausen, Ari Korhonen, Lauri Malmi, Myles McNally, Susan Rodger, and J. Angel Velazquez-Iturbide. Exploring the role of visualization and engagement in computer science education. *SIGCSE Bull.*, 35(2):131–152, June 2002.

[8] Juha Sorva, Ville Karavirta, and Lauri Malmi. A review of generic program visualization systems for introductory programming education. *Trans. Comput. Educ.*, 13(4):15:1–15:64, November 2013.

[9] Vesa Vainio and Jorma Sajaniemi. Factors in novice programmers' poor tracing skills. In *Proceedings of the 12th Annual SIGCSE Conference on Innovation and Technology in Computer Science Education*, ITiCSE '07, pages 236–240, New York, NY, USA, 2007. ACM.

Factors Influencing Computer Science Learning in Middle School

Shuchi Grover
Center for Technology in Learning
SRI International
Menlo Park, CA 94025
shuchi.grover@sri.com

Roy Pea
Graduate School of Education
Stanford University
Stanford, CA 94305
roypea@stanford.edu

Stephen Cooper
Computer Science Department
Stanford University
Stanford, CA 94305
coopers@stanford.edu

ABSTRACT

In this paper, we describe research conducted around a 7-week curriculum designed to introduce middle school students to computer science with a focus on algorithmic thinking and programming. The pedagogical ideas employed in this curriculum were drawn from past research. Empirical investigations over two studies in a public middle school in the US examined changes in students' understanding of algorithmic constructs and the factors affecting that learning. Multi-level analyses revealed that students in both studies (1) achieved substantial learning gains in algorithmic thinking skills and significant growth towards a more mature understanding of computing as a discipline, and (2) found certain CT ideas and constructs more difficult than others. Prior computing experiences and math and English ability were found to be predictors of learning outcomes. Extracurricular experiences with technology also appeared to impact outcomes.

Keywords

Middle School; Deeper Learning; Learning Factors; K-12 Computer Science Education; Computational Thinking.

1. INTRODUCTION

The rationale for introducing computing in K-12 in order to advance computational thinking (CT) is compelling [10,34,40]. While needs of high school students in the US are being prioritized through courses such as Exploring Computer Science (ECS) and AP CS Principles, there is a growing belief that experiences with computing must start at an earlier age. Middle school years are formative and key for cognitive and social development in the K-12 schooling journey especially with regard to future engagement with STEM fields [35]. Experiences with computing should therefore make middle school amenable to diverse future opportunities as part of students' possible selves.

While there has been some growth in structured middle school computer science (CS) curricula, the development of deeper, transferable CT skills in a classroom setting is yet to be empirically validated. The goal of this research was to address this through designing and empirically studying the use of a structured curriculum for middle school that leverages pedagogical ideas from the learning sciences and computing education research about how children can best develop algorithmic thinking and programming skills. We adopted an iterative process to design, refine, and study our introductory middle school CS course—*Foundations for Advancing Computational Thinking* (FACT) to empirically investigate students' development of CT skills.

This paper focuses on presenting our research around answering the following research questions—**RQ1:** ***What is the variation across learners in learning of algorithmic flow of control (serial execution, looping constructs, and conditional logic) through FACT; RQ2: What factors influence these learning outcomes?*** The paper is organized as follows. A survey of relevant related work presents a backdrop to the research framework and the rationale of FACT's curriculum, pedagogy and assessment design. The research methodology follows including a brief description of the pedagogical designs used to introduce students to computing and algorithmic thinking, and the empirical studies. The Results section provides results in the form of descriptive statistics and also describes the mixed-methods analyses that were used to examine what factors, such as prior experiences and learner backgrounds, explained the variance observed in learning outcomes. The paper ends with a discussion and synthesis of the main findings of this research as well as their implications.

2. RELATED WORK

Much of the CT research involving middle school children in the US has centered on introductory block-based computational tools such as Scratch, Alice, Agentsheets, Blockly, App Inventor etc. Engaging activities such as programming games and apps are used to foster fluency and motivation in computational problem solving. Tangible computational tools such as robotics kits and e-textiles (using Lilypad Arduino) have also been used and studied. Until recently, most of these have occurred in informal settings.

In the formal middle school context, research studies have been conducted as students engage with CT through game design in Alice and Agentsheets [4,28]. Some others have aimed to teach computational thinking in the context of middle school science [e.g. 32,38]. In Denner et al.'s work, students worked through a series of self-paced instructional exercises in Alice and then designed and developed their own games. Students were assessed using a specially designed assessment [37]. They summarize their experiences elsewhere by acknowledging that while computer game programming (CGP) in environments such as Alice have proved to be "a good strategy to attract underrepresented students to computing in middle school and to engage them in programming concepts and systems thinking, CGP does not automatically result in learning, and without some intention on the part of the teacher, it will not result in them learning specific programming concepts." [4]. Previous studies around children and

SIGCSE '16, March 02-05, 2016, Memphis, TN, USA
© 2016 ACM. ISBN 978-1-4503-3685-7/16/03…$15.00
DOI: http://dx.doi.org/10.1145/2839509.2844564

LOGO [19,22,25,26] endorsed the merits of such an approach and underscored that ***teachers as well as instruction play a substantial role in what and how students learn***.

In taking an approach focusing on teaching the foundational concepts of CS through the structured use of Scratch, FACT is similar to efforts in Israel and the UK [31,41]. Our pilot effort involved the design and evaluation of a 7-week "mini-course", to give students a brief introduction to CS and computational problem solving in order to raise interest and awareness in CS and serve as a good foundation for future computing experiences. More importantly, given its duration, FACT can potentially be taught as a unit in existing math, science or technology elective periods. Our work also employs pedagogy for a structured curriculum that makes the teaching of specific CS concepts and vocabulary more intentional, with the goal to consciously ***teach CS***. Since examining students' programming artifacts alone to assess learning can be misleading [19,23], we assess young learners' understanding of concepts of CS through designed assessments in addition to artifacts created by students for evidence of their understanding of computational concepts. This last aspect distinguishes FACT from other efforts in the US [30].

3. METHODOLOGY

This research effort involved two iterations that examined the use of FACT in a public middle school classroom setting. The first iteration was in a traditional face-to-face classroom setting, whereas the second iteration involved investigations on a blended model of learning using an online version of FACT designed and created on Stanford University's OpenEdX MOOC platform. The research involved designing the FACT curriculum; engineering a blended learning experience using an online version of FACT; and empirically investigating FACT's use in a classroom to answer the research question outlined earlier.

3.1 FACT Curriculum

The curriculum (Table 1) was inspired by the 36-week long ECS high school curriculum [8], and includes topics on algorithmic problem solving and programming (in Scratch) that the authors considered foundational and appropriate for middle school students. These map roughly to Units 1, 2 and 4 of ECS. The entire curriculum design effort was guided by goals for "deeper learning" [27], attending to the development of cognitive abilities in addition to interpersonal and intrapersonal abilities (such as collaboration and communication).

3.1.1 Features for Fostering Deeper Learning

To target deeper learning of algorithmic problem solving and to address issues in learning to program that novice programmers face [6,14,25,29], FACT's curriculum design leverages available learning sciences literature. The pedagogy uses a scaffolding and cognitive apprenticeship [2] approach to model the process of programming through the use of (worked) examples [16]. This includes modeling and constructing solutions to computational problems in a manner that reveals the underlying structure of the problem, and the process of composing the solution in pseudo-code or in Scratch. Drawing on past research [9], computing vocabulary and CT language are used during this scaffolding process. FACT also consciously engages with students' narrow perceptions of CS to help them see computing in a new light by using publicly-available videos (bit.ly/CS-rocks) exemplifying computing as a problem-solving discipline with applications in many real-world creative contexts and disciplines [12].

Table 1. 7-week FACT Course for Middle School

Unit 1	Computing is Everywhere! / What is CS?
Unit 2	What are algorithms & programs? Computational solution as a precise sequence of instructions.
Unit 3	Iterative/repetitive flow of control in a program: Loops
Unit 4	Representation of Information (Data and variables)
Unit 5	Boolean Logic & Advanced Looping
Unit 6	Selective flow of control: Conditional thinking
	Final Project (student's own choice; individual or pairs)

FACT emphasizes "learning by doing" [1] for students through a mix of directed projects and meaningful, open-ended projects in Scratch including a substantive culminating project that students were encouraged to do in pairs (Table 2). Frequent low-stakes multiple-choice formative assessments were designed to ensure learners stay engaged with the content and learning goals of the course, and to provide feedback both to the learners and the teacher. These also include questions inspired by Parson's puzzles [24]. FACT aims to foster a deeper understanding of foundational concepts by providing learners opportunities to work with plain English, pseudo-code as well as programs coded in Scratch. At occasional junctures during the course there are opportunities to examine the same algorithm put together in a language besides Scratch. Student learning was also assessed through the final open-ended game design project of choice. FACT's curriculum and assessments are detailed in earlier publications [13,14,15].

Table 2. Sample programming projects in Scratch

Programming Assignments	Algorithmic ideas
Share a recipe	Sequence of instructions
(Scratch) Make a life cycle of choice to use in a 6th grade science class	Serial execution
(Scratch) Draw a Spirograph from a polygon of choice	Simple nested loop (also, creative computing (CC))
(Scratch) Create a simple animation	*Forever loop*
(Scratch) Generic polygon maker	Variables; user input
Look inside Scratch code and explain the text version of code	Algorithms in different forms
(Scratch) Draw a 'Squiral'	Loops, variables (& CC)
Open-ended project (in pairs): Create a game using "Repeat Until"	*Loops ending with Boolean condition*
(Scratch) Maze game	Event handlers; Conditionals
(Scratch) Guess my number game	Loops, conditionals, variables, Boolean logic
(Scratch) Final project of choice	*All CT topics taught*

3.2 Study and Data Measures

Empirical studies were conducted in a public middle school classroom in Northern California. Two iterations (Study1 and Study2) of research were conducted with two different cohorts in the same 'Computers' elective class that met four days a week for 55 minute periods. The student samples comprised 7th and 8th grade students (Table 3; ELL="English Language Learners"). In Study1, the course was taught face-to-face by the first author. Study2 was conducted in the same classroom with a new cohort and used a refined version of FACT (based on learning from Study1) on OpenEdX for blended learning and comprised a mix of individual and collaborative activities. The regular classroom teacher, who did not have a background in CS or programming, was present in the classroom at all times assisting with classroom management and also "learning right alongside the students."

Table 3. Student samples in Study1 & Study2

Study	Mean Age	Male	Female	Grade 7	Grade 8	ELL	Special Ed.
1	12.9	21	5	15	11	4	2
2	12.3	20	8	16	12	3	1

3.2.1 Data Measures

The following constituted the main data measures:

- *Prior Experience Survey*: Students were given an extensive survey on prior experiences in technology and computational activities, especially programming.
- *CS Interest & Attitudes Pre-post Survey*: Inspired by [7]
- *Pre-Post Measures of CT*: Students were given pre-post tests that measured their understanding of computational concepts. The pretest and posttest used items from prior research involving middle school CS with Scratch [7] and included 6 out of 9 questions from the Israel National Exam described in [42]. We did not incorporate the other three questions, as we did not have details on them prior to our study's launch.
- *Course Experience Survey*: to gather feedback from learners for improvements for future iterations.
- *School data:* demographic information including age, gender, and academic placement (English, Math, special needs)

4. ANALYSIS & RESULTS

In order to answer RQ1, pre-post data were first analyzed separately for each study using descriptive statistics, paired *t-tests* and non-parametric tests to study within-subject differences from pre-to-post test. A comparative analysis was also conducted on the six questions of the posttest that were employed in the National CS Exam administered to about 4000 middle school students in Israel in 2012 [42].

Table 4. Pre- and Posttest Scores (out of 100), Study 1 & 2

	Pretest	Posttest		
Study	Mean (SD)	Mean (SD)	t-stat	p-value
1	36.3 (18.2)	79.4 (17.5)	-17.3	<0.001
2	28.1 (21.18)	81.6 (21.0)	-15.5	<0.001

Note: *Non-parametric Mann-Whitney (Wilcoxon) rank sum test was also conducted to test the difference between the pretest and posttest, and the results remained significant.*

Table 5. Posttest Scores by CT Topics, Study1 & Study2

	Study 1	Study 2		
	Mean (SD)	Mean (SD)	t-stat	p
Overall	78.6 (17.1)	81.6 (21.2)	-0.6	0.56
By CS Topic				
Serial Execution	97.4 (13.1)	91.1 (20.7)	1.4	0.18
Conditionals	84.5 (19.0)	84.9 (20.5)	-0.1	0.94
Loops	74.1 (21.9)	77.2 (26.3)	-0.5	0.64
CS Vocabulary	68.2 (17.9)	77.4 (22.2)	-1.7	0.10

*(**Note**: t-statistic and p-value refer to the test of difference in the mean scores for Study1 and Study2)*

Relevant learning outcomes pertinent to RQ1 are shown in Tables 4 and 5. On the posttest score, there was no significant difference between the studies. The pretest scores in the two studies were also not statistically different. The pre-to-posttest effect size (Cohen's *d*) on the CT test was roughly 2.4 in both studies. *Learners found serial execution to be easiest and loops, especially those involving variable manipulation, the most difficult to grasp* (Table 5). The comparative analysis with the results from the Israeli nationwide exam revealed comparable or slightly better performances by our students (Figure. 1; Question numbers are the same as in [42]). Some gender differences were observed with girls performing better than boys, however the small number of females in the samples precluded drawing deeper conclusions.

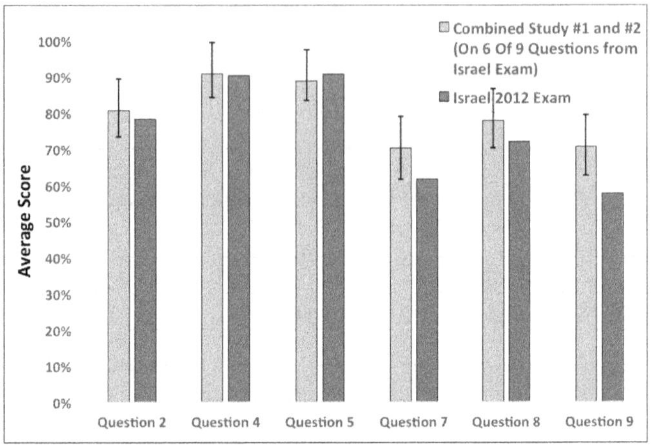

Figure 1: Comparison of Student Performance in Study1 & Study2 vs. 2012 Israel results (on 6 of 9 questions)

To answer RQ2, factor analyses on prior experience variables and multivariate regressions were conducted to determine which factors predicted outcome measures of interest (Section 4.1).

4.1 Factors Influencing Learning Outcomes

What factors explain these differences in learning outcomes? Learning is influenced by several factors, including learners' prior experience, interests and attitudes towards the subject being taught in addition to academic preparation, especially in foundational subjects such as mathematics and English [36]. While it is acknowledged that mathematics and English levels are often a function of learners' SES (socio-economic status), inclusion of SES variables was outside of the scope of this research (as was school context since both studies were conducted in the same school). In order to explain the variability, factor analyses and multivariate regressions analyses were carried out.

4.1.1 Rationale for combined regression analyses

Factor analyses and regressions were conducted on the combined sample from the two studies *to gain more statistical power with a larger sample size (N=54)*. The justification for combining the data was as follows: Since both studies were conducted in the same school and classroom, there were several similarities among the participants and school settings. Students in both studies came in with similar levels of knowledge of computing as tested by the pretest (there was no statistical difference between the studies). The two groups were similar in their mathematics and English abilities as measured by the STAR California state test, and the responses on the survey questions probing interests and attitudes towards CS both before and after the intervention were not statistically different between groups. Students' performances on the posttest were also not statistically different across the two studies (Table 5).

4.1.2 Factor Analysis on Prior Experience Survey

As a first step towards using multivariate regression analyses to explain the effects of the several possible independent variables on the main outcomes of interest, it was necessary to analyze several item-level responses on relevant questions (Table 6) in the prior experience survey for underlying patterns via exploratory factor analytic procedures. Factor analysis is a multivariate statistical approach commonly used for interpreting self-reporting questionnaires [39].

Table 6. Prior Experience Survey Items in Factor Analysis

Q5: (Yes/No) "Have you ever written a computer program?"

Q9: (9 items) "How many times have you ever created the following using some software on the computer?" [List]

Q11: (13 items) "How would you describe your level of experience with the following computer applications/equipment?" [List e.g. Scratch/Alice/Tynker]

Q12: (9 items) "How many times do you use a computer to do each of the following" [List e.g. play online multi-user games]

*Note: **Q9** measured depth of technology experience on a 4-point Likert scale– 1=never to 4=more than six times; **Q11** measured experience level on a 5-point Likert scale from 1="I don't know what it is" to 5="I'm an expert and can teach someone how to use it"; **Q12** measured frequency of computational and media creation on a 8-point Likert scale– 1=Never to 8=Several times a day*

Three main "prior experience factors" were found. We titled them *Coder*, *Media Creator*, and *Online Consumer* as described in Table 7. Pearson's correlation tests between the three factors indicated the correlation coefficient was less than 0.1 suggesting that these were 3 distinct types of students in the study sample. Pearson correlations also suggested that math ability levels (as measured by STAR scores) were significantly negatively correlated only to *Online Consumer*, and positively correlated with *Coder* and *Media Creator*. The implications of these correlational findings are discussed further in Section 5.

Table 7. Descriptions of Prior Experience Factor Variables

Prior Exp (PE) Factor	Description
PE Factor 1: *Coder*	Strong on programming experience. Especially strong components of factor 1 are a positive response on "have you ever programmed before?" and experience with coding languages.
Factor 2: *Media Creator*	Little to no coding experience but strong association with digital media creation activities such as creating digital movies, music, audio.
Factor 3: *Online Consumer*	Little to no experience with computer programming or creating digital media, however strong associations with playing computer & multi-user online games, watching movie videos.

4.1.3 *Multivariate Regressions*

Based on prior research [36], it was ascertained that the following variables could influence learning outcomes in FACT:

- Prior knowledge of computational constructs.
- Technology fluency and prior experience with computation.
- Interest in and attitudes towards CS.
- Academic preparation (as measured here by mathematics and English levels in STAR California State tests).
- Learning issues (English Language Learner, or ELL).
- Demographics (age and gender).

Some variables were dropped early on as they were not found to be significant predictors of outcomes of interest in either uni-variate or multivariate regressions with any combination of predictor variables. Age was one such variable. The stepwise regressions used to determine the best model thus included:

1. Mean of the CS attitudes survey items.
2. Mean of the 'future interest in CS' survey item calculated for each student.
3. Prior experience factors (the three factors identified above).
4. Most recent Math STAR test score.
5. Most recent English STAR test score.
6. ELL status.
7. Gender.
8. Pretest score (for posttest).

Following stepwise regressions, interest and attitudes variables were dropped due to lack of significance as predictors of outcome variables, as were gender and English STAR score. Table 8 presents the final full regression used to explain the variation in pretest and posttest scores.

Table 8. Final regression for factors influencing outcomes

	Posttest		Pretest	
Variable	**β**	**SE**	**β**	**SE**
Pretest	0.39^{***}	0.11	–	–
Math STAR	0.40^{**}	3.22	0.34^{**}	2.79
ELL	0.08	7.98	0.06	5.61
PE Factor1 (Coder)	0.14	1.79	0.62^{***}	3.10
PE Factor2 (Creator)	-0.01	2.07	0.13	1.64
PE Factor3 (Consumer)	-0.16	1.58	-0.02	1.53
Constant	–	13.82	–	13.39
N	54		54	
Adjusted R^2	0.53		0.49	

$^{*}p < 0.5$. $^{**}p<0.01$. $^{***}p<0.001$

4.1.4 *Performance Based on Prior Experience*

While prior programming experience as measured by the pretest was found to be relevant for the posttest, the three prior experience factors did not predict performance on the posttest. This suggested that FACT helped ***all students*** regardless of prior experience as measured by the self-report survey. To further examine how the prior experience factors affected learning outcomes, a median split was used to divide students into 'high' and 'low' groups for the 3 factors– "High Coder"/"Low Coder", "High Creator"/"Low Creator", and "High Consumer"/"Low Consumer". As expected, being a High Coder (as opposed to Low Coder) was beneficial for both pretest and posttest scores on the CT test. Since neither Media Creators nor Online Consumer factors were high on prior programming experience, it was also useful to examine how these sub-groups fared in the posttest. In general, learning gains were higher for High Creator than Low Creator students, and being a Low Consumer helped post-scores and learning gains more than being a High Consumer. These differences weren't significant, but were suggestive that perhaps significant relationships may emerge with larger samples.

5. DISCUSSION

Based on the quantitative results and analyses for the two studies, it appears that FACT helped all learners attain substantial gains in learning of basic algorithmic flow of control in computational solutions. Serial execution was the easiest to learn, as expected. *Between conditionals and loops, learners found loops harder to tackle.* Most of the assessment questions concerning loops required manipulation of variables as well, which seemed to be the hardest topic for students to grasp (based on OpenEdX dashboard data on formative quiz performances [11,15] and assigned programming activities). Both these aspects have been known to be particularly difficult for novice programmers [25,33]. Despite our conscious efforts, students struggled with these topics. Extra attention needs to be given as to how introductory courses could be improved to help learners build deeper understanding of variables and the ways in which they work in loops specifically, and in computational solutions, in general. Some of this may also be related to the level of math preparation as discussed below.

5.1 Prior Math and English Preparation

Regression analyses revealed math performance was a positively correlated predictor for CS posttest performance (even when controlling for the pretest). This correlation has been found in past research [21]. It is not entirely surprising given that abstraction is key to computing and a key skill taught in math [5,18]. Given the difficulties students had with loops and variables (which share a strong relationship with abstract and algebraic thinking) in comparison with conditionals, the link to prior math preparation needs to be probed further. This issue is also significant because students' mathematics preparation historically co-varies with socio-economic status and other indicators of diversity.

English Language Learner (ELL) status was a negative predictor for the text-heavy transfer test [discussed in 14,15]. However, ELL students showed high levels of motivation for their open-ended authentic final projects of choice. They performed better on the associated interviews even though their projects were on the lower end of the complexity scale compared to other class projects [15]. We hope to re-examine these aspects of our curriculum as we iterate on it and study it further with more diverse student populations. However, they do suggest that curricula must pay closer attention to diverse levels of math and English preparation and ensure that ***all*** learners succeed in introductory CS.

5.2 Out-of-school Technology Experiences

The curriculum helped all students achieve significant learning gains irrespective of prior experience (as measured by the self-report survey). Not surprisingly, prior programming experience as measured by the pretest was found to positively predict performance on the posttest. Regressing posttest performance on high and low levels of prior experience factors (that resulted from factor analyses on prior experience survey data) revealed that among students who did not have prior programming experience, those with experience in media creation generally did better than those that did not, and those that engaged only in online gaming and video watching (to the exclusion of programming or media creation activities (i.e. the *Online Consumers*), did worse. Having a high value for the *Online Consumer* factor was also correlated to poor mathematics and English ability (as measured by STAR tests). This perhaps points to other factors such as low SES and a lack of out-of-school experiences that may be considered intellectually enriching. More broadly, these results suggest that the nature of out-of-school technology experiences have a bearing on computational learning. These factors have important implications for curriculum and assessments design, and support the rationale for courses such as ECS that have a strong equity focus as we attempt to ensure ***computing for all***.

6. CONCLUSION & IMPLICATIONS

This research describes two studies that were conducted in a public school. The studies were conducted in an elective class, which meant learners (who were also mostly male) came into the course with generally high interest and motivation. Despite this limited generalizability, the research makes several unique contributions. It is perhaps the first structured online/blended introductory middle school curriculum that has been through rigorous empirical investigation, where computational thinking learning outcomes are measured through pre-post assessments. It is a curriculum that has been shown to result in learning gains (in the context in which it was studied) and to foster CT skills in middle school students as measured by assessment items used in prior research including a national CS exam in Israel. It serves as an example of course designed on an online platform that effectively employs an iterative research methodology to refine a curriculum aiming to foster learning in a blended classroom setting. The conscious attention devoted to teaching (and assessing) for transfer, as well as attending to perceptions of computing as a discipline through an engaging corpus of publicly available videos (presented in detail in prior publications [12, 15]), are also unique aspects of this research. Breaking down pre-posttest by algorithmic constructs to examine learning on these different aspects highlights targets of difficulty in middle school students. This research thus makes contributions to the design of curricula and assessments using block-based environments such as Scratch, Blockly, and Alice that are popularly used today.

The finding that students with low prior mathematics achievement experienced difficulties in learning CS in middle school has broad importance- it points to a need to build abstraction skills that math prepares students for. Other recent research also points to the relevance of English and math skills in environments such as Scratch for younger grades [17]. Future directions for this effort involve iterating on the curriculum to attend more closely to prior math preparation and to make the curriculum more accessible to all students by continuing to empirically examine its use with broader audiences of middle school students and teachers.

7. ACKNOWLEDGMENTS

We gratefully acknowledge grant support from the National Science Foundation (NSF #1343227 and NSF #0835854).

8. REFERENCES

[1] Barron B., & Daring-Hammond, L. 2008. How can we teach for meaningful learning? In Darling-Hammond, L.,et al. *Powerful learning: What we know about teaching for understanding*. San Francisco: Jossey-Bass.

[2] Brown, J. S., Collins, A., & Newman, S. E. 1989. Cognitive apprenticeship: Teaching the crafts of reading, writing, and mathematics. *Knowing, learning, and instruction: Essays in honor of Robert Glaser, 487.*

[3] Campe, S., Denner, J., & Werner, L. 2013. Intentional computing: Getting the results you want from game programming classes. *Journal of Computing Teachers.*

[4] Denner, J., Werner, L., & Ortiz, E. 2012. Computer games created by middle school girls: Can they be used to measure understanding of computer science concepts?. *Computers & Education, 58*(1), 240-249.

[5] Devlin, K. 2003. Why universities require computer science students to take math. *Communications of the ACM, 46*(9).

[6] du Boulay, B. 1986. Some difficulties of learning to program. *Journal of Educational Computing Research*, 2(1).

[7] Ericson, B., & McKlin, T. 2012. Effective and sustainable computing summer camps. In Proceedings of the 43rd ACM technical symposium on Computer Science

[8] Goode, J., Chapman, G., Margolis, J., Landa, J., Ullah, T., Watkins, D., & Stephenson, C. 2013. Exploring Computer Science. http://www.exploringcs.org/curriculum

[9] Grover, S. 2011. Robotics and engineering for middle and high school students to develop computational thinking, in *Annual Meeting of the AERA*, New Orleans, LA.

[10] Grover, S., and Pea, R. 2013. Computational Thinking in K–12: A Review of the State of the Field. Educational Researcher, 42(1), 38-43.

[11] Grover, S., Pea, R., & Cooper, S. 2014. Promoting active learning & leveraging dashboards for curriculum assessment in an OpenEdX introductory CS course for middle school. In *Proceedings of the first ACM conference on Learning@ scale conference* (pp. 205-206). ACM.

[12] Grover, S., Pea, R. & Cooper, S. 2014. Remedying Misperceptions of Computer Science among Middle School Students. *In Proceedings of the 45th ACM Technical Symposium on Computer Science Education.* ACM.

[13] Grover, S., Cooper, S., & Pea, R. 2014. Assessing computational learning in K-12. In *Proceedings of the 2014 conference on Innovation & technology in computer science education* (pp. 57-62). ACM.

[14] Grover, S., Pea, R. and Cooper, S. 2014. Expansive Framing and Preparation for Future Learning in Middle-School Computer Science. In Proceedings of the 11th ICLS (2014).

[15] Grover, S., Pea, R., Cooper, S. 2015. Designing for Deeper Learning in a Blended Computer Science Course for Middle School Students. *Computer Sc. Education*, 25(2), 199-237.

[16] Guzdial, M. 2009. How we teach Introductory Computer Science is wrong. Blog at *Communications of the ACM.*

[17] Hill, C., Dwyer, H. A., Martinez, T., Harlow, D., & Franklin, D. 2015. Floors and Flexibility: Designing a programming environment for 4th-6th grade classrooms. In Proceedings of the 46th ACM Technical Symposium on Computer Science Education (pp. 546-551). ACM.

[18] Kramer, J. 2007. Is abstraction the key to computing?. *Communications of the ACM, 50*(4), 36-42.

[19] Kurland, D. M., & Pea, R. D. 1985. Children's mental models of recursive LOGO programs. *Journal of Educational Computing Research, 1*(2), 235-243.

[20] Lahtinen, E., Ala-Mutka, K., & Järvinen, H. M. 2005. A study of the difficulties of novice programmers. *ACM SIGCSE Bulletin, 37*(3), 14-18.

[21] Lewis, C. M., & Shah, N. 2012. Building upon and enriching grade four mathematics standards with programming curriculum. In *Proceedings of the 43rd ACM technical symposium on Computer Science Education.* ACM.

[22] Mayer, R.E. 1989. The psychology of how novices learn computer programming. In E. Soloway & J.C. Spohrer (Eds.), Studying the novice programmer (pp. 129–159). Hillsdale, NJ: Lawrence Erlbaum

[23] Meerbaum-Salant, O., Armoni, M., and Ben-Ari, M., 2010. Learning computer science concepts with Scratch. In Proceedings of the Sixth International Workshop on Computing Education Research (ICER '10). ACM.

[24] Parsons, D., & Haden, P. 2006. Parson's programming puzzles: a fun and effective learning tool for first programming courses. In *Proceedings of the 8th Australasian Conference on Computing Education-Volume 52* (pp. 157-163). Australian Computer Society, Inc.

[25] Pea, R. D., & Kurland, D. M. 1983. On the cognitive prerequisites of learning computer programming. (Tech. Report No. 16). New York: Bank Street College of Education, Center for Children and Technology.

[26] Pea, R. D., & Kurland, D. M. 1984. On the cognitive effects of learning computer programming. New Ideas In Psychology, 2, 137–168.

[27] Pellegrino, J. W., & Hilton, M. L. (Eds.). 2013. *Education for life and work: Developing transferable knowledge and skills in the 21st century*. National Academies Press.

[28] Repenning, A., Webb, D., & Ioannidou, A. 2010. Scalable game design and the development of a checklist for getting computational thinking into public schools. In *Proceedings of the 41st ACM Technical Symposium on Computer Science Education (SIGCSE '10)*, 265–269. New York, NY: ACM.

[29] Robins, A., Rountree, J., & Rountree, N. 2003. Learning and teaching programming: A review and discussion. *Computer Science Education, 13*(2), 137-172.

[30] Schofield, E., Erlinger, M., & Dodds, Z. 2014. MyCS: CS for middle-years students and their teachers. In *Proceedings of the 45th ACM technical symposium on Computer science education* (pp. 337-342). ACM.

[31] Scott, J. 2013. The royal society of Edinburgh/British computer society computer science exemplification project. *Proceedings of ITiCSE'13*, 313-315.

[32] Sengupta, P., Kinnebrew, J. S., Basu, S., Biswas, G., & Clark, D. 2013. Integrating computational thinking with K-12 science education using agent-based computation: A theoretical framework. *Education and Information Technologies*, 1–30.

[33] Spohrer, J. C. & Soloway, E. 1986. Novice mistakes: are the folk wisdoms correct? *Communications of the ACM*, 29(7.

[34] Stephenson, C., Gal-Ezer, J., Haberman, B., & Verno, A. 2005. The new educational imperative: Improving high school computer science education. *Computer Science Teachers Association (CSTA), New York, New York.*

[35] Tai, R., Qi Liu, C., Maltese, A.V., Fan, X. 2006. Planning Early for Careers in Science. Science. 312(5777) 1143-1144

[36] Wang, M. C., Haertel, G. D., & Walberg, H. J. (1993). Toward a knowledge base for school learning. *Review of educational research*, *63*(3), 249-294.

[37] Werner, L., Denner, J., Campe, S., & Kawamoto, D. C. 2012. The Fairy Performance Assessment: Measuring Computational Thinking in Middle School. In Proceedings of the 43rd ACM Technical Symposium on Computer Science Education (SIGCSE '12), 215-220. ACM, New York, NY.

[38] Wilensky, U., Brady, C., & Horn, M. 2014. Fostering Computational Literacy in Science Classrooms. *Communications of the ACM. 57*(8): pp 17-21.

[39] Williams, B., Brown, T., & Onsman, A. 2010. Exploratory factor analysis: A five-step guide for novices. *Australasian Journal of Paramedicine, 8*(3). Retrieved from http://ro.ecu.edu.au/jephc/vol8/iss3/1

[40] Wing, J. 2006. Computational Thinking. Communications of the ACM. 49(3), 33-36.

[41] Zur Bargury, I. 2012. A new Curriculum for Junior-High in Computer Science. *ITiCSE'12,* pp. 204-208. ACM.

[42] Zur-Bargury, I., Pârv, B., & Lanzberg, D. 2013. A nationwide exam as a tool for improving a new curriculum. In Proceedings of ITiCSE'13 (pp. 267-272). ACM.

MyCS at 5: Assessing a Middle-years CS Curriculum

Brenda Castro, Terrence Diaz, Marissa Gee, Rebekah Justice, David Kwan,
Preethi Seshadri, and Zachary Dodds
Harvey Mudd College
301 Platt Blvd.
Claremont, CA 91711
{bcastro, tdiaz, mgee, rjustice, dkwan, pseshadri, dodds}@hmc.edu

ABSTRACT

This paper shares the five-year development and deployment of MyCS, a CS curriculum for "middle-years students," roughly in US grades 4-10. Consistent with many middle-years curricula, MyCS promotes positive individual identification with its field, CS, especially as it intersects with other facets of students' maturing identities. A detailed assessment of students' MyCS experiences reveal significant positive outcomes relative to a control group, as well as many neutral (no-distinction) results relative to the control. Feedback from teacher and administrators have refined MyCS and, perhaps more importantly, built curricular bridges to both elementary- and high-school CS. By tracing MyCS's assessment and evolution, this work highlights how two districts used a middle-years CS foothold from which to establish deeper, district-wide changes in identity.

Categories and Subject Descriptors

Social and professional topics - Professional topics - Computing education - K-12 education

Keywords

Middle-school CS; Computational Identity; K-12 CS; MyCS

1. MOTIVATION

Middle-years Computer Science, or *MyCS*, is an 18-week introductory CS curriculum targeting students in US grades 4-10. As described in [1], MyCS synthesizes well-established resources [2,3,4,5] along with original material in a semester-long course.

Successful approaches have integrated CS within existing facets of the middle-years curriculum, e.g. algebra [6] and science [7]. In contrast, MyCS offers a complete course that districts use as a stand-alone elective. Alternatively, its modules can supplement existing tech curricula, nudging students toward confidence in composing, as well as to consuming, computational resources. MyCS's primary goal is to promote a positive computational identity among its students.

Concretely, MyCS succeeds when its students say *"CS is something people like me do."* To date, over 4,000 students have taken MyCS-based courses in the curriculum's first five years; a number larger than that total are taking MyCS in '15-'16. In hopes of supporting other districts seeking to adopt or adapt CS for their middle-years students, this paper shares lessons distilled from MyCS's five-year evolution:

- MyCS's flexibility has enabled it to reach a more diverse student group than identify with CS at older ages. It supports a positive computational identity equitably across the student cohorts it has served.
- MyCS's modularity and graduated online resources support tentative teachers in building confidence in an unfamiliar subject -- at a pace they can tune to their liking.
- Far larger than the differential pre/post impacts between MyCS students and the control groups are the pre/post impacts it has had on its districts. Adopters have developed positive ***institutional*** identities vis-a-vis computing.

We next summarize MyCS's core curriculum and share the results of its assessments. Influenced by partnering districts' growing identification as *"places where **we** do CS,"* MyCS's curriculum has recently piloted transition materials that reach outward from its target age-range. From those efforts, we reflect on the conditions through which the "middle-years" might offer an especially fertile starting ground from which to grow a positive district-wide CS identity and CS program.

2. CURRICULUM

MyCS's curriculum emphasizes CS's breadth, opportunities for creative expression, and experiences in computational problem solving. For the past five years, MyCS has refined a computing course featuring conceptual, hands-on, and on-screen activities.

Often, the eighteen-week curriculum is expanded to a full year through deliberate pacing or through combining its material with an existing tech class. Professional development workshops have built enthusiasm and confidence for teaching CS in partnering districts, PUSD and KUSD, of Pomona, CA and Kauai, HI.

Detailed more thoroughly elsewhere [1], we offer here a brief summary of each of MyCS's six three-week modules. The first, "*What is CS?*," builds students' intuition about CS by making more deliberate and explicit their substantial prior experiences -- and assumptions -- about computers and software. The second module, "*A-maze-ing Scratch*," introduces students to Scratch through a gently graduated set of 100 mazes. "*Codes and Data*" challenges students to encode and decode messages of many forms, culminating in using binary to represent – and rebuild – a Lego tower of their own design. The fourth unit, "*Interactive Scratch,*" returns to programming by guiding message-sharing, story-staging, and game-creation. The fifth unit, "*Problem Solving and Algorithms*," offers a screen-free, hands-on introduction to algorithmic thinking, including searching and sorting. The final unit again spirals back: "*Algorithms in Scratch*" scaffolds students through decomposing problems and implementing solutions in what, we hope by term's end, is a programming environment in which they feel comfortable and confident.

SIGCSE '16, March 2–5, 2016, Memphis, TN, USA.
© 2016 ACM ISBN 978-1-4503-3685-7/16/03…$15.00 .
DOI: http://dx.doi.org/10.1145/2839509.2844643

Figure 1. Prompts and averages for *all* survey-takers (using a 1-6 Likert scale, with N=5475)

Date	Computing is fun.	I am good at computing.	Programming is Hard (Reversed)	I can become good at computing.	I'm interested in a career in computing.	I like the challenge of computing.	Computer jobs are boring. (Reversed)	I'm interested in more computing classes.	I'm more interested in computing now than I was last year.
Sep.	4.83	4.13	3.26	4.71	3.37	3.80	4.19	3.85	4.10
Dec.	4.80	4.08	3.40	4.66	3.41	3.83	4.21	3.90	4.20
May	4.81	4.23	3.37	4.61	3.45	3.88	4.17	3.90	4.26

3. ASSESSMENTS

Partnering districts' pilot and formal deployments of the course, both in part and in whole, have supported an assessment of MyCS student experience – especially as it overlaps with computational identity-building. In 2014-15, over 6000 student surveys were collected. Additionally, in the summer of 2015, MyCS ran three professional development workshops, reaching a total of 52 teachers, also pre/post surveyed.

3.1 Surveys and methods

Three times in 2014-15, in Sep., Dec., and May, partnering teachers asked their students to complete a nine-question survey elaborating computational identity. Figure 1 shows both the prompts and each season's average Likert responses on a scale from 1 to 6. Seven of the statements were phrased positively. We reversed the scores of the two negatively-phrased prompts, "*Programming is hard*" and "*Computer jobs are boring*" to provide a uniform measure of *positivity* in students' computational identity. For all of the analysis, higher scores represent a more positive view of CS. We note that we did *not* seek to measure students' pre/post changes in computational knowledge or skillsets.

The 6115 student responses were then anonymized, duplicates removed, and other invalid submissions deleted.[1] If a student submitted multiple responses in a single setting, we kept only the last. The cleaned data set consisted of 5475 responses.

During the week-long professional development workshops, pre/post surveys also tracked teachers' confidence with computing concepts and skills. Teachers reflected daily on the MyCS curriculum and its relevance/applicability to their classrooms.

3.2 Overall Results

As seen in Figure 1, responses were more often positive than negative, though not dramatically so. In general, even though students agreed that programming is difficult, they expressed enthusiasm about CS (being fun) and confidence in their own skills – and, more importantly, with even greater confidence in their *future* skills! While their attitudes did not change significantly over time, responses remained favorable throughout the three time periods.

We also separated all 5475 responses by self-identified gender; Figure 2 summarizes the results across time for each prompt. With MyCS's goal of inviting *all* identity-groups to take ownership of computing, the results are heartening. Young women consistently averaged significantly more positive responses to the computational identity questions, with $p<1.0e-6$. We note that, though the trend is positive, the results did not show significant changes over time between the young women's and men's cohorts.

It is crucial to note that the results of Figure 1 and Figure 2 *do not separate students who took MyCS from a control group*. Rather, we include those results here as a baseline snapshot – including some stereotype-defying distinctions – of the views of two quite diverse districts' middle-years students. Next we turn to how equitably MyCS reached different demographics within those districts, along with the differences (or lack thereof) between the students taking MyCS and the control cohort.

3.3 Comparative Results

To obtain the 5475 responses, our partnering teachers asked *all* of their students to share their reactions to the computational-identity prompts. This approach provided a large control group (whose classes included no computational components at all), as well as a cohort actively engaged in MyCS and/or some of its modules. In addition, it provides a natural control for variance between individual teachers: each teacher had students within the MyCS group and outside of it.

Among the students surveyed, 613 took a class that included the entire MyCS curriculum or several full units from it. We designated this group as the MyCS cohort. The control cohort comprised 3360 survey-takers who were in classes with little or no computational content. The other 1502 students were in classes with many full lessons from the MyCS curriculum, woven through existing curricula: these students were not included in the comparative results summarized in Figure 3. As the side-by-side distributions suggest, the MyCS cohort did report a significantly ($p<1.0e-10$) more positive computational identity than those in the control group.

However, the results showed *no* significant differences in the **gains** by the MyCS cohort relative to the control group. Reinforcing the data of Figures 1 and 2, ***all*** students, whether taking MyCS or not, increased their personal positive affiliations with computing over the past year – to about the same extent.[2] In fact, the one notable dip in positive sentiment among the MyCSers appeared for the prompt *"Programming is hard,"* i.e., students who spent considerable time programming did develop an appreciation for its challenges. Here, however, it seems that MyCS has helped those students keep programming's challenge in perspective: other facets of a positive computational identity remain.

[1] If either Taylor Swift or Iggy Azalea *did* take MyCS with us last year, we're afraid our analysis does not include their responses.

[2] Coincidentally, tech market indices followed this same trend.

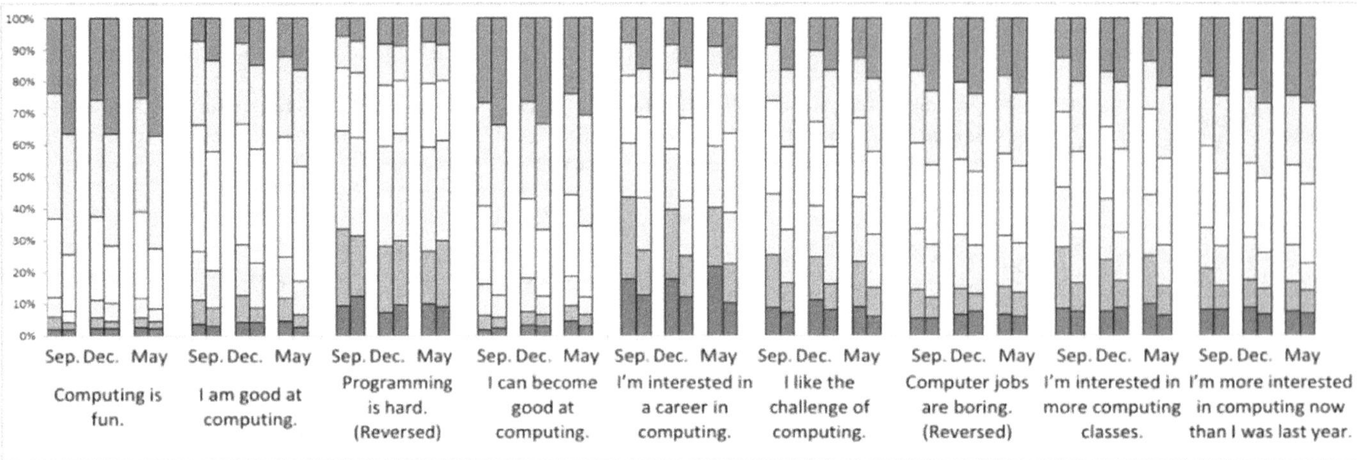

Figure 2. Computational identity responses over time separated by gender. Each column shows the distribution of Likert responses to each prompt, with the most positive scores (6) at top in dark green and the most negative (1) at bottom in dark red. Within each contiguous pair of columns, young women's answers are at right and young men's are at left. Averaging across prompts, female students expressed a significantly more positive computational identity ($p < 1.0e-6$)

One interpretation of these data is that overall positive sentiment toward CS was growing, perhaps particularly among adolescents. MyCS, then, offered an opportunity for especially enthusiastic students to pursue their computing interests, but did not lead to greater changes than the overall trend.

MyCS's long-term goal, however, is to reach students with less favorable views of computing and invite them to reconsider the field in a more personally positive way. More work remains.

3.4 Accessibility Results

Further, the possibility that MyCS is providing a home for computing-interested students is a cause for concern -- ***if*** it is perpetuating or reinforcing too-common stereotypes that only *some* groups of people identify with CS. Although MyCS's partnering districts serve a large number of students from backgrounds poorly represented in post-secondary CS, past research has demonstrated that simple co-location does *not* suffice to broaden CS's pipeline [8,9].

To assess how MyCS relates to the broadening *accessibility* to computing, we compare the demographics of students in the MyCS cohort with those in the control in Tables 1 and 2.

Table 1. Raw numbers and percentage-wise measures of the number of male and female students in MyCS and non-MyCS courses. MyCS's balance did not match the overall group's.

Gender	Control: Raw	Control: Percentage	MyCS: Raw	MyCS: Percentage
Female	1603	47.7%	263	42.9%
Male	1757	52.3%	350	57.1%

Table 1 shows that the students taking MyCS are to a larger extent male than female, even relative to the control cohort. This difference is likely due to individual student choices. At some schools MyCS is an option competing with other possible electives; at other schools, it is part of a technical curriculum that all students take. It is worth noting that, on average, the young women surveyed did not have less personal affiliation for computing, as Figure 2 attests. In addition, the 43/57 split, while not even, is noticeably more balanced than in some of the district's other electives, as reported by the teachers in MyCS's professional development workshops.

Table 2 shows that MyCS reached a larger proportion of students from racial and ethnic groups underrepresented (UR) in post-secondary CS. This testifies, in part, to the energy the districts and the teachers have invested in creating an inviting pathway into not only MyCS but all technical fields.

Table 2. Raw numbers and percentage-wise measures of the racial/ethnic background of students in MyCS and non-MyCS courses.

Race/ Ethnicity	Control: Raw	Control: Percentage	MyCS: Raw	MyCS: Percentage
Asian	310	9.2%	32	5.2%
Black/African American	67	2.0%	26	4.2%
Latina/o	1689	50.3%	386	63.0%
Native American	46	1.4%	9	1.5%
White	359	10.7%	59	9.6%
Multiracial	461	13.7%	22	3.6%
Other	429	12.8%	79	12.9%

We do note, albeit without a good explanation, that students identifying as *multiracial* did not participate in MyCS proportional to their overall numbers. Even so, the rate of participation across almost all of these demographic identities does suggest that MyCS can help provide an *intra*curricular opportunity for computing participation that avoids some of the segregation seen by other computing curricula and by some extracurricular or business-based delivery models [8,9].

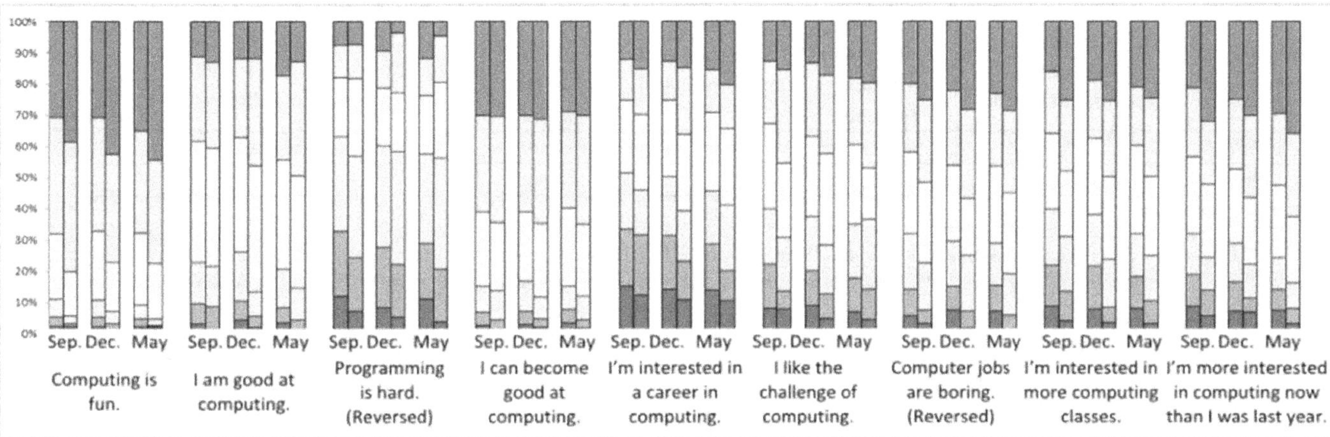

Figure 3. Changes in computational identity responses over time separated by whether the student was in a MyCS course (right-hand columns) or not (left-hand columns). Students in MyCS courses were significantly more positive than their peers about the field, but the gains (increased positivity) for MyCS students were *not* significantly greater than the gains for the control group.

3.5 Assessing the MyCS impact on teachers

One facet of the MyCS curriculum that, we believe, helps support a diverse group of students is its flexibility. Short term, most middle-years computing teachers will have a computing background almost wholly drawn from their professional-development (PD) experiences and their classroom experiments with teaching computing. Because of this, the primary goal of MyCS's PD workshops is teachers' confidence and comfort with *easing* into teaching computing.

Surveys of the 52 summer '15 PD workshop, summarized in Figure 4's distributions and Figure 5's numeric summaries, show that the group of teachers gained significantly in confidence with computing ($p<0.01$) for each skill queried.

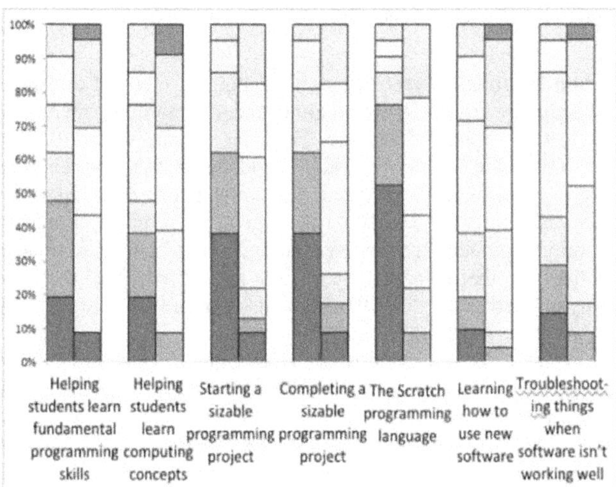

Figure 4. Teacher responses to surveys given before (left-hand columns) and after (right-hand columns) 2015's MyCS PD workshops. For all eight skills, teachers' confidence significantly increased over the course of the week.

In addition, teachers often depart the workshop reporting a desire to build their skills and understanding further. As one teacher commented on the final day, "This has opened a new world for us to expose to our students. We feel that preliminarily we can teach and integrate some of the concepts. We would love another year or two for more information and practice with computer science." Having a few teachers who are this enthusiastic can have an impact on entire schools and the numerous students they serve.

After a workshop, teachers are more enthusiastic about CS, and they express intent to share what they have learned with their school. One teacher shared, "MyCS and [this program] have had a huge positive impact on Fremont Academy. MyCS has help[ed] our Engineering teachers see the relevance of CS and it has shown them how to implement CS in the classroom. Just amazing!!! Thank you."

Although we realize that it's possible only in light of CS's still-maturing standards for external reporting at the middle-years level, we do strongly encourage teachers to adapt MyCS's resources to their specific situation and subjects. As a result, teachers have interlaced MyCS through all types of curricula, whether the class focuses on technology or not. Looking over the full five-year set of PD participants (N=145), of the teachers who attended the workshops and completed the surveys, a majority, 58%, have integrated some amount of MyCS in their classrooms – often in inspiring ways. For instance, one woodshop teacher has added MyCS's Arduino unit, part of the curriculum's bridge modules, asking his students to add programmatic motion and sensing to their projects. Other teachers dedicate a day a week from an existing tech-applications class, *CS Fridays*. Some science and math teachers integrate the screen-free lessons involving encoding and decoding into their science or math classes. English teachers have used the Scratch storytelling module to guide pairs of students in creating a scene summarizing a chapter from the current novel, resulting in a series of scenes following the book from beginning to end. Still other teachers use MyCS activities as warm-ups to start class or as rewards for students who finish work early!

3.6 Integrating qualitative teacher feedback

Through the workshops' daily routine of qualitative feedback, this diversity of teachers' voices and experiences has helped refine and expand MyCS's ability to reach a wide audience. One of the most difficult facets of MyCS for some teachers is developing confidence in using Scratch. Several teachers in 2015's early-summer PD noted this discomfort, e.g., "The Scratch game-building may be too difficult, and I would need training to teach this. It would be easier to start off with someone else's code," echoed by many other comments, as well.

Averages by questions	Helping students learn fundamental programming skills	Helping students learn computing concepts	Starting a sizable programming project	Completing a sizable programming project	The Scratch programming language	Learning how to use new software	Troubleshooting things when software isn't working well
Before	3.05	3.33	2.24	2.29	2.00	3.71	3.33
After	4.65	4.83	4.13	4.00	4.48	4.83	4.43
Difference	1.60	1.49	1.89	1.71	2.48	1.11	1.10

Figure 5. Average scores on a Likert scale from 1-6 of MyCS PD workshop participants' self-reported confidence in each of seven skills. Here, N=52 and the third row's differences are significant at the p<0.01 level for each skill.

To be sure, the "*Interactive Scratch*" module is MyCS's programming foundation, seeking to promote self-directed design, logical thinking, and collaborative expression. We updated the online curriculum using Scratch's new step-by-step and video tutorials, supplemented by the original starter projects. The curriculum now also leverages Colleen Lewis's Offline Scratch [offline] materials to support sound, art, and storytelling lessons, building gradually from others' code to creating one's own. The late-summer PD benefitted from these changes, e.g., with comments like, "Scratch: tutorials are easy to use. There's lots of potential there," and a large group of teachers leaving excited about using Scratch with their students.

MyCS's screen-free algorithms module (unit 5), in part, introduces searching and sorting. In early PD experiences the sorting activity moved too quickly, and many teachers reported feeling they did not grasp the explanations or examples, or purpose. Moreover, in an attempt to show the power of sorting algorithms, we increased the difficulty too quickly and left teachers feeling frustrated. The subsequent workshop recalibrated this experience, showing only two sorting algorithms, gradually building from basic examples to illustrate their processes and differences. After the workshops, the late-summer cohort reported a stronger grasp and greater confidence in this unit's material, in contrast to the early-summer group, who reported an impression of why sorting and searching were important but little confidence in their details.

4. BRIDGING BEYOND MyCS

One of the unexpected results of deploying a middle-years CS curriculum through two districts has been the change in the computational identities *of the districts themselves*. In fact, as Figures 2 and 3 attest, even absent significant intra-year gains in students' computational identities, inter-year gains in *institutional* computational identity have been substantial:

- After 2-3 years, both partnering districts sought to deploy MyCS at the elementary-school level; in 2015 Pomona opted to send a full PD cohort of 20 elementary teachers in order to start a district-wide rollout of computing.
- One district, too, found that the middle-years starting point was a gentle, low-overhead means to catalyze CS at the high-school level, resulting in a demand for a 2014 and 2015 "bridge" PD workshop, in which MyCS instructors added Python and Arduino materials to their repertoire. Those materials, in turn, are seeding an organic process of secondary-level CS development.

In this section, we share some of the "curricular bridges" that have grown out of the MyCS effort to bring in-school computing to both elementary and secondary classrooms of our partnering districts.

4.1 Textual programming: Python

As a result, 2014 saw the introduction of a week-long Python PD workshop run in parallel with PD for new MyCS instructors. Each unit of the Python curriculum begins with an interactive discussion, followed by hands-on practice with programming. Unit 1 of the Python curriculum provides an overview of data types and conditionals through creating multiple versions of rock-paper-scissors. An optional text adventure utilizes concepts such as user-input, strings, conditionals, and the `random` module. Unit 2 uses the Turtle library and loops, with activities ranging from composing functions to generate basic shapes to constructing more complex drawings such as checkerboards, targets, faces, wreaths, spirals, and pixelated grids.

Unit 3 parallels MyCS's encoding and decoding challenges with string and list operations to produce a "Pig Latin Generator," "Acrostic Decoder," "Letter Shifter Function," and "Prime Number Challenge." Again, similar to the latter units of MyCS, Python's Unit 4 consolidates the skills from previous units to discuss problem-solving algorithms in order to construct games such as a maze and tic-tac-toe. Hands-on challenges for the various units range from SET as a visual matching game that incorporates conditionals, to the human-pen drawing activity serving as a live preview of Turtle graphics to demonstrate how a computer will execute the code.

Python feedback Python piqued teacher engagement during our workshop by fostering anticipation and maintaining interest. As one teacher noted, "The Tic Tac Toe lesson would be very relatable to my students. This would be a fun and engaging lesson". We also incorporated numerous paper and discussion-based challenges to underscore the logical, step-by-step procedure behind computational processes. As with MyCS, teachers reacted positively to that balance, e.g., "I like the 'screen-free' stuff. The hands-on activities give the students a more tangible way of accessing the material."

The greatest challenge we faced was our daily time limit; even carefully structured, it is impossible for teachers to completely hone all the skills. Perhaps this is an equally important realization! One teacher remarked, "Everything was interesting. We just need more time." Another teacher admitted, the "most difficult [area] is the SYNTAX, SYNTAX, SYNTAX! The next most difficult thing is the SYNTAX still."

4.2 Hands-on Hardware: Arduino

Drawing from backgrounds across a variety of shop and professional-skills curricula, many teachers sought a MyCS extension that overlapped hands-on technical projects with project-based pedagogy and scheduling. The Arduino is a natural fit: it provides a pathway for creativity and hardware expression and, at heart, is a computational interface. Also a plus was the

Arduino's and its components' low cost, e.g., relative to Vex or Lego kits. All of the accessories in Figure 6 are part of the sequence of challenges provided. With servo motors, students can experiment with different types of wheels and determine which ones work better for their goals and chassis, i.e., a faster vehicle versus a sturdier vehicle.

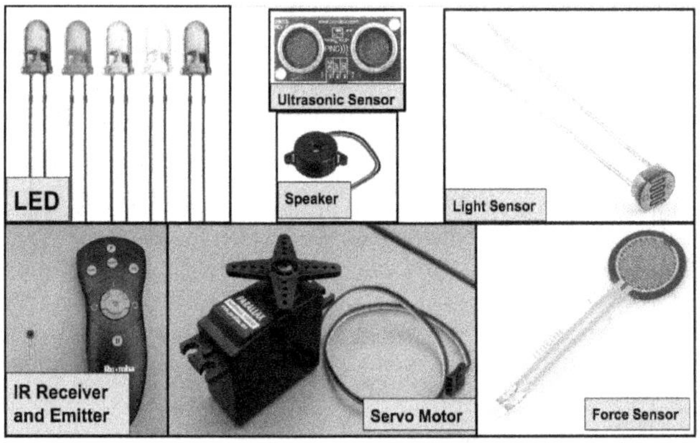

Figure 6. Hardware accessories compatible with the Arduino and used in the MyCS Arduino bridge-curriculum tutorials. Returning PD teachers can opt to supplement the content with Arduino or Python work. This, in turn, has led to deepening *institutions'* computational identities.

Accessibility via Ardublock To leverage the skills used in MyCS's Scratch-based curriculum, MyCS's Arduino curriculum uses Ardublock, a Scratch-like language in which syntax errors are not possible. Ardublock offers an important feature that Scratch does not, however: each time a block of code is compiled in Ardublock, it is converted into a text file (in Arduino's native Processing language) and then run. Far from a burden, this intermediate step exposes students to the underlying Processing code – and gives them the opportunity to re-edit and re-run that text file as many times as a student might wish. This provides an inviting – and unintimidating transition from block-based to text-based programming.

We have observed in workshops that attendees start with the block-based language and, at whatever pace they feel comfortable, start to modify the textual language rather than the block code. Usually, that experimentation leads to questions and exploration about how to use the text-based interface more effectively, as many students (and their teachers) find they are so much more efficient to specify and modify programs using text than blocks!

Arduino Feedback The MyCS Arduino tutorials provide scaffolded challenges that introduce hardware accessories in a natural order. First, LEDs support exploring programmed light patterns, then the photosensor enables creation of a light-meter or passing messages from one pair's Arduino circuit to another with both LEDs and photosensors. Servomotors mounted underneath the Arduino create a tethered robot, and an IR sensor/emitter allows the robot to be untethered but still remote controlled with an ordinary TV remote. The force sensor, speaker, and ultrasonic distance sensor add capabilities that allow student teams to build creative projects including theremins, piano-like instruments, or an alarm that someone's approaching or a door has moved.

During the workshops, teachers responded well to this progression, saying "My favorite [part] was the first day and learning about the very basics of the Arduino." An Arduino exhibition is a natural capstone to the unit; as one teacher noted, "the general idea to create a project is [an] excellent strategy."

5. PERSPECTIVE

In its adopting districts, the MyCS curriculum has evidenced both strengths and weaknesses relative to its original goals:

- By offering MyCS, partering districts have provided an opportunity to build computing skills and knowledge *in-school* to many more middle-years students than before it.
- Survey feedback to date does **not** show MyCS bolstering students' positive computational identities to a greater extent than a control cohort, but it **does** show that MyCS offers a home for engaging those students – from a representative cross-section of the surrounding district – who identify significantly more positively with computing.
- MyCS teachers and PD attendees are significantly more confident with computing skills after the experience, and are more likely than not to include computing in their classes.

Perhaps most importantly, MyCS has led to a deeper *institutional* identification with computing across its partner districts. The middle years already carry an expectation of transition, identity exploration, and, frankly, feeling awkward. As a result, those years are a safe place from which a district can experiment with the undeniable awkwardness of computing – and from which it can grow in the directions that best suit that district's teachers' and administrators' ambitions for their schools. In 2015-16 half of San Fransisco's middle schools will pilot MyCS, and we look forward to that chance to more deeply understand how to foster a positive computing identity among all middle-years students.

6. ACKNOWLEDGEMENTS

We thank the teachers, students, and administrators who have helped develop and refine MyCS. We thank Google's CS4HS initiative for supporting the pilot years of MyCS, and the NSF, though project #1240939, for enabling a careful assessment of the curriculum and substantially expanding its reach.

7. REFERENCES

[1] Schofield, E., Erlinger, M., and Dodds, Z., MyCS: CS for Middle-years Students and Their Teachers SIGCSE '14, Atlanta, GA, USA, pp. 337-342. www.cs.hmc.edu/MyCS

[2] Lewis, C. 2013. Scratch Offline. colleenmlewis.com/scratch

[3] Goode, J., Chapman, G., Margolis, J. (2012). Beyond Curriculum: The Exploring Computer Science Program. ACM Inroads. 3(2), 47-53.

[4] Bell, T., Witten, I., and Fellows, M. 2010. Computer Science Unplugged. URL: www.csunplugged.org

[5] code.org, accessed 10/23/2015

[6] Schanzer, E., Fisler, K., Krishnamurthi, S., and Felleisen, M. Transferring Skills at Solving Word Problems from Computing to Algebra Through Bootstrap SIGCSE '15, Kansas City, MO, USA, pp. 616-621.

[7] Lee, I., et al. Project GUTS URL: www.projectguts.org

[8] Sankar, P., Gilmartin, J., and Sobel, M. 2015. An Examination of Belongingness and Confidence among Female Computer Science Students. SIGCAS, 45 (2), Jul 2015, pp. 7-10.

[9] Margolis, J. Stuck in the Shallow End MIT Press, 2008.

“What Is a Computer?” What do Secondary School Students Think?

Shuchi Grover
SRI Education
333 Ravenswood Ave.
Menlo Park, CA 94025
shuchi.grover@sri.com

Daisy Rutstein
SRI Education
333 Ravenswood Ave
Menlo Park, CA 94025
daisy.rutstein@sri.com

Eric Snow
SRI Education
333 Ravenswood Ave
Menlo Park, CA 94025
eric.snow@sri.com

ABSTRACT
Nationwide, efforts are focusing on taking computer science (CS) to scale in high school classrooms through the Exploring Computer Science (ECS) and AP CS Principles (CSP) courses. Recent inroads are also being made to take structured introductory curricula to middle school classrooms. Often, a starting point for teaching CS in middle and high school is a discussion around the seemingly simple question “What is a computer?” The question is aimed to help learners understand through debate and discussion what makes a computer a computer. This paper reports our analysis of (a) middle school students’ discussions around this question, and (b) high school students’ responses to an assessment question measuring this understanding. Our analyses of students’ comments and responses reveal that a discussion around “what is a computer?” may be problematic for students, as it tends to focus on the tool, the “computer.” We suggest that the discussion needs re-framing to focus instead on *computing and computation*.

Keywords
K-12 Computer Science; Curriculum; Middle School: High School.

1. INTRODUCTION
There is a growing consensus that all children should learn computational thinking (CT) [24] and be offered introductory experiences in computer science in their K-12 school years. Computing and CT are seen as foundational to all modern STEM work [11]. Until recently, computationally rich experiences for learners were provided mainly through disparate efforts in after-school settings [19], or in place of computer literacy in schools. These early efforts paved the way for more systemic endeavors to take computer science (CS) to scale in high school classrooms through the NSF-supported Exploring Computer Science (ECS) curriculum and AP CS Principles (CSP) high school courses. Both ECS and CSP emphasize core disciplinary ideas of CS, the creative and collaborative aspects of computing, and enactment of authentic CT practices in the process of problem solving and design. Moreover, ECS is designed to level the playing field for diverse students with enthusiasm for computing, but little to no background; its curricular content and professional development directly address issues of interest and equity in computing for underserved populations. Although the needs of high school students across the US are being prioritized through pilot courses such as ECS and CSP, there is growing belief that experience with computing must start at an earlier age. Middle school is a key time for engagement with STEM fields [23]. Recent inroads in this space have been made through structured middle curricula e.g., Stanford University’s *Foundations for Advancing Computational Thinking* [8] and Harvey Mudd’s *MyCS* [21].

SIGCSE '16, March 02 - 05, 2016, Memphis, TN, USA

ACM 978-1-4503-3685-7/16/03…$15.00
DOI: http://dx.doi.org/10.1145/2839509.2844579

Prior research overwhelmingly shows lack of awareness of CS as a discipline among students [1,4,7,12,13,16, 25]. These studies suggest unequivocally that middle and high school students are completely unaware of what CS is about and often harbor negative stereotypes, and/or a “computer-centric” view of the discipline. This lack of awareness and misconceptions of CS likely impacts both students’ interests in CS and their course enrollment choices in high school and beyond [12]. One way to remedy the situation is to mold student conceptions of CS earlier in their education career [7]. As a result, several recent initiatives including curricular ones at the middle and high school level are aimed at building awareness about computing in addition to teaching computational problem solving.

An oft-used starting point for teaching CS in middle and high school curricula is a discussion around the question, “What is a computer?” It is aimed at helping learners discuss and discover the characteristics of a computer. It is considered a foundational question by some in CS, as it forms a backdrop to thinking about computing and recognizing that role that computers play in the world today. Despite its widespread use in recent curricula, much still isn’t known about secondary learners’ understanding of computers, how they respond to this question, or their pre-conceived notions about computers and digital devices. Knowing students’ prior knowledge and misconceptions around this question will be useful for secondary CS teachers.

This paper presents results from two independent studies that collected data pertinent to the question, “*What is a computer?*” The first study is situated in a middle school classroom that wrestled with this question before the start of an introductory CS and programming curriculum, and the second is in the context of Unit 1 of the ECS curriculum where students deliberate on this question in end-of-unit and end-of-course assessments.

2. Discourse around “*What Is A Computer?*”
ECS is designed around a definition of inquiry that focuses on a set of teaching and learning strategies through which students are expected and encouraged to help define the initial conditions of problems, utilize their prior knowledge, work collaboratively, make claims using their own words, and develop multiple representations of particular solutions [9,10,15]. ECS addresses the following topics over six units – Unit 1: Human-Computer Interaction; Unit 2: Problem Solving; Unit 3: Web Design; Unit 4: Programming; Unit 5: Computing and Data Analysis; and Unit 6:

Robotics. Days 1 and 2 of Unit 1 are dedicated to the topic, "What is a computer?" where "the concepts of computer and computing are explored through examples of each" [9]. Middle school curricula fashioned on ECS, such as *MyCS*, similarly start the introductory CS course sequence with a discussion and debate around "What is a computer?"

Teachers are encouraged to draw out student questions and responses. So, for a question such as "What is a computer?" the curriculum is designed to help students arrive at a working definition rather than be provided with one formal definition. All responses to the question are considered valid; it is through debate and discourse that students' thinking on the question is expected to evolve. These discussions are centered on questions such as "Is a cell phone a computer?," "Are mp3 players computers?," "What about appliances such as televisions, coffee makers, and washers?" The debate often involves the related question "why should an object be considered a computer?" which is meant to lead to a discussion around characteristics of computers. Coming to agreement on which characteristics are ***key*** to calling an object or device a computer helps formalize students' responses to the "What is a computer?" question. Such an organic discussion is central to the idea of "computational discourse" [6], where learners build competencies in CT and CT language [5] by *knowledge building discussions* in concert with engaging in computationally rich activities.

3. METHOD

This section describes our analyses of middle and high school students' responses to "What is a computer?" and related questions. We are drawing data from two independent research efforts—the first conducted with 7th and 8th graders in a public middle school classroom; and the second involving a pilot study of end-of-unit and end-of-course assessments created for ECS. We are working with two data sets in order to be able to highlight aspects of students' prior knowledge around this topic at different grade levels, and to describe middle school students' discussions and high school students' understanding of this concept.

3.1 Middle School Student Conceptions

The question guiding this research was: *What are students' commonly held notions of what a computer is and what sort of digital devices qualify as "computers"?*

3.1.1 Participants & Procedures

Students in a public middle school classroom in the San Francisco Bay Area were recruited to be part of an introductory CS intervention. The sample comprised 28 children from 7th and 8th grade (20 boys and 8 girls, mean age: ~12.3 years) enrolled in an elective class on "computer creations". IRB consent and assent were sought from parents and students. Of these, 16 were in 7th grade, and 12 in 8th grade. Four of the students in the class were students with special needs or learning difficulties. The classroom teacher wished to try out the online discussion board feature of Schoology, the learning management system in use by the school, with her students. It was therefore decided that prior to the start of the introductory CS course, the students would engage in online discussions around "What is a computer?" and related questions on their own with *little to no intervention on the part of the teacher or researcher. The researcher would follow the discussion closely as an observer, and then have face-to-face discussions with the class using students' ideas and talking points from the online discussion.* Using the online discussion board on their own allowed the students' discussions to flourish unfettered; it gave all students an equitable voice; and pre-empted any temptation a teacher would have had to express an opinion about students' incoming ideas about what is or is not a computer.

The following questions were posted on the discussion board. DP2 and DP3 were inspired by students' comments in response to DP1. The goal of DP1 was to extend students' thinking beyond what we traditionally think or talk about as computers before getting them to think of defining features of a computer (DP2) and then applying their feature-based criteria more broadly to other digital devices and appliances to discuss and debate DP3.

Discussion Prompt #1 (DP1): *What is a "computer"?*
Are iPads and tablets computers? Cell phones? What counts or does not count as a computer? How would you decide?
Discussion Prompt #2 (DP2): *What are the criteria or necessary features to call something a computer?*
Discussion Prompt #3 (DP3): *What are some devices that are digital that you don't think of as "computers"?*
Is a TV a computer? What about iPads? Or Smartphones? Or an ATM machine? What about Google Glass? What about the car GPS system? Or a microwave? Is an XBox a computer? How about DVD players or iPods? What about a digital thermostat? Any other devices you can think of?

Before students embarked on this activity, the teacher worked with the students and drew up etiquette-related "norms" for class online discussions. Students were asked to respond to DP1 during class time and any time until the next class period. The following week, DP2 and DP3 were added based on the types of discussions that emerged in response to DP1. Following online discussions in response to these prompts, the researcher had an in-class discussion around the ideas the children had discussed online. The focus of this experience report however is to present the initial notions that these students harbored around "computers," that were gleaned from the online discussions.

3.1.2 Results

The various prompts elicited varying amounts of engagement and responses. It is worth noting that DP2 and DP3 were posted almost at the same time. In response to the discussion prompts, DP1 had 69 posts, DP2 had 45 posts and DP3 had 111 posts. Comments in all 3 discussions were open coded to categorize the major themes around students' concepts of computers. The following broad categories emerged in DP1—

a) Students who argued that only what we call a ***computer*** in everyday parlance, is a computer; these students argued using attributes such as size to support their point
b) Students who argued around broader uses and functions to categorize computers; these students cited definitions from around the internet to justify their stance, and also saw parallels in the types of things accomplished between traditional computers, tablets and smartphones

Roughly 50% of the 69 posts were off-topic or comprised exchanges between the students that did not make a material contribution to the discussion. About 1/3rd of the meaningful comments were in category (a) above and almost all of the remainder were in (b). Table 1 describes how the discussion in response to DP1 started and how it ended. The exchanges reveal the 2 broad categories. They also reveal how, over the process of about 70 comments, students with vastly opposing stands began to converge somewhat at a consensus that things like size did not matter, nor what we call a computer, rather it was features and capabilities that defined what is or is not a computer. They also reveal that some students continued to have trouble seeing "computers" in a broader sense.

Table 1. Exchanges from start and end of DP1

DP1 discussion starts with this exchange
S1: Computers are the only thing that should be called a computer
S2: I disagree with S1 because computers can be other things
S1: I disagree with S2 cuz phones aint computers
S3: Smart phones are basically computers. They can process data almost as fast, and they have most of the features of the computer(ie: they can send emails and can run apps). The only thing that's different is the size and shape of them
S4: I agree with S3
S5: Not exactly tho
S6: We all have our opinions,But I honestly think COMPUTERS ARE COMPUTERS
S7: Agreed
S8: Actually, phones ARE computers because they do store data like what time our orthodontics appointments are at, and doctors appointments, what time we have to get up for school, ext.
DP1 discussion ends with this exchange
S2: Computers are bigger than phones, tables, and iPods
S8: I think they're all the same, just they come in different dimensions(sizes and shapes).
S9: I dont think they are computers for reasons as they can download different apps, computers can hold and use better apps also for computers you need internet and there is no 3g or 4g
S8: But isn't that what computers, IPads, and IPhones all do?
S10: it can help you do things and will help you do homework
S7: Yes, they can all be referred to as computers
S2: Computers come in many shapes and sizes
S6: i think that they can be called MINI computers IN A WAY
S11: I also think that they can be referred to as computers. They're all the same and all do the same things. Every time someone comes up with something new, they just make it look better, and everyone thinks its "so cool" cause it just brand new. ><
S12: I would say laptops, ipads, tablets, & smartphones are all computers; I was told a computer is anything electronic that can process and store data (and preferably connect to the internet)
S3: om·put·er kəm'pyootər/ noun 1. an electronic device for storing and processing data, typically in binary form, according to instructions given to it in a variable program. -Taken From Google Definitions-
S13: I was just about to say that
S14: I think computers and smart phones are different but still similar in some ways. They are different because you can use computers for more stuff like working on homework and writing computer programs. They are similar because they can both use the internet, play games, and watch videos.
S15: I think computers are everything that can store data and process information but because phones and iPads have different added functions they are given different names so we don't really think of them as computers.

It is interesting to note how students such as S6 come around to seeing devices such as phones and tablets as "MINI computers IN A WAY." However, it is worth noting that even the students whose comments were categorized in (b) were somewhat confused at various other points during the discussion. For example, S2 and S19 had the following to say (respectively)— *"Phone's are like computers but not computers because with computers u can do more stuff."* and "*[phones and tablets] kinda are computers but smaller versions but some can't do certain things that normal computers do tho."* Phrases such as "normal computers" and "like computers but not computers" suggest that since only certain devices are ***called*** computers while others that we're trying to characterize as computers, are not, the question itself may be problematic to think through.

Similar analyses of DP2 and DP3 revealed that common areas of confusion among these students stemmed from what features are needed for something to be a computer. Ability to connect to the Internet and/or have Wi-Fi triggered many exchanges between students. Close to 38% of all (meaningful) comments in DP2 and DP3 were related to whether Wi-Fi was a necessary feature. About 33% spoke of definitions of computers in the abstract (e.g. a device that can be programmed to carry out instructions); 13% mentioned components of computers (memory, hard disk, screen, etc.); and another 13% also referred to computers in terms of the tasks they do to help us ("saving photos"; "helping with homework"). The broad themes of the discussion revealed two main sources of confusion. (See Table 2).

1. *Connectivity*– Wifi and access to the internet was seen by many students as a key criterion for a device to qualify as a computer.

2. *Uses*– Can a device or appliance that clearly has other main functions (such as a car, microwave, TV, thermostat, ATM) be a "computer."

Table 2. Example exchanges from DP2 and DP3

Comments From DP2
S18: Everyone keeps saying that internet connection capabilities are necessary for a computer to be called a computer. I think that if you took a normal computer and never connected to the internet, i think you could still do a lot with it.
S16: Internet is NOT a criteria for being a computer. Neither is typing, as there are other ways to input data.
S1: Computers must store and process data as well as save photos and access the internet
S7: Bottom line is, anything that can store and process data and/or software is a computer. A desktop is a computer, an iPod is a computer, a laptop is a computer, an iPad can be a computer, a robot is a computer, a calculator is a computer, a GPS is a computer; anything that is related to the following is a computer.
Comments from DP3
S8: In my opinion, TVs aren't computers because they don't provide access to the internet, they let you watch the game tonight rather than let you surf the web.
S16: Does internet access have be a criteria?
S17: I don't think internet should be criteria.
S6: it should be a criteria
S6: i dont know why i just feel like it shouldd be. It just feels like every single device im on doesnt feel like a real computer without it because we depend on it so much nowdays, like to communicate, get work done, entertainment, etc.
S7: Everything except the microwave and the thermostat are computers.
S13: I think both the microwave and the thermostat are computers because the store and process information.
S12: How do they store info?
S16: It depends. Digital thermostats could conceivably be modified to store information (past temperatures), and some microwaves could "remember" settings. But then it becomes a question of whether that is a computer or a thermostat connected/monitored by a computer.
S7: Very true, I think that then they are just monitored by a computer and not really a computer themselves.
S1: I just don't feel like an xbox, PS, wii and non smart phones are computers they don't do things computers do. They do some of the stuff computers do but definitely not all of it

3.2 High School Student Conceptions

3.2.1 Participants & Procedures

The sample comprised 117 children from 9th and 10th grade enrolled in a year-long ECS course in a large urban school district in a Midwestern state in the U.S. IRB consent and assent were sought from parents and students. Data was not used from students who did not provide consent.

As mentioned in Section 2, the ECS curriculum is broken up into several units each of which build on ideas from previous units. The first unit, "Human Computer Interaction", provides an introduction to several topics related to computer science. The goals of Unit 1 include providing students with an introduction to the concepts of computers and computing, the worldwide web, the concept of data, and implications of different forms of communication. End-of-unit assessments were developed for the first four ECS units, as well as one additional cumulative assessment that covered concepts from all four units [20, 22]. The results discussed here are based on an analysis of student responses to one question on the Unit 1 end-of-unit assessment. The question provided students with a brief description of a microwave and then asked students to provide an argument for whether or not a microwave was a computer. We expected students to first identify a characteristic of a computer and then to explain why a microwave did or did not have that characteristic.

In the cumulative assessment, we took a different approach and instead of asking students to explain why something was a computer or not, we provided the students with a task. In this case designing and printing something using a 3-D printer and asked students whether or not the task was an example of computing, and if so, what aspect of the 3-D printing process was an example of computing. For both questions, points were assigned based on the explanation and not whether the student was able to correctly say if the task was or was not a computer or an example of computing. For the Unit 1 question, misconceptions of a microwave did not count against the students' score.

3.2.2 Results

On the Unit 1 assessment question, approximately 90% of students indicated that they believed a microwave was a computer. However, only about 2% were able to list two characteristics of a computer and appropriately relate them to a microwave. Examples of characteristics that we were hoping students would identify were—accepting inputs (to carry out a function—of heating food for a certain amount of time), producing outputs (based on inputs), storing information, and carrying out commands/processing information.

Table 3 lists a sample of responses that reveal that students had not completely understood the target concept. They identified characteristics that computers have but we did not believe they were ***key*** to the idea of computing and for something to be identified as a computer. The first four responses mention characteristics that a "typical" computer such as a desktop or laptop would have, but they are characteristics that not all computers have, or that objects that are not a computer may have. For example, an analog clock can display information, and a lamp uses electricity but we would generally not consider those to be computers. These responses show students focusing on trying to figure out what a microwave and a "typical" computer have in common, versus a broader view of computing and key features of computing devices. While most students answering "yes" for "Is a microwave a computer" indicates that students learned to broaden their definition of computers, it is not clear that students gained a deeper understanding of computing and computation.

Table 3. Example responses to ECS Unit 1 assessment

Response	*Computer Characteristic*	*Explanation*
R1	*Uses electricity to function*	*Most, if not all, computers function by using electricity as a source of energy*
R2	*Pre-set buttons*	*Has buttons like a computer that you can push how you think you want your food cooked*
R3	*Displaying Information*	*The microwave displays the amount of time remaining when it is in use.*
R4	*Screen*	*Microwaves and Computers both have screens. They are similar.*
R5	*Understands Math*	*A microwave understands if you press the button "add a minute" which is microwaves, it will add a minute to the original time.*

Table 4. Example responses to ECS summative assessment

Response	*Explanation*
R6	*It is a computing task because you have to design something and designing is part of computer science.*
R7	*It takes in data in the form of a virtual image then changes it into a physical mold.*
R8	*3-D printing is an example of a computing task because it was specific steps to achieve a goal. The printer does a step one by one in order just like a computer program would.*
R9	*Creating a 3-D object is an example of a computing task because you're using programs in the computer that tell weather or not or how you want the object to look.*
R10	*3-D printing is an example of a computing task because it uses a computer to tell the printer what to do.*

In R5, the student was making a connection between computers and mathematics. It is interesting to note that one of the goals of the unit is for students to gain an appreciation of the connection between mathematics and computer science. In this case, the student may also be thinking of a computer as something that computes and therefore discusses what it is that a microwave might compute. While one can see the effort to think of the aspects of computers beyond the physical aspects, the explanation falls short in that it isn't clear why "understands math" is an aspect of a computer. These examples highlight that students can come away from discussions about what a computer is without a clear understanding of key characteristics that warrant something being called a computer.

On the cumulative assessment, students were asked to explain why or why not 3-D printing was an example of a computing task. Some example responses are listed in Table 4. Only R6 indicates an understanding that computing was something beyond just the use of computers, and the idea that design is part of computer science. Responses R7 and R8 were more typical responses, as they related the 3-D printer process to the characteristics of a computer. In R7 the student described the process as taking input and producing output, while in R8 the student describes the process as that of following specific instructions. The last two responses suggest that some students believe that an example of a computing task is one that uses a computer.

In general, these responses are closer to the connections we hope students will make in an introductory CS curriculum as opposed to their responses for why a microwave is a computer. We also prefer the re-framing of the question to ask students about a "computing task" rather than whether an object is a "computer." This re-framing appears to encourage students to answer based on uses and not on the physical aspects of a computer.

4. DISCUSSION

The results for the middle school discussion highlight the value of the inquiry-driven curriculum. An approach such as this (and that ECS uses) builds off of socio-cultural learning theories that acknowledge that learning does not only occur in a vacuum; that students bring bodies of knowledge from their lives to the classroom. This includes preconceived notions that must be engaged. Doing so also helps teachers identify students' misconceptions—a first step in helping learners rectify them.

It is indeed fascinating to see students' thinking evolve in the online discussion to looking at characteristics as the defining criteria and deliberate what is or is not critical for a computer to perform different types of functions. That said, they show that the focus on ***calling*** something "a computer" (that is not a desktop or laptop computer) is problematic for students; they start to refer to certain things as "normal computers", especially when discussing other things that are not normally called computers, because the question forces them to argue whether or not other objects are "computers". High school students' performance in assessments dealing with this topic also reveals the same issue.

Students appear to have a conception of a computer, and even when they are asked through discussion to broaden this conception, the distinctions between general-purpose and special-purpose computing devices is not always apparent and they are unable to identify ***key characteristics*** of devices that enable computing. This is perhaps at the core of why some students in middle school struggled with the question, and spent so much time debating whether being able to access the internet was necessary for a device to be a computer. It is also why the high school students struggled with *"Is a microwave a computer?"*.

The different ways to conceive of a computer have led us to refine our ECS Unit 1 assessment question by providing the characteristics of a computer we would like students to focus on in their explanation. Upon reflection, we decided that it wasn't as important for students to remember a particular set of characteristics but more that they could take a set of characteristics and determine whether or not they enable computing. With the reworked item, we are shifting focus on *computing* rather than the *computer*.

One concern that we have after viewing the responses on the cumulative assessment is that some students did not seem to gain an appreciation of computing separate from a computer, and felt a device was involved in computing only because it used a traditional general-purpose computer. It may be the case that the discussion of computing (which came after that on computers) was framed or defined by the discussion of what makes a computer, and more time is needed to having students understand computing and computation rather than computers.

4.1.1 Rethinking the question to reframe the computer-centric conversation and mindset

Fellows and Parberry [2] famously said about getting kids excited about CS, "What would we like our children, the general public of the future, to learn about computer science in schools? We need to do away with the myth that computer science is about computers. Computer science is no more about computers than astronomy is about telescopes, biology is about microscopes or chemistry is about beakers and test tubes. Science is not about tools; it is about how we use them and what we find out when we do."

The name "computer science" itself is problematic [17] since (a) computer science is not simply the "science of computers", and (b) it leads to a misplaced fixation with computers. There have been countless articles written about this, and also moves to rename the discipline. In European universities, it is typically referred to as 'informatics', and "[to] avoid using the name of the machine in the title, [...] some use the word 'computing' instead" [3]. Not surprisingly, it has been shown in studies that student's misperceptions of computer science stem from these extremely "computer-centric" notions of the discipline. A majority of middle school children erringly think computer scientists mostly "build or fix computers", and some curricula make a concerted effort to draw children away from the machine-centric view of discipline to see computing in a broader light [7, 8].

How wise then is the decision then to start a curriculum focused on the big ideas of computing with the narrow question *"what is a computer?"* After all, is it so surprising that students in middle school call out on the absurdity of the question "is a microwave a computer?" It's not entirely illogical for a student to turn around and follow up that question with *"Why is a microwave called a microwave then?"* The problem lies in conflating the features of a device that uses computing to perform its functions with the object that we in everyday parlance identify as "computers". When asked to define a computer, one student in our middle school sample responded, "A screen with a keyboard that has a logo that says mac and pc," exemplifying this view.

CS is at its core a study of problems, problem solving, and the solutions that come out of the problem-solving process that can be carried out by a computational machine, and systems the bring together hardware *and* software to make this possible. We believe the focus should be on **computing**, **computation** and **computability**, not the ***computer***. It would be less confusing for students if they were expected to focus *on aspects of computing that are in use in the many digital devices that we do not even call computers* without phrasing the question as ***Is X a computer?*** We hypothesize that introductory curricula would be better served, with the question ***What is computing?*** and ***How is computing used*** *in different devices and appliances, as well as in the ways in which we do so many of our day-to-day activities such as communicating and collaborating?* "*What is computation*?" and follow up questions such as "*Can we say that the human body does computation?*" may also lead to rich thought and conversation. Even the ECS curriculum cites "what is computing?" as "possibly [the] more pertinent question" [9]. The discussion could also delve into what computer scientists do (hint: not all of their work involves programming or even computers!). This would help students get a better sense of the types of diverse fields and industries that computer scientists support. While we do think the discussion of "what is a computer" is important, this discussion might be better served once students have a broader understanding of computing and computation. An inquiry-based discussion around these more pertinent questions could be guided to include a discussion on key features of digital devices that make computing possible, and it is well within reason to assume that a robust discussion on the topic would organically also include a debate on features of computers. These hypotheses would need to be empirically tested.

5. CONCLUSION

This paper reports on middle and high school students' engagement with and understanding of the question "what is a computer?" Our findings indicate that the question (a) places a misplaced focus on the ***computer*** (rather than computing or computation) and (b) triggers confusion when students are expected to apply the definition to other devices and appliances. One of the goals of an introductory CS course is for the students to gain an appreciation of the discipline and to recognize that CS is more than just programming or using a computer. We are concerned that "What is a computer?" is the wrong starting point to achieve this learning goal as it does not do enough to move students away from thinking of computer science only in relation to computers. We want students to understand that different aspects of CS and computing are used in many different ways to solve real-world problems, model the world, and help us communicate and express ourselves. We urge educators to shift the initial focus of introductory courses to the deeper ideas of computing, computation and computability. While further research is needed to determine if our hypotheses bear out, we believe that a discussion around these ideas will likely allow students to start with a broader and more robust appreciation for CS as a discipline.

6. ACKNOWLEDGMENTS

We gratefully acknowledge grant support from the National Science Foundation (NSF #1343227 and #1240625).

7. REFERENCES

[1] Carter. L. 2006. Why students with an apparent aptitude for computer science don't choose to major in computer science. In *Proceedings of SIGCSE '06*, pages 27–3. ACM

[2] Fellows, M., & Parberry, I. 1993. SIGACT trying to get children excited about CS. *Computing Research News, 7.*

[3] Gal-Ezer, J., & Harel, D. 1998. What (else) should CS educators know?. *Communications of the ACM*, *41*(9), 77-84.

[4] Greening. T. 1998. Computer science: through the eyes of potential students. In Proceedings of the 3rd Australasian conference on Computer science education, pages 145–154, The University of Queensland, Australia, 1998. ACM.

[5] Grover, S. 2011. Robotics and engineering for middle and high school students to develop computational thinking, in *Annual Meeting of the AERA 2011*, New Orleans, LA.

[6] Grover, S. & Pea, R. 2013. Using a Discourse-Intensive Pedagogy and Android's App Inventor for Introducing Computational Concepts to Middle School Students. In *Proceedings of SIGCSE '13*. ACM.

[7] Grover, S., Pea, R. & Cooper, S. 2014. Remedying Misperceptions of Computer Science among Middle School Students. *In Proceedings of the 45th ACM Technical Symposium on Computer Science Education (SIGCSE '14).* New York, NY: ACM.

[8] Grover, S., Pea, R., Cooper, S. 2015. Designing for Deeper Learning in a Blended Computer Science Course for Middle School Students. *Computer Sc. Education*, 25(2), 199-237.

[9] Goode, J. & Chapman, G. 2015. Exploring Computer Science, 6th ed. Computer Science Equity Alliance.

[10] Goode, J., Chapman, G., & Margolis, J. 2012. Beyond curriculum: the exploring computer science program. *ACM Inroads*, *3*(2), 47-53.

[11] Henderson, P. B., Cortina, T. J., & Wing, J. M. 2007. Computational thinking. In *ACM SIGCSE Bulletin* (Vol. 39, No. 1, pp. 195-196). ACM.

[12] Hewner,M. and Guzdial.M. 2008. Attitudes about computing in postsecondary graduates. In Proceeding of ICER 2008, pages 71–78, Sydney, Australia. ACM.

[13] Hewner, M. 2013. Undergraduate conceptions of the field of computer science. In *Proceedings of the ninth annual international ACM conference on International computing education research* (pp. 107-114). ACM.

[14] Margolis, J., & Fisher, A. 2003. *Unlocking the clubhouse: Women in computing*. MIT press.

[15] Margolis, J., Ryoo, J., Sandoval, C., Lee, C., Goode, J., & Chapman, G. 2012. Beyond access: Broadening participation in high school computer science. *ACM Inroads, 3*(4), 72–78.

[16] Martin, C. D. 2004. Draw a computer scientist. In Working Group Reports on Innovation and Technology in Computer Science Education (ITiCSE-WGR'04). 11–12.

[17] Miller, B. N., & Ranum, D. L. 2011. *Problem Solving with Algorithms and Data Structures Using Python SECOND EDITION*. Franklin, Beedle & Associates Inc.

[18] Mitchell, A., Purchase, H. C., and Hamer, J. 2009. Computing science: What do pupils think? In *Proceedings of the 14th Annual Conference on Innovation and Technology in Computer Science Education (ITiCSE'09).* 353–353.

[19] Phillips, P., Cooper, S., and Stephenson, C. 2012. CSTA Voice Special Issue: K-8 Computer Science: Building a Strong Foundation.

[20] Rutstein, D., Snow, E., and Bienkowski, M. 2015. Computational Thinking Practices: Analyzing and Modeling a Critical Domain in Computer Science Education, in *Annual Meeting of the AERA 2015*, Philadelphia, PA.

[21] Schofield, E., Erlinger, M., & Dodds, Z. 2014. MyCS: CS for middle-years students and their teachers. In *Proceedings of the 45th ACM technical symposium on Computer science education* (pp. 337-342). ACM

[22] Snow, E., Bienkowski, M., and Rutstein, D. 2014. Supporting assessment practices in secondary computer science education, in *Annual Meeting of the CSTA 2014*.

[23] Tai, R., Qi Liu, C., Maltese, A.V., and Fan, X. 2006. Planning Early for Careers in Science. *Science. 312*(5777).

[24] Wing, J. 2006. Computational Thinking. *Communications of the ACM.* 49(3), 33-36.

[25] Yardi, S. and Bruckman, A. 2007. "What is computing?: bridging the gap between teenagers' perceptions and graduate students' experiences," in Proceedings of the third international workshop on Computing education research, (Atlanta, Georgia, USA), pp. 39–50.

A Multidisciplinary, Multifaceted Approach to Improve the Computer Science based Game Design Education: Methodology and Assessment

Chang Yun
University of Houston
Department of Computer Science
Houston, Texas, USA
cyun@uh.edu

Hesam Panahi
University of Houston
Bauer College of Business
Houston, Texas, USA
hpanahi@uh.edu

Zhigang Deng
University of Houston
Department of Computer Science
Houston, Texas, USA
Zdeng4@uh.edu

ABSTRACT

In this paper, we introduce a multidisciplinary and multifaceted pedagogical approach to enhance game design education in computer science curriculum and assess its effectiveness using outcomes from Microsoft US and World Imagine Cup competitions in the game design category. We offer team project-based courses that cover multiple disciplines such as computer science, art and animation, game design, production, and business and entrepreneurship. Our students gain fundamental knowledge and skills from the multidisciplinary approach and utilize them to undergo a systematic game development process over two semesters. We also implement a unique grading system that includes ranking duels to promote the competitiveness among students which ultimately improves the quality of every game designed in our courses. We successfully demonstrate the effectiveness of our approach with results from the Microsoft Imagine Cup competitions – dozens of our student teams have been nationally and internationally recognized in the past eight consecutive years.

Categories and Subject Descriptors

K.3.2 **[Computers and Information Science Education]**

General Terms

Design, Evaluation

Keywords

Education, Computer Science, Games Design, Imagine Cup

1. INTRODUCTION

As the number of gamers in US alone exceeds 155 million and has been increasing annually, the demand for more games in every genre and platform is also on the rise [8]. The rise of indie game startups to support this demand has prompted many educational institutions to open game design curricula to fulfill the needs for game designers in various disciplines. There are about 400 colleges in US that offer programs ranging from gaming courses to B.S/M.S./minor degrees and certificates [7]. The programs and corresponding curricula among colleges vary based on unique needs from the local gaming industry and/or the availability of resources. At University of Houston (UH), we offer four gaming courses in the computer science department to educate and train our students and guide them to pursue careers either in the traditional gaming industry or in the startup indie gaming industry.

Since UH only offers four game design related courses, it is necessary to design the curricula to be highly effective in training our students to become proficient entry-level game developers. For this reason, we design a multidisciplinary, multifaceted approach to improve our students' expertise and performance in game design and development.

Previously, Wolz et al. [21] introduced a curriculum where the students from various majors were taught game design by guest lecturers with multidisciplinary backgrounds for two semesters and were then required to produce individual games. While they selected the faculty members within their own institution as the guest lecturers, we invited most of our guest lecturers from the local gaming industry and other institutions except for guest lecturers in the business and entrepreneurship program. We placed the exception for this particular field since our institution has a nationally top-ranked entrepreneurship program with experienced entrepreneurs as faculty members. In addition, their multidisciplinary fields did not include the business and entrepreneurship as a part of their curriculum. We included this field in our curriculum since it can potentially benefit our students if they decide to pursue indie game startups. We also required our students to work on team projects as done by Bidarra et al. [3]. In the early years of our program, like Settle et al. [18], we required our students to focus on both individual and team projects. However, we later removed the individual projects from our curriculum to allow our students additional time to concentrate on their team projects. Bidarra et al. [3] permitted teams to have a large number of students but we limited the number to improve team logistics; we find that this leads to a more effective team game production process.

In order to assess the effectiveness of our approach, we decided to utilize our successes in national and/or international collegiate game design competitions as a primary parameter. We chose the Microsoft Imagine Cup to serve this purpose since it is a well-known student competition where students compete in both national and international settings. While Imagine Cup has been utilized as a foundation for computer science software capstone projects in the past [15], it has never been utilized as the tool to assess the effectiveness of game design programs before. For programs such as ours that offer a limited number of courses rather than a degree, it is difficult to find means to compare program quality with programs

SIGCSE '16, March 02 - 05, 2016, Memphis, TN, USA.

ACM 978-1-4503-3685-7/16/03$15.00
DOI: http://dx.doi.org/10.1145/2839509.2844582

offering degrees by utilizing conventional methods – human and material resources [17]. The competition provides opportunities for student teams from different game design programs at universities to compete head-on and demonstrate the strength of their program.

2. OUR METHODOLOGY

To maximize the effectiveness of our game design and development, we implement various mechanisms such as a unique course format, multidisciplinary coursework, one-on-one support, grading policies and assessments that can best serve our purpose.

2.1 Course Format

We design our courses as team-project oriented courses where qualified computer science students form teams and design a game in two semesters.

2.1.1 Qualification

Since our courses are listed as part of the computer science program, only computer science students are permitted to enroll them. For this reason, the courses are designed toward accommodating computer science students interested in learning about game development. However, we also permit computer technology, computer engineering or other major students with proficient programming skills to enroll.

Further, we also require enrolled students to be juniors, seniors or M.S./Ph.D. students. By allowing only qualified students to register, we ensure that they have sufficient computer science and programming skills to design their game – especially the core game engine. Another reason for not permitting freshmen and sophomores is to ensure that our courses do not get demoted to elementary programming courses. In the first few years of the program, lower level students (freshmen and sophomores) were able to register for the courses. Aside from obvious deficiencies in computer science and programming skills, they caused several problems in regard to work ethics, discipline and management skills. Consequently, they had a difficult time both in designing their own individual game and making reasonable contributions to their team game. For these reasons, we no longer permit the freshmen or sophomores in our classes.

2.1.2 Game Development Tools

Prior to 2012, we chose Microsoft XNA Game Studio as the primary game development tool for our students. The XNA is a programming environment Microsoft introduced to the public in 2006 [6] that "allows you to use Visual Studio to create games for Windows Phone, Xbox 360, and Windows" [13]. At the time, we selected the XNA because of its three advantages over other tools: (1) Relative ease of programming using Microsoft Visual C#, (2) shorter coding length (C# over C++) and time to create a game, and (3) capability to create cross-platform games for a PC, console (Microsoft Xbox 360), and mobile device (Microsoft Windows Phone/Zune Player). Although it was a relatively simple tool to design a game in the past, it still required our students to create and write the core game engine. Therefore, our students had to invest a significant portion of their total development time in producing a functional core engine alone. In 2013, we gradually transitioned away from XNA since Microsoft announced it was ending its support. We permitted our students to develop their games using either XNA or Unity Studio. Unity is a GUI-based application programming interface (API) that allows game developers easily create 2D/3D games in multiplatform settings [19]. Starting in 2014, we recommended they utilize Unity as the primary tool to develop their games. The major reason for choosing Unity was its multi-platform support. Unlike XNA that only allowed our students to produce their games for Microsoft-specific platforms, Unity supports most consumer platforms including Microsoft, iOS and Android.

2.1.3 Individual and Team Projects

In the first two years of our program, we required students to work on an individual game for two months. Our objective was to allow them to learn and experience the nature of the game design process and understand the fundamentals that every role required to produce a game. Afterward, we required them to form a team and produce a team-based game for the remainder of the course. However, we found that the difference between students entering the team project after completing their individual projects first or immediately starting the team project without first working on the individual projects was negligible. We also found that the students preferred to start the team project immediately so that they have more time to focus on developing their team game. The apparent benefits of starting with the individual project first were mostly covered in the team project as the students were required to understand roles and responsibilities and appoint themselves to the roles that were needed for their projects. Finally, we limited the number of team members to 4. As the size of the team increases, the workload it can handle increases. However, the size increase also contributes in increased logistical problems that potentially slow development processes when the number exceeds between 4 and 6. Furthermore, since Microsoft Imagine Cup competitions capped the maximum number of team members to 4, we adopted this rule as well.

2.2 Multidisciplinary Coursework

A successful game requires collaboration among a team of specialists from diverse disciplines such as computer science, art and animation, design, storytelling, audio and music, business and entrepreneurship, and legal. We aimed for our students to go beyond the traditional role of computer scientists in game development, which has been limited to developing a core game engine, artificial intelligence, network, and user interface (UI). We exposed them to the other aspects of developing a successful game which draws knowledge from the above disciplines. This required us teaching fundamentals from these disciplines so that our students can gain solid foundations that they can apply to develop successful games. In our program, we put a particular emphasis on the following disciplines: art and animation, design and production, and business and entrepreneurship.

2.2.1 Art and Animation

We cover fundamentals of game art concept and animation design as well as teaching skills in modeling, lighting, motion, and rigging using Autodesk Maya while learning how to tell a game story using the art assets. We require our students to create game-specific environments – including landscapes, terrains, objects, characters and structures. Finally, we cover advanced concepts in designing and producing computer-generated art and animation for the gaming environment.

2.2.2 Design and Production

The game design covers the creation of a blueprint for the game – developing game concepts and conveying these ideas to the rest of the team in a game design document (GDD) to turn the ideas into reality [16][14]. The role includes designing overall gameplays, user interface and user experience (UI/UX), and game levels including the world and environments, characters, and audio. We teach our students the process through the practice of research, critical analysis, brainstorming, and improvisation techniques to create ideas for an entertaining game. The discipline is especially important at the beginning of the project when the concept of the game is being established. On the other hand, game production covers various methods and techniques to complete the game project on time and budget without sacrificing the quality, number of features, and entertainment factors [4][14]. The discipline is important throughout the project. We cover these disciplines to ensure our students successfully design a well-conceived, fun game and complete it on schedule.

2.2.3 Business and Entrepreneurship

For the past decade, there has been major rise in indie game developers and subsequent startups in the video game industry. To accommodate those who are interested in the entrepreneurship, we dedicate several lectures in teaching the fundamentals of entrepreneurship and designing the simplified business plan using the lean canvas and the lean startup approach.

We cover this field for those who are interested in creating indie game startups in the future and equip them with the necessary knowledge and experience by the time they graduate. Although our program does not have a degree program specialized in game development and entrepreneurship [10], we offer our students support to pursue entrepreneurship in the indie game industry. If, after completing our courses, students wish to be exposed to more entrepreneurship resources, we connect them to the resources and infrastructure available at UH to help launch student startups.

The lean startup approach towards new ventures emphasizes continuous learning, customer development, and iteration. To apply this approach towards their game, students are required to draft a lean canvas, which covers the basic elements of a business model. They must then identify potential customer personas and validate their assumptions regarding their customer, pricing, and go-to-market strategy. In addition to business model development, students are required to pitch their game during the semester – preparing a pitch forces the students think about their game from a business and entrepreneurial perspective, and to learn to communicate aspects of their game in a simple, succinct, and engaging fashion.

2.3 Support

We regard the human factor as the most important factor in the game design process; personnel with experience and expertise offer constant guidance and recommendations to our students as they focus on producing their games throughout the semesters. For them to maximize the efficiency of their process and succeed in completing their game, we make available various support mechanisms from mentors, guest lectures, and teaching assistants.

2.3.1 Weekly Mentoring

In the early years of our game education, we learned that our students require consistent guidance throughout the semester outside the classroom setting as they work on their projects. Since 2009, we implemented a system where the instructor works as a mentor and meets with each individual team on a designated schedule at least an hour weekly.

At the beginning of the semester, the mentor takes a responsibility to guide and help them understand their constraints and try not to be overly ambitious about their games. Students without experience in game design always tend to be very ambitious in terms of the scenario, gameplay and/or number and scale of playable levels. The mentor first listens to the teams about their game development plan and assesses how many features and assets can be feasibly completed over the courses. The mentor then consults with the students and agrees on what essential game components they should prioritize and designate milestones accordingly. In the meantime, they categorize the rest as "nice-to-have" components and produce them if they have time left after completing "must-have" components.

After completing the planning and preparation stage (also known as the pre-production stage), the teams start developing the game and report their progress on various elements of the game such as the core game engine, assets and user interface (UI) to the mentor each week. The mentor assesses their progress and advises on how to improve quality without neglecting milestones/deadlines. The mentor suggests improving the gameplay by tweaking existing features or adding new features without causing major feature creep. Simultaneously, the mentor informs them to remove some features and/or the assets if they can potentially cause bottlenecks or if they are found to be too time consuming to complete. By providing regular feedback, the mentor guides the teams to improve their production efficiency to help guarantee the completion of the game with all anticipated features and assets included at the end of the semesters.

This out-of-class weekly meeting is valuable for the students since they can discuss the project with their mentor and ask questions, solicit inputs and/or provide comments.

2.3.2 Guest Lecturers

Throughout the semesters, we invite several guest lecturers with experience and proven expertise in various disciplines related to game design, either from the local gaming industry or from other academic institutions offering the game education. They offer fundamental knowledge by discussing their experiences, industry news, and advanced topics related to their fields of expertise. For example, we invited several faculty members from Guildhall at Southern Methodist University (SMU), who imparted their expertise in topics such as the game level design and arts. All our guest lecturers are invited from outside UH except for the field related to business and entrepreneurship since UH has a well-established business school with one of the top-ranked entrepreneurship programs in the nation according to Princeton Review and Entrepreneur Magazine in 2015 [11].

2.3.3 Teaching Assistant

In addition to having competent instructors and qualified lecturers, we are improving our student support by employing talented teaching assistants. For the past 6 years, we have made an effort to target our former game students who have received recognition at the national and/or world level.

Consequently, we have successfully recruited teaching assistants who have participated and ranked in the Microsoft Imagine Cup competitions. Below is the criteria to be qualified as teaching assistants in our courses in descending order:

1. Winners or finalists in US competition
2. Semi-finalists in World competition
3. Semi-finalists or honorable mentions in US competition

The teaching assistants with the above qualifications possess talent in the game design and project management skills thanks to their prior experiences in advancing to the US finals or US/World semifinals. They can offer information about their own game development experiences – both their successes and pitfalls – to ensure the students to work on their projects more effectively. In each year, our teaching assistants have successfully demonstrated their value in raising the quality of the games produced.

2.4 Grading Policies

The grade of each student is composed mainly of three items: homework assignments, a final presentation and two team duels. The first two items are trivial components that are widely utilized by most institutions in their game design courses. Unique to our program is a component called team duels: team duels increase the quality of the games produced.

2.4.1 Homework Assignments

The homework assignments are designed to help students prepare and schedule their team projects. They include preparing basic game design documents (GDD) and game development schedules in the pre-production and production stages. Since preparing these components are essential in developing and releasing a game successfully, we include them as assignments.

2.4.2 Final Presentation

At the end of the semester, each team is required to make a final presentation before a panel of judges whom we invite from the gaming industry and academia to provide feedback. The teams are required to present basic information about their games to the judges. After the presentation, they showcase their games and allow the judges to play them so that the judges can assess them based on multiple factors such as gameplay, entertainment value, usability, and production quality. At the end of the final presentation, the panel discusses each game and reaches a consensus on what grade should be awarded to the team. This grade is given to the team as a team grade. However, the team grade is one of two factors that determines individual grades. The second factor is their individual contributions to their team games throughout the semesters. This grading system allows each student to earn an individually deserving grade and prevents him/her to receive a high grade without making a meaningful contribution. As an example, we had some cases where everyone in a team received an 'A' grade while one member of the same team received a 'D' grade for the lack of contribution and effort.

2.4.3 Team Duels

The ranking duel system is designed to control and enhance the development progress, quality of assets and fun factor of the game that each team develops. Throughout semesters, the teams are expected to work a reasonable amount of hours (e.g. a minimum of 10 hours per member per week) and demonstrate effort to produce their games with the highest quality possible. Progress and achievements are judged in two dueling sessions known as the 'Rank D duel' and 'Rank C duel'. After we replaced intermediate presentations with the duel system, we observed the number of students enrolling our courses dropped by about 20%. However, it also greatly contributed in improving the quality of the games produced.

At the beginning of the semester, we classify the teams as D-rank teams, equivalent to the teams having a 'D' as their final grade. In designated weeks in late September and early October, we host a 'Rank D duel' where two D-rank teams duel by demonstrating their game components such as the core game, levels, features, assets, fun factor, and project quality in the presentations and demonstrations. The winning team of the duel advances to C-rank equivalent to the team having 'C' as its final grade. The lost team remains in D-rank and must duel against other D-rank teams during the designated weeks until it wins and advances to C-rank. However, we only allow each team to participate in the duel once per each class. The team that already participated and lost the duel in one class must wait until the next class to duel against another D-rank team.

We held the 'Rank C duel' about a month afterward, in a manner similar to the 'Rank D duel'. The winning teams advance to B-rank equivalent to having 'B' as their final team grades. These team ranks are carried into the final presentation where we determine the final team grades. Only B-rank teams are eligible to receive 'A' as their team grades at the end of the final presentation.

2.5 Assessments of Our Game Program

One way to assess the quality of our game education is to frequently engage with guest lecturers and judges from the gaming industry and academia with gaming programs who are given opportunities to meet with our students and assess their games. They can determine the competency of our students as potential future game developers and the effectiveness of our education: their assessments contribute significantly in improving our program continuously.

In addition, since the beginning of our game program, we continuously sought a novel method to learn where our program stood in national and international realms. We decided to utilize outcomes from annual game design competitions such as Microsoft Imagine Cup competition to assess the quality of our education. We let our students submit their games both to US and World Imagine Cup competitions and compete against student developers from other game programs in US and/or world. We monitored the outcomes from these competitions in each year to confirm the quality of our program. Having persistent successes by our students from the competitions validated the effectiveness of our pedagogical approach.

3. OUTCOMES AND EVALUATION

Microsoft Imagine Cup is a premier national and international student technology competition designed to challenge students to build software or games [12]. In terms of the game design competition, unlike the software design competition, the Imagine Cup is only one of few available competitions specifically designed for college students to compete in game design at national and international stages. We have led our students to compete in the game design category since 2007.

In addition to utilizing competitions to validate the effectiveness of our approach, we also utilized them to motivate our students to excel in developing their games. Instead of regarding their works merely as classroom projects in an isolated university classroom setting, our students perceived themselves as part of teams developing their games to compete against peer student competitors from US and/or world. This factor and their desire to be recognized encouraged the large majority of the students competing in the competition to invest more hours and efforts to produce high-quality games. The small number of the students who did not compete invested far less hours in their team games than those who competed. We observed that the parity between these two groups, in regards to the invested time, were more than 3 times. Subsequently, the quality and the fun factor of every game produced by the teams competing in Imagine Cup were far superior to those who did not.

Second, we utilized the competition as means for our students to assess their projects in the national and international settings by comparing their games with competitors' games from other institutions. They assessed their games by comparing multiple components including the game quality and fun factor. With information about past winners' games Microsoft provided to the public, our students compared their games with the winners' and led them to continue improving their games.

We also chose to incorporate Imagine Cup competitions into our curriculum since they fit well with our academic calendar. The US competition is composed with two semi-finals – one in fall and another in spring – where Microsoft selects half of the total finalists in each semi-final. Those who were selected as the finalist in any of two semi-finals are invited to the final competition in April – the District of Columbia in 2010, Redmond (WA) in 2011 and 2012, San Jose (CA) in 2013, online (virtual) in 2014, and San Francisco (CA) in 2015. Since we offered our courses in fall and spring, the competitions fit well for our students to schedule their developmental cycles around it and compete. According to the semi-final rule, the teams that are not selected as finalists after fall semi-final can improve their games and submit again in the spring semi-final for another chance to be selected as finalists. Thus, the teams have two opportunities to be selected as finalists.

In the US Imagine Cup, we achieved the following successes:

1. 2010 – 27,000 participants / Total 10 finalists
   a. Number of finalists from our program: 2 (20%)
   b. Final ranking: 2nd and 3rd
2. 2011 – 74,000 participants / Total 12 finalists
   a. Number of finalists from our program: 4 (33%)
   b. Final ranking: 1st and 2nd (Mobile) and 3rd (PC/Xbox)
3. 2012 – 113,000 participants / Total 12 finalists
   a. Number of finalists from our program: 3 (25%)
   b. Final ranking: 3rd (Mobile) and 4th (PC/Xbox)
4. 2013 – Total 4 finalists
   a. Number of finalists from our program: 2 (50%)
   b. Final ranking: N/A (Only 1st place winner announced)
5. 2014 – Total 2 finalists
   a. Number of finalist from our program: 1 (50%)
   b. Final ranking: 1st (Figure 1)
6. 2015 – Total 4 finalists
   a. Number of finalist from our program: 1 (25%)
   b. Final ranking: N/A (Only 1st place winner announced)

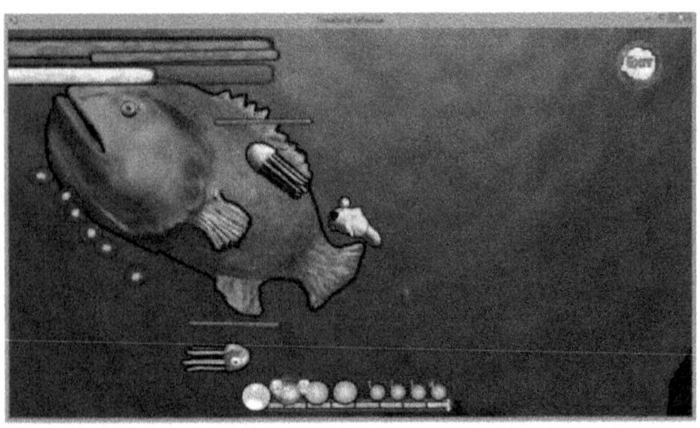

Figure 1. A gameplay screen of "Unnatural Selection", the 2014 US Imagine Cup winner and World Imagine Cup semi-finalist representing USA

The teams from our program has dominated the competition since 2010, the first year that the US Imagine Cup competition started the game design category. The number of finalists (13), winnings (two-1st places, two-2nd places, three-3rd places and one-4th place), and number of consecutive years the teams from our program successfully advanced to the final (6 consecutive years) are unprecedented in the competition's history. Our accomplishments in 2011 are especially noteworthy in terms of a number of finalists and winners. Figure 2 shows some of finalists and a mentor at the 2011 US Imagine Cup final. To our knowledge, our best competitor had a total of 2 finalists and had their gaming teams advancing to the final for two consecutive years. These results clearly validate the effectiveness of our pedagogical approach in leading our students to be highly competitive against their peers from other institutions for 6 consecutive years.

Figure 2. Some of US Imagine Cup finalists and mentors from our university attending the final

We also participated in the World Imagine Cup competition. Until 2012, the participants had to submit their products to three competition rounds: 1, 2 and 3 (semi-final). Only four teams were selected as finalists after round 3 and competed in the World final. Starting in 2013, only the 1st place winners from each local competition were selected as the world semi-finalist teams and competed to be selected as finalists. The teams were not permitted to submit their games in both national and world competitions separately. Instead, the only way to compete in the world competition is to win the local final (US competition in our case). Below is the list of our successes in the world competition:

1. 2008 – 1 semi-finalist ranked in top 25
2. 2009 – 1 semi-finalist ranked in top 100
3. 2010 – 4 semi-finalists ranked in top 48
4. 2011 – 6 semi-finalists ranked in top 50
5. 2012 – 9 semi-finalists ranked in top 200
6. 2014 – Sole semi-finalist representing USA

The unprecedented number of semi-finalists from our program between 2008 and 2014 also successfully demonstrates the quality of our game program in the international setting.

When we combine the number of our students making achievements and receiving recognitions both in the US and world competitions between 2008 and 2015, it becomes clear that a large majority of our students successfully demonstrated their ability as competent student game developers. This validates the effectiveness of our pedagogical approach that led to our students' successes for 8 consecutive years. Our success stories were published in various media. Multiple news channels from several local TV stations interviewed us every year between 2010 and 2014 – ABC in 2010 [1] and 2012 [2], CBS in 2011 [5], CW in 2013 [9] and FOX in 2014 [20].

Finally, Microsoft World Imagine Cup organizers recognized one of the authors, Yun, as one of the most successful game design educators and asked him to join judging teams to judge submitted games from all over the world. He assessed the quality of 15 games and recognized that the quality the top-tier games (two games he judged advanced to the final) were on par with the quality of the games that our students produced. His assessment was proven to be valid as 6 teams from our program advanced to the semi-final in 2011 competition.

4. CONCLUSIONS AND DISCUSSIONS

Our multidisciplinary and multifaceted approach successfully enhanced the quality our game design program. Our students attained fundamental knowledge and skills in multiple disciplines by the instructors and guest lecturers from the local game industry and other institutions with their own game design program. Utilizing these knowledge and skills to design games benefited our students as they offer insights on how the game design process is perceived and handled uniquely by different disciplines. This led to a clear division of roles and responsibilities among the team members from an early stage of the development process. Each team also recognized its capabilities/constraints and designed the game to a more realistic degree which resulted in successful completion of its game according to plans. Even after the completion of the courses, in collaboration with the business and entrepreneurship programs at UH, we offer the continual education, training and support from students who express interest in pursuing their own indie game startups. Our multifaceted approach also improved the strength of our courses. In regularly scheduled weekly meetings outside the classes, the mentor provided guidance, mentoring and recommendations to each team. He helped the students expedite their development by mitigating bottlenecks while directing them to choose and focus on essential features and improve the quality of the features and assets.

Teaching assistants who previously took our courses and won national and/or international recognitions significantly contributed in enhancing the students' game design skills and improving the quality of their games. The teaching assistants were greatly effective in assisting the students in each production phase of their projects by utilizing their own previous game design experiences. Further, using their own previous projects as standards, the teaching assistants contributed in helping the students to improve the quality and fun factors of the games.

The ranking duel system contributed significantly in improving the quality of games developed in our courses as it promoted competitiveness among the teams. Although the grade was the primary reason for our students becoming competitive, the nature of the duel and expectation to win pushed them to be further competitive and, consequently, promoted the major improvements in every game that was developed in our courses.

The effectiveness of our multidisciplinary and multifaceted approach was successfully validated in Microsoft US and World Imagine Cup competitions. In US competitions, our students advanced to the final for 6 consecutive years since 2010 and gained multiple records and winnings. In World competitions, they advanced to the semifinals 6 out of 8 years since 2009. Both records demonstrate the effectiveness of our unique approach that helped to educate our students and, consequently, led them to produce top-tier national/international games and achieve unprecedented records in Imagine Cup history.

5. REFERENCES

[1] Azad, S., Students Take Video Games to National Competition, ABC13 Eyewitness News, Houston, TX, (April 21, 2010).

[2] Barajas, E., UH Students Sweep Awards at Microsoft's Imagine Cup, ABC13 Eyewitness News, Houston, TX, (January 3, 2012).

[3] Bidarra, R., Boers, J., Dobbe, J., and Huijser, R., Bringing a pioneer games project to the next level, In Proceedings of 3rd International Conference on Game Development in Computer Science Education, (Feb. 27 – Mar. 3, 2008).

[4] Chandler, H. M. The Game Production Handbook, 2nd Ed., Jones and Bartlett Publishers, 2010.

[5] Clancy, A., Students At Imagine Cup Aim To Change World Through Technology, KIRO 7 News. Seattle WA, (April 12, 2011).

[6] Clingerman, G., Introducing XNA Game Studio Express, CODE magazine, EPS Software Corporation, Sept/Oct 2007.

[7] Entertainment Software Association (ESA), Colleges Video Game Program, http://www.theesa.com/about-esa/courses-certificates-degree-programs/, 2015.

[8] Entertainment Software Association (ESA), Essential Facts About the Computer and Video Game Industry, http://www.theesa.com/wp-content/uploads/2015/04/ESA-Essential-Facts-2015.pdf, 2015.

[9] Graber, J., Half of National Gaming Finalists are University of Houston students, CW39 TV NEWSFIX, Houston, TX, (June 10, 2013).

[10] Hogue, A., Kapralos, B., and Desjardins, F., The role of project-based learning in IT: A case study in a game development and entrepreneurship program, Interactive Technology and Smart Education, Vol. 8 (2), pp.120-134, 2011.

[11] Krier, J., Top Entrepreneurial Colleges Press Release – The Princeton Review & Entrepreneur Magazine Name The Top 50 Schools For Entrepreneurship Programs For 2015, http://www.princetonreview.com/press/top-entrepreneurial-press-release. (September 16, 2014);

[12] Microsoft, Imagine Cup Student Competition, http://www.imagnecup.com/, 2015.

[13] Microsoft, XNA Game Studio Refresh, Microsoft, https://msdn.microsoft.com/en-us/library/bb200104.aspx, 2012.

[14] Novak, J., Game Development Essentials: An Introduction, 3rd Ed., Delmar, Cengage Learning, 2012.

[15] Parrish, J., Bailey, J., and Jensen, B., Using the Imagine Cup SDI as the Foundation for Computer Science Capstone Projects, In Proceedings of the SIGCSE Conference 2010, pp. 68-71.

[16] Pedersen, R. E. Game Design Foundations, 2nd Ed., Wordware Publisher, 2009.

[17] Princeton Review, Top Game Design Methodology, http://www.princetonreview.com/college-rankings/game-design/methodology, 2015.

[18] Settle, A. Linhoff, J., and Berthiaume, A, A Hybrid Approach to Projects in Game Course, In Proceedings of 3rd International Conference on Game Development in Computer Science Education, (Feb. 27 – Mar. 3, 2008).

[19] Unity, What is Unity?, http://unity3d.com/unity, 2015.

[20] Watkins, A., UH Game Design Team Advances to World Competition, Fox 26 News, Houston, TX, (May 29, 2013).

[21] Wolz, U., Ault, C., and Nakra, T. M., Teaching game design through cross-disciplinary content and individualized student deliverables, Journal of Game Development. Volume 2 Issue 2, (Feb. 2007), pp. 19-31.

Design Insights into the Creation and Evaluation of a Computer Science Educational Game

Britton Horn
Northeastern University
bhorn@ccs.neu.edu

Christopher Clark
Northeastern University
clark.chris@husky.neu.edu

Oskar Strom
Northeastern University
strom.o@husky.neu.edu

Hilery Chao
Brown University
hilery_chao@brown.edu

Amy J. Stahl
Northeastern University
stahl.a@husky.neu.edu

Casper Harteveld
Northeastern University
c.harteveld@neu.edu

Gillian Smith
Northeastern University
gi.smith@neu.edu

ABSTRACT

Computer Science (CS) education at the middle school level using educational games has seen recent growth and shown promising results. Typically these games teach the craft of programming and not the perspectives required for computational thinking, such as abstraction and algorithm design, characteristic of a CS curriculum. This research presents a game designed to teach computational thinking via the problem of minimum spanning trees to middle school students, a set of evaluation instruments, and the results of an experimental pilot study. Results show a moderate increase in minimum spanning tree performance; however, differences between gender, collaboration method, and game genre preference are apparent. Based on these results, we discuss design considerations for future CS educational games focused on computational thinking.

CCS Concepts

•Social and professional topics → Computational thinking; Informal education; K-12 education; •Applied computing → Computer games;

Keywords

educational games; game design; computational thinking

1. INTRODUCTION

The computer science (CS) education community has spent much of its effort on introducing CS education earlier in the curriculum, in hopes to better prepare students for a world where procedural literacy and computational thinking is increasingly important [9, 13] as well as improve chronic issues of a lack of diversity in STEM fields, including CS at the university level and beyond [26]. Many of these efforts to reach younger students are done in informal contexts such as classroom visits, summer camps, and after-school programs [5, 7, 8]. The ACM has also recently proposed a set of computing education guidelines that can be integrated into a standard K-12 curriculum [25], and in the UK there are already efforts in place to teach computational thinking in primary and secondary schools [4].

Games have been a promising and popular component of many efforts to teach CS and broaden participation. At the middle school level, there are programs that encourage students to create games using simplified programming environments such as *Alice* [3] or *Scratch* [18]. Others are educational games especially designed to teach CS. However, the vast majority of these game-related outreach efforts tend to focus on the craft and practice of programming, rather than higher-level CS concepts [10].

With this in mind, we have developed *GrACE*, a puzzle game that aims to teach computational thinking–specifically, concepts of abstraction and algorithms [28]. The game teaches neither the structure nor syntax of programming. Instead, it is designed such that players must solve CS puzzles in an algorithmic manner, thus fostering computational thinking.

Puzzles in *GrACE* are built around the common CS problem of finding a graph's minimum spanning tree (MST). This problem was chosen due to the relative ease of mapping graphs onto spatial puzzles, the existence of many algorithms to solve the problem, and its property that even finding an incorrect solution (such as finding a spanning tree that is not minimal) still can involve computational thinking. Thompson and Bell also find the MST problem useful for mapping to a CS educational game due to the need for players to identify algorithms [23].

With this game, we explore the use of procedural content generation (PCG) to aid in computational thinking. Computer generated puzzles bring advantages including rapid puzzle creation and a guarantee all puzzles meet desired graph structure and aesthetic design constraints. Additionally, the incorporation of PCG means players can request new puzzles on demand increasing the amount of in-game content available to them to practice different strategies [21]. We conjecture that by seeing a larger variety of content,

SIGCSE '16, March 02-05, 2016, Memphis, TN, USA

DOI: http://dx.doi.org/10.1145/2839509.2844656

players receive a better understanding of the underlying concept [22]. We further believe that seeing content variety in a collaborative setting will push discussions among players toward abstracted solutions.

Our long-term goals are to come up with an appropriate puzzle design to foster computational thinking in middle school students and to study the educational benefit of including PCG in educational games. In this paper, we present the evaluation instruments and results of an experimental pilot study of the current design of *GrACE*. Our contribution is a set of design insights into how to construct and evaluate educational games that do not aim to specifically teach programming, but rather focus on high-level concepts.

2. RELATED WORK

Many game initiatives for teaching CS exist. Existing CS games frequently focus on teaching programming, either using actual code or a simulated programming-like set of tasks [10]. Those that do support multiplayer activities are typically competitive rather than collaborative, and rhetorically the games often position each player as a solitary character working alone towards a goal. In contrast, *GrACE* casts the player as a helpful character who needs to use their reasoning skills to help a friend, encouraging collaboration even though it is a single-player game.

The focus on competition in educational CS games is seemingly at odds with the value of collaboration in other aspects of CS education. Pair programming [27] is a common practice in introductory programming courses, with benefits to student learning arising from the ability to share strategies and point out potential errors during collaboration. Research in educational games in other fields, such as mathematics, shows competition can be more effective for achieving learning outcomes, but collaboration is still effective and can lead to greater student interest [11, 16].

Most educational games use content that was scripted by the human authors of the game. Procedural content generation (PCG) is the practice of "creating game content automatically, through algorithmic means" [24]. *Refraction* [20] is an example of a math education game that has procedurally generated puzzles. It uses PCG to create its puzzles both to ease authoring effort (by having the computer take on this design role) as well as make hard guarantees about the properties of levels from both an educational and aesthetic perspective. However, *Refraction* simply replaces a typical human-designed level with a computer-designed level; it does not take advantage of the existence of an on-demand puzzle designer during gameplay. *GrACE* uses similar technology to *Refraction* to generate its puzzles, and allows players to request new puzzles at the same difficulty level on demand throughout the game.

Our work examines differences in performance based on whether players had exposure to many different levels, as well as the impact on the use of PCG when players collaborate but are seeing different puzzles from each other. It has been argued that PCG may be useful for educational games through allowing players to explore alternate problems, and communicate abstracted strategies with each other [22].

3. METHODS

Based on our ideas of the potential for PCG for education and the possible mediating role of collaboration, we came up with the following three exploratory propositions:

Proposition 1. Experiencing variety leads to increased learning gains in computational thinking compared to no variety.

Propostion 2. Working in a collaborative context leads to increased learning gains in computational thinking than in an individual context.

Propostion 3. Experiencing variety in a collaborative context leads to increased learning gains in computational thinking compared to no variety in an individual context.

To explore these propositions and, more broadly, our game and evaluation design, we implemented an independent 2x2 factorial design as part of a pilot study. The two 2-level independent variables (IVs) are PCG (PCG vs. No-PCG) and Collaboration (Individual vs. Collaborative).

3.1 Participants

The experiment was implemented as part of a two week summer program at Northeastern University. This program selects 48 middle school talented students each year, and focuses on STEM content. The program historically supports underserved and underrepresented students with limited opportunities and is free of charge.

During the day of implementation, 43 students participated with the consent of their parents, 22 identifying as female and 21 as male. Ages ranged from 10 to 13 (M = 11.9, SD = 0.85). Four participants identified as Hispanic or Latino, 12 reported to be Asian, nine Black or African American, 12 White, and six as "other" (with four participants preferring not to answer).

3.2 Materials

All materials mentioned in this section are publicly archived.[1]

3.2.1 Game

GrACE has a nature-based theme, chosen as a result of focus testing with middle school students to determine the appeal of a variety of metaphors. The game is centered on two characters–a mouse and a rabbit–who are collecting vegetables. Vegetables (nodes) in the ground are connected by cracks (edges) that only the mouse can fit through. Edge weight corresponds to the amount of bunny energy needed to dig along a crack. Players control the mouse as it explores the map and flags cracks for the rabbit. To minimize the bunny's digging energy, players must find and flag the MST. An example can be seen in Fig. 1

Initially, players can only see the starting node and the nodes connected to it. The player chooses an edge to traverse at which point the next node and its connections are revealed. This mechanic discourages players from solving the puzzle visually by examining the entire graph at once. Instead, we designed the game around limited information exploration to encourage stepwise thinking and mimicry of MST solving algorithms.

We used two game versions in accordance with the PCG manipulation: one version with PCG and one without. The standard version contains 11 difficulty levels, each with a single associated puzzle pre-generated by the computer and the same across all instances of the game. These puzzles were each chosen at random from the set of levels used in the PCG version, to limit accidental biasing from including

[1]http://hdl.handle.net/2047/D20199448

Figure 1: Screenshot ©Northeastern University.

human-authored puzzles. Players can restart their puzzle and access previously played puzzles once completed. In addition, the PCG version allows for the possibility at anytime to press a "random" button to generate a new puzzle with the same difficulty level. We generated 100 puzzles for each level in advance, making the PCG version contain 1,100 puzzles in total. Level one contained two nodes and one edge to demonstrate basic game mechanics. Level 11 contained nine nodes and 16 edges.

Maps were created using a constraint-based, Answer Set Programming (ASP) method [19]. Graph constraints included the number of nodes and edges, minimum and maximum weights for edges, node connectivity, and a valid MST. Aesthetic constraints were the map size, distance between nodes, valid edge intersection angles, and various art tile layout rules. Constraints were separated so that future art implementations could have their own set of constraints swapped with the current set and not impact the core map generation.

The game was instrumented to track all player actions (e.g. placing or removing a flag, submitting an answer) and game states (e.g. mouse and bunny energy).

3.2.2 Questionnaires

The pre-questionnaire involved an adaptation of the 22-item New Computer Game Attitude Scale (NCGAS), which was developed to evaluate middle school students' attitudes toward educational games [12]. In our adaptation, we used the *Liking* and *Leisure* constructs, and adapted it to a 7-point Likert scale for consistency with our other measures. Liking (3 items; $\alpha = .760$) measures how much the students like playing video games; Leisure (5 items; $\alpha = .856$) measures the degree to which video games are incorporated in the leisure time of students.

On the post-questionnaire we included a scale on Game Experience to assess what students' opinions are of the game. We created two anticipated constructs, Enjoyment ($\alpha = .93$) and Difficulty ($\alpha = .78$), each with four 7-point Likert items. The post-questionnaire ended with demographics questions and questions about game-playing and school subject preferences, where students were requested to check any genre or topic that they liked.

3.2.3 Comprehension Test

The comprehension test was developed to measure conceptual understanding of the MST. Previous studies on computational thinking have included tests that made effective use of measuring change in students' conceptual understanding through design scenarios [2] or concept exams [14] specific to the software being tested. To allow for objective comparison across students, we provided a multiple choice assessment along the lines of the concept exams. In contrast to previous studies, we opted for questions not only about solving MST problems in the context of the specific software but also about solving MST problems with another metaphor and in an abstract manner. The goal with this is to measure knowledge transfer from the game to other contexts.

We created two tests, each with a different but similar puzzle for all three contexts: game, metaphor, and abstract. Each puzzle has three associated questions with four choice options for each question. Consistently across the puzzles, one question concerned the problem of adding a single edge, one about removing a single edge, and one about correcting an incorrect spanning tree. The questions were developed independently, validated by the three test question authors, and error-checked by a fourth researcher on the team.

Game. For these questions, we edited screenshots of random puzzles from the PCG version and constructed questions using similar language to that used in the game.

Metaphor. Here we adapted the "Muddy City" exercise from CS Unplugged [1]. In our adaptation, we simplified the language of this roads network problem because the students had to read it to themselves, and redid the artwork to make it clearer and easier to modify.

Abstract. These puzzles were based on a typical graph with nodes and edges that we referred to as circles and lines.

3.3 Procedure

This study was run as part of a "computational thinking" activity in the summer program. We randomly assigned students to a computer, and evenly distributed them across the conditions; however, due to a slightly lower turnout and one student opt-out, we had fewer students in both PCG conditions. We counterbalanced the comprehension test to rule out the difficulty of the test as a bias.

The experiment started in a single classroom where students received their pre-questionnaire, pre-test and lab assignment. Instructions for the game were then provided by a facilitator without mentioning the MST concept or the game's relationship to CS. One lab held all students in the individual condition, the other had students in the collaborative condition. We divided both spaces such that one half was assigned to the PCG condition and the other half to the No-PCG condition to minimize interference. Assigned pairs played next to each other and were encouraged to communicate and look at each other's screens. In the individual condition, students were discouraged from interacting. All facilitators followed a script instructing them how to respond during the questionnaires, tests and gameplay.

Students completed the post-questionnaire and post-test after the game, followed by a semi-structured discussion on the topic of CS and the MST concept in particular. The experiment took three hours, with one hour of gameplay.

4. RESULTS

For the purposes of this paper, we limit ourselves to reporting the main results that we derived on demographics, gameplay, and the performance on the comprehension test.

4.1 Demographics

The majority (61.9%) reported playing games more than 1-2 days a week. There were no strong preferences or dislikes of genres. Based on the preferences for school subjects, with 32 (74.4%) indicating a liking for math and 33 (76.6%) a liking for science, it is clear that this is a group with a bias towards STEM content. In terms of gender differences, boys reported to play more than girls, $\chi^2(1) = 4.39$, $p = .036$, $V = .371$. Boys further reported to like playing adventure and action games more so than girls, for both $\chi^2(1) = 10.5$, $p = .001$, $V = .495$. For school subjects, girls liked art and language and literature better, respectively $\chi^2(1) = 7.21$, $p = .001$, $V = .409$ and $\chi^2(1) = 6.89$, $p = .007$, $V = .400$. Boys, on the other hand, report liking technology better, $\chi^2(1) = 4.06$, $p = .044$, $V = .309$. No racial differences were observed in game and school subject preferences.

The results regarding game attitude suggest that the majority like games but are more spread in their opinion when it comes to the role of games in their leisure time. The variety in Leisure is partially a result of a difference in gender, $t(40) = -5.67$, $p < .001$, $r = .73$, with girls disagreeing more about its importance. This finding is consistent with the gender difference in frequency of playing.

4.2 Gameplay

Investigating the items associated with Enjoyment, it becomes clear that a strong majority agreed or strongly agreed they had fun and majorities further indicated they would recommend this to a friend, play it at home, and learned from it. Despite the enjoyment, in exploring the items associated with Difficulty, it shows that majorities thought it was frustrating, challenging, and hard. In contrast, the majority disagreed that they felt bored. No differences are found on gender and race, except for the Enjoyment item "I thought it was fun". It turns out girls ($Mdn = 5$, $IQR = 4\text{-}6$) agreed with this less than boys ($Mdn = 6.5$, $IQR = 5\text{-}7$), $U = 144$, $p = .047$, $r = .31$.

Both Liking and Leisure correlate with Enjoyment, respectively $r = .40$, $p = .009$ and $r = .309$, $p = .049$, which further suggests an initial predisposition is of influence in how the game is experienced. It is then not surprising to find that students who play more than 1-2 days a week enjoyed the game more than those who play less, $t(39) = 2.91$, $p = .006$, $r = .42$. Liking, leisure, and frequency of play do not relate to Difficulty.

There are aspects that do relate to Difficulty. Those who like puzzle and strategy games perceived less difficulty than those who do not, respectively $t(41) = 2.31$, $p = .026$, $r = .34$ and $t(40) = 2.73$, $p = .009$, $r = .40$. Interestingly, the same is true for students with a preference for sports games and physical education, respectively $t(21) = 2.54$, $p = .019$, $r = .48$ and $t(41) = 2.11$, $p = .041$, $r = .31$. This may suggest that these students like a challenge and have a different perception of difficulty. Surprisingly, it is students with an interest in simulation and role-playing games that scored higher on Enjoyment, respectively $t(40) = 2.41$, $p = .021$, $r = .36$ and $t(40) = 2.22$, $p = .032$, $r = .33$.

Regarding the conditions, it appears students in the PCG conditions agreed more with the Difficulty item "I felt frustrated", $t(41) = 2.47$, $p = .018$, $r = .36$. For the collaborative conditions it is interesting to note that it approaches significance for agreeing more on the Enjoyment item "I would recommend this game to a friend"(*.061*) and on the Difficulty item "I thought it was hard".

The game data revealed that students in the collaboration condition took longer to play the game with an average level time of 111 seconds ($SD = 33.3$) compared to individual participants' average of just 85 seconds ($SD = 28.5$), $t(40) = 2.67$, $p = .01$, $r = .39$. Somewhat related and nearing significance is that students in the individual condition ($Mdn = 11$, $IQR = 9\text{-}11$) were more likely to complete the final level than the collaboration condition ($Mdn = 9$, $IQR = 7.5\text{-}10.5$), $\chi^2(1) = 3.93$, $p = .056$. Every student was able to complete at least level 5 (4 nodes and 5 edges).

The "random" button was used a total of 125 times by the 19 students in the PCG group ($M = 6.58$, $SD = 6.74$). No statistically significant difference was seen between the collaboration and individual groups. The button was used most on Level 6 at 31 times (24.8%), followed by Level 8 at 25 (20%) and level seven at 23 (18.4%). The "random" was not used by seven students and—surprisingly—on Level 11.

4.3 Comprehension

Independent Samples T-tests show that there is no significant difference between the two versions on the total scores before and after the game, suggesting that the test versions are equal in difficulty. Test scores were calculated by providing one point per correctly answered question. Thus, with nine questions students could get a maximum score of nine points. Even though MST problem was likely unfamiliar to students, they performed quite well on the pre-test ($M_{pre} = 5.71$, $SD_{pre} = 2.13$) and marginally but significantly improved their performance on the post-test ($M_{pre} = 6.37$, $SD_{pre} = 2.33$), $t(41) = 2.40$, $p = .021$, $r = .35$. Of note is that the number of students with a perfect score increased from two (4.8%) to nine students (21%).

Table 1 provides an overview of the average improvement across conditions on the overall test and on the specific puzzles as well as kinds of questions. The table implies there are differences across the conditions. The collaborative conditions seem to improve less so than the individual ones, and this seems especially true for the collaborative condition with PCG, suggesting an interaction effect exists. No strong significant difference appears at first; however, in exploring the data a surprising finding was that students who liked the action genre ($M_{pre} = 5.61$, $SD_{pre} = 1.97$; $M_{post} = 6.88$, $SD_{post} = 1.92$) improved more than students who did not ($M_{pre} = 5.84$, $SD_{pre} = 2.36$; $M_{post} = 5.74$, $SD_{post} = 2.68$), $t(40) = 2.73$, $p = .009$, $r = .40$. None of the other demographics had such an influence. As boys liked the action genre more so than girls, we performed 2x2 ANCOVA analyses with PCG (PCG vs. No-PCG) and Collaboration (Ind. vs. Coll.) as between-subjects factors and with gender and action as covariates. On the total improvement this revealed a main effect of action, $F(1, 36) = 10.1$, $p = .003$, $\eta_p^2 = .22$, and Collaboration, $F(1, 36) = 4.69$, $p = .037$, $\eta_p^2 = .12$. The effects of gender ($p = .20$) and PCG ($p = .67$) were insignificant; however, the interaction effect between PCG and Collaboration approximates significance, $F(1, 36) = 3.64$, $p = .064$, $\eta_p^2 = .09$. The interaction effect is significant on the abstract puzzles specifically, $F(1, 37) = 5.36$, $p = .026$, $\eta_p^2 = .13$. As exemplified in Table 1, we can see that students in the individual condition with PCG improved more so than in the No-PCG conditions, whereas in the collaborative condition with PCG the performance seems to be less than in the No-PCG conditions.

Test Measure	Ind. x No-PCG (N=12)	Coll. x No-PCG (N=12)	Ind. x PCG (N=8)	Coll. x PCG (N=10)	Overall (N=42)
Total	1.08 (1.44)	0.67 (1.30)	1.13 (1.73)	-0.30 (2.31)	0.64 (1.73)
Game	0.50 (1.09)	0.17 (0.94)	0.63 (1.51)	0.30 (1.49)	0.38 (1.21)
Roads network	0.50 (0.52)	0.33 (0.78)	-0.25 (1.04)	-0.30 (1.33)	0.12 (0.97)
Abstract	0.08 (1.00)	0.17 (1.03)	0.75 (1.03)	-0.30 (0.95)	0.14 (1.03)
Addition	0.17 (0.86)	-0.08 (0.90)	0.50 (0.76)	0.00 (0.94)	0.12 (0.86)
Deletion	0.42 (0.90)	0.42 (0.90)	0.25 (1.16)	-0.10 (0.99)	0.26 (0.96)
Correction	0.50 (0.80)	0.33 (0.89)	0.38 (1.30)	-0.20 (0.92)	0.26 (0.96)

Table 1: Comprehension test improvement across conditions, in *M* (*SD*). The test is separated into three representations (original game aesthetic, road network metaphor and abstract) and three concepts (edge addition, edge deletion and completed tree correction). Conditions are broken down by Individual (Ind.) vs Collaboration (Coll.) and PCG vs No-PCG.

5. DISCUSSION

Our experience with designing the game, constructing instruments to evaluate it, and performing a pilot study has led to a number of design insights and areas for future study. It should be noted that the current study is limited by using a biased group of diverse but well performing students who are interested in STEM.

The potential of PCG and collaboration. With the results in this instance of *GrACE*, we must outright reject Proposition 2 since the opposite happened. The students in the collaboration conditions improved less. The possibility to discuss with partners does not outweigh playing more exercises, and it was noticeable that pairs played less and got less far. Future research should look into the communication between pairs and ways to better support collaboration through the game. Although an interaction effect seems to happen, it is also different than expected. PCG is only beneficial for those who play alone. For that reason we need to reject Proposition 3 about the multiplier effect of PCG and Collaboration too. However, we can partially accept Proposition 1. The current data provides an indication that when PCG is used in an individual context, increased learning gains are a result. The fact this is especially noticeable for the abstract puzzles is a promising result. Teaching abstract thinking is a difficult yet important skill to master, especially for students aspiring to a CS career.

Designing for collaboration. In keeping with other findings for educational games in non-CS STEM fields [11, 16], our findings suggest that players are more likely to recommend the game to a friend in the collaboration condition, yet perform better in the game in the individual condition. The goal of informal learning interventions is to be both engaging and educational. The Collaboration condition in *GrACE* does not involve students collaborating on the same puzzle, but rather collaborating to help each other with their own puzzles outside the game. In future versions of the game, we intend to explore ways to make this strategy-level collaboration more explicit and occur within the game in order to achieve a positive collaborative learning effect.

Placing content generation in context. A common argument in the game design and PCG community is that additional content leads to replayability and enjoyment [21]. However, our findings show that playing in the PCG condition leads to greater frustration. One possible explanation for this is that students who are struggling with one particular puzzle may generate new content hoping for an easier puzzle, but instead find one at the same difficulty level that is also challenging. While frustration may be linked to game enjoyment overall, this effect is something that requires more dedicated study. It is clear that the context in which PCG is used and how it is integrated into the game's overall mechanics must be carefully considered.

Fun vs. frustration Students reported a high rate of enjoyment for the game but also found it frustrating, challenging, and hard. This is perhaps tied to Papert's concept of "hard fun" in educational games: not that players find a game fun despite it being hard, but that they find it fun because it is hard [15]. While many educational games work to simplify concepts and offer extremely gentle introductions, with *GrACE* it seems that its difficulty is important for the enjoyment of the game. Our future work will include examining what specifically it is about the game that students find frustrating by looking at patterns in behavior from the game data, analyzing player demographics more in-depth, and testing additional iterations of the game.

Beyond gender: Understanding player profiles. Researchers have often discussed the importance of designing games that are accessible to girls, either by attempting to understand the design preferences exhibited by girls [6, 5] or by incorporating stereotypically feminine play styles and preferences into a game's design to make it "gender-neutral" [17]. However, our results show that while gender identity can influence player enjoyment, it is not alone responsible. Indeed, genre preferences (such as a preference for puzzle games, action games, or competitive sports games) have an impact on both experience and outcome performance, independent from gender. This points to the need for a deeper understanding of a target audience, refocusing design efforts away from looking at gender alone.

6. CONCLUSION

In this paper, we discussed the results from an experimental pilot study of *GrACE*, a game designed to foster computational thinking through PCG and collaboration, with the aim of retrieving design insights into the creation and evaluation of this CS educational game. While the game achieved a moderate improvement in the conceptual understanding of the MST problem, multiple unexpected insights were found such as the need for designing explicitly for collaboration, and the need to more deeply understand player profiles. These design insights are guiding our future work with *GrACE*, and can serve as guidelines for others interested in developing CS educational games.

7. ACKNOWLEDGMENTS

We want to thank the Northeastern STEM Center for Education for integrating our pilot study in their summer program and our external evaluators from TERC: Jim Hammerman and Audrey Martinez-Gudapakkam. This material is based upon work supported by the National Science Foundation under Grant No. 1422750.

8. REFERENCES

[1] T. Bell, I. H. Witten, and M. Fellows. *Computer science unplugged: An enrichment and extension programme for primary-aged children.* 2010. http://csunplugged.org/books.

[2] K. Brennan and M. Resnick. New frameworks for studying and assessing the development of computational thinking. In *Proceedings of the 2012 annual meeting of the American Educational Research Association, Vancouver, Canada*, 2012.

[3] S. Cooper, W. Dann, and R. Pausch. Alice: A 3-D tool for introductory programming concepts. *Journal of Computing Sciences in Colleges*, 15(5):107–116, 2000.

[4] A. Csizmadia, P. Curzon, M. Dorling, S. Humphreys, T. Ng, C. Selby, and J. Woollard. Computational thinking: A guide for teachers. Technical report, Computing At School, 2015.

[5] J. Denner, L. Werner, S. Bean, and S. Campe. The girls creating games program: Strategies for engaging middle-school girls in information technology. *Frontiers: A Journal of Women Studies*, 26(1):90–98, Jan. 2005.

[6] M. D. Dickey. Girl gamers: The controversy of girl games and the relevance of female-oriented game design for instructional design. *British Journal of Educational Technology*, 37(5):785–793, 2006.

[7] P. Doerschuk, J. Liu, and J. Mann. Pilot summer camps in computing for middle school girls: From organization through assessment. *SIGCSE Bull.*, 39(3):4–8, June 2007.

[8] C. Frieze. Diversifying the images of computer science: Undergraduate women take on the challenge! *SIGCSE Bull.*, 37(1):397–400, Feb. 2005.

[9] M. Guzdial. Education: Paving the way for computational thinking. *Commun. ACM*, 51(8):25–27, Aug. 2008.

[10] C. Harteveld, G. Smith, G. Carmichael, E. Gee, and C. Stewart-Gardiner. A design-focused analysis of games teaching computer science. In *Proceedings of Games+Learning+Society 10*, 2014.

[11] F. Ke and B. Grabowski. Gameplaying for maths learning: Cooperative or not? *British Journal of Educational Technology*, 38(2):249–259, 2007.

[12] E. Z.-F. Liu, C.-Y. Lee, and J.-H. Chen. Developing a new computer game attitude scale for Taiwanese early adolescents. *Journal of Educational Technology & Society*, 16(1):183–193, 2013.

[13] M. Mateas. Procedural literacy: Educating the new media practitioner. In D. Davidson, editor, *Beyond Fun*, pages 67–83. ETC Press, Pittsburgh, PA, USA, 2008.

[14] A. Munson, B. Moskal, A. Harriger, T. Lauriski-Karriker, and D. Heersink. Computing at the high school level: Changing what teachers and students know and believe. *Computers & Education*, 57(2):1836–1849, 2011.

[15] S. Papert. Does easy do it? Children, games, and learning. *Game Developer*, June 1998.

[16] J. L. Plass, P. A. O'Keefe, B. D. Homer, J. Case, E. O. Hayward, M. Stein, and K. Perlin. The impact of individual, competitive, and collaborative mathematics game play on learning, performance, and motivation. *Journal of Educational Psychology*, 105(4):1050, 2013.

[17] S. G. Ray. *Gender inclusive game design: Expanding the market.* Cengage Learning, 2004.

[18] M. Resnick, J. Maloney, A. Monroy-Hernández, N. Rusk, E. Eastmond, K. Brennan, A. Millner, E. Rosenbaum, J. Silver, B. Silverman, and Y. Kafai. Scratch: Programming for all. *Commun. ACM*, 52(11):60–67, Nov. 2009.

[19] A. Smith and M. Mateas. Answer set programming for procedural content generation: A design space approach. *Computational Intelligence and AI in Games, IEEE Transactions on*, 3(3):187 –200, Sept. 2011.

[20] A. M. Smith, E. Andersen, M. Mateas, and Z. Popovic. A case study of expressively constrainable level design automation tools for a puzzle game. In *Proceedings of the 2012 Conference on the Foundations of Digital Games*, Raleigh, NC, June 2012.

[21] G. Smith. Understanding procedural content generation: A design-centric analysis of the role of PCG in games. In *Proceedings of the 2014 ACM Conference on Computer-Human Interaction*, Toronto, Canada, Apr. 2014.

[22] G. Smith and C. Harteveld. Procedural content generation as an opportunity to foster collaborative mindful learning. In *Workshop on Games and Learning, co-located with Foundations of Digital Games 2013*, Chania, Greece, May 2013.

[23] D. Thompson and T. . Virtually unplugged: Rich data capture to evaluate CS pedagogy in 3D virtual worlds. In *Learning and Teaching in Computing and Engineering (LaTiCE), 2015 International Conference on*, pages 156–163, Apr. 2015.

[24] J. Togelius, G. Yannakakis, K. Stanley, and C. Browne. Search-based procedural content generation: A taxonomy and survey. *Computational Intelligence and AI in Games, IEEE Transactions on*, 3(3):172 –186, Sept. 2011.

[25] A. Tucker, F. Deek, J. Jones, D. McCowan, C. Stephenson, and A. Verno. ACM K-12 CS model curriculum, 2nd edition. Technical report, Computer Science Teachers Association, 2006.

[26] United States Department of Commerce. Women in STEM: A gender gap to innovation. Technical report, Aug. 2011.

[27] L. A. Williams and R. R. Kessler. All I really need to know about pair programming I learned in kindergarten. *Commun. ACM*, 43(5):108–114, May 2000.

[28] J. M. Wing. Computational thinking. *Communications of the ACM*, 49(3):33–35, 2006.

Experiences from an Experiential Learning Course on Games Development

Stephan Krusche
TU München
Munich, Germany
krusche@in.tum.de

Barbara Reichart
TU München
Munich, Germany
reichart.b@in.tum.de

Paul Tolstoi
TU München
Munich, Germany
tolstoi@in.tum.de

Bernd Bruegge
TU München
Munich, Germany
bruegge@in.tum.de

ABSTRACT

Games development brings fun into the software engineering curriculum, but it is a practical activity that educators cannot teach in traditional lecture-based environments. Including pedagogical aspects of problem-based, cooperative, blended and experiential learning is necessary to achieve a high learning experience.

In this paper we describe and evaluate a block course in which we ask students with almost no mobile application development experience to create games in just two weeks. We offer the course in two different modes, for beginners who learn games development, and for tutors who help us in the organization of the course and in the teaching activities.

Apart from games development and game design, students learn modeling, design patterns and software configuration management. They practice soft skills in team work, present their games to their classmates using Pecha Kucha and publish their games into the App Store. Our evaluations show that students appreciate the great learning experience.

Keywords

Software Engineering, Problem-based Learning, Blended Learning, Cooperative Learning, Interactive Tutorials

1. INTRODUCTION

Software engineering is an interactive and collaborative activity [23] that requires the practical application of knowledge [8, 20]. Educators struggle when teaching it in traditional lecture-based environments where activities take place in the front of the classroom. Lectures are usually similar to broadcasting, where essential education interactions are initiated by the teacher with only limited students participation. Self-guided learning, personal responsibility, practical relevance and individualization are important elements of a great learning experience. Several pedagogic theories have been developed that include these elements.

Problem-based learning is a technique to learn about a subject through the experience of problem solving. Educators facilitate learning by supporting, guiding, and monitoring this process [4]. *Cooperative learning* is an educational approach which aims to organize classroom activities into social learning experiences: Students work in groups to complete tasks collectively towards a common goal [12].

Blended learning allows students to learn through delivery of content and instructions via computer-mediated activities, digital and online media [10]. *Experiential learning* is the process of learning from experience, a methodology in which educators engage with students in direct experience to increase knowledge, develop skills, and clarify values [14].

We developed a course that includes a mix of these approaches and teaches software engineering concepts trough games development. While the combination leads to a more complex experience for educators, it lowers their stress and leads to higher satisfaction [2]. We base our teaching approach on a Chinese proverb, first mentioned by Confucius and adapted by Benjamin Franklin. In recent publications, an extended version of the proverb is mentioned: *"Tell me and I will forget. Show me and I will remember. Involve me and I will understand. Step back and I will act"* [15].

Explaining a concept only theoretically does not allow students to apply it. Therefore we include the idea of cognitive apprenticeship: an apprentice observes the skills of a master who shows how a concept works in practice. Clarifying the thinking process behind the application makes it easier for the apprentice to imitate the behavior [7]. Involving students in the learning process using interactive tutorials follows the idea of experiential learning. Students apply a concept on their own, in a way that fits to their own techniques, to understand the concept and its application. Including self-guided learning, self-improvement and problem-based learning lets students take the responsibility to solve a problem on their own using the concepts they learned before.

We teach students the ability to develop mobile application in a two-weeks block course. Compared to traditional games development, the development of mobile games is less complex [18]. This enables students to create playable mobile games within two weeks. Games development is a popular topic among computer science students and brings fun into software engineering [6, 22]. It has personal meaning-

SIGCSE '16, March 2–5, 2016, Memphis, TN, USA.

ISBN 978-1-4503-3685-7/16/03...$15.00
DOI: http://dx.doi.org/10.1145/2839509.2844599

fulness, hence it is easier for students to come up with their own ideas. Many students are interested in developing their own casual game and publish it into the App Store.

In this paper we show experiences from an experiential learning course on games development with up to 40 students. Section 2 describes the design of the course including learning objectives, organizational aspects, the schedule and the structure of an interactive tutorial. Section 3 shows experiences and observations during the conduction of several courses in the last years. We explain how to handle difficult situations and how tutors improve the learning experience. Section 4 shows findings of evaluations of the course, while Section 5 describes related work.

2. COURSE DESIGN

Creating and conducting a software engineering course on games development involves several aspects. The curriculum of the course needs to include topics like programming, the use of frameworks, game design, the application of design and architectural patterns, and user interface design. In this section we describe the course design starting with its learning objectives. We explain the organization including preparation, course and follow-up phase. We then describe details of the course phase, where students first attend interactive tutorials and then develop a mobile game in teams of two students. We finally explain structure and purpose of an interactive tutorial.

2.1 Learning Objectives

The learning objectives of the course support the seven outcomes described in the SE2004 recommendations for undergratuate software engineering curricula [19]: (1) show mastery of knowledge and skills necessary to begin practice, (2) work individually or in a team to develop quality software, (3) make appropriate trade-offs within cost and time limitations, (4) perform design in one or more domains, (5) demonstrate understanding and apply current theories, models, and techniques, (6) demonstrate soft skills such as negotiation, leadership, communication, (7) learn new models, techniques, and technologies as they emerge.

Depending on previous experience and interest, students participate in the course in two different modes: beginner and advanced. The beginner mode targets students who have not developed mobile applications or games before and have no experience with the programming language and the tools taught during the course. However, it is assumed that the beginners have basic knowledge of an object-oriented programming language and know how to model using UML. During the first week, the major focus is on learning the object-oriented programming language, the use of frameworks and the integrated development environment (IDE).

In addition to programming, the course includes concepts about design patterns and modeling to help the students structuring their source code and facilitating extensibility and reuse. Distributed version control allows the students to work collaboratively on source code. Another focus of the course are soft skills. The students practice communication with other developers, tutors, and teaching assistants (TA). Every team prepares and presents a presentation which is recorded. The students receive the videos and obtain feedback on content and delivery of their presentation.

The course does not focus on project management techniques like Scrum or planning poker, because the development teams consist of two students sitting next to each other. Including those topics would unnecessarily increase the complexity of the course. Such project management techniques only provide benefits in projects with an extended time period and a larger team as described in [17]. Instead, students work in pairs on a small prototype (using pair programming) for one week which encourages the cooperative learning process when working towards a common goal. This gives them enough confidence in their programming abilities, required to build larger applications, while at the same time not limiting them to mere implementation of small programming assignments. After the course, the students deepen their experience in capstone courses where they develop larger applications within a realistic context as described in [5]. Then the students also learn more about project management techniques.

In the advanced mode, students participate as tutors who already have acquired knowledge in the development environment, including programming language and tool chain. Tutors study one specialized and advanced topic such as sprite animation and prepare an interactive tutorial under the supervision of the TAs. They also learn about how to structure and teach the topic and how to present it as interactive tutorial. Tutors help beginners during development in the second week and deepen their knowledge about application and games development. All students learn about game design and the use of platform specific frameworks and have to deal with distributed version control to obtain the course material, to submit solutions to exercises and to work in teams during the development of the game. They practice their social and non technical skills such as working in a team, presenting, communicating and being proactive.

2.2 Organization

The course is organized by two TAs, one is responsible for the introduction to the programming language, the other one is familiar with games development. The TAs ask four to six students with experience in the programming language and tools to participate as tutors in order to help in the organization of the course. The course activities are shown in Figure 1. The TAs prepare the course starting about eight weeks in advance (colored orange in Figure 1). In the two weeks long course phase (green), all students attend full-time, typically before the semester starts. Finally there is a follow-up phase (blue) that is about six weeks long.

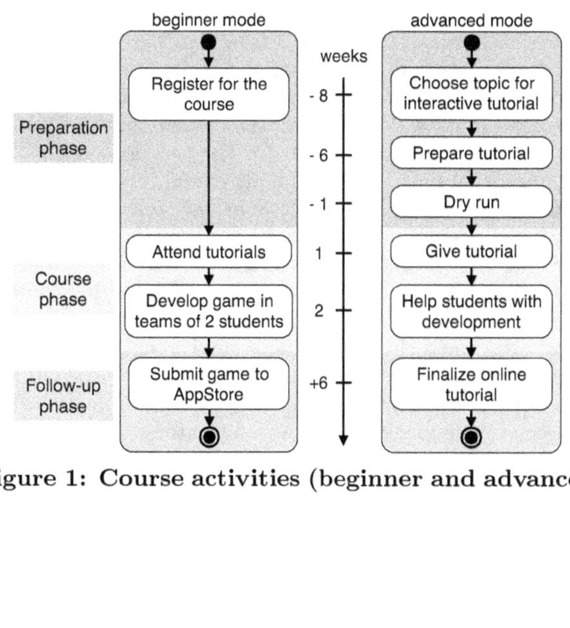

Figure 1: Course activities (beginner and advanced)

There are several reasons for conducting the course phase in two weeks. It is easier for TAs, tutors and students to keep focus and concentration high, when working full-time in the course. Developing a game in a short time is a huge motivating factor. TAs start to prepare the course at the end of the previous semester, when students apply for it. Undergraduate students (bachelor) have to be at least on the sophomore level to participate. Graduate students (master) also participate. The TAs can assume that participating students have learned enough about object-oriented programming and modeling. During registration the TAs tell the students that they can participate in the course in two different modes. In a short separate meeting, the TAs present the tutors possible advanced topics and distribute those, taking into account personal preferences.

Before the course starts, TAs supervise the tutors in creating one interactive tutorial using a master-apprenticeship approach. The tutors create an outline for the presentation and an idea for a sample project. Over several iterations they improve based on feedback and positive examples provided by the TAs. This process ensures that the tutor learns about the most important aspects in teaching. Furthermore it serves as quality control to ensure the content is correct and presented in an approachable manner.

One week before the course phase with all students, the tutors dry run their tutorial. They give the entire tutorial session as close to the final presentation as possible. TAs and other tutors participate in each dry run session, playing the role of beginners, so that the presenting tutor can observe them, discovering issues that could arise in the actual session. The tutor then receives detailed feedback on content and delivery. Details about the schedule of the course phase are described in the next section. In the follow-up phase, tutors write an online tutorial about their topic. Meanwhile, TAs help the beginners to submit their games into the App Store. While the submission is optional, usually all students are eager and finalize their game with respect to stability and feature completeness so that TAs can upload the game.

2.3 Schedule

The schedule of the course phase is shown in Figure 2. The goal of the first week is to teach basic as well as advanced concepts of the programming language and platform using interactive tutorials, which are described in more detail in the next section. TAs give 10-12, tutors give 4-6 tutorials. While TAs impart essential concepts required for games development in the first three days, tutors teach more specialized topics at the end of the week. The first day of the block course introduces students to distributed version control, so that they can obtain the course material, submit their solutions and collaborate in the second week. Then TAs start with basics about the programming language and the development environment, continue with intermediate language concepts like inheritance and closures and advance to graphic engine APIs. At the end of the first week, the programming assignment starts: the TAs ask the students to apply their newly gained knowledge by developing a game in one week until the end of the second week.

During the second week, the beginners develop a game in teams of two students. They choose their own game idea and receive feedback from TAs and tutors. The TAs ask the students to start with a simple idea they could actually develop in two days and that is extensible later on with features like leaderboards, achievements, particle effects or additional levels. A graphics designer from industry helps the students creating 2D and 3D graphics for their games. TAs also setup continuous integration and continuous delivery as explained in [16] and show the wallboard of the continuous integration server as shown in Figure 3. This ensures that the students always have a version in the repository that can be installed and tested on a real mobile device.

	Monday	Tuesday	Wednesday	Thursday	Friday
First week	Introduction to language & platform	Advanced language & platform concepts	Introduction to game development	Advanced game topics	Advanced game topics Programming assignment
Second week	Development of a game in teams of 2 students				Presentation and demo

Figure 2: Detailed schedule of the course phase

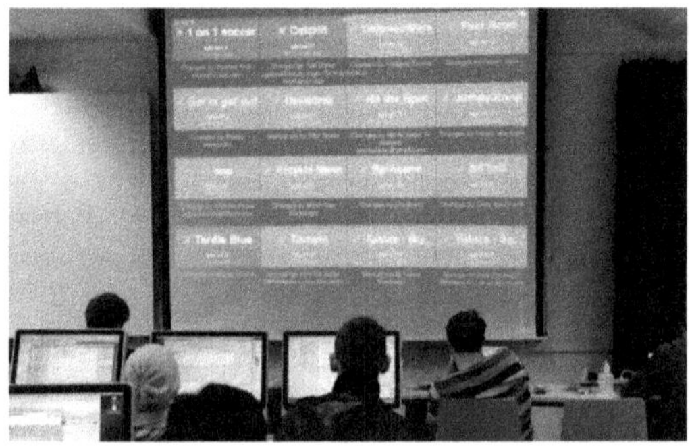

Figure 3: Wallboard with the status of the games

There is an intermediate milestone after two days, where the students present their ideas and current progress, and obtain feedback by the TAs. At the end of the second week, they present their game in a short Pecha Kucha [3] presentation. Presentations following the Pecha Kucha style have up to 20 slides each shown for exactly 20 seconds. The transition to the next slides is automatic and cannot be controlled manually. This presentation style requires the students to insert only simple graphics and only few text statements into one slide. It prevents the problem, that they talk too much on a boring slide, and have to rush on an interesting slide later in the talk. Not only the presenters, also the audience is more relaxed. It is easier for the TAs to control that students finish their presentation in time.

2.4 Interactive Tutorial

Each day of the first week includes three tutorial slots. An interactive tutorial is based on the idea of experiential and blended learning and consists of two parts. The first part is about 90 minutes long and includes theory intermixed with small exercises, each about 5-10 minutes long. The students learn concepts, then directly apply them and see step by step solutions afterwards. At the beginning of a tutorial, they download the slides to lookup concepts and solutions to these small exercises. After discussing the solution, the presenter also reflects on the concept and its application and tells the students when to use it. TAs and tutors directly help the students if they face problems during the tutorial.

The second part of the tutorial is an autonomous and problem-based learning exercise that is about 30 minutes long. Students have to solve this exercise on their own, challenging their understanding and participation in the first part by repeating concepts of the tutorial. TAs and tutors only explain the task, but do not show the solution. If students have serious problems with the autonomous exercise, the tutors repeat the concepts of the tutorial with them.

3. CASE STUDY

We describe observations and experiences from several courses in the last years in this section. We explain typical problems and how we addressed them. We show insights about the relationship between TAs, tutors and students and how an open atmosphere improves the learning experience.

The courses uses Apple's iOS platform to teach object-oriented programming with Objective-C - recently Swift - and games development. Playgrounds, lightweight live programming environments, allow students to explore and evaluate code interactively without the need to compile and without the full complexity of the IDE. They show immediate feedback and are ideal to introduce new programming or language concept to beginners. Figure 4 shows an example of a playground. In the left editor area, students type in code that is constantly evaluated so they get immediate feedback. In the middle, they see these evaluation results and can use the quick look feature to display more information. The timeline view on the right inspects the code and visualizes results of loops or animations.

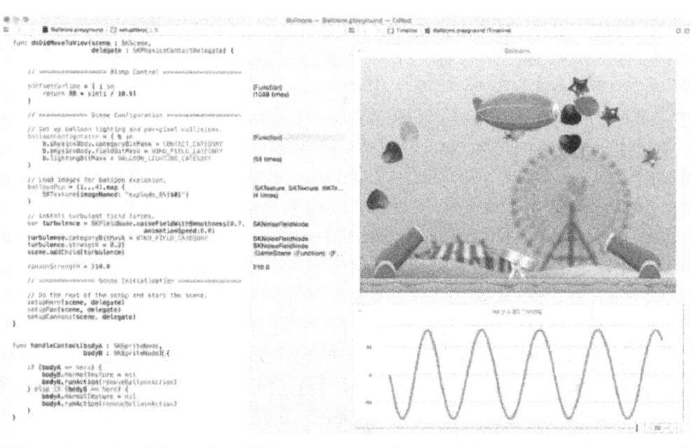

Figure 4: Xcode Playground: an interactive environment to experiment with Swift code [1]

Participating students have varying prior knowledge and experiences, forming a heterogeneous group. There are students with some experiences in mobile application development and students who never used the development environment before. To create a productive learning environment for all students, our interactive tutorials include easy exercises and optional advanced ones where even experienced students feel challenged. For such challenges it is necessary to combine knowledge from different sessions or to use the platform documentation to find the right solution. TAs introduce the delegation pattern and closures as an alternative, later the students need to be able to apply both techniques when they work with more advanced frameworks.

While experienced students solve more advanced exercises, TAs and tutors explain concepts again to less experienced students who need more time. TAs also ask students who finish exercises early to help their classmates to learn different ways of thinking and to consolidate the knowledge they just learned. If they are able to explain a concept to fellow students, they really understood it. Less experienced students need more time when interacting with the IDE, because they have to learn keyboard shortcuts and are initially unable to cope with the development tools. Due to the tight schedule some students cannot keep up with the pace of the course. In such cases, tutors help and motivate, especially if they experienced the same problems before.

Tutors have multiple responsibilities: They observe students and actively help them if they cannot follow the instructions. While helping students and experiencing their problems during the first sessions, the tutors get insights and can update their own tutorials to increase their usefulness. This includes adding small repetitions for important concepts of the course as well as adding hints to deepen the understanding. In the first week, the tutors also correct the submitted solutions of the students for the large exercises at the end of each tutorial and provide feedback. The course uses a distributed version control system for the submission of solutions which simplifies the correction of the tutors.

TAs ask students during an interactive tutorial to explain the rationale behind a solution because some students only copy and paste source code from the sample solution and do not try to understand the concept behind it. If tutors observe that students did not understand what they accomplished, they ask them to explain the solution. If students cannot explain the solution, because they did not understand it, the tutors explain the concept again to make sure the students can use it in later tutorials.

To improve the self-learning process of the students the tutors provide hints or references to documentation and slides. Another possibility is to refer to a prior solution and ask the students if they can adapt it to solve the current problem. Directly explaining the solution would reduce the sense of achievement for the students, but it is still better to help them instead of leaving them behind, especially because later sessions depend on the knowledge of previous ones. If students have difficulties, it helps to ask them to explain the problem in detail. During their own explanation of the problem, they suddenly understand it and a solution comes up to solve it. Hunt describes this process as Rubber Duck Debugging, an informal technique, where a developer explains his code, line-by-line, to a rubber duck [11].

Tutors assist the students in the game idea finding phase by asking questions about the main goal and core mechanics. We observed, that identifying core features of their game helps students to create a plan for the development. Asking questions encourages the students to think about their game idea and its potential flaws. This allows them to discard the game idea or to improve certain features, before they find out that the idea is not realizable during the actual development.

TAs ask students about feedback to improve the course. Tutors provide instant feedback during tutorials. Overall an open feedback culture is established where everyone should constructively criticize others and where feedback is not taken personal. While honest and detailed feedback is difficult for some of the students, they get used to it during the course and appreciate the idea of continuous improvement.

4. EVALUATION

We evaluated quality and usefulness of the tutorials and the course organization using surveys after three course instances with 24 beginners on average. This section describes the findings and limitations of these two evaluations.

4.1 Tutorial Evaluation

The first evaluation concerns the quality of interactive tutorials. We asked students in online surveys about the usefulness of each tutorial and about each speakers performance, for both, TAs and tutors. These surveys were completely anonymous and on average 75% of the students participated. The results are shown in Table 1.

Statement	Strong agree	Agree	Neutral	Disagree	Strong disagree
Objectives were clear	63%	33%	4%	0%	0%
Assignments supported objectives	58%	38%	4%	0%	0%
I learned new concepts	67%	25%	8%	0%	0%

Table 1: Results of tutorial evaluation

We asked the beginners about the amount of content, speed of delivery and difficulty of exercises of each tutorial. 79% of the beginners found the amount was right, only around 13% found it was too much content and 8% found it was too less. 84% found that the speed of the tutorial was right, while 8% found it too fast and 8% too slow. On average, 88% reported that the difficulty of the tutorial was right, only 8% found it was too hard and 4% found it was too simple. All tutorials had similar results in the survey. Therefore, we conclude that the quality of the tutorials was very high. We also asked open questions, e.g. about improvement recommendations. One student suggested to reduce the number of concepts in one tutorial and to have more repeating exercises instead.

4.2 Course Evaluation

The second evaluation concerns the general learning experience. We handed out the standardized paper based course evaluation of the university after the course and asked participants to fill it out anonymously. 76% answered 32 questions with a five point Likert answer scale. The results of different courses do not deviate significantly, so we combined them and present the most interesting findings.

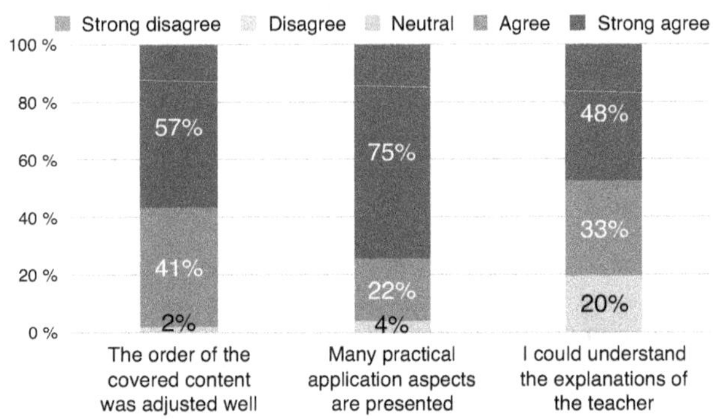

Figure 5: Evaluation of course difficulty

Figure 5 shows that almost all students agreed that the order of the covered content was adjusted well and that many practical application aspects are presented. About 80% of the students agreed that they could understand the explanations of the teacher, while only 20% had a neutral opinion.

Regarding the heterogeneous group of participants we think these are great results. Figure 6 shows that students considered the general difficulty of the course as high. We think it is important to challenge students instead of demanding too little from them. Speed of the content delivery was also considered too high based on the fact that the course is only two weeks long and that beginners with almost no development experience learn to develop a game. Students reported that the required prior knowledge was not too high to successfully participate in the course. We experienced no case yet where a student dropped out during the course which confirms that all students are motivated to pass the course.

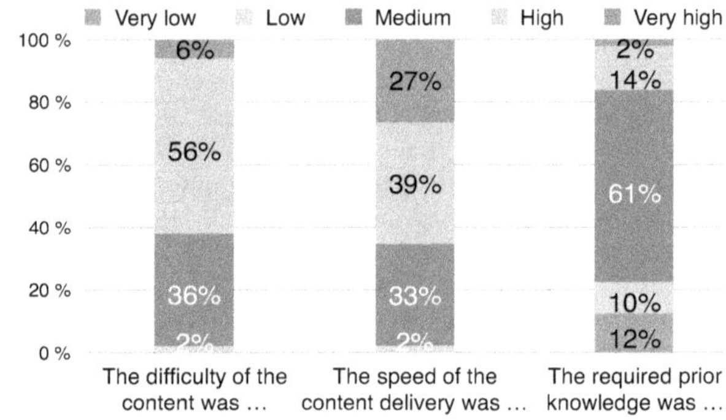

Figure 6: Evaluation of course content

68% evaluate the overall course as very good, 26% evaluate it as good and 6% evaluate it as neutral. No one evaluated it as bad or very bad. When we talked to students during and after the course we recognized that all of them really appreciated what they learned and that they can profit from the course in their future career. Most of the students participate in follow-up courses and are able to contribute greatly with the experiences they gained in this course.

4.3 Limitations

With this evaluation we aimed to explore whether students learned the concepts we taught, whether they found tutorials useful and whether speed and difficulty of the course was appropriate. We see threats to the validity of our evaluations and want to discuss them briefly. We might have the problem of selection bias because not all participants of the course took part in the questionnaires and the prior knowledge and experiences of the students were different.

We observed that experienced students found speed and difficulty of the course appropriate or sometimes too low, while inexperienced students usually found the tutorials too hard and too fast. We cannot guarantee that the distribution of experienced and inexperienced students were representative because not all students participated in the anonymous evaluation. However, in the discussions during and after the course the students agreed with our findings.

We were not able to measure the benefits of the learning techniques that we used. In general, the students agree that the mix of techniques such as experiential and blended learning is helpful, especially in contrast to traditional lectures. However, this is not an objective evaluation whether the particular technique is useful or not.

5. RELATED WORK

In this section, we describe related work. Eow et al. describe an approach where games development and appreciative learning enhance the creative perception of learners [9]. They studied 13-14 year old form one students and focused on creativity, while the course that we describe in this paper focuses on software engineering abilities. Jones describes a capstone course for undergraduates where students design and implement computer games [13]. He teaches a variety of computer science concepts but does not describe the application and benefits of pedagogic theories in his course.

Kurkovsky engages students through mobile game development early in the curriculum [18]. It enables students with limited programming experience to develop playable games within one course which is the same observation we made. While he describes different computer science areas that he covers in his course, he does not detail the educational approaches. Sweedyk and Keller use computer games as projects in their introductory software engineering course [22]. They focus on a detailed description of the developed games and describe how they meet the SE2004 learning outcomes [19], but leave out interesting details about which pedagogic theories they applied.

Smith et al. describe experiences with agile games development in a senior design course [21]. They found that emphasis on agile methods and fast releases is effective in aiding students to produce working games, however they do not explain pedagogic theories used in their course. Claypool and Claypool present how developing a game engages students to learn software engineering through games design [6]. They describe a linear teaching approach with 10 software engineering modules targeted to games design, but do not detail which pedagogic techniques they apply to teach these modules.

6. CONCLUSION

In this paper we described a practical two-weeks block course where we use different teaching aspects from problem-based, cooperative, blended and experiential learning. We teach students with almost no development experience to develop mobile games in two weeks. This brings fun into the software engineering curriculum and increases their skills in object-oriented programming. Each semester, more than 100 students apply for the course and want to learn software engineering with the help of games development. We continuously improve the learning experience of the students and get help by tutors in the organization of the course.

We further accompany the students after the final presentations to publish their games. Until now, they submitted 18 games into the iOS App Store. Our evaluations show that students appreciate a great learning experience with practical aspects that they can further use in their career. They improve their software engineering abilities, in particular object-oriented programming, and their soft skills with the help of games development and they have fun.

7. REFERENCES

[1] Apple. Introducing Swift, 2014. https://developer.apple.com/swift.

[2] R. Ben-Ari, R. Krole, and D. Har-Even. Differential effects of simple frontal versus complex teaching strategy on teachers' stress, burnout, and satisfaction. *International Journal of Stress Management*, 2003.

[3] A. Beyer. Improving student presentations pecha kucha and just plain powerpoint. *Teaching of Psychology*, 2011.

[4] D. Boud and G. Feletti. *The challenge of problem-based learning*. Psychology Press, 1998.

[5] B. Bruegge, S. Krusche, and L. Alperowitz. Software engineering project courses with industrial clients. *ACM Transactions on Computing Education*, 2015.

[6] K. Claypool and M. Claypool. Teaching software engineering through game design. In *SIGCSE Bulletin*, volume 37, pages 123–127. ACM, 2005.

[7] A. Collins, J. S. Brown, and A. Holum. Cognitive apprenticeship: Making thinking visible. *American educator*, 1991.

[8] T. M. Connolly, M. Stansfield, and T. Hainey. An application of games-based learning within software engineering. *British Journal of Educational Technology*, 38(3):416–428, 2007.

[9] Y. Eow, W. Ali, R. Mahmud, and R. Baki. Computer games development and appreciative learning approach in enhancing students creative perception. *Computers & Education*, 54(1):146–161, 2010.

[10] R. Garrison and H. Kanuka. Blended learning: Uncovering its transformative potential in higher education. *The internet and higher education*, 2004.

[11] A. Hunt and D. Thomas. *The pragmatic programmer: from journeyman to master*. Addison-Wesley, 2000.

[12] D. Johnson et al. *Cooperative Learning: Increasing College Faculty Instructional Productivity. ASHE-ERIC Higher Education Report*. ERIC, 1991.

[13] R. Jones. Design and implementation of computer games: A capstone course for undergraduate computer science education. In *Proceedings of the 31st SIGCSE Technical Symposium*, pages 260–264. ACM, 2000.

[14] D. Kolb et al. *Experiential learning: Experience as the source of learning and development*. Prentice-Hall, 1984.

[15] F. Korthagen et al. *Linking practice and theory: The pedagogy of realistic teacher education*. Routledge, 2001.

[16] S. Krusche and L. Alperowitz. Introduction of Continuous Delivery in Multi-Customer Project Courses. In *Proceedings of ICSE*. IEEE, 2014.

[17] S. Krusche et al. Rugby: An agile process model based on continuous delivery. In *Proceedings of the 1st Workshop on RCoSE*, pages 42–50. ACM, 2014.

[18] S. Kurkovsky. Engaging students through mobile game development. In *SIGCSE Bulletin*, pages 44–48. ACM, 2009.

[19] T. Lethbridge et al. Se2004: Recommendations for undergraduate software engineering curricula. *IEEE Software*, 23(6):19–25, 2006.

[20] D. Shaffer. Pedagogical praxis: The professions as models for postindustrial education. *Teachers College Record*, 106(7):1401–1421, 2004.

[21] T. Smith et al. Software engineering senior design course: experiences with agile game development in a capstone project. In *Proceedings of the 1st GAS Workshop*, pages 9–12. ACM, 2011.

[22] E. Sweedyk and R. M. Keller. Fun and games: a new software engineering course. In *SIGCSE Bulletin*, pages 138–142. ACM, 2005.

[23] J. Whitehead. Collaboration in software engineering: A roadmap. *FOSE*, 7(2007):214–225, 2007.

Nifty Assignments

Nick Parlante
Julie Zelenski
(moderators)
Stanford University
nick.parlante@cs.stanford.edu
zelenski@cs.stanford.edu

Baker Franke
Code.org
baker@code.org

Arvind Bhusnurmath,
Karen Her, and Kristen Gee
University of Pennsylvania|
bhusnur4@seas.upenn.edu
karenher@seas.upenn.edu
kgee@seas.upenn.edu

Eric Manley
Timothy Urness
Drake University
eric.manley@drake.edu
timothy.urness@drake.edu

Marvin Zhang, Brian Hou,
and John DeNero
University of California, Berkeley
zhangmarvin@berkeley.edu
brian.hou@berkeley.edu
denero@cs.berkeley.edu

Josh Hug
University of California, Berkeley
hug@cs.berkeley.edu

Kevin Wayne
Princeton University
wayne@cs.princeton.edu

Keywords
Education; assignments; homeworks; examples; repository; library; nifty; pedagogy

Abstract
I suspect that students learn more from our programming assignments than from our much sweated-over lectures, with their slide transitions, clip art, and joke attempts. A great assignment is deliberate about where the student hours go, concentrating the student's attention on material that is interesting and useful. The best assignments solve a problem that is topical and entertaining, providing motivation for the whole stack of work. Unfortunately, creating great programming assignments is both time consuming and error prone.

The Nifty Assignments special session is all about promoting and sharing the ideas and ready-to-use materials of successful assignments.

Each presenter will introduce their assignment, give a quick demo, and describe its niche in the curriculum and its strengths and weaknesses. The presentations (and the descriptions below) merely introduce each assignment. A key part of Nifty Assignments is the mundane but vital role of distributing the materials – handouts, data files, starter code – that make each assignment ready to adopt. The Nifty Assignments home page, http://nifty.stanford.edu, gathers all the assignments and makes them and their support materials freely available. If you have an assignment that works well and would be of interest to the CSE community, please consider applying to present at Nifty Assignments. See the nifty.stanford.edu home page for more information.

SIGCSE '16, March 02-05, 2016, Memphis, TN, USA
ACM 978-1-4503-3685-7/16/03.
http://dx.doi.org/10.1145/2839509.2844678

Greedy Mountain Paths (CS1) - Baker Franke
The basic premise: using a 2D array of elevation data representing a mountainous region of the U.S., find the "best" way to walk through the mountains. Topographic data lends itself nicely to graphical representations. Students write their own algorithms to find paths through the mountains (choosing their own level of complexity) and render them by drawing a colored line through the image. The initial suggestion for a path is to do a "greedy walk" from west to east, choosing a path that represents the least amount of change in elevation from step to step.

This assignment is great because it offers a context in which you can introduce 2D arrays and build quickly from typical array processing tasks to some very interesting and novel algorithms in a way that is approachable to introductory students while offering many different degrees of difficulty to choose from. While it can be a "big" 2D array assignment – covering file I/O, graphics, heuristics and greedy algorithms – there are many options for the instructor to scale it down or use components of the assignment to focus on a particular topic. The assignment is probably best situated in the latter half of a CS1 course, it assumes students have had "typical" experience programming up through linear processing of arrays.

Restaurant Recommendations (CS1) - Brian Hou, Marvin Zhang, and John DeNero
In this assignment, students apply basic machine learning concepts to predict user ratings and cluster restaurants around a university campus, using the Yelp Academic Dataset. The assignment primarily illustrates CS1 concepts such as data abstraction, sequence processing, and key-value pairs. The machine learning ideas are all introduced by the project text as a way of motivating course fundamentals.

The project builds a single interactive browser-based visualization. First, restaurants are clustered by location using the K-means algorithm. Second, ratings for restaurants (visualized using a color scale) are predicted using linear regression (one dimension only; no matrix inversions required). Test cases provided with the project ensure that these pieces combine correctly.

Interested students have a wide array of possible extensions. They can use the Yelp API to make recommendations based on their own Yelp ratings. To improve the accuracy of predictions, students can implement other regression techniques or extract better features. To improve the visualization, students can dive into web programming by using the Google Maps API to allow for more interactivity (e.g. zooming and dragging) or implementing variants of the main visualization (e.g. a weighted Voronoi diagram).

The niftiest aspect of the assignment is that students are exposed to the idea of machine learning in an intuitive and familiar setting, without math or confusing terminology. They particularly like the real-world application of recommending restaurants by analyzing large amounts of data.

Rack-O (CS1) - Arvind Bhusnurmath, Karen Her and Kristen Gee

The Rack-O assignment is based on a card game which is simple to explain but with enough complexity to make an interesting programming assignment. Rack-O is a card game that involves rearranging your hand of cards in order to have an increasing sequence. The cards are just numbered cards. There are no suits. The programming of this game can be easily done via manipulation of lists. We do the assignment in Python.

The overall goal for a student is to write a program such that a user can play Rack-O against a computer player. For the computer player, students are asked to come up with a strategy and then translate it into code.

What makes the assignment nifty is that students soon realize that strategies in this game are surprisingly easy to program. They spend a fair bit of time coming up with newer and more interesting ones. Some of the students take it upon themselves as a challenge to write a computer player that will beat the grader.

We also bring the physical game to the lab session in which this assignment is introduced. Most students have not seen it before and they have fun playing the physical version before programming it.

Movie Review Sentient Analysis (CS1/CS2) - Eric Manley and Timothy Urness

Sentiment analysis is a text mining task that attempts to figure out the general attitude (e.g. positive/negative attitude) conveyed by a particular piece of text. It can be used for things like analyzing product reviews or determining how the Twittersphere feels about a particular presidential candidate's debate performance.

For the assignment, students write sentiment analysis programs by training them on movie reviews from the Rotten Tomatoes website which have been manually labeled with a score of how positive or negative the review is. Their programs will be able to automatically determine that reviews like "The film was a breath of fresh air" have positive sentiment while reviews like "It made me want to poke out my eyeballs" carry negative sentiment.

The assignment is nifty because it involves real data used with a simple algorithm to achieve compelling results. It does not require any special libraries or software and can be adapted to emphasize a variety of different programming topics. We have used the assignment in CS1 (in both Java and Python) to emphasize file I/O, early control structures, accumulators/counters, and the min/max algorithm. We have used it in CS2 (in C++) to emphasize string manipulation and hash tables. It can also be used to introduce students to the increasingly popular discipline of data science within early programming courses, which was our primary aim in support of our new Data Analytics major. Assignment extensions involving validation, visualization, and algorithm improvement are all possibilities.

HugLife: Testing Creatures (CS1/CS2) - Josh Hug

Nearly every CS instructor has enjoyed watching little creatures running around a two-dimensional grid-based world, spreading across the grid gleefully or racing towards ecological catastrophe.

In HugLife, students program the AI and metabolic properties of competing species, and set them loose to vie for space. Naturally, any errors a student makes will be highly difficult to diagnose by simply running the simulation. Even minor errors can upset the delicate ecological balance of HugLife. Ultimately, the key lesson of this assignment is disciplined use of testing to support a complex system.

In the first part of the assignment, students write the code for the Plip species, a photosynthetic creature that slowly gains energy and replicates when it has become sufficiently plump. Then, before they're allowed to set their Plips loose on the world, they write a test suite that ensures that the Plips will behave properly. Finally, once the Plip has been tested, students are allowed to deploy them into the universe, which they will promptly fill with green goodness.

Students then repeat the exercise for the Clorus species, a blue carnivore that loves nothing more than consuming poor Plips. With our suggested AI rules and metabolic features, the system evolves into a not-quite stable equilibrium that can be addictive to watch. Students can tweak the existing creatures, or add new creatures of their own.

Most recently, this assignment was run as a two hour lab in Java that introduced testing of large systems. However, it can also be used as an introduction to inheritance and object oriented programming. Implementations available in Java and Python.

Autocomplete Me (CS2) - Kevin Wayne

Write a program to implement *autocomplete* for a given set of strings and weights. That is, given a query string, find all strings in the set that start with the query string, sorted in descending order of weight. Autocomplete is an important feature of many modern applications. For example, Google uses autocomplete to display suggestions in real time, as the user types a web search query.

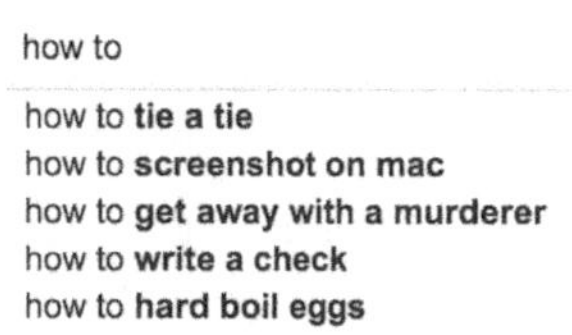

In one version of the assignment, students implement autocomplete by combining sorting with binary search. The built-in sort suffices for sorting the terms either by query or weight. However, the variant of binary search required is nonstandard (and not available in Java), so students must design and implement their own version. To enable the binary search, students must also implement an interesting custom order for the terms (comparing two strings lexicographically, but using only their first k characters). The assignment is nifty because

* It is a familiar and authentic application, for which performance is critical.
* It brings sorting and binary search—often dull and poorly motivated topics—to life.
* The accompanying interactive GUI and real-world datasets make it fun for students.
* It does not require any scaffolding code.

Demonstrations

Bringing Real-World Data and Visualizations Into Data Structures Courses Using BRIDGES

Kalpathi Subramanian, *University of North Carolina at Charlotte*
Jamie Payton, *University of North Carolina at Charlotte*
David Burlinson, University of North Carolina at Charlotte
Mihai Mehedint, University of North Carolina at Charlotte
Contact: krs@uncc.edu

This demo introduces participants to the concepts and application of BRIDGES, a software infrastructure designed to facilitate hands-on experience for solving traditional problems in introductory computer science courses using data from real-world systems that are of interest to students, such as Facebook, Twitter, and Google Maps. BRIDGES provides access to real-world data sets for use in traditional data structures programming assignments, without requiring students to work with complex and varied APIs to acquire such data. BRIDGES also helps the students to explore and understand the use of data structures by providing each student with a visualization of operations performed on the student's own implementation of a data structure. BRIDGES visualizations can be easily shared (via a weblink) with peers, friends, and family. Demo attendees will see (and possibly engage in) hands-on experience with BRIDGES and will have the opportunity to discuss how BRIDGES can be used to support various introductory computer science courses. Additionally, the demo will complement our oral presentation of our work at SIGCSE, by providing hands-on demonstrations of BRIDGES.

Keywords: data structure; visualization; retention

DOI: http://dx.doi.org/10.1145/2839509.2850512

ParseIT: A Tool for Teaching Parsing Techniques

Amey Karkare, IIT Kanpur
Nimisha Agrawal, IIT Kanpur
Contact: karkare@cse.iitk.ac.in

Compiler design is an important subject in the computer science curriculum for undergraduates. In a typical Compiler's course, about 15%–22% of the total time is spent on *syntax analysis* phase (also called *parsing techniques*). A number of concepts are introduced to explain the internals of parsers, for example first set, follow set, item set, goto and closure set, parse tables and the parsing algorithms, making the understanding difficult. While parser generators (YACC and its variants) allow the students to experiment with grammars, the working of the parser generated by the tools is still opaque.

We present **ParseIT**, a web based tool to help students understand the concept of parsing in an undergraduate Compiler Design course. Given a grammar, the tool generates multiple choice questions for concepts related to parsing. The tool evaluates students' attempts and provide hints for incorrect attempts. The hints are also generated in the form of specific questions about any correct choice that is missed or any incorrect choice that is selected. For grammars that can be parsed through the textbook LL or LR algorithms, an interesting form of hint generated is an input string that helps student identify incorrectly filled cells of a parsing table. The tool enables interactive and active learning of parsing concepts, resulting in a better understanding.

Keywords: Intelligent Tutoring; Education; Programming; Compilers

DOI: http://dx.doi.org/10.1145/2839509.2850513

SIGCSE'16, March 2–5, 2016, Memphis, TN, USA.
ACM ISBN: 978-1-4503-3685-7/16/03.

The Teaching Privacy Curriculum

Serge Egelman[1,2], Julia Bernd[1], Gerald Friedland[1], and Dan Garcia[2]
[1]International Computer Science Institute, Berkeley, CA, USA
{egelman,jbernd,fractor}@icsi.berkeley.edu
[2]University of California, Berkeley, CA, USA
{egelman,ddgarcia}@cs.berkeley.edu

ABSTRACT

A basic understanding of online privacy is essential to being an informed digital citizen, and therefore basic privacy education is becoming ever more necessary. Recently released high school and college computer science curricula acknowledge the significantly increased importance of fundamental knowledge about privacy, but do not yet provide concrete content in the area. To address this need, over the past two years, we have developed the Teaching Privacy Project (TPP) curriculum, http://teachingprivacy.org, which educates the general public about online privacy issues. We performed a pilot of our curriculum in a university course for non-CS majors and found that it was effective: weeks after last being exposed, students' privacy attitudes had shifted. In this paper, we describe our curriculum, our evaluation of it in the classroom, and our vision for future privacy education.

CCS Concepts

•Security and privacy → Human and societal aspects of security and privacy; •Applied computing → Education;

1. INTRODUCTION

Despite heightened attention to privacy issues in the popular media, accounts abound of people oversharing personal information online, with sometimes drastic consequences. These stories demonstrate that people still do not have a very good handle on what the specific problems are in sharing information, nor on the steps they can take to manage their privacy. We believe that in this day and age, a basic understanding of online privacy is key to both good cybersecurity practices and to becoming a good digital citizen.

Current computer science curricula aimed at high school and undergraduate students (e.g., the ACM's CS2013 [16] and AP CS:Principles [2]) acknowledge the importance of privacy education, but do not provide content or specific lesson plans. During outreach efforts stemming from our privacy research, many high school and college teachers have told us that they are eager to provide their students with guidance on online privacy, but feel unqualified to do so. In fact, a survey of 12-17 year olds found that 70% had sought outside advice on managing online privacy [11]. To fill this need, we began developing an online privacy curriculum to aid teachers in being able to offer their students actionable advice on how to better protect their personal privacy online. The *Teaching Privacy Project* (TPP) is a privacy education curriculum centered around ten principles and offers students descriptions of how they may be putting themselves at risk online, current threats to personal privacy, interactive demonstrations that illustrate the concepts, and guidance on what they can do to protect themselves.

Our online privacy curriculum is targeted at lay audiences, including high school and undergraduate students (i.e., non-computer science majors), and is accessible to the general public via our website, http://teachingprivacy.org. It is designed to not just convey comprehensive information about current threats to privacy, but to also empower students to do something about it. Rather than taking a prescriptive approach—telling our audience what services they should or should not use—our goal is to provide students with enough information so that they can make their own informed choices about their online privacy. We have been integrating and evaluating parts of TPP in our university's introduction to computer science for non-majors (CS10), which is one of a handful of university pilots of the AP CS:Principles class. CS10 is also the basis for professional development with wide participation from high school teachers. The integration of the TPP curriculum into CS10 has enabled teachers to feel more comfortable about teaching privacy concepts in their high school classrooms, as well as allowed us to receive feedback and improve our curriculum.

To have even broader impact on teachers, we are developing the Teachers' Resources for Online Privacy Education (TROPE), which is based on the TPP curriculum. In the TROPE project, we are building an online teachers' toolkit consisting of classroom-ready teaching modules that educators can use to teach young people about *why* and *how* to protect their privacy online. This way, teachers can easily integrate our curriculum into their classrooms, using as many of our explanatory videos, slide decks, classroom activities, discussion guides, and evaluation materials as they see fit. TROPE also features supporting materials for teachers with background information and guidance on how to employ the modules in the classroom. Our goal is to empower

SIGCSE '16, March 02 - 05, 2016, Memphis, TN, USA

ISBN 978-1-4503-3685-7/16/03...$15.00

DOI: http://dx.doi.org/10.1145/2839509.2844619

teachers to provide students with an understanding of some basic technical and social principles underlying how online privacy works, knowledge of effective techniques they can use to protect their privacy, and the motivation to use those techniques when interacting online.

In this paper, we provide an overview of other privacy education efforts (Section 2) and show that our curriculum is unique in its comprehensiveness and applicability to general audiences. In Section 3, we provide an overview of our curriculum and the teachers' toolkit. In Section 4, we describe our experiences teaching our curriculum in the classroom. Finally, we discuss future work to broaden our curriculum, improve our evaluation metrics, and widen our audience.

2. RELATED WORK

There are a number of existing providers that offer some classroom materials on online privacy, but none offer a comprehensive curriculum *per se*. Common Sense Media's *Digital Citizenship Curriculum* [6] includes among its offerings some privacy-related resources for elementary, middle-school, and high-school classrooms, such as videos and posters and lesson plans on oversharing, identity theft, and privacy policies. Fordham Law School's Center on Law and Information Policy has developed several middle-school lesson plans on privacy that include material on the relationship between security and privacy and the relationship between privacy and reputation management [5]. At the college level, Santa Clara University's *Your Privacy Online* resources cover privacy threats and privacy management from a law and ethics standpoint [13].

These materials are all of high quality—and, in fact, we include links to them on the teachingprivacy.org website—but they do not offer the combination of technical depth, comprehensive coverage of online privacy issues, and focus on U.S.-specific issues and high-school computer-science curriculum standards that we do. Interestingly, some of the most comprehensive efforts have come from Canada and the European Union, such as the privacy lesson plans from Media Smarts [14] (funded by the Privacy Commissioner of Canada) and Teachtoday [19] (funded by Deutsche Telekom).

The resources mentioned above come closest to the Teaching Privacy offerings in quality, scope, and technical grounding, but there are a few others worth noting simply because they are well-known, such as the NetSmartz [8] and Stay Safe Online [1] online-safety classroom materials, which provide some (relatively shallow) coverage of privacy. Several general providers of curriculum content also include some one-off lessons about one aspect of online privacy or another, but are not comprehensive.

In an attempt to locate online privacy curricula aimed at broad audiences, we also examined Massive Open Online Courses (MOOCs). We reviewed existing major providers of high-quality English-language MOOCs (e.g., Coursera, edX, Khan Academy, and Udacity), major universities that provide MOOCs on their own platforms (e.g., Stanford Online and UCLA), and a number of smaller providers (e.g., iversity, Udemy, and OpenLearn). There are several courses that cover privacy from legal, ethical, and policy perspectives (e.g., [20]), or that touch on privacy as it relates to best practices for technology designers (e.g., [18]) and professionals who handle private data (for example, in healthcare) or to cybersecurity and counterterrorism. However, to our knowledge, none offer courses to help non-experts understand the fundamental principles of managing online privacy. While edX and Coursera's introductory computer science offerings and Stanford Online's CS 101 [17] include discussions of Internet structure and cover some security topics, they do not include significant privacy content. In fact, among major providers, the content most similar to ours is edX's new BJCx [9]—which is led by Teaching Privacy's faculty consultant Dr. Dan Garcia and contains some of the Teaching Privacy content. But again, privacy is one topic among many, not the primary focus of the course.

In sum, we believe that our curriculum is unique in combining comprehensive coverage, alignment with U.S. curriculum standards, professional production quality, being accessible to a broad demographic, and grounding in technical expertise. In the next section, we describe the content of our curriculum.

3. THE CURRICULUM

The *Teaching Privacy Project* (TPP) started as an NSF education supplement to develop a set of interactive learning tools to help educators demonstrate what happens to personal information online, and the possible effects of sharing it. To provide context for the demonstrations that we developed, we identified *Ten Principles for Online Privacy* that describe at a high level how online privacy works, technically and socially. These principles form the basis of the TPP curriculum; each principle features an explanation of what it means, why it is important, relevant examples and demonstrations, as well as guidance on how certain privacy threats can be mitigated or outright avoided. The ten principles are as follows:

1. **You're Leaving Footprints**:
   Description: Your information footprint is not just what you intentionally post online. It consists of all of the information that you post or that others post about you, the hidden data attached to those posts by the services you use, the record of your online activities, and also the inferences that can be drawn from putting that collective information together.
   Guidance: Periodically check your privacy settings and update them to limit unintentional sharing.

2. **There's No Anonymity**:
   Description: Your information footprint on the Internet is like your body in the physical world: it defines your identity. Like seeing some part of your body, seeing some part of your information footprint – like the location of the device you're posting from or the pattern of your language – may allow someone to uniquely identify you, even when there is no name or other explicit identifier attached.
   Guidance: Don't do anything online that you wouldn't do in public.

3. **Information Is Valuable**:
   Description: Every piece of information, public or not, has value to somebody: to other people, to companies and organizations, or to governments. They will use your information however benefits them, which may be contrary to your interests—and possibly even embarrassing or dangerous to you.
   Guidance: If you're not sure how your information will be used, don't share it.

4. **Someone Could Listen**:
   Description: Unencrypted communication over the Internet works a lot like sending a postcard: it can be read by anybody along its route. Communication is routed through intermediary computers and systems, which are connected to many more computers and systems. Encryption, or encoding information so it appears scrambled to anyone who doesn't know the key, is a way to wrap a postcard in an envelope. While it can never be 100% secure, stronger encryption makes it harder for people to get to the contents.
   Guidance: Use strong passwords and only communicate sensitive information over secure channels.

5. **Sharing Releases Control**:
   Description: Any time you interact online, that information is recorded. As with in-person communication, once you've shared something, you can't control what happens to it – or how people will interpret it. Other people can repost or forward content to any audience without your permission, websites can sell information to other businesses, and data can be legally subpoenaed. Websites and search engines automatically pick up and duplicate content, making it impossible to "unshare" – the Internet never forgets!
   Guidance: Think before sharing online; ask yourself if you'd be comfortable becoming famous for it.

6. **Search Is Improving**:
   Description: Every day, more data is being put online. Search engines are getting better, allowing "deeper" searching of more types of data. Techniques for extracting and connecting information from different sources are getting more powerful. Furthermore, information that is not retrievable today may be retrievable tomorrow due to changes in terms of service, public policy, or privacy settings.
   Guidance: Monitor your information footprint.

7. **Online Is Real**:
   Description: Your online activities are as much a part of your life as your offline activities; they are interconnected and can affect your life and relationships in the same way.
   Guidance: Share online as if everyone could see it, and would interpret it in the worst possible way.

8. **Identity Isn't Guaranteed**:
   Description: Creating an identity on the Internet or impersonating somebody else is often just a matter of a few clicks. Currently, there is no foolproof way to match a real person with their online identity. This means that you can never be sure with whom you are communicating, and that someone could steal your online identity and impersonate you!
   Guidance: Before you share any information online, consider what you would be risking if the other party wasn't who you thought they were.

9. **You Can't Escape**:
   Description: Even if you're not actively using the Internet, someone else may be sharing information about you – intentionally or unintentionally. So, avoiding the Internet does not guarantee privacy.
   Guidance: Share what you've learned with your friends and family – it will improve your own privacy.

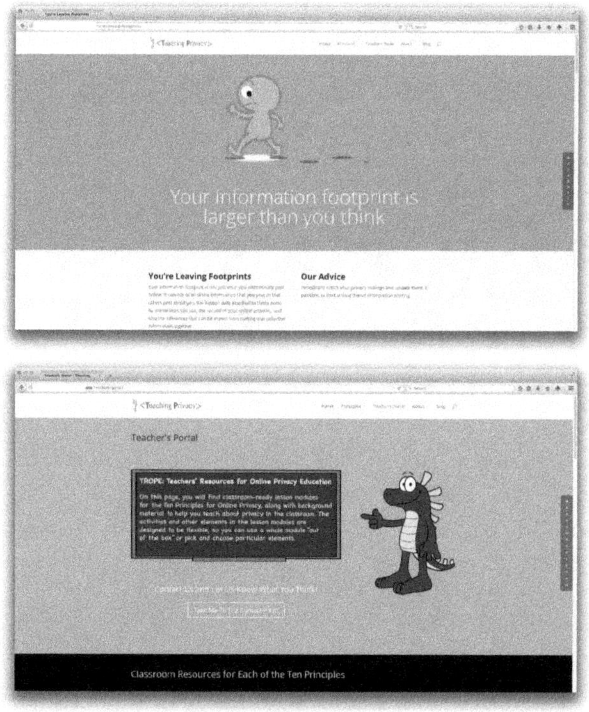

Figure 1: From the TPP website: (a) the principle "You're Leaving Footprints" (b) the Teachers' Portal.

10. **Privacy Requires Work**:
    Description: Most Internet technology is not designed to protect the privacy of those who use it; in fact, most technology providers make money by leveraging your private information. "Privacy policies" are generally written to protect providers from lawsuits, not to protect users' privacy. Laws and regulations cover only certain aspects of privacy and vary from place to place. So, like it or not, your privacy is your own responsibility, and requires your constant attention.
    Guidance: Encourage policymakers to develop comprehensive privacy regulations, educate yourself and others, and be proactive about protecting your privacy.

Taken as a whole, the principles demonstrate the general types of threats to privacy, how they occur, why organizations may exploit them, what the possible consequences are, and what people can do about it. The Teaching Privacy website, http://teachingprivacy.org/, features a separate page for each principle (Figure 1). Each page includes an easy-to-understand description of the underlying concepts; suggestions for actions people can take; questions that prompt broader thinking about the topic; and links to related resources. The principles are accompanied by reinforcing stories and interactive demonstrations. For instance, the *Ready or Not?* app illustrates the principle "You're leaving footprints." It allows a Twitter or Instagram username to be entered, and then shows a heat map and timeline of where and when that user recently posted, based on the geolocation metadata attached to their posts.

We are using this youth-oriented content as the basis for developing a teachers' portal, wherein high school, middle school, and college instructors can download classroom-

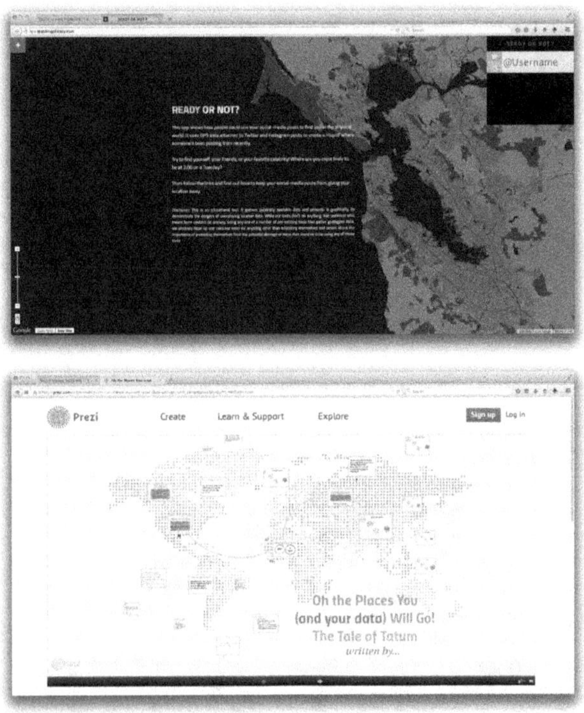

Figure 2: Two of the TROPE lesson elements: (a) the *Ready or Not?* app; (b) the *Oh the Places...* choose-your-own adventure class activity (draft).

ready learning modules and a teachers' guide. Our goal is to make our curriculum available *à la carte* so that teachers can integrate our materials into their lesson plans as they see fit. This effort, the Teachers' Resources for Online Privacy Education (TROPE), was also funded by NSF. It aims to provide teachers with the resources to teach young people about *why* and *how* to protect their privacy online. Each of the TROPE teaching modules is centered around one of the *Ten Principles for Online Privacy* and includes flexible lesson elements that can be used "out of the box" or adapted to supplement teachers' existing lesson materials. These elements include explanations (as slide decks and videos), discussion questions, classroom activities, homework assignments, quizzes, interactive demonstrations (Figure 2), and a glossary of terms. Each module is structured around the 5E constructivist learning model for lesson planning [3]:

- Engagement: Teachers pique students' interest in the topic by asking a question or telling a story to which students can relate.
- Exploration: Students play small-group games or perform exercises in which they explore the technical and social factors that underlie the principle(s), such as activities built around the interactive apps on the Teaching Privacy website.
- Explanation: Teachers use provided slide decks, written materials, and 5- to 10-minute high-quality videos explaining important concepts and effective protection techniques.
- Elaboration: Teachers can use additional discussion questions to encourage students to think about their online behavior; presentation content aimed at translating awareness into action; and suggested group activities or mini-projects.
- Evaluation: We provide assessment tools and follow-up questions so that teachers can measure student learning and we can receive feedback from teachers about the curriculum.

We are also developing supporting materials, including a teachers' guide that provides suggested lesson plans, as well as additional background information. In the future, we hope to develop additional online courseware, such as a Massive Open Online Course (MOOC) based around the TPP curriculum, to help teachers become familiar enough with our curriculum by first completing it themselves. Our goal is to ensure that teachers are comfortable with our content prior to using it in their classrooms.

All of the TROPE materials are released under a Creative Commons license and are being made available via a Teachers' Portal on http://teachingprivacy.org, where we also plan to implement a discussion forum to solicit teacher feedback and answer questions.

4. DISSEMINATION AND EVALUATION

The TPP curriculum and initial TROPE materials are currently being piloted and evaluated through CS10, UC Berkeley's introductory computer science course for non-majors. The course aims to increase the engagement of non-computer-science majors with technological concepts. CS10 is one of only a handful of university pilots for the Advanced Placement *CS:Principles* class (e.g., [10, 2]), and a prolific provider of professional development to high school teachers (with more than 175 teachers in the course's Piazza forum), so the Teaching Privacy Project curriculum is already influencing high schools at a national level. CS10 also has the distinction of being the only computer science course on campus with equal gender representation.

In this section, we discuss how we evaluated our curriculum by measuring its impact on students' privacy attitudes. We describe our method and results.

4.1 Methodology

During the Fall 2014 session of CS10, we piloted elements of the TPP curriculum and examined if they had an effect on students' privacy attitudes at the end of the course. Our hypothesis was that if our curriculum was effective, students would express stronger desires to exert control over their personal information. To test this hypothesis, we asked students to complete a privacy attitudinal scale before and after being exposed to our materials. During the first week of class, and after receiving IRB approval, we emailed the 309 students who were enrolled and asked them to complete an online survey. This initial survey provided a baseline metric of their privacy attitudes. During the final week of classes (week 14), we emailed students to ask them to complete a followup survey. The pre- and post- surveys were identical; the purpose was to observe whether any of their responses had changed over the course of the semester, after being exposed to our materials. Our privacy materials were presented to students during weeks 9 and 11, which means that by the time that they completed the post-survey, three weeks had passed since they had last been exposed to our materials in the classroom.

Our surveys consisted of a privacy attitudinal scale and an unrelated psychometric scale that is known to exhibit high internal reliability (as measured by Cronbach's α). For the privacy attitudinal scale, we created a hybrid scale by combining Malhotra et al.'s Internet Users Information Privacy Concerns (IUIPC) scale [12] with Buchanan et al.'s Privacy Concerns Scale (PCS), while removing redundant factors as determined by a previous study by Egelman and Peer [7]. This left us with 16 statements that participants rated using a 7-point Likert scale (from "strongly disagree" to "strongly agree"), which were grouped into four sub-scales (Appendix A): concerns about online fraud, online disclosure to companies, transparency and control, and dissemination by others.

Participants also completed the Need for Cognition (NFC) scale [4], which is a well-studied scale in the psychology literature that measures individuals' propensities to engage in "thoughtful" endeavors. We included this scale because it has been observed to have extremely high internal reliability, as measured by Cronbach's α (i.e., $\alpha > 0.8$), as well as remain relatively stable over time. We used the NFC scale as a reliability check for our other responses. Thus, if we observed low internal reliability amongst our sample or a statistically significant change, this would suggest that the responses to both scales are highly questionable and should be discarded (e.g., participants may not have been paying attention and made random selections).

4.2 Results

Of the 309 students enrolled in the class, 260 completed the pre-survey and 201 completed the post-survey. Because our IRB protocol did not allow us to collect personal identifiers, we asked participants to enter the last 5 digits of their university ID numbers so that we could link the pre- and post-surveys. Due to several participants omitting this step or entering non-matching numbers, we were only able to link 119 pre- and post-surveys. Thus, we consider our total response rate to be 38.5%, which we consider to be reasonably good for a voluntary survey with no incentives. Of our 119 participants, 64 were female (53.7% of 119), which did not observably differ from the gender balance of the entire class. Because this was an undergraduate population, we did not examine other demographic traits beyond gender (i.e., participants were likely to fall within the 18-22 age range and were unlikely to hold college degrees).

Based on the reliability of participants' NFC scores ($\alpha_{pre} = 0.86$ and $\alpha_{post} = 0.84$), our data suggests that participants were consistent and took the surveys seriously. We observed no statistically significant change in participants' NFC scores, as measured by a two-tailed Wilcoxon Signed-Ranks test ($\mu_{pre} = 3.52$, $\mu_{post} = 3.50$, $p < 0.826$).[1]

Examining participants' privacy scale responses, we did observe a statistically significant increase, as well as high internal reliability. Averaged across all four sub-scales, participants' scores increased from 5.17 (out of 7) to 5.34 ($\sigma_{pre} = 0.89$, $\sigma_{post} = 0.98$), which was statistically significant ($p < 0.021$). Thus, our hypothesis is supported, and the effect size is between small and medium ($r = 0.21$). Based on this result, we performed post-hoc testing to examine whether this effect was more prominent among any particular sub-scales. Across all four sub-scales, the only statistically significant difference was observed across the "Transparency and Control" sub-scale ($p < 0.003$), which remains significant after correcting for multiple testing, and exhibits a medium effect size ($r = 0.27$). Thus, our results suggest that after completing our curriculum, students exhibited a stronger desire to exert control over their personal information and for more transparency regarding how their information is used by others. This may suggest an increased desire to understand the contents of website privacy policies and/or control if and when companies send them marketing communications.

[1]Unless otherwise noted, we used the Wilcoxon Signed-Ranks test for all within-subjects comparisons in the remainder of this section.

5. DISCUSSION AND FUTURE WORK

Among university undergraduates, our curriculum appears to be effective. Our results show that three weeks after being exposed to our privacy education curriculum, students' attitudes about online privacy had remained changed: they stated an increased desire to have transparency and control over how their personal information is used. However, our work is far from complete. We are actively improving our website and increasing the amount of content that we provide to other educators through our Teachers' Resource for Online Privacy Education (TROPE). Eventually, we hope to develop a full-fledged MOOC so that we can reach much larger audiences of both students and teachers.

One limitation of our work, which applies to both the curriculum itself and the evaluation methodology that we discussed in Section 4, is that it is primarily geared towards those in high school and beyond. For instance, most middle school students (or those even younger) are unlikely to have privacy concerns surrounding business transactions! Yet, these students still experience issues relating to online privacy, just in different ways (e.g., social media usage). We recognize this need and are starting to develop a version of our curriculum that is applicable to a younger demographic, as well as more suitable evaluation metrics.

In addition to directly evaluating our materials in the classroom, we have also hosted several events, including a very popular interactive lab at our university's open house. We also conducted a privacy education workshop at the 2015 ACM SIGCSE conference, and this past summer, our university's NSA/NSF-funded GenCyber summer camp for K-12 students integrated our materials [15]. In addition to presenting our curriculum, we received feedback and on-the-ground stories from participating educators at both events.

We plan to conduct these outreach events regularly to continue to disseminate our materials and receive feedback from other educators. To date, the feedback that we have received about our curriculum has been very positive, because it genuinely appears to be filling a critical need.

6. ACKNOWLEDGMENTS

This work was made possible by the National Science Foundation under awards CNS-1065240 and DGE-1419319. We would like to thank the following contributors: Miranda Braselton, Megan Carey, Jaeyoung Choi, Alexis Conway, Isha Doshi, Henry Gan, Karina Goot, Blanca Gordo, Marian Harbach, Melia Henderson, Nicholas Henderson, Denise Huey, Fatima Ibrahim-Biangoro, Julie Ireton, Jeffrey Jacinto, James Jiang, Chan Kim, Justin Kim, Markus Krause,

Florin Langer, Jessica Larson, Itzel Martinez, Bryan Morgan, Regina Ongowarsito, Jeremy Orr, Marissa Pitta, Tim Radvan, Micky Prochaska Saglio, Gerardo Sánchez, Arany Uthayakumar, Melody Valdez, and Ketrina Yim.

7. REFERENCES

[1] N. C. S. Alliance. Stay safe online: Teach online safety. https://www.staysafeonline.org/teach-online-safety/. Website, accessed 12/3/2015.

[2] O. Astrachan, T. Barnes, D. D. Garcia, J. Paul, B. Simon, and L. Snyder. CS Principles: Piloting a new course at national scale. In *Proceedings of the 42nd ACM Technical Symposium on Computer Science Education (SIGCSE '11)*, pages 397–398, New York, NY, USA, 2011. ACM.

[3] R. Bybee, J. A. Taylor, A. Gardner, P. Van Scotter, J. Carlson, A. Westbrook, and N. Landes. The BSCS 5E instructional model: Origins and effectiveness. Technical report, Biological Sciences Curriculum Study, Colorado Springs, CO, 2006.

[4] J. T. Cacioppo, R. E. Petty, and C. Feng Kao. The efficient assessment of need for cognition. *Journal of personality assessment*, 48(3):306–307, 1984.

[5] Center on Law and Information Policy at Fordham Law School. Fordham CLIP volunteer privacy educators program. http://law.fordham.edu/assets/CLIP/2013_CLIP_VPE_Complete.pdf, 2013.

[6] Common Sense Media. K–12 digital citizenship curriculum. https://www.commonsensemedia.org/educators/curriculum. Accessed 12/1/2015.

[7] S. Egelman and E. Peer. Predicting privacy and security attitudes. *SIGCAS Comput. Soc.*, 45(1):22–28, Feb. 2015.

[8] N. C. for Missing & Exploited Children. Netsmartz workshop: Teaching materials. http://www.netsmartz.org/Resources. Website, accessed 12/3/2015.

[9] D. D. Garcia. The beauty and joy of computing (cs principles), parts 1–4. https://www.edx.org/course/beauty-joy-computing-cs-principles-part-uc-berkeleyx-bjc-1x#.VJFqqCdGzDw. edX.

[10] D. D. Garcia, B. Harvey, and L. Segars. CS Principles pilot at University of California, Berkeley. *ACM Inroads*, 3(2):58–60, June 2012.

[11] A. Lenhart, M. Madden, S. Cortesi, U. Gasser, and A. Smith. Where teens seek online privacy advice. Technical report, Pew Research Internet Project, 2013. http://www.pewinternet.org/2013/08/15/where-teens-seek-online-privacy-advice/.

[12] N. K. Malhotra, S. S. Kim, and J. Agarwal. Internet users' information privacy concerns (iuipc): The construct, the scale, and a causal model. *Information Systems Research*, 15(4):336–355, December 2004.

[13] Markkula Center for Applied Ethics, Santa Clara University. Your privacy online. http://www.scu.edu/ethics-center/privacy/.

[14] MediaSmarts, 2013. http://mediasmarts.ca/.

[15] National Security Agency. NSA's Cyber Camps Make Summer School Fun. https://www.nsa.gov/public_info/press_room/2015/gencyber_summer_camps.shtml, May 2015.

[16] T. J. T. F. on Computing Curricula (Association for Computing Machinery and I.-C. Society). Computer science curricula 2013. In preparation.

[17] N. Parlante. CS101. https://class.stanford.edu/courses/Engineering/CS101/Summer2014/about. Stanford Online.

[18] A. Pentland. Big data and social physics. https://www.edx.org/course/big-data-social-physics-mitx-mas-s69x#.VJFqWSdGzDw. edX.

[19] TeachToday, 2015. http://www.teachtoday.eu/.

[20] S. B. Wicker. Wiretaps to big data: Privacy and surveillance in the age of interconnection. https://www.edx.org/course/wiretaps-big-data-privacy-surveillance-cornellx-engri1280x#.VJFpwCdGzDw. edX.

APPENDIX

A. PRIVACY PREFERENCES SCALE

1. **Online Fraud**
   - I'm concerned that if I use my credit card to buy something on the internet my card could be mischarged.
   - I'm concerned that if I use my credit card to buy something on the internet my credit card number could be obtained/intercepted by someone else.
   - I'm concerned about online organizations not being who they claim they are.
   - I'm concerned about people online not being who they say they are.
   - I'm concerned that an email containing a seemingly legitimate internet address may be fraudulent.
   - I'm concerned about online identity theft.
2. **Online Disclosure to Companies**
   - When online companies ask me for personal information, I sometimes think twice before providing it.
   - It bothers me to give personal information to so many online companies.
   - It usually bothers me when online companies ask me for personal information.
3. **Transparency and Control**
   - Consumer online privacy is really a matter of consumers' right to exercise control and autonomy over decisions about how their information is collected, used, and shared.
   - A good consumer online privacy policy should have a clear and conspicuous disclosure.
   - Companies seeking information online should disclose the way the data are collected, processed, and used.
   - I believe that online privacy is invaded when control is lost or unwillingly reduced as a result of a marketing transaction.
4. **Dissemination by Others**
   - I'm concerned that an email I send someone may be printed out in a place where others could see it.
   - I'm concerned that an email I send may be read by someone else besides the person I sent it to.
   - I'm concerned that an email I send someone may be inappropriately forwarded to others.

A Reflective Approach to Assessing Student Performance in Cybersecurity Exercises *

Richard Weiss
The Evergreen State College
Olympia, WA 98505 U.S.A.
weissr@evergreen.edu

Michael E. Locasto
The University of Calgary
Calgary, Alberta, CA
locasto@ucalgary.ca

Jens Mache
Lewis & Clark College
Portland, OR U.S.A.
jmache@lclark.edu

ABSTRACT

Assessing student performance in cybersecurity labs and exercises is a difficult and time-consuming task. Simply recording the number of correct answers is inferior to in-depth assessment. Faculty are often best placed to offer expert feedback, advice, and guidance based on assessing student achievement and quality of performance for time-constrained exercises. Since this often takes place in the context of large classes and complex exercises, it can present obstacles to offering qualitative feedback. Yet, in some cases there is more information available that could simplify this task. This paper explores the use of command line history and visualization to add additional information and simplify the problem.

Categories and Subject Descriptors

C.2.0 [**Computer-Communication Networks**]: General—*Security and Protection*; K.3.2 [**Computer and Information Science Education**]: Computer science education

General Terms

Security, Measurement

Keywords

grading; assessment; cybersecurity; qualitative feedback; exercises; analysis skills; EDURange

1. INTRODUCTION

Because cyber security draws on so many subfields of computer science, it is inherently challenging for students to integrate this broad variety of knowledge, especially at the undergraduate level. Realistic cybersecurity exercises are not only difficult for students to master, but can also represent a significant amount of work for the instructor to adopt or design, test, and grade (i.e., assess). For both network and systems security, the learning objectives span multiple levels and areas of concern. They include acquiring both conceptual understanding as well as skills in applying theory to practice. Hence there are a wide variety of questions for students to explore. As a way of illustrating such variety, we list some examples of such questions related to network security (similar ones exist for systems security). This list is by no means complete: it is merely intended to provide some context for the types of exploration and analysis a student might undertake.

- What is the topology and content of a target network? What are the best ways to perform surveillance and auditing? (This is the topic that we focus on in this paper.)
- What are the vulnerabilities of a system? Which ones are serious?
- Has the network been compromised? If so, when and how and how can it be restored to safer state that eliminates the vulnerability that led to the problem?
- Have network resources been exhausted? Can we tell the difference between legitimate traffic and malicious traffic?
- Has sensitive data been exfiltrated? If so, when, which data, and how?

Even this brief list begins to reveal that teaching and testing a student's understanding of the issues at play is no simple affair. It is not just a question of whether students found a correct answer by applying the tools, but how they found the answer. We believe that we will be able to provide better feedback to students and better assess their work if we incorporate additional information about what they did in the exercise rather than just a numerical score based on the number of correct answers. In cybersecurity exercises in particular, there may be multiple paths to a correct solution, and how a student (or team of students) proceeds along these paths may involve backing up and correcting false assumptions. As instructors and assessors of student performance, we are most interested in seeing evidence of this kind of growth in student knowledge and competence [2, 4].

In order to answer questions like these, students often need to analyze complex systems and data, and the answers are not always simple. For example, to figure out if a process is doing something anomalous, one might need to look through a trace with hundreds of system calls. This requires that one understand what type of system calls there are and what they do. Following this example, one would become familiar with strace and its options, as well as process forking and interprocess communication.

We want to assess multiple types of knowledge: conceptual understanding of what the problems are and what tools to use to solve

*This work was partially supported by NSF grants 1141341, 1141314, 1516100, and 156730

SIGCSE '16, March 02 - 05, 2016, Memphis, TN, USA

ACM 978-1-4503-3685-7/16/03 ...$15.00.
http://dx.doi.org/10.1145/2839509.2844646

them, skills in using tools, analytical reasoning to correctly and thoroughly interpret extensive output. Written exams are a limited tool for doing this. Even skills-based tests can produce misleading results. It is possible for a student to copy a solution from the Web without really understanding it. There are several frameworks for hands-on exercises that have the potential to provide additional information for assessing operational and analytical skills relevant to security. Several are discussed in Section 2. In this paper, we look at a specific example implemented in EDURange where we collected this type of data, and we share our observations about what information we were able to extract.

2. RELATED WORK

There are many frameworks that are designed to teach cyber security through hands-on exercises. SecKnitKit and SEED provide VMs that the students download and use to perform specific tasks. Timchenko et al. [12] created VMs that they install in their lab. As such, they do not provide an opportunity to collect information about the problem-solving process. Modifying traditional Capture the Flag competitions such as CSAW and iCTF are challenging and time-consuming tasks [3]. Competitions such as CCDC and Packetwars [5] have access to these data, but they require significant infrastructure and are not something one could use in the classroom.

There are several cloud-based virtual environments that could be modified to capture user interactions in the classroom. The RAVE provides each student with access to several hosts that are configured for the labs in *Principles of Computer Security Lab Manual* [8]. NICE-challenges provides a more extensive environment with a collection of open-ended challenges that focus on security-related IT skills [7]. There are some exercises implemented in DETERlab [9]. EDURange provides a virtual environment in a public cloud with about six exercises, several of which have questions for students to answer [13].

Most of the computer science literature on assessment of learning seems to address programming and computational thinking. While this is a very important part of Computer Science, it does not address many of the aspects of security education. Many of the tasks that a penetration tester must perform involve understanding network protocols, and behaviors of operating systems and database management systems. Of course, there are issues related to secure coding practices and reverse engineering of executable code that require a solid understanding of programming concepts. Furthermore, there is great value in teaching students not to make simple coding mistakes [11]. Nevertheless, some researchers have tried to emphasize that programming is not just the ability to generate code; it may also be regarded as a way of thinking, decomposing, and solving problems ("Computing Curricula 2001", Marion et al [6]). As such, collecting data other than the final product, i.e. the program, is important for providing feedback to students.

The work on learning programming concepts that has inspired us has been Soloway [10]. This work assessed students learning to program on whether they learned the fundamental concepts. More recently, researchers have started to apply machine learning techniques to compare students to each other as a way of recognizing groups of students who are missing some of the concepts [1]. This approach has the advantage of being scalable. In that work, the researchers instrumented the Eclipse IDE so that every time the student compiled a file, it would save the list of API calls, the abstract syntax tree (AST), and the frequencies of key words. These features were used to compute the distances between any two programs. In addition to being able to predict exam scores, their pedagogical insight was that the development path contains more information than the resulting program.

3. THE EXERCISE

The exercise that we studied is a seemingly simple one of network reconnaissance. It asks students to determine the number of live hosts (if any) along with any running network services on those hosts in a network (different from their own) with roughly 2^{15} IP addresses. Students have an hour to complete the task, and it could take all of that time if not done efficiently. Each "path" that a student takes is a sequence of activities where the student executes programs to interact with the scenario environment. We record this path by capturing the Linux bash history of commands that the student enters.

There are also a few different levels for this exercise, depending on how much the students know about `nmap`. For example, in the simplest case, all of the hosts respond to ping, which can be used to do an efficient scan. At more difficult levels, some hosts may not respond to ping or even have open TCP ports. When the student is scanning for open ports, there could be a firewall that is blocking responses.

This exercise captures some key abilities, such as finding strategies for limiting the amount of data to be searched or finding faster, parallel ways of searching it. It also illustrates one of the ways in which cybersecurity relates to many specialties within computer science. This exercise could be used in a Networking class or Security class to (1) review basic network protocols (2) discuss topics such as netmasks, routing, IP addresses, (3) introduce scanning as "listening" to the sequences of packets that nmap produces in response to different requested scan types (4) discuss high-level strategies for efficient and/or quiet scanning.

4. DATA COLLECTION

For the reconnaissance exercise, we collected the bash histories from two classes at two different schools. There were a total of 24 teams of students. Each line was tagged with the primary command. Some commands were identified as *significant*, e.g. `nmap` was the primary command that we were looking for, and we identified that as significant. We also distinguish among different instances of significant commands by looking at the options that were used, e.g. `nmap -sn -n`. The sequence of commands that are typed by the student form a long list, which is generally difficult to interpret structurally. For purposes of visualization, we collapse commands that are similar, i.e. have similar options and arguments, into a single node in a directed graph. Although some temporal information is potentially lost, this gives a representation that can visually decompose the graph into chains and cycles that correspond to phases in the students' path, as can be seen in Figure 1. We also include some other commands such as `ls` or `grep` which are not specific to the task, but give potential information about what the student might be trying to do. One can decompose the graph into roughly four subgraphs. Sometimes a subgraph will correspond to a particular task or phase, such as finding all hosts or scanning ports on specific hosts. We did this for the teams and looked for patterns and similarities between the graphs.

5. RESULTS AND DISCUSSION

For each team, we analyzed the graphs of the nmap options that each team used and a qualitative summary of their activity along with a quantitative assessment of their scanning results (i.e., whether and to what extent they identified the correct target IP addresses and service ports). We then reflect on the difference between these two methods of assessing the quality and correctness of student performance in the context of a cybersecurity exercise.

Section 3 describes the exercise that faced each team. Although this exercise has the practical effect of teaching nmap-specific scanning knowledge, its primary formulation has the underlying goal (i.e., learning objective) of providing students with an opportunity to develop their analysis skills. In this case, the exercise presents students with a twofold opportunity to (1) plan their approach to scanning a large network (which has a very real time cost) and (2) understand what each of their expressed scans (via the command line parameters) is actually asking of the network based on the actual packet types or content used by nmap to initiate and execute the scan. Thus, the purpose of the exercise is to confront the student with these more sophisticated issues in addition to learning nmap "lingo."

Thus, in our assessment approach, we seek to comment on the teams' abilities to both learn about nmap's use *and* to use it effectively and efficiently (thereby demonstrating that they understand the tool's operation and effect on the network). This latter point is a crucial piece of our intended feedback to the student. Through the very design of the exercise and its inherent dependence on the significant amount of time needed to scan a large and mostly empty IP range, we are seeking to demonstrate to the student that they need to acquire an understanding of how the tool works, not merely the ways it is invoked in standard examples. The professional and pedagogical lesson we wish to drive home is that Computer Science education involves creativity, analysis, and problem solving – not the brute-force regurgitation of examples copied from the Web.

We designed the exercise to do this more effectively than any well-intentioned words of caution and warning, and our assessment will seek to point out and reinforce this lesson to the teams. It is precisely because of the subtle nature of this learning objective that we must (as instructors) engage in a more detailed study and evaluation of the students work – not just whether they "got the right answer" by returning a list of IP addresses. Hence, the need to provide better, more meaningful and professionally relevant feedback drives our need to approach assessment of these types of tasks with a more detailed analysis. In short, if we wish to raise the level of our students' learning, we have to raise the quality of our own assessment. Creating better learning outcomes does not simply rest on giving students more assignments, or more cleverly constructed assignments, but also in providing them with better constructed assessment of their performance. In the next subsection, we summarize the information we gained from the traces for some of the teams.

5.1 Qualitative Assessment

Team 1.

In one of the longest traces of the data set, this team begins by scanning a smaller subnet (the 10.0.0.0/18), perhaps realizing that the original task may take some time, and they place a bet that most hosts might reside in the 'beginning' or lower region of the /17 space. They then quickly switch to fairly aggressive ping scans of the entire /17. They find a handful of hosts, and attempt to ping and nmap these hosts (along with their own host and the router). This team does not ever seem to reach the full answer, but they do exhibit quite an appetite for nmap and seem to do a satisfactory job of exploring a range of the tool's options.

Team 2.

In an example of a brief scanning episode, Team 2 consults the nmap manual page and then a fairly aggressive ping scan of the entire /17. They also use the -n parameter to avoid DNS resolutions. They seem to find the host 10.0.0.6 early in the address space, concluding their very short trace (7 invocations of nmap in total) by aggressively default scanning this host. A somewhat mediocre attempt that stops at the first hint of reply from the simulated network.

Team 3.

Team 3's record is also fairly brief, but they show several noteworthy characteristics. They begin by applying nmap to their own host and consulting the manual documentation about nmap. This shows a good amount of willingness to explore the use of the tool before diving into the scan headlong. They initially use a default nmap scan of the entire /17; perhaps realizing this is taking too long, they attempt to switch to more verbose output and a scan that will report the OS type (a tempting option that is a distraction at this point in the game). They then seem to discover the '-T' parameter and execute increasingly aggressive scans. This is a good example of a team that improves, but in which a traditional approach to assessment would treat very harshly indeed. They demonstrated more progress than Team 2, even though they did not find any hosts In the graph we see a loop that includes reading the man pages and then invoking `nmap` again.

Team 4.

In the course of a medium-length trace, Team 4 manages to ping scan the entire /17 and move quickly on to aggressively (i.e., with the -T4 and -A options) scanning a set of individual IP addresses. They clearly solved the problem and understood the tool. The graph is much smaller than that for Team 1, but the complexity is hidden in the loops of length 1.

Team 5.

Team 5's trace amounts to a relatively small amount of work; they initiate a brute-force default scan of the entire /17, eventually redirecting output to a file. They spend the rest of the trace checking the status of this file with the `ls` command. Not much evidence of results or learning about the tool's operation. A relatively poor performance which we cannot yet chalk up to either ignorance of or over-confidence in the tool, although the unsophisticated use of nmap (i.e., default scan type, no use of -n) argues for the former case. The graph has some similarities to that of Team 4, except that the loop does not contain any of the significant commands.

Team 6.

Team 6 is a good example of a team that doesn't seem to get anywhere in terms of assembling a viable list of 'results', but they do spend a fair amount of time experimenting with and evolving the list of command line switches and parameters they pass to nmap.

Team 7.

One of the longer traces, team 7 also shows signs of modest command line expertise by starting scans in the background and redirecting output to files, occasionally checking the progress of this output. This team also consults the nmap documentation before initiating any scans. They begin with a brute-force scan of the /17 space; this scan eventually yields fruit, and they go on to scan individual machines. This team also seems to get deep into the task, because they end with attempts to scan for web servers (port 80) in the entire net and then attempt to figure out what a service running on a non-standard port on one of the hosts is. From the activity in this trace, this team looks (a) quite competent (if ultimately uninspired and sub-optimal) and (b) able to achieve the answer and explore some of the intended (i.e., purposefully configured) 'weirdness' in the simulated network.

Team 10.

Team 10 (graph not shown) does a large number of fast scans (-T5), each with slightly different options. They seemed to be preoccupied with specifying port ranges. This is a distraction because nmap does a good enough job at finding hosts using just a small number of ports. An explanation for why they did not find any hosts is probably that they did not wait for any of their scans to complete.

5.2 Recommendations

Assessing student work, particularly for certain kinds of interactive security exercises and labs, can be an onerous task for an instructor or TA that wishes to provide meaningful and in-depth feedback. Our experience turning student command sequences into graphs and writing up our observations leads us to see several ways in which these artifacts can be used in the classroom and for a variety of feedback.

1. **Use as peer feedback**. Get students and teams to exchange their own traces and talk through them with team members or other teams. Such peer feedback can be a low stress way of sharing experiences and results across teams without the pressure of being graded by an instructor or TA.
2. **Use as a class review artifact**. Anonymized traces and graphs can be used to spur whole-class discussion; each trace can be displayed and the pros and cons of the team's approach discussed by the entire class or lab section. This is similar to many code review activities.
3. **Use as contextualized feedback**. Getting students to improve their performance often requires them to understand where they went wrong and what alternatives could have led to better performance. Grading rubrics and score breakdowns often only communicate the relative weightings of different parts of assignments. In our approach, the graph augments the scoring rubric and individual feedback. Each student or team receives the annotated graph; the graph provides context and meaning to the rubric for the lab or assignment and a basis for interpreting the written feedback from the instructor and for self-reflection.
4. **Use as an instructor planning tool**. How students perform in clusters or groups can help inform the instructor where additional review or further reinforcement is needed; the graphs can show where common mistakes are made, or where students might have missed possible solutions to the problem at hand. In performing a reflective assessment of the exercise and attempting to explain what each team was doing, it often became apparent what each team's mental state might have been, and what information or insight they may have missed. This kind of reflection can lead the instructor to have some insight about hints or resources or unforeseen obstacles due to the design of the exercise.
5. **Use as a "live" scoring method for competitions**. Capture-the-flag style competitions are popular cybersecurity exercises. Such environments often benefit from a scoreboard, but showing (at least to the instructor) a graphical summary of each team's progress can help the instructor provide rapid feedback during the exercise itself. The utility of this approach is greatly enhanced if it can be largely automated. We note that the obvious analog here in programming courses is to an instructor reading and hand-grading hundreds or thousands of lines of code of a student program rather than just comparing output or running a few test cases. Such an approach is not scalable, and we are looking for ways to lighten the manual burden of this informal modeling of sequences of student behavior. Fortunately, the type of data we study is highly amenable to scripting and automated display.

5.3 Alternatives

One could suggest that a written exam could easily extract this type of information. One can design open-ended exams, but these are often very difficult and time-consuming to grade, especially for large classes or with little TA help. On the other hand, while they are easy to grade, there are problems with short-answer questions. In the case of network reconnaissance, we want to avoid asking students to memorize a set of commands that faculty deem as good a priori. We want to capture the process that students go through to find the answer because that is indicative of their ability to solve novel problems.

6. CONCLUSION

The key result that we have shown is that there is useful information in the bash history of students' commands that is not contained in the artifact that results from the completion of the set of tasks that was assigned. Teams 1, 4, and 7 did very well, but they used somewhat different approaches. Teams 3 and 6 did not find the answers, but met some of the learning goals. We did see one team that miraculously knew the IP addresses of the target hosts without seeming to scan the network. For this network reconnaissance exercise, whether or not students produced the correct answers, i.e. the correct IP addresses, ports and services, would **not** have been an accurate assessment of their understanding, e.g.,

1. By copying examples from the man pages or searching the Web, students could reproduce the right commands and options that will yield correct results.
2. Students could be on the right track to finding a good solution but run out of time or be missing just one piece of the solution.
3. Students may have understood the concepts but not have mastered all of the skills.

A significant amount of this information can be recovered from the history of what the students actually did in the course of their investigation. In all, this kind of informal modeling approach was practically useful for this exercise and generating meaningful feedback for the students.

Acknowledgments

We would like to thank Franklyn Turbak and Brian Fite for many suggestions and conversations about EDURange. We thank our students, especially Kahea Hendrickson, Isaak Yansane-Sisk, and Jeff Ladish. We also thank the reviewers for their useful and extensive comments.

7. REFERENCES

[1] Blikstein, P., Worsley, M., Piech, C., Sahami, M., Cooper, S., and Koller, D. Programming pluralism: Using learning analytics to detect patterns in the learning of computer programming. *Journal of the Learning Sciences 23*, 4 (2014), 561–599.

[2] Cooper, S., Nickell, C., Piotrowski, V., Oldfield, B., Abdallah, A., Bishop, M., Caelli, B., Dark, M., Hawthorne, E. K., Hoffman, L., Pérez, L. C., Pfleeger, C., Raines, R., Schou, C., and Brynielsson, J. An exploration of the current state of

information assurance education. *SIGCSE Bull. 41*, 4 (Jan. 2010), 109–125.

[3] Doupé, A., Egele, M., Caillat, B., Stringhini, G., Yakin, G., Zand, A., Cavedon, L., and Vigna, G. Hit'em where it hurts: a live security exercise on cyber situational awareness. In *Proceedings of the 27th Annual Computer Security Applications Conference* (2011), ACM, pp. 51–61.

[4] Endicott-Popovsky, B. E., and Popovsky, V. M. Application of pedagogical fundamentals for the holistic development of cybersecurity professionals. *ACM Inroads 5*, 1 (Mar. 2014), 57–68.

[5] Fite, B. The PacketWars Competition, 2015.

[6] Marion, B., Impagliazzo, J., St Clair, C., Soroka, B., and Whitfield, D. Assessing computer science programs: what have we learned. *ACM SIGCSE Bulletin 39*, 1 (2007), 131–132.

[7] Nestler, V. NICE challenge project, 2015.

[8] Nestler, V. *Principles of Computer Security Lab Manual*, 4 ed. McGraw-Hill Education, 2015.

[9] Peterson, P. A. H., and Reiher, P. L. Security exercises for the online classroom with deter. In *Proceedings of the 3rd International Conference on Cyber Security Experimentation and Test* (Berkeley, CA, USA, 2010), CSET'10, USENIX Association, pp. 1–8.

[10] Soloway, E., and Ehrlich, K. Empirical studies of programming knowledge. *Software Engineering, IEEE Transactions on SE-10*, 5 (Sept 1984), 595–609.

[11] Taylor, B., and Kaza, S. Security injections: Modules to help students remember, understand, and apply secure coding techniques. In *Proceedings of the 16th Annual Joint Conference on Innovation and Technology in Computer Science Education* (New York, NY, USA, 2011), ITiCSE '11, ACM, pp. 3–7.

[12] Timchenko, M., and Starobinski, D. A simple laboratory environment for real-world offensive security education. In *Proceedings of the 46th ACM Technical Symposium on Computer Science Education* (2015), ACM, pp. 657–662.

[13] Weiss, R. S., Boesen, S., Sullivan, J. F., Locasto, M. E., Mache, J., and Nilsen, E. Teaching cybersecurity analysis skills in the cloud. In *Proceedings of the 46th ACM Technical Symposium on Computer Science Education* (New York, NY, USA, 2015), SIGCSE '15, ACM, pp. 332–337.

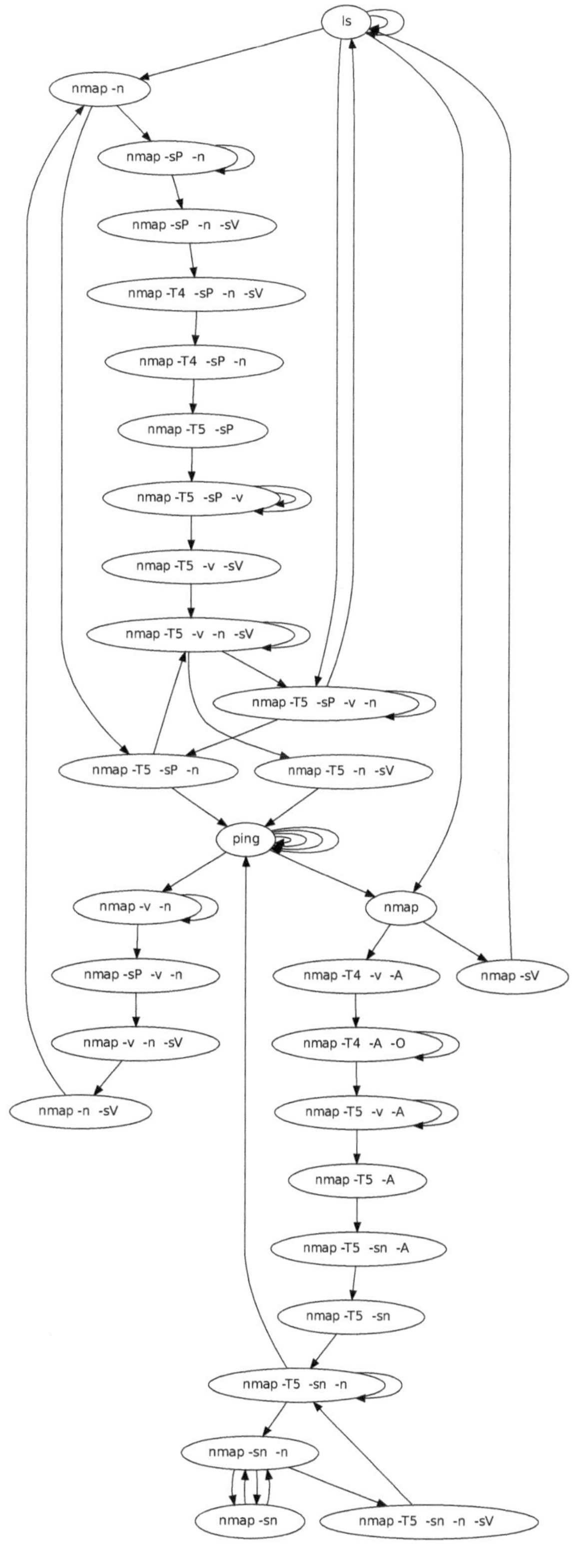

Figure 1: A directed graph of students' path

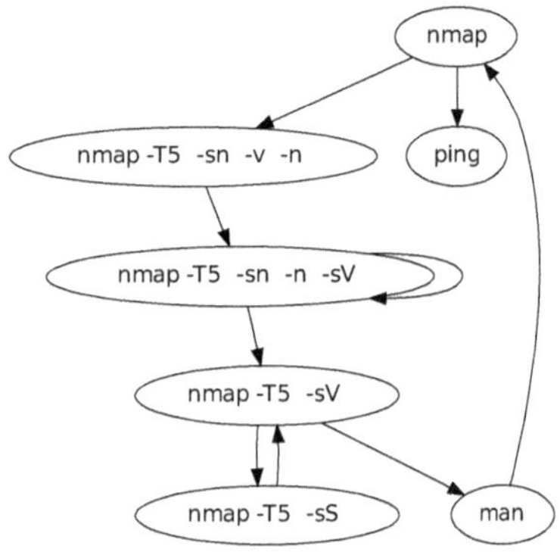

Figure 2: Team 2

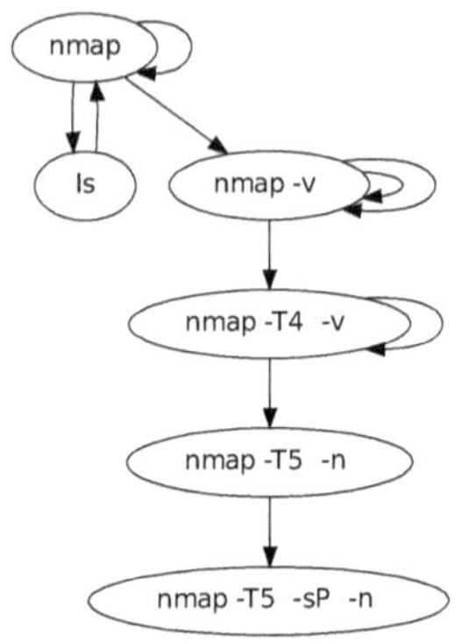

Figure 3: Team 3

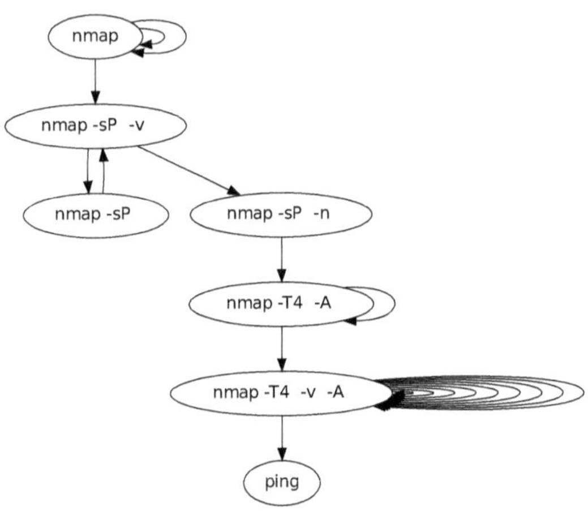

Figure 4: Team 4

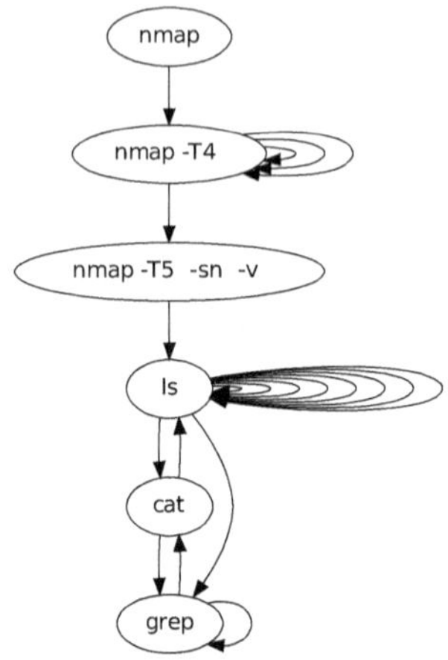

Figure 5: Team 5

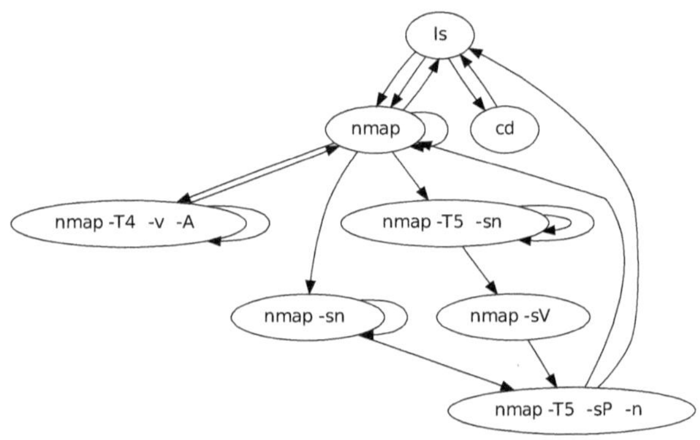

Figure 6: Team 6

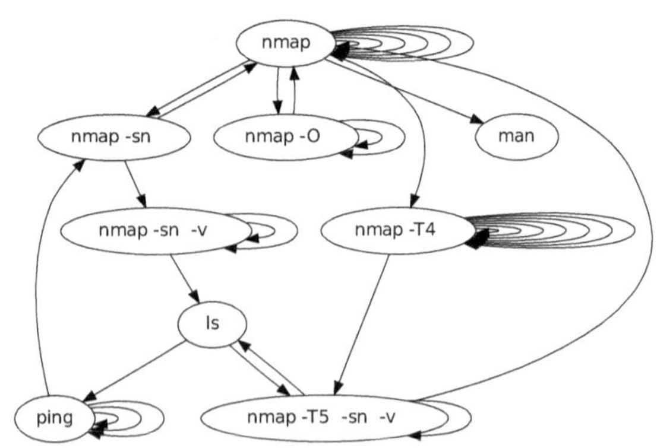

Figure 7: Team 7

Facilitating a Battle Between Hackers: Computer Security Outside of the Classroom

Nathan Backman
Buena Vista University
Storm Lake, Iowa, USA
backman@bvu.edu

ABSTRACT

Attack/Defend computer security contests require participants to leverage knowledge obtained from a variety of courses across a computer science curriculum, providing undergraduates with a novel and exciting opportunity to challenge both themselves and their peers. However, there are limited opportunities to participate in such contests and none of them is well suited for novices in computer security.

This paper describes the design of an Attack/Defend security contest that is geared towards undergraduates who have little exposure to computer security and require a more gentle introduction. We provide implementation details of the framework that supports this contest and offer lessons learned over the past three years in growing our contest into an intercollegiate event that is deployed on a cloud infrastructure to support multiple, concurrently operating contest sites which span three timezones.

Keywords

application security; hacking; capture the flag

1. INTRODUCTION

It is difficult to overstate the need for producing security-minded software developers. Addressing security issues late down the software development pipeline as an afterthought may lead to compromised systems and data. Software developers must practice defensive programming and be aware of the risks of the programming languages, libraries, frameworks, and systems they use. Additionally, researchers have learned that a firm grasp in offensive security[11] is an important step in better understanding the challenges inherent to computer security.

The need to further emphasize computer security in undergraduate programs was acknowledged in the ACM/IEEE Computer Science 2013 Curricula[10] through the inclusion of a new Knowledge Area named: *Information Assurance and Security*. Another way to support the development of computer security skills is by encouraging students to participate in extracurricular events and contests that feature these concepts – much like how the ACM International Collegiate Programming Contest[1] provides an opportunity for students to develop programming and algorithmic abilities.

SIGCSE '16, March 2–5, 2016, Memphis, TN, USA

DOI: http://dx.doi.org/10.1145/2839509.2844648

1.1 Capture The Flag

Computer security contests are not a new phenomenon and have existed in at least one popular form (Capture the Flag contests) since formalized in 1996 at the annual DEF CON[2] hacker convention. Capture The Flag (CTF) contests provide participants with the opportunity to identify and exploit vulnerabilities hidden within network-based applications (called *services*). Event organizers create custom services for these contests and purposely engineer into them at least one critical vulnerability. Successfully exploiting a vulnerability in a service will give an attacking team the opportunity to gain escalated privileges on the compromised service in order to acquire sensitive data (called a *flag*) stored within the service or on the computer. Teams report captured flags (typically represented as an ASCII string) back to a flag submission interface to redeem points. The flag will be validated for authenticity and teams will be rewarded with points for each flag they submit.

There are two main types of CTF contests: Jeopardy and Attack/Defend. In a Jeopardy contest, teams compete to exploit services hosted on computers that are controlled by the contest administrators. Contestants play only on the offensive and the administrators need only host a single set of services. Teams then compete to exploit as many services as they can as quickly as possible. In an Attack/Defend contest, each team is given control of their *own* computer and all of these computers are hosting an identical set of contest services. This places teams in a position to both defend the services on their own computer and attack the services hosted on the computers belonging to the other teams. To do this, teams will analyze the services (and their source code) to identify vulnerabilities that can lead to flag theft. Upon finding such a vulnerability, a team will fix (patch) that vulnerability in their own service and develop an attack to exploit that vulnerability in the services hosted on all of the other teams' computers. A successful exploit will result in the theft of flags which can be redeemed for points.

Attack-and-defend CTF contests offer a more rich experience by making teams look at application security comprehensively. Being able to identify vulnerabilities, understand the process of developing exploits, and patch these vulnerabilities are all incredibly important in the grand scheme of computer security. Understandably, facilitating an Attack/Defend CTF contest is more challenging that facilitating a Jeopardy CTF contest. The additional challenges include: 1) provisioning a computer (typically a virtual machine) for each team; 2) managing services, flags, and infrastructure support code on all computers; and 3) the need to incentivize teams to keep their services online and functional. Due to these additional development and production costs, Attack/Defend contests are quite a bit more rare than Jeopardy contests.

1.2 Related Work

To our knowledge, and at the time of writing, there are only two regularly occurring Attack/Defend CTF contests that are hosted from within the USA. They are: 1) the previously mentioned DEF CON CTF contest which is hosted by industry professionals in Las Vegas, draws in competitors of the highest caliber, and requires qualification by placing highly in one of a set of other CTF events (which have traditionally been Jeopardy contests); and 2) the iCTF[12] contest produced by academics from the University of California, Santa Barbara which is open only to educational institutions. iCTF is an internet-accessible event that has shown the capacity to host over a hundred teams with thousands of students in a single event. In their most recent event in 2015 [3], teams were required to contribute their own exploitable service to the contest in order to be eligible for participation. This would prove to be a barrier to entry for any participants who are novices in the area of computer security. Finally, there is an additional internet-accessible event hosted in Russia (RuCTFE[4]) that serves hundreds of teams that face a challenging set of services. In addition to these events, there are a small handful of other Attack/Defend CTF contests hosted in Europe and Asia that require a physical presence for participation. A managed list of regular occurring CTF events can be found at the CTFtime website[5].

EDURange[8] is a platform created to quickly deploy lab-based computer security exercises into the cloud with ease. Our CTF framework shares commonalities with this project in how we deploy exploitable services and labs as security exercises. For example, any one of our services could be easily deployed with EDURange to be used as a classroom exercise. With slight modifications, it could be possible to use EDURange to fully deploy an Attack/Defend CTF contest operating on our framework.

1.3 Outline

The remainder of the paper is organized as follows. Section 2 presents the motivation for our contest and describes the expansion of the event over the last three years. Section 3 describes the general format and design of our CTF contest. Section 4 provides an overview of contest services and how they must be structured for inclusion within our framework. Section 5 details the implementation of our framework. And, finally, Section 6 contains our conclusions, reflections, and areas for future work.

2. CONTEST DEVELOPMENT

As advocates for security, we encouraged our students to participate in Attack/Defend CTF contests to gain exposure to the discipline. Coming from a small, private liberal arts college, however, our students do not have a wealth of computer security classes with which to prepare themselves for such contests. In fact, prior to the production of our first CTF event we had never previously offered a course in computer security. This is not unusual for small, liberal arts colleges. Students originating from such colleges tend to have a more introductory skill set for computer security.

The few Attack/Defend CTF contests that exist tend to target and attract teams of an extremely high caliber. The problem sets (contest-provided exploitable services) can therefore be extremely challenging and often simply inaccessible to the security novice. There are not a wealth of these types of contests simply because the development and production costs of facilitating them are incredibly high. Therefore, those that exist tend to be facilitated by security professionals and computer security researchers who cater to advanced participants.

Seeing a need for a beginner's introduction to Attack/Defend CTF contests, we decided to produce such an event for our students. As educators, this prospect appealed to us because it provided an opportunity to integrate a large body of knowledge from our computer science curriculum into the contest-provided services. A collection of services can employ concepts from classes including: introductory programming, algorithms, operating systems, networks, database management systems, web application development, computer architecture, and potentially many more.

The integration of concepts from our curriculum into this extracurricular event provided our students with the unique opportunity to challenge their familiarity with the discipline of computer science as a whole within the context of software security. Students would look forward to subsequent contests as they matured through our computer science program to, loosely, measure themselves and to challenge both themselves and their peers.

2.1 Contest Expansion

We hosted our debut Attack/Defend CTF contest in 2013 on our campus at Buena Vista University (located in Storm Lake, Iowa) and accommodated 12 of our students arranged within 4 teams. Feedback from students was positive and they encouraged us to make this an annual event.

In 2014 we invited Whitworth University (located in Spokane, Washington) to participate with us remotely. The event included 39 students distributed across 10 teams. To accommodate both universities, our event was hosted on the Amazon Elastic Compute Cloud[6]. Web cams, microphones, and projectors were situated in the two separate contest sites to maintain a live audio/visual connection between the two universities throughout the duration of the contest. This created a "portal" between the two contest sites which allowed for an exciting environment and enabled friendly banter, taunts, and interactions between teams across sites. Again, feedback was positive and Whitworth University was receptive to being included in future events.

In 2015 we expanded yet again by inviting Taylor University (located in Upland, Indiana) to compete as a third remote site. We also invited students from nearby Northwestern College (Orange City, IA) to come compete at the Buena Vista University site. Ultimately there were 4 universities represented situated across 3 contest sites each in a different timezone and all sites again connected via web cams. Collectively, there were 70 student participants distributed across 14 teams. This event featured a bonus opportunity which allowed teams to "hack" into a black-box room accessible via a web interface in which lights, cameras, and USB missile launchers could be utilized to meet team-specific objectives. Again, feedback was positive and each university expressed an interest to return for future events in spite of a couple of hiccups that we faced in the administration of this event.

It is important to note that the other schools we invited to participate are also small, primarily undergraduate institutions without a wealth of security classes. At most, these institutions offered only an introductory computer security class (and this was often not the case). In fact only one of the participating institution offered a security class at the time of their first involvement in our contest and two universities have begun offering an introductory computer security course since their first involvement.

3. CONTEST FORMAT

This section presents the structure and format of our contest with notes on how the event has changed in successive iterations.

3.1 Team Composition

Some readers may have noticed that our participant count has not risen proportionally to our team count over the past three years. Due to the nature of the Attack/Defend contest, as the team count increases so does the work required in delivering exploits to other teams. This extra work can be circumvented through the automation of exploits but, frankly, many of our teams have not mastered the art of automation – especially the beginners who we are trying to attract. In an attempt to keep the team count from exploding, our most recent event has allowed for teams to participate with 4 to 6 students. This number of students per team seems manageable, not requiring extreme measures for coordination.

From the outset, this contest was designed to be a learning experience instead of a quick exhibition of skills like you might see in the ACM ICPC. With this in mind, each team was *required* to include a student that had not yet completed their first year of study in computer science. An initial and seemingly intuitive reaction would be that first-year participants would be completely out of their league in such a contest. Actually, and without exception, each first-year participant has told us this – that they were completely in over their head. However, when asked if they would recommend that future first-year students also participate, they, again without exception, recommended that they should.

We have found that including first-year students is a great way to get them connected with more senior students while building camaraderie within the major. These senior students have usually done a great job in finding ways for the first-year students to participate while offering insights along the way. It might be suggested that the addition of first-year students to a team may slow them down. While this is certainly possible, we again emphasize that our objective was to facilitate a learning experience rather than just an exhibition of skills. Also, due to the length of the contest, additional person-hours of support can be considered invaluable to assist in some tasks which are difficult to automate – launching exploits and submitting flags, for example.

3.2 Round-based Format

Our CTF contests takes place over a series of 1-hour rounds. At the beginning of each round, the contest framework will deliver new flags to each service on each computer. For example, if there are 4 teams and each team is hosting 6 contest services, 24 flags will be distributed at the beginning of the round with each computer receiving 6 flags (one for each service).

A team will only be rewarded points for capturing a specific flag once. Therefore, in a single round, with t teams and f flags, a team will be able to capture at most $(t-1)f$ flags per round. The fact that new flags are distributed at the beginning of subsequent rounds is very important. It allows teams to launch their exploits yet again to capture the newly distributed flags. The expectation of being hit with a fresh wave of exploits at the beginning of each round encourages teams to keep searching for ways to patch their services. Similarly the round-based format encourages teams to search quickly for vulnerabilities to develop exploits before the flags for the current round are replaced with new ones.

3.3 Contest Length

We have struggled to determine an appropriate length for our CTF contests. As the event is intended to be a learning experience, we want students to have plenty of time to investigate the services, research types of vulnerabilities, and develop exploits.

Our first contest had a length of 24 hours and was designed such that students could come and go as they pleased – the expectation was that students would take time off to eat and sleep. Well, our undergrads are stubborn and refused to heed suggestions to try to automate their exploits over the night. Instead, they were thrilled with the option of staying up through the night (or at least taking turns sleeping) to collect flags. In the following year, the contest kept its 24-hour time span but the contest was suspended for 8 hours at night to force students to take time off and sleep.

In our most recent contest, the invitation of a neighboring university to compete locally at our site resulted in shortening the contest. The new time format allowed for 4 hours of competition followed by a 1-hour break and then another 4 hours of competition. This format seemed to help to keep participants focused and adequately rejuvenated throughout the contest.

3.4 Scoring

Teams can score points in one of three ways.

1. **Capturing Flags**: By exploiting a service, a team will have an opportunity to steal a hidden flag. The flag can be redeemed for points through a flag submission interface.

2. **Keeping Flags**: At the end of a round, teams will be rewarded with defense points for keeping flags secure from other teams. For example, if a team is hosting a particular service that was exploited by only 2 of 10 other teams in a round, then they would receive defense points for each of the 8 teams that did *not* steal that flag in the round. A team that was exploited by all 10 other teams on a particular service would receive no defense points for that service.

3. **Maintaining Service Uptime**: In order to prevent teams from simply shutting down their services to prevent flag theft, we reward teams with points for service

uptime. Determining whether a service is up and functional is addressed in Section 4.4. All services on all team computers are checked to see whether they are functioning appropriately every 3 to 5 minutes over the duration of the contest. If a service is found to be functioning appropriately during an uptime check then the team hosting that service will receive uptime points.

Flag capture points and uptime points parallel the scoring mechanics of other Attack/Defense contests. We added points for keeping flags to reward teams that have done well patching services. We observed that some teams were able to patch many more services than they were able to exploit but they were not rewarded for their defensive capabilities. We now try to balance this dynamic by rewarding offensive as well as defensive successes.

4. CONTEST SERVICES

Services are developed for the contest with a couple of things in mind. We want to feature a broad range of programming languages, frameworks, and technologies and have students draw from their knowledge of a variety of concepts covered in the computer science curriculum. In the past, we have produced services that have been written using languages including: Python, Java, C, C++, Javascript, PHP, SQL, and Bash. Types of services we have created include: chat clients, social media sites, meme generators, file sharing programs, games, web servers, key-value data stores, and various other types of web applications and remote administrative tools.

When creating services for our first event, some of the services were really quite simple in size and scope. Such simple services did not leave a lot of room for creativity when it came to searching for vulnerabilities. That is, there were relatively few possible attack vectors worth investigating. Expanding on the size and scope of the services will ultimately require teams to do more investigative work to uncover vulnerabilities.

A recent example of a service we created is: HackerChat. This service was written in C and contained both client-side and server-side binaries. Clients would establish a TCP connection with a server and be presented with an IRC-like chat room and could chat with other clients connected to the server. This service could be exploited via buffer overflow. Overflowing the buffer containing the user's away message could overwrite the path the server maintained to a message-of-the-day file. Replacing this path with the path to the flag file could then enable the attacker to fetch the flag by prompting the server to print the contents of (what it believed to be) the message of the day file.

4.1 Vulnerabilities

Often, services are designed with a couple of vulnerabilities in mind. For example a content management system might be designed with a SQL injection vulnerability in mind or a C application might be designed to be vulnerable to a format string exploit. We typically try to include a wide range of vulnerability types across the set of services. Also, each service *should* ideally have more than just one vulnerability which can lead to flag theft. This can lead teams to wonder if they have found and patched all of the vulnerabilities within their services.

For the contest administrator, it can be exciting to see a team integrate a patch and thereby block a currently exploited vulnerability only to be exploited at a later time on that same service through a previously unknown vulnerability. We do not want students to rest easy just because they have found and patched a single vulnerability within a service. The potential for multiple vulnerabilities should keep teams on their toes and searching for extra vulnerabilities in the event that some of their previously developed exploits become blocked.

4.2 Flag Locations and Service Permissions

Each service must be written so that the vulnerabilities built into it can lead to the theft of its flag. All flags are stored in known locations. For example, if we have Services A, B, and C, then the following set of files would exist on each team's computer: `{/etc/flags/A, /etc/flags/B, /etc/flags/C}`. File permissions are set such that only the services to be exploited will have read access to their flag file. It is only by exploiting a service that you can leverage its permissions to gain read access to its flag file. Also, teams will never gain write-access to flag files – not even their own. This prevents teams from corrupting flags so that they fail validation when other teams capture and submit them.

We also allow flags to be stored in different ways as is appropriate for each particular service. For example, a content management system may store its flag in its back-end database under a field applicable to the site administrator. Then, perhaps via privilege escalation to administrator status or perhaps via SQL injection, an attacker may be able to fetch the flag from the database. In the event that a flag will be stored in such a service-specific way, then the location of that flag would be reported in the documentation for that service. Also, teams hosting services would have write access to these flags but we disincentivize teams from modifying their own flags with the threat of lost uptime points for corrupting service functionality.

In summary, teams should not be required to hunt for the flag – the locations of the flags will always be known – instead they must hunt for vulnerabilities that can let them gain access to a flag.

4.3 Minimizing Damage

We must be careful to restrict the kinds of havoc that an attacking team can inflict on the teams and services they exploit. For example, if an exploit allows one to execute arbitrary system commands on an opponents computer (such that `cat /etc/flags/A` would enable flag theft) then we want to prevent the attacking team from damaging or deleting other important service files. An exploit should not enable one team to impede the progress of another. Also, an exploit for one service should not be able to fetch flags from other service. Each service should be self-contained and vulnerable only to problems in its own code.

In our most recent contest, one team abused an exploit to delete all files relating to the attacked service on their opponents' VMs. This was ultimately a failure of the contest administrator and degraded the learning environment as well as the morale of the attacked teams. Their patches, progress, and exploits were repeatedly deleted. There is only so much an administrator can do to fix problems during the contest so every precaution must be taken to identify and remedy these issues prior to the start of an event.

4.4 Support Scripts

To integrate a service into the contest framework, a service author must also produce a series of scripts to support administrative functionality. These scripts are:

- **service-deploy**: A deployment script is used to install, configure, and start the service on a team's computer. Depending on the complexity of the service, this script may be as simple as copying files over to a working directory and executing a binary or involve something more complicated such as creating and initializing a MySQL database.
- **service-delete**: A service deletion script is used to remove all traces of the service from the computer. This will include deleting files, database, and terminating any running processes relevant to the service.
- **service-round-update**: This script must be written in order to facilitate any service's requirement to place a flag in a non-standard location. For example, this script may place the newly issued flag in a database if that would be appropriate for the service.
- **service-uptime-check**: This script is perhaps the most complicated of all. It reports back to the scoring system whether or not a running instance of the service is functioning appropriately. The definition of "functioning" here is ambiguous and left to the service writer to specify. Such a script will emulate standard and expected client behavior that the service is meant to facilitate. Should the service not respond in a way that the service author considers appropriate (for example by eliminating login functionality to prevent any form of privilege escalation – even when legitimate) then they will not receive uptime points. This script will report back one of three values: 1) **Online**: meaning that the service is deemed functional; 2) **Offline**: meaning that the service could not be contacted; and 3) **Malformed**: meaning that the service is active and responding but that it is not correctly facilitating legitimate user actions. This service status is displayed in a publicly available location for all teams to see after every uptime check. Teams can then take corrective measures when they notice that their service is not cooperating and they can also see which of the other teams' services are online and ready to be attacked.

The service-deploy and service-delete scripts are mainly used before the contest starts and after the contest ends. However, they also have a very important purpose during the contest. It is often the case that a team will somehow irreparably damage their own service – perhaps by deleting files, large portions of code, or making a change that they cannot undo. In such a scenario, their service status will likely go to "Offline" or "Malformed" and the team will quickly fall behind due to a loss of uptime points. We therefore provide a mechanism by which these scripts can be used to reset a service to a factory-default state.

5. CONTEST FRAMEWORK

We created our contest framework with the goal of facilitating a number of Linux virtual machines (VMs) to represent both the team computers and the administrative computer. In this model, we required only a single VM to be used for administrative purposes and one VM would be launched per team in the contest. Figure 1 provides a diagram of this architecture and we will elaborate on it in the following sections.

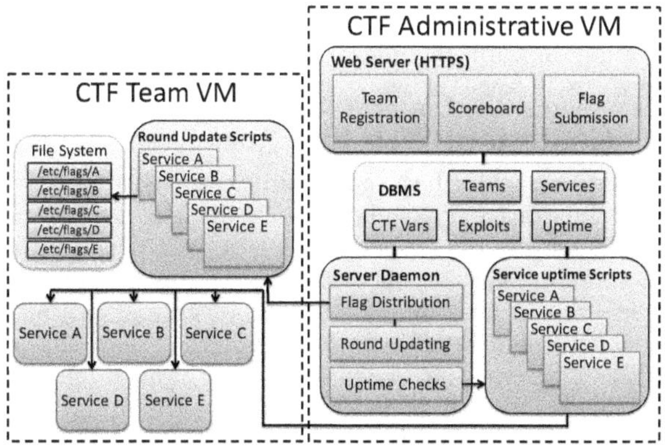

Figure 1: Architecture of the contest framework

5.1 Administrative VM

The administrative VM is responsible for hosting the contest website and for managing all updates to the state of the contest. The contest state is stored in a relational database and keeps track of team information (team name, password, VM IP address, etc.), service information (current flag, current uptime status, team ID, etc.), and a complete history of all scoring events (captures, defense points, uptime points). The database is relied upon heavily by both the contest website and the daemon that supports regular and ongoing administrative tasks.

The daemon triggers the beginning and end of the contest. Between these two points, the daemon had two additional tasks: 1) initiating new rounds; and 2) enforcing uptime checks. New rounds occur every hour on the hour. Once triggered it generates a new flag for every single service identified in the database and it then distributes those flags to the team VMs where those VMs would then locally run round-update scripts to integrate those flags. The uptime checks occur randomly once every three-to-five minutes throughout the duration of the contest. This variability was integrated to prevent teams from keeping their services off (and therefore immune to attack) except for when uptime checks were expected. The result of an uptime check is be immediately pushed to the database and assessed for points.

5.2 Team VMs

Team VMs are all spawned from the same image and contain all of the contest software. Prior to the start of the contest, we execute the service-deploy script to install and launch each of the services. With all services running, the team VM is only responsible for periodically executing round update scripts when commanded to do so by the administrative VM. This script integrates the new flags provided by the administrative VM. Occasionally these VMs would also be responsible for triggering the service-delete and service-deploy scripts when necessary to reset a service.

Teams otherwise have control over their team VM to investigate services, patch services, launch exploits, automate exploits, and do any additional development necessary. Team members connect to a VM its public, internet-accessible IP over ssh. All team members can then collectively work on the team's VM.

5.3 Contestant Web Interface

Teams interact with the game through a website hosted on the administrative VM. The website provides a basic scoreboard in which team standings are presented as well as a color-coded grid that depicts the uptime status of every service in the competition. Teams can quickly glance at this grid to determine when it was necessary to repair a service. We also graphed contest statistics over time to show flag accumulation as well as progression of defenses.

A nice and engaging feature of the website is that we designed a push-based mechanism to audibly inform teams immediately and verbally when flag captures occurred. On a flag capture, the speakers in the room would play a message akin to: "The Red Team has exploited Service B on the Green Team's server." This small feature was surprisingly effective at instantly changing the mood of the entire room!

In addition to reporting on the contest state, the website also featured a flag submission interface and a mechanism to ask for clarifications from the contest administrators. As the contest grew, it quickly became clear that disseminating important information and updates via web cam (aside from the opening briefing) was fraught with problems. We therefore implemented this clarification system to provide lasting records of posed questions similar to the system provided in the PC^2[7] programming contest platform.

6. CONCLUSIONS AND FUTURE WORK

We developed an Attack/Defend CTF contest and supporting framework to provide a more gentle introduction to the discipline for undergraduates who have had little exposure to computer security. Growing from 12 contestants, to 39, and then 70 has confirmed that there are other institutions that can benefit from this program and who are also interested in finding a way to encourage their undergraduates to seriously consider computer security.

To be frank, we have received a lot more interest from universities wishing to participate than we can currently handle under the umbrella of a single contest. Indeed, we face logistical challenges not faced by programs such as iCTF because of the fact that our demographic (our undergraduate teams) is less capable of scaling. If we were to permit the inclusion of well over 100 teams (as iCTF has done)[9] then our undergraduate teams would be burdened with carrying the logistical weight of exploiting a great deal more teams than they are likely capable of. Scaling in this way would shift our desired emphasis away from investigating vulnerabilities and developing exploits towards the menial work of applying developed exploits, recording and submitting flags, and attempting to automate scripts to do the same.

As we prepare for our next CTF contest in 2016, we plan to not introduce any additional sites or universities although we do expect the number of participants to increase due to growing exposure at those respective universities. Increasing the scale of our event beyond 16 teams or so will require a fundamental change to how the contest must be organized – and we flirted with that limit at our last contest. Before continued expansion we are considering implementing something akin to round-robin stages for the first half of the contest from which we can identify high performers and low performers that can be grouped together in subsequent stages. This would limit the number of targets each team must attack while grouping competitors of a similar skill level.

7. ACKNOWLEDGMENTS

We would like to thank our participating universities for their assistance and support in beta testing our framework and contest as we have expanded. This work was also supported by two Amazon AWS in Education Grants that funded deployment onto cloud services to support intercollegiate, cloud-based contests.

8. REFERENCES

[1] ACM International Collegiate Programming Contest, http://icpc.baylor.edu.

[2] DEF CON® Hacking Conference, A History of Capture The Flag at DEF CON, https://www.defcon.org/html/links/dc-ctf-history.html.

[3] The UCSB iCTF Competition, http://ictf.cs.ucsb.edu.

[4] RuCTFE, Online international challenge of information security, https://ructf.org/e.

[5] CTFtime.org: All about CTF (Capture the Flag), https://ctftime.org.

[6] Amazon Elastic Compute Cloud, http://aws.amazon.com/ec2/, Amazon.com, Inc.

[7] CSUS Programming Contest Control (PC^2), http://www.ecs.csus.edu/pc2/, California State University, Sacramento.

[8] S. Boesen, R. Weiss, J. Sullivan, M. E. Locasto, J. Mache, and E. Nilsen. Edurange: Meeting the pedagogical challenges of student participation in cybertraining environments. In *7th Workshop on Cyber Security Experimentation and Test (CSET 14)*, San Diego, CA, Aug. 2014. USENIX Association.

[9] N. Childers, B. Boe, L. Cavallaro, L. Cavedon, M. Cova, M. Egele, and G. Vigna. Organizing large scale hacking competitions. In *Proceedings of the 7th International Conference on Detection of Intrusions and Malware, and Vulnerability Assessment*, DIMVA'10, pages 132–152, Berlin, Heidelberg, 2010. Springer-Verlag.

[10] Joint Task Force on Computing Curricula, Association for Computing Machinery (ACM) and IEEE Computer Society. *Computer Science Curricula 2013: Curriculum Guidelines for Undergraduate Degree Programs in Computer Science*. ACM, New York, NY, USA, 2013.

[11] M. Mink and F. C. Freiling. Is attack better than defense?: Teaching information security the right way. In *Proceedings of the 3rd Annual Conference on Information Security Curriculum Development*, InfoSecCD '06, pages 44–48, New York, NY, USA, 2006. ACM.

[12] G. Vigna, K. Borgolte, J. Corbetta, A. Doupé, Y. Fratantonio, L. Invernizzi, D. Kirat, and Y. Shoshitaishvili. Ten years of ictf: The good, the bad, and the ugly. In *2014 USENIX Summit on Gaming, Games, and Gamification in Security Education (3GSE 14)*, San Diego, CA, Aug. 2014. USENIX Association.

A Programming Contest Strategy Guide

Aaron Bloomfield
University of Virginia
aaron@virginia.edu

Borja Sotomayor
University of Chicago
borja@cs.uchicago.edu

ABSTRACT

The ACM's International Collegiate Programming Contest (ICPC) is the world's oldest and largest programming contest. Although students can benefit both pedagogically and professionally from participating in this contest, participation in North America is far smaller than in the rest of the world, which we partially attribute to the perceived low payoff of participating in ICPC. We discuss the pedagogical benefits of participation in ICPC, which include higher student enthusiasm for computer science studies and better career prospects post-graduation, and present a set of cohesive strategies aimed at increasing involvement and success within the ICPC. For aspiring coaches and contestants, we also provide links and references for further study.

Categories and Subject Descriptors

K.3.m [**Computers and Education**]: Miscellaneous

General Terms

Algorithms, Measurement

Keywords

Programming contest, ICPC, Strategy

1. INTRODUCTION

There are many collegiate programming contests, but arguably the most prestigious is the ACM's International Collegiate Programming Contest[1] (ICPC), the largest and oldest programming contest in the world. The contest is open to undergraduate students and first year graduate students. Students form teams of three, coached by a faculty member – or someone designated by a faculty member – and compete in regional contests ("regionals") in the fall. In the 2014 regionals, the latest for which data is available as of publication time, there were 38,160 students from 2,534 institutions in 101 different countries. The top 128 teams from the regionals advance to the world finals, held most recently in Marrakesh, Morocco, in May 2015.

Although participating in the ICPC has the potential for winning large cash prizes and "bragging rights", it also offers students a number of pedagogical advantages, such as solidifying their understanding of core computer science concepts, often going beyond what is covered in a typical computer science major, as well as building many cross-cutting skills, such as effective teamwork.

However, despite the number of pedagogical and professional benefits, ICPC is not as popular or well known within ICPC's North American "super-region"[2] as in the rest of the world, where it is regarded as a highly prestigious competition. In fact, participation in North America lags behind that of the other ICPC super-regions, particularly Europe and Asia, and no North American team has won the world finals since 1999. In fact, since 2000, only teams from Russia, China, and Poland teams have won the world finals.

In this paper, we describe the pedagogical benefits of participating in ICPC and present a number of training and contest day strategies that we have used successfully with our own teams[3], and which we have seen consistently used by schools that regularly qualify for the world finals.

We are certainly not the first to present an article on programming contest strategy. Indeed, articles on this topic were appearing as early as the 1980's by Myers and Null [7]. Two valuable strategy guides are by Trotman and Handley [10], and by Khera, et. al. [4]. Manzoor provides a description focused on the common mistakes made during contests [5]. We have synthesized the wisdom of these articles, combined it with our successful experience in the last decade of competitions, and updated the strategies with recent advancements.

Our contributions to the literature are two-fold. Firstly, we have synthesized much of the extant literature on contest strategy, and presented it in a single, cohesive whole. Secondly, we present strategies for the contest itself, including training activities; much of the extant literature focuses on describing how to solve certain problems, rather than training and contest day strategies.

[1] `http://www.acmicpc.org/`

[2] ICPC defines this super-region as encompassing all the regional contests in the US and Canada, but not Mexico nor the Caribbean countries

[3] The authors have had considerable success over the last decade with coaching our respective teams. In the last eight years, the two authors have led their respective teams to the world finals in 14 of the 16 possible berths.

SIGCSE '16 March 02-05, 2016, Memphis, TN, USA

http://dx.doi.org/10.1145/2839509.2844632

2. CONTEST STRUCTURE

An ICPC-style programming contest is a five hour event in which teams of three students attempt to solve up to 12 provided programming problems using one of several allowed languages. Since the allowed languages at the world finals are Java, C, and C++, most of the North American regions allow only those three languages, although a few allow additional languages[4]. Each team has only a single computer with no Internet access. During the contest, teams submit their solutions using a contest submission system, and are then ranked according to how many problems they can solve and how quickly they can solve them (the ranking system is further explained below). During the contest, the solutions submitted by the teams are evaluated by several judges, with the help of an automated contest control system.

2.1 Contest Environment

The exact software environment on a team's computer varies by region, but is always known in advance. In general, contestants will have access to the compilers and interpreters for the allowed languages, and a number of text editors and debuggers, including IDEs such as Eclipse.

Since contestants have no access to the Internet, a selected number of electronic references are loaded onto the computers, typically language references (Java SDK API, a C++ STL reference, etc.), references for using editors, and system-specific references (how to print, etc.). On UNIX systems, contestants also have access to system documentation, including `man` pages.

Students are allowed to bring printed reference materials to the contest, with each region having its own rules on how much and what type of reference materials are admissible. Nearly all North American regions allow effectively unlimited amounts of reference material, while at the world finals each team is limited to a 25 page reference binder.

2.2 Problems

Problems are designed to test not just the team's programming abilities, but also their command of various computer science topics. A typical contest will present between 8 and 12 problems of varying difficulty.

The simpler problems usually require using, but not implementing, basic data structures covered in most introductory courses. The medium difficulty problems often cover the material taught in an upper division Algorithms course (dynamic programming, divide-and-conquer, greedy algorithms, graph algorithms, etc.). The most difficult problems will often combine multiple concepts from an Algorithms course – such as a max flow problem that requires dynamic programming and search space culling – or will require topics covered in advanced mathematics courses.

Steven Skiena's *Programming Challenges* book [9] provides a very detailed description of the typical types of problems that are often encountered in a regional contest, and describes how to solve these problems. Similarly, Steven Halim's *Competitive Programming* book [3] is similar in structure, but also provides more details on some topics and numerous solutions.

[4]Currently, the Greater NY region allows Ada, and the Southeast region allows Ada, C#, Fortran >= 90, Haskell, Lua, Pascal, Python 2&3, and Scala. In addition, many regions, not enumerated here, are now allowing Python.

2.3 Judgement of Solutions

Problems in programming contests are designed to accept input as plain text from standard input in a specific format, and similarly for its output (via standard output). For example, a simple problem could involve reading the input one line at a time, with each line containing a list of integers, and outputting the sum of the integers:

Input	Output
`10 20 30 40`	`100`
`5 10 5`	`20`
`10 0 7`	`17`
`0`	

A line of just '0' indicates the end of the input.

For each problem, teams are typically provided with simple test cases like the one above, mainly to provide an example the input/output format of the problem. Judges will use a separate collections of test cases (unknown to contestants), covering corner cases, largest and smallest inputs, etc., to test the solutions submitted by teams. The process of submitting solutions and judging them with the judges' test cases is handled by a "contest control system" like PC^2[5], KATTIS[6], or DOMjudge[7].

A solution is considered correct if and only if, given the judges' test cases, it produces the correct output within a given time limit. This time limit often precludes grossly inefficient solutions, such as brute force solutions. Any other outcome (such as producing incorrect output, raising an exception or a segmentation fault, etc.) results in the solution being marked as incorrect.

2.4 Scoring

During a contest, teams are ranked on a scoreboard based on a scoring metric that starts by looking at the number of problems solved: if team A solves more problems than team B, then team A will place higher than team B. When two teams solve the same number of problems, the tie-breaker is the total time taken to solve the problems. This is the sum, in whole minutes, of the time elapsed from the beginning of the contest until when each problem was solved successfully. So if a team solves problems at times 35, 90, and 140 (all in minutes; seconds are not counted), then their total time is the sum of those values, or 265. Any incorrect submission would additionally result in a penalty of 20 minutes. Note that the time (including penalties) is *only* counted if a problem is solved correctly; any problem not solved by the end of the contest does not contribute to the total time. ICPC defines an additional (and rarely invoked) tie-breaking rule if two teams have the same number of problems solved *and* have the same total time.

Due to how the scoring works, if a team was going to successfully solve n problems, then it will be strictly better to solve the easier ones (i.e., those that can be solved in less time) first, as that will lower the second metric of time.

Contest scoreboards can reveal trends and statistics that can be used to further analyze a team's performance. Manzoor provides a highly detailed description of analyses of both online submission systems and programming contest results [6].

[5]`http://www.ecs.csus.edu/pc2/`
[6]`https://kth.kattis.scrool.se/`
[7]`http://domjudge.sourceforge.net/`

3. PEDAGOGICAL BENEFITS

Although both the regionals and the world finals award prizes to the top teams (typically no cash prize for a regional, but with a grand prize of over $10,000 for the top team in the world finals), we have found that the vast majority of coaches and students are not motivated by these prizes. Instead, there are a number of pedagogical and professional benefits to participating in ICPC.

One important benefit is that the contest not only reinforces many concepts and skills that students see in computer science courses, but also builds a number of valuable cross-cutting skills. In preparation for a contest, ICPC contestants must hone their programming skills and have a solid grasp of data structures and algorithms, sometimes at a graduate level. Students are also exposed to many topics, such as advanced and esoteric algorithms, that are not typically covered in a classroom setting, requiring them to be independent learners who can research new topics and solve problems without the guidance of an instructor.

Furthermore, training for ICPC builds teamwork skills both inside the individual teams and between the teams. Inside a team, the three contestants must be able to collaborate on solving challenging problems. As we will explain later, team dynamic is as important as raw talent in the success of a team. Between the teams, students typically approach training as a cooperative competition: even though they must compete with each other during a contest (or a practice contest), they cooperate in all other aspects of training. For example, after a practice contest, a team that solves a problem that no one else solves is usually happy to explain their solution to the other teams. We have never witnessed ICPC teams hoarding resources or problem solutions to gain a competitive advantage over other teams in the same institution.

Participation in ICPC can also benefit the students' job prospects. Many current and former ICPC participants have told us that the skills they acquired through ICPC have been invaluable when applying for technical positions, specially those involving a "technical interview", which often requires candidates to solve complex programming and algorithmic problems on the spot.

4. TRAINING ACTIVITIES

Not surprisingly, the biggest factor that will help a team succeed is training. However, newcomers to ICPC tend to assume that working through programming problems is sufficient to prepare for the competition. Although that will certainly help contestants familiarize themselves with the style of problems found in ICPC, other forms of individual training are also important, along with training in teams.

There are many facets to selecting students who will work together well on a team; we discuss those strategies in Section 5.2, and focus on training strategies in this section.

4.1 Individual Training

Working through problems.

The best way of working through problems individually is to replicate, as much as is possible, the conditions of a programming contest, especially the automatic judging of solutions with test cases that the student is not privy to.

Fortunately, there are a number of online sites that provide exactly such a service. These include the UVa Online Judge[8] (from the University of Valladolid, Spain), with hundreds of regional problems; the Live Archive[9], a revamp of the previous site with many new problems; Open Kattis[10], the public version of the Kattis contest management system, with problems from contest all over the world; the companion site to the Programming Challenges[11] book (but note that this site cannot properly judge some problems); and TopCoder[12] and CodeForces[13], which have become popular lately as a contest training method.

As problems are solved, copies should be kept of the correct solutions, as this can help future students who are stuck on that problem. This is ideally done by the coach.

College courses.

Students participating in programming competitions need a solid understanding of many core computer science concepts, many of which are often easier to learn through collegiate courses than through self-study.

Contestants should plan to take some theory-based courses in computer science curricula, such as Algorithms and Theory of Computation. While both are of use, the former is somewhat more useful than the latter, largely because the material in a typical Algorithms course (dynamic programming, searches, etc.) is more viable to be made into a contest problem than the material in a typical Theory of Computation course (parsing, formal languages, etc.). If the opportunity to take both arises, then that is certainly the ideal. Computational geometry, combinatorics, and graph theory courses – sometimes taught by the mathematics department – are of use as well, as some problems will focus on those topics.

Many instructors use the ICPC-style of writing programs successfully in both Algorithms and Theory courses. One of the authors has done so in an Algorithms course at the University of Virginia, and similar concepts have been applied to Theory of Computation classes [8].

4.2 Team Sessions

Running practice contests.

Essential training includes running contests that replicate the conditions of real contests. We describe below the ways in which these conditions can be replicated.

Using real problem sets: When running a practice contest, there is no need to prepare problems specifically for the practice. It is much more useful to use problems from actual regional contests, especially those from regions where the difficulty of the problems is similar to one's home region. Most North American regional problem sets are good when practicing for a North American regional contest, while problem sets from other regions in the world should be used with care, as their difficulty tends to be closer to that of the world finals problems.

Most regionals provide their problem set and judging data online. With this data, a contest control system can be con-

[8] `http://uva.onlinejudge.org`
[9] `http://livearchive.onlinejudge.org`
[10] `https://open.kattis.com`
[11] `http://programming-challenges.com`
[12] `http://topcoder.com`
[13] `http://codeforces.com`

figured to judge the responses just as was done on the original contest. Some also provide a detailed scoreboard (i.e., not just the ranking of teams, but the exact problems solved and their times and penalties) that can be useful for post-contest analyses, and can show the team how they would have placed if they were competing in that regional.

Running five hour contests: Although five hours for a practice may seem excessive, it is important to avoid the temptation to run shorter practices. Five hour practices allow students to experience the stamina necessary to focus for that length of time. They also allow students to work through the four phases of a programming contest, described below.

Not all practices will be five hour practices. Indeed, two hour practices in the evenings are a popular option due to busy schedules. However, having as many five hour practices as possible is essential to becoming a competitive team.

Replicating the contest computer environment: As described earlier, a real ICPC contest will provide each team with a single computer with no Internet access and limited amounts of documentation. It is important to enforce, as much as possible, the same constraints they would encounter at a real contest, since students typically find it hard to "unplug" during a practice contest, or to limit themselves to using just a single computer. Using the same operating system, compilers, tools, submission system, and reference material that will be provided during the contest is also helpful.

Run contests with multiple teams: In our experience, practice contests with only one team are much less effective. When only one team is "competing", the temptation to get distracted or simply give up on the practice is much higher. It also means the team does not have access to a realistic scoreboard during the practice, which prevents them from making strategic decisions based on the state of the scoreboard. For example, if there is a problem that most of the other teams have solved, then it is likely an easier problem, and one that should be worked on earlier.

On the other hand, when multiple teams participate in a practice contest, there will be some friendly competition amongst them to see which team can solve more problems, and it provides a more realistic scoreboard. It also allows those teams to have a more productive discussion after the contest (see below), and share the insights that each team had on the various problems.

Problem discussion sessions.

Once a contest is done, the teams will have likely all solved different sets of problems. Some teams will have been unable to complete a problem that others were able to solve. If a team never understands how a problem is solved – either because they were unable to solve it or because it was not explained to them – then much pedagogical potential is lost.

Thus, having a discussion session after the contest is essential. There is often resistance, as students feel mentally tired after spending five hours working on the problems. Nonetheless, our students tend to feel that practices are not as useful unless they are followed by a problem discussion session.

During this discussion session, teams that solved a problem should explain their solution to the teams that did not solve it. This allows the teams who did not solve it to know if it was because of an incorrect theoretical approach, if they ran into implementation issues, or if they neglected to consider corner cases and boundary cases. These discussions also allow teams to understand how one would solve the problems that they were unable to attempt in the practice contest.

Reviewing official solutions.

Besides discussing problems in the context of a problem discussion session, teams should also review the official solutions provided by the authors of the problem set used in the practice contest. Most contests provide such solutions, and we tend to stay away from problem sets with no official solutions: if no team was able to solve a problem in a practice contest, it makes it harder to discuss its solution (or places the onus on the coach to come up with a solution).

4.3 Preparing the Reference Documentation

Before the actual contest, the team will need to assemble the reference documentation that they will bring with them to that contest. In regions with no limits on the amount of documentation, many teams invariably show up with backpacks filled to the brim with Algorithms books, programming books, and printed solutions to problems. However, quality is more important than quantity when preparing the reference material. In particular, Algorithms books are only useful if the students are *already* familiar with their contents (e.g., by having taken a course with that textbook). They should be regarded as a reference for algorithms that are too complex to memorize, and not as a source of new algorithms to be learned (and applied) during the contest itself.

Another useful strategy is for the team to write implementations of common algorithms (Dijkstra's shortest path, convex hull, etc.) in the language they are most familiar with, and bring printouts to the contest. This will allow them to quickly code those algorithms with a lower risk of making mistakes when reading them from pseudo-code in an Algorithms book or from notes. Similarly, solved problems from their practice sessions can also be valuable, as it is not uncommon to encounter problems that are very similar, or that take an existing problem and apply different constraints on it.

4.4 Continuity and Time Investment

While both individual and team training allow the students to gain experience and knowledge about the contest, that institutional knowledge is lost as soon as the students on that team graduate. Thus, it is crucial for there to be somebody who is actively involved in training the teams, allowing that accumulated knowledge to be retained across "generations" of teams. This is often a faculty member who acts as the coach, although this role is sometimes filled by community volunteers or graduate students, many of whom were involved with ICPC as undergraduates. Of all the competitive teams we are familiar with, and certainly all the teams we are familiar with that regularly qualify for the world finals, there is always someone to provide this form of continuity and to help coordinate and train the students.

Regardless of who fills the coach role, it will be a significant time investment. The most obvious time sink is the planning and running of the practice contests. In addition, retaining the knowledge in whatever format is desired (answer database, notes, etc.) will take time. We have found that an hour a week, in *addition* to the time coordinating the practices, is a reasonable estimate. Coordinating a practice usually takes one or two hours of work beyond the time of the practice itself (selecting the questions, preparing the submission system, etc.). Five hour practices are ideal, although it is also possible to have shorter practices on a regular basis, and hold five hour practices occasionally. Participating in online contests, often set up by experienced ICPC coaches, can help lower the time commitment by an individual coach. Likewise, involving graduate students, past ICPC contestants, or co-coaches can dramatically decrease the time required by the coach.

5. CONTEST STRATEGIES

In addition to proper preparation, a team should be familiar with how to approach the contest itself.

5.1 The Phases of the Contest

During the contest, contestants must make the most out of the five hours they are allotted, which can be challenging given the constraints under which they will be solving the problems – most notably having just one computer for the entire team. We hold that a programming contest, whether it be a local practice, a regional contest, or the world finals, is split into four distinct phases. Our terminology for the phases is loosely based on the terminology for chess games.

The opening: As soon as the contest starts, each team must determine which are the easiest problems – or, more specifically, the problems that can be solved the quickest. Since the time that each solved problem accrues is counted from the start of the contest, it is imperative to solve these short and easy problems first since it will result in a lower "total time taken" in the team's score, which may end up being the tie-breaker if the team solves the same number of problems as another team. This phase should not take more than a few minutes, and lasts until just *one* easy problem is identified, as the rest of the easy problems can be identified in the next phase. Many teams will split the problem set into thirds, and each contestant will look through one third of the problems.

The early game: After identifying at least one of the easy problems, one or two contestants should focus their attention on this problem (one if the problem is trivial to implement, two if it requires some discussion), while the other team member(s) simultaneously work on identifying the rest of the easy problems. Once all the easy problems have been identified, this phase is also used to identify the difficulty and the category of the remaining problems, ideally with a rough order in which the remaining problems will be attempted.

In this phase, the teams will be solving problems fairly rapidly. Checking the scoreboard is particularly useful in this phase, as it will help the team determine whether they correctly identified the easy problems (if they see other teams are submitting them), or if they chose a deceptively easy problem (if no other teams are attempting them, or there are many attempts but no correct solutions).

This phase lasts until all the easy problems have been attempted and ideally solved. The length of this phase will vary depending on the contest and the experience level of the team, but tends to last half an hour in regionals with an experienced team and a few easy problems.

The mid game: Once the easy problems have been attempted, it is time to return to those that were not solved successfully or start on the medium difficulty problems. Like the previous phase, the length of this phase will vary by contest and team experience. Due to the increased difficulty of the problems, submitted runs do not occur as often. This phase typically takes the most time in the contest.

The end game: The last phase is *not* necessarily to work on the hard problems. Any problems that were too hard to solve prior to this point are not likely to be solved in the little time remaining. Instead, this phase, typically lasting the last hour or half hour, is to focus on the problems that have been attempted in the previous phases, but not solved successfully. That being said, if all the easy and medium problems have been solved, then of course the team should move on to the hard problems.

The difficulty of the regional contests will vary considerably, and thus the length of the phases will vary considerably as well. Some particularly telling examples were in the 2009 regionals. In the Mid-Atlantic regional contest, the problems were difficult enough that only 48 of the 161 teams (30%) solved any problems, and only two teams solved more than three problems. Conversely, the Greater New York regional contest that same year was the opposite; this region in general tends to have great teams and easier problems. Thus, also in 2009, 9 of the 53 teams (17%) solved all 9 problems, and the top team solved them all in 1 hour and 41 minutes! Thus, in that contest, who qualified for the world finals was not a matter of how many problems were solved, but how fast they were all solved.

5.2 Team Dynamics

The reason that the contests are team-based, and not individual, is because teamwork is essential to solving the harder problems. This is perhaps the most overlooked part, as most college students are accustomed to working on programming problems individually. Yet forming a good team dynamic, and being able to work together constructively on a problem, is essential to success in a programming contest.

This is not to say the individual prowess of each team member is not important; in fact, individual work is very effective in the early game, and many experienced teams can solve several problems based on individual work alone. However, this strategy breaks down once the team has to deal with more difficult problems. In fact, many teams incorrectly assume that, as they learn more about programming and computer science, they will simply be able to individually solve more problems faster, and neglect working on the team dynamics necessary to solve the harder problems.

There are several team dynamics that teams can find useful. One common strategy is to have one person thinking about the next problem (working out the algorithm, sketching out pseudo-code, etc.), while the other two team members pair program the current problem. Once the current problem is submitted, the team members rotate – the "thinker" for the next problem starts pair programming with one other member, and the remaining member starts contemplating the problem to work on next.

However, pair programming is a bit of a mixed bag. On one hand, it will make it easier to catch simple mistakes, which can help prevent incorrect submissions, but it also ties up two people with the programming aspect, and thus only allows two problems to be worked on at a given time. If there were no paired programming, then the team could be working on three problems in parallel. We feel that less experienced teams will benefit from a pair programming strategy. More experienced teams will often not need it for the easier problems, although they should be able to tell when they do need to use it.

Intra-team relationships are critical as well. While the team need not all be best friends, they need to be friendly enough that they can (constructively) criticize each other's work without getting defensive. This exact issue has doomed some of our world finals teams.

5.3 Team Roles

There are many different proposals for how to split up the work that the team members do during a contest.

As mentioned above, some people propose that team members work on problems individually. This allows for maximum parallelization, as three problems can be worked on concurrently [1, 5]. However, this poses challenges for difficult problems, at which point the team members will have to work together.

Skiena and Revilla [9] define three roles: the coder, who is the primary programmer; the algorist, who is the one with the most theoretical knowledge, and the debugger, who helps determine why a program is not working correctly.

Lately, the most common strategy seems to be for teams to have members that take on *specialist* roles, where each member has experience with a particular set of problem types. When such a problem type comes up, that person will be the lead on solving that problem. Ernst discusses the specialist strategy, among other strategies [2].

We have adopted a hybrid of these different roles. In the early game, when the problems are easy, writing solutions in parallel is feasible, especially for experienced teams. Even then, however, pair programming can still help to reduce the number of errors in a program. As the problem difficulty increases, the teams often move more towards a specialist role. Training for the specialist is feasible, as each member can focus on older ICPC problems of those type(s). The specialist role setup effectively makes everybody an algorist, as defined by Skiena, but for a subset of the problem coverage. The dynamics of an individual team will determine who is the coder and debugger – it may well be the case that two or all three team members are equally proficient at those tasks.

5.4 Avoiding Tunnel Vision

One of the biggest problems that students face in the contest is the problem of tunnel vision. After several incorrect submissions for the same problem, students will often feel that they are really close to a correct answer, and that just a few more minutes of work and one more submission will achieve a correct answer. At some point, students need to move on to another problem, and come back to the one that is causing issues at a later point, hopefully with a fresher mind. Teams are typically allowed to print their code during a contest, and should do this to perform "offline debugging" of programs without utilizing the computer, so other team members can make progress on other problems.

We often tell our less experienced teams that after five unsuccessful submissions, then they must move on to a different problem. We do not feel that this rule is necessary for the more experienced teams, nor for any team in the world finals, as they should be experienced enough to avoid the tunnel vision trap on their own. However, for less experienced teams, this rule can help them avoid this trap, which has been the bane of many teams.

6. CONCLUSIONS

Our goal in this paper was to address the barriers limiting increased participation in ICPC, particularly barriers at individual institutions, who may struggle with how to start – and properly train – an ICPC program. We addressed the pedagogical benefits of an active ICPC program and presented concrete training activities and contest day strategies, in the hopes that this will help convince people to become more involved.

In our experience, participating in ICPC is a great experience for the students (and the coach!), as well as an enthusiasm generator, a way to encourage learning outside the classroom, and good preparation for going into the job market. Regardless of whether a team advances to the regionals or the world finals, ICPC can be a rewarding experience for all involved.

Acknowledgments

The authors would like to gratefully acknowledge the dedication and commitment of the ICPC staff and volunteers at the regional and world finals level. Participating in ICPC is a wonderful experience thanks to them.

We would also like to thank David Van Brackle and Godmar Back, who provided feedback on drafts of this article.

7. REFERENCES

[1] D. Chavey, T. L. Monrey, D. Van Brackle, and J. Werth. Preparing a team for the ACM scholastic programming contest (panel session). In *Proceedings of the 19th Annual Conference on Computer Science*, CSC '91, pages 701–, New York, NY, USA, 1991. ACM. Chairman-Bagert, Donald.

[2] F. Ernst, J. Moelands, and S. Pieterse. Programming contest strategies. *Crossroads*, 3(2):17–19, Nov. 1996.

[3] S. Halim and F. Halim. *Competitive Programming, 3rd Edition*. Lulu, 2013.

[4] V. Khera, O. Astrachan, and D. Kotz. The internet programming contest: a report and philosophy. In *Proceedings of the twenty-fourth SIGCSE technical symposium on Computer science education*, SIGCSE '93, pages 48–52, New York, NY, USA, 1993. ACM.

[5] S. Manzoor. Common mistakes in online and real-time contests. *Crossroads*, 7(5):4–4, July 2001.

[6] S. Manzoor. Analyzing programming contest statistics. *Southeast University, Dhaka, Bangladesh. http://acm. uva. es/p/13_Manzoor_rev. pdf*, 2006.

[7] D. Myers and L. Null. Design and implementation of a programming contest for high school students. In *Proceedings of the seventeenth SIGCSE technical symposium on Computer science education*, SIGCSE '86, pages 307–312, New York, NY, USA, 1986. ACM.

[8] N. V. Shilov and K. Yi. Engaging students with theory through ACM collegiate programming contest. *Commun. ACM*, 45(9):98–101, Sept. 2002.

[9] S. Skiena and M. Revilla. *Programming Challenges: The Programming Contest Training Manual.* Texts in Computer Science. Springer, 2003.

[10] A. Trotman and C. Handley. Programming contest strategy. *Computers & Education*, 50(3):821 – 837, 2008.

Datathons: An Experience Report of Data Hackathons for Data Science Education

Craig Anslow
Dept. of Computer Science
Middlesex University
London, UK
c.anslow@mdx.ac.uk

John Brosz
Libraries & Cultural Resources
University of Calgary
Calgary, Alberta, Canada
jdlbrosz@ucalgary.ca

Frank Maurer[1]
Mike Boyes[2]
[1]Dept. of Computer Science
[2]Dept. of Psychology
University of Calgary
Calgary, Alberta, Canada
{fmaurer,boyes}@ucalgary.ca

ABSTRACT

Large amounts of data are becoming increasingly available through open data repositories as well as companies and governments collecting data to improve decision making and efficiencies. Consequently there is a need to increase the data literacy of computer science students. Data science is a relatively new area within computer science and the curriculum is rapidly evolving along with the tools required to perform analytics which students need to learn how to effectively use. To address the needs of students learning key data science and analytics skills we propose augmenting existing data science curriculums with hackathon events that focus on data also known as *datathons*. In this paper we present our experience at hosting and running four datathons that involved students and members from the community coming together to solve challenging problems with data from not-for-profit social good organizations and publicly open data. Our reported experience from our datathons will help inform other academics and community groups who also wish to host datathons to help facilitate their students and members to learn key data science and analytics skills.

CCS Concepts

•**Social and professional topics** → *Computer science education; Information science education; Computing literacy;*

Keywords

Analytics, Community Engagement, Datathon, Data Science, Hackathon, Open Data

1. INTRODUCTION

Due to the ever increasing availability of data over recent years, acquiring key data science and analytics skills have become important areas of interest. The aim of data science is the extraction of knowledge from large volumes of data that are structured or unstructured [6]. There are many techniques of data science that require mastering such as analysis, capture, data curation, search, sharing, storage, transfer, visualization, and information privacy.

Many types of companies commonly use data science and analytics techniques to better understand the behaviour of their customers. Governments use analytics to better understand the impact of the policies they put in place. As companies, organizations, and governments begin to rely more and more on data for decision making the demand for data scientists will grow rapidly. A report by McKinsey Company stated by 2018, the US alone could face a shortage of up to 190,000 people with analytical skills as well as 1.5 million managers and analysts with the know-how to make effective data driven decisions [11]. Some columnists have even called data scientists "the sexiest job of the 21st century" [5].

Universities and schools are rapidly introducing courses and degrees on data science, however, they are still in their infancy and as of yet few students have degrees in this subject [15]. Some universities are establishing new interdisciplinary research institutes focusing on data science, for example in 2015 the Alan Turing Institute[1] was created which involves a number of leading UK universities. To address the challenge outside of academia many community based organizations are running events and focused groups to help people up skill and acquire key data science and analytics skills to complement their existing jobs.

We propose augmenting these practices and computer science curricula with hackathon events that focus on data also known as *datathons*. In this paper we present our experience at hosting four datathons over a two year period where students and members from the community came together to solve challenging problems with data from two not-for-profit social good organizations (SGOs) and publicly open data. The purpose of the datathons was for people to learn and put into practice new data science and analytics skills which they can then utilize for their studies and jobs. Another purpose lies in providing our partner SGOs that lack the expertise and resources to make use of data science and analytics, with data science knowledge and skills from within the community to better understand their data. This experience report about our datathons will help inform other academics and community groups who also wish to host datathons to help facilitate their students and members to learn key data science and analytics skills.

[1]https://en.wikipedia.org/wiki/Alan_Turing_Institute

SIGCSE '16, March 02-05, 2016, Memphis, TN, USA

DOI: http://dx.doi.org/10.1145/2839509.2844568

2. RELATED WORK

Cleveland first coined the term data science in 2001 [4]. The purpose for doing so was to help expand the technical areas of the field of statistics focusing on the data analyst. These areas included multidisciplinary investigations, models and methods for structuring data, computing with data, pedagogy, tool evaluation, and theory. Our work focuses on multidisciplinary investigations and pedagogy.

Data science has since become an active field within many parts of academia. To meet the demands for data scientists by prospective employers in businesses and governments universities are rapidly establishing data science and analytics courses and degrees to address these demands [5].

Anderson et al. [2] report on an undergraduate data science degree at the College of Charleston started in 2003. The program was initially called Discovery Informatics but later changed to Data Science in 2012 to address the shift in focus within academia. Some of the lessons they learned include that the name change helped improve program awareness, the benefits of allowing students to take courses from multiple disciplines, and that introductory courses in data science helped with retention. They also get students to participate in an online data science competition. Others have explored computer science courses with a focus on information security and analytics [9], big data analytics [10], healthcare informatics [20], and data science for software engineers [12].

Howe et al. [8] question the role the database community has within data science. They propose that they should be one of the main groups leading the conversation about data science especially given their close relationship with database users. They pose a number of questions to consider focusing on what data science is, what level to teach data science in the computer science (CS) curriculum, which areas of CS and elsewhere should be engaged in forming data science, and how to get industry involved in the classroom.

With regard to data science curriculum a number of universities have explored creating non-CS courses that have a data science focus. Sullivan [17] created a course for non-majors that provides a data-centric introduction to computer science. Varvel et al. [19] investigated iSchools and Library and Information Science to see how current programs and courses supported data science initiatives. They identified 475 courses in 158 programs at 55 schools that concentrated on data topics in courses and categorized the courses into data centric, data inclusive, digital, and traditional. They found a relatively small number of schools offering programs specifically designed to educate data professionals, but expect that to grow rapidly.

Gil [7] proposes topics for a course on data science for non-programmers and non-CS majors. The course outlines lessons on parallel and distributed computing where students learn the principles and benefits of these areas by practicing with workflows to understand key concepts.

Plaue and Cook [14] report on lessons learned from an interdisciplinary service course on data journalism which was a collaboration between the CS department and the college of journalism at their institution. The course was well received by students from a variety of backgrounds.

Topi [18] argues that data science involves multiple disciplines not just computer science, mathematics, and statistics, but should include others such as information systems. Topi also notes that the ACM Education Council has a group exploring the feasibility of launching an initiative to create data science curricular and degrees.

3. DATATHONS

We propose augmenting the data science curriculum with practical experience by having students participate in data hackathons also known as *datathons* to learn key data science and analytics skills. A datathon is an event similar to a hackathon where people come together over a certain time period, commonly a weekend, to work on problems with a specific dataset. There are a number of steps involved in a datathon including preparing, planning, recruiting participants, arranging an appropriate venue, preparing and documenting the data, logistics, and hosting the event. We describe the benefits of datathons and outline our experience at running four datathons. Datathons provide unique opportunities for computer science students to acquire experience in working with data, participate in interdisciplinary teams, communicate their ideas effectively, apply (or gain) project management skills, and engage with community organizations to work on real-world data problems.

Data science skills. Data science and analytics skills are important throughout computer science, whether in working directly with data, handling the data associated with software development such as testing results, as well as in communicating data to others. Additionally, datathons expose students to real-world data and its inherent problems such as reliability, lack of documentation, unused data fields, privacy, anonymization, incorrect data, and unstructured data.

Interdisciplinary teams. Many areas of computer science practice rely on teams working with non-computer scientists. The most prevalent example is that of requirements gathering with clients for development projects. In other areas, such as in game development or tools development for scientists, computer scientists work in partnership with professionals from other disciplines. Exposure to such environments will help computer scientists learn to communicate their capabilities, learn processes for working with these other professionals, and will deepen their understanding of their profession's strengths and weaknesses.

Communication skills. Beyond the communication inherent in working with other disciplines, participants also gain experience in communicating the goals or benefits of their projects when demonstrating results.

Project management skills. As with any project, developing a deliverable application or data analysis report within a short period of time will provide a venue to apply the planning, documentation, communication, resource management, and related skills that students have been taught (or will be formally taught) as part of their CS program.

Community engagement. Another important aspect of datathons is that they provide a point of engagement for departments, faculty, and students to work with community organizations on real-world data problems. Such events draw the interest of local media as well as businesses looking to hire graduates or engage in research.

4. CASE STUDIES

In our case studies we discuss two types of datathons where we report on a total of four datathon events (two of each type) held over a two year period. The first case study is a very data-focused approach where participants work with an outside organization's data, providing expertise in working with the data, and helping the organization answer questions that they lack the resources and skills to answer themselves. The second case study is a slight variation on a hackathon where the goal is to form teams and then create an app that makes use of specific, often public, datasets.

4.1 Data for Good

Calgary Data for Good (DFG)[2] is a local organization inspired by DataKind.org and is working for positive social action through "data in the service of humanity." DFG brings together data scientists with social good organizations (SGOs) through a collaborative approach that leads to shared insights, greater understanding, and positive action with data. DFG creates a network of data scientists from the community and universities to inspire new applications of data science skills and analytics in meeting the needs of SGOs.

DFG organizes regular meetups and datathon events for its members. These datathons are somewhat different than a typical hackathon. Rather than creating a specific application, the goal instead is to help the participating SGO make better use of their data. Due to back and forth with the SGO these datathons are much less of a self-contained event than hackathons, requiring a great deal of collaboration with the organization, preparation of their datasets, and in developing reasonably scoped objectives that can be accomplished by the group over the course of the datathon. Our datathons featured 30-50 volunteer data scientists working with datasets over a weekend.

While requiring much more organizational effort the involvement of the SGO in the datathons brings many benefits. It exposes participants to real, messy data, as well as the back-and-forth partnership effort needed to work with a client. The SGO also brings their mission and values, encouraging participants who might not be motivated by other factors (e.g., prizes, experience).

Recruiting an SGO is not necessarily as difficult as one might imagine. A common scenario among SGOs (particularly not-for-profit organizations) is possessing large amounts of data but lacking the resources or expertise to make use of it. These organizations gather a great deal of data to support grant applications, reporting requirements, and in tracking operations. However, typical non-profit funding usually includes very little or no support for administrative overhead, such as data management and analysis. This problem noted by Daniel Perron, IT Analyst for the 2015 SGO, *"We don't have the resources in house to break down all of this data, we have the reports, we have the raw data, but that doesn't really tell us what the trends look like"* [13]. Consequently these organizations make minimal use of their data but are often keen to see the data used to improve their efforts and organizational practices.

Due to the differing backgrounds of the participants in the datathons it is not possible to provide all of the software they might make use of. However participants, being interested and active in data science, in most cases had their own copies of the software tools they preferred. These tools and languages included C#, Excel, Python, R, Ruby, Splunk, SPSS, and Tableau. Most participants brought their own laptops and other equipment.

A key element at the datathons is making data accessible. As participants make use of a variety of tools, having the data converted to as many different formats as possible is helpful. In our experience CSV, Excel, and MS Access formats were the most used. It was also important to ensure data is available through physical transfer (external drives: flash, HDD) in case of network or server problems.

Another organizational point is separating the participants into teams to work on problems for the SGO. Naturally this separation is neither hard nor fixed. Our approach has been to do this based on tasks/objectives.

In 2014 the participating SGO was Sustainable Alberta. They organize a yearly national event tracking commuters and were interested in improving the experience of participating individuals and teams. The tasks created to address the SGO's needs were: improving information and statistics about groups that have participated for several years; create dashboards for participating individuals and teams; and examining ten years of historic data for trends in participation as well as analyzing behavior by community and geography. Groups varied from 3-15 members and a selection of findings was published by Anslow et al. [3].

The 2015 SGO was the Calgary Distress Centre, a 24-hour support, free crisis counseling and resource referral service. The SGO's objectives were expressed as six questions and participants were instructed to join whichever group they wished. Volunteer participants from the SGO attended and spread out with at least one representative per group. While this may not have been necessary, it was very helpful in obtaining on-the-spot context for the data. The questions were: does call content depend upon the time of day, what issues do Distress Centre personnel most successfully handle, do calls related to particular concerns change over time; are there monthly or seasonal patterns, are there correlations between call data and public datasets such as suicide rates or weather records, does interactive mapping show patterns in 211 informational calls (a separate local information service), and what is the difference in interactions between online chats and SMS texts? A summary of the findings has been compiled by DFG [1].

The creation of these tasks/objectives and preparing the data occurred through pre-event preparation. The organizers met several times with the SGO to ensure data was available, sufficiently anonymized, and documented. A larger meeting occurred two weeks in advance with a group of ten experienced participants. The data and objectives were described to this group and then were revised before the datathon based on the group's feedback. This feedback was essential in ensuring objectives were appropriately scoped and potentially answerable as well as that the dataset was sufficiently structured and documented.

The weekend of the years' events started Friday night with an introduction both in terms of motivation as well as a technical introduction to working with the dataset from SGO personnel (see Figure 1(a)). The remainder of the evening was social time for people to meet one another, ask questions, and start planning for the next day. Saturday started

[2]http://www.meetup.com/Data-for-Good-Calgary/

(a) Introductory social event. (b) A group exploring a dataset. (c) A group brainstorming together.

Figure 1: Datathons - illustrating different aspects of the datathons.

early; objectives were introduced, data access was provided, and groups were formed. People worked throughout the day (Figure 1(b)). Sunday consisted of a little more work; mostly time to gather results and assemble a presentation. Then each group presented their findings to the entire groups as well as the SGO attendees.

Feedback from both the SGOs and participants has been positive. The 2015 SGO noted that they have obtained several results: data is now shaped and formatted in a way that it can be more easily used and analyzed, a number of strong but preliminary results have been found that need to be validated; their organization can better perceive the value and power of data; they were introduced to a variety of useful tools; and they were connected to a group of knowledgeable volunteers [1].

Participants appreciated the experience, interfacing well with people from different disciplines: *"On Saturday morning, our team began putting that game plan into action, which proved a lot more difficult than anticipated. Different backgrounds meant we had different approaches to the data, so the first few hours were spent trying to get everyone's ideas heard, while simultaneously deciding how to modify the data into an appropriate format for the analyses. After lunch, everyone settled into a groove, talking quietly in nuclear groups and concentrating on their assignments"* [16]. Summarizing the experience Sabine Syeffarth also noted: *"I would highly recommend that anyone who has an interest in working as an analyst or data scientist take part in events like this. Apart from the great feeling you get by making a difference, it is also great to see how your own skills measure up against professionals. The benefit of the datathon is you can connect with people who have similar interests, learn new tools, and all in all, have a fun - albeit stressful - weekend!"* [16].

4.2 Canadian Open Data Experience

Data-focused hackathons are a popular means that local, regional, and federal governments are actively sponsoring to gather interest in open government data initiatives. These events aim to create apps that make use of recently released datasets. The events generated interest among developers and technology innovators in government datasets with the hope of creating useful and popular applications that will draw public interest and attention to these datasets.

Our involvement has been with the Canadian Government's Canadian Open Data Experience (CODE)[3] event. This event encourages developers to create applications using the Canadian government's open data portal[4]. While self-organized teams were free to explore the data ahead of the event; the event itself consisted of a 48-hour coding sprint at the start of which the desired application theme(s) were announced, and then the apps were developed.

We organized two hubs as part of CODE in 2014 and 2015. The 2014 theme for apps was "solving problems and increasing productivity through the use of open data." In 2015 there was the option of working towards one of three themes: youth employment, business opportunities, or healthy living. After the event a shortlist of fifteen finalist teams from across the country was created from which prize winners were selected: one for each application theme, a fan favourite, and a best student team. Participants had the option of working entirely on their own or at organized hubs where multiple groups worked in the same space.

In 2014[5] sixteen participants created four teams (Figure 1(c)). One team's app was selected as one of the 15 national finalists and presented their app for judges at the finals in Toronto. In 2015 fourteen participants formed five teams.

Organizationally these events are straightforward to organize as the data organization, event goal, and prizes were provided by the government event organizers. For our institution the key organizational elements were to locally publicize the event, recruit participants, and secure an appropriate space. The group structure and technologies were dependent on CODE's specifications. As this event was a competition we found it useful to provide programming both before and after to assist in group formation and to encourage post-event discussions on what they worked on.

The apps the teams built during CODE had to utilize the open data portal and many of them utilized visualization techniques and made web apps. One team built an app that explored which city is best in Canada based on economy, housing, weather, and crime data. One app looked at where crashes happen on roads in Canada and the best time to travel to avoid bad spots. Another app explored how not-for-profit organizations spend their funds. Finally, one app explored election data in the province of Quebec. All the students reported that it was a great activity to participate in, and one team stated: *"The CODE competition was in the core of what we believe in. It feeds into our skills as computer scientists in the sense that using data for the benefit of Canadians is the group's philosophy. It was a very good learning experience and it was a true measure of character, and we really pushed ourselves."*

[3]https://www.canadianopendataexperience.ca/

[4]http://open.canada.ca/

[5]https://www.youtube.com/watch?v=egw39gz9-tc

5. DISCUSSION

There are a number of aspects that we would like to draw upon based on our datathon hosting experience.

Interdisciplinary Teams. It is important to recruit a diverse set of participants in the datathons as working on data science teams requires interdisciplinary skills. It is critical that each group has access to people with different skill sets in order to solve the questions that are raised using different tools. Recruiting people beyond universities from community groups and other technical and user groups is important as it brings in fresh ideas, processes, and tools.

When recruiting it is important to emphasize that these events are learning environments and that prospective participants need not be experts, that whatever data skills they possess will be useful. To provide an anecdote from the 2015 datathon, one participant was worried about attending as they lacked statistics and visualization knowledge; however within their group this participant was able to perform that low-level parsing of the data that had the statistics and visualization experts in the group stumped. It is also important to ensure a core cadre of participants who have strong skills in certain areas as other participants can learn from those people with the specific skill sets such as statistics, data visualization, or data mining techniques. In the datathons we tailored several of the objectives to align with the known expertise of the groups.

Group Work. When forming groups it is important that participants are self-organized and that participants feel free to join and work in any group. Since these events are voluntary people are giving up their time to work on problems they are interested in. Hence if they are forced to do something they are unlikely to be engaged and go home early. However, it is possible to guide participants towards groups at the beginning by outlining the data science skills required to answer the questions associated with each task.

Data. A critical element for running a datathon is the data itself. The data that is made available during the datathon must be easily accessible for the participants. We found providing data through an internally hosted server on a database to be successful. Using cloud services such as DropBox allowed snapshots of the data to be available and made it easy for participants to share their findings. In order to make best use of the data it needs to be well structured, cleaned and anonymized. We found working with SGOs to accomplish this task requires significant time up-front as they were not used to doing these kinds of tasks with their data. Access and permission to the data must be made clear at the beginning of the datathon so participants know exactly what they can and cannot do with the data during and after the datathon. When working with open data as part of the datathons it was important that the students understand how to make best use of the data and what steps were involved in processing the data. In the events with open data there were fewer concerns as to what the participants did with the data post-datathon.

Goals. We found that for the datathons to be effective it was imperative that the SGO had specific goals up front at the beginning of the event. The goals that were defined were mainly geared towards the needs of the SGO, but it was also important to have realizable goals for the participants so they were able to accomplish significant results within the limited time of the event. The tasks that were selected helped the SGO meet their initial analytical enquiry goals. We found that both of the SGOs that participated were very happy with the results achieved.

Tools. We experienced that participants used a variety of tools to solve the problems as part of the datathons. Some used statistics focused tools such as R, SPSS, and MATLAB. Others used some visualization tools such as Tableau and Excel while participants who were developers used toolkits like D3 to develop visualizations and JavaScript UI frameworks to build dashboards. As part of the datathons we helped participants to learn some of these tools. To aid with tool learning we had break off groups run some mini tutorials to help others get up to speed with the tools.

Community Engagement. It was critical for the success of our datathons to partner with not-for-profit SGOs. Without these organizations participants would not have experienced real-world data problems when working with large and complex data sets. By working with these SGOs we had members from these organizations who were onsite during the datathon to help participants with all the specific questions they had about the data. This was also a profound effect for the members of these organizations who got new insights into how data scientists work with their data and the kinds of techniques they use in order to address the answers to the questions they seek.

Logistics and Planning. Particularly when working with SGOs, we found it very helpful a small group of data experts vet the data organization and documentation as well as the planned questions and tasks for the groups to ensure everything was on track. We began the majority of advertising and recruiting notices a month in advance through newsletters, posters, mailing lists, and so forth. Where possible we posted a reminder the week of the event. We found the best way to encourage participation was to have a recruitment event a couple of weeks prior to introduce the datathon. Having an introductory social evening the night before the actual event helped to set the stage of the datathons. During this introductory event the problems and objectives of the datathon were laid out to all participants which gave a useful overview on what needed accomplishing. This was a time for networking, allowing participants to start learning about one another and begin considering what they will do during the datathon. These events also provided participants the opportunity to ask all the questions they wanted to know before the datathon actually happened and for them to see what role they could play in making the datathon a success. The actual day of the event started with a short invigorating session to get the participants up to speed and then immediately working in the groups. We had checkins at the end of the day where teams reported what they had been working on. On the final morning we had all teams come back and give a formal presentation to the rest of the participants to demonstrate what outcomes they had achieved, and providing a cap-stone to the weekend. During the event it is important to have breaks for food. Given that people were volunteering their time, we found it more fitting to find a sponsor willing to donate some money towards food rather than having a user pay system. Participants felt they were more valued if there was someone else providing food.

Venue. We hosted our datathons in two locations; one in the department of computer science and the other in the library. From our feedback having the right venue makes the event more effective. If the room is not appealing or supportive of working in groups participants are less motivated to work. We found that it is useful to have a main room where everyone is welcome to hang out, network, and work together. This room was used for the introductory and presentation sessions. The room was configurable with chairs, tables, and several whiteboards for note-taking and planning. It was important that there sufficient power outlets and extension cables for participants to plug their equipment into. Given the nature of the datathon we found that groups needed space to have discussions, so we set up a number of break out rooms where smaller groups of people could work more closely together. We decided to use an adjoining room that had a kitchen for the food room where participants were freely available to come and go as they wanted. This allowed for a smooth transition from working on the datathon to some down time to take a break.

Media. We had a number of media agencies interested in the datathons which helped raise the profiles of some of the SGOs. It is important to get a representative of the group to speak and liaise with the media to make sure the right messages are being delivered about the importance of learning data science and analytical skills.

Things to Avoid. We that felt unlike many hackathons that it was best not to go all night; by making these events more compatible with travel times and family commitments we believe we were able to attract more diverse and experienced participants. We found that it was best to not group all technical people into one team and instead spread specialists out so that others can learn from their expertise. Rather than prescribe what participants worked on during the datathon we found it more effective for participants to have the freedom to work on what they wanted to. Lastly, for one of the early datathons we had a problem with all the data being on one server and experienced a single point of failure problem. Hence we recommend providing different aspects of the data from different servers as well as using cloud services such as DropBox when possible.

6. CONCLUSIONS

As data continues to grow within our lives, businesses, organizations, and governments there is a greater need to make sense of all the data. With this increase in data there is a need for people to learn and up-skill themselves with key data science and analytics techniques and tools to make better informed decisions. Universities are beginning to address this challenge by setting up new courses and degrees to support the new area of data science and analytics. We agree with universities diversifying their programs, and we encourage students and those who want to up-skill themselves to participate in data hackathons to get hands on experience with real-world data problems. In this paper we reported our experience at hosting four datathons that involved students and members from the community coming together to solve challenging problems with publicly open data and data from not-for-profit organizations. Our reported experience will help other academics and community groups who also wish to host datathons to promote data science.

Acknowledgments

Thanks to Data For Good Calgary (and Geoff Zakaib) for co-organizing the datathon. Many thanks to Sustainable Alberta Association and the Calgary Distress Center for their participation. This research was partially funded by Mitacs and supported by Project VALCRI, European Commission Grant FP7-IP-608142.

7. REFERENCES

[1] T. Al-towaitee. Distress center datadata technical summary. Data for Good Calgary Meetup Website, August 2015. http://goo.gl/7ciZnH.

[2] P. Anderson, J. Bowring, R. McCauley, G. Pothering, and C. Starr. An undergraduate degree in data science: Curriculum and a decade of implementation experience. In *SIGCSE*, pages 145–150. ACM, 2014.

[3] C. Anslow, B. Jackel, K. Mehmood, P. Fairie, A. D'Souza, M. Underwood, and K. Teh. CommuterVis: Towards understanding commuter behaviour. In *VIS Workshop on Business Visualization*. IEEE, 2014.

[4] W. Cleveland. Data science: An action plan for expanding the technical areas of the field of statistics. *ISI Review*, 69:21–26, 2001.

[5] T. Davenport and D. Patil. Data scientist: The sexiest job of the 21st century. Harvard Business Review, October 2012. https://hbr.org/2012/10/data-scientist-the-sexiest-job-of-the-21st-century/.

[6] V. Dhar. Data science and prediction. *Commun. ACM*, 56(12):64–73, Dec. 2013.

[7] Y. Gil. Teaching parallelism without programming: A data science curriculum for non-cs students. In *Workshop on Education for High-Performance Computing (EduHPC)*, pages 42–48. IEEE, 2014.

[8] B. Howe, M. Franklin, J. Freire, J. Frew, T. Kraska, and R. Ramakrishnan. Should we all be teaching "intro to data science" instead of "intro to databases"? In *SIGMOD*, pages 917–918. ACM, 2014.

[9] S. Kumar. Designing a graduate program in information security and analytics: Masters program in information security and analytics (MISA). In *SIGITE*, pages 141–146. ACM, 2014.

[10] A. Mahadev and K. Wurst. Developing concentrations in big data analytics and software development at a small liberal arts university. *J. Comp. Sci. Coll.*, 30(3):92–98, Jan. 2015.

[11] J. Manyika, M. Chui, B. Brown, J. Bughin, R. Dobbs, C. Roxburgh, and A. Hung Byers. Big data: The next frontier for innovation, competition, and productivity. McKinsey Global Institute, May 2011. http://www.mckinsey.com/insights/business_technology/big_data_the_next_frontier_for_innovation.

[12] T. Menzies, E. Kocaguneli, F. Peters, B. Turhan, and L. Minku. Data science for software engineering. In *ICSE*, pages 1484–1486. IEEE/ACM, 2013.

[13] M. Modjeski. Data for Good and Calgary Distress Centre to turn raw information into efficiencies. Metro Calgary, May 2015. http://goo.gl/OhoY23.

[14] C. Plaue and L. Cook. Data journalism: Lessons learned while designing an interdisciplinary service course. In *SIGCSE*, pages 126–131. ACM, 2015.

[15] R. Schutt and C. O'Neil. *Doing Data Science: Straight Talk from the Frontline*. O'Reilly Media, Inc., 2013.

[16] S. Seyffarth. Behind the scenes of a datathon! Cybera Tech Radar Blog, June 2015. http://goo.gl/m3QcMn.

[17] D. Sullivan. A data-centric introduction to computer science for non-majors. In *SIGCSE*, pages 71–76. ACM, 2013.

[18] H. Topi. Data science and information systems: Relationship of love or hate? *ACM Inroads*, 6(1):26–27, Feb. 2015.

[19] V. Varvel, E. Bammerlin, and C. Palmer. Education for data professionals: A study of current courses and programs. In *iConference*, pages 527–529. ACM, 2012.

[20] G. Zheeng, C. Zhang, and L. Li. Bringing business intelligence to healthcare informatics curriculum: A preliminary investigation. In *SIGCSE*, pages 205–210. ACM, 2014.

Teaching "Lawfulness" With Kodu

David S. Touretzky
Computer Science Dept.
Carnegie Mellon University
Pittsburgh, PA 15213
dst@cs.cmu.edu

Christina Gardner-McCune
Dept. of Computer & Info.
Science & Engineering
University of Florida
Gainesville, FL 32611
gmccune@ufl.edu

Ashish Aggarwal
Dept. of Computer & Info.
Science & Engineering
University of Florida
Gainesville, FL 32611
ashishjuit@ufl.edu

ABSTRACT

This paper introduces reasoning about lawful behavior as an important computational thinking skill and provides examples from a novel introductory programming curriculum using Microsoft's Kodu Game Lab. We present an analysis of assessment data showing that rising 5th and 6th graders can understand the lawfulness of Kodu programs. We also discuss some misconceptions students may develop about Kodu, their causes, and potential remedies.

CCS Concepts

•Social and professional topics → Model curricula; K-12 education; *Computational thinking;*

Keywords

Kodu Game Lab; formal reasoning; programming idioms

1. INTRODUCTION

We believe that mastery of *lawfulness* is an important but often overlooked computational thinking skill. In computing, formal laws (or rules) govern how expressions are evaluated, actions are sequenced, and state is updated. Often these rules deal with low level processes: languages such as Python or Java are only a bit more abstract than assembly language. Children's languages such as Scratch and Alice remove some sources of difficulty by providing a drag-and-drop GUI editor to prevent syntax errors, and a queryable graphics canvas that makes some program state readily apparent. But these environments provide few tools for helping children think about state. Likewise, tutorials for beginning Scratch and Alice programmers don't try to teach students to reason formally about the state changes they observe.

While a graphics canvas is somewhat useful for reasoning about state, with no physics and no intrinsic interactions among objects, nothing happens on Scratch's 2D or Alice's 3D canvas unless the programmer makes it happen. Interesting programs therefore require tedious detail that makes reasoning about them more difficult. Thus, graphics primitives alone are not as abstract or powerful as we would like for beginning programmers.

For children to demonstrate mastery of "lawfulness" in a computational framework they should be able to (1) state the laws, (2) explain program behavior by referencing the laws, and (3) apply the laws to predict future behavior from current state. Fortunately there is wide lattitude in what these laws can be. They don't have to describe low level primitives as in Python or Java, or – notwithstanding the graphics canvas – Scratch or Alice. For example, a set of objects can be referenced by specifying a pattern that they match rather than collecting and maintaining them in a subscripted data structure. To see what higher level laws look like, we will examine Microsoft's Kodu Game Lab [1] and its underlying computational principles.

Kodu worlds are three-dimensional environments with fluidly articulated characters. These characters are not merely graphics objects: they are semi-autonomous robots that perceive and act on the contents of a dynamically changing world. There is real physics, including gravity, inertia, friction, elastic collisions, complex lighting, wind, water, and waves. Actions in Kodu have built-in sound effects, collisions are always noisy, and when a character isn't doing anything else, it mumbles and fidgets amusingly. A handful of lines of Kodu code can produce highly engaging behaviors. Research presented in this paper will show that given the right tools, children are able to reason about these behaviors and demonstrate an appreciation of their lawfulness.

In the following sections we discuss various aspects of Kodu and four conceptual tools we employed to help children recognize "lawfulness". We then analyze assessment data from 23 rising 5th and 6th graders who attended a five session Kodu Camp. Finally, we identify two important misconceptions about Kodu rules, and their likely causes.

2. KODU SYNTAX

Kodu syntax is trivially simple. Each character has its own program, which is a set of up to 12 numbered pages. A page is an ordered list of rules. A rule consists of a WHEN phrase followed by a DO phrase, either of which can be empty. A non-empty phrase begins with a predicate or action tile and continues with zero or more argument/modifier tiles. These can appear in any order with a few exceptions.[1]

[1]The "random" tile takes distinct left and right arguments. And in operations involving scores, the first tile after the verb is required to be a score color and is treated specially. This is a recent change in Kodu syntax made in June 2015.

SIGCSE '16, March 2–5, 2016, Memphis, TN, USA.

DOI: http://dx.doi.org/10.1145/2839509.2844652

Finally, a rule's indentation level must be between 0 and one more than the indentation of the immediately preceding rule. That's it!

Kodu's GUI editor uses context-senstive menu selection rather than the drag-and-drop interface with fixed menus common in other visual languages. The menus only present options that are both syntactically and semantically legal at that point in the rule.

Although Kodu users can't make syntactic errors, it's still useful for them to think about syntax because it's an illustration of lawfulness. But a formal syntactic description like the one above is not easily digested by children. Touretzky created a set of plastic tile manipulatives whose colors and shapes reflect Kodu's syntactic constraints [6], as in Figure 1. The WHEN tiles are green, DO tiles are blue, and indentation levels are reified as yellow tiles.

Figure 1: Kodu tile manipulatives.

During a Kodu session with second graders, a child tried to use the manipulatives to make the improper rule "WHEN see apple DO eat apple", but the final tile wouldn't fit because the connector didn't match. Another child spontaneously corrected him by suggesting the "it" tile, which does fit, yielding the syntactically correct rule "WHEN see apple DO eat it" [6].

3. PRINCIPLES OF KODU COMPUTATION

Kodu's power comes in part from providing higher level primitives such as pattern matching — the mechanism of Kodu perception — and rich actions, such as giving a held object to another character with automatically generated motion and sound effects. Control structure is more subtle than in conventional languages because there is only one statement type: the conditional rule. Additional control comes from other sources: rule dependency relationships expressed through indentation, an arbitration scheme that mediates conflicting actions, an implicit variable binding mechanism with "it" and "me" tiles, and a "perform action once" modifier. There is no explicit iteration. Instead, all the rules on the currently active page run repeatedly, 50-100 times per second, until the character switches to a different page.

To teach students to reason about lawful behavior in Kodu, Touretzky formulated a set of "principles of Kodu computation" [5]. These principles (or laws) can either be taught explicitly or worked out by the children themselves through guided discovery. To illustrate the latter, consider the first problem posed in many Kodu tutorials: eating a bunch of apples scattered over a field. The solution comprises a single two-rule idiom, Pursue and Consume, discussed in section 4. Once they've learned the idiom and run the solution, children are asked how the kodu character chooses which apple to pursue first. They are encouraged to move the kodu and/or the apples and rerun the program. They quickly discover that the kodu always goes to the closest apple. This is the first principle. It is reinforced by having students restate it in written exercises, and by requiring them to apply it to predict the paths characters will take to consume various collections of objects. Formally, the first principle is "a rule always selects the closest matching object."

The second principle is that perceptual predicates like "see" or "bump" work by pattern matching, with additional tiles further constraining the match. So "see" matches any object other than the character itself; "see apple" matches apples; "see red" matches red things; and "see red apple" matches red apples, as does "see apple red".

The third principle is that an indented rule is only eligible to run if the parent rule is eligible and the parent's WHEN part is true. This principle, which produces block structure, is crucial for many Kodu idioms such as Do Two Things.

The fourth principle students learn is that when two rules specify conflicting actions, the earlier (lower numbered) rule wins. This principle makes the Default Value idiom possible.

These four are the most important principles, but there are many more, reflecting the richness of the language. The current list has more than 30. Together they capture many of the fine points of Kodu semantics. An example of a more subtle principle is: a character cannot "see" the object it is holding, but it can see objects held by others. (The "got" tile can be used in place of "see" to examine a held object.) Another more advanced principle is: "timers don't nest".

4. A KODU IDIOM CATALOG

Lawfulness is one interesting aspect of computation; another is the patterns in which primitives frequently combine. These patterns, or *idioms*, are a means of achieving higher level goals. Reasoning in terms of idioms instead of the component primitives is an example of abstraction, another important ingredient in computational thinking [8].

Touretzky created a catalog of Kodu idioms that students can draw upon [5]. They are depicted on a ring of flash cards (inspired by the Scratch Cards of Natalie Rusk [2]), and were given to each student at the start of every session. Each idiom has a name, a schematic illustration, sample code, and usage notes. Students were taught these idioms explicitly, and drilled on them in various ways. For example, they were asked to apply the idiom in a new situation. Or they were shown novel code fragments and asked to explain why each one does or does not qualify as an example of the idiom. Table 1 lists a few of these idioms.

The most basic idiom, which every Kodu student encounters when confronting a field of apples, is Pursue and Consume. Figure 2 shows the flash card. A pursue rule involves motion toward an object. A consume rule makes an object non-pursuable, either by destroying it as "eat" does, or by changing it to no longer match the perceptual pattern of the pursue rule. Kodu's repetitive execution of all the rules on a page takes care of the rest.

Students develop a more abstract understanding of Pursue

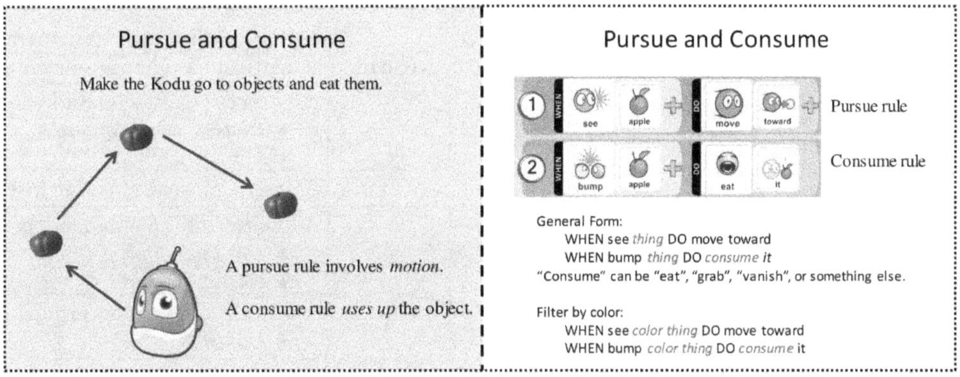

Figure 2: The Pursue and Consume idiom on a flash card.

Table 1: Some common Kodu idioms.

Name	Example
Pursue and Consume	Eat all the apples
Do Two Things	Eat an apple + play coin sound
Count Actions	Count the apples while eating
Default Value	Turn red if see octopus, else blue
Follow the Yellow Brick Road	Follow a path and react upon reaching the end
Let Me Drive	Steer character with joystick
Show Page As Color	Make a character's color indicate its current page
Parting Shot	Final action when killed or eaten

and Consume by exploring variants of the apple eating task. In one world they are asked to eat stars instead of apples. In another they are asked to grab (poisonous) blue apples instead of eating them; grabbing them makes them shrink and disappear. In yet another they pursue white or black huts and paint them blue, demonstrating that "consume" doesn't necessarily mean "remove".

An idiom is not just a code template; it's a rich semantic context in which to explore how primitives interact to achieve a result. We deepen students' understanding by asking them to give English definitions for "pursue" (to chase, or to proceed along a path) and "consume" (to eat or use up), and by having them predict the effects of altering parts of the idiom. For example, replacing "eat" with "boom" (explode) is fine, but replacing it with a non-consuming action such as playing a sound leaves the kodu stuck at the first object it pursued. A later exercise asks students for the opposite of pursue ("flee"), and then has them search for a movement action that will let the kodu flee an adversary. (Answer: "move away" instead of "move toward").

5. STATE MACHINES

State machines are among the most fundamental and ubiquitous concepts in computer science. They appear in digital logic design, formal languages, networking protocols, game programming, robot programming, and more. Learning to reason about state machines profoundly changes the way a person thinks about technology, from vending machines and traffic lights to smartphones and the Internet.

Kodu was inspired by behavior-based robotics [1] and is a natural state machine language. Each page functions as a state, with "switch to page" actions providing the transitions [3]. Some actual robot programming frameworks directly support state machines, but in conventional languages it falls to the programmer to implement them using a combination of conditionals and variables.

Kodu states are more complex than in most state machine languages because pages contain multiple conditional rules, all of which are embedded in an implicit while loop [7]. So it takes some effort to construct simple problems where multiple states are the most natural solution. One example is a world with red apples to be eaten and blue ones to be grabbed. With a single page and one "pursue apples" rule, the kodu will go to the closest apple no matter the color. With separate red and blue pursue rules, the rule ordering principle will cause the kodu to eat all the red apples first, before grabbing any blue ones, or vice versa. But if we want the kodu to alternate between red and blue apples, we must put the two pursue rules and their associated consume rules on separate pages and switch back and forth between them.[2]

To scaffold students' reasoning about state machines, they are taught the standard graphical notation using labeled nodes and arcs, and they practice mapping between Kodu code and state machine graphs. They are also shown how to use the graphs to reason about program behavior. For example, given the state machine in Figure 3, will the kodu ever eat another apple after grabbing a soccer ball?

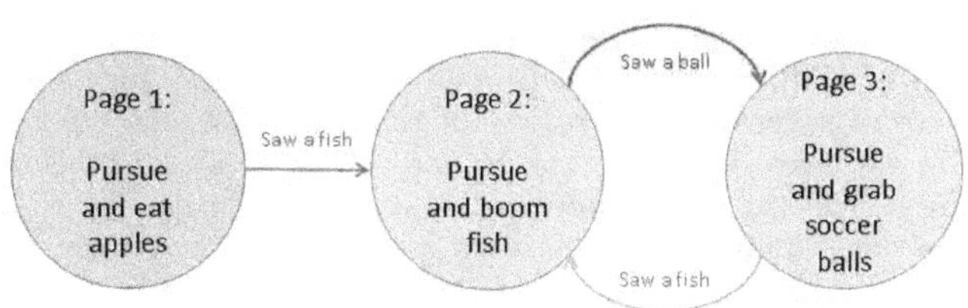

Figure 3: State machine reasoning problem.

Students use the Show Page As Color idiom to trace execution by having the kodu change its body color to indicate the current page. They also hand simulate a state machine, with one student playing the role of the kodu, to reinforce their understanding of page switching.

[2]We could instead use a variable to keep track of what color to pursue next, but that would just be implementing a state machine by hand, with more complicated rules.

6. METHODS

6.1 Participants

Twenty-three students participated in one of two week-long summer camps. Participants were recruited via emails to parents or teachers from the university's outreach office. There were 6 females and 17 males. The racial/ethnic breakdown was 14 White, 4 Asian/Indian, 1 Latino, 1 Multi-racial, and 1 Native American. All were rising 5th or 6th graders. 21 students completed the entire camp; 1 boy in each camp missed the last day.

4 out of 23 students indicated that they had not programmed prior to the Kodu Camp. 12 out of 23 students had participated in 2 or more computing programs, with 5 having participated in 5+ computing programs. Students who had programming experience reported a wide variety of experience types, but only one had worked with Kodu before. Over half of the students had used Scratch (n=12); none had used Alice; 9 had used Minecraft; 9 had participated in Hour of Code; and 5 had done robotics. Students also reported some experience in Python (n=7) and HTML and Javascript (n=4).

6.2 Structure of the Curriculum

The curriculum consisted of the first five modules and half of the 6th module described in Table 2. On most days students completed roughly the second half of one module and the first half of the next one. Each module focused on one or two idioms or computational principles, illustrated with a collection of pre-made worlds that presented some sort of game or challenge. With the first world the instructor introduced the topic of the module, using the flash cards and/or tiles as appropriate, and took the students through the solution. In the second world students were asked to apply the idea in a slightly different context on their own. A third world might be used to introduce supplementary material. Students then completed a paper assessment, and after handing in their pages, the instructor presented the correct answers. Students were then given a challenge world where they were asked to implement a variant of the idiom or key concept, or apply it to a slightly more complex case. Finally, each day ended with 30-45 minutes of free exploration where students could make their own worlds or play in the worlds they'd previously written.

The assessments contained a combination of fill in the blank, multiple choice, and open ended items. Questions were of several types: review of terms ("What new idiom did you learn today?"); recognition of rule types ("Is this a pursue rule or a consume rule?"); synthesis of rules ("Write the rules to pursue and consume green fish."); recognition of idioms ("Are the rules below an example of Default Value?"); and mental simulation ("Given the rules below, in what order will the kodu eat these apples?", or "What will happen if this rule's indentation is removed?").

6.3 Interactivity and Gamification

All the worlds require students to program the kodu to solve a problem autonomously. Initially students would run the world and passively observe the result. However, several taught themselves the Let Me Drive idiom and chose to guide the kodu with the game controller. This was fun but didn't demonstrate mastery of the concepts they were supposed to be learning. For the second camp, we compromised by introducing an additional character in some worlds that students could control while the main character solved the problem. In the Apple1X world, for example, while the kodu pursued and ate the apples, there was a flying fish that students were taught to make drivable. The flying fish could help the kodu by pushing apples toward it, or harrass it by bumping it or knocking apples away. It could even maneuver the apples to fall into a pit, making them unreachable by the kodu. The kodu "won" if it managed to eat 4 of the 5 apples; the flying fish "won" if it got 2 apples into the pit before time ran out. Gamification increased student engagement, seemingly without compromising learning goals.

Table 2: Kodu curriculum modules.

Module	Content (• *idioms in italics*)
1	Characters, objects, and rules • *Pursue and Consume* • *Let Me Drive*
2	Pattern matching: color filters
3	Indentation (rule dependency); Scores • *Do Two Things* • *Count Actions*
4	Conflict and rule ordering • *Default Value*
5	State machines • *Show Page As Color*
6	Paths • *Follow the Yellow Brick Road*

6.4 Data Analysis Procedure

To investigate students' understanding of the material, we analyzed their responses on the paper assessments. In Phase 1 we marked each response as correct or incorrect, and then used a grounded theory approach [4] to find trends and themes underlying the incorrect responses. Incorrect answers were coded and grouped by similarity, and each coded group was given a descriptive label.

In Phase 2 we further categorized incorrect responses based on possible causes of error: (1) confusing wording or structure of the question, (2) lack of understanding of a well-formulated question, (3) a misconception about Kodu computation, or (4) negative transfer from a previous activity or question. Questions that we believe had confusing wording or structure were excluded from further analysis. Responses that were left blank, or that did not properly address the question, were categorized as "lack of understanding". Responses were categorized as "misconceptions" when we found multiple instances of the incorrect answer across both camps, and when a plausible reason for the incorrect response could be identified.

A legitimate misconception should be recognizable by a consistent pattern of wrong answers across questions. In Phase 3 we assembled the evidence in support of each hypothesized misconception. Due to space limitations, we will focus here mainly on misconceptions about rule ordering.

7. FINDINGS

7.1 Evidence of Student Learning

Students demonstrated their understanding of lawfulness

by predicting the behavior of Kodu characters, applying idioms, and reasoning about rules. For example, in questions measuring students' knowledge of Kodu's matching behavior (Modules 1 and 3), 82% (n = 19) and 86% (n = 20) of students correctly indicated that the kodu always went to the closest apple. Similarly, in Modules 1 and 2, 86% (n = 20)and 91% (n = 21) of students correctly applied the Pursue and Consume idiom to new situations. In Module 3, 73% (n = 17) of students correctly identified Pursue and Consume and Count Actions in a novel code snippet. Prior programming experience was not a predictor of correct answers in assessments in any of Modules 1–4.

Predicting future behavior requires mentally simulating state changes, which all the students were able to do. In Module 1 they were shown a diagram of a kodu and five red apples (similar in format to Figure 4, top) and asked to label the apples with numbers to indicate the order in which the kodu would eat them. 91% (n = 21) got it right.

7.2 Misconceptions About Rule Ordering

Many students had difficulty mastering rule ordering in Kodu. The rules on a page run repeatedly; WHEN parts are evaluated in parallel and DO parts are performed sequentially if the WHEN part was true. If there are no conflicting actions, rule ordering is irrelevant. We tell students this explicitly. On the other hand, if rules do have conflicting actions, the earlier (lower numbered) rule prevails. So order does matter, but the rules do not constitute a sequential procedure. Several factors work against students assimilating this knowledge, discussed below.

```
Q2:  [1] WHEN see apple DO move toward
     [2] WHEN bump apple DO eat it

Q3:  [1] WHEN see red apple DO move toward
     [2] WHEN see blue apple DO move toward
     [3] WHEN bump apple DO eat it

Q4:  [1] WHEN bump apple DO eat it
     [2] WHEN see blue apple DO move toward
     [3] WHEN see red apple DO move toward
```

Figure 4: Module 4 rule ordering questions (presented to the students as tile sequences, not text).

Two pursue rules. Students did better on questions that required them to apply the rule ordering principle to an example program than on questions that discussed rule ordering in the abstract. Given the example programs in Figure 4, students were asked to label each apple with a number 1-4 to show the order in which it would be eaten. With the color-agnostic pursue rule (Q2), 78% (n = 18) correctly applied the "closest match" principle. With a slight a decrease in performance, this response rate is consistent with prior demonstration of ability to mentally simulate the Pursue and Consume rule. Correct responses resulted in a 1-2-3-4 (red, blue, blue, red) labeling pattern, reading left to right. Of the five wrong answers, two completely misunderstood the question, and three responded 1-2-4-3, which produced an alternating red/blue pattern even though the rule didn't mention color. The alternating red/blue pattern might be explained by misjudging the distances between the second apple and the third and fourth, which is consistent with a simple elliptical path from the kodu's initial position through all the apples.

With separate red and blue pursue rules in Q3 and Q4, 70% (n = 16) correctly predicted a 1-4-3-2 pattern (red, red, blue, blue) in Q3. When the rule order was reversed in Q4, the same 16 correctly predicted 4-1-2-3 (blue, blue, red, red), and were not confused by the consume rule preceding the pursue rules. Of the 7 students who answered incorrectly, the same two students who misunderstood Q2 misunderstood Q3 and Q4. Of the remaining 5 students who answered incorrectly, two students thought the pursue rules would alternate in both questions based on the rule order (Q3: 1-2-4-3 or red, blue, red, blue, and Q4: blue, red, blue, red). When there are two pursue rules, thinking of a page of rules as a sequential procedure is consistent with alternating between red and blue apples. These students had not alternated on Q2; they were among the majority who correctly applied "closest match".

Two students followed a "closest object" principle and ignored the color filters in Q3 and Q4, resulting in the same answer as Q2. One student apparently thought the rules would interfere with each other, resulting in the kodu either eating only the first red apple and stopping (Q3) or eating no apples (Q4).

None of the three students whose answers alternated with the single pursue rule in Q2 alternated on Q3 or Q4. Two of them actually got both Q3 and Q4 correct. The third used "closest object" for both. This suggests that their answers on Q2 may not have been deliberate alternation.

Abstract reasoning about rule ordering. When asked which of the two idioms Pursue and Consume and Default Value relied on rule ordering, only 34% (n = 8) answered correctly that only Default Value did, 12 thought that both did, 1 said neither did, and 2 said only Pursue and Consume did. When asked why rule ordering matters for some idioms and not others, only 5 wrote answers that had some flavor of correctness; 3 wrote answers that weren't obviously wrong but didn't mention rule priority or conflicting actions; 12 gave answers that were either irrelevant or incoherent; and 3 indicated they thought rules executed sequentially, e.g., "you need to pursue for rule 1 and consume for rule 2".

Pages as sequential procedures. Even after students had been taught about the rule cycle in module 3 (and had run a program that repeatedly increments a score, watching the value run up at a blistering rate), many had trouble overcoming the tendency to view a page of rules as a sequential procedure. There are several reasons for this.

First, the Kodu rule editor numbers the rules, giving them the appearance of sequential steps. These numbers serve no purpose in the interpreter: they are there solely as an aid to discussion. And it's indeed convenient to refer to rules by number. But sequential numbering wrongly suggests sequential execution.

A second, compounding factor is that our example programs order the rules in a logical way. Since you cannot consume something until you've pursued it, "pursue" comes first in the idiom name, on the flash card, and in sample code. We find that demonstrating that the behavior is the same when the rules are reversed may not suffice to overcome students' bias toward sequentiality.

Third, movement is continuous. When executing the idiom a character will perform a great many pursue steps (50-100 per second) before the consume step, but to a student who does not yet understand the Kodu rule cycle, it looks as if the character performed a single pursue step several seconds in duration, followed by a shorter consume step: a sequential procedure. This false sequentiality becomes apparent when there are multiple pursue rules, because they don't take turns as some students assumed. The second rule can only take effect when the first rule no longer finds something to pursue.

7.3 Indentation and Rule Dependency

In module 3 students used the Do Two Things idiom to make the kodu play a sound when it bumped and ate an apple (rules shown in Figure 1). In a second world they used the related Count Actions idiom to count how many red hearts the kodu ate. In both cases, students were prompted to remove the indentation of the play or count rule and observe that the kodu played the sound continuously, or the score ran up continuously at a high rate.

What we wanted students to understand was that indenting a rule makes it dependent on the parent rule having a true WHEN part. But what we saw from interactions with some students is that they may view indentation simply as a way to block unwanted behavior, without fully comprehending the mechanism.

Given the rules below, students were asked when the kodu would play the coin sound:

```
Q5:    [1] WHEN see ball DO move toward
         → [2] WHEN DO play coin
       [3] WHEN bump ball DO eat it
```

18 out of 23 correctly answered "when it sees a ball" or "when it moves toward the ball". Three gave incoherent or vague responses. And two said "when it bumps the ball", which suggested they may have attached the indented rule to the rule below instead of the rule above, as in [6]. An alternative explanation is that they weren't reasoning about rule dependency at all, and this was an example of negative transfer.

7.4 Negative Transfer From Past Experience

One type of evidence for mastery is a student successfully applying what they've learned to novel, atypical situations. This requires strict application of computational lawsrather than reasoning by analogy to earlier situations. In several instances where students gave incorrect answers, they appear to have made this type of mistake.

In the indentation example Q5 cited above, the coin sound plays for as long as the kodu sees a ball. But in all the examples students had seen of Do Two Things or its special case Count Actions, the additional action had been indented under a "WHEN bump ... DO eat it" rule whose action negates the condtion. This may have led two students looking at Q5 to expect that the coin sound would play once, when the ball was bumped and eaten, with indentation preventing unwanted repetition.

Errors resulting from stereotyped reasoning might be prevented by more exposure to atypical cases. For example, we could have a world where Do Two Things implemented a persistent action as in Q5 rather than a transitory one, illustrating that indentation does not prevent repetition.

A similar negative transfer situation arose with the state machine problem in Figure 3. In all the examples students had seen, each state had some sort of goal, such as to pursue and consume an object, and a transition occurred when the goal was satisfied. But in Figure 3, states pursue their respective goals repeatedly, and a transition is triggered by the appearance of a goal object for another state. When asked to turn this diagram into rules, some students mistakenly attached the transition rule to the consume rule rather than having it look for the other type of object.

8. CONCLUSIONS

The power and simplicity of Kodu facilitate teaching students to reason formally about program behavior. We described a novel curriculum that fosters an appreciation of lawfulness through a combination of tile manipulatives, explicit computational principles, named idioms, and state machine formalism. Students demonstrated an understanding of lawfulness in concrete situations, but did less well on more abstract questions.

Two potential misconceptions were identified that are unique to Kodu's style of computation, one concerning rule ordering, and the other rule dependency (indentation). Future designers of Kodu-based curricula will want to check for these misconceptions when gauging student understanding.

Acknowledgments

Funded by a gift from Microsoft Research. Thanks to Brooke Ley, Swati Priyam, and Shweta Venkateswaran, who served as TAs for the Kodu camps.

9. REFERENCES

[1] M. B. MacLaurin. The design of Kodu: A tiny visual programming language for children on the Xbox 360. In *Proceedings of POPL '11)*, pages 241–246, 2011.

[2] N. Rusk. Scratch cards. Available at <https://scratch.mit.edu/help/cards>, 2009.

[3] K. Stolee and T. Fristoe. Expressing computer science concepts through Kodu Game Lab. In *Proceedings of SIGCSE'11*, pages 99–104, 2011.

[4] A. Strauss and N. Corbin. *Basics of Qualitative Research: Techniques and Procedures for Developing Grounded Theory.* Sage, Thousand Oaks, CA, 1998. 2nd ed.

[5] D. S. Touretzky. Kodu resources page, 2014. Available at <http://www.cs.cmu.edu/~dst/Kodu>.

[6] D. S. Touretzky. Teaching Kodu with physical manipulatives. *ACM Inroads*, 5(4):44–51, 2014.

[7] D. S. Touretzky, D. Marghitu, S. Ludi, D. Bernstein, and L. Ni. Accelerating K-12 computational thinking using scaffolding, staging, and abstraction. In *Proceedings of SIGCSE'13*, pages 609–614, 2013.

[8] J. M. Wing. Computational thinking and thinking about computing. *Philos Trans A Math Phys Eng Sci*, 366(1881):3717–3725, 2008.

Towards a Common Framework for Evaluating Computing Outreach Activities

Adrienne Decker
Rochester Institute of Technology
2145 Golisano Hall
Rochester, NY 14623 USA
01-585-475-4653
adrienne.decker@rit.edu

Monica M. McGill
Bradley University
1501 W. Bradley Ave
Peoria, IL 61625 USA
01-309-677-4148
mmcgill@bradley.edu

Amber Settle
DePaul University
243 S. Wabash Ave
Chicago, IL 60604 USA
01-312-362-5324
asettle@cdm.depaul.edu

ABSTRACT

In the past six years, dozens of conference papers and journal articles have been presented in Association of Computing Machinery (ACM) and Institute of Electrical and Electronics Engineers (IEEE) educational forums concerning computing outreach activities. Nearly half of these (47.5%) appeared in SIGCSE venues. In this study, we used the free-form question "What type of data has been collected in formal, peer-reviewed research that has been conducted on computing outreach activities in recent years?" as a basis for a systematic literature review in these venues from 2009-2015. During the analysis of the articles, it was discovered that a majority of efforts focused on middle school and high school students, a majority of the reported events took place in the United States, and almost half had a goal of increasing gender diversity in computing. This paper summarizes the information about the studies, including their data collection techniques and the data that was collected. We also present a list of recommended practices for data collection, methodologies, and reporting for educational researchers engaged in these activities in an effort to provide comparative data and allow us as a community to more scientifically understand the impact that these activities are having on the participants.

Keywords

Outreach; Underrepresented groups in computing; Effectiveness; Literature Review

1. INTRODUCTION

At the 2015 Association of Computing Machinery (ACM) International Computing Education Research (ICER) conference, Jim Spohrer, the keynote speaker from IBM Global University Programs, highlighted the current shortage of technology workers and emphasized the exponential growth of this shortage that they anticipate in the next 10 to 40 years [18]. This has become a critical concern within the U.S., with the Gartner group and various Fortune 50 companies echoing the same sentiments [5].

While some say these concerns are driven by industry's desire to increase limits on H1-B visas that allow companies to hire foreign workers at significantly lower salaries, there are factors that still warrant consideration. The U.S. Department of Labor predicts a 17.7% increase in growth for computer occupations from 2012 to 2022. This is led by information security analysts (36.5%), computer system analysts (24.5%), and application software developers (22.8%), resulting in a need for 1,240,100 additional workers [3, 4].

At the same time, policy and decision makers have concluded that there is a lack of diversity within the field of computing and that this lack of diversity contributes to product performance challenges [12]. Much research has been conducted on this topic and industry profits of diverse teams have proven that diversity has an important role in creating better products [1, 13, 17].

In consideration of the above, industry and the government alike have poured millions of dollars of resources into outreach programs to address this issue [7, 11]. One primary goal has been to recruit and retain more students into the computing discipline through various outreach activities, with some efforts focusing primarily on the goal of broadening the participation of women and minorities [12]. Various outreach activities have been produced by academics and industry and have been primarily focused on students from Kindergarten through High School, with several of these programs (Code.org, Black Girls CODE, Girls Who Code, etc.) garnering national media attention [2, 16, 19].

But are these programs effective in recruiting and/or retaining students into studying computing? And are these programs effective in broadening the participation of women and minorities? Or simply, in industry terms, what is the return on investment and who is measuring the success of these activities?

Though industry may be measuring their effectiveness internally, the questions are valid and necessary to pose not only from a purely academic perspective, but also from the perspective of acknowledging and addressing the critical concerns voiced by government and by industry. Turning to reliable research available in computing education that reports on computing activities, the question becomes more basic: What data is reported and what types of successes do previous activities report?

To address these questions, we conducted a systematic literature review to determine what has been reported about the impact of computing outreach programs. After our initial experience with this data, we believed that more needed to be done to determine the impact of outreach activities on participant's choice of major and started towards that process [9].

However, the results of the literature review bear further discussion here. We conclude that a concerted effort must be made to collect data that can be compared and measured both in the long- and short-term and provide a framework for improving the quality of these studies. Therefore, the value of this study is two-fold and will be of

SIGCSE '16, March 02-05, 2016, Memphis, TN, USA

DOI: http://dx.doi.org/10.1145/2839509.2844567

interest to policy makers, those who invest time and resources in outreach activities, and researchers whose interests lie in broadening participation specifically or recruitment and retention in general.

2. METHODOLOGY

We undertook a systematic literature review to identify, evaluate, select, and synthesize results of high quality research involving computing outreach programs. To begin this initiative, we chose to primarily follow the framework developed by Khan, Kunz, Kleijnen, and Antes [8], with additional guidance from Petticrew and Roberts [15]. The framework has five foundational steps: frame the question, identify relevant work, assess the quality of the studies, summarize the evidence, and interpret the findings. This section describes the first three steps in detail, while the evidence summary and interpretation of the findings is presented in the following two sections.

2.1 Framing the research question

To begin the review process, a broad, free-form question was posed: "What type of data has been collected in formal, peer-reviewed research that has been conducted on computing outreach activities in recent years?" This question was carefully formulated to serve as a guide for identifying relevant work. Upon considering the research question, the following basic overarching characteristics were identified:

- Populations Studied—Students enrolled in computing outreach programs as defined by the researchers
- Interventions—Programs that exposed students to computing concepts
- Study designs—Quantitative, qualitative, or mixed methods studies
- Outcomes—Effects of the program on participants' behaviors, attitudes, skills, knowledge, or dispositions

2.2 Identifying relevant work

The ACM and Institute of Electrical and Electronics Engineers (IEEE) journal and conference publications have served as a reliable source for formal, blind, peer-reviewed computing education research for decades. Using this as a starting point for finding relevant literature, we further refined that to venues that emphasize education, identifying the following peer-reviewed journals and conference proceedings in electronic form as a reliable source for finding relevant research:

- SIGCSE Technical Symposium on Computer Science Education (SIGCSE)
- Frontiers in Education (FIE)
- Innovation and Technology in Computer Science Education (ITiCSE)
- International Computing Education Research Workshop (ICER)
- Taylor & Francis' Computer Science Education (CSE)
- Transactions on Computing Education (TOCE)

Publications from 2009 to 2015 inclusive[1] were considered. This resulted in 3,949 citations that were reviewed for relevance. An article was determined to be relevant if, upon human review, it had a title and abstract associated with outreach because it contained one or more of the actual or related identifying criteria: K-12, elementary school, high school, secondary school, after school clubs, summer camp.

After this initial search for relevance, 3,837 papers did not fit the criteria and were deemed irrelevant for the purposes of this review. This resulted in 112 articles to undergo a more thorough review. To evaluate these, the overarching characteristics were considered and collection points were created for organizing the data.

Table 1. Guidelines for identifying relevant work

Characteristic	Collection points
Populations Studied	Participant characteristics (age and/or grade in school, gender, ethnicity, location) Number of participants in study
Interventions	Goals and facets of the program
Study Designs	Research question Quantitative, Qualitative, Mixed Methods, or Other Longitudinal, cross-sectional, experimental, quasi-experimental, etc. Type of data collected (participants' behaviors, attitudes, skills, knowledge, or dispositions)
Outcomes	Results of the study

2.3 Assessing the quality of the studies

Data was collected for each point in Table 1 via a careful read of the 112 articles. Thirty-two of these did not use formal methods (quantitative or qualitative) to evaluate the impact of the associated outreach activities. Instead, these articles described the activity in general terms, provided advice on creating and implementing an activity, provided curriculum examples for these activities, or were work in progress papers that did not include any data or findings. This left 80 articles for in-depth review and analysis, both of which are discussed below.

3. RESULTS (SUMMARY OF EVIDENCE)

The next step in the systematic literature review was to summarize the evidence from our collection points of the remaining 80 articles. Table 2 provides an analysis of the venues for the papers by venue and year and note that the majority (47.5%) of the studies were published in SIGCSE forums over the last 6 years.

The papers were dominated by results from interventions in the U.S. (72%). Figure 1 shows the breakdown of where the interventions took place by country.

We converted the level of students in non-US activities to the U.S. system since that is where a majority of the interventions took place. A majority of the interventions (80%) were outreach efforts aimed at high school and/or middle school students. The others were aimed at various stages of students as outlined in Figure 2. Many outreach activities are aimed at broadening participation in computing by either increasing gender or ethnic diversity in computing. Of the interventions, 49% indicated that they were intended to increase gender diversity and 31% indicated that they were intended to increase ethnic diversity. There were also a number of interventions where the intentions were not at all clear

[1] FIE 2015 proceedings were not available at the time of writing and are not included.

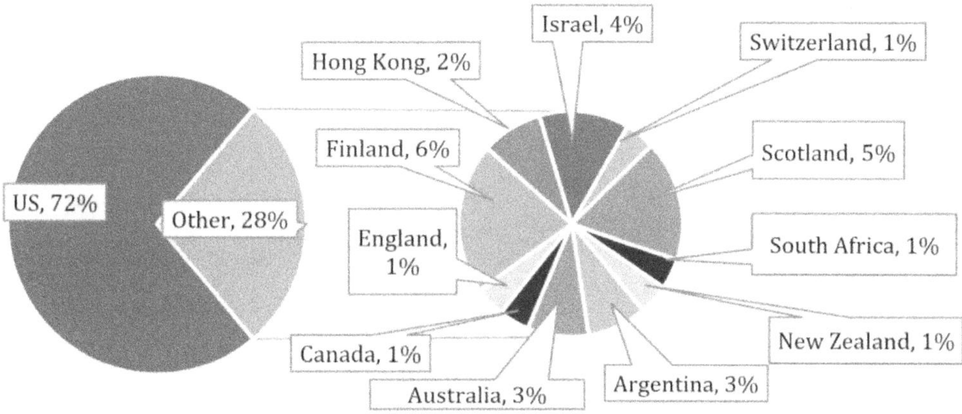

Figure 1. Countries where outreach activities took place

Table 2. Articles found by venue and year

	Number of articles meeting criteria							
	'09	'10	'11	'12	'13	'14	'15	Total
SIGCSE	10	5	3	4	7	5	3	37
FIE	2	3	2	3			n/a	10
ITiCSE	3	2	2		2	1	2	12
ICER				1		2	3	6
CSE			1	1	2			5
TOCE			9	1		1		11
Totals	15	10	17	10	11	9	8	80

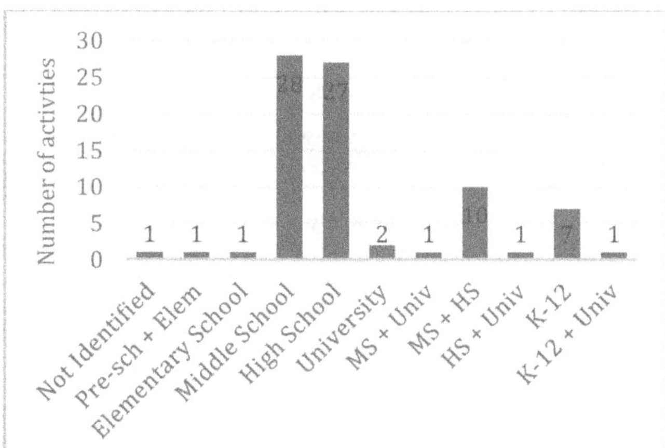

Figure 2. When outreach activities were offered

from the article. In fact, four of the articles (5%) were unable to be classified in either category. That is, the explanation of the intervention in the article did not allow for the ability for us to categorize them as either looking to improve diversity or not. Table 3 shows this breakdown.

The number of participants as reported by the interventions ranged from 2 to 9,999. Figure 3 shows in ranges the number of interventions that reported participants. The largest number of studies (11) had between 20-29 participants. The 16 studies (20%) that did not clearly report the total number of participants in the study are not included in Figure 3.

Table 3. Interventions designed to increase diversity

	Gender	Ethnic
Yes	39 (49%)	25 (31%)
No	37 (46%)	48 (60%)
Unknown	4 (5%)	7 (9%)

The gender of the participants was reported by 72.5% (58) of the studies. There were interventions that were single gender and interventions that were both genders. There were 22 studies (27%) that did not report the gender of the participants. Figure 4 shows the breakdown of gender in the interventions.

Of the activities that identified as mixed gender, 29 indicated the exact gender breakdown. Note that of those interventions previously identifying as attempting to address gender disparity (39), only 30 gave the exact gender breakdown of their interventions. Figure 5 shows percentages of female participation and how many studies were in each range.

The ethnicity of the participants was reported by 28 (35%) of the studies. There were only 3 studies (3%) that were strictly minority participation (two strictly Hispanic/Latino/Latina and one American Indian as reported by the articles). There were 25 studies (31%) that reported mixed ethnicity that included at least some minority participation. For those studies, the articles indicated the following races/ethnicities for the minority participants: American Indian or Alaskan Native; Asian; Asian/Pacific Islander; Black or African American; Filipino; Hispanic, Latino, Latina; Multi-racial; Other. There were 52 studies (65%) that did not indicate participant ethnicity.

The methodology of the studies is shown in Figure 6. Most of the studies were quantitative in nature (61%), but there was a significant amount of qualitative and mixed methods studies represented as well. For one of the studies, we were unable to classify its exact methodology from the description.

Table 4 breaks down the different types of data collected by the studies and the number of studies that collected this type of data. Computer science, information technology, and related disciplines are coded as "computing" for purposes of distinguishing the field.

Many of the studies collected data on more than one variable, so the studies were coded for each variable that was collected and reported. The most frequent data collected was participant attitudes towards computing (31% of studies). The second most frequent data collected was about interest in future study and/or careers in

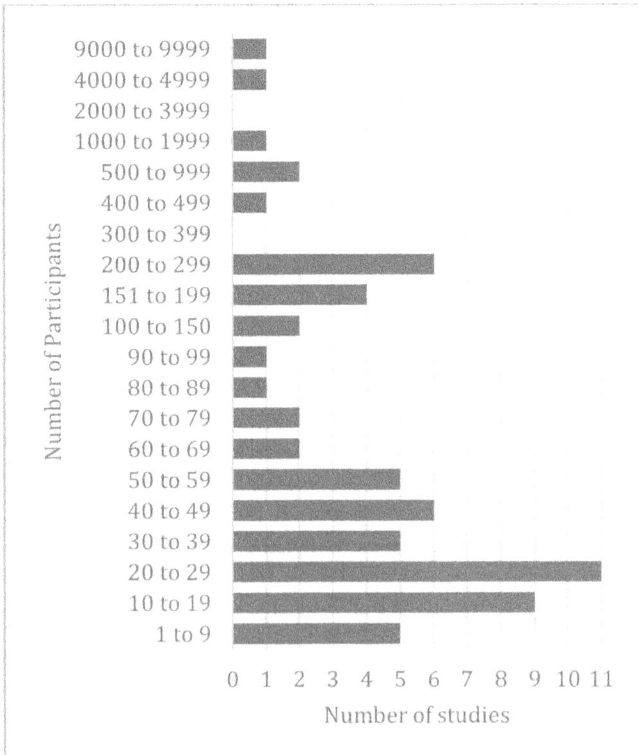

Figure 3. Number of participants in each study

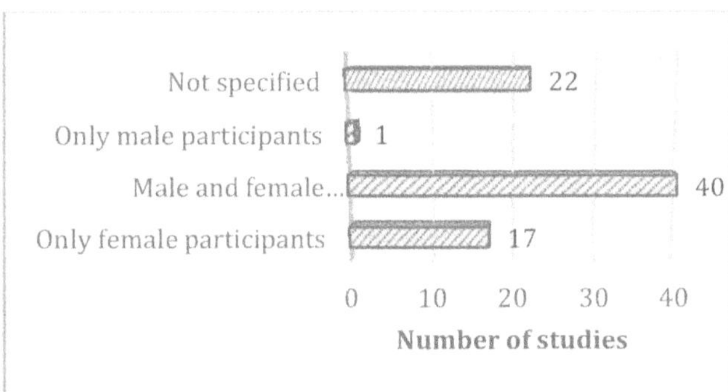

Figure 4. Breakdown of participants' gender in all studies

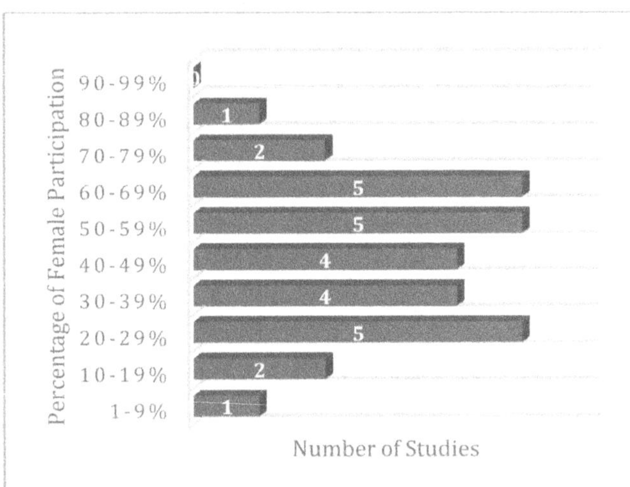

Figure 5. Female participation in mixed gender studies

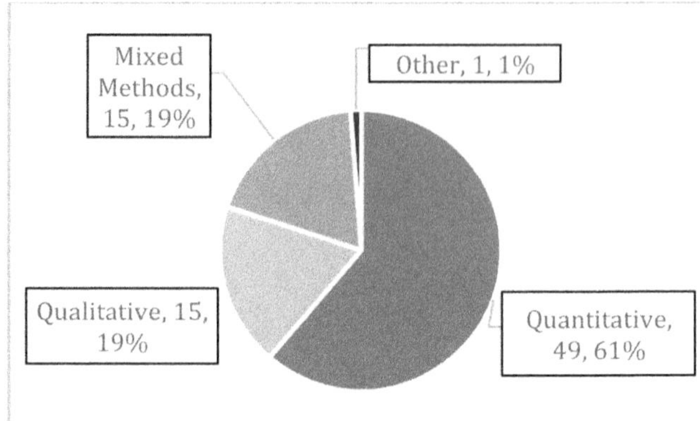

Figure 6. Study methodologies

computing (23%) and assessment of computing skills (23%) through some type of test.

Several studies were difficult to categorize. One study simply discussed the experiences of the students during the intervention, but not using a rigorous qualitative method. One study wanted to understand student differences by categorizing their personal study orientations. One study reported on the results of giving a university course as-is to high school students as an intervention. Finally, one study indicated that data was collected, but did not give information on what type or results.

Longitudinal data was only reported by 7 (8%) of the studies in the literature review. The durations of the longitudinal study were 9 months to 10 years, with an average duration of 4 years. The studies (short-term or longitudinal) all reported positive or neutral findings. There were no reports of negative findings for the outreach initiatives.

4. DISCUSSION

As noted previously, the question that this literature review was attempting to answer was, "What type of data has been collected in formal, peer-reviewed research that has been conducted on computing outreach activities in recent years?"

Upon analysis, we found that there was considerable data presented on outreach activities, but there is also missing data. First and foremost, there is little longitudinal evidence on the impact of these activities on the participants. Only 8% of the articles reflected a long-term study. In order to adequately address the larger question of the long-term effectiveness of these programs, more longitudinal studies are needed.

However, focusing on what has been reported, we see that the majority of the reported interventions are from the United States. The reason for this may be that the venues for publication are heavily US-centric. It should also be noted that this is the only category for which there are no ambiguities about the data. This is because the affiliation of the authors was used as a guide for determining location of the interventions. In many cases, the exact location for the interventions was not reported in the paper.

A majority of the interventions were aimed at middle school and high school students, which is not surprising given that several of the interventions were designed to increase student awareness of computing as a discipline, major, and career. There were a fair number targeting younger children--many target multiple age ranges or allow students to progress through them as they age.

Table 4. Summary of types of data collected by studies

Type of Data Collected	Number (Percent) of activities collecting
Attitudes towards computing	25 (31%)
Interest in future study of computing and/or interest in pursuing a career in computing	19 (23%)
Assessment of computing (programming) skills	19 (23%)
Perception of the field of computing	15 (18%)
Enjoyment of intervention	13 (16%)
General interest in computing	9 (11%)
Self-reported abilities with computing concepts	8 (10%)
Self-efficacy	4 (5%)
Number of majors in computing at university	4 (5%)
How material presented in intervention related to participants or the real world	4 (5%)
Relevance of computing	3 (3%)
Ability to express creativity with computing	3 (3%)
Engagement (general)	3 (3%)
Engagement with tools beyond the scope of the assigned task	3 (3%)
Assessment of spatial reasoning ability	2 (2%)
Participant GPA	2 (2%)
Motivation/persistence	2 (2%)
Completion of assigned task	2 (2%)
Assessment of other STEM skills	1 (1%)
Participant drop rate from computing program	1 (1%)
Identity within computing	1 (1%)
Belonging within computing	1 (1%)
Future enrollment in computing course	1 (1%)

Nearly half (49%) of the studies indicated that they were designed to increase either gender and/or ethnic diversity of the field of computing. However, only 31% indicated that increasing ethnic diversity was a goal. We know that both the lack of gender and ethnic diversity are problems in the field, but these numbers indicate that the problem of gender balance is being tackled more often than ethnic balance.

The number of participants in the studies varied greatly, but over half had less than 100 participants, and 36 (45%) had less than 50 participants. This is not surprising given the nature of these activities as summer camps or after school programs. The number of students corresponds to a typical size of a class/cohort or perhaps up to two classes. However, such small numbers and the lack of repetition of the intervention lead to problems for generalization of the activity's impact and effectiveness.

The measures of effectiveness varied across studies. Not surprisingly, participant attitudes about computing, potential further study of computing and interest in computing careers dominated the studies. Another highly measured outcome was participant knowledge about computing concepts, particularly programming constructs, which were considered by 23% of the studies. The way this data was collected varied from study to study, but for the most part, this data was collected using surveys that were created by the leaders of the interventions/studies.

The rigor in which results were reported varies considerably. While some report on the use of statistical means of analyzing the data, others report raw scores or means and indicate a raising or lowering of the means as success. Overwhelmingly, the studies reported positive or neutral findings. Because of the low numbers of participants for some of the interventions studied, statistical methods may not be viable for assessing the success of the intervention. However, case study or other rigorous qualitative methods could have been used in these cases. Except in a very few cases, qualitative studies simply gave anecdotes and observations about the intervention rather than following grounded theory or other acceptable qualitative study techniques.

Several studies did not clearly provide raw number or percentage for one or more pieces of data. There were studies where we were unable to categorize their intentions on increasing diversity of gender or ethnicity. For those that did indicate goals of increasing diversity, we discovered that a significant portion did not report on the exact gender or ethnic breakdown of participants. Furthermore, twenty percent of the studies did not clearly indicate the total number of participants in the interventions in any way.

As with any study, there are limitations. This literature review is focused on venues for academic researchers within the computing community. Research that does not appear in the aforementioned academic venues, like research from the National Center for Women in Technology (NCWIT) and the Girl Scouts of America, are not included in this study [10]. We evaluated articles in the selected venues, and these articles served as representation for the whole—though we recognize that there may be relevant articles in other venues. Further, despite our careful analysis, there may have been articles that should have been included, but were not. If a title did not seem to indicate an association with outreach activities, its abstract was not examined. Despite these limitations, the findings present an image of the quantity and quality of research being conducted and presented within the SIGCSE and larger ACM/IEEE community.

5. RECOMMENDATIONS

Based on this review as well as on standard research methods and practices defined by expert researchers [6, 8, 14, 15], we find that the results of these studies are difficult to compare and, in general, at best lack adequate data and at worst follow research methodologies that are weak and/or unsupported by formally accepted practices.

For reviewing, analyzing, and synthesizing qualitative data, particularly in grounded theory research, prescripting a framework or guidelines for such data contradicts accepted sound methodology. However, for quantitative data, studies with similar data collection techniques can provide a better pathway for cross-comparison and analysis of data. We therefore propose a basic framework to consider when conducting quantitative studies centered on computing activities designed to broaden the pipeline:

Preliminary steps

- Define overarching research question(s) to be studied
- Ensure that the data collection and reporting of data has been approved by your local institutional review board
- Consider variables outside of the study that may influence the outcomes and include these as part of your report
- Define data to be collected to provide answers to the research question

Data to be collected

- Collect basic demographic data on the participants, including gender, ethnicity, age, grade in school
- Collect any other unique characteristics about the participants that may influence the study (participated in

previous activities, were all gifted students, etc.)

- Use reliable, validated survey instruments, when possible, to gauge participant attitudes, self-efficacy, and skills if one or more of these are used to answer your research question(s)
- Consider the number of students in the group; statistical analysis such as a t-test typically requires 26 or more to be considered valid

Reporting

- Provide the research question and/or the purpose of the intervention (computing activity)
- Describe type of activity and where activity was held (including country)
- Provide amount of time participants were engaged in the activity (hours/days/weeks)
- Provide information on who ran the activity
- Provide data that was collected, reporting at a minimum the gender, ethnicity, age, and grade in school of participants, both in count and in percentages.
- For each piece of data collected, report count and percentages

Though there are many other ways to report data, and data collection is often very dependent on the nature of the study, these basic items may provide a measure of consistency among types of data that can be compared.

Even though these suggestions apply most acutely to quantitative studies, there are still many more things to be learned through rigorous approaches to qualitative studies surrounding the impact of outreach activities. While not highlighted explicitly in this paper, there were several very good examples of qualitative research exploring outreach initiatives. Given that our study shows that the number of participants in computing activities is generally low, sound qualitative methods when appropriate will enhance understanding of the personal impact on participants.

6. CONCLUSION

There is a significant number of outreach activities that are reported in the literature that impact a variety of different constituents across ages, countries, ethnicities, and gender. The activities are reporting impact on the participants through various metrics that are overwhelmingly positive. However, we did not find sufficient meta-evidence to conclude that, as a whole, computing outreach activities are effective, especially in the long-term.

This is in part due to the fact that we also uncovered many reports that are lacking in several details that are important from a research perspective for those interested in studying outreach efforts on a broader scale. We encourage conducting such studies to collect data that can be compared across programs. We also encourage researchers to track participants beyond the end of the activity. Though one-time activities can often provide a boost to a participants' self-efficacy or beliefs about computing, these can radically change over two years, two months, or even two days' time. By tracking longer periods, the results become more meaningful and will aid researchers in identifying practices that have higher success rates over the long-term.

7. REFERENCES

[1] Armstrong, C., Flood, P. C., Guthrie, J. P., Liu, W., MacCurtain, S., & Mkamwa, T. 2010. The impact of diversity and equality management on firm performance: Beyond high performance work systems. Human Resource Management, 49(6), 977-998.

[2] Bracy, C. 2013. Closing the Tech Industry's Gender Gap Requires Better Data. National Public Radio (NPR). Retrieved August 20, 2015 from http://n.pr/1WRblQt

[3] Bureau of Labor Statistics, U.S. Department of Labor, Occupational Employment Statistics, Employment by detailed occupation. Retrieved August 18, 2015 from http://1.usa.gov/1NSVkTT

[4] Bureau of Labor Statistics, U.S. Department of Labor, Occupational Employment Statistics, Fastest growing occupations. Retrieved August 18, 2015 from http://www.bls.gov/emp/ep_table_203.htm

[5] Charette, R.N. 2013. Is There a U.S. IT Worker Shortage? IEEE Spectrum, 3 Sep 2013. Retrieved August 20, 2015 from http://bit.ly/1V8d8ic

[6] Creswell, J.W. 2008. Educational Research. Planning, Conducting, and Evaluating Quantitative and Qualitative Research. Pearson Education, Upper Saddle River, New Jersey.

[7] Google Rise Awards. 2015. Retrieved August 19, 2015 from http://bit.ly/1zvi86f

[8] Khan, K.S., Kunz, R., Kleijnen, J., Antes, G. 2003. Five steps to conducting a systematic review. *J R Soc Med.* 96, 3, 118–121. http://www.ncbi.nlm.nih.gov/pmc/articles/PMC539417/

[9] McGill, M.M., Decker, A., and Settle, A. 2015. Does Outreach Impact Choices of Major for Underrepresented Undergraduate Students?. In *Proceedings of the eleventh annual International Conference on International Computing Education Research* (ICER '15). ACM, New York, NY, USA, 71-80.

[10] Liston, C., Petereson, K., Ragan, V. 2008. Evaluating Promising Practices in Informal Information Technology (IT) Education for Girls: Phase III: Women in IT – Survey Results. Retrieved July 2015 from https://www.ncwit.org/sites/default/files/resources/ncwit-gsusaphaseiiireport_final.pdf.

[11] National Science Foundation CE21 Award List. (2013). Retrieved May 16, 2013 from http://1.usa.gov/1JksPh4

[12] National Science Foundation, Increasing Accessibility to computer science education across the U.S., 2013. Retreived July 22, 2015 from http://1.usa.gov/1NSUZkc

[13] Page, Scott E. The difference: How the power of diversity creates better groups, firms, schools, and societies. Princeton University Press, 2008.

[14] Patton, M. (2002). Qualitative Research & Evaluation Methods. USA: Sage Publications.

[15] Petticrew, M., and Roberts, H. 2006. Systematic Reviews in the Social Sciences: A practical guide. Blackwell Publishing. Retrieved August 15 from http://www.cebma.org/wp-content/uploads/Pettigrew-Roberts-SR-in-the-Soc-Sc.pdf

[16] Richtel, M. 2014. Reading, Writing, Arithmetic, and Lately, Coding. New York Times. Retrieved August 20, 2015 from http://www.nytimes.com/2014/05/11/us/reading-writing-arithmetic-and-lately-coding.html?_r=0

[17] Slater, S.F., Weigand, R.A., and Zwirlein, T.J. 2008. The business case for commitment to diversity. Business Horizons, Vol(51)3, May-June 2008, pp. 201-209.

[18] Spohrer, J. 2015. Empowering Makers in the Cognitive Era. *In Proceedings of the eleventh annual International Conference on International Computing Education Research* (ICER '15). ACM, New York, NY, USA, 1-1. DOI=http://dx.doi.org/10.1145/2787622.2787623

[19] Westervelt, E. 2015. Disrupting Tech's Diversity Problem with a Camp for Girls of Color. National Public Radio (NPR). Retrieved August 20, 2015 from http://www.npr.org/sections/ed/2015/08/17/432278262/hacking-tech-s-diversity-problem-black-girls-code

Retention of Flow: Evaluating a Computer Science Education Week Activity

Alexander Repenning *
School of Education
University of Applied Sciences
and Arts Northwestern
Switzerland (FHNW)
Windisch, Switzerland
alexander.repenning@fhnw.ch

Ashok Basawapatna †
SUNY Old Westbury
Dept. Mathematics, Computer
& Information Science
Old Westbury, NY, USA
basawapatnaa@oldwestbury.edu

Dorit Assaf
School of Education
University of Applied Sciences
and Arts Northwestern
Switzerland (FHNW)
Windisch, Switzerland
dorit.assaf@fhnw.ch

Carmine Maiello
School of Education
University of Applied Sciences
and Arts Northwestern
Switzerland (FHNW)
Windisch, Switzerland
carmine.maiello@fhnw.ch

Nora Escherle
School of Education
University of Applied Sciences
and Arts Northwestern
Switzerland (FHNW)
Windisch, Switzerland
nora.escherle@fhnw.ch

ABSTRACT

High profile computer science education events such as the Hour of Code can reach millions of students but without proper evaluation it is not clear what motivational and educational consequences the participation has. If, for instance, participants' levels of motivation towards the end of an hour long activity are significantly fading, then their perception of programming to be "hard and boring" may actually get reinforced. By simply measuring how far participants progressed with their projects we have been able to collect retention data from thousands of participants in a way that allows us to interpret these data in terms of not only cognitive but also technical and practical activity challenges. Inflection points overlaying a negative exponential retention distribution serve as indicators of these challenges with potential impact on Flow. Retention of Flow is an evaluation approach to analyze computer science education activities, including interactive tutorials and online programming environments, with respect to cognitive as well as affective challenges.

*Department of Computer Science, University of Colorado, Boulder CO, USA

†School of Education, University of Applied Sciences and Arts Northwestern Switzerland (FHNW), Windisch, Switzerland

SIGCSE '16, March 02-05, 2016, Memphis, TN, USA

DOI: http://dx.doi.org/10.1145/2839509.2844597

1. INTRODUCTION

Recently, there have been encouraging developments in getting computer science and computational thinking into K-12 classrooms [25][5][24]. For example, Computer Science Education Week (CS EdWeek) that took place on December 7-13 2014, reached more than 100 million students through its Hour of Code activities [24]. Such broadened participation and excitement around computer science education affords opportunities to motivate, enrich, and empower great numbers of students with the 21st century skills necessary to succeed.

CS EdWeek activities expose massive numbers of students to programming mostly through visual languages in a cyberlearning context [3]. They are typically aimed at students with no prior programming experience, consequently the activities are highly scaffolded with interactive tutorials embedded in the exercise environment itself [15]. These interactive instructions allow students to proceed self-paced through the activity. Examples include games wherein programming is the main task, such as "Lightbot" [11] and "Code Combat", as well as more open-ended visual language environments in which students create artifacts such as "Scratch", "App Inventor" [15][21], and AgentCubes online. In "Lightbot", for instance, students program a robot that navigates around obstacles. Similarly, the official 2013 Hour of Code activity included a game wherein students used block programming to control angry birds characters towards a goal [15]. Activities like "Lightbot" and "Code Combat" usually consist of predetermined, puzzle-like tasks, that increase in complexity with each level by introducing more sophisticated programming concepts throughout the exercise. The 2013 Hour of Code "Scratch" exercise guides students through the creation of a Christmas card. The idea is to initially get students started with a highly scaffolded tutorial in order to introduce the basic functionality of the programming environment. The environment then provides an open enough programming palette to let the students eventually diverge from the tutorial and to proceed to create their own custom artifacts, such as an Android App with App Inventor, a custom Christmas card with Scratch, or a 3D game using AgentCubes online.

Massive exposure of students to computer science and programming activities is a first step towards motivating students and broadening participation. However, exposure itself is just the beginning of the story—the student activity-experience is also important. The hope is that students react to the activity as a "cliffhanger" wherein they are engaged at every step and are motivated to continue on after it being finished, opposed to having an "are we there yet?" disposition to the activity by being disengaged and simply waiting for the tutorial to be completed.

One might argue that regardless of the outcome, exposing as many students as possible to computer science is worthwhile. Research shows, however, that the first impression of computer science, especially at the middle school level, is crucial for students in deciding whether or not to continue subsequent pursuits of these activities [12][6]. These CS EdWeek activities can be a pivotal moment for hundreds of millions of students. If it is an unsatisfactory first experience, it could, actually, have negative implications for computer science education [7].

Even though answering these questions is vital for the discipline of computer science education, and the emergence of cloud-based programming environments enabling large data collection, there is not much state-of-the-art research yet that addresses these questions. One reason for the lack of research on massive exposure of students to computer science and programming activities might be the difficulty to collect data. Usually, there is little if any information on the participating students (e.g. age, gender, background) or the specific classroom contexts during these CS EdWeek Hour of Code events. We believe that despite these challenges we can still collect meaningful data, especially because we can exploit the large amount of data that participants of these events provide us. In this paper we will show that by looking at retention data, we can draw conclusions on the quality of the tutorial as well as learn about factors that lead to a student losing interest in the activity. A high student retention might be explained by several reasons: It can be high motivation leading to a cliffhanger effect but unfortunately it could also be a sign of high endurance to finish the tutorial despite boredom leading to the unpleasant "are we there yet?" experience. A low retention, however, might show a rather negative learning experience, be it due to overwhelming of the student which causes stress and anxiety, or technical challenges causing frustration, or under challenging causing boredom. These are examples of many other situations that might occur during these kind of education activities, which can cause a discontinuation of a student's Flow and consequently, loss of retention.

We designed and introduced an Hour of Code activity based on an existing Scalable Game Design (SGD) curriculum which has been developed for more than twenty years at the University of Colorado [20]. This curriculum is usually taught in a classroom context by teachers who have completed a thorough training in SGD of at least 25 hours. Through that curriculum students are exposed to computational thinking tools throughout their school year and the learning through game design activities are well embedded in an educational context. Conversely, Hour of Code activities are designed in a way as to enable teachers to introduce it in their classrooms without any previous training and to make it accessible for any student from the age of nine and older. Furthermore, we aimed at designing an activity that it is well scaffolded in the beginning to enable a low-barrier introduction to the programming environment but leaves room for open-endedness as the students reach the end of the tutorial, to hopefully give them a cliffhanger experience. Ideally, it will motivate students to continue working on their game projects at the same time it might inspire teachers to look more detailed into SGD or possible other computer science education curricula. Considering that we only get one hour to motivate students and teachers to continue being engaged in computer science education activities, it is of the essence that we evaluate the quality of the tutorial. It is the tutorial, after all, that guides students (and often teachers) through their first exposure to computer science and plays a crucial role in their first experiences with programming. We took the SGD curriculum and its programming environment AgentCubes online as resources to create our Hour of Code 3D Frogger activity. In this paper we do not evaluate the SGD curriculum and the AgentCubes online platform, as we refer to existing relevant evaluation and research publications [19][20]. We rather focus on our specific Hour of Code tutorial we created from these resources and evaluate it by looking into student retention. While we do not expect to provide final answers with this first study, we hope that both our approach and our findings will prove relevant and useful for further research in massive exposure of students to programming activities.

2. THE 3D FROGGER ACTIVITY

Based on the Scalable Game Design curriculum, we provided in 2014 a CS EdWeek Hour of Code 3D Frogger activity[1] that enabled students to create a game inspired by the 80's arcade game Frogger using the browser-based 3D environment AgentCubes online. The positive motivational aspects of this activity have already been established on the basis of experiences reported by thousands of students [20]. Notably, this included the first ever CS EdWeek activity launched in Switzerland and a pilot study in Mexico [8][9]. To support U.S., Mexico and all the participating Swiss cantons, the activity included an embedded tutorial video in English, Spanish, German, Italian, and French. This video provides step-by-step instructions to build a complete Frogger game, including custom characters that can be made from scratch, and employing programming pieces, such as conditions, actions and rules, to create in-game interactions between these characters. The agent gallery lists in-game characters called "agents" created by the user (in the this case a frog). Notably, students can create their own 3D characters by inflating 2D images (see Figure 1 Checkpoint 0: Frog is designed). The possibility to create custom characters and game worlds was found to be surprisingly important from a motivational point of view, due to an increased sense of ownership [19]. The embedded video tutorial walks students through the creation of a complete Frogger game. It is supplemented by an interactive table of its contents consisting of indexed links that allow students to (re-)access instructions for each single programming step. All in-game interactions are being implemented by "if-else" rules assigning actions to conditions (see Figure 1 Checkpoint 2: key

[1]http://www.csedweek.us (2015 version)

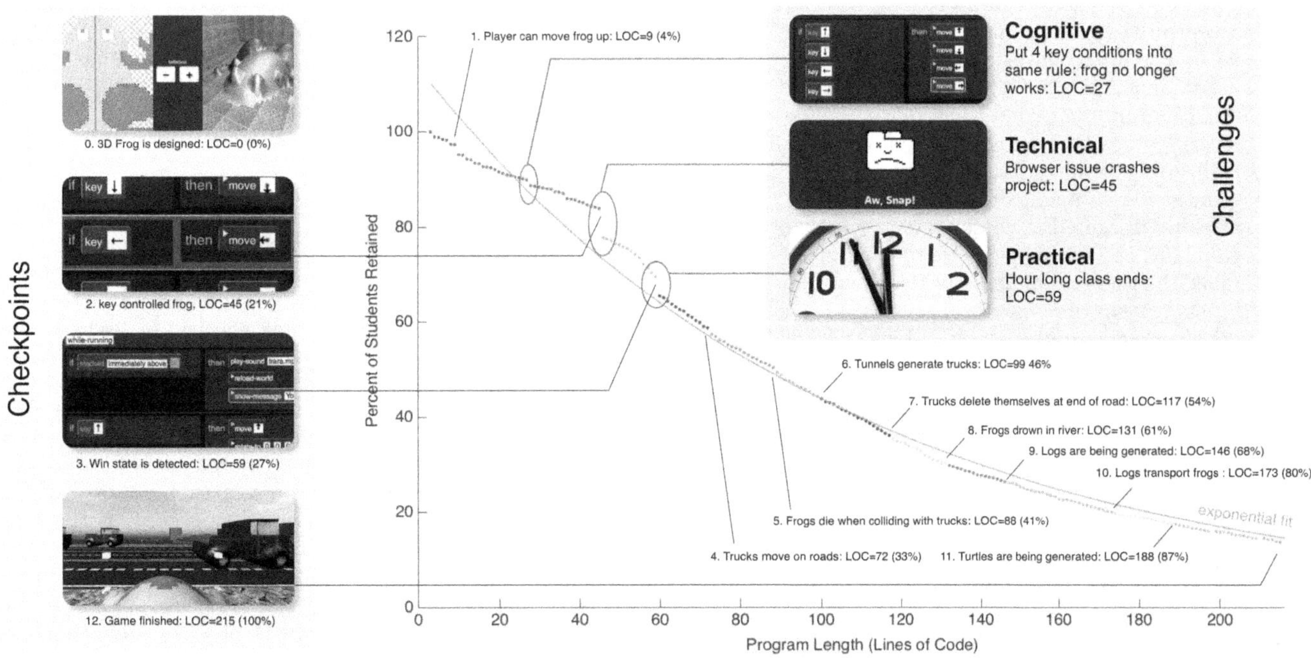

Figure 1: Retention graph for the Hour of Code 3D Frogger activity. The graph displays data of student projects with at least one line of code (LOC=1). The negative exponential fit curve is overlaid in blue. Program length corresponds to lines of code, or percentage of progress within the tutorial video. Color coded parts of the graph refer to subtasks including checkpoints within the embedded video tutorial. The identified inflection points on the graph refer to example challenges we found causing a drop of retention.

controlled frog). The conditions and actions palettes contain visual programming blocks that can be dragged into the behavior window, which is a work area that contains all rules. A more detailed description about the AgentCubes online game programming environment can be found under this reference [13]. The Hour of Code 3D Frogger activity is designed in an open-ended way, that means after the completion of the embedded video tutorial the students are able to make their game more complex by adding more agents and interactions on their own. AgentCubes online is cloud-based, which gives students the possibility to return working on their game (or create a new one) anytime later, for example from home.

3. RELATED WORK

As pointed out in the previous section there is little research that investigates the effects of large-scale exposure of students to computer science and programming activities in the context of events like the CS EdWeek. Among the few, the ones most relevant to this paper are those by Piech et al. [18] and Lee et al. [16]. Both studies employ a data-driven method to evaluate online programming activities and focus on student engagement which they correlate with retention. Specifically, Piech et al. claim "that data of how previous students navigated their way to the final answer can be leveraged to autonomously understand the landscape of such assessments and enable hints for future students," thereby potentially increasing future student retention. Lee et al. find that inserting in-game assessments after each level of their activity increases student retention. An important factor we need to consider in our analysis refers to those aspects that can potentially work against student retention, killing their motivation, making them quit the activity and thereby impeding their learning. Ko [14] has defined several learning barriers, which all refer to cognitive challenges. In online programming activities, which are typically characterized by a complex context where many practical and also technical factors play a vital role, we claim that there are many challenges and learning barriers which are not cognitive.

Massive Open Online Courses (MOOCs) have analyzed retention, including Survival Analysis techniques, to better understand at what point in time and why students might drop a course [23]. Though often on a larger time-scale, MOOC retention analysis shares many of the same challenges with the CS EdWeek activities stemming from the unknown populations of students who enroll. In recent studies, MOOCs have shown to be characterized by a negative exponential retention graph and, by some estimates, retain under 6.5%. In the future, the method presented here can be extended to MOOCs, for example, a programming class that assigns partially-scaffolded online assignments.

We strongly agree with Piech and Lee that student engagement is an important aspect of informal learning in computer science and programming, and that it can be correlated to retention, but we further claim that the scope of analysis needs to be broadened beyond issues of cognition. In particular, we claim that is important to include affective concerns [17] such as the framework of Flow [4]. Specifically, the framework we have utilized to keep students engaged in end-user programming is called the Zones of Proximal Flow [2]. The Zones of Proximal Flow starts with Csikszentmihalyi's diagram of Flow and inserts Vygotsky's Zone of Proximal Development [22] between the regions of Flow and Anxiety. The strategy employs this in an end-user programming context as follows. The teacher challenges students with a game creation activity matched to their skill level. However, throughout the course of the activity some students might drift towards Anxiety; at this point, scaffolding targeted at these students' Zone of Proximal Development hopefully guides them back into Flow. In order to make the theoretical Zones of Proximal Flow framework actionable, we have researched breaking down games in terms of constituent computational thinking skills and creating a path from games to simulations through a framework entitled Computational Thinking Patterns. We have also developed methods to assess computational thinking skills by validated automatic evaluation of student artifacts called Computational Thinking Pattern Analysis [1].

We employ three broad categories of challenges that could impact Flow. Cognitive challenges are challenges of understanding that may be caused by overly complex or simply confusing tutorial instructions. Technical challenges such as losing a network connection may seem trivial in nature but could be responsible for significant impact on Flow when for example the goal is to create a project and that project gets lost. Practical challenges, such as the end of class time, again, may result in significant impact on Flow. We do not claim for these categories to be exhaustive but from our experience with Scalable Game Design classroom observations [20], in schools around the USA, we find them to cover most of the cases that have measurable impact on students state of Flow.

4. METHODOLOGY

We can begin activity evaluation by employing the large numbers of participants to investigate retention of Flow. By analyzing student retention through the activity we can begin to identify potential problem areas in the activity. We calculated student retention based on the program length or lines of code (LOC) a student has created in AgentCubes online. Specifically, every time a user modifies their program for a given agent in AgentCubes online, by adding methods, rules, conditions, and actions, an XML file corresponding to that agent's programmed behaviors is modified on the server. Analyzing all the XML files corresponding to each agent allows for an operationalization of program length akin to a lines of code metric. Using this measure of program length, we can begin calculate student retention through the activity. At each program length (LOC), we can measure the number of students still retained in the activity by summing the number of games with lines of code greater or equal to that program length. For example, if a student programmed a game of length 80, then that student is counted from a program length of 0 to a program length of 80. To put another way, that student was *retained* until a program length of 80.

Following this measurement we looked at the relationship between this measure of retention and different levels of progression through the activity. Due to the highly scaffolded nature of the tutorial where every student initially implements the same code as well as the assumption that most of the students follow the tutorial, we can correlate lines of code to position in the tutorial video. We realize that students that did not follow the instructions of the tutorial and decided to program something else on their own might distort the data. However, with the large number of participants in events such as the CS EdWeek, we are able to collect data that drowns out this effect.

5. RESULTS

Figure 1 shows the retention graph for the Hour of Code 3D Frogger activity collected from 5,512 student projects in the context of CS EdWeek that took place in the U.S., Switzerland, and Mexico during December 7 - 13 2014. We solely include data of games that consists of at least one line of code (LOC=1). For this activity it implies that the first Frog keyboard "up" movement control has been implemented. Those datasets of student that only created a Frog agent (LOC=0) but didn't implement any behaviors were sorted out prior to analysis. The colored subsections of the graph displayed in Figure 1 represent each subtask of the embedded video tutorial. The first blue section is the Frog keyboard "up" movement control, followed by the orange subsection representing the implementation of all four keyboard directions i.e. "up", "down", "left", "right", and so on.

The Frogger game eventually is built by implementing each of these video tutorial subtasks. The x-axis of the retention graph represents the progress within the video tutorial, that means it is directly correlated to program length, or lines of code. The y-axis represents the percentage of students retained based on the number of projects that were included in the data, which equals number of students, assuming each student created and submitted only one project during this hour-long activity. The trend of retention is a negative exponential fit overlaid in black on the plot (goodness of fit: $r - squared = 0.993; F(1,212) = 31324.837, p < 0.01$).

The retention graph presents several inflection points where students tend to discontinue the activity. The analysis of the game artifacts of students who discontinued the activity at these inflection points revealed particularly interesting patterns that we categorize as cognitive, technical, and practical challenges. The inflection points give us feedback in which position of the video tutorial we lost a significant number of students and by identifying the nature of these challenges we can take measures to improve the quality of the activity. As follows we describe the three challenge categories through examples we found.

5.1 Cognitive Challenge

Cognitive challenges pertain to situations in which students' code included errors. For instance, by analyzing game artifacts of students who discontinued the tutorial at program length LOC=27 (Figure 1) we uncovered a programming error previously seen in classroom observations: It is the task to implement the Frog's keyboard movements in four directions "up", "down", "left", and "right". The correct implementation involves four separate "if-else" rules, each containing a keyboard event condition and a corresponding Frog moving action. That means, if the user hits one of the arrow keys on the keyboard, the respective "if-else" rule executes and lets the Frog to move into the desired direction. This Frog movement is a tutorial subtask which is represented in by the orange colored subsection of the retention graph in Figure 1. The correct implementation has a program length of LOC=45. The identified inflection point at LOC=27 within this subsection of the retention graph revealed that numerous students tried to implement the Frog movement by adding all four keyboard arrow conditions into one single "if-else" rule. By doing that, however, the code results in a different logic: for this rule to evaluate to true, all four conditions must be met corresponding to all four keyboard arrow keys being pressed at the same time (i.e. "up" AND "down" AND "left" AND "right"). This error is a typical problem for students, the difference of the correct and incorrect implementation in AgentCube online's visual user interface is only slight. Obviously, this is very frustrating for the students since they perceive to have everything implemented correctly according to the tutorial, but the Frog doesn't move at all. This kind of challenge we define as cognitive, it can emerge due to a misunderstanding of the mechanics of the programming environment, or because of more general problems. In this case, improvements of the programming environment or the activity must be considered.

5.2 Technical Challenge

Technical challenges correspond to problems such as networking issues, memory issues, and software bugs. Analyzing the inflection point discovered around program length LOC=45 revealed a common technical problem encountered by the participants. Specifically, students using the Internet Explorer browser would get an error message near this point when they tried to run their game. The instructions for the CS Ed Week activity specify that it works best with Chrome, Safari, or Firefox having WebGL enabled. However, this information is only shown at the beginning of the activity and requires the user to scroll down within the initial activity screen. The information will not show up again at a later point during the activity. When this Internet Explorer compatibility error occurs, the programmed Frog behavior is unreadable and there is no possibility to recover the student project without back-end server intervention. This is the point where the activity unfortunately must be quit, and it is not visible that it might be a browser issue. We assume that happened to a large number of students, the inflection point in the retention graph might correspond to this student loss.

5.3 Practical Challenge

Practical challenges refer to external environmental factors that affect student retention. In Figure 1 a practical challenge was identified at program length LOC=59. Now the student has implemented the frog win-state, that is the goal where the frog has to navigate to during the game. The student has created a minimal and simple functioning game where a user can navigate a Frog towards a goal using keyboard arrows. At this point the first three subtasks (colored blue, orange, and yellow) of the retention graph in Figure 1 have been implemented. This is a moment, where usually an hour has been passed and the class might have ended. Some teachers reserved additional class time, so that students had time to continue the activity.

6. DISCUSSION

It is not clear how to normalize retention. A very large number of people may come to some web-based activity only to instantly abandon it again because they did not really understand what they would get into. To that end, it often makes sense to define a minimal commitment point to define the 100% point of retention. Piech [18] normalizes his retention data by only counting the number of participants who complete the first of the 20 activities as 100%. Similarly, we only count the number of participants who have created a least one line of code and normalize them as 100%.

Assessing retention of Flow can be difficult because it is not clear what good or bad retention is. One measure could be the retention drop rate as defined by how much retention is dropping per time. In the case of hour of code activities, for instance, it could be argued that the hourly retention drop rate could be indicative of Flow. The 2013 Angry Birds activity analyzed by Piech [18] appears to have a retention drop of about 35% in one hour which is nearly identical to the retention drop of the 3D Frogger activity. However, the shape of the retention distribution appears to be qualitatively different. Angry Birds retention seems to drop linearly, whereas 3D Frogger drops negative exponential. Partially, this could be explained with the closed nature of the puzzle-based approach of Angry Birds, which only features 20 finite puzzles. 3D Frogger, in contrast, allows participants to continue due to its open ended nature. That is, when users do reach the end of the tutorial the activity does not necessarily have to end. Users keep a link to their project capturing not only the programming but also the 2D and 3D design work they have created. Additionally, they have full access to the programming environment and not just a limited subset. Data indicate that users do indeed continue along a trajectory suggested by the exponential fit curve presented in Figure 1 beyond the final checkpoint (LOC=215). This could be considered an indicator of Flow or perhaps even of the activity being a cliffhanger. Continuing beyond the end of the tutorial would not be possible with most puzzle-based approaches because users do not actually have the ownership of projects which they could continue.

A fundamental challenge in this research is to properly interpret inflection points and to correlate their manifestations with initial cause of a problem. Our retention data does exhibit a number of easily identifiable inflection points (Figure 1), but it is not always clear if these inflection points necessarily pinpoints the moment when the problem was caused. For instance, in the cognitive challenge example of Section 5.1, the temporal gap between making a programming mistake and its manifestation could be significant. This instance of a cognitive challenge is rooted in a confusion about how rules work. When participants create a faulty rule with all four key conditions and all four move actions in the same rule, they will not notice their mistake before they finish and test the frog cursor key control behavior. This mistake is a big Flow detractor manifesting itself significantly as an inflection point, because not only the move "right", move "left" and move "down" keys do not work, the originally move "up" rule stopped working as well. The possibility is high for a student to give up the activity at this point. In cases like this, the inflection point is several steps behind the programming step starting the problem, which makes debugging much more difficult. A potential solution for this particular cognitive challenge is to extend the programming tool with a proactive critiquing system that will catch these kind of programming errors as early as possible [10].

Data-driven research methodologies that are based on large numbers of participants afford new analytical approaches for meaningful interpretation. During the Computer Science Education Week in 2013, we reached nearly a quarter million participants. Each project consisted not only of code but also of individually created 3D agents that populated sometimes complex game worlds. For the purpose of employing this rich data collection as feedback to improve an activity, it is necessary to reduce this information significantly. With our methodology to investigate retention of Flow, we have gone to the extreme of reducing each project to a single "lines of code" indicator. To get meaningful retention data, is it necessary to get some kind of critical mass of participation as our retention of Flow approach may now scale down well.

7. CONCLUSION

We have shown in this paper that it is possible to evaluate open online programming activities that involve a large number of participants by looking at student retention. We collected data from thousands of students during 2014 CS EdWeek that took place in the U.S., Switzerland, and Mexico. The data showed the nature of student retention closely followed a negative exponential trend. Inflection points in the activity retention data indicated challenges which we could categorize as cognitive, technical, and practical. We demonstrated that these challenges might be responsible for a drop of Flow and consequently, loss of retention. As more and more learning tools are being cloud-based, our presented method can be used to improve similar activities that are highly scaffolded.

8. ACKNOWLEDGMENTS

This research has been funded by Swiss Hasler foundation and the National Science Foundation (G.No:1312129, 1138526). Any opinions, findings, and conclusions or recommendations expressed are those of the author(s) and do not necessarily reflect the views of these foundations.

9. REFERENCES

[1] A. R. Basawapatna, A. Repenning, and K. H. Koh. Closing the cyberlearning loop: Enabling teachers to formatively assess student programming projects. In *Proceedings of SIGCSE '15*, pages 12–17. ACM, 2015.

[2] A. R. Basawapatna, A. Repenning, K. H. Koh, et al. The zones of proximal flow: guiding students through a space of computational thinking skills and challenges. In *Proceedings of ICER '13*, pages 67–74. ACM, 2013.

[3] C. L. Borgman, H. Abelson, L. Dirks, et al. Fostering learning in the networked world: The cyberlearning opportunity and challenge. a 21st century agenda for the national science foundation. *Report of the NSF task force on cyberlearning*, 2008.

[4] M. Csikszentmihalyi. *Finding flow: The psychology of engagement with everyday life*. Basic Books, 1997.

[5] A. D'Alba, K. Huett, A. Remshagen, et al. ucode@ uwg: Building kids' interest in stem-c. In *Proceedings of SITE '15*, volume 2015, pages 96–99, 2015.

[6] J. Denner, S. Bean, and J. Martinez. the girl game company. *Afterschool Matters*, page 26, 2009.

[7] C. Duncan, T. Bell, and S. Tanimoto. Should your 8-year-old learn coding? In *Proceedings of WiPSCE '14*, pages 60–69. ACM, 2014.

[8] N. Escherle, D. Assaf, A. Basawapatna, et al. Launching swiss computer science education week. In *Proceedings of WiPSCE '15*, pages 11–16. ACM, 2015.

[9] N. Escherle, S. Ramirez-Ramirez, A. Basawapatna, et al. Piloting computer science education week in mexico. In *Proceedings of SIGCSE '16*. ACM, 2016.

[10] G. Fischer. Domain-oriented design environments. *Automated Software Engineering*, 1(2):177–203, 1994.

[11] L. A. Gouws, K. Bradshaw, and P. Wentworth. Computational thinking in educational activities: an evaluation of the educational game light-bot. In *Proceedings of ITiCSE '13*, pages 10–15. ACM, 2013.

[12] C. Hill, C. Corbett, and A. St Rose. *Why so few? Women in Science, Technology, Engineering, and Mathematics*. ERIC, 2010.

[13] A. Ioannidou, A. Repenning, and D. C. Webb. Agentcubes: Incremental 3d end-user development. *Journal of Visual Languages & Computing*, 20(4):236–251, 2009.

[14] A. J. Ko, B. Myers, H. H. Aung, et al. Six learning barriers in end-user programming systems. In *VL-HCC 2004 IEEE Symposium*, pages 199–206. IEEE, 2004.

[15] D. Kumar. Digital playgrounds for early computing education. *ACM Inroads*, 5(1):20–21, 2014.

[16] M. J. Lee, A. J. Ko, and I. Kwan. In-game assessments increase novice programmers' engagement and level completion speed. In *Proceedings of ICER '13*, pages 153–160. ACM, 2013.

[17] R. W. Picard, S. Papert, W. Bender, et al. Affective learning–a manifesto. *BT Technology Journal*, 22(4):253–269, 2004.

[18] C. Piech, M. Sahami, J. Huang, and L. Guibas. Autonomously generating hints by inferring problem solving policies. In *Proceedings of 2nd Conference on Learning@ Scale*, pages 195–204. ACM, 2015.

[19] A. Repenning, D. C. Webb, C. Brand, et al. Beyond minecraft: Facilitating computational thinking through modeling and programming in 3d. *IEEE Computer Graphics and Applications*, (3):68–71, 2014.

[20] A. Repenning, D. C. Webb, K. H. Koh, et al. Scalable game design: A strategy to bring systemic computer science education to schools through game design and simulation creation. *ACM Transactions on Computing Education (TOCE)*, 15(2):11, 2015.

[21] M. Resnick, J. Maloney, A. Monroy-Hernández, et al. Scratch: programming for all. *Communications of the ACM*, 52(11):60–67, 2009.

[22] L. Vygotsky, E. Hanfmann, and G. Vakar. *Thought and language*. MIT press, 2012.

[23] J. Williams, D. Paunesku, B. Haley, et al. Measurably increasing motivation in moocs. *In AIED 2013 Workshops Proceedings*, page 55, 2013.

[24] C. Wilson. Hour of code—a record year for computer science. *ACM Inroads*, 6(1):22–22, 2015.

[25] M. Yildiz and K. Scharaldi. Introduction to engineering and computer science in teacher education: Hour of code project. In *Proceedings of SITE '15*, volume 2015, pages 8367–8375, 2015.

Students' Initial Course Motivation and Their Achievement and Retention in College CS1 Courses

Duane F. Shell
Dept. of Educational Psychology
University of Nebraska-Lincoln
1-402-472-6981
dshell2@unl.edu

Leen-Kiat Soh
Dept. of Computer Science and Engineering
University of Nebraska-Lincoln
1-402-472-6738
lksoh@csse.unl.edu

Abraham E. Flanigan
Markeya S. Peteranetz
Dept. of Educational Psychology
University of Nebraska-Lincoln
1-402-472-8331
abrahamflangan@gmail.com
markeya.dubbs@huskers.unl.edu

ABSTRACT

The goal of this study was to investigate how students' entering motivation for the course in a suite of CS1 introductory computer science courses was associated with their subsequent course achievement and retention. Courses were tailored for specific student populations (CS majors, engineering majors, business-CS combined honors program). Students' goal orientations (learning, performance, task), perceived instrumentality (endogenous, exogenous), career connectedness, self-efficacy, and mindsets (growth or fixed) were assessed at the start of the course. Grades were significantly predicted from entering motivation; but prediction was highly variable across courses, ranging from not predicted for the engineering courses to highly predictable for the business-CS honors program. Course withdrawal was significantly predicted. Likelihood of withdrawing was decreased by future time career connectedness and learning approach goal orientation and increased by having an incremental theory of intelligence. Findings suggest that CS1 students who set learning approach goals for their classes have better academic outcomes and higher retention. Other motivational beliefs were inconsistent in their impacts and varied by course and student population. Except for students in an honors program, entering motivational beliefs weakly predicted achievement and retention, suggesting that impacts of the course itself on motivation and how motivation changes during the course are perhaps more important than student's initial motivation.

Keywords

Student motivation; Goal orientation; Retention; CS1 Achievement.

1. INTRODUCTION

In today's rapidly advancing technological environment, the need to attract and retain students in STEM majors is greater than ever before [22, 30]. Career opportunities in STEM-related fields are expected to grow at nearly twice the rate as non-STEM fields between 2008 and 2018 [22]. The need for more post-secondary students to major and graduate in STEM fields, especially computer science (CS), is widely recognized, [4, 22] and there is increasing need for computational thinking in CS and across the broader spectrum of STEM and non-STEM disciplines [29].

SIGCSE '16, March 02-05, 2016, Memphis, TN, USA
© 2016 ACM. ISBN 978-1-4503-3685-7/16/03…$15.00
DOI: http://dx.doi.org/10.1145/2839509.2844606

To address these needs, considerable effort has been focused on attracting and retaining students in CS. These include efforts to engage and motivate non-CS majors [7]; instructional strategies such as pair programming, peer-based instruction, and media computation [21]; using personal robots [16]; project-based instruction with different tracks [10]; and framing an appropriate classroom climate to reduce student anxiety about their status among peers and encourage them to co-learn and speak up in class [3]. But, despite these efforts, enrollment and persistence in CS continues to be problematic, with enrollments actually declining over the past decade [18].

This lack of progress indicates a need to better understand the motivations of students who are taking CS courses and how their motivation is contributing to their success and retention. Our purpose in this study was to investigate how students' motivation at the start of an introductory CS1 course was associated with their subsequent course achievement and retention.

2. THEORETICAL FRAMEWORK

Prior research has identified important aspects of motivation that are associated with academic achievement, engagement, and strategic self-regulation. These include goal orientation [9, 23, 24], future time perspective (FTP) [12, 13, 14], implicit intelligence or mindsets theory [5], and self-efficacy [2, 8].

In this study, we used a framework proposed by Shell et al. [24, also, 9, 19, 28] that examines course goals in three dimensions (learning, performance, and task) with each dimension having an approach and avoid component. Learning-approach goals are goals directed at learning new knowledge or gaining competence consistent with most past formulations of learning or mastery goals [23, 24]. Learning-avoid goals are deliberate goals to avoid learning of course material. Performance-approach goals reflect a desire to obtain favorable judgments of one's abilities by others or perform better than others in the class; whereas, performance-avoid goals reflect the desire to avoid negative judgments of one's ability or perform worse relative to others in the class. Task- or work-avoid goals reflect a desire to get through the class with as little time and effort as possible [19, 27, 28]. Task-approach goals reflect wanting to perform well on course assignments and tests [9, 19, 24, 28]. They differ from performance goals because they are about doing well without reference to normative performance or gaining positive or avoiding negative evaluations evaluation of competence. They also differ from learning goals in that students can have a goal to "do my work to the best of my ability" without any expectation that they will learn anything.

Studies in CS have found that learning (also known as mastery) approach goals were associated with higher achievement and retention, whereas, performance goals lead to lower achievement

[25] regardless of instructional approach (lecture vs peer instruction) [31]. Other studies in CS1 classes have shown that these goals change across the semester and that increase in task approach and decrease in learning avoid goals are associated with higher achievement and increase in learning approach goals is associated with higher metacognitive strategy use and deep learning [9].

Future time perspective (FTP) is a set of psychological constructs that together explain some differences in students' tendency to plan for the future, delay gratification, and make responsible life choices [13]. Connectedness refers to the ability to make connections between present activities and some future goal [14, 27]. Perceived Instrumentality (PI), is a person's perception of how useful a present task is for a future goal [12, 13]. In the school context, endogenous instrumentality reflects instrumentality of the course content for achieving personally meaningful future goals and outcomes. Exogenous instrumentality reflects a utilitarian connection between course grades and future goals. Students with high perceived instrumentality can see the connection between their current class activities and their more distant future academic, career, and life goals leading to increased motivation for their present learning in school [12, 13, 25]. Studies in CS classrooms have found that higher endogenous instrumentality is associated with higher achievement and exogenous instrumentality is associated with lower achievement, metacognitive strategies, and deep learning [25]

Implicit intelligence theories or mindsets have been shown to impact students' goals, motivation, and achievement [5]. Students who believe in a growth mindset that intelligence is malleable set learning goals, achieve better, and engage in better strategic self-regulation. Students who believe that intelligence is fixed and unchangeable are more likely to set performance-avoid goals and be at risk for learned helplessness [5]. Research has found that 50% of students in engineering fields had a fixed view of intelligence [11]. Studies in CS1 classes have found that growth mindset is associated with more and fixed mindset with less deep learning [25]. Also, both higher growth and fixed mindsets changed across the semester and were associated with lower achievement, contrary to expectations about growth mindsets [6].

Self-efficacy is defined as a person's subjective confidence in their capability of executing an action [2, 24]. Self-efficacy has been consistently identified as one of the most powerful motivators of human action. In a comprehensive synthesis of over 800 meta-analyses [8], it was identified as the strongest predictor of educational achievement. Studies have identified self-efficacy or similar confidence beliefs as key contributors to student choice of major and retention [2].

3. CURRENT STUDY

The goal of this study was to investigate how students' entering motivation was associated with their course achievement as measured by course grades, and their retention in the course. Prior research has found that students' motivation in introductory CS1 courses is associated with their course achievement and learning [9, 19, 25, 28]. Studies have shown that goal orientation and mindsets change across the semester [6, 9]. This prior work has looked primarily at during class motivation; it has not examined the goal orientations and motivation of students at the start of the class in-depth.

There are two reasons for looking at students' initial motivation for the course. *First*, students' initial motivation tells us something about why they chose to take the class. This can be important for attracting more students to CS and other STEM courses and majors. Knowing more about the motivation of students who take CS classes can help with targeting recruitment and promotion to students' motivational predispositions. *Second*, if poor performance and withdraw can be linked to students' initial motivation, it may be possible to identify students who are at risk by looking at their motivation at the beginning of class. That could allow instructors to potentially intervene earlier and to tailor interventions based on students' motivational characteristics.

4. METHODS

4.1 Participants

Participants were 274 students out of 305 total enrollees who consented to participation (229 men; 45 women; 153 freshmen, 62 sophomores, 30 juniors, 19 seniors, 10 other/unknown) from four courses in a suite of required introductory computer science courses (CS1) at a large Midwestern state university. Courses included one for CS majors (CSCE155A, 67 men, 9 women), one for a combined business/computer science honors program (RAIK183H, 20 men, 12 women), one for engineers with content tailored for engineering (CSCE155N, 60 men, 18 women), and one for a mix of computer engineering, other engineering, and general science majors (CSCE155E, 82 men, 6 women). Core content was the same for all courses, but courses were tailored for the different majors with different programming languages, lab exercises, and programming assignments. The study was approved by the University of Nebraska-Lincoln Institutional Review Board (IRB Number: 20120111818EP).

4.2 Measures

Further validation information for all goal orientation and motivation measures can be found in [5, 9, 12, 14, 19, 25, 26, 27, 28].

4.2.1 Goal Orientation

Students' course goal orientation was measured with an instrument used in prior studies [9, 19, 25, 28]. *Learning-approach goal orientation* (3 items) assesses goals for developing long-term, deep understanding of information and skills learned in the course (e.g., "Learning new knowledge or skills during the class just for the sake of learning them"). *Learning-avoid goal orientation* (3 items) assesses deliberate avoidance of long-term learning or retention of course information ("Getting a grade whether you remember anything beyond that or not"). *Performance-approach goal orientation* (3 items) assesses normative performance relative to other students and favorable assessments of ability by the instructor for ego protection (e.g., "Doing better than the other students"). *Performance-avoid goal orientation* (3 items) assesses avoiding negative performance evaluations and unfavorable assessments of ability by others (e.g., "Keeping others from thinking I am dumb"). *Task-approach goal orientation* (3 items) assesses efforts to achieve highly and do well on class assignments and activities without reference to normative comparisons (e.g., "Doing my best on course assignments and tests"). *Task-or work-avoid goal orientation* (3 items) assess deliberate intention to put forth minimal effort in the course (e.g., "Getting through this course with the least amount of time and effort"). Students rated goals on a 5-point Likert scale from 1 (*very unimportant*) to 5 (*very important*). Scores were computed as the mean score of the items in each scale. Cronbach alpha estimates were .73, .76, .71, .82, .82, and .77 for the learning approach, learning avoid, performance approach, performance avoid, task approach, and task/work avoid scales respectively.

4.2.2 *Future Time Perspective*

Future time perspective was measured by two instruments. *Career Connectedness* (11 items) assesses connections between a student's present and their future career goals (e.g., "One should be taking steps today to help realize future career goals; What will happen in the future in my career is an important consideration in deciding what action to take now) [14, 19, 27, 28]. Students indicated their agreement with each question using a 5-point Likert scale as follows: 1 (*strongly disagree*) to 5 (*strongly agree*). The career connectedness score was computed as the mean of the 11 items in the scale, with negative items reverse scored. Cronbach's alpha reliability estimate for the scale was .89.

Perceived instrumentality was measured with the Perceptions of Instrumentality Scale [12, 25, 28]. The scale measures both endogenous instrumentality (4 items; e.g., "What I learn in this CS1 will be important for my future occupational success") and exogenous instrumentality (4 items; e.g., "The only aspect of this class that will matter after graduation is my grade"). Students indicated their agreement with each question using a 5-point Likert scale from 1 (*strongly disagree*) to 5 (*strongly agree*). Scores are computed as the mean of the items in each scale. Coefficient alpha estimates for the endogenous and exogenous scales were respectively .91 and .91

4.2.3 *Mindsets*

Students' mindsets were measured with the Implicit Theories of Intelligence Scale [5]. The scale measures growth mindset (4-items; e.g., "No matter how much intelligence you have, you can always change it quite a bit") and fixed mindset (4-items; e.g., "You can learn new things, but you can't really change your basic intelligence"). Students indicated their agreement with each question on a 6-point Likert scale from 1 (*strongly disagree*) to 6 (*strongly agree*). Scores are computed as the mean of the items in each scale. Coefficient alpha reliability estimates for the incremental and entity scales were respectively .94 and .89.

4.2.4 *Self-Efficacy*

Students' self-efficacy was assessed using a questionnaire from [26]. Students were asked to rate their confidence in their knowledge of 12 computational thinking and CS topics with emphasis on application in their chosen field and enhancing creativity in their field ("Your ability to use computational algorithms to solve problems in your field;" "Your ability to conceptualize data in your field in ways that can be analyzed computationally"). Questions were based on the specific knowledge and skills taught and used during the CS1 courses. Ratings were done on a scale from 0 (*Completely Unconfident*) to 100 (*Completely Confident*). Self-efficacy scores were computed as the mean of the 12 items. The Cronbach's alpha reliability estimate was .94.

4.2.5 *Student Grades and Retention*

Students' course grades were obtained from University records. To standardize grades across courses, grades were converted to Z-scores within each course. Student retention was indicated by whether a student withdrew from the course.

4.3 Procedures

Data was collected during the first week of the fall 2014 semester in either course lecture sessions or course lab periods. All motivation measures test were administered on the Survey Monkey® Web platform.

5. RESULTS

5.1 Students' Entering Motivation

Mean scores for motivational variables are shown in Table 1. In relation to what are typically considered positive motivational orientations to these goals and beliefs [1, 2, 5, 13, 23, 24, 28], students in these CS1 classes as a group are approaching their class with highly positive motivation. They have high learning approach and task approach goal orientations with correspondingly low levels of learning and task avoid goal orientations. They also express moderate levels of performance approach and avoid goal orientations. They have high endogenous perceived instrumentality and low exogenous perceived instrumentality, along with high career future time connectedness. They express high incremental theory of intelligence and low entity theory. They express low self-efficacy but this is likely an accurate reflection of their computational thinking skills as this is their first college CS course.

Despite these generally positive motivations, there were significant differences in beliefs across the four courses. One-way ANOVA were done for each of the motivational variables. Results for these are indicated in Table 1. The most relevant differences are between the CSCE155N course for engineers and the other three courses. The other three courses are generally part of the students' major field or taken optionally because of the language used (C++ in the CSCE155E course). For the engineers in CSCE155N, the course is more like a foundational course that is not directly a part of their major [19]. Perhaps as a consequence of this not being directly in their major, these CSCE155N students express significantly lower learning approach goal orientation and endogenous instrumentality with correspondingly higher learning avoid goal orientation and exogenous instrumentality. They also have the lowest self-efficacy.

5.2 Prediction of Students' Course Grades

Multiple regression was used to predict students' within-course Z-score standardized grades. Because of the number of variables, a backward selection method was used to identify significant predictors. Regressions were done for all students combined and for each course separately because of differences between courses in motivational beliefs (Table 1). For all students, the regression for the final model was significant (R = .244, R^2 = .059, $F(4, 242)$ = 3.82, p = .005). Significant predictors were performance avoid goal orientation (β= .113), learning approach goal orientation (β = .198), endogenous PI (β = -.238) and exogenous PI (β = -.188).

There was considerable difference across the four courses. For CSCE155A, the course for CS majors, the final regression model was significant (R = .396, R^2 = .156, $F(5, 68)$ = 2.52, p = .037). Significant predictors were self-efficacy (β = -.258), fixed mindset (β = .270), performance avoid goal orientation (β = .217), endogenous PI (β = -.263), and exogenous PI (β = -.343). For CSCE155E, the course for a mix of computer engineering, other engineering, and science majors, the final regression model was significant (R = .282, R^2 = .080, $F(2, 72)$ = 3.12, p = .05), The only significant predictors were learning approach goal orientation (β = .340) and endogenous PI (β = .-.232). For CSCE155N, the course for engineers, no model achieved significant prediction (all variables: R = .324, R^2 = .105, $F(11, 58)$ = 0.618, p = .806), Although the prediction for CS majors in the CSCE155A was somewhat strong, prediction for the mixed course was marginal and prediction for the engineering majors was not present.

Table 1. Mean Scores of Variables and ANOVA Results

	All Students		CCE155A		CCE155E		CCE155N		RAIK183H	
Variables	*M*	*SD*	*M*	*SD*	*M*	*SD*	*M*	*SD*	*M*	*SD*
Course Grade	2.78	1.25	2.38	1.46	2.67	1.38	3.20	.83	2.99	.87
FTPS Career*	4.07	.57	4.18_a	.49	3.91_a	.62	4.10	.54	4.15	.57
Self-Efficacy*	49.49	19.24	50.87	19.57	48.20	19.36	46.18_a	18.36	57.83_a	18.34
Learning Approach GO*	4.51	.59	4.65_a	.41	4.59_b	.55	4.24_{abc}	.73	4.63_c	.46
Learning Avoid GO*	2.11	.83	1.86_a	.77	2.07_b	.84	2.52_{abc}	.76	1.83_c	.76
Performance Approach GO	3.22	.83	3.33	.81	3.22	.97	3.09	.73	3.26	.64
Performance Avoid GO	2.85	.99	2.90	.99	2.78	1.02	2.82	.94	2.98	1.07
Task Approach GO	4.64	.58	4.72	.42	4.66	.47	4.53	.83	4.71	.39
Task Avoid GO	2.25	.85	2.09	.77	2.37	.86	2.38	.86	1.98	.89
PI Endogenous*	4.22	.79	4.57_a	.62	4.32_b	.70	3.60_{ab}	.78	4.66_b	.36
PI Exogenous*	1.95	.83	1.80_a	.80	1.88_b	.81	2.34_{abc}	.82	1.48_c	.51
Growth Mindset	4.46	1.00	4.65	.94	4.33	1.06	4.45	.95	4.37	1.04
Fixed Mindset*	2.50	.99	2.22_a	.90	2.75_a	1.10	2.55	.87	2.42	.97

*Significantly different across courses at $p < .05$. Means with the same subscript are significantly different at $p < .05$ in Tukey tests.

In contrast to the poor prediction for the CSCE155 courses, prediction for RAIK183H, the course for business-CS honors majors, was very high. The final regression model was significant (R = .888, R^2 = .788, $F(7, 20)$ = 10.65, $p < .0001$), Significant predictors were learning approach goal orientation (β = .579), performance approach goal orientation (β = -.256), performance avoid goal orientation (β = .288), task approach goal orientation (β = -.872), endogenous PI (β = .877), growth mindset (β = .769), and fixed mindset (β = .811). Differences in the entering motivation of these students predicted almost all of the difference in their final grade.

5.3 Prediction of Students' Course Withdrawal

Logistic regression was used to predict students' withdrawal from the course. Twenty-two students withdrew from the four courses combined so the only analysis that could be done was for the entire sample. Withdrawal was significantly predicted (χ^2 (4) = 9.68, p = .021). Likelihood of withdrawing was decreased by future time career connectedness (β = -.845, OR = .429) and learning approach goal orientation (β = -.635, OR = .530) and increased by having a growth mindset (β = .506, OR = 1.66).

6. DISCUSSION

6.1 Students' Entering Motivation

The findings suggest that students *are primarily choosing to take their CS1 course because they see it as personally relevant to their future goals*. Whether they chose them voluntarily or not, students expected their CS1 course to contribute to their personal growth and development and help them achieve their future academic and career goals. While this might be expected for those students who have chosen CS majors, this pattern of motivation was also present for the engineering majors in CSCE155N who are taking the class as a foundational course. The engineering majors were somewhat less motivated by personal relevance and goals (lower learning approach goal orientation and lower endogenous PI) and somewhat higher utility motivation (higher exogenous PI), but still were primarily motivated by personal growth.

Most emphasis on motivating students to take CS and STEM courses and major in CS or other STEM disciplines is focused on getting students to buy into the motivational pattern and goals that these students have when they start the course [1, 3., 7, 11, 17, 24]. While their positive motivation likely is somewhat due to their having already chosen a CS or other STEM major, as they would be predisposed to be motivated toward STEM classes once their major was chosen, it also is possible that these students chose a STEM major because they had developed this positive motivation toward STEM subjects.

6.2 Prediction of Students' Course Grades

Although the expectation would be that these students' very positive entering goals and motivation would be associated with high achievement in the class [1, 19, 24, 25, 28], students' grades were *not* predicted by their goal orientations and motivation in consistent or expected ways. The honors program students in the RAIK183H course fit expectations from prior research very well. Goal orientation and motivation highly predicted their course grades, with over 75% of the variance in grades explained. This is an exceptionally high level of predictability for educational classroom research. Apparently for honors students, who generally have developed strong academic strategic self-regulatory skills, achievement outcomes follow from their motivation.

But, they also had associations that were contrary to what are usually seen as positive motivators of achievement. Higher performance avoid and lower task approach goal orientations were associated with higher grades. These patterns are not generally considered productive as performance avoid goals are usually associated with lower achievement [23] and goals to do one's best are typically seen as promoting greater engagement and learning. It is not clear why these honors students would have these contrary associations. They are high achievers who are typically seen by others as "smart", so we speculate that, because they achieve highly, it is possible that fear of failing is a productive motivator for them because they believe they will succeed. They are in a competitive program and environment and may actually thrive in this environment in ways other more average students do not. The RAIK183H students did not have overly high fixed mindset relative to their growth mindset, but although usually seen as contrary, both were positively predictive of grades. Prior research has established that fixed mindsets are not necessarily detrimental as long as students are achieving at high levels [5]. Perhaps for these high achievers, a fixed mindset does not have the same negative consequences that it has for more average students.

Prediction of grades for the other 155 students was considerably poorer than that for the RAIK183H course. The best prediction was for CSCE155A where about 16% of grade variance was explained. Only about 8% of variance was explained for CSCE155E, and grades were not predicted significantly at all for CSCE155N. These findings indicate that course achievement was generally unassociated with entering motivation and goals for students in these classes. Students in the 155 classes are more diverse academically, relative to the RAIK183H honor students, which may lessen the impact of student motivation on their grades. Prior research also has shown that students in the CSCE155E and CSCE155N classes also adopt a more diverse range of motivated strategic self-regulatory profiles with more students adopting profiles that are dysfunctional for attaining high grades [19, 28]. Studies have shown that goal orientations and mindsets change across the semester in introductory CS courses [6, 9]. Because these and other motivational constructs are sensitive to within-class experiences, perhaps what happens in the 155 classes leads to more changes in students' goals and motivation than in RAIK183H, reducing the impacts of their entering motivation.

Also, it is not clear why CSCE155A predictability was so low. Other studies have shown that they adopt similar motivated strategic self-regulatory profiles to the RAIK183H students, so they are maintaining positive approaches to learning throughout the semester [19, 28]. But, their course grades are more distributed than the RAIK183H class, so they are not as uniformly achieving in ways consistent with their entering motivation and goal expectations. This perhaps makes them more susceptible to changes in motivation and goals as a result of during class experience which would reduce the prediction from their entering goals and beliefs.

For these courses, the only result that followed expected prediction was the positive association for learning approach goal orientation in the total student sample and for CSCE155E. These findings reinforce the importance of learning approach goal orientation discussed in [24]. Other beliefs had very contrary associations. Like RAIK183H, performance avoid goals were positively predictive of grades for all students and for CSCE155A. Also, both endogenous PI (all students, CSCE155A, and CSCE155E), reflecting instrumentality for personal future goals, and endogenous PI (all students and CSCE155A), reflecting utility-based instrumentality, were negatively associated with grades. This means that *students who saw the course as important for achieving future goals achieved less well.*

6.3 Prediction of Students' Course Withdrawal

Few students withdrew from these introductory CS1 courses. Only 22 students withdrew. Retention in the course was predicted by having high learning approach goal orientation and high future career connectedness. So those *students who were more strongly connected to their future career and who set goals to deeply learn the course material for their personal growth and development were less likely to drop out.* However, contrary to expectations, students who adopted a growth mindset were more likely to drop out. Because students with a growth mindset see their ability and intelligence as changing through learning, perhaps they drop out because they did not think that they were learning anything meaningful. It also may be that while these students want to learn the material, they do not believe that learning it is worth the effort required. Studies using interview data have shown that students in CSCE155N do not typically see the course as valuable [26]. The pattern of beliefs predictive of withdraw mirrored those found for grades, suggesting that grades and retention are associated with similar motivational patterns.

7. CONCLUSIONS

Findings support that students taking introductory CS1 courses are coming to the course with the goal orientation and motivation necessary for success. But, except for an honors course, these positive entering goals and motivation did not always predict course achievement and retention in the ways that would be anticipated from prior research and theory.

Results confirm the centrality of learning approach goal orientation for successful learning and achievement [24]. Essentially, students will not learn if they do not set goals to learn the material and they will not develop sophisticated knowledge and expertise if they do not set goals to learn the material deeply. Learning approach goals were the *only* consistent positive predictor of grades and retention. Findings along with those by [31] suggest that *getting CS1 students to set learning approach goals and supporting these goals with positive learning experiences is critical to successful achievement and to retaining students in classes.*

Results for perceived instrumentality in contrast were the opposite of what would be expected. Except for the honors students in RAIK183h where endogenous PI was positively associated with higher grades, endogenous and exogenous PI were negatively associated with grades. These anomalous results may be because perceiving the course as being highly instrumental to future success produces higher anxiety. This may cause CS1 students who are not having success to shift into more dysfunctional patterns of strategic self-regulation [19, 28] that lead to lower achievement. Certainly these findings suggest a need to more fully understand the dynamics of perceived instrumentality across the semester.

Results for mindsets were similarly confounding. As was found by [6], h*aving* a growth mindset was positively predictive of grades for the RAIK183H honors student, but was not predictive for other classes. However, having a growth mindset also was positively predictive of withdrawing from the course. Contrary to general theory of intelligence beliefs and prior research in CS classes [6], a fixed mindset was positively predictive of grades for RAIK183H and CSCE155A. Prior research suggests that a fixed mindset is not necessarily problematic if a student perceives that they have high ability and achieves at a high level [5]. So *a fixed mindset may to be positive for the generally high achieving students in these classes.* The similarity of findings here and [6] call for more study of mindsets in introductory CS classes.

Results are important for CS educators trying to understand how to motivate student achievement and retention in CS courses. Findings suggest that students are coming to introductory CS courses with the positive motivational dispositions necessary to succeed. This is true whether they are CS majors or non-majors. Except for highly selective honors students, however, these entering motivations are not necessarily motivating course achievement. When coupled with research showing that students entering goals and motivation shift over the semester in introductory CS courses [6, 9, 17], our findings suggest that the focus needs to be on within-course motivational and instructional strategies. What instructors do affects students' motivation. However, as noted by [15] addressing motivation in CS courses is complex and will require going beyond simple instructional and motivational strategies, as even specifically targeted motivational/affective efforts may produce only limited effects [17, 20].

8. ACKNOWLEDGMENTS

This material is based upon work supported by the National Science Foundation under grant no. DUE-1431874.

9. REFERENCES

[1] Ackerman, P. L., Kanfer, R., & Beier, M. E. 2013. Trait complex, cognitive ability, and domain knowledge predictors of baccalaureate success, STEM persistence, and gender differences. *J. of Educ. Psychol.* 105. 911-927.

[2] Bandura, A. 1997. *Self-efficacy: The exercise of control.* New York, NY, US: W. H. Freeman/Times Books/ Henry Holt & Co.

[3] Barker, L. J., M. O'Neill, and N. Kazim 2014. Framing Classroom Climate for Student Learning and Retention in Computer Science. In *Proc. of the 45th ACM Technical Symposium on Comp. Sci. Educ. (SIGCSE'2014)*, 319-324.

[4] Committee on Prospering in the Global Economy of the 21st Century 2007. *Rising Above the Gathering Storm.* Washington, DC: National Academies Press.

[5] Dweck, C. S. 1999. *Self-Theories: Their Role in Motivation, Personality, and Development.* New York: Psychol. Press.

[6] Flanigan, A. E., Peteranetz, M. S., Shell, D. F., and Soh, L-K (2015). Exploring changes in computer science students' implicit theories of intelligence across the semester. In *Proc.of ICER'15 (Omaha, NE),* 161-168.

[7] Forte, A., and M. Guzdial 2005. Motivation and Nonmajors in Computer Science: Identifying Discrete Audiences for Introductory Courses. *IEEE Trans. on Ed.*, 48(2), 248-253.

[8] Hattie, J. 2009. *Visible learning: A synthesis of over 800 meta-analyses relating to achievement.* Oxford: Routledge.

[9] Hazley, M. P., Shell, D. F., Soh, L.-K., Miller, L. D., Chiriacescu, V. and Ingraham, E. 2014. Changes in student goal orientation across the semester in undergraduate computer science courses. In *Proc. 44th Annual Frontiers in Educ. (FIE) Conference*, (Madrid Spain), 2278-2285.

[10] Haungs, M., C. Clark, J. Clements, and D. Janzen 2012. Improving First-Year Success and Retention through Interest-Based CS0 Courses, in *Proc. 43rd ACM Technical Symposium on Comp. Sci. Educ.(SIGCSE'2012)*, 589-594.

[11] Heyman, G. , Martyna, B. and Bhatia, S. 2002. Gender and achievment-related beliefs among engineering students. *J. of Women and Minorities in Sci. and Eng.*, 8, 41-52.

[12] Husman, J. , Derryberry, W. P., Crowson, H. M. and Lomax, R. 2004. Instrumentality, task value, and intrinsic motivation: making sense of their independent interdependence. *Contemp. Educ. Psychol.* 29, 63-76.

[13] Husman, J. and Lens, W. 1999. The role of the future in student motivation. *Educ. Psychologist,* 34, 113-125.

[14] Husman, J. and Shell, D. F. 2008. Beliefs and perceptions about the future: a measurement of future time perspective. *Learn. and Individ. Differ.,* 18, 166-175.

[15] Kinnunen, P., and L. Maimi 2006. Why Students Drop Out CS1 Course?, in *Proc. of the Second International Workshop on Computing Education Research (ICER'2006)*, 97-108.

[16] McGill, M. M. 2012. Learning to Program with Personal Robots: Influences on Student Motivation. *ACM Trans. on Comp. Educ*,,12(1), article 4.

[17] McKinney, D., and L. F. Denton 2004. Houston, We Have a Problem: There's a Leak in the CS1 Affective Oxygen Tank. In *Proc. 35th SIGCSE Technical Symposium on Comp. Sci. Educ.*, 236-239.

[18] National Center for Education Statistics 2014. *Digest of Education Statistics.* Washington, DC: U.S. Dept. of Ed.

[19] Nelson, K.G., Shell, D.F., Husman, J., Fishman, E.J., and Soh, L.K. 2015. Motivational and self-regulated learning profiles of students taking a foundational engineering course. *J Eng Educ.*, 104, 74-100. DOI= 10.1002/jee.20066

[20] Ott, C., A. Robins, P. haden, and K. Shephard 2015. Illustrating Performance Indicators and Characteristics to Support Students' Self-Regulated Learning in CS1, *Comp. Sci. Educ.*, 25(2), 174-198.

[21] Porter, L., M. Guzdial, C. McDowell, and B. Simon 2013. Success in Introductory Programming: What Works?, *Communications of the ACM*, 58(8), 34-36.

[22] President's Council of Advisors on Science and Technology 2012. *Engage to excel: Producing one million additional college graduates with degrees in science, technology, engineering, and mathematics.* Washington, DC: Executive Office of the President of the United States.

[23] Senko, C., Hulleman, C. S. and Harackiewicz, J.M. 2011. Achievement goal theory at the crossroads: old controversies, current challenges, and new directions. *Educ. Psychologist,* 46, 26-47.

[24] Shell, D. F., Brooks, D. W., Trainin, G., Wilson, K., Kauffman, D. F., and Herr, L. 2010. *The Unified Learning Model: How Motivational, Cognitive, And Neurobiological Sciences Inform Best Teaching Practices.* Netherlands: Springer.

[25] Shell, D. F., Hazley, M. P., Soh, L-K., Ingraham, E. and Ramsay, S. 2013. Associations of students' creativity, motivation, and self-regulation with learning and achievement in college computer science courses. In *Proc. 43rd ASEE/IEEE Frontiers in Education Conference* (Oklahoma City, OK), 1637-1643.

[26] Shell, D. F., Hazley, M. P., Soh, L.-K., Miller, L. D., Chiriacescu, V. and Ingraham, E. 2014. Improving learning of computational thinking using computational creativity exercises in a college CS1 computer science course for engineers. In *Proc. 44th Annual Frontiers in Education (FIE) Conference,* (Madrid, Spain), 3029-3035.

[27] Shell, D. F. and Husman, J. 2008. Control, motivation, affect, and strategic self-regulation in the college classroom: a multidimensional phenomenon. *J. of Educ. Psychol.*, 100, 443-459.

[28] Shell, D.F. and Soh, L.K. 2013. Profiles of motivated self-regulation in college computer science courses: differences in major versus required non-major courses. *J. of Sci. Educ. and Tech.*, 22, 899-913.

[29] Wing, J. 2006. Computational Thinking. *CACM,* 49, 33-35.

[30] Xie, Y. and Killewald, A. A. 2012. *Is American science in decline*? Cambridge, MA: Harvard University Press. doi:10.4159/harvard.9780674065048

[31] Zingaro, D. 2015. Examining Interest and Grades in Computer Science 1: A Study of Pedagogy and Achievement Goals, *ACM Trans. on Comp. Educ*, 15(3), article 14.

Landscape of K-12 Computer Science Education in the U.S.: Perceptions, Access, and Barriers

Jennifer Wang
Google, Inc.
1600 Amphitheatre Pkwy.
Mountain View, CA 94043
+1-310-866-3258
jtw@google.com

Hai Hong
Google, Inc.
1600 Amphitheatre Pkwy.
Mountain View, CA 94043
+1-310-866-3258
haihong@google.com

Jason Ravitz
Google, Inc.
1600 Amphitheatre Pkwy.
Mountain View, CA 94043
+1-310-866-3258
ravitz@google.com

Sepehr Hejazi Moghadam
Google, Inc.
1600 Amphitheatre Pkwy.
Mountain View, CA 94043
+1-310-866-3258
shmoghadam@google.com

ABSTRACT

Through surveys of 1,673 students, 1,685 parents, 1,013 teachers, 9,693 principals, and 1,865 superintendents across the United States, this study explores perceptions, access, and barriers to computer science education at the K-12 level. We found most respondents were unable to distinguish computer literacy activities from computer science, with female, Black, or Hispanic respondents even less likely to do so. Perceptions of who does computer science were narrow and stereotypical (White, male, smart), but there was high value and demand for computer science across all populations, particularly among parents. Results indicate discrepancies in access to technology and computer science. Over 75% of principals reported their school did not offer computer science with programming/coding, but Hispanic students reported lower exposure to computers at home and in school and Black students and lower income students reported less access to computer science learning in school. Hispanic students and female students were also less likely to have learned computer science or have confidence to learn computer science compared to their counterparts. Finally, we explored barriers to access and identified a harsh disconnect: parent and student demand for computer science education was high while administrators' perceptions of this demand was low. Additionally, the most common barriers to offering computer science cited by principals and superintendents were the need to dedicate time to other courses and testing requirements and the lack of qualified teachers, with technology less common of a barrier.

CCS Concepts

K.3.2 [Computers and Education]: Computer and Information Science Education – computer science education.

Keywords

K-12; pre-university; pre-college; high school; middle school; teachers; principals; superintendents; parents; perceptions; knowledge; access; barriers; diversity; underrepresented minorities; Hispanic; Latino/a; Black; African American; income.

1. INTRODUCTION

Technical advancements and the expansion of professions in which computer science (CS) is relevant make it more important than ever for all students to have opportunities to learn CS. Research on underrepresented students in CS at the K-12 level is limited, as is research on key stakeholders in CS education including parents and administrators. We sought to understand the landscape and perceptions of CS for students and their influencers across the U.S. in order to inform outreach efforts and to advance CS education at the K-12 level.

This paper details the first year of a three-year study on the landscape of CS K-12 education in the U.S., surveying students, parents, teachers, principals, and superintendents. The goal of the study is to understand

- perceptions of CS,
- interest in and demand for CS,
- in- and out-of-school opportunities for CS,
- participation in CS, and
- barriers to providing and accessing CS opportunities.

2. RELEVANCE

The field of computer science has faced a major hurdle in expanding diversity in participation. At the high school level, Advanced Placement (AP) Computer Science A enrollment is low overall, but drastically lower for Blacks and Hispanics. For instance, among the 49 states with at least one student who took the computer science exam, 12 had no Black students participating in 2014 [1]. Of all the AP Computer Science A test takers in 2014, only 3.9% were Black and 8.8% were Hispanic, with dramatically lower pass rates for both Black (33.4%) and Hispanic (39.2%) when compared to the overall pass rate of 70.3% [1]. At the university level, only 11.4% of CS degrees were awarded to Blacks and 8.5% awarded to Hispanic students in 2012 [2]. And with the recent release of diversity data by top technology companies (e.g., Google, Microsoft, Facebook, Apple, Ebay, Pinterest, Pandora, LinkedIn), the lack of diversity is sounding the alarm for action.

Perceptions, encouragement, and exposure play important roles in the lack of participation and interest [3]. Carter [4] found that students chose not to study CS not because of lack of ability, but because of an incorrect or incomplete perception of the field. Fifty percent of students opposed CS because of their perception that computer scientists spend their days working in front of a computer. Furthermore, Cheryan et al. [5] found that a sense of belonging led to a greater likelihood of indicating interest in computer science. Stereotypes of computer scientists being male, "nerdy," and lacking social skills are pervasive. However, the authors found that students confronted with non-stereotypes about CS were more likely than students confronted with stereotypes to indicate an interest in majoring in CS.

Similarly, perceptions in one's own ability (i.e., self-confidence) have been found to be correlated with interest and participation.

SIGCSE '16, March 02-05, 2016, Memphis, TN, USA
ACM 978-1-4503-3685-7/16/03.
http://dx.doi.org/10.1145/2839509.2844628

Smith, Pasero, and McKenna [6] used data from Trends in International Mathematics and Science Study (TIMSS) and found that in fourth and eighth grade, boys had higher confidence than girls in science and were more likely to like science than girls. Cheong, Pajares, and Oberman [7] found that while teachers rated both boys and girls equally competent, girls rated themselves lower than boys on computer self-efficacy and self-concept. Girls' lower participation and interest in STEM and CS may also be explained by their lower confidence. In one study, Hispanic girls gained increased interest in computer careers, mediated by self-reported computing skills and confidence [8].

External influences involve encouragement from adults (parents, teachers, and other family and adult leaders) as well as peers [3]. Parental encouragement of science and mathematics in middle and/or high school increases the likelihood of a young adult pursuing [9] and persisting in STEM careers [10]. Teachers, as well as parents and peers, also play key roles as influencers [8].

In order to address issues of lack of awareness and exposure to CS, as well as negative perceptions that may discourage students from pursuing CS, we embarked on a study to understand the landscape of CS access for students in the United States. We sought to investigate the potential and interrelated factors of perceptions, encouragement, and exposure behind the low numbers of minorities pursuing computer science.

3. DATA SOURCES

This study details results from year one of implementation, surveying 1,673 students, 1,685 parents, 1,013 teachers, 9,693 principals, and 1,865 superintendents in the United States, as shown in Table 1.

Telephone interviews were conducted for students, parents, and teachers currently living in all 50 states and the District of Columbia using a combination of two sample sources: the Gallup Panel and the Gallup Daily tracking survey. The Gallup Panel is a proprietary, probability-based panel of U.S. adults selected using random-digit-dial (RDD) and address based sampling methods. The Gallup Panel is not an opt-in panel. The Gallup Daily tracking survey sample includes national adults with a minimum quota of 50% cellphone respondents and 50% landline respondents, with additional minimum quotas by time zone within region. Landline and cellphone numbers are selected using RDD methods. Landline respondents are chosen at random within each household based on which member had the most recent birthday.

Students and parents were representative of the U.S. population, with targeted, detailed data on underrepresented populations (Blacks and Hispanics). Students were in grades 7-12 and parents had students in grades 7-12. Student and parent interviews were conducted in both English and Spanish. Student and parent samples are weighted to correct for unequal selection probability and nonresponse. Student and parent data are weighted to match national demographics of age, gender, education, race, ethnicity and region. Demographic weighting targets are based on the most recent Current Population Survey. Black and Hispanic student and parent populations were targeted for a minimum sample for comparisons with White students and parents. Other races were included in the survey but were not used for comparison by race due to small sample sizes.

Teachers were also a representative sample, including teachers of 1st-12th grade, with approximately 20.6% teaching or having taught computer science. Teacher samples are weighted to correct for unequal selection probability and nonresponse. The data are weighted to match national demographics of age, gender, education, race, ethnicity and geographic region.

The population for principals was sampled from a list of 99% of U.S. public schools and approximately 30% of U.S. private schools. The population for superintendents was from a panel including more than 20% of all U.S. K-12 superintendents. The principal and superintendent populations were comprehensive, but not representative, with principals from all 50 states and the District of Columbia, and superintendents from all states except Hawaii and the District of Columbia.

Table 1. Methodology overview for the five populations.

Target Population	Methodology
Students *(nationally representative)*	***Mode***: Phone ***Respondents***: 1,673 • 234 Black • 262 Hispanic ***Response rates***: • Landline: 38% • Cell: 36%
Parents *(nationally representative)*	***Mode***: Phone ***Respondents***: 1,685 • 208 Black • 276 Hispanic ***Response rates***: • Landline: 29% • Cell: 35%
Teachers *(nationally representative)*	***Mode***: Phone ***Respondents***: 1,013 ***Response rates***: • Landline: 49% • Cell: 47%
Principals	***Mode:*** Online ***Respondents***: 9,693 ***Response rate***: 11%
Superintendents	***Mode***: Online ***Respondents***: 1,865 ***Response rate***: 14%

4. METHODS

The surveys for students, parents, teachers, and principals each lasted about 12 minutes, with 30-40 questions. Superintendents were surveyed as part of another regular online survey, with 10 closed-ended questions for this study. Table 1 shows the mode of surveys and respondents completing the surveys for the study.

After data were collected and demographic weighting applied, the data were coded and reviewed by response. Indices of related variables were created and analyzed using regression to understand trends across and within the surveyed populations.

5. RESULTS

5.1 Knowledge and Perceptions of Computer Science

Knowledge of computer science can influence perceptions; perceptions can influence who receives encouragement. Results on knowledge of computer science indicate that most respondents do not have a clear understanding of what computer science is and is not, and responses were varied. The most common misunderstanding was that CS includes creation of documents and presentations (77.6% of students, 64.3% of parents, 74.8% of teachers, and 63.4% of principals agreed) as well as searching the Internet (56.9% of students, 49.3% of parents, 63.8% of teachers, and 53.6% of principals agreed). In particular, female students, parents, and teachers are less likely than their male counterparts to correctly identify CS (see Figure 1).

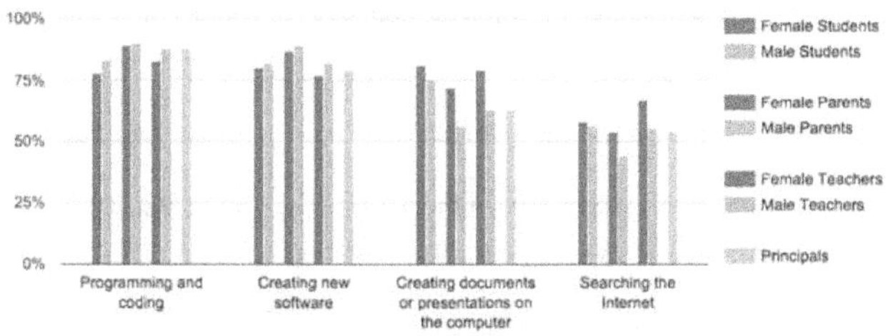

Figure 1. Computer science knowledge, by gender. Responses to the survey question gauging computer science knowledge, with respondents indicating whether these activities were part of computer science or not. Bars indicate the percentage of each population agreeing that the activity is part of computer science.

We also saw that Black and Hispanic students and parents were less likely to understand computer science than their White counterparts (see Figure 2). These misunderstandings could potentially contribute to underrepresentation of these groups in the field of computer science.

Encouragingly, a large majority of the respondents agreed that CS was important and had wide-impact and applicability. For instance, 82-94% of teachers, parents, and students agreed that people who do computer science work on fun and exciting projects, and 93% of students and parents agreed that people who do computer science make things that help improve people's lives. Furthermore, 81-96% of all five populations agreed that computer science can be used in many different types of jobs. Furthermore, most students (68%) and parents (79%) agreed that computer scientists have good-paying jobs.

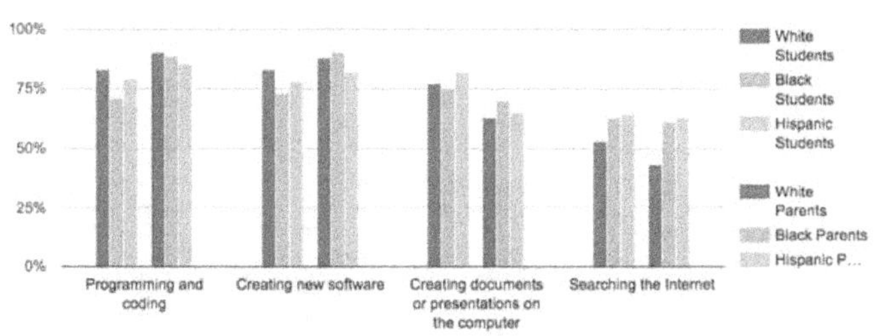

Figure 2. Computer science knowledge, by race. Responses to the survey question gauging computer science knowledge, with respondents indicating whether these activities were part of computer science or not. Bars indicate the percentage of each population agreeing that the activity is part of computer science.

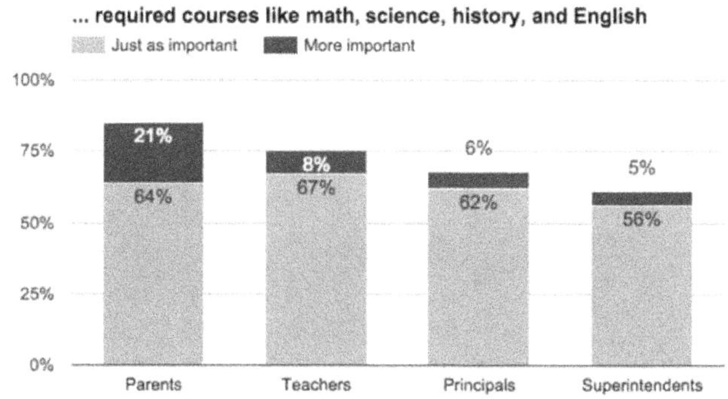

Figure 3. Responses to "Do you think offering opportunities to learn computer science is more important, just as important or less important to a student's future success than ... ?"

In particular, we see that a majority of parents, teachers, principals, and superintendents felt that computer science was just as important as or more important than required core classes, like math, science, history, and English (see Figure 3).

On the other hand, when considering perceptions of those who do do computer science, there is a clear distinction of those who do and do not. Almost half (48.5%) of students agreed that computer scientists need to be very smart. Teachers (62.3%) and principals (56.0%) agreed that students good at math and science would be more successful in computer science. However, only 42.2% of students rated themselves as skilled in math and 39.3% rated themselves as skilled in science. Only 54.2% of students stated that they were very confident they could learn computer science.

Gender biases were also prevalent. 73.7% of students, 64.1% of parents, and 63.4% of teachers think that boys are more interested

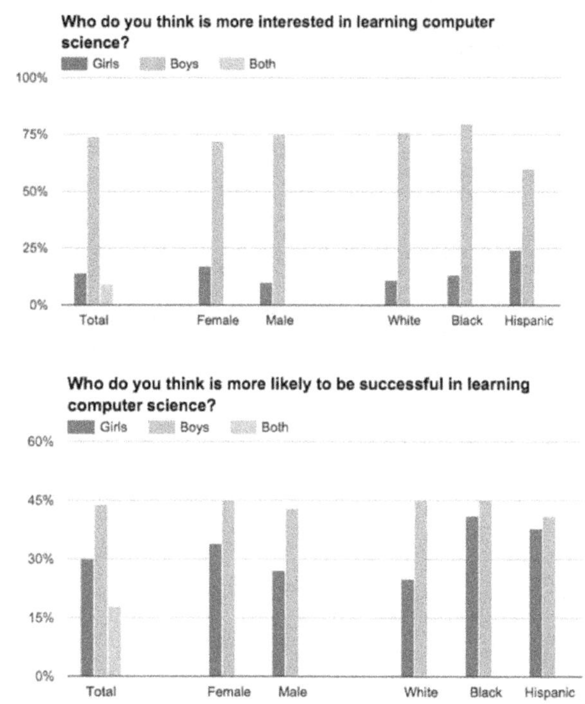

Figure 4. Student responses to items on interest and success in computer science, by gender and race.

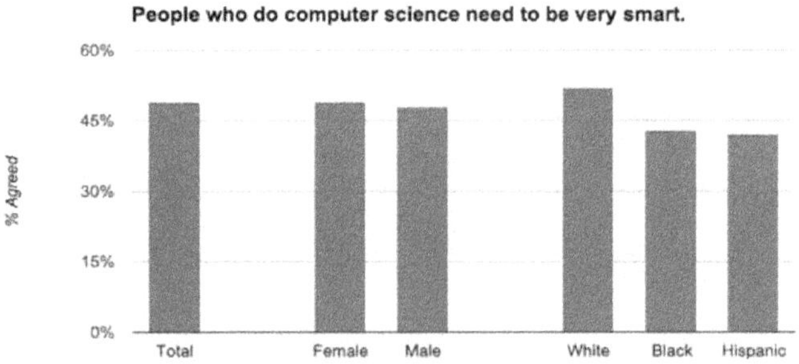

Figure 5. Percentage student agreement with "People who do computer science need to be very smart," by gender and race.

in CS than girls. And, 43.9% of students, 37.1% of parents, and 35.7% of teachers believe that boys would be more successful than girls in CS. These findings imply that many students may not be getting the encouragement to do computer science and many may not have the confidence to pursue learning computer science.

By demographic, we see that White and Black students are more likely than Hispanic students to say boys are more interested in learning CS. White students are the least likely to say girls are more likely to be successful in learning CS and the most likely to say you need to be very smart to do CS (see Figures 4-5). In other words, interestingly, White students are most likely to hold a stereotypical view of those in computer science, with respect to gender and mindset.

Not surprisingly, both students and parents perceive those who do computer science in the media as mostly white, male, and "wearing glasses." Considering this popular perception, Black and Hispanic students are less likely to have a sense of belonging in CS and, consequently, an interest in the field [5]. Further, with students' low ratings of their own skills in math and science, teachers and principals may be less likely to encourage these students to pursue CS. We saw that Hispanic students were less likely than White or Black students to rate themselves as skilled in science (28% of Hispanics, compared with 40% of Whites and 50% of Blacks). Perhaps the stereotypes of who does computer science is self-perpetuating, making the issue of diversity a deeply imbedded challenge. These findings point to the need to better shape CS learning environments and social influencers to be inclusive of all backgrounds.

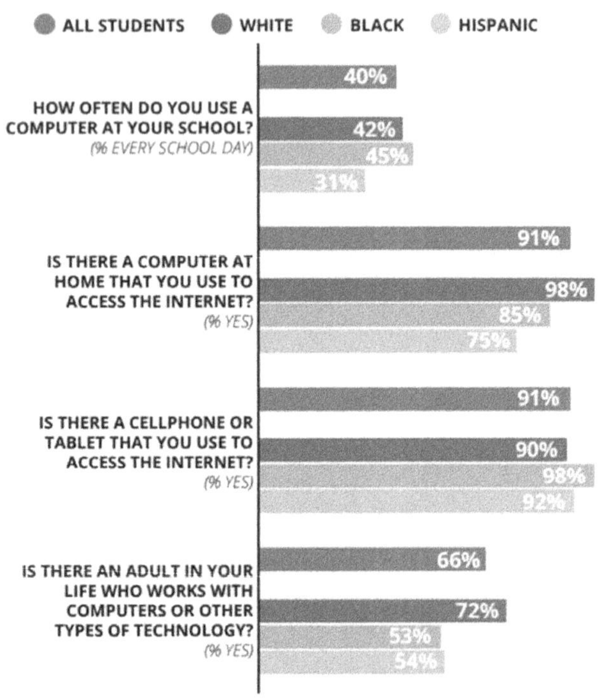

Figure 6. Student access to computer technology, by race.

5.2 Access to Technology and Computer Science

We now look at students' exposure to technology and computer science, as it may be influenced by students', parents', and educators' perceptions of the field. With regards to exposure to technology, Hispanic students are least likely to have exposure to computers at home and at school compared to Black and White students. Only 75% of Hispanic students report having access to a computer at home, compared to 85% of Black students and 98% of White students. At school, only 31% of Hispanic students report using a computer everyday, compared to 45% of Black students and 42% of White students. See Figure 6.

In terms of CS opportunities, over 75% of principals say their school offers no CS programming/coding classes. Black students, regardless of income, are less likely than White or Hispanic students to report opportunities to learn computer science at school, including dedicated CS classes, CS as part of other classes, and groups or clubs (see Figure 7). Hispanic students are also less likely than White students to report having dedicated computer science classes, but after accounting for household income, this effect diminishes. However, by income, lower income students are less likely to report access to CS learning opportunities.

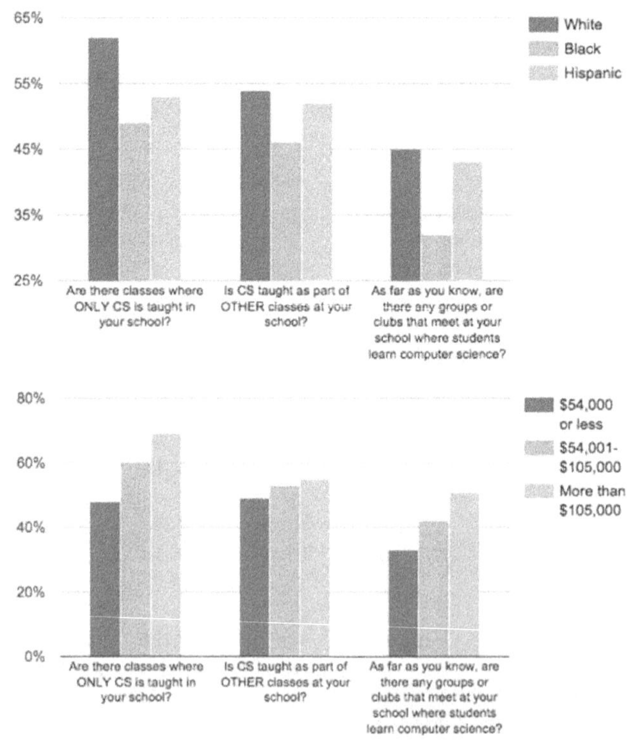

Figure 7. Student access to computer science learning in school, by race and income (% agree).

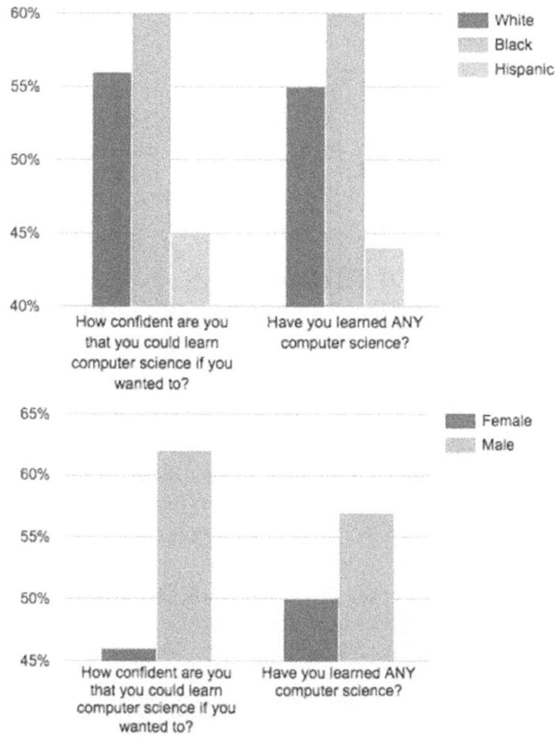

Figure 8. Student confidence (% very confident) and experience (% agree) in learning computer science, by race and income.

Of those students who had learned computer science, the most common means were in a class at school (73.1%) and on their own (55.8%). As shown in Figure 8, Hispanic students are the least likely to say they have ever learned computer science (44% compared to 60% Blacks and 55% Whites) and are the least likely to say they are very confident they could learn computer science if they wanted to (45% compared to 60% Blacks and 56% Whites). By gender, girls are less likely than boys to have learned CS or have confidence to learn CS (50% vs. 57% boys; see Figure 8).

For participation, teachers and principals indicated that students in CS classes are usually high-ability, white, and male. This confirms our findings on perceptions and stereotypes of those who do computer science, and implies the need to provide broader examples of those who do CS and encourage broader populations to participate.

5.3 Barriers to Access

To understand potential reasons for low access and exposure, we investigated barriers to offering CS. Surprisingly, we saw contrasting results between parent and student demand for CS and administrator perceptions' of parent and student demand. Demand, particularly from parents, was surprisingly high, with 90% agreeing that offering CS is a good use of their school's resources and 91% indicating that they would like their child to learn CS. 67% of parents and 56% of teachers even indicated that CS should be required, and 96% of students reported adults in their family would be supportive of their learning CS.

On the other hand, principals and superintendents did not believe there was high demand from parents. Over 50% of principals indicated demand from parents was low (with only 7% indicating demand was high) and 43.8% indicated demand from students was moderate, while 51.4% of superintendents indicated demand from parents was low (with only 6% indicating demand was high) and 49.1% indicated student demand as moderate. 30% of principals and 50% of superintendents indicated that low demand from parents and students was a barrier to offering CS. Furthermore, less than 30% of educators reported that CS is a top priority at their school or district. Interestingly, only 27.2% of teachers versus 82.9% of superintendents believed that computer

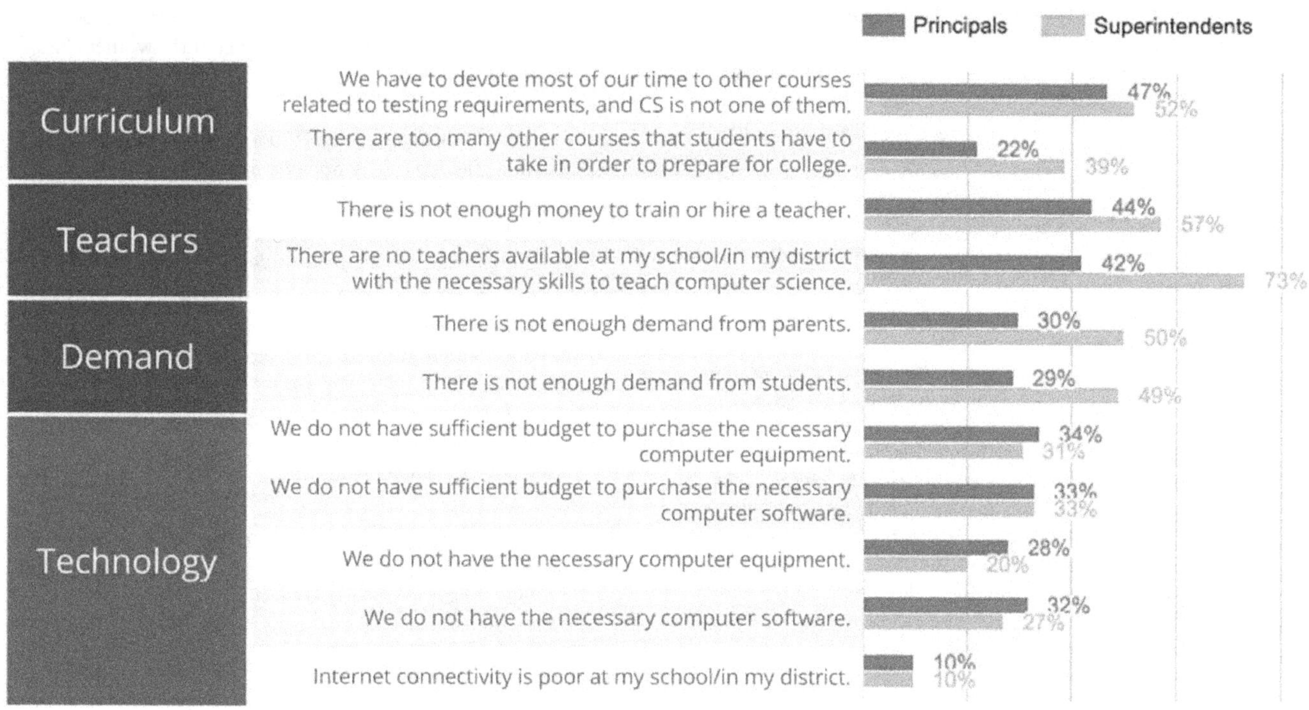

Figure 9. Barrier to offering computer science in their school or district (% agree).

science would be offered at their school in the next three years. And, many principals (41.5%) and superintendents (47.8%) did not indicate that students should be required to take a computer science course.

We also found the most common responses about barriers to offering CS were the need for qualified CS teachers and teaching support, cited by half of principals and superintendents (see Figure 9). Across teachers (82.8%), principals (79.3%), and superintendents (81.1%), there was strong agreement that teaching CS requires extensive training while 59.6% of teachers, 44.3% of principals, and 73.6% of superintendents indicated that they would need to hire a new teacher or could not identify a teacher already at the school to teach CS.

As schools prioritize and direct resources towards preparing for tests, testing requirements were cited as a barrier to offering CS by half of principals and superintendents. Testing was cited as the *main* barrier by 32.4% of principals and 23.6% of superintendents. Principals whose schools did offer CS most commonly (15.8%) cited "too many other courses students need to take" as the biggest barrier they had to overcome in order to offer CS.

Surprisingly, technology was not as common a barrier. Only 10% of administrators indicated access to Internet was a barrier and 20-33% mentioned software, equipment, and budget for technology as barriers.

An interesting opportunity arising from this need to dedicate resources to other required courses was that most teachers (66.6%), principals (70.0%), and superintendents (66.0%) indicated that it was a good idea to incorporate CS into other subjects.

6. SIGNIFICANCE

Overall, despite the positive image of CS careers and work, we still see a need for broader education on what CS is and is not among all populations, including educators. And, despite the high value and demand for CS from parents, the education infrastructure does not equitably provide all students with the desired exposure, possibly with insufficient encouragement and access for underrepresented populations. This may be due to the perceptions across populations that CS is only for certain types of people, as well as a lack of awareness of parent demands and lack of support for CS teacher training and flexibility in the curriculum. These indicate:

- A need to broaden perceptions of who does computer science as well as a need for greater awareness of biases;
- Educators should talk to parents and students, who should speak up about their demands;
- Computer science training resources that is inclusive of all students need to be made accessible, available, and known;
- Policymakers and administrators should consider strategies to be more supportive of computer science offerings, such as
    - more flexible curriculum and class schedules,
    - modifying requirements for standardized testing,
    - allowing computer science courses to count towards graduation and college admission requirements,
    - offering a variety of paths to learn computer science in and out of school, as well as through various means using computers, mobile devices, and without technology

Future research should further explore the possible connections between perceptions and its influence on those who may encourage and provide exposure to computer science students, as well as its influence on the students themselves to confirm our hypotheses as well as past studies (e.g., [4-5]). Research on equitable pedagogy in computer science can also help inform teaching and enlighten us on methods to lessen biases and discrepancies in exposure in order to create opportunities for all to advance with computer science.

7. ACKNOWLEDGMENTS

The authors would like to acknowledge the contributions of our colleagues at Google and Gallup: Chris Stephenson, Mo Fong, Cynthia English, Elizabeth Keating, Stephanie Kafka, Katherine Black, Brandon Busteed, and countless others.

8. REFERENCES

[1] College Board. (2014). AP Program Participation and Performance Data 2014. Retrieved from http://research.collegeboard.org/programs/ap/data/participation/ap-2014.

[2] National Center for Education Statistics (NCES). (2012). Bachelor's degrees conferred by postsecondary institutions, by race/ethnicity and field of study: 2010-11 and 2011-12. Retrieved from http://nces.ed.gov/programs/digest/d13/tables/dt13_322.30.asp.

[3] Wang, J., Hong, H., Ravitz, J., & Ivory, M. (2015). Gender Differences in Factors Influencing Pursuit of Computer Science and Related Fields. In *Proceedings of the 2015 ACM Conference on Innovation and Technology in Computer Science Education* (pp. 117-122). ACM.

[4] Carter, L. (2006, March). Why students with an apparent aptitude for computer science don't choose to major in computer science. In *ACM SIGCSE Bulletin* (Vol. 38, No. 1, pp. 27-31). ACM.

[5] Cheryan, S., Plaut, V. C., Handron, C., & Hudson, L. (2013). The stereotypical computer scientist: Gendered media representations as a barrier to inclusion for women. *Sex Roles, 69*(1-2), 58-71.

[6] Smith, T.J., Pasero, S. L. , & McKenna, C. M. (2014). Gender effects on student attitude toward science. *Bulletin of Science, Technology & Society, 34*(1-2), 7-12.

[7] Cheong, Y.F., Pajares, F. & Oberman, P.S. (2004). Motivation and academic help-seeking in high school computer science. *Computer Science Education, 14*(1), 3-19.

[8] Denner, J., Werner, L., Martinez, J., & Bean, S. (2012). Computing goals, values, and expectations: Results from an after-school program for girls. *Journal of Women and Minorities in Science and Engineering, 18*(3), 199-213.

[9] Fan, X. & Chen, M. (2001). Parental Involvement and Students' Academic Achievement: A Meta-Analysis. Retrieved from http://rd.springer.com/article/10.1023/A:1009048817385

[10] Dabney, K. P., Chakraverty, D., & Tai, R. H. (2013). The association of family influence and initial interest in science. *Science Education, 97*(3), 395-409.

CS Teacher Experiences with Educational Technology, Problem-Based Learning, and a CS Principles Curriculum

George Veletsianos
Royal Roads University
veletsianos@gmail.com

Bradley Beth
University of Texas at Austin
bbeth@cs.utexas.edu

Calvin Lin
University of Texas at Austin
lin@cs.utexas.edu

ABSTRACT

Little is known about how K–12 Computer Science (CS) teachers use technology and problem-based learning (PBL) to teach CS content in the context of CS Principles curricula. Significantly, little qualitative research has been conducted in these areas in computer science education, so we lack an in-depth understanding of the complicated realities of CS teachers' experiences. This paper describes the practices and experiences of six teachers' use of technology that was implemented to support PBL in the context of a dual enrollment CS Principles course.

Results from an early offering of this course suggest that (1) while CS teachers used technology, they did not appear to use it to support student inquiry, (2) local adaptations to the curriculum were largely teacher-centric, and (3) the simultaneous adoption of new instructional practices, technologies, and curricula was overwhelming to teachers. This paper then describes how these results were used to modify the curriculum and professional development, leading to increased teacher satisfaction and student success in the course.

1. INTRODUCTION

Most computer science curricula focus either on coding or technology applications (e.g., how to use the Microsoft suite of office productivity tools) rather than on the broader principles of computing and how computing impacts our world. For instance, recently, Code.org, a 501(c)(3) non-profit organization based in the US, launched several initiatives aiming to expand participation among underrepresented groups in computing. The goal of these initiatives is to increase exposure to computer programming in K–12 schools, and includes examples such as the following:

- The *Hour of Code*, a nationwide effort to introduce computer programming to students through participation in a variety of online tutorials. These tutorials are designed to give a brief overview of programming in the space of one hour and are targeted primarily toward K–8 students.

- Code.org promotional videos featuring industry leaders (e.g., founders of Microsoft, Facebook, Twitter, etc.), politicians, and celebrities advocating for learning computer science through writing code. These high-profile initiatives seek to encourage individuals to consider CS-related fields, but they equate computer science with *writing code*.

SIGCSE '16, March 02 - 05, 2016, Memphis, TN, USA

ISBN 978-1-4503-3685-7/16/03...$15.00

DOI: http://dx.doi.org/10.1145/2839509.2844645

Computer Science courses that focus on computer programming or applications are not engaging high school students [26]. To address its shortage of students and diversity, computer science education needs to address both the content and the pedagogies of introductory computer science courses. The paucity of K–12 CS courses that feature rich content, student-centered practices, and technology-enhanced environments is due in part to the lack of exemplary models and research. As a result, the CS education community lacks knowledge of teacher experiences with CS courses that make use of student-centered pedagogies. This paper addresses these gaps in the literature.

In particular, this paper makes the following contributions:

- We present the experiences of six high school teachers who implemented a dual enrollment CS Principles curriculum in 2012.

- We report three main findings: (1) Teachers made use of technology, but not to support student inquiry; (2) teachers largely did not adopt PBL pedagogies, except in a module that focused on programming; and (3) teachers were largely overwhelmed by the simultaneous adoption of a new curriculum, a new pedagogy, and new learning technology.

- We describe the subsequent changes to the curriculum and provide anecdotal evidence that these changes were effective in both improving teacher satisfaction with course content and pedagogy and increasing student completion rates for college credit.

The remainder of this paper is organized as follows. We first describe the course that the teachers implemented. Next we review relevant literature and the methods used to conduct this investigation. We conclude by presenting our findings and their implications.

2. BACKGROUND

Thriving in Our Digital World is an introductory high-school computer science course that uses an inquiry-based curriculum and a blended learning environment to improve the accessibility, rigor, and relevance of computer science. The course content is organized by a "framework of the principles and practices of computing" called CS Principles. Developed by the NSF and College Board, CS Principles covers a broader array of computer science than simply coding, including big ideas like programming and algorithms, but also other topics like data analysis, digital manipulation, and ethics. The course also strives to show students that computing is applicable to both local and global issues, and a variety of different fields. The curriculum uses student-centered practices and inquiry-driven pedagogies, like problem-based learning (PBL) based on the work of Krajcik and Blumenfeld [18] and the Jasper Woodbury Problem Solving Series [3].

The structure of *Thriving in Our Digital World* is modular, with a separate, overarching project driving each module's content [4]. Course modules begin with the presentation of a driving problem that situated the learning activities that follow. Students engage in authentic activities, collaborate with peers, and use technology to facilitate learning as they develop a product to address the question/challenge. Each problem is 'launched' via an anchor video [19] and students collaborate in small groups to develop their final solutions. Throughout each module, teachers also present content, provide mini-lessons and tutorials, implement formative assessments (e.g., peer collaboration evaluations), and orchestrate activities intended to support students in completing their projects (e.g., rubric checks). The learning environment itself is blended, with course materials (e.g., videos, guiding activities, rubrics, reading assignments, etc) organized within a Learning Management System (LMS), and face-to-face meetings occurring according to schools' regular bell schedules.

There are several reasons why this course appealed to high school administrators and teachers, including (1) its dual credit format (i.e. students who pass this course are able to apply the credits they earn towards their college education in the state in which this course was being developed), and (2) the nature of the content. The course has been designed in an iterative manner over a five-year period; this paper focuses on teachers' initial experiences with embedded learning technologies in the course and how these experiences informed subsequent course revisions.

3. RELATED WORK

Even though there is abundant literature on technology integration and inquiry learning, we do not have a clear understanding of how blended environments support inquiry learning specifically, especially in computer science education. Technology integration has been described as a "wicked problem," one which is complex and involves "the convoluted interaction of multiple factors, with few hard and fast rules that apply across contexts and cases" [22]. Mere access to technology does not necessarily result in effective technology integration [9], and efforts at technology integration are often limited to activities that aim at making known instructional approaches faster or cheaper [15]. Nevertheless, empirical research suggests that technology integration can create conditions that positively affect learning [3, 8, 16, 29]. A second-order meta-analysis of 25 meta-analyses and 1,055 individual studies for example, showed that learning outcomes are significantly and positively affected by learning technology integration in experimental research [27].

Effectively integrating instructional technology and inquiry-learning pedagogies into classroom instruction can be challenging. Numerous researchers have sought to articulate what teachers need to know in order to effectively integrate technology in their classrooms. One of the most popular frameworks over the last decade is the Technological Pedagogical And Content Knowledge (TPACK) framework [22]. Though Brantely-Dias and Ertmer [6] argue that the TPACK construct is both "too vague and too intricate" the framework purports that teachers should be knowledgeable of (1) their content area, (b) pedagogies that support learning of said content, and (3) how technology can support or facilitate content-specific pedagogies, and (4) the interactions between these three knowledge areas. This suggests that TPACK proficiency is more challenging to acquire than technological, pedagogical, or content knowledge proficiency alone. Furthermore, achieving TPACK proficiency may even be more difficult for teachers who adopt pedagogical approaches that are unfamiliar to them citees06. For example, PBL approaches invite teachers to take on unfamiliar roles (e.g., facilitating collaboration) and engage in unfamiliar activities (e.g., scaffolding problem-solving). Blended learning environments introduce additional challenges, too [11]. For instance, online course calendars must adjust to a variety of local events (e.g., state-mandated testing), and the amount of digital work produced by students can be prolific. Faced with such obstacles, teachers are likely to require tremendous support as they learn new pedagogical approaches that may conflict with pre-existing beliefs and practices [3].

While computer science teachers are likely to be proficient in their content area, the lack of CS-specific teaching methods courses and CS teaching certification programs across the U.S. [12, 30] suggests that CS teachers may lack content-specific pedagogical knowledge. This problem may be exacerbated by the fact that research on content-specific pedagogies for computer science education is minimal [14]. Likewise, research on the use of inquiry-based pedagogies in K–12 computer science classrooms is scant. An analysis of computer science education research shows that the plurality of computer science education research articles were program descriptions or contained only anecdotal evidence [24]. Our review of the literature on CS teachers' experiences in K–12 classrooms revealed a scarcity of relevant articles. In particular, we were able to locate empirical articles describing strategies that CS teachers employ to make CS interesting to students [5] and noting that it may be productive for teachers to view their interactions with students as connecting with a different culture [17]. We also located articles explaining how CS teachers experience the success of their students [7] and illustrating how they perceive the use of multiple choice assessments [25]. However, evidence of CS educators' experiences with inquiry learning in blended learning environments was minimal. Thus, more empirical research that examines CS educators' experiences and practices is necessary especially at a time when the CS community is seeking to increase the number of CS teachers and the effectiveness and diversity of CS education [2].

4. RESEARCH QUESTIONS

The field lacks an understanding of CS teacher practices and experiences with inquiry-driven learning and blended environments. This research project attempts to address this need by answering the following research question: How did teachers respond to a student-centered and technology-rich curriculum?

5. METHODOLOGY

5.1 Participants

In this initial pilot offering, six male computer science teachers were trained to teach *Thriving in Our Digital World* through a two week summer professional development and taught it in the following school year. Each agreed to participate in this study under the assigned pseudonyms Bob, Ken, Mark, James, Tyler, and Sam. As this was the first year of implementation, we targeted teachers with prior experience teaching high school computer science coursework.

Bob and Ken teach in small rural high schools, while Mark, James, Tyler, and Sam teach at high schools located in a large metropolitan area. Bob and Ken teach at predominantly white schools and have taught courses related to computer science for 15 and 20 years respectively. Mark has taught computer science related courses at an economically disadvantaged, ethnically diverse high school for five years. James has taught computer science at a magnet high school for less than five years, and at the same magnet school, Sam was teaching computer science for the first time. Tyler has taught computer science at a technology-based high school for less than five years. Tyler's school is infused with technology and utilizes a problem-based learning model school-wide. Tyler was an experienced problem-based teacher, whereas all other participants were novices to inquiry learning. Participants' classrooms each have a digital projector or interactive whiteboard, wireless Internet connections, and at least a 1:1 computing device to student ratio (desktop computer, laptop, or tablet). Class sizes ranged in size from 9 to 26 students.

5.2 Data Sources

To address the research questions, we collected qualitative data from classroom observations, teacher interviews, and student focus groups. Most computer science education research is quantitative in nature and frequently relies on experimental designs [24]. Qualitative methods are infrequently used in computer science education research [1, 10, 23], yet are capable of generating significant insights into the activities, practices, perceptions, ways of thinking, and overall lived experiences of computing education stakeholders. Our study is informed by six different classroom cases that include 14 one-to-one participant interviews, 28 observations of participants' classrooms, and numerous researcher field notes. Semi-structured teacher interviews were conducted at the beginning, in the middle, and at the end of the school year. Classroom observations occurred more regularly. Each interview lasted between 30 and 60 minutes, was audio-recorded and transcribed.

5.3 Data Analysis

Working within the interpretive research paradigm [21], data was analyzed using the constant comparative method [13]. Two researchers independently read and coded the data. With each new data that entered the analysis (e.g., a sentence, an interview), each researcher compared the data to existing codes and created new codes if necessary. After independent analyses were complete, researchers compared notes, discussed codes, and re-analyzed the data independently. Next, codes were combined to form themes and this process continued until consensus was reached and it was felt that data saturation[1] had been reached. Though the results presented are bound by the context within which the project was implemented, the results are presented using rich descriptions so as to enable readers and other researchers to judge the extent to which these results apply to their own contexts (c.f. Merriam [20]).

6. FINDINGS

Results from this investigation are presented in three themes. These themes capture some, but not all, of the experiences/activities of these six teachers. These themes are reported because they are novel in the CS education literature and bear significant implications for CS education.

6.1 Use of Technology in the Classroom

Although technology was integrated heavily into instruction as a result of the design of *Thriving in Our Digital World*, teachers did not use the technology scaffolds as prescribed. The learning technologies integrated into the curriculum were designed to be flexible so that order teachers could alter them as necessary (e.g., create/delete/moderate discussion board threads), and this flexibility resulted in both desired outcomes and unintended consequences.

Most integration efforts either replicated or amplified classroom practices, but they were rarely entirely transformative. At each school, students were online for the entirety of almost every class, so most work was completed and submitted digitally and asynchronously. Throughout the duration of the course all teachers accessed static content and assignment pages weekly, and in some cases daily. Some teachers altered these materials to better suit their needs. For instance, the online quiz feature of the blended environment was instrumental to Ken's course implementation, and he felt that the online quizzes helped learners succeed in the course. Ken created a static webpage within the LMS that contained a calendar of his class's daily activities and more:

> "I made up my own quizzes, and had [students] do additional stuff to get them prepared for that test."

Teachers also used digital tools in teacher-centric ways, such as when James and Sam requested or created supplementary Powerpoint presentations to deliver content to students on a regular basis. These efforts helped students and teachers remain organized, reduced paper usage in the classroom drastically, and provided another venue for access to course materials, but none of these activities transformed the teaching and learning process.

In general, most teachers utilized very few of the technology scaffolds to support inquiry-based and PBL learning pedagogies as intended, though many alternative integration efforts could clearly support PBL. Teachers tend to feel more comfortable integrating technologies that they are familiar

[1]Saturation is defined as the point at which researchers felt that additional analyses were yielding no new insights.

with than those that are strange to them. For instance, James already used Google Drive for classroom management and organization, but for *Thriving in Our Digital World*, he integrated into this course as a collaboration hub for groups, too. This helped James achieve his "really big goal that whatever we cover in class is easily available to students outside of class without having to use...district servers and stuff, which can be hard for students to access." Additionally, his students authored weekly blogs about the course, as they did in his other classes, allowing students to reflect on their learning. There was little need for him to facilitate online discussions via the discussion forums or to have groups collaborate using the various tools in the LMS, because he was already achieving the major goals he had set out to achieve using alternative means. Thus, use of these tools was rare, not just for James, but for the rest of the teachers as well. At the beginning of the school year, all teachers used the Discussions feature in the LMS to facilitate online discussions and group collaboration, but their usage practically ended after the initial module, with some teachers, like Ken, deleting the links to the discussions from the course outline, and other teachers, like Sam, avoiding them.

The blended environment seemed to support technology integration, but not inquiry learning or PBL instruction specifically.

6.2 Use of Pedagogical Innovation

Teachers often appeared to adapt the curriculum to meet instructional goals they deemed worthwhile, sometimes in ways that diverged from inquiry-based pedagogies. For instance, teachers integrated more lectures, homework, and quizzes than found in the original curriculum. James said that his "teaching philosophy centers around the idea that I want to get information across to the students as quickly as possible," so most of his course adoptions "centered around presentations." However, while many activities created by the teachers were teacher-centric, their pedagogical practices were inquiry-based and student-centered during the programming module of the pilot curriculum, which is the one module composed of the content most commonly associated with computer science instruction. Tyler, Bob, James, Ken, and Sam introduced pair programming, peer tutoring, and one-on-one tutorials to support self-paced learning activities in this module. The Programming activities required students to produce learning artifacts and included increased elements of student choice (e.g., program a virtual keyboard or a virtual paint palette) more often than in other modules. Students also progressed through the Programming module curriculum mostly at their own pace. According to Ken, "In the Programming unit [students] were able to just jump in and go, and I did not deliver a lesson, not once during that unit. I just didn't have to." Perhaps, teachers implemented more inquiry learning activities during this particular module, because they were more familiar with the content, they had greater experience in teaching programming, or because they simply enjoyed programming itself. Tyler for example said that he "did a lot of cheerleading for the Programming (module)" that he did not do for the previous modules.

6.3 Overwhelming Teachers with Changes

The simultaneous adoption of a pilot curriculum, PBL pedagogies, and blended learning environments appeared to overwhelm these teachers. Barriers to technology integration (e.g., classroom management skills), to the adoption of pilot curricula (e.g., learning new content), and to teaching in blended environments (e.g., organizing course materials and calendars) combined forces to inhibit instruction and exacerbate the challenges that teachers faced in their classrooms. For example, the challenges of classroom management associated with technology integration amplified the challenges of classroom management using student-centered pedagogies. For instance, James and Sam reported that they "got burnt out" by the quantity of online discussions, which they felt obligated to grade.

The adoption of new pedagogies, new content, and a new online learning environment required significant amounts of teacher preparation. All teachers mentioned spending more time preparing for this course than any other course, often struggling to stay ahead of the students. "I don't know how a busy person with a lot of kids [students] could teach this course," Bob conjectured. Mark said that "it can be overwhelming when you're throwing something new in there [that] you really haven't had a chance to get used to." James explained that he "probably went over (the lesson) the night before or the day of, hoping that I didn't find anything that was too wrong to be able to fix in that amount of time." Teachers had originally anticipated that the pilot curriculum would be ready to be implemented, but adopting curricular materials to local contexts took time. For instance, Tyler initially thought, "Great! You guys have done all the work for me," only later to realize "that there is a lot of work in taking others' stuff, and fitting it into what we usually do."

Teachers also yearned to learn the new content associated with the curriculum and explore the online materials prior to face-to-face class sessions and this imposed additional time demands. Sam "would love to have sat in on a course from someone that developed (this course's curriculum)," so that he could have discussions about the content and potential questions that his students might have had. Mark "didn't have enough time last summer to really get into (the curriculum), and be a month ahead of the kids." He would have preferred an opportunity to "turn [himself] into a student and do every single thing...that [he] would ask [his] students to do." Unfamiliarity with the content and pedagogies of the pilot curriculum hindered implementations, because teachers had to spend time learning the content and the instructional approaches associated with it. Furthermore, integrating new technologies and new pedagogies also required additional preparatory time. Bob felt the curriculum was "pretty open ended and it's hard on me to grade that kind of stuff."

None of these experiences happened in isolation, and as a result they compounded each other. The difficulties associated with simultaneous paradigm shifts are noteworthy and computer science developers should take into account the challenges that teachers may face when asked to engage in activities that require rethinking of content, pedagogy, and technology integration.

7. INNOVATIONS

These findings from the initial pilot of *Thriving in Our Digital World* have informed subsequent refinements to the course through (1) significant revisions in course design (further detailed in Veletsianos et al. [28]) and (2) an enhanced professional development sequence. The targeted areas of revision may be distilled to the following:

- **Daily usage of technology scaffolds is integrated into course expectations.** Rather than providing collaborative tools as course resources, explicit usage of discussion boards, wikis, and collaborative workspaces (e.g., Google docs) is detailed in the provided lesson plans, scope and sequence, and suggested assessments. Teachers are provided with scripted discussion seed questions and responses. Students are assessed on their use of collaborative spaces to create and submit group projects.

- **Pedagogical innovation is an explicit objective of professional development.** Rather than focusing solely on the student experience within the LMS, *Thriving in Our Digital World* professional development now devotes a significant portion of time to developing teacher-created artifacts. Teachers are provided guided practice in tailoring stock exercises to their student populations and sharing those innovations with other teachers remotely.

- **Professional development is approached holistically, emphasizing the overall course experience.** The initial professional development sequence preceding the pilot year of implementation was presented in a discrete subject format, where each of the course components were addressed in relative isolation. Our revised professional development curriculum now better integrates course components such as PBL, blended learning, and the course content through an extensive linear introduction to the course materials. This revision borrows heavily from the introductory module provided to students, explicitly introducing each of the core course components in the shared context of a unit project.

Although the effects of these innovations have not been directly studied, anecdotal evidence suggests that increases in teacher satisfaction and student success may be due in part to these targeted revisions. Teacher focus groups, surveys, and observation data analyzed by an external evaluator suggest that teacher confidence in both teaching the course content and implementing the course pedagogies (primarily PBL) greatly increased from year one to two of implementation. Whereas a majority of teachers expressed doubt over the efficacy of PBL and its connection to course content in the initial course offering, nearly all of the teachers in the subsequent year were overwhelmingly positive.

Additionally, student success as measured by completion rates for college credit rose dramatically from year one (72%) to two (88%). This increase is sustained over year three, where 86% of students completed the course with college credit.

8. CONCLUSION

This project examined the experiences and practices of a group of teachers asked to make rapid changes to their beliefs and practices about pedagogy, technology integration, and computer science content. Though past research shows that technology integration can support PBL, these cases reminds us that PBL and technology integration may also complicate each other under less favorable circumstances, such as when teachers are simultaneously responding to new pedagogies, curriculum, or technologies.

A significant implication of this research is the recognition that even though computer science teachers may be experts in computing, they may not necessarily be proficient in the use of educational technology. Teachers' expertise in computing, like software development or systems analysis, did not necessarily equate to expertise in technology integration for achieving desired learning outcomes. For instance, this group of teachers seemed unfamiliar with a few of the more commonplace learning technologies that were heavily integrated into the curriculum: Bob, Ken, and Mark lacked prior experience with social networking sites and had never used online collaborative documents prior to being asked to implement this curriculum. Computer science teachers likely need to develop their knowledge of how technology can enhance learning experiences and how it can support pedagogical innovation.

Computer science teachers tasked with implementing novel pedagogical practices require extensive support and assistance. Increased teacher satisfaction and student success after informed revisions to *Thriving in Our Digital World* curriculum and professional development bear this out. Future initiatives would benefit from considering teachers' beliefs, practices, content knowledge, technology knowledge, and readiness to adopt new pedagogical approaches. Equally important, given the dearth of research in CS teacher experiences and CS teacher preparation programs, more research on CS teachers' pedagogical practices and technology integration activities is both pressing and necessary.

9. ACKNOWLEDGMENTS

Thriving in Our Digital World is based upon work supported by NSF Grant DRL-1441009, NSF Grant CNS-1138506, and by the University of Texas at Austin's OnRamps college readiness program.

References

[1] V. L. Almstrum, O. Hazzan, M. Guzdial, and M. Petre. Challenges to computer science education research. In *Proceedings of the 36th SIGCSE technical symposium on Computer science education*, St. Louis, Missouri, USA, 2005. ACM.

[2] O. Astrachan, J. Cuny, C. Stephenson, and C. Wilson. The CS10K project: mobilizing the community to transform high school computing. In *Proceedings of the 42nd ACM Technical Symposium on Computer Science Education*, page 85. ACM, 2011.

[3] B. Barron, D. Schwartz, N. Vye, A. Moore, A. Petrosino, L. Zech, The Cognition, and Technology Group at Vanderbilt. Doing with understanding: Lessons from research on problem- and project-based learning. *The Journal of the Learning Sciences*, 7(3 and 4):271–311, 1998.

[4] B. Beth and C. Lin. Thriving in Our Digital World. *CSTA Voice*, 11(3):2–3, July 2015.

[5] J. Black, J. Brodie, P. Curzon, C. Myketiak, P. W. McOwan, and L. R. Meagher. Making Computing

Interesting to School Students: Teachers' Perspectives. pages 255–260. Proceedings of the 18th ACM Conference on Innovation and Technology in Computer Science Education, 2013.

[6] L. Brantley-Dias and P. A. Ertmer. Goldilocks and TPACK: Is the Construct "Just Right?". *Journal of Research on Technology in Education*, 46(2):103–128, 2013.

[7] A. Carbone, L. Mannila, and S. Fitzgerald. Computer science and IT teachers' conceptions of successful and unsuccessful teaching: A phenomenographic study. *Computer Science Education*, 17(4):275–299, 2007.

[8] L. ChanLin and K. Chan. PBL approach in web-based instruction. *Journal of Instructional Psychology*, 31:2, 2004.

[9] L. Cuban, H. Kirkpatrick, and C. Peck. High Access and Low Use of Technologies in High School Classrooms: Explaining an Apparent Paradox. *American Educational Research Journal*, 38(4):813–834, 2001.

[10] K. Deibel. Studying our inclusive practices: Course experiences of students with disabilities. In *Proceedings of the 12th Annual SIGCSE Conference on Innovation and Technology in Computer Science Education*, ITiCSE '07, pages 266–270, New York, NY, USA, 2007. ACM.

[11] R. Donnelly. Harmonizing technology with interaction in blended problem-based learning. *Computers and Education*, 54(2):350–359, 2010.

[12] J. Gal-Ezer and C. Stephenson. The current state of computer science in U.S. high schools: A report from two national surveys. *Journal for Computing Teachers*, Spring:1–5, 2009.

[13] B. Glaser and A. Strauss. *The discovery of grounded theory: Strategies for qualitative research.* Aldine Publishing Company, Chicago, 1967.

[14] M. Guzdial. Learning how to prepare computer science high school teachers. *Computer*, 44(10):95–97, 2011.

[15] J. Hughes, R. Thomas, and C. Scharber. Assessing Technology Integration: The RAT - Replacement, Amplification, and Transformation - Framework. *Paper presented at the Society for Information Technology and Teacher Education International Conference 2006, Orlando, Florida, USA*, 2006.

[16] S. Judge, K. Osman, and S. Yassin. Cultivating communication through PBL with ICT. *Procedia - Social and Behavioral Sciences*, 15:1546–1550, 2011.

[17] Y. Kolikant. Computer science education as a cultural encounter: a socio-cultural framework for articulating teaching difficulties. *Instructional Science*, 39(4):543–559, 2011.

[18] J. Krajcik and P. Blumenfeld. Project-Based Learning. In R. K. Sawyer, editor, *The Cambridge Handbook of the Learning Sciences*, pages 317–330. Cambridge University Press, Cambridge, UK, 2006.

[19] D. Kumar. Approaches to interactive video anchors in problem-based science learning. *Journal of Science Education and Technology*, 19(1):13–19, 2010.

[20] S. Merriam. What can you tell from an N of 1?: Issues of validity and reliability in qualitative research. *PAACE Journal of Lifelong Learning*, 4:51–60, 1995.

[21] S. Merriam. *Qualitative research in practice: Examples for discussion and analysis.* Jossey-Bass, San Francisco, CA, 2002.

[22] P. Mishra and M. Koehler. Technological pedagogical content knowledge: A framework for teacher knowledge. *Teachers College Record*, 108(6):1017–1054, 2006.

[23] L. Postner and R. Stevens. What resources do CS1 students use and how do they use them? *Computer Science Education*, 15(3):165–182, 2005.

[24] J. J. Randolph, G. Julnes, E. Sutinen, and S. Lehman. Computer science education research at the crossroads: a methodological review of computer science education research, 2000–2005. *Journal of Information Technology Education*, 7:135–162, 2007.

[25] S. Shuhidan, M. Hamilton, and D. D'Souza. Instructor perspectives of multiple-choice questions in summative assessment for novice programmers. *Computer Science Education*, 20(3):229–259, 2010.

[26] C. Simard, C. Stephenson, and D. Kosaraju. Addressing Core Equity Issues in K-12 Computer Science Education. *Report from The Anita Borg Institute, CSTA, and The University of Arizona*, 2010.

[27] R. M. Tamim, R. M. Bernard, E. Borokhovski, P. C. Abrami, and R. F. Schmid. What Forty Years of Research Says About the Impact of Technology on Learning: A Second-Order Meta-Analysis and Validation Study. *Review of Educational Research*, 81(1):4–28, 2011.

[28] G. Veletsianos, B. Beth, C. Lin, and G. Russell. Design Principles for Thriving in Our Digital World, a High School Computer Science Course. *Journal of Educational Computing Research*, in press.

[29] A. Walker, M. Recker, M. Robertshaw, J. Olsen, H. Leary, L. Ye, and L. Sellers. Integrating technology and problem-based learning: A mixed methods study of two teacher professional development designs. *The Interdisciplinary Journal of Problem-based-learning*, 5(2):70–94, 2011.

[30] A. Yadav and J. Korb. Learning to teach computer science. *Communications of the ACM*, 55(11):31, 2012.

Contextualized Teaching in the Lower Secondary Education Long-term Evaluation of a CS Course from Grade 6 to 10

Arno Pasternak
Fritz-Steinhoff-Gesamtschule Hagen
Technische Universität Dortmund
arno.pasternak@cs.tu-dortmund.de

ABSTRACT

In this paper we will report on the design, teaching and evaluation of a Computer Science course in the lower secondary education from grade 6 to grade 10 based on contextualised ideas.

With this study we are able to demonstrate that students can indeed be taught Computer Science as a (main) subject from early grades to the end of lower secondary education.

We will present quantitative and qualitative results. We will analyse the results of the course with the instrument of the *effect size d* [15] and draw first consequences.

So it becomes apparent that Computer Science can be taught just like any other science worth full curriculum credit even starting at the beginning of the lower secondary education.

CCS Concepts

•Social and professional topics → Computational thinking; Model curricula; K-12 education; Computing literacy;

Keywords

Lower Secondary Computer Science Education, Braided Teaching, Contextualised Teaching

1. INTRODUCTION

In an ACM study called 'Rebooting the Pathway to Success' Kaczmarczyk and Dopplick postulate: 'States should adopt a clear definition of rigorous computer science grounded in the CSTA K–12 Computer Science Standards.' [17, p.22] It is high time to install computer science in schools as a subject for all students.

The report demands correctly:

'2. All students should have access to, and be encouraged to complete, a rigorous computer science course in high school.
3. Rigorous computer science courses should count as a core high school graduation requirement in computer science, mathematics, or science.' [17, p.3]

SIGCSE '16, March 02 - 05, 2016, Memphis, TN, USA

ISBN 978-1-4503-3685-7/16/03...$15.00

DOI: http://dx.doi.org/10.1145/2839509.2844592

There are many people of the same opinion, not only computer scientists. This is demonstrated by initiatives like *www.code.org*. Nevertheless proper CS education in schools is still an exception.

This is not merely a special problem of the United States. All over the world CS has not the role in school demanded by social and economic developments. To install CS in schools, many teachers and specialized curricula are needed. Universities have to train teachers and universities and schools have to write, test and revise curricula.

With the help of the adminstration of a public school in Western Germany, we taught a CS (combined with Physics) course as a main subject course with full credits from the beginnung of this course in grade 6 to the final exams in grade 10.

We will report on the approach, content and result of this course in comparison to control groups.

1.1 Computational Thinking

In 2006 *Jeannette Wing* formulated the existence of *computational thinking* [31] similar to mathematical or physical thinking. Important parts of this computational thinking are the *abstraction and automation* of real processes in the world. In two workshops in 2010 and 2011 at the National Academy of Sciences validity and evidence of this thesis and the consequences for the education in schools were discussed [7, 8].

1.2 PISA - Report

Since the year 2000 the OECD has researched the quality of education all around the world in studies conducted by the organisation PISA[21, 22, 23]. A consequence of this research is the change from input- to the output-orientation aiming at students' *competences*.

In the following years the central state and the federal states in Germany shifted the educational standards and then the curricula of main subjects into a competence-orientated structure [1, 18]. In conformance with most other countries CS is not an important subject in Germany's school now. Consequently adminstrative structures published no standards for CS in school.

1.3 German educational standards for CS

The CS organisation *Gesellschaft für Informatik* took over the task and defined national standards for CS [1, 26] in 2008. One goal is to point out the importance of CS as a school subject. The basic approach of these standards were the US standards for Mathematics [20]. These standards for CS education are based on contents and processes.

1.4 CS around the world

We know that CS is one of the most important disciplines of the modern world, but this does not mean that it is taught as a subject in school especially in K-12. In many countries teachers and researchers try to change this situation. CS will be a mandatory subject in school only in a part of countries all over the world. Plenty of concepts of CS education are more a claim than fact. There is even less research about real CS education in schools. The good message is that in the last few years obviously a rethinking have taken place. In the following short paragraphs we describe the present situation in a few selected countries. The common sense is obviously now that *computational thinking* is a fundamental thinking of the modern world.

USA — The current curriculum from grade K to grade 12 was revised 2011 as 'CSTA K-12 Computer Science Standards' [28]. The items in this curriculum are organized as *strands* with CS content. Additionally in 2012 an initiative was started for CS in grade K-10 [4] The success of this initiative is the encreasing number of schools with an offer in CS education [5].

United Kingdom — In 2013 new curricula for CS were published. 'A high-quality computing education equips pupils to use computational thinking and creativity to understand and change the world.' [10] is the fundament of a new view of the subject CS. The new curricula started in September 2014. To implement it completely will take time for about ten years.

New Zealand — Between 2011 and 2013 CS was introduced as a school subject in New Zealand [2, 3]. CS has been a new subject for the last three years in high schools. After the first few years of CS education the evaluation is starting [30].

Israel — As early as 1998 a secondary school computer science curriculum was implemented in Israel. Contents are conceptual and applied topics and the addressed grades are 10 to 12. The curriculum distinguishes between students with 'limited interest' and students with more interest in CS [16].

The Netherlands — Similarly to Israel CS was introduced in the Netherlands in 1998 [27] as an elective subject. Only few students participate in these lessons in secondary education. In 2012 there was a rethink and a claim for CS as a compulsory subject based on *computational thinking* [12].

Germany — In Germany education is an issue of the federal states. Nevertheless there are existing nationwide education standards for the most important subjects. The German CS organisation GI definded the 'GI-Bildungsstandards' for CS for the lower secondary education [1]. The difficulties to implement CS in schools are described with examples in a case study for the federal state NRW in Germany [19].

To summarize our results we can conclude that in many important countries there was a new discussion about CS in schools with the intention to install CS as a compulsory subject for all students. Therefore it is recommendable to study experiences with real teaching of CS to confirm a curriculum.

1.5 Consequences

CS as a subject in schools will benefit from good and successful examples. In cooperation with a regular school in our district we designed and conducted a CS course from grade 6 to grade 10 over 5 years having now completed the first full 5-year cycle. In this paper a first view on the results of this CS course is reported.

2. BASIC CONCEPTS

Computer Science today consists of many subfields. There is a big danger of teaching a part of these subfields without any coherence. Students cannot achieve the *computational thinking* without a cohesion of these subareas. Thus it is vital to apply a theoretical concept to teach CS. The concept of *Strands and Braided Teaching* is a good response to this problem. This policy is based on the concept of a *strand*:

> 'A strand *is a sequence of items addressed in class that satisfies the following criteria:*
>
> *1. The items can be assigned to a well-defined subject matter (by their structure or their content).*
> *2. The subject matter is identifiable and recognizable to the students throughout the sequence.*
> *3. The subject matter is being presented from more than one point of view or embedded in more than one context.*
> *4. The sequence of items is addressed in more than one teaching unit.' [25]*

In figure 1 there are some examples at possible strands. These strands are a similar but not the same idea as the strands in the K-12-curriculum [28].

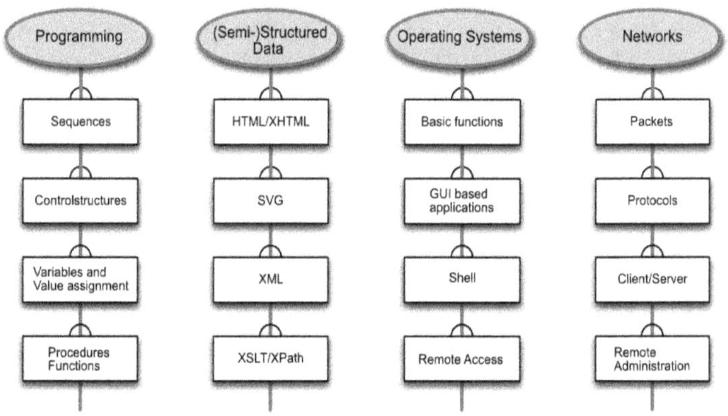

Figure 1: Possible Strands in CS-Education

More strands are possible, eg. multimedia (sound, video, graphic, animation), measuring, von Neumann architecture, etc.. The teacher chooses the suitable strands for the course.

The second idea is the *Braided Teaching* of these strands. The teacher organizes the contents of the strands in the single lessons with the aim of interlacing these different strands.

The third basic idea is to connect the lessons with the everyday life of the students. This means, that teachers have to teach lessons in a *contextualised* way. [13, 14, 9, 29] Most CS teachers have a mathematical or a physical background. Students today have a different background. Therefore it is necessary to guide students to CS without or only with a little Mathematics or Physics. It will be a great challenge for the teacher to find enough contexts, on the one hand,

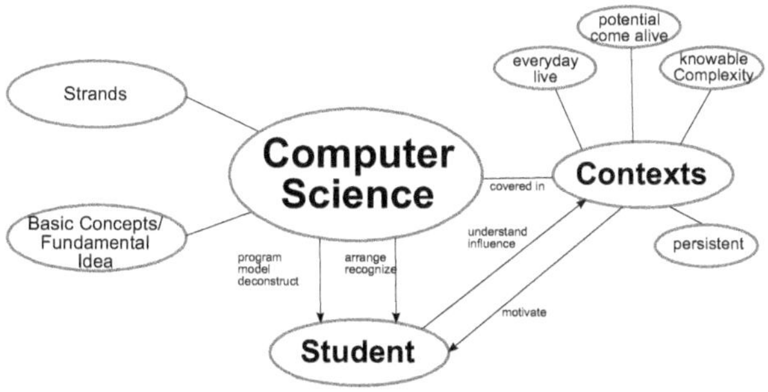

Figure 2: Contexts und Computer Science

and teach primarily the CS content of the concrete context on the other hand. The relation between context and CS is illustrated in figure 2.

A special problem is the contextualized teaching of programming. For computer scientists programming is an important part of CS. Young students know nothing about programming and often have not even seen any program. For example there is no relation between playing games with a computer and programming. Programming is not an everyday life context for students, nor is it for their parents and friends. Therefore it is necessary to find contact positions in a context for programming. We have decided to use the language `Tcl/Tk`, because it is relatively easy to create graphics with `Tcl/Tk` and you may combine programming assignments and operating system calls in the same script. John Ousterhout called this language a *glue* [24]. We used `Tcl/Tk` as such a glue in several contexts. Thus we have never had a programming course in these 5 years. Consequently students never had a special training for the basic structures and ideas of programming.

In 2009 CS teachers and researchers in Germany founded a group and a web page for *Computer Science in Contexts*[1] The very slow growth of this web page exemplifies how difficult it is to construct good examples for a contextualised teaching.

3. CURRICULUM IN A NUTSHELL

The goal of this course was to fill the educational standard matrix by using several strands. From the view of students, we work mainly in a context of everyday life. A short overview of the curriculum from grade 6 to grade 10 gives an insight into practical teaching. This curriculum contains only the CS items taught and not the concrete contexts.

The following example explains the embedding of CS items in a context considering strands. In grade 8 students visit companies in small groups to get some insight into the world of work. One of these entities was a telecommunication company where students were introduced into the distribution of data in networks and could have a look into the basement of the buildung containing a lot of fibre optic cables. Back in school students wanted to know what communication in fibre optic cables is all about. They were taught in this period in physical items like reflection and total reflection. This was the starting point for the context *Transmission of Data*. Students were taught in the representation of (decimal) numbers and characters (in a code like ASCII). Subsequently, the binary, octal and hexadecimal systems were worked out. Finally, we talked about security and safety in data communication. We also had a first look at simple examples at encryption. If these items are not embedded in a context, students not interested in Mathematics or Physics tend to be bored. However, if the teacher manages to implant contents in certain contexts, students do not recognize the items taught as parts of Physics or Mathematics. These contexts are made up of elements of several strands like Networks, Operating systems, Cryptologie, etc.

Let us have a short view on the curriculum of this course.

Grade 6 — The structure of the graphical desktop, the first small web page, storing files in a complex structure like a school net, working with graphics, concept of variables

Grade 7 — (Physical topics), drawing with scripts written in `Tcl/Tk`, digitalization of images, using gif-files in scripts

Grade 8 — Web pages (tables, links, images), animated graphics in `Tcl/Tk`, physical (optical) topics, technical communication in (fibre optic) networks, binary code and coding of numbers and strings, calculation in several systems,

Grade 9 — Hardware und operating systems, multi-users and multi-taskings systems, security of IT systems, colors, additive and subtractive color mixing, structure in networks: Web client and web server, protocol structures in networks: http, telnet, ports ...,

Grade 10 — Statical and dynamical web pages, communication between client and server, sound and notes, digitalisation of sound, creating a little digital synthesizer

Many times several strands like Programming, Multimedia, Networks, Structured Data were used from grade 6 to grade 10. Therefore students get a cohesive understanding of the ideas of CS.

4. BIOGRAPHY OF THE COURSE

The school where the course was given is a regular school in Germany with about 210 students per year from grade 5 to grade 10 and about 100 students per year from grade 11 to grade 13. Students may achieve all kinds of degrees. Due to the local competition of schools, this school has a lack of students with better preconditions. This seeming disadvantage simplifies the demonstration of students' quickly increasing competences in CS as well as its significance as a (main) subject for all students.

The course is an elective main subject for the students who choose one of four offers at the end of grade 5 starting with the beginning of grade 6. The course started with 27 students in 2009, 26 students graduated in grade 10 in 2015. Quantity and composition is representative for this school. One school year contains 38 weeks. Every week students have two lessons with 60 minutes. This course was a mixed course with Physics, so students have 60 minutes lessons in CS per week over the years.

5. QUALITATIVE EVALUATION

5.1 National CS Standards

The curriculum of this course is based on the national standards of CS in the lower secondary education [1]. We had to acknowledge that is was impossible to teach all items constituted in these standards due to a lack of time. An important example is a deeper insight into the cryptology with symmetrical and asymmetrical methods. This insight is

[1]http://www.informatik-im-kontext.de, 2015-06-29.

Mark	A	B	C	D	F
Quantity	1	7	9	8	0

Table 1: Marks at the end of grade 10

necessary for an understanding of encrypted communication in modern networks.

This is obviously not a problem of this course or a problem of teaching this course, it is a problem of these standards. In contrast to the standards in the other established subjects like Mathematics or mother language, CS is not taught nationwide. These standards will be and are a challange to the whole society and adminstration of schools. They are above all a theoretical construct and in the future we will have to revise these standards.

Most teachers involved in the construction of the standards are from schools where mainly students with higher precondition are instructed. Additionally, they have more experience with courses in grade 9 and 10. Students in lower grades need much more time to achieve the same objectives.

Additionally, both designers of educational standards and instructors of CS courses could gain teaching experience in courses with two lessons a week and students more interested in CS only in grades 9 and 10 in the last years.

Two lessons a week in two years is almost the same time as one lesson a week in five years. So we have overrated the possibilities of a CS course starting in the early grade 6. Additionally in this course it was the first time contents like multimedia were taught.

5.2 CS as a (Main-)Subject

Our aim is the implementation of CS as a mandatory subject in every kind of school. This compulsory elective with a normal quantity of students with a representative structure of this school allows us to conclude how just this claim is.

Students want to graduate successfully at the end of school. Table 1 shows the distribution of marks at the end of grade 10.

Students need an A or B mark to continue school in higher secondary education. The quantity of 8 students is similar to the other elective subjects in this age group. No student graduates with mark F. This supports the significance of CS as a main subject in the lower secondary education for all students. The broadly based distribution from A to D clarifies the possibility of a nuanced assessment in CS as a school subject.

6. QUANTITATIVE EVALUATION

6.1 Effect Intensity

Normally, researchers analyse the results of their study concerning statistical deviation between their research group and one or more control groups. This shows a potential effect of the intended aim. But this is obviously not sufficient.

John Hattie made an incredible research in pedagogical meta analysis based on about 250 million students [15]. He recognizes, that nearly all pedagogic studies reveal a significant statistical result. He introduces a linear measurement called the *effect size d* referring to Cohen's approach [6, p.274].

This *effect size d* [15, p.8] is defined as

$$d = \frac{\mu_1 - \mu_2}{\sigma}$$

where μ_1 is the mean of the outcome in the research group, μ_2 is the mean of the outcome of the control group and σ is the standard deviation of the pooled group. A second variety is: μ_1 is the mean at the beginning of the activity and μ_2 is the mean at the end of the activity. The aim is to get an effect size $d > 0.4$. With this effect size Hattie observes important insights in pedagogical efficiences.

It will be a good idea to introduce this effect size into the research of CS education. Thus this effect size enables us to categorize the teaching of the CS group.

6.2 Methodical Approach

The research group at the beginning comprised 27 students. We had one control group inside the same school with 26 students. Nobody in this group was taught in CS from grade 6 to grade 10 with the exception of an introduction into the school network and basics in word processing. Additionally, we analysed three groups with a total of 60 students in a different school and in addition two groups with about 55 students in a further school. These groups were taught partly in ICT. Students are asked to fill in a questionary with three types of questions three times in grade 6. Our goal is the learning of concepts corresponding to the ideas of *computational thinking* [31]. We want to know if the students have perceptions linked to these concepts. It is not easy to verify this with short questions. Therefore, at the end of the first year, we completed the study by interviewing most students with short *think aloud*-situations. In these interviews students point out their problem-solving competences by doing little exercises. These interviews agreed widely with the answers in the questionary. At the end of grade 9 and of grade 10 they answered the questionary again, which are questions about knowledge and opinions. While the basic of the research approach were the national standards in CS, the questions were orientated at the goal of these standards for the end of lower secondary education. This means that in the first survey as well as partly in the following questioning some questions could not be answered correctly. Therefore the results on the effect size were partly downgraded. In the following we will present a couple of results.

6.3 Summary of Knowledge

We asked in 29 questions about knowledge in the questionary. Students may choose *'It is correct'*, *'I agree'* or *'It is not correct'*, *'I don't agree'* or *'I don't know'*. We compare the effect size of the beginning of grade 6 to the effect size at the end of grade 6, and also of the beginning of grade 6 to the end of grade 10. The results are shown in table 2 and depicted in a 'Hattie-barometer' in figure 3. The CS group is abbrieviated with *CS*, the internal control group with CG_{int} and the external control group with CG_{ext}[2].

After elimination of three items not taught, we get the effects size as can be seen in the fourth line in table 2.

The effect size d of the computer science group is obviously larger than of both control groups. It is notable that the external control group CG_{ext} with a teaching in ICT has a worse effect size than the internal group without any

[2] At this moment we have only the statistical material from one of the two external schools.

Effect size	CS	CG_{int}	CG_{ext}
grade 6	0.26	0.15	0.15
from 6 to 10	0.55	0.40	0.27
... adjusted	0.61	0.34	0.29

Table 2: Effect size d from grade 6 to 10

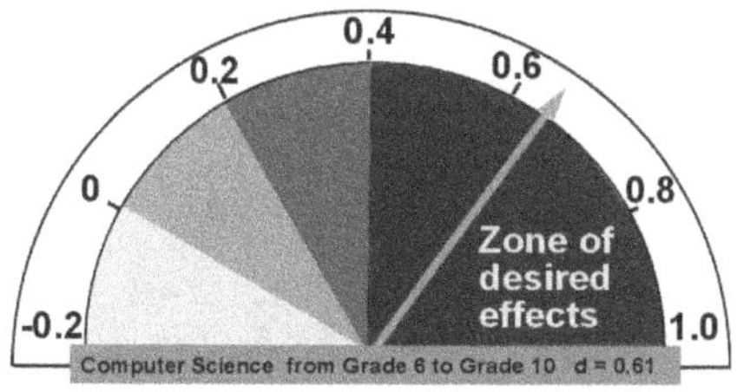

Figure 3: Barometer for Computer Science

teaching in CS or ICT. This points to the possible ineffictiveness of ICT. Nevertheless, the ability of the students in the external control group is not as high as in the internal control group.

The second variety of the effect size d is the comparison at the end of the research. The effect size between the CS group and the two control groups is listed in row 3 in table 3 and the adjusted effect size in shown in row 4 in table 3.

At the start of the CS course in grade 6 we observed a smaller effect size between the CS group and the control groups (cf. row 2 in table 3). It demonstrates that the students of the compulsory subject could rely on basic previous knowledge.

We conclude that students taught in CS as a subject in the lower secondary education have clearly better competences for the digital society, as measured by the outcomes defined in the national standards of CS.

6.4 Programming Knowledge

In CS we use programming as a tool. Scripting languages like `Tcl/Tk` reflect this position with their property as a *glue language* [24, p.25]. The goal in teaching CS is *computational thinking* [31], not programming in one or more languages. Nevertheless it is necessary and useful to achieve concepts and knowledge about programming languages and to have concrete competences in programming.

The question is: How to teach programming as a tool and not as the central item in CS? Our approach is teaching in contexts. There are a several forms of contextualised teaching: The lowest form is a problem-oriented lesson, the highest form is a special project. If these versions for teaching overlapped with everyday life, we called this teaching *contextualised teaching.*

Today students normally have no technical access to computers and computer science. Therefore programming cannot start and end on a technical level. Our starting point is, for example, a multimedia problem requiring a small script. Therefore students are taught programming. The ideas and competences of programming should be taught over a period of five years.

Effect size	CS - CG_{int}	CS - CG_{ext}
in Grade 6	0.26	0.25
in Grade 10	0.45	0.47
... adjusted	0.50	0.53

Table 3: Effect size d CS versus CG

Effect size	CS	CG_{int}	CG_{ext}
from 6 to 10	0.34	0.32	0.25

Table 4: Effect size d in programming

Effect size	CS - CG_{int}	CS - CG_{ext}
in Grade 6	0.09	0.11
in Grade 10	0.20	0.61

Table 5: Effect size d in programming CS – CG

The statistical data enable us to verify our approach. Nine of the twenty-nine questions require special background information about programming. Therefore these programming questions and their statistical outcome are examined separately. Table 4 shows the progress from grade 6 to grade 10 in the different groups and table 5 shows the effect size at the beginning and at the end of the course.

These tables show that students in all groups in grade 6 are comparable. In grade 10 all students have increased their competences. The difference between the groups is small. Only the external control group is an outlier. It is remarkable that in the CS group more students answered with *I don't know* rather than *I (don't) agree* than in the control groups. With concepts that we taught more intensely (eg. the *repeat structure*), students in the CS group answered often more correctly. Obviously, many students still feel unsure about this important part of CS.

A possible and a lucid explanation is the following reasoning. Hattie has researched the results of several forms of practice [15, p.184ff]. Such practice is normally a practice without any context. Therefore we have a problem. If we teach in contexts, and programming only has the role of a tool, there is no impact for an intensive training of the (newly learned) concepts of programming. But this intensive training is necessary if we want to produce sustainable competences.

Without giving up the idea of contextualised teaching, we have to acknowledge the demands for more practice in programming. Already in 1986 Dreyfus and Dreyfus recognized five degrees to acquire skills: novice, advanced beginner, competence, proficiency and expertise [11, p.21–36]. If you are a novice, you will learn this new skill with the help of instruction in a most context-free environment [11, p.21]. A good example of this situation is learning to drive a car [11, p.22]. You cannot learn driving in a short period of time. You have to practice for a lot of hours. In these training hours you do not learn in a context. You do not drive to your friends who live 30 miles away, for example. You will have no special contextualised training situations.

Our students are novices. According to Dreyfus, novices need instructions. Hattie's statistical results demand *Direct Instruction* (with an effect size of $d = 0.59$).

7. CONCLUSION

We have observed a CS group from the beginning of grade 6 to the end of grade 10 in lower secondary education in a German public school. The outcomes were compared with the outcomes of another group without CS lessons in this school, and about 60 student in another school. The approach was to introduce the ideas of computational thinking and concepts and structures of computer science based on the everyday life. Therefore is was useful to organize the curriculum items in strands and teach in contexts.

The results after five years show that CS is a possible subject in school for all students. The effect size of students of CS is obviously higher than the effect size of students without CS education.

Unfortunatly the effect size in programming skills is too low. This shows teaching the students to program alone in the area of the specific context has not the desired result. It is necessary to leave the context temporarily and teach programming context-free including suitable exercises to improve the programming skills. After studying programming it is reasonable to go back into the context.

It will be a future work to develop material for such a *teaching close to context*.

8. ACKNOWLEDGMENTS

This project took and still takes a lot of time. Special thanks go to *H. Danielsiek, R. Doherty, J. Fischer, N. Kirchheim, J. Kuhlmann, F. Kurpicz, A. Neuhaus, W. Paul, A. Thom, R. Thies and J. Vahrenhold* and we thank *G. Storkmann* and *S. Ruhkamp* as contact persons at the schools.

9. REFERENCES

[1] Arbeitskreis "Bildungsstandards"' der GI. *Grundsätze und Standards für die Informatik in der Schule.* LOGIN-Verlag, Berlin, 2008.

[2] T. Bell, P. Andreae, and L. Lambert. Computer science in new zealand high schools. In *Proceedings 12th Australasian Computing Education Conference (ACE 2010)*, ACE 2010, pages 15–22, Darlinghurst, Australia, Australia, 2010. Australian Computer Society, Inc.

[3] T. Bell, H. Newton, P. Andreae, and A. Robins. The introduction of computer science to nz high schools: An analysis of student work. In *Proceedings of the 7th Workshop in Primary and Secondary Computing Education*, WiPSCE '12, pages 5–15, New York, NY, USA, 2012. ACM.

[4] A. Briggs and L. Snyder. Computer science principles and the cs 10k initiative. *ACM Inroads*, 3(2):29–31, June 2012.

[5] Q. Brown and A. Briggs. The cs10k initiative: Progress in k-12 through "exploring computer science" part 1. *ACM Inroads*, 6(3):52–53, Aug. 2015.

[6] J. Cohen. *Statistical Power Analysis for the Behavioral Sciences.* L. Erlbaum Associates, 1988.

[7] Committee for the Workshops on Computational Thinking. *Report of a Workshop on The Scope and Nature of Computational Thinking.* National Academies Press, 2010.

[8] Committee for the Workshops on Computational Thinking. *Report of a Workshop on the Pedagogical Aspects of Computational Thinking.* National Academies Press, 2011.

[9] S. Cooper and S. Cunningham. Teaching computer science in context. *ACM Inroads*, 1(1):5–8, 2010.

[10] Department for Education. *Computing programmes of study: key stages 3 and 4 * National curriculum in England.* London, 2013.

[11] H. L. Dreyfus, S. E. Dreyfus, and T. Athanasiou. *Mind over machine: the power of human intuition and expertise in the era of the computer.* Computer science. Free Press, 1986.

[12] N. Grgurina, E. Barendsen, B. Zwaneveld, W. van de Grift, and I. Stoker. Computational thinking skills in dutch secondary education. In *Proceedings of the 8th Workshop in Primary and Secondary Computing Education*, WiPSE '13, pages 31–32, New York, NY, USA, 2013. ACM.

[13] M. Guzdial. Education: Teaching computing to everyone. *Commun. ACM*, 52(5):31–33, May 2009.

[14] M. Guzdial. Does contextualized computing education help? *ACM Inroads*, 1(4):4–6, 2010.

[15] J. Hattie. *Visible Learning: A Synthesis of Over 800 Meta-Analyses Relating to Achievement.* Taylor & Francis, 2008.

[16] O. Hazzan, J. Gal-Ezer, and L. Blum. A model for high school computer science education: The four key elements that make it! *SIGCSE Bull.*, 40(1):281–285, 2008.

[17] L. Kaczmarczyk and R. Dopplick. *Rebooting the Pathway to Success.* ACM, New York, USA, 2014.

[18] KMK der Bundesrepublik Deutschland. *Bildungsstandandards im Fach Physik für den mittleren Bildungsabschluss - Beschluss vom 16.12.2004.* Wolters Kluwer Deutschland - Luchterhand, Neuwied, 2005.

[19] M. Knobelsdorf, J. Magenheim, T. Brinda, D. Engbring, L. Humbert, A. Pasternak, U. Schroeder, M. Thomas, and J. Vahrenhold. Computer Science Education in North-Rhine Westphalia, Germany;A Case Study. *Trans. Comput. Educ.*, 15(2):9:1–9:22, Apr. 2015.

[20] NTCM. *Principles and Standards for School Mathematics.* Reston, USA, 2000. National Council of Teachers of Mathematics.

[21] OECD. *Measuring Student Knowledge and Skills A New Framework for Assessment: A New Framework for Assessment.* Measuring Student Knowledge and Skills A New Framework for Assessment. OECD Publishing, 1999.

[22] OECD, R. Adams, M. Wu, P. for International Student Assessment, O. for Economic Co-operation, and Development. *Pisa 2000 Technical Report.* OECD, 2002.

[23] OECD and U. Statistics. *PISA Literacy Skills for the World of Tomorrow Further Results from PISA 2000: Further Results from PISA 2000.* OECD Publishing, 2003.

[24] J. K. Ousterhout. Scripting: Higher level programming for the 21st century. *IEEE Computer*, 31:23–30, 1997.

[25] A. Pasternak and J. Vahrenhold. Braided teaching in secondary cs education: Contexts, continuity, and the role of programming. In T. Cortina and E. Walker, editors, *Proceedings of the 41st ACM Technical Symposium on Computer Science Education (SIGCSE 2010)*, pages 204–208. ACM, ACM Press, 2010.

[26] H. Puhlmann, C. Schulte, and T. Brinda. Bridging ICT and CS: educational standards for computer science in lower secondary education. In *Source ACM SIGCSE Bulletin archive, Volume 41, Issue 3*, pages 288–292, New York, 2009. ACM.

[27] V. Schmidt. *Vakdossier 2007 Informatica.* Fortbildung durch Selbststudium. SLO, Stichting Leerplanontwikkeling, Enschede, 2007.

[28] D. Seehorn, S. Carey, B. Fuschetto, I. Lee, D. Moix, D. O'Grady-Cunniff, B. B. Owens, C. Stephenson, and A. Verno. Csta k–12 computer science standards: Revised 2011. Technical report, New York, NY, USA, 2011.

[29] C. W. Starr, D. Bergman, and P. Zaubi. The development and implementation of a context-based curricular framework for computer science education in high schools. *SIGCSE Bull.*, 41(3):283–287, 2009.

[30] D. Thompson and T. Bell. Adoption of new computer science high school standards by new zealand teachers. In *Proceedings of the 8th Workshop in Primary and Secondary Computing Education*, WiPSE '13, pages 87–90, New York, NY, USA, 2013. ACM.

[31] J. M. Wing. Computational thinking. *Communications of the ACM*, 49(3):33–35, 2006.

Supporting Active Learning by Introducing an Interactive Teaching Tool in a Data Structures and Algorithms Course

Tommy Färnqvist* tommy.farnqvist@liu.se
Fredrik Heintz* fredrik.heintz@liu.se
Patrick Lambrix* patrick.lambrix@liu.se
Linda Mannila†* linda.mannila@abo.fi
Chunyan Wang* chunyan.wang@liu.se

*Department of Computer and Information Science
Linköping University
SE-581 83 Linköping, Sweden

†Department of Information Technologies
Åbo Akademi University
Joukahaisenkatu 3-5 A
FIN-20520 Turku, Finland

ABSTRACT

Traditionally, theoretical foundations in data structures and algorithms (DSA) courses have been covered through lectures followed by tutorials, where students practise their understanding on pen-and-paper tasks. In this paper, we present findings from a pilot study on using the interactive e-book OpenDSA as the main material in a DSA course. The goal was to redesign an already existing course by building on active learning and continuous examination through the use of OpenDSA. In addition to presenting the study setting, we describe findings from four data sources: final exam, OpenDSA log data, pre and post questionnaires as well as an observation study. The results indicate that students performed better on the exam than during previous years. Students preferred OpenDSA over traditional textbooks and worked actively with the material, although a large proportion of them put off the work until the due date approaches.

Keywords

active learning; e-textbook; interactive textbook; data structures and algorithms

1. INTRODUCTION

Traditionally, covering the theoretical foundations in a data structures and algorithms (DSA) course uses lectures followed by tutorials, where students practice their theoretical understanding on pen-and-paper tasks. In these courses, however, many concepts benefit from computer-based visualisation. Since the 1960s a multitude of tools and activities using visualisation have been developed for DSA courses, while didactic research investigating how to use such tools has become more common [13]. Until recently, though, there was no all-in-one way to integrate these tools into a traditional DSA course. Now, the open project OpenDSA [9, 14], aims at providing such an integrated tool. Some of its main features are the following. OpenDSA is an e-learning tool that provides textbook quality text with links to a dictionary of important terms. It provides many code examples and step-by-step algorithm visualizations. Understanding of algorithms is supported by simulation exercises for the algorithms. After each section and each chapter, there are quizzes with multiple choice questions based on the main concepts that have been covered. All examples, exercises and quizzes are randomly generated which allows a multitude of practice possibilities. Students can obtain hints as well as automated and immediate feedback on exercises and quizzes. Further, OpenDSA automatically stores extensive log data about the students' interaction with the system. For more details on how OpenDSA works and its features we refer to Fouh et al. [9].

In this paper, we present findings from a pilot study on using OpenDSA as the main material in a course on data structures and algorithms. We wanted to design a setting that builds on two main pedagogical principles: (1) *active learning* [4], where we, by employing a blended learning environment, could give students more responsibility and control over their own learning; and (2) *continuous examination* with individual and immediate feedback. We begin by briefly describing the rationale and pedagogical underpinnings for using OpenDSA in the course. Next, we present our study and the methods and data collection instruments used, after which we present and discuss the results. The paper is concluded with some ideas for future work.

SIGCSE '16, March 2–5, 2016, Memphis, TN, USA

© 2016 ACM. ISBN 978-1-4503-3685-7/16/03...$15.00

DOI: http://dx.doi.org/10.1145/2839509.2844653

2. PEDAGOGICAL RATIONALE

Active learning [4] builds on constructivist principles, which require that students are active participants in their own learning process [2]. Instead of viewing learning as passive transmission of information from the teacher to the students, learning is considered an active process, in which students themselves construct the knowledge by building further upon their prior knowledge. Moreover, both constructivism and active learning are related to the cone of experience developed by Dale in the 1940s [7]. This model suggests that students retain more information by what they do (90%) compared to what they read (10%), hear (20%) or observe (30%). Consistent with this model, Ramsden [12] suggests that most students cannot learn unless they are actively involved.

In addition to being actively involved in their studies, students also need feedback on their work – learning requires practice with frequent feedback [5]. To decrease the risk of students developing misconceptions that hinder learning it is important to discover and address them quickly [5]. Visualizations and interactive exercises have the potential to increase student engagement [10], and material that is perceived as engaging also drives students to invest more effort in studying it [15].

Lately, interactive and electronic study material has become increasingly popular, partly through the introduction of massive open online courses (MOOCs). Students are provided continuous access to different types of material, examples and exercises. From a teacher and research perspective, this kind of computer based, interactive material makes it possible to gather large amounts of data, ranging from time stamped interactions (e.g., page loads and button clicks) to performance on different types of tasks [11]. These data can be used to gain insight into student activity and learning.

The interactive exercises in OpenDSA engage students and give them increased opportunities for practicing their knowledge through practical hands-on work (analyzing problems, working with varying types of data structures, as well as applying algorithms to different structures). Furthermore, the summary questions at the end of each chapter give students a way of forming their own opinion on how well they succeeded in grasping the current concept. This is needed since learners tend to overestimate how much they have learned [3].

3. OUR STUDY

3.1 The Study Setting

At the start of their second year, the CS majors at Linköping University used to take a DSA course (TDDC70) comprising 6 ECTS credits. TDDC70 was a traditional monolithic course, with lectures, pen-and-paper based tutorials, and programming assignments. The course was assessed via a written exam at the end of the course for 4 credits, graded (fail, 3, 4, 5), and programming assignments for 2 credits, graded pass/fail. Since 2014 they instead take an 11 credit course (TDDD86) where the DSA contents is the same as in TDDC70 (with a few smaller additions), with the rest of the credits spent on teaching C++ and a small introduction to programming paradigms. It is in the TDDD86 course we have deployed OpenDSA.

Within the TDDD86 course we tried to discern how to best use the system and changes to the organisation of the course to create a blended learning environment in line with our aims. The goal was to support an active learning style among students by giving the students more responsibility for, and control over, their own learning, as well as employing continuous examination with individualised feedback.

One of the important criteria when designing the new version of the DSA course was to give students the opportunity to work at their own, albeit steady, pace, through continuous individual examination with immediate feedback. The mechanisms for this are already in place within OpenDSA, but to give the desired change more support, we also changed the examination of the course. Originally, the theoretical content of TDDD86 was supposed to be assessed by a written exam, comprising 5 ECTS credits, at the end of the course. We instead opted to split the exam credits in two parts: a two credit part for completing all assigned modules and exercises in OpenDSA, and a three credit part for an exam given at the end of the course. The OpenDSA exercises were to be completed by the students during non-scheduled time (compared to TDDC70, where tutorials were scheduled for doing paper-and-pen exercises). The new exam consisted of one computer-based part (using a small sample of the OpenDSA exercises used during the course) for which completion gave a passing grade (3) on the exam. For a higher grade (4, 5) the students needed to solve written problems testing deeper understanding of and connections between different DSA concepts.

3.2 Data Collection and Methodology

Our study involves data from four different sources; exam results, log data captured by the OpenDSA system, questionnaires, and an observation study. These are briefly described in the following:

3.2.1 Final Exam

We chose to include final exam results for TDDC70 from 2010–2013, since these had the same examiner as in TDDD86. Also, the written problems for a higher grade on the TDDD86 final exam were of the same types and estimated difficulty as the hardest types of problems used in the TDDC70 final exams.

3.2.2 Log Data

OpenDSA automatically stores extensive log data covering all interactions with the system. Hence, the data makes it possible to study aspects related to student behavior (how and when they study), student learning (performance on different types of exercises) and technical aspects (platforms and browsers used). A thorough overview of all data stored can be found on the OpenDSA web site (http://algoviz.org/OpenDSA/Doc/manual/DatabaseSchemas.html#exercise). The data can be used to investigate very specific issues related to these three areas. In this study, we have focused on log data related to student activity – how often they have used the material and at what times.

3.2.3 Questionnaires

To study the experience and attitude among the students toward interactive textbooks in general and our material specifically we conducted two online surveys. The first survey was distributed electronically to all the students at the start of the course and the second survey after the end of the course. The first survey was answered by 54 of 130 students (42%), while 35 students (27%) the second survey. Our experience from other studies in previous courses is that it is harder to get students to answer a questionnaire after the end of the course, there are of course also fewer active students as some have dropped out.

3.2.4 Observation study

We decided to use an observation study as it allows us to gather data in the specific setting to be studied [6], which in our case is that the students use the interactive book for studying. We used two nonparticipant observers. One of the observers has domain knowledge (former teacher in the area) while the other observer has no domain knowledge (language teacher). We expected the observers to focus on different things. The observers took descriptive as well as reflective notes.

Six students, five males and one female, participated in the observations. They were paid volunteers. For privacy reasons, in the remainder of this paper we refer to each student participating in the observation study as 'he'.

The students were each observed individually three times. In each session, the students worked on the chapters selected by the examiner and the observers together. The first observation was at the beginning of the term. The aim was to let the students become familiar with the observation. The chapter for the first session contained a large amount of text. The second session was arranged mid-term, while the third and final session was at the end of the term. The chapters for the second and third session required the students to be active and interact with the material. For the second and third session the students were asked not to work on the respective chapters before the sessions.

Each observation session lasted about 30 minutes. At the start of the first session the research project was introduced and students were asked about their expectations and concerns about using an interactive book. For each of the sessions the students were observed for about 25 minutes, during which they worked on the interactive online book. Students were also asked to think aloud. The observers sat back and observed the students' work methods and study patterns. In some cases the observers asked clarification questions. Furthermore, about 5 minutes at the end of the sessions were used for questions and discussions regarding the students' opinions about the interactive book, the comparison between learning using a traditional book and learning using the interactive online book, and whether, and if so, how the way of learning using the interactive book changed during the course.

4. FINDINGS

4.1 Exam Results

In Table 1 we can see the results on the final exam for different years in TDDC70 and TDDD86, respectively. Statistical calulations reveal that our experiment did not influence the average (passing) grade that much, but if we look at the proportion of students getting a higher than passing grade out of all students taking the exam, we have a significant increase when compared to the exams from 2010, 2012, and 2013 ($p < 0.02$, when looking at results from 2-sample χ^2-tests for equality of proportions). We also note that the 2011 TDDC70 exam has similar properties when compared to the other TDDC70 exams, but with a lower significance ($p < 0.05$).

4.2 Log Data

In total, the course had close to 145,000 exercise submissions and over 700,000 interactions. These data also include exercises taken as part of the exam and after it. If only considering exercises submitted during the course (September - December) and excluding exercises on the exam, students submitted almost 138,500 exercises.

	fail	3	4	5	avg	prop
TDDC70 2010	39	29	10	6	3.48	19 %
TDDC70 2011	19	42	21	3	3.41	28%
TDDC70 2012	59	25	8	2	3.34	10 %
TDDC70 2013	64	27	11	1	3.33	12 %
TDDD86 2014	0	71	30	15	3.51	39 %

Table 1: Number of students receiving different grades, average passing grade, and proportion of students receiving a higher than passing grade out of all students taking the exam.

Almost all (95%) of the students who were registered for the course submitted a solution to at least one exercise. On average students attempted 83 exercises (once or several times); only 12 students attempted less than 10 exercises (These students did not take the final exam and were otherwise quite inactive in the course). Most (98.5%) interactions with the system took place through a non-mobile operating system, with only a few students trying to use OpenDSA with Android or iOS.

Figure 1 shows the timely distribution of all exercise submissions (black) and overall interactions (grey) throughout the 24 hours in a day. Submission after the deadline did not give any course credit. Clearly, most activity has taken place in the late afternoon and early evening, but the system has been used over the entire span of a day.

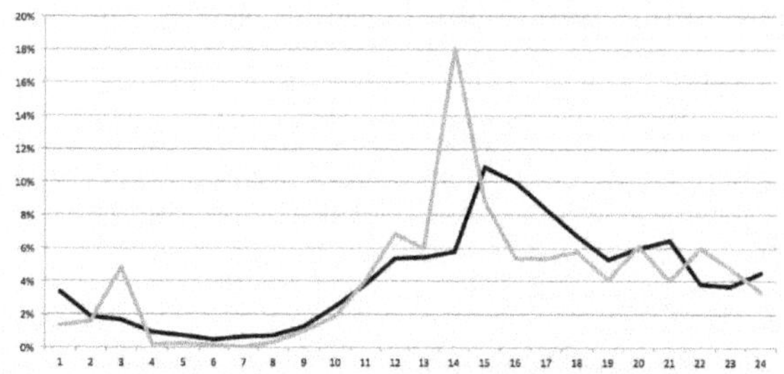

Figure 1: Hourly distribution of student activity with OpenDSA throughout the course

The data reveal that although students have been somewhat active throughout the course, the activity exploded in December. Figure 2 shows the distribution of when students submitted exercises during the fall period.

In December, most exercise submissions took place around the exam (December 19). The OpenDSA exercises included in the exam are not part of the data presented in Figure 3. In addition to this being the time of the exam, December 21 was the deadline for submitting the compulsory exercises for credit.

4.3 Questionnaires

4.3.1 *Previous experience with textbooks*

The questionnaires reveal that most students are used to reading textbooks, mainly for looking things up and for studying for an exam. The students have to a large degree been satisfied with earlier textbooks (15% is dissatisfied or very dissatisfied).

According to the students, the following properties charac-

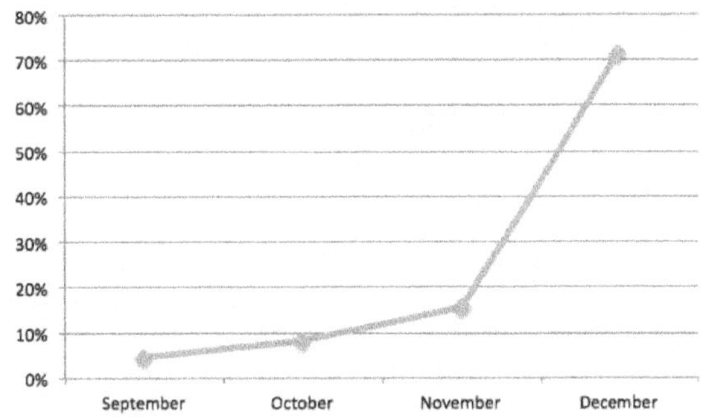

Figure 2: Monthly distribution of exercise submissions (not including exercises on the exam)

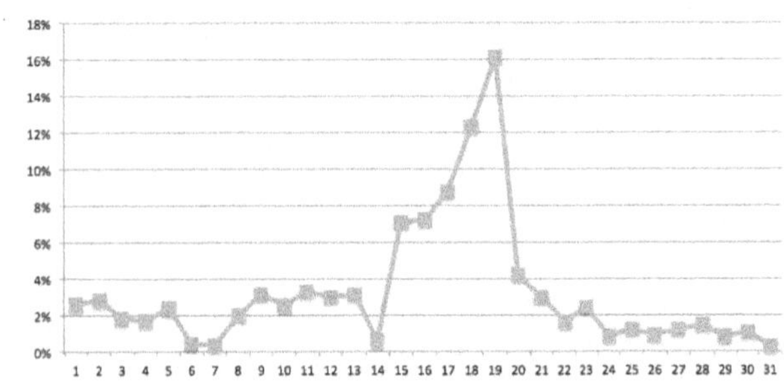

Figure 3: Daily distribution of exercise submissions in December (not including exercises on the exam)

terize a good textbook, here ordered from most important to least important: correct information, clear structure, good explanatory examples, clear pictures, suitable for the level of students and the course, correct language, nice layout and design.

4.3.2 Previous experience with e-books

Almost a third (30%) of the students had used e-books for other things besides studies, 39% also for studies and 31% had no previous experience. The benefits according to the students are: easier to navigate and find specific information, weightless, possible to enlarge the text, interactive and multimedia content, always available. The downsides according to the students are: tiring for the eyes, dependent on batteries, hard to get an overview of where you are, closer to distractions.

4.3.3 Experience with OpenDSA

Nearly two thirds (62%) of the students have studied the theory parts of OpenDSA at least once each week and 31% more than once a week. 54% of the students completed one or more exercises in OpenDSA at least once each week and 20% completed exercises more than once a week.

Most (89%) students were satisfied with OpenDSA and 49% of them were very satisfied. 71% of the students felt that their expectations were met and most (91%) of them prefer OpenDSA over a printed textbook. Only 3% prefers a printed textbook over OpenDSA, while the remaining students are indifferent.

Students were asked about the benefits and drawbacks with OpenDSA. Students were happy with the material always being accessible and appreciated the animations and interactivity which increases understanding. Students also found it good to have quizzes making it possible to check their own understanding. On the downside, students found some parts too long and were frustrated with the existence of bugs. Students also pointed out the need for an improved layout, in order to make it more clear what parts of the material are most relevant.

4.4 Observation Study

4.4.1 Initial expectations and worries

At the beginning of the first session, one student expected that the interactive book would be the same as a traditional text book but modernized (e.g., with interactive exercises). Two students expected that the interactive book will help or make them learn. Four students mentioned that they expect that they do not need to carry a book. Most of the students said that they have no worries regarding the use of the interactive book. Some students worried that there will be bugs and that there will be a lot of text. Some students worried that they may guess the answers to questions, and therefore not learn. One student usually skips large parts of text and worries that the exam may require that the students have read everything.

4.4.2 Observed work methods and study patterns

When using the interactive book, some students mark or use the mouse pointer to follow the text while reading. Several students adjust the screen to make it easier to read. Some students use pen and paper while reading, but several do not.

We observed that many students read a chapter from the beginning to the end, and do the exercises in turn. One student skims through the whole chapter to get an overview and then starts from the beginning. Another student reads the whole text first and then does the exercises. Several students skip text. They mentioned that they do not worry that they miss any important information. The students think that the important information will be in the tables, figures and interactive parts. This is consistent with Fouh et al. [8], who also found that, although ideally, students using OpenDSA should read most or all of the text, completing exercises as they go, many students skip directly to exercises only reading as required to get exercise credit (at least the first time they work on a particular piece of material).

We found that the dictionary was much appreciated and frequently used. Also, the students like the code examples.

Regarding the visualization of algorithms, we observed that some students go back and forth between the visualization and the text or code. However, some students go very fast through the visualizations and essentially just click through them. We also noted that students did not take advantage of the ability to run their own algorithm execution examples.

In general the students appreciated the interactive exercises. All students use the hints, but with different strategies. Some check all hints before answering. Some check hints only when answering wrong, and otherwise, they do not check the hints. Some check the remaining hints after answering correctly. We noted that some students try to guess the answers while others go back and forth between the exercises and the text. Sometimes students just click on all possible answers. One student said 'it takes too long to figure out the right answers'.

4.4.3 *Results from discussions with the students*

In the questions and discussions part of the sessions, most students said that they used the tool during the observation sessions in the same way as at home. This is important as it means that our observations are relevant for the real situation of how the students use the interactive book. One student mentioned that he usually works together with another student, because he likes discussions, which makes it easier to memorize.

With regard to when the students use the interactive book, most of the students usually use it after the lecture. One student mentioned that he works on several chapters at the same time.

Most students do not use additional materials. One student uses Wikipedia as a complement. Another student looked at other books in the beginning but found the interactive book to be better.

Regarding the positive aspects related to the interactive book, the students mentioned that the dictionary is very good because they do not have to go to another source to check the terminology. They like that there are many exercises and that they can redo exercises many times. They like the possibility to receive hints in the exercises and the fact that they can check answers, which helps their understanding. As one student said 'Even when you get the answers wrong, you still learn something'. Further, they thought that the code examples, the visualizations, and the overviews and introductions at the beginning of the chapter are good. Most negative comments regarding the interactive book are related to the presentation on the screen. The text format is not perfect and sometimes the students have to adjust the screen to make reading easier. Some students said it is hard to focus on the screen when they get tired. One student suggested introducing 'mini-content' pages that show an overview of the chapter that the student is working on. One student suggested using a pop-up dictionary instead of going to a new web page. Further, there are some bugs in the interactive books. Regarding the exercises some students found that some exercises require doing similar things too often and that some exercises need a better explanation. Some students want to have additional links from the exercises to other parts in the interactive book, so they would more easily know where to read when they failed an exercise.

Most students used the interactive book in the same way from the first session to the third session. One student mentioned that in the beginning he mainly guessed the answers to the exercises but realized that he did not learn much, and then changed his study method by spending more time on answering the questions in the exercises.

We discussed the difference in learning using a traditional book and the interactive book. Most students said that they usually do not read or like to read traditional books. With the interactive book, they are more active, and they feel they have to read the book. They would not read a traditional book until right before the examination, while with the interactive book, they read throughout the course because working with the interactive book is required for obtaining part of the credits of the course. The students said that they usually skip or do only some exercises in a traditional book and this right before the examination, while with the interactive online book, students are more active and do the exercises throughout the course because it is interesting and they get credits. The visualizations in the interactive book allow of immediate feedback on the correctness of the student's interpretation of the algorithms or exercises. With a traditional book, students would visualize with paper and pen, but would not be sure if it is correct. Finally, the students mentioned that they feel they learn deeper with the interactive book. One student thinks that is because they use more senses.

5. DISCUSSION

When looking at final exam results, one thing that stands out is that no students failed the exam in TDDD86, while quite a number of students failed the TDDC70 exams. Is this because the TDDD86 exam was easier? In a certain sense this is probably true, but at the same time it is a fact that 117 students finished all assigned OpenDSA exercises, and out of these 116 took the exam — meaning they were very well prepared for the OpenDSA part of the final exam. As we have no way of measuring how much drilling the TDDC70 students had done on the "easier" type of questions testing definitions and understanding of basic properties it is hard to make a fair comparison, but since the OpenDSA exercises were mandatory in TDDD86 and the students could work in their own pace continuously throughout the course, there is probably a big change in how much time the students have spent learning the basic concepts.

We have also seen, that there seems to be a change in how many students aspire for and obtain a higher grade on the final exam. Is this due to the fact that the TDDD86 students might have done more drilling than their TDDC70 counterparts? We certainly hope so — being more familiar with the properties of various data structures and their algorithms should make you better prepared to answer the harder questions requiring insight into how to combine different structures to solve algorithmic problems. However, we cannot rule out the possibility that the change in exam results is just due to the student group. To control for this we intend to make an analysis factoring in performance also on previous courses. A further confounding factor stems from other course acitivites; in TDDC70 the students did four mandatory programming assignments, while TDDD86 has eight mandatory programming assignments out of which six has clear algorithmic content. It could be the case that the higher exposure to solving more complex problems made the TDDD86 students significantly better prepared for those types of questions than the TDDC70 students. On the other hand, using OpenDSA enabled the examiner of the TDDD86 course to skip some lecture time used in TDDC70 to provide detailed demonstrations of data structure behaviour, leaving the TDDD86 students to do that kind of course work on their own, meaning that the TDDD86 students actually had less DSA lectures scheduled than the TDDC70 students.

The log data suggest that students actively used the material throughout the course. Having all students submitting on average solutions to nearly 90 exercises is a big improvement compared to using traditional material with a limited number of exercises to practice on. Students have also used OpenDSA continuously throughout the day and work week, suggesting that students have used it also outside university.

Nevertheless, the monthly and daily distribution of submissions (Figure 2 and 3) show that most activity took place around the final exam and the due date for submitting compulsory exercises for credit. This is in line with the findings of Fouh et al. [8], who found that students using OpenDSA tend to wait until the deadline before dealing with the tasks assigned. One thing to consider is hence, whether a more continuous formative assessment scheme, using, for instance, both OpenDSA exercises and a learning journal, could aid in helping students distribute their work more evenly.

The findings from the questionnaires show that the overall student experience with OpenDSA is very positive, 89% satisfied and 91% prefer OpenDSA over printed textbook, and the only issue is bugs. One student writes in a free text answer: 'When you get rid of the bugs this will be one of the best text books you can get. Animations in combination with text is very close to what you get from a good lecture.' The students also tend to spend more time with the material, can work in their own pace and keep a steady tempo through the course. Some comments from the students regarding this: 'I have learned more in less time, [...] [I] can go through the material in the pace that is needed.', 'The way the exercises were presented in OpenDSA made me spend more time with them after reading the chapter compared to a printed textbook, which is positive!' and 'Since there were mandatory exercises, and quite many, I read and did the exercises in the same pace as the lectures, which made it easier to study for the exam at the end and I had more knowledge and a better understanding.' We note that all of these findings have to be taken with a grain of salt, since especially the post survey had a low response rate.

Some main positive findings from the observation study are that (1) students prefer the interactive book over a traditional book, (2) the dictionary, visualizations and exercises (the interactive parts of the book) are appreciated and help students understand, and (3) the interactive book encourages students to work during the course.

The observations also revealed some issues that require special attention when using an interactive book: there are students that (1) skip text, (2) guess answers to exercises and (3) interact with the visualizations without learning.

6. FUTURE WORK

The findings presented in this paper indicate that the initial experience from the redesigned version of the DSA course, incorporating OpenDSA as the main material, has been positive. As stated above, OpenDSA collects a large amount of interesting data making it possible to study a multitude of interesting questions. Future work involves investigating, for instance, potential relationships between student activity in OpenDSA and exam performance. Also, the TDDD86 course is now (fall 2015) offered again using the same format, hence adding to the data available for analysis.

We are also interested in investigating how the log data can be used to guide the learning and the teaching in a dynamic way during the course, so called Just-in-Time Teaching [1]. For instance, for topics that from the log data are identified to be difficult, extra sessions could be scheduled.

7. ACKNOWLEDGMENTS

The authors want to acknowledge the timely and competent support provided by Cliff Shaffer and the OpenDSA team making this study possible, as well as the many helpful suggestions by the reviewers. The study was partially financed by funding for pedagogical projects at Linköping University, and by the pedagogical development group (PUG) at the Institute of Technology at Linköping University.

8. REFERENCES

[1] T. Bailey and J. Forbes. Just-in-time teaching for CS0. *SIGCSE Bulletin*, 37(1):366–370, 2005.

[2] M. Ben-Ari. Constructivism in computer science education. *SIGCSE Bulletin*, 30(1):257–261, 1998.

[3] R. Bjork, J. Dunlosky, and N. Kornell. Self-regulated learning: Beliefs, techniques, and illusions. *Annual Review of Psychology*, 64:417–444, 2013.

[4] C. C. Bonwell and J. A. Eison. *Active learning: Creating excitement in the classroom.* ASHE-ERIC Higher Education Report No. 1. George Washington University, 1991.

[5] J. D. Bransford, A. L. Brown, and R. R. Cocking, editors. *How People learn: Brain, mind, experience, and school.* National Academy Press, 1999.

[6] J. W. Creswell. *Educational Research: planning, conducting, and evaluating quantitative and qualitative research.* Pearson, 4th edition, 2012.

[7] E. Dale. *Audio-Visual Methods in Teaching*, chapter 4. Dryden Press, 1946.

[8] E. Fouh, D. A. Breakiron, S. Hamouda, M. F. Farghally, and C. A. Shaffer. Exploring students learning behavior with an interactive etextbook in computer science courses. *Computers in Human Behavior*, 41:478–485, 2014.

[9] E. Fouh, V. Karavirta, D. A. Breakiron, S. Hamouda, S. Hall, T. L. Naps, and C. A. Shaffer. Design and architecture of an interactive etextbook - The OpenDSA system. *Science of Computer Programming*, 88:22–40, 2014.

[10] C. D. Hundhausen, S. A. Douglas, and J. T. Stasko. A meta-study of algorithm visualization effectiveness. *Journal of Visual Languages & Computing*, 13(3):259–290, 2002.

[11] A. Korhonen, T. Naps, C. Boisvert, P. Crescenzi, V. Karavirta, L. Mannila, B. Miller, B. Morrison, S. H. Rodger, R. Ross, and C. A. Shaffer. Requirements and design strategies for open source interactive computer science ebooks. In *Proceedings of the ITiCSE Working Group Reports Conference on Innovation and Technology in Computer Science Education-working Group Reports*, ITiCSE -WGR '13, pages 53–72, 2013.

[12] P. Ramsden. *Learning to Teach in Higher Education.* Routledge, 1992.

[13] C. A. Shaffer, M. L. Cooper, A. J. D. Alon, M. Akbar, M. Stewart, S. Ponce, and S. H. Edwards. Algorithm visualization: The state of the field. *ACM Transactions on Computing Education*, 10(3):9:1–9:22, 2010.

[14] C. A. Shaffer, V. Karavirta, A. Korhonen, and T. L. Naps. OpenDSA: Beginning a community active-eBook project. In *Proceedings of the 11th Koli Calling International Conference on Computing Education Research*, pages 112–117, 2011.

[15] J. Sorva, V. Karavirta, and L. Malmi. A review of generic program visualization systems for introductory programming education. *ACM Transactions of Computing Education*, 13(4):15:1–15:64, 2013.

SEURAT_Edu: A Tool to Assist and Assess Student Decision-Making in Design

John Malloy
Computer Science and Software Engineering
Miami University
Oxford, Ohio, USA
malloyjm@miamioh.edu

Janet Burge
Mathematics and Computer Science
Wesleyan University
Middletown, CT 06459
+1 860-685-2413
jburge@wesleyan.edu

ABSTRACT

Decision-making is central to software development. Most problems do not have straightforward solutions but instead require assessing and evaluating multiple candidate solutions depending on the requirements (functional and non-functional) for the specific project. Real problems may have more than one valid solution and software engineering students need to be able to synthesize design alternatives and reason about them to make the best decision for the specific problem under consideration. The work described here uses a web-based system to administer rationale-based assignments where the students are required to explicitly present their rationale for a series of decisions and use the capabilities of the tool to justify their choices. Students using the tool report that it helped them consider more alternatives and put more thought into their decision-making process.

Keywords

Design Rationale; Decision-Making; Learning Management Systems; Bloom's Taxonomy

1. INTRODUCTION

As software developers, students need to be able to take the concepts they've learned in earlier classes and apply them to larger, more realistic problems in later ones (and in the real world after graduation). This is not always as straightforward as it sounds—real problems may have more than one valid solution and students need to be able to understand these problems, propose candidate solutions, and analyze the solutions based on a set of criteria that they have to discover as part of the process.

Many students find this challenging. Students may have difficulty dealing with problems where there is more than one right answer. They may also have difficulty objectively looking at alternatives when their preferences are biased in favor of past experience or personal goals that may not mesh with those of their client (such as how easy the solution is to code—a high priority for students who have demands on their time beyond the one class but not necessarily a priority for the client). This can be a problem if students fixate on a solution that may be less than optimal rather than explore new options.

One way to encourage generation and analysis of alternatives is to require that students create explicit argumentation documenting the decisions they need to make, alternatives considered, and the arguments for and against these alternatives. Argumentation-based design rationale is one mechanism for doing this. The rationale can be used to perform a simple numeric evaluation of the alternatives to encourage students to justify their choices.

We developed a web-based tool, SEURAT_Edu, to allow instructors to create rationale-based assignments suitable for students at different stages in the curriculum. The goal is to use these assignments to help them grow in their ability to identify, reason about, and select design alternatives. SEURAT_Edu integrates with existing Learning Management Systems (LMS) to make it easy for instructors to administer and evaluate student work.

This paper is structured as follows. Section 2 discusses related and prior work in educational research and using rationale in education; section 3 describes SEURAT_Edu, section 4 gives usability results from classroom use and section 5 provides a summary, conclusions, and future work.

2. RELATED AND PRIOR WORK

We designed SEURAT_Edu to help students become better designers by recording their rationale, something that has been shown to result in higher quality designs for inexperienced designers [1]. We observed that students found designing to be challenging and looked at existing models of student learning for help.

Two education models inspired this work. The first is Bloom's Taxonomy [2], a taxonomy of learning levels that is often used in formulating educational objectives. These levels are knowledge (memorizing concepts in a domain), comprehension (understanding these concepts), application (applying the facts to a new situation), analysis (reasoning about the concepts), synthesis (forming new concepts), and evaluation (assessing and judging using concepts and criteria). An argumentation-based approach appears to be a good fit for encouraging and assessing student ability to analyze and evaluate.

The second theory is the Perry scheme for Intellectual and Ethical Development [3]. Perry describes how students progress in development starting at dualism, where students believe there are always right or wrong answers, into multiplicity, where all options are equally valid, into relativism, and finally commitment.

SIGCSE'16, March 2–5, 2016, Memphis, TN, USA.
© 2016 ACM. ISBN 978-1-4503-3685-7/16/03…$15.00.
DOI: http://dx.doi.org/10.1145/2839509.2844555

Moving through these stages requires the ability to assess alternatives and make choices when faced with changing criteria.

In addition to student progression, evaluating alternatives also plays a role in encouraging creativity. One of the key stages in the creative process is ideation—the generation of multiple ideas. Ray McCall [4] discusses ideation in his work, but he combines it with evaluation. McCall believes that "intertwining ideation and evaluation promotes creativity in software design because feedback about consequences of design decisions challenges designers to devise new ideas."

In our earlier work, we performed a preliminary exploration of using argumentation to encourage exploration of alternatives [5] by comparing results of two design methods: using the Eclipse-based SEURAT (Software Engineering Using RATionale) plugin for rationale capture [6] and using Pugh Matrices [7] to capture alternatives and criteria. SEURAT provided the additional assistance of automatically assessing alternatives based on criteria while the Pugh Matrix was a more manual approach. The goal for using both tools was to encourage students to document their reasoning with the hope that this would cause them to delay making a decision until more analysis had occurred. Results showed that students using rationale-based approaches did not consider more alternatives (they were given a target number by the instructor) but these approaches did encourage reflection and were useful tools for faculty to identify where some of the difficulties were. This experiment only asked the students to provide rationale for a single decision.

Tang, et al. [1] conducted a study where participants were asked to apply design reasoning by capturing rationale both as they were designing and when prompted by interviewers. The designers in the experimental (rationale) group had more awareness of their own reasoning, considered usability throughout the process, were more likely to shift their initial design impression as they gained in knowledge, and did more backtracking to re-investigate previous decisions. The impact of using design reasoning was more apparent for less experienced participants (5 years of experience or less) than it was for more experienced designers.

Van Heersh, Avgeriou, and Tang [8] investigated the use of decision viewpoints as a way to encourage junior designers to investigate solution alternatives. They performed an experiment using four groups of software engineering students towards the end of their undergraduate education. They used three decision viewpoints in their study—a decision detail viewpoint, which gives information about architectural decisions that includes their rationale, a decision relationship viewpoint, that would include information about which decisions depend on (or are alternatives to) each other, and a decision forces viewpoint which gives the relationship between the decision and criteria (forces) that need to be considered when making architectural choices. They found that the latter viewpoints (forces and relationships) helped the students explore and evaluate design options and also helped them assess the results of combining different design options. The students did not like documenting the decision detail viewpoint and did not consider it useful for their own work but did say that they felt it would be helpful for subsequent developers who may take over the project in the future.

3. SEURAT_Edu

Our earlier work [5] used SEURAT to capture and evaluate rationale. SEURAT was designed to support software development and maintenance, not as a tool for assignment administration. This meant that using SEURAT had had a number of disadvantages.

1. *Eclipse Specific* – using SEURAT means using Eclipse. Students taking CS classes that are not using Eclipse are confused by the need to switch tools for the rationale-based assignments. We also want to eventually expand our experiments beyond computer science since decision-making is required in many other fields. Non-CS students and faculty would be unlikely to want to try the tool if it is designed only for software developers.
2. *Overly Complex* – SEURAT includes features designed to support software development that are not necessary for the classroom setting. A simplified version of the tool is easier for students and faculty to learn.
3. *Limited Access* – SEURAT uses a database local to the machine that Eclipse is installed on to store the rationale. This means that a student could only work on their rationale on a single computer in a computer laboratory with controlled access. This limited rationale use to small exercises and did not support capturing rationale as part of homework assignments.
4. *No Administration* – SEURAT is not set up to deliver pre-generated rationale to the students or to deliver rationale to faculty to be graded. Database expertise is required to ensure that students have access to rationale already in the database, either by installing an already populated database locally on each machine or by creating duplicate copies of the rationale in a shared database. There is no way to enforce deadlines with the tool. Analyzing student work is a challenge using SEURAT since the student database tables have to be accessible to the instructor. The instructor has to use SQL queries or to load the student data as a new SEURAT project in order to assess the rationale.

To address these issues, we developed a new system: SEURAT_Edu. SEURAT_Edu is purely web-based where rationale is stored in a shared MySQL database. It integrates with a variety of Learning Management Systems (LMSs) using the Learning Tools Interoperability (LTI) framework. This means that authentication and assignment administration are taken care of by the LMS. This means students do not need to register with a second system in order to complete rationale-based assignments but instead can access them directly through the LMS already used for the course. It also means that instructors can easily view the rationale trees just like the students—making it easy to view the rationale.

Moving to a web-based environment provides a tool that is not CS-specific but could be used in any subject area where faculty want students to develop and practice their skills at identifying and evaluating alternatives. Complexity was addressed by only implementing a subset of SEURAT's capabilities and the tool was designed to provide instructor support in developing and assessing assignments. The experiments described here were administered using a Sakai-based LMS (https://sakaiproject.org), but SEURAT_Edu has also been successfully integrated with Moodle.

3.1 Support for Assignment Creation and Administration

Rationale-based assignments can be tailored to the specific class needs and level of student by providing the students with starting rationale. SEURAT_Edu lets instructors create a set of "solution" rationale and then use that as the basis of a student version that may have some of the content modified or removed, as appropriate. The instructor is not required to have a complete rationale solution unless they prefer to start with one. The assignment due-date is set within SEURAT_Edu. Once the due-date has passed the students can view their solutions but no longer modify them. The instructor also can control if the assignment is visible to the students or not from inside SEURAT_Edu. Instructors can use SEURAT_Edu to view student submissions. Rationale in SEURAT consists of the following elements:

- *Requirements* – the system requirements, functional or non-functional, for something the students are required to design or define as part of the assignment. SEURAT_Edu also supports entering rationale for the requirements.
- *Decisions* – decision problems that the students need to solve as part of the assignment. Each decision can have either alternatives or sub-decisions, but not both.
- *Alternatives* – options considered as possible solutions for the decision problems posed by the assignment. Each alternative has arguments for and against it that are used to generate a score for the alternative. When creating alternatives, the user should not be filtering out solutions that they deem as bad, since we want to capture all options in the tool.
- *Arguments* – pros and cons of alternatives, or dependencies between alternatives. Each argument is about and contributes to its parent alternative while referring to a separate piece of rationale, like requirements, claims, or assumptions.
- *Claims* – criteria used in decision-making that were not explicitly given as requirements.
- *Assumptions* – reasons that the user believes to be true but is unsure about, or things that might change over time.

Figure 1 shows the types of rationale in their hierarchical structure.

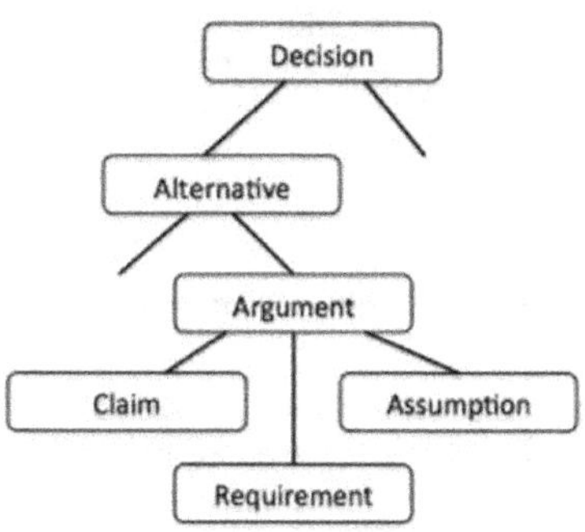

Figure 1. Rationale Types

Rationale is visualized using a tree format with colored icons differentiating between the different rationale elements. Rationale is entered via a form-based interface with default values provided for all fields except for the name of the rationale element. As rationale is entered, it is displayed in the rationale tree. Figure 2 shows a sub-set of a rationale tree giving a decision (How to persistently store data in the system), two alternatives, and some arguments.

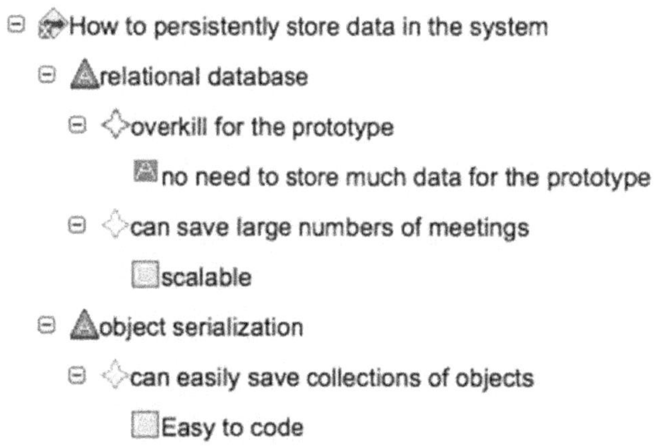

Figure 2.Rationale Tree in SEURAT_Edu

After creating the starter rationale, the instructor can then create a due-date for the assignment (the date after which the student will no longer be able to edit their rationale) and publish the rationale to the class through the LMS. The LMS uses the class roster to create copies of the rationale tree for each individual student so they can complete their assignments independently.

3.2 Support for Students Working on Assignments

The students use the starter rationale to complete the assignment designed by their instructor. They can view and edit the starter rationale and also add new elements. SEURAT_Edu encourages the students to use and complete the rationale by displaying its status. The rationale entered into SEURAT_Edu is evaluated by the system to look for errors in the rationale and/or errors in reasoning. These errors are shown in two places. One is in the rationale tree. There are small overlaid status icons to indicate where there are errors or warnings. One can be seen on the "How to persistently store data in the system" decision in Figure 2 – the small X (shown in red by the system) overlaying the lower left corner of the icon. The second place to see the results of the evaluation is in a Rationale Status Panel that lists all the errors and warnings. Figure 3 shows some initial errors given by SEURAT_Edu for the starting state of an assignment.

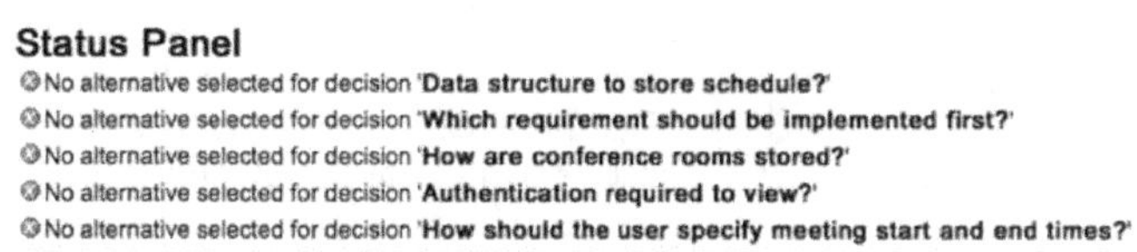

Figure 3.Rationale Status Panel

The rationale status is used by the students to see if the rationale that they have entered in their solution is consistent and complete. The following types of errors are detected and reported by SEURAT_Edu:

- *Requirement violation* (error) – an alternative has been selected where one of the arguments against it indicates that the alternative violates a requirement.
- *No alternative selected* (error) – the student has not selected an alternative for a decision problem.
- *Decision has too many selected alternatives* (error) – some decisions can be marked as multi-selection where more than

one alternative can be selected but for many only one choice is allowed. If only one choice is allowed but more than one alternative is selected an error will be reported.

- *Alternative has no arguments in its favor* – if a student selects an alternative without describing any reasons why, SEURAT_Edu reports this as an error.
- *A selected alternative requires that another alternative also be selected but it was not* (error) – if there are dependencies on alternatives and only one is selected by the student SEURAT_Edu will point out the error.
- *Duplicate arguments found* (warning) – if the same argument appears twice for an alternative that could be an error or could indicate that arguments are not given at a fine enough level of detail (for example, there could be two reasons why an alternative is "usable," in which case the specific reasons should be given rather than the more generic one appearing twice).
- *The highest rated alternative was not selected* (warning) – this appears if the alternative selected did not have as much support in the rationale as another alternative for the same decision. This means either a different choice should be made or more arguments for the current choice should be provided.

4. TOOL ASSESSMENT

SEURAT_Edu was used in three courses: a 200-level Data Structures (DS) course, a 200-level Software Engineering (SE) course and a 300-level Requirements Engineering (RE) course. The Data Structures course contained a laboratory exercise where the students used SEURAT_Edu to explore some design alternatives. This was an opportunity to test out the tool in a real educational setting and to dry-run our usability data collection. The survey instruments were re-written after this experiment because usability feedback on individual tool features turned out to be less interesting and useful than an assessment of the tool as a whole.

For the SE and RE classes, the same assignment was used in both so that responses could be compared. The RE course had the SE course as a pre-requisite so it was not possible to have a student taking both courses during the semester where the assessment was administered. Seventeen students participated from the SE class—ten second year students, four third year students, and three fourth year students. Nineteen students participated from the RE class—two second year students, seven third year students, seven fourth year students, and three fifth year students.

4.1 Assessment Structure

Each assignment had one in-class day (80 minutes) that consisted of four distinct parts:

- *Introduction/Waiver:* At the beginning of the class period, the instructor introduced the assignment and gave a brief explanation of why SEURAT_Edu was being used. Afterward, the students received waivers that they could optionally sign to allow their data to be analyzed. It was made very clear to the students that whether or not they released their data would have no impact on their grade for completing the assignment. Also attached to the waiver was a demographic survey.
- *Demonstration:* In addition to the actual class assignment, a demonstration assignment was created to teach the students how to use SEURAT_Edu. The demonstration consisted of walking the students through accessing the tool, viewing the assignment, and modifying rationale. The demonstration was conducted using a projector, while the students watched, asked questions, and made suggestions for rationale that could be entered for the demonstration assignment. The demonstration used party planning as an example rather than a technical problem to keep the focus on the tool rather than having students try to lean how to use the tool and how to understand the problem simultaneously.
- *Assignment:* After the demonstration, the students started the assignment in lab. As they worked, the instructor walked around to help answer questions about the assignment and to address any questions about SEURAT_Edu. It was not required that students finish the assignment during the class period. The assignment was structured this way to lessen the impact of learning effects on the rationale. We also did not want to penalize students who spent more time exploring the new tool rather than jumping right into completing the assignment.
- *Survey:* Students received usability surveys when there were only 10-15 minutes left in the class period. These surveys were used to gather student feedback on what aspects of the tool worked well and what aspects still needed work. The survey was given in class the day the assignment was given to ensure that only students who attended the demonstration were evaluating tool usability and to ensure that all students completed the survey. A disadvantage of this approach is that students were only making their judgments based on their initial in-class use.

4.2 Assignment

The students were given starter rationale for a conference room scheduling system. The assignment gave a brief description of the system, listing the five main user features (schedule meetings, delete meetings, view a weekly schedule for a room, and browse back and forth in time when viewing) as well as an administrative feature—the ability to add new conference rooms. The six features were listed as requirements in SEURAT_Edu. There were also three Claims given (easy to code, scalable, and quick access) and one Assumption (no need to store much data in the prototype).

The students were asked to complete the rationale for six decisions:

1. *"How to persistently store data in the system?"* The alternatives of "a RDBMS" or "object serialization" are given, along with fully specified rationale.
2. *"How are conference rooms stored?"* Two alternatives are given: "string giving the name" and "a conference room class".
3. *"Data structure to store schedule?"* Three alternatives are listed: ArrayList, linked list, and HashMap. There are no arguments given for any of the alternatives.
4. *"Which requirement should be implemented first?"* For this decision, the students are not given any alternatives although they do have the list of requirements.
5. *"How should the user provide start and end times?"* No alternatives are given.

6. *"Is authentication required?"* No alternatives are given.

The Rationale Status Panel displays errors and warnings from the rationale. The students are asked to complete the rationale so that there are no more errors or warnings—this means that an alternative must be selected for each decision and the selected alternative needs to have the same or more support indicated as its competing alternatives.

The starter-rationale was deliberately provided at different levels of completion:

- Fully specified rationale where the student only needed to make a choice.
- Decisions where alternatives were specified but where the students would need to use their own knowledge to specify arguments for and against the alternatives.
- Decisions where the students would need to specify both the alternatives and the arguments.

4.3 Survey Results

The students were given a survey towards the end of the lab session to ask them about their experience using SEURAT_Edu. We chose to administer it in the same class where the assignment started to ensure that only the students who had received training on the tool filled out the survey. Questions asked for answers on a Likert Scale, where answers ranged from Strongly Agree (SA) to Strongly Disagree (SD). The survey questions asked about both the usability and utility of the tool.

For usability, the students were asked if they agreed with the statement "It was easy to create/modify pieces of rationale." Responses from the two classes are shown in Figure 4. Most students agreed with that statement although six of the SE students were undecided and two from each class disagreed, although not strongly. One undecided student expressed tool usability concerns as did several of the disagreeing students. We do not know if the results might be different if the students had filled out this survey after completing the assignment rather than at the end of the class period where they were first introduced to the tool.

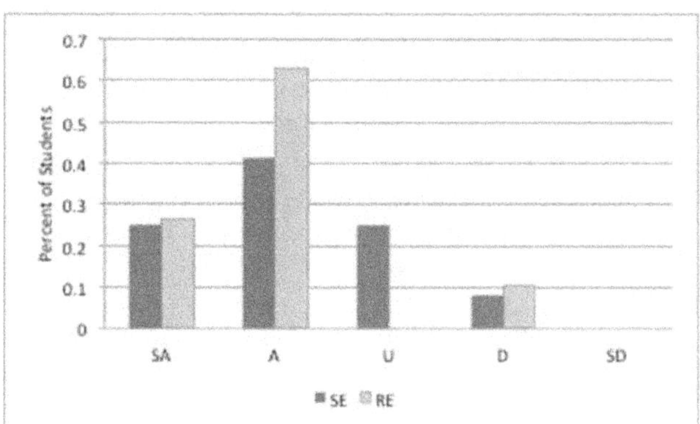

Figure 4. Easy to Create Rationale

Students were also asked if it was easy to see how the tool evaluated the alternatives (Figure 5). More students agreed than disagreed but for each class about a third were undecided. This could have been because they had only learned to use the tool that day. One SE undecided student said they would not have understood the tool without the demo and another did not understand how the numbers input into the argument were arrived at: "Some aspects were unclear. Why did I have to choose an importance/plausibility for arguments? What do these values mean? How can they be measured?" One of the SE students who disagreed that it was easy to see the evaluations gave the following reason: "I had a little trouble figuring out how each decision was evaluated with what I put in, but that could just be inexperience with the system."

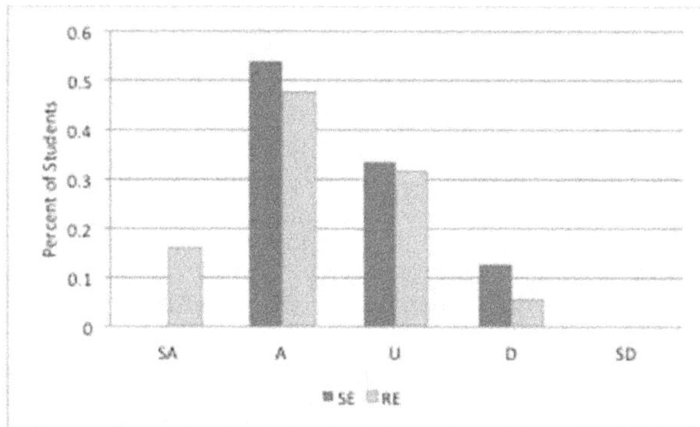

Figure 5. Easy to See Evaluations

We also asked four questions about the utility of the tool. First, the students were asked if they agreed or disagreed with the statement "SEURAT_Edu helped me consider more alternatives than I may have considered without it" (Figure 6). Most students agreed although there were still students who were undecided and a few who disagreed (although only one strongly). None of the undecided students gave a reason but one of the disagreeing students commented that they had to manually enter the alternatives (which was the point of the assignment).

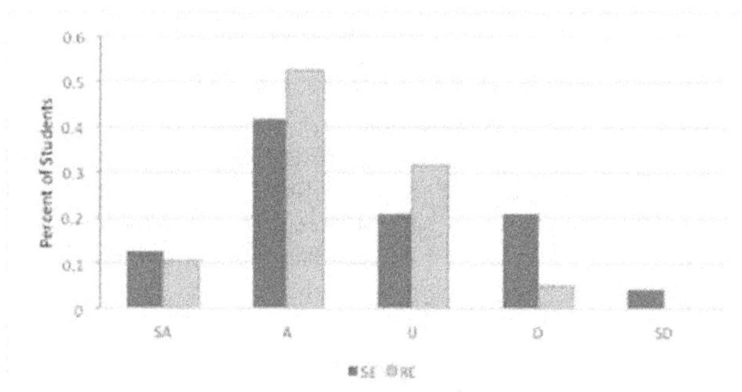

Figure 6. Helped Consider More Alternatives

The students were also asked if they agreed with the statement "SEURAT_Edu helped me put more thought into my decision-making" (Figure 7). Most students felt that it did. Some of the students who disagreed commented on the time required by the tool but it is interesting to note that the three SE students who disagreed all provided more alternatives and arguments than the average student, suggested that they put quite a bit of thought into their decision-making. The students were also asked to agree or disagree with the statement "I found SEURAT_Edu to be useful for this assignment" (Figure 8).

The majority of the RE students found the tool useful for the specific assignment and a little less than half of the SE students found the tool useful. The survey was given before the students had finished the assignment, which may have impacted the results. Two of the undecided SE students provided reasons—one felt the assignment was not large enough to need the tool and the other felt the assignment itself was too confusing.

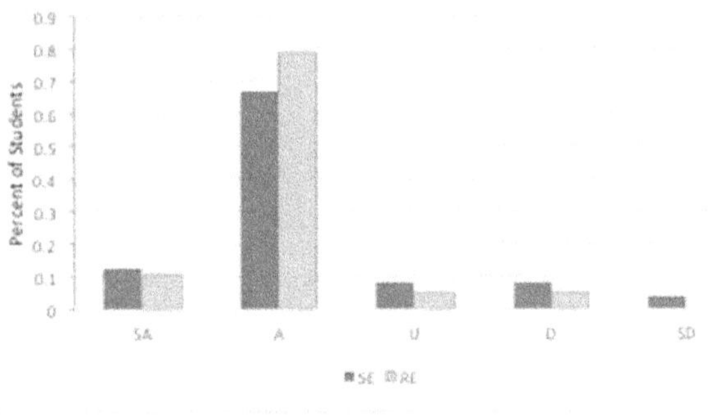

Figure 7. More Thought into Decision-Making

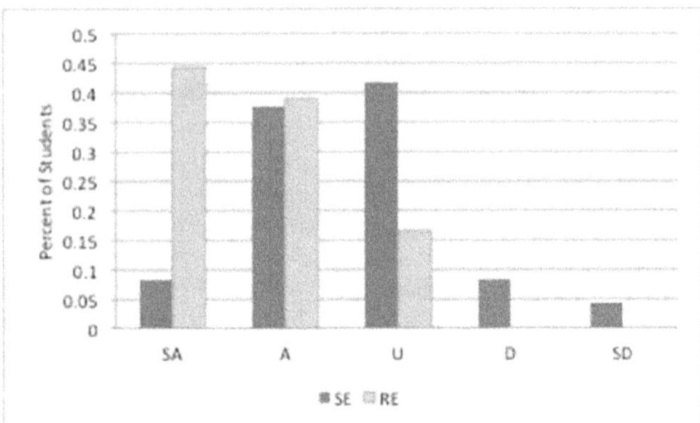

Figure 8. Usefulness for This Assignment

5. SUMMARY AND CONCLUSIONS

The results of the surveys suggest that most of the students did feel they considered more alternatives and made better decisions with the tool than they would have without the tool. The student survey results might have been different had the surveys been taken after the assignment was complete (when students would have been more familiar with the tool and the impact of just having learned to use it would be lessened) but we were concerned about students taking the survey who had not participated in training (all students were required to participate in the assignment but we only reported on results for those who were trained and who had consented to have their results used in the study). We suspect there would have been fewer undecided ratings if the students had more time with the tool although we can only speculate on the direction of those ratings.

We are currently extending SEURAT_Edu to allow group projects and to include analysis tools for use by the instructor and researchers. Analyzing the rationale requires either manual analysis of the student rationale or having direct access to the database to run SQL queries. Supporting common analysis queries will allow SEURAT_Edu to scale to larger classes to help instructors identify where students might have misconceptions about the material—such as not understanding some of the alternatives or how the criteria might apply. Our preliminary analysis highlighted some of these issues. For example, the software engineering instructor did not realize the course pre-requisites had new learning outcomes that no longer taught Java Collection classes like HashMap. This suggests an alternative use for SEURAT_Edu where students can have rationale-based assignments early in the course as way to determine where there might be gaps in prior knowledge that should be addressed at the start of the class.

We would also like to perform a longer study investigating the ability of the tool to help students progress in their reasoning abilities through the curriculum and to perform some controlled studies that assess performance on making design decisions assistance of with and without the tool.

While more work can and should be done to study the impact of using SEURAT_Edu, these initial experiments provided useful information on where there were gaps in student knowledge and where more time needed to be spent to address these issues. In particular, we uncovered a need to focus more on requirements prioritization. Using SEURAT_Edu to provide decision-centered assignments is a good start towards identifying where students may need more instruction and provide a springboard for discussion of these issues in class.

6. ACKNOWLEDGMENTS

This work was supported by NSF CAREER Award CCF-0844638 (Burge). Any opinions, findings, and conclusions or recommendations ex-pressed in this material are those of the author(s) and do not necessarily reflect the views of the National Science Foundation (NSF).

7. REFERENCES

[1] A. Tang, M. Tran, J. Han, H. vanVliet (2008). Design Reasoning Improves Software Design Quality, International Conference on the Quality of Software Architectures, pp. 28-42.

[2] B.S. Bloom (Ed.). (1956). Taxonomy of educational objectives: The classification of educational goals. New York: David McKay Company, Inc, 1956.

[3] W.G. Perry, Forms of intellectual and ethical development in the college years: A scheme. New York: Holt, Rinehart, and Winston, 1970

[4] R. McCall, "Critical Conversations: Feedback as a Stimulus to Creativity in Software Design." Human-Computer Interaction. 2013. Volume 20. 11-40.

[5] J. Burge, B. Brinkman, Using Rationale to Assist Student Cognitive and Intellectual Development, in Human Technology: An Interdisciplinary Journal on Humans in ICT Environments, Volume 6 (1), May 2010, 106–128

[6] J. Burge, D.C. Brown, "An Integrated Approach for Software Design Checking Using Rationale", Design Computing and Cognition '04, J. Gero (Ed.), Kluwer Academic Publishers, Netherlands, 2004, pp. 557-576

[7] S. Pugh, *Total design*. Wokingham, UK: Addison-Wesley Publishing Company, 1991.

[8] U. Van Heesch, P. Avgeriou, A. Tang, "Does decision documentation help junior designers rationalize their decisions? A comparative multiple-case study", Journal of Systems and Software, 86, 2013, pp. 1545-1565

Incorporating Analogies and Worked Out Examples as Pedagogical Strategies in a Computer Science Tutoring System

Rachel Harsley[1]
rharsl2@uic.edu

Nick Green[1]
ngreen21@uic.edu

Mehrdad Alizadeh[1]
maliza2@uic.edu

Sabita Acharya[1]
sachar4@uic.edu

Davide Fossati[2]
davide@fossati.us

Barbara Di Eugenio[1]
bdieugen@uic.edu

Omar AlZoubi[3]
oalzoubi@cmu.edu

[1]University of Illinois at Chicago, Chicago, IL, United States
[2]Emory University, Atlanta, GA, United States
[3]Carnegie Mellon University in Qatar, Doha, Qatar

ABSTRACT
Analogies and worked out examples are effective means of instruction in a wide variety of learning environments. However, the extent of their effectiveness in Computer Science (CS) education has not been fully explored. We extended our intelligent tutoring system (ITS) for CS data structures, ChiQat-Tutor, to incorporate worked out examples and analogy as teaching strategies. We compare three versions of the system: one that uses standard worked out examples, one that uses analogical worked out examples, and one that uses a pure analogical explanation with separate worked out examples. A study with 66 students showed that students using the standard worked out examples had greater learning gains than students in both analogy conditions. We also found that analogy can be less effective for students with higher prior knowledge. Additionally, we show that some interaction patterns highly correlate with student gains. Overall, the system implementation and results represent a step towards exploring the use of well-established instructional strategies in a computer science ITS.

Keywords
Intelligent Tutoring Systems; Analogy; Worked-Out Examples; Examples; Linked Lists; Computer Science Tutoring

1. INTRODUCTION
As demand for CS professionals rises, so does the importance of teaching computing with engaging, automated, and scalable methods [7]. One such method is the use of intelligent tutoring systems (ITSs). ITSs can provide adaptive feedback to students as they learn a topic. However, other teaching strategies in addition to feedback are possible. The goal of this paper is to analyze the impact of two of such strategies, namely worked out examples and analogy, on the effectiveness of an ITS for CS data structures.

SIGCSE'16, March 2–5, 2016, Memphis, TN, USA.
© 2016 ACM. ISBN 978-1-4503-3685-7/16/03…$15.00.
DOI: http://dx.doi.org/10.1145/2839509.2844637

ITSs provide several benefits to enhancing student learning, including: 1) avoid the one-to-many student teacher model and free teachers to more effectively triage student needs; 2) provide students with individual, customized support tailored to their level of proficiency; 3) allow students to reach common proficiency goals in an efficient and verifiable manner. ChiQat-Tutor aims to provide each of these benefits with the specific focus on CS education. The design of ChiQat-Tutor is informed by a corpus of interaction between students and human tutors. Analysis of tutors' teaching strategies and their effect on learning guide our implementation.

ChiQat-Tutor provides tutoring modules for several CS data structures and algorithms including liked lists, binary search trees, and recursion [5]. The focus of the current study is the linked list data structure module. The system presents a problem to a student in both textual and graphical representation (Figure 1). The student is required to programmatically solve the problem. Moreover, the system provides relevant positive and negative feedback to the student. Example problem types involve linked list node insertion and removal in addition to other more complicated operations.

The paper explores how changes in the instructional design implementation of the tutor affect student learning. Namely we implement and compare the following three strategies in terms of learning gain:

- worked out examples (WOE)
- analogy based worked out examples (AWOE)
- standalone analogy explanations with WOEs (A+WOE)

Moreover, we analyze the factors that contribute to learning gain in each condition and draw general conclusions on the strategies.

2. BACKGROUND
Worked Out Example (WOE): A worked out example is a problem whose solution is given to the student along with the steps for deriving the solution. Examples seem to play a central role in the early phases of cognitive skill acquisition [9]. Moreover, several studies showed the effectiveness of WOEs for learning in well-structured domains such as physics,

programming, and mathematics [9]. Further, WOEs have been implemented in tutoring systems and students achieved deeper conceptual understanding of concepts in comparison to their counterpart without WOEs [8].

In prior work we found moderate but significant correlations between WOE usage by tutors and learning gains in tutees [2]. An earlier experiment with the implementation of WOE in our tutoring system indicated that the intervention did not aid students' learning [3]. One of the possible reasons is that the system did not restrict students to sequential problem solving. Thus, the order in which students were introduced to problems may not have been consistent with the examples and their relevant conceptual principles introduced.

Analogy: Analogies capture parallels across divergent systems. Gentner defines analogies as “partial similarities between different situations that support further inferences” [4]. Analogy’s pivotal role in the learning process is well established and some researchers even consider it to be the core of cognition [6]. Gentner shows it can be especially helpful for learners lacking prior knowledge [4].

Our prior work in understanding analogy in CS tutoring dialogues found that the presence of analogical episodes correlated with student learning gains [1]. In our human tutoring corpus, common analogical mappings include comparison of linked lists to movie theatre lines, stacks to cafeteria trays and Legos, and a weaker mapping of binary trees to biological family trees. The tutor tended to initiate the analogical mapping and use it in two ways 1) as an introduction to a particular topic or 2) as a means to extend a problem.

3. SYSTEM DESIGN

ChiQat-Tutor is organized into four primary graphical interface components: 1) Problem View, 2) Feedback View, 3) State Space View, and 4) Command Panel (Figure 1). Unlike a prior study’s implementation of worked out examples, we require students to solve problems sequentially [3]. In this manner, students must first successfully solve the foundational problems before being able to advance to more complex problems. Thus, up to seven problems can be unlocked as a student successfully solves problems.

Once a student selects a problem, the linked list’s state space representation of the problem is depicted and students can enter code. Each valid line of code modifies the state space. Moreover, our system logs the correctness of code submission as well as the timing interaction influence the feedback of the tutor.

3.1 Worked Out Example (WOE)

The worked out example condition allows students to open an example that is relevant to the problem they are attempting to solve. The request for example button can be clicked at any time while a student attempts to solve a problem. Each problem has exactly one example. Students click to progress through the example, however, they may exit the example at any time by reselecting a problem.

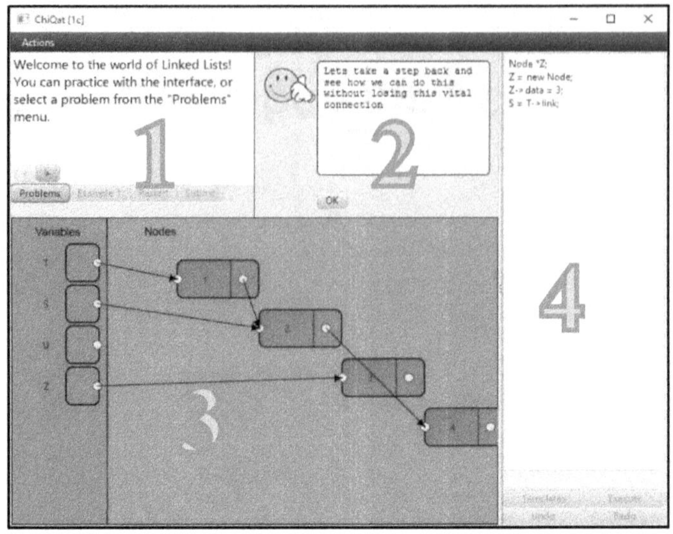

Figure 1. The GUI is split into four parts 1) Problem View 2) Feedback View 3) State Space View, and 4) Command Panel.

We designed the examples so that the principles needed to solve the related problem are illustrated in the example. It is then left to the student to perform the knowledge transfer to their specific problem and hopefully generalize the principles at large.

3.2 Analogical Worked Out Example (AWOE)

In the case of an analogical worked out example, the structure of interaction with the example is identical to the standard worked out example. However, the content of the example is based on an analogy as opposed to the pure linked list data structure. Given prior work analyzing a human CS tutoring corpus, the chosen analogy maps linked lists to a movie theatre line. A step of the analogical worked out example is depicted in Figure 3.

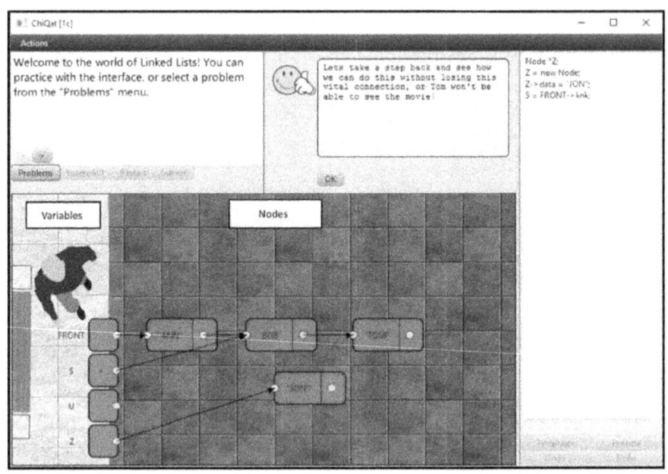

Figure 3. The image depicts another example of inserting a node into a list.

3.3 Analogical Explanation with Worked Out Example (A+WOE)

The second approach to integrate analogy is based on the fact that analogy is most likely to appear at the beginning of a human tutoring session [1]. Thus, when the linked list tutorial begins, the system displays a window describing an analogy of people standing in a line as depicted in Figure 5 (full analogy not shown).

In this condition, students are also able to explore the same WOEs used in the WOE condition.

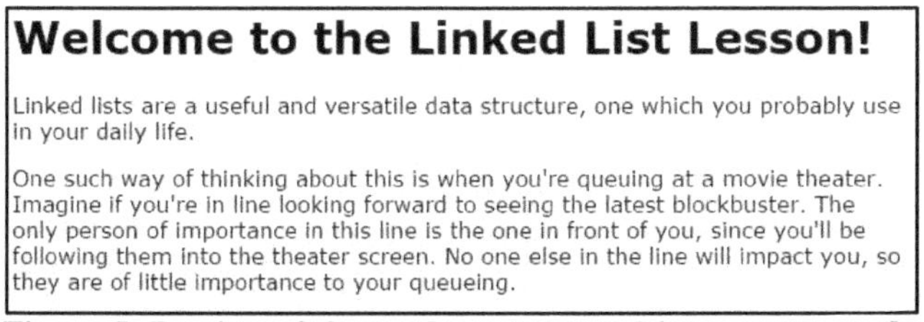

Figure 5. Portion of the analogy presented in a popup at the onset of the A+WOE condition.

4. EXPERIMENT

We conducted the experiment in a 2nd year CS programming course. The course focuses on software development tools and practices, and on the implementation of foundational data structures and algorithms such as stacks, linked list, and depth first search to solve real-world problems. For example, students are given a project to implement a linked list in C++ with support for insert, delete, and find operations. The following week they are required to implement a program which uses the linked list to store a waiting list for a restaurant.

Our experiments ran over four sections of the course, all taught by the same instructor and composed of a comparable mix of students. Students provided informed consent for the experiment. The students took a pre-test for 10 minutes; then they worked with ChiQat-Tutor for 40 minutes; finally they took a post-test (identical to the pre-test). Students' interaction with the system was continuously logged. There were three conditions with a total of 66 users; 23 (WOE), 21 (AWOE), and 22 (A+WOE).

Tests were graded between three independent graders, and their median score was selected. Both pre and post tests are identical and derived from prior work analyzing human CS tutoring dialogues. The first problem depicts the graphical state of a linked list. It is accompanied by code. Students are asked to describe visually and/or with words the state of the list after the accompanying code is executed. The second problem asks students to find the error in an almost exact replication of the code in problem one save for a semantically devised error. The third and final problem requires students to move the first node of the list depicted in problem one to the end of the list. We use use the following measure of learning gain to assist in our analysis of learning: *gain =post_test_score - pre_test_score.*

5. DISCUSSION/RESULTS

Of foremost importance in evaluating the system is the answer to the question of whether or not students have learned. Subsequent to this, is the question to what extent have they learned and finally what factors contributed to the learning. In answer to the primary questions, the students do learn in each of the conditions. The WOE condition achieves learning gains similar to those of the human tutoring corpus. The AWOE and the A+WOE seem to be lower in learning gain. However, ANOVA did not reveal an overall significant difference among the five groups when computing standard learning gain.

With the premise established that the system is effective in helping students learn, we aimed to further our analysis in terms of how learning occurs. In order to more deeply understand the features of the student interaction with the system, we exhaustively logged interactions. From the log files, several features have been analyzed using linear regression with each variable being used as a predictor of learning gain in several independent models.

Table 1. Learning gain of students in five conditions.

Tutor	N	Pre-test		Post-test		Gain	
		μ	σ	μ	σ	μ	σ
Human	54	.40	.26	.54	.26	.14	.25
ChiQat WOE	23	.41	.18	.55	.22	.14	.17
ChiQat AWOE	21	.50	.17	.61	.15	.11	.18
ChiQat A+WOE	22	.52	.21	.60	.23	.09	.21

Table 2. Features used in multiple linear regression models

Feature	Description
Collection_Duration	Time in milliseconds that the user used the system (from login to logout)
Example_Completed	User completed viewing the example
Example_Requested	User requested an example
Example_Started	An example has started to be played
Executing_ Example_Step	User clicked the 'next' button, moving an example to the next step
Feedback_Given	Feedback has been given to the user
Final_Pre	Pre-test score
Node_Clicked	User clicked on a node within the graphical problem solving area
Operation_Execution _Submitted	User submitted an operation, such as a line of code, for a problem
Operation_Redone	User elects to redo a step that was previously undone
Operation_Undone	User elects to undo a previously submitted step
Question_Answer_ Response	The system responded to an answer that the user has given to a posed question
Question_Given	A question has been posed to the user from the system
Solution_Submitted	A solution has been submitted for validation by the user to the system
Solved_Problems	Total number of problems the user solved
Template_Help_ Item_Selected	User clicked on a code template item in order to help them write code
Template_Help_ Requested	User requested to see all programming commands available in the system
Tutorial_Duration	Total duration that the user viewed a lesson tutorial
User_Acknowledge	User clicks the 'ok' button, signifying that they have acknowledged any feedback

The number of measured features (n=39) exceeds the number of examples per condition. Thus, we created a regression tree in order to determine important features in regards to learning gain.

From this point, we derived a linear additive model using the largest possible subset of important features capable of being added to the model. Given the result of the multiple regression analysis, we then found the minimum adequate model. This model is a reduction of the first model which aims to only keep features that are significant. Thus we show and discuss the statistically significant multiple linear regression model that selects a set of features resulting in the highest adjusted R^2. Of the initial 39 features, 27 were actually incorporated in the most explanatory models across the three conditions. The features and their descriptions are given in Table 2.

Table 3 and Table 4 show the statistically significant models we obtained as described above. ß are the best estimates of the coefficients of each and p shows the level of significance. R^2 explains how well features can describe variations in learning gain and it is given as well.

Table 3. Model for the WOE condition learning gain.

	ß	t value	p
(Intercept)	-9.816	-7.733	0.005 **
Feedback_Given	-.189	-2.150	.121
Collection_Duration	.002	2.662	0.07622 .
Operation_Undone	-.068	-1.342	.272
User_Acknowledge	.286	5.003	0.015 *
Executing_Example_Step	-.185	-5.195	0.014 *
Operation_Execution_Submitted	.111	4.664	0.019 *
New_Problem_Selected	.247	1.094	.354
Example_Started	-3.407	-2.106	.126
Example_Completed	2.644	1.568	.215
Example_Requested	1.357	2.216	.113
Problem_List_Requested	.247	2.100	.127
Final_Pre	-.111	-1.154	.332
Template_Help_Requested	.079	4.204	0.025 *
Lesson_Started	2.518	3.515	0.040 *
Node_Clicked	.060	7.276	0.005 **
Operation_Redone	-.567	-4.900	0.016*
Problem_Restarted	.326	1.749	.179
Question_Answer_Response	-.285	-1.770	.175
Solution_Submitted	-.276	-8.114	0.003 **

Signif. codes: 0 '***' 0.001 '**' 0.01 '*' 0.05 '.' 0.1 ' ' 1
Multiple R-squared: 0.9943, Adjusted R-squared: 0.9579

To our surprise, in the case of the worked out example condition, executing an example step is significantly negatively correlated to learning gain ($p<.01$). However, completing an example is positively correlated with a much larger coefficient. This seeming oxymoron may suggest that student use of the example signifies their lack of understanding of a particular principle. Thus, the further students explore an example, it may signify the depth of their uncertainty of a concept. This is also suggested by the much larger by the much larger positive correlation between example completion and learning gain. In a sense, if a student begins the example with uncertainty and completes the example, they learn the concept in question. However, if a student advances in examples without completing it, they may not attribute the same learning gain.

In general, submitting an operation for execution is significantly positively correlated with learning gain ($p<.01$). We also note that this submission does not account for whether the executed code is correct (syntactically or otherwise). Thus, in general, the more students attempt to find a correct solution, the more they learn. This is not the case for submitting a solution. Submission signifies that the student believes the entire problem has been solved. In fact, submitting entire solutions is strongly negatively correlated with learning gain ($p<.001$). This connection is clear because students with multiple solution submissions for the same problem are inherently missing some level of conceptual knowledge needed to solve the problem through they believe their work is viable to submit.

Also of interest is node clicks in the graphical representation of the list. This feature is strongly significantly correlated to learning gain ($p<.001$). It is not difficult to imagine that as students reason about either a worked out example or their own code, they rearrange the linked list nodes in ways that make sense for their understanding. This may help them internalize the conceptual principles. The high correlation of this feature serves as a testament to the power of the system to graphically represent the often difficult and abstract concept of linked lists.

The redo operation is significantly negatively correlated to student learning in the WOE condition ($p<.01$). The redo exemplifies student uncertainty about a concept. The student submits and operation, undoes the operation, then redoes the same operation.

Table 4. Model for the AWOE condition learning gain.

	ß	t value	p
(Intercept)	13.456	5.612	0.001 **
Final_Pre	-.947	-4.180	0.006 **
Template_Help_Requested	-.175	-1.968	0.097 .
Node_Clicked	.019	1.481	.189
Collection_Duration	-.004	-3.333	0.016 *
Template_Help_Item_Selected	.103	.944	.381
Starting_Lesson_Tutorial	-7.456	-1.686	.143
Tutorial_Duration	.107	2.729	0.034 *
Operation_Redone	.371	1.257	.255
Question_Given	1.242	1.904	.106
Operation_Undone	.189	3.869	0.008 **
Feedback_Given	.152	2.318	0.060 .
User_Acknowledge	-.139	-1.862	.112
Question_Answer_Response	-1.199	-1.839	.116
Executing_Example_Step	-.129	-2.364	0.056 .

Signif. codes: 0 '***' 0.001 '**' 0.01 '*' 0.05 '.' 0.1 ' ' 1
Multiple R-squared: 0.9434, Adjusted R-squared: 0.8113

Finally, in the WOE condition it is worth noting that the learning gain and pre-test score are not significantly correlated. This finding is important because it signifies that the system is able to influence learning gain irrespective of the prior knowledge of the student.

The regression analysis reveals a significant negative correlation between pre-test score and learning gain in the AWOE condition. Though the mean pre-test score for the AWOE (μ=.50) is slightly higher than the pre-test scores for the WOE condition ((μ=.41), the difference is not significant. This suggests that the AWOE attributes a ceiling effect on learning gain. This effect is explored further on in this section.

In the AWOE condition, requesting the template help is significantly negatively correlated to learning gain (p<.05). This correlation highlights that students are not internalizing the syntactic rules and are instead uncertain of what to code and the proper notation. They instead rely heavily on the system for assistance. This is further demonstrated by the difference in coefficients and significance of Template_Help_Item_Selected versus Template_Help_Requested. In essence, some students request template help much more often than they select a template from those provided. They attempt to use the templates as kick-starter for understanding but eventually end up performing multiple requests for templates and finally selecting a template.

An example of this pattern of interaction is given in Table 5. In this case, the student starts a lesson and immediately requests template help. The student again requests template help and then submits their code with a clear syntax error. After receiving feedback, the student requests further help and submits code, this time successfully. The student continues this cycle of requesting help one or more times, selecting a template, then submitting an operation throughout the lesson.

Table 5. Sample log of a student using "Template Help Requested" and "Template Help Item Selected"

Time	Action	Argument
15:49:54	Template Help Requested	
15:50:17	Template Help Requested	
15:50:18	Template Help Item Selected	? = new Node;
15:50:20	Operation Execution Submitted	3 = new Node;
15:50:21	Feedback Given	*omitted*
15:50:31	User Acknowledge	
15:50:37	Template Help Requested	
15:50:38	Template Help Item Selected	Node *?;
15:50:44	Operation Execution Submitted	Node *temp;

Further, undoing an operation attributes a significantly positive correlation to learning gain (p<.001). This feature allows students to remove a previously submitted operation. An undo represents a student's change in approach in regards to the problem. This may be representative of a student's newly found, deeper understanding of the problem goal and possible errors in their logic. Note, the undo cannot be a student attempting to correct syntactic errors as syntactic errors do not show up in the command panel as submitted code. Thus, we hypothesize the student may be attempting to solve higher order, semantic issues when an undue transpires.

In the final condition of A+WOE, the R^2 value is the lowest among the conditions (Multiple R-squared: 0.9827, Adjusted R-squared: 0.6376). Moreover, the model contains no significant predictors of learning gain. The model is not shown.

Table 6. Comparative overview of select features used in multiple linear regression models along with their role in each best fit regression model. (+) denotes positive correlation (-) denotes negative correlation. Significant correlations marked.

Feature	Learning Gain		
	WOE	AWOE	A+WOE
Collection_Duration	+ <.05	- <.01	+
Example_Completed	+		-
Example_Requested	+		
Example_Started	-		-
Executing_Example_Step	- <.01	- <.05	+
Feedback_Given	-	+ <.05	-
Final_Pre	-	- <.001	+
Node_Clicked	+ <.001	+	+
Operation_Execution_Submitted	+ <.01		-
Operation_Redone	- <.01	+	
Operation_Undone	-	+ <.001	+
Question_Answer_Response	-	-	-
Question_Given		+	+
Solution_Submitted	-		
Solved_Problems			+
Template_Help_Item_Selected		+	
Template_Help_Requested	+ <.01	- <.01	-
Tutorial_Duration		- <.05	
User_Acknowledge	+ <.01	-	+

Table 6 aims to provide a comparative look at the three conditions in terms of the factors that contribute to learning. A summary of findings follows:

- **Time on Task:** Interestingly, the amount of time spent with the system is significantly positively correlated with the WOE condition (p<.05), however, it is significantly negatively correlated with the AWOE condition (p<.01).
- **Examples:** Both the WOE and AWOE conditions show that executing example steps themselves significantly negatively correlate to learning.
- **Tutor Feedback**: In the AWOE condition, the volume of tutor feedback is significantly positively correlated to learning (p<.05). However, tutor feedback in the other conditions is negatively correlated to learning.
- **Prior Knowledge**: The pre-test score is very strongly significantly correlated to learning in the AWOE condition (p<.001). However, prior knowledge of the student in both the WOE and A+WOE conditions do not play a significant factor.
- **Graphical List Interaction**: In all conditions, interaction with linked list nodes is positively correlated with learning. In the WOE case the correlations is quite significant (p<.001).
- **Undo/Redo**: The undo behavior is positively correlated to student learning in both analogy conditions with a significant correlation in the AWOE condition (p<.001). However, the undo behavior is negatively correlated to learning for the WOE condition. Similarly, the redo behavior is significantly negatively correlated to learning in the WOE condition. Yet, in the AWOE condition it is positively correlated.

The strong negative correlation between the pre-test score and learning gain along with the conditional inference tree of both analogy conditions revealed an interesting split in users based on learning gain. The split occurred by dividing the users into those who scored <=5 (out of 15 max) on the pre-test and those who did not. A similar split occurred using the score cutoff of 7. We ran unpaired t-test to determine if the difference in learning gain was significant. The difference in learning gain was significant in each case (p=0.0006 and p= 0.0281 respectively). In comparison, the WOE condition did not have significant difference in learning gain with either threshold.

To make sense of this split, we performed t-test to compare the low pre-test analogy conditions with the low pretest WOE condition. We also conducted the same comparison for the high pre-test groups. The comparison of learning gains for WOE pre-test scores >5 and the combination of both analogy conditions pre-test scores >5 did not yield a significant difference (p= 0.1137). However, the threshold change of pre-test scores >7 did yield a significant difference (p= 0.0310). The significant difference suggests that the analogy conditions were least beneficial, and in fact damaging to students with higher prior knowledge in comparison to the standard WOE condition. Note, there was no significant difference in the low to low group comparisons.

6. CURRENT WORK/CONCLUSIONS

Work is ongoing to improve the ITS and ensure it incorporates the most effective strategies for helping students to learn CS. Our focus on foundational CS data structures and algorithms allows us to explore unchartered territories in the world of tutoring systems. Thus, the effectiveness of some common instructional designs seen in other fields have yet to be tested in our domain. In this study we expanded on prior work analyzing the use of analogy and worked out examples used by human tutors for CS. We integrated these strategies into our tutoring system in hope of 1) improving student learning gain and 2) understanding the factors that contribute to learning in each condition.

We explored three conditions: 1) worked out examples, 2) analogical worked out examples, and 3) standalone analogical explanations with worked out examples. To the benefit of students, our study shows that the system contributes to learning gains in all three conditions. However, the WOE condition exceeded the learning gain of the other two conditions and achieved gains comparable to a human tutor as well as prior best implementations of the tutoring system.

In general, we were able to create highly explanatory models of the three conditions. However, we caution the potential for the high number of factors and multiple comparisons to yield false positives in significance testing. With this in mind, we plan to evaluate individual factor manipulation for a more accurate understanding of the features relationship to learning gains.

The study showed that advancing through example steps in itself is not directly correlated to learning gains. However, completing the example is effective. In the case of the WOE, the more code students submit, regardless of correctness, the more they learn. Further, the study showed strong positive correlations between student exploration of the graphical linked list representation and learning across each condition. The analysis of this feature showcases the power of an ITS to adapt to individual users in regards to the code they submit, and their overall interaction with the problem.

Finally, the study shows that analogy is least beneficial to students with higher prior knowledge. However, students in the analogy condition attribute undo behavior that alludes to deeper understanding of concepts and correlates to learning gains. We are currently analyzing the abundance of log data to understand the intricacies of this behavior. Additionally, we are performing a finer grained analysis of analogy in regards to its benefits for particular concepts which can be extracted from each of the seven problems. A future implementation may prove analogy to be beneficial in certain cases.

7. ACKNOWLEDGEMENTS

This publication was made possible by NPRP grant 5-939-1-155 from the Qatar National Research Fund (a member of Qatar Foundation). The statements made herein are solely the responsibility of the authors.

8. REFERENCES

[1] Alizadeh, M., Di Eugenio, B., Harsley, R., Green, N., Fossati, D. and AlZoubi, O. 2015. A Study of Analogy in Computer Science Tutorial Dialogues. *Proceedings of the 7th International Conference on Computer Supported Education (CSEDU 2015)* (2015).

[2] Di Eugenio, B., Chen, L., Green, N., Fossati, D. and AlZoubi, O. 2013. Worked Out Examples in Computer Science Tutoring. *Artificial Intelligence in Education.* H.C. Lane, K. Yacef, J. Mostow, and P. Pavlik, eds. Springer Berlin Heidelberg. 852–855.

[3] Di Eugenio, B., Green, N., Alizadeh, M., Harsley, R. and Fossati, D. 2015. Worked-out Examples in a Computer Science Intelligent Tutoring System. *Proceedings of the 16th annual ACM SIGITE conference on Information technology education* (Chicago, IL, USA, Oct. 2015).

[4] Gentner, D. 1998. Analogy. *A companion to cognitive science.* (1998), 107–113.

[5] Green, N., AlZoubi, O., Alizadeh, M., Di Eugenio, B., Fossati, D. and Harsley, R. 2015. A Scalable Intelligent Tutoring System Framework for Computer Science Education. *Proceedings of the 7th International Conference on Computer Supported Education (CSEDU 2015)* (2015).

[6] Hofstadter, D.R. 2001. Analogy as the core of cognition. *The analogical mind: Perspectives from cognitive science.* (2001), 499–538.

[7] Monge, A.E., Fadjo, C.L., Quinn, B.A. and Barker, L.J. 2015. EngageCSEdu: Engaging and Retaining CS1 and CS2 Students. *ACM Inroads*. 6, 1 (Feb. 2015), 6–11.

[8] Schwonke, R., Renkl, A., Krieg, C., Wittwer, J., Aleven, V. and Salden, R. 2009. The worked-example effect: Not an artefact of lousy control conditions. *Computers in Human Behavior*. 25, 2 (Mar. 2009), 258–266.

[9] VanLehn, K. 1996. Cognitive Skill Acquisition. *Annual Review of Psychology*. 47, 1 (1996), 513–539.

Advanced Placement Computer Science Principles (APCSP): A Report from Teachers

Owen Astrachan
Duke University
ola@cs.duke.edu

R. Brook Osborne
Code.org
brook@code.org

Categories and Subject Descriptors

K.3.2 [**Computers and Education**]: Computer and Information Science Education – *computer science education*

General Terms

Standardization, Human Factors

Keywords

Computer Science Education; K-12Curriculum; APCS Principles; Curriculum; Professional Development

1. Summary

The AP CS Principles (APCSP) course begins as an AP course in 2016, fully realized after eight years with several presentations as part of SIGCSE conferences[1-3]. APCSP was designed to broaden participation in computer science in high school and beyond, and to be accessible to teachers who might be new to computer science, in some cases with limited previous experience in teaching courses in the area. The APCSP project has been grounded in an inclusive, community-driven approach to building a new course that is nearly unprecedented. Initially funded by the College Board and NSF, as this community of educators nears the official launch of APCSP the project has become more of a public/private partnership, garnering significant interest in building programs with NSF, non-profit, and industry support.

To understand how teachers new to computer science and/or new to APCSP might be able to launch a course that broadens participation at scale, to be part of what has been heralded as an effort to support 10,000 teachers in 10,000s schools, this special session is built on hearing directly from teachers who are in their first year of teaching APCSP, but who are teaching curricula developed by one of five projects that are part of a cohort working closely with the College Board in supporting APCSP. These projects have the potential to develop nationally, to support teachers with curricula and professional development, and to bring new teachers into the APCSP community, and by extension into the SIGCSE community. These five projects have been recognized by the College Board and the National Science Foundation as likely capable of such support. The projects are Project Lead the Way (PLTW)[4], Code.org[5], Beauty and Joy of Computing (BJC)[6], Mobile CSP[7], and Thriving in our Digital World[8].

SIGCSE'16, March 2–5, 2016, Memphis, TN, USA.
ACM ISBN: 978-1-4503-3685-7/16/03.
DOI: http://dx.doi.org/10.1145/2839509.2844677

2. Session Objectives

This session will address two broad objectives. The first is to provide attendees with up-to-date information about the APCSP course and exam and opportunities to understand several programs identified as exemplars in realizing the APCSP curriculum framework and preparing students for the exam. This objective will be realized using first-hand accounts from new teachers in these exemplar projects who have participated in professional development and who are offering the course.

The second objective is for session attendees to gain a deeper understanding of what supports are available, what opportunities there are for creating resources and professional development for teachers, and to participate in a discussion with teachers who are providing a report-from-the-field as we approach the launch of the APCSP course and exam in 2016-17.

3. Outline

Overview of APCSP (Owen Astrachan, 5 minutes)

We provide a brief overview of the AP CS Principles project: its design, implementation, and direction. We expect general familiarity with the project but include this overview to ensure that those in the audience are aware of recent changes regarding the scope and format of the exam. We also provide an explanation and a context for the projects that have been identified as those with the potential to supply support at scale to teachers and districts as APCSP projects that are recognized by the College Board.

Owen Astrachan is the PI of the CS Principles project. He works to help the community of educators working on this and related projects achieve their goals. He helps to coordinate CSP initiatives for the CS10K Community of Practice. He represents APCSP as part of professional development with cspdweek.org.

Supporting New Teachers (Brook Osborne, 5 minutes)

We report on the process from a first-hand viewpoint that has led to a partnership with College Board. We explain in general terms what a project that implements APCSP at scale must do to be recognized by College Board including curriculum development, pacing and planning guides, professional development, and the College Board audit process. We describe how professional development works to support new teachers, how curriculum development that adheres to the APCSP framework takes place, and what the rewards and challenges are in supporting new teachers taking on the import role of teaching a new AP course.

Brook Osborne is an Education Manager at Code.org, focusing on high school curriculum and PD. Previously, she worked with CSP Pilot teachers as the Pilot and Outreach Coordinator for three years as part of the College Board/NSF Pilot 2839509.2844677

Teacher Overview of Project (20 min)

In this first round of the teacher session, each teacher will provide a two-minute overview of the professional development they had in preparing for and in delivering their first year of APCSP, grounded in their experience as a teacher. Questions from the audience will follow these presentations, facilitated by the session organizers.

Rewards and Challenges (30 min)

In the second round each teacher will discuss for four minutes the rewards and challenges of teaching an APCSP course for the first time. Teachers will be asked to relate their stories to the pedagogies and practices of the APCSP approach they are using, rather than identifying rewards and challenges of teaching in general. Questions from the audience will follow these presentations, again facilitated by the session organizers.

Community Discussion (15 min)

The audience will have an opportunity to engage in a discussion of how the SIGCSE community can support APCSP, to perhaps address the challenges identified by the teachers. The stories of the teachers and the support provided for teachers by the participating projects will be the basis for the community discussion. We will ask the different communities in the audience to identify rewards and challenges that they anticipate or that they have experienced – particularly as colleges and universities begin and continue to support APCSP with courses that might receive credit or placement based on AP scores for the new APCSP course that will be received by students in the summer of 2017.

4. Project Overviews

We provide a brief context here for each of the projects represented in this session:

Project Lead The Way (PLTW)

PLTW's Computer Science and Software Engineering uses a project-based approach guided by real-world problems, and an interdisciplinary approach in providing students with opportunities to engage the curriculum framework using software and tools that are commonly used in industry.

Code.org

Code.org's APCSP curriculum is a student-centered, inquiry-based approach built on principles of equity and board access, with a programming environment (AppLab) and software tools expressly created for APCSP.

Beauty and Joy of Computing (BJC)

BJC is a project-based, programming-heavy curriculum that uses current events and readings to ground student creativity in using recursion and higher-order functions to emphasize concepts taken from the APCSP curriculum framework.

Mobile CSP

The Mobile CSP project engages students through the development of apps using AppInventor, a platform for creating mobile apps on Android devices. The Mobile CSP approach is grounded in practical and creative application of programming to solving problems identified by students in the course.

Thriving in Our Digital World

This program uses a problem-based approach to engage students in real-world problem solving using broad areas of Computer Science. The curriculum emphasizes a student-centered approach to mastering the curriculum framework.

5. Expectations

This special session is designed for all educators interested in better understanding the efforts around supporting the broadening participation goals of CS Principles. The varied approaches to these CSP programs have been developed using best practices in educational research, established pedagogical approaches designed to change how students learn, and in providing professional development opportunities for teachers. The partnerships represented in this special session continue a community-driven collaboration to support adoption by many different groups rapidly and at scale. These projects represent those currently working closely with the College Board and at scale nationally, or with the potential for such scale. Attendees will leave this session with a better understanding of the available resources and materials available from these projects.

6. Suitability for a Special Session

This proposal is well-suited for a special session because of the interactive presentation and discussion that will take place between the teachers and the audience. The round-robin nature of the teacher presentation, in which there is both presentation and dialog in discussing rewards and challenges is well-suited to the format described here, but not conducive to other formats that are part of SIGCSE sessions and panels.

7. References

[1] O. Astrachan, D. D. Garcia, B. Brown, J. Gray, R. Morelli, M. d. Jardins, et al., "Computer Science Principles Curricula: On-the-ground, adoptable, adaptable, approaches to teaching," in SIGCSE 46th Technical Symposium on Computer Science Education, Kansas City, MO, USA, 2015, pp. 176-177.

[2] O. Astrachan, R. B. Osborne, J. Gray, I. Lee, and C. Lee, "Diverse Learners, Diverse Courses, Diverse Projects: Learning from Challenges in New Directions," in SIGCSE, Atlanta, 2014.

[3] O. Astrachan, A. Briggs, L. Diaz, and R. B. Osborne, "CS Principles: Development and Evolution of a course and aCommunity," in SIGCSE, Denver, 2013.

[4] B. Brown. (2015, June 7, 2015). PLTW Computer Science, CSE. Available: https://http://www.pltw.org/our-programs/pltw-computer-science/pltw-computer-science-curriculum

[5] B. Franke and B. Osborne. (2015, June 7, 2015). Code.org Computer Science Principles. Available: http://code.org/educate/csp

[6] D. Garcia. (2015, June 7, 2015). Beauty and Joy of Computing (BJC). Available: http://bjc.berkeley.edu/

[7] R. Morelli. (2015, June 7, 2015). Mobile CSP. Available: http://mobile-csp.org/

[8] Calvin Lin. (2015). Thriving in Our Digital World. Available: http://www.cs.utexas.edu/~engage/

Special Session: Helping Students to Develop Communication, Teamwork, and Other Process Skills with POGIL

Clifton Kussmaul
Muhlenberg College
Allentown, PA 18104
kussmaul@muhlenberg.edu

Helen H. Hu
Westminster College
Salt Lake City, UT 84105
hhu@westminstercollege.edu

Tammy Pirmann
School District of Springfield Township
Erdenheim, PA 19038
tpirmann@gmail.com

SUMMARY

Employer surveys and other sources indicate that CS students need process skills such as communication, teamwork, critical thinking, and problem solving. Further, the AP CS Principles practices include communicating and collaborating. POGIL (Process Oriented Guided Inquiry Learning) can be used to teach these process skills in high school or college courses. Instead of sitting in lecture or working together with minimal guidance, student teams work through POGIL activities to discover concepts on their own, while the instructor circulates and facilitates learning of key concepts and the development of process skills. Structured roles help students learn to communicate and work in teams more effectively. In this special session, attendees will experience a POGIL activity, learn how process skills are developed and reinforced by POGIL (through a POGIL meta-activity), and see the range of activities available at http://cspogil.org. We will share POGIL activities and discuss how POGIL can transform CS classes at all levels, from high school to graduate-level classes, from small schools to large universities.

Categories and Subject Descriptors

K.3.2 [Computers and Education] - Computer and Information Science Education - Computer science education, information systems education, literacy, self-assessment

General Terms

Design, Experimentation

Keywords

Active Learning; Cooperative Learning; POGIL; Teams

1. OVERALL SESSION OBJECTIVE

After this session, attendees will be able to describe:

- What process skills are and why students need them.
- How POGIL activity structure, team roles, teacher facilitation, and other scaffolding can help students to learn content and process skills.
- Where to find field-tested POGIL activities for CS and how to learn more about facilitating POGIL activities.

SIGCSE '16, March 2–5, 2016, Memphis, TN, USA.
ACM 978-1-4503-3685-7/16/03.
http://dx.doi.org/10.1145/2839509.2844673

Employer surveys and other sources indicate that CS students need to develop communication, teamwork, problem solving, and other process skills (also called professional skills or soft skills). For example, a survey of IT job opportunities found high demand for communication skills, and high or moderate demand for analytical skills, problem solving, being a team player, and other similar skills [2]. Further, the AP CS Principles Computational Thinking Practices include *P5: Communicating* and *P6: Collaborating* [5]. Some teachers expect students to develop these process skills through team projects and other assignments. Others have a course to help students improve these skills [e.g. 1, 3, 4, 8].

Students can also develop these skills across the curriculum via Process Oriented Guided Inquiry Learning (POGIL). POGIL is a research-based instructional strategy that encourages students to collaboratively construct their own understanding of concepts [14]. In POGIL, student teams work together on specifically designed activities that guide students to discover principles on their own. When students discover concepts, they remember them better.

For example, a POGIL activity on unit testing might use the following structure. First, teams study several Java methods and answer questions about how they work and handle errors. Second, they complete a table of test inputs and expected outputs, and describe reasons to develop test cases. Third, they write simple test methods, compare the effort for manual and automated testing, and describe the implications for large software projects. Fourth, they answer questions that guide them to identify repetitive elements of test code, and describe key elements of a test framework. Fifth, they study a JUnit test class, answer questions about how it works and why unit test frameworks are useful. Sixth, they reflect on what they have learned and how they could improve in the future.

POGIL has been used successfully since the 1990s in high schools, colleges, and universities. Initially used in chemistry, POGIL has been used in biology, CS, engineering, math, and other areas. Research shows that students learn content better [13], have higher pass rates [15], and prefer POGIL over traditional lectures [7]. Students also believe that POGIL promotes critical thinking and other process skills, increases engagement, and improves understanding [6]. The POGIL Project (www.pogil.org) provides a variety of resources, including workshops to help faculty learn about POGIL practice and theory.

The session leaders have used POGIL in a range of courses (see statements below). One of us (Kussmaul) is the PI on a NSF TUES grant to develop and disseminate POGIL activities. Another of us (Hu) is the PI on an AAC&U TIDES grant to develop POGIL activities for a CS Principles course to be paired with courses in other departments to broaden the appeal of CS.

Two of us (Pirmann and Kussmaul) are collaborators on a Google CS4HS grant to create a community of practice for AP CS Principles teachers using POGIL activities.

2. SESSION OUTLINE

This special session will be experiential. As summarized below, we will start with a brief introduction to POGIL and its effectiveness. Next, teams of 3-4 attendees will work through a POGIL activity and experience it as students. Third, the teams will work through a POGIL meta-activity designed to help teachers understand how POGIL can affect student process skills. Fourth, session leaders and other teachers who have recently adopted POGIL will describe their experiences. The session will conclude with a question and answer discussion. We will share links to POGIL materials for CS and provide information about upcoming POGIL workshops.

#	Time	Content
1	5 min	Introductions and overview.
2	20 min	Complete a POGIL mini-activity
3	20 min	Complete a POGIL activity on process skills.
4	15 min	Successes and challenges.
5	15 min	Q&A and next steps.

2.1 Presenter Statement - Clifton Kussmaul

I have created and used POGIL activities in CS II, Software Engineering, AI, and other courses [12]. I often use Google Docs for the activities, so teams can edit collaboratively and copy text to and from other tools. A key benefit of POGIL is that I can observe, provide feedback, and support student learning of both content and process skills. I can also see where students have difficulty and adjust the activity for future classes.

2.2 Presenter Statement - Helen Hu

I have adopted POGIL in multiple CS courses, including a CS0 in App Inventor [9], a traditional CS1 in Java for CS majors [10], and a CS1 in Python for science majors [11]. My students discuss the importance of soft skills, and I use this to motivate the group work and POGIL learning teams. Although they may feel artificial at first, I find that emphasizing the POGIL roles improves the collaboration and teamwork. I have seen increases in student engagement levels as well as in my female students' pass rates [10]. Most of my POGIL activities are at http://tinyurl.com/CSPpogil and http://tinyurl.com/CS1pogil. I have started creating Instructor's Guides for each activity.

2.3 Presenter Statement – Tammy Pirmann

I have been using, adapting and creating POGIL activities for high school CS courses for several years. The process skills that are explicit in the CSTA K-12 CS Standards and the AP CS Principles framework are developed daily within a POGIL classroom. My students have many opportunities to practice collaboration, consensus building, communication, problem solving and critical thinking from within POGIL activities. Our POGIL-CSP team has created over twenty POGIL activities that align with the CS Principles Big Ideas and computational thinking practices.

3. EXPECTATIONS

This special session should appeal to teachers and instructors interested in incorporating more active learning in their classrooms. Attendees will experience how students discover computer science concepts for themselves while working through POGIL activities. They will learn how POGIL has been used in CS classrooms, how to access POGIL materials at http://cspogil.org, and how to learn more through POGIL workshops and regional meetings hosted by the National POGIL Office (https://pogil.org/events).

4. ACKNOWLEDGMENTS

This material is based upon work supported by a Google CS4HS grant for POGIL in CS Principles, multiple Google CS Engagement grants, National Science Foundation Grant DUE-1044679, and a grant from the AAC&U TIDES Institute and the Leona M. and Harry B. Helmsley Charitable Trust. We also acknowledge the National POGIL Office for encouragement and support.

5. REFERENCES

[1] K Abernethy, K Treu (2009) Teaching computing soft skills: an experiential approach. *J. of Computing Sciences in Colleges* 25(2):178-186.

[2] F Ahmed, LF Capretz, S Bouktif, and P Campbell. 2013. Soft skills and software development: A reflection from the software industry. In *International J. of Information Processing and Management*, 4(3):171-191.

[3] R Burns, L Pollock, T Harvey (2012) Integrating hard and soft skills: software engineers serving middle school teachers. In *Proc. of the ACM Tech. Symp. on Computer Science Education* (SIGCSE '12). 209-214.

[4] L Carter (2011) Ideas for adding soft skills education to service learning and capstone courses for computer science students. In *Proc. of the ACM Tech. Symp. on Computer Science Education* (SIGCSE '11). 517-522.

[5] College Board (2014) *AP Computer Science Principles: Curriculum Framework 2016-2017*. College Board.

[6] EP Douglas, CC Chiu (2009) Implementation of Process Oriented Guided Inquiry Learning (POGIL) in Engineering. *Advances in Engineering Education* 3(3).

[7] D Hanson, T Wolfskill. (2000) Process workshops - a new model for instruction. *J. of Chemical Educ.*, 77:120–130.

[8] Hazzan, G Har-Shai (2014) Teaching and learning computer science soft skills using soft skills: the students' perspective. In *Proc. of the ACM Tech. Symp. on Computer Science Education* (SIGCSE '14). 567-572.

[9] HH Hu and B Avery (2015) CS Principles with POGIL Activities as a Learning Community. In *Proc. of the 24th Annual CCSC Rocky Mountain Conference*.

[10] HH Hu, TD Shepherd. (2014) Teaching CS 1 with POGIL activities and roles. . In *Proc. of the ACM Tech. Symp. on Computer Science Education* (SIGCSE '14), 127-132.

[11] HH Hu, TD Shepherd. (2013) Using POGIL to help students learn to program. *Trans. on Computing Education* 13(3), 13.

[12] C Kussmaul (2012) Process oriented guided inquiry learning for computer science. In *Proc. of the ACM Tech. Symp. on Computer Science Education* (SIGCSE '12), 373-378.

[13] G McKnight (2011) Effectiveness of POGIL. Retrieved Sept. 1, 2011 from http://www.pogil.org/about/effectiveness.

[14] RS Moog, JN Spencer, eds. (2008) *Process-Oriented Guided Inquiry Learning*. Oxford University Press.

[15] A Straumanis, E Simons. (2006) Assessment of student learning in POGIL organic chemistry. In *Abstracts of Papers of the American Chemical Society*, vol 231.

Poster Session 1

Integrating Sustainability Concepts into Introductory Programming Courses

Jeffrey A. Stone, *Pennsylvania State University*
Contact: stonej@psu.edu

Sustainability, defined by Penn State University as "the simultaneous pursuit of human health and happiness, environmental quality and economic well-being for current and future generations", is becoming a more frequent theme in colleges and universities. There is currently little published research involving the use of sustainability-themed modules or courses in Computer Science. As part of an institutional effort to integrate sustainability concepts into undergraduate courses, the author constructed a series of projects and activities to educate students about sustainability issues in three distinct CS1-style courses for non-majors. These projects and activities involve traditional introductory topics (e.g. loops, arrays) but each focuses a specific sustainability-related issue or domain. Examples of project issues included the impact of acid rain; the construction of an optimal planting schedule; the impact of air pollution; the benefits of trees on air quality; and the benefits of water catchment systems. These projects and activities included a discussion of the sustainability concept at hand while providing the student an opportunity to demonstrate his/her knowledge of the particular language and algorithmic concepts. Supporting efforts include the integration of speakers on sustainability topics and a parallel effort by undergraduate researchers to create graphics and animations for the project concepts. This poster will describe the results of the pilot study, the lessons learned, and future adjustments.

Keywords: CS1; Sustainability; Social Impacts

DOI: http://dx.doi.org/10.1145/2839509.2850527

The Development of Internationalized Computational Thinking Curriculum in Hong Kong Primary Education

Gary K. W. Wong, *The Hong Kong Institute of Education*
Kening Zhu, *City University of Hong Kong*
Xiaojuan Ma, *The Hong Kong University of Science and Technology*
John Huen, Koding Kingdom
Contact: wongkawai@ied.edu.hk

Computational Thinking (CT) has been widely introduced and investigated in recent years, particularly in the U.S. since the born of visual, block-based, drag-drop programming environments such as Kodu, Scratch, Minecraft and App Inventor. Although the user interface is mainly in English, the characteristics of these easy-to-use, game-based, and interactive tools attract many teachers and researchers in the world to pay much attention to the possibilities and opportunities of introducing these tools to students. Recently, some primary school teachers in Hong Kong begin to independently introduce some of these programming tools to students at age 7 – 11 as a part of learning activities in their computer lessons. Their motives are similar but not the same, such as making a fun learning and teaching experience, motivating students for active and collaborative participation, and introducing CT concepts to develop generic skills (e.g. problem solving skills, creativity, and critical thinking). However, there is an absence of well-developed and planned curriculum for "coding education" to introduce computational thinking systematically to students in the local context with expected learning outcomes. Due to the uniqueness of K-12 curriculum in Hong Kong, the existing curriculum model in the U.S. may need to be customized and redesigned to become suitable for integrating into the curriculum in Hong Kong. In this poster, it describes the first proposed coding education curriculum in Hong Kong primary education (Primary 4 to Primary 6) with relevant objectives, structures, contents, and learning outcomes. A new pedagogical design framework for CT is introduced in this poster, which could be generalizable and yet to be evaluated. This new curriculum will serve as the curriculum guide to local teachers, and is the first research initiative of a three-year longitudinal study investigating the impact of CT activities to students particularly in Hong Kong. The experience of this curriculum development for CT concepts in K-12 education can inspire teachers and researchers in other parts of the world when adopting and internationalizing CT activities based on the curriculum model developed under the U.S. education.

Keywords: Computational thinking; K-12 curriculum development; International outreach for CS education; coding education

DOI: http://dx.doi.org/10.1145/2839509.2850528

A Holistic Sequence of Programming Assignments for CS2

Joanna Klukowska, *New York University*
Stewart N. Weiss, *Hunter College*
Contact: joanna.klukowska@acm.org

We present a sequence of programming projects for the CS2 introductory computer science course which provides a holistic experience for students in preparation for their future roles in any workplace in which software is developed, whether in academia, government, industry, or elsewhere. The progression of projects has several key features: (1) they are easily reused simply by changing the underlying input data set; (2) they offer a flexible degree of analysis objectives; (3) they take advantage of freely available open source data sets and encourage their use; (4) they are designed to be small models of the kinds of problems likely to be encountered outside of the classroom environment; (5) they facilitate the introduction of increasingly more sophisticated software testing concepts, starting with the most elementary; (6) a student who attempts to do them in earnest, even if unsuccessful, can still learn important lessons about the different facets of programming and problem solving; and (7) a student's understanding of the relationship between choice of data representation and performance

SIGCSE'16, March 2–5, 2016, Memphis, TN, USA.
ACM ISBN: 978-1-4503-3685-7/16/03

will likely mature if he or she successfully completes the assignments.

In our poster, we present the first and last assignments of the sequence that we have employed in a CS2 course, and discuss some results. We also show how these assignments can serve as a paradigm that may be used in other CS2-like courses. Many of the underlying concepts can also be applied to CS1-like courses as well as more advanced computer science courses.

Keywords: CS2; Data Analysis and Structures; Open Data; Programming Assignment; Software Testing

DOI: http://dx.doi.org/10.1145/2839509.2850532

Combating Perceptions of Computer Scientists: A Short-term Intervention

Shaundra B. Daily, University of Florida
Alison E. Leonard, Clemson University
Sophie Jörg, Clemson University
Sabarish V. Babu, Clemson University
Nikeetha DSouza, Clemson University
Dhaval Parmar, Clemson University
Kara Gundersen, University of Florida
Joseph Isaac, Clemson University
Serita Acker, Clemson University
Contact: shanib@ufl.edu

Fifty-four middle school girls were a part of weeklong program geared towards encouraging young women in STEM careers. During a two-day computer science intervention, we introduced students to our VEnvI software where students program virtual characters to perform choreography. During this time, students were introduced programming concepts: sequencing, loops, and variables. They also spent time performing to learn some of the movements in VEnvI and discussed different aspects of the VEnvI software design including motion capture & Unity 3D Development. The latter conversations were couched in relation to being a computer scientist. Data were collected from the students on the first day of the camp as well as at the end of the second day. Each student was given a piece of paper that only contained a code corresponding to her. The instructions were to write, "What do computer scientists do?" on one side of the page, and to draw a picture of a computer scientist on the other side.

Our findings suggest that, at least in the short term, this type of intervention can impact students' perceptions of computer science as well as broaden their perspectives of computer scientists. More students drew female computer scientists in the post-test and showed computer scientists working in teams rather than alone. Further, students' ideas of what computer scientists "do" shifted from fixing computers and making websites to creating, designing, and inventing with computers.

Keywords: computer science perceptions, girls, K-12

DOI: http://dx.doi.org/10.1145/2839509.2850533

SIGCSE'16, March 2–5, 2016, Memphis, TN, USA.
ACM ISBN: 978-1-4503-3685-7/16/03.

Coding, Designing, and Logistics: How Modes Affect Equity in Computer Science Education

Declan McClintock, *Michigan State University*
Niral Shah, *Michigan State University*
Contact: mcclin61@msu.edu

This poster delves into the interactions of pair programming students to observe the equality or inequality across three modes of discussion. These three modes are coding, designing and logistics. Coding being when students are discussing code, designing being the discussion of aesthetic aspects, and logistics being the discussion of saving or manipulating files. The students whose interactions are reviewed and assessed in this poster are participants in a three-week elementary computer science program taking place in Northern California in the years 2009, 2012, and 2013. The students' ages range between ten and eleven years old. This poster will compare and contrast specific interactions and examples to highlight how modes can present an interaction as equitable, inequitable, or both. The poster will also present tables to aid in the explanation of how one mode in an interaction can be equitable while the other two modes are not.

Keywords: Modes; Equality; Pair Programming

DOI: http://dx.doi.org/10.1145/2839509.2850534

Lights, Camera, but No Action: Exploring Affective Audio-Visual Features of Educational Videos

Abhay Doke, *Tata Research Development and Design Centre*
Niranjan Pedanekar, *Tata Research Development and Design Centre*
Contact: n.pedanekar@tcs.com

Several hundred Massively Open Online Courses (MOOCs) are available for students of Computer Science (CS) across the Internet. Yet, it has been observed that students exhibit a short attention span while watching MOOC videos. At the same time, as a viewer, they are likely to watch much longer movies and even educational films. In this poster, we propose that production of MOOCs needs to borrow certain affective features from more professionally produced educational films. To support this argument, we first present the results of a limited survey indicating an affective preference of users towards educational films over video lectures from MOOCs. Taking a cue from films in general, we present an analysis of certain affective audio-visual features of educational films vis-à-vis MOOC videos. These features include visual features related to the variety of color, number of scenes and movement, and audio features related to liveliness of speech. We then use these features to classify two groups of educational videos, and conclude that MOOC-like videos often tend to lack such affective audio-visual features. We also indicate possible directions of research in educational videos based on our initial findings.

Keywords: MOOC; Affective; Audio-visual, Educational Video

DOI: http://dx.doi.org/10.1145/2839509.2850535

Increasing Security Awareness in Undergraduate Courses with Labware

Michael Weeks, *Georgia State University*
Yi Pan, *Georgia State University*
Yanqing Zhang, *Georgia State University*
Contact: mweeks@cs.gsu.edu

This poster documents three approaches that we are undertaking to increase security awareness within undergraduate computer science classes. The first approach is a verbal password entry system, with surreptitious photos being taken when the mobile device is stolen. The second approach is a lab where students develop a password entry and verification system between a mobile device and a remote server. The third approach is a captcha system, where students implement a simple challenge that can be verified. Like password entry, the captcha communications must be secure and difficult to automatically manipulate. Unlike password entry, the captcha is meant to allow humans access while denying other computers.

Keywords: mobile security; undergraduate education; labware

DOI: http://dx.doi.org/10.1145/2839509.2850536

Visualizing Algorithm Analysis Topics

Mohammed F. Farghally, *Virginia Tech*
Eric Fouh, *Lehigh University*
Sally Hamouda, *Virginia Tech*
Kyu Han Koh, *Virginia Tech*
Clifford A. Shaffer, *Virginia Tech*
Contact: shaffer@vt.edu

Data Structures and Algorithms (DSA) courses are considered critical in any computer science curriculum. DSA courses emphasize topics related to procedural dynamics (how an algorithm works) and algorithm analysis (the algorithm's efficiency). Historically, algorithm visualizations (AVs) have dealt almost exclusively with portraying algorithm dynamics, and there are few examples of visualizations related to algorithm analysis topics. We have developed a new generation of visualizations that we term Algorithm Analysis Visualizations (AAVs) to convey algorithm analysis concepts. We present the motivation behind AAVs, and outlines a methodology for their evaluation. We present results from student surveys and the analysis of student interaction logs from the OpenDSA eTextbook used by several CS3-level classes during the period of Fall 2014 through Fall 2015. Initial results from Fall 2014 revealed that students were not spending enough time reading the algorithm analysis material presented as textual content. Our results from a preliminary deployment of AAVs in Spring 2015 showed that students interacted with AAVs for significantly longer than the control group spent reading the previous text-based algorithm analysis material. We will present additional results from our ongoing experiment in Fall2015 (control group without AAVs) and Spring2016 (test group with additional AAVs).

SIGCSE'16, March 2–5, 2016, Memphis, TN, USA.
ACM ISBN: 978-1-4503-3685-7/16/03

Keywords: eTextbooks; Data Structures; Algorithms; Interactive Content; Algorithm Analysis Visualization

DOI: http://dx.doi.org/10.1145/2839509.2850537

The Impact on Student Learning and Satisfaction When a CS2 Course Became Interactive

Steven Huss-Lederman, *Beloit College*
Contact: huss@beloit.edu

From 2013 to 2014, a fairly standard CS2 course was changed to a dynamic classroom using clicker questions and OpenDSA textbook (embedded animations with animated and multiple choice questions allowing instructor review of results). Through these changes, class time focused on conceptual ideas and discussion rather than the mechanics of data structures. The clicker questions were used to engage students by strategically asking questions that differentiated between correct ideas and common misconceptions. To assess these changes, surveys of central CS2013 topics were given to students in 2013 (before the changes) and in 2014 and 2015 (after the changes) where the course is offered each spring. Additionally, the drop rate and knowledge from assignments and exams were examined. The analysis showed that after the first year students showed greater learning gains and substantial decline in drop rate (57% to 27%) but found the course less valuable (class time, discussions and readings). In the second year there was a drop in learning gains, an even greater reduction in drop rate (12%) but students now found the course time more valuable than the first year. These results are attributed to regularly informing students in the third year to the reasons for the new methodologies and the fact that a greater diversity of students completed the course each year. The author hopes to engage others in a discussion of their experiences about interactive courses, and how clicker questions can be constructed to engage and educate our students.

Keywords: CS2; active learning; case study

DOI: http://dx.doi.org/10.1145/2839509.2850538

A Certification-Guided Course for Cloud Computing

Dahai Guo, *Florida Gulf Coast University*
Anna Koufakou, *Florida Gulf Coast University*
Contact: dguo@fgcu.edu

We are proposing an undergraduate course to introduce cloud computing technologies with guidance from an industry recognized certification: Amazon Certified Associate Developer. Today, cloud computing providers provide many services. For example, Amazon Web Services provide 46 broad types of services, without mentioning the combinations of these services. It is impossible to introduce all or even most of them in one course. This poster addresses the question of how to select an important and representative subset of cloud computing technologies for developing an undergraduate course on cloud computing. We propose to align our education with what the Amazon Certified Associate Developer certification covers. This certification addresses the core technologies that need to be mastered by software developers that use the Amazon Web Services, clearly the leader in cloud computing. The learning outcomes in the proposed course will be found to be consistent with the four domains identified by the certification.

Keywords: Cloud Computing; Certification

DOI: http://dx.doi.org/10.1145/2839509.2850539

Automated Analysis of Student Programmer Coding Behavior Patterns

Corey Ford, *California Polytechnic State University*
Clinton Staley, *California Polytechnic State University*
Contact: cstaley@calpoly.edu

Important information regarding the learning experience and relative preparedness of Computer Science students can be obtained by analyzing their coding activity at a fine-grained level, using an online IDE that records student code editing, compiling, and testing activities down to the individual keystroke. We report results from analyses of student coding patterns using such an online IDE. In particular, we gather data from a group of students performing an assigned programming lab, using the online IDE indicated to gather statistics. We extract high-level statistics from the student data, and apply supervised learning techniques to identify those that are the most salient prediction of student success as measured by later performance in the class. We use these results to make predictions of course performance for another student group, and report on the reliability of those predictions

Keywords: online IDE;automated evaluation;learning analytics;educational data mining;coding

DOI: http://dx.doi.org/10.1145/2839509.2850540

SPOCK – A System for Encouraging Interaction in Small Private Online Courses

Ryan Hardt, *University of Wisconsin – Eau Claire*
Grant Wuerker, *University of Wisconsin – Eau Claire*
Contact: hardtr@uwec.edu

Online courses are growing in popularity in the forms of Massive Open Online Courses (MOOCs), Small Private Online Courses (SPOCs), and flipped classrooms. Some MOOC interfaces provided by websites like Coursera, edX, Khan Academy and Udacity allow students to comment on lectures, but they do so using a different component than that used for consuming lecture content. Their comment systems are effectively message boards linked to by lecture pages. This component separation has been shown to create a cognitive overhead for students. Additionally, comments made in these systems typically apply to the lecture as a whole rather than to more finely-grained lecture content. Some SPOC interfaces allow fine-grained, timeline-based comments, but suffer from a "seeding" issue in which students who view the lecture early lack incentive to participate. Our system, the "Small Private Online Course Keeper" (SPOCK), is an online lecture environment for SPOCs. SPOCK is distinguished by (1) its tight integration between timeline-based lecture content and anonymous student questions, answers, and comments, (2) its use of gamification to encourage student interaction and address the seeding issue, (3) and by its loose coupling with lecture videos, which may be referenced from other websites like YouTube.

SIGCSE'16, March 2–5, 2016, Memphis, TN, USA.
ACM ISBN: 978-1-4503-3685-7/16/03

Keywords: SPOC; online courses; gamification

DOI: http://dx.doi.org/10.1145/2839509.2850541

Broadening the Path to Cybersecurity Profession in Predominantly Undergraduate and Liberal Arts Institutions

Xenia Mountrouidou, *Wofford College*
Xiangyang Li, Johns Hopkins University
Contact: mountrouidoup@wofford.edu

Cybersecurity is a broad, dynamic, and ever changing field that is difficult to be integrated into undergraduate Computer Science (CS) curriculum. In this poster, we will report our plan and progress on an ongoing NSF-funded three-year project. First, we develop manageable standalone course modules and labs to be integrated non-intrusively into the core Liberal Arts curriculum, and create two new Cybersecurity courses and a set of capstone projects for students motivated to pursue deeper Cybersecurity learning. With the Liberal Arts education in mind, these courses and modules will encompass law, policy, and societal impacts of Cybersecurity. Second, we use the Global Environment for Network Innovations (GENI) infrastructure in lab and project assignments to offer an active Cybersecurity learning experience for all students. This offers a solution to Predominantly Undergraduate Institutions that do not have the infrastructure or maintenance capability for sophisticated computer labs. This project is built on the collaboration between a Predominantly Undergraduate Liberal Arts college, Wofford College, and two primary research universities, Johns Hopkins University and University of South Florida that have well-known Cybersecurity programs.

Keywords: Cybersecurity; Liberal Arts Colleges; GENI; Experiential Learning; Undergraduate Education

DOI: http://dx.doi.org/10.1145/2839509.2850542

Leveraging Context to Create Opportunistic Co-Located Learning Environments

Stephen MacNeil, UNC Charlotte
Celine Latulipe, UNC Charlotte
Contact: smacnei2@uncc.edu

Active learning is becoming increasingly popular as a way to engage students and to provide social support. Providing social support is important because it has been shown to improve both student retention (Slavin 1990, Tinto 1987, Wenger 1999) and performance (Hsiung 2012, Kulkarni 2015, MacNeil 2015). Most forms of active learning use a flipped classroom model of teaching where students are expected to interact with materials, such as lecture videos, alone before class and then engage in active learning during class time (Lage 2000). In our previous work with team-based learning, students generally preferred learning in face-to-face teams (MacNeil 2016). To support co-located teams outside of class, we propose the design for a mobile app that is currently in development which uses students' location to form ad-hoc social learning opportunities for students that are located near each other. We take inspiration from flash teams, which create dynamic expert teams based on the availability of experts online (Retelny 2014). Our app will create teams based on the availability of students and their range of expertise, while leveraging additional context, such as student's location and intention. Students upload course topics that they are struggling with and a general geo-location. The app opportunistically pairs students and suggests that they arrange to meet based on either a geo-location match, a topic match, or preferably, both. In designing our prototype, we consider the possibility of suggesting exercises or assignments that students could work on together. Finally, we provide a brief discussion of the theoretical opportunities and challenges associated with using student's location for ad-hoc social learning.

Keywords: Context-aware; mobile app; co-located learning; flipped classroom; peer learning, social learning

DOI: http://dx.doi.org/10.1145/2839509.2850543

Student Perceptions of Success in Computer Science Senior Capstone Projects

Rick Parker, *Univ of Colorado at Boulder*
Contact: rick.parker@colorado.edu

We are studying how students navigate the school to work transition in the context of the CS senior capstone project course. We conducted semi-structured qualitative interviews with eleven of the seventy-two seniors completing their capstone project in the CS department at our institution. The interview instrument explores how students prioritized candidate projects during project selection, student perceptions of external evaluation, and self-evaluation of the success of their project experience. We used the concept of legitimate peripheral participation (LPP)[1] as a theoretical lens to inform the coding and interpretation of the qualitative data. LPP is a situated learning theory that highlights the importance of embedding learners within a community of practice. This embedding supports participants' development of their professional identities, and engages them in the use of tools and practices authentic to the community. Through analysis of the interview transcripts, we identified the following themes: 1) shift in authority from classroom to project sponsor, 2) the capstone experience serving as a knowledge integration forum, and 3) sufficient project scope to support a sense of ownership and transformative agency. These findings are consistent with a shift in identity from school-oriented to work-oriented, and highlight how the course lends legitimacy to the project work performed by the students. This poster represents preliminary research efforts into the questions of student identity formation within CS, and its impact on long term retention in the computer science discipline.

Keywords: capstone; computer science education; student perceptions

DOI: http://dx.doi.org/10.1145/2839509.2850544

Using Small Whiteboards to Engage Students in Active Learning

Victor Norman, *Calvin College*
Serita Nelesen, *Calvin College*
Contact: {vtn2,smn4}@calvin.edu

It is well known that active learning strategies, like Peer Instruction and Cooperative Learning promote deep learning of material in the classroom. These techniques are typically accomplished by having students use cell phones or laptops. However, research has also shown that use by students of these technologies detract from learning. In this poster we examine our low-tech solution: the use of inexpensive, handheld whiteboards in our classrooms. We provide examples of activities which make use of the boards, in contexts ranging from introductory programming to upper-level networking.

Keywords: active learning, peer instruction, whiteboards

DOI: http://dx.doi.org/10.1145/2839509.2850545

Design and Evaluation of a Course Module on Android Cipher Programming

Jinsheng Xu, *North Carolina A&T State University*
Xiaohong Yuan, *North Carolina A&T State University*
Ashrith Velma, *North Carolina A&T State University*
Contact: jxu@ncat.edu

Encryption is critical in protecting the confidentiality of users' data on mobile devices. However, research has shown that many mobile apps are not correctly using the ciphers, which makes them vulnerable to the attacks. The existing resources on cipher programming education do not provide enough practical scenarios to help students learn the cipher programming in the context of real world situations with programs that have complex interacting modules with access to networking, storage, and database. This poster introduces a course module that teaches students how to develop secure Android applications by correctly using Android's cryptography APIs. This course module is targeted to two areas where programmers commonly make many mistakes: password based encryption and SSL certificate validation. The core of the module includes a real world sample Android program for students to secure by implementing cryptographic components correctly. The course module will use open-ended problem solving to let students freely explore the multiple options in securing the application. The course module includes a lecture slide on Android's Crypto library, its common misuses, and suggested good practices. Assessment materials will also be included in the course module. This course

[1] Jean Lave and Etienne Wenger, Situated Learning: Legitimate Peripheral Participation, 1991.

SIGCSE'16, March 2–5, 2016, Memphis, TN, USA.
ACM ISBN: 978-1-4503-3685-7/16/03

module will be used and evaluated in a Network Security class. We will present the results of the evaluation in the conference.

Keywords: Android Cipher Programming; SSL; Password Based Encryption; Education; Hands-on Lab

DOI: http://dx.doi.org/10.1145/2839509.2850546

Building Pre-Service Teacher Interest in Computer Science Education through Mentoring Experiences

Kim C. Huett, *University of West Georgia*
Mary Alice Varga, *University of West Georgia*
Contact: khuett@westga.edu

K-12 teachers have an important role to play in introducing children to computer science. However, most teachers lack explicit training in computer science. This project explored questions related to the experiences of pre-service teachers as they mentored K-12 children in computer science in an informal learning environment. Through a grant-funded project at a comprehensive public university in the Southeastern United States, five pre-education major undergraduate students in an introductory education course learned basic computer programming, interacted with a K-12 computer science teacher around strategies for introducing computer science to kids, and mentored children in exploring computer science in an informal setting. Quantitative and qualitative analyses of the data suggest these experiences were effective in increasing student awareness of critical issues related to computer science education, increasing their knowledge and skills related to Scratch, increasing their self-perception as potential mentors in basic computer programming concepts, and increasing their attraction to STEM majors and endorsements.

Keywords: Pre-service teacher education; computer science education; mentoring; service learning; K-12

DOI: http://dx.doi.org/10.1145/2839509.2850547

Computing with a Community Focus: An App Inventor Summer Camp for Middle School Students

Lijun Ni, *University of Massachusetts Lowell*
Mark Sherman, *University of Massachusetts Lowell*
Diane Schilder, *Evaluation Analysis Solutions*
Fred Martin, *University of Massachusetts Lowell*
Contact: lijun.ni.gt@gmail.com

Recent work has demonstrated the power of providing relevant, meaningful contexts for computer science to broaden participation. In this poster, we present the design and evaluation of a one-week App Inventor summer camp for middle school students with an explicit focus on addressing local community needs. We recruited community partners to present their organization's work to students, and then we supported students in developing apps that would support these organizations' missions. Students successfully developed apps that were designed to address community issues. Students developed apps on topics ranging from local farmers' markets, healthy food and nutrition apps, invasive species, local trees, to providing users with information about recycling. At the end of the workshop, we conducted an in-depth interview study to examine its impact on students' attitudes and perceptions toward computer science, and supplemented this with results from project evaluation. Our results indicate that students had positive experience in learning, creating and sharing real apps for solving community problems. Focusing on local community needs can also help to motivate students' interest not only in creating apps as well as in learning more about computer science. After the camp, students became more confident in creating apps as well as in using apps to solve community problems, and the camps were successful in welcoming a diverse set of students into computing.

SIGCSE'16, March 2–5, 2016, Memphis, TN, USA.
ACM ISBN: 978-1-4503-3685-7/16/03.

Keywords: App Inventor; socially relevant computing; attitudes towards computing; middle school; summer camp

DOI: http://dx.doi.org/10.1145/2839509.2850548

Exploring Gamification to Teach Computer Science to Non-computer Science Related Major

Lorena B. Martinez-Elizalde, *ITESM*
Monica G. Duarte-Dominguez, *ITESM*
Contact: lorenamtze@itesm.mx

Engagement is a key factor in the process of teaching and learning any subject. Teachers have been facing this problem while teaching computer science at any level; we will be focusing on trying to engage college students from non-computer science majors. Solving problems with programming is a course taught to several majors varying from chemical engineering, through mechanical, physics, electronics, food and even innovation engineering all in the same class. Therefore, we decided to divide the class profiling the students into two roles: a) Mechanics, which showed proficiency on mathematics and critical thinking among the class and b) Pilots, who showed some gaps on their skills. Gamification is seen as a powerful strategy to influence and motivate people. The objectives of applying this kind of trend on a class are: The transformation of class activities into challenges, foster leadership of the participants, develop collaborative teams, reward efficiency and effort in the development of activities and foster meaningful learning experience. The poster will display our findings so far, since we are running the pilot test on this project. We will be assessing the feelings among students with a survey, and present the data analysis derived from the experience, and we will compare the results to a group that is taking the same class with a normal approach.

Keywords: Gamification; non-majors; college students; learning environments

DOI: http://dx.doi.org/10.1145/2839509.2850549

Using Learning Analytics to Trace Academic Trajectories of CS and IT Students to Better Understanding Successful Pathways to Graduation

Omaima Almatrafi, *George Mason University*
Huzefa Rangwala, *George Mason University*
Aditya Johri, *George Mason University*
Jaime Lester, *George Mason University*
Contact: oalmatra@gmu.edu

We present findings from a study examining students' course-taking pathways to graduation and identify the factors regarding course-taking choices that can affect students' performance. The data for the study was collected from two majors within an engineering school at a large public university: computer science (CS) and information technology (IT). Although we look in depth at CS students, we use the other data for a comparative analysis. CS and IT are the most popular and largest majors, respectively, at our institution with almost 2,500 undergraduate students enrolled in them. The results show that there are differences in specific patterns of courses and illustrate relationships between the frequent courses in each semester and the relationships between courses taken in two consecutive semesters. Some major insights from the analysis of trajectory of frequent courses for both groups include: low performers postponed some courses toward the end of the program, and take a collection of courses together that their counterparts do not usually take. This work has direct implications for advising of prospective and current students and can improve programs' curriculum and students' performance. In the next stage of this study we will compare trajectories of students who graduate with those of students who either leave CS and IT or take longer to graduate. This preliminary research is part of a NSF CISE/EHR funded grant project on "BigData and Education".

Keywords: Learning analytics; course-taking patterns; students' performance

DOI: http://dx.doi.org/10.1145/2839509.2850551

Promote Self-Efficacy in Learning of Mobile App and Security with real-world Relevant Laboratory

Kai Qian, *Kennesaw State University*
Dan Lo, *Kennesaw State University*
Wei Chen, *Tennessee State University*
Ying Qian, *East China Normal University*
Contact: kqian@kennesaw.edu

In this paper, we present an innovative, authentic, learning approach to mobile security through real-world-scenario case studies in computing field. The primary goal of this learning approach is to create an engagement and motivating learning environment that encourages all students in learning emerging technologies such as mobile software developments and its security concepts and practices. This approach provides students with hands-on laboratory practices on real-world mobile app developments and security. The laboratory consists of multiple modules covering Mobile App development, mobile security on cryptography, secure programming, network, database, Web app, mobile malware and spyware analysis. Each topic consists of a series of progressive sub-labs: a pre-lab, lab activities, and a student add-on post-lab.

The preliminary feedback from students is positive. Students have gained hands-on real world experiences on mobile security with Android mobile devices, which also greatly promoted students' self-efficacy and confidences in their mobile security learning.

Keywords: Mobile, Security, lab

DOI: http://dx.doi.org/10.1145/2839509.2850552

Data Science for All: An Introductory Course for Non-Majors, in Flipped Format

Lillian (Boots) Cassel, *Villanova University*
Darina Dicheva, *Winston Salem State University*
Christo Dichev, *Winston Salem State University*
Don Goelman, *Villanova University*
Michael Posner, *Villanova University*
Contact: lillian.cassel@villanova.edu

In this poster the authors report the approaches for presenting Data Science topics in Flipped Classroom mode, incorporating topics in Data Science into existing courses as well as in stand-alone courses. It provides an insight on listing of learning goals, central data science topics, content modules, and a framework for implementing a flipped classroom approach to introduce data science to students with limited technical backgrounds.

The presenters are NSF-funded investigators on a collaborative team of computer scientists and statistician to create flipped material for an introductory data science class.

After SIGCSE, materials described in the poster will be available in Ensemble, at http://computingportal.org/?q=VU-WSSU-DataScience

The poster will include a complete sample module, with emphasis on significant points related to addressing students with varying backgrounds, as well as guidance for use of the materials in a flipped classroom module. The poster will include a list of the modules that are available, and a link to the repository where they can be found.

The project includes a firm commitment to the flipped classroom format for instruction. The modules we produce include support for that learning style.

Keywords: Data Science

DOI: http://dx.doi.org/10.1145/2839509.2850558

SIGCSE'16, March 2–5, 2016, Memphis, TN, USA.
ACM ISBN: 978-1-4503-3685-7/16/03

Clashroom: A Game to Enhance the Classroom Experience

Shannon Duvall, *Elon University*
Dan Eagle, *Credit Karma*
Riese Narcisse, *Credit Suisse*
Thomas W. Price, *North Carolina State University*
Contact: sduvall2@elon.edu

Clashroom is a web-based fantasy game that was created to enhance the motivation and learning of a traditional classroom. It was created to address several drawbacks of other educational games by being broadly applicable to any course, requiring no class time, and allowing for optional rather than mandatory game play. Each player in the game is a dragon trainer, hoping to train a champion pet dragon. To gain skills and magical items for the dragon to use, players complete educational quests set up by the teacher. Players compete in weekly tournaments, where the quest rewards are vital to success. Because the gameplay and the learning material are decoupled, the game can be used for any subject at any level. After initial testing, students report that the game is fun and that the intrinsic rewards of a fun game are motivation enough for extra learning.

Keywords: Gamification; Game-based Learning; Educational Games; Education

DOI: http://dx.doi.org/10.1145/2839509.2850556

We Have Questions: Pedagogical, Technical, and Procedural Assistance Requests in a Large Computational Thinking Curriculum Research Project

Hilarie Nickerson, *University of Colorado – Boulder*
Jeffrey Bush, *University of Colorado – Boulder*
Yasko Chanoki Endo, *University of Colorado – Boulder*
Contact: hnickerson@colorado.edu

As teacher professional development efforts continue to scale to meet the growing demand for computer science educators, more individuals with little formal preparation in the discipline are seeking training. For this reason, it is important to understand the kinds of questions that these teachers, along with administrators and IT staff, are asking professional development providers. This research examines questions received by Scalable Game Design (SGD), a project that engages students in computing through game and simulation design activities. SGD has provided training for more than 300 teachers since 2009. We have found several dimensions of interest in the question pool. The major categories of questions received are pedagogical, technical, and procedural, and we present a generalizable taxonomy of question types plus specific examples. In addition, question content and questioner roles fluctuate throughout the professional development and classroom implementation cycle, from initial inquiries to requests regarding next steps. Knowledge of these factors can lead to adjustments in training content to reduce questions later on and potentially increase teacher confidence; moreover, this information can inform planning for support resources, an especially important activity when project growth is forecast. We also discuss how our support structures have changed over the life of the project and compare them to two other curriculum initiatives that rely on unique software environments. Our future work will investigate the characteristics of teachers who are asking particular kinds of questions, including their disciplinary backgrounds, experience in the classroom, familiarity with SGD, and instructional environments.

Keywords: Teacher Professional Development; Classroom Implementation; Experience Report; Scalable Game Design; Computational Thinking; Computer Science Education

DOI: http://dx.doi.org/10.1145/2839509.2850575

Autograding and Feedback for Snap*!*, A Visual Programming Language

Michael Ball, *UC Berkeley EECS*
Dan Garcia, *UC Berkeley EECS*
Contact: michael.ball@berkeley.edu

While text based languages have been (relatively) easy to grade automatically, visual programming languages have been largely left out of the equation. However, as the demand for introductory CS courses has recently grown, so too has the interest in CS courses that use visual programming languages, and thus the need for a scalable solution to providing student feedback. In this poster we present a system design for an autograder for Snap *!*, a visual programming language designed at UC Berkeley, inspired by Scratch. Creativity and open-ended responses are an important part of many CS0 courses, such as the Beauty and Joy of Computing, our autograder includes tools that allow instructors to build robust feedback mechanisms that handle a wide variety of student submissions. We also present our initial work to integrate this system into edX for a series of MOOCs as well as a prototype of integrating this tool into a traditional LMS on campus.

Keywords: Snap!; autograding; feedback, automated assessment; blocks programming; visual programming; LTI

DOI: http://dx.doi.org/10.1145/2839509.2850526

SIGCSE'16, March 2–5, 2016, Memphis, TN, USA.
ACM ISBN: 978-1-4503-3685-7/16/03

Poster Session 2

Combining Flipped Learning with Gamification to Improve Student Performance in a Data Structures Course

Darina Dicheva, *Winston-Salem State University*
Contact: dichevad@wssu.edu

Data Structures is one of the fundamental computing courses but also among those with the highest rate of drops and failures. Its importance for a timely completion of Computer Science college programs implies the need of employing innovative instructional methods and technologies to improve student engagement and performance. This poster presents an instructional method that leverages strategies from both flipped learning and gamification. The flipped classroom has been shown to effectively support active learning activities. Moreover, flipping a Data Structures classroom allows introducing programming labs in class, which is not typical for the standard way of teaching the course. However, the success of flipped learning depends crucially on the proper engagement of students in and outside of class. Here gamification can help. Gamification, defined as the use of game design elements in non-game contexts, has shown promises in shaping user behavior in desirable directions, which can be used to increase students' motivation and engagement in the learning process. The poster describes a gamified flipped learning approach and the author's experience and findings in using it in a Data Structures course at a minority university. In the proposed method, the in-class work features group problem solving and pair-programming labs. The employed gamification elements include accruing points, virtual currency, rapid feedback, unlocking content, freedom to fail, and social engagement. The measures used in assessing the effectiveness of the proposed approach include students' grades, information about class attendance and submission of lab assignments, and an attitudinal survey.

Keywords: Flipped learning; Gamification; Data Structures

DOI: http://dx.doi.org/10.1145/2839509.2850529

Assessing the Effectiveness of Experiential-Learning-Based Teaching Tools in Cybersecurity Courses

Xiaohong Yuan, *North Carolina A&T State University*
Jinsheng Xu, *North Carolina A&T State University*
Huiming Yu, *North Carolina A&T State University*
Junghee Kim, *North Carolina A&T State University*
Taehee Kim, *North Carolina A&T State University*
Contact: xhyuan@ncat.edu

The poster describes our project of Assessing the Effectiveness of Experiential-Learning-Based Teaching Tools in Cybersecurity Courses. We are assessing the effectiveness of experiential-learning-based teaching tools for 10 cybersecurity topics in five cybersecurity courses. For each topic, two teaching methods are selected: the control group teaching method, and the experimental group teaching method. The two teaching methods are compared to answer one of the two research questions: (1) Is using an experiential-learning-based teaching tool more effective in improving student learning than the traditional teaching method without using the teaching tool? (2) Is one experiential-learning-based teaching tool more effective than another experiential-learning-based teaching tool? We will assess the effectiveness of the teaching methods via three measures: (1) improvement in student learning outcomes, (2) improvement in student motivation in learning the topic, and (3) improvement in the student experience such as student enjoyment, satisfaction, and perceived difficulty in learning the topic. The knowledge gained from this research can be used by cybersecurity educators at other institutions to use effective teaching tools to improve cybersecurity education practices, which has the potential to increase the number of students well-prepared for entering cybersecurity careers.

Keywords: experiential-learning-based teaching tools; cybersecurity; assessment

DOI: http://dx.doi.org/10.1145/2839509.2850550

Teaching and Learning in an Introductory Undergraduate Programming Class: A Reflective Autoethnography

S. Zahra Atiq, *Purdue University*
Contact: satiq@purdue.edu

In scholarship of teaching and learning studies (SoTL), computer science (CS) educators have investigated the effectiveness of their teaching methods on students, but they have rarely investigated their own professional development. Some educators do examine their own practices through a process of reflection, but these informal self-reflection efforts have lacked scholarly rigor. A more rigorous study could be provided through the use of autoethnography. This poster presents an autoethnographic study by the author on the teaching of introductory computer programming courses. Through this study, which used five years of data, the author arrived at three main conclusions. First, the author found that students were able to learn new programming languages because the author emphasized self-learning and life-long learning in the classroom. Second, the author found that peer learning, in which one student explains ideas to another, benefits both students. Third, the author found that when educators mentor, support, and guide students, the students' motivation, engagement, and retention increase. Although these findings about effective practices confirm the results of previous studies, the autoethnographic method provides a new, credible way for educators to reflect and inform their practices.

Keywords: autoethnography; computer programming; reflection; research to practice

DOI: http://dx.doi.org/10.1145/2839509.2850553

SIGCSE'16, March 2–5, 2016, Memphis, TN, USA.
ACM ISBN: 978-1-4503-3685-7/16/03.

Eighteen Hours of Code with Fifth Grade Students

Katie Davis, *California Polytechnic State University-San Luis Obispo*
Zoë Wood, *California Polytechnic State University- San Luis Obispo*
John Wilcox, *Peabody Charter School*
Contact: kdavis22@calpoly.edu

Integrating programming and computer science into the K-12 curriculum is of national importance. This poster reports on our experience creating an eighteen-week lab curriculum for fifth grade students. Using Processing, an open source programming language and IDE that is built on the Java programming language, we developed and taught eighteen separate lab components introducing basic coding concepts appropriate for fifth grade. These lab modules were developed by a team consisting of a fifth grade teacher, a computer science master's student, and a computer science professor. The labs were taught to over 100 fifth grade students in the 2014-15 academic school year at a public school, Peabody Charter School. All coding labs produced visual output, either static scenes or animations. Topics included basic syntax with a large focus on two dimensional spatial reasoning, but also included three different modules focused on concepts from the fifth grade science curriculum. All curriculum is available at http://users.csc.calpoly.edu/~zwood/Outreach/PCS/PCS5.html. This poster breaks down the basic lab components developed and presents challenges and positive outcomes. In general, students enjoyed the exercises; the teacher observed that all students were eager to complete the labs. Prior to this experience the teacher had no programming knowledge and learned alongside the students each week. He continues to teach the Processing modules in the fifth grade for the 2015-16 school year.

Keywords: introductory programming; computer science education; K-12 education

DOI: http://dx.doi.org/10.1145/2839509.2850554

Multifaceted Efforts to Create an Inclusive Environment and Increase Diversity

Perry Fizzano, *Western Washington University*
David Hartenstine, *Western Washington University*
Contact: perry.fizzano@wwu.edu

The goal of increasing the representation of women and minorities in Computer Science is widespread and one to which we are strongly committed. There are several notable academic programs and professional organizations that are making headway on this goal themselves and are making resources available to others. While we have learned from others, we have also developed some novel approaches appropriate to our institution we feel are suitable for others.

In this poster, we outline the best practices that we've adopted and describe our novel approaches. Some of these efforts were funded by an NSF S-STEM grant which provided scholarships and supporting services for females pursuing degrees in Computer Science or Mathematics. Other ideas spawned independently of that grant and require few resources. Our efforts include: (1) actively recruiting female students (2) early advising and peer mentoring (3) creating a supportive department culture, paying special attention to underrepresented groups and first-generation students (4) developing teaching practices to increase freshmen interest and retain students through graduation (5) encouraging students to become members of the larger community (6) promoting professional and leadership development. We describe how the novel approaches we've developed contribute to these recognized best practices, report on our actions, and include our qualitative assessment of improved climate and quantitative results related to improved recruitment and retention. The human and financial resources required for each action item are indicated. Our ultimate goals are to share our approaches, learn from our colleagues, and to foster continued engagement.

Keywords: Diversity, Women in CS

DOI: http://dx.doi.org/10.1145/2839509.2850555

Deepening Learning in High School Computer Science through Practices in the NGSS

Marie Bienkowski, *SRI International*
Contact: marie.bienkowski@sri.com

High school computer science teaching can be informed by how science and engineering practices are defined in K-12 curriculum standards. In the United States, the Next Generation Science Standards (NGSS) are seen as broadly stated and widely accepted statements of what children should know about science and engineering to be literate citizens and to prepare for careers in STEM. While the NGSS do not identify practices for computer science, our experience is that the broadly defined engineering practices can serve as an appropriate framework for thinking about computational work. Our interpretation differs from efforts that use computation to teach science or mathematics, instead we apply NGSS approaches to teach computer science. We anticipate that K-12 teachers who are working with these standards as well as with the Common Core State Standards (CCSS) will find, as we have, a crossover from the emphasis in these standards on inquiry, argumentation, and overall deeper learning to the pedagogical orientation of curricula such as the high school introductory course Exploring Computer Science (ECS). This poster will show how a portion of the NGSS, carried over from the precursor Science and Engineering Framework and called the "Condensed Practices" can be used with activities in ECS to deepen student learning and help teacher adoption. Handouts will be available showing (1) knowledge, skills, and abilities for computational thinking, (2) curriculum guidance for teachers wishing to use the NGSS to inform ECS teaching and (3) suggestions for professional development in NGSS for computational thinking for all K-12 teachers.

Keywords: Exploring Computer Science; High School Computer Science; Engineering Design Practices

DOI: http://dx.doi.org/10.1145/2839509.2850557

SIGCSE'16, March 2–5, 2016, Memphis, TN, USA.
ACM ISBN: 978-1-4503-3685-7/16/03.

Replicating a Validated CS1 Assessment

Miranda Parker, *Georgia Institute of Technology*
Mark Guzdial, *Georgia Institute of Technology*
Contact: miranda.parker@gatech.edu

Validated assessments are important for teachers and researchers. A validated assessment is carefully developed to make sure that it is measuring the right things. Computing education needs more and better validated assessments. Validated assessments provide instructors with insight on how their students are doing in their class and provide researchers with insight on whether certain technologies and interventions are successful. Building high-quality, validated assessments is difficult. However, it is possible to *replicate* an existing validated assessment, and the new assessment can be validated against the original assessment. We need mechanisms to replicate assessments so that we can build more and more varied assessments for different audiences. We developed the Secondary CS1 Assessment (SCS1) as an isomorphic version of a previously validated assessment instrument for introductory computer science. In this poster we provide an overview for the process of replicating an existing valid knowledge assessment and validating the replication. Handouts will be provided with information about how to access and use the SCS1 Assessment.

Keywords: Assessment; CS1; validity; replication

DOI: http://dx.doi.org/10.1145/2839509.2850559

Assessing the Development of Computer Science Pedagogical Content Knowledge in the TEALS Program

Yvonne Kao, *WestEd*
Leigh Ann DeLyser, *CSNYC*
Aleata Hubbard, *WestEd*
Contact: ykao@wested.org

One of the critical barriers to increasing pre-collegiate computer science course offerings in the U.S. is a lack of qualified computer science teachers. Programs such as TEALS, a teacher preparation program pairing high school teachers with computing professionals to offer CS courses, provide opportunities for in-service teachers to gain experience teaching computer science. However, it is not clear whether the high school teachers develop sufficient pedagogical expertise to sustain high-quality computer science course offerings at their schools. Furthermore, the field of computer science education lacks valid and reliable ways of measuring pedagogical content knowledge (PCK), a construct that describes the knowledge teachers need for effective instruction. In this poster, the authors present these results from the first year of a three-year NSF grant to study how TEALS participation influences novice computer science teachers' PCK: 1) a theoretical framework describing the critical components of CS PCK, 2) the results of the first field test of a CS PCK assessment, including the psychometric properties of the assessment, and 3) a comparison of how teachers performed on the assessment at the beginning and end of their first year of computer science teaching and how they performed relative to their computing professional mentors.

SIGCSE'16, March 2–5, 2016, Memphis, TN, USA.
ACM ISBN: 978-1-4503-3685-7/16/03.

Keywords: computer science education; pedagogy; pedagogical content knowledge; high school; teacher preparation

DOI: http://dx.doi.org/10.1145/2839509.2850560

A Curiosity-Driven System for Developing Coding Literacy

Neeraj Chatlani, *Rollins College*
Daniel S. Myers, *Rollins College*
Contact: dmyers@rollins.edu

Coding literacy is the ability to understand a written computer program and interpret its functionality and output. Literacy is a valuable skill for programmers at all levels, because understanding written code requires developing and applying mental models of program execution. Previous work has shown that explicit instruction in program literacy is beneficial for new computer science students and aids the development of algorithmic thinking. This poster summarizes the authors' work-in-progress developing COLT: the Coding Literacy Trainer, a web-based adaptive tutorial system that provides instruction in the fundamentals of coding literacy and program interpretation to new computer science students. In addition to its pedagogical applications, COLT serves as a development platform for a novel theoretical foundation for adaptive teaching systems based on the concept of intrinsic curiosity. Inspired by the work of Lee et al. in the field of developmental robotics, a curiosity-driven system explores its complete knowledge environment in way that continually maximizes its learning progress. Thus, learners are driven to explore areas where they are currently making the greatest advances, while avoiding regions of the knowledge space that are either too simple to be interesting or too challenging to be approachable at the current time. The poster summarizes the theoretical background and implementation of the COLT system in a clear, easy-to-read format. A web-based version of COLT is currently under active development and slated for an open-source release in the spring of 2016.

Keywords: Coding literacy; Adaptive learning systems; Intrinsic curiosity; Computer science education

DOI: http://dx.doi.org/10.1145/2839509.2850561

Teaching Software Engineering Skills in CS1.5: Incorporating Real-world Practices and Tools

Sarah Heckman, *NC State University*
Jason King, *NC State University*
Contact: {sarah_heckman, jtking}@ncsu.edu

Students learn best in environments where they can meaningfully engage with materials that emulate real-world scenarios. Incorporating software engineering best practices and supporting tools in introductory courses provides students the opportunity to engage in course materials as a novice member of the profession. We support student engagement with industry tools to support software engineering best practices for tutorials, in-class labs, and programming projects. *The goal of the research is to improve student learning, engagement in the course and profession, and retention through the use of software engineering practices and tools that introduce students to the software engineering profession.* A prior study on the incorporation of in-class laboratories, supported with software engineering best practices, on linear data structures showed an increase in engagement, but did not show a difference on student learning when compared with active learning lectures. We are currently expanding the study by incorporating in-class laboratories across a full semester of a CS1.5 class at NC State University. The poster presents the preliminary results from Fall 2015.

Keywords: software engineering best practices; CS1.5; situated learning

DOI: http://dx.doi.org/10.1145/2839509.2850562

Designing and Refining of Questions to Assess Students' Ability to Mentally Simulate Programs and Predict Program Behavior

Ashish Aggarwal, *University of Florida*
Christina Gardner-McCune, *University of Florida*
David S. Touretzky, *Carnegie Mellon University*
Contact: ashishjuit@ufl.edu

Mental simulation is an important skill for program understanding and prediction of program behavior. Assessing students' ability to mentally simulate program execution can be challenging in graphical programming environments and on paper-based assessments. This poster presents the iterative design and refinement process for assessing students' ability to mentally simulate and predict code behavior using a novel introductory computational thinking curriculum for Microsoft's Kodu Game Lab. We present an analysis of question prompts and student responses from data collected from three rising 3rd - 6th graders where the curriculum was implemented. Analysis of student responses suggest that this type of question can be used to identify misconceptions and misinterpretation of instructions. Finally, we present recommendations for question prompt design to foster better student simulation of program execution.

Keywords: Computational Thinking; Kodu Game Lab; Program Simulation; Mental Simulation; K-12 CS Education & Curriculum; Instruction Design

DOI: http://dx.doi.org/10.1145/2839509.2850563

SIGCSE'16, March 2–5, 2016, Memphis, TN, USA.
ACM ISBN: 978-1-4503-3685-7/16/03.

Megas and Gigas Educate (MaGE): A Curricular Peer Mentoring Program

Heather Pon-Barry, *Mount Holyoke College*
Audrey St. John, *Mount Holyoke College*
Becky Wai-Ling Packard, *Mount Holyoke College*
Barbara Rotundo, *Mount Holyoke College*
Contact: ponbarry@mtholyoke.edu

The Megas and Gigas Educate (MaGE) program is a peer mentoring program being developed at Mount Holyoke College, a liberal arts college for women, for the introductory CS curriculum. Consistent with national trends, interest in CS is rising rapidly; current resources cannot meet demand while maintaining quality feedback and pedagogy. Supported by a Google Computer Science Capacity Award, MaGE has three main objectives: (1) to triple enrollment capacity over 3 years in introductory courses; (2) to increase enrollment and retention for women and other underrepresented groups; (3) to train students to educate, mentor, and support others in inclusive ways. Trained undergraduate students act as peer mentors to beginner students, providing close interaction and assisting with feedback. MaGE is currently being piloted in the introductory CS1 course. Enrolled students bring varying interests, including Art, History, Biochemistry, Economics and Engineering; most students have no prior programming experience. Each CS1 student is assigned a peer *Giga Education Mentor* (or GEM) in a 9:1 ratio. GEMs have undergone a rigorous training course that raises awareness of the role of social identity in learning, emphasizes active learning within computer science, and provides preparation for being technical peer mentors. While research supports the need for culturally-sensitive, inclusive training as part of the curriculum, we know of few peer-based models in CS that explicitly include this education. By building a diverse set of peer role models and connecting with the pre-existing co-curricular *Megas and Gigas* mentoring program, MaGE seeks to effectively engage underrepresented students in computing.

Keywords: Peer mentoring; diversity and inclusion; innovative curriculum design; recruiting and retaining students

DOI: http://dx.doi.org/10.1145/2839509.2850564

Pixels, Post-It's® and CS Principles

Jeffrey L. Popyack, *Drexel University*
William M. Mongan, *Drexel University*
Contact: popyack@drexel.edu

We describe an "unplugged" activity that exposes data structures and algorithms involved in image representation and compression, using multi-colored Post-It Notes®. We use Post-It's to illustrate how color images can be encoded and decoded so they can be stored efficiently on a computer and/or transmitted efficiently across a network. This provides an intuitive illustration of bitmaps and the GIF (Graphics Interchange Format), optimized with Lempel-Ziv compression. The algorithms are simple to explain and comprehend, and simultaneously appeal to the participants' sense of art and creativity while demystifying advanced computing concepts and computer graphics.

We describe two sample exercises which make use of these concepts. In one exercise, teams of participants create messages with Post-It's, encode them and send them to other teams for decoding. In another exercise, a larger image is encoded and broken into letter paper-sized smaller images to be decoded and reassembled by a group.

This activity has proven to engage participants with a wide variety of backgrounds, and provides the background needed for further exploration and discussion of Computer Science Principles, specifically the Big Ideas of Creativity, Abstraction, Data and Information, and Algorithms.

Keywords: CS Principles; Unplugged; Hands-On

DOI: http://dx.doi.org/10.1145/2839509.2850565

Adventures in K-5 STEM Outreach Using the NAO Robot

Steve Hadfield, *United States Air Force Academy*
Chris Coulston, *Pennsylvania State Univ. - Erie*
Marissa Hadfield, *Academy School District 20*
Lillian Warner, *United States Air Force Academy*
Contact: steven.hadfield@usafa.edu

The humanoid NAO robot continues to win both hearts and imaginations with its lifelike appearance and behaviors. Its consistent growth in popularity, an increasing wealth of free behaviors, and the intuitive Choregraphe development environment provide educators and developers with exceptional opportunities to motivate interest in STEM disciplines and breach impediments such as perceptions that such technology is simply too hard. In this poster, the authors discuss a variety of experimental uses of the NAO robots for K-5 STEM Outreach. Initial development and demonstrations focused on generating enthusiasm for both robotics and programming. Dancing and exercising behaviors from Notre Dame University's F.U.N. Lab and Aldebaran Robots easily integrated into voice-controlled Choregraphe demonstration scripts. Faculty and undergraduate students directed this enthusiasm to motivate engagement in Hour of Code programming activities. The team also utilized the NAO robots in small group settings within a K-5 Response To Intervention (RTI) program where demonstrations were followed by having the children interactively experiment with the robots stimulating imagination, creativity, curiosity, and problem solving skills as well as confidence and self-esteem. Next the RTI children actually programmed the robots using a story-based methodology and the powerful while intuitive building block programming constructs of Choregraphe. The team's on-going development efforts focus on expanding the repertoire of available behaviors to include interactive math games and foreign language educational dialogs. Results from use of these new behaviors will be presented at the SIGCSE Symposium. The team is also working to measure attitudinal, conceptual understanding, and math and language skills improvements.

Keywords: STEM; Outreach; K-5; robots; RTI; NAO

DOI: http://dx.doi.org/10.1145/2839509.2850566

SIGCSE'16, March 2–5, 2016, Memphis, TN, USA.
ACM ISBN: 978-1-4503-3685-7/16/03.

Engaging School Counselors, Creating Computing Allies

Sarah Hug, *University of Colorado Boulder*
Jane Krauss, *NCWIT*
Contact: jkrauss@mahonia.us

When counselors become advocates for computing they can have significant impact in recruiting youth in the field through their administration of course assignments and engagement in career exploration with students. A recent study of counselors' academic backgrounds, work priorities, and current perspectives and practices regarding advising in computing has implications for educators and others interested in building cooperative relationships with counselors. The study took place as an activity of the *Counselors for Computing (C4C)* program. C4C leverages the National Center for Women & Information Technology (NCWIT)'s organizational membership, applies evidence-based approaches for professional development, and monitors and adjusts practices to make inroads into CS education through school counselor engagement. In an effort to tailor existing professional development for counselors to the realities of their complex roles in schools, C4C asked 80 counselors to describe their background academic experiences, the schools in which they work and the ways they spend their time at work. In addition, study participants were asked to describe their current counseling practices regarding computing, the extent to which computing was taught in their schools and their preferred methods of receiving professional learning. Understanding the ways in which school counselors interact with youth, parents, administrators, teacher colleagues and other stakeholders may assist K12 computing educators in their efforts to collaborate with counselors in a shared effort to recruit and retain youth in their courses. In this poster presentation the authors will a) frame the problem of counselor readiness to guide toward computing, b) describe the current experiences of school counselors with regard to computing education and career guidance, c) detail how counselors' current work assignments and backgrounds can inform professional learning and relationships in support of pathways to computing careers, and d) show sample messaging and resources computer science educators can use to inform counselors and other school professionals about opportunities for youth in computing.
Laptop Recommended. It is recommended that participants bring a laptop computer to this workshop

Keywords: counselor; computer science education; equity

DOI: http://dx.doi.org/10.1145/2839509.2850567

OnRamp to Parallel and Distributed Computing

Samantha S. Foley, *Univ. of Wisconsin-La Crosse*
Joshua Hursey, *Univ. of Wisconsin-La Crosse*
Daniel Koepke, *Univ. of Wisconsin-La Crosse*
Justin Ragatz, *Univ. of Wisconsin-La Crosse*
Jason Regina, University of Wyoming
Contact: ssfoley@cs.uwlax.edu

Computer science students must understand parallel and distributed computing (PDC) concepts to be effective computer scientists in the workforce, as reflected in the ACM Curriculum guidelines. Communities of CS educators are creating educational modules, and making parallel computer environments (PCEs) available to educators who are integrating PDC concepts into their existing curriculum. Even with these resources there is a barrier to entry for students to use PCEs, namely the unfamiliar and complex system software ecosystem of modern PCEs. The OnRamp project lowers that barrier to entry for exploring PDC concepts on a variety of PCEs while also providing a path for students to learn how to be productive on the native PCE. OnRamp is designed to be a general-purpose web portal for supporting the exploration of PDC concepts that harnesses the existing educational resources created by the CS education community. It coaches students through interactive modules that teach them about PDC concepts and PCEs while allowing them to launch parallel applications from day one. As students become more comfortable with running parallel applications on PCEs, OnRamp transforms into a reference guide as they graduate to using the native PCE. This poster describes the motivation, design, and some motivating use cases for the project. We hope that this poster inspires parallel and distributed computing educators to use OnRamp in their courses.

Keywords: parallel and distributed computing; web portal; learning environment.

DOI: http://dx.doi.org/10.1145/2839509.2850568

Teaching Computational Thinking Through Bio-Design

Johanna Okerlund, *UNC Charlotte*
Orit Shaer, *Wellesley College*
Celine Latulipe, *UNC Charlotte*
Contact: jokerlun@uncc.edu

We are developing ways to teach computational thinking through interaction with tangible digital tools for synthetic biology. Inspired in part by Jeannette Wing's (Wing 2008) notion of the essence and pervasiveness of computational thinking, a growing community within SIGCSE is exploring tools that encourage computational thinking that don't use traditional computer science terminology or computer programming (Basawapna 2013, Daily 2014, Freeman 2014, Miller 2014, Wolz 2011). However, that community has not yet explored how to teach computational thinking through bio-design. Synthetic biology is a relatively new research field where scientists engineer living organisms to exhibit new behaviors. Biologists arrange and combine BioBricks, sequences of DNA that exhibit a behavior, sense an environmental factor, or indicate the beginning or end of a larger sequence. Bio-design not only incorporates traditional principles of computational thinking (abstraction, modularity, design/build/test), but also introduces new challenges that force the user to apply these principles in new ways. Interacting with biology can thus 1) help deepen understanding for people who are proficient in computational thinking, 2) provide a platform for introduction to computational thinking for the first time. Because most bio-design is performed in a wetlab by experienced biologists, we focus now on designing and developing low-barrier digital tools for interacting with biology. We present SynFlo (Okerlund 2016), a tangible interactive system for bio-design that mimics a real-life biological wetlab protocol and we discuss the properties of SynFlo and bio-design in general that encourage computational thinking.

Keywords: Computational thinking; Tangible interaction; Biology

DOI: http://dx.doi.org/10.1145/2839509.2850569

User Experience and Feedback on the RPI Homework Submission Server

Andrea Wong, *Rensselaer Polytechnic Institute*
Eric Tran, *Rensselaer Polytechnic Institute*
Joe Jung, *Rensselaer Polytechnic Institute*
Ben Shaw, *Rensselaer Polytechnic Institute*
Marina Espinoza, *Rensselaer Polytechnic Institute*
Beverly Sihsobhon, *Rensselaer Polytechnic Institute*
Melissa Lindquist, *Rensselaer Polytechnic Institute*
Samuel Breese, *Rensselaer Polytechnic Institute*
Matthew Peveler, *Rensselaer Polytechnic Institute*
Barbara Cutler, *Rensselaer Polytechnic Institute*
Contact: wonga6@rpi.edu

The Rensselaer Polytechnic Institute (RPI) Homework Submission Server is an ongoing, open-source project used to collect, compile, and automatically grade programming homework for students in our introductory and sophomore computer science classes. It allows viewing of homework, lab, test, and overall grades and late submissions and excused absences on homework. Our first hypothesis is that an electronic submission server is the preferred way for students to submit their coding homework because it provides immediate feedback about the correctness of their code and ensures fair, consistent grading since their code is compiled and run with the same test cases, on the same computer. Our second hypothesis is that students appreciate courses with a flexible policy for late submission of homework, allowing them to use a specific number of "late days" throughout the semester without penalty. We recently conducted a survey to test these hypotheses and will incorporate specific feedback from the students as we continue development and expand the server to more courses at RPI and other universities.

Keywords: CS1/2, Open Source

DOI: http://dx.doi.org/10.1145/2839509.2850570

Guiding Career Development Prior to Capstone Experiences

Deborah Knox, *The College of New Jersey*
Contact: knox@tcnj.edu

A new course, Computer Science Professional Development Seminar, engages students in reflective self-discovery and career planning, and also facilitates attainment of student outcomes assessment data for continual improvement of our program. Prior to requiring this half-semester course, students selected when to attend colloquia and various presentations. This strategy did not insure that students had a common exposure to topics. Though this course is titled as a professionalism course, this poster describes broader content coverage. Lifelong learning, ethical professionalism, and social media are included. The learning experiences in this course encourage students to establish an early commitment to their

SIGCSE'16, March 2–5, 2016, Memphis, TN, USA.
ACM ISBN: 978-1-4503-3685-7/16/03.

personal career development. Additionally, students are guided to increase their awareness of social issues and professional practice knowledge areas from CS2013. Targeted to the second-year (sophomore) population, this course helps connect the students with our departmental community and leads the students to better understand expectations and capstone opportunities. During this course, students receive mentorship by upper-class students, alumni, faculty, staff, and outside computing professionals. Since the course is required, students are afforded dedicated time to expand their understanding of professionalism, to learn about many opportunities for undergraduates, to reflect on case studies and on their intended career path, and to advance their preparations for the next step of their career.

This annual course has been offered four times. We strive to keep section enrollments at seminar level to facilitate discussion and to promote community. Some events with outside speakers require one common meeting of all sections. Course management strategies are offered.

Keywords: professionalism; career development; mentoring; lifelong learning; ethical professionalism

DOI: http://dx.doi.org/10.1145/2839509.2850571

Bigger Isn't Better When It Comes to Online Computer Science Teacher Communities

Mackenzie Leake, *Stanford University*
Colleen Lewis, *Harvey Mudd College*
Contact: mleake@cs.stanford.edu

Dozens of online communities have been developed to support high school computer science (CS) teachers by providing them with CS teaching resources. However, these sites have failed to meet teachers' needs and are widely underused. Despite this underutilization, organizations continue to create new communities with content that overlaps with the materials provided within existing communities. Our research explores the barriers to CS teachers' engagement with online resources and their attitudes toward online communities. We find that teachers are frustrated by the time and difficulty required to navigate the sites and find useful information. It appears the barriers to accessing these resources cannot be overcome by creating additional large, multipurpose communities. Even though it seems that having large communities would be valuable for increasing access to resources, our research indicates teachers prefer smaller, more specialized communities. We are eager to discuss ideas for designing new communities that provide more relevant content for teachers in a way that is easy for them to find.

Keywords: CS teachers; online communities; online resources

DOI: http://dx.doi.org/10.1145/2839509.2850573

SIGCSE'16, March 2–5, 2016, Memphis, TN, USA.
ACM ISBN: 978-1-4503-3685-7/16/03.

The Sol y Agua Project: Enhancing Middle School Education through Computing with an Emphasis on Simulation and Data Science

Ann Gates, *The University of Texas at El Paso*
Monika Akbar, *The University of Texas at El Paso*
Mary Kay Roy, *The University of Texas at El Paso*
Florencia Larsen, *The University of Texas at El Paso*
Ivonne Lopez, *The University of Texas at El Paso*
Christian Murga, *The University of Texas at El Paso*
Angel Ortega, *The University of Texas at El Paso*
Jesus Tellez, *The University of Texas at El Paso*
Rebecca Urbina, *The University of Texas at El Paso*
Contact: faramos2@miners.utep.edu

Data Science, the field of data extraction, manipulation, and analysis in order to derive knowledge or insight, is becoming an essential component of effective management and planning for industrial, research, scientific, and social communities. With the goal of engaging middle-school students in the important field of Data Science, the Sol y Agua project is developing a computer game based on regional environmental issues explored through data analysis. The Sol y Agua project will augment the learning environment of middle school students by incorporating simulation and data science to existing curricula in the form of an interactive educational game. The game has a theme of water sustainability and stewardship with an emphasis on information analysis, negotiation, and decision-making. The game will also immerse students in regional issues concerning biodiversity, sustainability, and the human impact on the environment. This video game will allow students to analyze and interpret data, and make informed decisions about water conservation and sustainability. Simulation and data visualization allow students to perform simulated, environmentally-conscious planning and virtual experiments. Using simulations allows students to easily and inexpensively gather data from the virtual environment. Data visualization allows us to quickly represent this data in new, meaningful, and engaging ways.

Keywords: Data visualization; Interactive Learning Environments; Simulation; Video-Game; Middle School Education

DOI: http://dx.doi.org/10.1145/2839509.2850574

An Expert System for the Prediction of Student Performance in an Initial Computer Science Course

Michael Kuehn, University of North Dakota
Jarred Estad, University of North Dakota
Jeremy Straub, University of North Dakota
Tom Stokke, University of North Dakota
Scott Kerlin, University of North Dakota
Contact: michaelkuehn12@gmail.com

There are many factors that play a part in how a student performs during a course. Some of these factors can be looked at in hindsight to help suggest why a student may or may not have done well in class. This poster assesses the potential of predicting student performance in an introductory computer science class using information about students' preparation, attitudes and study habits. An expert system has been utilized for this purpose. The expert system accepts data related to seven different categories of preparation, belief and attitude and, through the partial activation of multiple rules, predicts an outcome for each student on the post-test (which should correlate with and is used as a surrogate for the student's final course grade). This poster presents our findings and correlation between certain factors relevant to students' success. It shows how these factors can be used to predict a student's grade and discusses the significance of being able to do so. Thus far, the results from the first sample of data appear promising. The work has shown that certain groups of self-assessment questions have clearly out performed other groups in predicting final test grades. The use of expert system techniques to predict student grades can provide an insight on different factors that affect student performance. Knowledge of characteristics that may lead to poor performance allows instructors to potentially identify students who may be at risk of a low grade and need supplemental instruction, tutoring or other support at the outset of the semester.

Keywords: Computer science education; educational assessment; course outcome prediction; student learning

DOI: http://dx.doi.org/10.1145/2839509.2850576

A Web-based Environment for Developing and Utilizing Teaching Languages for Novice Computer Science Students

Benjamin J. Kruger, *Northeastern State University*
Richard Matzen, *Northeastern State University*
Contact: kruger@nsuok.edu

First year Computer Science students must face the dual challenge of learning to think algorithmically while simultaneously assimilating the complex and often unintuitive syntax of their first programming language. Mitigating this problem has been an active research area for decades, spawning a number of programming languages intended for students. While some such teaching languages have achieved a measure of popularity, both in the classroom and for general purpose programming, none has achieved ubiquity, which suggests there is no silver bullet. To this end, we present a suite of open source software including (1) a web-based toolkit for developing and modifying teaching languages using parsing expression grammars, (2) C Spot Run, a simple imperative teaching language built with the toolkit and informed by empirical research in intuitive syntax, and (3) a web-based development environment enabling the student to complete programming assignments directly from a web browser, eliminating complicated compiler installation and configuration. These artifacts are the first steps in an ongoing project intended to serve not only as a classroom tool, but also as a platform for the observational and experimental study of programming languages in classroom settings. By analyzing source code and metadata, common syntactic obstacles may be exposed and empirical studies of syntax can be verified in the classroom.

Keywords: Parsing Expression Grammars; PEG; PEG.js; Teaching Languages; Language Design; CS1; Open Source

DOI: http://dx.doi.org/10.1145/2839509.2850577

FunWithSound: A Music Composition and Synthesis Library for Processing

David Hovemeyer, York College of Pennsylvania
Contact: dhovemey@ycp.edu

FunWithSound is a music composition library for Processing which makes it easy for students in creative computing and introductory programming courses to create music compositions with a small amount of code. Building upon Processing's considerable strengths in the domain of visual art, FunWithSound extends Processing to support music creation.

Keywords: music; music synthesis; Processing

DOI: http://dx.doi.org/10.1145/2839509.2850530

Exploring the Role of Computer Science in the Liberal Arts

Gary R. Skuse, Rochester Institute of Technology
Daniel A. Walzer, University of Massachusetts, Lowell
Contact: grssbi@rit.edu

There is a growing body of evidence that indicates that many students would benefit from coursework in computer science regardless of their academic majors. While there are obvious advantages to learning computer science for students in the quantitative and analytical fields that comprise the STEM disciplines, the advantages to other students are less obvious. In order to investigate the impact of computer science principles and methods on students in the liberal arts we convened a workshop of faculty comprised of an equal number of participants from each discipline, i.e. computer science and the various liberal arts. We identified a clear need to better understand the computational needs of liberal arts students and faculty and we identified opportunities for computer scientists and liberal arts students and faculty to work together to better prepare students in both disciplines and better support faculty research in the liberal arts.

Keywords: Liberal Arts; disciplinary convergence; career nimbleness; multidisciplinary collaboration

DOI:http://dx.doi.org/10.1145/2839509.2850531

SIGCSE'16, March 2–5, 2016, Memphis, TN, USA.
ACM ISBN: 978-1-4503-3685-7/16/03.

Birds of a Feather 1

Universal Access to Computing Education

Richard E. Ladner, *University of Washington*
Brianna Blaser, *University of Washington*
Andreas Stefik, *University of Nevada, Las Vegas*
Daniela Marghitu, *Auburn University*
Contact: blaser@uw.edu

Approximately 10% of computer science and engineering majors have a disability of some kind. Students with disabilities are more likely to drop out of the major than those without disabilities. This BOF will bring together individuals who are interested in increasing the representation of students with disabilities in computing and improving their success. Participants will share strategies and promising practices to help each other do a better job of including these students in our classes and research projects. Resources, including those produced by AccessComputing (uw.edu/accesscomputing) and AccessCS10K (uw.edu/accesscomputing/accesscs10k), will be shared.

Keywords: Disability; broadening participation; universal design; accessibility

DOI: http://dx.doi.org/10.1145/2839509.2850474

Updates to the ABET Computing Accreditation Criteria

Allen Parrish, *The University of Alabama*
Stan Thomas, *Wake Forest University*
Contact: allen.parrish@ua.edu

The ABET Computing Accreditation Commission (CAC) has been involved in a multi-year process to update the accredAitation criteria to incorporate a new framework for outcomes assessment, as well as to update the specific program criteria in computer science, information systems and information technology. Of the program criteria revisions, the computer science criteria are the most heavily revised, with the goal of achieving some degree of consistence with the CS2013 Report. This Birds of a Feather session is designed to discuss the philosophy behind the criteria changes, and present a draft of the revised criteria for review and comment. The session will promote attendee participation via small group discussions, thereby providing the opportunity for participants to provide input on the revised criteria. The session will also solicit feedback to ABET on computing accreditation in general, and on the overall accreditation process.

Keywords: accreditation; outcomes assessment; model curricula.

DOI: http://dx.doi.org/10.1145/2839509.2850475

SIGCSE'16, March 2–5, 2016, Memphis, TN, USA.
ACM ISBN: 978-1-4503-3685-7/16/03

Fostering Computational Creativity through *Computing in the Arts*: A Community of Educators

Susan Reiser, *UNC Asheville*
Rebecca Bruce, *UNC Asheville*
Jennifer Burg, *Wake Forest University*
Bill Manaris, *College of Charleston*
Contact: reiser@unca.edu

Do you teach or are you interested in teaching digital media? Do you work in a digital media degree program or department? This BOF will explore different ways of merging computer science and the arts. We invite you to apply to attend our creative, collaborative *Computing in the Arts* community of CS educators this summer at our NSF-funded faculty workshop. Additionally, we want to learn what you teach in digital media, and how your program is structured. Is it part of Computer Science, Art, Mass Communications, New Media, or something else? High schools in many states require no computing education beyond studying office suite software. However, these same students are experienced and enthusiastic digital media users. *Computing in the Arts* degree programs can harness this interest and experience, facilitating both critical and creative thinking. Computing theory and practice can be applied in art and, at the same time, be informed by artistic concepts and methods. Moreover, art theory and practice can be enriched by computational methods and techniques.

Keywords: Computing in the Arts; Digital Media; Embedded Systems; New Media; STEAM

DOI: http://dx.doi.org/10.1145/2839509.2850476

Birds of a Feather: Teaching with Alice

Donald Slater, *Carnegie Mellon University*
Wanda Dann, *Carnegie Mellon University*
Stephen Cooper, *Stanford University*
Contact: dslater@cmu.edu

This session is for anyone currently using Alice Level 2 and/or Alice Level 3, or those exploring the possibility of using Alice in their curriculum. The discussion leaders and attendees will share teaching strategies, tips, and techniques with each other and those new to Alice. This is an opportunity to share assignments and pointers to web sites to access instructional materials, such as syllabi, student projects, exams, and other resources. There will be a special emphasis on the new Alice 3 to Java textbook and accompanying support materials, how Alice supports the transition to Java, and mapping Alice 2 and Alice 3 curriculum standards and guidelines.

Our goals for this session include:

- Review of the new Alice 3 to Java textbook and support materials, and issues related to helping students transition from Alice and other block-based tools to Java ad other traditional programming languages.
- Discuss learning standards and objectives encountered in the use of Alice in different environments and educational contexts.

- Allow educators using Alice to share exemplary assignments and teaching strategies.
- Provide an opportunity for those thinking about using Alice to ask questions as they determine how it may be most useful in their particular situation.
- Foster the development of community by allowing Alice teachers to connect and become resources for each other throughout the year.
- Allow educators to interact with Alice team members to learn more about the latest features of Alice 3 and Alice 2.

Keywords: Alice; Alice 2; Alice 3; Java; NetBeans; pre-APCS; pre-CS1; animation; 3D Graphics; Introduction to Programming

DOI: http://dx.doi.org/10.1145/2839509.2850477

Computer Science: Small Department Initiative

Catherine Bareiss, *Olivet Nazarene University*
Contact: cbareiss@olivet.edu

Faculty members in a small department (5 FTE or less) face special challenges and strengths because of their size. This BOF is a time for faculty to meet and discuss ways to meet the shared challenges and take advantage of their strengths. The actual topics covered will be based on those attending. Possible topics might include: sharing classes, increasing enrollment, general education, and specialized courses.

Keywords: small department

DOI: http://dx.doi.org/10.1145/2839509.2850478

Researching Programming Education with Blackbox

Amjad Altadmri, *University of Kent*
Neil C. C. Brown, *University of Kent*
Contact: nccb@kent.ac.uk

The Blackbox project collects data from opted-in users of the BlueJ beginners' Java IDE. This data includes source code edits, compilation results, and use of various tools within BlueJ (such as the debugger). Interested researchers may sign up either to use the global database, and/or to use Blackbox as a data collection platform for their local BlueJ-based studies. Blackbox has been running for over two years and contains the results of over 100 million compilation events from over 1 million users. Over 50 researchers have already signed up for access to the data.

This session will allow interested researchers, whether already using Blackbox or not, to come together and talk to each other and to the Blackbox team about using the Blackbox data in their research. The Blackbox team will provide a brief overview of the project, and the research opportunities it provides, followed by lots of time for questions and discussion.

Keywords: BlueJ; Blackbox

DOI: http://dx.doi.org/10.1145/2839509.2850479

Mentoring Student Teaching Assistants for Computer Science

Charles Garrod, *Carnegie Mellon University*
Jeffrey Forbes, *Duke University*
Colleen Lewis, *Harvey Mudd College*
Peter-Michael Osera, *Grinnell College*
Contact: charlie@cs.cmu.edu

Institutions small and large often use student teaching assistants (TAs) to provide office hours, tutor students, and grade student work, and the quality of a course's TAs can greatly affect the quality of the course. In this BOF we will discuss the training we provide to prepare TAs for their course duties and the mentoring we provide to foster their role as future educators. Improving the effectiveness of TA training and mentoring can have an immediate impact on the quality of teaching, potentially improve retention and diversity in computer science, and have a long-term impact on all aspects of our field as our current students and TAs progress through their industry and academic careers. Our goal is to provide a forum for you to disseminate your TA mentoring practices and for you to hear the mentoring practices of others, with the goal to develop a collection of best practices for TA training and mentoring for computer science. This BOF is appropriate for professors or instructors of any computer science course or summer program that uses undergraduate or graduate student teaching assistants.

Keywords: teaching assistants; student mentoring

DOI: http://dx.doi.org/10.1145/2839509.2850480

Practical Methods for Broadening Participation Through Student Engagement in CS1/CS2 Courses

Beth A. Quinn, *National Center for Women & Information Technology*
Alvaro E. Monge, *California State University, Long Beach*
Lecia Barker, *University of Texas at Austin*
Leo Porter, *University of California, San Diego*
Daniel Zingaro, *University of Toronto, Mississauga*
Contact: beth.quinn@ncwit.org

While the overall number of students interested in computer science is increasing, the number of women and other underrepresented groups remains low. Research suggests that engaging and meaningful introductory courses are important to broadening participation in computing (e.g., Barker et al, 2014). But what makes a CS course engaging or meaningful to a more diverse group of students? How does one integrate actionable, effective practices into introductory CS courses? This BoF will convene instructors of CS1/CS2 to discuss ways of engaging all students in introductory computing courses. Discussion leaders will use the Engagement Practices Framework developed by NCWIT's EngageCSEdu

SIGCSE'16, March 2–5, 2016, Memphis, TN, USA.
ACM ISBN: 978-1-4503-3685-7/16/03

interdisciplinary project team to structure the discussion. The Framework is a set of teaching practices that research suggests helps attract and retain women and other underrepresented students in CS. Interestingly, these techniques tend to also engage and retain ALL students. All peer-reviewed materials in the new EngageCSEdu collection (https://www.engage-csedu.org/) employ at least one of these practices. The group will explore examples from the collection (e.g., homework, assignments) and discuss how to effectively implement these practices--and to avoid common pitfalls--in their courses. ***Participants are encouraged to bring laptops in order to access the EngageCSEdu collection during the session.***

Barker, L. J., Hovey, C. L., & Thompson, L. D. (2014). Results of a large-scale, multi- institutional study of undergraduate retention in computing. Proceedings of the 44th Annual Frontiers in Education Conference (pp. 1693-1700). IEEE, New York, NY. doi:10.1109/FIE.2014.7044267

Keywords: diversity; pedagogy; introductory courses; active learning

DOI: http://dx.doi.org/10.1145/2839509.2850481

A Town Meeting: SIGCSE Committee on Expanding the Women-in-Computing Community

Gloria Childress Townsend, *DePauw University*
Contact: gct@depauw.edu

In January 2004, we organized the second SIGCSE Committee ("Expanding the Women-in-Computing Community"). Our annual Town Meeting provides dissemination of information concerning successful gender issues projects, along with group discussion and brainstorming, in order to create committee goals for the coming year. We select projects to highlight through listserv communication and through our connections with NCWIT, ABI, ACM-W, CRA-W, etc. This year we will highlight ACM-W Chapters and ACM-W Celebrations of Women in Computing.

Keywords: Gender Issues

DOI: http://dx.doi.org/10.1145/2839509.2850482

SIGCSE Reads: Time for Book Discussion

Rebecca Bates, *Minnesota State University, Mankato*
Valerie Summet, *Emory University*
Contact: bates@mnsu.edu

Have you read any of the common reads for SIGCSE 2016? Now's your chance to talk about them! Two books: The Diamond Age: Or, A Young Lady's Primer by Neal Stephenson (Bantam Spectra, 1995) and Ancillary Justice by Ann Leckie (Orbit, 2013) as well as two short stories: "A Logic Named Joe" by Will F. Jenkins (Street and Smith, 1946) and "Seven Years from Home" by Naomi Novik (Clarksworld Magazine, 2014) were proposed at the end of the 2015 conference. If you're interested in science fiction, whether on a personal, academic, or pedagogical level, come join us in this BoF and discuss one or more of the two books and two stories. We'll provide potential topics and discussion questions targeting how to incorporate these books into a CS course, but the discussion will be open. The BoF will close with a discussion of potential books for the 2017 conference.

Keywords: Science fiction; computer science; computer science education.

DOI: http://dx.doi.org/10.1145/2839509.2850506

Teaching Track Faculty in CS

Mark Sherriff, *University of Virginia*
Daniel Garcia, *University of California, Berkeley*
Contact: sherriff@virginia.edu

Many computer science departments have chosen to hire faculty to teach in a teaching-track position that parallels the standard tenure-track position. These teaching-track positions include the possibility for promotion, longer-term contracts and greater pay as demonstrated by excellence in teaching, educational material development, and service. Since this type of position is relatively new in CS departments, the expectations and responsibilities for such faculty varies from one university to another, but they certainly differ from the traditional tenure-track positions. This birds-of-a-feather is designed to gather educators who are currently in such a position to share their experiences as members of the faculty of their departments and schools, and to provide opportunities for schools considering such positions to gather information. In past sessions, we have laid the groundwork for keeping this community together through online discussions and consolidating information about teaching-track positions at various universities together into an online database.

Keywords: Non-tenure track faculty; teaching faculty

DOI: http://dx.doi.org/10.1145/2839509.2850485

POGIL in Computer Science for Beginners and Experts

Chris Mayfield, *James Madison University*
Saturnino Garcia, *University of San Diego*
Helen Hu, *Westminster College*
Clif Kussmaul, *Muhlenberg College*
Tammy Pirmann, *School District of Springfield Township*
Contact: mayfiecs@jmu.edu

Process-Oriented Guided Inquiry Learning (POGIL) is a research-based instructional strategy with a proven history across STEM disciplines. In a POGIL classroom, teams of students work on activities that are specifically designed to guide them to construct their own understanding of key concepts. At the same time, students develop process skills such as communication, teamwork, problem solving, and critical thinking. POGIL incorporates practices shown to be particularly helpful for students from underrepresented populations. In a POGIL classroom, teachers are facilitators, not lecturers. Multiple studies have shown that students in POGIL

SIGCSE'16, March 2–5, 2016, Memphis, TN, USA.
ACM ISBN: 978-1-4503-3685-7/16/03

classes do better on common exams and in subsequent courses. For more information, see http://cspogil.org and http://pogil.org. This BOF will (1) enable people unfamiliar with POGIL to ask questions and learn more, and (2) bring together experienced POGIL practitioners to share experiences, concerns, ideas, and insights. As in a POGIL classroom, we will discuss topics in small teams and report out to the larger group.

Keywords: Active Learning; Cooperative Learning; Inquiry Learning; Teams

DOI: http://dx.doi.org/10.1145/2839509.2850486

Preparing to Teach Humanitarian Open Source

Heidi J. C. Ellis, *Western New England University*
Stoney Jackson, *Western New England University*
Gregory W. Hislop, *Drexel University*
S. Monisha Pulimood, *The College of New Jersey*
Gina Likins, *Red Hat*
Contact: ellis@wne.edu

Student participation in Humanitarian Free and Open Source Software (HFOSS) projects offers great learning opportunities for students, including: designing, coding, testing, documentation, collaboration and other professional skills. Humanitarian projects also foster understanding of computing's potential social impact. However, working with any open source project – including HFOSS projects – presents some challenges to instructors. Identifying appropriate assignments, creating meaningful rubrics, mapping the academic schedule to a project's release cycle, and eliciting engagement from the HFOSS project community are just a few of the potential hurdles to overcome. This BOF will be led by a diverse group of faculty who have encountered and overcome these challenges. The organizers and other attendees will share approaches to student involvement in HFOSS as well as the challenges they've encountered and how they've overcome them. Faculty who are interested in involving students in real-world projects will be able to ask about topics including use of HFOSS in a range of courses including introductory courses, project selection, structuring courses and assignments, and gaining university buy-in, while making connections with more experienced faculty in this area. Participation of an open source community member will add perspective from open source communities.

Keywords: Humanitarian Free and Open Source Software

DOI: http://dx.doi.org/10.1145/2839509.2850487

SIGCSE'16, March 2–5, 2016, Memphis, TN, USA.
ACM ISBN: 978-1-4503-3685-7/16/03

CS Ed PhD Students Unite!

Briana B. Morrison, Georgia Institute of Technology
Contact: bmorrison@gatech.edu

The number of PhD students researching Computer Science Education worldwide is growing. This is an organized opportunity for all those attending the largest Computer Science Education Conference to meet one another. All attendees will be invited to introduce themselves along with their institution and focus of research. They may also propose the most important question to be answered by the BOF. After introductions the attendees will have the opportunity to discuss research goals, job opportunities and career trajectories, future conference and publication plans, and even compare advisor stories. Undergraduates and masters students interested in a CS Ed PhD are also encouraged to attend and ask questions. Attendees will determine the best way to stay connected and everyone will be given the opportunity to opt-in for future communications.

Keywords: CS Education Research; PhD; Student

DOI: http://dx.doi.org/10.1145/2839509.2850488

Defining Concepts, Practices, and Standards for K-12 CS

Pat Yongpradit, *Code.org*
Deborah Seehorn, *CSTA*
Tammy Pirmann, *CSTA*
Irene Lee, *Massachusetts Institute of Technology*
Bryan Twarek, *San Francisco Unified School District*
Contact: Pat@code.org

Our community has been seeing explosive interest and growth in K-12 computer science education. With this, a common question from states and school districts arises: What should students learn in a K-12 computer science pathway? We in the community are routinely asked to provide input on what is critical for students to learn at various grade levels.

Code.org, CSTA, ACM, and lead states have kicked off the development of a framework for states and districts creating a K-12 pathway in computer science. The framework, called Framing K-12 CS, is not about developing standards (that will be left up to the CSTA/states to do), but rather a more high-level framework that can guide states or districts who want to then design their own curriculum, standards, assessments, or teacher certification programs. The framework would identify the core themes, practices, and (within each theme) learning statements that detail CS literacy when exiting certain grade spans (ex: exit competencies at grades 2, 5, 8, and 12). The CSTA and Code.org are aligning the development of this framework and the current CSTA standards revision. K-12 practitioners, researchers, states, districts, industry, and non-profit organizations have been involved throughout the development.

This BOF will allow the CS education community to get an internal community preview of the framework before the larger public review period later in the Spring, and discuss its relationship to the CSTA standards. The BOF will include the opportunity to give input and ask questions.

Keywords: concepts; practices; standards; K12; education; computational thinking; teachers

DOI: http://dx.doi.org/10.1145/2839509.2850494

Industry Strength Tools for Software Engineering: What Works, What is OverKill?

Karen Jin, *University of New Hampshire Manchester*
Bonnie MacKellar, *St John's University*
Contact: mackellb@stjohns.edu

Many, if not most, computer science majors plan a career in some aspect of the software development industry. Software development in industry is characterized by extensive use of tools and specialized software to support large scale projects, such as Git, Maven, Gradle, Jenkins, Hibernate, and Spring. We want our students to have exposure to industry strength tools and systems, but want to avoid having our courses overwhelmed by tools with steep learning curves. In this session, we plan to discuss questions and issues that are raised when choosing, installing, teaching, and using industrial strength tools and frameworks in software project courses. Bring your suggestions for favorite tools and frameworks, ideas on learning activities, and support materials. Some of the questions we might tackle: How do we identify tools that support our course learning objectives? How do we find the time and resources to learn the tools? How do we work with our IT staff in installing and configuring the tools? How many tools and systems should we use in a project course, and when do we merely start overwhelming the students? And finally, what works?

Keywords: capstone projects, software development tools, software engineering education

DOI: http://dx.doi.org/10.1145/2839509.2850499

SIGCSE'16, March 2–5, 2016, Memphis, TN, USA.
ACM ISBN: 978-1-4503-3685-7/16/03.

Birds of a Feather 2

How Do You Teach Debugging? Resources and Strategies for Better Student Debugging

Colleen M. Lewis, *Harvey Mudd College*
Chris Gregg, *Tufts University*
Contact: lewis@cs.hmc.edu

"Why doesn't my code work?" Instructors and TAs hear this question day in and day out during introductory computer science courses, and beyond. Students arguably have a harder time learning how to debug their own (and others') code than they do in learning how to plan and write the code in the first place. Debugging strategies are difficult to teach, and there are pros and cons to different debugging methods (e.g., print statements vs. gdb vs. Googling). This BoF will elicit strategies for teaching debugging to CS students, and we will discuss the benefits of introducing certain tools earlier or later in the curriculum. We will also discuss how to assess whether students are able to debug code effectively. All suggestions will be posted on CSTeachingTips.org for dissemination (See tinyurl.com/CSTT-TAs for tips from SIGCSE 2015). We welcome attendance from seasoned and novice instructors, and from teaching assistants.

Keywords: Undergraduate, debugging, pedagogy, assessment

DOI: http://dx.doi.org/10.1145/2839509.2850473

Supporting Students of Color in Learning Computer Science

Jakita Thomas, PhD, *Spelman College*
Shaundra B. Daily, PhD, *University of Florida*
Mikala Streeter, *Mikala Streeter Preparatory School*
Contact: mpstreeter@gmail.com

Recent statistics from diversity reports released by major tech companies have reminded us that people of color account for a tiny fraction of technical and overall employees; reinforcing that the industry is white male dominated. In this session we intend to utilize our previous experiences in order to discuss a variety of issues including: How might we create environments in our classrooms and programs for students of color to see themselves in the tech industry? How might we combat negative industry stereotypes that could discourage students from trying computer science? How might we connect them with culturally aware industry mentors and companies? For students who want to code but don't want to necessarily enter the tech industry, how might we engage them in computer science work that connects to their cultures and interests, and shows them that they don't need to be a white male in order to be a great coder? What are culturally relevant projects that have been shown to engage students of color? What are models of programs that connect with the values and goals of the students we work with? What has been found to *not* work? What other social, cultural and non-technical academic considerations should we keep in mind - e.g. families not valuing tech as much as medicine or sports careers, language barriers for ESL students, low reading/math abilities for low-income students? What non-traditional ideas might we try with our students to improve their long term success not just short term exposure?

Keywords: diversity, students of color, cultural relevance

DOI: http://dx.doi.org/10.1145/2839509.2850483

Current Initiatives and Future Directions of the Computer Science Teachers Association (CSTA)

David Reed, *Creighton University/CSTA*
Mark R. Nelson, *CSTA*
Contact: davereed@creighton.edu

The Computer Science Teachers Association (CSTA) is a member organization of more than 21,000 educators and supporters of K-12 computer science. It was formed by and is affiliated with ACM, but serves as an independent non-profit with a mission to support K-12 CS teachers and promote computer science education. The past year has been a landmark one for CSTA, with the hiring of a new Executive Director, Dr. Mark R. Nelson, as well as a number of new initiatives. These initiatives include a new Website, expanded member benefits, new partnerships and advocacy programs, and a greater emphasis on professional development and research. This session will provide a brief overview of some of these initiatives, as well as introduce plans for the organization that are currently in development. The majority of the session will be an open forum in which attendees will be encouraged to voice their opinions and provide feedback to the Executive Director and members of the CSTA Board of Directors in attendance. Current CSTA members, along with any SICGSE attendees who have an interest in K-12 CS education, are encouraged to attend, learn about CSTA's efforts, and share experiences that can guide the future of CSTA and K-12 CS education.

Keywords: K-12 CS Education, Computer Science Teachers Association, CSTA.

DOI: http://dx.doi.org/10.1145/2839509.2850489

Web Programming

Marty Stepp, *Stanford University*
Allison Obourn, *University of Washington*
Jessica Wolk, *Microsoft Research*
Victoria Kirst, *Google*
Contact: stepp@cs.stanford.edu

Several times in the past few years we have held BoF sessions about teaching web programming at the college level. Our feedback indicates that the most valuable aspect of the past sessions was simply to get everyone together for an exchange of ideas and information, so this will be the focus of the session again. We'd like to bring together two groups of web programming instructors: Newcomers who have not yet taught this material before (or are just starting) and want to soak up information, and veterans who have

SIGCSE'16, March 2–5, 2016, Memphis, TN, USA.
ACM ISBN: 978-1-4503-3685-7/16/03.

now taught it and have insights to share with the group. Newcomers can ask questions about materials, languages and technologies to use, what works and what doesn't, and so on. Veterans can share tips from the classroom and helpful resources. We can also discuss the latest technologies such as HTML, ECMAScript/JavaScript, iPhone/iPad, Android, and web application frameworks such as Node.js, Rails, AngularJS, and more.

Keywords: Web Programming; Classroom Resources; College Teaching

DOI: http://dx.doi.org/10.1145/2839509.2850490

Mathematical Reasoning in Computing Education: Connecting Math We Teach with Writing Correct Programs

John Dougherty, *Haverford College*
Joseph Hollingsworth, *Indiana University Southeast*
Joan Krone, *Denison University*
Murali Sitaraman, *Clemson University*
Contact: jholly@ius.edu

Computing students often have difficulty understanding the relevance of the math we teach, though educators appreciate the significance. This BoF will discuss ways to connect this math with what computing students think they should be doing: programming. This BoF will focus on the benefits (and perils) of connecting math to the development of correct programs with the goal of motivating the relevance of the math-related portion of the ACM/IEEE Computer Society CS2013 curriculum. The discussion will continue the spirit and essence held by the *math-thinking* working group, a distributed working group of approximately 170 people who have been promoting and clarifying the importance of mathematics in computer science education.

Keywords: discrete math curriculum; software engineering; program correctness; formal methods; software verification

DOI: http://dx.doi.org/10.1145/2839509.2850491

Exploring Learning Analytics for Computing Education

Christopher D. Hundhausen, *Washington State University*
Adam S. Carter, *Washington State University*
Contact: hundhaus@wsu.edu

Computing educators have become increasingly interested in learning analytics, which involves collecting and analyzing data on students' learning processes and outcomes for the purpose of improving learning and instructional practices. A variety of computer programming environments enable the automated collection of log data on students' programming processes. In addition, log data on students' online social behavior can be easily collected. All of these data can be analyzed alongside data on students' learning outcomes in order to identify correlations between learning processes and outcomes, and ultimately to better tailor instruction to students' needs. This BOF will provide a platform for discussing the emerging field of learning analytics within the context of computing education. The following questions will serve as a starting point for our discussions: (1) What types of data should we be collecting on computing students? (2) How can we best analyze these data in order to gain meaningful insights into students' learning processes? (3) How can we design effective instructional interventions based on the data we collect and analyze?

SIGCSE'16, March 2–5, 2016, Memphis, TN, USA.
ACM ISBN: 978-1-4503-3685-7/16/03

Keywords: learning analytics; learning management systems; computer science education

DOI: http://dx.doi.org/10.1145/2839509.2850492

Handling Very Large Lecture Courses: Keeping the Wheels on the Bus II

Josh Hug, *UC Berkeley*
Daniel D. Garcia, *UC Berkeley*
Contact: hug@cs.berkeley.edu

As classes grow beyond hundreds or even a thousand students, instructors must come to grapple with handling course logistics at scale. Otherwise mundane tasks can no longer be handled in an ad hoc way, and standard course design challenges become more acute. Just to name a few issues, the instructor might have to contend with: Providing timely effective feedback for students, exam scheduling, recruiting and managing a teaching staff that consists of dozens of people, ensuring consistency of grading, identifying and providing interventions for struggling students, providing a consistent policy for makeup work, and creating diverse course content (e.g. lab, HW, discussion section) that allows for an efficient path to mastery for each student regardless of diverse backgrounds and ability. If you have good ideas for handling these issues you'd like to share, or just want to learn what others are doing, come join us! Discussion will ideally include staffing techniques, technologies (including automated assessments), and ways of developing course content. A master list of such tips will be compiled and provided to the SIGCSE community.

Keywords: large lecture courses; course logistics; instructional technologies; automated assessments

DOI: http://dx.doi.org/10.1145/2839509.2850493

Setting Quantifiable Goals for Broadening Participation in Computing

Kate Lockwood, *University of St. Thomas*
Maureen Doyle, *Northern Kentucky University*
Contact: aklockwood@stthomas.edu

The National Center for Women & Information Technology (NCWIT) works with faculty at all stages of the pipeline to create measureable change at their educational institutions. While faculty are typically committed to this work, they often do not have the time or expertise to create clear, measureable goals that can be assessed and reported to funders or administration. In this BoF, participants will work with NCWIT-developed change tracking tools, and social scientists to develop goals for their home institutions. To gain the most out of the session, please bring your Internet enabled device to try hands-on activities during the session..***Laptop is recommended.***

Keywords: Broadening participation

DOI: http://dx.doi.org/10.1145/2839509.2850495

Computer Science Summer Camps: Making Summer Programs Fun and Sustainable

David E. Johnson, *University of Utah*
Contact: dejohnso@cs.utah.edu

Higher education has the opportunity (and often the mandate) to provide STEM outreach to their communities. Summer camp programs are one mechanism for providing quality CS learning experiences to a wide audience. This BOF will provide a platform for discussing strategies to make summer camps fun and sustainable. What are camp topics have been successful? How is funding obtained and sustained? Nationally, technology camps run the gamut from small, one-week programs to large camps that serve hundreds. The proposer will share his experience developing the University of Utah GREAT camps (www.cs.utah.edu/~dejohnso/GREAT), which have over 700 students attend one-week camps and hopes the BOF will attract others with their own experiences.

Keywords: summer camps; outreach

DOI: http://dx.doi.org/10.1145/2839509.2850496

Leveraging CS Teachable Moments in the Maker Movement

Jennifer (Ginger) Alford, *Trinity Valley School & Fort Worth Museum of Science and History*
Erik Brunvand, *University of Utah*
Contact: gralford@acm.org; elb@cs.utah.edu

The growing do-it-yourself movement relies heavily on electronics, code, and data. Abundant resources and low cost materials result in people of all ages seeking to learn how to master these modern creative supplies. We will discuss how computer science educators might tap into teachable moments provided by this voluntary, informal, enthusiastic movement to promote formal computer science study.

The success of introducing formal computer science skills in the context of computing as a creative tool has been well established in the areas of media computation and digital art. It is natural to extend this idea to computing as a tool for creating physical objects and for interacting with the physical world in different ways. This discussion will focus on examples of creative projects that expose topics in computer science, including microcontrollers, 3D printing, laser cutting, toy hacking, and environmental sensing. The session will emphasize the types of computer science concepts that naturally tie into each project. Attendees are encouraged to share their own project experiences and to reflect on lessons learned, accessibility of concepts, and practical issues of class management.

Keywords: CS1; open source; maker movement; Arduino; physical computing;

DOI: http://dx.doi.org/10.1145/2839509.2850497

Brainstorming Data Science as a Fluency Course for Non-Majors and as a New Specialization

Lillian (Boots) Cassel, *Villanova University*
Don Goelman, *Villanova University*
Darina Dicheva, *Winston Salem State University*
Heikki Topi, *Bentley University*
Contact: Lillian.cassel@villanova.edu

Data Science programs are emerging in many areas and are related to many disciplines. This includes sciences, social sciences, business, journalism, history, and any other area dealing with massive amounts of data. Some institutions are establishing majors or minors in data science while others need to incorporate some level of introduction to relevant topics within the context of other coursework. The BOF will engage SIGCSE participants who have views on the content and role of courses and programs in data science. Two existing NSF sponsored projects will seed the discussion. One of the projects investigates the use of flipped classroom instruction for course material in data science, with significant attention to what can be done with a minimum of prerequisites. The other project produced a workshop to elicit opinions from a number of perspectives on what are the core elements of data science and how the subject is seen by different disciplines. Results from the workshop will be available at SIGCSE. With these as a starting point, participants in the Birds of a Feather session will explore the emerging field of data science and its relationship to computer science education.

Keywords: Data Science, Flipped Classroom

DOI: http://dx.doi.org/10.1145/2839509.2850498

Competency Based Education in Lower-Division Computer Science Taught at Community Colleges

Amardeep Kahlon, *Austin Community College*
Linda Smarzik, *Austin Community College*
Mary Kohls, *Austin Community College*
Contact: akahlon@austincc.edu

Many community colleges are looking at Competency Based Education (CBE) as a way to increase student recruitment, engagement, completion, and transfer to baccalaureate programs. In addition, colleges are looking at CBE as a way to reduce costs as well as provide students with clear, marketable skills for employment. CBE is particularly suited to computer science due to the nature of the discipline where well-defined, measurable outcomes can be designed and implemented. Is your college

SIGCSE'16, March 2–5, 2016, Memphis, TN, USA.
ACM ISBN: 978-1-4503-3685-7/16/03

exploring a curricular redesign using CBE? Do you want to know what CBE is and how to implement a CBE curriculum in computer science? This BoF will host a discussion on planning, implementation, and scale-up of CBE programs. Besides learning about CBE, this BoF will provide attendees with a chance to connect with others trying to implement CBE programs so that they can share knowledge, share resources, and form future collaborations. The recent CS2013 curricular guidance will also be discussed as an important resource for developing CBE in CS.

Keywords: Distance Learning; Competency Based Education; Community College

DOI: http://dx.doi.org/10.1145/2839509.2850500

Assessment of Security Knowledge, Skills and Abilities using Hands-On Exercises in 2016

Richard Weiss, *The Evergreen State College*
Michael E. Locasto, *The University of Calgary*
Jens Mache, *Lewis & Clark College*
Blair Taylor, *Towson University*
Elizabeth Hawthorne, *Union County College*
Siddharth Kaza, *Towson University*
Ambereen Siraj, *Tennessee Tech University*
Contact: weissr@evergreen.edu

We see teaching cybersecurity through hands-on, interactive exercises as a way to engage students. However, we also want to assess how much students are learning from these exercises, and the exercises themselves could be used to assess what students know. Creating new hands-on exercises requires significant preparation on the part of the instructor. As a community we have begun to share exercises and discuss what works and what problems students and instructors have encountered. The purpose of this BOF is two-fold: 1) to continue to bring together instructors who have developed hands-on exercises with those who would like to use them, and 2) extend the discussion to include assessment of student learning.

We recognize that few CS programs can afford new required courses, so we will discuss ways to integrate security-related exercises into existing ones. This could include networking, OS, computer architecture, programming languages, software engineering, algorithms and programming (CS0, CS1, CS2). The questions we will ask are, "What exercises have you tried? What are your experiences? What are you looking for? What are the learning goals for your students? How do you assess them?"

Recent hiring forecasts indicate that there is still a tremendous need for skilled information security experts. Security is one of the core areas in the ACM/IEEE COMPUTER SCIENCE 2013 Curricula. It is particularly important to share stories from the classroom (what worked and what didn't), discuss ethical hacking, discuss how to teach and evaluate analytical skills, and discuss how we know if we are making a difference. We plan to share experiences, practices and ongoing efforts, including our own (e.g., our teaching experiences, Security Injections, the Security Knitting Kit project, The EDURange project and our dissemination of other infosec interactive exercises such as SEED labs). Both Security Injections and EDURange have features that address assessment.

Keywords: security; laboratory exercises; hacker curriculum; secure coding; cybersecurity

DOI: http://dx.doi.org/10.1145/2839509.2850501

Student ICTD Research and Service Learning Abroad

Joseph Mertz, *Carnegie Mellon University*
Contact: joemertz@cmu.edu

This BOF is intended to allow faculty interested in global service learning, Information and Communication Technology and Development (ICTD) research, and other cross-cultural experiences an opportunity for information sharing. It takes a lot to get students out into the field. Challenges include developing partnerships, negotiating agreements, vetting the safety of destinations, identifying sources of funding, navigating the logistics of immunizations, visas, accommodations and flights to less-traveled places, reassuring parents as to the wisdom of their child's participation, managing development partner expectations, advising students' activities, and many more. And how can these experiences be evaluated? This BOF will provide a venue for sharing experiences, information, and identifying potential new collaborations. We will discuss means for sharing best practices, news, materials, and project artifacts. We will also explore opportunities for collaborating on projects and joint proposals.

Keywords: Global Service Learning; ICTD; ICT4D; International Development; HFOSS; Humanitarian Computing; Computers and Society; Internships; Field Research; Ethical Computing; Consulting; Study Abroad; Student/Faculty Exchanges; International Experiences

DOI: http://dx.doi.org/10.1145/2839509.2850502

Increasing Programming Contest Participation for Fun and Profit

Aaron Bloomfield, *University of Virginia*
Borja Sotomayor, *University of Chicago*
Contact: aaron@virginia.edu

Programming contests have a number of pedagogical benefits: they reinforce many concepts and skills that students see in computer science courses, build cross-cutting skills such as teamwork, and can improve job prospects by better preparing students for technical job interviews.

The largest and oldest inter-collegiate programming contest in the world is the ACM's International Collegiate Programming Contest (ICPC). Participating in this contest can be fun and instructive for students, but some schools are discouraged from participation because of the large hurdles involved in forming an effective programming contest team, or in making an existing team more effective.

SIGCSE'16, March 2–5, 2016, Memphis, TN, USA.
ACM ISBN: 978-1-4503-3685-7/16/03

A key to success for coaches and teams is to connect with existing individuals who are involved in the process and learn from them, as it is very hard to initiate effective involvement with no external help. This birds-of-a-feather will bring together existing ICPC coaches with other faculty who want to start such a programming contest team, or who want to improve their existing teams.

Discussions will include issues that prevent greater participation in the North American super-region, as well as the overall international ICPC climate. Extensive links to existing resources – both online and published – will be provided, as well as a means for coaches to foster networking and communication. Strategy guides, including an article in this year's SIGCSE conference, will be discussed and distributed.

Keywords: Programming contest; ICPC; Strategy

DOI: http://dx.doi.org/10.1145/2839509.2850503

Providing Impactful Professional Development Teachers Can Implement

Kathy Menchaca Isbister, *Stanford University*
Contact: menchaca@cs.stanford.edu

This session is for K-12 (primary/secondary) educators who would like to talk about what types of professional development would be most relevant to them. It is also for curricular innovators who offer CS professional development to share how successful their attendees have been at implementing the strategies learned through their programs, and if attendees were able to use any materials the program provided in their own classrooms. We welcome an open and positive dialogue on opportunities for improvement in professional development offerings, and a celebration of successful strategies. The discussion leaders will share their own experience with the NSF funded Adventures in Alice workshops to prompt dialogue, and will encourage all attendees to actively participate in the session by sharing their own experiences, concerns, and triumphs.

Keywords: K-12 education; professional development

DOI: http://dx.doi.org/10.1145/2839509.2850504

SIGCSE'16, March 2–5, 2016, Memphis, TN, USA.
ACM ISBN: 978-1-4503-3685-7/16/03

Wednesday Workshop

CReST-Security Knitting Kit: Ready to Use Teaching Resources to Embed Security Topics into Upper Division CS Courses

Ambareen Siraj, *Tennessee Tech University*
Sheikh Ghafoor, *Tennessee Tech University*
Contact: asiraj@tntech.edu

Information Assurance and Security has been designated as a new knowledge area in the new ACM/IEEE-CS Curricula 2013. This is not a trivial task to accomplish, especially with lack of resources. With support from NSF (Award# DUE-1140864), we have developed a set of readily available resources called SecKnitKit (Security Knitting Kit, www.secknitkit.org), which offers a suite of instructional material for non-security faculty (faculty whose primary teaching/research focus is not security) to integrate security in upper division CS courses such as operating systems, software engineering, computer networks and databases. As part of the NSF CReST (CyberWorkshops: Resources and Strategies for Teaching Cybersecurity in Computer Science, DUE-1438861, www.crest4cs.org) project, this workshop will introduce CS faculty to the SecKnitKit resources that can be easily adaptable into any standard CS curriculum. The participants will receive access to all SecKnitKit materials (instructional and assessment) of interest and demonstrated use of the active learning exercises. *Each participant will receive $125.00 stipend for his/her time. Requires a Windows or Mac laptop. Enrollment is limited to 28 participants who teach at least one of these courses: operating systems, software engineering, computer networks and databases).*

Keywords: Security, security education, ACM/IEEE-CS Curricula 2013

DOI: http://dx.doi.org/10.1145/2839509.2844702

Making Music with Computers: Creative Programming in Python

Bill Manaris, *College of Charleston*
Tobias Kohn, *ETH Zürich*
Contact: manarisb@cofc.edu

This is an introduction to creative software development and music making in Python. This material is intended for CS0/CS1 courses and for courses at the intersection of computing and the arts. The workshop will introduce music making activities for teaching traditional CS1 topics, GUIs, event-driven programming, and connecting to external devices (e.g., smartphones, digital pianos) via MIDI and OSC (Open Sound Control). Participants will be introduced to Jython Music (**http://jythonMusic.org**), a library of Python modules for creative programming and music making, and will be making their own music artifacts a few minutes later. Intended audience: Computer science educators interested in teaching creative programming and computational thinking for CS0, CS1, introductory courses in the intersection of computing and the arts, and courses intended to attract and retain new CS majors. Some familiarity with Python expected. Each participant will receive a copy of (1) handouts to be used during the workshop, (2) sample student assignments and projects, (3) API documentation, (4) all required software, and (5) numerous sample programs. **Laptop required (with Java JDK 7 or higher)**. All other software will be provided. Headphones are recommended.

Keywords: music; creative programming; Python; CS0/CS1; MIDI; audio; OSC (open sound control); image manipulation; graphical user interfaces; event-driven programming; computing and the arts.

DOI: http://dx.doi.org/10.1145/2839509.2844707

A Web-Based IDE for Teaching with Any Language

Dan Armendariz, *Harvard University*
David J. Malan, *Harvard University*
Nikolai Onken, *Cloud9 IDE, Inc.*
Contact: danallan@cs.harvard.edu

This workshop introduces participants to CS50 IDE (cs50.io), a web-based integrated development environment based on Cloud9 (c9.io). Not only does the IDE enable students to work on programming projects within a browser, without need for local downloads or installations, it also provides students with an integrated terminal window and full sudo privileges. Underneath the hood is a Docker "container" that allows students to experiment with the underlying Ubuntu Linux OS, installing and configuring software at will, adapting it to their particular projects' needs. The IDE supports any compiler, interpreter, or other software that can be installed via a Linux command-line, while the IDE itself provides a fully-featured text editor for text files and source code that reside on the underlying instance. The Cloud9 GUI is fully extensible through a plugin system and is leveraged by CS50 IDE to provide additional functionality for students. Among the additional features implemented through this mechanism are a GUI-based file submission system, an optional "less comfortable" mode that simplifies the GUI to provide a scaffolded experience for students new to programming, and a GUI front end for the GNU Project Debugger, a CLI debugger for many languages, including C. This workshop will highlight useful features of the IDE in the context of classrooms (including the collaborative nature of a workspace to allow pair programming or provide alternative one-on-one instruction), provide tips for writing or adapting assignments based on its architecture, and introduce developing plugins for full customization.

Keywords: CS50; Cloud9; IDE; GDB; Docker; debugger; linux; cloud-based IDE

DOI: http://dx.doi.org/10.1145/2839509.2844712

SIGCSE'16, March 2–5, 2016, Memphis, TN, USA.
ACM ISBN: 978-1-4503-3685-7/16/03.

High Yield in the Short Term: Planning Strategically to Get Women into your Major

Lecia J. Barker, *University of Texas at Austin*
Leisa D. Thompson, *University of Virginia*
Contact: lecia@ischool.utexas.edu

Most academic departments have outreach efforts to inform potential students and the public about their computing majors. Most participate in events and produce materials to communicate with students, teachers, parents, and employers. Often, however, these recruiting efforts are attended in an opportunistic way rather than strategically. Often, little thought is given to the return on investment of this nontrivial use of scarce resources (money, time), the message conveyed to the particular audience, or to tracking outcomes. In this workshop, participants will develop an actionable plan for increasing the enrollment of qualified women into their undergraduate majors. The workshop philosophy is that departments should accomplish the greatest return on investment, in the shortest time to bring benefits, with the smallest resource commitment. After all, recruiting women is rarely one's "day job." Using research-based materials developed by the National Center for Women & Information Technology (NCWIT) and ideas shared by NCWIT's Academic Alliance members, the presenters will provide information, a planning structure, resources, and activities to support participants in developing a strategic plan to improve the gender diversity of their undergraduate majors.

Keywords: Recruitment, attracting, women in computing

DOI: http://dx.doi.org/10.1145/2839509.2844691

Guiding Students to Discover CS Concepts and Develop Process Skills using POGIL

Clifton Kussmaul, *Muhlenberg College*
Helen H. Hu, *Westminster College*
Chris Mayfield, *James Madison University*
Contact: kussmaul@muhlenberg.edu

This workshop is for anyone who teaches CS, and introduces process-oriented guided inquiry learning (POGIL) in computer science. In a POGIL classroom, teams of 3-5 learners work on activities with active facilitation by the teacher. Through scripted inquiry and investigation, learners discover concepts and construct their own knowledge. Using assigned team roles and other scaffolding, learners develop process skills and individual responsibility. In a POGIL classroom, the teacher is not a lecturer, but a facilitator who helps to ensure that all students are engaged and able to achieve the learning objectives. POGIL activities have a particular structure based on learning cycles. POGIL is a research-based instructional strategy, and studies show that it can significantly improve student performance. Workshop participants will work through POGIL activities as students. Participants will also work through meta-activities that use POGIL and are designed to help teachers learn core POGIL concepts, practices, and benefits. POGIL materials for a variety of CS concepts will be shared. More information is available at http://pogil.org and http://cspogil.org, including sample activities for CS1, CS2, and other courses. Laptops optional.

Keywords: Active Learning; Cooperative Learning; Inquiry Learning; POGIL; Teams

DOI: http://dx.doi.org/10.1145/2839509.2844683

SIGCSE'16, March 2–5, 2016, Memphis, TN, USA.
ACM ISBN: 978-1-4503-3685-7/16/03.

Engage, Energize and Empower Your Students with Team-Based Learning

Lenore Horowitz, *University at Albany*
George Berg, *University at Albany*
Kimberly Van Orman, *University at Albany*
Contact: lhorowitz@albany.edu

Even when we believe the research that shows that active learning is particularly helpful to both engage and empower students—they learn better, they learn deeper and it addresses issues of diversity—it's often not clear to us how we can implement it while keeping the quality of our course high. At UAlbany, courses taught using TBL including: computer programming, data structures, databases, web programming, networking and others. TBL is a structured method that can help instructors improve student learning and energize their classrooms.

Team Based Learning (TBL) is an approach to course design that takes advantage of research into what helps students learn. Students work in permanent teams and course meetings are organized around application exercises. Courses are divided into units, and students are held responsible for the core reading in a beginning-of-unit test taken both as individuals and as teams. Application exercises conform to core principles ("4S"): Teams all work on the SAME problem, teams make a SPECIFIC choice, the problem must be SIGNIFICANT, and the teams must make a SIMULTANEOUS report of answers. A variant of the "flipped classroom," the TBL course spends far less time "covering the material" in class, allowing course time to be spent on skill development and feedback on student work. In this hands-on workshop, participants will experience a model TBL learning sequence and learn active learning techniques that they can adopt in any classroom while learning the basics of the TBL method.

Keywords: team-based learning; active learning; Computer Science teaching

DOI: http://dx.doi.org/10.1145/2839509.2844700

Teaching Parallel Computing Concepts with OpenMP

Joel C. Adams, *Calvin College*
Richard Brown, *St Olaf College*
Elizabeth Shoop, *Macalester College*
Contact: adams@calvin.edu

OpenMP is an industry-standard, platform-independent parallel programming library built into all modern C and C++ compilers. Unlike complex parallel platforms, OpenMP is designed to make it relatively easy to add parallelism to existing sequential programs, as well as write new parallel programs from scratch. In this fun, interactive, hands-on workshop, participants will use OpenMP to learn about a variety of parallel programming concepts, including *single program multiple data* (SPMD) execution, *fork-join* threading, *parallel loops*, *parallel blocks*, *atomic execution*, *mutual exclusion*, and others. Participants will explore 15 short programs designed to help students understand specific parallel concepts, plus several longer programs in which OpenMP is used to solve significant problems. The workshop includes: (i) an introduction to OpenMP, (ii) self-paced hands-on experimentation with the OpenMP programs, and (iii) a discussion of how OpenMP may be used to achieve parallel computing objectives in CS 2013. Participants will also view visual examples that let students see parallelism happening in real time. Participants will need a laptop with an SSH client (e.g., BitVise, PuTTY), or a laptop with a compiler that supports OpenMP (e.g., gcc 4.2 or later, Visual Studio 2008 or later); Linux, Mac, and Windows laptops will be supported. Knowledge of a C-family language (e.g., C, C++, Java, ...) may be helpful but is not required to benefit from the workshop. All materials from this workshop will be freely available from *csinparallel.org*.

Keywords: computer science; education; multicore; multithreading; OpenMP; parallel; patterns; shared-memory; teaching; thread; visualization; TSGL; workshop.

DOI: http://dx.doi.org/10.1145/2839509.2844670

Using OpenDSA eTextbooks in Your Class

Clifford A. Shaffer, *Virginia Tech*
Thomas L. Naps, *University of Wisconsin-Oshkosh*
Susan H. Rodger, *Duke University*
Contact: shaffer@vt.edu

The OpenDSA eTextbook system provides a practical way for instructors to adopt algorithm visualizations (AVs), state machine simulations, and interactive practice exercises into a variety of courses, including CS2, Data Structures, Algorithms, Programming Languages, and Formal Languages. An OpenDSA eTextbook can be used either as a complete replacement for your traditional textbook and assignments or as supplemental readings, auto-graded assignments, or student practice. In this workshop, we present use cases from successful adoption of OpenDSA into existing courses. We will guide you past the real-life hurdles and pitfalls that get in the way of using AVs, interactive exercises, and simulators. We show you how to adopt OpenDSA exercises, how to configure existing OpenDSA materials to suit your needs, and provide an overview of how to create new AVs or exercises. This workshop is about letting you engage students with highly interactive materials in ways that you have said for years that you wanted to do.

Keywords: eTextbooks; Data Structures; Algorithms; Formal Languages and Automata; Programming Languages; Interactive Content; Algorithm Visualization

DOI: http://dx.doi.org/10.1145/2839509.2844687

SIGCSE'16, March 2–5, 2016, Memphis, TN, USA.
ACM ISBN: 978-1-4503-3685-7/16/03.

Reading and Writing Like Computer Scientists: How to Promote Critical Thinking and Student Engagement

Mark E. Hoffman, *Quinnipiac University*
Jerod Weinman, *Grinnell College*
Contact: mark.hoffman@quinnipiac.edu

This workshop introduces participants to an informal writing process that promotes student engagement and critical thinking with easily-assessed, low-stakes assignments. Unlike the formal writing typically used in software development or capstone courses to demonstrate knowledge, informal writing supports student learning (i.e., writing as thinking). Participants will use the Prioritize, Translate, and Analogize (PTA) Process in a model assignment; discuss how it works; and use it to develop a writing assignment. Participants will receive materials for the workshop assignment, samples of prompts employing the PTA process in a variety of courses, and other support materials. Participants are encouraged to bring an assignment idea to develop at the workshop. The workshop is intended for computer science instructors who want to learn about strategies for integrating writing in their courses to engage students and improve their critical thinking while limiting time for instruction and evaluation. No laptop is required.

Keywords: Writing; Communication Skills; Critical Thinking; Student Engagement; Low-Stakes Assignments

DOI: http://dx.doi.org/10.1145/2839509.2844694

Lego-based Case Studies for Teaching Software Engineering Concepts throughout the Curriculum

Stan Kurkovsky, Central Connecticut State University
Contact: kurkovsky@ccsu.edu

Lego Serious Play (LSP) is an experiential and highly creative process designed to facilitate strategic planning, team building, and problem solving using Lego bricks. In the LSP methodology, team members use their intelligence both as individuals and as a group to build simple models representing various concepts in response to a question posed by the faculty facilitator. Discussing the models helps students communicate valuable aspects of their own understanding and interpretation of the problem at hand, explore the team dynamics, and reduce the complexity of many projects.

This workshop is intended for faculty interested in teaching undergraduate and graduate software engineering and related courses. This workshop will also benefit all other faculty (including high school teachers) looking for ways to supplement their course material with engaging and playful hands-on activities aimed to strengthen the teamwork, oral communication, problem solving, and design skills of students. LSP-based hands-on activities discussed during the workshop focus on a single software engineering topic including requirements engineering, architectural design, software testing, software dependability, project planning and management, design patterns, etc.

Workshop participants will learn the basic principles of LSP and participate in two hands-on activities illustrating how LSP can be used to teach software engineering concepts in an engaging context. Participants will receive the necessary Lego kits, which they can keep after the workshop. Laptop is not required for this workshop.

This work is supported in part by a 2015 ACM SIGCSE Special Project grant. More information at http://www.cs.ccsu.edu/~stan/sigcse2016/.

Keywords: Software engineering; Lego; Lego Serious Play; LSP; case study

DOI: http://dx.doi.org/10.1145/2839509.2844699

Peer Instruction in Computing: A Focus on Student Learning

Daniel Zingaro, *University of Toronto*
Leo Porter, *University of California, San Diego*
Quintin Cutts, *University of Glasgow*
John Glick, *University of San Diego*
Joe Hummel, *University of Illinois at Chicago*
Cynthia Lee, *Stanford University*
Jaime Spacco, *Knox College*
Contact: daniel.zingaro@utoronto.ca

Recent work in computing has converged on a collection of complementary findings suggesting the value of the Peer Instruction (PI) pedagogy. Compared to lecture, PI has been shown to decrease fail rates, increase final exam grades, and increase engagement and enjoyment. In PI, students work together to exchange perspectives and use clickers to answer challenging conceptual questions in the presence of a knowledgeable instructor.

In our efforts to mentor potential PI adopters, we note difficulties bootstrapping PI uptake at new institutions and new departments. In this workshop, our main goal is to support potential adopters in the process of shifting from lectures to PI. In recent months, we have contributed materials for many freely-available PI courses, and led a successful 3-day NSF-funded PI workshop. We will work with participants and their existing lecture-based resources to begin considering the ways that PI can enhance student learning.

Instructors interested in increasing engagement in any CS course may attend. Participants are encouraged to bring current lecture materials. Laptop optional.

Keywords: peer instruction; student learning; clickers; active learning

DOI: http://dx.doi.org/10.1145/2839509.2844690

How to Launch a STARS Computing Corps Cohort to Improve Retention and Broaden Participation in Computing

Jamie Payton, *University of North Carolina at Charlotte*
Tiffany Barnes, *North Carolina State University*
Contact: payton@uncc.edu

The STARS Computing Corps is a national alliance with the mission to grow a diverse community of computing leaders. STARS serves as a framework for integrating civic engagement into college computing departments with the goals of broadening participation of underrepresented groups in computing, recruiting K-12 students into the computing pipeline, and retaining students in computing majors. The STARS approach to broadening the participation of women and under-represented minorities in computing is based on research that has shown the value of creating a community and sense of identity. The Corps creates such a community across multiple institutions, including women's and historically black colleges and universities, with members that share the core values of becoming responsible leaders who use their computing skills for social benefit. Each cohort of students and faculty at a STARS member university collaborates with local K-12 schools and industry partners to conduct computing-related outreach, service, and research that can broaden participation in computing. These local cohorts help to build community within and across STARS member institutions, retain students in college degree programs in computing, recruit new students into computing, educate local K-12 teachers, counselors, students, and parents about computing, and build bridges with local industry and community organizations. This workshop will provide hands-on training for new schools to learn how to begin and build a STARS Computing Corps cohort on their own campus.

Keywords: broadening participation in computing; gender and diversity; civic engagement; outreach

DOI: http://dx.doi.org/10.1145/2839509.2844698

SIGCSE'16, March 2–5, 2016, Memphis, TN, USA.
ACM ISBN: 978-1-4503-3685-7/16/03.

Friday Workshops

A Hands-On Introduction to the Internet of Things

Bill Siever, *Western Illinois University*
Michael P. Rogers, *Northwest Missouri State University*
Contact: bsiever@gmail.com

The Internet of Things (IoT), considered by many to be the next big revolution in computing, refers to the trend to include networking and computing in a wide range of devices, such as watches, appliances, health monitors, toys, etc. Including IoT applications early in the curriculum may serve multiple pedagogical purposes, such as demonstrating social relevance, (e.g., health monitoring applications) and motivating other CS topics (e.g. distributed systems, networking, OOP, event driven programming, computer organization, and databases).

This workshop will introduce participants to basic terms and technologies behind IoT. Participants will then work through a hands-on, classroom-ready exercise to build a complete IoT solution. The embedded portion of this solution, based on the popular Arduino platform (hardware provided), will be targeted at students who have completed CS1. The completion of a mobile app that interacts with the embedded devices will require CS2 skills.

Participants should have an interest in IoT or be interested in engaging assignments for both introductory and upper level students. Participants are asked to bring a laptop computer and a recent mobile device, with appropriate software tools installed. Links to these tools, as well as a list of compatible mobile devices, will be provided. Most Android and iOS devices made within the last three years are suitable.

Keywords: Internet of Things; Mobile Apps; Mobile

DOI: http://dx.doi.org/10.1145/2839509

Introducing Secure Coding in CS0, CS1, and CS2

Blair Taylor, *Towson University*
Siddharth Kaza, *Towson University*
Contact: skaza@towson.edu

The CS 2013 curriculum includes Information Assurance and Security as a pervasive knowledge area. However, introducing security in lower level courses is challenging because of lack of appropriate teaching resources and training. This workshop, part of the Cybersecurity Resources and Strategies for Teaching (CReST) project, www.crest4cs.org, will provide a well-tested strategy for introducing secure coding concepts in CS0, CS1, and CS2. We will introduce attendees to secure coding through hands-on exercises, and provide self-contained, lab-based modules designed to be injected into CS0-CS2 with minimal impact on the course (www.towson.edu/securityinjections). Participants will be encouraged to bring in their own syllabus and labs to modify to include secure coding concepts. The first 15 participants will be reimbursed for the workshop cost on attendance. *Laptop recommended.*

Keywords: CS0; CS1; CS2; Secure Coding; Security Injections

DOI: http://dx.doi.org/10.1145/2839509.2844684

Building on Blocks: Getting Started with Frames in Greenfoot 3

Amjad Altadmri, *University of Kent*
Neil C. C. Brown, *University of Kent*
Contact: nccb@kent.ac.uk

Blocks-based programming has become a very popular technology for teaching introductory programming in schools, but it still faces some issues as learners progress. The large transition gap between blocks-based and text-based programming is a source of worry for many educators. However, the difficulties learners have with developing and maintaining progressively larger and more complex programs in block-based systems force teachers to move students on to text-based systems rather than remain with blocks.

Greenfoot 3 introduces *frame-based* programming, a hybrid of blocks-based and text-based programming. Frame-based programming adds comprehensive keyboard support, along with several other usability improvements aimed at removing frustrations for intermediate and experienced programmers, while also providing a way to fill the gap in the transition process.

This workshop will show how to teach introductory programming using the new frame-based editor from Greenfoot 3. We will help the participants to explore the new editor in a hands-on session, accompanied by explanations of its distinctive features and how they have been designed to overcome the friction and niggles present in current blocks-based editors, while also providing pedagogical guidance for learners. ***Participants should bring their own laptop with the latest version of Greenfoot installed, available from* www.greenfoot.org**

Keywords: Frame-based editing; Greenfoot

DOI: http://dx.doi.org/10.1145/2839509.2844693

Rubricking Like a Boss: Writing and Using Rubrics for Faster, Fairer Grading of Student Assignments

Don Blaheta, *Longwood University*
Adrienne Decker, *Rochester Institute of Technology*
Contact: blahetadp@longwood.edu

Educators responsible for coordinating a staff to grade a large volume of exams or projects have learned, sometimes the hard way, the importance of writing good rubrics: they keep the graders on track, grading equitably, consistently, and quickly. But these benefits of a well-written rubric extend also to those of us without a grading staff, even to single classrooms of twenty or so students. Good rubrics will change your life!

SIGCSE'16, March 2–5, 2016, Memphis, TN, USA.
ACM ISBN: 978-1-4503-3685-7/16/03.

In this workshop, we will present various principles we have found to write effective analytic rubrics for student programming work, helping to keep our grading unbiased and to assess the student work more quickly. We will show specific examples of good rubrics, and then participants will jointly grade some sample work according to a shared rubric, discussing what works and what doesn't. Finally, participants will break into small groups to workshop a rubric for an assignment they've given in their own class. Most examples will be at the CS1/CS2 level (and CS1-only educators are welcome), but some of the discussion will address higher-level courses as well.

Participants should bring the specification/handout for a programming assignment they have recently given in class (which need not be CS1/CS2), and are encouraged (if possible) to bring a small number of handed-in student solutions for that assignment. Laptops are not necessary unless that's how the participant is bringing or accessing their student solutions.

Keywords: rubric; programming; grading

DOI: http://dx.doi.org/10.1145/2839509.2844704

Permeating Data Visualization in CS Courses

Aaron Cadle, *Fort Worth Country Day School*
Ira Geenberg, *Southern Methodist University*
Deepak Kumar, *Bryn Mawr College*
Ursula Wolz, *RiverSound Solutions*
Dianna Xu, *Bryn Mawr College*
Contact: riversoundsol@gmail.com

Since 2007, we have successfully designed and implemented a computational art based context for introductory computing courses at both the undergraduate and high school level, leveraging the Processing development environment. Students learn to create data visualizations ranging from simple time series and heatmaps to word clouds, treemaps, and map-based geographical data visualizations. We have noticed two emerging trends; increased student engagement and interest in the visualization of data, and a resurgence of the web as a media-rich platform. This workshop builds on lessons learned from the creative coding classroom during these past 8 years. Working with the Processing environment, as well as its web-based implementations Processing.js and P5.js, attendees will explore approaches to visualizing data, applicable to CS courses ranging from high school to upper level interdisciplinary courses that would benefit from visualizations. Attendees will learn how to connect to online data streams, input, parse, visualize, and ultimately interact with the data, in both 2D and 3D. We will demonstrate the basic principles of creative coding and its applicability to teaching core structures and theory for the computing classroom. We will demonstrate how to seamlessly translate data visualizations from the desktop to web-based implementations--enabling the development of an online portfolio. This hands-on workshop will balance formal presentations with hands on opportunities for attendees to develop a series of short data visualizations, including a web-based portfolio of their work. Basic familiarity with Java and/or JavaScript is expected, prior experience with Processing is helpful but not essential. Laptops required.

Keywords: visualization; cs curriculum; creative computation; Processing

DOI: http://dx.doi.org/10.1145/2839509.2844695

Learn CS1/2 by Playing and Building Commercial Grade Casual Games

Kelvin Sung, *Univresity of Washington Bothell*
Rob Nash, *Univresity of Washington Bothell*
Jason Pace, *Univresity of Washington Bothell*
Contact: ksung@uw.edu

Designed specifically for instructors of university or high school Introductory Java Programming Classes (CS1/2) with no background in videogames or computer graphics, and based on our original casual game designs, this workshop will: (1) lead participants through structured gameplay sessions; (2) analyze how game mechanics contribute to player engagement; (3) map core game logic and mechanics to programming constructs taught in CS1/2 classes (e.g., conditionals, loops); (4) guide participants to develop simplified versions of these games based on our custom APIs and using CS1/2 programming constructs; (5) present sample teaching materials based on the games that are being used in our own classrooms, including: lecture materials, hands-on worksheets, and programming assignments; and (6) discuss our experiences using the materials, including what worked and what to avoid. Our games are innovative twists on popular casual genres (e.g., a Breakout variant using the z-plane, and a Zuma variant with user-movable paths) and we're currently enhancing the educational versions for commercial release. We've developed custom APIs for our games that are readily accessible to new programmers based on the successful Game-Themed CS1/2 project. Participants of this workshop will gain the confidence to build similar games, examine approaches to developing teaching materials based on the games and APIs, and understand the challenges inherent to this approach. Students will have the unique opportunity to play with commercial-quality game demos while using CS1/2 concepts to build games that are fun and appropriate for all ages.

Keywords: Computer Science Education, Assignment Design, Casual Games, CS1/2

DOI: http://dx.doi.org/10.1145/2839509.2844713

CSinParallel: Using WebMapReduce to Teach Parallel Computing Concepts, Hands-on

Richard Brown, *St. Olaf College*
Elizabeth Shoop, *Macalester College*
Joel Adams, *Calvin College*
Contact: rab@stolaf.edu

Map-reduce computation is the on-ramp to data-intensive cloud computing, and arguably the most widely deployed form of parallel/distributed computing. Participants will carry out exercises designed for students at CS1, intermediate, and

SIGCSE'16, March 2–5, 2016, Memphis, TN, USA.
ACM ISBN: 978-1-4503-3685-7/16/03.

advanced levels that introduce data-intensive scalable computing concepts using WebMapReduce (WMR), a simplified open-source interface to the dominant Hadoop map-reduce programming environment. WMR supports programming in a choice of languages including Python, Java, C++, and C#. Besides a hands-on experience with introductory teaching materials, the workshop includes an overview of teaching advanced map-reduce programming using WMR, and a comparison of WMR to direct Hadoop programming. All materials will reside on csinparallel.org, and the demonstration WMR system is reservable for participants' courses. Intended audience: CS instructors. Web-enabled laptop required.

Keywords: CSinParallel, WebMapReduce, WMR, map-reduce, parallel computing, parallelism, distributed computing, education, parallel design patterns, curriculum, design patterns, exemplars, CS1, advanced courses, parallel and distributed computing

DOI: http://dx.doi.org/10.1145/2839509.2844688

MUzECS: Block-based Arduino Programming for Exploring Computer Science

Dennis Brylow, *Marquette University*
brylow@mscs.mu.edu

The inexpensive Arduino makes for an attractive embedded platform in introductory courses. Its many variants, open source tools, and well-established hobbyist community support a staggering breadth of possible uses. In this workshop, we concentrate on block-based programming of the Arduino, providing a smooth path for Scratch programmers to expand into the wider world of sensors, actuators, and embedded systems. The MUzECS curriculum is designed to be an inexpensive replacement for the costly final robotics module of Exploring Computer Science (ECS), but also has clear applicability to Advanced Placement Computer Science Principles (AP CSP) and even college undergraduate courses. The session will introduce the Arduino Leonardo board, detail various "shield" extensions that are available, and present the tools and resources needed for high school or college instructors to get started. Demonstration activities will focus on ECS-style lessons that build programmable musical instruments. Laptop required.

Keywords: ECS; Arduino; ArduBlock; digital music; block-based programming; K-12 computer science.

DOI: http://dx.doi.org/10.1145/2839509.2844708

SIGCSE'16, March 2–5, 2016, Memphis, TN, USA.
ACM ISBN: 978-1-4503-3685-7/16/03.

How to Plan and Run Summer Computing Camps - Logistics

Kristine Nagel, *Georgia Gwinnett College*
Nannette Napier, *Georgia Gwinnett College*
Krishnendu Roy, *Valdosta State University*
Contact: knagel@ggc.edu

This workshop will provide details on how to plan and run non-residential, week-long computing summer camps for 4th–12th grade students. Georgia Tech has been offering computing summer camps since 2004. These camps are financially self-sustaining and effective. Items used in the camps include: CS Unplugged, LightBot, Scratch, Alice, LEGO robots (WeDo, NXT, EV3, and Tetrix), EarSketch, and App Inventor. Georgia Tech helped start other computing camps at eleven other colleges and universities in Georgia from 2007 to 2010 as part of Georgia Computes! NSF BPC grant. Since 2014, as part of the Expanding Computing Education Pathways (ECEP) NSF grant we have also helped institutions start or expand summer computing camps in South Carolina, Massachusetts, and California.

The workshop will include presentation about application forms, a timeline, sample agendas, sample flyers, budget plans, a planning checklist, suggested projects, surveys, pre and post-tests, evaluation results, lessons learned, and more. **Laptops are recommended** for this workshop.

Keywords: Summer camps; diversity; K-12; outreach; broadening participation; informal learning

DOI: http://dx.doi.org/10.1145/2839509.2844706

K–12 Teacher Support for Computer Science Principles: An Introduction to the UTeach Course, *Thriving in Our Digital World: AP*

Jeff Mickel, *The UTeach Institute*
Bradley Beth, *The University of Texas at Austin*
Contact: mickel@uteach.utexas.edu

Thriving in Our Digital World: AP provides high school teachers a complete, classroom-ready curriculum, including custom online resources and flexible curricular materials, designed to satisfy the College Board's requirements for its new course, AP Computer Science Principles. Organized in a series of project-based modules, the course focuses on current areas of research among real-world computer scientists, including Big Data, digital manipulation, and data security.

Beginning in Summer 2016, UTeach—the highly successful STEM teacher preparation program that began at The University of Texas at Austin in 1997 and is now being replicated nationwide—will offer professional development, ongoing support, and incentives for teachers to teach the course. UTeach's PD model encourages the participation of teachers with a variety of backgrounds and levels of experience, and leverages participating teachers' diverse areas of expertise to improve PD and support opportunities for all participants. Individuals who teach *Thriving in Our Digital World: AP* will join a national community of educators dedicated to improving K–12 computer science education and better engaging girls and other historically underrepresented groups in computing.

K–12 educators and school and district administrators should plan to attend this hands-on workshop. Presenters will engage participants in demonstration lessons and activities, and participants will leave with materials and handouts that are directly relevant to K–12 computer science classrooms. Laptops are required.

Keywords: Computer Science Education; K–12 Education; Computer Science Principles; Thriving in Our Digital World; Advanced Placement

DOI: http://dx.doi.org/10.1145/2839509.2844709

Conducting Educational Research in the Computer Science Classroom: Choosing the Appropriate Research Design to Address Your Research Questions

Aman Yadav, *Michigan State University*
Contact: *ayadav@msu.edu*

This workshop will provide CS educators with tools to conduct educational research. Primary objectives of this workshop are: (1) learn basic principles of research design; (2) learn about various types of research designs: qualitative vs. quantitative; experimental vs. quasi-experimental; case studies, survey; and (3) to practice designing research. This workshop will help participants make informed decisions when faced with limitations of educational research and collect empirical evidence about what works in the classroom. In addition, we will also discuss how to develop robust student outcome measures, such as surveys and tests. The workshop will be beneficial to participants who have not yet done all of these activities as well as those who have some background in educational research. Participants will be provided with material on research designs.

Keywords: Educational Research; Research Design

DOI: http://dx.doi.org/10.1145/2839509.284468

AP CS Principles and The Beauty and Joy of Computing Curriculum

Daniel D. Garcia, *University of California, Berkeley*
Tiffany Barnes, *North Carolina State University*
Michael Ball, *University of California, Berkeley*
Emil Biga, *Millard North High School*
Josh Paley, *Gunn High School*
Marnie Hill, *J.H. Rose High School*
Nathan Mattix, *Piedmont High School*
Parisa Safa, *Urban School of San Francisco*
Sean Morris, *Albany High School*
Shawn Kenner, *Sharon High School*
Contact: ddgarcia@cs.berkeley.edu

The Beauty and Joy of Computing (BJC) is a CS Principles (CSP) course developed at UC Berkeley, intended for high school juniors through university non-majors. It was twice chosen as a CSP pilot, and both the College Board and code.org have endorsed it. Since 2011, we have offered professional development to over 240 high school teachers. Our guiding philosophy is to meet students where they are, but not to leave them there. It covers the big ideas and computational thinking practices required in the AP CSP curriculum framework using an easy-to-learn blocks-based programming language called Snap! (based on Scratch), and powerful computer science ideas like recursion, higher-order functions and computability. Through the course, students learn to create beautiful images, and realize that *code itself* can be beautiful. Having fun is an explicit course goal. We take a "lab-centric" approach, and much of the learning occurs through guided programming labs that ask students to explore and play. In this workshop, we will provide an overview of BJC, share our experiences as instructors of the course at the university and high school level, provide a glimpse into a typical week of the course, and share details of potential crowd-funded summer professional development opportunities. ***This is a hands-on workshop. Laptops are required, and all "handouts" will be digital.***

Keywords: BJC; Beauty and Joy of Computing; CS Principles; Computer Science Principles; Professional Development; Broadening Participation; CS10K

DOI: http://dx.doi.org/10.1145/2839509.2844714

SIGCSE'16, March 2–5, 2016, Memphis, TN, USA.
ACM ISBN: 978-1-4503-3685-7/16/03.

Saturday Workshops

JavaScript Applications for CS0/CS1: Getting Hands-on with Code.org's App Lab

Baker Franke, *Code.org*
Sarah Filman, *Code.org*
Brook Osborne, *Code.org*
Contact: baker@code.org

App Lab (https://code.org/applab) is Code.org's rapid-prototyping environment for creating HTML, CSS, and JavaScript-powered web applications. It was created as part of a rich set of instructional resources designed for teachers of the new AP Computer Science Principles (CSP) course. Yet, App Lab far exceeds the needs of CSP, and would be an appropriate learning environment for students in any CS0/CS1 class, even at the university level. App Lab gives novice programmers access to capabilities previously reserved for courses that require sophisticated tech setup and knowledge of both front and backend web development, server-side scripting, databases, etc.

Rather than focusing on curriculum, this workshop will focus on how App Lab works as a programming tool in its own right, and how it was designed to aid and motivate student learning. Participants will get hands-on time with some of App Lab's more advanced features guided by a Code.org product manager, while working with the education team to help understand the educational philosophy that went into its development. Participants will come away with exemplars that highlight App Lab's possibilities, practice with some of its richer features, and do a hackathon to create something to share with each other (and the world)! Finally, we will end with a discussion about how best to integrate App Lab into existing courses.

App Lab was developed as part of collaboration between Code.org and David Bau (Google), creator of PencilCode.net.

A laptop is required for this session. All other materials will be provided.

Keywords: App Lab; Code.org; JavaScript; CS0; CS1; Programming Environment; Web Development

DOI: http://dx.doi.org/10.1145/2839509.2844692

Programming Web Services on the Cloud with Node.js

Ariel Ortiz, *Tecnologico de Monterrey, Campus Estado de Mexico*
Contact: ariel.ortiz@itesm.mx

Web services (a.k.a. web APIs) allow developers to build web and mobile applications using data from multiple online sources. This workshop is aimed at CS instructors that wish to teach how to use and write web services using Node.js on a cloud development environment. Node.js is an open source JavaScript platform that is currently used by companies like PayPal, DowJones, Walmart, Netflix, and Yahoo. Over 120 companies in the fortune 500 are not only using, but embracing Node.js in their everyday operations. Using and writing web services in Node.js is significantly easier than using other environments based on languages such as C# or Java. Because we will be using a cloud platform, all our tools are readily available through any modern web browser, thus eliminating the hassle related to installing a complete standalone development environment. Teaching web API design with Node.js on the cloud provides our students a relevant real life technical skill. Workshop participants will use the free service provided by Cloud9 IDE (https://c9.io/) to learn how to write scalable RESTful web services using Node.js, the Express web framework, MySQL, and jQuery. Participants should have a working knowledge of HTML, JavaScript, and SQL. Additional information available at: *http://node.arielortiz.info/* **Laptop required.**

Keywords: Web development; Web services; JavaScript; Node.js

DOI: http://dx.doi.org/10.1145/2839509.2844703

Teaching Robotics Using ROS

Nathan Sprague, *James Madison University*
Ralph Grove, *James Madison University*
Contact: spragunr@jmu.edu

The deployment of autonomous and semi-autonomous robots is likely to increase dramatically over the next decade. Recent autonomous vehicle prototypes illustrate both the rapid progress of the underlying technology and the commercial possibilities of robotics. The next few years are likely to see increased interest in robotics among both students and employers.

The Robot Operating System (ROS) is an open-source software framework for developing robotics applications. It has become a standard platform with a wide range of supported robots and a vibrant software ecosystem.

This workshop will provide a hands-on introduction to ROS. Participants will have the opportunity to write ROS-based Python programs to control a Turtlebot educational robot. We will discuss the benefits and challenges of using ROS in an undergraduate robotics course. The workshop is intended for CS educators with an interest in teaching robotics. Laptops will be provided. No experience with ROS or Python is required.

Keywords: Robotics; ROS

DOI: http://dx.doi.org/10.1145/2839509.2844701

SIGCSE'16, March 2–5, 2016, Memphis, TN, USA.
ACM ISBN: 978-1-4503-3685-7/16/03.

AP Computer Science Principles Performance Task: *Create – Applications from Ideas*, Approaches to Programming Collaboratively. It's a Hackathon Workshop!

Lien Diaz, *College Board*
Richard Kick, *Newbury Park High School*
Andrew Kuemmel, *Madison West High School*
Contact: ldiaz@collegeboard.org

The AP Computer Science Principles assessment model comprises two main components: 1) an end-of-course AP Exam (i.e., a paper-pencil, multiple choice questions); and 2) a through-course assessment that includes two (2) performance tasks in which students complete during class time. This workshop focuses on content and skills included in one of the through-course assessment performance tasks: *Create – Applications from Ideas*. In this task, students are expected to collaborate with another student in the development process of writing a program, and because each student will submit her/his own program for AP scoring purposes, students are also expected to be able to continue working on their program individually. To obtain the knowledge and skills students will need to be successful with this performance task, students can consider practicing various possible ways to write programs individually and collaboratively. That said, teachers can support student success with this performance task by considering different ways to teach how to develop programs collaboratively (beyond Pair Programming). In this workshop, participants will experience different collaborative programming techniques to develop a program. This workshop is meant for programmers "from beginners to experts". In addition, participants will reflect on the collaborative process, thereby learning some of the essential knowledge and skills that students will need to obtain in order to successfully complete the *Create* performance task. **Laptop Recommended**. It is recommended that participants bring a laptop computer to this workshop

Keywords: Advanced Placement, AP, AP Computer Science Principles, performance task, programming, collaboration

DOI: http://dx.doi.org/10.1145/2839509.2844711

Scaling up for CS10K: Teaching and Supporting New Computer Science High School Teachers

Tiffany Barnes, *North Carolina State University*
Jamie Payton, *University of North Carolina - Charlotte*
Daniel D. Garcia, *University of California at Berkeley*
Contact: tmbarnes@ncsu.edu

Increasing need for computing expertise in our everyday lives and in the workforce, paired with declining enrollments in computing by women and underrepresented minorities have made it critical to provide students with experiences in computing before college. CS10K is a national effort to engage 10,000 high school teachers in teaching computer science across the United States. With CS10K projects working on this goal since 2012 having prepared less than 1000 teachers for teaching computer science in high school, there is a need to scale professional development opportunities to local communities. College and university computing faculty have the unique preparation and call for community engagement that make it a win-win to support local high school teachers in learning to teach computer science. We will use the STARS model of building university-based communities that broaden participation in computing, adapted to the context of supporting K12 teachers to become change agents and educators prepared to teach computer science. In this workshop, participants will learn how to implement scalable team-based professional development for K12 teachers new to teaching computer science. We will provide resources to recruit, plan, and support small groups of new teachers to teach the new CS Principles course that will become an Advanced Placement course in 2016-2017. ***Laptops for attendees are optional.***

Keywords: Scalable; Professional Development; CS Principles

DOI: http://dx.doi.org/10.1145/2839509.2844705

App Development for All! Learn the Hybrid Development Model and How Scaffolded Projects can Bring App Development to your Classes

David P. Hayes, *Lane Tech College Prep HS, Chicago*
Dale F. Reed, *University of Illinois at Chicago*
Contact: dphayes@cps.edu

In this workshop, participants will learn how to build custom, data-driven mobile apps using the hybrid model and how to scaffold app development projects to focus students' efforts on specific lesson, unit or assignment goals. It is intended for post-secondary or late secondary educators who want to increase student engagement by including app projects in their courses. With new tools and techniques, barriers to implementation have been reduced: in the hybrid model, developers use HTML5, CSS and Javascript - along with libraries enabling access to mobile device features such as accelerometer, camera, contacts, etc - to quickly develop apps and to distribute them on multiple platforms. Participants will learn how to create app interfaces using the Bootstrap Mobile framework, how to compile their apps using PhoneGap, and how to pull data from public APIs into their apps. Participants will also learn how to use Google tools to quickly create a web service, giving students greater capacity to design and develop relevant, engaging and useful apps. ***Participants will need a laptop or will need to work with a colleague and should have at least a rudimentary knowledge of HTML, CSS and Javascript.***

Keywords: mobile; appdevelopment; scripting; web; data; engagement; APIs

DOI: http://dx.doi.org/10.1145/2839509.2844710

SIGCSE'16, March 2–5, 2016, Memphis, TN, USA.
ACM ISBN: 978-1-4503-3685-7/16/03.

Mixing Code and 3D Printers with Madeup

Chris Johnson, *University of Wisconsin, Eau Claire*
Heather Amthauer, *University of Wisconsin, Eau Claire*
Ryan Hardt, *University of Wisconsin, Eau Claire*
Peter Bui, *University of Notre Dame*
Contact: johnch@uwec.edu

Madeup is a text- and blocks-based programming language for making things up—literally. Programmers write sequences of commands to move and turn through space, tracing out printable 3D shapes with algorithms and mathematical operations. The language is designed to teach computation from a tangible, first-person perspective and help students integrate computation back into the physical world. Madeup joins a crowd of existing teaching tools, including Scratch, Alice, and many others, all of which aim to make computing more accessible to new learners. What sets Madeup apart from existing projects is its physical product. The model that a programmer creates does not remain virtual. It can be printed, felt, carried in a pocket, and handed to a parent or friend---all of which may make computation real and relevant in the eyes of the programmer. In this workshop, we empower educators to use the freely-available and browser-based Madeup programming environment in their classrooms. Participants are to bring their own laptops with a browser that supports WebGL and should expect to learn actively.

Keywords: 3D printing; media computation; syntonic learning

DOI: http://dx.doi.org/10.1145/2839509.2844682

Infusing Cooperative Learning into Early Computer Science Courses to Support Improved Engagement

Owen Astrachan, *Duke University*
Jeff Gray, *University of Alabama*
Fran Trees, *Rutgers University*
Contact: fran.trees@cs.rutgers.edu

Many new curricula and tools have been developed recently to promote the exciting opportunities available in computer science. However, curriculum and supporting tools alone do not drive engagement – the most interesting and innovative curriculum can still be taught in a disengaged manner, leading to lost opportunities for broadening the appeal and interest in computing across a diverse student population. The learning science literature on Cooperative Learning (CL) has been shown to increase class participation and student learning, while also promoting diversity in a manner that supports the differentiated instruction needed to engage students who have mixed abilities. This workshop will demonstrate how the best practices of CL can be applied in early CS courses (e.g., AP CS Principles AP CS A, or CS1). Workshop participants will be introduced to the CL structures that have been used in many different disciplines across multiple age/grade levels. These structures will be used to demonstrate specific applications toward computer science concepts. The workshop itself will be taught in a cooperative learning style so that participants can understand the dynamics and structure of a CL classroom. This workshop is intended for two types of educators: 1) K-12 teachers currently teaching AP CS A, CS Principles (CSP), or other introductory programming courses and 2) university faculty currently teaching CS 1 or other introductory computer science courses.

Keywords: cooperative learning; broadening participation; student engagement

DOI: http://dx.doi.org/10.1145/2839509.2844696

SIGCSE'16, March 2–5, 2016, Memphis, TN, USA.
ACM ISBN: 978-1-4503-3685-7/16/03.

Solving the Cloud Computing Impasse with MBaaS

Michael P. Rogers, *Northwest Missouri State University*
Bill Siever, *Western Illinois University*
Contact: mprogers@mac.com

Students raised on tablets and smart phones have a lot of expectations: data that is instantly available on all of their devices; social media integration so they can share that data with their friends; and push notifications, so that responses from their friends get the attention that they deserve. Unfortunately, the vendor-specific technologies required to make this magic happen are daunting, to put it mildly, well beyond the scope of a beginning mobile computing course. However, the last 2 years has seen the emergence of a new technology, Mobile Backend as a Service (MBaaS), that is vendor-agnostic and suitable for novice developers. This workshop will provide a hands-on introduction to this technology. Participants will be provided source code for Pigs Ahoy!, an implementation of the famed dice game Pig that lacks cloud storage and social media integration. During the course of the workshop, participants will add that functionality, and in the process of doing so, acquire a sufficiently detailed knowledge of MBaaS that they can confidently incorporate it into their classes. Because MBaaS is vendor-agnostic, participants may work on either iOS or Android versions of Pigs Ahoy!: full instructions will be provided in both Swift and Java, as well as snapshots of Pigs Ahoy! at various stages of completion, so that no one need fear being left behind. There are multiple MBaaS providers, and they offer similar capabilities and approaches. We will concentrate on the most popular, parse.com.

Keywords: Mobile Computing; Mobile Backend As A Service; Cloud Storage; Social Media

DOI: http://dx.doi.org/10.1145/2839509.2844685

Reviewing NSF Proposals: Learn about Effective Proposal Writing via the Review Process

Michael Erlinger, National Science Foundation
Paul Tymann, National Science Foundations
Contact: ptymann@nsf.gov

This workshop focuses on the NSF proposal review process. Via close examination of the review process, participants gain an understanding of how to write good reviews and how to improve their own proposal writing. The workshop covers the following topic areas: the proposal review process from submission of a proposal to award or decline; elements of a good review; NSF merit criteria (intellectual merit and broader impacts); elements of a good proposal; and how to volunteer to review proposals.

The workshop uses a structured guided-interactive methodology to lead participants through each topic by introducing related issues, engaging participants in group exercises designed to explore and share their understanding of the issues, and then providing some "expert" opinion on these issues. Good and bad examples and a Top Ten List of Do's and Don'ts will be provided.

Keywords: grant writing; proposal review

DOI: http://dx.doi.org/10.1145/2839509.2844689

Transition to Java Using Alice 3

Donald Slater, *Carnegie Mellon University*
Wanda P. Dann, *Carnegie Mellon University*
Contact: dslater@cmu.edu

This workshop, designed for pre-AP, Introduction to Programming, Programming for non-majors, and CS1 Java courses, will introduce the tools in Alice 3 that are specifically designed to support a transition to Java and will provide experience with the software, a new textbook, and the available course materials. The workshop offers hands-on experience in programming with Alice 3 and Java, together. Participants will see how to use Alice 3 to build virtual worlds and how to transfer these programs into a Java IDE. The workshop will also explore curricular design and implementation. Alice 3 uses built-in tools including a Java language display that dynamically updates and displays the Java syntax as students build their Alice project, and a plugin for a Java IDE that allows students to start their projects in Alice and then continue their work by writing Java code. These tools allow students to develop animations and simple games using objects in a truly object-oriented style.

Additional Information: **Laptop (Mac or Windows) Required:** *Alice 3* is not available for mobile platforms. A mouse is highly recommended, but not absolutely required. A copy of the software and presentation materials will be given to participants.

Keywords: Alice; Alice 3; Java; NetBeans; pre-APCS; pre-CS1; animation; 3D Graphics; Introduction to Programming

DOI: http://dx.doi.org/10.1145/2839509.2844697

SIGCSE'16, March 2–5, 2016, Memphis, TN, USA.
ACM ISBN: 978-1-4503-3685-7/16/03.

Student Research Competition

Applying Formal Models of Instructional Design to Measurably Improve Learning in Introductory Computing

Austin Cory Bart, *Virginia Tech*
Contact: acbart@vt.edu

Software Engineers apply systematic techniques to formalize requirements, build tests, and plan out complex architectures. However, few Computer Science Educators bring the same rigorous methods to the design of their students' learning experiences. Educational theories of Instructional Design (compatible with a wide range of popular educational theories) bridge this gap by emphasizing meaningful assessment, identification of instructional objectives, and analysis of the learners; unfortunately, these theories have been neglected within Computer Science Education. I have applied the Dick & Carey Model of Instructional Design in two formal case studies to create new learning modules with extensive documentation, detailed components, and clear results. In fact, my formal evaluations of my materials with real learners suggest that students had average learning gains of up to 43%. More crucially, however, the model provided key opportunities to improve the instruction a priori and posteriori. My major contribution in this research is not the generation of new instructional materials, but the demonstration of the raw potential of this methodology for curriculum development.

Keywords: Instructional Design; Dick & Carey; Formal Methods; Teaching

DOI: http://dx.doi.org/10.1145/2839509.2851050

Learning to Program Using Online Forums: A Comparison of Links Posted on Reddit and Stack Overflow

Caroline D. Hardin, *University of Wisconsin- Madison*
Matthew Berland, *University of Wisconsin- Madison*
Contact: caroline.hardin@wisc.edu

While the USA struggles with a demand for computer programming education which exceeds the capacity of formal educational opportunities, online resources dedicated to programming are growing rapidly. One valuable way to measure the usefulness of these online resources is to examine the links posted in the forums of CS learning communities. We scraped and analyzed over 80,000 posts from two popular forums (Reddit and Stack Overflow), and found that how these communities use and talk about CS learning resources (such as books and tutorials) demonstrated their differing priorities. These results have much to suggest to both novices and teachers.

Keywords: Reddit; Stack Overflow; Online Community; Technical Forum; Computer Science Education

DOI: http://dx.doi.org/10.1145/2839509.2851051

Open Sourcing the Classroom

Mike Izbicki, *UC Riverside*
Contact: mike@izbicki.me

This project describes an experimental course on open source software construction. The course has two twists on the standard project-based software construction course. The first twist is simple: all projects are developed and released on GitHub. The second twist is more radical: the course uses an "open source textbook." The textbook is hosted in a git repository that students are required to contribute to throughout the term. Contributions range from minor typo fixes to adding entire chapters. Currently, 88% of the textbook is written by students, including many of the assignments. We use student surveys, participation in social networking sites like GitHub, and web traffic logs to determine that these assignments had a positive effect on students' future contributions to the open source community.

Keywords: open source; git; education

DOI: http://dx.doi.org/10.1145/2839509.2851052

A Wavelet Transform Module for a Speech Recognition Virtual Machine

Euisung Kim, *Minnesota State University, Mankato*
Contact: euisung.kim@mnsu.edu

This work explores the trade-offs between time and frequency information during the feature extraction process of an automatic speech recognition system using wavelet transform features instead of Mel-frequency cepstral coefficients. The Speech Recognition Virtual Kitchen toolkit (www.speechkitchen.org) is used as the framework for implementing wavelet modules in a virtual machine loaded with the Kaldi recognition system. The SRVK toolkit is a computing resource that provides virtual machines for a variety of research and education purposes. Results comparing different wavelets and feature extraction approaches will be presented. The resulting virtual machine, which allows straightforward comparisons of signal processing approaches, is freely available for research and educational use.

Keywords: Speech recognition, wavelets, virtual machines

DOI: http://dx.doi.org/10.1145/2839509.2851053

SIGCSE'16, March 2–5, 2016, Memphis, TN, USA.
ACM ISBN: 978-1-4503-3685-7/16/03.

Monitoring – An Intervention to Improve Team Results in Software Engineering Education

Maíra Marques, *Universidad de Chile*
Contact: mmarques@dcc.uchile.cl

Software engineering education is currently being taught in many universities with a hands-on approach, where students have to learn to develop software in teams, intending to simulate industry, to minimize the gap between what universities teach and what industry needs. The industry "simulation" that a university performs in software engineering courses is a good approach but it is normally undermined by student bad behaviors (free-riding, social loafing and student syndrome), which leads to lower team performance and lower team motivation. In this work I propose the use of reflexive weekly monitoring (RWM) to mitigate these students' bad behaviors that can disrupt team results. The use of the RWM in the past two semesters in a software engineering course, has improved teams' results in terms of both, project and final grades.

Keywords: software engineering education; monitoring

DOI: http://dx.doi.org/10.1145/2839509.2851054

Pair Programming for Teaching Mobile Development

Mohammed Seyam, *Virginia Tech*
Contact: seyam@vt.edu

Pair Programming is an agile practice that has numerous studies showing its benefits for education. The emergence of mobile software design education raises questions about the effectiveness of Pair Programming in this evolving field. Developing for mobile is different than regular desktop/web development in three major areas: having more than one screen to work on (i.e. computer screen and mobile device screen), connectivity issues (dealing with Bluetooth, GPS and location data, smart watches, and sensors), and User Experience (UX) issues. Our research probes unique challenges for Pair Programming when used in mobile software design classes, focusing on five mobile design topics: dealing with interface and data managements (as in fragments), using camera, handling multi-device connectivity, using sensors and collecting GPS data, and using microphones and speakers. The study highlights successes and challenges for Pair Programming for mobile applications, with the objective of providing a set of recommendations for instructors considering using Pair Programming in their mobile development classes.

Keywords: Computer Science Education; Pair Programming; Mobile development

DOI: http://dx.doi.org/10.1145/2839509.2851055

SIGCSE'16, March 2–5, 2016, Memphis, TN, USA.
ACM ISBN: 978-1-4503-3685-7/16/03.

Community and Collaboration in an All-Female, Immersive Computer Science Program

Jeff Stern, *University of Michigan*
Contact: jeffster@umich.edu

Girls Who Code is a national nonprofit that operates after-school and summer programs to engage female students with computer science with the goal of reaching gender parity in the field. The Girls Who Code teaching philosophy and curriculum is designed around four major components: (1) developing a breadth of technical and computational thinking skills, (2) building on students' prior interests, (3) providing authentic exposure to mentors and real computer science projects, and (4) cultivating a community-focused classroom. Using qualitative and quantitative data collected from more than 1,500 students that have participated, this work explores the impact of Girls Who Code's intervention and the value of building community for effective computer science education.

Keywords: Gender; Collaboration; Community; Girls Who Code

DOI: http://dx.doi.org/10.1145/2839509.2851056

Implementing K-Means Clustering and Collaborative Filtering to Enhance Sustainability of Project Repositories

Matthew Steuerer, *The College of New Jersey*
Contact: steuerm1@tcnj.edu

Websites for dissemination of grant-funded projects can quickly become unsustainable once funding ends since they require significant human intervention to ensure that data are current and reliable. CABECTPortal is a website that maintains information about research projects that involve interdisciplinary pedagogical collaborations. It leverages social computational concepts and a machine learning algorithm, specifically k-means clustering, to improve the sustainability of dissemination efforts by engaging the research community in the process. Usability design concepts are integrated with throughout the site to enhance user motivation and engagement. This poster will present the machine learning algorithms that were implemented for the recommendation system used in CABECTPortal. Acknowledgment: This project is based on work supported by the National Science Foundation under NSF DUE Award# 1141170. Any opinions, findings and conclusions or recommendations expressed in this material are those of the authors and do not necessarily reflect the views of the National Science Foundation (NSF).

Keywords: Social computational system; sustainability; collaboration; computational thinking

DOI: http://dx.doi.org/10.1145/2839509.2851057

Web-based Visual Programming for Media Computation Using Blockly

Jake Trower, *University of Alabama*
Contact: jatrower@crimson.ua.edu

Tunely and Pixly are web-based programming environments for media computation built using the Blockly visual programming editor library. These language environments were inspired by Georgia Tech's Media Computation approach and allow images (Pixly) and sounds (Tunely) to be transformed programmatically. Tunely and Pixly provided an approachable environment to students who have little to no experience in programming, and allow younger students to explore programming in a fun way without the challenges and frustration of learning syntax in a textual language. This SRC poster summarizes the design and implementation of these languages. We also briefly introduce initial work on integrating an accessibility tool to allow children with disabilities to explore these opportunities.

Keywords: visual programming language; Blockly; media computation; image processing; sound processing

DOI: http://dx.doi.org/10.1145/2839509.2851058

An Evaluation of Cluster 3.0 as a General Tool for Principal Component Analysis

Alex Bender, *Eastern Mennonite University*
Contact: alex.bender@emu.edu

In computer science experimentation, more researchers have begun using Principal Component Analysis (PCA). Discerning how to apply this mathematical technique, however, can be confusing; papers in this area tend to focus on results rather than the methodology in using PCA. Consequentially, reproducing or verifying PCA results is difficult without prolonged communication with the authors. Our larger goal with this work is to create a general descriptive methodology for PCA usage and give examples of how widely available programs are used to provide a resource for discipline-specific researchers. Here we focus on utilization of the program Cluster 3.0 with an experiment from our chemistry department.

Keywords: Principal Component Analysis; Software Evaluation; Cluster 3.0

DOI: http://dx.doi.org/10.1145/2839509.2851059

SIGCSE'16, March 2–5, 2016, Memphis, TN, USA.
ACM ISBN: 978-1-4503-3685-7/16/03.

Detecting Insider Attacks with Video Websites using Distributed Image Steganalysis

C. Francis-Christie, *Kennesaw State University*
Contact: stxbfrancis@gmail.com

The safety of information inside of cloud networks is of interest to the network administrators. In a new insider attack, the inside attackers merge confidential information with videos using digital video steganography. The video can be uploaded to video websites, where the information can be distributed online, where it can cost firms millions in damages. Standard behavior based exfiltration detection does not always prevent these attacks. This form of steganography is almost invisible. Existing compressed video steganalysis only detects small-payload watermarks. We develop such a strategy using distributed algorithms and classify videos, then compare existing algorithms to new ones. We find our approach improves on behavior based exfiltration detection, and on the existing online video steganalysis.

Keywords: Security and Privacy; Firewalls; Insider Exfiltration; Online Video; Video Steganography; Video Steganalysis;

DOI: http://dx.doi.org/10.1145/2839509.2851060

Programming by Voice to Support Hour of Code for Children with Motor Disabilities

Caitlin Hanley, *University of Alabama*
Contact: crhanley@crimson.ua.edu

Every December, Code.org provides a set of Hour of Code exercises as part of CS Education week. However, motorically challenged students may be unable to participate because they cannot use the mouse and/or keyboard to interact with the Blockly-based Graphical User Interface and drag-and-drop programming environment. Programming by Voice (PBV) allows users to interact with block-oriented programming environments by speaking their program, rather than using a keyboard and mouse. The Myna tool, a PBV tool that was originally designed for the Scratch programming language, has been modified to work with the Code.org programming environment. Children with a mobility disability can use this tool to experience Code.org's educational opportunities.

Keywords: programming by voice; accessibility; motor disabilities; Code.org; computing education

DOI: http://dx.doi.org/10.1145/2839509.2851061

The Role of Chronology in Analyzing Introductory Programming Assignments

Kayla Holcomb, *Abilene Christian University*
Nevan Simone, *Abilene Christian University*
Contact: kmh12c@acu.edu

Entry-level college programming courses have high failure rates, which lead to high dropout rates for associated majors. These courses typically cover fundamental programming concepts for students to master in order to succeed in their majors. When attempting to perceive a student's competency, instructors often utilize Automated Assessment Tools, but most tools do not fully record student progress in assignments. Access to the student's problem solving steps can provide educators a more complete understanding of the student's thought process. Our tool tracks the student's steps and sequencing while attempting to complete assignments. With this resource, teaching methodologies can be modified to more effectively foster successful problem-solving strategies within early programming courses.

Keywords: Problem Solving; Automated Assessment Tool; CS1; Programming Concepts; Sequencing

DOI: http://dx.doi.org/10.1145/2839509.2851062

A Simple Line Game with Real-Time Visualization of the Internal Data Structure

John Huff, Ohio University
Contact: jh571912@ohio.edu

Designing tools for K-12 computer science education poses a unique and difficult challenge. The focus should be on teaching broad computer science concepts in an engaging way. Other approaches have involved visualizing data structures and algorithms. However, these approaches aren't very engaging. By applying the principles of universal design for learning, we created an interactive visualization tool for a simple line game. This visualization tool has several ways to represent the same data structure, and is much more engaging than other approaches to teaching computer science concepts. We are still conducting research on the effectiveness of this tool, but our preliminary results look promising

Keywords: Data Structure Visualization; Web Game; k-12 education; Education tool; Universal design

DOI: http://dx.doi.org/10.1145/2839509.2851063

3D-Printed Animatronic Hand with Wireless Mirroring Glove and Precision Control

Cyrus Xiyuan Liu, *Wake Forest University*
Contact: liux212@wfu.edu

This project was motivated by a desire to learn about 3D printing, Arduinos, and Bluetooth by implementing a prosthetic or animatronic hand. The goal was to make the animatronic hand mirror the gestures of a human hand inside a sensor-equipped glove. The animatronic hand serves as a prototype of a prosthetic human hand, or a robotic hand that can operate in dangerous areas. The project has five elements: 1. 3D modeling and printing the hand parts and the casings for the entire system; 2. assembling the joints with strings attached to servomotors; 3. two Arduino boards programmed such that the prosthetic hand mirrors the finger motions of a sensor-equipped glove worn by a human; 4. Bluetooth communication between the sensors on the glove and the Arduino board, which moves the fingers of the prosthetic hand by pulling strings attached to the servomotors; and 6. experiments on the completed hand to refine the relationship between the Arduino commands and the precise motions of the finger joints. Future work is also expected to implement electro-sensors on upper muscles with the intention of controlling the prosthetic hand based on the detected electrical signals in the muscles.

Keywords: 3D printing; Arduino; Bluetooth; prosthetics

DOI: http://dx.doi.org/10.1145/2839509.2851064

Robotic Navigation through Gesture Based Control

Nickolas McCarley, *University of Alabama*
Contact: nwmccarley@crimson.ua.edu

Robotic Navigation Through Gesture Based Control (RNTGBC) assists people who may not be able to operate a smart device using their fingers. These individuals might face limitations due to physical disabilities or may be in a job where their fingers are not free to operate the smart device. For this project, a motion sensor was used in combination with a robot. The sensor was used to capture gestures and operate the robot. The tools used are the Leap (a device that reads 3D gesture motion), the Sphero (a remote controlled rolling ball), and a laptop. RNTGBC uses the Leap device to control the Sphero with hand gestures. This technology is important because navigation through gestures can be adapted towards larger contexts, such as helping someone in a wheelchair move around or assisting someone who does not have their hands available when performing a job task.

Keywords: Robot; Navigation; Assistance; Accessibility

DOI: http://dx.doi.org/10.1145/2839509.2851065

Advances in Phylogenetic-based Stemma Construction

Andrew Miller, *The College of New Jersey*
Nathan Gould, *The College of New Jersey*
Dimitris Papamichail, *The College of New Jersey*
Contact: millea18@tcnj.edu

An ultimate goal of traditional textual criticism is the reconstruction of the archetype of a given work. By comparing differences and similarities among multiple versions of the work, the interrelations among existing and hypothetical ancestral versions can be naturally presented as a tree, in which a branch represents derivation of a new version. We will present our investigation into the generation of phylogenetic trees with extant manuscripts at both leaves and internal nodes of the tree, and discuss algorithms for promoting leaf nodes to ancestral positions while optimizing the tree construction objective, based on the maximum parsimony criterion.

Keywords: Phylogenetics; Stemmatics; Computational Biology

DOI: http://dx.doi.org/10.1145/2839509.2851066

SIGCSE'16, March 2–5, 2016, Memphis, TN, USA.
ACM ISBN: 978-1-4503-3685-7/16/03.

Syntactic Hint Generation for Introductory Programming Problems

Aayush Mudgal, *Indian Institute of Technology Kanpur*
Contact: mudgal@cse.iitk.ac.in

We provide an extension to the existing data-driven tutoring system, ITAP (Rivers and Koedinger 2014) to provide personalized help to students. The existing ITAP framework relies on abstract syntax trees and works only on compilable code, we extend the framework to work even with uncompilable code. We use an iterative correction technique that locally corrects code by manipulating tokens in the vicinity of an erroneous token, using a specially designed parser. It utilizes the power of a LALR (1) parser to identify the erroneous token, and suggests the possible expected token at that position. We utilize this information to iteratively modify the code to reach to a compilable state. This compilable state is then fed as an input to the ITAP, and the received hints are then coupled suitably.

Keywords: Intelligent Tutoring System, Syntax hints, Automatic Hint Generation

DOI: http://dx.doi.org/10.1145/2839509.2851067

Novel Logical Reasoning Tutor

Matthew Pfister, *Clemson University*
Contact: mpfiste@clemson.edu

In a sudden push for at-home learning, various simulation programs have been created to allow students to explore academic concepts in a variety of fields. But computer scientists are still forced to rely on trial-and-error test cases when trying to understand a tricky piece of code. In this poster the author reports on the results of a novel web-based educational tool that teaches coding through logical reasoning. Students are challenged to postulate symbolic relationships between generalized parameters within example code, and the tool evaluates the correctness and relevance of these answers within the context. Students may take comfort that their knowledge of the topic is comprehensive since the verification process takes into account all possible edge cases for parameter values.

Keywords: Logical reasoning tutor; Online eductional tools; Computer science education

DOI: http://dx.doi.org/10.1145/2839509.2851068

Loop Invariants: Learning to Help Teach

Caleb Priester, *Clemson University*
Contact: calebhpriester@gmail.com

Loop invariants are a key component in developing code for verification, but many students struggle to grasp how to arrive at one that will remain true at the beginning and end of each iteration as well as be sufficiently strong to prove subsequent assertions reliant on the outcome of the loop. The focus of this research is to provide professors with a clearer idea of the difficulties students face in developing suitable loop invariants by using automated verification tools and collecting data in the background as students develop invariants in a series of isolated studies. This information will help professors to better allocate teaching time in order to best teach students the fundamentals of identifying correct loop invariants and developing verifiable code using tools.

Keywords: Loop invariants; formal verification; data analysis

DOI: http://dx.doi.org/10.1145/2839509.2851069

Mobile Security via Reverse Tether

Donna Young, *Kennesaw State University*
Contact: dyoung2@students.kennesaw.edu

Mobile security risks are increasing at an alarming rate. By using reverse tethering, the security of a desktop firewall, router, and ISP safeguards can be leveraged to keep mobile devices safe and free from malicious code and attacks. The software technology needed is currently in the initial stages of development and will protect users' personal information from being accessed through a vulnerability in the mobile platform.

Keywords: Mobile security; Reverse tethering

DOI: http://dx.doi.org/10.1145/2839509.2851070

SIGCSE'16, March 2–5, 2016, Memphis, TN, USA.
ACM ISBN: 978-1-4503-3685-7/16/03.

Author Index

www.ingramcontent.com/pod-product-compliance
Lightning Source LLC
LaVergne TN
LVHW082344011026
849160LV00024B/1042
* 9 7 8 1 4 5 0 3 4 4 6 8 5 *